The Good Guide to Britain 1999

Edited by Alisdair Aird

Deputy Editor: Fiona May

Associate Editors: Karen Fick, Robert Unsworth

Research Officer: Rachel Martin

Walks Consultant: Tim Locke

Additional Research: Fiona Wright

EBURY PRESS
LONDON

Please send reports to:

The Good Guide to Britain
FREEPOST TN1569
WADHURST
E Sussex
TN5 7BR

This edition published in 1998 by
Ebury Press
Random House, 20 Vauxhall Bridge Road
London SW1V 2SA

1 3 5 7 9 10 8 6 4 2

ISBN 0 09 186354 6

Typeset from author's disks by Textype Typesetters, Cambridge
Printed and bound in Great Britain by Mackays of Chatham, plc

CONTENTS

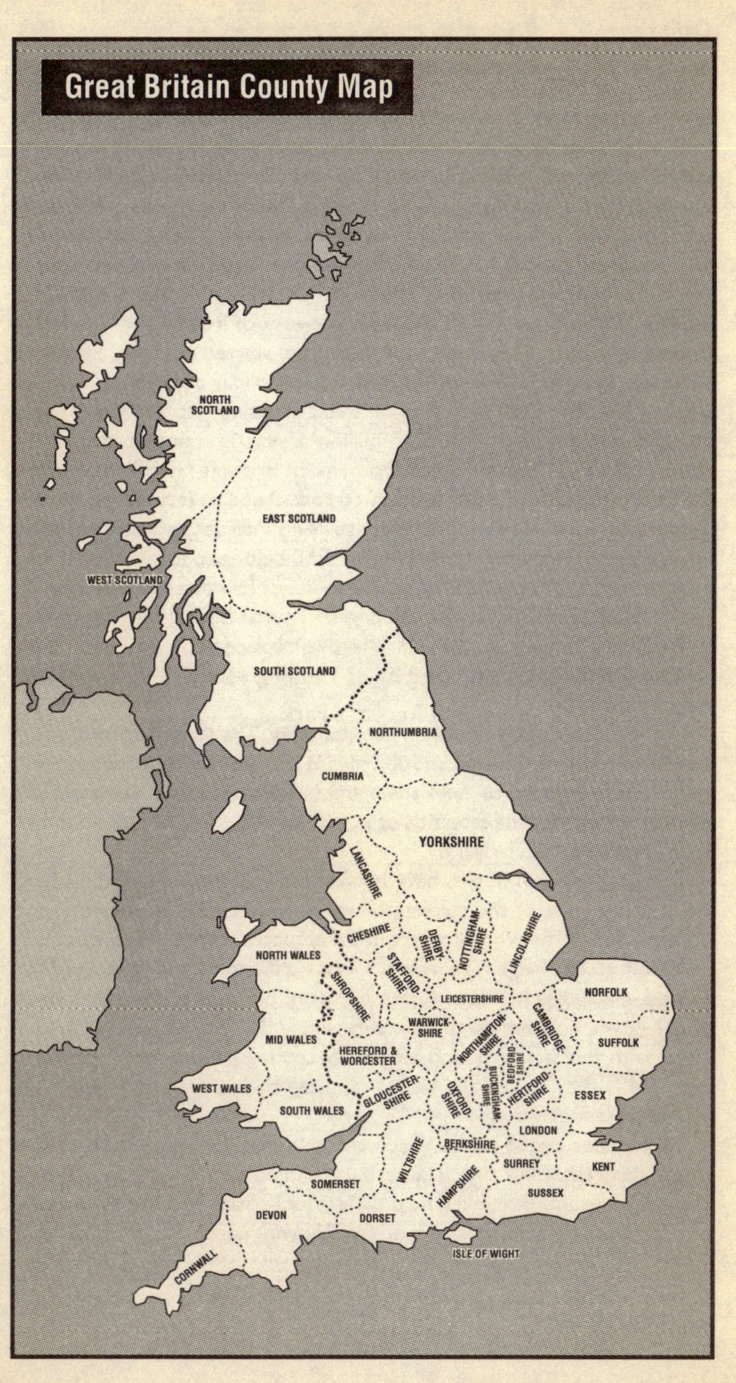

Great Britain County Map
NORTH SCOTLAND
EAST SCOTLAND
WEST SCOTLAND
SOUTH SCOTLAND
NORTHUMBRIA
CUMBRIA
YORKSHIRE
LANCASHIRE
CHESHIRE
DERBY-SHIRE
NOTTINGHAM-SHIRE
LINCOLNSHIRE
NORTH WALES
STAFFORD-SHIRE
SHROPSHIRE
LEICESTERSHIRE
NORFOLK
CAMBRIDGE-SHIRE
WARWICK-SHIRE
NORTHAMPTON-SHIRE
SUFFOLK
MID WALES
HEREFORD & WORCESTER
BEDFORD-SHIRE
BUCKINGHAM-SHIRE
HERTFORD-SHIRE
WEST WALES
GLOUCESTER-SHIRE
OXFORD-SHIRE
ESSEX
SOUTH WALES
LONDON
BERKSHIRE
WILTSHIRE
SURREY
KENT
SOMERSET
HAMPSHIRE
SUSSEX
DEVON
DORSET
ISLE OF WIGHT
CORNWALL

INTRODUCTION

Britain's tourist industry has an uncanny knack for shooting itself in the foot. With enormous natural advantages, and by far the world's greatest concentration of interesting places to visit, it has repeatedly shunned opportunities of making the most of these. There's a wonderful range of accommodation, but squabbling between English, Welsh and Scottish tourism organisations has killed off hopes of a single national star system to help and inform consumer choice. A lynch-pin of Britain's appeal for holidays and outings was its excellent network of free museums – but in the last few years all too many of them have started charging. Efforts to advertise and promote Britain's tremendous holiday possibilities are very weak: against the £260 million a year spent on selling people who live here holidays abroad, only some £37 million a year is spent on promoting British holidays. One and a half thousand of Britain's historic buildings – the buildings that make our scenery so special and so interesting – are in such urgent need of repair that they are falling into decay (and not all have negligent private owners, either – over 250 belong to local councils, and many others to government or official bodies). Now that the Government has decided to stop paying for the English Tourist Board, has the industry immediately jumped in with an effective replacement, to co-ordinate tourism initiatives on a national basis? You've guessed – no, of course, it hasn't. And so on.

We shouldn't really complain about all this. The lack of co-ordination and absence of effective promotion means that people need independent guides such as ours to help them track down Britain's extraordinary holiday riches. But the latest twist in the sorry saga of Britain's botched tourism does particularly irk.

This year tourism bosses have been squealing loudly about the effects on their business of the strong pound, which they say is pricing British holidays out of the world market. It's undoubtedly true that the pound's current high exchange rate makes it more difficult to sell *anything* British abroad – including holidays. A crucial part of the answer must be to hold prices down. So what do the tourism people do? You've guessed again – faced with the strong pound effectively costing people from abroad an extra 16%, they've actually been increasing their prices on top of that, instead of reducing them.

Of 20 most visited places which charge admission, none has cut their prices this year. Only two (Canterbury Cathedral and London's Natural History Museum) have even held their prices steady. All the others have increased their prices, as shown on the following page.

	% increase
Bath's Roman Baths	5.0
Drayton Manor Park	5.3
Alton Towers	5.4
Chessington World of Adventures	5.6
London Zoo	6.2
Chester Zoo	6.3
Legoland	6.7
Windsor Castle	8.0
Madame Tussaud's	8.8
Edinburgh Castle	9.1
Science Museum	9.2
Kew Gardens	11.1
Warwick Castle	11.2
Tower of London	11.8
Thorpe Park	11.9
St Paul's Cathedral	14.3
Granada Studios Tour	15.4
Blackpool Tower	19.0

These increases average 9.5% – against an increase in retail prices generally of only 3%. Our spot checks on lesser-known places suggest that such big price increases are also common among them.

Such steep increases are uncomfortable for all of us. But for foreign visitors, coupled with the pound's strength, they mean that British holiday attractions now carry the equivalent of a 25% price increase. In our view, British attractions are so good that they could easily have shrugged off the effects of the strong pound on its own. But the dogged way that tourism bosses have forced up prices on top of that, in their relentless search to extract the last possible penny from their customers, will undoubtedly put off a great many potential visitors.

All this makes our search for real value in British holidays even more rewarding this year than usual. One direct contribution we can make is with our Discount Vouchers (see **Using the Guide** and tear-out voucher card for details). We asked the places that we reckon are really good value for family outings if they'd co-operate with us in offering our readers a discount. Nearly 250 of them agreed, usually allowing one child free admission for two adults paying.

Our choice as **Family Attraction of the Year** is Chatsworth in Derbyshire – a glorious place in lovely surroundings, with plenty of interest and action for children now, and a good-value family pass.

Heritage Building of the Year is Dover Castle in Kent: this magnificent clifftop fortress brings its story vividly to life, spanning centuries and wars from Roman and Norman times to the present – and again, there's a good-value family ticket.

Garden of the Year is the imaginatively restored Lost Gardens of

Heligan near Mevagissey in Cornwall – a Victorian paradise that's been lovingly reclaimed from wilderness, and has all sorts of secrets and surprises like the living sculptures created there by Cornish artist Sue Hill.

Zoo of the Year is Chester Zoo – Britain's biggest, always with something new, in attractive gardens; it scores particularly highly for the near-natural conditions in which it keeps the animals, with a striking roster of breeding successes.

National Museum of the Year is the National Fishing Heritage Centre in Grimsby (Lincolnshire) – an enthralling and, at times, devastating insight into the trawlerman's tough life.

Living Museum of the Year is Archaeolink at Oyne in East Scotland. This new place is not nearly as big as other memorably lively recreations of the past such as Blists Hill at Ironbridge (Shropshire), the North of England Open-air Museum at Beamish (Northumbria), the Weald and Downland Open-air Museum at Singleton (Sussex), the Black Country Living Museum at Dudley (in our Warwickshire and West Midlands chapter) or the Welsh Folk Museum just outside Cardiff (Wales). But it makes up for this in enthusiasm and vividness, and is thoroughly good fun for children.

Local Museum of the Year is the Judges Lodgings in Presteigne (Wales) – an enthusiastic recent restoration of the judge's living quarters and of the Victorian court, with the important difference from many such places in that you're encouraged to try out the seats, beds and so forth yourself.

Experience of the Year is Big Bob, the London Balloon; on its 500-foot tether by the Thames, it gives an extraordinary view over London – plus the experience of going up in a balloon at a very small fraction of the price of conventional balloon rides.

Tour of the Year is the memorable boat trip deep underground through the floodlit channels of the Speedwell Cavern near Castleton (Derbyshire), ending in a vast vault of a chamber with an eery bottomless pit.

Scariest Ride of the Year is Oblivion at Alton Towers in Staffordshire – 160 seconds of heart-stopping, hurtling terror that screams to its end in a headlong sheer drop.

Children's Outing of the Year is Eureka! in Halifax (Yorkshire); brilliantly designed to catch and hold children's attention, its series of galleries encourages them to explore all sorts of topics and activities – and try their hands at them.

The year has seen some excellent new start-ups, with Lottery money making more of an impact as we approach the Millennium. The National Glass Centre in Sunderland (Northumbria) and the new Ikon Gallery in Birmingham are two of our favourites, and the National Centre for Popular Music in Sheffield (Yorkshire) and Our Dynamic Earth Centre in Edinburgh look extremely promising. Recent years have seen a revolution in aquarium design, turning them from gloomy rows of samey and empty-looking fishtanks into exciting confrontations with dazzling underwater worlds. Europe's biggest has now opened in Ellesmere Port (Cheshire):

Blue Planet – it's our choice as **New Attraction of the Year**.

Remember when bed & breakfast places were the poor relation of the holiday accommodation business? Things have changed dramatically since then. Today, many of the most attractive and comfortable establishments that we include in our **Where to stay** sections are B & Bs. These range from simple cottages through beautifully set farms to wonderful country houses, with as much comfort as the hotels we list – and often more individuality. Outstanding among these are the privately owned individual homes linked together in the Wolsey Lodges scheme. These lovely houses are so charming that Wolsey Lodges are our **Accommodation of the Year**.

For the future, the Government's commitment to more pedestrianisation in London's main tourist areas is very welcome. So is the Government's promise of further funding to support free admission to museums and galleries – the target is that during 1999 the main museums should start admitting children free, that during 2000 they should start admitting pensioners free, and that during 2001 they should stop charging the rest of us.

We have absolutely no doubt that free admission is a duty for publicly funded museums and galleries. It's ridiculous for them to shut away national and other public collections almost as if they're *not* public, as if they are just for privileged scholars to peruse in private – or for people who are prepared to pay. Already, some of those which have started charging in recent years (and seen their visitor numbers plummet as a consequence) are starting to mutter darkly about closing bits off if they have to let people in free, or about opening less frequently. Such threats need firm rebuttal. So we hope that the promised watchdog body, to check that the public gets good value from Government funding of museums and galleries, will make unrestricted access a priority.

In the fight to bring back free admission and to make sure that museums and galleries are giving their public good value, the National Art Collections Fund has played a vital role in focusing official attention on value for money. That is why we name as **Heritage Man of the Year** its Director, David Barrie.

Alisdair Aird

Using the Guide

The Counties

England has been split alphabetically into county chapters. Scotland and Wales have each been covered in single chapters, and London appears immediately before them at the end of England.

Where to stay

In each section, hotels, inns and other places to stay such as farmhouses are listed alphabetically.

The price we show is the total for two people sharing a double or twin-bedded room with its own bathroom, for one night in high season. It includes full English breakfast (unless only continental is available, in which case we say so), VAT and any automatic service charge that we know about. So the price is the total price for a room for two people. We say if dinner is included in this total price. It is included in some of the more remote places, especially in Scotland and Wales, and may also be in some other places where the quality of the food is a main attraction; in these cases, the establishment concerned does not normally offer B & B on its own. In some of the places we list, some or occasionally even all the bedrooms share bathrooms; we say if this is the case.

An asterisk beside the price means that the establishment concerned assured us that that price would hold until the end of summer 1999. Many establishments were unable to give us this assurance; this last year, bedroom prices outside London have been holding very steady, but to be on the safe side it would be prudent to allow for an increase of around 5% by then. In London, allow 10%.

A few hotels will do a bargain break price at weekends even if you're staying for just one night. If so, that's the price we give, and we show this with a **w** beside the price. Many more hotels have very good-value short break prices, especially out of season, if you stay a minimum of at least two nights; if you plan to stay in one area rather than tour around, it's well worth asking if there's a special price for short breaks when you book. Many hotels also offer short-notice bargains which don't appear on their tariffs if they are underbooked on a particular night, so as to fill their rooms even at a discount. So, especially if you are not booking in advance, ask what price they can quote you for that particular night.

If there's a choice of rooms at different prices, we always give the cheapest, and if we know that maybe the back rooms are the quietest or the front ones have the best views or the ones in the new extension are more spacious then we say so. If you want a room with a sea view or whatever, you should always ask specifically for this, and check whether it costs extra.

If the hotel closes for any day or part of the year, we say so. But especially in outlying areas hotels have been known to close at other times if their business is very slack. And this last year or two we've found some go out of business altogether. So don't head off into an area where there are no nearby alternatives without checking by telephone first.

We always mention a restaurant if we know the inn or hotel has one. Note that we always commend food if we have information supporting a positive recommendation. So a bare mention that food is served shouldn't be taken to imply a recommendation of the food.

Where to eat

The price in **bold type** is for one person having a typical three-course restaurant meal with half a bottle of wine, including any automatic service charge. So double it to get a meal for two. The second price, in normal type after the |, is for a more informal single-dish meal, if that's available.

We list any scheduled closing dates. We have found quite a few instances of unscheduled closures in the last year or two, and recommend booking if your plans would be thrown into turmoil by finding a place unexpectedly closed. Moreover, many of the restaurants we list are very popular, and without a booking you may find there's no room for you.

If you want a good meal out in any area, look at the places to stay as well as the restaurants, especially in country areas. When we praise a hotel or inn for its food, that means it's well worth consideration as a place for a good meal out. In some parts of the country, it's in these hotel restaurants that you'll find the best food.

Our brief mentions of places to eat in the text of the **To see and do** sections are based on our own inspections or firm recommendations from readers.

Children

We asked all hotels, restaurants and other places to stay in and eat at which have full entries in the *Guide* whether they allow children. If the entry doesn't mention children, that means the establishment has told us that it welcomes them, with no restrictions. If there are restrictions (either an age limit, or segregated early evening meals for them), we spell these out. We have found that very occasionally establishments turn out in practice to be more restrictive about children than they claim. And of course managements change, and so do their policies. If you are travelling with children, to avoid misunderstandings it's always worth checking ahead that there will be no problem. Please let us know if you find any difference from what we say. Obviously, too, you should bear in mind the character of the hotel or restaurant, as described, and in relation to your own children. While some children might fit perfectly into the atmosphere of a dignified and old-fashioned country house, others might be fractiously ill at ease there – no fun for you, or for the other guests.

Locations

Generally, we list places to see (and hotels and restaurants) under the name of the nearest village or town. We use **BOLD CAPITALS** to name the locality, and **bold type** like this to name the establishment. If the village is so small that you probably wouldn't find it on a road map, we've listed it under the name of the nearest sizeable village or town instead.

Places well known in their own right – famous castles, great houses, for example – are sometimes shown in **BOLD CAPITALS** instead of the locality name.

The maps use the same locality name as the text.

We include places in their true geographical locations – so if a village is actually in Buckinghamshire that's where we list it, even if its postal address is via some town in Oxfordshire.

Days Out

In each chapter except London, we have suggested several full days out, based around places or walks that we recommend in the main text, and which are close enough together to fit well into a day. Most of the itineraries we have suggested make very full days indeed. While a determined and energetic sightseer might well pack everything into one long day, we expect most people would prefer to treat each day out as a sort of mini-menu, picking the things they'd enjoy most and skipping over the rest.

Calendar

Each chapter ends with a list of events we have been able to pin down dates for in 1999; even so, some of these dates are provisional, so best to phone the numbers shown for confirmation if your holiday depends on it.

On Heritage Open Days, not included in the Calendars, many notable buildings will be open to the public which are normally closed. The main date for England and Wales is National Heritage Weekend, 11–12 September, when some 2,000 properties will be open. As we go to press individual details are undecided, but if 1998 was anything to go by they will range from intriguing follies through all sorts of official and office buildings to even the Chancellor of the Exchequer's office. For regional directories write to Civic Trust, 17 Carlton House Terrace, London, SW1Y 5AW with six 2nd-class stamps; for Wales, ring (01222) 484606.

On London Open House Weekend, 18–19 September, there will be free admission to around 100 buildings; in 1998 these included Lloyds of London, Lancaster House, St Pancras Hotel and Bushy House. For more details write to London Open House, PO Box 6984, London, N6 6PY.

The Scottish equivalent will be Doors Open Days – again during September, but precise dates were undecided as we went to press; ring (0141) 221 1466.

Prices and other factual details

Information about opening times and so forth is for 1999. In some cases establishments were uncertain about these when the *Guide* went to press during the late summer of 1998; if so, we say in the text. (And of course there's always the risk of changed plans and unexpected closures.) When we say 'cl Nov–Mar' we mean closed from the beginning of November to the end of March, inclusive; however when we say 'cl Nov–Easter' we mean that the establishment re-opens for Easter.

Where establishments were able to guarantee a price for 1999, we have marked this with an asterisk. In many cases establishments could not rule out an unscheduled price increase, and in these cases – i.e. no asterisk against the price – it's probably prudent to allow for a 5% increase in around April 1999. If you find a significantly different price from that shown, *please let us know.*

Our discount voucher

Places to visit which have a symbol immediately after their name have said they will honour our discount voucher until the end of 1999 (or of course the end of their season, if they close earlier). To get the discount, you must hand one of the vouchers in at the admissions kiosk; there are six vouchers on the tear-out card in the centre of the book. Usually, the discount is that one child will be admitted free for two adults paying the full price. Please check the text for that entry carefully. If there are any variations from the usual, or any special conditions, we spell them out within brackets immediately after the symbol. Please also note the general conditions on the voucher itself.

National Trust

NT after price details means that the property is owned by the National Trust, and that for members of the Trust admission is free. There is a similar arrangement for properties owned by the National Trust for Scotland (NTS); the two Trusts have a reciprocal arrangement, so that members of one may visit the properties of the other free. Membership is therefore well worth while if you are likely to visit more than a very few properties in the year – quite apart from its benefit to the Trusts' valuable work. NT membership is £28 a year (£48 for joint membership); details from National Trust, PO Box 39, Bromley, Kent BR1 1NH; (0181) 315 1111. NTS membership is £26 (£42 for a family); details from National Trust for Scotland, 5 Charlotte Sq, Edinburgh EH2 4DU; (0131) 226 5922.

Friends of Historic Houses

The Friends of Historic Houses Association has NT-style membership offering free entry to 283 historic houses and gardens in private ownership throughout Britain – including a high proportion of those we recommend which aren't NT, English Heritage or any other national equivalent. Membership is £28 a year (£40 for joint membership), so you only have to go to four or five houses and you've got your money back. Details from Historic Houses Association, Heritage House, PO Box 21, Baldock, Herts SG7 5SH; (01462) 896688.

English Heritage

A similar membership scheme now gives free access to those EH properties (about half) which charge admission. It costs £25 (£40 for two adults, £43 for a family). Details from English Heritage Membership Dept, PO Box 1BB, London W1A 1BB; (0171) 973 3000. CADW (for Wales) (01222) 500200 and Historic Scotland (0131) 668 8600 have similar schemes.

Other money savers

In the relevant sections we mention any notable travel bargains and other sightseeing bargains we know of, such as the London for Less discount card scheme – so popular in the four years it's been running that it's now been extended to Edinburgh, Bath and York, where the discount cards are particularly good value. You can save the cost of it almost straightaway, and it covers some of the main attractions rather than just peripheral ones. It's also worth knowing about the Slow Travel Networks, especially if you're young and on a budget. Very popular with backpackers from overseas, these are coach runs linking all the main tourist cities around the country – a £119 ticket gets you the whole circuit, though you can get on or off at any stage for as long as you like – there's no time limit, and the drivers are very flexible; (0171) 373 7737.

Map references

Most place names are given four-figure map references, looking like this: NT4892. The NT means it's in the square labelled NT on the map for that area. The *first* figure, 4, tells you to look along the grid at the top and bottom of the NT square for the figure 4. The *third* figure, 9, tells you to look down the grid at the side of the square to find the figure 9. Imaginary lines drawn down and across the square from these figures should intersect near the locality itself.

The second and fourth figures, the 8 and the 2, are for more precise pinpointing, and are really for use with larger-scale maps such as road atlases or the Ordnance Survey 1:50,000 maps, which use exactly the same map reference system. On the relevant Ordnance Survey map, instead of finding the 4 marker on the top grid you'd find the 48 one; instead of the 9 on the side grid you'd look for the 92 marker. This makes it very easy to locate even the smallest village.

Disabled access

We always ask establishments if they can deal well with disabled people. We mention disabled access if a cautious view of their answers suggests that this is reasonable, though to be on the safe side anyone with a serious mobility problem would be well advised to ask ahead (many establishments made clear that this helped them to make any special arrangements needed). There may well be at least some access even when we or the establishment concerned have not felt it safe to make a blanket recommendation – again, well worth checking ahead. There are, of course, many places where we can't easily make this sort of assessment – particularly the less formal 'attractions' such as churches, bird reserves, waterside walks and viewpoints. In such cases (which should be obvious from the context) the absence of any statement about disabled access doesn't mean that a visit is out of the question, it simply means we have no information about that aspect. We're always grateful to hear of readers' own experiences. An important incidental point: many places told us that they would give free admission to a wheelchair user and companion.

Our web site – new

We are working on a new Internet web site which we hope will be open at least in its first version by the time this book is published. It will use and we hope combine material from *The Good Guide to Britain* and its sister publication *The Good Pub Guide* in a way that gives people who do not yet know the books at least a taste of them. We also hope that we can use it to give readers of the books extra information (and allow them to report quickly to us), and hope to expand and improve the site significantly (for instance with pictures of places to visit or stay in) over the next year or two. You can try the site yourself at www.goodguides.com.

Changes during the year – please tell us

Changes are inevitable during the course of the year. Managements change, and so do their policies. We very much hope that you will find everything just as we say. But if you find anything different, please let us know, using the report card in the middle of the book, the forms at the end of the book, or just a letter. For letters posted in Britain you don't need a stamp: the address is *The Good Guide to Britain*, FREEPOST TN1569, WADHURST, E. Sussex TN5 7BR.

Reports

This *Guide* depends very heavily indeed on readers reporting back to it. In that sense it's very much a collaborative venture: and the more people that send us reports, the better the book will be. So please do help us by telling us about places you think should be added to the book, or removed from it, or even just confirming that places still deserve their entry. We try to answer all letters (though there may be a delay – and between the end of May and October we put all letters aside until after the end of the hectic editorial rush). People who help us do get a special offer discount price on the next edition. There's a note on the sort of information we need at the back of the book, with report forms; and a tear-out report card in the middle of the book.

SYMBOLS

We have used the same symbols in the text and on the maps to pick out all the main types of places to visit. Though you don't need to pay any attention to the symbols, you can if you like use them to scan the text or a map quickly, to see what castles, say, or gardens a particular area has. These are what we have used the symbols to denote (they are repeated on the last page of this book so that you can refer to them quickly):

★ Attractive village or town
Interesting house – anything from an intimate cottage to the stateliest of stately homes
Castle, ruined abbey or other romantic ruin
More or less archaeological site such as Roman remains, Neolithic stone circles, early medieval maze, Iron Age hill fort
Church, cathedral, minster, inhabited abbey
Watermill, windmill or other type of mill
Nature conservation, including wildlife reserves
Bird reserve, bird centre (including falconry)
Zoo, safari park, anywhere keeping exotic animals
Farm animals, farm park, country centre, farm museum; also a vineyard
Anything to do with fish, including both fishing and aquariums
Butterfly park
Garden, plant centre, arboretum, landscaped park
Walk
Wood, forest
Viewpoint
Orchard, fruit farm, pick-your-own
Cave, cavern
Museum
Art gallery, sculpture park, notable painting collections
Boat museum
Air museum
Motor museum
Open-air museum (including industrial museums)
Heritage centre such as Jorvik Centre in York
Steam locomotives, railway
Boat trip
Amusement park, theme park, leisure park, permanent funfair
Craft centre or craft workshop: potters, glass-blowers, weavers, etc
Factory visit (including power station visits and breweries)
! Anything odd, unusual or decidedly different
London Underground
Surface rail – former British Rail
Our special offer discount (see details above and on the tear-out card in the middle of the book)

Some places embrace all sorts of different attractions in just the one locality. With these, instead of cluttering the maps with all sorts of different symbols, we show a ✪ on the map.

On the maps, a bed symbol indicates recommended places to stay; a knife-and-fork symbol indicates recommended places to eat.

Bedfordshire

Some first-class family days out.

Woburn Abbey deserves its fame. This constantly developing complex has plenty to keep all sorts of people interested, and more than enough for a day visit – from the exciting safari park to the quieter glories of the abbey and its collections. Whipsnade also makes an outstanding family day out. On an altogether smaller scale, Woodside Farm at Slip End and Toddington Manor have great family appeal. The attractive village of Old Warden is a good focus for an outing, with an interesting collection of veteran aircraft and a romantic wilderness garden. The Cecil Higgins gallery in Bedford has an exceptional collection of paintings, and the Stockwood craft museum, near Luton, is a bit different. There are some charming villages to stroll through.

Dunstable Downs have decent walking and remarkable views, though otherwise the county's scenery is generally not memorable. The relative flatness is a boon to cyclists; a tourist board leaflet details good circular cycle routes. You can get this from local tourist information centres, which stand out in this county for their wide range of helpful information. Another good leaflet is their timetable for 'Step This Way', a year-round programme of weekend activities and guided walks through some of the prettier villages and countryside.

Where to stay

FLITWICK TL0335 **Flitwick Manor** *Church Rd, Flitwick MK45 1AE (01525) 712242* **£160,** plus special breaks; 15 comfortable, thoughtfully decorated rms. 17th-c country house surrounded by interesting gardens; with a log fire in the entrance hall, comfortable lounge and library, and a smart restaurant with fine French wines and delicious food using lots of fresh fish and home-grown and local produce; tennis, putting, croquet; children over 12 in evening restaurant; limited disabled access.

LEIGHTON BUZZARD SP9225 **Swan** *High St, Leighton Buzzard LU7 7EA (01525) 372148* **£59.50w;** 38 rms. Handsome Georgian coaching inn with a pleasant lounge, relaxed bars, and an attractive restaurant with English cooking.

SANDY TL1749 **Highfield Farm** *Great North Rd, Sandy SG19 2AQ (01767) 682332* **£50;** 6 rms (2 in former stables), 4 with own bthrm. Neatly kept whitewashed house set well away from the A1 and surrounded by arable farmland; friendly and helpful owner, an open fire in the comfortable sitting room, and communal breakfasts in the pleasant dining room.

WOBURN SP9433 **Bell** *Woburn, Milton Keynes, Bucks MK17 9QD (01525) 290280* **£70,** plus wknd breaks; 24 attractively decorated rms, some with antiques. Lovely old inn, carefully restored, with beamed restaurant, popular bar, and good food; also, residents' own lounge and bar.

Please let us know what you think of places in the *Guide*. Use the report forms at the back of the book or simply write us a letter.

To see and do

Bedfordshire Family Attraction of the Year

WOBURN SP9632 **Woburn Safari Park** An especially entertaining new feature at this superior park – attractively set in 300 acres of the grounds of Woburn Abbey – is the walk-through monkey enclosure, where 22 friendly and inquisitive squirrel monkeys clamber about all over the place; luckily they provide special monkey-proof bags at the entrance to protect belongings from burrowing fingers. The highlight of any visit is still the drive-through safari, but pick your day carefully: readers who've visited on bank holidays have found themselves in traffic jams so slow-moving it's ruined their enjoyment, so it's probably best to avoid coming then if you can. At quieter times, the excitement of seeing lions and tigers through your own car windscreen can be hard to beat, but don't expect the animals to sit by the side of the road waiting for you to drive past; you may not see exactly what you'd hoped to first time round. Children love spotting rhinos, giraffes and the other usual suspects, but keep your eyes skinned and the guidebook handy and you may catch a glimpse of something a bit different, like the shy but distinctively marked bongo. Rather than go down the theme park road, Woburn has kept most of its subsidiary features wildlife-related, so once out of the car, the mixture of hands-on animal attractions in the Wild World leisure section should easily fill a big chunk of the day for most families. You can feed elephants over the fence of their enclosure, go right up to the pygmy goats, or watch lively penguin feeding and sealion shows. The walk-through aviary at Rainbow Landing is fun: carry a nectar cup in your hand and multicoloured lorikeets will swoop down for a taste. A well constructed indoor adventure playground is shaped like Noah's Ark, and there's a separate play area for younger children – not to mention swan-shaped boats gliding across the lake. Several features are under cover, but you'll definitely get more out of it on a dry day, especially in school holidays when there are extra events and activities for children. Meals, snacks, shop, disabled access; cl wkdys Nov–Feb; (01525) 290407; £10.50 (£7 children, free for under-3s).

AMPTHILL PARK TL0239 Former hunting grounds of Henry VIII, surprisingly heathy but landscaped by Capability Brown, with lovely trees and a water-lily lake. The Chequers, towards nearby Houghton Conquest, does decent pub lunches.

BEDFORD TL0449 Despite its long history this is really a straightforward modern town. There are decent riverside gardens and a few nice buildings, and the Corn Exchange (St Paul's Sq) has a bronze bust of Glenn Miller, who made many of his morale-boosting broadcasts from here. The very rewarding **Cecil Higgins Art Gallery & Museum** (Castle Close) is the most outstanding attraction, boasting the kind of paintings most other museums can only dream about, inc great works by Turner, Constable, Rembrandt, Matisse, Picasso and Dali. The Victorian mansion's beautifully furnished rooms make it look as if the family that lived here have just popped out; lots of thought has gone into the displays, and nothing seems unnatural or out of place. An award-winning extension has collections of local lace, glass and ceramics. Snacks, shop, disabled access; cl am Sun, all Mon (exc pm bank hols), 25–26 Dec, 1 Jan, Good Fri; (01234) 211222; free. The town **museum** next door is more traditional; cl am Sun, all Mon, and 25 Dec; free. John Bunyan lived around here for most of his life and the **museum** (Mill St) dedicated to his life has significantly expanded, moving into a new building in the grounds of the church where he was minister. Snacks, shop, disabled access; cl Mon, Dec–Mar; (01234 213722); free. There's also a trail around Bunyan-related sites in the town. Lincolns (Goldington Green) is an interesting old place for lunch; Nicholls (Embankment) is more lively.

BROMHAM TL0050 **Bromham Mill** (Bridge End) Picturesque, working 17th-c watermill on the River Ouse, with summer milling demonstrations, and a gallery with local art and crafts. Snacks, shop, disabled access to ground floor only; open Sun, pm Weds–Sat, and bank hols, Mar–Oct; (01234) 824330; £1.50. The Swan is a popular food pub.

COLMWORTH TL1160 **Bushmead Priory** Ruins of a late 12th-c Augustinian priory, well preserved, with medieval wall paintings and a timber-framed roof. Open wknds and bank hols, July and Aug; (01234) 376614; £1.75.

DUNSTABLE DOWNS TL0019 Very popular with kite-fliers and gliders at weekends or in summer. There's a countryside centre (cl Mon and winter wkdys), 2 car parks, and lots of space to run around. There are great views from a spectacular escarpment path, amid ancient grasslands, and the downs can be linked to a circuit incorporating Whipsnade village and the nearby Tree Cathedral – the best walk in Beds. **Five Knolls** here is an important Bronze Age burial mound, excavated by Agatha Christie's husband Sir Mortimer Wheeler, and Gerald Dunning. The Horse & Jockey (on the A5183) is a good family food pub. Dunstable itself has little to detain visitors, though the remarkable priory church incorporates part of a 12th-c abbey (where Henry VIII's first marriage was dissolved). The Old Sugarloaf (High St) is useful for lunch.

ELSTOW TL0546 The county's finest village, with a splendid core of fine old timbered houses by the green. John Bunyan was born nearby and baptised in the attractive church, which has an unusual detached tower and a 'Pilgrims Progress' window. The **Moot Hall**, an outstanding brick and timber medieval market house, has a collection of Bunyan's works and a reconstruction of his writing room. Shop; cl am, all Mon (exc bank hols) and Fri, and Nov–Mar; £1. The Three Tuns at Biddenham is the closest good place for lunch.

FELMERSHAM SP9957 A lovely church by a medieval tithe barn, a fine old thatched pub and some other attractive old houses, with the River Ouse below. Nearby Pavenham is also pretty, with a stroll down to the river.

HARROLD SP9456 Pretty riverside village with 13th-c church and packhorse bridge, and an early 19th-c lock-up on the village green. Nearby, the **Harrold-Odell Country Park** is highly recommended for birdwatching; it's especially good for waterfowl, particularly in winter, and Bedfordshire County Council publish a circular route incorporating 3 waymarked walks up to 13 miles long from here. Snacks, disabled access; visitor centre cl Mon and Tues (exc bank hols); (01234) 720016; free. The Magpie is useful for lunch, and, in Odell, so is the Bell.

LEIGHTON BUZZARD RAILWAY SP9224 (Billington Rd) Fine collection of over 50 locomotives from around the world, with a fleet of 11 steamtrains to trundle you through gently varied countryside. The

Days Out

Fresh air and animals: Walk on Dunstable Downs; Tree Cathedral, Whipsnade; lunch at the Bell, Studham (or picnic at Whipsnade); Whipsnade Wild Animal Park or Woodside Farm, Slip End.

Woburn – and more: Toddington Manor; lunch at the Rose & Crown, Ridgmont, the Red Lion at Milton Bryan, or in Woburn; Woburn Abbey and deer park, or Woburn Safari Park.

Bedfordshire's quieter side: Elstow; Bromham Mill; lunch at the Swan, Bromham, or the Bell in Odell; stroll in Harrold-Odell Country Park.

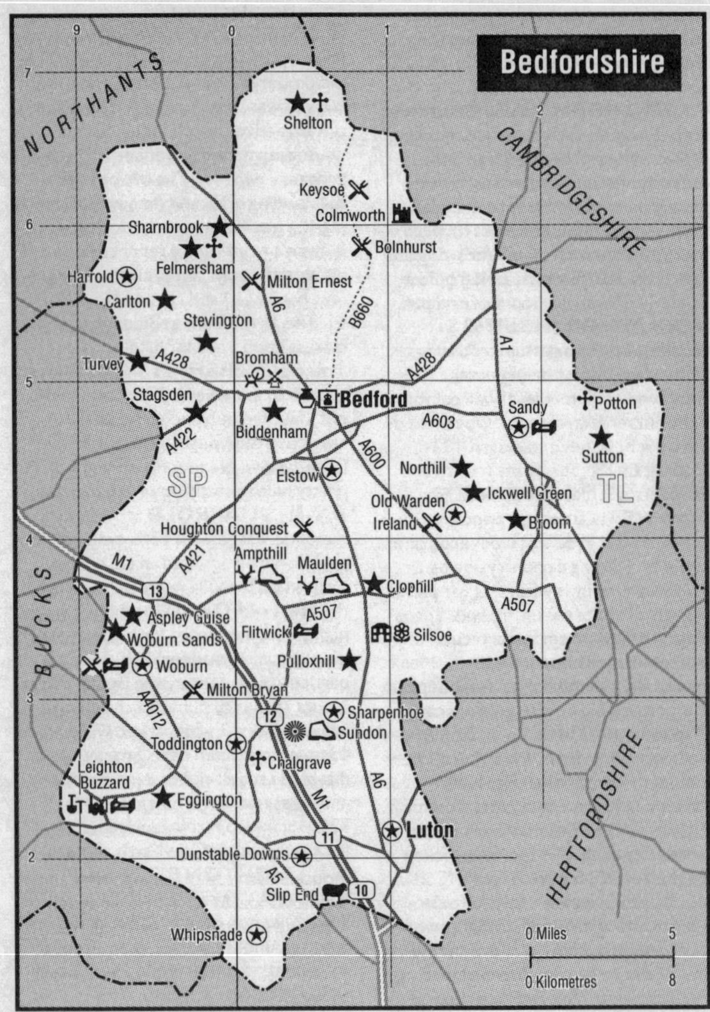

Stonehenge Works terminus has industrial heritage displays. Snacks, shop, disabled access; open Sun and bank hols Easter–Sept, plus Weds Jun–Aug, Tues, Thurs and Sat in Aug, and wknds in Dec; (01525) 373888 for timetable; £4.50. The Globe in Linslade is a nicely set, canalside food pub, with pleasant nearby walks.

LUTON TL0820 The town of Luton itself has few attractions for visitors, but **Stockwood Craft Museum and Gardens** (Stockwood Country Park, Farley Hill) is ideal for a restrained and uncomplicated day out. Besides a museum there are several lovely period garden settings (inc a 17th-c knot garden and a Victorian cottage garden), a refreshingly witty sculpture garden, and an adjacent children's play area. Also here, the **Mossman Collection** of restored old vehicles includes plenty of vintage cars. Pony and cart rides through the park at weekends. Snacks, shop, disabled access; cl Mon (exc bank hols), and wkdys Nov–Mar; (01582) 738714; free.

MAULDEN WOOD TL0538

Ancient woodland with a picnic site, marked walks and muntjac deer.

★ ✝ ❀ ⌂ **OLD WARDEN** TL1343 Well worth a visit in its own right, this attractive village was built deliberately quaintly in the 19th c. The village church has a number of European wood carvings, inc some from the private chapel of Henry VIII's wife, Anne of Cleves. Most people are drawn here by the **Shuttleworth Collection** ⊡ of nearly 40 working historic aeroplanes covering the early history of aviation, from a 1909 Blériot to a 1942 Spitfire, in purpose-built hangars on a classic grass aerodrome. Several exhibits are the only surviving examples of their type, and it's worth trying to go on one of the days when some of them are flown (usually the 1st Sun of the month and Sat evenings, May–Oct). Meals, snacks, shop, disabled access; cl 2 wks at Christmas; (01767) 627288; £6, higher charges on flying days. The **Swiss Garden** nearby is an early 19th-c romantic wilderness garden, with pretty vistas and colourful trees and shrubs – a nice place for a stroll. Meals, snacks, shop, disabled access; open Sun and bank hols Jan–Oct, plus pm daily Mar–Sept; (01234) 228671; £2.50. New entrance, now approached from Old Warden Park via **Shuttleworth Mansion** which will be open some days in the summer. The Hare & Hounds is a useful food pub.

❀ ♈ ✈ ♧ ⌂ **SANDY** TL1847 **The Lodge** This elegant, 19th-c, Tudor-style house is the RSPB's HQ, and isn't open to the public, but is surrounded by formal gardens, a newly developed wildlife garden, and a nature reserve covering 106 acres of heath, lake and woodland, with plenty of birds, animals and trails spread all over. Perfect for watching rare species undisturbed, but even if birdspotting's not your thing, this is a relaxing place to wander through, especially nice in spring when the woods are carpeted with bluebells. Snacks, shop, some disabled access; cl 25–26 Dec; (01767) 680551; £2.50 (free for RSPB members). The Locomotive nearby is handy for lunch, and in the town the King's Arms is good.

❀ ♧ ⊓ ❀ ⌂ **SHARPENHOE CLAPPERS** TL0629 Steep-sided downland with chalkland flora and butterflies, crowned with a fine beechwood and Iron Age hill fort; the area is owned by the NT and is laced with paths.

★ ✝ **SHELTON** TL0368 Pretty little cottages, Hall and rectory grouped around the quite delightful church, with 13th-c decoration inside, wall paintings, and a 14th-c font on 7 legs.

⌂ ❀ **SILSOE** TL0935 **Wrest Park** (off the A6) Inspired by French châteaux, the 19th-c house has several ornately plastered rooms open to visitors, but it's the enormous formal gardens that are the main attraction. They go on for over 90 acres and give a good example of the changes in gardening styles between 1700 and 1850. Perhaps best of all is the Great Garden, designed by the Duke of Kent between 1706 and 1740 and later modified by Capability Brown, with lovely views down the water to the baroque pavilion. Snacks, shop; open wknds and bank hols Apr–Sept; (01525) 860152; £2.95. The George Hotel is a friendly place for family lunches.

♞ **SLIP END** TL0718 **Woodside Farm and Wildlife Park** ⊡ (Mancroft Rd) Very good for children, with plenty of friendly and feedable farmyard animals, a playground and tractor rides; you can handle rabbits and collect eggs straight from the hen house. Also rare breeds, poultry and wildfowl, and a farm shop. They sell pets and poultry, along with all the accessories you'll need to look after them. Meals, snacks, shop, disabled access; cl Sun, 25–26 Dec, 1 Jan; (01582) 841044; £2.30. The Farmer's Boy at Kensworth, an appealing family-minded pub, is not far.

❀ ⌂ **SUNDON HILLS COUNTRY PARK** TL0528 Sheep-cropped downland with good views and marked walks (some quite steep).

★ **SUTTON** TL2247 Notable for its picturesque, steeply humped packhorse bridge, looking more like a part of Devon or Derbys; ironically, cars have to use a more ancient crossing, the shallow ford beside it. A decent pub nearby is named after John o' Gaunt, the village's former owner.

TODDINGTON MANOR TL0029 (Park Rd) Readers warmly recommend this well set place for its rare breeds centre and gardens, with pleached lime walk, herbaceous borders, and herb and rose gardens. Children are given treasure hunt sheets, and nets and buckets for pond-dipping. Lovely woodland walks, vintage tractor collection, and weekend cricket matches in front of the house. Snacks, shop, plant centre, disabled access; open Weds–Sat May–July, wknds in Aug; (01525) 873924; £3.75. The village green is attractive, there are unusual carvings on the church, and decent food is to be found at the Bedford Arms.

! WHIPSNADE TL0017 **Whipsnade Wild Animal Park** Plenty of space for the animals at this splendid 600-acre zoo; the elephant paddock is reckoned to be Europe's biggest. Altogether 2,500 creatures roam the beautiful downs-edge parkland, from tigers, lions, giraffes and rhinos to monkeys, wallabies, peafowl and Chinese water deer. You'll need a full day to see everything, and it's too big to get round completely on foot – you can drive round the perimeter road and walk from various stopping-points, or there's an open-topped tour bus, but the best way of getting around is on their railway, which takes you past herds of Asian animals. Younger visitors enjoy the elephant walk, penguin feed, and sealion demonstrations, and there's a hands-on Children's Farm, as well as indoor Discovery Centre with dwarf crocodiles, snakes and spiders. Play areas include a bear-themed maze. Meals, snacks, shop, disabled access; cl Nov–Jan; (0990) 200 123; £8.90. Tucked just off the village road is the **Tree Cathedral**, trees planted in the plan of a cathedral in the 1930s to create a most unusual war memorial. The Bell at Studham is the best nearby place for lunch; the Old Hunter's Lodge is also very handy.

★ **WOBURN** SP9632 **Woburn Abbey and Deer Park** One of England's grandest stately homes – everything from the lovely English and French 18th-c furniture to the splendid range of silver seems to have the edge over most assemblages elsewhere, and the art collection, taking in sumptuous paintings by Rembrandt, Van Dyck and Gainsborough, is outstanding (where else can you see 21 Canalettos in just one room?). The 3,000 acres of surrounding parkland were landscaped by Humphrey Repton, and today are home to several varieties of deer. Swans, ducks and other waterfowl on the lake, and a newly developed aviary with free-flying budgies (a particular enthusiasm of a previous Duke of Bedford); also a pottery and huge antiques centre. Meals, snacks, shop, disabled access by arrangement; cl Nov–Dec and wkdys Oct and Jan–Mar; (01525) 290666; £7.50 (the antiques centre is 20p extra). *See separate Family Panel on p. 2 for adjoining* **Woburn Safari Park**. The crowds come to Woburn for these 2 major attractions, but it's worth a look in its own right, with some lovely 18th-c houses and decent antique shops. The Red Lion at Milton Bryan has good-value food.

★ **Other attractive villages** include Aspley Guise SP9335, spacious Biddenham TL0249 (nice 12th-c church), Broom TL1743, Clophill TL0837, Eggington SP9525, Northill TL1546, Sharnbrook SP9959 (interesting specialist shops), Pulloxhill TL0634 and Turvey SP9452 (the

We welcome reports from readers

This *Guide* depends on readers' reports. Do help us if you can – in return, we offer a discount on the next edition to people who've helped us with reports for it. Tell us what you think about places already in it, and anything extra you think we should say about them. And send us your ideas for inclusion in the next edition: places to visit, eat at or stay in, attractive drives or walks, maybe even unusual interesting shops you know of. Use the card in the middle, the report forms at the end, or just write – no stamp needed: *The Good Guide to Britain*, FREEPOST TN1569, Wadhurst, E Sussex TN5 7BR.

interesting church has Saxon origins); all have pubs we can recommend for lunch. Carlton SP9555 and (with good wooded walks nearby) Woburn Sands SP9235 are also pleasant. Ickwell Green TL1545 nr Northill is well worth a look, too, with its colourful thatched houses around a broad green; Stagsden SP9849 is attractive, with thatched houses and strolls in the woods nearby. Stevington SP9853 has a handsomely restored windmill, and a holy well opposite the handsome church.

† Other **churches** worth investigating include Chalgrave TL0027 and Potton TL2449 (it's the gravestones that are worth the visit).

Where to eat

BOLNHURST TL0859 **Olde Plough** *(01234) 376274* Pretty 15th-c cottage, with a comfortably spacious lounge bar, woodburning stove in the public bar, dining room and upstairs restaurant; enjoyable daily specials, well kept real ale, and a pretty garden. **£18.65**|£6.50.

HOUGHTON CONQUEST TL0441 **Knife & Cleaver** *(01234) 740387* Civilised, 17th-c dining pub with a welcoming bar, blazing winter fire, attentive service, and stylish bar food (lovely fresh fish and shellfish); 24 good wines by the glass, well kept real ales, good choice of whiskies, no smoking conservatory restaurant, and a neat garden; cl pm Sun, 27–30 Dec; disabled access. **£29**|£6.25.

IRELAND TL1341 **Black Horse** *(01462) 811398* Busy, attractively refurbished, beamed pub in a lovely setting; interesting, good-value food (fresh fish towards end of week), welcoming staff; disabled access. **£20**|£5.

KEYSOE TL0762 **Chequers** *(01234) 708678* Friendly and unpretentious village local with 2 comfortably modernised beamed bars; consistently good food in the vegetarian choices, and, on Friday, fresh fish dishes; well kept beer; cl Tues; disabled access. **£16.25**|£6.

MILTON BRYAN SP9730 **Red Lion** *(01525) 210044* Relaxed, comfortable pub with a spotless, beamed bar area; fresh flowers, good, popular food inc quite a few fresh fish dishes and very good-value OAP weekday lunches; real ales, pretty hanging baskets and plenty of seats on both terrace and lawn. **£19.75**|£7.50.

MILTON ERNEST TL0156 **Strawberry Tree** *Radwell Rd (01234) 823633* 18th-c thatched cottage with low beams and open fires; very good, interesting lunchtime and evening food (using the best ingredients) from a sensibly short menu in the no smoking dining room, and very popular afternoon teas, too; cl Mon, Tues, all Jan; disabled access. **£40**|£10.

WOBURN SP9433 **Paris House** *(01525) 290692* Lovely black and white timbered house in Woburn's deer park, serving enjoyable Anglo-French food with exotic touches and a mainly French wine list; a neat garden for pre-meal drinks; cl Mon, Feb; disabled access. **£49**|£15

Special thanks to M and J Back, Anna Power, Michael Sargent.

Bedfordshire Calendar

Some of these dates were provisional as we went to press. Please check information with the telephone numbers provided.

FEBRUARY

16 **Toddington** Shrove Tuesday Ceremony: *just before midday* children gather on Conger Hill, with ears to the ground listening for the witch frying her pancakes (01582) 471012

27 **Bedford** Festival of Music, Speech and Drama – *till 6 Mar* (01234) 720481

MARCH

28 **Leighton Buzzard** Teddy Bears' Outing at Leighton Buzzard Railway (01525) 373888

APRIL

2 **Leighton Buzzard** Easter Steam Weekend at Leighton Buzzard Railway – *till Mon 5* (01525) 373888

3 **Whipsnade** Easter Weekend at the Wild Animal Park – *till Mon 5 (01582) 872171*

24 **Silsoe** St George's Day Festival at Wrest Park – *till Sun 25 (01767) 682728*

MAY

1 **Whipsnade** Steam Event at the Wild Animal Park – *till Mon 3* (01582) 872171

13 **Dunstable Carnival** (01582) 607895; **Ickwell Green** May Festival (01767) 640588; **Wilden** May Day Celebration (01234) 77185

34 **Luton** Open Garden at Seal Point, Wendover Way (01582) 611567

30 **Bedford** Combined Athletics Union Championship at the Athletic Stadium – *till Mon 31* (01234) 351115

31 **Luton** Carnival (01582) 876005

JUNE

1 **Luton** Open Garden *(see 4 May for details)*

13 **Luton** Festival of Transport at Stockwood Park (01582) 876083

16 **Ampthill** Music Festival – *till Sun 27* (01525) 714049

19 **Flitwick** Carnival (0171) 250 9920

26 **Luton** Festival at Lewsey Park (01582) 402034

JULY

2 **Cranfield** Air Rally and Exhibition at Cranfield Airfield – *till Sun 4* (01273) 461616

4 **Bedford** 'Lazy Sunday': free festival with live bands, children's entertainment, street theatre and circus (01234) 360601

6 **Luton** Open Garden *(see 4 May for details)*

11 **Bromham** Show (01234) 825684

Bedfordshire Calendar (cont.)

AUGUST

1 **Leighton Buzzard** Model Event at Leighton Buzzard Railway (01525) 373888
3 **Luton** Open Garden *(see 4 May for details)*
7 **Bedford** Proms in the Park (01234) 269099; **Whipsnade** Teddy Bear Weekend at the Wild Animal Park – *till Sun 8* (01582) 872171
28 **Bedford** British Athletic League Cup Final at the Athletic Stadium – *till Sun 29* (01234) 351115; **Biggleswade** Bedfordshire Millennium Celebration: the last 1,000 years of the county, inc re-enactments, re-created village square, Bedfordshire at war and lots more at Shuttleworth Park – *till Mon 30* (01767) 602499
28 **Kempston** Fun Day (01234) 300848
30 **Biddenham** Show at St James School Field (01234) 211668

SEPTEMBER

4 **Leighton Buzzard** Autumn Steam-up at Leighton Buzzard Railway – *till Sun 5* (01525) 373888; **Woburn** Craft Show at the Abbey – *till Sun 5* (01525) 290666
7 **Luton** Open Garden *(see 4 May for details)*
11 **Luton** Country Show at Stockwood Park – *till Sun 12* (01582) 876005
17 **Bedford** Bunyan Fair – *till Sat 18* (01234) 267422

OCTOBER

6 **Bedford** Beer Festival at the Corn Exchange – *till Sat 9* (01234) 364796

NOVEMBER

5 **Luton** Fireworks at Popes Meadow (01582) 876083
6 **Podington** Fireworks and Drag Racing at Santa Pod Raceway – *till Sun 7* (01234) 782828
24 **Bedford** Christmas Lights Switch On (01234) 215226

DECEMBER

9 **Bedford** Victorian Fair – *till Sat 11* (01234) 215226

BERKSHIRE

Interesting days out; quieter countryside in the west – good relaxing breaks.

Legoland has quickly established itself as a favourite day out for children; they also really enjoy the Look Out discovery park in Bracknell. Furthermore, there are quite a few lower-key places for enjoyable family outings. The county's greatest draw is Windsor Castle, and the town has plenty to fill a day or more's busy sightseeing. For a complete change of pace nearby, Dorney Court is a fine ancient building with the deep charm of a proper family home.

The main tourist places are in the east of the county. This also includes some gloriously lush scenery. Windsor Great Park, the Savill Garden and the Valley Gardens have memorable vistas, and can be returned to again and again without exhausting their possibilities. Between Marlow and Henley is perhaps the finest stretch of the Thames, with easy towpath sauntering and plenty of boating activity. In holiday time the river does get very busy, but is idyllic on a fine early summer or autumn afternoon.

In the west, the innovative Wyld Court Rainforest, at Hampstead Norreys, and Beale Park, at Lower Basildon, are most rewarding for anyone with an interest in wildlife. This part of Berkshire has quite a good range of walking possibilities, from gentle strolls to long hikes, and with some comfortable and attractive places to stay in, as well as plenty of decent food, it makes for a relaxing short break.

Its rolling downland and civilised small villages linked by pleasant minor roads make for attractive drives – the Lambourn Valley and Lambourn Downs, the B4009 and B4494, and the back road from Pangbourne to Aldworth are among the best.

Besides the county's great racecourses, horse-lovers can choose between opposite ends of the speed scale, at Lambourn and at Littlewick Green. The rural life museum on the edge of Reading is one of the best in Britain.

Where to stay

BRAY SU9079 **Monkey Island** *Bray, Maidenhead SL6 2EE (01628) 23400* ***£149,** plus special breaks; 26 comfortable rms. Set on an island in the River Thames and reached only by footbridge or boat, this 18th-c former fishing lodge, built by the 3rd Duke of Marlborough, is made up of 2 smart white buildings surrounded by beautifully kept gardens with peacocks, ducks and geese; some fine original features, inc an original painted ceiling in the lounge showing monkeys in 18th-c sporting gear; helpful, friendly staff, and enjoyable food in the restaurant overlooking the water; cl lunchtime 25 Dec for 3 wks.

EAST ILSLEY SU4981 **Crown & Horns** *East Ilsley, Newbury RG16 0LH (01635) 281205* **£48;** 8 rms, some in converted stable block. Lively and friendly old pub in horse-training country; with beamed rooms, a pretty paved stable yard, interesting bar food, and lots of whiskies.

HAMSTEAD MARSHALL SU4165 **White Hart** *Hamstead Marshall, Newbury RG20 0HW (01488) 658201* **£75;** 6 beamed, comfortable rms in converted barn. Civilised country inn in a quiet village; with a log fire open on both sides in the L-shaped bar, a partly no smoking restaurant, good Italian food (the daily specials are the thing to go for), decent Italian wines, and friendly service; also, a very pleasant walled garden; cl 25–26 Dec, 1 Jan, 2 wks summer.

HUNGERFORD SU3368 **Bear** *Charnham St, Hungerford RG17 0EL (01488) 682512* ***£93w,** plus special breaks; 41 comfortable, attractive rms with antiques and beams in older ones. Civilised hotel with fresh flowers, open fires, and a stuffed bear; decent food in the bar, and a relaxing restaurant; disabled access.

HUNGERFORD SU3368 **Marshgate Cottage** *Marsh Lane, Hungerford RG17 0QX (01488) 682307* ***£48.50;** 9 individually decorated rms. Family-run little hotel backing on to the Kennet & Avon Canal; with residents' lounge and bar, and seats overlooking water and marsh, and more in the sheltered courtyard; plenty to see nearby; children over 5; disabled access.

LAMBOURN SU3278 **Lodge Down** *Lambourn, Newbury RG17 7BJ (01672) 540304* **£45;** 3 rms. Country house in lovely grounds with views over the gallops of Lambourn Downs; open fire in the spacious, elegant sitting room, friendly owners, and good breakfasts around a communal table; visits to stables on request; tennis court and swimming pool.

MAIDENHEAD SU8783 **Beehive Manor** *Cox Green Lane, Maidenhead SL6 3ET (01628) 20980* ***£60;** 3 rms. Carefully preserved Tudor house run by 2 sisters; with huge beams, linenfold panelling, stained glass, latticed windows, and a sheltered garden; home-baked bread for breakfast, eaten around a big, polished, communal table, and light suppers by arrangement; cl Christmas; children over 12.

MAIDENHEAD SU8783 **Fredricks Hotel & Restaurant** *Shoppenhangers Rd, Maidenhead SL6 2PZ (01628) 635934* **£198;** 37 luxurious rms, many with garden views. Smart, red brick hotel close to the centre and next to the greens of Maidenhead Golf Club; champagne on arrival in reception, with its stylishly modern chandeliers and marble waterfall; plush cocktail bar, fine professional cooking in the luxurious restaurant, and good, formal service from the long-standing staff; lush wintergarden overlooking the gardens; cl Christmas–New Year; disabled access.

PANGBOURNE SU6376 **Copper** *Church Rd, Pangbourne, Reading RG8 7AR (0118) 984 2244* **£90w;** 22 rms, most overlooking gardens. Timbered and creeper-covered coaching inn, with a warm and relaxing atmosphere, comfortable sitting room, smart lounge, and good food and wine; disabled access.

STREATLEY SU5980 **Swan Diplomat** *High St, Streatley, Reading RG8 9HR (01491) 873737* **£86,** plus special breaks; 46 attractive rms, many overlooking the water. Well run, friendly riverside hotel with comfortable, relaxing lounges, and consistently good food in the attractive restaurant; popular leisure club, restored Magdalen College barge, and a flower-filled garden; disabled access.

WINDSOR SU9676 **Oakley Court** *Windsor Rd, Water Oakley, Windsor SL4 5UR (01753) 609988* **£150,** plus special breaks; 115 spacious, individually furnished rms. Splendid Victorian country-house hotel in 35 acres of grounds by the Thames, with a 9-hole golf course, croquet lawn, tennis, fishing, boating, and health club; log fires in the elegant lounges, a panelled library, and very good cooking in the relaxed bistro and more formal restaurant; has featured in 200 films – notably the St Trinians series and Hammer House Dracula films; disabled access.

YATTENDON SU5574 **Royal Oak** *The Square, Yattendon, Newbury RG16 0UF (01635) 201325* **£129,** plus special breaks; 5 pretty rms. Elegant and comfortable old inn in a peaceful village; fresh flowers and a log fire in the prettily decorated panelled bar, a relaxed atmosphere, interesting modern food, real ales, and a good wine list; also, a pleasant walled garden.

To see and do

BERKSHIRE Family Attraction of the Year

☺ **WINDSOR** SU9676 **Legoland** (B3022, 2m SW of the town centre; shuttle-bus from the station at Windsor and Eton Riverside, which connects with London Waterloo) Now firmly established as one of the most visited attractions in the country (and our favourite Berkshire place for families for the third year running), this truly imaginative theme park just about manages to live up to its considerable hype – especially if you're under 12. Particularly impressive is that, far from resting on its laurels, it continues to add new rides and attractions, including this year a delightful roller-coaster, with dragon-themed cars flying through a knight's castle, and the more sophisticated Mindstorms Centre, where children over 9 can create robotic models (entrance by timed ticket, so best to sort out your slot as soon as you arrive). Don't be put off by the price: comparatively speaking it's not bad value, as you'll need a full day to stand even a chance of seeing everything. If you'd prefer not to rush, a 2-day ticket is only £3.50 extra. As at any theme park you can expect a fair amount of standing in line, though you can avoid this as much as possible by booking in advance – you'll miss the long wait at the entrance, and be able to plan beforehand which bits you most want to see (essential for getting the best out of the place). It also removes the risk of not seeing anything at all – they close the doors when they feel there are enough visitors. The park is divided into several differently themed areas (all built with those amazingly versatile coloured building bricks), with the driving school at Lego Traffic one of the most popular; children who best negotiate the simulated roads and traffic systems earn their own driving licence. The Wild Woods is ideal for lively boys: its Rat Trap is a first-class labyrinth of wooden walkways, climbing nets and slides, and the Pirate Falls is an excellent steep water-chute. This section gets very busy mid-afternoon, so it's a good idea to head here straight away in the morning. Younger children enjoy the colourful Duplo Gardens, while My Town has some jolly fairground rides, a circus, and some splendidly put-together scenes and tableaux in the Explorer's Institute. Best of all though is Miniland, where 20 million Lego bricks charmingly re-create Amsterdam, Brussels, London and Paris in miniature, with moving people, vehicles and animals, and wonderful attention to detail (even down to the 'Mind the Gap' on the London Underground). Several snack bars and restaurants (and very good picnic area), decent shops, good disabled access; open daily from wk before Easter–end of Oct, (01753) 626111; £16 (£13 children).

WINDSOR SU9676 Well worth an expedition (though full of other visitors), the town is dominated by its famous castle, the largest inhabited one in the world. The little streets to the south have many pretty timber-framed or Georgian-fronted houses and shops. The High St, by contrast, is wide and busy. **Legoland** (*see separate Family Panel above*) is a huge draw for children. You can walk by the Thames (for example, from Home Park, beyond the station) or across to Eton. The good evening racecourse is best approached by boat – shuttle services run from Barry Avenue Promenade; telephone (01753) 865234 for race dates. The Trooper in St Leonard's Rd and Two Brewers in Park St (handy for the Royal Mews) are useful for a bite to eat, but for a better meal we'd recommend going out to the Thatched Tavern in Cheapside – convenient for the various Windsor Park attractions. Both the Union and Oxford Blue are decent pubs in the quieter nearby Thames-side village of Old Windsor.

! WINDSOR CASTLE SU9776 A mass of towers, ramparts and pinnacles, this splendid palace is the official residence of the monarch, though it's changed considerably since William the Conqueror built his original wooden fort here. Henry II constructed the first stone buildings, inc the familiar Round Tower, from the top of which, on a good day, you can see 12 counties. For many the highlight is the magnificent **St George's Chapel**, a splendid example of Perpendicular architecture, with intricate carvings on the choir stalls, fine ironwork, an amazing fan-vaulted ceiling, and the arms and pennants of every knight entered into the Order of the Knights of the Garter. This is closed Sun and occasional other dates, often at short notice – best to check on the telephone number given below. The **State Apartments**, used for ceremonial and official occasions, are decorated with carvings by Grinling Gibbons and ceilings by Verrio, and are full of superb paintings from the Royal Collection (inc notable Rembrandts and Van Dycks), porcelain, armour, and exceptionally fine furniture. This area (which may be closed when the Queen is in residence) was badly damaged by the disastrous fire in 1992, but you'd hardly know it now, with St George's Hall restored beyond its former glory. Entrance to **Queen Mary's Doll's House**, an exquisite creation by Edwin Lutyens, built for Queen Mary in the 1920s, with perfectly scaled furniture and decoration, is now also included in the general admission price. Shop, disabled access; (01753) 831118 or (01753) 868286 ext 2235 for full details of opening times; £9.50 (£7.50 when St George's Chapel is closed). The guards generally change daily Mon–Sat (alternate days only in winter), at 11 o'clock – again, telephone for exact dates.

Windsor Dungeons (opposite the castle) Waxworks give a graphic illustration of the often barbaric forms of punishment faced by criminals over the last 600 years. Shop, disabled access; cl 25 Dec; (01753) 865555; £4.50, children £3.00 or £1.50 if under 12 with an adult.

Frogmore House SU9677 (Home Park) This lesser known former Royal residence is definitely worth catching on one of its few open days – usually spring and summer bank hols; (01753) 868286 ext 2347 for dates,(children under 8 not admitted). It was a favourite with Queen Victoria, who is buried in a mausoleum in the grounds (open annually on Weds nearest to 24 May), alongside her beloved Albert.

Savill Garden SU9770 (Wick Lane, Englefield Green – where the Sun is a good place for lunch) On the eastern edge of Windsor Great Park, 35 peaceful acres taking in woodland, a formal rose garden, rock plants, herbaceous borders and so forth, and punctuated with a number of rare trees, shrubs and perennials. The range of colours can be quite dazzling. Perhaps best in spring, but quite stunning at any time of year. Meals, snacks, good shop with plant sales, disabled access; cl 25–26 Dec; (01753) 860222; £3.80.

Valley Gardens SU9769 Lovely for a relaxing stroll, with over 400 acres of woodland – 50 of which are devoted to rhododendrons, making this the largest planting of the species in the world. Also an outstanding collection of trees and shrubs, a heather garden, waterfowl lakes, and attractive landscaping. It's free for pedestrians (the mile-long walk from Savill Garden is pleasant), though cars can enter by a gate on Wick Rd, Englefield Green, for a fee of £3 (change needed for the automatic barrier).

Days Out

Regal splendour: Windsor Castle (get there early to avoid the crowds); stroll into Windsor Great Park; lunch at Oakley Court, Windsor – or drive to the Fish in Bray (Old Mill Lane) or the Thatched Tavern, Cheapside; Eton College.

Orchids and exotica: Walk by the Thames at Streatley; Wyld Court Rainforest, Hampstead Norreys; lunch at the White Hart there, or at the unspoilt Bell in Aldworth; Beale Park, Lower Basildon.

Windsor Great Park SU9672 Miles of well kept parkland, so sensitively landscaped that it takes the occasional surprising find (statues, even a totem pole) to remind you that it's not natural. It's the only real prospect in this eastern part of the county for walks that'll make you feel genuinely exercised.

Virginia Water SU9768 Very beautiful, particularly in autumn; and the Long Walk gives glorious perspectives of Windsor Castle. Best access via Valley Gardens or Savill Garden car parks.

ETON SU9677 So close to Windsor it's pretty much part of it. There is a restrained and decorous High St with a mix of interesting old shops and houses. Its glory, however, is **Eton College**, the famous public school, whose stately Tudor and later buildings in graceful precincts are marvellously calm during the school's holidays. The chapel is an outstanding late Gothic building in the Perpendicular style, and a museum tells the story of the school from its foundation in 1440 up to the present, with fascinating videos on life for pupils here today (inc Prince William). Bizarre information is turned up by the various historical documents – in the 17th c, for example, smoking was compulsory for all scholars as a protection against bubonic plague. The Brewhouse Gallery has some good watercolour drawings and changing exhibitions, and next door there's an exhaustive collection of Egyptian antiquities. Shop, some disabled access; cl am in term-time, and all Oct–Mar; (01753) 671177; from £2.50 (more for guided tours). The college runs residential courses in summer on topics as diverse as rowing and choral singing. The Eton Wine Bar (High St) is very good.

Other things to see and do

BOATING ON THE THAMES SU9084 Though busy in summer, this is a lovely stretch of the river, flowing through lively towns and villages, past grand houses in imposing grounds to idyllic reaches by steep quiet woodland – with islets where you can picnic. A particularly pretty trip is from

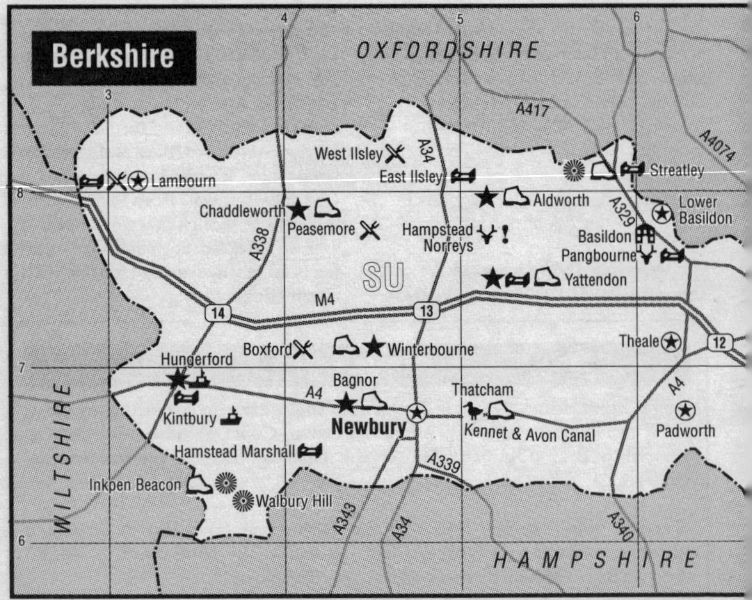

Wargrave to Henley to Medmenham Abbey to Hambleden, Hurley and Marlow Reach. A good shorter stretch is Cliveden Reach (the 2 miles between Cookham and Boulter's Lock). As well as motor launches, you can hire very attractive (not to mention silent and quite environmentally friendly) electric launches, though for the purists – and the energetic – only a rowing boat will do. Bray Boats in Maidenhead, (01628) 637880, have small boats/motor launches ranging from £20 an hour to around £150 a day; they also run half-hour or 2-hour trips as far as Cookham. Kris Cruisers in Datchet have rowing boats from £5 an hour and electric launches from around £13 – they do good discounts during the week; (01753) 543930. A recorded information service (updated weekly) has details of events and estimated conditions on the river; (0118) 953 5520.

❀ **ARBORFIELD** SU7566 **Henry Street Garden Centre** Specialist rose and bedding-plant grower, with a well stocked garden centre. From Jun–Sept you can wander through the fragrant rose fields. Meals, snacks, shop, disabled access; (0118) 976 1223; free. The George & Dragon over at Swallowfield is good for lunch.

! ASCOT SU9268 **Royal Ascot** Probably the most famous racecourse in the world, though most visitors spend as much time watching the people as the horses. The 4-day Royal Meeting in mid-Jun is still one of the highlights of the English season; to try for admission to the Royal Enclosure, British citizens should apply to Ascot Races (Royal Enclosure and Members' Stand), St James's Palace, London SW1; foreign citizens to their embassy. For the other stands, contact the racecourse; tickets must be booked in advance and are available from 1 Jan. Plenty of other top-class races throughout the year, when ticket prices range from £7 to £34 depending on the enclosure (the Silver Ring is the cheapest). Meals, snacks, shop, disabled access; (01344) 622211 for dates. The Thatched Tavern at Cheapside is the best nearby place for lunch.

† BISHAM CHURCH SU8485 Well worth a look; sitting on a seat in the churchyard by the Thames on a fine evening is rather special.

☺ ♧ ⛫ ❀ ! † **BRACKNELL** SU8666 Few find much to delight them in the town itself, but it's worth tracking down the **Look Out** (off the B3430,

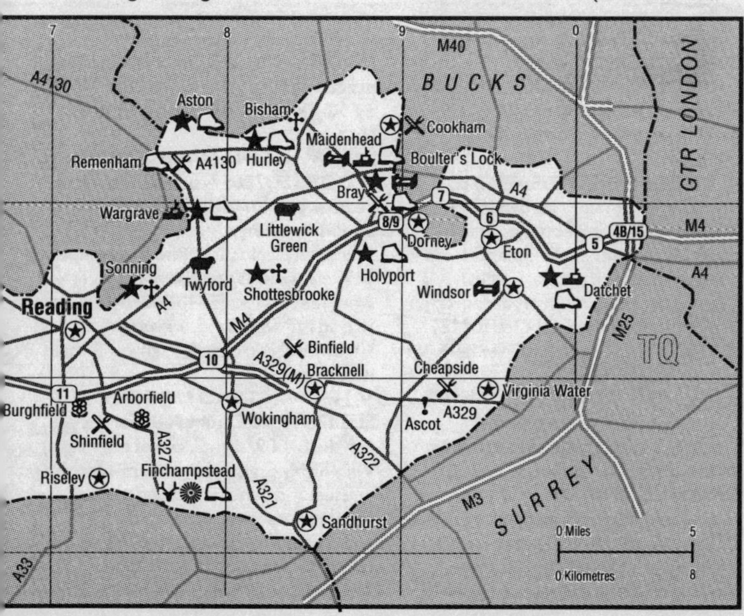

southern edge of Bracknell) a lively centre that's the starting-point for 2,600 acres of woodland. Families love the hands-on science centre, now very much the main feature of the place, and a very full timetable of events includes some particularly well organised children's activities. Mainly conifer plantations, the forest is full of nature trails and wildlife (as well as an Iron Age hill fort); as the name suggests, there's an elevated platform with good views of the surrounding area. You can hire mountain bikes and the many tracks, some based on Roman Roads, allow long though not particularly varied walks and rides. Meals, snacks, shop, disabled access; cl Christmas wk; (01344) 868222; £3.50. Across the road **Coral Reef** is an unusually wacky swimming pool complex, great for younger members of the family; the Wild Water Rapids are the best bit. Meals, snacks, shop, disabled access; wkdys outside school holidays slides operate only from 3.30pm, £4.95. **Easthampstead church** is notable for the fine pre-Raphaelite stained glass by William Morris, Edward Burne-Jones and others (as is the one NE of here at Cranbourne). The Old Manor (Grenville Pl, High St) has decent food all day, and there's a dry-ski centre with toboggan run at the Leisuresport Complex at Amen Corner.

BOULTER'S LOCK SU9082 An excellent starting-point for leisurely strolls by the River Thames (head upstream).

BURGHFIELD SU6668 **Old Rectory** Plantsman's garden inc oriental rarities and cottage-garden plants. Plant centre selling plants from other gardens in the area, snacks, disabled access to most of garden; open last Weds of month Feb–Oct; (0118) 983 3200; *£2. The Hatch Gate here is a friendly pub for lunch.

★ **COOKHAM** SU8985 The village, leading down to the Thames, is attractive, and has several decent pubs of which Uncle Tom's Cabin at Cookham Dean is the current pick. Cookham really made its mark on Stanley Spencer and his art: it was his birthplace and he spent most of his working life here. The rewarding little **Stanley Spencer Gallery** (King's Hall) has a good range of his unique work, with highlights inc *The Last Supper* and the curious *Christ Preaching at Cookham Regatta*. Shop, disabled access; cl wkdys Nov–Easter; (01628) 520890; *50p. There are plenty of opportunities in this area for walks combining the Thames with its hinterland, including great views from the chalk escarpment of Winter Hill. **Cock Marsh** (NT), by the Thames, is a fine lowland marsh, with breeding wading birds and wetland flora. Paths in this area are very well kept, and it is hard to lose the way seriously, although woodland walking sometimes means you have to keep your eyes skinned for arrow markers painted on trees.

DORNEY SU9279 **Dorney Court** Engaging, partly 15th-c, timber-framed manor house with pleasant gardens and some very fine furniture, as well as the Elizabethan Palmer Needlework tapestry. The same family have lived here for over 450 years. In the 16th-c they grew the first pineapple raised in England, and still have pick-your-own fruit and vegetables every day in season (usually daily Jun–Sept – discounts on Mon, Tues or Weds). There's also a plant centre, with plants from Blooms of Bressingham, and teas with their own honey. Open pm Mon–Thurs Jun–Aug, pm bank hols and preceding Suns in May; (01628) 604638; £4.50. The Eton Wine Bar in Eton is fairly handy for lunch.

FINCHAMPSTEAD RIDGES SU7863 A steepish chunk of heather and pinewood, not big but with a good natural character, nice views and sheltered picnic spots; the fine avenue of Wellingtonias just above it is well worth seeing too. To the north, Simons Wood NT woodland, with a walk to Heath Pool and Devil's Highway Roman Road, now a track.

! **HAMPSTEAD NORREYS** SU5376 **Wyld Court Rainforest** (on the B4009, slightly out of the village) Very highly praised by readers – an unusual and quite fascinating tropical rainforest reconstructed under glass, with thousands of weird-looking plants currently in danger of extinction. They're spread over 3 different areas,

Lowland Tropical, Amazonica and Cloudforest, each with its own climate and atmosphere. Particularly strange are the giant 8-ft lily pads (best from Jun–Oct), which start each year the size of a pea, and the orchid collection is exceptional. Quite a few of these plants can't be seen anywhere else in Europe. Also squirrel monkeys, varied fish, and terrapins. As it's so warm, this is particularly handy on a cold day. Snacks, good shop (with plants for sale), mostly disabled access (though hard work in gravel car park); cl 25–26 Dec; (01635) 200221; £3.50. The White Hart has good-value food.

★ **HUNGERFORD** SU3368 Attractive small town with some interesting antique shops (there's a large arcade on the High St), some general, others specialising in items as diverse as fireplaces, kitchen furnishings and billiard tables; antique fairs in the town hall. There are **canal trips** from the wharf in summer. The Tally Ho towards the motorway is a friendly place for lunch.

INKPEN BEACON SU3562 The high escarpment between here and Walbury Hill gives some dramatic Ridgeway walking; best reached from the minor road south of Inkpen (where the Swan is handy for lunch). The gibbet on top of the hill is a macabre relic from highwayman days. Immediately south lie some lovely rolling downlands, laced with gentle and mostly well marked tracks, field paths and woodland paths overlapping into Hants and Wilts.

KINTBURY SU3866 **Horse-drawn barge trips** 1½-hour trips along the restored Kennet & Avon Canal; from Easter–Sept; (01635) 44154; £4.40.

! † **LAMBOURN** SU3278 Quiet, streamside, racehorse-training village below the downs. **Lambourn Trainers' Association** (Windsor House) Guided tours around this successful racehorse training centre; you meet individual horses and see them put through their paces. Wear suitable shoes, and you must make an appointment. Shop, disabled access; open 10–12 noon, daily exc Sun and bank hols; (01488) 71347; *£5.87. The parish **Church of St Michael and All Angels** is worth a look (originally Norman, with Perpendicular additions), and the Hare & Hounds (on the B4000 S), with strong racing connections, is good for lunch. Nearby, up on the downs off the Lambourn–Kingston Lisle rd (OS Sheet 174 SU329827), the **Seven Barrows** Bronze Age cemetery has at least 32 barrows – a spectacle even for the uninitiated.

LITTLEWICK GREEN SU8580 **Courage Shire Horse Centre** (A4, 2 miles W of Maidenhead) You can go right up to the horses at this friendly place, and watch them being groomed and plaited up; also small animals and birds, working forge on some days, and a children's playground. Meals, snacks, shop, disabled access; cl Nov–Feb; (01628) 824848; £3.

LOWER BASILDON SU6179 **Beale Park** (Church Farm) Good, reliable and informative wildlife gardens, with a varied range of birds and mammals – many rare. Just about all their animals were born here in conditions as near as possible to the wild. The surroundings are lovely, and there's a lot going on: added attractions include a narrow-gauge railway, a model boat collection with exhibits displayed both in and out of the water, paddling pools and a children's playground. Readers get a great deal of pleasure from coming here. Meals, snacks, shop, disabled access; cl Christmas–Feb; (0118) 984 5172; £4. In summer there are short river cruises and you can get a boat to here from Caversham Bridge in Reading (2 hours each way, £7 return).

Basildon Park (off the A329) Elegant, Bath-stone Palladian mansion with delicate plasterwork on the ceilings and walls, an unusual Octagon Room, and an intriguing collection of rare seashells in the Shell Room. Outside are old-fashioned roses, a pretty terrace, and pleasant grounds beyond. The classical frontage is particularly impressive. Summer teas, light lunches wknds and bank hols, shop, disabled access to garden and grounds only; open pm Weds–Sun and bank hols, Apr–Oct; (0118) 984 3040; £4, £1.60 grounds only; NT.

NEWBURY SU4667
Busy shopping town famed for its notorious bypass, which should by the time of publication be complete and reducing congestion in the centre. Some nice old parts, with interesting older buildings among the High St shops. **St Nicolas** is a fine early 16th-c Perpendicular church with a magnificent pulpit. West Mills is the best evocation of the town's 18th-c prosperity, and leads to the attractively rejuvenated canal. **Boat trips** occasionally run from the old wharf, beyond the market square on the other side of the High St; (01635) 44154. The handsome **West Berkshire Museum** (The Wharf) is good on the Civil War battles fought here, and on the development of ballooning; open Mon–Sat, exc Weds in term-time, plus pm Sun and bank hols Apr–Sept; free. The town has an excellent **racecourse**, with mid-week and weekend races all year; (01635) 40015 for dates; prices from £4–£17. **Donnington Castle** (just N off the B4494) This is actually the tall, ruined medieval gatehouse of a much larger fortress destroyed in the Civil War. The walled gardens at **Hollington Nurseries** (Woolton Hill) are tranquil and relaxed; snacks, shop; open Mar–Sept, Thurs–Sat; *£1. The waterside Lock Stock & Barrel has reliable food all day.

PADWORTH SU6067
Kennet & Avon Canal Visitor Centre (Aldermaston Wharf) Set in a nice little house beside the canal, exhibitions on the history and usage of the waterway, and useful information on things to do along its various stretches. Snacks (in picnic garden), shop, limited disabled access; cl am Sun, and Nov–Mar; (0118) 971 2868; free. Nearby, quietly placed **Padstow church** feels very ancient and peaceful, and the Round Oak has decent food. The canal has been well restored in the last few years, and is now very pleasant to stroll or cycle along – some would say the Berks bits are the prettiest. *See also Hungerford, Kintbury and Newbury entries for boat trips*. And besides other places we mention, there's good access from Aldermaston Wharf SU6067, Marsh Benham SU4267, Thatcham SU5167 and Woolhampton SU5767, all of which have decent pubs. The railway makes a useful method of return, after a walk along the canal from Hungerford to Kintbury, for example.

PANGBOURNE SU6376
Pangbourne Meadow Traditional meadow by the Thames, scythed after flowering and seeding to preserve its wide range of wild flowers. The attractive riverside Swan has food all day, and the village has some decent shops; it was the home of Kenneth Grahame, who perhaps found inspiration around here for *The Wind in the Willows*.

READING SU7173
Berkshire's county town, largely 19th-c red brick, and not really a tourist town, but with museums worth visiting. The **abbey ruins** in Forbury Gardens are worth a look if passing. In West St, Vicars & Sons is an old-fashioned game butchers', established in the 19th c; an interesting shop with good food. For the extravagant, a **balloon trip** gives a very different view of Berks; lift off from town-centre parks daily (weather permitting) in summer, dawn and dusk; (0181) 840 0108; £115. Sweeney & Todd in Castle St has excellent-value home-made pies, and the canalside Fisherman's Cottage (Kennet Side – walk through from Orts Rd off King's Rd) is also very popular for lunch. The well organised **Blake's Lock Museum** (Gasworks Rd) concentrates on Reading's waterways, trade and industries, with a reconstructed bakery (the town was well known for biscuit-making), barber's shop and printer's workshop, and a Victorian turbine house. Shop, disabled access; open pm wknds and bank hols, plus all day Tues–Fri in school hols; (0118) 939 0918; free. The **Museum of Reading** (Blagrave St), in a showy neo-Gothic building, has hands-on displays, good reconstructions, and a unique Victorian copy of the Bayeux Tapestry. Meals, snacks, shop, disabled access; cl Mon and am Sun; free. Away from the centre, you won't find a better exploration of life in the English countryside over the last couple of centuries than the **Museum of Rural**

Life (University of Reading, Whiteknights Park; 2m SE on the A327; SU7371), taking in farm tools, rural crafts, and domestic room settings. Shop, disabled access; cl 1–2pm, all Sun and Mon, and 25 Dec–1 Jan; (0118) 931 8663; *£1.

Remenham SU7684 A good start for gentle strolls along the Thames towpath, showing to full effect the river's nostalgic qualities of boating and Edwardian England. There are spectacular period riverside mansions towards Maidenhead. This reach is the course of the Henley Regatta; you can instead start from Henley itself (coming back over the bridge).

RISELEY SU7164 **Wellington Country Park** (off the B3349 Reading–Basingstoke rd) Plenty for families in this big country park; the 350 acres of meadows, woodland and lakes include marked nature trails, a miniature railway, deer park, a collection of small domestic animals, and an adventure playground. You can fish and hire rowing and pedal boats on the lake. Meals, snacks, shop, some disabled access, cl Nov–Feb; (0118) 932 6444; £3.70. The George & Dragon at Swallowfield does good lunches.

SANDHURST SU8361 **Trilakes Country Park and Fishery** (Yateley Rd) Not just for fishermen, these attractive lakes and surrounding park and woodland have lots of animals and birds, some of which you can feed. Shetland pony rides for children on summer Suns, and in spring you can bottle-feed the lambs. Also a model railway. Meals, snacks, shop, limited disabled access; cl wkdys Nov–Mar; (01252) 873191; £2, £7 fishing. The Bird in Hand at Little Sandhurst is useful for lunch.

† ★ **SHOTTESBROOKE CHURCH** SU8377 A magnificent 14th-c building, unusually set in a park just E of Waltham St Lawrence – itself an attractive quiet village with an ancient centre.

★ † **SONNING** SU7575 A charming village, with a pleasant walk through the churchyard and past the lovely **church** to the River Thames, and to Sonning Lock.

STREATLEY HILL SU5580 The NT car park below here gives access to NT downland for fine views over the Thames valley. The long-distance downs-top Ridgeway Path, one of the oldest tracks in England, follows surfaced farm roads in places hereabouts, but takes in some quiet countryside.

THATCHAM MOOR SU5066 Surprisingly, the largest area of inland freshwater reed beds in England; lots of birds (some rare), moths, and marshland and aquatic plants. Car park S of the A4. The **Nature Discovery Centre** (Muddy Lane, Lower Way) explains more about the environment and has a good programme of special events. Snacks, shop, disabled access; cl Mon; free.

THEALE SU6271 **Englefield House** (A340) The striking house itself is open only to groups, but the surrounding woodland is attractive, with interesting trees, water and formal gardens, and deer park. Some disabled access; open Mon all year, plus Tues–Thurs Apr–July; (0118) 930 2221; £2. The Old Boot over in the pretty village of Stanford Dingley has very good food these days.

TWYFORD SU7975 **Thames Valley Vineyard** (Stanlake Park, B3018) English wines made by a pioneering blend of tradition and technology. Snacks, shop; cl am Sun, 25 Dec–2 Jan; (0118) 934 0176; free. Just off the A4, **Rocks Country Wines** (Loddon Park Farm) produce a range of country wines, liqueurs, mead and cordials, with tastings and a walled herb garden. Cl am wknds; (0118) 934 2344; free. The Bull nr the Thames at Sonning is pleasant for lunch.

WOKINGHAM SU8068 **Holme Grange Craft Village** (Heathlands Rd) Expanding craft centre with paintings, sculpture, rugs, and even a circus shop; Widget, the pot-bellied pig, is a favourite with children. Snacks, disabled access; cl 25 Dec–1 Jan; (0118) 977 6753; free. Heathlands Rd has a couple of farm shops and pick-your-own plots; the Crooked Billet on Gardeners Green, Honey Hill, just SE of Wokingham, is a friendly place for lunch. Just south of town on the B3016 S, turning right at Wick Hill opposite the B3430, the woods of **California Country Park** are very useful for young children to let off steam.

★ ⌂ **Other attractive villages**, all with decent pubs and pleasant local walks, include Aldworth SU5579, Aston SU7884, Bagnor SU4569 (with a well regarded theatre in a lovely old watermill), Bray SU9079, Chaddleworth SU4177, Datchet SU9876, Holyport SU8977, Hurley SU8283, Wargrave SU7878, Winterbourne SU4572 and Yattendon SU5574.

Where to eat

BINFIELD SU8571 **Stag & Hounds** *(01344) 483553* Little, low-beamed rooms with log fires, interesting furnishings and pictures, and some fine sporting prints; a bustling atmosphere, real ales, decent wines, daily papers, and lots of good modern daily specials – plenty of fish and vegetarian dishes, too. **£21**|£7.75.

BOXFORD SU4271 **Bell** *(01488) 608721* Civilised and neatly kept, mock Tudor village inn with a long snug bar, a nice mix of racing pictures and smaller old advertisements, and interesting bric-à-brac; rather smart restaurant, thoughtful modern cooking, well kept real ales, and decent wines; bdrms. **£20.50**|£8.

BRAY SU9079 **Fat Duck 1** *High St (01628) 580333* Really innovative food cooked with immense care and based on traditional French cooking (some perfectly cooked, more straightforward dishes as well) in this black and white former pub; a relaxed if slightly sophisticated feel, knowledgeable helpful staff, and a well chosen wine list; cl 2 wks Christmas; disabled access. **£55**|2-course lunch £17.50.

BRAY SU9079 **Fish** *Old Mill Lane (01628) 781111* Relaxed dining pub with 2 stylish rooms and a no smoking conservatory, candles and fresh flowers; friendly service, particularly good fish dishes and other adventurous food inc lovely puddings, real ales, and New World wines; cl pm Sun, Mon, Christmas; children over 12 in evening; disabled access. **£29**|£5.95.

BRAY SU9079 **Waterside Ferry Rd** (01628) 620691 Famous restaurant with rooms, on a quiet stretch of the Thames, with big windows overlooking the water; exquisitely presented, superb classical French cooking using the best luxury ingredients, lovely puddings, fine French cheeses, an outstanding (if pricey) wine list, and impeccable service; pretty bdrms; cl pm Sun (in winter), Mon, am Tues, 26 Dec–27 Jan, 5–8 Apr; children over 12; disabled access (restaurant only). **£37.50**.

CHEAPSIDE SU9469 **Thatched Tavern** *Cheapside Rd (01344) 620874* Smartly civilised dining pub (not actually thatched!) with low old beams, polished flagstones, and a big inglenook; pretty gingham cloths on the tables in the long dining room, a large choice of good food inc local game and fresh fish, well kept real ales, and polite, friendly service. **£22.45**|£10.50.

LAMBOURN SU3278 **Hare & Hounds** *(01488) 71386* Stylish dining pub in the heart of horse country; with colourful and idiosyncratically decorated rooms leading off the narrow bar, imaginative food, well kept real ales, decent wines, and friendly service. **£23.50**|£10.50.

PEASEMORE SU4577 **Fox & Hounds** *(01635) 248252* Tucked-away pub with hunting prints and fox masks in the 2 bars; a relaxed atmosphere, enjoyable bar food, real ales, and a wide range of wines; cl Mon. **£23**|£5.50.

REMENHAM SU7683 **Little Angel** *(01491) 574165* Cosy little restaurant with good seafood, a splendid range of wines by glass, and helpful service; also bar food and well kept real ales in the old, low-beamed and panelled bar; floodlit terrace. **£25**|£6.

SHINFIELD SU7368 **L'Ortolan** *Church Lane (0118) 988 3783* Smartly refurbished Victorian rectory with 2 plant-filled conservatories; exceptional and innovative French cooking inc delicious puddings and a fine cheeseboard, an excellent wine list, and courteous service; cl pm Sun, Mon; disabled access. **£30**.

WEST ILSLEY SU4782 **Harrow** *(01635) 281260* Popular, white-tiled village inn overlooking the duck pond and green; with good bar food (you can take the pies home, too), no smoking dining area, and real ales; notable children's play area with lots of animals; no food winter pm Sun; disabled access. **£21.50**|£8.50.

Special thanks to Heather Martin, E G Parish, Roger Stamp.

Berkshire Calendar

Some of these dates were provisional as we went to press. Please check information with the telephone numbers provided.

JANUARY

2 **Savernake** Forest Icicle Hot-air Balloon Meet – *till Sun 3* (01672) 562277

MARCH

7 **Riseley** Husky Day at Wellington Country Park (0118) 932 6444
12 **Eton** English Chamber Orchestra at Eton School (01753) 671169
20 **Burchett's Green** Lambing Weekend at Berkshire College of Agriculture – *till Sun 21* (01628) 824444

APRIL

2 **Lambourn** Lambourn Racing Stables Open Day (01235) 751693
4 **Riseley** Easter Fun Days at Wellington Country Park – *till Mon 5* (0118) 932 6444
25 **Taplow** Horse Show (01628) 868196
30 **Reading** Real Ale Festival at King's Meadow – *till 2 May* (0118) 939 0375

MAY

1 **Newbury** Steam Funtasia at the Showground – *till Mon 3* (01663) 732750; **Wokingham** Festival Week – *till Sat 8*; with May fair in the town centre on *Mon 3*, with Green Man, Sun God, and maypole dancing (01344) 423147
3 **Riseley** Pet Day at Wellington Country Park (0118) 932 6444
5 **Windsor** Frogmore Gardens and Mausoleum Open Day – *till Thurs 6* (01483) 211535
8 **Newbury** Spring Festival – *till Sat 22* (01635) 32421; Windsor Savill Garden Plant Fair (01784) 435544
13 **Windsor** Royal Horse Show at Windsor Home Park – *till Sun 16* (0171) 370 8206
16 **Burchett's Green** Country Fair and Open Day at Berkshire College of Agriculture (01628) 824444
22 **Reading** Children's Festival: free events – *till 6 June* (0118) 939 0375
29 **Wokingham** French Market – *till Sun 30* (0118) 978 1985
31 **Sandhurst** Donkey Derby at Memorial Hall (01252) 879060

JUNE

4 **Reading** Caversham Folk Festival: free event – *till Sun 6* (01734) 390373
5 **Burchett's Green** Garden Open Day at Berkshire College of Agriculture (01628) 824444
6 **Newbury** Summer Fair at Watermill Theatre (01635) 46044
11 **Hungerford** Music from the Movies with fireworks at Littlecote House (01625) 575681
12 **Woodley** Carnival (01734) 344117
14 **Windsor** Garter Ceremony at St George's Chapel after procession from Windsor Castle (apply for limited tickets between *1 Jan* and *28 Feb* to the Superintendent, Windsor Castle, SL4 1NJ)

Berkshire Calendar (cont.)

15 **Ascot** Royal Ascot at the Racecourse – *till Fri 18* (01344) 622211
26 **Chieveley** Garden and Leisure Show at Newbury Showground – *till Sun 27* (01635) 247111; **Hurst** Country Fayre and Horse Show – *till Sun 27* (0118) 934 5253; **Reading** Waterfest (0118) 939 0375

JULY

2 **Bracknell** Festival at the Wilde Theatre – *till Sun 4* (01344) 427272
3 **Bracknell** Music Festival – *till Sun 4* (01344) 427272
10 **Sandhurst** Royal Military Academy Open Days – *till Sun 11* (01276) 412273
19 **Sunbury–Abingdon** Swan Upping on the River Thames: colourful 13th-c ceremony of swan-marking by Swan Masters and their assistants – *till Thurs 22* (01628) 523030
22 **Reading** Real Ale and Jazz Festival – *till Sat 24* (0118) 939 0375
23 **Reading** WOMAD at Rivermead – *till Sun 25* (0118) 939 0375
24 **Ascot** Diamond Day at the Racecourse (01344) 622211
25 **Windsor** International Polo Tournament at Windsor Smiths Lawn (01784) 434212

AUGUST

1 **Riseley** Heckfield Horticultural Show at Wellington Country Park (0118) 932 6444
3 **Windsor** International Three-day Event at Windsor Great Park – *till Weds 4* (01753) 860222
8 **Riseley** Pet Day at Wellington Country Park (0118) 932 6444
13 **Basildon** Themed concert and fireworks, and jazz concert and fireworks on *Sat 14* at Basildon Park (01494) 528051; **Knowl Hill** Steam Fair – *till Sun 15* (01628) 823393
27 **Reading** Rock Festival – *till Mon 30* (0118) 939 0375
28 **Bracknell** Country and Western Festival: live music, line dancing and tuition, gun fight at the OK Corral, North & South Re-enactment Society, 1880s camp, Indian village, cancan girls, at Moss End – *till Mon 30* (01344) 874787; **Newbury** Orchid Fair at Jarvis Elcot Country Hotel – *till Sun 29* (01626) 352233; **Windsor** Savill Garden Plant Fair (01784) 435544
29 **Spencers Wood** Swallowfield Horticultural Show – *till Mon 30* (0118) 988 3575
30 **Bray** Wick Littlewick Show (01628) 30622

SEPTEMBER

4 **Riseley** Shetland Pony Show at Wellington Country Park (0118) 932 6444
5 **Spencers Wood** Wokingham and Reading Agricultural Show (0118) 973 2232
18 **Chieveley** Newbury and County Show at Newbury Showground – *till Sun 19* (01635) 247111; **Windsor** and **Eton** Festival – *till 3 Oct* (01753) 623400
25 **White Waltham** Royal East Berkshire Ploughing Match and Show at Shottesbrooke Farm (01628) 822559
26 **Burchett's Green** Shrub Sunday at Berkshire College of Agriculture (01628) 824444

Berkshire Calendar (cont.)

OCTOBER

3 **Wokingham** Victorian Day: arts, crafts and entertainments at the Holme Grange Craft Village (0118) 977 6753

NOVEMBER

6 **Reading** Fireworks at King's Meadow (01734) 390358
28 **Wokingham** Winter Carnival and Victorian Street Fair (0118) 978 1985

DECEMBER

5 **Woodley** Winterland Street Party (0118) 969 0356

We welcome reports from readers

This *Guide* depends on readers' reports. Do help us if you can – in return, we offer a discount on the next edition to people who've helped us with reports for it. Tell us what you think about places already in it, and anything extra you think we should say about them. And send us your ideas for inclusion in the next edition: places to visit, eat at or stay in, attractive drives or walks, maybe even unusual interesting shops you know of. Use the card in the middle, the report forms at the end, or just write – no stamp needed: *The Good Guide to Britain*, FREEPOST TN1569, Wadhurst, E Sussex TN5 7BR.

Buckinghamshire

Some great houses and gardens, beautiful Chilterns countryside.

Plenty of grandeur here: Waddesdon Manor, Ascott at Wing, Claydon House at Middle Claydon and the memorable landscape gardens of Stowe and Cliveden. Other less flamboyant favourites include Bletchley Park with its friendly and untouristy memories of World War II secrets, the Chiltern Open-Air museum at Chalfont St Giles and the medieval manor house at Chenies. For families, the Roald Dahl Gallery in Aylesbury and Odds Farm Park at Wooburn Common are both outstanding; many adults enjoy the Bucks Goat Centre at Stoke Mandeville, the unusual zoo at Weston Underwood, and Bekonscot model village in Beaconsfield as much as children do.

The Chiltern Hills give the south of the county a special charm: quiet valleys, lovely tucked-away villages with pretty brick and flint houses, endless walking possibilities. This scenery is at its peak in spring and autumn through to November, when the beechwoods are at their most beautiful. Some of the most appealing stretches of the Thames are in this area – the finest reaches of all are best seen from a boat.

Where to stay

ASTON CLINTON SP8712 **Bell** *London Rd, Aston Clinton, Aylesbury HP22 5HP (01296) 630252* **£79,** plus special breaks; 20 comfortable rms, some in main building with antiques, some (more modern but spacious) in converted stables around a flower-filled courtyard. Early 17th-c coaching inn with an elegant panelled drawing room, flagstoned smoking room, restaurant with pretty murals and excellent modern French cooking, and formal but kind service; attractive, mature gardens; disabled access.

AYLESBURY SP8213 **Hartwell House** *Oxford Rd, Aylesbury HP17 8NL (01296) 747444* ***£195,** plus special breaks; 46 rms, some huge and well equipped, others with four-posters and fine panelling, and 10 secluded suites in separate building with private garden and statues. Elegant Grade I listed building with Jacobean and Georgian façades, wonderful decorative plasterwork and panelling, fine paintings and antiques, marvellous Gothic central staircase, a splendid morning room and library; exceptional service and excellent food; 80 acres of parkland with a ruined church, lake and statues, and spa with indoor swimming pool, saunas, gym and so forth, as well as an informal restaurant; croquet, fishing; children over 8; dogs accepted; good disabled access.

FAWLEY SU7586 **Walnut Tree** *Fawley, Henley-on-Thames, Oxon RG9 6JE (01491) 638360* **£50;** 2 rms with showers. Popular dining pub in a lovely spot with the Chilterns all around; attractively furnished bars, and imaginative food and decent wines in the separate restaurant and no smoking conservatory.

HAMBLEDEN SU7886 **Stag & Huntsman** *Hambleden, Henley-on-Thames, Oxon RG9 6RP (01491) 571227* ***£55;** 3 old-fashioned rms. Peaceful, brick and flint pub opposite the church in a very pretty village, surrounded by Chilterns beechwoods; with a compact, half-panelled lounge, large fireplace, attractively simple public bar and cosy snug; good food, well kept real ales, and a spacious, pretty garden (summer barbecues).

MARLOW SU8586 **Compleat Angler** *Marlow Bridge, Marlow SL7 1RG (01628) 484444* **£193,** plus special breaks; 65 pretty, individually furnished rms overlooking garden or river. Famous Thames-side hotel with a comfortable panelled lounge and a balconied bar; spacious, beamed restaurant with a marvellous view, imaginative food, and friendly, prompt service; tennis, croquet, coarse fishing and boating; disabled access.

MURSLEY SP8128 **Richmond Lodge** *Mursley, Milton Keynes MK17 OLE (01296) 720275* **£48;** 3 attractive rms, some with own bthrm. Carefully run Edwardian house surrounded by big neat garden, with tennis and croquet; open fire in the sitting room, lovely breakfasts (super dinner if ordered in advance), and friendly owners; no smoking; cl Christmas; children over 6.

TAPLOW SU9185 **Cliveden** *Taplow, Maidenhead SL6 0JF (01628) 668561* **£255** room only (plus £5.50 per person paid to the National Trust); 38 luxurious, individual rms with maid unpacking service and a butler's tray. Superb Grade I listed stately home with gracious, comfortable public rooms, fine paintings, tapestries and armour, and a surprisingly unstuffy atmosphere; lovely views over the magnificent NT Thames-side parkland and formal gardens (open to the public); daily-changing imaginative food in the 2 no smoking restaurants, with lighter meals in the conservatory, friendly breakfasts around a huge table, and impeccable, bright staff; pavilion with swimming pool, gym and so forth, tennis, squash, croquet, riding, coarse fishing, and boats for river trips; disabled access.

WINSLOW SP7627 **Bell** *Market Sq, Winslow, Buckingham MK18 3AB (01296) 714091* **£52;** 41 rms. Elegant, black and white timbered inn with beams and open fires, a plush hotel bar, all-day coffee lounge, decent bar food, and good lunchtime carvery in the restaurant; also, a pleasant inner courtyard; disabled access.

WOOBURN COMMON SU9187 **Chequers** *Kiln Lane, Wooburn Common HP10 0JQ (01628) 529575* ***£92.50,** plus special breaks; 17 stripped pine rms in mock Tudor wing. Popular inn with a cheerful, traditional atmosphere in the cosy, low-beamed bar, standing timbers and alcoves, log fires and comfortable sofas, and well kept real ales; tasty food in the busy dining room, nice breakfasts, and a spacious garden.

We welcome reports from readers

This *Guide* depends on readers' reports. Do help us if you can – in return, we offer a discount on the next edition to people who've helped us with reports for it. Tell us what you think about places already in it, and anything extra you think we should say about them. And send us your ideas for inclusion in the next edition: places to visit, eat at or stay in, attractive drives or walks, maybe even unusual interesting shops you know of. Use the card in the middle, the report forms at the end, or just write – no stamp needed: *The Good Guide to Britain*, FREEPOST TN1569, Wadhurst, E Sussex TN5 7BR.

To see and do

BUCKINGHAMSHIRE Family Attraction of the Year

WOOBURN COMMON SU9387 **Odds Farm Park** Great value, efficiently run and notably friendly, this cheery rare breeds centre was developed especially with children in mind. They can go right up to the cattle, pigs, sheep and poultry, and join in daily activities such as bottle-feeding the lambs, hand-milking the goats, or collecting the chickens' eggs. Most pens and enclosures have signs written in a way that younger visitors will understand, and quite a bit of thought has gone into the indoor and outdoor play areas. They won't necessarily be doing every activity every day (so best to check first if there's something you'd particularly like to do), but there's always plenty going on, even in winter, when everything takes place under cover (the animals are in snugger barns and sheds then). Each month, extra weekend events have a different theme, from sheepdog demonstrations in Apr and sheep-shearing in May, to an indoor play barn in Nov, and Father Christmas in Dec; they may also have occasional donkey rides (50p extra). Younger children can pet the rabbits and guinea-pigs in the pets' corner, while older ones can learn a lot about farm life – they work hard to make sure the displays are instructive as well as fun. Plenty of space for picnics. It's not an enormous place, but is all the better for not being overly developed, and children usually find it an endless source of fascination and interest. Snacks, shop, disabled access; cl 25–26 Dec, and Mon–Weds mid-Nov–Feb; (01628) 520188; £3.50 (£2.50 children over 2). If you don't live too far away and have children particularly wild about animals, an annual ticket is £17.50 (£12.50 children).

!AYLESBURY SP8113 Roald Dahl lived in Bucks for most of his life and the **County Museum** (St Mary's Sq, Church St) celebrates the connection with a gallery of hands-on displays that use Dahl's characters to teach children about insects, light and any number of other topics. Visitors can crawl through the tunnel of Fantastic Mr Fox, discover Willy Wonka's inventions, and even go inside the Giant Peach to find out what things look like under the microscope. Also a good collection of regional art and a walled garden. Meals, snacks, shop, good disabled access; cl am Sun and 25–26 Dec (Dahl gallery cl until 3pm wkdys in term-time); (01296) 331441; £3.50 (£1 without Dahl gallery). The Bottle & Glass, out on the A418 at Gibraltar, is the closest decent dining pub.

! BEACONSFIELD SU9391 **Bekonscot Model Village** (Warwick Rd) Popular with readers, this miniature portrayal of rural Britain in the 1930s includes scaled-down churches, castles, zoo and even a racecourse, as well as a gauge-1 model railway. Snacks, shop, disabled access; cl Nov–mid-Feb; (01494) 672919; £3.60. The Greyhound is handy for lunch.

BLETCHLEY SP8633 **Bletchley Park** (turn off the B4034 at Eight Bells pub, then turn right into Wilton Ave) During World War II, 12,000 men and women worked in and around this Victorian mansion, cracking German codes. It now has a series of genuine and untouristy wartime exhibitions and displays, warmly praised by contributors. Some of the code-breaking bits are a little technical, but there's plenty more to see, inc a toy collection, landscaped grounds, wartime fire engines and a working tank. It's a shame they've had such trouble trying to raise funds to develop the site. Snacks, shop, disabled access; open alternate wknds; (01908) 640404; *£3.50. The Crooked Billet (Westbrook End, Newton Longville) has decent food.

! BOARSTALL SP6214 **Boarstall Duck Decoy** Displays and working demonstrations of one of only 3 remaining 17th-c, working duck decoys. Also woodland walks and nature trail. Open wknds and bank hols, plus 4–7pm Weds, Apr–Aug; (01844) 237488; £2.10; NT. Brill is the nearest useful place for lunch.

BOOKER SU8390 **Blue Max Collection** (Wycombe Air Park) The 15 or so aircraft here, inc a 1917 Sopwith Camel and 1940 Battle of Britain Spitfire, are all veterans of films or TV, from *Indiana Jones* to *Poirot.* There are some displays of film props and memorabilia. Snacks, shop, disabled access; open Weds and Sun, Apr–Nov; (01494) 529432; £2.75. The Chequers at nearby Wheeler End seems a very appropriately chatty sort of place for lunch.

★ **BRADENHAM** SU8297 This pretty village is surrounded by ancient woodland, with pleasant strolling possibilities.

★ **BRILL** SP6514 The **windmill** (open pm summer Suns) is in a magnificent position right on the edge of the Chilterns, with distant views across Oxford; there's been a mill on this site for over 700 years. In the distinctive and quietly attractive village, the Pheasant (with a view of the windmill) is good for lunch. There's a decent walk up nearby Muswell Hill, or along the ridge and down to Boarstall.

BROUGHTON SP8414 **Oak Farm Rare Breeds Park** (off the A41, E edge of Aylesbury) Friendly little working farm, with animals to feed, walks and nature trails. Snacks, shop; open Weds–Sun (plus bank hol Mons) Apr–Sept; (01296) 415709; *£2.50. The Chequers in Weston Turville has enjoyable food.

! **BUCKINGHAM** SP6934 Quite a lot of attractive early 18th-c brick buildings, and much of the nostalgic charm of a once-important town that has been eclipsed by rivals (in this case Aylesbury and Milton Keynes). **Old Gaol Museum** (Market Hill) Small local history museum in an extraordinary, early Gothic Revival gaol, with a good audio-visual show in an intact original cell. Shop; open Mon–Sat Apr–Dec, plus pm Sun Apr–Sept; (01280) 823020; £1. The thatched Wheatsheaf out at Maids Moreton is nice for lunch.

BURNHAM BEECHES SU9485 A supreme example of a Chilterns beechwood, splendid in spring and autumn colours, and with maybe a glimpse of deer; maps are posted throughout the forest, but it is quite easy to lose one's bearings. The main starting-point is at East Burnham Common car park, opposite the west end of Beeches Rd at Farnham Common. There are several decent pubs dotted around the forest.

CHALFONT ST GILES TQ0193 **Chiltern Open-air Museum** (Newland Park, Gorelands Lane) A good few traditional Chilterns buildings that would otherwise have been demolished have found their way here in the last 20 years, painstakingly dismantled and rebuilt again piece by piece. Dotted about the 45 acres are structures as diverse as an Iron Age house, a Victorian farmyard, an Edwardian public convenience and a 1940s prefab, several containing displays on their original use; also an

Days Out

Nature managed, manicured – and liberated: Odds Farm Park; Cliveden; picnic at Burnham Beeches; Church Wood Nature Reserve (lunch options: Cliveden for the grand, Blackwood Arms, Littleworth Common, for the merry).

A stroll into hellfire: Chilterns woodland walk from Bradenham to West Wycombe, lunch at the George & Dragon there; West Wycombe Park, Hell Fire Caves.

Some Chilterns history: Chiltern Open-air Museum and Milton's Cottage, Chalfont St Giles; lunch at the Red Lion, Chenies; walk in Chess Valley.

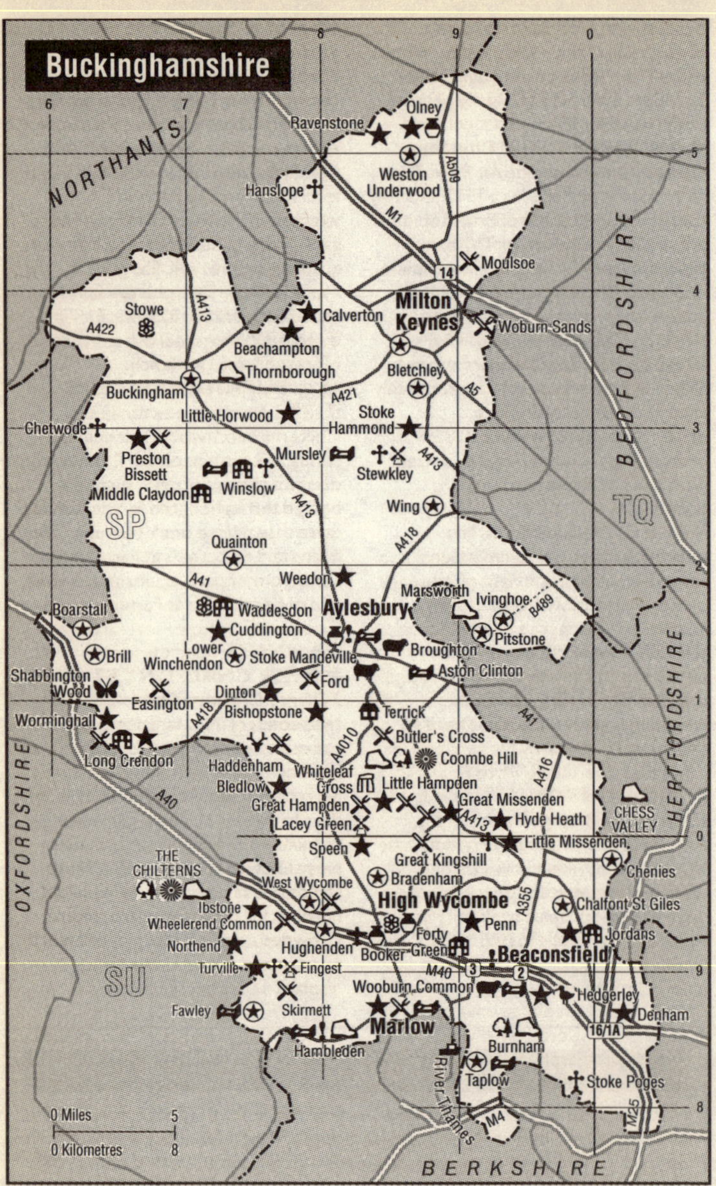

adventure playground and nature and sculpture trails through the parklands. Usually extra events and activities on Suns and bank hols. Snacks, shop, some disabled access; open Apr–Nov, pm Tues–Fri and all day wknds and bank hols; (01494) 872163; £4. **Milton's Cottage** (Deanway, SU9893) The writer brought his family to this timber-framed 16th-c cottage to escape the Plague in 1665, and while here completed *Paradise Lost* and began *Paradise Regained*. Displays of first editions, other rare books and memorabilia, and a charming cottage garden full of plants and flowers mentioned by Milton in his poetry. Shop, disabled access to ground floor; cl 1–2pm, all Mon (exc bank hols), and Nov–Feb; (01494) 872313; £2. The Ivy House (London Rd) has decent food.

CHENIES TQ0198 **Manor House** Rewarding 15th-c house with Tudor rooms, doll collection, tapestries, priest's hole, and a 13th-c crypt; the gardens include a physic garden, herbs and a maze. Home-made teas, shop (good for dried flowers and herbs); open pm Weds, Thurs and bank hols Apr–Oct; (01494) 762888; £4.50 house and garden, £2.20 garden only. The neighbouring **church** has the rich family monuments of the Bedfords (viewed through a glass panel), 15th-c brasses, and a Norman font. The Red Lion is handy for lunch.

CHESS VALLEY TQ0298 Shared between Bucks and Herts, this is miniature and unspoilt, and handily reached from Chalfont & Latimer station on the Metropolitan Underground line. Chenies and Latimer in Bucks, and Sarratt just over the Herts border, are the villages to head for.

CHETWODE CHURCH SP6429 A handsome church, notable for its fine Early English windows.

THE CHILTERNS SU7295 The well wooded Chiltern Hills offer plenty of easy-going walks, with a good scattering of rural pubs and pretty villages, though sometimes you have to choose your path carefully to avoid the numerous suburban developments. Even so, it's easy to escape into idyllic landscapes which some rate above all others for weekend walks; we pick out several of the best places under their own names. The escarpment, where the hills drop sharply down to the plain, gives some very distant views, for instance from above Bledlow (decent pub here). The signposted Ridgeway takes in the most dramatic features.

CHURCH WOOD SU9786 On the edge of the immaculate village of Hedgerley, this is a nature reserve managed by the RSPB, with over 80 species of birds in 34 acres.

COOMBE HILL SP8506 The highest point in the Chilterns, with its Boer War Memorial (an excellent place for views – and for kite-flying). Wendover Woods with some well marked nature trails are adjacent. The town of Wendover (the Red Lion Hotel here is walker-friendly) gives nearby access, or you can follow paths from Ellesborough and sneak views of Chequers, the Prime Minister's country retreat (emphatically private); an alternative path in is from Dunsmore.

FAWLEY SU7684 **Fawley Court** Not the typical English stately home it appears to be; though it does boast some fine Wyatt interiors and an elaborate ceiling by Grinling Gibbons, it's owned by a Polish religious group, and has a unique museum dedicated to their homeland, particularly strong on Polish military history. The grounds (landscaped by Capability Brown) run down to the river, and you can stay here, B & B or half and full board. Shop, limited disabled access; open pm Weds, Thurs and Sun Mar–Oct (exc wks of Easter and Whitsun); (01491) 574917; £2. The Walnut Tree has very good food.

FINGEST CHURCH SU7791 This brick and flint church is famous for its huge Norman tower with a twin saddleback roof. The Chequers, opposite, is nice for lunch, and, below the landmark windmill to the north, this is a particularly delectable valley – try the road round through Turville.

FORTY GREEN SU9291 **The Royal Standard of England pub** stands out as a quite remarkable old building, full of interesting furniture. Crowded at weekends, it's well worth a quiet prowl during the week.

HADDENHAM SP7408 **St Tiggywinkles Wildlife Hospital Visitor Centre** (Aston Rd) Should be open by the time this book reaches the shops; all outdoors, in gardens with enclosures for the animals that they can't release back into the wild, inc hedgehogs, ducks, badgers and foxes. Shop; (01844) 292292; phone for admission and opening times. The church end of the village is very attractive.

! **HAMBLEDEN** SU7886 Charming Chilterns village; for **Thames walks** the attractive footbridge over the weir below is the best starting-point on the Bucks bank.

HANSLOPE CHURCH SP8046 Attractive in its own right, but the most striking feature is its unusually tall spire.

HIGH WYCOMBE SU8693 The sprawling, suburban-looking town grew around the furniture industry, starting with chair-making using beechwood from the Chilterns. **Wycombe Museum** (Castle Hill House), housed in an 18th-c house, has an unusual collection of the various styles of chair produced nearby, as well as pretty landscaped gardens. Shop; disabled access to ground floor; cl Sun and bank hols; (01494) 421895; free.

HODGEMOOR WOODS SU9693 (W of Chalfont St Giles) This ancient woodland has 3 colour-coded nature trails, giving enjoyable walks of varying lengths.

HUGHENDEN SU8695 **Hughenden Manor** The home of Benjamin Disraeli until his death in 1881, this imposing old house still has many of the former Prime Minister's books and other possessions, as well as related memorabilia, portraits of friends, and formal gardens; he's buried in the grounds. Snacks, shop, some disabled access; open pm Weds–Sun and bank hols, Apr–Oct, wknds only in Mar; (01494) 532580; £4, garden only £1, NT. The Red Lion at Great Kingshill does good fish lunches, and there's a pleasant walk over from the Le De Spencers Arms on Downley Common.

★ **IVINGHOE** TQ0120 Attractive old village, the 18th-c **Ford End Watermill** (Station Rd) is the only remaining working watermill in the county. An unusual feature is the sheep wash, a special pool into which sheep were dropped and cleaned to make shearing easier. Shop; open pm Sun and bank hols May–Sept, with milling (water level permitting) 3–5pm on bank hols and 2nd Sun in May, Jun, July and Sept; £1. The Rose & Crown does fresh bar lunches. This enclave is a fragment of Bucks almost encircled by Herts, so see that chapter for nearby attractions.

IVINGHOE BEACON SP9616 This 230-metre-high (760-ft) hill has splendid views (especially to the north – they say you can see 8 counties) and an Iron Age earthwork on top. It's a protruding finger of the Chilterns, and the finish of the long-distance Ridgeway Path which begins in Wilts. The slopes, too steep for ploughing, comprise woodland, scrub and unspoilt downland. The Old Swan at Cheddington is the nearest good pub.

★ **JORDANS** SU9791 Interesting, quiet, tree-filled village built mainly this century in honour of the first 17th-c Quaker meeting-place here – a simple, evocative building. The nearby Mayflower Barn is built with timbers from the famous ship.

LACEY GREEN SP8100 **Smock Mill** (off the A4010) The oldest surviving smock mill in the country, and indeed the third oldest windmill of any type, built in 1650 at Chesham and moved here in 1821. It's been well restored. Open pm Sun and bank hols May–Sept; (01844) 343560; 70p. The Pink & Lily does decent food – and has kept its little tap room much as Rupert Brooke enjoyed it. Other well restored windmills can be seen at nearby Pitstone (*see entry below*) and Loosley Row (SP8100). The mill at Ibstone (SU7593) is unusual for having 12 sides.

★ **LITTLE MISSENDEN** SU9298 The **church** of this pretty village has some wall paintings from the 12th c and some pre-Norman traces, and the village itself has charming old timbered and tiled houses. The attractive old Crown does good sandwiches.

★ **LONG CRENDON** SP6909 The cottages in the High St are very pretty, some little changed since the village was a rich wool centre in the 15th c. The **courthouse** is a particularly lovely timber-framed building, early 15th-c; probably built as a wool store. Open wknds, bank hols and pm Weds, Apr–Sept; £1; NT. The Angel is a worthwhile dining pub.

★ **LOWER WINCHENDON** SP7312 This secluded old place has carefully restored houses and a charming, simple church; the walk over the hill to Upper Winchendon gives interesting views.

MARSWORTH SP9114 Interesting **canal walk**, past an imposing flight of locks; there's a useful family pub at Startops End.

MIDDLE CLAYDON SP7125 **Claydon House** The wonderfully

over-the-top rococo décor is the prime attraction of this mainly 18th-c house – quite a surprise given the classical simplicity of the exterior. Highlights are the carvings by Luke Lightfoot and the fantastic walls, ceilings and overmantels, though there are also portraits by Lely and Van Dyck, and mementos of Florence Nightingale, a frequent guest. The original owner's tastes were considerably richer than his pockets; but though his ambitious plans for the house eventually bankrupted him, his family still live here. Snacks, disabled access to ground floor; open pm Sat–Weds Apr–Oct; (01296) 730349; £4; NT. The Seven Stars between Twyford and Calvert is a pleasant place for lunch.

MILTON KEYNES SP8239 Britain's largest New Town is perhaps also the most successful example of the idea, with roads well laid out to keep traffic moving easily and well away from pedestrians, and a lot of greenery. Locals are proud of the remarkable number of public sculptures dotted around, from the endearing Wounded Elephant to the famous concrete cows in a field on the N side of the H3 road (Monks Way, or A422), nr the A5 junction. There's a swish shopping centre at Midsummer Boulevard, named for its alignment with the summer solstice. The **Milton Keynes Museum of Industry and Rural Life** (Southern Way, Wolverton) re-opened last summer and now includes Victorian and Edwardian room settings, a schoolroom, a steamtram, print shop and a new transport hall. Snacks, shop, disabled access; open pm Weds–Sun, Apr–Oct; (01908) 316222; *£3, family ticket £6. The **City Discovery Centre** (Bradwell Abbey) tells you all you could need to know about the New Town development (lots of slides, maps and old photographs), in a 16th-c farmhouse in the 17-acre grounds of a former abbey. Also a 14th-c barn and chapel, medieval fishponds, herb gardens and a nature trail. Meals, snacks, shop, disabled access; open wknds Apr–Sept, and all year Mon–Fri, but advisable to phone in advance to avoid large school groups; (01908) 227229; free. Not far from here, **Willen Lakeside Park** (Brickhill St, SP8839) has 2 lakes – one with water sports, hotel and restaurant, and the other for birdwatching; also a Japanese peace pagoda built by Buddhist monks, turf maze and a nature trail. Tucked around the city are various villagey corners, and the Swan (Broughton Rd in the Old Village) and the canalside Black Horse, at Great Linford, are both pleasant retreats for lunch.

★ **OLNEY** SP8851 Pleasant, stone-built, extended village with a Thursday market and the enthusiastically run **Cowper and Newton Museum**, in the former home of hymn-writer William Cowper. Several of his possessions, manuscripts and poems are on display, along with some belonging to his friend John Newton, curate of Olney and composer of *Amazing Grace*. There's a notable lace-making exhibition, and a restored period summerhouse in the little garden. Shop; cl 1–2 pm, all Sun and Mon, and Christmas–Feb; (01234) 711516; £2. There's a nice riverside stroll to the Robin Hood at Clifton Reynes; the Bull, HQ for the town's famous Shrove Tuesday pancake race, is an alternative for lunch, as are the Swan and Two Brewers.

PITSTONE SP9416 As well as a decent little **agricultural museum** (open some summer Suns and bank hols; 01296 662151) and an interesting old **church**, this small village has the oldest **windmill** in the country, built in 1627. Open pm Sun and bank hols Jun–Aug; *£1, NT. You can hire canal boats for a day from the wharf (over the B489; the Duke of Wellington has reasonably priced food), and there are nice canal walks from there to the Red Lion or White Lion at Marsworth.

QUAINTON SP7419 **Bucks Railway Centre** (Quainton Rd station) One of the largest collections of engines and rolling stock we know of, with examples from all over the world attractively displayed in a restored country station; also vintage steamtrain rides, workshops, miniature railway, and a small museum. Regular half-day steam driving courses (not cheap at £135, but people come away converted for life). Snacks, picnic area, shop; open Sun and bank hols Easter–Oct, plus Weds Jun–Aug; (01296) 655720; £3.50 (£4.50 bank hols). On the edge of the green is a particularly tall **tower mill**; you can watch the continuing restoration work. Open am Sun and bank hols; (01296) 655348; £1. Waddesdon is the closest good place for lunch. The prominent viewpoint of **Quainton Hill** is one of the main features on the 30-mile North Bucks Way, a long-distance footpath from Chequers Knap above Great Kimble to Wolverton in Milton Keynes; the Way also runs past Waddesdon.

SHABBINGTON WOOD SP6210 (nr Oakley) This has been designated a Site of Special Scientific Interest because of its rich butterfly habitats; a special butterfly trail has been created to help you spot some of the 40-odd species here.

† **STEWKLEY** SP8426 The **church** in this unusually long village has good examples of late Norman work. The village also has 2 decent pubs, and hour-long **balloon trips** over the whole county; (01525) 240451; £125 a person.

STOKE MANDEVILLE SP8309 **Bucks Goat Centre** (Layby Farm, just off the A4010) Goats galore as well as a pig, poultry, sheep, donkeys and pets; you can feed the animals (they sell bags of cut-up vegetables in the shop). Many animals are under cover, so good for a rainy day. Donkey rides most weekends. Also a plant nursery, farm shop (with cheese and fudge made from goats' milk), pet shop and a specialist motor bike shop. Meals, snacks, disabled access; cl Mon (exc bank hols); (01296) 612983; £2.50. The Chequers over at Weston Turville does decent lunches.

† **STOKE POGES CHURCH** SU9782 The graveyard inspired Thomas Gray's elegy (he's buried here); the church itself has 17th-c stained heraldic glass in the 16th-c chapel.

STOWE SP6737 Stunning **Landscape Gardens** stretch over a staggering 580 acres, first laid out between 1713 and 1725. Capability Brown was head gardener for 10 years, and the monuments and temples that adorn the grounds are by the likes of James Gibb, Sir John Vanbrugh and William Kent. Several suitably grand events throughout the year, but at any time this is a spectacular place to visit, the scale of its artistry quite staggering. Snacks, shop, disabled access (inc electric-powered cars at no extra charge). Open daily during school hols (inc over Christmas), plus Mon, Weds, Fri and Sun mid Apr–Oct; (01280) 822850; £4.40; NT. The house itself (a public school since 1923) is open pm daily (exc Sat) during the Easter and summer hols (not bank hols or Easter wk); you may feel it's outclassed by its surroundings, though it is very elegant from the outside; £2. The Bull & Butcher at Akeley has a good-value buffet lunch (not Sun, when the Wheatsheaf at Maids Moreton would be a reasonable substitute).

★ **TAPLOW** SU9185 **Cliveden** Nearly 400 acres of lovely formal gardens, woodland and parkland overlooking the Thames. The magnificent house used to belong to the Astors and is now a luxury hotel (and extremely enjoyable as such), although non-resident visitors can see 3 of the rooms with their family portraits and elegant furnishings and décor. Meals and snacks (not Mon or Tues), shop, very good disabled access; gardens open daily Apr–Sept, house open only Thurs and Sun Apr–Oct from 3–6pm; (01628) 605069; £4.80, house £1 extra; NT. The village too is attractive.

TERRICK SP8308 **Chiltern Brewery** (B4009) Small, traditional brewery with guided tours at noon every Sat. Shop, disabled access; cl 25–26 Dec, 1 Jan; tour £3.50.

THAMES BOATING SU8586 Marlow Reach is lively and attractive, and a good centre for trips in either direction (see *Berkshire chapter*). Salters (01865) 243421 operate 40-minute cruises May–Sept, £3.75. The Compleat Angler right on the river is a fine place for lunch; on a humbler plane the Two Brewers, back over the bridge, and the Hare & Hounds, out towards Henley, are good bets.

THORNBOROUGH BRIDGE SP7433 (on the A421) A 4½-mile walk starting and ending here, and well described in a leaflet from Bucks

County Council, takes in a mill, the site of a medieval village, and the Buckingham Arm Canal. Leaflets free from information centres, or from the County Hall; (01296) 382845. There's good sustenance at the Lone Tree.

WADDESDON SP7316 **Waddesdon Manor** The most spectacular of the mansions built for Baron Ferdinand de Rothschild. Plenty of rooms to see, each as lavish as the last, and filled with a dazzling array of furnishings, porcelain, portraits and other objects; there's an unrivalled display of Sèvres china. Improvements continue: parts of the Bachelors' Wing are now fully restored and open for the first time. Quite splendid, late Victorian formal gardens surround the house, and a cast-iron rococo aviary is still in use. The fabled wine cellars have huge vintage bottles, and a collection of labels designed or painted by some of the century's greatest artists. A very satisfying place to visit, but it does get busy; they operate a timed ticket system for the house (can be bought in advance, but £2.50 booking charge), so if you arrive too late, it's possible you won't get in at all. Good meals and snacks, shop, disabled access; house open Thurs–Sun, Apr–Oct, plus Weds and bank hols in July and Aug; grounds open Weds–Sun Mar–20 Dec; (01296) 651282; £9, Bachelors' Wing £1, £3 grounds only; NT. No under-5s in house. The Five Arrows does very good lunches (and has some fine Rothschild wines in all price ranges).

★ **WEEDON** SP8118 This is a lovely little village, well worth walking around for the variety of its 17th- and 18th-c houses.

★ ! † **WEST WYCOMBE** SU8294 The whole village was bought by the NT in 1929 when it was threatened with road-widening. It's still beleaguered by traffic, and you risk getting run over as you step back to admire the architecture along the village street. **West Wycombe Park** 300 acres of beautifully laid out parkland surround this splendid 18th-c Palladian house, unaltered since its completion. The magnificent rooms have a good collection of tapestries, furniture and paintings, and the Italianate painted ceilings are particularly notable. Snacks, shop; some disabled access; open pm Sun–Thurs, Jun–Aug, plus grounds only pm Sun, Weds and bank hols in Apr and May; (01628) 488675; £4.40, £2.60 grounds only; NT. **Hell Fire Caves** Great fun, these spooky old caves were extended in the 1750s by Sir Francis Dashwood to provide work for the unemployed. Legend has it that the Hell Fire Club he founded met in the tunnels for their drinking, whoring and sorcery. Once through the atmospheric Gothic entrance, the tunnels extend for about a third of a mile underground, and are filled with colourful models and tableaux. Underground café, shop; cl wkdys Nov–Feb; £3. **St Lawrence Church**, on the site of an Iron Age fort, was crowned by Dashwood with a golden ball so big (it can seat 6 people) that it, too, served as a meeting-place for the Hell Fire Club. The view from the top of the tower is impressive, and the church's interior has a number of unusual features. The busy George & Dragon in West Wycombe is handy for lunch. A visit here can be easily combined with a walk into the beechwoods just N; the pretty village of Bradenham makes a good objective for longer circular walks.

! **WESTON UNDERWOOD** SP8650 **Flamingo Gardens and Zoological Park** Not just flamingos, but a notable collection of rare and endangered birds from all over the world, inc unusual pink-backed pelicans, vultures, cockatoos and toucans. Also mammals such as bison, llamas and a unique herd of white wallabies. William Cowper wrote many of his poems in the area now patrolled by peacocks and cranes, and extracts appear on several of the statues and urns. Popular with readers; the staff are particularly helpful. Shop; disabled access, open pm Weds–Sun and bank hols May–Jun and Sept, pm daily July and Aug; (01234) 711451; *£4.50. The village is attractive, with Cowper's Oak good value for lunch.

WHITELEAF CROSS SP8203 A large, ancient hill cross dug out of the chalk on the Chilterns escarpment, above which is a Neolithic barrow. The

Red Lion below is nice for lunch, and the houses of the surrounding hamlet are quite pretty.

WING SP8922 **Ascott** Another Rothschild mansion, its black and white timbers and jutting gables quite a contrast to the luxuriant opulence of nearby Waddesdon. Once again, it's crammed full of treasures, but it feels more like a home and less like a museum; indeed it's still lived in. Ming and K'ang Hsi porcelain, paintings by Hogarth, Rubens and Gainsborough, Dutch art by Hobbema, Cuyp and others, and French and Chippendale furniture. The 260-acre grounds have extensive gardens with rare trees and shrubs, and some intriguing astrological topiary. Open Apr and Sept, pm Tues–Sun, plus garden only May–Aug, Weds and last Sun in month; (01296) 688242; £5.40, garden only £4; NT. **All Saints Church** has a fine monument to Sir Robert Dormer (died 1552), a 10th-c apse, crypt and nave, and a 12th-c font. The Queen's Head has good-value home cooking.

WINSLOW SP7727 **Winslow Hall** Striking house almost certainly designed by Wren, and unusually surviving without any major structural changes. A modest but friendly place, with a collection of Chinese art. Open pm bank hol wknds Easter–Aug, plus pm Weds and Thurs July and Aug, or by appointment; (01296) 712323; £5. **Keach's Meeting House,** nr the Market Sq (SP7627), is a fine example of a 17th-c dissenters' chapel; you'll need to get the key from Wilkinson's the estate agent on Market Sq, or from Mrs Williams, (01296) 712387. The Bell is useful for lunch.

WOOBURN COMMON SU9387 *See separate Family Panel on p.26 for* **Odds Farm Park**.

★ **Other attractive villages**, all with decent pubs, include Beachampton SP7737 (with a stream along the main street), Bishopstone SP8010 (pleasant country walks), Bledlow SP7702 (which has a Norman church with early wall paintings), Calverton SP7939, Cuddington SP7311, Denham TQ0386, Dinton SP7611, Great Missenden SP8901, Hedgerley SU9686, Hyde Heath SU9399, Ibstone SU7593, Little Hampden SP8503, Little Horwood SP7930, Marlow SU8586, Northend SU7392, Penn SU9193 (interesting church), Preston Bissett SP6529, Ravenstone SP8450, Speen SU8399, Stoke Hammond SP8829, Turville SU7690 (perhaps the most lovely valley of all here) and Worminghall SP6308.

Where to eat

BUTLER'S CROSS SP8406 **Russell Arms** *(01296) 622618* Although unremarkable from outside and having a straightforward bar which has standard pub furnishings, this surprises with its very good fresh fish dishes and other inventive food, excellent puddings, real ales, decent wines, and friendly service; a pleasantly relaxed atmosphere and a small, but light and airy dining room; no food pm Sun, Mon. **£25**|£10.

EASINGTON SP6810 **Mole & Chicken** *(01844) 208387* Country dining pub with a very attractively furnished, beamed bar, winter log fires, and a nice mix of people; particularly good food served by neatly dressed young staff, a chatty atmosphere, and a fine range of drinks; cl 25 Dec; disabled access. **£25**|£5.95.

FORD SP7709 **Dinton Hermit** *(01296) 748379* Cosy, tucked-away pub with a log fire in the comfortable lounge and a traditional public bar with an inglenook woodburner; good, home-made lunchtime bar food and a more elaborate evening menu, real ales, and a sheltered garden opposite; no food pm Sun, cl Mon, no food Tues, cl 2 wks July; children must be well behaved; disabled access. **£16.50**|£5.50.

GREAT HAMPDEN SP8401 **Hampden Arms** *(01494) 488255* Comfortable 2-room country pub by the cricket green; with a civilised atmosphere, a decent choice of freshly cooked food, real ales, friendly and efficient young licensees, and a tree-sheltered garden; handy for nearby walks; cl 24–25 Dec; partial disabled access. **£20**|£4.95.

GREAT KINGSHILL SU8798 **Red Lion** *(01494) 711262* Little brick and flint cottage with simple furnishings and good fresh fish from the friendly Spanish landlord; decent house wines; cl Mon. **£19.50**|£7.50.

GREAT MISSENDEN SO8901 **George** *(01494) 862084* Attractive 15th-c inn originally built as a hospice for the nearby abbey; with beams, alcoves and a big log fire in the cosy 2-roomed bar; popular, good-value food, quick, cheerful service, and a no smoking restaurant; pretty bdrms; cl pm Sun, pm 25–26 Dec. **£15**|£5.75.

HADDENHAM SP7408 **Green Dragon** *(01844) 291403* Civilised dining pub with particularly imaginative food in its 2 thoughtfully decorated, high-ceilinged rooms; a French brasserie-type atmosphere, well chosen wines, real ales, a winter log fire, and seats outside on the big, sheltered terrace; children over 6; disabled access. **£25**|£7.

LITTLE HAMPDEN SP8503 **Rising Sun** *(01494) 488393* Secluded upmarket dining pub with invariably good and interesting food, decent wines and real ales; attractive terrace, and rewarding walking country; bdrms; cl pm Sun, Mon (open am bank hols). **£22**|£4.95.

LONG CRENDON SP6909 **Angel** *Bicester Rd (01844) 208268* Carefully restored 17th-c dining pub with big sofas in the comfortable lounge; very good, interesting food in both the bar and restaurant, real ales, and friendly staff; cl pm Sun; disabled access. **£30**|£9.95.

MARLOW SU8586 **Burgers** *The Causeway (01628) 483389* Long-standing, family-run place serving breakfast, morning coffee, lunch and afternoon tea – as well as a spacious shop selling home-baked bread, cakes, pastries, scones, confectionery, and chocolates; take-away sandwiches, too; cl Sun, bank hols, Christmas; disabled access. £4.

MOULSOE SP9041 **Carrington Arms** *(01908) 218050* Well refurbished, old brick house with comfortable, traditional furnishings; delicious meat and fish displayed in a refrigerated glass case, with friendly staff who guide you through what is on offer (it is then sold in pounds and ounces and cooked on a sophisticated indoor barbecue), separate bar menu as well, and an oyster bar; well kept real ales, a decent range of wines inc champagne by the glass, and good coffee; bdrms. **£23.50**|£7.25.

PRESTON BISSETT SP6529 **White Hart** *(01280) 847969* Friendly, 18th-c thatched and timbered house with 3 cosy little rooms, traditional atmosphere and furnishings, real ales and a dozen malt whiskies; tasty, often interesting bar food inc lunchtime snacks, and chatty, helpful staff. **£21.45**|£8.95.

SKIRMETT SU7790 **Frog** *(01491) 638996* Appealing pub with the atmosphere of a smart country local, and a nice mix of comfortable furnishings and an open fire in the neat, beamed bar area; good, popular and interesting food, efficient service, a no smoking restaurant, real ales and a fair range of wines; also, a lovely garden; bdrms. **£21.65**|£8.95.

WEST WYCOMBE SU8394 **George & Dragon** *High St (01494) 464414* Striking, partly Tudor inn with a cheerful, bustling atmosphere in the rambling main bar, a big log fire, and popular food inc very good home-made pies; a big, peaceful garden; bdrms (not Christmas, New Year or Easter). **£18**|£6.75.

WHEELEREND COMMON SU8093 **Chequers** *(01494) 883070* Pleasant old pub with welcoming licensees, a fine inglenook, simple furnishings, and small hunting prints in the little bar; good-value, homely bar food, and well kept real ales; cl pm Sun, Mon; disabled access. **£15.50**|£5.

WOBURN SANDS SP9235 **Spooners** *61 High St (01908) 584385* Smart, pretty restaurant with good-value French and English cooking, and a welcoming atmosphere; worthwhile snacks downstairs; cl Sun, Mon, 10 days Aug, 10 days from 24 Dec; disabled access. **£25**|£7.50.

Special thanks to Mrs P A Beaumont, Paul Kennedy, George Atkinson.

Buckinghamshire Calendar

Some of these dates were provisional as we went to press. Please check information with the telephone numbers provided.

FEBRUARY

14 **Milton Keynes** Brass Band Festival at Stantonbury Leisure Centre (01908) 510809
16 **Olney** Pancake Race: since 1455 (01234) 711392

APRIL

4 **Quainton** Circus Fun Days at Bucks Railway Centre – *till Mon 5* (01296) 655720
9 **Winslow** New Orleans and Classic Jazz Festival at the Bell Hotel and other venues, inc a street parade – *till Sun 11* (01296) 730575
10 **Wendover** Music Festival (01296) 622805
24 **High Wycombe** Arts Festival – *till 29 May* (01494) 528226
30 **Chalfont** St Giles Live Craft Show at Chiltern Open-air Museum – *till 3 May* (01494) 871117

MAY

2 **High Wycombe** Carnival (01494) 522808; near **Wendover** Whitchurch Morris Men at Coombe Hill *at 6.30am* (01865) 766191
3 **Ivinghoe Milling** Demonstrations at Ford End Watermill, Ford End Farm (01582) 600391; **Pitstone** Pitstone Green Farm Museum Open Day (01296) 662151; **Quainton** May Day Fair (01296) 655348
8 **Wendover** Music Festival (01296) 622805
9 **Ivinghoe** National Mills Day: milling at Ford End Watermill, Ford End Farm (01582) 600391
20 **High Wycombe** Mayor-making and Weighing at the Guildhall (01494) 421134
31 **Chalfont St Giles** Rare Breeds Show at Chiltern Open-air Museum (01494) 871117; **Ivinghoe** Milling at Ford End Watermill, Ford End Farm (01582) 600391; **Pitstone** Pitstone Green Farm Museum Open Day (01296) 662151; **Quainton** Bus Rally at Bucks Railway Centre (01296) 655720

JUNE

7 **Stony Stratford** Music and Performing Arts Festival – *till Sun 13* (01908) 566407
11 **Quainton** Thomas the Tank Engine and Friends at Bucks Railway Centre – *till Sun 13* (01296) 655720
12 **Wendover** Music Festival (01296) 622805
13 **Ivinghoe** Milling at Ford End Watermill, Ford End Farm (01582) 600391; **Pitstone** Pitstone Green Farm Museum Open Day (01296) 662151
18 **Great Linford** Waterside Festival: free theatre, music events and park entertainments – *till Sun 20* (01908) 662928
19 **Marlow** Regatta (01491) 575478

Buckinghamshire Calendar (cont.)

JULY

2 **Milton Keynes** International Festival – *till Sun 4* (01908) 610564
3 **Aylesbury** Massed Morris Men in Market Sq, *at 10am* (01865) 766191; **Buckingham** Summer Music Festival – *till Sat 10* (01280) 814080; **Prestwood** Chiltern Traction Engine Steam Rally – *till Sun 4* (01923) 262845; **Stowe** North Bucks Show at Stowe Park (01280) 812038
10 **Wendover** Music Festival (01296) 622805
11 **Ivinghoe** Milling at Ford End Watermill, Ford End Farm (01582) 600391; **Pitstone** Pitstone Green Farm Museum Open Day (01296) 662151
17 **Burnham** Carnival at Burnham Park (01628) 605772

AUGUST

7 **Middle Claydon** Lanternlight Concert at Claydon House (01296) 738511
8 **Pitstone** Pitstone Green Farm Museum Open Day (01296) 662151
9 **Chalfont St Giles** Experience Medieval England: living history at Chiltern Open-air Museum – *till Sun 15* (01494) 871117
30 **Ivinghoe** Milling at Ford End Watermill, Ford End Farm (01582) 600391; **Pitstone** Pitstone Green Farm Museum Open Day (01296) 662151; **Quainton** Vintage Transport Rally at Bucks Railway Centre (01296) 655720; **Stony Stratford** Town Fair: stalls, Morris dancers, children's events (01908) 563143; **Winslow** Show: parade, horses and horticultural show (01296) 713023

SEPTEMBER

2 **Weedon** Buckinghamshire County Show at Weedon Park (01296) 483734
4 **High Wycombe** Show – *till Sun 5* (01494) 529179
11 **Quainton** Thomas the Tank Engine and Friends at Bucks Railway Centre – *till Sun 12* (01296) 655720; **Winslow** National Mare Show at Addington Equestrian Centre – *till Sun 12* (01296) 713663
12 **Ivinghoe Milling** at Ford End Watermill, Ford End Farm (01582) 600391; **Pitstone** Pitstone Green Farm Museum Open Day (01296) 662151; **Stowe** Landmark Trust Open Day at Gothic Temple: not open to the public at any other time of the year (01628) 825925
16 **Thame** Agricultural Show (01844) 212737
19 **Chalfont St Giles** Transport Day at Chiltern Open-air Museum (01494) 871117; **Wolverton** Fête (01908) 563143

OCTOBER

9 **Chalfont St Giles** Harvest Celebration at Chiltern Open-air Museum – *till Sun 10* (01494) 871117
31 **Chalfont St Giles** Halloween Event at Chiltern Open-air Museum – (01494) 871117

Buckinghamshire Calendar (cont.)

NOVEMBER

5 **Downley** Torchlight Procession and Bonfire (01494) 421892

11 **Fenny Stratford** Firing the Poppers: since 1730 in celebration of St Martin, patron saint of Fenny Stratford church; poppers are quart-size metal vessels filled with gunpowder and fired with a hot rod (01908) 372825

DECEMBER

5 **Chalfont St Giles** Victorian Christmas at Chiltern Open-air Museum (01494) 871117

We welcome reports from readers

This *Guide* depends on readers' reports. Do help us if you can – in return, we offer a discount on the next edition to people who've helped us with reports for it. Tell us what you think about places already in it, and anything extra you think we should say about them. And send us your ideas for inclusion in the next edition: places to visit, eat at or stay in, attractive drives or walks, maybe even unusual interesting shops you know of. Use the card in the middle, the report forms at the end, or just write – no stamp needed: *The Good Guide to Britain*, FREEPOST TN1569, Wadhurst, E Sussex TN5 7BR.

Cambridgeshire

Cambridge is a great city for a short visit; the county has two excellent family attractions, and quite a lot to interest older people.

The city of Cambridge is an easy day out from London. Arguably Britain's most attractive ancient university city, it has lots of interesting places to visit, and a grace and charm that make for delightful short stays. Its museums are outstanding. It's at its best during the university terms, as it's the college students who put life and context into the medieval lanes, buildings and gardens. In summer, when it is host instead to foreign language students, its popularity with coach tours means that particular places can suddenly overflow with visitors, so perhaps the best time of all is spring or autumn. In winter, both city and county can be very chill.

In the continually developing Duxford Air Museum and Linton Zoo the county has two first-class family attractions, easily reached from the M11 – as is stately Wimpole Hall. Other family favourites include the Peakirk waterfowl garden (now attractively reworked), the Hamerton wildlife centre, the Nene Valley Railway between Wansford and Peterborough, and the Sacrewell country centre at Thornhaugh. Flag Fen just east of Peterborough is an intriguing window on prehistoric life around here – and on the intricate detective work needed to piece it together. Older people like quiet Ely with its graceful cathedral, Anglesey Abbey at Lode, and Elton Hall. There are some lovely villages to stroll through, often with fine churches.

The countryside is a touch monotonous for most people – especially the north's flat silt fens and vast level fields. But there are those who love the misty bleakness in autumn, say, and this area has a lot to offer birdwatchers. Wicken Fen has a much broader appeal, showing what the area was like before intensive agriculture took over; the Prickwillow Drainage Engine Museum gives another interesting slant on these fenland landscapes. To the west, the land is drier and more rolling, with stonebuilt villages more reminiscent of Leicestershire.

Cambridgeshire's Tourist Information Centres are among the best – very helpful with information, maps and trails.

Where to stay

CAMBRIDGE TL4658 **Arundel House** *53 Chesterton Rd, Cambridge CB4 3AN (01223) 367701* **£72;** 105 comfortable rms, 6 without bthrm, some overlooking the river. Carefully preserved terrace of fine early Victorian houses overlooking the River Cam and parkland; comfortable, attractive bar with 2 fires, elegant restaurant, large and airy plant-filled conservatory, good imaginative food, and seats in the pleasant garden.

CAMBRIDGE TL4658 **Cambridge Lodge** *Huntingdon Rd, Cambridge CB3 0DQ (01223) 352833* **£72.50;** 13 rms, 10 with own bthrm. Mock-Tudor house on the outskirts, with open fire in relaxed and comfortable lounge, friendly service, and good freshly prepared food in popular restaurant; cl Christmas–New Year.

DUXFORD TL4745 **Duxford Lodge** *Ickleton Rd, Duxford, Cambridge CB2 4RU (01223) 836444* **£80w;** 15 good-sized rms. Carefully run Victorian hotel in an acre of neatly kept gardens; a restful little lounge, spacious bar, relaxed atmosphere, and enjoyable modern cooking in the airy restaurant; cl 25–30 Dec; disabled access.

ELY TL5380 **Lamb** 2 *Lynn Rd, Ely CB7 4EJ (01353) 663574* **£84;** 32 comfortable rms. Pleasant, neatly kept old coaching inn nr cathedral; with 2 bars, enjoyable food in attractive restaurant, very friendly staff, and good car parking.

HUNTINGDON TL2371 **Old Bridge** *1 High St, Huntingdon PE18 6TQ (01480) 452681* **£89.50,** plus wknd breaks; 25 excellent rms. Creeper-covered Georgian hotel with prettily decorated lounge, and log fire in panelled bar; imaginative British cooking and extensive wine list in the partly no smoking restaurant and more informal lunchtime room (pretty murals), and quick courteous service; riverside gardens.

LITTLE GRANSDEN TL2754 **Gransden Lodge Farm** *Little Gransden, Sandy, Beds SG19 3EB (01767) 677365* **£40;** 5 rms. Set on a working farm of 860 acres with pedigree Gelbwieh cattle, this friendly house has a big lounge, dining room, and gardens with fish ponds; no evening meals (plenty of pubs and restaurants locally).

NEEDINGWORTH TL3472 **Pike & Eel** *Needingworth, St Ives, Huntingdon PE17 3TW (01480) 463336* **£60;** 9 rms. Very peaceful riverside spot with spacious lawns and marina, roomy plush bar, big open fire and easy chairs in smaller room, glass-walled restaurant, carvery, real ale, good breakfasts, and friendly staff.

SIX MILE BOTTOM TL5757 **Swynford Paddocks** *Six Mile Bottom, Newmarket, Suffolk CB8 0UE (01638) 570234* **£127,** plus wknd breaks; 15 individually furnished rms with good bthrms. Gabled mansion in neat grounds, with carefully furnished panelled rooms, fresh flowers and log fires, a relaxed atmosphere, good food, and friendly service; tennis, putting, croquet, and giant chess.

STILTON TL1689 **Bell** *High St, Stilton, Peterborough PE7 3RA (01733) 241066* ***£59w;** 20 rms. Elegant, carefully restored coaching inn with attractive rambling bars, big log fire, generous helpings of good food using the famous cheese (which was first sold from here), and seats in the sheltered cobbled and flagstoned courtyard; cl 25 Dec.

WANSFORD TL0799 **Haycock** *Wansford, Peterborough PE8 6JA (01780) 782223* **£99w,** plus special breaks; 50 attractively decorated rms. Old-fashioned golden stone inn with relaxed, comfortable, carefully furnished lounges and pubby bar; pretty lunchtime café, smart restaurant with good food, excellent wines and efficient friendly service; garden with boules, fishing and cricket; disabled access. The little village it dominates is attractive, with a fine bridge over the Nene, and a good antique shop.

We welcome reports from readers

This *Guide* depends on readers' reports. Do help us if you can – in return, we offer a discount on the next edition to people who've helped us with reports for it. Tell us what you think about places already in it, and anything extra you think we should say about them. And send us your ideas for inclusion in the next edition: places to visit, eat at or stay in, attractive drives or walks, maybe even unusual interesting shops you know of. Use the card in the middle, the report forms at the end, or just write – no stamp needed: *The Good Guide to Britain*, FREEPOST TN1569, Wadhurst, E Sussex TN5 7BR.

To see and do

CAMBRIDGESHIRE Family Attraction of the Year

LINTON TL5546 **Linton Zoological Gardens** (B1052, just off the A604) There's a real emphasis on conservation and breeding at this friendly family-run zoo, and though it's a wonderful place for visitors it's reassuring to see that the animals always come first. Current residents include giant tortoises, snow leopards, a couple of Grevy's zebras, Sumatran tigers, and tarantula spiders, all housed in enclosures as close to their natural habitats as possible. The tigers might peer through a glass window back at you – quite a thrilling experience – and it's intriguing getting a real bird's-eye view of the domestic goings-on of cockatoos, parrots and owls, courtesy of strategically placed closed-circuit cameras. They do very interesting animal encounters, and hands-on demonstrations: children who find stroking an owl too tame should get more excited at the prospect of posing for a picture with a boa constrictor wrapped round their necks. As at most places, these events vary from day to day, so best to check in advance exactly what's going on – and make a note of the times when you arrive. Covering 16 acres, the prettily landscaped grounds are becoming a draw almost in their own right; they put in 10,000 bedding plants every year. They usually have pony rides and a bouncy castle in school holidays and on sunny summer wknds, and an enjoyable family quiz trail is always available. Several picnic areas (some under cover), a playing field for letting off steam, and a play area ideal for younger children (not so thrilling for older ones). There are plenty of bigger zoos around the country (you can easily see everything here at a relaxed pace in half a day) but the honest and friendly approach somehow makes this more rewarding than most. Summer snacks, shop, disabled access; cl 25 Dec; (01223) 891308; *£4.50 (£3.50 children aged 2–13).

CAMBRIDGE TL4458 Quieter and prettier than Oxford (which the colleges here were founded to escape), the centre is dominated by ancient and graceful university buildings: you get a real sense of centuries of study. It still has the character of a small old-fashioned market town, almost untouched by the modern world; Cambridge's hi-tech light industry is kept firmly on the outskirts. Between the colleges and university buildings are numerous less imposing but attractive old buildings, often grouped together quite picturesquely. The architecture has a striking diversity (continuous development of the colleges means that most have either much loved or maligned modern blocks), though isn't always shown off at its best, thanks to layers of muck and grime that rather spoil some of the libraries and faculty buildings. Happily, one of the most delightful parts of town, **the Backs**, where the river snakes through the colleges, never looks less than charming, with its delightful lawns, trees, college gardens, punts gliding past the weeping willows and sometimes even grazing cattle opposite King's. Don't try to drive around town; there really is no parking, and apart from the pedestrianised centre there's a frustrating tangle of congested one-way streets. Head for one of the big NCPs or a Park and Ride. If you don't plan to take a car at all, it's worth noting that the railway station is far from central, although there is a frequent bus service into the historic centre. Chauffeured trishaws offer a pleasant alternative way to get around. For a first-time visit, the Tour Bus (about an hour) is a good introduction. Walking tours set off from the Tourist Information Centre (Wheeler St) 5 times a day in summer. Cyclists will enjoy the towpaths here; nettle-free, and safe if you have children with you. Quite a few shops are that bit different and worth popping into. In term-time, there are countless events; any college noticeboard will show what's on. West Road concert hall has outstanding acoustics, while a concert in one of the smaller college chapels can be a charmingly intimate experience.

CAMBRIDGE COLLEGES TL4458 The colleges look private, but you can usually wander into the courtyards (not at exam time, and expect to be charged by many during the summer). Be warned, though, college porters will get terribly agitated if you even look at the grass let alone accidently step on it. Several of the dining halls and chapels are worth seeking out. The largest, finest and richest college is Trinity, where the imposing Great Court is usually open to the public and the Wren Library (open wkdys 12–2pm) in Nevilles Court is definitely worth a visit. King's is probably the best known, with its magnificent chapel (see below); and is pleasant to walk through. Gonville & Caius (pronounced 'keys') is small and slightly snooty, but very pretty. Queens' has a half-timbered courtyard and an eye-catchingly gaudy painted hall, as well as the famous Mathematical Bridge (reputedly built without any bolts or fastenings, until curiosity got the better of some engineers who dismantled it and found they couldn't put it back together in the same way). Peterhouse is the oldest, founded in 1284; the buildings carry their years very gracefully, although these days its deer park is devoid of deer. St John's has the very photographed Bridge of Sighs. Jesus, a bit off the main beat, is huge and grandly impressive, and Emmanuel has notable gardens. Clare and Trinity Hall are smaller yet charming colleges, next to each other by the Backs.

† **King's College Chapel** TL4458 The annual Festival of Nine Lessons and Carols has made the interior and something of the atmosphere familiar to most visitors, but you're still not fully prepared for the grandeur and scale of the fan-vaulted ceiling, or the miraculously preserved 16th-c stained glass. The overall effect is marred slightly by the unique dark oak screen added by Henry VIII, but the chapel's other famous feature – Rubens's *Adoration of the Magi* – is quite breathtaking. Try to attend choral evensong at 5.30pm Tues–Sat in term-time, or one of the Sun services (10.30am and 3.30pm). Shop, disabled access; cl most of Sun during term-time, and 24 Dec–3 Jan; (01223) 331155; £3.

University Botanic Garden TL4557 (Cory Lodge, Bateman St) Founded in 1762 and moved to its present site in 1831, now covering 40 acres, with some marvellous mature trees, a geographic rock garden, scented garden, water and winter gardens, and many rare plants inc several National Collections. Rarely crowded, and very pleasant to stroll through. Snacks, shop, disabled access; cl 25–26 Dec, (01223) 336265; £1.50.

Fitzwilliam Museum TL4457 (Trumpington St) This is a wonderful place, a grand and impressive building, crammed with more dazzling treasures than you could hope to examine in one visit. Downstairs are Greek, Egyptian and Roman antiquities, European ceramics, English glass, carvings, and armour, while upstairs paintings include

Days Out

Cambridge: Climb Great St Mary's Tower for the view; King's College Chapel and colleges; lunch in the Eagle, Bene't St; on sunny days punt (or walk) along the Cam to the tearoom at Granchester – otherwise the University Botanic Garden, and Fitzwilliam Museum.

A busy family day: Duxford Airfield/American Air Museum; lunch at the Pear Tree, Hildersham; Linton Zoo.

Country life: Willers Mill Wildlife Park and Docwra Manor gardens, Shepreth; stroll through Foxton and Barrington – lunch at the Royal Oak there; Wimpole Hall, Home Farm and/or stroll in the estate; if it's the last Sun of the month you may have time to fit in Bourn windmill.

works by Titian, Canaletto and French Impressionists; if you've not been for a couple of years you'll be pleased to hear both galleries are now open all day. Decent café, shop, disabled access; cl Mon (exc bank hols), 24 Dec–1 Jan, Good Fri; (01223) 332900; free.

OTHER CAMBRIDGE MUSEUMS TL4558 Most of the town's other museums have a rather academic bent, but are no less rewarding for that: the **Sedgwick Museum** (Downing St) is the university geology museum, with an outstanding collection of fossils, and rocks from Darwin's journey in HMS *Beagle*. The curator not so long ago proved that iguanadons were put together differently from how scientists had previously thought; the bones of his museum's 20-ft specimen have not been rearranged for historical reasons although theoretically, he claims, it is currently in agony. Shop, limited disabled access; cl 1–2pm, pm Sat, all day Sun, Christmas–New Year, Easter; (01223) 333456; free. Down the same street is the **Museum of Archaeology & Anthropology** (open pm Tues–Sat, cl Christmas, Easter) and a **Museum of Zoology**, where a 70-ft whale skeleton hangs above the entrance inside (cl wknds and 1–2pm outside term-time; free). The **Museum of Classical Archaeology** on Sidgwick Ave has one of the few surviving collections of casts of Greek and Roman sculpture (cl wknds; free), while the various scientific instruments and apparatus at the **Whipple Museum of Science** (Free School Lane) quickly make you thankful we need no longer rely on sundials and abacuses (open pm wkdys; free).

CAMBRIDGE & COUNTY FOLK MUSEUM TL4459 (2–3 Castle St) Useful exploration of local life in handsome 16th-c former inn nr river. Shop; cl winter Mons; (01223) 355159; £2.

KETTLE'S YARD (Castle St, Cambridge) Lively arts centre with temporary exhibitions in the gallery and permanent displays in the avant-garde yet surprisingly welcoming house, taking in 20th-c paintings and sculptures (interesting St Ives connections), lovely 18th-c furniture and oriental carpets, and collections of shells and stones. Lots of activities and workshops, several designed especially for the blind or hard of hearing. Devotees say the sunlight on winter afternoons illuminates the exhibits to extraordinary effect. Shop, some disabled access; cl am, all day Mon (except bank hols); (01233) 352124; free.

Of the many churches here, it's worth noting **St Bene't's**, one of the city's oldest, the popular **Holy Sepulchre** or Round Church (which has brass rubbing), and **Great St Mary's** with its fine roof and good city views from the tower.

The many **secondhand bookshops** are worth a look. Heffers children's bookshop is particularly good, and the general bookshops are as fine as you'd expect in this university town. There's often a craft fair on St John's Green. Many attractive **snack places** include Clowns (King St, off Sidney St), Roof Garden (top floor of Arts Theatre – side entrance in St Edward's Passage opposite King's), Boards (down a floor), the tiny Little Tea Room (All Saints Green), Copper Kettle (King's Parade), King's Pantry (King's Parade), and Browns (Trumpington St). Decent **riverside pubs** include the Anchor (Silver St Bridge), Boathouse (Chesterton Rd), Fort St George (Midsummer Common) and Mill (Mill Lane). The best pubs away from the river are the smoke-free Free Press (Prospect Row) and atmospheric Eagle (Bene't St).

PUNTING TL4458 The only way to travel, though if your skills in this department were picked up in Oxford you'll find they do things a little back to front here. You can punt right along the Backs, and even down to Grantchester, a pleasant little village still much as described in Rupert Brooke's poem of the same name, with the civilised Orchard Tea Gardens (lovely in summer – and does other drinks too, inc champagne) and 3 pubs. Hire punts from Scudamores on Mill Lane or other stations along the water; prices are generally around £10 an hour (£25 if you require a chauffeur). Bumps races (several rowing eights start off in a line and have to catch up with the one in front) take place on the river in Feb, Jun and July.

TOWPATH WALKS TL4459 From Magdalene Bridge right in Cambridge itself there's a pleasant walk by the towpath out into the meadows – tranquil, with only punts as far as the lock. Beyond that, you could walk as far as Ely, with oarsmen setting an altogether more vigorous tone – though the Ancient Shepherds or Plough at Fen Ditton might be a gentler target. Another pleasant stroll out – in the opposite direction – from Cambridge is the walk along the Cam to Grantchester.

Other things to see and do

★ ✝ **BARNACK** TF0704 Barnack has interesting dotted-about clusters of stonebuilt houses, a windmill, a part-Saxon church, and a fine pub (the Millstone).

★ **BARRINGTON** TL3949 Superb village green surrounded by pretty timbered houses, interesting church and a good pub; the nearby village of Foxton is especially interesting if you know the book *The Common Stream* by Rowland Parker (an intricate account of the village through the ages).

BOURN TL3158 The working **windmill** here is thought to be the oldest trestle post mill in the country. Usually open pm last Sun of month, Mar–Oct; (01223) 243830; £1. The Duke of Wellington has good food.

✝ **BURWELL CHURCH** TL5866 This handsome and airy building has a fine oak roof. The attractive village also has a restored **windmill**.

★ ✝ **CASTOR** TL1298 Now that it's bypassed, this ancient village is settling into a pleasantly relaxed mood. It has a fine **church**, several handsome thatched stonebuilt houses, and 2 pleasant pubs – both thatched too.

COTON ORCHARD TL4059 (Madingley Rd) Busy 60-acre site with garden centre, pick-your-own soft and top fruits, orchard, and small vineyard. Snacks, farm and gift shop, some disabled access; (01954) 210234; free.

✝ **CROYDON CHURCH** TL3149 quietly charming, a proper country church with a timeless feel. The Queen Adelaide is a popular dining pub.

DEVIL'S DITCH TL5765 This miles-long ancient embankment lets you fuel a walk with thoughts of whether it was built to fight off the Romans, or some centuries later to protect the riches of East Anglia from Midlands warlords. A good start or finish might be the King's pub in Reach TL5666, at its N end: expert German cooking. It's not much of a topographical feature, and is crossed by one or two very busy roads.

✝ **DUXFORD AIRFIELD** TL4546 Very handy from Cambridge, this branch of the Imperial War Museum is home to Europe's best collection of military and civil aircraft, with over 140 flying machines from flimsy-looking biplanes to state-of-the-art Gulf War jets. Children particularly enjoy the fun hands-on section, where they can go into the cockpits of some exhibits, and preserved hangars, control towers and operations rooms create something of the atmosphere Duxford must have had when it was a working World War II air base. Also a realistic hi-tech flight simulator re-creates a Battle of Britain dogfight, the prototype Concorde, a summer narrow-gauge railway, pleasure flights, and an adventure playground; air shows in summer – phone for details. Meals and snacks (or plenty of space for picnics), shop, disabled access; cl 24–26 Dec; (01223) 835000; £7.

ELTON HALL TL0892 From the back a splendid 'gothick' fantasy, this is a fascinating lived-in house dating back to Tudor times, with lovely furnishings, porcelain and paintings, inc works by 15th-c Old Masters and Gainsborough and Constable. The library has a Prayer Book that belonged to Henry VIII (his writing is inside), and the gardens are especially pleasant in summer when the roses are in bloom. Adjacent garden centre and tearoom; open pm 23–24 May, pm Weds Jun–Aug, plus pm Thurs and Sun July–Aug, and pm 30 Aug;

(01832) 280468; £4.50, £2.50 garden. The Black Horse in the pretty village is very handy for lunch.

✝ **ELY** TL5480 Busy little market town with good shops and some lovely old buildings; it well repays a leisurely stroll. The main attraction is the **cathedral**, one of England's most striking, its distinctive towers dominating the skyline for miles; especially good views coming in on the Soham Rd. Complete by the late 12th c, it was restored in a surprisingly sympathetic manner mainly in the mid-19th c. The façade, covered in blind arcading, is fantastic, but most remarkable perhaps is the Octagonal Tower, over 400 tons suspended in space without any visible means of support; it looks especially impressive from inside. The Lady Chapel has the widest medieval vault in the country, the walls carved with hundreds of tiny statues which were all somewhat brutally beheaded in the Reformation. The splendid Norman nave seems even longer than it really is because it's so narrow. Also not to be missed are a couple of elaborately sculpted medieval doors – and see if you can spot the railwayman's epitaph, with its unique imagery. Evensong every day except Weds, at 5.30pm. Meals, snacks, shop, disabled access; (01353) 667735; £3.50. Inside the cathedral the **Stained Glass Museum** preserves fine medieval and more modern stained glass rescued from redundant buildings and churches. Good displays on how the windows are made, and a bonus is the unusual view down over the church; open daily, (01353) 667735; £2.50. The Prince Albert, handy for the cathedral, has a nice garden. The town **museum** (Old Gaol, Market St) has displays on Hereward the Wake, who led the Anglo-Saxon resistance to the Norman Conquest from here. Shop; disabled access; cl Mon (exc bank hols); (01353) 666655; £1.80. **Oliver Cromwell's House** (St Mary's St, Ely) Next to the unexpectedly grand church of St Mary's, this fine old house was the home of Oliver Cromwell and his family from 1636 until shortly before he became Lord Protector. Period furnished rooms, useful videos (one on the draining of the fens), and information centre in the downstairs front room. Shop; cl winter Suns, 25–26 Dec, 1 Jan; (01353) 662062; £2.50. The Cutter out at Annesdale off the A10 is an attractively placed riverside family pub.

★ **FULBOURN** TL5256 This is an attractive largely thatched village, with a windmill on the Cambridge rd, a good farm shop with pick-your-own fruit, and a pretty church; a path eastwards takes you to the wooded line of the Fleam Dyke, a miles-long Dark Ages defence earthwork.

GOG MAGOG HILLS TL4953 Not exactly a towering range, these are worth a passing visit; among tall trees you can trace the main rampart and ditch of **Wandlebury Iron Age fort**, and there are good views of distant towers and spires of Cambridge.

GRAFHAM WATER TL1667 Fishing and sailing, cycle hire, nature reserve with birdwatching hides and trails (you'll see a lot more birds in winter), exhibition centre. There's an attractive waterside path along the northern shore. Snacks, good disabled access; car parking charge; (01480) 812154. The Wheatsheaf at West Perry is a popular refreshment stop and, if you're travelling on the B661 from here to Staunton, look out for the roadside stall at the Dillington crossroads – excellent pickled onions and the like, reasonably priced.

HAMERTON WILDLIFE CENTRE TL1481 A favourite of several of our correspondents (some of whom seem to make monthly visits as there is always something new to see), an expanding centre providing sanctuary for over 120 different kinds of animal, some extinct in the wild. Enclosures of meerkats, wallabies, wolves, gibbons, cheetahs and many more, inc the only breeding group of two-toed sloths in the country. Frequent exchanges with other zoos, so the inmates change quite often. Regular visitors recommend bringing wellies in winter, though there are concrete paths. Not much under cover but if it rains they will give you free tickets to come back another day. Sensibly priced tearoom (cl winter),

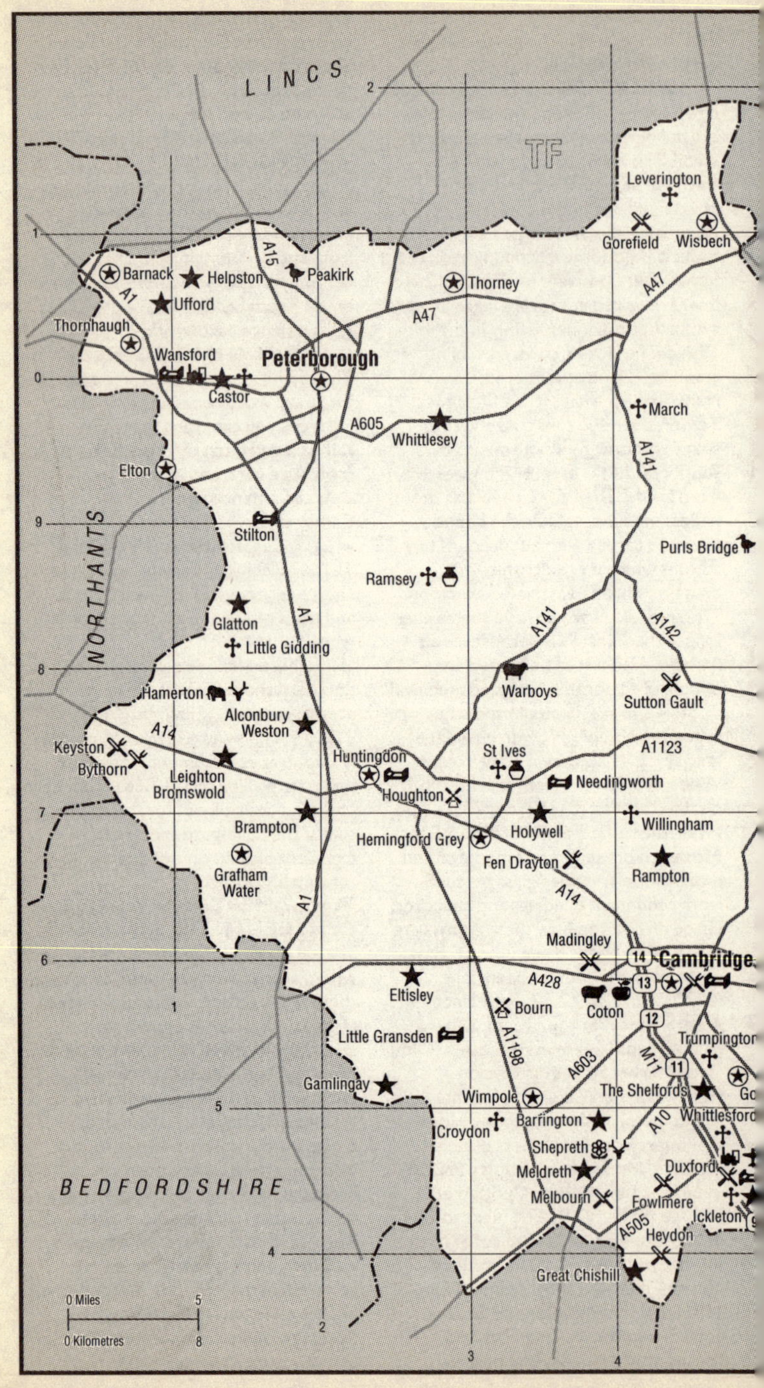
LINCS
TF
NORTHANTS
BEDFORDSHIRE
Leverington
Gorefield
Wisbech
Barnack
Helpston
Peakirk
Thorney
Ufford
Thornhaugh
Wansford
Peterborough
Castor
March
Whittlesey
Elton
Stilton
Purls Bridge
Ramsey
Glatton
Little Gidding
Hamerton
Warboys
Sutton Gault
Alconbury Weston
Keyston
Bythorn
Leighton Bromswold
Huntingdon
St Ives
Needingworth
Houghton
Brampton
Hemingford Grey
Holywell
Willingham
Grafham Water
Fen Drayton
Rampton
Madingley
Cambridge
Eltisley
Bourn
Coton
Little Gransden
Trumpington
Gamlingay
Wimpole
The Shelfords
Croydon
Barrington
Whittlesford
Shepreth
Meldreth
Duxford
Melbourn
Fowlmere
Ickleton
Heydon
Great Chishill
A1
A15
A47
A605
A141
A142
A14
A1123
A428
A1198
A603
M11
A10
A505
0 Miles 5
0 Kilometres 8

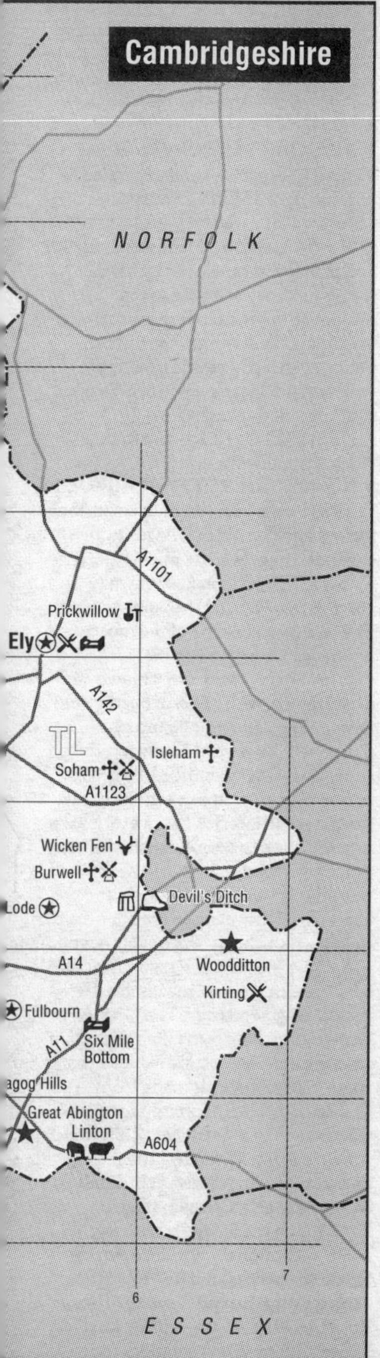

shop, disabled access (when dry); cl 25 Dec; (01832) 293362; £4.50. The Green Man over at Leighton Bromswold is a useful food stop.

★ ✝ ⌂ ✕ **HEMINGFORD GREY** TL2970 Charming village with a peaceful view of the church over the willow-bordered river (the odd church tower is the result of its spire being lopped off by an 18th-c storm); one stone house among the thatched brick ones is Norman and said to be England's oldest. Nearby Hemingford Abbots is also pretty, and the Axe & Compass here is useful for lunch. The **River Ouse** between Hemingford Grey and St Ives is a popular weekend stamping-ground, with **Houghton Mill** as a charming set piece – a lovely building in pretty setting; the Three Horseshoes nearby has decent food.

HUNTINGDON TL2371 After considerable recent growth the old centre now feels a bit sidetracked, but has one or two fine buildings such as the George, a particularly handsome Georgian coaching inn. Two of Huntingdon's MPs can claim to have run the country for a while, and the **Cromwell Museum** (Grammar School Walk) commemorates the first. The restored Norman building is where the future Lord Protector went to school (as did Pepys), and many of his possessions are on display. Shop; cl 1–2pm , all day Mon, am winter Suns and wkdys, 24–26 Dec; (01480) 425830; free. The Old Bridge is a good civilised place for lunch. **Hinchingbrooke Country Park** (a couple of miles W, TL2271) is good for a walk, a run-about, or a picnic. Guided walks and events start at the visitor centre most wknds, and there are water sports on the lake. Snacks, disabled access; (01480) 451568; free. Neighbouring **Hinchingbrooke House** (now a school) is where some reckon Cromwell and Charles I met as children; it's usually open bank hols and pm summer Suns (£1). The Olde Mill opposite is a delightfully set family dining pub.

★ ✝ **ICKLETON** TL4944 This attractive village has a fine church, with Roman columns as bases for its arches, and interestingly carved pews. The churchyard is lovely, and around the church and small green are several beautiful old houses – often a good deal older than their Georgian refacing suggests.

✝ **ISLEHAM CHURCH** TL6474 Attractive from the outside, but its best feature is its wonderful roof.

✝ **LEVERINGTON CHURCH** TF4411 The tower and its spire are noteworthy, as is the very unusual 2-storey 14th-c porch.

LINTON TL5546 *See separate Family Panel on p.41* for the **Zoological Gardens**. Not far from here towards Balsham is **Chilford Hall Vineyard**, a friendly 18-acre winery with interesting old buildings and tours on the hour; cl Nov-Easter; (01223) 892641; £4.50 (inc tastings and a little souvenir glass). The Pear Tree in Hildersham does decent family food.

✝ **LITTLE GIDDING CHURCH** TL1281 Archetypal small-village country church, well worth a look inside; if it's closed, ask at the farmhouse.

LODE TL5362 **Anglesey Abbey** All that remains of the original priory is a medieval undercroft, but the handsome 17th-c house has an engaging collection of clocks and eclectic range of furniture and paintings; it's definitely worth pausing at Constable's view of the Thames and the landscapes by Claude. The bookshelves in the library are made from Rennie's Waterloo Bridge. The lovely gardens were laid out in Georgian style from 1926 by the first Lord Fairhaven, and a restored **watermill** in the grounds still produces flour; the famous drifts of snowdrops are usually at their best in late Feb. Varied events and activities, inc highly regarded open-air theatre and opera. Meals, snacks, shop, some disabled access; house open pm Weds–Sun and bank hols late Mar–mid-Oct, grounds open from 11am (and are also open Mon and Tues most of July and Aug). Shop, restaurant and plant centre; (01223) 811200; £5.80 (£6.80 Sun and bank hols), £3.40 grounds only; NT. The Red Lion at attractive Swaffham Prior does decent fresh food.

✝ **MARCH** TL4195 Pleasant country town, market day Weds; a good base for exploring the Fens. **St Wendreda's church** with its wonderful angel roof was described by Betjeman as being 'worth cycling 40 miles in a headwind to see'. The Stars (Wimblington Rd) has decent food.

PEAKIRK TF1606 **Waterfowl World** Reorganised and expanded, it now has over 150 different species of waterfowl inc rare and unusual breeds, all in a lovely setting. Most were reared in captivity and can be fed by hand – always fun; they sell corn in the gatehouse but the birds seem to prefer bread, so take some along. A good outing even if you're not exactly a twitcher, fascinating if you are. Snacks, shop, disabled access; cl 24–25 Dec, (01733) 252271; £3.50. The Ruddy Duck is popular for lunch.

✝ **PETERBOROUGH** TL1998 Has preserved much of its long history and fine old buildings, though it expanded hugely in the mid-1970s and is now a thriving industrial town (with a good pedestrianised shopping centre). The **cathedral** is one of the most dramatic in the country, its extraordinary west front a medieval masterpiece, with a trio of huge arches. Despite the damage inflicted by Cromwell (he is said to have looked on approvingly as prayer books were torn up and the organ smashed), the richly Romanesque interior has preserved its original fabric to a remarkable degree; especially worth a look are the elaborately vaulted retrochoir and the fine early 13th-c painted wooden nave ceiling – though you'll probably need good light and glasses to see this at its best. Snacks, shop, some disabled access; £3 guided tour. The **City Art Gallery** and **Museum** (Priestgate) among other interesting exhibits has some unusual models made from fishbones by Napoleonic prisoners of war (open Tues–Sat; free). **Railworld** (Oundle Rd) is a friendly little railway museum; cl wknds Nov–Feb; £2.50. **St Margaret's Church** (Fletton, TL1896) on the S edge of the city, has some exceptionally fine little Anglo-Saxon sculptures, and just W of the centre **Longthorpe Tower** (Thorpe Rd, TL1698) is a 13th–14th-c fortified house with rare wall paintings (open wknds and bank hols Apr–Oct; £1.30). Charters (by Town Bridge) is an enjoyable floating pub/restaurant in a converted barge. The best place for lunch is some miles outside the town – the Haycock, along the A47 at Wansford. **Flag Fen** (2m E at Fengate) Fascinating and well organised prehistoric site, with excellent Bronze Age museum displaying finds from the ongoing excavations. In summer you should be able to watch archaeologists painstakingly uncovering more secrets, and a reconstructed Bronze Age farm (including primitive breeds of sheep and pigs) puts the discoveries in context. Snacks, shop, disabled access; cl 25 Dec–1 Jan; (01733) 313414; £3.50. **Ferry Meadows Country Park**, 4 miles W off the A605 (TL1329), is useful for children to let off steam; 500 acres with children's play areas, 2 big lakes with watersports and boat trips, bird reserves, pony and trap rides, miniature railway, 2 golf courses and pitch and putt.

PRICKWILLOW DRAINAGE ENGINE MUSEUM TL5982 The story of water, pumping and fen drainage in the area since the last Ice Age, especially interesting when the engines are running; phone for dates. Snacks, shop, disabled access; open daily Apr–Oct, and wknds Nov and Mar; (01353) 688360; £2 (£3 when engines running).

PURLS BRIDGE TL4787 Highly recommended for diehard birdwatchers; there's an RSPB reserve off the B1093 with several hides (one with disabled access) and big mugs of coffee – more substantial sustenance in the Ship overlooking the reserve.

✝ **RAMSEY** TL2984 **Abbey Gatehouse** The ruins of an ornate Gothic gatehouse with buttresses and friezes, along with the 13th-c Lady Chapel (all that's left of the abbey itself); cl Nov–Mar; free. Some of the stone from the abbey is thought to have made up the nearby local history **museum** (open pm Thurs and Sun Apr–Sept; £1). The Cross Keys at Upwood (where there's a windmill) has good-value food.

✝ **ST IVES** TL3171 Pleasant little town, with a graceful church, small local museum, and walks by the curving river. There's an unusual tiny chapel on the old bridge, rising straight out of the water; key from museum. In the town, the Royal Oak does generous food, and the riverside Pike & Eel out at Needingworth is attractively placed for lunch.

★ **THE SHELFORDS** TL4552 The interlinked villages of Great and Little Shelford will reward a slow stroll for those with an eye for architectural detail, and even a quick drive through will show up several delightful timbered houses.

SHEPRETH TL3948 **Willers Mill Wildlife Park** Genuine little wildlife rescue centre with all sorts of unwanted or injured animals and birds. There's a monkey house, and fish farm where the koi will feed from your hand; pony rides summer weekends. The entrance isn't that well signed, so keep an eye out. Snacks (in elevated treetop café), shop, disabled access; cl 25 Dec; (01763) 262226; *£3.95. The tranquil gardens at **Docwra Manor** nearby are at their best Apr–Jun but always have a variety of unusual plants growing and for sale. The highlight is perhaps the lovely intimate walled garden. Disabled access (although gravel paths may be hard work); open Weds and Fri, plus Apr–Oct pm 1st Sun of month; (01763) 261557; £2. The Plough is useful for lunch.

✝ **SOHAM** TL5872 As well as a rather grand **church**, this has 2 surviving mills – you can buy flour ground here.

✝ **THORNEY** TF2804 Rises from the flatlands like an island – which it was, when this was all half-submerged marsh. Much older than most villages in the area, it has a Norman-modified Saxon church on its green, and some interesting yellow-brick workers' houses put up by the Duke of Bedford. The friendly **Heritage Museum** has good displays, and organises tours of the village and abbey. Shop; open pm wknds Easter–Oct, or by appointment; (01733) 270908; museum free, tours £1.50. The Rose & Crown does freshly made food.

THORNHAUGH TF0700 **Sacrewell Farm and Country Centre** (off the A47)

Based around an old working watermill, demonstrations and displays of rural crafts, tools and machinery, as well as garden, a maze and nature trails, lots of animals, and pick-your-own fruit in season. Pleasantly simple and undeveloped, this is a friendly place, well liked by visitors, and very organised for children. Snacks, shop, disabled access; (01780) 782254; £3. Wansford is very handy for lunch.

✝ TRUMPINGTON CHURCH TL4454 Attractive in its own right, but perhaps most famous for having the second oldest memorial brass in England.

WANSFORD TL0997 **Nene Valley Railway** 15-mile round trip on steam trains through delightful countryside to Peterborough. Also a fine collection of steam locomotives and rolling stock, and a small museum. The railway is a favourite with film-makers. Meals, snacks, shop, disabled access; cl Mon exc bank hols, best to phone for train times, (01780) 784444; £2 site admission (refundable against train fare), £7.50 for the train. It's easy to extend this into an all-day trip by breaking your journey at one of the country parks alongside stations en route, or by taking a stroll around Peterborough (see entry above). At the Wansford end (pretty village), the Haycock is particularly good for lunch.

WARBOYS TL3583 **Grays Honey Farm** (Cross Drove, 5m NE of Warboys, off the A141) Buzzing little place with bees at work in an observation hive, an ingenious model railway, aviary, and guinea pig sty. Tearoom (speciality honey ice-cream), shop (lots of honey-based products), disabled access; cl Sun and Mon (exc bank hols) and Nov–Mar (though shop usually open then); (01354) 693798; free.

✝ WHITTLESFORD CHURCH TL4748 The interior is a rich testament to the former agricultural wealth of this area. The Tickell Arms, a little way off, is a most unusual pub.

WICKEN FEN TL5670 (Lode Lane) The last of the undrained fens, surrounded in plastic to prevent its drying out. Outstanding for birdwatching (there are hides), the marshy and open fen landscape is one of the oldest nature reserves in the country, originally safeguarded in 1899 as an example of what the fens were like before they were turned over to intensive agriculture. Beautiful at all times of year, it's home to a remarkable range of plants, insects, birds and other wildlife; some good trails (one for wheelchairs), along with the last fenland windpump (moved here from elsewhere), and a tiny fen cottage. Snacks, shop, disabled access; cl 25 Dec; (01353) 720274; £3.50; NT. The Maid's Head overlooking the pretty village green is a handy dining pub.

✝ WILLINGHAM CHURCH TL4070 Lots to notice here: outside are the fine tower and spire, and inside it has many early wall paintings, and some fine early screens.

WIMPOLE HALL TL3350 (off the A603) One of the most striking mansions in the whole of East Anglia, mainly 18th-c, with an imposing and harmonious Georgian façade, lovely *trompe l'oeil* chapel ceiling, and rooms by James Gibbs and Sir John Soane. Best of all are the 360 acres of parkland, designed by several different notable landscapers inc Capability Brown and Repton; the remains of a medieval village are under the pasture. Good programme of concerts and events in the hall or grounds. Meals, snacks, shop; open mid-Mar–Oct, pm wknds, pm Tues–Thurs, and bank hols, plus pm Fri in Aug; (01223) 207257; £5.50 (£2 gardens only); NT. Sir John Soane also designed the thatched and timbered buildings of adjacent **Wimpole Hall Farm**, when it was at the forefront of agricultural innovation. Machinery and tools are displayed in a restored barn, and there are rare farm animals and heavy horse wagon rides. Snacks, shop, disabled access; open as Hall, plus mornings, winter wknds, and Fri in Jun and July; £4.20; NT. A joint ticket is £7. The surrounding park is open all year: the estate welcomes walkers free of charge to the extensive paths and tracks through its farmland and woodland, past a folly and up to a surprisingly elevated ridge path. Start either from the main car park here, or walk over the hill from Great Eversden.

The Queen Adelaide at Croydon is a good-value comfortable dining pub.

WISBECH TF4609 **Peckover House** Lovely early 18th-c house with rococo decoration, contemporary art exhibitions, and a 2-acre Victorian garden with kitchen garden and greenhouses – where orange trees are still fruiting after 250 years. Afternoon teas when house open; open Apr–Oct, pm Weds, wknds and bank hols, plus garden only pm Mon, Tues and Thurs; (01945) 583463; £3.20 (£2 on garden only days), NT. An honest and thorough **local history museum** (Museum Sq) has several early manuscripts, and an exhibition on the slave trade (cl Sun, Mon; free). The North Brink along the River Nene has handsome Georgian houses (among them the Rose and – better for food – Red Lion are both decent pubs).

★ **Other attractive villages** include Alconbury Weston TL1776, Brampton TL2170, Eltisley TL2659, Helpston TF1205 (John Clare's village), Elton TL0893, Glatton TL1585, Leighton Bromswold TL1175, Gamlingay TL2452, Great Abington TL5348, Great Chishill TL4239 (well restored windmill), Holywell TL3370, Meldreth TL3746, Rampton TL4268, Ufford TF0904 (the surrounding area can be lovely at bluebell time), Whittlesey TL2797 and Woodditton TL6659.

Where to eat

BYTHORN TL0575 **White Hart** *(01832) 710226* Civilised dining pub with friendly welcome, several linked smallish rooms, magazines and cookery books to read, open fire, imaginative food, real ales, and a sensible wine list; cl pm Sun, Mon, 26 Dec–1 Jan. **£20.50**|£7.50.

CAMBRIDGE TL4658 **Twenty Two** *Chesterton Rd (01223) 351880* Simple and pretty candlelit evening restaurant with good modern cooking inc lovely puddings from a set menu, a fine wine list, and friendly service; cl Sun, Mon, 1 wk Christmas; children over 12. **£27.50**.

DUXFORD TL4745 **John Barleycorn** *(01223) 832699* Pretty, early 17th-c thatched country pub, attractively furnished, with quietly chatty bar, good food and courteous service; fine hanging baskets and flower-filled back garden; no children. **£21**|£4.60.

ELY TL5380 **Old Fire Engine House** *25 St Mary's St (01353) 662582* Former fire engine station next to the cathedral with good hearty English cooking inc nice puddings, an interesting wine list, simple furnishings and a relaxed atmosphere, and large walled garden; also, an art gallery; cl pm Sun, bank hols, 10 days from 24 Dec; disabled access. **£28**|£4.50.

FEN DRAYTON TL3368 **Three Tuns** *(01954) 230242* Pretty thatched inn with 2 inglenook fireplaces and heavy Tudor beams and timbers in its unpretentious and cosy bar; well kept real ales, generous helpings of good bar food, and a neat back garden with children's play equipment; children until 8pm only; disabled access. **£13**|£4.75.

FOWLMERE TL4245 **Chequers** *(01763) 208369* Civilised old coaching inn with smartly dressed waiters, ambitious food in the galleried restaurant, good puddings, and excellent wines; 2 warm comfortably furnished rooms with an open log fire, some interesting photographs of local World War I and World War II airfields, and a no smoking conservatory overlooking the neat garden; cl 25 Dec; disabled access. **£20.85**|£4.90.

GOREFIELD TF4211 **Woodmans Cottage** *(01945) 870669* Very cheerfully run busy village pub with up to 50 puddings as well as a wide choice of other good food in the spacious modernised bar, a comfortable eating area, and separate restaurant; cl pm 25 and 26 Dec; well-behaved children only; disabled access. **£16.50**|£4.

HEYDON TL4340 **King William IV** *(01763) 838773* Bustling village pub with nooks and crannies in the rambling rooms, neatly kept agricultural implements on standing props, wall timbers and dark oak beams, log fire; good bar food inc interesting vegetarian dishes, well kept real ales, and friendly efficient staff. **£21**|£7.95.

KEYSTON TL0475 **Pheasant** *(01832) 710241* Pretty thatched former smithy, full of character, with a nice civilised atmosphere, a relaxed bar with informal service, a slightly more formal no smoking room with linen napkins, delicious imaginative food, a particularly good wine list, real ales, and friendly service; cl pm 25 Dec; disabled access. **£25**|£6.95.

KIRTING TL6857 **Queens Head** *(01638) 731737* Peacefully set and charming 16th-c pub discreetly refurbished in period style, with delicious imaginative food from a splendid blackboard, decent wine list and real ales. **£21.20**|£8.95.

MADINGLEY TL3960 **Three Horseshoes** *(01954) 210221* Smart thatched dining pub with a relaxed if civilised atmosphere, open fire in the charming bar, an attractive conservatory, very good imaginative food, well kept real ales, and good wine list (many by the glass inc champagne); pretty summer garden. **£25**|£6.50.

MELBOURN TL3844 **Pink Geranium** *Station Rd (01763) 260215* Very pretty 16th-c thatched cottage, pink inside and out, with consistently good sophisticated cooking, a cosy and relaxed atmosphere, a carefully chosen wine list with helpful notes, cottagey garden, and chauffeur service; good-value set lunches, and cookery courses, too; cl Sun and Mon; disabled access. **£45.50**|£7.

MELBOURN TL3844 **Sheene Mill** *(01763) 261393* Lovely late 17th-c watermill on the River Mel and just 200 yards from its sister restaurant, the Pink Geranium; relaxed and informal bar and conservatory, airy restaurant decorated in yellow and terracotta with pretty blue dining chairs around yellow-clothed tables, and lovely gardens with seats on the terrace; delicious modern cooking inc vegetarian and fish dishes, and light lunches or snacks; bdrms; cl 26 Dec; disabled access. **£28**|£10 2 courses.

SUTTON GAULT TL4279 **Anchor** *(01353) 778537* Popular dining pub with gas lamps and candles in 4 heavily beamed rooms (2 are no smoking), log fires, stripped pine furniture, delicious home-made food, real ales, very good wine list (10 by the glass), and riverbank tables; bdrms; cl 25–26 Dec; must book in advance for children; disabled access. **£26.50**|£6.50.

Special thanks to Michael and Jenny Back, Helen Dixon, John and Sally Clarke.

We welcome reports from readers

This *Guide* depends on readers' reports. Do help us if you can – in return, we offer a discount on the next edition to people who've helped us with reports for it. Tell us what you think about places already in it, and anything extra you think we should say about them. And send us your ideas for inclusion in the next edition: places to visit, eat at or stay in, attractive drives or walks, maybe even unusual interesting shops you know of. Use the card in the middle, the report forms at the end, or just write – no stamp needed: *The Good Guide to Britain*, FREEPOST TN1569, Wadhurst, E Sussex TN5 7BR.

Cambridgeshire Calendar

Some of these dates were provisional as we went to press. Please check information with the telephone numbers provided.

JANUARY

8 **Whittlesey** Straw Bear Festival: folk song, music and dance *on Fri 8*, street procession and evening barn dance *on Sat 9*, straw bear burning *on Sun 10* (01733) 208245

FEBRUARY

Lode Snowdrops at Anglesey Abbey most weekends (01223) 811200

MARCH

13 **Arrington** Lambing Weekend at Wimpole Hall and Home Farm – *till Sun 14* (01223) 207257

20 **Arrington** Lambing Weekend at Wimpole Hall and Home Farm – *till Sun 21* (01223) 207257; **Alwalton** National Shire Horse Show at the East of England Showground – *till Sun 21* (01733) 234451

27 **Arrington** Lambing Weekend at Wimpole Hall and Home Farm – *till Sun 28* (01223) 207257; **Thriplow** Daffodil Weekend: gardens open, crafts, rural pursuits – *till Sun 28* (01763) 208132

APRIL

4 **Elton** Garden Show at Elton Hall – *till Mon 5* (01832) 280468

23 **Alwalton** National Motorhome Show at the the East of England Showground – *till Sun 25* (01733) 234451; **Peterborough** Pageant inc St George's Day Celebrations, jousting, helicopter rides, town criers' contest and much more – *till Sun 25* (01733) 700035

MAY

2 **Alwalton** Truckfest at the the East of England Showground – *till Mon 3* (01733) 234451

3 **Stilton** Cheese Rolling Contest: wooden replicas are rolled down the high street; stalls and Mayday celebrations (01733) 241206

15 **Wisbech** Open Weekend: private historical buildings open to the public – *till Sun 16* (01945) 583263

22 **Alwalton** British Motorcyclists Federation Rally: largest outdoor motorcycle festival in Europe at East of England Showground – *till Sun 23* (0116) 254 8818

30 **Cambridge** Trinity College Choir sing from the college towers *from noon*, and from lamplit punts on the river *from 8.45pm* (01223) 338400; **Waterbeach** Medieval and Country Food and Historic House Cuisine at Farmland Museum and Denny Abbey – *till Mon 31* (01223) 860988

JUNE

6 **Duxford** Air Display at the Airfield (01223) 835000

Cambridgeshire Calendar (cont.)

12 Peterborough Kite Festival at Ferry Meadows Country Park – *till Sun 13* (01733) 700718

18 Alwalton East of England Show at the East of England Showground – *till Sun 20 (01733)* 234451

23 Cambridge Midsummer Fair on Midsummer Common; funfair – *till Mon 28* (01223) 463363

27 Waterbeach English Heritage Event at Farmland Museum and Denny Abbey (01223) 860988

28 Cambridge GrassRoots 99 at the Cambridge Drama Centre: festival of new writing – *till 24 July* (01223) 322748

30 Wisbech Rose Fair: flower festival, jazz, musical entertainments, stalls and cream teas – *till 3 July* (01945) 583263

JULY

2 Peterborough Cathedral Festival: concerts, music, jazz and dance – *till Sat 10* (01733) 343342

3 Arrington Jazz & Blues Fireworks Concerts at Wimpole Hall and Home Farm – *till Sun 4* (01223) 207257; **Cambridge** Open Studios: around 200 exhibiting members at various venues – *till Sun 4, also Sat 10–Sun 11, Sat 17–Sun 18, Sat 24–Sun 25* (01223) 249394; **Duxford** Air Show at the Airfield – *till Sun 4* (01223) 835000

4 Ely Riverside Gala and Raft Race at Willow Walk (01353) 662062; **Waterbeach** Knights Templar Tours at Denny Abbey – *also on Sun 11* (01223) 860988

5 Peterborough American themed fête at Thorpe Hall (01733) 330060

9 Ely Folk Festival: family dance and music event – *till Sun 11* (01353) 740999

10 Witcham World Pea Shooting Championships: stalls and games (01353) 778363

14 Peterborough Open-air Shakespeare: *Twelfth Night* at Thorpe Hall (01733) 330060

16 Cambridge Open-air Family Pop Concert (free) at Parker's Piece (01223) 463363

17 Cambridge Big Day Out: free family day with bands, performers, displays, fireworks at Parker's Piece (01223) 463363

20 Alwalton East of England Championship Dog Show at the East of England Showground – *till Thurs 22 (01733)* 234451

24 Waterbeach Rare Breeds at Farmland Museum and Denny Abbey – *till Sun 25* (01223) 860988

30 Cambridge Folk Festival: one of Europe's top acoustic festivals – *till 1 Aug* (01223) 457000; **Wansford** Jazz Festival at the Haycock Hotel – *till 1 Aug* (01780) 782223

31 Alwalton Faith 99: large gathering of mixed denominations at the East of England Showground – *till 7 Aug* (01733) 234451; **Peterborough** Fireworks Concert at Thorpe Hall (01733) 330060

AUGUST

14 Arrington Open-air Concerts at Wimpole Hall and Home Farm – *till Sun 15* (01223) 207257; **Peterborough** Summer Regatta – *till Sun 15* (01733) 563966

24 Peterborough CAMRA Beer Festival on the river embankment: over 200 real ales – *till Sun 29* (01733) 574331

Cambridgeshire Calendar (cont.)

29 **Waterbeach** '30s on the Farm' at Farmland Museum and Denny Abbey – *till Mon 30* (01223) 860988

SEPTEMBER

5 **Duxford** Air Display at the Airfield (01223) 835000
11 **Haddenham** Steam Rally inc heavy horse show – *till Sun 12* (01487) 841893; **Peterborough** National Heritage Day: free entry to Thorpe Hall (not usually open) – *till Sun 12* (01733) 330060; **Wisbech** Open Weekend: private historical buildings open to the public – *till Sun 12* (01945) 583263
25 **Waterbeach** Medieval and Country Games at Farmland Museum and Denny Abbey – *till Sun 26* (01223) 860988
27 **Soham** Pumpkin Fair: pumpkins, sunflowers and large vegetables (01223) 236236

OCTOBER

10 **Duxford** Air Display at the Airfield (01223) 835000
31 **Waterbeach** Halloween and Sugar Beet at Farmland Museum and Denny Abbey (01223) 860988

NOVEMBER

5 **Cambridge** Fireworks at Midsummer Common (01223) 463363
21 **Ely** County Brass Band Championships (01353) 662062
25 **Peterborough** Christmas Street Festival (01733) 452280

DECEMBER

5 **Peterborough** Victorian Christmas Fair at Thorpe Hall (01733) 330060
11 **Peterborough** Christmas Tree Concert and Fair at Thorpe Hall (01733) 330060

We welcome reports from readers

This *Guide* depends on readers' reports. Do help us if you can – in return, we offer a discount on the next edition to people who've helped us with reports for it. Tell us what you think about places already in it, and anything extra you think we should say about them. And send us your ideas for inclusion in the next edition: places to visit, eat at or stay in, attractive drives or walks, maybe even unusual interesting shops you know of. Use the card in the middle, the report forms at the end, or just write – no stamp needed: *The Good Guide to Britain*, FREEPOST TN1569, Wadhurst, E Sussex TN5 7BR.

CHESHIRE

Rich variety of scenery and plenty of places to visit – yet not too touristy.

Chester – very pedestrian-friendly – has beautifully restored and preserved medieval buildings, lots of interest, and a lively feel. The city's tourist information department couldn't be more helpful.

Chester Zoo (always something new, from baby elephant and hippo to the innovative bat cave) is one of the county's big attractions. The new Blue Planet Aquarium in Ellesmere Port is Europe's largest (the boat museum there is also fun), and other top days out include romantic Peckforton Castle, the lively and burgeoning Styal industrial heritage site, Tatton Park at Knutsford (lovely grounds, working historic farm), Lyme Park near Disley, and on a smaller scale the entertaining Mouldsworth motor museum (not just cars).

Other rewarding places include Tabley House, Arley Hall near Northwich, Little Moreton Hall at Scholar Green, Gawsworth Hall, Norton Priory in Runcorn, the Ness botanic gardens, and the spectacular garden centre at Bridgemere. Jodrell Bank, and Catalyst in Widnes, science in intriguing packages, and Macclesfield and Bollington take you vividly back to their mill-town days.

There's great variety of countryside, from the picturesque castle-topped wooded hills of the west, through the lush parkland, leafy lanes and meres (shallow lakes) of the central plain to the eastern more rugged Peak District scenery – small steep stone-walled pastures, shaggy sheep, deep twisty valleys, austere moorland. There are many charming thatched and timbered villages, and an intricate network of canals takes in some of the most interesting countryside, with well kept towpaths.

Industry is largely confined to the Mersey, with chemical works at Northwich and engineering around Crewe.

Where to stay

BEESTON SJ5459 **Wild Boar** *Whitchurch Rd, Beeston, Tarporley CW6 9NW (01829) 260309* **£85,** plus special breaks; 37 rms with complimentary extras such as fresh fruit and sherry. Attractive half-timbered 17th-c former hunting lodge, carefully extended over the years, beneath the 12th-c castle; with relaxed and comfortable bars and lounges, enjoyable food in the beamed restaurant, and good, helpful service; disabled access.

BICKLEY MOSS SJ5549 **Cholmondeley Arms** *Bickley Moss, Malpas SY14 8BT (01829) 720300* **£60,** plus special breaks; 6 rms with showers. Airy converted Victorian schoolhouse close to castle and gardens; lots of atmosphere, very friendly staff, interesting furnishings, open fire, excellent imaginative bar food, and a very good choice of wines; disabled access.

CHESTER SJ4166 **Castle House** *23 Castle St, Chester CH1 2DS (01244) 350354* **£44,** plus special breaks; 5 comfortable rms, 3 with own bthrm. Small, carefully preserved 16th-c guest house in the middle of the city, with helpful, friendly owners, and fine breakfasts.

COTEBROOK SJ5765 **Alvanley Arms** *Cotebrook, Tarporley CW6 9DS (01829) 760200* **£50;** 3 rms. Handsome creeper-covered Georgian inn with pleasant beamed bars (one area is no smoking), big open fire, a chintzy little hall, generous helpings of good food, and a garden with pond and geese.

FULLERS MOOR SJ4166 **Frogg Manor** *Fullers Moor, Nantwich Rd, Broxton, Chester CH3 9JH (01829) 782629* **£100,** plus special breaks; 6 lavishly decorated rms. Enjoyable Georgian manor house full of ornamental frogs and antique furniture; with open fires, restful upstairs sitting room, little bar, old-time music, and good English cooking in the elegant dining room which leads to a conservatory overlooking the gardens; dogs by arrangement; cl 1 Jan.

HIGHER BURWARDSLEY SJ5256 **Pheasant** *Higher Burwardsley, Chester CH3 9PF (01829) 770434* **£70,** plus special breaks; 10 rms in comfortably converted sandstone-built barn. Pretty half-timbered 17th-c inn on top of Peckforton Hills with marvellous views, interesting decorations, a huge fireplace, and a parrot called Sailor in the attractive old-fashioned bar, no smoking conservatory, good food, and friendly staff; lots of walks nearby; disabled access.

HIGHER WYCH SJ4943 **Mill House** *Higher Wych, Malpas SY14 7JR (01948) 780362* **£36;** 1 rm. Very welcoming and friendly B & B in former farmhouse on the Welsh/English border with relaxed atmosphere and good breakfasts – evening meals by arrangement; self-catering cottage; cl Dec.

HOOLE SJ4368 **Hoole Hall** *Warrington Rd, Hoole, Chester CH2 3PD (01244) 350011* **£113.50,** plus special breaks; 97 well equipped rms, some no smoking. Extended and attractively refurbished 18th-c hall with 5 acres of gardens, good food in 2 restaurants, and friendly service; good disabled access.

MACCLESFIELD SJ9271 **Sutton Hall** *Bullocks Lane, Sutton, Macclesfield SK11 0HE (01260) 253211* **£90;** 10 marvellous rms. Welcoming and secluded historic baronial hall, full of character, stylish rooms with tall black beams, stone fireplaces, suits of armour and so forth, friendly service, and good food; can arrange clayshooting/golf/fishing.

MACCLESFIELD FOREST SJ9471 **Hardingland Farm** *Macclesfield Forest, Macclesfield SK11 0ND (01625) 425759* **£39;** 3 rms. Neatly kept Georgian stone farmhouse set in the Peak National Park with wonderful views, an elegantly furnished lounge and Regency-style dining room; helpful owners, and delicious food using their own lamb and beef; cl Dec–Feb; no children.

MOBBERLEY SJ7879 **Laburnum Cottage** *Knutsford Rd, Mobberley, Knutsford WA16 7PU (01565) 872464* **£50;** 6 pretty rms, 3 with own bthrm. Neatly kept and friendly no smoking house set in flower-filled landscaped garden with croquet; a relaxed atmosphere in the comfortable lounge with log fire and books, generous breakfasts, and the new owners offer evening meals; disabled access.

MOLLINGTON SJ3870 **Crabwall Manor** *Parkgate Rd, Mollington, Chester CH1 6NE (01244) 851666* **£95w;** 48 very comfortable, individually decorated rms. Partly castellated historic hotel in landscaped grounds with restful, attractive day rooms, open fires, very good modern British cooking in the elegant restaurant, and friendly, professional service; disabled access.

POTT SHRIGLEY SJ9479 **Shrigley Hall** *Shrigley Park, Pott Shrigley, Macclesfield SK10 5SB (01625) 575757* **£130,** plus special breaks; 150 smart, well equipped rms, some with country views. Set in over 260 acres of parkland, this impressive country house has a splendid entrance hall with several elegant rooms leading off, enjoyable food in the Orangery and restaurant, and good service from friendly staff; championship golf course, fishing, tennis, and leisure centre in former church building; plenty to do nearby; disabled access.

PRESTBURY SJ9077 **White House** *The Village, Prestbury, Macclesfield SK10 4HP (01625) 829376* **£87w;** 11 individual, stylish and well equipped rms with antiques, in separate brick manor. Exceptionally friendly and pretty restaurant-with-rooms (new bedrooms, another lounge, and an orangery added this year) – lots of plants, silk and lace, and very good modern British cooking; breakfast in small conservatory lounge or in room; cl 25 Dec.

ROWTON SJ4564 **Rowton Hall** *Whitchurch Rd, Rowton, Chester CH3 6AD (01244) 335262* **£95,** plus wknd breaks; 42 attractive rms; 18th-c country house in 8 acres of award-winning gardens, with conservatory lounge, comfortable bar, log fires and a relaxed atmosphere; leisure club with swimming pool, gym, sauna and solarium; may be cl over Christmas; disabled access.

SANDBACH SJ7661 **Old Hall** *Newcastle Rd, Sandbach CW11 0AL (01270) 761221* **£70w;** 14 comfortable rms. Fine Jacobean timbered hotel with lots of original panelling and fireplaces, relaxing lounge, pianist, friendly welcome, and popular restaurant; disabled access.

SANDIWAY SJ6071 **Nunsmere Hall** *Tarporley Rd, Sandiway, Northwich CW8 2ES (01606) 889100* **£140w;** 36 individually decorated rms. Luxurious lakeside hotel on wooded peninsula, with elegantly furnished lounge and library, oak-panelled cocktail bar, very good modern cooking, and a warm welcome from courteous staff; children over 10 in evening restaurant; disabled access.

TARPORLEY SJ5563 **Swan** *50 High St, Tarporley CW6 0AG (01829) 733838* **£72.50;** 20 rms. Well managed Georgian inn with a good mix of individual tables and chairs in the attractive bar, well kept real ales, decent wines, and quite a few malt whiskies; good food from brasserie menu with lighter lunchtime choices, nice breakfasts, and friendly staff; disabled access.

TILSTON SJ4651 **Tilston Lodge** *Tilston, Malpas SY14 7DR (01829) 250223* ***£60;** 3 thoughtfully equipped rms. Warmly friendly and beautifully restored Victorian house in 16 acres with a collection of rare breed farm animals; comfortable and attractive public rooms, open fire in the dining room, and good breakfasts; evening meal by arrangement.

WESTON SJ7352 **White Lion** *Main Rd, Weston, Crewe CW2 5NA (01270) 500303* **£59;** 16 comfortable rms. Pretty 17th-c timbered inn with low beams (several no smoking areas), a friendly, relaxed atmosphere, well kept real ales, and popular food; own bowling green; no accommodation 25–26 Dec.

WETTENHALL SJ6261 **Boot & Slipper** *Wettenhall, Winsford CW7 4DN (01270) 528238* **£48;** 4 attractive rms with showers. Cosily refurbished 16th-c coaching inn on small country lane; with low beams and open fire in quiet bars, a relaxed friendly atmosphere, and good breakfasts.

WHEELOCK SJ7559 **Grove House** *Mill Lane, Wheelock, Sandbach CW11 0RD (01270) 762582* **£60w;** 8 rms. Family-run Georgian restaurant-with-rooms with a relaxed homely atmosphere, quietly furnished lounge and restaurant, personal, friendly service, and very good modern cooking in popular restaurant; plenty to do nearby; cl Christmas–New Year; partial disabled access.

WORLESTON SJ6556 **Rookery Hall** *Worleston, Nantwich CW5 6DQ (01270) 610016* **£120w,** plus special breaks; 45 individually decorated rms. Fine early 19th-c hotel in 200 acres of lovely parkland; with elegant lounges, log fires, intimate panelled restaurant with enjoyable food, and friendly service; disabled access.

We welcome reports from readers

This *Guide* depends on readers' reports. Do help us if you can – in return, we offer a discount on the next edition to people who've helped us with reports for it. Tell us what you think about places already in it, and anything extra you think we should say about them. And send us your ideas for inclusion in the next edition: places to visit, eat at or stay in, attractive drives or walks, maybe even unusual interesting shops you know of. Use the card in the middle, the report forms at the end, or just write – no stamp needed: *The Good Guide to Britain*, FREEPOST TN1569, Wadhurst, E Sussex TN5 7BR.

To see and do

CHESTER LSJ4166 One of Britain's most rewarding cities, Chester was the site of an important fort in Roman times, and later plentiful river traffic kept it rich. The old centre is ringed by a medieval **town wall** that's more complete than any other in Britain. You can walk the whole way round, enjoying marvellous views; there are summer exhibitions in some of the towers along the way. Partly because of the limit set by the wall, the centre of town is an easy place to get around on foot, not too big, and with the main streets pretty much free of cars (there may be a few buses), although in summer the sheer numbers of tourists and shoppers can still make them appear congested. Guided walks leave the tourist information centre on Town Hall Square at 10.45am each day. If you're driving in, you'll be shunted round to one of the big car parks, and you may have to queue a while to get a space. Chester's racecourse, the Roodee, is the oldest in the world; it still has fashionable races in May, and a summer Sun meet that's become a lively event for families. The trendiest restaurants in town are currently Nico's Brasserie (Dark Row) and Bensons (Lower Bridge St). The quaint Albion (Park St) has good food, and Watergates (Watergate St), in a fine medieval crypt, is useful for lunch. The ancient Blue Bell (Northgate St) has been licensed to sell alcohol since 1494.

The Rows SJ4066 Giving Chester's heart a magnificently Tudor look, these are sets of timbered 2-storey shops – with open upper arcaded galleries – radiating from the central Cross. Parts are thought to be at least 700 yrs old. Besides being attractive to look at and charming to walk through, they form the heart of the city's shopping centre (and include a useful pub, the Boot, on Eastgate Row N). Watergate is one of the finest stretches, with some of Chester's most glorious timber-framed buildings, though more fine buildings jetty out over the pavement in Lower Bridge St (for instance, the late 17th-c Falcon, once a house used by the Duke of Westminster's ancestors but now a good pub), and in St Werburgh St off Eastgate (built in the 1890s, despite their Elizabethan look). Several of the attractions described below are in the Rows.

† **Chester Cathedral** SJ4066 Not unlike an ordinary church at first glance, this is far more impressive inside, with some marvellous medieval carving in and above the choir stalls, and some fine vaulting. Many of the former abbey buildings survived the Reformation, so the precincts still include peaceful arcaded flagstoned cloisters, a medieval chapter house, and older Norman parts inc a refectory – brought back into use as an excellent café (pianist Tues, Fri and Sat lunchtimes). There are quiet cobbled Georgian lanes around Abbey Square, behind the cathedral a little way down Northgate.

Roman Chester SJ4066 Remains include some broken Roman columns in a neat and peaceful garden running along the town wall by the gate at the bottom of Pepper St. Nearby is the excavated part of a very large Roman amphitheatre – probably big enough to seat nearly 10,000 people. Other relics can pop up in unexpected places: Spud-U-Like and Miss Selfridge show off well preserved sections of hypocaust.

Dewa Roman Experience SJ4066 (Pierpoint Lane, off Bridge St) Re-creation of Chester's Roman heyday, with the sights, sounds and smells of streets, fortresses, and even bathhouses. It starts off as though you're on board a Roman galley, and at the end is an exhibition of Roman, Saxon and medieval relics found on the site. Shop, disabled access; cl 25–26 Dec; (01244) 343407; *£3.95.

Grosvenor Museum SJ4066 (Grosvenor St) The surprising highlight is an award-winning gallery of huge Roman tombstones. A passage from here leads to a Georgian house with restored Georgian and Victorian rooms, an art gallery, and displays of locally made silver and furniture. Snacks, shop; cl am sun, Good Fri, 24–26 Dec, 1 Jan; (01244) 321616; free. They also have a little outpost, the

Chester Heritage Centre, in a former church on Bridge St Row; (01244) 317948; cl am Sun; £1.25, free if you're a Chester resident.

On the Air SJ4066 (Bridge St Row) Evocative exhibition of radio equipment and broadcasts from the 1920s through to the 1990s, with reconstructed 1920s living room, 1930s shop, and wartime air raid shelter brought to life with period recordings. Displays of television and other broadcast equipment too – you can play on the cameras. Shop (sells vintage radios), good disabled access; cl Sun and Mon from Christmas–Easter; (01244) 348468; *£1.95.

Toy Museum SJ4065 (Lower Bridge St Row) One of the best such collections we've come across, not least because of the hard-to-beat assemblage of Matchbox cars and toys (the company's HQ are here). Lots of Dinky toys and Hornby trains, as well as dolls, teddies, and some vintage amusement machines. Shop (good for dolls house furniture); cl 25–26 Dec, 1 Jan; (01244) 346297; *£2.

Chester viewpoints SJ4066 The tree-shaded Groves look out to the medieval bridge over the River Dee – very photogenic and a pleasant place for a stroll or picnic. The bridge at the N end of Northgate gives a close view of the so-called Bridge of Sighs over the canal far below. Several companies operate ½hr boat trips along here.

Chester Castle SJ4065 Though now largely moated by car parks and occupied by civil servants, this has some impressive buildings, both medieval and grand-manner late 18th-c.

Chester Zoo (will admit 1 child with every 1 paying adult) SJ4170 (A41, 2m N) The biggest zoo in Britain, and undoubtedly one of the best. Its several thousand animals are housed in spacious near-natural enclosures spread over 80 acres of glorious gardens, with 11 miles of pathways. They put a great deal of effort into successful breeding; on our last visit an elephant, camel and a giraffe were among the new arrivals. Highlights include Chimpanzee Island (feeding time 2.15pm), the Tropical House, the bat cave (complete with free-flying bats) and the penguin pool with underwater viewing panels. The lions are fed between 1.30pm and 3pm (not Fri) and the sea lions at 10.30am, 2.30pm and 2.40pm; times may change. In summer a waterbus can ferry you between the attractions, or there's an overhead train that zips around the grounds (both £1 extra). Meals, snacks, shops, good disabled access; cl 25 Dec; (01244) 380280; £8.50.

Days Out

Gems of the South Wirral: Ellesmere Port aquarium and/or boat museum; lunch at the Wheatsheaf, Raby; Ness Gardens; Parkgate, Little Neston and Burton villages, with walk along the Dee estuary.

Romance of the Peckforton Hills: Peckforton and Beeston castles; lunch at the Cholmondeley Arms, Cholmondeley or Pheasant, Higher Burwardsley; Cholmondley Castle gardens or walk in Peckforton Hills.

Other things to see and do

CHESHIRE Family Attraction of the Year

! **ELLESMERE PORT** SJ4174 **Blue Planet Aquarium** (signed off the A5117 W of M53, J10) Opening only a couple of months before we went to press (with the Queen as one of its first visitors), this splendid new aquarium is in the same family as the excellent Deep Sea World at North Queensferry in Scotland, and very much in the same vein – but a lot bigger, and far more elaborate. The most obviously dramatic feature is the 71-metre (233ft) walk-through tunnel, surrounded by sharks, stingray, and 3½ million gallons of water; a moving walkway lets you trundle along gawping without having to look where you're going. But we were equally impressed by the number of well informed and helpful 'presenters' as they call them – knowledgeable staff on hand at each exhibit to answer questions and give talks at various times of the day. Many of them are marine biologists who really do know their stuff. Also standing out are the particularly useful talks and shows in the Aquatheatre, rather like a cinema with the screen replaced by a window into one of their biggest tanks; divers regularly go down to feed the creatures, and have microphones to chat with the audience as they do it. The main sections represent water environments and their occupants from trout streams to mangroves, with touchpools in some areas giving children the chance to handle starfish and the like. As well as fish they have plenty of reptiles and insects, with some rather dubious hands-on opportunities: holding a toad isn't too bad, but who would have thought touching hissing cockroaches would prove so popular? Also a couple of caymans (crocodile cousins), and several slide shows. Most displays are at a height younger children can appreciate, and there's free face-painting. Check show and feeding times when you arrive so you don't miss them, and try to and get to the Aquatheatre a little before displays are due to start to bag a good seat. As at any aquarium, there can be slight congestion around some of the remarkable creatures, but there's enough space to stop that being a problem. Meals, snacks, shop, good disabled access; cl 25 Dec; (0151) 357 8800; *£7.50 (£5 children over 3). They do various family tickets, better value the more children you have; two adults and two children is £23.95, but muster up four children and it's £28.95. The aquarium is next to the huge factory shopping village Cheshire Oaks.

ARLEY HALL & GARDENS SJ6780 The dramatic-looking house is Victorian Jacobean, but the same family has lived on the estate for over 500 years, so there are older furnishings and mementos. Outside, the award-winning grounds include walled, scented, and herb gardens, shrub rose collection, a more informal woodland area, and craft workshops; also an interesting private chapel. Meals, snacks, shop and nursery, disabled access; open April to Sept, Tues–Sun, house open pm Tues and Sun only; (01565) 777353; £3.60 grounds and gardens, hall £2.50 extra. From the car park, tractor and trailer rides take you to nearby **Stockley Farm**, a friendly working dairy farm that's ideal for children. Open pm Weds, Sat, Sun and bank hols Apr–Sept, plus daily exc Mon in Aug; (01565) 777323; £3.

† ★ **ASTBURY** SJ8461 This is a delightful village, and its church is well worth a look with a graceful detached spire, spectacular roofing, and rich carving.

AUDLEM WHARF SJ6543 For walkers, a good access point for the **Shropshire Union Canal** which threads through this area giving interesting stretches for strolls; just outside the village is an impressive flight of over a dozen locks.

★ † **BARTHOMLEY** SJ7752 This charming village has lots of thatch, black and white timbering, quiet up-and-down lanes, and a fine church.

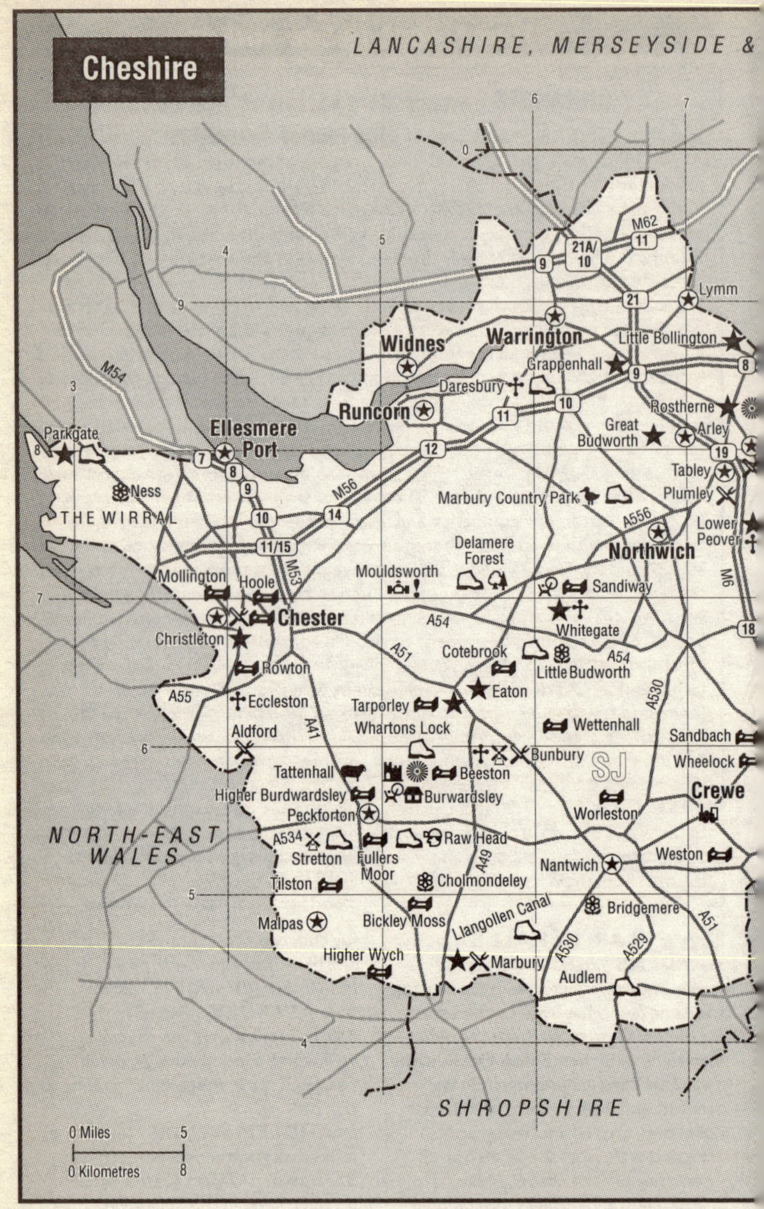

BEESTON CASTLE SJ5459
Wonderful views from this ruined 13th-c fortress, perched atop dramatically rising crags, and said to be where Richard III left buried treasure. Good exhibition. Snacks, shop; cl 24–26 Dec, 1 Jan; (01829) 260464; £2.70. The pub of the same name, handy for the canal, does good-value generous food.

★ **BOLLINGTON** SJ9377
Well worth a stroll: handsome stone mill-town buildings, unchanged 19th-c

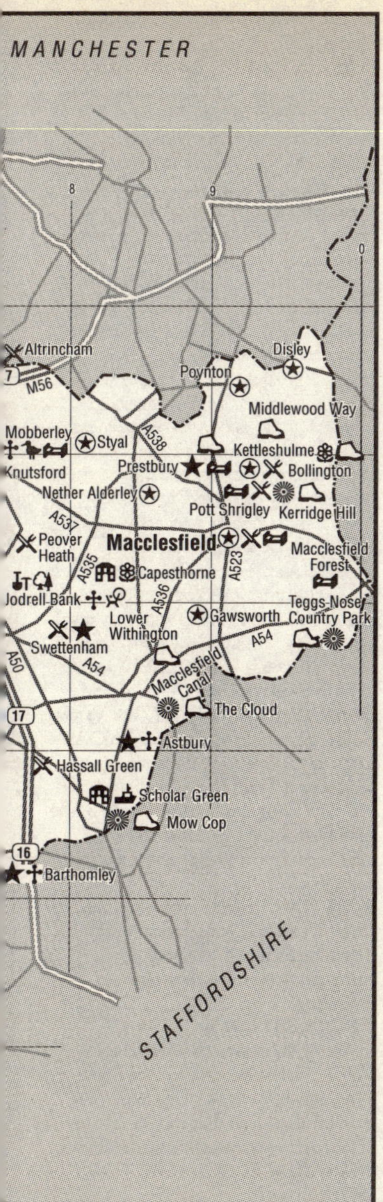

shops and houses, and overhead a great stone aquaduct and its later rival the railway viaduct. Useful pubs include the Church House and Vale. In summer you can hire bikes along a traffic-free 10-mile stretch of the **Middlewood Way** bordering the Peak District (£5 for 3 hours – £9 full day), (01625) 572681. Just outside, the Cheshire Hunt in Spurley Lane at Pott Shrigley is a good place for lunch, and nr it you can pick up the long-distance **Gritstone Trail** for walks among high stone-walled pastures. The Poachers (Ingersley Rd) or Redway (Kerridge) are good start points for the viewpoint Kerridge Hill *(see entry below)* just E of the town.

BRIDGEMERE GARDENS SJ7243 (A51) A garden-lover's paradise – 25 acres of gardens (inc the WI cottage garden), plants, glasshouses, and garden furniture, with more plants in more varieties than anywhere else in Britain (indoor and outdoor), and professional help on hand for any sort of query. Best to visit in the morning before the coach parties arrive. Good meals and snacks, excellent shop, disabled access; cl 25–26 Dec; (01270) 520381; free (exc Garden Kingdom, £1.50).

BUNBURY SJ5758 Bunbury has pretty cottages around its 14th-c church, and a well restored 19th-c watermill.

BURWARDSLEY SJ5257 **Cheshire Candle Workshops** Lots of improvements to the facilities here in recent years, but still the same popular demonstrations of candle-making and other crafts, and a big craft shop. Meals, snacks, disabled access; cl 25 Dec; (01829) 770401; free. The Pheasant is good for lunch, with great views.

CAPESTHORNE HALL SJ8473 18th-c family home of the Bromley-Davenports, who have lived on the site since Domesday; fine paintings include Lowry's unusual interpretation of the house's striking exterior, and there's a good collection of Roman and Greek busts and vases. Also a lovely Georgian chapel and 60 acres of gardens and woodland. Snacks, disabled access; open pm Weds, Sun and bank hols Mar–Oct; (01625) 861221; £4.50, £2.50 garden only. The Blacksmiths Arms at Henbury (A537 towards Macclesfield) is a decent family dining pub, if you don't want the longer trip to the Dog over at Peover Heath.

CHOLMONDELEY CASTLE GARDENS SJ5351 Very pretty to

stroll through, with acres of colourful ornamental gardens around elegant castle buildings (not open). Also fine woodland and lakeside walks, llamas and entertaining pygmy goats among the rare breeds, and an ancient private chapel. Famously it's pronounced Chumley. Snacks, shop and plant centre; open pm Sun, Weds, Thurs and bank hols Apr–Sept; (01829) 720383; £2.50. The Cholmondeley Arms is excellent for lunch.

★ **CHRISTLETON** SJ4465 Though now almost part of Chester, this is still very much a distinct village, with a classic green, pond, almshouses, and medieval packhorse bridges.

THE CLOUD SJ9063 There are good hilly walks here, and the craggy summit, with steep drops to the Cheshire Plain, gives grand views; the Coach & Horses at Timbersbrook is a useful nearby pub.

CREWE SJ7055 A 19th-c railway town, smartened up a lot in the last decade or two, with bargains, especially china in the market, a pedestrianised centre, colourful Queen's Park and useful foyer restaurant in the Victorian theatre. The Crewe Arms is good-value for a comfortable lunch. **Railway Age** (Vernon Way, Crewe) Rapidly developing exhibition with one of the widest ranges of preserved electric and diesel locomotives in the country, along with models, miniature and standard gauge railways and other displays. Some disabled access; cl Nov–mid-Feb; (01270) 212130; £2.50 wkdys, £3.50 wknds (when there's more going on).

† **DARESBURY CHURCH** SJ5882 The **Alice in Wonderland** stained-glass window commemorates Lewis Carroll, who was born here. There are pleasant canalside strolls, and the Ring o' Bells is useful for lunch.

DELAMERE FOREST SJ5571 Several square miles of mainly coniferous plantation, with some older oak and other woodland, inc plenty of open stretches and picnic places, and some small stretches of reedy water. A section of the 30-mile **Sandstone Trail** long-distance path takes in much of the best bits, with good access from several places including Delamere SJ5669 and Hatchmere SJ5672, with decent, prettily placed pubs in both villages.

DISLEY SJ9682 **Lyme Park** Wonderful country estate outside this pleasant hillside village. The Hall at its centre is a magnificent blend of Elizabethan, Georgian and Regency architecture and styles. Tours are unguided, so you can take your time looking at the intricate carvings, and lovely tapestries, paintings and furniture. There's a particularly grand staircase, and a fine collection of English clocks. Around the house (its exterior was used as Pemberley in the BBC's *Pride and Prejudice*) are 17 acres of Victorian gardens with orangery, sunken Dutch garden and wilderness garden, and a sprawling ancient park with herds of red deer and nature trails. Pleasant walk down to the canal. Snacks, shop, disabled access (with notice); house and gardens open Apr–Oct, garden cl am Wed and Thurs, house cl all am plus Wed and Thurs, gardens also open some winter wknds – best to ring for dates; the park is open all year; (01663) 762023; £3.30 per car to go in the park, then £4 house and garden, £2 garden only; NT. The White Horse is a useful food stop (with OAP lunch days). The long-distance **Gritstone Trail** starts from the Park and runs along the western flanks of the Peak District. It's well marked and offers a few days' walking of the highest quality.

★ **EATON** SJ5763 Eaton is a classic Cheshire village, with unassuming but charming picture-postcard combinations of thatch, stone and timbering.

† **ECCLESTON** SJ4162 This romantically eclectic estate village was built in the last century for the Duke of Westminster, with a richly expansive sandstone church that's a culmination of Victorian ecclesiastical architecture.

ELLESMERE PORT SJ4076 **Boat Museum** (Dockyard Rd) Nicely set in a historic dock complex, a huge floating collection of canal boats, as well as steam engines, a blacksmith's forge, workers' cottages, stables, big indoor exhibitions, and boat trips. Meals, snacks, shop, disabled access; cl winter Thurs and Fri, 24–26 Dec;

(0151) 355 5017; £5.40. Parts of the surrounding docks have been redeveloped with craft workshops and the like. The Woodland (Chester Rd) is a useful pub/restaurant (with its own bowling green). On the S edge of town (nr M56 junction 10) **Cheshire Oaks** claims to be Europe's biggest factory outlet shopping village, with familiar brands and good bargains. *See separate Family Panel on p.61* for the new nearby **Blue Planet Aquarium.**

★ **GAWSWORTH** SJ8969 **Gawsworth Hall** Exceptionally pretty timbered manor house dating back to Norman times, the former home of Mary Fitton, possibly the Dark Lady of Shakespeare's sonnets; plenty of fine furniture, stained glass, pictures and sculptures. In summer the open-air theatre has a well chosen range of concerts and plays; good gardens and park too. Snacks, shop; cl am, and all Oct–Mar; (01260) 223456; £3.80. The village has fine houses in parkland, ponds, an interesting church, and an unusual unspoilt farm pub, while the Sutton Hall Hotel over at Sutton Lane Ends is quite handy for lunch.

★ **GRAPPENHALL** SJ6386 This attractive village is worth a visit for the ancient grinning cat on its church tower; there are peaceful canalside strolls here.

★ **GREAT BUDWORTH** SJ6677 Set in attractive rich countryside, this is a quaint purpose-built estate village; the church is imposing (as is the pub), and there are many pretty cottages.

JODRELL BANK SCIENCE CENTRE AND ARBORETUM SJ7970 Plenty to do at this lively place, which has developed quite a lot over the last few years. The centrepiece is still the huge radio telescope, the second largest in the world and as big as the dome of St Paul's, but they also have a fun Science Centre, with hands-on displays and exhibitions examining subjects as diverse as plants, prisms and planets. Outside is an arboretum with 2,500 types of tree, as well as nature trails, picnic spots, and an Environmental Discovery Centre. Regular shows in the Planetarium. Meals, snacks, shop, disabled access; cl Mon Nov–mid-Mar, 22–25 Dec and 4–9 Jan; (01477) 571339; *£4.30. The Dog at Peover Heath is quite handy for lunch.

KERRIDGE HILL SJ9477 Above Bollington, and with fine views, this is topped by the curious folly known as White Nancy. Good walks here, and to the E – where the quaint Highwayman pub (B5470 N of Rainow) also has good views, and is handy for the long-distance **Gritstone Trail** path.

KETTLESHULME SJ9970 **Dunge Valley Gardens** (off the B5470) Colourful gardens in Peak District countryside, especially good for rhododendrons (May/Jun), roses and unusual perennials. Teas, plant sales, limited disabled access; cl Sept–Mar; (01663) 733787; *£3 wknds and bank hols, *£2.50 wkdys (refundable if £10 spent on plants). The Crag Inn nearby in its untypically leafy valley at Wildboarclough does decent food, and fits well with a walk to the Three Shires Head and the summit of Shutlingsloe.

KNUTSFORD SJ7578 Despite obvious present-day prosperity and some rather heavy traffic, this has a pleasantly old-world feel, with lots of striking Georgian and other period buildings. It quickly conjures up schoolday memories of reading Mrs Gaskell's *Cranford*, its alias. On the northern edge, **Tatton Park** is a busy estate with a handsome neo-classical Georgian mansion at its centre. Magnificent collection of furnishings, porcelain and paintings (inc 2 Canalettos) in the opulent state rooms, and restored kitchens and servants' quarters; the Medieval Old Hall hints at the long history of the estate. The lovely grounds boast an Edwardian rose garden, Italian and Japanese gardens, orangery and fern house, leading to a big country park with mature trees, lakes, signposted walks and deer and waterfowl; you can fish, hire bikes, or take a carriage ride. There's also a **Home Farm** that works as it did 60 years ago, with vintage machinery and rare breeds of animals; children's playground. You could easily spend most of an undemanding day here (good family activities in summer school hols), or take a carload for a picnic in the park. Meals, snacks, shop, some disabled access; park and gardens open all year (except winter Mons), rest cl Mon (exc bank hols), all Nov–Mar (exc farm open Sun), mansion and old hall also cl am (mansion open some wknds Dec with seasonal decorations); (01565) 750250; entry to park £3 per car (free for cyclists and pedestrians), then £2.80 for the mansion or gardens, and £2.50 for the farm or old hall. An all-in ticket is £8.50; NT (though as the site is managed by the county council members still have to pay for all exc the mansion and garden). Tabley House *(see entry below)* is just outside the town, over the M6.

★ **LITTLE BOLLINGTON** SJ7286 This peaceful hamlet gives strolls by the Bridgewater Canal and in Dunham Massey deer park.

LITTLE BUDWORTH SJ5867 **Cheshire Herbs** Award-winning specialist herb nursery growing and selling over 200 different varieties from agrimony to yellow melilot. Shop; cl 25 Dec–2 Jan; (01829) 760578; free. The Shrewsbury Arms has good-value food. **Little Budworth Common** This country park is a strong (and oddly refreshing) contrast to most of this area's richly manicured countryside: poor wild heath with young bogs and scrawny birch woods.

LLANGOLLEN CANAL SJ5947 Relaxing for gentle and pretty waterside walks, with access, for example, at Wrenbury; the good Dusty Miller dining pub here has an interesting lifting bridge by it.

★ † **LOWER PEOVER** SJ7474 Many people's favourite Cheshire village: cobbled lanes, glorious 14th-c black and white timbered church, quiet watermeadows and a fine pub.

† **LOWER WITHINGTON** SJ8169 **Welltrough Dried Flowers** (signed off the A34) Well praised by readers, a helpful and friendly dried flowers specialist based on a working dairy farm, with waterfowl and calves for children. Snacks, shop, cl 25–27 Dec, 1–3 Jan, free. Further along the A34 at Marton is a simple 14th-c shingle-roofed black and white timbered **church** in unpromising surroundings; there's a **craft centre** adjacent.

★ **LYMM** SJ6887 There are pretty cottages in **The Dingle**, and you can take **boat trips** on the Bridgewater Canal, for example from the new Admiral Benbow pub at Agden Wharf. The stroll up to the lake at Lymm Dam is pleasant.

MACCLESFIELD SJ9173 Away from the modern shopping streets are plenty of fine old buildings associated with the early industrial revolution and the silk industry; the restored weavers' cottages on **Paradise Street** with their wide garret windows are of special note. Behind St Michael's Church is a more ancient core with quaint little cobbled alleys, the famous 108 steps, and fine views across the town to the Pennines. The **Silk Museum** (Roe St) is the best place to learn about the industry; good audio-visual and some fine examples of the end product, also town trail leaflets. Snacks, shop, some disabled access; cl am Sun, 24–26 Dec, 1 Jan, Good Fri; (01625) 613210, £2.60. Nearby **Paradise Mill** (Park Lane) is good fun; enthusiastic guides (many of whom are former silk workers) demonstrate the silk production process on the mill's restored handlooms, and room settings give a good idea of 1930s working conditions. Shop, good disabled access; cl am, Mon (exc bank hols), 24–26 Dec, 1 Jan, Good Fri; (01625) 618228; £2.60. Joint ticket with the Silk Museum £4.60. **West Park Museum** (Prestbury Rd) Small but recently refurbished, with a decent range of decorative arts, some interesting Egyptian antiquities and bird paintings by Charles Tunnicliffe. West Park adjacent is pleasant and has one of the largest bowling greens in the country. Shop; cl am, all day Mon (exc bank hols), 24–26 Dec, 1 Jan, Good Fri; free. The teashop at Arighi Bianci is highly recommended. The Sutton Hall Hotel just S is best for lunch. 3 or 4 miles NW of the town, **Hare Hill** (off the B5087) has acres of lovely parkland with walled garden, pergola and fine spring flowers. Some disabled access; open daily mid-May–Jun (for rhododendrons and azaleas), Weds–Sun and bank hols Apr and

July–Oct; £2.50; NT. A footpath leads to Alderley Edge (*see Nether Alderley, below*).

MACCLESFIELD CANAL SJ8965 With good more or less level towpath walks, this tracks through fine high countryside from the Cheshire county boundary nr Disley to pass Bollington, Macclesfield and Congleton, with plenty of access points. One of the most interesting places is S of the A54 just W of its junction with the A523, where a staggering flight of 10 locks leads down to a sturdily elegant iron aqueduct.

† ★ **MALPAS** SJ4847 The most striking thing in this attractive place is the extraordinarily uplifting ceiling in its 14th-c hilltop church. There's also a fragmentary castle ruin nearby, as well as pretty cottages and almshouses, and some grander buildings.

★ **MARBURY** SJ5645 Some delightful landscapes open up in this village, with an attractive church, lake, wood and canal.

MARBURY COUNTRY PARK SJ6576 (nowhere near the above village) With some quiet short walks, this gives on to the extensive **Budworth Mere**, with sailing, and herons, ducks, grebes and coots pottering around the rushes; good pubs nearby at Comberbach (pronounced Comberbatch) and Great Budworth.

MIDDLEWOOD WAY SJ9482 A sort of linear country park nr Macclesfield, this runs along a former railway; attractively bordered with wild flowers and trees, with tracks too for cyclists (bicycle hire at Lyme Park or Bollington) and horse rides (can also be hired by the hour, about £10); several decent pubs in Bollington, one at Whiteley Green.

† **MOBBERLEY** SJ7979 **Hillside Ornamental Fowl** (Damson Lane) Excellent private collection of wildfowl with rare species such as magpie geese, white-headed stifftail and the Abyssinian black duck, as well as aviaries of softbills, flamingos and other exotic birds. Children should enjoy the penguin pool, and they have a pair of white wallabies. Undercover picnic area, snacks, shop; open Easter–Oct exc Thurs; (01565) 873282; £4.50. The **church** has a magnificently carved Tudor rood screen. The Church Inn is useful for lunch.

! **MOULDSWORTH** SJ5070 **Motor Museum** (Smithy Lane) Splendid changing collection of cars, everything from vintage Bentleys to gleaming Ferraris, with several dozen other vehicles in between. It's notably friendly, and you really don't have to be a car fiend to enjoy it – the 1930s art deco building and its grounds are very attractive in themselves, and there's plenty to amuse children, with quizzes, play areas and space to run around. There's also a collection of unusual teapots, many from the 1920s and 1930s. Disabled access; open pm Sun and bank hols Mar–Nov, plus pm Weds July and Aug; (01928) 731781; £2.50. The White Lion at Alvanley is a popular nearby dining pub.

MOW COP SJ8557 Right on the Staffs border is a shaggy, steep hill with a castellated folly on top, and a rock pinnacle left by former quarrying; rich views over Cheshire (the village just behind, which is in Staffs, is a reminder of the contrast with Cheshire's richness). Worth a look if passing.

† **NANTWICH** SJ6552 A pedestrian-only centre protects the splendid 14th-c **church**, with its exceptional carved choir stalls; look out for the devil forcing open a nun's mouth, and the wife threatening her husband with a ladle. Much of the town, destroyed by a firestorm in 1583, was rebuilt then in intricate black and white timbering, and with countless window-boxes in flower in spring and summer is a fine sight especially around the centre. Quite a few decent antique shops, and the ancient and central Crown does good snacks and lunches. As most of S Cheshire's roads seem to intersect at the town, traffic can be a problem.

Stapeley Water Gardens (A51 about a mile SE) The world's largest and best-regarded watergarden centre with display pools, fountains (the dancing ones are popular with younger visitors), waterfalls, gardens, coldwater and tropical fish, and a huge heated glasshouse with many of their 350 different water lilies (at their best Jun–Sept), piranhas, sharks, palms and parrots. Plenty of gifts (lots for fishermen) as well as plants, and frequent special events. Meals, snacks, shop, disabled access; (01270) 623868; gardens free, palm house £3.35. **Firs Pottery** (Aston; A530, about 5m towards Whitchurch) Friendly place organising one-day pottery workshops (half-days for children). Booking essential; (01270) 780345; £25 for a day course, inc lunch and tea and coffee (£10 children, during school hols). A good shop sells all sorts of useful pots, and the nearby Bhurtpore does good food. Readers enjoy the vast array of different flavours of ice-cream available at **Snugbury's Ice-Cream Farm** (A51 N); cl 25–26 Dec, 1 Jan.

NESS GARDENS SJ3075 **Liverpool University Botanic Gardens** (Neston) Extensive collection of specimen trees and shrubs, herbaceous plants, renowned heather, rock, rose and water gardens; visitor centre, good children's adventure playground, and picnic area. Meals, snacks, shop and plant sales, disabled access; cl 25 Dec (open till dusk in summer); (0151) 353 0123; £4. Parkgate is handy for lunch.

NETHER ALDERLEY MILL SJ8476 Lovely 15th-c watermill with carefully preserved atmosphere, and restored working waterwheels. The Victorian machinery still grinds flour (water supplies permitting). Open pm Weds, Sun and bank hols Apr–Oct, plus pm Tues, Thurs, Fri and Sat Jun–Sept; (01625) 523012; £2; NT. Nearby **Alderley Edge** SJ8677 (not to be confused with the straggling suburban settlement named after it), rises high out of the plain, with good walks through the woodland and fine views of the higher hills to the E. The local caving-club members are working towards opening some of the former copper mines which honeycomb the area.

NORTHWICH SJ6674 Cheshire is the only British county to produce salt on a large scale, and much of it comes from here. This **Salt Museum** (London Rd) has the industry pretty well covered; microscopes let you see the intricacy of each crystal. Snacks, shop, limited disabled access; cl am wknds, all day Mon (exc bank hols and in Aug), 24–26 Dec; (01606) 41331; £1.85. You can follow the Salt Heritage Trail around some of the other buildings. From the Quay there are cruises down the river. The Smoker at Plumley (A556 E) is a reliable dining pub.

★ **PARKGATE** SJ2879 This interesting village is the country's only inland seaside resort, the Dee estuary having retreated since its palmy days at the end of the 18th and early 19th c. Before that, it was a more important port than Liverpool, and there's an eerie charm in sitting in the Boathouse or Red Lion on the 'Promenade', looking out over the marshes to the distant waters and the Welsh hills. A similar sense of stranded time can be had at the Harp by the ruined marshside quay nr Little Neston; you can walk between the two (and on to Ness Gardens, *see entry left*) along the Dee estuary 'coastal' path.

PECKFORTON CASTLE SJ5357 It seems bizarre to talk about a medieval Victorian castle, but that's exactly what this is, built in 1840 using authentic medieval plans. It's the only intact medieval-style castle in the country, unique in showing what such a place was like in its prime. Rising majestically from its wooded hilltop, it has all the features you'd expect – forbidding gatehouse, ramparts, and broad battlements – as well as fine views over the Cheshire plain. There may be people in period costume, and readers tell us they have some quite outstanding cobwebs. Snacks, shop; cl mid-Sept–Easter; (01829) 260930; *£2.50. The Beeston Castle at Beeston is handiest for lunch, though there's a good hill walk over to the Pheasant at Higher Burwardsley.

PECKFORTON HILLS SJ5256 These are tracked by a particularly fine section of the 30-mile **Sandstone Trail**, with splendid views of real and real-looking romantic castles, and good pubs usefully placed at Bulkeley and Higher Burwardsley. The Trail offers very varied scenery, following the romantically wooded sandstone ridges, crags and outcrops stretching from Overton in the N (the church here is pretty, and the Ring o' Bells is a most attractive pub, with Mersey views) to the Shropshire border S of Malpas (the ancient Bell o' the Hill pub nr Tushingham down there is a useful stop).

POYNTON SJ9183 **Brookside Garden Centre** (Macclesfield Rd) A splendid miniature railway chuffs its way through an authentically detailed circuit in a pretty garden setting to a replica West Country station, packed with railway memorabilia. Also pottery and birds of prey. Parking is not always easy. Meals, snacks, shop, disabled access (not train); railway runs wknds all year plus Weds Apr–Sept and daily mid-July and Aug; (01625) 872919; train 50p, garden centre free. A mile away at Higher Poynton, Coppice Fruit Farm has pick-your-own. The pleasant stretches of the Middlewood Way (*see above*) around the Poynton inclines are underrated, and the Boars Head here is a good-value refreshment stop.

★ **PRESTBURY** SJ9077 Very prosperous-feeling now, with leafy surroundings, good shops, and for refreshment the smart Legh Arms and homelier Admiral Rodney. There are pleasant riverside walks to the S, along the Bollin.

RAW HEAD SJ5154 From the A534 nr Harthill a section of the 30-mile **Sandstone Trail** ascends Raw Head, the most spectacular natural feature of the central Cheshire ridge, with sandstone cliffs weathered into bizarre shapes, and a cave to explore.

★ **ROSTHERNE** SJ7483 As well as charming brick cottages along its quaint cobbled pavement, this picture-postcard village gives a lovely view over one of the county's broadest meres from the graveyard of its attractive timbered church.

RUNCORN SJ5182 The main reason for visiting this New Town is **Norton Priory Museum & Gardens** (Tudor Rd, Manor Park, SJ5583), a lovely 12th-c priory that developed into a Georgian stately home, with exhibitions on medieval monastic life, and demonstrations of tile-making, carving and sculpture. Outside is an enchanting 18th-c walled garden, and beautiful woodland gardens. Snacks, shop, disabled access; cl am, 24–26 Dec, 1 Jan, walled garden cl Nov–Feb; (01928) 569895; £3. More centrally the Sun pm **miniature train rides** in the park on Stockham Lane (Halton) are popular with children. There are views from the nearby ruins of **Halton Castle** up on its grassy hill.

SANDIWAY SJ6070 **Blakemere Craft Centre** (Chester Rd) Much better than average craft centre around restored Edwardian stable block, with 18 interesting shops, aquatic centre, and good food hall. Wknd craft fairs, meals, snacks, disabled access; cl Mon (exc bank hols); (01606) 883261; free.

SCHOLAR GREEN SJ8358 **Little Moreton Hall** (A34 N) One of Britain's best-preserved half-timbered buildings, its splendid black and white exterior pretty much unchanged since built in 1580, and covered with such a profusion of lines the effect is almost dizzying. The inside, though largely unfurnished, has some interesting features too, especially the wainscoted Long Gallery, Great Hall and chapel. There's a re-creation of a typical 17th-c knot garden – and make sure you don't miss the built-in dog kennel. Regular open-air theatre and concerts. Meals, snacks, shop, disabled access to ground floor only; open pm Weds–Sun late Mar–Oct, then pm wknds up to Christmas; (01260) 272018; £4; NT. The Brownlow Arms nearby or Rising Sun in Scholar Green itself are popular for lunch. **Heritage Narrow Boats** at Kent Green have electric narrow boats to hire by the day; cl Nov–Easter; (01782) 785700; £50–£75 wkdys for up to 12 people (£65–£90 wknds) – very satisfying, gliding along in silence.

STRETTON SJ4453 The working **watermill** in lovely countryside here still produces corn, powered by 2 ancient wheels. Shop, some disabled access; cl am, all day Mon, and Oct–Mar (open wknds only Apr and Sept); (01606) 41331; *£1.75. The Cock o' Barton up on the A534 is quite useful for lunch (and a good base for walks – as is the Farndon Arms in the attractive Dee-side village of Farndon).

STYAL SJ8383 **Quarry**

Bank Mill and Country Park One of the best and most extensive places in the country to get to grips with the Industrial Revolution – you can easily spend the best part of a day here. The 18th-c cotton mill that's the centrepiece still produces cloth (you can buy it in the shop); besides demonstrations of spinning and weaving, lively exhibitions look at factory conditions for the millworkers and their bosses. Thanks to a lottery grant an 1840 beam engine has been fully restored and installed in the original engine house. A new hands-on exhibition explains the project, while the 50-ton working waterwheel remains an impressive sight. The surrounding village has carefully preserved workers' cottages, chapels and shop; at the apprentice house enthusiastic guides in period dress explain the lifestyle and 12hr working days faced by young pauper children, you can even try out their beds (there are timed tickets in operation here, so it makes sense to see this bit at the start of your visit). Good woodland and riverside walks in the park, lots of events throughout the year. Meals, snacks, shop, disabled access (recently improved through the park); cl winter Mons, apprentice house cl am wkdys and Mon during school terms; (01625) 527468; all-in ticket £5.50, mill only £4.20, apprentice house only £3.50; NT. The Ship is pleasant for lunch.

★ **SWETTENHAM** SJ8067 One of Cheshire's tucked-away comfortable villages – rich paddocks with wrought-iron fences, daffodils in spring in a dell by an old mill, a good dining pub (the Swettenham Arms) behind the partly 13th-c church.

! TABLEY SJ7277 **Tabley House** (off the A5033) Probably the finest Palladian House in the NW, with a splendid collection of paintings. Sir John Fleming Leicester (whose family lived here for over 800 years) was the first great collector of British art, and, though his plans to turn his home into a National Gallery came to nothing, most of the works he assembled are still here, inc pictures by Turner (the one of a pineapple shows why he is remembered for his landscapes), Reynolds, Henry Thompson and James Ward. Snacks, shop, very good disabled access (though they prefer notice); open Apr–Oct, pm Thurs–Sun and bank hols; (01565) 750151; £4. **Tabley Cuckoo Clock Collection** (Old School House, Nether Tabley) A unique collection of these and other mechanical timepieces from all over the world. At the moment there are 500 rare and beautiful clocks, most of them working, but the number constantly increases as the owners nip off to Europe to track down more (they have recently acquired 3 working historic fairground organs). Because of this (and as it takes time to get them all going) the exhibition is open only by appointment. Shop, disabled access; (01565) 633039; £3.50. The Smoker at Plumley is good for lunch.

★ **TARPORLEY** SJ5562 Largely bypassed and quietly attractive, with very individual shops inc antique shops; the Rising Sun is a fine pub, the Swan a well restored old coaching inn.

TATTENHALL SJ5059 **Cheshire Cheese Experience** (Drumlan Hall Farm) Demonstrations of cheshire cheese-making in purpose-built dairy; which stages of the process you see depends on the time of day you visit, but a museum fills you in on the rest. Shop, disabled access; cl 25 Dec, 2 wks in Jan; no cheese-making Tues or Weds; (01829) 770924; £1. The adjacent **Ice-Cream Farm** has samples of another flavoursome dairy product, and you can see the cows being milked; cl 2 wks end Jan; (01829) 770995; free. The Egerton Arms down the A41 at Broxton is a good lunch stop.

TEGGS NOSE COUNTRY PARK SJ9472 Cheshire's hilly eastern edge forms part of the Peak District, and offers some grand views westwards towards N Wales. This country park has a useful summer information centre, and good walks with far views, punctuated by relics of the former quarrying here. By the turn off the A537, the Setter Dog is a good pub. From the park, a well marked track (part of the long-distance Gritstone Trail) heads off S into the **Macclesfield Forest**, with steep, deep green pine plantations around neatly walled small reservoirs; on the far side of this the isolated Leathers Smithy E of Langley is a warmly welcoming moorside refuge with superb views, and the Stanley Arms tucked away at Bottom of the Oven is also good.

WARRINGTON SJ6087 Not an inspiring town for visitors, but its unusually lively **Museum & Art Gallery** (Bold St) has decorated skulls and shrunken heads, an Egyptian mummy, a toy-packed nursery, and a number of outsize beetles and other creepy-crawlies. Snacks, shop, disabled access; cl Sun and bank hols; free. **Gulliver's World** Theme park very similar to its sister park in Matlock Bath (*see Derbyshire chapter*), with rides and entertainment aimed at the under 12s. Snacks, shop, disabled access; open wknds Apr–Oct, daily June–mid-Sept and during school hols; (01925) 444888; £5.80. The Ferry at Fiddlers Ferry down by the Mersey off the A562 at Penketh is prettily placed for lunch – and for remote-feeling walks.

WHARTONS LOCK SJ5360 With a handy family dining pub nearby, a good place for walks along the **Shropshire Union Canal**; this is a charming section, winding through the richly wooded farming country below Beeston Castle.

★ † **WHITEGATE** SJ6168 An interesting village, with thatched houses around the village green, fragmentary remains of what was once the biggest Cistercian monastery in the whole of England opposite its church, and a lakeside walk along a nearby derelict railway.

WIDNES SJ5183 Another town that rarely tops visitor itineraries, but well worth a special trip for **Catalyst** (Mersey Rd), an award-winning centre exploring the chemical industry and how it affects our lives – children who enjoy museums where you poke, press and push things will really get a lot out of it. It's presented in a splendidly entertaining way, with interactive games and displays such as the Game of Health, which involves travelling from the past to the present without falling victim to any deadly diseases. A glass lift whisks you up to a rooftop observatory with splendid views. There's an adjacent waterside park, with wildlife and brightly coloured fishing boats. Meals, snacks, shop, disabled access; cl Mon exc bank hols (may be open Mon in school hols), 24–26 Dec, 1 Jan; (0151) 420 1121; £4.35.

Where to eat

ALDFORD SJ4159 **Grosvenor Arms** *(01244) 620228* Sizeable Victorian pub, attractively decorated, with huge panelled library and several quieter rooms, airy conservatory, good interesting food from a daily-changing menu, well kept real ales, lots of New World wines (and malt whiskies), and a large elegant sun-trap terrace and neat lawn; best to get there early. **£18.75**|£5.95.

ALTRINCHAM SJ7788 **Juniper** *21 The Downs (0161) 929 4008* Smart but informal-feeling restaurant with wooden floor and ceiling and an Italian mural; beautifully presented modern cooking (super fish), lovely puddings, good cheeses, a carefully chosen and interesting wine list, and efficient service; downstairs bar, too; cl am Sat, Sun, am Mon. **£39.50**|£12.

BOLLINGTON SJ9377 **Mauro's** *88 Palmerston St (01625) 573898* Friendly Italian restaurant with lots of good pasta, excellent fresh fish and lovely puddings; cl am Sat and Sun, Mon, 25–26 Dec and 1 Jan; disabled access. **£27**|£4.95.

BUNBURY SJ5758 **Dysart Arms** *Bowes Gate Rd (01829) 260183* Informal but smart dining pub with good interesting food, well kept real ales, decent wines by the glass, friendly neat staff, comfortable seats in cosy small areas, convivial atmosphere, no smoking area, and tables on the terrace and in garden. **£22.15**|£8.95.

CHESTER SJ4166 **Francs** *14 Cuppin St (01244) 317952* Cheerful timbered brasserie on 2 floors of old converted warehouse with very good French country food; partial disabled access. **£20**|£5.95.

CHESTER SJ4166 **Garden House** *1 Rufus Court, off Northgate St (01244) 320004* First-floor restaurant in handsome Georgian building with good interesting food; cl Sun, bank hols, and Christmas. **£28**|£5.25.

CHESTER SJ4166 **Old Harkers Arms** *1 Russell St, under Mike Melody Antiques, off City Rd (01244) 344525* Attractive conversion of an early Victorian canal warehouse with lofty ceiling, tall windows and well spaced tables and chairs; lots to look at, a comfortably busy atmosphere, friendly and efficient staff, a changing choice of nicely presented, sometimes unusual food (inc interesting sandwiches), well kept real ales, and New World wines; cl pm 25 and 26 Dec; no children; disabled access. **£19**|£6.

HASSALL GREEN SJ7858 **Canal Centre and Tearoom** *(01270) 762266* 200-year-old house with tearoom offering breakfasts, snacks, lunches, cream teas, and evening restaurant – and you can sit on the lawn and watch the narrow boats going through the locks; gift shop and towpath walks; bdrms. **£17.50**|£4.95.

KNUTSFORD SJ7578 **Belle Epoque Brasserie** *60 King St (01565) 633060* Popular restaurant with rooms decorated in art nouveau style with lavish drapes, marbled pillared alcoves, and smartly set tables; enthusiastic friendly staff and lovely modern cooking; cl Sun, bank hols; children over 9. **£25**|£11.50.

MACCLESFIELD SJ9173 **Dorothy's Tea Shoppe** *72 Chestergate (01625) 503733* Enjoyable afternoon tea (as well as morning coffee and light lunches), in a beamed building above Gatehouse Antiques, close to the Heritage Centre; cl Sun, Weds, bank hols. **£11.75**|£4.50.

MARBURY SJ5645 **Swan** *(01948) 663715* Friendly creeper-covered pub in attractive village, with an open fire in the neatly kept comfortable lounge, interesting food (well liked daily specials), good ales and whiskies and friendly service; nice walks to Llangollen Canal; cl am Mon; disabled access. **£22**|£6.

PEOVER HEATH SJ7973 **Dog** *(01625) 861421* Set on a quiet lane, this bustling pub has been refurbished and extended this year to include 2 big no smoking areas, a cosier, comfortable taproom with darts and pool, open fires, well kept real ales, a good choice of whiskies, a comprehensive wine list, and well liked food; bdrms. **£17.50**|£3.95.

PLUMLEY SJ7175 **Smoker** *(01565) 722338* Popular thatched 16th-c pub with open fires and comfortable sofas in 3 well decorated connecting rooms; good, swiftly served food, a wide choice of whiskies, well kept real ales, and friendly service; big garden; disabled access. **£18.50**|£6.95.

POTT SHRIGLEY SJ9478 **Cheshire Hunt** *(01625) 573185* Isolated stone pub with several rambling small rooms, solid furnishings, beams and flowers, good bar and restaurant food and no noisy games machines or piped music; seats outside with country views; cl am Mon except bank hols; disabled access. **£20**|£5.50.

SWETTENHAM SJ8067 **Swettenham Arms** *(01477) 571284* Tucked-away country dining pub with 3 spacious beamed bar areas, winter log fires, nice furnishings and a huge range of very popular food; no smoking restaurant and real ales; disabled access. **£21**|£4.95.

Special thanks to E G Parish, Philip Pritchard, L Cherry, Dave and Deborah Irving, Miss A Cleworth, P Kidwell.

Please let us know what you think of places in the *Guide*. Use the report forms at the back of the book or simply write us a letter.

Cheshire Calendar

Some of these dates were provisional as we went to press. Please check information with the telephone numbers provided.

Chester Public Proclamations by the Town Crier *12 noon* at the Cross – *every Tues–Sat, Apr–Oct* (01244) 402445
Chester Band Concerts by the River *2pm and 3.30pm and 4pm and 6pm* at the Edwardian Bandstand in the Groves – *every Sat and Sun and Bank Hol Mon, May–Sept* (01244) 402445
Chester Guided walk of Roman Chester *1.45pm* from Chester Visitor Centre and *2pm* from the Town Hall – *every Thurs, Fri and Sat, Jun–Aug* (01244) 402445
Chester Ghost Walk *7.30pm*, Chester Visitor Centre – *every Thurs, Fri and Sat, May–Oct* (01244) 402445
Chester Guided Musical Walking Tour from Town Hall – *third Sun of month, Jun–Oct* (01244) 402445
Chester Guided Literary Walking Tour from Town Hall – *last Sun of month, Jun–Oct* (01244) 402445
Chester Races at the Roodee – *4 and 6 May, 2 and 23 Jun, 9, 10 and 25 July, 20 and 21 Aug, 22 Sept* (01244) 323170

JANUARY

6 **Knutsford** Antiques Fair at Tatton Park – *till Sun 10* (01270) 878519
23 **Nantwich** Holly Holy Day: re-enactment of the Battle of Namptwyche in1643 (01270) 610983

FEBRUARY

27 **Chester** Folk Day at Hoole Community Centre (01244) 320424

MARCH

15 **Warrington** Fleadh: Irish Festival at Parr Hall – *till Sat 20* (01925) 442362

APRIL

2 **Ellesmere Port** Traditional Boat Gathering at the Boat Museum – *till Mon 5* (0151) 355 5017; **Nantwich** Jazz & Blues Festival inc Kenny Ball – *till Mon 5* (01270) 625283
3 **Knutsford** Easter Festival at Tatton Park: circus, fair, fun-on-the-farm, living history – *till Mon 5* (01565) 654822
10 **Macclesfield** Rainbow Craft Fair: over 200 stands at Capesthorne Hall – *till Sun 11* (01625) 861221
18 **Sandbach** Transport Festival (01270) 764499
23 **Chester** Pentice Court: full ceremonial and traditional gathering of Chester Guildsmen and procession to the Guildhall (01244) 320431

MAY

1 **Knutsford** Royal May Day Festival: pavements are carpeted with elaborate sand patterns, procession, horse-drawn tableaux, morris dancers, maypole dancers, fireworks (01565) 633074

Cheshire Calendar (cont.)

3 **Sandbach** Elizabethan Market (01270) 763231
4 **Chester** May Festival: racing at the Roodee racecourse – *till Thurs 6* (01244) 323170
8 **Knutsford** Angling Fair at Tatton Park – *till Sun 9* (01565) 654822; **Marbury** Merry Days: falconry, raft racing – *till Sun 9* (01270) 610983
15 **Chester** Lord Mayor's Parade (01244) 324324 or 402126; **Chester** Festival and Vintage Cars at the Roodee (racecourse) – *till Sun 16* (01244) 375283
22 **Chester** Regatta – *till Sun 23* (01244) 335593; **nr Nantwich** Reaseheath College Open Weekend: nature trails, gardening, tractor rides, animals and pets, sheepdog displays – *till Sun 23* (01270) 625131
23 **Chester** Classic Car Run from Eastgate Street (01572) 717273; **Macclesfield** Kit Car Show at Capesthorne Hall (01625) 861221
26 **Willaston nr Nantwich** World Worm Charming Championships at the Primary School (01606) 661528
28 **Chester** Garrison Beating Retreat at Castle Square (01244) 390958; **Kelsall** Chester Folk Festival at the Morris Dancer Pub (01244) 320424
30 **Audlem** Carnival (01270) 811467; **Ellesmere Port** Model Tug Towing at the Boat Museum (0151) 355 501731; **Knutsford** Street Fair (01565) 632611; **Northwich** Regatta (01606) 862862; **Runcorn** Town Park Show (01928) 576246

JUNE

3 **Neston** Ladies Day: afternoon procession in period costume (0151) 336 3104
6 **Knutsford** Orchid Show at Tatton Park (01565) 654822
12 **Ness** Garden Festival at Ness Botanic Gardens – *till Sun 13* (0151) 353 0123
13 **Knutsford** Music from the Movies and fireworks at Tatton Park (01625) 575681
17 **Gawsworth** Open-air Festival: concerts and plays at Gawsworth Hall – *every Weds–Sat till Aug 14* (01260) 223456
18 **Middlewich** Folk & Boat Festival – *till Sun 20* (01606) 836896
19 **Appleton Thorn** Bawming the Thorn: traditional procession and festivities during which children bawm (dance round) a hawthorn tree, originated when a knight went on the crusades with an offshoot of the Glastonbury Thorn (01925) 266764; **Chester** Midsummer Watch Parade: re-creation of medieval procession inc family of 4 Chester giants, ship of fools, angels, devils and mythical beasts – *till Sun 20* (01244) 348365
22 **Tabley** Cheshire Show at the Showground – *till Weds 23* (01829) 760020
25 **Ellesmere Port** Classic Car Show at the Boat Museum (0151) 355 5017; **Knutsford** Antiques Fair at Tatton Park – *till Sun 27* (01270) 878519
26 **Arley** Garden Festival at Arley Hall – *till Sun 27* (01565) 777353; **Ness** Open-air Concert at Ness Botanic Gardens (0151) 353 0123

JULY

Sutton Open-air Opera at the Civit Hills Opera – *till end Aug* (01260) 252322
2 **Warrington** Walking Day: long processions wind round the town originally to draw people away from the races (01925) 444400 ext 2143

Cheshire Calendar (cont.)

3 **Arley** Fireworks Concert at Arley Hall (01565) 777353; **Knutsford** American Car Show at Tatton Park – *till Sun 4* (01565) 654822; **Northwich** Carnival (01606) 862862; **Runcorn** Carnival (01928) 580366

4 **Chester** River Carnival and Raft Race (01244) 324888

10 **Warrington** Steam Fair at Grappen Hall – *till Sun 11* (01751) 473780

16 **Chester** Summer Music Festival with international performers – *till Sat 31* (01244) 320722; fringe festival (01244) 321496; **Macclesfield** Popular Music Open-air Concerts at Capesthorne Hall – *till Sat 17* (01625) 861221

17 **Widnes** Halton Show at Spike Island – *till Sun 18* (0151) 424 2061

22 **Knutsford** RHS Flower Show at Tatton Park – *till Sun 25* (01270) 878519

25 **Chester** Family Day at the Racecourse: children's entertainment, music and fun (01244) 323170; **Macclesfield** Classic Car Show at Capesthorne Hall (01625) 861221; **Warrington** Street Theatre Festival: free entertainment *also Sun 1 and Sun 8 Aug* (01925) 442362

28 **Nantwich** and South Cheshire Agricultural Show at Dorfold Hall Park (01270) 780306

31 **Knutsford** Firework Concert at Tatton Park (01565) 654822

AUGUST

7 **Chelford** Astle Park Traction Engine Rally – *till Sun 8* (01751) 473780

15 **Knutsford** Medieval Fair: re-enactments, craft displays at Tatton Park (01565) 654822; **Macclesfield** Forest Chapel, Rushbearing Ceremony (01625) 504114; **Macclesfield** Family Fun Day: free day, two arenas, parachute drop, 250 stalls at West Park (01625) 504114; **Rainow** Rushbearing Ceremony at the Parish Church (01625) 572013

22 **Over Peover** Game and Angling Fair at Peover Hall: gun dogs, parade of hounds, fly-fishing demonstration, birds of prey (01565) 733847

28 **Crewe and Nantwich** Carnival at Queen's Park – *till Sun 29* (01270) 610983; **Ellesmere Port** Model Boat Convention at the Boat Museum – *till Mon 30* (0151) 355 5017; **Knutsford** Steam Engine Rally at Tatton Park – *till Sun 29* (01565) 654822; **Poynton** Show at Poynton Park (01625) 504114

SEPTEMBER

4 **Crewe and Nantwich** Folk Festival – *till Sun 5* (01270) 663120; **Knutsford** Fireworks Concert at Tatton Park (01625) 575681

8 **Knutsford** Antiques Fair at Tatton Park – *till Sun 12* (01270) 878519

11 **Malpas** Yesteryear Rally – *till Sun 12* (01978) 780749

18 **Knutsford** Wood Weekend: demonstrations, displays and sales at Tatton Park – *till Sun 19* (01565) 654822; **Macclesfield** Rainbow Craft Fair: over 200 stands at Capesthorne Hall – *till Sun 19* (01625) 861221

OCTOBER

2 **Ellesmere Port** Tugs and Pushers at the Boat Museum *till Sun 3* (0151) 355 5017

3 **Chester** Literature Festival: guest authors, readings and workshops – *till Sun 17* (01244) 319985

Cheshire Calendar (cont.)

NOVEMBER

6 Chester Fireworks at the Roodee racecourse (01244) 375283

27 Ellesmere Port Christmas Craft Fair at the Boat Museum: Santa and narrow boat grotto – *till Sun 28* (0151) 355 5017

DECEMBER

2 Chester Lantern Parade (01244) 348365

4 Knutsford Lancastrian Theatre Organ Christmas Concert at Tatton Park (01565) 654822

9 Chester Lantern Parade (01244) 348365

11 Lymm Dickensian Christmas: locals in costume, craft fairs (01925) 753272

We welcome reports from readers

This *Guide* depends on readers' reports. Do help us if you can – in return, we offer a discount on the next edition to people who've helped us with reports for it. Tell us what you think about places already in it, and anything extra you think we should say about them. And send us your ideas for inclusion in the next edition: places to visit, eat at or stay in, attractive drives or walks, maybe even unusual interesting shops you know of. Use the card in the middle, the report forms at the end, or just write – no stamp needed: *The Good Guide to Britain*, FREEPOST TN1569, Wadhurst, E Sussex TN5 7BR.

Cornwall

Britain's best coastline, from sandy family resorts to wild majestic cliffs; masses of family attractions, some spectacular gardens, quaint fishing villages, a fine choice of places to stay.

Attractive seaside villages and towns are the highlight here – often really lovely, with friendly local people. Generally well sheltered, they can be pleasantly mild when other parts of the West Country are cold. Even in summer they manage to keep their charm, as the strolling crowds never quite override the natural local character. Coupled with them is magnificent coastal scenery. Readers like the south coast best – very sheltered, with wonderful places to stay in, and more gently picturesque than the north. East of the Lizard Point are plenty of interesting little coves, winding estuaries and creeks rich in bird life, and boat and fishing trips from virtually every harbour. There are some dramatic cliffy stretches too, interspersed with fine sandy beaches, especially west of the Lizard.

The north coast scores for uncomplicated family beach holidays, around the attractive town of St Ives, and between Padstow (appealing combination of fishing port and resort) and lively Newquay (Cornwall's biggest resort, increasingly a surfing centre). This stretch is an almost continuous line of resort developments, with plenty of family attractions nearby.

There are much wilder stretches of coast, too. West of St Ives are rugged stretches of windswept empty moorland clifftops, with a hinterland exceptionally rich in well preserved visible archaeology Bronze Age burial chambers and standing stones, Iron Age hill forts and village sites, ancient stone crosses. Small rather withdrawn-looking granite villages and farmsteads among wind-beaten pastures give this western part a rather clannish feel, almost like the more nationalistic parts of Wales; but though visitors are clearly seen as outsiders, the locals are far from unfriendly. Another stretch of wild grandeur is up towards Devon, north of commercialised Tintagel – towering precipices, dramatic surfing beaches and much completely unspoilt seaboard, with no development, little car access, just wildlife, wind, waves and the occasional walker. Port Isaac and Boscastle are the pick of this part's few settlements.

A great range of enjoyable family outings is topped by the Flambards theme park near Helston (entertaining for all ages). There's plenty to occupy children at Paradise Park in Hayle and the Dobwalls adventure park, and lots of good animal places elsewhere – the monkey sanctuary near Looe stands out, and the friendly and uncommercial-feeling animal centre at Trecangate is a favourite with readers.

Cornwall's great gardens, at their best in late spring but gorgeous at almost any time, are quite unlike those elsewhere in England – altogether more exotic, almost subtropical: see Caerhays, Madron, Mawnan Smith,

Mevagissey, Probus and Trelissick. Cotehele, near Calstock, is Cornwall's loveliest house, and Lanhydrock House, Trerice, Antony House at Torpoint and the fairy-tale castle on St Michael's Mount off Marazion are also well worth visiting.

Away from the sheltered south-east, the inland parts are largely treeless, with rolling pasture and moorland. Windswept Bodmin Moor is the county's most untouched inland area. In the more exposed spots the towering alloy propellers of the new windfarms are becoming a striking landscape feature.

In high summer Cornwall's better for long stay-put holidays than for short breaks or touring: with lots of traffic on the narrow roads (and some serious parking problems), getting there, back and around can overshadow a short summer visit. On a longer holiday, it's surprisingly easy to escape the crowds that go with the big family attractions, honey-pot fishing villages and famous beaches. With 500 miles of coastal walks here, much of the land owned and beautifully preserved by the National Trust, you can always quickly escape into solitude. Incidentally, few roads actually follow the coast – good for walkers, if disappointing for drivers (or cyclists). The relatively warm sea makes Cornwall popular bathing country in summer: we pick out reliably clean beaches in the text.

Out of high season, Cornwall comes into its own for those prepared to spend the time getting there: lots to do, a very relaxed pace of life, and attractive prices. Late May and early June is an ideal time for a short break here, with the scenery at its best, and relatively few other visitors. In spring and early summer, the tall roadside hedged banks which block the view from many byroads compensate by being virtual walls of wild flowers. September and October is seal pup time. From London, you should allow about five hours' driving out of season to get well into the county; it's about three hours from Bristol, across just a couple of counties. The A30 is now a good fast long-distance route (much better than the A390).

If you'd rather avoid the roads altogether, a Cornish Rail Rover ticket is good value for eight days' (which don't have to be consecutive) unlimited train journeys throughout the county for around £35; you can also get a ticket for three days.

The Isles of Scilly are ideal for a really quiet and relaxing holiday, with Penzance the quickest jumping-off point.

Where to stay

BODINNICK SX1352 **Old Ferry** *Bodinnick, Fowey PL23 1LX (01726) 870237* **£60;** 12 comfortable and spacious rms, most with own bthrm and river views. 400-year-old inn in lovely situation overlooking Fowey estuary, with back flagstoned bar partly cut into the rock, real ales, comfortable lounge with French windows opening onto a terrace, and decent food in bar and little evening restaurant; pool in games room; quiet out of season.

BOTALLACK SW3633 **Botallack Manor Farm** *Botallack, St Just in Penwith, Penzance TR19 7QG (01736) 788525* **£46;** 3 rms. Blissfully quiet and friendly 17th-c local granite farmhouse on working farm, with medley of furnishings in comfortable lounge, good breakfasts with home-baked bread, and safe walled garden; marvellous cliff walks, ruined mines and small coves; no pets.

BURYAS BRIDGE SW4429 **Rose Farm** *Chyanhal, Buryas Bridge, Penzance TR19 6AN (01736) 731808* **£38,** plus winter breaks; 3 delightfully furnished rms. Relaxed, informal, friendly farmhouse tucked away down remote country lane with excellent breakfasts around big table; can see animals (working farm), and children love it; cl Christmas for 3 days.

CALSTOCK SX4368 **Danescombe Valley** *Lower Kelly, Calstock PL18 9RY (01822) 832414* **£185w inc dinner** – they do B & B only during the week; 5 airy rms with river views. Lovely small Georgian house with first-floor verandah and fine views over a wooded bend on the River Tamar, warmly friendly owners, quiet relaxing atmosphere, open fires, flowers, books (no TV), and delicious food using fresh local produce (not during the week); Cotehele House (NT) is just 15 mins' walk; cl Nov–Mar; children over 12.

CARNE BEACH SW9038 **Nare** *Carne Beach, Veryan, Truro TR2 5PF (01872) 501279* **£202,** plus special breaks; 36 lovely rms to suit all tastes – some stylish ones look over the garden and out to sea. Attractively decorated and furnished hotel in magnificent clifftop position with secluded gardens, outdoor and indoor swimming pools, antiques, fresh flowers and log fires in the airy, spacious day rooms, very good food inc wonderful breakfasts, and run by staff who really care; very good for quiet family hols, with safe sandy beach below; cl 4 Jan–1 Feb; disabled access.

CONSTANTINE BAY SW8574 **Treglos** *Constantine Bay, Padstow PL28 8JH (01841) 520727* **£102,** plus special breaks; 44 light rms, some with balcony. Quiet and relaxed hotel close to good sandy beach, and in the same family for 30 years; comfortable traditional furnishings, log fires, good food, friendly helpful staff, sheltered garden, indoor swimming pool, pool and snooker, and children's playroom; lovely nearby walks; self-catering apartments; cl mid-Nov–mid-Mar; disabled access.

CRACKINGTON HAVEN SX1396 **Manor Farm** *Crackington Haven, Bude EX23 0JW (01840) 230304* ***£60;** 4 pretty rms. Lovely Domesday-listed no smoking manor surrounded by 25 acres of farmland and carefully landscaped gardens, with antiques in 4 lounges, a log fire, a house-party atmosphere, games room, big breakfasts, and a fine 4-course dinner at 7pm; cl 25 Dec; no children.

CRANTOCK SW7960 **Highfield Lodge** *Halwyn Rd, Crantock, Newquay TR8 5TR (01637) 830744* ***£42;** 11 rms, most with en suite shower. Close to a super beach, this neatly kept no smoking sea-view house offers a friendly welcome, a hearty breakfast, a licensed bar serving snacks, and plenty to do nearby; no pets.

EAST LOOE SX2553 **Woodlands** *St Martin's Rd, East Looe PL13 1LP (01503) 264405* **£40;** 4 rms. Attractive Victorian country house overlooking the river estuary by quiet woodland, with helpful owners, good breakfasts, and evening meals on request; ; cl Christmas; children over 7.

FALMOUTH SW8032 **Penmere Manor** *Mongleath Rd, Falmouth TR11 4PN (01326) 211411* ***£93,** plus special breaks; 37 spacious rms. Run by the same owners for 27 years, this quietly set Georgian manor has 5 acres of sub-tropical gardens and woodland, heated outdoor swimming pool, giant chess, croquet, and leisure centre with indoor swimming pool, mini-gym and sauna, and woodland fitness trail; particularly helpful friendly staff and enjoyable food (inc menu dedicated to lobster dishes) in restaurant and informal bar; cl 24–27 Dec.

FOWEY SX1252 **Carnethic House** *Lambs Barn, Fowey PL23 1HQ (01726) 833336* ***£64,** plus special breaks; 8 rms. Warmly friendly Regency house in lovely gardens with heated swimming pool, badminton and putting; a relaxed and informal atmosphere, very helpful owners, attractive lounge, and good home-made food (local fish is popular); cl Dec–Jan; limited disabled access.

FOWEY SX1252 **Marina** *The Esplanade, Fowey PL23 1HY (01726) 833315* **£76,** plus special breaks; 11 rms, several with lovely views (some with balcony). Homely, friendly hotel in fine position overlooking the River Fowey and the open sea (private access from secluded walled garden); comfortable lounge, dining room

overlooking the water, good food, and helpful service; cl Jan/Feb.
GERRANS BAY SW8937 **Pendower Beach House** *Gerrans Bay, Ruan High Lanes, Truro TR2 5LW (01872) 501241* **£108,** plus special breaks; 15 rms. Family-run hotel dating back to the 16th c in 8 acres by lovely sandy beach, with superb sea and coastal views, and plenty of seats on sunny terrace; a relaxed, friendly atmosphere in attractive and comfortable rooms, good food in cosy restaurant (super fresh local fish and shellfish), and tennis court; cl end Oct–Mar; disabled access.
GILLAN SW6527 **Tregildry** *Gillan, Helston TR12 6HG (01326) 231378* ***£60 inc dinner,** plus special breaks; 10 good rms with fine views over Falmouth Bay. Elegantly refurbished hotel in 4 acres with private access to the cove below; spacious comfortable lounges, fresh flowers and books, a restful atmosphere, very good food in attractive restaurant, and courteous helpful service; cl Nov–end Feb; children over 8.
GUNWALLOE SW6522 **Halzephron** *Gunwalloe, Helston TR12 7QB (01326) 240406* **£59;** 2 cosy rms. 500-year-old former smugglers' inn run by knowledgeable and friendly Cornish couple; good food in bar areas and bistro-style restaurant, open fire, and fine views of Mount's Bay; lots of walks, nearby beaches, golf, and boating; cl 24–25 Dec; no children.
LAMORNA COVE SW4524 **Lamorna Cove** *Lamorna Cove, Penzance TR19 6XH (01736) 731411* **£69;** 12 well furnished rms, most with cove views. Comfortable, beautifully placed hotel looking over gardens to the sea, with homely rooms, light airy restaurant using fresh local food (especially seafood), very good attentive service, and outdoor heated swimming pool; marvellous walks; cl end Oct–end Feb, but open 4 days at Christmas and 4 days at New Year.
LITTLE PETHERICK SW9172 **Old Mill Country House** *Little Petherick, Wadebridge, PL27 7QT (01841) 540388* **£61;** 7 rms. 16th-c corn mill in lovely riverside gardens with waterwheel and other original features; lounges, enjoyable breakfasts in beamed dining room and attentive service; plenty of places nearby for evening meals; cl Nov–Feb; no children.
LOOE SX2252 **Talland Bay** *Talland, Looe PL13 2JB (01503) 272667* **£108,** plus special breaks; 19 charming rms with sea or country views. Down a little lane between Looe and Polperro, this restful partly 16th-c country house has lovely subtropical gardens just above the sea; comfortable drawing room with log fire, smaller lounge with library, fresh flowers, courteous service, good food in pretty oak-panelled dining room, and pleasant afternoon teas; heated outdoor swimming pool, putting, croquet; cl Jan–Feb; children over 5 in evening restaurant (high tea for younger ones); dogs by prior arrangement.
MAWNAN SMITH SW7728 **Meudon** *Mawnan Smith, Falmouth TR11 5HT (01326) 250541* **£140,** plus special breaks; 29 well equipped comfortable rms in separate wing. Run by the same caring family for over 30 years, this is an old stone mansion with a newer wing set in beautiful subtropical gardens laid out by Capability Brown; fine views from the dining room, comfortable lounge with log fire and fresh flowers, good English cooking, and old-fashioned standards of service; cl Nov–Feb; dogs by arrangement (not in public rooms); limited disabled access.
MAWNAN SMITH SW7728 **Nansidwell Country House** *Mawnan Smith, Falmouth TR11 5HU (01326) 250340* ***£135,** plus special breaks; 12 individually decorated rms. Comfortable creeper-covered granite house in wonderful woodland garden with sea views and direct access to good beach; comfortably elegant rooms with log fires, fresh flowers, and books; fine food inc home-grown produce and home-made jams and breads in excellent restaurant, and hard-working, enthusiastic owners; cl Jan; children over 6 in evening restaurant (high tea available); disabled access.
MAXWORTHY SX2592 **Wheatley Farm** *Maxworthy, Launceston PL15 8LY (01566) 781232* **£44,** plus special breaks; 4 attractive rms with showers. In the same family for 5 generations, this working sheep and dairy farm has comfortable, pretty furnishings, log fires, good 4-course evening meals using local produce in spacious dining room, hearty breakfasts, games room with table tennis and toys,

animals to visit, pony rides, and safe play area for children; self-catering cottages too; cl Nov–Mar.

MITHIAN SW7450 **Rose-in-Vale Country House** *Mithian, St Agnes TR5 0QD (01872) 552202* **£80,** plus special breaks; 18 pretty rms. Secluded and quietly set Georgian house in 4 acres of neatly kept gardens, with comfortable spacious day rooms, a friendly atmosphere, helpful, long-standing local staff, and good food in enlarged dining room; ducks in ponds and trout steam, outdoor swimming pool, badminton and croquet; cl Jan–Feb; children over 7 in evening in public rooms and restaurant (high tea for smaller ones); well behaved dogs welcome; disabled access.

MULLION SW6719 **Polurrian** *Mullion, Helston TR12 7EN (01326) 240421* ***£168 inc dinner,** plus special breaks; 39 rms, some with memorable sea view. White clifftop hotel in lovely gardens with path down to sheltered private cove below; a restful atmosphere in the comfortable lounges and bright cocktail bar, fresh flowers, good food using fresh local ingredients (pianist and sea views in the dining room), enjoyable breakfasts, leisure club with heated swimming pool, and heated outdoor pool, badminton, tennis, mini-golf, squash and croquet; good with children (hotel nanny for babies and toddlers); cl Jan; disabled access.

NEWLYN SW4628 **Higher Faugan** *Newlyn, Penzance TR18 5NS (01736) 62076* ***£89,** plus special breaks; 12 attractive rms with garden and sea views. Country house in 10 quiet acres with outdoor swimming pool, tennis and putting green; pleasantly old-fashioned restful sitting rooms, helpful owners, and good home-made food using fresh local produce in the cosy dining room (incorporating original Edwardian conservatory); disabled access.

PADSTOW SW9175 **Treverbyn House** *Station Rd, Padstow PL28 8AD (01841) 532855* **£60;** 3 rms with lovely views over the Camel estuary. Carefully restored Edwardian house opposite the famous Seafood Restaurant, with friendly owners, open fires in comfortable public rooms, and good breakfasts; cl Christmas.

PELYNT SX2055 **Jubilee** *Pelynt, Looe PL13 2JZ (01503) 220312* ***£59,** plus special breaks; 9 rms. Neat 16th-c inn with Queen Victoria mementos, oak tables and a mix of comfortable seats under the beams in the relaxed lounge bar; log fire, gleaming brass and fresh flowers, and good waitress-served bar food; a well equipped play area.

PENDEEN SW3834 **Trewellard Manor Farm** *Pendeen, Penzance TR19 7SU (01736) 788526* ***£21;** 3 rms, 2 with own bthrm. Victorian house in lovely coastal spot, with log fire in guest lounge, outdoor summer swimming pool, and fine walks all round; self-catering also; cl Christmas.

PENZANCE SW4730 **Abbey Hotel** *Abbey St, Penzance TR18 4AR (01736) 66906* **£100,** plus winter breaks; 7 charming rms. Stylish little 17th-c house close to harbour, with marvellous views, relaxed atmosphere in comfortable drawing room full of flowers, fine paintings and antiques, a good set menu in small restaurant, and pretty garden; cl 2 wks Christmas; children over 5.

PILLATON SX3664 **Weary Friar** *Pillaton, Saltash PL12 6QS (01579) 350238* ***£50,** plus special breaks; 12 rms. Pretty 12th-c inn by church in pleasantly remote village with lots of character in its 4 knocked-together rooms (one no smoking); attractive furnishings, well kept real ales, and good food in both bar and restaurant.

POLPERRO SX2051 **Landaviddy Manor** *Landaviddy Lane, Polperro, Looe PL13 2RT (01503) 272210* ***£48,** plus special breaks; 7 pretty rms. Attractive and carefully furnished no smoking 18th-c manor house with fine views over 2 acres of peaceful gardens and the bay beyond; comfortably furnished lounges, open fire, a relaxed atmosphere and Aga-cooked breakfasts in beamed dining room; cl mid-Oct–mid-Mar; no children.

POLPERRO SX2051 **Old Mill House** *Mill Hill, Polperro, Looe PL13 2RP (01503) 272362* **£45,** plus special breaks; 8 attractive rooms. Pretty white cottagey pub with a civilised feel, solid stripped pine furniture on polished boards, log fire in big fireplace, fishing boat pictures, well kept real ales, good enjoyable food inc fresh fish (no food winter lunchtimes) in cosy little bistro, and friendly service; fishing trips/boating outings arranged.

PORT ISAAC SX0080 **Port Gaverne** *Port Isacc PL29 3SQ (01208) 8802441* ***£106,** plus special breaks; 17 comfortable rms. Lovely place to stay and an excellent base for the area (dramatic coves, good clifftop walks, and lots of birds); big log fires in well kept bars, relaxed lounges, decent bar food, good restaurant food, and fine wines; also restored 18th-c self-catering cottages; cl early Jan–mid-Feb; children over 7 in restaurant; dogs allowed.

QUINTRELL DOWNS SW8560 **Manuels Farm** *Quintrell Downs, Newquay TR8 4NY (01637) 873577* ***£40;** 4 rms, 2 with own bthrm. Comfortable and relaxed 17th-c farmhouse with log fires, candlelit dinners, and pretty garden; good for children – they can bottle-feed calves, collect eggs and so forth (free babysitting); cl Christmas/New Year.

RUAN HIGH LANES SW9039 **Crugsillick Manor** *Ruan High Lanes, Truro TR2 5LJ (01872) 501214* **£80,** plus special breaks; 3 rms. One of the loveliest houses in Cornwall, this Queen Anne manor is extended from a pre-Elizabethan farmhouse and surrounded by a big quiet garden with wooded valley views; log fire in drawing room with Napoleonic ceiling, candlelit dinners in 17th-c dining room using home-grown produce where possible, fine breakfasts, and charming owners; self-catering cottages in grounds with excellent disabled access, where children welcome; cl Christmas/New Year; children over 12 in main house.

ST AUSTELL SX0553 **Boscundle Manor** *Tregrehan, St Austell PL25 3RL (01726) 813557* ***£130,** plus special breaks; 12 rms. Mainly 18th-c rambling manor with country house atmosphere in its low-beamed and carefully furnished rooms, enjoyable food, a good wine list, and breakfasts in pretty conservatory; 14 acres of grounds inc 2 acres of terraced gardens, croquet, outdoor heated swimming pool, indoor swimming pool, golf practice area with 2 greens and 2 all-weather teeing positions, barn with gym, snooker, table tennis and darts, and outside badminton; woodland walks, too; self-catering cottage; cl Nov–late Mar.

ST BLAZEY SX0654 **Nanscawen House** *Prideaux, St Blazey, Par PL24 2SR (01726) 814488* ***£74;** 3 spacious, pretty rms overlooking the garden. Attractive creeper-covered no smoking Georgian house in 5 acres of quiet grounds, with helpful owners, big drawing room with small bar, and plenty of places to eat nearby in the evening; heated outdoor swimming pool and outdoor whirlpool bath; cl 25–26 Dec; children over 12.

ST IVES SW5140 **Blue Hayes** *Trelyon Ave, St Ives TR26 2AD (01736) 797129* **£74,** plus special breaks; 9 rms, most with own bthrm. Long-standing and friendly guest house in wonderful clifftop position overlooking the sea; quiet flower-filled garden leading to beach; comfortable rooms, and enjoyable food; cl end Oct–Mid-Mar; children over 5.

ST IVES SW5140 **Countryman** *Old Coach Rd, St Ives TR26 3JQ (01736) 797571* ***£55,** plus special winter breaks; 6 rms. Small friendly no smoking hotel in 2 acres of gardens, with log fire in comfortable lounge, bright flower-filled breakfast room, and cosy little restaurant; walks, golf and Tate Gallery nearby; children over 7.

ST IVES SW5140 **Garrack** *Burthallan Lane, St Ives TR26 3AA (01736) 796199* **£94,** plus wknd breaks; 18 rms, some in more modern wing. Friendly no smoking hotel in 2 acres of gardens with wonderful sea views; cosy lounges with antiques, books and open fires, a fine collection of paintings by Newlyn artists, family room, restaurant with good food inc fresh shellfish, helpful staff, and indoor leisure centre (heated outdoor swimming pool, too); disabled access.

ST IVES SW5140 **Kandahar** *11 The Warren, St Ives TR26 2EA (01736) 796183* **£48;** 5 rms with sea views, some with shared bthrm. No smoking B & B in splendid water's-edge position looking over the harbour and up the coast to Newquay, with comfortable old-fashioned lounge and good breakfasts in small dining room overlooking the sea; cl mid-Nov–mid-Mar; children over 6; no pets.

ST IVES SW5140 **Skidden House** *Skidden Hill, St Ives TR26 2DU (01736) 796899* **£78;** 8 rms. Small warmly welcoming 16th-c hotel nr beach, with carefully cooked food in cosy dining room, quiet no smoking lounge with small library, and comfortable bar; you may be asked for a large deposit; cl Dec; dogs welcome by prior arrangement; disabled access.

ST KEYNE SX2564 **Old Rectory** *St Keyne, Liskeard PL14 4RL (01579) 342617* ***£58,** plus special breaks; 9 comfortable rms. Friendly family-run hotel in 3 acres, with open fire in comfortably furnished lounge, cosy bar, good homely atmosphere, and enjoyable food; cl Christmas/New Year; children over 12; pets by prior arrangement; disabled access.

ST KEYNE SX2460 **Well House** *St Keyne, Liskeard PL14 4RN (01579) 342001* **£130,** plus special breaks; 9 good rms with fine views. Light and airy Victorian country house with warmly friendly owner, courteous staff, comfortable drawing room, cosy little bar, and particularly good food and fine wines in dining room overlooking terrace and lawns; 3 acres of gardens with hard tennis court, swimming pool and croquet lawn; children over 8 in evening restaurant.

ST MARTIN SX2655 **Bucklawren Farm** *St Martin, Looe PL13 1NZ (01503) 240738;* ***£44,** plus special breaks; 6 rms. Spacious farmhouse on 500-acre dairy and arable working farm with coastal and sea views, croquet and putting in the big garden, large homely lounge, south-facing sun lounge, and farmhouse cooking using home-grown and local produce; cl Nov–Mar; children over 5.

ST MAWES SW8433 **Rising Sun** *St Mawes, Truro TR2 5DJ (01326) 270233* **£59,** plus special breaks; 8 rms. Small attractive hotel in popular picturesque waterside village, with harbour views, large comfortable newly refurbished lounge bar area, airy conservatory, charming terrace.

ST WENN SW9665 **Wenn Manor** *St Wenn, Bodmin PL30 5PS (01726) 890240* ***£80;** 4 rms. Carefully restored and friendly restaurant with rooms, tucked away among rolling hills in 4 acres of wooded grounds; panelled bar with inglenook fireplace and deep well, candlelit dining room with 2 open log fires, a Garden Room for light lunches, and good, fresh food; croquet; cl Christmas; children over 12.

SALTASH SX4258 **Erth Barton** *Saltash PL12 4QY (01752) 842127* **£68;** 3 rms. Lovely old manor house with its own chapel, peaceful rooms with lots of books, pictures and big fireplaces, good enjoyable food, birdwatching in the surrounding estuaries, and riding (you can bring your own horse); children over 12.

SENNEN SW3425 **Land's End Hotel** *Sennen, Land's End, Penzance TR19 7AA (01736) 871844* **£99,** plus special breaks; 33 elegant airy rms, many with splendid sea views. Comfortable hotel right on the clifftop with fine sea views, good food in attractive conservatory-style restaurant, elegant seating areas, informal bar with lots of malt whiskies, and helpful staff.

TREGADILLETT SX2983 **Eliot Arms** *Tregadillett, Launceston TL15 7EU (01566) 772051* ***£50,** plus special breaks; 3 rms, 2 with own bthrm. Friendly creeper-covered old house with fascinating collections (72 antique clocks inc 7 grandfathers, 400 snuffs, hundreds of horse brasses and so forth), and very good food with plenty of fish and interesting daily specials; cl 25 Dec; dogs by arrangement.

TREGASWITH SW8963 **Tregaswith Farmhouse** *Tregaswith, Newquay TR8 4HY (01637) 881181* **£44,** plus special breaks; 3 pretty, homely rms. 18th-c house with beams and antiques on smallholding breeding horses (pony rides) and rare poultry; good breakfasts and proper country cooking; dogs welcome by arrangement.

TREGONY SW9245 **Tregony House** *Tregony, Truro TR2 5RN (01872) 530671* ***£44,** plus winter breaks; 5 individually furnished rms, some with own bthrm. Partly 17th-c no smoking house with very friendly and helpful owners, big breakfasts and good evening meals in low-beamed dining room, cosy sitting room with open fire, and pretty cottagey garden; cl Dec/Jan; children over 7.

TRELIGHTS SW9979 **Long Cross** *Trelights, Port Isaac PL29 3TF (01208) 880243* ***£46,** plus special breaks; 12 rms, some with sea view. Well modernised, family-run Victorian house with lively bar (real ales, folk evenings, darts and pool), home-made food inc Indian dishes and seafood kebabs, cream teas, and interesting period 'garden of secrets' – attractive plants in carefully restored interlocking hedged enclosures snugged down against the winds (*see Port Isaac entry in* **To see and do** *section, below*); disabled access.

TRENALE SX0688 **Trebrea Lodge** *Trenale, Tintagel PL34 0HR (01840) 770410*

***£80,** plus special breaks; 7 pretty rms with views across fields to the sea. Handsome manor house with log fire and honesty bar in comfortable smoking room, elegant first-floor drawing room, and good set dinner in oak-panelled dining room; lots of walks; cl Jan–mid-Feb; children over 12; dogs welcome by prior arrangement.

WATERGATE SX2354 **Harescombe Lodge** *Watergate, Looe PL13 2NE (01503) 263158* ***£44,** plus special breaks; 3 cosy rms. Friendly and carefully modernised 18th-c house with waterfalls and old stone bridges in quiet garden, and good breakfasts; half an hour's walk along river path into Looe; no children.

WIDEGATES SX2858 **Coombe Farm** *Widegates, Looe PL13 1QN (01503) 240223* ***£56,** plus special breaks; 10 comfortable rms. Warmly welcoming and relaxed no smoking country house in 10 acres of garden, meadows, woods and streams with distant sea views, outdoor swimming pool, and a stone barn with table tennis and snooker; plants, log fires and antiques in sitting room, hearty English breakfasts, enjoyable set evening meals, and honesty drinks tray; cl Nov–end Feb; children over 12; disabled access.

To see and do

CORNWALL Family Attraction of the Year

☺ ✝ **HELSTON** SW6626 **Flambards** (off the A394 at the S edge of town) A clear cut above the average theme park, this beautifully kept leisure park usually delights adults at least as much as children. Fairground rides and play areas gel rather well with nostalgic displays and interesting exhibitions, and there's easily enough to keep everyone happy for most of the day. Prices are good value, and they've added quite a few new attractions in recent years, including a weather station with live satellite pictures from space. For older visitors the best bit is probably the very good reconstructed Victorian village; once just 3 rooms, it now has over 50 authentically furnished and stocked houses, shops and settings, complete with cobbled streets, carriages and other period pieces. Also a state-of-the-art time travel exhibition from the Big Bang to the present day, a life-size 'Britain in the Blitz' street, a collection of aircraft, and displays on topics as varied as wedding fashions 1820–1970 and this year's solar eclipse. Younger children are especially well catered for, with good play areas to suit various ages (inc toddlers), a petting zoo, and a lively parrot show. Older children should enjoy the adventure playground and interactive science centre, and especially the rides, which range from a hornet-styled roller-coaster to a log flume and hairy Demon Drop Slide. The award-winning gardens have experts on hand in the garden centre most afternoons, and in summer they have occasional evening firework displays. Well organised facilities for baby changing and so on. Meals, snacks, shop, disabled access; cl Nov–Easter, and Mon and Fri at the start and end of the season; (01326) 564093; £6.99, £4.50 children 3–6, £5.99 children 7–11 – all prices lower off-season or from mid-afternoon. A very good-value family ticket is £20 for 4 people of any age, and they have excellent deals on return visits.

✝ **ALTARNUN** SX2281 The **church** has an enchanting set of 16th-c carved bench ends, much humanity and humour. The unpretentious Rising Sun just N does decent simple food. Nearby **Wesley's Cottage** just off the A30 at Trewint, the world's smallest Methodist place of worship, has a primitive time-warp room used by Wesley in 1744.

BEDRUTHAN STEPS SW8469 (off the B3276 from Newquay to Padstow) Really special, with their dramatic rock pinnacles, cliffs and lovely sandy coves. A splendid place for walks.

BODMIN SX0667 **Bodmin & Wenford Railway**

(Bodmin General Station, St Nicholas St) Restored steam locomotives take you back to the glory days of the Great Western Railway when hordes of holiday-makers travelled this route to the sun. As well as enjoying the view, you can stop off for pleasant woodland walks. Regular trains connect with Bodmin Parkway station. Snacks, shop, disabled access; cl Jan–late Mar, and Nov, with a limited service in Oct and Dec best to phone for train times; (01208) 73666; £5. **Bodmin Gaol** (Berrycombe Rd) The former county prison, built in 1778, with spooky underground dungeons; the Crown Jewels were stored here in the First World War. Meals and snacks (pub on site), shop; (01208) 76292; £3. There's a sacred well in the churchyard of St Petroc's church. **Pencarrow** (Washaway, off the A389 3m NW) Notable 18th-c house with fine paintings and furniture, rococo ceiling in the music room, and, perhaps the highlight, 50 acres of lovely formal and woodland gardens with over 600 different rhododendrons and an acclaimed conifer collection. Also marked trails, children's play area, peacocks, chickens and other birds, craft centre and ancient British encampment. Snacks, shop, disabled access; open all day Jun–mid-Sept pm Easter–May and mid-Sept–mid-Oct; (01208) 841369; £4. The Borough Arms (on the A389) is good value for lunch.

BODMIN MOOR SX1875 This windswept expanse is not as richly endowed as Dartmoor for walking, and much is boggy and rough. It does have its own bleak character, with strange tors, prehistoric traces, wind-bent trees, granite walls, lonely lakes, and, despite official denials, continuing tales of black panthers. The main A30 actually gives more striking views of the moor than the small side roads, which tend to burrow along wooded coombs or between rather high dykes or walls. Riding is popular on the moor, and quite a few stables on or around it cater for all levels of ability.

! BOLVENTOR SX1876 **Potter's Museum of Curiosity** Set in the little complex that's sprung up around Jamaica Inn, the pub immortalised by Daphne du Maurier, this is a bizarre Victorian collection of stuffed animals and other assorted oddities. Rather than simply displaying them in cases, Mr Potter constructed elaborate tableaux around the bodies brought to him by local farmers, with the animals positioned as if they were tiny humans. Guinea pigs play cricket, rabbits sit in a classroom, and squirrels carouse in a pub in this weird little world while the Kittens' Wedding has to be seen to be believed. Meals, snacks, shop, disabled access; cl Jan; (01566) 86838; £2.50. The pub itself is still atmospheric despite the developments. Just S on the A30, **Colliford Lake Park** has plenty going on for families – rare breeds of birds, cattle, poultry, and sheep, indoor and outdoor pets, adventure play areas, undercover assault course, museum, and lakeside walks. Meals, snacks, shop, some disabled access; cl Oct–Easter; (01208) 821469; £3.50. About a mile away, Dozmary Pool is one of two Cornish lakes that claim to be where a legendary arm rose from the depths and reclaimed Excalibur (the other is

Days Out

Island escapade: St Michael's Mount; Penzance – lunch at the Turk's Head; Flambards, nr Helston.

Lost gardens and a remote coast: Mevagissey; Charlestown; lunch at the Crown, St Ewe; the Lost Gardens of Heligan; Portloe and Veryan villages.

Animal magic and a look at the past: Looe; Monkey Sanctuary; Polperro (walk in from Talland Bay), lunch at the Old Mill House or Crumplehorn Mill; Lanreath folk museum and church.

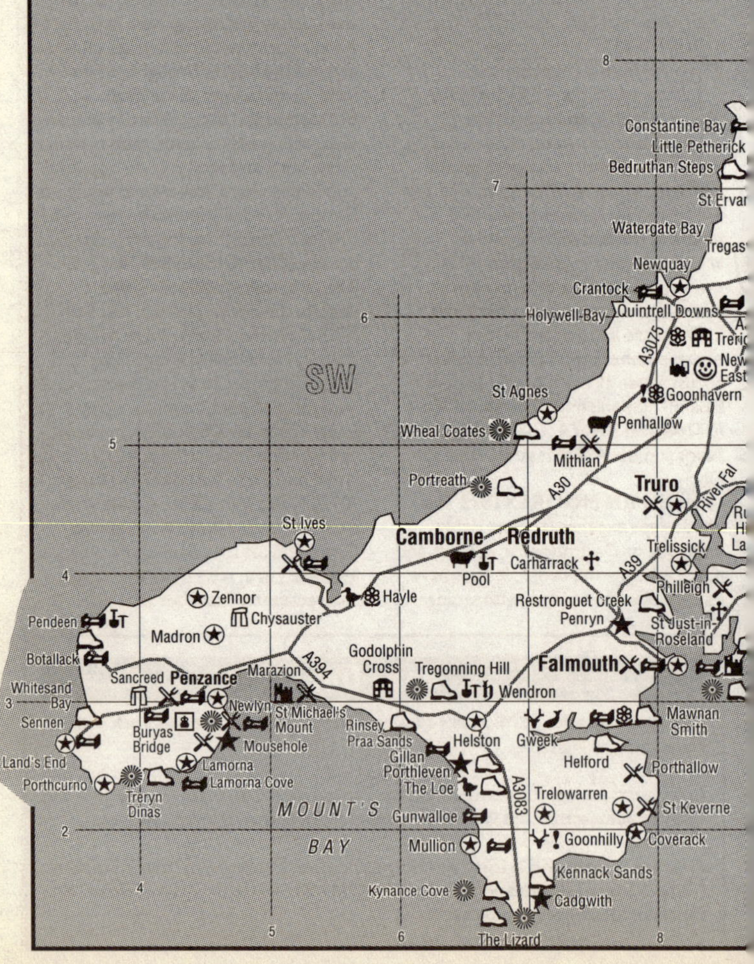
Cornwall
ATLANTIC OCEAN
SW
Constantine Bay
Little Petherick
Bedruthan Steps
St Ervan
Watergate Bay
Newquay
Crantock
Holywell Bay
Quintrell Downs
A3075
Goonhavern
St Agnes
Wheal Coates
Penhallow
Mithian
Portreath
A30
Truro
River Fal
St Ives
Camborne
Redruth
Trelissick
Pool
Carharrack
A39
Zennor
Hayle
Philleigh
Pendeen
Chysauster
Restronguet Creek
Penryn
St Just-in-Roseland
Madron
Botallack
Godolphin Cross
A394
Marazion
Sancreed
Penzance
Tregonning Hill
Falmouth
Whitesand Bay
Wendron
Newlyn
St Michael's Mount
Sennen
Buryas Bridge
Rinsey
Praa Sands
Helston
Gweek
Mawnan Smith
Mousehole
Gillan
Land's End
Lamorna
Porthleven
Helford
Porthallow
Porthcurno
Lamorna Cove
The Loe
A3083
Treryn Dinas
Trelowarren
MOUNT'S BAY
Gunwalloe
St Keverne
Mullion
Goonhilly
Coverack
Kennack Sands
Kynance Cove
Cadgwith
The Lizard

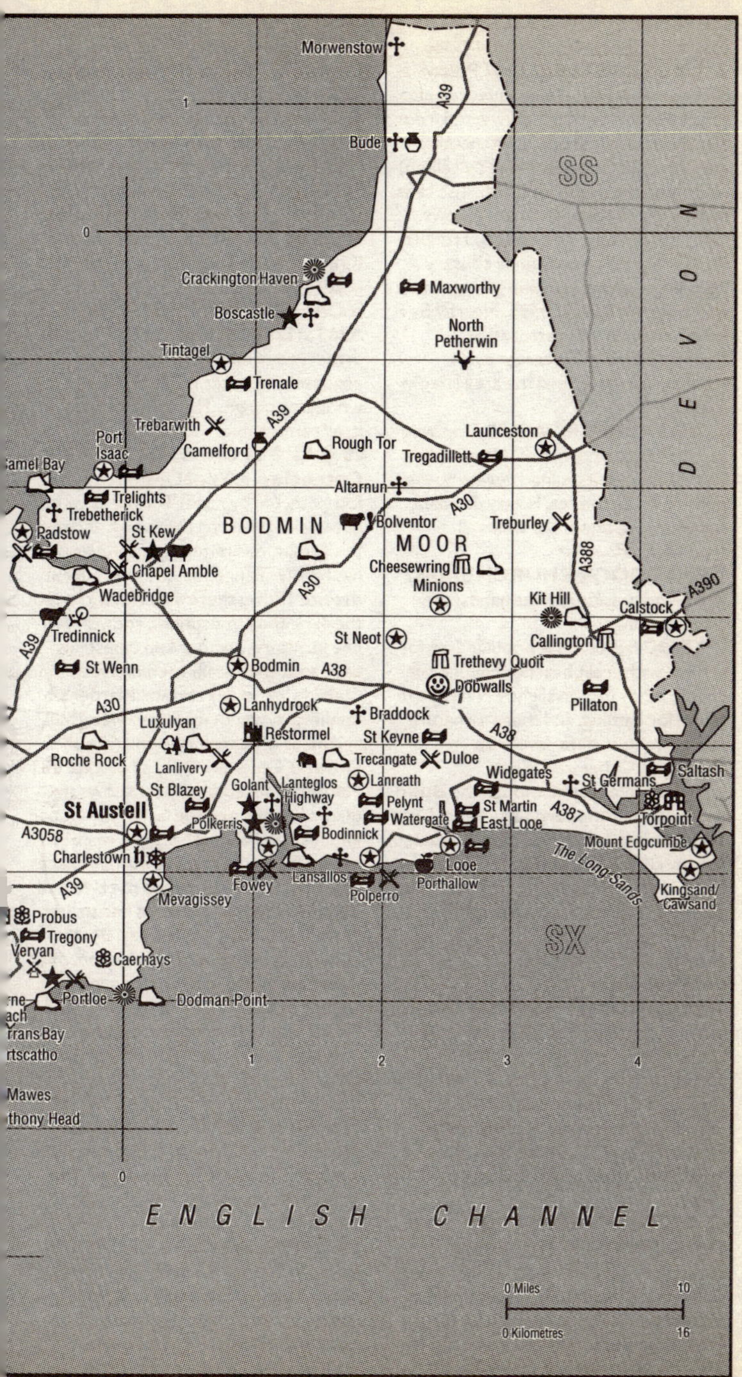
Morwenstow
Bude
SS
Crackington Haven
Maxworthy
Boscastle
North Petherwin
Tintagel
Trenale
Trebarwith
Port Isaac
Camelford
Rough Tor
Launceston
Tregadillett
Altarnun
Trelights
Trebetherick
Padstow
St Kew
BODMIN
Bolventor
MOOR
Treburley
Chapel Amble
Cheesewring
Minions
Wadebridge
Kit Hill
Calstock
Tredinnick
St Neot
Callington
St Wenn
Bodmin
Trethevy Quoit
Dobwalls
Lanhydrock
Pillaton
Braddock
Luxulyan
Restormel
St Keyne
Roche Rock
Trecangate
Duloe
Lanlivery
Widegates
St Germans
Saltash
St Blazey
Golant
Lanteglos Highway
Lanreath
Pelynt
St Martin
Torpoint
St Austell
Polkerris
Watergate
East Looe
Bodinnick
Mount Edgcumbe
Charlestown
Fowey
Lansallos
Looe
Polperro
Porthallow
The Long Sands
Kingsand/ Cawsand
Mevagissey
Probus
Tregony
Veryan
SX
Caerhays
Portloe
Dodman Point
DEVON
A39
A30
A38
A388
A390
A387
A3058
ENGLISH CHANNEL
0 Miles 10
0 Kilometres 16

Loe Pool near Porthleven), and it's an easy starting point for Bodmin Moor.

★ ✝ **BOSCASTLE** SX0991 Pretty harbour with 16th-c pier squeezed into a rocky creek, cottages converted from warehouses, gift shops, a witchcraft museum; the Cobweb and (a stiff climb) Napoleon are useful for lunch. The cliffs nearby afford some fascinating views. Not far from here at Trevalga, Tredole Farm will arrange coastal or country **horse and pony trekking**; non-riders welcome; (01840) 250495. Nearby **St Juliot church** was restored by Thomas Hardy in his career as an architect; he described the area later in *A Pair of Blue Eyes*.

BOTALLACK SW3632 On a wild day this rugged corner of West Cornwall, with its ruined engine house right down by the sea, is very dramatic, and there are fine steep walks all around.

✝ **BRADDOCK CHURCH** SX1662 Well worth visiting for its handsome wood carvings.

✝ **BUDE** SX2106 A popular area for surfing, with great beaches beyond the dunes; Sandy Mouth slightly N has clean water for bathing, and there's a nature trail close to surfers' favourite Duckpool. Otherwise it's an unremarkable resort, though the **Bude & Stratton Museum** (The Wharf) is a decent rainy-day retreat (shop, disabled access; cl Oct–Easter; 50p). The Falcon Hotel does good-value quick food. The carved bench ends up at **Poughill church** (pronounced Poffle) are entertaining; the Preston Gate is a decent pub here.

★ **CADGWITH** SW7214 This picturesque village on its pretty cove has photogenic fish stores, thatched cottages, and a decent pub. A rewarding short stroll on the coast path leads S to Chynhalls Point past the aptly named Devil's Frying Pan, where the waves foam into a spectacular collapsed cavern.

CAERHAYS CASTLE GARDENS SW9741 Relatively undiscovered, these magnificent spring gardens are beautifully set around the back of a striking castle, with lovely coastal views. Renowned especially for their rhododendrons, magnolias and camellias, they're easily combined with a visit to the now better-known Lost Gardens of Heligan (they do a map showing how to get between the two). Good afternoon teas, shop, some disabled access; open wkdys from mid-Mar to around the end of May; (01872) 501144; £3.50. The Crown over at St Ewe does good lunches, but depending on where you're coming from the King's Arms at Tregony up on the main road might be handier.

CALLINGTON SX3769 (off the A388 S) **Dupath Holy Well** The best-preserved of many in Cornwall, its unappetising water is said to cure whooping cough. The town is not in itself remarkable.

CALSTOCK SX4268 **Cotehele** (1m W of Calstock by footpath, 6m by road) Tucked away in a network of twisting roads high above the Tamar, this rambling granite house has hardly changed since it was built in the late 15th c; there's no electricity, so the dark and atmospheric rooms with fine furniture, armour and tapestries have an authentically medieval feel. Outside are lovely terraced gardens, a medieval dovecot, restored watermill, and miles of peaceful woodland walks. Down at Cotehele Quay a National Maritime Museum outpost shows the quay's history, and the last of the Tamar ketch-rigged barges has been restored here. One of the most rewarding places to visit in Cornwall, but so over-visited that the National Trust has had to limit entrance to 600 people a day. Best to come midweek out of high season, or at least early in the morning, to avoid a wait or even outright disappointment. Meals, snacks (tearoom in pleasant riverside setting with good cream teas), shop; house cl Fri and Nov–Mar, mill as house but cl am, garden open daily all year; (01579) 351346; £5.60, £2.80 garden and mill only; NT. Pleasant walks along the Tamar from the village. The unusual Who'd Have Thought It at St Dominick is good for lunch.

CAMEL BAY SW9280 On the E side, sand dunes suddenly give way to a rocky headland, Rumps Point, which can be walked round in an hour or so; or at low tide there's a pleasant sandy walk between Rock and Polzeath (which has one of Cornwall's best beaches, popular with surfers).

♁ **CAMELFORD** SX1083 Locals will tell you this is the site of Camelot, and send you a mile N to the otherwise unremarkable Slaughter Bridge, where Arthur supposedly fell at his last battle. Far more interesting is the **British Cycling Museum** (Camelford Old Station on the B3266 N) Comprehensive (and still growing) collection of over 400 bicycles, tricycles and even a 5-wheeled Hen & Chickens bike, ranging from an original 1819 hobby-horse through boneshakers and penny-farthings to the hi-tech bikes of today. The couple who run it met through cycling, and really know their stuff. Outside they even have a sculpture made from old bicycles. Shop, disabled access; usually cl Fri and Sat; (01840) 212811;*£2. **North Cornwall Museum & Gallery** (The Clease) Good exploration of regional life over the past century, with displays of cider-making and farming, and collections of pottery and even early vacuum cleaners. Shop; cl Sun and Oct–Mar; (01840) 212954; £1.50. The Masons Arms has good-value food.

† **CARHARRACK** SW7341 The **church** has an exhibition on Cornish Methodism and John Wesley, who preached at the chapel that used to stand here. Disabled access; open am Mon–Thurs, or by appointment; (01209) 820381; free. Wesley preached more regularly at nearby **Gwennap Pit**, which still has services (2.30pm Suns in July and Aug), and a visitor centre. Centre cl Oct–May, am Sat and all day Sun, the peaceful grass amphitheatre itself is open all the time; free. The Fox & Hounds at Lanner is useful for lunch.

❄ ⚓ **CHARLESTOWN** SX0351 A picturesque working china clay port, with sailing ships as well as modern cargo boats; it's much used as a film/TV setting, featuring in *Poldark* and ITV's *Moll Flanders* and there are plans to leave sets intact for summer visitors. Two square-rigged sailing ships, stars of many films inc *1492: Conquest of Paradise* may be in the harbour. The **Shipwreck & Heritage Centre** is good for local history (cl Nov–Feb; £3.95). The Harbour Inn is useful for lunch.

🏛 ⛰ **CHEESEWRING** SX2775 (Bodmin Moor) A striking megalithic tomb, the massive stones now left high and dry by a fall in the soil level over thousands of years, its several improbably overhanging granite slabs making an appealing camera subject with Bodmin Moor stretching into the distance. There is a clear track to the nearby Hurlers stone circles.

🏛 **CHYSAUSTER ANCIENT VILLAGE** SW4735 (off the B3311 N of Gulval) On a windy hillside overlooking the coast, these stunted remains of 8 courtyard houses give some impression of village life 2,000 years ago. The site is also notable for its large untreated meadow, popular with wild birds, and, depending on the season, bright with bluebells, heather or unusual orchids. Snacks, shop; cl Nov–Mar; (0831) 757934; £1.60.

★⛰ ❋ **COVERACK** SW7818 An attractive coastal village, with a decent pub. A rewarding walk takes you down to Black Head and maybe beyond, or to Lowland Point, for dramatic views of the Manacles – striking offshore rocks.

⛰ ❋ **CRACKINGTON HAVEN** SX1496 With a superbly sited dining pub, the Coombe Barton, to set you up (or reward you afterwards), this has a good walk to **High Cliff**, Cornwall's highest.

☺ **DOBWALLS ADVENTURE PARK** SX2165 (off the A38) Good theme park with lively attractions inc steam and diesel train rides along a 2-mile stretch of miniature American-style railroads, aerial cableways, and lots of excellent play areas (outdoors and under cover), with their Skydome a complex climbing frame of latticed ropework – particularly unusual. Also weekly sheepdog trials in the summer hols, and an interesting wildlife gallery. Meals, snacks, shop, disabled access; cl Oct–Easter and maybe Fri; (0800) 521812; £5.25. The Highway is useful for lunch.

❋ ⛰ **DODMAN POINT** SX0039 Reached from Gorran Haven, or one of the closer car parks (for instance, at Hemmick Beach), this allows a round walk mainly along clifftops.

★ ⛴ ❄ ♜ ✽ **FALMOUTH** SW8132
The county's biggest town has a huge natural harbour full of sailing boats of every description, big sea-going ships, little passenger ferries (to St Mawes and Truro – great fun) and boat trips; it's also a busy but pleasant shopping centre with some nice old-fashioned streets, ships' chandlers and a good bustling atmosphere, though surprisingly few sea views. Broad avenues of spiky-leaved dracaena trees away from the centre give it a quite foreign feel. A **maritime museum** opposite Marks & Spencer on Market St has lots of seafaring history; cl Sun; £1.50. The Quayside and Chain Locker by the inner harbour do useful food, and the Warehouse is an enjoyable waterside restaurant. The A39 here from Truro can be tiresomely slow. **Pendennis Castle** (1m SE) Superb views from this well preserved fort, one of Henry VIII's chain of coastal defences. Snacks, shop, some disabled access; cl 24–26 Dec, 1 Jan; *£3.

★ ♜ ⌂ **FOWEY** SX1251
(pronounced Foy) Steep, lively and bustling, in an exceptional riverside position, with pretty views from up the hill on either side, some interesting shops in its maze of quaint alleys and tiny lanes, and a choice of good-value food pubs – the King of Prussia, Ship and Galleon. The harbour has yachts to ocean-going ships, also a car ferry to Bodinnick, and a foot ferry to Polruan, the similarly steep little harbourside hamlet opposite with lovely views of Fowey (both have decent pubs). **St Catherine's Castle** is a ruined stronghold built by Henry VIII, restored in the mid-19th c; free. The NT owns most of the coastline in these parts, so count on clean beaches; just around from the harbour, the secluded cove at Lantic Bay (reached by a steep coastal path) is particularly attractive. A popular circular route takes walkers across on the Bodinnick car ferry, then follows the path through the steep creekside woods round to Polruan, and comes back on the foot ferry.

⌂ **GODOLPHIN CROSS** SW6031
Godolphin House 15th-c house of the Earls of Godolphin, well known for its colonnaded front, and gardens dating back to Tudor times. Teas, shop (plants and herbs for sale), some disabled access; open pm Thurs and bank hols May–Sept (all day Thurs in Aug, with a break for lunch) as well as pm Tues July–Sept; (01736) 762409; *£3. The Queen's Arms down at Breage (where the church has medieval paintings) does decent food.

★ ✝ **GOLANT** SX1254 This waterside village has its attractions – particularly the **church**, unusual for its complete 15th-c fittings.

! ❀ **GOONHAVERN** SW7853
World in Miniature The world's landmarks at a fraction of the normal cost and size and some much larger dinosaurs. Beautiful gardens with thousands of plants, and children's fairground rides. Meals, snacks, shop, disabled access; cl Nov–Mar; (01872) 572828; £4.75.

! ♈ **GOONHILLY SATELLITE EARTH STATION** SW7221 Very un-Cornish, this space-age complex is one of the planet's foremost telecom centres, and the vast dishes rising out of the heath are an awesome sight. In the control room you can see information and images sent out and received from all over the world, while the visitor centre lets you operate one of the tracking dishes yourself. Also bus tour round the site (which is a nature reserve), audio-visual show, and free internet surfing. Well presented, earnest and interesting, though not ideal for younger children. Meals, snacks, shop, disabled access; cl Nov–Easter; (0800) 679593; £3.99. The B3293 past here and the byroad to Kuggar are unusual for Cornish roads, in giving some quite distant views. The White Hart at St Keverne is the best place around for lunch.

♈ ♪ **GWEEK** SW7027 **National Seal Sanctuary** Biggest seal sanctury in Europe with dozens of injured or orphaned seals that they hope to be able to release back into the wild, all with their own names and character traits. Underwater observatories, feeding time fun, guided woodland walks, play area, as well as donkeys, ponies and goats, a new audio visual display and a nature trail. Snacks, shop, disabled access; cl 25 Dec; (01326) 221361; £5.50. The Gweek Inn, with home-made food, is handy, and the Trengilly Wartha at Nancenoy is excellent for lunch, with a pleasant walk down to Scotts Quay on the creek.

HAYLE SW5536 **Paradise Park** Headquarters of the World Parrot Trust, with the colourful birds showcased to spectacular effect in the huge Parrot Jungle, a splendid mix of waterfalls, swamps and streams. Plenty of other exotic and rare birds, and lots of animals too, some of which you can feed at the Fun Farm. Entertaining penguin and otter feeding displays, children's quiz trails, and a big play area, with bird of prey displays in summer (not Sat), and a narrow-gauge railway gently rattling through the park. Adults may prefer the Victorian walled garden (lovely clematis arches in May), or the pub that brews its own real ale. Snacks, shop (with plant sales), disabled access; (01736) 753365; £5.50, with return tickets just £1. The Towans, just N in St Ives Bay, is a good clean beach.

HELFORD SW7526 There's an undemanding coast path E to **Dennis Head** and beyond. This NE part of the Lizard is appreciably leafier than the rest of the peninsula, with some intricate coves.

! **HELSTON** SW6527 World-famous for its annual Furry Dance, it has a popular Sat market and a little **Folk Museum** in the Old Butter Market (cl Sun, pm Weds, Christmas week; free). *See separate Family Panel on p.84* for **Flambards**. The simple Blue Anchor pub has a 15th-c working brewhouse which you can usually look round at lunchtime; the best food nearby is at the Halzephron at Gunwalloe, off the A3083 S – a good road with views, and usually signs of action from the Culdrose helicopter base.

KENNACK SANDS SW7316 (just E of Kuggar) One of the cleanest beaches in Britain, with beautifully clear water; it can get crowded.

★ ✝ **KINGSAND/CAWSAND** SX4350 Appealing seaside village with higgledy-piggledy charm; the Halfway House and Rising Sun both have good local fish. There are great cliff walks, especially to **Rame Head**, jutting far out at the E end of Whitsand Bay and capped by a primitive **hermitage chapel**.

KIT HILL SX3771 (off the A390 N of Callington) With a huge chimney stack and mine shafts, this gives breezy walks, and impressive views across to Dartmoor.

KYNANCE COVE SW6813 A particularly fine beach below the spectacular cliffs a long walk down from the car park, but well worth it for the strange rock formations, caves and sandy coves. There are lovely views from the cliff walk S.

LAMORNA SW4424 The cove is pretty, with good walks along the coast path. There's a good view of the **Merry Maidens** stone circle from the B3315. The Lamorna Wink is useful for lunch, and **Lamorna Pottery** has a garden with acclaimed cream teas. Meals, snacks, shop, disabled access; cl mid-Jan; (01736) 810330; free.

LAND'S END SW3425 The most westerly point of England, with wild and blustery walks along dramatic clifftops, and on a clear day views out as far even as the Isles of Scilly. You may not be able to stand and contemplate it on your own – the 200-acre site has been extensively developed for families in the last few years, and it's become almost like a theme park, with 'multi-sensory experiences', gift shops, craft centres, farm animals and burger bars. It's not as bad as it sounds – the exhibitions and hi-tech displays are a useful enough introduction to the folklore of the area, and there's plenty to amuse children. An RSPB observation hide has information on the coastline's wildlife. Meals, snacks, neat shopping arcade, good disabled access; cl 25 Dec; (01736) 871501; £7.95 for all attractions, less off-season. A public right of way goes through here to Land's End itself, so you're not obliged to buy a ticket if you just want to walk to the end of England. The same goes for the fine cliff walks in both directions – the one to Sennen is lovely, and the cove there is worth looking around. Some of the wildest and most formidable cliffs in Britain are between here and Treen.

LANHYDROCK HOUSE SX0863 A staggering 49 rooms to visit in this splendid old house, well liked by readers; the highlight is the Long Gallery, with its magnificently illustrated Old Testament scenes – it's one of the few original 16th-c parts left, as a disastrous fire in the 19th c resulted in major changes and refurbishments. Do leave time to explore the pretty formal **gardens** and grounds; it's a lovely walk down to the river and back through the woods. Good meals and snacks, shop and plant sales, disabled access; house cl Mon (exc bank hols) and Nov–Mar, grounds cl Nov–Feb; (01208) 73320; £6.20, £3.10 grounds only; NT. The Crown down at Lanlivery is most enjoyable for lunch, in a Jane Austen village setting with an interesting church.

★ † **LANREATH** SX1856 Pretty village with some remarkable woodwork in its exceptional medieval **church**. The **Folk Museum** is most fun for its summer demonstrations and workshops – corn dolly making (Mon), Cornish pasty crimping (Weds) and egg decorating (Fri); all activities 2–4pm. Snacks, shop, disabled access; cl Nov–Easter; (01503) 220321; *£2.50. The Punch Bowl has a fascinating old bar.

† **LANSALLOS CHURCH** SX1751 The attraction here is inside – the ancient carved bench ends, each individual but all sharing a style.

† **LANTEGLOS HIGHWAY CHURCH** SX1453 A curiosity, Perpendicular but not – subsidence has left the arches at drunken angles.

LAUNCESTON SX3285 The most attractive inland town in Cornwall, with winding old hillside streets and an untouristy feel; it was once Cornwall's capital. **Launceston Steam Railway** 2-ft gauge line on the trackbed of the old North Cornwall Railway, running through 2½ miles of scenic valley – on sunny days in an open carriage; also engine displays, model railway, and transport museum. A recent extension provides access to the region's network of footpaths. Snacks, shop, disabled access; open Easter, then Sun and Tues until spring bank hol Sun–Fri spring bank hol – Sept, Sun and Tues Oct, and some trains Dec wknds; (01566) 775665 for times; £5.20. The museum in Georgian **Lawrence House** (Castle St) has useful displays on the town's past; cl wknds and mid-Oct–Mar; free. Set on a Norman motte, the ruined 12th- and 13th-c hilltop **castle** is substantial and commanding – it was captured 4 times during the Civil War. Shop, some disabled access; cl Nov–Mar; £1.60. The White Hart does popular food. **Trethorne Leisure Farm** (Kennards House, off the A30 3m W) 140-acre working dairy farm good for children, who can milk Daisy the cow, walk the miniature ponies, play with the rabbits, take a pony ride or bottle-feed the lambs. Also birds of prey, ten pin bowling, good 18-hole golf course, and big indoor and outdoor play areas. Meals, snacks, shop, disabled access; cl Sun (exc golf); (01566) 86324; £4.50, golf £17 round.

THE LIZARD SW7012 This peninsula S of Helston is famous as the most southerly part of mainland Britain, and though the inland parts can be rather flat and dull and not really worth extended walks, the coastline is altogether more attractive. The NT have improved the area around Lizard Point, the southern tip, in recent years, and it's a good start for bracing cliff walks in either direction, with good views. Readers very much enjoy exploring the Lizard's dramatic western and eastern edges. The W side has mighty cliffs, with roads down to beautiful Mullion Cove and Kynance Cove. The E side is more sheltered and lusher, with wooded creeks. **Lizard village** itself is pretty uninspiring (there's a very civilised pub, and they sell interesting local serpentine rock carvings), but is well placed for longer walks encompassing Church Cove to the E and Kynance Cove to the W. On top and inland the Lizard is disappointing, a big flat peninsula although the Goonhilly satellite station is a remarkable landmark.

THE LOE SW6424 Cornwall's largest lake, a haven for waterfowl, is blocked from the sea by an NT shingle bank called Loe Bar (only breeding place of the rare sandhill rust moth –

and favourite place of worship of a German evangelical sect); a path leads round the lake. There's a coast walk from here to Gunwalloe fishing cove (and to Porthleven).

LOOE SX2553 Seaside resort packed with tourist shops, teashops and pubs, but with a nice easy-going atmosphere even in high season. The old fishing village with its picturesque harbour and narrow little back streets is now immersed in tourism, and is the shark-fishing place (on 'shark-fishing' trips you watch others doing the catching). You may see a locally caught shark on ice at the **Living from the Sea Exhibition** (Buller Quay); also local lobsters and shellfish in an aquarium. Disabled access; cl 12.30–1pm, all day Sat in low season, and all Nov–Easter; £1.75. From the quay there are summer **boat trips** to nearby St George's Island and further. **Looe Monkey Sanctuary** (signed off the B3253 at No Man's Land) is one of the most fascinating places in the county; established in 1964, its wooded grounds are home to the world's first colony of Amazon woolly monkeys to breed successfully outside their natural habitat. You can get right up to the animals, all born here, and talks give an intriguing insight into the dynamics and politics of the monkey community. Meals, snacks, shop, disabled access; cl Fri, Sat, and Oct–Easter; (01503) 262532; £4. The Olde Salutation has plenty of atmosphere and good simple food; the Smugglers is a decent friendly restaurant, and the quayside Trawlers has very good unusual seafood.

LUXULYAN SX0558 The village has an attractive church, and from the village you can walk along the lush wooded valley to the S, strewn with huge granite boulders and crossed by an impressive viaduct; if you feel adventurous you can climb up the valley to the top of the viaduct.

MADRON SW4431 **Trengwainton Garden** (on the B3312) The name in Cornish means 'Farm of the Spring' and it does always seems to be spring at this lovely place, the climate favouring plants not usually found outside in England. Magnolias, azaleas, rhododendrons, unusual southern hemisphere trees and shrubs inc a delightful tree-fern grotto, walled gardens, good views to Mount's Bay and the Lizard. Cream teas, shop, interesting plant sales; open Sun–Thurs (and Good Fri) Mar–Oct, (01736) 362297; £3; NT. The King William IV has good-value basic food. The road across to **Morvah** passes a very photogenic prehistoric burial chamber at Lanyon Quoit; a bit further along by a phone box a signed path on the right takes you to a great Bronze Age stone hoop at Men-An-Tol, and the lane opposite leads to **Chun Castle**, an Iron Age fort with great views, close to Chun Quoit, a Bronze Age burial chamber. In a few miles walkers can take in all these sights, the cliff path, and the moors close to the ruin of Ding Dong Mine.

MARAZION SW5130 **St Michael's Mount** There's something particularly awe-inspiring about this medieval castle, rising majestically from the sea. On gloomy or stormy days the picturesque silhouette seems even more dramatic. The little island is reached by ferry (it doesn't go in bad weather), or at low tide on foot along a causeway; the walk up to the castle, still the home of the family which acquired it in 1660, is quite steep. Fine Chippendale furniture, plaster reliefs, armour and paintings, audio-visual show. Summer meals, snacks, shop; open wkdys and most wknds Apr–Oct, best to phone for winter opening; (01736) 710507; £3.90; NT (members may have to pay some wknds). The Cutty Sark has decent food.

MAWNAN SMITH SW7627 **Trebah Garden** This steeply wooded ravine garden, well liked by readers, is widely reckoned to be one of the finest in the world. At times it really feels as if you've strayed into a benign, exclusive jungle. Huge subtropical tree ferns and palms, giant gunnera, lots of blue and white hydrangeas, 100-year-old rhododendrons, some fine rare trees. Several activities for children, and at the bottom end a private beach on the Helford River – good for a picnic or secluded swim. Snacks, shop (plants for sale); (01326) 250448; *£3.50. **Glendurgan** Lovely subtropical garden in valley above Helford River, started by Alfred Fox in 1820; fine shrubs from all over the world, mature trees, walled garden and restored laurel maze. Shop, snacks; cl Sun, Mon (exc bank hols), Good Fri, all Nov–Feb; (01326) 250906; £3.20; NT. The village itself is pretty, and the Red Lion is good for lunch. From nearby Mawnan a fine if blowy stretch of the coast path takes you around Rosemullion Head and on N to Maenporth, where there's a sheltered sandy cove with decent modern pub/restaurant.

★ **MEVAGISSEY** SX0144 This bustling place is a picturesque fishing village much expanded into quite a commercialised resort, but fun, with hillside cottages, narrow streets, gift shops, and a busy working harbour. The Ship and Fountain are worthwhile pubs, and the harbourside Mr Bistro does mainly fresh fish. **Lost Gardens of Heligan** (off the B2373, just NW, SX9946) Forgotten and neglected between 1914 and 1991, these highly acclaimed gardens have now been fully restored. Some very fine mature trees, Victorian walled gardens, lots of rhododendrons, lakes, and big collection of tree ferns, bamboos and palms. It's a friendly place, and they're more than happy to talk about their work. Snacks, shop/nursery, disabled access; cl 24–25 Dec; (01726) 844157; £4.50. Back in town, the **World of Model Railways** (Meadow St) has over 50 model trains trundling through a realistic little world that takes in Cornish china-clay pits, ski resorts, fairgrounds, towns and country. Shop, some disabled access; cl wkdys Nov–Easter; (01726) 842457; £2.75. There's a decent **folk museum** in an 18th-c boat-builder's shed on East Quay; cl am Sat and am Sun and Oct–Easter; *50p.

MINIONS SX2571 The highest village in Cornwall. Above, the **Hurlers** are 3 Bronze Age stone circles the central one still has 14 stones standing. Close by is the **Rillaton Barrow** where the lovely Rillaton gold cup (now in the British Museum) was found, along with other interesting relics. There is a clear track to the nearby Cheesewring; not far off, the track between Sharptor and Kilmar Tor gives fine views.

† **MORWENSTOW** SS2015 The **church**, in an idyllic setting, has Norman arches and 16th-c bench ends, with shipwrecked sailors' headstones in the graveyard. A driftwood shack built by a Victorian parson for contemplation over the impressive cliffs is preserved by the NT. The Bush is an interesting old pub, and the rectory tearoom is delightful.

MOUNT EDGCUMBE SX4552 (on the B3247 E of Kingsand) A short walk up from the Cremyll pedestrian ferry from Plymouth, this mansion was reconstructed after World War II bombing, with period furniture and (the main attraction) acres of lovely gardens and parkland, divided into English, French and Italian sections. Great views to Plymouth. Meals, snacks, shop, disabled access; house cl Mon (exc bank hols), Tues, and Oct–Mar (but park and gardens open then, free); (01752) 822236; £4. The charmingly furnished Edgcumbe Arms by the ferry has good-value food.

★ **MOUSEHOLE** SW4626 Attractive working fishing village with steep little roads – too many summer visitors, but lovely out of season, with spectacular Christmas lights in the little harbour; the harbourside Ship (with good-value bedrooms) is fun for lunch.

★ † **MULLION** SW6719 This attractive village has an enjoyable family pub (the Old Inn) and a possibly unique feature in its church – a dog flap. You can hire bicycles at Atlantic Forge (£5 half-day, £7 day); (01326) 240294 – open all year, but check first out of season. This is a good way to explore the Lizard. **Mullion Cove** This dramatic fusion of rock, sand and sea is most rewardingly reached by a there-and-back walk along the cliff from Porth Mellin; for the energetic, the extension S to Kynance Cove is outstanding.

NEWLYN SW4629 Cornwall's busiest working fishing port; it's great fun watching the boats come in. There's an unusual art deco swimming pool, and an excellent and occasionally rather avant-garde **art gallery** (New Rd) in a lovely coastal setting with fine views; cl Sun, 25 Dec, 1 Jan; (01736) 363715;

donations. At Christmas the fishermen decorate the harbour and its boats with spectacular lights. The Dolphin and Fisherman's Arms are useful for lunch.

NEWLYN EAST SW8655

Lappa Valley Steam Railway and Leisure Park 15-in gauge steam train trips through pretty countryside to an old lead mine, currently being restored. It's surrounded by parkland with lakes, woodland walk, a maze, and play areas; a section of the old branch line leads to a soft ball golf course. Meals, snacks, shop, some disabled access; cl Nov–Easter, limited opening in Oct – best to check train times; (01872) 510317; £5.80, covers fare and all attractions exc golf. The backstreet Pheasant has good home cooking.

NEWQUAY SW8261

Now famed as England's surfing capital, a thorough-going seaside resort with excellent safe golden beaches below fine cliffs; Crantock Beach is the best and least crowded, with great views from the Bowgie family pub up on West Pentire headland. There's no shortage of souvenir shops, an alcohol-free zone declared on the streets, theme parks on the edge, and older houses around the harbour; there's decent food all day at the Fort Hotel (Fore St). Thanks in part to the surfers, the town has quite a cheery young feel these days. Fistral Beach is reckoned by some to be the best surfing beach in Europe; a couple of surfing schools here can get beginners started. **Newquay Zoo** (Trenance Leisure Park, off the A3075 Edgcumbe Ave) The emphasis is very much on conservation here, with carefully designed enclosures for monkeys, penguins, lions and tortoises, as well as gardens, and summer activities. Feeding displays are well timetabled so there's something to see throughout the day. Also children's farm, play areas, and a maze. Meals, snacks, shop, disabled access; (01637) 873342; £4.75. You can get a joint ticket to **Water World**, a lively fun pool on the same site. **Sea Life Centre** (Town Promenade) Another in the reliable chain – a see-through tunnel creates the illusion of walking along the sea bed, and bubble windows bring you face to face with fish, sea horses and sharks. Meals, snacks, shop, some disabled access; cl 25 Dec; (01637) 872822; £4.95. **Holywell Bay Fun Park** (off the A3075 SW) Active children should enjoy the go-karts, bumper boats, rides, indoor play area, golf; cl Oct–March; (01637) 830095; separate charges for various attractions. **Dairyland** (on the A3508 4m SE) Much expanded since it first opened 20 years ago, this bustling dairy farm is a huge favourite with families. Its showpiece remains the daily milking sessions, when cows step aboard a bizarre merry-go-round milking machine and are milked to the strains of classical music. Also well labelled nature trails, farm park, rural bygones, brass rubbing centre and plenty of activities for children. Meals, snacks, shop, disabled access; cl Nov–Mar (exc around Christmas); (01872) 510246; £5.20.

NORTH PETHERWIN SX2889

Tamar Otter Park Friendly place breeding otters then releasing them into the wild; it's fun to watch the attractive Asian short-clawed otters playing. Three species of deer roam free, and there are waterfowl lakes, wallabies, and nature trails. The otters are fed at noon and 3.30pm. Snacks, shop, disabled access; cl Nov–Mar; (01566) 785646; £4.50.

★ **PADSTOW** SW9175 Quaint streets, old buildings clustered around the working fishing harbour, and attractive slate houses; Rick Stein's restaurants are currently drawing the crowds (you'll need to book well in advance). The Golden Lion, London Inn and Old Custom House are useful for lunch. The Camel estuary is popular for sailing: gentle dreamy scenery with lots of little boats. Plenty of good clean beaches near here; Constantine Bay is the best, and popular with surfers. The B3276 has the best roadside coastal views in this part of Cornwall.

Prideaux Place Still a lived-in family home, this fine old house has changed little since it was built in the late 16th c. Highlights include the elegant ceilings, atmospheric library and the intricate biblical tableaux in the Great Chamber. Notable concerts and special events in the grounds. Snacks, shop, disabled access to ground floor only; open pm

Sun–Thurs Easter–mid-Oct (may be subject to change, best to phone); (01841) 532411; £4. **Shipwreck Museum** (South Quay) Not far from the town's little harbour, a collection of relics and tales of the plentiful shipwrecks along this coast. Shop, disabled access; usually open Mar–Oct; (01726) 69897; £3.95.

PENDEEN SW3733 **Levant Mine** (on the B3306) Unusual mine beneath the sea, powered by the oldest steam engine in Cornwall, all explained by knowledgeable and enthusiastic staff. Shop; open Easter and May bank hols, Weds–Fri and Sun in Jun, Sun–Fri July–Sept; (01736) 786156; £3; NT. The nearby Pendeen Watch lighthouse is worth a look, and the Radjel is useful for something to eat.

PENHALLOW SW7650 **Callestock Cider Farm** Traditional working cider farm producing scrumpy, country wines and jam, with seasonal demonstrations, and friendly horses, rabbits, goats, pigs and donkeys. Also cider museum with ancient presses, and hives of the bees needed for pollination. Summer snacks, shop (with samples of everything they make); cl Sun (exc mid-June–mid- Sept), and Dec–Jan; (01872) 573356; free, £2 for museum and tractor ride. The Miners Arms at Mithian is useful for lunch.

★ **PENRYN** SW7834 Appealing waterside village, quite sizeable, with pretty houses dropping down to the estuary.

PENZANCE SW4730 The area's main shopping centre, a pleasantly relaxed town by the sea. The prettiest part is Chapel St, where there's a decent **Maritime Museum** (cl Sun; £2), the extravagantly designed early 19th-c Egyptian House deserves a passing look, and the Turk's Head is a good pub. Harris's restaurant on New St has good local fish. **National Lighthouse Centre** (Old Buoy Store, Wharf Rd, Penzance) Easy to spot thanks to the big buoys outside, this has an excellent collection of lighthouse equipment, and a good audio-visual display on what it was like to live in one; a typical room is reconstructed, with original curved furniture. Many of the staff are ex-lighthouse personnel so a good source of information and anecdote and there is a lighthouse opposite. Shop, disabled access; cl Nov–Easter; (01736) 360077; £2.50. The paintings in the **District Museum & Art Gallery** (Morrab Rd) are worth a look – mainly by the Newlyn school. Snacks, shop, disabled access; cl Sun (exc pm July–Aug); £2 (free Sat). In summer you can take **boat trips** around the coastline or across to the Isles of Scilly, and there are regular **helicopter flights** to the islands.

★ **POLKERRIS** SX0952 Little seaside hamlet – scarcely more than the waterside inn – with terrific view, almost even better in winter, across St Austell Bay from well restored ancient quay.

★ ! **POLPERRO** SX2150 Almost unbelievably pretty, tiny streets around a very quaint sheltered fishing harbour, little cottages perched on rocks once a busy smuggling place, now some enjoyable craft shops tucked away, one or two tourist attractions, oddities like the shell-encrusted Shell House, and unspoilt harbourside fishermen's locals; the Old Mill House is the nicest pub, and Crumplehorn Mill does decent food. The beaches around here are some of England's cleanest. It gets very busy in summer, with little electric buses (or horse and cart) shuttling in from the out-of-village car park. A sensible alternative to sweating out summer traffic jams to the village itself is to park instead in Talland Bay, for an easy 1-mile walk along the coast to enter this harbour feeling you've earned it. The **Land of Legend & Model Village** (The Old Forge, Mill Hill), with a model railway and scaled-down version of Polperro, is a useful enough distraction for children; cl Nov–Easter; (01503) 272378; £2.50.

POOL SW6741 **Cornish Engines** (on the A3047) Developing site based around 2 big beam engines, originally used for pumping water from tin and copper mines. Shop, visitor centre; cl Oct–Mar; (01209) 216657; £3; NT. The Cornish Choughs (at Treswithian, just off the far end of the Camborne bypass) has interesting food inc good fresh fish. At Treskillard a little way S of Pool (SW6739) Lower Gryllis

Farm has an uncommercialised **shire horse farm**; most displays are indoors, and there are working blacksmith and wheelwright's shops. Meals, snacks, shop, disabled access; open Sun–Fri, Easter–Sept, and Sun and Tues in Oct; (01209) 713606; £3.50.

★ ⛰ ❀ **PORT ISAAC** SX0080 Delightful steep fishing village, a favourite with many: tiny streets, and houses hanging high over the pretty harbour – the Golden Lion's terrace overlooks it. Park at the top and walk down (at low tide you can park on the beach). There are some particularly fine stretches of cliffs for walking around here, and just up the coast Port Gaverne is a beautiful NT cove. Slightly inland at Trelights (but with good views down to the sea) the prettily restored **Long Cross Victorian Gardens**, intricately hedged against the sea winds, have interesting granite and water features, a maze, and playground and pets corner for children. Meals, snacks, plant sales; (01208) 880243; £1.40.

PORTHALLOW SX2251 This is snugly set above a little fishing harbour with a beautifully set pub, the Five Pilchards; the beach is notoriously polluted, and swimming in the sea is not recommended. A friendly little **vineyard** here has self-guided tours, free samples of their wines and cider, and a particularly tasty birch country wine; cl 1–2pm, all day Sun, and Nov–Easter; (01326) 280050; free.

! ⛰ **PORTHCURNO** SW3822 **Minack Theatre & Exhibition Centre** There are few better backdrops for plays than the one at this famous little open-air theatre – dramatic cliffs and blue sea stretching into the distance make a magical setting. Varied summer season, and an exhibition on the life of Rowena Cade, the remarkable woman who built the theatre, cut into these steep cliffs, with her own hands. Tickets go on sale in May, but aren't for particular seats – if you've booked you'll still need to get there early to bag the best. Evening shows are more atmospheric. Shows are cancelled only in extreme conditions, so take a waterproof. Snacks, shop, disabled access; performances May–Sept, exhibition cl Jan–Feb and during matinees; (01736) 810181; shows £6, exhibition £2. The secret wartime communications centre in the underground tunnels here is now the **Museum of Submarine Telegraphy**. Don't let the name put you off – it's good deal more interesting than you'd think. Meals, snacks, shop, disabled access, cl Sat, Sun and Nov–Easter; (01209) 612142; £3.50. Porthcurno's lovely silver sands among Cornwall's best beaches are now the property of the NT, in common with so much of the coastline round here. If you walk their length, be careful not to get cut off by high tide. The Logan Rock at Treen is handy for lunch, and there are good cliff walks.

★ ⛰ **PORTHLEVEN** SW6225 Pretty working fishing village; the Ship built into the cliffs is a good pub, and the long stretch of rocky beach S is a good walk if the surf's not beating in too fiercely.

★ ⛰ **PORTLOE** SW9339 Tiny unspoilt village wedged into a precipitous cove, with splendid cliff walks in rugged scenery, and stiffish climbs on to Nare Head; good teashop/small restaurant.

⛰ ❀ **PORTREATH** SW6545 A good base for long bracing clifftop walks, with a decent pub; along this whole section of coast, between St Ives Bay and Trevose Head (nr Padstow), the coast path is rich in rugged views, and very rewarding to those with sturdy legs.

★ ⛰ **PORTSCATHO** SW8735 Very sheltered fishing village with a picturesque little harbour, and some fine nearby beaches excellent for families. The Plume of Feathers is popular for lunch. Virtually the whole of Gerrans Bay around here is good easy walking, with some lovely clifftop stretches; there's a good sandy stretch at Pendower Beach.

PRAA SANDS SW5828 A popular summer family beach.

❀ **PROBUS** SW9247 **Trewithen** (off the A390 towards Grampound, where the Dolphin has good-value food) Justly famous landscaped gardens, with many rare trees and shrubs. The early 18th-c house is a little unfairly overshadowed by what's outside, and is an interesting obviously lived-in family home. Snacks, rare plants for sale, disabled access; gardens open Mar–Sept (cl Sun exc Apr and May), walled garden open as house, house open pm Mon and pm Tues Apr–July (and Aug bank hol); (01726) 883647; £6.20, £3 gardens only.

RESTORMEL CASTLE SX1060 Very well preserved Norman castle with notable round keep and fine views over Fowey valley. Lots of flowers in spring. Snacks, shop, limited disabled access; cl Nov–Mar; (01208) 872687; £1.60. The Royal Oak in Lostwithiel is good for lunch.

RESTRONGUET CREEK SW8137 Though the waterside village is mainly of no great age, its pub the Pandora has a lovely location – you can park in Mylor Bridge for a leisurely 2-mile waterside walk there and back, or drive all the way.

RINSEY SW5927 The coast path passes 2 magnificently sited **ruined mine** buildings, Wheal Prosper and Wheal Trewavas (tin and copper), both now maintained by the NT.

ROCHE ROCK SW9959 This small but picturesque crag is worth the short walk from the B3274, with a 14th-c ruined ivy-covered chapel built into it, and a ladder up (decent pub nearby, past the station).

ROUGH TOR SX1284 (pronounced Roe Tor) The summit, reached from a signed car park off the A39 nr Camelford, gives views of Brown Willy, the highest point in Cornwall.

★ **ST AGNES** SW7150 A former mining town, now with a holiday role; some attractive steeply terraced cottages, fine cliff scenery nearby, and great views from the top of 630-ft St Agnes Beacon, just W of town. **Presingoll Barns** (Penwinnick Rd) Craft centre with demonstrations of pottery, candle and fudge-making, good picnic areas; cl 25–26 Dec; (01872) 553007; free, small charge for pottery tuition or candle-dipping.

ST ANTHONY HEAD SW8431 On the E side of the Fal estuary, by the **Zone Head lighthouse**, this has superb views, and easy walks along low, level cliffs; parking at the head itself, or nr Porth Farm on the way down.

† **ST AUSTELL** SX0352 The centre of the china-clay industry and a busy modern shopping town. **Holy Trinity church** has a fine tower and interesting font, and you can tour the **St Austell Brewery** on Trevarthian Rd (booking recommended); (01726) 66022; £4, inc samples of beer. The area N is a strange bleak moonscape of whitish spoil heaps with metallic blue lakes dotted among them; the B3279 St Stephen–Nanpean gives some of the best views over this. Up here off the A391 is the **Wheal Martyn Museum**, an interestingly restored 19th-c clay works showing the 200-year history of china-clay production. Working waterwheels and other equipment, steam locomotives, nature trails with a spectacular viewpoint over a huge clay pit, and children's adventure trail. Meals, snacks, shop; cl Nov–Mar; (01726) 850362; £4.25 (a good-value family ticket gets 2 adults and up to 4 children in for £11.50). **Automobilia** (St Stephen, on the A3058 about 4m W of St Austell) Over 50 cars, motorcycles and other vehicles from 1904 to the 1960s, inc a vintage Bentley and Aston Martin, with a permanent auto-jumble that vintage-car owners may find useful. Snacks, shop, disabled access; cl Sat in Apr, May and Oct, and all Nov–Mar; (01726) 823092; £3.25.

ST ERVAN SW9170 **Animal Playland** (off the A39) Friendly and unspoilt working farm with rare animals and poultry; lots of pigs (the piglets may race up to greet you) – even Iron Age types descended from wild boar; ferret racing and tractor rides. One of the things that stands out here is the genuine and uncommercialised feel. Teas, shop; cl Sat and Oct–Easter; (01841) 540606; *£3.50. The Ring o' Bells over at St Issey is useful for lunch.

† **ST GERMANS** SX3657 The **church** has a wonderful Norman doorway and particularly fine east window; worth a look if you're passing this waterside village. There's a good view towards Port Eliot, a stately home designed by John Soane (not open).

★ **ST IVES** SW5039 A pretty place, despite the summer crowds, with its attractive working harbour and narrow streets and alleys (the cobbled

Fore St is the prettiest). It has good wide beaches, and plenty of bird life along the Lelant Saltings (RSPB reserve). Its popularity with artists is best explored at the **Tate Gallery St Ives**, which can take a lot of the credit for the town's increasing popularity in recent years (in its first 18 months an extra £16 million was pumped into the local economy). Works by the familiar St Ives-school names are regularly joined by new displays of 20th-c art with a Cornish connection. It's an impressive building, outside and in, fully exploiting its spectacular cliffside setting – views are best from the café. Meals, snacks, shop, disabled access; (01736) 796226; £3.50. The adjacent **Barbara Hepworth Museum & Sculpture Garden** is a tranquil escape from the holiday hordes, devoted to the artist's work and life, with sculptures in the house, studio and subtropical garden, as well as photographs and letters. Shop; *£3. Other works by Hepworth are dotted about the town. Besides the Pig 'n' Fish (*see* **Where to eat** *section, below*), the waterside Sloop (interesting pictures for sale) does reliable food. The best beach for surfers is Porthmeor slightly N, while in the other direction the B3306 to Land's End has great coast and moorland views. Out of season, when the caravan and camp sites are empty, the magnificent sands around St Ives Bay are well worth walking, with good cliff walks to the W.

† **ST JUST-IN-ROSELAND** SW8435 An unspoilt spot, its **church** in an idyllic creekside setting; the steep graveyard is like a lost subtropical garden – well worth a visit on a quiet sunny day, or in spring with the baby rooks blethering and the smell of wild garlic. The words on the inscribed stones by the path seem quite fitting.

★ **ST KEVERNE** SW7921 Set around a little square, this is a pleasant village with a good dining pub, the White Hart – and a lovely little **working farm** just S at Tregellast Barton, undeveloped and tranquil, with pleasant walks through woods and meadows, afternoon milking (4.30pm), and a good farm shop with samples of their unusually flavoured ice-cream; phone for opening times; (01326) 280479; free. There's a good walk to Lowland Point, for dramatic views of the Manacles – striking offshore rocks.

★ **ST KEW** SX0276 Delightful quiet leafy village with old-fashioned feel, and agreeably low-key **Donkey and Pony Sanctuary;** cl Nov–Easter; (01208) 841710; £3.75. The St Kew Inn is a nice place for a meal.

ST MAWES SW8433 Very pretty harbourside and estuary views, a long waterfront to stroll along, clean bathing waters, a foot-passenger ferry to Falmouth and other boat trips (full of yachtsmen and others in summer, lots of guesthouses). The 16th-c **castle** is remarkably well preserved; cl winter Weds and Thurs; £2.50. The Victory does good-value lunches. The ferry across to St Anthony allows some remote and unspoilt views and walks. The King Harry chain-drawn car ferry on the B3269 N of St Mawes is a favourite family crossing, and on the way the Roseland at Philleigh is one of Cornwall's nicest pubs.

† **ST NEOT** SX1867 The village **church** is well known for its early stained glass, and also has an unusual stone vault in the south porch. Nearby ancient remains include the 5 impressive **Brown Gelly Barrows** and some hut circles. **Carnglaze Slate Caverns** are big long-abandoned mining chambers, with a lake at the far end of one; guided tours; cl Sat; £3. The London Inn is good for lunch.

SANCREED SW4129 **Carn Euny Ancient Village** Dating from the 1st c, substantial traces of a little village of stone courtyard houses, and a 66-ft underground passage leading to a circular chamber (some very minor roads to get here).

† **TINTAGEL** SX0688 A tourist trap since the 19th c, but well worth penetrating for **Tintagel Castle**. Forgetting the myths and legends, these dramatic 12th- and 13th-c ruins have a spectacular setting and unrivalled views. A good start is from Rocky Valley, a craggy valley leading from the B3263 to the sea. Try to come out of season, when the crowds are fewer and the mist and crashing waves add a touch of mystery. There's quite a lot of climbing

involved, and the often steep steps among the crags can be slippery in wet weather. A small exhibition makes the most of the case for a connection with King Arthur (boosted by the 1998 find of a 6th-c house plaque with a similar name). Shop; cl 24–26 Dec; (01840) 770328; £2.80. A Land Rover service can ferry you to the site from the village at regular intervals throughout the day. The Cornishman is useful for lunch, and the parish **church** worth a look. Arthurian legends are taken as fact at **King Arthur's Great Halls** (Fore St), built by a custard magnate in the 1920s, and while there's no denying the impressive craftsmanship (especially in the 72 stained glass scenes), it's done too seriously to be anything more than a time-filler on a rainy day. Decent shop, disabled access; cl 25 Dec; (01840) 770526; £2.50. **Old Post Office** Small saggy-roofed 14th-c manor used in the 19th c as a post office: Shop; cl Nov–Mar; (01840) 770024; £2.20; NT.

TORPOINT SX4156 A pleasant ferry ride from Devonport in Plymouth (it's a lot harder to get to by road). **Antony House** (2m NW) The finest Classical house in Cornwall, little changed since the early 18th c, with interesting contents and paintings in its panelled rooms; also riverside gardens redesigned by Humphrey Repton, and a dovecot. Snacks, shop, disabled access to ground floor only; open pm Tues–Thurs and bank hols Apr–Oct, plus Sun Jun–Aug; (01752) 812191; £4, woodland garden £2.50; NT.

† **TREBETHERICK** SW9277 **St Enodoc Church** Tucked well away from the roads under a seaside hill off the Rock road, looking out to Padstow Bay. A nice stroll from the village, it's the burial place of John Betjeman. Daymer Bay near here is a very clean and attractive beach, and as it's so shallow ideal for families wanting a paddle. The Carpenters Arms is useful for lunch, and down on the water at Rock the Mariners Hotel has lovely views over to Padstow.

TRECANGATE SX1759 **Porfell Animal Land** Delightfully unspoilt and friendly, with deer, wallabies, racoons, lemurs, meerkats and a capybara called Bart, as well as rabbits, guinea pigs, goats, ducks and chickens in 15 acres of sloping fields and woodland. Readers very much enjoy the peaceful and remote feel. Snacks, shop, disabled access; cl Nov–Easter; (01503) 220211; £3.50. The Ship over at Lerryn is fairly handy for lunch and often has good watercolours for sale; the stepping stones over the river there are a hit with children, and good circular walks are signed from the car park.

TREDINNICK SW9270 **Shire Horse Adventure Farm** Far more to this busy complex than just the magnificent horses: there's a children's farm, an exhibition of rural antiquities, nature trails, watermill and working craftsmen, and very big indoor and outdoor adventure playgrounds. The horses are displayed in an indoor arena, and you can see them being groomed in their stables – along with Shetland ponies. Lots for all ages, but ideal for children. Meals, snacks, shop, disabled access; cl Nov–Easter and Sat in Oct; (01841) 540276; £5.80. The Ring o' Bells at St Issey is handy for lunch.

TREGONNING HILL SW6029 Takes only a few minutes to climb but has an impressive view; here in 1746 William Cookworthy made the first discovery of china clay in England, and went on to make porcelain.

TRELISSICK GARDEN SW8339 (on the B3289) Woodland park with beautifully kept gardens of camellias, magnolias and hydrangeas, also subtropical garden and other unusual plants; wonderful views of the King Harry Passage and over to Pendennis Castle. There's a pretty orchard, and good walks in the surrounding woodland. Meals, snacks, shop, disabled access; cl am Sun, and all Jan and Feb; (01872) 862090; £4; NT. The NT have 4 holiday cottages on the estate. The Punch Bowl & Ladle at Penelewey on the King Harry Ferry road is popular for lunch.

TRELOWARREN SW7223 This **manor house** is worth a look for its elaborate Strawberry Hill gothick chapel (open pm Weds and bank hols only), and the surrounding estate (open all the time, free) has plenty going on, inc woodland walks, craft shops and pottery, campsite, summer Thurs evening concerts, and good meals and snacks in the Yard Bistro.

TRERICE SW8458 Pretty Elizabethan house with unusual gables, and elaborate plasterwork ceilings in the magnificent Hall and Great Chamber. Fine furnishings from the 17th and 18th c, notable paintings, early embroideries, Oriental and English porcelain, and in the grounds an unusual collection of lawnmowers; lovely colourful gardens with Cornish fruit trees. Snacks (in a barn with activities for toddlers), shop, very good disabled access; cl Sat and Tues (exc Aug), and all Nov–Easter; (01637) 875404; £3.80; NT. The Two Clomes at Quintrell Downs is quite handy for lunch.

TRERYN DINAS SW4022 The most stunning of Cornwall's headlands, capped by the precariously balanced Logan Rock; it's a fairly easy walk from the Logan Rock pub (good food) in Treen.

TRETHEVY QUOIT SX2568 (St Cleer) This is a very photogenic megalithic tomb, its massive stones now left high and dry by a fall in the soil level over thousands of years. The Crows Nest down near Darite is handy for lunch.

TRURO SW8244 A busy but civilised town with good shops; Lemon St is a particularly fine Georgian street, and Boscawen St is cobbled. **Royal Cornwall Museum** (River St) Tales of local characters such as Black John of Tetcott, an 18th-c dwarf whose party piece was apparently tying mice together by their tails, swallowing them whole, and then pulling them up again. New natural history and textile galleries this year. Meals, snacks, shop, disabled access; cl Sun, bank hols; (01872) 272205; £2.50. The **cathedral** is one of the newer Anglican ones, designed in 1880 in Early English style and finished in 1910; the twin spires of the west front are handsome, and pop up dramatically from behind shops and houses. Just outside the centre **Bosvigo** (Bosvigo Lane) is a charming plantsman's garden, with most colour Jun–Aug; small nursery; open Weds–Sat Mar–Sept; (01872) 275774; *£2. The Old Ale House, Wig & Pen and William IV are all good for lunch.

VERYAN SW9139 Lovely village famous for its 5 devil-proof thatched round houses; also a water garden sheltered by holm oaks. Nearby, 16th-c **Melinsey Mill** is a nicely restored watermill in a lovely setting, with good afternoon teas. The prettiest approach is to walk along the streamside 'Secret Valley' from Pendower Beach (off the A3078 S) rather than go from the village itself.

WADEBRIDGE SW9673 The disused railway track between Wadebridge and Padstow is a level 6m along the edge of the Camel estuary, with banks of wild flowers, birds, and lovely views between cuttings – you can walk or cycle (bike hire at either end), or picnic on the small beaches at low tide. Those with less energy could park at Wadebridge, walk to Padstow, have lunch and get the bus back (2.30pm from the old station). You might then walk on through scenic countryside beyond Bodmin (worth stopping at Helland pottery, just by the path at Helland Bridge).

WENDRON SW6831 **Poldark Mine & Heritage Centre** A fun feature of this old tin mine is its underground post box, the deepest in Britain. More serious attractions include a tour of the mine, an 18th-c village, a film on the history of Cornish mining, old cottages, collection of working beam engines, and plenty of children's amusements. Varied enough to interest most members of the family. Meals, snacks, shop, limited disabled access; cl Nov–Mar; (01326) 563166; £4.95.

WHEALE COATES SW6949 One of the most photogenic mine ruins on the Cornish coast; for walkers, the diversion up St Agnes Beacon is well worth it for the commanding views.

WHITESAND BAY SW3526 Long expanses of wonderfully clean sands below the cliffs here give good walks, stretching away N of Sennen Cove (very popular with surfers; the Old Success here has a great view).

ZENNOR SW4537 **Wayside Folk Museum** Readers enjoy this decent little local history museum which has chatty descriptions and information scattered through the exhibits; you should be able to see the wheel of the adjacent watermill gently turning. Teas, shop (specialising in Cornish books and crafts); cl Nov–Easter, and Sats in Oct; (01736) 796945; £2. The **church** is best seen in its granite landscape from the hills above. The Tinners Arms is useful for lunch. Around here you can walk for miles without seeing another soul; **Gurnard's Head** juts dramatically into the Atlantic, and the hotel there is a good base for cliff walks (with unusual bar snacks).

Where to eat

Several of the hotels and inns recommended as good places to stay are also good for diners eating out (*see* **Where to stay** *section, above*).

CHAPEL AMBLE SW9975 **Maltsters Arms** *(01208) 812473* Popular family-run pub with attractively knocked together rooms (one is no smoking), flagstones, beams and a big stone fireplace, good interesting food inc lots of fish, 20 wines by the glass, well kept real ales, and helpful friendly staff; cl pm 25 Dec; children in family room or over 8 in restaurant; disabled access. **£26**|£5.95.

DULOE SX2358 **Olde Plough House** *(01503) 262050* Very neatly kept pub with lovely slate floor in both communicating bar rooms, 3 woodburners, a mix of pews and chairs, good interesting food inc fishy specials, real ales, sensibly priced wines, and attentive service. **£15.35**|£4.85.

FALMOUTH SW8032 **HMS Ganges** *Mylor Yacht Harbour (01326) 374320* Not actually a ship (though obviously named after one), this friendly little restaurant looks across the River Fal and specialises in fresh fish and seafood; good choice of wines from around the world at reasonable prices, and helpful service; cl pm Sun, Feb; disabled access. **£24.50**|£4.95.

FALMOUTH SW8032 **Pennypots** *Maenporth Beach (01326) 250251* Attractively decorated and airy evening restaurant with fine views across Falmouth Bay, a strong emphasis on beautifully presented really fresh local fish and shellfish dishes (lovely non-fishy things too), delicious puddings, an extensive wine list, and deft attentive service; cl Sun, Mon, 4 wks winter; disabled access. **£33.50**.

FOWEY SX1252 **Food for Thought** *Town Quay (01726) 832221* Generous helpings of carefully presented food in quayside evening restaurant – fine fish and some simple as well as other elaborate dishes, lovely puddings; cl Sun, Jan–Feb; children over 10. **£26**.

LANLIVERY SX0759 **Crown** *(01208) 872707* Pretty 12th-c inn with friendly licensees, a rambling series of rooms with open fires, a chatty atmosphere, good food using home-grown and local produce, well kept real ales, and a nice garden; disabled access. **£15**|£4.50

MITHIAN SW7450 **Miners Arms** *(01872) 552375* Secluded Tudor pub with lots of character, fine old furnishings and warm winter fires, popular food, a no smoking dining room, real ales, and friendly service. **£16**|£4.50.

MOUSEHOLE SW4726 **Cornish Range** *(01736) 731488* Friendly restaurant, neatly kept, with nice atmosphere and carefully cooked food inc plenty of good local fish dishes and enjoyable puddings; cl winter Mon–Weds; disabled access. **£25**.

NEWLYN SW4628 **Smugglers** *12–14 Fore St (01736) 331501* In a fine setting on the edge of the fishing-boat harbour, this simply furnished little restaurant has candles on pine tables, a friendly atmosphere, and an interesting menu inc delicious fresh fish and super puddings; cl 25–26 Dec, 1 Jan; partial disabled access. **£16**.

PADSTOW SW9175 **St Petroc's** *4 New St (01841) 532700* Attractive little hotel (under the same ownership as the Seafood Restaurant) with good quickly served food from a short menu (mostly fish), a sensible wine list, and friendly atmosphere; cl Mon, Christmas; disabled access. **£27.45**.

PADSTOW SW9175 **Seafood** *Riverside (01841) 532485* Wonderfully fresh seafood straight from the boats in busy (and famous – hence having to book so far in advance) airy quayside restaurant, good puddings, nice cheeses, a long, interesting and fairly priced wine list, and friendly service; conservatory for aperitifs; bdrms; cl Sun, 19–26 Dec; children over 6; limited disabled access. **£40 dinner, £34 lunch**|£6.20.

PENZANCE SW4730 **Harris's** *46 New St (01736) 364408* Long-standing and boldly decorated cosy restaurant in a narrow cobbled street, with good enjoyable food using local produce (popular fish and shellfish), well liked puddings, and a decent wine list; cl Sun, 3 wks in winter. **£28**|£6.50.

PHILLEIGH SW8639 **Roseland** *(01872) 580254* Friendly little 17th-c pub with good winter fire, lots of rugby and rowing prints, a relaxed atmosphere, well kept real ales, and good popular home-made food; disabled access. **£15**|£4.75.

POLPERRO SX2051 **Kitchen** *The Coombes (01503) 272780* Cottagey, informal no smoking evening restaurant with really enjoyable interesting food inc vegetarian and daily-changing fresh fish dishes (lovely fresh lobster and crab), and good-value wines; cl Sun, Nov–Easter; children over 12. **£23**.

POLPERRO SX2051 **Plantation Café** *The Coombes (01503) 272223* Popular beamed tea shop with good cream teas, a wide choice of interesting teas inc herbal and fruit, lunchtime sandwiches, and evening meals; cl Nov–Apr; disabled access. **£12.75**|£4.75.

PORTHALLOW SW7923 **Taranaki Tea Rooms** *(01326) 280671* Lovely flower-filled tropical gardens with seats under covered pergola or in conservatory; home-baked scones and cakes, cream teas and light lunches (super crab sandwiches) all prepared by friendly owner; no licence but you can bring drinks from nearby pub; cl Oct–Good Fri; partial disabled access. **£6.50**|£3.

PORTLOE SW9339 **Tregain** *The Post Office (01872) 501252* Small friendly no smoking restaurant serving interesting well cooked food using local produce inc daily specials (fresh fish in the evening and lovely home-made crab soup at lunchtime), light lunches and super cream teas, a decent wine list, and local cider; 2 bdrms; cl pm Sun (exc bank hol wknds), Nov–Mar. **£25**|£5.

ST IVES SW5140 **Pig 'n' Fish** *Norway Lane (01736) 794204* Simply decorated restaurant with attractive modern pictures, lots of good interesting fish dishes (some meaty ones, too), and a French wine list; cl Sun, Mon, best to phone for Nov–Feb; no children. **£26.50**|£5.50.

ST IVES SW5140 **Porthminster Beach Café** *(01736) 795352* Bustling, popular café open all day for morning coffee with home-baked pastries, cream teas, light lunches and more substantial evening meals offering good Mediterranean cooking (nice daily specials) using local produce, and a wide choice of coffees and teas; kind to children; cl Oct–Mar; disabled access. **£17**|£5.

ST KEVERNE SW7921 **White Hart** *The Square (01326) 280325* Well liked inn with beams, an open fire, a mix of simple furniture on the bare boards, a relaxed chatty atmosphere, enjoyable food inc good fresh fish, well kept real ales, and seats outside in the garden; disabled access. **£25**|£5.

ST KEW SX0276 **St Kew** *(01208) 841259* Rather grand-looking stone pub with a friendly welcome, nice old-fashioned furnishings, good popular food, and peaceful garden. **£18.45**|£6.95.

ST MICHAEL'S MOUNT SW5130 **Sail Loft** *The Harbour (01736) 710748* Converted boat house with enjoyable home-made cakes, Cornish cream teas, more substantial meals, and friendly service; no smoking; cl Nov–Easter; disabled access. **£14.25**|£4.50.

TRURO SW8244 **Old Ale House** *7 Quay St (01872) 271122* Appealing, bustling and friendly back-to-basics pub, popular with a good cross-section of people, with interesting bric-a-brac and engaging old furnishings, up to 24 real ales, and enterprising, freshly prepared and very cheap food from a spotless kitchen. **£12.50**|£4.50.

TREBARWITH SX0585 **Port William** *(01840) 770230* Fresh fish from local fishermen in this marvellously placed old harbourmaster's house (other good food, too), nautical decor, and lovely sunsets; bdrms; cl 25 Dec; disabled access. **£20**|£5.

TREBURLEY SX3477 **Springer Spaniel** *(01579) 370424* Lovely relaxed atmosphere in main-road pub with totally home-made interesting food inc delicious puddings (some home-grown produce), very friendly service, simply furnished bars, well kept real ales, and attractive no smoking restaurant. **£20**|£4.50.

Isles of Scilly

The islands, about 30 miles west of Land's End, are charmingly unspoilt and a great place for utter relaxation. They have beautiful scenery, an almost subtropical climate, and a variety of shorelines giving excellent coastal walks. In a lazy day you can comfortably walk round the largest, St Mary's, which is just 6 square miles. Tresco and St Agnes are the other main populated ones, though that means small undeveloped communities rather than any towns or big settlements. There are over 100 islands in all, some just strange-shaped rocks jutting out of the sea, their only visitors seals, dolphins and puffins.

You can get there from Penzance by ferry (around £30 day return) or more spectacularly by helicopter, a 20-minute ride with really beautiful views of the Cornish coast and of the islands (return fares start at around £60). The islands also have their own little airline Skybus which leaves from Land's End, Newquay or Exeter several times a day. The trip from Land's End is quickest and cheapest (from £40 return; no flights Sun). They also do packages in conjunction with InterCity – (01736) 787017 for details.

Where to stay

TRESCO SV8915 **Island** *Tresco, Isles of Scilly TR24 0PU (01720) 422883* **£258 inc dinner;** 48 rms, many with balconies and terrace overlooking gardens or sea. Tiny private island, renowned for its wonderful subtropical Abbey Gardens and reached by helicopter or boat – hotel's tractor-drawn bus (no cars allowed though bike hire available) takes you to spacious, very friendly modern hotel with colonial-style bar, library, fine food and wine, panoramic views, swimming pool, and private beach; cl Nov–Feb; no dogs.

HUGH TOWN SV9010 **Tregarthens** *Hugh Town, St Mary's, Isles of Scilly TR21 0PP (01720) 422540* **142 inc dinner;** 33 rms, most with sea views. Magnificent views over the harbour and outer islands of Samson, Bryher and Tresco from this extended and modernised hotel, first opened in 1848; neatly kept rooms, good food and pleasant service; cl late Oct–mid-Mar; no dogs.

PELISTRY BAY SV9311 **Carnwethers Country House** *Pelistry Bay, St Mary's, Isles of Scilly TR21 0NX (01720) 422415* ***£94 inc dinner** (good-value weekly terms, too); 9 rms. Well run no smoking country guesthouse nr very fine beach, with an acre of lovely gardens, heated swimming pool, and croquet; lounge with helpful books about the islands, well stocked bar, good freshly cooked set 4-course dinner using local produce served at 6.30pm, sound wine list, and games room with pool table and table tennis; sauna; lots of coastal walks; cl Oct–Apr; children over 8.

Special thanks to Dave and Deborah Irving, Annabella Martin, Mrs N Holtum, Mrs L Phillips, Mr and Mrs W Crawford, Dr A J Dobson, Ian and Jacqui Ross, Mrs S Bagnall.

Please let us know what you think of places in the *Guide*. Use the report forms at the back of the book or simply write us a letter.

To see and do

As each of the islands is so small, few apart from Tresco have many specific attractions – visitors come mainly to 'get away from it all', and there can be a refreshing feeling of complete isolation. By far the best activity is walking – there are plenty of white sandy beaches to stroll along (the sea is clean but cold), or unusual plants and birds to track down. Hiring bikes is another good way of exploring and enjoying the scenery. Thanks to the climate – the name means Sun Isles – flowers come out early, and spring and autumn sunsets can be particularly beautiful. A good plan is to island-hop – there are regular ferries between the larger islands, though it can prove expensive. Every Fri evening and some Weds in summer you can watch the racing of the traditional 6-oar gigs that used to dash out to shipwrecks.

❋ **BRYHER** SV8715 A tiny quiet place, even by Scilly standards. The S bay has lots of wild flowers, and Watch Hill has wonderful views. The Hell Bay Hotel is good value.

❋ **ST AGNES** SV8708 The most south-westerly community in the British Isles, joined to a smaller island called Gugh by a sandbar, awash at high tide. The sheltered cove here is especially popular. The 17th-c lighthouse is the second oldest in Britain. The views from here out to the rocks and islets are very atmospheric especially when you remember more ships have been wrecked here than anywhere comparable in the world.

❋ **ST MARTIN'S** SV9315 A narrow rocky ridge with flowers stretching down to the main attraction – the extensive beaches, very popular for picnics. There's a diving school, and the St Martin's Hotel has lovely sunset views.

ST MARY'S SV9010 The hub of Scilly Isles life, though its centre, Hugh Town, is little more than a village by mainland standards. Most ferries and planes arrive here, and you can get **pleasure cruises** from the Old Quay out to the bird and seal colonies on the outer islets and islands; there are fishing trips from here too. There's a **Museum**, and 9-hole putting green with fine views. The **Longstone Papers Past Exhibition** has a huge collection of archive newspapers; open am Mon–Fri, May–Aug; free. The Bishop & Wolf is a pleasant pub, and the Atlantic Hotel has a good pub part. Up in the N at Bant's Carn there's a burial chamber and ancient village. Back down S, walk out to Peninnis Head for good views of the Wolf and Bishop's Rock lighthouses. Just along the coast is **Star Castle**.

TRESCO SV8914 The highlight here is the amazing **subtropical garden** around the grounds of the abbey, begun in 1834, which, despite storms, contains a magnificent collection of exotic plants, bananas even. Also in these grounds is **Valhalla**, a collection of carved figureheads from wrecked ships, many dating back to the 17th c. Helicopters from Penzance land just outside the garden gate, so it's possible (though not cheap) to come here for just a day. The southern parts of the island are mainly sandy, but in the north it's more wild and rugged, with the remains of castles of both Charles I and Oliver Cromwell, and a cave known as Piper's Hole. Cycling and walking are real pleasures – not least because there aren't any cars. The New Inn, embellished with a mystery cargo of pine planking which washed ashore recently, has good food inc seafood.

Where to eat

ST AGNES SV8807 **Turks Head** *The Quay, Isles of Scilly (01720) 422434* Idyllically placed pub (a pleasant place to stay) with outstanding views over sweeping bay, real ales, decent wines, good food inc fresh fish, cream cakes/ices all afternoon, evening barbecues; you can take food down to the beach; cl Nov–Feb; disabled access. **£16**|£5.50.

Cornwall Calendar

Some of these dates were provisional as we went to press. Please check information with the telephone numbers provided.

JANUARY

1 **Bodmin** Brown Willy Run (01326) 317534; **Mawnan Smith** Trebah Icicle: charity swim at Trebah Garden (01326) 250448; **St Ives** Exhibition: works from the collection, and *An Artist's Project*: Eric Cameron at the Tate Gallery – *till end Apr* (01736) 796226

25 **Saltash** Music & Speech Festival – *till Fri 29, also 1–5 Feb* (01752) 843073

FEBRUARY

8 **St Ives** Hurling the Silver Ball: the town and its people are divided in two and *at midday* a ball is thrown by the mayor from the town hall into the crowd below who carry, fight or secrete the ball to their own half (01736) 797840

13 **Mawnan Smith** Dinosaur Trail at Trebah Garden – *till Sun 21* (01326) 250448

16 **St Columb Major** Hurling the Silver Ball: town and country residents battle in the streets with shop windows boarded up; the town goal is a small stone trough and the country goal is 1m N on the road to Wadebridge – *also Sat 27* (01872) 274057

27 **Wadebridge** Music & Speech Festival *also 5–7 Mar* (01208) 863731

MARCH

5 St Piran's Day: various processions and church services in honour of the patron saint of Cornish tinners; **Newquay** British Surfing Association Championships – *till Sun 7* (01736) 360250

7 **Mawnan Smith** Daffy Down Dilly Day at Trebah Garden (01326) 250448

8 **Truro** County Music Festival – *till Sat 13* (01872) 573338

13 **Perranporth** Land Yachting Regatta – *till Sun 14* (01326) 376191

17 **Cornwall** Festival of Spring Gardens: over 70 gardens open – *till end May* (01872) 274057

21 **Truro** Wildlife Photographer of the Year at the Royal Cornwall Museum – *till 25 Apr* (01872) 272205

27 **Falmouth** Spring Flower Show – *till Sun 28* (01326) 311277

APRIL

1 **Mawnan Smith** Easter Egg Hunt at Trebah Garden – *till Sun 18* (01326) 250448

2 **Bodmin** Thomas the Tank Engine at Bodmin General Station – *till Mon 5* (01208) 73666; **Marazion** Windsurfing National Racing Championship – *till Mon 5* (01705) 468182

4 **St Endellion** Easter Music Festival – *till Sun 11* (01208) 850463

5 **Helston** Easter Celebration at Flambards Village (01326) 573404

6 **Hayle and Gwithian** British Wave Championship – *till Sun 11* (01705) 468182

16 **Mevagissey** Festival of Flowers at the Lost Gardens of Heligan – *till Sun 18* (01726) 845100; **Padstow** Fish Festival *till Sun 18* (01841) 533449

Cornwall Calendar (cont.)

24 **Camborne** Trevithick Day: traction engine rally, traditional Cornish dancing, street parades (01209) 712941

30 **Boscastle** Beer Festival and Duck Race – *till 3 May* (01840) 250202

MAY

1 **Newquay** English National Surfing Championships – *till Mon 3* (01271) 890421; **Newquay** Great Cornwall Balloon Festival – *till Sun 2* (01637) 872211; **Padstow** Obby Oss Celebrations: May song, man in large full-skirted horse costume with other strangely dressed characters (01841) 533449; **St Mary's** Isles of Scilly World Pilot Gig Championships – *till Mon 3* (01720) 422536

3 **Calstock** Revels (01822) 834418

7 **Fowey and St Austell** Daphne du Maurier Festival of Arts & Literature – *till Sun 16* (01726) 274324

8 **Helston** Flora Day: from early morning dance *at 8.20am*, with Hal-an-Tow and ancient Furry Dance later (01326) 565431

9 **Bodmin Moor** Ten Tors Walk (01208) 72793

15 **Bude** March *at 10.30am* preceding re-enactment of the Battle of Stamford Hill (1643) at **Stratton** – *till Sun 16* (01288) 354886

17 Betjeman Week (tours to various venues) – *till Fri 21* (01726) 66232

20 **Wall** Music Festival – *till Sat 22* (01736) 850420

27 **Porthcurno** Minack Theatre Festival – *till mid-Sept* (01736) 810181

28 **Calstock** Festival – *till 5 Jun* (01822) 832653

29 **Newquay** Surfing Festival – *till Mon 31* (01736) 360250; **Truro** Exhibition: Matisse; and Jazz at the Royal Cornwall Museum – *till 27 Jun* (01872) 272205

30 **Bodmin** Steam & Diesel Gala at Bodmin General Station – *till Mon 31* (01208) 73666; **Launceston** Steam Engine Rally – *till Mon 31* (01566) 776544

JUNE

6 **Mawnan Smith** D-Day Commemoration at Trebah Garden (01326) 250448

10 **Wadebridge** Royal Cornwall Show – *till Sat 12* (01208) 812183

17 **Penzance** Golowan Festival: traditional sea and land festival, with theatre, street theatre, Celtic arts, carnival and fireworks, with Mazey Eve on *Fri 25* and Mazey Day *on Sat 26* – *till Sun 27* (01736) 332211

19 **Mawnan Smith** Midsummer Music Festival at Trebah Garden (01326) 250448; **Redruth** Murdoch Day: street entertainment – *till Sun 20* (01209) 210038

21 **Liskeard** Carnival Week – *till Sat 26* (01579) 341343

26 **Bodmin** Cornwall Theatre & Heritage Festival – *till 3 July* (01208) 787975

27 **Mevagissey** Feast Week – *till 3 July* (01726) 74014

30 **Truro** Jazz Festival – *till 4 July* (01872) 222202

JULY

3 **Bodmin** Riding & Heritage Day (01208) 76616; **Bude** Surf & Rock: rock festival and surfing competition – *till Sun 4* (01736) 360250

4 **Newquay** 1900 Week: Victorian entertainments inc processions, flora dance, fireworks – *till Fri 9* (01637) 878735

Cornwall Calendar (cont.)

10 **Merrymeet** Liskeard Country Show at Trengrove Farm (01579) 343125; **St Austell** White Gold Festival: street entertainment, clay dances, art and musical events – *till Sat 17* (01726) 74269
12 **Stithians** Show (01872) 240113
14 **St Day** Feast Day Celebrations (01209) 820639
15 **Launceston** Agricultural Show at Kennards House (01566) 777777
17 **Camborne** Show (01209) 842228; **Lanhydrock** Jazz in the Park at Lanhydrock House (01208) 73320
27 **St Endellion** Summer Music Festival – *till 6 Aug* (01208) 850463

AUGUST

1 **Falmouth** Carnival Week – *till Sat 7* (01326) 319126; Contemporary Art at Falmouth Art Gallery to coincide with the eclipse of the sun (01326) 313863
2 **Helston** Blues Brothers Firework Show at Flambards Village – *also Weds 11, Mon 16, Mon 23 and Mon 30* (01326) 573404
4 **St Keverne** Ox Roast inc torchlight procession (01326) 280487
6 **Tintagel** Re-enactment of the Battle of Camlann (AD 450): field opens *at 2pm – till Sun 8* (01840) 770050
7 **Falmouth** Regatta Week inc parade of old wooden sailing boats – *till Sat 14* (01326) 211555; **Newquay** RAF St Mawgan International Air Day (01637) 872201; **Paignton** Regatta – *till Mon 16* (01803) 558383
9 **Marhamchurch** Revels: procession and country dancing (01288) 361391
11 **Camelford** Agricultural Show (01840) 213761; **Cornwall** Total Eclipse of the Sun (01872) 274057
14 **Bude** Carnival (01288) 355100
15 **Fowey** Royal Regatta and Carnival Week – *till Sat 21* (01726) 832047
20 **St Agnes** West of England Steam Engine Society Rally – *till Sun 22* (01872) 74057
26 **Newquay** British National Surfing Championships – *till Mon 30* (01736) 360250
27 **Bodmin** Thomas the Tank Engine at Bodmin General Station – *till Mon 30* (01208) 73666; **Wadebridge** Folk Festival *till Mon 30* (01208) 831123
28 **Looe** Vintage Steam Rally at Bray Farm, Normansland – *till Mon 30* (01503) 240520; **Newquay** Surfers Against Sewage Ocean Festival – *till Mon 30* (01872) 553001; **Penryn** Town Fair (01326) 374763
28 **Bude** Jazz Festival: over 150 events, mostly trad jazz with street parades – *till 4 Sept* (01288) 356360
29 **Stithians** Cornish Game & Country Fair (01872) 273366
30 **Bude** Lifeboat Day (01288) 355100; **Newlyn** Fish Festival (01736) 363499; **Ruan Minor** Kennack Sands Horse Show (01326) 290824

SEPTEMBER

4 **Bodmin** Thomas the Tank Engine at Bodmin General Station – *till Sun 5* (01208) 73666; **Hayle** Cornish Gorsedd: celebration of the Cornish language inc traditional dancing and bards (01726) 833402; **Helston** Harvest Fair – *till Mon 6* (01326) 563167; **Mawnan Smith** Seafood Festival at Trebah Garden – *till Sun 5* (01326) 250448
11 **Lanlivery** Vintage Rally and Country Fair – *till Sun 12* (01208) 873986
13 **St Ives** Festival: folk, jazz and poetry – *till Sat 25* (01736) 796883

Cornwall Calendar (cont.)

18 **Mawnan Smith** Plant Sale at Trebah Garden – *till Sun 19* (01326) 250448

OCTOBER

6 **Callington** Honey Fair; ancient street fair (01579) 350230
13 **Perranporth** Lowender Peran Celtic Festival at Ponsmere Hotel: Cornish folk culture – *till Sun 17* (01872) 553413
23 **Mawnan Smith** Halloween Horror Trail at Trebah Garden – *till Sun 31* (01326) 250448
30 **Helston** Halloween Firework Display at Flambards Village – *till Sun 31* (01326) 573404

NOVEMBER

10 **Camelford** Carnival (01840) 212200
15 **Camborne** Music Festival – *till Sat 20* (01209) 711455
24 **St Austell** Music & Speech Festival – *till Sat 27, also Mon 29–Dec 4* (01726) 72982

DECEMBER

12 **Mawnan Smith** Santa Trail at Trebah Garden – *also Sun 19 and Weds 22* (01326) 250448
23 **Mousehole** Tom Bawcock's Eve: trad event with lamplit boats and stargazey pie to celebrate the man who saved the town from starving by going out in a storm to catch fish (01326) 312300

We welcome reports from readers

This *Guide* depends on readers' reports. Do help us if you can – in return, we offer a discount on the next edition to people who've helped us with reports for it. Tell us what you think about places already in it, and anything extra you think we should say about them. And send us your ideas for inclusion in the next edition: places to visit, eat at or stay in, attractive drives or walks, maybe even unusual interesting shops you know of. Use the card in the middle, the report forms at the end, or just write – no stamp needed: *The Good Guide to Britain*, FREEPOST TN1569, Wadhurst, E Sussex TN5 7BR.

Cumbria

England's most beautiful area (and highest mountains); outstanding access to the countryside, excellent places to stay in, masses of interest for all ages.

The most beautiful landscapes are concentrated thickly around the central area, especially around Ambleside and Windermere. Both places are quite intensively developed for visitors and very busy indeed in summer; Keswick too has lots going on for all ages. These parts really come into their own at quieter times of year – you need a degree of peace and quiet to enjoy the beauty of the delicious central area between Windermere and Grasmere.

There's tremendous variety among the lakes and the hills around them. Windermere, the longest and busiest lake, has always been a general favourite; it's picturesquely dotted with villas built by Victorian magnates, and has masses of accommodation on its east side. Ullswater approaches the grandeur of Scottish lochs, and has some excellent (if not cheap) places to stay right by the lake shore; Buttermere and Crummock Water also have scenery on the grand scale, perhaps without quite matching Ullswater's scenic perfection. Derwent Water wavers charmingly between highland and lowland in flavour, and its islands and manageable proportions make it a favourite for idle boating as well as for bankside strolls. Coniston Water, quite well wooded, also appeals to both boaters and walkers, with some fine views – in some ways it's a junior version of Windermere, smaller and quieter. Wast Water, England's deepest lake, is austere, surrounded by towering screes. Bassenthwaite Lake is altogether gentler, lowland in feel. Some much smaller lakes, notably Grasmere, Rydal Water and Elterwater, are idyllic.

The National Trust controls over a quarter of the land in the Lake District National Park. So preservation of and access to the countryside here is first class (and it's an area where membership of the Trust really pays off in terms of free admission).

The best coastal scenery is around Morecambe Bay in the south. The west coast is untouristy, with miles of unfrequented beaches (as well as some run-down-looking places, and the big nuclear power plant at Seascale, which has an excellent visitor centre).

There are lots of interesting places to visit, including many good craft shops. We'd recommend a look at Hawkshead, Troutbeck and Cartmel, and among the many other places of interest we'd pick out the great houses and impressive gardens of Holker Hall at Cark-in-Cartmel, Levens Hall and Sizergh Castle (all in the south), Muncaster Castle in the west, and, towards the north, Dalemain House at Dacre, friendly Mirehouse near Bassenthwaite, and Hutton-in-the-Forest at Skelton. Many of these are given special charm by a degree of intimacy and personal contact that's missing from many places further south – and this is particularly true of smaller houses, such as Townend at Troutbeck, or those connected with literary figures. The Wordsworth trail at Grasmere and Rydal is heavily trodden in summer, but extremely well managed; specially rewarding at quieter times. The bobbin mill at Finsthwaite is surprisingly interesting, Ravenglass has a fine steam railway, and the Maryport steamships are intriguing.

Cumbria is very good territory for children who get a kick out of doing outdoor things. Families who need more in the way of amusements laid on have tended to enjoy other areas more, but the growing list of enjoyable family attractions here is now reaching a level where there's really plenty to keep most children entertained. Some particularly good places (which many adults like too) are the Lakeside Aquatarium, well organised farm centres at Morland, Bassenthwaite and a new one (with ostriches) at Langwathby, the wildlife parks at Milnthorpe and Dalton-in-Furness, the cheery sheep centre near Cockermouth, and perhaps the vast collection of reptiles at Amazonia in Bowness. Many young children very much enjoy the Beatrix Potter centre in Windermere, and the Lowther Leisure Park at Hackthorpe will keep most amused for the best part of a full day.

Among such a wealth of what one might call 'classic' visitor attractions, the few less conventional ones, such as the Seascale nuclear visitor centre and the Buddhist temple at Ulverston, stand out all the more strikingly; and Whitehaven's heritage centre, the Beacon, is fascinating for anyone with a weather obsession – all too easy to acquire in Lakeland.

You could stay here for weeks every year of your life and never walk the same path twice – so our walks' suggestions are really just initial pointers. Also, many of the recommended places to stay here have been chosen for the grand walks right from their doorsteps. There's an excellent choice of places to stay, many of which serve really good food. We have gone out of our way to recommend places that are strong on peace and quiet; there's a splendid range of styles and prices.

For a quiet break with plenty of walking easily accessible, the Langdales, particularly Great Langdale, and Borrowdale are outstanding. The west is even quieter, separated from the central Lake District by high ridges with tortuous roads over the few passes. British rock-climbing was born over here, with England's highest mountain, Scafell Pike, surrounded by other awesome peaks – serious walking country.

Another area where you can reckon on peace and quiet even in summer is the part east of the M6. This is one of England's least-known areas, and though overshadowed by the Lake District proper has a lot of charm, and some excellent-value places to stay in. Quiet river valleys shelter below more dramatic open country and high moors, and there are some attractive and untouristy places to visit. Much of the high country is too bleak and boggy for most walkers, but moorland roads give drivers good views (e.g. the A683 Kirkby Lonsdale–Kirkby Stephen, B6260 Tebay–Appleby, B6413 Lazonby–Brampton, A689 Brampton–Alston roads). The railway crossing the moors between Carlisle and Settle is perhaps the best way of all of seeing this unusual part of England.

Lakeland generally is at its best out of season. May (sheets of wild flowers on the hills) and June are ideal: more sun, no crowds. The views are often clearest (and the ground firm and dry for walkers) in October and November, though afternoons are short then. In the summer holidays and at other peak times, crowds make the best places less enjoyable, and indeed put a real strain on the environment. If you're determined to go at that time of year, you've more chance of finding peace in the west, or over by the Pennines, east of the M6. For all but the hardiest and expert outdoorsmen, winter up here is too bleak for pleasure – unless you plan to stay indoors. Whenever you come, bring something waterproof – the Lake District has more annual rainfall than any other part of the country.

Public transport in the Lakes is good and useful for round-trip long walks; information service (01228) 812812. Local information leaflets offer plenty of choice of well guided walks; information too from National Park visitor services (01539) 446601, and from the flourishing Cumbria Wildlife Trust (01539) 432476, which controls many reserves. Bicycles can be hired by the day in the main towns (considering the scenic grandeur, you can cycle for a surprisingly long way, at least in the central area, without having to struggle up steep hills). Many places offer riding: around £10 an hour for adults, £8 for children.

Where to stay

ALSTON NY7246 **Lovelady Shield** *Nenthead Rd, Alston CA9 3LF (01434) 381203* **£163 inc dinner,** plus special breaks; 12 rms. In a lovely setting with the River Nent running along the bottom of the garden (tennis and croquet), this handsome country house has a tranquil atmosphere, courteous staff, and log fires in the comfortable rooms (no smoking in sitting room or restaurant); very good food inc fine breakfasts; cl Jan; dogs by prior arrangement.

AMBLESIDE NY3804 **Rothay Manor** *Rothay Bridge (Coniston Rd), Ambleside LA22 0EH (015394) 33605* **£170 inc dinner,** plus special breaks; 18 attractive rms, many overlooking garden. Family-run, Regency-style country house in neatly kept, mature grounds; log fires and fresh flowers in the quietly civilised, comfortable day rooms, very good English food in the no smoking dining room, a thoughtful wine list, super big breakfasts, and helpful, friendly service; windsurfing/waterskiing, etc, close by, free use of nearby leisure club; cl Jan; good disabled access.

AMBLESIDE NY3804 **Rowanfield Country House** *Kirkstone Rd, Ambleside LA22 9ET (015394) 33686* ***£60,** plus special breaks. 7 rms. Charming, carefully restored Lakeland house looking across Lake Windermere to the distant hills; with a woodburner in the comfortable and attractively furnished sitting room, enjoyable and interesting food at 7pm in the flagstoned and candlelit dining room (bring your own wine), super breakfasts, and friendly owners; cl mid-Nov–Mar, but open Christmas and New Year; children over 8.

AMBLESIDE NY3804 **Wateredge** *Borrans Rd LA22 0EP (015394) 32332* ***£104,** plus special breaks; 22 good, comfortable rms. Beautifully placed, warmly welcoming hotel with neat gardens running down to Lake Windermere (embarkation point for cruising the lake); light and airy lounges, good meals in the cosy, beamed, no smoking dining room, and excellent service; cl mid-Dec–mid-Jan; children over 7; dogs by prior arrangement.

APPLEBY NY6921 **Appleby Manor** *Roman Rd, Appleby CA16 6JB (01768) 351571* ***£122,** plus special breaks; 30 well equipped rms in original house (the nicest), coach house annexe or modern wing. Very friendly, family-run hotel with fine views over Appleby Castle and the Eden Valley; log fire in one of the 3 comfortable lounges, relaxed bar with a wide range of whiskies, excellent service, and good, interesting food in the panelled restaurant; also, a leisure centre; cl 25–26 Dec; disabled access.

BARBON SD6282 **Barbon Inn** *Barbon, Carnforth LA6 2LJ (015242) 76233* **£60;** 10 simple but comfortable rms, some with own bthrm. Small, friendly village inn in a quiet spot below the fells; relaxing bar, traditional lounge, good meals in the candlelit dining room, and helpful service.

BASSENTHWAITE LAKE NY1930 **Pheasant** *Bassenthwaite Lake, Cockermouth CA13 9YE (017687) 76234* **£90,** plus special breaks; 20 rms. Civilised hotel with a delightfully old-fashioned pubby bar, restful lounges with open fires, antiques, fresh flowers and comfortable armchairs; interesting gardens merging into the surrounding fellside woodlands; cl pm 24 Dec, 25 Dec; disabled access.

BORROWDALE NY2413 **Seatoller House** *Borrowdale, Keswick CA12 5XN (017687) 77218* ***£58;** 9 spotless, comfortable rms. Friendly house-party atmosphere in this 17th-c house that has been a guesthouse for over 100 years; self-service drinks and board games in the comfortable lounges (no TV), and a good no-choice, fixed-time, hearty dinner (not Tues) served at 2 big oak tables; packed lunches; 2 acres of grounds and many walks from the doorstep as the house is at the foot of Honister Pass; cl Nov–Mar; children over 5.

BOWLAND BRIDGE SD4289 **Hare & Hounds** *Bowland Bridge, Grange-over-Sands LA11 6NN (015395) 68333* **£50,** plus special breaks; 15 attractive rms, mostly with own bthrm. Friendly, extended village inn below the fells; with a welcoming landlord (ex-international soccer player), log fires, beams and stone walls in the lounge bar, a cosy residents' lounge, open fires, and a sheltered garden.

BOWNESS SD4097 **Linthwaite House** *Crook Rd, Bowness-on-Windermere, Windermere LA23 3JA (015394) 88600* **£130,** plus special breaks; 18 individually decorated rms, some with lake views. Stunningly set Lakeland house in 14 acres of immaculate gardens overlooking Lake Windermere, and with their own tarn fishing; comfortable, stylish furnishings in the engaging day rooms, an easy-going atmosphere, very good service, and most enjoyable, modern British cooking in the cosy candlelit restaurant; croquet, putting, golf practice hole; children over 7 in evening restaurant; disabled access.

BRAMPTON NY5361 **Farlam Hall** *Hallbankgate, Brampton (on the A689 S) CA8 2NG (016977) 46234* ***£220 inc dinner,** plus special breaks; 12 comfortable rms. Charmingly Victorian (though parts are much older) and very civilised country house with log fires in the spacious lounges, and excellent, attentive service; good 4-course dinner, marvellous breakfasts, and peaceful, spacious grounds with a croquet lawn and a small pretty lake; cl Christmas–New Year; children over 5; dogs by prior arrangement.

BRANDLINGILL NY1626 **Low Hall** *Brandlingill, Cockermouth CA11 0RE (01900) 826654* **£60;** 3 pleasant rms. Beautifully sited, partly 17th-c farmhouse below Whinlatter Pass and close to Cockermouth; with a big, peaceful garden, log fires and books in the lounges, and super farmhouse breakfasts inc 20 different teas, home-made oatcakes, muesli, and preserves; no smoking; children over 10.

BUTTERMERE NY1817 **Bridge Hotel** *Buttermere, Cockermouth CA13 9UZ (017687) 70252* ***£96,** plus special breaks; 22 rms. Comfortable hotel surrounded by some of the best steep countryside in the county; with a beamed bar (the flagstoned part is popular with walkers), log fire and deep armchairs in the sitting room, and good food in both the bar and no smoking restaurant; real ales, decent malt whiskies, and a friendly atmosphere; self-catering also.

CARLISLE NY4056 **Number Thirty-one Howard Place** *31 Howard Pl, Carlisle CA1 1HR (01228) 597080* ***£60;** 3 well equipped, individually decorated rms. Carefully restored, no smoking Victorian townhouse with a relaxed and informal atmosphere, open fire and plenty of books in the cosy lounge, and delicious, interesting food using the best local produce; breakfast with home-baked bread, home-made preserves and home-made Cumberland sausages; and helpful, courteous owners; cl Dec–Mar; no children.

CARTMEL SD3879 **Uplands** *Haggs Lane, Cartmel, Grange-over-Sands LA11 6HD (015395) 36248* **£142 inc dinner,** plus special breaks; 5 pretty rms. Comfortable Edwardian house in 2 acres of garden with views over towards Morecambe Bay; attractively decorated rooms, and helpful service; the main draw is undoubtedly the richly imaginative food in the no smoking dining room; cl 1 Jan–1 Mar; children over 8; well behaved dogs welcome.

CASTERTON SD6379 **Pheasant** *Casterton, Carnforth LA6 2RX (015242) 71230* **£68**, plus special breaks; 10 comfortable rms, most with countryside views. Small civilised inn with a pleasant atmosphere, a cosy residents' lounge, no smoking garden lounge, and cheerful staff; good food in the panelled dining room, and a small but sound wine list; dogs allowed; disabled access.

CATLOWDY NY4677 **Bessiestown Farm** *Catlowdy, Longtown, Carlisle CA6 5QP (01228) 577219* **£47;** 4 rms. Friendly farmhouse (mainly no smoking) on a small beef and sheep-rearing farm close to the Scottish Borders; with 2 comfortable lounges, good home-made food and big breakfasts in attractive dining room, indoor heated swimming pool, and a games room; self-catering also; well behaved children.

CROOK SD4695 **Wild Boar** *Crook, Windermere LA23 3NF (015394) 45225* ***£82;** 36 rms. Comfortable, well run, extended hotel with period furnishings and log fires at its ancient core; attentive service, and good food in the no smoking dining room; free access to the nearby leisure club and discounts on watersports.

CROSBY ON EDEN NY4559 **Crosby Lodge** *High Crosby, Crosby on Eden, Carlisle CA6 4QZ (01228) 573618* ***£100,** plus wknd breaks; 11 spacious rms (2 in stable conversion). Imposing and carefully converted country house in attractive, mature grounds; with comfortable and appealing individual furnishings, a good choice of tasty food in both the bar and no smoking restaurant, and friendly, long-established owners; surrounded by nice countryside; cl 24 Dec–mid-Jan; limited disabled access.

DENT SD7187 **Sportsmans** *Cowgill, Dent, Sedbergh LA10 5RG (01539) 625282* **£44;** 6 rms with shared bthrm. Unassuming, comfortable pub notable for its wonderful position in Dentdale by the River Dee, with the viaduct of the Settle–Carlisle railway close by, and walks in all directions; open log fires and good-value, home-made food; well behaved dogs allowed.

DOCKRAY NY3921 **Royal** *Dockray, Matterdale, Penrith CA11 0TT (017684) 82356* **£58,** plus special breaks; 10 rms. Friendly, family-run hotel with open fires in the big, modernised, open-plan bar, good-value, hearty meals, and well kept beers; in a fine spot between hills and lake, with walks from the doorstep; children must be well behaved; partial disabled access.

ELTERWATER NY3305 **Britannia Inn** *Elterwater, Ambleside LA22 9HP (015394) 37210* ***£70,** plus winter breaks; 13 rms, most with shower, some in quiet annexe opposite. Simple, charmingly traditional pub in fine surroundings opposite the village green; happy, friendly atmosphere, hearty home cooking inc superb breakfast, comfortable no smoking lounge and a bustling bar, real ales; pleasant walks; cl 25 Dec, pm 26 Dec; well behaved dogs allowed.

ESKDALE GREEN NY1400 **Bower House** *Eskdale Green, Holmbrook CA19 1TD (019467) 23244* **£64,** plus wknd breaks; 24 comfortable rms, some in annexe. Relaxed and pleasantly isolated old stone inn with a nicely tended, sheltered garden; lounge bar with a log fire and a separate one with sofas and easy chairs, several bar rooms; popular, good-value food inc wonderful puddings, a no smoking restaurant, and friendly staff; disabled access.

FAR SAWREY SD3893 **Sawrey** *Far Sawrey, Ambleside LA22 0LQ (015394) 43425* ***£58;** 18 rms. Friendly hotel, well placed at the foot of Claife Heights; with simple pubby and smarter bars, friendly staff, decent, straightforward food, and seats on a pleasant lawn with good views of Lake Windermere; cl Christmas; kind to children; dogs allowed; partial disabled access.

GARRIGILL NY7441 **Crossgill Farmhouse** *Garrigill, Alston CA9 3HE (01434) 381383* **£40;** 3 rms, 2 with own bthrm. 18th-c, former-shooting lodge on a hill overlooking the River Tyne; with an open fire in the lounge, good home cooking, and friendly owners; no evening meal pm Weds; no smoking; cl Apr and Christmas.
GARRIGILL NY7441 **George & Dragon** *Garrigill, Alston CA9 3DS (01434) 381293* **£37;** 4 small rms, shared bthrm, but clean and comfortable. Friendly 17th-c pub on a dead-end road in beautiful countryside; with an informal, flagstoned bar, stone and panelled dining room, a log fire in the lovely fireplace, and good service; children over 10.
GRANGE-OVER-SANDS SD4077 **Graythwaite Manor** *Fernhill Rd, Grange-over-Sands LA11 7JE (015395) 32001* ***£85,** plus special breaks; 21 individually furnished rms, many with fine views. Set in flower-filled landscaped gardens with views over Morecambe Bay, this comfortable hotel (run by the same family since 1937) has a particularly relaxed and friendly atmosphere; elegantly furnished lounges with flowers and antiques, open fires, and carefully prepared food in the attractive, no smoking dining room; cl 4–22 Jan; no dogs; disabled access.
GRASMERE NY3406 **Michael's Nook** *Grasmere, Ambleside LA22 9RP (015394) 35496* **£170 inc dinner,** plus winter breaks; 14 lovely rms. Beautifully furnished hotel with fine antiques, paintings and rugs (the owner is a former antiques' dealer); lovely flowers, comfortable sofas by open fires in the cosy bar or elegant drawing room, and excellent food; landscaped garden with specimen rhododendrons, and good walks; also, Great Danes and exotic cats; free use of indoor pool and health facilities at the nearby Wordsworth Hotel (under the same ownership, and listed below); children by arrangement, but no under-7s in evening restaurant.
GRASMERE NY3406 **Swan** *Grasmere, Ambleside LA22 9RF (015394) 35551* **£78;** 36 rms, most with fine views. Smart and friendly 17th-c hotel in beautiful fell-foot surroundings; with beams and inglenooks, an elegant, no smoking dining room, and an attractive garden; lovely walks; partial disabled access.
GRASMERE NY3406 **Wordsworth** *Grasmere, Ambleside LA22 9SW (015394) 35592* **£179,** plus special breaks; 37 comfortable, pretty rms. Well run hotel, right in the village and next to the churchyard where Wordsworth is buried; stylish lounges and airy restaurant overlooking landscaped gardens, a relaxed conservatory and popular pubby bar, friendly service, enjoyable food; heated indoor pool, mini-gym and sauna; good disabled access.
GRIZEDALE SD3494 **Grizedale Lodge** *Hawkshead Hill, Grizedale, Ambleside LA22 0QL (015394) 36532* ***£75,** plus special breaks; 9 no smoking rms. Friendly, comfortable hotel in the middle of the magnificent Grizedale Forest, with lots of walks from the front door; log fire in the lounge bar, imaginative fresh food in the attractive restaurant, and big breakfasts; children under 5 provided with high tea at 5.30pm; disabled access.
HAWKSHEAD SD3598 **Drunken Duck** *Barngates, Hawkshead, Ambleside LA22 0NG (015394) 36347* **£75,** plus special breaks; 9 rms. Very friendly, popular inn alone in 60 hillside acres; with several cosy rooms, open fires, and views of Lake Windermere in the distance; home-brewed ales, good, interesting food, and a no smoking restaurant; fishing in private tarn; cl pm 25 Dec; limited disabled access.
HAWKSHEAd SD3598 **Highfield House** *Hawkshead Hill, Hawkshead, Ambleside LA22 0PN (015394) 36344* **£76,** plus winter breaks; 11 good rms. Welcoming Victorian country house set in a spacious woodland garden with fine views (good walks from the door); open fire in the comfortable lounge, a cosy bar, and generous food inc packed lunches and children's high tea; cl Jan.
IREBY NY2439 **Overwater Hall** *Ireby, Carlisle CA5 1HH (017687) 76566* **£84,** plus special breaks; 12 rms. Relaxed and friendly, family-run hotel in 18 acres of gardens and woodland; with a log fire in the elegant, comfortable drawing room, and good, imaginative food in the cosy dining room; lots of nearby walks; children over 7 in restaurant (high tea 5pm); well behaved dogs welcome; cl first 2 wks Jan.
KENDAL SD5293 **Low Jock Scar** *Selside (6m from Kendal), Kendal LA8 9LE (01539) 823259* ***£55;** 5 rms, most with own bthrm. Relaxed and friendly little

country guesthouse in 6 acres of garden and woodland; with a residents' lounge, and good home cooking (picnic lunches on request); no smoking; cl Nov–end Feb; children over 12.

KESWICK NY2618 **Shu-le-Crow** *7 Penrith Rd, Keswick CA12 4HF (017687) 75253* ***£38;** 3 attractive rms. Pink-washed, no smoking, 18th-c cottage with plenty of original features; cheerful owners who can advise on local walks, and super breakfasts (vegetarian options); plenty of places to eat nearby; no children.

KESWICK NY2618 **Stakis Lodore** *Derwent Water, Keswick CA12 5UX (017687) 77285* ***£116,** plus special breaks; 75 well equipped rms. Long-standing but well updated, big holiday hotel with lots of facilities in 40 acres of lakeside gardens and woodland; open fires in the comfortable day rooms, and an elegant restaurant; leisure club, tennis and squash, outdoor swimming pool, games room and lots for children such as a nursery with NNEB nannies, remote control cars, Sega computer games, babysitting, baby-listening service, and high teas; spacious self-catering house too.

KESWICK NY2624 **Swinside Lodge** *Newlands, Keswick CA12 5UE (017687) 72948* **£88,** plus special breaks; 7 comfortable rms. Victorian hotel in own grounds and surrounded by wonderful, unspoilt scenery at the foot of Catbells, and a few minutes from the shores of Derwent Water; with hearty breakfasts and super home-made evening meals in the candelit dining room, helpful, friendly service, and 2 relaxing sitting rooms; cl Dec–Jan; children over 12.

KIRKCAMBECK NY5269 **Cracrop Farm** *Kirkcambeck, Brampton CA8 2BW (016977) 48245* **£50;** 3 rms overlooking garden and open fields. Friendly Victorian farmhouse on 425 acres, with stock animals and very good marked farm trails (they are keen on conservation); comfortable and homely rooms, tasty, traditional breakfasts (other food arranged in advance), games room and sauna; no smoking; cl Christmas; children over 12.

LANERCOST NY5664 **Abbey Bridge** *Lanercost, Brampton CA8 2HG (016977) 2224* **£60;** 7 simple rms, most with own bthrm. Beautifully placed, small country inn, in a quiet spot nr the ancient priory; decent food in the informal, converted forge, which also houses a cheerful bar; pleasant staff; cl 25 Dec; disabled access.

LANGDALE NY2906 **Old Dungeon Ghyll** *Great Langdale, Ambleside LA22 9JY (015394) 37272* **£66,** plus special breaks; 15 rms, some with shared bthrm. Friendly, simple and cosy walkers' and climbers' inn, dramatically surrounded by fells, wonderful views and terrific walks; comfy residents' lounge and popular food – best to book for dinner if not a resident; cl 3 days over Christmas.

LINDALE SD4280 **Greenacres** *Lindale, Grange-over-Sands LA11 6LP (015395) 34578* ***£52,** plus special breaks; 5 appealing rms. Charming 19th-c cottage with a friendly atmosphere, pretty sitting room, conservatory, log fire, and good, home-made food and big breakfasts in the cosy dining room; packed lunches on request; cl Christmas–New Year.

LITTLE LANGDALE NY3204 **Three Shires** *Little Langdale, Ambleside LA22 9NZ (015394) 37215* **£72,** plus special breaks; 10 rms. Family-run, stone-built country inn with beautiful views; comfortably old-fashioned residents' part, and a separate walkers' bar with real ales; decent food, and pretty gardens; cl Jan.

LORTON NY1525 **New House Farm** *Lorton, Cockermouth CA13 9UU (01900) 85404* **£70,** plus special breaks; 4 rms with wonderful hillside views. Friendly, no smoking, 17th-c house (not a working farm) in 15 acres of grounds; with beams and rafters, flagstones and open fires, and 2 residents' lounges; very good food inc game and fish caught by the owner, home-made scones and preserves, and a thoughtful wine list; lots of nearby walks; children over 12.

MUNGRISDALE NY3731 **Mill Hotel** *Mungrisdale, Penrith CA11 0XR (017687) 79659* **£120 in dinner;** 9 rms, most with own bthrm. Very friendly, small streamside hotel, beautifully placed in a lovely valley hamlet hidden away below Blencathra; an open fire in the cosy and comfortable sitting room, good, imaginative 5-course evening meals, and a small, carefully chosen wine list; cl Nov–Feb; dogs welcome by arrangement; disabled access.

POOLEY BRIDGE NY4724 **Sharrow Bay** *Pooley Bridge, Penrith CA10 2LZ (017684) 86301* **£290 inc dinner;** 26 lovely rms with antiques, books, and games, mostly with own bthrm. Country house hotel in a quiet, idyllic spot by Ullswater; with lovely views of both the lake and mountains, and showing the years of loving care the owners have put into the distinctive style, furnishings and décor; unobtrusively attentive service and excellent English cooking in the 2 contrasting dining rooms; cl Dec–late Feb; no children.

RAVENSTONEDALE NY7204 **Fat Lamb** *Cross Bank, Ravenstonedale, Kirkby Stephen CA17 4LL (015396) 23242* **£60,** plus special breaks; 12 comfortable rms. Welcoming moorland inn set in beautiful open countryside; a log fire and good local photographs in the cheerfully modernised, 2-room bar, and decent food; 17 acres of land, 7 of which is nature reserve; very good disabled access.

RYDAL WATER NY3606 **White Moss House** *Rydal Water, Grasmere, Ambleside LA22 9SE (015394) 35295* **£144 inc dinner,** plus special breaks; 7 thoughtfully furnished rms in main house, plus separate cottage let as one unit with 2 rms. Bought by Wordsworth for his son, this attractive, stripped-stone country house, set in charming, mature grounds overlooking the lake, has a comfortable lounge, and fine, no-choice, 5-course meals in the pretty, no smoking dining room; also, an excellent wine list; free use of hotel rowing boat, free fishing and free use of local leisure club; cl Dec–Feb; not suitable for toddlers.

ST BEES NX9712 **Queens** *Main St, St Bees CA27 0DE (01946) 822287* **£45;** 15 rms. Set in an attractive village with a marvellous beach, this 17th-c hotel has 2 bars with real ales and over 100 whiskies; beams and log fires, generous helpings of good food in the dining room or no smoking conservatory, a garden with fine views, and friendly staff.

TALKIN NY5557 **Hullerbank** *Talkin, Brampton CA8 1LB (016977) 46668* **£42;** 3 rms. Comfortable and very friendly, no smoking, Georgian farmhouse in unspoilt countryside; with a relaxed atmosphere in the homely lounge, and good food using home-grown and local produce inc home-produced lamb (packed lunch on request); cl Christmas–New Year; children over 12.

THIRLMERE NY3116 **Dale Head Hall** *Thirlmere, Keswick CA12 4TN (017687) 72478* ***£80,** plus special breaks; 9 pretty rms, most with lake views. Peaceful, partly 16th-c country house in lovely lakeside grounds; with comfortable lounges, a log fire, friendly owners, and home-cooked food using produce grown in own walled garden; children over 10 for evening meals; cl Jan.

TIRRIL NY5126 **Queens Head** *Tirril, Penrith CA10 2JF (01768) 863219* **£45,** plus special breaks; 7 lovely rms, most with own bthrm. Bustling inn with flagstones and exposed floorboards in the bar; a spacious back restaurant (mostly no smoking), low beams, black panelling, an inglenook fireplace and old-fashioned settles in the older part; interesting food inc snacks and OAP specials, and well kept real ales.

TROUTBECK NY4103 **Mortal Man** *Troutbeck, Windermere LA22 3PL (015394) 33193* **£122 inc dinner;** 14 rms. Spotlessly kept, relaxing inn surrounded by marvellous scenery; with a partly panelled bustling bar, big open fire, dark beams, and picture windows in the restaurant; well kept real ales, good food, lovely breakfasts, and friendly staff; cl mid-Nov–mid-Feb; children over 5.

WASDALE HEAD NY1808 **Wasdale Head** *Wasdale Head, Seascale CA20 1EX (019467) 26229* ***£78;** 9 simple, but warmly comfortable, pine-clad rms. Old flagstoned and gabled walkers' and climbers' inn, in a magnificent setting surrounded by steep fells; with civilised day rooms, popular home cooking for 7.30pm dinner, good wine list, huge breakfasts, and a cheerfully busy public bar; self-catering cottages; disabled access.

WATERMILLOCK NY4522 **Leeming House** *Watermillock, Ullswater, Penrith CA11 0JJ (017684) 86622* **£160,** plus special breaks; 40 cosseting rms, many with beautiful views. Well run, extended hotel in 20 acres of quiet lakeside grounds; with log fires in the comfortable lounges, a cosy panelled bar, fine food in the lovely, no smoking dining room, and courteous service; boating and fishing; high teas for young children; good provision for disabled.

WATERMILLOCK NY4522 **Old Church** *Watermillock, Penrith CA11 0JN (017684) 86204* **£85,** plus special breaks; 10 rms, some with lovely Ullswater views. Attractive, 18th-c Lakeland house peacefully situated in waterside gardens; with log fires in civilised day rooms, kind service, and excellent English dinners at 8pm in the no smoking dining room; rowing/windsurfing boats; cl Dec–Feb.

WATERMILLOCK NY4522 **Rampsbeck Country House** *Watermillock, Ullswater, Penrith CA11 0LP (017684) 86442* **£116;** 21 rms. Run by friendly, helpful people, this 18th-c hotel is set in 18 acres by Ullswater; an open fire in the cosy sitting room, French windows into the garden from the plush, comfortable lounge, and carefully prepared food in the attractive dining room; croquet; lots to do nearby; cl Jan–mid-Feb; children over 8 in evening restaurant.

WATER YEAT SD2989 **Water Yeat** *Water Yeat, Ulverston LA12 8DJ (01229) 885306* **£53,** plus special breaks; 5 chintzy rms with lovely views. Attractively converted and very neatly kept 17th-c farmhouse by Coniston Water, set in 3 acres of garden and woodland; with an especially relaxing atmosphere, a log fire in the lounge, generous breakfasts, wonderful food in the heavily beamed dining room (much loved locally), and super hosts; cl mid-Dec–mid-Feb; children over 4.

WINDERMERE SD4199 **Fir Trees** *Lake Rd, Windermere LA23 2EQ (015394) 42272* ***£56;** 8 attractive, spotless rms inc 2 big family ones. Well run and comfortable, no smoking, Victorian house with an informal and relaxed atmosphere; antiques, fine prints and fresh flowers, warm and helpful service (detailed suggestions of what to do), and good hearty breakfasts.

WINDERMERE SD4199 **Holbeck Ghyll Country House** *Holbeck Lane, Windermere LA23 1LU (015394) 32375* **£170 inc dinner,** plus special breaks; 20 individual rms with fresh flowers and complimentary sherry and many with fine views; 6 rms in new building (could be self-catering). Charming, warm and friendly country house in mature landscaped gardens and 5 acres of woodland overlooking Lake Windermere; with tennis court, putting green and croquet – their labradors like to walk with you; immaculate, comfortable lounges with antiques and panelling, log fires, billiard room, and very good food (vegetarian too) and wine in the oak-panelled restaurant; health spa; children over 8 in evening restaurant; disabled access.

WINDERMERE SD4199 **Langdale Chase** *Windermere LA23 1LW (015394) 32201* **£130;** 29 rms, many with marvellous lake views. Welcoming, family-run hotel in a lovely position on the edge of Lake Windermere, with waterskiing and bathing from the hotel jetty; tennis, croquet, putting and rowing, and afternoon tea on the terraces; gracious oak-panelled rooms with antiques, paintings, fresh flowers and open fires; very good food (huge breakfasts, too), and friendly service; disabled access.

WINDERMERE SD4199 **Miller Howe** *Rayrigg Rd, Windermere LA23 1EY (015394) 42536* **from £160 inc dinner,** plus special breaks; 12 comfortable, well equipped rms, many with fine views. Splendid, immaculately kept, Edwardian country house set high over the lake, with unbeatable views from the day rooms, conservatory and sloping garden; excellent evening meals, a remarkably wide-ranging New World wine list with helpful tasting notes, and super breakfasts; children over 8; cl Jan.

WINTON NY7810 **Bay Horse** *Winton, Kirkby Stephen CA17 4HS (017683) 71451* **£35;** 3 clean, good-value rms. Well kept, unpretentious moorland pub in a lovely setting; with welcoming, low-ceilinged rooms, friendly owners, and good, generous home cooking; well behaved children over 5.

WITHERSLACK SD4384 **Old Vicarage** *Witherslack, Grange-over-Sands LA11 6RS (015395) 52381* **£130 inc dinner,** plus special breaks; 15 individually decorated rms, some in the modern Orchard House are more spacious and have their own woodland terraces. Late Georgian vicarage in 5 acres of peaceful gardens and woodland; with 2 comfortable lounges, a log fire, good, interesting food in the cosy restaurant, inc home-made bread, cakes and preserves, and hearty breakfasts; tennis and lots of surrounding walks; dogs welcome by arrangement.

To see and do

AMBLESIDE NY3704 A busy holiday-oriented shopping centre inc excellent outdoor equipment shops strung along its central one-way system, with the quaintest information centre in the Lakes – the little NT shop in the tiny stone Bridge House over Stock Ghyll by the main car park. In the side lanes above here are one or two attractive older buildings. Traditional **glass blowing** at Adrian Sankey, Rydal Rd; good demonstrations and shop, but no pressure to buy; (015394) 33039. **Hayes Garden World** (Lake Rd) is a big garden centre in landscaped gardens; café, disabled access. The Queen's Hotel is good value for lunch.

Stagshaw (Waterhead, just S) Hillside woodland garden with lovely lake views, mature camellias, rhododendrons, magnolias and heathers; best in spring. Open daily Apr–Jun, then by appointment July–Oct; (015394) 35599; £1.30; NT. Parking is very limited. There's little left of the **Roman fort** in nearby Borrans Park.

Brockhole NY3901 (on the A591 S of Ambleside, or by launch from town pier) Recently revamped National Park information centre in a country house with well landscaped gardens and attractive lakeside grounds; also audio-visual show, exhibitions, and an adventure play area. Special talks and events throughout the year. Meals, snacks, shop, disabled access; visitor centre cl Nov–Mar, gardens and grounds open all year; (015394) 46601; free, but charge for parking.

Wansfell Pike NY3904 Gained by a path from the town, this is toylike in size compared with the bigger fells, but the view is as good as from many more imposing peaks.

KENDAL SD5192 A real town as opposed to a tourist centre, busy, with hectic traffic, but lots of small closes leading off the main street, some of them attractively restored to give a feel of what the place was like in the 18th-c heyday of the wool-weaving industry. The mint cake that takes its name from here comes in a surprising number of varieties. The Gateway (Crook Rd) is a decent newish pub/restaurant. **Brewery Arts Centre** (Highgate) Good changing events and exhibitions, café, bar, and a landscaped garden; (01539) 725133 for what's on. K Shoes have a **factory shopping centre** at Netherfield (cl 25 Dec). Lakeland Canoes (Hollins Lane, Burneside) hire them by the day, and will take them to and fro for you. **Webbs Garden Centre** (Burneside Rd) is big, with lots of plants; decent café, disabled access.

Abbot Hall (Kirkland) Beautifully restored Georgian house with period furniture, silver, china and glass and, most importantly, an art collection that reflects Kendal's importance in the 18th c as the centre of an artists' school, and includes works by Ruskin, Turner, Constable, and especially George Romney. Meals, snacks, good craft shop, disabled access; cl 31 Jan–12 Feb; (01539) 722464; £2.80 (or £1 if you have visited one of Kendal's other 2 museums). The **Museum of Lakeland Life & Industry** behind has lovingly re-created period rooms, shops and workshops, and an almost palpable feel of the past. Subjects as diverse as shoe-making, Arthur Ransome and Postman Pat. Some disabled access; hours and prices as above.

Kendal Museum SD5193 (Station Rd) Less immediately appealing than the town's other museums – comprehensive but mostly traditional; lots of realistically mounted stuffed animals, and a gallery devoted to the work of Alfred Wainwright, the walkers' guru. Shop, disabled access to ground floor only; (01539) 721374; cl Sun and 24 Dec–11 Feb; prices as above.

Kendal Castle SD5292 Ruin on a small hill on the E edge of town, the birthplace of Henry VIII's wife Catherine Parr. There's little more now than parts of the outer wall with some towers – but children enjoy it, and there are fine views. A humbler building associated with it is the **Castle Dairy** (Wildman St), an unspoiled Tudor house with some period furniture, inc the oldest bed the V & A have ever recorded. It's a restaurant, but they are happy to let people look around.

Quaker Tapestry Exhibition (Friends Meeting House, Stramongate) Bayeux-style tapestry history of the Quaker movement, also embroidery demonstrations. Shop, disabled access; cl Sun and Nov–Mar; (01539) 722975; £2.75.

KESWICK NY2623 The tourist centre of the northern Lakes, handy for Derwent Water, with lots of Victorian villas (many of them now guesthouses and small hotels) outside quite a traditional centre, with small cobbled closes running off the main streets. It's full of breeches, boots and backpacks in high season, with good outdoor equipment shops, and is a routine stop on coach tours. The Dog & Gun and older-fashioned George Hotel are very popular for lunch, with the Pheasant, out towards Crosthwaite, also worthwhile. The **Wild Strawberry** is a quaint tearoom with an upstairs gallery; cl Tues and Weds. **Lakeside Tea Gardens** (Lake Rd) have home baking, lots for children, pleasant modern furniture and crockery inside and a garden with trees and chaffinches; cl about 5pm. George Fisher (Borrowdale Rd) is a useful big outdoors shop. The back road around Swinside is pretty, and in clear weather is worth following up the gauntly formidable Keskadale Pass.

Cars of the Stars (Standish St) Unusual collection of cars from film and TV dating back to Laurel & Hardy's Model T Ford, taking in Chitty Chitty Bang Bang, the Batmobile and cars used by James Bond and Postman Pat along the way. Shop, disabled access; cl Jan and part of Feb; (017687) 73757; £3.

Keswick Museum (Fitzpark, Station Rd) Thoroughly traditional; the Poets' Corner stands out. Shop, disabled access; cl Nov–Easter; (017687) 73263; £1.

Pencil and teapot museums Pencils and collectable teapots are both made in Keswick; the museum alongside the Derwent pencil factory (Southey Works) is surprisingly interesting, with some unexpected exhibits (shop, disabled access; cl 25–26 Dec, 1 Jan; £2); while the only shape you won't see among the often ludicrous examples at the Teapottery (Central Car Park Rd) is the traditional one we all have in our kitchens (shop, some disabled access; cl 25–26 Dec, 1 Jan; free).

Castlerigg Stone Circle NY2822 (just E of Keswick) This Neolithic monument is well preserved, and gives photogenic perspectives of the mountains (the best times for pictures are morning and evening); take a map to identify the peaks it aligns with. The site is owned by the National Trust, and there's a brief explanation of the stones' history.

Friar's Crag NY2622 An easy walk S from here, this gives exquisite views of Derwent Water, with more prospects unfolding as you walk up to Castlehead Wood (there's more direct access to this from a car park on the B5289 S of Keswick).

Walla Crag NY2721 (off the B5289 S) A steep walk up above Great Wood (often teeming with red squirrels), this gives fairly high views over Derwent Water; a moorland path heads to the photogenic Ashness Bridge, from where a rewarding return walk is one down to the shore and back again.

PENRITH NY5130 A real locals' rather than tourists' town, and the biggest in Lakeland. It's very much a northern country town, with solid stone streets, farmers from far and wide descending on its Skirsgill agricultural market to beef about Brussels (Tues, sometimes Fri too in late summer/autumn), and genuinely traditional Lakeland shops selling real fudge and toffee, rich cakes (Birketts), local cheeses (Grahams), prize Cumberland sausages (Cranstons), local antiquarian books, and cheap and sturdy country clothes. John Norris (21 Victoria Rd) is the outstanding fishing/outdoor wear shop, with something for everyone; good prices. A **museum** on Middlegate is a useful introduction to the area, and the George does decent lunches. Six miles out of Penrith in Whinfell Forest (NY5728) **Oasis Holiday Village** is the Rank Organisation's Center Parcs-style holiday village. It's been very well thought out as far as visitors are concerned (and for the red squirrels – rope bridges save them from the traffic), and for small groups the lodges are pretty good value; (0990) 086000.

Penrith Castle NY5129 Built in the 14th c as a defence against Scottish raids, and the home of Richard III when he was Duke of Gloucester. The ruins are surrounded by a park; free.

Brougham Castle NY5329 (off the A6 S) A sturdy Norman ruin on steep lawns above riverside sheep pastures; climb to the top of the keep for the best view. Traces of Roman remains too, with a small exhibition of tombstones. Snacks, shop; cl Nov–Mar; (01768) 862488; £1.90. **Brougham Hall Craft Centre** nearby has 13 different craft workshops inc metal workers, furniture restoration and chocolate-makers, in the attractive stone courtyard of a 15th-c Hall. Plenty to see around the house and grounds inc a Cromwellian chapel and a collection of dolls and dolls' houses; currently undergoing a massive restoration. Meals, snacks, shop, disabled access; cl 25 Dec; (01768) 862488; £2 suggested donation.

Wetheriggs Pottery NY5326 (Clifton Dykes, signed off the A6 S) Interesting and very smart working pottery – one of the oldest in the country – with a 19th-c steam engine and equipment; children can try their hands at the wheel, and there's a play area, birds of prey and rare breeds of pig. Restaurant, shop, disabled access; 25–26 Dec, 1 Jan, Mon and Tues from Oct–Mar; (01768) 892733; free.

WINDERMERE/BOWNESS SD4199/SD4096 An extensive, largely Victorian development of guesthouses and small hotels spreads up between the older village of Bowness and the hillside station. It has a touristy feel right through the year, especially around the main street down to the steamer piers. In Bowness itself, there is an inner core of narrower much older streets and buildings – one of the most ancient is the engaging Hole in t' Wall pub. **Horse-riding** can be arranged from Wynlass Beck Stables (bottom of Patterdale Rd). The tourist information centre on Victoria St has a useful range of locally produced crafts if you haven't time to look properly, and the Birdcage (College Rd) is a good antique shop – mostly small things, especially lamps.

Steamboat Museum NY4097 (Rayrigg Rd) Nearly three dozen gleamingly restored, graceful antique steamboats, inc the 1850 SL *Dolly*, the oldest mechanically powered steamboat in the world, and the record-breaker *Miss Windermere IV*. Also a few boats that comfortably predate steam, and events like vintage boat rallies and model boat regattas. Snacks, shop, disabled access; cl Nov–Mar; (015394) 45565; £3. For an extra £4.75, there are stately 50-minute tours of the lake on the silent steam launch *Osprey* or *Swallow*, weather permitting.

! World of Beatrix Potter SD4097 (Old Laundry, Crag Brow, Bowness) Much enjoyed by young children, delightfully detailed re-creations of characters and scenes from *Peter Rabbit* and other tales. Some bits have smells, so you can get more of the atmosphere of Mrs Tiggy-Winkle's laundry or nasty old Mr McGregor's potting shed. Meals and snacks (in the Tailor of Gloucester's kitchen), shop, disabled access; cl 25 Dec, and probably last 3 wks Jan; (015394) 88444; £2.99.

Amazonia Fascinating changing collection of reptiles – all shapes and sizes including snakes, crocodiles and brightly coloured lizards. All housed among koi and turtle ponds, waterfalls and free-nesting tropical birds. Meals, snacks, shop, disabled access; cl 25 Dec,

1 Jan; (015394) 48002; *£3.95.

Lake Windermere The most popular boating lake, so the easiest on which to hire rowing boats and other vessels. Lots of launches, of all sorts of shapes and sizes, run cruises of varying lengths from Bowness Bay, Ambleside, Waterhead and (not Nov–Mar) Newby Bridge. The pick of the sightseeing boat trips are those from the steamboat museum (see *above*). The pier at the S end of the lake is the terminus for the Haverthwaite steam railway.

Rowing boats can be hired from the Bowness Bay Boating Company. They also have motorboats and a number of launches – at least one of which is equipped to take disabled people; (015394) 43360 to check. Lake Holidays Afloat do motorboats too; around £50 for a full day.

A pleasant place to hire rowing boats (not Nov–Easter) is **Fell Foot Park**, nr Newby Bridge, an 18-acre park with plenty of room for lakeside picnics; café and shop (cl Nov–Easter), some disabled access; (015395) 31273; parking charges (from £1.50), rowing boats £5 per hour for 2 people; NT. They can provide details of boating and fishing on other NT waters.

Lakeland Sailing at Ferry Nab, Bowness, do day, weekend or longer cruises and courses on large sailing yachts; from £50 a day. Windsurfing or waterskiing can be arranged at Low Wood Water Sports Centre, Windermere. Windsurfing, canoeing or dinghy sailing Mar–Oct at Windermere Sailing Centre, Rayrigg Rd, Windermere.

The chain ferry linking the ferry road below Bowness with the Hawkshead road below Far Sawrey is a utilitarian way of taking to the water; but though it runs every 20 mins and saves miles of driving, queues mean that it saves time only out of season.

Orrest Head SD4199 A short steep walk (half-hour each way) from opposite the station, giving spectacular views over Lake Windermere and the Pennines, lovely at sunset.

Other things to see and do

CUMBRIA Family Attraction of the Year

! **MILNTHORPE** SD5078 **Lakeland Wildlife Oasis** (off the A6 S) Millions of years of evolution flash before your eyes at this lively jungle house, a fascinating cross between zoo and museum. Children can have plenty of fun here, crawling along a tunnel leading into the meerkat enclosure (their heads pop up in a little dome while the cheery little creatures scamper round outside), or touching snakes, lizards and tortoises. Their animal handling sessions aren't just at set times: you can hold some creatures just about all through the day, and it's worth asking whether it's possible to touch any of the others, as helpful staff are usually happy to introduce more adventurous visitors to tarantulas and other creepy-crawlies. The range of wildlife is quite extensive, with everything from starfish and monkeys to the less often seen flying foxes and poison arrow frogs. Butterflies, bats and birds fly around the exotically planted tropical halls, and there are interactive displays to design your own mammal or weigh a whale. Other activities include fossil-rubbing and an animal rubber-stamping trail. Entertaining, friendly and informative, this can fill 2 or 3 hours without any difficulty. Though there are some animals outside (and a picnic lawn), most of the exhibition is under cover, so it's ideal for the area's not entirely reliable climate, and a good bet for winter school holidays. Snacks, shop, disabled access; cl 25–26 Dec; (015395) 63027; £4.50 (£2.50 children). The family ticket is good value at £12.50, covering entry for 2 adults and 3 children.

† **ABBEY TOWN** NY1751 **Holme Cultram** (on the B5302 Wigtown–Silloth) Remains of a formidably rich Cistercian abbey – extraordinarily grand for this quiet village. The New Inn at Blencogo has good food – must book (016973) 61091.

ALSTON NY7146 Interesting, little well weathered Pennine town, with a surprising number of pubs up and down its very steep, cobbled main street (the Angel is best). **South Tynedale Railway** is the chief attraction here, with diesel and occasionally steam vintage narrow-gauge train trips along a lovely winding valley. They plan to open a service up to Kirkhaugh in Northumberland. Teas, shop, disabled access by arrangement; open wknds and bank hols Apr–Oct, daily Jun–Sept (exc Mon and Fri Jun and Sept), and some wknds in Dec – best to ring for timetable; (01434) 381696; fares from £2.50. **Gossipgate Gallery** (The Butts) Local art and crafts, with changing exhibitions and a good big shop. Tea garden, disabled access (though no facilities); cl Jan–mid-Feb, and some wkdys Feb–Mar and Nov–Dec; (01434) 381806; free. **Hartside Nursery** (A686 W, NY6943) Beautifully placed alpine nursery, with a small streamside garden and rare plants for sale; it's quite a draw for birds and wildlife. Shop, some disabled access with notice; cl am wknds and bank hols, and all Nov–Feb (exc by appointment); (01434) 381372.

★ **APPLEBY** NY6820 An attractive riverside village; the main street, rising from the harmonious 12th-c church to the castle, is still a grand sight despite the cars, with a good few handsome buildings inc a lovely courtyard of almshouses. Pleasant strolls by the River Eden. The Royal Oak is most enjoyable for lunch. **Appleby Castle Conservation Centre** One of the best-preserved Norman keeps in the country (the rest of the buildings are later additions); terrific views from the ramparts. The Clifford family lived here for nearly 700 years, though they moved later to the grander house next door, the great hall of which has antiques, paintings and Chinese porcelain on display. The main feature of the attractive grounds is the big collection of birds, waterfowl and farm animals, in a lovely setting above the river; also brass rubbing, exhibitions and falconry displays. Meals, snacks, shop, limited disabled access; cl Nov–Easter; (017683) 51402; £3.

ARNSIDE SD4578 A good start for the 20-minute train trip along the N shore of Morecambe Bay to Ulverston: long viaducts, stupendous views. Nearby **Arnside Knott** looks across Morecambe Bay to the southern Lakeland fells, with very rewarding views for walkers. The Ship at nearby Sandside also has glorious views.

Days Out

Industrial time-warp by Windermere: Sculpture trail in Grizedale Forest; Hawkshead, lunch up at the Drunken Duck, Barngates; Stott Park Bobbin Mill; steamer trip on Windermere from Lakeside; Lakeside & Haverthwaite Railway; Lakeside Aquarium.

A Cumbrian farmhouse and Ullswater's landscapes: Ambleside; Townend, Troutbeck – lunch at the Queen's Head; steamer from Glenridding to Howtown, and walk back along shore of Ullswater; Aira Force (with children, afternoon could include Lowther Leisure Park at Hackthorpe instead of the walk, after lunch at the Punch Bowl, Askham).

Rainy day options: Levens Hall or Sizergh Castle; lunch at the Strickland Arms or the Hare & Hounds, Levens; Kendal – especially Museum of Lakeland Life and Industry or Abbot Hall Art Gallery, and walk up to the castle.

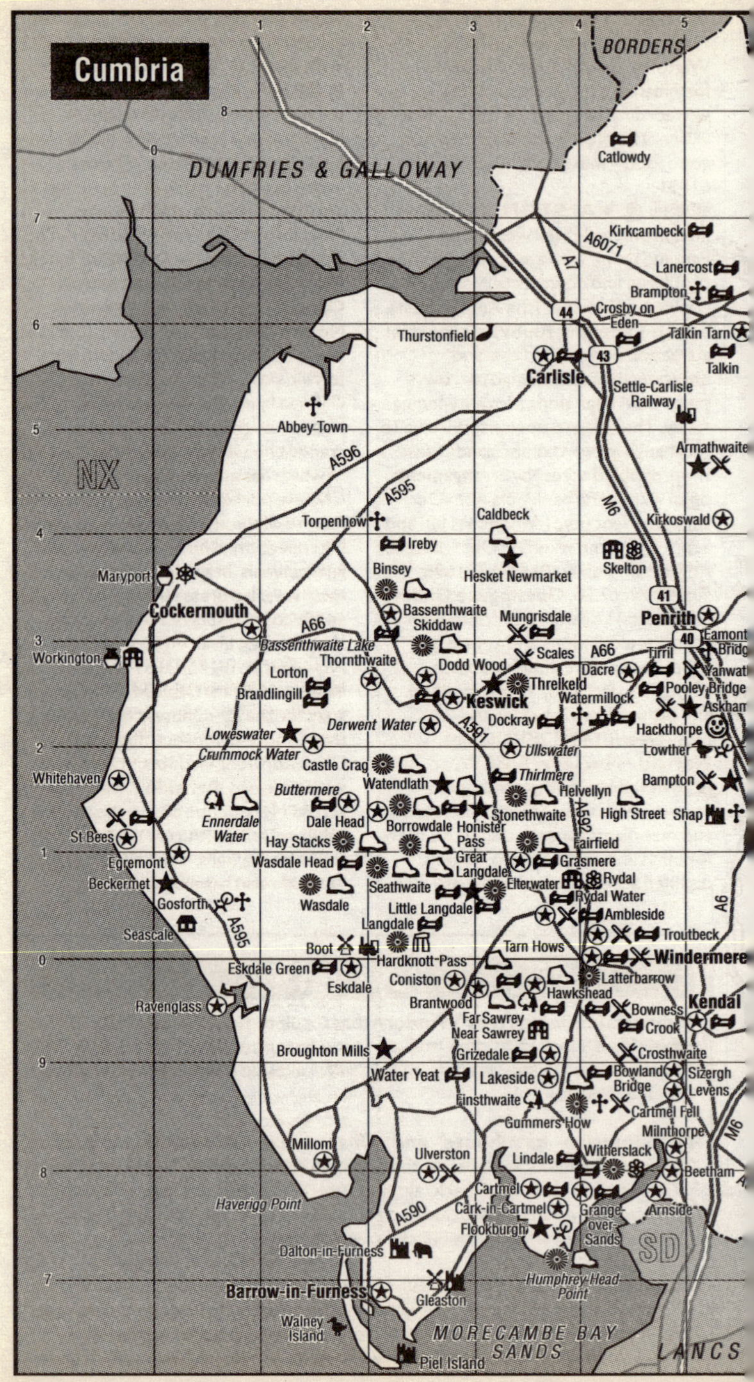
Cumbria
DUMFRIES & GALLOWAY
BORDERS
Catlowdy
Kirkcambeck
Lanercost
Brampton
Crosby on Eden
Talkin Tarn
Talkin
Thurstonfield
Carlisle
Settle-Carlisle Railway
Abbey Town
Armathwaite
A596
A595
Torpenhow
Caldbeck
Kirkoswald
Ireby
Skelton
Binsey
Hesket Newmarket
Maryport
Cockermouth
Bassenthwaite
Skiddaw
Mungrisdale
Penrith
Eamont Bridge
A66
Bassenthwaite Lake
Thornthwaite
Scales
Workington
Lorton
Dodd Wood
Dacre
Tirril
Yanwath
Brandlingill
Threlkeld
Pooley Bridge
Keswick
Watermillock
Askham
Derwent Water
Dockray
Hackthorpe
Loweswater
Ullswater
Lowther
Crummock Water
Castle Crag
Thirlmere
Bampton
Whitehaven
Watendlath
Buttermere
Helvellyn
High Street
Shap
Ennerdale Water
Dale Head
Borrowdale
Honister Pass
Stonethwaite
St Bees
Hay Stacks
Great Langdale
Fairfield
Egremont
Wasdale Head
Grasmere
Beckermet
Seathwaite
Elterwater
Rydal
Wasdale
Rydal Water
Gosforth
Little Langdale
Ambleside
Langdale
Troutbeck
Seascale
A595
Boot
Hardknott Pass
Tarn Hows
Windermere
Eskdale Green
Eskdale
Coniston
Latterbarrow
Hawkshead
Ravenglass
Brantwood
Bowness
Kendal
Far Sawrey
Near Sawrey
Crook
Grizedale
Crosthwaite
Broughton Mills
Water Yeat
Lakeside
Bowland Bridge
Sizergh
Levens
Finsthwaite
Cartmel Fell
Gummers How
Milnthorpe
Millom
Lindale
Witherslack
Ulverston
Beetham
Cartmel
Haverigg Point
Cark-in-Cartmel
Grange-over-Sands
Arnside
A590
Flookburgh
Dalton-in-Furness
Humphrey Head Point
Barrow-in-Furness
Gleaston
Walney Island
MORECAMBE BAY SANDS
Piel Island
LANCS
A6071
A7
M6
A591
A592
A6
NX
SD

★ **ASKHAM** NY5123 An attractive village in fine scenery, with not one but 2 village greens – each with a good pub.

★ **BARBON** SD6282 An unpretentious village given appeal by its fine setting, just below the fells; the road up to Dent, Dent Head and Deepdale reaches beautifully deep into the hills. The Barbon Inn is good.

BARROW-IN-FURNESS SD1969 The town shows the effects of the virtual collapse of shipbuilding in this country, on which it depended. The mainline **railway** from here to Whitehaven hugs the coast and has good views, missed by the road, though in the other direction the A5087 to Ulverston has fine views across Morecambe Bay. The Black Dog (Broughton Rd, Dalton) does decent food all day. **Dock Museum** (North Rd) Futuristic-looking museum exploring how Barrow developed from a tiny hamlet to the biggest iron and steel centre in the world, before becoming renowned for shipbuilding; displays range from simple fishing boats to Trident submarines. An extension includes interactive displays and an adventure playground. Snacks, shop, good disabled access; cl Mon (exc bank hols), Tues; (01229) 894444; free. **Furness Abbey** (slightly NE, towards Dalton, SD2171) Impressive, warm sandstone, Norman remains of the one-time second richest monastery in England, with lovely arched cloisters, peaceful lawns, and views of a pretty valley. Small museum, disabled access; cl winter Mon and Tues, 24–26 Dec; (01229) 823420; £2.50.

BASSENTHWAITE NY2332 Attractive, close-set little village – the 12th-c parish church is 3m S; the Sun is an enjoyable pub. Escorted woodland **horse-riding** can be arranged from £12 an hour; (017687) 76949 for details. You can hire rowing boats on Bassenthwaite Lake. **Mirehouse** (off the A591 S) The family that still live in this modest 17th-c house once had excellent literary connections, so the fine rooms have mementos of Wordsworth, Carlyle and Tennyson among others. There may be piano recitals in the music room, and on

Weds in Jun, July and Sept they usually have displays of lace-making. Interesting garden (bee/butterfly plants), as well as peaceful lakeshore grounds, lakeside church, and woods with well thought out adventure play areas. Lots to do, with a surprising number of activities for children – they may even let them sound the gong. Good home cooking in ex-mill tearoom, shop, disabled access; open Easter–Oct, house pm Sun and Weds, plus pm Fri in Aug; phone for winter opening; (017687) 72287; £3.50, garden only £1.50. **Trotters and Friends Animal Farm** (Coalbeck Farm) Excellent for families; children can join in feeding and milking, and there are plenty of other opportunities to get close to the animals. The 23-acre deer park is pleasant for a picnic, and there are birds of prey and a reptile house. Indoor areas make it a good bet on drizzly days. Meals, snacks, shop, disabled access; cl wkdys Nov–Mar; (017687) 76239; £3.30. Readers tell us they know of few nicer sites for a caravan than the one at Englethwaite Hall nr here.

BEETHAM SD4979 **Heron Cornmill and Museum of Papermaking** Well organised working watermill which dates back to 1096, though the current building is 18th c; new exhibition on baking. The big paperworks next door has displays of paper-making. Snacks, shop; cl Mon (exc bank hols), and Oct–Easter; (015395) 65027; £1.50. Beetham itself is attractive, with an interesting **church**, and the Wheatsheaf is good for lunch.

BINSEY NY2235 A pathless lump of a hill, but it rewards walkers with splendid views of the Lakes and Solway Firth (and into southern Scotland) by virtue of its geographical isolation.

BOOT NY1801 The steam railway from Ravenglass ends here, at Dalegarth station. **Eskdale Watermill** Guided tours of an attractively set, 16th-c, working 2-wheeled mill, with a picnic area nr woodland waterfalls. Snacks, shop; cl Mon (exc bank hols), and Oct–Mar; (019467) 23335; £1.25. Dalegarth Falls here are lovely. The Burnmoor Inn, very well placed for walkers, has extremely good-value food; the Bower House and King George IV, further down Eskdale at Eskdale Green, are also worthwhile.

BORROWDALE NY2517 Many people's favourite Lakeland base for walks, with good paths along or just above the River Derwent, especially from Grange (useful teashop). For lazier souls, the drive along the B5289 gives glorious views. Other prized walks giving or leading to fine views include mossy Johnny Wood (from Rosthwaite or Seatoller, where there's an NT centre exc in winter), and the 2 famous waterfalls, both best after rain, Taylorgill Force and Lodore Falls (behind Lodore Hotel).

† **BRAMPTON** NY5563 **Lanercost Priory** (signed away from town) Impressive and extensive remains of a Norman priory, built with stone recycled from Hadrian's Wall. Shop, some disabled access; cl Nov–Mar; £1.90. The nave, picturesquely framed by an arch, was restored in the 18th c as a red sandstone church, and now has stained glass by William Morris and Burne-Jones. The Abbey Bridge Inn by the priory has good food.

BRANTWOOD SD3195 Ruskin's rambling Victorian house, with lots of his furniture, books and paintings. It's appealingly unstuffy, but the real attraction is the surroundings and setting, especially the very extensive, informal, hillside woodland gardens (best in late May/Jun). Good hour's walk on the nature trail, and mouth-watering views of lake and fells. Meals, snacks, good shop, disabled access (grounds steep in places); cl winter Mon and Tues and 25–26 Dec; (015394) 41396; £3.90.

BROUGH NY7914 **Castle** Classic ruined Norman fortress, in a romantic setting on moors above the village, with great views; free. The Golden Fleece is useful for lunch.

BUTTERMERE NY1815 A splendid, varied, flat walk circles the lake, with glorious views, plenty of safe opportunities for children to let off steam, and even a tunnel; the weather has to be really savage to spoil it. Parking at Gatescarth. The Bridge

Hotel in the little village is good for lunch, and you can hire **rowing boats**. Rannerdale Knotts NY1618, best reached by a walk via Low Bank, gives fine views of Crummock Water and the hills surrounding it. The green slatey fells N offer keen walkers superlative routes along high ridges: Whiteless Pike, Causey Pike, Crag Hill and Grasmoor are among the most exciting points.

CALDBECK NY3239 John Peel's grave can be found in the churchyard here, and the Oddfellows Arms has good generous food. There's a pretty drive to attractive Mungrisdale; alternatively, a pleasant stroll to a peaceful spot with a waterfall called the Howk.

CARK-IN-CARTMEL SD3577 **Holker Hall** Opulently built and furnished, mainly Victorian mansion with an appealingly unstuffy feel despite the beauty. The glorious 25-acre formal and woodland gardens are among the best in the country, with spectacular water features, a rose garden, rhododendron and azalea arboretum and rare plants and shrubs. Also a deer park, entertaining motor museum, falconry displays and adventure playground – enough to take up quite a lump of the day. Meals, snacks, shop, disabled access; cl Sat and Nov–Mar; (015395) 58328; £3.35 gardens, grounds and exhibitions; Hall, motor museum and bird of prey centre extra. The nearby Engine is useful for lunch.

CARLISLE NY3956 A sizeable town, not an obvious holiday destination, but plenty to interest the visitor, with several quietly attractive old buildings (and a very helpful visitor centre in one of them, the Old Town Hall). **Tullie House** (Castle St) Great fun: dramatic displays of Border history, using state-of-the-art techniques of sight, sound and smell. Children especially find lots to do, from exploring mine tunnels to trying out a Roman crossbow. The ground floor has a more conventional art gallery/museum. Meals, snacks, shop, disabled access; cl am Sun, 25 Dec; (01228) 534781; £3.50 (get there between 10 and 11am and it's half-price). The unpretentious little **cathedral**, founded in 1122 and severely damaged in the Civil War, has fine stained glass; try to go on a bright morning when the sunlight comes streaming colourfully through the east window. Also medieval carvings inc the Brougham Triptych, painted panels and stonework, and crypt treasury. Meals, snacks, good shop (some tasty local foods), disabled access (exc to restaurant); free. The extensive medieval **Castle**, rather gaunt and forbidding, is surprisingly well preserved considering its violent history. Interesting period furnished rooms, a portcullised gatehouse, lots of staircases and passages, and centuries of prisoners' carved graffiti in the dungeons; good views from the ramparts. Snacks, shop; cl 24–26 Dec, 1 Jan; (01228) 591922; £2. The **guildhall** in Green Market is a handsomely restored medieval timbered hall; worth a look inside if passing – some displays inc interesting guild silver (open Easter–Sept, pm Thurs–Sun; 50p). **St Cuthbert's Church** is remarkable for its mobile pulpit. The Crown & Mitre (English St) has a good-value lunchtime buffet, and there's decent home cooking in the Black Lion out at Durdar, where the attractively placed racecourse has meetings every month exc July; (01228) 522973 for dates. The **Settle–Carlisle Railway** running up Ribbledale and into the Cumbrian Pennines, stopping at Dent station, Garsdale Head, Kirkby Stephen, Appleby, Langwathby and other Eden Valley villages, is a memorable 70 miles of grand scenery, best from Appleby to Settle (described more fully under Settle in our **Yorkshire** chapter); (0345) 484950 for times and fares.

★ **CARTMEL** SD3778 Picturesque little alleys lead off the delightfully harmonious central square – especially the one out through the former **priory gatehouse**. The **priory church**, which towers massively over the village, is an interesting mix of architectural grandeur from 12th to 16th c, inc fine carving. Lots of arts and crafts in the village. The Cavendish Arms is good for lunch.

CARTMEL FELL SD4189 In a wonderful, tucked-away country location, the **church** here has interesting early pews and a fine triple-decker pulpit. The Masons Arms is deservedly popular for lunch. The road here from Winster is very pretty.

CASTERTON SD6279 Brontë fans will want to see **Casterton School**; attractive pre-Raphaelite stained glass and paintings in the **church** result from enthusiastic Brotherhood holidays here. The Pheasant is good.

CASTLE CRAG NY2416 This impregnable-looking pinnacle can be reached by a path winding up the back from Grange. It's a challenging hike, but gives terrific lake views.

COCKERMOUTH NY1130 Quietly attractive riverside town, increasingly worth a holiday visit, with a wide range of places to visit. **Wordsworth House** (Main St) The poet's happy childhood home, a handsome, restored 18th-c townhouse with fine furniture, pictures by friends and contemporaries, original panelling, and a walled garden above the river. Well worth a visit in its own right as well as for its Wordsworth associations, and interesting to see how different it is from the places he lived in later on. Snacks, shop; cl wknds (exc Sats July and Aug or before bank hols), and Nov–Mar; (01900) 824805; £2.80; NT. Next door the **Printing House** is a working print museum with a good range of historic presses and equipment; you can try out various printing methods. Disabled access; cl Sun; (01900) 824984; £2.50. **Jennings Brewery** Tours of traditional Castle Brewery, where the water for brewing is still drawn from the well that supplied the castle at the time of the Norman Conquest. Shop; tours 11am and 2pm wkdys Mar–Oct (plus maybe 12.30pm in summer hols), and 11am and 2pm Sat Apr–Sept – booking advisable; (01900) 823214; £3. No children under 12. **Cockermouth Motor Museum** next door has a changing range of vehicles, audio-visual displays, and a model race track for children. Snacks, shop, disabled access; cl Jan and winter wkdys; (01900) 824448; £3. **Castlegate House Gallery** (Castlegate) Friendly, lived-in Georgian house opposite the castle, with a walled garden, Adam ceiling and sales of paintings and crafts. Cl Thurs, Sun, and Jan and Feb; (01900) 822149; free. **Toy and Model Museum** (Market Pl) Expanding collection of mainly British toys from this century; shop, limited disabled access; cl Dec and Jan exc by appointment; (01900) 827606; *£2.40. **Lakeland Sheep and Wool Centre** (off the A5086 slightly S, NY1129) Entertaining live show starring 19 different species of sheep and maybe a few geese; they demonstrate shearing and sheepdog trials, and an adjacent exhibition is a worthwhile introduction to the area. Show times 10.30am, noon, 2pm, and 3.30pm; no shows Mon or Tues from Easter–mid-Nov; meals, snacks, shop, disabled access; cl 25 Dec; (01990) 822673; show *£3, exhibitions free. The comfortable Trout does decent food.

CONISTON SD2997 Unpretentious village at the foot of its mountain, the Old Man. The Black Bull does filling food all day. From Spoon Hall, there's **pony-trekking** on the fells above; cl Nov–Easter; (015394) 41391; from £11 an hour. An opulent Victorian steam yacht sails daily end Mar–Oct, from Coniston Pier, Brantwood and Park-a-Moor; (015394) 41288 for times – best to ring between 9 and 10.30am or you're likely to get the answerphone. You can hire rowing or other boats from the boating centre run by the National Parks, 15 minutes' walk from the village; cl Nov–Mar; (015394) 41366; rowing boats from £5 an hour (£1 each extra person), motorboats from £10, electric boats £12.50. **Coniston Water walks** There's a lovely path on the W side, S of Coniston; you can combine this walk with one on a higher-level route along the Walna Scar 'road' (an ancient hard track closed to through traffic) beneath the **Old Man of Coniston**, the outstanding viewpoint of the vicinity. Climb the Old Man from Coniston, go up past the remains of copper mines, and return down the Walna Scar road.

CRUMMOCK WATER NY1520 The scenery is less rewarding than around Buttermere, but it's not to be sniffed at. A good start for a walk is the car park by **Lanthwaite Wood**, off the

B5289 towards Loweswater at the N end; there's a pretty view from the hill above the wood. You can hire rowing boats on this lake, and if you're keen to swim in one of the lakes this is probably the best.

DACRE NY4626 **Dalemain House** Largely Elizabethan despite the Georgian façade, and with a number of even older features, so an appealing variety of periods and styles. Some rooms are grand, others are charming, with splendid furnishings and paintings and a good deal for children to enjoy. Particularly interesting Chinese Room with hand-painted wallpaper. There's an adventure playground, and deer in the carefully landscaped **park**, with lake and mountain views. Atmospheric restaurant, shop, plant centre, limited disabled access; cl Fri and Sat, and Oct–Mar; (017684) 86450; £5, grounds only £3. The village **church** has pre-Norman sculpture, and quaint medieval stone bears in the graveyard. The King's Arms in Stainton is nice for lunch.

DALEHEAD NY2215 From Howtown there's a good walk up Martindale (where the **church** has attractive primitive stonework), then up over the fells to Bedafell Knott and down into Patterdale; hard work, but gorgeous views, Herdwick sheep, buzzards and ring ouzels.

DALTON-IN-FURNESS SD2273 **South Lakes Wild Animal Park** Rapidly expanding 14-acre wildlife centre, well placed for fine views of the entire Furness peninsula. Animals such as wallabies, antelope, racoons, coatis and porcupines, and a 4-acre section with pheasants and ducks wandering free and waiting to be fed; also a nature trail, lakeside walks, miniature railway, and pets corner. It's a very committed place, taking part in a number of international breeding programmes. Meals, snacks, shop, some disabled access; cl 25 Dec; (01229) 466086; £4.75. The village also has a rather austere square **castle**; the Black Dog (Broughton Rd) has decent food.

★ **DENT** SD7087 Inside the modern outskirts is a delightful, steep cobbled village, a rewarding end to an attractive drive – though now on the tourist trail, so busy in summer. The welcoming Sun brews its own beer, and the church is well worth a look. E of the village, towards Denthead, Colin Gardner (Stone House, Cowgill; cl wknds) makes traditional furniture. Dentdale has easy to middling walks, in the shadow of Whernside.

DERWENT WATER NY2523 With all its inlets and little islets, this is a pleasant place for pottering about in boats. It has gorgeous lakeside scenery, romantic little islets, ancient woodland, and a variety of mountain backdrops. You can hire rowing boats and launches in Keswick (not Nov–Easter), from around £5 per hour. Regular launches run all year from Keswick to half a dozen points around the lake. Walks along the lake's western shore, best reached from car parks off the back road between Grange and Swinside, can be combined with the more demanding walk up Catbells for the best lake views.

DODD WOOD NY2427 (off the A591 N of Keswick) Marked walks through the woods, or on open hillside, with Bassenthwaite views.

EGREMONT NY0110 Dominated by its very ruined Norman **castle**; as so often, the gatehouse is the best preserved part. **Lowes Court Gallery** Georgian house with local arts and crafts for sale; cl Sun, pm Weds and pm wkdys Jan and Feb; (01946) 820693; free. Just SE on the A595, the **Florence Mine Heritage Centre** is based around what was the last working iron ore mine in Europe. Tours of the pit at 10.30am and 1.30pm, and a visitor centre with reconstructions of pit life at the turn of the century. Snacks, shop, disabled access to visitor centre; cl Nov–Easter; (01946) 820683; £6.50 pit tour, £1 visitor centre.

★ **ELTERWATER** NY3204 Idyllically placed village, with lake views. The Britannia is very popular for lunch. The B5343 past here gives awesome mountain views; you can keep on a poorer, steeper road, passing nr pretty Blea Tarn, and coming back down through the gentler Little Langdale.

ENNERDALE WATER NY1016 Gentle walks by the lake (no boating) and through forestry, with high peaks above; the Fox & Hounds at Ennerdale Bridge is a good pub.

ESKDALE NY1700 Excellent for walks, especially around Boot. Here, a prime objective is the **Stanley Ghyll Force** waterfall, approached by a series of bridges and visible from a dizzying view-platform high above. From Trough House Bridge car park nr the waterfall, you can walk along one side of the river to Doctor Bridge, then return the other side, for an easy route – with delectable views throughout. Other walks take you up towards the open fells (the landlord of the Burnmoor Inn is helpful with route suggestions). You can use the Ravenglass & Eskdale Railway as part of a round trip.

FAIRFIELD NY3511 Rewarding for determined fell-walkers, climbed by a horseshoe layout of ridges from Rydal.

FAR SAWREY SD3895 Between the ferry here and the Wray Castle estate to the N can be found the cream of Windermere's waterside strolls, along the lake's western shore. The estate is a large NT tract with general public access. The forested slope rising from this shore has several well signposted routes, with Far Sawrey and Near Sawrey villages and Latterbarrow worthwhile objectives for circular walks.

FINSTHWAITE SD3788 **Stott Park Bobbin Mill** (just N) Set in coppiced woodland, this former water-and-steam mill made wooden cotton reels from 1835 right up to 1971; enthusiastic guides give excellent demonstrations of 19th-c industrial techniques. The mill is still powered by steam Tues–Thurs: the lathes look lethal. Snacks, shop, disabled access; cl Nov–Mar; (015395) 31087; £2.90. The Swan at Newby Bridge is attractively set for lunch.

★ **FLOOKBURGH** SD3675 This peaceful village has excellent potted local shrimps, and a decent craft shop.

GLEASTON SD2671 Well restored working **watermill** in peaceful surroundings, with a working corn mill, and leather-making demonstrations. Meals, snacks, shop, some disabled access; cl Mon; (01229) 869244; *£1.50. The ruins of a partly built medieval castle are nearby.

GOSFORTH NY0603 The churchyard has a 10th-c carved **cross**, one of Britain's finest; there are more ancient, carved, hogback tombstones in the church. The working pottery may let you try making a pot (only in school hols); good shop. Cl Mon Oct–May and Tues and Weds Jan–Feb, 25–26 Dec.

GRANGE-OVER-SANDS SD4077 This sedately old-fashioned resort is the start for summer guided walks over **Morecambe Bay Sands**, oddly other-worldly; glistening tidal flats, quick-stepping patrols of wading birds, distant hills, grisly tales of people and horses sucked under – a guide really is essential; phone Cedric Robinson, the official guide appointed by the Queen, on (015395) 32165 for times. **Hampsfield Fell** is a pleasant walk up through the woods from here, giving terrific views over the bay from its limestone pavements and summit 'hospice' inscribed with 19th-c words of wisdom.

★ **GRASMERE** NY3407 The pretty village swarms with visitors in summer, most of them here to see **Dove Cottage** – still much as Wordsworth had it in his most creative years (he completed *The Prelude* here), with sister Dorothy's journals and his extensive cottage garden. Informative guided tours cope well with the bustle; in early morning (opens 9.30am) out of season you may get some space to yourself. The place always was crowded; barely big enough for 2, with the poets' children and friends it often had a dozen or more people living here. The adjoining **Wordsworth Museum**, included in the price, has changing exhibitions and possessions of the poet and his family and friends, as well as a reconstructed Lakeland kitchen. Meals, snacks, shop; cl last 3 wks Jan and first wk Feb, 24–26 Dec; (015394) 35544; £4.40. Wordsworth is buried in the graveyard of the robust old church, which has quite an unusual interior. Sarah Nelson's gingerbread shop by the church is wonderfully old-fashioned. The Traveller's Rest (A591) is our current pick for lunch. The lake itself, with Rydal Water and Elter Water, is the very heart of picturesque Lakeland. All 3 are famous for their lovely settings, and there are pleasant walks all around; you can even link all 3 together in a long afternoon's walk filled with glorious views. The walk up the good track to Easedale Tarn from Grasmere takes you into a fine valley; the lake itself is romantically set below rocks.

GREAT LANGDALE NY2806 Dominated by the awesome Langdale Pikes, this is the area's main centre for more serious fell-walking in grand scenery. One very popular shorter walk here is up the good track to Stickle Tarn, from the car park by the Stickle Barn (useful for refreshments), and Bow Fell and Crinkle Crags are 2 longer fell walks. Wainwright's, in the not specially graceful settlement of Chapel Stile off the B5343, another useful refreshment place, is particularly popular with many of our contributors as a base for walks along here.

GRIZEDALE FOREST PARK SD3394 Woodland trails from short strolls to half-day walks, punctuated by often hard-to-spot timber and rock sculptures. These trails are good when rain cuts off more open views; the sculptures are set in various spots throughout the plantations (map from visitor centre). Lots of other activities: craft centre, decent information centre, bookable deer observation hides, orienteering, bike hire (it's an ideal area for cycling), and adventure play area. In all, 6 or 7 square miles of mainly coniferous hillside timber to get lost in. Some disabled access; (01229) 860373; parking charge, £1 for 3 hours. A highlight is the Theatre in the Forest; (01229) 860291 for what's on. The Eagle's Head at Satterthwaite (some winter closures) is good value for lunch, and the back roads through this area are quiet and pleasant.

GUMMERS HOW SD3988 An easy 20-minute climb from the road, for a fine lake view.

HACKTHORPE NY5224 **Lowther Leisure and Wildlife Park** (signed off the A6 S of Penrith) Plenty to keep children up to around 11 amused for most of the day (the pace is too sedate for teenagers). Some features have a refreshingly old-fashioned appeal: there's a circus with trapeze and clown acts, and the rides are more along the lines of a traditional funfair than gravity-busting rollercoasters. The attractive parkland has a developing wildlife area, as well as puppet shows, boating, miniature train rides, challenging play areas, and an archery range. Meals, snacks, shop, disabled access; open wknds Easter–spring bank hol, then daily till early Sept; (01931) 712523; £6.95. The Punch Bowl at Askham does interesting food.

HADRIAN'S WALL NY5664 Surviving traces of this far less known western section of the Roman wall can be reached on well signed paths from the lanes between the A69 and the B6318 N of Brampton.

HARDKNOTT PASS NY2101 **Hardknott Roman Fort** Quite well preserved and interestingly restored, but most notable for its staggering lonely position high in the mountains; magnificent views to sea and even the Isle of Man. The drive up here is not for the faint-hearted – it's very steep and twisting, through this pass and Wrynose Pass, but the scenery makes it worthwhile; the Woolpack Inn at Bleabeck just W is good value.

★ **HAWKSHEAD** SD3598 Don't miss this virtually unchanged Elizabethan Lakeland village, with sturdy outside walls, and sheltered, flower-filled inner courtyards. Though very popular with summer visitors, even at its busiest it has a pleasantly foreign 'different' feel, and the fact that cars are kept out helps a lot. The church has some eye-catching early 18th-c murals. The **Beatrix Potter Gallery** (Main St) has a generous, annually changing selection of the original illustrations of *Peter Rabbit* and other favourites, as well as rather different, more acutely (almost acidly) observed drawings. A timed ticket system keeps it uncrowded – during holiday periods you may have to wait to get in. Shop; cl Fri, Sat, and Nov–Mar; (015394) 36355; £2.80; NT. The **Old Grammar School**, now a museum, is worth poking your nose into, if only to see where Wordsworth carved his name on a desk (he attended from 1779 to 1783); limited disabled access;

cl 12.30–1.30pm, am Sun, and Nov–Easter; £1.50. The best nearby pub for lunch is the Drunken Duck up at Barngates. There's trout **fishing** and **boat hire** on nearby Esthwaite Water, the largest stocked lake in the region.

HAY STACKS NY1913 To the S of Buttermere and high above it, this is a challenging walk, but a rewarding one for the changing views, continuing on to Fleetwith Pike.

HELVELLYN NY3415 This famous Lakeland landmark is most easily (and crowdedly) tackled from Thirlmere, but much more exciting when reached from Glenridding and **Striding Edge**, where the path follows a narrow rocky edge (mild scrambling needed – best ascended rather than descended) above a great post-glacial corrie; it's a day's severe walking, for perhaps the grandest and certainly the most popular of all Lakeland panoramas, with dramatic ridges leading off for miles.

HIGH CUP NICK NY7426 A great scoop in the ridge of the Pennines, this is one of the most dramatic features in the whole of the range, and well worth the long but easily followed walk from Dufton, where the Stag is open all day in summer.

HIGH STREET NY4515 One of Lakeland's great fell walks, this is a Roman ridge road, reached best from Hawes Water reservoir (the hotel here is a good stop).

HONISTER PASS NY2213 From the top of the pass, stout-hearted and well equipped walkers can tackle Brandreth, and perhaps head on via Windy Gap for the least taxing ascent of **Great Gable**. Even if you decide not to go the whole way, the views in clear weather are spectacular.

HOWGILL FELLS SD6897 Bold 2,000-footers, empty and tough-going even for hardened walkers; the easiest walks into them are up Winder from Sedbergh, and from the A683 N of Sedbergh to majestic **Cautley Spout** waterfall.

HUMPHREY HEAD POINT SD3874 This ¾-mile-long headland protruding into the sea gives walkers stunning views of Morecambe Bay.

★ † **KIRKBY LONSDALE** SD6178 Small and usually quiet town of considerable character, with interesting old yards and ginnels and nice country shops; it's more lively on Thurs country-market day. Behind the fine **Church of St Mary** is a pretty stretch of the River Lune, good for walking or just lazing about – even swimming if it's hot. Along here, 87 steps lead up to Ruskin's View, a beautiful panorama over the Lune Valley, appealing countryside little visited by tourists. The Snooty Fox has decent food.

★ **KIRKOSWALD** NY5541 This attractive village has the ruins of a 13th-c **castle**, views towards the Pennines, and a useful pub.

LAKESIDE SD3787 The steamer stop at the S end of Lake Windermere, and the starting-point for the **Lakeside & Haverthwaite Railway**, a short steamtrip running up to Haverthwaite. There's a small collection of steam and diesel locomotives. Meals, snacks, shop, disabled access; trains daily May–Oct; (015395) 31594 for times; £3.40 return. By the steamer stop, the imaginatively laid out **Lakeside Aquarium** vividly demonstrates the story of a local river. You can walk in see-through tunnels along a re-created lake bed, with the area's animal (including otters), insect, bird and plant life all around, and there's a water lab with microscopes for close-up examinations of tadpoles, plankton and larvae. Snacks, shop, disabled access; cl 25 Dec; (015395) 30153; £4.95. **Graythwaite Hall Gardens** (2m N, SD3791) Well kept late Victorian garden, strong on rhododendrons and late-spring-flowering shrubs. Open Apr–Jun only; (015395) 31248; £2. The White Hart at Bouth does good food.

LANGWATHBY NY5633 **Eden Ostrich World** (Langwathby Hall Farm) Pigs, shire horses, ducks, geese and, of course, ostriches at this friendly farm. Meals, snacks, shop, disabled access; cl Oct–Easter; (01768) 881661; *£3.75.

LATTERBARROW SD3699 A dwarf in comparison to the great Lakeland fells, but elevated enough above a relatively low-lying area to give views over Windermere and Langdale.

LEVENS HALL SD4985 (on the A6) Impressive Elizabethan mansion based around an older core, with fine carved oak chimney-pieces, ceiling plasterwork, Spanish leather panelling, period furnishings and interesting paintings. The magnificent topiary **gardens** in their original layout of 1692 are perhaps the highlight; the fantastic shapes really standing out against the ancient grey stone of the house. Also model and other **steam engines** (pm only; in steam, bank hols and some summer Suns), play area, grand beech trees, and a deer park. Snacks, plant sales, shop, disabled access to grounds only; open Sun–Thurs, Apr–mid-Oct (plus gardens open wkdys in Oct); (015395) 60321; £5.20, grounds only £3.80. The Hare & Hounds is good for lunch.

LONG MEG AND HER DAUGHTERS NY5737 There's access off the lane N of Little Salkeld to this quaintly named **stone circle.**

LOWTHER NY5323 **Lakeland Bird of Prey Centre** Set in the huge Victorian walled garden at Lowther Castle, hawks, eagles, owls, buzzards and falcons, with flying displays at 11.30am, 2pm and 4pm. Also a craft gallery. Teas, shop, disabled access; cl Nov–Feb; (01931) 712746; £4.50.

MAIDEN WAY NY6433 The back road from Langwathby on the A686 through Skirwith to Kirkland leads to a **Roman road**, still sound for walkers, which plunges northwards into the bleak high Pennines, giving a great feeling of solitude. There are other walks from the clusters of sheep farms along the foot of the Pennines between here and Appleby.

MARYPORT NY0337 Small port with 18th- and 19th-c streets; the harbour has been smartly redeveloped in recent years, though sadly has yet to revitalise the town's fortunes. **Senhouse Museum** (The Battery, Sea Brows) Impressive collection of Roman military altar stones and inscriptions, dug from the former fort next door from the 1570s onwards, making it one of the oldest collections of antiquities in the country; also other artefacts, inc a Celtic serpent stone. Snacks, shop, disabled access; open Fri–Sun all year, plus Tues and Thurs Apr–Oct, bank hols, and daily July–Sept; (01900) 816168; £1.50. There's a straightforward **maritime museum** on Senhouse St (cl Sun exc pm in summer, and maybe lunchtimes especially in winter; free) and an **aquarium** on South Quay (snacks, shop, disabled access; £3.80). The 2 fully restored **steamships** in Elizabeth Dock have been re-opened by a group of enthusiastic volunteers, who bought them from the council for £1; best to check opening times on (01900) 815954; £1.50. The B5300 N has good views across to Scotland.

MILLOM SD1779 Not much of a town, but there's an interesting **church**, and **ruined castle** around what's now a farm (A5093 N: ask at the house for permission to look round the ruins). A decent **folk museum** on St George's Rd (cl Sun, and mid-Sept–Apr – exc Easter; £1). S of the town, a broad lagoon built to protect former mineworks is now a bird reserve, the loneliness exaggerated out of season when the nearby unsmart but enjoyable little resort of Haverigg SD1678 (great beaches, good sailing and fishing) has closed down; the Harbour Inn has decent, cheap food, and there are pleasant walks in the wild flower dunes.

MILNTHORPE SD5078 *See separate Family Panel on p. 122 for the* **Lakeland Wildlife Oasis**. The Wheatsheaf at Beetham and Blue Bell at Heversham are both good for lunch; the B5282 to Arnside has quiet estuary and mountain views.

MORLAND NY6022 **Highgate Farm and Animal Trail** Cheerful farm with plenty of fun activities from cuddling bunnies and egg-collecting to pony rides, and pig-feeding and sheep-racing; also falconry displays and an indoor play barn with go-karts and a sandpit. Snacks, shop, disabled access; cl Nov–Easter; (01931) 714347; £4.95.

NEAR SAWREY SD3795 **Hill Top** Small, remote, 17th-c farmhouse, kept exactly as it was when owned by Beatrix Potter, who wrote many of her stories here. Or at least as it was – apart from the tourists; the NT (great beneficiaries of Potter's generosity) feel the place is over-visited, and are keen to reduce visitor numbers – there's a daily limit of 800. It's so small they don't allow many people in at once, so if you do decide to visit be prepared to queue. Shop (the turnover is higher than at any other NT shop); cl Thurs, Fri, and Nov–Mar; (015394) 36269; £3.80; NT. The old-fashioned, NT-owned Tower Bank Arms (with nicely furnished bedrooms) is pictured in *The Tale of Jemima Puddle-Duck.*

PIEL ISLAND SD2363 Small island shared by a basic inn and a grand 14th-c ruined fortress commanding Barrow harbour and Morecambe Bay. It's reached by ferry (by arrangement only in winter) from Roa Island nr Barrow.

RAVENGLASS SD0896 Pretty sailing harbour by the well sheltered Esk estuary; in summer a local fishing boat sells freshly caught fish on the shore. **Ravenglass & Eskdale Railway** England's oldest narrow-gauge steamtrains, lovingly preserved, with open carriages chugging up 7 miles of unspoilt valley to Dalegarth; admirers say it's the most beautiful train journey in England. Cafés at each end, and a small museum at Ravenglass. Shop, disabled access (with notice); cl most wkdys Dec–mid-Feb, but best to phone for train times and dates; (01229) 717171; £6.30 return. Good 3-hour summer walk back from Boot (walks booklets from stations). The so-called **Walls Castle** just outside the village is actually a Roman bath-house; its walls stand taller than any other building of its age so far north. **Muncaster Castle, Gardens & Owl Centre** (A595 1m E) The same family have lived in this grand old house since 1208 – and will continue to do so as long as a magical glass drinking bowl remains intact. Extended over the centuries (especially in the 19th) from its original tower, its elegant rooms have rich furnishings and décor, inc fine Elizabethan furniture and embroidery. Entertaining Walkman tour, and glorious Esk and mountain views from the terrace. The lovely 77-acre grounds are particularly rich in species rhododendrons, and also have unusual trees, nature trails, an adventure play area, lots of rescued birds of prey, and a new owl centre with a closed-circuit TV of nesting owls, along with talks and flying displays every afternoon at 2.30pm (Apr–Oct), weather permitting. The house is being fully renovated and a new playground has been added. Meals, snacks, shop and plant centre, good disabled access; house open pm daily (exc Sat), garden and owl centre open all year; (01229) 717614; £5.20, just garden and owl centre £3.50. The fell above has nice views. A well restored working **watermill** (A595 NE) has Victorian machinery, and flour for sale. Cl Nov–Mar (exc wknds); (01229) 717232; £1.60. They also do good-value B & B.

† **RAVENSTONEDALE** NY7203 The village is notable more for its pleasant riverside scenery than for its buildings – apart from the unspoilt **church** which escaped Victorian refitting; longitudinal pews, 3-decker pulpit, steeply pitched gallery (steep stairs up), and a fine east window memorial to the Fothergill family (one was the last female Protestant martyr to be burned at the stake). Choose a bright day for the best light. The Black Swan and King's Head both have decent food.

RYDAL NY3606 **Rydal Mount** (off the A591) Wordsworth's sister Dorothy described Rydal as 'a paradise' when the family moved here from Grasmere in 1813; they stayed for the rest of their lives. The house itself is rather modest, with family portraits and period furniture, and it's what's outside that really stands out – the good-sized garden is still much as the poet laid it out, consciously picturesque, with original ideas that people are still rediscovering today. The setting is lovely, overlooking mountains and lakes, and they often have readings of the poetry it inspired. Shop; cl Tues Nov–Mar, and the last 3 wks of Jan; (015394) 33002; *£3. Decent campsites nearby. The Glen Rothay Hotel does respectable lunches.

ST BEES NX9511 **cliffs and birds** The Cumbrian coast has one particular lure for walkers and birdwatchers: the cliff path between Whitehaven and St Bees – each town has a railway station. From the beach car park NW of St Bees, an easy walk takes you up the nature-reserve sandstone headland, famous for its bird life, and with magnificent sea and hill views.

ST WILFRED'S CHURCH NY5128 (on the B6262 E of Eamont Bridge) A striking exception to the usual Lakeland rule of simplicity in churches, it is filled with magnificent furnishings inc Continental treasures; candlelit.

SEASCALE NY0204 **Sellafield** (off the A595) Several million pounds have been lavished on the imaginative exhibitions and displays at this nuclear power visitor centre. Not everyone approves of the pro-nuclear PR, but children certainly enjoy the hands-on, Disney-style approach to the industry, and there's still no entrance charge for any of the attractions. Meals, snacks, shop, disabled access; cl 25 Dec; (019467) 27027; free. Seascale itself has a pleasant beach, and a singularly scenic golf course, where every hole offers views of the sea or the mountains; the third tee ironically puts Sellafield into the same frame as a ring of prehistoric stones.

SEATHWAITE NY2109 Determined fell-walkers enjoy the unspoilt packhorse track from here over **Styhead Pass** down into Wasdale. The summit of the pass is a starting-point for a fiercely dramatic route up Scafell Pike.

SEDBERGH SD6390 Hardy small town at the foot of the Howgill Fells, with a helpful Yorkshire Dales National Park Centre on Main St (cl Dec–Easter). It's recently replaced its picturesque cobbles with an ordinary surface – much to the chagrin of the National Parks and English Heritage, who only a few years ago paid for new cobbles. **Holme Farm** (Middleton, just SW) 2pm tours of a traditional hill farm, with plenty of young animals and a nature trail. They do occasional evening tours with a badger watch. Disabled access; cl Oct–Feb exc by arrangement; (015396) 20654; £2. You may be able to camp here. The Dalesman is good for lunch.

SHAP NY5514 **abbey** (left towards Keld, off the A6 going N out of village) The best feature is the unspoilt and undeveloped riverside seclusion; the abbey itself is very ruined, but you can trace the 13th-c layout in some detail. Nearby, **Keld Chapel** is a lonely, untouched, shepherds' church in a riverside hamlet, and the gated Swindale road signed off the Bampton road nr Rosgill is pretty. The Greyhound is good value for lunch.

SIZERGH CASTLE SD5087 Lovely lakeside house, over the centuries harmoniously extended from its original sturdy 14th-c tower by the family who have lived here for generations. Fine Tudor and Elizabethan carving, panelling and furniture, Jacobite relics, and terraced gardens surrounding a grand flight of steps to water. Lots to interest a gardener, inc an enormous rock garden, Japanese maples, watergarden, wild flowers, and daffodils in the crab-apple orchard; the autumn colours are lovely. Snacks, shop, disabled access to garden; open pm Sun–Thurs Apr–Oct; (015395) 60070; £4, garden only £2; NT. The **Barn Shop** (Low Sizergh Barn) has plenty of fresh farm foods (cheese, meat, ice-cream, sausage and bread), and other local produce inc Morecambe Bay shrimps. Also a craft shop and pick-your-own strawberries. The tearoom overlooks the milking parlour, and they hope soon to bottle and sell the milk themselves. Cl Mon Jan–Mar; (015395) 60426; free. The Strickland Arms, owned by the NT, is handy for lunch.

SKELTON NY4635 **Hutton-in-the-Forest** (on the B5305) Some say this formidable mansion was the castle of the Green Knight of Arthurian legend. Grandly extended in the 17th c from its 14th-c peel tower core, then castellated more recently, it has a magnificent panelled gallery. A terraced garden runs down to the lake; there's an 18th-c walled formal garden, and a more romantic Victorian garden with grand trees, dovecot and woodland nature walk. Snacks, shop; garden open daily (exc Sat), house open pm Thurs, Fri and Sun Apr–Sept, plus Easter wknd and all bank hols; (017684) 84449; £4, garden only £2.50.

SKIDDAW NY2629 One of Cumbria's great peaks, but more accessible than many – quite an easy haul up from Applethwaite, for far views.

★ **TALKIN TARN** NY5457 Lovely lake with partly wooded shores, peaceful mountain views, plenty of space for strolling; a nature trail, orienteering and rowing boats; disabled access, teas. The village is pretty; the Blacksmith's Arms is popular for food.

TARN HOWS SD3299 An easy hour's walk from Hawkshead, this is a gorgeously photogenic small lake; particularly beautiful on a still clear autumn day (in summer it is somewhat spoiled by the crowds).

TEMPLE SOWERBY NY6128 **Acorn Bank** Richly planted terraced and walled garden with 250 varieties of medicinal and culinary herbs, clematis, unusual old fruit trees, and herbaceous borders; the steep wild garden drops down to a stream. A mill down here has been restored, and the wheel turns at weekends. This is a lovely spot at daffodil time. Shop, disabled access; cl Nov–Mar; (017683) 61893; £2.20; NT. The B6412 to Lazenby and then the back road through the Eden Valley to Armathwaite and on up to Wetheral gives delicious quiet views.

THORNTHWAITE NY2225 **Thornthwaite Galleries** Fine art, pottery and other crafts, as well as teas, summer try-your-hand-at-it demonstrations, and a play area. Snacks, shop, disabled access (but no facilities); cl Tues and Dec–Feb; (017687) 78248; free. **Thornthwaite Forest** The first-ever Forestry Commission plantation: walks through it, and up to the fells above (with lake and mountain views), are best started with a visit to the Whinlatter Visitor Centre (on the B5292, above Braithwaite). This has good explanatory forestry displays, shop, forest maps, teas. The Coledale Inn at Braithwaite is useful for lunch (and walkers).

★ **THRELKELD** NY3325 Attractive village, with decent food at the Salutation; the B5322 to Thirlmere is pretty, with a very photogenic view of Clough Head from the Brigham/Keswick side road, turning off just past Yew Tree Farm.

THURSTONEFIELD NY3156 Lough Fishery (B5307) hire tackle and boats (one suitable for disabled) for **trout fishing** on a well stocked, sizeable lake in peaceful woodland; cl Nov–mid-Mar; (01228) 576552.

† **TORPENHOW CHURCH** NY2039 A formidably Norman building, striking in itself, but worth looking at closely for the even older Roman masonry.

★ **TROUTBECK** NY4002 Delightful settlement of ancient farms strung along a steep valley. One of these, **Townend**, is the perfectly preserved home of a comfortably off, very traditional farming family who lived here for 300 years till the 1940s, the house showing little change over all that time. Solid, simple, unshowy comfort, and a sensible, down-to-earth and entirely self-sufficient layout. This is one of several such beautifully placed 'statesmen's' farms making up this lovely village below high fells. Cl am, all Mon (exc bank hols) and Sat, and Nov–Mar; (015394) 32628; £2.80; NT. **Holehird** (off the A592 S) The Lakeland Horticultural Society's hillside garden – 5 acres of well grown plants in wide variety, inc National Collections of hydrangeas and some other families; lovely views. Open all year, but manned in summer only; (015394) 46008; donations (they rely on these to maintain the gardens). Rookin House Farm has accompanied **horse-riding**, beginners welcome; (017684) 83561; £10 an hour. The quaint Queen's Head is good.

ULLSWATER NY4421 Here elegant Victorian steamers converted to diesel run between Pooley Bridge, Howtown and Glenridding; disabled access, cl Dec–Mar. Sailing dinghies can be hired by competent sailors from the sailing school at Glenridding (017684) 82541; cl winter. Rowing and other boats can be hired from Tindals in Glenridding; (017684) 82393; around £5 per hour, motorboats around £10.

The eastern shore is outstanding for walking; there are many different views, with a rewarding combination of waterside stretches and higher ground – from which to see more sweeping vistas. On the best and most popular stretch, Howtown–Patterdale–Glenridding, you will meet quite a few other people in summer (when it can be combined with the steamer for a round trip; best to take the steamer on the way out in case the service is cancelled). The charmingly old-fashioned Howtown Hotel makes good respite in a stunning setting, and Hallin Fell nearby gives an aerial view of the lake.

Aira Force Waterfall is the best-known walk destination on the western side – a pleasant if rather populated stroll of a mile or so, from the car park on the A592 just NE of the A5091 junction, through NT lakeshore woods to the waterfall itself, and the 'gothick' folly of Lyulphs Tower, with Wordsworth's daffodils a bonus in spring; the waterfall is at its best after rain or on a misty morning. Restaurant and shop, £1.20 parking charge.

ULVERSTON SD2877 On weekdays you can visit the factory of **Cumbria Crystal** (Lightburn Rd), and watch the craftsmen blowing, cutting and (Mon–Thurs) engraving; £1. The factory shop (cl Sun) is good value, with cheap seconds; disabled access. The Pork Pie Shop at the north end of Market Pl is very good indeed, while the Doll's House Man (Furness Galleries, Theatre St) makes doll's houses, farms, wooden animals and so on, and usually has examples on display. The **Heritage Centre** on Lower Brook St has local history displays (cl Sun, and winter Weds; £2). **Laurel & Hardy Museum** (Upper Brook St) The owner of this unique exhibition (a former mayor) really knows his subject, and it's his obvious enthusiasm that makes this one of Lakelands's best-loved attractions. Fittingly in Stan Laurel's home town, with delightfully informally presented mementos and all-day films. Shop, disabled access; cl Jan; (01229) 582292; £2. There are guided tours of **Conishead Priory** (Priory Rd), open pm most summer wknds; £2, and in the grounds you can visit a brand new Buddhist temple. The Rose & Crown (King St) has decent food, and the Bay Horse out at Canal Foot is ideal for lunch.

WALNEY ISLAND SD1869 Over the bridge from Barrow, this has some long roads of low houses, but is mostly a windswept sweep of duney grass, very offshore-feeling. Nature reserves at both ends, with excellent birdwatching and interesting plants. The George has worthwhile food.

WASDALE NY1808 The start for many magnificent fell walks, inc the ascents of Great Gable and Scafell Pike; one less taxing walk is straight up the head of the valley to the summit of Black Sail Pass and back. Apart from around the interesting churchyard, it's not so good for gentle strolls, and parking at Wasdale Head can be a problem in summer or at holiday times. Besides the Wasdale Head Hotel, the Screes lower down is a useful stop for food.

★ **WATENDLATH** NY2716 This lovely 'lost village' is little more than a tarn, a farm and a very modest café. There is a narrow road up from the B5289 by Derwent Water, but the village makes a very rewarding destination for a walk over the hills – for instance from Rosthwaite, where the Scafell is a fine walkers' local.

WATERMILLOCK NY4422 The **church** is worth stopping at for its evocative photographs of all its 1930s parishioners. **Sailing dinghies** can be hired by competent sailors from Ullswater Marina here.

★ ! **WHITEHAVEN** NX9718 Planned as an 18th-c industrial town and major port, this interesting place is being restored after a decline. The harbour is attractive at high tide (a bit dirty at low tide). Michael Moon's **bookshop** (now in Lowther St) has a vast and rewarding second-hand stock, the best in the Lakes; cl Sun, bank hols, and Weds Jan–Easter. There are some other interesting shops in side streets, and the Richmond (Hensingham) is useful for lunch. The town's history is excellently covered at **The Beacon** (West Strand), but what really makes this friendly heritage centre worth a look is the Met Office Weather Gallery on the top floor, full of hi-tech monitoring and recording equipment, and excellent hands-on displays explaining how weather forecasts are put together. The building itself is striking, with nice views over the town and harbour from the top floor. Shop, disabled access; cl Mon (exc bank hols) and 25 Dec; (01946) 592302; *£3.80. Just S at Sandwith, the Lowther Arms is recommended by readers for good homely food and accommodation, handy for the coast-to-coast walk.

WITHERSLACK SD4384 **Halecat Garden** (A590) Fine example of modern landscaping with nice views from the mainly herbaceous garden; plants for sale (especially hydrangeas). Mostly disabled access; cl all Sat and am Sun; (015395) 52229; free.

WORKINGTON NY0028 **Helena Thompson Museum** (Park End Rd) Some antique and Georgian costumes, as well as pottery, silver, furniture and local history, in period surroundings; cl Sun; (01900) 62598; free. **Workington Hall** (Curwen Park, NE) Former mansion, now a ruinous hulk around a Norman tower, in a public park – an odd conjunction. A famous letter by Mary Queen of Scots to her cousin Elizabeth I was written here. Shop; cl 1–2pm, am wknds, all Mon (exc bank hols), and Nov–Easter; (01900) 735408; 90p. Cobbled Portland Sq is pretty, and the Alamin Indian restaurant (Jane St) is worthwhile.

★ **Other attractive villages** in fine scenery, all with pleasant pubs, include Armathwaite NY5146, Bampton NY5118, Beckermet NY0207, Broughton Mills SD2290, Crosby Ravensworth NY6215 (Maulds Meaburn is also pretty), Garrigill NY7441, Hesket Newmarket NY3438, Langwathby NY5734 and Stonethwaite NY2613. The comfortable Kirkstile Inn at Loweswater NY1222 deserves a mention for its glorious setting.

For Birdoswald Roman Fort at Gilsland, *see Northumbria chapter* (the **goat farm** at Holme View nearby sells prize-winning traditional cheeses).

Where to eat

AMBLESIDE NY3804 **Sheila's Cottage** *The Slack (015394) 33079* 250-year-old cottage and converted barn run by the same owners for over 30 years, with 2 menus – one for light lunches and snacks, another for more substantial meals; popular afternoon tea, too; cl Sun, Jan. **£28**.

APPLEBY NY6921 **Royal Oak** *(017683) 51463* Warm, friendly and very popular, partly 14th-c coaching inn; with good and imaginative food, huge breakfasts, a fine range of beers, and carefully chosen wines; comfortable bdrms. **£21.40**|£6.95.

ARMATHWAITE NY5146 **Dukes Head** *(016974) 72226* Comfortable and friendly inn in an attractive village; a civilised lounge bar, coal fire, tasty home cooking, well kept real ales, and decent wines; bdrms. **£21.50**|£5.

ASKHAM NY5123 **Punch Bowl** *(01931) 712443* Bustling pub attractively set by a village green; with an interestingly furnished rambling bar, an open log fire, friendly atmosphere, generous helpings of good bar food, and well kept beers; cl pm 25 Dec; disabled access. **£16**|£6.50.

BAMPTON NY5118 **St Patricks Well** *(01931) 713244*. Imaginative food in unpretentious surroundings (also simple, good-value bdrms); no children later in evening; cl winter am Mon; **£16**|£5.25.

BOWNESS SD4097 **Hole in t' Wall** *(015394) 43488* Lively, intriguingly ancient Lakeland pub, with a friendly welcome for all; lots to look at, a fine log fire, good, home-made food, well kept real ales and home-made lemonade; can be busy in summer; no food pm Sun. **£15.75**|£5.75.

BOWNESS SD4097 **Porthole** *3 Ash St (015394) 42793* Long-established, bustling bistro with consistently good evening meals (mainly Italian); a genuine personal touch to the service, simple furnishings, and decent wine – a reliably enjoyable evening out; cl am Sat, Tues, mid-Dec–mid-Feb; limited disabled access. **£28**|£7.50.

CARTMEL FELL SD4288 **Masons Arms** *(015395) 68486* Old-fashioned building in an unrivalled setting with wonderful views; superb range of beers inc own-brew and interesting Continental real ales, and very popular food with many vegetarian options; self-catering accommodation; cl 25 Dec. **£20.30**|£6.95.

CROSTHWAITE SD4491 **Punch Bowl** *(015395) 68237* Prettily set Lakeland inn concentrating very much on excellent food; an interesting series of nicely furnished rooms with a good pubby atmosphere, well kept real ales, and friendly service; bdrms; cl 25 Dec. **£21**|£5.25.

DENT SD7187 **Stone Close** *Main St (015396) 25231* Cottagey, 17th-c teashop with pine furniture on the flagstones, cast-iron ranges, beams, and local crafts; home-made meals served from mid-morning until early evening, inc delicious cakes and pastries, and a relaxed, friendly atmosphere; bdrms, plus self-catering cottage next door; cl mid-week Nov–Feb. **£10.50**|£4.

KIRKBY LONSDALE SD6278 **Snooty Fox** *(015242) 71308* Rambling inn with plenty of interest to look at in the various relaxed pubby rooms; good interesting food, a no smoking dining annexe, well kept beers, and a pretty garden; cl pm 25 Dec; children must be well behaved; disabled access. **£20**|£4.95.

MELMERBY NY6237 **Shepherds** *(01768) 881217* Friendly place in an unspoilt sandstone village; with popular, home-made food inc a marvellous range of cheeses, delicious puddings, and lots of daily specials using only local produce; quick and amiable table service; cl 25 Dec; fair disabled access. **£15**|£6.

MELMERBY NY6237 **Village Bakery** *(01768) 881515* Converted stone barn selling wonderful organic bread and cakes for cream teas; super breakfasts (until 11am) and good, home-made restaurant food using produce grown organically behind the bakery; craft gallery upstairs; cl 25–26 Dec, 1 Jan; and at 2pm in Jan and Feb. **£20.35**|£4.

MUNGRISDALE NY3630 **Mill** *(017687) 79632* Friendly inn in a high secluded valley; with an open fire in the simply furnished main bar, and a separate restaurant; enjoyable home-made food inc home-baked bread, vegetarian and vegan dishes, and a wide choice of cheeses, well kept real ales, 10 wines by the glass, and really friendly, helpful service; there is a separate Mill Hotel in the same hamlet. **£18.85**|£7.95.

ST BEES NX9611 **Seacote Hotel** *Beach Rd (01946) 822777* Lovely views and headland walks; with decent food in the pleasant roomy bar or restaurant; welcoming to children. **£16**|£4.

SCALES NY3427 **White Horse** *(017687) 79241* Cosy and isolated farmhouse inn in a dramatic setting under Blencathra, a perfect haven after walks; best to book as the generously served food, using fresh local produce, is very popular; cl Mon, cl Nov–Apr. **£16.85**|£5.90.

TROUTBECK NY4103 **Queens Head** *(015394) 32174* Gabled 17th-c coaching inn with a rambling bar, some fine antique carving, and 2 roaring log fires; helpful, friendly staff, and extremely popular, first-class bar food, and well kept real ales; bdrms; cl 25 Dec. **£22**|£5.50.

ULVERSTON SD2978 **Bay Horse Hotel and Restaurant** *Canal Foot, past Glaxo (01229) 583972* Civilised and nicely placed inn overlooking Morecambe Bay; with beautifully presented, innovative food (interesting vegetarian choices and well hung Scotch steaks), well kept real ales and a good wine list; bdrms; children over 12; cl am Mon. **£35**|£8.50.

WINDERMERE SD4199 **Rogers** *4 High St (015394) 44954* Intimate, well liked little evening restaurant with beautifully presented and individualistic, French-based cooking; candlelit tables, helpful service and good-value set menus; cl Sun. **£20**.

YANWATH NY5128 **Gate** *(01768) 862386* Unpretentious village local, with really good inventive food, well kept real ales, and obliging service; log fire in the simple chatty bar, and a no smoking dining room. **£18.50**|£5.80.

Special thanks to Stewart Mackie, Ian Smith, Mrs M I Paton, Sue Wrathalls, E G Parish, A J Clark, Faye Hammill, Mrs Abigail Burgess, Roger Ashley.

Cumbria Calendar

Some of these dates were provisional as we went to press. Please check information with the telephone numbers provided.

Medieval rushbearing ceremonies mark the time when earthen church floors were covered with straw and sweet-smelling herbs for warmth and cleanliness. Rushes are carried into the church in a colourful procession, followed by children (bearing flowers and garlands) and the town or village band with merry-making and thanksgiving.

JANUARY

1 **Kirkby Stephen** Nine Standards Fell Race (017683) 71199
22 **Grasmere** Book Collectors' Festival at Dove Cottage – *till Sun 24* (015394) 35544

FEBRUARY

5 **Keswick** Queen's Hotel Jazz Festival – *till Sat 6* 017687) 73333
7 **Grasmere** Wordsworth Winter School at Dove Cottage: residential course of lectures, seminars and poetry – *till Fri 12* (015394) 35544

MARCH

20 **Ambleside** Daffodil and Spring Flower Show – *till Sun 21* (015394) 3225227
27 **Coniston** English Lakes Hotels Coniston 14: very scenic road race (015394) 41367

APRIL

2 **Barrow-in-Furness** Model Railway and Transport Exhibition at Forum 28 Main Hall – *till Sun 4* (01229) 583595; **Grasmere** Cumbria Local Artists' Annual Art Exhibition and Sale – *till Sun 11* (015394) 32963
3 **Furness** Morris Men: Easter Mummers Play in the South Lakes villages – *till Mon 5* (01229) 587120; **Whittington** Point to Point (015242) 21175

MAY

2 **Carlisle** Spring Flower Show at Bitts Park – *till Mon 3* (01228) 23203
3 **Penrith** May Day Gala (01768) 866147
8 **Barbon** National Speed Hill Climb for racing, sports and vintage cars at Barbon Manor (01539) 740777; **Carlisle** Spring Orchid Show at Carlisle College (016977) 2476
9 **Gleaston** National Mills Day at Gleaston Watermill: blacksmith, clog dancers (01229) 869244
21 **Keswick** Jazz Festival – *till Sun 23* (017687) 73333
29 **Coniston** Water Festival – *till 6 Jun* 015394) 41707; **Wasdale Head** La'al Cumbrian Beer Festival: local beers and ceilidh band – *till Mon 31* (019467) 26229; **Workington** Fair inc an historical pageant at Curwen Park (01900) 604078
31 **Kendal** Medieval Market (015395) 63595

Cumbria Calendar (cont.)

JUNE

2 **Appleby-in-Westmorland** Horse Fair at Fair Hill: gypsies from all over Europe gather on Fair Hill for this 300-year-old event with fortune telling, racing and spectacular horse, carriage and van sales on the last 2 days – *till Weds 9* (017683) 51177

4 **Cark-in-Cartmel** Garden and Countryside Festival at Holker Hall and Gardens: festival gardens, lectures and demonstrations, plus a steel band and children's play area – *till Sun 6* (015395) 58838

12 **Grange-over-Sands** Edwardian Festival – *till Sun 13* (015395) 34026

13 **Brough** Hound and Terrier Show: classes for working dogs and gun dogs, plus children's pets, and a dry-stone walling competition at Castle Garth (017683) 51921; **Carlisle** Carnival (01228) 625444

19 **Cockermouth** Carnival (01900) 824173

20 **Barrow-in-Furness** Gala: dancing, vintage vehicles and stunt cars (01229) 835123; **Flookburgh** Charter Fair (015395) 58421; **Keswick** Carnival (017687) 73189

27 **Endmoor** Country Fayre: ring events, wrestling (015395) 67858; **Patterdale** Ullswater Country Fair (01539) 723531

29 **Warcop** Rushbearing (017683) 41774

JULY

3 **Ambleside** Rushbearing (015394) 33205; **Cockermouth** Festival – *till Sat 31* (01900) 823608; **Musgrave** Rushbearing (017683) 41355; **Whitehaven** Carnival (01946) 66307

4 **Distington** West Cumbria Vintage Vehicle and Machinery Rally at Hayes Farm (01900) 871637

10 **Appleby** Town Carnival and Sports – *till Sun 11* (017683) 53056; **Grange-over-Sands** Lakeland Rose Show – *till Sun 11* (015395) 32375; **Maryport** Carnival (01900) 813171

17 **Brampton** Live 99: international line-up of roots music inc workshops (01228) 534781; **Carlisle** Cumberland County Show at Rickerby Park: music, children's entertainment, vintage vehicles, air and animal displays (01228) 560364; **Cleator Moor** Sports (01946) 811656; **Keswick** Convention: 124-year-old Bible convention – *till Sat 31* (017687) 72589

23 **Appleby** Jazz Festival at Appleby Castle – *till Sun 25* (017683) 51052

24 **Flookburgh** Cumbria Steam Gathering: arena events, circus – *till Sun 25* (015242) 71584; **Penrith** Agricultural Show at Brougham Hall Farm (01931) 713325

25 **Coniston** Country Fair (015395) 52314

28 **Ulverston** North Lonsdale Show at Bardsey Park (01229) 585140

29 **Ambleside** Sports: traditional Lakeland sports (015394) 45531

30 **Grasmere** Lake Artists' Society Summer Exhibition – *till 10 Sept* (015394) 35628

31 **Barbon** Motorcycle Speed Hill Climb at Barbon Manor (01539) 727828; **Cockermouth** Agricultural Show (01946) 692798; **Grasmere** Wordsworth Summer Conference at Dove Cottage: residential course of lectures, seminars and poetry – *till 13 Aug* (015394) 35544

Cumbria Calendar (Cont.)

AUGUST

1 **Silloth** Trawler Race (016973) 31358
4 **Cartmel** Agricultural Show (01539) 722777
5 **Ings** Lake District Sheepdog Trials at Hill Farm (015394) 33721 or (017684) 82260
6 **Ambleside** Summer Flower Show and Craft Fair: 3 marquees – *till Sun 8* (015394) 32904; **Lowther** Horse-driving Trials and Country Fair at Lowther Castle – *till Sun 8* (01931) 712378
7 **Grasmere** Rushbearing (015394) 35245
8 **Grange-over-Sands** Yorkshire Dales and English Lakes Historic Vehicle Run (015395) 34026
10 **Kirkby Lonsdale** Lunesdale Show (015396) 20471
12 **Appleby** Agricultural Show (01931) 714571
14 **Dalston** Agricultural Show (01228) 523034
16 **Langdale** Country Fair (01229) 837680
18 **Gosforth** Agricultural Show (019467) 24652
20 **Grasmere** Traditional Sports with Lakeland wrestling, hound trails, mountain bike and fell races inc English Hill Championship (015394) 32127
21 **Hutton-in-the-Forest** Skelton Horticultural and Agricultural Show at Old Park: vintage vehicle parade, equestrian and driving events, 140 stands, music (017684) 83032
25 **Kirkland** Ennerdale and Kinniside Show at Leaps Field (01946) 861391
26 **Crosby Ravensworth** Agricultural Show (01931) 715382
27 **Kendal** Folk Festival at the Brewery Arts Centre – *till Sun 29* (01539) 725133; also **Kendal** Gathering: music, theatre, vintage vehicles, torchlight procession – *till 12 Sept* (01539) 720040
28 **Broughton-in-Furness** Millom and Broughton Agricultural Show (01229) 772556; **Dufton** Agricultural Show and Sheepdog Trials (017683) 62015
29 **Cark-in-Cartmel** MG Rally at Holker Hall (015395) 58838; **Eskdale Green** Fête (019467) 23319; **Kentmere** Sheepdog Trials (01539) 821550; **Silloth** Wagon Pull: teams of 10 pull wagons along Criffel St (016973) 31257
30 **Keswick** Agricultural Show (016973) 23418; **Ravenglass** Country Fair and Sheepdog Trials at Muncaster Castle (01229) 717608; **Silloth** Carnival (016973) 31257

SEPTEMBER

3 **Wasdale Head** Beer Festival: live music, up to 50 real ales – *till Sun 5* (019467) 26229
4 **Kirkby Lonsdale** Victorian Fair: vintage vehicles, street entertainers, fair and dancing – *till Sun 5* (015242) 71237; **Lowick** Show (01229) 861420; **Ulverston** Market Charter Festival – *till Sat 18* (01229) 462334
9 **Crooklands** Westmorland County Show: around 240 trade stands (015395) 67804
10 **Kendal** Torchlight Procession: 2-mile-long procession with over 100 illuminated floats, plus classic cars (015395) 63018
16 **Loweswater** and **Brackenthwaite** Agricultural Show (01900) 85294
18 **Egremont** Crab Fair inc world gurning (pulling a face) championships, greasy pole, and pipe-smoking contest (01946) 821554

Cumbria Calendar (cont.)

19 Rosthwaite Borrowdale Shepherds' Meet and Show (017687) 77678
25 Boot Eskdale Show (019467) 23170
26 Urswick Rushbearing (01229) 587913

OCTOBER

9 Wasdale Head Show and Shepherds' Meet (019467) 25340
16 Ravenglass Thomas the Tank Engine at Ravenglass & Eskdale Railway – *till Sun 17* (01229) 717171
18 Windermere Powerboat Record Attempts at Low Wood Watersports Centre – *till Sun 24* (015394) 42595

NOVEMBER

7 Cockermouth Firework Display (01900) 823608; **Whitehaven** Cumbria Brass Band Association Annual Open Contest in the Civic Hall (01946) 61955
18 Santon Bridge Biggest Liar in the World Competition at the Bridge Inn (01946) 67575

DECEMBER

5 Keswick Victorian Fair (017687) 71337

We welcome reports from readers

This *Guide* depends on readers' reports. Do help us if you can – in return, we offer a discount on the next edition to people who've helped us with reports for it. Tell us what you think about places already in it, and anything extra you think we should say about them. And send us your ideas for inclusion in the next edition: places to visit, eat at or stay in, attractive drives or walks, maybe even unusual interesting shops you know of. Use the card in the middle, the report forms at the end, or just write – no stamp needed: *The Good Guide to Britain*, FREEPOST TN1569, Wadhurst, E Sussex TN5 7BR.

DERBYSHIRE

Beautiful scenery and some great days out – plenty to fill a holiday at any age; very good places to stay in.

The White Peak area, picturesquely cut by the intricate channels of the dales, has an abundance of generally gentle walking – and is very rewarding for drivers too. High, flat pastures have small fields of rich grassland enclosed by silvery stone walls, clusters of often very photogenic pale stone farm buildings, and small old-fashioned villages. In summer the most lovely dales do have almost a crocodile of walkers snaking along them, though even then you can find quiet areas. The limestone is laced with remarkable underground caverns: Poole's Cavern in Buxton the most striking, the Heights of Abraham in Matlock Bath a great family draw, Treak Cliff Cavern the best of those around Castleton. Further north, up in the High Peak, the scenery becomes bleaker and more forbidding – daunting for all but the most committed walker, though exhilarating for drivers – the A6024, A628 (rather slow), A57, A5002, A624 and A625 all have outstanding views.

Some highlights include the tramway museum at Crich, the enjoyable Peak Rail at Darley Dale, Lea Gardens (especially in late spring), and Bolsover Castle and Eyam Hall. Best of all are the stately homes: charming Haddon Hall and Sudbury Hall, and magnificent Chatsworth (with an amazing adventure playground now), Hardwick Hall, Calke Abbey and Kedleston Hall.

There's plenty of variety, with unusual places like proto-industrial Cromford, or ruined Wingfield Manor at South Wingfield. Families have plenty of entertainment, especially around Matlock (the Riber Castle wildlife park is a strong draw); the American Adventure theme park at Ilkeston is a reliable family day out, and people love the Chestnut Centre nature park at Chapel-en-le-Frith.

Where to stay

ASHBOURNE SK1846 **Callow Hall** *Mappleton Rd, Ashbourne DE6 2AA* (01335) 343403 **£115,** plus special breaks; 16 lovely, well furnished rms, excellent bthrms. Friendly and relaxed Victorian mansion up long drive through grounds with fine trees, surrounded by marvellous countryside; comfortable drawing room with open fire, fresh flowers and period furniture, very good traditional food using home-grown produce, excellent breakfasts, and kind hosts; good private fishing; cl Christmas, 1 wk Feb; disabled access.

ASHFORD IN THE WATER SK1969 **Riverside House** *Fennel St, Ashford in the Water, Bakewell DE4 1QF* (01629) 814275 ***£120,** plus special breaks; 15 individually decorated pretty rms. Creeper-covered Georgian house in delightful village, with attractive riverside gardens; a relaxed house-party atmosphere, antiques and log fires in cosy sitting rooms, fine modern English cooking, and good service; children over 8; disabled access.

BAKEWELL SK2272 **Hassop Hall** *Hassop, Bakewell DE45 1NS* (01629) 640488 **£98.90,** plus winter breaks; 13 gracious rms. Mentioned in the Domesday Book, in lovely parkland surrounded by fine scenery, this handsome hotel has antiques and oil paintings, an elegant drawing room, oak-panelled bar, good food and friendly service; tennis and croquet; no accommodation 3 nights over Christmas; partial disabled access.

BASLOW SK2572 **Cavendish** *Baslow, Bakewell DE45 1SP* (01246) 582311 **£134.20,** plus winter wknd breaks; 23 spotless, comfortable and individually furnished rms (varying in size). Charming hotel with magnificent views over Chatsworth estate; most attractive, well furnished day rooms (some furnishings come from Chatsworth), open fires and fresh flowers, fine food in 2 restaurants, very courteous staff; limited disabled access.

BASLOW SK2572 **Fischer's Baslow Hall** *Calver Rd, Baslow, Bakewell DE4 1RR* (01246) 583259 ***£100,** plus special breaks; 6 comfortable, pretty rms. Handsome Edwardian manor house with individually chosen furnishings and pictures, open fires, fresh flowers and plants; beautifully presented fine food using the best ingredients (some home-grown and lots of game and fish) in airy dining room or in lunchtime Café Max, and courteous attentive service; cl 25–26 Dec; children over 12 in evening restaurant.

BIGGIN-BY-HARTINGTON SK1559 **Biggin Hall** *Biggin-by-Hartington, Buxton SK17 0DH* (01298) 84451 ***£59,** plus special breaks; 18 spacious rms with antiques, some in converted 18th-c stone building and in bothy. Cheerfully run 17th-c house in quiet grounds with a very relaxed atmosphere, 2 comfortable sitting rooms, log fires; freshly cooked straightforward food with an emphasis on free-range wholefoods served at 7pm in the attractive dining room, and packed lunches if wanted; children over 12; limited disabled access.

BIRCH VALE SK0286 **Waltzing Weasel** *New Mills Rd, Birch Vale, Stockport SK12 5BT* (01663) 743402 **£65,** plus special breaks; 8 lovely rms. Attractive traditional inn with open fire, some handsome furnishings, daily newspapers and plants in the civilised bar, very good food using the best seasonal produce in charming back restaurant (fine views), excellent puddings and cheeses, obliging service; children over 7; disabled access.

CASTLETON SK1583 **Bargate Cottage** *Market Pl, Castleton, Sheffield S30 2WG* (01433) 620201 ***£43;** 4 well equipped rms. Lovely old cottage, beautifully restored by charming owners (who are full of local knowledge), with beams, inglenook fireplace, delicious breakfasts, enjoyable evening meals, super packed lunches, and pretty terraced garden; no smoking; cl 25 Dec; children over 12.

DOVE DALE SK1452 **Peveril of the Peak** *Dove Dale, Ashbourne DE6 2AW* (01335) 350333 **£100,** plus special breaks; 46 rms. Relaxing hotel in pretty village, with comfortable sofas and log fire in the lounge, modern bar and attractive restaurant overlooking the garden, and good English cooking; tennis; wonderful walking nearby; disabled access.

DOVERIDGE SK1134 **Beeches** *Doveridge, Ashbourne DE6 5LR* (01889) 590288 **£56;** 10 rms with home-made biscuits, fruit and flowers. 18th-c farmhouse on working farm (can watch the milking and meet the animals), with an open fire in the rustic beamed bar, several cosy beamed eating areas with original brickwork, good English food, and hearty breakfasts; cl Christmas; partial disabled access.

GLOSSOP SK0394 **Wind in the Willows** *Derbyshire Level, Sheffield Rd, Glossop SK13 9PT* (01457) 868001 **£85;** 12 individual rms with thoughtful extras. Set in 5 acres of grounds on the edge of the Pennines, this early Victorian house has a restful atmosphere in its tranquil, traditionally furnished sitting rooms; enjoyable set dinners (the restaurant is not open to the general public), particularly good breakfasts, and charming, helpful service; adjoining golf course; cl Christmas; children over 10.

GRINDLEFORD SK2478 **Maynard Arms** *Main Rd, Grindleford, Sheffield S30 1HP* (01433) 630321 **£73,** plus special breaks; 10 rms. Comfortable hotel with log fire and good Peak District views from the first-floor lounge, smart welcoming bar, interesting choice of food, particularly attentive service; good walks nearby.

HATHERSAGE SK2381 **George** *Hathersage, Sheffield S30 1BB* (01433) 650436 **£98.50,** plus special breaks; 19 pretty rms (the back ones are quietest). Substantial and comfortably modernised old inn with an attractive airy lounge, beamed friendly bar, popular food, and a neat flagstoned back terrace by rose garden; good walks all around.

HOPE SK1783 **Underleigh House** *Edale Rd, Hope, Castleton S30 2RF* (01433) 621372 ***£70,** plus special breaks; 6 thoughtfully decorated rms with own teddy bear.

In unspoilt countryside, this spotlessly kept converted barn has fine views from the comfortable sitting room, hearty breakfasts and very good home-made evening meals enjoyed around communal table in flagstoned dining room, friendly cheerful owners (who used to run a successful restaurant), and neat gardens; children over 12.

HOPTON SK2553 **Henmore Grange** *Hopton, Wirksworth DE4 4DF* (01629) 540420 **£55;** 11 rms, 9 with own bthrm. Friendly and carefully modernised stone-built farmhouse and renovated farm buildings with lots of original features; old-fashioned hospitality, and a garden designed to attract butterflies; disabled access.

KIRK IRETON SK2650 **Barley Mow** *Kirk Ireton, Ashbourne DE6 3JP* (01335) 370306 **£42;** 5 rms. 17th-c walkers' inn with lots of woodwork in straightforward series of interconnecting bar rooms, and solid fuel stove in beamed residents' sitting room; close to Carsington Reservoir; cl Christmas wk.

MATLOCK SK3060 **Riber Hall** *Matlock DE4 5JU* (01629) 582795 **£115,** plus special breaks; 14 lovely beamed rms with antiques, chocolates, and baskets of fruit. Elizabethan manor house in pretty grounds surrounded by peaceful countryside, with antique-filled heavily beamed rooms, and fresh flowers; 2 elegant dining rooms with reliable food and fine wines, and tennis and clay pigeon shooting; children over 10.

MONSAL HEAD SK1871 **Monsal Head Hotel** *Monsal Head, Bakewell DE4 1NL* (01629) 640250 **£60,** plus special breaks; 8 very good rms. Comfortable and enjoyable small hotel in marvellous setting high above River Wye with horsey theme in bar (converted from old stables), Victorian-style restaurant, well prepared decent food, and good service; cl 25 Dec; dogs by prior arrangement.

ROWLAND SK2072 **Holly Cottage** *Rowland, Bakewell DE45 1NR* (01629) 640624 **£40,** plus special breaks; 2 rms, shared bthrm; 200-year-old no smoking cottage on a quiet lane, surrounded by peaceful rolling countryside; with an open fire in the large lounge, wood-burning stove in panelled hall, an attractive dining room, excellent breakfasts with home-made rolls, bread and preserves, lovely gardens, and friendly black labrador; lots of walks; cl Nov–Dec.

ROWSLEY SK2566 **Peacock** *Rowsley, Matlock DE4 2EB* (01629) 733518 **£110,** plus special breaks; 16 comfortable rms. Handsome early 17th-c hotel by lovely trout river (private fishing in season), with well kept gardens, friendly staff, interesting old-fashioned inner bar, spacious comfortable lounges, and very popular restaurant.

SHIRLEY SK2141 **Shirley Hall Farm** *Shirley, Ashbourne DE6 3AS* (01335) 360346 **£40;** 3 rms, 2 with own bthrm. Timbered and part-moated farmhouse on family-run dairy/sheep/arable farm; with homely sitting room, fine breakfasts, and private coarse fishing and lots of walks; self-catering cottages; nearby pub for evening meals; cl for Christmas; children over 10.

SHOTTLE SK3149 **Dannah Farm** *Bowmans Lane, Shottle, Belper DE56 3DR* (01773) 550273 ***£70,** plus special breaks; 9 rms with old pine and antiques. Carefully restored and friendly Georgian farmhouse with 2 comfortable sitting rooms, and popular imaginative cooking in the attractive no smoking dining room; calves, ducks, hens, lambs in spring, Vietnamese pot-bellied pigs and farm dogs and cats; cl 25–26 Dec; children over 10.

We welcome reports from readers

This *Guide* depends on readers' reports. Do help us if you can – in return, we offer a discount on the next edition to people who've helped us with reports for it. Tell us what you think about places already in it, and anything extra you think we should say about them. And send us your ideas for inclusion in the next edition: places to visit, eat at or stay in, attractive drives or walks, maybe even unusual interesting shops you know of. Use the card in the middle, the report forms at the end, or just write – no stamp needed: *The Good Guide to Britain*, FREEPOST TN1569, Wadhurst, E Sussex TN5 7BR.

To see and do

DERBYSHIRE Family Attraction of the Year

! **Chatsworth** SK2670 (off the B6012) An elaborate new adventure playground has considerably broadened the already wide family appeal of this splendidly grand house, prettily set on the banks of the River Derwent. The well thought out facilities appeal to most ages, with sand and water play areas for younger children, and ropewalks and commando wires for older ones. Another highlight for children is the farmyard, with friendly demonstrations showing how they work the extensive estate, and plenty of opportunities to get close to cows, sheep, pigs and horses. Children can feed the fish in the trout-rearing tanks, and there's a milking demonstration every day at 3.30pm. The house itself has been home to the Duke of Devonshire's family for nearly 450 years. Sumptuously furnished, the 17 rooms on display show off a superb collection of fine arts, including memorable paintings by Rembrandt and Van Dyck, and all sorts of intriguing decorative details; there are usually less people around as the afternoon wears on. A set of 9 Regency rooms is usually open for a small extra cost. The lovely gardens cover over 100 acres and are full of surprises, with a maze, and brass bands playing on pm summer Suns. The surrounding park was landscaped by Capability Brown, and covers 1,000 acres; well marked walks and trails. You might have expected Chatsworth's considerable charms to have most interest for older visitors, but children themselves are surprised at how much they get out of coming here; the range of activities is varied enough to keep most families entertained for the bulk of the day. Meals, snacks, shops, garden centre, disabled access to garden only; cl Nov–mid-Mar; (01246) 582204. The best value for families is the £25 family pass, which gets 2 adults and up to 4 children into the house and garden, farmyard, and adventure playground (you don't have to go to all of these on the same day). Otherwise, individual ticket prices are £6.25 for the house and garden (£3 children), £3.60 garden only (£1.75 children), and £3 for just the farmyard and adventure playground. Also in the grounds, at Stud Farm, a mile and a half from the house towards Pilsley, is one of England's best farm shops, and the estate village of Edensor SK2469 opposite the main gate is a marvellous mix of styles, with fine views from the lane leading up out of it.

ALKMONTON SK1839 **Bentley Fields Open Farm** Unspoilt traditional livestock farm stretching over 245 acres; they milk their cows at 1 and 4pm. In spring you may see calving or lambing – or chicks pecking their way out of their eggs. Teas, shop, some disabled access; open daily Easter wk and May half term, bank hol Suns and Mons; (01335) 330240; £1.50. The Holly Bush over at Church Broughton is quite handy for lunch.

ASHBOURNE SK1846 A good few interesting Georgian buildings in the streets off the hillside market-place, especially leading to its elegantly proportioned **church**, which has a famous white marble statue of a sleeping child. **Derwent Crystal Centre** (Shaw Croft) Quality glassworks and engravers, with demonstrations and factory shop. Disabled access; cl winter Suns, 25–26 Dec, 1 Jan; (01335) 345219; free. The Gingerbread Shop sells the town's long-standing speciality. Smiths Tavern and the White Lion are good for lunch. The B5056 towards Bakewell and B5053 to Wirksworth have characteristic views. **Tissington Trail** This path for walkers and cyclists follows a disused railway track from Ashbourne up to Parsley Hay on the A515, where it joins the similar **High Peak Trail** from Buxton to nr Cromford. You can hire cycles in Ashbourne, or from Parsley Hay Cycle Hire, Parsley Hay.

★ **ASHFORD IN THE WATER** SK1969 One of the area's more appealing villages.

BAKEWELL SK2168 Away from the traffic this is a civilised small town, especially around the church. You can still get those raspberry tarts here, though there has been some dispute over the original recipe – two shops have claimed rights to the authentic Bakewell Pudding, and the case even went to court. **Old House Museum** (Cunningham Place, Bakewell) Folk collection in the 16th-c former home of pioneer industrialist Richard Arkwright, still with its original wattle-and-daub interior walls and open-timbered chambers. Cl am, and Nov–Mar; (01629) 813165; £2. The Castle Hotel and Aitch's are useful for lunch. 3m W, the surface remains of **Magpie Mine**, last worked in 1958 and stabilised in the 1970s, give a good idea of a 19th-c lead mine; free.

BIRCHOVER SK2362 The starting point for an extraordinary walk over **Stanton Moor**, where among quarry workings and prehistoric burial mounds are the Nine Ladies stone circle, a folly tower and a huge boulder known as the Cork Stone, equipped with metal steps for the courageous and adorned with at least 4 centuries' worth of graffiti (the earliest we found was 1613); there are good views into Darley Dale from the edge of the escarpment. Behind the Druid Inn in Birchover are **Rowtor Rocks**, a gritstone outcrop into which one Rev Eyre cut steps, benches and a stone armchair for contemplation.

BOLSOVER SK4770 The original ruined **castle** dates back to the 12th c, but was rebuilt in 1613 as a spectacular mock castle – about 200 years ahead of this fashion. Battlements and turrets outside, and inside allegorical frescoes, fine panelling and ornate fireplaces. Snacks, shop, some disabled access; cl winter Mon and Tues, 24–26 Dec; (01246) 823349; £2.95, inc Walkman tour. Just on the other side of the M1 at Sutton Scarsdale (and in fact looking down on the motorway), the ruins of a once-grand 17th-c hall are quite evocative.

★ † **BRADBOURNE** SK2152 Appealing Dales village, with an ancient Saxon cross outside its **Norman church**.

BUXTON SK0673 Much changed, but it still has some handsome buildings dating from its days as a flourishing spa, with Georgian terraces (the Crescent is a noble Georgian streetscape) and a restored Edwardian opera house. St Ann's Well is the only direct reminder of its water-based heyday – you can take the water for free here but, be warned, it's naturally warm. Many of the grander buildings come back to life during the town's excellent annual festival. The **Museum & Art Gallery** on Terrace Rd is a useful introduction to the area (cl Mon and winter Sun; £1). **Poole's Cavern** (Buxton Country Park, Green Lane) The best show cave in the Peak District and the longest in Britain, a spectacular natural limestone cavern in 100 acres of woodland, with well lit stalactites and stalagmites, and exhibitions on caves, woodland and Romans. As in other caverns, wrap up well. Snacks, shop, limited disabled

Days Out

Tram treat: Cromford village (or in spring/early summer Lea Gardens); lunch at the Derwent, Whatstandwell; Crich Tramway Museum.

Heights and depths: Matlock Bath, for Riber Castle Wildlife Park and the Heights of Abraham (inc cable car); lunch at the Boat House (A6 S); Peak District Mining Museum, Temple Mine, Peak Rail (*see Darley Dale entry on p.152*).

Aristocratic eye-catcher: Chatsworth House and Gardens; lunch at the Devonshire Arms, Beeley; Edensor village; stroll by the River Derwent in Chatsworth estate.

access; cl Nov–Feb; (01298) 26978; £4.20. **Grin Low Woods** (just S of town) are well landscaped, with mature woodland and the Victorian folly of Solomon's Temple (good views from the top), though it's not always open. The Clubhouse (Water St) is good for lunch.

CALKE ABBEY SK3622
One of the most rewarding NT properties in Britain, an unusual baroque mansion still in pretty much the same state as when the last baronet died here in 1924. You might expect the splendidly decorated rooms with their fascinating displays (inc an extensive natural history collection), but it's quite a surprise to find the more dilapidated corridors and areas where family possessions were just bundled together in heaps. This gives you a better appreciation of how the Abbey was a much-loved family home – and of how things forgotten in the attic can quickly become social history. Also extensive wooded parkland and walled gardens. Meals, snacks, shop, disabled access; cl Thurs, Fri, and Nov–Mar, house usually cl am; (01332) 863822; £4.90, garden only £2.20 – there's a £2 vehicle charge on entering the park, refundable on entry to the house (which has a timed ticket system); NT. The Hardinge Arms at Kings Newton is quite handy for lunch, and the cosy Saracen's Head at Heath End has good sandwiches.

CASTLETON
SK1482 Very much geared to visitors, and filled with walkers and cavers in summer; plenty of cafés, and shops selling expensive worked pieces of the Blue John fluorspar that's found only in the nearby mine workings. A small **Blue John Museum** in one of the Cross St craft shops has some magnificent examples. The village's attractive dark stone buildings (one of the most impressive now a youth hostel), are dominated by the ruins of **Peveril Castle**, built high above in the 11th c – magnificent views. Shop; cl Mon and Tues from Nov–Mar, 24–26 Dec; (01433) 620613; £1.75. **Peak Cavern** Right in the village, this is the biggest natural cavern in the county and really does seem huge – the entrance hall is so large it used to house an entire village. From there it's a ½-mile walk along lighted subterranean passageways to the Great Cave, 45 × 27 metres (150ft wide, 90ft long). By the time you reach the Devil's Dining Room you'll be nearly 140 metres (450ft) underground. Snacks, shop; cl wkdys Nov–Easter; (01433) 620285; £4.50. **Blue John Cavern** (Buxton Rd) Containing 8 of the 14 known veins of Blue John, this has been the main source of the precious stone for nearly 300 years. It's an impressive example of a water-worn cave, over a third of a mile long, with chambers 45 metres (150ft) high. Snacks, shop; (01433) 620638; £5. **Speedwell Cavern** (Winnats Pass – the former A625 W, SK1382) Very atmospheric former lead mine, with 105 steps down to a ½-mile underground boat trip along floodlit passages, finishing in a cathedral of a cavern with an impressive 'bottomless pit'. Good fun, though you may have to queue. Shop; (01433) 620512; cl 25 Dec; £5. **Treak Cliff Cavern** (off the former A625 W) Informative tours of the first Blue John mine, worked since 1750, with rich veins of the mineral and quite staggering stalactites and stalagmites. Well placed lights create spooky shapes and atmospheric shadows. The entrance is narrow, and it's quite steep, but this is a favourite with readers. Snacks, shop; cl 25 Dec, but worth checking first in winter; (01433) 620571; £4.95. The Rose Cottage, Castle, Olde Nag's Head and Peak all do decent food, and in the pretty nearby village of Hope, the Cheshire Cheese is good. The B6061 to Sparrowpit (where the Wanted Inn has good-value home cooking) has fine views. The most varied **walks** in the High Peak are found around Castleton and Hope. The great walk here takes in Castleton, the Lose Hill/Mam Tor ridge, the caves, and Winnats Pass; Mam Tor is so shaly and prone to landslips that it's dubbed the Shivering Mountain – the abandoned section of the A625 is a testament to the victory of the mountain over man. Cave Dale is an optional side trip from the back of Castleton. Quarrying has had an unfortunate effect on the local landscape in the area, and limits walks further afield, though there are some

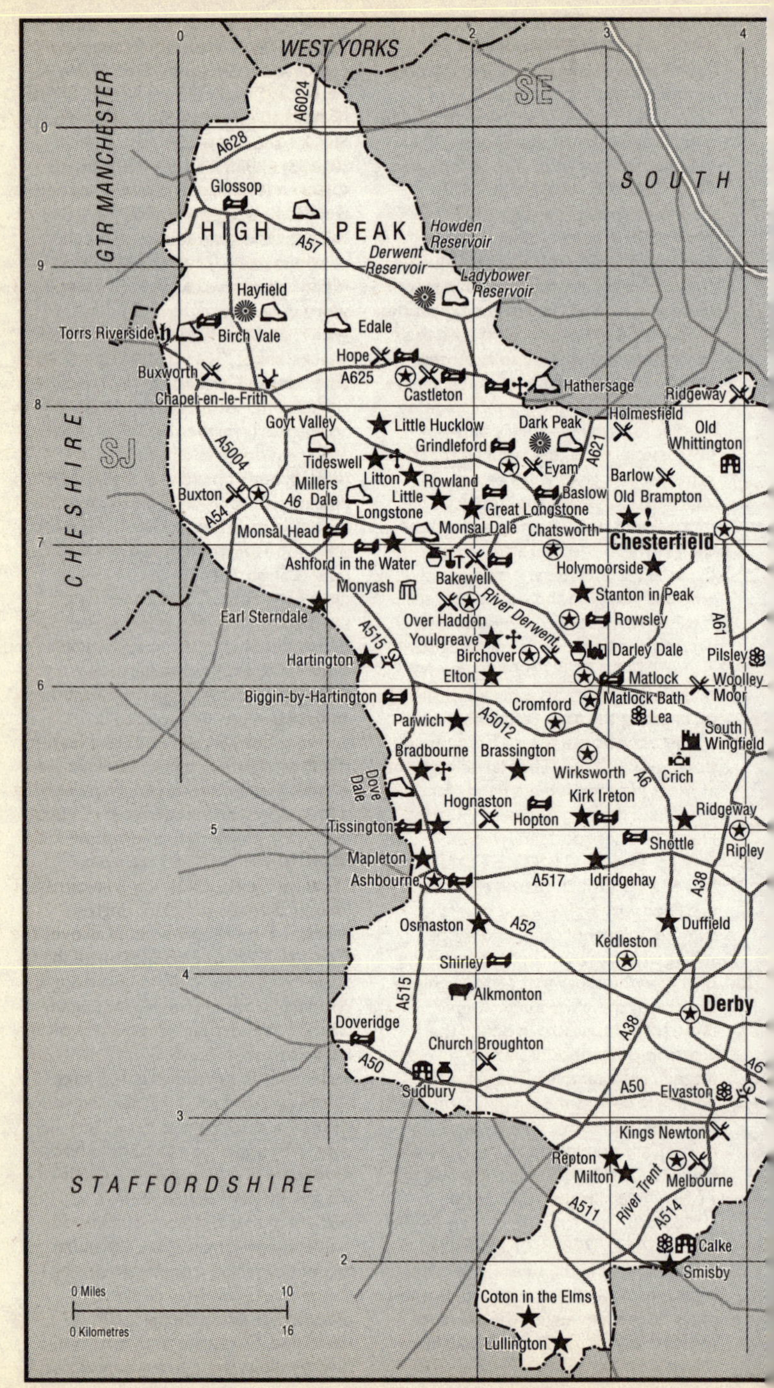
WEST YORKS
SE
GTR MANCHESTER
SOUTH
HIGH PEAK
CHESHIRE
SJ
STAFFORDSHIRE
A6024
A628
Glossop
A57
Howden Reservoir
Derwent Reservoir
Ladybower Reservoir
Hayfield
Torrs Riverside
Birch Vale
Edale
Hope
A625
Castleton
Hathersage
Buxworth
Chapel-en-le-Frith
Ridgeway
Holmesfield
Old Whittington
Goyt Valley
Little Hucklow
Dark Peak
A621
A5004
Tideswell
Grindleford
Eyam
Barlow
Millers Dale
Litton
Rowland
Baslow
Old Brampton
Buxton
A6
Little Longstone
Great Longstone
A54
Monsal Head
Monsal Dale
Chatsworth
Chesterfield
Ashford in the Water
Bakewell
Holymoorside
Monyash
Stanton in Peak
Earl Sterndale
River Derwent
Over Haddon
Rowsley
A61
A515
Youlgreave
Birchover
Darley Dale
Pilsley
Hartington
Elton
Matlock
Woolley Moor
Biggin-by-Hartington
Cromford
Matlock Bath
Lea
Parwich
A5012
South Wingfield
Bradbourne
Brassington
Dove Dale
Wirksworth
A6
Crich
Hognaston
Kirk Ireton
Hopton
Ridgeway
Tissington
Shottle
Ripley
Mapleton
Ashbourne
A517
Idridgehay
A38
Osmaston
A52
Duffield
Kedleston
Shirley
A515
Alkmonton
Derby
Doveridge
Church Broughton
A38
A50
Sudbury
A50
Elvaston
A6
Kings Newton
Repton
Milton
Melbourne
River Trent
A511
A514
Calke
Smisby
Coton in the Elms
Lullington
0 Miles 10
0 Kilometres 16

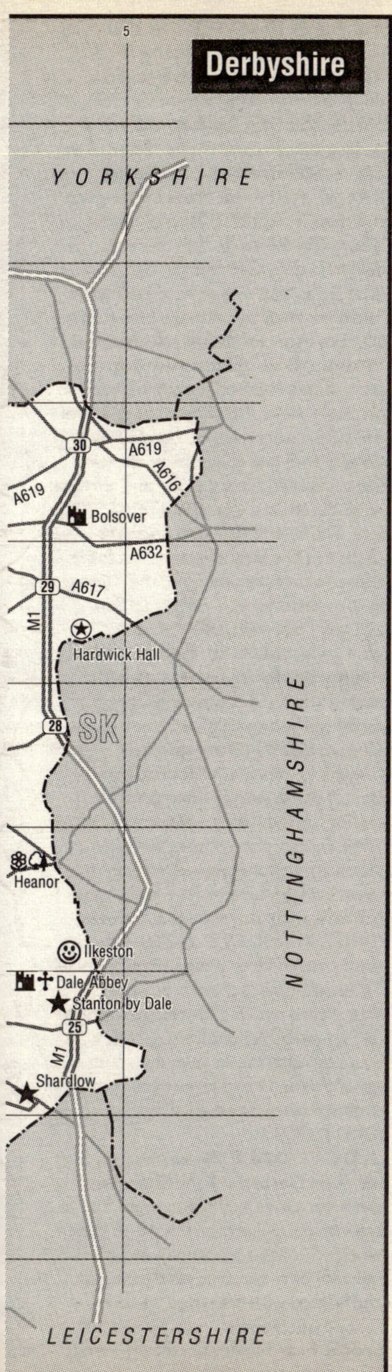

pleasant walks to be had in the gentler high pastures of the limestone country to the S.

CHAPEL-EN-LE-FRITH SK0580 **Chestnut Centre** (A625) Warmly recommended conservation park, concerned especially with breeding otters and barn owls, but other animals and birds of prey too. Good observation platforms. Snacks, shop; cl wkdys Jan and Feb; (01298) 814099; £4.50. The Cross Keys has decent food (all day Sun).

★ **CHATSWORTH** SK2670 (off the B6012) *See separate Family Panel on p.147* for the stately home. Around Chatsworth are 2 more most attractive small estate villages, Baslow and Beeley (which has a good food pub). The B6012 (busy in summer) has pleasant views.

CHESTERFIELD SK3871 Not a tourist town, but its largely 14th-c **church** has a really striking leaning spire, and is a rich building inside; the town **museum** (Corporation St) has the full angle on it. The Victorian market hall has flourishing markets every day exc Tues and Sun (junk Thurs, street entertainment summer Sats). Nearby **Grassmoor Country Park** is a pleasant place to stroll; fishing lake. The Derby Tup (Sheffield Rd) is an enjoyable ale house with good-value simple food.

CRICH SK3455 **National Tramway Museum** A favourite of many correspondents: lovingly restored vintage trams from all over the British Isles and beyond, many of them in working order and running along a 1-mile period street overlooking the Derwent Valley. Unlimited rides on the vehicles, and very good indoor exhibitions and displays. They have a guide book in Braille. Meals, snacks, shop, some disabled access; cl Fri Apr–May and Sept–Oct (exc school hols), and Nov–March; (01773) 852565; £5.90. The Derwent over at Whatstandwell on the A6 has good-value food. The village is pronounced 'Cry', not 'Critch', and is the setting for TV's *Peak Practice*.

CROMFORD SK2956 A good example of an 18th-c cotton-milling village, little developed after its original building, and rewarding to stroll through. **Cromford Mill** (Mill Lane) is where Richard Arkwright established the world's first successful water-powered cotton mill in 1771 – the beginning of the factory age; several craft shops. Wholefood restaurant, shop, disabled access; cl 25 Dec; (01629) 825776; site free, tours £2. Carefully preserved North St is the first true industrial street in the world (built in 1777). The restored **canal** is a quiet and attractive early Industrial Revolution setting with a restored steam-powered pumping house and a fine aqueduct over the river; pleasant walks along here, and horse-drawn barge trips in summer; branching off at Roystone Grange is an archaeological trail. The **High Peak Junction Workshops** out here have exhibitions and a film (cl winter wkdys; 50p). The Boat has well priced food. The A5012 to Grangemill gives evocative views.

DALE ABBEY SK4338 Abbey ruins, Hermits Cave and remarkable All Saints church, part of which was formerly the village inn; the Carpenters Arms has good-value food, and the village is attractive.

DARLEY DALE SK2762 **Peak Rail** Blooming private railway, very popular with readers. Trains run between here and Matlock, then on to Rowsley. The eventual aim is to run as far as Buxton. Wknd restaurant car, shop, disabled access; usually open wknds all year (not Sat in depths of winter), plus most days in summer hols, but best to check times; (01629) 580381; £5. The nearby **Red House Working Carriage Museum** has a collection of vehicles and equipment, some of which you can ride in. Also horse and pony rides – booking essential. Teas, disabled access; cl 25 Dec; (01629) 733583; £2.50. The Grouse (A6 N) is handy for a snack.

DARK PEAK SK2575 The E edges include the abrupt ramparts of Curbar Edge and Froggatt Edge, popular with rock-climbers and easily accessible from the road. Birchen Edge and Wellington's Monument are obvious objectives for walkers from the Robin Hood at Curbar.

DERBY SK3536 A big busy city, but not too daunting for a visitor to penetrate, and has several things worth visiting; it's got far more open spaces than you'd expect, and a pedestrianised centre. The 16th-c tower of the **cathedral** is the second highest in the country; the rest of the building was replaced in the 18th c. Bess of Hardwick is buried in the vaults, and there's a delightful early Georgian screen. Shop, disabled access; £2 suggested donation. The quaint nearby Olde Dolphin (Queen St) has bargain food all day. **Industrial Museum** (Full St) Restored early 18th-c silk mill and adjacent flour mill, with probably the world's finest collection of Rolls-Royce aero engines, and a Power Gallery with lots of hands-on displays. Shop, disabled access; cl Sun and am bank hols, 25–28 Dec, 1 Jan; (01332) 255308; free. The town **Museum and Art Gallery** (The Strand) stands out for its collections of porcelain and the paintings by local artist Joseph Wright (cl Sun, 25 Dec, 1 Jan; free), and you can get a good idea of 18th-c domestic life at **Pickfords House** (Friargate), with period furnished rooms and Georgian garden (cl Sun and 25 Dec; free). **Royal Crown Derby** (Osmaston Rd) Cheerfully informative tours of bone-china factory, with a visitor centre tracing the industry's development from 1748. Snacks, shop (lots of bargain seconds); visitor centre open daily; no tours bank hols, no tours wknds, bank holidays or factory shut-down weeks; (01332) 712800; £5.25 (£2.50 without tour) – no children under 10 on tours. A Tudor grammar school in St Peter's churchyard is now a **Heritage Centre** (cl Sun and bank hols; free). Ghost walk tours through the city's tunnels and other themed tours leave here 7pm in summer; booking essential on (01332) 299321.

DOVE DALE SK1452 Shared between Derbyshire and Staffs, with the River Dove as the boundary, this is the most popular of all the dales. Partly wooded, it has a beautifully varied mixture of water, trees and pastures, and is lined with crags and curiously shaped outcrops of rock. To see fewer people, head further upstream. Handy nearby refreshment places are the

Okeover Arms at Mapleton (with a domed church, and a nice riverside walk to Thorpe), the Coach & Horses at Fenny Bentley and (to be found on the Staffs side) the Izaak Walton Hotel nr Ilam (cosier inside than it looks from out).

EDALE Famous as the start of the 256-mile **Pennine Way** to the Scottish border, with a good information centre and a couple of hikers' pubs. It tends to be packed with expectant long-distant walkers on Sunday mornings. For a taste of the Dark Peak proper, this can be the start for ½-day walks that quite quickly take you up through the stone-walled pastures of the valley on to the edge of the dark plateau above. The track signed as the alternative Pennine Way route up Jacob's Ladder is easier to find, and has more to see, than the official Pennine Way plod across a huge blanket bog.

ELVASTON CASTLE COUNTRY PARK SK4032 (B5010) 200 acres of lovely 19th-c landscaped parkland, with formal and Old English gardens, wooded walks, and wildfowl on the ornamental lake. Also museum with traditional craft workshops, and nature trails. Meals, snacks, shop, disabled access; open all year, but museum cl Mon, Tues, and Nov–Apr; (01332) 571342; museum £1.20, car park 70p wkdys, £1.30 wknds. Shardlow is convenient for lunch.

★ **EYAM** SK2276 Attractive secluded village with a dark past: in the Great Plague sick villagers confined themselves here for fear of infecting people outside – plaques record who died where, and stones on the village edge mark where money was disinfected (recent uncharitable suggestions that over the centuries too much has been made locally of what was actually just a later measles epidemic have been firmly refuted). **Eyam Hall** Sturdy-looking 17th-c manor house, still very much a family home, with furniture, portraits and tapestries, fine Jacobean staircase and impressive flagstoned hall. Small craft centre in the stables. Good meals and snacks (wonderful home-made cakes), shop, some disabled access; house open Weds, Thurs, Sun and bank hols Easter–Oct, craft centre open daily exc Mon; (01433) 631976; £3.75 – timed ticket system. The Miners Arms is very good for lunch. Just up the B6521 at Upper Padley, **Padley Chapel** is an interesting 15th-c revival, effectively restored in 1933.

GOYT VALLEY SK1077 Well wooded valley with its 3 miles of reservoirs. It's a man-made landscape, but nonetheless charming for walks or picnics; reached off the A54 W of Buxton.

HADDON HALL SK2066 One of the most perfectly preserved medieval manor houses in England, still with its 12th-c painted chapel, 14th-c kitchen, and banqueting hall with minstrels' gallery. Some rooms can seem rather bare (there aren't many furnishings or pictures), but a bright spot is Rex Whistler's painting of the house in the silver-panelled long gallery. It's a particularly pretty location in summer when the long terraced rose gardens are in full bloom. Several films and TV adaptations have had scenes shot here in recent years. Meals, snacks, shop; cl Oct–Mar; (01629) 812855; £5.50. In the pretty village of Over Haddon (SK2066) the **Lathkill Dale Craft Centre** (Manor Farm) has plenty of craft shops and demonstrations, and a café; cl 25 Dec; (01629) 813589; free. The Lathkil Hotel is good for lunch, and nearby roads have attractive views.

HARDWICK HALL SK4663 The marriages of the redoubtable Bess of Hardwick couldn't necessarily be described as happy but she certainly did very well out of them, the fourth leaving her enough money to build this triumphant Elizabethan prodigy house. The beautifully symmetrical towers are crowned with the monogram ES, and there's an amazing expanse of glass (her sight was dimming). Also fine tapestries and needlework, large park, and gardens laid out in the walled courtyard. Meals, snacks, shop, disabled access; open Apr–Oct, house cl am, and all day Mon (exc bank hols), Tues and Fri; (01246) 850430; £2 vehicle charge to enter the grounds, refundable against full tickets –

£6 house and garden, £2.70 garden only, operating on a timed ticket; NT. Not far from this 'new' house is the shell of **Hardwick Old Hall**, the first house that Bess built; (01246) 850431; £2.30 (NT members free). A joint ticket is available for both houses. Also on the estate is a restored watermill (another £1.50, NT). The park is attractive for walks, and at the end of it the Hardwick Inn, also NT-owned, is useful for lunch.

★ **HARTINGTON** SK1260 This attractive village has a good cheese shop selling local stilton, and a pottery on Mill Lane.

† **HATHERSAGE** SK2281 Charlotte Bronte wrote Jane Eyre here. The **church** is the legendary site of Little John's grave. It's a good village for walkers and climbers, with pleasant walks including the attractive moorland, pastures and woodland making up Longshaw, near the Fox House Inn up on the Sheffield road; or, closer and gentler, down along the River Derwent towards Grindleford. Besides the George, the Plough (A622) is useful for lunch. The B6001 S is a pleasant drive.

HAYFIELD SK0387 This moorland village and its attractive nearby smaller sister Little Hayfield have good walks around them, both up towards Kinder Scout and to the Lantern Pike viewpoint in the opposite direction. There's also a popular walk or cycle ride – the **Sett Valley Trail** – along a hillside former railway to New Mills, looking down on the mill buildings by the River Sett. There's a handy bike shop in Hayfield itself, and an information centre for the Trail. The Lantern Pike Inn in Little Hayfield could hardly be more welcoming.

HEANOR SK4545 **Shipley Country Park** Medieval estate developed and landscaped in the 18th c, with 600 acres of woodland, lakes and fields. A pleasant place to wander, with railway lines transformed into leafy walkways; you can hire bikes (daily July–Aug, wknds Easter–Nov, £4 for 2 hours). Snacks, shop, disabled access; visitor centre cl 25 Dec; (01773) 719961; free.

HIGH PEAK SK1092 These dark moors are one of England's great wildernesses. They have few easy circular routes, but are largely very bleak indeed, and often consist of private grouse moor with no right of public access. The car park at the top of Snake Pass (A57 Glossop–Hathersage) is near the centre of the biggest of the National Trust's moorland holdings here, giving free access to the miles of Hope Woodlands (there aren't actually many trees).

☺ **ILKESTON** SK4444 **American Adventure** (Pit Lane) Excellent theme park with around 100 rides and attractions; all supposedly have an American theme, though this can be rather tenuous – ever so English Sooty stars in a Wild West show. Highlights include dropping 13 metres (42ft) at 62mph on the Nightmare Niagara triple log flume, and the Missile, a stomach-churning roller-coaster that twists and turns at unfeasible angles, before going the whole route again backwards. Live shows include a Wild West saloon and a Mexican fiesta, and there's a huge indoor play area for younger children. Meals, snacks, shops, good disabled access; cl Nov–Mar; (01773) 531521; £12.99.

KEDLESTON HALL SK3140 This 18th-c Palladian mansion is thought by many to be the finest example of Robert Adam's work – it's certainly the least altered. Interesting objets d'art, original furnishings, good collection of paintings, and a museum of items collected by Lord Curzon when he was Viceroy of India. Adam designed a charming boathouse and bridge in the park outside, which also has extensive formal gardens with marvellous rhododendrons, and long woodland walks. Meals, snacks, shop, disabled access (best to phone in advance); open Apr–Oct, house pm Sat–Weds, grounds daily and wknds Nov–Dec; (01332) 842191; £4.70, or £2 per vehicle for just the park; NT. The Cock at Mugginton is fairly handy for something to eat.

LADYBOWER RESERVOIR SK1788 Pretty enough to drive past; also the lane up to the car park by the Derwent Reservoir (with a summer minibus service beyond to Howden Reservoir) gives plenty of easy waterside-forest **walking** on the relatively sheltered stone-walled slopes of the upper parts of Derwent Dale, with access to the higher moors for better views – for example, up on to Win Hill, or on a kind day on to the formidable Derwent Moors to the E. The Ladybower pub down on the main road is useful.

LEA GARDENS SK3258 Beautiful woodland gardens with rhododendrons inc rare species and cultivars, azaleas and rock plants. Home-baked snacks, shop and garden centre, some disabled access; open 20 Mar–4 July; (01629) 534380; £3.

★ **THE LONGSTONES** SK1871 Little Longstone and nearby Great Longstone are charming steep stonebuilt villages, and the back road from Baslow through here to Tideswell is a pretty drive. The White Lion has decent food.

MATLOCK SK3059 **Riber Castle Wildlife Park** (off the A615 at Tansley) Specialising in rare breeds and endangered species of birds and animals (it's renowned for its lynx), a 25-acre park set high up on Riber Hill in the grounds of ruined Riber Castle. Excellent views; you find yourself looking down on the Heights of Abraham (*see Matlock Bath entry*). Wrap up well – even in summer the wind can make it feel rather chilly. Snacks, shop, disabled access; cl 25 Dec; (01629) 582073; £4.50. The Boat House is good value for lunch, with interesting walks. The A615 E and B5056 and B5057 W are good drives.

MATLOCK BATH SK2958 Pleasantly busy place, with lots to do and attractive illuminations by the river on autumn evenings. A spectacular wooded cliff looks across the lower roadside town to pastures by the Derwent; up the side of the gorge, quiet lanes climb steeply past 18th- and 19th-c villas. **Peak District Mining Museum and Temple Mine** (Temple Rd) Lively exploration of mining, with a unique early 19th-c water-pressure pumping engine, and interactive display on the pitfalls of working in a mine. Also tours of the old Temple Mine workings, and the chance to pan for minerals – they found a tiny amount of gold not so long ago. Snacks, shop, disabled access; cl 25 Dec; (01629) 583834; £2.

Heights of Abraham Derbyshire is full of stunning show caverns, but few can boast as thrilling an introduction here: cable cars whisk you up from the Derwent Valley to a 60-acre country park, with dramatic views over the ancient limestone gorge (not to mention a railway and the busy A6). At the end of the 5-minute trip a multimedia show explains how the rock was formed 325 million years ago, then guides escort you into the 2 show caverns. Outside are nature trails, the Prospect Tower to climb, dinosaur displays and a few play areas (inc a maze), as well as great views and nicely laid out woodland walks; usually Punch & Judy shows or similar entertainments. Meals, snacks, shop, some disabled access; open daily Easter–Oct and some winter wknds (best to check first as dates can depend on the weather); (01629) 582365; £6.20. **Gulliver's Kingdom and Royal Cave** (1m S, off the A6) Family theme park with chair lift and hectic rides, cave tour, and cowboy and ghost towns; it's aimed at the under 13s so don't expect white knuckles. Meals, snacks, shops; open wknds and school hols Easter–Oct; (01629) 580540; £5.55. The **Aquarium and Hologram Gallery** (cl winter wkdys; £1.80) is a useful family attraction if you're staying in the area. The Temple Hotel (Temple Walk) has great views and decent food.

MELBOURNE SK3825 This pleasant small town has a good relaxed feel and villagey lanes; the White Swan and Railway Hotel are good for lunch. The **church** of St Michael and St Mary is impressive, more like a cathedral than an ordinary parish church. **Melbourne Hall** Behind its 18th-c façade, this grandly extended house dates back in part to the 13th c, and has twice been the home of British prime ministers; fine pictures and furnishings. Glorious formal gardens with fountains, pools, and famous yew tunnel; interesting craft centre (open all year). Meals, snacks, shop, disabled access; Hall open pm daily in Aug (exc first 3 Mons), plus gardens open pm Weds, Sat, Sun and bank hols Apr–Sept; (01332) 862502; £2.50 (additional charge for gardens).

MILLERS DALE SK1573 The B6049 N off the A6 SE of Buxton gives access to **Millers Dale**, just past the little village of that name (the Anglers Rest is a decent pub); upstream of Monsal Dale (*see entry below*), this is rather less visited but also a lovely spot for walks – as is its continuation Chee Dale.

MONSAL DALE SK1771 This winding valley is the outstanding place for walks in this central part of the White Peak area, its pastoral quality emphasised by the disused limestone cotton mills along the way. It's especially lovely in May and June, with wild flowers enriching the pastures along the broader stretches, but don't expect to have it to yourself. There's good access from the A6 a couple of miles towards Buxton from Ashford in the Water; and from Monsal Head (handy hotel), where a disused railway viaduct adds interest and forms part of the **Monsal Trail** that runs along a former railway from Wye Dale E of Buxton to Coombs Road viaduct S of Bakewell. W of Millers Dale station, the trail leaves the old railway and takes a stepping-stone route along the river beneath the towering cliffs of Chee Tor before rejoining the railway track.

MONYASH SK1566 Quiet village with good-value home cooking at the Bull's Head, and (2m S) the mysterious **Arbor Low stone circle**.

★ ! **OLD BRAMPTON** SK3371 The village itself is attractive, and has one special curiosity: count the minutes between one and two o'clock on its church clock.

OLD WHITTINGTON SK3874 **Revolution House** (High St) Innocuous-looking thatched cottage, 300 years ago the birthplace of what came to be known as the Glorious Revolution. Good audio-visual display, period rooms and furniture. Disabled access to ground floor only; open Good Fri–2 Nov; (01246) 453554; free. The White Horse is useful for lunch.

★ **OSMASTON** SK2043 This village of pretty thatched cottages has a pleasant path through a lakeside park.

PILSLEY SK4264 **The Herb Garden** Big main garden with lots of herbs and old English roses, smaller gardens specialising in rare medicinal herbs, pot pourri or lavender. Teas, shop; cl mid-Sept–mid-Mar; (01246) 854268; £1. Pilsley itself is a charming village.

RIPLEY SK4151 **Midland Railway Centre** (Butterley station) Regular steam-train passenger service through country park, and developing railway museum. Meals, snacks, shop, disabled access; cl 25 Dec; best to ring for train timetable, (01773) 570140; £6.95 (£7.95 bank hols). It's good for families – not only are there a few animals on the adjacent farm (you can visit here free without having to go on the railway), but 2 children are admitted free with every adult ticket. **Denby Pottery Visitor Centre** (B6179 S) Guided factory tours (10.30am and 1pm – not Fri or wknds; booking essential) show the intricate skills of potters and craftsmen. Big factory shop, and children's play area. Meals, snacks, shop, disabled access; cl 25–26 Dec; (01773) 743644; full tours £3.75, otherwise £2.75. The Excavator on the A610 out at Buckland Hollow is a good-value family dining pub.

ROWSLEY SK2565 **Caudwell's Mill and Craft Centre** Working 19th-c flour mill, powered by water turbines, with crafts such as glass-blowing and wood-turning. Meals, snacks, shop; cl wkdys Jan and Feb; (01629) 734374; mill £2.50, craft centre free. Rowsley also has an interesting **stone circle** called the Nine Ladies. The Grouse & Claret does decent food (all day wknds).

★ **SHARDLOW CANAL BASIN** SK4430 Attractive, with some handsome former wharf buildings – one now an antiques warehouse, another, the Malt Shovel, a good pub.

SOUTH WINGFIELD SK3754 **Wingfield Manor** (B5035) Substantial ruin with virtually complete banqueting hall, tower and undercroft. The 16th-c Babington Plot is thought to have been hatched here, leading to the final downfall of Mary, Queen of Scots. Used as a filming location for Zeffirelli's Jane Eyre Shop; cl Mon and Tues, winter wkdys, 1–2pm winter wknds, 24–26 Dec; (01773) 832060; £2.95, inc Walkman tour. The White Hart at

Moorwood Moor has reasonably priced food.

SUDBURY HALL SK1532 Individual but attractive Stuart mansion with elaborate carving, frescos, murals and plasterwork in splendidly elegant rooms; the interiors featured in the BBC's Pride and Prejudice as the home of Mr Darcy. It's worth a visit just for the excellent **National Trust Museum of Childhood**, which has a chimney climb for sweep-sized children. You can play with some exhibits, and at wknds the schoolroom is staffed by an Edwardian teacher. Meals, snacks, shop, disabled access; open pm Weds–Sun (and bank hol Mons) Apr–Oct, plus museum open pm wknds till Christmas; (01283) 585305; £5 for everything, or £3.50 house and grounds or museum only; NT. The Boar's Head Hotel is useful for lunch.

† ★ **TIDESWELL** SK1575 The spacious 14th-c **church** is known as the Cathedral of the Peak; the village is attractive, and this is good walking country. The B6049 across Millers Dale has nice views.

★ **TISSINGTON** SK1752 The Peak District's most beautiful village, its broad main street wonderfully harmonious, with wide grass verges, handsome stone houses inc a Jacobean hall (guided tours pm Mon–Weds Jun and July; best to book (01335) 350501; £4.50) and an interesting church. The grey stone gardener's cottage is familiar from many calendars. Garden centre, decent homely café.

TORRS RIVERSIDE PARK SJ9984 This deep gorge below New Mills is a good place to potter among the ivy-covered remains of former mills and other industrial relics; the canal basin undergoing restoration over at Buxworth is interesting, with a very enjoyable pub. The **Goyt Way** is a track heading N towards and beyond Marple SJ9588, partly following the Peak Forest Canal – a pretty walk.

WIRKSWORTH SK2755 **National Stone Centre** (Porter Lane) 330 million-year-old tropical lagoons and limestone fossil reefs, as well as an exhibition, guided fossil trails, and activities like gem-panning or fossil-rubbing. Snacks, shop, some disabled access; cl 25 Dec; (01629) 824833; £1.80. **Wirksworth Heritage Centre** (Crown Yard, Market Pl) Attractive old silk and velvet mill, with displays on quarrying and local customs like well dressing and clypping the church, and a few children's activities. Meals, snacks, shop; cl Mon (exc bank hols and mid-July–mid-Sept), Tues (exc Apr–mid-Sept), and all Nov–mid-Feb; (01629) 825225; £1. Slightly N at Middleton, **Middleton Top Engine House** is home to a beam engine built in 1829 to haul waggons up a steep incline on the Cromford & High Peak Railway. Snacks, shop, disabled access; engine in motion first wknd of month and bank hol wknds; cl wkdys Oct–Mar; (01629) 823204; £1. There's cycle hire out here, with the High Peak Trail (see *Ashbourne*) dipping exhilaratingly down the great incline to reach the Cromford Canal at High Peak Junction; good for walkers, too. The Knockerdown Inn out on the B5035 is pleasant for lunch, and the **Carsington Reservoir** (good visitor centre, watersports, enjoyable walks, cycling, etc) out that way is beginning to tone into the landscape.

★ † **YOULGREAVE** SK2164 Charming dales village, with an interesting **church**.

RIVER DERWENT SK2666 You can walk along pleasant stretches where Izaak Walton fished, either upstream from Rowsley, or from the B6012 N of there at the Calton Lees car park – there's open access to Chatsworth Park on this W side of the river, which is particularly lovely.

RIVER TRENT SK3427 This impresses with its silent power – perhaps Britain's most formidable river. Ingleby is one good access point – for example, from the big garden of the John Thompson pub, which brews its own beer.

★ **Other attractive villages** include Brassington SK2354, Coton in the Elms SK2415, Duffield SK3443, Earl Sterndale SK0967, Elton SK2261, Holymoorside SK3469, Idridgehay SK2849, Kirk Ireton SK2650, Little Hucklow SK1678, Litton SK1675, Lullington SK2513, Mapleton SK1648 (domed church, nice riverside walk to

Thorpe), Milton SK3126, Parwich SK1854, Repton SK3026, Ridgeway SK3551, Smisby SK3419, Stanton by Dale SK4638 and Stanton in Peak SK2464.

⛰ Decent country pubs perfectly placed for walkers include the Miners Arms at Milltown, Ashover SK3561 (despite quarrying), Peacock at Barlow SK3474, Robin Hood at Baslow SK2572 (handy for the ridge of Baslow Edge), King's Head at Bonsall SK2858 (very child-friendly, by the Limestone Way), Bowling Green at Bradwell SK1781 in Smalldale, the Barrel on the ridge at Bretton SK2077, Church at Chelmorton SK1170, Beehive at Combs SK0478 (lovely valley), Bridge at Ford SK4080, Chequers just below Froggatt Edge SK2476, Queen Anne at Great Hucklow SK1878, Royal Oak at Millthorpe SK3276, Miners Arms at Milltown SK3561, Bull's Head at Monyash SK1566, Grouse at Nether Padley SK2577, New Napoleon by Ogston Reservoir SK3761, Little Mill nr Rowarth SK0189 (particularly for Lantern Pike), Queen's Arms at Taddington SK1472 and Bull's Head at Wardlow SK1874 (for well wooded Cressbrook Dale).

Where to eat

BAKEWELL SK2168 **Byways** *Water Lane (01629) 812807* Olde-worlde tearoom with several separate areas, a roaring log fire, well presented good-value food from snacks to meals, and warmly friendly staff. £3.

BAKEWELL SK2168 **Renaissance** *Bath St (01629) 812687* Overlooking a little walled garden where fresh herbs are grown, this beamed restaurant serves imaginative French dishes inc gourmet specials and a fresh fish of the day, and delicious puddings; friendly service; cl pm Sun, Mon, first 2 wks Jan, 1st 2 wks Aug; disabled access. **£24.89**|£5.99.

BARLOW SK3474 **Trout** *(01742) 890893* Refurbished dining pub with plenty of brocaded banquettes and neat tables, beamery and old-world prints, a proper pubby part and second dining room; good, genuinely home-made food inc delicious puddings, no smoking restaurant, well kept real ales, and quick competent service. **£18.25**|£7.50.

BIRCHOVER SK2462 **Druid** *(01629) 650302* Pleasantly remote creeper-covered dining pub with huge choice of very popular abd interesting food (best to book), well kept real ales, good friendly service, bustling little bar with big coal fire, no smoking garden room, and spacious and airy 2-storey dining extension; children under 5 must leave by 8pm; cl 25 Dec. **£24**|£8.

BUXTON SK0673 **Coffee Bean Café** *50 Spring Gardens (01298) 27345* Small bustling café, long and narrow, with old tea and coffee advertisements, 15 types of coffee, all-day breakfasts, savouries and light lunches, and delicious cakes; cl evenings; disabled access. £3.95.

BUXTON SK0673 **Old Sun** *High St (01298) 23452* Refurbished old coaching inn with several small cosy rooms leading off the central bar, open fires, low beams, comfortable leather armchairs and chesterfields, fresh flowers and carefully chosen bric-à-brac; a decent choice of real ales, a dozen wines by the glass, good adventurous food inc excellent puddings, and friendly staff. **£16.45**|£6.95.

BUXWORTH SK0282 **Navigation** *(01663) 732072* Very welcoming extended pub by the former canal basin, with low-ceilinged rooms, plenty to look at, good fires, well kept real ales, good-value generous food, and cheerful staff; tables on sunken flagstone terrace; disabled access. **£15**|£4.

CASTLETON SK1583 **Rose Cottage** *Cross St (01433) 620472* Friendly village cottage with lots of summer flowering baskets, pretty garden, lunchtime home-made snacks and meals and afternoon cream teas; cl Fri, Jan; disabled access. £3.50.

CHURCH BROUGHTON SK2033 **Holly Bush** *(01283) 585345* Neat brick village pub, nicely refurbished, with well kept real ale and good-value, home-made, simple but decent food in bar and separate dining room; no food pm Sun; disabled access. **£13**|£4.

EYAM SK2276 **Eyam** *Tea Rooms The Square (01433) 631274* Family-run teashop with sandwiches, salads and good cream teas, and lots of speciality teas; cl Mon, Dec, wkdys Nov, Jan, Feb; partial disabled access. £3.50.

EYAM SK2276 **Miners Arms** *Water Lane (01433) 630853* Carefully refurbished pub with a restful atmosphere in its 3 little plush beamed rooms; good, interesting lunchtime food served by attentive staff, well kept ales, and decent nearby walks; bdrms; cl pm Sun, am Mon, first 2 wks Jan; disabled access. **£21.90**|£5.50.

HOGNASTON SK2350 **Red Lion** *(01335) 370396* Carefully renovated open-plan, oak-beamed dining pub with a friendly welcome and relaxed atmosphere, an attractive mix of candlelit tables on ancient flagstones, 3 open fires, a collection of teddy bears, well presented, imaginative food (book at wknds), well kept real ales, and attentive staff; bdrms. **£20.60**|£8.95.

HOLMESFIELD SK3277 **Robin Hood** *(01742) 890360* Rambling former farmhouse with open fires, and a neat extended comfortable lounge; generous helpings of good food inc interesting daily specials, real ales, and friendly staff; good Cordwell Valley walks. **£20**|£5.50.

HOPE SK1783 **Cheshire Cheese** *Edale Rd (01433) 620381* 16th-c village pub with 3 cosy beamed rooms, each with its own coal fire; well kept real ales, a decent choice of house wines, good food (especially evenings), obliging service, and 2 small no smoking dining rooms. **£20**|£4.35.

KINGS NEWTON SK3826 **Hardinge Arms** *(01332) 813808* Civilised friendly pub with beams, open fires and comfortable rambling rooms, popular lunchtime carvery and other enjoyable bar food, and well kept real ales; disabled access. **£15**|£5.50.

MELBOURNE SK3825 **Bay Tree** *4 Potter St (01332) 863358* Small family-run and cottagey restaurant with beams and simple furnishings, carefully presented popular food (Sun lunch is booked up weeks ahead), and thoughtful, relaxed service; cl am Sat, pm Sun, Mon, 2 wks in summer. **£40**|£7.

OVER HADDON SK2066 **Lathkil** *(01629) 812501* Busy, civilised pub in lovely walking spot, with open fires, beams and comfortable furnishings, good food and well kept real ales, and helpful service; cl 25 Dec; children lunchtime only. **£23**|£7.

RIDGEWAY SK4081 **Old Vicarage** *(0114) 247 5814* Big Victorian house in lovely gardens with a marvellously relaxing, welcoming atmosphere, cosy sitting room for pre-dinner drinks and beautifully presented, quite exceptional cooking using home-grown produce in the candlelit dining room or light and airy less formal conservatory; cl am Sat, pm Sun, Mon; disabled access. **£35.50**.

WOOLLEY MOOR SK3661 **White Horse** *(01246) 590319* Popular old pub run by very friendly people – and much liked by locals; very good food using best local produce, lots of daily specials, decent wines and beers, a new conservatory, lovely view from the garden (pleasant Ashover Valley walks), good play area; disabled access. **£13.50**|£4.25.

Special thanks to Nicholas Heath-Brown, Mr and Mrs S J Pyke, B M Eldridge, Sheena Grosset, Mrs Abigail Burgess, Joy and Peter Heatherley.

We welcome reports from readers

This *Guide* depends on readers' reports. Do help us if you can – in return, we offer a discount on the next edition to people who've helped us with reports for it. Tell us what you think about places already in it, and anything extra you think we should say about them. And send us your ideas for inclusion in the next edition: places to visit, eat at or stay in, attractive drives or walks, maybe even unusual interesting shops you know of. Use the card in the middle, the report forms at the end, or just write – no stamp needed: *The Good Guide to Britain*, FREEPOST TN1569, Wadhurst, E Sussex TN5 7BR.

Derbyshire Calendar

Some of these dates were provisional as we went to press. Please check information with the telephone numbers provided.

Many villages here decorate their wells and springs with flower-petal pictures in annual festive Well Dressings. Originally a pagan water-worshipping ceremony, this is now part of the Christian calendar. A procession led by the clergy and a blessing of the wells usually initiates a week of village celebrations. To avoid the crowds go a day or two before the actual ceremony for a good close view of the elaborate flower pictures which should stay fresh for almost a week. Some of the best are Chesterfield, Eyam, Tissington, Wirksworth and Youlgreave.

FEBRUARY

16 **Ashbourne** Shrovetide Football Game: free-for-all between unlimited number of Up'ards and Down'ards (from above and below Henmore Brook) who compete to get the ball to goals 3 miles apart along the brook – *till Weds 17* (01335) 343666

APRIL

5 **Chesterfield** Easter Market and Entertainment (01246) 207777

MAY

3 **Chesterfield** May Day Market and Gala (01246) 207777
8 **Chatsworth** Angling Fair at Chatsworth House – *till Sun 9* (01263) 711736
9 **Doe Lea** Airbourne Parade at Hardwick Hall and National Mills Day at Stainsby Mill (01246) 850430
13 **Tissington** Well Dressing – *till Weds 19* (01335) 390246
16 **Elvaston** Derbyshire County Show at Elvaston Castle Country Park (01332) 571342
29 **Ashbourne** Derbyshire Steam Fair at Hartington Moor Showground – *till Mon 31* (01663) 732750; **Ashford in the Water** Well Dressing – *till 6 Jun* (01246) 345777; **Brackenfield** Well Dressings: 5 displays (01629) 534767; **Castleton** Ancient Garland Ceremony: ancient pagan fertility ceremony with Celtic origins now encompassing Oak Apple Day – King wears a beehive-shaped flower headdress and is accompanied by consort on horseback with girls in white dresses bedecked with fresh flowers; the procession stops and dances outside the 6 village inns (01433) 620571; **Chester Green** Well Dressing (01332) 673210; **Middleton-by-Youlgreave** Well Dressing – *till 4 Jun* (01246) 345777; **Wirksworth** Well Dressing – *till 5 Jun* (01246) 345777
31 **Bamford** Sheepdog Trials (01433) 651624; **Chesterfield** Spring Bank Holiday Market and Street Entertainment (01246) 207777

JUNE

4 **Eyam** Well Dressing with Carnival (01433) 630935
26 **Chatsworth** Flower and Garden Show at Chatsworth House – *till Sun 27* (01328) 830367

Derbyshire Calendar (cont.)

27 **Church Gresley** Festival of Leisure: free family event at Maurice Lea Memorial Park (01283) 228094

JULY

3 **Dove Holes** Beer and Jazz Festival – *till Sun 4* (01298) 814722; **Elvaston** Steam Rally at Elvaston Castle Country Park – *till Sun 4* (01332) 571342; **Glossop** Carnival and Country Fair at Manor Park – *till Sun 4* (01457) 868996

10 **Pleasley** Well Dressing and Flower Festival – *till Weds 14* (01623) 810775

14 **Buxton** Well Dressing – *till Mon 19* (01298) 25106

24 **Buxton** Jazz Festival inc parade (01625) 528336; **Stoney Middleton** Well Dressing – *till 2 Aug* (01433) 631590

27 **Chesterfield** Medieval Market and Street Entertainment (01246) 207777

28 **Buxton** Gilbert and Sullivan Festival: competition, masterclasses, costumed parade – *till 14 Aug* (01298) 72190

31 **Bonsall** Well Dressing and Carnival Week – *till 7 Aug* with World Championship Hen Racing *on 7 Aug* (01629) 825685; **Tansley Cromford** Steam Rally at Highacres Farm – *till 1 Aug* (01629) 824263

AUGUST

4 **Bakewell** Show: biggest show in the county – *till Thurs 5* (01629) 812736

11 **Ashover** Agricultural and Horticultural Show (01246) 863412

28 **Ashbourne** Derbyshire Country Show at Hartington Moor Showground – *till Mon 30* (01663) 732750; **Foolow** Well Dressing – *till 4 Sept* (01433) 630602

29 **Crich** Festival of Transport at the National Tramway Museum – *till Mon 30* (01773) 852565; **Eyam** Plague Commemoration Service in Cucklet Dell (01433) 630935

30 **Chesterfield** August Bank Holiday Market, Street Entertainment and evening Fireworks (01246) 207777; **Hope** Show and Sheepdog Trials (01433) 620905

SEPTEMBER

4 **Chatsworth** Country Fair at Chatsworth House – *till Sun 5* (01328) 830367; **Glossop** Victorian Weekend – *till Sun 5* (01457) 666233

5 **Derby** Concert at Darley Park (01332) 715608

7 **Chesterfield** Well Dressing Demonstration at Peacock Centre Courtyard – *till Sat 11* (01246) 345777

11 **Chesterfield** Well Dressing at several locations inc Crooked Spire Church – *till Sat 18* (01246) 345777

25 **Little Hayfield** Sheepdog Trials and Country Show at Spray House Farm – *till Sun 26* (01663) 733644

NOVEMBER

5 **Chesterfield** Fireworks at Whittington Moor (01246) 345777/8

Devon

Devon has a splendid range of places to stay in, great scenic variety, masses of things to do and see, and some very good food. There are lovely gardens, delightful thatched villages clustered around ancient church and equally ancient pub, glorious vistas of coast and moor, some lively museums, lots of country life, and vintage steamtrains puffing through gorgeous river valleys. We have divided these riches into three areas: Exeter and East Devon (classic family holiday country, with Exeter a charming small city); South Devon and Dartmoor (wonderful scenery, the widest range of interesting places to visit – good all year); and North Devon and Exmoor (a quieter appeal than other parts, less touristy but plenty of interest).

Outstanding day-out treats for children are Crealy at Clyst St Mary (East Devon), and in South Devon the Plymouth Dome, Paignton Zoo and the Woodland Leisure Park at Blackawton. Moreover, even 'adult' places generally have a lot to entertain children too – Buckland Abbey in South Devon is a fine example. And vice versa – many family-orientated places can keep adults smiling as well, such as the Big Sheep near Bideford or the Gnome Reserve near Bradworthy (North Devon), with its unexpectedly appealing plantings. Devon also boasts the country's most enjoyable 'attraction shop' the one attached to Buckfast Abbey at Buckfastleigh (South Devon).

Some of the best views in the county are from trains; besides the steam lines, the standard railway Devon Rover is a good deal, with unlimited train journeys in the area at a reduced rate for either a week or any three days out of seven.

Exeter and East Devon

Enjoyable seaside resorts, interesting places to visit – including Exeter itself.

Exeter is civilised and attractive, with a lot to see; all its museums are interesting and particularly well organised. Served by fast trains and the M5, it can be reached quickly from far away – and good roads bring the other parts of Devon within comfortable reach for a day out.

Exmouth is the liveliest and biggest of this coast's four main family beach resorts, and doubles as a working port. Seaton, quieter, is a more typical family resort, with much less of a beach. Budleigh Salterton, the quietest, is rather retiring and genteel. Sidmouth is slightly busier, with a good deal of character as well as plenty for families – the broadest all-round appeal. Branscombe is the prettiest place on this coast.

Inland, coastal downs give a gently varied landscape of charming wooded valleys with views and high pastures between, and several attractive villages. North of the A30/A35 is more self-contained farmland, mainly well hedged traditional stock and dairy farms.

Besides places mentioned in the main introduction, Killerton, the working-mill museum at Uffculme, and Bicton Park gardens at East Budleigh are all favourites here – as is Ottery St Mary.

Where to stay

CHARDSTOCK ST3004 **George** *Chardstock, Axminster EX13 7BX (01460) 220241* ***£49.50;** 4 rms. Neatly thatched old village inn with character furnishings, beams and old gas lamps, a quietly chatty feel, and good food in bar and restaurant; good walks nearby; children over 12.

EXETER SX9292 **Edwardian** *30–32 Heavitree Rd, Exeter EX1 2LQ (01392) 276102* ***£49,** plus special breaks; 13 individually furnished rms, some with four-posters. Popular guesthouse close to cathedral and city centre, with pretty lounge, enjoyable breakfasts in attractive dining rooms, and warmly friendly and knowledgeable resident owners; plenty of places nearby for evening meals; cl 25–26 Dec.

EXETER SX9292 **St Olave's Court** *Mary Arches St, Exeter EX4 3AZ (01392) 217736* ***£70w,** plus special breaks; 15 well equipped rms. Handsome Georgian-style house just 400 yards from the cathedral in its own walled garden, with a warm welcome from helpful friendly staff, comfortable rooms, imaginative evening meals in candlelit restaurant, and super breakfasts; disabled access.

EXETER SX9292 **White Hart** *66 South St, Exeter EX1 1EE (01392) 279897* **£84,** plus special breaks; 60 modern but slightly dated rms. Rather splendid 14th-c inn with lots of different eating areas (winebar-type as well as a proper restaurant), marvellous atmospheric bar, open fires, beams, antiques, good range of wines, friendly service, attractive courtyard with proper barbecues, and enjoyable breakfasts; cl 24–26 Dec.

GITTISHAM SY1398 **Combe House** *Gittisham, Honiton EX14 0AD (01404) 540400* **£98,** plus winter breaks; 15 individually decorated, pretty rms with lovely views. Peaceful Elizabethan country hotel (new owners this year) in gardens with lawns and shrubbery, and walks around the 3,000-acre estate; elegant day rooms with antiques, pictures and fresh flowers, a happy relaxed atmosphere, good food using some home-grown produce, and fine wines; young children have own supper; cl 2 wks end Jan–mid-Feb; dogs by prior arrangement.

HIGHER BULSTONE SY1988 **Bulstone** *Higher Bulstone, Branscombe, Sidmouth EX12 3BL (01297) 680446* **£75,** plus special breaks; 12 rms, 6 with own bthrm. In over 3 acres and surrounded by fields, this is a super place for family holidays – with both parents' and children's needs catered for; completely no smoking; lots of facilities and friendly staff.

LYMPSTONE SX9984 **River House** *The Strand, Lympstone, Exmouth EX8 5EY (01395) 265147* **£80,** plus special breaks; 3 pretty rms. Warmly welcoming restaurant-with-rooms with marvellous river views from big picture windows, good imaginative food (wonderful fresh fish and interesting vegetable dishes) in first-floor restaurant using some home-grown produce, thoughtfully chosen wines, and kind service; practical cookery courses, too; cl 25–27 Dec, 1–2 Jan, restaurant cl pm Sun and Mon (though open if residents want to eat and for private parties of 6 or more); children over 6; limited disabled access.

MEMBURY ST2703 **Lea Hill Hotel** *Membury, Axminster EX13 7AQ (01404) 881881* **£98,** plus special breaks; 11 rms, inc 2 suites, in carefully converted barns, mostly with private garden areas or terraces. Set in 8 acres in lovely countryside, this thatched 14th-c longhouse has comfortable beamed rooms, a convivial bar, relaxed and friendly owners, good evening meals, and nice breakfasts; well behaved dogs by special arrangement.

SIDFORD SY1390 **Blue Ball** *Sidford, Sidmouth EX10 9QL (01395) 514062* **£40;** 3

rms with nice touches like free papers, fruit and fresh flowers (shared bthrm – hoping to open 3 with own bthrm). Welcoming thatched 14th-c inn run by the same family since 1912, with lovely winter log fire in low partly panelled lounge bar, heavy beams, lots of bric-à-brac, no smoking snug, very friendly service, and decent food inc hearty breakfasts; dogs by arrangement.

STOCKLAND ST2404 **King's Arms** *Stockland, Honiton EX14 9BS (01404) 881361* **£40**; 3 rms. Cream-faced thatched pub with elegant rooms, open fires, first-class food in bar and evening restaurant (especially fish), and interesting wine list; skittle alley, live music pm Sun; no accommodation 24 Dec–1 Jan; well behaved children only.

WHIMPLE SY0497 **Woodhayes** *Whimple, Exeter EX5 2TD (01404) 822237* **£95;** 6 lovely spacious rms. Big Georgian country house in neat grounds, with comfortable, quietly decorated lounges, small library, open fires, flagstoned bar and pretty dining room; fine food, afternoon teas, and excellent breakfasts; tennis, croquet; cl 2 wks over Christmas/New Year; children over 12.

To see and do

★ ⛴ **EXETER** SX9292 Though large parts of the centre were devastated by World War II bombing, some choice streets and buildings survive, with picturesque partly Tudor narrow lanes leading from the mainly pedestrianised High St into the serene tree-shaded cathedral close. The atmosphere is distinctive – relaxed and liberal yet responsible, buoyed up by the thriving university. In the centre, modern shops are integrated into the old layout very discreetly indeed. With many smaller churches, decent book and other shops, pubs and so forth nearby, this is a very pleasant part for browsing around. Particularly attractive streets include Southernhay at the end of the close, and Stepcote Hill, a picturesque detour from Fore St. The Quay, beyond the streams of fast traffic on the ring road (there are quiet underpasses), has become lively and entertaining, with handsomely restored buildings, resurgent cafés and pubs (the Prospect is good), and a growing number of craft shops and the like; the Old Quay House has a visitor centre with audio-visual show. Apart from the White Hart (*see* **Where to stay** *section above*), civilised pubs and wine bars with decent food include the sumptuous Imperial (New North Rd), Ship (14th-c, Martins Lane), Well House (The Close – cathedral view and Roman well), Papermakers (very foody; Exe St) and Prospect (Quay). There are **boat trips** down the ship canal to Exminster; or you can walk down, passing the Double Locks (a favourite pub) and ending at the Turf Hotel looking out over the estuary. The quickest way into the city from either the M5 or the A38 is to keep on round to the westbound A30 and go into the city from the Alphington roundabout.

† **Exeter Cathedral** England's finest example of decorated Gothic architecture, with its magnificent nave soaring to the fan-vaulted roof, and intricately carved choir stalls; the misericords are thought to be the longest in the country. It boasts the longest Gothic vault in Europe, superbly atmospheric. Lots of colourfully embroidered cushions, chronologically illustrating English and local history. The façade has 3 tiers of sculpted figures, inc Kings Alfred, Canute and William I. Meals, snacks, shop, disabled access; guided tours 11am and 2.30pm wkdys, just 11am Sat; £2 suggested donation.

! Underground Passages (entrance via Boots Arcade, High St) An unusual medieval attraction, this atmospheric network was built in the 13th c to bring water into the city; there's an introductory exhibition and video, then a guided tour of the tunnels themselves, still much as they were centuries ago. The guides are enthusiastic and can be very entertaining. Flat shoes are recommended. On Sats they do longer tours for those who want to go into the more creepy and constricted parts – great fun, but be prepared to get muddy then. Shop; cl am wkdys (exc July–Sept and school hols), all day Mon (exc school hols) and Sun; (01392) 265887; £2.50 (£3.50 July and Aug).

Exeter Guildhall This medieval municipal building with its ornately colonnaded Elizabethan façade is one of the oldest still in use; it has displays of civic regalia and so on; cl 1–2pm, pm Sat (and all day some Sats in winter), all day Sun and bank hols, and during civic functions; free.

St Nicholas's Priory (Mint Lane) 11th-c Benedictine monastery with unusual Norman undercroft, Tudor room and 15th-c kitchen. Shop, disabled access to ground floor only; open 3–4.30pm Mon, Weds and Sat Easter–Oct (guided tour last Tues of month); occasionally cl for private functions; (01392) 265858; free.

Royal Albert Memorial Museum and Art Gallery (Queen St) Wonderful Gothic exterior, notable displays of regional silver, African carvings, archaeology, paintings and natural history. Snacks, shop, disabled access; cl Sun, Good Fri, 25–26 Dec and 1 Jan; (01392) 265858; free.

Other things to see and do

★ **BEER** SY2289 Rather cottagey resort village, still with fishing boats pulled up on the shingle beach (summer boat hire, too), and a stream channelled down the main street. **Pecorama Pleasure Gardens** Fun for railway-lovers, with models and train collections in the house, and outside a miniature steam and diesel passenger line with stunning views of the bay. Also crazy golf, aviary, children's maze and assault course, a big new garden, live entertainment and maybe children's pony rides. Meals, snacks, shop, mostly disabled access; cl pm Sat, Sun (exc Jun–Aug), and outdoor features cl Oct–Easter (exc Oct half-term); (01297) 21542; £3.50 (less for just outside features). The village was famous from Roman times for its cavernous whitestone quarries, which can be visited, and the B3174 inland passes lots of Bronze Age burial mounds. The Anchor Hotel has good fresh local fish, and readers have also found good-value B & B at the Dolphin.

✝ ★ **BRANSCOMBE** SY1988 The **church** has a magnificently carved oak gallery, and a Norman tower with distinctive stair-turret. The village is notably pretty – a series of largely unspoilt thatched hamlets strung along a lovely seaside valley. The Masons Arms is good, as is the NT Old Bakery tearoom opposite the unique NT thatched smithy. Various tracks loop down to the coast path – rewarding here, over Hooken Cliff then down through the Hooken undercliff: a tremendous jumble of collapsed chalk.

★ ✝ ! **BROADCLYST** SX9897 Pretty thatch and cob village, with a marvellous old church, photogenic outside, interesting in. The Red Lion has good food – and the post office has a unique computer information kiosk.

☺ **CLYST ST MARY** SY0090 **Crealy** (Sidmouth Rd) This bustling family complex seems to get bigger every year. There's plenty to amuse children of all ages, from bumper boats and go-karts to a farm where you can milk the cows

Days Out

Sheltered combes and dramatic undercliff: Sidmouth, inc donkey sanctuary; Branscombe, lunch at the Masons Arms, look at church, smithy, NT bakery/tearoom; Branscombe Mouth – walk along Hooken Cliffs and through undercliff.

Otter potter and Exe exploits: Bicton Park, East Budleigh or (at Ottery St Mary) Cadhay; Otterton Mill Centre; Topsham – lunch at Passage House; A la Ronde, Exmouth.

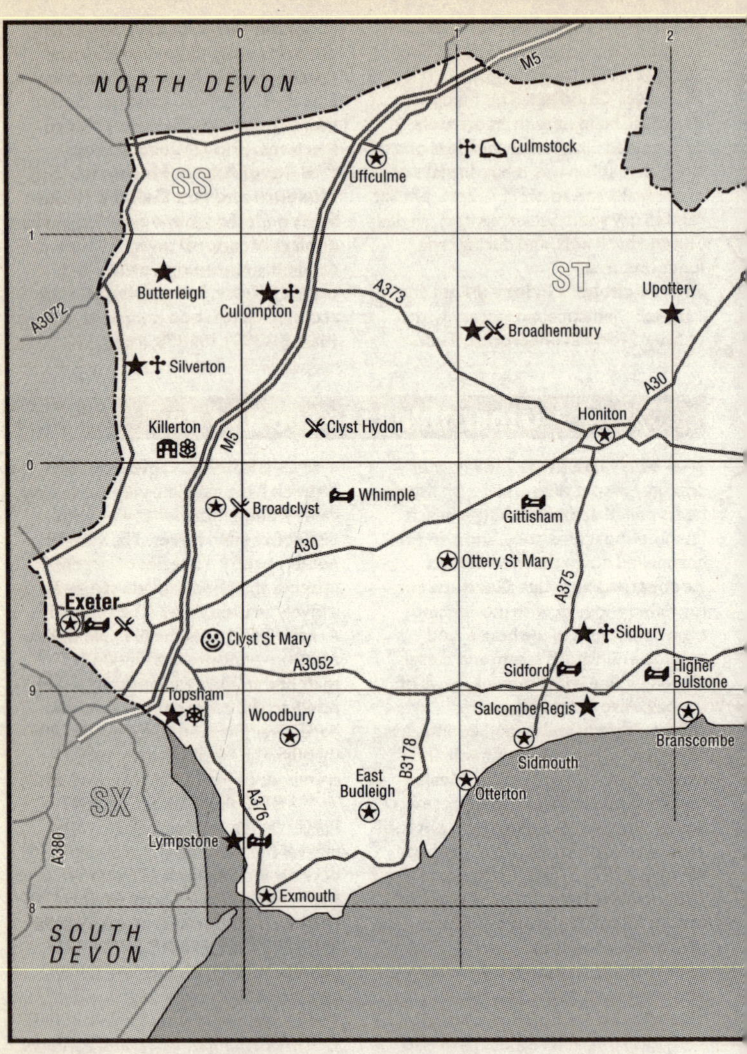

(and always meet baby animals). Many of the attractions are indoors, inc some of the animals and a very good and varied adventure playground, with lots of slides (one has a practically vertical drop) and things to swing on. Other features include pony rides and lakeside walks, and they have a particularly wide range of special events and activities (usually on summer Suns) from pirates' treasure hunts to conker championships. Meals, snacks, shop, disabled access; (01395) 233200; cl 24–26 Dec; £4.50. If you don't want to eat in the park, the Half Moon has decent food.

✝ ★ **CULLOMPTON** ST0207 The **church** is notable for its remarkable painted screen; the busy little town has an attractive feel.

✝ ⌂ **CULMSTOCK** ST1013 The village has a handsome **church**, a prettily placed old pub, and a pleasant riverside walk to Uffculme.

❀ ✺ ★ **DALWOOD** ST2400 **Burrow Farm Gardens** (½m or so off the A35; turn off for Taunton Cross) Part of this 5-acre site has been created

from an ancient Roman clay pit, and there are spacious lawns, borders and unusual shrubs and trees as well as a woodland garden, pergola walk with old-fashioned roses, and super views. Cream teas, snacks, nursery; cl Oct–Mar; (01404) 831285; £2.50. The pretty Tuckers Arms in the attractive village is good for lunch.

DOWLANDS CLIFFS SY2889 The steeply tumbled brambly wooded wilderness of this undercliff 3m E of Axmouth has numerous small birds.

EAST BUDLEIGH SY0684 Attractive and quietly placed cob and thatch village; the pleasant **church** has fascinating Jacobean carved pew ends – some grotesque, some hilarious, some frankly rude. **Bicton Park Garden** 50 acres of lovely gardens, shrubs, lakes and woodland. A futuristic-looking glass Palm House turns out to be early Victorian, and has a fine collection of tropical trees and plants; also fuchsia, geranium and orchid houses, bird garden, pinetum, and magnificent Italian gardens. Snacks, shop and plant centre, disabled access; cl Nov–Easter; (01395) 568465; £3.50. Nearby, the entirely separate gardens of **Bicton College of Agriculture** are of great if rather more specialised appeal; long monkey-puzzle avenue through parkland, rich collection of magnolias, camellias and flowering cherries, national pittosporum and agapanthus collections, and 17-acre arboretum with woodland garden. Snacks, plant centre; cl winter wknds, 25 Dec, Good Fri; (01395) 568353; £2. The Sir Walter Raleigh has good food.

EXMOUTH SY0080 Good family seaside holiday town, worth a visit for its lively harbour and marina, its long sandy beach and its stately church. Summer cruise trips go from the harbour up to Topsham, and there are sea fishing trips from the clock tower (they supply rod and bait); (01395) 222144 for both. **Great Exmouth Model Railway** (Sea Front) Home to the world's biggest 00 gauge model railway, nearly 1½m of track indoors with outside trains running round a pond of koi carp. It took 14 years to build and is constantly updated; some of the detail is amazing, right down to the birds in the trees. Shop, some disabled access; cl Nov–Easter; (01395) 278383; £2.25. **A la Ronde** (on the A376 2m N, SY3083) Extraordinary 16-sided house, built around 1795 and decorated in part with feathers, seashells, seaweed and sand. A charmingly whimsical place, the outside looking not entirely unlike a giant biscuit barrel. Meals, snacks, shop; cl Fri, Sat, and all Nov–Easter; (01395) 265514; £3.20; NT. **World of Country Life** (Sandy Bay, SY0279) 40 acres of decent family-based activities, with friendly animals, adventure playground and undercover play areas, safari rides through deer and llama paddocks, reconstructed Victorian street, classic motorcycle collection, crafts, steam engines, and falconry centre (no displays Sat, exc July and Aug). Meals, snacks, shop, disabled access; cl Nov–Easter; (01395) 274533; £5.25. The Seafood Restaurant (Tower St) has nothing but the freshest fish and shellfish; the Grove (attractive seafront garden) and seafront Deer Leap are useful too. **High Land of Orcombe** Reached by the shore road E out of Exmouth (SY0279) and protected against campsite encroachment by its NT ownership; offers walkers a short stroll with sea views.

HONITON ST1600 Some handsome Georgian buildings along this country town's long high street, and some interesting shops. The Red Cow (High St) is good value for lunch. The 13th-c **Allhallows Museum** (High St) has displays of Honiton lace, with lace-making demonstrations in Jun, July and Aug. Shop, disabled access to ground floor only; cl Sun, and Nov–Easter; (01404) 44966; £1. Fine views from the A375 S and from **Hembury hill fort**, a walk up from the A373 NW.

KILLERTON SS9700 Best of all in spring, 15 acres of beautiful hillside gardens, shrub borders and planted beds, with an impressive avenue of beech trees. The 18th-c house has an annually changing costume exhibition in period furnished rooms, but it's the gardens that really give the place its special appeal. Meals, snacks, shop and plant centre, good disabled access (with buggies round the grounds); house cl Tues, and all Nov–mid-Mar; (01392) 881345; £4.50, £3.50 garden only; NT. The Three Tuns in Silverton has decent food, especially vegetarian, and readers recommend the antiques centre at nearby Hele (towards Bradninch).

★ **OTTERTON** SY0785 **Mill Centre** Working watermill still grinding flour for the bread, cakes and pies sold on the premises. Also craft workshops, display of East Devon lace, and interesting evening events. Meals and snacks (restaurant cl winter wkdys), shop and garden centre; cl 25–27 Dec; (01395) 568521; *£2. The village is pretty, and the King's Arms has a good choice of food (with a lovely evening view from the back garden).

★ ! **OTTERY ST MARY** SY1095 Restrained small town – or extended village – with some attractive old buildings around its interesting twin-towered church. The circular **tumbling weir** by an 18th-c mill signed off Mill St is unusual, and photogenic. The London Inn is useful, and the Otter Nurseries (award-winning lavatories) have good plants. **Cadhay** (just NW, SY0996) Beautiful Tudor and Georgian manor house, with fine timbered 15th-c roof in its Great Hall, and unusual Court of Sovereigns – a pretty courtyard with statues of various monarchs. Disabled access to garden and downstairs; open pm Tues–Thurs July and Aug, plus Sun and Mon spring and Aug bank hol; (01404) 812432; *£3. Nearby **Escot Aquatic Centre and Gardens** (Parklands Farm, Escot, SY0898) has tropical and coldwater fish from koi carp to piranhas, as well as rabbits and other pets, otters (fed at 11am and 3pm), Victorian walled rose garden, wild boar enclosures, walks, views and parkland. Also wetlands and waterfowl park, birds of prey, play area and pet centre with all you'll need for any kind of pet, inc the animals themselves. Meals, snacks, shop, disabled access; cl Mon Jan–Mar and 25–26 Dec; (01404) 822188; £2.95.

! **SEATON** SY2490 **Music Fun Centre** A unique place, where you can try your hand at playing any kind of musical instrument – you don't even have to have picked it up before. Woodwind, brass, percussion, keyboards, they've got the lot – though they tell us bagpipes are what most people want to have a go at. Booking essential, (01297) 445803; *£2. **Lyme Bay Cider** (Manor Farm; on the A3052 just N) Vintage equipment and free tastings; cl Sun; (01297) 22887; free. Open-top trams run from Seaton to Colyton, where the Kingfisher is a good pub; back in town, the Fisherman's Inn (Marine Crescent) has decent food all day.

★ † **SIDBURY** SY1391 A pretty village, with a charming **church**, and a good pub nearby at Sidford.

★ SIDMOUTH SY1287
Attractive old streets running back from the grander Regency seafront. It was a fashionable upper-class resort in the early 19th c, and many of the town's buildings show undoubted architectural verve – there's very little seaside tat. The pebbly beach has fishing boats pulled up on it, and the town is protected by warm red sandstone cliffs; it stretches back along the river valley, though away from the sea the buildings are less interesting. The Old Ship has good value food. The dedicated **donkey sanctuary** is a useful free attraction for families readers report an unbelievable number of donkeys. The **heritage centre** (in a fine Regency house on Church St, cl am Sun and Mon and all Nov–Easter) organises summer walking tours round the town, Tues and Thurs at 10.15am.

★ † **SILVERTON** SS9502 An attractive village, with a particularly handsome **church**.

★ **TOPSHAM** SX9688 Old-world seaside village, well worth a quiet potter, its buildings showing its past importance as a port – as do its large number of good pubs and inns. The Passage House is currently the best for food, and readers like the fresh fish at the Galley restaurant. There's a small maritime museum.

★ † **UFFCULME** ST0612 A large pleasant village above the River Culm, with a magnificent carved screen in the attractive **church**. **Coldharbour Mill Working Museum** Every stage in the production of wool, in a well restored 18th-c mill building. Also restoration of a steam engine, and one of the largest tapestries in the world – for a donation you can add your own stitch. Meals, snacks, shop, limited disabled access; cl winter wknds, and at least a wk at Christmas; (01884) 840960; £5. The B3397 to Culmstock and then the turn to Hemyock is a pretty drive; beyond at Clayhidon the Half Moon has good food, by a footpath to the Blackdown Hills visitor centre.

★ **WOODBURY** SY0387
Off the B3180 E are miles of heath with some pinewoods – a place to get away from people even in high summer (red flags warn if there's firing on one section which is a shooting range). From the highest points, near the road, there are views along the coast and to Dartmoor. The wooded **hill fort** right by the road is worth a look; it's a bit eerie tracing the ramparts through the beech trees. The village itself is attractive, with a good pub.

★ **Other attractive villages**, all with decent pubs, include Axmouth SY2591, Broadhembury ST1004, Butterleigh SS9708, Chardstock ST3004, Lympstone SX9984, Salcombe Regis SY1488, Tytherleigh ST3103 and Upottery ST2007.

Where to eat

BEER ST2389 **Anchor** *(01297) 20386* Largish inn just up from the beach, this spreading place has a 2-roomed characterful public bar, pleasant lounge, large no smoking restaurant, particularly good fresh fish dishes, elaborate non-fishy things, and bar snacks; well kept real ales, good wines, and a relaxed, chatty atmosphere; bdrms. **£23.55**|£6.

BROADCLYST SX9897 **Red Lion** *(01392) 461271* Ochre-washed pub in quiet village setting with popular food, very good wines, heavy-beamed long bar, and skittle alley. **£13.50**|£5.20.

BROADHEMBURY ST1004 **Drewe Arms** *(01404) 841267* Charming 15th-c pub in attractive village with carved beams and handsome stone-mullioned windows in the bar, several other interesting rooms, excellent fresh fish dishes, lovely puddings, well kept beers, fine wines, and lovely garden; disabled access. **£25**|£8.10.

CLYST HYDON ST0301 **Five Bells** *(01884) 277288* Charming spotless thatched pub, with very good food inc fresh fish in long bar divided by standing timbers, warmly friendly service, and lovely cottagey gardens; cl pm 25–26 Dec; children over 6 in evening restaurant; disabled access. **£22.50**|£6.

DALWOOD ST2400 **Tuckers Arms** *(01404) 881342* Delightful thatched medieval longhouse with fine flagstoned bar, lots of beams, log fire in inglenook, woodburner, a good mix of dining chairs, window seats and wall settles, huge collection of miniature bottles, well prepared enterprising bar food and lots of colourful hanging baskets; bdrms; disabled access. **£18.95**|£5.95.

EXETER SX9190 **Double Locks** *Canal Banks, Alphington (01392) 256947* Friendly and very relaxed lockside country pub, popular with students, with good simple bar food (all day), summer barbecues, and up to 10 real ales on handpump; no children; disabled access. £4.75.

EXETER SX9292 **Lambs** *15 Lower North St (under the iron bridge) (01392) 254269* 18th-c house close to the cathedral and cheerfully run by knowledgeable staff, with well balanced menu using fresh seasonal local produce – everything from nibbles to breads and puddings is totally home-made; thoughtful wine list; cl am Sat, all day Sun and Mon, 2 wks Aug. **£24**|£11.

EXETER SX9292 **St Martin's Café Bar** *Cathedral Close (01392) 310130* Attached to the Royal Clarence Hotel and overlooking cathedral precinct; attractive, light and airy with lots of pine, helpful young service, relaxed atmosphere, and enjoyable food usefully served all day (from breakfast until last orders 11pm). £5.

South Devon and Dartmoor

Marvellous scenery, charming villages, very interesting places to visit, Torbay; beautiful places to stay in.

Contrasting with the promenades, low cliffs, bright gardens and palm trees of Torbay and its English Riviera is the more intimate coast to the south and west – small coves, stretches of cliff, sheltered boating creeks and estuaries cut deeply into the hills, and relaxed welcoming small towns such as Dartmouth and Totnes. Another contrast is inland Dartmoor, a magnificent brooding wilderness, with excellent walking and all sorts of points of interest – especially its strange-shaped tors and its prehistoric remains. Around its edges are many lovely valleys and villages, delightful to explore. Elsewhere are well hedged hilly pastures, steeply wooded valleys and occasional vivid red-earth fields.

Besides places mentioned in the main introduction, top attractions here are Morwellham Quay, the steam railway between Buckfastleigh and Totnes (perhaps combined with a river trip), magnificent Saltram near Plympton, Coleton Fishacre garden, Powderham Castle, Castle Drogo at Drewsteignton, Lydford Gorge on Dartmoor, Buckland Abbey and the Garden House at Buckland Monachorum, Overbecks garden near Salcombe, the friendly medieval farmhouse at Malborough, and the Dunstone shire horse centre. Plymouth has plenty to fill a rainy day, including a fine new aquarium and interesting redevelopment of former Defence Ministry land.

Please let us know what you think of places in the *Guide*. Use the report forms at the back of the book or simply write us a letter.

Where to stay

ASHBURTON SX7569 **Holne Chase** *Ashburton, Newton Abbot TQ13 7NS (01364) 631471* ***£125,** plus winter breaks; 17 comfortable and individually furnished rms, many with views over the Dart valley, some split-level suites in converted stables. Marvellously peaceful former hunting lodge to Buckfast Abbey in 70 acres with sweeping lawns and plenty of woodland walks, a mile of Dart fishing, shooting and riding on Dartmoor; cheerful welcoming owners, comfortable public rooms with log fires, very good modern English cooking using home-grown vegetables, and enjoyable breakfasts and afternoon teas (home-made breads, marmalades and so forth); children over 10 in evening restaurant; disabled access.

AVETON GIFFORD SX6947 **Court Barton Farmhouse** *Aveton Gifford, Kingsbridge TQ7 4LE (01548) 550312* ***£44;** 7 rms, 6 with own bthrm. Pretty creeper-clad 16th-c farmhouse on 300 acres of arable land, with cosy homely lounge, log fires, a warm welcome, farmhouse breakfasts, and flower-filled garden; cl Christmas.

BANTHAM SX6643 **Widcombe House** *Bantham, Kingsbridge TQ7 3AA (01548) 561084* ***£56;** 3 well equipped neat rms. In lovely countryside with fine views down to the sea, this modern no smoking house is spotlessly kept and very relaxing, with very good breakfasts and delicious evening meals in their new dining room using home-grown produce; cl Nov–Feb; no children.

BLACKAWTON SX8050 **Normandy Arms** *Blackawton, Totnes TQ9 7BN (01803) 712316* ***£50,** plus special breaks; 5 pretty rms. Quaint, friendly pub in quiet village, with cosy main bar, log fire, some interesting displays of World War II battle gear, generous food in bar and restaurant, real ales, and seats in garden.

BOVEY TRACEY SX8178 **Edgemoor Hotel** *Haytor Rd, Bovey Tracey, Newton Abbot TQ13 9LE (01626) 832466* ***£92.50,** plus special breaks; 17 charming rms. Ivy-covered country house in neatly kept gardens on the edge of Dartmoor, with comfortable lounge and bar, log fires, good food in elegant restaurant, and high tea for children under 8; cl 1st wk Jan; children over 8 in restaurant; dogs welcome.

BURGH ISLAND SX6443 **Burgh Island** *Burgh Island, Bigbury-on-Sea TQ7 4BG (01548) 810514* **£218 inc dinner;** 14 art deco seaview suites, most with balconies. Extravagantly decorated and restored 1929 hotel on cut-off small island – access by hotel Land Rover (or foot) at low tide, and on seagoing summer tractor-on-stilts at high tide; domed palm court, sun lounge, classic cocktail bar, art deco furniture, kind helpful hosts, good food, and super breakfasts. Tennis, mini-gym, snooker, water sports, natural pool and private beach, walks, and sea fishing. Island has 14th-c pub – and summer day crowds. Hotel cl Jan and wkdys Feb; no dogs.

CHAGFORD SX7087 **Easton Court** *Sandy Park, Chagford, Newton Abbot TQ13 8JN (01647) 433469* ***£90,** plus special breaks; 8 rms. Creeper-clad thatched 15th-c house with beams, inglenook fireplace, granite walls, and big library (literary connections inc Evelyn Waugh writing *Brideshead Revisited* here); cosy bar, charming sitting room, good breakfasts, delicious evening meals in candlelit restaurant; cl Jan; children over 12; disabled access.

CHAGFORD SX7087 **Gidleigh Park** *Chagford, Newton Abbot TQ13 8HH (01647) 432367* **£355 inc dinner,** plus winter breaks; 15 opulent and individual rms with fruit and flowers. Exceptional luxurious Dartmoor-edge mock Tudor hotel with deeply comfortable panelled drawing room, wonderful flowers, conservatory overlooking the grounds (40 acres, with walks straight up onto the moor), log fires, particularly fine cooking and a good wine list, and caring staff.

DARTINGTON SX7762 **Cott** *Dartington, Totnes TQ9 6HE (01803) 863777* **£65,** plus special breaks; 6 character rms. Pretty and very warmly friendly ancient inn with fine thatched roof (the longest in southern England), heavy-beamed communicating rooms with open fires and flagstones, good lunchtime buffet and interesting evening food (lots of fresh fish), real ales and quite a few wines by the glass, and friendly cats; no smoking restaurant, seats on terrace, and fine nearby walks; cl 25 Dec; children over 5.

DARTMOUTH SX8751 **Ford House** *44 Victoria Rd, Dartmouth TQ6 9DX (01803) 834047* ***£75,** plus special breaks; 4 individually decorated rms. Nr the harbour, this Regency town house has a log fire in the comfortable drawing room, antiques, good interesting food using fresh local produce eaten round a big table, delicious breakfasts, helpful service, and sheltered garden; you can take over the whole house for a wknd party; cl Oct–Apr.

DARTMOUTH SX8751 **Royal Castle** *11 The Quay, Dartmouth TQ6 9PS (01803) 833033* **£96,** plus special breaks; 25 individually furnished rms. Well restored mainly Georgian hotel (part 16th-c) overlooking inner harbour – great views from most rooms; lively and interesting public bar with open fires and beams, quiet library/lounge with antiques, drawing room overlooking quayside, winter spit-roasts in lounge bar, elegant upstairs seafood restaurant, decent bar food, and friendly staff.

DODDISCOMBSLEIGH SX8586 **Nobody** *Doddiscombsleigh, Exeter EX6 7PS (01647) 252394* ***£64;** 7 rms, some in a Georgian manor house 150 yards down the road, and most with own bthrm. Friendly, atmospheric 16th-c pub with beams, heavy wooden furniture, and inglenook fireplace in the attractively furnished 2-roomed lounge bar, an outstanding cellar running to 800 wines and 250 malts, and popular food in bar and restaurant inc huge range of Devon cheeses; good views from garden, and the church is worth visiting for fine stained glass; cl 25–26 Dec; no children.

GALMPTON SX6840 **Burton Farm** *Galmpton, Kingsbridge TQ7 3EY (01548) 561210* ***£52;** 9 rms, most with own bthrm. Welcoming working farm in lovely countryside with dairy herd and pedigree sheep (guests welcome to look around and help); traditional farmhouse cooking using home-produced ingredients; no smoking; cl Christmas.

GOVETON SX7546 **Buckland-Tout-Saints** *Goveton, Kingsbridge TQ7 2DS (01548) 853055* **£90,** plus special winter breaks; 13 luxurious period rms. Handsome Queen Anne mansion in 6 well kept acres of gardens with croquet/putting; relaxing rooms with antiques, fine panelling and plasterwork, chintzy furniture and roaring log fire, imaginative food using good local produce in lovely no smoking restaurant, notable wines, and excellent personal service; cl Jan; children over 6 in restaurant; dogs by arrangement.

HAYTOR SX7677 **Bel Alp House** *Haytor, Newton Abbot TQ13 9XX (01364) 661217* ***£120,** plus special breaks; 8 spacious rms. Handsome Edwardian country house with elegant drawing room, comfortable sitting room, log fires, friendly atmosphere, and fine careful cooking in pretty restaurant; wonderful views and peaceful garden; disabled access.

HAYTOR VALE SX7677 **Rock** *Haytor Vale, Newton Abbot TQ13 9XP (01364) 661305* **£61,** plus special breaks; 9 rms. Civilised old inn on the edge of Dartmoor National Park, with good food (inc fresh fish), a mix of visitors and locals in the 2 rooms of the panelled bar, open fires, no smoking restaurant, courteous service, and big garden; walking, fishing, riding and golf nearby.

HAZELWOOD SX7148 **Crannacombe Farm** *Hazelwood, Loddiswell, Kingsbridge TQ7 4DX (01548) 550256* ***£38;** 2 rms. Quietly set and comfortable Georgian farmhouse on working stock farm in a lovely unspoilt valley, with prize-winning cider, and hearty food; no smoking; babysitting; cl Christmas.

HOLNE SX7069 **Church House** *Holne, Newton Abbot TQ13 7SJ (01364) 631208* **£50,** plus special breaks; 4 rms, 3 with own bthrm. Medieval Dartmoor-edge inn with comfortable and interesting pine-panelled lounge bar, freshly prepared food using local produce, restaurant, decent wine list, pleasant service, and lots of good walks close by.

HOLNE SX7069 **Wellpritton Farm** *Holne, Ashburton TQ13 7RX (01364) 631273* ***£38;** 4 pretty rms, 3 with own bthrm. Small friendly Dartmoor farm with lots of animals, comfortable sitting room, good food (packed lunches on request), and small swimming pool; children over 5 (younger by arrangement, out of season).

HOPE COVE SX6739 **Hope Cove** *Hope Cove, Kingsbridge TQ7 3HH (01548) 561233* **£53,** plus special breaks; 7 rms with fine sea views. Neatly kept and welcoming little hotel in tranquil spot with sandy beaches and plenty of walks; lovely views from lounge or dining room, helpful owners and staff, and enjoyable food; cl Oct–Mar; children from 6; no dogs.

KINGSTON SX6347 **Dolphin** *Kingston, Kingsbridge TQ7 4QE (01548) 810314* ***£49;** 3 rms. Peaceful 16th-c inn with several knocked-through beamed rooms, a warmly welcoming atmosphere, a small no smoking area, very good home-made food, and real ales; tracks down to the sea.

LEWDOWN SX4486 **Lewtrenchard Manor** *Lewdown, Okehampton EX20 4PN (01566) 783256* **£105,** plus special breaks; 9 well equipped rms with fresh flowers and period furniture. Lovely Elizabethan manor house in garden with fine dovecot, surrounded by peaceful estate with shooting, fishing and croquet; dark panelling, ornate ceilings, antiques, fresh flowers, and log fires, a friendly welcome, relaxed atmosphere, and candlelit restaurant with very good food; children under 8 by arrangement; disabled access.

LIFTON SX3885 **Arundell Arms** *Lifton PL16 0AA (01566) 784666* ***£90,** plus special breaks; 28 well equipped rms, 5 in annexe over the road. Carefully renovated old coaching inn with 20 miles of its own waters – fishing is the main thing; comfortable sitting room, log fires, very good food in smart restaurant, decent wines, and kind service from local staff; cl 2 days over Christmas; dogs welcome away from restaurant and river bank.

LYDFORD SX5184 **Castle** *Lydford, Okehampton EX20 4BH (01822) 820242* ***£62;** 10 individually decorated rms, most with own bthrm. Very well run charming Tudor inn with particularly friendly staff, lots of interesting antiques and furnishings in lounge areas (one overlooks pleasant garden with covered terrace), log fires, beams and flagstones, lovely food, well kept real ales and decent wines; pets corner; next to castle and nr gorge; cl pm 25 Dec.

MALBOROUGH SX7037 **Soar Mill Cove** *Malborough, Salcombe TQ7 3DS (01548) 561566* ***£164 inc dinner,** plus special breaks; 21 comfortable rms, some opening onto garden. Neatly kept single-storey building in idyllic spot by peaceful and very beautiful cove on NT coast (excellent walks), with lovely views, extensive private grounds, tennis/putting, and warm indoor pool; outstanding service, log fires, very good food (marvellous fish), and thoughtful early-evening children's meal; cl Dec–beginning Feb (open Christmas and New Year); small, mature, well behaved dogs by arrangement; disabled access.

MORETONHAMPSTEAD SX7586 **Great Sloncombe Farm** *Moretonhampstead, Newton Abbot TQ13 8QF (01647) 440595* ***£42;** 3 rms – the big double is the favourite. Lovely 13th-c farmhouse on a working dairy and stock farm, with friendly owners, carefully polished old-fashioned furniture, decent food, log fires, a relaxed atmosphere, and good nearby walking and birdwatching; no smoking; children over 8; dogs by arrangement.

MORETONHAMPSTEAD SX7585 **White Hart** *Moretonhampstead, Newton Abbot TQ13 8NF (01647) 440406* **£60,** plus special breaks; 21 rms. Comfortable former Georgian posting house, interesting furnishings in civilised lounge bar and hall, lively back bar, good bar food, and no smoking restaurant; well placed for Dartmoor; children over 10.

PRESTON SX8574 **Sampsons Farm** *Preston, Newton Abbot TQ12 3PP (01626) 354913* ***£65;** 10 rms, most with own bthrm. Thatched 14th-c longhouse with beams, panelling and big open fires in cosy sitting rooms, a very relaxed welcoming atmosphere, most enjoyable food in popular restaurant, and lots of nearby walks; self-catering too; children over 3; disabled access.

SALCOMBE SX7337 **Tides Reach** *South Sands, Salcombe TQ8 8LJ (01548) 843466* **£126,** plus special breaks; 38 rms, many with estuary views. Unusually individual resort hotel run by long-serving owners in pretty wooded cove by the sea, with airy luxurious day rooms, big sea aquarium in cocktail bar, good restaurant food using fresh local produce, friendly efficient service, and squash, snooker, leisure complex, health area, and big heated pool; windsurfing etc, beach over the lane, and lots of coast walks; cl Dec and Jan; children over 8; disabled access.

SANDY PARK SX7189 **Mill End** *Sandy Park, Chagford, Newton Abbot TQ13 8JN (01647) 432282* ***£80,** plus special breaks; 17 neat rms, most with views. Quietly set former flour mill (carefully restored this year) with waterwheel in neatly kept grounds below Dartmoor; comfortable newly refurbished lounges, carefully prepared interesting food and fine breakfasts, and good service; well behaved dogs welcome away from public rooms; partial disabled access.

SOUTH ZEAL SX6593 **Oxenham Arms** *South Zeal, Okehampton EX20 2JT (01837) 840244* ***£60,** plus special breaks; 8 rms, 7 with own bthrm. Grandly atmospheric old inn dating back to 12th c and first licensed in 1477 (a neolithic standing stone still forms part of the wall in the TV room); elegant beamed and panelled bar with chatty relaxed atmosphere and open fire, decent food and wines; and charming small garden (formerly a monastery's); well behaved dogs welcome.

STAVERTON SX7964 **Sea Trout** *Staverton, Totnes TQ9 6PA (01803) 762274* **£68;** 10 cottagey rms. Comfortable pub in quiet hamlet nr River Dart with 2 relaxed beamed bars, log fires, popular food in bar and airy dining conservatory, and terraced garden with fountains and waterfalls; cl Christmas.

STOKE GABRIEL SX8457 **Gabriel Court** *Stoke Gabriel, Totnes TQ9 6SF (01803) 782206* **£77,** plus special breaks; 19 rms, some in former hay lofts. In a walled Elizabethan garden, this attractive family-run manor has quiet relaxing lounges (winter log fire), enjoyable traditional English food, and courteous helpful staff; outdoor heated swimming pool and grass tennis court; dogs welcome.

TEIGNMOUTH SX9473 **Thomas Luny House** *Teign St, Teignmouth TQ14 8EG (01626) 772976* ***£70,** plus special breaks; 4 pretty rms with flowers and books. Lovely little no smoking Georgian house nr fish quay, with open fires in spacious, comfortable drawing room and elegant dining room, a relaxed friendly atmosphere, enjoyable food round big dining table, and sunny walled garden; cl Jan; children over 12.

TWO BRIDGES SX6175 **Prince Hall** *Two Bridges, Yelverton PL20 6SA (01822) 890403* **£80;** 9 attractive, spacious rms. Surrounded by Dartmoor National Park, this tranquil 18th-c country house is run by caring friendly owners and their helpful staff; lovely views from convivial bar, comfortable sitting room, and cosy dining room, open fires, very good evening meals, enjoyable breakfasts, and lots of fine walks; cl end Dec–2nd wk Feb; children over 8 in evening dining room; partial disabled access.

To see and do

DARTMOOR SX5880 Classic moorland, where distant vistas of changing greens and browns fade into the austere grey-blues of far shoulders and edges. The moor is punctuated with all sorts of interesting focal points and features: numerous easily traceable prehistoric remains; strange wind-sculpted, eroded granite tors which crown many of the slopes; the little streams that thread over boulders; tamed watercourses where leats or miniature canals (dating back to the 16th-c one cut by Drake to supply Plymouth) curl carefully round the contours; sheltered valleys cut into the moors, where white houses crouch among sycamores and oaks, occasional higher clusters of much more stunted oaks mark abandoned tin-mine workings with ruined wheelhouses, and shaggy ponies hope for a hand-out. Good roads over the moor are the B3212 and B3357, and the back road towards Ashburton off the B3344 just NW of Manaton. The main information and visitor centres are at Princetown on Tavistock Rd, (01822) 890414, and at Postbridge on the B3212, (01822) 880272. Dartmoor is outstanding for walking, but mist can come down very suddenly, so on the open moor you must carry a compass and your waterproofs. A lot of the moor is a long way from the road, hence rather inaccessible. There are more paths for walkers than the right-of-way network suggests, but don't assume a right of way marked on the OS map will be visible on the ground (the black dashed lines on these maps are generally more reliable). Old mineral railways and cart tracks make for some good walkers' routes. There are plenty of things to head for, to give a moorland walk a sense of purpose – most obviously, one of the many tors of naked rock rising out of the moor (beware: the rounded rocks can be a good deal more slippery than they look). The surrounding villages are well worth exploring: typically, thatched white-plastered stone cottages clustered round an ancient stone church beside its church-house inn. The towns ringing the moor have useful facilities. A big chunk of NW Dartmoor is used by the Ministry of Defence for firing practice; it's marked by red and white posts, and you can go in when there are no red lights or red flags. We pick out below some particularly nice spots:

BEL TOR CORNER SX7071
Dr Blackall's Drive This specially created carriage drive to New Bridge gives splendid views of the Dart valley, and is among Dartmoor's finest paths for walkers.

BOWERMAN'S NOSE SX7480
This quaint tor, looking snootily out over a patchwork of pastures, makes a pleasant objective for a Dartmoor walk.

† **BRENTOR CHURCH** SX4881
(above the back road from Lydford–Tavistock, just S of North Brentor) 12th-c, one of England's smallest churches, notable for its lonely hilltop position with remarkable coast and Dartmoor views.

† **BURRATOR RESERVOIR**
SX5568 This gives a 5-mile walk in beautiful woodland and moorland surroundings. **Sheepstor church** on the way has interesting memorials to the Brookes family, former rajahs of Sarawak.

DARTMEET CLAPPER BRIDGE SX6773 By the road, this attractive ancient stone packhorse bridge is a popular place for strolling.

DEVONPORT LEAT SX5670
Easily reached off the B3212 Yelverton–Princetown, this watercourse, still largely complete, was first engineered 200 years ago to give Devonport a water supply. A path along the gently graded channel takes in some remote scenery in Dartmoor's western moors, and makes getting lost quite difficult.

FINGLE BRIDGE SX7489
From the Angler's Rest a lovely 'Fisherman's Path' winds along a wooded stretch of the River Teign; you can return at high level on the 'Hunter's Path', passing nr Castle Drogo and gaining tremendous views.

GREAT MIS TOR SX5676
In the lonely terrain N of Dartmoor Prison, this gives walkers panoramic views over much of the moor – though access may be barred by army firing practice (red flags give warning).

GRIMSPOUND SX6980
By a stream, this is one of the most impressive of Dartmoor's **ancient sites**, with a fine old lichened granite cross nearby to mark the way for later medieval travellers; great views from the round walk to Widecombe.

HAYTOR ROCKS SX7577
This fortress-like collection of rocks makes a striking and popular objective for walks; nearby is an abandoned quarry served by an unusual 19th-c tramway with grooved-granite rails. Not far from here **Hound Tor** SX7478 is majestic, monumental and a good destination for a walk, with an interesting excavated abandoned medieval village nearby. **Honeybag Tor** SX7278 has marvellous views over Widecombe and though the OS map doesn't show this, there's a path back to Hound Tor, along the spine of the ridge.

★ **LUSTLEIGH** SX7881 One of the most attractive villages in the whole of England, with charming riverside walks in utterly unspoilt woodland around it. Primrose Cottage is hotly tipped for cream teas, and the Cleave Inn is good. The ridge path to landmark **Hunter's Tor** SX7682 gives panoramic views of Lustleigh Cleave and the Bovey valley.

! **LYDFORD GORGE** SX5084
Spectacular gorge formed by the River Lyd cutting into the rock, causing boulders to scoop out potholes in the bed of the stream. Walks along the ravine take you to dramatic sights such as the White Lady waterfall and the

Devil's Cauldron whirlpool (summer crowds around this bit). Children like it but need to be watched carefully, and paths can be narrow and slippery. Snacks (in ingeniously designed tearoom), shop; most parts cl winter; (01822) 820441; £3.20; NT. The forbidding ruined **castle** has a daunting 12th-c stone keep, its upper floor once used as a court, and the lower as a prison; free. The Castle Inn is very good.

MEAVY SX5367 (pronounced 'Mewy' locally) Attractive village, where the parish still owns the (good) pub. The clear wooded River Meavy has some pleasant spots for strolling (another useful pub for walkers here is the Skylark at Clearbrook).

POSTBRIDGE CLAPPER BRIDGE SX6478 By the road, this ancient stone packhorse bridge is an attractive – and in summer very popular – focus for Dartmoor strolls, often complete with hopeful ponies.

RIVER PLYM SX5866 The upper valley has numerous visible hut circles, stone rows and cairns: interesting for walks.

SHOVEL DOWN SX6686 These open moorland expanses harbour some of Dartmoor's richest concentrations of antiquities. You'll need a map just to find the car park at Scorhill, SW of Gidleigh and W of Chagford; from there, a path brings you out onto the moor within sight of **Scorhill stone circle**. Close by are stone slab bridges over clear brooks; among the litter of rocks by one river is the **Teign Tolmen**, a natural boulder through which the water has gouged a perfectly circular hole. You can walk over to nearby **Kes Tor**, close to which is the **Long Stone** and a fine stone row of about 2500–1500BC.

VIXEN TOR SX5474 Towering up from the bracken, this looks unclimbable, but is quite easily reached from behind. This area of the **Walkham valley** is relatively lush and green, and walkers can explore the old railway tracks which once served local quarries.

★ † **WIDECOMBE IN THE MOOR** SX7176 One of the most visited villages on Dartmoor, immortalised by the trip of Uncle Tom Cobbleigh and all to Widecombe Fair. The granite-carved village sign shows them all crowded onto their old grey mare. The **church**, known as the Cathedral of the Moors, has a distinctive, disproportionately high tower. The adjoining 16th-c church house, now the church hall, is worth a look. Next door, the **Sexton's Cottage** is an NT and National Park information centre and gift shop; cl Jan. The Post Office Stores has good ice-cream and local honey. The reconstructed Olde Inne in the village is very popular with tourists, but for more of a Tom Cobbleigh flavour try the Rugglestone Inn just S. The **Shilstone Rocks Riding Centre** organises horse-riding over Dartmoor, beginners welcome. Disabled access; (01364) 621281; from £12 an hour.

YES TOR SX5890 Up in the lonelier northern part of the moor, this landmark gives great views over Dartmoor. This area of Okehampton Common is the highest terrain in southern England, though (as throughout this northern area) access is often barred by army firing practice – look out for red flags on approach roads.

★ **DARTMOUTH** SX8751 Charming waterside small town with many exceptional buildings, especially around the inner harbour. Though so popular, it's kept its own strong character, and stays very much alive through the winter. Cobbled Bayards Cove, with old fort and steep wooded hills behind, is particularly photogenic, as is pedestrianised Foss St. Markets Tues, Fri: Old Market is picturesque. The Royal Naval College is a striking building. Interesting shops, plenty of waterside seats, lots of action on the river. Parking in summer can be trying: best to use good Park & Ride on the B3207 Halwell Rd.

Please let us know what you think of places in the *Guide*. Use the report forms at the back of the book or simply write us a letter.

River trips to Totnes pass some of Devon's prettiest scenery, much of which can't be seen on foot or by car; you can combine this with steamtrains or a connecting bus back which saves hearing the commentary a second time. You can also go on circular tours of the surrounding area. There may still be boats in winter – tel (01803) 832109 to check; £6 return to Totnes. Also quaint car and pedestrian ferries to Kingswear and the A379 (can be a 2-hour car wait at peak summer times).

Dartmouth Castle (slightly SE, off the B3205) Classic late 15th-c battlemented fortress, virtually intact, with cannon and later gun batteries, and great views out into the Channel. Snacks, shop; cl winter Mon and Tues; (01803) 833588; £2.50. In summer a little ferry leaves the South Embankment for here every 15 minutes or so. Otherwise it's an enjoyable and fairly gentle 20-minute walk from Dartmouth itself, though the immediate hinterland is unremarkable.

St Saviour's church Lots of charming detail, well worth a close look, inc altar, pulpit, painted rood screen, brasses on chancel floor, elaborate 14th-c hinges on south door.

Dartmouth Museum (Duke St) Well restored 17th-c timbered house, with mainly nautical displays; cl Sun, 25–26 Dec; *£1. **Henley Museum** (Anzac St) Smaller but interesting – and currently undergoing a major refurbishment to increase its appeal to children; cl wknds and Oct–Easter; free.

Newcomen Engine House (Royal Ave Gardens) Huge steam-powered atmospheric beam-engine pump, thought to be the world's oldest, worked 1720–1913. Shop, disabled access; cl Sun Nov–Mar and Christmas; (01803) 834224; *50p.

PAIGNTON SX8861 Largely a typical resort, with long promenade between good sandy beach and green; the little harbour is pretty, with working fishing boats as well as yachts. The original inland core has an attractive red sandstone church with some interesting buildings nearby, especially **Kirkham House**, a handsome sandstone Tudor merchant's house with lofty hall. The formal and subtropical lakeside gardens at **Oldway** are colourful; on summer wkdy mornings there may be guided tours of the Versailles-style colonnaded mansion at their centre. Attractive Elberry Cove between Paignton and Brixham is altogether quieter. Decent places for lunch include the Blagdon Inn (off the A385), Embassy (Colin Rd), Isaac Merritt (Torquay Rd) and Ship (Totnes Rd).

Paignton Zoo (St Michael's) Well run and shown, with over 1,300 animals and birds (many of them breeding) in 75 acres of beautifully planted surroundings; it's perhaps the country's most visually appealing zoo. Recent improvements include new ape, giraffe and elephant enclosures, and more additions are planned during the next couple of years. Also lakeside miniature railway, and splendid hands-on animal education centre for children. Lots of events and feeding displays throughout the day. Meals, snacks, shop, good disabled access; cl 25 Dec; (01803) 557479; £6.75.

Paignton & Dartmouth Steam Railway (Queen's Park Station, Torbay Rd) One of the nicest such trips we know of – GWR steamtrains run from here right by the sea along Tor Bay (halts at Goodrington Beach, which has closer parking, and Churston), then along the Dart estuary to Kingswear. The front Pullman coach is less crowded, and there's a model railway at the Paignton end. You can combine this with a boat Dartmouth–Totnes, and bus Totnes–Paignton. Snacks, shop, disabled access; cl Nov–Feb (exc parts of Dec), and some wkdys and Sats out of season; (01803) 555872 for timetable; £6.10 return.

PLYMOUTH SX4753 Apart from the area round the Barbican, most of the old bits of the city were destroyed in the war, and in parts it is like lots of other busy modern towns. There are some interesting escapes from the bustle, and in places the Hoe has something of the feel of smaller seaside promenades, with great views out over the Sound; decent food at the Waterfront bar/restaurant. A statue of Drake is a reminder that he's supposed to have played his famous game of bowls here; there's still a bowling green close by. A tour bus can take you to the main attractions, though it's perhaps more fun on one of the **boat trips** run by Tamar Cruises from Mayflower Steps, off Madeira Rd, Barbican; (01752) 822105. There are also boats from here to the **Mountbatten Peninsula**, a former Ministry of Defence area now open to the public; you can walk along the breakwater, which goes right out into the Sound with views back towards the city. The ferries over to Torpoint in Cornwall put Antony House and Mount Edgcumbe in very easy reach. The Bank (behind the Theatre Royal) does good-value food all day, and the Tourist Information Centre is one of the most efficient we've come across.

Plymouth Barbican Carefully restored since the war, a series of narrow twisty streets of old buildings W of working Sutton Harbour; photogenic, and evocative even in wet weather. New St is its oldest core, and the waterside Ship has decent food. The next 6 attractions are all round here.
Prysten House (Finewell St) The city's oldest house, an austere late 15th-c granite building with galleried courtyard. Unpretentious but quite atmospheric restored rooms feature a model of 17th-c Plymouth, and several yards of an ambitious tapestry showing American colonisation; cl Sun, and Nov–Mar; (01752) 661414; 70p.
St Andrew's church (St Andrew St) Bombed but lovingly restored, with stained glass by John Piper illustrating the city's history.
Merchant's House (St Andrew St) Well restored 16th-c jettied house, telling the city's day-to-day history in displays themed on tinker, tailor, soldier, sailor; also early Victorian apothecary's shop and schoolroom. Shop; cl 1-2pm, Sun, Mon (exc bank hols), and Oct–Mar; (01752) 264878; 90p.
Black Friars Distillery (60 Southside St) Photogenic home of Plymouth Dry Gin, now the only English gin still made in its original distillery, founded in 1793. The building itself dates back much further, and has had periods as a monastery and a prison; tours include demonstrations of production, a film of the town's history and of course a sample of the gin itself. Shop; cl Sun, and Nov–Easter; (01752) 665292; £2.75.
Elizabethan House (32 New St) Splendid timber-framed Tudor sea-captain's house, with period furniture; cl Mon, Tues, and all Nov–April; £1. There's an Elizabethan garden just down the road at number 39.
Fish Market Redeveloped as a new visitor centre: glass-blowing demonstrations by Dartington Crystal, and exhibitions on the local area. Large shop, disabled access; cl 25–26 Dec, Easter Sun; free.
Plymouth Dome (The Hoe) State-of-the-art evocation of Plymouth's past and present using feel-part-of-it technology – you can stroll along lively Elizabethan streets, dodge press gangs, meet Drake and the Pilgrim Fathers, and come bang up to date with satellite and radar monitoring of current harbour action and weather. Good fun as well as interesting, and well worth 2 hours (you may have trouble parking nearby for longer than that). Particularly good for families – children don't mind learning about a place's heritage when it's presented like this. Snacks, shop, good disabled access; cl 25 Dec; (01752) 603300; £3.95 (inc admission to Smeaton's Tower).
National Maritime Aquarium There are literally hundreds of fish at this new aquarium, from all round the world, inc freshwater, British coastal, tropical and some Carribean sharks. The discovery pool, an open-topped rock pool area, should prove popular with children. Meals, snacks, shop, disabled access; cl 25 Dec; (01752) 600301; £6.50.

Smeaton's Tower (The Hoe) Colourfully striped 18th-c former Eddystone Rocks lighthouse, moved here 110 years ago, with a good view from the top if you like steps; cl Nov–Mar, and maybe in bad weather; (01752) 600608; 75p.

Royal Citadel (The Hoe) Unrivalled views of city and sea from the ramparts of this magnificent 17th-c battlemented fortress. The gateway is striking, and the barracked parade-ground is still in use; admission by guided tour only, at 2pm and 3.30pm May–Sept, starting from the main gate get tickets at least 15 minutes earlier from the Dome or the Tourist Imformation Centre; (01752) 775841; £3.

City Museum (Drake Circus) Well shown collections of mostly West Country interest. Shop, disabled access; cl Sun, Mon (exc bank hols); free.

Crownhill Fort (Crownhill Fort Rd) Just N of town, the biggest and least altered of Plymouth's Victorian forts, though from the road it looks little more than a wooded hill. Used by the army right up to 1986, it's been well restored by the Landmark Trust, with barrack rooms, underground tunnels, secret passageways, and lookout towers to explore; children can run around quite freely, and there's an adventure playground. You can stay here in a Victorian officer's flat (open all year), and have the run of the place after dark. Snacks, shop, limited disabled access (lots of steep steps); cl Nov–Mar; (01752) 793754; £2.75.

TORQUAY SX9163 The busiest of the area's resorts, good for evening strolling, with palm trees and rocks, promenades, colourful gardens, decorous guest houses and huge hotels, broad Victorian streets and expensive shops. The sheltered beaches round here are cleaner than many along this coast. Summer bustle centres around the attractive harbour, with lots of shops, boat trips, and an aquarium. In summer a **cliff railway** takes care of a dizzy swoop from Oddicombe Beach to the high wooded clifftop (around 60p each way). The quaint Hole in the Wall (Park Lane) and smart new London (Strand) do good-value food.

Kents Cavern (Ilsham Rd, Wellswood) The oldest directly dated archaeological site in Britain; continuing excavations often make scientists reconsider their theories about prehistoric life. Good guided tours really bring out the mystery of the caves, and colourful stalagmites and stalactites add to the eerie atmosphere. In summer they do spooky evening tours (booking essential). Very well presented, and definitely worth an hour or so if you're in the area. Special visits at Christmas. Summer snacks, shop, disabled access (with prior notice); cl 25 Dec; (01803) 215136; £4, £4.75 evening tours.

! **Model Village** (Hampton Ave, Babbacombe) Hundreds of 1:12 scale buildings in 4 acres of miniaturised landscape, beautifully done. Try coming at dusk between Easter and Oct, when the scenes are prettily floodlit. Snacks, shop, good disabled access; cl 25 Dec; (01803) 328669; £4.20 – a little pricey, but it's probably the best of its type (you may also have to pay for parking). The beach here has safe bathing water, and the Cary Arms (Beach Rd) is good.

Torre Abbey (King's Drive) Some of the earlier parts of the abbey remain, inc the medieval sandstone gatehouse and ruined Norman tower, but they've been eclipsed by the later house with its 17th-, 18th- and 19th-c period rooms. The main feature now is the art gallery, along with a showy garden and palm house and an Agatha Christie room, full of possessions of the locally born author. Snacks, shop; cl Nov–Mar; (01803) 293593; £2.75.

Bygones (Fore St, St Marychurch) Enthusiastically reconstructed life-sized Victorian street, with well stocked period shops and rooms, model railway, and re-created World War I trench, replete with sound effects and cooking smells. Open till 10pm (6pm Fri and Sat) in summer. Café, shop; cl 25 Dec; (01803) 326108; *£2.95.

Torquay Museum (529 Babbacombe Rd) Finds from ancient

local caves, local history, Victoriana and a cannon that turns out to be a clock, designed to fire its charge at midday. Shop; cl am Sun and winter wknds; (01803) 293975; £2.

★ **Cockington** Winding lanes of olde-worlde thatched cottages and bric-à-brac/craft shops in sheltered village with millpond etc, well preserved by Torbay Council; adjoining 500-acre park. The Drum pub (a useful stop) was designed to match by Lutyens in 1934. Terribly pretty, and very touristy in season, with open horse-drawn carriages.

★ **TOTNES** SX8060 Busy in summer, but still keeping most of its charm even then, particularly early in the morning. The picturesque Elizabethan area known as **The Narrows** is very atmospheric, especially along the High St down to the arch at the top of Fore St, with quaint pillared arcades. On Tues May–Sept many traders wear Elizabethan costume, and the main streets are closed to traffic then, delighting visitors but infuriating some local traders. There's a working harbour (*see Dartmouth entry above for excellent river trips*), and you can walk some way downstream on either side of the River Dart. Behind the church of St Mary's (which has a super rood screen), several rooms in the 11th-c **guildhall** may be open; it was originally part of a Benedictine priory. Perhaps unexpectedly, Totnes has quite a New Age flavour; there's even a flotation tank to wash away city stresses. The Kingsbridge Inn (Leechwell St), Royal Seven Stars Hotel (Fore St) and Albert (Bridgetown) have decent food, though the Cott at nearby Dartington easily merits the extra distance. The **South Devon Railway**, which stops here, is described under Buckfastleigh entry (*see below*).

Totnes Castle Part Norman, part 14th-c, these classic circular remains were lucky enough to avoid any battles, so the keep is pretty much intact. There's a tree-shaded inner lawn, and lovely views of the town and down to the river. Shop; cl winter Mon and Tues (and maybe lunchtimes then); (01803) 864406; £1.60.

Totnes Museum (70 Fore St) Stately Elizabethan merchant's house with galleried courtyard, herb garden, and display on the inventions of Totnes boy Charles Babbage, creator of one of the earliest computers. Shop, disabled access with prior arrangement; cl wknds, and Nov–Mar; (01803) 863821; *£1.50.

Devonshire Collection of Period Costume (43 High St) Period costumes and accessories from the 18th c to the present, from high fashion to ordinary work clothes, with changing annual exhibitions. Shop; cl wknds, and Nov–Apr; *£1.50.

Bowden House (Ashprington Rd, S) Tours by costumed guides of handsomely restored grand Tudor and baroque rooms (plenty of weaponry, and well documented tales of ghosts), and separate **photography museum** with still and moving pictures (inc cartoons) in attractive grounds. Snacks, shop, disabled access to museum only; open pm Mon–Thurs and bank hol Suns from April–Oct; (01803) 863664; £4.60.

We welcome reports from readers

This *Guide* depends on readers' reports. Do help us if you can – in return, we offer a discount on the next edition to people who've helped us with reports for it. Tell us what you think about places already in it, and anything extra you think we should say about them. And send us your ideas for inclusion in the next edition: places to visit, eat at or stay in, attractive drives or walks, maybe even unusual interesting shops you know of. Use the card in the middle, the report forms at the end, or just write – no stamp needed: *The Good Guide to Britain*, FREEPOST TN1569, Wadhurst, E Sussex TN5 7BR.

Other things to see and do

DEVON Family Attraction of the Year

☺ **BLACKAWTON** SX8052 **Woodland Leisure Park** (off the A3122)
For children who like to run around and let off steam this is one of the best days out in Devon. The emphasis is firmly on fairly traditional family fun – no major surprises or hugely elaborate rides, but good-value activities and entertainment that children up to around 12 or 13 can spin out for most of the day. A highlight for children at the upper end of the age range is the Twister, an exhilarating spiralling and plunging water-coaster – be prepared to get wet; there are several similar waterchutes nearby, and a very exciting toboggan run, the Tornado. Younger children enjoy the small zoo with wallabies, llamas and foreign birds. Well thought out play schemes range from a commando-style assault course to indoor areas for toddlers, with plenty of slides, swinging tyres and rope bridges in between. A nicely put together new Wild West town is aimed at the under 6s, with miniature bellows in the forge, and a slide down from the mine. There's also a honey farm with millions of bees behind glass, as well as a tractor yard, paddling pool, pedal karts, and twice daily falconry displays. Clowns, jugglers and other entertainers are usually on hand at weekends or during school holidays, and they have particularly good activities around midsummer, Hallowe'en and weekends up to Christmas. There's a fair bit under cover, but you'll get most out of it on a dry day. It's the kind of place that adults enjoy vicariously, though there are boats on the lake and plenty of quieter areas for woodland walks. They don't allow dogs, but do provide kennels. Meals, snacks, shop, disabled access; open wknds and school hols and daily mid-Mar–mid Nov; (01803) 712598; £4.95 (children £4.60); a family ticket for 2 adults and 2 children is £17.95.

★ **ASHBURTON** SX7370
Probably the best of the small towns around Dartmoor, with distinct character. The **River Dart Country Park** (Holne Park) is pleasant for walking or fishing, with adventure playgrounds for children. Snacks, shop; cl Oct–Mar; (01364) 652511; £4.50.

BANTHAM SANDS SX6643
A gentle walk from Bantham through dunes (good picnic spots) to the broad stretch of rivermouth sand facing Burgh Island. You can go on above the rocks S, for views of Bolt Tail and the coves between.

BERRY HEAD SX9356
Tremendous coast, sea and shipping views from former quarry, now a country park; squat lighthouse, formidable Napoleonic War battlements with cannon (and guardhouse café), nature trail taking in kittiwakes and guillemots on cliffs, uncommon plants.

✝ **BERRY POMEROY CASTLE**
SX8361 (off the A385 just E of Totnes; keep on past village) Reputedly Devon's most haunted castle, hidden away on a crag over a quiet wooded valley. Appropriately spooky Norman gatehouse and walls around the ruins of an imposing and unexpected Tudor mansion, with an interesting 15th-c fresco inside. The lawns in front are ideal for a picnic. Snacks, disabled access; cl Nov–Mar; (01803) 866618; £2.10. The red sandstone 15th-c village **church** is worth a look on the way; there's an odd monument in the Seymour Chapel. The road through here from Ashburton via Littlehempston and on to Stoke Gabriel is a pleasant drive.

BICKINGTON SX7972 **Gorse Blossom Railway Adventure Park**
Unlimited rides on 7¼in gauge steam railway through acres of woodland; also nature trails, play areas, and outdoor model railway in Swiss mountain setting. Meals, snacks, shop, some disabled access; cl Nov–Easter; (01626) 821361; *£4.50. The Toby Jug is useful for lunch.

BLACKAWTON SX8052
See separate Family Panel on p. 181 for **Woodland Leisure Park**. The George and Normandy Arms are good.

BOLT HEAD/BOLT TAIL SX6937 6 miles of one of the best coast-path sections, with remote exposed clifftops, glorious coves, far views, well preserved Iron Age earth ramparts on Bolt Tail; all NT. Best access is via Overbecks, Soar Mill Cove or Hope Cove.

BOVEY TRACEY SX8178 An unassuming small Dartmoor-edge town. The Devon Guild of Craftsmen have a good varied **craft centre** at Riverside Mill (cl winter bank hols; £1.25 for exhibitions). **Teign Valley Glass & House of Marbles** (Pottery Rd) Demonstrations of glass-blowing at factory specialising in marbles, with a fantastic array of these and some interesting marble runs in its museum. Meals, snacks, shop, disabled access; no glass-blowing Sat and winter Suns; (01626) 835358; free. The **Lowerdown Pottery** (off the B3344) does fine decorated pottery; open by appointment only; (01626) 833408; free. The Cromwell Arms does generous food. Nearby **Yarner Woods** SX7778 still has a good nature trail, despite hundreds of acres nearby being torched by arsonists in spring 1997 – the first signs of strong regrowth are very heartening.

★ **BRIXHAM** SX9256 Busy fishing port, perhaps the prettiest of the riviera resorts, with some attractive narrow streets on the hill above. Lots of activity (and summer seaside shops and cafés) in the harbour, inc (for no apparent reason) a full-size reconstruction of Drake's *Golden Hind*, and summer boats around Tor Bay. The local history **museum** (Bolton Cross) has something of a maritime emphasis (cl all day Sun, pm Sat, and all Nov–Easter; £1.20). The quaint Quayside Inn is handy for lunch, and Shoalstone beach near here has some of the cleanest bathing water in the UK. The finest part of Devon's south coast for walkers is between here and Plymouth. **Scabbacombe Head** offers a blowy but rewarding day's walk from Brixham to Kingswear, 12 miles of stunning wild scenery (and some steep climbs), passing the oasis of Coleton Fishacre gardens.

✝ **BUCKFASTLEIGH** SX7467 **Buckfast Abbey** Originally established in 1018 but after the Dissolution of the Monasteries left abandoned until 1882, when it was refounded by 4 remarkable monks, who then did most of the rebuilding work themselves over a period of 32 years. It's now one of the most visited religious sites in Britain, with an interesting exhibition, and several services each day. An excellent shop sells not just their own famous honey, but goods produced at other Benedictine monasteries around Europe, inc Bavarian beer, French cakes, and Irish linen; many people feel this alone is worth a special journey. Good meals and snacks, disabled access; guided tours (01364) 642519; free. **South Devon Railway** GWR steamtrain trips through lovely unspoilt scenery along the wooded River Dart (some of which is hard to see any other way). It now stops just outside Totnes

Days Out

The Dart's changing moods: Totnes; South Devon Railway to Buckfastleigh (via Butterfly Park and Dartmoor Otter Sanctuary, after lunch at the Kingsbridge Inn, Totnes), or river trip to Dartmouth (lunch there at the Carved Angel, Billy Budds, Cherub or Royal Castle, then a town walk along the coast path S from castle to Bolt Tail and Bolt Head).

Dartmoor ponies, Uncle Tom Cobbleigh and all: Miniature Pony Centre, North Bovey; Widecombe in the Moor; lunch at the Rock, Haytor Vale; strolls from the road to Hound Tor and Haytor; North Bovey and Lustleigh villages – cream tea at Primrose Cottage, Lustleigh.

as well as at Staverton, and they do tickets combining it with a Dartmouth–Totnes river trip; also a small museum, play area and a chance to see the ongoing restoration of rolling stock. Usually every 1½ hours in summer, less often at other times; open daily Easter hols and mid-May–mid-Oct, best to check dates in between; (01364) 642338 for timetable; £5.90. The Dartbridge opposite is a popular family dining pub. The trains call at the **Butterfly Park & Dartmoor Otter Sanctuary** (Dart Bridge Rd): watch otters swimming and playing from an underwater viewing tunnel, or see them on land in the 6 big landscaped enclosures; summer feeding times 11.30am, 2pm and 4.30pm. Also undercover tropical garden with free-flying butterflies and moths. Meals, snacks, shop, disabled access; cl Nov–Feb; (01364) 642916; £4.45. **Pennywell Farm Centre** (Lower Dean, off the A38 just S) Friendly and unfussy, with over 750 animals in 80 acres, as well as lovely scenery, wildlife viewing hides, and falconry demonstrations. Different events every half-hour, from milking and feeding to ferret-racing and worm-charming, so always something for children to get involved in; also play areas, a new assault course, pony and donkey rides and a new corner where children can try out crafts like basket-weaving. Meals, snacks, shop, disabled access; cl Nov–Mar (exc Feb half-term and Dec wknds); (01364) 642023; £4.95.

BUCKLAND MONACHORUM SX4866

Buckland Abbey The home of Francis Drake until his death in 1596, and of his family until 1946. They still have the famous drum said to sound whenever England is in danger, as well as craft workshops, herb knot garden, a new thyme garden, good walks, and entertaining summer activities for children. In Aug for a small extra charge you can play bowls on the lawn. Meals, snacks, shop, disabled access to ground floor only; cl Thurs, and Nov–Mar exc pm wknds; (01822) 853607; £4.30, £2.20 grounds only; NT. **Garden House** Profusion of unusual plants beautifully laid out in warm garden sheltered by picturesque partly ruined walls of former abbey buildings. They recently added a spring garden, quarry garden, rhododendron walk and wild flower meadow. Teas Apr–Sept, interesting plant sales; cl Nov–Feb; (01822) 854769; *£3.50. The Drake's Manor is good for lunch.

! BURGH ISLAND SX6544

Connected at low tide by a causeway to Bigbury-on-Sea (undistinguished for much save its clean sandy beaches); spectacular cliffs on the seaward side, a true island and quite remote-seeming when the tide's in. At high tide an odd giant tractor-on-stilts wades back and forth with passengers. The Pilchard is a quaint seaview pub, and you can windsurf or fish nearby.

★ CHAGFORD SX7087 A large village, quite busy, and an attractive jumping-off point for the moor; even the bank is thatched, and the 2 old-fashioned general stores are fun. The Ring o' Bells is good for lunch, and the Buller's Arms is useful too. If you eat at the luxury country-house hotel **Gidleigh Park**, you can stroll around their lovely grounds, with colourful woodland walks and watergarden, and immaculate more formal gardens.

★ CHUDLEIGH SX8678

Despite the 1807 fire which destroyed lots of the buildings, this is a pleasant old wool town with pretty cottages in narrow, winding lanes. **Rock Garden and cave** 3-acre wild garden, with a good range of birds and wildlife. The cave has some interesting calcite formations, and they have started digging in search of legendary larger caverns. From the pretty neighbouring waterfall it's a short walk up Chudleigh Rock for dramatic vistas of the surrounding countryside and moors. Snacks, nursery, craft shop, limited disabled access; cl Christmas, and some bits may be cl in winter; (01626) 852134; *£2. **Ugbrooke Park** (off the A380 just SE) An interesting early example of the work of Robert Adam, in lovely Capability Brown parkland. Delightfully informal guided tours (2pm and 3.45pm). Teas, disabled access; open pm Sun, Tues, Weds, Thurs and bank hols mid-July–early Sept; (01626) 852179; £4.20.

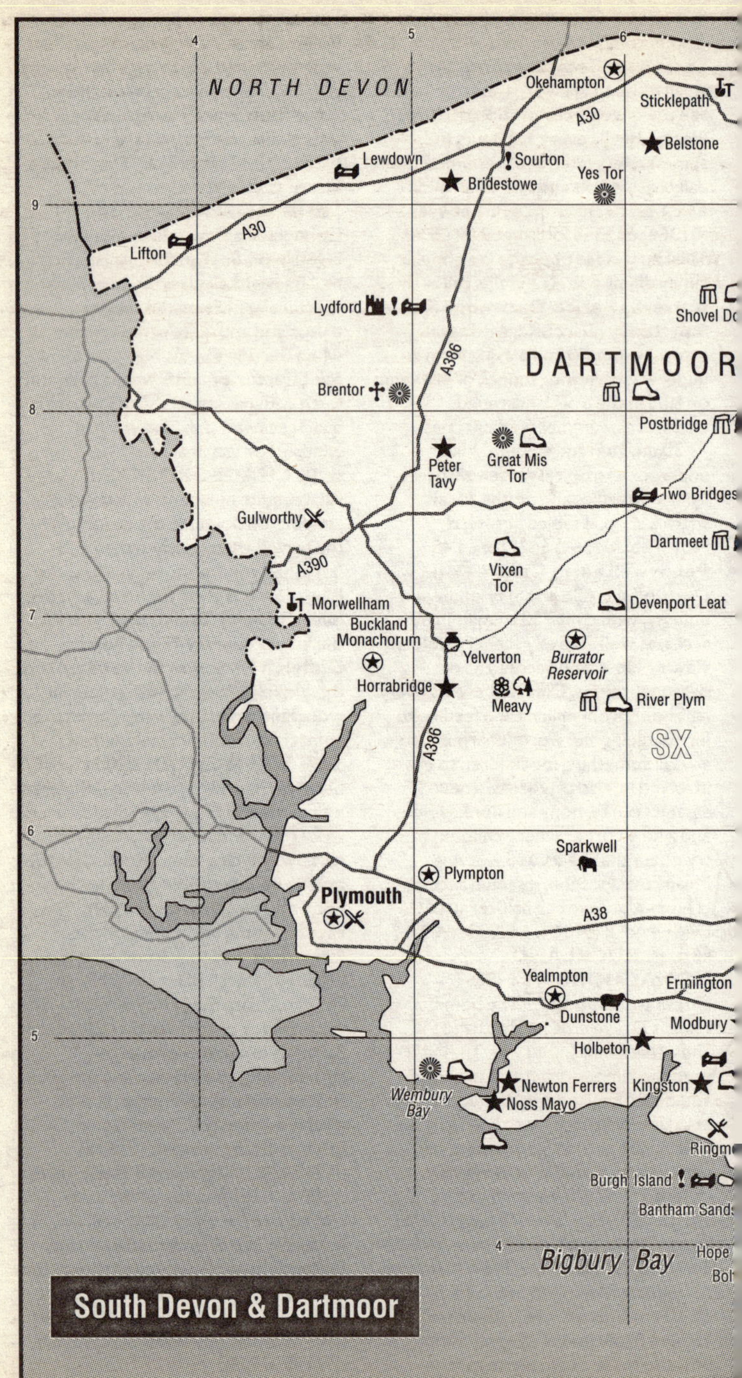

NORTH DEVON
Okehampton
Sticklepath
A30
Belstone
Sourton
Lewdown
Bridestowe
Yes Tor
Lifton
A30
Lydford
Shovel Dc
DARTMOOR
A386
Brentor
Postbridge
Peter Tavy
Great Mis Tor
Two Bridges
Gulworthy
Dartmeet
A390
Vixen Tor
Morwellham
Devenport Leat
Buckland Monachorum
Yelverton
Burrator Reservoir
Horrabridge
Meavy
River Plym
SX
A386
Sparkwell
Plympton
Plymouth
A38
Yealmpton
Ermington
Dunstone
Modbury
Holbeton
Newton Ferrers
Kingston
Wembury Bay
Noss Mayo
Burgh Island
Bantham Sands
Bigbury Bay
South Devon & Dartmoor

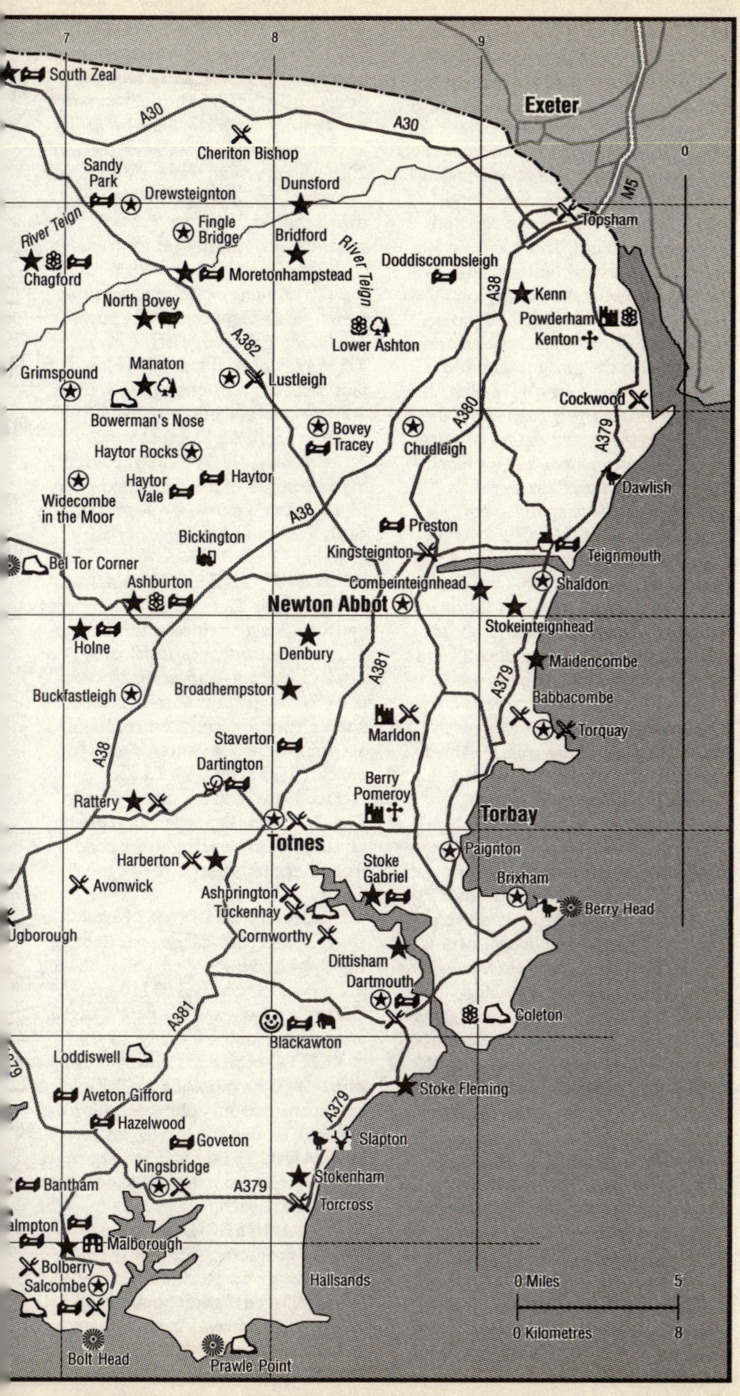
South Zeal
A30
Exeter
Cheriton Bishop
Sandy Park
Drewsteignton
Dunsford
Topsham
M5
River Teign
Fingle Bridge
Bridford
Chagford
Moretonhampstead
Doddiscombsleigh
A38
Kenn
Powderham
Kenton
North Bovey
Lower Ashton
A382
Grimspound
Manaton
Lustleigh
Cockwood
Bowerman's Nose
Bovey Tracey
Chudleigh
A380
A379
Haytor Rocks
Haytor Vale
Haytor
Dawlish
Widecombe in the Moor
Bickington
Preston
Kingsteignton
Teignmouth
Bel Tor Corner
Ashburton
Combeinteignhead
Shaldon
Newton Abbot
Stokeinteignhead
Holne
Denbury
Maidencombe
A381
Buckfastleigh
Broadhempston
Babbacombe
Marldon
Torquay
Staverton
Dartington
Berry Pomeroy
Rattery
Torbay
Totnes
Paignton
Harberton
Stoke Gabriel
Brixham
Avonwick
Ashprington
Tuckenhay
Berry Head
Ugborough
Cornworthy
Dittisham
Dartmouth
Coleton
Blackawton
Loddiswell
Stoke Fleming
Aveton Gifford
Hazelwood
Slapton
Goveton
Kingsbridge
Stokenham
Bantham
A379
Torcross
Malborough
Bolberry
Salcombe
Hallsands
0 Miles 5
0 Kilometres 8
Bolt Head
Prawle Point

COLETON FISHACRE SX9051 (3m E of Kingswear, off Lower Ferry Rd at Tollhouse) D'Oyly Carte's romantic and lush subtropical garden, with 20 colourful acres dropping down to a pretty cove; formal terraces, walled garden with stream-fed ponds, unusual trees and shrubs, grassy woodland paths. Snacks, shop, limited disabled access; open Weds, Thurs, Fri and Sun Apr–Nov, plus bank hols and pm Sun in Mar; house open occasionally, phone to check; (01803) 752466; £3.30 (house £1 extra); NT. More ambitious marked paths beyond the gardens take you along the cliffs, showing how wild this part was before the garden was planted. The Ship in the pretty waterside village of Kingswear is quite useful for lunch, and the Dart Valley Railway runs between the village and Paignton.

DARTINGTON SX7862 **Cider Press Craft Centre** (Shinners Bridge) Cluster of 16th- and 17th-c buildings with craft shops, farm foods, herbs and such, and restaurants, inc a good vegetarian one. The surroundings add a lot to the attraction, with nearby medieval great hall on photogenic lawned courtyard, sculpture gardens, and streamside nature trail. Disabled access; cl Suns Christmas–Easter; (01803) 864171; free. The Cott, excellent for lunch, is close by.

DAWLISH SX9576 Old-fashioned small resort with modern developments and camps outside; red sandstone cliffs, good beach, waterside parks with black swans, small summer museum, prom, pier; the mainline railway cut through the cliffs right by the water is striking. **Dawlish Warren** SX9879 Sandy grassy spit (with golf course) largely blocking in the Exe estuary, with glistening tidal flats full of wading birds, and dunes with some rare plants. In summer get well out to the point, to avoid the crowds and caravan parks at the station end; in winter it's splendidly wild and blowy, with thousands of ducks, brent geese and waders (even avocets) congregating at high tide to wait till the mudflats show again. Visitor centre cl winter wkdys; free, but they do guided summer nature walks for about £1.50; (01626) 863980 for times. The Mount Pleasant out here has decent food.

★ **DREWSTEIGNTON** SX7290 Above this charming village is impressive granite **Castle Drogo**, designed by Lutyens and built earlier this century as a bizarre and brilliantly inventive mixture of medieval style and 20th-c luxury, with cunningly disguised radiators and amazing details even in the kitchen and lavatory. Lovely grounds with yew hedges form an outer barbican. Good guided walks through the surrounding woodland, and super views – it's 275 metres (900 ft) up overlooking the gorge of the River Teign. Meals, snacks, shop; cl Nov–Mar, plus castle cl Fri (though garden, shop and tearoom still open); (01647) 433306; £5.20 £2.40, garden and grounds only; NT. A well signposted minor road W of the village takes you to **Spinster's Rock**, a well preserved easily accessible Neolithic burial chamber.

DUNSTONE SX5951 **National Shire Horse Centre** Shire horses and foals, waggon rides, smithy and saddlery, butterfly house, falconry displays (pm only), adventure playground and pets corner. Meals, snacks, shop and craft centre, disabled access; maybe cl in winter, phone to check; (01752) 880268; £3.95, reduced rates and displays in winter. The Dartmoor Union in Holbeton is quite handy for lunch, and the road from there to Noss Mayo has good views.

† **ERMINGTON** SX6353 Notable for the crooked 14th-c stone spire above the church tower – Victorian rebuilding preserved the tilt. The B3210 from Totnes is pretty, and the First & Last is an attractive pub.

† **KENTON** SX9583 A delightful **church**, its harmonious medieval sandstone masonry photographing well against blue sky; fine carving inside.

★ **KINGSTON** SX6347 There are several walks from the village down to an unspoilt beach.

★ † **KINGSBRIDGE** SX7344 Small town of character, with pretty cobbled lanes diving off steep Fore St, arcaded shops, pillared market house (market day Weds), interesting monuments in the church, boats on the tidal estuary (and ferry to Salcombe); the waterfront

Crabshell is very popular for seafood. **Cookworthy Museum** (Fore St) In a 17th-c grammar school, this reopens in March after a major refurbishment; from then it will be cl Sun, and all Nov–Mar; (01548) 853235; admission charge not decided as we went to press. At the head of the nearby creek, pretty South Pool has a fairly interesting **church**, with a delightfully ghoulish story attached, and a good pub.

LODDISWELL SX7248 Cross the river by the lane towards Woodsleigh for a quiet walk upstream by riverside pastures and woods towards Topsham Bridge.

LOWER ASHTON SX8382 **Canonteign Falls & Country Park** Pleasant country park covering 80 acres of ancient woodland, with a spectacularly high waterfall; also lakes, wildfowl, and children's commando course. Meals, snacks, shop; cl mid-Nov–Mar (exc Sun and Feb half-term); (01647) 252434; £3.50. The Manor pub in the village is useful for lunch (no children inside).

★ **MALBOROUGH** SX7037 **Yarde Medieval Farmhouse** (just outside, towards Salcombe) Although it's somewhat dilapidated – a programme of restoration proceeds as finances allow – readers enjoy visiting this attractive old farmhouse complete with brewhouse and stables; also Shetland ponies, goats, hens, ducks and a pets corner. Tea and cakes; open pm Sun, Weds and Fri, Easter–Oct; (01548) 842367; £2. In the lovely village the Old Inn is popular for food.

★ **MANATON** SX7580 A pretty village, with the private riverside woodland around **Becky Falls** (off the B3344 to Bovey Tracey) useful enough for undemanding family walks if you don't plan to take advantage of the countryside proper. Meals, snacks, shop, some disabled access; cl Nov–mid-Mar (exc wknds, weather permitting); (01647) 221259; £3.25. The prettily placed Kestor has decent food.

MARLDON SX8962 **Compton Castle** (1m N, off the A3022; or off the A381 at Ipplepen turnoff) Formidably fortified and rather picturesque 14th- and 16th-c manor around courtyard with portcullised entrance, particularly interesting for its completeness. The exterior was used as Willoughby's house in the recent film of *Sense and Sensibility*. Very limited disabled access; open Mon, Weds and Thurs Apr–Oct, cl 12.15–2pm; (01803) 827112; £2.80; NT. The Church House Inn is handy for lunch.

★ **MODBURY** SX6551 Attractive buildings especially in steep Church St, with a photogenic church at the top and pretty Exeter Inn at the bottom. Brownston St is quite interesting too, especially the ornate water conduit at the top.

MORWELLHAM QUAY SX4470 Thriving and meticulously researched open-air museum in lovely countryside, with costumed guides convincingly re-creating the boom years when Morwellham was the greatest copper port in the empire. The restored cottages come complete with pigs in the backyard, and you can watch the work of a blacksmith, a cooper, coachmen and quay workers. Also rides into the mines, horse-drawn carriages, and lovely walks. Very popular in school hols – a visit can easily last all day. Meals, snacks, shop, some disabled access; cl 24 Dec–2 Jan; (01822) 832766; £7.95 (reduced price and operations in winter). The Ship (part of the centre) is good, with period waitresses and drinks.

NEWTON ABBOT SX8670 A working town rather than a holiday centre, but several interesting places here or nearby. **Tuckers Maltings** (Teign Rd) One of the few remaining working malthouses in the country, and the only one open to the public – every year they produce enough malt for 15 million pints of beer. Tours show all aspects of malting (you can touch the grain and taste the malt), and they've recently set up their own brewery. There's a hands-on section for children. Meals, snacks, shop with large range of speciality bottled beers; last guided tour starts 3pm (3.45pm July–Sept and bank hols), cl Nov–Easter; (01626) 334734; £4.20 (inc sample of beer). **Plant World** (St Marychurch Rd, Coffinswell, SX8869) Unusual 4-acre garden built and planted as a giant map of the world, with the countries containing their correct native plants, trees and flowers – many of them quite rare in this country, but flourishing in the mild Devon climate. Also plant centre (with seeds of some of the rarest plants), old-fashioned English garden and fine views from picnic area. cl Weds and Oct–Mar; (01803) 872939; *£1. The Linny in the attractive village is a charming old thatched pub. **Bradley Manor** (off the A381 S, SX8470) Peaceful 15th-c house nr stream through extensive wood-fringed grounds; quiet walks. Open pm Weds Apr–Sept; £2.60; NT. **Orchid Paradise** (Forches Cross, A382, SX8473) Colourful place, with lots of rare and endangered species in elaborate indoor reconstructions of their natural habitats. Snacks, nursery and shop, disabled access (but no facilities); cl winter bank hols; (01626) 352233; £1.50.

★ **NEWTON FERRERS/NOSS MAYO** SX5548 Picturesque twin villages on very sheltered rocky wooded creek of Yealm estuary; besides modern development, there are some attractive whitewashed cottages. Lots of yachting in summer. The Old Ship, Dolphin and Swan are all pleasant places for lunch. There are attractive waterside walks from here, then beyond to Gara Point and exposed cliff; largely NT. This can be reached in sections via the Noss Mayo–Holbeton coastal ridge road.

★ **NORTH BOVEY** SX7184 A delightful peaceful spot, not usually invaded by tourists: oak-shaded green with mounting block, stone cross, pump, ancient cottages and attractive pub. **Miniature Pony Centre** (Wormhill Farm) Lots of friendly and engaging tiny ponies, happy to give children steady rides. Also bigger horses, pigs, donkeys, pigmy goats, bird garden, and good adventure playground. The setting is lovely. Meals, snacks, shop, good disabled access; cl Nov–Mar; (01647) 432400; £4.75.

OKEHAMPTON SX5895 This Dartmoor-edge working town has a couple of things worth stopping for. The **castle** tower on a steep grassy mound above the river is remarkable above all for the way it stays standing – a balancing act of ruined masonry zigzagging up into the sky. It's the biggest medieval castle in Devon, with sections dating from the 11th to the 14th c; good woodland walks. Snacks, shop; cl Nov–Mar; (01837) 52844; £2.30. **Museum of Dartmoor Life** (West St) Well converted old watermill with interactive displays on local life, Tourist Information Centre and working craft studios next door. Tearoom, shop, some disabled access; cl Sun (exc Jun–Sept) and all Nov–Easter; (01837) 52295; £1.90.

★ **PLYMPTON** SX5255 **Saltram** (2m W, off the A38/A379 at Marsh Mills roundabout) Magnificent mostly 18th-c mansion still with pretty much all the original contents, especially notable for its unaltered Robert Adam rooms. George II furnishings, decoration and paintings (strong on Reynolds, who as a regular guest advised on which other pictures to buy), interesting period kitchen, stately garden with orangery, and parkland by wooded Plym estuary. The house has attracted lots of extra visitors since starring as Norland Park in *Sense and Sensibility*. Meals, snacks, shop, local-art/crafts gallery, disabled access; cl Fri, Sat, and all Nov–Mar (house cl am); (01752) 336546; £5.60, £2.60 garden only; NT. The old town around St Maurice Church is worth a look if you're here: attractive partly arcaded streets, very ruined motte and bailey castle, decent food at the George.

POWDERHAM CASTLE SX9684 The ancestral home of the Earls of Devon, badly damaged in the Civil War but elaborately restored in the 18th and 19th c. The richly decorated state rooms were used in the film *The Remains of the Day*. Spectacular rose garden, home to Timothy the 156-year-old tortoise, spring woodland garden, a secret garden especially designed for children with ducks, rabbits, guinea pigs and chinchillas, and broad deer park with views over the Exe estuary. Good guided tours, and lots of special events. Meals, snacks, shop, some disabled access; cl Sat, and Nov–Easter;

(01626) 890243; £4.95. The ancient waterside Anchor has good seafood.

PRAWLE POINT SX7735 Impressive scenery: wind-blasted gorse, grass and thrift above low but fierce cliffs, lending itself to a round walk, with a useful network of green lanes leading inland to the village of East Prawle (good food at the Freebooters Arms).

SALCOMBE SX7438 Steep narrow-streeted fishing village, full of enjoyable holiday bustle in summer, with lots of souvenirs, bric-a-brac, boating shops, teashops and pubs overlooking the sea, nearby beaches and coves, **boat trips** and boat hire. Besides the Foot in the Plate and Spinnaker restaurants, the Ferry, Fortescue and Victoria are all popular for food. **Overbecks** (South Sands; also signed from Malborough) Named after the eccentric research chemist who lived here until 1937; among his possessions and inventions you can still see the Rejuvenator which he claimed 'practically renewed' his youth. For most the chief attraction is the luscious subtropical gardens, with terraced plantings among woodland, many rarities and plenty of palms and citrus fruits; outstanding late May–Jun for the magnolias, but worth a trip any time of year. Glorious views out to sea; also colourful statue garden, picnic belvedere and collections of dolls and lead soldiers. Snacks, shop; cl Sat and Nov–Mar; (01548) 842893; £3.80, £2.60 garden only; NT. Mill Bay near here has one of the area's safest bathing beaches.

★ **SHALDON** SX9372 Interesting and colourful mix of seaside houses spanning 200 years of architectural fancy; some lovely corners especially down by the water away from the centre, also much older cottages in Crown Sq. The waterside Ferryboat has decent food. High grassy sandstone Ness overlooks the sea and Teignmouth, with a tunnel cut by the 19th-c landowner to a sheltered beach; the beautifully set Ness House up here is useful for food. **Wildlife Trust** (Ness Drive) Nicely low-key breeding collection of rare and endangered foreign birds, and small mammals inc monkeys; cl 25 Dec, 1 Jan; (01626) 872234; £2.50. The **botanic gardens** are pleasant, with lots of rare shrubs and trees and nice views; free. The A379 to Maidencombe has sea views.

SLAPTON SANDS SX8343 One of the finest beaches in the country, 6 miles of almost straight shingle N of the lighthouse at Start Point, backed by hills in the S and by road, shingle bank, lake (Slapton Ley nature reserve, with marked nature trail) and marsh, then low cliffs, in the N. Good for out-of-season desolation, sheltered from west winds, with a storm-ruined village at Hallsands, and salvaged tank memorial to a US Normandy landings practice disaster at Torcross.

! **SOURTON** SX5390 **Highwayman** An extraordinary pub, one bar recalling a galleon, the other a sort of fairy-tale fantasy, and the garden demonstrating yet more exuberant imagination – all meticulously done by the owners.

SPARKWELL SX5858 **Dartmoor Wildlife Park** Various animals inc big cats (feeding time 3.30pm) in 30 acres of countryside. Also falconry centre with displays at 12 and 4pm, adventure playground and picnic area. Snacks, shop, disabled access; (01752) 837209; *£5.95.

STICKLEPATH SX6494 **Finch Foundry** No longer producing the sickles, shovels and tools for which it was known in the 19th c, but the waterwheels and machinery are all still working. Snacks, shop, disabled access; cl Tues, and Nov–Mar; (01837) 840046; £2.60; NT. The thatched Devonshire Inn in the village is good value.

★ **STOKE GABRIEL** SX8457 Steep village above a sheltered side-pool of the Dart estuary, with 14th-c church (with ancient yew) and Church House (pleasant for lunch) perched prettily on a high cobbled terrace.

TEIGNMOUTH SX9473 A popular resort for family holidays with the feeling of a more leisurely age. Good beaches, windsurfing and so on, some handsome 19th-c streets and active docks, and a decent local history **museum** (cl Oct–Apr; £1).

TUCKENHAY SX8156 This gives a pretty 1-mile stroll E along wooded Bow Creek, from the Maltsters Arms – good food here.

WEMBURY BAY SX5148
A walk here gives good views, starting from Wembury past the church at the start of NT clifftops; woods and pastures on the opposite shore, Plymouth shipping in the distance.

YEALMPTON SX5751
Kitley Caves Tours of stunning illuminated caves, and above ground 50 acres of pretty woodland and riverside walks. Lots of varieties of plants, shrubs and trees, and displays of Stone Age relics found in the caves. Snacks, shop; cl Nov–Easter; (01752) 880885; £3.50. The Rose & Crown does decent food. Nearby is a good **farm shop**, and seasonal pick-your-own fruit and veg (inc courgettes, spinach and pumpkins).

YELVERTON SX5167
Paperwieght Centre (Buckland Terrace) Odd collection of hundreds of glass paperweights, all sizes and designs, inc collector's pieces. Shop, disabled access; open wknds and daily Apr–Oct and Dec; (01822) 854250; free. The Rock (on the A386) is a good family pub.

★**Other attractive villages** with good pubs include Belstone SX6293, Bridestowe SX5189, Bridford SX8186, Broadhempston SX8066, Combeinteignhead SX9071 (besides the Wild Goose in the village, the waterside Coombe Cellars is outstanding for families), Denbury SX8168, Dittisham SX8654, Dunsford SX8189 (traditional cidermaking in summer), Harberton SX7758, Holbeton SX6150, Holne SX7069, Horrabridge SX5169, Kenn SX9285 (charming church), Maidencombe SX9268, Moretonhampstead SX7585, Peter Tavy SX5177, Rattery SX7461, Ringmore SX6545, South Zeal SX6593, Stokeinteignhead SX9170, Stokenham SX8042 (sea views from the Stoke Fleming road – Stoke Fleming SX8648 has some of the best beaches in the country).

Where to eat

ASHPRINGTON SX8156 **Durant Arms** *(01803) 732240* Friendly gable-ended dining pub with 2 attractive bar rooms, several open fires, good bar food, well kept beers, and friendly service. **£17**|£5.25.

AVONWICK SX7157 **Avon Inn** *(01364) 73475* Popular dining pub with comfortable fairly modern furnishings, a wide range of good food inc lots of interesting pasta dishes, plenty of fish, and lovely puddings, good Italian wines, well kept real ales, and pleasant riverside garden; disabled access. **£24**|£5.95.

BABBACOMBE SX9365 **Tea Rose Tea Rooms** *Babbacombe Downs Rd (01803) 324477* Charming small tearoom with inside and outside tables set in a garden opposite the sea, with waitresses in period dress, generous cream teas, and snacks; disabled access. £3.25.

BANTHAM SX6643 **Sloop** *(01548) 560489* Nr sandy beach (good for surfing), this 16th-c nautical village inn has good bar food inc lots of fish, hearty breakfasts, and decent beers and wines; bdrms and self-catering cottages. **£19.50**|£4.80.

BOLBERRY SX6939 **Port Light** *(01548) 561384* Popular even on dismal winter wkdys, this clifftop former RAF radar station (easy walk from Hope Cove) is warmly friendly with good home-made food in attractive bar and restaurant, super sea views, woodburner, and good outdoor children's play area; bdrms; cl winter Tues, and all Jan. **£20.80**|£5.95.

CHERITON BISHOP SX7793 **Old Thatch** *(01647) 24204* Welcoming 16th-c inn with good bar food from big menu, interesting puddings, and friendly service; bdrms. **£15**|£4.

COCKWOOD SX9780 **Anchor** *(01626) 890203* Friendly pub by the harbour with small low-ceilinged rambling rooms and lots of good fresh fish dishes – 30 ways of serving mussels, 12 of serving scallops, 10 of oysters, and so forth; no smoking restaurant, well kept real ales, 10 wines by the glass, and 50 malt whiskies. **£17.35**|£6.

CORNWORTHY SX8255 **Hunters Lodge** *(01803) 732204* Welcoming country local with a 2-roomed low-ceilinged bar, cottagey restaurant with 17th-c fireplace, popular food from an extensive menu, well kept real ales, and plenty of seats outside. **£22**|£5.25.

DARTMOUTH SX8751 **Carved Angel** *2 South Embankment (01803) 832465* Black and white timbered restaurant, airy and attractive, overlooking the quay, with wonderful meals using carefully chosen absolutely fresh produce – superb fish, delicious puddings and lovely cheeses; fine wines in every price range, and a smart yet friendly atmosphere; no smoking; cl pm Sun, Mon, 1 wk Christmas, 6 wks from 1 Jan; children under 5 free; disabled access. **£55.50 dinner, £37.50 lunch**.

DARTMOUTH SX8751 **Cherub** *10 Higher St (01804) 832571* Dartmouth's oldest building (already 300 years old when Sir Francis Drake used it), this has a bustling bar, liked by locals, an upstairs dining room, decent food, and well kept ales; children in upstairs restaurant only. **£19**|£3.95.

GULWORTHY SX4472 **Horn of Plenty** On the *A390 just W of Tavistock (01822) 832528* On the edge of Dartmoor in quiet flower-filled gardens, this relaxed Georgian no smoking restaurant-with-rooms has excellent, carefully cooked food using top quality local produce inc lovely puddings and cheeses (wonderful breakfasts, too), a good wine list, warmly friendly service, and vine-covered terrace for aperitifs; comfortable bdrms; cl am Mon, 25–26 Dec; no children; disabled access. **£38.50 dinner**|£10.50 2 courses.

HARBERTON SX7758 **Church House** *(01803) 863707* Ancient village pub with magnificent medieval panelling, attractive old furnishings, generous helpings of interesting daily specials, well kept beers, and decent wines; bdrms; children in family room; cl pm 25-26 Dec, 1 Jan. **£20**|£4.95.

KINGSBRIDGE SX7344 **Crabshell** *The Quay, Embankment Rd (01548) 852345* Famous old dining pub, very popular for its lovely waterside position and fresh local fish; quick friendly staff, well kept real ales, decent wines, and warm winter fire; disabled access. **£22**|£9.25.

KINGSTEIGNTON SX8773 **Old Rydon** *(01626) 354626* Cosy old pub with wide choice of constantly changing imaginative bar food, big winter log fire, well kept real ales, helpful service, and prettily planted dining conservatory. **£26**|£6.40.

LUSTLEIGH SX7881 **Primrose Cottage** *(01647) 277365* Thatched cottage by the old village church with seats in riverside garden, clotted cream teas, lovely home-made cakes and pastries, and tasty all-day light meals; cl Tues, and mid-Dec–mid-Feb. **£13**|£6.

MARLDON SX8663 **Church House** *(01803) 558279* Well run bustling pub with several different attractive bar areas, candles on tables, bare boards, hops and dried flowers, characterful restaurant, good popular food inc interesting daily specials and themed food evenings, well kept real ales, and seats outside; bdrms. **£16.75**|£6.25.

PLYMOUTH SX4755 **Chez Nous** *13 Frankfort Gate (01752) 266793* Informal and friendly French bistro with careful cooking of fresh local produce, especially fresh fish and fine puddings; some distinguished wines, and friendly atmosphere; cl am Sat, all day Sun and Mon, 3 wks Feb, 3 wks Sept; partial disabled access. **£42**.

RATTERY SX7461 **Church House** *(01364) 642220* One of Britain's oldest pubs, with big open fires, friendly customers and staff, good bar food, decent wines and beers, fine malt whiskies, and nice dog and cats; peaceful setting; disabled access. **£15**|£3.85.

RINGMORE SX6545 **Journey's End** *(01548) 810205* Partly medieval inn in pretty setting with thatched servery in panelled bar, open fire, a warm welcome, well kept beer, and nice fresh food; good-value bedrooms; cl 3–6pm daily. **£17.50**|£4.50.

SALCOMBE SX7338 **Foot in the Plate** *Russell Court (01548) 842189* Bustling and enjoyable evening restaurant with relaxed atmosphere, a good choice of pasta and Greek dishes, and music from around the world; cl Sun, and all winter; well behaved children over 5; disabled access. **£18**.

SALCOMBE SX7338 **Spinnaker** *(01548) 843408* Relaxed waterside restaurant with good fresh local fish and shellfish (some meat also), lunchtime bar snacks, and nice puddings; cl Sun, Mon, all Dec and Jan (exc open Christmas wk). **£21**|£5.

TOPSHAM SX9688 **Georgian Tea Room** *Broadway House, 35 High St (01392) 873465* 18th-c house with pretty embroidered tablecloths and fresh flowers, lunchtime meals inc a popular roast on Tues, Thurs and Sun – also snacks, cream teas, home-made cakes and cookies, a wide range of teas and coffees, home-made lemonade and so forth. £4.

TORCROSS SX8241 **Start Bay** *(01548) 580553* Notable and very popular fresh seafood generously served in busy thatched pub overlooking 3-mile pebble beach; farm cider; family room; cl pm 25 Dec. **£17.30**|£5.

TORQUAY SX9264 **Mulberry Room** *1 Scarborough Rd (01803) 213639* Popular no smoking restaurant-with-rooms, with good interesting food using local produce, and very enjoyable home-made cakes and scones for afternoon tea; cookery demonstrations; bdrms; cl Mon, Tues; disabled access. **£15**|£5.95 2 courses.

TORQUAY SX9264 **The Table** *135 Babbacombe Rd (01803) 324292* Pretty little restaurant in white terraced house with excellent modern cooking (lots of fish and shellfish), a relaxed atmosphere, super bread, and good-value wines; cl 2 wks beginning Feb, 2 wks end Mar; children over 11. **£32.50**.

TOTNES SX8060 **Greys Dining Room** *96 High St (01803) 866369* No smoking Georgian house with pretty china on a handsome dresser and partly panelled walls, lots of teas plus herb and fruit ones; sandwiches, salads and omelettes as well as lots of cakes and set teas; cl Weds; no pushchairs. £6.

TUCKENHAY SX8156 **Maltsters Arms** *(01803) 732350* Very well run creekside pub with enthusiastic friendly owners, particularly good interesting food – though they are keen to keep it as a pub where people also feel comfortable dropping in for a drink – well kept real ales, 12 wines by the glass, and relaxed, airy bars; seats by the water; super bdrms. **£19.20**|£6.95.

UGBOROUGH SX6755 **Anchor** *(01752) 892283* Friendly pub, with oak beams and log fire, a wide choice of very good food inc unusual things such as ostrich, alligator, emu and bison, lots of fresh fish, courteous service, and well kept real ales. **£22**|£5.50.

North Devon and Exmoor

Outstanding coastal scenery, particularly below Exmoor; quieter than South Devon, but plenty of interest.

Outside the few resorts and the legendarily pretty Clovelly and Combe Martin, the area is largely untouched by tourism, with long stretches of coast which are empty even in summer, and a magnificent coast path. Even Ilfracombe, the main resort, is not too trippery; it's pleasant and distinctive, with plenty for families, and stays active all year. The lower-key beach resorts such as Woolacombe and Westward Ho! go into mothballs when the season's over, their marvellous beaches then ideal for lonely walks; elsewhere there are fine bracing cliff walks.

Some favourite places to visit here are Arlington Court, Bickleigh Castle, the woodland gardens at Rosemoor near Torrington, Knighthayes Court at Bolham, Lynton, Hartland Quay, and for children the Big Sheep near Bideford and quirky Gnome Reserve near Bradworthy.

Exmoor itself is full of interest for walkers (and drivers), and quieter in summer than Dartmoor. Though part lies in Somerset, we've covered the whole of the moor area in this chapter (some places such as Dunster within the boundary of the National Park but outside the moor itself are described in the Somerset chapter). Other inland parts are largely secluded farmland; the twisty wooded Taw valley (A377) is pretty.

Where to stay

ASHWATER SX3895 **Blagdon Manor** *Ashwater, Beaworthy EX21 5DF (01409) 211224* **£110;** 7 pretty rms. Carefully restored and tranquil 17th-c manor in 8 acres (croquet and 4-hole practice golf course) surrounded by rolling countryside; beams and flagstones, log fires, fresh flowers, lovely food in a dinner-party atmosphere, and kind staff; cl Christmas; no children.

BISHOP'S TAWTON SS5630 **Halmpstone** *Bishop's Tawton, Barnstaple EX32 0EA (01271) 830321* ***£100,** plus special breaks; 5 pretty rms. Quietly relaxing small country hotel with log fire in comfortable sitting room, enjoyable food in panelled dining room, good breakfasts, caring service, an attractive garden, and nice views; no children.

BUCKLAND BREWER SS4220 **Coach & Horses** *Buckland Brewer, Bideford EX39 5LU (01237) 451395* **£40;** 2 rms above bar (so could be noisy for children until 11.30pm). Welcoming well preserved 13th-c thatched village pub with cosy beamed bar, log fires in inglenook fireplaces, enjoyable food, dining room, and pleasant garden; cl pm 25 Dec; children over 8; no dogs.

CADBURY SS9005 **Beers Farm** *Cadbury, Exeter EX5 5PY (01884) 855426* **£32;** 2 rms. Set in several acres with lovely views across to the Raddon Hills, this non-working, no smoking farm is quiet and comfortable with friendly helpful owners, and good breakfasts; packed lunches on request; lots to do nearby.

CHITTLEHAMHOLT SS6420 **Highbullen** *Chittlehamholt, Umberleigh EX37 9HD (01769) 540561* ***£95,** plus special breaks; 35 comfortable and elegant, often spacious rms in main building and various attractively converted outbuildings. Victorian Gothic mansion set in huge wooded parkland and gardens with lots of wildlife, fishing (several beats), 9-hole golf course, indoor tennis court and swimming pool, table tennis, and squash court; consistently good food in intimate restaurant overlooking the valley, busy little bar, library, and relaxed informal service (no reception, you ring a bell and wait); children over 8; no dogs.

CLAWTON SX3599 **Court Barn** *Clawton, Holsworthy EX22 6PS (01409) 271219* ***£80,** plus special breaks; 8 individually furnished rms. Charming country house in 5 pretty acres with croquet, 9-hole putting green, small chip-and-putt course, and tennis and badminton courts; comfortable lounges, log fires, library/TV room, good service, imaginative food and award-winning wines (and teas), and a quiet relaxed atmosphere; cl 2–12 Jan; dogs allowed away from public rooms.

DULVERTON SS9127 **Ashwick House** *Dulverton, Somerset TA22 9QD (01398) 323969* ***£96,** plus special breaks; 6 peaceful rms with thoughtful extras. Quietly set Edwardian house in 6 lovely acres overlooking the Barle valley, with personal service from caring owner, comfortable old-fashioned furnishings, fresh flowers, log fires, and candlelight; enjoyable food, hearty breakfasts (which can be taken on the south-facing terrace), and a really relaxing atmosphere; children over 8; disabled access.

EAST BUCKLAND SS6731 **Lower Pitt** *East Buckland, Barnstaple EX32 0TD (01598) 760243* ***£70;** 3 comfortable rms. Quiet, pretty stone farmhouse with log fire in cosy lounge, good well presented food using herbs and veg from own garden, simply furnished dining room and attractive conservatory, and friendly service; good cycling/walking from the door; cl 25–26 Dec; children over 12.

HATHERLEIGH SS5404 **Pressland House** *Hatherleigh, Okehampton EX20 3LW (01837) 810871* **£42,** plus special breaks; 6 rms overlooking the gardens or open countryside. Relaxed and friendly Victorian house in neat grounds with views to Dartmoor, 2 attractive lounges, good homely food, and small wine list; lots to do nearby; cl Dec–Feb; children over 12.

HATHERLEIGH SS5404 **Tally Ho** *Market St, Hatherleigh, Okehampton EX20 3JN (01837) 810306* **£50,** plus wknd breaks; 3 rms. Friendly and interesting old inn with genuinely old-fashioned fittings, good food and own-brew beers.

HAWKRIDGE SS8530 **Tarr Steps** *Hawkridge, Dulverton, Somerset TA22 9PY; off the B3223 towards Hawkridge, N of Dulverton; (01643) 851293* **£116 inc dinner,**

plus special breaks; 11 rms, most with own bthrm. Former Georgian rectory in 11 acres of gardens, surrounded by 500 acres of land with rough shooting and trout-filled river, riding, and clay-pigeon shooting; carefully refurbished comfortable drawing room with log fires and flowers, oak-panelled bar, good food in attractive dining room (popular locally) using own organic vegetables, a relaxed happy atmosphere, and friendly staff; self-catering cottage also; cl 12 days beginning Feb; well behaved dogs; disabled access.

HEDDON'S MOUTH SS6549 **Heddon's Gate** *Heddon's Mouth, Parracombe, Barnstaple EX31 4PZ (01598) 763313* **£126 inc dinner,** plus special breaks; 14 comfortable rms named for their original use, many with views. Victorian country house hotel in interesting large gardens on the edge of Exmoor, with marvellously relaxed and friendly atmosphere, refurbished sitting room with lovely views, good library/Victorian morning room, attractive dining room, very good home cooking inc 6-course dinners and proper afternoon tea, and friendly helpful service; cl 3 Nov–Easter; children welcome if able to eat at 8pm (no special meals for them); dogs by prior arrangement; disabled access.

HORNS CROSS SS3823 **Lower Waytown** *Horns Cross, Bideford EX39 5DN (01237) 451787* **£47;** 3 rms. Beautifully converted barn and roundhouse in 5 acres of grounds with ornamental waterfowl on stream-fed pond; round sitting room with beams and inglenook fireplaces, and lovely breakfasts in big dining room; no smoking; self-catering cottages; cl Christmas/New Year; children over 12.

KNOWSTONE SS8223 **Masons Arms** *Knowstone, South Molton EX36 4RY (01398) 341231* **£55;** 4 rms. Delightfully unspoilt 13th-c thatched pub with very individual character, relaxed friendly service, good homely bar food, restaurant, decent wines and nice garden; nearby walks; cl Christmas; dogs welcome.

LYNMOUTH SS7249 **Rising Sun** *Mars Hill, Lynmouth EX35 6EQ (01598) 753223* **£98;** 16 comfortable and cosy rms. Historic thatched 14th-c inn with lovely views over the little harbour and out to sea, oak-panelled dining room, beamed and panelled bar with uneven oak floors, good food and wines, charming terraced garden, and lots of nearby walks; children over 7.

LYNTON SS7149 **Bear Hotel** *Lydiate Lane, Lynton EX35 6AJ (01598) 753391* **£48,** plus special breaks; 9 rms. Under new owners, this friendly hotel has 2 comfortable and very neatly kept lounges, a blazing log fire, good varied breakfasts and candlelit dinner.

LYNTON SS7149 **Highcliffe House** *Sinai Hill, Lynton EX35 6AR (01598) 752235* **£84;** 6 well equipped attractive rms. Carefully refurbished no smoking Victorian house with wonderful views over Lynton, the sea, and wooded countryside; comfortable sitting room with log fire, conservatory, good food in candlelit dining room, and kind staff; cl Dec and Jan; no children.

MARTINHOE SS6648 **Old Rectory** *Martinhoe, Parracombe, Barnstaple EX31 4QT (01598) 763368* **£95;** 8 rms. Set on the edge of Exmoor in 3 acres of secluded gardens, this welcoming little hotel has a comfortable drawing room, small library and airy vinery (much of the furniture made by the owners' son), very good English cooking in elegant dining room, and carefully chosen wines; no smoking; lots of wildlife and fine walks; cl Nov–Feb; no children; disabled access.

MORCHARD BISHOP SS7707 **Wigham** *Morchard Bishop, Crediton EX17 6RJ (01363) 877350* **£138 inc dinner,** plus special breaks; 5 rms. Picturesque thatched longhouse on 30-acre farm with house-party atmosphere, 2 sitting rooms, big log fires, snooker room, dining room with honesty bar, and good set dinner and breakfasts using home-grown fruit and veg, home-made butter, breads and jams, and their own free-range eggs; no smoking and no pets (they have their own); outdoor heated swimming pool; children over 8.

NORTHAM SS4429 **Yeoldon House** *Durrant Lane, Northam, Bideford EX39 2RL (01237) 474400* ***£90,** plus special breaks; 10 cosy rms. At the end of a long private drive, this quietly set hotel by the River Torridge has a warmly friendly and relaxed atmosphere, a comfortable lounge where you can enjoy a complimentary sherry before dinner, good food using local produce in the attractive dining room, and helpful service; lots to do nearby; cl 25 Dec.

OAKFORD SS9121 **Newhouse Farm** *Oakford, Tiverton EX16 9JE (01398) 351347* ***£40,** plus special breaks; 2 rms. 17th-c longhouse on edge of Exmoor, part of a farm with beef suckler cows and a small flock of friendly sheep; cottagey sitting room, inglenook fireplace, beams, and country dining room serving home-made food inc good bread, pâtés and puddings; cl Christmas; no children or pets.

PORLOCK SS8846 **Oaks** *Doverhay, Porlock, Minehead, Somerset TA24 8ES (01643) 862265* ***£90,** plus special breaks; 9 airy and pretty rms. Particularly welcoming and spotless Edwardian country house looking down from Exmoor to Porlock Bay, with surrounding lawns and oak trees, a relaxed atmosphere and log fire in comfortable lounge, and good unpretentious cooking in attractive no smoking restaurant; cl Nov–mid-Mar; children over 8.

PORLOCK SS8846 **West Porlock House** *Porlock, Minehead, Somerset TA24 8NX (01643) 862880* ***£50;** 5 rms. Nicely proportioned no smoking former manor house in 4 acres, with spacious carefully furnished rooms, and kind personal service; cl Dec and Jan; children over 6.

SELWORTHY SS9346 **Hindon Farm** *Selworthy, Minehead, Somerset TA24 8SH (01643) 705244* ***£40;** 3 rms, 1 with own bthrm. Relaxed and friendly working farm with sheep, pigs, calves, goats and horses (you can help if you want), lots of lovely walks around the farm or further afield, and large lawn with stream and ducks; attractive sitting and dining rooms, log fires, fine breakfasts, and games barn with snooker, table tennis, darts and fancy dress; they can arrange riding or you may bring your own horse; self-catering wing also; cl Christmas/New Year; dogs welcome.

SHEEPWASH SS4806 **Half Moon** *Sheepwash, Beaworthy EX21 5NE (01409) 231376* ***£57.50,** plus special breaks; 16 rms. Civilised heart-of-Devon hideaway in colourful village square with 10 miles of private salmon, sea trout and brown trout fishing on the Torridge, a neatly kept friendly bar, solid old furnishings and big log fire, good wines, lovely evening restaurant, and lunchtime bar snacks; dogs welcome; disabled access.

SOUTH MOLTON SS7527 **Whitechapel Manor** *Whitechapel, South Molton EX36 3EG (01769) 573377* **£110,** plus special breaks; 11 pretty rms. Carefully restored Grade I listed Elizabethan manor in large grounds with magnificent Jacobean carved oak screen in the entrance hall, fine panelling, beams and log fires, relaxed atmosphere in cosy bar and comfortable lounge, excellent thoughtful service, fine modern cooking as well as home-made breads, jams and marmalade, and carefully chosen wines; handy for Exmoor.

WEST BUCKLAND SS6531 **Huxtable Farm** *West Buckland, Barnstaple EX32 0SR (01598) 760254* ***£50,** plus special breaks; 6 rms. 16th-c farmhouse surrounded by carefully converted listed stone buildings, open fields, fine views, sheep, chickens, rabbits and Squeak the Shetland pony; candlelit dinner with wholesome home-made food using home-grown produce, home-made wine and bread, and relaxing sitting room; sauna, fitness room, tennis court, games room, and outside children's play area with swings, sandpit and Wendy house; cl Dec and Jan; disabled access.

WEST PORLOCK SS8746 **Bales Mead** *West Porlock, Somerset TA24 8NX (01643) 862565* ***£58;** 3 comfortable rms with sherry, fresh flowers, and thoughtful little extras. This quiet and relaxing no smoking Edwardian house has lovely Exmoor views towards the sea, a particularly pretty little garden, charmingly decorated sitting room with log fire and baby grand piano, super breakfasts (no evening meals), and friendly, helpful owners; cl Christmas/New Year; no children.

WITHYPOOL SS8435 **Westerclose Country House** *Withypool, Minehead, SomersetTA24 7QR (01643) 831302* **£69,** plus special walking breaks; 10 rms. Family-run 1920s hunting lodge with moorland views and 9 acres of gardens and paddocks; comfortable lounges, relaxed atmosphere, and good, interesting food using local produce; cl Jan and Feb; dogs welcome.

To see and do

EXMOOR SS7739 Excellent walking, less busy than Dartmoor in summer. In some places it's been more tamed than Dartmoor – drained and resown with richer-growing grasses for better pasture. But it's still a wild place, with hawthorns and low oak trees bent and gnarled by the winds, and (unlike Dartmoor) wild deer. Where it drops away sharply to the sea, fast streams and rivers cut deeply into beautiful wooded valleys. It's rewarding territory for drivers, with plenty of good views; the B roads are generally less congested. Below are some of the best spots.

BADGWORTHY WATER SS7945 This Exmoor stream is the focus of a walkers' path from Malmsmead which takes you into the very heart of Lorna Doone country – it gets wilder and more remote with every step southwards (the surrounding moors provide a handful of return routes).

★ **DULVERTON** SS9127 The main town for Exmoor is a civilised place, with a handsome old stone market house, and a fine bridge over the river which has cut this steeply wooded valley. The Lion Hotel is useful for lunch, and the area's main information centre is at the S end of Fore St, (01398) 323841.

DUNKERY HILL SS8941 Exmoor's great ridge walk, with Dunkery Beacon as its high point surveying a huge chunk of south-west England and South Wales (as tramping boots have worn 3 feet off the top of the Beacon, walkers are now asked to take a bag of stones and earth up to deposit there). A good place to leave the car is Webbers Post (which is also good for local pottering). The Hill can also be incorporated into longer walks from Horner Woods or Luccombe.

★ † **EXFORD** SS8538 Prettily set in a sheltered valley by a small streamside green; the **church** up the hill a bit is well worth a look. The White Horse and Crown are useful for lunch. The peace of inland Exmoor is perhaps best appreciated from along paths by the rivers. A notable stretch of the Exe is between here and Winsford.

HEDDON'S MOUTH CLEAVE SS6549 This secretive wooded combe runs up through the rugged seaside moorland hills by the sea W of Lynton. This and others like it are prime territory for walkers. There's a good walk down from the beautifully placed Hunters Inn W of Martinhoe, and another fine one in this area is the terraced walkway known as the Ladies' Mile which runs along a charming valley nr Trentishoe.

MALMSMEAD SS7748 The Exmoor Natural History Society run leisurely 2-hour strolls through the striking scenery around their **Natural History Centre** every Weds from mid-May–early Sept at 2pm. Very enthusiastically done, and especially worth knowing about as they're free (inc a cup of tea afterwards for a small donation); Mrs Waite has full details on (01643) 703470. The best way of finding the Centre is from the County Gate National Park centre on the A39. Jan Ridd brought his bride Lorna Doone round here in the eponymous novel. The Exmoor Sandpiper at Countisbury up towards Lynton has decent food.

★ † **PARRACOMBE** SS6644 A lovely little village worth visiting in its own right, but particularly interesting is **St Petroc's church**, completely unspoilt medieval fabric with Georgian interior; locked Nov–Easter, but key available from custodian then. The Fox & Goose is useful for lunch.

★ † **SELWORTHY** SS9146 Gloriously unspoilt village with groups of white thatched cottages around a prettily planted hillside green looking out over Exmoor, and trees behind. The **church** is a gem, with a fine waggon ceiling with roof bosses. **Selworthy Beacon** give walks with excellent views.

TARKA TRAIL SS7241 Not yet complete, this long-distance signed path will eventually run to nearly 200 miles linking Exmoor, Dartmoor and the north Devon coast, following the route of Henry Williamson's *Tarka the Otter* – and is most enjoyable with a copy of the book. One beautiful section is the route around **Pinkworthy Pond** and the

Chains, reached from the car park a couple of miles along the B3358 E of Challacombe (where the Black Venus is good).

TARR STEPS SS8632 The River Barle's most famous feature, the finest of all the stone and slab clapper bridges for packhorses. The path along the river, which runs between Simonsbath and Dulverton, is uneven and surprisingly slow going in places.

WATERSMEET SS7448 Paths run eastward out of Lynton along the River Lyn to Watersmeet (1½m E), where the Farley Waters tumble down to meet the East Lyn in a series of rocky cascades among steeply picturesque oak woods (there's a discreet NT refreshment pavilion here). **Watersmeet House** The 19th-c fishing lodge itself is not particularly remarkable (though it has interesting local wildlife displays), but the estate that surrounds it really is attractive – a perfectly relaxing wooded valley, with the house at the meeting point of the rivers. Just right for an afternoon's pottering (and forming one of the best parts of the Tarka Trail long-distance walk), though some of the walks can be steep. Meals, snacks, shop; cl Nov–Mar; (01598) 753348; free; NT. Another scenic path leads high above the same valley along its south side, and riverside paths head on further upstream to the prettily set Rockford Inn (a good base for walks – food finishes at 2pm). Just N of Watersmeet, the **Foreland Cliffs** are the highest in the country – a good walk with dramatic views.

★ **WINSFORD** SS9035 Quiet and attractive village below high hills, with the River Exe lacing through its countless bridges. The carefully restored Royal Oak is good for lunch.

Other things to see and do

★ **ALLERFORD** SS9047 Pretty stonebuilt village with lovely packhorse bridge, and enthusiastic **West Somerset Museum of Rural Life** (cl am Sat, Sun exc school hols, and mid-Oct–Easter, £1) with summer craft demonstrations. **Bossington Farm Park** Friendly place with rare breeds, pony rides, baby animals for children to feed, and birds of prey. B & B in the 15th-c farmhouse. Snacks, shop, disabled access; cl Nov–Feb; (01643) 862816; *£4.50.

★ **APPLEDORE** SS4630 A pretty centre of narrow cottagey streets off the quayside road which looks out over the Taw estuary, and ship- and boat-building in the yard just upstream. There's a pedestrian ferry over to Instow. The **North Devon Maritime Museum** (Odun House, Odun Rd) is good, exploring a different topic in each room. Shop, disabled access to ground floor only; cl 1–2pm, and Nov–Easter; (01237) 422064; £1. The Royal George has lovely views and decent food, and the Beaver is also good for lunch.

ARLINGTON COURT SS6140 (on the A39) From its Victorian heyday up to 1949 Rosalie Chichester filled this early 19th-c house with model ships, stuffed birds, holiday souvenirs – in fact anything she could get her hands on; her assemblages have been watered down since, but there's still quite a fascinating medley. Covering 3,500 acres, the grounds have attractive landscaped gardens and a number of Shetland ponies and sheep, along with a Victorian garden and conservatory, woodland and lakeside nature trails, and an unusual collection of carriages and horse-drawn vehicles (rides available). Meals, snacks, shop, disabled access; cl Sat (exc bank hol wknds), and Nov–Mar; (01271) 850296; £5.10, £2.80 garden only; NT. The Pyne Arms at East Down is useful for lunch.

ASHFORD SS5235 **Butterfly House & Gardens** Well looked after collection of tropical butterflies, with plenty of plants and birds, and 2 acres of landscaped gardens outside. Meals, snacks, shop, disabled access; cl Nov–Easter; (01271) 342880; £2.50, gardens free. The Ring of Bells at Pilton is useful for lunch.

★ **BARNSTAPLE** SS5533 The main regional shopping centre, with a good deal of unforced charm in the older parts. Interesting buildings include an imposing 18th-c colonnaded arcade on the Great Quay, a lofty Victorian market hall (market days Tues and Fri), almshouses behind the church, more off the square by the long old stone bridge, and some interesting shops. It's still a working port, though in a very small way now. **Museum of North Devon** (The Square) Some interactive displays, and an exhibition on the local environment. Shop; cl pm Sat, am Sun, all day Mon, 25–26 Dec and bank hols; (01271) 346747; £1 (free Sat). **Brannams Pot Factory** (Roundswell Industrial Estate) Guided tours of big pottery (their terracotta pots are indispensable to many gardeners) with a chance to throw your own. Meals, snacks, shop, disabled access; no tours wknds, but shop open Sat and summer Sun; (01271) 343035; £3.50. The best nearby pub is the Chichester Arms up in Bishop's Tawton. On Pilston Causeway there's a good **sheepskin shop**; you can tour the adjacent factory. **Disused railway paths** Sections of the former track from here and Bideford can be walked or cycled (local bicycle hire £5 a day, more for mountain bikes). The best section is the one through Instow and Bideford up to the Puffing Billy at the former Torrington Station. In autumn and winter particularly this gives close views of the wading birds massed on the tidal sands of the estuary, and year-round the section up to Torrington is very attractive. The surviving mainline Exeter–Barnstaple line (known as the **Tarka Line**), mostly tracking along closer to the River Taw than the road does, is one of the finest of all train rides for scenery.

BICKLEIGH CASTLE SS9306 Charming moated and fortified manor house, still very much a family home; the 11th-c chapel is said to be Devon's oldest complete building. Also medieval hall, armoury and guard room, Tudor bedroom, 17th-c farmhouse, and exhibitions on maritime history and the Civil War. All done with great enthusiasm, and with a fair bit to amuse children. Good cream teas, plant sales in the Victorian walled garden, shop, limited disabled access; open pm Weds, Sun and bank hols Easter–May then pm daily (exc Sat) till early Oct; (01884) 855363; £4. The Fisherman's Cot is a beautifully placed riverside dining pub.

★ **BIDEFORD** SS4526 Quiet hillside town now bypassed, with notable medieval bridge and some pleasant old streets, partly pedestrianised, behind the Quay. The day-trip boat for Lundy (a good long day) sails from here year-round, though not every day, and only rarely in March. One of the oldest streets is Bridgeland St, and up towards the top of Bridge St there are quite a few antique or antiqueish shops. The Joiners Arms (Market Sq) has decent food, and readers recommend the Vagabond Cavalier (Cooper St) for good-value Italian meals. **The Big Sheep** (on the A39 2m W) Exuberant sheep centre, best known for its splendidly entertaining sheep steeplechasing (usually around 3.20pm), when sheep with knitted jockeys on their backs race 200 yards from their field towards the prize of extra food. Even better are the duck trials half an hour later, miniature sheepdog trials with the sheep replaced by ducks; there are more traditional sheepdog demonstrations too. Other events and displays take in everything from shearing and bottle-feeding to

Days Out

Picture-book scenes on a wild coast: Rosemoor Garden, Torrington; Clovelly – Hobby Drive toll road, Buck's Mills village, Milky Way, lunch at the Red Lion; Hartland Quay, and a walk along the cliffs in either direction; Hartland Abbey.

Village Exmoor: Allerford and Selworthy villages; a stroll from the road up Dunkery Beacon; Exford; lunch at the Royal Oak, Withypool; Winsford; Tarr Steps for a stroll by the river (good picnic spot); Dulverton.

milking, with plenty of opportunities to get close to the animals (lambs are born throughout the year, so there are always some to cuddle). Decent adventure play area, and a couple of puppet shows. Lots under cover, and it's particularly good value – tickets are valid for unlimited return visits for a week. Home-made meals and snacks (good teas), shop, disabled access; (01237) 477916; *£4.50. The Thatched House family dining pub at Abbotsham is handy for lunch.

BOLHAM SS9615
Knightshayes Court Lovely woodland garden with acres of unusual and even unique plants, especially lovely in spring but a glory at any time of year. Alpine and more formal gardens, ancient yew topiary, attractive walks, and good Exe valley views. The spooky-looking house itself is extravagantly ornate Victorian Gothic, with elaborate painted ceilings and décor and a newly restored minstrels' gallery. The original plans were even more over the top, but when the horrified owner saw them he sent the architect packing. Meals, snacks, shop and plant centre, disabled access; cl Nov–Mar, plus house cl Fri (exc Good Fri); (01884) 254665; £5.10, £3.50 garden only; NT. The Rose & Crown over at Calverleigh is a pleasant place for lunch.

! **BRADWORTHY** SS3515
Gnome Reserve (West Putford, 2¼m E) One of the most delightfully silly places in the area, woodland and wild flower meadows populated by hand-painted and individually modelled pixies. They lend you gnome hats and fishing rods so that resident gnomes will think you're one of them. The setting is pretty (flowers and plants are labelled), and small children love it. Shop; cl Nov–mid-Mar (exc shop); (01409) 241435; £1.75. Coming from the N you could stop for something to eat at the thatched Farmers Arms at Woolfardisworthy. The village is a pleasant jumping-off point for walks, with some quiet local strolls on the common, or over by the Tamar Lake a couple of miles SW.

BRATTON FLEMING SS6638
Exmoor Steam Railway (Cape of Good Hope Farm) Enthusiastically run family-owned narrow-gauge railway with half-sized steamtrains winding through a mile of countryside, and a small display of traction engines. Meals, snacks, shop, disabled access; cl Fri (exc mid-July–Aug), Sat, and Nov–Mar (exc Dec specials); (01598) 710711; £3.50. The White Hart is useful for lunch.

BRAUNTON BURROWS
SS4532 This vast nature reserve expanse of great swelling dunes is easily reached from the B3231 W of Braunton (red flags warn if there's shooting on the range here). In Braunton itself **Elliott Gallery** is an extensive craft centre (cl Sun, plus Thurs–Sat in winter; £1, 50p in winter). The Mariners Arms in South St is a useful pleasantly untouristy pub, and the Coffee Shoppe (Copperfields) has good local seafood.

THE BROWNSHAMS SS2825
These isolated farmhouses, now NT property, give walkers good quiet access to the woods, cliffs and clifftop farmland W of Clovelly.

BULL POINT SS4646 There's a lighthouse here, and dramatic cliff walks between here and Morte Point; the Ship Aground public house by the interesting church in Mortehoe is useful.

† **CALVERLEIGH** SS9214 An attractive village with a fine **church** and decent pub.

CHITTLEHAMPTON SS6127
Cobbaton Combat Collection (off the A377) Growing private collection of British and Canadian World War II vehicles, quite tightly packed under cover but looking ready for action; also mock-ups of wartime scenes, wartime memorabilia, and play area with Sherman tank. Summer snacks, shop, some disabled access; open daily Apr–Oct, best to ring for winter opening; (01769) 540740; £4. The Exeter Inn at Chittlehamholt has good food.

★ **CLOVELLY**
SS3124 One of Devon's most famous views, down the very steep old cobbled street, free from traffic and with flower-covered cottages either side, to the tiny harbour below. It's a delightful village, best appreciated out of season. At any time of year you'll have to park up at the top, outside the village, then pay £2 to

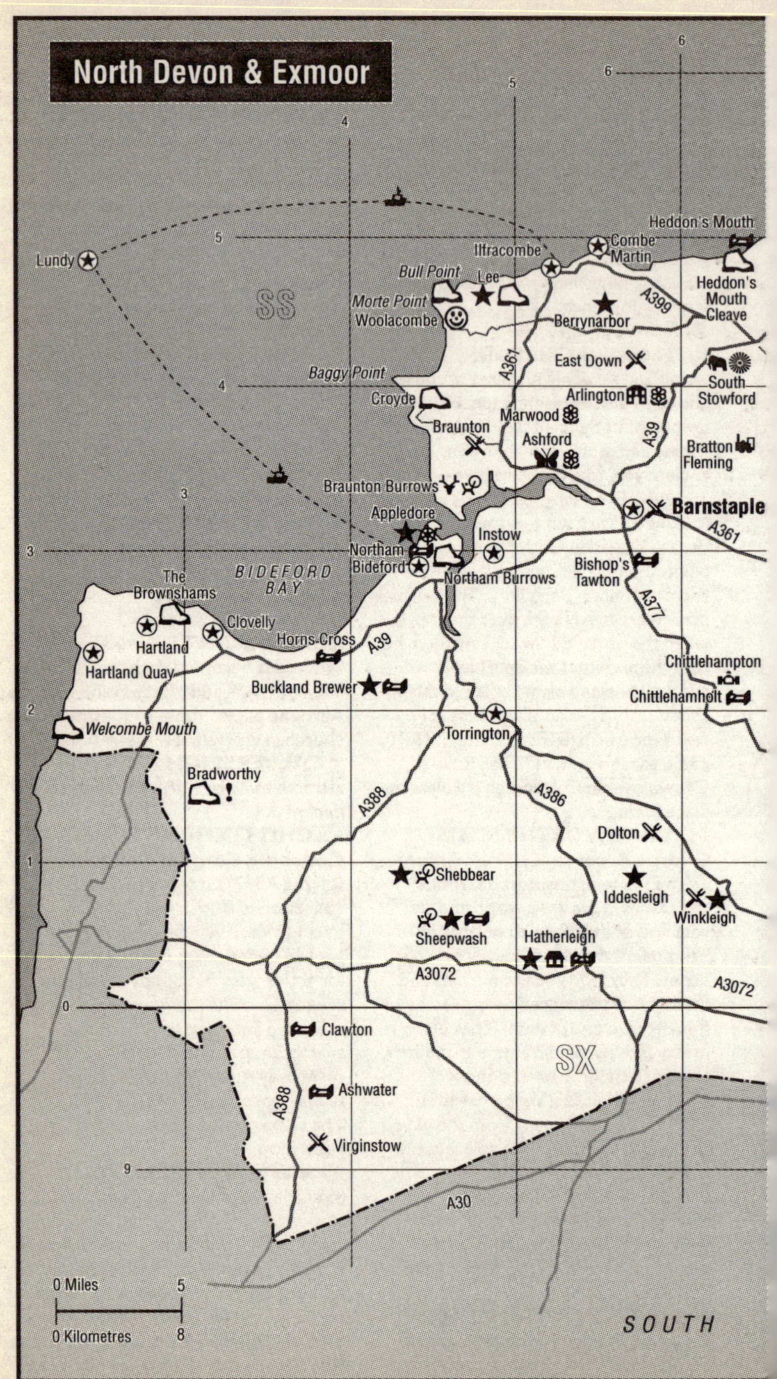
North Devon & Exmoor
Lundy
Heddon's Mouth
Combe Martin
Ilfracombe
Bull Point
Lee
Heddon's Mouth Cleave
Morte Point
Woolacombe
Berrynarbor
A399
East Down
South Stowford
Baggy Point
A361
Croyde
Arlington
Marwood
Braunton
Ashford
A39
Bratton Fleming
Braunton Burrows
Barnstaple
Appledore
A361
Instow
Northam
Bideford
Northam Burrows
Bishop's Tawton
BIDEFORD BAY
The Brownshams
Clovelly
A377
Hartland
Horns Cross
A39
Hartland Quay
Chittlehampton
Buckland Brewer
Chittlehamholt
Torrington
Welcombe Mouth
Bradworthy
A388
A386
Dolton
Shebbear
Iddesleigh
Winkleigh
Sheepwash
Hatherleigh
A3072
A3072
Clawton
SX
SS
Ashwater
A388
Virginstow
A30
0 Miles 5
0 Kilometres 8
SOUTH

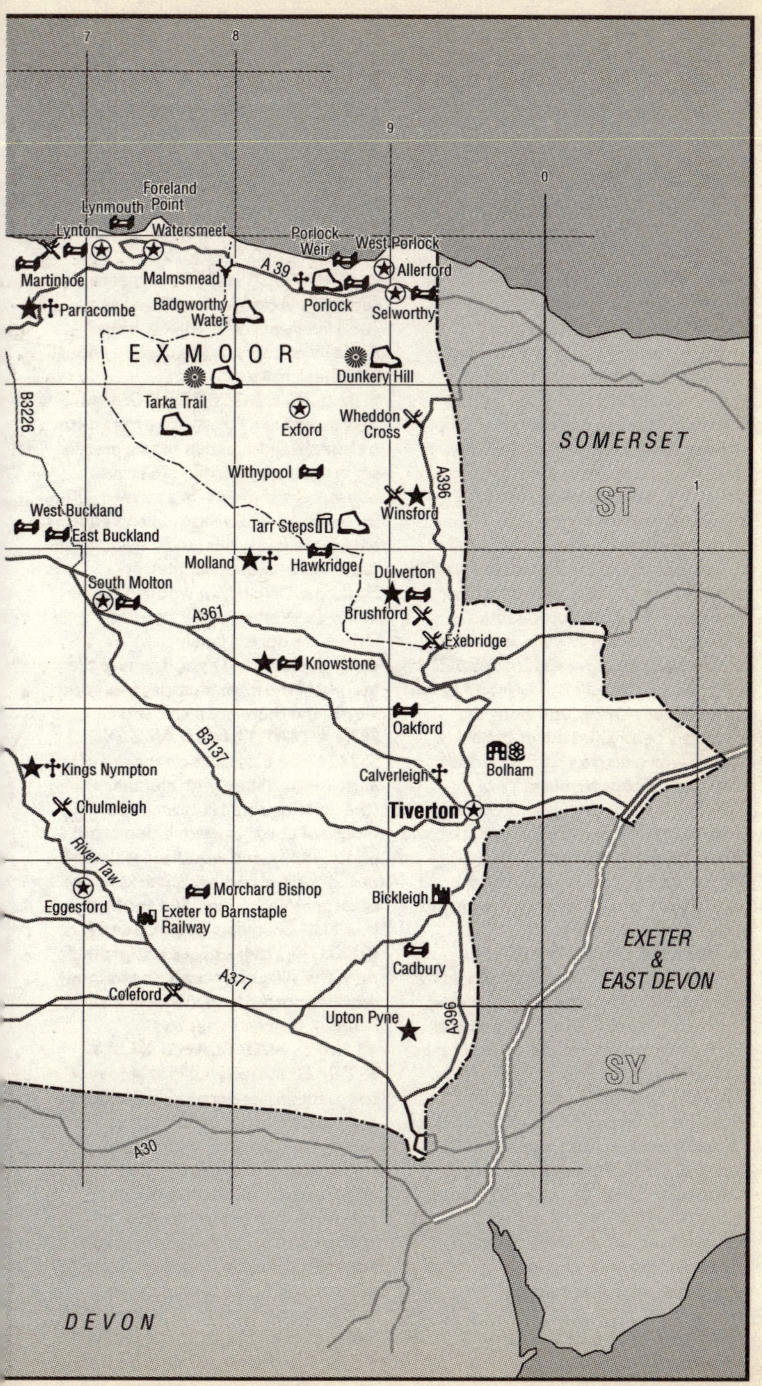

Foreland Point
Lynmouth
Lynton
Watersmeet
Martinhoe
Malmsmead
Parracombe
Badgworthy Water
Porlock Weir
West Porlock
Allerford
A 39
Porlock
Selworthy
EXMOOR
Dunkery Hill
B3226
Tarka Trail
Exford
Wheddon Cross
SOMERSET
Withypool
A396
Winsford
ST
West Buckland
East Buckland
Tarr Steps
Molland
Hawkridge
Dulverton
South Molton
Brushford
A361
Exebridge
Knowstone
Oakford
B3137
Bolham
Kings Nympton
Calverleigh
Chulmleigh
Tiverton
River Taw
Eggesford
Morchard Bishop
Bickleigh
Exeter to Barnstaple Railway
EXETER & EAST DEVON
Cadbury
A377
Coleford
Upton Pyne
A396
SY
A30
DEVON

pass through a turnstile, and walk down. The Red Lion down by the quay is pleasant; if you can't face the climb back up a Land Rover can drive you back from behind here (summer only, £1.40). You may be able to get boats to Lundy in summer. The parkland gardens of **Clovelly Court** have tranquil sea views, and a fine walled garden and restored Victorian greenhouse. Open Apr–Sept; (01237) 431200; *£1.50. **Milky Way** (Downland Farm) One of the biggest covered attractions in the region, losing a bit of its original character as it grows, but still friendly, and very good for families. They guarantee all children will be able to feed a lamb or kid, and there's also cow-milking, a working pottery, golf driving nets, laser clay pigeon shooting, birds of prey (twice-daily displays, not Sat), sheepdog training centre (no demonstrations Sun) and a little railway. Good indoor and outdoor play areas and the new Clone Zone interactive ride game. Snacks, shop, disabled access; cl wkdys Nov–Mar (exc during school hols); (01237) 431255; £5.50. Up towards the A39 is a big Iron Age hill fort, Clovelly Dykes, and along the coast the beachside hamlet of Buck's Mills is well worth a visit. The woods, cliffs and clifftops farmland W of Clovelly is attractive walking country. The moorland road down from Stibb Cross on the A388 via Woolfardisworthy is good, and the woodland Hobby Drive toll road is the area's best coast drive.

★ ! **COMBE MARTIN** SS5846 A string of former smallholdings and cottages scattered down a lovely sheltered valley, with an odd pub, the Pack of Cards, built to celebrate a cards win – 4 floors, 13 doors, 52 windows. There's a little fishing harbour in the shingly cove between the cliffs, and the Dolphin and Fo'c'sle are useful for lunch. **Combe Martin Wildlife & Dinosaur Park** (on the A399) Good range of animals and birds over 20 acres of woodland, inc a pair of rare snow leopards, and meerkats in a huge desert enclosure. Also meticulously researched life-size dinosaurs, some of which move and roar – like the towering *Tyrannosaurus rex*. New themed train ride through gardens with rare and tropical plants, and there's a petting zoo for children. Meals, snacks, shop; cl Nov–Easter; (01271) 882486; £5.95. **Combe Martin Motorcycle Collection** (Cross St) British bikes displayed against old petrol pumps, signs, garage equipment and other motoring nostalgia. Shop, disabled access; cl Nov–mid-May; (01271) 882346; *£2.50.

CROYDE SS4439 A magnet for surfers, this clean-sand village has a good family pub, the Thatch. Baggy Point W of here has a path good enough for wheelchairs.

† **EGGESFORD** SS6711 This quiet Taw Valley village has a 14th-c **church**, and a garden centre prettily set in the walled garden of a ruined house; refreshments on a terrace with lovely views. The village is also a good base for inland walks (and a stop on the Barnstaple–Exeter rail line): in Flashdown Wood, up wooded Hayne Valley to Wembworthy (the Odd Wheel is a decent family pub), or through Heywood Wood, where the mound of the former castle gives good views (and there are picnic sets).

HARTLAND ABBEY SS2424 Fine old house on the site of an Augustinian abbey, with elegant rooms (the drawing room is modelled on the House of Lords), an exhibition of old photography, and woodland walks in peacock-filled parkland. Snacks, shop; open pm Weds, Thur, Sun and bank hols May–Sept, plus Tues July and Aug; (01237) 441264; £3.50, £1.50 grounds only. The village has **craft shops** inc a working pottery and Windsor chair maker (children's sizes too).

HARTLAND QUAY SS2324 Grand isolated spot at foot of toll road, on jagged coast which looks a dramatic cross between illustrations for geology textbooks and ones for a shipwreckers' manual. On the way down detour to **Docton Mill**, an extensive interestingly planted sheltered streamside garden, largely naturalised, beside an ancient restored watermill. It's especially attractive in spring. Snacks (good cream teas), plant sales; cl Nov–Feb; (01237) 441369; £2.75. They have a couple of bedrooms you can stay in. Down by the sea is a wonderfully maritime old inn, and the **museum** covers 4 centuries of shipwrecks – even big ships still go down here – and smuggling; cl Oct–spring bank hol (exc Easter); 50p. For walkers, the cliffs around here are much more dramatic than those at nearby Hartland Point (which also has a toll gate). Just S at Spekes Mill Mouth the sea-eroded valley leaves the river spewing down the cliff in a seaside waterfall.

★ **HATHERLEIGH** SS5404 An attractive hillside village – even the church slopes – with fine inns (the Tally Ho, brewing its own beer, and the George) and a good **pottery** (20 Market St).

★ † **ILFRACOMBE** SS5147 Picturesque resort around busy harbour sheltered by high cliffs, with terraces of late Victorian boarding houses and small hotels looking out over it from their perches among the trees of the steep bay. There are period resort buildings and gardens, and even tunnels cut through the rock to a former Victorian bathing place. The 14th-c chapel above the harbour mouth has doubled as a lighthouse for over 450 years; the lifeboat station can be visited (donation requested). The town **museum** (Runnymede Gardens) is cheerful and enthusiastic, if unsurprising (cl wknds in winter; £1). **Holy Trinity Church** (Church St) is worth a look for its richly carved 15th-c waggon roof, one of the most striking in the area. The Royal Britannia (down by the harbour) has good-value food, and we can also recommend the George & Dragon. In summer the paddle steamer *Waverley* or the traditional cruise ship *Balmoral* run cruises from the pier to Lundy, Minehead, and other places – even as far as Swansea. **Hele Mill** (on the A399 just E, SS5447) Well restored early 16th-c mill still producing wholemeal flour. Pottery demonstrations and the chance to throw your own pot. Snacks, shop; cl Nov–Mar; (01271) 863185; *£2. Bicclescombe Park (on the A361 just S) has a restored 18th-c **cornmill**; the Coach House nearby has decent food. **Watermouth Castle** (off the A399, 3m E) Billed as 'Devon's Happy Castle', this is a fine 19th-c structure overlooking the bay, transformed into a world of gnomes, goblins, trolls and fairy tales, with slides, carousels and a musical water show. Very much for families, with young children the ones who'll enjoy it most. Snacks, shop, disabled access; cl Sat, plus Fri at the start and end of the season, and all Nov–Easter; (01271) 867474; £5.25. The best cliff walks are to the W of the town, towards Lee Bay. **Old Railway** This disused railway trail above the town is popular with walkers and cyclists, with a tunnel, interesting plants, and attractive scenery inc the Slade Reservoirs. For a one-way walk it's best to do it in reverse, for better views – and it's downhill all the way; Red Bus 31 or Filers 303 up from the town to Lee Bridge or Lee Cross (or to the Fortescue Hotel for a preliminary bracer).

INSTOW SS4728 At the mouth of the Torridge estuary, this has an expanse of tidal sands, with dozens of moored boats beached on them at low tide. The Boathouse has good food and views. **Tapeley Park** (Westleigh) The very pretty Italianate garden with rococo features and walled kitchen garden is the main draw, though there's also a pets corner, play area, and woodland walk. Lovely views down to the sea. Teas and snacks in period dairy, plant sales, disabled access; cl Sat, and Nov–Easter; (01271) 342371; £2.80.

★ † **KING'S NYMPTON** SS6819 An attractive village with a fine **church** and decent pub.

★ **LEE** SS4846 This pretty village in a sheltered woody valley has an attractive ancient pub, the Grampus. There are good cliff walks between the bay and Ilfracombe.

LUNDY DAY TRIPS SS1344 (boat from Bideford or, in summer, Ilfracombe) Well worth considering if you're in Devon for more than just a few days. The island's best known for the migrant birds that come here in spring and autumn, but the remoteness and loneliness is also a powerful draw – the permanent population is around a dozen. Lovely walks along its 7 miles of formidably high cliffs, windswept rough pastures, small church, evocative castle ruins, 2 lighthouses (one the highest in

Britain), wandering goats, small Soay sheep and ponies, and the chance of seeing seals (especially in autumn), the introduced small sika deer, and, in Apr and May, the island's trademark puffins. Accommodation can be arranged through the Landmark Trust (01628) 825925. The Marisco Tavern is a good place to eat. The return boat trip (about 2¼ hours each way) is about £25; (01237) 423365 for sailing times.

★ ⛰ ✿ ☗ **LYNTON** SS7249 Merging into its harbourside extension, Lynmouth, down at the bottom of the cliff railway track, this delightfully situated steep village tucks into the wooded seaside gorge where the East and West Lyn tumble down to the sea. The most delightful walks in North Devon are around here. Lynton clearly shows its origins as a Victorian resort in one of the many areas then known as Little Switzerland, with hillside villas now quiet boarding houses, photogenic corners and some older cottages. Pretty cottages down by the little tidal harbour, as well as craft shops and so forth (there's a friendly hands-on pottery); lots of trippers during the day in summer. **Lyn and Exmoor Museum** (Market St) In the old part of the upper village, this engagingly simple museum is in an 18th-c cottage with a scale model of the former Lynton–Barnstaple narrow-gauge railway (you can still walk much of its track bed). Shop; cl 12.30–2 pm, Sat, and Nov–Easter; £1. **Glen Lyn Gorge** Carefully restored after the tragic flood of 1952, with pretty walks and an exhibition on water power. Exhibition cl Nov–Mar, gorge cl 26 Dec and possibly in bad weather; (01598) 753207; £2. They have decent holiday flats and cottages in a peaceful setting. The Olde Cottage Inne (on the B3234 – a lovely walk up the Lynway from Sinai Hill) is useful for lunch, and the Rising Sun down by the harbour has a good restaurant. Reached by an easy coast path from Lynton, the **Valley of the Rocks** is a great valley bowl with steep crags and pinnacles of rock dividing it from the sea (and a dreadful unscreened car park smack in the middle). You can also approach by paths over Hollerday Hill (wooded, but opens out dramatically on top). **Watersmeet** (*see Exmoor entry, above*) is also within easy reach.

❀ **MARWOOD HILL GARDENS** SS5437 (off the A361 from Barnstaple–Braunton) 18 well kept and colourful acres inc rare trees and shrubs, small lakes, extensive bog garden, clematis, camellias, alpines and eucalyptus, and national collections of astilbes (best in July) and Tulbaghia. Cream teas Sun and bank hols, plant centre, some disabled access; cl 25 Dec; *£2. The New Ring o' Bells at Prixford is very handy for lunch.

★ ✝ **MOLLAND** SS8028 An attractive village with a fine **church** and decent pub.

⛰ **NORTHAM BURROWS** SS4430 Dunes, sand slacks and meres behind a pebble ridge, with the Atlantic rollers swinging in along the rock-strewn Saunton Sands beyond – deserted out of season and stimulating then for lonely walks; in summer a popular family beach.

⛰ ✝ **PORLOCK** SS8846 A lot of traffic, but some attractive cottages with distinctive lighthouse-like chimneys and thatched roofs. The nearby harbour of **Porlock Weir** is much quieter though it does get a lot of summer visitors; decent food at the thatched Ship. There are long walks along the coast: heading W along the shore at the foot of the wooded cliffs, even the most avid pebble-hunter would find all he wanted. Another good walk is through the woods up to the tiny and quite isolated **Culbone church**.

★ ✿ **SHEBBEAR** SS4409 Interesting and attractive tucked-away village, with the odd Devil's Stone by the green (and a decent pub named after it), and a working wood-fired pottery.

★ ✿ **SHEEPWASH** SS4806 Quiet village with cob and thatch houses around the green; the Half Moon is good for lunch. A mile N is **Duckpool Cottage**, a traditional wood-fired pottery.

☗ ! 🏛 **SOUTH MOLTON** SS7126 An attractive central square and imposing church and its farming roots show in the Thurs cattle market. The 18th-c guildhall has a local history

museum (cl Fri, Sun, and Dec–Feb; free), and monthly art-and-craft shows. The Castle at George Nympton has generous home cooking. **Quince Honey Farm**(North Rd) The biggest wild bee farm in the world, with observation hives looking right into the centre of the colonies. Snacks, shop (lots of honey and their own beeswax skin and hair care products); cl Nov–Easter (though shop stays open); (01769) 572401; £2.95. **Hancock's Devon Cider** (Clapworthy Mill, 3m SW) Exhibition and film showing how they produce their good scrumpy. It's a nice spot for a picnic. Snacks, shop, good disabled access; cl 1–2pm, all day Sun, and Oct–Easter; (01769) 572678; £1.95.

SOUTH STOWFORD SS6540 **Exmoor Zoological Park** (off the B3226 N of Bratton Fleming) Good-sized collection of rare and endangered creatures, many of which breed successfully throughout the year. Children can feed the smaller animals or play on the assault course, and there are good views from the well landscaped grounds. Snacks, shop, disabled access; cl 25–26 Dec; (01598) 763352; £4.25. The Old Station House at Blackmoor Gate is a pleasant dining pub.

TIVERTON SS9512 Formerly prosperous wool town, well worth wandering round; **St Peter's Church** is magnificently decorated with rich carving, and other grand buildings include the Jacobean council offices. The handsome **castle** was built in 1106 as a royal fortress dominating the River Exe, and still has its Norman tower and gatehouse, as well as an interesting clock collection and one of the best assemblages of Civil War armour and arms. You can stay in apartments in the oldest parts of the building. Shop; open pm Sun and Thurs Easter–Sept, plus pm Mon–Weds July and Aug; (01884) 253200; £3. A 19th-c school on St Andrew St houses the local history **museum,** with two waterwheels, an excellent railway gallery and a new display about the work of the wheelwright (cl Sun, and Christmas–Jan; *£1). The 4 showrooms of the **Tiverton Craft Centre** showcase the work of over 170 local craftsmen; cl Sun; (01884) 258430; free. In summer there are 2½-hour **horse-drawn boat trips** along the attractively restored canal from the wharf; booking advisable, (01884) 253345; £6. Rowing boats for hire and motor-boat trips too, and they can sort out fishing permits.

TORRINGTON SS4919 Quiet dairy-farming town on a ridge above the River Torridge, with some attractive buildings inc 14th-c Taddiport Chapel (for a former leper colony), the imposing Palmer House, and a rather grand church built to replace the original blown up in the Civil War. There are good views from the neatly mown hill above the river, and other nearby strolls on the preserved commons surrounding the town. The Black Horse is useful for lunch. RHS **Garden Rosemoor** (off the B3220 just S) A wonderful place, constantly being developed and updated by the Royal Horticultural Society; marvellous rare trees, shrubs, and other plants in charmingly landscaped sheltered woodland setting, rose, stream and bog gardens, foliage and plantsman's garden, and trails for children. Meals, snacks, a new picnic area, smart shop, disabled access; cl 25 Dec; (01805) 624067; £4. **Dartington Glass** (Linden Close) On wkdys you can tour the factory (last tour 3.15pm); there's a useful visitor centre, and a shop with well priced goblets and decanters. They get very busy on wet days in summer – best to phone and check tour availability. Meals, snacks, disabled access by prior arrangement; no tours bank hols or 2 wks at Christmas, shop cl 25–26 Dec, Easter Sun; (01805) 626242; £2.75. **The Downes** (on the A386 towards Bideford, nr Monkleigh) Fine big woodland garden with interesting flowering trees and shrubs and lovely landscaped lawns. Wknd teas, plant sales; open Easter–early Jun, then by appointment till Sept; (01805) 622244; *£2. You can stay in a self-contained wing of the Georgian house.

★ **UPTON PYNE** SX9197 Readers particularly enjoy this unspoilt village, the basis of Barton in Jane Austen's *Sense and Sensibility*.

⛱ **WELCOMBE MOUTH** SS2118 Rather a rough drive down, but an attractive spot, and the cliffs around have possibilities for wild coast walks.

☺ **WOOLACOMBE** SS4843 The beach here is particularly nice, and its Atlantic breakers now draw quite a few surfers. The Rock at Georgeham and Mill at Ossaborough are pleasant for lunch, and the back road to Mortehoe is scenic. **Once Upon A Time** (Old Station; on the B3343 inland) Run by the same people as Watermouth Castle at Ilfracombe, this is a super place for children up to about 11, with lots of rides and other activities; there's a driving school that even offers tests. Meals, snacks, shop, disabled access; cl Sat, plus Fri at start and end of season, and all Oct–Easter; (01271) 867474; £2.55 (£4.95 children).

★ **Other attractive villages** with decent pubs include Berrynarbor SS5646, Buckland Brewer SS4220, Iddesleigh SS5708, Knowstone SS8223 and Winkleigh SS6308.

Where to eat

BARNSTAPLE SS5533 **Lynwood House** *Bishop's Tawton Rd (01271) 343695* The same family have run this no smoking restaurant-with-rooms for 29 years and the elegant Victorian dining room specialises in popular fresh local seafood (though meaty and vegetarian dishes are covered, and there's also a lighter menu); bdrms; cl am Sat, all day Sun, 1–4 Jan. **£30**|£6.85.

BRAUNTON SS4836 **Squires** *Exeter Rd (01271) 815533* First-class fish and chip take-away and restaurant with really excellent fish, good wines, friendly service and attractive airy surroundings; cl Sun (but open school summer hols then), 25–26 Dec, 1 Jan; disabled access. £4.

BRUSHFORD (Somerset) SS9225 **Carnarvon Arms** *(01398) 323302* Good English bar and restaurant food and friendly staff in comfortable and individual sporting hotel with its own stabling, fishing and shooting; bdrms; disabled access. **£31**|£6.

CHULMLEIGH SS6814 **Bakehouse** *South Molton St (01769) 580137/580074* Thatched 16th-c merchant's house with lots of beams, a flower-filled courtyard, and dining room serving morning coffee, light lunches and afternoon teas (plus breakfast and dinner for residents); bdrms; cl Mon, 2 wks Feb; disabled access. **£21**|£5.

COLEFORD SS7701 **New Inn** *(01363) 84242* Comfortable thatched 14th-c inn, good interesting food, extensive wine list, well kept real ales, 4 nicely furnished areas, winter log fire, and attractive garden with stream; bdrms; cl 25–26 Dec; disabled access. **£24.65**|£6.95.

DOLTON SS5712 **Union** *(01805) 804633* Relaxed and friendly old pub with good interesting genuinely home-made food using first-class produce, well kept real ales, and decent wines; comfortable little lounge, characterful lower bar with chatty drinking area and tables for eating, and charming owners; bdrms. **£18.95**|£6.95.

EAST DOWN SS5941 **Pyne Arms** *(01271) 850207* Popular pub with lots of nooks and crannies in low-beamed bar, small no smoking galleried loft, games area, good food, and well kept real ales; cl 25 Dec; no children. **£17**|£6.70.

EXEBRIDGE SS9224 **Starlight Express** *Lakeside Caravan Park (01398) 324028* Bustling little restaurant (you can't actually see the caravans) with enjoyable food, decent wines, and friendly service. **£17.70**|£7.50.

LYNTON SS6549 **Lee Cottage** *Lee Abbey (01598) 752621* Charming cottage run by the Christian community from Lee Abbey, in pretty terraced streamside gardens with coast views; a few seats inside but plenty on the lawns and verandah; all the scones, bread and cakes used in the snacks and cream teas are home-made; no smoking; cl Sun (and Mon in Jun), and mid-Sept–mid-May. £1.85.

VIRGINSTOW SX3792 **Percy's at Coombeshead** *(01409) 211236* Carefully renovated 16th-c longhouse in 40 acres which provide some of the organic produce used in the no smoking restaurant, somewhere to enjoy good, imaginative modern cooking (super bread and puddings) and a well chosen wine list; comfortable, spacious bdrms; children over 10; disabled access. **£29**|£12.

WHEDDON CROSS (Somerset) SS9238 **Rest & Be Thankful** *(01643) 841222* Helpful staff and varied bar food in comfortably modern 2-room bar with 2 good log fires, big jug collection, and aquarium; restaurant; good bdrms; cl 25 Dec; disabled access. **£17**|£5.75.

WINKLEIGH SS6308 **Pophams** *Castle St (01837) 83767* Tiny bustling place for morning coffee and lunch – bring your own wine with particularly good freshly cooked food, and relaxed happy atmosphere; cl Sun, Mon, Tues, and all Feb; no children. **£25**.

WINSFORD (Somerset) SS9034 **Royal Oak** *(01643) 851455* Beautiful thatched inn in quiet spot with attractively furnished cosy bars, a smartly civilised atmosphere, log fire, good home-made bar and restaurant food, well kept real ales, and friendly staff; lots of surrounding walks; bdrms; disabled access. **£25**|£7.65.

Special thanks to Miss C Pardey, Julie Watson, Mr and Mrs W Crawford, Mrs H Woodfield, Caroline and Richard Nocton, J and M Back, D J Wallington, Catharine Gilson, S Barber.

We welcome reports from readers

This *Guide* depends on readers' reports. Do help us if you can – in return, we offer a discount on the next edition to people who've helped us with reports for it. Tell us what you think about places already in it, and anything extra you think we should say about them. And send us your ideas for inclusion in the next edition: places to visit, eat at or stay in, attractive drives or walks, maybe even unusual interesting shops you know of. Use the card in the middle, the report forms at the end, or just write – no stamp needed: *The Good Guide to Britain*, FREEPOST TN1569, Wadhurst, E Sussex TN5 7BR.

Devon Calendar

Some of these dates were provisional as we went to press. Please check information with the telephone numbers provided.

JANUARY

2 **Clyst St Mary** Antiques Fair at Westpoint: about 500 stands – *till Sun 3* (01392) 446000
3 **Clyst St Mary** Baby Pets & Animal Day at Crealy Park (01395) 233200
7 **Clyst St Mary** Caravan & Camping Show at Westpoint – *till Sun 10* (01392) 446000
16 **Exmouth** RSPB Cruise on the River Exe to view the wintering avocets – *also Sun 17, Sat 30 and Sun 31* (01392) 432691
29 **Clyst St Mary** Indoor Motocross at Westpoint – *till Sun 31* (01392) 446000

FEBRUARY

6 **Exeter** Antiques Fair at the Exeter Livestock Centre: about 430 stands (01392) 256847
13 **Exmouth** RSPB Cruise on the River Exe to view the wintering avocets – *also Sun 14, Sat 27 and Sun 28* (01392) 432691
16 **Clyst St Mary** Holiday on Ice at Westpoint – *till Sun 21* (01392) 446000
21 **Clyst St Mary** Baby Pets & Animal Day at Crealy Park (01395) 233200
24 **Exeter** Taste of the West Food & Drink Fair at Exeter Livestock Centre – *till Thurs 25* (01392) 256847

MARCH

6 **Clyst St Mary** Antiques Fair – *till Sun 7 (see 3 Jan)*
14 **Exmouth** RSPB Cruise on the River Exe to view the wintering avocets *also Mon 15* (01392) 432691
24 **Clyst St Mary** Taste of the West Food & Drink Fair at Westpoint – *till Thurs 25* (01526) 398198
26 **Lynton** Jazz Festival – *till Sun 28* (01271) 372064

APRIL

2 **Clyst St Mary** Easter Egg Hunt at Crealy Park – *also Sun 4 and Mon 5*, (01395) 233200; **Exeter** Lands End Trial Start: 300 mile classic trial for motorcycles and cars (01359) 270954
3 **Exeter** Antiques Fair *(see 6 Feb)*
15 **Newton Abbot** Beer Festival at Tuckers Maltings: over 120 West Country real ales – *till Sun 18* (01626) 334734
22 **Exeter** American Square Dancing Convention at St George's Hall – *till Sat 24* (01392) 265118
25 **Clyst St Mary** Toy & Train Collectors Fair at Westpoint – (01526) 398198; also Fireworks at Crealy Park (01395) 233200

Devon Calendar (cont.)

MAY

1 **Clyst St Mary** Antiques Fair – *till Sun 2 (see 2 Jan)*; **Dartmouth** Music Festival – *till Sun 2* (01803) 834224

2 **Blackawton** International Festival of Worm Charming (01803) 834224; **Clyst St Mary** Lost Toys Treasure Hunt at Crealy Park – *till Mon 3* (01395) 233200; **Exeter** Great West Run (01392) 265118; **Modbury** May Week – *till Sun 9* (01548) 830159

3 **Uffculme** Sheep Show: coloured and rare breeds at Coldharbour Mill Working Wool Museum (01884) 840960

6 **Torrington** May Fair (01805) 622441

13 **Holsworthy** Agricultural Show (01409) 253979

20 **Clyst St Mary** County Show at Westpoint – *till Sat 22* (01392) 444777

21 **Torquay** English Riviera Dance Festival: world champion cabaret, sequence and social dancing – *till 5 Jun* (01895) 632143

22 **Babbacombe** Devon Art Society Exhibition & Sale at St Anne's Institute Hall – *till 6 Jun* (01803) 328141; **Brixham** Heritage Festival: live music, dance displays, fireworks – *till Sun 30* (01803) 855262

28 **Combe Martin** Hunting of the Earl of Rone *from Fri at 6pm, then every day – till Mon 31* when effigy is captured, seated facing backwards on a donkey and after procession with fool and hobby horse is thrown into the sea (01271) 882524

29 **Torquay** Power Boat Race from Cowes – *till Sun 30* (01803) 297428

31 **Stockland** Country Fair & Donkey Derby (01404) 881447

JUNE

5 **Exeter** Antiques Fair *(see 6 Feb)*

12 **Beer** Steam & Model Festival at Pecorama Pleasure Gardens – *till Sun 13* (01297) 21542

13 **Salcombe** Festival (01548) 843546

19 **Brixham** Trawler Race & Quay Festival (01803) 882325; **Exeter** Blues Festival (01392) 265118

20 **Clyst St Mary** Model Boats at Crealy Park (01395) 233200; **Ivybridge** Vintage Rally at Challonsleigh Farm (01752) 896253

23 **Kenton** Phillips Fine Art Sale at Powderham Castle – *till Weds 30* (01626) 890243

26 **Ashburton** Carnival Week – *till 3 July* (01364) 652142; **Bovey Tracey** Devon Guild of Craftsmen Exhibition at Riverside Mill – *till S5 Sept* (01626) 832223; **Buckland Monachorum** Craft Fair – *till Sun 27* (01822) 853607

27 **Clyst St Mary** Teddy Bears' Picnic at Crealy Park (01395) 233200

JULY

2 **Exeter** Festival: cathedral concerts, open-air jazz, theatre, comedy, street entertainment, fireworks concert – *till Sun 18* (01392) 265118

3 **Clyst St Mary** Antiques Fair – *till Sun 4 (see 2 Jan)*; **Kenton** Horse Trials at Powderham Castle – *till Sun 4* (01626) 890243

6 **Exeter** Open-air Shakespeare at Roguemont Gardens – *till Sat 31* (01392) 265118

10 **Kenton** Historic Vehicle Gathering at Powderham Castle – *till Sun 11* (01626) 890243

Devon Calendar (cont.)

14 **Clyst St Mary** South West Qualifier for Crufts at Crealy Park – *till Fri 16* (01395) 233200

17 **Barnstaple** Green Man Festival: procession, market, street battle and re-enactment of the meeting of the Green Man with the prior (01271) 375776; **Clyst St Mary** classic Bike show at Westpoint – *till Sun 18* (01526) 398198; **Kingsbridge** Fair Week with Traditional Glove Hanging Ceremony *on Weds 21* Carnival Procession *on Sat 24* (01548) 856440.

19 **Dartmouth** Town Week – *till Sun 25* (01803) 835200

20 **Honiton** Hot Penny Ceremony & Fair (01404) 43716

23 **Kenton** Fireworks Concert at Powderham Castle (01626) 890243

24 **Tiverton** Mid-Devon Show at Hartnoll Farm (01884) 821815

25 **Salcombe** Town Regatta: inc fireworks – *till Sat 31* (01548) 843927; **Torbay** Carnival – *till 1 Aug* (01803) 297428

26 **Clovelly** Agricultural Show at Thornery Farm (01409) 241273

29 **Berry Pomeroy** Totnes & District Show (01803) 863168

30 **Sidmouth** International Folk Festival: one of Europe's largest, with dance, concerts and carnival – *till 6 Aug* (01296) 393293

AUGUST

1 **Clyst St Mary** Dolls & Miniature Show at Westpoint (01526) 398198; **Salcombe** Yacht Club Regatta – *till Fri 6* (01548) 843927

4 **Landkey** North Devon Show at Plym's Farm (01769) 560205

5 **Honiton** Agricultural Show (01404) 891763; **Kenton** English National Sheepdog Trials at Powderham Castle – *till Sat 7* (01626) 890243

7 **Cornwood** Agricultural & Horticultural Show (01752) 837667; **Exeter** Antiques Fair *(see 6 Feb)*; **Shaldon** Water Carnival (01626) 872842

8 **Clyst St Mary** Pirates' Treasure Hunt at Crealy Park (01395) 233200

14 **Babbacombe** Devon Art Society Exhibition & Sale at St Anne's Institute Hall – *till Sun 29* (01803) 328141; **Exeter** Roman Weekend – *till Sun 15* (01392) 265118; **Kingsbridge** Vintage Machinery Show at Sorley Cross – *till Sun 15* (01548) 852939; **South Zeal** Dartmoor Folk Festival – *till Sun 15* (01837) 840162

20 **Brixham** Regatta – *till Sun 22* (01803) 852861

21 **Dalwood** Country Fair: costume parades, street market, medieval banquet (01404) 881676; **Torbay** Royal Regatta – *till Weds 25* (01803) 299772

22 **Clyst St Mary** Toy & Train Fair at Westpoint (01526) 398198; **Topsham** Town Fair – *till Sat 28* (01392) 265118

24 **Totnes** Orange Races in the main street (01803) 863714

26 **Dartmouth** Royal Regatta: Red Arrows, fireworks, barrel rolling – *till Sat 28* (01803) 832435; **Moretonhampstead** Carnival (01647) 440145

28 **Clyst St Mary** South West Motorcycle Show at Westpoint – *till Sun 29* (01526) 398198; **Hope Cove** Fun Weekend – *till Mon 30* (01548) 853195

30 **Brixham** Fish Market Open Day (01803) 859123

SEPTEMBER

4 **Clyst St Mary** Antiques Fair – *till Sun 5 (see 2 Jan)*; **Kingsbridge** Agricultural Show (01548) 853195

5 **Exe** Struggle Raft Race (01884) 252336

8 **Newton Abbot** Ancient Cheese & Onion Fayre: sample local cheese and wines (01626) 353567

Devon Calendar (cont.)

12 **Plymouth** Landmark Trust Open Day at Crownhill Fort: not usually open to the public (01628) 825925
18 **Exeter** Antiques Fair *(see 6 Feb)*

OCTOBER

9 **Buckland Monachorum** Tudor Living History at Buckland Abbey – *till Sun 10* (01822) 853607
15 **Lynton** Jazz Festival – *till Sun 17* (01271) 72064
16 **Exeter** Antiques Fair *(see 6 Feb)*
17 **Endsleigh** Landmark Trust Open Day at Pond Cottage: not usually open to the public (01628) 825925
28 **Bampton** Fair (01884) 255255
30 **Clyst St Mary** Antiques Fair *(see 2 Jan)*
31 **Clyst St Mary** Halloween Party at Crealy Park (01395) 233200; **Exeter** Guided Ghost Tour (01392) 265118

NOVEMBER

5 **Ottery St Mary** Rolling of the Tar Barrels: since 1688 (01404) 812252
19 **Kenton** Antiques Fair at Powderham Castle – *till Sun 21* (01626) 890243
20 **Kingsbridge** Illuminated Carnival (01548) 853195
27 **Exeter** Antiques Fair *(see 6 Feb)*; also Grand Illuminated Procession (01392) 276619

DECEMBER

11 **Clyst St Mary** Father Christmas at Crealy Park – *every day till Thurs 23* (01395) 233200
31 **Exeter** Millennium Ball at University of Exeter: family celebration inc bands, groups and entertainers celebrating music through the centuries, and fireworks (01392) 263552

We welcome reports from readers

This *Guide* depends on readers' reports. Do help us if you can – in return, we offer a discount on the next edition to people who've helped us with reports for it. Tell us what you think about places already in it, and anything extra you think we should say about them. And send us your ideas for inclusion in the next edition: places to visit, eat at or stay in, attractive drives or walks, maybe even unusual interesting shops you know of. Use the card in the middle, the report forms at the end, or just write – no stamp needed: *The Good Guide to Britain*, FREEPOST TN1569, Wadhurst, E Sussex TN5 7BR.

Dorset

Family appeal, traditional resorts with character – also lots of interest for adults, and unspoilt coast and countryside.

Bournemouth has miles of good beaches, with a civilised and spacious spread of comfortably sedate resort areas and leafy suburbs (and Poole's bustling waterfront for contrast); the new aquarium here is very well done. Other smaller places – notably Weymouth and Lyme Regis – have a lot to offer families who want something a bit different. Children also particularly enjoy the Monkey World at Wool and the costume museum in Blandford Forum, while the tank museum at Bovington Camp appeals to many. The fact that Dorset is fossil country is reflected by a number of dinosaur centres; the one in Dorchester is the best.

Dorset's inland countryside has a subtle understated appeal, with secluded valleys, narrow lanes threading through peaceful farmland and tucked-away villages (Milton Abbas is best of all). The central area's chalk uplands, cut by intricate valleys, give some splendid high viewpoints. The west's intimate farming country feels very untouched by passing time. Thomas Hardy's books (and films of them) are vividly conjured up by particular villages and tracts of countryside. Dorchester, Sherborne, Beaminster, Shaftesbury and Blandford Forum are interesting country towns. Forde Abbey at Thorncombe and the gardens and swannery at Abbotsbury are outstanding places to visit, and other rewarding places include Corfe Castle, Mapperton Gardens near Beaminster, Kingston Lacy near Wimborne, Athelhampton House, and Compton Acres Gardens in Poole.

The coast is lovely, with some marvellous views. Much of it is quiet and unspoiled (especially along the rugged Isle of Purbeck), with the coast path going the length of the county. The tremendous sweep of the Chesil Beach, its pebbles and boulders immaculately graded by millennia of storms, is emphatically not for swimmers – the undertow will suck you straight down – but with its long lagoon behind is very interesting for beachcombers and nature-lovers. The heathland west of Poole Harbour, partly planted with conifers, has a quite different character – largely flat tank-training ground west of Weymouth, but a more interesting roaming ground for nature-lovers towards Studland Bay.

An Explorer ticket is a good buy if you're going to be doing much travelling on buses.

Where to stay

ABBOTSBURY SY5785 **Ilchester Arms** *Abbotsbury, Weymouth DT3 4JR (01305) 871243* **£52.85;** 10 comfortable rms. Handsome old stone inn nr abbey; log fire in the rambling beamed bar decorated with hundreds of swan pictures, breakfasts in attractive no smoking conservatory, restaurant, pleasant staff; plenty of walks; no accommdation Christmas; disabled access.

BOURNEMOUTH SZ0991 **Langtry Manor** *26 Derby Rd, Eastcliff, Bournemouth BH1 3QB (01202) 553887* ***£99.50,** plus special breaks; 28 pretty rms, some in the manor, some in the lodge. Built by Edward VII for Lily Langtry, with lots of memorabilia, relaxed public rooms, and good food inc an Edwardian dinner every Sat evening; disabled access.

BRIDPORT SY4692 **Britmead House** *West Bay Rd, Bridport DT6 4EG (01308) 422941* **£60,** plus special breaks; 7 rms. Extended Victorian hotel with lots to do nearby; comfortable lounge overlooking the garden, attractive dining room, good food using fresh local produce, and kind, helpful service; self-catering bungalow; children over 5; dogs by prior arrangement; disabled access.

CORFE CASTLE SY9681 **Knitson Old Farmhouse** *Corfe Castle, Wareham BH20 5JB (01929) 422836* ***£40;** 3 rms, shared bthrm. Big ancient cottage on working farm with sheep and Jersey cows, a large garden with hens, pigs and horses; comfortable sitting room with flagstones and woodburner, and good evening food by arrangement using home-reared pork and lamb served in the spacious kitchen; no smoking; cl Jan.

CRANBORNE SU0513 **Fleur-de-Lys** *Cranborne, Wimborne BH21 5PP (01725) 517282* ***£50,** plus special breaks; 8 rms. Nicely placed old creeper-clad pub with oak-panelled lounge bar, simply furnished beamed public bar, and decent food; cl 24–25 Dec.

DORCHESTER SY6890 **Casterbridge** *49 High East St, Dorchester DT1 1HU (01305) 264043* ***£68,** plus weekend breaks; 15 rms. Small Georgian hotel in town centre with modern annexe across little courtyard, elegant drawing room, cosy library, and attractive dining room and conservatory; no evening meals (lots of nearby restaurants); cl 25–26 Dec; disabled access.

DORCHESTER SY6890 **Kings Arms** *High East St, Dorchester DT1 1HF (01305) 265353* **£56.85,** plus special breaks; 31 rms – the Lawrence of Arabia and the Tutenkhamun suites are extraordinary. Smart, thriving coaching inn made famous by Hardy; different menus in restaurant, coffee shop and bar, old-fashioned public bar with real ales, live music twice a week; disabled access.

DORCHESTER SY6789 **Maiden Castle Farm** *Dorchester DT2 9PR (01305) 262356* **£40;** 4 rms, most with own bthrm. Victorian farmhouse on big working farm set beneath the prehistoric earthworks from which it takes its name; views of the castle and countryside, and comfortable, traditionally furnished sitting room which overlooks the garden.

EAST KNIGHTON SY8185 **Countryman** *East Knighton, Dorchester DT2 8LL (01305) 852666* **£50;** 6 rms. Attractively converted pair of old cottages with open fires and plenty of character in the main bar, no smoking family room, generous food in carvery restaurant, and courteous staff; cl 25 Dec.

EVERSHOT ST5403 **Summer Lodge** *Evershot, Dorchester DT2 0JR (01935) 83424* **£165,** plus special breaks; 17 big, individually decorated rms. Beautifully kept and peacefully set former dower house with lovely flower displays in the comfortable and elegantly furnished day rooms, excellent food using the best local produce in a most attractive restaurant overlooking the pretty garden, delicious breakfasts and afternoon tea, and personal, caring service; outdoor swimming pool, tennis and croquet; dogs by prior arrangement and away from public rms; partial disabled access.

FARNHAM ST9515 **Museum** *Farnham, Blandford Forum DT11 8DE (01725) 516261* **£65;** 4 rms in converted stables. Traditional civilised old country inn in thatch and stone village; with inglenook fireplace and classical music in lounge bar, attractive conservatory, very good food inc excellent breakfasts, and sheltered terrace and garden; cl 25 Dec; disabled access.

FLEET SY6280 **Moonfleet Manor** *Fleet, Weymouth DT3 4ED (01305) 786948* **£130;** 40 rms. Handsome stuccoed Georgian manor with a very relaxed atmosphere, friendly and helpful staff, Edwardian furnishings, log fires and plants, enjoyable food in restaurant and Verandah Bar, lots to do for adults and children, residents' nightclub in Georgian cellars, and lovely countryside; disabled access.

GILLINGHAM ST8026 **Stock Hill** *Wyke, Gillingham SP8 5NR (01747) 823626* ***£240 inc dinner,** plus special breaks; 9 lovely, very comfortable rms. Marvellously relaxing, carefully run Victorian manor house in 11 acres of wooded grounds; with antiques and paintings in opulent day rooms, particularly welcoming service, and excellent food in the no smoking restaurant using home-grown herbs and veg, local meat and fish; all-weather tennis court, croquet; children over 7.

HALSTOCK ST5407 **Halstock Mill** *Halstock, Yeovil BA22 9SJ (01935) 891278* ***£50;** 4 rms. Attractive 17th-c house quietly set in 10 acres with lots of surrounding walks; log fire in cosy beamed lounge, pleasant little dining room, and good food using home-grown fruit and veg, local fish and cheese; stabling; cl Christmas; children over 5.

LODERS SY4994 **Loders Arms** *Loders, Bridport DT6 3SA (01308) 422431* ***£45;** 2 rms. Carefully refurbished pub in pretty village; friendly, unspoilt atmosphere, interesting food in small restaurant, comfortable bar with log fire and a nice mix of customers; good beers and wines, and a skittle alley.

LOWER BOCKHAMPTON SY8290 **Yalbury Cottage** *Lower Bockhampton, Dorchester DT2 8PZ (01305) 262382* **£72,** plus special breaks; 8 rms overlooking garden or fields. Very attractive, family-run 16th-c thatched house with a relaxed, friendly atmosphere; low beams and inglenook fireplaces in the comfortable lounge and dining room; carefully cooked, often imaginative food, good wines.

MILTON ABBAS ST8001 **Hambro Arms** *Milton Abbas, Blandford Forum DT11 0BP (01258) 880233* **£55;** 2 rms. Pretty and popular old inn in beautiful village; with beamed front lounge, log fire, popular food, and prompt, friendly service; children over 14.

POOLE SZ0590 **Inn in the Park** *Pinewood Rd, Branksome Chine, Poole BH13 6JS (01202) 761318* **£42;** 5 comfortable rms. Small friendly hotel well off the tourist track, with nice steep walks down to the sea, lots of pine in the residents' area, attractive dining room, decent small bar specialising in well kept real ales, good-value bar food, and a small sunny terrace.

POOLE SZ0190 **Mansion House** *Thames St, Poole BH15 1JN (01202) 685666* ***£125,** plus special breaks; 28 cosy rms with lots of little extras. Close to waterfront, this civilised old merchant's town house has a lovely sweeping staircase, antiques in the pretty residents' lounge, a cosy cocktail bar, good food in the attractive restaurant, and courteous, old-fashioned service.

SHAFTESBURY ST8622 **Old Rectory** *St James, Shaftesbury SP7 8HG (01747) 853658* ***£62;** 3 rms. Elegant 18th-c house with a friendly informal atmosphere, comfortable sitting room with log fire, very good food and an interesting wine list, a sunny conservatory, and quiet walled garden; cl Christmas.

STURMINSTER NEWTON ST7814 **Plumber Manor** *Hazelbury Bryan Rd, Sturminster Newton DT10 2AF (01258) 472507* **£95,** plus special breaks; 16 very comfortable rms. Handsome 17th-c house in quiet countryside, with tennis and trout stream; warm fires, resident labradors, good uncomplicated food, a relaxed atmosphere, and friendly helpful service; cl Feb; dogs allowed away from public rms; children welcome by prior arrangement; disabled access.

SYDLING ST NICHOLAS SY6399 **Lamperts Cottage** *Sydling St Nicholas, Dorchester DT2 9NU (01300) 341659* ***£40;** 3 little attic rms, shared bthrm. Charming, mainly no smoking 16th-c thatched cottage in unspoilt village; friendly welcome from helpful owner, good breakfasts in a beamed dining room with huge inglenook fireplace and bread oven, and a pretty garden; children over 8.

UPLYME SY3293 **Amherst Lodge Farm** *Uplyme, Lyme Regis DT7 3XH (01297) 442773* ***£50,** plus special breaks. 4 rms. Comfortable long house surrounded by 140 acres of gardens, woodlands, fields and 8 lakes – rod room, coarse and trout fishing; relaxed, friendly country-house atmosphere, oak-panelled lounge with fire, books and magazines, and enjoyable evening meals; self-catering also; cl Christmas; no children.

WAREHAM SU9287 **Priory** *Church Green, Warham BH20 4ND (01929) 551666* **£140,** plus special breaks; 19 very comfortable rms – the best being in the converted boathouse with its own landscaped gardens. Beautifully converted medieval buildings in 4 acres of carefully kept riverside gardens; 2 elegant lounges with antiques (pianist Sat evening), delicious English cooking served in the converted abbot's cellar (exceptional English cheese board), and genuinely welcoming service; disabled access.

WEST BEXINGTON SY5387 **Manor** *West Bexington, Dorchester DT2 9DF (01308) 897616* **£90,** plus special breaks; 13 cottagey rms. Handsome and civilised old stone hotel mentioned in Domesday Book and in a pleasant setting not far from beach; relaxed, informal atmosphere, comfortable lounge, popular pubby cellar bar, log fires, good bar food, excellent restaurant, friendly service.

WIMBORNE MINSTER SZ0199 **Beechleas** *Poole Rd, Wimborne Minster BH21 1QA (01202) 841684* **£89,** plus special breaks; 9 attractive, comfortable rms. Carefully renovated Georgian house with open fires in the cosy sitting room and charming dining room, airy conservatory, enjoyable Aga-cooked food using organic produce, nice breakfasts, and friendly, helpful owners; cl 24 Dec–11 Jan.

YETMINSTER ST5910 **Manor Farmhouse** *High St, Yetminster, Sherborne DT9 6LF (01935) 872247* **£50;** 3 rms. Fine, carefully modernised, no smoking 17th-c building with beams and oak panelling, inglenook fireplaces, helpful owners, and good traditional cooking; no children or dogs; partial disabled access.

To see and do

BOURNEMOUTH SZ0890 Still has something of the 'very salubrious air' that Queen Victoria recommended to Disraeli. Neatly kept streamside gardens in the centre, a pier that's one of the few to look as fresh as when it was built, long promenades below the low cliff, and miles of well organised sandy beach (no dogs in summer, and children's activities then). The best beaches, with water safe for swimming, are at Southbourne and Durley Chine (the Durley is a good seaside dining pub). All this, along with the mild climate and a good local orchestra, has made the town expansively popular both as a civilised place to retire to and as a centre for regular development, so it's a big, busy town surrounded by suburbs, with tall modern buildings and monumental traffic schemes. But down by the sea you're well insulated from all of that. And the western residential suburbs of Westbourne and particularly Branksome Park (it's virtually impossible to tell here when Bournemouth becomes Poole) are quiet, with pinetree valleys winding down to the sea. Butlers Crab & Ale House (Old Christchurch Rd) is useful, and the Moon on the Square (Exeter Rd) is good value.

Oceanarium (Pier Approach, West Beach) An impressive range of fish from around the world at this new aquarium complex, with an emphasis on the environment and conservation. Snacks, shop, disabled access; cl 25 Dec; (01202) 311993; £5.60.

! **Dinosaur Discovery** (Expocentre, Old Christchurch Lane) A family favourite, full of computerised displays, fossils, and bones comparing the prehistoric beasts to more familiar mammals. Shop; (01202) 293544; £2.95. Two other exhibitions in the same building offer a similar mix of fun and education: **Mummies** looks at ancient Egypt and mummification, and the **Dorset Teddy Bear Museum** takes in teddies of all ages, shapes and sizes; times and prices as above.

Shelley Rooms (Boscombe Manor, Beechwood Ave) Small museum devoted to the life and work of the poet, especially the later part of his life. Disabled access; cl am, all Mon, 25–26 Dec, Good Fri; (01202) 303571; free. Shelley's heart is buried beneath the impressive tombstone of Mary Shelley in St Peter's churchyard.

Hengistbury Head SZ1790 By far the best place close to Bournemouth for a stroll: not a long walk, but the feeling of space and views are outstanding.

POOLE SZ0190 Merging indistinguishably into Bournemouth on the edges, its centre is wholly distinct, with a more lively feel, especially around The Quay. The broad natural harbour is still busy with the comings and goings of boats and small ships (several decent pubs to watch them from – the nautical Portsmouth Hoy is best for lunch); launch ferries around the harbour, and out to Brownsea Island. There are interesting old buildings along here; the streets behind, some pedestrianised, are well worth strolling through.

Poole Pottery (The Quay) Distinctive china has been produced here since 1873. Good factory tours, and a museum and film; you can have a go at throwing and decorating your own pot, and even smash up a few plates. Other craft demonstrations too. Restaurant with harbour views (open evenings), shop, disabled access; cl 12.30–1.30pm, 25 Dec, and some winter wknds, phone to check; (01202) 666200; *£3.50.

! Poole Aquarium Complex (Hennings Wharf, The Quay) Busy indoor centre with an enormous 00 gauge model railway as well as the aquarium, also smuggling and space exhibitions, and insectarium. Good for families on rainy days. Meals, snacks, shop; cl 25 Dec; (01202) 686712; *£4.75.

Waterfront Museum (High St) Recent funding cuts have forced this museum to reduce the size of its displays, but there are still 2 floors of well laid out local history. Teas, shop, disabled access; (01202) 683138; cl Nov–Easter; £3.25 (part of the ground floor may be open free in winter). During August a ticket includes entry to next door **Scaplen's Court**, a well restored medieval merchant's home with exhibitions upstairs.

Compton Acres Gardens SZ0589 (Canford Cliffs) Perhaps Poole's outstanding attraction, with lovely statuary among fine plants landscaped in an eclectic variety of styles – the Japanese garden is the foremost in Europe. Good views of the hills and Poole harbour. Sat is the least busy day to visit. Meals, snacks (decent crêperie), shop and plant sales, disabled access; cl Nov–Feb; (01202) 700778; £4.75. The Nightjar has decent food.

Splashdown SZ0494 (Tower Park, 2m NE on the A3049) Good for children, a water park with 11 rides and slides (indoor and out), inc a near-vertical drop in total darkness. Snacks; cl from 2pm winter wkdys (in peak periods they may have limits on how long you can stay); (01202) 716123; £5.50.

Chain ferry From Sandbanks, by the harbour mouth, to the Studland side – a spectacular entrance to Dorset proper; it's quickest to go as a foot passenger or by bus (they have priority). The beach at Sandbanks is regularly lauded as one of the best in Britain.

BROWNSEA ISLAND SZ0287 Unspoilt 500-acre island in the middle of the huge natural harbour, famous as the site of the first scout camp in 1907. Lots of birds (inc peacocks), animals and butterflies in heath and woodland (you may spot red squirrels), large heronry, nature reserve, and fine views back towards the coast from its beaches. It's a really splendid place to explore. Guided walks 2.45pm daily in July and Aug, and from mid-July to mid-Aug may be open-air Shakespeare or opera. Snacks, shop, disabled access; cl Oct–Mar; (01202) 707870; £2.40; NT. Ferries to the island run every half hour from Poole Harbour (£3.80 return, takes half an hour) or Sandbanks (£2.50 return, only takes 6 minutes); don't forget to check the time of the last one back.

CHRISTCHURCH SZ1592 At the 'Hampshire' end of the Bournemouth complex, with attractive Georgian brick buildings in its old centre, a restored watermill, and a quay looking out over the yachting harbour, busy in summer. Hengistbury Head overlooking the harbour and reached from the Bournemouth side is a popular place for strollers, with traces of an Iron Age hill fort (good beach here too). On the other side of the harbour mouth, long beaches stretch way into Hampshire from the vast Mudeford car park (the Haven House by the sea here is well worth knowing for its unrivalled position, and there's an excellent fishmonger nearby). Pleasant walking out of season.

Christchurch Priory Magnificent medieval monastic church, at well over 90 metres (300ft) the longest parish church in the country; very striking inside, with remarkable carving. The 'Miraculous Beam' apparently fitted in the roof only with divine assistance, so prompting the renaming of the borough to Christchurch (it used to be called Twynham). Free recitals most Thurs lunchtimes. Shop, snacks on recital days; disabled access; £1 suggested donation. The church has a small museum open in the summer, and good views from the tower (50p) – though with 176 spiral steps you have to earn them.

Christchurch Castle All that remains is a ruined keep, and the ruins of the Norman house probably used by the castle constable. It's quite well preserved, with one of the earliest chimneys in the country, and an ancient midden by a millstream; free.

Red House Museum & Gardens (Quay Rd) Georgian house with local history, dolls and costumes, and walled herb garden. Shop, disabled access to ground floor only; cl am Sun, Mon (exc bank hols), Christmas wk; (01202) 482860; £1.

! Big Top Jousting (Arena, Stony Lane) A good distraction for children (especially in poor weather), a lively 2-hour spectacle, under cover, with mock jousting. On tournament mornings you can usually visit the horses in their stables. Shows at 3pm daily July and Aug, and 7.30pm Thurs and other dates May, Jun and Sept, best to ring; (01202) 483777; £6.

WEYMOUTH SY6878 Elegant 18th- and 19th-c terraces along its curving esplanade, and some older buildings in the narrower, partly pedestrianised streets behind. The harbour is lively, with big ferries leaving from the outer quay, and the town's inner ring road running one-way around the inner harbour. The Old Rooms has good-value food and interesting harbour views. On the far side of the harbour the narrow streets of the old town are worth exploring; there's a **Tudor house** on Trinity St. The resort has a good beach, and lots of lively family attractions.

Sea Life Park SY6880 (Lodsmoor Country Park) One of the most elaborate in the excellent Sea Life Centres chain. Stunning marine displays and touch pools, also a Shark Academy, with fun interactive games and quizzes leading to a scholarship, and a splendid outdoor play area. Meals, snacks, shop, disabled access; cl 25 Dec; (01305) 788255; £5.95.

! Deep Sea Adventure (Custom House Quay) Fascinating look at underwater exploration, shipwrecks, and the search for buried treasure, with lots of interactive displays. There's an exemplary exhibition on the *Titanic*, and a first-class indoor play area taking up most of the second floor (extra charge). Meals, snacks, shop, disabled access; cl 24–26 Dec; (01305) 760690; £3.50

Brewers Quay In the heart of the Old Harbour, this is a skilful conversion of harbourside Victorian brewery into shopping and leisure complex, with plenty of good year-round activities: the **Timewalk** imaginatively re-creates scenes from the town's history (limited disabled access), there's a craft market, ten-pin bowling, lively hands-on science centre, even a microbrewery – so the building has come full circle. Several places to eat, and good specialist shops; cl 25–27 Dec, and a couple of wks late Jan; (01305) 777622; centre free, charges for some attractions.

Nothe Fort (Barrack Rd) Interesting armed Victorian fort on 3 levels, spread over a staggering 70 rooms. Children can clamber over some of the vehicles and guns, and there are fine views of the harbour and coast. Snacks, shop, disabled access; open daily mid-May–Sept, Easter hols and Oct half-term, plus pm Sun and bank hols rest of year; (01305) 787243; *£3. Good views too from the garden of the Nothe Tavern (tasty fresh fish), and the pleasant nearby Nothe Gardens.

DORCHESTER SY6990 Thriving country town, with busy shopping streets and Weds market, and several worthwhile antique and print shops. Though most of the more attractive Georgian buildings are just out of the bustle, there are a few distinguished buildings on the main streets, inc the timbered building of **Judge Jeffreys' Lodgings** in High West St; he stayed here during his notorious Bloody Assizes. The trial of the Tolpuddle Martyrs also took place on High West St, in the **Shire Hall**; the room is preserved as a memorial, and is open wkdys in summer hols, as are some of the cells. There are one or two traces of the Romans' occupation, including the fragmentary remains of a town house behind the County Hall, and of an amphitheatre on Weymouth Ave. Not far from here **Eldridge Pope's Victorian Brewery** has tours at 11am and 1pm on summer Weds, or you may be able to join a pre-booked tour at other times; (01305) 251251 to check.

Thomas Hardy lived here for most of his life, using the town as the centre of events in *The Mayor of Casterbridge* (the eponymous mayor supposedly living in what's now Barclays Bank). Among the places still associated with the author is **Max Gate** (Alington Ave, 1m E on the A351), the house he designed and lived in from 1885 to his death in 1928, and where he wrote *Tess* and *Jude the Obscure*. You can see only the drawing room (the study has been moved to the County Museum), but the gardens are fascinating, not least because they inspired so much of Hardy's poetry. Shop, disabled access; open pm Sun, Mon and Weds Apr–Sept; (01305) 262538; £2.10; NT. The Trumpet Major food pub is very handy.

Hardy's Cottage SY7292 (Higher Bockhampton, just off the A35, 3m E) The writer's 1840 birthplace is just outside town; the thatched house hasn't changed much since; cl Fri and Sat and all Nov–Mar; (01305) 262366; £2.50; NT. The surrounding heath is now largely forested. You can walk into the plantations, and just SE of the cottage are stretches of open heathland, much as Hardy knew it, on Black Heath and Duddle Heath, parts of the 'untamed and untameable' Egdon Heath of his novels. A path leads to the river at Lower Bockhampton, and a nature trail leads from the cottage to Thorncombe Wood.

County Museum (High West St) Hardy's study from Max Gate has been reconstructed here, and there's a display on his namesake, Nelson's flag-captain at the Battle of Trafalgar. Quite a traditional museum, though very comprehensive. Shop, disabled access to ground floor only; cl Sun (exc July and Aug), 25–26 Dec, Good Fri; (01305) 262735; £3. Along in High East St the King's Arms Hotel, full of Hardy associations, is a good place for lunch.

! **Dinosaur Museum** (Icen Way) The best of Dorset's dinosaur-related exhibitions, a well displayed and entertaining collection very much designed with younger visitors in mind. Although it is quite small there are full-size skeletons and reconstructions, lots of opportunities to handle bones, fossils and the like (not many exhibits have barriers), and fun activities like Dinosaurs and You, where you put in your height and weight and the computer works out how you compare with a couple of dinosaurs. Look out for the intriguing Dinosaurid – a Canadian expert's idea of what dinosaurs would have evolved into if they hadn't become extinct. Shop, some disabled access; cl 24–26 Dec; (01305) 269880; £3.50 (£2.25 children). A similar approach is found at the **Tutankhamun Exhibition** (High West St), re-creating the discovery of ancient treasures using a mix of sights, sounds and smells; details as Dinosaur Museum.

Keep Military Museum (Bridport Rd) More interesting than most military museums, in handsome Victorian barracks gatehouse; splendid views from the battlements. Shop, disabled access; cl Sun, 24 Dec–2 Jan; (01305) 264066; £2.50.

Maiden Castle SY6889 (off the A354, S of Dorchester) One of the best examples of an Iron Age fort, a massive series of grassy ridges covering 47 acres. It's so vast that the tour of its grassy ramparts almost qualifies as a fully fledged walk.

Other things to see and do

DORSET Family Attraction of the Year

! Abbotsbury Swannery SY5982 For over 600 years this sheltered spot has been home to a colony of friendly mute swans, and it's the only place in the world where you can see such a group nesting. With up to a thousand swans around it can be an amazing spectacle, particularly from late May through to the end of June, when the cygnets are hatching. Hundreds of the fluffy little creatures cover the paths and waterways then, and rather than look at them from a distance you're right in the thick of the action, with eggs hatching immediately beside you. There's plenty going on at other times of the year too: from the summer until the early autumn the cygnets develop into the feathered equivalent of a gawky adolescent, at the end of this period clumsily making their first attempts to fly. And from late March to the end of April the swans choose the best sites for their nests, ready for the whole process to begin again. An audio-visual show fills in the gaps. All year there are mass feedings of the herd at noon and 4pm; they sometimes choose a visitor to help, and it can be rather dramatic – certainly a far cry from the average trip to feed the swans. The swan herd may also let children touch some of the cygnets. There are a few displays along the way, with an ugly duckling trail to keep younger children amused, and interesting reed-bed walks; also the country's oldest duck decoy. Note that the lavatories are at the entrance to the car park, rather than in the swannery itself. A visit here typically lasts about 1½ hours, though if you combine it with the other attractions in the village, it's easy enough to spend a whole day around Abbotsbury. Sunny weather adds considerably to the experience (and the views). Children love it when the swans come right up to them. Obviously dogs aren't allowed. Restaurant (reached by a little bridge), shop, good disabled access; cl Nov–Feb; (01305) 871684; £4.80 (children aged 5–15 £2.50). A family ticket (2 adults, 2 children) is £12.50.

ABBOTSBURY SY5982 Delightful Dorset village with several worthwhile places to visit. *See separate Family Panel above* for **Swannery. Subtropical Gardens** 20 acres of beautiful woodland with the very mild coastal climate letting rare and record-breaking plants and trees flourish; they claim the tallest cultivated rose in the world. The central walled garden in spring is a mass of azaleas, camellias and rhododendrons. Also woodland trail, aviary and play area. Meals, snacks, shop and plant centre, some disabled access; cl 25–26 Dec; (01305) 871387; £4.20 summer, less in winter. The 14th-c hilltop **chapel** (not always open), with a bare earth floor, belonged to the abbey, of which there are a few medieval fragments around the church. A huge medieval thatched **tithe barn** now houses a friendly children's farm and a display of Chinese terracotta warriors. Shop, disabled access; (01305) 871817; £3.50. After visiting one of Abbotsbury's attractions you get discounts on the others. The village also has an **oyster farm** (cl am winter), and the Ilchester Arms is good for lunch. Abbotsbury is the start for strolls around Chapel Hill and on to the massive shingle bank of Chesil Beach (exhausting to walk any distance along). Paths leading N give lovely views from the chalk downs, as does the B3157 W.

ARNE SY9788 Relatively undiscovered village with a good toy museum, quiet beach and nature trail.

ASHLEY HEATH SU1006 **Moors Valley Country Park** Good for families, nearly 400 hectares of forest, with river and lakeside walks, fishing, nature trails, plenty of wildlife, narrow-gauge steam railway, unusual treetop walkway, and 18-hole golf course. Meals, snacks, shop, disabled access; cl 25 Dec; (01425) 470721; £3.50 car parking charge (£1.50 after 4pm), free winter wkdys (£1.50 wknds then).

ATHELHAMPTON HOUSE SY7794 (A35) Magnificent 15th-c house, built on the legendary site of King Athelstan's palace. The great hall has a fantastic roof. You'd never know now there was a disastrous fire here in 1993 – most of the beautiful furnishings and contents (even much of the panelling) were saved, and are back in their original positions. Acres of wonderful formal and landscaped gardens with rare plants, topiary and fountain pools. Meals, snacks, shop, disabled access; open daily (exc Sat) Mar–Oct, Sun only Nov–Feb; (01305) 848363; *£4.90 house and gardens, £3 garden only. The Martyrs at Tolpuddle has good home cooking.

BEAMINSTER ST4700 **Parnham** (A3066 towards Bridport) Surrounded by 14 acres of lovely gardens, this fine Tudor mansion is famous as the home of John Makepeace, the furniture-maker. His workshop is open, with completed pieces shown around the house, along with exhibitions by other craftsmen. The mix of modern furniture with period rooms is refreshingly different. Also formal gardens and play area. Meals, snacks, shop, mostly disabled access; open Apr–Oct, Sun, Tues–Thurs, and bank hols; (01308) 862204; *£4. The nearby woods of Hooke Park are pleasant for a stroll; you can get a combined ticket with the house. **Mapperton Gardens** SY5199 (off the B3163 E,) Several delightful acres of terraced hillside gardens in the grounds of a 16th-c manor house; specimen trees and shrubs, fountains, grottoes, fishponds, orangery, good walks and views. Occasional musical events in summer. Shop, some disabled access; cl am, and all Nov–Feb; (01308) 862645; *£3. **Horn Park** ST4602 (A3066 N) Unusual plants in series of gardens with bluebell woods, ponds, wild flowers and good views. They've begun work on an arboretum. Teas, plant sales, some disabled access; open pm Sun–Thurs Apr–Oct; (01308) 862212; *£3. In Beaminster, the Greyhound has decent food.

BERE WOOD SY8794 At the W end of Bloxworth, this fine bluebell wood is at its best in May; the track can be followed right through to Bere Regis.

† **BERE REGIS** SY8494 The **Church** here has the finest timbered roof in Dorset, with extraordinary carved figures; 20p in a slot lights these up to remarkable effect. It also contains the Turberville tomb and window mentioned in *Tess of the d'Urbervilles*. The Drax Arms is good value for lunch.

★ **BLANDFORD FORUM** ST8806 Georgian market town, rebuilt in 1731 after the older buildings were destroyed by fire – very interesting to walk round. **Mrs Penny's Cavalcade of Costume** (The Plocks) Wide-ranging collection of clothes in Georgian Lime Tree House; children can try on copies of some of the exhibits. Snacks, shop, limited disabled access; cl Tues, Weds; (01258) 450388; £3. The Greyhound has a popular restaurant, and Nelson's has decent food. Out at Blandford Camp the lively **Royal Signals Museum** looks at the history of army communications, with a new exhibition for children on codes and code breaking (cl wknds exc May–Sept; £3).

! † **BOVINGTON CAMP** SY8288 **Tank Museum** Over 260

Days Out

Monkey business: Monkey World, Wool; lunch at the Countryman, East Knighton; Bovington Camp Tank Museum – or walk from Lulworth Cove.

Fossils and Forde Abbey: Boat trip from Lyme Regis; lunch at the Pilot Boat there; Forde Abbey, Thorncombe.

Poole and its unique island: Poole, Compton Acres Gardens; lunch at Portsmouth Hoy; boat trip to Brownsea Island; Sandbanks beach.

armoured fighting vehicles from 23 countries, some of which you can go inside, as well as tank simulators (the screen can be a bit fuzzy), costumes, medals, weapons and videos. Many of the tanks are put through their paces, complete with gunfire (12 noon Thurs July–Sept); there may be armoured vehicle rides on summer wknds, and their Battle Day, the last Sun in July, is quite a spectacle. There's an exhibition on Lawrence of Arabia, and an assault course for children. Meals, snacks, shop, disabled access; cl Christmas wk; (01929) 405096; £6. A mile or so up the road **Clouds Hill** is where Lawrence lived as a private in the tank corps, and his sleeping-bag, furniture and other memorabilia can be seen in the 3 ascetic little rooms on display. Open pm Weds, Thurs, Fri, Sun and bank hols Apr–Oct; £2.30; NT. The very child-friendly Countryman at East Knighton has good food, and the church windows over at Moreton are spectacular.

BRADFORD PEVERELL SY7191 **New Barn Field Centre** Authentic re-creation of Iron Age homestead, complete with animals and so on; also a working potter, wildflower reserve and nature trails. Summer meals and snacks, shop, some disabled access; cl Oct–Easter; (01305) 268865; £3.50.

BRIDPORT SY4692 Still the country's main rope producer, and its old harbour is now the busy fishing port of nearby West Bay, a restrained small resort (where the West Bay Hotel has good local seafood). **The Harbour Museum** (Salt House, West Bay) has rope- and net-making displays, with free activity sheets for chidren (cl Nov–mid-May; £1).

BROADWINDSOR ST4302 **Good craft and design centre** in former farm buildings; woodworkers, hatters, painters and so forth. Meals, snacks, shop, disabled access; cl 23 Dec–1 Mar; (01308) 868362; free. The B3164 W to Birdsmoorgate and then the B3165 through Marshwood (good country pub) is an unspoilt scenic drive through a little-known valley.

BULBARROW HILL ST7705 Memorable viewpoint on the narrow lanes just S of Woolland, especially on a summer evening with the sun going down over Somerset. Around here, a scenic drive runs from Piddletrenthide through Plush (the Brace of Pheasants is a very good lunchtime stop) and Mappowder to Hazelbury Bryan, then through Ansty and Melcombe Bingham, to turn right at Cheselbourne for Piddletrenthide again.

★ **CERNE ABBAS** ST6701 Attractive village with a fine church, fragments of the old abbey, a remarkable collection of good pubs (the Red Lion and Royal Oak are the best), and its famously indelicate prehistoric giant cut into the chalk above, best seen from the main road N. The National Trust took a dim view when he acquired a £40,000 pair of plastic blue jeans one night in May 1998 as a publicity stunt for a new range of jeans. There's a working **pottery** (cl winter Mons) on the way up to the giant; above it, the old Dorchester–Middlemarsh ridge road has some bracing views.

CHETTLE HOUSE ST9513 Fine baroque country house, with beautifully laid out gardens, vineyard and gallery; various craft wknds and special events. Snacks, disabled access to garden; cl Tues, Sat, and mid-Oct–Easter; (01258) 830209; *£2.50. The Bugle Horn at Tarrant Gunville is handy for lunch.

CHICKERELL SY6580 **Bennetts Water Gardens** (Putton Lane) Eight acres of landscaped lakes renowned for their summer water lilies – over 100 varieties; also a new museum covering local history and the gardens and Chickerell brickworks. Home-made teas, shop, disabled access; open Tues-Fri Apr–Oct, plus Sats Apr–Sept, and Suns Apr–Aug; (01305) 785150; £3.95.

★ **CORFE CASTLE** SY9681 The **castle** is the most spectacular ruin in the area, and gives superb views from its dramatic hilltop position. The site is remarkably atmospheric considering how little of the castle is left, and it's great fun clambering over the ancient stones. Meals, snacks, shop; cl 25–26 Dec; (01929) 481294; £3.80; NT. **Model Village** Set in attractive gardens, with a

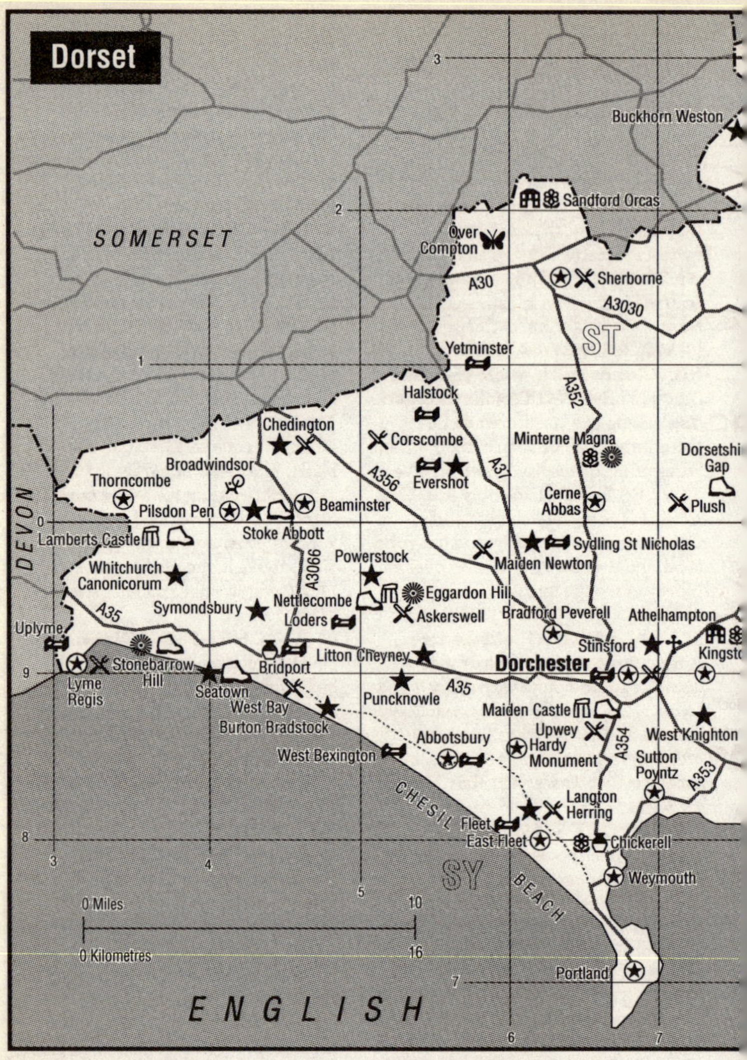

faithful reconstruction of what the Norman castle looked like before the Parliamentarians destroyed it in 1646; cl Oct–Easter; (01929) 481234; *£2. The Swanage Railway (*see entry below*) now runs to here; a joint ticket is available. A Tudor building on West St has a decent local history **museum**, with dinosaur footprints; cl wkdys Nov–Mar; free. Parking can be a problem in this attractive ancient small town in summer. The Halfway at Norden Heath (on the A351 towards Wareham) has good food. The road W through Church Knowle is pretty.

❀ **CRANBORNE** SU0513 A peaceful place, with the Fleur-de-Lys a good pub well known to Hardy and the subject of an entertaining poem by Rupert Brooke (framed inside). **Cranborne Manor Gardens** Splendid 17th-c gardens originally laid out by Tradescant; Jacobean mount garden, herb garden, lovely river garden and avenues of beech and lime. Particularly attractive in spring. Snacks, shop and garden centre,

disabled access; gardens open Weds only Mar–Sept, garden centre daily all year; (01725) 517248; *£3. The B3078 has good country views, as does the minor road crossing it to Three Legged Cross and the Gussages.

CRANBORNE CHASE ST9116 Shared between Dorset and Wilts, with good walking and some fine views, especially around Ashmore.

DELCOMBE WOOD ST7805 A lovely bluebell wood, sheets of colour in May; the public track just skirts the W edge of the wood.

DORSETSHIRE GAP ST7403 The downland W of Binghams Melcombe is attractive for walkers; the dry ground of the Gap comes as a pleasant surprise on those days when it seems as if all Dorset is turning to chalky mud. Despite the ultra-English charm of much of inland Dorset – chalk downs, sleepy thatched villages, clumps of beechwoods and fine views – the area is surprisingly little walked, so field routes are often not obvious, careful map-reading is necessary, and even then sometimes the longer paths can be difficult to follow.

EAST FLEET SY6380 Interesting, particularly for the tiny ruined church which was wrecked by a legendary 1824 storm. Swans nest nearby on the great lagoon, enclosed by Chesil Beach, which was used for trying out the World War II dam-busting bouncing bomb; now a peaceful spot, with lots of other birds too. The vicinity's pleasant walks are especially interesting if you've read J M Faulkner's *Moonfleet*. The Elm Tree at Langton Herring is handy for lunch.

EDMONDSHAM SU0611 **Dorset Heavy Horse Centre** (well signed from Verwood) Cheery place with 5 different breeds of huge heavy horse, and miniature Shetland ponies at the other extreme as well as llamas, miniature donkeys and pygmy goats. Snacks, shop, disabled access; (01202) 824040; £3.95, may be less out of season. For an extra £12 an hour you can go for a tolt on an Icelandic horse (the tolt is said to be the most comfortable gait of all). The Albion is handy for lunch.

EGGARDON HILL SY5494 Iron Age hill fort with wonderful views and impressive ramparts.

HAMBLEDON HILL ST8412 Formidable Iron Age hill fort in a commanding position just above Child Okeford.

HARDY MONUMENT SY6187 As hideous as it is prominent, this commemorates Nelson's admiral, not the Dorset author. This high heathland above Portesham (where the King's Arms has decent food) gives walkers views over the entire sweep of the Dorset coast. A track along Bronkham Hill SE from the car park feels truly ancient, with prehistoric burial mounds flanking it. If you don't feel like leaving the car, the Black Down road passing the Monument towards Martinstown also gives fine views.

★ **HINTON ST MARY** ST7816 Attractive village with a superb manor house and striking medieval tithe barn.

! **HURN** SZ1197 **Alice in Wonderland Maze** (opposite Bournemouth Airport) Enthusiastic place with a maze made up of 5,200 bushes cut into shape of Alice characters; also play areas, croquet lawns, herb gardens, theatre, a few rides, farmyard with rare breeds, and pick-your-own fields with berries, beans, potatoes, courgettes and sweetcorn. Lots of thought and effort have been put into the site. Meals, snacks, shop, some disabled access; open Easter–Oct (wknds only from mid-Sept); (01202) 483444; £3.75. The Avon Causeway Hotel does decent food.

KIMMERIDGE BAY SY9179 A lovely spot with intriguing rock strata, kept quieter than it might be by the toll. The New Inn up at Church Knowle is good for lunch.

KINGSTON SY9579 From here there's an easy level path to **Hounstout Cliff**; fortify yourself beforehand at the Scott Arms, a good family pub with superb views of Corfe Castle. Turn left at the end and you are into Dorset fossil country, presided over by the primitive hermitage chapel on St Aldhelm's Head; the path here is of the switchback sort, and the chalk mud can make it tough going in wet seasons.

KINGSTON MAURWARD PARK SY7191 Very close to Dorchester, but feeling like the heart of the countryside, with peaceful woodland and lakeside walks, visitor centre, farm park (children can feed the animals), and plenty of garden variety inc Elizabethan and Edwardian gardens, Penstemon and Salvia national collections. Snacks, shop, some disabled access; cl Nov–Easter; (01305) 215000; £3.

LAMBERTS CASTLE SY3799 This unspoiled **hill fort** is charming for strolls, especially in late summer when the heather is out; it's quite hard to spot the turning from the road.

★ **LYME REGIS** SY3492 Charming old seaside town, with rather an elegant, steep main street, interesting side streets, sheltered esplanade and lively little fishing and yacht harbour. The town gets very busy in summer, but it is worth braving the crowds. The sea has been cleaned up by a new sewage treatment plant, tempting some quite varied animals to make the occasional visit. A coast path snakes W through an intriguing nature-reserve undercliff, still subject to landfalls; this is a celebrated area for fossils and flora (several shops sell fossils, with show collections too). There are pleasant walks in the valley. The Pilot Boat on the front is the best place for lunch; the enjoyable old Royal Standard has a lit terrace by the beach. **Dinosaurland** (Coombe St) An excellent collection of fossils, and they can tell you about any you may have at home. They do 2-hour fossil walks along the beach. Shop; cl 25–26 Dec; (01297) 443541; £3.20, guided beach walks £4.50 (booking recommended). **Marine Aquarium** (The Cobb) Decent family-run aquarium right on the historic harbour wall, with local history exhibits too; disabled access; cl Nov–Easter; (01297) 443678; £1.30. The Jane Austen cliffside gardens (partly cl during 1998 after a landslip as yet unstabilised) have peaceful sea views.

MILTON ABBAS ST8001 Lovely thatched village built in the 18th c to replace an earlier one which had spoilt the view from the big house; the 17th-c almshouses were moved here at the same time. Pleasant stroll past the lake through the Capability Brown park to the fine 15th-c **abbey church** of a former Benedictine monastery (it now serves the public school in the nearby house). There's an attractive signed walk over the lane to a former chapel in the wood. Another pleasant walk through the abbey estate leads into **Green Hill Down Nature Reserve**, and a longer walk continues NW to **Bulbarrow Hill** (*see entry above*), which looks far into Somerset and Wilts. **Rare Poultry, Pig and Plant Centre** (Long Ash Farm, just W on the Ansty rd) 10 breeds of pig and piglets, all sorts of unusual poultry inc hens laying eggs in dazzling blues and browns, baby chicks to touch, and local crafts. Snacks, shop, limited disabled access; cl Mon–Weds (exc bank hols), and Oct–Easter (exc Sun); (01258) 880447; £2. The road through the pretty Winterbornes to Okeford Fitzpaine has good downland views.

MINTERNE MAGNA ST6604 **Minterne Gardens** (Minterne House, A352) Beautiful landscaped gardens, with lakes, cascades, streams, rare trees and impressive spring shows of azaleas, rhododendrons and spring bulbs; the autumn colours can be quite spectacular. Open April–Oct; (01300) 341370; £3. The road W up Gore Hill and Batcombe Hill to Holywell has memorable views.

NETTLECOMBE SY5295 This sleepy village is in charming walking country, little touched by agricultural improvement – delectable downland and valley landscapes, with a reasonably good path network – and a good pub.

NINE BARROW DOWN SY9982 The main Purbeck ridge, this has far-ranging two-way views – good from a car, and also a good goal for walks from Corfe Castle.

OVER COMPTON ST5916 **Worldlife and Lullingstone Silk Farm** Superb collection of butterflies, flying free in reconstructions of their natural habitat inside Elizabethan Compton Hall. The silk farm demonstrates production of English silk used for coronations and royal weddings. Snacks, shop, some disabled access; cl Sat and all Oct–Mar; (01935) 474608; £3.95.

OWERMOIGNE SY7685 **Mill House Cider Museum** 18th- and 19th-c equipment, and video demonstrating the process. Also collection of locally made 18th- and 19th-c clocks. Shop with local ciders; cl Dec 25–mid-Jan; (01305) 852220; £1.50 cider museum, £2 clocks, £2.90 both. The beautifully placed Sailors Return at East Chaldon is good value for lunch.

PILSDON PEN ST4101 Ideal for those who want a rewarding view in a very short stroll – Dorset's highest point, capped by a **hill fort**, and looking over Lyme Bay and N towards the Mendips. Reached within minutes from the layby.

PORTLAND SY6973 This odd, much-quarried promontory with its narrow neck and long naval connections gives tremendous views from its peak. Nearer at hand, the remarkable sea defences of Portland Harbour laid out below are a fine sight – and you may glimpse Britain's first prison ship for generations moored off here. The **castle** was built under Henry VIII to defend the south coast. New audio tour, snacks, shop, limited disabled access; cl Nov–Mar; (01305) 820539; £2.30. From the car park you may be able to watch helicopters landing and taking off from the naval base next door. A cottage used by Hardy in *The Well-Beloved* (Wakeham St) is now a local history **museum**, founded by Dr Marie Stopes, the birth control pioneer (cl 1–1.30pm, all Weds and Thurs, and all Nov-Mar; (01305) 821804; £1.65). The Pulpit, handy for a stroll to the lighthouse and cliffs, is useful for lunch.

SANDFORD ORCAS ST6221 **Manor House** Interesting, lived-in Tudor manor house, largely unaltered since the 16th c, with fine furnishings and family portraits, and pleasant gardens, at their best May and Jun. Open Easter Mon, then pm Sun and all Mon May–Sept; (01963) 220206; *£2.50. The Queen's Arms at Corton Denham has decent food.

★ **SEATOWN** SY4291 This seaside hamlet has some charming stone cottages and a perfectly placed seaside pub. There's a steep walk up to the **Golden Cap**, the highest point on the county's coast, and another good walk along to the New Inn at Eype. Just inland, the village of Chideock is pretty – or would be, if it wasn't sadly ripped in half by the busy A35.

★ **SHAFTESBURY** ST8623 Hilltop town with good views from Castle Hill and Park Walk; there are several craft shops and workshops. The most famous street is Gold Hill – thatched cottages stepped down a steep cobbled street, familiar from those Hovis TV advertisments. At the bottom, St James (where the Two Brewers is the town's best family food pub) is attractive. You can still see the foundations of the **abbey** set up by Alfred the Great; excavated remains from the site can be seen at an adjacent, newly refurbished **museum**, along with an Anglo-Saxon herb garden. Shop, disabled access; cl Nov–Easter; (01747) 852910; £1. At the top of Gold Hill the **local history museum** includes a mummified cat found during the rethatching of a local cottage, an 18th-c fire engine and a collection of old farm implements. Shop, disabled access to ground floor only; cl Oct–Easter; (01747) 852157; £1.

★ **SHERBORNE** ST6316 An attractive town to wander through, given a feeling of unchanging solidity by the handsome stone medieval abbey buildings that mix in with later ones of the public school here, and by many other fine old buildings in and near the main street. The **abbey** itself is a glorious golden stone building with a beautifully vaulted nave; at the Dissolution the townspeople raised the money to buy it, and it's been the parish church ever since. Locals remain very much involved in its fortunes, recently winning their campaign to rid the church of a 19th-c stained-glass window by Pugin, in which Old Testament prophets were said to resemble Mr Blobby. **Sherborne Castle** (just E) Striking old house built by Sir Walter Raleigh in 1594, standing out particularly for its wonderful period furnishings, though there are also interesting paintings and porcelain. Outside are gardens designed by Capability Brown, and beautiful parkland with an enormous lake. Snacks, shop; open pm Thurs, Sat, Sun, and bank hols Easter–Oct; (01935) 813182; £4.80 house and gardens, £2.40 grounds only. Directly across the water **Sherborne Old Castle** is the original 12th-c castle, now a beautifully evocative ruin. Good for a picnic, and especially appealing in Apr when the dry ditch is full of wild primroses. Shop, disabled access (but no facilities); cl 1–2pm, winter Mon and Tues, 24–26 Dec; (01935) 812730; £1.60. **Sherborne Museum** (Abbeygate House, Church Ave) An eclectic collection includes a reconstruction of the old castle in its heyday, as well as a Victorian dolls' house and Roman remains. Shop, disabled access to ground floor only; cl am Sun, Mon (exc bank hols), and Nov–Easter; (01935) 812252; £1. The unspoilt Digby Tap (handy for the abbey but no food Sun) and Skippers (Horsecastles) are useful for lunch. Several craft shops include a working saddlery in the main street.

STAPEHILL ABBEY SU0500 Just right for a relaxed, unhurried afternoon, a 19th-c Cistercian abbey (the nuns moved out in 1989, although the chapel has been preserved) now houses craft workshops and exhibitions on monastic life; acres of park and landscaped gardens with waterfalls and woodland walk, and a play area and farm animals for children. Meals, snacks, shop, disabled access; cl Mon and Tues Oct–Easter, Christmas and all Jan; (01202) 873060; £4.80 (less in winter). **Knoll Gardens** (Stapehill Rd) Rare and exotic plants in various colourfully themed gardens, with over 4,000 different named species, many of which can be bought in the rapidly developing nursery. Meals, snacks, shop and garden centre, disabled access; cl Jan, Feb, and Mon and Tues in Mar; (01202) 873931; £3.40. Adjacent Trehane Nurseries have a great range of camellias. The Barley Mow at Colehill is a good food pub.

★ **STINSFORD** SY7191 On the Thomas Hardy trail: he featured the village as *Mellstock*, and at the church his heart is buried beside the body of his first wife.

★ **STOKE ABBOTT** ST4500 With thatched houses, a good deal of charm, and a pleasant pub, this offers walkers attractive and undisturbed surrounding countryside, with a reasonably good path network.

STONEBARROW HILL SY3893 Reached by a steep narrow road just E of Charmouth, this has good easy walking, fine sea and inland views, a disabled WC, and NT shop in season.

STUBHAMPTON ST9214 The bridleway along Ashmore Bottom to Ashmore is well worth exploring; can be muddy in a wet spring.

STUDLAND SZ0482 The most remarkably varied short walk in Dorset. In a couple of hours you can take in Ballard Down (huge views over Poole Harbour), Old Harry Rocks (tooth-like chalk pinnacles detached from the cliff) and the Agglestone (a rock standing solitary on Dorset's largest surviving heath). The **beach** is lovely – there's a charge to go on it in summer (less after 2pm), when 2 areas are set aside for dog owners and car parking is expensive exc for NT members; behind is a nature reserve, with a NT visitor centre with snacks and shop nearby, and decent food at the Manor House Hotel (where Churchill and Eisenhower watched D-Day rehearsals).

★ **SUTTON POYNTZ** SY7083 This attractive thatched village, with a decent pub, has a good path to the nearby village of Osmington (also thatched, pretty and with a good pub). The path gives views of the **White Horse** – an equestrian portrait of George III etched into the hillside. You can walk back along the Dorset coastal path, which here leads along the top of the downs rather than along the coast itself.

SWANAGE SZ0278 Fairly quiet 19th-c resort, which, for reasons hotly disputed by locals, seems to be losing much of the sand from the northern end of its beaches. **Swanage Railway** Steamtrains run 6 miles to Corfe Castle (a joint ticket is available): a nice way of approaching the ruins – or you could walk there and ride back. The Swanage station has an exhibition of old railway memorabilia, and, more unusually, a travel agency where the commission goes to the railway's upkeep. (Parking is easier at the Norden end of the line.) Snacks, shop, disabled access; cl winter wkdys exc school hols, best to ring for timetable; (01929) 425800 for train times; £6. The seaview Mowlem Theatre restaurant (Shire Rd) is good. On the edge of Swanage **Durlston Country Park** has spectacular clifftop scenery and unspoilt countryside, with good views from the headland, the **Great Globe** (a 40-ton global representation in Purbeck marble), and good spots to watch seabirds, butterflies or deer (let them know if you see dolphins, seals or whales). Snacks, shop, good disabled access (they have a little buggy for bumpy ground); information centre cl wkdys Nov–Mar; (01929) 424443; free, but a parking charge of around £2 in summer (less in winter).

TARRANT KEYNSTON ST9104 **Keynston Mill Fruit Farm** Interesting vineyard and farm shop, with 21 different kinds of pick-your-own. Meals and snacks; cl winter Mon, wkdys Jan–Mar: (01258) 452596; free. The True Lovers Knot has decent food and a big garden.

THORNCOMBE ST3504 **Forde Abbey** The extensive gardens here really are special, with glorious trees and shrubs, a fine collection of Asiatic primulas, many interesting plants, and sweeping lawns. The striking abbey buildings still retain some of the features of the original 12th-c Cistercian monastery, but it was modernised in 1500 by Abbot Chard, and it's his Great Hall and Tower that remain. Cromwell's Attorney-General later turned the abbey into a house, and the interior has changed little since, with magnificently furnished rooms, unusual plaster ceilings and a set of Raphael tapestries. Meals and snacks (in 12th-c undercroft), shop, disabled access to gardens only; house open pm Weds, Sun and bank hols Apr–Oct, garden and nursery all year; (01460) 220231; £5, £3.75 garden only. Thorncombe Wood is awash with bluebells in spring. The George over at Chardstock is the closest good place for lunch.

TOLPUDDLE SY7894 Famous for the agricultural workers who were transported to Australia after they united to improve their working conditions and terms of employment. The **Martyrs' Tree** under which they supposedly met still remains, and there's a little **museum** between the 6 cottages built by the TUC as a memorial. Shop, disabled access by arrangement; cl Mon, Christmas wk; (01305) 848237; free. The Martyrs pub is useful for lunch.

★ **TYNEHAM ABANDONED VILLAGE** SY8880 On the army's Purbeck firing ranges (open holidays and most wknds), this is quite poignant; there's an explanatory exhibition in the former church.

✝ **WAREHAM** SY9287 This largely modern town has a few striking old buildings, inc the **church** of St Martin's, with a finely carved memorial to Lawrence of Arabia. The church of Lady St Mary not far from the Quay has the coffin of Edward the Martyr, murdered at nearby Corfe Castle in 978. There are 2 very traditional old inns, the Black Bear and King's Arms; another, the Quay, is in a fine position. **Blue Pool** (Furzebrook, 3m S, SY9282) Peaceful beauty spot with curious colour changes in the water whenever the weather alters, from light green to blue to suddenly a rich turquoise; it's bluest on an overcast day. Also 25 acres of heathland with rare plants and animals. Snacks, shop, some disabled access; facilities and museum cl Oct–Easter, site cl Dec–Feb; (01929) 551408; £2.80. The attractive road over the West Creech Hills may sometimes be closed for army firing practice.

✝ **WEST LULWORTH** SY8280 A lovely spot, though hardly undiscovered (parking can be a nightmare), just above a very beautiful cove with extraordinary nearby rock formations; the thatched Castle Inn is useful for lunch. The 17th-c **Lulworth Castle** has been fully restored, and its SE tower has splendid views over the wooded park; the formal gardens are a nice spot for a picnic. The Catholic chapel was the first to be built in England after the Reformation, and an Anglican church was built in part by Thomas Hardy, about whom there's an exhibition inside. Meals, teas, shop, limited disabled access; open daily Apr–Oct, best to check winter opening; (01929) 400352; £3. The Lulworth Equestrian Centre can arrange **horse-riding**; (01929) 400396; around £10 an hour. The **cove** itself is really best appreciated out of season. There's a classic mini-walk W along the cliffs to Durdle Door, a natural arch eroded by the sea; the unusually shaped rocks are surrounded by particularly good beaches. Inland is prairie-like monotony, and it is best to return the same way. Exhibitions on smuggling and country wines in the **Lulworth Cove Heritage Centre** (cl 25 Dec; free – may be charge for parking nearby). E of Lulworth Cove is army training land, which means high-security fences and dire warning notices, but you are allowed in most wknds and daily in Aug and during Easter (keep to the paths). Information boards by road junctions off the A351 and A352 nr Wareham give opening times; or ring (01929) 462721 ext 4824 and ask for the Guardroom. The coast walk between Lulworth Cove and Kimmeridge Bay is very strenuous but excellent, heading past the surreal 'fossil forest' (formed of petrified algae that once clung to tree-trunks) to Mupe Bay. Another path ascends Bindon Hill, looking down over the semi-circular cove.

WIMBORNE MINSTER SZ0199 Georgian houses (and decent antique shops and auctions) in the narrow central streets around the **Minster** – a fine, well preserved, largely Norman church with contrasting red and grey masonry, twin towers, and a brightly coloured jack striking the clock bell every quarter. Inside, is an interesting Norman crypt, a distinctive astronomical clock and the original chained library. **Priest's House Museum** (High St) Historic town house with carefully researched period rooms; regular cooking displays in the Victorian kitchen, and a charming walled garden. Summer teas, shop, disabled access to ground floor and garden; cl Sun (exc pm Jun–Sept and bank hol wknds), and Nov–Mar; (01202) 882533; £2. Dormers (Hanham Rd) and the Cross Keys (Victoria Rd, W) are best for lunch. **Kingston Lacy** (Now on the B3082, SU9702) Impressive 17th-c mansion later remodelled by Charles Barry, with grand Italian marble staircase and superb Venetian ceiling; outstanding paintings such as the *Judgement of Solomon* by Sebastiano del Piamtino, and others by Titian, Rubens and Van Dyck. The enormous grounds have landscaped gardens, a herd of Red Devon cattle in the park, and summer concerts and plays. Lovely snowdrops in Feb and early Mar. Meals, snacks, shop, disabled access to park and gardens; open Apr–Oct, house cl am and Thurs, Fri; (01202) 883402; £6, £3 grounds only; NT. **Walford Mill** (Stone Lane) Former 18th-c flour mill with exhibitions and local crafts. Meals, snacks, shop, disabled access; cl 25–26 Dec, 1 Jan, and Mons Jan–Mar; (01202) 841400; free. **Merley House** Fine 18th-c mansion with interesting plaster ceilings and excellent collection of 5,000 model toy cars and aeroplanes. Snacks (July and Aug only), shop, limited disabled access; open for temporary exhibitions in spring and early summer (ring for exact dates) and daily July–Sept; (01202) 886533; £1.50. Just W of town at Pamphill is a good big farm shop, and just E there are pleasant country walks around the Fox & Hounds at Little Canford. The once formidable hill fort of **Badbury Rings**, just off the B3082 NW, is associated by some with King Arthur. It's a good strolling ground with an impressive range of wild flowers; if you feel more energetic, a **Roman road** lets you strike out for miles N.

WOOL SY8589 **Monkey World** (off the A35 towards Bere Regis) Enthusiastic rescue centre for apes and chimps being gradually reintroduced to natural surroundings; very enjoyably laid out for visitors. In addition to the biggest group of chimpanzees you'll see outside Africa, they usually have ring-tailed and ruffed lemurs, barbary macaques, capuchins and vervets, all roaming and climbing freely in decent-sized open enclosures. Keepers give useful talks, and you can see baby chimps playing in their nursery. There's quite a range of play areas, with an extensive 15-stage obstacle course (parents are quick to see the irony in putting it close to the main chimp enclosure), and mini-motor bikes and jet boats; there may be a clown in summer. Meals, snacks, shop, disabled access (a few steep paths); cl 25 Dec; freephone (0800) 456600; £5.25. The village itself was used by Thomas Hardy as the ancient seat of the d'Urbervilles. The Seven Stars at East Burton has decent food (and a playground).

★ **WORTH MATRAVERS** SY9677 In this prettily set coastal hamlet the unpretentious Square & Compass has lovely views, and is a good base for coastal walks. Nr here, the rock pool at Dancing Ledge is said to have been cut by a local schoolmaster.

★ **Attractive villages** with decent pubs include Buckhorn Weston ST7524, Burton Bradstock SY4889, Chedington ST4805, Church Knowle SY9481, Evershot ST5704, Farnham ST9515, Fiddleford ST8013, Kingston

SY9579, Langton Herring SY6182, Litton Cheyney SY5590, Loders SY4994, Powerstock SY5196, Puncknowle SY5388 (pronounced Punnel), Sydling St Nicholas SY6399, Symondsbury SY4493, Tarrant Monkton ST9408, West Knighton SY7387 and Whitchurch Canonicorum SY3995 (fine church).

Where to eat

ASKERSWELL SY5292 **Spyway** *(01308) 485250* Former smugglers' look-out with exceptional value, very popular bar food, lots of salads and cheesecakes; nice views, big garden, walks nearby; no children under 14 inside; cl Mon exc bank hols. **£14.50**|£5.

CHEDINGTON ST4805 **Winyards Gap** *(01935) 891244* Comfortable pub with marvellous views and nearby walks; a wide choice of good bar food inc lots of fresh fish, vegetarian choices, home-made puddings, daily specials, and children's menus; self-catering flats in converted barn; cl pm Mon Nov–Mar; disabled access. **£14**|£5.50.

CHRISTCHURCH SZ1593 **Splinters** *12 Church St (01202) 483454* Fine old building nr priory with 3 attractively decorated rooms; good, imaginative modern cooking, lovely chocolatey puddings, a fine British cheese choice, good-value wines, and friendly helpful owners; also run Pommery's (next door) with a delicatessen and lively upstairs café bar; cl pm Sun, Mon. **£35**|£4.95.

CHURCH KNOWLE SY9481 **New Inn** *(01929) 480357* Very attractive partly thatched old pub with 2 nicely furnished main bar areas, lots of bric-à-brac, log fires, relaxing dining lounge, very good fresh fish (and other food), well kept ales, decent wines, and a skittle alley; camping in field behind (need to book). **£18.50**|£7.50.

CORSCOMBE ST5015 **Fox** *(01935) 891330* Cosy thatched pub, very much a traditional family-run place, with lovely polished copper pots and pans, scrubbed pine tables, candles in champagne bottles, open fires in one room and woodburner in another; particularly good food (especially daily specials), well kept real ales, local cider, and a good wine list; nice surrounding walks; well behaved children welcome; bdrms. **£21**|£4.95.

DORCHESTER SY6890 **Potter In** *19 Durngate St (01305) 260312* All-day food inc English breakfast, enjoyable lunchtime meals and snacks, afternoon tea, a walled garden for summer, open fire and fresh flowers, and a friendly welcome; disabled access. £2.50.

EAST MORDEN SY9195 **Cock & Bottle** *(01929) 459238* Popular dining pub with several beamed communicating areas, a nice mix of old furnishings, and a good log fire; enjoyable food inc interesting daily specials with plenty of fish and seasonal game, well kept beers and good wines. **£20.50**|£8.50.

LANGTON HERRING SY6182 **Elm Tree** *(01305) 871257* Busy pub in pretty thatched village, with copper, brass and bellows on the walls of the beamed main rooms, a traditionally furnished dining extension, a good range of interesting daily specials, real ales, flower-filled garden, and nearby walks. **£19.90**|£7.50.

LYME REGIS SY3492 **Pilot Boat** *(01297) 443157* Welcoming place across from the beaches, with a bustling atmosphere, light comfortable dining bar decorated with fishing and nautical memorabilia, good food, no smoking restaurant, and decent wines and liqueurs; disabled access. **£18**|£6.50.

MAIDEN NEWTON SY5997 **Petit Canard** *Dorchester Rd (01300) 320536* Welcoming little restaurant with simple furnishings; good, very interesting food – grilled kangaroo, quite a few Eastern influences, fine puddings, and a well chosen wine list; cl am, Sun, Mon, 1st wk Jan, 1st wk May; children over 7. **£30**.

MARNHULL ST7718 **Blackmore Vale** *(01258) 820701* Relaxed and friendly old pub with nice home-made bar food, decent beer and wine, and a log fire and interesting furnishings in the comfortably modernised bar; you can eat in the garden where one of the tables is thatched; children over 14. **£17**|£4.45.

PLUSH ST7102 **Brace of Pheasants** *(01300) 348357* Long, low 16th-c thatched cottage with a civilised but relaxed atmosphere, good solid furnishings, fresh flowers and a nice log fire in the airy beamed bar; interesting food, well kept real ales; swings and an aviary in the garden; children in the family room; disabled access. **£22.50**|£5.75.

SHERBORNE ST6316 **Pheasants** *24 Greenhill (01935) 815252* Georgian restaurant with rooms in attractive town; friendly staff, enjoyable modern English cooking, good breakfasts; cl Mon, 2 wks mid-Jan; well behaved children welcome; disabled access. **£29**|£15 3 courses Sat/Sun only.

STURMINSTER NEWTON ST7814 **Red Rose** *Market Cross (01258) 472460* Long-standing, family-run lunchtime restaurant with proper English cooking; very relaxed and happy, popular locally; cl evenings, Sun; disabled access. **£5.50**|£3.50.

SWANAGE SZ0278 **Galley** *9 High St (01929) 427299* Enjoyable little evening restaurant, not far from the seafront, with emphasis on fresh local fish and game, good and reasonably priced wines, and helpful service; cl 3 wks Nov, 1 Jan–Easter; no children. **£23.50**.

TARRANT MONKTON ST9408 **Langton Arms** *(01258) 830225* Thatched 17th-c pub in a pretty village; wide choice of fresh home-made food (inc popular children's menu), bistro restaurant, well kept beers, decent wines, cosy bar, open fire, and a skittle alley; comfortable bdrms; children in family room; disabled access. **£25**|£5.50.

UPWEY SY6684 **Old Ship** *7 Ridgeway (01305) 812522* Pretty, whitewashed cottagey pub with very good bar food, well kept beer, a fine range of wines, and friendly service; cl 24 Dec. **£11.50**|£3.50.

UPWEY SY6684 **Wishing Well** *(01305) 814470* Nice little restaurant, popular locally, with good, interesting lunchtime food and afternoon tea, and friendly service; bring your own wine; open 10am–6pm; cl mid-Jan–Feb; disabled access. **£12.50**|£5.50.

WEST BAY SY4590 **Riverside** *(01308) 422011* Well placed and friendly restaurant with excellent, locally caught fish and shellfish (also a few meat dishes), and helpful service; cl pm Sun, Mon exc bank hols, and Dec–Mar; disabled access. **£25**|£5.

WIMBORNE MINSTER SZ0199 **Cloisters** *40 East St (01202) 880593* Friendly restaurant with pleasant décor and enjoyable food inc breakfast with home-made marmalade, lunchtime snacks and meals, and afternoon tea; cl 4 days Christmas; disabled access. **£15.25**|£4.

WORTH MATRAVERS SY9677 **Worth Café and Craft Centre** *(01929) 439360* Welcoming converted barn with enthusiastic staff, nice home-made lunches (lots for vegetarians) and cakes, and good, locally made crafts; walkers welcome; cl Tues, Jan; disabled access. £5.50.

Special thanks to G Bennett, T R Turner, K H Frostick, Mrs H Jaggers, Chris Reeve, J S M Sheldon.

We welcome reports from readers

This *Guide* depends on readers' reports. Do help us if you can – in return, we offer a discount on the next edition to people who've helped us with reports for it. Tell us what you think about places already in it, and anything extra you think we should say about them. And send us your ideas for inclusion in the next edition: places to visit, eat at or stay in, attractive drives or walks, maybe even unusual interesting shops you know of. Use the card in the middle, the report forms at the end, or just write – no stamp needed: *The Good Guide to Britain*, FREEPOST TN1569, Wadhurst, E Sussex TN5 7BR.

Dorset Calendar

Some of these dates were provisional as we went to press. Please check information with the telephone numbers provided.

JANUARY

23 Sherborne Aber Valley Male Voice Choir and Brass Band in the Abbey (01935) 815341

FEBRUARY

1 Weymouth 'Quakers' Exhibition at Brewers Quay – *till 11 Apr* (01305) 765262

16 Corfe Castle Marblers' and Stonecutters' Day to enforce rules laid down in 1651. At noon the church's pancake bell summons the company from the Fox Inn to the Town Hall. After the meeting a football is kicked along the old road to Ower Quay (each participant carrying a pint of beer and loaf of bread) to preserve an ancient right of way used in the shipping of marbles (01929) 422885

22 Weymouth Story Telling and Poetry Festival – *till 5 Mar* (01305) 765265

MARCH

1 Stapehill Craft Fair at the Abbey (01202) 861686

6 Weymouth Music Festival (01305) 765265

27 Weymouth Easter Festival at Brewers Quay – *till 11 Apr* (01305) 785747

29 Bournemouth Flower Festival – *till 1 Apr* (0171) 828 5145

APRIL

2 Athelhampton Craft Show at Athelhampton House – *till Mon 5* (01305) 848363

MAY

2 Bovington Dorset Children's Show at the Tank Museum: rare breeds, arena events (01929) 405096; **Corfe** English Civil War Society, the Siege of 1643 at Corfe Castle – *till Mon 3* (01929) 481294; **Sherborne** Ascension Day: abbey choir sing from the roof of the abbey tower *at 7am* (01935) 815341; **Weymouth** International Beach Kite Festival: 175ft kites, stunt kite teams, children's workshop: firework and night kite-flying display *Sun evening – till Mon 3* (01305) 785747

3 Cerne Abbas Wessex Morris Men dance on Giant Hill *at 7am* (01305) 251481

13 Abbotsbury Garland Day inc blessing of the sea (01305) 251481

15 West Lulworth Country Gardening Festival at the Castle – *till Sun 16* (01929) 552740

16 Weymouth Vintage Motorcycle Rally and Display (01305) 785747

29 Wareham Saxon Festival – *till Mon 31* (01929) 552740

30 Athelhampton Flower Festival at Athelhampton House – *till 3 Jun* (01305) 848363; **Weymouth** Oyster Festival at the Olde Harbour; also Dorset Tour: vintage and classic vehicle rally (01305) 785747

Dorset Calendar (cont.)

31 **Blandford** Georgian Fayre and Town Criers' Competition (01258) 480808; **Weymouth** Trawler Race and Water Carnival (01305) 785747

JUNE

9 **Weymouth** Jazz Festival at Brewers Quay – *till Sun 13* (01305) 785747

12 **Netherbury** Open Gardens – *till Sun 13* (01308) 488270; **West Bay** Traction Engine Rally – *till Sun 13* (01308) 424901; **West Lulworth** Open-air Concert at the Castle (01929) 552740; **Weymouth** International Military and Veterans Festival inc Remembrance Parade with over 90 military and historic vehicles – *till Fri 18* (01305) 785747

19 **Abbotsbury** Gardens Festival at the Sub tropical Gardens – *till Sun 20* (01305) 871387; **Ashmore** Filly Loo: country dancing round the village pond (01747) 853514; **Cerne Abbas** 20–30 Gardens Open – *till Sun 20* (01300) 341311; **Dorchester** Carnival (01305) 785747

26 **Abbotsbury** Jazz Night at the Subtropical Gardens (01305) 871387; **Bournemouth** Music-makers Festival: free amateur events, parades, tattoo – *till 10 July* (01202) 451718; **Cattistock** 20 Gardens open, vintage cars and aeroplanes at Chalmington Manor (01300) 320226

27 **Beauminster** Gardens Open Day (01308) 862675; **Bovington** Wessex Road and Custom Car Show at the Tank Museum (01929) 405096

JULY

1 **Bovington** Firepower Mobility: tank battles in the arena – *every Thurs at noon in July* (01929) 405096; **Poole** Family Fun and Entertainment on Poole Quay – *every Thurs evening July–Aug* (01202) 253253

2 **Lyme Regis** Jazz Festival – *till Sun 4* (01297) 442138

3 **Christchurch** Festival – *till Sun 4* (01202) 471780; **Shaftesbury** Gold Hill Fair – *till Sun 4* (01308) 424901

4 **Athelhampton** MG Owners Rally at Athelhampton House (01305) 848363; **Frampton** Village Fête (01300) 320394

10 **Puddletown** Carnival (01305) 848625; **Yetminster** Fair: Yetties concert, art exhibition, street market, dancing (01935) 872940

17 **Tolpuddle** Rally: trade union banners, speeches (01202) 294333; **Weymouth** International Maritime Modelling Festival – *till Sun 18* (01305) 785747

20 **Christchurch** Open-air Shakespeare at Priory Gardens – *till Sat 31* (01202) 471780; **Poole** Fireworks Concert at Upton Country Park – *till Thurs 22* (01202) 253253

23 **Brownsea Island** Open-air Production of *A Midsummer Night's Dream* – also *Mon 26, Weds 28, Fri 30 and 2, 4 and 6 Aug* (01929) 552740; **Kingston Maurward** 50th Anniversary at Kingston Maurward House (01305) 215000

25 **Lyme Regis** Lifeboat Week: Red Arrows, opera and fireworks – *till 1 Aug* (01297) 443724

28 **Portesham** Possum Fez Wik: traditional fair week (appears in Hardy's *Under the Greenwood Tree*) – *till 1 Aug* (01305) 871316

30 **Weymouth** National Beach Volleyball Championships – *till 1 Aug* (01305) 785747

Dorset Calendar (cont.)

AUGUST

1 **Puddletown** County Arts and Crafts Association Exhibition at St Mary's School – *till Thurs 5* (01202) 553113
2 **Weymouth** Firework Display – also on *Mon 9, Wed 18, Mon 23, Mon 30* (01305) 785747
5 **Bovington** Firepower Mobility: tank battles in the arena – *every Thurs at noon in Aug* (01929) 405096
8 **Bridport** Trawler Race (01308) 424901; **Weymouth** National Lifeboat Day (01305) 785747
14 **Bridport** Carnival Procession (01308) 422884; **Lyme Regis** Carnival – *till Sat 21* (01297) 442138; **Christchurch** Regatta – *till Sat 21* (01202) 471780
15 **Poole** Powerboat racing (01202) 707227
18 **Motcombe** Gillingham and Shaftesbury Agricultural Show (01747) 823955; **Weymouth** Carnival: Red Arrows, procession, fireworks (01305) 772444
20 **Weymouth** Real Ale and Cider Festival at the Rugby Club – *till Sat 21* (01305) 785747
22 **West Lulworth** Classic Car Event at the Castle (01929) 552740
26 **West Bay** Melplash Agricultural Show (01308) 423337
28 **Abbotsbury** Open-air Opera at the Subtropical Gardens (01305) 871387; **Athelhampton** Craft Show at Athelhampton House – *till Mon 30* (01305) 848363; **Shaftesbury** Moto Guzzi: motorbike rally – *till Sun 29* (01747) 852514; **Studland** Country Fair (01929) 552740
31 **Bournemouth** Festival of lights: light show set to music – *till Sept 3* (01202) 451700

SEPTEMBER

1 **Tarrant Hinton** Great Dorset Steam Fair: 30th anniversary, 500-acre site, steam funfair – *till Sun 5* (01258) 860361
2 **Bovington** Firepower Mobility: tank battles in the arena – *every Thurs at noon in Sept* (01929) 405096
4 **Dorchester** Agricultural Show at Came Park – *till Sun 5* (01305) 264249
11 **Corfe** Archaeology Weekend: activities and living history at Corfe Castle – *till Sun 12* (01929) 481294; **Poole** French Street Market at Poole Quay – *till Sun 12* (01202) 253253
16 **West Lulworth** National Flower-Arranging Festival at the Castle – *till Sun 19* (01929) 552740
19 **Weymouth** Vintage and Classic Car Rally at Weymouth Pavilion (01305) 765265

OCTOBER

2 **Bovington** Model Show at the Tank Museum (01929) 405096; **Shaftesbury** Carnival (01747) 854327
9 **Gillingham** Carnival (01747) 853514
11 **Sherborne** Pack Monday Fair (01935) 813343
23 **Corfe** Civil War Garrison at Corfe Castle – *till Sun 24* (01929) 481294; **Weymouth** Halloween Festival at Brewers Quay – *till Sun 31* (01305) 785747

Dorset Calendar (cont.)

NOVEMBER

5 **Weymouth** Fireworks on the beach (01305) 785747
6 **Mudeford** Fireworks (01202) 471780
15 **Weymouth** Christmas Festival at Brewers Quay – *till 24 Dec* (01305) 785747
28 **Christchurch** Winter Carnival: Snow Queen procession (01202) 471780

DECEMBER

9 **Bridport** Christmas Festival (01305) 267992; **Weymouth** Victorian Shownight (01305) 785747
25 **Weymouth** Harbour Swim (01305) 785747

We welcome reports from readers

This *Guide* depends on readers' reports. Do help us if you can – in return, we offer a discount on the next edition to people who've helped us with reports for it. Tell us what you think about places already in it, and anything extra you think we should say about them. And send us your ideas for inclusion in the next edition: places to visit, eat at or stay in, attractive drives or walks, maybe even unusual interesting shops you know of. Use the card in the middle, the report forms at the end, or just write – no stamp needed: *The Good Guide to Britain*, FREEPOST TN1569, Wadhurst, E Sussex TN5 7BR.

Essex

Quietly attractive countryside and villages in the north and on the coast, some good days out; traditional seaside resorts.

Some fine family outings include Colchester's excellent zoo, the toy museum and reconstructed Norman castle at Stansted, the wildlife park at Widdington and several well organised farm parks and private railway centres.

For adults, Saffron Walden is a delightful small town, with magnificent Audley End nearby. There are fascinating gardens at Elmstead Market, Lamarsh (plenty to keep children occupied here), and Rettendon. Colchester has excellent museums, and other appealing places include Layer Marney Tower, Coggeshall, Burnham-on-Crouch, Finchingfield, Dedham and Castle Hedingham. Many of the churches are well worth a look. The secret Cold War command centres at Kelvedon Hatch and Mistley have a chilling fascination – touched with relief that we seem to have stepped back from that brink.

North Essex has a real East Anglian flavour. Driving through, you pass lots of attractive houses right by the road, often with fine old timbering and distinctive colourwashed plasterwork – the intricate patterning is known as pargeting. The landscape gem is the Stour Valley, but a question-mark hangs over the survival of Constable's famous landscapes under the tide of mass tourism. The Blackwater/Crouch coast has a surprisingly remote feel, given the closeness of densely urban South Essex.

Where to stay

BROXTED TL5827 **Whitehall** *Church End, Broxted CM6 2BZ (01279) 850603* **£119,** plus special breaks; 25 pretty rms. Fine Elizabethan manor house in lovely walled gardens, with outdoor swimming pool and tennis court; restful, spacious lounge, and a smaller, cosier one with log fire, pleasant bar, good food in big timbered restaurant, and friendly service; cl 26–31 Dec; disabled access.

BURNHAM-ON-CROUCH TQ9595 **White Harte** *Burnham-on-Crouch CM0 8AS (01621) 782106* ***£50;** 19 rms, 11 with own bthrm. Old-fashioned 17th-c yachting inn on quay overlooking the River Crouch with its own jetty; high ceilings, oak tables, polished parquet, sea pictures, panelling; residents' lounge, decent bar food, and restaurant; cl Christmas.

COGGESHALL TL8422 **White Hart** *Market End, Coggeshall, Colchester CO6 1NH (01376) 561654* **£97,** plus weekend breaks; 18 attractive rms. Family-run, 15th-c hotel with beamed lounge bar and residents' bar, log fires, friendly staff, and good food in both the bar and restaurant; cl 25–26 Dec.

DEDHAM TM0432 **Maison Talbooth** *Dedham, Colchester CO7 6HN (01206) 322367* **£140,** plus special breaks; 10 luxuriously furnished rms. Tranquil Victorian country house in fine Constable country, with deeply comfortable seating and fresh flowers in the elegant lounge; very good, imaginative food in lovely timber-framed restaurant overlooking river and gardens, and marvellous breakfasts; partial disabled access.

DEDHAM TM0533 **Marlborough Head** *Dedham, Colchester CO7 6DH (01206) 323250* **£55;** 3 rms. Comfortable, old-fashioned, early 18th-c inn in heart of

Constable's home village; unusual carved woodwork in central lounge, and a wide choice of interesting food; cl 25 Dec.

DUDDENHOE END TL4536 **Duddenhoe End Farm** *Duddenhoe End, Saffron Walden CB11 4UU (01763) 838258* ***£42;** 3 rms. 17th-c no smoking farmhouse with inglenook fireplaces and beams, visitors' lounge and separate dining room; cl Christmas; children over 12.

MALDON TL8407 **Blue Boar** *Silver St, Maldon CM9 4QE (01621) 852681* **£80,** plus weekend breaks; 28 comfortable rms. Fine 14th-c coaching inn with cosy little beamed and oak-panelled rooms, roaring log fires, good food (nice breakfasts), and friendly staff; limited disabled access.

RICKLING GREEN TL5029 **Cricketers Arms** *Rickling Green, Saffron Walden CB11 3YG (01799) 543210* **£60;** 10 rms, some in modern block behind. Cheerful family-run pub by the village green, with cricketing mementos, beamed bar with open fires, home-made food in bar and attractive restaurant; handy for Stansted Airport; partial disabled access.

THAXTED TL6031 **Swan** *Thaxted, Dunmow CM6 2PL (01371) 830321* **£60;** 22 comfortably modernised rms. Four-gabled late 15th-c inn with views towards the church and almshouses; pleasantly pubby big bar area with nice warm atmosphere, well kept real ales, and good food.

WEST MERSEA TM0012 **Blackwater** *West Mersea, Colchester CO5 8QH (01206) 383338* ***£60,** plus special breaks; 9 pretty rms. Creeper-covered hotel with neat little sitting room, fresh flowers, attractive beamed restaurant with good, mainly French food (emphasis on fresh fish), the relaxed and informal Mussel Pan Bistro which specialises in mussels, big breakfasts, and friendly service; cl 5–25 Jan.

To see and do

ESSEX Family Attraction of the Year

Colchester Castle TL9925 (Castle Park, off High St) Older children with even a passing interest in Colchester's bloodthirsty history really enjoy visiting this exemplary museum. Lots of effort has been put in to make it interesting and entertaining for families, so as well as several dramatic audio-visual shows and interactive displays, you can try on a toga or Roman helmet, or touch 2,000-year-old pottery excavated nearby. The Norman castle itself has the biggest Norman keep in Europe, and stands on the site of a colossal Roman temple (you can still see the vaults). The fall of the temple came when Boudicca burned the town in AD 60, and they've made a valiant attempt to bring those moments to life, as they have with some other grisly moments in the castle's history: Matthew Hopkins, the infamous Witchfinder General, interrogated so-called witches in the prison here, and you can hear a dramatisation of one of the forced confessions. Some of the exhibits in the prison section aren't really ideal for younger children. More traditional displays include an Egyptian mummy, a splendid collection of Roman glass and jewellery, and some remarkably preserved Roman military tombstones; also brass-rubbing. Museums have very much gone out of fashion in recent years, replaced on the whole by less demanding multi-sensory experiences, so it's nice to see a place like this successfully combining a realisation that children like to use their imaginations with a desire to encourage them to do it for themselves. It's worth paying the £1 extra for a guided tour of the castle, taking you up on the roof as well to the vaults and chapel. Good shop, mostly disabled access (not to the the castle itself); may be cl some Suns – best to check first; (01206) 282931; *£3.60 (children 5–15 £2.30). A family ticket for 2 adults and 2 children is £9.50.

★ **BATTLESBRIDGE** TQ7894 Attractive village, popular antiques and crafts centre, walks to the head of the Crouch estuary, and a good pub.

BILLERICAY TQ6991 **Barleylands Farm** (A129 SE) Expanding series of attractions, from farm animals and rural life displays to working glassworks, craft studios and miniature railway (summer Sun only). Meals, snacks, shop, disabled access; cl Mon Oct–Mar; (01268) 282090; *£3. The nearby Duke of York (South Green) has decent food.

BLACKWATER ESTUARY TL9610 Vast skies, with boats and bird life punctuating the flat sea and landscapes; the pick of local walks include paths along the dykes from Tollesbury, and towards isolated St Peter's Chapel from Bradwell-on-Sea. The Chequers at Goldhanger is another good starting-point. Like other parts of this low-lying much indented coast, the immediate hinterland is generally too dull to make circular walks worthwhile – usually best to come back the way you went.

★ † **BRADWELL-ON-SEA** TL9907 Worth the long drive for the sense of being right out on the edge of things – the timeless emptiness if anything exaggerated by distant views of vast industrial installations. The walk eastwards down the old Roman road across the marshes takes you to a little restored **Saxon chapel** right on the sea wall, the scene of an annual pilgrimage in July.

BRAINTREE TL7622 **Working Silk Museum** (South St) Silk production demonstrated from start to finish, in a well restored old mill building; the hand looms they use are over 150 years old. Shop, disabled access; cl lunchtimes, wknds and bank hols; (01376) 553393; £3. The Green Dragon just S at Young's End has good food.

★ **BURNHAM-ON-CROUCH** TQ9595 Attractively old-fashioned yachting station, lively in summer (packed around the Aug bank hol for its regatta), but nice in winter too, with rigging clacking forlornly against the masts of those yachts left to ride at anchor offshore. There are pleasant walks along the banks of the River Crouch. The White Harte on the quay is good for lunch and there is a decent little **craft centre** (where they filmed some episodes of *Lovejoy*) at Blake End, a little W on the A120.

Mangapps Farm Railway Museum (B1021 towards Southminster) Friendly and growing collection of vintage rolling stock and railway memorabilia. They now have a station formed from railway buildings from sites all over East Anglia and steamtrain rides along 1½ miles of track. Mostly under cover; open pm wknds, daily in Aug and Easter; (01621) 784898; *£4. Further along, The Limes is a decent **farm shop**, with nature trails and pick-your-own.

★ † **CASTLE HEDINGHAM** TL7736 The town, which has some attractive buildings, is named for the Norman **castle** which dominates it, the magnificent 4-storey keep towering above the surrounding trees. Exceptionally well preserved, it still has its roof, banqueting hall and minstrels' gallery. Teas, shop; cl Nov–Easter (exc some wknds Oct); (01787) 460261; £4. The **church** has grand Norman masonry and interestingly carved choir seats. There's a good working pottery in St James St, and the Bell is good for lunch.

Colne Valley Railway Museum (Yeldham Rd, A1017 N) Lovingly restored Victorian railway buildings with a collection of vintage engines and carriages; short steamtrain trips pm Sun mid-Mar–mid-Oct, and pm Weds and Thurs in hols; diesel rides pm Tues, Fri and Sat in school hols. Meals on Pullman coaches, snacks, shop, limited disabled access; cl 23 Dec–Feb; (01787) 461174; *£5, *£2 when trains not running. The B1058 towards Sudbury then left through Gestingthorpe and the Belchamps is a pleasant excursion.

CHAPPEL TL8927 **Knights Farm** (Swan St) Everything for the dried-flower enthusiast, plus other local crafts. The prettily sited Swan has good food, in sight of the Chappel Viaduct (reputedly the biggest brick structure in Europe), and there's a decent **railway museum** – maybe rides on a short demonstration line. Shop, disabled access; cl 25–26 Dec; £4.50 (£2.50 non-steam days).

✝ **CHELMSFORD** TL7007 A big busy city with little for visitors, but its 15th-c **cathedral,** consecrated as such only in 1914, has particularly harmonious Perpendicular architecture.

★ **CLACTON** TM1714 Roomy, family seaside resort, with long stretches of gently shelving sandy beach and all the usual amusements. The Robin Hood (London Rd) is the best family dining pub in the area.

★ **COGGESHALL** TL8422 Attractive small town with a good few antique shops, and **Paycocke's** (West St), a fine timber-framed medieval merchant's home with unusual panelling and carvings, and a pretty garden behind. Open pm Tues, Thurs, Sun and bank hols Apr–Oct; (01376) 561305; £2; NT. The Fleece next door has decent food. There's a working **pottery** along the street, and the Woolpack out by the church is a magnificent timbered building. 12th-c **Grange Barn** (Grange Hill, B1024 S) is the oldest surviving timber-framed barn in Europe, originally part of a Cistercian monastery. Disabled access; hours as Paycocke's; £1.50, or joint ticket with Paycocke's £3; NT. **Marks Hall** TL8524 (B1024 N) Gradually being restored, this estate gives attractive and undemanding strolls. There's a massive 13th-c oak, and a developing arboretum. Teashop, shop, disabled access; cl Mon, and Nov–Easter; (01376) 563796; £3 per car.

✝ **COLCHESTER** TL9925 Britain's oldest recorded town, the capital of Roman Britain. See *separate Family Panel on p. 237* for **Colchester Castle**, which has helpful map-leaflets to guide you to the town's most interesting places; tours leave the tourist information centre (Queen St) at 11am (Jun–Sept; £2). You can trace the Roman wall (the Hole in the Wall, Balkerne Gardens, is a decent pub built into the one surviving fragmentary gatehouse). The High St has handsome buildings, some extravagantly timbered, and plenty more historical buildings inc **St Botolph's**, the oldest Augustinian priory in the country; readers have enjoyed the contemporary **art gallery** at No. 74. A clutch of interesting museums nearby includes the **Natural History Museum** and **Hollytrees Museum** on the High St, the latter featuring lots of toys, costumes and curios from the last 2 centuries, and round the corner in Trinity St the **Tymperleys Clock Museum**, a particularly unusual selection in a lovely 15th-c house; there's something very special about coming here and hearing all the ticking. All 3 museums cl lunchtime, all Sun and Mon, clock museum also cl Nov–Mar; (01206) 282931; all free. Children like **Rollerworld** (Eastgates), the only international-standard roller-skating rink in Britain; evenings only during the week, cl Mon; from £3.20; also Quasar and ten-pin bowling. The Rose & Crown (East St) is popular for lunch. **Bourne Mill** (just off the B1025 S) Delightfully quaint restored watermill by pretty millpond, worth a look from the outside even when it's not open. Open pm Sun and Mon bank hol wknds, plus pm Sun and Tues July and Aug; (01206) 572422; £1.50; NT.

COLCHESTER ZOO TL9522 (Maldon Rd, Stanway, 2m E of Colchester by the B1002) One of the country's most satisfying zoos: over 170 rare and endangered species housed in glass-panelled enclosures as close to their natural habitats as possible, with a particularly good timetable of events and demonstrations. Children can join in feeding the seals and elephants, and there are good play areas (best is the splendid Kalahari Capers under-cover complex). Activities such as face-painting and brass rubbing are included in the price, as well as Punch and Judy and magic shows. Meals, snacks, shop, some disabled access (a few steep hills); cl 25 Dec; (01206) 330253; £7.50 (good-value annual tickets and a 5% discount if there is a paying child in the group).

✝ **COPFORD** TL9222The **church** IS worth a visit, particularly for its well restored 12th-c wall paintings.

CRESSING TL7918 **Cressing Temple** (Witham Rd) Medieval barns with exhibitions on medieval husbandry, surrounded by a new 16th-c-style garden. Snacks, shop, disabled access; cl Sat and all Nov–Easter; *£3.

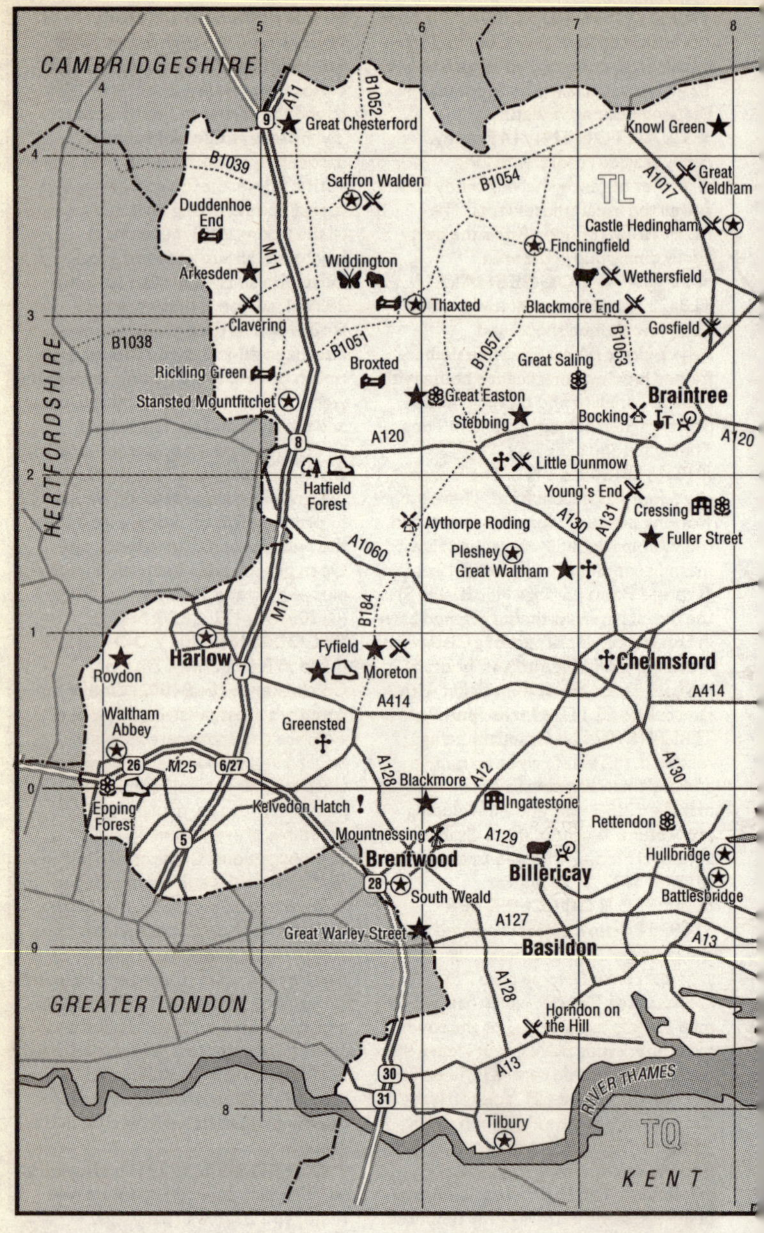

★ ✝ ⌂ ✿ 🐄 **DEDHAM** TM0533
Several fine old buildings, especially the 15th-c flint **church**, its pinnacled tower familiar from so many Constable paintings. There's also the school Constable went to, and good walks through the protected riverside meadows to his father's mill at Flatford (across the river lock, so in Suffolk, and described in that chapter). Worries about the hordes of visitors the Constable connection attracts have led

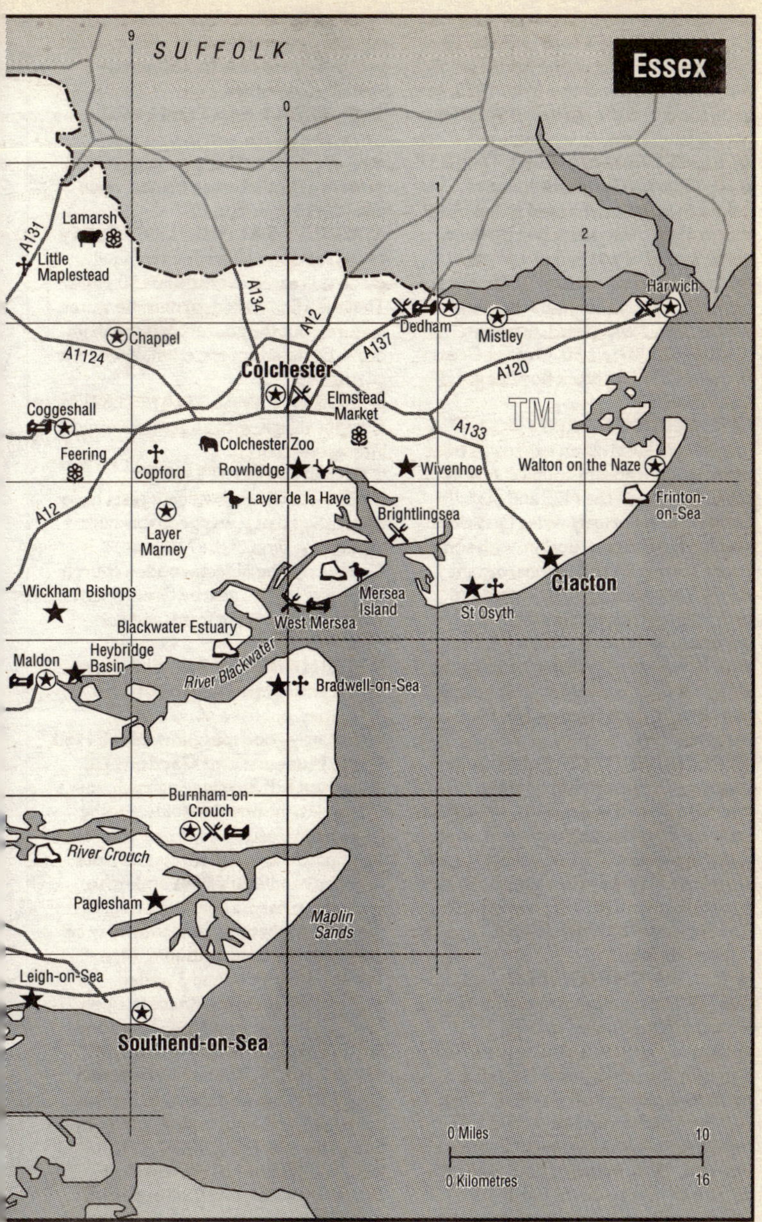

local tourist boards to cut down on the publicity they give the village in their literature. The **Art and Craft Centre** (High St) has a number of crafts, growing collection of dolls houses, stained glass workshop and candle making; cl Mon–Jan-Mar; 50p.

Dedham Rare Breeds Farm (Mill St) Nicely undeveloped 16-acre farm, where children can feed the animals (bags of feed provided); pony rides at wknds and during school hols. Snacks, shop, some disabled access; cl Oct–Mar; (01206) 323111; £3.35. The handsome Marlborough Head, a wool merchant's house dating from 1475, has good food, and the partly medieval Sun here is useful too.

ELMSTEAD MARKET TM0623 **Beth Chatto Gardens** A riot of colour in summer; it's hard to believe that in 1960 these attractive gardens were 4 acres of wasteland. Lots of gardening ideas, and unusual varieties of plants for sale. Cl Sun, bank hols and winter Sats, 2 wks over Christmas; (01206) 822007; £2.50. Over at Great Bromley, the Old Black Boy has good-value food.

EPPING FOREST TQ4197 A magnificent survival, an expansive tract of ancient hornbeam coppice, mainly tucked between the M25 and outer London; miles of leafy walks (and rides – you can hire horses locally), with some rough grazing and occasional distant views. There are so many woodland paths that getting lost is part of the experience; the long-distance Forest Way is, however, well marked. On the W side there's a pleasant diversion to High Beach, from where a few field paths lead SW.

FEERING TL8620 **Feeringbury Manor** (Coggeshall Rd) Fine big riverside garden with ponds, streams, a little waterwheel, old-fashioned plants and bog gardens. Disabled access; open am wkdys May–July (exc bank hols), or by appointment; (01376) 561946; £2. The Sun towards Kelvedon has interesting food.

★ **FINCHINGFIELD** TL6734 The county's prettiest village, with charming houses spread generously around a sloping green with a stream and pond; just off stands a pristine-looking small windmill. The Fox (one of the most attractive buildings) is useful for lunch. There's a pleasant, easily followed path along the stream to nearby Great Bardfield which also has a windmill, and charming cottages.

FRINTON-ON-SEA TM2419 A pleasant family seaside resort, with long stretches of gently shelving sandy beach; it's a quieter place than its neighbour Clacton. Beyond, the blowy open space of The Naze is pleasant for strolling, especially out of season when you're likely to have its 150 acres virtually to yourself.

★ **GREAT EASTON** TL6025 Attractive village, worth strolling through. Nearby there are pleasant gardens at Little Easton Manor; open pm Thurs May–Sept; £2.

GREAT SALING TL7025 **Saling Hall Gardens** 12 acres of tranquil gardens created over the last 50 years. There is a fine walled garden and water features, but the aboretum is the main draw. Disabled access; cl am, Weds and all Aug–Apr; £2.

★ † **GREAT WALTHAM** TL6913 Pleasant village, with an attractive and interesting church.

† **GREENSTED** TL5302 **St Andrew's Church** Recent tests have established that it was probably built around the time of the Norman Conquest – the oldest wooden church in the world. The nearby Green Man at Toot Hill has decent food (and fine wine).

HARLOW TL4611 A New Town, and not perhaps top of most itineraries, but has a couple of surprisingly good museums. **Mark Hall Cycle Museum and Gardens** (Muskham Rd) Bewildering assortment of bicycles, inc one that folds, another made from plastic – even one where the seat tips forward and throws its rider over the handlebars if the brakes are applied too hard; as we went to press they told us that this collection may be moved to the town museum. Also Tudor herb garden and 3 walled gardens. Shop, disabled access; open Mon–Fri (museum cl Mon, Thurs and Fri) and 3rd Sun of each month; (01279) 439680; *£1.75. The town **museum** (Third Ave) has an important Roman collection, and a butterfly garden. Shop; open Thurs–Sat (exc 12.30–1.30pm); free. The 1st floor of the townhall houses the **Gibberd Collection**, a surprisingly fine collection of British modern art, inc works by Graham Sutherland, Elizabeth Blackadder and John Nash, to name but a few. Open wknds and bank hols; free.

HARWICH TM2430 **The Redoubt** Circular fort built in 1808 in case of invasion by Napoleon, with 3 small museums. Shop; cl Sept–Apr; (01255) 503429; *£1. Harwich's 2 lighthouses both have small museums, one a **maritime museum** (times as above; 50p), the other a collection of vintage radios and televisions (times as above; £1). Also a little lifeboat museum (times as above, 50p), and summer cruises around the harbour. From the A120 W there's an unusual sight for this part of Essex – a tall narrow **windmill** (actually an interloper, as it was brought from Suffolk).

HATFIELD FOREST TL5320 (just S of Stansted Airport) An unexpected survivor, ancient mainly hornbeam woodland, with a nature trail and boating lake.

HULLBRIDGE TQ8193 **Jakapeni Farm** Small rare breeds park, specialising in pigs and sheep, with lake fishing (£2.50 a day). Snacks, shop, disabled access; open Sun and bank hols Easter–Oct; (01702) 232394; £1.75. The Bull at nearby Hockley has decent food, and is handy for walks in Hockley Woods.

INGATESTONE HALL TQ6598 Interesting old house, nothing too remarkable but enthusiastic tours by the family that live here, and lovely grounds. Teas, shop; open pm wknds, bank hols and Wed–Fri in school hols Apr–Sept; (01277) 353010; £3.50. The Cricketers Arms out at Mill Green is a handy food pub.

! KELVEDON HATCH TQ5599 **Secret Nuclear Bunker** (off the A128) Who'd have thought that a 3-storey Cold War underground complex lay beneath this innocuous 1950s bungalow? Knowledgeable tours through all parts of this clinically self-sufficient little world, done with real relish, but you can't help feeling relieved when you're back in the surrounding woodland. Snacks, shop; cl Mon–Weds Nov–Feb; (01277) 364883; *£5. The Black Horse in Pilgrims Hatch is a good, handy dining pub.

LAMARSH TL8836 **Paradise Centre** (Twinstead Rd) Fascinating for gardeners, with a very wide variety of unusual plants beautifully laid out and for sale, particularly woodland ones; also miniature goats, bantams and play area. Open wknds and bank hols Easter–Oct, or by appointment; (01787) 269449; *£1.50. The Lion is good for lunch, and the Bures–Henny Street rd is a pretty drive.

LAYER DE LA HAYE TL9517 **Abberton Reservoir Wildfowl and Visitor Centre** (B1026) Popular wetland stop for wildfowl; observation room and hides, nature trails, and events for families in summer. Snacks, shop, disabled access; cl Mon; (01206) 738172; £1 suggested donation (more for special events). The Donkey & Buskins (on the B1026) is handy for a meal.

LAYER MARNEY TOWER TL9217 The mansion here was never completed, but its 8-storey Tudor gatehouse is one of the most striking examples of 16th-c architecture in Britain. Formal gardens, a rare breeds farm, medieval barn, farm shop and deer park. Tearoom, shop, disabled access to grounds; cl am, all day Sat, and Oct–Mar; (01206) 330784; *£3.25.

★ **LEIGH-ON-SEA** TQ8385 Though attached to Southend, this has a quite distinct character, altogether more intimate, with wood-clad buildings and shrimp boats in the working harbour; Ivy Osborne's cockle stall here is justly famous, and the Crooked Billet overlooking the water is useful.

† **LITTLE DUNMOW** TL6521 The **church** is unusually stately for such a relatively small village – it's the surviving part of a priory founded in 1106; key from the good Flitch of Bacon pub.

† **LITTLE MAPLESTEAD** TL8234 **Church** Very different from most in the area – an unusual round building modelled on the Holy Sepulchre in Jerusalem.

† **MALDON** TL8507 An ambitious tapestry commemorating the 1,000th anniversary of the crucial Battle of Maldon is housed in the **Maeldune Centre** (Market Hill/High St); shop, (01621) 851628; £1.50. The Millennium Gardens are named for the same event, and re-create what a garden might have looked like at the time of the battle. Also a **church** with an unusual triangular tower, some decent shops, a couple of small museums, and a

riverside stroll past the golf course to the pretty weir by Beeleigh Abbey. **Hythe Quay** is full of life, and the best chance to see one of the classic Thames barges with its ox-blood sails in action.

MERSEA ISLAND TM0012 Linked to the mainland by a little causeway, which can get covered by the tide; much of its coast is a shoreside National Nature Reserve, and there's a bracing coastal walk from East Mersea along the sea-dyke overlooking the Colne estuary. It does feel very much an island, and away from the extended village of West Mersea, popular for retirement homes, there are few people about out of season (in summer the caravan parks bring in lots of families). The Willow Lodge has good food; the Blackwater and Fox are good value too.

! † **MISTLEY** TM1230 **Essex Secret Bunker** (B1352) Much of its original equipment has been returned by the government and other groups, so the operations centre at this nuclear war command centre looks especially authentic. Odd seeing something so contemporary consigned to history, especially when similar establishments are still in operation. Snacks, shop, disabled access; cl Dec–Jan and wkdys Oct–Mar; (01206) 392271; £4.75. **Animal Rescue Centre** (New Rd) Very friendly; Ping and Pong the Vietnamese pot-bellied pigs may come to greet you as you go in. Snacks, shop, disabled access; £2.50. (01206) 396483. The village has the remains of a Robert Adam church. If you come by train, don't miss the splendid station buffet at Manningtree.

★ **MORETON** TL5306 Attractive village; helpfully the pubs here usually have a leaflet detailing an interesting walk.

★ **PLESHEY** TL6614 This attractive village has a ruined castle, charming churchyard, country walks and a good pub.

RETTENDON TQ7899 RHS **Garden Rettendon** (Hyde Hall) 8 acres of year-round hillside colour, with woodland garden, big rose garden, ornamental ponds, shrubs, trees, and national collections of malus and viburnum. Meals and snacks in thatched barn, plant sales, limited disabled access; cl Nov–Mar; (01245) 400256; £3. The Barge at Battlesbridge is quite handy for lunch.

RIVER CROUCH walks TQ8596 The Ferryboat Inn down at the end of the lane through North Fambridge is a good base for lonely waterside **walks**.

★ **ROWHEDGE** TM0221 The village itself is well worth a visit; and nearby is a nature reserve among former gravel workings at Fingringhoe.

★ † **ST OSYTH** TM1215 Pretty village distinguished by the remarkable crenellated flint gateway leading to **St Osyth Priory**. The buildings and grounds beyond are lovely but as we went to press were up for sale and closed to the public. The White Hart towards Point Clear has decent food, and, not too far away, the beach at Brightlingsea is probably the county's best.

★ † **SAFFRON WALDEN** TL5438 The region's finest small town, with prime examples of warmly colour-washed pargeting throughout. Walking around to look at the buildings, you'll be tempted into one of the many antique shops (or David Prue, the fine cabinet-maker in Radwinter Rd; cl wknds). The grand airy **church** has a magnificent spire, the very ruined **castle** up on a grassy

Days Out

Pargeting extravaganza: Audley End; Saffron Walden – lunch at the Eight Bells there; Arkesden, Clavering.

Inland from the Blackwater: Beth Chatto Gardens, Elmstead Market; Layer Marney Tower; Abberton wildfowl centre, Layer de la Haye; lunch at the Sun, Feering; Feeringbury Manor garden there; Thames barges at Maldon; Wivenhoe, Rowhedge, Wickham Bishops villages.

mound is worth prowling around, and children will enjoy the maze on the Common. Notable natural history section in the town **museum** as well as social history and toys and dolls; good disabled access; cl am Sun and bank hols, 24–25 Dec; (01799) 510333; £1. The Eight Bells does good food. **Bridge End Gardens** (Bridge St) Pleasant early Victorian gardens with rose garden, formal Dutch garden, kitchen garden and an atmospheric wilderness leading to a little grotto. You'll need to get a key from the tourist information centre (Market Pl) to explore the yew tree maze. Disabled access; cl 25 Dec; free. **Audley End House** (B1383, 1m W of Saffron Waldon) Spectacular Jacobean mansion and former Royal palace remodelled by Robert Adam, serenely surrounded by splendid gardens landscaped by Capability Brown from the town you can walk straight into the park. Nothing inside can compete with the quite breathtaking façade, but it's not for want of trying there are around 30 rooms to see, crammed with fine furnishings and art. Suitably grand concerts and other events in the grounds. Snacks, shop, disabled access to gardens and ground floor; cl Mon (exc bank hols), Tues, and Oct–Easter; (01799) 522842; £5.75, £3.50 grounds only. The town has a goodish network of tracks for walks around it, extending into Audley End's parkland. Longer rambles can take in Newport (more pargeting), and Wendens Ambo. The B184 to Chipping Ongar is a nice country drive; about 4m along Grace's Farm Shop at Wimbish is good, with pick-your-own in summer. Another good drive is the B1053 to Braintree.

SOUTHEND-ON-SEA TQ8885 Traditional seaside resort long favoured by East Londoners, with many of the attractions you'd expect. Most famous is the pier, the longest in the world, excellent for fishing, with a museum and happily a restored train service – it's a long walk there and back. **Central Museum and Planetarium** (Victoria Ave) The only planetarium in the SE outside London, with a local history museum too. Shop; cl Sun and bank hols (planetarium also cl Mon and Tues); (01702) 330214; planetarium £2.25, museum free. **Sea Life Centre** (Eastern Esplanade) Fun way of exploring underwater life, with bubble-windows to make it seem as if you're in there with the sea creatures, and walk-through tunnel along reconstructed seabed. Children like the shark exhibition. Meals, snacks, shop, disabled access; cl 25 Dec; (01702) 462400; £4.95. **Southchurch Hall Museum** (Park Lane) An unexpected find, a medieval moated manor house in an attractive park, with period room settings, and fun talks on Tudor life inc lute demonstrations every am Sat. Shop, limited disabled access; cl 1–2pm, all Sun and Mon; (01702) 467671; free, talks £1.50. **Prittlewell Priory Museum** (Priory Park, slightly N of centre) 12th-c Cluniac priory in nice grounds, with eclectic collections of local and religious history; details as Southchurch Hall. Like many such resorts, Southend in winter has a special appeal for people who wouldn't like it in summer – seafront shops by the endless promenade looking closed for ever, the sea itself a doleful muddy grey. Readers enjoy the Westcliff part of town, with its decent art gallery (cl 1–2pm, Sun and Mon, free). Summer **boat trips** include occasional runs on a vintage paddle-steamer: (01634) 827648 for dates. There are year-round ferries to Felixstowe.

★ **SOUTH WEALD** TQ5992 Attractive village; the Tower Arms is a decent food pub. **Old Macdonald's farm park** (Weald Rd) Very extensive range of animals, with 30 breeds of sheep alone. Demonstrations, nature trails and craft displays, and plenty of opportunities to stroke the animals. Meals, snacks, shop, disabled access; cl 25–26 Dec; (01277) 375177; £2.75. Nearby is a **country park** with deer enclosure, lakes, woods, and visitor centre.

STANSTED MOUNTFITCHET TL5024 **House on the Hill Toy Museum** The biggest, privately owned toy collection in the world, with over 30,000 toys, games and playthings from Victorian times to the 1970s; entertaining and well thought out displays, lots of them animated. There are a few coin-operated slot machines and puppet shows, and a good collectors' shop. All indoors, so good in any weather; cl mid-Dec–mid-Jan; (01279) 813237; *£3.50. **Mountfitchet Castle and 1066 Village** Authentically reconstructed Norman castle and village, complete with thatched houses, and deer, sheep, goats and chickens wandering around between them. The castle includes a small chunk of the original, and dummies show gruesome examples of torture and punishment. Snacks (and space for picnics), shop, disabled access; cl mid-Nov–mid-Mar; *£4.50. It's under the same management as the toy museum 5 minutes' walk up the hill. The well preserved 18th-c **windmill** still has much of its original equipment (though isn't working). Open pm 1st Sun of month Apr–Oct, plus pm every Sun in Aug, and pm bank hol Sun and Mon; 50p. The Cricketers Arms at nearby Rickling Green is good for lunch.

★ ✝ **THAXTED** TL6131 This engaging small town has a graceful, airy **church** (Holst was organist here) with a tremendous spire, several handsome buildings inc nearby almshouses, a fine **guildhall** (small local museum), and a restored **windmill**. The **Raven Armoury** (on the B184 towards Dunmow) does hand-forged steel and weaponry. The 15th-c Swan has decent food.

TILBURY FORT TQ6475 Well preserved 17th-c fort with unusual double moat; good views of the Thames estuary. The most violent episode in its history was a 1776 cricket match that left three dead. Snacks, shop, some disabled access; cl Mon and Tues Oct–Mar, 24–26 Dec; (01375) 858489; £2.30. For an extra £1 you can fire a 1943 3.7 anti-aircraft gun – irresistible for several children of our acquaintance. A pleasant 3-mile walk along the Thames reaches **Coalhouse Fort** TQ6976 (off the A1013, Orsett–Stanford-le-Hope; open last Sun of month and bank hols Nov–Feb; £2).

✝ **WALTHAM ABBEY** TL3800 Despite the surrounding housing developments, the centre has some handsome buildings – especially the **Abbey Church** with its famous peal of 13 bells (and a museum in the crypt). Associated ruins include part of a Norman cloister, and the bridge dates back to the abbey's time. **Epping Forest District Museum** (Sun St) Lively holiday activities for children, in 2 timber-framed old houses. Shop, limited disabled access; open pm Fri–Tues; (01992) 716882; free. **Lee Valley Farm Park** (2m N on the B194) Takes in Hayes Hill children's farm with plenty of traditional animals, a pet centre and play area, and Holyfield Hall working farm and dairy, with 150 cows milked every afternoon at 2.45pm, and seasonal events like sheep-shearing and harvesting. Snacks, shop, disabled access; (01992) 892781; £2.75.

WALTON ON THE NAZE TM2623 There's a pleasant walk northwards from this quiet seaside town, along the coast, round the tip of The Naze – with views of shipping entering and leaving Harwich and Felixstowe – to a **nature reserve** harbouring migrant birds, with a nature trail.

WETHERSFIELD TL7229 **Boydells Dairy Farm** Working dairy farm where you may be able to join in milking the goats and cows – or even the sheep. Also working beehives, various other animals, and ice-lollies made from their own sheep yoghurt. Snacks, shop, disabled access; open Fri–Sun mid-Apr–Sept, plus pm Weds and Thurs Jun, July and Sept, and pm daily during school hols; (01371) 850481; £2.50.

WIDDINGTON TL5431 **Mole Hall Wildlife Park** Family-run place with wide variety of animals around moated manor house. Otters a speciality, but also free-roaming wildfowl, deer paddock and butterfly house. Summer snacks, shop, some disabled access; cl 25 Dec; (01799) 540400; £4.50 in summer, less in winter when butterfly house is closed. The Fleur-de-Lys is a popular food pub.

Windmills Good ones are to be seen at Aythorpe Roding TL5815, Bocking TL7527 and Mountnessing TQ6397.

★ **Other attractive villages**, all with decent pubs, include Arkesden TL4834, Blackmore TL6001, Fuller Street

TL7416, Fyfield TL5606, Great Chesterford TL5143, Great Warley Street TQ5890, waterside Heybridge Basin TL8707, Knowl Green TL7841, Paglesham TQ9293, Roydon TL4109, Stebbing TL6624, Wickham Bishops TL8412 and Wivenhoe TM0321.

Where to eat

BLACKMORE END TL7430 **Bull** *(01371) 851037* Comfortable, tucked-away dining pub with pretty cottagey restaurant area, good snacks, excellent meals, interesting choice of wines; cl Mon exc bank hols; children in restaurant. **£20**.

BRIGHTLINGSEA TM0816 **Coffee Pot** *Victoria Pl (01206) 305738* Spotlessly clean, with very good breakfast, lunch and tea – everything is freshly made daily; helpful and friendly staff; cl pm, Sun; disabled access. £3.25.

BURNHAM-ON-CROUCH TQ9595 **Contented Sole** *80 High St (01621) 782139* Long-standing, family-run restaurant very popular for consistently good, imaginative food with an emphasis on fine seafood; wine tastings all year; cl pm Sun, Mon, 4 wks from 24 Dec, 2 wks Sept; disabled access. **£42**|£11.95 2 courses.

BURNHAM-ON-CROUCH TQ9595 **Crooked Cottage Tea Rooms** *1 The Quay (01621) 783868* 17th-c beamed fishermen's cottages, with seats in the summer rose garden; nice cream teas with home-made cakes and a huge choice of teas, and friendly service; cl Mon (exc bank hols), mid-week Nov–Mar. £3.75.

CASTLE HEDINGHAM TL7835 **Bell** *St James's St (01787) 460350* Interesting old coaching inn with a log fire in the beamed lounge bar, traditionally furnished public bar, quickly served decent food, and a lovely big walled garden behind; cl pm Mon or Sun in winter. **£15**|£6.

CLAVERING TL4731 **Cricketers** *Wicken Rd (01799) 550442* Attractive and cosy L-shaped dining pub with low beams, 2 open fires, and a wide choice of imaginative, well presented food in the bar and restaurant; pretty bdrms; cl 25–26 Dec; disabled access. **£29**|£3.50.

COLCHESTER TM0025 **Clowns** *61 High St (01206) 578631* Huge helpings of nice, straightforward food in this clean, spacious restaurant; good children's menu, too; disabled access. **£17.50**|£4.25.

COLCHESTER TM0025 **Warehouse Brasserie** *12 Chapel St N (01206) 765656* Bustling brasserie on several levels with really enjoyable food using organic produce, a relaxed and chatty atmosphere, good service, and an eclectic wine list; very good-value set meals; cl pm Sun; disabled access. **£20**|£3.95.

DEDHAM TM0533 **Mallard** *Riverside Cottage, Mill Lane (01206) 322066* Unlicensed little riverside restaurant with a homely relaxed atmosphere and good straightforward food; cl Mon–Tues, 2–20 Jan. **£21.50**|£6.

FYFIELD TL5606 **Black Bull** *(01277) 899225* Prettily lit and vine-covered dining pub with nice, interesting food in low-beamed communicating rooms, well kept real ales, a welcoming atmosphere, and seats and an aviary in the garden. **£17.75**|£7.25.

GOSFIELD TL7829 **Green Man** *(01787) 472746* Smart restauranty pub with relaxed, chatty atmosphere, impeccable service, 2 little bars and no smoking dining room; super food inc marvellous lunchtime cold buffet and delicious puddings, well kept real ales and decent wines, many by the glass. **£17.75**|£7.

GREAT YELDHAM TL7638 **White Hart** *Poole St (01787) 237250* Striking Tudor inn with an attractive garden, beams and oak panelling in refurbished rooms (one is no smoking), exceptionally good and inventive food (very good-value set 3-course menu), and fine wines; cl pm Sun, Mon; disabled access. **£25**|£7.95.

HARWICH TM2632 **Pier at Harwich** *The Quay (01255) 241212* Delicious fish and chips and smarter fish dishes in an attractive building overlooking the Stour and Orwell estuaries; cl pm 25–26 Dec. **£38.50**|£5.95.

HORNDON ON THE HILL TQ6683 **Bell** *(01375) 673154* Flower-decked medieval inn with welcoming licensees, an open-plan beamed bar with polished oak floorboards and flagstones; carefully prepared imaginative food, 5 real ales, good choice of wines; restaurant cl 25–26 Dec; no children. **£25**|£8.95.

LITTLE DUNMOW TL6521 **Flitch of Bacon** *(01371) 820323* Friendly pub with a small, attractively furnished, timbered bar, a sensibly small range of good, unpretentious bar food, popular Sunday buffet, and real ales; comfortable bdrms. **£17.50**|£6.50.

SAFFRON WALDEN TL5438 **Eight Bells** *Bridge St (01799) 522790* Handsome Tudor inn with lots of daily specials in splendidly timbered weekend restaurant, well kept real ales, a good choice of wines by the glass, and friendly service. **£20**|£3.95.

WEST MERSEA TM0112 **Willow Lodge** *108 Coast Rd (01206) 383568* Large, busy restaurant with a wide range of excellent food inc lots of fresh fish; cl pm Sun, Mon; well behaved children welcome; disabled access. **£20**|£6

WETHERSFIELD TL7131 **Dickens** *The Green (01371) 850723* Mainly 17th-c, very popular restaurant in quiet country spot; lovely modern cooking, fine wines, very good service; cl pm Sun, Mon, Tues; disabled access. **£25**.

YOUNG'S END TL7319 **Green Dragon** *(01245) 361030* Well run dining pub, restaurant area with attractive, understated barn theme (no smoking section), an extensive range of very good, interesting bar food, well kept real ales, plenty of seats in the back garden. **£18.65**|£7.25.

Special thanks to Mr and Mrs R A Sceats.

We welcome reports from readers

This *Guide* depends on readers' reports. Do help us if you can – in return, we offer a discount on the next edition to people who've helped us with reports for it. Tell us what you think about places already in it, and anything extra you think we should say about them. And send us your ideas for inclusion in the next edition: places to visit, eat at or stay in, attractive drives or walks, maybe even unusual interesting shops you know of. Use the card in the middle, the report forms at the end, or just write – no stamp needed: *The Good Guide to Britain*, FREEPOST TN1569, Wadhurst, E Sussex TN5 7BR.

Essex Calendar

Some of these dates were provisional as we went to press. Please check information with the telephone numbers provided.

JANUARY

10 **Lee Valley Park** Bird Race: who can spot the most birds in one day (01992) 717711
29 **Harwich** Film Festival – *till Sun 31* (01255) 676381

FEBRUARY

19 **Old Harlow** Viola Festival at St John's Arts and Recreation Centre – *till Sun 21* (01279) 442447

APRIL

2 **Chappel** Thomas the Tank Engine at East Anglian Railway Museum – *till Mon 5* (01206) 242524; **Stanford-le-Hope** Stationary Engine Rally at Walton Hall Farm Museum – *till Mon 5* (01375) 671874; **Walton** Folk Festival – *till Mon 5* (01255) 256155
4 **Billericay** Family Day at Barleylands Farm – *till Mon 5* (01268) 532032

MAY

2 **Billericay** May Madness at Barleylands Farm – *till Mon 3* (01268) 532032
3 **Dovercourt** Tour de Tendring: cycle Rally (01255) 256168
9 **Colchester** Classic Vehicle Rally at the Colchester Institute, Sheepen Road (01206) 718000
11 **Benfleet** European Beer Festival at Runnymede Hall – *till Sat 15* (01268) 792711
12 **Chelmsford** Cathedral Festival – *till Sat 22* (01245) 359890
16 **Battlesbridge** Classic Car Show (01268) 575000; **Epping** Air Show at North Weald Airfield (01992) 522210; **Great Leighs** Essex Young Farmers Show at the Essex Showground (01245) 362411
21 **Epping** Aerofair at North Weald Airfield – *till Sun 23* (01992) 522210
29 **Southend-on-Sea** Air Show: free event – *till Mon 31* (01702) 215465
30 **Billericay** May Madness at Barleylands Farm – *till Mon 31* (01268) 532032; **Chelmsford** Opera Festival *till 12 Jun* (01245) 606636

JUNE

5 **Chappel** Model Railway Exhibition at East Anglian Railway Museum – *till Sun 6* (01206) 242524; **Thaxted** Morris Ring: annual meeting of over 200 morris men, massed dancing in the morning – *till Sun 6* (01371) 831024
6 **Southend-on Sea** Brass Band Competition (01702) 215118
12 **Braintree** Carnival (01376) 551969; **Southend-on-Sea** Water Festival – *till Sun 13* (01702) 215465
18 **Great Leighs** Essex County Show at the Essex Showground – *till Sun 20* (01245) 362412; **Thaxted** Festival: classical and jazz concerts, workshops – *weekends till 11 July* (01371) 831421

Essex Calendar (cont.)

19 **Brentwood** Strawberry Fair: vintage vehicles, swing orchestra, morris dancing at Shenfield Common (01277) 201111; **Castle Hedingham** Thomas the Tank Engine at the Colne Valley Railway – *till Sun 20* (01787) 461174; **Harwich** Festival: inc special openings of historic buildings, concerts – *till Sun 27* (01255) 880590; **Maldon** Blackwater Barge Match: historic vehicles race on River Blackwater, best at Maldon Quay in the afternoon (01621) 851147

25 **Old Leigh and Southend-on-Sea** Folk Festival: more than 350 free music and dance events – *till Sun 27* (01702) 215465

26 **Castle Hedingham** Thomas the Tank Engine at the Colne Valley Railway – *till Sun 27* (01787) 461174; **Harwich** Festival – *till 4 July* (01245) 437748

27 **Canvey Island** Castle Point Show at Waterside Farm Showground (01268) 792711

JULY

4 **Battlesbridge** Motorcycle Rally and bike jumble (01268) 575000; **Clacton-on-Sea** Classic Vehicle Show (01255) 256155

10 **Manningtree** Tendring Hundred Show at Lawford Park (01206) 571517

15 **Cressing** Festival of Early Music at Cressing Temple Barns – *till Sun 25* (01376) 584903

17 **Chappel** Meccano Exhibition at East Anglian Railway Museum – *till Sun 18* (01206) 242524

24 **West Bergholt** Historic Vehicle Show: about 500 entries – *till Sun 25* (01206) 271253

25 **Southend-on-Sea** Classic Car Run (01702) 215455

28 **Southend-on-Sea** Jazz Festival – *till 1 Aug* (01702) 215120

AUGUST

8 **Great Leighs** Essex Heavy Horse Show at the Essex Showground (01787) 237880

13 **Southend-on-Sea** Carnival Week – *till* illuminated Carnival Procession and Fireworks *on Sat 21* (01702) 215118

14 **Chelmsford** V99: rock concert at Hylands Park – *till Sun 15* (01245) 606985;

21 **Purleigh** English Wine Festival at New Hall Vineyards: country skills fair and family events – *till Sun 22* (01621) 828343

26 **Clacton-on-Sea** Air Show: Red Arrows – *till Fri 27* (01255) 423400

27 **Brentwood** Festival – *till 19 Sept* (01277) 201111; **Chelmsford** Spectacular at Hylands Farm: open-air concerts, street entertainment, fringe tents – *till Mon 30* (01245) 606977; **Clacton-on-Sea** Jazz Festival – *till Mon 30* (01245) 423400; **Great Leighs** International Custom Car Show – *till Mon 30* (01384) 392742

28 **Southend-on-Sea** Sailing Barge Race (01702) 215465

SEPTEMBER

4 **Orsett** Horticultural and Agricultural Show at the Orsett Showground (01708) 224666

8 **Chappel** Beer Festival: about 120 beers and ciders at the East Anglian Railway Museum – *till Sat 11* (01206) 242524

Essex Calendar (cont.)

11 Billericay Essex Steam Rally and Craft Fair at Barleylands Farm: over 300 stands – *till Sun 12* (01268) 532032
17 Brentwood International Blues Festival – *till Sun 19* (01277) 201111
19 Brentwood Town and Country Show (01277) 201111
26 Battlesbridge Vintage Vehicle Rally (01268) 575000

OCTOBER

3 Colchester Countryside Open Day at High Woods Country Park: historic re-enactments, rare breeds, activities (01206) 853588
29 Saffron Walden Folk Festival – *till Sun 31* (01799) 528046
30 Chappel Halloween Party and Steam Fair at the East Anglian Railway Museum (01206) 242524

NOVEMBER

6 Canvey Island Fireworks at Waterside Farm Showground (01268) 792711
11 Southend-on-Sea Christmas Lights (01702) 215465
27 Southend-on-Sea Victorian Christmas in the High St – *till Sun 28* (01702) 215120

DECEMBER

5 Chappel Santa Steam Days at the East Anglian Railway Museum, also *Sat 11, Sun 12, Sat 18, Sun 19* (01206) 242524

We welcome reports from readers

This *Guide* depends on readers' reports. Do help us if you can – in return, we offer a discount on the next edition to people who've helped us with reports for it. Tell us what you think about places already in it, and anything extra you think we should say about them. And send us your ideas for inclusion in the next edition: places to visit, eat at or stay in, attractive drives or walks, maybe even unusual interesting shops you know of. Use the card in the middle, the report forms at the end, or just write – no stamp needed: *The Good Guide to Britain*, FREEPOST TN1569, Wadhurst, E Sussex TN5 7BR.

Gloucestershire

Idyllic Cotswold villages and countryside, lots of interesting places to visit, excellent places to stay in.

This is one of the best parts of Britain for a relaxing short break, with good food and lovely places to stay in. It's the countryside above all which delights – especially the rolling hills themselves, with their traditional dry stone-walled fields, occasional beechwoods, meandering streams, and beautiful villages of warm golden-tinted stone picturesquely roofed in heavy stone slabs. Many villages have handsome medieval churches, and their cottages and houses don't hide away behind gardens and high walls, but tend to be right by the road. Often, there's a strip of daffodil-planted grass between pavement and road (the area is particularly attractive in spring), and sometimes a little stream. The one snag is that the Cotswolds tend to be expensive – particularly in the north. In the summer they do attract a great many visitors, though even then you can find delightful villages that have escaped the crowds – especially in the south.

Chipping Campden, Cirencester, Northleach, Painswick and Stow-on-the-Wold are all handsome Cotswold towns bulging with sightseeing possibilities – and antique shops; Tewkesbury too is attractive. Gloucester – a busy modern city – has a great deal to reward a day visit. Nearby Cheltenham still has a considerable degree of Regency elegance (and good events – they're packing special energy into the literature festival this year). It's a useful base for exploring the area; the tourism office does a good leaflet detailing how to get to most Cotswold attractions by public transport.

This county's strongest appeal is to adults, with plenty of marvellous outings. Snowshill Manor, Stanway House, Sudeley Castle near Winchcombe, the Chedworth Roman villa, and the visible restoration of the never-finished Gothic mansion at Nympsfield are particular favourites, and the Nature in Art collection at Twigworth is very special. Some of the county's gardens and parks are unforgettable, especially Kiftsgate near Mickleton, the arboretums at Westonbirt and Batsford near Moreton-in-Marsh, and, particularly in late May, the gardens of Lydney Park.

Among the best family days out are the friendly farm and animal park at Blockley, the farm park at Kineton, the country park at Tockington, steam railways at Lydney and Toddington, and for younger children the clever Treasure Train at Coleford. Many children join adults in enjoying the birds of prey centres at Batsford and outside Newent. The Slimbridge wildfowl centre is outstanding for all ages. Bourton on the Water, despite the crowds, is well worth a visit by old and young alike, with Birdland, the enterprising new Dragonfly Maze, and other appealing places in charming surroundings. For something a bit different, the Clearwell caverns are an adventure – not to mention the Coopers Hill cheese-rolling race if the safety police lift their ban on this ancient tradition (see *Calendar*).

For cyclists, the Cotswolds are great – quiet village-to-village lanes with ever-changing views. Campus Holidays hire out bikes and can arrange your route and accommodation; (01242) 250642. Extended walks over the Cotswold plateau are not always rewarding, with unchanging views of arable fields often the rule. However, there are plenty of really enjoyable walks through choice scenery, with the long-distance Cotswold Way between Chipping Campden and Bath tracing through much of the best.

Away from the Cotswolds, some less well known parts are delightful (and generally cheaper): the tortuously steep hills and valleys around Stroud, the quiet watermeadows of the upper Thames, the unspoilt orchard and farming countryside around the Severn Valley (so few river crossings that the little villages down by the west bank, with few people passing through, have a very secluded and unchanging feel). The Forest of Dean has a unique landscape: hilly woodland, much of it ancient, that shows many traces of the way it has provided a livelihood for the people living around it (the newly opened free-miner colliery near Coleford is particularly interesting). The Forest is flanked by a spectacular stretch of the Wye Valley, and its woodland colours are at their best in late May and autumn.

Where to stay

BIBURY SP1106 **Bibury Court** *Bibury, Cirencester GL7 5NT (01285) 740337* **£98.90;** 19 individual rms. Lovely peaceful mansion dating from Tudor times, in beautiful gardens, with an informally friendly atmosphere, panelled rooms, antiques, huge log fires, conservatory, and good imaginative food; cl Christmas.

BIBURY SP1106 **Swan** *Bibury, Cirencester GL7 5NW (01285) 740695* **£150,** plus special breaks; 18 very pretty individually decorated rms. Handsome creeper-covered hotel on the River Coln with private fishing and attractive formal gardens, lovely flowers and log fires in carefully furnished comfortable lounges, a cosy no smoking parlour, good food in opulent dining room, nice breakfasts, and attentive staff; disabled access.

BLEDINGTON SP2422 **Kings Head** *The Green, Bledington, Chipping Norton, Oxon OX7 6XQ (01608) 658365* ***£65;** 12 rms (2 over the kitchen can be noisy). Very nicely placed 15th-c Cotswold inn by duck-filled stream with cheery log fire in atmospheric bar, lounge overlooking garden, good food in bar and attractive, partly no smoking restaurant, and friendly service; cl 24–25 Dec; limited disabled access.

BROADWELL SP2027 **College House** *Chapel St, Broadwell, Moreton-in-Marsh GL56 0TW (01451) 832351* **£60;** 3 lovely big rms, 2 with own bthrm. 17th-c house with large inglenook fireplace in flagstoned sitting room, good breakfasts, and delicious evening meals – which can be eaten on the terrace in summer; no children.

BROOKTHORPE SO8312 **Gilberts** *Gilberts Lane, Brookthorpe, Gloucester GL4 0UH (01452) 812364* **£48;** 4 rms. 400-year-old house with woodburning stove and games in sitting room, organic produce from the surrounding smallholding used for delicious breakfast (own honey and eggs); relaxed atmosphere; non smokers preferred.

BUCKLAND SP0836 **Buckland Manor** *Buckland, Broadway, Worcs WR12 7LY (01386) 852626* ***£195,** plus special breaks; 13 sumptuous rms. Really lovely 13th-c building in 10 acres of beautifully kept gardens, comfortable lounges with magnificent oak panelling, flowers and antiques; elegant restaurant with fine food using home-grown produce; outdoor swimming pool, riding, tennis, croquet, putting; children over 12.

CHARINGWORTH SP2039 **Charingworth Manor** *Charingworth, Chipping Campden GL55 6NS (01386) 593555* **£170;** 26 lovely rms with thoughtful extras. Early 14th-c manor with Jacobean additions set in fine grounds, with mullioned windows, antiques, log fires and heavy oak beams in relaxing sitting room; good modern cooking in charming restaurant, excellent breakfasts, and friendly staff; billiards, leisure spa with indoor swimming pool, and all-weather tennis court; dogs by arrangement.

CHELTENHAM SO9522 **Hotel on the Park** *Evesham Rd, Cheltenham GL52 2AH (01242) 518898* ***£109,** plus special breaks; 12 lovely rms. Warmly welcoming and handsome Regency house with elegantly furnished drawing room and dining room, pretty flowers and antiques; imaginative food in stylish restaurant – good breakfasts, too; children over 8.

CHELTENHAM SO9421 **Lypiatt House** *Lypiatt Rd, Cheltenham GL50 2QW (01242) 224994* **£60,** plus wknd breaks; 10 attractive rms. Carefully restored Victorian house in its own grounds, open fire, books and plants in light comfortable drawing room, little conservatory bar, and friendly, personal service.

CHIPPING CAMPDEN SP1539 **Eight Bells** *Chipping Campden GL55 6JG (01386) 840371* ***£45;** 2 rms. Neatly restored heavy-beamed 14th-c pub by church; three log fires; interesting food with fresh local produce, decent wines and beers, friendly staff, and pleasant courtyard; cl 25 Dec; disabled access.

CHIPPING CAMPDEN SP1539 **Noel Arms** *High St, Chipping Campden GL55 6AT (01386) 840317* **£99,** plus special breaks; 26 comfortable, recently refurbished rms. Bustling 14th-c inn with comfortable traditionally furnished small lounge areas, open fire, armour and antiques, conservatory, restaurant, and decent wines; disabled access.

CLEARWELL SO5708 **Tudor Farmhouse** *Clearwell, Coleford GL16 8JS (01594) 833046* **£58,** plus special breaks; 13 cottagey rms. Carefully restored Tudor farmhouse and stone cottages with landscaped gardens and surrounding fields, lots of beams, sloping floors and oak doors; delicious food in candlelit restaurant, and friendly staff; cl 1 wk over Christmas.

CLEARWELL SO5708 **Wyndham Arms** *Clearwell, Coleford GL16 8JT (01594) 833666* ***£75,** plus special winter and wknd breaks; 17 well equipped rms. Smart and neatly kept old country inn with comfortable beamed bar, open fire, particularly good food (much home-grown), good service, and friendly dogs; disabled access.

CORSE LAWN SO8330 **Corse Lawn House** *Corse Lawn, Gloucester GL19 4LZ (01452) 780771* ***£100,** plus special breaks; 19 pretty, individually furnished rms. Magnificent Queen Anne building with comfortable and attractive day rooms, a distinguished restaurant with good interesting food and excellent wines (there's a less pricey bistro-style operation too), warmly friendly staff, a relaxed atmosphere, and 12 acres of surrounding gardens and fields; dogs welcome; cl 24–26 Dec; disabled access.

GREAT RISSINGTON SP1917 **Lamb** *Great Rissington, Cheltenham GL54 2LP (01451) 820388* **£60w,** plus special breaks; 14 pretty rms – several are suites with own lounge. Civilised 17th-c inn with sheltered hillside garden, cosy 2-roomed bar, residents' lounge with log fire, good nearby walks; cl 25–26 Dec; dogs by prior arrangement.

GREET SP0230 **Manor Farm** *Greet, Cheltenham GL54 5BJ (01242) 602423* **£45;** 3 rms. Carefully restored 16th-c manor house on mixed farm, with fine views, big garden and croquet; also, self-catering cottages; cl Christmas.

HAZLETON SP0818 **Windrush House** *Hazleton, Cheltenham GL54 4EB (01451) 860364* ***£48;** 4 rms, 2 with own bthrm. Warmly friendly and neatly kept no smoking guest house with exceptionally good, imaginative food, lovely breakfasts, and traditional furnishings; cl mid-Dec–mid-Feb; no children, no dogs.

KINETON SP0926 **Halfway House** *Kineton, nr Guiting Power, Cheltenham GL54 5UG (01451) 850344* **£36;** 3 rms, shared bthrm. Friendly little stone pub with a good mix of customers, a warm fire, farm tools and pictures in the unpretentious bar, tasty food inc themed nights, and well kept real ales.

LITTLE BARRINGTON SP2012 **Inn For All Seasons** *Little Barrington, Burford, Oxon OX18 4TN (01451) 844324* ***£79;** 10 rms. Handsome old inn with low beams, stripped stone and flagstones, a big log fire, old prints; particularly good fresh fish and other food, well kept real ales and wines, lots of malt whiskies, and a pleasant garden surrounded by good walks; cl 25–26 Dec.

LITTLE RISSINGTON SP1819 **Touchstone** *Little Rissington, Cheltenham GL54 2ND (01451) 822481* ***£38;** 3 rms with thoughtful extras. Attractive traditional Cotswold stone house with very friendly owners, good breakfasts in dining room with doors on to terrace, lots of nearby walks; children over 7; cl Dec–Jan.

LOWER SLAUGHTER SP1622 **Lower Slaughter Manor** *Lower Slaughter, Cheltenham GL54 2HP (01451) 820456* **£215;** 15 luxurious, well equipped rms. Grand 17th-c manor house with 4 acres of neatly kept grounds, a 15th-c dovecot, all-weather tennis court, croquet, and indoor pool; lovely flower arrangements, log fires, fine plaster ceilings, antiques and paintings; excellent modern cooking and award-winning wines in the elegant restaurant, and attentive welcoming staff; children over 12.

LOWER SWELL SP1725 **Old Farmhouse** *Lower Swell, Cheltenham GL54 1LF (01451) 830232* **£72,** plus special breaks; 12 rms, some in main building but most in various barns, stables and outbuildings, and all with own bthrm. Peaceful and unpretentious 16th-c manor farm with log fire in lounge bar, good interesting food using fresh local produce, a thoughtful wine list, friendly staff, and walled rose garden; restaurant.

MORETON-IN-MARSH SP2032 **White Hart Royal** Moreton-in-Marsh *GL56 0BA (01608) 650731* **£73;** 19 good rms. Busy and comfortable partly 15th-c inn with interesting Civil War history, oak beams, stripped stone, big inglenook fire in lounge area just off main bar, friendly helpful staff, well kept real ales, decent food in bar and pleasant restaurant, and quick welcoming service; attractive courtyard; disabled access.

NAILSWORTH ST8599 **Egypt Mill** *Nailsworth, Stroud GL6 0AE (01453) 833449* ***£75,** plus special breaks; 18 comfortable airy rms. Carefully converted 16th-c watermill with original millstones and lifting equipment in the spacious lounge, a split-level restaurant, ground floor bar where 2 waterwheels can be seen, good freshly made food, friendly service, and seats in the waterside gardens; disabled access.

NORTH CERNEY SP0208 **Bathurst Arms** *North Cerney, Cirencester GL7 7BZ (01285) 831281* **£45;** 5 refurbished rms. Civilised and handsome old inn with lots of atmosphere, notably friendly staff, a nice mix of polished old furniture, warm fires, very good food, good wines, and attractive garden running down to river.

NORTH NIBLEY ST7596 **New Inn** *Waterley Bottom, North Nibley, Dursley GL11 6EF (01453) 543659* **£35;** 2 rms, shared bthrm. Simple inn with character landlady, wholesome home-made food, plentiful breakfasts, several interesting ales, neatly kept garden, small orchard, good nearby walks; cl Christmas–New Year; no children.

NORTHLEACH SP1114 **Market House** *The Square, Northleach, Cheltenham GL54 3EJ (01451) 860557* **£44;** 4 rms, mostly shared bthrm. Pretty 400-year-old stone house with flagstones, beams and inglenook fireplace, and good breakfasts; cl Dec–Jan; children over 12.

ODDINGTON SP2225 **Horse & Groom** *Oddington, Moreton-in-Marsh GL56 0XH (01451) 830584* **£65,** plus special breaks; 7 quaint and comfortable rms. Attractive, well run inn in pretty Cotswold village with handsome old furnishings, big log fire, candlelit dining room, and lovely garden with watergarden and large play area; small well behaved dogs by arrangement.

PAINSWICK SO8609 **Painswick Hotel** *Kemps Lane, Painswick, Stroud GL6 6YB (01452) 812160* **£150;** 20 well equipped comfortable rms. 18th-c Palladian mansion – once a grand rectory – with fine views, antiques and paintings in the elegant rooms, open fires, good food using the best local produce, and a relaxed friendly atmosphere; garden with croquet lawn.

PARKEND SO6108 **Edale House** *Folly Rd, Parkend, Lydney GL15 4JF (01594) 562835* **£45,** plus wknd breaks; 5 rms, most with own bthrm. Georgian house opposite cricket green and backing on to Nagshead Nature Reserve, with comfortable sitting room, very good food in attractive dining room (overlooking the garden), and a relaxed atmosphere; self-catering cottages; cl Jan; children over 12.

PUCKRUP SO8836 **Puckrup Hall** *Puckrup, Tewkesbury GL20 6EL (01684) 296200* **£130,** plus special breaks; 84 comfortably spacious rms. Handsome Regency mansion in over 140 acres of parkland with its own par 71, 18-hole golf course, and leisure club inc indoor swimming pool, crèche, gym and so forth; elegant lounge with fine plasterwork, relaxed bar overlooking croquet lawn, and good food in four different dining areas; disabled access.

ST BRIAVELS SO5605 **George** *St Briavels, Lydney GL15 6TA (01594) 530228* ***£40;** 3 rms, plus special breaks. Pleasant old pub in particularly interesting village overlooking 12th-c castle, with 3 rambling rooms, big stone fireplace, a Celtic coffin lid dating from 1070 (found in a fireplace here and now mounted next to the bar counter), cosy dining room, and good food; outdoor chessboard.

SHURDINGTON SO9218 **Greenway** *Shurdington, Cheltenham GL51 5UG (01242) 862352* **£140,** plus special breaks; 19 well equipped, spacious and pretty rms. Very well run, lovely 16th-c manor house with antiques, fresh flowers and comfortable seats in the attractive drawing room, cosy cocktail bar, particularly good modern British cooking, excellent wine list, attentive service, and neatly kept gardens; children over 7; limited disabled access.

STOW-ON-THE-WOLD SP1925 **Grapevine** *Sheep St, Stow-on-the-Wold, Cheltenham GL54 1AU (01451) 830344* **£148,** plus special breaks; 22 well furnished rms. Warm, friendly and very well run hotel with antiques, comfortable chairs and a relaxed atmosphere in the lounge, a beamed bar, and good food in the attractive sunny restaurant with its 70-year-old trailing vine.

STOW-ON-THE-WOLD SP1925 **Old Stocks** *The Square, Stow-on-the-Wold, Cheltenham GL54 1AF (01451) 830666* **£74,** plus special breaks; 18 rms. Well run 16th/17th-c Cotswold stone hotel with cosy welcoming small bar, beams and open fire, good food, friendly staff, and sheltered garden; cl 19–29 Dec; disabled access.

STOW-ON-THE-WOLD SP1925 **Royalist** *Digbeth St, Stow-on-the-Wold, Cheltenham GL54 1BN (01451) 830670* ***£70;** 12 rms. Ancient hotel with good claims to origins in 10th c, family-run, friendly and full of character; log fire in charming lounge, cosy beamed bar, all-day coffee shop, good home-made bar food; disabled access.

THORNBURY ST6390 **Thornbury Castle** *Thornbury, Bristol BS12 1HH (01454) 281182* **£150;** 20 opulent rms, some with big Tudor fireplaces or fine oriel windows. Impressive and luxuriously renovated early 16th-c castle with antiques, tapestries, huge fireplaces and mullioned windows in the baronial public rooms, 2 restaurants (one in the base of a tower), fine cooking, extensive wine list (inc wine from their own vineyard), thoughtful friendly service, and vast grounds; cl 4 days Jan; children over 12; partial disabled access.

UPPER SLAUGHTER SP1523 **Lords of the Manor** *Upper Slaughter, Cheltenham GL54 2JD (01451) 820243* **£130,** plus special breaks; 27 rms carefully furnished with antiques, Victorian sketches and paintings. Warmly friendly hotel with mid-17th-c heart (though it's been carefully extended many times), lovely views over 8 acres of grounds from very comfortable library and drawing room, log fires, fresh flowers; fine modern English cooking in attractive candlelit restaurant overlooking the original rectory gardens, good breakfasts, and kind service.

VINEY HILL SO6506 **Viney Hill Country Guest House** *Viney Hill, Blakeney GL15 4LT (01594) 516000* ***£48,** plus special breaks; 6 well furnished, comfortable rms. Delightful old no smoking farmhouse in lovely countryside with very pretty garden, 2 cosy lounges (one with TV), lots of books and local information, decent evening meals and good breakfasts, and friendly efficient service; very good walking all around.

WESTONBIRT ST8589 **Hare & Hounds** *Westonbirt, Tetbury GL8 8QL (01666) 880233* **£92,** plus special breaks; 31 comfortable rms. Cotswold stone hotel in 10 acres of grounds with 2 tennis courts, squash and croquet; a pleasant old-fashioned bar, relaxed spacious and comfortable lounges, open fires, good food, friendly service, table tennis, and snooker; limited disabled access.

WILLERSEY SP1039 **Old Rectory** *Church St, Willersey, Broadway, Worcs WR12 7PN (01386) 853729* ***£65,** plus special breaks; 8 attractive, well equipped rms. Quietly set and friendly 17th-c house opposite church (nice walks from the churchyard), with a log fire in dining/sitting room and pretty flower-filled walled gardens with an ancient mulberry tree; good breakfasts, but no evening meals – though several places nearby; cl Christmas; children over 8; disabled access.

WINCHCOMBE SP0327 **Sudeley Hill Farm** *Winchcombe, Cheltenham GL54 5JB (01242) 602344* **£44;** 3 no smoking rms. Friendly 15th-c farmhouse on working mixed farm with log fires, guest sitting room, and dining room overlooking the large garden; cl Christmas; no dogs.

WINCHCOMBE SP0228 **Wesley House** *High St, Winchcombe, Cheltenham GL54 5LJ (01242) 602366* **£75,** plus special breaks; 5 cosy rms with showers. Pretty half-timbered 15th-c house with quiet friendly atmosphere, log fire in comfortable lounge, and good food in attractive beamed restaurant; cl 14 Jan–9 Feb.

WINSTONE SO9509 **Winstone Glebe** *Winstone, Cirencester GL7 7JU (01285) 821451* ***£58;** 3 rms. Small Georgian rectory in quiet countryside with 5 acres of gardens and paddocks, tennis, lots of surrounding walks, friendly hosts, traditional furnishings, and delicious food (by arrangement); dogs welcome; cl Christmas.

WITHINGTON SP0315 **Halewell Close** *Withington, Cheltenham GL54 4BN (01242) 890238* ***£87;** 6 beamed and comfortable rms. Lovely old Cotswold stone house, dating back to the 15th c, with relaxed house-party atmosphere, beamed sitting room, late breakfasts, and good English food in the panelled dining room; high tea for children; 50 acres of grounds inc big garden with stone terraces, heated outdoor swimming pool, and fish in trout lake and on River Coln; riding can be arranged; children and dogs by arrangement; good provision for the disabled.

To see and do

GLOUCESTER SO8318 A busy modern city despite its long history – you have to search out the old buildings among today's big shops (for instance the splendid timber-framed house tucked down a passageway off 26 Westgate St). The Tourist Office at St Michael's Tower (itself a fine ancient building at the central Cross) is particularly good at sending you off well equipped for the hunt. The Waterfront (Llanthony Rd, S end of docks), and – all handy for the cathedral – Fountain, New Inn and Tailors House (Westgate St) are useful for a quick lunch.

Gloucester Docks The revitalised waterfront deserves much of the credit for the city's tourism renaissance; guided walks, summer boat trips along the canal or as far as Tewkesbury (contact National Waterways Museum (01452) 318066), and also the unusually interesting **Soldiers of Gloucester Museum** (cl Mon exc Jun–Sept and bank hols; (01452) 522682; £3.50), and a big **antiques centre**, with 110 varied antique shops in Dickensian arcades (cl am Sun; free wkdys, 50p wknds and bank hols). The next two attractions are both here:

National Waterways Museum The story of Britain's inland waterways, and the first heyday of these docks after the opening of the Gloucester & Berkeley Canal. It's a lively place, with a good deal to amuse children, who can even try their hand at steering a narrow boat. New galleries are to be added following a substantial Lottery grant. Snacks, shop, good disabled access; cl 25 Dec; (01452) 318054; £4.50.

Robert Opie Collection Museum of Advertising and Packaging SO8218 (Albert Warehouse) Great for nostalgia-lovers, an enormous and quite fascinating assembly of packets, tins, bottles, posters, street signs and more from Victorian days onwards. Also continuous showing of vintage TV commercials. Snacks, shop, disabled access; cl winter Mons, 25–26 Dec; (01452) 302309; *£3.50.

Gloucester Cathedral In 1330 the Abbot astutely purchased the remains of murdered Edward II, and the resulting stream of pilgrims paid for elaborate rebuilding in an early example of Perpendicular style, which towers majestically over the city's more recent buildings. Lovely fan-vaulted cloisters, the second largest medieval stained-glass window in the country, and a fine collection of church plate in the Treasury. Meals, snacks, shop, disabled access; (01452) 528095; donations. Not far from here are the remains of 9th-c **St Oswald's Priory**, the city's oldest structure, and other ecclesiastical remains inc **Greyfriars** and **Blackfriars**, the latter pretty much unchanged since the 13th-c, with a rare scissor-braced roof.

Prison Museum (Barrack Sq) The only museum of its type attached to a fully operational prison (it's in the old Gate Lodge), with interactive videos and displays on life behind bars from the 19th c to the present. Shop (selling goods made by inmates of various jails), some disabled access with prior arrangement; cl Sun, Oct–Easter; (01452) 529551; £1.

Folk Museum (Westgate St) Social history in a group of Tudor and Jacobean timber-framed houses; Victorian classroom, reconstructed ironmonger's shop and now a toy gallery. In summer there may be Gloucestershire Old Spot pigs in the yard. Shop, limited disabled access; cl Sun exc July–Sept; (01452) 526467; £2 (Gloucester residents free).

City Museum and Art Gallery (Brunswick Rd) Local history (inc the oldest known backgammon set), and paintings by Gainsborough and Turner. Shop, disabled access; cl Sun exc July–Sept; (01452) 524131; £2. Guided tours of the ancient **City East Gate** leave here every hour on Sats May–Sept; 40p.

House of the Tailor of Gloucester (College Ct) Inspiration for Beatrix Potter's story, now with new exhibition and shop. Disabled access downstairs; cl Sun and bank hols; £1.

Jet Age Museum SO8921 (Airport, Cheltenham Rd E) The working surroundings make this collection seem more ready for action than some; children can climb into some of the cockpits; cl Christmas week and 1 Jan; (01452) 330761; £3.

Robinswood Hill Country Park SO8416 (2m S) A little outcrop of the Cotswolds, with 250 acres of walks and trails, a wildlife information centre (fun talks and events), and wonderful views of the city from the summit. Snacks, shop, disabled access; (01452) 303206; free. Not far away is a dry ski slope.

Farm shop at Over (1m W) A good one, with local produce and pick-your-own in summer.

FOREST OF DEAN SO6212 The Forest of Dean has a unique landscape: hilly woodland with many traces of the way it has provided a livelihood for the people living around it. It's flanked by a spectacular stretch of the Wye Valley, and its woodland colours are at their best in late May and autumn. Still largely ancient oak woodland despite encroaching pine plantations, the forest rolls over many miles of hilly countryside, giving plenty of space – even in summer you can often have much of the woods to yourself. There are ponds, streams with stepping stones, cattle and maybe fallow deer, sudden distant views, the humps and gouges that mark ancient iron workings, the tracks of abandoned railways and tramways, and still one or two of the freeminers, who've been digging coal by hand from surface seams for hundreds of years. The forest scenery has most impact on those prepared to delve into its past a bit – a good start is the **heritage centre** at Upper Soudley; the forest is well equipped with car parks, picnic sites and trails. Around the edges the scenery changes to a patchwork of steep pastures – also very attractive. It's well worth getting a forest map, either from the Dean Heritage Centre or direct from the Forestry Commission in Coleford, (01594) 833057; these outline walks, and the best spots for views or picnics. The information centres can also provide details of canoeing, caving, cycling or fishing in the forest. The B4432 to Symonds Yat gives some good views, the B4228 down past St Briavels is a pleasant country road, and the little lanes around the edges of the Forest are rewarding drives – but you need a large-scale map.

Forest sights and walks The **Sculpture Trail** takes a 4-mile route passing nearly 20 specially commissioned sculptures hidden deep in the forest (from picnic site nr the comfortable Speech House Hotel SO6611). **Conifer arboretum** SO6212 This makes an interesting change from the Forest's predominantly broad-leaved trees; nr Speech House. **Kidnalls Forest Trail** SO6205 is a good way of tracking down some early industrial sites. **Foundry Wood Trail** passing Soudley fish ponds SO6212 gains some fine views. Signed paths ensure easy route-finding up to the open summit of **May Hill** SO6921, where on a clear day you can see the Cotswolds, Malverns, Welsh Marches and Severn Estuary. You can track the remarkably durable paving of a **Roman road** SO6508 just off the B4431 at Blackpool Bridge. **Nagshead RSPB Nature Reserve** SO5909 is a good place to see deer and other wildlife.

Symonds Yat Rock SO5615 Perhaps the Forest of Dean's most spectacular feature, where the River Wye rolls around a monumental wooded cliff barrier, a favourite spot with peregrine falcons; tremendous views in all directions from the top, and at the bottom a ferry runs between 2 inns.

Wye Valley SO5309 The river on the W side of the Forest cuts through a gorge giving some very picturesque views. As there are few crossing points, and the scenery away from the gorge is relatively unspectacular, walks along it are generally of the there-and-back sort, along the Offa's Dyke Path.

Other things to see and do

GLOUCESTERSHIRE Family Attraction of the Year

BLOCKLEY SP1634 **Sleepy Hollow** (Draycott Rd) Really excellent value, and nicely unspoilt and friendly, this 25-acre farm park has especially good informative talks and displays throughout the day. A highlight is the Big Cat demonstration at 3pm, when a mixture of animals not currently shown in the park's main enclosures are brought out by keepers who've clearly established a terrific bond with the beasts. You can arrange to meet a cub, a unique opportunity that helps the animals get used to meeting different people. Other sessions standing out are the raccoon and pig feeding sessions, the otter playtime, and the snake encounter; times vary, but are posted by the entrance. They also have a calendar of events that takes in sheep shearing, fun days, and guest visits from wolves and tiny stallions. The main enclosures are particularly strong on pigs, with ring-tailed lemurs, deer and bagot goats added last year, and plenty of sheep, waterfowl, and other creatures. You can walk in some of the enclosures (lambs, chickens, and some of the goats), and there may be shire horse cart rides in the main season (weather permitting, 50p extra). If you want to feed any of the animals, they sell special pellets (30p a bag). Best to bring wellies if it's rained recently, though some of the talks are indoors. Not overly developed – and all the better for that – this is the kind of place where asking questions can really pay off: the helpful staff are very enthusiastic about their subject. There's a picnic area, with play equipment aimed at younger children, and nice walks in the surrounding woodland – particularly when the bluebells are out. Animal-minded families can happily spend up to half a day here (longer if it's hard to drag young children away from the indoor pet area), quite a bargain considering how low the admission is. Snacks, shop; cl mid-Nov–mid-Mar; (01386) 701264; *£2.95 (children 3–15 £1.60).

ARLINGHAM SO7011 **St Augustine's Working Farm** (B4071) Friendly working dairy farm with cows, pigs, goats, hens, sheep and rabbits, all of which children can go right up to (quite a few feeding opportunities). Snacks, shop, some disabled access; cl Mon (exc bank hols) and all Oct–Easter; (01452) 740277; *£3. The Ship at Upper Framilode nearby has decent food in an attractive setting.

ASHLEWORTH SO8125 A **tithe barn** of some note, and a very traditional pub right on the River Severn, that's been in the same family for centuries.

BARNSLEY HOUSE GARDENS SP0805 (B4425) Lovely little herb, vegetable and knot gardens, fruit trees and decorative plants, laburnum and lime walks and 18th-c summerhouses; especially attractive spring blossom and autumn colours. Plant sales, some disabled access; cl Sun; (01285) 740281; £3.50. The Village Pub is good.

BELAS KNAP SP0125 There's a pleasant walk up these steep grassy slopes, for great views, from the enjoyable Craven Arms in Brockhampton; you can divert past some surprising ruins of a Roman villa tucked away in nearby woods.

BERKELEY ST6899 **Berkeley Castle** (off the A38) Excellently preserved castle, very much a family home, but still keeping a flavour of its days as a Norman fortress. Impressive paintings, furnishings and silver, fine old keep and Great Hall, terraced gardens, park, extensive butterfly farm – and the dungeon where Edward II was murdered in 1327. Snacks, shop, limited disabled access; open Tues–Sun Apr–Sept (cl am Sun, and am daily in Apr), plus Mons July and Aug, and pm Sun in Oct; (01453) 810332; £5.20, £1.95 butterfly farm. **Jenner Museum** (High St) Largely unchanged Georgian home of Edward Jenner, who discovered the smallpox vaccine here and gave free vaccinations from the thatched hut in the attractive grounds. Shop, some disabled access; cl am, all Mon exc bank hols, Oct exc Sun, and Nov–Mar; (01453) 810631; *£2.20. **Cattle Country** (off the B4066 E) has various cattle including American bison, yaks, and you can feed the wild boar; also farm trail and large adventure playground. Snacks, shop, disabled access; open wknds and school hols Easter–Sept; (01453) 810220; £3.50. The Pickwick at Lower Wick is a popular dining pub.

★ **BIBURY** SP1106 One of the most popular villages in the area, with lovely golden streamside houses; summer crowds can rather blunt its appeal. **Trout Farm** Long-established working farm breeding rainbow trout in 20 ponds. You can feed the fish, or try to catch your own. Snacks, good shop; cl 25 Dec; (01285) 740215; £2. **Arlington Mill** The 18th-c machinery of this well restored watermill is demonstrated every day, with guided tours by arrangement. Meals, snacks, shop; cl 25 Dec; (01285) 740368; £2. The **River Coln** lets you approach Bibury more quietly and prettily, along

Days Out

Meet the animals and ride the train: Stroll up Cleeve Hill from Cleeve Common (good for kite-flying); lunch at the Hollow Bottom, Guiting Power or the Halfway House, Kineton; Cotswold Farm Park there; steamtrain trip from Toddington or Winchcombe.

The great forest: Forest of Dean Sculpture Trail; lunch at the Wyndham Arms, Clearwell; Clearwell Caves; Symonds Yat Rock, walk along Wye Gorge S to Biblins suspension bridge.

Sanctuaries along the Severn Estuary: Frampton Court; lunch at the Bell, Frampton on Severn; Wildfowl and Wetlands Trust, Slimbridge.

the path from the toll-house just S of Coln St Aldwyns. This route takes you in by the mill and bridge over the Coln itself. By the same trout-stream, a pleasant drive links other villages that are just as engaging, but bypassed by most visitors, particularly Coln St Aldwyns SP1405 (the New Inn is excellent) and Quenington SP1404 (a decent village pub). On the far side of Bibury the back road tracking along the river passes through a string of pleasant little villages such as Coln Rogers, Coln St Dennis and Yanworth (particularly attractive at daffodil time), eventually reaching pretty Withington SP0315 (delightful pub right on the stream).

BIRDSWOOD SO7418 **Old Ley Court** (Chapel Lane) Working farm producing double and single Gloucester cheese – you can watch them make it on Tues and Thurs, 9.30–11.30am and 12.30–4pm, (01452) 750225; £1.50. The Apple Tree at nearby Minsterworth is a pleasant dining pub, and the lane past it leads to a good quiet spot for watching the Severn Bore *(see Westbury on Severn)*.

★ **BLOCKLEY** SP1634 *See separate Family Panel on p.259* for **Sleepy Hollow** animal park. The Crown in the pretty village is a smart place for lunch.

BOURTON-ON-THE-HILL SP1732 **Bourton House** Unusual plants inc tender ones in attractive garden around fine old house (not open). Teas in 16th-c tithe barn, shop; open pm Thurs and Fri late May–Oct; £3. The Horse & Groom does decent food. **Sezincote** (off the A424 about 1m S) Exotic onion-domed forerunner of Brighton Pavilion, stunning from the outside, less interesting inside. Also classic early 19th-c watergarden, and a more recent Indian-style garden to match the building. Garden open pm Thurs, Fri and bank hols (cl Dec), house open pm Thurs and Fri May–July and Sept; £4.50, £3 garden only. Children are not allowed in the house.

★ **BOURTON-ON-THE-WATER** SP1620 One of the best-known Cotswold villages, but disfigured by sprawly crowds in summer unless you get there very early in the morning – when it's enchanting. There is a wealth of attractions aimed at visitors. **Birdland** (Rissington Rd) Rare and exotic birds on banks of meandering River Windrush, inc one of the biggest colonies of penguins outside America. Snacks, shop, disabled access; cl 25 Dec; (01451) 820480; £4. **Cotswold Motor Museum and Toy Museum** (Sherbourne St) In an old watermill, cars and motorcycles from vintage years to 1950s, along with advertising signs, automobilia, and toy collection. It's the home of Brum the children's TV character. Shop, disabled access; cl Dec–Jan, plus occasional winter wkdys; (01451) 821255; *£1.75. The price includes entry to the adjacent **Village Life Exhibition**, with recreated Edwardian rooms, village shop, and blacksmith's forge. **Model Village** (High St) Charming replica of the village, modelled from Cotswold stone in the 1930s at 1:9 scale, complete with working waterwheel and music in the church. Good home-made food (and lovely river view) in adjacent welcoming Old New Inn, shop; cl 25 Dec; (01451) 820467; *£2. **Perfumery Exhibition** (Victoria St) Aromatic displays and demonstrations of perfume-making and scent extraction, with scented garden. Shop, disabled access; cl 25–26 Dec; (01451) 820698; £2. **Dragonfly Maze** A new attraction; you follow clues on engraved flagstones to find your way through a yew tree maze to an ornate central pavillion filled with charming animated sculptures. Shop, disabled access; open daily in summer, best to check in winter; (01451) 822251; *£2. **Folly Farm Waterfowl** (3m W on the A436) Lakes and pools with 160 species of waterfowl, as well as friendly ducks, geese and poultry, and hand-reared animals. Good for children, and a nice spot for a picnic (or to camp). Their lavender fields are in full bloom in July. Snacks, shop, disabled access; cl 25 Dec; (01451) 820285; *£3.50. The Old Manse has decent food and garden tables overlooking the Windrush; the riverside Parrot & Alligator is good, too. The best walk out of Bourton-on-the-Water is the exit by the church, heading out W past the school and over the old railway line, then following the lanes and tracks S of Upper Slaughter to

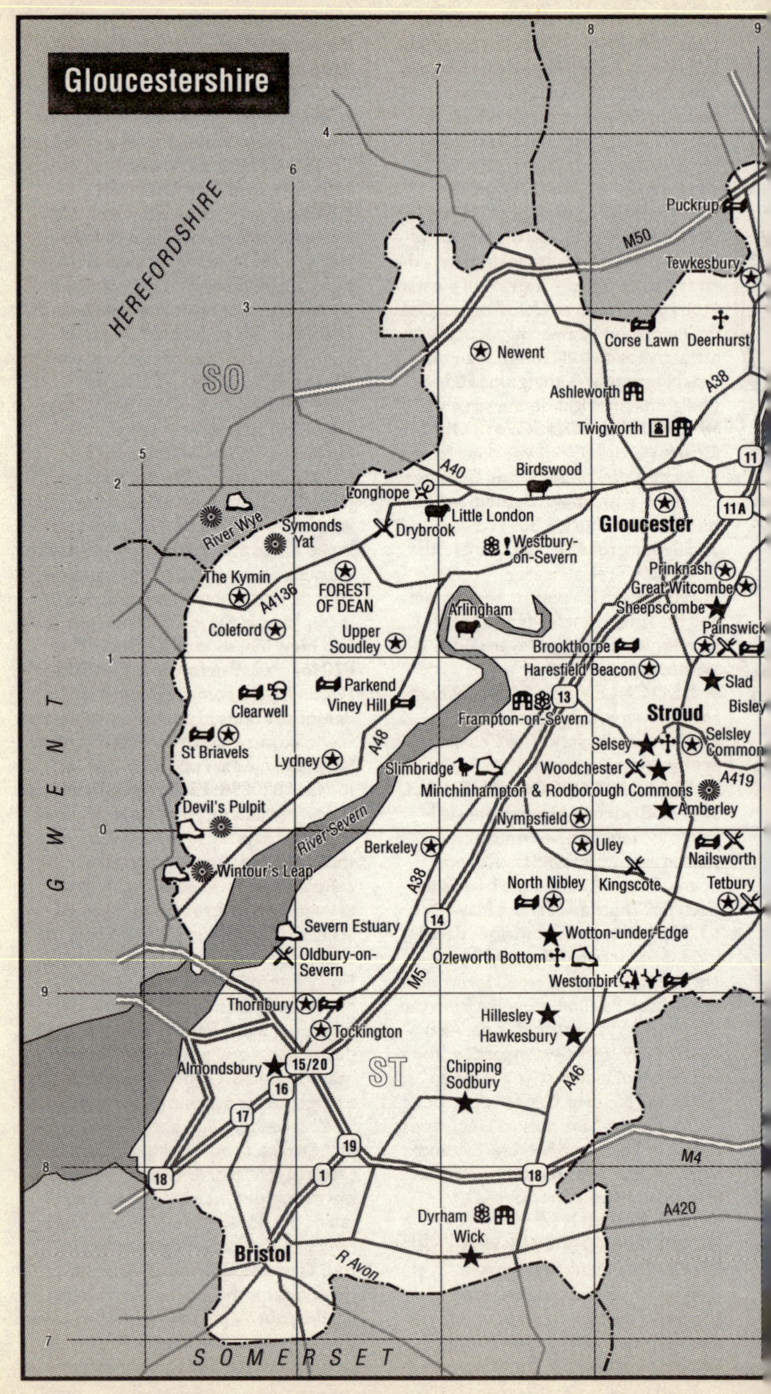
Gloucestershire
HEREFORDSHIRE
SO
GWENT
SOMERSET
ST
Puckrup
M50
Tewkesbury
Corse Lawn
Deerhurst
Newent
Ashleworth
A38
Twigworth
Birdswood
A40
Longhope
Little London
Drybrook
Gloucester
Westbury-on-Severn
River Wye
Symonds Yat
The Kymin
A4136
FOREST OF DEAN
Coleford
Upper Soudley
Arlingham
Prinknash
Great Witcombe
Sheepscombe
Painswick
Brookthorpe
Haresfield Beacon
Slad
Parkend
Viney Hill
Clearwell
St Briavels
Lydney
A48
Frampton-on-Severn
Stroud
Bisley
Selsey
Selsley Common
Woodchester
A419
Slimbridge
Minchinhampton & Rodborough Commons
Amberley
Devil's Pulpit
Nympsfield
River Severn
Berkeley
Uley
Nailsworth
Wintour's Leap
Kingscote
Tetbury
North Nibley
Severn Estuary
Wotton-under-Edge
Oldbury-on-Severn
Ozleworth Bottom
M5
Westonbirt
Thornbury
Tockington
Hillesley
Hawkesbury
Almondsbury
Chipping Sodbury
A46
M4
Dyrham
Wick
A420
Bristol
R Avon

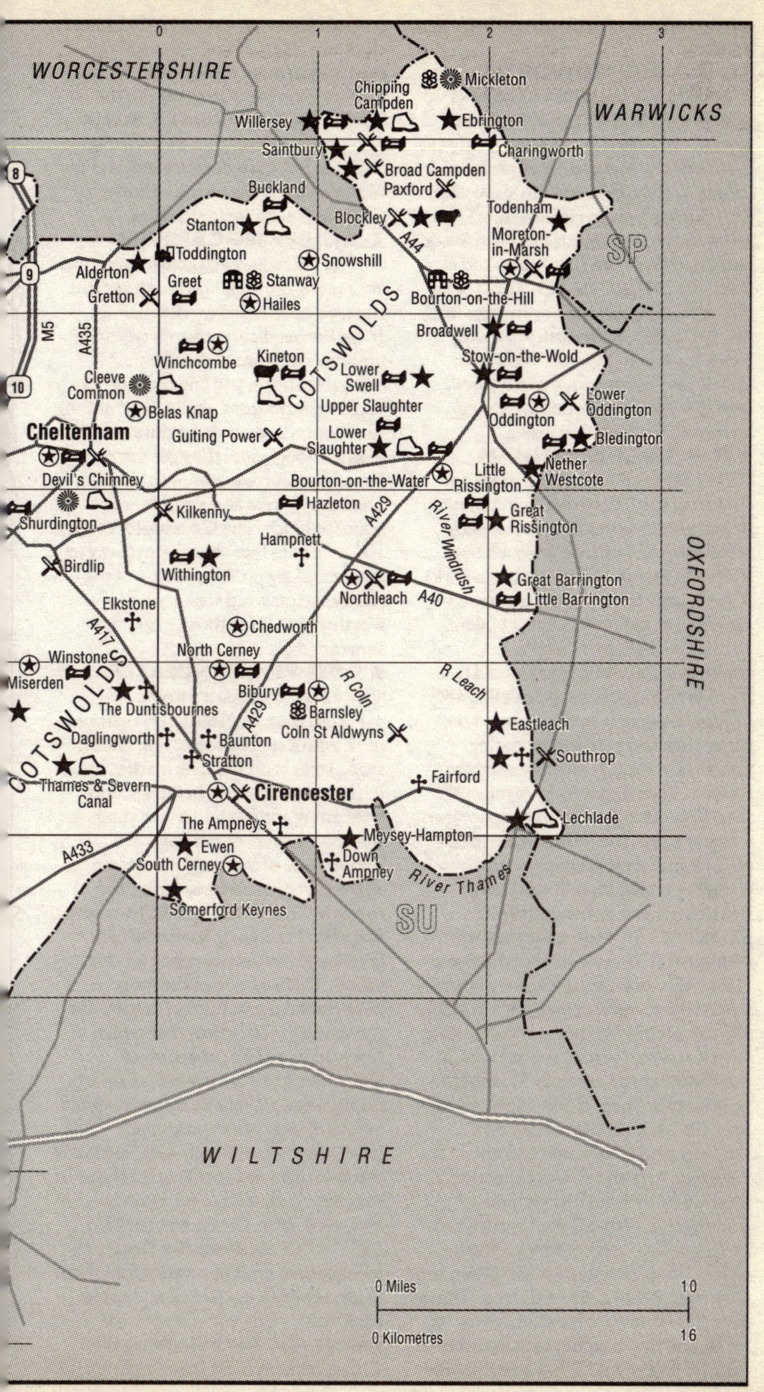
WORCESTERSHIRE
WARWICKS
OXFORDSHIRE
WILTSHIRE
Mickleton
Chipping Campden
Willersey
Ebrington
Saintbury
Charingworth
Broad Campden
Paxford
Buckland
Stanton
Blockley
Todenham
Moreton-in-Marsh
SP
Toddington
Snowshill
Alderton
Greet
Stanway
Gretton
Hailes
COTSWOLDS
Bourton-on-the-Hill
A44
M5
A435
Broadwell
Winchcombe
Kineton
Lower Swell
Stow-on-the-Wold
Cleeve Common
Upper Slaughter
Lower Oddington
Oddington
Belas Knap
Cheltenham
Guiting Power
Lower Slaughter
Bledington
Devil's Chimney
Bourton-on-the-Water
Little Rissington
Nether Westcote
Hazleton
Kilkenny
Shurdington
A429
River Windrush
Great Rissington
Hampnett
Birdlip
Withington
Northleach
A40
Great Barrington
Little Barrington
Elkstone
Chedworth
A417
North Cerney
Winstone
Miserden
R Coln
R Leach
Bibury
The Duntisbournes
Barnsley
Eastleach
Coln St Aldwyns
Daglingworth
Baunton
Southrop
Stratton
Fairford
Thames & Severn Canal
Cirencester
Lechlade
The Ampneys
Ewen
Meysey-Hampton
A433
South Cerney
Down Ampney
River Thames
Somerford Keynes
SU
0 Miles
10
0 Kilometres
16
0
1
2
3
8
9
10

rejoin the River Windrush and back to Bourton.

★ **CHEDWORTH ROMAN VILLA** SP0513 The best example of a 2nd-c Roman house in Britain, excavated in 1864 and nicely set in secluded woodland. Well preserved rooms, bath houses and 4th-c mosaics, with smaller remains in museum. Shop, some disabled access; cl Mon (exc bank hols), and Dec–Feb (exc first wknd in Dec); (01242) 890256; £3.20; NT. The Mill at Withington and Seven Tuns in pretty Upper Chedworth are quite handy for lunch – and the walk from each is very picturesque and unspoilt, with Chedworth Woods providing further scope for short walks.

★ **CHELTENHAM** SO9523 Beautiful spa town useful for exploring the Cotswolds, for shopping, or just admiring the elegant Regency architecture of its tree-lined avenues. **Pittville Pump Room** (Pittville Park) A short walk from the centre, generally regarded as the town's finest building, 19th-c Greek Revival with a colonnaded façade and balconied hall. It's easy to imagine the place's Regency heyday, especially strolling round the super park and gardens, or during concerts in the July music festival; on summer Suns they may have musical teas. You can still sample the spa water – rather salty. The museum has local history and notable costume and jewellery collections. Shop, limited disabled access; cl Tues; (01242) 523852; *£1.50. **Holst Birthplace Museum** (Clarence Rd) Nr the Pump Room, this interesting Regency house is where the composer was born in 1874; you can see his first piano. Worthwhile even if you're not mad about Holst, as the rooms are all carefully furnished in period style. Shop; cl Sun, Mon and bank hols; (01242) 524846; £1.50. **Art Gallery and Museum** (Clarence St) Excellent Arts and Crafts collection inspired by William Morris, fine paintings inc 17th-c Dutch works, and rare porcelain and ceramics. Meals, snacks, shop, disabled access; cl Sun and bank hols; (01242) 837431; free. These days Cheltenham is best known for its races, and the racecourse at Prestbury Park (N on the A435) has an exhibition on Gold Cup winners; (01242) 513014; cl wknds; free. Lots of antique shops, especially around the Montpellier area. Taylors wine bar (Cambray Pl), the Restoration (Grosvenor St), Beehive (Montpellier Villas) and Beaufort Arms (London Rd) have decent food, and the well run café in the beautiful Imperial Gardens is suitable for families.

★ **CHIPPING CAMPDEN** SP1539 Extremely attractive town, with interesting old buildings inc an ancient covered open-sided market hall, a grand Perpendicular church typical of the area's rich 'wool churches', enjoyable shops, and fine old inns. Many of our contributors would put it among the country's most delightful small towns, though until they get the cars out of the centre not all would agree. The Lygon Arms and Volunteer are good for lunch. The **Cotswold Way**, a 100-mile path from here all the way to Bath, carefully picks out some of the choicest Cotswold scenery – a worthwhile aid for those planning a shorter stroll.

★ ✝ **CIRENCESTER** SP0202 A busy country town, particularly on its Mon and Fri market days, with a succession of fine Cotswold stone streets off the long market place. It has many attractive buildings, and interesting antique and other shops inc traditional country saddlers, etc. Though one of the most handsome of all the Cotswold towns, it isn't too touristy. The **Church of St John the Baptist** (Market Pl) is wonderfully grand, and has a striking late Gothic tower. This was one of the most important cities in Roman Britain, and the spacious **Corinium Museum** (Park St) has a fine collection of antiquities from the period (all clearly displayed and labelled). Reconstructed period dining room and kitchen (complete with menus), with Saxon and medieval galleries too. Snacks, shop, excellent disabled access; cl am Sun, Mon Nov–Mar, Christmas; (01285) 655611; *£2.50. **Brewery Court** 16 independent craft businesses and shops in former brewery (cl Sun and some bank hols), along with theatre, gallery and café. Also worth a look are the 12th-c remains of **St John's Hospital**, the **Norman arch**, and the various well preserved wool merchants' houses. Cecily Hill, one of the town's most attractive streets, gives on to the pleasant strolling-ground of Cirencester Park. Decent places for lunch include the Slug & Lettuce, Corinium Court, Tatyans (Chinese) and (very local but good value) Golden Cross.

CLEARWELL CAVES SO5708 (off the B4228) Tours of huge caverns, a source of ore from the Iron Age right up to 1945; deeper trips for the more adventurous. It's quite a labyrinth, with many miles of passageways, so stout shoes recommended. Lively themed displays down here at Christmas. Snacks, shop; cl Nov, and 24 Dec–end Feb; (01594) 832535; £3.50. The Wyndham Arms is good for lunch, and though the village is not in itself particularly pretty it's a very good centre for the lovely surrounding countryside.

CLEEVE COMMON SO9924 The steep grassy slopes of the W escarpment of the Cotswolds make for some of the area's best walking. This, the highest point of the Cotswolds, has breezy, unkempt grassland on its open expanses and can be reached either from the nearby village of Cleeve Hill on the A46, or integrated into a long circular walk past Belas Knap long barrow and through the Sudeley Castle estate into Winchcombe.

COLEFORD SO5710 **Great Western Railway Museum** Converted Coleford GWR goods station with several large-scale model steam locomotives, relics, photographs and a Victorian ticket office; very much a private collection, enthusiastically presented, and manned by helpful volunteers. Cl Sun and Mon, otherwise varied opening times, phone to check but it's best Sat pm; (01594) 833569; *£2. **Puzzle Wood** (just off the B4228 S) Pleasant for a stroll: wooded paths arranged in a puzzle, landscaped in the 19th c nr remains of Roman iron mines. Snacks, shop; cl Mon (exc bank hols), and Nov–Easter; (01594) 833187; £2.50. Across the road is the **Treasure Train**; steam trains along a ¾-mile stretch of narrow-gauge track, with children solving clues that lead to treasure along the way. There are 4 stops, with footpaths through the woods nearby. Snacks, disabled access; open wknds and bank hols Easter–Oct, maybe Tues–Thurs and Sat too in summer hols; (01594) 834991; £2.95 for unlimited train journeys, plus £1.50 for the treasure trail. The Dog & Muffler at Joyford is a pretty place for lunch; good walks nearby. **Hopewell Colliery** (B4226 W) 45-min underground tours of the 'free' mine guided by ex-miners, and display of mining tools and equipment. You'll need sturdy shoes and warm clothing. Snacks, shop; cl Nov–Mar; (01594) 810706; £3.

✝ **DEERHURST** SO8729 Ancient remains here include **Odda's Chapel**, a restored 11th-c chapel discovered as part of a farmhouse, and the **Priory Church of St Mary**, a mainly Saxon church with a lovely atmosphere and some intriguing original carvings and features. The Farmers Arms at Apperley is a good dining pub (brewing its own beers).

DEVIL'S CHIMNEY SO9418 On the Cotswold Way, a viewpoint rock pinnacle amid old quarries on Leckhampton Hill, perched above Cheltenham.

DEVIL'S PULPIT ST5499 A great viewpoint on the Offa's Dyke Path, where trees frame a perfect vista of Tintern Abbey far below on the opposite bank of the Wye.

DYRHAM PARK ST7475 Set in an ancient park grazed by fallow deer, this fine William & Mary house has hardly changed since the late 17th c. The interiors have Dutch-style furnishings, Delft ware, Dutch bird paintings and a remarkable *trompe l'oeil* by Hoogstraten. Meals, snacks, shop, disabled access to ground floor; house cl am, all day Weds and Thurs, and all Nov–Mar, park open all year; (0117) 937 2501; £5.40, £2.80 garden and deer park only; £1.70 deer park only; NT. The Bull at Hinton Dyrham and Crown at Tolldown (A46) are handy for lunch.

★ **EASTLEACH** SP2005 Delightful Cotswold village; a lovely ancient clapper bridge links the two Norman churches, very photogenic at daffodil time. The Victoria has good food.

FAIRFORD SP1501 Pleasant riverside meadows, and a wonderful 15th-c Perpendicular **church**, well known for its remarkable medieval stained glass (inc a fascinating depiction of Hell), and comical misericords. The Bull has decent food.

FRAMPTON ON SEVERN SO7407 **Frampton Court** Elegant lived-in Georgian house, with original furniture, porcelain and paintings, and fascinating gardens. The 18th-c orangery has been converted into self-catering holiday flats. Disabled access; personal tours all year by appointment, (01452) 740267; £4. The village green is said to be the largest in the country, with the orangery on one side, and the civilised Bell (good range of food) on another. Nearby the Gloucester & Sharpness Canal passes grand colonnaded lock-keepers' houses by pretty swing bridges.

GREAT WITCOMBE SO9014 The outlines of a substantial **Roman villa** can still be traced here, around a courtyard, with several mosaics and evidence of an underfloor heating system. The Royal George at Birdlip has decent food, and the Golden Heart at Brimpsfield is good. **Crickley Hill Country Park** (just N) has a few ancient sites, as well as nature trails, lovely clearly marked woodland walks, and fine views. Some disabled access; visitor centre cl winter; (01452) 863170; free.

HAILES ABBEY SP0430 (B4632) Graceful ruins of 13th-c Cistercian abbey, once a centre for pilgrims who flocked to see a phial containing what they believed to be Christ's blood. Walkman tour, shop, some disabled access; cl winter wkdys; (01242) 602398; £2.50; NT. The Harvest Home at Greet has the best food nearby, but Hayles Fruit Farm down the road is good for snacks, and has pick your own.

HARESFIELD BEACON SO8108 (3m NW of Stroud) 450 acres of NT woodland and grassland on the Cotswold escarpment, with spectacular views; free, and just a short ascent from the road.

KINETON SP0926 **Cotswold Farm Park** (off the B4077, E) Full of delightfully odd-looking species of sheep, cattle, pigs, goats, horses and poultry, this is particularly well organised as far as children are concerned. Rabbits and piglets to cuddle and feed, good safe rustic-themed play areas, and a designated children's shop, with items from 5p to around £2 at the most. You can easily spend most of a day here; nature trails and woodland walks are ideal for a break from the animals, and there are 19 acres to picnic, kick a ball around, or relax on the grass. Lots under cover, so still good when the weather isn't perfect (best to wear wellies then). Meals, snacks, shop, disabled access; cl Oct–Feb; (01451) 850307; £3.50. The Halfway House does decent food. Nearby Guiting Power is attractive, sensitively restored and genuine, with pleasant walks; the Hollow Bottom there is good.

! THE KYMIN SO5212 Can be climbed from May Hill; at the summit is the Naval Temple, a quaint rustic conceit put up in 1800 to commemorate admirals of the Napoleonic Wars.

★ LECHLADE SU2199 Graceful village with one or two decent antique shops, a good traditional toyshop, pleasant walks, and access to the quiet reed-fringed Thames for footpath walks – especially along to Kelmscot in Oxon. The Trout along the A417 at St John's Bridge has lovely riverside tables.

LITTLE LONDON SO6918 **Angora Goat and Mohair Centre** (Blakemore Farm) Unusual goat farm with shop selling clothes made from their fleeces; other animals too. Snacks, shop, disabled access; cl Mon (exc bank hols) and Tues, 24 Dec–Jan; (01452) 830630; £1. The Red Hart at Blaisdon is attractive for lunch.

LONGHOPE SO6818 **Harts Barn Flower and Craft Centre** Smart craft workshops, inc dried flowers, jewellery and ceramics, in an attractive Norman hunting lodge. Courtyard tea room; cl Mon exc bank hols; (01452) 830954; free.

★ LOWER SLAUGHTER SP1622 With its sister village Upper Slaughter, this is perhaps the prettiest village in Britain – a perfect harmony of stone, water, grass and trees. It's not as overwhelmed by summer visitors as its nearby rival Bourton-on-the-Water, though it certainly gets its fair share. The riverside stroll from Lower to Upper Slaughter is a leisurely mile or so; to make a longer walk for a circuit of a couple of hours, you can follow the signposted Warden's Way.

LYDNEY SO6304 **Dean Forest Railway** (New Mills, slightly N) Lots of locomotives, wagons and equipment at the station, and steam trips through the forest (mainly just wknds, best to ring for dates). Snacks, shop, disabled access; static displays open all year; (01594) 843423; £3.50. The Woodman at Parkend, handy for the stop there, has decent food and good nearby walks. **Lydney Park** Extensive sheltered spring garden rich with flowering shrubs, rhododendrons, azaleas and magnolias; also lakes and deer park. Tucked away among the trees are the remains of a Roman temple, and a museum with finds from the site, inc the astonishingly intricate Lydney dog. Snacks, shop, plant sales; open Sun, Weds and bank hols Easter–early Jun; (01594) 842844; £2.40 (£1.40 Weds).

MICKLETON SP1743 **Kiftsgate Court Garden** (off the B4081) Renowned for its old-fashioned roses (best Jun and July), inc the largest rose in England, but with many other rare plants, shrubs and trees, good views across the Vale of Evesham, and that special feel that comes from generations of care by a gifted gardening family. Snacks, rare plant sales; open pm Weds, Thurs, Sun and bank hols, Apr–Sept, plus pm Sat Jun and July; (01386) 438777; £3.50. **Hidcote Manor Garden** (adjacent) Series of small gardens separated by walls and hedges of different species, with rare shrubs, trees and roses. Very popular even midweek, despite the price. Meals, snacks, good shop, some disabled access; cl Tues (exc Jun and July), Fri and Nov–Mar; (01386) 438333; £5.50; NT. The Kings Arms is good value for lunch.

MINCHINHAMPTON AND RODBOROUGH COMMONS ST8699 900 acres of open land with fine views and a wide range of wildlife; NT, free. The Old Lodge on Minchinhampton Common has good food, and the steep lanes all around are interesting drives.

★ **MISARDEN PARK** SO9308 Views over the wooded Golden Valley from handsome gardens of 17th-c manor house (not open), with Lutyens topiary, mature shrubs and trees, and colourful walled garden. Nursery, some disabled access; open Tues–Thurs Easter–Sept; (01285) 821303; £3. Also woodland trail down by the river. The quiet village is charming, with decent food in the Carpenters Arms.

★ ✝ **MORETON-IN-MARSH** SP2032 Attractively bustling old place, once an important linen weaving centre and coaching town, now with popular Tues market. For food we recommend the White Hart Royal and Redesdale Arms. **Wellington Aviation Museum** (Broadway Rd) World War II aircraft pictures, sculpture and related material. Shop, disabled access; cl 12.30–2pm, all day Mon, 25 Dec, Jan; (01608) 650323; £1.50. **Batsford Arboretum** (Batsford Park, just NW) Well grown private collection of over 1,000 rare and beautiful species of tree spread over 50 acres; hundreds of maples, 90 different magnolias, flowering cherries. Best in May and autumn, but relaxing any time. Meals, snacks, garden centre, disabled access; cl Nov–Feb; (01608) 650722; £3.50. **Cotswold Falconry Centre** (Batsford Park) Flying demonstrations throughout the day, with a chance to handle some of the birds. Closed-circuit TVs give a bird's-eye view of life in the nest. Snacks, shop, disabled access (but no facilities); open Mar–Nov; (01386) 701043; £3. The Park is also home to plenty of deer.

NEWENT SO7225 Small country town with some timbered buildings which have a bit of a Worcestershire or Herefordshire look. **Shambles Museum of Victorian Life** (Church St) Enthusiastic re-creation of Victorian cobbled square, with shops and furnished tradesman's house. Shop, limited disabled access;

cl Mon (exc bank hols), Jan–mid- Mar; (01531) 822144; £3.45. The George opposite is handy for lunch. **National Birds of Prey Centre** (Gt Boulsdon, just S) Exceptional collection of birds of prey, with flying displays and breeding aviaries. Meals, snacks, shop, some disabled access; cl Dec–Jan; (01531) 820286; £4.75. The Yew Tree at Cliffords Mesne a bit further on this road has decent food, and is handy for May Hill. You can tour two local vineyards. **Three Choirs Vineyard** (off the B4215 towards Dymock, SO7129) is now one of the 6 largest in the country; meals, snacks, shop, disabled access; cl 23 Dec–6 Jan; tastings free, tour and exhibitions £2.75. **St Annes Vineyard** (Oxenhall, off the B4221, SO7126) grow and sell 100 varieties of vine, and make wines; cl some winter wkdys, best to check on 01989 720313; free.

★ NORTH CERNEY SP0207 **Cerney House Gardens** Expansive old garden behind 13th-c church, with old roses, trees, shrubs, walled and herb gardens, a few animals (they make tasty goat's cheese), and a new watergarden. The surrounding woods are lovely at bluebell time. Teas, shop, some disabled access; open pm Tues, Weds and Fri Mar–Sept; (01285) 831300; £3. The village is attractive, and the Bathurst Arms is good for lunch.

NORTH NIBLEY ST7496 **Hunts Court** Informal gardens with over 400 varieties of old roses, plus unusual shrubs and other plants; fine views. Plant sales, disabled access; open Tues–Sat (though cl Aug), plus spring bank hols and usually last 3 Suns in Jun and first 2 in July; (01453) 547440; £1.50. The walk up to the Tyndale Monument gives even better views, and the Black Horse is handy for lunch.

★ † ! NORTHLEACH SP1114 Fine example of an unspoilt small wool town, with a particularly interesting **church**, renowned for its collection of brasses. They recently installed an automatic winder to the church clock, allowing retirement for the man who'd faithfully wound it for the last 65 years. **Keith Harding's World of Mechanical Music** (Oak House, High St) Captivating collection of clocks, musical boxes and automata in old wool merchant's house, displayed and played in period settings. It's quite spooky watching the instruments work themselves. Shop, good disabled and blind access; cl 25–26 Dec; (01451) 860181; £5. **Countryside Collection** (Fosseway) Decent collection of rural bygones; cl am Sun, and all Nov–Mar; £2.50. The Red Lion and Wheatsheaf Hotel are both pleasant for lunch.

! NYMPSFIELD SO8000 **Woodchester Mansion** (B4066) Construction of this splendid unfinished Gothic mansion was inexplicably abandoned virtually overnight in 1870. It's being repaired but not finished, and you can usually see traditional building techniques like stonemasonry. Five species of bat add to the atmosphere; excellent guided tours. No children inside, for safety reasons. Snacks, shop, disabled access to ground floor only; open first wknd of month Apr–Oct, plus bank hol wknds; (01453) 860661; £3.50. The village is attractive, and you should be able to explore the surrounding valley, recently purchased by the NT. The walk up Coaley Peak gives tremendous views over the Severn Valley.

★ † ODDINGTON SP2325 Charming Cotswold village; the 11th-c **church** has an interesting mural, and there are pleasant walks, especially from the Fox at Lower Oddington – very good food there, too.

† OZLEWORTH BOTTOM ST7992 This valley, not far from Wotton-under-Edge, has a nostalgically forgotten quality about it, providing an interesting walk between Lasborough Manor and Ozleworth Park, with its unusual Norman **church** endowed with a hexagonal tower.

★ † PAINSWICK SO8609 Delightful little town sometimes referred to as the 'Queen of the Cotswolds'. There's been a settlement here since Celtic times, and **Painswick Beacon** has the remains of the earliest structures; it's a short ascent from the road, with great views towards the Malvern Hills. Plenty of old buildings to look at, such as the 15th-c **post office** and the **Church of St Mary** with its fine tombs and fascinating churchyard – 99 immaculately clipped yews forming gateways and canopies, interesting tombstones, drifts of wild cyclamen in Sept. Also antique shops and craft workshops. **Painswick Rococo Garden** (The Stables, Painswick House) Careful restoration of sizeable 18th-c garden to match a 1748 painting showing its fanciful mix of precisely trimmed hedging, paths and shrubs, unrestrained trees, a newly planted maze and slightly zany garden buildings. Pleasant vistas, children's walks – a cheery-feeling place. Snacks, shop, plant sales, some disabled access; cl Mon, Tues, and Dec; (01452) 813204; £3. The Royal Oak is popular for lunch.

PRINKNASH SO8713 **Prinknash Abbey and Pottery** (off the A46) Unusual 20th-c Benedictine monastery and earlier house, now home to the world-famous pottery; you can watch production from the viewing gallery. Snacks, shop, disabled access; cl 25–26 Dec, Good Fri; (01452) 812239; £1 for pottery tours. The abbey buildings aren't to everyone's taste but the grounds are attractive, with good views over the Severn Vale. **Prinknash Bird Park** Exotic pheasants, peacocks and other birds, as well as deer, goats and waterfowl; most animals feed from your hand (the fallow deer are particularly friendly). Snacks, shop; cl 25–26 Dec, 1 Jan, Good Fri; (01452) 812727; *£3. The Black Horse in the very steep village of Cranham has enjoyable food.

★ **ST BRIAVELS** SO5504 Attractive and unusual small village focused on the ruins of its 13th-c castle (the inhabited part is a youth hostel), with a steeply grassy former moat and views from the ramparts of the curtain wall. The George is good for lunch, and Mr McGubbin in the **craft shop** has devised various circular walks.

★ **SELSLEY** SO8203 Strung-out Cotswold village in the steep country just S of Stroud; William Morris, Maddox-Brown, Burne-Jones and Rossetti all worked on the **church windows.**

SELSLEY COMMON SO8303 **Herb Garden** This sizeable place has cream teas on Sun and bank hols, and a good nursery. Open pm Tues–Sun and bank hols Apr–Sept, or by appointment; (01453) 766682; £1. They also have a herb shop just up the A46 in Nailsworth (which also has plenty of trails around its old mills). The grassland common itself is quite high, with good views and pleasant walks; the Bell is a handy refreshment stop.

SEVERN ESTUARY ST6196 This makes for some lonely walks along the sea wall, with power station cooling towers and the vast Severn bridges emphasising the emptiness of the tidal flats. The White Hart in Littleton-upon-Severn, the Anchor in Oldbury-on-Severn and right by the embankment the Windbound at Shepperdine are useful starting points. Further upstream Arlingham is locked within a big bend of the Severn, about a mile from the river, with the river path looking across to the Forest of Dean.

★ **SHEEPSCOMBE** SO8910 Delightful Cotswold village, clinging to picturesque hillsides; the cricket ground's so steep that fielders can scarcely see the bowler.

SLIMBRIDGE SO7204 **Wildfowl and Wetlands Trust** (off the A38) The first of the Wildfowl and Wetlands Trust's 8 centres, and still the best, this enormous place is a lot more than just a bird and nature reserve. Thoughtfully upgraded in recent years (with more to come thanks to a hefty grant from the Millennium Commission), it shows off probably the world's most comprehensive collection of geese, swans and ducks, as well as 6 species of flamingo (you won't see so many anywhere else in Europe), and a tropical house that re-creates the sights, sounds and smells of a rainforest. Children explore wetland environments by pond-dipping and seeing what they help fish out of the water magnified on TV screens. Also quite a few computer and video displays and games, and extra events and talks in the school hols. In winter up to 8,000 wild birds fly in; several of the excellent hides and viewing facilities are heated then. Some birds can be fed by hand. Meals and snacks, shop, binocular hire, disabled access; cl 25 Dec; (01453) 890065; £5.25 (free to WWT members). The Tudor Arms by the swing bridge across the canal is useful for food, and the village post office has details of pleasant little walks.

SNOWSHILL MANOR SP0933 It looks like an ordinary Cotswold manor house, but inside is one of those extraordinary collections of ephemera great eccentrics somehow amass. Each room is carefully themed, full of maybe toys, musical instruments, bikes hanging from the ceiling – and even suits of Japanese samurai armour, spookily arranged to look like a group of warriors meeting in the gloom. There's a charming cottage garden, and you can stay in one of 3 cottages. Meals, snacks, shop and secondhand books by the entrance; open pm Weds–Mon Apr–Oct; (01386) 852410; £5.50; NT. This is one of the Trust's busier properties, and there's a timed ticket system; try to come midweek or out of season. The nearby Snowshill Arms is popular for lunch (busiest 12–1.15pm), and the drive by the River Windrush to Ford, Kineton and charming Naunton SP1123 is delightful.

SOUTH CERNEY SU0496 **Cotswold Water Park** 2,000 acres of lakes with facilities for angling, windsurfing, sailing and other watersports, country parks and walks, birdwatching and nature reserves. Snacks at some lakes, disabled access; some activities cl winter; (01285) 861459; £4 (£2 wkdys) car parking, free in winter. **Butts Farm** (1m NE, on the A419) Notably friendly, with a good range of animals for children to feed, and daily pony or cart rides and goat milking. Snacks, shop, disabled access; cl Mon and Tues outside school hols, phone for winter opening; (01285) 862205; £2.95. The Eliot Arms in the prettily preserved 16th-c village has good food.

★ † **SOUTHROP** SP2003 Charming Cotswold village that really comes into its own when the daffodils appear, with a delightful riverside **church**.

★ **STANTON** SP0734 One of the prettiest Cotswold villages, very small – and rarely overrun with visitors. The best views over it are from the Mount pub, up the steep no through road beyond the village centre. The Cotswold Way is well marked to 2 equally timeless nearby villages, Stanway and Buckland; field paths and farm track let you detour to Snowshill, and from there it's a pleasant 3-mile walk to Broadway just over the Herefs & Worcs border.

STANWAY HOUSE SP0632 One of the most beautiful 16th-c manor houses in the country, a cluster of gabled buildings popping up unexpectedly from the countryside, with charming and clearly lived-in rooms. The early 18th-c grounds have fine trees and interesting buildings, inc a folly pyramid on a steeply wooded hill. Open pm Tues and Thurs Jun–Sept; (01386) 584469; £3.50.

★ **STOW-ON-THE-WOLD** SP1925 Handsome market town with fine stone buildings around its square and in the surrounding narrow lanes, and a good few antique shops, book shops and so forth. It's something of an antidote to the more sweetly pretty Cotswold villages, on quite a high plateau and altogether more austere in style – not for nothing was it known as 'Stow on the Wold, where the wind blows cold', and the ancient stocks on the village green add a touch of quaint severity. The Queen's Head is the best pub for lunch.

TETBURY ST8993 A splendid raised **market house**, some interesting little lanes, quite a few antique shops and craft workshops, and decent food in the Crown. **Chavenage** (2m NW) Friendly unspoilt 16th-c manor house with entertaining tours by the owner. It's a popular location for TV programmes, providing a backdrop for characters from Poirot to Mr Blobby. It recently featured in the BBC's *Berkeley Square*. Shop, disabled access to ground floor only; open pm Easter Sun and Mon then pm Thurs, Sun and bank hols May–Sept; (01666) 502329; £3. Out this way the Gumstool (A46/A4135) has very good food. The pretty gardens at **Hodge's Barn** (Shipton Moyne, 2m S) are warmly praised by readers.

★ † **TEWKESBURY** SO8832 Severnside town, site of the last battle in the Wars of the Roses in 1471, still full of attractive half-timbered medieval buildings in a maze of little alleyways.

Two of these old places now house **museums**. Most impressive is the **abbey**, its massively confident Norman tower one of the finest in existence. Also splendid vaulting, some 14th-c stained glass, and regular concerts. The historic Bell Hotel and (simpler) ancient Black Bear and Berkeley Arms are useful for lunch.

★ THAMES & SEVERN CANAL SO9303 The rich, steeply sheltered valleys around Stroud make up a complicated landscape, seen to best advantage, for example, between Chalford and Sapperton. The derelict canal here is atmospherically overgrown, although its towpath survives as an attractive wooded walkway; the Crown in Frampton Mansell SO9292 or Daneway at Sapperton SO9303 are useful jumping-off points in pretty villages.

★ † THORNBURY ST6094 **Oldbury Power Station** Tours of nuclear power station, with hands-on displays, multi-media show, and nature trail. Shop, disabled access (not on tour); cl winter Sats, 24 Dec–1 Jan; (01454) 419899; free. The Anchor in pretty Oldbury-on-Severn has good food (the church on the nearby knoll is unusual; pleasant walks).

TOCKINGTON ST6187 **Oldown** (B4461) Lively country park with good adventure play areas for older children – lots of rope bridges, tube slides and climbing nets. Play area for younger children too, though they'll probably get more out of the animals and demonstrations at the farm. Several picnic areas, pleasant walks, summer pick-your-own, and excellent farm shop – organic meat, local cheeses, home-made honey and so on. Meals, snacks, shop, disabled access; cl Mon (exc bank hols), and most parts cl winter (exc shop and restaurant); (01454) 413605; £4. The quiet village itself is attractive, with good value food in the Swan.

TODDINGTON SP0432 **Gloucestershire–Warwickshire Railway** Steam and diesel train trips through about 6 miles of quiet countryside, departing from restored GWR stations either here or at Winchcombe (*see entry below*). Snacks, shop, good disabled access (though watch out for the potholes in the car park); phone for timetable (01242) 621405; £6.50. They stop nr the Harvest Home at Greet and Royal Oak at Gretton, both doing good food.

TWIGWORTH SO8223 **Nature in Art** (Wallsworth Hall, A38) In an imposing Georgian mansion, a very enjoyable growing collection of well displayed paintings, sculpture, and mosaics inspired by nature – more interesting than you'd expect – artists represented include Picasso, Henry Moore and Graham Sutherland. Good meals and snacks, shop, disabled access; cl Mon (exc bank hols), 24–26 Dec; (01452) 731422; £3.10.

★ ULEY ST7898 Attractive former weaving village with some 18th-c or older stone houses; the Old Crown is good value (ditto its bedrooms), and a good base for walkers. **Uley Tumulus** (off the B4066 N) Quite daunting 55-metre (180ft) long burial mound known as Hetty Pegler's Tump, with stone central passage and 3 burial chambers; key from nearby house. **Owlpen Manor** (B4066, just E) Charming Tudor manor house, with lovely formal gardens and peaceful woodland. Restaurant; open pm daily (exc Mon) Apr–Oct; (01453) 860261; £4.25. Good views from this road.

UPPER SOUDLEY SO6513 **Dean Heritage Centre** (Camp Mill) Useful introduction to the Forest of Dean, set around an old watermill in pretty wooded valley. Plenty going on, inc a working beam engine, a collection of clocks, craft displays, adventure playground, and occasional traditional charcoal burning. Meals, snacks, shop, disabled access; cl wkdys Nov–Jan; (01594) 822170; £3.30.

! WESTBURY-ON-SEVERN SO7114 **Westbury Court** Formal Dutch garden with canals, yew topiary, etc, restored to its 18th-c layout using pre-1700 cultivars inc old fruit varieties. Disabled access; cl Mon (exc bank hols), Tues, Good Fri, and all Nov–Mar; (01452) 760461; £2.70; NT. The Red Lion has good generous food, by the **church** with its unusual detached tower. The village is a good spot for catching the Severn Bore – a tidal wave surging upstream at high tide, sometimes 2 metres (6ft) high around the spring and autumn equinoxes. The National Rivers Authority produces a calendar listing the best times and places to catch the phenomenon, with a rating of how spectacular it's likely to be; (01684) 850951.

WESTONBIRT ARBORETUM ST8588 Over 18,000 numbered trees and shrubs fill the 17 miles of pathways at this magnificent collection, begun in 1829. Outstanding in spring and autumn, but worth a stop any time, with lots of wildlife hidden away amongst the trees. Meals, snacks, shop, disabled access; open all year, though visitor centre cl late Dec–Feb; (01666) 880220; £3.50. The Hare & Hounds is handy for food.

★✝ **WINCHCOMBE** SP0228 Very peaceful and photogenic – once the capital of Mercia, now worth a stop for a look at the **church** with its grotesque gargoyles, or just to soak up the tranquil atmosphere. **Folk and Police Museum** In the Old Town Hall, this has a sometimes surprising collection of British and international police uniforms (cl Sun, and Nov–Mar; 80p). **Railway Museum and Gardens** (Gloucester St) Victorian garden full of lovingly rescued railway memorabilia inc booking office, working signals and signal box. Snacks, shop, disabled access; usually open wknds Easter–Sept and daily in school hols in between (exc cl 1–2 wks in Aug); (01242) 620641; £2.25. The Old Corner Cupboard and Plaisterers Arms (High St) have good value food, and there are interesting craft and other shops here. **Sudeley Castle and Gardens** (off the B4632) Delightful old house, once lived in by Catherine Parr, the luckiest of Henry VIII's wives. The remains of the original medieval castle were skilfully blended into a 19th-c reconstruction. Rich furnishings, porcelain and tapestries, and notable paintings by Turner, Van Dyck and Rubens. The 8 gardens are splendid, and include a knot garden constructed using flowers shown on a 16th-c tapestry on view in the library. Meals, snacks, shop and specialist plant centre, disabled access to garden; cl Mon and all Nov–Feb; (01242) 604357; £5.50, £4 gardens only. There's a working **pottery** nearby (cl winter Suns).

WINTOUR'S LEAP ST5496 A highlight of the Offa's Dyke Path: a sheer cliff over the Wye N of Chepstow with dizzy views downwards.

★ **WOTTON-UNDER-EDGE** ST7693 Charming small town, with a fine Schreider organ in its church, a new little **heritage centre**, and some handsome old buildings; the B4058 is a good drive.

★**Other attractive villages**, all with decent pubs, include Alderton SP0033, Almondsbury ST6084, Amberley SO8401, Bisley SO9005, Bledington SP2422, Broad Campden SP1637, Broadwell SP2027, the Duntisbournes SO9709, Ebrington SP1840, Ewen SU0097, Great Barrington SP2013 (good cheap bedrooms at the Fox, lovely walks), Great Rissington SP1917, Lower Swell SP1725, Meysey Hampton SU1199, Nether Westcote SP2120, Slad SO8707 (the setting for Laurie Lee's *Cider With Rosie*), Somerford Keynes SU0195, South Woodchester (particularly for the views) SO8302, Todenham SP2436, Wick ST7072 (pleasant walks) and Willersey SP1039. Though there's no pub to recommend there, Saintbury SP1139 is a winner when the daffodils are out. The B4060 N of Chipping Sodbury ST7282 and the side roads through Hawkesbury ST7786 and Hillesley ST7689 take you through attractive Cotswoldy scenery.

✝ Many villages have most **attractive churches**, few of them as yet locked. Cirencester is a good base for planning circuits of these. One such group E of the town consists of Ampney Crucis SP0602, Ampney St Peter SP0801, Ampney St Mary SP0802, Down Ampney SP1097 (Vaughan Williams was the vicar's son), Hampnett SP1015 and Northleach SP1114. Another group, NW of Cirencester, has Elkstone SO9612, Duntisbourne Abbots SO9707, Duntisbourne Rouse SO9806, Daglingworth SO9905 (with its finely preserved Saxon carving of Christ on the cross), Stratton SP0103, Baunton SP0204 and North Cerney SP0208.

Guided horse-riding SO8412 Ongers Farm at Brookthorpe organises this, (01452) 813344, from around £9 an hour.

Where to eat

BIRDLIP SO9214 **Kingshead House** *(01452) 862299* 17th-c former coaching inn with lovely English/French cooking using the best fresh produce (home-grown herbs), impeccable service, and good wines; cl pm Sun, Mon; disabled access. **£33**|£8.

BLOCKLEY SP1634 **Crown** *(01386) 700245* Smart and civilised Elizabethan stone inn with very good food in bar or one of 2 restaurants (marvellous fresh fish), lots of good wines, comfortable lounge bar, attractive split-level hotel bar; children allowed if well behaved; pretty bdrms; disabled access. **£20.90**|£8.95.

BROAD CAMPDEN SP1637 **Bakers Arms** *(01386) 840515* Atmospheric granary in tranquil village with very good-value bar food (inc children's menu), a fine range of real ales, cosy beamed bar, log fires, friendly cats, pleasant service, and nice garden; cl 25 Dec, pm 26 Dec. £4.50.

CHELTENHAM SO9421 **Le Champignon Sauvage** *24–26 Suffolk Rd (01242) 573449* Classic French cooking in quietly and simply decorated restaurant with helpful service and good thoughtful wine list; cl am Sat, Sun, 2 wks in summer, Christmas–New Year, all bank hols; disabled access. **£24.50 lunch**.

CHIPPING CAMPDEN SP1539 **Forbes Brasserie** *High St (01386) 840330* Fine 17th-c hotel with stylish and attractive brasserie offering good interesting meals and light snacks plus morning coffee and afternoon tea – more formal restaurant, too; pretty bdrms; cl 3 days Christmas; partial disabled access. **£16**|£6.50.

CIRENCESTER SP0201 **Swan Yard Cafe** *6 Swan Yard (01285) 641300* Popular with shoppers, this small simple café is nicely decorated with dried flowers, china and knick-knacks (all for sale); friendly service, and tasty very good-value food (inc vegetarian); disabled access. **£12**|£4.50.

COLN ST ALDWYNS SP1405 **New** *(01285) 750651* Civilised ivy-covered inn with beautifully presented restaurant-standard food served in a relaxed pubby atmosphere, attractively decorated rooms, a central log fire, well kept real ales and good wines, a no smoking restaurant, and split-level garden; nice surrounding countryside and walks; comfortable bdrms; no children under 10 in restaurant. **£26.50**|£7.95.

DRYBROOK SO6518 **Cider Press** *(01594) 544472* Enjoyable little country restaurant specialising in delicious interestingly cooked fresh fish, often using home-grown herbs; free-range meat dishes, too, plus lovely puddings and cheeses, and reasonably priced wines; cl Tues (open Sun/Mon by prior arrangement), early Jan; disabled access. **£25**.

GRETTON SP0131 **Royal Oak** *(01242) 602477* You can arrive at this popular pub by steamtrain at wknds to enjoy the good-value food in the long series of flagstoned or bare-boarded rooms; beams, dim lighting from candles in bottles, entertaining medley of furnishings, and friendly young service; cl 25–26 Dec; disabled access. **£20**|£5.95.

GUITING POWER SP0924 **Hollow Bottom** *(01451) 850392* Beamed pub run by licensees with racing connections, log fire in main bar, flagstoned public bar, friendly staff, good fresh food, well kept beer, separate restaurant, and good nearby walks. **£20**|£4.50.

KILKENNY SP0018 **Kilkeney Inn** *(01242) 820341* Comfortable dining pub, airy and spacious, with extended and modernised bar (drinking area at one end), lovely food that changes twice daily (best to book), well kept ales, excellent range of wines, and no smoking dining conservatory; disabled access. **£20**|£6.95.

KINGSCOTE ST8196 **Hunters Hall** *(01453) 860393* Civilised creeper-covered old inn with some fine old furniture and big log fires in high-beamed connecting rooms, good bar and restaurant food, excellent breakfasts, and quite a few wines by the glass; big garden with play area; bdrms; disabled access. **£19.50**|£5.95.

LOWER ODDINGTON SP2325 **Fox** *(01451) 870555* Carefully restored elegant inn with well presented, imaginative food, a superb wine list, well kept real ales, fresh flowers and open fire in neat rooms, a lovely dining room, and a relaxed atmosphere; cl 25 Dec, 31 Dec; disabled access. **£19**|£3.95.

MORETON-IN-MARSH SP2032 **Marsh Goose** *(01608) 652111* Cotswold stone house with local artists' work on the walls in the several eating areas, especially good inventive cooking inc good-value and popular set lunch, more elaborate evening meals, lovely puddings, a thoughtful wine list, and quick, young staff; weekly cookery lessons; cl pm Sun, Mon; disabled access. **£32**|£12.

NAILSWORTH ST8599 **William's Bistro** *3 Fountain St (01453) 835507* Marvellous delicatessen with good-value bistro in a back extension; cheerful and informal atmosphere and décor, delicious interesting fish dishes (a few non-fishy things too), efficient service even when really busy, and fairly priced wines; cl Sun, Mon, Tues after bank hols, Good Fri, 2 wks over Christmas. **£25**.

NORTHLEACH SP1114 **Red Lion** *Market Pl (01451) 860251* Good-value, well presented simple food in comfortable and friendly pub, popular Sun roast, open fire, no food pm Mon; disabled access. **£16**|£4.50.

OLDBURY-ON-SEVERN ST6092 **Anchor** *Church St (01454) 413331* Attractively modernised village pub with good-value daily-changing bar food, enterprising puddings, friendly service, and no smoking dining room; busy wknds; cl 25 Dec and pm 26 Dec; children in dining room and garden only; disabled access. **£14**|£4.

PAINSWICK SO8609 **Country Elephant** *New St (01452) 813564* Popular little restaurant open for morning coffee and summer afternoon tea as well as lunch and dinner; delicious interesting food, good wines, and friendly service; no smoking in restaurant but you can smoke in bar/lounge; big summer garden; cl Sun, Mon, Christmas; disabled access. **£17 lunch, £21 dinner**|£3.

PAXFORD SP1837 **Churchill** *(01386) 594000* Under the same ownership as the Marsh Goose, Moreton-in-Marsh, quaint Cotswold stone pub with newish restaurant extension, small side drinking bar with a proper pubby feel, good log fire, assorted tables and chairs on flagstones, particularly good interesting modern cooking, well kept real ales, good wines. **£20.95**|£9.50.

SOUTHROP SP1903 **Swan** *(01367) 850205* Civilised creeper-covered old stone-tiled pub in pretty village, with good interesting food inc delicious ice-creams, a respectable wine list, no smoking restaurant, friendly service, and log fires; cl pm Sun. **£20**|£3.85.

TETBURY ST8993 **Gumstool** *(01666) 890391* Bustling pubby bistro (actually part of rambling Calcot Manor) with stripped pine, flagstones, and hop bines, neatly modern furnishings, a relaxed but civilised atmosphere, particularly good, interesting food, well kept real ales, a thoughtful choice of wines by the glass, and good service; comfortable bdrms. **£21.15**|£7.70.

WOODCHESTER SO8302 **Ram** *(01453) 873329* Bustling cheerful pub with spectacular valley views from terrace, attractive beamed bar, good bar food, prompt friendly service, and lots of real ales; partial disabled access. **£12.40**|£4.95.

Special thanks to Patricia Laws, Mr and Mrs Matthews, M and J Back, Peter Neate, B M Eldridge, Arthur and Margaret Dickinson, J Spencer, Darren and Pippa Horrell, Lynn Sharpless, Bob Eardley, Mrs Turley, Gavin Smith, Val Dickens, J A Byfield, Andrew and Celia Rose.

Please let us know what you think of places in the *Guide*. Use the report forms at the back of the book or simply write us a letter.

Gloucestershire Calendar

Some of these dates were provisional as we went to press. Please check information with the telephone numbers provided.

JANUARY

9 Mickleton Great British Pudding Festival at Three Ways House, home of the Pudding Club – *till Fri 22* (01386) 438429

30 Stow-on-the-Wold Cotswold Antiques and Fine Arts Festival: over 30 talks by international experts – *till 5 Feb* (01451) 831082

FEBRUARY

5 Cheltenham Folk Festival – *till Sun 7* (01242) 522878

MARCH

16 Cheltenham National Hunt Racing Festival inc Gold Cup – *till Thurs 18* (01242) 513014

20 Tewkesbury Cheltenham Bach Choir at the Abbey (01684) 850959

APRIL

3 Yanworth Easter Egg Hunt at Chedworth Roman Villa – *till Mon 5* (01242) 890256

9 Cheltenham Jazz Festival – *till Sun 11* (01242) 521621

10 Gotherington Midland Hillclimb Championship at Prescott Hill – *till Sun 11* (01242) 673136

30 Minchinhampton Craft Fair at Gatcombe Park – *till 3 May* (01529) 414793

MAY

1 Gotherington British Hillclimb Championship at Prescott Hill – *till Sun 2* (01242) 673136; **Upton upon Severn** Folk Festival – *till Mon 3* (01684) 594200

2 Coleford Steam and Vintage Rally at Speech House (01989) 562602; **Randwick** Cheese Rolling – after church service *at 10.30am* three cheeses are blessed and rolled anticlockwise round the church three times. One cheese is cut and distributed, the other two are kept till the following Sat when they are rolled down a slope to open the Randwick Wap (*see below*) (01453) 766782

8 Randwick Wap (see Randwick Cheese Rolling above): carnival, maypole and morris dancing (01453) 766782

13 Bisley Blessing of the Wells at the Parish Church (01452) 770056

15 Tewkesbury Tewkesbury Choral Society at the Abbey (01684) 850959

30 Gloucester Town and Country Show at the Showground – *till Mon 31* (01242) 256446

31 Brockworth Coopers Hill Cheese Rolling: locals chase cheeses down steep hill *from 6pm (see chapter intro)* (01452) 421188; **Tetbury** Woolsack Races: teams of men and women race up and down steep Gumstool Hill carrying 65lb woolsacks, medieval market and street entertainers (01452) 425673

Gloucestershire Calendar (cont.)

JUNE

4 **Chipping Campden** Robert Dovers Cotswold Olimpick Games at Dovers Hill: trad sports, bands, dancing, torchlight procession, then *on Sat 5* Scuttlebrook Wake with street entertainment, morris dancing and procession (01384) 274041

5 **Gotherington** Classic Car Hillclimb at Prescott Hill – *till Sun 6* (01242) 673136; **Yanworth** Archeology Activity Weekend at Chedworth Roman Villa – *till Sun 6* (01242) 890256

19 **Cirencester** Festival of Music and the Arts – *till 4 July* (01285) 657181

26 **Gotherington** Midland Hillclimb Championship at Prescott Hill – *till Sun 27* (01242) 673136; **Tewkesbury** Herb Day at the Abbey (01684) 850959

JULY

3 **Chedworth** Dry Stone Walling Competition and Church Fête (01242) 820482; **Cheltenham** International Festival of Music, and Fringe Festival – *till Sun 18* (01242) 521621; **Hailes** Music Festival – *till Weds 28* (01242) 602379; **Stroud** Show at Stratford Park (01453) 751191; **Tewkesbury** Carnival – *till Sun 4* (01684) 295027

10 **Tewkesbury** Medieval Fayre – *till Sun 11* (01684) 294939

13 **Cheltenham** Cricket Festival – *till Sun 25* (0117) 9245216

17 **Stroud** Rolling: international brick and rolling pin throwing competition (01453) 882039

24 **Fairford** International Air Tattoo – *till Sun 25* (01285) 713300; **Gloucester** Festival inc Folk Roots Festival, street theatre, fireworks concert – *till 7 Aug* (01452) 396605; **Guiting Power** Festival of Music: classical, jazz and opera – *till Sat 31* (01242) 603912; **Yanworth** National Archeology Days at Chedworth Roman Villa – *till Sun 25* (01242) 890256

AUGUST

1 **Painswick** Gloucestershire Guild of Craftsmen Exhibition – *till Tues 31* (01285) 760356

2 **Tewkesbury** Musica Deo Sacra at the Abbey – *till Sun 8* (01684) 850959

7 **Gotherington** Vintage Sports Car Club Hillclimb at Prescott Hill – *till Sun 8* (01242) 673136

21 **Fairford** Steam Rally and Show – *till Sun 22* (01285) 655011; **Tibberton** Horticultural Society Show (01452) 790424

22 **Temple Guiting** Open Day at David Nicholson's Racing Stables (01386) 584209

30 **Berkeley** Hunt Agricultural Show (01453) 54335; **Moreton-in-Marsh** Horse Trials at Springhill Estate (01789) 720144

SEPTEMBER

4 **Gloucester** Barton Fair (01452) 421188; **Gotherington** British and Midland Hillclimb Championship at Prescott Hill – *till Sun 5* (01242) 673136; **Moreton-in-Marsh** Agricultural and Horse Show (01608) 651908

Gloucestershire Calendar (cont.)

11 Stow-on-the-Wold Day of Dance: morris dancing around the town *from 11am* (01451) 831082

12 Frampton on Severn Country Fair (01452) 740698

18 Yanworth Archeology Activity Weekend at Chedworth Roman Villa – *till Sun 19* (01242) 890256

19 Painswick Ancient Clypping Ceremony at St Mary's Church (01452) 812334

25 Cirencester Cotswold Country Fair – *till Sun 26* (01285) 652007

OCTOBER

8 Cheltenham International Festival of Literature: 50th anniversary – *till Sun 24* (01242) 227979

9 Tewkesbury Mop Fair: mainly a fun fair (01684) 295027

NOVEMBER

27 Cheltenham Festival of Christmas Lights: street party (01242) 522878

DECEMBER

26 Gloucester Mummers and morris dancers in the Cathedral Precincts and New Inn Courtyard *at midday* (01453) 759921

We welcome reports from readers

This *Guide* depends on readers' reports. Do help us if you can – in return, we offer a discount on the next edition to people who've helped us with reports for it. Tell us what you think about places already in it, and anything extra you think we should say about them. And send us your ideas for inclusion in the next edition: places to visit, eat at or stay in, attractive drives or walks, maybe even unusual interesting shops you know of. Use the card in the middle, the report forms at the end, or just write – no stamp needed: *The Good Guide to Britain*, FREEPOST TN1569, Wadhurst, E Sussex TN5 7BR.

HAMPSHIRE

Plenty for all ages; the New Forest is particularly attractive, good countryside elsewhere too.

Some first-class family outings here include the continually developing Marwell Zoo at Colden Common, the Sea Life Centre in Portsmouth, the working Iron Age farm at Chalton, the imaginative Hawk Conservancy at Weyhill, the lovely Watercress Railway Line from Alresford, the cheerful Hollycombe Steam Collection near Liphook, the nature park and neighbouring farm park near Ashurst, and the farm park near Andover. For younger children, Paultons Park *(see Family Panel)* is an excellent treat.

Many children get a tremendous kick out of the richly shown ship and warfare heritage that's concentrated around Portsmouth, and there's much to interest adults in this vein. More peacefully, there are some magnificent houses and gardens. Beaulieu with its great range of subsidiary attractions, Broadlands near Romsey, Breamore, Hinton Ampner, the fully restored Vyne at Sherborne St John, Stratfield Saye and the tranquil ruins of Basing House are all very rewarding. The grounds of waterside Exbury are irresistible in late spring, Mottisfont Abbey has wonderful old-fashioned roses, and Houghton Lodge, just upriver towards Stockbridge, is a peaceful spot. Spinners at Boldre is an exciting newer garden, and the gardens and arboretum at Ampfield are very fine. The Sandham Memorial Chapel at Burghclere is thought by some to be the greatest masterpiece of 20th-c British art.

The New Forest countryside, mainly rolling heathland, is great for free-form wandering among ponies and deer. Its coast has sheltered yachting harbours, the pleasant waterside town of Lymington with warm Georgian buildings (the rest of Hampshire's coastline is largely built up), and the interesting Bucklers Hard.

Further inland, a broad belt of gentle countryside stretches from Andover, Stockbridge and Romsey along the Test Valley in the west, through Winchester and Alresford, to Alton and Petersfield in the east. This is a quietly charming mix of rolling, blowy, chalk downland, a patchwork of hedged fields and clumps of steep beechwood, the rich valleys of the clear chalk streams, and attractive small villages often of brick and flint.

Winchester has a charming old quarter around its cathedral, and plenty of opportunities for strolls nearby; a possibility for a quiet city break.

Where to stay

BEAULIEU SU3902 **Montagu Arms** *Palace Lane, Beaulieu SO42 7ZL (01590) 612324* **£119,** plus special breaks; 24 individually decorated rms. Attractive, creeper-clad hotel with a lovely terraced garden; comfortable sitting room, conservatory lounge, very good food in the beamed restaurant, and attentive staff; their health club is in the village; they also run the village shop, post office and bakery; children over 5 in evening restaurant (high tea for little ones).

CHERITON SU5828 **Flower Pots** *Cheriton, Alresford SO24 0QQ (01962) 771318* **£45;** 5 rms. Unspoilt and quietly comfortable village local, run by a very friendly family; with 2 pleasant little bars, a log fire, decent bar food, own-brew beers, and old-fashioned seats on the pretty lawns.

EASTLEIGH SU4317 **Park Farm** *Stoneham Lane SO50 9HS (01703) 612960* ***£35;** 3 rms, shared bthrm. Lots of country walks around these converted coaching stables, coarse fishing in their own lake, and evening meals by arrangement.

HURSTBOURNE TARRANT SU3954 **Esseborne Manor** *Hurstbourne Tarrant, Andover SP11 0ER (01264) 736444* ***£120,** plus special breaks; 15 individually decorated rms. Small, stylish Victorian manor with a calm and relaxed atmosphere; a comfortable lounge and snug little bar, good modern cooking, and friendly staff; neat gardens with tennis, croquet and golf; disabled access.

LYMINGTON SZ3094 **Efford Cottage** *Everton, Lymington SO41 0JD (01590) 642315* ***£44,** plus special breaks; 3 comfortable rms. Spacious family home nr the New Forest; really marvellous 4-course breakfasts with freshly baked bread and home-made jams, optional evening meals, and good parking; children over 12; well behaved pets welcome by arrangement.

LYMINGTON SZ3097 **Passford House** *Mount Pleasant Lane, Lymington SO41 8LS (01590) 682398* **£115,** plus special breaks; 55 neatly kept, pretty rms. Attractive hotel by the New Forest; with a comfortable, panelled lounge (3 others, too), cocktail bar, open fires, and excellent service; 9 acres of gardens and parkland,with indoor and outdoor swimming pools, tennis, croquet and putting.

LYMINGTON SZ3295 **Stanwell House** *High St, Lymington SO41 9AA (01590) 677123* **£95;** 31 pretty rms. Handsome townhouse with a comfortable, attractively furnished lounge, cosy little bar, and good, imaginative food; also, a pretty, walled back garden; 50-ft yacht for charter.

LYNDHURST SU3107 **Parkhill** *Beaulieu Rd, Lyndhurst SO43 7FZ (01703) 282944* **£126,** plus special breaks; 20 carefully furnished rms, some overlooking the lawns. 13th-c hunting lodge, rebuilt by the Duke of Clarence in the 18th c, in parkland with fine views; comfortable lounges, antiques, flowers, and a civilised atmosphere; good food in the attractive dining room, and friendly, professional staff.

MIDDLE WALLOP SU2837 **Fifehead Manor** *Middle Wallop, Stockbridge SO20 8EG (01264) 781565* **£90,** plus special breaks; 15 spacious rms. Friendly and comfortable, old brick manor house in several acres of lovely gardens; with a restful atmosphere, pleasant small lounge and bar, fine food in the candlelit restaurant, enjoyable breakfasts, and friendly staff; croquet; disabled access.

MOCKBEGGAR SU1609 **Plantation Cottage** *Mockbeggar, Ringwood BH24 3NL (01425) 477443* ***£50;** 2 rms. Charming, 200-year-old cottage with 3 acres of gardens and paddocks; nice breakfasts; no smoking; lots of pubs and restaurants nearby; self-catering cottage; no children.

NEW MILTON SZ2293 **Chewton Glen** *Christchurch Rd, New Milton BH25 6QS (01425) 275341* **£230;** 52 really beautiful rms. Luxurious hotel in lovely grounds; with fine antiques in the sumptuous day rooms, excellent modern French cooking, and very good service; gardens with a 9-hole golf course, swimming pool, tennis (2 indoor courts as well) and croquet; also a health club with indoor swimming pool, gym, saunas, treatment rooms; children over 7; disabled access.

NEW MILTON SZ2497 **Yew Tree Farm** *Bashley Common Rd, New Milton BH25 5SH (01425) 611041* ***from £60;** 2 lovely spacious rms. Marvellously comfortable and well run traditional thatched smallholding on the edge of the New Forest; with a small cosy hall, and friendly welcome; extensive breakfasts (taken in the bedroom), and good, home-made dinners (if required) using top quality produce; riding nearby; no smoking, children or dogs.

PORTSMOUTH SZ6299 **Fortitude Cottage** *51 Broad St, Old Town, Portsmouth PO1 2JD (01705) 823748* ***£46;** 3 neat and attractive rms. Comfortable B & B in a cottage named after an old ship, with a pretty, beamed breakfast room overlooking fishing boats; no evening meals, but places nearby; cl 25–26 Dec; no children.

PORTSMOUTH SZ6399 **Sally Port** *High St, Old Town, Portsmouth PO1 2LU (01705) 821860* **£65,** plus special breaks; 10 rms. Beautifully kept, 16th-c inn in a quiet spot, with good food and very friendly, efficient service; said to have been a favourite of Nelson's.

ROCKBOURNE SU1117 **Shearings** *Rockbourne, Fordingbridge SP6 3NA (01725) 518256* **£52;** 3 rms, plus garden annexe. Beside a winter stream, this warmly welcoming and pretty, 16th-c thatched cottage has inglenook fireplaces, ancient beams (some nearly 1,000 years old), and a comfortable sitting room; good pub just up the road; cl mid-Dec–end Jan; children over 12; no dogs.

ROMSEY SU3321 **Spursholt House** *Salisbury Rd, Romsey SO51 6DJ (01794) 512229* ***£46;** 3 rms with antiques, fireplaces and sofas. Lovely welcoming house, with a beautiful garden and a view of Romsey Abbey; an open fire in the characterful sitting room, no evening meals, and warm, friendly owners; cl Christmas–New Year.

ROTHERWICK SU7155 **Tylney Hall** *Rotherwick, Basingstoke RG27 9AZ (01256) 764881* **£135,** plus special breaks; 110 comfortable, well equipped rms. Grand Victorian mansion in 66 acres of gardens and parkland; with gracious day rooms, ornate plasterwork, oak panelling, oil paintings, and log fires in the big ornate fireplaces; interesting food in the candlelit restaurant, and good, attentive service; tennis, golf, indoor and outdoor swimming pools, gym and sauna; disabled access.

SPARSHOLT SU4431 **Lainston House** *Sparsholt, Winchester SO21 2LT (01962) 863588* ***£164,** plus wknd breaks; 38 spacious, individually decorated rms. Close to Winchester, this elegant William and Mary hotel has 63 acres of fine parkland, a relaxing lounge, panelled bar and restaurant, fresh flowers and paintings; a notable wine list, and good British cooking; disabled access.

SWAY SZ2798 **Nurses Cottage** *Station Rd, Sway, Lymington SO41 6BA (01590) 683402* ***£90 inc dinner,** plus special breaks; 3 rms. Small, immaculately kept cottage with a comfortable lounge and dining room, enjoyable evening food using seasonal produce, and a thoughtful wine list; hearty breakfasts, very helpful owner, and a neat garden; cl mid-Nov–mid-Dec; children over 10.

WICKHAM SU5711 **Old House** *The Square, Wickham, Fareham PO17 5JG (01329) 833049* **£90,** plus special breaks; 9 rms. Lovely, early Georgian house under the same charming owners for 27 years; with beamed and panelled rooms, antiques, fresh flowers, and open fires; reliably good French cooking in the restaurant (once the timber-framed outhouse and stables), and a pretty back garden; cl 2 wks Aug, 1 wk Christmas, 1 wk Easter.

WINCHESTER SU4729 **Hotel du Vin & Bistro** *14 Southgate St, Winchester SO23 9EF (01962) 841414* **£85;** 23 rms, real quality, and each sponsored by a well known wine company, with relevant paintings, labels and old photographs. An engaging, early 18th-c townhouse with enthusiastic owners and hard-working staff; a deeply comfortable sitting room, 2 relaxed and pretty eating areas with good, bistro-style cooking and an exceptional wine list; also, a lovely walled garden for summer dining; disabled access.

WINCHESTER SU4828 **Wykeham Arms** *75 Kingsgate St, Winchester SO23 9PE (01962) 853834* ***£79.50;** 13 well equipped, attractive rms. Very well run, smart old town inn, close to the cathedral; with very interestingly furnished buoyant bars, and 2 small dining rooms serving an excellent, daily-changing menu (very good breakfasts, too); fine wines (lots by the glass), and prompt, friendly service; several no smoking areas; no children; cl 25 Dec.

To see and do

⛴ † **PORTSMOUTH** SU6299 An island town, with just 2 roads and the motorway bridging it and its residential/resort part Southsea to the mainland – traffic can be very slow indeed on the main approaches. Its great claim on the imagination is its place at the heart of English naval history, with the Old Town and the Historic Dockyard of particular interest to visitors, on either side of the ferry berths and well away from the traffic. Overlooking the narrow harbour neck, Georgian buildings on an old-fashioned cobbled hard give a good feel of the old days, and the little inner Camber Harbour still has fishing boats. A **waterbus** (Apr–Oct) goes around the harbour, and over to Gosport. By the harbour, the Still & West is a beautifully placed food pub, and the Dolphin's a nice place in the old High St behind. The harbour is starting a huge redevelopment programme, the centrepiece of which will be a 165-metre (540-ft) tower. The **cathedral**, dating from the 13th c to the present, is a delightful departure from the traditional layout.

HM Naval Base The main stop for most visitors, with lots to see. It houses **HMS *Victory***, the ***Mary Rose***, **HMS *Warrior***, and the **Royal Naval Museum**. The flagship is of course HMS *Victory*, still in commission, and manned by regular serving officers. Guided tours bring those Trafalgar days very close, and include the spot where Nelson died. The raising of the *Mary Rose* from the Solent silt where it had sat for 437 years provided a wealth of material and information about the Tudor period. The discoveries are well shown in an airy hall, while the great oak hull itself is in a separate shed, sprayed almost constantly to prevent the timbers from drying out. HMS *Warrior*, when launched 140 years ago, was the most fearsome battleship in the world; she's been immaculately restored, and is manned by tars in period uniform. Again, tours are very vivid. The **Royal Naval Museum**, in handsome 18th-c dockside buildings, has lively displays on the development and history of the Navy up to and beyond the Falklands War (or, as it's called here, the South Atlantic Campaign). Lots of Nelson memorabilia, and a very jolly gallery looking at popular images of the sailor. Each ship costs £5.75 to visit individually (though the HMS *Victory* ticket also includes entry to the museum, which on its own costs £3), but if you want to see more than one it's well worth getting the all-in ticket at £14, which covers all 3 ships and the museum. The site – which itself costs nothing to enter, after a security check – has a restaurant and shop, and there's disabled access to all the ships; (01705) 870999.

D-Day Museum (Clarence Esplanade, Southsea) The most notable of the museums devoted to Portsmouth's fighting history; it vividly recalls and explains the Normandy landings from the point of view of both sides. Very realistic in places you almost panic when the sirens sound. There's a remarkable 272-ft D-Day embroidery inspired by the Bayeux Tapestry. Snacks, shop, disabled access; cl am Mon Nov–Mar, 24–26 Dec; (01705) 827261; £4.75.

! † Royal Marines Museum (Eastney) This vigorous place couldn't be more different from the usual military exhibitions – lively re-creations of major amphibious actions, a junior commando assault course, and a jungle room with real snakes and scorpions. Meals, snacks, shop, disabled access; cl Christmas; (01705) 819385; £3.75.

Royal Garrison church (French St) Roofless now, this once-grand place was where Charles II was married in 1662; usually open Mon–Weds, but best to make an appointment, (01705) 527667.

Harbour Fortifications The fortifications in defence of Portsmouth Harbour, here, around Gosport, and up on Portsdown, give a remarkably complete picture of the development of defensive strategy from Tudor times to the fears of French invasion in the 1860s, though they have more appeal to people interested in warfare than to those who like the romantic idea of a regular 'castle'. **Southsea Castle and Museum** is the best place to start, built in 1545 as part of Henry VIII's coastal defences. Good displays on Portsmouth's military history, and some splendid fish-bone model ships made by Napoleonic prisoners-of-war. Snacks, shop; cl wkdys Nov–Mar, 24–26 Dec; (01705) 827261; £2. On the seaward side of Southsea are sturdy Tudor and later towers, bastions and batteries, alongside the resort's gardens and entertainments, giving interesting sea views. Good guided walks around the

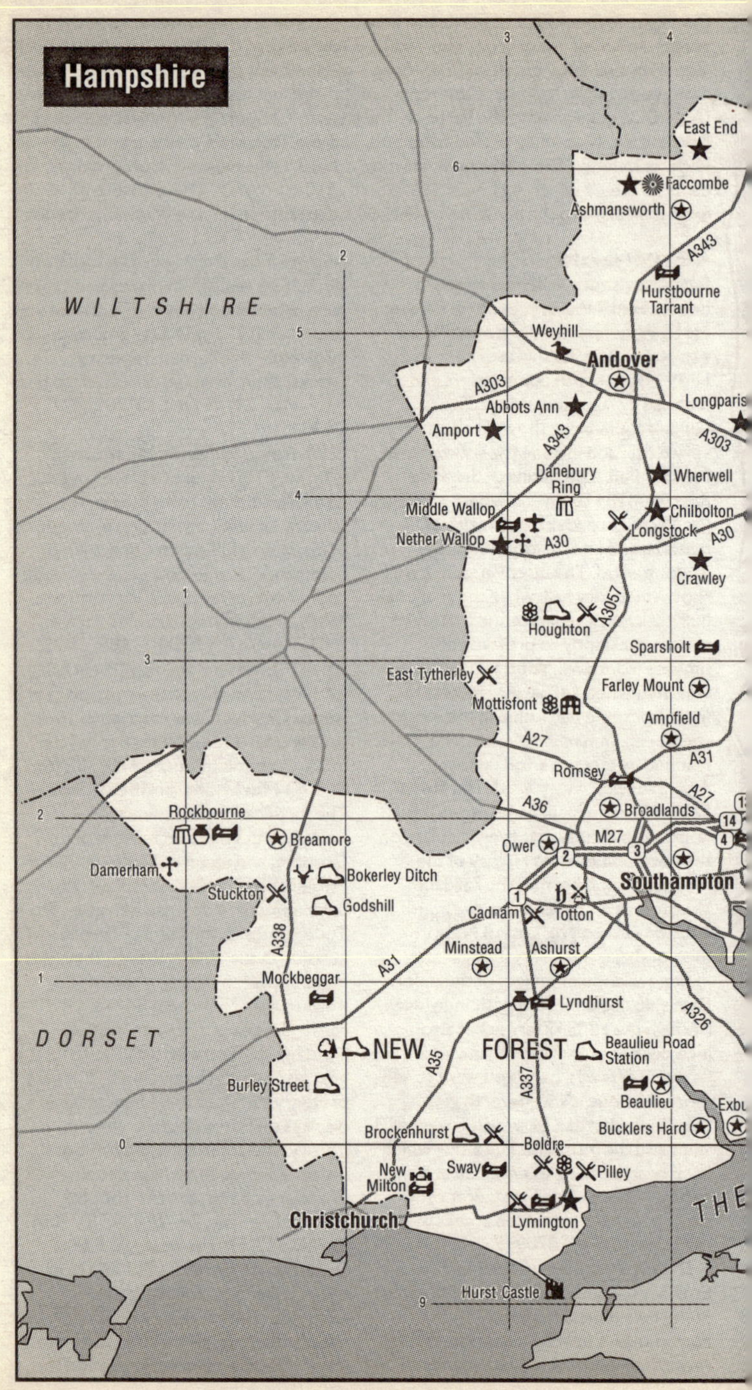
Hampshire
WILTSHIRE
DORSET
East End
Faccombe
Ashmansworth
Hurstbourne Tarrant
Weyhill
Andover
Abbots Ann
Amport
Longparish
Danebury Ring
Wherwell
Chilbolton
Middle Wallop
Nether Wallop
Longstock
Crawley
Houghton
Sparsholt
East Tytherley
Farley Mount
Mottisfont
Ampfield
Romsey
Broadlands
Rockbourne
Breamore
Ower
Damerham
Bokerley Ditch
Stuckton
Southampton
Godshill
Cadnam
Totton
Minstead
Ashurst
Mockbeggar
Lyndhurst
NEW FOREST
Beaulieu Road Station
Burley Street
Beaulieu
Bucklers Hard
Brockenhurst
Boldre
Sway
Pilley
New Milton
Christchurch
Lymington
Hurst Castle
A343
A303
A30
A3057
A27
A31
A36
M27
A338
A35
A337
A326

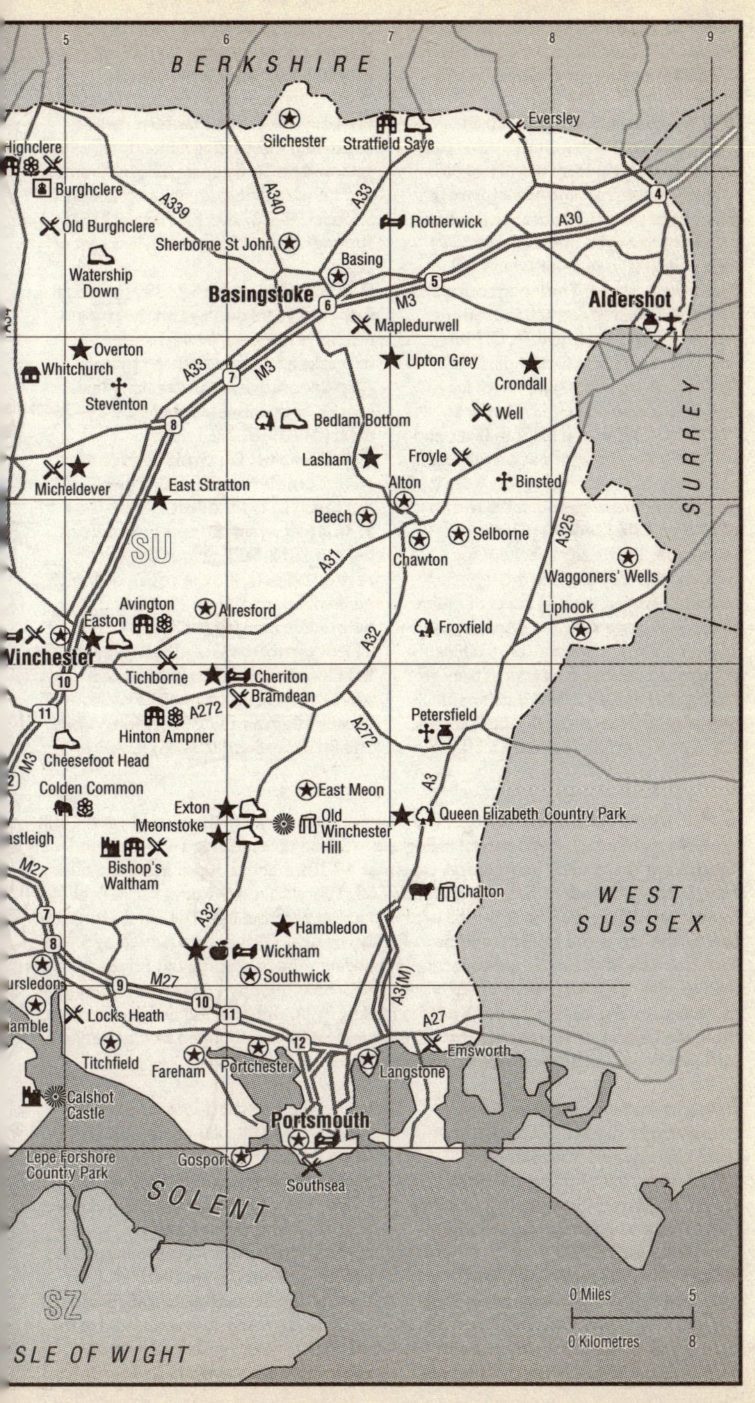

BERKSHIRE
SURREY
WEST SUSSEX
SOLENT
ISLE OF WIGHT
SU
SZ
Highclere
Burghclere
Old Burghclere
Watership Down
Silchester
Stratfield Saye
Eversley
Sherborne St John
Rotherwick
Basing
Basingstoke
Aldershot
Mapledurwell
Overton
Whitchurch
Steventon
Upton Grey
Crondall
Well
Bedlam Bottom
Lasham
Froyle
Binsted
Alton
Micheldever
East Stratton
Beech
Selborne
Chawton
Waggoners' Wells
Liphook
Avington
Easton
Alresford
Froxfield
Winchester
Tichborne
Cheriton
Bramdean
Hinton Ampner
Petersfield
Cheesefoot Head
Colden Common
East Meon
Exton
Meonstoke
Old Winchester Hill
Queen Elizabeth Country Park
Eastleigh
Bishop's Waltham
Chalton
Hambledon
Wickham
Southwick
Bursledon
Locks Heath
Hamble
Titchfield
Fareham
Portchester
Langstone
Emsworth
Calshot Castle
Portsmouth
Lepe Forshore Country Park
Gosport
Southsea
A339
A340
A33
A30
M3
A31
A32
A272
A3
A325
M27
A3(M)
A27
0 Miles 5
0 Kilometres 8

Tudor fortifications and the best parts of the Old Town leave the Square Fort at 2.30pm on Sun (not late Sept–mid-Apr).

Spitbank Fort Wind up an exploration of Portsmouth's naval past with the boat trip from the Naval Base to this granite, iron and brick fortress a mile out to sea. Its 2 floors are linked by a maze of passages, and there's a 130-metre (420-ft) deep well which still draws fresh water. The inner courtyard is now a sheltered terrace for summer refreshments from the café. Cl Mon (exc bank hols), and Oct–Apr; (01329) 664286; £6 inc boat trip. Ferries leave the pontoon beside HMS *Warrior* at 12.15pm, 1.30pm and 2.45pm (Sat), and you can stay overnight out on the fort if you really do want to get away from it all (great views from comfortable rooms).

Sea Life Centre (Clarence Esplanade, Southsea) Excellent for families, this is one of the most hi-tech of these centres, with all sorts of multi-sensory experiences and displays, and an exciting shark encounter. Children complete a scratchcard trail as they go round, and there's a new indoor soft play area. Snacks, shop, disabled access; cl 25 Dec; (01705) 734461; £5.50 (they'll stamp your hand and let you come back later in the day). **Boat trips** round the harbour from nearby.

Cumberland House Natural History Museum (Eastern Parade, Southsea) Interesting collections, with a splendid butterfly enclosure in summer, and full-size dinosaur reconstructions. Shop; cl 24–26 Dec; (01705) 827261; £2 summer (butterfly season), less rest of year.

City Museum SZ6399 (Museum Rd) Very good displays on the city's history, in an astonishing former barracks a bit like a French château. Also decorative art and crafts. Meals, snacks, shop, disabled access; cl 24–26 Dec; (01705) 827261; free.

Dickens' Birthplace Museum (Old Commercial Rd, main town) Restored to the modest middle-class style it had when the author was born here in 1812. Still various Dickens-related objects, inc the couch on which he died. Shop; cl Nov–Mar (exc 3 wks before Christmas); (01705) 827261; £2.

Portsmouth Guildhall (Guildhall Sq) Contains what's said to be the world's biggest glass mural. Free tours, usually 10am and 11.30am Mon, Weds and Fri, Apr–Sept; (01705) 834092.

★ **WINCHESTER** SU4829 The compact and fascinating medieval centre still has 2 city gates intact; it was capital of England in Saxon times. Guided walks around the sights from the tourist information centre at 10.30am and 2.30pm Mon–Sat during May–Sept (2.30pm only in Apr and Oct); £2.50. There's a multi-storey car park at the top of the High St, or a Park & Ride nr the junction with the M3. The most attractive part of the city is the glorious and peaceful **Cathedral Close**, surrounded by a very harmonious and distinguished collection of buildings; the handsome old Eclipse Inn, nr the NE edge, is a useful refreshment break. The Brooks Shopping Centre has a few jolly dioramas and displays on the city's history (cl Sun; free), with the chance for children to make their own Roman mosaic. There are pleasant walks up rounded **St Catherine's Hill**, which has a small medieval turf maze and traces of a hill fort.

Regimental Museums Anyone interested in military history will enjoy the 3 Light Infantry museums in Winchester, but of these only the Gurkha Museum (Romsey Rd) could be said to have a wider appeal; cl Sun, Christmas wk; *£1.50.

✝ **Winchester Cathedral** Awesome and full of interest – one of Europe's finest, with the longest of all Gothic naves, and quite a mixture of architectural styles. Among many rare books and manuscripts in its library is a wonderful 12th-c illuminated Bible, while the sculpture gallery contains some outstanding late Gothic work. William of Wykeham paid for much of the rebuilding, so his tomb is appropriately the finest; also memorials and monuments to Jane Austen, King Canute and St Swithin. Good guided tours, and a first-rate visitor centre in the 16th-c coach house, with very appetising meals and snacks (not cheap) and a distinguished shop; £2.50 suggested donation.

Close by are the appreciable remains of Wolvesey Castle, the original Bishop's Palace begun in the 12th c, and beside it (not open, but a handsome sight), the present Bishop's Palace of 1684. The best way out of the cloisters is through the medieval King's Gate, which includes the upper-floor church of St Swithin. This takes you into Kingsgate St, calm and old-fashioned, with an excellent dining pub, the Wykeham Arms. Down on the left, a lovely riverside path takes you along to the City Mill and a mighty statue of King Alfred.

Winchester College All along Kingsgate St are buildings connected with this, the oldest school in the country. Most of the original school buildings remain intact, especially around the grand 14th-c chapel and its calm, tilting cloisters with a delightful 2-storey chantry in their centre, and a glimpse of the warden's garden through one gate. Good shop in the former tuck shop, some disabled access; guided tours Apr–Sept, cl 1–2pm, am Sun (winter tours by appointment only); (01962) 621217; £2.50.

Winchester Castle All that now remains is its huge 13th-c Great Hall, where Raleigh was tried and condemned to death; hanging off one wall is a round table they call King Arthur's (actually much the same date as the castle, and painted with its Arthurian scenes later). The roof, stone parapets and stained glass windows are being restored – work is due to finish in Jan. A small but interesting garden is laid out on the lines of what might have been there in the 13th c. Shop, disabled access; cl 25–26 Dec; (01962) 846476; free.

Westgate Museum (High St) Local history above a formidable medieval city gate – the panorama of the city and countryside is rewarding. Shop; cl 1–2pm Sat, am Sun, Mons in Oct, Feb and Mar, and all Nov–Jan; (01962) 869864; 30p.

Guildhall Gallery (Broadway) Refurbished 19th-c building with changing exhibitions of fine art, crafts and photography. Snacks, shop, disabled access; cl am Sun and Mon (all Mon in winter), Good Fri, 25–26 Dec, 1 Jan; (01962) 848269; free.

Winchester City Museum (The Square) Well organised local history and archaeology exhibits, inc a Roman mosaic. Shop, limited disabled access; cl 1–2pm Sat, am Sun, Mon Oct–Mar, 25–26 Dec; (01962) 863064; free.

City Mill (Bridge St) Restored 18th-c working watermill, with timbered and raftered ceilings and a pretty little island garden. Cl Mon (exc bank hols) and Tues, wkdys in Mar, and all Nov–Feb; (01962) 870057; £1; NT.

St Cross SU4727 A short stroll along the watermeadows by the River Itchen. Very attractively set around 2 quadrangles, the quaint 15th-c almshouses still provide bread and ale to travellers who ask at the massive gate (you have to ask for 'wayfarer's dole'). 19th-c scandals here inspired Trollope's *The Warden*. Summer snacks, shop, disabled access; cl winter 12.30–2pm in winter, Sun, 25 Dec, Good Fri; £2. The Bell out here is useful for lunch.

NEW FOREST SU2605 The New Forest countryside has enormous charm. Only parts of it are in fact wooded; the rest is unspoilt rolling heathland. Walkers can head off in virtually any direction without worrying about trespassing. Once away from the roads, it does give a great feeling of untrammelled space. Children like it: there are free-running ponies and deer, and plenty of scope for generally running riot without coming to grief.

This unchanging blend of woodland and heath covers nearly 150 square miles, designated a royal hunting preserve by William the Conqueror not long after the Battle of Hastings. The 2 best drives are the slow back road from Brockenhurst N through Bolderwood and then round past Linwood to Rockford, and the road from Brockenhurst to Burley; main roads can get very busy around the more popular areas, especially on summer weekends.

Still with quite a medieval feel, the ancient woodlands are very atmospheric to stroll through, especially when you come across an unexpected sunlit leafy glade.

It's most fun just to potter around, but you'll also get a lot out of a guided tour with people who've lived or worked in the forest all their lives; (01703) 282269 for details. Many of them have ancient forest rights and privileges, such as letting their pigs forage for acorns. The path network in the New Forest is remarkably comprehensive, and in most places there's no obligation to stick to rights of way (of which there are very few). There are no obviously defined hills, and long walks in the eastern woodlands, many of which are coniferous, can become monotonous. Further W, the scenery is more intricate and a touch more varied. It is often a good idea to use routes which have plenty of landmarks to guide the way; the heath and forest can be fiendishly disorienting. Besides the ponies, you may see fallow deer, especially at the Bolderwood Deer Sanctuary (and in the woods, very occasionally, the smaller, shyer roe deer; even in some places red deer).

The best walks alternate mixed forest with heathland; isolated ponds and country pubs provide focal points. Good starting-points include **Brockenhurst** SU2902 (also bicycle hire at around £9 a day – the forest is a fine place for cycling), **Beaulieu Road Station** SU3506 (for its surrounding, remote-feeling heaths), **Burley Street** SU1904 and **Godshill** SU1714. In summer you can usually go on guided badger-watch evenings; (01425) 403412. The **Museum and Visitor Centre** at Lyndhurst is also a worthwhile place to start, and has details of water sports, riding and campsites. Handy pubs include the Royal Oak at Bank, Red Lion at Boldre (nr Roydon Woods nature reserve), Royal Oak at Fritham, Forester's Arms at Frogham, High Corner Inn or Red Shoot nr Linwood, Royal Oak at North Gorley, Alice Lisle at Rockford, Sir Walter Tyrell at Upper Canterton, Turf Cutter's Arms at East Boldre and Filly at Setley.

Other things to see and do

HAMPSHIRE Family Attraction of the Year

☺ 🐄 🐦 ❀ 🍴 ! **OWER** SU3116 **Paultons Park** With quite a few things added over the last couple of years, this agreeable family theme park is a nicely varied day out; it's hardly Alton Towers, but younger children especially enjoy its mix of gentle rides, gardens, animals, birds and wildfowl, spread out over 140 acres. Typical rides are the Runaway Train rollercoaster and a spin on the Whirly Copter or teacups, plus go-karts (the only thing with an extra charge). There are bumper boats, seasonal clown shows, radio-controlled cars, and several good play areas, many ideal for toddlers. Cheery animated dinosaurs and scenes from *The Wind in the Willows* might seem a little old-fashioned for sophisticated tastes, but are well put together and delight small children; there's a festive display along the same lines during the weekends before Christmas. The attractive grounds have quieter corners for woodland or lakeside strolls, a hedge maze, and a couple of neatly landscaped gardens; there are plenty of tropical and other birds dotted about, and a small petting zoo. Next to the village life museum is a more unusual Romany Experience, with the sights, sounds and smells of traditional gypsy life. Children over 12 won't get quite so much out of it, but younger ones can be entertained here for half a day or more without too much trouble; there are several decent places to eat. As flamingos breed only when they're surrounded by large numbers, mirrors have been installed to make them think they're part of a bigger flock. Meals, snacks, shop, disabled access; cl wkdys Nov and Dec (exc Christmas specials), and all Jan and Feb; (01703) 814442; £8.50 adults (£7.50 children under 14; children under 1 metre tall are free – though they can't go on everything). There's a range of family tickets, starting at £22.50 for 2 adults and 1 child.

✝ ♁ **ALDERSHOT** SU8651
Airborne Forces Museum (Browning Barracks) The best of Aldershot's profusion of military museums (most of which are of rather specialist appeal), looking at the parachute forces. Lots to take in, with very traditional displays. Snacks, shop, disabled access; cl Christmas and 1 Jan; (01252) 349619; £2.50. **Military Museum** (Queen's Ave) Quite well done, exploring the development of the local military camps and their impact on civilian and military life. Shop, disabled access; cl Christmas–New Year; (01252) 314598; *£2.

ALRESFORD SU5832
Watercress Line (Special discount not applicable to Thomas the Tank Engine events, Santa Specials or Dining Trains.) One of the nicest steam railways in the country, with 10-mile trips between Alresford and Alton through wonderful countryside and its watercress beds. They try to create a pre-war feel, with stations decked out accordingly. Their Thomas the Tank Engine weeks around Easter and in Aug are extraordinarily popular; several railways organise something similar, but the Thomas here is unusual in being built to the design and proportions in the books, and there may also be other characters such as James the Red Engine, Diesel and the Fat Controller. Properly called the Mid-Hants Railway, it has connections to Waterloo. Meals, snacks, shop, disabled access; phone for timetable, (01962) 734866, no trains Nov–Jan (exc Santa specials); £7.50. On some weekdays you can combine it with a visit to the modern Bass brewery at the Alton end, usually open only to groups (01420) 541177. Alresford itself is a charming little town, from the Roman ponds teeming with wildfowl in Old Alresford to the so-called New Alresford founded around 1200; good antiquarian bookshop here. The Globe overlooking the ponds does decent lunches, and the Café Cressdon is pleasant. The Itchen road W through Ovington and Easton is pretty, the B3046 N shows high Hampshire farmland well, and the old road E, past Ropley and Monkwood, to Steep gives a fine downland impression.

ALTON SU7139 The terminus of the Watercress Line from Alresford. **Allen Gallery** (Church St) Superb collection of pottery, and a little herb garden. Some disabled access; cl Sun, Mon; (01420) 82802; free. The town brewery is commemorated in a **museum** on the High St; a **church** bears scars from one of the last battles of the Civil War. The French Horn (The Butts) is a friendly food pub.

AMPFIELD SU3824
Sir Harold Hillier Gardens and Arboretum (Jermyns Lane, off the A31) Impressive collection of trees and shrubs, the biggest of its kind in Britain, covering 160 beautifully landscaped acres. Full of colour and surprises all year, and good walks and events (especially first Sun of month). Summer meals, snacks, nursery, disabled access; cl Christmas bank hols; (01794) 368787; £4 (£3 Nov–Mar). The White

Days Out

Army and Navy: D-Day Museum and Sea Life Centre, Southsea; lunch at the Still & West (Bath Sq, nr the waterfront), Portsmouth; boat trip to Spitbank Fort; HMS *Victory* or *Mary Rose*; or spend a full day at Portsmouth's Historic Dockyard.

Escape to the forest: New Forest Museum and Visitor Centre, Lyndhurst; Furzey Gardens, Minstead; picnic in the New Forest, or lunch at the Trusty Servant, Minstead; stroll or mountain bike ride in the New Forest, or Bolderwood/Rhinefield Ornamental Drives; Spinners garden, Boldre.

Hampshire's watery fringes: Bucklers Hard; lunch at the Master Builder's House there; Beaulieu National Motor Museum, or Exbury Gardens; if there's time, stroll in Lepe Country Park.

Horse nearby is a comfortable lunch break, and there are nice walks in Ampfield Woods.

ANDOVER SU3645 **Museum of the Iron Age** Nr the church at the top of the impressive High St of this very extended country town, the museum looks particularly at finds from nearby Danebury Ring, giving a vivid impression of life for the pre-Roman Celts. Snacks, shop, limited disabled access; cl Sun (exc pm summer), Mon (exc pm bank hols); (01264) 366283; £1.50. There's an adjacent more general **museum** (open same hours, free). **Test Valley Tapestry** (Weyhill Rd, B3402) The local authority's conference room houses this remarkable work, each of its many panels embroidered by a different village to show a scene relating to that community; generally open Mon lunchtimes and pm last Thurs of each month – best to phone (01264) 364144 ext 3453 to check; free. **Finkley Down Farm Park** (just NE, SU3847) Well laid out working farm with a wide range of animals and poultry inc rare breeds; they encourage you to touch the tamer animals, and there are varied activities every half-hour. Also a countryside museum, adventure playground and picnic site. Readers rate this very highly, and it has lots for children (inc space for them to run around). Snacks, shop, disabled access; cl Nov–Mar; (01264) 352195; £3.80. There are well stocked **trout fishing** lakes around Andover, such as Rooksbury Mill. Poplar Farm (on the A343 at Abbotts Ann) is a useful food stop.

★ **ASHMANSWORTH** SU4157 An attractive village, Hampshire's highest; good walks and a decent pub. There are fine views from many of the lanes around here – best explored by car.

ASHURST SU3310 **New Forest Otter and Owl Park** (Longdown; off the A326 nr Marchwood) Redevelopment of the former New Forest Nature Quest with a large collection of otters, owls and other indigenous wildlife; also, woodland nature trails. Meals, snacks, shop, disabled access; cl 25 Dec; (01703) 292408; £4.75. The neighbouring **Longdown Dairy Farm** (Deerleap Lane) is a friendly place with plenty of animals to feed; their herd of Jersey cows is milked from 2.30pm every day. There's a small play area. Snacks, shop, disabled access; cl Nov–Easter; (01703) 293326; £4. The Pilgrim is an attractive thatched dining pub.

AVINGTON PARK SU5332 Georgian mansion with Tudor origins, set in lovely parkland. Teas in the orangery, disabled access; open Sun and bank hols May–Sept; (01962) 779260; £3.

BASING HOUSE SU6652 Peaceful ruins of what was once the country's largest house, destroyed during a 2-year siege during the Civil War. Also remnants of a Norman castle, a 16th-c barn, dovecots, an exhibition explaining the eventful history of the site, and a newly created 17th-c garden. Shop, disabled access; open pm Weds–Sun and bank hols Apr–Sept; (01256) 467294; £1.50. Nice walks from here along the River Loddon; the Gamekeepers at pretty nearby Mapledurwell is handy for lunch.

! **BEAULIEU** SU3802 Justifiably popular family day out, its centrepiece still the **National Motor Museum**, a collection that has grown from humble beginnings to become one of the most comprehensive in the world. Other features have a motoring theme too, inc a hands-on gallery about how cars work, and Wheels, probably the highlight for children – you sit in a pod-like vehicle and trundle through 100 years of motoring. For an extra £2, a simulator ride gives you a more robust driving experience. A monorail whizzes round the grounds, and in summer they usually have a daily Disneyland-style parade of vintage vehicles. Also go-kart-style mini-bikes, radio-controlled cars, and some hi-tech arcade-style driving games. Meanwhile the Palace House is a fine old mansion based around the gatehouse of the huge Cistercian Abbey that stood here until the Reformation (still with what are thought to be the original monastic fan-vaulted ceilings). The surrounding lakeside parkland and gardens are rewarding to explore, with ruins of other abbey buildings, and an exhibition on the monks who lived here. Meals, snacks, shops, disabled access; cl 25 Dec; (01590) 612123; £8.75 In the village facing the Palace House gates, the Wine Press is popular for lunch, and a marked trail leads from it down to Bucklers Hard.

BEDLAM BOTTOM SU6246 Pleasant, partly wooded valley walks, particularly pretty in spring, just W of Ellisfield SU6345 (where the Fox has good food), with more downland walks above.

BEECH SU6838 **Alton Abbey** (signed off the A339) The home of a community of Benedictine monks in peaceful woodland, so a relaxing place for a stroll. The grounds have mature specimen trees and shrubs, especially rhododendrons and azaleas. The traditional Sun at Bentworth does decent food.

BINSTED SU7740 **Church** where Field Marshal Montgomery is buried; after the war he lived a mile away at Islington Mill – a pretty spot. The Cedars has worthwhile food.

BISHOP'S WALTHAM PALACE SU5517 Impressive ruins of the Bishop of Winchester's majestic 12th-c palace, with the remains of state apartments round a cloister court, and William of Wykeham's Great Hall and tower. Shop, disabled access to ground floor; cl Nov–Mar; (01489) 892460; £2. The Barleycorn (Basingwell St) has decent food, and the downs N of here between Owslebury, Beauworth and Warnford give scenic drives.

BOKERLEY DITCH SU0419 This dyke acted as a bulwark from raiders into Dorset in the 4th c; still impressive to walk along, it marks the county boundary and can be reached by walking up from Martin SU0619. Towards Pentridge Hill is a nature reserve.

BOLDRE SZ3298 **Spinners** (School Lane) Wonderful gardens created since the 1960s. The nursery is famed for its rare trees (especially maples and magnolias), shrubs and plants. Some disabled access; gardens open Tues–Sat mid-Apr–mid-Sept, or by appointment; nursery open all year exc Sun and Mon Sept–Apr; (01590) 673347; £1.50. The Red Lion (no children) is good for lunch.

★ **BREAMORE HOUSE** SU1519 Late Elizabethan manor house, with fine furnishings, tapestries and paintings (mainly 17th- and 18th-c Dutch school), and a better than average countryside museum. Children aren't left out – there's a mysterious mizmaze cut in the turf and an adventure playground. Snacks, shop, disabled access; open pm Tues, Weds and Sun Apr–Sept, plus Thurs and Sat May–Sept, and daily in Aug; (01725) 512468; *£5. The village has many thatched houses, and is a pleasant walk from Breamore House. The home cooking at the Horse & Groom at Woodgreen is enjoyable, with more lovely wood and riverside walks.

BROADLANDS SU3520 (just S of Romsey) Elegant Palladian mansion by the River Test, in beautiful landscaped grounds. Fine furnishings and paintings, and a good exhibition on former resident Earl Mountbatten. You can fish on an adjacent stretch of the River Test. Snacks, shop, disabled access; open pm mid-Jun–mid-Sept; (01794) 516878; £5. The nearby Old Horse & Jockey and (afternoon teas too) Three Tuns have worthwhile food. Mountbatten is buried in the interesting 13th-c **Romsey Abbey**, bought by the townspeople for their parish church at the Dissolution. There are some notable Saxon crosses and a 16th-c panel painting.

★ **BUCKLERS HARD** SU4099 Very pretty little waterside village, with long, red-roofed cottage rows flanking a wide, grassed waterside street. It was once an important centre for shipbuilding, and the **Maritime Museum** tells the story of the industry, right up to the voyages of Sir Francis Chichester. You have to pay to come into the village, though admission includes entry to the museum and the various other exhibitions and reconstructions dotted around, inc the carefully restored 18th-c homes of a shipwright and labourer, and a typical inn scene complete with costumed figures, smells and conversation. Meals, snacks, shop; cl 25 Dec; (01590) 616203; £3.20. There are summer boat trips, and the Master Builder's House is useful for lunch. A pleasant 2½-mile riverside walk takes you to Beaulieu, run by the same people.

BURGHCLERE SU4761 **Sandham Memorial Chapel** Stanley Spencer's moving masterpiece, built in memory of H W Sandham, killed in the First World War. The final resurrection scene is especially dramatic, best on a bright day as the room is quite dark. Cl Mon (exc bank hols when cl following Weds instead), Tues, wkdays Nov and Mar and all Dec–Feb; (01635) 278394; *£2; NT. The Carpenter's Arms opposite is pleasant for lunch, with superb views.

BURSLEDON SU4911 **Manor Farm Country Park** (Pylands Lane) Woodland and riverside walks based around a traditional working farm, with lots of animals, crafts and activities, inc a forge and a wheelwright. Meals, snacks, shop, mostly disabled access; park open all yr, farm cl winter exc Sun and Feb half-term; (01489) 787055; £3.50. There may be **boat trips** on some summer Sats from here along the Hamble. Bursledon also has a **windmill**; open Sun and summer Sats. The Jolly Sailor is a beautifully placed food pub.

CALSHOT CASTLE SU4802 Down past the oil refineries and power stations, this Tudor fort stands on the end of the spit of land beyond the tidal mudflats at the end of Southampton Water; splendid views of the shipping and the Isle of Wight. The Jolly Sailor, at Ashlett Creek nr Fawley, is a pleasant waterside food pub.

CHALTON SU7117 **Butser Ancient Farm** (Bascombe Copse) Reconstructed Iron Age farm, with crops, animals, crafts and demonstrations. You can try your hand at grinding corn on a stone, and there's a Celtic maze (planted with period herbs). Shop, disabled access; cl Nov–Easter; (01705) 598838; £2.50. The ancient Red Lion is handy for lunch.

CHAWTON SU7037 **Jane Austen's House** Unpretentious 17th-c house where the author lived and worked between 1809 and 1817, still with some of her letters and possessions. Rooms are furnished in period style, and the pleasant garden is nice for picnics. Good bookshop, disabled access to ground floor and garden; cl wkdys Jan and Feb, 25–26 Dec; (01420) 83262; *£2.50. The Greyfriar opposite has reasonably priced food, and there are enjoyable walks here. Just up the road, Chawton House, the former home of Jane Austen's brother Edward, is to become a centre for the study of early English women's writing.

CHEESEFOOT HEAD SU5327 (locally pronounced Chesford) Good for walks; a natural amphitheatre where Eisenhower and Montgomery addressed the troops before the Normandy invasion.

★ **CHILBOLTON** SU3940 An attractive village with a decent pub; the common is being carefully preserved.

COLDEN COMMON SU5121 **Marwell Zoo** (off the A333 towards Bishop's Waltham) Too many supposedly conservation-minded animal attractions still shove their animals into overcrowded cages or enclosures, so it's particularly nice to find one like this where – at least in places – the tables are turned; visit the lemurs and they'll be enjoying plenty of space and freedom while you watch from covered walkways. Other well conceived viewing areas include a glass wall at the end of the tiger enclosure (so they can jump up at you in perfect safety) and underwater windows into the penguin pool. The Tropical House is impressive – it takes 2 hours each day to water the plants. It's the turn of the giraffes to get a new home this year. Children can join in Animal Encounters during the summer holidays, maybe handling a snake or riding a camel, and touch tables allow you to feel things you wouldn't normally be able to get close to – lion and tiger skins, for example. The thousand acres of parkland are attractively laid out, with particularly pleasant picnic areas, a good adventure playground and road and rail trains to whisk you between the different enclosures. Meals, snacks, shop, good disabled access; cl 25 Dec; (01962) 777406; £8. On the downs above, the Ship at Owslebury is nice for a family lunch – quieter than the big, nearby Fishers Pond.

DAMERHAM CHURCHYARD SU1016 Well worth a Feb visit, to see the carpet of snowdrops.

DANEBURY RING SU3237 Iron Age hill fort rich in (excavated) remains. The Peat Spade, at Longstock to the E, has good food.

★ **EAST MEON** SU6822 This appealing village has a splendid Norman **church**, and a decent pub. Many woods in this part of Hampshire fill with snowdrops in February; Warnford SU6223 is a good example.

★ **EASTON** SU5031 This attractive village, with a nice pub, is well placed for pleasant Itchen Valley walks.

EXBURY GARDENS SU4200 Wonderful 200-acre, landscaped woodland gardens on the east bank of the River Beaulieu, with a splendid rock garden, heather garden and river walk, and, above all, the Rothschild collection of rhododendrons, azaleas, magnolias and camellias – one of the world's finest, at its best in May and early Jun. Meals, snacks, shop, disabled access; cl Nov–Feb; (01703) 891203; price varies with the season, from £3.30 in summer, to £4.80 in spring. Nearby **Lepe Country Park** is a nice place for a coastal stroll, with good views and lots of natural habitats. The Jolly Sailor, at Ashlett Creek nr Fawley, is quite handy.

★ **EXTON** SU6020 Beautifully set by the River Meon under the downs, this attractive village (with a decent pub) has good walks nearby.

★ **FACCOMBE** SU3957 Bright with daffodils in spring, this attractive village has a pleasant pub, and great views from Pilot Hill.

FAREHAM SU6007 **Fort Nelson** (Downend Rd) Built in 19th c in response to fears of the French, this now houses the Royal Armouries Museum of Artillery, which they like to call the noisiest museum in the world. Certainly enough booms, blasts and crashes to please most children (guns are fired at noon and 3pm), and you don't have to be interested in weaponry to enjoy it. Wafting smells create a period atmosphere, and there are lots of underground tunnels to explore. Views of Portsmouth Harbour from the ramparts. Meals, snacks, shop, disabled access; cl winter wkdys; (01329) 233734; £4.25. You can get a joint ticket with Submarine World *(see Gosport entry, below)*. The Osborne View out at Hill Head has superb views, with pleasant walks nearby.

GOSPORT SZ6299 **Submarine World** (Royal Navy Submarine Museum, Haslar Jetty Rd) The highlight here is the tour of the beached World War II submarine HMS *Alliance*, still in full working order, and fascinating inside to small boys of any age. More conventional features include an audio-visual show giving the flavour of diving into the depths. Snacks, shop, some disabled access; cl 24 Dec–1 Jan; (01705) 529217; *£3.75. **Fort Brockhurst** A good overview exhibition of how the various forts protected Portsmouth; the Dolphin (Fort Rd) has popular food. You can get a waterbus across to Portsmouth (Apr–Oct), and the sea at Stokes Bay is probably Hampshire's cleanest for swimming in.

FARLEY MOUNT SU4229 Attractive for walks – downland and woodland, with good views.

FROXFIELD GREEN SU7124 In May much of the woodland here is carpeted with bluebells, as are other nearby woods – for example at East Tisted SU7032 and Ropley SU6431.

★ **HAMBLE** SU4806 This pleasant village in *Howards Way* country has interesting views of the yachts, and you can walk a long way upriver or towards the Solent; the simple Olde Whyte Harte has decent food. There's a friendly little ferry, taking about 10 people at a time, to Warsash, where the riverside Rising Sun has good food, and there's a wildfowl nature reserve just N (this makes for an interesting ferry-aided circular walk). Nearby Netley has a coastal **country park** and the extensive ruins of a 13th-c abbey.

HIGHCLERE CASTLE SU4360 (best approached from the A34 rather than Highclere itself) Magnificent pastiche of a medieval castle, impressively grand inside and out. Elaborate saloon and main staircase, a desk that belonged to Napoleon, and a Van Dyck of Charles I. Exhibitions of

Egyptian relics (the 5th earl discovered Tutankhamun's tomb with Howard Carter), and horse-racing (the current earl is the Queen's racing manager). The lovely gardens and grounds include a Victorian tropical conservatory and a walled garden. Meals, snacks, shop and plant centre; open Tues–Sun July–Sept, plus bank hol wknds; (01635) 253210; £6, gardens only £3. The Yew Tree (on the A343 S of village) is a good-value dining pub.

HINTON AMPNER SU5927 Attractive Georgian house, but it's the grounds that impress most, with tranquil 20th-c shrub gardens. Teas, disabled access; gardens open 15 and 22 Mar (good for daffodils), then pm Tues, Weds, wknds and bank hols Apr–Sept; house open only pm Tues and Weds, and Sat and Sun in Aug; (01962) 771305; £4 house and garden, garden only £3; NT. The neighbouring Hinton Arms now has good food.

HOUGHTON SU3433 **Houghton Lodge Gardens** (just SW of Stockbridge) Pretty and very peaceful gardens running down to the River Test, with fine trees and lawns, topiary peacocks and a topiary dragon that breathes 'steam'. An intriguing hydroponicum demonstrates how to grow plants without soil. Weekend snacks, plant sales (especially good on fuchsias), disabled access; open Mar–Sept, all day Weds, wknds and bank hols, and pm other wkdys; hours may change in 1999, phone to check (01264) 810177; £2.50. The Boot has decent food; walks by this lovely stretch of the Test, or up on the downs.

HURST CASTLE SZ3189 One of the most sophisticated fortresses around when built by Henry VIII, on a little spit commanding the Solent, and best reached on foot or by boat from Keyhaven (there's a pleasant walk from the 17th-c Gun pub – good-value food). Fortified again in the 19th-c, it still has 2 huge 38-ton guns. Summer snacks, shop; cl wkdys Nov–Mar, 24–26 Dec, 1 Jan; (01590) 642344; £2.50.

★ **LANGSTONE** SU7104 Thatched cottages, an old tidal mill, and a couple of decent pubs looking out over the thousands of acres of silted harbour – winter sunsets are memorable. Swans float up at high tide, with oyster-catchers and droves of darting dunlins on the low-tide mudflats. Interesting walks along the old sea wall.

LIPHOOK SU8330 **Bohunt Manor** Lovely woodland gardens owned by the Worldwide Fund for Nature, with a watergarden, roses and herbaceous borders, lakeside walk, and unusual trees and shrubs. Disabled access; (01428) 722208; *£1.50.

Hollycombe Steam Collection (Midhurst Rd, SU8529) Huge collection of steam-driven equipment, from paddle-steamers to an entire Edwardian fairground, including the big wheel. Sometimes open evenings when the fairground is delightfully lit. Traction engine rides, and woodland steamtrain trips. Snacks, shop; open pm Sun and bank hols Easter–mid-Oct, and usually daily mid-July–Aug; (01428) 724900; £5.50. The nearest place for a good lunch is the Red Lion over at Fernhurst.

★ **LYMINGTON** SZ3295 Handsome and relaxed waterside town, very popular in summer with yachting people; it has quite a number of attractive Georgian buildings and some good shops. The Chequers down Ridgeway Lane, S of Pennington, has decent food; the Angel (High St) and Toll House (A337) are also useful. You can get ferries to the Isle of Wight from here, and the B3054 to Dibden Purlieu is a pretty road.

LYNDHURST SU2908 The tourist centre of the New Forest, as well as the main shopping town for people living here, so lots of tea shops, cafés, etc.

New Forest Museum (High St) From outside it looks like a modern supermarket, but inside there are very good themed displays and an audio-visual exploration of the forest's history and wildlife, and a 7½-metre (25-ft) embroidery. Decent children's features too. Shop, disabled access; cl 25 Dec; (01703) 283914; £2.75. The car park has a good information centre for the area. The Royal Oak, in the pretty village of Bank just outside, has a fair choice of worthwhile food.

★ **MEONSTOKE** SU6119 An attractive village, with a decent pub. The road from here down through

Soberton runs by the River Meon, and is quiet enough to suit walkers; the old Meon Valley railway line nearby is now open as a walkway.

✈ **MIDDLE WALLOP** SU3038 **Museum of Army Flying** One of the country's best military museums, exploring man's efforts to fly. Kites, balloons, vintage aircraft, World War II gliders, and interactive displays. Some exhibits still soar occasional weekends. Meals, snacks, shop, disabled access; cl Christmas wk; (01980) 674421; *£3.90.

❀ ★ ✝ **MINSTEAD** SU2711 **Furzey Gardens** Eight peaceful, heather-filled acres, with a developing young arboretum, around a charming, 16th-c thatched cottage and local craft gallery. Snacks, plant sales, limited disabled access; cl 25–26 Dec; (01703) 812464; *£3 (£1.50 winter). The village is quiet and pretty, with a fine old church at the top of the hill; the Trusty Servant by the green has good food.

❀ **MOTTISFONT ABBEY** SU3227 12th-c priory salvaged from the Reformation as a delightful family house, in wonderful, peaceful surroundings. The gardens are a delight, housing a national collection of old roses (largely scented). You can usually see a few of the rooms, inc one richly decorated by Rex Whistler. Meals, shop, good disabled access; open pm Sat–Weds Apr–Oct, and daily during the rose season (usually the end of Jun); (01794) 340757; £4, £5 in rose season; NT. The Bear & Ragged Staff up on the A3057, does good-value food all day, and the road along the Test through Houghton and on to the attractive village of Wherwell is pretty.

★ ✝ **NETHER WALLOP** SU2936 An attractive sleepy village with an interesting Saxon church; surprisingly, Leopold Stokowski died here, not in Hollywood. The Five Bells is a pleasantly modest place for lunch.

NEW MILTON SZ2394 **Sammy Miller Museum** (Bashley Manor) Well regarded changing collection of fully restored motor cycles, many the only surviving examples of their type in the world. Snacks, shop, disabled access; cl 25–26 Dec; (01425) 620777; £3.50. There's an adjacent craft shop.

❀ **OLD WINCHESTER HILL** SU6420 This **hill fort** gives wide views of Hampshire, the Solent and Isle of Wight, with nature trails through natural downland that's never been ploughed and resown; fairly busy on fine weekends, wonderfully remote on a blustery spring or autumn weekday. The George & Falcon at Warnford is popular for food.

★ **OVERTON** SU5149 There's a charming drive along the B3400 to Hurstbourne Priors and the B3048 to Wherwell; Overton though quite large is an attractive stop along the way, with a decent pub.

☺ ! **OWER** SU3116 *See separate Family Panel on p.286 for* **Paultons Park**. The White Hart at Cadnam is good.

✝ **PETERSFIELD** SU7423 **Bear Museum** (Dragon St) Teddies, dolls and toys in a nursery setting. Children (or anyone else for that matter) can cuddle the exhibits; shop; cl Mon and Sun (exc Christmas); (01730) 265108; free. There's an interesting **church** on Market Sq, and the Good Intent does good lunches.

✝ **PORTCHESTER CASTLE** SU6204 The imposing high walls and towers stretching right down to the waterfront were originally part of a 3rd-c Roman fort – they're the best example of their type in Europe. Other remains include a 12th-c church and 14th-c great tower, and what's left of a palace built by Richard II. Snacks, shop, disabled access; cl 25–26 Dec; (01705) 378291; £2.50. The nearby Cormorant has good-value food.

★ **QUEEN ELIZABETH COUNTRY PARK** SU7117 Lots going on all year, with woodland walks and rides (stables at the park), open downland, a new adventure play trail, and events like Easter-egg-rolling. You can hire bikes or arrange horse-riding (01705) 599699. Shop and café (cl wkdys Nov–Mar); (01705) 595040; £1.50 parking charge Sun and bank hols, £1 rest of wk. The excellent Five Bells at Buriton is nearby.

ROCKBOURNE SU1117 **Roman villa** (off the B3078) Remains of the largest known Roman villa in the area, found by chance 50 years ago by a farmer digging out a ferret. Interesting mosaics in the museum. Snacks, shop, disabled access; cl am wkdys exc July and Aug, and all Oct–Mar; (01725) 518541; £1.50. In the charming thatched village, the Rose & Thistle is good for lunch.

SELBORNE SU7433 **Gilbert White's House** (The Wakes) Naturalist Gilbert White's impressive 18th-c home, furnished in period style. The extensive gardens are being restored to their original form, and separate galleries commemorate Captain Oates and Frank Oates. Teas and 18th-c style snacks, shop, plant sales, disabled access to ground floor and garden; cl winter wkdys, Christmas; (01420) 511275; *£3.50. The Queen's Hotel is handy for lunch. There are good pockets of scenery nearby – the countryside White recorded in such detail. The zigzag path he created with his brother in 1753 still climbs Selborne Hanger. The hangers hereabouts are beechwoods which cling to the abrupt escarpments; Noar Hill close by has been designated a nature reserve for its chalkland flora. From Selborne churchyard, a path leads into The Lythe, a wooded hillside that was another favourite haunt of White's.

SHERBORNE ST JOHN SU6356 **The Vyne** The Tudor mansion with its splendid 17th- and 18th-c embellishments is now fully open after major restoration work, with some rooms on view for the first time. The gardens include a 19th-c walled garden and a newly designed summerhouse garden; there are pleasant woodland walks. Snacks, shop, disabled access; cl am, Mon (exc bank hols), Tues, and Nov–Mar, house also cl Apr and May; (01256) 881337; £2; NT.

SILCHESTER SU6262 The site of the Roman town Calleva Atrebatum has been excavated nearby; 1½ miles of city wall to walk along (tricky in places), as well as a 9,000-seat amphitheatre, 12th-c church on the site of the Roman temples, and a **museum** with a small collection of finds from the site. The Calleva Arms (with a family dining conservatory) does cheap lunches, and sells helpful guides to the site; the Red Lion at Mortimer West End is a good dining pub.

SOUTHAMPTON SU4111 Known earlier this century (through its shipping importance) as the Gateway to the World, this huge bustling town rather unexpectedly has one of the 3 best-preserved medieval town walls in the country. The best stretch is along the western side of the old core, around from the magnificent partly Norman **Bargate** (which has a small local museum); there are usually guided walks along here on Sun mornings, or you can walk it yourself at any time. Lots of other old buildings dotted around the less appetising modern townscape, though if you're short of time it's best to concentrate your efforts on the area around St Michael's Sq, Bugle St and perhaps the old High St. Parking around the centre is metered. The quayside nearest here has been cleaned up, with modern café-bars overlooking yachting berths. **Maritime Museum** (Bugle St) A fine 14th-c warehouse with an impressive timber ceiling, and useful displays on the history of the port. Especially good on the great liners. Shop, disabled access to ground floor only; cl 1–2pm, am Sun, Mon, Christmas; (01703) 635904; free. You may be able to visit the pretty 15th-c **Tudor house** on the same road (it has been closed for restoration). The ancient nearby Duke of Wellington has decent food. **God's House Tower** (Winkle St) An early 15th-c prototype gun battery, now housing an archaeology museum with displays on the city's Saxon forebear, Hamwic; cl 12–1pm, and otherwise as Maritime Museum. The nearby bowling green is said to be the oldest in the world. **Hall of Aviation** (Albert Rd S) Various aircraft of local interest – inc prototype helicopters and the Spitfire. Shop, disabled access; cl am Sun, winter Mons (exc bank and school hols), Christmas; (01703) 635830; *£3. **City Art Gallery** (Civic Centre, Commercial Rd) Extensive and distinguished collection of British and European paintings and sculptures from the last 600 years, with particular emphasis on the 20th c; highly praised by readers. Meals, snacks, shop, disabled access; cl am Sun, Mon, 24–26 Dec and Good Fri; (01703) 632601; free.

★ ⛰ ❁ **SOUTHWICK** SU6208 This attractive village, with a decent pub, is well placed for good walks on Portsdown Hill – fine views.

✝ **STEVENTON CHURCH** SU5447 12th c, with a memorial to Jane Austen, who was born in the village.

STRATFIELD SAYE SU6962 (off the A33) A grateful nation granted the Duke of Wellington the money to buy this 17th-c house after Waterloo. Perhaps surprisingly, the duke had a taste for French furniture, lots of which is still here – as is his splendid funeral carriage, and his hearing aid (needed after prolonged exposure to cannons). Snacks, shop, disabled access; cl am, all day Fri, wkdys and bank hols May and Sept, all Oct–Apr; (01256) 882882; *£5. The elegant Wellington Arms has good food. There are pleasant walks on Heckfield Heath E of the estate, and Wellington Country Park in Berks is nearby.

TITCHFIELD ABBEY SU5305 Ruined 13th-c abbey, almost overshadowed by the grand Tudor gatehouse built after the Dissolution. Some of Shakespeare's plays were reputedly first performed here. Disabled access; cl 25 Dec; free. The riverside Fisherman's Rest opposite is a good pub/restaurant, and there's a fine walk by the old canal to the coast at Meon Shore nr Hill Head.

TOTTON SU3612 **Eling Tide Mill** (Eling Toll Bridge) There's been a mill on this causeway for over 900 years, and the present one still uses tidal energy to produce flour. Heritage centre, snacks, shop, disabled access to ground floor only; cl Mon, Tues, and 25 Dec ring for milling times, which of course depend on the tide; (01703) 869575; £1.50. In unpromising surroundings, the Anchor on Eling Quay is a decent, cheap place for something to eat.

WAGGONERS' WELLS SU8534 A series of hammer ponds, a legacy of the medieval Wealden iron industry, set in charming, heathy woodlands in a valley N of Liphook, and perfect for a picnic. Paths skirt these NT-owned ponds, which are a haven for wildlife.

WATERSHIP DOWN SU4956 (SW of Kingsclere) The home of the rabbits in the novel by Richard Adams – their final adventure was down at Freefolk, where the local pub often has live rabbits. Pleasant, partly wooded walks through this area.

WEYHILL SU3046 **Hawk Conservancy** One of the best birds of prey centres we've come across and a very good-value family day out; you can handle some of the birds, and there are regular flying displays (the best at 2pm). An exciting study centre with hands-on computers, wild flower meadow, ferret racing in school hols and a toddlers' play area. Snacks, shop, disabled access; cl Nov–Feb; (01264) 772252; £5.50. The Weyhill Fair is handy for lunch, and the lanes N take you into a particularly unspoilt corner of Hants.

WHITCHURCH SU4648 **Silk Mill** Working silk mill, (they produce fabric for theatrical costumes, interior designers and historic houses) using Victorian machinery and traditional processes. Prettily set on an island in the River Test; you can watch the trout or feed ducks. Snacks, shop; cl Mon exc bank hols; (01256) 892065; £2.50 (guidebook is a little pricey).

★ **WICKHAM** SU5711 An attractive village despite the traffic, notable for its huge village square; at nearby Droxford there's a good farm shop with pick-your-own.

★ **Other attractive villages** with decent pubs include Abbots Ann SU3243, Amport SU2944, Cheriton SU5828, Crawley SU4234, Crondall SU7948, East End SU4161 (the one nr Highclere), East Stratton SU5439, Hambledon SU6414, Lasham SU6742, Longparish SU4344, Micheldever SU5142, Upton Grey SU6948 and Wherwell SU3941.

Please let us know what you think of places in the *Guide*. Use the report forms at the back of the book or simply write us a letter.

Where to eat

BISHOP'S WALTHAM SU5517 **Old Granary** *Brook St/Bank St (01489) 896352* Cosy restaurant with friendly service, simple French and other international dishes, and decent wines; cl pm Sun, Mon, last 2 wks Jan. **£20**|£5.95.

BOLDRE SZ3198 **Red Lion** *(01590) 673177* Very busy, friendly refurbished pub with 4 black-beamed rooms, interesting bric-à-brac and bygones; impressive bar food, a fine choice of wines by the glass, and well kept beer; prompt service; worth getting there early; no children; disabled access. **£22.40**|£6.90.

BRAMDEAN SU6127 **Fox** *(01962) 771363* Welcoming 17th-c dining pub, with famous fox masks in the modernised and neatly cared for open-plan bar; lots of good fish (other food, too), an extensive wine list, well kept real ales, and obliging service; no children; cl 25 Dec. **£22.15**|£8.95.

BROCKENHURST SU2902 **Le Poussin** *The Courtyard, Brookley Rd (01590) 623063* Popular little restaurant with carefully cooked, interesting food using the best local produce; good cheeses and puddings, friendly service, and chicken-themed decorations; cl Mon and Tues; disabled access. **£35**.

BROCKENHURST SU2902 **Thatched Cottage** *16 Brookley Rd (01590) 623090* Charming, 400-year-old, thatched cottage with a cosy beamed lounge, good dried and fresh flower arrangements, and a pretty restaurant; enjoyable, well presented, imaginative food served by friendly staff; super cream teas in the neat garden, morning coffee too; cl pm Sun, Mon, Jan; children over 12. **£45**.

CADNAM SU2913 **White Hart** *(01703) 812277* Big, multi-level dining lounge with good, solid furnishings; a wide choice of interesting food, inc fine daily specials and tempting puddings, well kept real ales and decent wines; goat, horses and dogs on the premises; cl 25–26 Dec; disabled access. **£20**|£5.

EAST TYTHERLEY SU2928 **Star** *(01794) 340225* Friendly country local by the village cricket field; homely furnishings, log fires, and a no smoking lower lounge bar; pretty no smoking restaurant with a pleasantly informal atmosphere, enjoyable home-made food inc good daily specials, well kept real ales, and smart, efficient staff; garden and skittle alley; bdrms. **£16.20**|£5.95.

EMSWORTH SU7405 **36 On The Quay** *South St (01243) 375592* Very good French cooking in this charming quayside restaurant, with helpful service and a sound wine list; cl am Mon, am Sat, Sun, 2 wks Jan, 1 wk Oct; children over 2. **£26.50 lunch, £39.45 dinner**|£16 2-course lunch.

EVERSLEY SU7662 **New Mill** *New Mill Rd (0118) 973* 2277 16th-c watermill by the Blackwater River with a working waterwheel and grinding equipment; big windows overlooking the river and its wildlife, open fires and candlelit tables, and a good range of interesting, carefully cooked food; more informal, beamed and flagstoned grill room, with a simpler menu (and cheaper); thoughtful wine list with many by the glass; cl am Sat; partial disabled access. **£30** restaurant, **£20** grill room.

FROYLE SU7542 **Hen & Chicken** *(01420) 22115* Old coaching inn with interconnecting rooms, hops on beams, candles on tables, and daily papers; neat staff serving imaginative food, a partly no smoking restaurant, well kept real ales, and a big garden with children's play equipment. **£22.65**|£9.25.

HIGHCLERE SU4358 **Yew Tree** *Hollington Cross, on the A343 S (01635) 253360* Plush, L-shaped dining bar with a big log fire, enterprising food, and friendly licensees; good, unobtrusive waitress service, well kept real ales and decent wines; also a restaurant; bdrms. **£21**|£6.75.

HOUGHTON SU3432 **Boot** *(01794) 388310* Friendly, well run dining pub with simple décor; popular bar and restaurant food, well kept real ales, and pleasant service; cl Mon, no food pm Sun; disabled access. **£30**|£6.

LOCKS HEATH SU5006 **Jolly Farmer** *Fleet End Rd (01489) 572500* Thriving old inn with plenty of character, and small rooms with lots of country bric-à-brac; a wide choice of quickly served food, well kept real ales, and neat, friendly staff; disabled access. **£15**|£5.95.

LONGSTOCK SU3536 **Peat Spade** *(01264) 810612* Lively, popular dining pub with an airy, attractive bar, Toby jugs around the fire, and an elegant little dining room with a no smoking area; imaginative, enjoyable food, well kept real ales, and decent wines; bdrms. **£23.25**|£8.

LYMINGTON SZ2996 **Gordleton Mill** *Silver St, Hordle (01590) 682219* 300-year-old converted watermill with lovely romantic gardens (you can sit on the terrace and enjoy an aperitif by the water); comfortable and attractive interior, exquisitely presented, exceptional modern cooking, and a marvellous wine list; comfortable bdrms; cl pm Sun, Mon, Jan; children over 7. **£47**.

MAPLEDURWELL SU6851 **Gamekeepers** *(01256) 322038* Interesting old pub in a lovely thatched village; with a wide choice of enterprising food, good-value wines, friendly service, and a separate, more upmarket restaurant; cl pm Sun, 25–26 Dec; disabled access. **£20**|£6.50.

MICHELDEVER SU5138 **Dever Arms** *(01962) 774339* Attractive country pub, with a simply decorated beamed bar, woodburners at each end, and solid furniture; generous helpings of interesting food, inc lots of good daily specials, well kept real ales, and decent wines; seats on the terrace and by the cricket green; disabled access. **£19**|£6.95.

OLD BURGHCLERE SU4658 **Dew Pond** *(01635) 278408* Beautiful, 16th-c country house with log fires and a friendly atmosphere; imaginative food using fresh local produce on a frequently changing small menu – good game, fish and lovely puddings; no smoking; cl Sun, Mon, 2 wks Jan, 2 wks Aug; children over 5; disabled access. **£32**.

PILLEY SZ3298 **Fleur de Lys** *(01590) 672158* The oldest pub in the New Forest (an inn since 1096), with plenty of atmosphere and a huge inglenook fireplace; well kept real ales, good wines and farm cider, and a wide range of carefully prepared, interesting food, inc vegetarian dishes and fish, plus a thoughtful children's menu; also, a pretty garden. **£21.99**|£8.99.

SOUTHSEA SZ6499 **A Fistful of Tacos** *Albert Rd (01705) 293474* Evening restaurant with good Californian/Mexican food; cl 24–26 Dec, 1 Jan; partial disabled access. **£15**.

SOUTHSEA SZ6698 **Tenth Hole** *Eastern Parade (01705) 830009* Bustling café by the pitch-and-put; snacks, light lunches and generous teas served by the friendly staff; cl Jan; no very young children; disabled access. £4.25.

STUCKTON SU1613 **Three Lions** *(01425) 652489* Warmly welcoming restaurant with an informal atmosphere, a neat airy bar, and fresh flowers; very imaginative food inc forest fungi and lovely puddings, a fine wine list, superb breakfasts, and charming owners; good atmosphere and friendly, efficient service; cl pm Sun, Mon, last 2 wks Jan, first wk Feb; disabled access; comfortable bdrms. **£35**|£13.50 2-course lunch.

TICHBORNE SU5730 **Tichborne Arms** *(01962) 733760* Attractive, thatched country pub in rolling countryside; with very good and imaginative bar food, delicious puddings; big garden; cl pm 25 and 26 Dec; no children; disabled access. **£14.55**|£5.50.

WELL SU7646 **Chequers** *(01256) 862605* Neatly kept and rather smart country pub with a relaxed atmosphere, snug rooms, beams, and lots of 18th-c country-life prints; very good bar food; partial disabled access. **£15**|£6.25.

WINCHESTER SU4829 **Cathedral Refectory** *Visitors' Centre, Inner Close (01962) 853224* Excellent, totally home-made food in a bright, airy, modern conservatory; lovely breads and soups, afternoon cream teas, and a good children's menu; friendly and informal atmosphere, and nice staff; cl 25–26 Dec, 1 Jan, Good Fri; disabled access. £3.75.

Special thanks to Mrs Brenda Harris, M and J Back, B M Eldridge, Graham James, Phyl and Jack Street, Mark Holman, Mrs R Cox, Canon and Mrs D Hutchinson, Mrs C Lilley.

Hampshire Calendar

Some of these dates were provisional as we went to press. Please check information with the telephone numbers provided.

FEBRUARY

13 **Winchester** Children's Festival – *till Fri 19* (01962) 840222
16 **Sway** Shrove Tuesday Pancake Race: Station Rd (01590) 683402

MARCH

13 **Highclere** Country Lifestyle Fair at the Castle – *till Sun 14* (01635) 253210

APRIL

2 **Gosport** Easter Folk Festival at Thorngate Halls – *till Mon 5* (01705) 545294
11 **Beaulieu** Boat Jumble at the National Motor Museum (01590) 612345; **Micheldever** Fly-in at Popham Airfield (01256) 397733
16 **Winchester** Folk Festival – *till Sun 18* (01962) 840222

MAY

1 **Aldershot** Show at Rushmoor Arena – *till Mon 3* (01264) 771055; **Portsmouth** Lord Mayor's Show (01705) 828112
2 **Southsea** Heavy Horse Parade at Castle Field Arena – *till Mon 3* (01705) 834146
3 **Micheldever** Aero/Auto Jumble, Fly-in and Classic Car Rally at Popham Airfield (01256) 397733
8 **Beaulieu** Auto Jumble and Classic Car Show at the National Motor Museum – *till Sun 9* (01590) 612345
9 **Basingstoke** Festival of Transport at War Memorial Park (01256) 845682; **Micheldever** Fly-in at Popham Airfield (01256) 397733
15 **Netley Abbey** Flower Festival Garden Show at Royal Victoria Park – *till Sun 16* (01703) 455157
29 **Netley Abbey** Conservation Week at Royal Victoria Park – *till 6 Jun* (01703) 455157
30 **Highclere** Southern Counties Game and Country Fair at the Castle – *till Mon 31* (01635) 253210

JUNE

5 **Basingstoke** Kite Festival at War Memorial Park – *till Sun 6* (01256) 845682; **Mottisfont** Open-air Opera at the Abbey (01794) 340757
7 **Bishop's Waltham** Festival – *till Sun 13* (01962) 840222
13 **Beaulieu** Mini Cooper Rally at the National Motor Museum (01590) 612345; **Micheldever** Fly-in at Popham Airfield (01256) 397733
19 **Beaulieu** Motor Show at the National Motor Museum – *till Sun 20* (01590) 612345; **Wickham** Midsummer Weekend: street entertainers, carnival – *till Sun 20* (01329) 833808
26 **Basingstoke** Balloon Festival at War Memorial Park – *till Sun 27* (01256) 845682; **Fordingbridge** Carnival (01425) 657491
28 **Northington** Opera at Northington Grange: new outdoor opera festival in the Orangery – *till 18 July* (0171) 246 7567

Hampshire Calendar (cont.)

JULY

2 **Winchester** Festival – *till Sun 11*, inc the Hat Fair – *till Sun 4* (01962) 840222

3 **Beaulieu** Fireworks Concert at the National Motor Museum (01590) 612345; **Gosport** Carnival (01705) 522944

10 **Horndean** Hampshire Country Fair and Sheepdog Trials at Queen Elizabeth Country Park (01705) 595040

11 **Micheldever** Fly-in at Popham Airfield (01256) 397733

14 **Mottisfont** Open-air Play at the Abbey – *till Sat 24* (01794) 340757

16 **Sherborne St John** Craft Fair with entertainments at The Vyne – *till Sun 18* (01344) 874787

17 **Fordingbridge** Show (01425) 652223; **Winchester** Show – *till Sun 18* (01962) 866556

18 **Alton** Agricultural Show at Froyle Park (01420) 563492

21 **Winchester** Southern Counties Cathedral Festival – *till Sat 24* (01962) 840222

24 **Southampton** Balloon and Flower Festival – *till Sun 25* (01703) 832755

27 **Brockenhurst** New Forest and County Show at New Park – *till Thurs 29* (01590) 622400

31 **Hedge End** Carnival and Gala Show (01489) 785041

AUGUST

6 **Portsmouth** and **Southsea** Show on Southsea Common: arena events, circus and farm trail – *till Sun 8* (01705) 834146

8 **Micheldever** Fly-in at Popham Airfield (01256) 397733

13 **Mottisfont** Open-air Jazz at the Abbey – *till Sat 14* (01794) 340757; **Netley Abbey** Hampshire Show at Royal Victoria Park – *till Sun 15* (01703) 455157

21 **Netley Abbey** Hobbies Fair at Royal Victoria Park – *till Sun 22* (01703) 455157

28 **Highclere** Craft Fair at the Castle – *till Mon 30* (01635) 253210; **Southsea** International Kite Festival – *till Mon 30* (01705) 834553

29 **Catherington** Country Show: arena events, show jumping, cars – *till Mon 30* (01705) 592520; **Highclere** Horse Trials at the Castle – *till Mon 30* (01635) 253210

30 **Emsworth** Show (01243) 378804; **Gosport** Vintage Vehicle Rally (01705) 351624

SEPTEMBER

4 **Alresford** Agricultural Show at Tichborne Park (01962) 733887; **Beaulieu** International Auto Jumble at the National Motor Museum – *till Sun 5* (01590) 612345

10 **Southampton** International Boat Show at Western Esplanade – *till Sun 19* (01784) 473377

11 **Fordingbridge** Patronal Festival Floral Carpet: floral carpet of around 10,000 flowers, church tower open – *till Sun 12* (01425) 653163; **Romsey** Show at Broadlands Park (01794) 517521

12 **Micheldever** Fly-in at Popham Airfield (01256) 397733

17 **Winchester** Literature Festival – *till Sun 26* (01962) 840222

Hampshire Calendar (cont.)

OCTOBER

10 Micheldever Fly-in at Popham Airfield (01256) 397733
15 Sway Village Autumn Festival inc Wine Weekend – *till Sun 17* (01590) 683402
25 Titchfield Carnival (01329) 846166

NOVEMBER

6 Netley Abbey Fireworks at Royal Victoria Park (01703) 455157; **Winchester** Fireworks and Torchlight Parade (01962) 840222

DECEMBER

3 Highclere Christmas Fair at the Castle – *till Sun 5* (01635) 253210
26 Crookham Village Mummers Plays: *from midday* outside the Black Prince, Chequers and Queen's Head (01252) 811151

We welcome reports from readers

This *Guide* depends on readers' reports. Do help us if you can – in return, we offer a discount on the next edition to people who've helped us with reports for it. Tell us what you think about places already in it, and anything extra you think we should say about them. And send us your ideas for inclusion in the next edition: places to visit, eat at or stay in, attractive drives or walks, maybe even unusual interesting shops you know of. Use the card in the middle, the report forms at the end, or just write – no stamp needed: *The Good Guide to Britain*, FREEPOST TN1569, Wadhurst, E Sussex TN5 7BR.

Hereford and Worcester

Classic unspoilt English countryside with appealing small towns, lovely villages, great gardens.

This is a splendid area for restorative short breaks – lots of peace, classic unchanging scenery. The Malvern Hills stand out, though as you head west the Herefordshire countryside becomes almost bewitchingly untouched – not at all showy, but the sort of idyllic world that elsewhere tends to survive only in people's memories. Not many tourists or country-cottagers have penetrated that area, even at the height of summer, yet there's an abundance of art galleries and bookshops (Hay-on-Wye, that town-sized bookshop, is an attractive drive just over the Welsh border), and excellent natural cooking using local produce.

The main appeal is decidedly adult – beautiful black and white villages, civilised and attractive small towns, quiet scenic drives, good craft centres, inspiring walks with long gentle views, and an exceptional number of fine gardens ranging from small ones such as Kingstone Cottages or relatively young ones such as the one at Kimbolton to products of several generations such as Hergest Croft near Kington. Eastnor Castle, Berrington Hall at Ashton, Lower Brockhampton House, Great Witley with its extraordinary ruin and splendid church, Croft Castle, Hanbury Hall (with several other places to visit nearby), Goodrich Castle, Dinmore Manor and the buildings museum at Bromsgrove make pleasant outings, and there are several enjoyable cider farms. The new horse refuge at Hoarwithy is engaging.

The east of the area has the most family outings; Bewdley in particular has plenty for children to enjoy. Elsewhere, the expanding farm park at Kington is a great favourite, and two specialised places liked by many children are the pig centre at Linley Green and the Domestic Fowl Trust at Ullington.

Hereford is engaging and relaxing, with plenty of varied attractions – the cathedral has a splendid display of its great treasures. Worcester is a much busier city, but has interesting finds among its more workaday bustle – the Commandery is exceptional. Ledbury, Broadway, sober Great Malvern and Evesham are all attractive, with several appealing places to visit. Kington, Leominster and Ross-on-Wye are also agreeable to wander around.

The orchards make blossom time (usually April through early May) and harvest time (September) attractive: local tourist board trails make it easy to see the best of this, especially in the Vale of Evesham – rich farmland and orchard country, full of farm shops. There's an abundance of fresh local asparagus in May. In winter big log fires and generous central heating are the rule – people here really seem to appreciate their warmth.

Where to stay

ABBERLEY SO7367 **Elms** *Stockton Rd, Abberley, Worcs WR6 6AT (01299) 896666* **£110;** 16 comfortable rms. Lovely Queen Anne mansion with fine views from the well kept grounds, elegant restful drawing room with antiques, log fires and flowers, very good food and wines in airy restaurant, and friendly efficient staff.

BRIMFIELD SO5267 **Roebuck** *Brimfield, Ludlow, Shropshire SY8 4NE (01584) 711230* ***£60;** 3 rms. Civilised dining pub with good food in elegant modern no smoking restaurant and panelled bar, open fires, caring staff, well kept real ales and good wine list; cl 25–26 Dec.

BROADWAY SP0937 **Broadway** *The Green, Broadway, Worcs WR12 7AA (01386) 852401* **£95,** plus special breaks; 20 well kept rms. Lovely 16th-c building, once a monastic guesthouse, with galleried and timbered lounge, cosy beamed bar, attractively presented food served by attentive staff in airy comfortable restaurant, and seats outside on terrace.

BROADWAY SP0839 **Collin House** *Collin Lane, Broadway, Worcs WR12 7PB (01386) 858354* **£88,** plus special breaks; 7 warm, comfortable and quiet rms. Golden stone 16th-c Cotswold house in 3 acres of gardens, orchard and meadow, with restful public rooms, oak beams, log fires, very good English food and carefully chosen wines in candlelit beamed restaurant with mullioned windows, and friendly helpful service; cl 5 days at Christmas.

BROADWAY SP0937 **Lygon Arms** *High St, Broadway, Worcs WR12 7DU (01386) 852255* **£193,** plus special breaks; 65 lovely period rms (some more modern, too). Handsome hotel where Oliver Cromwell and King Charles I stayed, with interesting old beamed rooms, oak panelling, antiques, log fires, fine traditional food in the Great Hall with minstrels' gallery and heraldic frieze, excellent service, and charming garden; health spa; disabled access.

BROMSBERROW HEATH SO7333 **Grove House** *Bromsberrow Heath, Ledbury, Herefs HR8 1PE (01531) 650584* **£69;** 3 spacious rms, 2 with four-posters. Wisteria-clad 15th-c manor house with dark panelling, open fires, beams, fresh flowers and polished antiques, and good evening meals at huge dining table using home-grown produce; 13 acres, hard tennis court, and neighbour's outdoor swimming pool; cl Christmas/New Year.

CAREY SO5631 **Cottage of Content** *Carey, Hereford HR2 6NG (01432) 840242* **£48;** 3 rms. Very pretty medieval country cottage in peaceful setting, with flagstoned and timbered bars, friendly atmosphere, enjoyable food, well kept real ales, a good wine list, and seats on flower-filled front and back terraces; cl 25 Dec.

CHADDESLEY CORBETT SO8873 **Brockencote Hall** *Chaddesley Corbett, Kidderminster, Worcs DY10 4PY (01562) 777876* ***£125,** plus special breaks; 17 individually decorated rms. Grand country-house hotel in 70 acres with half-timbered dovecot and lake; large, airy and attractively furnished rooms, conservatory lounge with garden views, elegant restaurant with good modern French and English cooking, and excellent service; no dogs; disabled access.

EVESHAM SP0443 **Evesham** *Coopers Lane, off Waterside, Evesham, Worcs WR11 6DA (01386) 765566* ***£92,** plus special breaks; 39 spacious rms. Comfortably modernised and cheerfully run hotel with warmly friendly relaxed atmosphere, lots of facilities for children, very good food (especially the lunchtime buffet) from jokey menu, a huge range of spirits, indoor swimming pool, and croquet; cl 25–26 Dec; pets welcome (not in public rooms); partial disabled access.

EYTON SO4761 **Marsh** *Eyton, Leominster, Herefs HR6 0AG (01568) 613952* ***£130,** plus special breaks; 4 individually decorated comfortable rms with garden views. Carefully restored 14th-c timbered country hotel with quietly relaxing atmosphere in prettily furnished beamed rooms (fine medieval hall), enjoyable food using lots of home-grown herbs, good wines, and colourful big garden; cl 3 wks Jan; children over 12.

FOWNHOPE SO5734 **Green Man** *Fownhope, Hereford HR1 4PE (01432) 860243* ***£56,** plus special breaks; 20 rms. Attractive Tudor inn with impressive oak-beamed lounge (the residents' lounges are no smoking), log fire, and generously served popular bar food; disabled access.

FRITH COMMON SO6970 **Hunthouse Farm** *Frith Common, Tenbury Wells, Worcs WR15 8JY (01299) 832277* **£36;** 3 rms. 16th-c timbered farmhouse on 180-acre arable and sheep farm in lovely countryside; friendly atmosphere, oak beams and open fires, and home-made cake served on arrival in the guest sitting room; cl Christmas; children over 8.

GRAFTON SO4936 **Grafton Villa Farm** *Grafton, Hereford HR2 8ED (01432) 268689* ***£42;** 3 rms. Characterful early 18th-c farmhouse with panoramic views, friendly dogs, open fire in lounge, and enjoyable hearty breakfasts using their own free-range eggs; cl Nov–Feb; disabled access (and self-catering cottage accessible also).

HARVINGTON SP0548 **Mill** *Anchor Lane, Harvington, Evesham, Worcs WR11 5NR (01386) 870688* **£96;** 21 comfortable rms overlooking grounds. Handsome Georgian hotel in 8 acres of parkland with 180 metres (600ft) of river, mooring for guests' boats, fishing, hard tennis court, and heated outdoor swimming pool; carefully refurbished airy lounges with open fires, courteous helpful staff, fine imaginative food using fresh local produce, thoughtful wine list with helpful notes, and good breakfasts; cl 24–28 Dec; children over 10.

HIMBLETON SO9459 **Phepson Farm** *Himbleton, Droitwich, Worcs WR9 7JZ (01905) 391205* **£40;** 4 rms. Relaxed and friendly 17th-c farmhouse on 170-acre working farm with beef and sheep; comfortable lounge, good breakfasts in separate dining room; self-catering apartment; cl Christmas/New Year; pets by arrangement; partial disabled access.

KEMERTON SO9437 **Upper Court** *Kemerton, Tewkesbury, Glos GL20 7HY (01386) 725351* ***£85,** plus special breaks; 6 rms, plus others in cottages. Lovely Georgian Cotswold manor with Domesday watermill, lake (lots of wildfowl and free fly fishing in season), and dovecot in 15 acres of fine gardens; outdoor heated swimming pool, tennis court, croquet, and boating; relaxed atmosphere and many antiques (the owners run an antiques business and there is always something for sale) in elegant rooms, very good food using home-grown produce, and nice breakfasts; cl Christmas; dogs by arrangement; good disabled access.

KINGTON SO3156 **Penrhos Court** *Kington, Herefs HR5 3LH (01544) 230720* **£95,** plus special breaks; 19 elegant rms. Beautifully restored 13th-c hall in 6 acres, with fine beams and flagstones and very good carefully cooked food using home-grown herbs and vegetables; medieval banquets, too; cl Jan; disabled access.

KINNERSLEY SO3349 **Upper Newton Farmhouse** *Kinnersley, Hereford HR3 6QB (01544) 327727* ***£44,** plus special breaks; 4 prettily decorated rms with hand-crafted items. 17th-c farmhouse in the middle of a working farm, with log fires, beams, sloping floors, good food (inc vegetarian) using fresh farm veg; colourful garden and lots of walks; no smoking or pets; self-catering cottage.

LEDBURY SO7137 **Feathers** *High St, Ledbury, Herefs HR8 1DS (01531) 635266* **£89.50,** plus special breaks; 24 carefully decorated rms making the most of the old beams and timbers. Very striking mainly 16th-c black and white hotel with a relaxed atmosphere, log fires, and comfortable lounge hall with country antiques, beams and timbers; particularly enjoyable food and friendly service in Fuggles bar, good wine list, and a fine mix of locals and visitors.

LEYSTERS SO5762 **Old Vicarage** *Leysters, Leominster, Herefs HR6 0HS (01568) 750208* ***£64;** 2 rms. Comfortable and friendly 17th-c farmhouse with Victorian additions, in 18 acres with a sizeable garden and all-weather tennis court, surrounded by the unspoilt north Herefordshire hills; antiques, good food using home-baked bread eaten around a big dining table; cl Christmas/New Year; children over 12; no dogs.

LITTLE WITLEY SO7763 **Ribston House** *Little Witley, Worcester WR6 6LS (01886) 888750* **£60;** 3 cottagey rms. Charming old farmhouse with a Georgian façade, antiques, pictures and fresh flowers; little guest sitting room with log fire, enjoyable food using home-grown vegetables, welcoming, kind owners who will act as your guide if you wish, and tranquil grounds (with llamas!).

MALVERN SO7647 **Cowleigh Park Farm** *Cowleigh Rd, Malvern, Worcs WR13 5HJ (01684) 566750* ***£46;** 3 rms. Carefully restored and furnished black and white timbered 13th-c farmhouse in own grounds, surrounded by lovely countryside, with good breakfasts and light suppers or full evening meals (prior booking necessary); self-catering also; cl Christmas/New Year; children over 7.

MALVERN WELLS SO7845 **Cottage in the Wood** *Holywell Rd, Malvern Wells, Worcs WR14 4LG (01684) 575859* ***£89.50,** plus special breaks; 20 compact but pretty rms, some in separate nearby cottages. Family-run Georgian dower house with quite splendid views across the Severn Valley (marvellous walks from the grounds), antiques, log fires, comfortable seats and magazines in public rooms, and modern English cooking and an extensive wine list in attractive no smoking restaurant.

OMBERSLEY SO8463 **Crown & Sandys Arms** *Ombersley, Droitwich, Worcs WR9 0EW (01905) 620252* **£48;** 6 no smoking rms, most with own bthrm. Civilised and pretty Dutch-gabled inn with good views from garden, comfortable lounge bar with beams, timbers, log fires and maybe daily newspapers, and good popular food inc lots of fish; cl 24–30 Dec; no dogs.

ROSS-ON-WYE SO6024 **Brookfield House** *Ledbury Rd, Ross-on-Wye, Herefs HR9 7AT (01989) 562188* **£43,** plus special breaks; 8 rms, some with own bthrm. Part Queen Anne and part Georgian house with sunny terrace and little garden with a view over the town, very friendly welcoming owners, log fire in lounge, and super breakfasts in big airy breakfast room; children over 8; pets allowed.

RUCKHALL COMMON SO4539 **Ancient Camp** *Ruckhall Common, Hereford HR2 9QX (01981) 250449* **£65;** 5 rms, 2 with river views. Smart country inn in pleasantly remote spot with good views of River Wye and beyond from the terrace; beamed and flagstoned bar, good bar and restaurant food (not pm Sun or Mon); no children; disabled access.

ULLINGSWICK SO5849 **Steppes** *Ullingswick, Hereford HR1 3JG (01432) 820424* **£80,** plus special breaks; 6 spacious, pretty rms in barn and restored stone stable. Attractive 17th-c country house hotel with heavy beams, flagstones and inglenook fireplaces in cellar bar, lounge and dining room; very good food, fine breakfasts, and hospitable owners; cl 2 wks before Christmas and Jan; children over 10.

UPTON SNODSBURY SO9454 **Upton House** *Upton Snodsbury, Worcester WR7 4NR (01905) 381226* **£68;** 2 well equipped pretty rms. Carefully run 12th-c village manor house with beams and log fires, comfortable sitting room, good food in unlicensed dining room, new conservatory, helpful owners, pretty flower-filled garden, and outdoor heated swimming pool; cl Christmas and Easter; no children; kennel facilities for dogs.

WEOBLEY SO4051 **Olde Salutation** *Market Pitch, Weobley, Hereford HR4 8SJ (01544) 318443* ***£65;** 4 rms. Friendly 500-year-old inn with good bar and elaborate restaurant food, quiet lounge with standing timbers and log fires, and small public bar; also self-catering cottage; children in cottage only.

WICKHAMFORD SP0642 **Wickhamford Manor** *Wickhamford, Evesham, Worcs WR11 6SA (01386) 830296* ***£60;** 3 rms. Striking timbered manor, first mentioned in the Domesday book, in 20 acres with 12th-c dovecot and lake, big log fire in beamed drawing room, good breakfasts in the flagstoned kitchen, dinner by arrangement, and a really warm welcome from the friendly owners; tennis and fishing; self-catering cottage; cl Christmas/New Year; children over 12.

WOOLHOPE SO6135 **Butchers Arms** *Woolhope, Hereford HR1 4RF (01432) 860281* ***£39;** 2 neat, attractive rms with fruit and chocolates (shared bthrm). Family-run 14th-c timbered building with low oak beams and log fires in bars, friendly staff, lots of flowers, and decent food (good breakfasts); lovely surrounding walks.

To see and do

★ **HEREFORD** SO5039 Grew as a regional market centre, and still has its busy livestock and general market every Weds. For the rest of the week it feels very quiet-paced and old-fashioned, its streets (some pedestrianised) lined with handsome Georgian and other buildings (Church St is medieval). Guided walks leave the tourist information centre every day from May–mid-Sept at 10.30am (2.30pm Sun). Wye-side walks give a pleasing view of the city, its spires and towers. The Bay Horse, Saxtys and the Green Dragon Hotel are useful for lunch.

† **Hereford Cathedral** Nicely placed by the Wye, this largely Norman building has a lovely 13th- and 15th-c chapel, as well as the country's biggest chained library (the second biggest is at All Saints church, at the opposite end of the main street) and the famous Mappa Mundi, the largest surviving 13th-c world map. There's a splendid new interpretative exhibition, with some computer displays; the map itself is shown in a specially dimmed room to preserve it. Meals, snacks, shop, disabled access; some parts cl Sun, occasional lunchtimes, Good Fri, 25 Dec; (01432) 359880; cathedral free, exhibition £4. Guided tours at 11am, 1pm and 2.30pm (£1.50).

Cider Museum (Pomona Pl) Cider-making down the ages, with huge 17th-c French press, original cellars, and a working cider-brandy distillery – the first licensed for over 250 years. Shop, limited disabled access; cl winter Mon, 25–26 Dec and 1 Jan; (01432) 354207; £2.20.

Bulmer's Cider Mill (Plough Lane) This enormous modern plant has tours and tastings. Shop; cl wknds, bank hols and mid-Dec–Feb, tours (10.30am, 2.15pm, 7.30pm) by appointment; (01432) 352000; *£2.95, *£3.95 joint ticket with cider museum above.

Old House (High Town) Glorious Jacobean house with period furnishings and paintings. Shop, limited disabled access; cl Sun, Mon (exc bank hols), 25–26 Dec, 1 Jan and Good Fri; (01432) 364598; free.

Churchill House Museum (Venns Lane, northern outskirts) Regency house in fine grounds, with good local history, room settings, and 18th- and 19th-c furniture, costumes and paintings. Shop, some disabled access; will be under new management by the time we go to press so best to check opening times; (01432) 267409; free.

Waterworks Museum (Broomy Hill) Restored Victorian pumping station, with giant steam pumping engines, and smaller handpumps; you can try working some. Snacks, shop, disabled access; open pm last Sun of month, Apr–Sept, plus bank hols; (01432) 361147; *£2.

City Museum & Art Gallery (Broad St) Natural history and archaeology, interesting bee-keeping display, and changing art exhibitions. Shop, disabled access; cl Mon and winter Suns; (01432) 364691; free.

WORCESTER SO8554 Though a busy commercial centre, this has some splendid medieval buildings dotted about, with lots of half-timbered houses, particularly around Friar St and New St. Plenty of shops, inc some nice specialist ones and cafés in Hopmarket Yard, a former coaching inn; the King Charles I (New St) serves good meals and the Farriers Arms (Fish St, nr cathedral) has good snacks. You can tour the handsome Georgian guildhall (not Sun).

Commandery (Sidbury) The only museum in the country wholly devoted to the English Civil War, in striking timber-framed 15th-c building. Lots of weaponry, spectacular audio-visual shows and life-size talking figures re-creating events from the war. Unusual special events and military displays, and brass rubbing centre. Meals, snacks, shop; cl am Sun, 25–26 Dec, 1 Jan; (01905) 355071; £3.50.

Museum of Worcester Porcelain (Severn St) The country's oldest continuous producer of porcelain, with wkdy factory tours (no children under 11), and rare 18th-c porcelain in the excellent museum which continues to be improved and extended. Meals, snacks, shop, disabled access to museum only; cl 25–26 Dec and Easter Sun; (01905) 23221; tour £4, museum £2. The Potter's Wheel opposite has decent food.

Worcester Cathedral Founded on the site of a Saxon monastery, in a calm and peaceful setting overlooking the river. It took from 1084 to 1375 to build, and has an attractive 14th-c tower, Norman crypt, and the tombs of Prince Arthur and King John, the latter topped by the oldest royal effigy in the country. Lots of Victorian stained glass, and some monastic buildings. Guided tours in summer. Snacks, shop, some disabled access; £2 suggested donation.

Greyfriars (Friar St) Beautiful carefully restored medieval timber-framed town house (still lived in), with delightful walled garden. Open pm Weds, Thurs and bank hols, Apr–Oct; (01905) 23571; £2.40; NT.

Tudor House (Friar St) 15th-c, housing a **museum of local life**. Shop, some disabled access; cl Thurs, Sun, 25–26 Dec, 1 Jan, Good Fri, Easter Sun; (01905) 722349; free.

City Museum & Art Gallery (Foregate St) Local and natural history, with River Severn gallery and several children's activities. Meals, snacks, shop, disabled access; cl Thurs, Sun, 25 Dec, Good Fri and around other public holidays – best to check; (01905) 25371; free.

Worcester Woods Country Park (just E off the A442) 140 acres of ancient woodland on the edge of the city; not as interesting as woodlands elsewhere, but useful for strolling if you don't want to leave the city. Snacks, shop, disabled access; cl 25–26 Dec, 1 Jan; (01905) 766492; free.

Bennetts Farm Park SO8352 (Lower Wick) Working dairy farm with animals, wknd milking parlour and vintage machinery museum in pretty 16th-c farm buildings. Walks and fishing in season. Snacks (inc their own ice-cream), shop, disabled access; (01905) 748345; *£3.

Other things to see and do

HEREFORD & WORCESTER Family Attraction of the Year

KINGTON SO3055 **Small Breeds Farm Park** (Kingswood – off the A4111 S) Since last year this friendly little farm has greatly improved its wet-weather facilities: all the animals can be displayed under cover if it's raining, and there's a heated barn for picnics. Also new is an enclosure for an extended family of playful chipmunks, and a pair of red squirrels. It can't compete with the bigger wildlife parks or zoos in terms of size or elaborate visitor facilities (it covers only 4 acres), but more than makes up in its genuine enthusiasm and relaxed atmosphere. Many of the animals – mostly miniature and rare or unusual – can be fed by hand, and there are plenty of rabbits and guinea pigs to pet and fuss. The views and setting are a bonus, and the extensive collections of owls and waterfowl are housed in an attractively landscaped garden. Quite a few of the animals have distinctive characteristics and personalities. A particular favourite is Dorrie, the miniature Dexter cow, who even on tiptoe is just 81cm (32in) high; she has a strapping daughter, Delores. Numpy the giant milky eagle owl likes to be stroked by visitors, while Flo-Jo the goose (easy to spot by her luminous green beak) can take quite a fancy to male visitors over 50. There are also pigs, goats, tortoises and pheasants. You won't need to spend more than half a day here, but it's the kind of place people like to come back to (they often spot parents returning without the children). Father Christmas is usually here in December. Snacks, shop, disabled access; cl Nov, and Jan–Easter; (01544) 231109; £3 (£1.75 children).

ABBERLEY HILLS SO7567 (nr Stourport) Little visited by walkers but rewarding for them: partly wooded, with good views.

ABBEY DORE SO3830 Primarily the impressive surviving part of a once-huge 12th/13th-c Cistercian abbey church, with Early English features and an awesome stone altar. **Abbey Dore Court Garden** Attractive riverside lawns and gardens, with good views across to the ruins. Snacks (in 17th-c stables), disabled access; cl Weds, and mid-Oct–Feb; (01981) 240419; *£2.50.

★ **ABBOTS MORTON** SP0255 Charming village, with lovely church and decent pub.

ALMELEY SO3351 Early 18th-c half-timbered Quaker Meeting House, contemplative feel; key in porch.

ASHTON SO5164 **Berrington Hall** (on the A49) Elegant late 18th-c neo-Classical house, very elaborate inside, with beautiful décor and furnishings (mostly French), charming nursery, and interesting examples of 'downstairs' life in Georgian dairy and laundry. The grounds were landscaped by Capability Brown, and the house was built by his son-in-law. Pleasant circular walk through the park (July–Oct only); new play area and children's orienteering course. Meals, tearoom, shop, disabled access; open pm Fri–Sun and bank hols Apr–Oct, plus pm Weds and Thurs May–Sept, and daily July and Aug; (01568) 615721; £4, £1.80 garden only; NT. The Stockton Cross Inn (on the A4112 NE of Leominster) is good.

† ★ **ASHTON UNDER HILL** SO9938 Charming black and white timbered houses and a good Norman church; made all the more attractive by the brooding backdrop of Bredon Hill.

★ **BEWDLEY** SO7874 Attractive small town, with riverside walks and interesting side streets. The Little Pack Horse (old High St) is full of character. **Severn Valley Railway** Splendid steamtrain trips through the Wyre Forest and the Severn valley between Kidderminster and Bridgnorth in Shropshire, with lots going on – this railway is run with great verve. The station has a fine model railway. Meals, snacks, shop; trains daily May–Sept and most other wknds (01299) 403816 for timetable; £9.20 for full trip. **Bewdley Museum** (Load St) An 18th-c row of butchers' shops houses this local history museum; cl Nov–Mar; £2. **West Midlands Safari & Leisure Park** (Spring Grove, on the A456 just E) Very much a full day out, with the main attraction the drive-round animal reserves, home to over 40 species of rare and exotic animals. Some animals may come right up to your car, but others will watch nonchalantly from a distance; happily, you can go round as often as you like, so if you don't see what you want it's easy to give it another go later on. Admission also covers the sea lion show, reptile house, and pets corner, but you'll have to pay extra for the leisure park, which has around 30 rides from gentle carousels to a roller-coaster and popular log flume. The undercover Dome shows cartoons throughout the day. Meals, snacks, shop, disabled access; cl Nov–Mar; (01299) 404604; £4.95 animals, £6.25 for limitless ride wristband.

Days Out

The great train ride: Trip on the Severn Valley Railway, Bewdley; lunch at the Little Pack Horse there; stroll around Bewdley; Witley Court.

Black and white villages: Weobley, Pembridge and Eardisland villages; lunch at the Riverside, Aymestrey; Croft Castle; walk through Leinthall Common to Croft Ambrey.

Wye cornucopia: Ross-on-Wye; Hoarwithy church; lunch at the Cottage of Content, Carey; Brockhampton church; Weston's cider farm, Much Marcle; Goodrich Castle.

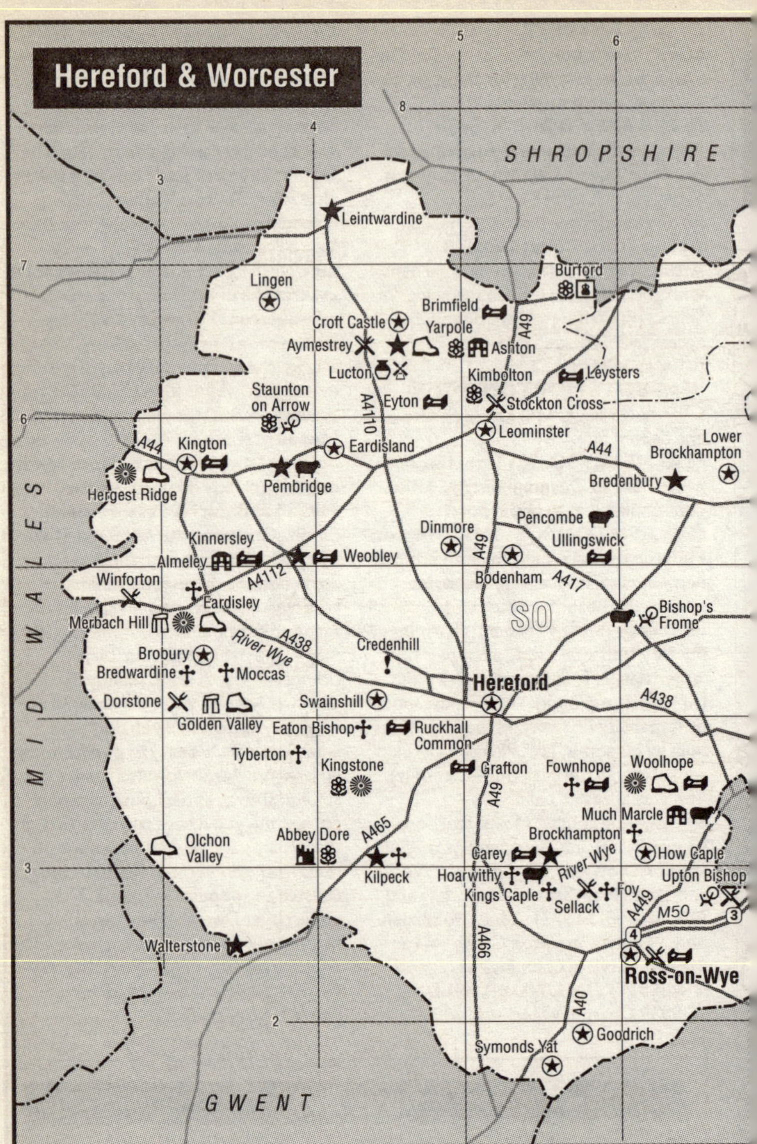

BISHOP'S FROME SO6647
Hop Pocket Hop Farm Traditional hop farm, its hundred acres a hive of activity in the harvest season. Tours of kilns by arrangement, pretty gardens, and big craft shop – you can buy hop bines, and hop pillows (a favourite with poor sleepers). Snacks, disabled access; cl am Sun, Mon (exc bank hols), and Tues–Thurs Jan and Feb; (01531) 640323; tours £2.50. The Green Dragon is a good pub.

BLAKESHALL SO8381
Kingsford Country Park 200-acre park with pine forests, birch groves and plenty of walks and trails (inc one for the disabled). Very nice unspoilt feel – even the signposts and picnic tables are made at the sawmill here.

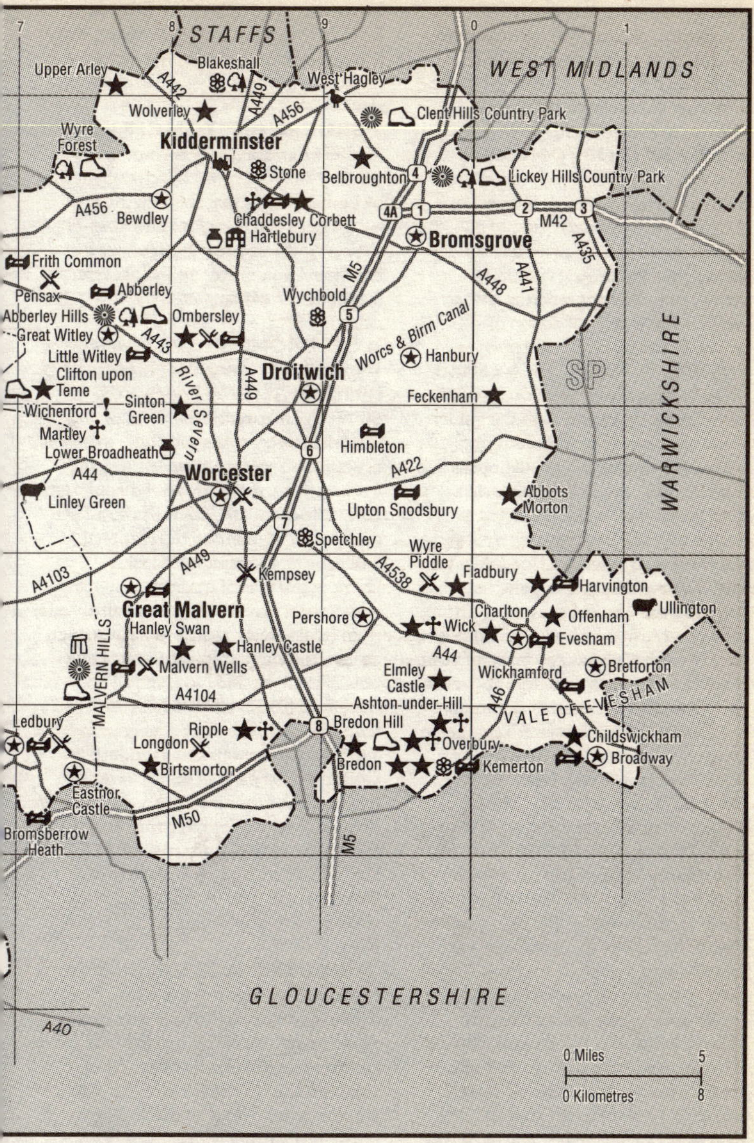

BODENHAM SO5151 **Queenswood Country Park & Arboretum** 170 acres of woodland and arboretum with over 500 tree varieties; also wildlife displays and good views. Meals, snacks, shop and information centre, disabled access; café cl 25–26 Dec; (01568) 797052; free, though car park 50p. The Three Crowns between Ullingswick and unspoilt Little Cowarne has very good food.

★ **BREDON** SO9236 Attractive village above River Avon, with magnificent medieval tithe barn and good pub.

BREDON HILL SO9339 The Vale of Evesham's one notable feature for walkers. It's an outlier of the Cotswolds, distinctively rounded and on cloudy days rather ominous. It's easily reached from Overbury, but the best walk over it is from Bredons Norton to Elmley Castle.

★ † **BRETFORTON** SP0944 One of the prettiest black and white thatched villages, with an interesting church and a splendid medieval pub, the Fleece, left to the NT after being in the same family for several centuries; a proper pub, it's kept much as it was, with a magnificent collection of Jacobean oak furniture and pewter.

★ **BROADWAY** SP0937 An exceptionally harmonious stone-built Cotswold village, with the golden stone and uneven stone-tiled roofs perfectly blending the grand houses and the humbler cottages together, in a long, grass-lined main street. It's decidedly on the coach-tour trail, very busy indeed in summer. Fine things for sale in extraordinarily expensive antique shops, and a very grand old inn, the Lygon Arms, with a useful side wine bar. The other places recommended in the **Where to stay** section, above, do good bar lunches; a good escape from the tourists is the Crown & Trumpet in Church St, and the Buckland Manor does good teas. **Broadway Teddy Bear Museum** (High St) Decent collection of old bears and toys. Shop; cl 25–26 Dec; (01386) 858323; £1.50. **Broadway Tower** (off the A44 SE) Above the village, this late 18th-c folly has marvellous views that on a clear day – with the help of the telescope – are said to stretch over 12 counties. There are exhibitions on the history of the tower and regular visitor William Morris, while the country park around it has farm animals and nature trails. Meals, snacks, shops, some disabled access; cl Nov–Mar; (01386) 852390; £2 tower only, £3 tower and park. The A44 W is good for produce stalls; Chapel Hill nursery about ½m W has good-value plants for sale.

BROBURY SO3344 **Brobury House Gallery** 8 acres of semi-formal gardens with fine views; also watercolours and prints for sale. Disabled access (but no facilities); cl Sun, 25–26 Dec; (01981) 500595; gardens £2.50, gallery free. They do B & B in the smart Victorian house, with fishing permits available. The Portway nr Monnington on Wye is a useful food stop.

† **BROCKHAMPTON CHURCH** SO5931 Extraordinary turn-of-the-century Arts & Crafts church designed by Lethaby; note that this is in the little village between Hereford and Ross-on-Wye, not the estate near Bromyard between Leominster and Worcester (*see Lower Brockhampton entry, below*).

BROMSGROVE SO9468 **Avoncroft Museum of Historic Buildings** (Stoke Prior; on the B4091 S) Threatened buildings of historical interest are carefully re-erected and restored here – anything from a 14th-c monastic roof through an 18th-c dovecot and ice-house to a 1946 prefab, not to mention the National Collection of Telephone Kiosks. Demonstrations of traditional building techniques, maybe wknd miniature train rides. Meals, snacks, shop, disabled access; cl Mon (exc July, Aug and bank hols), Fri in Mar and Nov, and all Dec–Feb; (01527) 831363; £4.25. The Country Girl here does generous food and is handy for walks on Dodderhill Common; the parish council have mapped out other walks too. Bromsgrove proper has a thoroughly traditional local history **museum** (cl Sun; £1.20) and **Daub & Wattle's Pottery**, a largely unchanged pottery building with displays and shop (cl Sun, Mon).

BURFORD SO5868 **Burford House Gardens** (off the A456, W of Tenbury Wells) Delightfully set by the River Teme, these tranquil gardens are the home of a national collection of clematis. Lots of other colourful plants, and the ground floor of the Georgian house is open as a contemporary art gallery. Meals, snacks, plant sales, disabled access; cl 25–26 Dec and 1 Jan; (01584) 810777; £2.50.

★ **CAREY** SO5630 Delightful tucked-away village, with a charming pub.

★ † **CHADDESLEY CORBETT** SO8973 Despite the trunk road an attractive village, with a decent pub and a fine partly Norman **church**.

★ **CHILDSWICKHAM** SP0738 This streamside village has some delightful timbered stone cottages.

CLENT HILLS COUNTRY PARK SO9380 A fine high hillscape for walkers, open and exhilarating, with waymarked routes. The Holly Bush at Clent is a good lunch break.

★ **CLIFTON UPON TEME** SO7161 A pleasant village, with lots of quiet strolls above the orchards.

! **CREDENHILL** SO4443 **Escargot Anglais** (on the A480) Part of the National Snail Farming Centre, with snail trails showing various species (even hairy ones) and exhibitions. Shop, open summer wknds and Mon, Thurs and Fri by appointment only; (01432) 760218; £2.50. The Bell at Tillington does more orthodox food.

CROFT CASTLE SO4565 The walls and turrets date from the 14th and 15th c, but the inside is mostly 18th-c, with an interesting staircase and plastered ceilings. Attractive parklands with avenue of 350-year-old chestnuts. New tearoom, shop, disabled access; open pm Weds–Sun and bank hols May–Sept, plus wknds Apr and Oct; (01568) 780246; *£3.20; NT. The picturesque Bell at Yarpole is handy for lunch. You can walk around the Castle's estate on the brackeny expanse of Leinthall Common, a quiet corner of Herefordshire scattered with cottages, and scale the modest heights of Croft Ambrey, an Iron Age **hill fort** with a view into Shropshire.

DINMORE MANOR SO4850 Hilltop manor house with spectacular views of surrounding countryside. Grand hall, good stained-glass collection, and farm animals in the grounds. Perhaps most interesting is the ancient chapel, incongruously placed between a rock garden and a venerable yew tree. Plant centre, disabled access; (01432) 830322; £3. Nearby Green Acres has organically grown pick-your-own fruit and veg; **Dinmore Fruit Farm** has a very wide choice of apple varieties, as well as more conventional pick-your-own.

! † **DROITWICH** SO8963 Famous as a spa town; you don't drink the water here, you float in it. The **brine baths** on St Andrew's Rd are just the thing after an exhausting day's sightseeing; cl 25–26 Dec, (01905) 794894; *£6 (inc sauna). Interesting buildings include the timbered houses around the High St and the **Sacred Heart Church** with its fine stained-glass mosaics. The **heritage centre** (Victoria Sq) has an unusual exhibition on radios and broadcasting, and brass rubbing. Shop, disabled access; cl Sun and bank hols; (01905) 774312; free. The Firs out at Dunhampstead (just SE) is a pleasant dining pub.

★ **EARDISLAND** SO4158 Gorgeous riverside black and white village; the spectacularly wonky weather-vane on one ivy-clad dovecot has been at that angle for years. The friendly Cross Inn has decent food. **Burton Court** (on the A44 just S) Interesting old house with 14th-c great hall, collections of ship models, costumes and natural history specimens. Also working model fairground, and pick-your-own. Teas, shops, disabled access; open pm Weds, Thurs, wknds and bank hols May–mid-Sept, or evenings by arrangement; (01544) 388231; *£2.50.

† **EARDISLEY CHURCH** SO3149 12th-c font with wonderfully vivid carvings of sinner being wrested from the clutches of evil.

EASTNOR CASTLE SO7336 (just E of Ledbury) Splendid neo-Gothic castle, especially dramatic in autumn, when the virginia creeper that all but envelops the stirring battlements turns a fierce red. Designed by Pugin, the richly decorated rooms are breathtaking, with fine collections of armour, tapestries, furniture and paintings. The attractive grounds have an arboretum, 300-acre deer park, woodland walks, adventure playground, children's maze and garden centre. Meals, snacks, shop; open Sun and bank hols Easter–early Oct, and wkdys in July and Aug; (01531) 633160; *£4.50. Eastnor village's thatched post office is lovely.

★ **ELMLEY CASTLE** SO9841 Very old-fashioned village below Bredon Hill, with attractive houses strung out between its lovely church and the millpond.

★ **EVESHAM** SP0343 The pedestrianised market square has some fine buildings around it inc a 12th-c **abbey gateway**; the church's striking 16th-c bell tower is well preserved, and some altogether more ruined remnants in the town park beyond lead to riverside meadows. The tourist information centre is in another attractive abbey building, the Almonry, a Tudor timbered house with craft shows, small museum, and nice gardens. The Royal Oak (Vine St) is useful for lunch, and the Green Dragon (Oat St) visibly brews its own ales. In April or early May the orchard drive through Harvington, the Lenches, Badgers Hill, Fladbury Cross, Wood Norton and Chadbury is pretty. **Farm shops** around here are good for all manner of local produce inc eggs, jams, pickles and trout as well as fruit and veg, but the highlights of the year are asparagus in May and apples and particularly plums in Sept.

★ **FECKENHAM** SP0061 Attractive green and some fine Georgian red brick.

★ **FLADBURY** SO9946 This appealing village offers walks by the River Avon, a 9th-c Saxon cross, and a handsome Georgian village green.

GOLDEN VALLEY SO3141 The B4348/B4347 is a pretty drive, with particularly satisfying walks in the surrounding hills; the tucked-away village of Dorstone has an impressive prehistoric burial mound nearby (and Herefordshire's oldest pub). The remoter roads parallel to this, to the W, are also well worth the drive, through Clodock (delightful church) and Michaelchurch Escley (another good pub down by the river), or passing Craswall.

GOODRICH CASTLE SO5719 Readers are very fond of this proper-looking 12th-c castle, built using the same red sandstone rock it stands on so that it seems almost to grow out of the ground. Still plenty to see, with towers, passageways, dungeon and marvellous views of the surrounding countryside. Shop; cl 24–26 Dec; (01600) 890538; £2.95. These formidable ruins are a feasible objective for stout-hearted walkers from Symonds Yat – or could be a start point for Wye valley gorge walks. The nearby Hostelrie has decent food, and the Crown off the B4228 at Howle Hill (not Mon) is good.

★ † **GREAT MALVERN** SO7745 Elegant hillside spa town with easy access to inspiring hill scenery; the B4232 from Upper Colwall to Wynds Point has some of the best high views, while the B4218 on the E side gives several good views of the hills themselves. A good few craft workshops include musical instrument-makers such as Hibernian Violins, Players Ave; cl wknds. The Foley Arms and Mount Pleasant Hotel have decent food, and good views. **Malvern Museum** (Abbey Rd) The splendid former gateway of a Benedictine monastery houses a museum with displays on local history, Malvern spring water, and the life of Sir Edward Elgar. Shop; cl Weds in term time, all Nov–Easter; (01684) 567811; £1. The beautifully symmetrical **priory** just along the road has a notable collection of medieval wall tiles. **Barnards Green House** On the E side of the Malvern Hills, this has an attractive garden with a wide range of gardening ideas around a gracious 17th-c house (not open). The owner is an authority on dried flowers. Teas, plant sales, disabled access; open pm Thurs Apr–Sept, a couple of Suns in Apr, Jun and Aug, and other times by appointment; (01684) 574446; *£2. The nearby Bluebell is useful for lunch. **Picton Garden** (Old Court Nurseries, Walwyn Rd, Colwall) On the W side of the Malvern Hills, this has a nicely laid out cottagey collection of hardy plants and shrubs, best in summer, with a national collection of asters (late summer/autumn) and rock garden. Plant sales, disabled access; cl Mon, Tues, and Nov–Mar; (01684) 540416; £2. The Chase Inn at Upper Wyche is handy for lunch.

† **GREAT WITLEY** SO7765 **Witley Court** Astonishing ruined shell of Jacobean house transformed into an Italianate palace by the Earl of Dudley, and partly destroyed by fire in 1937. It's an elaborate place, with enormous Perseus fountain, and

balustraded garden – very atmospheric to wander through. Overlooking the lake beside it, a gloriously baroque church is no less dramatic, and one of the county's great finds; it has splendid paintings and stained glass around the largely papier-mâché interior. Snacks, shop, some disabled access; cl 24–26 Dec; (01299) 896636; £3.10. The Hundred House is handy for lunch. **Eastgrove Cottage Garden** (Sankyns Green, off the A443 E, towards Shrawley) Interesting and unusual hardy and tender perennial plants in a cottage-garden setting by ancient timbered house (not open). Good plants for sale, disabled access; open pm Thurs–Mon Apr–July, then pm Thurs–Sat Sept–mid-Oct; (01299) 896389; *£2.

HANBURY HALL SO9463 18th-c country house with outstanding painted ceilings and staircase, fine porcelain, and contemporary ice-house and orangery in grounds. The formal gardens are being carefully restored. You can book rooms in the Lodge on the edge of the estate. Snacks, shop, some disabled access; open pm Sun–Weds Apr–Oct; (01527) 821214; £4.30, £2.50 garden only; NT. The **church**, high on a hill, has superb views over the countryside. The Gate Hangs Well (Woodgate) has a good carvery. **Jinney Ring Craft Centre** (on the B4091 Droitwich Rd) Various craft workshops in beautiful timbered barns, from pottery to violin-making; some wknd courses. Meals, snacks, shop, some disabled access; cl Mon exc bank hols; (01527) 821272; free.

★ **HANLEY CASTLE** SO8342 Well worth a stop, a rustic little place around a great cedar tree, with an unusually unspoilt pub.

★ **HANLEY SWAN** SO8142 An attractive village, with a pleasant traditional pub by the village green and duck pond.

HARTLEBURY CASTLE SO8371 The official residence of the Bishops of Worcester since 850, now part of the **County Museum**; you can visit some of the elegant state rooms Tues–Thurs. Snacks, shop, some disabled access; museum cl am Fri and Sun, all Sat, Dec, Jan and Good Fri; (01299) 250416; £2.20 (inc state rooms).

★ **HARVINGTON** SP0549 One of the area's oldest villages, brilliantly black and white.

HERGEST RIDGE SO2756 Reached via a cul-de-sac from Kington, this is north-west Herefordshire's answer to the Malvern Hills – and like them (allegedly) inspired Elgar, in this case to write his *Introduction and Allegro for Strings*, as well as Mike Oldfield with his album *Hergest Ridge*, and the less-known composer Moeran with his *Sinfonietta*. It's another of those ridges for walkers who can't decide whether they prefer the gentle lowland textures of England or the more rugged offerings of Wales. The walk gets better with every step, as the wide ridge tapers into horseback width at the far end, above Gladestry in Powys.

† **HOARWITHY** SO5429 **Glenda Spooner Farm** This friendly and caring place used to be the home of the jockeys Michael and Peter Scudamore. Now a centre for the International League for the Protection of Horses, with care and rehabilitation for equine victims of maltreatment. Some disabled access; open wknds and bank hols; (01953) 498682; free. The **church** is remarkably Italianate, full of mosaics, etc.

† **HOW CAPLE COURT** SO6130 11 acres of peaceful formal and woodland Edwardian gardens overlooking the river, with old roses and unusual perennials for sale. Snacks; cl wknds Oct–Feb; (01989) 740626; £2.50. Also interesting medieval church and fabrics shop. The Green Man at Fownhope is popular for food.

★ **KEMERTON** SO9437 **The Priory** Big garden richly planted with colourful borders; also cool streamside plantings, handsome trees and shrubs. Plant sales; open pm Thurs May–Sept plus half a dozen Suns (when they do teas); (01386) 725258; £2.50 (less in May and Jun). There are other pretty stone-built houses in this attractively leafy village below Bredon Hill. The Crown is useful for lunch.

KIDDERMINSTER SO8376 Not an alluring place to visit, but a terminus of the Severn Valley steam railway (see *Bewdley entry, above*), with a cheerful replica of Edwardian station refreshment rooms.

✝★ **KILPECK CHURCH** SO4430 This small Norman church in a delightful little hamlet has amazing sandstone carving inside and out, beautifully preserved (except for the more uncomfortably pagan bits which prudish Victorians tried to remove).

❀ **KIMBOLTON** SO5161 **Stockton Bury Gardens** (on the A4112 S) Attractive and developing garden complex, now covering 4 acres, good for a gentle wander. Plant sales, disabled access; cl am, all Mon (exc bank hols) and Tues, plus Nov–Mar; (01568) 613432; *£2.50.

❀ ❁ **KINGSTONE COTTAGES** SO4235 (off the A40) Charming, exuberant cottage garden, not to be missed at midsummer for its profusion of old-fashioned pinks and border carnations. Also fine views, and tucked-away little grotto – looking out it seems as though you're waist-high in water. Unusual plants for sale; open wkdys early May–late Jun, or by appointment; (01989) 565267; £1. Not too far from the Ancient Camp Inn at Ruckhall.

★ ⌂ ❀ ♧ **KINGTON** SO2956 Attractive border town by the River Arrow, well placed for walks – for instance, the **Mortimer Trail**, a waymarked 30-mile path to Ludlow, with loop walks off, e.g. at Shobdon SO4062 and Wigmore SO4169. This gives a good sample of the hilly, unspoilt landscape of northern Herefordshire. The Queen's Head has good-value food and brews its own ales. NE of town at Bradnor Hill, the Kington Golf Club (in 240 acres of NT-owned land) is the highest in the country, and has good views. **Hergest Croft Gardens** (just W, off the A44) The splendid result of inspired work by several generations of keen gardeners; some of the centenarian rhododendrons in the woods are of almost incredible size. Famous kitchen garden with colourful flowerbeds, and the national collections of birches and maples. Snacks, shop, some disabled access; cl am, and all Nov–Easter; (01544) 230160; £2.75. *See separate Family Panel on p.306* for **Small Breeds Farm Park** at Kingswood.

★ ⛫ ✝ ♜ ♧ **LEDBURY** SO7138 The spaciously leisured High St has some fine buildings: the old **Market House**, the **Feathers Hotel** and **Ledbury Park House** are famous for their well balanced 15th- and 16th-c timbering, and there are plenty of similar structures. From the Market House an exceptional alley of ancient jettied buildings leads to the partly Norman **Church of St Michael & All Angels**, with an unusual spire tower detached from the main building, and its carillon ringing out a well known hymn every third hour. The **Old Grammar School** along here has been restored as a heritage centre (cl Nov–Easter). The council offices must be the only ones in the country decorated with medieval wall-paintings; you can see these any wkdy between 11am and 2pm; free. There are craft workshops, antique shops, the national Playmobile specialist and a decent book shop, and the Feathers has good food. The road N through Wellington Heath towards Mathon has some good views.

★ **LEINTWARDINE** SO4074 Appealing riverside village notable for its church – much bigger than usual for this county; the nicely placed Lion has good-value bedrooms.

★ ✝ ⛫ **LEOMINSTER** SO4958 An attractive centre, the medieval streets almost lined with black and white timbered houses. The red **priory church** still has many of its original Norman features, and the handsome old Talbot has decent food. **Herefordshire Cheesemaking** (on the A44, 2m W) You can watch cheese being made by hand using traditional methods. Snacks (inc ploughman's with their own cheese), shop, disabled access; shop and café cl winter Sun and Mon (cheese-making Mon, Weds and Fri only, 10am–2.30pm); (01568) 720307; £1.25.

⌂ ♧ ❁ **LICKEY HILLS COUNTRY PARK** SO9975 A good example of the interesting topography W of Birmingham: high (rising to over 300 metres or 1,000ft), and densely wooded, a fragment of primeval forest, with the views suddenly opening out over the sprawling city; waymarking makes the maze of paths and tracks less confusing.

★ ❀ ⛰ **LINGEN** SO3667 Attractive village prettily set among hills, with Kim Davis's renowned alpine nursery and garden, and a walk linked to the Mortimer Trail *(see Kington entry, above)*.

LINLEY GREEN SO6953 **Pig Pen** (Hareley Farm) Fun working pig farm, with lots of piglets to handle (lambs too in early spring), tours of pens and yards, play area, and woodland nature trails. Bring wellies when it's muddy. Snacks, shop, disabled access; open pm daily mid-Easter–Sept and autumn half-term; (01886) 884362; £2.50.

LOWER BROADHEATH SO8157 **Elgar's Birthplace Museum** (Crown East Lane) Modest cottage (with modern red-brick annexe, and controversial plans for enlargement) where the composer was born in 1857; now, as he wanted, a museum of his life and work, with displays of musical scores and letters, and the desk where he did his writing. Shop, disabled access to ground floor; cl am in winter, all Weds, and mid-Jan–mid-Feb; (01905) 333224; £3. You can pick up routes and information here about the Elgar Trail around the area, and the Bear & Ragged Staff over at Bransford is a very suitable place for lunch.

❀ **LOWER BROCKHAMPTON** SO7055 Idyllic timber-framed and moated 14th-c manor house in attractive secluded countryside. Particularly interesting 15th-c gatehouse, and the ruins of a 12th-c chapel. Shop, some disabled access; cl Mon exc bank hols, Tues, and Nov–Mar; (01885) 488099; £2; NT. The Trust also owns the adjacent 1,720-acre **Brockhampton Estate**, with splendid views from its park and woodlands, and marked trails inc a sculpture one. The Talbot at Knightwick is a nice place for lunch.

LUCTON SO4263 **Mortimer's Cross Mill & Battle Centre** Charming watermill on banks of River Ludd, still in working order, with exhibition on the decisive Wars of the Roses battle fought here in 1461. Open pm Thurs, Sun and bank hols Apr–Sept; (01568) 708820; *£2. The Riverside at Aymestrey has good food.

⛰ **MALVERN HILLS** SO7641 Forming a splendid backdrop to the Vale of Evesham, these offer good walking. From a distance they look a formidable mountain range, but seem to get milder and more welcoming as you approach. The gentle up-and-down path along their spine makes one of England's great ridge walks, with the Cotswolds and Midland plain on one side and wilder Wales on the other. The **Herefordshire Beacon**, capped by ramparts of an Iron Age hill fort, is easily reached from the car park on the A449 nr Little Malvern. Great Malvern is well placed for the **Worcestershire Beacon**, the highest point of the range (425 metres or 1,395ft), and for long circular walks. The Chase Hotel at Upper Wyche and Malvern Hills Hotel by the British Camp car park on Wynds Point are also useful start or finish points. Ledbury and Eastnor are good bases for rambles into the attractive western slopes.

✝ **MARTLEY CHURCH** SO7559 Notable for its 13th-c wall-paintings.

⛰ **MERBACH HILL** SO3143 Reached by driving up from Bredwardine, and then walking from the top of the lane, this gives a view right over the Black Mountains, Herefordshire and Radnorshire. A short stroll along the lane SE brings you to **Arthur's Stone**, a prehistoric burial chamber.

MUCH MARCLE SO6433 **Weston's cider farm** Still alongside the family house, this has an engaging combination of modern equipment and old-fashioned atmosphere. Enthusiastic guided tours, liberal tastings, interesting ciders and perries. Meals, snacks, good shop with wide range of ciders, tours by appointment; cl Sun and pm Sat; (01531) 660233; *£3. The nearby Slip has good dishes of the day and outstanding gardens; the memorial monuments in the village church are unrivalled in the area. **Hellens** (just opposite) Unspoilt manor house dating from the 13th c; you can see the portrait of Catherine of Braganza that convinced Charles II to marry her. Teas; open pm Sat, Sun, Weds and bank hols Easter–Sept; (01531) 660668; £3.50.

★ **OFFENHAM** SP0546 Still has its original gaily striped maypole in its wide black and white main street; a nice village.

OLCHON VALLEY SO3029 Perhaps the remotest place in Herefordshire, a magnificent dead-end valley beneath the eastern flank of the Black Mountains. From the well signed picnic site nr Longtown a path heads up the Black Hill, an exciting knife-edge ridge, its end-on aspect strikingly triangular – this bit is known as the Cat's Back; after the trig point you can make a circuit by dropping down from the very head of the Olchon valley, or carrying on over peaty terrain to join the Offa's Dyke path.

★ **OMBERSLEY** SO8463 Attractive mix of handsome black and white timbered houses with elegant Georgian brick; a choice of good pubs, too.

★ † **OVERBURY** SO9537 Immaculate stone-built estate village, with older buildings and fine church.

★ **PEMBRIDGE** SO3958 One of Herefordshire's most striking black and white villages, full of fine timbered buildings inc a medieval market hall, the ancient New Inn, and a lovely church with an unusual detached belfry where you can watch the clock mechanism. Just S is **Dunkerton's cider farm** SO3955 (Luntley), using ancient traditional local cider-apple and pear cultivars for distinctive ciders and perries; welcoming atmosphere, free tastings, and good restaurant; cl Sun.

PENCOMBE SO5951 **Shortwood Family Farm** Working farm ideal for children, with hands-on afternoon activities like milking Daisy or feeding the pigs and calves. Good play area. Snacks, shop; cl Oct–Easter (though open Oct half-term for cider-making); (01885) 400205; *£3. The Three Crowns at Ullingswick has very good food.

★ † ! **PERSHORE** SO9445 Very much a working town, the 'capital' of the fruit- and vegetable-growing area around it. It's a pleasant place, largely Georgian, with an impressive **abbey** and walks by the River Avon. The Brandy Cask (Bridge St) has good-value food and brews its own beer. Heading out along the A4104 SW, when you've passed the Oak in Defford, keep your eyes skinned for a group of cottages on your right; the last, surrounded by farm animals and without an inn sign, is the **Monkey House**, a uniquely old-fashioned cider tavern (cl pm Mon, Tues).

★ † **RIPPLE** SO8737 An appealing village, with finely carved choir seats in its imposing largely 13th-c church.

★ **ROSS-ON-WYE** SO5924 Picturesquely perched on a sandstone cliff by the river, with twice-weekly markets at the striking 17th-c **market hall**. The lower riverside part has attractive waterside walks; the Hope & Anchor here has decent food, and Oat Cuisine (Broad St) has substantial vegetarian food. There are pleasant woodland walks in Penyard Park, SE of the town. **Button Museum** (Kyrle St) A unique place, far more interesting than you would expect, with some extraordinarily intricate workmanship as well as some real curiosities; shop, disabled access; cl Nov–Mar; £1.50.

SPETCHLEY PARK GARDENS SO8953 (on the A422) 30 acres of lovely gardens, with sweeping lawns and herbaceous borders, rose lawn, and interesting trees and shrubs. The adjacent park has both red and fallow deer. Snacks, disabled access (but no facilities); cl Sat, am Sun, all Mon (exc bank hols), and Oct–Mar; (01905) 345213; £2.90. The Berkeley Knot is handy for lunch.

STAUNTON ON ARROW SO3560 **Horseway Herbs** (Horsewayhead Cottage) Friendly little place to wander around, with herbs sold as both plants and crafts; they also sell home-made pickles and jams. Snacks, disabled access; cl Weds, all Nov–Mar; (01544) 388212; free. The New Inn at Pembridge is good.

STONE SO8675 **Stone House Garden** Unusual walled garden with colourful plants, especially climbers and tender flowering shrubs; interesting plant sales. Disabled access; open Weds–Sat Mar–Oct; (01562) 69902; £2. The Fox at Chaddesley Corbett has a popular carvery.

SWAINSHILL SO4341 **Weir Gardens** (Garden Cottage, off the A438) Delightful riverside gardens at their best in spring, with displays of bulbs set in woodland trails, and fine views from clifftop walks. Paths can be steep in places. Open Weds–Sun (and bank hols) mid-Feb–Oct; £1.80; NT. The Ancient Camp at Ruckhall is quite handy.

! **SYMONDS YAT** SO5517 Shared with Glos on the other side of the river, this is a spectacular bend of the River Wye through a steep wooded rock gorge, where peregrine falcons nest (the RSPB have a demonstration area); splendid Wye views, nature trails; 2 inns on either side of the river are linked by a hand-pulled ferry, and there's ample (walkers would say over-generous) parking – cheapest nr the Royal Hotel. It's a big tourist draw. **Jubilee Park** This centres on a hedge maze created for the Queen's Silver Jubilee in 1977; and lively maze museum tells the history of similar labyrinthine creations. Meals, snacks, shop, disabled access; cl wkdys Mar and Oct and all Nov–Feb; (01600) 890360; £2.80. On the same site, the **Splendour of the Orient** has oriental watergardens and a new indoor tropical garden area with scenes from fairy tales. Some wknd events such as martial arts displays or talks on feng shui. Snacks, shop (specialising in cane furniture), disabled access; cl Dec 25–26; (01600) 890668; *£2.90. There's potential for more ambitious walks into the gorge, where an old railway line follows the river; to the SW an entertainingly rickety wire-mesh suspension bridge at the Biblins gives access to the west bank, in addition to the chain ferry at Symonds Yat village.

ULLINGTON SP1147 **Domestic Fowl Trust** (just N of Honeybourne, E of Evesham) A friendly place with rare breeds of sheep, hens, ducks, geese and turkeys, plus young chicks for children to handle (all year), new adventure playground and an indoor play area planned. You'll need wellies on wet days. Summer snacks, shop, limited disabled access; (01386) 833083; £2.50.

UPTON BISHOP SO6327 **Wobage Farm craft workshops** Several potters, a furniture-maker, wood-carver and jeweller; open wknds only; (01989) 780233; free. The Moody Cow is a good individual lunch stop.

★ **WEOBLEY** SO4051 In the very top rank of Herefordshire's black and white villages, with its long sloping green, and idyllic stroll out past the bowling green to the church; the Olde Salutation is good for lunch.

WEST HAGLEY SO8979 **Falconry Centre** (Hurrans Garden Centre, Kidderminster Rd, S) Frequent flying displays of hawks, owls and other birds of prey; short falconry courses. Shop, some disabled access; cl 25–26 Dec; (01562) 700014; *£2.50. The Holly Bush (on the A491 towards Bromsgrove) has popular fresh food.

! **WICHENFORD** SO7759 Unusually constructed timber-framed wattle and daub 17th-c **dovecot** with nearly 600 nesting boxes; recently restored. Open daily Apr–Oct, winter by appointment; (01684) 850051; 60p; NT.

★ † **WICK** SO9645 This riverside village has attractive houses and a good church.

★ **WOLVERLEY** SO8279 Steeply gabled cottages below a brick-built hilltop church, and the decent cliffside Lock Inn by the quaint Staffs & Worcs Canal.

WOOLHOPE SO6135 The elevated country around here has a good variety of scenery for walkers; the views from Ridge Hill E and the more densely wooded hills nr Mordiford are among the highlights.

WYCHBOLD SO9165 **Webbs Garden Centre** (on the A38 towards Bromsgrove) One of the best in the country, attractively laid out, with a massive choice of things to buy, fine amusements for children and good disabled access. The thatched café is exemplary; cl 25–26 Dec; (01527) 861777.

WYRE FOREST SO7574 This major broadleaved woodland, on the Shropshire border, has numerous Forestry Commission trails (leaflets available from the Visitor Centre; the Royal Forester nearby, if open, is useful for lunch).

★ **YARPOLE** SO4765 The church of this attractive streamside village has an uncommon free-standing medieval bell tower, and a signed walk linked to the Mortimer Trail *(see Kington entry, above)*.

★ **Other attractive villages**, all with decent pubs, include Belbroughton SO9277, Birtsmorton SO7936, Bredenbury SO6156 (despite the main road), thatched Charlton SP0145, Sinton Green SO8160, Upper Arley SO7680 (the Severn Valley Railway from Bewdley stops at a station over the River Severn footbridge) and Walterstone SO3425 (peaceful walks).

✝ Quiet country drives can link several **attractive churches**, such as Bredwardine SO3344, Moccas SO3543, Tyberton SO3839 and Eaton Bishop SO4439; or perhaps Fownhope SO5834, Kings Caple SO5528 and even Foy SO5928 with Brockhampton and Hoarwithy.

Where to eat

AYMESTREY SO4265 **Riverside** *(01568) 708440* Black and white timbered riverside inn with rambling beamed bar, some fine furniture, log fires and a relaxed atmosphere, good ambitious food, well kept own-brewed beers, decent wines, and obliging service; good bdrms. **£15.95**|£4.95.

DORSTONE SO3141 **Pandy** *(01981) 550273* Cosy half-timbered ancient pub, very relaxed and friendly, with good imaginative food (lots of fresh fish and game), beamed and flagstoned rooms, well kept beers, and woodburner; partial disabled access. **£15**|£3.95.

KEMPSEY SO8548 **Walter de Cantelupe** *(01905) 820572* Popular roadside pub with friendly relaxed bar, quite a mix of furniture, flowers and candles on tables, a good big fireplace, well kept real ales, a good choice of wines by the glass, and hard-working young landlord. **£16.75**|£6.25.

LEDBURY SO7137 **Market Place** *(01531) 634250* Pleasant bustling restaurant open all day for morning coffee, lunch and afternoon tea with home-made cakes, flans and puddings; cl pm, 25–26 Dec, 1 Jan. **£12**|£2.50.

LONGDON SO8433 **Hunters** *(01684) 833388* Friendly rather civilised place with good imaginative food in smart heavy-beamed restaurant and small dining room, 2 comfortable bars with flagstones and a woodburning stove, well kept beer and nice wines, and 6 acres with dogs, rabbits and ponies. **£19.90**|£5.

MALVERN WELLS SO7742 **Croque-en-Bouche** *221 Wells Rd (01684) 565612* Boldly decorated Victorian house with delicious carefully cooked evening food from a shortish menu with marvellous puddings and cheeses, and an exceptional wine list – must book; open pm only Thurs–Sat; cl 1 wk May, 1 wk Sept, Christmas. **£30**.

OMBERSLEY SO8463 **Kings Arms** *(01905) 620142* Big black-beamed and timbered Tudor pub with comfortably informal rambling rooms, various nooks and crannies full of stuffed animals and birds, rustic bric-à-brac and 4 open fires; excellent varied bar food, well kept real ales, and seats in sheltered courtyard and terrace. **£20**|£7.75.

PENSAX SO7468 **Bell** *(01299) 896677* Unspoilt and friendly 19th-c pub with good food, several changing real ales, open fires, and dining room extension with a fine view over the hills to Wyre Forest; cl am Mon except bank hols and summer holiday period; disabled access. **£19**|£6.50.

ROSS-ON-WYE SO5924 **Pheasants** *52 Edde Cross St (01989) 565751* Homely little restaurant with cosy lounge, good interesting food, nice cheeses, and relaxed atmosphere; cl Sun, Mon, 25 Dec–2 Jan; well behaved children welcome. **£35**.

SELLACK SO5526 **Lough Pool** *(01989) 730236* Attractive black and white timbered cottage in lovely countryside, with log fire in cosy beamed room and excellent tasty bar food; cl 25 Dec, pm 26 Dec; disabled access. **£20**|£3.25.

STOCKTON CROSS SO5261 **Stockton Cross** *(01568) 612509* Heavy-beamed long bar with old-fashioned feel, a huge log fire and woodburner, solid furnishings, wide choice of enjoyable food, well kept beer, and good welcoming service; seats in garden; cl pm Mon; children over 6. **£22**|£6.50.

UPTON BISHOP SO6326 **Moody Cow** *(01989) 780470* Merry place with several snug separate areas, a pleasant medley of stripped country furniture, big log fire, no smoking rustic candlelit restaurant and second small dining room, a good choice of enjoyable food, and well kept beers. **£19.70**|£7.75.

WINFORTON SO2946 **Sun** *(01544) 327677* Very friendly and neatly kept little pub with beamed rooms, woodburners, particularly good interesting food, and sheltered garden; good bdrms; cl winter Tues, pm Tues in summer; children over 10. **£21.85**|£7.50.

WORCESTER SO8454 **Browns** *24 Quay St (01905) 26263* Most attractive and spacious warehouse conversion with big windows overlooking river, excellent modern cooking inc fish and vegetarian dishes, and good wines; cl am Sat, pm Sun, 1 wk Christmas; well behaved children over 8; disabled access. **£18.50 3-course lunch, £34.50 dinner**.

WORCESTER SO8554 **King Charles II** *29 New St (01905) 22449* Inn from which King Charles II made his escape through the back door, closely pursued by Cromwell's forces; enjoyable food, open fires, and a relaxed atmosphere in downstairs restaurant and upstairs bar; cl Sun, 25–26 Dec. **£25**.

WYRE PIDDLE SO9647 **Anchor** *(01386) 552799* Relaxing 17th-c pub with lovely views across lawn and river and on over the Vale of Evesham; friendly little lounge with log fire, comfortable bar, and good popular food. **£21**|£7.

Special thanks to Mrs A D Buckley, Mr and Mrs Matthews, E G Parish, Linden Miller, Arthur and Margaret Dickinson, Dr and Mrs D E Awbery, B M Eldridge, Graham James, Mrs A Griffiths.

We welcome reports from readers

This *Guide* depends on readers' reports. Do help us if you can – in return, we offer a discount on the next edition to people who've helped us with reports for it. Tell us what you think about places already in it, and anything extra you think we should say about them. And send us your ideas for inclusion in the next edition: places to visit, eat at or stay in, attractive drives or walks, maybe even unusual interesting shops you know of. Use the card in the middle, the report forms at the end, or just write – no stamp needed: *The Good Guide to Britain*, FREEPOST TN1569, Wadhurst, E Sussex TN5 7BR.

Hereford & Worcester Calendar

Some of these dates were provisional as we went to press. Please check information with the telephone numbers provided.

JANUARY

23 Great Malvern Worcs & Malvern Dog Show at the Three Counties Showground (01684) 584900

FEBRUARY

27 Great Malvern Mid-Western Gundog Show at the Three Counties Showground (01684) 584900

MARCH

6 Worcester Music & Dance Weekend: living history at the Commandery – *till Sun 7* (01905) 355071

27 Leominster Easter Parade (01432) 260621

APRIL

2 Ross-on-Wye Real Ale Festival at the Crown & Sceptre – *till Mon 5* (01989) 562765; **Worcester** Living History Encampment at the Commandery – *till Mon 5* (01905) 355071

23 Redditch Medieval Street Fair – *till Sat 24* (01527) 64252

MAY

1 Upton upon Severn Folk Festival – *till Mon 3* (01684) 594200

2 Cropthorne Open Gardens Day: 18–20 gardens open – *till Mon 3* (01386) 860674; **Eastnor** Spring Country Craft Fair at Eastnor Castle – *till Mon 3* (01531) 633160

3 Kington Flower Fair at Hergest Croft Gardens (01544) 230160; **Leominster** May Fair (01568) 616460

7 Bromyard Spring Festival – *till Thurs 13* (01432) 260621; **Great Malvern** Spring Gardening Show at the Three Counties Showground – *till Sun 9* (01684) 584900

9 Nr Pershore Worcestershire Wildlife Trust Open Day at Tyddesley Wood Nature Reserve (01386) 554719

22 Droitwich Spa Arts Festival – *till 5 Jun* (01386) 565000; **Pershore** Horticultural College Open Day (01386) 552443

29 Upton upon Severn Oak Apple Day Celebrations – *till Mon 31* (01684) 594200; **Worcester** Oak Apple Festival at the Commandery: celebration of the Restoration of Charles II – *till Mon 31* (01905) 355071

30 Bretforton Silver Band Asparagus Auction at the Fleece (01386) 832717; **Pershore** Town Carnival – *till Mon 31* (01386) 565000

31 Eastnor Steam Fair & Country Show at Eastnor Castle (01531) 633160; **Pershore** Town Carnival (01386) 553233; **Ross-on-Wye** Bank Holiday Festival (01989) 563164

Hereford & Worcester Calendar (cont.)

JUNE

5 **Eastnor** Flower & Garden Show at Eastnor Castle – *till Sun 6* (01531) 633160; **Kington** Festival – *till Sun 20* (01544) 230743; **Leominster** Festival – *till Sun 13* (01568) 612874
12 **Broadway** Arts Festival – *till Sat 26* (01386) 565000
15 **Great Malvern** Three Counties Agricultural Show at the Three Counties Showground – *till Thurs 17* (01684) 584900
18 **Hereford** Flower Festival at the Cathedral – *till Sun 20* (01432) 260621
19 **Brockhampton** Poetry & Picnic at Lower Brockhampton (01885) 488099; **Bromsgrove** Charter Fair: starts festival week which runs *till carnival procession on Sat 26* (01527) 876663; **Kidderminster** Carnival (01562) 751634
20 **Hindlip** Agricultural College Open Day (01386) 552443
25 **Abbey Dore** Music Festival at Dore Abbey – *till Sun 27* (01981) 750315; **Upton upon Severn** Jazz Festival – *till Sun 27* (01684) 594200
26 **Tewkesbury** Herb Day at the Abbey (01684) 850959
29 **Canon Pyon** Traherne Festival – *till Weds 30* (01432) 260621

JULY

2 **Brockhampton** Evening of Music at Lower Brockhampton (01885) 488099
3 **Bromyard** Gala – *till Sun 4* (01432) 260621; **Pershore** Midsummer Brass Festival (01386) 552071
8 **Ledbury** Poetry Festival – *till Sun 18* (01531) 636147
9 **Eastnor** Art of Living Decorative Arts Fair at Eastnor Castle – *till Sun 11* (01531) 633160
10 **Evesham** River Festival & Illuminated Boat Rally – *till Sun 11* (01386) 442338; **Madley** Festival – *till Sun 18* (01981) 550293
11 **Kidderminster** Open Gardens Day: 12 gardens open (01562) 755817
16 **Eastnor** Malvern Classic Mountain Bike Rally at Eastnor Castle – *till Sun 18* (01531) 633160
23 **Welland** Steam Rally – *till Sun 25* (01684) 594200
24 **Pembridge** Show (01544) 388414
26 **Pershore** Dance Festival – *till Fri 30* (01386) 860266
29 **Eardisley** Village Spectacular – *till Sat 31* (01432) 260621
30 **Hereford** Beer Festival at the Spread Eagle – *till 1 Aug* (01432) 260621

AUGUST

2 **Tewkesbury** Musica Deo Sacra Week at the Abbey – *till Sun 8* (01684) 850959
7 **Ross-on-Wye** Carnival (01989) 562768; **Tenbury Wells** Show (01584) 810666
8 **Eastnor** Herefordshire Country Fair at Eastnor Castle (01531) 633160
14 **Eastnor** Model Spectacular at Eastnor Castle – *till Sun 15* (01531) 633160; **Pershore** Flower & Craft Show (01386) 554235
16 **Eastnor** Children's Fun Week at Eastnor Castle – *till Fri 20* (01531) 633160
19 **Ross-on-Wye** International Festival – *till Mon 30* (01989) 563330
21 **Worcester** Three Choirs Festival at the Cathedral – *till Fri 27* (01905) 28854

Hereford & Worcester Calendar (cont.)

22 **Leominster** Family Fun Day (01432) 260621
27 **Hereford** Beer Festival at the Barrels – *till Mon 30* (01432) 268430
28 **Abbey Dore** Welsh Male Choir at Dore Abbey (01981) 240075; **Great Comberton** Flower Show (01386) 710529; **Upton upon Severn** Water Festival – *till Mon 30* (01684) 594200
30 **Brockhampton** Civil War Re-enactment at Lower Brockhampton (01885) 488099; **Ledbury** Carnival (01531) 633172; **Madresfield** Agricultural Show at Home Farm (01684) 576604; **Ross-on-Wye** Regatta (01989) 564100; **Wychavon** Angling Competition (01386) 565000
31 **Eastnor** Hot Air Balloon Meet at Eastnor Castle – *till 1 Sept* (01531) 633160

SEPTEMBER

4 **Eastnor** Living History at the time of the Wars of the Roses at Eastnor Castle – *till Sun 5* (01531) 633160
10 **Hereford** Photography Festival – *till 14 Oct* (01432) 344039
11 **Kington** Show (01432) 260621
12 **Wychavon** Festival of Brass (01386) 41648
17 **Bromyard** Folk Festival – *till Sun 19* (01531) 670249
18 **Redditch** Carnival (01527) 64252
25 **Great Malvern** Autumn Show at the Three Counties Showground – *till Sun 26* (01684) 584900
26 **Leominster** Apple & Fruit Festival: tastings, competitions, live music (01568) 616348

OCTOBER

2 **Eastnor** Christmas Craft Fair at Eastnor Castle – *till Sun 3* (01531) 633160; **Malvern** Autumn in Malvern Festival – *till Sun 10* (01684) 569721
16 **Much Marcle** Big Apple Weekend – *till Sun 17* (01432) 260621

NOVEMBER

11 **Leominster** Victorian Street Fair (01432) 260621
27 **Bromyard** Christmas Lights & Festivities – *till Sun 28* (01432) 260621; **Leominster** Christmas Lights (01432) 260621

Please let us know what you think of places in the *Guide*. Use the report forms at the back of the book or simply write us a letter.

Hertfordshire

Some pleasant outings, patches of quiet countryside.

Though much of the county is built up, there are attractive villages and good escapes into protected countryside. Highlights for most adults are the Henry Moore sculpture garden at Much Hadham and in summer the rose gardens just outside St Albans which itself is rewarding to visit, especially for its Roman remains. The zoological museum at Tring is remarkably intriguing. Good family outings include Knebworth, Standalone Farm on the edge of Letchworth and the friendly wildlife park at Broxbourne.

Where to stay

CHIPPERFIELD TL0401 **Two Brewers** *The Common, Chipperfield, Kings Langley WD4 9BS (01923) 265266* **£78.90w;** 20 comfortable rms. Comfortable and very neatly kept country hotel with relaxing views of pretty village green, dark-beamed main bar with cushioned antique settles, bow-windowed lounge with comfortable sofas and easy chairs, open fires, and good bar and restaurant food; pleasant nearby walks; disabled access.

ST ALBANS TL1407 **White Hart** *Holywell Hill, St Albans AL1 1EZ (01727) 853624* **£60;** 11 rms, most with own bthrm. Comfortable and civilised former coaching inn with 2 bar areas, antique panelling, handsome fireplaces and furnishings, residents' lounge reached by barleytwist staircase, courteous friendly service, and good restaurant.

To see and do

ST ALBANS TL1407 Though modern shops dominate your first impressions, corners of real antiquity are tucked away between and behind them. This was one of the most important Roman towns in northern Europe, and has some fine, well excavated remains in peaceful surroundings. There are other notable buildings: the tourist information office in the Town Hall, Market Pl, has helpful guide maps. Down between the abbey gate and the park, the Fighting Cocks is based on an ancient building which had some connection with the abbey, and its interesting layout includes the clearly discernible shape of a cockpit. In the quietly attractive, largely Georgian St Michael's St, the Rose & Crown is very civilised, and the Six Bells is on the site of a Roman bath-house, though not visibly so. The Cock (Hatfield Rd) is worth looking out because of its bizarre history; its floors were found to rest on thick foundations of human bones. Worth a look if you're nearby are the **museum** (Hatfield Rd), covering the town's post-Roman history (disabled access to ground floor; cl am Sun, 25 Dec; free), and **Grebe House** in the park nr Verulamium, a regional nature trust HQ with a woodland garden (cl wknds and bank hols; free). The B651 N towards Hitchin is quite a scenic country drive.

Verulamium This was the Roman city; its remains are down in the south-west corner of town, past the cathedral and attractive park (coming from outside, most easily reached by the A4147 off the Hemel Hempstead exit from the M1, junction 7). The place to start is the excellent **Verulamium Museum** (St Michael's St), with its lively interpretation of everyday Roman life, as well as jewellery, wall-paintings and domestic items found nearby. Shop, disabled access; cl am Sun, 25–26 Dec; (01727) 819339; £2.80. Follow signs from here into the adjacent playing fields: an unassuming brick building looking like changing rooms houses the carefully restored mosaic floor and hypocaust underfloor heating system of an excavated villa; free. Further on is a good section of the Roman town wall.

Roman theatre Most impressive; not large compared with some others (room for 1,600), but taking into account its good state of preservation it's unique. Shop, limited disabled access; cl 25 Dec, 1 Jan; (01727) 835035; £1.50.

St Albans Cathedral Up on a mound, this has good views; its 11th-c reddish exterior uses flint recycled from the Roman remains. Once the country's premier abbey, it suffered after the Reformation, and its fortunes didn't revive until Victorian times. It was touched up a lot then, but the majestic interior does have some earlier features, inc 13th- and 14th-c paintings in the long nave, and some Saxon transept pillars. Meals, snacks, shop, disabled access; cathedral free, £1.50 for audio-visual show. The great 14th-c **abbey gatehouse** beyond leads down to a neat park, its lake and willow-edged stream packed with ducks.

Medieval clock tower This striking free-standing stone building has a bell, striking on the hour, even older than the tower itself. Exhibitions on the way up and fine views from the top; open wknds and bank hols Easter–mid-Sept; 25p. Nearby, French Row is a narrow alley of striking timbered buildings jettied out over the street, right by a modern shopping centre. The Fleur de Lys pub here is a remarkable medieval building.

Organ Museum (Camp Rd, 2m E of centre) Tuneful collection of automatically operated organs and other musical instruments, inc Wurlitzer and Rutt theatre organs. Recitals every Sun 2–4.30pm, and concerts once a month. Shop, disabled access (but no facilities); open pm Sun only; (01727) 869693; £2.

Gardens of the Rose (Chiswell Green; on the B4630 S) The showgrounds of the Royal National Rose Society, with over 1,600 cultivars, many in mass plantings. Plenty of interesting cultivation trials going on, new roses from all over the world, lots of clematis, and a new iris garden. Snacks, shop, disabled access; open Sun and bank hols Apr–May and all Jun–Sept; (01727) 850461; £4. The Holly Bush at nearby Potters Crouch has decent food (not Sun).

Kingsbury Watermill 16th-c watermill half a mile from the city on the River Ver, still with one working waterwheel and a museum. Good meals, snacks, shop, disabled access; cl 25 Dec; (01727) 853502; *£1.10.

Gorhambury TL1107 2 miles out of St Albans (the other side of Verulamium's park) but peaceful enough to make you think it's the heart of the country, an 18th-c house with an extensive assemblage of 17th-c family portraits, and some 16th-c enamelled glass. Open pm Thurs May–Sept; (01727) 855000; £4.

Days Out

Distinctly East Anglian: Braughing; Westmill – lunch at the Sword in Hand there, or the Jolly Waggoner, Ardeley; Cromer windmill (limited opening); Benington village and Benington Lordship (limited opening).

Romans and roses: St Albans Abbey; Verulamium Roman town, amphitheatre and museum; lunch at the Waffle House (St Michael's St), St Albans; Gardens of the Rose.

Other things to see and do

HERTFORDSHIRE Family Attraction of the Year

TRING SP9211 **Zoological Museum** (Akeman St, off High St) Part of the Natural History Museum, this remarkable place is quite different from most of the animal attractions we recommend: for a start, all the residents here are stuffed, and displayed in very traditional glass cases. For children even slightly interested in wildlife it's fascinating, not least because they can get so much closer to the creatures here than they ever could anywhere else. It's quite a thrill standing right next to a tiger or lion, even though it's not moving – you can't help thinking that any minute it's going to leap at you out of the case. Based on the remarkably eclectic collections of the second Lord Rothschild, started when he was a little boy, the museum has thousands of preserved mammals, insects, birds, fish and reptiles, with probably more species on display than anywhere else in the world. There are domestic dogs, giant tortoises and dressed fleas, but most intriguing are the cases showing off now-extinct creatures such as the zebra-like quagga, or huge giant moa. It's all much as it was when first opened to the public in 1892, and though children will be busily concentrating on the animals, older visitors may pick up something of the period atmosphere you get in a place like the Pitt-Rivers Museum in Oxford. Some might find it a little eerie, and if the idea of looking at weird and wonderful creatures in cases doesn't immediately appeal then you won't get too much out of it, but it holds most visitors spellbound for a couple of hours. They don't have a tearoom, but there are places to picnic, one outside. Shop, limited disabled access; cl am Sun, and 23–26 Dec; (01442) 824181; £2.50, £1.25 children over 5 (under 5s are free, but some might find the displays slightly startling). Entry is free after 4pm wkdys, and 4.30pm wknds and bank holidays, though as it shuts at 5pm you'd have to dash round a bit to see everything then.

ALDENHAM TQ1695 **Country Park** Plenty of space for children to run around in, with adventure play area, nature trails and a herd of longhorn cattle.

★ **ALDBURY** SP9612 A perfect village green, stocks, etc, attractive houses, teas, 2 good pubs; good walks nearby.

★ **ARDELEY** TL3027 Attractive thatched village with good food at the Jolly Waggoner, and a pleasant quiet drive along the lane down through Wood End, Haultwick and Dane End. This rolling countryside is very rural, with quite an East Anglian flavour: some of Hertfordshire's best walking territory. **Cromer windmill** (just NW) Partly 13th-c, lovingly restored, the last remaining post-mill in the county. In Mar 1998 the sails turned for the first time since 1920. Open pm Sun, bank hols and alternate Sats mid-May–Aug; (01992) 504331; *£1.20.

★ **ASHWELL** TL2639 Attractive village with some fine houses and an unusually tall church tower; the Bushel & Strike just beside it and the Three Tuns are both useful for lunch.

★ **AYOT ST LAWRENCE** TL1916 Delightful little backwater, with a very picturesque 12th-c ivy-covered **ruined church**; the existing **church** is an incongruously grand neo-Grecian affair. **Shaw's Corner** Much as it was when GBS lived here, 1906–1950; Shaw devotees will enjoy seeing his exercise machine, pen, spectacles, and even the soft Homburg he wore for 60 years. The tiny writing shed at the bottom of the garden was designed to revolve and so maximise sunlight. Open pm Weds–Sun and bank hols, Apr–Oct; (01438) 820307; £3.20; NT. The Brocket Arms is an enjoyably old-fashioned inn. The village is conveniently close to link to a walk along the River Lea, which has been dammed at Brocket Hall to form a lake (in view from the public right of way). Shorter walks can start from the Waggoners at Ayot Green; an

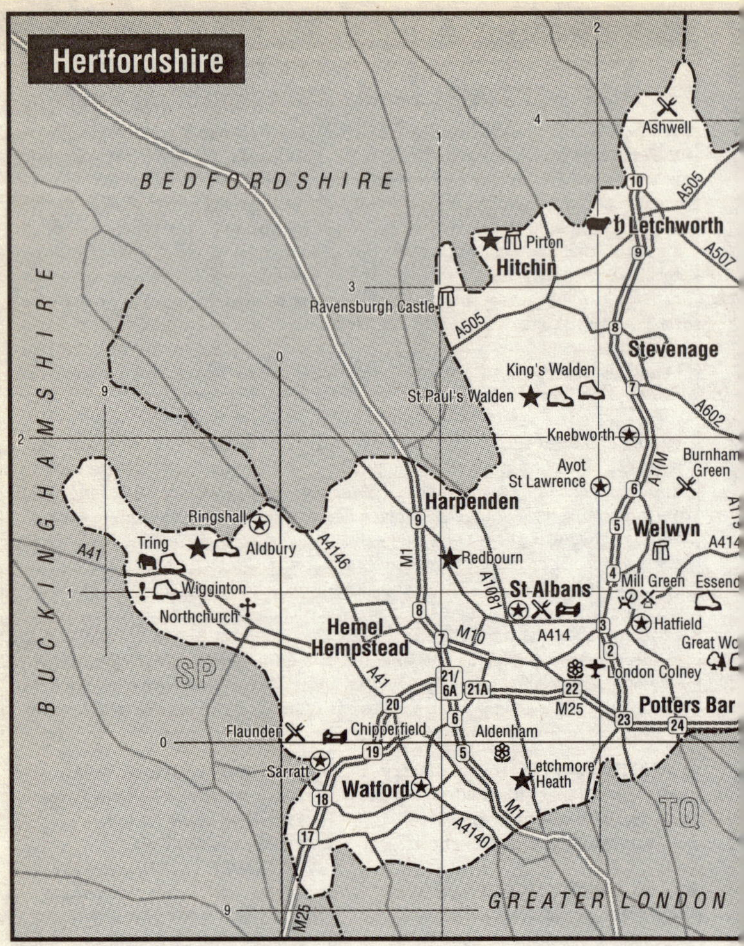

abandoned railway line is open to walkers and forms a useful link.

BENINGTON LORDSHIP TQ2923 7 acres of Edwardian terraced gardens with many unusual plants, fine herbaceous borders, roses and rock garden, and a particularly lovely splash of snowdrops in spring. The grounds include a very picturesque early 19th-c 'Norman' ruined gatehouse, actually put together from stones of the genuinely Norman ruined moated keep. Snacks; open pm Weds Apr–Sept and Sun Apr–Aug, plus pm bank hols, 3rd Sun in Oct for plant sales, and some dates Feb/Mar for snowdrops – ring for details; (01438) 869668; *£2.70. The village is one of the county's prettiest and most interesting, its church lovely when the snowdrops are out. The handsome old Bell has generous food. The countryside around offers some of Hertfordshire's better walking.

★ † **BRAUGHING** TL3924 (pronounced Braffing) Attractive village with pretty 14th-c riverside church; decent pub.

BROXBOURNE TL3306 **Paradise Wildlife Park** (White Stubbs Lane, W) Friendly little zoo and leisure park with lions, monkeys, camels and zebras, events from meeting the python to feeding the lions, and adventure playground, crazy golf,

woodland walk and paddling pool. Meals, snacks, shop, disabled access; cl 25 Dec; (01992) 468001; £6. The Coach & Horses at Newgate Street does enjoyable food, and there are good woodland walks around here.

ESSENDON TL2708 The mildly hilly, partly wooded country around here is popular with weekend walkers, with pleasantly varied village-to-village paths.

★ **GREAT AMWELL** TL3612 Pretty conjunction of church, pre-Norman Emma's Well and pool with islets. The Van Hage Garden Co have an unusually lively **garden centre** here, good for an afternoon out, with children's farm, and plenty to look at in addition to their excellent range of plants. Miniature railway some summer wknds. Meals, snacks, shops, disabled access; (01920) 870811; free.

★ **GREAT HORMEAD** TL4029 An attractive village, plenty of thatch and timbering.

GREAT WOOD TL2704 (off the B157 N of Northaw; the Two Brewers is a useful stop) Pretty walks in ancient woodland.

† **HATFIELD HOUSE** TL2308 In extensive parkland, this great Jacobean house was built in 1611 on the site of a childhood home of Elizabeth I; the splendid State Rooms include portraits of the queen, and even her silk stockings, perhaps among the earliest worn in this country. Also the National Collection of Model Soldiers, with over 3,000 exhibits. The scented garden and knot garden contain plants that were typical between the 15th and 17th c. Meals, snacks, shop, disabled access; open Apr–Sept, park and gardens every day, house cl am and all day Mon exc bank hols. No guided tours Sun or bank hols; (01707) 262823; £5.70, £3 park and garden only. The nearby **church** has a window by Burne-Jones and the attractive village of Old Hatfield has a fine old pub (the Eight Bells). Beyond is the New Town that has taken the Hatfield name.

HERTFORD TL3212 Some quiet older parts include the old main Fore St, which has handsomely pargeted buildings one of them the relaxing old Salisbury Arms Hotel. There are several antique shops in St Andrew St (one in a fine 15th-c house). The so-called **castle** is in fact the 15th-c gatehouse for Edward IV's original moated castle, carefully restored and now occupied by the council; open pm 1st Sun in month May–Sept; free. The extensive riverside grounds (with the massive flint walls of Henry II's castle) are always open. **Hertford Museum** (Bull Plain) Cheery local history museum, in an elegant 17th-c building; it has a graceful Jacobean knot garden. Shop, disabled access to ground floor and garden; cl Sun, Mon (exc bank hols), 25–26 Dec and Good Fri; (01992) 582686; free. McMullens Brewery is a striking riverside Victorian building.

The Old Barge by the Lee Navigation Canal has a wide choice of vegetarian food among other dishes. Nearby Hertingfordbury is attractive, between river and beechwoods.

KING'S WALDEN TL1623 This quiet village and the rolling farmland around it is pleasant walking territory.

! KNEBWORTH HOUSE, GARDENS & COUNTRY PARK TL2221 The house at the centre of this 250-acre park was originally a straightforward Tudor mansion, but was spectacularly embellished by Victorian author Edward Bulwer-Lytton; he wanted it to be a castle fit for the romantic characters in his novels. Still a lived-in home, the grand rooms include a splendid Jacobean great hall, and mementos of former guests like Dickens and Churchill. The gardens were designed by Lutyens, and include a herb garden laid out to plans by Gertrude Jekyll; also a deer park, maze and miniature railway. There's an exceptionally good adventure playground – in addition to the usual wooden climbing equipment and so forth there are quite a few exciting slides, inc the monorail suspension slide (which basically means you hang on to a rope and then slide down back to the ground), and the twisting Corkscrew. Meals, snacks, shop, limited disabled access; open wknds and school hols Easter–Sept, house cl am and all day Mon, and occasionally for special events; (01438) 812661; £6 for everything, £4 grounds only (including playground and railway). Along the outer edge of the park is the pretty little hamlet of Old Knebworth; the Lytton Arms here is a good pub.

LETCHWORTH TL2232 The country's first garden city, begun in 1903. The **First Garden City Heritage Museum** (Norton Way S), set in the architects' charming Arts & Crafts-style thatched cottages, shows the thinking behind this uniquely 20th-c idea. Shop, disabled access; cl Sun, 25–26 Dec; (01462) 482710; *£1. The nearby Three Magnets (Leys Ave) is a fine new pub. **Standalone Farm** (Wilbury Rd) Simple and unfussy working show farm, best for younger children with a genuine interest in animals. Milking demonstrations every day at 2.30pm, and in Mar and Apr (definitely the best time to come) you can bottle-feed new-born lambs (usually at 12 and 4pm). Also pigs, free-range chickens and rare breeds of poultry wandering round the farmyard, exhibition barn with working beehive, model dinosaurs and various creepy-crawlies, outdoor play area, and 170 acres of farmland, with walks and arboretum. Shire horse wagon rides wknds and school hols. Teas, shop, disabled access; cl Oct–Feb (exc autumn half-term); (01462) 686775; £2.70.

LONDON COLNEY TL1902 **De Havilland Heritage Museum** (next to Salisbury Hall, off the B556) The Mosquito bombers were developed here in secret from 1939, and now the site houses a collection of 20 different de Havilland aircraft, as well as engines and other memorabilia. Snacks, shop, disabled access; open Mar–Oct, pm Tues, Thurs and Sat, all day Sun and bank hols; (01727) 822051; £4. There are pretty riverside gardens down by the bridge. **Aylett Nurseries** (on the A414 N) Enthusiastically run garden centre specialising in geraniums, fuchsias and especially their award-winning dahlias. Meals, snacks, disabled access; cl 25–27 Dec, Easter Sun; (01727) 822255. The trial grounds for the dahlias are at **Bowmans Farm**, 5 minutes away by car – you can walk round free from Aug to the first frost of autumn. The farm itself has become quite a draw, not least because of its huge **farm shop**, practically a supermarket (though cheaper for most things), with an enormous range of produce. Also animals, tractor rides, lakeside walks, and play areas. Meals, snacks, disabled access; cl 25–26 Dec; (01727) 821253; shop free, farm £3.75.

MILL GREEN TL2309 **Mill Green Museum** Well restored working watermill with craft demonstrations most Suns Apr–Sept and Sats July and Aug, from paper-quilling to love-spoon carving. Shop, disabled access to ground floor only; cl am wknds, all day Mon, milling Tues, Weds and pm Sun; (01707) 271362; free.

★ MUCH HADHAM TL4319 **Henry Moore Foundation**

The excellent sculpture garden here is very enjoyable. Several works are displayed in the studios where they were made, while the larger ones are shown off against a backdrop of woodland, pasture and hedgerows. Open wkdys only for 90-minute guided tour at 2.30pm, must book; (01279) 843333; £3. The village is attractive, with fine Tudor and Georgian houses, a good specialist nursery (Hopleys), and an enjoyable family dining pub (Jolly Waggoners). **Forge Museum** (High St) Based around a working blacksmith, the story of such craftsmen through the ages, with an unusual bee shelter in the Victorian-style garden. Snacks, shop, some disabled access; open Fri–Sun in summer, in winter by appointment on wkdys only; (01279) 843301; 80p.

NORTHCHURCH SP9609 Largely swallowed up in Berkhamsted, but notable for the ancient church where Peter the Wild Boy is buried; the George & Dragon is handy for lunch.

★ **PIRTON** TL1431 Attractive village; the green is actually the remains of a Norman motte and bailey.

RAVENSBURGH CASTLE TL1029 Up in the woods above Hexton, this is an easily traced Iron Age hill fort.

RINGSHALL SP9912 **Ashridge Estate** Right on the county border and nr Whipsnade Zoo in Beds, 4,000 acres of unspoilt woodlands and open spaces. Plenty of deer and other wildlife (inc the dormouse, though you won't see it in daylight), and a monument erected for the Duke of Bridgewater. Teas summer wknds, shop and information centre, disabled access; monument and facilities cl am, Fri, and Nov–Mar; (01442) 851227; monument £1; NT. The Greyhound and Valiant Trooper at Aldbury just below are good for lunch.

★ **ST PAUL'S WALDEN** TL1922 Birthplace of the Queen Mother, a quiet village in good rolling walking country.

★ **SARRATT** TQ0498 Long and attractive village green; the church is partly Saxon, and the Cock nearby is good. There are pleasant unspoilt walks from here into the Chess Valley in Bucks.

SAWBRIDGEWORTH TL4815 **Keksy's Farm** (off the A1184) Working farm with sheep, cattle, poultry, rabbits and rare breeds of pig; there's coarse fishing on the river, and a campsite. Disabled access; cl Oct–Easter; (01279) 600896; £2. The George IV (nr the station) has a good restaurant, and the Coach & Horses up at Thorley Street is a good-value family food pub.

SCALES WOOD TL4133 (nr Anstey) A useful strolling ground.

★ **STANDON** TL3822 Has some good timbered buildings in its curving High St.

TRING SP9211 *See separate Family Panel on p.325* for the **Zoological Museum**. Tring has a choice of **canal towpath walks** from nr the Grand Junction Arms pub (on the B488 at Bulbourne), where the Grand Union Canal has a part-abandoned offshoot, the Wendover Arm, and the still-operational Aylesbury Arm. (There's also canal access from the Boat down Ravens Lane in Berkhamsted SP9807, the Fisheries at Boxmoor TL0306 and the King's Head at Hunton Bridge TL0800.) For more ambitious walkers, the Royal Hotel on Station Rd stands by the Ridgeway long distance path, which heads off W right across southern England. The Cow Roast (on the A4521 towards Berkhamsted) has good food (and popular family barbecues).

! **WARE** TL3513 **Scott's Grotto** (Scotts Rd) Built in the 1760s by the poet John Scott, one of the finest bits of romantic gothickry in the world, extending 20 metres (67ft) into the hillside under a modern housing development, with underground passages and chambers decorated with flints, shells, stones and minerals. Wear flat shoes and bring a torch. Open pm Sat and bank hols Apr–Sept, or by appointment; (01920) 464131; donation requested. Several private gardens running down to the quiet River Lee have antique gazebos over the water, neatly restored with crisp white paintwork. The A10 N of here is quite a pleasant road, with decent food at the Sow & Pigs.

WATFORD TQ1097 **Cheslyn Gardens** An unexpected pleasure in this largely modern urban area, with 3½ acres of woodland and formal gardens, and an aviary; cl 25–26 Dec; free. From Cassiobury Park there are **canal boat trips** along the Grand Union Canal on bank hols and pm Sun Easter–Sept, plus Tues and Thurs in Aug; (01438) 714528; £4.50. The local **museum** (High St) has a display on the Watford Home Guard, the basis for the TV series *Dad's Army*. Shop, disabled access; cl 1–2pm Sat, all day Sun, bank hols; free.

WELWYN TL2315 **Roman Baths** (just off the A1(M), junction 6 – head towards Welwyn on the A1000, and counting the motorway slip roundabout as the first roundabout go nearly all the way round the second roundabout; the car park is through 2 5-barred gates) Excavated before the construction of the A1 and since then rather ingeniously preserved within the motorway embankment, this Roman bath house is all that remains of a 3rd-c villa. Very good condition, with explanatory displays. Shop, disabled access; cl am wkdys Jan–Nov (exc bank and school hols), all Dec, and occasional other dates; (01707) 271362; *£1.

★ **WESTMILL** TL3627 A happy combination of neat green, tiled cottages and fine old church; the Sword in Hand has decent food, and there are pleasant walks nearby.

! **WIGGINTON** SP9310 The landlord of the Greyhound here is very helpful with suggestions for walks; the 18th-c summerhouse in the woods is an odd find.

★ **Other attractive villages**, all with decent pubs, include partly thatched Barley TL3938, Cottered TL3129, Letchmore Heath TQ1597, Redbourn TL1012 (despite motorway noise Church End with its workhouse and Norman church is pretty) and Rushden TL3031.

Walking in Hertfordshire
Large areas are taken up by the northwards spread of London with continuous swathes of development, and by the first early 20th-c New Towns, the garden cities of Letchworth and Welwyn, and their more modern successors Hatfield, Hemel Hempstead and Stevenage. But between and beyond these are green windows of carefully preserved farmland and some more wooded countryside – good if not outstanding walking country. Elsewhere are large chunks of prairie-like arable farmland, but a positive point is that field paths are often in remarkably good condition and very adequately waymarked. Pubs handy for walks include the Clarendon Arms at Chandler's Cross TQ0698, Two Brewers on Chipperfield Common TL0401, Fish & Eels at Dobbs Weir TL3808 nr Hoddesdon, Bricklayers Arms and Green Dragon at Flaunden TL0100, Alford Arms at Frithsden TL0110, Huntsman at Goose Green TL3509 (for Hertford Heath), Cross Keys at Gustard Wood nr Wheathampstead TL1716, Five Horseshoes at Little Berkamsted TL2908, Cabinet at Reed TL3636, Harvest Moon at Thorley TL4718 and White Lion at Walkern TL2826.

Where to eat

ARDELEY TL3026 **Jolly Waggoner** *(01438) 861350* Friendly and pretty little pub with lots of woodwork, civilised relaxed atmosphere, carefully prepared food in bars and restaurant, good range of wines, well kept Greene King ales, and attractive garden; cl Mon; children over 7. **£29**|£5.

ASHWELL TL2639 **Bushel & Strike** *(01462) 742394* Popular dining pub with cheerful open-plan bar, neatly laid tables, a wide choice of good food in charming Edwardian conservatory restaurant, well kept real ales, friendly staff, and seats on terrace and in garden; cl pm Sun. **£20**|£7.75.

BURNHAM GREEN TL2616 **White Horse** *(01438) 798416* Thriving and civilised dining pub with attractive original black-beamed part by bar counter, big 2-floored extension (no smoking downstairs), very good-value food, friendly service from uniformed staff, and well kept real ales. **£18**|£4.95.

FLAUNDEN TL0101 **Bricklayers Arms** *(01442) 833322* Cottagey pub with roaring log fires, snug low-beamed rooms, bar snacks and more elaborate restaurant food (which can be eaten anywhere in the pub), good range of real ales and wines, and friendly efficient service; it does get busy at weekends. **£24.25**|£9.

ST ALBANS TL1307 **Waffle House** *Kingsbury Watermill, St Michael's St (01727) 853502* Little restaurant attached to mill (see **To see and do** *section, above*), serving delicious sweet and savoury waffles; riverside terrace; disabled access. **£10**.

WATTON AT STONE TL2919 **George & Dragon** *High St (01920) 830285* Civilised pub first licensed in 1603, with antiques, open fires, daily newspapers, friendly efficient service, first-class imaginative food in bar (good-value daily specials) and no smoking restaurant, and good house wines; cl 25 Dec; children must be well behaved. **£25**|£6.

WESTMILL TL3627 **Sword in Hand** *(01763) 271356* In a very attractive village, this 14th-c colour-washed pub is full of character, with exposed beams, log fires, and traditional-style furniture; partly no smoking dining room has nice views over garden and church, food is well presented and very good, ales are well kept, wines are decent, and there are plenty of seats on the terrace and in the garden, with a play area for children. **£19.45**|£7.50.

Special thanks to Bob and Maggie Atherton, C Patton, Mr M Brown, Charles Bardwell, Sylvia Fountain.

We welcome reports from readers

This *Guide* depends on readers' reports. Do help us if you can – in return, we offer a discount on the next edition to people who've helped us with reports for it. Tell us what you think about places already in it, and anything extra you think we should say about them. And send us your ideas for inclusion in the next edition: places to visit, eat at or stay in, attractive drives or walks, maybe even unusual interesting shops you know of. Use the card in the middle, the report forms at the end, or just write – no stamp needed: *The Good Guide to Britain*, FREEPOST TN1569, Wadhurst, E Sussex TN5 7BR.

Hertfordshire Calendar

Some of these dates were provisional as we went to press. Please check information with the telephone numbers provided.

St Albans Living Roman History at the Verulamium Museum *every second weekend in the month* (01727) 819339

JANUARY

1 **St Albans** New Year's Day Family Concert at the Cathedral (01727) 860780

FEBRUARY

14 **Hatfield** Snowdrop Sunday at Hatfield House – *also Sun 21* (01707) 262823

MARCH

6 **Hatfield** Listed Building Show at Hatfield House – *till Sun 7* (01707) 262823

MAY

1 **Hertford** Music Festival – *till Mon 31* (01992) 503129
3 **Hertford** Art Society Annual Open Exhibition – *till Sat 15* (01438) 723535
6 **Hatfield** Living Crafts: over 500 craftspeople at Hatfield House – *till Sun 9* (01705) 426523
15 **Rickmansworth** Festival Week – *till Sat 22* (01923) 772325
22 **Rickmansworth** Canal Festival – *till Sun 23* (01923) 778382
29 **Elstree** Country & Western Festival at Aldenham Country Park – *till Mon 31* (01344) 874787; **Redbourn** County Show – *till Sun 30* (01582) 792626
30 **New Mill** Canal Festival at Tring Wharf – *till Mon 31* (01442) 823378

JUNE

13 **Hatfield** *Much Ado About Nothing* at Hatfield House (01707) 262823; **Stevenage** Day inc arena events (01438) 766751
19 **Borehamwood** Carnival Parade (0181) 207 1382; **Hatfield** Festival of Gardening: lectures, guided tours, flower marquee, arena events at Hatfield House – *till Sun 20* (01707) 262823
25 **Chiswell Green** Gilbert & Sullivan in the Marquee at The National Rose Society (01727) 850461
26 **Borehamwood** Elstree Film Day (0181) 207 1382

JULY

3 **Borehamwood** Families Day: free event, arena, fair, stalls in Meadow Park (0181) 207 1382; **Chiswell Green** Open-air Concert at The National Rose Society (01727) 850461
4 **Hemel Hempstead** Lark in the Park: family fun day (01442) 260161; **Wilstone** Whitchurch Morris Men dancing outside the Half Moon *at noon* (01865) 766191

Hertfordshire Calendar (cont.)

10 Hatfield Folk Dance Festival at Hatfield House (01707) 262823
11 Chiswell Green Open-air Theatre at The National Rose Society – *till Sat 17* (01727) 850461
17 Hatfield Tudor Revels: reproduction of a busy Tudor village inc jousting and working crafts to celebrate the 500th anniversary of the building of the Old Palace in Hatfield Park at Hatfield House – *till Sun 18* (01707) 262823
18 Hemel Hempstead Carnival (01442) 260161
31 Chiswell Green National Show of Miniature Roses at The National Rose Society – *till 1 Aug* (01727) 850461

AUGUST

1 Knebworth Fireworks Concert at Knebworth House (01625) 575681
6 Hatfield Pottery & Ceramics Festival at Hatfield House – *till Sun 8* (01707) 262823
8 Hoddesdon Broxbourne Folk Festival (01992) 441946
13 Elstree Craft Fair at Aldenham Country Park – *till Sun 15* (01344) 874787; **Chiswell Green** Big Band Concert at The National Rose Society (01727) 850461
14 Chiswell Green concert at The National Rose Society (01727) 850461; **Hatfield** Organic Gardening Weekend at Hatfield House – *till Sun 15* (01707) 262823;
21 Hatfield Fireworks Concert at Hatfield House (01707) 262823
27 Chiswell Green Opera in the Marquee at The National Rose Society – *till Sat 28* (01727) 850461
30 St Albans Carnival (01727) 853046

SEPTEMBER

4 Watford Show (01923) 213971
10 Hatfield Fireworks Concert at Hatfield House – *till Sun 12* (01707) 262823
23 Letchworth CAMRA Beer Festival at Plinston Hall – *till Sat 25* (01462) 455976

OCTOBER

30 Hatfield Halloween Fireworks Party at Hatfield House (01707) 262823

NOVEMBER

5 Borehamwood Fireworks (0181) 207 1382
7 Hatfield Autumn Colours: gardens open at Hatfield House (01707) 262823
19 Hertford Medieval Night: street entertainers, stalls (01992) 551214

Please let us know what you think of places in the *Guide*. Use the report forms at the back of the book or simply write us a letter.

Isle of Wight

Good beaches, some of Britain's best weather, lots of interesting family events and places to visit; also under-rated coast and countryside, quiet off-season breaks.

In high summer there's plenty of scope for traditional family holidays here – and plenty of people enjoying them, with the main resorts and places to visit getting very busy. Away from the main tourist haunts, however, much of the island is surprisingly unspoilt and little visited. The most attractive scenery is in the west, the largest concentration of things to do in the east.

The family attractions here don't really go in for the new-fangled displays and technology that you can find on the mainland. The most satisfying children's outings are firmly traditional: Blackgang Chine, and its Robin Hill stablemate near Arreton (free return visits within 7 days now), and Brickfields Horse Centre at Binstead (pigs perform there too). Quite a few other enjoyable visits centre on animals or birds, particularly the Amazon Adventure at Newchurch and the bird and animal attractions at St Lawrence. Arreton has lots around it to entertain families. Osborne House at East Cowes is a highlight for many older people, and the new dinosaur museum near Brighstone brings interesting real-life authenticity to fossil hunting.

Outside the main holiday season the island feels fresh, uncrowded and leisurely. The coastal walks are the finest in south-east England – worth coming just for these. Inland are long curving chalk ridges (tracks often follow the crests) and forestry plantations with many signposted woodland trails. Many of the more child-oriented places close for six months over winter.

The crossing takes about 30 minutes – half that for the Portsmouth–Ryde catamaran, even less for the Southsea Hovercraft. Readers like the Lymington–Yarmouth trip best (you'll need to book in summer). Foot fares start at £7.90, cars from around £35 – though the very cheapest fares are usually at pretty anti-social times: (0990) 827744 for bookings from Portsmouth to Fishbourne or Ryde, and Lymington to Yarmouth; (01703) 334010 for Southampton–Cowes; (01705) 811000 for Hovercraft Southsea–Ryde (from £8.20 day return).

Once you're there, prices are rather on the low side compared with the mainland, and for longer stays some hotels do good-value package deals that include the ferry fare.

The island bus service is excellent, especially between May and September; a week's bus pass is good value, as is a daily Rover road/rail ticket.

Where to stay

BONCHURCH SZ5777 **Lake** *Shore Rd, Bonchurch, Ventnor PO38 1RF (01983) 852613* ***£54,** plus special breaks; 20 rms. Early 19th-c country house in 2 acres of pretty gardens, with lots of flowers and plants in 3 light and airy lounges (one is an attractive conservatory); bar, restaurant and enjoyable food; cl Nov–Feb; children over 3; dogs by prior arrangement.

BONCHURCH SZ5778 **Winterbourne** *Bonchurch, Ventnor PO38 1RQ (01983) 852535* **£136 inc dinner;** 14 rms, most with own bthrm, many with sea views and some in the coach house. Charming creeper-covered house with 4 acres of pretty grounds inc waterfalls, a stream, and small heated swimming pool; restful day rooms, good food in attractive restaurant, and friendly staff and resident owners; Charles Dickens wrote *David Copperfield* here; cl Nov–Mar; dogs welcome.

CHALE SZ4877 **Clarendon** *Chale, Ventnor PO38 2HA (01983) 730431* ***£74;** 15 rms inc 3 suites, plus winter special breaks. Warmly friendly hotel (and very well run Wight Mouse family pub, attached) with engaging helpful owners, lots of charm and character, comfortable sun lounge and cocktail bar, good food, wines and real ales, and an extraordinary collection of whiskies; excellent for families; disabled access.

RYDE SZ6092 **Ryde Castle** *Esplanade, Ryde PO33 1JA (01983) 563755* **£80;** 20 rms, many with sea views, and some quite modern. 16th-c castle with comfortable lounge, tapestries, a good bar, friendly helpful staff, enjoyable food in galleon-look restaurant, and excellent breakfasts.

ST LAWRENCE SZ5476 **Lisle Combe** *Bank End Farm, Undercliffe Drive, St Lawrence, Ventnor PO38 1UW (01983) 852582* ***£37;** 3 rms; shared bthrm. Elizabethan-style farmhouse in 5-acre coastal garden with great sea views, friendly courteous staff, and lovely paintings and furniture – it was once the home of poet Alfred Noyes and is still owned by the family; they keep their own rare breeds and waterfowl park, and are close to coves and beaches; must book months ahead (it's so popular with return customers); self-catering cottage; cl Christmas/New Year; no dogs.

SEAVIEW SZ6291 **Seaview** *High St, Seaview PO34 5EX (01983) 612711* ***£85,** plus special breaks; 16 attractively decorated rms, some with sea views and private drawing rooms. Small, friendly and spotlessly kept hotel with fine ship photographs in the chatty and relaxed front dining bar, an old-fashioned characterful back bar, good imaginative bar food, and a highly regarded evening restaurant; proper high tea for children; cl Christmas for 3 days; children over 5 in evening restaurant.

SHANKLIN SZ5779 **Luccombe Chine House** *Luccombe, Shanklin PO37 6RH (01983) 862037* **£76,** plus special breaks; 6 rms, all with four-posters and sea or garden views. Very friendly small hotel at the end of a long drive and surrounded by large wooded grounds – you can watch foxes and badgers at night taking food left for them on the lawn; homely lounge with help-yourself drinks tray, beams and inglenook fireplaces, very good food in cosy dining room; good walks; cl Dec and Jan; no children.

SHORWELL SZ4582 **Westcourt Farm** *Shorwell, Newport PO30 3LA (01983) 740233* ***£36;** 3 rms. Fine Elizabethan manor connected to a farm of 250 acres, with comfortable lounge/dining room, and a restful atmosphere; no smoking; lots of surrounding walks; cl Nov–Mar; children over 12.

VENTNOR SZ5577 **Royal** *Belgrave Rd, Ventnor PO38 1JJ (01983) 852186* **£90;** 55 well equipped rms. Friendly Victorian hotel with fine sea views, neat gardens with heated outdoor pool, spacious and comfortable day rooms, good food in attractive restaurant, and helpful service; disabled access.

YARMOUTH SZ3589 **Bugle** *The Square, Yarmouth PO41 0NS (01983) 760272* ***£66;** 8 rms, most with own bthrm (best to have one not above the lively bar). Bustling inn with bar decorated like the stern of a galleon, other panelled rooms, a friendly atmosphere, good bar and restaurant food, children's room, and sizeable garden; restaurant cl Sun and Mon; well behaved dogs welcome.

YARMOUTH SZ3589 **George** *Quay St, Yarmouth PO41 0PE (01983) 760331* **£120;** 17 comfortable rms. Pleasantly relaxing panelled bars, one with nautical theme, log fires, good food, prompt, courteous service, own gardens to private beach, and own fishing operation in Yarmouth and St Vaast.

To see and do

ISLE OF WIGHT Family Attraction of the Year

☺ ❄ ⛹ **BLACKGANG** SZ4876 **Blackgang Chine** This 40-acre leisure park is a useful retreat for families, especially those with younger children. Very much a fine weather outing, it's been livened up a bit in the last year by the addition of an enjoyable high speed water chute ride, and they've introduced an excellent policy on return visits: each ticket allows free entry for a second visit within 7 days. Perhaps the most interesting parts are the maritime museum at the restored quayside, with whale skeletons and a collection of shipwreck memorabilia, and the complete replica of a Victorian sawmill, inc working steam and oil engines. Lots of effort has been put into the displays and models of dinosaurs, goblins, and nursery rhyme scenes dotted around the gardens; as at its stablemate, the Robin Hill Country Park (*see Arreton entry, below*), the representations of a Wild West town, pirate ship and fairyland castle have been done with a fair bit of flair and panache, if not the high-tech wizardry you can now find in comparable mainland places. Small children can find plenty to interest them as they wander round, especially on summer evenings, when thousands of coloured lights add sparkle to even the more dated displays. The park is open till 10pm then, and we'd say that's definitely one of the most enjoyable times to visit. Also fossils and gemstones, a hedge maze, and several play areas, including one for toddlers. Meals, snacks, shop, some disabled acess; open Mar–Oct; (01983) 730330; £5.50 (children 3–13 £4.50). A family ticket (2 adults, 2 children) is £18.

☺ ❄ 🏠 🏰 **ALUM BAY** SZ3085 The beach here is famous for its multi-coloured sands from the different rock strata in the cliff that runs down to it; 20 shades of pinks, greys and ochres, showing up brightest after rain. The High Down Hotel towards Totland has decent food. **Needles Pleasure Park** Otherwise unremarkable clifftop pleasure park which stands out for its spectacular chairlift down to the beach, with wonderful views along the way. They sell little glass tubes with the sands carefully layered inside (or you can make your own). Meals, snacks, shop, disabled access; cl Nov–Mar; (01983) 752401; park entry free (though car parking is £3), then individual charges for attractions (return trip on the chairlift is £2.50). Glass-blowing demonstrations at adjacent **Alum Bay Glass** (not Sat or winter Sun; 80p); there's also a good factory shop. **Needles Old Battery** From Needles Pleasure Park it's a ¾-mile walk to this 19th-c Palmerstonian fortress (you can't go by car); the parade-ground shows off two 12-ton gun barrels salvaged from the sea, and there is a World War I exhibition. A longish underground tunnel leads to a look-out spot that gives stunning views of the Needles themselves, a group of wave-battered chalk pinnacles, and their lighthouse. Snacks; cl Fri and Sat (exc July and Aug), and Nov–Mar; (01983) 754772; £2.50; NT.

✝ 🏛 ⛁ ⚘ ☺ **ARRETON** SZ5386 A pleasant place with a delightful 13th-c **church** (which has a brass-rubbing centre). The White Lion is good for lunch, and the cross-island Wootton Bridge–Niton back road through here has quietly attractive views. **Arreton Manor** Lovely old mellow stone house, dating from around 1600, with splendid period furnishings and panelling, collections of lace and dolls, and the **National Wireless Museum** – Marconi made his pioneering experiments nearby. Meals, snacks, shop; cl, Sat (exc bank hol wknds), am Sun and Nov–Easter; (01983) 528134; £3. The nearby **Country Craft Village** has craft workshops, pub, and restaurant with home baking. **Haseley Manor** The largest and oldest manor house open on the island, some parts dating from 1310. The enthusiastic owners have put a lot of effort into restoring the place, and the 20 or so

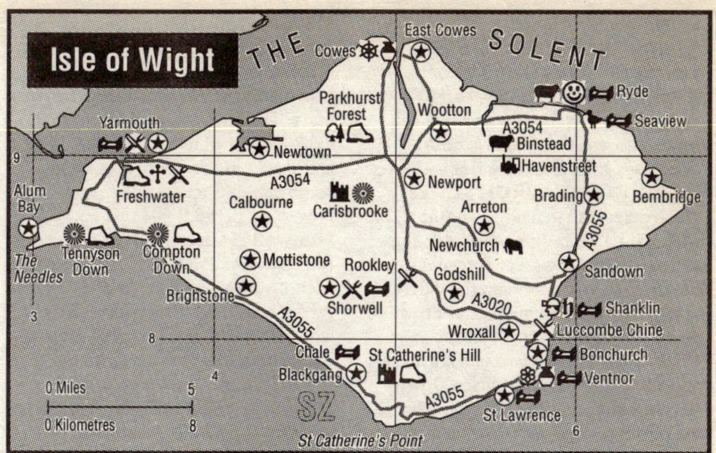

rooms are carefully decorated in period style. Also reconstructed 18th-c farm with animals, herb gardens, pottery and adventure playground, so a popular family day out. Snacks, shop, disabled access; cl Nov–Easter; (01983) 865420; £4.30. **Robin Hill Country Park** (Downend) A very useful retreat for families, particularly those with younger children. Like its stablemate Blackgang Chine it has a few rather dated-looking representations of trolls and the like, but scores more highly for activities and play areas, inc quite a few new slides, underground tunnels and assault-course style equipment. Paths and wooded trails wind through 88 acres, and there's a toboggan run, a pitch and putt course, look-out tower, wooden maze (like walking round lots of high garden fences), and plenty of space for football, basketball or just wandering round. Best in fine weather (most features are outdoors). Meals, snacks, shop, disabled access but rather hilly; cl Nov–Mar; (01983) 527352; £3.95 (you can return free within the next week).

BEMBRIDGE SZ6488
Even in summer this is quiet for a coastal place, though with plenty going on in its yachting harbour, and a lifeboat station nearby. Though most of Wight's east coast is heavily developed, with the coastal path sometimes following roads and skirting large residential areas, Bembridge has the best opportunities for walks. Out on the Foreland the magnificent rock pools would keep any beachcomber happy for hours. The Crab & Lobster (Forelands) has good seafood and fabulous views. There's also a good walk S to Culver Cliff, for more views. **Shipwreck Centre & Maritime Museum** (Sherbourne St) 6 galleries of salvage and shipwreck items, and tales of pirates and mermen. Shop, disabled access ground floor only; cl Nov–Mar; (01983) 872223; £2.35. **Bembridge Windmill** nearby is the only surviving windmill on the island, built in 1700 and used until 1913. Shop; cl Sat (exc Easter Sat and July–Aug) and Nov–Mar; £1.30; NT.

BINSTEAD SZ5792 **Brickfields Horse Country** (Newnham Rd)
2 daily parades of horses in the indoor arena (12 and 3.30pm), livened up by the appearance of a medieval knight, and a cowboy and Indian, who chase each other around firing pistols and flinging tomahawks. Also tours of stables, wagon rides, rabbits and guinea pigs, and a collection of Shetland ponies. This year they have branched out into pigs, with pig races 3 times a day. Show-jumping displays from 7pm on summer Weds (car boot sales Mon evenings), and on 3 evenings in mid-Dec they put on a spectacular Christmas show, which might include a pantomime and a Shetland pony Grand National. Meals, snacks, shop, disabled access; cl 25–26 Dec; (01983) 566801; *£4.50. The old White Hart at Havenstreet is handy and

a useful place for lunch.

❋ **BLACKGANG** SZ4876 *See separate Family Panel on p.336* for **Blackgang Chine** fantasy park. The Wight Mouse at Chale is an excellent family pub, and the A3055 in both directions gives fine sea and coast views.

† ❋ ⛰ **BONCHURCH** SZ5778 Much quieter than nearby Ventnor, with leafy lanes hugging the steep slopes and passing an unexpected tree-shaded pond; steep steps connect the different levels, and there's a quiet cove down below the cliff. The small 13th-c **church** has a lovely peaceful graveyard, and above the cliff St Boniface Down has tremendous views. The Bonchurch Inn is rather unusual, with its Italian landlord and food. For several miles along this section of coast, the cliffs have been and to some extent still are subject to massive landslides. The **Undercliff** is formed from the irregular masses of earth which have come to rest below, with often rocky chasms between each other and the cliff itself. Sometimes planted and sometimes with profuse natural vegetation, the resulting scenery is unlike anything else on the island, with quite a subtropical aspect. Some of the attractions along here we've listed in the St Lawrence entry, below. **Bonchurch Down** above has unsightly radar installations but gives walkers fine views.

★ † ⛫ ❋ **BRADING** SZ6086 Busy and attractive with interesting monuments in its Norman **church**, and a pretty graveyard. The Bugle is a useful family food pub. The remains of a **Roman villa** have good mosaics (cl Nov–Mar; *£2.50). **Lilliput Doll & Toy Museum** (High St) Excellent private collection, with over 2,000 exhibits starting from 2000 BC, and examples of almost every seriously collectable doll in Britain. Shop, disabled access (though there are 2 steps); cl 25 Dec; (01983) 407231; £1.55. **Isle of Wight Waxworks** (High St) In the partly 11th-c Ancient Rectory Mansion, this has an adjacent collection of stuffed animals and birds, and summer candle-carving demonstrations. Shop, mostly disabled access; (01983) 407286; £4.50.

Morton Manor (off the A3055 S) Friendly partly 13th-c manor house, set in lovely landscaped gardens with ornamental ponds and Elizabethan turf maze. The little vineyard has an exhibition of winemaking relics. Meals and snacks in new tearooms, shop, some disabled access; cl Sat, and Nov–Mar; (01983) 406168; £3.50. **Nunwell House & Gardens** (West Rd, off the A3055 NW) Lovely lived-in 16th-c house with 5 acres of charming gardens, and interesting furniture and family memorabilia. Charles I spent his last night of freedom here. Snacks, shop; cl am, all Thurs–Sun, and all Oct–Jun; (01983) 407240; £4 (including guide book), £2.50 garden only. The road out over Bembridge Down to Culver Cliff gives fine views, especially from the Culver Haven pub at the end.

! ⛰ ❋ **BRIGHSTONE** SZ4381 **Dinosaur Farm** (on the A3055 SE) One of most important dinosaur skeletons to be found in the UK was discovered here in 1992. An enthusiastic museum is dedicated to the find and you can watch the experts at work, preparing the bones for scientific research and display. Snacks, shop, disabled access; open Thurs and Sun Easter–Sept, plus Tues and Fri July and Aug; (01983) 740401; £1.75. The hills N of here represent some of the pick of the island's scenery, for walkers; the Countryman on Limerstone Rd is a good refreshment break, with fine views from the front garden down to the sea.

★ † ⌂ ✗ **CALBOURNE** SZ4186 Attractive village with photogenic streamside thatched cottages, 13th-c **church**, and an enjoyable working **pottery**; cl Sun Jan–Easter; shop open but no demonstration summer Suns and 2 wks at Christmas; *50p. It's worth getting here early to avoid the coach tours. Fine views from the Blacksmiths Arms, a good family pub on the B3401 E. **Calbourne Watermill & Rural Museum** (on the B3401) A 6-metre (20ft) waterwheel still powers this 17th-c mill, and the grounds have tame peacocks. Home-baked snacks, shop with stoneground flour, etc, some disabled access; cl Nov–Easter; (01983) 531227; £3.

CARISBROOKE CASTLE SZ4888 Ruins of the only medieval castle on the island, between 1647 and 1648 home to the imprisoned Charles I (his daughter died here in 1650). Some later buildings behind the imposing gatehouse and walls, and entertaining demonstrations of how donkeys drew water from one of the medieval wells. Snacks, shop, disabled access to ground floor; cl 24–26 Dec; (01983) 522107; £4. The Eight Bells above the waterfowl lake has decent food and Solent views.

COMPTON DOWN SZ3785 Another good place for walks on this south coast, a hogsback grassy hill E of Freshwater Bay; circular walks can take in the coast path along Compton Bay – one of the island's best beaches, not touristy, with impressive cliff views (NT car park).

COWES SZ4995 Stylish and lively, very much centred on its yachting connections, with interesting buildings and shops inc fascinating ships' chandlers in the long narrow High St, and the battery of over 20 brass cannons used to start the yacht races down by the harbour. The Union (Watchhouse Lane) has good-value food. Seafaring collections at the small **maritime museum** in the public library on Beckford Rd (cl Thurs and Sun, Christmas and 1 Jan; free), and at the pretty **Sir Max Aitken Museum** (open Tues–Sat May–Sept; *£1).

EAST COWES SZ5194 **Osborne House** (1m SE) Queen Victoria's favourite residence, where she died in 1901; the state and private apartments haven't changed much since. Designed to resemble an Italian villa, by Prince Albert with professional help from Thomas Cubitt, it's a striking place. Albert and his wife were also responsible for the original layout of the fine gardens, which seem filled with every conceivable English tree. A horse-drawn carriage conveys you in style to the Swiss cottage, where the royal children learnt cooking and gardening. Snacks, shop, disabled access to ground floor only; open daily Apr–Oct, phone for winter opening; (01983) 200022; £6.50. Down on the River Medina, the beautifully placed Folly Inn has an appropriately nautical atmosphere. Nearby **Whippingham church** was another of Prince Albert's designs, more eccentric than Osborne House: a bizarre mix of different styles.

FRESHWATER SZ3386 A very extended rather sprawling village, with a charming quiet core. The picturesque thatched **church** (built this century) includes quite a few Tennyson family memorials, and beyond it a causeway crosses the head of the Yar estuary. The Red Lion has good food, and the Vine has a pleasant terrace for warm days. There are fine walks nearby, and Hill Farm has riding.

★ ! **GODSHILL** SZ5281 Best appreciated in winter, when the coach parties that descend on the teahouses and quaint little streets have gone home. Plenty of famously pretty thatched cottages, and a 15th-c **church**, with interesting 15th-c wall-painting. The Cask & Taverners has good food. **Godshill Model Village** Painstakingly recreates Shanklin, its Chine valley and Godshill in miniature (there's even a model model village), and is nicely floodlit on summer evenings. Shop, disabled access; cl Nov–Feb; (01983) 840270; £2.25. **Old Smithy Tourist Centre** Based around a former blacksmith's forge, this has an aviary of exotic birds, and a garden in the shape of the island itself. Snacks, shop (with local crafts), disabled access; cl 25–26 Dec, gardens cl Oct–Mar; (01983) 840364; 80p. The **Nostalgia Toy Museum** (High St) has lots of post-war toys and die-cast model cars; cl Nov–Easter; £1.25. The **Natural History Centre** (High St) has a decent collection of fossils and minerals and some tropical fish and sea shells; shop, disabled access; cl Jan and Feb; *£1.25. There's a good walk via the Worsley Trail onto Stenbury Down (radio masts, but redeemed by wide views), then back via the atmospherically ruinous Appuldurcombe House (see *Wroxall entry, below*) and passing through a huge estate gateway.

HAVENSTREET SZ5589 **Isle of Wight Steam Railway** Well restored railway with very pleasant 10-mile trip from Wootton to Smallbrook Junction nr Ryde (where you can change directly onto main line trains). Vintage engines and rolling stock, and related memorabilia displayed in the old gasworks. Meals, snacks, shop, disabled access if accompanied; open Apr–Oct, phone for timetable; (01983) 884343; £5.50. The Island Line day ticket (around £7) includes the steam railway with travel on all regular trains on the island. The White Hart does good generous food.

★ **MOTTISTONE** SZ4083 Charming old village with a well in the centre of the green; even the bus shelter is stone-built. The Bluebell Wood opposite the church is lovely in spring. **Mottistone Manor** The attractive gardens are open pm Weds and bank hols Apr–Sept; on fine days there are teas; (01983) 740552; £2; NT. The medieval and Elizabethan manor house itself is open Aug bank hol only.

NEWCHURCH SZ5685 **Amazon World** (Watery Lane) Expanding collection of the kind of animals you'd find in an Amazon rain forest, with lively jungle and village settings; an effective mix of entertainment with environmental awareness. Also animal petting area and adventure playground. Meals, snacks, shop, disabled access; cl 25 Dec; (01983) 867122; £4.50. The village is quiet, with a photogenic church; the Pointer beside it has decent home cooking.

★ † **NEWPORT** SZ5089 The island's capital, with a good deal of character, some fine old Georgian houses, and warm red brick 18th-c buildings down by the quay. It's the main place on the island for antique shops. The parish **church of St Thomas** is worth a look – it has an interestingly carved Jacobean pulpit and a 19th-c memorial to Charles I's daughter. The 17th-c Wheatsheaf nearby is good for lunch. The Quay Arts Centre (Sea St) has craft fairs some Sats. **Newport Roman Villa** (Cypress Rd) Well preserved baths and reconstructed rooms on the site of a 3rd-c Roman villa, with an informative museum; also Roman garden. Shop; cl Sun and all Nov–Mar; (01983) 529720; £2. The back road to Brading has pleasant views.

NEWTOWN SZ4290 For a while this was the island's capital, but began a slow decline after a disastrous fire in 1377, and eventually faded out altogether – what used to be rich merchants' streets are now just grassy tracks. The **Old Town Hall**, rebuilt in 1699 but now left stranded and unusually isolated from any houses, is all that's left to mark the once thriving town; open pm Mon, Weds and Sun Apr–Oct, plus pm Tues and Thurs in July and Aug, Good Fri and Easter Sat; £1.20; NT. A boardwalk leads within minutes into the heart of a **nature reserve**, with walks around the tranquil Norfolk-like creeks of the Newtown/Clamerkin estuaries (but there are few circular routes). The New Inn at Shalfleet, open all day in summer, has good seafood.

PARKHURST FOREST SZ4891 Just W of the prison, this is a couple of miles across, with plenty of signposted paths and a good chance of seeing red squirrels.

RYDE SZ5992 Now the biggest town here, with a long triple pier, good sandy beaches, and a full set of holiday-resort amusements – just right for a straightforward family holiday. Free tours and tastings at the **Rosemary Vineyard** on Smallbrook Lane; (01983) 811084.

ST CATHERINE'S HILL SZ4978 Capped by the ruins of a 14th-c oratory, a short walk up from the coast path further E; you can walk on along a ridge to the prominent Hoy's Monument at the far end of St Catherine's Down. The coast path meanwhile skirts the undercliff of St Catherine's Point, the isle's southern tip, which has a modern working lighthouse; there are several other paths through the undercliff here.

ST LAWRENCE SZ5476 **Rare Breeds & Waterfowl Park** (Lisle Combe, Undercliff Drive) Good rare breeds centre in really lovely setting, covering 30 secluded coastal acres. They are building new walk-through aviaries and have smaller animals for younger children (inc a guinea pig village). Meals, snacks, shop, disabled access (they prefer notice); cl winter wkdys and 25 Dec; (01983) 852582; £3.50. They do B & B in the attractive old house. **Isle of Wight Glass**, Demonstrations (not wknds), lovely displays, and shop. Disabled access (but no facilities); cl winter wknds and 2 weeks at Christmas; (01983) 853526; 60p.

SANDOWN SZ6084 All the usual things for a family beach holiday – pier, boat trips, canoeing lake, discos – and a fine beach. You can usually tour the partly underground winery of **Adgestone Vineyard** on Upper Rd, but must book; (01983) 402503; free. **Sandown Zoo** Rare and endangered animals like tigers, panthers and leopards, as well as a notable collection of poisonous snakes and primates. Summer meals and snacks, shop, disabled access; cl Nov–mid-Feb (exc wknds); (01983) 403883; £4.90. **Museum of Geology** (High St) Small but interesting collection of local fossils and rocks, with recently excavated dinosaur fossils. Shop, some disabled access; cl Sun, 25–26 Dec and 1 Jan; (01983) 404344; free. This year the collection should show the benefits from a £1 million grant from the Millennium Commission.

SEAVIEW SZ6291 A timelessly quiet retreat, with sedate streets of unassuming villas; the Seaview Hotel does very good lunches. **Flamingo Park** (Springvale, just W) Hundreds of birds in spacious landscaped grounds; some can be fed by hand. Meals, snacks, shop, disabled access; cl Nov–Easter; (01983) 612153; £4.25.

SHANKLIN CHINE SZ5881 Quite glorious natural gorge with magnificent 14-metre (45ft) waterfall. A heritage centre gives details of rare flora, nature trails and life in Victorian Shanklin. Snacks, shop, some disabled access; cl mid-Oct–Easter; (01983) 866432; *£2. Down on the beach, the thatched Fisherman's Cottage is useful for lunch (open all day in season, cl Nov–Mar), and up at the top the Chine Inn is a good-value family pub (no food Sun evening, Tues or Sat).

★ **SHORWELL** SZ4583 One of the few really pretty villages on the island to have escaped a flood of tourist interest, with charming streamside thatched cottages and a fine church; the attractive Crown is very good for lunch. **Yafford Mill Farm Park** (just S) Fun: a seal lives in a special enclosure beside the millpond of the working 18th-c watermill, various species of waterfowl fill the pools of the stream, and rare breeds of sheep and cattle graze along its banks. Also nature trails, wagons and traction engines (sometimes in steam), an adventure playground across the lane and a newly constructed 2ft 6in gauge railway. Meals and snacks, shop, disabled access; cl 25 Dec; (01983) 740610; £3.50.

TENNYSON DOWN SZ3285 On Wight's west tip, the best place of all for walkers here: a friendly grassy ridge and cliff walk rolled into one, with views over most of the island and across to the mainland. You pass the monument to Alfred Lord Tennyson (who lived nearby and loved this place),

Days Out

Tennyson's strolling ground: Yarmouth; Newtown Old Town Hall and nature reserve; lunch at the Eight Bells, Carisbrooke; Carisbrooke Castle; Calbourne; walk on Tennyson Down from Alum Bay, or visit Needles Old Battery – or the dinosaur museum nr Brighstone.

Thatched cottages and a ruined mansion: Godshill; Appuldurcombe House, Wroxall; lunch at the Spyglass, Ventnor; St Lawrence Rare Breeds & Waterfowl Park; Shorwell.

Queen Victoria's retreat: *either* Brickfields Horse Country, Binstead and Isle of Wight Steam Railway (described under Havenstreet) *or* Bembridge windmill and stroll on Culver Cliff; lunch at the Seaview Hotel, Seaview; Osborne House.

and the walk culminates in spectacular fashion above the Needles. You can walk the entire ridge from Freshwater Bay (summer bus service from Alum Bay to bring you back), or make a round walk from Alum Bay car park, past the Needles Old Battery and along to the monument, then up onto Headon Warren before going down to Alum Bay. The High Down Hotel (on the B3322) is another start point.

VENTNOR SZ5476 Relatively untouristy little town up on the cliff, the fairly restrained and decorous seafront down below linked to it by a tortuously steep loop of road; between them perched on ledges among the trees is quite a number of Victorian villas – many of them still private houses rather than guesthouses. Its great pride is the **Botanic Garden**, where an exceptional collection of subtropical plants makes the most of the mild climate (gardens free, 50p for temperate house); the Garden Tavern here has decent food and sea views. **Museum of Smuggling History** In the Botanic Garden (or more correctly under it) this demonstrates the tricks smugglers past and present have used to sneak in wool, brandy, tobacco or drugs. Meals, snacks, shop; cl Oct–Easter; (01983) 853677; *£2.20. There are two decent local history museums: the **Heritage Museum** on Spring Hill (limited disabled access; cl 12.15–2pm, pm Weds and Sat, all Sun, and Nov–May; 50p), and the **Longshoreman's Museum** on the Esplanade (cl Jan and Feb; *50p). The Spyglass is an interesting pub with superb sea views.

WOOTTON SZ5290 A terminus for the **steam railway** *(see Havenstreet entry, above)*. It has an attractive partly Norman **church**. The Sloop down overlooking the creek is a reliable food pub. **Butterfly World** (Staplers Rd) A tropical butterfly house, next to a 5-acre garden centre with watergardens and fountains; snacks, shop, disabled access (but no facilities); cl Nov–Easter; £3.60.

WROXALL SZ5480 **Appuldurcombe House** (off the B3327 W) Intriguing shell of Palladian house, nestling among grounds beautifully landscaped by Capability Brown. You can still catch something of the atmosphere of the days when this was one of the grandest houses on the island. The stables have been converted into holiday cottages, and they plan to open a falconry centre here in April 1999. Snacks, shop, some disabled access; cl Nov–Mar; (01983) 840188; £2.

YARMOUTH SZ3589 A lively place, its old harbour busy with yachts in summer. The **castle** was built as part of Henry VIII's coastal defences; it's in an excellent state, and you can see the Master Gunner's surprisingly homely parlour and kitchen. Outside, the open gun platform has good views of the harbour. Shop, disabled access to ground floor; cl Nov–Mar; (01983) 760678; £2. The Wheatsheaf here is popular for lunch. **Fort Victoria Country Park** Surrounding a 19th-c fortress, this has good views down over the Solent, as well as 50 acres of woodland and a mile or so of pebbly beach. In the grounds are a maritime heritage centre (£1), excellent aquarium (£1.90) and planetarium (£2). Snacks, shop, disabled access (exc planetarium); not all parts open winter – best to check first; (01983) 760860; park free. The adjacent **Fort Victoria model railway** is reckoned to be the biggest in the country, and the only one completely controlled by computer. Good shop; open Easter–Sept; (01983) 761553; £3. The unspoilt reed-fringed **Yar estuary** is skirted by a footpath along the former railway line S.

Where to eat

FRESHWATER SZ3487 **Red Lion** *(01983) 754925* Carefully run, civilised pub with comfortably furnished open-plan bar, lots of local pictures and photographs, open fires, an interesting and extensive range of food, real ales, nice little wine list, and seats outside; no children. **£19.50**|£7.50.

LUCCOMBE CHINE SZ5880 **Dunnose Cottage Tea Rooms** *(01983) 862585* 16th-c thatched cottage in 3 landscaped acres, all-day breakfasts, cream teas, snacks, good-value 3-course lunch, and lots of different teas; cl pm, and all Oct–Easter. **£12.95**|£5.

ROOKLEY SZ5083 **Chequers** *(01983) 840314* Comfortable lounge with easy chairs and settees by the end fire, lively public bar, large no smoking family room with exceptionally good facilities for children, and an extensive choice of consistently good bar food. **£16.60**|£5.65.

SHORWELL SZ4583 **Crown** *(01983) 740293* The big back garden with its trout-filled stream, ducks, doves and lilies is nice in summer, and there's an extended beamed lounge with log fire, good food, and friendly staff; disabled access. **£12**|£5.50.

YARMOUTH SZ3589 **Jireh House** *St James's Sq (01983) 760513* 17th-c guesthouse with friendly owners, a relaxed atmosphere, and a range of home-made meals, snacks and afternoon tea inc daily specials and fresh fish; cl Nov–just before Easter; disabled access (restaurant only). **£9.50**|special afternoon tea £5.50.

YARMOUTH SZ3589 **Wheatsheaf** *Bridge Rd (01983) 760456* Handy for the ferry, this inn has 4 comfortable and spacious eating areas inc airy conservatory with wide choice of good food (daily specials are the best choice), well kept beers and quick, friendly service; cl 25 Dec, pm 26 Dec; children in harbour lounge and conservatory. **£15**|£3.

Special thanks to P Wood.

We welcome reports from readers

This *Guide* depends on readers' reports. Do help us if you can – in return, we offer a discount on the next edition to people who've helped us with reports for it. Tell us what you think about places already in it, and anything extra you think we should say about them. And send us your ideas for inclusion in the next edition: places to visit, eat at or stay in, attractive drives or walks, maybe even unusual interesting shops you know of. Use the card in the middle, the report forms at the end, or just write – no stamp needed: *The Good Guide to Britain*, FREEPOST TN1569, Wadhurst, E Sussex TN5 7BR.

Isle of Wight Calendar

Some of these dates were provisional as we went to press. Please check information with the telephone numbers provided.

FEBRUARY

16 **Yarmouth** Pancake Races (01983) 760015

APRIL

5 **Brook** Easter Steam-up and Vintage Ploughing Match at Compton Farm (01983) 740215

MAY

1 **Mottistone** Dance at Dawn by morris men at the Longstone *at 5am* (01983) 882143

2 **Round the Island** Bicycle Island Randonnee: cycle round the Island from any of 6 starting points (01983) 526774

13 **Ventnor** Music for Fun Festival at St Catherine's church – *till Sun 16* (01983) 854564

28 **Bembridge** Festival – *till street fair on Mon 31* (01983) 872175

31 **Whitwell** Crab Fair at the Rugby Club: stalls, fresh crabs (01983) 855794

JUNE

1 **Arreton** Historical Re-enactments at Arreton Manor – *till Sun 13* (01983) 528134

5 **Shorwell** Open Gardens: up to 17 gardens open – *till Sun 6* (01983) 551304

11 **Binstead** Heavy Horse & Rural Life Festival at Brickfields Horse Country – *till Mon 14* (01983) 566801

20 **Niton** Mackerel Fair (01983) 551348

26 **Cowes** Round the Island Yacht Race: over 1,000 yachts (01983) 296621; **Wootton** Isle of Wight Sheepdog Trials at Littletown Dairy Farm – *till Sun 27* (01983) 882001

JULY

3 **Newport** Art in the Park: art exhibition at Church Litten Park (01983) 823822

10 **East Cowes** Victorian Festival (01983) 281524

17 **Ryde** Festival Regatta – *till Sun 18* (01983) 613247; **St Helens** Jazz on the Quay (01983) 874625

24 **Northwood** County Show at the Showground – *till Sun 25* (01983) 740485

28 **Sandown** Carnival (01983) 402024

30 **Mottistone** Open-air Jazz at Mottistone Manor Gardens – *till Sat 31* (01983) 741020

31 **Cowes** Week – *till 7 Aug* (01983) 295744

Isle of Wight Calendar

AUGUST

1 **Shanklin** Carnival Week – *till Sun 8* with processions *on Weds 4 and Sat 7* and fireworks *on Thurs 5* (01983) 862117

18 **Shanklin** Regatta (01983) 862422; **Ventnor** Carnival Procession (01983) 855019

21 **Arreton** Garlic Festival at the Fighting Cocks Crossroads: biggest festival on the island with arena events, arts and crafts, circus, live bands – *till Sun 22* (01983) 865450

25 **Sandown** Illuminated Carnival (01983) 402024

26 **Newport** Carnival Procession – *also on Sat 28* (01983) 526595

27 **Havenstreet** Island Steam Show (inc live bands) at Isle of Wight Steam Railway – *till Mon 30* (01983) 882204

30 **St Helens** Carnival (01983) 873240

SEPTEMBER

18 **Ryde** Garden Show – *till Sun 19* (01983) 568867

NOVEMBER

5 **St Helens** Bonfire (01983) 872948

DECEMBER

23 **East Cowes** Christmas in the Square: evening charity stalls and entertainments (01983) 281524

Please let us know what you think of places in the *Guide*. Use the report forms at the back of the book or simply write us a letter.

Kent

Masses to do and see for all ages, attractive, quite intricate countryside; good seaside resorts – old-fashioned without being jaded.

The north-east coast resorts date from pre-railway Victorian days, when well-to-do Londoners came by boat. When the early coastbound railways took people further afield, these forerunners – most notably Broadstairs – settled into a tranquillity that at least to a degree they've kept till today. Inland, the Weald (roughly west of the M20) has peaceful and intimate landscapes of little hills and valleys, small pasture fields and oak woods, and villages with attractive tile-hung and weatherboarded houses, early medieval stone-built churches, and a good smattering of antique shops, teashops and so forth – pleasant territory for pottering about by car. The North Downs between the M20 and the M2, also north of the M25/M26, are more open; the best parts are above Wye. The flatlands of Romney Marsh have a certain bypassed-by-time appeal. Incidentally, much of east Kent's orchard country tends to be lined by very high hedges that make country drives less interesting.

Dover is excellent for a family day out, with its splendid castle and well done White Cliffs Experience. The zoos at Lympne and Bekesbourne are also outstanding family attractions, and there's lots more in the county to entertain children (the 'Tamworth Two' have now gone to ground at the farm park at Matfield, and there are several other really friendly animal and rare breeds centres – the one at Woodchurch is outstanding). Many (boys, particularly) will love the historic Chatham dockyard, which also has a strong adult appeal. There are several enjoyable steam railways – the Romney Hythe & Dymchurch is delightfully quaint.

Canterbury has many fine buildings besides the cathedral itself, including two interesting heritage centres, and well shown Roman remains. Many excellent gardens are headed by grand Groombridge (lots for families here) and Hever, romantic Sissinghurst and (near Lamberhurst) Scotney Castle. The comprehensive Brogdale fruit tree collection near Faversham and the unusual organic gardens at Yalding are quite eye-opening. Even the most avid appetite for stately homes won't be sated by the remarkable choice here, led by Leeds Castle, Knole near Sevenoaks, Penshurst Place, Squerryes Court and Chartwell near Westerham, Ightham Mote and Hever Castle. Darwin's Downe House near Westerham is an interesting newcomer. Among less conventional places, the bizarre *memento mori* in Hythe church, the extraordinary collections at Birchington, the Finchcocks collection of keyboard instruments at Goudhurst, the Hop Farm at Beltring, the bird park at Wingham, and the ruined houses and birds of prey centre at Eynsford all stand out – and most have plenty to entertain children.

Where to stay

BIDDENDEN TQ8435 **Bishopsdale Oast** *Biddenden, Ashford TN27 8DR (01580) 292321* **£50;** 3 large, homely rms with king-size beds and country views. Large double-kiln oast house in 4 acres of wild and cultivated gardens, with beams and original features; good breakfasts and imaginative dinner inc an excellent cheeseboard, eaten on terrace or in dining room, and friendly owners; cl Christmas; children over 12.

BOUGHTON LEES TR0147 **Eastwell Manor** *Eastwell Park, Boughton Lees, Ashford TN25 4HR (01233) 219955* **£170,** plus special breaks; 23 prettily decorated, spacious rms. Fine Jacobean-style manor (actually built in the 1920s) in 62 acres, with grand oak-panelled rooms, open fires, comfortable leather seating, antiques and fresh flowers, very good service and extremely good food in the atmospheric restaurant; snooker, croquet, pitch-and-putt, riding, tennis and lots of walks; disabled access.

BOUGHTON MONCHELSEA TQ7849 **Tanyard** *Wierton Hill, Boughton Monchelsea, Maidstone ME17 4JT (01622) 744705* **£105;** 6 lovely beamed rms. Appealing medieval yeoman's house with fine views, beams and log fires in the cosy day rooms, restaurant in 13th-c part of building (open to non-residents, too), and 10 acres of landscaped gardens; cl 3 wks late Dec–early Jan; children over 6.

CANTERBURY TR1457 **Cathedral Gate** *36 Burgate, Canterbury CT1 2HA (01227) 464381* ***£76.50,** plus special breaks; 24 rms, 12 with own bthrm and some overlooking cathedral. 15th-c hotel with bow windows, massive oak beams, sloping floors, antiques and fresh flowers, and a quiet, restful atmosphere.

CANTERBURY TR1457 **Thanington** *140 Wincheap, Canterbury CT1 3RY (01227) 453227* ***£68,** plus special breaks; 15 rms linked to the main building by Georgian-style conservatory. Thoughtfully run and warmly welcoming hotel with elegant little rooms, games room, walled garden, and indoor swimming pool; cl 25 Dec.

CHARING HEATH TQ9247 **Barnfield** *Charing Heath, Ashford TN27 0BN (01233) 712421* **£40;** 5 beamed rms, shared big bthrm. Delightful early 15th-c farmhouse with fine beams, big open fires, comfortable sitting rooms, lots of books, antiques and homely knick-knacks, good breakfasts, friendly owners, and a big garden; cl Christmas.

CHARTHAM TR0953 **Thruxted Oast** *Mystole, Chartham, Canterbury CT4 7BX (01227) 730080* ***£78;** 3 charming rms. Carefully converted 18th-c oast house surrounded by hop gardens and orchards, with pretty terrace and croquet; breakfast served in big farmhouse kitchen; picture-framing workshop and fine country walks; cl 25 Dec; children over 5.

CHIDDINGSTONE HOATH TQ4842 **Hoath House** *Penshurst Rd, Chiddingstone Hoath, Edenbridge TN8 7DB (01342) 850362* **£45;** 3 rms, 1 with own bthrm. Wonderful medieval house that has been added to over the years, with huge beams and plastered walls in the sitting room, family portraits, open fire in the library, heaps of interest and atmosphere, homely suppers, kind, welcoming owners, and a big garden with fine views; cl Christmas/New Year.

EAST PECKHAM TQ6651 **Roydon Hall** *East Peckham, Tonbridge TN12 5NH (01622) 812121* **£110;** 25 rms, some with own bthrm. Fine Tudor manor offering vegetarian B & B (vegetarian lunch and light supper by arrangement); 10 acres of woodlands and garden, original oak panelling in the public rooms, and regular meditation courses; no smoking.

FRITTENDEN TQ8041 **Maplehurst Mill** *Mill Lane, Frittenden, Cranbrook TN17 2DT (01580) 852203* **£70;** 3 rms with views over the water and surrounding countryside. Carefully restored 18th-c watermill attached to 15th-c mill house, with original machinery, millstones and waterwheel, big comfortable drawing room; delicious, imaginative food using home-grown organic produce in beamed and candlelit dining room; 11 acres of gardens and grounds and heated outdoor swimming pool; no smoking; no dogs; children over 12; disabled access.

GOUDHURST TQ7237 **Star & Eagle** *High St, Goudhurst TN17 1AL (01580) 211512* ***£55;** 11 character rms, 9 with own bthrm. Striking medieval inn with comfortable Jacobean-style furnishings in heavy-beamed day rooms, pretty views, polite staff, good food, and well kept ales.

GROOMBRIDGE TQ5337 **Crown** *Groombridge, Tunbridge Wells TN3 9QH (01892) 864742* ***£38;** 4 rms, shared bthrm. Carefully preserved Elizabethan inn on village green, with snug, atmospheric timbered bar rooms, a log fire in the big brick inglenook, and traditional furnishings; good popular food, well kept beers, good-value house wines, and quick service; children over 4.

LITTLESTONE TR0825 **Romney Bay House** *Coast Rd, Littlestone, New Romney TN28 8QY (01797) 364747* **£70,** plus winter breaks; 11 rms. 1920s house on a private road facing the sea with log fire in comfortable drawing room, first-floor 'look-out' with telescope, games and library, charming, friendly owners and a relaxed atmosphere; enjoyable set evening meal, afternoon teas, and garden with tennis court and croquet; golf close by; cl 1 wk Christmas; no children.

MARDEN TQ7341 **Tanner House** *Goudhurst Rd, Marden, Tonbridge TN12 9ND (01622) 831214* ***£40;** 3 rms (showers). Quietly set Tudor farmhouse on small, family mixed farm with residents' lounge, inglenook dining room, a large garden, and walks and picnic areas around farm; they breed shire horses; cl Christmas; children over 5; no pets.

PENSHURST TQ5342 **Swale Cottage** *Old Swaylands Lane, Penshurst, Tonbridge TN11 8AH (01892) 870738* ***£62,** plus winter breaks; 3 beamed rms. Careful conversion of 13th-c Grade II listed barn and hayloft, with beams and an inglenook fireplace in the sitting room, good breakfasts, and cottage garden; not far from Hever; no smoking; dogs by arrangement; children over 10.

PLAXTOL TQ6054 **Jordans** *Sheet Hill, Plaxtol, Sevenoaks TN15 0PU (01732) 810379* ***£60;** 3 rms, shared bthrm. 15th-c no smoking house with leaded windows and beams, a warm fire in the inglenook fireplace, good breakfasts, and pretty garden; lots to see nearby; cl mid-Dec–mid-Jan; children over 12.

PLUCKLEY TQ9243 **Dering Arms** *Pluckley, Ashford TN27 0RR (01233) 840371* **£40;** 3 rms, shared bthrm. Dutch-gabled old inn with friendly and relaxed attractive bars, and wonderful food with emphasis on fish and game; monthly vintage-car rally; cl 26–27 Dec.

PLUCKLEY TQ9145 **Elvey Farm** *Pluckley, Ashford TN27 0SU (01233) 840442* **£59.50,** plus special breaks; 9 rms, some in the oast house roundel, some in original barn and stable block. 15th-c farmhouse in secluded spot on 75-acre working family farm, with timbered rooms, inglenook fireplace, and French windows from lounge onto sun terrace; ample play areas for children; well behaved pets welcome.

ST MARGARET'S AT CLIFFE TR3444 **Wallett's Court** *St Margaret's at Cliffe, Dover CT15 6EW (01304) 852424* **£65,** plus special breaks; 10 rms, 2 in converted stable block with gentle views. Fine old manor house with 13th-c cellars, beams, antiques, comfortable seating and open fires, helpful service, charming owners, marvellous food, and swimming pool; cl 4 days over Christmas; very close to ferries; limited disabled access.

SHIPBOURNE TQ5952 **Chaser** *Stumble Hill, Shipbourne TN11 9PE (01732) 810360* **£65;** 15 rms. Colonial-style building with porticoed front in a lovely spot by the village church and green; comfortable and homely atmosphere in the well kept bar, and a wide range of attractively presented good food in both the bar and the beamed restaurant.

SISSINGHURST TQ8037 **Sissinghurst Castle Farm** *Sissinghurst, Cranbrook TN17 2AB (01580) 712885* ***£54,** plus special breaks; 5 rms, some with own bthrm. Gabled Victorian farmhouse in the grounds of Sissinghurst Castle, with spacious rooms, a pretty garden, and farm shop; farm is mostly arable with cattle and sheep; cl Christmas; children over 5.

SMARDEN TQ8742 **Chequers** *Smarden, Ashford TN27 8QA (01233) 770217* ***£50;** 5 rms, 3 with own bthrm. Comfortable olde-worlde pub full of character, with beams and log fire, a varied choice of good, reasonably priced food, and nice breakfasts; cl 25 Dec.

TENTERDEN TQ8733 **Brattle House** *Watermill Bridges, Tenterden TN30 6UL (01580) 763565* ***£68;** 3 rms. Partly 17th-c tile-hung house, said to have been the home of Horatia, illegitimate daughter of Nelson and Lady Hamilton; set in 11 acres of garden, meadow and woodland; charming owners, low-beamed residents' sitting room, good breakfasts in conservatory, and delicious, imaginative dinners in candlelit dining room; no smoking; cl Christmas and New Year; no children.

TUNBRIDGE WELLS TQ5839 **Hotel du Vin & Bistro** *Crescent Rd, Tunbridge Wells TN1 2LY (01892) 526455* ***from £85;** 31 very attractive, individually decorated rms with CD players, satellite TV and power showers. Handsome sandstone building, extended in the 19th c, with a relaxed atmosphere in the 2 rooms of the bar, comfortable sofas and chairs in the lounge rooms, good modern cooking in the airy, high-ceilinged and informally French-feeling restaurant, and particularly good wines; disabled access.

TUNBRIDGE WELLS TQ5739 **Spa** *Mount Ephraim, Tunbridge Wells TN4 8XJ (01892) 520331* ***£144,** plus weekend breaks; 74 comfortable rms. Run by the same family for 3 generations, this Georgian hotel, in 14 acres of landscaped gardens, has a comfortable and quietly decorated, partly no smoking lounge, a popular and attractive bar, good food in Regency-style restaurant, a nice old-fashioned atmosphere and friendly, long-serving staff; leisure centre with indoor heated swimming pool, gym, beauty salon, sauna, Jacuzzi, and solarium, and floodlit hard tennis court; disabled access.

WEST MALLING TQ6757 **Scott House** *High St, West Malling ME19 6QH (01732) 841380* ***£69;** 3 pretty little rms. No smoking Georgian town house (from which the family also run an antique business) with a big comfortable lounge, good breakfasts in the dining room, a friendly atmosphere, and helpful owners; cl Christmas; children over 10.

To see and do

CANTERBURY TR1457 One of Britain's most satisfying places to visit – but as around 100,000 visitors arrive each day in summer you'll find it much more pleasant out of season. Redevelopment after World War II air-raid damage has been rather unsympathetic, but there's still a wealth of historic buildings tucked away in narrow medieval streets. The centre is largely pedestrianised, with good car parks on the fringes (and a reliable Park & Ride). Interesting guided walks leave from the Visitor Information Centre, 34 St Margaret's St (11.30am and 2pm, 2pm only in winter); if you're making your own way, don't miss Palace St, Burgate with the Buttermarket Sq, and St Peter's St, all of which have fine buildings. You can follow quite a lot of the ancient city wall on a walk passing the remains of the Norman castle (not open). The city's Roman and ecclesiastical heritage is well known, but there are other remains here too, notably a prehistoric tumulus in Dane John Garden. The Canterbury Tales (off St Peter's St) is the best pub for lunch.

† Canterbury Cathedral
Dramatically floodlit in summer, this spectacularly lives up to expectations – for the most overwhelming first impression, it's best approached from Queningate. The earliest parts are Norman, with much added in the 15th c. Rewarding features are everywhere – an airily impressive nave, fascinating stained glass, the Bell Harry Tower, lovely cloisters, and the shrine of Thomas à Becket, murdered here in the 12th c. The crypt has some wonderfully grotesque carvings, full of strange animals and fantastic fighting monsters. Shop, disabled access; may be cl for services at certain times, limited opening Sun; £2.50 – note this isn't a donation, you'll be charged this (even on Sun) just to enter the precincts, and there are additional charges for everything from guided tours to visiting the lavatory. This is intended to reduce the sheer pressure of numbers visiting. In the precincts are fine buildings connected to the cathedral, inc the

ruins of the former monastery in Green Court, and the impressive Norman Staircase. Not far outside is the medieval King's School (The Borough).

St Augustine's Abbey (Longport) Founded at the end of the 6th c, but most of the remaining ruins date from the Benedictine rebuilding in the 11th. Impressive new museum; shop, disabled access; cl 24–26 Dec, 1 Jan; (01850) 293822; £2.50.

Canterbury Heritage Museum (Stour St) In the medieval Poor Priests' Hospital (look out for the magnificent oak roof), a splendid interpretation of the city's history, with deft use of lavishly up-to-date display technology inc holograms, leaving many vivid visual impressions – one of the most rewarding places in SE England. There's a Ruper Bear gallery. Shop, disabled access to ground floor only; cl Sun (exc pm Jun–Oct), Good Fri and Christmas wk; (01227) 452747; £2.20. Hidden away through an arch is charming Greyfriars, above the River Stour, the remains of the first Franciscan settlement in the country.

Roman Museum (Longmarket) Spendidly extended and updated underground museum, by the remains of a Roman town house; lively reconstructions of a market and aromatic kitchen, as well as lots of hands-on and hi-tech displays. The house's mosaic floor is very well displayed. Shop, disabled access; cl Sun (exc Jun–Oct), Good Fri and Christmas wk; (01227) 785575; £2.20.

! The Canterbury Tales (St Margaret's St) Well put together, Chaucer's characters brought enthusiastically to life with smells, sound effects and lively celebrity voices. Meals, snacks, very good and unusual shop, disabled access (prior notice preferred); cl 25 Dec; (01227) 454888; £4.95. They also organise evening ghost tours (phone for details). The **Chaucer Centre** on St Peter's St also has an interesting shop, and may be displays ; cl Sun, 25 Dec; free.

West Gate Museum (St Peter's St/St Dunstan's St) The city's last remaining fortified gatehouse, built in the late 14th c, with interesting cells, and excellent views from the battlements. Children can do brass rubbing or try on replica armour. Shop; cl 12.30–1.30pm, all day Sun, Good Fri, Christmas wk; (01227) 452747; 90p.

Royal Museum and Art Gallery (High St) Fine porcelain, glass, clocks and watches, Roman and Anglo-Saxon jewellery, and Victorian animal paintings by T S Cooper. Shop, disabled access; cl Sun, Good Fri and Christmas wk; (01227) 452747; free.

† **St Martin's Church** TR1457 (North Holmes Rd) The country's oldest church in continual use; the Venerable Bede says it was built by the Romans, and there are certainly Roman bricks in the walls.

The Roman road S to the coast (B2068) is a good drive.

We welcome reports from readers

This *Guide* depends on readers' reports. Do help us if you can – in return, we offer a discount on the next edition to people who've helped us with reports for it. Tell us what you think about places already in it, and anything extra you think we should say about them. And send us your ideas for inclusion in the next edition: places to visit, eat at or stay in, attractive drives or walks, maybe even unusual interesting shops you know of. Use the card in the middle, the report forms at the end, or just write – no stamp needed: *The Good Guide to Britain*, FREEPOST TN1569, Wadhurst, E Sussex TN5 7BR.

Other things to see and do

KENT Family Attraction of the Year

Dover Castle TR3241 A quite splendidly preserved fortress on a commanding cliff, this magnificent place packs in a real variety of things to see, and it's easy for half a day or longer to fly by without your realising. Imaginative displays bring scenes from the site's history vividly to life, giving the stories a human touch that make them easy for most ages to understand. The properly forbidding Norman keep is the finest surviving example of its type, and there are fantastic views over the English Channel from its roof. A new exhibition dramatically re-creates an early 13th-c siege, and there's a good children's activity area, with interactive displays and brass rubbing. Beneath the massive walls and towers is a network of secret underground tunnels that played a vital role in World War II; for many the evocative and very well put together guided tour of this part of the castle is the highlight of a visit. As the lights dim you can hear the bombers overhead, and other effects clearly show what it was like to be stationed down here in 1940. Also within the castle walls are a Roman lighthouse that uses a 4th-floor brazier as a guide light (it's one of the tallest Roman structures still standing), a 74-metre (242ft) well, and a restored Saxon church. A walk round the battlements gives interesting views of the comings and goings down in the harbour (something which captivates small children); you can get an audioguide to listen to as you stroll. There's plenty of space to run around – the site covers 79 acres – and a land-train links the main attractions. A picnic site is splendidly placed on the Admiralty Lookout. Various battle re-enactments and other lively special events throughout the year. Few places cover so many different periods and events so well, and to our minds this is undoubtedly one of the best and most enjoyable historic sites in the whole country. Meals, snacks, shop, disabled access; cl 24–26 Dec; (01304) 211067; £6.60 (£3.30 children). A family ticket, covering 2 adults and up to 3 children, is very good value at £16.50.

ASH TR2858 has a handsome partly 12th-c **church**.

AYLESFORD TQ7258 **Aylesford Priory** Often referred to as the Friars, these carefully restored 13th/14th-c buildings are once again the home of a group of Carmelite monks. Fine cloisters and chapels, sculptures and ceramics by modern artists, working pottery, and beautiful grounds. Snacks, shop; cl Good Fri; (01622) 717272; free. The Little Gem pub is very quaint and ancient. **Kits Coty House** (Aylesford, towards the A229, TQ7460) A massive Stone Age tomb chamber which 'mightily impressed' Pepys when he saw it; free.

BARHAM TR1947 **Elham Valley Vineyards** Friendly little vineyard in pretty sheltered valley; guided tours and tastings (£2.50); sales, good craft shop, disabled access; cl am Sun, Christmas wk; (01227) 831266. The Duke of Cumberland has decent food, and the B2065 through this valley is a pretty drive.

BEDGEBURY PINETUM TQ7233 Lakeside landscaped valley full of magnificent conifers, with walks up through forest plots designed to try out the commercial possibilities of all sorts of little-known species. Snacks, shop; visitor centre cl wkdys Jan and Feb; (01580) 211044; £2.20. The Bull at Three Leg Cross, Ticehurst is useful for lunch.

BEKESBOURNE TR1956 **Howletts Wild Animal Park** The first of John Aspinall's 2 excellent wildlife parks (the other is at Lympne, see entry below), well spread over lovely grounds. A highlight is the world's largest colony of breeding gorillas, though there are also deer, antelope, leopards, bison and a herd of breeding elephants. Meals, snacks,

shop, disabled access; cl 25–26 Dec; (01227) 721286; £8.90. The good King William IV in nearby Littlebourne has a comparably exotic menu.

BELTRING TQ6746 **Hop Farm Country Park** (off the A228) A popular and very well organised family outing, based around the largest surviving group of Victorian oast houses and galleried barns. Clearly laid out exhibitions on hop-farming, rural bygones and somewhat incongruously the water industry, easy nature trails, animals (they have more than you'll find in quite a few farm parks), falconry displays, shire horses, pottery, and special events most summer wknds. Snacks, shop, some disabled access (not into oast houses); (01622) 872068; £5. Brookers next door has decent food in a smart conversion of another oast house – used for drying hops (though usually now converted into homes), these buildings with their tall white cowls turning with the wind are a trademark of the Weald of Kent and E Sussex.

BEWL WATER TQ6733 Boating and fishing, picnic areas, and cycle hire (and a great adventure play area); can be very busy on bank hols; £3.80 parking charge summer wknds

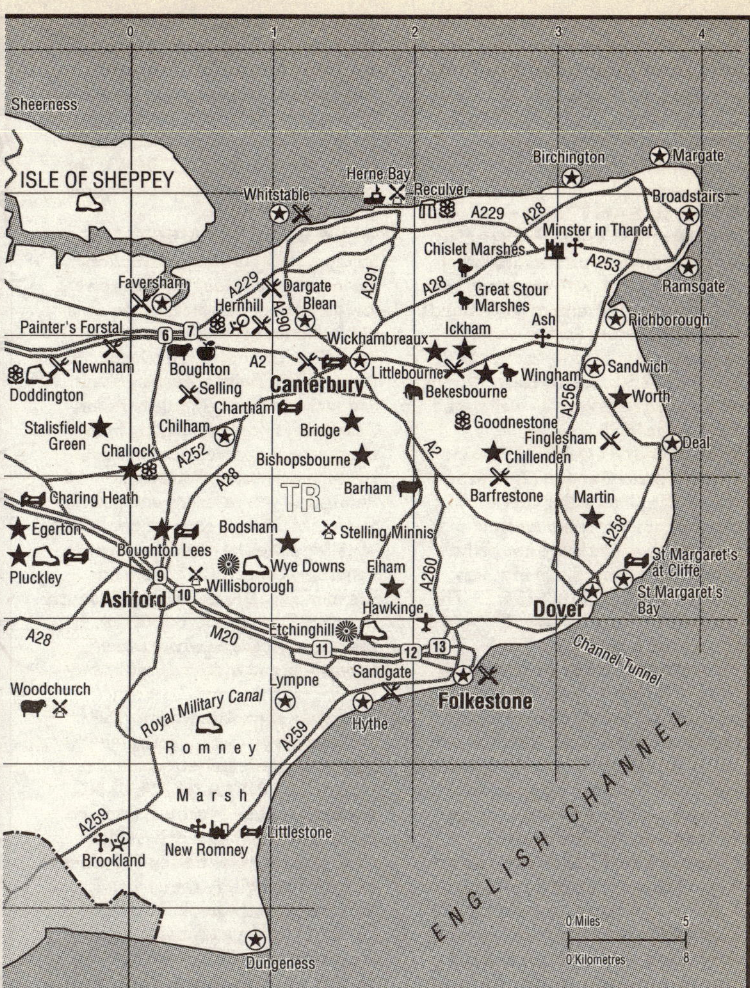

and bank hols, less at other times. The reservoir, dissected by the Kent/Sussex boundary, is skirted by a 14-mile path around its banks.

BIDDENDEN TQ8538
Attractive village with several interesting old houses on the S side of the High St, and a handsome 13th-c **church** with a bold tower. The Red Lion has decent food. **Biddenden Vineyards** (Benenden rd) Thriving wine- and cider-producing vineyard. All-year tastings, harvesting in Oct and bottling in Mar. Snacks, shop, disabled access (but no facilities); cl am Sun and all Sun Jan and Feb, 24 Dec–2 Jan; (01580) 291726; free.

BIRCHINGTON TR3068
Quex House and Gardens and Powell-Cotton Museum (off the A28) Fascinating museum attached to fine Regency house with furnished period rooms. 9 galleries display the collections of Victorian explorer and naturalist Major Powell-Cotton, with hundreds of well mounted animals, ethnic artefacts and oriental art. The walled gardens are being restored, and the grounds have an unusual early 19th-c bell tower with bizarre wrought-iron spire (open unusual Suns in summer). Summer snacks, shop, disabled access;

open Tues–Thurs, Sun and bank hols Apr–Oct (house open pm only), plus gardens and museum open Sun in Mar, Nov and Dec; (01843) 842168; £3.50, £2.50 in winter. The Morton's Fork Hotel inland at Minster does worthwhile lunches, and the Minnis Bay beach is good.

BLEAN TR1161
Druidstone Wildlife Park (A290) Farmyard animals, parrots and other animals and birds, with woodland trails, and a couple of adventure playgrounds (one for under 5s). Snacks, shop, disabled access; cl Nov–Easter; (01227) 765168; *£3.50. Nearby Blean Woods are a nature reserve, with well signed walks in the RSPB area.

BOROUGH GREEN TQ6356
Great Comp Garden (2m E at St Mary's Platt) Interesting collection of trees, shrubs, herbaceous plants and heathers, with fine lawns and paths. Snacks, plant shop, disabled access; cl Nov–Feb; (01732) 886154; £3. The Plough at Ivy Hatch a few miles S is a good restaurant.

BOUGH BEECH TQ4846
Nature Reserve At the N end of the reservoir, with wildlife exhibitions in a 19th-c oast house. Open Weds, wknds and bank hols Apr–Oct; (01732) 750624; free. The Wheatsheaf has good food, and there are pleasant walks around here.

BOUGHTON TR0459
Farming World (Nash Court) Friendly farm with traditional and rare breeds and heavy horses, tractor and wagon rides, nature trails, adventure playground, walled garden, and pick-your-own fruit and veg (Jun–Oct). Meals, snacks, farm shop, disabled access; cl Nov–Feb; (01227) 751144; £3. The White Horse at Boughton Street has decent food all day.

BRASTED TQ4852 **Emmett's Garden** (Toys Hill, 3m S) Charming hillside shrub garden with magnificent views – it's the highest garden in Kent. Full of bluebells in spring and a riot of colour in autumn. Teas, shop, some disabled access; open wknds, Weds and bank hols Apr–Sept; (01732) 868381; £3; NT. The quaint Fox & Hounds out here has good cheap snacks, and there are good walks; back in the village are quite a few antique shops.

★ **BRENCHLEY** TQ6840
Marle Place Pretty garden around a fine 17th-c house (not open), with interesting scented plants in the walled garden, woodland walk, and showy bantams. Teas, some disabled access; cl Nov–Mar; (01892) 722304; £3. The village has some attractive old houses and a venerable inn.

★ **BROADSTAIRS** TR3967
Still appealingly unspoilt, attractively meandering up among the trees on the low hill behind, with pleasant gardens, old-fashioned bathing-huts on its central beach, and a good relaxed atmosphere. There are fishing boats and yachts in the lively little harbour, 7 sandy bays (Joss Bay, slightly E from the centre, is excellent for families), refreshing clifftop walks (even to Ramsgate if you're feeling energetic), and lots of Dickens connections ('Our watering place', he called the town). Bandstand concerts at 2.30pm on summer Suns. **Bleak House Museum** (Fort Rd) Dickens's favourite seaside residence, where he wrote *David Copperfield*, and which he used as the title for another novel. Lots of his belongings and related memorabilia, plus displays on local wrecks and smuggling. Shop, some disabled access; cl Dec–Feb; (01843) 862224; £2.50. **Dickens House Museum** (Victoria Parade) Former home of Miss Mary Strong, the basis for Betsey Trotwood in *David Copperfield* – the parlour is furnished as in the book. Also more of Dickens's letters and possessions. Shop; cl am, all mid-Oct–Mar; (01843) 862853; £1. The quayside Tartar Frigate has harbour views from its upstairs seafood restaurant.

† **BROOKLAND** TQ9825
Philippine Village (A259 SW) Unique centre selling crafts from the Philippines, with occasional special events. Open daily Whit–Sept and wknds Easter–Whit, other times by arrangement; (01797) 344616; free. The Walland Marsh here is an extension of Romney Marsh; the sign off the A259 to the Woolpack leads you to a particularly good pub with the right sort of atmosphere for the area. **Fairfield church** TQ9626 (just NW) Quite alone in the marsh, a tent-roofed

brick and timber building remarkable for its utterly lonely surroundings; attractive inside.

CHALLOCK TR0152 **Beech Court Gardens** Peaceful gardens surrounding a medieval farmhouse; lots of spring and autumn colour, with firs and pines reflecting the designer's admiration for Inverewe in Scotland. Teas in oast house, plant sales and craft shop, disabled access; cl am Fri and wknds, and all Nov–Easter; (01233) 740735; *£2.50. The 17th-c Chequers by the village green has good-value food.

CHATHAM TQ7666 **Historic Dockyard** Excellent 80-acre working museum set in the most complete Georgian dockyard in the world. Lots to see and do: the Wooden Walls exhibition uses sights, sounds and smells to show how 18th-c warships such as HMS *Victory* were built here, and there's an exhibition on the RNLI, with 15 lifeboats. Also restorations, rope-making demonstrations, craft workshops, and lively events. A visit here can easily fill most of the day. Meals, snacks, shop, disabled access; open daily Apr–Oct, plus wknds and Weds in Nov, Feb and Mar; (01634) 823800; £6.20. You can get a ticket that includes **boat trips** on the paddle steamer *Kingswear Castle*, and may be able to tour the submarine *Ocelot* moored in Chatham Maritime. **Fort Amherst** (Dock Rd) Perhaps the finest surviving 18th-c fort in the country, with massive ditches, gun emplacements, a warren of tunnels and a firing gun battery. 18 acres of parkland, and live re-enactments the first 3 Suns of each month. Meals, snacks, shop; cl 25–26 Dec, 1 Jan; (01634) 847747; £4. The Command House below by the water does limited but decent food.

★ **CHIDDINGSTONE** TQ5045 A favourite Kentish village (as seen in *A Room with a View*), an unspoilt cluster of Tudor houses and buildings owned by the NT, in lovely countryside. The church and the mysterious stone which one story claims gives the village its name are worth a look. The Castle Inn is good for lunch. **Chiddingstone Castle** 17th-c house rebuilt in castle style at the start of the 19th c; renowned paintings and antiquities from England, Egypt and the Orient, inc fine collections of Japanese swords and Buddhist art. The landscaped grounds have been restored, and you can fish in the lake (£8 a day). Snacks, shop, some disabled access; open pm Weds, Thurs, Fri, Sun and bank hols May–Sept, Sun only in Apr and Oct; (01892) 870347; £3.50, £4 Sunday.

★ **CHILHAM** TR0653 The lovely village square is the prettiest in Kent, and several antique shops reflect its popularity with visitors – in summer, get there early to catch it at its most photogenic. The Woolpack just down the hill is useful for lunch. **Badgers Hill Farm and Cidery** (New Cut Rd, towards Selling) Cheerily unspoilt spot, with cider-making, local crafts, a barrel merchant, free-roaming pigs (you may find them in the shop) and other animals, play area, and pick-your-own apples (10 types, Aug–Oct). Farm shop, disabled access; cl 24 Dec–Feb; (01227) 730573; free.

CHISLET MARSHES TR2366 Thousands of geese and ducks; duck food by the bag from the nice little Gate Inn at Boyden Gate.

CLIFFE MARSHES TQ7279 N of Rochester, these are bounded by a long sea wall cum footpath which feels (and is) extraordinarily remote and not a little surreal – perhaps the best Thames estuary walk in N Kent.

★ **COBHAM** TQ6668 A good mix of unspoilt buildings from various centuries – an excellent place to walk round (as Dickens liked to do). The partly 13th-c **church** is worth examining, with its magnificent brasses and tombs, as is the 14th-c **New College**, like a miniature Oxford college but far less known to visitors (free). The Leather Bottle has decent food, interesting Dickens memorabilia and a good garden. **Cobham Hall** The Earls of Darnley once lived in this impressive place, now a girls' school. The décor is quite splendid in parts (some notable marble fireplaces), and the lovely grounds are being restored. Snacks, shop; open pm selected dates Mar, Apr, July and Aug; (01474) 824319; *£3. **Owletts** At the S end of Cobham, this modest 17th-c yeoman's house has an interesting staircase – and in the garden the grandest bird bath we've ever seen. Open pm Weds and Thurs Apr–Sept; (01892) 890651; *£2; NT.

CRANBROOK TQ7736 A very good working **windmill**, picturesquely set almost in the centre, still grinds corn. They've recently bought the workshop behind with the aid of a lottery grant and after restoration intend to open it with displays on the mill's history. Open pm Sat and bank hols Apr–Sept, plus pm Sun mid-July–Aug; donations. The attractive miniature town, with largely unspoilt lanes of tile-hung buildings, also has a friendly local-history museum, and for picnics Perfect Partners (Stone St) is the best delicatessen for many miles. The walk to Sissinghurst and back is a pleasant way of joining 2 very interesting places.

★ **DEAL** TR3752 Once the busiest harbour in SE England, and Caesar's landing point in 55 BC; now pleasantly understated seaside resort, full of pretty little streets and alleys but beware of vigilant traffic wardens. The seaview King's Head (Beach St) has good-value food (and bedrooms). **Deal Castle** The biggest in Henry VIII's chain of coastal defences, uniquely shaped like a Tudor rose with every wall rounded to deflect shot. Good audio tour, shop, some disabled access; cl Mon and Tues in winter; (01304) 372762; £3. **Walmer Castle** (just S) Another of Henry VIII's coastal defence fortresses, later the official residence of the Lord Warden of the Cinque Ports (one was the Duke of Wellington, who left behind his famous boot). It became more stately home than fortress, with rooms furnished in 18th-c style, and pretty gardens laid out mainly by a niece of William Pitt (there's a new one dedicated to the Queen Mother). Snacks, shop, some disabled access; cl Mon and Tues in winter, wkdys Jan and Feb, and whenever the Lord Warden is in residence (usually over Christmas); (01304) 364288; £4. **Time-Ball Tower** (Victoria Parade) Museum of time, telegraphy and maritime communication, with time-ball dropping on the hour. Shop; open July and Aug (not Mon); (01304) 360897; £1.20.

DODDINGTON PLACE TQ9357 Grand garden with formal plantings, old-fashioned rock garden, rhododendrons in woodland, broad views, and delightfully peaceful atmosphere. Plant sales, café, disabled access; open Weds, bank hols, and pm Sun May–Sept; (01795) 886101; £2.50. The George at Newnham is nice for lunch, with good walks nearby.

! **DOVER** TR3241 *See separate Family Panel on p.351* for **Dover Castle**. The busiest ferry port in Europe, Dover is not in itself an attractive town but has several fascinating places to visit, reflecting the vivid history it owes to its strategic importance. Blakes (Castle St) is useful for lunch, and there is fast, helpful service at Valentino's on Townland St. **White Cliffs Experience** (Market Sq) Refreshingly lively museum where children can press, poke and push things, and inadvertently learn about Dover's history while they're doing it. Splendid Roman Encounter and World War II section, as well as 20-minute animatronic show bringing the town's history to life. In summer there may be outdoor activities like archery. Snacks (and picnic site), shop, disabled access; cl 25 Dec; (01304) 214566; £5.50. The same site also has a more conventional museum, and a gallery based around the Bronze Age boat discovered during roadworks in 1992 should open this summer. **Old Town Gaol** (High St) Hi-tech effects re-create courtroom scenes and life in a Victorian prison; they'll even lock you (albeit briefly) in a tiny cell. Shop, disabled access; cl Mon and Tues; (01304) 242766; £3.45. **Grand Shaft** An unusual spiral stone staircase which links top and bottom of Dover's famous cliffs; open Tues–Sun July–Aug; £1.20. **Crabble Corn Mill** (Lower Rd) Beautifully restored working 19th-c watermill. Snacks (made with their own flour), shop; open Sun all year, plus wknds and bank hols Easter–Oct, and Weds–Fri mid-July–mid-Sept; (01304) 823292; tours *£2. **Roman Painted House** (New St) Well preserved remains of Roman hotel with unique wall paintings and panels, and elaborate underfloor heating system. Brass rubbing, shop, disabled access; cl Mon, and Nov–Mar; (01304) 203279; £2. The **White Cliffs** themselves give an exhilarating walk (and interesting views of the harbour – you can even see France on a clear day) from Dover Castle to St Margaret's at Cliffe, passing the Roman lighthouse above Dover, and a curious scaled-down windmill at St Margaret's at Cliffe. There's a bus back to Dover (no point making a circuit, as the inland scenery here is not worthwhile), or you can press on to the Rising Sun or Zetland Arms at Kingsdown, or to Deal.

DUNGENESS TR0817 Fascinatingly odd, a real curiosity and quite foreign-feeling, its acres of shingle colonised by fishing shacks and railway carriages converted into homes (Derek Jarman used to live here and you can see his garden). It's a terminus for the little steam railway described under New Romney. And there are more pebbles than you could ever imagine. **Dungeness Information Centre and Power Stations** Tours of either the A or the B nuclear power station, with interactive displays, videos, and nature trail. Snacks, shop, disabled access to visitor centre only; open daily Mar–Sept, phone for winter opening; no children under 5, as everyone has to wear a hard hat; (01797) 321815; free. **Dungeness Nature Reserve** RSPB, on the shingle headland, interesting for its unusual plants and in late spring for the nesting terns. Snacks, shop, disabled access; cl Tues, 25–26 Dec; £2.50, RSPB members free. **Old Dungeness Lighthouse** Fine views from the top of its 167 steps; shop; cl wkdys Mar–May and Oct, and all Nov–Easter; £2.20. The friendly Britannia nearby has fresh local fish.

ETCHINGHILL TR1638 The long-distance **Saxon Shore Path** gives some good views and interesting walks. A section starting here crosses under an old railway line, heads up an unspoilt dry valley, and leads along the top of the slope for sightings of Dungeness and the French coast (Cap Gris Nez in Picardy).

EYNSFORD TQ5465 **Eynsford Castle** Norman knight's fortress with impressive 9-metre (30ft) walls, and remains of the hall and ditch; free. There are organised trails from the nearby countryside centre along the River Darent and into woods above the golf course. The Malt Shovel has good seafood. **Lullingstone Castle** Historic family mansion with fine state rooms, great hall, staircase and library, and beautiful grounds. The 15th-c gate tower was one of the first buildings to be made entirely of brick. Snacks, shop, disabled access; open pm wknds and bank hols July–Sept plus Sun Apr–Jun; (01322) 862114; *£3.75. **Lullingstone Roman Villa** (just SE, off the A225) Remains of rather well-to-do 1st- and 2nd-c family's villa, with exceptionally well preserved floor mosaics and an extensive bath complex. Also an early Christian chapel – the only one so far found in a private house. Snacks, shop, some disabled access; cl 24–26 Dec; (01322) 863467; £2.30. **Eagle Heights** Birds of prey centre, good in any weather as many displays are indoors (outdoor ones at 12 noon and 3pm). You can handle snakes and reptiles and meet the owls. Snacks, shop, disabled access; cl wkdys Dec–Feb; (01332) 866466; £4.

★ **FAVERSHAM** TR0161 Photogenic small town ideal for a stroll: plenty of colour-washed timbered old buildings such as the Elizabethan grammar school and the Guildhall (one of the few raised market halls still to shelter stallholders in the pillared market court beneath it – Tues/Fri/Sat). The Albion (Front Brents) has good food, and just N of the town, a track off the road to Oare leads to a remote waterside pub, the Shipwrights Arms: charming setting on summer evenings. **Fleur de Lis Heritage Centre** (Preston St) 16th-c building with enthusiastic volunteers, colourful displays, reconstructions and a working vintage-telephone exchange. Shop (good for Kent books), disabled access to ground floor only; cl Sun, Oct–Mar; (01795) 534542; *£1.50 for museum. Walking tours of Faversham leave here at 10.30am every Sat Apr–Sept (75p). **Chart Gunpowder Mills** (Westbrook Walk) Well restored old gunpowder mills, reputedly the last left in the country. Small shop; open pm wknds and bank hols Apr–Oct;

donations. **Brogdale Trust** (Brogdale Rd, S of the A2) Mammoth fruit farm, beautiful but baffling to stroll through, its 30 acres of orchards producing hundreds of distinct varieties of every hardy fruit imaginable; there are 2,500 variants of apple alone. The shop sells trees, bushes and flowering plants, as well as crops from pears, plums and cherries to cobnuts, quinces and medlars. Meals, snacks, disabled access; orchards cl Nov–Apr, though shop and tearoom open then; (01795) 535286; £2.50. **Belmont** (Throwley, 4m SW of Faversham, TR9856) A pleasant 18th-c mansion in well placed parkland, with a walled garden, and collection of unusual clocks – one looks like a church steeple. Snacks, shop, disabled access; open pm wknds and bank hols Easter–Sept; (01795) 890202; £5, £2.75 garden only.

FOLKESTONE TR2335 Despite much development of this major cross-Channel port, there is an intact pre-19th-c area called the Bayle around the interesting old **church** – very pretty and Kentish. The part around the harbour, previously a picturesque warren, was badly bombed in World War II, but the fish stalls there contribute authentic local colour, the Old High St has a Cornish-type quaintness, and Carpenters (The Stade) has good fresh fish. The remains known as **Caesar's Camp** in fact long pre-date the Roman invasion. Particularly pleasant is a walk along The Leas, a clifftop expanse of lawns and flower gardens with good views. A water-balanced cliff lift operates between here and the seafront. You can watch sweet- and rock-making in the afternoons (exc Weds and Sun) at **Rowlands Confectionery** on the Old High St; free. The **Rotunda Amusement Park** has traditional fairground rides, crazy golf and roller coasters, with lots under cover. Just E on the B2011 the **Battle of Britain Memorial** is a huge stone figure looking out in comtemplation across the Channel, giving an extraordinary air of calm solemnity. Snacks, shop, disabled access; cl Nov–Apr; (01303) 276697; free (parking £1). The **Warren** is an intriguingly jungly tumbledown undercliff, reached from the East Cliff at Folkestone by a walk out past the Martello Tower; once there you can cross a railway footbridge and reach the shore, or go up a flight of steps and on to the clifftop, to return along the cliffs past the Memorial. The cliff path also makes for a good bracing walk from Folkestone all the way to Dover for the train or bus back.

GILLINGHAM TQ7669 The town has a partly Norman **church**, and the **Royal Engineers Museum** (Brompton Barracks) is more appealing than you might think, with sound effects, art and oddities brought back from various countries, and also a Harrier jump jet. Snacks, shop, disabled access; cl Fri, 25–26 Dec, 1 Jan; (01634) 406397; £3. Off the A2 between here and Boughton Street village, any of the little lanes take you deep into orchard country, with foody pubs at Dargate, Selling and Eastling; blossom-time Apr and early May, many farm shops with local apples Sept onwards.

GOODNESTONE PARK TR2653 Old-fashioned roses in traditional walled garden recalling Jane Austen's stays in the fine 18th-c house (not open). Also woodland garden with good trees. Teas Weds and Sun May–Aug, nursery, disabled access; cl Tues, Sat, and Nov–Mar; (01304) 840107; £2.50. The Fitzwalter Arms has good-value food.

★ **GOUDHURST** TQ7237 Charming Wealden village, with quite a few antique shops and so forth, and spectacular views from the graveyard of the 14th-c hilltop church (but during the day too much traffic for comfort). The Spread Eagle up by the church, one of the village's most handsome old buildings, is useful for lunch. **Finchcocks** (off the A262 W) The early Georgian house and its lovely gardens are attractive, but the main draw is the big collection of working keyboard instruments from the 17th c onwards. Some of these are played whenever the house is open, the well organised recitals really adding to the atmosphere. Snacks, shop, some disabled access; open pm Weds and Thurs in Aug, as well as pm Sun and bank hols Easter–Sept; (01580) 211702; £5.50. The Green Cross Inn up by the main road has good home cooking.

GREAT STOUR MARSHES TR2462 Interesting for their thousands of geese and ducks; access from the good Grove Ferry pub just off the A28 near Upstreet.

GROOMBRIDGE PLACE GARDENS TQ5337 (B2110) Beautiful walled gardens, among the country's most spectacular and best developed for visitors, around 17th-c moated mansion (not open), the parkland and forest inspiring generations of artists and writers. Drunken topiary garden, oriental garden, rose garden, sculpture garden (the flower-pot men are in a different league to Bill and Ben), paths patrolled by peacocks and the moat guarded by black swans. The developing fantasy wilderness is best for children, complete with magic pools, teepees, gipsy caravans and atmospheric wind chimes. Families are in general better provided for than at most gardens, with play areas, birds of prey, and canal boat and tractor rides. Snacks, gift shop; cl Nov–Mar; (01892) 863999; £5.50. Nr the entrance, the prettily placed Crown does good food.

HADLOW TQ6249 **Broadview Gardens** Opened in spring 1997 after several years' careful design and planting, a good mix of traditional and imaginatively themed gardens put together by horticulturists at neighbouring Hadlow College; the atmospheric Heaven and Hell Garden is one of our favourites. National collections of hellebores and Japanese anemones, and a well stocked plant centre. Meals, snacks, shop, disabled access; cl Nov–Mar; (01732) 850551; £2. Hadlow's church has the interesting Hop Pickers Memorial, dedicated to the 30 hop pickers who one wet day in 1853 drowned on their way back from the fields; the enormously tall folly of Hadlow Tower is worth a look – there are plans to replace the elaborate top dismantled after the 1987 storms. The Artichoke has decent food.

HAWKINGE TR2039 **Kent Battle of Britain Museum** Plenty of aeroplanes, and extensive collection of relics and memorabilia of British and German aircraft involved in the fighting, inc relics of more that 600 crashed aircraft. Snacks, shop, some disabled access; cl Nov–Easter; (01303) 893140; *£3. The Valiant Sailor at Capel le Ferne (A20) saves you going into Folkestone for lunch.

HERNE BAY TR1868 Not terribly exciting, but a decorous and spaciously laid out 19th-c resort. Mike Turner runs **boat trips** around the bay and out to see seals from May–Oct; best to book for the seal trip, (01227) 366712. The Richmond and Old Ship, on or just off the front, both have decent food. The **windmill** may be open, but as we went to press it was without sails and its future was in doubt.

HERNHILL TR0659 **Mount Ephraim Gardens** 7 acres of pleasant gardens, with Japanese rock garden, topiary garden, watergarden, woodland walk and small vineyard; good views. Teas (not Tues), craft shop; open pm mid-Apr–Sept; (01227) 751496; £2.50. There's a craft centre on Sun. By the church and small green of this charming village, the ancient Red Lion has decent food.

! HEVER CASTLE AND GARDENS TQ4745 In 30 acres of beautiful gardens, the double-moated 13th-c castle has hardly changed externally since Anne Boleyn lived here as a child. Inside it's a different story, as the rooms were magnificently restored by the Astor family at the start of this century. Antiques, furnishings and art from all over Europe, and an exceptional collection of astonishingly detailed miniature houses, furnished and decorated in authentic period styles. The grounds are a draw in their own right, with lakes, Italianate garden with antique sculptures, walled rose garden and maze. New summer splashing water maze and adventure playground. Meals, snacks, shop, good disabled access to gardens; cl Dec–Feb, castle cl am; (01732) 865224; £7, £5.50 gardens only. The Henry VIII is popular for lunch.

! HYTHE TR1634 This hillside town, served by the classic **Romney Hythe & Dymchurch Light Railway** (*see New Romney entry, below*), is well worth a look, with attractive old houses in its narrow

High St and the pretty lanes around the church. **St Leonard's Church crypt** houses an amazing collection of 2,000 skulls and 8,000 thigh bones, dating from before 1500 and all neatly arranged on shelves or carefully stacked in a large heap (cl am Sun, lunchtime, and Oct–Apr; 50p). From the junction of Station Rd (B2065) and Mill Lane a path leads through parkland up to **Saltwood Castle**, which still has its impressive medieval curtain wall. And there are walks along the towpath of the Royal Military Canal, to West Hythe and beyond. The beach stretches to Sandgate, also pleasant to stroll through (the Ship and, closer to Hythe, the Clarendon up a steep cobbled lane have decent food).

IDE HILL TQ4851 With nice pubs and picture-book green, this is on the scarp slope of the lower greensand escarpment, and on the Greensand Way: a good walking area.

IGHTHAM MOTE TQ5853 (off the A227, 2m S of Ightham) Lovely medieval manor house, still with its surrounding moat, a unique survival that looks especially beautiful on a sunny day. Fascinating great hall, Tudor chapel and 14th-c crypt, while the drawing room has a striking Jacobean fireplace, frieze and windows. Pretty courtyard, garden and woodland walks. The North West Quarter and upper floor of the house are now open after one of the National Trust's largest ever restoration projects. Snacks, shop, some disabled access (more later in year); cl am Tues, Sat, and all Nov–Mar; (01732) 810378; £4.50; NT. The Plough at Ivy Hatch does good meals; the Harrow on Common Rd is cheaper and more informal.

ISLE OF SHEPPEY TR0469 Walkers may enjoy the E end, with a path along the sea dyke S from Leysdown-on-Sea to Shell Ness, at the mouth of the Swale.

LAMBERHURST TQ6835 **Scotney Castle** (A21 just S of Lamberhurst) Beautiful 19th-c gardens surrounding the ruins of a small 14th-c moated castle, with impressive rhododendrons, azaleas and roses – a really romantic place. Shop, some disabled access (they recommend a strong pusher); open Weds–Fri and pm wknds and bank hols Apr–Oct, castle open same hours May–mid-Sept; (01892) 891081; £3.80; NT. A public footpath strides through the estate's woods and pastures, which can form a basis for circular walks from Kilndown to Lamberhurst and back. The Brown Trout, on the B2169 nearly opposite Scotney Castle entrance, has good fish. **Owl House Gardens** (off the A21 NE of Lamberhurst) 16 acres of sweeping lawns, flowers, shrubs and fruit trees around timber-framed 16th-c wool smugglers' house; sunken watergardens and woodlands. Shop, disabled access; cl 25 Dec, 1 Jan; (01892) 890230; *£4. **Lamberhurst Vineyard** (Ridge Farm) One of the biggest vineyards in SE England; no tours but you can wander round and taste the wines. Shop, disabled access; cl Christmas wk; (01892) 890286; free. Also, a useful if short public path skirts the vineyards. The attractive village of Lamberhurst still awaits its bypass. **Bayham Abbey** (2m W of Lamberhurst, just over the Sussex border) Impressive ruins of 13th-c Premonstratensian abbey and gatehouse in pretty wooded valley. Shop, disabled access; cl 25 Dec and wkdys Nov–Mar; (01892) 890381; £2. The Elephant's Head at Hook Green is a useful nearby pub.

! LEEDS CASTLE TQ8353 Long renowned as one of the loveliest castles in the country, perfectly placed on 2 little islands in the middle of a lake in 500 acres of landscaped parkland. It dates from the 9th c, and was converted into a royal residence by Henry VIII. Lots of paintings, furniture and tapestries, and a unique dog-collar museum in the gatehouse. The enormous grounds have gardens (a new one is due to open in 1999), a maze and grotto, duck enclosure and aviary (well liked by readers), even a golf course; as this suggests, it's a busy place, not quite as idyllic as it appears from a distance, but very satisfying for a day out. Special events from wine festivals to open-air concerts. Meals, snacks, shop, good disabled access; cl 25 Dec, and the day before evening ticketed events (3 days a year, usually the last wknd in Jun, the first in July and the one nearest 5 Nov, but best to check first); (01622) 765400; £8.80, £6.80 park and gardens only. The Pepper Box nr Ulcombe is the best nearby place for lunch.

LYMPNE TR0935 **Port Lympne Wild Animal Park, Mansion and Gardens** Set in wonderful ornamental parkland around a well restored house, Port Lympne and its sister park Howletts are well known for their genuinely dedicated approach to looking after rare or endangered animals; they are kept in enclosures as close to their natural habitat as possible (and eventually returned to the wild if possible), and, more controversially, a real bond is developed between keeper and animal. There's a lot to see, paths can be steep and there are 300 acres altogether, so the free Safari Shuttle trailers between enclosures is a welcome improvement. Particular highlights include the new 2-acre moated gorilla enclosure, and the country's largest breeding herd of black rhino. Also tigers, elephants, lions and wolves, and occasional special talks and events. The house has a number of unusual features, inc the Hexagonal Library used to sign the Treaty of Paris after World War I, but most remarkable must be the incredible Tent Room by Rex Whistler; there's also a room entirely covered by a mural showing SE Asian animals and birds. Meals, snacks, shop; cl 25–26 Dec; (01303) 264646; *£7.99. **Lympne Castle** Fortified medieval manor house remodelled in Edwardian times, with good views from Norman tower. Open Mon–Thurs and occasional Suns Jun–mid-Sept; (01303) 267571; £2. The Botolphs Bridge Inn just S has decent home cooking.

MAIDSTONE TQ7555 Busy modern town, but worth penetrating for its good museums. The Minstrel (Knightrider Rd) is a useful wine bar, and the Muggleton (King St) an exemplary new pub converted from a very grand Victorian building in conjunction with English Heritage. You may be able to go on a **boat trip** along to Allington. **Archbishop's Palace** (Mill St) Striking edifice used by the Archbishops of Canterbury as a stopping-place on their way from London. You can visit the Great Hall and other rooms; cl 25–26 Dec; (01622) 663006; free. In the stables is the **Tyrwhitt Drake Museum of Carriages**, a notable collection of horse-drawn vehicles. Shop, disabled access to ground floor only; cl am winter, 25–26 Dec; (01622) 754497; £1.50. The site also includes the old parish **church** of All Saints. **Maidstone Museum & Art Gallery** (St Faith's St) Handsome Elizabethan manor house with period original room settings. Snacks, shop, some disabled access; cl am Sun, 25–26 Dec; (01622) 754497; free.

MARDEN TQ7444 This attractive village has a 12th/14th-c ragstone **church** with a unique white weatherboarded tower, and other buildings going back to the 14th-c. **Marden Meadow** (Staplehurst Rd) A lovely unimproved hay meadow, alive with wild flowers and butterflies in late spring and early summer. The Wild Duck just S (Pagehurst Lane) has good food.

MARGATE TR3571 A touch of seaside brashness here, but huge grants from the European Union are helping to bring back the resort's palmy days, and there's plenty for families, inc excellent sandy beaches. The Old Town Hall (Market Pl) has a local history **museum** (cl winter wknds; *£1), and nearby is a well preserved **Tudor house**, open only on special occasions, but worth a look from outside. **Shell Grotto** (Grotto Hill) An unexpected puzzle is this 185 sq metres (2,000 sq ft) of winding underground passages and exquisitely decorated tunnels leading to a mysterious ancient shell temple, thought to be the only one in the world. No one really knows its origins or what it was for. Shop; cl Nov-Easter; (01843) 220008; £1.50. **Margate Caves** These huge caverns are atmospheric with wall paintings and spooky shapes and shadows; (01843) 220139; times and price as Grotto. **Dreamland Theme Park** Completely redeveloped by its current owners, and once through the inauspicious entrance is a very satisfactory and well laid out fairground;

phone for opening (01843) 227011. To the E of town on College Rd there's a working **windmill** (open pm Easter Sun, pm Sun May–Sept and Thurs evening July and Aug, 60p).

MATFIELD TQ6543 **Badsell Park Farm** (Crittenden Rd) Run by a charity looking after disabled young people, this appealing place has rare breeds of cattle, pigs (inc Bonnie and Clyde, the runaway Tamworths), goats and sheep, a new reptile house, tractor and pony rides (60p), maze, and nature trail. Meals, snacks, shop, disabled access; cl 25 Dec; (01892) 832549; £4.50. The Standings Cross Inn and Wheelwrights Arms both have decent food.

MEOPHAM WINDMILL TQ6365 Unusual both for its 6 sides and for the fact that its base is a meeting-place for the parish council. Shop; open pm Sun May–Aug; *70p. The Cricketers prettily set on the green is a useful chain-food pub.

✝ **MINSTER IN THANET** TR3164 **Minster Abbey** Site of one of the earliest nunneries in the country, with ruins and cloisters of the 7th-c building. The current house is still run by Benedictine nuns. Shop, some disabled access; open 11am–noon, then 2–4.30 pm, am only Oct–May, cl Sun and pm Sat; (01843) 821254; free.

✝ **NEW ROMNEY** TR0724 **Romney Hythe & Dymchurch Railway** The world's smallest-scale public railway, with 13½ miles of 15in-gauge track between Hythe and Dungeness. The station has a toy and model museum with 2 magnificent model railways. Engines are often changed en route, and the carriages are comfortable. Well run and friendly, it's quite a favourite with readers. Snacks, shop, disabled access (they prefer notice); trains daily Apr–Sept, wknds Oct and Mar ring for timetable; (01797) 362353; £8.60 full fare (but wide range of lower ones). **Romney Marsh** The most unspoilt corner of Kent, flat country laced with drainage ditches and isolated farmsteads: St Mary in the Marsh has a small but attractive **church** (where E Nesbit aka Mrs Edith Hubert-Bland is buried), and a good flagstoned pub – the Star.

ONE TREE HILL TQ5653 Reached from an NT car park S of Godden Green, this gives walkers a grand view over the Weald. From here the Greensand Way (look for GW markers) follows the very edge of the lower greensand escarpment which dips gently down to Ightham Mote, 2m E; Ivy Hatch and Stone Street have handily placed pubs to make this into a circuit.

★ ✝ **OTFORD** TQ5159 This charming village has a ruined archbishop's palace, and pleasant walks along an easy track to the attractive nearby village of **Shoreham**, which has a lovely church. There are decent pubs in both villages. The downlands to the E give scope for longer walks across Magpie Bottom and past Romney Street.

OTHAM TQ7953 **Stoneacre** Lovely half-timbered 15th-c manor house, restored in 1920s, with charming cottage garden. Open pm Weds and Sat Apr–Oct; (01622) 862871; £2.50; NT.

★ **PENSHURST** TQ5244 A pretty village, with antique shops, teas and so forth, and, above all, **Penshurst Place**, a great medieval manor house, unchanged since the Sidney family first came here centuries ago and an enchanting sight even from the road. Interesting combination of architectural styles, huge chestnut-beamed baronial hall, extensive collections of portraits and furnishings, toy museum, and marvellous formal gardens with nature trails and adventure playground. Meals, snacks, shop, disabled access to grounds (inc a garden for the blind); house cl am, wkdys in Mar, all Nov–Feb; (01892) 870307; £5.70, grounds only £4.20. The Leicester Arms in the village is handy for lunch. **Penshurst Vineyards** (Grove Rd) Self-guided tours, tastings and various animals inc rare breeds of sheep. Cl Christmas wk, and wknds Jan and Feb; (01892) 870255; £1.50 to see animals. The Bottle House and the Rock out in this direction are also both well worth tracking down if you're walking in this attractive area, which has some of the Weald's most luscious lowlands, predominantly pasture, the cottages characteristically tile-hung, and the paths just elevated enough to gain charming views. As with much of the rest of the area, route-finding for walks is fiddly and patient map-reading is in order. One of the best circular routes, passing several good pubs, is Penshurst–Chiddingstone Hoath–Chiddingstone.

PLAXTOL TQ6154 **Old Soar Manor** An ancient oak door at this 13th-c knight's dwelling has graffiti spanning the ages, and there's also a very well preserved chapel and barrel-vaulted undercroft; cl Oct–Mar; free; NT. This general area is attractive orchard country, not too hedged, with good-value apples from the farm shops from Sept onwards; many here also have fresh cobnuts in Sept. The old Kentish Rifleman (Silver Hill, Dunks Green) has enjoyable food and a good garden.

★ **PLUCKLEY** TQ9245 This attractive village has had quite a flood of visitors since *The Darling Buds of May* was filmed here; well marked walks, good pubs for refreshment.

★ **RAMSGATE** TR3864 Quietly civilised seaside resort, with some elegantly colonnaded Georgian buildings and other fine houses up on the cliffs (Pugin, the architect of the Houses of Parliament, designed the church – where he's buried – and the house next door), and a historic harbour (bustling now with its yacht marina and Hoverport). Churchills (The Paragon) has harbour views and good-value food. **Maritime Museum** (Pier Yard) Good collection of historic ships and boats in a handsome early 19th-c clock-house on the harbour (cl wknds Oct–Mar; £1.50). **Motor Museum** (West Cliff Hall, The Paragon) Vintage cars, motorbikes and bicycles in cheerful period settings (cl Dec–Mar exc Sun; £2.50).

RECULVER ROMAN FORT TR2269 Built in the 3rd c, this was well preserved until the 18th c, when cliff erosion collapsed some of it into the sea; some parts remain, though it's the proud pair of tall Saxon towers of the former church on the mound above the beach that stay in the memory. Surrounding these remains is a **country park**, with a visitor centre (cl Mon exc bank hols, plus Tues Sept–Mar and Mon–Sat Oct–Mar); free.

RICHBOROUGH ROMAN FORT TR3260 Another evocative ruined Roman castle – lots of walls and foundations, and a small museum. Snacks, shop, disabled access; cl Mon and Tues Nov and Mar and all wkdys Dec–Feb; (01304) 612013; £2.50 (inc Walkman tour).

ROCHESTER TQ7468 A busy town, but well worth walking round, with several attractive buildings besides those we mention; one of the quaintest is Kent's oldest pub, the Coopers Arms (St Margaret's St; cheap lunches), and many of those on the High St are featured in Dickens's novels. **Rochester Cathedral** Spectacularly Norman, with original richly carved door, vaulted crypt, St Gundolph's tower, tombs and effigies and huge 15th-c window. The choir sings Evensong at 5.30pm wkdys, 3.15pm wknds. Snacks, shop, good disabled access; £2 suggested donation. **Rochester Castle** One of the best examples of 11th-c military architecture – dramatic too; the great square keep looks a little like the Tower of London, only more forbidding. Shop; cl 24–26 Dec; (01634) 402276; £3.50. **Charles Dickens Centre** (High St, Rochester) Late Tudor house used in both *Pickwick Papers* and *Edwin Drood*, with scenes and characters from the author's books brought vividly to life using impressive hi-tech effects. Shop; cl Christmas; (01634) 844176; £3.50 **Guildhall Museum** (High St) Impressive decorated plaster ceilings, and some hands-on exhibits for children. Disabled access to ground floor only; cl 24–26 Dec; free. **Gad's Hill School** (Higham, on the A226 NW) Dickens fans should also try to visit this, the only house the writer ever owned. He wrote many of his novels here, and his first sight of the house, many years before he lived there, is described in *A Christmas Carol*. Meals, snacks, shop; open pm 1st Sun of month Easter–Oct, plus bank hol Suns, during Broadstairs' summer and Christmas Dickens festivals, and other times – out of school hours – by arrangement, (01474) 822366; £2.50.

ROLVENDEN TQ8331 Good walking territory, with consistently appealing Wealden scenery, a **windmill** and oast houses gracing the landscape.

ROYAL MILITARY CANAL TR0634 Built along the N fringe of Romney Marsh as a defence against Napoleon, this forms a section of the Saxon Shore Way long-distance path; you can combine it with a path along the escarpment at Lympne Castle.

ST MARGARET'S BAY TR3844 **Pines Garden and Bay Museum** (Beach Rd) 6 acres of trees, shrubs, flowers and an ornamental lake, with small local history museum. Disabled access; museum cl am, Mon and Tues and all Sept–May, garden only cl 25 Dec; (01304) 852764; *£1.50. The spectacularly sited Coastguard is useful for refreshments. **South Foreland Lighthouse** (St Margaret's Bay) Clifftop exhibition on Marconi, who used the lighthouse in his early radio experiments, and excellent views from the top. Open pm wknds and bank hols Apr–Oct; £1.50; NT.

SANDHURST TQ7828 Fine 14th-c **church** with good views from the graveyard. **Sandhurst Vineyard** (Hoads Farm, Crouch Lane) has tours of vineyard and hop gardens; hop picking in Sept. Tastings and shop; cl am, and Jan–Easter exc by arrangement; (01580) 850296; free. They do B & B in a 16th-c farmhouse. **Tile Barn Nursery** (Standen Street, Iden Green, TQ8030) The only nursery in the world to specialise in wild cyclamen, with 4 greenhouses filled with over two dozen miniature species, most of them hardy, in flower Sept–Apr. Usually cl Sun–Tues, best to ring first to check; (01580) 240221. The 17th-c Woodcock signed nearby has decent food. E of Sandhurst an attractive round walk runs from Burnt House Farm on the A268, via Cledge Wood and Marsh Quarter Farm to the Kent Ditch and the River Rother, to take you round to Bodiam Castle in Sussex, and back via Northlands Farm and Silverden.

SANDLING TQ7558 **Museum of Kent Life** (Lock Lane) The story of the Kent countryside, entertainingly told over 27 acres, taking in farming tools, crafts, gardens, animals, and a working oast house. A fair bit for children, and special events at least every other wknd. Snacks, shop, disabled access; cl Nov–Mar; (01622) 763936; £3.95. Nearby, a well restored 17th-c barn on Bluebell Hill has information on the area's nature reserves; cl Jan; (01622) 662012; free. The King's Arms in the pretty neighbouring village of Boxley does decent lunches, with pleasant walks nearby.

SANDWICH TR3358 Pleasant quiet town with a surprising number of medieval remains, inc some sections of the old town wall and 3 handsome medieval **churches**, one part-Norman. In its day it was one of England's main commercial ports; the sea has now left it far behind. The best timbered buildings are in Strand St, with some by the attractive former quay on the River Stour (the old Bargate is very photogenic). **White Mill** (on the A257 just outside town) A cheerful place with a little folk museum; they've just had a Heritage grant so may expand and be open longer hours – at present open am Fri and Sun, plus pm Sun and bank hols Easter–mid-Sept; (01304) 612076; £1. The St Crispin in the pretty village of Worth just S, not far from the sands, is pleasant for lunch.

SEVENOAKS TQ5453 This commuters' town has little to see apart from the handsome old buildings of Sevenoaks School. However, the area around it has more walking potential than a glance at the OS map might suggest. The terrain is complicated, the Wealden villages unspoilt to a remarkable degree, and the path network dense and very well kept. Orchards, hop gardens, and tile-clad, timber-framed cottages and oast houses set the Kentish theme. Newcomers may be surprised to find such attractive and deeply rural countryside so close to London. **Knole** (just E) Originally a simple medieval manor house, this was transformed into a palace by a 15th-c Archbishop, Henry VIII, and several generations of the Sackville family. It's now a magnificent set piece, the largest – some would say the grandest – still lived-in private house in the country. It's a calendar house, with 365 rooms, 52 staircases and 7 courtyards. Outside are 26 acres of attractive grounds and a 1,000-acre deer park. Wrap up well: some of the beautifully furnished rooms can get a little chilly. Meals, snacks, shop, some disabled access; open pm Weds–Sun and bank hol Mon Apr–Oct; the garden is open only on the first Weds of each month May–Sept; (01732) 450608; £5, £2.50 car park; NT. The Park is criss-crossed with public paths and tracks encompassing the deer park, as well as the great house itself. The Buck's Head at nearby Godden Green has decent food. **Wildfowl reserve** (Bradbourne Vale Rd) 135 acres of lakes, ponds, woodland and reedbeds, several viewing hides and a satisfying nature trail. Snacks, shop, disabled access; open Weds, Sat, Sun and bank hols; (01732) 456407; £3. **Riverhill House Gardens** (A225 S) Hillside gardens with rose and shrub terraces, woodland walks among fine trees, rhododendrons, bluebells in spring, and fine views. Teas, plant sales; open pm Sun and bank hol wknds Apr–Jun; (01732) 458802; £2.50.

SISSINGHURST GARDEN TQ8037 Several charming gardens themed according to season or colour and cared for by obviously loving hands, all offset by the lovely tall-towered Elizabethan gatehouse (not open). Get there early – a timed ticket sytem is in operation, and they may close once capacity has been reached. Meals, snacks, shop, disabled access; cl am wkdys, all day Mon, and Oct–Mar; (01580) 712850; £6; NT. The Three Chimneys towards Biddenden is useful for lunch.

SMALL HYTHE TQ8930 **Smallhythe Place** (B2082) Handsome half-timbered house, now a museum of the life of former resident Dame Ellen Terry. Charming rose garden. Open pm Sat–Weds Apr–Oct; (01580) 762334; £3; NT. **Tenterden Vineyard and Herb Garden** (Spots Farm) Acres of vines, attractive lakes ideal for picnics, winery, herb garden, agricultural museum and new children's adventure trail. Meals, snacks, shop, some disabled access; cl 25–26 Dec, 1 Jan; (01580) 763033; free. **Wittersham windmill** (B2082 S) The tallest post mill in Kent; open pm Sun and bank hols May–Sept, £1. Further down the B2082 the Crown at Stone in Oxney is a good dining pub.

STAPLEHURST TQ7842 **Iden Croft Herbs** (Frittenden Rd) Peaceful walled herb gardens, thyme rockery, and gardens designed for the blind or disabled. Snacks, plant sales; cl winter Suns; (01580) 891432; *£1.50 gardens. The Lord Raglan (Chart Hill Rd) has reasonably priced food.

STELLING MINNIS TR1446 Working **windmill**, open pm Sun and bank hols Apr–Sept; 50p.

★ **TENTERDEN** TQ8833 Busy but attractive small town with lots of charming old buildings, especially 17th- and 18th-c character cottages on the N side of the very broad High St. A few antique shops, and the striking 15th-c Woolpack has good food. **Kent & East Sussex Railway** (A28 W) Steam trains from here to Northiam in Sussex, with lovely Wealden views; the line is being extended to Bodiam in Sussex. Meals, snacks, shop, disabled access; no trains Jan – (01580) 765155 for timetable; £6.50. There's a small local history **museum** further up the road (open pm wknds Mar–Oct, pm Mon–Thurs Apr–Oct, plus Fri mid-July–Aug; 75p).

TONBRIDGE TQ5946 **Tonbridge Castle** (just off the High St) A splendid Norman castle with good displays in 13th-c gatehouse, dramatic views from the battlements, and pleasant gardens. Shop; cl 25–26 Dec, 1 Jan, but lottery grant pending so best to phone to check; (01732) 770929; *£3. The commuter town is perked up a bit by the distinguished buildings of Tonbridge School, and with an outdoor area the **swimming pool** is a cut above the average municipal baths. In summer you can hire river rowing boats.

TROTTISCLIFFE TQ6561 (pronounced Trosley) There's a good walk E to the **Coldrum Stones**, a 4,000-year-old burial chamber, with an extension on to the North Downs (Trosley Country Park), densely wooded except on the steep slope itself. A problem for walkers elsewhere around here is that as you head E the farmland soon gets arable, with tedious slogs over ploughed fields.

TUNBRIDGE WELLS TQ5838 A busy commuters' shopping centre nowadays, but parts still show its former character as a genteel spa town. The allegedly health-restoring water still trickles through the Pantiles, the former centre of the town, full of elegant buildings and interesting shops. You can try the water at the Chalybeate Spring here, 25p a glass; cl Nov–Mar. The **church** of King Charles the Martyr is an interesting chapel built in the late 17th c for the gentry visiting the Pantiles; it has a remarkable plaster ceiling. Above the Pantiles the hillside Common is pleasant for strolls, with plenty of trees and rocks. **A Day at the Wells** The town's Georgian heyday elaborately re-created using very up-to-date display technology. Shop, disabled access (prior notice preferred); cl 25 Dec; (01892) 546545; £4.65. **Museum & Art Gallery** (Civic Centre, Mount Pleasant Rd) Examples of Tunbridge ware, the area's speciality small-scale woodware. Shop, disabled access; cl Sun and bank hols; (01892) 526121; free. **Spa Valley Railway** (Old West Station, by Sainsburys off the A26 just S of the centre) Developing railway running steam train trips as far as Groombridge. Best to ring (01892) 537715 for timetable; £3.50 return. **High Rocks** (off the A264 just W) On the edge of town, this former Stone Age camp has impressive sandstone formations in scenic woodland; take care when wet; cl 26 Dec; (01892) 515532; £2. The pub out here (with a stop on the steam railway) has good jazz nights.

UPCHURCH CHURCH TQ8467 13th c, with a unique 'candle snuffer' tower. An attractive village, with a decent pub.

UPNOR CASTLE TQ7570 Well preserved Elizabethan castle famous for failing to protect the Medway from the Dutch in 1667; attractive turrets, gatehouse and windows. Snacks, shop; open Apr–Sept; (01634) 718742; £3.50. Up towards the Thames marshes, the Black Bull at Cliffe has authentic Malaysian food.

WEST KINGSDOWN TQ5763 Largely Saxon **church**, given great appeal by its unique tranquil setting, in the middle of a wood. The yew tree by the west door looks very old indeed.

WEST MALLING TQ6857 Attractive village, most of which is a conservation area thanks to its many old timbered houses and wells; lots of nice alleyways to explore. Particularly worth a look are the **abbey**, one of the country's oldest ecclesiastical buildings, and **St Leonard's Tower**, a fine Norman tower from an 11th-c castle. **Manor Park Country Park** Lots of wildlife in its lake and copses, with children's play area and plenty of space to run round; cl 25 Dec; £1 parking Sun and bank hols, 50p other days.

WESTERHAM TQ4454 This pleasant country town is perhaps best known to visitors for Chartwell nearby, but it has other

Days Out

Weatherboarding and pantiles: Tenterden, and steamtrain trip on the Kent & E Sussex Railway; lunch aboard (Sun only), or at the Three Chimneys, Biddenden; Biddenden Vineyards; Sissinghurst; Cranbrook.

Journey to the end of the Earth: Folkestone harbour and The Leas; lunch at the Clarendon, Sandgate; perhaps stroll from Hythe town centre to Saltwood Castle; Romney Hythe & Dymchurch Railway from Hythe to Dungeness.

The White Cliffs: Dover Castle; lunch at Blakes (Castle St); White Cliffs Experience, or walk along the cliffs to St Margaret's Bay.

handsome houses on its doorstep, and pleasant walks in the surrounding countryside. **Quebec House** Gabled boyhood home of General Wolfe with exhibitions on his life and the battle that made his name. Open pm Tues and Sun Apr–Oct; (01892) 890651; £2.50; NT. **Squerryes Court** Overshadowed by its more famous neighbour Chartwell but to some people more satisfying, this fine 17th-c manor house overlooks attractive grounds and has excellent collections of paintings, china and furniture. The garden was first laid out in 1689 and is being painstakingly restored; some of the magnificent lime trees are as old as the house. Teas, shop; open pm Weds, wknds and bank hols Apr–Sept; (01959) 562345; £3.90, grounds only £2.40. **Chartwell** (off the B2026 S) The home of Winston Churchill until his death. Still much as he left them, the rooms are full of his possessions and reminders of his career, and the gardens are very attractive, with the famous black swans on the lakes. Though this is one of the NT's most popular houses (entry is by timed ticket), you need at least a passing interest in the statesman really to enjoy it. Meals, snacks, shop, disabled access; house and garden cl Nov–Mar, all Mon and Tues (exc bank hols and Tues July and Aug); (01732) 866368; £5.20 house and garden, gardens only £2.60, 50p; NT. This is good walking country. **Downe House** (Luxted Rd; TQ4360, 4½ miles N via Cudham – so in fact over the Greater London boundary) Bought by English Heritage in 1996, this attractive former home of Charles Darwin is now open to the public after extensive restoration costing £2 million. Darwin lived here with his family for 40 years during which he wrote most of his major works inc *On the Origin of Species*. Filled with his personal belongings, notes and journals, the ground floor is much as it was when the Darwins were in residence, while upstairs is an exhibition on Darwin's life and work. Restoration of the garden is still in progess. Snacks, shop, disabled access; cl Mon, Tues, all Feb and 24–26 Dec; essential to pre-book on (0870) 6030145; £5.

WHITSTABLE TR1066 The focus here is still very much the busy working harbour; the town **museum and gallery** (Oxford St) explores its maritime history and traditions. Shop, disabled access; cl 1–2pm, Weds and Sun, Good Fri, Christmas wk; free. **Oyster Fishery Exhibition** (East Quay) Looks at the traditional Kentish industry of oyster fishing, with live shellfish, and hands-on seashore exhibit for children. Shop, disabled access (though no facilities); cl Nov–Mar; (01227) 272003; £1.50. They sell fresh oysters (which you can order by mail), and a recipe book with ideas for cooking them. Pearsons fish restaurant is good value. **Chuffa Trains Railmania Museum** (High St) Small, friendly and ideal for children, with model trains and other toys to play on. Model-railway shop; cl Sun, Weds, bank hols; (01227) 277339; *£1.50. Unusually, the shingle beach is privately owned, by the Oyster Fishery.

WILLESBOROUGH WINDMILL TR0342 Working, open pm wknds Easter–mid-Oct; *£1.

★ **WINGHAM BIRD PARK** TR2558 Endangered birds from around the world, with the emphasis on breeding and conservation; they now have a large walk-through aviary. Also racoons, wallabies and other animals, and a good adventure playground (made from recycled materials). Snacks, shop, disabled access; cl 25–26 Dec; (01227) 720836; *£3.50. The village is attractive, with decent food in 2 medieval inns, the Dog and Red Lion.

WOODCHURCH TQ9534 **South of England Rare Breeds Centre** Acres of Kentish farmland with one of the largest collections of rare farm animals in Europe; lots of pigs, cattle, horses, goats and poultry. All nicely undeveloped and friendly, with plenty for children to touch and fuss (and a paddling pool and play area for letting off steam). In summer there are lots of special events. Meals, snacks, shop, disabled access; cl winter Mons, 24–25 Dec; (01233) 861493; £3.25. **Woodchurch Windmill** Well restored, still grinding corn for demonstrations, and its sails turning whenever it's open. Shop; open pm Sun and bank hols Easter–Sept; (01233) 860043; *£1.

⛰ ❀ **WYE DOWNS** TR0746 Some of Kent's nicest walks are on the North Downs not that high, but steep enough along the escarpment to give some great views. The Wye Downs, designated a nature reserve for their chalkland flora that includes a variety of orchids, look across the orchards below to both the Thames Estuary and the Channel. The road above Wye through Hastingleigh, Bodsham Green, Sole Street and along the Crundale Downs is a nice drive.

❀ **YALDING ORGANIC GARDENS** TQ6949 (B2162 just S of Yalding) Interesting series of gardens maintained by the Henry Doubleday Research Association, the organic farming and gardening organisation (*see also Ryton Gardens in Warwickshire chapter*); each looks at how people have cultivated land in a given period, from medieval physick gardens to modern organic vegetable plots. Open wknds Apr and Oct, Weds–Sun May–Sept, and Easter and bank hols; (01622) 814650; £2.50. The Walnut Tree is a handy food stop.

★ **Other attractive villages**, all with decent pubs, include Addington TQ6559, Bishopsbourne TR1852, Bodsham TR1045, Boughton Lees TR0247, Bridge TR1854, Challock TR0050, Chillenden TR2653, Egerton TQ9047, Elham TR1743, Harvel TQ6563, Ickham TR2257, Leigh TQ5446, Martin TR3346, Offham TQ6557, Shipbourne TQ5952, Smarden TQ8842, Speldhurst TQ5541, Stalisfield Green TQ9553, Sutton Valence TQ8149, West Peckham TQ6452, Wickhambreaux TR2158, Worth TR3356 and Wrotham TQ6159.

Pubs useful for walkers include the Bald Faced Stag at Ashurst TQ5038, Woolpack at Benover TQ7048, Pepper Box at Fairbourne Heath above Ulcombe TQ8550, Woodman on Goathurst Common TQ4952, Buck's Head at Godden Green TQ5555, Ringlestone Inn TQ8755 N of Harrietsham, Rock at Hoath Corner TQ4943, Cock at Ide Hill TQ4851, Cock at Henley St nr Luddesdown TQ6667, Kentish Horse at Markbeech TQ4742, Horns and Bull at Otford TQ5359, Fox & Hounds at Toy's Hill TQ4751, Harrow at Warren Street TQ9253 and Rising Sun at Woodlands TQ5560.

Where to eat

BARFRESTONE TR2650 **Yew Tree** *(01304) 831619* Chatty and relaxed pub tucked away by pretty Saxon church in country hamlet; old pine and hops, second little bar with French windows on to the garden, and a cosy dining room; good bar food (daily specials inc local game), 7 real ales, and 7 fresh coffees; disabled access. **£12**|£5.

BIDDENDEN TQ8438 **Claris's** *High St (01580) 291025* Charming no smoking 15th-c tearoom and gift shop with beams and inglenook fireplaces, lace tablecloths, a little garden, and home-made cakes and savouries all day; cl Mon, 3 wks Jan. £3.90.

BIDDENDEN TQ8238 **Three Chimneys** *A262 W (01580) 291472* Atmospheric country pub with small beamed rooms, log fires, and imaginative food from a large, seasonally changing menu; cl 25–26 Dec; children in garden dining room only. **£18.15**|£6.95.

CANTERBURY TR1556 **La Bonne Cuisine** *Canterbury Hotel, 71 New Dover Rd (01227) 450551* Run by the same family for over 20 years, this neat little hotel is warmly friendly and comfortable and serves beautifully presented and very good French food in the cheerfully yellow dining room; attractive bdrms. **£22**.

CANTERBURY TR1457 **Sully's** *High St (01227) 766266* Part of the County Hotel, this slightly old-fashioned-looking restaurant has good, imaginative, seasonally changing cooking inc 2- and 3-course set menus (plenty of choice), and a generous lunchtime roast; disabled access. **£29.50 dinner, £23.50 lunch**|£9.95.

DARGATE TR0861 **Dove** *(01227) 751360* Well liked pub with popular, imaginative food and well kept real ales; rambling rooms with good winter fire, plenty of seats on the bare boards, and a sheltered, pretty garden. **£20.75**|£9.

EDENBRIDGE TQ4445 **Honours Mill** *87 High St (01732) 866757* Charmingly converted watermill with lots of beams in the downstairs bar and upstairs restaurant; nice interesting food (the weekday set menus are popular and good value), and a mainly French wine list; cl am Sat, pm Sun, Mon, 2 wks Christmas. **£26 dinner, £15.50 lunch.**

FAVERSHAM TR0161 **Albion** *(01795) 591411* Creekside pub (nice walks) with a pleasant chatty atmosphere in the airy open-plan bar, perfectly kept beer and a sensible choice of very imaginative food from French chef; lots of outside seats for summer evenings; disabled access. **£18**|£6.25.

FINGLESHAM TR3353 **Crown** *(01304) 612555* Pleasant 16th-c country pub, attractively refurbished, with a wide choice of reasonably priced bar food, popular old-world restaurant with inglenook fireplace and flagstones, and good, friendly service; cl pm 25 Dec. **£16**|£4.75.

FOLKESTONE TR2335 **Paul's** *2a Bouverie Rd W (01303) 259697* Popular, enjoyable restaurant run by the same owners for well over 20 years, with very imaginative food inc good fish, game and vegetarian options, and a decent wine list; cl 1 wk Christmas; disabled access. **£22.20**|£4.95.

HERNHILL TR0660 **Red Lion** *(01227) 751207* Pretty Tudor inn next to the church, with long, narrow, beamed and flagstoned interior, nice interesting bar food, well kept real ales, and upstairs restaurant. **£20**|£7.75.

HOLLINGBOURNE TQ8455 **Dirty Habit** *(01622) 880880* Early 15th-c inn with quite a bit of character in the various rooms, panelled and candlelit dining room with an interesting mix of seats, good and enjoyable bar food, well kept real ales, a relaxed atmosphere, and friendly staff. **£21**|£8.95.

IVY HATCH TQ5854 **Plough** *(01732) 810268* Relaxed and friendly tile-hung house with good, imaginative and constantly changing food (inc separate fish menu), interesting wines and well kept beers, and efficient service; cosy bar areas, elegant conservatory restaurant, and nearby walks; best to book; disabled access; cl pm Sun. **£20**|£7.50.

LANGTON GREEN TQ5439 **Hare** *(01892) 862419* Popular and civilised dining pub with light, airy, knocked-through rooms, a chatty atmosphere, imaginative, generously served food from a menu that changes twice daily, attentive waitress service, and decent wines and beers; outside terrace; children in restaurant (not in bar); cl pm 25 Dec, pm 1 Jan; partial disabled access. **£22.80**|£5.95.

LITTLEBOURNE TR2057 **King William IV** *4 High St (01227) 721244* Friendly inn with straightforward character and décor but with good, freshly prepared, interesting food like ostrich and kangaroo, very good service, well kept real ales, interesting wines; bdrms. **£22**|£7.95.

NEWNHAM TQ9557 **George** *(01795) 890237* Distinctive 16th-c pub with friendly staff, imaginative food using fresh local produce, well kept beers, and good wines; no food pm Sun, Mon; children allowed, disabled access. **£18.50**|£7.50.

PAINTER'S FORSTAL TQ9958 **Read's** *(01795) 535344* Excellent restaurant with a comfortable bar and airy dining room, and lovely views from the back terrace; exceptionally good, innovative English cooking using the best local ingredients, wonderful puddings, a marvellous wine list, and neat young staff; cl Sun, Mon; disabled access. **£28.50 wkdys, £42.50 wknds.**

PENSHURST TQ5142 **Bottle House** *Coldharbour Rd (01892) 870306* Relaxed and friendly 15th-c pub with huge beams, stone pillars, and big windows in the unpretentious bars, lots of old sewing machines, excellent popular food, efficient service, and well kept local ales; cl 25 Dec. **£20**|£4.95.

PENSHURST TQ5242 **Spotted Dog** *Smarts Hill (01892) 870253* Quaint tiled house with fantastic views over Penshurst Place from the terrace, particularly good food from a constantly changing menu, excellent wines and real ales, popular restaurant, and fine inglenook and a bustling atmosphere in the neatly kept beamed and timbered bar; cl pm Mon, 25–26 Dec. **£20.50**|£8.25.

RINGLESTONE TQ8755 **Ringlestone** *(01622) 859900* Welcoming atmosphere in interestingly decorated, deservedly popular country pub, with very good, interesting food, especially the hot and cold lunchtime buffet (no chips or fried food), and lots of real ales and country wines; cl 25 Dec; bedrooms. **£28**|£5.75.

SANDGATE TR1934 **La Terrasse** *Sandgate Hotel, Wellington Terrace, The Esplanade (01303) 220444* Smart Victorian hotel and restaurant overlooking a pebbled beach, with open fires and fresh flowers, excellent classic French cooking and a fine wine list, and helpful, knowledgeable staff; attractive bdrms; cl pm Sun, Mon, Jan. **£27.50 wkdys, £36.50 wknds.**

SELLING TR0455 **Rose & Crown** *Perry Wood (01227) 752214* Quietly civilised, tucked-away woodland pub (good walks) with a relaxed atmosphere, lots of beams, hops and interesting corn-dolly work, a huge fireplace, comfortably cushioned seats, friendly, helpful service, good, generously served food, well kept real ales, and decent wines; children in restaurant/family room; limited disabled access. **£18.65**|£6.

SISSINGHURST TQ7937 **Rankins** *The Street (01580) 713964* Interesting, enjoyable food from a fixed evening and Sun lunch menu in pretty white clapboarded cottage, inc lovely puddings and vegetarian choices; no smoking until food service has finished; cl Mon, Tues; children by prior arrangement; partial disabled access. **£29.25.**

TENTERDEN TQ8833 **Kent & E Sussex Railway** *Tenterden Town Station (01580) 765155* Steam-hauled and ornately decorated Pullman dining car with good English food (Sun lunch/afternoon tea/dinner) served by authentically dressed stewards; great fun; cl Jan–Feb; children on selected services; disabled access. **£26**|£3.50.

TUNBRIDGE WELLS TQ5839 **Sankeys** *39 Mount Ephraim (01892) 511422* Excellent fresh fish and seafood cooked in all sorts of ways in several cosy and relaxed restaurant rooms, very good wines, real ales, and friendly service; cheaper lively downstairs cellar wine bar too (get there early for a seat), and seats in the walled garden; cl Sun. **£21.50**|£8.50.

TUNBRIDGE WELLS TQ5839 **Thackeray's House** *85 London Rd (01892) 511921* Civilised detached house with 2 beamed upstairs rooms, pretty paintings, a mix of tables with crisp white cloths, very relaxed, comfortable atmosphere, friendly but carefully professional service, interesting and enjoyable food, and very good house wines; downstairs, the small wine bar does simpler food; cl pm Sun, Mon, Christmas. **£35**|£10.

ULCOMBE TQ8550 **Pepper Box** *Fairbourne Heath (01622) 842558* Cosy old country pub with low beams and standing timbers in friendly, homely bar, comfortable sofa and armchairs by splendid inglenook fireplace, very good, imaginative food, well kept real ales, and efficient, courteous service; nice views from the garden. **£20.45**|£7.50.

WHITSTABLE TR1066 **Pearsons** *(01227) 272005* Consistently good, very fresh seafood in homely upstairs restaurant; kind and quick service – even when very busy; bustling traditional pub downstairs; cl 25 Dec. **£20**|£6.95.

Special thanks to Mr and Mrs G Howard, I W Hughes, Mr and Mrs R Marshall, E G Parish.

We welcome reports from readers

This *Guide* depends on readers' reports. Do help us if you can – in return, we offer a discount on the next edition to people who've helped us with reports for it. Tell us what you think about places already in it, and anything extra you think we should say about them. And send us your ideas for inclusion in the next edition: places to visit, eat at or stay in, attractive drives or walks, maybe even unusual interesting shops you know of. Use the card in the middle, the report forms at the end, or just write – no stamp needed: *The Good Guide to Britain*, FREEPOST TN1569, Wadhurst, E Sussex TN5 7BR.

Kent Calendar

Some of these dates were provisional as we went to press. Please check information with the telephone numbers provided.

JANUARY

1 **Leeds** New Year's Day Treasure Trail at the Castle (01622) 765400

FEBRUARY

15 **Leeds** Historical Story-telling at the Castle – *till Fri 19* (01622) 765400

MARCH

6 **Dover** Film Festival – *till Weds 10* (01304) 212268
27 **Penshurst** Armada: Penshurst Place in 1588 as it prepares for the Spanish Invasion – *till Sun 28* (01892) 870307

APRIL

2 **Beltring** Easter Capers at the Hop Farm – *till Mon 5* (01622) 872068; **Sandling** Easter Chicken Hunt at the Museum of Kent Life – *till Mon 5* (01622) 763936
3 **Leeds** Celebration of Easter at the Castle – *till Mon 5* (01622) 765400
4 **Chatham** Mad Hatter's Tea Party: characters from *Alice in Wonderland*, magic show, fun and games at the Historic Dockyard – *till Mon 5* (01634) 812551; **Penshurst** Easter at Penshurst Place: trailer rides, stories and eggs – *till Mon 5* (01892) 870307
6 **Folkestone** Children's Fun Festival – *till Sat 10* (01303) 255070
17 **Leeds** Greenhouse Weekend: meet the groundsmen at the Castle – *till Sun 18* (01622) 765400
18 **Penshurst** Concert at Penshurst Place (01892) 870307
23 **Broadstairs** St Peter's Millennium Egg-Rolling Competitions (01843) 861020
30 **Folkestone** East Garden Coast Dance Festival at Leas Cliff Hall – *till 3 May* (01303) 253193

MAY

1 **Hever** May Day Celebrations at the Castle – *till Mon 3* (01732) 865224; **Penshurst** Weald of Kent Craft Show at Penshurst Place – *till Mon 3* (01892) 870307; **Rochester** Sweeps Festival: processions, morris dancers, ceilidhs, street entertainment – *till Mon 3* (01634) 843666
2 **Sandling** May Day Celebrations at the Museum of Kent Life – *till Mon 3* (01622) 763936
3 **Broadstairs** May Day Fête (01843) 865230; **Whitstable** May Day Celebrations (01227) 763763
7 **Canterbury** World Cup Cricket Fixtures (01227) 456886
9 **Canterbury** World Cup Cricket Fixtures (01227) 456886; **New Romney** Steam & Diesel Gala at Romney, Hythe & Dymchurch Railway (01797) 362353
15 **Leeds** Festival of English Food and Wine at the Castle – *till Sun 16* (01622) 765400

Kent Calendar (cont.)

18 Canterbury World Cup Cricket Fixtures (01227) 456886

23 Ramsgate Spring Festival: classical, jazz and popular concerts, street entertainment, children's events – *till 6 Jun* (01843) 580994

29 Deal East Kent Garden Show at Castle Community School – *till Mon 31* (01304) 201644; **Dover** Festival: street entertainment, dance – *till 5 Jun* (01304) 872058; **Hever** Medieval Entertainments at the Castle – *till Mon 31* (01732) 865224; **Sellindge** Steam Special at Hope Farm – *till Mon 31* (01303) 813000

30 Goudhurst Spring Fair at Finchcocks – *till Mon 31* (01580) 211702; **Penshurst** Classic Car Show at Penshurst Place – *till Mon 31* (01892) 870307; **Sandling** Family Fun Weekend at the Museum of Kent Life – *till Mon 31* (01622) 763936; **Woodchurch** Piggy Picnics: pig obstacle course, races, puppet shows at the Rare Breeds Centre – *till Mon 31* (01233) 861493

31 Broadstairs Medieval Day (01843) 861020; **Leeds** Family Maze and Garden Week at the Castle – *till 6 Jun* (01622) 765400; **Penshurst** Wool Race: demonstration of sheep shearing, spinning, weaving and knitting at Penshurst Place (01892) 870307

JUNE

3 Leeds Flower Festival at the Castle – *till Sun 6* (01622) 765400; **Rochester** Dickens Festival: Victorian costumed parade, street entertainers, *son et lumière*, fireworks – *till Sun 6* (01634) 843666

5 Biggin Hill International Air Fair – *till Sun 6* (01959) 572277

6 Herne Bay Heavy Horse Parade (01227) 742690; **Ramsgate** The Great Bucket and Spade Vintage Car Run: over 300 vehicles (01843) 583333

19 Broadstairs Dickens Festival – *till Sat 26* (01843) 601364; **Lydd** Carnival Day (01797) 320892; **Westerham** Big Band Fireworks Concert at Chartwell (01732) 866368

20 Beltring Motorcycle Show at the Hop Farm (01622) 872068; **Lamberhurst** Vintage Car Rally at Bewl Water (01892) 890661

26 Leeds Open-air Concert at the Castle (01622) 765400

30 Leeds Children's Promenade Concert at the Castle (01622) 765400

JULY

3 Ash Carnival (01304) 812662; **Beltring** Kent Steam and Vintage Vehicle Rally at the Hop Farm – *till Sun 4* (01622) 872068; **Dover** Carnival (01304) 872074; **Folkestone** Napoleonic Re-enactment at Martello Tower, East Cliff – *till Sun 4* (01516) 486592; **Ightham** Songs from the Shows: open-air concert at Ightham Mote (01732) 810378; **Leeds** Open-air Concert at the Castle (01622) 765400; **Ramsgate** Ships' Open Days at Ramsgate Royal Harbour – *till Sun 4* (01843) 587765

4 Broadstairs Horse Show (01843) 865819; **Herne Bay** Punch & Judy Day (01227) 742690; **Penshurst** Falconry at Penshurst Place – *every Sun in July and Aug* (01892) 870307

7 Broadstairs Fireworks Display – and *every Weds evening in July and Aug*

8 Lamberhurst Open-air Opera and Concert at Scotney Castle – *till Sun 11 (or may run Thurs 15–Sun 18)* (01892) 891081

10 Penshurst Balloon Fiesta: balloons take off at 6am and 6pm – *till Sun 11* at Penshurst Place (01892) 870307

11 Sandling Historic Commercial Vehicle Gathering at the Museum of Kent Life (01622) 763936

Kent Calendar (cont.)

15 Detling Kent County Show – *till Sat 17* (01622) 630975
17 Lamberhurst Firework & Laser Concert at Bewl Water (01892) 890661; **Penshurst** Classical Concert at Penshurst Place (01892) 870307
18 Birchington Carnival Procession (01843) 846785
22 Canterbury Kent Beer Festival: over 80 real ales and ciders, live bands – *till Sat 24* (01227) 463478
23 Beltring Invicta Military War & Peace Show at the Hop Farm – *till Sun 25* (01622) 872068; **Ramsgate** Carnival Fair – *till* Procession on *Sun 25* (01843) 593413
24 Dartford Festival – *till Sun 25* (01322) 343242; **Lamberhurst** Have-a-go Weekend at Bewl Water: sailing, windsurfing, canoeing, archery and more – *till Sun 25* (01892) 890661; **Penshurst** Elizabethan Revelry at Penshurst Place – *till Sun 25* (01892) 870307; **Whitstable** Regatta and Oyster Festival: landing of oysters and parade – *till 1 Aug* (01227) 265666
28 Broadstairs and Ramsgate Viking Festival inc Viking ship – *till 1 Aug* (01843) 225511; **Tunbridge Wells** Scandals at the Spa – Georgian Festival in the Pantiles – *till 1 Aug* (01892) 515675
29 Ramsgate Children's Open Day at Ramsgate Royal Harbour (01843) 587765
31 Birchington Fireworks Concert (01843) 232281; **Penshurst** Elizabethan Revelry at Penshurst Place – *till 1 Aug* (01892) 870307; **Ramsgate** Harbour Heritage Festival – *till 29 Aug* (01843) 587694

AUGUST

1 Margate Carnival Procession (01843) 293733
4 Canterbury Cricket Week – *till Sun 8* (01227) 456886
6 Broadstairs Folk Week: international shows, torchlight procession – *till Fri 13* (01843) 604080; **Penshurst** Outdoor Jazz at Penshurst Place (01892) 870307
7 New Romney Country Fair inc carnival and arena (01797) 364600; **Sandling** Woodland and Traditional Crafts at the Museum of Kent Life – *till Sun 8* (01622) 763936; **Whitstable** Carnival (01227) 273436
8 Broadstairs Carnival Procession (01843) 585456
14 Beltring Heavy Horse Show at the Hop Farm – *till Sun 15* (01622) 872068; **Brasted** *The Blues Band* at Emmett's Garden (01892) 890651; **Detling** Transport and Country Fair: over 1,000 exhibits – *till Sun 15* (01622) 630975; **Margate** East Kent Kite Fair at Palm Bay – *till Sun 15* (01843) 224593; **Ramsgate** International Sailing Week – *till Sat 21* (01843) 591766
15 Herne Bay Carnival (01227) 742690
18 Hythe Venetian Fête: floodlit river carnival on the Royal Military Canal (01303) 266024
20 Margate Festival of Fun – *till Sun 22* (01843) 225511
21 Folkestone Carnival (01303) 220889
22 Penshurst *Much Ado About Nothing* at Penshurst Place (01892) 870307; **Westgate on Sea** Carnival Procession (01843) 296548; **Woodchurch** Rare Breeds Show and Country Fair at the Rare Breeds Centre (01233) 861493
25 Broadstairs Water Gala (01843) 863225
26 Dover Pageant at Dover College – *till Sat 28* (01304) 201711
28 Goudhurst Eighteenth-century Gala: concerts and dancing at Finchcocks – *till Mon 30* (01580) 211702; **Rochester** Norman Festival: re-enactments throughout the town inc encampment in castle grounds – *till Mon 30* (01634) 843666

Kent Calendar (cont.)

30 Tunbridge Wells Sedan Chair Race in the Pantiles (01892) 515675

SEPTEMBER

3 Folkestone Shepway Festival: airshow, fireworks and motoring pageant – *till Sun 5* (01303) 852321

4 Faversham Hop Festival – *till Sun 5* (01795) 585601; **Sandling** Beer & Hop Festival at the Museum of Kent Life – *till Sun 5* (01622) 763936

5 Ramsgate Victorian Street Fair (01843) 596288

6 Ramsgate Model Ships Rally at Westcliff (01843) 585951

10 Deal Sea Shanty Festival – *till Sun 12* (01304) 872058; **Goudhurst** Finchcocks Festival: opera and chamber music played on period instruments – *every wknd till 3 Oct* (01580) 211702

11 Leeds Balloon & Vintage Car Weekend at the Castle – *till Sun 12* (01622) 765400

18 Boughton Farming Festival at Farming World – *till Sun 19* (01227) 751144

20 Folkestone Kent Literature Festival at the Metropole Arts Centre – *till Sat 25* (01303) 255070

25 Folkestone Euromilitaire: one of the world's largest military modelling displays inc bands, war-gaming and re-enactments at Leas Cliff Hall – *till Sun 26* (01303) 253193

OCTOBER

2 Folkestone Model Railway Exhibition at Leas Cliff Hall – *till Sun 3* (01303) 253193

3 Penshurst Classical Concert at Penshurst Place (01892) 870307

8 Goudhurst Autumn Fair at Finchcocks – *till Sun 10* (01580) 211702

9 Canterbury Festival: classical, jazz, folk, blues, street entertainment, children's events, fireworks – *till Sat 23* (01227) 452853; **Folkestone** Southern Counties Brass Band Competition at Leas Cliff Hall – *till Sun 10* (01303) 253193; **Sandling** Apple & Cider Festival at the Museum of Kent Life – *till Sun 10* (01622) 763936

18 Leeds Festival of Autumn Flowers and Produce at the Castle – *till Sun 24* (01622) 765400

23 Broadstairs Celebrity Connections Family Festival – *till Fri 29* (01843) 868718

NOVEMBER

6 Leeds Fireworks at the Castle (01622) 765400; **Sandling** Fireworks at the Museum of Kent Life (01622) 763936

DECEMBER

4 Rochester Dickensian Christmas: street theatre, children's shows, carol singers – *till Sun 5* (01634) 843666

13 Leeds Christmas at the Castle – *till Fri 24* with open-air carol service *on Fri 17* (01622) 765400

31 Dover, Deal and Walmer Fireworks, Beacon Lighting, Torchlight Processions (01304) 872057; the South Foreland Lighthouse, Dover will see the first light of dawn in England on 1 Jan 2000 (01304) 852463

Lancashire

Good value and rich variety, with a lot of surprises.

Both for holidays and for outings there's great variety here, from lively family entertainment and Blackpool's summer high spirits to unspoilt moorland and charming quiet villages, from the mass of interesting things to do in Manchester and Liverpool to a good range of days out elsewhere. Places to stay and eat out offer particularly good value, and the people are really warm-hearted.

Manchester and Liverpool are both splendid for day visits, especially on summer weekends, with grand Victorian buildings, and all sorts of attractions. Both have very good public transport. This year Liverpool perhaps has the edge, with its refurbished Tate Gallery, bargain Eight Pass joint admissions ticket and a particularly helpful tourist office (not to mention the opening of the McCartney family home, and a new visitor centre at Anfield); while Manchester is rebuilding parts of its centre, and multi-million-pound refits mean major gallery and museum closures there.

Elsewhere, the re-creation of 1900s life at Wigan Pier is quite engrossing, and other choice places include the Birkenhead warships, Bury's steam railway, Hoghton Tower, Leighton Hall, the Martin Mere wildfowl centre, the safari park at Prescot, Rufford Old Hall, and the Leighton Moss nature reserve above Silverdale. Family favourites are the Camelot theme park at Charnock Richard, and, in Manchester, the Granada studios and the science and industry museum.

There's glorious countryside even just outside the big cities, where the South Lancancashire moors have plenty of scope for exhilarating drives and walks, and bewitched Pendle Hill has always held the imagination. Other areas of fine countryside include the great whaleback of Longridge Fell, the wooded Beacon Fell country park, the magnificent Pennine moorland of the Forest of Bowland, and the peaceful and little-visited Silverdale/Arndale area up beyond the attractive town of Lancaster.

The area has some lovely stretches of sand, and, of course, its famous traditional seaside resorts. Blackpool, with more visitors each year than the whole of Spain, has lots of discos, fun pubs and so forth, as well as its vivid array of entertainments – more a place for young adults to have summer fun than for family beach holidays. Out of season, when those long stretches of beach and dune are empty, they have a certain lonely charm, and there's an element of fascination about the treacherous tidal sands of Morecambe Bay.

Where to stay

ASHWORTH VALLEY SD8512 **Leaches Farm** *Ashworth Valley, Rochdale OL11 5UN (01706) 41117* ***£36;** 3 rms, shared bthrm. 17th-c hill farm with really wonderful views, massive stone walls, beams and log fires; cl Christmas and New Year; children over 8 and dogs by arrangement.

BILSBORROW SD5039 **Guy's Thatched Hamlet** *Bilsborrow, Preston PR3 0RS (01995) 640010* ***£48,** plus wknd breaks; 53 smartly modern rms. Bustling complex by the canal; thatched tavern, restaurant and pizzeria, outside terrace, play area and craft shops; good base for exploring the area; open all day; cl 25 Dec; disabled access.

BLACKPOOL SD3037 **Imperial** *North Promenade, Blackpool FY1 2HB (01253) 623971* **£150,** plus special breaks; 183 well equipped rms. Fine Victorian hotel overlooking the sea; with spacious and comfortable day rooms, lots of period features, and a full health and fitness club with indoor swimming pool, gym, jacuzzi, steam and sauna room and solarium free to residents; disabled access.

BROMLEY CROSS SD7213 **Drop Inn** *Hospital Rd, Last Drop, Bromley Cross BL7 9PZ (01204) 591131* **£99;** 86 rms. Big, well equipped Rank hotel complex cleverly integrated into an olde-worlde pastiche village, complete with a stone-and-cobbles street of gift and tea shops, bakery, etc., even a spacious, creeper-covered pub with lots of beamery and timbering; popular, one-price hot and cold buffet, and heavy tables out on the attractive flagstoned terrace; disabled access.

BURY SD8313 **Normandie** *Elbut Lane, Birtle, Bury BL9 6UT (0161) 764 3869* ***£69;** 23 attractive rms. Unpretentious hotel high on the Pennines, with fine views; homely lounge and a snug bar, excellent French and English restaurant food, fine wine list, and friendly, professional service; cl 2 wks from 26 Dec, 1 wk over Easter; disabled access.

CAPERNWRAY SD5371 **New Capernwray Farmhouse** *Capernwray, Carnforth LA6 1AD (01524) 734284* ***£64;** 3 comfortable rms. Pretty, 300-year-old, former farmhouse, with helpful and friendly owners; cosy lounge, stone walls and beams, and candlelit dinner in what was the dairy; they offer personally conducted tours; children over 10; cl Nov–Mar.

CHIPPING SD6343 **Gibbon Bridge** *Chipping, Preston PR3 2TQ (01995) 61456* **£100,** plus special breaks; 30 rms, inc 22 split-level suites overlooking gardens. Family-owned country hotel with beautiful landscaped gardens (plus popular bandstand featuring local bands); attractively presented food in the spacious, airy restaurant and adjoining conservatory, a quiet relaxing atmosphere, fine wines, and helpful service; health and gym area; a good base for walking and short driving trips; licensed for marriages, they have a thriving trade in civil weddings; good disabled access.

COLNE SD8741 **Higher Wanless Farm** *Red Lane, Colne BB8 7JP (01282) 865301* ***£42;** 2 rms, one with own bthrm. Warmly welcoming farmhouse with beams, log fires and lovely surrounding farmland used mainly for the breeding of shire horses, as well as sheep; cl mid-Dec–mid-Jan; children over 3.

COWAN BRIDGE SD6475 **Hipping Hall** *Cowan Bridge, Kirkby Lonsdale, Carnforth LA6 2JJ (01524) 271187* **£88,** plus special breaks; 7 pretty rms, 5 in main hotel, 2 cottage suites across courtyard (can be self-catering). Relaxed country-house atmosphere and delicious food in this handsome small hotel, with help-yourself drinks in the conservatory; an open fire, lovely beamed Great Hall with minstrels' gallery where guests dine together, and 4 acres of walled gardens; fine walks from the front door; cl Nov–Feb; children over 12.

DARWEN SD7222 **Old Rosins** *Pickup Bank, Hoddlesden, Darwen BB3 3QD (01254) 771264* **£62.50,** plus wknd breaks; 15 well equipped rms. Friendly old pub tucked below the moors, ideal as a base for exploring the area; good views from cosy open-plan bar, interesting bar and restaurant food; partial disabled access.

HURST GREEN SD6937 **Shireburn Arms** *Hurst Green, Blackburn BB7 9QJ (01254) 826518* ***£60,** plus special breaks; 18 rms. Lovely 17th-c country hotel with a refined but friendly atmosphere, an airy and neatly modernised bar, a comfortable lounge, and open fires; well presented, enjoyable food in the restaurant, good service, and fine view of the Ribble Valley from the conservatory; disabled access.

LANGHO SD7034 **Northcote Manor** *Northcote Rd, Langho, Blackburn BB6 8BE (01254) 240555* **£110;** 14 attractive rms with antiques, bric-à-brac and board games, reached up a fine staircase. In pretty countryside, this neatly kept, red brick Victorian house is more of a restaurant with rooms; beams and oak panelling, big log fires, and 2 comfortable lounges; wonderful breakfasts, and delicious food in the civilised dining room; cl 25 Dec, 1–2 Jan; partial disabled access.

MANCHESTER SJ8397 **Victoria & Albert** *Water St, Manchester M3 4JQ (0161) 832 1188* **£99w, £149 mid-week,** plus special breaks; 156 rms, individually styled and named after TV programmes. Carefully converted Victorian warehouse opposite Granada TV studios (free entry if staying here); with original iron pillars, oak beams and exposed brickwork, particularly good service, and a comfortable bar overlooking the river; imaginative food in both the restaurant and all-day brasserie; disabled access.

WADDINGTON SD7243 **Backfold Cottage** *The Square, Waddington, Clitheroe BB7 3JA (01200) 422367* ***£42;** 3 rms. Tiny 17th-c cottage in a cobbled street; beautifully furnished with antiques, very good service, and candlelit evening meals (bring your own wines); nice nearby walks; children at owner's discretion.

WADDINGTON SD7144 **Peter Barn** *Cross Lane, Waddington, Clitheroe BB7 3JH (01200) 428585* ***£44,** plus special breaks; 3 lovely rms. Converted old stone tithe barn with a beamed sitting room, antiques, and lovely home cooking; warmly welcoming owners and a gentle atmosphere; surrounded by a delightful garden, fine walking country; cl Christmas/New Year; children over 6.

WHITEWELL SD6546 **Inn at Whitewell** *Whitewell, Clitheroe BB7 3AT (01200) 448222* ***£79.50;** 11 refurbished rms, some with open peat fires. Civilised stone inn in the Forest of Bowland; an attractive setting and grounds with views down the valley; interesting period furnishings, plenty of room, good food, fine wines, and unusual facilities such as an art gallery and 6 miles of trout, salmon and sea trout fishing; friendly dogs welcome.

YEALAND CONYERS SD5074 **Bower** *Yealand Conyers, Carnforth LA5 9SF (01524) 734585* ***£52;** 2 attractive rms. Charming, little, no smoking, Georgian house in a big garden with views of Ingleborough and the surrounding hills; friendly owners (keen bridge players), an open fire and piano in the comfortable sitting room, and enjoyable food served around a large table in the dining room; children over 12; dogs by prior arrangement.

To see and do

LIVERPOOL SJ3590 One of the world's most imposing waterfronts – the fine 19th-c buildings which mark Liverpool's past as one of the world's great ports have in the last few years taken on a cleaner and prouder look. At the same time a good few varied family attractions have opened. Many are covered by the excellent-value National Museums and Galleries on Merseyside Eight Pass: admission to any one of the 8 attractions in the scheme (£3, £1.50 concessions) allows unlimited visits for a year to that and the other 7 attractions. The Philharmonic (Hope St) is probably the country's grandest late Victorian pub; nearby, the Everyman Bistro has good-value food. You can tour the city's trademark Liver Building on wkdys Apr–Sept by arrangement, (0151) 236 2748, though it's best viewed from one of the famous ferries across the Mersey, which leave regularly from Pier Head. The real commuter ferries operate half-hourly during rush hours (£1.70 return); the rest of the day the boats are hourly and aimed at visitors, with a commentary (£3.30 return).

† LIVERPOOL CATHEDRALS Unusually, both Liverpool's cathedrals were built this century, in widely differing styles. Walk along Hope St (the heart of the city's 18th-c area, with many Georgian brick terraces) to the impressive and more obviously modern **Metropolitan Roman Catholic cathedral**, designed by Frederick Gibberd after a vast earlier scheme by Lutyens ran out of money; blue light from the 16-sided glass tower reflects evocatively on the marble inside. The **Anglican cathedral** looks much older, but was completed only in 1978. Britain's biggest, it's undeniably powerful, though its soaring proportions and cavernous scale make it impersonal. Both have good concerts.

Albert Dock Spectacular restoration of previously redundant warehouse buildings by the river, now a lively complex of shops, cafés and exhibitions, with entertainers, performers, events, boat trips and, of course, Fred's weather map. The Pump House, one of the renovated buildings, is good for lunch, and the next few attractions are housed in the complex – you can easily base a whole day around a visit here.

Tate Gallery (Albert Dock) Refurbished and extended in 1998, with plenty of sculptures, paintings and various special events. All very well presented with especially good use of natural light, though not really for traditionalists. Meals and snacks (in new café), shop, disabled access; cl Mon exc bank hols; (0151) 709 3223; free, though £3 for special exhibitions.

! Beatles' Story (Albert Dock) Bouncy (and pricey) tribute to the local boys made good and the sights and sounds of the 60s, inc a reconstruction of the Cavern Club. Shop, disabled access; cl 25–26 Dec; (0151) 709 1963; £6.45. Beatles' fans (considering the price, you need to have been really devoted) can also go on a 2-hour tour in a Magical Mystery Tourbus around related city sites – it leaves the Albert Dock daily at 2.20pm, calling at the Clayton Sq shopping centre at 2.30pm; (0151) 709 3285; *£9.50.

Merseyside Maritime Museum (Albert Dock) Huge museum spread over 6 floors, with boats, ships, craft demonstrations and a lively interpretation of what it was like for the millions who travelled from here to the New World. It takes in the **Museum of Liverpool Life**, vividly re-creating social history from the last century or so, and the **Customs and Excise Museum, Anything to Declare** – a lot more fun than it sounds, with an intriguing look at concealment techniques, and even demonstrations by sniffer dogs. A gallery on transatlantic slavery has bitterly divided local historians, who disagree on Liverpool's true role in the slave trade. Meals, snacks, shop, disabled access; cl 24–26 Dec, 1 Jan; (0151) 478 4499; £3 – Eight Pass (*see details above*).

Walker Art Gallery (William Brown St) One of the finest art collections outside London, with especially notable Italian, Dutch and Pre-Raphaelite works. Snacks, shop, disabled access; cl am Sun, 1 Jan, 24–26 Dec; (0151) 478 4199; Eight Pass (*see details above*).

! Liverpool Museum (William Brown St) You could spend hours at this excellent museum and still not see everything. There's an aquarium, a particularly good planetarium (shows 3.15pm, plus 1.15pm, 2.15 and 4.15pm wknds; cl Mon), and a hands-on natural history centre (pm only, cl Mon). Snacks, shop, disabled access; cl am Sun, 23–26 Dec, 1 Jan; (0151) 207 0001; Eight Pass (*see details above*). Just along the road you can tour one of the biggest public libraries in Europe (not Sun or bank hols); (0151) 225 5445 to book; free.

Paul McCartney's home (20 Forthlin Rd, Allerton) Despite protests from neighbours, last summer the NT opened this 1950s terraced council house, the former home of the McCartney family. John, Paul and George met, rehearsed and wrote many of their earliest songs here inc *Love Me Do* and *I Saw Her Standing There*. Open Sat and summer Weds, Thurs and Fri; essential to book (0151) 486 4006, access by minibus from Speke Hall (*see entry on p.393*) only; £4.50 (NT members £1.50).

Western Approaches (Rumford St) Evocatively restored underground command centre for the World War II Battle of the Atlantic; a labyrinth of rooms covering over 4,500 sq metres (over an acre) under the city's streets. Snacks, shop; cl Fri, Sun, and Nov–Mar; (0151) 227 2008; *£4.75.

! Liverpool Football Club (Anfield Rd) The new visitor centre and Anfield tours are a must for the faithful. There are cups, trophies, programmes and other treasured memorabilia as well as films of the club's finest hours. The tour takes in the grounds, dressing room and pitch – you can even sit on the manager's bench. Snacks, shop, disabled access; visitor centre cl 25 Dec; no tours on match days and booking essential (0151) 260 6677; £8 (visitor centre only £5).

Sudley (Mossley Hill Rd) Interestingly unspoilt Victorian house with good gardens, attractive furniture, and paintings by Turner and the Pre-Raphaelites. Weekend snacks, disabled access to ground floor only; cl am Sun, 23–26 Dec, 1 Jan; (0151) 207 0001; Eight Pass (*see details above*).

Croxteth Hall and Country Park (5m NE, SJ4094) Period displays in this Edwardian house, and a working farm, Victorian walled garden, miniature railway, and country walks in the grounds – makes a pleasant family trip out. Meals, snacks, shop, some disabled access; house cl Oct–Easter, park open all yr; (0151) 228 5311; park free, house, farm and garden £3.50, house or farm only £1.75.

† **MANCHESTER** SJ8398 Ambitious works on the redevelopment of the city centre, backed by huge government grants, will greatly enhance Manchester's already significant appeal. It's packed with interesting places to visit, and on a fine weekend or summer evening, strolling around the very impressive buildings is already a real pleasure; Albert Sq is one of the finest areas, with the great Albert Memorial (predating London's), several key cultural centres, and some lively café-bars. The **town hall** is a massively impressive piece of Victoriana, facing colourful summer gardens; there may be guided tours in summer. The **cathedral** is a very wide, 15th-c church, with notable choir stalls; the small medieval centre around it, and Shambles Sq (subject to some construction closure during the Arndale rebuilding), deserve a look, as do Exchange St and St Ann's Sq. The Castlefield area by the basin where the Bridgewater and Rochdale canals meet is interesting: restored warehouses, viaducts and the like, lots of lively redevelopment inc a tramway and a wonderfully light and airy new footbridge, also the good Dukes 92 pub (maybe street theatre outside) – and, not far off, on the other side of the GMEX exhibition centre, the very smart new Bridgewater concert hall. By contrast, the Rochdale canal towpath is a fascinating seamy-side walk. The city will soon have the nation's largest Marks & Spencer's, there's a vast new shopping centre with a 20-screen cinema at Trafford Park to the N, and young trendies head to Afflecks Palace on Church St for 4 floors of antique clothing, records, etc. Mash & Air (Chorlton St) also draws the young and fashionable, thanks to its unusual own-brew beers and equally distinctive food. Chinatown here, incidentally, is the second largest Chinese community in England: lots of authentic restaurants and a Chinese Arts Centre. It's surprisingly quick getting across the city, and the Metrolink trams quickly cover much of Greater Manchester. The City Art Galleries (Mosely St) are closed this year for major refurbishment and expansion. *See also separate entries for Salford and Prestwich.*

John Rylands Library (Deansgate) One of the city's most remarkable buildings – magnificently neo-Gothic. Small exhibitions and tours by arrangement; cl Sun and am Sat and Christmas–New Year; (0161) 834 5343; entrance and tours free as we went to press, although charges for tours were under review.

☺ **Granada Studios Tour** (Water St) The behind-the-scenes studio tour at this lively place has quickly become eclipsed by the other attractions, and it's now practically a theme park. Most features are based on TV programmes that Granada produce (inc the new Gladiators Skytrack), though there are exceptions: the Alien motion-master ride, for example. Other highlights include a replica of the House of Commons, an interactive mystery based on *Cracker*, and the exterior sets for the *Sherlock Holmes* series, *Moll Flanders* and, of course, *Coronation Street*. You'll find plenty of people peering through the letterboxes of the latter, and there's usually an appearance by a member of the cast. The main shows and exhibitions each last around half an hour, so check the times of what's on as you arrive – some bits overlap, and you'll need to do a bit of planning (seeing everything once takes 7½ hours). Meals, snacks, shop, disabled access; open daily July and Aug, but maybe cl Mon and Tues and possibly other days in winter, best to check; (0161) 833 0880; £14.99.

! Museum of Science and Industry (Castlefield) Enormous museum on the site of the oldest passenger railway station in the world, hours of things to do, and plenty to touch and fiddle with. Highlights include the power hall, air and space gallery (with an exciting simulator), interactive science area, the reconstructed sewer in the underground exhibition on sanitation, an electricity gallery – this bit alone covers 4 storeys – and a new £1 million gallery exploring Manchester's textile industry. Enough to keep most families intrigued and entertained for the bulk of the day, and if you don't feel like paying for the Granada Studios' tour you can glimpse the famous Street from the power hall. Meals, snacks, shop, disabled access; cl 24–26 Dec; (0161) 832 2244; *£5, car parking £1.50. The nearby White Lion (Liverpool Rd) has good-value food.

Gallery of English Costume (Platt Hall, Rusholme) The best museum of its kind, housed in a Georgian mansion, with comprehensive displays of fashion over the last 400 years. Displays change regularly – though, like the styles themselves, eventually come back. Shop, disabled access to ground floor only; cl Sun, Mon; (0161) 224 5217; free.

Whitworth Art Gallery (Oxford Rd) British watercolours from Sandby to Turner, plus modern paintings and sculpture, and unusual collections of textiles and wallpaper. Meals, snacks, shop, disabled access; cl am Sun, Good Fri, Christmas wk; (0161) 275 7450; free.

Manchester Museum (Oxford Rd) Good Japanese collection, as well as Egyptian relics, and a beehive. Partly closed in 1999 for major renovations, so best to phone for opening times. Shop, limited disabled access; (0161) 275 2634; free.

Pankhurst Centre (62 Nelson St, Chorlton on Medlock) Emmeline Pankhurst launched the Suffragette Movement from this Georgian semi, now with a period-furnished parlour and an interestingly planted garden. Meals, snacks, shop, disabled access; cl wknds and bank hols; (0161) 273 5673; free.

Manchester Jewish Museum (Cheetham Hill Rd, A665 1 m N) In a former synagogue, the story of Manchester's Jewish community over the last 200 years, with fascinating recorded recollections of life earlier this century. Shop, some disabled access; cl Fri, Sat and Jewish hols; (0161) 834 9879; £2.75. The Derby Brewery Arms is a classic Mancunian pub, with good-value snacks.

Museum of Transport (Boyle St, Cheetham) Around 80 vintage local buses and other vehicles, as well as photographs, tickets and memorabilia – even historic bus stops. Snacks (Sat and Weds only), shop, disabled access; open Weds, Sat, Sun and bank hols; (0161) 205 2122; £2.50.

Manchester United Museum and Tour Centre (Old Trafford) Purpose-built football museum, covering the club's history from its foundation in 1878 to the more recent glory days. Hundreds of exhibits (changing almost as frequently as their strip) and tours of the ground (not match days, and limited on the days before). Snacks, shop (not unjustifiably they call it a megastore), disabled access; cl Mon (exc bank hols), 25 Dec; (0161) 877 4002; £7.50 tour and museum, museum only £4.50.

Please let us know what you think of places in the *Guide*. Use the report forms at the back of the book or simply write us a letter.

Other things to see and do

Lancashire Family Attraction of the Year

WIGAN SD5805 **Wigan Pier** (Wallgate) This dynamic and entertaining wharfside centre re-creates local life in the early 1900s, with scenes from the period put together with real energy and verve. It's an ingenious mix of museum and theatre, with professional actors performing in reconstructed settings over the main 3 floors of exhibits; they bring vividly to life everything from a night at the Palace of Varieties to a day at the seaside. You get a tangible impression of what it was like at the turn of the century, and though there's something of an educational bent (it's a popular school outing), it's done in a fun way that children really enjoy. Oddly, younger visitors particularly like the Victorian schoolroom, and its disciplined approach to teaching, but also get a lot out of the reconstructed mine – as close as you're likely to get to the feel of the pit face without actually going underground. Other scenes well illustrate the home and work environments of mill workers and owners, and there might be demonstrations of basket-weaving or clog-making. They recently added a well thought out interactive area for the under-7s, themed as a yard, equipped according to census material of 1881; toys, clogs and other hands-on exhibits, and story-telling at selected times. Water buses take you across the river to a fully restored mill and engine house, with the world's largest working mill steam engine, and there are pleasant canalside walks and gardens. Maybe jazz on the last Sun of the month, various events and activities on other days. Mostly under cover, this has enough to keep families busy for the bulk of the day. The nicest place for lunch is the reconstructed period pub (named after Orwell, who originally turned the old Wigan Pier music-hall catch phrase into what's virtually become shorthand for social history – and was surprisingly an Old Etonian). Meals, snacks, shop, disabled access; cl Fri (exc Good Fri), 25 Dec; (01942) 323666; £5.10 (£4.10 children). A good-value family ticket, covering 2 adults and 2 children, is £14.50.

ACCRINGTON SD7627
Haworth Art Gallery and Museum (Haworth Park, Manchester Rd) Notable for its collection of Tiffany glass, said to be the biggest in Europe (an Accrington man used to manage the Tiffany studios). Nice setting, with a nature trail through the grounds. Cl am, all Mon and Tues, 25–26 Dec, 1 Jan and Good Fri; (01254) 233782; free.

ALTRINCHAM SJ7587
Dunham Massey Hall (off the B5160 W) 16th-c moated manor house extensively remodelled in the 18th c, with impressive silverware, paintings and furnishings, and a restored kitchen, pantry and laundry. The largely unaltered grounds have plenty of deer, formal avenues of trees, and a working Elizabethan saw mill (usually Weds and Sun only). Concerts and events even in winter when the house is closed. Meals, snacks, shop, some disabled access; open Sat–Weds Apr–Oct, house cl am; (0161) 941 1025; £5 house and garden, £3 garden only; NT. The Vine at Dunham Woodhouses has popular home cooking.

BARNOLDSWICK SD9046
Bancroft Mill Engine The last working steam mill in the area – not that long ago Barnoldswick had 13. Snacks, shop, disabled access; open most Sats for static viewing, (01282) 813932 for dates of steamdays; *£1.50. The Fanny Grey (B651 towards Colne) has decent food.

BARROWFORD SD8639
Pendle Heritage Centre Growing local history centre, with 18th-c walled gardens, a small farm, country trails, a 14th-c barn with a pot-bellied pig, and an exhibition on the Pendle witches – the house itself looks appropriately witchy. Snacks, shop, disabled access; cl 25 Dec;

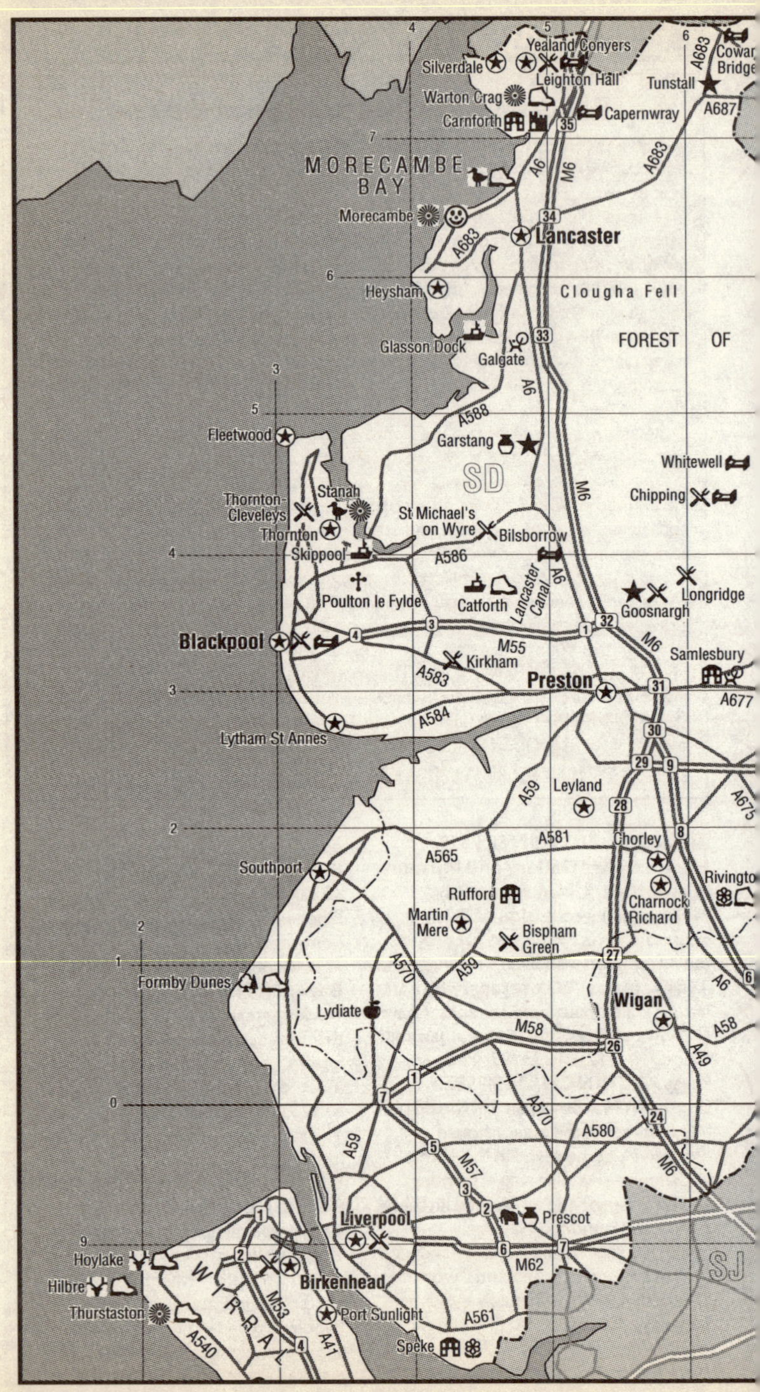

MORECAMBE BAY
Silverdale
Yealand Conyers
Leighton Hall
Warton Crag
Carnforth
Capernwray
Tunstall
Cowan Bridge
Morecambe
Lancaster
Heysham
Clougha Fell
Glasson Dock
Galgate
FOREST OF
Fleetwood
Garstang
SD
Whitewell
Chipping
Thornton-Cleveleys
Stanah
Thornton
St Michael's on Wyre
Bilsborrow
Skippool
Poulton le Fylde
Catforth
Lancaster Canal
Longridge
Goosnargh
Blackpool
Kirkham
Samlesbury
Preston
Lytham St Annes
Leyland
Chorley
Southport
Rufford
Martin Mere
Bispham Green
Charnock Richard
Rivington
Formby Dunes
Lydiate
Wigan
Liverpool
Prescot
Hoylake
Hilbre
Thurstaston
WIRRAL
Birkenhead
Port Sunlight
Speke
SJ

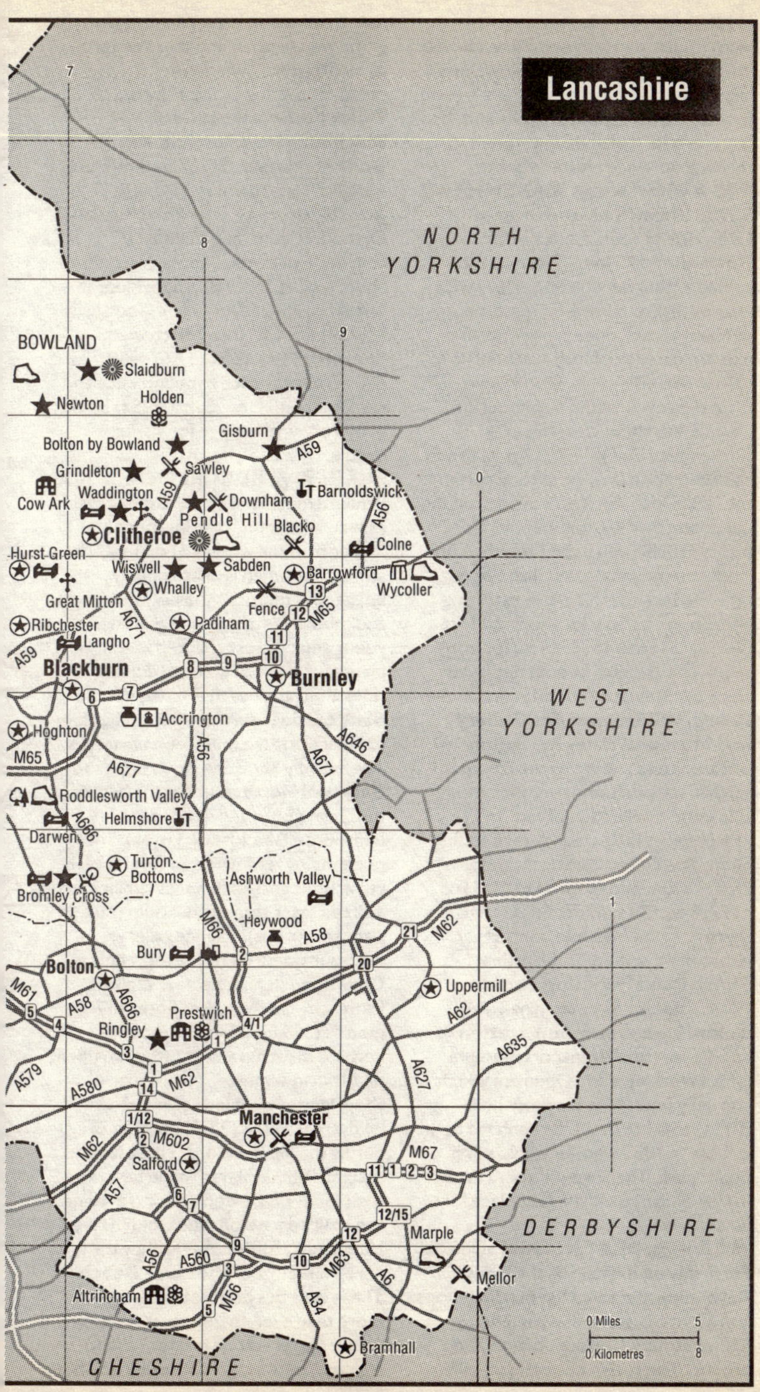
Lancashire
NORTH YORKSHIRE
WEST YORKSHIRE
DERBYSHIRE
CHESHIRE
BOWLAND
Slaidburn
Newton
Holden
Gisburn
Bolton by Bowland
Grindleton
Sawley
Cow Ark
Waddington
Downham
Barnoldswick
Pendle Hill
Blacko
Clitheroe
Colne
Hurst Green
Wiswell
Sabden
Barrowford
Wycoller
Whalley
Great Mitton
Fence
Ribchester
Padiham
Langho
Blackburn
Burnley
Accrington
Hoghton
Roddlesworth Valley
Helmshore
Darwen
Turton Bottoms
Ashworth Valley
Bromley Cross
Heywood
Bury
Bolton
Uppermill
Prestwich
Ringley
Manchester
Salford
Marple
Mellor
Altrincham
Bramhall
0 Miles 5
0 Kilometres 8

(01282) 661701; £2. This is picturesque, evocative countryside; the **church** at nearby unspoilt Newchurch has the witches' grave, and there's good food at the Forest Inn at Fence and the Bay Horse at Roughlee – a stone's throw from Alice Nutter's home.

BIRKENHEAD SJ3288 Waterfront views over to Liverpool, of course, but a surprise in **Birkenhead Priory** (Priory St), a ruined 12th-c Benedictine priory with a notable visitor centre. Shop, some disabled access; open pm wknds all yr, plus pm daily (exc Mon) in school hols; (0151) 666 4010; free. Good views from the tower of the neighbouring church. **Historic warships** (Birkenhead Docks) HMS *Plymouth* and the Submarine *Onyx* both took part in the Falklands War. You can peep up the periscope on the *Onyx*, and there's plenty for children to fiddle with. A few ladders to negotiate, but don't be put off – readers find this a very satisfying afternoon out. Snacks, shop; cl 24–26 Dec; (0151) 650 1573; £4.50 for both ships. The German U-boat displayed alongside spent the last 50 years on the seabed. **Williamson Art Gallery and Museum** (Slatey Rd) English watercolours and art by the Liverpool school, sculpture and ceramics, model ships, and a collection of cars and motorcycles in a period garage setting. Shop, disabled access; cl am, and all Mon, 25 Dec and Good Fri; (0151) 652 4177; free. On summer Suns in Aug, there are generally free concerts at either the museum or the priory. **Shore Road Pumping Station** (Woodside, nr ferry terminal) This unusual **steam pumping station** has an adjacent small transport museum with a working tram. Open pm wknds, and daily (exc Mon) in school hols; (0151) 650 1182; *£1. Birkenhead Park laid out in 1853 was the world's first public park. The Shrewsbury Arms out in Claughton Firs is the best place for lunch.

BLACKBURN SD6828 Put firmly on the map by the Industrial Revolution, the town has bustling shops and a market, some fine buildings, and lots of beautiful unspoilt countryside around. The parish **church** (actually now a cathedral) is very handsome – grand yet elegant – and there are plans to incorporate a window commemorating Diana, Princess of Wales, in one of the towers. **Blackburn Museum and Art Gallery** (Museum St) Quite a mixture – English watercolours, Japanese woodblock prints, Greek and Russian Orthodox icons, and a fantastic collection of beetles, some pretty scary. Shop, disabled access; cl Sun, Mon, am Tues–Fri, 25–26 Dec, 1 Jan, Good Fri; (01254) 667130; free. **Witton Country Park** (off the A674 W) 480 acres of attractive countryside to explore; cl am Mon–Sat; (01254) 55423; park free, small charge for visitor centre.

BLACKPOOL SD3036 Britain's most loved and loathed seaside resort, in summer offering more bed spaces than the whole of Portugal. The atmosphere then is unashamedly boisterous (it's pretty dreary in winter), and though it's now more geared to young adults, most children love it, with plenty for them to do from donkey rides along the beaches to days at the **Sandcastle** leisure complex. The tram to Fleetwood is a must for tram freaks. The friendly Ramsden Arms opposite Blackpool North station is the best of the town's pubs and has good-value bedrooms. **Blackpool Tower** The outstanding landmark has several lively attractions geared towards families, inc a circus, laser shows, aquarium (rare giant sea turtles), science gallery, dinosaur ride, a lift to the top, replica Crown Jewels and the new Walk of Faith – a 5-cm thick glass floor, 117 metres (385 ft) above the ground. Perhaps most fun at night (they're open till 11pm in summer). Meals, snacks, shop, limited disabled access; cl winter wkdys; (01253) 622242; £5.95, more during the Illuminations. These famous autumn light displays are the best of their kind – if you don't mind travelling at a snail's pace along the Golden Five Hundred Yards (or Mile as they call it here). **Blackpool Pleasure Beach** These days this dominates the town more than ever, thanks to its monster rollercoaster – at 72 metres (235 ft) high and quite reasonably called the Big

One, its coaches run at a speed of up to 85mph. Crowded and noisy, with a sprawling mass of over 145 other breathtaking rides, the amusement park is year after year Britain's most visited attraction. Meals, snacks, shops, disabled access; open daily Easter–Oct and wknds Mar; (01253) 341033; individual prices for rides, or books of tickets (around £20). **Coronation Street Experience** (opposite the Pleasure Beach) Reconstructed version with sets and props from the programme, and a 15-minute Sooty Show; cl winter wkdys; (01253) 299555; £5.99, so pretty much for fans only. **Sea Life Centre** (Golden Mile Centre) Broadly similar to others in the chain, but with a bonus: one of the biggest displays of tropical sharks in Europe, with a walk-through tunnel underneath, so you feel you're in there with them. Meals, snacks, shop, disabled access; cl 25 Dec; (01253) 622445; £5.50 (they stamp your hand so you can come back later that day).

Grundy Art Gallery (Queen St) This decent gallery away from the crowds is proof that there's more to Blackpool than ice-creams and eyesores. Shop, disabled access but no facilities; cl Sun and bank hols; free. **Blackpool Zoo** (East Park Drive) Over 400 animals in 32 acres of landscaped gardens. The big cats are usually fed at 11.45am (not Fri), the sealions at 11am and 3pm, and the penguins at 2.30pm. Meals, snacks, shop, disabled access; cl 25 Dec; (01253) 765027; £6.

BOLTON SD7109
Quite a few places to visit here, and you can tour **Warburtons Bakery** (Hereford St) by arrangement, Tues–Thurs only; (01204) 523551; free. **Smithills Hall** (Smithills Dean Rd) Interesting (though much restored) old manor house with a 14th-c Great Hall and splendid panelled drawing room. There are ambitious plans to develop the site as a 'living history' exhibition. Shop, disabled access to ground floor only; cl am Sun, Mon (exc bank hols), all Oct–Mar; (01204) 841265; £2 (£3 joint ticket with Hall i' th' Wood). **Hall i' th' Wood** (Crompton Way) 15th-c house, where Samuel Crompton developed his Spinning Mule in 1779; it was refurnished by the first Lord Leverhulme in 1902. Details as Smithills Hall. **Museum and Art Gallery** (Le Mans Crescent) Quite good, with Egyptian mummies, lots of watercolours and 20th-c sculpture. Shop, disabled access; cl Weds, Sun and bank hols; free. The King's Head (Junction Rd, Deane), with a bowling green behind, is useful for lunch, as is the restaurant of the Queen's Moat House – an interesting church conversion.

BRAMALL HALL SJ8886
One of the finest houses in the area (particularly from the outside), a splendid, timber-framed, 14th-c Hall with rare 16th-c wall paintings and furniture, and extensive parkland; there was a fair bit of prettifying restoration in the last century. Meals, snacks, shop, disabled access to ground floor; open pm wknds all yr, plus pm wkdys Easter–Dec (not Mons Nov and Dec); (0161) 485 3708; £3.50, park free. The Davenport Arms at Woodford does decent lunches.

BROMLEY CROSS SD7213 (N of Bolton) **Last Drop Village** Pastiche of an 18th-c village, very rustic and quaint, with cottages, shops, a decent pub and craft centre. The B6391 and old Roman road through Edgworth N of here are fine moorland roads, as are the A675 N of Bolton itself (good detours off at Belmont), and the A666 to Darwen.

BURNLEY SD8530
The **canal wharf** (Manchester Rd), which has a small museum, allows short towpath walks along the Leeds & Liverpool Canal, giving a vivid impression of the towering old weaving mills; the raised canal embankment across the valley is a remarkable sight. **Towneley Hall** (A646 S) A striking 14th-c building housing a decent museum (cl Sat, am Sun, Christmas; free – but subject to review in 1999). **Rockwater Bird Conservation Centre** (Foxstones Lane, Cliviger – above Mereclough SE of Burnley, SD8831) Expanding collection taking in pheasants, bantams, foreign birds and owls as well as rabbits, chipmunks and miniature sheep. Children can feed some animals. Snacks, disabled access

(but no facilities); cl Mon (exc bank hols), wkdys Mar and Oct, all Nov–Feb; (01282) 415016; £2.50. Nearby **Cliviger Gorge** has pleasant walks, with a stream, woodland and farmland; moors above. The Kettledrum at Mereclough has good home cooking, and the moorland roads around it are attractive – especially the old packhorse road from Mereclough up Stansfield Moor; nice views from the back road angling off SE from the A52 to the junction of the A671 and B6238.

BURY SD8010 **East Lancs Railway** (Bolton St Station) Well regarded by enthusiasts, a scenic 17-mile steam journey along the pretty Irwell Valley; you can get on or off along the way. Meals, snacks, shop, disabled access; open wknds, bank hols, and other dates July and Aug; (0161) 764 7790 for timetable; £6 full return. The Lord Raglan up at Nangreaves (off the A56/A666 N) has great moorland views and hearty food.

CARNFORTH SD4970 The dilapidated station at this otherwise unremarkable little town starred in *Brief Encounter* in 1945; Railtrack have been developing the site to capitalise on the connection. A mile or so N are the ruins of a 14th-c manor house, **Warton Old Rectory**.

CATFORTH SD4735 **Lancaster Canal** Between Preston and Carnforth, this is ideal for boating – 40 miles without a single lock; often through quiet countryside, with herons and even occasional kingfishers – best in spring or early summer, with ducklings and cygnets bobbing about, and lambs in the fields alongside. In summer, boats can be hired by the day here (01772) 690232; there's a decent teashop. This is a good spot too for pleasant towpath walks.

CHARNOCK RICHARD SD5415 **Camelot** New management, so there may be changes at this 130-acre park themed around the mythical world of Camelot and Arthurian legend – the rides and shows have on the whole been carefully thought out to fit in with this; one of the rollercoasters hurtles around a pseudo-medieval castle, and a dizzying swing-boat ride is in the shape of Excalibur. In Pendragon's Plunge, you sit in an inflatable boat and drop 9 metres (30 ft) through a series of twists and turns at speeds of up to 25mph; there are 3 different routes. New attractions include a driving school for younger children. As well as the rides, there are displays of falconry and jousting in a full-sized arena, a very good rare breeds farm, and dozens of other attractions. Meals, snacks, shop, disabled access; open wknds and school hols Apr–Oct, and daily Jun–Aug; (01257) 453044; £12.99 (though frequent discounts).

CHORLEY SD5718 **Astley Hall** (Astley Park) Unusual, timber-framed, 16th-c house with very elaborate carvings and plasterwork, interesting pottery and paintings, and extensive gardens and woodland. It was used in the TV adaptation of *Moll Flanders*. Shop, disabled access to ground floor only; cl am, Mon (exc bank hols) and Mon–Thurs Nov–Mar; (01257) 262166; £2.80, free for Chorley residents. The Malt 'n' Hops behind the town station is useful for a bite to eat.

CLITHEROE SD7441 Bustling old market town: every Weds evening hundreds of poultry and small livestock enthusiasts come to the auctions, some from as far away as Scotland. The High St is dominated by the **castle** perched on its limestone rock. One of the oldest buildings in Lancs, it has one of the smallest Norman keeps in the country. The **castle museum** has an extensive geology exhibition, and good views of the Ribble Valley. Shop, limited disabled access; cl Thurs and Fri Mar–Apr and Oct–Dec, and all mid-Dec–Feb; (01200) 424635; £1.40. Cowmans Famous Sausage Shop (Castle St) has an incredibly wide range of traditional and speciality sausages. The Starkie Arms below is handy for lunch, and readers like the sculpture trail in Bungerley Park. There's a lovely drive through Bashall Eaves, the Trough of Bowland and Quernmore.

COW ARK SD6845 **Browsholme Hall** Unpretentious-looking Tudor house on the edge of the Forest of Bowland, with a surprisingly rich range of contents. Good guided tours by members of the family. Snacks, shop; open pm Easter and spring bank hol wknds, plus pm Fri–Sun in Aug; (01254) 826719; £3. The Inn at Whitewell in one direction and Red Pump at Bashall Eaves in the other offer a choice of good places to eat.

★ **DOWNHAM** SD7844 Below Pendle Hill, carefully preserved and outstandingly pretty, on the side of a steep pasture valley with a stream winding along the bottom.

FLEETWOOD SD3448 Developed as a rather elegant 19th-c resort, with landscaping by Decimus Burton, plenty of smart buildings, a lively harbour (summer boat trips), an excellent market, 2 elegant if not entirely practical lighthouses (one's in the middle of the street), a decent summer museum (cl Nov–Easter, all day Weds exc July–Sept, and am Mon, Thurs and wknds; £1.10), a factory shopping centre, and trams from Blackpool right through the town. The architecturally interesting North Euston Hotel, by the terminus, is a safe bet for food. The Marine Hall exhibition centre on the front has a decent bar (the Wyre – no food) with excellent views of the harbour and Morecambe Bay.

FOREST OF BOWLAND SD6650 Magnificent Pennine moorland, less visited than most areas of comparable scenery, as much of the moorland, privately owned, has been closed to walkers, with only a few paths crossing the impressive massif that forms some of the county's most significant scenery. Development in some of the villages (also in private hands) is controlled too strictly for any significant expansion of holiday accommodation – let alone a proliferation of camp sites and so forth. These restrictions make the area particularly appealing for people who want peace and quiet, and there are now more than 3,000 acres of Access Areas, where you can wander at will over the moors, subject to agreement restrictions displayed at car parks and access points; these areas include Clougha Pike reached from Quernmore SD5259, and Fair Snape Fell, Saddle Fell and Wolf Fell reached from Chipping SD6143 or Bleasdale SD5745. Rights of way also give walks above Tarnbrook Wyre SD5855, and up Dunsop Fell from Slaidburn SD7152 or Dunsop Bridge SD6550. Beacon Fell Country Park SD5642 is atmospheric to wander through, and there are some pleasant walks around the Coronation Arms at Horton SD8550. The Bowland Pathfinder bus service is geared to walkers, linking Preston, Clitheroe and Beacon Fell Information Centre, and meeting trains on the Manchester–Carlisle line; (01995) 640557 for times. There's also a useful network of camping and bunkhouse barns for long-distance walkers.

FORMBY DUNES SD2808 Reached from the NW edge of Formby, a large tract of sweeping sandy dunes which in some areas is being stabilised by pine plantations; broad beaches and good walks through the adjacent pinewoods, made interesting by the chance of seeing and even feeding red squirrels (you can buy nuts here). Best in spring and autumn – can be busy in summer; parking in some places may cost £1.50, but keep looking – a number of other spots are free.

GALGATE SD4855 **Canalside Craft Centre** Converted farm buildings with various crafts, inc a wood-turner producing unusual clocks, barometers and bowls; canalside seating. Cl Mon; (01524) 752223; free. The Plough has decent food.

★ **GARSTANG** SD4945 Quite an attractive small market town, with a good deal of canal activity (and a fine aqueduct crossing the River Wyre). The entertaining waterside Owd Tithebarn (with a canal museum upstairs) is fun for lunch, and the **Discovery Centre** (High St) is a useful introduction to the area's natural history.

GLASSON DOCK SD4456 Once an important port for Lancaster, this still has the occasional coaster berthing, but is mainly a lively summer boating place now, in pleasant countryside. The Victoria on the dock is a popular dining pub, as is the 17th-c Stork up on the A588.

† **GREAT MITTON CHURCH** SD7139 Attractive, with an outstanding range of memorial tombs.

HELMSHORE TEXTILE MUSEUMS SD7821 (Holcombe Rd) 2 stone mills with comprehensive collections of textile machinery, much still in working order. Easily one of the best textile museums in the country, but if social history and machinery aren't your things it's unlikely to convert you. Snacks, shop, disabled access; cl am, all Sat, and Nov–Easter; (01706) 226459; £3. The Duke of Wellington on the B6232 W of Haslingden is a reliable family dining pub in fine surroundings, with more views further on that road.

HEYSHAM POWER STATIONS SD4160 Hi-tech, interactive exhibition on electricity generation, with tours of a power station and nuclear reactor, and a 25-acre nature reserve. This is the most elaborate of Nuclear Electric's visitor centres. Tours by arrangement (ring for details); it may be worth booking in summer. Snacks, shop, disabled access; cl Sat, and Nov–Easter; (01524) 855624; free. A tremendous contrast is the quaint, squint-walled, little village **church**, partly Saxon, with a Norse-carved, hogback tombstone inside. The unusual waterside Golden Ball at Heaton with Oxcliffe, off the Lancaster road (may be cut off by very high tides), is fun for lunch.

HEYWOOD SD8510 **Corgi Heritage Centre** (53 York St) Hundreds of die-cast model vehicles from pre-war cars to James Bond's Aston Martin – even a turning Magic Roundabout; of course it's all a huge plug for the company that makes them, but fascinating for collectors. Shop, disabled access; cl Tues and Sun, bank hols; (01706) 365812; free. The Egerton Arms, off the B6222 Bury road is a good moorland dining pub.

HILBRE SJ1887 The biggest of 3 tidal islands which you can reach on foot at low tide from West Kirby; Hilbre is a **nature reserve**, once popular with sunbathers, now visited mainly by birds and occasional seals. Make sure you know the tide times – (0151) 648 4371 – as it's easy to be stranded out here.

HOGHTON TOWER SD6226 (A675) Splendid, 16th-c, fortified hilltop mansion, with grand state rooms and royal bedchamber, and a collection of dolls and dolls' houses. The gardens are lovely (particularly the rose garden) and the surrounding grounds offer wonderful views of the sea, moors, Lakeland hills and Welsh mountains. Meals, snacks, shop; open pm Sun and Mon bank hol wknds, plus Mon–Thurs and pm Sun July–Sept; (01254) 852986; £1 parking and grounds, £2.50 house. The Royal Oak at Riley Green has decent food.

HOLDEN SD7749 **Holden Clough Nursery** Old-fashioned nursery with a thoroughly up-to-date approach to raising interesting plants, in the Victorian kitchen garden of Holden Clough Hall; beds of alpines, trough gardens, herbaceous perennials, shrubs and rhododendrons and maybe RHS special events. Disabled access; cl 12–1pm, Mon and most Suns, 25 Dec–1 Jan; (01200) 447615; free. The Copy Nook has good food, and is a useful stop for walkers.

HOYLAKE BEACH SJ2088 These sweeping sands are beautiful, with an unusual partly tidal **nature reserve** at Red Rocks, N of the golf links.

HURST GREEN SD6939 **Stonyhurst College** Magnificent 16th-c manor house, now home to the famous Catholic boarding school. You can see the library, chapel, other historic rooms and the extensive grounds. Snacks, shop, limited disabled access; open pm Aug exc Fri, gardens usually open 20 July–24 Aug; (01254) 826345; £4, garden only £1. The Punch Bowl and Bayley Arms have good food, with fine Ribble Valley walks nearby.

LANCASTER SD4761 Friendly and relaxed despite the grandeur of many of its stone buildings; ambling down the cobbled streets and alleyways (much is pedestrianised), it's hard to believe this was once a major West Indies shipping port. These days the water traffic is more sedate, with punts for hire and **canal cruises** in summer. The Farmhouse Tavern (part of Scale Hall, A589 Morecambe road) has good food, and other places worth knowing for lunch include the George & Dragon (nr

River Lune) and the canalside White Cross. **Lancaster Castle** Dramatic, 12th-c Norman fortress famous for hangings and witch trials, owned by the Queen as Duke of Lancaster. Part of it is still used as a prison, but the cells, tower and 18th-c Gothic Revival Shire Hall can all be visited. Shop; open wknds Apr–Oct, and wkdys when Court not in session – usually around school hols but best to check; (01524) 64998; £3.50. **Priory Church** Dates back to before the Conquest, though the present hilltop building is mainly 14th/15th c; very interesting medieval choir stalls, needlework and Anglo-Saxon cross fragments. Snacks, shop, some disabled access; cl winter lunchtimes; free. Nearby are the remains of a **Roman bath-house**. **Maritime Museum** (St George's Quay) Up-to-date look at the local maritime trade and fishing industry; the audio-visual show is good fun. Snacks, shop, disabled access; cl am Nov–Easter, 25 Dec and 1 Jan; (01524) 64637; £2 (free to local residents). **Judges' Lodging** (Church St) 17th-c house with well restored period rooms, plenty of Gillow furniture, and a museum of childhood. Shop, open pm Easter–Oct (exc Sun), maybe all day in summer hols; (01524) 32808; £2. Other decent collections at the firmly traditional **City Museum** on Market Sq, in a very grand, Georgian, former town hall (cl Sun, 24 Dec–1 Jan; free), and at the **Cottage Museum**, opposite the castle, furnished in the style of an early 19th-c artisan's house (open pm Easter–Sept; *75p). **Ashton Memorial** (Williamson Park) A magnificent folly clearly visible from the motorway, set in 38 acres of lovely landscaped parkland; splendid views from the upper galleries. Displays on Edwardian life, and a butterfly house with a good collection of plants and lepidoptera, as well as free-flying birds and various creepy-crawlies. Snacks, shop, disabled access; cl 25–26 Dec, 1 Jan; (01524) 33318; £2.95.

LEIGHTON HALL SD4874 A notably friendly welcome at this neo-Gothic mansion (more restrained inside), still the home of the Gillow family and with early examples of their furniture. The grounds have a collection of birds of prey, nature trails, and beautifully kept gardens. The setting is lovely, with Lakeland hills rising up behind. Snacks, shop, disabled access; cl am, all Sat and Mon (exc bank hols), Oct–Apr; (01524) 734474; £3.60. The nearby New Inn at Yealand Conyers has excellent food.

LEYLAND SD5422 **British Commercial Vehicle Museum** (King St) Now slightly jazzed up with sound effects, and over 90 perfectly restored British wagons, buses, trucks, vans, fire engines and even a Popemobile, shining so much you'd think they were new. Snacks, shop, disabled access; Open Sun, Tues, Weds and bank hols Apr–Sept, Sun only Oct; (01772) 451011; £4. The sturdy 16th-c **Old Grammar School** (Church Rd) has changing local history displays; open pm Thurs, all Tues and Fri, and am Sat; free. **Worden Park** has art displays and 9 varied craft workshops, and walks, gardens, a maze, and miniature golf. Leyland also has a pleasant little town trail, and the 15th-c church has some fine stained glass. The friendly little Rose & Crown (A581 S) has decent basic food.

LYDIATE SD3604 Pick-your-own is popular throughout this flat coastal area, with soft fruit the speciality, late Jun to Aug; **Lydiate Fruit Farm** (Pilling Lane) has a good farm shop in attractive, 18th-c, former stable buildings.

LYTHAM ST ANNE'S SD3228 Decorous seaside town that seems a world away from nearby Blackpool. It has a splendidly restored **windmill** by the promenade in the centre of Lytham green (cl 1–2pm, Mon and Fri, and all Oct–Apr exc Easter; free), and a small **Lifeboat Museum** next door (open Tues, Thurs and wknds, plus Weds July and Aug; free). The Taps is a good real ale pub here. **Toy and Teddy Bear Museum** (Clifton Drive N, St Anne's) Porritt-built Victorian building with a big collection of nostalgic children's items. Good shop, some disabled access; open wknds, school hols, and bank hols all year, plus Weds–Fri Whit–Oct; (01253) 713705; £2.50. A sand dune **nature reserve** stretches opposite.

MARPLE SJ9688 **Peak Forest Canal** The towpath soon leaves suburbia for green countryside; N is the famous set of Marple locks and aqueduct over the River Etherow. To the S, you can leave the canal at Strines and climb on to Mellor Moor.

MARTIN MERE SD4214 **Wildfowl and Wetlands Centre** (off the A59) Thousands of wild geese, swans, ducks and flamingos regularly visit the re-created natural open water habitats at this important 376-acre centre. Some birds will feed straight from your hand. Good visitor centre, well organised walks, lively activities for children and an adventure playground, and plenty of instructive and entertaining events. Meals, snacks, shop, disabled access; cl 25 Dec; (01704) 895181; £4.50. The canalside Ship at Lathom is very popular for lunch. **Windmill Animal Farm** (Fish Lane, Holmeswood, just N) This friendly 40-acre place has animals and their babies to feed (inc rare breeds), tractor rides, a miniature railway, and an adventure playground. Snacks, shop, disabled access; cl wkdys mid-Sept–Easter; (01704) 892282; £2.50.

MORECAMBE SD4264 5 miles of promenade and more of beaches to stroll along at this cheery resort, with pretty sunsets over the bay. The Dog & Partridge (Bare) has decent fresh food. **Frontierland** (Morecambe) Wild West theme park with 30 family rides and attractions (inc a circus), and spectacular views across the bay from the top of the bizarre Polo Tower, designed to look like end-to-end tubes of sweets. Meals, snacks, shop, disabled access; cl Nov–Easter and some other days outside high season; (01524) 410024; £8.95 (less in low season).

MORECAMBE BAY SD4666 Vast mudflats and sands, home to 200,000 wading birds. Walks over them are easiest from the Cumbrian side, though guided walks also go from Hest Bank (details from local tourist information centres; the galloping tides and quicksand do make a guide essential).

PADIHAM SD8034 **Gawthorpe Hall** Early 17th-c manor house with fine panelling and moulded ceilings, minstrels' gallery, and a Jacobean long gallery. Important collections of costume, embroidery and lace, and paintings from the National Portrait Gallery. Snacks, limited disabled access; house cl am, Mon (exc bank hols), Fri, and Nov–Mar, grounds open all yr; (01282) 771004; £2.90; NT. The hilly cobbled alleys in the town's centre are now a conservation area.

PENDLE HILL SD8240 An excellent network of paths lets you walk round and almost all over it. Although Pendle's witch-persecuting days are happily over, the place still has a haunting elemental appeal. The view that enraptured George Fox, the founder of the Quakers, is as good as ever. The quickest way up is from Barley village.

PORT SUNLIGHT HERITAGE CENTRE SJ3384 Sets the scene for this most famous of the garden villages built by 19th-c philanthropists, contriving something better than the appalling squalor of northern England's factory towns. Historically important as the precursor of garden cities, garden suburbs and New Towns, it's perfectly preserved, with groups of mock-Tudor cottages, swathes of greenery and parkland: no two groups of houses are alike. Useful village trail leaflets; also period soap packaging (you can buy soap in replica wrappings). Shop, some disabled access; cl winter wknds, Christmas and New Year; (0151) 644 6466; 40p. **Lady Lever Art Gallery** (Port Sunlight) Lord Leverhulme, who had built his Sunlight Soap factory here, donated the village its outstanding gallery. Recently refurbished, it has interesting Victorian paintings inc Turners and Pre-Raphaelites – many adapted for use in soap ads, to the fury of the artists. Meals, snacks, shop, disabled access; cl am Sun, 23–26 Dec, 1 Jan; (0151) 645 3623; £3 for an Eight Pass ticket, covering 7 other galleries in the area (see *Liverpool entries*). Nearby Thornton Hough was also built by Lord Leverhulme, as a mock-Tudor estate village – Port Sunlight on a much smaller scale; the Seven Stars there is useful for lunch.

POULTON LE FYLDE SD3539 Quite an attractive pedestrianised market square, with a lovely church (as others in Lancs, looking a good deal older than in fact it is), and several useful places to eat – the Old Town Hall is particularly good value.

PRESCOT SJ4793 **Knowsley Safari Park** 5-mile drive through very natural-looking reserves of lions, tigers, rhinos, monkeys and other animals; they have the biggest herd of African elephants in Europe. Also a pets corner and miniature railway. Meals, snacks, shop, disabled access; cl wkdys Nov–Feb; (0151) 430 9009; £12 per car – load in all your friends and it's very good value indeed. If you have to pass through the town, the **museum** (Church St) has an interesting collection relating to the area's former clock-making industry; cl 1–2pm, am Sun, Mon (exc bank hols), Tues, Good Fri, 25–26 Dec, 1 Jan; (0151) 430 7787; free. The Clock Face is a pleasant old mansion-house pub here.

✝ **PRESTON** SD5329 The town has 2 decent museums: the impressive if rather dour Greek revival **Harris Museum and Art Gallery** on Market Sq (cl Sun and bank hols; free), and the **County Museum** on Stanley St (cl Thurs, Sun and bank hols; *£1.10). There's a good big market (the space is used for car boot sales instead on Tues and Thurs); Wall Street (Fishergate) has decent food. The **Railway Centre** from Southport is due to reopen as the **Ribble Steam Railway** in Preston Marina, early in 1999. **Moor Park Observatory** is open most Thurs evenings (exc the second of the month) Sept–Mar (not Dec); (01772) 257181 to check. **Church of St Mary** (Penwortham) 14th-c chancel, and the scant remains of a motte and bailey castle in the churchyard; nearby the Fleece (Liverpool Rd) is useful for lunch. The polished white granite temple of the Mormons' oldest missionary branch is now a landmark by the M61 (junction 8).

PRESTWICH SD8104 **Heaton Hall** Splendidly decorated, 18th-c neo-Classical house in extensive, well used, public parkland; fine paintings, plasterwork and furniture, an unusual circular Pompeiian room, and various recitals and temporary exhibitions. Disabled access; probably cl 12–1pm, all Mon and Tues, and Oct–Easter, phone to check; (0161) 773 1231; free. The Victorian Woodthorpe by the main gate has decent food.

★ ✝ **RIBCHESTER** SD6535 Attractive little town, many of its buildings incorporating masonry plundered from the former Roman town here: the White Bull pub, with good food, has a couple of Tuscan pillars for its porch and an excavated Roman bath-house behind. **Roman Museum** On the site of a fort occupied between the 1st and 4th c, with lots of coins, pottery and the famous Ribchester helmet. Shop, disabled access; cl 25 Dec; (01254) 878261; £1.35. The 15th-c **church** also stands on the site of the Roman fort, and looks as if it uses much salvaged material from it. **Stydd Nursery** (Stoneygate Lane) There are excavated Roman granaries behind this nursery specialising in old-fashioned roses and hardy perennials; some disabled access; cl am (exc Sat), all Mon, 25–26 Dec, 1 Jan and Good Fri; (01254) 878797; free.

★ **RINGLEY** SD7605 Unexpected corner so close to the urban areas – village stocks and an ancient bridge over the Irwell (and a decent pub).

RIVINGTON RESERVOIRS SD6215 These attractive waters just outside Horwich make good walking territory. Lower Rivington Reservoir has a waterside path along its eastern edge, and a curious mock-up of Liverpool castle, built in 1912, as an adornment to the vast and atmospherically decayed gardens of Lever Park, which cover the hillside. A trail guides you around the undergrowth and up to the Pigeon Tower, within a few minutes of Rivington Pike, the summit. The Great House Barn is the place to start, with a decent information centre, maps and guides.

RODDLESWORTH VALLEY SD6622 Good woodland walks from the Royal Arms at Tockholes, and maybe on to the ruins of Hollinshead Hall and its restored curative well.

RUFFORD OLD HALL SD4616 Lovely, timber-framed, Tudor house built by the Hesketh family in the 16th c, with an intricate hammerbeam roof in the Great Hall, and impressive collections of 17th-c Lancashire oak furniture, and 16th-c arms, armour and tapestries. Some later rooms too. Snacks, shop, limited disabled access (no facilities); cl am, all Thurs and Fri, and Nov–Mar; (01704) 821254; £3.50, garden only £1.70; NT. The Robin Hood, just the other side of Mawdesley, has good home cooking.

★ **SABDEN** SD7737 Attractive village, with a decent antiques centre, on the slopes of Pendle Hill; linked by a scenic drive to another charming Pendle Hill village, Pendleton.

SALFORD SJ8198 Merging almost imperceptibly into Manchester, this owes its distinct place in the popular consciousness mainly to the works of L S Lowry. The city recently received a £64-million Lottery grant to build a giant arts centre, which as well as other features will be able to show its entire collection of his works. The waterside Mark Addy (Stanley St) has a great choice of cheeses and pâtés. **Museum and Art Gallery** (Peel Park) A fine showing of L S Lowry paintings, also a nostalgic reconstructed industrial street scene, with some wonderfully over-the-top period advertisements. Snacks, shop, disabled access; cl 25–26 Dec, 1 Jan, Good Fri; (0161) 736 2649; free. **Mining Museum** (Eccles Old Rd) Georgian building with 2 reconstructed mines, and displays showing the history and development of coal mining. Snacks, shop; cl 12.30–1.30pm, am Sun, Sat; (0161) 736 1832; free. **Ordsall Hall Museum** (Ordsall Lane) Timbered Tudor manor house with local history exhibits and a Victorian farmhouse kitchen. Shop, some disabled access; cl 12.30–1.30pm, am Sun, Sat, Good Fri, 25–26 Dec; (0161) 872 0251; free.

SAMLESBURY HALL SD6130 Well restored, half-timbered, 14th-c manor house, with good changing exhibitions and craft demonstrations, and sales of antiques. Meals, snacks, disabled access to ground floor only; cl Mon exc bank hols, Jan; (01254) 812010; £2.50. The Myerscough Hotel (A59) is pleasant for lunch.

★ **SILVERDALE** SD4875 A little-visited peaceful oasis, up beyond the attractive town of Lancaster: hilly countryside well suited both to walkers and to drivers, and a coastline that's particularly interesting to birdwatchers and naturalists. The small town looks out over the tidal sands to the Cumbrian hills, with streets of quiet houses and a church that looks 14th-c, but was built barely a century ago. Various crafts are sold at the Georgian buildings of the **Wolf House Gallery** (Gibraltar), which also has an adventure playground and a courtyard garden. Snacks; cl 1–2pm, all Mon and wkdys Christmas–Easter. There are nice woodland walks behind the town, and the Silverdale Hotel on Shore Rd is worth knowing. **Leighton Moss Nature Reserve** (off the Yealand Redmayne Rd) RSPB reserve with several roomy hides by reed beds where bitterns, bearded tits and marsh harriers breed; good walks and views. Guided wildlife outings on Tues and Thurs evenings in Aug. Meals, snacks, shop, disabled access; cl 25 Dec; (01524) 701601; £3.75 (RSPB members free). The Moss is also crossed by a (free) public footpath. Nearby, **Yealand Conyers Friends' Meeting House** is unobtrusively charming, in a quiet and pleasant village; the New Inn here is an outstanding dining pub.

SKIPPOOL SD3540 Lots of yachting activity in an attractive boating area, with a decent small café.

★ **SLAIDBURN** SD7152 A perfectly preserved Forest of Bowland village: charming stone cottages, a green with the River Hodder running by, and, at the opposite end, an early 18th-c schoolhouse and a church with a very 18th-c feel inside. Readers enjoy the Whiteholme Victorian Tearooms and the Hark to Bounty is good for lunch and has comfortable bedrooms. The B6478, and the narrow road N past Stocks Reservoir have appealing views.

★ **SOUTHPORT** SD3217 Smartish Victorian seaside resort, long famed as the most pleasant shopping town in the area, and as the place where the sea doesn't come in. In fact it comes in as often as anywhere else, but doesn't stay quite as long; this could be due to the famously mucky beach – for cleaner shores try slightly S at Formby.

The promenade is set back quite a way from the sea, and looks over a man-made lake with boats. From here there are bracing trips down the pier, either on foot or on the little train, and there are plenty of good summer activities inc pleasure flights over the sands. Lord St is the elegant main shopping street; there's an excellent antiquarian bookshop down the Wayfarers Arcade just off it.
Pleasureland is a typical fairground, its wooden rollercoaster well regarded by connoisseurs (£11 wristband for all rides). **Southport Zoo** (Princes Park) Has one of the few snow leopards to be bred in captivity in the West and a new tropical wader aviary. Snacks, shop, some disabled access; cl 25 Dec; £3. **Atkinson Art Gallery** (Lord St) Specialises in 19th- and 20th-c watercolours, oil paintings, prints and sculpture. Shop, disabled access; cl pm Thurs and Sat, all Sun, bank hols; (01704) 533133; free. **British Lawnmower Museum** (Shakespeare St) Fully restored and often bizarre machines from the 1830s to the present, inc one of the first racing lawnmowers – the curator used to be a champion. Shop; cl Sun and bank hols; (01704) 535369; *£1. **Churchtown** (SD3618) Southport's villagey oldest part, with a number of pretty thatched cottages, and the lakeside **Botanic Gardens**, which are very attractive as well as being interesting to plantsmen; boats to hire, fernery, pets corner, and a local history **museum** (open 11–3pm Tues–Fri and pm wknds and bank hols; free). Just opposite, **Meols Hall** is worth a look for its paintings, inc works by Ramsey, Reynolds, Romney and Poussin. Disabled access; open pm 14 Aug–14 Sept; (01704) 28326; *£3. The Hesketh Arms across from the main gate is good for lunch.

SPEKE HALL SJ4282 (nr Liverpool Airport) Built around a square courtyard, one of the most beautifully timbered black and white houses in the country; the inside is mainly Victorian, though there's a vast Tudor Great Hall. Restored Victorian garden. Snacks, shop, disabled access; house open pm exc Mon Apr–Oct, plus wknds Nov–mid-Dec, garden open pm exc Mon all yr; (0151) 427 7231; £4, grounds only £1.40; NT. They do occasional roof tours to show how the timbers were put together.

STANAH SD3542 Out on the Wyre estuary, this has a stretch of waterside country with reed beds, birds and views, attractive despite the ICI chemical works in the background. On the opposite bank, over the toll bridge past Poulton, the Shard Bridge Inn at Hambleton is nicely placed for lunch.

THORNTON WINDMILL SD3342 (B5412) This restored working windmill has a good range of craft shops alongside; also, an excellent teashop, summer weekend entertainments, even a little clog museum.

THURSTASTON SJ2484 **Wirral Country Park** From here the best bits of the Merseyside Wirral's attractive NW corner are linked by a 12-mile footpath running down to the Cheshire parts, with views across to the Welsh mountains from the edges of the Dee, and some unusual NT heathland. The Irby Mill at nearby Irby has decent food.

TURTON BOTTOMS SD7315 **Turton Tower** 15th-c Renaissance house with Elizabethan buildings and an earlier peel tower; mostly a museum inside, but there is a couple of period rooms, and a major collection of carved wood furniture. It was interestingly extended by followers of the Romantic and later Arts and Crafts movements. Formal Victorian gardens. Snacks, shop; open daily May–Sept (cl 12–1pm for lunch, and am wknds), pm Sat–Weds in Mar, Apr and Oct, and just pm Sun Nov and Feb; (01204) 852203; *£2. The Strawbury Duck, just N at Entwistle, is prettily placed for lunch.

★ **UPPERMILL** SD9905 This whole area of mill settlements in steep valleys cut through the moors is full of interest, and Uppermill itself is one of the most attractive places. **Saddleworth Museum & Art Gallery** (High St) Based around an old mill, and volunteers occasionally dress up in appropriate garb. They've worked hard to liven up visits for families. Shop, limited disabled access; (01457) 874093; £1.25. Up above the town is a lonely moorland church, with good walks around it and an ancient pub opposite. Fine drives around here include the A635 over Saddleworth Moor, and the B6197 Delph–Grains Bar, then the A672 or A640 over the moors.

✝★ **WADDINGTON** SD7243 Forest of Bowland village, with a fine **church**, and a lovely drive from Longridge.

❁ **WARTON CRAG** SD4973 (just N of Carnforth) Fine views over Morecambe Bay and the coast, and enjoyable walking.

✝ **WHALLEY ABBEY** SD7336 Striking remains of a 14th-c Cistercian abbey – the monks' quarters, rather than the church which has virtually disappeared – in the grounds of a 16th-c manor house used as a religious retreat (they do B & B). 2 gatehouses are intact, and there's a visitor centre. Snacks, shop, disabled access; cl Christmas and New Year; (01254) 822268; £1.50. The separate 13th-c parish **church** has interesting woodwork and 3 ancient Celtic-Scandinavian crosses. The Freemasons Arms at Wiswell does good food.

WIGAN SD5805 *See separate Family Panel on p.381* for **Wigan Pier**. The Old Pear Tree on Frog Lane does decent lunches. **Haigh Hall Country Park** (just N) 250-acre country park with guided walks, nature trails, a beautifully set golf course, craft centre, walled gardens and miniature railway. Meals, snacks, shops (one excellent for golfers), some disabled access; (01942) 832985; park free, charges for parking and attractions.

WYCOLLER PARK SD9339 Lancashire Brontë country (the ruined hall at Wycoller features in *Jane Eyre*), with walks along a beck to Clam Bridge, an Iron Age slab, and up to Foster's Leap, a finely placed crag.

★ **Other attractive villages**, all with decent pubs and great surrounding scenery, include Goosnargh SD5537, Tunstall SD6173 (Brontë church) and Wiswell SD7437. Particularly pretty ones in or on the edges of the Forest of Bowland are Bolton by Bowland SD7849 (with a fine church), Gisburn SD8248, Grindleton SD7545 and Newton SD6950.

Pubs well placed for walkers include the Hare & Hounds at Abbey Village SD6422, Pack Horse at Affetside SD7513, Black Dog at Belmont SD6716, the Dog at Belthorn SD7224, White House on Blackstone Edge SD9716, Owd Betts at Cheesden on Ashworth Moor SD8316, Ram's Head nr Denshaw SD9710, Diggle Hotel at Diglea Hamlet above Diggle itself SE0008, Wright Arms at Egerton SD7114, Strawbury Duck by Entwistle Station SD7217, Bull's Head on Grains Bar SD9608, Duke of Wellington on the B6232 W of Haslingden SD7522, Egerton Arms off the narrow Ashworth Rd above Heywood SD8513, Green Man at Inglewhite (nr Beacon Fell) SD5440, New Drop on Longridge Fell SD6439, the Romper at Ridge End above Marple SJ9686, the Kettledrum at Mereclough SD8632, the Highwayman at Nether Burrow SD6275 (pretty stretch of the Lune Valley), Old Rosins at Pickup Bank, Old Hoddlesden SD7222, the Roebuck on Roebuck Low SD9606 and the Railway at White Coppice SD6118. Up on the moors, many of these are closed during lunchtime Mon–Thurs.

Days Out

Liverpool walkabout: Museums in William Brown St, Roman Catholic cathedral; lunch at the Philharmonic (Hope St); Anglican cathedral; walk via Rodney St and Hanover St to Albert Dock; Tate Gallery or Merseyside Maritime Museum; walk to Royal Liver Building for ferry across Mersey to Birkenhead and back; walk back to William Brown St via Water St and Dale St.

Pennine heritage: East Lancs Railway, Bury; lunch at the Lord Raglan, Nangreaves; Helmshore Textile Museums (not Sat).

Industrious Manchester: Town Hall; walk Rochdale Canal towpath from Princess St to the junction with the Bridgewater Canal in Castlefield area; lunch at Dukes 92, Castle St; Museum of Science and Industry, or Granada Studios Tour.

Where to eat

Manchester and Liverpool both have plenty of good ethnic restaurants.

BIRKENHEAD SJ3288 **Pastime Restaurant** *42 Hamilton Sq (0151) 647* 8095 Popular restaurant in a handsome Victorian building; with enjoyable food (the fixed-price menu is good value), a relaxed atmosphere, and friendly, helpful service; cl Mon. **£23**|£5.

BISPHAM GREEN SD4813 **Eagle & Child** *(01257) 462297* Striking, 3-storey, dark brick pub with a civilised, mainly open-plan bar, fine old stone fireplaces, oriental rugs and some coir on the flagstones, and handsome oak settles; imaginative food, well kept real ales, and friendly service; bowling green and croquet behind. **£20.50**|£7.

BLACKO SD8542 **Moorcock** *(01282) 614186* Isolated old stone inn with wonderful views from the big picture windows in the spaciously comfortable lounge bar; good, generous food (lovely lamb dishes), and efficient, friendly service; disabled access. **£15**|£4.95.

BLACKPOOL SD3036 **September Brasserie** *15–17 Queen St (01253) 623282* Not far from the seafront and set above a hairdresser's, this busy little airy restaurant's open-view kitchen does particularly good and inventive food; a short menu with ideas from all over the world (inc lovely puddings); also a thoughtful wine list; cl 1 wk summer, 1 wk winter. **£18.50**|£6.80.

CHIPPING SD6243 **Dog & Partridge** *Hesketh Lane (01995) 61201* Spotlessly kept and relaxed dining pub with a comfortable main lounge, cosy winter log fire, and a good choice of enjoyable food (inc fine home-made chips); real ales, and quite a few wines and malt whiskies. **£18**|£6.50.

DOWNHAM SD7844 **Assheton Arms** *(01200) 441227* Popular pub among peaceful pastures in a prettily preserved village; with a rambling beamed bar, reasonably priced, generous bar food (lots of good fresh fish dishes), well kept real ales, and decent wines; disabled access. **£17**|£5.95.

FENCE SD8237 **Forest** *(01282) 613641* Comfortable pub with heavy panelling, lots of paintings, vases, plates, books and a big open fire; no smoking restaurant with varied and inventive food, a decent choice of wines, and friendly, helpful service. **£22.45**|£8.95.

GOOSNARGH SD5537 **Bushells Arms** *Church Lane (01772) 865235* Friendly, modernised pub close to Chingle Hall; with an excellent range of imaginative food from a constantly changing menu, and a good selection of wines; cl occasional Mon, 25 Dec; well behaved children only; partial disabled access. **£14.50**|£5.

KIRKHAM SD4232 **Cromwellian** *16 Poulton St (01772) 685680* Tiny evening restaurant in a 17th-c house, with consistently good, interesting food from a fixed-price menu; thoughtful wine list, too; cl Sun and Mon, 1 wk Feb, 1 wk Oct. **£22.50**.

LIVERPOOL SJ3589 **Bechers Brook** *29a Hope St (0151) 707 0006* Popular Georgian restaurant, close to the theatres; with a downstairs bar, and a restaurant decorated with Canadian ethnic art; interesting modern cooking (pre-theatre suppers also), a carefully chosen wine list, and friendly staff; cl am Sat, Sun, Christmas, bank hols; disabled access. **£32**|£8.75.

LONGRIDGE SD6137 **Paul Heathcotes** *104 Higher Rd (01772) 784969* Pretty restaurant with flowers, beams and candlelit tables in little interconnected rooms; exceptional, modern British cooking, marvellous puddings, and exemplary service; cl Mon, and am Tues, Weds Thurs and Sat. **£55 dinner, £35 lunch**.

MANCHESTER SJ8497 **Little Yang Sing** *17 George St (0161) 228 7722* Very busy and popular basement restaurant, with super Chinese food (very good casseroles, vegetarian dishes, and dim-sum), a children's fixed menu, decent wines, and friendly service; cl 25 Dec. **£25**|£6.50.

MANCHESTER SJ8499 **Mark Addy** *Stanley St, Salford (0161) 832 4080* Smart pub in converted boat waiting-rooms, with a good range of food – though its choice of 50 different cheeses is the main feature; extremely big helpings, doggy-bags provided; bread and cheese £3.50.

MANCHESTER SJ8497 **Mash & Air** *40 Chorlton St (0161) 661 6161/1111* In a converted canalside mill are 2 restaurants on 4 floors, with a micro-brewery in the middle and 3 real ales to sample; Mash is informal and serves 'smart' pizzas from wood-fired ovens, grilled sandwiches, salads and so forth; cl 25–26 Dec; disabled access. **£22**|£6. Air (evenings only) is more formal and decorated in stylish blues with lots of modern art; imaginative modern cooking with influences from all over the world, plenty of New World wines, and good service; cl Sun, bank hols; disabled access. **£36**.

MANCHESTER SJ8491 **Royal Oak** *729 Wilmslow Rd, Didsbury (0161) 445 3152* Busy pub with an exceptional choice of cheeses from around the world – rare to be given less than a pound; no children; bread, cheese or pâté and salad £3.50 (not wknds).

MANCHESTER SJ8398 **Simply Heathcotes** *Jackson Row, Deansgate (0161) 835 3536* Stylish modern restaurant with high ceilings, polished wood floors, loud colours on the walls, and contemporary furniture; up-to-the-minute, brasserie-style cooking inc very good-value set lunches, a fine wine list, and efficient service; cl 25 Dec, 1 Jan, bank hol Mons; disabled access. **£32.20**.

MANCHESTER SJ8497 **Yang Sing** *3 Charlotte St* (they aim to get back to 34 Princess St – destroyed by a fire – by May 1999) *(0161) 236 2200* Exceptionally good Chinese food using the best fresh ingredients (tanks of live fish, too), wonderful dim-sum, and some unusual dishes among the traditional Cantonese specialities; good-value set meals, a bustling atmosphere, and efficient service; must book ahead; cl 25 Dec; disabled access. **£21.50**.

MELLOR SJ9888 **Oddfellows Arms** *73 Moor End Rd (0161) 449 7826* Fine old building with low ceilings, open fires and a chatty atmosphere in 2 flagstoned rooms; no smoking restaurant, and a wide range of interesting food, inc lots of different types of fresh fish. **£17**|£7.25.

ST MICHAEL'S ON WYRE SD4641 **Mallards** *Garstang Rd (01995) 679661* Well run and busy little restaurant in a former village smithy; with reliable straightforward food, good-value wines, and helpful service; cl am exc Sun, plus 1 wk Jan, July, Oct; disabled access. **£24.50**.

SAWLEY SD7746 **Spread Eagle** *(01220) 441202* Attractive, 16th-c hotel with fine views over the River Ribble and valley from its big picture windows; a bustling bar, thoughtful wine list, and particularly good, interesting modern food in the comfortable dining area; partial disabled access. **£25**|wkdy 2-courses £5.95.

THORNTON-CLEVELEYS SD3541 **River House** *Wyre Rd, Skippool Creek (01253) 883497* Delightful restaurant with long-serving owners; very good, honest cooking using the freshest local ingredients, and a decent wine list; fresh flowers, log fires and fine views; bdrms; cl Sun; children over 7, must be well behaved. **£40**.

YEALAND CONYERS SD5074 **New Inn** *(01524) 732938* Ivy-covered stone dining pub, with a log fire in the little beamed bar, and 2 communicating, cottage dining rooms; novel daily specials, fine salads served with the meals, friendly professional service, decent wines, well kept ales and home-made lemonade; also, and a sheltered side lawn. **£15.95**|£4.95.

Special thanks to Phil and Dilys Unsworth, Margaret and Arthur Dickinson, E G Parish, Derek and Sylvia Stephenson.

Please let us know what you think of places in the *Guide*. Use the report forms at the back of the book or simply write us a letter.

Lancashire Calendar

Some of these dates were provisional as we went to press. Please check information with the telephone numbers provided.

JANUARY

8 **Liverpool** Speke Hall open to the public – *also on Mon 11 and Mon 18* (0345) 585702

7 **Liverpool** St George's Hall open to the public: the unique floor with over 30,000 Minton tiles will be uncovered – *till Sat 9* (0151) 707 2391

11 **Lancaster** New Year's Eve Old Calendar Walk: torchlit walk round the historic town with re-enactments, *starts 7pm* from John o'Gaunt Gateway (01524) 32878

FEBRUARY

12 **Manchester** Vienna Symphony Orchestra at Bridgewater Hall (0161) 907 9000

16 **Manchester** Chinese New Year in Chinatown – *till Thurs 18* (01625) 618333

25 **Lancaster** Valentine's Day Old Calendar Walk (*see Jan 11 for details*); **Liverpool** Chinese New Year Celebrations in Chinatown (0151) 708 8854

MARCH

1 **Manchester** Spanish Film Festival at the Cornerhouse – *till Weds 31* (0161) 200 1500

22 **Liverpool** Town Hall open to the public: grade I building with 3 of the finest chandeliers in Europe – *till 9 Apr* (0151) 707 2391

APRIL

1 **Burnley** Blues Festival – *till Mon 5* (01282) 430005

2 **Lancaster** Maritime Festival at the Maritime Museum and St George's Quay: sea songsters, shanty men and entertainments – *till Mon 5* (01524) 582394

3 **Bacup** Britannia Coconut Dancers – colourful, elaborately costumed, black faced clog dancers *from 9am*, thought to be pirate dances brought with miners moving north from Cornwall (01706) 226590

5 **Preston** Egg-rolling in Avenham Park (01772) 253731

8 **Aintree** Race Meeting inc Grand National – *till Sat 10* (0151) 523 2600

16 **Newton-le-Willows** Book Fair at Haydock Park – *till Sat 17* (0161) 764 4488

23 **Accrington** Lancashire Food Festival (01254) 380298

MAY

1 **Manchester and surrounding districts** International Festival of Street Arts: inc steel bands, outdoor theatre, and a torchlight procession – *till Mon 31* (0161) 224 0200

4 **Lancaster** St George's Day Old Calendar Walk (*see Jan 11 for details*)

Lancashire Calendar (cont.)

10 Manchester Cricket World Cup: Scotland v Lancashire at Old Trafford (0161) 877 4002
12 Manchester Cricket World Cup: Pakistan v Lancashire at Old Trafford (0161) 877 4002
13 Lancaster May Day Old Calendar Walk (*see Jan 11 for details*)
15 Accrington Clog-dancing Festival – *till Sun 16* (01254) 380298
28 Blackpool Dance Festival: championships open to the world – *till 4 Jun* (01253) 625252
30 Manchester Cricket World Cup: West Indies v Australia at Old Trafford (0161) 877 4002; **Haigh** Wigan Motor Show – *till Mon 31* (01942) 832895
31 Oldham Festival – *till 12 Jun* (0161) 911 4072

JUNE

6 Garstang Myerscough College Open Day (01995) 640611; **Morecambe** Carnival (01524) 414379
8 Manchester Super Six: World Cup cricket (0161) 282 4020
12 Burnley King Cotton Carnival: family fun day – *till Sun 13* (01282) 437840; **Lune Valley** Studio Trail: a dozen artists open their studios – *till Sun 27* (015242) 21520; **Manchester** Lord Mayor's Parade (0161) 234 5209
13 Burnley Show (01282) 699843
16 Manchester Cricket World Cup: Semi-finals at Old Trafford (0161) 877 4002
18 Liverpool Mersey Festival: around the river and Albert Dock – *till Mon 21* (0151) 233 6351
19 Lancaster and **Morecambe** National Music Weekend – *till Sun 20* (01524) 582828

JULY

2 Carnforth Fireworks Concert at Leighton Hall (01625) 575681
3 Liverpool Cathedral Festival – *till Sun 18* (0151) 709 6271
4 Lancaster Midsummer Eve Old Calendar Walk (*see Jan 11 for details*); **Warton** American Independence Day Celebrations (01524) 32878
10 Lancaster and **Morecambe** One-man Band Shebang – *till Sun 11* (01524) 582828; **New Brighton** Wirral Show – *till Sun 11* (0151) 677 8943; **Wigan** Jazz Festival – *till Sat 17* (01942) 825677
17 Blackpool Kids Megafest – *till 8 Aug* (01253) 625212; **Morecambe** Summerbreeze 99: jazz and soul music festival – *till Sun 18* (01524) 582828
18 Fleetwood Tram Sunday: large transport festival, bands and side shows (01253) 876525
23 Carnforth Fireworks Concert at Leighton Hall (01625) 575681
24 Morecambe Peripatetic Promenaders – *till Sun 25* (01524) 582828
30 Chorley Royal Lancashire Show at Astley Park – *till 1 Aug* (01254) 813769; **Lancaster** and **Morecambe** Streetbands Festival – *till 1 Aug* (01524) 582828; **St Helens** Show at Sherdley Park: circus, live bands, stalls – *till 1 Aug* (01744) 456991

AUGUST

1 Blackpool Carnival (01253) 693661; **Liverpool** Brouhaha Festival: street performers' festival – *till Tues 10* (0151) 709 3334

Lancashire Calendar (cont.)

7 **Garstang** Agricultural Show (01772) 717418; **Morecambe** Festival of Light and Water – *till Sun 8* (01524) 582801
14 **Rochdale** Rushbearing Ceremony – *till Sun 15* (01706) 356592
15 **Lancaster** and **Morecambe** Latin American Folklore Festival and Carnival – *till Weds 18* (01524) 582828; **Southport to Blackpool** Commercial Vehicle Rally (01204) 308253
18 **Burnley** Open-air Theatre at Towneley Park – *till Sun 22* (01282) 437840
19 **Southport** Flower Show at Victoria Park – *till Sat 21* (01704) 547147
20 **Newton-le-Willows** Book Fair at Haydock Park – *till Sat 21* (0161) 764 4488
21 **Saddleworth** Rushcart Festival: morris dancing – *till Sun 22* (01457) 834871
22 **Cleveleys** Jubilee Day (01253) 860375
26 **Carnforth** Burton, Milnthorpe and Carnforth Show (01524) 701066; **Liverpool** International Beatles Festival – *till Tues 31* (0151) 236 9091
27 **Colne** Rhythm and Blues Festival: over 700 bands on 7 stages – *till Mon 30* (01282) 661234; **Morecambe** Worldbeat Weekend – *till Sun 29* (01524) 582828
29 **Colne** Street Festival – *till Mon 30* (01282) 661682; **Lancaster** Carnival (01524) 33318; **Liscard** Alive: free pop festival (0151) 637 1341
30 **Hoylake** Lifeboats Open Day inc aircraft displays at the Promenade (0151) 647 6780; **Lancaster** Georgian Festival Fair: sedan chair-carrying championships (01524) 32878; **Liverpool** Matthew Street Festival: free music festival (0151) 236 9091

SEPTEMBER

3 **Blackpool** Illuminations – *till 7 Nov* (01253) 625212; **Fleetwood** Fylde Folk Festival: over 125 events – *till Sun 5* (01253) 872317
4 **Preston** Lancashire Vintage and Country Show at Hamilton House Farm – *till Sun 5* (01772) 687259
11 **Preston** Maritime Festival: rally of yachts and canal boats, Royal Navy displays, fireworks, and live music – *till Sun 12* (01772) 558111; **Rochdale** Heritage Open Days: buildings open – *till Sun 12* (01706) 356592
18 **Parkgate** Horse Trials and Country Fair – *till Sun 19* (0151) 336 4169
19 **Morecambe** Heritage Gala: traditional entertainments, vintage vehicles, and aerial displays (01524) 582803

OCTOBER

1 **Manchester** Food and Drink Festival – *till Sun 10* (0161) 228 2900
10 **Lancaster** Michaelmas Day Old Calendar Walk (*see Jan 11 for details*)
17 **Blackpool** British Freestyle Dance Championships (01253) 478203

NOVEMBER

5 **Newton-le-Willows** Book Fair at Haydock Park – *till Sat 6* (0161) 764 4488
6 **Lancaster** Fireworks and Beacon Lighting (01524) 32878
10 **Lancaster** Halloween Old Calendar Walk (*see Jan 11 for details*)
12 **Wirral** International Guitar Festival – *till Sun 21* (0151) 647 2366

Lancashire Calendar (cont.)

18 **Blackpool** British National Dance Championships – *till Sat 20* (01253) 478203

DECEMBER

1 **Burnley** Early Music Festival – *till Sat 11* (01282) 437840
17 **Lancaster** St Nicholas's Day Old Calendar Walk (*see Jan 11 for details*)

We welcome reports from readers

This *Guide* depends on readers' reports. Do help us if you can – in return, we offer a discount on the next edition to people who've helped us with reports for it. Tell us what you think about places already in it, and anything extra you think we should say about them. And send us your ideas for inclusion in the next edition: places to visit, eat at or stay in, attractive drives or walks, maybe even unusual interesting shops you know of. Use the card in the middle, the report forms at the end, or just write – no stamp needed: *The Good Guide to Britain*, FREEPOST TN1569, Wadhurst, E Sussex TN5 7BR.

LEICESTERSHIRE AND RUTLAND

Sweeping country views, grand houses and castles, some unusual places to visit – and not too many tourists.

Leicester sets an excellent example with its policy of keeping museums and similar places free; it's a good place for day visits, with lots to see – often out of the ordinary. Elsewhere, great houses and castles in attractive parkland and fine scenery make this a pleasant area for a civilised break. The sweeping countryside particularly suits scenic drives or cycle rides, especially in the east: graceful patches of woodland, plenty of charming stone-built villages to potter through, delightful churches. Many of the less busy roads stride along old coach routes, with broad views. There are quite a few worthwhile walks, too – and you get out into unspoilt countryside very quickly from the built-up areas, even from busy Leicester itself.

Rutland Water has the look of a huge natural lake, pleasant to walk along the water's edge with quite a lot to see and do around it, including nature reserves, boat hire and boat trips, a butterfly centre, Rutland's engaging capital Oakham, the Cottesmore railway museum, and the late Geoff Hamilton's gardens near Exton.

Favourite family outings include Twycross Zoo (good for apes), the Coalville discovery park and the steam railway near Market Bosworth. Among several enjoyable farm parks, the friendly, well organised one at Oadby stands out, and people also very much like the one near Oakham.

Information centres here are very helpful, and bus services excellent.

Where to stay

EMPINGHAM SK9508 **White Horse** *Main St, Empingham LE15 8PS (01780) 460221* ***£63,** plus special breaks; 13 pretty rms, some in a delightfully converted stable block. Popular, refurbished old pub handy for Rutland Water; relaxed and friendly atmosphere, big helpings of excellent food inc fine breakfasts, coffee and croissants from 8am, and cream teas all year; log fire, an attractive restaurant and efficient, friendly service; cots/high chairs; disabled access.

GLOOSTON SP7394 **Old Barn** *Main St, Glooston, Market Harborough LE16 7ST (01858) 545215* **£49.50;** 3 rms. Attractively restored 16th-c pub with civilised décor and an open fire in the beamed main bar; a charming little restaurant, super inventive food (some produce from their kitchen garden), good breakfasts, and decent real ales; pleasant walks nearby; well behaved children and dogs allowed.

HAMBLETON SK9107 **Hambleton Hall** *Hambleton, Oakham LE15 8TH (01572) 756991* **£195;** 15 luxurious rms. In beautiful grounds by Rutland Water, this grandly restored Victorian manor house has elegant day rooms with fine views, antiques, open fires and exceptional flower arrangements; professional and friendly staff, wonderful food in the no smoking restaurant, a stimulating wine list, and a marvellously pampering atmosphere; no babies in restaurant (exc for breakfast); disabled access.

KINGS MILLS SK4127 **Priest House** *Kings Mills, Castle Donington DE74 2RR (01332) 810649* **£109;** 45 good rms, some in annexe. At the end of a country lane in a pretty spot by the River Trent, this extended, partly 11th-c building has a

Gothic tower and arched windows and doors; there's a huge Adam fireplace in the comfortable library, a cheerful bar, and a restaurant overlooking the river; cl 27–30 Dec.

MARKET HARBOROUGH SP7387 **Three Swans** *21 High St LE16 7NJ (01858) 466644* **£70w,** plus special breaks; 50 rms. Fine old coaching inn with a plush lounge bar, attractive conservatory and a glorious courtyard; very friendly, helpful staff, and good food; disabled access.

MEDBOURNE SP7992 **Nevill Arms** *Medbourne, Market Harborough LE16 8EE (01858) 565288* **wkdys £50, wknds £39.95;** 8 rms. Bright and busy, old mullion-windowed inn just across a footbridge over the stream; excellent food, lots of bar games, friendly and prompt service, and an inglenook log fire; cl 25 Dec; disabled access.

OAKHAM SK8608 **Whipper-In** *Market Pl, Oakham LE15 6DT (01572) 756971* ***£71,** plus special breaks; 24 rms. Attractive and well run, 17th-c stone coaching inn with an oak-beamed and panelled lounge opening into a pleasant cosy eating area; log fires, good food in the cosy restaurant, and well kept ales; disabled access.

PACKINGTON SK3512 **Springs Hydro** *Packington, Ashby-de-la-Zouch LE65 1TG (01530) 273873* **£130** inc massage and free use of all facilities, plus special breaks; 58 rms. Britain's first purpose-built health hydro with all the amenities; good healthy food, and friendly staff; cl 20–27 Dec; no children; disabled access.

ROTHLEY SK5712 **Rothley Court** *Rothley, Leicester LE7 7LG (0116) 237 4141* **£107.90;** 34 rms (the ones in the main house have more character). Mentioned in the Domesday Book, this carefully run manor house, with its beautifully preserved 13th-c chapel, has some fine oak panelling, open fires, a comfortable bar, conservatory, a terrace and garden; courteous staff; disabled access.

SAXELBYE SK7020 **Saxelbye Manor House** *Church Lane, Saxelbye, Melton Mowbray LE14 3PA (01664) 812269* ***£42;** 3 rms, 1 with own bthrm. Attractive old house (parts several hundred years old) with marvellous Victoriana, and a long passage leading to a fine Elizabethan oak stairway built in the old stone stairwell; helpful, friendly owner, and very good traditional evening meals and breakfasts; cl Nov–Mar.

STAPLEFORD SK8118 **Stapleford Park** *Stapleford, Melton Mowbray LE14 2EF (01572) 787522* **£193.87;** 51 lavishly decorated rms, plus cottage. Luxurious country house, extravagantly restored, in lovely large grounds; with lots of mahogany, opulent furnishings, fine oil paintings and an impressive library; good restaurant food, enthusiastic American owner, and a warmly welcoming staff; health spa, indoor swimming pool, riding, stabling, tennis, croquet, miniature golf (and a newly opened golf academy), coarse fishing, clay-pigeon shooting, hunting; cots/babysitting; dogs welcome; disabled access.

STRETTON SK9416 **Ram Jam Inn** *Great North Rd, Stretton LE15 7QY (01780) 410776* ***£66.10;** 7 comfortable and well equipped rms. Actually on the A1, this civilised place has a comfortable, airy, modern lounge bar blending into a wine-bar-like eating area; a good choice of food quickly served all day, and a useful small wine list; cl 25 Dec.

UPPINGHAM SP8699 **Lake Isle** *16 High St East, Uppingham, Oakham LE15 9PZ (01572) 822951* ***£69,** plus special breaks; 12 rms with home-made biscuits, sherry and fresh fruit, and 2 cottage suites. In a charming market town, this 18th-c restaurant with rooms has an open fire in the attractive pink-walled lounge, a little bar (once a barber's where the schoolboys had their hair cut), excellent food in the pine-walled country restaurant (delicious breakfasts, too), and a fine, carefully chosen wine list; also, a small and pretty garden.

Please let us know what you think of places in the *Guide*. Use the report forms at the back of the book or simply write us a letter.

To see and do

Leicestershire Family Attraction of the Year

TWYCROSS SK3305 **Twycross Zoo Park** (A444) Recently celebrating its 35th birthday, this cheery place is best known for its collection of primates, with an enormous range of apes, gibbons, orang-utans, and chimpanzees – every shape, size and species. But there are plenty of other animals too, inc giraffes, sealions, elephants and penguins; the reptile house is 20p extra. In the summer there are animal talks, demonstrations and feeding sessions; times are posted nr the entrance and they announce everything over the public address system. It's not huge (you're never really more than 5 minutes away from your car), so is easy to get round at a leisurely pace, though it can get crowded on summer afternoons. There's a decent picnic area, and an adventure playground for younger children (it's a bit tame for over-10s). In winter slightly less goes on, except in the run up to Christmas when they have an enthusiastically put-together grotto. Most animals are under cover if it rains, though you'll get more out of it on a dry day. Friendly and committed, its slightly low-key feel – compared to some of the country's bigger zoos – seems to add to the appeal. Meals, snacks, shop, disabled access; cl 25 Dec; (01827) 880250; £5.50 (£3.50 children).

ARNESBY WINDMILL SP6192 Handsomely preserved, well worth a look.

ASHBY CANAL SK3707 The towpath offers good countryside walking, with green fields and stone-arched bridges, as well as coots, moorhens, herons and maybe even the flash of a kingfisher. The best parts run from the tunnel under Snarestone SK3409 past Gopsall Park, and then on through Shackerstone and Congerstone to pass Shenton Park SK3800 on an embankment, before heading into Warwicks and its junction with the Coventry Canal. It also makes an ideal walking link between Bosworth battlefield and the steam railway to the N.

ASHBY-DE-LA-ZOUCH SK3516 **Castle** The Norman core and its 15th-c extension were largely destroyed in the Civil War, but the ruins are impressive, and the adjoining fields were the setting for Sir Walter Scott's *Ivanhoe*. Bring a torch for the underground passage. Shop, limited disabled access; cl 24–26 Dec, and winter Mon and Tues; (01530) 413343; £1.70. There's a little **museum** (Easter–Sept) by the tourist information centre on North St, and the Royal Hotel has a good-value carvery.

BEACON HILL COUNTRY PARK SK5114 A good surviving chunk of the former vast Charnwood Forest hunting park. The hill itself (above Woodhouse Eaves) is one of the best viewpoints in the area – an intriguing mix of the industrial and the very rural; it's a popular local beauty-spot, rising almost like a volcano above its lower woodland slopes. From the 245-metre (800-ft) summit, the Jubilee Walk heads N and E through partly wooded country. A trail S makes a small circuit around Broombriggs Farm, with boards explaining farming methods by the path. The Wheatsheaf is handy for lunch.

BELVOIR CASTLE SK8133 Pronounced 'Beaver', this is best from the outside, a glorious fantasy of turrets and battlements, pinnacles and towers, surrounded by terraced gardens peopled with sculptures. Inside, only a couple of rooms are grand enough to impress, and some of the contents are starting to look a little shabby. Meals, snacks, shop, limited disabled access – it's quite a walk up the hill; cl Mon (exc bank hols), Fri, and Oct–Mar; (01476) 870262; £5. The Peacock, at Redmile not far off, is excellent for lunch. Good drives on fine old coach roads centre on Belvoir: for instance, from Long Benington (Lincs) through Bottesford,

Harby and Hose, or via Knipton down through Eastwell and past Gromston all the way to Barrow upon Soar.

BOTTESFORD CHURCH SK8139 Full of elaborate tombs and monuments; they had to raise the roof to fit them all in.

BRADGATE COUNTRY PARK SK5210 On the edge of Newtown Linford, this extensive tract of the former vast hunting park of Charnwood Forest is little changed over the last 750 years. At its heart are the ruins of the 15th-c home of Lady Jane Grey, and a visitor centre tells her sad story. Shop, limited disabled access; visitor centre cl am, Mon, and all winter wkdys; (0116) 234 1850; pay and display parking, visitor centre £1.20. The entrance off the B5328 N of Cropston has better lavatories than the main entrance on the B5327. Fallow deer still roam these heathy slopes among the rock outcrops, and there's general access, plenty of waymarked paths, and lots of opportunities for picnics. Nearby Cropston Reservoir has waterfowl. The Pear Tree in Woodhouse Eaves has good food.

BREEDON ON THE HILL CHURCH SK4023 On an interesting, partly quarried, Iron Age hill fort, this has some unique Anglo-Saxon carvings.

BURROUGH HILL SK7510 There's an enjoyable path along its escarpment. The summit has splendid views, and an imposing Iron Age hill fort, its high ramparts still largely intact (50p parking charge).

CHARNWOOD FOREST SK4515 The friendly Bull's Head (on the former B587 Whitwick–Copt Oak road), with a big garden and lots of animals, has fine views over surviving remnants of this former vast hunting park, popular for walks; the Copt Oak pub itself, over on the B591, is also a useful base for walks.

! **CLIPSHAM** SK9716 **Yew Tree Avenue** (just E, off the Castle Bytham Rd) Delightfully quirky avenue of 150 yew trees, clipped in sometimes bizarre shapes to represent animals, characters and events; free. The surrounding woods are full of deer (not to mention bluebells in spring), and the Olive Branch has decent food.

! **COALVILLE** SK4114 **Snibston Discovery Park** (Ashby Rd) Busy 100-acre centre based around a former colliery (the first shaft was sunk by George and Robert Stephenson), with fun exhibitions and interactive displays on a hugely varied range of topics connected to science and industry. Children like the Science Alive gallery best, with plenty of hands-on experiments and activities (inc the illusion of cycling with a skeleton), while similarly organised galleries look at transport, mining, and fashion. The landscaped grounds include a huge play area and nature reserve, with extra charges for golf, fishing and tours of the mine workings by former pitmen. Snacks, shop, disabled access; cl 25–26 Dec; (01530) 510851; *£4.75. The Bull's Head, above Whitwick, is a popular family food pub.

COTTESMORE SK8913 **Rutland Railway Museum** Nearly 40 industrial steam and diesel locomotives, and 60 other wagons and vehicles used in the ironstone quarries and industry. Occasional steamrides, and quite a nice lineside walk to the old Oakham Canal. Open wknds and bank hols – best to tel (01572) 813203 for dates of steamdays; *£2.50. The Sun is useful for lunch.

DESFORD SK4704 **Tropical Bird Gardens** (Lindridge Lane) Pleasant 5-acre woodland garden with over 50 different species, many in walk-through aviaries; the free-flying macaws are particularly spectacular and may even perch on your shoulder. Cl Oct–Mar (01455) 824603; *£3.

DONINGTON LE HEATH MANOR HOUSE SK4212 One of the very rare examples of an almost untouched medieval manor house, pretty much unaltered since it was built in 1280. Developing 17th-c style gardens inc a decorative maze. Snacks, shop; disabled access to ground floor only, cl 25 Dec, 1 Jan; (01530) 831259; free.

DONINGTON PARK SK4225 **Donington Collection** World's largest private collection of single-seat racing cars, with vehicles driven by all the greats, and related memorabilia. The price means you really have to be a racing fan to appreciate it. Meals, snacks, shop, disabled access; cl 25–26

Dec, 1 Jan; (01332) 811027; £7. The Nag's Head is a good dining pub.

EXTON SK9110 **Barnsdale Plants and Gardens** (The Avenue) Familiar to viewers of *Gardeners' World*; they were developed on the programme by the late Geoff Hamilton. The interesting plants are grown organically using peat-free compost, and there are plenty of useful ideas and techniques. Nursery, disabled access; cl Nov–Feb; (01572) 813200; £5. S of here, towards the A606, the Barnsdale Lodge Hotel has good food, comfortable bedrooms and a neighbouring antiques centre. In the opposite direction, Exton village is a handsome collection of thatched houses around a tree-studded green; the attractive **church** is beautifully placed in a park, and the Fox & Hounds has decent home cooking.

EYEBROOK RESERVOIR SP8595 Rewarding for birdspotters and fishermen, though as it has no hides or facilities appeals mainly to true enthusiasts.

FOXTON SP6989 **Canal museum** Next to an interesting staircase flight of locks, and based around the extraordinary, Victorian, steam-powered boat lift built to avoid using the lock and so save water – now being restored. Shop, some disabled access; cl winter Mon and Tues; (0116) 279 2657; site free, museum £1.50. Bridge 61 at the bottom of the locks has basic food and welcomes children (lots of ducks – take plenty of bread). The locks are a good focus for Grand Union Canal towpath walks. The reservoir over at Saddington is a pretty spot, and the Queen's Head there is a popular dining pub.

GADDESBY CHURCH SK6812 Notable for its elaborate 13th-c workmanship.

HINCKLEY SP4594 **Burbage Common and Woods** (off the A47, just E) Ancient forest with lots of footpaths (some accessible by wheelchair), observation hides, and spectacular flora. Visitor centre open Sun, pm Sat, and pms summer exc Weds; (01455) 633712; free.

KEGWORTH SK4826 The Cap & Stocking is an interesting old tavern, at the start of a pleasant drive through the Leakes, Wysall, Widmerpool, Kinoulton, Colston Bassett (just over the Notts border – the Martins Arms is the best lunch stop of all), Granby and Orston.

KIBWORTH HARCOURT WINDMILL SP6894 The county's only remaining post mill, a fine example from the early 18th c. The Three Horseshoes is useful for lunch. The old coach road through Kibworth from Uppingham (another nice little town with a well known school and an old church) and on to Kilby, Counteshorpe and Cosby is a rewarding drive.

KING'S NORTON CHURCH SK6800 A graceful Gothic Revival building.

KIRBY MUXLOE CASTLE SK5204 Peaceful 15th-c ruins, barely used by their original owner before he was executed. Shop, disabled access; open wknds and bank hols (exc 1–2pm) Apr–Nov; (0116) 238 6886; £1.75. The Royal Oak is handy for lunch.

LEICESTER SK5804 In this busy city's mix of ancient and modern, it's the modern which makes the most immediate impression. But a bit of digging around among the shops, office blocks and traffic schemes does turn up reminders of its long and varied past – most notable among some fine old buildings is the 14th-c Guildhall. The city's staunch defence of free entrance to museums, etc., while places elsewhere are increasingly demanding a fee, is most attractive. Good ones include **Newarke Houses** (The Newarke), where there's a quiet period garden, and the **Leicestershire Museum and Art Gallery** (New Walk), which has a collection of German Expressionist art that for this country must be unique, and a Discovery Room with interactive displays for children; both open as Jewry Wall. **Jewry Wall Museum and Site** (St Nicholas Circle) Site of 2nd-c Roman baths, the courtyard now excavated to reveal porticoes and shops sheltered by the remains of a massive stone wall. Excellent collections of mosaic pavements and painted wall plaster. Shop, disabled access with prior arrangement; cl am Sun, 25–26 Dec;

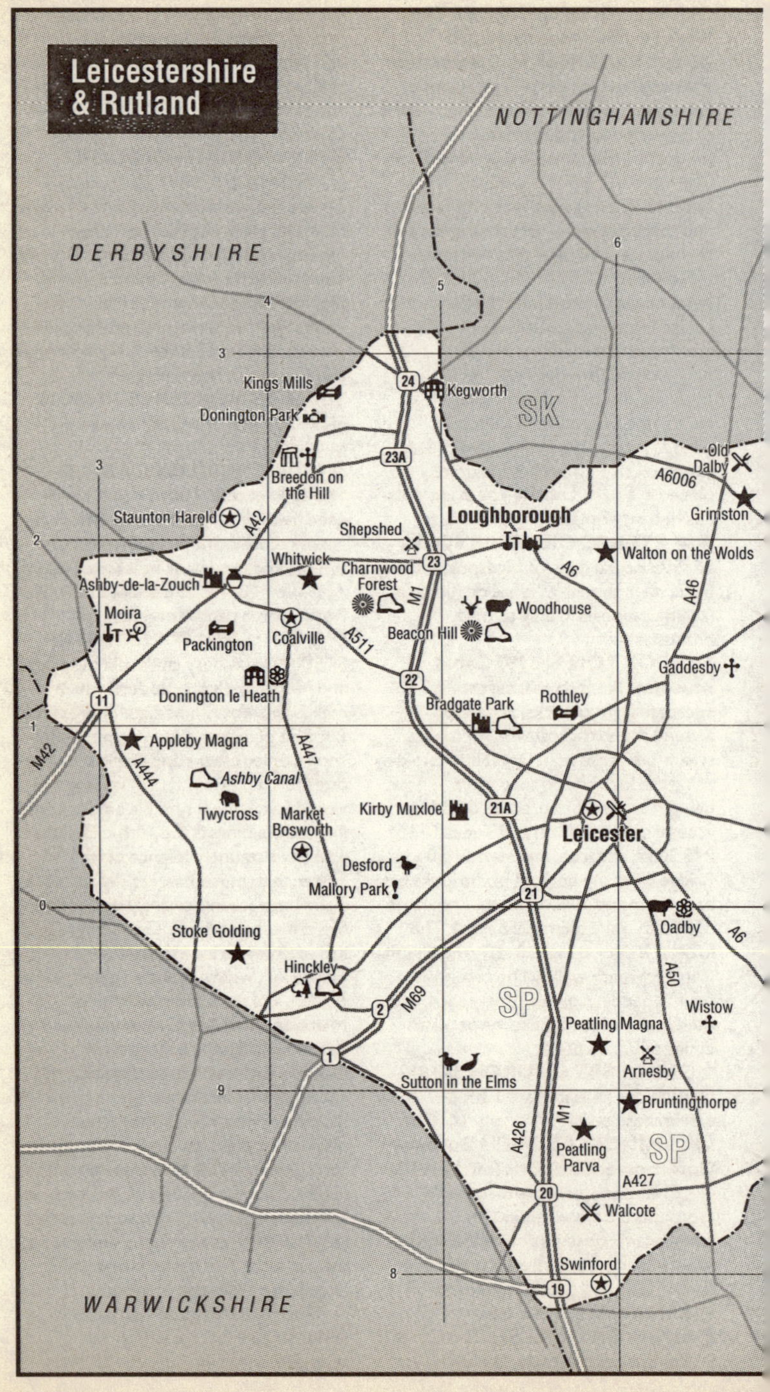

Leicestershire & Rutland
NOTTINGHAMSHIRE
DERBYSHIRE
WARWICKSHIRE
Kings Mills
Donington Park
Kegworth
SK
Breedon on the Hill
Staunton Harold
A42
Shepshed
Loughborough
Old Dalby
A6006
Grimston
Walton on the Wolds
Ashby-de-la-Zouch
Whitwick
Charnwood Forest
M1
A6
A46
Woodhouse
Moira
Packington
Coalville
A511
Beacon Hill
Gaddesby
Donington le Heath
Bradgate Park
Rothley
Appleby Magna
M42
A444
A447
Ashby Canal
Twycross
Market Bosworth
Kirby Muxloe
Leicester
Desford
Mallory Park
Oadby
A6
Stoke Golding
Hinckley
M69
SP
A50
Wistow
Peatling Magna
Arnesby
Sutton in the Elms
Bruntingthorpe
A426
Peatling Parva
A427
Walcote
Swinford

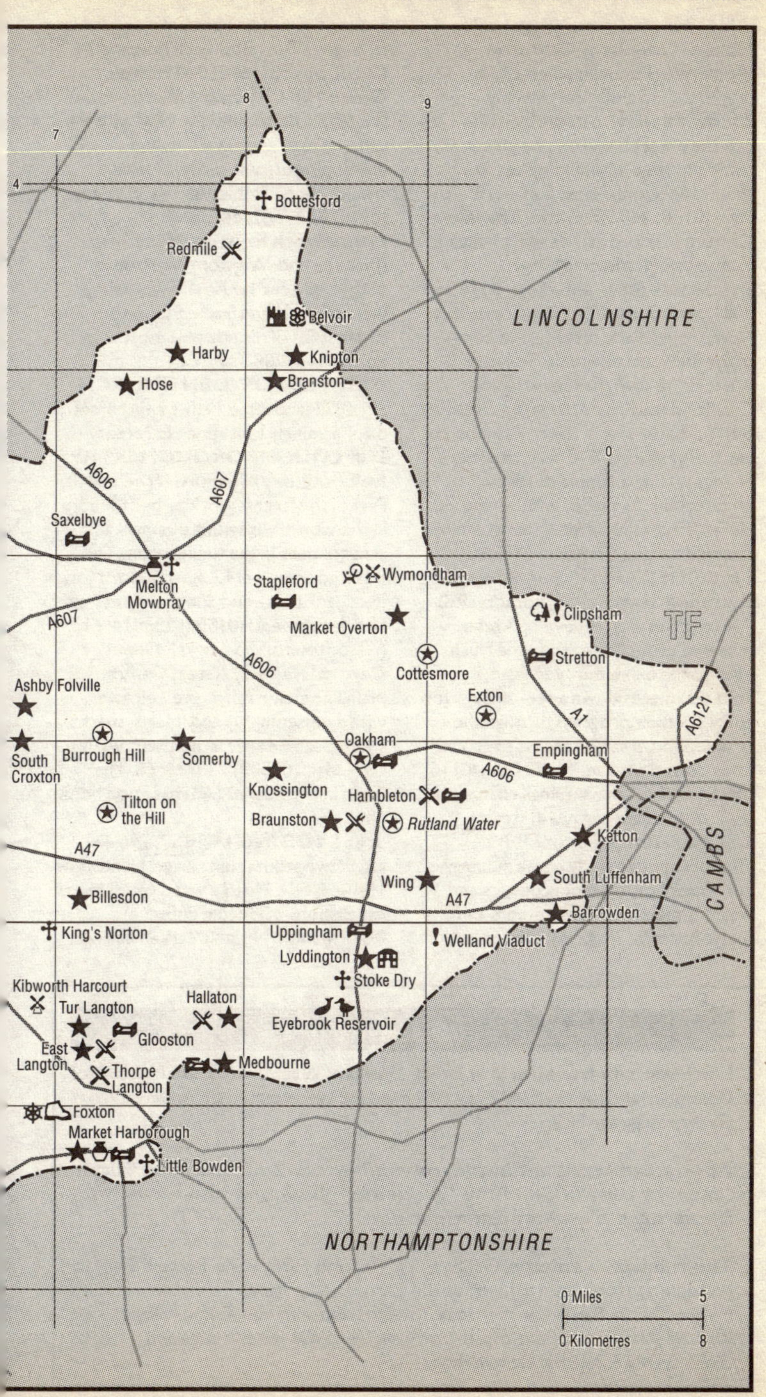
LINCOLNSHIRE
NORTHAMPTONSHIRE
CAMBS
TF
Bottesford
Redmile
Belvoir
Harby
Knipton
Hose
Branston
A606
A607
Saxelbye
Melton Mowbray
Stapleford
Wymondham
Clipsham
Market Overton
Stretton
Cottesmore
Exton
A1
A6121
Ashby Folville
Burrough Hill
Somerby
Oakham
Empingham
South Croxton
Knossington
Hambleton
Tilton on the Hill
Braunston
Rutland Water
Ketton
A47
Wing
South Luffenham
Billesdon
Barrowden
King's Norton
Uppingham
Welland Viaduct
Lyddington
Stoke Dry
Kibworth Harcourt
Tur Langton
Hallaton
Eyebrook Reservoir
East Langton
Glooston
Thorpe Langton
Medbourne
Foxton
Market Harborough
Little Bowden
0 Miles 5
0 Kilometres 8

(0116) 247 3021; free. **Wygston's House Museum of Costume** (Applegate) Reconstructed 1920s draper's shop and entertainingly displayed English costume from the 17th c to the present; you may be able to try some on. Shop, disabled access to ground floor only; cl am Sun and 25–26 Dec; (0116) 247 3056; free. The **Jain Centre** (Oxford St) has some fantastic examples of traditional Indian architecture (open pm wkdys; 0116 254 3091; donations). The Hindu temple on Narborough Rd is reckoned to be one of the finest outside India. Towpath walks along both the Grand Union Canal and the River Soar give a relatively tranquil back view of the city's industrial life. **Belgrave Hall** (Church Rd, city's N edge) A fine example of 18th-c architecture, furnished with period pieces. Charming gardens. Shop, limited disabled access; cl am Sun, 24–26 Dec, 1 Jan; (0116) 266 6590; free. **Abbey Pumping Station** (Corporation Rd) Also out this way, redeveloped as a museum of public health; in the Flush With Pride exhibition, you flush imitation faeces down a see-through loo to follow their progress through the drains. Shop, disabled access to ground floor only; cl am Sun, 24–25 Dec; (0116) 299 5111; free (maybe small charge on days when beam engines in steam). **Gas Museum** (Aylestone Rd) Comprehensive study of the industry and its application, from cookers and washing machines to hairdryers and magic lanterns. Shop, disabled access to ground floor only; open pm Tues–Fri (though cl Tues after bank hols and 24 Dec–1 Jan); (0116) 250 3190; free. **Gorse Hill City Farm** (Anstey Lane) Friendly little community farm with the usual animals and activities, and a developing organic garden. Meals, snacks, shop, disabled access; cl Weds; (0116) 253 7582; donations. **Framework Knitters Museum** (Bushloe End, Wigston) A restored 18th-c knitters' house and workshop, with original hand frames. Open pm Sun and first Sat of month, plus most bank hols; (0116) 288 3396; £1.

† **LITTLE BOWDEN CHURCH** SP7487 Handsome 12th-c church, set off charmingly by its fine old rectory.

LOUGHBOROUGH SK5419 **Bell Foundry Museum** (Freehold St) Part of the largest working bell foundry in the world, with a quite remarkable array of bells in the tuning room. Shop, disabled access; cl 12.30–1.30pm, Mon (exc bank hols), and Sun and winter exc by arrangement; (01509) 233414; £1, (£3 for tour of the works). **Great Central Railway** (Great Central Rd) Main line steam railway to Leicester, with a museum this end. Meals, snacks, shop, disabled access; no trains wkdys Oct–Mar; (01509) 230726; £8. The Swan in the Rushes (A6) has good home cooking.

★ **LYDDINGTON** SP8796 An attractive stone-built village. Handsome 15th-c **Bede House** was a residence of the Bishops of Lincoln until the Reformation. Notable carved ceilings,

Days Out

Leicester city freebies: Jewry Wall Museum; Wygston's House Museum of Costume; lunch at Welford Place (Welford Pl); Leicestershire Museum and Art Gallery; Belgrave Hall.

Apes, steamtrains and battleground: Twycross Zoo; lunch at the Cock at Sibson or the Belper Arms at Newton Burgoland; steamtrain from Shackerstone to Bosworth Battlefield.

The miniature county: Oakham, inc Rutland Farm Park; Rutland Railway Museum at Cottesmore; lunch at the Barnsdale Lodge at Barnsdale; antiques centre there; Barnsdale Gardens towards Exton, then Exton village – or Rutland Water for a boat trip and/or walk along the water's edge and a visit to the Butterfly & Aquatic Centre there.

15th-c glass, and a tranquil garden. Shop, disabled access to ground floor only; cl 1–2pm, and Nov–Mar; (01572) 822438; £2.30. The Old White Hart is nice for lunch.

! **MALLORY PARK** SK4500 Motor sport meetings every wknd Mar–Oct, a splendid spectacle for enthusiasts. Meals, snacks, shop, disabled access; (01455) 842931; from £7. The Royal Arms at Sutton Cheney is the nearest good eating place.

MARKET BOSWORTH SK4000 Site of the deciding action in the Wars of the Roses, when Richard III's defeat led to the Tudors' seizing of the English throne. The **Bosworth Battlefield Visitor Centre and Country Park** has explanatory films and exhibitions, as well as a detailed trail following the sites of the fighting (now thought to be ever so slightly out). Also an exhibition of armoury from the *Mary Rose*. Meals, snacks, shop, disabled access; cl am wkdys (exc bank hols and during July and Aug), and all Nov-Mar; (01455) 290429; £2.80. The Royal Arms at nearby Sutton Cheney has decent food. Market Bosworth village itself is interesting to walk through, and the Black Horse (by the market square alms houses) has good-value food. **Battlefield Steam Railway Line** From Shackerstone through Market Bosworth to Shenton by Bosworth Battlefield, a rather nice return trip of just over 9 miles. There's a Victorian tearoom at the Shackerstone end (open Tues–Sun), and some displays. Trains usually wknds and bank hols Mar–Oct, plus Weds and Fri in summer, (01827) 880754 for timetable; £5 return.

★ **MARKET HARBOROUGH** SP7387 An attractive market town which used to specialise in the production of corsets; bizarre, florid and even agonising examples can be seen in the town **museum** (cl am Sun; free). The centre has some fine old Georgian buildings, and above them the gracefully soaring 14th-c spire of the church. The Three Swans Hotel does good lunches.

† **MELTON MOWBRAY** SK7519 Stilton cheese, pork pies and the Quorn hunt all originate in this little town, which also has a particularly distinguished church, St Mary's. **Melton Carnegie Museum** (Thorpe End) celebrates Melton Mowbray's fashionable 19th-c days; cl am Sun; free. Dickinson & Morris (Nottingham St) still make the pies to a traditional recipe and Websters' dairy in Saxelbye (SK6921) is a good place to buy Stilton. In the next village of Grimston, the Black Horse has a remarkable collection of cricket memorabilia.

MOIRA FURNACE SK3115 (B5003 W of Ashby) 19th-c blast furnace and foundations of an engine house and casting shed, with a few craft workshops in the grounds. They have just got major funding to restore the furnace, lime kilns and 1,200 yards of canal, and create a play area and sculpture trail. Snacks, shop, disabled access; cl Mon, Tues, and Nov–Apr; (01283) 224667; free. The new **Heart of the National Forest Visitor Centre** is along the same road, showing progress on the ambitious plan for vast new tracts of traditional broadleafed woodland. The Rawdon Arms out here is useful for lunch, and the Ashby Canal towpath links the furnace to the attractions listed under Market Bosworth.

OADBY SK6102 **Farmworld** (Gartree Rd) Nicely set in charming countryside (but very quick to get to from Leicester), this is a particularly well organised working farm with a good range of traditional farm animals and rare breeds. You can feed most of the inhabitants (they sell food, but don't mind you bringing sensible offerings from home), and they usually have some kind of baby or young animals all year round; milking displays most days, and decent play areas for younger children. Meals, snacks, shop, disabled access; cl 24 Dec–3 Jan; (0116) 271 0355; £4. **Botanic Gardens** (Stoughton Drive South) Around student halls of residence, these university gardens are 16 acres filled with a wide variety of plants in different and delightful settings, inc a hardy fuchsia collection. Plant sales, disabled access; cl wknds and bank hols; (0116) 271 7725; free. The Grange Farm (Florence Wragg Way) has imaginative food.

★ **OAKHAM** SK8608 Rutland's small and attractive county

town, with a good sense of country bustle about it, and one or two interesting antique shops. By the church, the 17th-c Wheatsheaf has decent food, and Barnsdale Lodge (just off A606 E) does worthwhile lunches. **Oakham Castle** The magnificent Norman banqueting hall is all that's left of the building, but earthworks and walls give a good idea of what it must have been like. The hall itself is decorated with a droll collection of extraordinary horseshoes, some grossly opulent, some simply enormously oversized. Shop, disabled access; cl am Sun, Mon (exc bank hols), 25–26 Dec, Good Fri; (01572) 723654; free. **Rutland County Museum** (Catmose St) The emphasis is on rural life, though there are some Roman and Saxon finds. Snacks, shop, disabled access; cl am Sun, 25–26 Dec and Good Fri (01572) 723654; free. **Rutland Farm Park** (Uppingham Rd) Well liked by readers, with various breeds of cattle, pig, sheep and poultry, as well as old farm equipment, a play area, and shortish but pretty strolls round the woodland and stream, with fine trees and Victorian rockeries. Snacks, shop, disabled access; cl Mon (exc bank hols), wkdys Apr–May and all Oct–Mar; (01572) 756789; *£2.50. There's a fine drive through Ashwell, Wymondham and Waltham on the Wolds to Harby.

RUTLAND WATER SK8707 Europe's biggest man-made lake, oddly shaped, with a number of attractions. On the N side of the lake are nature trails, an unusual drought garden created by the late Geoff Hamilton, places to hire bikes, and hourly **boat trips**. The White Horse at Empingham is good for lunch, and other handy dining places are the Finches Arms at Hambleton (the best views over the water), and the Noel Arms at Whitwell. You can fish in various parts, and there's a fishing centre down at Normanton, as well as a small **museum** in a church modelled on London's St John's, Smith Sq. The refreshingly informal Normanton Park Hotel here has decent food. **Butterfly & Aquatic Centre** (off the A606 Empingham–Whitwell road, SK9308) Next to the main Rutland Water information centre, there's a butterfly house with a good water feature, and various other insects and reptiles; also a video on the reservoir's construction in the 1970s. Meals, snacks, shop, disabled access; cl Nov–Mar; (01780) 460515; £2.95. **Rutland Water Nature Reserve** This 9-mile reserve is divided into 2 parts. The part at Egleton (SK8707) is aimed at the more serious birdwatcher (with a comfortable, purpose-built observation centre – several breeding pairs of ospreys have now been settled here, the first in England for generations). Varied talks, walks and events; (01572) 770651; open usually every day (£3, less after 2pm). The Lyndon part (off the Lyndon–Manton road, SK8905) is for the general public (with a useful visitor centre, and maybe summer Sun crafts). Varied talks, walks and events; (01572) 770651; open wknds all year, plus wkdys exc Mon in summer (£1.20). A path totalling 24 miles tracks around the water's edges – information centres have details of shorter trails. The little-publicised walk from Hambleton touring the peninsula, which protrudes into the reservoir, is the best.

SHEPSHED WINDMILL SK4618 Handsomely preserved, well worth a look.

★ **STAUNTON HAROLD** SK3720 (off the B587 N of Ashby) In this pretty village the **Ferrers Centre** has good craft shops around a striking Georgian courtyard and special events most summer Suns (cl Mon exc bank hols and 2 wks at Christmas; free). The **church** out here (owned by the NT) was one of the few built during the Commonwealth; open pm Sat–Weds and bank hols Apr–Sept, plus pm wknds in Oct. *See Derbyshire chapter for nearby* **Calke Abbey**.

SUTTON IN THE ELMS SP5093 **Falconry Centre** (Mill on the Soar, Coventry Rd) Flying demonstrations of owls, hawks, falcons and buzzards; they really try to get the audience involved. On the same site are a fishing lake and a thriving family dining pub. Meals, snacks, shop, disabled access; cl Mon, and 25 Dec; (01455) 285924; *£2.

SWINFORD SP5879

Stanford Hall and Motorcycle Museum 5,000 books line the library of this handsome 17th-c house, an elegant place that still keeps a cosy lived-in atmosphere. Highlights are the painted ceiling in the ballroom, the portraits that accompany the winding grand staircase, and a good costume collection. The excellent motorcycle museum is in the grounds, which also have a lovely 14th-c church with splendid stained glass, a walled rose garden, Sunday craft centre, and a replica of the first successful flying machine in the country. Meals, snacks, shop, limited disabled access; open pm wknds, bank hols and Tues after bank hols, Easter–Sept; (01788) 860250; house and grounds £3.80, grounds only £2.10, motorcycle museum £1 extra. The Cherry Tree at Catthorpe (cl Mon/Tues lunchtime) has good-value food.

TILTON ON THE HILL SK7505 **Halstead House Farm** (Oakham Rd) Specialist poultry farm, with a few animals as well as the birds, nature trail, fishing lake and gardens. They recently added miniature ponies, and do tractor rides. Meals, snacks, well stocked farm shop (game and other fresh meats), disabled access; cl Mon, and all Oct–Mar; £2.70. The village **church** is notable, and the Rose & Crown is handy for lunch.

TWYCROSS SK3305 *See separate Family Panel on p.403* for **Twycross Zoo Park**. The Cock at Sibson is attractive for lunch.

! WELLAND VIADUCT SP9197 (nr Seaton) One of the area's most striking sights: the country's longest viaduct, nearly a mile long, swooping across the valley pastures.

WOODHOUSE SK5415 **Whatoff Lodge** (E towards Quorn) A decent nature trail starts from this working farm, where there's an exhibition of rural bygones and some farm animals. Snacks, shop, disabled access; cl Mon (exc bank hols), and mid-Oct–mid-Mar; (01509) 412127; £2.50. The Pear Tree at Woodhouse Eaves is the best nearby place for lunch.

WYMONDHAM WINDMILL SK8518 One of only 4 6-sailed mills in the country, with a tearoom and craft shops (cl Mon, and winter wkdys); free.

★ **Other attractive villages,** all with decent pubs, include Appleby Magna SK3109, Ashby Folville SK7011, Barrowden SK9400, Billesdon SK7202, Branston SK8129, Braunston SK8306, Bruntingthorpe SP6089, East Langton SP7292, Grimston SK6821, Hallaton SP7896, Harby SK7531, Hose SK7329, Ketton SK9704 (good walks), Knipton SK8231, Knossington SK8008, Market Overton SK8816, Medbourne SP7993 (interesting church too), Peatling Magna SP5992 and Parva SP5889, Somerby SK7710 (the Old Brewery pub brews very fine ales), South Croxton SK6810, South Luffenham SK9402, Stoke Golding SP3997, Tur Langton SP7194, Walton on the Wolds SK5919, Whitwick SK4316, and Wing SK8902, notable for its small medieval **turf maze**. Stoke Dry SP8596 and Wistow SP6496 also have fine **churches**.

Pubs useful for walkers here include the the Pear Tree and Bull's Head in Woodhouse Eaves SK5214; and, all handy for canals, the George & Dragon at Stoke Golding SP3997, Soar Bridge in Barrow upon Soar SK5717, the Griffin at Congerstone SK3605, and the Navigation at Kilby Bridge SP6097. The Cove Inn, spectacularly overlooking the Stoney Cove diving centre nr Stoney Stanton SP4894, is another attractive spot for something to eat.

Where to eat

BRAUNSTON SK8306 **Blue Ball** *(01572) 722135* Said to be Rutland's oldest pub, this popular place puts much emphasis on the well presented and imaginative food; well kept real ales, several wines by the glass, interesting furnishings, a pleasant, informal atmosphere, and very good service even when busy. **£18.95**|£5.25.

BRAUNSTON SK8306 **Old Plough** *(01572) 722714* Attractive place with a pubby atmosphere, traditional bar with heavy beams, and a stylishly modern, no smoking conservatory; good choice of well presented meals, decent beers and a well noted wine list; also, seats out under fruit trees; boules. **£20.50**|£7.95.

EAST LANGTON SP7292 **Bell** *(01858) 545278* Pretty, creeper-covered inn with a warm inviting atmosphere, log fire and plain wooden tables in the long stone bar; good and imaginative food from a seasonally changing menu, OAP weekday lunches, a no smoking dining room, well kept real ales, and friendly, efficient service. **£21**|£8.25.

HALLATON SP7896 **Bewicke Arms** *(01858) 555217* Thatched cottage by the village green; with a warm welcome and traditional feel in its 2 beamed bar rooms, generous helpings of popular food inc fine puddings, well kept real ales, and friendly service; they've now opened a tearoom and gift shop in the converted stables, and a small farm park walk; cl 25 Dec; bdrms; no dogs. **£18**|£4.45.

HAMBLETON SK9007 **Finches Arms** *(01572) 756575* Delightfully placed pub overlooking Rutland Water; with stylish cane furniture and paintings (for sale) in both the bar and more modern, no smoking restaurant; good, interesting, upmarket food with a Mediterranean slant, and real ales; bdrms. **£23.40**|£8.50.

LEICESTER SK5804 **Welford Place** *9 Welford Pl (0116) 247 0758* Once a Victorian gentlemen's club, this friendly place offers full meals in the civilised, high-ceilinged restaurant; also has a spacious bar with enjoyable food served all day – breakfast, snacks and light meals, morning coffee and afternoon tea; efficient service; disabled access. **£19.25**|£6.50.

OLD DALBY SK6723 **Crown** *(01664) 823134* Rather smart former farmhouse, with a wide range of drinks (a dozen real ales, lots of malt whiskies, and an interesting wine list); imaginative and completely fresh food (no freezers, microwaves or chips); several little black-beamed rooms, open fires, and a large, no smoking dining room; plenty of tables on a terrace and the big, sheltered lawn. **£25**|£6.95.

REDMILE SK7935 **Peacock** *(01949) 842554* Atmospheric little village house below Belvoir Castle, with extremely popular, imaginative and enjoyable food in both the bar and the pretty, no smoking restaurant; well kept real ales, nice wines, and courteous, friendly service; open fires, attractive conservatory. **£20.65**|£7.25.

THORPE LANGTON SP7492 **Bakers Arms** *(01858) 545201* Extended thatched pub with a warm and friendly welcome, simple furnishings, and very good, nicely presented food (need to book well ahead); helpful service, well kept beer, a decent choice of wines, and a no smoking snug; cl Mon, am wkdys, pm Sun; children over 12. **£24.75**.

WALCOTE SP5683 **Black Horse** *(01455) 552684* Big helpings of authentic Thai food cooked by the Thai landlady, unusual drinks, a chatty and unpretentious atmosphere, big open fire, and a no smoking restaurant; and outside seats for summer; must book; cl am Mon–Tues am (open bank hols); children in dining area only; disabled access. **£16.50 for 5-course meal**|£6.25.

Special thanks to Mr and Mrs Hadley, M and J Back, B M Eldridge, Graham James.

We welcome reports from readers

This *Guide* depends on readers' reports. Do help us if you can – in return, we offer a discount on the next edition to people who've helped us with reports for it. Tell us what you think about places already in it, and anything extra you think we should say about them. And send us your ideas for inclusion in the next edition: places to visit, eat at or stay in, attractive drives or walks, maybe even unusual interesting shops you know of. Use the card in the middle, the report forms at the end, or just write – no stamp needed: *The Good Guide to Britain*, FREEPOST TN1569, Wadhurst, E Sussex TN5 7BR.

Leicestershire Calendar

Some of these dates were provisional as we went to press. Please check information with the telephone numbers provided.

JANUARY

9 **Castle Donington** Antiques Fair: 200 stands at the International Exhibition Centre – *till Sun 10* (01332) 812919

FEBRUARY

6 **Castle Donington** Antiques Fair – *till Sun 7 (for details see 9 Jan)*
27 **Castle Donington** Toy and Train Fair: 350 stands at the International Exhibition Centre – *till Sun 28* (01332) 812919

MARCH

6 **Castle Donington** Antiques Fair – *till Sun 7 (for details see 9 Jan)*
7 **Leicester** Jazz Festival – *till Sat 13* (0116) 250 6131
13 **Castle Donington** Lotus Show at the International Exhibition Centre – *till Sun 14* (01332) 812919
27 **Loughborough** Food and Country Shopping Fair at Beaumanor Hall – *till Sun 28* (01509) 217444
28 **Castle Donington** Collectors' Fairs at the International Exhibition Centre (01332) 812919

APRIL

4 **Cottesmore** Steam Open Day at the Rutland Railway Museum – *till Mon 5* (01572) 813203
5 **Hallaton** Bottle Kicking, and Hare-pie Scrambling: teams compete to get 3 small kegs of beer across 2 streams a mile apart (01858) 468106; **Kegworth** Charter Market (01530) 411767
17 **Castle Donington** Antiques Fair – *till Sun 18 (for details see 9 Jan)*

MAY

2 **Bruntingthorpe** Open Day at the Airfield (0116) 247 8040; **Cottesmore** Steam Open Day at the Rutland Railway Museum – *till Mon 3* (01572) 813203; **Loughborough** County Show at Dishley Grange Farm – *till Mon 3* (01509) 646786
3 **Castle Donington** Medieval Street Market (01332) 810432
9 **Leicester** Historic Transport Pageant at Abbey Park (0116) 222 4040
15 **Castle Donington** Toy and Train Fair – *till Sun 16 (for details see 27 Feb)*
23 **Burley on the Hill** Rutland County Show (01664) 223876; **Leicester** Early Music Festival – *till 12 Jun* (0116) 270 9984; **Leicester** Historic Transport Pageant at Abbey Park (0116) 270 4040
29 **Castle Donington** Antiques Fair – *till Sun 30 (for details see 9 Jan)*
30 **Belvoir** Civil War Siege Group at the Castle – *till Mon 31* (01476) 870262; **Cottesmore** Steam Open Day at the Rutland Railway Museum – *till Mon 31* (01572) 813203
31 **Loughborough** Carnival (01509) 218113; **Melton Mowbray** Show: arena events, Royal Air Force and bands (01664) 480992

Leicestershire Calendar (cont.)

JUNE

6 **Brooksby** Open Day and Horse Event at Brooksby College (01664) 434291
7 **Little Casterton** Stamford Shakespeare Company Summer Season at Rutland Open-air Theatre, Tolethorpe Hall – *till 28 Aug* (01780) 754381
11 **Leicester** International Music Festival – *till Sun 20* (0116) 247 3043
12 **Market Harborough** Carnival (01858) 462626
19 **Hinckley** Carnival (01455) 637356; **Loughborough** Summer Steam Gala at Great Central Railway – *till Sun 20* (01509) 230726
27 **Belvoir** Jousting at the Castle (01476) 870262; **Swinford** American Civil War Society at Stanford Hall (01788) 860250

JULY

3 **Breedon on the Hill** Open Gardens: 20 gardens – *till Sun 4* (01332) 862099
10 **Wymeswold** Rempstone Steam and Country Show – *till Sun 11* (01509) 213102
11 **Market Bosworth** Show and National Sweetpea Society Show (01530) 271169
16 **Peckleton** Festival – *till Sun 25* (01455) 822604
18 **Measham** Ashby Show at Measham Lodge Farm (01283) 229225
25 **Belvoir** Jousting at the Castle (01476) 870262; **Swinford** Vintage Motorcycle Club Founders' Day Rally at Stanford Hall (01788) 860250
31 **Castle Donington** Toy and Train Fair – *till 1 Aug* (*for details see 27 Feb*)

AUGUST

7 **Castle Donington** Antiques Fair (*for details see 9 Jan*); **Leicester** Caribbean Carnival at Victoria Park (0116) 253 0491; also Abbey Park Festival – *till Weds 11* (0116) 252 7350
13 **Ashby-de-la-Zouch** Fireworks Concert at Calke Abbey – *till Sat 14* (01332) 863822
14 **Swinford** Fireworks Concert at Stanford Hall (01788) 860250
20 **Egleton** British Birdwatching Fair at Rutland Water – *till Sun 22* (01780) 460321
21 **Market Bosworth** Living History and Battle Re-enactment at the Battle Field – *till Sun 22* (01455) 290429
22 **Leicester** Castle Park Festival – *till Sun 29* (0116) 253 2569
29 **Belvoir** Jousting at the Castle – *till Mon 30* (01476) 870262; **Cottesmore** Steam Open Day at the Rutland Railway Museum – *till Mon 30* (01572) 813203
30 **Packington** Open Gardens: up to 10 gardens (01530) 412012

SEPTEMBER

4 **Shackerstone** Steam and Canal Festival – *till Sun 5* (01827) 880754
11 **Castle Donington** Antiques Fair – *till Sun 12* (*for details see 9 Jan*)

Leicestershire Calendar (cont.)

OCTOBER

2 **Castle Donington** Toy and Train Fair – *till Sun 3 (for details see 27 Feb)*
9 **Castle Donington** Antiques Fair – *till Sun 10 (for details see 9 Jan)*
16 **Loughborough** Thomas the Tank Engine at Great Central Railway – *till Sun 17* (01509) 230726

NOVEMBER

6 **Coalville** Fireworks at Snibston Discovery Park (01530) 510851; **Leicester** Bonfire Night at Abbey Park (0116) 252 7350
13 **Castle Donington** Antiques Fair – *till Sun 14 (for details see 9 Jan)*
28 **Castle Donington** Collectors' Fairs at the International Exhibition Centre (01332) 812919

DECEMBER

11 **Castle Donington** Antiques Fair – *till Sun 12 (for details see 9 Jan)*
27 **Castle Donington** Toy and Train Fair – *till Tues 28 (for details see 27 Feb)*

We welcome reports from readers

This *Guide* depends on readers' reports. Do help us if you can – in return, we offer a discount on the next edition to people who've helped us with reports for it. Tell us what you think about places already in it, and anything extra you think we should say about them. And send us your ideas for inclusion in the next edition: places to visit, eat at or stay in, attractive drives or walks, maybe even unusual interesting shops you know of. Use the card in the middle, the report forms at the end, or just write – no stamp needed: *The Good Guide to Britain*, FREEPOST TN1569, Wadhurst, E Sussex TN5 7BR.

Lincolnshire

Lovely houses, castles, churches and villages, well away from the crowds, with some real surprises – and of course the famous seaside resorts.

Away from the traditional family beach resorts, this huge county has another very appealing and largely undiscovered side, with a lot to offer a touring holiday or get-away-from-it-all break. With generally low prices, it's good value, and tourist information centres here tend to be particularly helpful.

Lincoln itself is an interesting city with plenty to see and a glorious cathedral; Stamford and Boston, too, have a good deal of character. North and east of Lincoln, the rolling Wolds countryside makes for enjoyable drives on uncrowded roads, punctuated by attractive villages and charming small towns, and by soaring church spires. Some very striking houses and castles are led by Burghley House on the edge of Stamford, Belton House, and Tattershall and Grimsthorpe castles, with lesser-known delights such as Doddington Hall, Gunby Hall gardens and the great gardens at Harlaxton now being restored. The National Fishing Heritage Centre in Grimsby is a real eye-opener, and the new Time Trap there is a lively hands-on exploration of life in the old days. The cheerful entertainment museum at Whaplode St Catherine's is fun, and the ruined abbey at Thornton Curtis is a little-known romantic gem. There's RAF nostalgia at Coningsby and East Kirby.

For families, there's plenty to do, with well arranged and lively country parks at Elsham Hall and Normanby Hall, heavy horses at Great Steeping, and seals at Mablethorpe and Skegness. Warm escapes on those days when east winds blow from the North Sea include the butterfly park at Long Sutton, and the largely under-cover amusement park at Ingoldmells.

Around the Wash and up the coast towards Wainfleet and Coningsby, the land is very flat, reclaimed from the sea: in springtime the endless bulbfields around Spalding burst into spectacular bloom. Throughout the county's farmland, huge fields of arable crops can be rather tedious for walkers; speeding past more quickly in a car, bus or train, you're more aware of the shape of the countryside, giving it more appeal.

In winter, Lincolnshire can be very chilly.

Where to stay

ALFORD TF4576 **White Horse** *29 West St, Alford LN13 9DG (01507) 462218* **£40,** plus special breaks; 10 prettily furnished and comfortable rms. Picturesque thatched 16th-c inn, carefully restored over the years, with a plush beamed lounge, a good range of well prepared reasonably priced food, and friendly staff.

BINBROOK TF2195 **Hoe Hill** *Swinhope, Market Rasen LN8 6HX (01472) 398206* **£50;** 3 rms. Comfortable late 18th-c farmhouse in attractive countryside, with a big sitting room, and doors opening on to a terrace and croquet lawn; hearty breakfasts with home-made bread and marmalade in the elegant dining room, and particularly good evening meals (by prior arrangement); cl Jan; children over 5.

BOURNE TF0919 **Bourne Eau House** *30 South St, Bourne PE10 9LY (01335) 350287* ***£70;** 3 rms. Handsome house, partly Elizabethan, partly Georgian, with beams and inglenook fireplaces, good dinners in the elegant dining room, and enjoyable breakfasts; friendly owners; cl Christmas and Easter.

BUSLINGTHORPE TF0985 **East Farm House** *Middle Rasen Rd, Buslingthorpe, Lincoln LN3 5AQ (01673) 842283* ***£42,** plus special breaks; 2 rms. 18th-c farmhouse surrounded by family farm, with beams, stripped pine, log fires, a relaxed atmosphere, and good breakfasts; tennis and lots of walks; self-catering cottage; cl Christmas.

DYKE TF1022 **Wishing Well** *Dyke, Bourne PE10 0AF (01778) 422970* ***£49;** 8 rms, most with own bthrm. The wishing well is at the dining end of the long rambling bar – heavy beams, dark stone, brasswork, candlelight and a big fireplace; good popular food, helpful service, and a friendly atmosphere; disabled access.

EAST BARKWITH TF1581 **Bodkin Lodge** *Grange Farm, Torrington Lane, East Barkwith, Market Rasen LN8 5RY (01673) 858249* ***£45;** 2 pretty ground-floor rms. Run by the same warm and friendly family as Grange Farm, this carefully extended bungalow has a comfortable sitting room with books, fresh flowers, an open fire and a baby grand piano, good breakfasts in a big dining room (evening meals by arrangement); award-winning wildlife farmland trails from the door, and marvellous country views; cl Christmas–New Year; children over 10.

FULLETBY TF2973 **Old Rectory** *Fulletby, Horncastle LN9 6JX (01507) 533533* **£40;** 5 rms. Lovely house with a 16th-c heart, in 5 acres on the edge of the Wolds looking over to Lincoln cathedral; comfortable sitting room with an open stone fireplace and French windows to the garden, good breakfasts in separate dining room, evening meals by prior booking, and welcoming owners; no smoking; dogs by arrangement; cl Christmas–New Year; no children.

HOLBEACH TF3426 **Pipwell Manor** *Washway Rd, Saracens Head, Holbeach, Spalding, PE12 8AL (01406) 423119* ***£40;** 3 rms. Handsome 18th-c farmhouse, welcoming and spotless, with a log fire in the comfortable sitting room, a pretty panelled dining room, good breakfasts with their own eggs and home-made preserves, and a conservatory; no children, no smoking and no pets; cl Christmas and New Year.

LINCOLN SK9771 **Carline** *1–3 Carline Rd, Lincoln LN1 1HL (01522) 530422* ***£41;** 12 well equipped rms. Spotlessly kept and comfortable double-fronted no smoking Edwardian guesthouse 5 minutes from the cathedral, with helpful and cheerful long-serving owners, quiet sitting rooms, and fine breakfasts; cl Christmas and New Year; no baby facilities.

LINCOLN SK9871 **D'Isney Place** *Eastgate, Lincoln LN2 4AA (01522) 538881* **£72,** plus special breaks; 17 charming rms. Friendly 18th-c hotel with lovely gardens, nr the cathedral; fine furniture, friendly owners and a relaxed and homely atmosphere, good breakfasts served in the rooms; partial disabled access.

STAMFORD TF0306 **George** *71 St Martins, Stamford PE9 2LB (01780) 750700* **£100,** plus special breaks; 47 rms. Historic ancient former coaching inn with quietly civilised atmosphere, and welcoming staff; sturdy timbers, broad flagstones, heavy beams and massive stonework, open log fires; wonderful food in the garden lounge (tempting help-yourself buffet), restaurant and courtyard (in summer), excellent range of drinks – very good-value Italian wines, well kept walled garden and sunken lawn where croquet is played; disabled access.

WHAPLODE TF3323 **Guy Wells** *Eastgate, Whaplode, Spalding PE12 6TZ (01406) 422239* ***£40;** 3 rms. In a country garden, this Queen Anne house is surrounded by the friendly owners' daffodil and tulip fields and glasshouses (cultivated spring flowers) – you can buy bulbs; low beams, a woodburning stove, pretty furnishings in sitting room, and very good food using their own vegetables and free range eggs; no smoking; cl 25 Dec; children over 5.

WINTERINGHAM SE9322 **Winteringham Fields** *Winteringham, Scunthorpe DN15 9PF (01724) 733096* ***£80;** 7 pretty, chintzy rms with period furniture (3 off courtyard). Thoughtfully run restaurant-with-rooms in a 16th-c manor house with comfortable and very attractive Victorian furnishings, beams and open fires; really excellent inventive food in no smoking dining room, fine breakfasts, and warm, friendly service; cl 1 wk March, 1 wk Aug, 2 wks Christmas; children over 8 (babies allowed).

To see and do

LINCOLN SK9771 The cathedral and castle, both very striking, share the central hilltop, with enough old buildings around them to keep a sense of unity. There's a lot to appeal up here, and in the steep streets (Steep Hill, and Strait St) of ancient buildings running down from them to the 15th-c Stonebow Gate at the top of the High St below. This lower part of the town is much more of a normal bustling shopping and working centre, though even here are a good few interesting old buildings – inc several Saxon churches and the Norman guildhall. The **Greyfriars Exhibition Centre** (Broadgate) – formerly the County Museum – is in a lovely 13th-c Franciscan building (open Weds–Sat; free). Behind the cathedral and castle the Adam & Eve is a nice old pub. There are good views from the A607 to Grantham.

† **Lincoln Cathedral** Many people reckon this to be England's finest. The original building was largely destroyed in an 1185 earthquake, but the magnificent west front survived, and after nearly a century of rebuilding it was complete by 1280. The triple towers rise spectacularly above the nearby rooftops, and are beautifully lit at night. The carvings and stained glass are stupendous, and the architecture gracefully harmonious. Snacks, shop, disabled access; £3 suggested donation. The ruins of the once formidable Bishop's Palace are close by.

Lincoln Castle In beautiful surroundings on a formidable earthwork, this was originally built in 1068 for William the Conqueror, but only 2 towers and 2 impressive gateways date back to then. One of only 4 remaining originals of Magna Carta is on show, and the ramparts give super views. A 19th-c prison has suitably gruesome exhibits; its chapel is unusually designed so that none of the congregation could see each other. Snacks, shop, mostly disabled access; cl 25–26 Dec, 1 Jan; (01522) 511068; *£2.50.

Roman remains These include the high wall along Westgate, and the largely reconstructed Newport Arch N of the cathedral (it had survived intact until a 1964 disagreement with a lorry); the canal between Lincoln and the River Trent is also Roman – you can walk out into the country along it.

Museum of Lincolnshire Life (Burton Rd) County life over the last couple of centuries, well illustrated in big former barracks. Snacks, shop, disabled access; cl am winter Suns, 24–27 Dec, 1 Jan, Good Fri; (01522) 528448; £2. A lawn in the courtyard makes a good picnic area.

Usher Gallery (Lindum Rd) Attractive gallery with fine watches, porcelain and miniatures, Tennyson memorabilia, and Peter de Wint watercolours. Snacks, shop, disabled access; cl am Sun, 25–26 Dec, 1 Jan, Good Fri; (01522) 527980; *£2.

! **Incredibly Fantastic Old Toy Show** (Westgate) Growing collection of old toys and end-of-pier amusements, close to both the cathedral and castle, so a good treat for unwilling culture buffs. Shop, disabled access; open Tues–Sat plus pm Sun and bank hols Easter–Sept, wknds plus Tues–Fri in school hols Oct–Dec; (01522) 520534; *£1.90.

The Lawn In 1820 this was the county's first lunatic asylum; now its landscaped grounds include hands-on history and archaeology, an aquarium and an exotic glasshouse, and a restaurant, coffee shop and bar. Cl 25–26 Dec; (01522) 560330; free.

Other things to see and do

Lincolnshire Family Attraction of the Year

GRIMSBY TA2609 **National Fishing Heritage Centre** (Alexandra Dock) Unexpectedly lively, this outstanding museum is far more interesting than you might initially have imagined. Fascinating displays provide the full experience of a trawlerman of the mid-1950s, taking you from the back streets of Grimsby to the fishing grounds of the Arctic Circle and back, complete with smells and sensations as well as sights and sounds. Children particularly enjoy the moving deck, where you really do feel as though you're on a boat out at sea, with freezing winds blowing into your face. The Trawlers at War exhibition has similarly lively experiences: you'll get sunk from the deck of a minesweeper, and depth-charged as you retreat into the safety of the control room. There are hands-on opportunities all around the centre, with several activities for younger children – guessing the weight of the rations, or tying knots in the knot room. Everything in the main centre is under cover, but outside there are guided tours of a real trawler, the *Ross Tiger*, led by a former trawlerman. When you see the cramped sleeping quarters it's hard to imagine spending 3 weeks on a boat like this as part of a crew of 12. Watch out for the engine room: it's very noisy. Plenty of special events and extra activities in the summer, from craft exhibitions to pirate days. Snacks, shop, disabled access (not to *Ross Tiger*); cl 25–26 Dec, 1 Jan; (01472) 323345; *£4.50 for centre and trawler (£3.50 children), £3.50 for just one (£2.50 children). Family tickets are available, also one adding entry to **Time Trap** *(see Grimsby, below)*. The Heritage Centre is easily the must-see of the town's attractions: on its own you'll need at least 2 hours to see it properly, but combined with the trawler tour and Time Trap you could easily fill up 4 hours or more.

ABY TF4179 **Claythorpe Watermill and Wildfowl Gardens** Pretty spot around 18th-c watermill, the grounds full of ornamental wildfowl and poultry, and animals such as rabbits and a miniature pony. Fun to wander through the woods. Meals, snacks, shop, mostly disabled access; cl Nov–Feb; (01507) 450687; £3. The Vine in pretty South Thoresby is a civilised place for lunch.

ALFORD TF4575 Pleasant town with some attractive brick and thatch buildings, and a summer craft market (Fri). **Alford Manor House** (West St) is now a folk museum; cl Nov–Easter; £1.25. There's a tall restored 5-sailed **windmill** on the road towards Sutton on Sea (open Tues, Sat, pm Sun, and bank hols all year, plus Weds–Fri Aug–Sept and Fri Oct; £1.50), and another a little further along at Bilsby. W of here, just N of the A16/A1104 junction, the Bluestone Heath hill road past South Ormsby and on to the A157 W of Louth is a splendid scenic drive.

ALKBOROUGH SE8821 Overlooks the confluence of the Trent and Humber from a high (for this area) scarp called The Cliff; walks along it on a path leading S to the attractive village of Burton upon Stather.

ASWARBY CHURCH TF0639 Delightfully set in a well tended park.

BARTON-UPON-HUMBER TA0222 **Barton Clay Pits** Informative country park based around former clay pits, with nature reserves, walks, fishing (extensive reed beds), sailing – and good views of the Humber Bridge. Limited disabled access; visitor centre open wknds and bank hols Easter–Sept; (01652) 633283; free. **Baysgarth House** (Caistor Rd) This handsome 18th-c house has well displayed local history, esp good on rural crafts. Shop, disabled access to ground floor only; cl Mon (exc bank hols)–Weds, 25–26 Dec, 1 Jan; (01652) 632318; free.

BELTON HOUSE SK8844 Splendid Restoration-period mansion

with wonderful carvings, ornate plasterwork, and sumptuous furnishings, paintings and ceramics. The thousand-acre deer park has an orangery and a formal Italian garden. Meals, snacks, shop, limited disabled access; open pm Weds–Sun and bank hols Apr–Oct, grounds open 11am; (01476) 566116; £5; NT. The relaxing Brownlow Arms in picturesque Hough on the Hill has good-value food.

BOSTON TF3243 Once the country's second-largest seaport, this little town has some pretty spots and handsome historic buildings. Most famous is the **Boston Stump**, the graceful tower of the magnificent 14th-c church St Botolph's. Climb to the top for far views over this flat landscape – it's the second-tallest parish church in the country; the inside is spectacular too. Another prominent feature of the skyline is the **Maud Foster Mill**, the tallest working windmill in the country, and surely one of the most photogenic. The Kings Arms opposite has lovely views of it, and cheap food; Goodbarns Yard (Wormgate) is a popular central pub/restaurant. **Boston Guildhall Museum** (South St) In 1607 this was the prison of the Pilgrim Fathers after their unsuccessful attempt to flee to Holland (they did, of course, eventually escape further afield, taking this town's name with them). Displays cover this and the rest of the town's history. Shop, disabled access to ground floor only; cl Sun (exc pm Apr–Sept), Christmas and New Year; (01205) 365954; £1.25. The surroundings (and the Lincs coast generally) are too flat for driving to be very interesting around here, and side roads which look clear on a map can turn out to be tryingly slow in practice, with agricultural vehicles trundling along slowly and muddily; the B1183 and B1192 aren't bad.

BOURNE WOOD TF0721 (on the A151 just outside Bourne) Sheltered woodland good for a gentle stroll, with plenty of bird life, and busy at weekends with locals exercising their dogs; parking charge. In the town's market place, there's decent food in the Angel Hotel, opposite an interesting antique shop.

BRANDY WHARF TF0197 **Cider Centre** (on the B1205 SE of

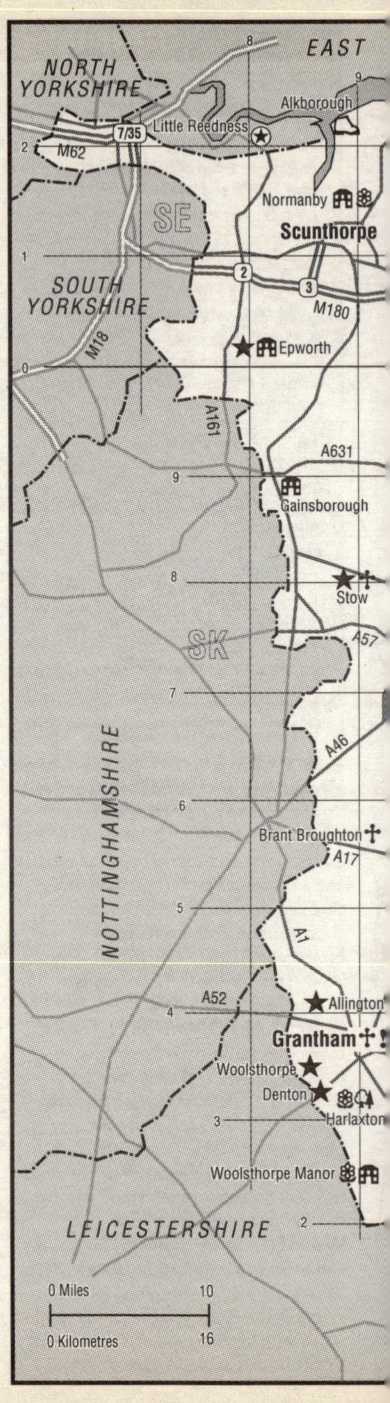

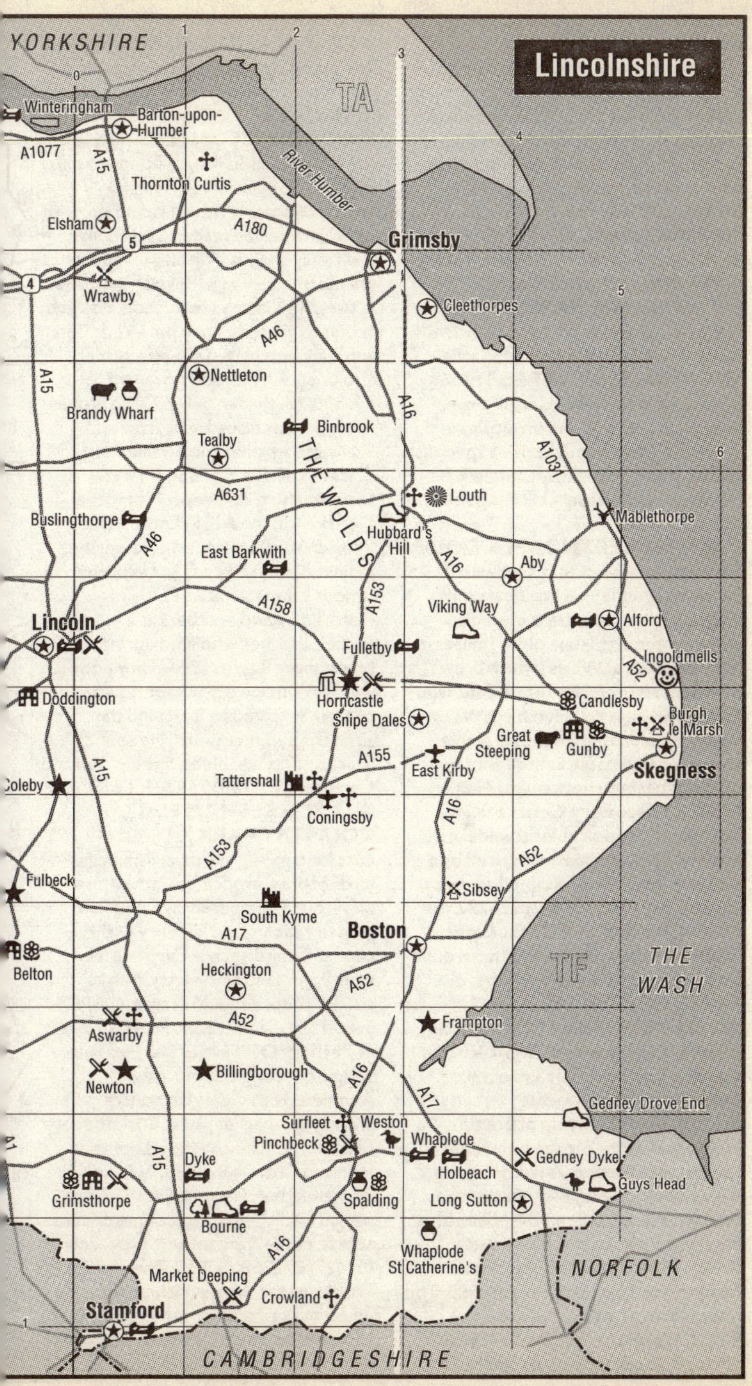
Lincolnshire
YORKSHIRE
TA
TF
Winteringham
Barton-upon-Humber
A1077
A15
Thornton Curtis
River Humber
Elsham
A180
Grimsby
Wrawby
Cleethorpes
A46
Nettleton
A15
Brandy Wharf
A16
Binbrook
Tealby
THE WOLDS
A1031
A631
Louth
Mablethorpe
Buslingthorpe
Hubbard's Hill
A46
East Barkwith
A16
Aby
A153
A158
Viking Way
Lincoln
Alford
Fulletby
Ingoldmells
A52
Doddington
Horncastle
Candlesby
Snipe Dales
Burgh le Marsh
Great Steeping
Gunby
A15
A155
East Kirby
Skegness
Coleby
Tattershall
Coningsby
A16
A153
A52
Fulbeck
Sibsey
South Kyme
A17
Boston
Belton
Heckington
THE WASH
A52
Frampton
A52
Aswarby
Newton
Billingborough
A16
A17
Gedney Drove End
Surfleet
Weston
Pinchbeck
Whaplode
Gedney Dyke
A15
Dyke
Holbeach
Guys Head
Grimsthorpe
Spalding
Long Sutton
Bourne
A16
Whaplode St Catherine's
NORFOLK
Market Deeping
Crowland
Stamford
CAMBRIDGESHIRE

Scunthorpe) Pleasingly zany 18th-c riverside cider house with up to 60 different varieties; also orchard and small museum. The enthusiastic owner really knows his stuff. Meals and snacks (not Mon), shop, disabled access; open licensing hours, though cl winter Mon lunchtimes; no chidren under 14; (01652) 678364; free.

BRANT BROUGHTON SK9154 The elegant and very tall **church spire** is, a landmark for miles around.

BURGH LE MARSH TF4965 Has a notable **church**, and a **windmill** nearby has unusual left-handed sails.

CANDLESBY HERBS TF4567 (Cross Keys Cottage) Good range of herb plants for sale and on display in the garden; cl Mon; free. There's a specialist cactus grower at nearby Candlesby House, and the Royal Oak has good home cooking.

CLEETHORPES TA3108 Big traditional seaside resort with extensive, gently shelving tidal sands, and a surprisingly ancient **church** among some attractive older houses in its original core. Willys (which brews its own beer) is useful for lunch. **Fuchsia Fantasy** (Kings Rd) Hundreds of varieties of fuchsia, and other plants according to season; limited winter opening, best to check on (01472) 883075. **Discovery Centre** (Kings Rd) Hands-on look at local wildlife; its unusual spiral shape was inspired by a seashell. Teas, shop, disabled access; cl 25–26 Dec, 1 Jan; (01472) 323232; £1.80. **Cleethorpes Coast Light Railway** (Kings Rd) Gentle trip around local scenery; not winter wkdys; (01472) 604657; *£1.80.

CONINGSBY TF2257 **Battle of Britain Memorial Flight Visitor Centre** (on the A153) Subject to operational commitments you can see the aircraft of the Battle of Britain Memorial Flight – inc the only flying Lancaster in Europe. A visitor centre has exhibitions. Summer snacks, shop, disabled access; cl Sun, some Sats, bank hols, and 2 wks over Christmas; (01526) 344041 – check first if you hope to see a particular aircraft; £3. The **church** has what's said to be the biggest dial of any clock with a single hand. Just out of town, the interesting old Leagate Inn is useful for lunch.

CROWLAND CHURCH TF2410 The imposing remains of a once-great abbey, part of which is still used as the parish church.

DODDINGTON HALL SK9070 (on the B1190) Striking lived-in Elizabethan mansion, unchanged externally since it was built, and still with its original walled gardens, gatehouse and family church. The elegant rooms are mostly Georgian. Regular concerts in the Long Gallery. Teas, shop, disabled access to gardens; open pm Weds, Sun and bank hols May–Sept, plus garden also open Sun Mar and Apr; (01522) 694308; £4, garden only £2. The Stones Arms prettily placed in nearby Skellingthorpe has good-value food.

EAST KIRBY TF3563 **Lincolnshire Aviation Heritage Centre** (on the A155) Enthusiastic World War II collection on a wartime airfield. The highlight is *Just Jane,* the famous Lancaster NX611 lovingly restored by two brothers as a memorial to their brother who died during the Nuremberg Raid in 1944. They hope it will fly again one day but for now are content with taxiing it around the airfield in summer (a stirring sound). Snacks, shop, disabled access; cl Sun and Christmas; (01790) 763207; £3.50.

ELSHAM HALL COUNTRY PARK TA0311 Lots for families – farmyard animals, birds of prey, arboretum, adventure playground, puppet shows, craft and garden centres, and falconry with regular flying displays. Carp will feed from your hand at the jetty. Meals, snacks, shop, disabled access; cl mid-Sept–Mar; (01652) 688698; *£3.95.

★ **EPWORTH** SE7803 Pleasant village, the centre of the Isle of Axholme, with Georgian houses around the market place. **Old Rectory** (Rectory St) The childhood home of John and Charles Wesley, built in 1709 by their father. Restored in 1957, with period furnishings. Shop, some disabled access; cl 12–2pm, am Sun, Nov–Feb; (01427) 872268; *£2.50. They do B & B. Thanks to the Wesley connection, the whole village has become something of a Methodist centre; the Red Lion has decent food, especially vegetarian.

★ **FRAMPTON** TF3239 Perhaps the prettiest Fenland village.

GAINSBOROUGH SK8189 **Old Hall** (Parnell St) Restored medieval manor house with interesting great hall and original kitchen. Good Walkman tour. Snacks, shop, disabled access to ground floor only; cl Sun (exc pm Easter–Oct), 25–26 Dec, 1 Jan, Good Fri; (01427) 612669; £2.50. The Trent Port is useful for lunch, and the lane N along the Trent embankment gives views of the flood plain of this powerful brooding river; the Jenny Wren at Susworth is another good stop.

GEDNEY DROVE END TF4828 **Sea Walk** A good way of seeing the Wash is from the sea wall dyke, reached from a car park here; you can follow it to the mouth of the Nene.

† ! **GRANTHAM** SK9136 **Two rarities** The unusually tall church spire here is commemorated in an early 19th-c jingle: 'Grantham, now two rarities are thine, A lofty steeple and a living sign'. The living sign is the hive with living bees – descended from those of that time – still used as an inn sign by the good Beehive pub on Castlegate.

GREAT STEEPING TF4364 **Northcote Heavy Horse Centre** Magnificent horses showcased from 11am, with harnessing demonstrations, grooming and wagon rides. Snacks, shop, disabled access; open Sun and Tues–Thurs Apr–Sept, plus Mon and Fri July and Aug; (01754) 830286; £4. The Bell at Halton Holegate has good home cooking.

GRIMSBY TA2609 *See separate Family Panel on p.419 for* **National Fishing Heritage Centre**, which is doing so much to draw visitors to the town – formerly the world's largest fishing port, and now in its decline working hard to develop an appeal for visitors. At **Time Trap** in the prison cells of the Town Hall the town's social history also gets lively treatment. Interactive games and rather jolly displays cover the building of the docks and the struggle for women's suffrage – and you can see what it's like to be locked in a prison cell (open pm only, cl Sun; £2.50 adults, free on Fri). The *Lincoln Castle*, a paddle-steamer moored in Alexandra Dock, is now a good-value floating restaurant, and Leons (Alexandra Rd) does good fresh fish. The Abbeygate Centre has reasonably priced antique shops, also upstairs craft workshops inc lace-making; café. Alfred Enderby's smoked fish house (Fish Docks Rd) demonstrates traditional methods of smoking salmon, haddock and cod; cl Sun, most Sats and 2 wks at Christmas; (01472) 342984 to check.

GRIMSTHORPE CASTLE TF0422 A patchwork of styles from its medieval tower and Tudor quadrangle to the baroque north front by Vanbrugh; the state rooms and galleries have especially fine furnishings. Outside are formal gardens and parkland with a lake (you can take a tour with the ranger in his Land Rover), and red deer tame enough for children to feed. Meals, snacks, shop, some disabled access; open Sun, Thurs and bank hols Easter–Sept, plus Mon–Weds in Aug, house cl am; (01778) 591205; £6 all-in, £3 just castle or garden. The Five Bells at Edenham is a good dining pub (and handy for walkers).

GUNBY HALL TF4666 (the Gunby nr Spilsby; off the A158) Interesting neat red brick William III house, with fine oak staircase and clock collection; especially worth visiting for the 9 acres of splendid gardens, said to be Tennyson's 'haunt of ancient peace'. Open pm Weds (plus garden only pm Thurs) Apr–Sept; £3.50, £2.50 garden only. The Royal Oak at Candlesby is handy.

GUYS HEAD TF4925 **Peter Scott Walk** A 10-mile walk E from the mouth of the Nene, with its twin lighthouses either side. Scott used to come here to study and paint wildfowl. It leads along the dyke into Norfolk, with access from a car park on the Nene's E bank.

HARLAXTON MANOR GARDENS SK8832 (on the A607) Around 45 acres of classical gardens, built in the early 19th c to rival the finest in Europe, now being restored. Rose and herb gardens in 6-acre walled garden, and nature trails through surrounding woodland. The stunning mansion at the estate's heart takes on a gorgeous golden glow in the late afternoon sun. Snacks, shop; cl Mon (exc bank hols), and Nov–Mar; (01476) 592101; £3. The Red House over at Knipton is a good dining pub.

HECKINGTON TF1443
Understated but pleasant small town, its well restored **windmill** the only one in Britain with 8 sails; shop (selling their flour and locally made bread and ginger cake); open pm Sun mid-Sept–mid-July, plus Thurs–Sat and bank hols mid-Apr–mid-July, and daily mid-July–mid-Sept; (01529) 461919; *£1. Nearby the Pearoom is a decent **craft centre**, and the Nags Head is good for lunch. The **church** still has many of its orginal 14th-c fittings.

★ **HORNCASTLE** TF2569
Attractive market town popular for antiques, with 30 shops in the Bridge St Antiques Centre. You can still see parts of the town's **Roman wall**. Old Nicks (North St) has a decent carvery, and the Bull (Bull Ring) is also good value. Some 3 miles N the 'High Street' forking off the A158 is a good drive, following an Iron Age trackway up to Caistor. The A153 to Louth gives rolling Wolds views. Another pretty drive here includes Scrivelsby and its vast deer park, Belchford (Blue Bell useful for lunch), Fulletby (perhaps a stroll on the footpaths here), Somersby (Tennyson's birthplace – his bust is in the church), Old Bolingbroke (castle ruins), Spilsby (delicatessen in the quiet market place with its statue of Sir John Franklin), and, if you've made good time, Wainfleet and Boston.

HUBBARD'S HILL TF3186
A walk SW from Louth; not in fact a hill, but a river valley – surprisingly deep for the Wolds.

INGOLDMELLS TF5666 **Fantasy Island** (£10 free ride vouchers when you purchase £10 worth of ride vouchers) (Sea Lane) Just opposite the beach, this is more elaborate than your average fairground and ideal in any weather – 95% of the rides and other features are inside, with thatched buildings and palm trees nestling under a giant pyramid. Europe's longest rollercoaster – the length of the Humber Bridge – is due to open here in April; other highlights include a new volcano theme ride, the IMAX simulator's 3 rollercoaster type experiences (the screen is all around you, and your seat slides towards it as well as shaking about all over the place), the balloon flight, with authentically created computer-controlled balloons soaring around the pyramid, a sail-through aquarium, and two water rides – one quite long, the other rather wet. Meals, snacks, shop, disabled access; open wknds Mar–Apr, daily in Easter hols and May–Oct; (01754) 872030; free admission, then rides separately charged.

★ **LITTLE REEDNESS**
SE8022 Attractive village with 14th-c **church**, Ouse walks; RSPB **nature reserve** just E at Blacktoft Sands marshes.

LONG SUTTON TF4324
Butterfly and Falconry Park One of Britain's biggest walk-through tropical houses, with hundreds of butterflies flying free. Also creepy-crawly little insectarium, reptiles, snakes, wildflower meadows, and twice-daily falconry displays. A well organised place. Snacks, shop, disabled access; cl Nov–Mar; (01406) 363833; £4.20. The parish **church spire** is unusual for the hundreds of tons of lead sheathing it. The 17th-c Olde Ship has good home cooking.

LOUTH CHURCH TF3387
This very elegant 16th-c building has the tallest spire of any parish church in Britain. The tower can be climbed on summer afternoons; hundreds of steps for a fabulous view.

MABLETHORPE TF4987
Animal Gardens and Seal Trust (North End) Rescued seals unable to return to the wild find a permanent home here, along with monkeys, parrots, porcupines, llamas, emus, wild cats and many other animals. It's right by the beach. Snacks, shop, mostly disabled access; cl Nov–Easter; (01507) 473346; £3.50.

NETTLETON TA0900
Potterton & Martin's **nursery** (Moortown Rd) has unusual and interesting plants – mainly alpines and small bulbs; (01472) 851714. Just S towards Normanby le Wold, Caistor Top is the highest point on the Wolds, at 550 metres (1,805ft), with bracing walks. The Nickerson Arms over at Rothwell has decent food.

NORMANBY HALL COUNTRY PARK SE8816 (B1430) Pleasant spot with grazing deer, lots of wildfowl, nature trails, some interesting sculptures, a newly restored Victorian kitchen garden and a farm museum in its 350 busy acres. Period rooms in the Regency mansion. Meals, snacks, shop, disabled access to ground floor only; house and museum cl am and all Oct–Mar, park open all year; (01724) 720588; £2.50 (North Lincs residents half price). The Sheffield Arms at Burton upon Stather has decent food.

PINCHBECK TF2425 **Tropical Forest** (Rose Cottage Water Garden Centre, just N of Spalding) One of the biggest displays of tropical and subtropical plants in the country. Snacks (summer only and not Mon), shop, water garden centre, disabled access; cl 25–26 Dec; (01775) 710882; £2.45.

SIBSEY TF3551 (on the A16 N of Boston) The village has a couple of **windmills**, one of them a splendidly restored 6-sailed model with fine views from the top.

SKEGNESS TF5663 Built as a late 19th-c resort, this has been an archetypal one, with the first Butlin's Holiday Camp just up the coast; the beach has clean bathing water. **Natureland Seal Sanctuary** (North Parade) Rewarding place renowned for its seal-rescuing activities. It's fascinating to watch the seals performing tricks – they aren't trained in any way, they just like showing off. Also other animals inc crocodiles, snakes and a tarantula, aquarium, and free-flying tropical butterflies (May–Oct). Snacks, shop, disabled access; cl 25–26 Dec, 1 Jan; (01754) 764345; £3.70. **Church Farm Museum** (Church Rd Sth, Skegness) Good recreation of daily farm life at the end of the 19th c, with craft demonstrations, and quite a few Lincoln longwool sheep. Snacks, shop, disabled access; cl Nov–Apr; (01754) 766658; £1. The comfortable old Vine Hotel on the southern edge of the town was here long before the resort, welcoming Tennyson among others; it's pleasant for lunch.

SNIPE DALES TF3368 Country park and nature reserve, managed by the county council, covering 210 acres rich in bird and plant life; the country park is a 90-acre area of pine woods, while the adjacent nature reserve has a trail leading through 2 valleys and to a viewpoint over the Wolds.

SOUTH KYME TF1650 A fine 14th-c battlemented tower stands alone in a meadow quite nr the road.

SPALDING TF2624 **Ayscoughfee Hall Museum and Gardens** (Church Gate, Spalding) Spooky-looking medieval manor house, with social history museum, and 5 acres of gardens and ancient yew hedges. Meals, summer snacks, shop, disabled access to ground floor only; museum cl winter wknds, gardens open all year; (01775) 725468; free. All around this area, the flat fields by the roadside are a mass of spring colour, first daffodils and then a multicoloured sea of tulips – very Dutch. The riverside Lincolnshire Poacher is useful for lunch.

STAMFORD TF0307 John Betjeman considered this England's most attractive town. Within the medieval walls are no fewer than 500 listed buildings, inc a good number of attractive medieval **churches** – particularly All Saints in the centre, St George's with excellent 15th-c stained glass, and St Mary's nearby. The George, one of the town's grandest buildings with some parts going back to Saxon times, is excellent for lunch. **Stamford Museum** (Broad St) Includes life-size figures dressed in the clothes of Tom Thumb (only 1 metre – 3ft 4in – tall) and Daniel Lambert, a portly fellow who weighed 218 kg (50 stone) when he died on a racing outing here. Shop, disabled access to ground floor only; cl Sun (exc pm in summer), 25–26 Dec; (01780) 66317; free. **Burghley House** A 20-minute walk from Stamford's centre leads to this splendid mansion, built by William Cecil and still the home of his family. The exterior is Tudor at its most solidly showy, but the state rooms inside are largely baroque, with wonderful frescoes by Antonio Verrio – the Heaven Room is astonishing. The peaceful grounds, where the Burghley Horse Trials are held, were landscaped by Capability Brown. Meals, snacks,

shop, limited disabled access; cl early Oct–Mar (though gardens may open some dates in Apr for spring flowers display); (01780) 52451; £5.85.
Tolethorpe Hall (off the A6121 N) has Europe's biggest **open-air theatre** in its grounds, with a covered auditorium and a good Shakespeare season; (01780) 54381.
✝★ **STOW** SK8881 The **church** is notable for its fantastic Saxon arches; the Cross Keys in the attractive village has good unusual food.
✝ **SURFLEET** TF2528 The tower and spire of the church lean alarmingly.
✝ **TATTERSHALL CASTLE** TF2056 The 15th-c **castle** has a magnificent 30-metre (100ft) turreted keep, with fine heraldic chimneypieces on each of the 4 storeys; there's a double moat with peacocks and waterfowl. Snacks, shop (with food for the birds), some disabled access; open Sat–Weds Apr–Oct, pm wknds Nov and Dec; (01526) 342543; £2.70; NT. The airy 15th-c **church** is also attractive, and just off the A153 towards Sleaford, on the left before you reach Tattershall Bridge, is a preserved steam engine which worked at keeping this area of the fens drained for nearly a century. The Abbey Lodge Hotel (on the B1192 towards Woodhall) has good food, and the woods nr Woodhall are good for picnics.
✝ **TEALBY** TF1590 The best example of that Lincolnshire speciality – colourful **village cottage gardens**, easily seen from the road. Here, a great variety of neat and charmingly planted gardens front the stonebuilt cottages, some thatched, on the main street, running down from the 12th-c **church** to a watersplash near a watermill, and there is more colour in the quaintly named side lanes. The 14th-c Kings Head has good food.
✝ **THORNTON CURTIS** TA1118 **Thornton Abbey** (on the East Halton road) The ruins of this 12th-c Augustinian abbey, very atmospheric with its worn spiral stone stairs and dark corridors, are well worth a visit. Also small exhibition in magnificent 14th-c gatehouse. Disabled access (not into gatehouse); grounds open daily, gatehouse open only pm 3rd Sun in month, plus pm 1st Sun Apr–Sept; free.
VIKING WAY TF3072 Long-distance path helping village-to-village walks, with 'Tennyson country' a popular focus (Tennyson was born at the rectory in Somersby TF3472, when his father was rector at adjoining Bag Enderby); the Black Horse at Donington on Bain TF2382 and the 2 Tealby pubs are handy stops.
WESTON TF2924 **Baytree Owl Centre** (A151) Expanding collection of owls and other birds, with displays in a big arena (12 noon and 3pm), and maybe red squirrels; some birds can be handled. This year there is a new creepy-crawly house. Good meals and snacks, shop, disabled access; cl 25–26 Dec, 1 Jan; (01406) 371907; *£2.50. It's part of a busy little complex, with ducks and rabbits in a landscaped glasshouse, good garden centre, and play area; also donkeys and a mule in a paddock by the car park – regular visitors tell us the latter can't resist carrots.
WHAPLODE ST CATHERINE'S TF3219 **Museum of Entertainment** (Millgate, off the B1165) Unusual and quirky collection tracing the development

Days Out

The best of Lincoln: Lincoln Cathedral; Castle; explore Steep Hill area – lunch at the Wig & Mitre or Browns Pie Shop there; Usher Gallery; Museum of Lincolnshire Life; Incredibly Fantastic Old Toy Show.

Those in peril: Fishing heritage centre, Grimsby; fish lunch at Leons there, or eat on board the *Lincoln Castle*; trawler visit, and Time Trap.

Showpiece stonebuilt town: Stamford; lunch at the George there; Burghley House, or Grimsthorpe Castle.

of entertainment from barrel and church organs to puppets and phonographs, taking in a history of the fairground along the way. Many exhibits are working (there are organ concerts throughout the summer), and the owners clearly love their subject. Snacks, shop, disabled access; open pm Sun–Thurs July–Sept, plus Easter wknd and pm Sun Easter–Jun; (01406) 540379; *£2.50.

WOOLSTHORPE MANOR SK9224 (the Woolsthorpe nr Colsterworth) The birthplace of Isaac Newton, where he later conducted some of his more important experiments. Geometry workings said to be in his handwriting are scratched into the plasterwork – and of course the garden has a venerable apple tree. Open pm Weds–Sun Apr–Oct; (01476) 860338; £2.50; NT.

WRAWBY TA0209 The village has a working **windmill**, open bank hols and some Suns Jun and July – ring Mrs Day to check, (01652) 653699; £1.

★ † **Other attractive villages**, all with decent pubs, include Allington SK8540 (despite the nearby A1), Billingborough TF1134, Coleby SK9760, Denton SK8632, Fulbeck SK9450, Newton TF0436 and Woolsthorpe SK8435 (the one nearest to Grantham). Readers recommend the woods at Stapleford SK8857 for picnics (especially when the rhododendrons are in bloom). Castle Bytham SK9819 has decent views and a duckpond, with nature trails in nearby woods. Langton by Partney TF3970 has an attractive church.

Where to eat

ASWARBY TF0639 **Tally Ho** *(01529) 455205* Handsome 17th-c stone inn with beams and open fire in country-style bar, a gently civilised atmosphere, papers to read, good enjoyable food inc fine puddings, well kept real ales, good house wines, and an attractive pine-panelled restaurant (best to book); bdrms. **£17**|£6.50.

GEDNEY DYKE TF4126 **Chequers** *(01406) 362666* Warmly welcoming and spotlessly kept small pub with lots of fresh fish and seafood and a wide choice of other good interesting cooking, an open fire, elegant dining conservatory, well kept beer, decent wines, and polite, helpful service. **£22**|£8.95.

GRIMSTHORPE TF0423 **Black Horse** *(01778) 591247* Large open fire and rustic atmosphere in a narrow bar, a cosy Buttery Bar with another open fire, and intimate candlelit dining room – all with excellent food and decent wine; friendly staff; children over 14. **£28**|£5.50.

HORNCASTLE TF2669 **Magpies** *73–75 East St (01507) 527004* Popular well run restaurant with a relaxed atmosphere and very good French cooking using top quality fresh local ingredients; cl Sun Mon, am Sat, 2 wks Aug. **£30**|£6.

LINCOLN SK9771 **Browns Pie Shop** *33 Steep Hill (01522) 527330* Spectacular, really interesting pies (and lots of other food), helpful staff, comfortable seats and pleasant traditional atmosphere; cl 25 Dec and 1 Jan. **£19**|£4.50.

LINCOLN SK9771 **Jews House** *15 The Strait (01522) 524851* Small, intimate and elegantly furnished evening restaurant in one of the oldest buildings in the city, with very good imaginative food, well schooled friendly service, and upstairs coffee lounge for those who want to smoke after the meal; cl lunchtimes, Sun, Mon. **£30**.

LINCOLN SK9771 **Wig & Mitre** *30 Steep Hill (01522) 535190* Attractively restored 14th-c building with imaginative food served all day (breakfast too), excellent puddings, an elaborate restaurant menu, interesting wine list, and consistently efficient prompt service; disabled access. **£19.25**|£5.50.

MARKET DEEPING TF1309 **Caudle House** *High St (01778) 347595* Georgian house with 2 small dining rooms and a little bar area, and friendly helpful staff (the waitresses wear Victorian dress); a good choice of carefully cooked food, and a thoughtful wine list; bdrms; open Thurs–Sat pm, am Sun – but will cater for residents at any time; children over 8. **£26**.

NEWTON TF0436 **Red Lion** *(01529) 497256* Full of charm and character, this civilised pub specialises in an imaginative cold buffet (which comes in small, medium or large helpings) plus other hot dishes, 4 roasts on Sat evening and Sun lunchtime, well kept real ales, friendly service, and a neat well sheltered garden with a good play area; cl 25 Dec; disabled access. **£20**|£7.50.

PINCHBECK TF2225 **Ship** *Northgate (01775) 723792* Friendly pub with a comfortable small lounge and dining area, helpful service, good-value bar food, smarter restaurant, and real ales; cl pm 25–26 Dec; disabled access. **£20.45**|£5.

Special thanks to Mrs B Burgess, M and J Back.

We welcome reports from readers

This *Guide* depends on readers' reports. Do help us if you can – in return, we offer a discount on the next edition to people who've helped us with reports for it. Tell us what you think about places already in it, and anything extra you think we should say about them. And send us your ideas for inclusion in the next edition: places to visit, eat at or stay in, attractive drives or walks, maybe even unusual interesting shops you know of. Use the card in the middle, the report forms at the end, or just write – no stamp needed: *The Good Guide to Britain*, FREEPOST TN1569, Wadhurst, E Sussex TN5 7BR.

Lincolnshire Calendar

Some of these dates were provisional as we went to press. Please check information with the telephone numbers provided.

JANUARY

6 **Haxey** Haxey Hood Game: created in the 13th-c by Lady de Mowbray whose hood was blown away and retrieved by labourers, the game resembles rugby played with leather hoods. Procession of players, colourfully dressed Boggans, king and fool (01302) 735385

23 **Spalding** Motorbike '99: arena events at Springfields – *till Sun 24* (01775) 713253

24 **Lincoln** Great Australian Breakfast: celebration of Australia Day inc fancy dress, music (01522) 881188

FEBRUARY

4 **Spalding** Flower Show at Springfields – *till Sun 7* (01775) 713253

14 **Spalding** Toy and Train Collectors Fair at Springfields (01775) 713253

21 **Spalding** Antiques Fair at Springfields (01775) 713253

27 **Grimsby and Cleethorpes** Lincolnshire Literature Festival – *till 6 Mar* (01472) 323004

MARCH

28 **Gainsborough** Craft Fair at Gainsborough Old Hall (01427) 612669

APRIL

2 **Cleethorpes** Dance Festival – *till Sun 11* (01472) 323004

3 **Alford** Easter Gala Weekend: vintage cars, military vehicles, town criers, carnival – *till Mon 5* (01507) 462541

4 **Lincoln** Victorian Prison Open at the Castle: re-enactments – *till Mon 5* (01522) 881188; **Spalding** Easter Gifts and Open Gardens at Springfields – *till Mon 5* (01775) 713253

10 **Tetford** Flower Festival – *till Sun 11*

11 **Spalding** Toy Tractor Fair at Springfields (01775) 713253

17 **Belton** Horse Trials at Belton House – *till Sun 18* (01476) 566116

30 **Lincoln** Folk Festival – *till 3 May* (01522) 569434

MAY

1 **Alford** Morris Men Dance at Dawn at the Windmill (01507) 462136; **Spalding** Flower Festival and Country Fair: famous flower-float parade through the town, and entertainment at Springfields – *till Mon 3* (01775) 713253

2 **Gainsborough** Living History Weekend at Gainsborough Old Hall – *till Mon 3* (01427) 612669

3 **Spilsby** May Carnival (01790) 753273

16 **Belton** Family Fun Day at Belton House (01476) 566116

19 **Tallington** Beer Festival at Barholm Road Showfield – *till Sat 22* (01780) 763063

Lincolnshire Calendar (cont.)

22 **Tallington** Steam and Country Festival – *till Sun 23* (01780) 763063
28 **Alford** Craft Market at Manor House Gardens – *till Mon 31* (01507) 270241; **Cleethorpes** Folk Festival – *till Mon 31* (01472) 323004
29 **Ealand** Crowle Agricultural Show (01724) 710463; **Normanby** Horse Trials at Normanby Hall – *till Sun 30* (01724) 720588
30 **Carrington** Steam and Vintage Rally – *till Mon 31* (01205) 270241
31 **Woodhall Spa** Agricultural Show (01526) 352896

JUNE

5 **Cleethorpes** Festival of Transport – *till Sun 6* (01472) 323004
6 **Messingham** Show (01724) 763004
12 **Old Bolingbroke** Classics at Old Bolingbroke Castle (01507) 609289
19 **Grantham** Carnival – *till Sun 20* (01476) 574484
20 **Appleby** Country Fair: jousting, falconry (01724) 733602
23 **Grange-de-Lings** Lincolnshire Show at the Lincolnshire Showground – *till Thurs 24* (01522) 524240
26 **Stamford** Music from the Movies with Fireworks at Burghley House (01625) 575681; **Waddington** RAF Waddington Air Show: foreign aircraft and display teams, Red Arrows, service displays, crafts, funfair – *till Sun 27* (01522) 726100

JULY

2 **Grimsby** International Jazz Festival – *till Sun 4* (01472) 323004
3 **Burgh le Marsh** Carnival (01754) 810474
10 **Lincoln** Water Carnival at Brayford Pool – *till Sun 11* (01522) 881188
11 **Spilsby** Show (01790) 752566
17 **Barton** Carnival – *till Sun 18* (01652) 635330; **Skegness** Illuminations Switch On (01754) 764821
18 **Louth** Grand Carnival Parade, crafts, art exhibition and music (01507) 606574; **Mablethorpe** District Show (01507) 472496; **Spalding** Vintage Vehicle and Classic Car Show at Springfields (01775) 713253
21 **Sutton-on-Sea** Carnival and Parade – *till Sun 25* (01507) 472496
23 **Old Bolingbroke** Exhibition and Sale of Paintings by Lincolnshire Artists – *till Sun 25* (01507) 526636; **Spalding** Country Music Festival at Springfields – *till Sun 25* (01775) 713253
24 **Belton** Fireworks Concert at Belton House (01476) 566116; **Cleethorpes** Carnival Week *till 1 Aug* with Parade on *Fri 30* (01472) 323004; **North Somercotes** Carnival and Horticultural Show – *till Sun 25* (01507) 358474
25 **Mablethorpe** Illuminations Switch On, also District Show (01507) 472496
31 **Lincoln** Family Fun Weekend: arena, music events at the Lawn – *till 1 Aug* (01522) 881188; **Stamford** Fireworks Concert with Dancing Waters at Burghley House (01625) 575681; **Sutton-on-Sea** Horticultural Society Annual Show (01507) 441284

AUGUST

1 **Revesby** Country Fair (01205) 365213
2 **Partney** Sheep Fair (01754) 810477

Lincolnshire Calendar (cont.)

6 **Lincoln** Outdoor Concerts – *till Sun 8* (01522) 881188
8 **Mablethorpe** Carnival Week – *till Sun 15* (01507) 472496; **Skegness** Carnival Week – *till procession on Sat 14* (01754) 764821
21 **Cleethorpes** Kits Festival – *till Sun 22* (01472) 323004; **Grange-de-Lings** Steam and Vintage Rally at the Lincolnshire Showground – *till Sun 22* (01507) 605937; **Lincoln** Steam Spectacular at the Lincolnshire Showground – *till Sun 22* (01522) 524240
22 **Lincoln** Concert at Lincoln Castle (01625) 575681
28 **Barkston Heath** National Model Flying Championships at RAF Barkston Heath – *till Mon 30* (0116) 244 0028; **Boston** Show at Central Park – *till Sun 29* (01205) 368966
29 **Lincoln** Victorian Prison Open at the Castle: re-enactments – *till Mon 30* (01522) 881188
30 **Epworth** Agricultural Show (01427) 872571; **Spilsby** Medieval Day (01790) 753273

SEPTEMBER

2 **Stamford** European Championships Horse Trials at Burghley House – *till Sun 5* (01780) 752131
4 **Coningsby** and District Show – *till Sun 5* (01526) 342333
19 **Epworth** Festival of the Plough: horse ploughing competitions, steam roundabouts, vintage cars, sheepdog trials (01427) 872659
24 **Woodhall Spa** Festival – *till Sun 26* (01526) 353775

OCTOBER

9 **Corby Glen** Sheep Fair – *till Mon 11* (01476) 550502
15 **Spalding** Country Music Festival at Springfields – *till Sun 17* (01775) 713253

NOVEMBER

5 **Cleethorpes** Fireworks (01472) 323111
6 **Lincoln** Fireworks at City Football Ground (01522) 881188; **Spalding** Model Railway Exhibition at Springfields – *till Sun 7* (01775) 713253
20 **Spalding** Crafts and Entertainments at Springfields – *till Sun 21* (01775) 713253
27 **Gainsborough** Craft Fair at Gainsborough Old Hall – *till Sun 28* (01427) 612669

DECEMBER

9 **Lincoln** Christmas Market – *till Sun 12* (01522) 881188

NORFOLK

Interesting outings, timeless unspoilt north coast, Broads boating, civilised cathedral city, good range of beach resorts.

North Norfolk has a great deal of unspoilt charm, untouristy and traditional-feeling, with a real sense of place from its Dutch-gabled buildings, flint walls, broad sweeps of sea, saltings and sky, and the odd windmill. A path runs the length of the coast, with often hundreds of birds in sight at a time, big enough and distinctive enough to excite even non-ornithologists. There's a real get-away-from-it-all feel, and inland too, this part has the same sort of appeal (though the weather is often kinder on the coast). Hunstanton and Cromer are civilised seaside resorts with a good deal of individuality, and there are many attractive smaller places.

Further down, the coast is dotted with beach resorts, some large and lively (most obviously, Great Yarmouth), some relaxed and more individual.

Away from the north, the countryside is not in itself a big draw – much is flat and repetitive. It's excellent for cycling, though, with quiet lanes, attractive villages and country churches, and fair views (and lots of roadside snowdrops in spring). Driving along the twisty coastal A149 is pleasant out of season – though not much fun in summer. The best parts – the winding rivers and reed-fringed meres of the Broads – are best seen from a boat, but we've also picked out some good bits for landlubbers.

Many of the most enjoyable places to visit appeal to children as well as adults. Boat trips from Blakeney to see the seals sum up the timeless simplicity of North Norfolk's appeal. Other enjoyable family days out include The Village at Burgh St Margaret, the tropical centre in Great Yarmouth, and Bressingham's steam museum and gardens. Other places for steam enthusiasts are Aylsham, Sheringham, Wells-next-the-Sea, Forncett St Mary and (our own favourite) Thursford Green. Some really unusual outings include the watergardens at South Walsham, the dinosaur park at Weston Longville, the ancient sites at Cockley Cley and Grimes Graves, and the elderly fighting vehicles at Weybourne. Among the many wildlife, zoo and farm parks here, those at Great Witchingham, Filby, Banham, Snettisham and Welney stand out. And of course there are the great Norfolk mansions: Blickling Hall, Holkham Hall, Houghton Hall, Felbrigg Hall, and Sandringham, less grand than other royal residences – people like its more personal feel.

Norwich is a distinguished yet lively cathedral city, not overly touristy, yet with plenty to see.

Please let us know what you think of places in the *Guide*. Use the report forms at the back of the book or simply write us a letter.

Where to stay

BANNINGHAM TG2129 **Wheelers Meadow** *Colby Rd, Banningham, Norwich NR11 7DY (01263) 733325* ***£45;** 3 rms, 1 with own bthrm. Attractive country house in pretty gardens, with residents' sitting room, open fires, tasty evening meals, good breakfasts with their own eggs and home-made preserves, real ales (brewed on the premises), and friendly owners; plenty to do nearby.

BLAKENEY TG0243 **Blakeney Hotel** *Blakeney, Holt NR25 7NE (01263) 740797* **£158,** plus special breaks; 59 very comfortable rms, many with views over the salt marshes and some with their own little terrace. Overlooking the harbour with fine views, this friendly hotel has appealing public rooms, good food, and very pleasant staff; indoor swimming pool, saunas, spa bath, billiards room, and garden; good disabled access.

BLICKLING TG1728 **Buckinghamshire Arms** *Blickling, Norwich NR11 6NF (01263) 732133* **£50,** plus special breaks; 3 rms with four-posters, one with own shower. Handsome Jacobean inn in the grounds of Blickling Hall; with a civilised atmosphere, helpful staff, interesting food in both the bar and restaurant (best to book), nice breakfasts, well kept ales and good wines.

BURNHAM MARKET TF8342 **Hoste Arms** *The Green, Burnham Market, King's Lynn PE31 8HD (01328) 738777* **£76,** plus special breaks; 20 comfortable rms. Handsome inn on the green of a lovely Georgian village; with a smartly civilised atmosphere, attractive bars, some interesting period features, stylish food in the conservatory and restaurant, inc morning coffee and afternoon tea, well kept real ales and good wines; professional and friendly staff.

DOWNHAM MARKET TF6103 **Crown** *Bridge St, Downham Market PE38 9DH (01366) 382322* **£44.50,** plus special breaks; 10 rms. 17th-c coaching inn with an interesting history, low beams, flagstones and a roaring log fire, restaurant in the former stables, and a welcoming, cheerful landlord.

GREAT BIRCHAM TF7632 **Kings Head** *Great Bircham, Kings Lynn PE31 6RJ (01485) 578265* **£59;** 5 rms. Old-fashioned and rather grand-looking Victorian country inn with an unassuming lounge, a quiet pleasant atmosphere and a good log fire; cheerful Italian landlord, reliable and generous bar food (quite a few Italian specialities and tempting puddings), a no smoking dining area, decent wines and well kept beers; also a big side lawn with seats and playthings.

GRIMSTON TF7022 **Congham Hall** *Grimston, King's Lynn PE32 1AH (01485) 600250* **£140,** plus special breaks; 14 individually decorated rms. Warmly welcoming and handsome Georgian manor in 40 acres, inc herb, vegetable and flower gardens (herbs for sale and garden open to the public), outdoor swimming pool, tennis court, paddock, orchards, and a cricket pitch – also, walks leaflets available; lovely drawing room, a pretty orangery formal restaurant with excellent modern cooking (lighter lunches in the bar), and exemplary service; children over 12.

KING'S LYNN TF6120 **Tudor Rose** *St Nicholas St, King's Lynn PE30 1LR (01553) 762824* **£50,** plus special breaks; 14 refurbished rms. Attractive, half-timbered 15th-c inn with an interesting medieval door; friendly and chatty atmosphere, decent food in the bar and a no smoking raftered restaurant, and good breakfasts; disabled access.

MORSTON TG0043 **Morston Hall** *Morston, Holt NR25 7AA (01263) 741041* ***£120,** plus special breaks; 6 comfortable rms with country views. Attractive 17th-c flint-walled house in a tidal village; lovely quiet gardens, beams and open fires in the 2 small lounges, hard-working and friendly owners, very good modern English cooking, a thoughtful small wine list, and super breakfasts; croquet; cl Jan.

MUNDFORD TL8093 **Crown** *Crown St, Mundford, Thetford IP26 5HQ (01842) 878233* ***£49.50;** 16 good rms. Friendly small village pub, originally a hunting inn and rebuilt in the 18th c, with an attractive choice of good-value, straightforward food, very welcoming staff, happy atmosphere, and well kept real ales; disabled access.

NORWICH TG2208 **Beeches** *4–6 Earlham Rd, Norwich NR2 3DB (01603) 621167* ***£76,** plus special breaks; 25 quiet rms. 2 listed Victorian mansions and an extension only 10 minutes' stroll from the city centre but standing in 4 acres of

English Heritage Victorian gardens; with a relaxed and informal atmosphere, friendly resident owners, enjoyable food in bistro-style restaurant, and good breakfasts; cl Christmas; no children; disabled access.

PULHAM MARKET TM1986 **Old Bakery** *Church Walk, Pulham Market, Diss IP21 4SJ (01379) 676492* **£46;** 3 rms. 16th-c, no smoking house with lots of beams and timbers, inglenook with a fine log fire in the lounge, good breakfasts, enjoyable evening meal, and a friendly atmosphere; cl Christmas/New Year.

SOUTH LOPHAM TM0381 **Malting Farm** *Blo'Norton Rd, South Lopham, Diss IP22 2HT (01379) 687201* ***£44,** plus special breaks; 3 well furnished rms, 1 with own bthrm. Welcoming, no smoking, Elizabethan farmhouse on a working dairy farm, with woodburners in the inglenook fireplaces in both the sitting and dining rooms, big breakfasts with home-baked bread and preserves around a large table, and small play area with toys; the owner's passion is embroidery, patchwork, spinning and quilting; cl Christmas/New Year.

SPROWSTON TG2512 **Sprowston Manor** *Wroxham Rd, Sprowston, Norwich NR7 8RP (01603) 410871* **£110,** plus special breaks; 94 individually decorated, spacious rms. Extended 16th-c manor house in 10 acres of parkland surrounded by Sprowston Park golf course; comfortable day rooms, fine food in the elegant orangery and attractive restaurant, leisure club with palms and stone balustrades, poolside bar, health spa; disabled access.

STOKE HOLY CROSS TG2302 **Salamanca Farm** *Stoke Holy Cross, Norwich NR14 8QJ (01508) 492322* ***£40;** 4 rms. Mainly Victorian farmhouse (parts are much older) just a short stroll from the River Tas; with guests' lounge, spacious dining room, big garden, and farm shop; cl 15 Dec–15 Jan.

SWAFFHAM TF8109 **Strattons** *Ash Close, Swaffham PE37 7NH (01760) 723845* ***£90,** plus special breaks; 7 interesting, pretty rms. Warmly welcoming, elegant Queen Anne house (no smoking throughout), with delicious English food using home-grown herbs and vegetables from a family smallholding, and a carefully chosen wine list illustrated with Mrs Scott's own watercolours; comfortable drawing rooms with open fires and lots of china cats, dried flowers, and books; big cupboard full of toys and games for children; cl 25–26 Dec, 2 wks in summer; dogs welcome.

THORNHAM TF7343 **Lifeboat** *Thornham, Hunstanton PE36 6LT (01485) 512236* ***£72,** plus special breaks; 12 pretty rms, most with sea views. Well placed by coastal flats, with a very cosy atmosphere – especially in winter, when there are 5 fires and antique paraffin lamps; good food in both the bar and elegant restaurant; partial disabled access.

THORPE MARKET TG2434 **Elderton Lodge** *Thorpe Market, North Walsham NR11 8TZ (01263) 833547* **£80,** plus special breaks; 12 rms. 18th-c shooting lodge and dower house for the adjacent Gunton Hall estate, lots of original features such as old gun cabinets and fine panelling, a comfortable lounge bar, conservatory, restaurant with good food using fresh fish and game from the estate, and 6 acres of mature grounds overlooking herds of deer on the 1,000 acres of Gunton Park; children over 6; disabled access.

TITCHWELL TF7543 **Titchwell Manor** *Titchwell, King's Lynn PE31 8BB (01485) 210221* ***£110,** plus special breaks; 16 rms. Comfortable hotel, handy for the nearby RSPB reserve; with an open fire, magazines and good naturalists' records of the wildlife, a cheerful bar, and a pretty no smoking restaurant with French windows on to the sheltered, neatly kept walled garden; very good food (especially fish), and particularly helpful licensees and staff; lots of pleasant walks and footpaths nearby; dogs welcome (bdrms only, £2.50); cl last 2 wks Jan; disabled access.

WARHAM TF9441 **Three Horseshoes** *Warham, Wells-next-the-Sea NR23 1NL (01328) 710547* **£48;** 4 rms, one with own bthrm. Basic but cheerful local with a marvellously unspoilt traditional atmosphere in its 3 friendly and gaslit rooms; simple furnishings, a log fire, very tasty, generous helpings of bar food, decent wines, home-made lemonade, and very well kept real ales; bdrms are in the Old Post Office adjoining the pub, with lots of beams and a residents' lounge dominated by an inglenook fireplace; cl 25–26 Dec; no children; partial disabled access.

WINTERTON-ON-SEA TG4919 **Fishermans Return** *The Lane, Winterton-on-Sea, Great Yarmouth NR29 4BN (01493) 393305* ***£50;** 3 characterful rms, shared bthrm. Traditional 300-year-old pub in a quiet village, close to the beach; with warmly welcoming owners, a relaxed lounge bar, open fire, good home-made food inc fresh fish (fine crabs), enjoyable breakfasts, and a sheltered garden.

To see and do

NORWICH TG2308 Busy but civilised, the old centre has quite a concentration of attractive streets and buildings, with all sorts of surprises in the narrow streets and lanes that still follow its medieval layout; Elm St is especially handsome, and there are plenty of antique shops and so forth. Even the more commercial/industrial centre N of the River Wensum has fine patches (such as Colegate), and the main shopping areas are closed to traffic. Fortunately the visually disappointing university is hidden away out on the W edge, though in term-time its students do bring a good bit of life into the centre. Norwich is the home of Colmans mustard, and the Mustard Shop (Bridewell Alley) has some varieties you may not have come across before. The ancient Adam & Eve (Bishopgate) is good for lunch, and the riverside Ribs of Beef (Wensum St) is also useful.

Norwich Castle (Castle Meadow) This impressive four-square Norman fortress dominates the city from its hill. Guided tours of the dungeons, battlements and 12th-c keep, and **museum** with displays of art (with particular emphasis on the Norwich School), silverware (for which the town was famous) and ceramics. Don't miss the natural history gallery if you like stuffed birds. Snacks, shop, disabled access; cl am Sun, Good Fri, 25–26 Dec, 1 Jan (but probably closing for refurbishment towards the end of the year so best to check); (01603) 223624; £3.20 July–Sept, otherwise £2.30. Linked to this museum via an underground passage is a former courtroom in the historic Shirehall, now a regimental museum.

Norwich Cathedral Basically medieval, the church has some fine features from later periods – the flying buttresses, for example, and the late 15th-c vaulted roof, spire and west window with Victorian glass. The Norman cloisters are the largest in the country, rebuilt after a serious riot between city and cathedral in 1272, and remarkable for the 400 bosses carved with scenes of medieval life (there are hundreds more in the cathedral itself, though less easy to see). Snacks and shop (not Sun), disabled access. Free guided tours leave the Information Desk at 11am wkdys and Sat, and 2.15pm wkdys only. The extensive precincts make an awe-inspiring impression: great medieval gateways firmly exclude the modern city from these closes, medieval alleys and secluded gardens, with all sorts of varied buildings from the cottages of Hooks Walk through the finer houses in the Upper Close to the buildings of Norwich School. The best view of the cathedral is from the river by Pulls Ferry; it's not easy to see from other parts of the town.

Bridewell Museum (Bridewell Alley) 14th-c building used as a prison from 1583 to 1828, now with exhibits on the town's trade and industries, and reconstructed turn-of-the-century shops. Cl Sun, Mon, and Oct–Mar; (01603) 667228; £1.30.

Dragon Hall (King St) Well preserved medieval merchant's hall, with a splendid timber-framed roof, intricate carvings, cellars, vaulted undercroft, and some finely painted roundels. Shop, limited disabled access; cl wknds exc summer Sats, 22 Dec–2 Jan, bank hols; (01603) 663922; *£1.50.

Medieval churches Literally dozens of them, in great variety, these are one of the city's joys. Perhaps the finest of all is St Peter Hungate (Princes St), an impressive 15th-c church with grand hammerbeam roof, museum of church art and brass-rubbing centre.

Inspire Hands On Science Centre Popular with readers, in medieval St Michael's church (Coslany St) – hence the witty name. Snacks, shop, disabled access; cl Mon, Christmas week; £3. The **Puppet Theatre** in St James Church (Whitefriars) is another useful diversion for children; (01603) 629921; from £5.

Boat trips From the River Wensum you can clearly see how some of the city's older buildings were designed for water-borne traffic, rather than road transport.

Sainsbury Centre for Visual Arts (University of East Anglia, off the B1108 W of centre) Striking Norman Foster building with notable 19th- and 20th-c European art, and a fascinating range of ethnographic art, inc African tribal sculpture, and Egyptian and Asian antiquities. Meals, snacks, shop, disabled access; cl Mon, 23 Dec–2 Jan; (01603) 592467; £2.

THE BROADS TG3017 Norfolk's network of linking waterways is undoubtedly best seen from a boat. Cruising on the Broads is generally a week-long affair, but could be worked into a short-stay holiday; the boats nowadays have every mod con and are easy for even a novice to handle, but it's a chilly pastime until summer's well established. Wroxham, with its neighbour Hoveton, is a main centre for boat hire, and like the other main centre Horning is probably better thought of as a base for longer spells afloat than short breaks or day trips (though there are paddle-boat cruises from Horning). If you want a boat for just the day, the quieter reaches of the more northern Broads would probably suit you better – say, from Barton Turf TG3522, Hickling TG4122, Stalham TG3724 or Wayford Bridge TG3424. Or for a quick taste you can combine a boat trip with the trains on the **Bure Valley Railway** at Aylsham.

The Broads are not easy to visit on foot or by car; few paths get close enough, and once away from the waterside and fenny woodlands you are immediately into the flat, humdrum agricultural landscapes found in much of the rest of the area. There is some scope for strolling along rivers, with pumping-mills, birdlife and the boating scene being the principal features.

Places to watch the boating activity from on land include Horning TG3417 (perhaps from the Swan or the Ferry, busy Chef & Brewer pubs; there's also some scope for walking along the canalised parts of the River Bure nearby), Hickling TG4122 (pleasant path along the N shore), Bramerton TG2905 (Wood's End pub), attractive Coltishall TG2719 (the Rising Sun pub is on a pretty bend of the River Bure; bike hire from nearby Just Pedalling), Dilham TG3325 (the Crown), Itteringham TG1430 (the quaint Walpole Arms), Stokesby TG4310 (the Ferry House), Surlingham TG3006 (another Ferry House – there's still a rowing-boat ferry here; nearby Coldham Hall is a pub with lovely riverside gardens), Sutton Staithe TG3823 (Sutton Staithe Hotel, a lovely quiet spot), Geldeston TM3891 (long track to the Lock, a remote candlelit pub by the River Waveney) and Ormesby St Michael TG4715 (the Eel's Foot pub here has attractive waterside lawns).

BERNEY ARMS WINDMILL TG4605 Across the water from Burgh Castle and amazingly remote, this and its nearby pub can be reached not by road but either by boat or train from Great Yarmouth, or as a worthwhile objective for a long walk with a real sense of adventure, across the marshes from Wickhampton or Halvergate, passing other former windpumps. The 7-storey mill dates from the 19th-c when it was used to drain water from the marshes; cl 1–2 pm, and Oct–Mar; (01493) 700605; *£1.50. There's also scope for walking by reedy Breydon Water, the estuarine channel of the River Yare between here and Great Yarmouth.

★ **NEATISHEAD** TG3520 This attractive village, with a decent pub, gives access to **Barton Broad** nature reserve.

RANWORTH BROAD TG3514 One of the few broads the

cruise boats can't get to. A **conservation centre** here has nature trails and displays of local and natural history; snacks, shop, disabled access; cl Nov–Mar; free. There may be guided tours of the local wildlife on summer Suns; best to book, on (01603) 270479. The village **church** has the best painted rood screen in the county.

RIVER THURNE TG4117 The towpath by its canalised parts gives one of the few opportunities for Broadland waterside walks.

SOUTH WALSHAM TG3713 **Fairhaven Garden Trust** Charming wooded watergardens set beside the private South Walsham Inner Broad, the waterways linked by little bridges. Rare plants, masses of rhododendrons among the flowers and a tree – the King Oak – said to be 900 years old. It's an extensive place, running to some 230 acres, inc a big **bird sanctuary** – to visit this part you need permission from the warden. Boat trips every half hour. Snacks, shop, disabled access – but paths are quite uneven; open Easter wk then Tues–Sun plus bank hols May–Sept, cl am Sat; (01603) 270449; £3. The Ship has good home cooking.

STRUMPSHAW MARSH TG3306 (off Low Rd, Brundall) Partly drained water meadows and fen between woodland and River Yare, with RSPB hides for watching marsh birds inc harriers and bearded tits, winter geese, and maybe swallowtail butterflies in Jun; £2.50 (RSPB members free). The Yare Inn in Brundall is popular for food.

Other things to see and do

Norfolk Family Attraction of the Year

GREAT WITCHINGHAM TG0818 **Norfolk Wildlife Park** (on the A1067) Saturday is a particularly good family day at this cheerful wildlife centre: 2 children get in free with every paying adult then, making it exceptional value. It's a good bet on other days too, though don't expect big, wild animals – the 40 acres of attractive parkland are filled with the kind of creatures typically found in Britain and Europe, so foxes, wild boar and Dartmoor ponies rather than elephants, lions and tigers. In spring they have around 500 heron nests up in the trees, and an unusual feature is a tower you can climb up to be on their level; you'll see most in Mar or Apr. They also have glass windows looking into a badger set, but do remember these engaging creatures are nocturnal, so if you visit in the morning they'll probably be asleep (they move around a bit more in the afternoon). There's a rabbit and guinea-pig village for younger children, and you can wander among the wallabies; they sell feed bags (don't bring your own). The 2 big play areas appeal most to slightly older children, with tyres, rope swings and the like. It takes a couple of hours to walk round and see everything, though obviously if you get a lot out of animals it's easy to stay longer – some people bring a picnic and stay most of the day. Meals, snacks, shop; cl Nov–Mar; (01603) 872274; £4 (£2.50 children aged 4–15).

ATTLEBOROUGH TM0292 **Peter Beales Rose Nursery** A specialist in old-fashioned roses that you won't find for sale elsewhere; you can wander around the 3 acres of gardens; cl Sun in Jan; (01953) 454707). The 15th-c **church** is interesting, with an unusual round tower and a screen decorated with the arms of the 24 bishoprics in England when it was built. The Griffin and White Lodge have decent food.

AYLSHAM TG1926 **Bure Valley Railway** Steam trains along 9 miles of narrow gauge track between here and Wroxham; you can combine the journey with a 1½-hour cruise on the Broads. The stock isn't very old, but the people are friendly and the journey is good value. Snacks, shop, disabled access; trains Apr–Oct, best to ring for timetable; (01263) 733858; £6.90 full return (£10.75 inc Broads cruise).

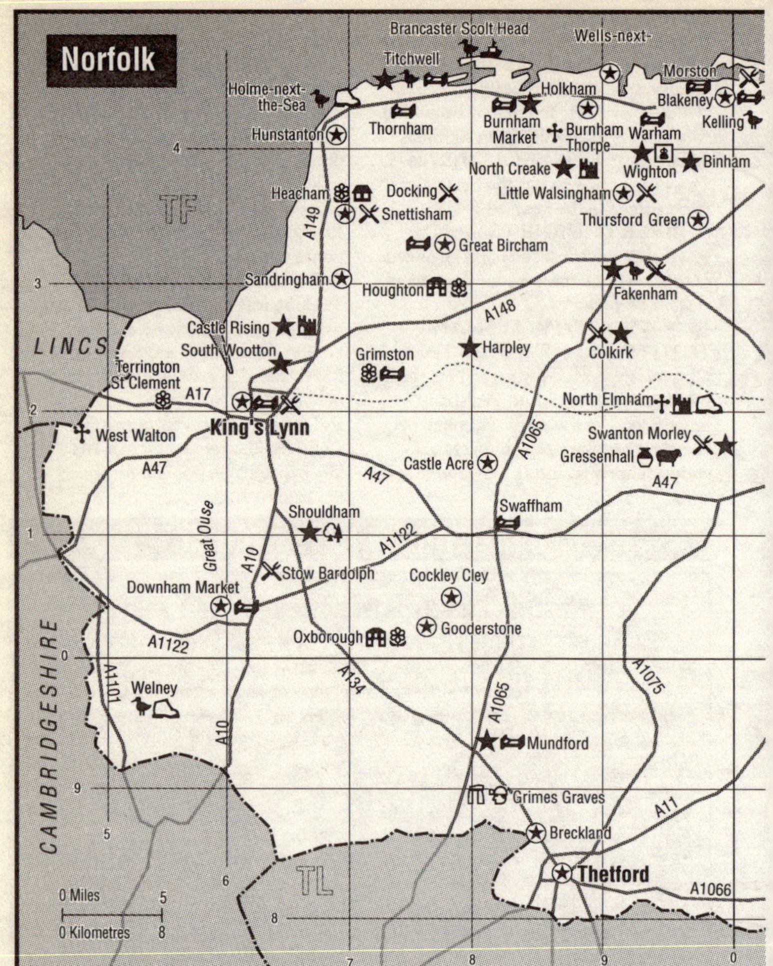

BACONSTHORPE CASTLE TG1336 The gatehouses, curtain walls and towers are all that's left of this moated and semi-fortified 15th-c house, but displays show what it must have looked like in its glory. A very pretty peaceful spot, with swans on the lake adding to its charm; free. You can find information booklets at the nearby post office. The Hare & Hounds on the way to Hempstead is useful for lunch.

BANHAM ZOO TM0587 (The Grove) Over 20 acres of parkland and garden with rare and endangered species, particularly monkeys and apes. Also an indoor activity centre, ice-cream parlour, play area, putting green and across the road a **craft centre** around a cobbled courtyard. Helpful explanatory notes, and feeding times spread throughout the day. Regular visitors tell us it gets better with every visit. Meals, snacks, shop, disabled access; cl 25–26 Dec; (01953) 887771 ext 217; £6.50 (crafts free). The King's Head opposite the medieval market hall in New Buckenham, has inexpensive home cooking.

BEACON HILL TG1841 (nr Cromer) The only place of any height (a humble 90 metres, 300ft) on the North Norfolk coast; the coastal

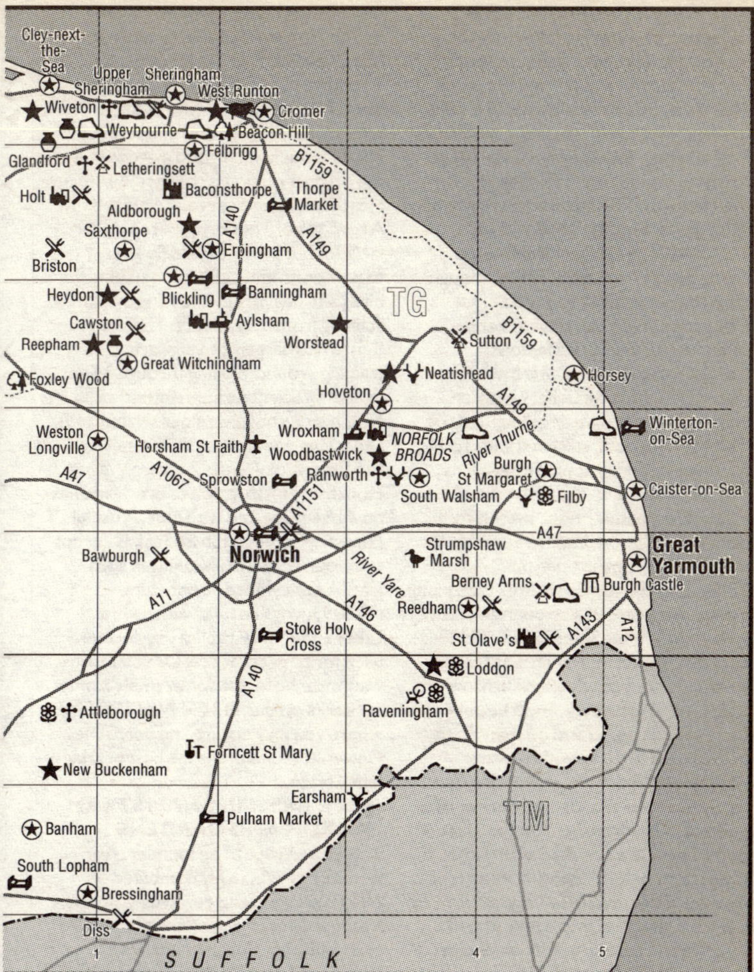

path here detours over the sandy heath and through woodlands.

BLAKENEY TG0044 **Seal Boat Trips** Boats leave from Morston Quay slightly W of Blakeney on the A149 coast rd once or twice a day from Mar–Oct (times depend on the tide), and on most winter wknds; when the tide allows you'll also find trips wending their way down the creek from the little harbour at Blakeney itself. Most last 2 hours, which takes in an hour or so exploring the NT-owned bird reserve at **Blakeney Point** (nice for walks and edged by a good stretch of the North Norfolk Coastal Path, although the shingle bank needs patience and is hard on the ankles; pleasant dunes at the far end). The highlight comes just before that, when the boat goes past the sandbanks at the end of the Point, where dozens of grey and common seals lie basking happily in the sun. Several different operators run boats, with the smaller ones owned by the Beans our favourites. Booking is recommended (especially in summer, when there are crowds of visitors waiting on the quay), on (01263) 740038. £4. Local information centres have full details of operators and times. Crabbing is fun from here, and surprisingly successful. Also a (free) collection of waterfowl down by the harbour, long breezy walks, unspoilt flint cottages, broad sky and sea vistas. There's a good dyke walk to Cley-next-the-Sea, with the birds on the mudflats for company. Blakeney has a very good teashop; besides the Blakeney Hotel, the Manor and White Horse are good.

BLICKLING HALL TG1728 (B1354) Magnificent house dating mainly from early 17th c, though the hedges that flank it may be older. Dramatic carved oak staircase and splendid paintings (inc a famous Canaletto), but best of all is the 38-metre (125-ft) Long Gallery with its ornate Jacobean plaster ceiling, and the Chinese bedroom, still lined with 18th-c hand-painted wallpaper. The gardens and grounds are lovely, with several miles of footpaths. Meals, snacks, shop, plant centre, good disabled access (a lift in the house); house open pm Thurs–Sun and bank hols Apr–Oct, plus Tues in Aug, garden also open am, daily in Aug and winter Sun; (01263) 733084; £6, £3.30 garden only; NT. There's a pleasant walk from the Buckinghamshire Arms (good for lunch), and free public access to the **parkland** on the W side of the pike-filled lake with its water birds, with large tracts of woodland and pasture, as well as a disused railway line, perhaps even kingfishers on the River Bure. There are circular walks within the park, and the **Weavers Way** long-distance path can be used as part of a link from the parkland to take in walks through and around the **Wolterton Park** and **Mannington Hall** estates, both owned by the Walpoles, who have opened up a network of paths in the area extending NW to **Holt Country Park**. The Saracen's Head on the edge of Wolterton Park is a very civilised dining pub.

BRANCASTER/SCOLT HEAD TF7944 Miles of dunes, flat coastal saltings, broad tidal beaches: a fine lonely place, largely National Trust and full of birds – Scolt Head island is an important breeding ground, and in good weather a boat takes people across from Brancaster Staithe. Incidentally, all along this coast the wading birds, surprisingly approachable, are best seen on a falling tide. The Jolly Sailors and White Horse are useful for lunch.

BRECKLAND Around Thetford, this is a region originally of poor, flat, sandy heathland with scattered shallow meres and scrubby mixed woodland. A good place to see the original version is the East Wretham Heath **nature reserve** TL9188 off the A1075 NE of Thetford: limited visitor facilities but plenty of wild flowers, nature trails, and hides for watching the birds and deer; free. The **Pingo Trail**, starting from Stow Bedon TL9596, is an 8-mile path largely through army training ground, passing through 3 Sites of Special Scientific Interest (inc Cranberry Rough, an alder swampland), and taking you along a disused railway line before joining the Peddars Way at Hockham Heath. Much of Breckland has now been forested with pine. A useful Forestry Commission leaflet has 7 maps of colour-coded trails taking in such features as Lynford Arboretum (TL8293: dogs not allowed), Lynford Lakes and a metal replica stag formerly used for target practice. Or you can just walk into the forest, for example from car parks on the A134 NW of Thetford, where you may disturb roe deer. The Crown at Mundford is the best nearby lunch place.

BRESSINGHAM STEAM MUSEUM AND GARDENS TM0880 (A1066) The founder, Alan Bloom, has effectively combined his two interests at this rewarding site. The 6 acres of informal gardens are planted with 5,000 species and cultivars of alpines and perennials in island beds, with lots of the dwarf conifers Bloom has done so much to popularise. Then there's the excellent steam collection, inc 50 road and rail engines, mostly restored to working order, and a charming fairground carousel. 4 steam-hauled trains run through the charming countryside and parts of the garden (all may not be in steam out of high season). Meals, snacks, shop, disabled access; cl Nov–Mar, and museum also cl wkdys in Oct; (01379) 687382; £4.50. The Garden House is handy for lunch.

BURGH CASTLE TG4705 You can still see sections of the massive walls of this coastal Roman fortress, built in the 3rd c to protect the coast from Saxon marauders; free. The Church Farm Inn overlooking the Yare and Waveney has decent food.

BURGH ST MARGARET TG4513 **The Village** (A1064) Delightful, if idealised, pastiche of a 19th-c village: old-fashioned fairground rides (inc traditional Victorian gallopers), candle-making and other crafts, and amusing live shows – the puppet show effectively blends marionettes with people. Also silent comedy films in the 1920s concert hall, miniature railway, steam-hauled trailer rides, working sawmill, collections of vintage motorbikes and other vehicles, woodland walks, and decent adventure play area. Meals, snacks, shops, disabled access; cl Nov–Mar; (01493) 369770; *£5.95 (*£2.75 Sat, when less going on: no crafts or live shows).

★ **BURNHAM MARKET** TF8342 Handsome and opulent village with a fine green, and gatehouse and 13th-c priory remains; the Hoste Arms is a good dining pub.

† **BURNHAM THORPE** TF8541 This hamlet's strong Lord Nelson connections include a pub named after him, with interesting related memorabilia. The lectern in the village church uses wood from HMS *Victory*, and the church has other Nelson mementos.

CAISTER-ON-SEA TG5012 Like the other settlements down this coast, Caister plays host to a good many summer visitors, with all the usual attractions, inc long sandy beaches. It's also got a lifeboat station, right by the beach. The town has various remains of an excavated **Roman fort** inc one gateway and a town wall. **Caister Castle** This moated ruin is set back from the town, a little way inland. Falstaff (the original behind Shakespeare's creation) built it on returning from Agincourt; its walls surround a 30-metre (98-ft) tower. The grounds contain a **motor museum** with a good collection of vehicles from 1893 onwards. Snacks, some disabled access; open daily exc Sat mid-May–Sept; (01572) 787251; £4.50.

★ † **CASTLE ACRE** TF8115 A delightful village, with an 18th-c feel along the tree-shaded walk of Stocks Green (the Ostrich here is handy for lunch). The sparse ruins of a great **Norman Castle** are still awe-inspiring. **Castle Acre Priory** Extensive ruins of a Cluniac building built by William the Conqueror's son-in-law, inc the fine arcaded west front of the 11th/12th-c church, and a chapel and 15th-c gatehouse; good Walkman tour. Well laid out, and very picturesque. Snacks, shop, some disabled access; cl winter Mon and Tues, 24–26 Dec, and maybe 1–2pm for lunch; (01760) 755394; £2.95. The site is on the Peddars Way, a Roman road following the track of an earlier herding way. West Acre, 2 or 3 miles W, has a few further priory remains, and (like Castle Acre itself) picturesque fords over the River Nar. A few miles N, some private woodland opens for 3 wks in late spring for its magnificent azaleas.

★ **CASTLE RISING** TF6624 **Castle** Massive earthworks surround this fine Norman keep, a marvellous setting for the summer jousting they occasionally stage here. Shop; cl winter Mon and Tues, 24–26 Dec; (01553) 631330; £2.30. By the church and almshouses in the attractive village the Black Horse is a popular dining pub.

† **CLEY-NEXT-THE-SEA** TG0443 Handy for the bird-sanctuary marshes towards the Blakeney Point sandspit, a pleasant village with a magnificent **church**. The neatly restored **windmill** is a more obvious landmark, and has great views from the top (open pm Easter–Oct; £1.50), as well as very good accommodation. There's a long pebbly beach, and the Three Swallows has decent food.

† ! **COCKLEY CLEY** TF8004 Lots of interesting historical things to see around this village (pronounced to rhyme with 'fry'). There's a **museum** in a 17th-c cottage, nature reserve, carriage collection, and 7th-c Saxon church, but most unusual is the **Iceni village**, built as and where it was believed to exist 2,000 years ago. Snacks, shop, disabled access; cl Nov–Easter; (01760) 724588; £3.30 covers all attractions. The Twenty Churchwardens is handy for lunch.

† **CROMER** TG2242 Popular seaside resort since Victorian times,

with lovely sandy beaches, more sun than average, bustling markets, golf courses, interesting shops and galleries and lots of entertainments. The pier is one of the last in the country to present an end-of-pier show – very popular, so worth booking early. The tower of the imposing **church** on Church St – Norfolk's tallest – gives spectacular views of the surrounding countryside. A good local history **museum** next door is spread over 5 19th-c fishermen's cottages (cl Mon lunch, am Sun, Good Fri, 23–26 Dec, 1 Jan; £1.20), and on the prom a small **Lifeboat Museum** looks at local lifeboatman Henry Blogg, who over 53 years saved 873 lives (cl Nov–Apr; free). Nearby you often find dressed crabs for sale; the crab boats still work from here, and Cromer crabs are the best on England's E coast. The seafront Bath House has decent food.

DOWNHAM MARKET TF5903 **Hermitage Hall** (Bridge Farm, A1122 just W) Based around an old chapel used by pilgrims on the way to Walsingham, now with mementos of local boy Nelson (inc letters, birth certificate and death mask), small collection of cars, Victorian street, and gentle walks down to the Ouse. Snacks, shop, disabled acess; normally open pm Weds, Fri and Sun, Easter–Dec; (01366) 383185; *£4. There's an adjacent animal sanctuary.

EARSHAM TM3188 **Otter Trust** (off the A143) This charitable trust works towards reintroducing otters to rivers from which they've disappeared; they're displayed here in a natural environment. They're obviously cheerful and intelligent, but don't perform on demand and you may have to wait a while to see anything. Snacks, shop, disabled access; cl Nov–Mar; (01986) 893470; £4.50. The Green Dragon in Bungay is a heartening retreat if they don't show.

ERPINGHAM TG2032 **Alby Crafts and Gardens** 4 acres of interesting shrubs, plants and bulbs, with a museum devoted to lace, another concentrating on bottles (over 2,000 of them, mainly from regional brewers), bee observation hive, and crafts inc woodturning and stained glass. Very good roses and lilies in July. Meals, snacks, shop, mostly disabled access; cl Mon (exc bank hols), all wkdys mid-Jan–mid-Mar (lace museum also cl Sat); (01263) 761226; crafts and lace museum *free, gardens *£1.50, bottle museum *50p. The Ark, and the Saracen's Head out at Wolterton (at the start of a pleasant 2- or 3-hour circular walk), are both very good for lunch.

★ **FAKENHAM** TF9429 A pleasant market town; the comfortable Wensum Lodge Hotel has good food (as does the prettily set Sculthorpe Mill off the A148 just W), and the roads N pass through attractive villages.

Pensthorpe Waterfowl Trust (Pensthorpe, A1067) Good-sized collection of wild and exotic waterfowl, many of them rare. The visitor centre has displays of wildlife art and photography. Also woodland, meadow, lakeside and riverside nature trails, adventure playground, and very good talks and events. Meals, snacks, shop, disabled access; cl wkdys Jan–Mar, 25 Dec; (01328) 851465; £4.50.

FELBRIGG HALL TG1939 Magnificent 17th-c house in splendid grounds, inc an orangery with a fine collection of camellias, and a colourfully restored walled garden overlooked by a dovecot. The house is decorated with paintings and furnishings from the 18th c, and has a wonderful Gothic library. Lots of events, with something going on at the stable block most Sun afternoons. Meals, snacks, shop, disabled access; hall and gardens cl Thurs, Fri, and Nov–Mar, hall also cl am; (01263) 837444; £5.40, garden only £2.20; NT. There's public access to the 1,700-acre wooded grounds (cl 25 Dec only), landscaped by Repton, with their fine mature trees and lake.

FILBY TG4612 **Thrigby Hall Wildlife Gardens** 18th-c park filled with Asian animals and birds, with tropical and bird houses, tree walk, willow pattern garden, and ornamental wildfowl on the lake. Also a huge jungly swamp hall where crocodiles doze under water. Readers enjoy coming here – though warn of queues on summer wknds. Summer snacks, shop, disabled access; (01493) 369477; *£5.50.

FORNCETT ST MARY TM1694 **Industrial Steam Museum** Unusual collection of 8 giant stationary steam engines rescued from all over the country, inc one that used to open Tower Bridge. Snacks, shop, disabled access; open 1st Sun of month, May–Nov, when the engines are in steam; (01508) 488277; £3.50 (2 children free with every adult). The Bird in Hand, over at Wreningham, is a good-value dining pub.

FOXLEY WOOD TG0522 A big block of ancient woodland, mainly deciduous and grown naturally for many centuries; lovely woodland spring flowers.

GLANDFORD TG0441 **Shell Museum** Curious little museum housing the often very beautiful seashells and other interesting objects collected by Sir Alfred Jodrell, who lived in nearby Bayfield Hall. Some disabled access; cl lunchtimes, all day Sun and Mon (exc bank hols), and Nov–Feb; (01263) 740081; £1.50. The King's Head at Letheringsett is quite handy for lunch.

★ † **GOODERSTONE** TF7602 Attractive village, with decent pub, ancient **church** and nearby **watergardens**.

★ **GREAT BIRCHAM WINDMILL** TF7632 Not far from Houghton Hall, this striking mill is on that Norfolk rarity, a hill – so one of the few places with views. They sell bread baked at the mill's own bakery. Snacks, shop, some disabled access; cl Oct–Easter, tearooms and bakery also cl Sat; (01485) 578393; £2.25. You can hire bikes. The village is attractive, with an art gallery, and the King's Head Hotel (unpretentious despite being a favourite with Sandringham shooting parties) is good for lunch.

GREAT WITCHINGHAM TG0818 *See separate Family Panel on p.437* for **Norfolk Wildlife Park**. The Old Brewery House in Reepham is the nearest good place for lunch.

! † **GREAT YARMOUTH** TG5307 A cross between working town and resort, this still has a busy fishing harbour – used too as a port of call by the Broads cruising boats. There are lots of holiday entertainments, particularly good for families (there's a decent fairground) and some attractions that might well tempt older visitors into the town if they were nearby. The best pubs here are the White Lion (King St) and Red Herring (Havelock Rd).

The **Maritime Museum of East Anglia** (Marine Parade) looks at the local fishing industry, with some more incongruous features inc a mummified hand and Indian scalp; times as Elizabethan House Museum below; (01493) 745526. **Sea Life Centre** (Marine Parade) Displays of the kinds of marine life found on the Norfolk coast, as well as underwater tunnels through shark-infested oceans and tropical fish. Meals, snacks, shop, disabled access; cl 25 Dec; (01493) 330631; £5.50. **Amazonia** (Marine Parade) Cousin to similar centre at Bowness up in Cumbria, an indoor tropical paradise with reptiles, insects, butterflies and birds; they have a 4-metre (13-ft) alligator, a python well over 7 metres (24ft) long, and an iguana named Levi. Snacks, shop, disabled access; cl 25–26 Dec; (01493) 842202; *£3.75. **Merrivale Model Village** (Wellington Pier Gardens) Attractive landscaped gardens with children's rides and remote-controlled cars, and the exceptionally detailed village – featuring a railway, radio-controlled boats and over 200 models. Meals, snacks, shop, disabled access; cl Nov–Easter; (01493) 842097; £2.80. **Elizabethan House Museum** (South Quay) Recently refurbished, this is a patchwork of historical detail – built in 1596, it has a Georgian façade, 16th-c panelled rooms and, among features from later periods, some rooms decorated and furnished in 19th-c style, and a functional Victorian kitchen. Shop, disabled access to ground floor only; open 2 wks at Easter, then daily exc Sat Jun–Sept; (01493) 745526; £1.90. The last surviving steam drifter, the *Lydia Eva*, divides her time between here and Lowestoft – if she's by South Quay she can usually be visited Easter–Oct; donations.

The 14th-c **church** of St Nicholas, at the top end of the market place, has an exceptionally wide nave, and an impressive west front. The 13th-c

Tolhouse Museum (Tolhouse St) used to be the town's gaol and courthouse (you can still see the dungeons). It now has local history, and a brass-rubbing centre; times as Elizabethan House Museum; (01493) 745526; 80p. **Old Merchant's House** (Row 117) 17th-c house standing among the narrow lanes or Rows nr the waterfront, with some well restored rooms. Shop; cl 1–2pm, and all Oct–Mar; (01493) 857900; *£1.85.

GRESSENHALl TF9716 **Norfolk Rural Life Museum and Union Farm** Re-creation of a typical 1920s farm, with rare breeds of sheep, pigs, cattle and poultry, and working reconstructions of agricultural life. Meals, snacks, shop, disabled access; cl am Sun, Nov–Easter; (01362) 860563; £3.80. The White Horse at Longham has good-value food.

GRIMES GRAVES TL8189 Bring a torch to this Breckland site, as you can climb into one of the 300 pits and vertical shafts which lead down into the galleries – some around 10 metres (33ft) deep – where the Neolithic people mined their flint; the landscape around is pitted by their efforts. No lavatories at the site, but there are some within a mile. Shop; cl 1–2pm, all day Mon and Tues Nov–Mar, Christmas; (01842) 810656; £1.75.

GRIMSTON TF7022 **Congham Hall Herb Garden** In summer this has around 500 different herbs, in traditional layouts, with many unusual varieties for sale; open 2–4 pm Apr–Sept (cl Sat); free.

HEACHAM TF6837 **Norfolk Lavender** (Caley Mill) The largest lavender-growing and distilling operation in the country, along with a national collection of lavender species and cultivars. The guided tour (daily spring bank hol–Sept) really adds interest, and at harvest time they may drive visitors out to the fields. Also rose and herb gardens. Snacks (inc their lavender and lemon scones), shop, disabled access; cl 25–26 Dec, 1 Jan; (01485) 570384; tours (mid-July–mid-Aug) £1.50, £3.95 by minibus. The Gin Trap at Ringstead (with a decent nearby art gallery) and Rose & Crown at Snettisham both have good food.

★ **HEYDON** TG1127 Delightfully unspoilt, tucked-away village, with a green that time seems to have passed by, and good food at the Earle Arms.

HOLKHAM HALL TF9143 Splendid Palladian mansion in grand and very extensive tree-filled grounds with an ornamental lake, temple, obelisk and 18th-c walled garden. Sumptuously furnished state rooms, with fine paintings by Claude, Rubens, Van Dyck and Gainsborough. An ancestor of the present owner was Thomas Coke, whose revolutionary farming techniques are described in an exhibition in the porter's lodge; there's also a pottery. Snacks, shop, limited disabled access; open pm Sun–Thurs, and bank hols Easter–Oct; (01328) 710227; £6 for everything, £4 hall only. Walkers have free access to this coastal estate's driveways; the parkland is a bit sombre, but impressively landscaped. The Victoria Hotel is handy for lunch. The beach has a bird reserve (and a nudist section). There is a car park quite close to the beach, where pine trees meet the sands; this coastal section of the North Norfolk Coastal Path is good for lonely walks – westwards any summer crowds rapidly thin out. From **Overy Staithe** a particularly fine stretch of the path follows a zigzagging dyke – saltmarsh on one side, neat farmland on the other – to the dunes and sandy beach, which never quite looks the same from one day to the next.

HOLME-NEXT-THE-SEA TF6943 From the sandy beach there's a 2-mile walk past a rewarding **bird sanctuary** and saltings to Thornham – another good bird-watching place. Another more serious walking possibility is the **Peddars Way** which starts here – an inland link from the coastal path, running from Holme down through Castle Acre and then in a strikingly straight beeline right across the county to Knettishall Heath nr Thetford, following ancient-feeling green ways and quiet lanes. Earnest walkers may find there is a little too much road-walking to sustain interest.

HOLT TG0738 Pleasant little town with some handsome Georgian buildings; Nicholsons in the High St sells anything from clothes to antiques, and has a useful, continental-style licensed café. The terminus of the **North Norfolk Steam Railway** from Sheringham.

HORSEY TG4622 A quiet corner of the coast, below sea level – among the places most at risk of flooding if the sea defences are breached. There's a good path to the dunes and the sea from the lane past the Nelson Head (good food). On the other side of the main road, **Horsey Windpump** is a restored drainage windmill, now in full working order. Teas, small shop; cl Oct–Mar; £1.20; NT. This is a good area for a **varied round walk**: a path along quiet reed-fringed Horsey Mere (NT, with wildfowl and otters) and the New Cut to another former drainage windmill – the marshes on the far side of the cut seem alive with birds. Then you can either walk straight back to the village, or for a total contrast join the beach for sea views nr Horsey Corner.

HORSHAM ST FAITH TG2114 **Norwich Aviation Museum** (Old Norwich Rd) Enthusiastic displays of local aeronautical history, with aircraft (there's a Vulcan bomber), engines, and other paraphernalia; on the edge of Norwich Airport, so a good view of the live article too. Snacks, shop; cl Mon and winter wkdys; (01603) 625309; *£2.50. The thatched Chequers in the pretty village of Hainford has good food.

HOUGHTON HALL TF7928 Built for Robert Walpole and obviously designed to impress, this is a spectacularly grand Palladian mansion set in charming parkland. The state rooms were decorated and furnished by William Kent, and house an important collection of 20,000 model soldiers and other militaria. Heavy horses, Shetland ponies and llamas in the stables. Snacks, shop, disabled access; open pm Thurs, Sun and bank hols Easter–Sept; (01485) 528569; £6. Driving along the C- road nr North Pole farm you may spot unusual herds of white deer. The 17th-c Duke's Head at West Rudham has good home cooking.

HOVETON HALL GARDEN TG3120 Large and attractive spring woodland garden with daffodils and rhododendrons, lakeside walk, walled and old-fashioned herbaceous garden and kitchen garden. You can stay in a wing of the house. Teas, plant sales, disabled access; open Weds, Fri, Sun and bank hols Easter–mid-Sept; (01603) 782798; *£3. The Black Horse is useful for lunch. **Wroxham Barns craft centre** (Tunstead Rd) Good for families, with several craft workshops in 18th-c restored farm buildings, as well as a children's farm and traditional fair. Meals, snacks, shop, play area, disabled access; cl 25–26 Dec; (01603) 783762; £2 for farm, otherwise free.

HUNSTANTON TF6740 Clean, fresh and well kept resort with gently shelving tidal sands (donkey rides still), summer boat trips, and pleasant dune walks past the golf course up to the **bird reserve** on Gore Point. **Sea Life Centre** (Southern Promenade) An ocean tunnel at this excellent place brings you face to face with deep-water creatures as well as octopuses and toothy conger eels. Meals, snacks, shop, disabled access; cl 25 Dec; (01485) 533576; £5.35. **Oasis** Standing out among the typical resort entertainments is this giant leisure park on the prom with tropically heated indoor and outdoor pools and both towering and toddler aquaslides (cl Dec–Feb; £3). On a clear day you can see Boston's Stump across the Wash, and the low cliffs around the town are quite colourful, with different rock strata. The Ancient Mariner (part of Le Strange Hotel, Old Hunstanton) is good value, opposite an interesting craft gallery, and the Marine Bar (St Edmund's Terrace) has decent food all day.

KELLING TG0942 **Falconry Centre** (Weybourne Rd) Over a hundred or so kestrels, sparrowhawks and owls, as well as rarer peregrine falcons and redtail hawks; flying displays midday, 2pm and 4pm (weather permitting). Meals, snacks, shop, disabled access; cl winter Mon; (01263) 712235; £3.50. The attached Kelling Park Hotel is friendly and reasonably priced.

KING'S LYNN TF6120 Once England's fourth-largest town, it's quieter now, with pleasant corners, some attractive Georgian brick buildings and a few much older places such as the 17th-c Custom House on the quay by the River Purfleet, the 15th-c **church** of St Nicholas (Chapel Lane; attractive for festival concerts), the South Gates, Red Mount Chapel and the 2 medieval guildhalls. The first of these, the 15th-c **St George's Guildhall** (King St), is now the town's theatre, and home of the King's Lynn Festival; the tourist information centre has details of tours, (01553) 763044. **Old Gaol House** (also Saturday Market Pl) Lively journey through the town's rich history; with spirited models, and spooky sights, sounds and smells, this is particularly good for children. Shop, disabled access; cl Weds and Thurs from Nov–Easter, 25–26 Dec and 1 Jan; (01533) 763044; *£2.20 (inc audio tour). The tour includes the 14th-c King John Cup and other fabulous examples of civic paraphernalia housed in the undercroft of the handsome medieval Trinity Guildhall (not open to the public). **Trues Yard** (North St) Restored old fishermen's cottages giving a good picture of life here in the last century, when families of up to 11 were often squeezed into 2 little rooms. Snacks, shop, mostly disabled access; cl 25 Dec–1 Jan; (01553) 770479; £1.90. **Town House Museum** (Queen St) More social history; cl Sun exc pm May–Sept, and bank hols; £1.20. **Lynn Museum** (Old Market Sq) Includes the skeleton of a Saxon warrior, and a surprisingly interesting collection of medieval pilgrims' badges (cl Sun and Mon; 80p). On Tues the main market place has some good craft stalls. The Tudor Rose between there and St Nicholas is good for lunch, and the Globe Hotel on the market place itself is good value.

LETHERINGSETT TG0638 The **church** has an unusual round tower. A restored **watermill** in a pretty setting still mills flour from local wheat; cl 1–2pm, Sun (exc school and bank hols), Mon, and pm Sat in winter; demonstrations pm every day; (01263) 713153; £2.75 during demonstrations, otherwise £1.75. The King's Head is pleasant for lunch.

LITTLE WALSINGHAM TF9336 Once as popular a centre of pilgrimage as Canterbury, thanks to a replica of the Virgin Mary's home in Nazareth. Things tailed off when Henry VIII destroyed the priory and its shrine in 1538, but picked up again earlier this century. **Walsingham Abbey Grounds** Plenty of remains of the 12th-c building, inc the abbey gates, great arch, part of the refectory and the holy Wells. Pleasant gardens and woodland walks, with masses of snowdrops in early spring. Open via the Shirehall Museum and Tourist Information Centre in summer (joint tickets available), or the estate office in winter (office hours only); (01328) 820259; £2.50. **Shirehall Museum** Emphasis on the pilgrimage to Walsingham; displays are in an almost perfect Georgian courtroom complete with original fittings. Shop, limited disabled access; cl Sun, and Oct–Easter; 75p. The Bull Inn is a good place, with plenty of pilgrimage customers. The terminus of the **steam railway** from Wells-next-the-Sea.

★ **LODDON** TM3695 **Reads Nursery** (Hales Hall, off the A146 SE) Specialising for the last century in unusual conservatory plants, inc a good range of lemon, orange and other citrus fruits, also nut trees, etc. Disabled access; cl Mon (exc bank hols), Sun exc pm Jun–Sept, 25 Dec–5 Jan; (01508) 548395; nursery free, barn and garden £1.50. The village is attractive, and the 17th-c Swan has home-made food.

★ **NEW BUCKENHAM** TM0890 A fine village, largely medieval, with a decent pub.

★ **NORTH CREAKE** TF8539 **Creake Abbey** All that remains of this early 13th-c Augustinian priory is the crossing and E arm, but it's still worth a passing look, and the village is charming. Cartwrights at South Creake has good food.

✝ **NORTH ELMHAM CHURCH** TF9821 An attractive 13th-c building, odd in that there's a step down into it; a little further N are the interesting ruins of a **Saxon cathedral**, and there are pleasant walks. The King's Head has good food.

OXBURGH HALL TF7401 Henry VIII stayed in this pretty moated manor house in 1487, and the room is now decorated with wall hangings worked by Mary Queen of Scots. Unfortunately, most of the house was thoroughly refurbished during Victorian times, but the gatehouse remains as an awe-inspiring example of 15th-c building work, 24 metres (80ft) high. The garden has a colourful French parterre. Meals, snacks, shop, disabled access; cl am, Thurs, Fri, and Nov–Mar, garden also open some wknds Mar; (01366) 328258; £4.80, £2.40 garden only; NT. The Bedingfeld Arms opposite has decent food.

RAVENINGHAM HALL GARDENS TM3996 Interesting collection of rare shrubs, shrub roses, traditional kitchen garden, arboretum, and Victorian conservatory. Teas Sun and bank hols; open pm Easter Sun and Mon, Sun and bank hols May–July; (01508) 548222; *£2. **Raveningham Craft Workshops** (Beccles Rd) Victorian farm buildings with furniture-making, piano workshop, antiques and other workshops; teas; free. Loddon is the best nearby place for a meal.

REEDHAM TG4202 **Pettitts Feathercraft and Animal Adventure Park** You can still watch the demonstrations of feather craft, though they've become a little swamped by the other attractions here, inc aviaries, a gnome village, American-style locomotive ride around the grounds, big adventure playground, miniature horse stud, deer-petting park and crazy golf. Meals, Snacks, shop, some disabled access; cl Sat, and Nov–Easter (exc bank hols); (01493) 701094; £6.35. The waterside Ferry is popular for lunch, and the little car ferry here is fun.

★ **REEPHAM** TG0922 This attractive large village or small town has some worthwhile shops, a fine old inn (the Old Brewery House) and a **nostalgia collection** in the station.

ST OLAVE'S PRIORY TM4599 Ruins of 13th-c Augustinian priory; you can still see the fine brick undercroft in the cloister – a remarkable early use of this material; free. The riverside Bell is very old indeed, though much modernised.

SANDRINGHAM TF6928 Many people come to this part of the county for its connection with the Royal Family. **Sandringham House** was bought by Queen Victoria for her son Edward in 1862 and has become famous as the Royal Christmas residence; the 19th-c building is filled with their portraits and those of their European counterparts, and has various gifts presented to the family over the years. Unlike at their other homes, you can see most of the rooms the family use, so there's a much more intimate feel than you'd get at Windsor or Buckingham Palace; expect queues though. The grounds and surrounding country park are lovely, with nature trails, adventure playground, and the parish Church of St Mary Magdalene. Lovely rhododendrons in the woods May/Jun. Meals, snacks, shop, disabled access (a train runs between the entrance to the grounds and the house); open Easter–Sept, exc during summer Royal visit – best to check for dates; (01553) 772675; £4.50, £3.50 grounds and museum only. In summer, pick-your-own lets you sample fruit that might otherwise have graced the Royal table. There's free access to **Sandringham Country Park** with its majestic trees and glades, a notable parkland walking area. The Feathers towards Dersingham is useful for lunch.

SAXTHORPE TG1332 **Mannington Gardens** The most beautiful feature of these gardens is the summer rose display, but 20 miles of footpaths around the hall and woodland are open all year (£1 parking). Snacks, shop, disabled access; gardens open pm Sun May–Sept plus Weds–Fri Jun–Aug; (01263) 874175; £3. Paths lead to the pleasant grounds of Wolterton Park. The riverside Walpole Arms in the pretty nearby village of Itteringham has good food.

SHERINGHAM TG1543 The working fishing harbour has some old buildings around it, though there's a lot of more modern building up behind. The beach is nice, and the Two Lifeboats has good sea views (as well as decent food inc fresh fish). **North Norfolk Railway** Full-size steam railway, chugging through over 5 miles of lovely coastal scenery to Holt. Plenty of railway memorabilia at the Sheringham station, and a collection of steam engines and vintage rolling stock. Meals, snacks, shop, disabled access; steamtrains Mar–Dec; (01263) 822045 for timetable; £6.50 full return journey. **Sheringham Park** This extensive parkland, gloriously landscaped by Humphrey Repton (it was his favourite work), gives excellent coastal views from its waymarked walks and viewing towers. Also mature trees and fine azaleas and rhododendrons (best late May/Jun), with good walks to the coast. A restored steam-powered sawmill operates some wknds; Snacks, disabled access; (01263) 823778; free, but parking £2.50; NT.

★ **SHOULDHAM** TF6709 Just N of this attractive village, with a decent pub, are **nature trails** in pleasant woods.

SNETTISHAM TF6833 **Park Farm** Working farm offering good insight into seasonal farming operations – lambing, shearing, and red deer calving. Lots of animals, plus impressive adventure playground, craft centre and mini golf. Meals, snacks, shop, disabled access; cl some days in winter, so best to check first out of season; (01485) 542425; £3.95 for either farm or 45-minute guided ride around deer park, £7 for both. Pretty walks nearby, as well as a nature reserve down by the beach. The Rose & Crown is a good dining pub.

SUTTON WINDMILL TG3923 The most striking mill in Norfolk and the tallest in Britain, 9 floors high; shop; cl Oct–Mar; (01692) 581195; *£3. Other fine examples are at Acle TG3910, Little Cressingham TF8600 and Paston TG3135.

TERRINGTON ST CLEMENT TF5519 **African Violet Centre** Wide range of plants besides the African violets it has developed so successfully as house plants; the owner is also a priest, and takes services in a former packing shed here. Good tearoom; (01553) 828374. The Woolpack at Walpole Cross Keys has decent food.

THETFORD TL8683 **Ancient House Museum** Early Tudor house with fine oak ceilings, now a local history museum with small period herb garden behind. Shop; cl 12.30–1pm, Sun (exc pm in summer); (01842) 752599; free exc July and Aug, when 80p. **Thetford Priory** Ruins of 12th-c Cluniac monastery; you can easily make out the full ground plan of the cloisters, and the 14th-c gatehouse still stands; disabled access; free. **Warren Lodge** 15th-c flint former hunting lodge, worth a look. The Bell and Thomas Paine are both civilised places for lunch.

THURSFORD GREEN TF9734 **Thursford Collection** Bouncy collection of musical organs, whether barrel, street or fairground. Most are demonstrated every day, and the Wurlitzer cinema organ also stars in daily concerts. Showmen's steam engines too, plus 2-ft- gauge steam railway, adventure playground, and Venetian Gondola switchback ride. Meals, snacks, shop, disabled access; cl am and Oct–Easter; (01328) 878477; £4.50.

★ **TITCHWELL** TF7544 This pleasant coastal village has a good RSPB reserve nearby; besides the Manor Hotel, the Three Horseshoes has good-value food and bedrooms.

† **UPPER SHERINGHAM** TG1441 The 14th-c **church** in this quiet flintstone village is very attractive, and the Red Lion is a pleasant stop. Footpaths from here lead to Sheringham Park.

★ **WELLS-NEXT-THE-SEA** TF9142 Pleasant and rather gracious little village-sized town; don't be fooled by the name – the sea is a mile away these days, though there's a particularly good stretch of the North Norfolk Coastal Path from here to **Overy Staithe**, where the sandy beach never looks quite the same from one day to the next. **Wells & Walsingham Light Railway** Passing through delightful countryside, this railway is remarkable for being the longest in Britain to use a 10¼-inch-gauge track, with a steam locomotive built specially for it a few years ago. Snacks, shop, some disabled access; cl Oct–Easter; (01328) 856506 for times; *£5 return. The Crown is good for lunch.

WELNEY TL5393 **Wildfowl and Wetlands Trust** (Hundred Foot Bank) Excellent 1,000- acre wild bird reserve, with numerous hides, spacious observatory, and a floodlit lagoon. In winter the sights include up to 4,000 migratory Bewick's swans and numerous species of duck; it can be busy then, and you'll need to wrap up well. In spring the emphasis switches to waders and other birds. There's a summer nature trail, and interesting conducted summer evening walks. Snacks, shop, disabled access; cl 25 Dec; (01353) 860711; *£3.25. In winter some local roads can be flooded, and then you can approach it only from the E. The nearby towering hydraulic gates of **Denver Sluice** (TF5800) that control water levels in these parts are quite a sight. The Jenyns Arms there, with peacocks in its riverside gardens, is a pleasant lunch stop.

★ **WEST RUNTON** TG2042
Norfolk Shire Horse Centre
Extensive collection of draught horses and moorland and mountain ponies (they have 9 breeds). You can hire riding horses by the hour, and there's a children's farm (though some readers feel the aviaries and hutches are a little crowded). Meals, snacks, shop, disabled access; cl Sat (exc maybe July and Aug), and Nov–Easter; (01263) 837339; *£4.50. The seaside village itself is attractive, and the Village Inn is useful for lunch.

✝ **WEST WALTON CHURCH**
TF4713 A textbook example of early Gothic architecture; just about all of it dates from the mid-13th c, and there's a cool elegance throughout. The King of Hearts (good for lunch) holds the key.

! ☺ **WESTON LONGVILLE**
TG1017 **Dinosaur Park** (A1067) 300 acres of unspoilt woodland with life-sized reconstructions of dinosaurs lying in wait around every corner – good for children to appreciate properly how big some of these beasts were. Also a maze, adventure playground (inc a 'climbasaurus') and rural bygones. Snacks, shop, disabled access; cl Nov–Easter; (01603) 873397; £4.50. The Parson Woodforde has popular food.

WEYBOURNE TG1043
Muckleburgh Collection (on the A149) World War II fighting vehicles and other soldierly relics on the site of a former military camp, once the lynch-pin of defences on this coast. Tank demonstrations every Sun, bank hols and wkdys during summer school hols. Meals and snacks (in NAAFI-style café), shop, disabled access; cl Nov–mid-Feb; (01263) 588210; *£4. The Dun Cow overlooking the Salthouse marshes has decent food, with a nearby shack selling very fresh shellfish and samphire. Salthouse and Kelling back heathy hinterlands, allowing walkers a mix between this and the unvaryingly straight coast.

★ **WIGHTON** TF9439 Pleasant village in an attractive coastal area, where the sculptor Henry Moore lived for a while; the Carpenters Arms is a decent pub, and there's a good **art gallery**. A stop on the steam railway between Wells and Walsingham.

WINTERTON-ON-SEA TG4919
One of the quieter seaside resorts on this coast, with a gentle villagey feel, and a particularly good beach over the dunes – nice for a wander by the sea; the 17th-c Fisherman's Return is very pleasant for lunch.

Days Out

Tanks, shells and fairground organs: Muckleburgh Collection, Weybourne (more peacable option: Kelling falconry centre); lunch at the White Horse, Blakeney; Glandford shell museum; Thursford Collection; Letheringsett watermill (if open).

Landscapes of the Broads: Fairhaven Garden Trust, South Walsham, or rent a boat from Wroxham; lunch at the Ferry, Reedham; walk along the River Yare, or take a boat or train from Great Yarmouth to Berney Arms windmill.

To the manor born: Walk in Mannington Hall/Wolterton Park estates, Saxthorpe; visit Mannington Hall gardens if open; lunch at the Saracen's Head, Wolterton, or the Buckinghamshire Arms, Blickling; Blickling Hall.

★ **WOODBASTWICK** TG3215 This picturesque thatched estate village includes Woodfordes Brewery, one of Britain's best microbreweries; the Fur & Feather dining pub is the brewery tap.

WROXHAM TG3017 The main centre for **Broads boat cruising**, with several boat-hire firms – a good place to watch the boating activities from dry land, or to use as the start of a longer cruising holiday. It can be very congested in summer. **Barton House Railway** (Hartwell Rd, Wroxham) Miniature railway through a big riverside garden; open pm 3rd Sun of month in summer, 40p. Boats leave for here from Wroxham Bridge (80p). The Bell has kept more character than many places around, and the more modern Hotel Wroxham has excellent boating views.

★ **Other attractive villages** here, all with decent pubs, include Aldborough TG1834, Binham TF9839, Colkirk TF9126, Harpley TF7825, Mundford TL8093, South Wootton TF6422, Swanton Morley TG0116, Wiveton TG0342 and Worstead TG3025. Decent pubs in attractive coastal areas include the Red Lion at Stiffkey (pronounced 'Stukey') TF9743 and Three Horseshoes at Warham TF9441.

Where to eat

BAWBURGH TG1508 **Kings Head** *Harts Lane (01603) 744977* Bustling old pub with friendly licensees, 4 linked rooms with low beams and standing timbers, a big log fire and a woodburner; generous, attractively presented food (the weekly specials are much liked), a no smoking restaurant, and well kept real ales. **£17.45**|£6.

BLAKENEY TG0243 **White Horse** *4 High St (01263) 740574* Small hotel nr harbour (if that's not too grand a word), with a long cosy bar, a good mix of customers, efficient and friendly service; good, well presented food inc local fish, reasonably priced wines, and an attractive evening restaurant; bdrms. **£20**|£6.

BRISTON TG0632 **John H Stracey** *(01263) 860891* Neatly kept, well run country dining pub with a wide choice of well cooked and fairly priced bar food, popular restaurant, speciality evenings, comfortable seats and log fire, well kept real ales, and friendly licensees; comfortable bdrms; partial disabled access. **£20**|£6.

CAWSTON TG1422 **Grey Gables** *Norwich Rd (01603) 871259* Very good English cooking using fresh local produce in this little Georgian evening restaurant, with a log fire in the comfortable lounge, pleasant service, and a fine wine list; lunch by arrangement; bdrms; cl 24–26 Dec; children over 5. **£21**.

CAWSTON TG1422 **Ratcatchers** *Eastgate (01603) 871430* Popular dining pub with a huge choice of good, freshly prepared food (so there may be a wait) inc fresh fish and home-made bread, chutneys, stocks and herb oils; open fires, real ales, country wines, an L-shaped beamed bar, and a cosy candlelit dining room too; cl 25–26 Dec; disabled access. **£20**|£5.95.

COLKIRK TF9126 **Crown** *(01328) 862172* Unpretentious, friendly village pub with open fires, solid country furniture, pleasantly informal, no smoking dining room; good, promptly served food (nice daily specials inc vegetarian choices), well kept real ales, decent wine list, and a helpful landlord; own bowling green behind. **£16**|£6.25.

DISS TM1279 **Salisbury House** *Victoria Rd (01379) 644738* Victorian country house in pleasant gardens, with fresh flowers and period décor; a good choice of interesting food on the monthly changing menu in the relaxed bistro, a set menu in the more formal restaurant, a decent choice of mainly French wines, and friendly, helpful service; bdrms; cl am Sat, Sun, Mon, 2 wks summer; disabled access. **£29 restaurant, £22 bistro**.

DOCKING TF7637 **Hare Arms** *(01485) 518402* Attractive and individually decorated pub with entertaining bric-à-brac, 2 smallish main bar rooms, a log fire, enjoyable and interesting food, well kept ales, and decent wines. **£17.85**|£7.25.

ERPINGHAM TG1931 **Ark** *The Street (01263) 761535* Lovely individual food inc home-made bread and home-grown vegetables in a simple relaxed cottage with a log fire and courteous service; bdrms; cl Christmas week, Mon, am Tues–Sat, pm Sun; disabled access. **£23.50**.

ERPINGHAM TG1631 **Saracen's Head** *Wolterton (01263) 768909* Comfortably civilised inn with simple, stylish 2-room bar, a nice mix of seats, log fires and fresh flowers; excellent and inventive food inc good-value 2-course Sun supper and 3-course monthly feasts, very well kept real ales, interesting wines, and a charming, old-fashioned gravel stableyard; good bdrms; cl 25 Dec; limited disabled access. **£22**|£4.50.

FAKENHAM TF9129 **Wensum Lodge** *Bridge St (01328) 862100* Brick-built former grain store by the river, with a very roomy, relaxed and civilised bar, 2 beamed dining rooms (one no smoking), interesting food inc sandwiches and filled baked potatoes served all day, real ales, and attentive service; bdrms; disabled access. **£17.50**|£5.75.

HEYDON TG1127 **Earle Arms** *(01263) 587376* 17th-c inn (Norfolk's only fully licensed pub theatre) in lovely village, with 2 individually furnished rooms opening off the small lobby, interesting bric-à-brac, tiny and homely dining room, no smoking, simple conservatory; very good and interesting food (lunchtime dishes all £4.95), well kept real ales, a decent wine list, and a friendly, enthusiastic licensee. **£18.70**|£4.95.

HOLT TG0738 **Owl Tea Rooms** *White Lion St (01263) 713232* Georgian building with a bakery and tearooms behind; home-made bread, scones, quiches and pies served on plates made by the owners, organic local vegetables, daily specials and vegetarian choices, home-made preserves, and good cream teas; cl Sun, bank hols; disabled access. **£10.75**|£3.50.

KING'S LYNN TF6119 **Rococo** *11 Saturday Market Pl (01553) 771483* Delicious, imaginative modern cooking using fresh local produce, in a pretty dining room with lots of fresh flowers and paintings; also a cosy lounge area, relaxed atmosphere, good informal service, and decent wines; cl Sun, am Mon, Christmas–New Year; disabled access. **£33.50 dinner, £19.50 lunch**|£3.

LITTLE WALSINGHAM TF9336 **Old Bakehouse** *33 High St (01328) 820454* In an attractive medieval village, Georgian-fronted house with high beams in the main restaurant, a smaller dining room with a brick oven dating from 1550, and a downstairs bar; sound cooking with plenty of choice, reasonably priced French wines; bdrms; cl Sun, Mon, Tues (but for residents, no food only on Mon), 2 wks Jan/Feb, 1 wk Jun, 1 wk Nov; children by arrangement. **£29**.

NORWICH TG2208 **Adlards** *79 Upper St Giles St (01603) 633522* Warm and friendly, quietly decorated restaurant serving delicious, carefully thought-out food from a menu that changes daily; lovely puddings, fine service, and a good wine list; cl Sun, am Mon, 25–30 Dec. **£39**|£11.

REEDHAM TG4001 **Ferry** *(01493) 700429* Perfectly placed pub beside River Yare, with plenty of tables to watch boats or swans (good moorings), a secluded back bar with a fine log fire, long front bar with big picture windows, a no smoking restaurant, and very popular, good food; disabled access. **£17.65**|£4.10.

SNETTISHAM TF6834 **Rose & Crown** *Old Church St (01485) 541382* Pretty white cottage with a nice traditional layout to the 4 bustling bars; log fires, 5 real ales, 20 wines by the glass, good daily specials as well as the standard menu, afternoon teas, colourful garden, and an adventure playground; disabled access. **£17.50**|£5.

ST OLAVES TM4599 **Priory Farm** *(01493) 488432* Good interesting food inc fresh fish and children's menu; right by St Olave's Priory; open all day Jun–Sept, cl 26 Dec; disabled access. **£20**|£4.95.

STOW BARDOLPH TF6205 **Hare Arms** *(01366) 382229* Good-value, quickly served, interesting lunchtime bar food in a pleasantly refurbished country pub with cheerful licensees; prompt and courteous service even when busy, fresh flowers, a separate, elegant evening restaurant, and a big conservatory for children (not allowed in main bar; must be over 10 in restaurant); cl 25–26 Dec. **£21.75**|£6.75.

SWANTON MORLEY TG0117 **Darbys** *Elsing Rd (01362) 637647* Cosy, beamed country pub decorated with lots of farm tools and so forth; very well kept real ales, good, generously served and often interesting bar food (the beef comes from their own farm), log fire, friendly staff, a children's room and an adventure playground; also bdrms, self-catering, camping, caravan site, horse facilities, country trails; disabled access. **£16.50**|£5.

UPPER SHERINGHAM TG1542 **Red Lion** *(01263) 825408* Relaxing little flint cottage with 2 quiet, small bars, simple furnishings, a big woodburner, and newspapers to read; very good food inc quite a few fish dishes, well kept real ales and over 60 whiskies. **£17.70**|£6.95.

Special thanks to M and J Back, Anne Deane, Ian Phillips.

We welcome reports from readers

This *Guide* depends on readers' reports. Do help us if you can – in return, we offer a discount on the next edition to people who've helped us with reports for it. Tell us what you think about places already in it, and anything extra you think we should say about them. And send us your ideas for inclusion in the next edition: places to visit, eat at or stay in, attractive drives or walks, maybe even unusual interesting shops you know of. Use the card in the middle, the report forms at the end, or just write – no stamp needed: *The Good Guide to Britain*, FREEPOST TN1569, Wadhurst, E Sussex TN5 7BR.

Norfolk Calendar

Some of these dates were provisional as we went to press. Please check information with the telephone numbers provided.

JANUARY

1 **Felbrigg** New Year's Day Walk at Felbrigg Hall (01263) 837444

APRIL

2 **Blickling** Country Skills and Working Crafts Show at Blickling Hall (01263) 734711

MAY

1 **King's Lynn** May Garland: large double hoop of flowers, ribbons and beads, with a doll in the middle, is carried through town accompanied by ox horns (01553) 768930

8 **Blickling** Norfolk Food and Drink Festival at Blickling Park – *till Sun 9* (01625) 575681

13 **Norwich** Festival of Early Music – *till Sun 23* (01603) 766129

15 **Norwich and Norfolk** Artists' Open Studios: exhibitions and over 150 professional artists' studios – *till Sun 30* (01603) 614921; **South Walsham** Candelabra Primulas Weeks at Fairhaven Garden Trust – *till Sun 16* (01603) 270449

22 **Bergh Apton** Sculpture & Literature Trail – *also on Sun 23, Sun 30, Mon 31, 5 and 6 Jun* (01508) 480696

30 **Downham Market** Festival – *till 6 Jun* with carnival *on Mon 31* (01366) 387440

JUNE

6 **Wymondham** Carnival (01263) 579114

11 **Hunstanton** Festival of Arts – *till Sun 27* (01485) 532516

12 **Sandringham** Lilliput Lane Collectors Fair at Sandringham House – *till Sun 13* (01553) 772675

13 **Norwich** LEAP: Festival of Dance – *also on Weds 16–Sat 19* (01603) 614921

19 **Blickling** Open-air Classical Concert at Blickling Hall (01263) 731660

25 **Norwich** Open-air Theatre Festival: over 30 performances in parks and open spaces – *till 24 July* (01603) 666071

26 **Sandringham** Country Show and Horse-driving Trials at Sandringham House – *till Sun 27* (01553) 772675

27 **Caister-on-Sea** Carnival (01493) 846342; **Felbrigg** Agricultural Bygones Day at Felbrigg Hall (01263) 837444; **Hunstanton** Carnival (01485) 532516

30 **Norwich** Royal Norfolk Show – *till 1 July* (01603) 748931

JULY

3 **Martham** Carnival – *till Sun 4* (01493) 846342

8 **Wymondham** Festival of Music, Dance, Drama inc Tudor Fair and re-enactments to commemorate the 450th anniversary of the peasant rebellion – *till Sun 11* (01953) 605469

Norfolk Calendar (cont.)

9 **Norwich** Lord Mayor's Weekend Celebrations: carnival floats, music, fireworks – *till Sun 11* (01603) 666071
10 **Sandringham** Fireworks Concert at Sandringham House (01553) 772675
16 **Wheeting** Steam Rally – *till Sun 18* (01842) 810317
17 **Blickling** Lakeside Jazz and Blues at Blickling Hall – *till Sun 18* (01263) 731660; **Congham** World Snail Racing Championships (01485) 532516; **Hunstanton** Street Organ Festival – *till Sun 18* (01485) 532516; **Norwich** Tudor Fair at the Cathedral (01603) 632224; **Wells-next-the-Sea** Country Fair at Holkham Hall – *till Sun 18* (01263) 711736
22 **King's Lynn** Festival of Music and the Arts – *till Sat 31* (01553) 774725
28 **Sandringham** Flower Show inc arena events at Sandringham House (01553) 772675
30 **Worstead** Festival – *till 1 Aug* (01603) 666071

AUGUST

1 **Caister-on-Sea** Lifeboat Day and Fête (01493) 846342; **Gorleston-on-Sea** Raft Race and Clifftop Gala Event (01493) 846342; **Norwich** Free Music Festival at Waterloo Park: 2 stages, entertainers, dance, children's area (01603) 212137
5 **Hingham** Festival: home of Abraham Lincoln's ancestors celebrates its American links – *till Sun 8* (01953) 850111
7 **Burgh Castle** American Cars and Harley Davidson Show – *till Sun 8* (01493) 846342
8 **Hemsby** Lifeboat Day (01493) 846342
15 **Great Yarmouth** Carnival (01493) 846342
18 **Cromer** Carnival (01263) 512497
20 **Blickling** Fireworks Concert at Blickling Hall – *till Sat 21* (01263) 731660
28 **Filby** Fun Weekend – *till Mon 30* (01493) 369308
30 **Blickling** Aylsham Agricultural Show at Blickling Hall (01263) 732432

SEPTEMBER

5 **Hemsby** Herring Festival: helicopter rides, morris men at Hemsby Beach (01493) 731606

OCTOBER

1 **Norfolk and Norwich** Festival – *till Sun 17* (01603) 662661
16 **South Walsham** Autumn Colours at Fairhaven Garden Trust – *till Sun 31* (01603) 270449
25 **Norwich** CAMRA Beer Festival at St Andrew's Hall and Blackfriars Hall – *till Sat 30* (01603) 666071
31 **Blickling** Halloween Tours at Blickling Hall (01263) 734711

NOVEMBER

13 **Norwich and Norfolk** East Coast Jazz Festival – *till Sat 27* (01603) 660352
29 **Norwich** *Swan Lake*: performed by all-male dance company at the Theatre Royal – *till 4 Dec* (01603) 630000

NORTHAMPTONSHIRE

Little-known charming countryside with fine houses and grounds; not so much family interest.

Althorp is now known to all the world as the childhood home and final resting place of Diana, Princess of Wales: it's one of an unrivalled concentration of great houses in grand surroundings in this archetypal Shire – Rockingham Castle, Canons Ashby, Deene Park, Cottesbrooke Hall and Boughton House, with more lovely grounds to wander through at Castle Ashby, Holdenby House and Coton Manor. These give a touch of grandeur and distinction to a quiet and civilised break here. The scenery is relaxing – gently appealing, partly wooded landscapes, villages built of red or honey-coloured stone, the fine churches of the Nene Valley.

Wicksteed Park on the edge of Kettering is a good treat for children, and Sulgrave Manor's living history events are most enjoyable for people of any age. Other places with wide appeal are the canal museum at Stoke Bruerne, and on sunny summer days the dragonfly centre near Oundle.

Where to stay

ASHBY ST LEDGERS SP5768 **Olde Coach House** *Ashby St Ledgers, Rugby CV23 8UN (01788) 890349* ***£70,** plus special breaks; 6 rms. In an attractive thatched stone village, this busy old inn has rambling atmospheric rooms, a winter log fire, and fine food in both the bar and partly no smoking dining room; also well kept beer, smiling service, and big gardens with a good play area; cl 25 Dec.

BADBY SP5559 **Windmill** *Badby, Daventry NN11 3AN (01327) 702363* **£59,** plus special breaks; 8 rms. Traditional, carefully modernised thatched stone inn with beams, flagstones and a huge inglenook fireplace in the front bar, cosy comfortable lounge, good and generously served bar and restaurant food, and decent wines; fine views of the pretty village from the car park.

CASTLE ASHBY SP8659 **Falcon** *Castle Ashby, Northampton NN7 1LF (01604) 696200* **£92.50;** 17 nicely decorated rms. Smart hotel in attractive, preserved village, with stone walls and hops on the dark beams in the 16th-c cellar bar, an open fire, and real ales; restaurant overlooking the pretty garden, good breakfasts, and a welcoming landlord; children over 10 in evening restaurant; disabled access.

EAST HADDON SP6668 **Red Lion** *East Haddon, Northampton NN6 8BU (01604) 770223* ***£80;** 5 rms. Welcoming and popular golden stone inn with pretty gardens, a neat, white-panelled lounge, small public bar, pretty restaurant, high quality, daily-changing food, and nice breakfasts; disabled access.

OLD SP7873 **Wold Farm** *Old, Northampton NN6 9RJ (01604) 781258* **£50;** 5 rms, 4 with own bthrm. No smoking 18th-c house at the heart of a beef and arable farm; with spacious and interesting rooms, hearty breakfasts in the beamed dining room, and attentive, welcoming owners; also a log fire, snooker table, and 2 pretty gardens.

OUNDLE TL0488 **Talbot** *New St, Oundle, Peterborough PE8 4EA (01832) 273621* **£104,** plus special breaks; 39 most attractive big rms. Mary Queen of Scots walked to her execution down one of the staircases now in this carefully refurbished 17th-c hotel; attractive and cosy lounges, big log fires, good food in the timbered restaurant, and a garden.

PAULERSPURY SP7245 **Vine House** *100 High St, Paulerspury, Towcester NN12 7NA (01327) 811267* ***£66;** 6 individually decorated rms. 300-year-old building with carefully preserved original features, and a relaxed, welcoming atmosphere; cosy bar with an open fire, and very good modern English cooking (inc home-made bread and petits fours) in the attractive restaurant; pretty cottage garden; cl 24 Dec–3 Jan.

SUDBOROUGH SP9682 **Vane Arms** *High St, Sudborough, Kettering NN14 3BX (01832) 733223* **£45;** 3 rms. Cheerful, relaxed thatched pub on a picturesque village street; with a comfortable main bar, inglenook fireplaces, friendly and helpful staff, a no smoking upstairs restaurant, and a marvellous range of real ales.

To see and do

Northamptonshire Family Attraction of the Year

☺ **Wicksteed Park** SP8777 (S edge of Kettering) All the more welcome in an area looking after adults rather better than it does children, this big amusement park was one of the first of its type, set up in 1921 when they introduced boating facilities on the lake. Some older features still remain (an antique roundabout, for example), though in the last few years they've been joined by more modern attractions, inc a monorail, roller-coaster, and films in the Cine 2000 dome. It's still relatively low-key compared to other leisure parks – thrill rides here are mainly of the dodgems, ferris wheel and pirate ship school – but for many visitors that's precisely the appeal, and there's enough to keep children up to around 12 amused for quite some time. You can still row on the lake, and the grounds are very pleasant for a stroll or a picnic, with a pitch and putt course, various well laid out gardens, an aviary, paddling pools, and free play areas for younger children. Dogs are welcome on a lead. Their home-made ice-creams are very tasty. Meals, snacks, shop, disabled access; open daily Easter–early Sept, then wknds and school hols in Oct; (01536) 512475; £4 parking charge (less wkdys out of high season, or after 3pm), then you buy vouchers for the rides (not all of which have to be used on the same day), or a wristband with 1 day's unlimited rides for £10.50 children, £6 adults.

† ★ **ALTHORP** SP6864 The home of the Spencer family since 1508, remodelled several times, especially in the 17th and 18th c, and now best known as the resting place of Diana, Princess of Wales. You can't see the grave itself, on an islet in the Oval Lake, in a small arboretum just NE of the house, but you can view the lake, and Earl Spencer has spent £3 million converting the stable block into a museum/memorial to his sister, filled with her personal possessions, favourite clothes, video footage of her life and some of the thousands of books of condolences sent to Kensington Palace on her death. It's been done with great restraint and dignity. The house itself has a splendid collection of furnishings and porcelain, and paintings by Rubens, Van Dyck and Lely. Snacks, shop, some disabled access; open pm daily July and Aug but only by advance booking; (01604) 7702097 or (01604) 592020; £9.50. The attractive **church** is on the edge of the park; fine views from the churchyard. The village, Great Brington, is charming, and the Fox & Hounds has good food and lots of character. On the far side of the estate there's public access to wildlife-filled pine woods and heathland known as Harlestone Firs, pleasant for walking.

BOROUGH HILL SP5962 The best views in the region, from above the golf course; an Iron Age hill fort shares the top with a formidable array of television and telecommunications masts, but on a clear day the views are tremendous.

† **BRIXWORTH CHURCH** SP7471 Particularly fine Anglo-Saxon church, one of England's oldest – mostly 7th c with much re-used Roman material. The George has cheap food.

† **BRIGSTOCK** SP9485 The **church** has a Saxon tower, and a bell that used to be rung three times a day to

help anyone lost in the woods; the Green Dragon is useful for food. **Brigstock Country Park** Good for a wander, especially around wildlife-filled Fermyn Woods on the edge; it can be a little muddy. **Lyveden New Bield** (off Lyveden Rd, some miles E; SP9885) Started in 1595 but abandoned unfinished after the owner Sir Thomas Tresham's son died in the tower. Intriguing and unusual, it was intended to celebrate the Passion of Christ, and is shaped like a Greek cross; the Elizabethan watergardens are open some Suns in July; (01832) 205358; £1.70; NT. It's a half-mile walk from the car park.

CANONS ASHBY SP5750 (B4525) Exceptional little manor house, more northern-looking than Midlands, beautifully restored with Elizabethan wall paintings and glorious Jacobean plasterwork. The formal gardens have also been carefully restored over the last 20 years to reflect the layout of the early 18th c. A reasonably sized park has a hilltop 12th–14th-c priory church. Brewhouse café, shop, disabled access; open pm Sat–Weds and bank hols Apr–Oct; (01327) 860044; £3.60; NT – it's one of their busier properties. The Olde House at Home, at Moreton Pinkney, is handy for lunch.

CASTLE ASHBY HOUSE SP8659 Only the gardens can be visited, but the Elizabethan house is well worth seeing from outside – splendidly palatial, at the end of a magnificent mile-long avenue nearly 300 years old. The gardens include grand Victorian terraces, sweeping lawns, Italianate gardens with an orangery, and lakeside parkland that may well be the prolific Capability Brown's most enduring achievement. Disabled access; cl 25 Dec; (01604) 696696; £2.50. The **church** in the park is very attractive; there's a public path to it. Restored farm buildings nearby house a **Craft Centre and Rural Shopping Yard** (cl Mon). The Falcon in the handsomely preserved estate village has good food (and attractive bedrooms), and the drive through Cogenhoe, Whiston, Grendon and Easton Maudit is pleasant.

CHAPEL BRAMPTON SP7366 **Northampton & Lamport Railway** (Pitsford Rd) Enthusiastic little railway, with short Sun train rides (01604) 820327; £2.60. Its name is a proud commitment to growth northwards, but for now the 14-mile walk and cycle way through pretty countryside by the line is a very pleasant foretaste. The Brampton Halt here has decent food.

COTON MANOR SP6771 (Guilsborough, off the A428) Attractive views from charming gardens around 17th-c stonebuilt manor house (not open); interesting plantings, and watergardens with flamingos, cranes and ornamental waterfowl wandering freely. The neighbouring woods are lovely at bluebell time. Good meals and snacks, plant sales, disabled access; open pm Weds–Sun Easter–Sept; (01604) 740219; £3.50. Besides the Grooms Cottage here, the Red Lion at East Haddon is good for lunch.

COTTESBROOKE HALL SP7174 Very attractive Queen Anne house, reputedly the model for Jane Austen's *Mansfield Park*, with a renowned collection of mainly sporting and equestrian paintings. The lovely garden has formal borders, venerable cedars, greenhouses, an extensive wild garden, and a separate cottage garden. Teas, unusual plant sales, disabled access to gardens only; open pm Thurs and bank hols Easter–Sept, plus pm wknds in Sept, garden also open pm Tues, Weds and Fri Easter–Sept; (01604) 505808; *£4, garden only *£2.50.

CROUGHTON CHURCH SP5433 Handsome church with unusual murals, dating from 14th/15th c.

DEENE PARK SP9592 (off the A43) Lord Cardigan who led the Charge of the Light Brigade lived in this beautifully kept partly Tudor house; there's a high-spirited contemporary portrait of him in full-attack gallop. Extensive parklands with woodside and lakeside walks, and gardens reflecting continuing interest by the owners over the generations. Cream teas, shop, some disabled access; open pm Sun Jun–Aug, plus Sun and Mon of bank hol wknds Easter–Aug; (01780) 450223; £4.50. The Queen's Head opposite the church in the pretty village of Bulwick has good-value food. **Kirby Hall** (W of

Northamptonshire
LEICESTERSHIRE
WARWICKSHIRE
BUCKINGHAMSHIRE
OXFORDSHIRE
Rockingham
Corby
Geddington
Rushton
Rothwell
Harrington
Welford
Kettering
Naseby
Guilsborough
Cottesbrooke Hall
Lamport
Coton
Old
Little Harrowden
Kilsby
Brixworth
Pitsford Water
East Haddon
Holdenby
Ashby St Ledgers
Great Brington
Chapel Brampton
Sywell
Mears Ashby
Althorp
Harlestone
Earls Barton
Knightley Way
Northampton
Ecton
Whiston
Borough Hill
Dodford
Grendon
Badby
Grand Union Canal
Great Houghton
Castle Ashby
Hellidon
Upper Stowe
Everdon
Bugbrooke
Denton
Farthingstone
Gayton
Horton
Yardley Hastings
Preston Capes
Litchborough
Roade
Salcey Forest
Canons Ashby
Towcester
SP
Stoke Bruerne
Paulerspury
Grafton Regis
Sulgrave
Thorpe Mandeville
Middleton Cheney
Passenham
Evenley
King's Sutton
Croughton
M1
M45
A5
A6
A14
A43
A45
A361
A422
A427
A428
A508
A509
A5199
A6003
15
15A
16
17
18
19

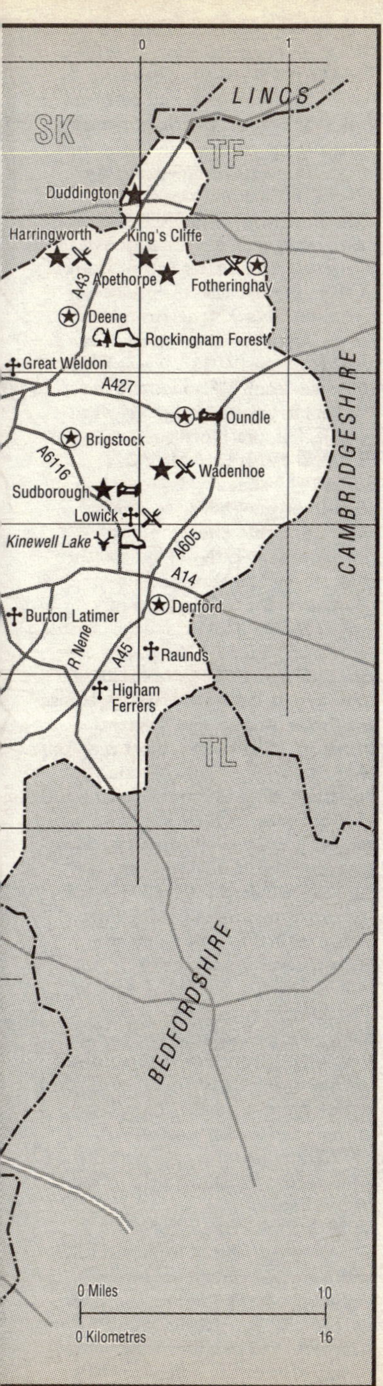

Deene) Splendid Elizabethan ruin with a bizarre mixture of styles; from some angles it still looks intact – even close up. The 17th-c gardens are being restored, and it's a tranquil spot for a picnic. Shop, disabled access; cl wkdys Nov–Mar; (01536) 203230; £2.50 (inc Walkman tour).

✝ **DENFORD CHURCH**
SP9976 Attractive in any event (like so many other churches along this river valley); doubly worth a visit for its nature-reserve churchyard by the River Nene, with waterside walks from here.

★ ✝ **FOTHERINGHAY** TL0793
Lovely village with interesting historical displays in the charming if slightly out-of-proportion 14th-c **church** across a watermeadow from the River Nene. It was part of a small pre-Reformation college and doubles as a memorial to the House of York, with some interesting heraldry. There's only a fragment left of the **castle** where Mary Queen of Scots was imprisoned, beside the castle mound. The Falcon is excellent for lunch.

★ ✝ **GEDDINGTON**
SP8982 The very well preserved elaborate 13th-c cross was erected by Edward I where Queen Eleanor's funeral cortège rested on its way to Westminster. The photogenic packhorse bridge is even older, and there's a 12th-c church. **Boughton House** (off Grafton Rd, SE) Impressively grand old place often compared to Versailles (some of its treasures were in fact made for there). Richly furnished and decorated, with gorgeous mythical scenes painted on the ceilings, and works by El Greco, Murillo and Caracci lining the walls. Excellent armoury, beautiful parklands, and adventure playground and garden shop. Snacks, shop, disabled access; grounds open pm May–mid-Sept (exc Fri), house pm Aug only; (01536) 515731; £4, grounds only £1.50.

GRAND UNION CANAL The towpath is popular for country walks, with access among other places from the Royal Oak at Blisworth SP7253, Admiral Nelson (Dark Lane) at Braunston SP5466, New Inn at Buckby Wharf SP6065, Navigation Inn at Thrupp Wharf nr Cosgrove SP7843, and Wharf Inn in Welford SP6481.

★ **HARRINGWORTH** SP9197 This attractive village is famous for its 82-arch **railway viaduct**.

HOLDENBY HOUSE GARDENS SP6967 In Elizabethan times this was one of the biggest houses in the country, and the extensive grounds have been restored in the original style. Also reconstructed 17th-c farmstead, play area and children's farm. *The Woman in White* was filmed here recently. Snacks, shop, disabled access; Open pm daily exc Sat Apr–Sept; (01604) 770074; £2.75. An adjacent falconry centre is open the same times. The house itself (with its unique piano collection) is open only Easter, spring and Aug bank hol Mons; £4.

KETTERING SP8777 See *separate Family Panel on p.456* for **Wicksteed Park**; the Red Lion at Cranford St John just E of here has good-value food. **Manor House Museum** (Sheep St) and the adjacent **Alfred East Gallery** are worth a look if passing; the former has free children's activities in school hols (and a famous mummified cat). Both cl Sun and bank hols; free.

KINEWELL LAKE SP9979 Well managed local **nature reserve** around former gravel-pit lakes by the River Nene; pleasant walks.

KNIGHTLEY WAY SP5559 Pleasant 12-mile walk from the attractive village of Badby, through an area where gorgeous orange-coloured stone adds to the charm of buildings; it's well waymarked to Greens Norton. The finest part is between Badby Wood and Fawsley Park, where the path drops to Capability Brown's landscaped lakes by the hall and attractive estate church. In May, the Badby Wood bluebells are lovely.

LAMPORT HALL SP7574 (on the A14) Mainly 17th- and 18th-c house in spacious park, with tranquil gardens containing a remarkable alpine rockery – the home of the first garden gnomes, only one of which now survives. Frequent antique fairs, concerts and other events. Snacks, shop, disabled access to ground floor only; open pm Sun and bank hols Easter–Oct, plus in Aug guided tours daily at 3.30pm (exc Sun); (01604) 686272; £3.80. The Swan, with great views, has good-value food.

! NASEBY SP6877 The owner of Purlieu Farm has made a model of the Civil War's crucial **Battle of Naseby**, using many hundreds of model soldiers, with a 10-minute commentary; open pm bank hol Sun and Mon and by appointment, (01604) 740241; £1. The nearby Fitzgerald Arms is a good-value dining pub. One **battle monument** (Sibbertoft Rd) marks the position of Cromwell's New Model Army before his devastating counter-attack; there's another on the B4036 towards Clipston (this road from W Haddon and on to Market Harborough in Leics gives a good feel of rural Northants).

NORTHAMPTON SP7560 This shoe-making town has some interesting buildings. Among several fine **churches**, the most notable are the 12th-c Holy Sepulchre (one of only 4 remaining round churches in the country), the very grand central All Saints, and the ornate Norman St Peter's in Marefair by the dual carriageway. The Welsh House (now a china shop) and Hazelrigg House are also very handsome. **Central Museum** (Guildhall Rd, Northampton) Home to a remarkable collection of boots and shoes, inc an elephant's boot, Margot Fonteyn's ballet shoes, Roman sandals, and Queen Victoria's wedding slippers. Shop, disabled access; cl am Sun, 25–26 Dec; (01604) 639415; free. A social history museum in Abington Park is set in the 15th-c home of Shakespeare's granddaughter; cl am, Mon exc bank hols, 25–26 Dec; free. The county's Enterprise Agency runs many good guided factory visits, most free, ranging from big shoe companies and places like Carlsberg or Barclaycard to helicopter-makers, narrow-boat builders and blacksmiths; tel (01604) 671200 and ask for their 'Tours of the Unexpected' brochure; all tours must be pre-booked.

★ **! OUNDLE** TL0488 Charming and elegant stonebuilt town with a graceful church and several antique shops. The ancient Ship does decent food. **Barnwell Country Park** (just S) A good spot for a walk, with a variety of birds; the waterside Mill is a pleasant place for lunch. **National Dragonfly Museum** (just SE – coming from town take a right at the A605 roundabout) At pretty Ashton Mill, this unique place has dramatic feeding sessions, several different habitats, and a TV microscope link to the larvae under the water. Fully grown dragonflies put on their best shows on sunny days, though it's a rewarding place in any weather. Teas, shop, disabled access; open wknds and bank hols 13 Jun–27 Sept; (01832) 272427; £2.80. Ashton itself is attractive.

PITSFORD WATER SP7669 Praised for birdwatching, especially in winter when wildfowl flock to the northern part of the lake; the southern part is popular for fishing. The White Swan at Holcot has decent food.

ROCKINGHAM CASTLE SP8691 (A6003) Lovely old house still tucked away behind the curtain wall of the original Norman fortress – effective enough to resist repeated assaults in the Civil War. The site of the keep is now a rose garden, but the outline of the 2 baileys and the drum towers survive, and the later Elizabethan house has a good range of furnishings and art. Meals, snacks, shop, limited disabled access; open pm Sun, Thurs, and bank hols Easter–Sept, also Tues in Aug or after bank hols; (01536) 770240; *£4.20, garden only £2.70.

ROCKINGHAM FOREST SP9892 Pleasant back roads through the former Forest of Rockingham give quiet views of a particularly attractive part of the county. This part is good for walks, too, with enough country houses scattered around it to spice interest, and grey-stone cottages are a local feature; on its NW edge the Exeter Arms at Wakerley, a former hunting lodge, gives access to both Wakerley Woods (nice for a picnic) and the Welland Valley.

! **RUSHTON** SP8283 **Triangular Lodge** (1m W) Late 16th-c oddity designed by same man as Lyveden New Bield, nr Brigstock: 3 walls, 3 windows and 3 gables on 3 levels, and a 3-sided chimney, to represent the Holy Trinity; cl Nov–Mar; (01536) 710761; £1.30. The Thornhill Arms in the pretty village does decent food. **East Carlton Country Park** a few miles NE (SP8389) is a pleasant spot for strolls, with a few **craft workshops** nr the entrance.

SALCEY FOREST SP8051 A couple of miles of ancient forest, largely oak, now managed for nature conservation, with well marked trails inc one good for wheelchairs.

STOKE BRUERNE SP7449 **Canal Museum** Close to a flight of locks on the Grand Union Canal, with fine old canal buildings (inc a popular pub, the Boat), and lots happening on the water, this is a handsome former corn warehouse housing a good collection of canal memorabilia, inc a reconstructed traditional narrow boat complete with immaculately packed-in colourful furniture and crockery. Also boat trips through nearby tunnel. Shop, limited disabled access; cl winter Mon, 25–26 Dec; (01604) 862229; £2.90. Good towpath walks from here.

Days Out

Grand Union heritage: Walk the towpath and/or take a canal boat trip from Stoke Bruerne; canal museum, and lunch at the Boat Inn there; Canons Ashby; walk Knightley Way from Everdon, through Badby Wood and to Fawsley Park.

Gardens after lunch: Lunch at Grooms Cottage, Guilsborough; Coton Manor gardens; then (depending on day) choice of Cottesbrooke Hall gardens, Lamport Hall gardens, Holdenby House gardens or (half-hour drive) Boughton House gardens.

Around the Nene: Stroll in Barnwell Country Park; Oundle (and National Dragonfly Museum if open); lunch at the Mill, Oundle, or at the Falcon, Fotheringhay; Fotheringhay; Elton Hall (*see* **Cambridgeshire** *chapter*).

SULGRAVE MANOR SP5545 (off the B4525) The ancestral home of George Washington's family, this modest manor has exceptionally good special events, when the whole place returns to how it would have been during a particular period. People in period costume go about their daily business, and children can take part in a wide range of activities from wassailing or helping in the kitchen at Christmas, to joining in the harvest during the Apple Day Festival. Still worth a visit on non-event days, several relics of Washington (he never lived here – it was his great-great-grandfather who emigrated to America), as well as elegant rooms and well kept gardens. Meals, snacks, shop, disabled access; open wknds Mar–Dec, and pm wkdys (exc Weds) Apr–Oct, may be cl 1–2pm; (01295) 760205; £3.75. Just down the road, the Star is enjoyable for lunch.

SYWELL COUNTRY PARK SP8365 (off the A4500 towards Mears Ashby) Woodland and lakeside walks, play areas, and a little wildlife display; you can fish on the reservoir.

TOWCESTER SP6948 This small town (pronounced 'toaster'), despite some light industry on the edge, has a pleasantly villagey feel, with attractive Georgian and Victorian buildings.

UPPER STOWE SP6456 **Old Dairy Farm Craft Centre** Sheep, pigs, peacocks, ducks and donkeys, as well as craft workshops, antiques, classic clothes, farm shop and wool collection. Well organised, and decent views – though it can be muddy. Restaurant, snacks, shop, disabled access; cl 2 wks from 25 Dec; (01327) 340525; free, exc special wknds.

The Globe at Weedon is good for lunch.

✝ The county is notable for its lovely stonebuilt **churches**, many with elegant spires visible a long way off and a memorable feature of the county's landscape – particularly along the valley of the River Nene. Besides those mentioned above we'd suggest Ashby St Ledgers SP5768, Burton Latimer SP9075, Dodford SP6160 (striking memorials), Earls Barton SP8563 (fine Saxon tower), Easton Maudit SP8858, Great Weldon SP9289, Higham Ferrers SP9669, King's Sutton SP4936, Lowick SP9780, Middleton Cheney SP4941, Passenham SP7739 (17th-c murals), Raunds SP9972, Rothwell SP8181 and Whiston SP8460. With many of these, the village is well worth seeing, too.

★ **Other attractive villages**, all with decent pubs, include Apethorpe TL0295, Badby SP5658, canalside Bugbrooke SP6757, Denton SP8358, Duddington SK9800, Ecton SP8263, Evenley SP5834, Farthingstone SP6155 (Knightley Way walks), Gayton SP7054, thatched Grafton Regis SP7546, Great Houghton SP7958, Grendon SP8760, Harlestone SP7064, Harrington SP7779, Hellidon SP5158 (pleasant walks nearby), Kilsby SP5671, Litchborough SP6353, Little Harrowden SP8771, Mears Ashby SP8466 (narrow lanes of thatched cottages), Sudborough SP9682, Thorpe Mandeville SP5344, riverside Wadenhoe TL0383, Welford SP6480 and Yardley Hastings SP8656. We'd also recommend rather Cotswoldy King's Cliffe TL0097, and 2 lovely, mellow, orange ironstone villages, Preston Capes SP5754 and Everdon SP5957.

Where to eat

FARTHINGSTONE SP6155 **Kings Arms** *(01327) 361604* In a pretty village, this handsome 18th-c stone building has homely comfortable sofas and armchairs, a huge log fire in the small atmospheric bar, lots of decorative plates and pictures, a spacious dining area, a wide choice of good, imaginative food, well kept real ales, decent wines and friendly licensees; decent nearby walks; cl Mon, am Tues. **£17.15**|£6.95.

FOTHERINGHAY TL0593 **Falcon** *(01832) 226254* Stylish but relaxed old country pub with a good mix of customers, comfortable lounge with fresh flowers and fireplaces each end, no smoking conservatory and dining room, and little tap bar for locals; excellent food from a varied and interesting menu, well kept real ales, and a fine wine list; neat garden. **£19**|£7.

GREAT BRINGTON SP6664 **Fox & Hounds** *(01604) 770651* Golden stone, thatched village inn with lots of old beams, big flagstones and bare boards, an attractive mix of country tables and chairs, 2 fine log fires, and lots of bric-à-brac; a good range of real ales, country wines, a sensibly short choice of good, freshly cooked food (especially the game), and sheltered tables in the paved courtyard and side garden. **£20**|£7.

GUILSBOROUGH SP6771 **Grooms Cottage** *Coton (01604) 740219* Attractively converted stable block, serving good English food in the lovely gardens (open to the public) of Coton Manor (not open); open Easter–Oct for light lunches Weds–Sat, and from Sept–Easter, evening meals Fri, Sat, and for Sun lunch; disabled access. **£14.75**|£5.

HARRINGWORTH SP9197 **White Swan** *Seaton Rd (01572) 747543* Neatly kept, stonebuilt Tudor pub, with generous helpings of enjoyable food; comfortable lounge/dining area, a quieter dining room, and friendly staff; bdrms. **£18**|£4.50.

HORTON SP8154 **French Partridge** *Newport Pagnell Rd (01604) 870033* Lovely little evening restaurant run by the Partridges for over 30 years; consistently excellent food (marvellous puddings), a relaxed atmosphere, and fine wines; cl Sun, Mon, 2 wks Christmas, 2 wks Easter, 3 wks summer; well behaved children only; disabled access. **£35 for 4 courses.**

LOWICK SP9780 **Snooty Fox** *(01832) 733434* Imposing 17th-c inn with a roaring log fire, dark oak beams and neat, attractive dining chairs around well spaced tables in the atmospheric 2-roomed lounge; very good food from a changing blackboard menu, well kept real ales, and plenty of picnic-sets on the grass. **£17.90**|£6.95.

ROADE SP7551 **Roadhouse** *16 High St (01604) 863372* Attractive, popular restaurant with long-standing owners; comfortable surroundings, courteous service, reliably good and enjoyable food, and reasonably priced wines; new bdrms; cl pm Sun, am Mon, Sat; disabled access. **£30**|3-course lunch £15.

SULGRAVE SP5545 **Star** *Manor Rd (01295) 760389* Hospitable, small, creeper-covered pub with good seasonal food, friendly staff, lots to look at, well kept real ales, and a no smoking restaurant; bdrms; no children. **£22.50**|£6.95.

WADENHOE TL0183 **Kings Head** *Church St (01832) 720024* In an attractive village of thatched stone houses, this welcoming pub has seats among willows by the River Nene, a bar with woodburner and pale pine furniture, and a little beamed dining room; particularly good, imaginative evening and winter lunchtime food (summer lunchtime is limited to soup and sandwiches or ploughman's), well kept real ales, an extensive wine list, pleasant service, and magazines to read. **£18.50**|£7.

Special thanks to M and J Back, Norma and Keith Bloomfield.

We welcome reports from readers

This *Guide* depends on readers' reports. Do help us if you can – in return, we offer a discount on the next edition to people who've helped us with reports for it. Tell us what you think about places already in it, and anything extra you think we should say about them. And send us your ideas for inclusion in the next edition: places to visit, eat at or stay in, attractive drives or walks, maybe even unusual interesting shops you know of. Use the card in the middle, the report forms at the end, or just write – no stamp needed: *The Good Guide to Britain*, FREEPOST TN1569, Wadhurst, E Sussex TN5 7BR.

Northamptonshire Calendar

Some of these dates were provisional as we went to press. Please check information with the telephone numbers provided.

FEBRUARY

6 **Sulgrave** Chamber Music Concert in the Grand Hall at Sulgrave Manor (01295) 760205

MARCH

6 **Sulgrave** Chamber Music Concert in the Grand Hall at Sulgrave Manor (01295) 760205

13 **Hunsbury Hill** Northamptonshire Model Railway Exhibition at Abbey Centre (01604) 580844

14 **Sulgrave** Gardeners' Day: demonstrations, exhibitions at Sulgrave Manor (01295) 760205

APRIL

2 **Sulgrave** Festival of Easter Customs and Traditions at Sulgrave Manor – *till Mon 5* (01295) 760205

4 **East Carlton** Fun Day at East Carlton Countryside Park (01536) 402551; **Elton** Garden Show at Elton Hall – *till Mon 5* (01832) 280468; **Lamport** Antiques Fair at Lamport Hall – *till Mon 5* (01604) 686272

10 **Sulgrave** Chamber Music Concert in the Grand Hall at Sulgrave Manor (01295) 760205

MAY

1 **Daventry** Arts Festival – *till Mon 31* (01327) 302486; **Sulgrave** American Civil War Re-enactment at Sulgrave Manor – *till Mon 3* (01295) 760205

2 **Lamport** Craft Fair at Lamport Hall – *till Mon 3* (01604) 686272; **Oundle** Open Day at Short Wood Wildlife Trust Reserve: bluebells and guided walks, entrance by Southwick water tower, 2m N of Oundle – *till Mon 3* (01832) 226243

9 **Daventry** Country Day: demonstations of country crafts at Daventry Country Park (01327) 871100

15 **Wellingborough** 21st Waendel Walk: international walking, swimming and cycling event – *till Sun 16* (01933) 229777

29 **Braunston** Boat Show: historic boats, parade and fireworks – *till Mon 31* (01788) 890666; **Rothwell** Street Fair – *till 5 Jun* (01536) 710897; **Sulgrave** The American Frontier: see the America that confronted Colonel John Washington when he emigrated in 1656, at Sulgrave Manor – *till Mon 31* (01295) 760205

30 **East Carlton Fête** at East Carlton Countryside Park – *till Mon 31* (01536) 402551; **Lamport** Country Festival at Lamport Hall: field events, steam engines, vintage cars – *till Mon 31* (01604) 686272; **Rockingham** Antiques Fair at the Castle – *till Mon 31* (01536) 770240

Northamptonshire Calendar (cont.)

JUNE

3 **Northampton** Nunn Such Island Beer Festival at Beckets Park: over 60 real ales, live entertainment – *till Sat 5* (01604) 702374
4 **Northampton** National Street Rod Association at Billing Aquadrome – *till Sun 6* (01727) 824259
5 **Cottesbrooke** Rolls Royce Enthusiasts Club Rally at Cottesbrooke Hall – *till Sun 6* (01604) 505808
12 **Northampton** Arts and Music Festival – *till Sun 20* (01604) 238791; **Sulgrave** Tudor Living History at Sulgrave Manor – *till Sun 20* (01295) 760205
13 **Lamport** Doll Fair at Lamport Hall (01604) 686272
18 **Northampton** American Auto Club: thousands of American cars, bands and side shows at Billing Aquadrome – *till Sun 20* (01948) 830754
19 **Corby** Carnival (01536) 402551; **Flore** Flower Festival: about 7 open gardens, over 60 flower displays in the church – *till Sun 20* (01327) 341264; **Rockingham** Craft Fair at the Castle – *till Sun 20* (01536) 770240; **Rushton** Tresham Trail Guided Walk: a strange collection of buildings, some incomplete, erected by the architect and landowner Sir Thomas Tresham, from Triangular Lodge – *till Sun 20* (01604) 730325
20 **Cottesbrooke** Open Garden Day at Cottesbrooke Hall (01604) 505808

JULY

3 **Hollowell** Steam and Heavy Horse Show – *till Sun 4* (01604) 505422; **Sulgrave** American War of Independence: meet George Washington and soldiers of the period at Sulgrave Manor – *till Sun 4* (01295) 760205
4 **Castle Ashby** Country Fair: over 100 stands, ring events (01604) 696521
10 **Corby** Highland Gathering at West Glebe Park: UK's longest running games (01536) 402551 ext 8006
11 **Silverstone** British Grand Prix (01327) 857271
16 **Northampton** Land Rover off-road at Billing Aquadrome: arena events, largest off-road course in Britain – *till Sun 18* (01379) 890056; also Town Show – *till Sun 18* (01604) 238791; **Oundle** International Festival of Music – *till Sun 25* (01832) 272026
17 **Rockingham** Open-air Theatre: *Twelfth Night* at the Castle (01536) 770240; **Rushton** Tresham Trail Guided Walk – *till Sun 18*, see *19 Jun* for details
25 **Lutterworth** Vintage Motorcycle Club Rally at Stanford Hall (0116) 2884619
31 **Sulgrave** Festival of Needlework at Sulgrave Manor – *till 8 Aug* (01295) 760205

AUGUST

7 **Blakesley** Agricultural Show at Seawell Grounds (01327) 359821; **East Carlton** Transport Gala at East Carlton Countryside Park – *till Sun 8* (01536) 402551

Northamptonshire Calendar (cont.)

13 **Sulgrave** *The Rivals*: outdoor theatre at Sulgrave Manor – *till Sun 15* (01295) 760205
20 **Northampton** Hot-air Balloon Festival – *till Sun 22* (01604) 238791
21 **Rushton** Tresham Trail Guided Walk – *till Sun 22*, see *19 Jun* for details
28 **Sulgrave** Seven Years War: living history at Sulgrave Manor – *till 3 Aug* (01295) 760205
29 **Lamport** Antiques Fair at Lamport Hall – *till Mon 30* (01604) 686272; **Northampton** Dog Agility Stakes at Billing Aquadrome (01788) 817267

SEPTEMBER

11 **Lamport** Craft Fair at Lamport Hall – *till Sun 12* (01604) 686272; **Nassington** Living History at Prebendal Manor House – *till Sun 12* (01780) 782575; **Northampton** Heritage Open Days: free classic bus tour and admission to several venues (01604) 238775
18 **Sulgrave** Harvest Home: traditional harvest festival inc morris dancers and mummers at Sulgrave Manor – *till Sun 19* (01295) 760205
22 **Northampton** Festival of Music at the Church of the Holy Sepulchre – *till Sun 26* (01604) 231800

OCTOBER

2 **Sulgrave** Tudor Living History at Sulgrave Manor – *till Sun 10* (01295) 760205; also Chamber Music Concert in the Grand Hall
3 **Lamport** Doll Fair at Lamport Hall (01604) 686272
10 **Oundle** World Conker Championships (01832) 272735
16 **Rockingham** Craft Fair at the Castle – *till Sun 17* (01536) 770240
23 **Lamport** Craft Fair at Lamport Hall – *till Sun 24* (01604) 686272; **Sulgrave** Apple Day Festival at Sulgrave Manor – *till Sun 24* (01295) 760205

NOVEMBER

5 **Corby** Fireworks and torchlight procession (01536) 402551
6 **Sulgrave** Chamber Music Concert in the Grand Hall at Sulgrave Manor (01295) 760205
14 **Sulgrave** Embroidery Day: displays based on the Elizabethan embroideries project at Sulgrave Manor (01295) 760205

DECEMBER

4 **Sulgrave** Traditional Christmas Customs at Sulgrave Manor – *till Sun 5, also Sat 11–Sun 12, Sat 18–Sun 19 and Mon 27–Fri 31* (01295) 760205; also Chamber Music Concert in the Grand Hall
26 **Moulton** Mummers Play and Morris Dancing on Stocks Hill (01604) 646818

Northumbria

Grand unspoilt scenery, some outstanding places to visit, awesome castles and monuments – especially Hadrian's Wall; very good value.

Northumberland and County Durham include great sweeps of largely unspoilt scenery, quiet and uncrowded even in summer. Prime spots are the beautiful landscapes of North Tynedale, Coquetdale and Teesdale, and the rolling empty grassy uplands of the Cheviot Hills. There are majestic stretches of rocky sandy coast, with a coast path covering the finest sections. Kielder Water is now an attractive recreational area, in a part of Northumbria that's otherwise so little visited as to seem almost an undiscovered country. Peaceful lower landscapes are enlivened by streams and woodland, solid stone country buildings, and unhurried small market towns. The area is very good both for walking and for driving, with little traffic (outside the Tyneside/Teesside industrial areas).

Durham is one of England's most rewarding cities for a short stay, with plenty to see besides its magnificent cathedral. Newcastle is becoming a really lively place to visit, with the bonus of good free museums and galleries.

This is one of the very best parts of Britain for anyone interested in times past. Hadrian's Wall, striding indomitably across England for nearly 2,000 years, is a staggering sight, with Roman forts and engrossing reconstructions and interpretations. Historic highlights elsewhere are Bede's World in Jarrow, the re-created 18th-c port at Hartlepool, and above all the remarkable reconstruction of North of England life a hundred years ago, at Beamish – a fascinating living museum.

Children really enjoy many of these places; a special treat for them is Newcastle Discovery – and it's free. The spectacular new National Glass Centre in Sunderland has a lot to captivate children as well as adults. Good days out for older people include the Bowes Museum at Barnard Castle (an absolute treasure-trove) and Cragside at Rothbury (a magnificent stately home in glorious surroundings – with plenty to keep children amused). Alnwick, Warkworth and Lindisfarne are favourites among an abundance of classic castles, with Bamburgh, Raby at Staindrop and Chillingham (with its ancient white cattle) also very enjoyable. Among delectable villages, Ford and Etal stand out for interesting features.

People up here are among Britain's friendliest, and prices are low. May and June are the best months, with long evenings (stay away from inland waters in summer, unless you're midge-proof). September can be delightful, but autumn tends to set in quite fiercely in October, and winter is bleak.

Where to stay

ALNMOUTH NU2411 **Marine House** *1 Marine Rd, Alnmouth, Alnwick, Northumberland NE66 2RW (01665) 830349* **£84 inc dinner,** plus special breaks; 10 rms. 17th-c stone hotel by golf links, with fine sea views, a log fire and plenty of books in traditional upstairs residents' lounge, cosy bar, and enjoyable freshly prepared food in cheerfully decorated no smoking dining room; self-catering also; cl Jan; children over 7; well behaved dogs welcome.

BAMBURGH NU1834 **Lord Crewe Arms** *Fore St, Bamburgh, Northumberland NE69 7BL (01668) 214243* **£74,** plus special breaks; 24 comfortable rms, 21 with own bthrm. Relaxing and comfortable old inn, beautifully placed in charming coastal village below castle, with entertaining bric-à-brac and log fire in back bar, no smoking plush lounge, and good bar and restaurant food; cl end Oct–Easter; children over 5.

CAMBO NZ0383 **Shieldhall** *Cambo, Wallington, Morpeth, Northumberland NE61 4AQ (01830) 540387* **£47;** 4 well equipped suites, each with its own entrance. 18th-c stone house and carefully converted farm buildings around a courtyard, with antiques and other interesting furnishings (Mr Robinson-Gay is a fine cabinet-maker), library, bar, and cosy lounge with French windows opening on to the neatly kept big garden; enjoyable freshly produced food in candlelit beamed dining room; cl Dec and Jan; children over 10.

CHOLLERFORD NY9170 **George** *Chollerford, Hexham, Northumberland NE46 4EW (01434) 681611* **£110,** plus special breaks; 47 well equipped rms. Quiet hotel with fine gardens sloping down to the river, 17th-c bridge over the North Tyne visible from the candlelit restaurant, and thoughtful attentive service; swimming pool and leisure club; disabled access.

CORNHILL-ON-TWEED NT8742 **Tillmouth Park** *(just NE) Cornhill-on-Tweed, Northumberland TD12 4UU (01890) 882255* ***£120,** plus special breaks; 14 spacious, pretty rms with period furniture. Solid stone-built country house in 15 acres of parkland (fishing on the River Till, rod and drying room), with comfortable relaxing lounges, open fires, a galleried hall, and good food in bistro or restaurant; lots to do nearby; cl 26 Dec; dogs welcome.

COTHERSTONE NZ0119 **Fox & Hounds** *Cotherstone, Barnard Castle, Durham DL12 9PF (01833) 650241* **£55;** 3 no smoking rms. Attractive building in lovely setting overlooking Teesdale village green, with alcoves, local photographs and open fire in comfortably furnished cosy beamed bar, good food in no smoking dining room, and courteous friendly service; handy for walks; cl 25 Dec.

CROOKHAM NT9138 **Coach House** *Crookham, Cornhill-on-Tweed, Northumberland TD12 4TD (01890) 820293* **£36;** 9 individual rms with fresh flowers and nice views, 7 with own bthrm. 17th-c farm buildings around a sunny courtyard, airy beamed lounge with comfortable sofas and big arched windows, good breakfasts, enjoyable dinners, and very warmly friendly and helpful owner; lots to do nearby; cl Nov–Easter; good disabled access.

DURHAM NZ2742 **Georgian Town House** *11 Crossgate, Durham DH1 4PS (0191) 386 8070* ***£50;** 7 pretty rms, some overlooking the cathedral. Attractive Georgian listed house with extravagantly comfortable sitting room, attractive airy conservatory dining room, and friendly atmosphere; cl Christmas.

DURHAM NZ2742 **Royal County** *Old Elvet, Durham DH1 3JN (0191) 386 6821* **£130,** plus special breaks; 150 attractive well equipped rms. Close to the city centre with views of the castle and cathedral, this extended hotel has pleasant furnishings, original Tudor beams, panelling and unusual stained glass ceiling, several restaurants, and lots of leisure facilities; disabled access.

GATESHEAD NZ2560 **Eslington Villa** *8 Station Rd, Low Fell, Gateshead, Tyne & Wear NE9 6DR (0191) 487 6017* **£69.50,** plus wknd breaks; 12 rms. Extended comfortable Edwardian house in quiet residential area with some original features, lounge with comfortably modern furniture and bay windows overlooking garden, good food in conservatory restaurant, and a friendly atmosphere; cl 25–26 Dec, bank hols; disabled access.

GREENHEAD NY6667 **Holmhead** *Hadrian's Wall, Greenhead, Carlisle, Cumbria CA6 7HY (01697) 747402* **£42,** plus special breaks; 4 cosy rms with showers. Family home, built of Wall stones, once a farmhouse but now a comfortable B & B with moorland, wildlife, Hadrian's Wall and Roman castles all nearby; airy lounge with TV at one end, small bar at the other; games and children's toys, good freshly prepared food using farm and local produce eaten family-style around candlelit oak table, and pretty garden with a stream and games (table tennis and snooker in garage); also self-catering; cl 2 wks in winter; disabled access.

GRETA BRIDGE NZ0813 **Morritt Arms** *Greta Bridge, Barnard Castle, Durham DL12 9SE (01833) 627232* **£72.50,** plus special breaks; 26 rms. Smartly old-fashioned coaching inn where Dickens stayed in 1838 to research for *Nicholas Nickleby* – one of the interesting bars has a colourful Dickensian mural; comfortable lounges, fresh flowers, good open fires, and pleasant garden; coarse fishing; no children in evening dining room; pets allowed; disabled access.

HALTWHISTLE NY7366 **Ald White Craig** *Shield Hill, Haltwhistle, Northumberland NE49 9NW (01434) 320565* **£44;** 2 rms. Homely and neatly kept 17th-c croft overlooking South Tyne valley, with prize-winning sheep, rare cattle, dogs, cats and poultry, coal fire and local information in beamed sitting room, good breakfasts around central table in dining room; plenty of walks; self-catering cottages; cl Nov–Mar; no children.

HAYDON BRIDGE NY8366 **Hadrian Lodge** *(just N) Haydon Bridge, Hexham, Northumberland NE47 6NF (01434) 688688* **£36;** 8 comfortable rms, some with own bthrm. Attractive modern stone-built lodge in 18 acres of pasture close to Hadrian's Wall, with summer residents' bar, family tearoom, a self-catering kitchen, small launderette, and 2 trout lakes with rods for hire; self-catering cottages, bunkrooms, and caravan/camp site.

HEADLAM NZ1818 **Headlam Hall** *Headlam, Darlington DL2 3HA (01325) 730238* ***£75,** plus wknd breaks; 36 pretty rms, in the main house and adjacent coach house, plus 2 bdrm cottage in village. Peaceful Jacobean mansion in 4 acres of carefully kept gardens with little trout lake, tennis court, small golf practice area, and croquet lawn; elegant rooms, a fine carved oak fireplace in the main hall, good traditional food in the 4 individually decorated rooms of the restaurant, and courteous staff; indoor swimming pool, snooker and sauna; cl 24–25 Dec; disabled access.

HIGH FORCE NY8828 **High Force Hotel** *High Force, Barnard Castle, Durham DL12 0XH (01833) 622222* ***£45;** 6 rms. Close to England's highest waterfall (after which it's named), this is a cheerful and friendly place with log fires in relaxing bars, good service, straightforward food, a microbrewery, and lots of malt whiskies; it includes a mountain rescue post; no pets.

KIRKWHELPINGTON NY9684 **Cornhills** *Kirkwhelpington, Newcastle upon Tyne NE19 2RE (01830) 540232* ***£45;** 3 rms, some with own bthrm. Big no smoking Victorian farmhouse on large stock-rearing farm with marvellous views towards the coast and the Tyne valley, lots of original features, a comfortable lounge, good breakfasts (local pubs for evening meals), and indoor and outdoor games for children; self-catering also; cl Apr.

LONGFRAMLINGTON NU1301 **Embleton Hall** *Longframlington, Morpeth, Northumberland NE65 8DT (01665) 570249* **£85;** 13 comfortable, pretty and individually decorated rms. Charming hotel in lovely grounds surrounded by fine countryside, with a particularly friendly relaxed atmosphere and courteous staff; neat little bar, elegant lounge, log fires, excellent-value bar meals, and very good food in the attractive dining room; disabled access.

LONGHORSLEY NZ1496 **Linden Hall** *Longhorsley, Morpeth, Northumberland NE65 8XF (01670) 516611* **£125,** plus special breaks; 50 individually decorated rms. Georgian hotel in 450 acres of landscaped park with coarse fishing, clay pigeon shooting, mountain biking (bike hire available), new 18-hole golf course, pitch and putt, croquet, jogging routes, giant chess, and lots of leisure facilities inc big swimming pool; pubby bar, elegant drawing room, and good food in attractive restaurant; children in main restaurant early evening only; disabled access.

ROMALDKIRK NY9922 **Rose & Crown** *Romaldkirk, Barnard Castle, Durham DL12 9EB (01833) 650213* **£82,** plus special breaks; 12 rms – those in the main house have lots of character. Smart and interesting old coaching inn by green of delightful Teesdale village, with Jacobean oak settle, log fire, old black and white photographs, and lots of brass in the beamed traditional bar, a cosy residents' lounge, very good popular food in bar and fine oak-panelled restaurant, and well kept real ales and wines; cl 25–26 Dec; disabled access.

SEAHOUSES NU2232 **Olde Ship** *Main St, Seahouses, Northumberland NE68 7RD (01665) 720200* **£75,** plus special breaks; 16 rms, inc 4 apartments. Thriving harbourside inn with small rooms full of nautical items and fishing memorabilia, windows looking out towards the Farne Islands, comfortable residents' lounge, popular bar food, 5 real ales, and good service; ideal for coastal walks; cl Dec and Jan; children over 10.

SLALEY NY9757 **Rose & Crown** *Slaley, Hexham, Northumberland NE47 0AA (01434) 673263* ***£45;** 3 attractively modernised rms. Traditional village inn with mugs hanging from the beams, popular food in bar and restaurant, and friendly service; lots to do nearby.

STANNERSBURN NY7286 **Pheasant** *Stannersburn, Hexham, Northumberland NE48 1DD (01434) 240382* ***£58,** plus special breaks; 8 rms. Beautifully located unpretentious 17th-c stone inn close to Kielder Water and its quiet forests, with a traditional comfortable lounge, simple public bar, a happy mix of customers, good food inc excellent fresh veg and enjoyable Sun lunch, well kept real ales, a fine choice of malts, good welcoming service, nice breakfasts, and picnic sets in streamside garden; cl 25–26 Dec; disabled access.

WEST WOODBURN NY8986 **Bay Horse** *West Woodburn, Hexham, Northumberland NE48 2RX (01434) 270218* **£40;** 5 rms. Pretty, welcoming 18th-c coaching inn with curious Roman stone in garden which runs down to River Rede (trout and salmon fishing), comfortable open-plan bar with open fire, and good standard food in airy dining room.

WOLSINGHAM NZ1037 **Greenwell Farm** *Wolsingham, Tow Law, Bishop Auckland, Durham DL13 4PH (01388) 527248* ***£45,** plus special breaks; 6 rms in comfortably converted stone barn. 300-year-old farmhouse with fine views, sitting and dining rooms, good food using naturally reared meats and locally grown produce, and spring lambs, calves and chicks; nature trail and conservation areas; you can bring your own horse or mountain bike; self-catering cottage; cl Christmas and New Year; disabled access.

To see and do

★ ⛴ **DURHAM** NZ2742 The old part is largely pedestrianised, with attractive cobbled alleys and narrow medieval lanes, and fine medieval buildings among the Georgian and later ones, particularly around the 12th-c pedestrians-only Elvet Bridge (where the Regatta tearooms have decent food). There are several medieval churches, and interesting little shops. This ancient core stands on a crag defended by an almost complete loop of the River Wear, with a rewarding riverside path going from Prebends Bridge up to South St (with some of the best views of the cathedral's magnificent pinnacled towers), recrossing the river by Silver St bridge. You can hire rowing boats nr Elvet Bridge, which is also the departure point for launches. The Hogshead (Saddler St) is a handy central place for something to eat; the best-value food is out at the Duke of Wellington (A167 S of Nevilles Cross).

✝ **Durham Cathedral** Huge, and probably England's finest, a fiercely beautiful and unusually well preserved Norman building, breathtaking inside; it was the first in Britain to use pointed arches. St Cuthbert's shrine is here, and they say that the Lady Chapel owes its odd position at the west end to his hatred of women; every time they tried to build it in the right place his spirit apparently caused the foundations to collapse. Try to spot the unique bronze knocker that seems to have a cheery grin. Rare books and manuscripts in the 15th-c monks' dormitory. Meals, snacks, shop, disabled access; monks' dormitory open 10am–3.30pm Mon–Sat, 12.30–3pm Sun (80p),

Treasury cl am Sun (£2). The close behind the cathedral has some handsome old houses.

Durham Castle Developed from an early Norman motte and bailey. Still a proud building, with original chapel and 13th-c great hall; now used for university accommodation – you can stay here. Guided tours Mon, Weds and wknds 2–4.30 pm in term-time, usually every day in hols – best to check first; (0191) 374 3800; £3.

University Museum of Archaeology On the river bank below the cathedral's south-west corner, a former fulling mill with finds from the city and surrounding area. Shop; cl am, and in winter cl Tues and Weds; (0191) 374 3623; £1. Also along these banks is a sculpture of the Last Supper, carved by Colin Wilbourn from 13 trees that died of Dutch elm disease.

Oriental Museum (Elvet Hill) Remarkable displays of everything from plates, carvings, and paintings to costumes and mummies. Shop; cl 1–2pm pm, am wknds, Christmas–New Year; (0191) 374 7911; £1.50.

University Botanic Gardens (Hollingside Lane) Hugely enjoyable 18-acre garden in mature woodland with exotic trees from America and the Himalayas, tropical house, cactus house and visitor centre, and unusual sculpture garden. Snacks, shop, disabled access; cl Christmas–New Year; (0191) 374 2671; *£1.

St Mary le Bow church (The Bailey) The heritage centre has exhibitions on the city's history. Shop, disabled access; cl am (exc July and Aug), wkdys in Apr and May, and all Oct–Mar; 90p.

Houghall College Gardens (Shincliffe Rd) The county's main horticultural training centre, with 10 acres of hardy plants, a watergarden, woodland garden, Alpine rock garden, parterre and arboretum. This area records some of the lowest temperatures in the country so if it grows here, it'll grow anywhere. Snacks, plant sales, disabled access; (0191) 386 1351; free.

Durham Art Gallery (Aykley Heads) Good gallery with unusual temporary exhibitions, and adjacent regimental museum. Snacks, shop, disabled access; cl am Sun, Mon (exc bank hols), 25–26 Dec, 1 Jan; (0191) 384 2214; £2.

Finchale Priory NZ2947 (3m NE, minor rd off the A167) St Godric chose this site in 1110 as a place to meditate, and it's still a pleasant spot for contemplation, beside the graceful ruins of the 13th-c church.

NEWCASTLE UPON TYNE NZ2563 This big industrial conurbation is far from being conventionally pretty, but has a strong vibrant atmosphere, and several excellent free museums. Its best parts are grouped very compactly high above the River Tyne with its three great bridges – particularly what has become almost the city's trademark, the two-decker High Level Bridge for road and rail designed by Robert Stephenson in the 1840s. The Metro system makes it quick and straightforward to get around, and to the attractions noted under North and South Shields, Tynemouth and Whitley Bay; a one-day Day Rover ticket (from stations or the tourist information centre) costs around £3 and is good for all Metro trips and stations (and the ferry between North and South Shields). You can still trace some stretches of the medieval city wall, especially from St Andrew's church along the cobbled lane west of Stowell St – Chinese restaurants around here – and past the Heber Tower along Bath Lane. Grey's Monument is now closed to the public – people were throwing pennies and stones from the top and causing damage below. Fitzgeralds down the street is useful for a bite to eat. Steep alleys and steps lead from the centre down to The Quay, the oldest part of town, with several unexpected and quaintly attractive timber-framed medieval buildings; one of the oldest, the Cooperage, is a good pub. Downstream, east of the 1920s Tyne Bridge, an area of refurbished 19th-c wharf buildings is enjoyable to walk through, with crafts and bric-à-brac on Sun, and a useful pub for food – the Bonded Warehouse. This whole quayside area is gradually being redeveloped on a most impressive scale, with plans for a huge arts complex, and funding heading towards £200 million.

Another stylish quayside warehouse conversion, the Waterline (by the New Law Courts) has good food, as does the Fog on the Tyne overlooking the St Peter's Basin marina. Besides the pubs mentioned above, the handsome Crown Posada (The Side, off Dean St) and the Duke of Wellington (High Bridge) are pleasantly civilised.

✝ **Newcastle Cathedral** The 14th/15th-c Anglican cathedral is worth a look (cl most of Sun); a dramatic new stone sculpture by Stephen Cox now occupies the Chapel of the Incarnation.

Newcastle Castle This Norman building gave the city its name; a lot still remains. It's a little spoiled by the main railway line which cuts the gatehouse off from the keep, but as much of the fortress was rediscovered only during the railway's construction it seems a little churlish to complain. Shop; cl Mon, 25 Dec, 1 Jan, Good Fri; (0191) 232 7938; *£1.50.

Newcastle Discovery (Blandford Sq) Not so long ago this thriving complex housed a standard collection of displays on science and engineering, but now has galleries and interactive features on subjects more likely to appeal to the whole family: it's the biggest and busiest museum in the area. Pride of place goes to the 30-metre (100-ft) *Turbinia*, once the fastest ship on the seas, shown off in a splendid new multimedia gallery. The interactive Science Factory has plenty to push, press and poke: TV effects create the illusion of flying down the Tyne, and there's a soft play area for very young children, and lots of mirrors, magnets and microscopes to fiddle with. Other galleries offer a similarly hands-on look at the history of the city (inc the early days of Newcastle United), fashion, shipbuilding, army life, and local inventors. Meals, snacks, shop, disabled access; cl am Sun, 25–26 Dec, 1 Jan, Good Fri; (0191) 232 6789; free.

Bessie Surtees' House (Sandhill) Well renovated timbered Jacobean house, with elaborate plaster ceilings and carved panelling; cl wknds and bank hols; (0191) 261 1585; free.

Laing Art Gallery (New Bridge St) Notable temporary exhibitions and excellent children's gallery, the activities well designed to encourage young children to think about shapes, texture and patterns. Free guided tours of the main galleries 11.30am Sat; cl am Sun, 25–26 Dec, 1 Jan, Good Fri; (0191) 232 7734; free.

Hancock Museum (Barras Bridge) Very good natural history museum, with magnificent collections of stuffed birds and mammals. Again, lively temporary exhibitions, and plenty for children. Meals, snacks, shop, disabled access; cl am Sun, 25–26 Dec, 1 Jan, Good Fri; (0191) 222 7418; £3.50–£3.95 (price varies according to exhibitions).

Museum of Antiquities (The University) Particularly good on Roman remains, with reconstructions of various points along Hadrian's Wall. The displays have been reorganised in a very user-friendly fashion. Shop, disabled access by arrangement; cl Sun, 24–26 Dec, 1 Jan, Good Fri, (0191) 222 7846; free.

HADRIAN'S WALL NY7868 An amazing sight, if you've never seen it before. It's extraordinary to imagine those Roman military engineers, so far from their warm homeland, building this remarkable construction through such inhospitable surroundings. Many of its 73½ miles run along the natural crag of the great Whin Sill, making it that much more formidable; the overall sense of grandeur is a definite part of the appeal. The stone wall itself, with its turret watchtowers, milecastles and more sporadic forts, defines the north side of a narrow frontier zone, bounded on its south side by an equally remarkable ditch between turf ramparts; a military road runs between wall and ditch. It was this whole installation rather than just the wall itself which the Romans used to control trade and cross-border travel. The B6318 following the military road is a fine drive, with some of the best views of the Wall. This road also gives walkers easy access to the line of the Wall, with numerous car parks on the way. There's not a lot of point trying to make walks into circuits: all the interest is along the Wall itself, although in places you may prefer to drop down beneath the switchback Whin Sill, which itself can be quite tiring. The views are bleak and exhilarating. Even in fine summer weather the wind can be chilly, so go well wrapped up. English Heritage are cutting back on the publicity for some sites – thousands of marauding tourists have caused more damage than centuries of harsh weather and unstable politics ever managed. In summer a tourist bus runs between Hexham and several of the main sites (and even as far as Carlisle), and you can get on or off at any of the stages along the way; ring (01434) 605225 for times. The best place to eat near the main sites is the Milecastle Inn on the B6318 NE of Haltwhistle; the Robin Hood at East Wallhouses, on the B6318 NE of Corbridge, is also useful.

Carrawbrough NY8571 **Mithraic Temple** Three 3rd-c altars to Mithras were found here, on the line of the Roman wall nr the fort of Brocolitia. They're now in Newcastle's Museum of Antiquities, but you can see replicas in their original setting.

Cawfield Crags NY7166 One of the best-preserved sections of the Wall.

Chesters NY9170 (on the B6318, slightly W of Chollerford) The best-preserved example of a Roman cavalry fort in Britain, in an attractive riverside setting. In the bathhouse you can see exactly how the underfloor heating system worked, and a museum has sculptures and inscriptions from here and elsewhere. Snacks, shop, disabled access; cl 24–26 Dec; (01434) 681379; £2.70. The Hadrian Hotel at Wall (on the A6076 S) has good-value food.

Corbridge Roman Site NY9864 (slightly NW of town) Granaries, portico columns and what may be the legionary HQ survive among these 3rd-c remains. The adjacent museum has the magnificent Corbridge Lion. Shop, limited disabled access; cl winter Mon and Tues, and maybe lunchtimes; (01434) 632349; £2.70. The village (or very small town) is attractive, above the Tyne; the Black Bull is good for lunch. Brocksbushes Farm (2m E) has pick-your-own fruit and a farm shop; (01434) 633400.

Cuddys Crag NY7567 Perhaps the most beautiful section of the Wall, very photogenic and giving glorious views.

Birdoswald Roman Fort NY6166 Overlooking the Irthing Gorge W of Gilsland (and in fact just over the Cumbrian border), this is one of the most impressive sites on Hadrian's Wall, partly because it has so many features in such a small area, and partly for its grand views. Good visitor centre; snacks, shop, some disabled access; visitor centre cl Nov–Mar; (016977) 47602; £1.95. The **goat farm** at Holme View nearby sells prize-winning traditional cheeses.

Greenhead Roman Army Museum NY6767 (Carvoran) Entertaining and informative intrepretation of what it was like to be a Roman soldier, with everything you could possibly want to know about his training, pay, and off-duty hobbies. Snacks, shop, disabled access; cl mid-Nov–early Feb; (016977) 47485; £2.80.

Housesteads Roman Fort & Museum NY7969 (on the B6318) The best-known and most visited section of the Wall (and also one of the best-preserved), pretty much slap bang in the middle. It owes its fine state of preservation partly to the fact that while other stretches were being used as a handy source of free recycled quality masonry, this fort was base camp for a powerful group of border bandits; woe betide anyone who tried to use their fortifications as material for cowsheds or churches. A museum has altars, inscriptions and models, and there are good walks in either direction. Snacks, shop; cl 24–26 Dec; (01434) 344363; £2.70.

Once Brewed NY7567 (Steel Rigg) Very useful National Park Information Centre, handy for Housesteads and Vindolanda, with exhibitions and audio-visual presentations. Guided walks leave from here (though not every day). Snacks, shop, disabled access; cl Nov–Easter; (01434) 344396; free. The walk from here to Housesteads offers some of the best views of the Wall; it's only 3 miles but is up and down so can take up to 2½ hours.

Vindolanda NY7766 (Bardon Mill) Started well before the Wall itself, this Roman fort and frontier town soon became a base for 500 soldiers. Full-scale reconstructions, lots of well preserved remains, possibly further excavations in progress. The adjacent museum has a fascinating selection of hand-written letters and documents found on the site, inc party invitations, shopping lists and a note that could have been written by many a modern mother: 'I have sent you socks and two pairs of underpants.' Shop, snacks, disabled access to museum but not site; cl late Nov–mid-Feb; (01434) 344277; £3.50.

Walltown Crags NY6766 One of the best-preserved sections of the Wall.

Other things to see and do

Northumbria Family Attraction of the Year

SUNDERLAND NZ3957 **National Glass Centre** (Liberty Way) Of much wider appeal than you'd initially think, this dazzling new £16 million exhibition is one of the first high-profile Lottery-funded attractions to open its doors (and in this case windows) to the public. A cross between gallery, museum and factory visit, it focuses on how glass is made and used all around the world, and is surprisingly captivating for a couple of hours if you're anywhere nearby. Full of light and colour, the myriad displays are quite bewitching in places. It's in a striking glass structure on a sloping site alongside the River Wear; you can walk along the glass roof, looking down on the exhibitions below – the makers claim it can take the weight of 30,000 people, though were slightly embarrassed when a few mystery cracks appeared last summer. A highlight for visitors over 9 is the chance to have a go at glass-making yourself, with a range of classes and workshops (£5 extra). Don't be daunted by the exquisite creations of their resident glassmakers: several companies are based here, so the skilled craftsmen you can watch at work have had plenty of practice. The main exhibition areas are fascinating, particularly the Kaleidoscope Gallery, which explores the more imaginative ways glass is used, from time-lapse photography to a hall of mirrors. Britain's first stained glass was made nr Sunderland 1,300 years ago, so there are plenty of examples of this and other decorative glasswork. Younger children haven't been forgotten: several exhibits are interactive, with computer displays and activities, and trails and quizzes. In school holidays and every other Sat they have extra things for children, such as painting and story-telling. The centre opened only a couple of months before we went to press, but in that time managed to experience more than its fair share of bad luck and publicity, with newspaper reports of chef temperament in the restaurant, and even snipers taking out some of the windows. Meals, snacks, good shop, disabled access; cl 25 Dec, 1–14 Jan; (0191) 515 5555; *£3.50 (children £2).

ALLENDALE NY8352 The B6305/B6295 is a great scenic drive; lots of walks up there, and good stops at the King's Head in Allendale town and entertaining Allenheads Inn further up.

★ **ALNMOUTH** NU2410 Pleasant town with attractive beaches, good coastal walks, a lot for summer visitors; the Saddle has good food.

ALNWICK NU1813 Busy town at the heart of prosperous farming country, with some attractive old streets nr the market square. The hillside **church** of St Michael and All Angels above the river is a perfect example of a complete Late Gothic building. The Market Tavern has bargain food. **Alnwick Castle** The 'Windsor of the North' dates back to the 11th c, and is the second-largest inhabited castle in the country. Stone soldiers stand guard on the battlements, and inside all is Italian Renaissance grandeur, with a magnificent art collection taking in works by Titian, Van Dyck and Canaletto, and an outstanding Claude. Also famous collection of Meissen china, Roman remains, children's playground. Landscaped grounds by Capability Brown. Meals, snacks, shop; cl Fri, and Oct–Easter; (01665) 510777; £5.95. **Hulne Park** NU1615 Excellent for gentle parkland walks; dogs not allowed. Don't miss the whimsical Brizlee Tower and hermit's cave.

★ **AMBLE** NU2604 This attractive small town has a solid old fishing harbour, and new yacht marina; RSPB **boat trips** around nearby Coquet Island with its colourful eider ducks and puffins.

AYDON CASTLE NZ0066 13th-c, and remarkably well preserved, in a lovely setting. Snacks, shop, some disabled access; cl Nov–Mar; (01434) 632450; £1.90.

★ **BAMBURGH** NU1835 **Bamburgh Castle** Stunning huge square Norman castle on a cliff above the sea, its clock serving as timekeeper for the cricket green in the attractive village below. Despite the forbidding exterior, the inside is very much a lived-in stately home, with armour from the Tower of London. Snacks, shop; cl Nov–Mar; (01668) 214515; £3.50. **Grace Darling Museum** (Radcliffe Rd) Pictures and mementos of the local heroine, inc the boat in which Grace and her father rescued 9 survivors from the wrecked SS *Forfarshire*. Shop, disabled access; cl am Sun and all Nov–Easter; free (donations to RNLI). There's a neo-Gothic shrine to Grace Darling in the yard of the interesting 13th-c **church**. The Lord Crewe Arms is well placed for lunch.

★ **BARNARD CASTLE** NZ0416 Pleasant market town, still coming to life on Weds market day, with several attractive buildings. In the centre, the Golden Lion and Old Well have good-value food. **Castle** These dramatically set 12th-c ruins include the original keep and the 14th-c hall. Shop, disabled facilities; cl winter Mon and Tues and maybe lunchtmes, 24–26 Dec, 1 Jan; (01833) 638212; £2.20 (inc audio tour). **Bowes Museum** A beautiful French-style chateau in 20 acres of meticulously kept formal grounds. The 40 rooms are filled with sumptuous fine arts and an outstanding display of paintings by Canaletto, Goya, El Greco and others; also children's room and local history section. Relatively few people find their way to this treasure-house, though it's one of the most worthwhile places to visit in the entire country. Meals and snacks (summer only), shop, disabled access; cl am Sun and over Christmas, but winter closure is under discussion; (01833) 690606; £3.90. **Rokeby Park** (just SE) Elegant 18th-c villa in a fine setting, most famous for its *Rokeby Venus* by Velasquez (the original is now in the National Gallery). The best of the other pictures is probably Pellegrini's *Venus disarming Cupid*. Open May bank hols and the following Tues, then pm Mon and Tues Jun–2nd Tues in Sept; (01833) 637334; £3.50. The Morritt Arms nearby does good meals. **Egglestone Abbey** Downstream from Barnard Castle, this is reached by a couple of miles of enjoyable riverside walk – or by car. Substantial remains inc gracefully arched windows, and some remnants of the monastic buildings; disabled access; free. The charming gorge scenery around Barnard Castle makes for good walks – wooded, romantic and unmistakably lowland in character. The valley path W eventually climbs above the river and follows field routes towards Cotherstone. The B6278 to Stanhope and Edmundbyers is a fine drive.

★ **BEADNALL** NU2329 On Northumberland's underpopulated coast, this attractive village has boats on the beach, and an interestingly restored waterside limekiln; nearby Benthall is also pleasant.

BEAMISH NZ2154 **North of England Open Air Museum** This amazingly ambitious 300-acre museum exhaustively re-creates life in the North of England at the turn of the century. No detail is overlooked, and there's something for everyone in the 5 main sections: a town with shops, houses, businesses and pub, colliery village with mine, chapel, cottages and school, manor house with formal gardens and orchard, railway station, and home farm with animals and craft demonstrations (ducks and geese wander round for extra authenticity). Costumed interpreters really bring the place to life. Children can wander at their leisure, touching everything, and joining in most of the activities, from hoops and hopscotch to schoolroom lessons (bad handwriting is rewarded by a light rap on the knuckles). A Victorian fairground has rides inc a Hall of Mirrors (small extra charge), and working trams and buses link the different areas. Meals and snacks (inc period pub), good shops, some disabled access; cl Mon and Fri Nov–Mar, and 2 wks over Christmas; (01207) 231811; £8, or £3 late Oct–Mar when only the town and tramway are open. The Shepherd & Shepherdess not far from the gate is useful for lunch, as is the more individual Beamish Mary (follow the sign from the A693 to No Place & Cooperative Villas).

† **BELLINGHAM** NY8383 (pronounced Bellingjum) A small country town with an attractive 13th-c **church**, stone-roofed to protect it against arson-minded Border raiders; there's a pretty walk just N of the town, to Hareshaw Linn's 9-metre (30-ft) cascade. The Cheviot Hotel does decent food. This is the main town in North Tynedale, one of the least-known parts of Northumberland, with good scenic drives. Between the Pennines and the Cheviots, it's a peaceful unspoilt valley surrounded by wild moorland, with fine scenery and a really unrushed atmosphere – very relaxing.

BELLISTER NY7063 This NT estate has a **ruined castle** and peel tower; good for gentle walks, with year-round access to the paths.

BELSAY HALL, CASTLE & GARDENS NZ1078 (on the A696) The same family have lived here for nearly 600 years, first in a medieval castle, then a Jacobean manor house and finally a grand mansion designed to look like a Greek classical

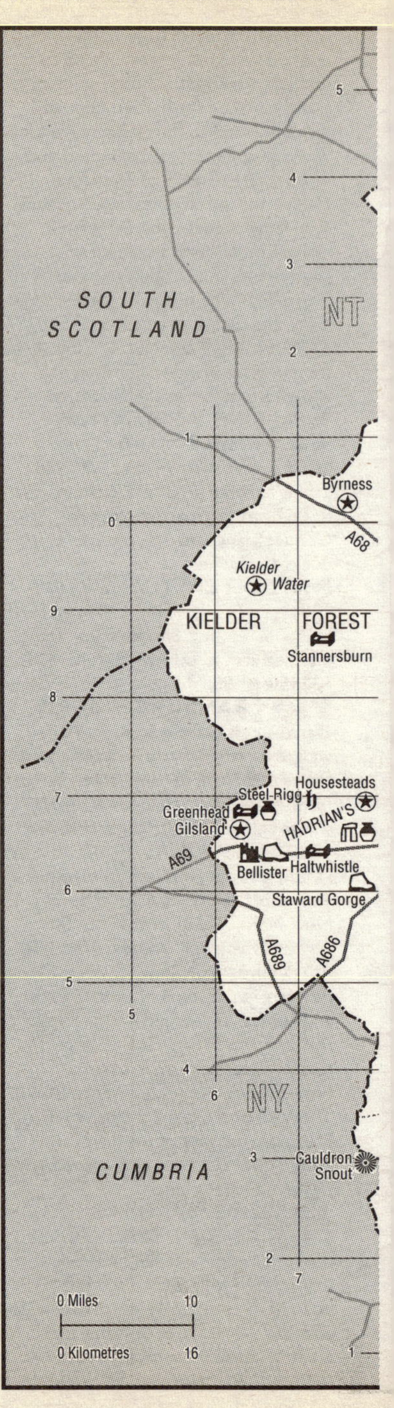

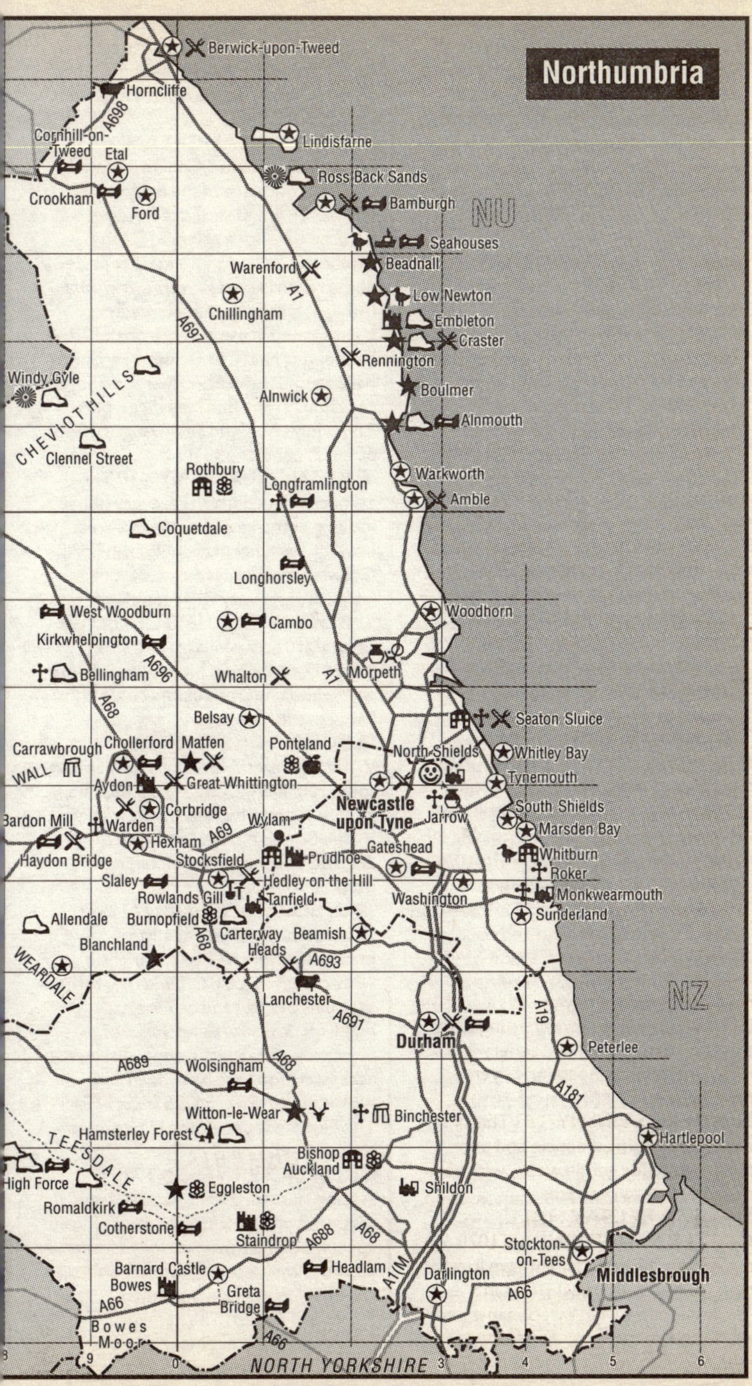
Northumbria
Berwick-upon-Tweed
Horncliffe
Cornhill-on-Tweed
Etal
Crookham
Ford
Lindisfarne
Ross Back Sands
Bamburgh
NU
Seahouses
Beadnall
Warenford
Low Newton
Chillingham
Embleton
Craster
Rennington
Windy Gyle
CHEVIOT HILLS
Boulmer
Alnwick
Alnmouth
Clennel Street
Rothbury
Warkworth
Longframlington
Amble
Coquetdale
Longhorsley
Woodhorn
West Woodburn
Cambo
Kirkwhelpington
Bellingham
Whalton
Morpeth
Seaton Sluice
Belsay
Carrawbrough
Chollerford
Matfen
Ponteland
North Shields
Whitley Bay
WALL
Aydon
Great Whittington
Tynemouth
Newcastle upon Tyne
Jarrow
South Shields
Corbridge
Bardon Mill
Warden
Wylam
Marsden Bay
Hexham
Haydon Bridge
Stocksfield
Prudhoe
Gateshead
Whitburn
Roker
Slaley
Hedley-on-the-Hill
Washington
Monkwearmouth
Rowlands Gill
Tanfield
Sunderland
Allendale
Burnopfield
Carterway Heads
Beamish
Blanchland
WEARDALE
Lanchester
NZ
Durham
Peterlee
Wolsingham
Witton-le-Wear
Binchester
Hamsterley Forest
Hartlepool
TEESDALE
Bishop Auckland
High Force
Eggleston
Shildon
Romaldkirk
Cotherstone
Staindrop
Stockton-on-Tees
Barnard Castle
Headlam
Middlesbrough
Bowes
Darlington
Greta Bridge
Bowes Moor
NORTH YORKSHIRE
A698
A697
A1
A696
A68
A69
A693
A691
A689
A19
A181
A688
A1(M)
A66

temple – all can still be seen, but the mansion is strangely eerie: there's no furniture and in some rooms no floors either. The 30 acres of landscaped parkland are especially agreeable, with rhododendron garden, formal terraces and woodland walks. Snacks, shop, disabled access; cl 24–26 Dec; (01661) 881636; £3.60. The Highlander has good food.

★ **BERWICK-UPON-TWEED** NT9953 Largely unspoilt, this has some handsome 18th-c buildings and a fine 17th-c church; most people who come here seem to while away a bit of time watching the swans on the River Tweed. Alternatively, look out over the sea from the Rob Roy (Spittal Rd), which has good local fish. The town has an extraordinary trio of bridges, and deserves to be approached by walking along the Tweed: there are paths on both banks, starting from the East Ord picnic site by the A1 road bridge. The **town ramparts**, impressively intact, were a masterpiece of 16th-c military planning. Partly grassed over and easy to walk, they give good views. **Berwick Barracks** (The Parade) Britain's oldest surviving purpose-built barracks, now a local history museum and gallery, with an interesting exhibition on the British soldier. Snacks, shop, disabled access; cl winter Mon and Tues and maybe lunchtimes, 24–26 Dec, 1 Jan; (01289) 304493; £2.50. **Wine & Spirit Museum** (Palace Green) The mainland base of Lindisfarne mead and country wine makers, with a collection of objects from the wine and spirits industries, working potter, home-made pot-pourri, and Victorian chemist shop. Snacks, shop, disabled access; cl Sun and Christmas wk; (01289) 305153; free.

BINCHESTER ROMAN FORT NZ2031 Quite a lot left of this 1st-c 10-acre fort, inc the best-preserved military baths in the country, with an exceptional hypocaust system. Interesting events inc days when you can sample Roman food. Shop, disabled access; cl Oct–Easter; (01388) 663089; £1.50. **Escomb Church** nearby was built in the 7th c of stone from the fort. A 3rd-c fort can be seen a few miles S at Piercebridge (where the riverside George, with its famous grandfather clock which stopped when the old man died, is useful for lunch); finds from both sites are shown at the Bowes Museum in Barnard Castle.

BISHOP AUCKLAND NZ2130 **Auckland Castle** The main country residence of the Bishops of Durham, a grand series of buildings entered through a splendid Gothic gatehouse in the town's market place. Some rooms are relatively stark, but a highlight is the chapel, splendidly transformed in the 17th c from a 12th-c banqueting hall. The attractive grounds have an unusual 18th-c deercot. Shop; open pm Fri and Sun May–Sept, plus Thurs July–Aug, and Sat in Aug; (01388) 601627; £3.

★ **BLANCHLAND** NY9650 The archetypal border village, every house looking a stronghold, alone in a great bowl of magnificent scenery; the Lord Crewe Arms here is an interesting hotel, in parts very ancient indeed.

★ **BOULMER** NU2613 One of several attractive villages and small towns dotted down Northumberland's scenic and underpopulated coast, this has active fishing boats.

BOWES CASTLE NY9913 Within the earthworks of a Roman fort, these remains include a great Norman keep, 3 storeys high; free. A few miles W the Bowes Moor Hotel, one of England's highest, is a welcoming moorland oasis.

BURNOPFIELD NZ1857 **Gibside** Marvellous Palladian mausoleum for the Bowes family in 18th-c landscaped park, with the rather sad ruins of a hall and other estate buildings dotted around. Miles of pleasant walks. Snacks, shop, disabled access; cl Mon (exc bank hols) and Nov–Mar; (01207) 542255; £3; NT. The Highlander at White le Head has decent food.

BYRNESS NT7702 A good start for getting up to **Chew Green Roman Camps** – little-visited spectacular earthworks alone in wild country, well repaying the stiff walk up the Pennine Way through the Redesdale Forest. The Pennines up here contain a great many more unspoilt prehistoric and other archaeological remains – useful goals for walkers in these magnificent hills, often yielding remarkable views. Some areas N of the A68 (which as it approaches the Scottish border is a remarkably dramatic drive) and W of the B6341 may temporarily be put out of bounds by army training.

CAMBO NZ0283 **Wallington House** Built in 1688 and altered in the 1740s, with fine plasterwork and porcelain, and works by the Pre-Raphaelite circle which often congregated here in the house's 19th-c cultural glory days. Showpiece fuchsias in the conservatory, and 100 acres of lawns, terraces, lakes and woodland landscaped by Capability Brown. Meals, snacks, shop, plant centre, new adventure playground, disabled facilities; house cl am, all Tues, and Nov–Mar, grounds and garden open all year; (01670) 774283; £4.80, £2.80 grounds only; NT. There is free access to the huge surrounding estate, laced with footpaths and inc prehistoric sites and more parkland.

CAULDRON SNOUT NY8128 Beyond High Force, the Pennine Way rewards walkers with some truly wild landscape as the Tees rushes along a gorge beneath Cronkley Scar and tumbles down Cauldron Snout, a 60-metre (200-ft) cascade which can be reached from the dam at Cow Green Reservoir (where there is also a nature trail). The pleasant Langdon Beck Inn is a short drive or walk below the dam.

CHEVIOT HILLS NT9716 Part of the Northumberland National Park, the Cheviots are strikingly empty and solitary, with only the characteristic local breed of hardy sheep for company in most places – for walkers who really want to escape other people.

CHILLINGHAM CASTLE NU0525 Striking old castle dating from 12th c, full of antiques, tapestries, arms and armour. Formal gardens, woodland walks, lake, and splendid country views; occasional concerts and special events. Brave souls can rent one of their haunted rooms. Snacks, shop; cl am, Tues (exc July and Aug), and Oct–Apr; (01668) 215359; £3.90. The Percy Arms at Chatton is good for lunch. **Chillingham Wild Cattle Park** The famous large-horned white cattle have been here for 700 years, the only ones of their kind still uncrossed with domestic breeds. As they're potentially aggressive, tours are led by a warden. Bring binoculars for a closer view. Snacks, shop, limited disabled access; cl 12–2pm, am Sun, all Tues, and Nov–Mar; (01668) 215250; £2.50. **Ross Castle** Above the park, this hill fort has great views.

CHOLLERFORD NY9070 **Hexham Herbs** (on the B6318, nr Chesters; *see under Hadrian's Wall on p.473*) Over 800 varieties beautifully laid out in attractive walled gardens; also old-fashioned roses, many other plants, and woodland walk. Shop, some disabled access, plant sales; telephone for winter opening; (01434) 681483; *£1.50.

CLENNEL STREET NT9207 Ancient drove road leading from Coquetdale, a good walking route into the Cheviots – lonely grassy moors (boggy in parts when it's wet), drystone walls, sheep, dark conifer plantations. You can pick up the route nr Alwinton, and there's a pretty way back, beside the River Alwin.

COQUETDALE NY9799 Northumberland's most scenic drive is the B6344 following the river past Brinkburn Priory to Rothbury, then W on the B6341 past Hepple, then turning right on the unclassified road past Holystone and Alwinton. Picturesque walks around Holystone (where the Salmon is a useful stop), increasingly desolate up towards Blindburn.

★ **CRASTER** NU2519 Tidal fishing harbour, good kippering factory, excellent pub, and magnificent clifftop walk to Dunstanburgh Castle (*see Embleton entry, below*).

! † **DARLINGTON** NZ2815 **Railway Centre & Museum** Interesting museum in carefully restored North Rd Station, part of which is still used for train services. Exhibits inc Robert Stephenson's 1825 *Locomotion*, which pulled the first passenger steamtrain on a public railway. Steam rides some summer wknds. Snacks, shop, disabled access; cl 25–26 Dec, 1 Jan; (01325) 460532;

£2.10. An extraordinary **brickwork locomotive**, a 40-metre (130-ft) approximation of the pre-war record-breaking *Mallard* complete with clouds of bricky steam, stands by Morrisons supermarket; worth its £760,000? St Cuthbert's (Church Row) is an interesting Early English **church**.

★ **EGGLESTON** NY9923 Attractive moorside Teesdale village, with **Eggleston Hall Gardens** a good example of an updated 19th-c country-house garden, with rare and unusual trees, shrubs, perennials and other plants. They sell plants, organically grown herbs, and fruit and vegetables from the walled kitchen garden. Snacks, some disabled access; (01833) 650403; 50p, or £1 for a season ticket (money refunded if you buy a plant).

EMBLETON NU2521 **Dunstanburgh Castle** Screeching seagulls add to the atmosphere at these imposing ruins on the cliff above the North Sea; Turner painted the scene 3 times. Snacks, small shop; cl winter Mon and Tues, 24–26 Dec, 1 Jan; (01665) 576231; £1.70; NT. The comfortable hotel named after the castle does good-value meals. The NT also owns much of this stretch of coastline, inc the pleasantly bracing walk to Craster – one of the finest sections of the Northumbrian coast path.

★ **ETAL** NT9239 Pretty row of white cottages running down to a ford across the river, with a working forge and good thatched pub. A terminus of the **Heatherslaw Light Railway** (see *Ford entry below*). **Etal Castle** Good Walkman tours guide you round these evocative 14th-c ruins; also exhibition on Border history. Shop, disabled access to exhibition area; cl Nov–Easter; (01890) 820332; £2.50.

★ **FORD** NT9338 Built as a model estate-workers' village, for Ford Castle; very attractive, with one or two craft workshops, a well restored working cornmill – cl winter; (01890) 820338; *£2.50 – and the friendly Heatherslaw Bakery making good use of the resulting flour. You can also hire bikes. **Lady Waterford Hall** is well worth a look. Used as the village school until 1957, it has murals (recently restored using lottery money) showing the children of the village and their families as characters from well known Bible stories; cl 12.30–1.30pm and all Nov–Mar; £1.75. **Heatherslaw Light Railway** Steam or diesel journeys on narrow-gauge railway to Etal, along pretty valley of the River Till. Snacks, shop, disabled access; cl Nov–Easter, exc some wknds before Christmas; (01890) 820317 for times; £3.50.

! **GATESHEAD** NZ2162 Not yet the area's most appealing stop for visitors, though a £100 million Tyneside arts complex, partly funded by Lottery money and inc a massive contemporary arts centre, should open in 2000. Meantime, the **Metro Centre** (on the A1 just W) is a useful rainy-day outing from Newcastle, a vast modern shopping and leisure complex with several different themed undercover areas, all sorts of fairground attractions (better for younger children than teenage thrill-seekers), and even a Roman Catholic church. Do remember exactly where you put your car – there are 12,000 parking spaces. The **Shipley Art Gallery** on Prince Consort Rd is worth a look (cl am Sun; free), and the Keelmans riverside walk (off South Shore Rd) is quite pleasant. You'll find it difficult to miss the Angel of the North NZ2657, towering over the A1 with a 52-metre (169-ft) wingspan.

HAMSTERLEY FOREST NZ1231 5,000 acre fellside forest with good walks, cycle routes, 4-mile forest drive, and visitor centre with local wildlife exhibitions (cl Nov–Easter); (01388) 488312; forest drive £1.50 a car. The Cross Keys at Hamsterley is a useful base.

HARTLEPOOL NZ5132 Developing several lively new attractions likely to put it firmly on the tourist map. **Historic Quay** At the old docks, this vivid open-air re-creation of an 18th-c port has painstakingly reconstructed furnished houses, market, prison, and fully stocked shops. Also a couple of film shows, and dramatic (and noisy) exhibition on fighting ships. Lots to see, exceptionally well done. Meals, snacks, shop, disabled access; cl 25 Dec, 1 Jan; (01429) 860888; £4.95. The next-door Jacksons Wharf has decent food.

HMS *Trincomalee* berthed nearby is the world's second-oldest floating warship; cl 25–26 Dec, 1 Jan; (01429) 223193; £2.50. **Museum of Hartlepool** (The Marina) More excellent largely maritime reconstructions, and the well restored paddle steamer *Wingfield Castle* has now moved here (it's used in part as a café). Meals, snacks, shop, disabled access; cl 25–26 Dec, 1 Jan; (01429) 222255; free. The town also has some remains of its medieval wall, and a factory shopping mall. **Hartlepool Nuclear Power Station** (3m S) The visitor centre has lively displays and tours (best to book). Shop, disabled access; cl Sat, winter Sun, 25–26 Dec, 1 Jan; (01429) 853888; free.

★ ⛨ ✝ **HEXHAM** NY9364 A pleasant market town, not too big, with some attractive stone buildings. The County Hotel is a standby for lunch. **Border History Museum** Formerly the country's first purpose-built prison; colourfully charts the chequered contacts between the English and Scots. Shop; cl Sun, Weds–Sat Nov and Feb–Easter, and every day Dec and Jan; (01434) 652351; £1.75. **Hexham Abbey** Founded around 674 by St Wilfrid, once the largest church N of the Alps. The bulk dates from the 12th c, though there are 2 splendid Saxon survivals – the superbly atmospheric crypt, and the throne of the Bishop (St Wilfrid's Chair or Frith stool). The choir still descend the unique Night Stairs for services. Summer snacks, shop, disabled access; free, but donations welcome.

HIGH FORCE NY8828 England's most powerful **waterfall**, dropping into a craggy cauldron at the end of a striking wooded gorge – you'll have to pay around 50p (on top of parking) for the short path from the B6277 for the best view. From Bowlees visitor centre you can make more of a walk of it, first detouring N to Gibson's Cave, a pretty waterfall at the top of a gorge, and then heading S to cross the Tees for an easy 2 miles upriver, passing Low Force on the way. The nearby High Force Hotel has decent food (and the highest brewery in England).

HORNCLIFFE NT9450 **Chain Bridge Honey Farm** Over 1,000 bee colonies, a good visitor centre, and honey-based products for sale; cl am Sun, and wknds Nov–Apr; (01289) 386362; free.

✝ ⛨ **JARROW** NZ3365 **St Paul's Church & Monastery** The Venerable Bede lived here for most of his 7th/8th-c life, producing the 37 books that encompass much of what is known of life in early Christian England. Along with the other half of the monastery, St Peter's, at nearby Monkwearmouth, the site is still a major Christian shrine. Very little remains of the original monastery, but there's Saxon stained glass in the church, and the chancel incorporates one of the earlier chapels. A museum in adjacent Georgian Jarrow Hall has finely carved Anglo-Saxon stones, more stained glass, and excavated relics. The whole developing site is now known as **Bede's World**, with an authentically re-created 11-acre period farm and new museum/visitor reception centre. Meals, snacks, shop, some disabled access; cl am Sun, all day Mon (exc bank hols), Christmas wk; (0191) 489 2106; £3.

KIELDER WATER NY6293 This huge reservoir has opened up a remote part of the Borders; an attractive drive from Bellingham. It's an interesting shape, modelled by the steep folds of the land, and is already beginning to look as if it's always been tucked away in these pine-blanketed hills. Reivers of Tarset hire boats and canoes: rowing boats from £4 for half an hour, motor boats from £10; (01434) 250203. Visitor centres can supply fishing permits. You can rent log cabins around the lake by the week; (01502) 500500. **Tower Knowe Visitor Centre** (NY6986) Down at the foot of the Water, with an exhibition and useful information about the area and its wildlife. Meals, snacks, shop, disabled access; cl 25–26 Dec, 1–2 Jan; (01434) 240398; centre free, exhibition £1. **Cruises** start from here too, and call all around the lake (takes about an hour and a half). **Leaplish Waterside Park** (slightly round to the W, NY6587) Another good starting point, with lots to do in summer, inc plenty of water sports, trails, and canoe and other **boat hire**; (01434) 250203.

Bakethin Conservation Area Up at the top (NY6392), particularly rewarding for wildlife. **Kielder Castle** (NY6393) This 18th-c hunting lodge built for the Duke of Northumberland is now a very good Forest Enterprise visitor centre with exhibitions, closed-circuit TV birdwatching and a sculpture trail. Shop, meals and a play area; (01434) 250209; cl wkdys Nov–Christmas and all Christmas–Easter; free. Regular guided walks from here into the great surrounding tract of Kielder Forest – miles of pine trees with a good chance of seeing red squirrels, as well as deer. There are also self-guided forest walks (easy to follow) from half a dozen or more points along the road through; and a 12-mile forest drive. The friendly Kielder Bikes, who hire bicycles, have their main shop in the village of Kielder itself, opposite the Castle (01434) 250392, and also hire from Hawkhope car park NY7088; they're good for repairs too. A good mountain bike costs around £8 for 3 hours; the area has been well developed for cycling. The Pheasant at Stannersburn and Blackcock at Falstone have good food.

LANCHESTER NZ1243 **Hall Hill Farm** (on the B6296 SW) Friendly working farm with lots of animals, nature trails, riverside walk and trailer rides. Snacks, shop; cl Sat, and Sept–Mar (exc Suns in Sept, Oct and maybe Dec – best to check); (01388) 730300; £3. The Queen's Head is good for food.

LINDISFARNE NU1242 Otherwise known as Holy Island, this important centre for Christian pilgrims is linked to the mainland by a causeway which you can drive (or walk) over at low tide. Tide tables are posted at each end, or tel (01289) 389200; check these carefully – the causeway is impassable for 2 hours before high tide and 4 hours after. If you want to visit a particular attraction, make sure that the tide and the opening times match on the day you want to go. There are nature-reserve dunes, fishermen's huts made of upturned former boats, old limekilns, a small extended village with tourist cafés and pubs, and good views from the close-grazed grassy crags. The Ship is useful for more conventional refreshment. The 3-mile walk around the island's shores is easy but fascinating.

Lindisfarne Priory In the 7th c St Aidan and monks from Iona replanted the seeds of Christianity in Dark Age England from here. These early monks were driven out by Vikings, so it's the extensive remains of a later 12th-c church you can see today; a very peaceful and romantic spot, with graceful red sandstone arches bordered by incongruously neat lawns. Shop, disabled access to visitor centre; cl 24–26 Dec; (01289) 389200; £2.70.

Lindisfarne Castle The rather lonely and austere exterior belies what's within; the 16th-c fortress was restored by Lutyens for the editor of *Country Life* in a suitably monolithic quasi-medieval style. Sumptuous furnishings include a fine collection of antique oak furniture, and there's a walled garden designed by Gertrude Jekyll to protect against the North Sea winds; cl am, Fri (exc Good Fri), and Nov–Mar; (01289) 389244; £4; NT. It's a mile's walk from the car park.

St Aidan's Winery Home of Lindisfarne Mead, a fortified wine made from grapes, honey, herbs and water from an island well. They make honey too, and the shop has British beers, ciders and cheeses, as well as local pottery and jewellery. Shop; cl winter wknds, 19 Dec–5 Jan, and other times according to tide; (01289) 389230; free.

† **LONGFRAMLINGTON** NZ1199 **Brinkburn Priory** Well preserved 12th-c church (thanks to some Victorian restoration), still with medieval grave slabs, font and double piscina. Occasional services and concerts. Shop, some disabled access; open pm Apr–Sept; (01665) 570628; £1.50. The Granby is useful for lunch.

★ **LOW NEWTON** NU2325 Charming seaside village on a fine stretch of little-visited coast, with a **bird reserve** nearby. The Joiners Arms in High Newton has famous fish and chips.

! **MARSDEN BAY** NZ3965 (nr South Shields) The **nature reserve** here gives one of the few reasonable coastal walks in industrial Tyneside. Nearby the **Grotto** (on the A183) is unique: a lift (or a hundred or so steps) down to a pub cut into the seaside cliffs.

★ **MATFEN** NZ0370 One of the prettiest inland villages in Northumbria, with a riverside village green – and a good pub.

MONKWEARMOUTH NZ4057 **St Peter's church** Sister church of St Paul's at Jarrow, its early years equally well documented by the Venerable Bede. Much of the original Saxon church still remains, inc the west wall and tower. A striking Colin Wilbourn sculpture outside commemorates the church's 7th-c founder Benedict Biscop. **Railway Museum** (Monkwearmouth Station) As well as trains, the chance to learn to drive a bus; cl am Sun; (0191) 567 7075; free.

MORPETH NZ2086 The clock tower here is one of only 8 non-church bell towers in Britain; it has only one hand, but still rings the curfew every night. The Tap & Spile, open all day, has good-value food. **Morpeth Chantry Bagpipe Museum** (Bridge St) Harmonious collection of small pipes and bagpipes from around the world. Headphones explain the difference between a rant and a reel. Shop; cl Sun; (01670) 519466; *£1.50. Good **craft centre** next door (cl Sun).

NORTH SHIELDS NZ3568 **Stephenson Railway Museum** (Middle Engine Lane) Excellent, with steamtrain trips along a short section of the North Tyneside Railway, as well as displays on the development of steam and a collection of rolling stock, inc George Stephenson's *Billy*. Last year they were open wknds from May–Sept, but best to ring for 1999 opening, (0191) 200 7145; site free, £2 steam trips. **Wet 'n' Wild** (Royal Quays) Children like this well heated indoor water park with exciting flumes and slides (one has a *very* steep drop); cl some days in Nov and Dec; (0191) 296 1333; £6.50 wknds and school hols, less at other times. The Magnesia Bank (Camden St) has good-value food.

PETERLEE NZ4338 **Castle Eden Dene** The biggest of Durham's wooded coastal ravines, now a picturesque nature reserve with 12 miles of footpaths over 550 acres; free.

PONTELAND NZ1577 **Kirkley Hall Gardens** (2m NW towards Morpeth) Attractive and thoughtfully maintained, with lots of herbaceous perennials, Victorian walled garden, pretty sunken garden, woodland garden and unusual trees and shrubs. Plant sales, disabled access; cl Oct–Mar; (01661) 860808; £1.50. Nearby Milbourne has a good farm shop with pick-your-own.

PRUDHOE CASTLE NZ0963 12th/14th-c ruined castle on an impressive mound (the name means 'proud hill') overlooking the Tyne, once the stronghold of the powerful Percy family. Remarkable restored gatehouse, and exhibition in nearby 19th-c manor house. Snacks, shop, disabled access; (01661) 833459; cl Nov–Apr; £1.70. The Feathers at Hedley on the Hill does good wknd food.

ROKER NZ4058 The interesting **church** was designed by leading members of the Arts & Crafts movement.

ROSS BACK SANDS NU1339 One of the finest sections of the Northumbrian coast path – splendid windswept solitude, looking out to Holy Island.

ROTHBURY NU0501 **Cragside** Opulent Victorian mansion of Lord Armstrong, the armaments king, with spectacular rooms and some of the amazing gadgets he designed. Best of all are the miles of well wooded landscaped grounds, with lakes, glorious rhododendrons, showy formal garden, and a walk illustrating the various elements of the hydro-electric scheme he devised to light the house. Meals, snacks, shop, disabled access (inc fishing pier on trout lake); cl Mon exc bank hols, and Nov–Mar; house cl am; garden, grounds and visitor centre open selected days in winter; (01669) 620333; £6, £3.80 grounds only; NT. The Newcastle Hotel and Queen's Head have decent food. The **Rothbury Terraces** have excellent gentle parkland walks.

ROWLANDS GILL NZ1456 **Derwentcote Steel Furnace** (on the A694 between Rowlands Gill and Hamsterley, where the Cross Keys does good-value food) The earliest and most complete steel-making furnace to have survived, with an exhibition on steel production. Shop, disabled access; open pm 1st and 3rd Sun of month, Apr–Sept; (01207) 562573; free.

SEAHOUSES NU2232 An unpretentious seaside resort, with amusement arcades and so forth – and a busy fishing harbour, overlooked by a good interesting pub, the Olde Ship. From Apr–Sept, weather permitting, **boat trips** around the Farne Islands let you see the eider ducks, thousands of other seabirds, and grey seals. Breeding season for the birds is usually around May–July, though perhaps a little later for the seals, whose plaintive-voiced pups stay on shore for only a few weeks. Most boats cost around £7. Landing on the NT-owned islands is extra (from £3; £3.90 at breeding times). The NT has an information centre about the islands on Main St, cl winter Mon and Tues; (01665) 721099.

SEATON SLUICE NZ3276 **Seaton Delaval** Vanbrugh's Palladian masterpiece, a splendid design of central porticoed main block and massive outer wings. Not all the interior has survived unscathed, and much of the original park and grounds has been submerged by surrounding developments. Snacks, shop; open pm Weds, Sun and bank hols May–Aug, plus Thurs July–Aug; (0191) 237 3040; £3. The buildings around the Norman **church** are attractive, and the Waterford Arms nr the low-key seafront does generous fresh fish.

SHILDON NZ2326 **Timothy Hackworth Railway Museum** (Hackworth Cl, just SE) Restored home of early railway pioneer, with working replica of *Sans Pareil* in goods yard, and occasional passenger rides along 400 yards of original Stockton & Darlington track bed. Snacks, shop, limited disabled access; cl Mon (exc bank hols), Tues, and Nov–Easter; (01388) 777999; *£1.50.

SOUTH SHIELDS NZ3667 **Arbeia Roman Fort** (Baring St) Huge variety of remains, as well as re-created scenes of camp life, museum with excellently displayed finds, and plenty for children to enjoy. Snacks, shop, some disabled access; cl Sun exc pm Apr–Sept; (0191) 456 1369; free, £1 for **Time Quest** (splendid hands-on archaeology exhibition). **Museum & Art Gallery** (Ocean Rd) Just round the corner, this also has some hands-on exhibitions; open as Arbeia; (0191) 456 8740; free. Kirkpatricks (Ocean Rd) is a comfortable dining pub, and the Marsden Rattler (South Foreshore) is an enjoyable seafront bar complete with 2 original railway carriages.

STAINDROP NZ1221 **Raby Castle** Imposing fortress with Saxon origins; vast medieval hall, 14th-c kitchen, and dazzling Victorian octagonal drawing room – now restored to its original splendour. From the outside – where there are walled gardens and a deer park – it looks just as a castle ought to. Snacks, shop (selling oven-ready game from the estate); open bank hol wknds from Easter, Weds and Sun May and Jun, and Sun–Fri July–Sept, castle pm only; (01833) 660202; £4, £1.50 park and gardens only. The village is pretty. Up at Butterknowle the Malt Shovel has good-value food, evenings and wknd lunchtimes.

STAWARD GORGE NY8063 Part of the **Allen Banks** estate (NT), with year-round access to the paths along the wooded River Allen – frequented by roe deer – and a ruined peel tower.

STOCKSFIELD NZ0762 **Cherryburn** (slightly E at Mickley) Well preserved 18th-c farm, the birthplace of artist and naturalist Thomas Bewick, with an exhibition on his life. A nice spot, with farmyard animals, craft demonstrations, and good valley views. Shop, some disabled access; cl am, all day Tues and Weds, and Nov–Mar; (01661) 843276; £2.80; NT. The Highlander at Ovington is good value.

STOCKTON-ON-TEES NZ4419 **Green Dragon Museum** (Theatre Yard) Local history inc a good audio-visual presentation on the birth of the railways here in 1825. Shop, some disabled access (prior notice please); cl Sun and bank hols; (01642) 674308; free. There's a railway heritage trail round the town. **Preston Hall Museum** (on the A135 Stockton–Yarm, NU4215) Very well constructed Victorian high street and period rooms, plus working craftsmen, aviary, and woodland and riverside walks. Snacks, shop, disabled access to ground floor only; cl am Sun, 25–26 Dec, Jan 1, Good Fri; (01642) 781184; £1. On the same site **Butterfly World** has a re-created jungle environment with hundreds of exotic butterflies flitting between the trees, rocks and waterfalls. Shop, disabled access; cl Nov–Feb; (01642) 791414; £2.90. Slightly E along the river, the surprisingly graceful Tees Barrage keeps polluted tidal water from mixing with water from the hills, moors and valleys, which it's hoped will simulate watersports in the area.

☺ **SUNDERLAND** NZ3957 *See separate Family Panel on p.474* for **National Glass Centre**.

TANFIELD RAILWAY NZ2057 The world's oldest surviving railway, built in 1725 to carry coal to the Tyne, and set in a picturesque wooded valley. Steamtrains still chuff along the route, and you can get off by a wooden gorge spanned by **Causey Arch**, the earliest railway bridge. There's a collection of locomotives, and they often have a blacksmith forging new parts for restoration work. Summer snacks, shop, disabled access; trains usually run every Sun, plus Weds and Thurs in summer hols, and bank hols; (0191) 274 2002 for timetable; fares from £3.50. The Potters Wheel in Sunniside at the other end has decent food.

TEESDALE NY9425 The best of County Durham's scenery; the B6277 below its moors and on to Alston in Cumbria is one of the finest drives in England. Upper Teesdale has much of the best walking in the Durham Pennines, and is famous for its limestone flora, inc rare arctic alpine species and the unique Teesdale violet; Widdybank Fell is a National Nature Reserve. The attractive villages of Middleton-in-Teesdale, Romaldkirk (there's an especially distinguished church here), Eggleston and Cotherstone all have good pubs and inns. A rewarding side track is to the cosy Strathmore Arms in Holwick.

! **TYNEMOUTH** NZ3769 **Castle & Priory** Evocative clifftop ruins, high above the Tyne estuary. Little remains of the once-rich 11th-c Benedictine priory beyond its stirring nave and chancel, and the spooky gravestones outside. Even less is left of the 11th/14th-c castle, but it's unusual to find 2 such ruins next to each other, and it's a great spot for picnics. Shop, disabled access; cl winter Mon, 24–26 Dec, 1 Jan; (0191) 257 1090; £1.70. The Salutation (Front St) is comfortable for lunch. **Tynemouth Sea Life Centre** (Grand Parade, Beaconsfield) The same reliable mixture as at their other centres, with a spectacular underwater tunnel surrounded by shark-infested water, and the unique Jelly Lab, demonstrating the life cycle of a jellyfish. Meals, snacks, shop, disabled access; cl 25 Dec; (0191) 257 6100; £4.50.

† **WARDEN CHURCH** NY9166 (just N of Hexham) Down a lane by the Tyne, a fine example of the sturdy northern churches that had to do double duty as holy places and watchtowers to warn of Border raiders.

★ † ! **WARKWORTH** NU2405 The main street of this quietly picturesque small town rises attractively from the riverside 12th-c Norman **church** with its finely vaulted chancel to the striking **castle** on its hill above the River Coquet. It's virtually complete, so wandering round the crooked passageways and dark staircases is wonderfully atmospheric. Events here were immortalised in Shakespeare's *Henry IV*. Shop; cl 1–2pm in winter, 24–26 Dec; (01665) 711423; £2.70. **Warkworth Hermitage** Prettily placed a short way upstream, this 14th-c cell of retreat is cut into the sandstone cliff, with some crude wall-carvings and a tiny vaulted chapel; on Weds, Sun and bank hols Apr–Sept a boat can take you, £1.50. The Hermitage Hotel and Masons Arms are useful for lunch; there are one or two antique shops, and this stretch of coast has some lovely beaches.

WASHINGTON OLD HALL NZ3156 (The Avenue) Well restored stone-built 13th-c manor, for several hundred years the home of George Washington's family, though his ancestors had been established elsewhere (notably Sulgrave Manor in Northants) for quite a while by the time he was born. They're re-creating a Jacobean formal garden. Snacks, shop, disabled access to ground floor only; open Sun–Weds Mar–Oct; (0191) 416 6879; £2.50; NT. The unspoilt old village comes as a real surprise when you've penetrated the surrounding New Town. The Washington Arms is good value for lunch, and there's a small **mining museum** down Albany Way (free). **Wildfowl & Wetlands Centre** (District 15, off the A1231 E) 100 acres with hides, well laid out walks, adventure play area, and very good visitor centre. Some birds will feed from your hand (you can buy bird food – worth it to see the flamingos squabbling over every mouthful). Meals, snacks, shop, disabled access; cl 25 Dec; (0191) 416 5454; £4.25. In summer the River Wear ferry from Sunderland stops here.

WEARDALE NY8242 This gave much of County Durham's wealth, with lead and iron mining along its length and in the moors above. There's little reminder of those days now, but the A689 is a memorable drive. **Killhope Lead Mining Centre** Probably the best-preserved lead-mining site in Britain, and unmissable if you're at all interested in industrial history. Equipped with hard hat and lamps, you're led through the mine's dark, chilly passageways to a huge underground waterwheel. Snacks, shop; cl Nov–Mar; (01388) 537505; £3.40 for surface exhibitions, £5 inc mine trip. A **riding centre** at Low Cornriggs Farm has lessons, guided rides along scenic former packhorse routes, and farmhouse B & B; (01388) 537600. **Weardale Museum** (Ireshopeburn) Near the source of the river, this re-creates life in this high valley's heady lead-mining days, and has an exhibition on John Wesley, who often preached next door. Shop; cl am, all day Mon and Tues (exc in Aug), and Oct–Easter; (01388) 537417; £1. Along the dale is a string of attractive villages such as Stanhope (the valley's 'capital', with a curious fossil tree stump in the churchyard) and Wolsingham (good-value food at the Black Bull), as well as pleasant waterside and moorland walks. The Golden Lion at St John's Chapel, open all day in summer, is a useful stop. The diversion to **Rookhope** NY9442 is worthwhile: fine alpine plants nursery, small craft centre, decent pub, and more good walks.

WHITBURN NZ4064 **Souter Lighthouse** Built in 1870, this was the most advanced lighthouse of the day, the first to be powered by electricity; it still has period rooms and equipment. Meals, snacks, shop, disabled access (but not to tower); cl Fri, and all Nov–Mar; (0191) 529 3161; £2.50; NT. The NT also owns the Leas, the spectacular stretch of coastline around here, leading to Marsden Rock with its colony of kittiwakes, cormorants and fulmars. The Jolly Sailor has decent food.

Days Out

The Great Wall of Northumbria: Birdoswald Roman fort; Greenhead Roman Army Museum; lunch at the Milecastle Inn, on the B6318 NE of Haltwhistle; Vindolanda frontier town; Housesteads Roman fort, and walk along Hadrian's Wall; or skip the walk and look at Chesters Roman fort.

Gems of Teesdale: Barnard Castle, and the Bowes Museum; lunch at the Fox & Hounds, Cotherstone or the Rose & Crown, Romaldkirk; nature trail from Bowlees visitor centre to Gibson's Cave; High Force; walk from Cow Green Reservoir to Cauldron Snout.

Island eye-openers: Boat trip to the Farne Islands from Seahouses; lunch at the Olde Ship, Seahouses; Bamburgh Castle; Holy Island (time visit to catch low tide).

WHITLEY BAY NZ3575 **St Mary's Lighthouse** On St Mary's Island, reached by a causeway at low tide. Good views from the top – to tempt you up the 137 steps, a camera relays the image to a colour TV at the bottom. Shop; cl all Nov–Mar, and possibly other times depending on the tide; (0191) 200 8650; *£2. When the lighthouse is closed the island is worth a visit for the rock pools alone, and is visited all through the year by a wide range of birds. The Shiremoor House Farm up on Middle Engine Lane, New York (handy too for North Shields and Tynemouth) has some of the best food in this area – good value.

WINDY GYLE NT8515 The high summit by a fine ridge section of the Pennine Way, along the English/Scottish border – the best of the Way's long, lonely plod over the Cheviots' grassy moors. You have to walk some way from the road to reach this main ridge: start from Coquetdale and walk along the Street, an ancient drovers' track. Gradients are mild but the peaty ground can get boggy after rain; not all routes are defined on the ground, but stone boundary walls and forest plantations are useful guides.

★ **WITTON-LE-WEAR** NZ1631 **Low Barns Nature Reserve** 100-acre reserve with nature trails, woodland, grassland, lake and lots of interesting wildlife. Snacks, shop, good disabled access; cl 25–26 Dec, 1 Jan; (01388) 488728; free. The village is attractive, with a tree-lined sloping green; the Victoria is useful for lunch.

WOODHORN COLLIERY MUSEUM NZ2889 (Queen Elizabeth II Country Park) Former colliery buildings re-creating life in the pit and the communities around it. Also short trips on narrow-gauge railway, displays of art by local miners, craft workshops and woodland walks. Meals, snacks, shop, some disabled access; cl Mon (exc bank hols) and Tues; (01670) 856968; free, though charge for railway. **Woodhorn church** Partly Saxon and Norman, said to be the oldest on this coast; it has a local history museum and wknd craft demonstrations. Shop, disabled access; cl Mon (exc bank hols), Tues, and all Nov–Apr; (01670) 817371; free.

WYLAM NZ1264 **Stephenson's Birthplace** The single room open here is the NT's least visited property, some days attracting nobody at all (open pm Thurs, Sat, Sun and bank hol Mon, Apr–Oct; 80p); the Fox & Hounds (a short walk along the old railway track) and Boathouse have good-value food.

Where to eat

AMBLE NU2604 **Charlie's Chip Shop** *Albert St (01665) 710206* Popular family-run restaurant serving chips with fish, chicken and pies; vegetarian options and children's dishes, plus a take-away service. £4.50.

BAMBURGH NU1835 **Copper Kettle Tea Rooms** *21 Front St (01668) 214315* 18th-c cottage nr castle, with beams, panelling, and copper implements; sandwiches, baked potatoes and salads, as well as home-made cakes and biscuits, a fine range of teas inc many fruit and herb ones, and a good choice of other drinks; no smoking; cl end Oct–mid-Mar; limited disabled access. £3.50.

BERWICK-UPON-TWEED NU0052 **Foxtons** *26 Hide Hill (01289) 303939* Lively bistro with good, imaginative and varied food that changes daily, good wine list, and friendly service; cl Sun, bank hols; children over 8. **£22**|£4.80.

CARTERWAY HEADS NZ0452 **Manor House** *(01207) 255268* Simple slate-roofed stone house with pleasant view over moorland pastures, good popular food from a wide, changing menu, and a friendly atmosphere. **£21.85**|£8.

CORBRIDGE NY9864 **Valley** *Old Station House, Station Rd (01434) 633434* Extremely friendly Indian restaurant in attractively converted sandstone station house, with wide choice of very good Indian food and kind service; also, a special train service for parties from Tyneside with uniformed escort and free travel, and your order is phoned ahead to be ready on arrival – good fun; cl lunchtimes, cl Sun. **£20**.

CRASTER NU2519 **Craster Restaurant** *(01665) 576230* Upstairs restaurant overlooking the harbour with candles on tables, exceedingly welcoming staff, and huge helpings of fairly priced really fresh fish – they have their own smoking yard, too; cl Oct–May; well behaved children. £7.50.

DURHAM NZ2643 **Bistro 21** *Aykley Heads House, Aykley Heads (0191) 384 4354* Former 17th-c farmhouse, now a light and airy Mediterranean-style restaurant with pine dining chairs on wooden or flagstoned floors, a good choice of very enjoyable interesting modern cooking, a thoughtful wine list, and professional but relaxed service; cl Sun; disabled access. **£28.50**|£8.50.

GREAT WHITTINGTON NZ0071 **Queen's Head** *(01434) 672267* Simple stone inn with 2 beamed, comfortable and neatly furnished rooms, a wide choice of good interesting food, no smoking restaurant, log fires, well kept real ales, decent wines, and quite a few malt whiskies. **£20.90**|£6.50.

HAYDON BRIDGE NY8464 **General Havelock** *(01434) 684283* Very civilised old stone terraced house with stripped-stone back dining room overlooking the Tyne, good if limited lunchtime food and interesting evening meals, well kept real ales, good wines by the glass, pleasant service, and friendly local atmosphere; cl Mon, 1st 2 wks Jan, 1st 2 wks Sept; disabled access. **£25 for 4 courses**|£8.50.

HEDLEY ON THE HILL NZ0759 **Feathers** *(01661) 843607* Little stone local with 3 neatly kept traditional bars, woodburners, straightforward furnishings, a charming, relaxed and welcoming atmosphere, imaginative meals (not wkdy lunchtime), and well kept real ales; disabled access. **£13.65**|£5.

MATFEN NZ0370 **Black Bull** *(01661) 886330* Striking creeper-covered stone building by village green with fresh, well presented tasty bar food in spacious Turkey-carpeted main bar, very good restaurant menu, log fires, and efficient service; comfortable bdrms; no food pm 25 Dec, 26 Dec or 1 Jan; disabled access. **£20**|£4.95.

NEWCASTLE UPON TYNE NZ2563 **Courtney's** *5–7 The Side, Quayside (0191) 232 5537* Popular little waterside restaurant with very enjoyable international modern cooking, nice puddings, good service, and a decent wine list; cl am Sat, Sun, bank hols. **£40**|2-course lunch £9.95.

NEWCASTLE UPON TYNE NZ2666 **Fisherman's Lodge** *Jesmond Dene (0191) 281 3281* Once the town residence of Lord Armstrong and in a quiet spot down a long drive, this popular restaurant has an attractive bar and elegant dining room, and specialises in delicious fresh seafood – though the local meat and lovely puddings are quite a draw too; professional service and reasonably priced wines; cl am Sat, Sun, bank hols; children over 9 in evening; disabled access. **£36 dinner, £24 lunch**.

RENNINGTON NU2119 **Masons Arms** *(01665) 577275* Friendly, well run old coaching inn with good-value generously served bar food inc nice daily specials; comfortably modernised beamed lounge bar, friendly helpful staff, real ales, and decent breakfasts; bdrms; children over 5 in evening. **£15**|£5.

SEATON SLUICE NZ3477 **Waterford Arms** *(0191) 237 0450* Popular dining pub with comfortable homely bar, separate restaurant, a no smoking area, very good enjoyable food with a strong emphasis on fresh fish, real ales, and friendly service; bdrms. **£20.35**|£7.25.

WARENFORD NU1328 **Warenford Lodge** *(01668) 213453* Very individual old, though rather modern-feeling, dining pub with stripped stonework, big stone fireplace, comfortable extension with woodburner, really good attractively presented, imaginative food, and decent wines; children in evening dining room only; cl Mon, am Tues–Fri; limited disabled access. **£20**|£4.70.

WHALTON NZ1281 **Beresford Arms** *(01670) 775225* Civilised bar and dining room serving very good reasonably priced genuine home cooking, well kept real ales, and friendly staff; cl pm winter Suns; disabled access. **£18.70**|£6.95.

Special thanks to A J Clark, Mrs J M Best, D A Harris, John Prescott.

Northumbria Calendar

Some of these dates were provisional as we went to press. Please check information with the telephone numbers provided.

FEBRUARY

16 **Alnwick** Shrovetide Football at the Castle: ball is thrown from battlements and piped in procession to pastures where the game is played (01665) 510665; **Newcastle** Chinese New Year: lion and unicorn dance procession and fireworks – *till Thurs 18* (0191) 261 0691

APRIL

9 **Morpeth** Northumbrian Gathering: festival of Northumbrian traditions – *till Sun 11* (01670) 513308

10 **Gateshead** Spring Flower Show at Gateshead Central Nurseries – *till Sun 11* (0191) 477 1011

MAY

1 **Berwick-upon-Tweed** Riding the Bounds: colourful groups of horse riders head out of town for an afternoon of fun and races (01289) 330044

2 **Newcastle** Green Festival at Leazes Park (0191) 232 1750; **West Allerdean** Country Fair at West Allerdean Farm (01289) 308589

8 **Durham** World Cup Cricket Warm Up Match: Scotland v Durham (0191) 387 1717; **Newcastle** National Performance & Sports Car Show at Telewest Arena (0191) 260 5000

10 **Durham** World Cup Cricket Warm Up Match: Pakistan v Durham (0191) 387 1717

15 **Houghall** Farm & Garden Event at Durham College of Agriculture – *till Sun 16* (0191) 386 1351

16 **Berwick-upon-Tweed** Border Marches Festival: circular walks through the Tweed valley (01289) 330044

20 **Durham** World Cup Cricket Match: Pakistan v Scotland (0191) 387 1717

26 **Barnard Castle** Carnival – *till parade on Mon 31* (01833) 637637

27 **Durham** World Cup Cricket Match: Australia v Bangladesh (0191) 387 1717

28 **Berwick-upon-Tweed** Mayfair: music, stalls – *till Mon 31* (01289) 303677

29 **North Shields** Fish Quay Festival: international street theatre, world music stage, Irish stage, children's village, parade, fireworks – *till Mon 31* (0191) 200 5415

31 **Bishop Middleham** Countryside Fair at Island Farm (01388) 424200; **Corbridge** Northumberland County Show inc arena events at Tynedale Park (01434) 344443; **Rothbury** Street Fair (01669) 620574

JUNE

1 **Darlington** Cycling Festival – *till 31 July* (01325) 388584

5 **Allendale** May Fair: carnival, bands (01434) 683269

12 **Durham** Regatta – *till Sun 13* (0191) 384 0615; **Stamfordham** South Tyne Engine Society Steam & Vintage Rally at Ouston Airfield – *till Sun 13* (01434) 321029

Northumbria Calendar (cont.)

18 **Newcastle** Hoppings: funfair at Town Moor – *till Sun 27* (0191) 454 6239
19 **Ovingham** Goose Fair: morris and country dancing, Northumbrian pipes (01661) 832822
26 **Darlington** Carnival – *till Sun 27* (01325) 253686
27 **Alnwick** Medieval Fair: costumed re-enactment, duckings, courts – *till 3 July* (01665) 605004; **Darlington** National Music Day: live bands in Market Square (01325) 388584

JULY

3 **South Shields** Cookson Country Festival: free family festival – *till 8 Aug* (0191) 427 1717; **Sunderland** International Kite Festival – *till Sun 4* (0191) 514 1235
7 **Barnard Castle** Outdoor Theatre & Fireworks – *till Sat 10* (01833) 650623
10 **Durham** Miners' Gala: colourful march culminating in Trade Union rally on racecourse (0191) 384 3515; **Whitley Bay** Jazz Festival – *till Sun 11* (0191) 281 2935
16 **Whitley Bay** North of England Motorshow (0191) 516 0085
17 **Durham** County Show at Lambton Park (0191) 388 5459; **Rothbury** Traditional Music Festival (01669) 620718
18 **Middlesbrough** Mela: Asian festival (01642) 263839
20 **Tynemouth** Pageant at the Castle & Priory – *till Sat 24* (0191) 251 4022
23 **Burnopfield** Open-air Concert at Gibside: a tribute to Queen (01670) 774691
24 **Burnopfield** Open-air Concert at Gibside (01670) 774691
25 **Seaham** Carnival (0191) 581 8034
29 **Gateshead** World Veteran Track & Field Championships – *till 8 Aug* (0191) 477 1011
31 **Gateshead** Summer Flower Show at Gateshead Central Nurseries – *till 1 Aug* (0191) 477 1011

AUGUST

6 **Saltburn-by-the-Sea** International Festival of Folk Music, Dance & Song – *till Sun 8* (01947) 840928
7 **Alnwick** International Music Festival – *till Sun 8* (01665) 602682; **Hartlepool** Headland Carnival (01429) 279850; **Sunderland** International Airshow: largest airshow in the country – *till Sun 8* (0191) 510 9317
14 **Billingham** International Folklore Festival: up to 10 countries represented – *till Sat 21* (01642) 393911; **Hartlepool** Show at Grayfield Recreation Ground: arena events, vintage vehicles – *till Sun 15* (01429) 523420; **Slaley** Show: traditional agricultural show at Townhead Field (01434) 673530
20 **Alnwick** Horse Driving Trials at the Castle – *till Sun 22* (01668) 217329
27 **Cambo** Open-air Concert at Wallington House – *till Sat 28* (01670) 774691
28 **Consett** Show at Allensford Park: festival of music and theatre – *till Mon 30* (01207) 218000; **St John's Chapel** Weardale Agricultural Show (01388) 537398
29 **Newcastle** Mela: Asian Festival – *till Mon 30* (0191) 211 6232
30 **Blanchland** and Hunstanworth Show (01434) 675799; **Seahouses** Lifeboat Fête (01668) 214256

Northumbria Calendar (cont.)

SEPTEMBER

4 **Berwick-upon-Tweed** Military Tattoo – *till Sun 5* (01289) 307427; **Wolsingham** Agricultural Show & Country Fair at Scotch Isle Farm – *till Mon 6* (01388) 527862

6 **Darlington** Railway Carnival at Darlington Railway Centre & Museum – *till Sun 12* (01325) 388584

11 **Bowes** Agricultural Show (01833) 637059; **Gilsland** Agricultural Show (01697) 747651; **Ingram** Agricultural Show (01665) 578361; **Stanhope** Agricultural Show at Unthank Park – *till Mon 13* (01388) 528642

12 **Whitfield** Country Fair & Vintage Rally (01434) 345313

18 **Darlington** Championship Dog Show at South Park – *till Sun 19* (01325) 312484; **Eggleston** Agricultural Show at High Shipley Farm (01833) 638749

19 **Darlington** Rhythm & Blues Day: live bands in Market Square (01325) 388584

OCTOBER

2 **Houghton-le-Spring** Feast: tournaments, parades – *till Sun 10* (0831) 458774

3 **Bardon Mill** Landmark Trust Open Day at Causeway House: not usually open to the public (01628) 825925

5 **Middlesbrough** Writearound: festival for writers and readers – *till Fri 22* (01642) 243425

9 **Alwinton** Border Shepherds Show (01669) 630246; **Northumberland** Music Week: wide variety of traditional music and events at various venues – *till Sun 17* (01670) 533923

NOVEMBER

4 **Bishop Auckland** Fireworks & Music at Town Recreation Ground (01388) 765555

5 **Newcastle** Comedy Festival – *till Sat 20* (0191) 230 4406

6 **Darlington** Firework & Laser Spectacular at South Park (01325) 388413; **Hartlepool** Firework & Music Display at Seaton Carew (01429) 869706

DECEMBER

4 **Durham** Christmas Festival – *till Sun 5* (0191) 386 3050

31 **Allendale** Baal Festival: villagers parade in costume carrying burning tar barrels (01434) 683763

Please let us know what you think of places in the *Guide*. Use the report forms at the back of the book or simply write us a letter.

NOTTINGHAMSHIRE

Some good family outings, fine landscapes and low prices; Nottingham is well worth a visit.

The county has some charming and interesting villages, and one or two attractive old towns such as Newark and Southwell. Nottingham itself merits exploration: lively and stimulating; its Galleries of Justice are exceptional. Newstead Abbey is the county's surviving great house. The mansions and families which gave the name of the Dukeries to the countryside in the north are long gone, but broad tracts of landscaped wooded parkland remain; Clumber Park is a choice example.

This is of course Robin Hood country, and parts of Sherwood Forest remain; the World of Robin Hood at Haughton is an excellent-value family outing. Other real treats for young children are Sundown Adventureland at Rampton and White Post farm at Farnsfield, while most ages find Creswell Crags intriguing – especially on cave tour days.

Where to stay

GRINGLEY ON THE HILL SK7390 **Old Vicarage** *Gringley on the Hill, South Doncaster, Yorks DN10 4RF (01777) 817248* ***£56,** plus special breaks; 3 rms. Pretty house in 3 acres with fine views; comfortable sitting room, delicious food using some home-grown produce, and friendly owners; a flower-filled garden, tennis court and super views; cl 24–26 Dec, 31 Dec–1 Jan; dogs by prior arrangement.

LANGAR SK7234 **Langar Hall** *Langar, Nottingham NG13 9HG (01949) 860559* ***£85;** 10 lovely rms, some in wing and courtyard as well. Fine country house in spacious grounds; beautifully furnished, elegant rooms, a pillared dining hall with paintings for sale, antiques and fresh flowers, and a relaxed, informal atmosphere; lively and friendly owner, and very good food; regular theatricals and murder weekends; dogs by arrangement.

SOUTHWELL SK7053 **Old Forge** *Burgage Lane, Southwell NG25 0ER (01636) 812809* ***£54,** plus special breaks; 5 rms. 200-year-old, former blacksmith's house with a welcoming owner and interesting furnishings; super breakfasts in the conservatory overlooking the Minster, light suppers on request, and a pretty terrace; well behaved dogs welcome.

SOUTHWELL SK7053 **Saracens Head** *Market Pl, Southwell NG25 0HE (01636) 812701* **£70;** 30 well kept rms. Interesting old hotel (Charles I spent his last free night here) with an ancient-feeling, beamed main bar; pleasant staff, straightforward bar lunches, and a restaurant.

To see and do

NOTTINGHAM SK5739 At weekends and on summer evenings it quickly loses its big-city character, and is then easy to park in and stroll through, without the rush of traffic along its inner ring road. The parts around the parish church (interesting carvings) and the Lace Market are particularly attractive. Sadly the fascinating Lace Hall itself has closed (after failing to get a Lottery grant). The tourist information centre on Smithy Row has a useful ½-hour introduction to the town (Mon, Fri and Sat only). An Explorer Pass covers entry to the main attractions, valid for a year. Besides the museums described below, the **Museum of Costume and**

Textiles (43–51 Castle Gate; cl Mon exc bank hols, Tues, 24 Dec–1 Jan; free) is well worth a look. Useful lunch places are Fellows Morton & Clayton (Canal Rd; brews its own beer), the quaint old Bell (Angel Row), the Limelight (attached to the Playhouse) and Lincolnshire Poacher (Mansfield Rd).

Nottingham Castle Up on the summit, this dates from the 17th c, but the gateway is from an earlier 13th-c fortress. It now houses an appealing **museum**, with a history of the site and the subterranean passageways – the rock on which old Nottingham stood is honeycombed with hundreds of galleries, cellars and tunnels (an old pub nearby, the Olde Trip to Jerusalem, has a fascinating bar bored right into the rock). Meals, snacks, shop, disabled access; cl 24 Dec–1 Jan; (0115) 915 3700; £2 wknds and bank hols, free wkdys.

Cave tours Tours usually leave the castle daily (exc Sun) at 2pm and 3pm (and 4pm in summer), but have recently been suspended because of a rockfall, so call (0115) 915 3700 first. They're quite strenuous. £1.

Caves of Nottingham (Drury Walk) This is a tour with taped commentary of the 700-year-old caverns beneath a busy modern shopping centre, through an underground tannery, Victorian slum, air-raid shelters, and pub cellars. Shop; cl 24–26 Dec, 1 Jan; (0115) 924 1424; *£2.95.

Galleries of Justice (Shire Hall, High Pavement) The grim realities of a 19th-c trial and prison life are re-enacted with real verve at this growing centre, set around 2 Victorian courtrooms in use right through to 1986. The award-winning centrepiece – designed very much to entertain children – is called Condemned, and begins with visitors being given a criminal identity number before being sent to trial in the Criminal Court. It's hardly giving the game away to say that the verdict is always guilty. 'Prisoners' are then taken down to the cells, where costumed interpreters posing as prison warders lead them to their fate. Nicked is a similar new police station experience where visitors can help to solve a murder. Meals, snacks, shop, some disabled access; cl Mon (exc bank hols) and 24–26 Dec; (0115) 952 0555; Condemned *£7.95.

Brewhouse Yard Museum (Castle Boulevard) Spread over 5 17th-c houses with period rooms and reconstructions, this has very good interactive displays on local life, and several features designed with children in mind (the Feely Boxes are fun). Award-winning historic roses in the cottage garden. Shop, some disabled access; cl winter Fri, 25–26 Dec; (0115) 948 3504; £1.50 wknds and bank hols, otherwise free.

Lace Centre (Castle Rd) This pretty 15th-c house has lace hanging from almost every beam, much of it for sale. Lace-making demonstrations pm summer Thurs. Some disabled access; cl 25–26 Dec; (0115) 941 3539; free.

Wollaton Hall (Wollaton Park, 3m W) Splendidly ornate Tudor house with the city's natural history collection. The 500-acre grounds are a delight. Shop, some disabled access; cl 24 Dec–1 Jan; (0115) 915 3900; free wkdys, £1.50 wknds and bank hols (£2 inc adjacent industrial museum). The **Industrial Museum** (Courtyard Buildings) looks once again at lace-making, along with other local industries. Open Sun; phone for steamdays (0115) 915 3910; £1.50.

Tales of Robin Hood (Maid Marian Way) Cars carry you through the sights, sounds and smells of a re-created medieval Sherwood Forest, and a film looks at the truth behind the stories. Pretty much for insistent children only – otherwise you might be better going out to Haughton (*see entry below*). Meals, snacks, shop, disabled access; cl 25–26 Dec; (0115) 948 3284; *£4.50.

! Green's Mill and Science Centre (Windmill Lane, Sneinton) Good for families: the restored tower mill still produces flour, and you can try grinding corn on part of an old millstone. Among the exhibits at the hands-on Science Centre next door is a weather satellite receiver showing pictures live from space. Shop, disabled access; cl Mon (exc bank hols), Tues, and 24 Dec–1 Jan – tel (0115) 915 6878 to check if the mill is working; free.

Djanogly Art Gallery (University Arts Centre, University Park, SW of centre) Good temporary exhibitions; cl am Sun, am bank hols, Christmas; (0115) 951 3189; free.

Attenborough Nature Reserve SK5235 Unusual, down by Beeston, with worthwhile birdwatching at the extensive, partly wooded lakes; on the far side, a path runs along a narrow spit of land dividing them from the mighty River Trent. The Manor at Toton is a pleasant nearby dining pub.

Other things to see and do

Nottinghamshire Family Attraction of the Year

RAMPTON SK7978 **Sundown Adventureland** (Treswell Rd; N of the A57) Over the last year, quite a few readers with young children have written to us full of praise for this cheerful little leisure park. Designed for children up to 10 (and best for those between around 4 and 8), it's full of life-size representations and tableaux of stories and fairy tales, from the Wild West to the Three Little Pigs, taking in witches, wizards, dungeons and dragons along the way. There are 3 gentle rides – the Boozy Barrel Boats and the Rocky Mountain Train are the best – as well as a few animals, and several themed play areas, one under cover (height restrictions apply in here). At Christmas they have delightful seasonal displays, accompanied by carol singers, morris dancers or Punch and Judy shows, and Santa gives every child a present (not everything else is working then). Most of it is outdoors, so best on a dry day. It's definitely not the kind of place to bring an older sister or brother (they'd be bored stiff), but very young children find it enchanting, and the length of a visit depends very much on the limits of your child's imagination. Snacks (mostly fast food), shop, some disabled access; cl 25–26 Dec, 1 Jan, and all Jan wkdys; (01777) 248274; £4.25 everyone over 2.

BEACON HILL SK7490 Above the Chesterfield Canal at Gringley on the Hill, magnificent views in all directions; you can make out the towers of Lincoln Cathedral on a clear day.

★ **BLYTH** SK6185 An attractive small town, with interesting wall paintings in the **church**; the White Swan's good for lunch. **Hodsock Priory Gardens** (off the B6045 S) Especially lovely at snowdrop time; open 4 or 5 weeks Feb/Mar, and other days throughout the year; (01909) 591204; plant sales; *£3.

CANAL WALKS There's scope for quiet **towpath walks** by the Chesterfield Canal, nr the Boat at Hayton SK7284; or the Grantham Canal, nr the Plough at Hickling SK6929.

CLUMBER PARK SK6375 One of the great former Dukeries estates, nearly 4,000 acres of farmland, parks, lake and woodland, with an interesting walled garden, and the longest lime avenue in Europe, almost 2 miles long. The estate has outstanding walks, enough for a full-day excursion. You can also hire bikes. Meals, snacks, shop, disabled access; park open all yr, some parts cl winter; (01909) 476592; £3 per car; NT.

★ **COSSALL** SK4743 Attractive village in D H Lawrence country: he was engaged to a girl who lived in Church Cottage. But the government has just approved a huge open-cast mine in the fields they used to roam here (the county council had been blocking the plans, to safeguard the landscape).

CRESWELL CRAGS SK5474 Stone Age man lived in the caves and rock shelters of this limestone gorge right by the Derby border (the village is actually over in Derbys). Even on days with no cave tours it's an intriguing prehistoric site, with a good **visitor centre**, reconstructions of Ice Age family life, and other displays and activities. They sometimes have children's stories in one of the caves

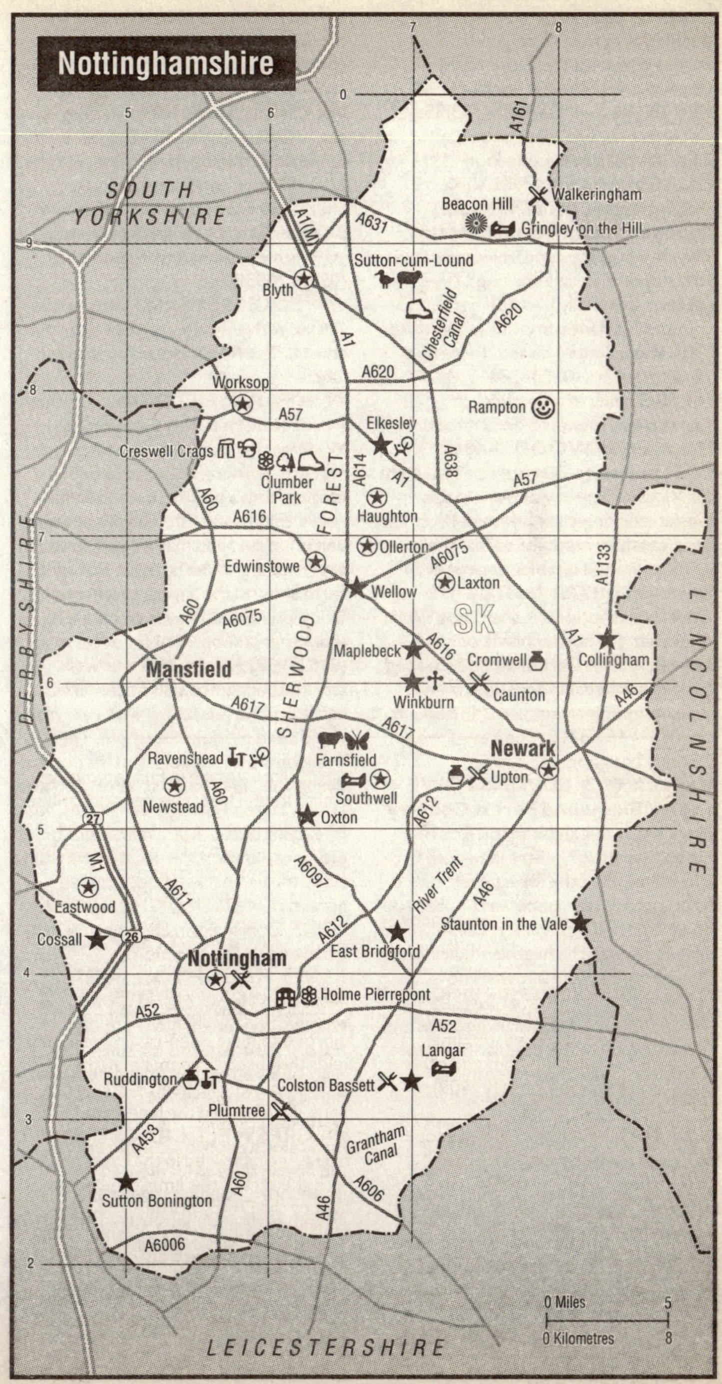
Nottinghamshire
SOUTH YORKSHIRE
DERBYSHIRE
LINCOLNSHIRE
LEICESTERSHIRE
SHERWOOD FOREST
Walkeringham
Beacon Hill
Gringley on the Hill
Sutton-cum-Lound
Blyth
Chesterfield Canal
Worksop
Rampton
Elkesley
Creswell Crags
Clumber Park
Haughton
Ollerton
Edwinstowe
Wellow
Laxton
SK
Maplebeck
Cromwell
Collingham
Mansfield
Winkburn
Caunton
Newark
Ravenshead
Farnsfield
Upton
Newstead
Southwell
Oxton
River Trent
Eastwood
Cossall
Staunton in the Vale
East Bridgford
Nottingham
Holme Pierrepont
Langar
Ruddington
Colston Bassett
Plumtree
Grantham Canal
Sutton Bonington
0 Miles 5
0 Kilometres 8

(booking required). Picnic area, shop, disabled access; cl Nov–Jan exc Sun – best to check for cave tour dates (usually every wknd at least); (01909) 720378; site free, cave tours £1.95. Take a torch. The Greendale Oak at Cuckney has good-value food.

CROMWELL SK7961 **Vina Cooke Museum of Dolls and Bygone Childhood** (Old Rectory) Thousands of toys and objects related to childhood, in an imposing 17th-c rectory. Especially lively on Easter Mon, with morris dancers, crafts and the like. Teas, shop, limited disabled access; cl 12–2pm, all Fri; (01636) 821364; *£2.50. The Great Northern at Carlton-on-Trent has decent food.

EASTWOOD SK4647 **D H Lawrence Birthplace Museum** (8a Victoria St) He was born in this typical working-class house in 1885; it's been carefully restored to how he knew it. Shop, limited disabled access; cl 24 Dec–1 Jan; (01773) 763312; £1.75. Craft workshops next door (not Weds, or pm Sats). Another home of Lawrence's, on Garden Rd, is furnished as he described it in *Sons and Lovers*; open by appointment with Mr Roberts on (0151) 653 8710. The Yew Tree at Brinsley has good-value food.

EDWINSTOWE SK6267 **Sherwood Forest Country Park** With an exhibition on Robin Hood, the visitor centre is a good springboard for the forest itself, only a fraction of what it once was (it used to cover a fifth of the county) but still miles across, though the heathland that Robin himself would have known is now largely either farmland or forestry plantation. Good waymarked paths and footpaths, the most popular being to the Major Oak (a huge tree in the forest's heart). Meals, snacks, shop, disabled access; park free, car park £1.50 wknds, bank hols and all Aug. **Sherwood Forest Art and Craft Centre** nearby has 17 craft studios housed in a mid-18th-c coach house and stables. **Sherwood Forest Farm Park** (Lamb Pens Farm) Unusual breeds of traditional farm animals, pets corner, and colourful waterfowl on a sizeable lake. Home-baked teas, shop, disabled access but best to phone in advance; cl wkdys Oct, all Nov–Mar; (01623) 823558; £3.75. Near the village church (supposedly where Robin Hood and Maid Marian were married), the Black Swan is handy for something to eat. The best drive is the B6034 N towards Worksop, then the right turn to Carburton and Clumber Park. Sherwood Forest has one of England's 3 Center Parcs, a rewarding place to stay with excellent leisure facilities; (0990) 200300.

★ **ELKESLEY** SK6875 Attractive village, with a working potter near the church. The Robin Hood is useful for lunch.

FARNSFIELD SK6257 **White Post Modern Farm Centre** (1m W) Great for children, a bustling, modern, working farm with exhibits ranging from a mouse town to llamas, quails, snakes and fish. The pig-breeding unit is fun, and you may be able to watch eggs hatching in the huge incubator. The Farm Show in the barn is a highlight. Good play areas, heated picnic barn, snacks, farm shop, disabled access; (01623) 882977; £4.25. Their well stocked pet centre sells mice, gerbils, hamsters and rats, along with everything you'd need to look after them. The Waggon & Horses at Halam is a popular dining pub. **White Post Wonderland** (1m W) Useful enough for families, with free-flying butterflies, a maze, indoor play area, junior rollercoaster and train rides. Meals, snacks, shop, disabled access; cl 24–26 Dec; (01623) 882773; *£3.25. Combs Farm Shop nearby is a good one (cl Sun and Mon).

! **HAUGHTON** SK6872 **World of Robin Hood** With an emphasis on fun that may put off historical purists, this is a splendidly enjoyable re-creation of medieval life, putting the Robin Hood stories in their historical context. They've meticulously constructed an entire medieval village, with moated drawbridge, cobbled streets and authentic shops and houses. There are costumed guides and plenty for children, inc a Disneyish version of the legends inside the castle for younger children, a small animal farm, and play area. Outside is a deer park and owl sanctuary, with summer activities such as archery. Meals, snacks, shop, some disabled access; cl Nov–Feb; (01623) 860210; £3.95. The Robin Hood at Elkesley has good-value food.

HOLME PIERREPONT HALL SK6339 Early Tudor manor house with interesting early 15th-c timbers, and an elaborate parterre in the formal courtyard garden. Teas, shop, disabled access to gardens only; phone for opening; (0115) 933 2371; £3, garden only £1.50. The Round Oak in Radcliffe on Trent has decent food.

! **LAXTON** SK7267 Unique for keeping the pattern of its **medieval farming**, with different villagers each owning strips of the 3 great fields. You can walk the grass paths or sykes which divide groups of these strips, and the Dovecote, a good pub, has an exhibition in the yard explaining the system. The **church** has a fine 15th-c screen.

★ **MAPLEBECK** SK7160 Delightfully rustic village; the Beehive's a classic country tavern, and nearby Woodborough and Lambley are also worth a look.

★ **NEWARK** SK7953 Attractive old market town with some interesting buildings in its side streets, a fine **church**, and walks by the River Trent with summer **boat trips**. The Old King's Arms (Kirkgate) is useful for lunch. Useful museums include the **Museum of Social and Folk Life** on Millgate (cl am wknds and bank hols; free), and the local history collection on Appletongate (cl 1–2pm, Thurs, and Sun exc summer pms; free). **Newark Castle** The ruins date from the 11th c, and there's still a fair bit to see; it was destroyed during the Civil War, then had periods as a cattle market and bowling green. The gardens are being relaid as they were in Victorian times. Good explanatory displays at the **Gilstrap Heritage Centre** in the grounds; cl 25–26 Dec, 1 Jan, Easter; free. **Air Museum** (Winthorpe, NE of Newark, SK8256) Over 40 assorted aircraft inc rare jet fighters and bombers; half the exhibits are under cover, so fine all year round (and the Willow Tree, over at Barnby in the Willows, is handy for lunch). Snacks, shop, disabled access; cl 24–26 Dec; (01636) 707170; £3.50.

NEWSTEAD ABBEY SK5454 (off the A60) Splendid former home of Lord Byron, in gorgeously romantic grounds, with many of his possessions. Rooms are decorated in a variety of styles from medieval through to Victorian, and there are substantial remains of the original abbey. Meals, snacks, shop, limited disabled access; cl am and Oct–Mar; (01623) 793557; house and gardens £4, gardens only £2. There are fears that mining below the house may cause problems in 1999. The Horse & Groom, in the attractive nearby village of Linby, is a useful stop.

OLLERTON SK6567 **Ollerton Mill** (Market Pl) The county's only working watermill, still producing flour as it did in the early 18th c, in a pleasant setting. Award-winning teas (teashop often open when mill isn't), shop; mill working pm Sun and bank hols Apr–Sept; (01623) 822469; £1.50. The Hop Pole, in the pretty market place, has good-value food. **Rufford Country Park** (off the A614 S) Pleasant lakeside spot on the edge of Sherwood Forest, with the ruins of a 12th-c abbey, craft centre and family activities most summer wknds (£1.50 car park charge).

★ **OXTON** SK6251 Attractive village; the lane up the hill N below the power lines leads to an Iron Age hill fort.

☺ **RAMPTON** SK7978 *See separate Family Panel on p.494* for **Sundown Adventureland**.

RAVENSHEAD SK5654 **Longdale Craft Centre** (Longdale Lane) Very good craft centre, partly set out as a Victorian village street, with rows of period workshops and a small museum. Decent restaurant, disabled access; cl 25–26 Dec; (01623) 794858; free. **Papplewick Pumping Station** (Longdale Lane) A working Victorian waterworks with 2 beam engines; best to ring for steamdays, though open for static displays pm most wknds and Weds Easter–Oct; (0115) 963 2938; £1.50 (£3 steamdays). The Burnstump, in the nearby country park, is a good-value family dining pub; the Little John (B6020) has decent food too.

RIVER TRENT This gives a tremendous sense of power even when it's on its best behaviour, sliding swiftly and massively along; its occasional floods are devastating, and most years it claims lives. Villages giving pleasant access to it include Laneham SK8076 and Thrumpton SK5031; decent pubs and inns in good riverside spots include the Hazleford Ferry at Bleasby SK7149, Lazy Otter in Wyke Lane, Farndon SK7651, Bromley Arms at Fiskerton SK7351, Unicorn Hotel at Gunthorpe SK6844 and the Ferry at Wilford SK5637.

RUDDINGTON SK5732 **Framework Knitters' Museum** (Chapel St) In restored 19th-c workshops, cottages and frameshop, this explores the industry for which Nottinghamshire was once famous. Besides reconstructed cottages, you can see the machinery working, inc the bizarre circular sock-knitting machines. Snacks, shop; cl Sun–Tues (exc pm Sun Easter–Sept), Weds and Fri, and all Dec–Easter; (0115) 984 6914; £1.50. The **Village Museum** (Easthorpe St) has reconstructed Edwardian shops (open Weds, Thurs, Sat, Easter–Sept; £1).

★ † **SOUTHWELL** SK7053 An attractive town around a magnificent 12th-c **Minster**, a fine sight from miles around (especially at night when it's floodlit), and glorious to walk through. Fine leaf carvings and a lovely choir screen; it's worth catching one of the regular concerts. There's a smart new visitor centre. This small quiet town is the home of the Bramley apple, developed by Henry Merryweather in the last century. One of the original trees still prospers at his descendant's garden centre on Halam Rd, with a small exhibition on the subject. The Bramley Apple next door is good for lunch. There's a **fruit farm** in the grounds of nearby Norwood Park.

SUTTON-CUM-LOUND SK6985 **Wetlands Waterfowl Reserve and Exotic Bird Park** (off Loundlow Rd) Lagoons full of birds from ducks and swans to flamingos, and many more wild birds, inc parrots in the surrounding countryside. Also owls, foxes, llamas, wallabies, prairie dogs and a children's farm. Meals, snacks, shop, disabled access; cl 25 Dec; (01777) 818099; *£2. The canalside Boat at Hayton has decent food.

UPTON HALL SK7254 Includes a museum of clocks and timepieces from marine chronometers to the first telephone speaking clock. Some exhibits are over 300 years old, so don't expect them to keep perfect time. Snacks, shop, disabled access; open pm (exc Sat) Apr–Oct; (01636) 813795; *£2.70. The French Horn and Cross Keys have good food.

★ **WELLOW** SK6665 An attractive village, unusual for its permanent maypole – which used to be the trunk of a Sherwood Forest tree, but is now metal. It stands on the only genuine village green in the county, kept that way since the village was founded in the 12th c (all the others were just open spaces used by the villagers and itinerant traders for buying and selling, which have been grassed over since all that stopped). The Olde Red Lion is good for lunch.

★ † **WINKBURN** SK7158 Attractive village; unusually, its simple 12th-c village church was formerly a temple of the Knights Hospitaller.

† **WORKSOP** SK5880 **Mr Straw's House** (7 Blyth Grove) One of the NT's most unusual properties, an ordinary 1920s semi, left untouched by 2 brothers who inherited it when their parents died. Even the calendar remains

Days Out

Robin Hood country: Creswell Crags; Sherwood Forest Country Park, Edwinstowe; picnic there, or lunch at the Black Swan; walk or hire a boat or bike in Clumber Park; or World of Robin Hood, Haughton; or Mr Straw's House, Worksop (timed ticket needed).

The mighty Minster: Southwell Minster; lunch at the French Horn, Upton or at the Burnstump, Papplewick; Upton Hall or Newstead Abbey.

unturned. A fascinating time-capsule, it's open by pre-booked timed ticket only (Tues–Sat Apr–Oct), but it really is worth taking the trouble to obtain one, and by limiting numbers the Trust ensure that you can get a really good feeling of what it was like to live here; (01909) 482380; £3.50. The **town museum** has a display on the Pilgrim Fathers (cl Sun and pm Thurs and Sat; free), and the **priory church** is worth a look for the elaborate scrollwork on its 12th-c yew door; there's an art gallery and tearoom in the gatehouse. The Newcastle Arms (Carlton Rd) has good-value food.

★ **Other attractive villages** include Collingham SK8663, East Bridgford SK6943 (the Reindeer serves decent fresh fish), Sutton Bonington SK5025, and, with their more 'Leicestershire-ish' character, Colston Bassett SK7033 (the Haby Lane dairy makes good Stilton), and Staunton in the Vale SK8043.

Where to eat

CAUNTON SK7459 **Caunton Beck** *Main St (01636) 636793* Built in 1820, and carefully restored using reclaimed oak and Elizabethan timbers; roomy and welcoming, with an open fire and a wide range of food, from breakfasts to sandwiches to traditional and imaginative modern dishes, right through the day; friendly staff, a good wine list and real ales; disabled access. **£19.25**|£6.95.

COLSTON BASSETT SK7033 **Martins Arms** *School Lane (01949) 81361* Civilised, rather smart pub with particularly good and imaginative food in both the bar and restaurant (lovely puddings); well kept real ales, a decent choice of malt whiskies, quite a few wines by the glass, an open fire, and smart, uniformed staff; no children; disabled access. **£23**|£6.95.

NOTTINGHAM SK5740 **Lincolnshire Poacher** *Mansfield Rd (0115) 941 1584* Cheerful town pub with really tasty home-made food using fresh local produce (inc lots of vegetarian dishes); interesting real ales, good ciders, lots of whiskies and a wine of the week; pleasant service, a big wood-floored bar with breweriana, lively smaller bar, and a chatty back snug; popular with young people in the evening. **£16.40**|£4.95.

NOTTINGHAM SK5739 **Sonny's** *3 Carlton St, Hockley (0115) 947 3041* Bustling, popular brasserie with a pleasant mix of customers, an airy modern feel, and very good, up-to-date food using influences from all over the world; a well chosen wine list, and friendly service; cl bank hols; disabled access. **£25**|£4.95.

PLUMTREE SK6132 **Perkins Restaurant and Bar** *Station Rd (0115) 937 3695* Delightfully converted old railway station, with very popular and fresh delicious food (strong French influence); excellent, friendly service, and good wines; cl pm Sun, Mon, Christmas; children over 7. **£22.70**|£9.75 wkdy 2-course lunch.

UPTON SK7354 **French Horn** *(01636) 812394* Friendly and bustling dining pub with a neat and comfortable open-plan bar, a nice relaxed atmosphere, and imaginative food, inc very good daily specials and lots of puddings; well kept real ales, several wines by the glass, friendly and efficient service; also, a big sloping back paddock. **£17**|£6.25.

WALKERINGHAM SK7792 **Three Horseshoes** *(01427) 890959* Warmly welcoming distinctive pub, rather like a French *logis*, with quite amazing flowers and hanging baskets (using 9,000 plants); a wide choice of often inventive food, and well kept real ales. **£17.60**|£6.60.

Special thanks to A J Travers, Mrs S C Bailey, Roger Cooper, Mrs M Joseph, Mrs B Burgess, J A Smalley.

Please let us know what you think of places in the *Guide*. Use the report forms at the back of the book or simply write us a letter.

Nottinghamshire Calendar

Some of these dates were provisional as we went to press. Please check information with the telephone numbers provided.

FEBRUARY

1 **Winthorpe** Antiques Fair: largest in Europe at Newark Showground – *till Tues 2* (01636) 702627
13 **Winthorpe** Craft Fair at Newark Showground – *till Sun 14* (01636) 702627
28 **Newark** Doll Fair, Miniature and Teddy Bear Fair at Kelham Hall (01480) 216372

APRIL

3 **Newark** Craft Fair at Thoresby Park: about 30 stands – *till Mon 5* (01636) 605111
12 **Winthorpe** Antiques Fair – *till Tues 13 (see 1 Feb for details)*
16 **Sutton Bonington** National Folk Music Festival – *till Sun 18* (01296) 415333

MAY

3 **Mansfield** May Day Market (01623) 656656
7 **Winthorpe** Nottingham County Show at Newark Showground – *till Sat 8* (01636) 702627
29 **Nottingham** City Show inc free music festival, shire horse show, bus and commercial vehicle rally at Wollerton Park – *till Mon 31* (0115) 915 5555
30 **Newark** Steam Fair at Thoresby Park – *till Mon 31* (01636) 605111
31 **Wellow** Maypole Dancing (01623) 824545

JUNE

4 **Newark** Fest Noz: music, dancing, workshops and concerts at Thoresby Park – *till Sun 6* (01636) 605111
6 **Clipstone** Fun Day at Vicar Water Country Park (01636) 708265; **Nottingham** New, Vintage and Classic Car Rally at Wollerton Park (0115) 915 5555; **Southwell** Countryside Festival at Brackenhurst College (01636) 817034
7 **Winthorpe** Antiques Fair – *till Tues 8 (see 1 Feb for details)*
12 **Nottingham** Steam Spectacular at Wollerton Park – *till Sun 13* (0115) 915 5555
17 **Calverton** Annual Art and Craft Convention: over 150 artists and craft designers demonstrate, exhibit and sell their work – *till Sun 20* (0115) 965 3479
19 **Winthorpe** Kit Car Show at Newark Showground – *till Sun 20* (01636) 702627
26 **Ollerton** Ceramics Fair at Rufford Country Park – *till Sun 27* (01623) 822944; **Watnall** Nottingham Steam and Country Show at Front Park – *till Sun 27* (0115) 928 9149
28 **Edwinstowe** American Theme Week at Sherwood Forest Craft Centre – *till 4 July* (01623) 824033

JULY

7 **Winthorpe** Americana: American show with cars and music at Newark Showground – *till Sun 11* (01636) 702627

Nottinghamshire Calendar (cont.)

9 **Upton** Annual Clock and Watch Fair at Upton Hall, the British Horological Institute's headquarters: inc clock- and watch-making demonstrations, wood-turning, dial-painting and the Institute's collection open to the public – *till Sun 11* (01636) 813795

10 **Mansfield** Mardi Gras – *till Sun 11* (01623) 656656; **Newark** Vintage Tractor Rally at Thoresby Park: about 30 stands – *till Sun 11* (01636) 605111; **Nottingham** Craft Fair at Wollerton Park – *till Sun 11* (0115) 915 5555

11 **Newark** Doll Fair, Miniature and Teddy Bear Fair at Kelham Hall (01480) 216372

24 **Nottingham** Pop Concert at Wollerton Park (0115) 915 5555

29 **Edwinstowe** Summer Fun at Sherwood Forest Craft Centre – *till 2 Sept* (01623) 824033

AUGUST

2 **Edwinstowe** Robin Hood Festival at Sherwood Forest Visitor Centre – *till Sun 8* (01623) 823202

7 **Nottingham** Riverside Festival: free event with street theatre, carnival, fireworks, world music and steam organs at Victoria Embankment – *till Sun 8* (0115) 915 5555

9 **Winthorpe** Antiques Fair – *till Tues 10* (*see 1 Feb for details*)

14 **Sutton in Ashfield** Show at Lawn Pleasure Grounds – *till Sun 15* (01623) 450000

29 **Mansfield** Horticultural Show (01623) 656656; **Watnall** Moorgreen Country Show: classic cars, shire horses, and heritage marquee – *till Mon 30* (01773) 711767

30 **Newark** Classic Car Show at Thoresby Park (01636) 605111

SEPTEMBER

30 **Cropwell Butler** Ploughing Match inc trade stands (01949) 836566

OCTOBER

3 **Nottingham** Asian Religious Festival at the Castle (0115) 915 5555

7 **Nottingham** Goose Fair: largest funfair in the country – *till Sat 9* (0115) 915 5555

8 **Newark** Endurance Horse and Pony Society at Thoresby Park – *till Sun 10* (01636) 605111

18 **Winthorpe** Antiques Fair – *till Tues 19* (*see 1 Feb for details*)

28 **Nottingham** Robin Hood Pageant at the Castle – *till Sun 31* (0115) 915 5555

31 **Newark** Doll Fair, Miniature and Teddy Bear Fair at Kelham Hall (01480) 216372

NOVEMBER

5 **Nottingham** Bonfire Night (0115) 915 5555

13 **Winthorpe** Craft Fair at Newark Showground – *till Sun 14* (01636) 702627

17 **Nottingham** Christmas Lights Switch-on (0115) 915 5555

Nottinghamshire Calendar (cont.)

29 **Edwinstowe** Christmas Events at Sherwood Forest Craft Centre – *till 4 Dec* (01623) 824033

DECEMBER

6 **Winthorpe** Antiques Fair – *till Tues 7* (see *1 Feb for details*)

We welcome reports from readers

This *Guide* depends on readers' reports. Do help us if you can – in return, we offer a discount on the next edition to people who've helped us with reports for it. Tell us what you think about places already in it, and anything extra you think we should say about them. And send us your ideas for inclusion in the next edition: places to visit, eat at or stay in, attractive drives or walks, maybe even unusual interesting shops you know of. Use the card in the middle, the report forms at the end, or just write – no stamp needed: *The Good Guide to Britain*, FREEPOST TN1569, Wadhurst, E Sussex TN5 7BR.

Oxfordshire

Richly varied countryside, plenty of delightful places for adults to visit, some good family days out; Oxford itself is a vibrant mix of medieval buildings and modern bustle.

Blenheim Palace by the attractive small town of Woodstock is the county's great showpiece, with memorable lakeside grounds, and all sorts of things going on to entertain families. Children as much as adults enjoy the lively Cogges Farm Museum in Witney, and the Cotswold Wildlife Park at Burford, the bird and animal collection at Ipsden, and the model landscape at Long Wittenham are all good family outings; while on a warm day you can't beat a Thames boat trip – this area has some of the finest river scenery.

Most of the county's other attractions are suited more to adults than to children. The new rowing museum in Henley is a must for aficionados (while Greys Court just outside has a gentler appeal). Broughton Castle, Chastleton House, Dorchester Abbey, Rousham House, Stonor House, Buscot Park, Mapledurham House and Kelmscott Manor head a substantial list of rewarding old houses and other interesting buildings. Steam enthusiasts won't want to miss the railway collection at Didcot.

Oxford itself has masses to see – a great many striking buildings, the colleges themselves, the art collections of the Ashmolean Museum, the unusual Curioxity, and the intriguing Pitt Rivers ethnology museum, to name but a few; the university's botanic garden is the oldest in the world. The tourist office is particularly helpful – though one of the hardest to get through to on the phone.

Many of the villages and small towns are very rewarding, with picturesque stone houses (up in the north-west corner many glow with a glorious golden stone), and plenty of antique and craft shops. The countryside has considerable variety, from the edge of the Cotswolds in the west to the fringes of the Chilterns in the east, with some sweeping downland in the south.

It's a prosperous county, with a fine choice of hotels and good food – at a price.

Where to stay

ASTHALL SP2811 **Maytime** *Asthall, Burford OX18 4HW (01993) 822068* **£62.50,** plus bargain breaks; 6 quiet rms. Attractive, 16th-c Cotswold stone inn, with a comfortable and relaxing dining bar, good food and decent wines, huge breakfasts; worth taking an early spring-morning walk through the pretty village, across the fields to Swinbrook and back along the river; disabled access.

BAMPTON SP3102 **Morar** *Weald, Bampton OX18 2HL (01993) 850162* ***£44,** plus special breaks; 3 rms. Warm, friendly and neatly kept, modern stone house (no smoking), with helpful and knowledgeable owners (keen gardeners, barn dancers, morris dancers and church bell ringers); separate lounge and dining room, lovely English cooking in winter using home-grown produce (home-made bread and preserves, too); also, a pretty, flower-filled, big garden, and pet sheep, goat and cats; cl Jan and Feb; children over 6.

BURFORD SP2512 **Burford House** *High St, Burford, OX18 4QA (01993) 823151* **£80,** plus winter breaks; 7 cosy, individually decorated rms. Attractive, 14th-c Cotswold stone and beamed building, with 2 comfortable lounges (one for residents only), log fires, and super breakfasts; lots of plants in the pretty stone courtyard; children over 10.

BURFORD SP2512 **Lamb** *Sheep St, Burford OX18 4LR (01993) 823155* **£100,** plus special breaks; 15 rms. Very attractive, 500-year-old Cotswold inn with a lovely, restful atmosphere; spacious, beamed, flagstoned and elegantly furnished lounge, a civilised public bar, bunches of flowers on the oak and elm tables, 3 winter log fires, antiques, and very good food in the airy restaurant; pretty little walled garden; cl 25–26 Dec.

CHARLBURY SP3519 **Bell** *Church St, Charlbury, Chipping Norton OX7 3PP (01608) 810278* **£95,** plus special breaks; 13 comfortable rms. Small, neatly kept, 17th-c hotel with a warm and friendly atmosphere; quiet and civilised flagstoned bar, a huge open fire, short choice of interesting bar lunches, decent restaurant, well kept real ales, and good breakfasts.

CHURCH ENSTONE SP3724 **Crown** *Mill Lane, Church Enstone, Chipping Norton OX7 4NN (01608) 677262* **£49.50;** 4 well appointed rms, 3 with own bthrm. Cotswold stone inn in a pretty village; with an attractive horseshoe bar, conservatory, friendly atmosphere and staff, good food in both the bar and restaurant, and decent breakfasts; Heritage barn nearby can be viewed by appointment.

CLANFIELD SP2802 **Plough** *Bourton Rd, Clanfield, Bampton OX18 2RB (01367) 810222* **£95,** plus special breaks; 6 lovely rms. Rose-clad, 16th-c Cotswold stone manor house, with armchairs and sofas in the relaxed, beamed lounge bar, and an open fire; friendly, helpful staff and very good food in the elegant restaurant; children over 12.

CLIFTON SP4831 **Duke of Cumberlands Head** *Clifton, Banbury OX15 0PE (01869) 338534* **£60;** 6 rms in sympathetic extension. Pretty, thatched, 17th-c stone inn with a friendly atmosphere; very good food in both the bar and back restaurant, enjoyable breakfasts, a log fire, well kept beers and wines, and helpful service; tables in garden.

CLIFTON HAMPDEN SU5495 **Plough** *Clifton Hampden, Abingdon OX14 3EG (01865) 407811* **£75;** 6 rms with four-posters. Quaint little no smoking village pub close to the Thames, run by an obliging and idiosyncratic Turkish couple; with a marvellously relaxed and friendly atmosphere, cosy bar with beams and panelling, 2 civilised lounge areas, and good fresh food in both the bar and restaurant.

CROPREDY SP4646 **Old Manor** *Cropredy, Banbury OX17 1PS (01295) 750235* **£54;** 3 rms, 1 with own bthrm. In a historic village, this lovely old place has 2 acres of garden and orchard, a moat with ducks and geese, and Gloucester old spot pigs in the fields bordering the Oxford Canal; guests' sitting room with games and books, breakfast in the 15th-c dining room with antiques, clocks and more books, and several dogs and cats; self-catering barn; private motor museum; cl Christmas–New Year; disabled access.

DORCHESTER SU5794 **George** *High St, Dorchester, Wallingford OX10 7HH (01865) 340404* **£80,** plus special breaks; 20 characterful rms. Lovely 500-year-old building with a medieval dining room, a comfortably old-fashioned and civilised bar, ancient beams, and a big fireplace; good wines, interesting food, pleasant service; first used as a brewhouse for the Norman abbey opposite; disabled access.

GREAT MILTON SP6202 **Manoir aux Quat' Saisons** *Great Milton, Oxford OX44 7PD (01844) 278881* ***£249,** plus winter breaks; 32 opulent rms. Luxurious Jacobean manor in 27 acres of parkland and lovely gardens, with a heated pool and kitchen garden (providing many of the cooking ingredients); sumptuous lounges with fine furniture, beautiful flowers and open fires, a new conservatory, exemplary service, and exquisitely presented, superb food (at a price); residential cookery courses; disabled access.

HENLEY-ON-THAMES SU7481 **Hernes** (out towards Rotherfield Greys), *Henley-on-Thames RG9 4NT (01491) 573245* **£70,** plus special breaks; 3 rms. In big gardens and grounds surrounded by farmland, this peaceful, no smoking, family house has a 16th-c core; comfortable sitting room with panelled ceiling, family portraits, and good breakfasts – dinner by arrangement; cl Dec–mid-Jan; no children.

HENLEY-ON-THAMES SU7682 **Red Lion** *Hart St, Henley-on-Thames RG9 2AR (01491) 572161* **£137,** plus special breaks; 26 rms, some with river views. Handsome, family-run and neatly kept, 16th-c riverside hotel with comfortable public rooms; very good, interesting food in the elegant, Regency-style restaurant, and particularly helpful, warm and friendly staff.

HORTON-CUM-STUDLEY SP5912 **Studley Priory** *Horton-cum-Studley, Oxford OX33 1AZ (01865) 351203* ***£140,** plus special breaks; 18 rms. Once a Benedictine nunnery, this lovely, 12th-c Elizabethan manor stands in 13 wooded acres; fine panelling, 16th- and 17th-c stained-glass windows, antiques and open fires in the elegant drawing room and cosy bar, and seasonally changing menus in the attractive restaurant; grass tennis court and croquet.

KELMSCOT SU2599 **Plough** *Kelmscot, Lechlade, Gloucs GL7 3HG (01367) 253543* ***£50;** 8 comfortable rms. Pretty little inn nr the Thames, with an attractively traditional small bar, ancient flagstones, stripped stone walls and a relaxed, chatty atmosphere; a larger, cheerfully carpeted back bar, log fires, a wide choice of food, and well kept real ales; lots of nearby walks and the Oxfordshire cycleway is easily accessible, too; no rooms 24–30 Dec; children over 10.

KINGHAM SP2523 **Mill House** *Station Rd, Kingham, Chipping Norton OX7 6UH (01608) 658188* ***£100,** plus special breaks; 23 good rms with country views. Carefully renovated, 17th-c flour mill in 7 acres with a trout stream; comfortable, spacious lounge, an open log fire in the lounge bar, and original features such as 2 bread ovens; a cosy, popular restaurant, and very good, interesting food; disabled access.

KINGSTON BAGPUIZE SU3997 **Fallowfields** *Southmoor, Kingston Bagpuize, Abingdon OX13 5BH (01865) 820416* **£95;** 10 rms. Delightful, Gothic-style, no smoking, old manor house with elegant and relaxing sitting rooms, and open fires; good Aga-cooked food (using home-grown produce) in the attractive dining room, and 2 acres of pretty gardens with outdoor heated swimming pool and tennis court; children over 10.

LITTLE WITTENHAM SU5692 **Rooks Orchard** *Little Wittenham, Abingdon OX14 4QY (01865) 407765* ***£50;** 2 rms. Comfortable 17th-c house in lovely gardens by a nature reserve and Wittenham Clumps; with beams, inglenook fireplaces, decent breakfasts (evening meals by arrangement), welcoming owners, and a babysitting service; dogs by arrangement.

LONG HANBOROUGH SP4214 **Old Farmhouse** *Station Hill, Long Hanborough, Witney OX8 8JZ (01993) 882097* **£43;** 2 rms, 1 with own bthrm. Welcoming, no smoking, 17th-c house with lots of charm, stone walls and beams; homely sitting rooms with inglenook fires, a conservatory, fine breakfasts with home-made preserves, and enjoyable meals using home-grown produce; also, a pretty cottagey garden; Oxford is only a 10-minute train ride away, and plenty to do nearby; cl Christmas; children over 12.

MINSTER LOVELL SP3211 **Hill Grove Farm** *Crawley Dry Lane, Minster Lovell, Witney OX8 5NA (01993) 703120* ***£44;** 2 rms. Friendly B & B on a family-run, 300-acre mixed working farm; homely lounge and sun room, good breakfasts, and nice views and walks; no smoking; cl Christmas.

MOULSFORD SU5983 **Beetle & Wedge** *Ferry Lane, Moulsford, Wallingford OX10 9JF (01491) 651381* **£120,** plus special breaks; 10 pretty rms, most with lovely river view. Civilised riverside hotel where Jerome K Jerome wrote *Three Men in a Boat* and where H G Wells lived for a time (it was the Potwell in *The History of Mr Polly*); informal, old beamed Boathouse bar and a lovely conservatory dining room (both with first-rate food), a carefully chosen wine list, open fires, and fresh flowers; riverside terrace and waterside lawn with moorings, and a warmly welcoming atmosphere; pleasant nearby walks; disabled access.

OXFORD SP5009 **Cotswold House** *363 Banbury Rd OX2 7PL (01865) 310558* **£64;** 7 comfortable rms with showers. Beautifully kept modern, no smoking, Cotswold stone house with particularly helpful owners; residents' lounge, very good breakfasts, pretty flowers throughout, and a neat back garden; cl 10 days at Christmas; children over 5.

OXFORD SP5106 **Old Parsonage** *1 Banbury Rd OX2 6NN (01865) 310210* **£150;** 30 lovely rms. Handsome and civilised 17th-c parsonage, fairly central, with very courteous staff; good breakfasts and excellent light meals in the cosy bar/restaurant, small lounge, open fires and fine paintings, and a pretty little garden; they have their own punt and provide picnics; cl 25–26 Dec.

OXFORD SP5204 **Pine Castle** *290/292 Iffley Rd OX4 4AE (01865) 241497* **£65,** plus wknd breaks; 8 rms. Small, family-run Edwardian hotel with a comfortable, cosy lounge, and enjoyable breakfasts in the small restaurant; cl Christmas wk.

OXFORD SP5106 **Randolph** *Beaumont St OX1 2LN (01865) 247481* **£180.50,** plus special breaks; 110 rms. Fine, neo-Gothic, Victorian hotel facing the Ashmolean Museum; with elegant and comfortable day rooms, a grand foyer, graceful restaurant with lovely plasterwork ceiling, and a cellar wine bar; disabled access.

SHENINGTON SP3642 **Top Farm House** *Shenington, Banbury OX15 6LZ (01295) 670226* **£40;** 2 rms, shared bthrm. 18th-c farmhouse by the village green; with oak beams, inglenook fireplaces, a residents' sitting room, and decent breakfasts.

SHILLINGFORD SU5991 **Shillingford Bridge** *Ferry Rd, Shillingford, Wallingford OX10 8LZ (01865) 858567* **£95,** plus special breaks; 42 rms. Riverside hotel with own river frontage, fishing and moorings; spacious, comfortable bars and an attractive, airy restaurant (all with fine views); squash, outdoor heated swimming pool, and Sat dinner-dance; disabled access.

SHIPTON-UNDER-WYCHWOOD SP2717 **Lamb** *Shipton-under-Wychwood, Chipping Norton OX7 6DQ (01993) 830465* **£75;** 5 comfortable rms. Ancient Cotswold stone pub with a relaxed and civilised atmosphere, open log fire, highly polished furniture and newspapers to read in the beamed bar; good food in the no smoking restaurant, and enjoyable breakfasts.

SHIPTON-UNDER-WYCHWOOD SP2717 **Shaven Crown** *Shipton-under-Wychwood, Chipping Norton OX7 6BA (01993) 830330* **£82,** plus special breaks; 8 comfortable rms. Densely beamed, ancient stone hospice built around a striking medieval courtyard with old-fashioned seats on cobbles, lily-pool and roses. Impressive medieval hall with a magnificent lofty ceiling, sweeping stairway and old stone walls, and a log fire in the comfortable bar; intimate, candlelit restaurant, a well chosen wine list, friendly service, a warm and relaxed atmosphere; also, a bowling green; children over 5 in evening dining room; disabled access.

SHIPTON-UNDER-WYCHWOOD SP2717 **Shipton Grange House** *Shipton-under-Wychwood, Chipping Norton OX7 6DG (01993) 831298* ***£60;** 3 rms. Carefully converted, no smoking, Georgian coach house and stables; with elegantly furnished sitting rooms, good breakfasts, a friendly welcome, and an attractive walled garden; cl Christmas; children over 12.

STONOR SU7388 **Stonor Arms** *Stonor, Henley-on-Thames RG9 6HE (01491) 638345* **£105,** plus special breaks; 10 pretty rms. Carefully restored, 18th-c hotel with imaginative food in 2 elegant restaurants, each with a pretty conservatory; relaxed, flagstoned bar, and friendly staff; disabled access.

UFFINGTON SU3089 **Craven** *Fernham Rd, Uffington, Faringdon SN7 7RD (01367) 820449* ***£60,** plus special breaks; 6 pretty rms, some with own bthrm. Most attractive, 17th-c thatched house with a beamed sitting room, log fire in the inglenook, antiques, and a friendly, relaxed atmosphere; good food in the beamed farmhouse kitchen, and lots of nearby walks; disabled access.

WOODSTOCK SP4416 **Feathers** *Market St, Woodstock OX20 1SX (01993) 812291* ***£105,** plus special breaks; 22 individually decorated rms. Lovely old building with a relaxing drawing room and study, open fires, and first-class, friendly staff; a gentle atmosphere, daily-changing imaginative food inc lovely puddings, and a sunny courtyard with attractive tables and chairs.

WOODSTOCK SP4416 **Holmwood** *6 High St, Woodstock OX20 1TF (01993) 812266* **£70;** 2 pretty rms, both with their own sitting room. Early 18th-c Cotswold stone house with oak beams and antiques, an attractive dining room, and friendly, helpful owners; no smoking; cl Jan; children over 12.

To see and do

OXFORD SP5105 First impressions can be a bit frenetic: the ancient university buildings with their medieval lanes and scholarly corners are surrounded by a bustling, largely industrialised town, with a formidable amount of traffic. The one-way system and difficulties in parking away from the NCPs combine to make it a driver's nightmare; if you don't come by train or coach, it may be best to leave your car at one of the Park & Rides around the ring road. Otherwise, the tourist information centre does a useful car park map, with times and prices. For first-time visitors, hop on and off **tour buses** from St Aldates, High St, Gloucester Green or Pembroke College take in all the best sites and last about 1½ hours (£6–£9). Many of the city's oldest or most interesting buildings are grouped around the Bodleian Library, the Sheldonian Theatre and the splendid domed Radcliffe Camera (also a library). This partly cobbled central university area is most attractive, but does sometimes get so packed with visitors that the noise puts students off their exams. In the streets and lanes leading off, the honey-coloured stone makes for a harmony that unites different styles and different centuries. There are a few good shops dotted about; Blackwells is the main bookseller, with several branches around the Broad St area (the secondhand section in the main branch is well used by students, and their music shop on Holywell St is rewarding). Nr the station, the **Oxford Antique Trading Co** has 80 dealers under one roof.

OXFORD COLLEGES Most allow visitors into at least some of their quads (courtyards), and have a wonderful, timeless appeal. One of the few they failed to impress was William Cobbett, who wrote in his *Rural Rides* that he 'could not help reflecting on the drones that they contain, and the wasps they send forth'. The colleges are all separate bodies with little in common, each firmly maintaining its own dons, rules and traditions; the university itself is little more than an administrative umbrella. Several now charge admission, notably Christ Church, New, Magdalen, Trinity and Brasenose. Access may be more limited in term-time. A few may let you in only with a guide, so a good way of making sure you see a cross-section is to join one of the walking tours that leave the tourist information centre (Old School, Gloucester Green) every day at 10.30am, 11am, 1pm and 2pm; £4. Afternoon tours are the best, but get there early – places are limited. Guided walks may also leave from the Catte St/High St corner. Ideally, it's worth trying to explore at your own pace away from the crowds – again, afternoons are best, with more colleges open then. Besides colleges we pick out individually, more are tucked down some of the town's prettiest streets, such as charming **Exeter, Jesus** and **Lincoln** down Turl St, and **Corpus Christi** and **Oriel** around Merton Lane and Oriel Sq. This last college has a very attractive and unusual entrance to its dining hall. **Trinity** on Broad St is very grand. Around Radcliffe Sq **Brasenose** is quaint (and has good views of the surrounding skyline from its quads), and **Hertford** has its Bridge of Sighs over New College St, in itself worth exploring for some more unusual and less busy views and an interesting look at the gargoyles on the backs of some of the buildings. **Worcester** has particularly nice **gardens**, and many of the other colleges' private Fellows' gardens not usually open to visitors can be seen under the National Gardens Scheme.

Magdalen College The most beautiful college, its tower a dramatic sight for visitors entering the city from the S. The quads and cloisters are very pleasant to stroll through, but the chief attraction is the **deer park**, an unexpected haven in the heart of the bustling city. Addison's Walk, a path around this meadow (you can't go in), is in spring a mass of snowdrops and daffodils, then has hundreds of thousands of fritillaries in later spring, and after that the deer. Over a small bridge is the Fellows' Garden with a small ornamental lake – a very peaceful, sheltered spot.

Christ Church The best known college, a magnificently stately place begun by Cardinal Wolsey in the 16th c, but soon taken over by Henry VIII. The main entrance into the front quad is through Tom Tower, designed by Christopher Wren and named after its famous bell that rings out 101 times at 9 o'clock every night – in less liberal times, the hour when students were due back in their rooms. The hall is worth a look, with its remarkable hammerbeam roof, paintings of alumni and benefactors by all the most expensive portrait-painters of the period, and the long tables laid out with silver for meals; there may be teas here some afternoons. The elaborate little **cathedral** is England's smallest, and doubles as the college chapel. It has some excellent stained glass by Burne-Jones, fantastic pendant vaulting in the choir, and some of the original Norman priory work. Entry into the college may be limited on Suns. A hidden treasure unnoticed by most visitors is the college's **picture gallery** (Canterbury Quad), with an important collection of old master paintings and drawings, and various temporary exhibitions. Shop; cl 1–2pm, am Sun, and Christmas and Easter wks; guided tours Thurs at 2.15pm; (01865) 276172; *£1.

New College Impressive chapel, atmospheric, wisteria-covered cloisters, and parts of the old city wall.

Merton College The most ancient buildings, with the country's oldest library (tours available).

Keble College (Parks Rd) Brightly Victorian and very red-brick, with perhaps the most famous Pre-Raphaelite painting of all, Holman Hunt's *Light of the World*, in its chapel.

St Edmund Hall The only surviving medieval college, complete with a Norman crypt.

University College Harmonious buildings – and an interesting monument to Shelley despite having thrown him out.

Ashmolean Museum (Beaumont St) The country's first museum, and still one of its finest, opened in 1683 and rehoused in this imposing building from 1845. Well arranged galleries inc marvellous European paintings, an extensive collection of Pre-Raphaelite pictures, a representative range of work by French Impressionists, and antiquities from ancient Egypt, Greece and Rome. Meals, snacks, shop, disabled access; cl am Sun, Mon (exc pm bank hols), first wk of Sept (St Giles Fair), Christmas wk; (01865) 278000; free.

Bodleian Library (Broad St) One of the oldest in Europe, its splendidly grand quad dominated by the Tower of the Five Orders. Most of it is closed to the public, but guided tours take in the beautifully vaulted 15th-c Divinity School, which shows some of the library's treasures, and, for the first time this year, the Chancellor's Court and Convocation House. Tours every 10 minutes, and additional tours of Duke Humfrey's Library, the oldest reading room, usually at 10.30am, 11.30am, 2pm and 3pm; (01865) 277188; no children under 14, excellent shop, limited disabled access (notice preferred); cl some bank hols and last wk of Aug; £2.50, Duke Humfrey's Library £3.50. Altogether the library houses over 5,500,000 books, going down 6 storeys under the centre of the city.

Sheldonian Theatre (Broad St) A grand classical building, with a lovely painted ceiling. In its time it's been used for parliaments, and nowadays university ceremonies are held here; you may see gowned students heading for these on some weekends, though the theatre is closed to the public then.

Pitt Rivers Museum (Banbury Rd) Shrunken heads, totem poles and fertility rites – a fascinating, close-packed ethnological museum off the tourist track, with art and ingenuity from all cultures and periods. The million or so exhibits range from Captain Cook's Pacific Islands collection and 18th-c ship models to severed fingertips and an Eskimo coat made from seal intestines. Everything is displayed in firmly traditional cases or drawers, with neatly handwritten labels, and there's still something of the Victorian atmosphere it must have had when it originally opened. Shop, limited disabled access; cl am, Sun, a few days over Christmas and Easter; (01865) 270927; free. The adjacent **Balfour Building** has a gallery of archaeology and a large collection of musical instruments.

University Museum (Parks Rd) Victorian Gothic structure specialising in natural history – outstanding if solidly earnest collection, enlivened by a working beehive in summer; cl am, Sun, some days over Easter and Christmas; free.

History of Science Museum (Broad St) Excellent if rather scholarly collection of national importance, in one of the city's nicest old buildings (cl am, Sun, Mon, and a wk at Christmas and Easter; free). An extensive refurbishment programme means some parts may be closed.

Oxford Botanic Garden (High St) Britain's oldest botanic garden, founded in 1621, with 8,000 species of plant from all over the world. It's a lovely place to sit for a while, or wander through on the way to the river. Disabled access; cl Good Fri and 25 Dec; (01865) 276920; £2. They also administer the University Arboretum at Nuneham Courtenay.

Christchurch Meadow An unspoilt expanse of green astonishingly close to the busy city streets. You can gaze across the fields of grazing longhorn cattle to the spires in the distance, or walk under overhanging trees along the banks of the river to the boathouses; college eights row from here all year, in just about any weather.

Oxford Story (Broad St) Europe's longest dark ride, with cars designed as desks taking you through a cheerful and well researched re-creation of university history, complete with sights, sounds and smells. A useful introduction to the city (especially for families), though no substitute for the real thing. Good shop (you can just visit here using the entrance on Ship St), disabled access; cl 25 Dec; (01865) 790055; £5.50. In summer you can get a ticket which also includes entry to Magdalen and New College (£7.75).

! **Oxford Covered Market** (High St) A maze of stalls with something different at every turn; chic boutiques, speciality shops, cafés and old-fashioned butchers and poultry merchants. The Oxford Sandwich Co do excellent take-away sandwiches here, and Ben's Cookies are a favourite with students.

! **Curioxity** (Gloucester Green) The Old Fire Station complex houses a theatre and this **interactive science gallery** where visitors can experiment with the exhibits. The staff are helpful, and several sets of parents have told us it kept their children captivated for a full hour. Meals, snacks, shop; open wknds and daily during school hols; (01865) 794494; *£2.10. This area, interestingly rejuvenated with trendy shops, cafés and a bustling Weds market, was once one of the less desirable parts of town. Not far from here, among the fashionable shops and boutiques of Little Clarendon St, George & Davies is a good ice-cream parlour.

Bate Collection of Musical Instruments (St Aldates) Outstanding – and constantly developing – collection of early keyboards, woodwind, brass, percussion and other instruments, inc a complete Japanese gamelan. Shop, mostly disabled access; cl am, wknds (exc am Sat during term-time), and a few days at Christmas and Easter; (01865) 276139; free.

Oxford Museum of Modern Art (Pembroke St) Modern art museum with the sort of exhibitions and displays not often found in galleries outside London. Open till 9pm Thurs. Good meals and snacks, good bookshop, disabled access; cl Mon, and 2 wks between exhibitions – worth checking; (01865) 722733; *£2.50.

Museum of Oxford (St Aldates) Interesting little local history museum, with re-created rooms, maps and period music. Shop; cl Sun (exc July–Oct) and Mon; (01865) 815559; £1.50, free for county residents.

Oxford Castle Mound There isn't much of the Norman castle left save a tower and crypt of the castle church, and an underground well chamber, but the mound gives quite good views over the city and its surroundings. The Museum of Oxford may arrange tours, phone (01865) 815559.

St Michael at the North Gate (Cornmarket St) Oxford's oldest building, a Saxon church with displays of silver, clocks and bells; great views from the tower. Cl 1–2pm and during services, 25 Dec and Good Fri; *£1.50.

St Mary's Church (High St) Interesting university church with fine views, and a nice – if busy – café in the crypt; cl am Sun; £1.50.

Carfax Tower Right at the traditional centre of Oxford, all that remains of a 14th-c church; good views, and the bells in the tower are interestingly designed. Shop; cl 25 Dec–1 Jan; £1.20.

Punting and boat trips Good fun in sunny weather; once you've got the knack it's a very nice way of spending a lazy afternoon. You can hire boats from Magdalen Bridge or Folly Bridge; usually £8–£10 an hour – you'll have to put down a big deposit. Salters run steamer trips from Folly Bridge to Abingdon.

Rotunda Museum of Antique Dolls' Houses (Grove House, Iffley Turn – 2m S of centre) Private collection of over 40 elaborate houses, dating from 1720 to 1900, with period furniture, carpets and dinner services (no under-16s; open pm 1st Sun of month May–Sept; £2). Iffley's Norman **church** is one of the county's finest.

University Parks There are countrified walks almost from Oxford's city centre. The Parks (primarily playing fields) are the closest place for a good stroll – and in summer you can watch first-class cricket matches for free.

Waterside walks Port Meadow SP5007 is the best outlying area for Oxford walks, an expanse of waterside common land with grazing horses and flocks of geese, which extends N from Jericho and can be reached on the far side of the Oxford Canal via Walton Well Rd, crossing the Thames and turning right along the W bank. Just beyond the far end of Port Meadow is the ruin of 12th-c **Godstow Nunnery**, where Fair Rosamund the mistress of Henry II is buried; nearby, the riverside medieval Trout pub is touristy but very attractive, and there are often peacocks around here. A second well sited riverside pub, the thatched Perch at Binsey, is another popular walking objective in this direction; at the church, just beyond, a **holy well** dedicated to St Margaret used to draw thousands of pilgrims. The Rivers Thames and Cherwell cut strikingly rural corridors through the city, though walks along the Cherwell may be impeded by closed college gates. They are most likely to be open in mid-afternoon.

Iffley Meadows SP5204 These are conserved for wildlife, and in late spring are a sea of purple snakes-head fritillaries.

Ruskin walk From the big garden of the Fishes pub at North Hinksey SP4905, a footpath towards Oxford partly follows a causeway built originally by John Ruskin to give students experience of healthy outdoor labour.

We welcome reports from readers

This *Guide* depends on readers' reports. Do help us if you can – in return, we offer a discount on the next edition to people who've helped us with reports for it. Tell us what you think about places already in it, and anything extra you think we should say about them. And send us your ideas for inclusion in the next edition: places to visit, eat at or stay in, attractive drives or walks, maybe even unusual interesting shops you know of. Use the card in the middle, the report forms at the end, or just write – no stamp needed: *The Good Guide to Britain*, FREEPOST TN1569, Wadhurst, E Sussex TN5 7BR.

Other things to see and do

Oxfordshire Family Attraction of the Year

WITNEY SP3609 **Cogges Farm Museum** (Church Lane) Entertaining as well as informative, this 20-acre site shows what it was like to live on a farm in Victorian times. First stop for families is usually the farmyard, where you can meet horses, donkeys, cows, pigs, ducks and chickens, with daily feeding displays, and demonstrations of agricultural techniques. There's a period dairy and a walled garden. The manor house dates from the 13th c, and in recent years has been very well restored; it's furnished as it would have been in Victorian times, and they've tried hard to re-create the feel of those days. In the afternoons, follow the tantalising baking smells to the kitchen and you can chat to the cook about what she's making. There's an activities room where children can try on Victorian costumes and play with traditional toys and games. One of the barns has an exhibition on Witney blankets, and they have demonstrations of the 18th-c loom most Tues, Fris and Suns. Various other craft demonstrations throughout the week (spinning Tues, lace-making Weds and Thurs, butter-making Sun), and a busy programme of events and activities that takes in everything from sheep-shearing and corn-dolly-making to visits from the Sealed Knot or Punch and Judy; the events on Advent weekend are fun. The orchard is a nice spot for picnics, and the woodland and riverside are delightful for a gentle stroll. All done with great enthusiasm and attention to detail, this can be really rewarding if you're at all interested in farms or history – it might seem a bit worthy if you're not. Meals, snacks, shop (good for free-range eggs and other farm produce), mostly disabled access; cl am wknds, all Mon (exc bank hols), and all Nov–Mar (exc Advent wknd); (01993) 772602; £3.25 (£1.75 children 3–16). A family ticket (2 adults, 2 children) is £9.

★ **ABINGDON** SU4997 Attractive Thames-side town, until 1974 the county town of Berks. Much expanded around its old partly pedestrianised core, which still has a fine old gatehouse, several attractive old buildings and almshouses around the impressive 15th/16th-c Wren-style **Church of St Helen** (off Thames St), a good **museum** in the 17th-c former county hall (free), and the unusual **Church of St Mary**, wider than it's long. The remains of the partly Norman Benedictine **abbey**, once the second most powerful in England, have been restored, part now housing a local theatre. The riverside Old Anchor is prettily placed for lunch; the Mill House, part of the medieval town bridge, also has decent food.

★ **ARDINGTON** SU4388 Attractive small village; good dining pub, and several craft workshops in the Home Farm buildings.

BANBURY SP4540 The busy shopping town was actually without its famous cross for some 250 years, between the Puritans destroying it in 1602 and the construction of its replacement in 1859. In the graveyard is the tomb from which Jonathan Swift borrowed the name Gulliver for his traveller. There's a decent local history **museum** (cl Sun and winter Mons; free), and the Reindeer and the Wine Vaults, both in Parsons St, are useful for lunch. The B4035 towards Sibford Ferris runs through attractive hilly farmland, with good summer pick-your-own; the loop N through North Newington, Shutford and Epwell is pleasant too.

BENSON VETERAN CYCLE MUSEUM SU6292 Private collection of over 500 bicycles from between 1818 and 1930; open mornings Easter–Sept by appointment with Mr Passey, on (01491) 838414; free. Down by the river at the Cruiser station you can hire boats by the day or the hour; (01491) 838304. The footpath beyond the weir bridge leads to Wallingford. The Home Sweet Home at Roke is a charming dining pub.

BIX BOTTOM SU7285
Warburg Reserve Wild-flower-rich rough grassland and ancient beechwood, good for wild orchids and butterflies, besides birds and maybe deer. The Fox (A423) is nice for lunch. The **Oxfordshire Way** long-distance path includes a short walk with a palpable sense of peace, from the lane past Bix Hall to Valley End Farm.

BROUGHTON CASTLE
SP4138 (B4035 SW of Banbury) Striking early 14th–16th-c house with a proper moat and gatehouse, originally owned by William of Wykeham. Exceptional oak panelling, period furniture, and Civil War relics. Some rooms have bare stone walls under elaborately plastered ceilings, an unusual combination that works rather well. Snacks, shop, disabled access to ground floor only; open Easter, then mid-May–mid-Sept pm Weds, Sun and bank hols, plus Thurs July and Aug; (01295) 262624; £4. There's a decent village **museum**, and the Roebuck at North Newington is a good dining pub.

BURFORD SP2512
Lovely little Cotswold town with interesting shops and teashops along its pretty main street. The **church** is intriguing, with a super graveyard, and 17th-c graffiti by some of the 400 Leveller mutineers imprisoned here by Cromwell. The town also has an interesting little **museum** (open pm Apr–Nov; 50p), and is full of attractive pubs: the best for food and atmosphere is the Lamb, and the Mermaid serves food all day. **Widford church** (just E) Very simple, but notable for three things – its medieval wall paintings, the remains of a Roman pavement at the west end of the chancel, and its surroundings, a former village that save one solitary house has now virtually disappeared. **Cotswold Wildlife Park** (Bradwell Grove, A361 S of Burford) A thoroughly reliable family day out well liked by readers, with animals, birds and reptiles from all over the world in spacious re-creations of their natural environment, inc a new walk-through aviary. Also an aquarium, tropical and insect houses, brass-rubbing centre, adventure playground and summer train rides, in acres of attractive parkland.

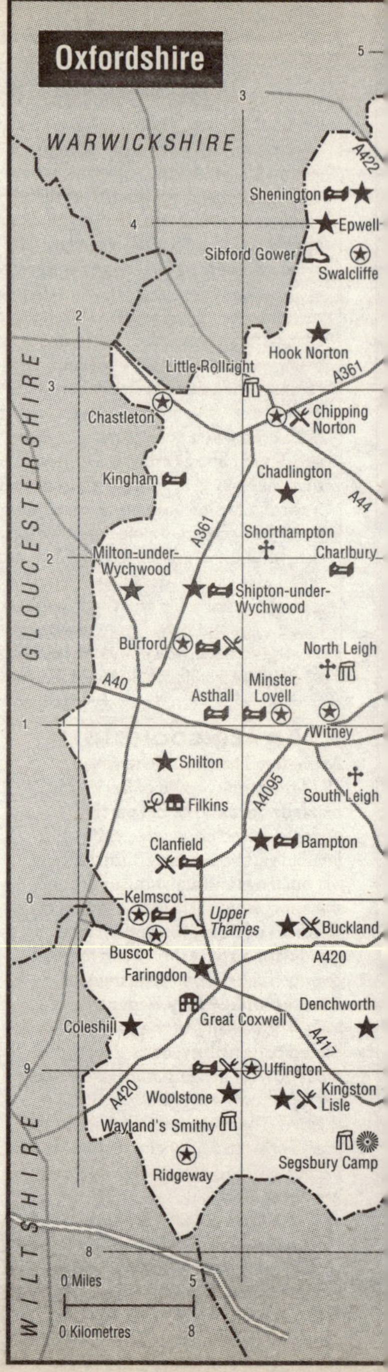

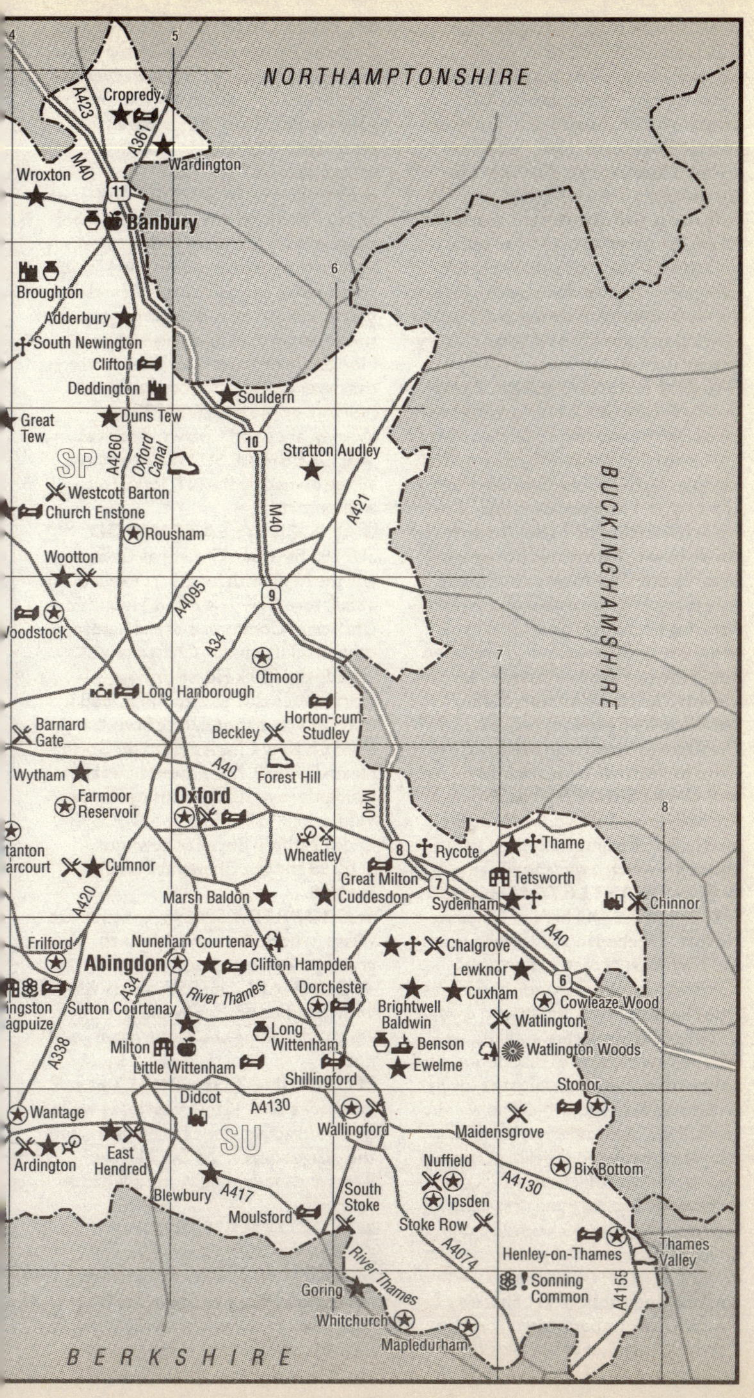
NORTHAMPTONSHIRE
BUCKINGHAMSHIRE
BERKSHIRE
Cropredy
Wardington
Wroxton
Banbury
Broughton
Adderbury
South Newington
Clifton
Deddington
Souldern
Great Tew
Duns Tew
Stratton Audley
Oxford Canal
SP
Westcott Barton
Church Enstone
Rousham
Wootton
Woodstock
Otmoor
Long Hanborough
Horton-cum-Studley
Barnard Gate
Beckley
Forest Hill
Wytham
Farmoor Reservoir
Oxford
Wheatley
Rycote
Thame
Tetsworth
Great Milton
Cuddesdon
Sydenham
Chinnor
Cumnor
Marsh Baldon
Frilford
Nuneham Courtenay
Chalgrove
Abingdon
Clifton Hampden
Lewknor
Dorchester
River Thames
Brightwell Baldwin
Cuxham
Cowleaze Wood
Sutton Courtenay
Watlington
Long Wittenham
Benson
Watlington Woods
Milton
Ewelme
Little Wittenham
Shillingford
Stonor
Didcot
Wantage
Wallingford
Maidensgrove
SU
Ardington
East Hendred
Nuffield
Bix Bottom
Blewbury
South Stoke
Ipsden
Moulsford
Stoke Row
Henley-on-Thames
Thames Valley
Sonning Common
Goring
Whitchurch
Mapledurham
M40
A423
A361
A4260
A421
A4095
A34
A40
A420
A338
A4130
A417
A4074
A4155
11
10
9
8
7
6
4
5

Meals, snacks, shop, disabled access; cl 25 Dec; (01993) 823006; £5.50. Burford does get very busy indeed with visitors, and it's worth noting that several smaller and altogether quieter nearby villages are, in their way, as pretty: **Taynton**, the **Barringtons** (just over the Gloucs border), **Fulbrook**, **Swinbrook** and **Asthall**. All except the first have the additional attraction of a decent pub. There are attractive walks between these, along the River Windrush for much of the way – back roads along the Windrush Valley give pleasant drives, too.

BUSCOT PARK SU2496 (on the A417) 18th-c house made really special by the amazing collection of art and furnishings amassed by its owners; paintings by Reynolds, Gainsborough, Rembrandt, Murillo and several of the Pre-Raphaelites (inc a splendid series by Burne-Jones), with some more recent pictures too. The attractive grounds have formal watergardens and a mouth-watering kitchen garden, and maybe pick-your-own in summer. Teas; open Apr–Sept, pm Weds–Fri and every 2nd and 4th wknd in the month; (01367) 240786; £4.40, grounds only £3.30; NT. The Thames-side Trout (off the A417 towards Lechlade) is popular for lunch.

★ † **CHALGROVE** SU6396 Attractive small village, with notable medieval wall paintings in the 11th-c **church** – which owns the village pub.

CHASTLETON HOUSE SP2429 (off the A44 NW of Chipping Norton) Opened in 1997 after 6 years and £3 million of restoration, this handsome Jacobean manor house was little changed by the family who owned it 1605–1991, really feeling like a well lived-in family house of that period, and not oversmartened despite the lovely plasterwork, beautiful oak and walnut furnishings, embroideries, Jacobite glassware, and even the Bible Charles I took to the scaffold. Peaceful Jacobean gardens inc a topiary and first-class croquet lawn. Car park up hill from house. Open Apr–Oct pm Weds–Sat; (01608) 674284; £4.80, must have pre-booked timed ticket; NT. There's pleasant walking between this village, Cornwell and (just inside Gloucs) Adlestrop.

CHINNOR SP7500 **Chinnor and Princes Risborough Railway** 4-mile train trips into Bucks, most weekends Apr–Sept, some steam-hauled – ring (01844) 353535 for timetable and prices (you may need to book for special events).

★ **CHIPPING NORTON** SP3127 Pleasant, old, stone-built wool town with an unusually wide market place, pretty church, some fine 17th-c almshouses, antique shops, Victorian theatre, and a summer local history **museum** in the Co-op Hall (cl am, all Mon exc bank hols; *£1). The Chequers has decent food. The roads to Hook Norton, or the B4026/B4022 to Witney, are good Cotswoldy drives.

★ **COLESHILL** SU2393 Attractive village owned by the NT; lots of nice walks nearby.

COWLEAZE WOOD SU7295 Between Christmas Common and the M40, with forest art exhibits on a sculpture trail. The Fox & Hounds on Christmas Common is useful here, and other useful pubs for Chilterns walks include the Black Horse or Four Horseshoes at Checkendon SU6683, the Highwayman at Exlade Street SU6582, King Charles Head on Goring Heath SU6678, Five Horseshoes at Maidensgrove SU7288, Rising Sun on Witheridge Hill nr Highmoor SU6984, Olde Leathern Bottel at Lewknor SU7198 and the Crown at Pishill SU7389.

★ **CROPREDY** SP4646 An attractive village, where you may find sheep grazing the raised churchyard.

★ **CUXHAM** SU6695 A pretty village, with thatched houses by the stream which runs along beside the road; good pub.

DEDDINGTON SP4631 This still has traces of its 12th-c **castle**, as well as some attractive stone buildings around the village square; the Deddington Arms and Holcombe Hotel are handy for lunch.

DIDCOT SU5290 **Railway Centre** The biggest collection anywhere of Great Western Railway stock, housed under cover, inc 20 steam locomotives, a diesel railcar and lots of passenger and freight rolling stock. Snacks, shop, disabled access;

open wknds all year and wkdys Easter–Sept, best to ring for steamday dates, usually every Sun and Weds in summer hols; (01235) 817200; £4–£6.50 depending on event. The town itself more or less sprang up around the railway sheds.

DORCHESTER SU5894 **Dorchester Abbey** Impressive and well preserved old abbey, with a 12th-c nave and rare lead font. The tower was rebuilt in 1605 and has a 14th-c spiral staircase, as well as an exceptional Jesse window from the same period, and some mosaic-like 12th-c glass in other windows. The adjacent former guesthouse now houses a little **museum**. In summer, they do very individual, ever-so-English teas (pm Weds–Sun), all home-made and quite addictive. Shop, disabled access; museum cl Mon, am Sun, wkdys in Oct and all Nov–Apr; free. The whole Thames-side village is a lovely place to explore, with interesting antique shops. The **River Thames** has pleasant walks starting and finishing here; you can cross at Day's Lock, and a short walk brings you to **Wittenham Clumps** (alternative access from adjacent car park), a pair of hillocks which look across the Chilterns and Berkshire Downs. The George and Fleur de Lys do good lunches.

★ **EWELME** SU6491 One of Oxfordshire's prettiest and most unspoilt villages.

FARMOOR RESERVOIR SP4405 Trout fishing, sailing, birdwatching, and other activities, though you'll need a permit; (01865) 863033 for details and prices.

FILKINS SP2207 **Cotswold Woollen Weavers** Friendly working woollen mill with demonstrations of traditional production methods in 18th-c buildings. Snacks, well stocked shop, some disabled access; (01367) 860491; cl am Sun, 25–31 Dec; free. The Five Alls and Lamb are useful for lunch.

FOREST HILL SP5807 Above Oxford, this gives several pleasant walks from the White Horse pub.

FRILFORD SU4397 **Millets Farm Centre** Pick-your-own fruit, animals, walks, and an unusually extensive farm shop which takes in a bakery, delicatessen, garden centre, and wine merchant; cl 25 Dec; (01865) 391625.

GREAT COXWELL BARN SU2693 As noble as a cathedral according to William Morris, a 13th-c stone-built tithe barn 46 by 13 metres (152ft long, 44ft wide), with beautifully crafted timbers supporting the roof; 50p.

★ **GREAT TEW** SP3929 The most charming village in the area (some would say in all England). It's an outstanding series of golden stone 17th- and 18th-c cottages, some thatched and others with stone-slabbed roofs, around an attractive sloping green and among ancient trees, with wooded slopes above; the Falkland Arms here is a classic country tavern.

★ **HENLEY-ON-THAMES** SU7781 Pleasant, well heeled Thames-side town famed for its summer regatta. You can usually see other rowing races or practices on the river throughout the year, or hire your own boats on (01491) 572035. A stunning new building by Mill Meadows houses the new **Museum of Rowing**. As well as comprehensive displays on the sport, it focuses on the Regatta and the history and life of the river itself. Meals, snacks, shop, disabled access; cl 25–26 Dec, 1 Jan; (01491) 415600; £4.95. The informal Anchor (Friday St) and Little White Hart (Bell St) are good-value pubs nr the river, and the Three Tuns (Market Pl) does food all day. **Greys Court** (Rotherfield Greys, 3m W of Henley, SO7283) An attractive gabled Jacobean house with interesting ruins of its medieval predecessor; the gardens are even more alluring, with white and rose gardens, ancient wisterias, a kitchen garden, wheelhouse, icehouse and brick maze. Teas, bookstall, some disabled access; open Apr–Sept, house pm Mon, Weds and Fri, garden pm daily exc Thurs and Sun; (01491) 628529; £4.40, gardens only £3.20; NT. The village **church** is delightful, and the Maltsters Arms dining pub has lovely country views, and good nearby walks. The B480 to Watlington is a pleasant Chilterns drive.

! **IPSDEN** SU6386 **Wellplace Zoo** Mainly a bird park, but also animals such as lambs, goats, otters, donkeys and monkeys. You can feed several of them, so good for children. Snacks, shop, disabled access; cl wkdys Oct–Easter; (01491) 680473; £2. Ian Smith can arrange **horse-drawn waggon rides** through these pretty Chilterns fringes; most fine summer days he runs 2-horse waggons from Darkwood Farm, Park Corner on a local pub tour; (01491) 641324. Even by car, these are pleasant Chilterns drives – for instance the loop S of Nettlebed through Highmoor Cross, Stoke Row and Nuffield.

KELMSCOTT MANOR SU2599 The summer home of William Morris until his death in 1896, now with one of the best assemblages of Morris memorabilia, standing out all the more for its domestic setting. Works by other Pre-Raphaelite artists include splendid paintings by Rossetti, who initially shared the lease. Snacks, shop, disabled access to ground floor only; open Weds (exc 1–2pm) and pm 3rd Sat of month Apr–Sept; (01367) 252486; £6. The mid-Aug village fête in the grounds is a nicely old-fashioned occasion. The Plough, in the peaceful little Thames-side village, is good, and there's a straightforward Thames-side walk of a mile and a half E to the Swan at Radcot Bridge.

KINGSTON BAGPUIZE SU4098 **Kingston House** (off the A415) Charming 17th-c manor house, remodelled in the early 18th c, with lovely panelling, attractive furnishings and a friendly, unstuffy feel; peaceful garden with mature flowering shrubs, woodland walks, and a Georgian gazebo. Snacks, shop; usually open pm bank hol wknds, and occasional other summer pms – best to ring for exact dates; (01865) 820259; *£3.50, garden only *£1. The Hinds Head has good-value food.

LITTLE ROLLRIGHT SP2931 **Rollright Stones** Dramatic and mysterious Bronze Age stones, chiefly in a circle about 30 metres (100ft) across, now thought to date from between 1500 BC and 2000 BC; legend has it that the stones are a king and his men tricked by a witch into falling under her spell, and petrified. It's supposed to be impossible to count them as you can never tell where you started – which must have been frustrating for the estate agent when the stones were put on the market a couple of years ago. The Gate Hangs High, nr here, is useful for lunch.

LONG HANBOROUGH SP4314 **Oxford Bus Museum** Around 40 vehicles, from Oxford horse trams to more modern machines up to the 1960s, some roadworthy, others being restored. Disabled access; open Sun only; (01993) 883617; *£3. The Hand & Shears at Church Hanborough is now a very good dining pub.

LONG WITTENHAM SU5493 **Pendon Museum of Miniature Landscape and Transport** Charming exhibition with a highly detailed model railway and meticulously researched model 1930s village scenes; modellers working on the exhibits are always happy to chat. Snacks, shop; open pm wknds and bank hols Jan–Nov, plus pm Weds July and Aug; (01865) 407365; £3. The Machine Man and riverside Plough are handy for lunch.

★ **MAPLEDURHAM** SU6776 Very attractive little community with lovely beechwoods full of birds; the nicest way to reach it is by boat from the Caversham Promenade at Reading (summer wknds only). **Mapledurham House** An impressive Elizabethan mansion in pretty parkland running down to the Thames, with paintings and family portraits, great oak staircases, and moulded Elizabethan ceilings. In the grounds is the last **watermill** on the Thames to use wooden machinery, still producing flour, bran and semolina. Also riverside walks and an island with picnic area. Teas, shop, disabled access to ground floor only; open pm Sat, Sun and bank hols Easter–Sept; (0118) 972 3350; £5 house and watermill, house only £4, watermill only £3. You can stay in a number of lovely cottages on the estate (some thatched).

MILTON MANOR SU4892 Elegant 17th-c manor house with a splendid Strawberry Hill 'gothick' library, an interesting chapel, walled garden, and unusual collections of teapots and fine china. Open bank hol wknds and daily in Aug; (01235) 831287; £4. The Admiral Benbow has decent food. The **cherry orchards** around Milton Hill are a fine sight when the white blossom is out in spring, and around July roadside stalls sell fresh cherries – the Grove Farm Shop (A4130) is especially friendly.

MINSTER LOVELL SP3211 One of the prettiest and most unspoilt old villages in the area; there's an attractive 15th-c **church** and village green, and a 15th-c bridge over the River Windrush narrow enough for the Welsh drovers to use for counting the sheep in the flocks they brought this way each year. The smart Old Swan does good light lunches. **Minster Lovell Hall** Imposing and attractively set, this was being used as ramshackle farm buildings until its 'restoration' as neat ruins in the 1930s. Macabre stories about the 15th-c Hall usually involve people being shut up in various places and forgotten about until their skeletons are discovered much later. Open every day, free. There's a well restored medieval dovecot nearby.

NORTH LEIGH SP3813 **Roman villa** Occupied between the 2nd and 4th c, when it was a very grand place with several dozen rooms, it's now just a few neat but poignant traces, in a very pleasant wooded setting; free. The medieval village **church**, with a Saxon tower, is lovely inside, and the Woodman is popular for lunch.

NUFFIELD PLACE SU6787 The home of Lord and Lady Nuffield 1933–1963, with the original 1930s furnishings. Very good gardens with mature trees and shrubs, inc rhododendrons, lawns, a pond and rockery, as well as Lady Nuffield's own Wolseley and a display of vintage cars. Teas, limited disabled access; open pm 2nd and 4th Sun each month May–Sept; (01491) 641224; £3. The Crown has reasonable food.

NUNEHAM COURTENAY SU5599 **Oxford University Arboretum** (A4074) Fine conifers and other trees over 55 acres, as well as plants like rhododendrons that won't grow in the soil of Oxford itself. Some disabled access; cl wknds Nov–Apr, and 2 wks at Christmas; free. About half a mile away, the roses at Notcutts Garden Centre are a blaze of summer colour easily seen from the road; decent meals here, though perhaps pricier than at some garden centres.

OTMOOR SP5614 Several square miles of flatland, so poorly drained that in very wet weather its river actually flows backwards, and interesting to walk through. Because serious farming is virtually out of the question, it does have more natural wildlife than most places in the county; there are several paths. The Abingdon Arms at Beckley, with enjoyable food, is one starting-point (and there's a good farm shop on the B4027 from Stanton St John); the Nut Tree at Murcott does excellent steaks. The pick-your-own fruit farm at Elsfield has nice views over the wilderness, and a very wide range of varieties.

OXFORD CANAL The towpath is shadowed by the railway, so you can walk the canal from one village to another, for example from Lower Heyford SP4824 to Nethercott SP4820, and return by train. There's also access from the Jolly Boatman at Thrupp SP4816.

RIDGEWAY SU2885 Nr the N crest of the downs, the Ridgeway tracks right across from Wilts to Berks. This broad grassy trackway was used as a herding highway for some 2,000 years before the Romans came, and after the break-up of the Roman Empire came back into use for the same purpose, well into medieval times. It's now part of the long-distance path network, and gives good walking with fine views. A particularly atmospheric short stretch nr Compton Beauchamp SU2787 takes in the ancient sites of Wayland's Smithy, the White Horse and Uffington Castle.

ROUSHAM HOUSE SP4824 Nicely unspoilt 17th-c house embellished by court artists and architects, and remodelled in the 18th c by William Kent to give the external appearance of a Gothic Tudor mansion. It still has Civil War shooting holes in the door. Excellent, 18th-c, classically landscaped garden with buildings, cascades, statues and vistas in 30 acres of hanging woods above the River Cherwell, and walled flower and vegetable gardens. No children under 15. Some disabled access to grounds;

house open pm Weds, Sun and bank hols Apr–Sept, gardens open daily all year; (01869) 347110; house £3, garden £3. There's a 12th-c church. The Red Lion at Steeple Aston is very good for lunch (no children here, either).

† **RYCOTE** SP6604 (off the A329) Peaceful little 15th-c private **chapel**, later visited by both Elizabeth I and Charles I. The wedding scene in the recent TV production of *Jane Eyre* was filmed here. Shop, disabled access; open pm Fri–Sun bank hols Apr–Oct; £1.60. The Bull at Great Milton has decent food.

SEGSBURY CAMP SU3883 Extensive Iron Age hill fort, later used by the Romans, with fine views; reached by the dead-end lane up past the Sparrow in Letcombe Regis.

★ **SHIPTON-UNDER-WYCHWOOD** SP2717 Old houses around a lovely big sloping green, 2 good inns (one very ancient), and an interesting bookshop.

† **SHORTHAMPTON CHURCH** SP3220 Notable for its fine wall paintings.

SIBFORD GOWER SP3537 There are pleasant Cotswold walks nr this quiet village; the thatched Wykham Arms is good for lunch.

! **SONNING COMMON** SU7079 **Herb Farm** (Peppard Rd) Extensive range of herb plants and products, with over 3,200 different varieties in the display garden. There's an impressive maze (summer only), and agricultural displays in a restored granary. Summer snacks, shop, disabled access; cl Mon; (0118) 972 4220; free, £1 for maze. The Butcher's Arms is a useful dining pub with weekend family entertainment.

† **SOUTH LEIGH CHURCH** SP3908 Notable wall paintings.

† **SOUTH NEWINGTON CHURCH** SP4033 Also has fine wall paintings; may be locked, but you can get the key from College Farmhouse next door.

★ **STANTON HARCOURT** SP4105 **Manor House** The medieval great kitchen has no chimney – the smoke from ovens and fireplaces collected in the cone of the roof and drifted out through wooden louvres. The gardens too are striking, with neat lawns and topiary, and a wilder wooded area. Teas, shop, disabled access; usually open pm Thurs and Sun fortnightly from mid-Apr–Sept, plus bank hols – best to check first; (01865) 881928; £4, garden only £2.50. The village is attractive, and the Harcourt Arms nearby does good meals.

STONOR HOUSE AND PARK SU7489 Even older than the stately Tudor façade suggests, with beautiful furnishings, paintings, sculptures and tapestries, and mementos of Jesuit scholar Edward Campion, one of the many Catholic recusants who found refuge here during the Reformation. The lovely gardens have an unusual exhibition of sculpture from Zimbabwe, and there's a wooded deer park. Snacks, shop; open pm Sun and bank hols Apr–Sept, plus pm Weds May–Sept, pm Thurs July and Aug, and pm Aug bank hol Sat; (01491) 638587; £4.50, chapel and garden only £2.50. The smart Stonor Arms is useful for lunch. The deer park is skirted by an attractive right of way from the village, and you can link this with the famous and unusual Maharajah's Well in the charming vilage of Stoke Row SU6883; or for a longer Chilterns walk you can continue E to Turville SU7690 in Bucks.

★ **SUTTON COURTENAY** SU5093 An attractive village to stroll through, with things to look out for – like Asquith and Orwell, unlikely bedfellows in their final rest in the graveyard.

★ **SWALCLIFFE BARN** SP3737 (B4035, Swalcliffe) Well preserved tithe barn, with much of its medieval half-cruck timber roof intact. There's a display of agricultural and trade vehicles. Disabled access; open pm Sun and bank hols Apr–Oct; free. The village is pretty, and the Stag's Head has good food.

★ † **SYDENHAM** SP7301 A charming village, and a lovely church.

TETSWORTH SP6801 For many years an atmospheric coaching inn, the 16th-c Swan on the High St is now an unusual **antique centre**, with top-of-the-range antiques and furnishings well displayed in period rooms and meandering corridors. More like visiting a house than a shop, with the contents priced at anything from £15 to £5,000. Similarly stylish restaurant attached; cl 25–28 Dec; (01844) 281777. The Lion on the Green has good-value food.

★ ✝ **THAME** SP7006 Well worth a look for its splendid range of unspoilt architecture. The very wide main street has escaped any significant development this century, and has medieval timber-framed buildings next to stately Georgian houses; the 13th-c **church** is attractive. The 15th-c Birdcage Inn used to be the town lock-up; the Rising Sun, Abingdon Arms and Six Bells are useful for a bite to eat – though the best nearby place for lunch is the Mole & Chicken at Easington, out past Long Crendon.

THAMES VALLEY Shared with Berks and Bucks, this has a classic, very English sort of beauty, with boating scenes, superb trees and riverside architecture. Riverside walks on the Oxon side are possible only in places, notably between Henley-on-Thames and Sonning – for instance to Shiplake Lock from the Plowden Arms at Shiplake SU7678; you can also get down to the Thames from the attractive Perch & Pike at South Stoke SU5983.

★ ✝ **!** **UFFINGTON** SU3089 Charming village, with decent food at the Fox & Hounds. Opposite here is John Betjeman's former home Garrard Farm, which you can rent in summer, (01328) 851155; as warden of **St Mary's Church**, he made sure its oil lamps were preserved. **Tom Brown's School Museum** (Broad St) Young Mr Brown's schooldays were based on those the author Thomas Hughes passed here; there's an exhibition on his life and work. Shop; open pm wknds May–Oct; 60p. **Uffington Castle** High above the village, this Iron Age fort covered 8 acres but had only one gateway; great views over the vale below. On the hillside, a 115-metre (375-ft) **white horse** carved into the chalk is now thought to be around 3,000 years old; it's a striking design, very Celtic. If you stand in the centre of the eye and turn around 3 times with your eyes closed, any reasonable wish will be granted. This is one good setting-off point for the Ridgeway. The flat-topped little hill below is said to be where George killed the dragon. A bit over a mile E, off the B4507, the turning off up towards the downs opposite the Kingston Lisle road almost immediately passes a cottage on the left, which has outside a huge pitted flint rock, locally known as the blowing stone: if you blow in the right hole and in the right way you can produce a splendid deep blast of sound. The pub named after it has good food.

UPPER THAMES W of Oxford, the Thames flows through low-lying country, giving the sort of walk you enjoy more for the people you're with than the scenery itself. Quiet riverside strolls can start or finish at the Trout at Tadpole Bridge SP3300 (on the unclassified road Bampton–Buckland), the Maybush at Newbridge SP4001 (on

Days Out

Amble round Oxford: Walk through Christ Church quads and meadow; Botanic Garden; Magdalen College; walk past Radcliffe Camera and the Bodleian Library; lunch at the Turf Tavern; walk along Holywell St and Broad St; Ashmolean Museum – or spend the afternoon punting along the river from Magdalen Bridge or Folly Bridge, or walking out along the Oxford Canal to Port Meadow, for an early evening drink at the Trout, Godstow.

Cotswolds tones: Walk in the park of Blenheim Palace, Woodstock, or hire a boat; lunch at the Feathers Hotel in the town; Roman villa, North Leigh; Minster Lovell; Burford.

Victorian farming, world wildlife: Cogges Farm Museum, Witney; lunch at the Lamb, Burford; Cotswold Wildlife Park.

the A415; the Rose Revived here is worth knowing for its big Thames-side lawn), and the Talbot nr the Swinford toll bridge SP4408 (on the B4044).

WALLINGFORD SU6089 Ruins of a 13th-c **castle** on a hill, the history of which can be found at the nearby **museum** (High St), which also has a very good sight-and-sound history of the area complete with a reconstructed Victorian street. Shop; cl am (exc Sat), Mon (exc bank hols), winter Suns, and all Dec–Feb; (01491) 835065; £1.75. Plenty of places to hire boats or fish around here.

WANTAGE SU3987 Historic town where King Alfred was reputedly born; recently much expanded, though there's an attractive quiet corner by the 13th/15th-c **church** with its raised graveyard, and, in Newbury St, 17th-c almshouses have a courtyard cobbled with bones. **Vale and Downland Museum Centre** (Church St) has well displayed local history and geology exhibits as well as the local tourist information centre. Meals, snacks, shop, limited disabled access; cl am Sun, Mon, Good Fri, Christmas; (01235) 771447; free (although in 1999 there may be a charge for the newly refurbished main gallery). The downland roads S into Berks have fine views. **Venn watermill** (A338 N) Regularly used working corn mill; open 2nd Sun in month Apr–Oct; £1.

WATLINGTON WOODS SU7093 A mass of bluebells in spring, this steep edge of the Chiltern Hills gives great views.

WAYLAND'S SMITHY SU2885 Midway along the Ridgeway between the Uffington White Horse and the B4000 above Ashbury (where the Rose & Crown is ideally placed for walkers), this was even in Saxon times reputed to be the forge of a magic blacksmith, who would invisibly shoe your horse overnight if you left it there with a silver coin – and exact horrid penalties if you tried to slip by without paying. It's an impressive place, alone on the downs, an excavated **Neolithic burial chamber** rather more than over 5,000 years old, made with massive sarsen stones each weighing several tons; free.

WHEATLEY SP5805 The unusual octagonal **windmill** is open by appointment, (01865) 874610; free. Just S at Garsington, Jennings Farm Shop has a wide range of produce as well as craft workshops and a working blacksmith's forge. Garsington has decidely smart open-air operas (though spoilsport locals have occasionally tried to drown them out with strimmer and mower noise); the French-run Three Horseshoes there is good.

WHITCHURCH SU6377 An attractive little village, with nice walks nearby; the Greyhound does good-value food. **Boze Down Vineyard** (B471 N of Whitchurch) Free tastings pm wknds, and guided tours by appointment; (0118) 984 4031; *£5. Path Hill Farm on Goring Heath nearby has a shop selling organic products.

WITNEY SP3609 *See separate Family Panel on p.511* for **Cogges Farm Museum**. Saxon kings used to hold their meetings, or witans, here – hence the name. It was a prosperous town in the Middle Ages, and is well known for its blankets, made here ever since. Quiet and relaxed, with picturesque stone buildings, the market square still with its ancient butter cross and 17th-c clock, and quite a few interesting old buildings such as the 13th-c church and 18th-c blanket hall. Just off Church Green, you can see the excavated foundations of a 12th-c palace of the Bishops of Winchester (pm wknds only, free).

WOODSTOCK SP4416 Civilised and prosperous small town, with good antique shops and fine stone buildings. The Feathers Hotel, Bear Hotel and cheaper Queen's Own and Star are all decent places for lunch. **Oxfordshire County Museum** (Fletcher's House) Elegant townhouse with pleasant gardens and nice displays, although a large portion will be closed for refurbishment until summer 2000. Snacks, shop, disabled access; cl am Sun, Mon; (01993) 811456; *£1. **Blenheim Palace** Undoubtedly one of the most impressive stately homes in the country. Given to the Duke of Marlborough by Queen Anne as a reward for his military achievements, the house itself covers 14 acres, and the grounds stretch for well over 2,000. Churchill was born here and there's a straightforward exhibition on his life. Highlights include the sumptuous state rooms and 56-metre (183-ft) Long Library, along with plenty of opulent furnishings and sculpture; tours leave every 5–10 minutes. The very extensive grounds, landscaped by Capability Brown, are full of interesting paths and tracks; you can picnic. Also a butterfly house, miniature railway and play areas with swings, ropes and slides. An extra £1 adds a hedge maze, putting green, and model village based on Woodstock and its surroundings. You can hire rowing boats (£1 a person for 30 mins) or arrange coarse fishing on the lake, and at weekends they have a bouncy castle. There's enough space to absorb the crowds (Sun is busiest, Weds is popular with overseas students); the house usually gets quieter after about 3pm. You can avoid having to wait for tickets by arriving early; though most parts are closed till 10.30am, the gates and ticket office open at 9am. Meals and snacks (3 different restaurants), several shops and a plant centre, some disabled access; house cl Nov–mid-Mar, grounds open all yr; (01993) 811325; £8, grounds only £5 per car. There is also a public right of way through the huge estate, with pleasant walks in, for example from the attractive village of Combe. The graveyard of nearby **Bladon church**, where Churchill is buried, has views over the grounds.

★ **WOOLSTONE** SU2987 An attractive village in the Vale of the White Horse; Thomas Hughes reputedly wrote *Tom Brown's Schooldays* in the bar of the White Horse here.

★ **WYTHAM** SP4708 Charming unspoilt village, all houses owned and preserved by Oxford University; good dining pub.

★ **Other attractive small towns and villages** here, all with decent pubs, include Adderbury SP4635, Bampton SP3103, Blewbury SU5385, Brightwell Baldwin SU6595, Buckland SU3497, Chadlington SP3222, Church Enstone SP3724, Clifton Hampden SU5495, Cuddesdon SP5903, Cumnor SP4603, Denchworth SU3791, Duns Tew SP4528, East Hendred SU4588 (interesting church), Epwell SP3540, Faringdon SU2895, Goring SU6080, Hook Norton SP3533, Kingston Lisle SU3287, Lewknor SU7198, Marsh Baldon SU5699, Milton-under-Wychwood SP2618, Shenington SP3742, Shilton SP2608, Souldern SP5131, Stratton Audley SP6026, Wardington SP4945, Wootton SP4320 and Wroxton SP4142.

Where to eat

ARDINGTON SU4388 **Boars Head** *(01235) 833254* Civilised and upmarket dining pub with a friendly new licensee; 3 neatly kept and simply decorated rooms, low beams, bare boards, and fresh flowers; particularly good wines, well kept real ales, imaginative, regularly changing food; pleasant nearby walks; no food pm Sun, cl Mon; disabled access. **£20.50**|£8.

BARNARD GATE SP4010 **Boot** *(01865) 881231* Friendly dining pub with an interesting collection of celebrities' boots; impressive choice of good, generous food in the bar and partly no smoking restaurant, prompt and friendly service, decent wines, well kept beers, and a big log fire. **£22.95**|£9.

BECKLEY SP5611 **Abingdon Arms** *(01865) 351311* Busy dining pub with a sensibly short seasonal choice of really interesting food, well kept ales, and a good range of wines; a comfortably modernised, simple lounge with pretty flowers on the tables, a smaller public bar, pleasant garden and floodlit terrace; no children; cl pm Sun for food. **£20**|£6.75.

BUCKLAND SU3498 **Lamb** *Lamb Lane (01367) 870484* Extended, 18th-c stone dining pub in a tiny village; very popular and imaginative food changing seasonally, good-value house wines from a predominantly French wine list, real ales, and smart, helpful service; comfortable bdrms; good walks nearby; cl 25–26 Dec. **£26**|£5.95.

BURFORD SP2512 **Mermaid** High St *(01993) 822193* Busy pub with a handsome Tudor frontage, an attractive, long narrow bar with flagstones, stonework and some panelling, pretty dried flowers; a no smoking dining conservatory and upstairs restaurant, good food inc cream teas usefully served all day, well kept real ales, and courteous, efficient staff; no children in the bars. **£15**|£4.95.

CHALGROVE SU6396 **Red Lion** *(01865) 890625* Delightful pub owned by the local church since the 17th c; with a traditional atmosphere, stylish simple furnishings, a log fire and old woodburner, carefully collected prints and period cartoons; well kept real ales, decent wines, imaginative and very well presented food, a helpful landlord, and a no smoking back dining room; no food pm Sun; cl pm 25 Dec; disabled access. **£20**|£5.95 2-course wkdy lunch.

CHINNOR SU7598 **Sir Charles Napier** *Spriggs Alley*, (up on the escarpment) *(01494) 483011* Decidedly civilised place with excellent food in the stylish back restaurant, champagne on draught, a huge wine list, and freshly squeezed pink grapefruit or orange juice; smartly relaxed little bar with homely furnishings, log fire, delicious food from a short bar menu, and real ales; croquet lawn; cl pm Sun, Mon, 3 wks after Christmas; children over 7 in evening; partial disabled access. **£30**|£5.75.

CHIPPING NORTON SP3127 **Chavignol** *7 Horsefair (01608) 644490* A move lock, stock and barrel from Lovells at Windrush Farm, Minster Lovell to this Cotswold stone cottage with its open fires and beams; really excellent meals inc super cheeses and puddings in a friendly and relaxed atmosphere; cl Sun, Mon, 3 wks Jan. **£42**.

CLANFIELD SP2802 **Clanfield Tavern** *(01367) 810223* Pretty village inn with new licensees; a no smoking conservatory linking to a barn, well kept ales, decent wines, and imaginative home-made food; several flagstoned, heavy-beamed and stone-walled small rooms leading off the main bar, and a handsome stone fireplace; cottagey restaurant. **£20**|£8.50.

CUMNOR SP4604 **Bear & Ragged Staff** *(01865) 862329* Smart old pub with roaring log fires in the comfortably rambling, softly lit bar, and a civilised atmosphere; well presented, good food (the dining area is no smoking), well kept real ales, several wines by the glass, and pleasant, obliging service; cl Christmas and New Year; disabled access. **£25**|£10.

EAST HENDRED SU4688 **Wheatsheaf** *(01235) 833229* Attractive black and white timbered, 16th-c village pub with a good mix of locals and visitors; high-backed settles, some panelling and an inglenook fireplace, very enjoyable, interesting food, well kept real ales, and decent wines. **£17.20**|£6.50.

KINGSTON LISLE SU3287 **Blowing Stone** *(01367) 820288* Popular pub with a brightly modernised bar, simple furnishings, fresh flowers and newspapers, and a comfortable lounge; restaurant and conservatory, imaginative, carefully prepared food, real ales and a very good choice of wines. **£23.50**|£9.

MAIDENSGROVE SU7288 **Five Horseshoes** *(01491) 641282* 17th-c little brick house with a log fire in the rambling bar/bistro, good, often imaginative food, decent wine list, well kept real ales, and a walkers' bar; surrounded by Chilterns beechwoods; summer barbecues in the nice garden; cl 25 Dec; children must be well behaved; partial disabled access. **£22**|£6.50.

NUFFIELD SU6787 **Crown** *(01491) 641335* Attractive, brick and flint pub in fine countryside; with roaring log fires, a wide choice of food, comfortable atmosphere, well kept beers, decent wines and prompt, friendly service; cl pm Sun Oct–Mar; disabled access. **£20**|£4.95.

OXFORD SP5106 **Café Moma** *Museum of Modern Art, Pembroke St (01865) 722733* Clean, light and very popular self-service café in the basement; simple modern furnishings, exhibitions on walls, largely vegetarian food from a blackboard, excellent cakes, and efficient, friendly service; open till 5pm (till 9pm Thurs only); cl Mon, bank hols; disabled access. **£10.65**|£4.50.

OXFORD SP5107 **Gees** *61a Banbury Rd (01865) 553540* Relaxed, airy atmosphere; fresh herbs and spices to enliven interesting vegetarian pastas, wild mushrooms and so forth, as well as good meat and fish dishes, decent, unusual wines; in a genuine old conservatory; cl 25–26 Dec. **£26**|£9.75 3-course lunch.

OXFORD SP5007 **Le Petit Blanc** *71–72 Walton St (01865) 510999* Very popular, stylish and airy 2-room brasserie open all day for breakfast, lunch, afternoon tea and dinner; from the smarter room you can see into the kitchen and watch the preparation of the extremely good Mediterranean food; friendly service and helpful notes against each wine listed; children very welcome; cl 25 Dec; disabled access. **£23**|£7.75.

As well as these, the city is full of useful stop-offs. The ancient Turf Tavern in Bath Pl between Holywell St and New College Lane is the most interesting pub, and other decent pubs include the ancient Bear (Alfred St), the enjoyably studenty King's Arms (Holywell St), Eagle & Child (St Giles; with Tolkien/C S Lewis connections), the unspoilt old Rose & Crown (North Parade) and the handily central White Horse (Broad St). The Victoria Arms at Old Marston, with a big garden on the Cherwell, is a popular punters' destination. The Pizza Express (Golden Cross) is in a surprisingly interesting medieval building.

SOUTH STOKE SU5983 **Perch & Pike** *(01491) 872415* Attractive flint pub with a relaxed atmosphere, comfortable seats, open fires, a nice assortment of tables, and civilised touches such as linen napkins, bone-handled cutlery and old napkin rings; good and innovative food; cl pm Sun, 25 Dec, pm 26 Dec; no children in the bar; partial disabled access. **£26**|£6.25.

STOKE ROW SU6884 **Crooked Billet** *(01491) 681048* Open-plan, beamed dining pub with a relaxed and homely atmosphere (rather like a French country restaurant); log fires, a wide choice of good, interesting food inc a vegetarian menu, decent wines and real ales; also, a big garden by Chilterns beechwoods. **£25**|£4.95.

UFFINGTON SU3087 **Britchcombe Farm** *(01367) 820667* Working farm in a lovely spot below White Horse Hill; afternoon cream teas on Sat, Sun and bank hol Mons with home-made scones, cakes and so forth; very friendly service, log fire in winter, tables outside among the geese and sheep in summer; some fruit and vegetables, home-made mohair knitwear and crafts, caravan for hire, and certified camping/caravan site; disabled access. £5 tea and scones for 2.

WALLINGFORD SU6089 **Annie's Tearooms** *79 High St (01491) 836308* Prettily decorated and friendly, no smoking, 17th-c house serving morning coffee, lunches with a home-made daily dish, and afternoon tea inc a fine choice of home-made cakes and quite a few teas; cl Weds, Sun (Oct–Jun); disabled access. £3.90.

WATLINGTON SU6894 **Chequers** *Love Lane (01491) 612874* Cheerful, cosy old pub with low beams, candlelight, nice old chairs and antique tables; conservatory, wide choice of good, popular food, real ales, and a pretty garden; no food pm Sun, cl 26 Dec; children in conservatory only. **£19**|£5.50.

WESTCOTT BARTON SP4325 **Fox** *(01869) 340338* Lovely, stone-built village pub with enjoyable, authentic Italian food cooked by the Italian landlord and his brother; a relaxed little bar with hops on low beams, open fires, high-backed settles and pews on the flagstones; an elegant restaurant, well kept ales, and espresso and cappuccino coffee; pleasant garden with wooden play fort. **£16.25**|£5.25.

WOOTTON SP4319 **King's Head** *(01993) 811340* Pretty, 17th-c Cotswold stone pub with a civilised and beamed no smoking lounge; a nice mix of furniture, an open log fire, very good, imaginative food inc lovely puddings, well kept real ales, and decent wines. **£24.25**|£6.95.

Special thanks to Mark Smith, W Stockton, Joan Olivier, Stewart Mackie, S Goodwin, Dr and Mrs D E Awbery.

Please let us know what you think of places in the *Guide*. Use the report forms at the back of the book or simply write us a letter.

Oxfordshire Calendar

Some of these dates were provisional as we went to press. Please check information with the telephone numbers provided.

FEBRUARY

21 **Oxford** Chinese New Year Celebrations at the Town Hall (01865) 204188

MARCH

5 **Didcot** Thomas the Tank Engine at the Railway Centre – *till Sun 7* (01235) 817200
6 **Woodstock** Winston Churchill Memorial Concert at Blenheim Palace (01993) 811325

APRIL

5 **Steeple Aston** Spring Flower Show (01869) 340512
31 **Oxford** Lord Mayor's Parade and Show at South Park (01865) 790260

MAY

1 **Oxford** May Morning: Magdalen College choir sings from Magdalen Tower, morris dancing in Radcliffe Sq and Broad St (01865) 726871; **Wallingford** Regatta – *till Sun 2* (01491) 836517; **Woodstock** Craft Fair at Blenheim Palace – *till Mon 3* (01283) 820548
3 **Whitchurch** May Fair inc morris dancing (01865) 766191
13 **Oxford** Beating the Bounds: starts at the Church of St Michael at the Northgate (01865) 726871
15 **Oxfordshire** Art Weeks: 300 open studios and exhibitions – *till 6 Jun* (01865) 430582

JUNE

12 **Woodstock** Fireworks Concert at Blenheim Palace (01993) 811325
13 **Banbury** and District Show (01295) 252535
19 **Abingdon** Election of the Mayor of Ock Street (since the fight over an ox in 1700), new mayor is chaired down Ock St, plus morris dancing into evening (01235) 522711; **Thame** Festival – *till* Carnival *on Sat 26* (01844) 215650; **Wallingford** Carnival (01491) 836594; **Woodstock** Carnival at Quarry Park (01993) 811495
26 **Banbury** Steam and Vintage Vehicle Rally – *till Sun 27* (01295) 730272
30 **Henley-on-Thames** Royal Regatta – *till 4 July* (01491) 572153

JULY

2 **Whitchurch** Weekend of Dance inc morris men – *till Sun 4* (01865) 766191
3 **Uffington** White Horse Show – *till Sun 4* (01367) 242191
4 **Hook Norton** Rural Fair (01608) 737336
8 **Caversfield** Bicester and Finmere Show (01280) 848327

Oxfordshire Calendar (cont.)

15 **Waterperry** Arts and Crafts in Action at Waterperry Gardens: over 300 crafts people and fine artists from around the world – *till Sun 18* (0171) 381 3192

17 **Hook Norton** Beer Festival at the Pear Tree Inn (01608) 737482

19 **Sunbury–Abingdon** Swan Upping on the River Thames: colourful traditional ceremony – *till Fri 23* (01628) 523030

AUGUST

8 **Caversfield** Bicester and Finmere Show (01280) 848327

15 **Woodstock** Rolls Royce Enthusiasts' Rally at Blenheim Palace (01993) 811325

28 **Woodstock** Oxfordshire Craft Fair at Blenheim Palace – *till Mon 30* (01993) 811325

30 **Steeple Aston** Summer Flower Show (01869) 340512

SEPTEMBER

9 **Woodstock** Blenheim International Horse Trials at Blenheim Palace – *till Sun 12* (01993) 813335

12 **Abingdon** Works Car Show (01235) 555552; **Banbury** Carnival (01295) 252535

16 **Thame** Agricultural Show at the Showground (01844) 212737

OCTOBER

1 **Didcot** Thomas the Tank Engine at the Railway Centre – *till Sun 3* (01235) 817200

9 **Shillingford** British National Ploughing Championship – *till Sun 10* (01302) 852569

13 **Banbury** Michaelmas Fair – *till Fri 15* (01295) 259855

DECEMBER

10 **Didcot** Thomas the Tank Engine at the Railway Centre – *till Sun 12* (01235) 817200

We welcome reports from readers

This *Guide* depends on readers' reports. Do help us if you can – in return, we offer a discount on the next edition to people who've helped us with reports for it. Tell us what you think about places already in it, and anything extra you think we should say about them. And send us your ideas for inclusion in the next edition: places to visit, eat at or stay in, attractive drives or walks, maybe even unusual interesting shops you know of. Use the card in the middle, the report forms at the end, or just write – no stamp needed: *The Good Guide to Britain*, FREEPOST TN1569, Wadhurst, E Sussex TN5 7BR.

SHROPSHIRE

Interesting and unusual – and largely unspoilt.

Shropshire, particularly in its southern parts, has very attractive unspoilt scenery – the old-fashioned England which elsewhere exists only in memory, imagination and the books of P. G. Wodehouse. Drives and walks pass attractive buildings in stone or black and white timbering, and offer sleepy views from a set of uncommonly distinctive hills.

Many family days out here fit well into this rustic pattern. There are quite a few appealing open farms: the one at Preston on the Weald is particularly good value, considering how long it holds people's attention, and the very traditional one at Acton Scott is also much enjoyed. Ludlow Castle has a lively and surprising mix of ancient fortress with modern holograms. The Ironbridge museums are among Britain's most enjoyable days out, with enough variety to hold anyone's attention – and plenty to entertain children at lively open-air Blists Hill. Hawkstone Park is another exceptionally enjoyable and unusual place. Other outstanding attractions include Shrewsbury Quest (Shrewsbury is full of interest), the expanded aerospace museum at Cosford, and the Severn Valley steam railway out of Bridgnorth. Wenlock priory, Boscobel House (good guided tour) and Benthall Hall at Broseley (charming garden) are favourites with older people. There are charming places to stay in.

Where to stay

ALL STRETTON SO4595 **Jinlye** *Castle Hill, All Stretton, Church Stretton SY6 6JP (01694) 723243* **£54,** plus special breaks; 8 spacious comfortable rms with lovely views. Charming 16th-c house in large grounds surrounded by National Trust land, with log fires in the comfortable lounges (one has an inglenook fireplace, lots of heavy beams, and a mix of interesting furniture), good home cooking in big no smoking dining room, enjoyable breakfasts, friendly owners; children over 12; disabled access.

BISHOP'S CASTLE SO3288 **Castle** *Market Sq, Bishop's Castle SY9 5BN (01588) 638403* **£60;** 6 spacious rms with fine views, some with own bthrm. Standing on the site of the old castle keep, this enjoyable 18th-c hotel has good fires, a relaxed and friendly atmosphere, lovely home-made food, well kept beers, and welcoming owners; cl 24–25 Dec.

BOURTON SO5996 **Bourton Manor** *Bourton, Much Wenlock TF13 6QE (01746) 785531* **£110,** plus special breaks; 8 rms. In landscaped grounds surrounded by pretty countryside, this extended 16th-c manor house has comfortably old-fashioned rooms with lots of panelling, a convivial bar, open fires, and very good service from friendly staff; most enjoyable food; partial disabled access.

CLUN SO2881 **New House Farm** *Clun, Craven Arms SY7 8NJ (01588) 638314* ***£45;** 2 rms. Remote 18th-c farmhouse nr the Welsh border with plenty of surrounding hillside walks; homely rooms with copper pans and decorative plates on the walls, plenty of books, a country garden, and a helpful, friendly owner; enjoyable home-cooked evening meals, packed lunches, good breakfasts; cl Nov–Easter; children over 5.

CRESSAGE SJ5604 **Cholmondeley Riverside** *Cound, Cressage, Shrewsbury SY5 6AF (01952) 510900* **£65;** 6 rms. Neatly converted 17th-c inn overlooking an exceptionally pretty stretch of the River Severn, with church pews, cushioned settles and oak tables in the civilised, roomy bar, wicker chairs in the conservatory with more out on the terrace; good imaginative food, well kept beers, a fine choice of wines, and a relaxed friendly atmosphere; coarse fishing.

DIDDLEBURY SO5085 **Delbury Hall** *Diddlebury, Craven Arms SY7 9DH (01584) 841267* **£85;** 3 rms. Beautiful stately Georgian house in 80 acres of landscaped parkland with ornamental duck on the lake, trout fishing, flower-filled gardens, and a hard tennis court; large hall with fine oak staircase, spacious drawing room, sitting room and snooker room, enjoyable food using their own vegetables, milk, eggs, hand-churned Jersey butter, a good wine list, and hearty breakfasts.

GRETTON SO5195 **Court Farm** *Gretton, Cardington, Church Stretton SY6 7HU (01694) 771219* ***£48;** 3 rms. Large, comfortable no smoking stone-built farmhouse on 325-acre mixed farm; a warm welcome, with a big woodburner in the inglenook fireplace and good food using home-grown and local produce; self-catering also in adjacent stables; cl Nov–Feb; no children or pets.

HANWOOD SJ4409 **White House** *Hanwood, Shrewsbury SY5 8LP (01743) 860414* ***£60;** 6 rms, 3 with own bthrm. Charming 16th-c black and white half-timbered house with 2 sitting rooms, breakfasts using their own eggs, enjoyable evening meals with some home-grown produce (must pre-book); 2 acres of garden; no children.

HOPESAY SO3883 **Old Rectory** *Hopesay, Craven Arms SY7 8HD (01588) 660245* ***£70;** 3 comfortable rms, one with own sitting room. 17th-c rectory with lovely 2-acre garden overlooking Hopesay Hill (NT); comfortable drawing room with a log fire and a baby grand piano, and an attractive dining room; excellent home cooking, and hearty breakfasts with home-baked bread; no smoking; cl Christmas–New Year; no children.

HOPTON WAFERS SO6376 **Crown** *Hopton Wafers, Kidderminster Worcs DY14 0NB (01299) 270372* **£75,** plus special breaks; 7 rms. Attractive creeper-covered stone inn in pleasant countryside, with an interestingly furnished bar, and inglenook fireplace; enjoyable food, decent house wines, beers and malt whiskies, friendly efficient service; streamside garden.

KNOCKIN SJ3321 **Top Farmhouse** *Knockin, Oswestry SY10 8HN (01691) 682582* **£40;** 3 pretty rms. Most attractive Grade I listed black and white timbered house dating back to the 16th c, with friendly owners; lots of timbers and beams, a log fire in the restful, comfortable drawing room, good breakfasts in the large dining room, and an appealing garden; snooker; children over 12.

LLANFAIR WATERDINE SO2476 **Red Lion** *Llanfair Waterdine, Knighton LD7 1TU (01547) 528214* ***£50;** 3 comfortable refurbished rms, 1 with own bthrm. In beautiful countryside overlooking the River Teme and landscaped river banks, this pub has a heavily beamed convivial lounge bar with a big open fire, small black-beamed tap room, a little dining room and a terrace dining room with fine views; good big breakfasts, affable service and a determinedly traditional atmosphere – no noisy machines, music or children.

LONGVILLE SO5393 **Longville Arms** *Longville, Much Wenlock TF13 6DT (01694) 771206* ***£45,** plus special breaks; 5 comfortable rms in converted stables with showers; fresh flowers and home-made biscuits. Warmly friendly inn with 2 spacious bars, well kept real ales, a wide range of enjoyable food, superb breakfasts, and a neat terraced side garden; cl 25 Dec; partial disabled access.

LUDLOW SO5174 **Feathers** *Bull Ring, Ludlow SY8 1AA (01584) 875261* **£98.50,** plus special breaks; 40 comfortable rms. Striking hotel with exquisitely proportioned and intricately carved timbered frontage, Jacobean panelling and carving, period furnishings; artistically presented restaurant dishes, decent food in bar; efficient pleasant service; limited disabled access.

LUDLOW SO5175 **Unicorn** *Lower Corve St, Ludlow SY8 1DU (01584) 873555* **£50;** 5 comfortable, beamed and timbered rms, most with own bthrm. Pleasantly refurbished family-run inn with huge log fires; good popular food in bar and relaxing restaurant (inc vegetarian and vegan dishes), excellent breakfasts, real ales, attentive service; riverside terrace; cl 25 Dec.

LUDLOW SO5174 **Wheatsheaf** *Lower Broad St, Ludlow SY8 1PQ (01584) 872980* ***£40,** plus special breaks; 5 comfortable oak-beamed rms with showers. Attractively furnished small 17th-c pub spectacularly built into a medieval town gate; traditional atmosphere, 2 log fires, lots of hops, timbers, and exposed stone walls; wide range of good food in bar and no smoking restaurant (super steaks), real ales and farm ciders, and friendly owners.

MUCH WENLOCK SO6299 **Talbot** *High St, Much Wenlock TF13 6AA (01952) 727077* **£90,** plus special breaks; 6 rms. Dating from 1360 and once part of Wenlock Abbey, this converted 18th-c malthouse is very civilised, with pretty flowers, log fires, and prints; pleasant staff; good food in the no smoking restaurant and bar, and well kept real ales.

NORTON SJ7200 **Hundred House** *Bridgnorth Rd, Norton, Shifnal TF11 9EE (01952) 730353* **£99,** plus special breaks; 10 cottagey rms (some with a swing and lavender-scented sheets). Carefully refurbished mainly Georgian inn with quite a sophisticated feel; neatly kept bar with old quarry-tiled floors, beamed ceilings and oak panelling, and handsome fireplaces, elaborate evening meals using the inn's own herbs, friendly service, good bar food, excellent breakfast and afternoon tea; delightful garden, no dogs.

RHYDYCROESAU SJ2430 **Pen-y-Dyffryn** *Rhydycroesau, Oswestry SY10 7JD (01691) 653700* ***£74,** plus special breaks; 10 rms. Handsome Georgian stonebuilt rectory in 5 acres with lovely views of the Welsh hills, log fires in both comfortable lounges, and a relaxed friendly atmosphere; good food using the best local ingredients, trout fishing, hill-walking and riding (shooting can be arranged); well behaved dogs welcome; cl Jan; disabled access.

SHREWSBURY SJ4917 **Albright Hussey** *(off the A528 N) Ellesmere Rd, Broad Oak, Shrewsbury SY4 3AF (01939) 290571* **£95,** plus special breaks; 14 lovely rms. Fine moated medieval manor house, partly timber-framed and partly stone and brick, in 4-acre garden; particularly good food in timbered and panelled restaurant, and excellent service; children over 3; disabled access.

SHREWSBURY SJ4417 **Fitz Manor** *(off the B5067 NW) Bowmere Heath, Shrewsbury SY4 3AS (01743) 850295* **£50;** 3 rms, shared bthrm. Lovely black and white timbered 15th-c manor house with oak panelling and a log fire in the comfortable sitting room, a big dining room with antiques, paintings and parquet flooring; good enjoyable evening meals, big breakfasts, friendly owners, and outdoor heated swimming pool.

STREFFORD SO4485 **Strefford Hall Farm** *Strefford, Craven Arms SY7 8DE (01588) 672383* ***£42;** 3 rms. No smoking Victorian stonebuilt farmhouse surrounded by 360 acres of working farm; woodburner in the sitting room; good breakfasts (evening meals by arrangement); lots of walks; cl Christmas–New Year.

WENLOCK EDGE SO5796 **Wenlock Edge Inn** *Hilltop, Wenlock Edge, Much Wenlock TF13 6DJ (01746) 785678* ***£70,** plus special breaks; 3 rms, showers only (served by 190-ft well). Popular and cheerfully welcoming family-run inn by the Ippikins Rock viewpoint, with lots of walks through the NT land that runs along the Edge; chatty and relaxed atmosphere; good fresh home-made bar food inc old-fashioned puddings, fine breakfasts, and wide range of drinks; 2nd Mon evening of month is story-telling night; cl Christmas; children over 8; partial disabled access.

WOOLSTASTON SO4698 **Rectory Farm** *Woolstaston, Church Stretton SY6 6NN (01694) 751306* ***£44;** 3 comfortable rms. Lovely half-timbered 17th-c farmhouse on the lower slopes of the Long Mynd, with fine views, friendly welcome, a big beamed lounge, a cosy TV room; hearty breakfasts; no evening meals; cl Dec–Feb; children over 12; no dogs.

WORFIELD SO7595 **Old Vicarage** *Worfield, Bridgnorth WV15 5JZ (01746) 716497* ***£107.50,** plus special breaks; 14 pretty rms. Restful and carefully restored Edwardian rectory in 2 acres, with 2 airy conservatory-style lounges; very good interesting food in the no smoking restaurant, a fine wine list, and warm friendly helpful service; good disabled access.

WROCKWARDINE SJ6212 **Church Farm** *Wrockwardine, Telford TF6 5DG (01952) 244917* ***£50;** 5 individual well equipped rms, most with own bthrm. Friendly Georgian farmhouse on a very ancient site overlooking the attractive garden and church; with a relaxed atmosphere, particularly good caring service, beams and a log fire in the lounge; good daily changing food in the traditionally furnished dining room; cl Christmas; children over 10.

To see and do

Shropshire Family Attraction of the Year

Ludlow Castle SO5174 Dating from around 1086, this splendid fortress has a properly 'castle-ish' feel; throughout the year various events and activities make it fun for families, such as the birds of prey displays and face painting on summer Weds. Other events might include food fairs, conker championships, battle re-enactments and plays at the open-air theatre (there's always Shakespeare during the Ludlow Festival). The list of events can change, so ring the number below to find out exactly what's on when. A more unusual draw for children is the hologram exhibition in the dungeon, with the good-sized collection of laser-generated images and illusions forming a dramatic contrast to the ancient Norman walls. Highlights include the seemingly endless hole in the ground on the first floor, and the section where you can swap heads with whoever's with you; many of the other holograms change quite dramatically as you walk past them. As for the castle itself, lots of original parts survive, inc the Norman keep, and the chapel with its unusual circular nave. The towers and battlements on their wooded crag over the River Teme have wonderful views, and children of all ages can get quite a buzz from exploring them. The mix of ruins and hi-tech holograms works rather well, and you can easily spend a happy couple of hours combining the two – more if there's something else going on. The castle has quite an illustrious history: for a while it was a royal palace, and the ill-fated Prince Arthur lived here with his bride Catherine of Aragon for a short time before his death. It was abandoned around the start of the 18th c. Shop, mostly disabled access; cl 25 Dec, Jan wkdys; (01584) 873355; entry to castle £2.50 (£1.50 children), hologram show £1.50 (children 50p).

ACTON BURNELL CASTLE SJ5301 Ruined red sandstone manor house built in the 13th c, but almost abandoned by 1420; disabled access; free. The Plume of Feathers at Harley is fairly handy for lunch.

ACTON SCOTT WORKING FARM SO4589 (off the A49) Vivid introduction to traditional rural life, with plenty of rare breeds, and crops cultivated using old rotation methods; all the work is done by hand or horse power, with period farm machinery. Lots of craft demonstrations, and daily butter-making. Unusually, this is a farm aimed just as much at adults (maybe more) as at children. Meals, snacks, shop, disabled access; cl Mon (exc bank hols), and Nov–Mar; (01694) 781306; £3.25. The most convenient place for lunch is the Green Dragon at Little Stretton.

ATCHAM SJ5409 **Attingham Park** Splendidly grand, late 18th-c house on the site of an old Roman town, with an imposing 3-storey colonnaded portico. The extensive picture gallery was designed by Nash, who made imaginative use of early curved cast iron and glass for the ceiling; attractive mature gardens and deer park outside. Snacks, shop, disabled access by prior arrangement; grounds open daily, house open pm Sat–Weds and bank hol Mons Apr–Oct; (01743) 709203; house and grounds £4, grounds only £1.50 ; NT. **Attingham Home Farm** Rare breeds and traditional farm machinery; you can watch the milking of the Jersey cows (3.30pm), and play with the pets. Farmhouse teas, shop, limited disabled access; cl am, Thurs and Fri (exc school hols), and Oct–Easter; (01743) 709243; £2.50. The Cholmondeley Riverside towards Cressage has good food.

BILLINGSLEY SO7183 **Rays Farm Country Matters** Traditional farm in pleasant countryside with pigs, sheep, cattle, miniature ponies, llamas, and a good collection of owls and other animals. Pleasant woodland walks, and indoor and outdoor picnic areas. Snacks, shop, disabled access; cl wknds in Jan; (01299) 841255; *£3.25. Both pubs in nearby Chelmarsh have decent food and lovely reservoir views; the Chelmarsh–Highley road is a nice drive.

BISHOP'S CASTLE SO3288 Historic little market town with some fine Elizabethan and Georgian buildings, railway and local history museums, good shops, and the curious House on Crutches. It's handy for exploring Offa's Dyke. The Three Tuns has a unique Victorian tower brewhouse, still in use – you can usually arrange a tour, (01588) 638797.

BOSCOBEL HOUSE SJ8308 Interesting old house renowned for sheltering Charles II after the Battle of Worcester, with an unusually well preserved 17th-c garden and cobbled courtyard, and 19th-c décor giving a romanticised view of the king's drama. Good guided tour. Meals, snacks, shop, disabled access to gardens only; cl winter Mon and Tues, 24–26 Dec, Jan; (01902) 850244; £3.95. The **Royal oak** here is said by some to have been the hiding place of the king, by others to be a descendant, and by still others to be just a fine old tree. The Bell in Tong is good for lunch, and Weston Park at Weston under Lizard (Staffs) is nearby. **White Ladies Priory** (just SW of Boscobel) The ruins of an Augustinian nunnery destroyed in the Civil War; free.

★ **BRIDGES** SJ3600 Pleasant quiet village, with a good pub and nearby walks.

★ **BRIDGNORTH** SO7193 On the Severn, this old market town is picturesque without being touristy. It's divided into the High Town and Low Town, with steps between the two – though it's easier (and more fun) to take the hair-raising **Cliff Railway**. On the way down you pass some small caves that people lived in till 1856 (they're not open, but labelled). As well as some handsome red brick, High Town has lots of fine timbered buildings, such as the odd town hall built on a sandstone-arched base that straddles the road in the high street. **Castle** Largely destroyed in the Civil War, but part of the keep remains, left at a scary tilt by the constant bombardment; the grounds are now a park with good views – the best views are from Castle Esplanade. The unusual **church** on nearby East Castle St was designed by Thomas Telford. **Costume and Childhood Museum** (Newmarket Building) Lots of old costumes, dolls, and a Victorian nursery. Not open every day (usually cl Tues), but if you find them shut, next door Beryl's Pantry has a key and can let you in; *£1.25. Useful pubs for food here are the Bear (Northgate; not Sun) and Punch Bowl (on the B4364; good carvery, great views). **Severn Valley Railway** The leading standard-gauge steam railway, with a great collection of locomotives, a splendidly lively atmosphere, and trips through beautiful scenery; for details *see entry under Bewdley, in Hereford and Worcester*. The Railwayman's Arms in the station is an atmospheric place for a snack. **Daniels Mill** (on the B4555, 1m S) Working cornmill still powered by its big waterwheel; a picturesque old place, run by the same family for 200 years. Snacks, shop; open pm wknds, Weds and bank hols Easter–Sept; (01746) 762753; £2. **Midland Motor Museum** (off the A458 SE) Over 100 well restored sports cars, racing cars and motorcycles, in converted stables in the beautiful grounds of Stanmore Hall. Snacks, shop, disabled access; cl 25 Dec; (01746) 762992; *£3.50. The grounds also have a caravan site.

BROSELEY SJ6701 **Benthall Hall** (just NW) Well liked by readers, an Elizabethan sandstone house with fine oak woodwork and panelling, decorative plasterwork, interesting garden, and 17th-c church (services 3.15pm most Suns). Some disabled access; open pm Weds, Sun and bank hols Apr–Sept; (01952) 882159; £3, garden only £2; NT. The Foresters Arms is useful for lunch.

BROWN CLEE HILL SO5986 Aptly named, this is Shropshire's highest point at nearly 550 metres (1,800ft). It has a disappointingly flat top but offers walkers a certain solitary grandeur.

† **BUILDWAS ABBEY** SJ6404 (on the B4378) Beautiful remains of 12th-c Cistercian abbey – apart from the roof it's practically all still here. Snacks, shop, some disabled access; cl Nov–Mar;

*£1.75. It's right next to the gigantic cooling towers of a power station, which this close seem to have a geometrical beauty of their own. The Meadow coming out from Ironbridge has decent food.

BURY DITCHES SO3283 Iron Age ring fort, high on a hill, with superb views of S Shrops and N Herefords.

CAER CARADOC SO4794 (E of Church Stretton) This hill has a pleasingly compact summit, and the pick of the local views. The best start for walks is Hope Bowdler, not far from Shropshire's oldest pub, the Royal Oak in pretty Cardington.

★ **CHIRBURY** SO2698 An attractive village, with a famously haunted graveyard.

★ ✝ **CLAVERLEY** SO7993 An attractive village of black and white timbered houses. The church has impressive medieval wall paintings.

✝ **CLEOBURY MORTIMER** SO6775 Civilised small town, most notable perhaps for its church's **crooked spire**, though timbered Tudor buildings among its more elegant Georgian ones are picturesque. A restored **watermill** produces its own stoneground flour. The 16th-c Kings Arms has good value food (and comfortable bedrooms).

★ **CLUN** SO3080 Attractive stonebuilt village on the edge of the **Clun Forest**, a peaceful pastoral area of rolling partly wooded hills. The ruined Norman **castle** gives fine views from its mound; free. Down by the River Clun, the 16th-c stone bridge is very picturesque. The Sun and White Horse are useful for lunch.

✝ **COSFORD** SJ7805 **Royal Air Force Museum** (on the A41) One of the country's best aviation museums, a spectacular collection of carefully arranged aircraft inc the Victor and Vulcan bombers, Hastings, York and British Airways airliners, and the last airworthy Britannia, as well as lots of missiles and a display of engines. A large extension, inc an art gallery, should be open by summer 1999. Snacks, shop, disabled access; cl 24–26 Dec, 1 Jan; (01902) 374872; £5. There's a decent farm shop on Holyhead Rd, and the Bell at Tong is a reliable family dining pub.

ELLESMERE WALKS SJ4035 There are several meres or lakes nr Ellesmere – the mere by Ellesmere itself, Blake Mere, and Cole Mere, which has a country park around it. This is close enough to the Shropshire Union Canal to include a walk along the towpath, with Colemere village SJ4332 a suitable starting place.

GRINSHILL HILL SJ5223 This gives walkers much wider views than you'd expect from its modest height, and has quite an atmospheric summit, where woods open out by sheer quarried rock-faces.

HARMER HILL SJ4921 **Pim Hill Farm** (Lea Hall; on the A528 S) Organic farm with rare breeds, picnic site, a friendly donkey called Jenny, a shire horse called Blossom, and well priced produce shop. Snacks from their own bakery; cl 25 Dec; (01939) 290342; free. The Bridgewater Arms has decent family food.

✝ **HAUGHMOND ABBEY** SJ5214 (off the B5062 E of Shrewsbury) Extensive ruins of an Augustinian abbey, inc a fine Norman doorway in the chapter house, some interesting sculpture, and well preserved lodgings and kitchens. Good for picnics. In the grounds are some plants unique to the area. Shop, some disabled access; open Easter–Sept; (01743) 709661; £1.75.

! **HAWKSTONE PARK** SJ5628 This remarkable steeply wooded 18th-c parkland has been restored after a period of neglect; spectacular views from the monuments dotted around its 100 acres. Highlights include the ruins of a medieval red castle, intricate arches and pathways, and a fantastic underground grotto with tales told by an eerily convincing laser-powered animatron. The full circuit can easily take up to 3 hours and the path isn't always easy going, so wear sensible shoes (and you may need a torch for some of the caves and tunnels). The BBC filmed their *Chronicles of Narnia* here. Meals, snacks, shop, limited disabled access; cl wkdys Nov–Mar; (01939) 200300; £4.50. The Caspian Bar of the Hawkstone Park Hotel has good-value food.

★ **HODNET** SJ6128 Several attractive half-timbered houses here, and some interesting old books in the church. **Hodnet Hall Gardens** 60 acres of lovely landscaped gardens with spacious lawns, lush pools, plants and trees; the astonishingly decorated tearoom is full of big-game trophies. Snacks, shop, disabled access (prior notice preferred); cl am, Mon, and Oct–Mar; (01630) 685202; £3. The Bear Hotel opposite is good for lunch.

★ **IRONBRIDGE** SJ6703 This steep town, with intriguing hillside paths and narrow lanes, was the birthplace of the Industrial Revolution: it was Abraham Darby's use here of coke instead of charcoal for smelting which made mass-production of iron possible. Well set among the woods and grassy slopes of the Severn Gorge, it was known only as Coalbrookdale until the Darbys built the **iron bridge** across the river that today gives the town its name. As their industry took off they produced the world's first iron rails, boats, trains, and wheels, and for quite some while the valley was the biggest iron-making area in the world. Attractively placed by the riverside, the Meadow, Woodbridge and Olde Robin Hood, and (all handy for Maws craft centre and the Coalport Museum) the Boat and Half Moon at Jackfield and the Shakespeare at Coalport are all useful for lunch; there's a pleasant terraced walk between the river and the Golden Ball (Wesley Rd, off Madeley Hill). For a fuller restaurant meal, the Coracle in the village square is nice. **Ironbridge Gorge Museum** (voucher only valid when purchasing Passport Ticket, see below) Many of the former industrial sites now make up this outstanding network, one of the most satisfying places to visit in the whole country, scattered over 6 miles along the gorge. 50-acre **Blists Hill** is the highlight, and the part children like best – a complete reconstructed Victorian village, showing everything from the offices, houses and machinery to the school, pubs, pigsties and swingboats; it's the biggest open-air museum of its kind. Costumed staff add authenticity, and there are extra activities in the school hols. The other main sections include museums devoted to the river, and the iron, china and tile-making

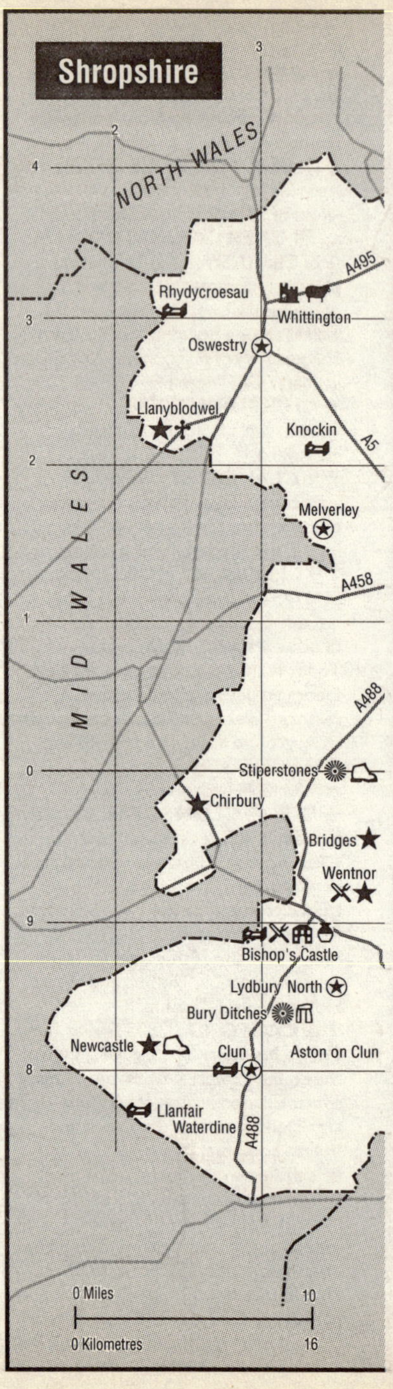

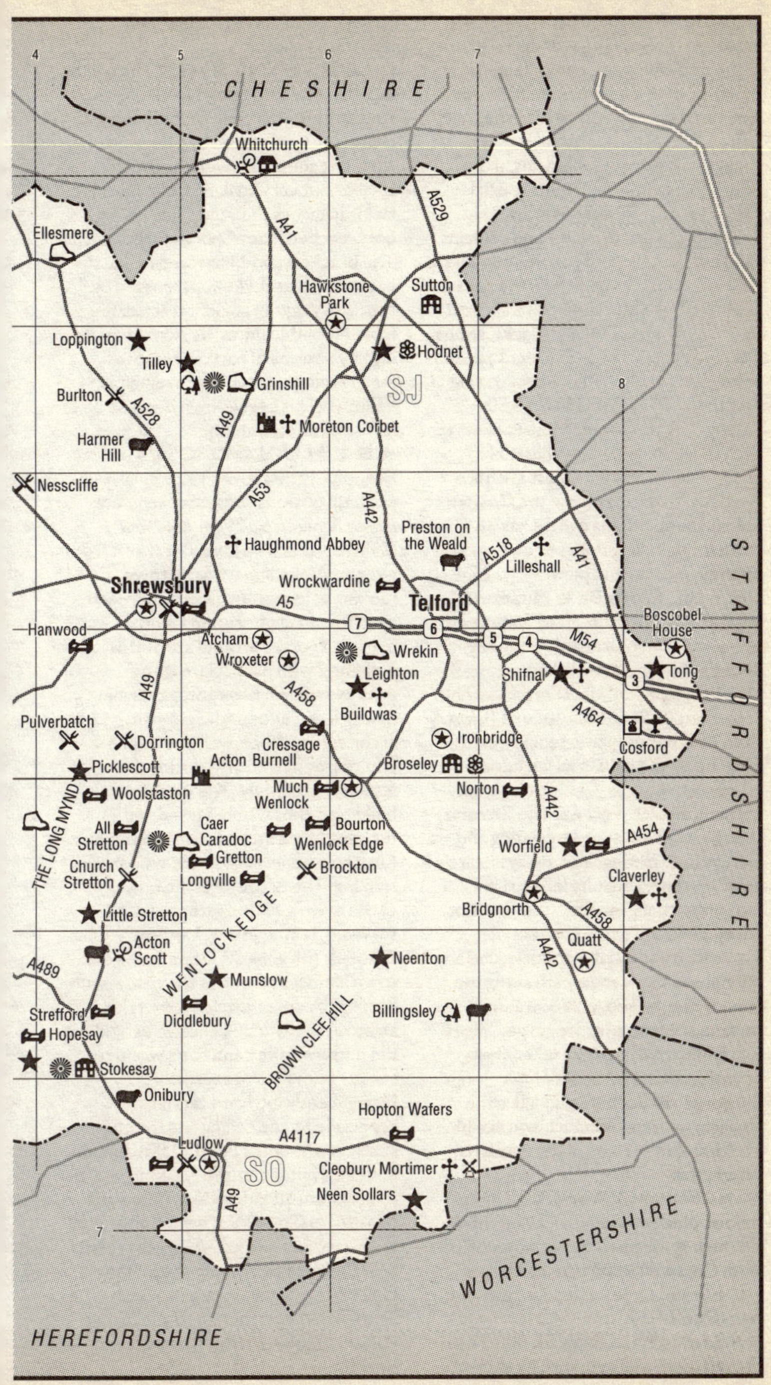
CHESHIRE
STAFFORDSHIRE
WORCESTERSHIRE
HEREFORDSHIRE
SJ
SO
Whitchurch
Ellesmere
Hawkstone Park
Sutton
Loppington
Hodnet
Tilley
Grinshill
Burlton
Moreton Corbet
Harmer Hill
Nesscliffe
Preston on the Weald
Haughmond Abbey
Lilleshall
Shrewsbury
Wrockwardine
Telford
Boscobel House
Hanwood
Atcham
Wroxeter
Wrekin
Leighton
Shifnal
Tong
Buildwas
Pulverbatch
Dorrington
Cressage
Ironbridge
Cosford
Picklescott
Acton Burnell
Broseley
Woolstaston
Much Wenlock
Norton
THE LONG MYND
All Stretton
Caer Caradoc
Bourton
Wenlock Edge
Worfield
Gretton
Church Stretton
Longville
Brockton
Claverley
Little Stretton
WENLOCK EDGE
Bridgnorth
Acton Scott
Quatt
Neenton
Munslow
Strefford
Diddlebury
BROWN CLEE HILL
Billingsley
Hopesay
Stokesay
Onibury
Hopton Wafers
Ludlow
Cleobury Mortimer
Neen Sollars
A41
A529
A528
A49
A53
A442
A518
A5
M54
A458
A464
A454
A489
A4117

industries, with some beautifully restored houses (and wonderful echoes in the brick kilns at Coalport) and a newly opened pipeworks in Broseley. You need only buy tickets for the parts you're interested in (useful leaflets suggest a variety of itineraries, from 3 hours to a whole day), but a special offer Passport Ticket covering everything is good value – and remains valid indefinitely until you've seen all the bits you want. On bank hols the sites are linked by a bus, otherwise it's best to drive (or walk). Meals, snacks, shops, disabled access; cl 24–25 Dec, 1 Jan and some parts cl Nov–Mar – best to ring first then; (01952) 433522; £9.50 Passport Ticket, or individual tickets to each museum available – Blists Hill is around £6.50. **Maws Craft Centre** Across a footbridge from the Coalport tile museum, this big centre has 26 workshops selling things as diverse as pottery, puzzles and pictures (cl 25 Dec; free). **Teddy Bear Museum** Next to the Museum of the River, with bears and other furry animals made here by the long-established Merrythought Co; cl 25 Dec; free. The **Museum of Steel Sculpture** (Cherry Tree Hill) has dramatic sculptures inspired by the industrial heritage in 10 attractive acres. Cl Mon exc bank hols and all Dec–Feb; £2. The **Severn Gorge** itself has such fascinating and picturesque (though not always exactly pretty) scenery that its industrial monuments cry out for a tour on foot. Steep lanes and paths connect Ironbridge and Coalbrookdale, and an old railway track and a path along the base of Benthall Edge Wood assist walking routes along the gorge. A fine linear walk can be taken from Broseley, descending NW into the gorge via Corbett's Dingle to Coalport. From Coalport, you could even follow the river all the way S to Bridgnorth.

† **LILLESHALL ABBEY** SJ7314 Very impressive ruins of 12th-c abbey in pleasant setting surrounded by yew trees – it's a nice spot for a picnic, peaceful and undisturbed; open wknds Apr–Oct; £1.30.

★ † **LLANYBLODWEL** SJ2422 This attractive village, with its ancient riverside pub, has an exuberantly decorated church.

LONG MYND SO4294 The partly heather-covered Long Mynd, England's southernmost grouse moor, has great character (undimmed by a huge fire early last summer), with the much smaller but very striking Caer Caradoc facing it across the valley. For walks, it's best reached from Church Stretton. The bracken-and-bilberry-clad massif has a flat plateau-like top, crossed by the Port Way, an ancient track dating from Neolithic times. Its sides are cut into by a series of narrow remote-feeling valleys, of which Cardingmill Valley (NT) is best known because of its relative accessibility.

★ † **LUDLOW** SO5174 Beautiful 12th-c town, its original grid plan still obvious today. *See separate Family Panel on p.529* for **Ludlow Castle** – there's a lovely view of it from over at Whitcliffe, with the town looking at its best from this approach road from Wigmore and Leinthall Starkes. Dotted around are 500 listed buildings, with particularly good examples down Broad St, a charming mixture of Tudor and Georgian architecture. Book well in advance if you're planning to visit during the festival in early July. The most famous building is the lavishly carved and timbered **Feathers Hotel** on the Bull Ring; some parts inside are almost as striking. The Broadgate, the only one of the town's 13th-c gates to have survived, is interesting. **Ludlow Church** (off King St) Dominating the town almost as much as the castle, with its magnificent pinnacled tower; it's in an attractive tranquil enclave behind the old buttermarket, and has a wonderful sense of timeless peace inside. Magnificently intricate carvings, especially on the ceiling and the choir stalls. In winter it's open 12.30–3pm on Sun only, but in summer you can visit all day (exc am Sun). **Ludlow Museum** (Castle St) Good local history museum; cl 1–2pm, Sun exc Jun–Aug, Nov–Mar; *£1. Quite a few antique shops; the Unicorn is the nicest pub for lunch. The town is overlooked by the rather volcanic-looking Titterstone Clee to the NE.

LYDBURY NORTH SO3485 **Walcot Hall** Fine Georgian house built for Clive of India; free-standing ballroom, stable yard with matching clock towers, big walled garden, and arboretum with good rhododendrons, azaleas and specimen trees. Disabled access; usually open pm bank hol Mon and the preceding Sun, and by appointment; (0171) 581 2782; £2.50. You can stay in various wings, and they can arrange fishing and riding.

MELVERLEY SJ3316 **St Peter's Church** This beautiful black and white structure was rebuilt in 1406 after Owain Glyndwr burned the previous one; it has a fine Jacobean pulpit and chain Bible. The stables of the Old Rectory have a **craft centre**; open Sun–Tues. The Old Three Pigeons over at Nesscliffe has good food and all-day coffee, with Kynaston Cave and good cliff walks nearby.

MORETON CORBET CASTLE SJ5623 Destroyed by Parliament in 1644, but you can still see a small 13th-c keep and the substantial ruins of the once-grand Elizabethan house; free. There are some elaborate tombs in the adjacent **church**; the 18th-c Raven at Tilley up towards Wem is a good dining pub.

★ **MUCH WENLOCK** SJ6200 Lovely little medieval market town, with lots of timbered and jettied buildings. The Talbot is good for lunch. **Much Wenlock Priory** Has its origins in the 7th c, but it's the magnificent remains of the 11th-c building and later additions you can see today. The chapter house has remarkably patterned interlaced arches. Shop; disabled access; sometimes cl 1–2pm, winter Mon and Tues, 24–26 Dec, 1 Jan; £2.30 (inc Walkman tour). **Much Wenlock Museum** Local history and new displays on geology and natural history, in the Old Market Hall; cl 1–2pm, Sun exc Jun–Aug, all Oct–Mar; 50p. **Wenlock Edge** (SO5695) This very long smooth hill is wooded (and much quarried) along its flanks, but has possibilities for walks. The B4371 along it has good views.

★ **NEWCASTLE** SO2482 An attractive village, with good local walks, and a decent pub.

ONIBURY SO4378 **Wernlas Collection of Rare Poultry** (Green Lane, W of the A49) Incredible numbers of chickens and bantams, also rare pheasants and unusual European species, as well as pigs, donkeys and goats. About 6,000 chicks hatch each year, so usually some for children to handle or feed. Snacks, shop; cl Mon (exc mid-July–mid-Sept and bank hols), 25 Dec; (01584) 856318; £3. The Hollybush is handy for lunch.

OSWESTRY SJ2929 **Cambrian Railway Museum** and **Oswestry Cycle Museum** (Oswald Rd) Joint museum with lots of old bicycles and a history of cycling (especially good on Dunlop), as well as steam engines and railway memorabilia; one locomotive may be in steam bank hols last Sun of month. Snacks, shop, some disabled access; cl 25 Dec; (01691) 671749; £1. The Butchers Arms has good-value food, and the Wynnstay Hotel is a comfortable refuge. **Old Oswestry** (just N) Impressive Iron Age hill fort covering 68 acres. The elaborate western defensive entrance and 5 ramparts remain; free. **Old Racecourse** (on the B4580, 2 or 3m W, SJ2630) A high stretch of common with splendid views into Wales.

★ **PICKLESCOTT** SO4399 Attractive tucked-away village, with a delightfully placed ancient pub, and good walking nearby.

PRESTON ON THE WEALD SJ6814 **Hoo Farm Animal Kingdom** Exceptionally good-value, traditional working farm, with enough to keep families with very young children happy for a sizeable chunk of the day. All the ingredients you'd expect, from bottle feeding the lambs and milking demonstrations to a petting corner, egg collecting and nature trails, as well as several more unusual features, such as ostriches, pheasant-rearing, and a big walk-in beehive, where a glass window lets you watch the bees at work. Also sheep-racing (summer afternoons at 3pm, not Fri), with a tiny Tote for betting. There's a Christmas tree plantation and a Christmas tree maze, with a story for toddlers to follow as they go round;

Father Christmas is here in Dec. Picnic and play areas, and occasional spinning demonstrations. Snacks, shop, disabled access; cl Mon Sept–mid-Oct and 24 Dec–24 Mar; (01952) 677917; £2.95. The Tayleur Arms over at Longdon upon Tern is a decent family dining pub.

QUATT SO7487 **Dudmaston** (off the A442) 17th-c house with the old flower-painting collection of Francis Darby of Coalbrookdale, modern art, and lakeside and woodland walks in the extensive parkland. Meals, snacks, shop, disabled access; open pm Weds and Sun Apr–Sept; (01746) 780866; house and garden £3.50, garden only £2.50; NT. There's usually free pedestrian access to the woods all year. Nearby, the Lion at Hampton Loade is a good jumping-off point for walks by the River Severn (with a quaint ferry crossing to a stop on the Severn Valley Railway – *see Bridgnorth entry, above*).

★ † **SHIFNAL** SJ7407 Much expanded under the influence of nearby Telford, but still with a villagey heart and attractive buildings, inc an interesting church and some good food pubs such as the Star (Market Pl) and Jaspers (Victoria Rd).

★ **SHREWSBURY** SJ4912 The central street layout is still largely medieval, with oddly named streets (Shoplatch, Murivance, Wyle Cop), and plenty of quiet corners up narrow alleys and courtyards among its more modern shops and offices. It's rich in striking architecture, both Tudor timbering and Georgian brick, with a signposted trail between some of the more interesting buildings. Around The Square numerous buildings reflect the medieval wool fortunes, inc the old market hall; in the adjacent High St, Owens Mansion and Irelands Mansion are fine half-timbered houses worth looking at from outside. Even McDonalds is in a medieval building. The walk up Castle St is worth while, passing the original Grammar School building and the half-timbered Council House Court. Nearby the **church of St Mary** has one of the tallest spires in England. 12th-c **Shrewsbury Castle** guards the narrow neck of land between the river's loop. It was refurbished by Thomas Telford in 1790, though still has parts of the earlier building. The **Shropshire Regimental Museum** has recently reopened here after a terrorist attack in 1992. The grounds are attractive. Shop, some disabled access; cl Mon (exc bank hols) and winter Suns; (01743) 358516; £3, grounds free. **Clive House Museum** (College Hill) Old town house associated with Clive of India, with excellent displays of Coalport and Caughley porcelain, fine paintings in period rooms, and walled garden. Shop, disabled access to ground floor only; cl Mon (exc bank hols), winter Suns, 2 weeks at Christmas, but best to phone to check – as we went to press the long-term future of this museum was uncertain; (01743) 354811; £2. **Rowley's House Museum** (Barker St) Impressive timber-framed building with social and natural history, and some interesting Roman remains. Shop, disabled access to ground floor only; hours as Clive House; (01743) 361196; £3. **St Julian's Craft Centre** (St Alkmunds Sq) Among other interesting shops in this part of town is an excellent craft centre in a 12th-c church, with several cheery workshops, a bustling craft fair every Sat, and a good restaurant (especially useful for vegetarians). Some disabled access; cl Sun; (01743) 353516; free. **Shrewsbury Quest** (Abbey Foregate) Delightful reconstruction of medieval monastic life, loosely based around the Brother Cadfael books by Ellis Peters (set in medieval Shrewsbury). You can create your own decorated manuscript or try your hand at ancient games and crafts. The carefully researched period herb garden is a draw in its own right – quite a few poisonous plants despite the lovely smell. Meals and snacks (some inspired by medieval recipes), shop, disabled access; cl 25 Dec, 1 Jan; (01743) 243324; £4.25. Just opposite, the impressive 14th-c **abbey** includes a statue of Edward III, and a memorial to Wilfrid Owen. The original town is almost entirely ringed by a loop of the Severn (quiet waterside paths and parks, and you can hire boats along some stretches). Places to mention for food include the riverside Armoury (Victoria Quay) and Boat House (New St/Quarry Park), also the Three Fishes (Fish St), cheery Dun Cow Pie Shop (Abbey Foregate), Castle Vaults (Castle Gates), Coach & Horses (Swan Hill/Cross Hill), stately Lion Hotel (Wyle Cop) and Cromwells (Dogpole). Heading SW from Shrewsbury, the old coach road through Longden and Pulverbatch is an attractive drive – great views the further you go.

STIPERSTONES SO3799 The rather eery Stiperstones are outcrops of harder quartzy rock leaving strange-shaped boulders, tors and crests on the skyline – and strange tales among the people living nearby. The ridge is crowned by dramatic rocks and has a splendid view; a short walk from a nearby car park (you can make an interesting 8½ mile circuit with a stop at the More Arms at Hope), or you can take the longish walk up from the former lead-mining village of Snailbeach SJ3702.

STOKESAY CASTLE SO4381 (off the A49) One of the finest examples of a medieval manor house, 13th-c, in a notably charming setting. The hall with its cruck-framed roof and early English windows is just as it was 700 years ago, and there's a timbered Tudor gatehouse. Good views from the top of the tower, and excellent Walkman tour. Summer snacks, shop; cl 1–2pm, all Mon and Tues Nov–Mar, plus 24–26 Dec; (01588) 672544; £2.95. The pub named after the 'castle' in nearby Craven Arms has good-value family food.

SUTTON SJ6631 **Old Colehurst Manor** (S of Mkt Drayton) 17th-c, beautifully restored by its Danish owner, though you need to stay here to get the full experience; (01630) 638833.

WHITCHURCH SJ5440 **Rocking Horse Workshop** (Cottage Farm, Tilstock Rd) Here you can watch the production and restoration of traditional rocking horses. Shop; cl 25 Dec and maybe wknds, they may move in the next year so best to phone to check; (01948) 666777; free.

WHITTINGTON SJ3131 **Park Hall Working Farm Museum** (off the A5) Powerful shire horses still work the land here as they have for decades. The Victorian stables have livestock from that period inc cattle, sheep and several breeds of pig, and there's lots of vintage farm machinery and equipment. Snacks, shop, disabled access; usually cl Fri (exc July–mid-Sept), all Nov–Easter, but may change – best to check first; (01691) 652175; £2.50. Nearby are the handsome remains of a 13th-c **castle**, with good value food at the Olde Boot alongside.

WREKIN SJ6108 (just W of Telford – and towering boldly over it) The Wrekin is no Everest (an easily attained 407 metres, 1,334ft), but because it's so isolated on the edge of the Shropshire uplands it offers walkers a huge panorama, spanning places over 100 miles apart; just below, the Huntsman in Little Wenlock is handy for refreshment.

WROXETER ROMAN CITY SJ5607 One of the country's most important Roman sites, though the majority of the remains are buried under fields. There's a well preserved colonnade and municipal bath, with useful explanatory boards, and the

Days Out

Follies and other surprises: Hawkstone Park; bar lunch at the Hawkstone Park Hotel, or the Bear Hotel, Hodnet; Hodnet Hall gardens; Moreton Corbet Castle; walk up Grinshill Hill.

Planes and trains: Royal Air Force Museum, Cosford; lunch at the Bell, Tong; Bridgnorth–Severn Valley Railway there.

The quintessential Marches: Stokesay Castle; Ludlow; lunch at the Unicorn, Olive Branch or Merchant House there; Clun; Bishop's Castle.

museum has a good range of finds from the town (then Britain's fourth biggest) and the earlier fortress. Snacks, shop; some disabled access; cl Mon and Tues Nov–Mar, 25 Dec, 1 Jan; (01743) 761330; £2.95. The Horseshoes at Uckington is a decent family dining pub.

Wroxeter Roman Vineyard Friendly little place producing several wines; also lavender farm, rare breeds, and some interesting glacial stones – not to mention a Roman wall. Teas, shop (with various lavender-based products), disabled access; cl Oct–Mar, shop open all year; (01743) 761888; £3.

★ **Other attractive villages**, with decent pubs, include Aston on Clun SO3982, Leighton SJ6105, Little Stretton SO4392, Loppington SJ4729, Lydbury North SO3586, Munslow SO5287, Neen Sollars SO6672, Neenton SO6488, Tilley SJ5027, Tong SJ7907, Wentnor SO3893 and Worfield SO7696.

Local tourist information centres have details of **imaginative trails** around the region, centring on the work of Thomas Telford, haunted villages, the novels of Ellis Peters, and sites connected with King Arthur (recent theories suggest the mythical king was a 5th-c warlord ruling from a post-Roman city here – possibly Wroxeter). They also have **balloon trip** details.

Where to eat

BISHOP'S CASTLE SO3288 **Three Tuns** *(01588) 638797* Bustling lively atmosphere in simply furnished, beamed bar rooms, own-brewed beer from the handsome Victorian brewhouse, newspapers to read, a good mix of customers, and good home-made bar food. **£17**|£6.50.

BROCKTON SO5793 **Feathers** *(01746) 785202* Stylish stone pub with charming atmospheric beamed rooms (one no smoking), a restauranty atmosphere, and a conservatory; very good interesting food using fresh seasonal produce, and well kept real ales. **£21.85**|£9.50.

BURLTON SJ4526 **Burlton Inn** *(01939) 270284* Attractively restored pub with 3 cottagey connecting rooms, fresh flowers, magazines to read, winter open fires, very attractively presented interesting food from a seasonal menu, well kept real ales, and helpful staff. **£20.90**|£8.

CHURCH STRETTON SO4593 **Acorn Wholefood** *26 Sandford Ave (01694) 722495* Simple, unpretentious family-run restaurant with friendly service in several no smoking rooms; good filling food (mostly vegetarian), delicious puddings and soups, and cream teas with a choice of 25 teas; cl Tues, Weds (open Weds during school hols), 2 wks Feb, 2 wks Nov–Dec. **£10**|£2.95.

DORRINGTON SJ4702 **Country Friends** *(01743) 718707* Cosy half-timbered restaurant with good interesting food inc lovely puddings and British cheeses with home-made bread; bdrms; cl Sun, Mon, two wks mid-July. **£33**|£8.70.

LUDLOW SO5175 **Merchant House** *Lower Corve St (01584) 875438* Two simply furnished and decorated rooms in friendly and relaxed Jacobean house; exceptionally good food (wonderful fish and fine game) from a set 3-course (3 choices) menu, good-value interesting wines, and competent service; cl Sun, Mon, 2 wks spring, 1 wk Christmas; children must be well behaved. **£34**.

LUDLOW SO5174 **Olive Branch** *Old St (01584) 874314* Cheery wholefood restaurant in 17th-c former inn with a changing range of good lunchtime meals and snacks inc often inventive vegetarian meals, and teas with home-made cakes and scones; cl pm. **£11.05**|£5.10.

NESSCLIFFE SJ3818 **Old Three Pigeons** *(01743) 741279* Bustling dining pub in 2 acres with all sorts of birds as well as a Russian tank and other military hardware (which they often lend to museums or shows); 2 traditional bar areas with log fires and cushioned wall sofas, separate restaurant; very good meat and fish dishes, friendly service and well kept real ales; cl Mon in winter. **£22.50**|£8.

PULVERBATCH SJ4202 **White Horse** *(01743) 718247* Bustling, welcoming country pub with beams and heavy timbering in several rambling areas, plates, pewter mugs and a collection of antique insurance plaques; well kept beers, decent wines by the glass, 115 malt whiskies, and good, homely food served by friendly efficient staff; disabled access. **£15**|£4.95.

SHREWSBURY SJ4912 **Armoury** *Victoria Quay (01743) 340525* Recently converted warehouse with big arched windows overlooking river; lots of old prints and documents, cabinets with shells and explosives, corks and bottle openers; a good range of well kept real ales, 25 wines by the glass, 70 malt whiskies, and good interesting bistro-style food. **£22**|£8.95.

SHREWSBURY SJ4912 **Castle Vaults** *16 Castle Gates (01743) 358807* Mexican restaurant attached to an ancient timbered pub, with generous helpings of good-value food; bdrms; cl pm Sun, 25–26 Dec. **£20**|£3.25.

SHREWSBURY SJ4912 **Poppy's** *8 Milk St (01743) 232307* Lovely 17th-c building with really fine timbers in an upstairs room, plenty of space for shoppers on the ground floor and in the courtyard, and a little room for smokers; good enjoyable lunches and popular morning coffee and afternoon tea; cl Sun; disabled access. **£12.95**|£4.45.

WENTNOR SO3892 **Crown** *(01588) 650613* 16th-c inn in a quiet village with beams, standing timbers, a good log fire, a collection of china and glass, and a mix of tables set for eating in the main area, and a snug end with comfortable sofas; a good choice of enjoyable food, and a cosy, beamed no smoking restaurant; well kept real ales, decent wines, helpful friendly staff, and fine views of the Long Mynd from seats on the neat back lawn. **£29.50**|£8.

Special thanks to Dr and Mrs D E Awbery, M and J Back, P Gurnett, Miss Vicky Collier, Graham James.

We welcome reports from readers

This *Guide* depends on readers' reports. Do help us if you can – in return, we offer a discount on the next edition to people who've helped us with reports for it. Tell us what you think about places already in it, and anything extra you think we should say about them. And send us your ideas for inclusion in the next edition: places to visit, eat at or stay in, attractive drives or walks, maybe even unusual interesting shops you know of. Use the card in the middle, the report forms at the end, or just write – no stamp needed: *The Good Guide to Britain*, FREEPOST TN1569, Wadhurst, E Sussex TN5 7BR.

Shropshire Calendar

Some of these dates were provisional as we went to press. Please check information with the telephone numbers provided.

MARCH

27 **Hawkstone Park** Mountain Bike Race (competitors must book in advance) – *till Sun 28* (01939) 200300
28 **Cosford** Shropshire Scale Modellers Exhibition at Aerospace Museum (01902) 374112

APRIL

2 **Hawkstone Park** Easter Egg Hunt – *till Mon 5* (01939) 200300; **Ironbridge** Easter Fair and Van Rally: Living History at Ironbridge Gorge Museum, Blists Hill – *till Mon 5* (01952) 433522
9 **Shrewsbury** Children's Book Festival – *till Sun 11* (01743) 350761
10 **Hawkstone Park** Narnia Weekend – *till Sun 11* (01939) 200300
17 **Bridgnorth** Model Engineering Weekend at Severn Valley Railway – *till Sun 18* (01299) 403816
24 **Bridgnorth** Spring Steam Gala at Severn Valley Railway – *till Sun 25* (01299) 403816

MAY

2 **Newport** Shropshire Game Fair at Chetwynd Park – *till Mon 3* (01588) 672708
3 **Acton Scott** Vintage Club Rally at Acton Scott Working Farm (01694) 781306
7 **Church Stretton** Mary Webb Weekend: local folklore, talks and walks at the Thresholds Centre – *till Sun 9* (01694) 751411
8 **Shrewsbury** Regatta – *till Sun 9* (01743) 350761
9 **Hawkstone Park** Circus Workshop (01939) 200300
14 **Hawkstone Park** Shakespeare in the Park (01939) 200300
15 **Bridgnorth** Friends of Thomas the Tank Engine at Severn Valley Railway – *till Sun 16* (01299) 403816
21 **Shrewsbury** Shropshire and West Midlands Show at Shropshire and West Midlands Showground – *till Sat 22* (01743) 362824
23 **Hawkstone Park** Morris Dancers (01939) 200300
24 **Bridgnorth** Friends of Thomas the Tank Engine at Severn Valley Railway – *till Tues 25* (01299) 403816
28 **Bridgnorth** Haydn Festival – *till 6 Jun* (01952) 825235
29 **Ludlow** Craft Fair at the Castle: dancing, children's tent, hands-on area – *till Mon 31* (01588) 650307
30 **Hawkstone Park** Arthurian Battle – *till Mon 31* (01939) 200300
31 **Shrewsbury** Fun Day in the Quarry: stalls, funfair and arena entertainments (01743) 350761

JUNE

5 **Acton Scott** Sheep Shearing at Acton Scott Working Farm – *till Sat 6* (01694) 781306
6 **Hawkstone Park** Local Artists Day (01939) 200300

Shropshire Calendar (cont.)

12 **Bridgnorth** Heavy Horse Weekend at Severn Valley Railway – *till Sun 13* (01299) 403816

13 **Cosford** Royal Air Force Open Day at Aerospace Museum (01902) 374112; **Hawkstone Park** Trails of the Unexpected (01939) 200300

19 **Bishops Castle** Midsummer Rejoicing: rushbearing festival with morris dancing and procession – *till Sun 20* (01588) 638467; **Ludlow** Festival – *till 5 July* (01584) 875070 and Fringe Festival (01584) 873611; **Shrewsbury** Carnival and Show (01743) 350761

26 **Hawkstone Park** Antiques and Memorabilia Weekend – *till Sun 27* (01939) 200300; **Shrewsbury** International Music Festival – *till 2 July* (01743) 244255; Abbey Fair (01743) 232723

27 **Ellesmere** National Triathlon (01743) 255071

JULY

3 **Bridgnorth** 1940s Weekend at Severn Valley Railway – *till Sun 4* (01299) 403816

4 **Bishop's Castle** Carnival (01588) 638462; **Hawkstone Park** American Independence Day Celebrations (01939) 200300;

9 **Bishop's Castle** Real Ale Festival – *till Sat 10* (01588) 638462; **Much Wenlock** Olympiad – *till* Athletics on *Sun 11* (01952) 727615

10 **Hawkstone Park** Jazz and Fireworks (01939) 200300

11 **Shrewsbury** World Music Day: open-air bands at the Castle (01743) 231142

16 **Much Wenlock** International Storytelling Festival – *till Sun 18* (01952) 883936

17 **Hawkstone Park** Shakespeare in the Park – *till Sun 18* (01939) 200300; **Ratlinghope** Music at Leasowes Bank – *till Sat 31* (01743) 790769

24 **Acton Scott** Herb Weekend at Acton Scott Working Farm – *till Sun 25* (01694) 781306; **Bishop's Castle** Agricultural Show (01588) 638462; **Church Stretton and South Shropshire** Arts Festival – *till 7 Aug* (01694) 723402; **Wem** National Sweet Pea Society and Wem Sweet Pea Festival: celebration of 300 years of the Sweet Pea – *till Sun 25* (01948) 840779

31 **Bridgnorth** Le Rive Gauche Festival – *till 1 Aug* (01746) 763257

AUGUST

1 **Acton Scott** Falconry at Acton Scott Working Farm (01694) 781306

5 **Burwarton** Show (01746) 787535

7 **Oswestry** Show (01691) 654875

13 **Shrewsbury** Flower Show at Quarry Park: one of England's largest flower shows – *till Sat 14* (01743) 364051

21 **Ironbridge** Victorian Love Story at Ironbridge Gorge Museum, Blists Hill – *till Mon 23* (01952) 433522; **Minsterley** Show (01743) 790767

27 **Bridgnorth** Folk Festival – *till Sun 29* (01746) 768813

29 **Bicton** County Steam Engine Rally at Onslow Park – *till Mon 30* (01694) 723799; **Hawkstone Park** Victorian Fun – *till Mon 30* (01939) 200300

30 **Ironbridge** Coracle (traditional boats) Regatta (01952) 432769; **Ledbury** Carnival (01531) 636147

Shropshire Calendar (cont.)

SEPTEMBER

10 Ellesmere Festival – *till Sun 12* (01691) 622097; **Shrewsbury** Real Ale Festival at the Music Hall – *till Sat 11* (01743) 244255

11 Ludlow and Marches Food and Drink Festival – *till Sun 12* (01588) 650307

18 Bishops Castle Michaelmas Fair: vintage vehicles, morris dancing – *till Sun 19* (01588) 638462

19 Acton Scott Traditional Harvest Festival at Acton Scott Working Farm (01694) 781306

25 Bridgnorth Autumn Steam Gala at Severn Valley Railway – *till Sun 26* (01299) 403816

26 Acton Scott Crafts in Action at Acton Scott Working Farm (01694) 781306

OCTOBER

10 Bridgnorth Classic Vehicle Day at Severn Valley Railway (01299) 403816

15 Bridgnorth Diesel Gala at Severn Valley Railway – *till Sun 17* (01299) 403816

16 Acton Scott Steam Threshing in Action at Acton Scott Working Farm – *till Sun 17* (01694) 781306

23 Acton Scott Cider and Perry Making Weekend at Acton Scott Working Farm – *till Sun 24* (01694) 781306

27 Hawkstone Park Halloween Ghost Hunt – *till Sun 31* (01939) 200300

30 Acton Scott Steam Threshing in Action at Acton Scott Working Farm – *till Sun 31* (01694) 781306; **Ironbridge** Ghostly Gaslight at Ironbridge Gorge Museum, Blists Hill (01952) 433522

NOVEMBER

6 Ironbridge Traditional Bonfire Night at Ironbridge Gorge Museum, Blists Hill (01952) 433522

28 Bridgnorth Santa Special Trains at Severn Valley Railway (01299) 403816

DECEMBER

4 Bridgnorth Santa Special Trains at Severn Valley Railway – *till Sun 5, also on Sat 11, Sun 12, Sat 18 and Fri 24* (01299) 403816

Please let us know what you think of places in the *Guide*. Use the report forms at the back of the book or simply write us a letter.

SOMERSET

Good value for a short or longer holiday, with all sorts of places to visit, and lots of interest from unspoilt countryside through charming and distinctive villages and small towns to fascinating cities.

Somerset has an enviable combination of subtly interesting scenery with a great many enjoyable places to visit, for all ages. Favourites include the indoor jungle at Washford, Dunster and its castle, Wells (a charming largely unspoilt small cathedral city), magnificent Montacute House, the friendly animal centre at East Huntspill, the Fleet Air Arm museum at Yeovilton, Glastonbury with its Arthurian legends, Hatch Court at Hatch Beauchamp, and enjoyable cider mills at Dowlish Wake and Bradford-on-Tone. There are lovely gardens, at attractive Castle Cary (Hadspen), Barrington Court, East Lambrook and Cheddon Fitzpaine (Hestercombe), and the unusual rose time-trail in Wells. On the coast, Minehead is a pleasant traditional resort, with a long steam railway line below the Quantocks (there's another smaller but very friendly steam line inland at Bitton), and Weston-super-Mare and Clevedon have their attractions.

Bath is a very rewarding city for a short break – sophisticated, mellow, graceful and elegant, with plenty to see. Bristol too has all sorts of things to pack a day visit with interest, including the first-class hands-on science discovery centre and a splendid zoo, both excellent for families; with the usual range of big-city problems, however, it's less appealing as a place to stay in.

Excluding Exmoor (discussed separately, in the **Devon** chapter), the brooding Mendips have the county's most interesting walks, along their edges and particularly in the great limestone gorges. Cheddar Gorge and the Wookey Hole caves bring summer crowds and are best visited at quieter times – though even in summer there are much less populated parts of the Mendips (such as Ebbor Gorge, and the plateau of poor windswept sheep pasture on top, pocked with unseen caverns used by potholers, and more visible Bronze Age funeral barrows). Over in the west the countryside feels more secluded and self-contained, with each small valley of the Quantocks seeming a private world, and the Blackdown Hills charmingly untouristy, too – classic quiet English countryside with some lovely villages.

The dead-flat vivid green marshy pastures of the Somerset Levels provide an interesting contrast, rewarding for wildlife and for traditional crafts such as basket-making. Towards the east, richer, more rolling farmland with small valleys and wooded hillsides offers some gentle country drives.

Throughout, there are delightful villages, and the countryside is dotted with a profusion of landmark church towers, pinnacled, turreted and gargoyled. Many churches, particularly in the west, have very finely carved 15th- and 16th-century bench ends, with fascinating figures, beasts and fertility symbols; also fine oak waggon roofs, brass candelabras and carved screens. In the hillier parts, buildings are generally of stone, varying in colour and character from the Cotswold style of the north-east, through the pale limestones of the Mendips and the golden warmth of south Somerset's Hamstone, to the rugged and stolid greys of the hamlets tucked into the green folds of the Quantocks.

Somerset tourist information centres have a great deal of helpful material.

Where to stay

BARWICK ST5613 **Little Barwick House** *Barwick, Yeovil BA22 9TD (01935) 423902* **£89,** plus special breaks; 6 rms. Carefully run listed Georgian dower house in 3½ acres, with a lovely relaxed atmosphere, log fire in cosy lounge, excellent food using local produce, a thoughtful wine list, super breakfasts, nice afternoon tea with crumpets, and particularly good service; 2m S of Yeovil; cl Christmas/New Year; dogs by arrangement.

BATH ST7464 **Badminton Villa** *10 Upper Oldfield Park, Bath BA2 3JZ (01225) 426347* ***£58,** plus special breaks; 4 rms. Big no smoking Victorian house with marvellous city views, comfortable lounge, good breakfasts, and helpful friendly owners; cl 1 wk Christmas; children over 5.

BATH ST7465 **Brocks** *32 Brock St, Bath BA1 2LN (01225) 338374* ***£60,** plus special breaks; 6 rms. Georgian house with fine breakfasts in big dining room, lounge area, helpful staff, and good central position; cl 2 wks Jan.

BATH ST7463 **Haydon House** *9 Bloomfield Park, Bath BA2 2BY (01225) 427351* **£70,** plus special breaks; 5 good rms with sherry and home-made shortbread. Deceptively unassuming-looking Edwardian house with comfortable, elegant and restful rooms, antiques, excellent breakfasts (no evening meals), warmly welcoming owners, and pretty garden; no smoking; children by arrangement.

BATH ST7565 **Old Boathouse** *Bath Boating Station, Forester Rd, Bath BA2 6QE (01225) 466407* ***£50;** 5 rms. Edwardian boating station with black and white timbered verandah overlooking river, free launch to Bath centre, punts and rowing boats for hire, sitting room with river views, and separate restaurant; cl Christmas; partial disabled access.

BATH ST7464 **Paradise House** *86-88 Holloway, Bath BA2 4PX (01225) 317723* ***£65,** plus special breaks; 8 rms (room 6 has a super view). Classically elegant early 18th-c hotel, lovingly restored, with marvellous views over the city, pretty breakfast room, restful drawing room, log fire, spacious walled gardens; peaceful, though only 7 minutes' walk to the centre; cl 5 days over Christmas; disabled access.

BATH ST7465 **Queensberry** *Russel St, Bath BA1 2QF (01225) 447928* **£135,** plus special breaks; 29 lovely rms. 3 beautifully decorated Georgian town houses in quiet residential street, with comfortable, restful drawing room, open fire, attractive modern restaurant (the Olive Tree; see **Where to eat** *section, below*) and professional service; cl 1 wk Christmas.

BATH ST7465 **Royal Crescent** *16 Royal Crescent, Bath BA1 2LS (01225) 739955* **£199** rm only, plus special breaks; 45 luxurious rms. Elegant Georgian hotel in glorious curved terrace, with comfortable antiques-filled lounges, very attractive garden room (with own menu), open fires and lovely flowers; excellently presented, very well prepared fine food in the Dower House Restaurant, impeccable service; outdoor pool and croquet; children over 7 in evening restaurant; disabled access.

BATH ST7565 **Villa Magdala** *Henrietta Rd, Bath BA2 6LX (01225) 466329* **£80,** plus winter breaks; 17 comfortable rms. Overlooking Henrietta Park, this elegant Victorian house is close to the centre and has good breakfasts in the attractive dining room, a spacious comfortable lounge, and friendly helpful staff.

BATHFORD ST7866 **Eagle House** *Church St, Bathford, Bath BA1 7RS (01225) 859946* **£44,** plus special breaks; 8 comfortable big rms, 2 in cottage. Lovely Georgian house with an informal friendly atmosphere, particularly helpful owners, open fires, spacious drawing room and smaller sitting room, good breakfasts, and big garden with fine views; grass tennis court in summer; very good for families; 3m from Bath; cl 20 Dec–2 Jan.

BEERCROCOMBE ST3120 **Frog Street Farm** *Frog St, Beercrocombe, Taunton TA3 6AF (01823) 480430* **£50,** plus special breaks; 3 rms. Peaceful 15th-c listed farmhouse deep in the countryside on big working farm, with beams, fine Jacobean panelling, inglenook fireplaces, warmly friendly owner, delicious food (much produce from the farm, local game and fish; bring your own wine) and good breakfasts; cl Nov–Feb; no children.

CANNINGTON ST2538 **Blackmore Farm** *Cannington, Bridgwater TA5 2NE (01278) 653442* ***£40;** 4 rms. Grade I listed manor house dating from 15th c with garderobes, beams and stone archways, good breakfasts around a huge table in the Great Hall, and log fire in comfortable sitting room; no evening meals; disabled access.

DUNSTER SS9943 **Luttrell Arms** *High St, Dunster, Minehead TA24 6SG (01643) 821555* **£95,** plus special breaks; 27 rms. Comfortably modernised Forte hotel in ancient building of great character with individual atmosphere, friendly service, good popular food and interesting evening meals; Civil War cannon emplacements in the garden; close to Exmoor National Park; limited disabled access.

HATCH BEAUCHAMP ST3020 **Farthings** *Hatch Beauchamp, Taunton TA3 6SG (01823) 480664* **£80,** plus special breaks; 9 rms with thoughtful extras. Charming little Georgian house in 3 acres of gardens, with open fires in quiet lounges, and good food using fresh local produce; they can arrange golf and other activities.

HINTON CHARTERHOUSE ST7759 **Homewood Park** *Hinton Charterhouse, Bath BA3 6BB (01225) 723731* **£135;** 19 lovely rms. Charming Victorian hotel on the edge of Hinton Priory ruins, with flowers, oil paintings and fine furniture in graceful relaxing day rooms, elegant restaurant with very good imaginative food (honey from their own bees – you can help them collect it), and 10 acres of gardens and woodlands; tennis, croquet; disabled access.

HOLFORD ST1541 **Combe House** *Holford, Bridgwater TA5 1RZ (01278) 741382* ***£72,** plus special breaks; 16 rms. Warmly friendly former tannery (still has waterwheel) in pretty spot, with comfortable rooms, log fires, good home-made food, and relaxed atmosphere; heated indoor swimming pool, sauna, croquet, and tennis court.

HOLFORD ST1541 **Quantock House** *Holford, Bridgwater TA5 1RY (01278) 741439* ***£40;** 3 rms. Thatched 17th-c house with large cottagey garden, big inglenook in residents' lounge, delicious English cooking (evening meals by arrangement) and a friendly welcome; cl 25 Dec; well behaved pets allowed.

HUNSTRETE ST6461 **Hunstrete House** *Hunstrete, Pensford, Bristol BS18 4NS (01761) 490490* **£170,** plus special breaks; 23 individually decorated rms. Classically handsome mainly 18th-c country-house hotel on the edge of the Mendips in 92 acres inc walled garden and deer park; comfortable and elegantly furnished day rooms with antiques, paintings, log fires, fresh flowers from the garden, a tranquil atmosphere, excellent service, and very good enjoyable food using produce from the garden when possible; lovely gardens, croquet lawn, heated swimming pool, all-weather tennis court, and nearby riding; disabled access.

KILVE ST1543 **Meadow House** *Sea Lane, Kilve, Bridgwater TA5 1EG (01278) 741546* ***£80,** plus special breaks; 10 rms, 5 in cottage in courtyard. Beautifully kept Georgian house with relaxed atmosphere, fresh flowers, antiques and comfortable seats; traditional English food using their own fruit and veg, and a fine wine list; landscaped gardens, croquet, streamside walks, and sea fishing (5 minutes away); a smugglers' passage is said to run from the hotel to the church.

LANGLEY MARSH ST0728 **Langley House** *Langley Marsh, Wiveliscombe, Taunton TA4 2UF (01984) 623318* **£112.50,** plus special breaks; 8 individually decorated pretty rms. Spotless Georgian house with 16th-c heart, charming lounge and dining room, antiques, fresh flowers, log fires, friendly service, very good carefully cooked food using home-grown herbs and veg, and 4 acres of lovely landscaped gardens; croquet; dogs by arrangement.

LANGPORT ST4226 **The White House** *The Hill, Langport TA10 9QZ (01458) 250892* **£40;** 2 rooms (one with lovely view), shared bthrm. Attractive house with charming owners, a drawing room with open fire in the hamstone fireplace, fine rugs on the polished wooden floor, and lots of pictures and antiques; a snug study with TV, good full breakfasts with home-made marmalade taken in dining room with French windows leading to conservatory, and marvellous views over the Somerset Levels.

LOWER VELLOW ST0938 **Curdon Mill** *Lower Vellow, Williton, Taunton TA4 4LS (01984) 656522* **£60,** plus special breaks; 6 smallish but pretty and individually furnished rms. Charming, beautifully furnished no smoking hotel between the Quantocks and the Brendon Hills with 200 acres of working farm to wander over, a lovely garden, very good evening meal in antique-filled dining room, substantial breakfasts, and friendly staff (and other guests); the waterwheel and mill shaft have been carefully preserved and still work; outdoor heated swimming pool; civil marriage licence; children over 8.

LUXBOROUGH SS9737 **Royal Oak** *Kingsbridge, Luxborough, Watchet TA23 0SH (01984) 640319* **£50;** 10 simple rms, most with own bthrm. Unspoilt and interesting old pub in idyllic spot, chatty and friendly beamed bar with log fire, good choice of well kept real ales, good food in bar and restaurant (plenty of game), and well liked breakfasts.

MIDDLECOMBE SS9545 **Periton Park** *Middlecombe, Minehead TA24 8SW (01643) 706885* **£84,** plus special breaks; 8 rms (3 no smoking) with views of surrounding countryside. Fine Exmoor-edge Victorian country house with comfortable lounge, books, log fire, a relaxed atmosphere, friendly service, and good food in panelled no smoking dining room; pleasant walks nearby, and they can arrange shooting, fishing or riding at the adjacent riding centre; cl Jan; children over 12; dogs in 1 rm only; disabled access.

NORTH PERROTT ST4709 **Manor Arms** *North Perrott, Crewkerne TA18 7SG (01460) 72901* ***£48,** plus special breaks; 8 rms in restored coach house inc a fine panelled and beamed one. Comfortable and attractive 16th-c inn with friendly helpful licensees, beams, exposed stone and inglenook fireplace, good home-made food in small restaurant and bar, and garden with play area; free coarse fishing, free entry to some south Somerset gardens; disabled access.

POLSHAM ST5142 **Southway Farm** *Polsham, Wells BA5 1RW (01749) 673396* ***£37;** 3 rms. Friendly Georgian farmhouse between Wells and Glastonbury with open fire in comfortable lounge, attractive dining room, good breakfasts and pretty garden; cl Dec and Jan.

ROADWATER ST0337 **Wood Advent Farm** *Roadwater, Watchet TA23 0RR (01984) 640920* ***£45;** 4 rms. Relaxed, spacious farmhouse on 340-acre working farm within Exmoor National Park; log fire in comfortable lounge, good country cooking using their own produce in attractive dining room (with woodburner); grass tennis court, outdoor heated swimming pool, and fishing, clay pigeon and pheasant shooting; children over 10.

SEAVINGTON ST MARY ST4014 **Pheasant** *Seavington St Mary, Ilminster TA19 0QH (01460) 240502* **£90,** plus special breaks; 8 comfortable pretty rms. Carefully converted and spotlessly kept thatched 17th-c former farmhouse with open fire in low-beamed bar, enjoyable food in attractive candlelit restaurant, and a quiet landscaped garden.

SOMERTON ST4828 **Lynch Country House** *4 Behind Berry, Somerton TA11 7PD (01458) 272316* **£49;** 5 prettily decorated rms. Carefully restored homely Georgian house with books in comfortable lounge, and good breakfasts (no evening meals) in airy room overlooking tranquil grounds and lake with black swans and exotic ducks; also self-catering cottages; cl Christmas.

STANTON WICK ST6161 **Carpenters Arms** *Stanton Wick, Pensford, Bristol BS18 4BX (01761) 490202* **£69.50;** 12 rms. Warm and attractively furnished tile-roofed inn converted from a row of miners' cottages, with big log fire, woodburner, wide choice of good food inc generous breakfasts, well kept beers, and friendly efficient staff.

STOGUMBER ST1037 **Hall Farm** *Stogumber, Taunton TA4 3TQ (01984) 656321* **£37;** 6 rms. Old-fashioned B & B with optional evening meals (bring your own wine) – wonderfully unpretentious, with warmly friendly staff; cl Christmas; well behaved dogs welcome; disabled access.

STOKE ST GREGORY ST3527 **Rose & Crown** *Woodhill, Stoke St Gregory, Taunton TA3 6EW (01823) 490296* **£38;** 3 rms with shared bthrm, plus 2 rms in annexe. Very friendly 17th-c cottagey inn with a cosy and pleasantly romanticised stable theme, generous helpings of particularly good-value food in no smoking dining room, excellent breakfasts, decent wine list, efficient service from hard-working family in charge, and popular skittle alley.

STON EASTON ST6254 **Ston Easton Park** *Ston Easton, Bath BA3 4DF (01761) 241631* **£345,** plus special breaks; 21 really lovely rms. Majestic Palladian mansion of Bath stone with beautifully landscaped 18th-c gardens and 26 acres of parkland; elegant day rooms with antiques and flowers, attractive no smoking restaurant with good food (much grown in the kitchen garden), fine afternoon teas, library and billiard room, and extremely helpful, friendly and unstuffy service; babies and children over 7 welcome by prior arrangement; no dogs in rooms (though have kennels).

TAUNTON ST2224 **Castle** *Castle Green, Taunton TA1 1NF (01823) 272671* **£127,** plus special breaks; 44 lovely rms. Appealingly modernised partly Norman castle (its west front almost smothered in wisteria), with fine old oak furniture, tapestries and paintings in comfortably elegant lounges, really excellent modern English cooking, good breakfasts, a range of good-value wines from a thoughtful list, efficient friendly service, and pretty garden; dogs by arrangement; disabled access.

WELLS ST5445 **Infield House** *36 Portway, Wells BA5 2BN (01749) 670989* **£49,** plus special breaks; 3 comfortable rms (best view from back rm). Carefully restored no smoking Victorian town house with period furnishings, unusual paperweight collection, elegant lounge (with lots of local guides), good breakfasts in dining room with Adam-style fireplace (no evening meals), and friendly personal service; cl 1 wk Jan; children over 12; no pets (they have a cheery labrador).

WOOKEY HOLE ST5347 **Glencot House** *Glencot Lane, Wookey Hole, Wells BA5 1BH (01749) 677160* **£85;** 13 rms, many with four-posters or half-testers. In 18 acres of gardens and parkland (and with its own cricket pitch), this Jacobean-style Victorian mansion has some fine wood panelling, carved ceilings, antiques and flowers in the public rooms and hallways, a relaxed friendly atmosphere, and good food in the restaurant; fishing, table tennis, and snooker; lots to do nearby; cl Christmas.

We welcome reports from readers

This *Guide* depends on readers' reports. Do help us if you can – in return, we offer a discount on the next edition to people who've helped us with reports for it. Tell us what you think about places already in it, and anything extra you think we should say about them. And send us your ideas for inclusion in the next edition: places to visit, eat at or stay in, attractive drives or walks, maybe even unusual interesting shops you know of. Use the card in the middle, the report forms at the end, or just write – no stamp needed: *The Good Guide to Britain*, FREEPOST TN1569, Wadhurst, E Sussex TN5 7BR.

To see and do

★ **BATH** ST7564 For many this is England's most rewarding old town, though its throngs of summer visitors tend to mask its charms a bit then. Parts not to be missed include the great showpieces of 18th-c town planning, Queen Sq, The Circus and the Royal Crescent; the quieter Abbey Green and cobbled Abbey St and Queen St; and the great Pulteney Bridge (there's a fine view of it from the bridge at the end of North Parade, or the riverside Parade Gardens, where brass bands play in summer). Many places enjoyably recall the days of Beau Nash and the building of Bath as a fashionable resort; other draws go back to the Roman baths, and come right up to date with the city's interesting and unusual shops (not to mention the ambitious new spa building being designed by the architect of Waterloo's Eurostar terminal, for the Millennium). The narrow little lanes between the main streets can be fascinating. Our favourite places to visit are the Roman baths, Pump Room, Museum of Costume at the Assembly Rooms, Building of Bath Museum, Industrial Heritage Centre, No 1 Royal Crescent, and Bath Abbey. The American Museum on the edge of the city at Claverton is very special.

In summer lots of informal eating places have tables outside. Good pubs with decent food include the Old Green Tree (Green St), Crystal Palace (Abbey Green) and Saracen's Head (Broad St). Good street markets are in Bartlett St (daily), junk to top-drawer antiques, often buzzing with dealers from elsewhere; Guinea Lane (very early am Weds), antiques changing hands quickly; and Walcot St flea market (Sat, occasionally Sun), good bargains. On the first Sat of the month there is a farmers' market with lots of fresh fruit and veg by Green Park Station. The beautifully restored historic Theatre Royal presents more pre-West End productions than anywhere else in the country.

Don't try to drive around the city: Bath's streets were laid out for travel by sedan chair, not car, and a tortuous one-way system seems designed to deter drivers rather than to make traffic flow more easily. Inadvertently park your car in the wrong place and it may be quickly towed away, despite a lack of proper warnings. Walking around Bath is anyway a delight; there are flat parts, though to make the most of it you have to be prepared to slog up some of the steeper streets. Readers particularly enjoy the somewhat irreverent Bizarre Bath walking tours that leave the Huntsman Inn on North Parade Passage at 8pm daily, Apr–Sept (£3.50) – more street theatre than a typical tour.

The rush of a day trip doesn't do justice to the host of things worth seeing; it is best to stay, preferably out of season. On summer days crowds of trippers and school parties tend to spoil the best-known parts, and if you want to visit during Bath's early summer Festival, book accommodation well ahead. If you're staying, the Bath for Less card is a good investment (£4 for 2 people for 4 days), with discounts on some attractions (inc the baths) and restaurants; it's on sale at tourist information centres.

Roman Baths Founded by AD 75, and undoubtedly one of Britain's most remarkable Roman sites. They were built for pilgrims visiting a temple to Minerva constructed around a sacred hot spring. After this the spring played a dual role – as both a focus for worship, and a reservoir supplying the baths with spa water. The baths were all but forgotten until the 18th c, when workmen chanced upon a bust of Minerva, and it was not until 1878 that most of what you see today was uncovered. The main baths are pretty much intact, though some of the columns are 18th- and 19th-c reconstructions; in August they're open at night and quite beautifully floodlit. A **museum** shows finds made during excavations, inc the bust of Minerva and a remarkable gorgon's head pediment (thought by some authorities to depict not a gorgon at all but King Bladud, father of Lear and aeronaut extraordinaire), and a model of the site as it would have appeared in the 4th c.

Meals, snacks, shop, some disabled access (though not to baths themselves); cl 25–26 Dec; (01225) 477785; £6.30, inc audio-guide.

Pump Room This stylish 18th-c mecca for the fashionable was built directly above the Roman temple courtyard; you can catch a glimpse of the baths next door. It now houses a restaurant serving morning coffee, lunches and teas to the gay strains of the Pump Room trio. You can sample the hot spa water, which always comes out at 46.5°C (116°F).

Bath Abbey Particularly renowned for its fan vaulting, the current building is the third great church to be built on this site, begun in 1499. The Elizabethans called it the Lantern of the West because of its profusion of stained glass. Most impressive is the great east window, depicting 56 scenes from the life of Christ. On one side of this is a finely carved memorial to Bartholomew Barnes (1608), and on the other the beautiful medieval carving of the Prior Birde chantry. Restoration work has been returning the interior's gradually blackened Bath stone to its more appealing honey colour. Shop, disabled access; cl 24–26 Dec, 1 Jan, Good Fri; £2 suggested donation. A very good exhibition on the abbey's history is in the adjacent carefully restored 18th-c vaults. Disabled access; cl Sun; (01225) 422462; £2. In summer there may be walking tours from the abbey churchyard (usually around 10.30am and 2pm).

No 1 Royal Crescent The most splendid example of the architecture that sprang up in the town's Georgian heyday. In 1768 it was the first house built in Bath's most regal terrace, and has 2 floors restored and beautifully furnished in period style. Shop; cl Mon (exc bank hols), and Dec–mid-Feb; (01225) 428126; *£4. The current glut of tour buses is now damaging the Crescent (and disturbing the residents) and there are plans to close one end to traffic – it's certainly best seen on foot.

Georgian Garden (Gravel Walk) Nr Queen Sq, another striking reminder of the period, this re-creates the original layout and the kind of plants that would have been used in a small town garden in the 1760s. Given the high ratio of walking-space to plants, the emphasis back then was clearly on strolling and chatting rather than horticulture itself; cl wknds and bank hols, and all Nov–Apr; free.

Building of Bath Museum (The Vineyard, The Paragon) Fascinating displays on how John Wood and others transformed the town and its architecture, with full-scale reconstructions, original tools, and a fabulous model of the entire city, lighting up when you press the buttons. Shop, disabled access but no facilities – and those who have difficulty walking might notice the floor's slight unevenness; cl Mon (exc bank hols), and Dec–mid-Feb; (01225) 333895; *£3.

Herschel House & Museum (New King St) Interesting Georgian home and workplace of William Herschel, the astronomer (and composer), with period rooms, models of his telescopes, and other scientific equipment. He discovered the planet Uranus from the back garden. Book shop; cl am, and wkdys Nov–Mar; (01225) 311342; £2.50.

Holburne Museum (Gt Pulteney St) Fine old building displaying the decorative and fine-art collection of Sir Thomas William Holburne (1793–1874), as well as lots of 20th-c art and crafts. Meals, snacks, shop, disabled access; cl am Sun, winter Mons, and all mid-Dec–mid-Feb; (01225) 466669; *£3.50.

Industrial Heritage Centre (Julian Rd) The highlight is the engaging **Mr Bowler's Business**, an elaborate re-creation of a factory first established in 1872, providing various services from plumbing and engineering to gas-fitting and bell-hanging. Everything is just as it was then, inc the antique soda fountain that turned out such intriguingly named drinks as Hot Tom and that distant harbinger of today's alcopops, Cherry Ciderette. Snacks, shop, some disabled access by arrangement; cl wkdys Nov–Easter; (01225) 318348; £3.50.

Museum of Costume & Assembly Rooms (Bennett St) Dazzling – over 200 figures dressed in original costumes from the late 16th c to the present, one of the most impressive displays of fashion and fashion accessories in the world. It's housed in the Assembly Rooms built in 1771 by John Wood the Younger, where the audio-guide has a particularly entertaining commentary – listen out for the bun fight. Summer coffee, shop, disabled access; cl 25–26 Dec, and Assembly Rooms may be cl other dates for functions; (01225) 477752; £3.80. Along the same street is a small **museum of East Asian art**.

Postal Museum (Broad St) First-class exploration of the development of the postal system since the 16th c, inc a full-scale replica Victorian post office; it was from here that the world's first stamp was sent in 1840. Snacks, shop, disabled access to ground floor only; cl am Sun; (01225) 460333; £2.50.

Book Museum (Manvers St) First and early editions of authors who lived or worked in Bath, especially Jane Austen and Charles Dickens; there's a reconstruction of Dickens's study at Gad's Hill on the other side of England. A good chunk of the exhibition is devoted to the history and art of bookbinding, and adjoining this is the shop of **George Bayntun**, who has been binding and selling antiquarian books for 50 years; cl 1–2pm pm, pm Sat, all day Sun and bank hols; (01225) 466000; *£2.

Royal Photographic Society (The Octagon, Milsom St) 5 galleries with major international exhibitions and displays on photographic history, inc the first picture ever taken. Meals, snacks, shop, disabled access (not to restaurant); cl 25–26 Dec; (01225) 462841; *£2.50 (free to members).

Sally Lunn's Kitchen (North Parade Passage) Reputedly the oldest house in Bath, a charming, partly timbered medieval structure, still preserving in its cellars the 17th-c kitchen of Sally Lunn, who created her famous brioche bread buns here. Meals and snacks (inc of course the buns, made to a secret recipe), shop; cl 25–26 Dec; (01225) 461634; *30p.

Victoria Art Gallery (Bridge St) European Old Masters and 18th- to 20th-c British paintings and drawings, as well as decorative arts inc porcelain, glass and watches. Disabled access to ground floor only; cl am Sun, all day Mon, 25–26 Dec and most bank hols; (01225) 477233; free.

Beckford's Tower (Lansdown Rd) Italianate tower with fine views from the top, and a little museum commemorating the well travelled collector William Beckford. It's closed for restoration until summer 1999, phone for opening details; (01225) 460705. NW are good strolling grounds on Lansdown Hill, with the Cotswold Way making the most of the escarpment views as it skirts Bath racecourse, and passes the Grenville Monument to a 1643 Civil War battle.

Boat cruises These leave Pulteney Bridge landing stage at a quarter to and a quarter past the hour (not Oct–Easter). Boats and punts can be hired in summer from the Boating Station on the River Avon, Forester Rd, Bathwick: (01225) 466407. The revivified **Kennet & Avon Canal** is one of Bath's pleasures, with quiet towpath walks along to Bathampton (where the George is popular for lunch); it has quite a few colourful narrowboats in summer. You can cycle right into the centre along the Avon Cycleway, cycle tracks converted from the old Bath & Bristol railway.

! **Balloon trips** Hot-air balloons give a good view of the city as it's shown in the great architectural drawings. They take off, subject to weather, from the Royal Victoria Park; (01225) 466888; from £115.

Prior Park Landscape Garden ST7662 (Ralph Allen Drive, off the A3062 S) In a sweeping valley, these striking 18th-c landscaped gardens are being comprehensively restored by the National Trust after a period of neglect. Capability Brown and Alexander Pope helped local entrepreneur Ralph Allen with the original design, and there are plenty of unique ornamental features (inc 18th-c graffiti on the Palladian bridge). Woodland walks offer unusual views over Bath. Note you can't drive all the way here: there's no nearby car parking (planning permission to keep the property open depends on an anti-car transport scheme). You can walk from town, but the hill is very steep, so best to take the number 2 or 4 bus; cl am, all day Tues, 25–26 Dec, and

1 Jan; (01225) 833977; £3.80 (£1 off if you show a bus or train ticket); NT. There's decent food at the Cross Keys over on Midford Rd.

American Museum in Britain ST7864 (Claverton Manor, just SE) Quite a contrast to the rest of Bath's attractions, a fascinating illustration of American history and life, in lovely gracious surroundings. 18 rooms are fully furnished and decorated to re-create the style of American homes from the 17th to the 19th c, while the grounds include a replica of part of George Washington's garden at Mount Vernon, and an American arboretum. Collections of folk art and patchwork quilts, with sections on Native Americans and Shakers, and good special events. Well liked by readers, it's the only museum in the country completely devoted to our colonial cousins. Snacks, shop, some disabled access; cl am, all day Mon (exc Aug and bank hols), and Nov–Mar; (01225) 460503; £5.

BRISTOL ST5873 Too busy an industrial city to use as a base for an enjoyable stay, this has masses of things to fill a lively day visit. It's easily reached from Bath – or from one of the cosseting nearby country-house hotels we list in the **Where to Stay** section, above; day visits are helped by good rail connections, and the motorway that plunges right into the city's heart. The city's prosperity still stems from its port, though aerospace now predominates among many other manufacturing interests. There are some striking buildings around the centre, notably the Corn Exchange and the Old Council House on Corn St, and on Broad St the Grand Hotel (1869), the Guild Hall (1843) and the art nouveau façade of the former Edward Everard printing house. The Theatre Royal, opened in 1766, is one of the oldest working theatres in the country. The best part for leisurely strolls is the elegant suburb of Clifton, with handsome Georgian terraces and its famous suspension bridge. Useful central places for a cheapish lunchtime bite are the Bridge (Passage St), Commercial Rooms (Corn St) and Le Chateau (Park St). A 250-mile cycleway now links Bristol with Padstow in Cornwall, keeping off roads as much as possible.

Bristol Docks Being attractively restored, with distinctive blue and yellow **ferries** (Apr–Sept) linking several points. The old part around King St, between the waterfront and the Bristol Old Vic, has quiet cobbled streets of Georgian buildings, pleasant to wander through, and elsewhere some of the bigger warehouses (and even the boats) are being pressed into service as museums, café-bars and the like. The **Arnolfini**, a big former tea warehouse, is now a contemporary arts complex with bar, restaurant, exhibitions, cinema, theatre and so forth.

Industrial Museum (Princes Wharf) Housed in a converted dockside transit shed, and especially good on transport, with locally built steam locomotives and aircraft (inc a mock-up of Concorde's flight deck), and a good look at the development of the port. Shop, disabled access; cl Thurs, Fri, and in winter usually all wkdys; (0117) 925 1470; £1.05.

SS *Great Britain* On the dockside a small steam railway will whisk you on summer wknds along the old cargo route to and from this ship, designed by Isambard Kingdom Brunel as the first iron, screw-propelled, ocean-going vessel, and a real departure from what had gone before. It's being restored, after a half century or so lying neglected in the Falkland Islands, and you can see various curiosities inc the captain's bath. Snacks, shop; cl 24–25 Dec; (0117) 926 0680; £4.50. This includes entry to the **Maritime Heritage Centre**, with reconstructions and original machinery illustrating the city's long history of ship-building. The nearby diesel-powered firefloat *Pyronaut* (1934) and Fairbairn steam-crane (1876) operate on occasional summer wknds.

Historic boat trips Also moored here is the 1860s steam-tug *Mayflower*, which has interesting trips round the docks every hour on alternate wknds in summer. It only takes 12 passengers so best to book with the Industrial Museum; £2.50. From Apr–Oct the **pleasure steamers** *Waverley* and *Balmoral* run fairly frequent day cruises from here, along the Avon and Severn or to Devon, Wales or Lundy; (0117) 926 0767 for programme. The *Balmoral* has surprisingly well kept real ale in its bar.

† **Bristol Cathedral** On the other side of the water, this was originally an Augustinian monastery, founded on what's supposedly the spot where St Augustine met the Celtic Christians in the early 7th c. It's a real mix of architectural styles, and perhaps the country's most splendid example of a hall church, where the nave, choir and aisles are all the same height. Highlights include the Chapter House (one of the finest Norman rooms in Britain), and the candlesticks given in thanks by the privateers who rescued Alexander Selkirk (whose adventures inspired Daniel Defoe to write *Robinson Crusoe*). Snacks, shop, some disabled access.

† **St Mary Redcliffe** (Redcliffe Hill) Elizabeth I described this as 'the goodliest, fairest and most famous parish church in England'. Most of the current building dates from the late 13th c, inc the wonderful hexagonal outer porch. Notable features include the tomb of Admiral Sir William Penn, the father of the man who founded Pennsylvania, and the Handel Window, where 8 passages of the *Messiah* commemorate the great composer's ties with this church. Snacks Mon–Thurs, disabled access (through south door). Free organ recitals Thurs lunchtimes during term-time.

† **Lord Mayor's Chapel** (Park St) Rare civic church, with glorious 16th-c stained-glass windows, floor tiles and fan-vaulted ceiling; guided tours 11am and 2pm.

† **John Wesley's Chapel** (Horsefair) Incongruously set in a shopping centre, but much as it was when Wesley preached here (from the famous double-decked pulpit upstairs); the oldest Methodist chapel in the world, built 1739, rebuilt 1748. Guided tours by arrangement. Shop, disabled access to ground floor only; cl Sun; (0117) 926 4740; free (tour £2.50).

† **Christmas Steps** This famously old-fashioned alley is quaintly lined by steep buildings. At the top is the tiny late 15th-c **Chapel of the Three Kings of Cologne** (the 'three kings' are the three wise men whose shrines are in Cologne cathedral); the warden of the nearby almshouses can let you in. And at the bottom is the lodge of **St Bartholomew's** – all that remains of the 13th-c hospital and almshouse which once stood on this site. This is a good area for shops selling antiques, stamps and old books.

Red Lodge (Park St) The house was altered in the 18th c, but on its first floor still has the last surviving suite of 16th-c rooms in Bristol, as well as a wonderful carved stone chimney piece, plasterwork ceilings and fine oak panelling. They occasionally open the reconstructed Tudor-style garden. Open Sat–Weds and most bank hols Apr–Oct; (0117) 921 1360; £1.05. There are several elegant Georgian streets nearby, notably Great George St, where the **Georgian House**, built in 1790 for a wealthy sugar merchant, is a fine illustration of a typical town house of the day. 3 floors are decorated in period style, inc the below-stairs area with kitchen, laundry and housekeeper's room. Times and price as for Red Lodge; (0117) 921 1362.

† **Cabot Tower** The attractive park at the end of Great George St is an urban nature reserve, and its tower rewards those willing to climb the hundreds of steps with probably the best views of the city. Snacks, cl 25 Dec; free. Nearby **St George's** has good Fri lunchtime concerts, usually with seats available on the day, but best to check on (0117) 923 0359.

Bristol City Museum & Art Gallery (Queens Rd) Good collections of fine and applied art, archaeology, geology, and history – well worth a look. Snacks, shop, disabled access; (0117) 922 3571; £2.10. The neo-Gothic Wills Memorial tower next door is a distinctive landmark.

! **Exploratory Hands-on Science Centre** (by Temple Meads Railway Station) Probably the best of its kind, this hugely enjoyable science centre is as much fun for adults as it is for children. Altogether there are around 150 hands-on experiments (or plores as they call them), presenting science in an appealingly accessible and relevant way: light and vision are illustrated by walk-in kaleidoscopes and distorting mirrors, racing cars are operated by pulleys, and you can make your own electricity or launch a hot-air balloon. The sound and music gallery is fun: you stand inside a giant acoustic guitar and feel the vibrations as its strings are plucked, or play an enormous walk-on keyboard. A new gallery looks at the human body. There are computers for surfing the Net, and plenty of staff on hand to help with any of the displays. The StarDome planetarium (75p extra) is usually open wknds and school hols, but tickets for here sell fast and seats are limited; best to get your ticket for this bit as soon as you arrive, and note you'll crawl or crouch to get inside. Snacks (wknds and school hols only), shop, disabled access; cl Christmas wk; (0117) 907 9000; £5.

Harveys Wine Museum (Denmark St) Unique collection of antique corkscrews, decanters, glasses, bottles, furniture and other items associated with the production and serving of wine, housed in the medieval cellars of this wine company. There's a very good shop, and you may occasionally be able to join one of the guided tours with tutored tastings. Cl Sun and bank hols and occasionally at other times; (0117) 927 5036; £4 (inc a glass of sherry).

★ **CLIFTON** The quiet side of Bristol, with some fine late 18th- and 19th-c terraces, an antiques market (The Mall, cl Sun and Mon), a big park right on the spectacular Avon gorge facing the NT woodlands on the crags opposite, and the remarkably modern-looking suspension bridge, based on an 1836 design by Brunel and finished in 1864; a Victorian girl leapt off here after a tiff with her boyfriend, but was saved when her huge skirts acted as a parachute. The Somerset House (Princess Victoria St) is useful for something to eat.

Bristol Zoo Gardens (Clifton Down; easily reached by buses 8, 9, 508 and 509 from the city centre) One of the most enjoyable zoos in the country, excellent value, lots to see, and plenty of well thought out children's activities. Highlights include the new Gorilla Island, walk-through aviary, Bug World, and Twilight World, with wide-awake rats, mice and other nocturnal animals, even a walk-through bat enclosure. Good adventure playground, activity centre with face-painting, brass-rubbing and so on, and animal encounters spread through the day. A bonus is that everything is spread through beautifully laid out gardens, with spacious lawns and colourful borders. Meals, snacks, shop, disabled access; cl 25 Dec; (0117) 973 8951; £6.90.

Blaise Castle Estate ST5678 (Henbury, 4m NW, off the B4047) A spacious and locally popular undulating park with some woodland and refreshments. The late 18th-c house is now a branch of the City Museum, with lots of carefully explained farming equipment, and collections of costume and dolls. The castle itself is a Gothic folly built in 1766 within the now scarcely discernible ramparts of an Iron Age hill fort. Shop; museum cl Thurs and Fri, and all Nov–Mar, park open daily; (0117) 950 6789; free. Nearby Blaise Hamlet is an NT-owned estate village designed by John Nash.

We welcome reports from readers

This *Guide* depends on readers' reports. Do help us if you can – in return, we offer a discount on the next edition to people who've helped us with reports for it. Tell us what you think about places already in it, and anything extra you think we should say about them. And send us your ideas for inclusion in the next edition: places to visit, eat at or stay in, attractive drives or walks, maybe even unusual interesting shops you know of. Use the card in the middle, the report forms at the end, or just write – no stamp needed: *The Good Guide to Britain*, FREEPOST TN1569, Wadhurst, E Sussex TN5 7BR.

Other things to see and do

Somerset Family Attraction of the Year

! **WASHFORD** ST0441 **Tropiquaria** (on the A39 – easy to spot by tall radio masts) The idea of handling tarantulas and boa constrictors makes many adults squirm, but is the kind of thing that children love, and there are plenty of opportunities for it at this enjoyable place, an amazing transformation of a 1930s BBC transmitting station. The broadcasting equipment has been moved to another part, and the main hall converted into an indoor jungle with high waterfall, tropical plants, free-flying birds and weird and wonderful animals – the more dangerous ones caged. You can touch all sorts of creatures: plenty of snakes and lizards, maybe a millipede if you're lucky. There's an aquarium beneath the hall, while out in the landscaped gardens are birds, lemurs, chipmunks, guinea pigs and wallabies, as well as a sand pit, trampolines, and a couple of good play areas. For many people the highlight of a visit has nothing to do with the wildlife: there's a delightful puppet theatre below the café, with 20-minute marionette and shadow puppet shows that most visitors find quite charming. A bell signals the start of each show and it's worth heading straight there as soon as you hear it – shows are usually hourly in summer, but at other times they're much less frequent, and by thinking you can head there later you may end up missing it altogether. Some days out of season have no shows at all, so it's worth checking first. Another intriguing feature is a collection of vintage radios and televisions, so there's a real mix of things to see that can easily take up most of a morning or afternoon. In summer you'll find Sat less busy than Sun, and there are picnic areas both inside and outside; more to do on a dry day, but enough to merit a visit even if it's wet. Meals, snacks, shop, disabled access (not to aquarium); open daily Easter–Oct, then wknds and school hols Nov, Feb and Mar, and 28 Dec–3 Jan; (01984) 640688; £4.25 (children £2.80). A family ticket for 2 adults and 2 children is £13.

★ **AXBRIDGE** ST4354 Pleasant small town with an appealing largely medieval square and narrow winding high street, unusual around here for its jettied timber-framed buildings. The rambling old Lamb on the corner of the square is good for lunch. **King John's Hunting Lodge** (High St) Actually built around 1500 so having no connection with King John (nor in fact with hunting) – but no less attractive for that. It houses a local history museum. Disabled access to grounds; open pm Easter–Sept; (01934) 732012; donations; NT.

BARRINGTON COURT ST3918 Magnificent series of gardens influenced by Gertrude Jekyll, inc rose garden and traditional walled kitchen garden (they sell the produce). The splendid 16th-c house shows off the reproduction furniture of Stuart Interiors. Meals, snacks, plant centre, disabled access; open Apr–Sept exc Fri; (01460) 241938; £4.20; NT. The village itself is attractive, and the Royal Oak does good lunches.

BERROW ST3054 **Animal Farm Country Park** (Red Rd, N) Good fun for children, with animals and conservation trails, trampolines and play areas. Meals, snacks, shop, disabled access; cl 25 Dec (maybe other dates too in winter); (01278) 751628; £3.50. There's a small **nature reserve** in the nearby sand dunes. The Red Cow at Brent Knoll has good food.

★ † **BISHOPS LYDEARD** ST1729 Attractive village, interesting church with handsome carving.

BITTON ST6770 **Avon Valley Railway** (Bitton Station) Friendly little railway extending lines along the old Midland Railway towards Bath. Snacks, shop, disabled access; open wknds and bank hols, steamtrains Sun May–Sept, plus bank hols and Christmas; £3.

BRADFORD-ON-TONE ST1722 **Sheppy's Cider** (Three Bridges) The Sheppys have been making cider here since the early 19th c, and you can follow the entire process over the 370-acre farm. Tastings in the shop, and a little museum. Snacks, shop, disabled access; cl Sun (exc 12–2pm Easter–Christmas); (01823) 461233; £1.75. The White Horse has good food.

BREAN DOWN ST2958 Protruding into the Bristol Channel between Weston-super-Mare and acres of holiday camps, this gives the best coastal walk in east Somerset, relatively unspoilt – especially as a local authority plan to develop the fort on top as a tourist attraction has just foundered (the National Trust pointedly didn't give their support, and no Lottery money was forthcoming).

BRENDON HILLS SS9738 These give breezy walks with long views; the Royal Oak at Luxborough is a good base.

★ † **BRENT KNOLL** ST3450 The attractive village has a church with remarkable carved bench-ends; the Red Cow is a good dining pub. A path leads up to the prominent summit giving the village its name.

BRIDGWATER ST3036 Once through the industrial outskirts, some central bits are worth seeing: Castle St is the finest early 18th-c street in the county. **Admiral Blake Museum** (Blake St) Now the local history museum, this picturesque house was the birthplace of the Admiral in 1598, and shows his personal possessions (inc his sea chest) and a diorama of his great victory over the Spaniards at Santa Cruz. Shop; cl Sun, Mon, Christmas and New Year; (01278) 456127; free.

★ † **BRUTON** ST6834 Fascinating little town; worth looking out for are the Bartons, narrow alleys leading down from the High St to the river (crossed by footbridge or stepping stones). **St Mary's Church** is on the site of a medieval Augustinian priory and abbey – the old abbey wall with its buttresses still stands in Silver St. The church has a spectacular altarpiece, and in the chancel is a fine effigy of Sir Maurice Berkely, a great survivor who was standard-bearer to Henry VIII, Edward VI and Queen Elizabeth. Interesting and individual shops – antiques, books and prints. The Castle Inn is good for lunch. The drive up towards Alfred's Tower gives some open views.

† **BURNHAM-ON-SEA** ST3050 In summer a bustling inexpensive family seaside resort, with wide beaches, sandy dunes, and the usual holiday facilities. Its plain-looking **church** surprises with its collection of Grinling Gibbons carvings from the long-demolished Palace of Whitehall in London.

BURRINGTON COMBE ST4858 An easy walk by the B3134 (the best drive through the Mendips), this great steeply wooded limestone gorge on the north flank of the Mendips can be combined with walks up on to Black Down for memorable views in all directions, and over the heather and cranberry tops to Dolebury Warren, where the site of an Iron Age hill fort marks a splendid Mendip viewpoint. Other useful starting points for Mendips walks include the Crown at Churchill, Swan at Rowberrow and Ring o' Bells at Compton Martin.

BURROW BRIDGE ST3428 **Somerset Levels Basket Centre** (Lyng Rd) Sells baskets made from materials cut on the surrounding Levels; they have other crafts, maybe demonstrations. Shop, disabled access; cl Sun, and 25 Dec–1 Jan; (01823) 698688; free. The Rose & Crown at East Lyng has good food.

CADBURY CAMP ST4572 This Iron Age hill fort makes a good destination for a walk from the engaging Black Horse in Clapton-in-Gordano, by a lane past the church, which leads to a footbridge high over the M5. This should not be confused with the more famous Cadbury Castle down towards Yeovil.

CANNINGTON COLLEGE HERITAGE GARDENS ST2539 Extensive gardens inc over 10,000 different types of plant, with 8 national collections, display and ornamental beds, tropical and subtropical glasshouses, and gardens of bees and butterflies; cl am, and Nov–Easter; (01278) 655000; *£2.25. The Malt Shovel at Bradley Green has decent food, and there's a nice drive to Nether Stowey via Combwich and Stogursey.

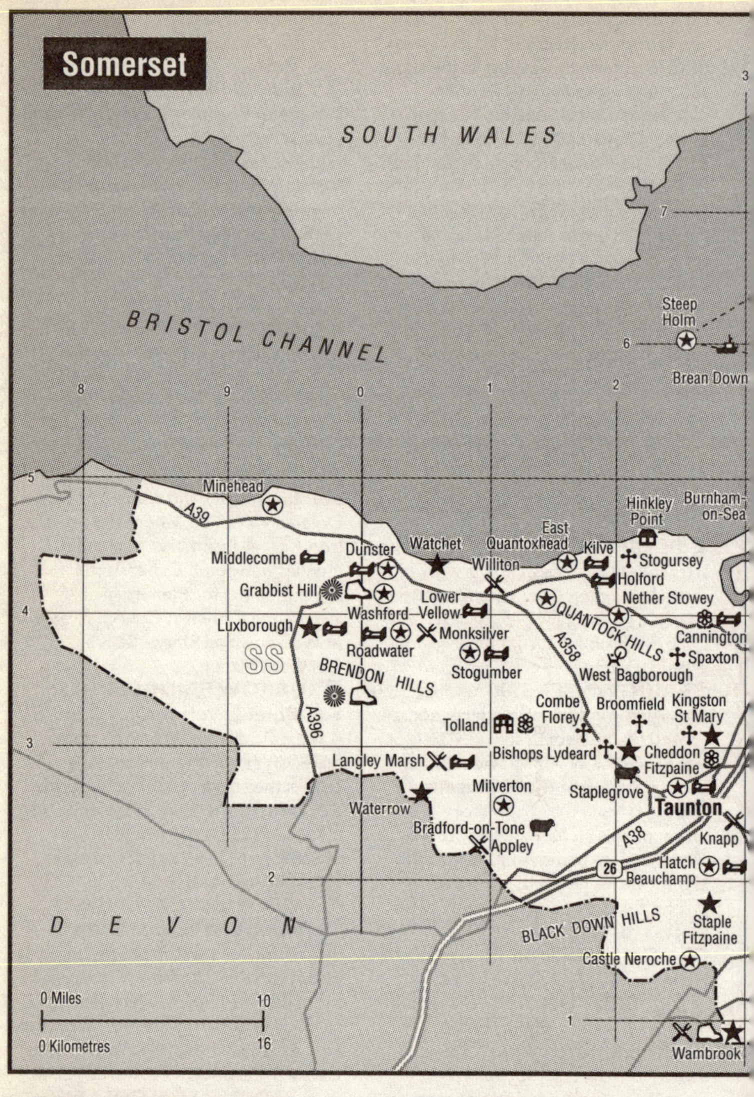

★ CASTLE CARY

ST6432 Very attractive – basically a medieval market town, now with a useful range of traditional family-run shops and crafts and antique shops. The 18th-c **Roundhouse** is Britain's smallest prison, and the local museum is worth a look. The George, a comfortable old thatched coaching inn, has good food. **Hadspen Gardens** (off the A371 2m SE) Beautiful 8-acre gardens surrounding fine 18th-c house; many old favourite plants, but also lots of exotics. A delightful 17th-c walled garden has all sorts of herbaceous plants and old-fashioned roses, and there's a lily pond and ancient flower meadow. Teas (Sun only), nursery, some disabled access; open Thurs–Sun Mar–Sept; (01749) 813707; £2.50. **Castle Cary Vineyard** (Honeywick, just E) Produces award-winning wines and welcomes visits (cl am Sun, and Nov–Apr).

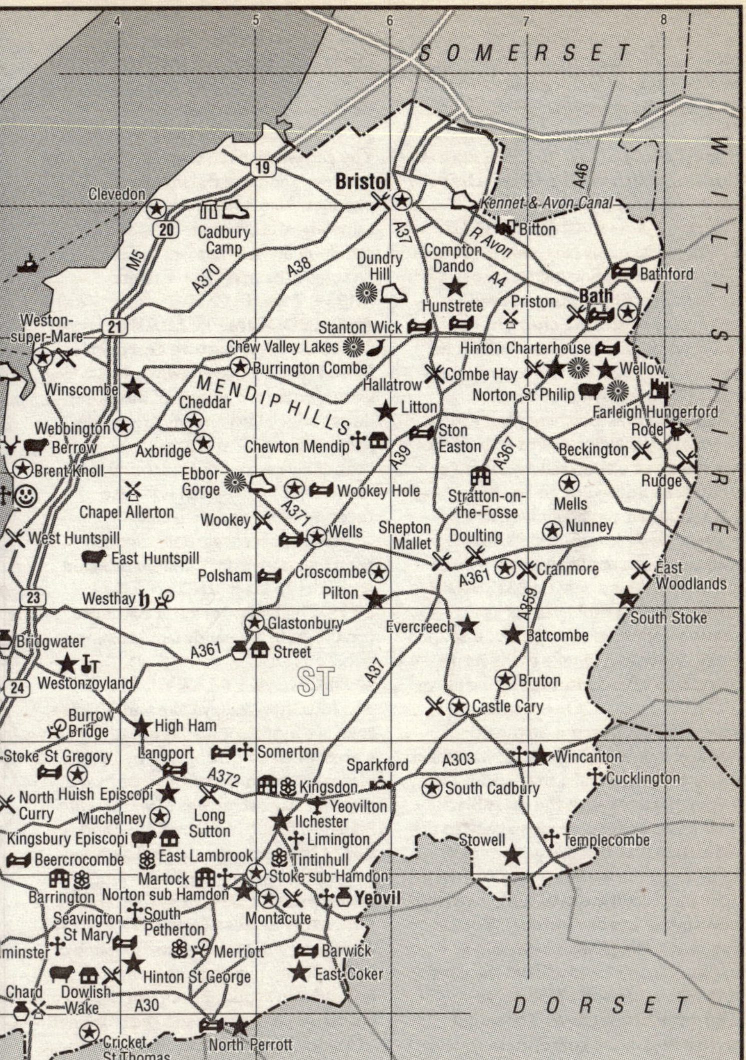

CASTLE NEROCHE ST2715 This isolated ruined Norman fortification, with more the aspect now of a hill fort than a castle, is the central feature of well marked woodland walks down towards the Blackdown Hills S of Taunton; fine views at the top.

CHAPEL ALLERTON ST4150 **Ashton Windmill** The only complete mill left in Somerset, built in the 18th c, with splendid views over the Cheddar Gorge and Somerset Levels. Open pm Sun and bank hols Easter–Sept, plus pm Weds July–Sept; (01934) 712694; free.

CHARD ST3108 The local history **museum** (High St) has good displays on local industries such as lace-making, and a bizarre collection of artificial limbs. Shop, disabled access; cl Sun (exc July and Aug), and Nov–Apr; (01460) 65091; *£2. There are a couple of places to hire bikes; the local tourist board does good cycle routes. **Forde Abbey**, just over the Dorset border and described in that chapter, is particularly worth visiting. **Hornsbury Mill** (just N) 200-year-old watermill, with landscaped watergarden, trout lake, and play area; you can stay here. Meals, snacks, shop, disabled access; cl Jan; (01460) 63317; *£2. Past here at Combe St Nicholas the Green Dragon has good-value food.

CHEDDAR

ST4553 In its older part, this extended village has a very fine market cross, with some interesting shops and a tall-towered 14th/15th-c **church**. The Galleries is quite useful for lunch, and outside are roadside strawberry stalls and pick-your-own in summer. Cheddar gets astonishingly busy then, when every building seems to be either a tearoom or a shop selling cheese or cider. **Cheddar Gorge** The area's big attraction, a magnificent limestone gorge with picturesque cliffs, formed when a cavern roof collapsed. You can just walk up the dramatic B3135 road through, which rapidly loses its commercialised trappings. But it's much more rewarding to take paths rising either side of the entrance to the gorge and make a circuit. One path climbs from the Toy Museum on the north side and follows Gorge Walk waymarks above Cheddar Cliffs; after about 1½ miles you go through the quiet Black Rock Nature Reserve, drop back to the road, then take the West Mendip Way up through the woods opposite, fork right and skirt the top of the gorge (the views into it are hair-raising). You can also reach this viewpoint via the 274 steps of Jacob's Ladder from the road at the Cheddar end of the gorge. **Cheddar Showcaves** 2 beautiful caves beneath the gorge; quite cathedral-like, with spectacular stalagmites and stalactites joining to form columns. Also an exhibition devoted to 'Cheddar Man', Britain's oldest complete skeleton, with a re-creation of his world of 9,000 years ago. Good clifftop walks, and plenty of activities for children, inc the lively Crystal Quest. Meals, snacks, shop; cl 24–25 Dec; (01934) 742343; £6.90. The more daring can don hard hats and boiler suits for what they call Adventure Caving Expeditions; £7.50 (no under-12s). **Cheddar Gorge Cheese Co Rural Village** (The Cliffs) Shops and traditional crafts based around a factory that thanks to its location claims to make the only genuine Cheddar cheese in the world. You can watch each stage of the 7-hour process, and taste the matured product. Also fudge-making, scrumpy sampling, and crafts inc lace- and candle-making. Meals, snacks, shops, disabled access; cl Nov–Easter; (01934) 742810; £2.50.

CHEDDON FITZPAINE

ST2428 **Hestercombe Gardens** Raised walks, sunken lawns and a watergarden are all part of the grand design which Lutyens and Gertrude Jekyll created for this garden (now beautifully restored) set around the Somerset Fire Brigade HQ – also recently reopened intriguing landscaped secret gardens. Snacks, shop (inc plant sales), limited disabled access; cl 25 Dec; (01823) 413923; £3.25. The Bathpool Inn at Bathpool (on the A38) is a handy family dining pub.

CHEW VALLEY LAKES

ST5760 Chew Valley Lake and Blagdon Lake are more popular as breathing places for people living nearby than as places for visitors from afar; both are pleasant large stretches of water, with managed fishing, and the B3130 and B3114 have pleasant views. The New Inn at Blagdon is nicely set for lunch.

CHEWTON MENDIP ST5952

Chewton Cheese Dairy (Priory Farm) Another traditional cheese dairy, one of the few to mature their cheeses properly, so producing not just the characteristic rind but also the true depth of flavour. They start at 7.30am and go on till 3pm, with the best time to watch between 11.30am and 2.30pm. A video shows the stages you may have missed. Meals, snacks, farm shop, disabled access; no cheesemaking Thurs or Sun; cl 25–26 Dec, 1 Jan; (01761) 241666; £1 (guided tour £2.50, 11.30am–1.45pm, not Thurs or Sun). The 15th-c **church tower** is perhaps the most magnificent in any village in the area. The Waldegrave Arms has decent food.

CLEVEDON

ST4071 The Victorian **pier** has been

lovingly restored (it partly collapsed in 1970) and was officially reopened in May 1998. It is pleasant for a stroll. Upstairs, above the tollhouse, a gallery sells paintings, and there are sailings and fishing from the pier itself. Shop, disabled access; cl Weds Oct–Mar, and 25 Dec; (01275) 878846; *75p. Round the corner in Waterloo House is a **heritage centre**; 60p. Good views from Church Hill, and in Moor Lane the **Clevedon Craft Centre** has 15 varied workshops and a tearoom; some parts cl Mon. The Little Harp and Moon & Sixpence are seafront family dining pubs with sea views to Wales.
Clevedon Court (on the B3130 just E) Most of the original structure of this manor house, built in 1320, is still intact, though there are interesting additions from other periods inc a charming 18th-c garden. Thackeray wrote part of *Vanity Fair* here. Snacks; open pm Sun, Weds, Thurs and bank hols Apr–Sept; (01275) 872257; £4; NT.
† **COMBE FLOREY CHURCH** ST1531 Charming church with attractive carvings; Evelyn Waugh lies buried outside.
★ ❋ **COMBE HAY** ST7359 This charming steep village has a good pub, and the road to Monkton Combe gives good views.
CRANMORE ST6643
East Somerset Railway Steam trips along what's known as the Strawberry Line, as well as engine shed and workshops, with 9 steam locomotives and rolling stock, and art gallery with wildlife paintings by David Shepherd who founded the railway. Meals, snacks, shop, disabled access; open daily, though trains don't run every day – best to ring for timetable; (01749) 880417; £5.50, less when no trains running. The Strode Arms in this quiet and pleasant village is very good for lunch.
Cranmore Tower Good views from the top of this folly; cl Oct–Mar; £1.
CRICKET ST THOMAS ST3708 The leisure park on the great estate here, familiar from *To The Manor Born* and *Mr Blobby* (although Noel Edmonds has now relocated his *Crinkley Bottom*), has lovely parkland, 600 wildlife park animals, and plenty more to amuse children. As we went to press it seemed likely that it would be bought by Warner, with further leisure developments inc a hotel. Plans were not yet finalised but parts of the estate will probably be closed at the beginning of 1999. Best to phone to check for opening and prices; (01460) 30755.
★ † ❋ **CROSCOMBE** ST5844 Attractive village, with great 17th-c woodwork in its 15th-c church. The walk to Wells gives unforgettable views of the cathedral.
† **CUCKLINGTON CHURCH** ST7527 13th-c, with small side chapel for St Barbara, whose sacred well is further down in the village.
DOWLISH WAKE ST3712
Perry's Cider Mills They've been making cider here for centuries, and between Oct and Nov you can watch it being produced. The cider mill is in a group of thatched 16th-c buildings around a yard with brightly painted old farm wagons and so forth. Enthusiastically run, with a video on cider-making, liberal tastings and half a dozen different ciders for sale, in old-fashioned earthenware flagons if you want. Shop, disabled access; cl 25–26 Dec, 1 Jan; (01460) 52681; free. The nearby New Inn is very good for lunch.
❋ **DUNDRY HILL** ST5666 Just S of Bristol's suburbs, this gives walkers views over the city, Chew Valley and Blagdon lakes and the Mendips.
★ † ! ❋ **DUNSTER** SS9943 Well worth a day of anybody's time, with fine medieval houses along the wide main street below the wooded castle hill, as well as a handsome octagonal former yarn market and market cross, a lovely 15th-c priory **church** with particularly tuneful bells, and a well established **doll museum** in the Memorial Hall (cl Oct–Mar; 50p). The National Park Information Centre is a useful stop for Exmoor visitors. The handsome old Luttrell Arms Hotel is good for lunch, and there's a wealth of tearooms. **Old Dovecote** (St George's St) In summer you can go right up this 12th-c dovecot, special for still having its potence or revolving ladder, used for harvesting the plump squabs from the nesting boxes.
Dunster Castle Dramatically set in a 28-acre park rich with exotic flora and

even subtropical plants, the castle was largely rebuilt in the 19th c, but has older features such as the 17th-c oak staircase and gallery with its brightly painted wall hangings. Excellent views. Shop in 17th-c stables, limited disabled access (a buggy avoids the steep climb up the hill); castle cl Thurs, Fri, and all Nov–Mar (gardens open all year); (01643) 821314; £5.20, garden and park only £2.80; NT. **Dunster Watermill** Well restored 18th-c mill still grinding and selling flour; teas in a pleasant riverside garden; cl Sat (exc July and Aug), and all Nov–Mar; (01643) 821759; *£2.

★ **EAST COKER** ST5412 Charming quiet village; T S Eliot's ashes are buried here, and the Helyar Arms has good-value food.

EAST HUNTSPILL ST3345 **Secret World** (New Rd Farm) Very friendly family-run working farm, with an emphasis on wildlife rescue (especially badgers). The best feature is the unique observation badger set in the Nocturnal House, with glass viewing panels to watch the creatures' life underground. Also farm trail, barn owls, lots of other animals, adventure playground, and special events. Meals, snacks, shop, disabled access; cl Jan; (01278) 783250; £4.75. You can hire bikes here too (without having to go into the farm). The Crossways Inn over at West Huntspill is a popular lunch place.

EAST LAMBROOK MANOR GARDEN ST4318 This well loved cottagey garden around a 15th-c house (not open) is now Grade I listed; it was started by Walter and Margery Fish in 1937, and Mrs Fish described the process in her book *We Made A Garden*, which became immensely popular. They keep a national collection of geraniums. Plant sales, shop; cl Sun, and all Nov–Feb; (01460) 240328; £2.50.

★ † **EAST QUANTOXHEAD** ST1343 Delightful village with archetypal duckpond, tiny church with fine oak carvings, and walks to the coast.

EBBOR GORGE ST5248 If you like Cheddar Gorge but don't like the souvenirs, coach parties and all, then Ebbor Gorge is for you. It's the same sort of thing, above Wookey Hole, but altogether quieter and more unspoilt. It has an attractive nature trail, and a good walk runs from Wookey Hole through the Gorge to Pen Hill for panoramic views. The Hunters Lodge and New Inn up around Priddy have sensibly priced food.

FARLEIGH HUNGERFORD ST8057 Extensive ruins of 14th-c **castle**, with monuments in the chapel to the Hungerford family, who once owned the land from here to Salisbury. Picnics welcome, shop, limited disabled access; cl winter Mon and Tues, and 24–26 Dec; (01225) 754026; *£2.30 inc audio tour. The Hungerford Arms has decent food.

★ ! **GLASTONBURY** ST4938 Tales of King Arthur can be found all over the country, but are especially prominent here; they like to say that bones reinterred in the abbey in 1191 were those of Arthur and Guinevere. The best approach is by the B3151, showing the town below the famous Tor. Glastonbury has quite a New Age feel, probably due to all the legends. The George & Pilgrims, its medieval carved façade one of the sights of the town, is quite useful for lunch, and the Who'd A Thought It has good-value food. The bypass has made the town much more pleasurable. **Glastonbury Abbey** These noble ruins are said to mark the location of the birth of Christianity in this country. The story goes that Joseph of Arimathaea struck his staff into Wearyall Hill, where it took root. Offshoots of the tree, the famous Glastonbury Thorn, have flourished to this day and there's a fine specimen in the parish churchyard. He is also said to have brought with him the Holy Grail (Jesus's Last Supper platter, used by Joseph to receive His blood at the cross), which Arthur's knights heroically sought through so many famous stories. The remains of the church date mainly from 1524, though the Lady Chapel is much older, and massive roof timbers and richly decorated gable ends and porches testify to the enormous wealth of the order who ran it. An interpretation area has a good range of stories connected with the site. Summer snacks, shop, disabled access; cl 25 Dec; (01458) 832267; £2.50. **Chalice Well** (Chilkwell St) Legend has it that the Holy Grail was hidden here, now set in a colourful 2½-acre garden; the spring has apparently possessed healing powers ever since. True or not, it's a nice peaceful spot. Shop, disabled access; (01458) 831154; £1.50. **Somerset Rural Life Museum** (Chilkwell St) Housed in the Abbey Barn and outbuildings, with displays of traditional regional skills such as cider-making, peat-cutting and basket-weaving. Also orchard, rare breeds, and bee garden with hives. Summer snacks, shop, some disabled access; cl Sun, Mon; (01458) 831197; £2. **Glastonbury Tribunal** (High St) Glastonbury was formerly an island rising from a vast inland lake, and you can almost see this from the top of the Tor, the highest point of the hills and ridges among which the little town nestles, with fantastic views. Excavations here have revealed a prehistoric **lake village** covering 3 or 4 acres below it, consisting of nearly a hundred mounds surrounded by a wooden palisade. Lots of items and timbers from the village have been unusually well preserved thanks to the waterlogged state of the site, and some of the finds, providing a fascinating insight into the life of the settlement, are displayed in this fine 15th-c town house. The tourist information centre is here too, and there's some notable plasterwork in the lower back room. Shop, limited disabled access; cl 25–26 Dec; (01458) 832954; *£1.50.

GRABBIST HILL SS9843 Not as famous as Exmoor's Dunkery Hill (and less frequented), but it does give rewarding views, and can be climbed from nearby Dunster.

† **HATCH BEAUCHAMP** ST3021 **Hatch Court** Fine Palladian mansion with impressive hall, walled kitchen garden, deer park, plenty of china and small military museum. It's one of those places where the family takes real care showing you round, enlivening the tour with lots of anecdotes. Teas (Thurs only), disabled access to garden; house open pm Thurs mid-Jun–mid-Sept, garden open all day Mon–Thurs mid-Apr–Jun, plus Fri July–Sept; (01823) 480120; £3.50, garden only £2.50. The church is attractive, and the Hatch Inn good value.

HINKLEY POINT POWER STATION ST2146 The visitor centre has displays and interactive videos on how electricity is generated, also on local ecology and wildlife (several nature trails nearby); tours by arrangement, (01278) 652461. Snacks, shop, disabled access; cl winter Sat, Christmas wk; free.

★ **ILCHESTER** ST5222 Charming, with a useful range of well stocked little shops. Used to be a Roman town, and one of the houses has a piece of Roman paving. The whole of the green fronting the town hall is said to be the burial ground of plague victims. The comfortable Ilchester Arms has good food.

† **ILMINSTER CHURCH** ST3614 Magnificent 15th-c tower, all turrets, pinnacles and gargoyles.

KENNET & AVON CANAL ST6470 Attractively restored, with a good footpath alongside, it runs from Bristol through Hanham (where the Lock & Weir is a charmingly placed pub), Saltford and Bath to the spectacular aqueduct at Avoncliff (and beyond, across Wiltshire and into Berkshire).

KINGSBURY EPISCOPI ST4321 **Somerset Cider Brandy Co** England's first fully licensed cider distillery, with huge copper stills, oak vats and wooden presses, and traditional cider orchards to stroll through. Maybe tastings of their cider brandy. Shop, limited disabled access; cl Sun, 25–26 Dec; (01460) 240782; free. The village green has an ancient lock-up, and the Wyndham Arms is useful for lunch.

KINGSDON ST5226 **Lytes Cary Manor** Most of the surviving building dates from the 16th c, though there are interesting earlier features inc the 14th-c chapel, and the Great Hall with its 15th-c stained glass. The gardens were designed and stocked by Henry Lyte, a notable Elizabethan horticulturist, and are being brought back to their original state. Plant sales, disabled access to garden only; open pm Mon, Weds and Sat Apr–Oct; (01985) 847777; £4, garden only £2; NT. The Kingsdon Inn does good home cooking.

★ † **KINGSTON ST MARY** ST2229 Pretty village, with attractive church.

† **LIMINGTON CHURCH** ST5422 Interesting for its effigies of the Giverney family, dating back to the 1300s.

† **MARTOCK** ST4619 The magnificent **church** has a splendid roof; also look out for the old court house turned into a grammar school by William Strode in 1661, with the inscription above the door 'Martock neglect not your opportunities' in English, Latin, Hebrew and Greek. The Fleur de Lis in Stoke sub Hamdon is useful for lunch.

★ † **MELLS** ST7249 Delightful and venerable stone-built village, with marvellous church and graveyard, charming ancient inn, pleasant walks nearby.

MERRIOTT ST4412 **Scotts of Merriott** Perhaps the last of the big general retail nurseries to raise and grow most of their own trees and shrubs, on 90 acres – a sea of colour when the 500 varieties of roses are in flower in July. Shop; cl 25 Dec, Easter Sun; (01460) 72306; free. In the village **D B Pottery** (Highway Cottage, Church St) makes attractive teapots and other stoneware; (01460) 75655; free. The Lord Poulett on the attractive main street of nearby Hinton Street George is good for lunch.

★ † **MILVERTON** ST1225 The parish church has some fine carving, and the charming High St has a little pottery.

MINEHEAD SS9646 There's an easily missed area of sloping streets and thatched cottages around the church, with Church Steps a quaint steep back lane. Around this original fishing village is a spacious resort, its beach and promenade sheltered by the wooded hills to the NE. It has the usual attractions, a lively harbour (long-running sea wall repairs should finish in 1999), a sizeable holiday camp (due for a £43 million revamp this year), and a modern shopping area; there are plans to build England's first new pier for many years. The Old Ship Aground has good-value food and pleasant harbour views. There's an unusual **pottery shop** (cl 12–1.30pm) on Park St, and a little **shoe factory** you can visit on North Rd (cl 1–2pm and wknds exc am Sat). From the harbour you may be able to catch the pleasure steamer *Waverley* or *Balmoral*, along the Bristol Channel or to Lundy Island. The clifftop Blue Anchor at the end of the B3191 has decent food and great views. **West Somerset Railway** Steamtrains run from here along the coast to Watchet, then inland to Bishops Lydeard – a splendid long run stopping at several little stations. Meals, snacks, shop, very good disabled access, with a specially adapted coach; station open daily but no trains Mon and Fri in Apr, May and Oct, and none except Santa specials Nov–Feb, best to ring (01643) 707650 for timetable; £8.60 full return fare.

MONKSILVER ST0737 **Combe Sydenham Country Park** (on the B3188) Halfway through a 40-year restoration plan, 580 acres of Exmoor-edge woodland, with walks and trails, corn mill, play areas, and trout fishing. On summer Mon, Thurs and Fri they sometimes do tours of the 16th-c house. Park cl Sat, and Nov–Mar; (01984) 656284, £2 car park, charges for some features (£4 house tour, £4 coarse fishing). The Notley Arms is excellent for lunch.

MONTACUTE HOUSE ST4917 Magnificent 16th-c honeyed stone house in beautiful little village, with a wealth of interesting tapestries, furniture, paintings and ceramics, set in rooms with decorated ceilings, ornate fireplaces and fine wood panelling. A highlight is the collection of Tudor and Jacobean paintings from the National Portrait Gallery. Impressive formal gardens. Meals, snacks, shop, disabled access to grounds only; cl am, Tues and Nov–Mar; (01935) 823289; £5.20, garden only £2.90; NT. The park is open to walkers. Village features worth seeing include the Borough (a charming square of 2-storey houses), and Abbey Farm and the Monk's House – all that remains of the Norman priory destroyed during the Dissolution. The Phelips Arms is good for lunch.

† **MUCHELNEY ABBEY** ST4224 The abbey was founded in the

9th c (perhaps earlier), but the well preserved ruins date from the 15th, inc part of the cloister, and the abbot's lodging with its splendidly carved fireplace. Shop, limited disabled access; cl Oct–Mar; (01458) 250664; £1.60. The tiny 14th-c priest's house opposite is worth a quick look (open pm Sun and Mon Apr–Sept; £1.60; NT) as is the unusual painted ceiling in the **church**. The **John Leach Pottery** has a small display in the abbey, with the main showroom a couple of minutes' drive S; cl lunchtime, pm Sat, and Sun. The Wyndham Arms at Kingsbury Episcopi is handy for lunch.

★ ❋ ⌂ 🏛 🏠 NETHER STOWEY ST1939 An appealing large village with winding streets, handy for both Exmoor and the Quantocks, with good views over the Levels from the mound of the former Norman castle. The **Quantock Hills Information Centre** in Castle St is a valuable source of information. The tiny road up wooded Cockercombe crossing the ridge to Crowcombe (which has a delightful church and decent inn) gives a lovely sense of the Quantocks' feeling of peace and timelessness, and easy access for walks on the moorland tops – a different world, where ancient trackways lead past prehistoric cairns and burial mounds. From up here Exmoor, the Bristol Channel, South Wales and the Mendips are in sight. **Coleridge Cottage** (Lime St) Little changed since Coleridge moved here in 1796; he lived here with a pig or two, and his friends the Wordsworths resided in considerably more style not far away – both families were regarded with suspicion by the local population. Open pm Tues, Weds, Thurs and Sun, Apr–Oct; (01278) 732662; £1.70; NT. The Cottage Inn at Keenthorne just E is a useful lunch stop.

🐄 ❋ NORTON ST PHILIP ST7756 **Norwood Rare Breeds Farm** 🎟 (on the B3110) Friendly organic farm on high open land with plenty of traditional and rare breeds, nature trails, and good views. You can go right up to the animals, and watch the pigs being fed. Meals, snacks, good farm shop, disabled access; cl Oct–Easter; (01373) 834356; *£3.50. Refurbishments in the George, one of the most interesting ancient inn buildings in Britain, have just uncovered some rare medieval wall paintings. The B3110 has some steep intricate views.

🏰 ★ ✝ NUNNEY CASTLE ST7345 This 14th-c fort was reduced to ruins in the Civil War, but has one of the deepest moats in the country; the moat and its feeder stream running through the green of this quaint and quiet village are jostling with ducks. The castle's layout and round towers were supposedly modelled on France's Bastille; free. There's a small covered market place just above the stream, and nearby are 18th-c weavers' cottages. The **church**, as usual in so many Somerset villages, is well worth a look.

✠ PRISTON MILL ST6961 (Priston Mill Farm) In charming countryside, a working watermill once run by the monks of Bath Abbey. Good explanations of how it works, as well as play areas, pets corner, trailer rides, nature trails and a tithe barn. A relaxing place, good for families. Meals, snacks, shop; open bank hol Mon and the preceding Sun, plus pm Thurs in Aug; (01225) 423894; £2.50.

⌂ 🌳 🏛 ✝ ❋ QUANTOCK WALKS The Quantock Hills have the most for walkers in west Somerset (short of Exmoor). Their secretive quality is illustrated by the dense broad-leafed woodlands on the north side, where shady combes display splendid spring and autumn colours. The village of Holford ST1541 is a good starting point: the paths begin with helpful signposts, though you may soon get bemused by the complexity of the path junctions. Holford Combe is reasonably easy to find, and a map will get you to the ancient hill fort site capping Dowsborough, from where a moorland track leads gently N to Holford. Another good approach is from Kilve ST1442, from where you can take a path to and along the coast, then through East Quantoxhead to the north Quantock slopes for a remarkably varied circuit. The west slopes, less wooded than the north-east side, have some attractive valleys enclosed by plunging slopes, with tracks along the bottom: Bicknoller ST1139 with its fine church (good carvings) is an attractive start, the Blue Ball at Triscombe ST1535 another useful port of call. The roads on this side generally have the best views. *See also Nether Stowey entry, above.*

RODE BIRD GARDENS ST8053 Around 200 species of colourful and exotic birds flying through 17 acres of grounds, with ornamental lakes, ponds and masses of trees and shrubs. Also pets corner and woodland miniature railway (Easter–mid-Sept). Summer meals, snacks, shop (inc sales of clematis, of which they have a notable collection), disabled access; cl 25 Dec; (01373) 830326; £4.50. The Woolpack at Beckington has good food.

† **SOMERTON** ST4928 Built in light grey stone, this market town has a 17th-c market cross and fine old Georgian buildings in the quiet main square, where the Globe has decent food. **St Michael's church** is stupendous, its roof supposedly created by monks of Muchelney from 7,000 fetter pieces, among which is a beer barrel – apparently a reference to Abbot Bere.

★ **SOUTH CADBURY** ST6325 An attractive scatter of golden cottages huddle around the church with its striking gargoyled tower; Waterloo Crescent is a distinctive row of farmworkers' cottages built in 1815. **Cadbury Castle** Its Arthurian connection is the main draw. The legendary king and his knights are still said to sleep below the turf of this huge hill fort, waking on Christmas Eve to ride down along what's long been known as King Arthur's Hunting Causeway, and through the village on their pilgrimage to Glastonbury. The castle, covering about 18 acres, is in fact a massive Iron Age camp: many relics have been found there – especially Roman artefacts. It's quite a steep climb, and can be muddy; stout walking shoes recommended. The nearby Sparkford Inn is a nice place for lunch. Compton Pauncefoot just E is pretty.

† **SOUTH PETHERTON** ST4317 The **church** has the second-highest octagonal tower in the country.

SPARKFORD ST6127 **Haynes Motor Museum** (on the A359) Huge collection of gleamingly restored vintage and classic cars and motorcycles; you should be able to see some being test-driven. Meals, snacks, shop, disabled access; cl 25 Dec, 1 Jan; (01963) 440804; £4.95. The Sparkford Inn has a good carvery.

★ **STAPLE FITZPAINE** ST2618 Pretty village with a fine pub; a quiet drive with good views loops along the south edge of Staple Hill then crosses the B3170 to run over Culmhead (where the Holman Clavel is a good stop), along the Blackdown Hills and past the Wellington Monument.

STAPLEGROVE ST2027 **Staplecombe Vineyards** Friendly little vineyard, with self-guided tours of the fields, then back at the house a cheery couple happy to chat. Open pm exc Sun Apr–Oct, or by appointment; (01823) 451217; free. Avoiding Taunton, the Kingfisher at Bishops Lydeard does decent lunches.

STEEP HOLM ST2260 A small island a few miles offshore, its 50 acres a nature reserve teeming with rare plants, wildlife and historic remains. Terrific views from the rugged cliffs. You can get snacks out here, and there's a shop in former Victorian barracks, but it's not really suitable for the disabled. Boat trips to the island run from Knightstone Causeway, Weston-super-Mare, Apr–Oct – Mrs Rendell has dates and times on (01934) 632307; all-day trip £12.

★ † **STOGUMBER** ST0937 Charming village with cottage gardens, an unblemished main street, and an interesting **church**; the White Horse has good food. **Bee World & Animal Centre** (just S of Stogumber Station) Rather jolly bee farm with observation hives, useful enough exhibition, and plenty of rare breeds and farm animals, some of which children can stroke. Also play area, a new crazy golf course, nature trails, and children's pony rides. Staff are helpful and friendly, and you can see trains pass on the West Somerset Railway (*see Minehead entry, above: combined tickets available*). Good meals and snacks, shop, disabled access; cl Nov–Easter; (01984) 656545; £3.15.

† **STOGURSEY CHURCH** ST2042 Exceptional Norman church with

charming carved 15th- and 16th-c pew ends – fascinating figures, faces and grotesques.

STOKE ST GREGORY ST3326 **Willow & Wetlands Visitor Centre** (Meare Green Court, towards North Curry) Shows how this area – the most important wetland in England – developed from marsh and swamp, and looks at its wildlife and industries, especially willow-growing and basket-making (of which there may be demonstrations). Shop, some disabled access; cl Sun; (01823) 490249; free. **English Basket Centre** (Curload, towards Athelney) Produces baskets from its own willow plantations, as well as art charcoal. Also working blacksmith and display of willow sculptures. Shop, disabled access; cl pm Sat, all day Sun, bank hols; (01823) 698418; free. The Rose & Crown at Woodhill is popular for lunch.

STOKE SUB HAMDON ST4717 The former 14th- and 15th-c **priory** manor house has long since vanished, but its fine thatched barn and the screens, passage and Great Hall of the chantry can still be seen; free. The Fleur de Lis is a good place for lunch. Between here and Montacute is a striking folly, St Michael's Tower; it's one of three, all built by neighbouring friends in the 18th c – whenever one had a flag up it was an invitation for the others to go round for a hearty evening. **Ham Hill Country Park** 140 acres of grassland and woodland, full of wildlife and plants. The hill has provided the stone for many of the villages in the area, producing that distinctive warm honey-coloured look. The elevated area of old stone quarries gives walkers splendid views; you can go E from here on paths past St Michael's Hill, topped by an 18th-c pepperpot tower, to Montacute.

STRATTON-ON-THE-FOSSE ST6550 Notable for the spectacular modern (though not modern-looking) Downside Abbey.

STREET ST4836 Clarks Shoes have been made here for quite some while now, and their **shoe museum** on the High St has examples of footwear from Roman times to the present, along with machinery and advertising material. Shop, disabled access; cl Christmas week; (01458) 443131; free. Behind here **Clarks Village** is an attractively laid out multiple-outlet factory shopping centre; some real bargains, plenty of snacks.

TAUNTON ST2224 Busy and prosperous shopping country town with a lively Sat cattle market. It's not of great visual distinction; the best bit is Hammet St, a short street of 18th-c red brick terraces leading to the county's biggest **church**, which has an exceptionally ornate roof, lovely pinnacled tower and lofty Perpendicular chancel. The Tudor House on Fore St is attractive. Just behind Riverside Pl the **Shakespeare Glassworks** may have demonstrations of glassblowing, and in Bath Pl **Makers** is a decent craft shop selling local hand-made crafts (cl Sun). The Masons Arms in Magdalene St is good for lunch (not Sun). **Somerset County Museum** Fine museum, housed in part of the former castle (whose 13th-c portcullised gate-tower is absorbed into the County Hotel). Shop, disabled access to ground floor only; cl Sun, Mon (exc bank hols), 25–26 Dec, Good Fri; (01823) 355455; £2.20. **Somerset Cricket Museum** (Priory Bridge Rd) Another old building, thought to have been the gatehouse for the priory that once stood on the cricket ground: bats, balls and blazers, cards, cuttings and caps, and a cricketing reference library too. Some disabled access; open wkdys Apr–Oct, plus wknds when there's a match on; (01823) 275893; £1.

TEMPLECOMBE ST7022 Ancient village with stocks still in place; the name comes from the medieval order of Knights Templar, dedicated to the protection of the Holy Sepulchre and pilgrims to it. The church, supposedly founded by King Alfred's daughter, houses a 13th-c painting of Christ, found by accident in an outhouse 30 years ago; possibly an early copy of the Turin Shroud, which the Knights Templar may have had in their possession for a while.

TINTINHULL HOUSE GARDEN ST5020 Colourful and attractive 1930s formal garden sheltered by walls and hedges, around 17th-c house with Queen Anne façade (not open). Teas, some disabled access; open pm Weds–Sun May–Sept; (01935) 822545; £3.70; NT. The nearby Crown & Victoria is good.

TOLLAND ST1131 **Gaulden Manor** (on the B3224) Nicely tucked away medieval manor house distinguished for its early plasterwork. The gardens are pleasant too, with a rose garden and bog garden. Teas, shop, plant sales, disabled access; open pm Sun, Thurs and bank hols Jun–Aug; (01984) 667213; £3.80.

★ **WAMBROOK** ST2908 Attractive village, in quiet countryside suiting both walkers and cyclists; the Cotley Inn here is good.

WASHFORD ST0441 *See separate Family Panel on p.554* for **Tropiquaria**. The nearby station on the steam line from Minehead has a little **railway museum** devoted to the old Somerset & Dorset Railway; cl Nov–Feb; (01984) 640869; £1. **Cleeve Abbey** (signed S) Remarkably well preserved 12th-c Cistercian abbey, the gatehouse, dormitory and refectory all in good condition. Fine timbered roof, detailed wall paintings and traceried windows, and an exhibition on monastic life. Snacks, shop, some disabled access; cl winter Mon and Tues, winter lunchtimes, 24–26 Dec; (01984) 640377; £2.50. The Notley Arms at Monksilver is the closest good place for a meal.

★ **WATCHET** ST0743 This small working port has fishing boats and coasters using its tidal harbour, and enough industry to keep it from being too touristy – though it's by no means unattractive. The West Somerset Hotel has good cheap food.

WEBBINGTON ST3855 **Forgotten World** Romany museum and working wheelwright's shop, with brightly coloured carriages and caravans, and an Edwardian fairground. Snacks, shop, disabled access; open Weds–Sun Easter–Sept, daily July–Aug; (01934) 750841; £2. There are pleasant walks on the hills above here. Best reached by a path from Compton Bishop ST3955, **Crook Peak** ST3855 is one of the outstanding Mendip viewpoints; the high ground E can be explored via the West Mendip Way over Wavering Down – this long-distance path along the plateau is signed all the way from Wells to Weston-super-Mare.

★ † **WELLS** ST5546 With a population of only 9,500 this delightful place wouldn't normally even qualify as a big town, but in fact it's England's smallest city. **Wells Cathedral** Stunning structure right in the centre, its 3 towers stretching up against the Mendip foothills. The spectacular west front is reckoned by many to be the finest cathedral façade in the country; dating from the 13th c, it carries 293 pieces of medieval sculpture. Unmissable oddities inside include the wonderful scissor-shaped inverted arches, the north transept's 14th-c clock where horsemen still joust every quarter of an hour, and the fine carvings in the south transept, inc various victims of toothache and 4 graphic scenes of an old man stealing fruit and getting what for. The embroidered stallbacks in the choir (1937–48) are a riot of colour, and the library, with documents dating back to the 10th c, is at 51 metres (168ft) the longest medieval library building in England. Evensong is at 5.15pm wkdys (not Weds), 3pm Sun. Meals, snacks, shop, disabled access; £3 suggested donation. The **Vicar's Close**, linked by the 15th-c Chain Gate to the cathedral itself, is said to be one of the oldest complete medieval streets in Europe; the cathedral's Vicars Choral still live here. **Bishop's Palace** Moated and fortified, approached through a 14th-c gatehouse; it's quite dramatic going across the drawbridge. The beautiful series of buildings still has some original 13th-c parts, notably the banqueting hall and undercroft, as well as several state rooms and a long gallery hung with portraits of former bishops. The grounds are the site of the wells that give the town its name, producing on average 150 litres (40 gallons) of water a second. Also lovely gardens, decent arboretum and a rather clever pair of swans, trained to ring a little bell under the gatehouse window when they're hungry (so many people feed them in summer that this isn't terribly often). Snacks, disabled access to ground floor; open Tues–Fri plus bank hols and pm Sun Easter–Oct, daily in Aug; (01749) 678691; £3, maybe more for special exhibitions. **Wells Museum** (Cathedral Green) Tudor building with good local history museum inc notable embroidery samplers, and stone figures originally on the west front of the cathedral, but now too fragile to be returned there. Disabled access to ground floor only; cl winter Mon and Tues; (01749) 673477; £2. There are a good few other attractive old buildings, many now used as offices and shops (inc several antique shops), and several grouped around the Market Pl; the City Arms and Fountain near here are good for lunch, and there's a big cheese shop not far away. **Time Trail of Roses** (Westfield Rd) is unusual: a small ½-acre garden with over 1,500 different varieties of rose all planted in date order of their introduction to this country; teas; cl am, Mon, Tues, Aug and all mid-Oct–Apr; £2.75 (nearest parking is Tucker St). The B3139 through Wedmore and side roads off it give a good feel of the dead flatness of the Somerset Levels.

WEST BAGBOROUGH ST1733 Tiny village well placed below the Quantocks, with a traditional working **pottery**, and fresh generous food (and comfortable bedrooms) at the Rising Sun.

WESTHAY ST4241 **Peat Moors Visitor Centre** (Shapwick Rd) In the heart of the peat-cutting area of the Somerset Levels, with an excellent exhibition on the topic, and a reconstructed Iron Age village. Craft demonstrations most summer wknds. Snacks, shop, disabled access (but no facilities); cl Nov–Feb; (01458) 860697; £2.25. The Olde Burtle Inn over past Catcott Burtle has good fresh fish.

WESTON-SUPER-MARE ST3161 Friendly family seaside resort, its Latin epithet added in the 19th c in an attempt to be one up on the fashionable French resorts. **Time Machine** (Burlington St) Actually a fairly unsurprising local history museum, focusing mainly on Victorian domestic life, with reconstructed shops and lots of seaside displays; it includes adjacent Clara's Cottage, a typical Westonian home of the 1900s with period kitchen, parlour and bedroom. Snacks, shop, disabled access to ground floor only; cl 25–26 Dec, 1 Jan; (01934) 621028; £2.50. **Heritage Centre** (Wadham St) More local history; cl Sun; £1. **Sea Life Centre** (Marine Parade) Another in the reliable chain, right by the beach, with walk-through underwater tunnel, and plenty of sharks. Meals, snacks, shop, disabled access; cl 25 Dec; (01934) 641603; £3.95. The seafront Pavilion (Knightstone Parade) is a rather stylish family dining place, and there are pleasant walks (and a toll road) through the woods around the Iron Age fort above the town. The quietest beaches are to the N, around Sand Bay. **International Helicopter Museum** (on the B3146, which was the A370) An unexpected find with over 50 helicopters and autogyros on

Days Out

Uniquely Bath: Building of Bath Museum; Museum of Costume; No 1 Royal Crescent; lunch at the Beaujolais (Queen Sq) or the Old Green Tree (Green St); Roman baths; tea in the Pump Room.

Bristol-fashion: SS *Great Britain* and Maritime Heritage Centre; Exploratory Hands-on Science Centre; Bristol Zoo – picnic here; Clifton suspension bridge.

Natural wonders of the Mendips: Burrington Combe (walk on to Dolebury Warren if time); Cheddar Gorge (take the Jacob's Ladder steps up the south side, hold on to something, and look down into the gorge); lunch at the Lamb, Axbridge or the Burcott Inn, Wookey; Wookey Hole Caves; Ebbor Gorge.

display, and a realistic simulator. On the 2nd Sun each month (exc Jan and Feb) they have an Open Cockpit Day, when some helicopters are opened up for visitors to inspect. Snacks, shop, disabled access; cl 25–26 Dec, 1 Jan; (01934) 635227; £3.

★ **WESTONZOYLAND** ST3534 A pretty village with a **steam pumping station**, open Suns Apr–Oct, in steam 1st Sun of month, static most other wks. Also open pm Thurs Jun-Aug; steam days £2.50, otherwise £2.

★ † **WINCANTON** ST7128 Fine Georgian houses and many of the multitude of inns and hotels survive from the coaching era; many still have old coach-entry gates. The **church porch** has a medieval relief of St Eligius. The cheerful Nog (South St) has decent food.

WOOKEY HOLE ST5347 **Wookey Hole Caves & Papermill** Guided tours of half a mile of dramatic subterranean tunnels and caverns, using remote-controlled lighting and special effects to spotlight the geological features and bring to life associated history and myths. Just along the river the papermill demonstrates paper production, and also houses an authentic Edwardian fairground, Magical Mirror Maze and an Old Penny Arcade. A bustling place, all under cover, so ideal when the sun's not shining. Meals and snacks, shop, disabled access exc to caves; cl 17–25 Dec; (01749) 672243; £6.70. The Burcott Inn nearby is good for lunch, and Burcott has a working **watermill**; cl Mon and Tues, maybe milling tours at wknds; £2.

† **YEOVIL** ST5515 Little to interest visitors, but the **Museum of South Somerset** (Hendford) is worth a look if you're passing, with a good range of local history and reconstructed Roman and Georgian rooms (cl Sun and Mon, plus winter Sats; free); there's a dry-ski centre and partly 14th-c **church**.

† **YEOVILTON** ST5423 **Fleet Air Arm Museum** (Royal Naval Air Station, off the A359) Big place concentrating on the story of aviation at sea from 1908, and the history of the Royal Naval Air Service. Lively displays on the WRNS, the Falklands and Gulf wars, jets and helicopters, as well as nearly 50 historic aircraft, and lots of models, paintings, weapons and photographs. A new exhibition on supersonic flight opens in May 1999. Viewing galleries look out over the aircraft using this busy base. Also adventure playground, and hi-tech flight simulator. You could easily spend a good few hours here. Meals, snacks, shop, disabled access; cl 24–26 Dec; (01935) 840565; £6.80. The Kingsdon Inn is the best nearby place for lunch.

† **Other interesting churches** with fine carvings include Broomfield ST2231 and Spaxton ST2237.

★ **Particularly attractive villages**, all with decent pubs, include Batcombe ST6838, Compton Dando ST6464, Evercreech ST6438, Hinton St George ST4212, Huish Episcopi ST4226, Litton ST5954, Luxborough SS9837, North Perrott ST4709, Norton sub Hamdon ST4615, South Stoke ST7641 (picturesque views from the steep nearby lanes), Waterrow ST0425, and Wellow ST7458. High Ham ST4320, Pilton ST5940, Stowell ST6822 and Winscombe ST4157 are also well worth a visit.

Where to eat

APPLEY ST0621 **Globe** *(01823) 672327* Cheerfully run unspoilt 15th-c pub with a relaxed chatty atmosphere, generous helpings of good interesting food inc adventurous specials and vegetarian meals, and super puddings; no smoking dining room; cl am Mon exc bank hols. **£25**|£6.25.

BATH ST7464 **Beaujolais** *5 Chapel Row, Queen Sq (01225) 423417* Bustling wine bar with naughty postcards and so forth on the walls, a conservatory area, enjoyable French food, cheerful staff, and small summer courtyard; cl Sun, 2 wks Jan. **£25.50 supper, £13.80 lunch**|£6.80.

BATH ST7465 **Hole in the Wall** *16 George St (01225) 425242* Popular restaurant with a simply but attractively furnished main room plus another no smoking stylish room, imaginative modern cooking from a varied menu, excellent wine list, and good service; cl Sun; disabled access. **£30**|£6.

BATH ST7464 **Old Green Tree** *12 Green St (01225) 448259* Genuinely unspoilt pub with bustling, cheerful atmosphere in its 3 oak-panelled little rooms, a no smoking back bar, several well kept real ales, lots of malt whiskies, a nice little wine list with a dozen by the glass, and good home-made lunchtime bar food; cl am Sun, 25–26 Dec, Jan, Easter Sun. **£14.80**|£4.80.

BATH ST7465 **Olive Tree** *Russel St (01225) 447928* Light and airy no smoking basement restaurant in the Queensberry Hotel; stylishly simple modern décor, friendly helpful service, super Mediterranean cooking (delicious fish and tempting puddings), and good-value wines; cl am Sun, 1 wk Christmas; partial disabled access. **£35 dinner**|£11.50 2-course lunch.

BATH ST7564 **Rajpoot** *4 Argyle St (01225) 466833* Exceptionally good carefully cooked Indian food in attractively decorated restaurant, particularly good service (you are met at the door by a colourfully uniformed doorman), and used by stars of screen and stage; cl 25–26 Dec; disabled access (by arrangement). **£19**|£6.95.

BECKINGTON ST8051 **Woolpack** *(01373) 831244* Relaxed and welcoming old inn with an attractive no smoking lounge, antique furnishings, a lively flagstoned public bar with a good log fire, cosy candlelit no smoking dining room, good interesting food from a short regularly changing menu, well kept real ales, good, reasonably priced wines, and cheerful helpful service; comfortable bdrms; cl Christmas; children over 5. **£20.75**|£7.

BRISTOL ST5873 **Bowlers** *40 Alfred Pl, Kingsdown (0117) 924 5026* Under new management, this little restaurant specialises in interesting organic food – meaty and vegetarian dishes; cl am Sat, Sun, Mon, 1 wk Christmas, 1 wk Easter. **£20**|£5.

BRISTOL ST5872 **Harveys** *12 Denmark St (0117) 927 5034* Attractive restaurant in 13th-c wine cellars with lots of interesting memorabilia (old sherry casks, wine bottles, and old silver and glassware), very good imaginative food, an exceptional cheese board, friendly knowledgeable staff, and a wonderful wine list; cl am Sat, Sun, 1 wk Feb, 2 wks Aug; children over 8. **£45**.

BRISTOL ST5772 **Howards** *1a–2a Avon Crescent, Hotwells (0117) 926 2921* Charming friendly restaurant in 2 Georgian terraced houses – smarter upstairs restaurant and more relaxed downstairs bistro, with enjoyable seasonal cooking inc set-priced meals, and good-value wines; cl am Sat, am Sun, bank hols. **£30**|£6.75.

BRISTOL ST5873 **Markwicks** *43 Corn St (0117) 926 2658* Elegant restaurant in the vaults of an old bank building, delicious daily-changing French and English cooking (first-class fish, lovely puddings), a carefully chosen wine list, and good friendly service; cl am Sat, Sun, Mon, 1 wk Christmas, 1 wk Easter, 2 wks Aug. **£29.50 dinner, £22.50 lunch**.

BRISTOL ST5672 **Neil's** *112 Princess Victoria St, Clifton (0117) 973 3669* Cosy restaurant with friendly owner and a good choice of imaginative food; cl Sun, Mon, 16 days over Christmas. **£18.95**.

CASTLE CARY ST6432 **George** *(01963) 350761* Thatched coaching inn with huge black elm mantelbeam said to be over a thousand years old over log fire in beamed front bar, civilised relaxed atmosphere, no smoking restaurant and inner no smoking bar, well kept ales, decent house wines, good interesting food, and pleasant staff; bdrms. **£25**|£4.95.

COMBE HAY ST7359 **Wheatsheaf** *(01225) 833504* Popular country pub in a pretty setting, with pleasantly old-fashioned rooms, a big log fire, shuttered windows, reliably good food (plenty of game and fish), well kept real ales, decent wines, and friendly staff; cl 25–26 Dec; disabled access. **£25**|£4.50.

CRANMORE ST6743 **Strode Arms** *(01749) 880450* Neatly kept former farmhouse with charming country furnishings, newspapers to read, log fires in handsome fireplaces, generous helpings of good interesting food in bar and restaurant, well kept real ales, and decent wines; cl pm winter Suns; children in restaurant only; disabled access. **£20**|£4.

DOULTING ST6445 **Waggon & Horses** *(01749) 880302* 18th-c inn with stone-mullioned latticed windows, rambling bar with interesting pictures for sale, 2 no smoking rooms, a wide choice of enjoyable robustly flavoured food (good fresh seafood Thurs and Fri), decent house wines, cocktails, real ales, and a lovely big walled garden with some remarkably fancy fowl (they sell the eggs), horses and a goat; big raftered gallery for art shows and classical music. **£19.80**|£7.

DOWLISH WAKE ST3712 **New Inn** *(01460) 52413* 17th-c stone pub with hops and old-fashioned furnishings in spotlessly kept dark-beamed bar, woodburner in inglenook, a no smoking family room, good enjoyable bar food, well kept real ales and Perry's ciders, and pleasant back garden; no food pm winter Suns; children in family room. **£20**|£5.50.

EAST WOODLANDS ST7944 **Horse & Groom** *(01373) 462802* Small civilised pub on the edge of the Longleat estate with pleasant little bar, comfortable lounge, sizeable no smoking dining conservatory, good, well presented food, well kept real ales, good wines by the glass, helpful service, and seats in attractive garden. **£21.50**|£4.35.

HALLATROW ST6356 **Old Station** *(01761) 452228* Extraordinary pub packed with a formidable collection of bric-à-brac in its dimly lit bars, a handsome beer counter with well kept real ales, a mix of furniture, surprisingly good enjoyable food (given the style of the place), and a no smoking railway carriage restaurant in a garden with a well equipped play area; bdrms. **£19.70**|£7.

KNAPP ST3025 **Rising Sun** *(01823) 490436* Fine 15th-c longhouse with friendly atmosphere, stripped beams and stonework, inglenook fireplaces, good food with a strong emphasis on fish, well kept real ales, farm ciders, a decent wine list, and welcoming staff (and dogs); bdrms; some disabled access. **£23.25**|£8.

LANGLEY MARSH ST0729 **Three Horseshoes** *(01984) 623763* Unpretentious red sandstone pub with short, changing choice of imaginative food (inc vegetarian dishes and always a game casserole), veg from their own garden, no chips or fried food, a wide choice of often unusual real ales, farm ciders, no fruit machines or pool tables, skittle alley, beer garden, and sloping back garden with play area and farmland views; good nearby walks; cl winter Mon; children must be well behaved. **£15**|£4.50.

LONG SUTTON ST4625 **Devonshire Arms** *(01458) 241271* Imposing solid stone inn with tall gables and mullioned windows, a cosily old-fashioned front bar and smart restaurant with a friendly relaxed atmosphere, a flagstoned back bar, well kept beers, decent wines, good coffee, and interesting daily-changing food; bdrms. **£20**|£5.95.

MONKSILVER ST0737 **Notley Arms** *(01984) 656217* Relaxed and friendly pub with characterful beamed L-shaped bar, candles and fresh flowers, woodburners, particularly good popular food, interesting puddings, well kept beers, and neatly kept cottagey garden running down to a swift clear stream; cl last wk Jan/1st wk Feb; disabled access. **£13.50**|£5.

MONTACUTE ST4916 **Milk House** *The Borough (01935) 823823* Lovely old golden stone evening restaurant with antiques, a big open fire, and friendly welcome; very good interesting food (using home-grown produce), and a reasonably priced wine list; bdrms; cl Sun, Mon, Tues and all Nov–Apr; well behaved children only. **£25**.

NORTH CURRY ST3125 **Bird in Hand** *(01823) 490248* Friendly village pub with flagstones, beams, timbers and log fires, a proper public bar, interesting enjoyable food using organic vegetables (à la carte meals in winter only served Fri and Sat evenings), free hors d'oeuvres Sun lunchtime, separate restaurant with conservatory, good choice of real ales (festival May and Oct), and a thoughtful choice of wines. **£18.25**|£7.

RUDGE ST8251 **Full Moon** *(01373) 830936* Attractive rustic pub with friendly licensees, a lot of character in the different rooms, a gently upmarket atmosphere, small flagstoned dining room (and separate plush restaurant), generous helpings of good bar food inc a bargain 3-course set lunchtime and early evening meal, and well kept real ales; comfortable bdrms; disabled access. **£24**|£8.

SHEPTON MALLET ST6143 **Blostins** *29 Waterloo Rd (01749) 343648* Friendly little candlelit evening bistro with consistently good, interesting food inc lovely puddings, and fairly priced wines; cl Sun, Mon, 2 wks Jan, 2 wks July. **£21**.

WAMBROOK ST2907 **Cotley** *(01460) 62348* Bustling country pub with a relaxed, happy yet rather smart atmosphere, 2-room no smoking dining area, a no smoking separate restaurant, open fires, good, really enjoyable food (especially daily specials for large and smaller helpings), well kept real ales, a good choice of wines, a children's play area in the garden, and lots of nearby walks; good bdrms; disabled access. **£18.50**|£5.45.

WEST HUNTSPILL ST3145 **Crossways** *(01278) 783756* Popular dining pub with buoyant atmosphere and plenty of space, enjoyable food (especially daily specials), well kept real ales, and decent wines; comfortable bdrms; cl 25 Dec; disabled access. **£14**|£5.

WESTON-SUPER-MARE ST3261 **Reflections** *22 Boulevard (01934) 622454* Informal family-run restaurant, a good but ordinary café at lunchtimes (exc Sun, when decent set lunch), but transformed Thurs, Fri and Sat evenings with elaborate and well presented high quality meals; cl pm Sun–Weds, 1 Jan for 2 wks. **£23.50**|£4.25.

WILLITON ST0741 **White House** *Long St (01984) 632777* Charming shuttered Georgian hotel under the same owners for over 30 years, with antiques and more modern furnishings, paintings and ceramics, very good enjoyable carefully cooked food using the best local produce, and a fine choice of reasonably priced wines; good breakfasts; bdrms; cl Nov–mid-May; disabled access. **£39**.

WOOKEY ST5145 **Burcott** *(01749) 673874* Little roadside pub, close to Wells, neatly kept and friendly with 2 simply furnished small front bars, an open fire, a roomy, attractive back restaurant, nice bar food, well kept real ales, and a sizeable garden. **£22**|£7.

Special thanks to A G Morris, Kevin Flack, Peter Neate, Jenny and Michael Back, Dr and Mrs A K Clarke, Miss Vicky Collier, Ian and Jacqui Ross, Mrs Norsworthy.

We welcome reports from readers

This *Guide* depends on readers' reports. Do help us if you can – in return, we offer a discount on the next edition to people who've helped us with reports for it. Tell us what you think about places already in it, and anything extra you think we should say about them. And send us your ideas for inclusion in the next edition: places to visit, eat at or stay in, attractive drives or walks, maybe even unusual interesting shops you know of. Use the card in the middle, the report forms at the end, or just write – no stamp needed: *The Good Guide to Britain*, FREEPOST TN1569, Wadhurst, E Sussex TN5 7BR.

Somerset Calendar

Some of these dates were provisional as we went to press. Please check information with the telephone numbers provided.

JANUARY

23 **Shepton Mallet** Antiques Fair: up to 500 stands at the Royal Bath & West Showground – *till Sun 24* (01775) 768661

31 **Shepton Mallet** Collectors Toy Fair: up to 350 stands at the Royal Bath & West Showground (01373) 452857

FEBRUARY

6 **Shepton Mallet** Bristol Classic Car Show at the Royal Bath & West Showground – *till Sun 7* (0117) 907 1000

26 **Bath** International Literature Festival – *till 6 Mar* (01225) 463362

MARCH

19 **Minehead** Steam Gala at West Somerset Railway – *till Sun 21* (01643) 704996

27 **Shepton Mallet** Antiques Fair – *till Sun 28 (see 23 Jan for details)*

APRIL

2 **Claverton** Easter Egg Hunt at the American Museum – *till Mon 5* (01225) 460503

3 **Dunster** Easter Egg Hunt at Dunster Castle (01643) 821314

5 **Wells** Daffodil Fair inc Civil War battle, egg rolling, street fair (01373) 812898

18 **Shepton Mallet** Collectors Toy Fair *(see 31 Jan for details)*

24 **Hatch Beauchamp** Plant Hunters Fair: rare plant fair at Hatch Court (01823) 480120

30 **Minehead** Hobby Horse Celebrations: old May Day custom, Hobby Horse dances round the streets – *till 3 May* (01643) 702624

MAY

1 **Bath** Spring Flower Show at Royal Victoria Park – *till Mon 3* (01225) 462231; **Shepton Mallet** South West Custom & Classic Bike Show at the Royal Bath & West Showground – *till Sun 2* (01749) 823260; **Yeovil** Abbey Hill Steam Rally at the Showground – *till Mon 3* (01935) 863603

2 **Frome** Guided Walk of historical sites (also by appointment) (01373) 463494

3 **Long Ashton** North Somerset Show at Ashton Court (0117) 964 3498

6 **Badminton** Horse Trials at Badminton House – *till Sun 9* (01454) 218272

7 **Cheddar** Jazz Festival: about 15 bands – *till Sun 9* (01934) 742610

8 **Shepton Mallet** Antiques Fair – *till Sun 9 (see 23 Jan for details)*

16 **Wells** Finish of the Mendip Tour Classic Car Rally on the Cathedral Green (01749) 675486

21 **Bath** International Music Festival – *till 6 Jun* (01225) 463362

29 **Bath** Jazz Weekend – *till Mon 31* (01225) 462231

31 **Watchet** Spring Festival (01984) 631495

Somerset Calendar (Cont.)

JUNE

2 **Shepton Mallet** Royal Bath & West Show at the Royal Bath & West Showground – *till Sat 5* (01749) 822200
6 **Frome** Guided Walk *(see 2 May for details)*
13 **Long Ashton** Bristol Motor Show and Historic Transport Pageant at Ashton Court Estate (0117) 934 3542; **Shepton Mallet** Collectors Toy Fair *(see 31 Jan for details)*
19 **Claverton** Native American Weekend at the American Museum – *till Sun 20* (01225) 460503
20 **Yeovil** Country & Game Show (0976) 606910
25 **Glastonbury** Festival – *till Sun 27* (01749) 890470

JULY

2 **Wells** Big Bands on Cathedral Green – *till Sat 3* (01749) 670687
3 **Claverton** Independence Day Celebrations at the American Museum – *till Sun 4* (01225) 460503; **Shepton Mallet** Truckfest at the Royal Bath & West Showground – *till Sun 4* (01775) 768661
4 **Frome** Guided Walk *(see 2 May for details)*; **Watchet** Carnival (01984) 633344
9 **Banwell** Wild West Week: over 2,000 cowboys and Indians, live bands – *till Sun 25* (01934) 822383
10 **Minehead** Friends of Thomas the Tank Engine at West Somerset Railway – *till Sun 11* (01643) 704996; **Montacute** Horse Trials at Montacute House – *till Sun 11* (01963) 34694
17 **Blackford** Healing Weekend: complementary therapies in 4 acres of garden at Corner Cottage – *till Sun 18* (01934) 712957; **Yeovilton** International Air Day (01935) 456751
30 **Weston-super-Mare** Helicopter Fly-in: static displays, flights, variety show, fair – *till 1 Aug* (01934) 822524
31 **Claverton** French Indian War Re-enactment at the American Museum – *till 1 Aug* (01225) 460503

AUGUST

1 **Frome** Guided Walk *(see 2 May for details)*
7 **Bishops Lydeard** Vintage Vehicle Rally at West Somerset Railway – *till Sun 8* (01643) 704996; **Nunney** Street Fair (01373) 836322
13 **Glastonbury** Open Air Fireworks Concert at Glastonbury Abbey – *till Sat 14* (01749) 890470
14 **Montacute** Cycle Festival at Montacute House – *till Sun 15* (01935) 823289; **Yeovil** Festival of Transport: largest display of vintage vehicles in Europe – *till Sun 15* (01963) 34532
15 **Shepton Mallet** Mid-Somerset Show at the Royal Bath & West Showground (01749) 880494
18 **Priddy** Sheep Fair: colourful event (01749) 672552
20 **Dunster** Show (01398) 341490
27 **Wiveliscombe** Beer & Music Festival – *till Sun 29* (01984) 624285
28 **Bristol** Jazz on King Street – *till Mon 30* (0117) 927 7137

Somerset Calendar (Cont.)

SEPTEMBER

3 **Shepton Mallet** National Amateur Gardening Show at the Royal Bath & West Showground – *till Sun 5* (01460) 66616

5 **Frome** Guided Walk *(see 2 May for details)*

10 **Minehead** Vintage Steam Rally at West Somerset Railway – *till Sun 12* (01643) 704996

11 **Shepton Mallet** Countryside Cavalcade: country show at the Royal Bath & West Showground – *till Sun 12* (01458) 446645

15 **Frome** Cheese Show (01373) 463600

25 **Frome** Carnival (01373) 467271; **Shepton Mallet** Antiques Fair – *till Sun 26 (see 23 Jan for details)*; **Wellington** Illuminated Carnival (01823) 662339

29 **Bridgwater** St Matthew's Fair: sale of sheep and ponies *on Weds* street traders and funfair *daily – till 2 Oct* (01278) 427652

OCTOBER

2 **Weston-super-Mare** Speed Trials and Vintage Sprint – *till Sun 3* (01934) 888800

9 **Chard** Carnival (01460) 64209

10 **Shepton Mallet** Collectors Toy Fair *(see 31 Jan for details)*

16 **Castle Cary** Carnival (01935) 813101; **Taunton** Illuminated Carnival and Cider Barrel Rolling Race (01823) 336344

23 **Wincanton** Carnival (01963) 34037

29 **Wells** Festival of Literature – *till Sun 31* (01749) 673385

NOVEMBER

4 **Bridgwater** Guy Fawkes Illuminated Carnival: one of Europe's most spectacular parades with floats up to 100ft long with thousands of lights (01278) 429288

6 **North Petherton** Guy Fawkes Illuminated Carnival *(see Bridgwater above)*

8 **Burnham-on-Sea** Guy Fawkes Illuminated Carnival *(see Bridgwater above)*

9 **Weston-super-Mare** Western National Chrysanthemum Exhibition at the Winter Gardens – *till Weds 10* (01934) 510151

10 **Shepton Mallet** Guy Fawkes Illuminated Carnival *(see Bridgwater above)*

12 **Wells** Guy Fawkes Illuminated Carnival *(see Bridgwater above)*

13 **Glastonbury** Guy Fawkes Illuminated Carnival *(see Bridgwater above)*

15 **Weston-super-Mare** Guy Fawkes Illuminated Carnival *(see Bridgwater above)*

20 **Shepton Mallet** Antiques Fair – *till Sun 21 (see 23 Jan for details)*

DECEMBER

3 **Dunster** By Candlelight – *till Sat 4* (01643) 702624; **Shepton Mallet** Crafts for Christmas at the Royal Bath & West Showground – *till Sun 5* (01775) 768661

4 **Minehead** Santa Specials at West Somerset Railway – *till Sun 5, also on Sat 11–Sun 12, Sat 18–Sun 19 and Thurs 23–Fri 24* (01643) 704996

5 **Shepton Mallet** Collectors Toy Fair *(see 31 Jan for details)*

Staffordshire

Good-value family outings, some lovely countryside.

Staffordshire has lots of scope for entertaining family days out. Alton Towers is a great family outing, with something to appeal to everyone, and each year keeps on top of the competition with new highlights (this year their scary sheer-drop Oblivion ride). Other family favourites here include the free working farm at Amerton, and the friendly steam railway at Blythe Bridge. Even 'adult' places here such as garden centres, for example the one at Eccleshall, include lots to appeal to children, as do Tamworth Castle, and those splendid great houses in equally splendid grounds, Shugborough and Weston Park at Weston under Lizard. The Potteries around Stoke-on-Trent are full of industrial museums and showplaces that fascinate anyone even remotely interested in china – now with a Wedgwood bus service to help you get around them. Even non-gardeners really enjoy Biddulph Grange Garden.

The north-east gives beautiful walks and drives in parts of the Peak District, including glorious Dove Dale, the Manifold Valley and Churnet Valley. Further south, industry is increasingly dominant, but even here Cannock Chase has miles of fine landscape, and the canal network allows some unusually attractive walks.

Where to stay

BETLEY SJ7847 **Adderley Green Farm** *Heighley Castle Lane, Betley, Crewe CW3 9BA (01270) 820203* ***£36;** 3 rms, 1 with bthrm. Georgian farmhouse on big dairy farm with good breakfasts in the homely dining room, and a large garden; fishing on an adjoining farm; cl Christmas/New Year; children over 5.

BLACKSHAW MOOR SK0161 **Three Horseshoes** *Buxton Rd, Blackshaw Moor, Leek ST13 8TW (01538) 300296* **£60,** plus special breaks; 6 rms. Large, well appointed family-run pub with lots of nooks and crannies, open fire, and a no smoking area; good atmosphere, generous food served by young friendly staff in a separate candlelit restaurant, well kept real ales, and a decent wine list; cl 23 Dec–2 Jan.

CAVERSWALL SJ9542 **Caverswall Castle** *Caverswall, Stoke-on-Trent ST11 9EA (01782) 393239* **£65;** 3 oak-panelled rms with four-posters. Castle dating from 1270 with turrets, dungeon, portcullis and moat; lots of atmosphere, fine panelling and paintings, comfortable, restful day rooms, grand dining room, and a big billiards room; indoor swimming pool and 2 lakes for fishing; cl Dec–Jan; disabled access; self-catering in restored stone turrets.

CHEADLE SK0044 **Ley Fields Farm** *Leek Rd, Cheadle, Stoke-on-Trent ST10 2EF (01538) 752875* ***£36;** 3 rms. Listed Georgian farmhouse on a working dairy farm in lovely countryside with lots of walks; traditional furnishings in both the lounge and dining room, good home cooking, and a friendly welcome; cl Christmas.

CHEDDLETON SJ9651 **Choir Cottage** *Ostlers Lane, Cheddleton, Leek ST13 7HS (01538) 360561* ***£55;** 2 pretty rms in an adjacent cottage. 17th-c, no smoking cottage with comfortable lounges, an attractive dining room with country views, nice breakfasts, evening meals by prior arrangement; cl Christmas/New Year; children over 5.

ECCLESHALL SJ8329 **St George** *Castle St, Eccleshall, Stafford ST21 6DF (01785) 850300* **£60w,** plus special breaks; 9 rooms. Friendly little hotel with an open fire in the relaxed bar, ales from their own microbrewery, and good food in the bistro.

OAKAMOOR SK0544 **Bank House** *Farley Lane, Oakamoor, Stoke-on-Trent ST10 3BD (01538) 702810* **£66;** 3 lovely big rms. Carefully restored country home in neat gardens on the edge of the Peak District National Park and with lovely views; log fire in the comfortable drawing room, library, piano in the inner hall, and most enjoyable food using home-grown and local produce – super home-made breads, brioches, pastries and jams and marmalade at breakfast; friendly dog and cats; lots to do nearby; cl Christmas wk.

OAKAMOOR SK0747 **Tenement Farm** *Three Lows, Ribden, Oakamoor, Stoke-on-Trent ST10 3BW (01538) 702333* ***£50;** 8 rms with showers. Comfortable, no smoking house on traditional beef and sheep farm surrounded by fine countryside; with an airy, homely lounge, licensed bar, and a sunny conservatory; also self-catering cottage; cl Nov–Mar.

ROLLESTON ON DOVE SK2327 **Brookhouse Hotel** *Brookside, Rolleston on Dove, Burton upon Trent DE13 9AA (01283) 814188* **£99,** plus wknd breaks; 21 comfortable rms with Victorian brass or four-poster beds. Handsome, ivy-covered William and Mary brick building in 5 acres of lovely gardens; with comfortable, antique-filled rooms, and good food in the elegant little dining room; children over 12; disabled access.

WARSLOW SK0858 **Greyhound** *Warslow, Buxton SK17 0JN (01298) 84249* ***£33;** 4 clean and comfortable rms with shared bthrms. Warm, welcoming atmosphere in this comfortably refurbished slated stone inn handy for the Peak district; generous helpings of home-made food inc hearty breakfasts, live Sat evening entertainment; cl 24–25 Dec; children over 12.

WETTON SK1055 **Olde Royal Oak** *Wetton, Ashbourne DE6 2AF (01335) 310287* ***£35,** plus wknd breaks; 4 rms. Shuttered old stone village inn in lovely NT walking country; with a warm and cheerful welcome, an attractive older part that leads into a more modern-feeling area, open fires, country furniture, sun lounge overlooking a small garden, decent food, and nice breakfasts; children by arrangement.

We welcome reports from readers

This *Guide* depends on readers' reports. Do help us if you can – in return, we offer a discount on the next edition to people who've helped us with reports for it. Tell us what you think about places already in it, and anything extra you think we should say about them. And send us your ideas for inclusion in the next edition: places to visit, eat at or stay in, attractive drives or walks, maybe even unusual interesting shops you know of. Use the card in the middle, the report forms at the end, or just write – no stamp needed: *The Good Guide to Britain*, FREEPOST TN1569, Wadhurst, E Sussex TN5 7BR.

To see and do

Staffordshire Family Attraction of the Year

Alton Towers SK0743 (off the B5032) There isn't anywhere that compares with this 200-acre giant. One reason for Britain's top paid attraction's continued success is that they're never content to rest on their laurels, each year adding increasingly elaborate rides and features. Last year a whole new area, the X-Sector, opened around a typically terrifying new roller-coaster, Oblivion, a £12 million horror that climaxes with a 70mph vertical drop. Lasting just under 3 minutes, and unsuitable for anyone under 1.37 metres (4ft 6in), Oblivion has quickly become one of the most popular rides, even after a hiccough soon after opening when a fault left 16 passengers poised over its most precarious point for almost an hour. Another ride spins you round 3 complete loops before leaving you dangling 15 metres (50ft) above ground (accompanied by jets of water from handily placed fountains); and Nemesis whisks you through unfeasible angles at a greater G-force than that faced by astronauts during a space shuttle launch. In the last few years they've deliberately set out to appeal to whole families rather than just daredevil teenagers. Storybook Land, for example, has quite a range of gentle rides aimed at children up to around 7; toddlers love the singing barn. There are dozens of other distractions, from log flumes and rowing boats to live shows such as *Peter Rabbit on Ice*, and lovely extensive gardens that anywhere else would probably be worth a visit in their own right. There's even a splendidly zany (but thoroughly comfortable) hotel, with a bizarre cross between a galleon and a hot-air balloon in the lobby, and a room which keeps dishing out chocolate; you'll need to book well in advance for themed rooms, such as the Peter Rabbit burrows. Expect queues at the most popular rides – on a summer afternoon an hour's wait for Nemesis is not at all uncommon, though queues tend to shorten late in the day. Other rides have an average wait of around 10 minutes. It's not cheap, and you'll need the whole day and some fairly organised planning to get the most out of it, but the presentation and facilities are excellent – if you don't normally like theme parks you may be pleasantly surprised. They usually end the season with a spectacular firework display. Meals, snacks, shops, disabled access (on most rides too); open mid-Mar–early Nov; (01538) 702200; £19.50 (£15.50 children). A family ticket for 2 adults and 2 children (or 1 adult and 3 children) is £59, a saving of up to £11 (you can book this in advance).

ALTON SK0742 *See separate Family Panel above* for **Alton Towers**. The Talbot is useful for lunch. There are very pretty **Churnet Valley** walks from here or Oakamoor SK0545 (where the attractive Old Blazing Star does food), especially through Hawksmoor and Greendale to pass the broad fishponds in wooded Dimmings Dale and come back down to the river past an old smelting mill – and a good café called the Ramblers Retreat (cl Mon). Hawksmoor Wood is an attractive nature reserve.

★ **ABBOTS BROMLEY** SK0824 Quite a lot of attractive buildings, with pleasant countryside. The Crown has decent food.

BIDDULPH GRANGE GARDEN SJ8858 (Grange Rd) Quite charming High Victorian garden, extensively restored; divided by its founder into a number of smaller themed gardens to house specimens from all over world. Also a display by Spode on the history of the Willow Pattern plate, and how its design was used in the Chinese garden. Snacks, shop; cl am wkdys, all day Mon (exc bank hols), Tues, and Nov–Mar (exc wknds Nov–mid-Dec); (01782) 517999; £4 (£2 Nov–Dec); NT. You can get a joint ticket with Little Moreton Hall, 6 miles away in Cheshire.

BLYTHE BRIDGE SJ9441 **Foxfield Steam Railway** 5 miles through scenic

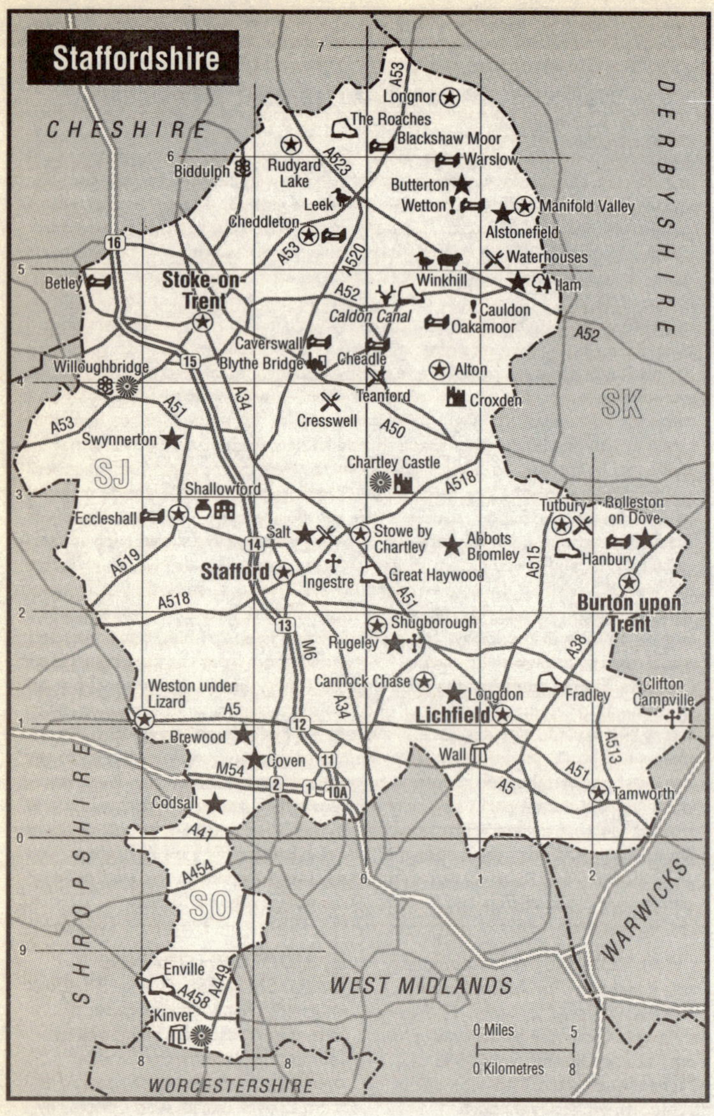

countryside; a return ticket gives unlimited travel for the whole day (exc during special events). Staff are particularly friendly, and there's a collection of locomotives and rolling stock. Open wknds and bank hols Apr–Sept; (01782) 396210; £3.90. The Izaak Walton at Cresswell does a good lunch.

★ **BREWOOD** SJ8808 Charming small town, with many attractive Georgian and older buildings.

BURTON UPON TRENT SK2523 This town is dominated by its connections with the brewing industry, and the **Bass Museum** (Horninglow St) explores this topic in some detail – with an emphasis on Bass and the company's shire horses. You can tour the brewery (no under-13s); also indoor and outdoor play areas. Summer special events and occasional lunchtime brass-band concerts. Meals, snacks, shop, disabled access; cl 25–26 Dec, 1 Jan; (01283) 511000; £4. By contrast, the little **Burton Bridge Brewery** shows brewing at the very opposite end of the scale. The Queen's Hotel is a comfortable place for lunch, as is the Marquis Suite carvery at the New Talbot Hotel on Anglesey Rd. The Boat House at Stapenhill has river and wetland views (boat trips leave on the hour from the ferry bridge from midday onwards in summer). Nearby Rangemore has a good **garden centre**, with farm animals for children.

CALDON CANAL SK0348 The most attractive canal in Staffordshire, with many miles of interesting towpath walks. There's usually something happening at the Froghall Wharf canal terminus (maybe inc horse-drawn barge trips – (01538) 266486), and a rather special canal walk to Consallforge (unusual remote pub here). The nearby Nature Park continues this strange lost-valley scenery. There's also access to the canal from the Boat pub at Cheddleton SJ9752, and the Holly Bush at Denford nr Leek SJ9553.

CANNOCK CHASE SK0215 Miles of lovely woodland and rolling heath, threaded with quiet side roads – the breathing space for the more industrial part of Staffordshire. Dotted around the 17,000 acres are Iron Age hill forts, nature trails, streams, pools and springs, and lovely spots for picnics or dramatic views; fallow deer are often seen. There's an information centre at Marquis Drive, and decent campsites. The canalside Moat House at Acton Trussell does good food. There are good views towards the Welsh borders from the heights N of Broadhurst Green SJ9815, and the German war cemeteries nr here are rather moving. **Castle Ring** SK0412 is a large hill fort giving walkers views over the forests to the Trent Valley.

! **CAULDON** SK0749 Notable for its pub, the **Yew Tree**; a very unpretentious place packed with an extraordinary and delightfully higgledy-piggledy collection of remarkable bygones, especially mechanical music.

CHARTLEY CASTLE SK0228 (just over 6m W of Uttoxeter) A fine old ruin, with good views.

CHEDDLETON SJ9752 **Flint Mill** (Cheadle Rd) Fully preserved 17th- and 18th-c water mills, with a little museum. They are undertaking a major programme of restoration this year thanks to a Lottery grant; shop; cl am most wkdys, 25–26 Dec, 1 Jan; free. Readers praise the **Old School Craft Centre** nearby; it has a pleasant tearoom. **Churnet Valley Railway** (Station Rd) Small steam locomotive museum in Victorian station building, complete with signal box and engine sheds. Short steam and diesel runs in attractive surroundings. Snacks, shop; open wknds Easter–mid-Oct, plus Weds in Aug and for various special events (inc in Dec); trains running Sun Apr–Oct, plus Sat July and Aug and Weds in Aug; (01538) 360522; £3.90 (less when no trains running). The canalside Boat does decent lunches.

† **CLIFTON CAMPVILLE CHURCH** SK2510 One of those rare country churches that seems practically perfect in every way.

★ **CODSALL** SJ8604 Notable in summer for its profusion of lupins. Moors Farm has a good farm shop and small restaurant.

CROXDEN ABBEY SK0639 Ruins in quiet surroundings, with some towering arches surviving. The Raddle at Hollington is a good family country pub.

ECCLESHALL SJ8329 **Fletchers Garden Centre** (Bridge Farm, Stone Rd) Plenty to amuse children, inc adventure playground, falconry displays, aquatic centre, animals, crazy golf and (summer wknds and bank hols) a miniature railway; (01785) 851057. The St George (Castle St) has good home cooking and brews its own beer, and on the other side of town the Star out at Copmere End, is prettily set overlooking the lake.

ENVILLE SO8287 The Cat here is a useful place to join the way-marked **Staffordshire Way** footpath.

FRADLEY JUNCTION SK1513 The **Trent & Mersey Canal** gives less opportunity for towpath walks than other Staffordshire canals, but with lots happening on the water (and a waterside pub) this is a good spot for a stroll.

GREAT HAYWOOD SJ9923 There are interesting **canal walks** from here, with the longest **pack-horse bridge** in Britain nearby.

HANBURY SK1728 The Cock pub is a start for several attractive walks, inc a poignant one to the vast crater left by the 1944 Fauld bomb dump explosion, a tragedy understandably not much publicised at the time.

★ **ILAM** SK1350 Attractive estate village, in lovely countryside. Wooded Ilam Park shows the Manifold Valley at its most sheltered.

† **INGESTRE CHURCH** SJ9824 Designed by Christopher Wren – perhaps the finest small 17th-c church outside London.

KINVER SO8582 (the one right over in the W) Interesting village, with some of Britain's only rock houses nearby, still lived in 30 years ago; there are good views from the Iron Age fort on the ridge above.

LEEK SJ9856 Nearby Coombe Valley has an RSPB **bird reserve**; shop, disabled access; (01538) 384017; free. The A53 high moorland road N has good views, and E of here the B5053 gives an excellent impression of the dales country (the Jervis Arms at Onecote is a good family stop).

★ † **LICHFIELD** SK1109 The attractive centre is largely pedestrianised, with many 18th-c and older buildings among the more modern shops (and antique shops). The **cathedral**, with its 3 graceful spires and close with lovely buildings around it, is magnificent inside, and its west front is memorable, especially at dusk or in the dark when shadows seem to bring the profusion of statues to life. Wonderful illuminated gospels in the chapter house. **Samuel Johnson Birthplace Museum** (Breadmarket St) Dr Johnson was born here in 1709; the house is now furnished in period, with many mementos of him. Shop; cl Sun Nov–Jan; (01543) 264972; £1.40. **Heritage Centre** (Market Sq) Worth a look, in a sympathetically restored chapel site; cl 25–26 Dec, 1 Jan; £1.50. You may be able to go up to the viewing platform in the spire, which has splendid views of the surrounding countryside (£1). On summer Sats you can see the remains of a 16th-c gaol behind the Guildhall (Bore St); 30p. The Queen's Head (Queen St) has a fine choice of cheeses.

★ † **LONGNOR** SK0865 This attractive small town, despite its grand church, has a pleasantly villagey feel (and a good craft centre).

MANIFOLD VALLEY SK1350 This has many good walks, with fewer of the sensational rock features that abound in Dove Dale, but plenty of charm – more or less steep riverside pastures, ancient woodland in the narrower, steeper gorges, waterside caves; there's good access to the hills above it, such as Wetton Hill, which have attractive views. The best viewpoint of all, not to be missed, is Thor's Cave, high above the dale. The branch off up Hamps Dale is extremely pretty. There are good pubs nearby at Warslow, Wetton and Hulme End.

THE ROACHES SJ9963 These form an impressive western barrier at the edge of the Dark Peak; this is perhaps the most exhilarating of several moorland walks from the side roads off the A53 N of Leek. A walk here can be combined with the path through the unspoilt Dane Valley to Danebridge on the Cheshire border; hidden in the woods above the Dane is Lud's Church – not a church, but a miniature chasm reputed to have been a hiding place for religious dissenters.

RUDYARD LAKE SJ9459 Though man-made, it's perhaps one of Staffordshire's prettiest sights (a certain Mr Kipling liked it so much he named his son after it); you can hire a boat and perhaps have a steamboat ride, there's a miniature railway (Mar–Oct), and the muddy marshland provides a haven for wading birds. The meadows and forested slopes above are pleasant for walks and picnics.

★ † **RUGELEY** SK0418 Quite a few attractive old buildings, inc a beautiful 12th-c **church**.

SHALLOWFORD SJ8729 **Izaak Walton Cottage** (Worston Lane) Smartly re-thatched home of the author of *The Compleat Angler*, with displays on the development of angling, a period herb garden and picnic orchard. Shop, limited disabled access; cl Mon (exc bank hols), and Nov–Mar; (01785) 760278; £1.75. The Worston Mill at Little Bridgeford is attractive for lunch.

SHUGBOROUGH

SJ9921 (A513) Imposing ancestral home of the Earls of Lichfield, begun in the late 17th c and enlarged in the 18th; magnificent state rooms, restored working kitchens, interesting marionette collection, exhibition of the present Earl's photography, even a new small brewery. The park has a variety of unusual neo-classical monuments, working rare-breeds farm, and a restored corn mill. Meals, snacks, shop, disabled access; open Easter–Sept, plus Sun in Oct; (01889) 881388; entry to estate £1.50 (payable by NT members), museum and servants' quarters £3.50 (NT members £2.50), house £3.50, farm £3.50 (NT members £2.50); NT. An all-in ticket is quite expensive at £8 – better value on one of their special event days, when there are more activities (such as hands-on Victorian cookery displays) for no extra cost. The canalside Wolseley Arms towards Rugeley is a handy food stop.

STAFFORD SJ9223

Greengate St has what's said to be the biggest timber-framed house in the country, built with local oak in 1595; period room settings and an information centre. The Picture House (Bridge St/Lichfield St) has decent food all day. **Stafford Castle** (A518 SW) Norman remains, rebuilt in the Gothic Revival style in the early 19th c, then allowed to fall into disrepair. Good visitor centre, and a medieval herb garden. Teas Sun only, shop, disabled access to visitor centre; (01785) 57698; cl Mon (exc bank hols), 25–26 Dec, 1 Jan; £1.75. **Shire Hall Gallery** (Market Sq) Handsome former county hall complete with grand courtrooms used until 1992; exhibitions of art, craft and photography, and a good craft shop; cl Sun and bank hols; (01785) 278345; free.

STOKE-ON-TRENT

SJ8745 **The Potteries** These five linked towns within the Stoke-on-Trent conurbation still produce some of the finest china and pottery in the country. You can tour several of the factories, and most have museums or a visitor centre; local buses and a service operated by Wedgwood (see below) link them all, taking you through a memorable urban landscape, the buildings clinging to small steep hills. One hilltop enclave, Penkhull SJ8644, even preserves an undisturbed village feel despite the urbanisation all around. **Gladstone Pottery Museum** (Uttoxeter Rd, Longton, SJ9242) Particularly engrossing, a complete Victorian pottery made much more appealing to families over the last few years, with lively demonstrations and interpretation. It's very much hands-on, and even hands-in – they're quite keen to get your fingers round the clay. It's quite possible to spend up to half a day here. Meals, snacks, shop, mostly disabled access; cl Christmas week; (01782) 319232; £3.75. **Royal Doulton Visitor Centre** (Nile St, Burslem, SJ8749) Potted history of the famous fine china company, with craft demonstrations, and a well displayed collection of Royal Doulton figures. Factory tours wkdys at 10.30am, 1.15 and 2.45pm (no 2.45pm

Days Out

The Dove's giant rockery: Walk into Dove Dale from Alstonefield; lunch at the George, Alstonefield; Ilam; drink at the Yew Tree, Cauldon.

A look at the Potteries: Gladstone Pottery Museum, Longton; lunch at the Plough, Etruria; Etruria Industrial Museum; visitor centre at Spode (factory tour most days), Royal Doulton or Wedgwood.

Transports of delight: Caldon Canal (Froghall Wharf) for a walk or horse-drawn barge trip; or a trip on the Foxfield steam railway, Blythe Bridge; lunch at the Izaak Walton, Cresswell; Chartley Castle (for the view); Amerton working farm, Stowe by Chartley.

tour Fri), booking recommended; no under-10s. Good shop, disabled access to visitor centre only; cl Christmas, and no tours on factory and bank hols – best to check first; (01782) 292434; visitor centre and tour £5.75, visitor centre only £3. **Spode** (Church St, Stoke, SJ8745) The birthplace of fine bone china, this is the oldest manufacturing ceramic factory in the Potteries. A museum has rare and precious pieces, especially in the beautifully laid out Blue Room, and you can have a go at making a piece yourself. Meals, snacks, factory shop, disabled access; no tours pm Fri or wknds, though shop and visitor centre open wknds; tours by appointment, (01782) 744011; £4 inc factory tour, or just visitor centre and museum £2.50. **Wedgwood Visitor Centre** (Barlaston, SJ8839) The story of that favourite item on wedding lists; art gallery, museum, reconstruction of Wedgwood's original 18th-c Etruria workshops and the chance to watch present-day potters at work. Full factory tours by arrangement. Meals, snacks, shop, disabled access; cl 25–26 Dec; (01782) 204141; £3.25 (tours £7.25). They run a bus service between the different Potteries attractions; £4 day pass. **Potteries City Museum and Art Gallery** (Bethesda St, Hanley, SJ8847) Excellent: more pottery and porcelain, plus other local history. Meals, snacks, shop, disabled access; cl am Sun, 25 Dec–1 Jan; (01782) 232323; free. **Ford Green Hall** (Smallthorne, SJ8850) An interesting little 17th-c house with occasional informal performances of period music, cl am, Fri, Sat and 25 Dec–1 Jan; (01782) 233195; £1.50. **Etruria Industrial Museum** (Lower Bedford St, Etruria, SJ8646) Based around the only surviving steam-powered potter's mill in the country, grinding materials right up to 1972. It's been well restored, and there's a working blacksmith. Museum open Weds–Sun all year (exc Christmas), engine in steam one wknd a month Apr–Dec, usually the 1st, but best to check; (01782) 287557; £1.50. The Plough (off the A53 opposite the festival site in Etruria) does decent lunches.

STOWE BY CHARTLEY SJ9927 **Amerton Farm** Working dairy farm with milking at 4pm, farm shop, trails, garden centre, craft workshops, pottery, wildlife rescue centre and a little steam railway (Sun and bank hols Apr–Oct, diesel summer Sats). Meals and snacks (with cream and ice-cream made on the premises), shop, disabled access; cl 25–26 Dec; (01889) 270294. This busy place stands out all the more because admission is free (£1.50 for wildlife centre, £1 train). The Plough opposite is handy for lunch.

TAMWORTH SK2003 A decent town trail links a number of historic buildings; there's also a unique indoor ski slope with real snow. **St Editha's church** has windows by William Morris. **Tamworth Castle** (off Market St) Glorious mixture of architectural styles from the original Norman motte and bailey walls through the Elizabethan timbered hall to the fine Jacobean state apartments. Perhaps more museum than historic home, but plenty to see, with a fair amount to please children, inc high-tech talking heads. Shop, disabled access to ground floor; cl am Sun, 24–26 Dec; (01827) 709626; £4. **Drayton Manor Park** (off the A4091 S) Popular theme park, with 50 rides and attractions inc a small zoo, and Europe's only stand-up roller-coaster. Meals, snacks, shop, disabled access; cl Nov–Mar; (01827) 287979; entry to park £3, rides extra, or £10 for a wristband giving unlimited rides. The good Twycross Zoo is a few miles E, just over the Leics border.

★ **TUTBURY** SK2129 Pleasant village: the Norman church has a notable west doorway and elaborate carvings; also 2 crystal works, craft shops, an attractive ruined castle with good views, and the Olde Dog & Partridge with decent food.

WALL ROMAN SITE SK0806 (Watling St) An important military base from around AD 50; excavations began in the 19th c and revealed one of the most complete Roman bath-houses in the country. Good audio-tour, and finds from the area. Shop; cl 1–2pm, and all Nov–Mar; (01543) 480768; £1.75. The Black Bull at Shenstone is useful for lunch.

WESTON UNDER LIZARD SJ8010 **Weston Park** (A5) Striking richly decorated 17th-c house, with a fine collection of paintings inc works by Van Dyck, Rubens,

Gainsborough and Constable, and Disraeli letters that still somehow catch the imagination. The deer park and grounds, landscaped by Capability Brown, feature a restored 18th-c terrace garden, brightly planted broderie garden, and interesting trees and shrubs; in the last century it took 37 gardeners to look after it all. Also play area, pets corner, and miniature railway through the woodland. Meals, snacks, shop, some disabled access; open Easter, then wknds and bank hols mid-Apr–mid-Sept, plus Tues–Thurs mid-Jun–Aug, and daily in summer hols; (01952) 850207; £5, park and gardens only £3.50. The Bell at Tong is a reliable food pub; there are several interesting places close by, just over the Shrops border.

! WETTON SK1055 Adventurous souls can enrol at the **Peak District School of Hang Gliding**; (01335) 310257; 2-day courses start at around £85.

WILLOUGHBRIDGE SJ7539 **Dorothy Clive Garden** (A51) Woodland gardens created by the late Colonel Harry Clive in memory of his wife; at their best perhaps in spring and early summer, but lovely all year. Rhododendrons, azaleas, old roses, watergarden, rock garden and stunning views of the surrounding countryside. Tearoom with good home-made cakes, disabled access; cl Nov–Mar; (01630) 647237; £2.80. The Falcon in Woore does good food.

WINKHILL SK0551 **Blackbrook World of Birds** Unusual species and aviaries, as well as waterfowl, insects and reptiles, and a children's farm – all much enjoyed by readers. Tearooms, shop, disabled access (although paths are steep); cl wkdys Nov–Mar; (01538) 308293; £4.50. At pretty Waterhouses nearby you can hire bikes from the Old Station Car Park, (01538) 308609; around £5.70 for 3 hours. The prettily set Cross there has decent food – or treat yourself at the Old Beams.

★ **Other attractive villages**, with decent pubs, include Alstonefield SK1355, Butterton SK0756, Coven SJ9006, Longdon SK0714, Rolleston on Dove SK2427, Salt SJ9527 and Swynnerton SJ8535.

There's good canal access from the decent pubs at Amington SK2304 (the Gate), Armitage SK0816, Gnosall Heath SJ8220, Norbury Junction SJ7922, Filiance Bridge in Penkridge SJ9214, Shebdon SJ7626 (great echoes under the aqueduct) and Wheaton Aston SJ8412.

Moseley Old Hall nr Wolverhampton is listed in the *Warwickshire* chapter.

Where to eat

CRESSWELL SJ9739 **Izaak Walton** *(01782) 392265* Very neatly kept, upmarket dining pub with 2 prettily decorated bar rooms and impressively good food (particularly the daily specials); mostly no smoking; cl 25–26 Dec; disabled access. **£18**|£2.95.

SALT SJ9627 **Holly Bush** *(01889) 508234* Thatched house dating in part from the 14th c, with pretty hanging baskets and a big back lawn, some ancient beams in several cosy spreading areas, a more modern back extension, and coal fires; extremely good popular food (the daily specials are the thing to go for), Sunday roasts, well kept ales, and friendly, efficient service. **£17.75**|£7.50.

TEANFORD SK0040 **Ship** *Cheadle Rd (01538) 722253* Busy little local with a generous choice of tasty home-made food (especially bread and puddings), changing daily specials, and a good-value Sun lunch; friendly staff; cl Mon; disabled access. **£17**|£5.95.

TUTBURY SK2128 **Olde Dog & Partridge** *(01283) 813030* Popular carvery in half-timbered dining inn with a stylish layout; well kept beers, good wines, and friendly, helpful service; nice bdrms; cl pm 25–26 Dec, pm 1 Jan; disabled access. **£20**|£3.95.

WATERHOUSES SK0850 **Old Beams** *Leek Rd (01538) 308254* Very pretty cottage surrounded by flowers and creepers, with oak beams, antique furniture, and a cosy, friendly atmosphere; excellent, carefully cooked food, and good service; bdrms; cl am Sat, pm Sun, pm Mon and Tues; disabled access. **£23**|£6.

Special thanks to M and J Back, Jerrold Thomas, B M Eldridge, Philip Pritchard, Mrs V Richmond, Miss Vicky Collier, Neil and Nicola Embrey, E G Parish.

Staffordshire Calendar

Some of these dates were provisional as we went to press. Please check information with the telephone numbers provided.

Many villages here decorate their wells and springs with flower-petal pictures in annual festivals called Well Dressings. For more information see the Derbyshire Calendar.

JANUARY

1 **Stafford** West Midlands Antique Show: about 200 stands at the County Showground – *till Sun 3* (01785) 258060
15 **Lichfield** Beer Festival at Guildhall – *till Sat 16* (01543) 262223
29 **Stafford** Antiques Show: about 400 stands at the County Showground – *till Sun 31* (01785) 258060

FEBRUARY

10 **Lichfield** Garrick Drama Festival – *till Sat 13* (01543) 254021
16 **Lichfield** Shrovetide Fair: pancake race and colourful procession in Market Square (01543) 250011

MARCH

11 **Stafford** West Midlands Antiques Show at the County Showground – *till Fri 12* (01785) 258060
13 **Stafford** Sports and Kit Car Show at the County Showground – *till Sun 14* (01737) 225857
20 **Uttoxeter** Grand National at the Racecourse (01889) 562561
21 **Stafford** Antiques Show at the County Showground (01785) 258060

APRIL

4 **Weston under Lizard** Festival of Transport at Weston Park – *till Mon 5* (01952) 850201
10 **Milford** Gamekeepers' Fair at Shugborough – *till Sun 11* (01889) 881388
23 **Lichfield** St George's Day Court: light-hearted gathering at the Guildhall (01543) 250011; **Weston under Lizard** Horse Trials at Weston Park – *till Sun 25* (01952) 850201
24 **Stafford** Classic Bike Show at the County Showground – *till Sun 25* (01785) 258060

MAY

1 **Stafford** West Midlands Antiques Show at the County Showground – *till Sun 2* (01785) 258060
2 **Weston under Lizard** Craft Fair at Weston Park – *till Mon 3* (01952) 850201
3 **Newborough** Well Dressing (01283) 575430
16 **Milford** Dressage Festival at Shugborough (01889) 881388
24 **Newcastle-under-Lyme** Carnival (01782) 717717
29 **Milford** Spring Craft Show at Shugborough – *till Mon 31* (01889) 881388
31 **Lichfield** Court of Arraye at the Guildhall: traditional ceremony to start Lichfield Bower Day: carnival and displays (01543) 250011

Staffordshire Calendar (cont.)

JUNE

2 **Stafford** County Show at the County Showground – *till Thurs 3* (01785) 258060
4 **Weston under Lizard** Open-air Shakespeare at Weston Park – *till Sun 6* (01952) 850201
5 **Stoke-on-Trent** Canal Festival at Etruria Industrial Museum – *till Sun 6* (01782) 233144
6 **Fradley** Curborough Sprint Course Open Day: free introduction to against-the-clock racing (01543) 264280
16 **Lichfield** Shakespeare in the Park – *till Sat 19* (01543) 254808
18 **Lichfield** Folk Festival – *till Sun 20* (01889) 582908
19 **Mayfield** Well Dressing – *till Sun 20* (01335) 342863; **Milford** Fireworks Concert at Shugborough (01889) 881388; **Weston under Lizard** Model Air Show and German Shepherd Dog Show at Weston Park – *till Sun 20* (01952) 850201
24 **Lichfield** Real Ale, Jazz and Blues Festival at the Rugby Club – *till Sun 27* (01543) 262223
26 **Weston under Lizard** Hovercraft Championships at Weston Park – *till Sun 27* (01952) 850201
27 **Uttoxeter** Family Day at the Racecourse (01889) 562561

JULY

2 **Stafford** Festival inc Open-air Shakespeare at the Castle – *till Sat 17* (01785) 223181
3 **Lichfield** Cajun Festival (01543) 262223; **Milford** Gardeners' Show at Shugborough – *till Sun 4* (01889) 881388; **Uttoxeter** Carnival at the Racecourse (01889) 564085
9 **Lichfield** International Arts Festival – *till Sun 18* (01543) 257298
10 **Burton upon Trent** Regatta and Riverside Show – *till Sun 11* (01283) 221333; **Lichfield** Medieval Market (01543) 418413
11 **Lichfield** Community Arts Fringe Festival – *till Sat 17* (01543) 262223
17 **Weston under Lizard** Balloon Night Glow at Weston Park – *till Sun 18* (01952) 850201
18 **Milford** Goose Fair at Shugborough (01889) 881388
24 **Milford** Fireworks Concert at Shugborough (01889) 881388

AUGUST

1 **Milford** Victorian Street Market at Shugborough (01889) 881388
7 **Betley** Show (01782) 717717; **Weston under Lizard** American Civil War Re-enactment at Weston Park – *till Sun 8* (01952) 850201
12 **Weston under Lizard** Music Festival at Weston Park – *till Sun 15* (01952) 850201
17 **Ilam** Dove Dale Sheepdog Trials – *till Weds 18* (01283) 812245
22 **Milford** Fireworks Concert at Shugborough (01889) 881388
28 **Milford** Craft Show at Shugborough – *till Mon 30* (01889) 881388
29 **Weston under Lizard** Town and Country Fair at Weston Park – *till Mon 30* (01952) 850201

Staffordshire Calendar (cont.)

SEPTEMBER

6 **Abbots Bromley** Horn Dance: ancient ritual dance (01283) 840224

11 **Lichfield** Sheriff's Ride: riding the bounds (01543) 250011; **Weston under Lizard** Midland Game and Country Sports Fair at Weston Park – *till Sun 12* (01952) 850201

16 **Burton upon Trent** Festival inc barrel rolling and heavy horse parade – *till Sun 26* (01283) 563761

18 **Lichfield** Open Day at Samuel Johnson Birthplace Museum and Samuel Johnson Birthday Celebrations (01543) 250011; **Weston under Lizard** Midland Game and Country Sports Fair at Weston Park – *till Sun 19* (01952) 850201

23 **Burton upon Trent** Beer Festival at the Town Hall – *till Sat 25* (01283) 569310

OCTOBER

4 **Burton-upon-Trent** Statutes Fair – *till Tues 5* (01785) 277335

8 **Weston under Lizard** Horse Trials at Weston Park – *till Sun 10* (01952) 850201

9 **Milford** Christmas Craft Fair at Shugborough – *till Sun 10* (01889) 881388

NOVEMBER

5 **Stafford** National Chrysanthemum Society Show at the County Showground – *till Sat 6* (01785) 258060

7 **Weston under Lizard** Bonfire and Fireworks at Weston Park (01952) 850201

18 **Burton upon Trent** Christmas Lights Event (01785) 277335

24 **Newcastle-under-Lyme** Christmas Lights Switched On (01782) 717717

26 **Tutbury** Christmas Lights Event (01785) 277335

DECEMBER

7 **Milford** Christmas at Shugborough – *till Fri 10* (01889) 881388

SUFFOLK

Charming quiet scenery, with some beautiful villages and unspoilt coast; good for a peaceful break.

Suffolk's gentle scenery makes for a relaxing break, and several of its villages are really special, especially Long Melford, Lavenham, Cavendish and Clare with their classic, harmoniously colour-washed, timbered buildings. The first two in particular have plenty of places to visit. Many other less famous villages and small towns have glorious churches, appealingly timbered and plastered buildings, attractively restored windmills – and lots of antique shops. There are rewarding buildings such as Euston Hall, Somerleyton Hall, Ickworth at Horringer and Framlingham Castle, with delightful gardens at most of these, and also at Coddenham, Helmingham Hall, Little Blakenham, Rougham Green and Stanton. Bury St Edmunds has a good range of interesting places to visit, and anyone interested in racehorses could spend a very enjoyable weekend based at Newmarket. The collection of music machines at Cotton is great fun.

Constable country, around East Bergholt by the border with Essex, has had more than a comfortable share of summer visitors, but it is very pretty, and people interested in traditional British painting can easily combine visits to Flatford Mill, Christchurch Mansion in Ipswich (free) and Gainsborough's House in Sudbury.

Even in summer you can walk for miles along fairly empty unspoilt beaches and long stretches of coastal bird country: these wide sea and skyscapes are very restorative. Southwold, Walberswick, Aldeburgh and Orford are ideal for a seaside stay in understated civilised surroundings.

All this sounds pretty grown-up, and Suffolk's special strength is as a place for quiet adult holidays. But there are some real family highlights too. The re-creations of Tudor life at Kentwell Hall in Long Melford are tremendous fun for any age, and the open-air museum at Stowmarket is excellent for an undemanding family day out. The wildlife park at Kessingland, particularly strong on African animals, is another family favourite. Children also enjoy the various attractions at West Stow, and there are several good farm and country centres. Lowestoft, England's busiest fishing port, doubles as a summer beach and boating resort, and has plenty to do; Felixstowe is another place successfully combining commercial port with low-price family beach resort.

Suffolk is excellent for cycling – quiet back roads, lots of villages, gentle gradients, and a very low accident rate.

Where to stay

ALDEBURGH TM4656 **White Lion** *Market Cross, Aldeburgh IP15 5BJ (01728) 452720* **£93,** plus special breaks; 38 rms, some with sea view. Popular, rather smart, 16th-c, family-run seafront hotel with comfortable lounges, 2 bars, log fires, and good food in the panelled and beamed restaurant; cheerful, friendly staff.

BILDESTON TL9949 **Crown** *Bildeston, Ipswich IP7 7EB (01449) 740510* **£39,** plus special breaks; 15 rms, most with own bthrm. Lovely, timber-framed Tudor inn with a comfortable, well furnished, beamed lounge, open fires, good food in the popular restaurant, and welcoming, courteous service; attractive, 2-acre, informal garden; also, a resident ghost; disabled access.

BURSTALL TM0944 **Mulberry Hall** *Burstall, Ipswich IP8 3DP (01473) 652348* ***£38;** 3 comfortable rms, shared bthrm. Once owned by Cardinal Wolsey, a lovely old farmhouse with a fine garden; an inglenook fireplace in the big beamed sitting room, and excellent food (ordered in advance) in the pretty little dining room; very good breakfasts with home-baked bread, helpful and friendly owners; cl Christmas–New Year.

BURY ST EDMUNDS TL8564 **Angel** *Angel Hill, Bury St Edmunds IP33 1LT (01284) 753926* **£98,** plus special breaks; 42 individually decorated rms. Thriving, creeper-clad, 15th-c country-town hotel with particularly friendly staff; comfortable lounge and a relaxed bar, log fires and fresh flowers, and good food in the elegant, newly refurbished restaurant and downstairs medieval vaulted room (Mr Pickwick enjoyed a roast dinner here).

BURY ST EDMUNDS TL8564 **Twelve Angel Hill** *12 Angel Hill, Bury St Edmunds IP33 1UZ (01284) 704088* **£75,** plus wknd breaks; 6 individually decorated rms. Warmly welcoming, mainly early 19th-c house (no smoking); with a cosy oak-panelled bar, comfortable sitting room, good breakfasts in the separate dining room, and period furniture; also, a pretty, little walled garden; cl Jan; no children.

CAMPSEA ASHE TM3255 **Old Rectory** *Campsea Ashe, Woodbridge IP3 0PU (01728) 746524* **£69,** plus special breaks; 9 comfortable and pretty rms. Very relaxed and welcoming Georgian house by the church; with a log fire in the comfortable, restful drawing room, and lovely food from a set menu in the summer conservatory or more formal, no smoking dining rooms with more log fires; fine wine list, and peaceful gardens; cl Christmas; dogs allowed (not in dining rooms).

FRAMLINGHAM TM2863 **Crown** *Market Sq, Framlingham, Woodbridge IP13 9AN (01728) 723521* **£65,** plus special breaks; 13 comfortable rms. Bustling and friendly, little black and white Tudor coaching inn with a pleasantly old-fashioned feel; a comfortable lounge with an open fire, cosy bar with heavy beams and another log fire, good food in both the bar and restaurant, and helpful staff; also, an attractive, small courtyard.

HADLEIGH TM0242 **Edgehill** *2 High St, Hadleigh, Ipswich IP7 5AP (01473) 822458* **£60,** plus special breaks; 8 pretty rms. Friendly, family-run Tudor house with a Georgian façade; comfortable, carefully restored rooms, personal service, traditional English cooking in the no smoking dining room, and an attractive walled garden with croquet; cl Christmas.

HARTEST TL8353 **The Hatch** *Pilgrims Lane, Cross Green, Hartest, Bury St Edmunds IP29 4ED (01284) 830226* **£55;** 3 rms. Pretty, 15th-c thatched cottage, Grade II listed, on the pilgrims' way to Bury; lovely beamed drawing room with antiques, separate dining room for enjoyable breakfasts, a conservatory, seats out on the terrace and a pretty garden; no evening meals, but the nearby Crown does good food; the charming owners did run Hancocks in Kent, and many of their former guests have happily found their way here; cl Christmas; children over 9 (though babies welcome); disabled access.

HIGHAM TM0335 **Old Vicarage** *Higham, Colchester CO7 6JY (01206) 337248* **£56;** 3 rms. Charming Tudor house nr a quiet village, with very friendly owners; pretty sitting room with fresh flowers, log fire and antiques, enjoyable breakfasts in the attractive breakfast room, and neatly kept grounds with river views, tennis court and swimming pool (unheated).

HINTLESHAM TM0743 **College Farm** *Hintlesham, Ipswich IP8 3NT (01473) 652253* ***£40;** 3 rms, 1 with own bthrm. Late 15th-c, no smoking house on a farm, with a neat garden; comfortably furnished rooms, lots of beams, log fire in the inglenook fireplace, good Aga-cooked breakfasts in the separate dining room, and friendly owners; walks around the farm (beef and arable), and riding and golf nearby; cl mid-Dec–mid-Jan; no pets; children over 10.

HINTLESHAM TM0843 **Hintlesham Hall** *Hintlesham, Ipswich IP8 3NS (01473) 652334* **£150,** plus special breaks; 33 lovely rms. Magnificent mansion, mainly Georgian but dating from Elizabethan times, in 175 acres with big walled gardens, 18-hole golf course, outdoor heated swimming pool, tennis, trout fishing and croquet; there's also snooker, a sauna and steam room; restful and comfortable day rooms with books, antiques and open fires, fine modern cooking in several restaurants, a marvellous wine list, and exemplary service; well behaved children over 10 in evening restaurant.

HITCHAM TL9751 **Hill Farmhouse** *Bury Rd, Hitcham, Ipswich IP7 7PT (01449) 740651* **£44;** 3 rms. Georgian/Victorian farmhouse with an adjoining 15th-c timbered cottage, in 3 acres with ducks on 2 ponds, croquet and badminton; a residents' sitting room and separate dining room, dried flowers in the inglenook fireplace, home-grown vegetables (where possible) and eggs used in the imaginative dinners (on Tues and Thurs, set meals only), bring your own wine; good breakfasts; cl Nov–Feb.

LAVENHAM TL9149 **Angel** *Market Pl, Lavenham, Sudbury CO10 9QZ (01787) 247388* ***£65,** plus special breaks; 8 comfortable rms. 15th-c inn with original cellar and pargeted ceiling, several Tudor features such as a rare shuttered shop window front, and a civilised atmosphere; good food in both the bar and restaurant (they smoke their own meat and fish), lots of decent wines, several malt whiskies, well kept real ales, thoughtful and friendly service; maybe live classical piano pm Fri; cl 25–26 Dec; disabled access.

LAVENHAM TL9149 **Swan** *High St, Lavenham, Sudbury CO10 9QA (01787) 247477* **£139.90;** 46 rms. Handsome and comfortable Elizabethan hotel, with lots of cosy seating areas, interesting historic prints, and alcoves with beams, timbers, armchairs and settees; good food in the lavishly timbered restaurant (actually built only in 1965), afternoon teas, an intriguing little bar, and friendly, helpful staff; disabled access.

LAWSHALL TL8654 **Brighthouse Farm** *Melford Rd, Lawshall, Bury St Edmunds IP29 4PX (01284) 830385* ***£40;** 3 rms. Homely B & B in this timbered Georgian farmhouse; log fires, lounge and games room, good breakfasts in the charming dining room, landscaped gardens and farm trail; self-catering and camping also.

LONG MELFORD TL8645 **Bull** *Hall St, Long Melford, Sudbury CO10 9JG (01787) 378494* **£100,** plus special breaks; 25 rms, ancient or comfortably modern. An inn since 1580, this fine black and white hotel was originally a medieval manorial hall; handsome and interesting carved woodwork and timbering, large log fire, an old weavers' gallery overlooking the courtyard, and old-fashioned and antique furnishings; a lovely calm atmosphere, good food, and pleasant, friendly service; beautiful village.

MILDENHALL TL7074 **Riverside** *Mill St, Mildenhall, Bury St Edmunds IP28 7DP (01638) 717274* ***£82,** plus special breaks; 21 rms. 18th-c country house by the River Lark, with a relaxed restaurant overlooking the lawns, a comfortable bar, welcoming staff, enjoyable food, and real ales; croquet, and boats to hire; bridge wknds.

NEEDHAM MARKET TM1053 **Pipps Ford** *Norwich Rd, Needham Market, Ipswich IP6 8LJ (01449) 760208* **£57,** plus winter breaks; 7 pretty rms with antiques and fine old beds, 4 in converted Stables Cottage. Lovely 16th-c farmhouse in a quiet garden surrounded by farmland, and alongside an attractive river; with log fires in the big inglenook fireplaces, and good, imaginative food in the conservatory with subtropical plants (some meals can be communal); home-baked bread, home-produced ham and pork, and own honey, eggs and preserves, with organically home-grown vegetables and herbs; cl Christmas–New Year; children over 5; disabled access.

NEWMARKET TL6463 **White Hart** *High St, Newmarket CB8 8JP (01638) 663051* **£49.95;** 22 rms. Comfortable hotel with racing pictures and an open fire in the spacious lounge, traditional restaurant, and reliable bar food; friendly staff, front bar where the trainers meet, and a solid back cocktail bar where they take their more important owners.

ROUGHAM TL9063 **Ravenwood Hall** *Rougham, Bury St Edmunds IP30 9JA (01359) 270345* **£83,** plus special breaks; 14 comfortable rms with antiques, some rms in mews. Tranquil Tudor country house in 7 acres of carefully tended gardens and woodland; with a log fire in the comfortable lounge, cosy bar, good food in the timbered restaurant with its big inglenook fireplace (home-preserved fruits and vegetables and home-smoked meats and fish), a decent wine list, and helpful service; croquet, heated swimming pool and hard tennis court; disabled access.

SOUTHWOLD TM5076 **Crown** *High St, Southwold IP18 6DP (01502) 722275* **£68;** 12 rms. Outstanding old inn with excellent, imaginative food in the no smoking restaurant and a smart but relaxed main bar; inventive breakfasts, lots of interesting, properly kept wines by the glass, well kept real ales, and friendly, helpful staff; cl 2 wks beginning of Jan.

SOUTHWOLD TM5076 **Swan** *Market Pl, Southwold IP18 6EG (01502) 722186* **£97,** plus special breaks; 45 rms, most with own bthrm. 17th-c hotel with a comfortable and restful drawing room, upstairs reading room, convivial bar, and good food in the elegant, no smoking dining room; fine wines, well kept real ales (the hotel backs on to Adnams Brewery), and polite, helpful staff; no dogs in main hotel; limited disabled access.

STOKE-BY-NAYLAND TL9836 **Angel** *Stoke-by-Nayland, Colchester CO6 4SA (01206) 263245* **£59.50;** 6 comfortable rms. Civilised and elegant dining pub in the Stour Valley; with Tudor beams in the cosy bar, stripped brickwork and timbers, fine furniture, a huge log fire and a woodburner; decent wines, and particularly good, imaginative and reasonably priced bar food; cl 25–26 Dec; children over 8.

WANGFORD TM4679 **Angel** *Wangford, Beccles NR34 8RL (01502) 578636* **£49;** 6 rms. Neatly kept and handsome, Georgian-faced, 17th-c inn with a light and airy bar, no smoking restaurant, good-value dishes of the day and Sun lunch; well kept real ales, decent house wines, pleasant staff, and a garden.

WESTLETON TM4469 **Crown** *The Street, Westleton, Saxmundham IP17 3AD (01728) 648777* **£94.50;** 19 quiet, comfortable bdrms. Smart, extended country inn in a lovely setting with pleasant nearby walks; comfortable bar, no smoking dining conservatory, restaurant, a wide range of good food (nice breakfasts, too), log fires, several well kept real ales, and decent wines; pretty garden with an aviary and floodlit terrace.

WOODBRIDGE TM2548 **Seckford Hall** *Woodbridge IP13 6NU (01394) 385678* **£110,** plus special breaks; 32 rms. Handsome Tudor mansion in 34 acres of gardens and parkland with a trout-filled lake and putting; there's also a leisure club with an indoor heated pool and gym; fine linenfold panelling, huge fireplaces, heavy beams, plush furnishings and antiques in the comfortable day rooms, and good food and service; cl 25 Dec; well behaved dogs welcome; disabled access.

WORLINGTON TL6973 **Worlington Hall** *Worlington, Bury St Edmunds IP28 8RX (01638) 712237* **£65,** plus special breaks; 9 comfortable rms with decanter of sherry, fruit and fresh flowers. 16th-c former manor house in 5 acres of grounds, with a 9-hole pitch-and-putt course; comfortable panelled lounge bar with a log fire, good food in the relaxed, candlelit bistro, and friendly staff.

We welcome reports from readers

This *Guide* depends on readers' reports. Do help us if you can – in return, we offer a discount on the next edition to people who've helped us with reports for it. Tell us what you think about places already in it, and anything extra you think we should say about them. And send us your ideas for inclusion in the next edition: places to visit, eat at or stay in, attractive drives or walks, maybe even unusual interesting shops you know of. Use the card in the middle, the report forms at the end, or just write – no stamp needed: *The Good Guide to Britain*, FREEPOST TN1569, Wadhurst, E Sussex TN5 7BR.

To see and do

Suffolk Family Attraction of the Year

LONG MELFORD TL8647 **Kentwell Hall** (off the A134) The enthusiastic re-creations of Elizabethan life in this beautiful moated Tudor mansion are great fun for families; best of all is the early summer Great Annual Re-creation, when for 3 weekends 250 costumed volunteers do everything as closely as possible to the way they would have behaved in the house's 16th-c heyday, but other smaller events throughout the season are as rewarding. We went to last year's High Summer event around the August bank hol, finding the house and grounds full of hard-working Tudors cooking period meals in the kitchen, playing instruments in the Great Hall, baking bread in the moathouse, cleaning out the stables, or simply sitting in a corner waiting to draw visitors into conversation. They don't just look the part, they sound it too, diligently adopting 16th-c speech patterns that once at their post they refuse to give up: it would be nice to think that our spectacularly unimpressive attempts at archery were due to a failure to understand the period instructions. It really is worth taking the trouble to chat to the various characters as you stroll round: they truly know their stuff, and are particularly good at capturing the interest of children – just as many youngsters huddled around a woman talking them through her clothes as were to be seen fussing the Tamworth pigs in the farm buildings. Lots of time and effort has been put into restoring the house, but don't expect everything you see to be original or even particularly old: the chief appeal of most rooms is as a backdrop to what's going on in them, and though some parts have a friendly lived-in feel, no part of the inside can match the quite glorious exterior. There's enough going on for inquisitive families to spend at least half a day here, with space for picnics, and refreshments in the undercroft, or maybe on the cedar lawn (where a spit roast makes for an unusual lunch). The **Calendar** at the end of this chapter has dates of 1999 events; you can visit at other times too, but there's not much going on then, and children might find it rather dull. Snacks, shop, disabled access; house open pm Sun Mar–Oct, and daily Easter wk and mid-July–Sept, with Tudor re-creations on several wknds Apr–Sept; (01787) 310207; most re-creations cost around £7.50 (£5 children 5–15), though the Great Annual one is £11 (£7.25 children). On non-event days, entry is £5.10, or £3 garden and farm only.

★ **ALDEBURGH** TM4656 Quaint fishing village with a shingle beach where the fishermen still haul in and sell their catch, and a much-loved boating pond; touristy, but in a quiet way. **Moot Hall** 16th-c brick and timber, with an outside staircase; scene of the trial in Britten's *Peter Grimes*. It has displays on maritime history and coastal erosion, and finds from the Anglo-Saxon ship burial at Snape. Shop; open wknds Apr and May, daily Jun–Oct (cl am exc July and Aug); (01728) 452730 *50p. Composer Benjamin Britten and his companion the singer Peter Pears are buried side by side in the churchyard. The attractively placed Cross Keys, White Lion and Mill are all good for lunch. There's an RSPB reserve just N at North Warren.

ALDRINGHAM TM4461 **Craft Market** 3 extensively stocked galleries of local crafts and fine art. Teas, disabled access; cl 12–2pm Sun (all am winter Suns), 25–28 Dec, 1 Jan; (01728) 830397; free. The Parrot & Punchbowl has decent food.

ASHBOCKING TM1855 **James White's Cider Mill** (Helmingham Rd) Cider- and apple-juice-making and tasting, with pick-your-own in season. Snacks, shop; best to check first wknds and bank hols; (01473) 890111; free. The Barley Mow over at Witnesham has reasonable food.

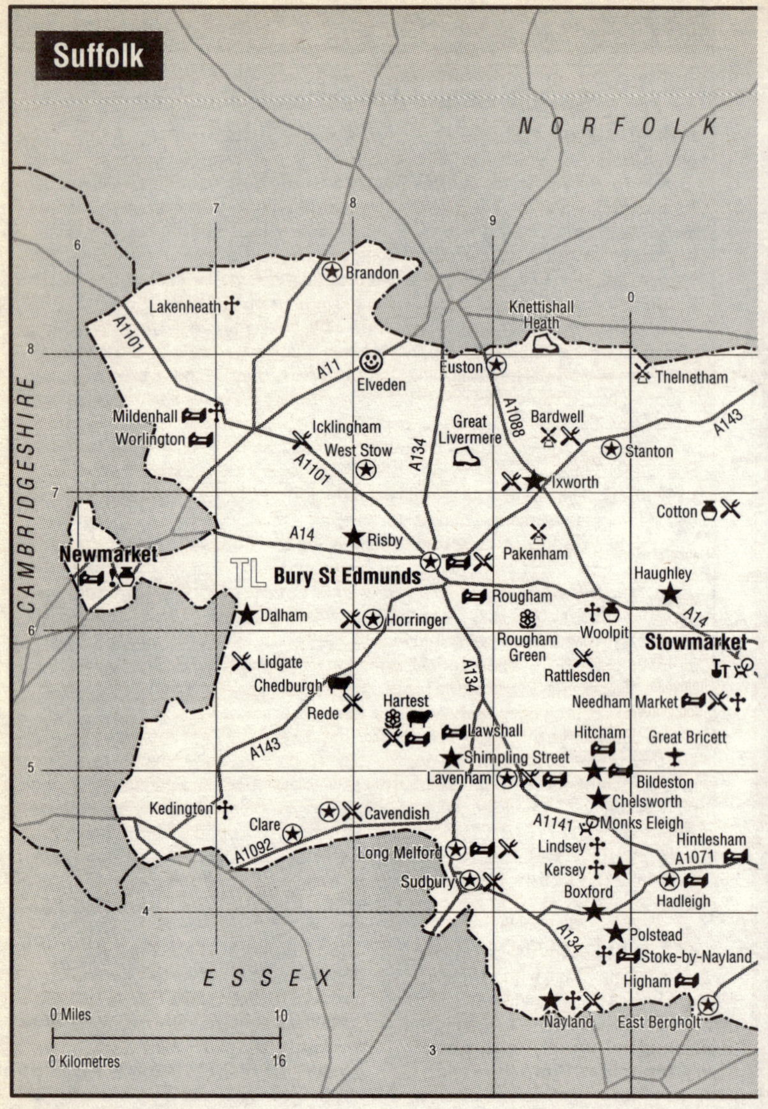

BARDWELL WINDMILL
TL9473 An attractive sight; open for visits at least summer Suns. The village green, with an ancient church opposite the 16th-c pub, is pleasing, too.

BECCLES TM4290 **William Clowes Print Museum** (Newgate) Interesting look at the development of printing from 1800 onwards, with a wide range of machinery, woodcuts and books. Shop; open 2–4.30pm wkdys Jun–Sept, or by appointment; (01502) 712884; free. Down the same road is a decent local history **museum**; cl am, Mon (exc bank hols), Nov–Mar. The riverside Waveney House Hotel has good-value food.

BLYTHBURGH CHURCH
TM4575 Magnificent, in a lovely setting above the marshes; small working pottery nearby.

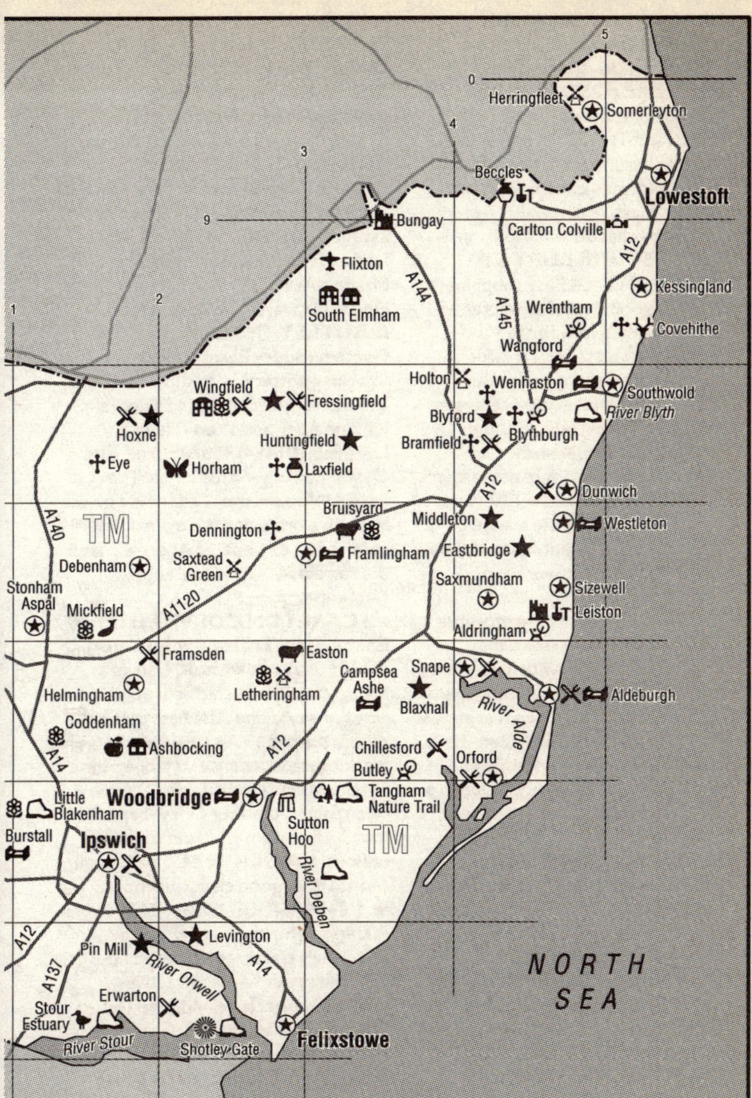

† BRAMFIELD CHURCH TM4073 Interesting, with an unusual detached round tower.

BRANDON TL7886 **Brandon Heritage Centre** (George St) Brandon used to be the centre of the Stone Age flint industry, so among the local history here is a reconstructed flint-knappers' workshop; also displays on the fur industry and Thetford Forest. Shop, disabled access; open Sat, pm Sun, and bank hols, Easter–Oct, plus Thurs; *50p. **Brandon Country Park** Largely pinewoods, pleasant for strolls; for a car-borne impression of Thetford Heath, the best road is the B1106.

BRUISYARD TM3266 **Bruisyard Vineyard** (signed off the B1119 Framlingham road) Picturesque 10-acre vineyard producing decent

English wine, with a herb garden, watergardens and woodland picnic area. Meals, snacks, shop, some disabled access; cl 25 Dec–mid-Jan; (01728) 638281; £3.50.

BUNGAY TM3389 In the centre of this historic small market town are the ruins of its Norman **castle**, with twin towers and massive flint walls. The Green Dragon has decent food.

★ **BURY ST EDMUNDS** TL8464 Busy shopping town with a good deal of character, quite a few attractive Georgian and earlier houses, and several antique shops. Jun–Sept walking tours usually leave the tourist information centre at 2.30pm Mon, Tues, Thurs, Fri, and 11am Weds and Sun. **Abbey precincts** Little remains of the former medieval abbey beyond the 12th- and 14th-c gatehouses, but the tranquil gardens are very pleasant, and a **visitor centre** in Samson's Tower has a history of the site. Cl Nov–Mar; (01284) 763110; free. The pretty little Nutshell nearby (Traverse) is the country's smallest pub, with long church connections – cl Sun and Holy Days. The **cathedral** gained that status only in 1913; parts are 15th c, but the hammerbeamed ceiling is 19th c, and work still goes on. The nearby Queen's Head (Churchgate St) has good food. Another fine old church, **St Mary's** (Crown St), has the tomb of Mary Tudor. The handsome **Theatre Royal** on Westgate St is Britain's third oldest working theatre, built in 1819 by William Wilkins, the designer of London's National Gallery. It's owned by the NT, and you can look round when productions or rehearsals are not in progress (not Sun or bank hols); (01284) 769505. **Manor House Museum** (Honey Hill) Georgian mansion with a marvellous collection of watches, clocks and other timepieces, as well as period costumes and quite a few hands-on displays. A seemingly innocuous pair of breeches fell into this category not so long ago; they'd been worn by Mr Darcy in the TV adaptation of *Pride and Prejudice* and had to be put under guard when female visitors wouldn't stop stroking them. Snacks, shop, disabled access; cl Mon (exc bank hols), Good Fri, 25–26 Dec; (01284) 757072; *£2.70, less for locals. **Art Gallery** (Market Cross) A fine Robert Adam building with changing exhibitions and a decent craft shop. Cl Sun, Mon, wk between exhibitions, Christmas; (01284) 762081; 50p. **Greene King Brewery** (Westgate St) Brewery tours Mon–Thurs; booking essential, (01284) 714382; £5. The Linden Tree (Out Northgate St), Mason's Arms (Whiting St) and Cupola House (Traverse) do decent food.

BUTLEY TM3751 **Butley Pottery**(Butley Barns, Mill Lane) Working pottery, with shop, tearoom and restaurant; cl Mon and Tues (exc July and Aug), and Wed–Thurs Dec–Feb; (01394) 450785; free. The Oyster pub is good for lunch. The B1084 Woodbridge–Orford is a quietly attractive drive, and the even quieter back road S to Capel St Andrew passes the remains of a medieval abbey gatehouse.

CARLTON COLVILLE TM5090 **East Anglia Transport Museum** (B1384 SW of Lowestoft) Lots of lovingly restored vehicles around 3 acres of woodland. The best part is the reconstructed 1930s street scene with working trams, trains and trolley-buses. Snacks, shop, some disabled access; open Easter, then Suns May–Sept, Sats Jun–Sept, and pm wkdys in summer hols; (01502) 518459; £4. The Crown (A146) does good cheap lunches.

★ **CAVENDISH** TL8046 A lovely sight, its green framed by colourfully plastered timbered houses, with the tower of the attractive medieval **church** behind. The 16th-c Bull has good-value food. **Cavendish Manor Vineyards** and Nether Hall (Peacocks Rd) 15th-c manor house nicely surrounded by vineyards; interesting old paintings in the house, tours and tastings in the vineyard. Shop; cl 25 Dec; (01787) 280221; *£2.50. The A1092 from Clare goes on to Long Melford with a back road on to Lavenham – 3 lovely villages. The back roads N of here are also pleasant drives, passing colour-washed houses.

CHEDBURGH TL8058 **Rede Hall Farm Park** (A143 just E) Working farm based around agricultural life in the 1930s–50s, with rare breeds, huge working horses and seasonal activities. Snacks, shop, disabled access; cl Oct–Mar; (01284) 850695; £3. A little further E, the Plough at Rede has good food.

★ ✝ ♜ ⛫ **CLARE** TL7645 Another of the area's very special timber and plaster villages, with a huge and beautiful **church**, the sketchy ruins of a **castle** on an Iron Age earthwork above the River Stour, some remains of a 13th-c Augustinian priory, and little modern intrusion; nature trails around the castle. There's a 3-storey antiques warehouse, and the Swan and Clare Hotel have decent food.

❀ **CODDENHAM** TM1252 **Shrubland Park Gardens** Stunning Victorian gardens inc a formal terrace and wild woodland garden. There's a magnificent conservatory and enchanting follies inc a Swiss chalet. Snacks, limited disabled access; open pm Sun and bank hols Apr–Aug; (01473) 830221; £2.50. The Sorrel Horse at Barham is useful for lunch.

COTTON TM0667 **Mechanical Music Museum and Bygones** Lots of instruments and musical items inc organs, street pianos, polyphons, gramophones, even dolls, fruit bowls and a musical chair. Their pride and joy is a Wurlitzer theatre pipe organ in a reconstructed cinema. Teas, shop, disabled access (but no facilities); open pm Sun Jun–Sept, plus the 1st Sun in Oct, a fair organ enthusiasts' day; (01449) 613876; £3. The Trowel & Hammer is handy for lunch.

✝ **COVEHITHE CHURCH** TM5281 Attractive building; this stretch of coast is good for nature walks, especially out of season.

★ ✝ **DEBENHAM** TM1763 This attractive village has a fine, partly Saxon **church**, and a **pottery** (Carters Ceramics, Low Rd), specialising in teapots. Cl Sun (exc pm summer), and they don't make pots at wknds; (01728) 860475.

✝ **DENNINGTON CHURCH** TM2866 Interesting and attractive – with excellent sermons; pleasant surroundings.

♜ **DUNWICH** TM4770 Once quite a sizeable town, but most has now slipped slowly under the sea. Some say that on quiet nights, with a swell running after a storm, they can hear submerged church bells tolling.

Dunwich Museum (St James St) Small but very interesting, on the village's gradual erosion; open pm wknds Mar–Easter, then daily Easter–Oct, free. There are some fragmentary ruins of a friary up on the cliffs. Excellent coastal walks along the cliffs, beaches and heathland of Dunwich Heath, which has a NT tearoom (£1.50 parking charge).

✝ **EAST BERGHOLT** TM0733 **Bridge Cottage, Flatford** A 17th-c cottage nr the mill immortalised by Constable, with a good interpretative centre for his paintings. Teas (highly recommended by readers), shop; cl Mon and Tues (exc Jun–Sept), and Jan–Feb, limited opening in Dec, best to phone; (01206) 298260; free; NT. Guided walks through areas that inspired his work leave here several times a day May–Sept, but fill quickly (£1.80). You can hire rowing boats for trips along the River Stour. The mill itself and its famous partner **Willy Lott's Cottage** are owned by the NT and leased by them to the Field Studies Council. You can see inside only by taking part in their arts courses or popular wildlife-watching wknds; (01206) 298283. The King's Head nearby is attractive for lunch, and the church with its uncompleted tower has a unique, 16th-c, timber-framed bell cage. From the village, the walk along the watermeadows by the Stour is East Anglia's most famous and well worthwhile – picturesque views immortalised by Constable. There is no real point in leaving the path to make a circular route. Elsewhere, the Stour Valley's attractive villages don't quite compensate for the humdrum scenery in between; although you can find field paths, it's difficult to work these into round walks. This Constable country is shared with Essex, around Dedham.

EASTON FARM PARK TM2758 Friendly farm with milking demonstrations in a Victorian dairy and its more modern counterpart alongside; also, rare breeds, a working blacksmith, an adventure playground and nature trails. Readers with very small children have found the gravel paths tricky with pushchairs. Meals, snacks, shop, disabled access; usually cl Mon (exc bank hols and July–Aug), and all Oct–mid-Mar; (01728) 746475; £4. The quaint White Horse has decent food, and the Wickham Market–Debenham back road through here via Brandeston and Cretingham has some attractive views.

ELVEDEN TL8080 **Center Parcs,** a relaxing place to stay on the edge of – indeed, virtually part of – Thetford Forest, with excellent leisure facilities; (0990) 200300.

EUSTON HALL TL8978 (A1088) Elegant old house built by Charles II's Secretary of State Lord Arlington. The highlight is probably the excellent art collection, with several portraits of the Merry Monarch and his family and court, inc works by Lely and Van Dyck. The grounds were laid out by John Evelyn, William Kent and Capability Brown, so reflect centuries of development, with stately terraced lawns, fine trees, a lake, lovely rose garden and classical temple. Teas in former kitchen, shop, disabled access to grounds and tearoom; open pm Thurs Jun–Sept; (01842) 766366; £3. The Six Bells at Bardwell has good food.

EYE CHURCH TM1473 Beautiful stonework and rood screen.

FELIXSTOWE TM2832 Quite a busy port, with a ferry (passengers, not cars) across to Harwich, and further afield to Zeebrugge. Thanks to its beaches and relatively dry climate it's developed into a popular, low-price, family resort. 18th-c **Landguard Fort** is well worth a look and has displays on local history; open Sun and bank hols May–Sept; (01394) 286403; £2. Along the coast N, past another Martello tower, golf course and quiet sand dunes, is the gently attractive and altogether quieter little settlement of Felixstowe Ferry, with another foot-ferry across the estuary of the River Deben, and good local seafood in the waterside Victoria.

FLIXTON TM3288 **Norfolk and Suffolk Aviation Museum** (Homersfield Rd) Aircraft and related items from the Wright brothers to the present day, with aeroplanes outside and in the Blister Hangar. Shop, disabled access; open Sun and bank hols Easter–Oct, plus usually Tues–Thurs in summer hols; (01986) 896644; donations. The Green Dragon in Bungay is useful for food.

FRAMLINGHAM TM2863 The sloping market square is attractive, and the Crown at its head does decent food. The **church** has an excellent hammerbeam roof. **Framlingham Castle** (B1116) 12th c, is where Mary I heard that she had become Queen. Unusually the entire curtain wall has survived (you can walk all the way along it), and there are 13 towers, some 17th-c almshouses, and an array of Tudor chimneys. Good views, and an interesting museum. Snacks, shop, disabled access to ground floor only; cl 25–26 Dec; (01728) 724189; £2.95. The B1116 to Fressingfield is quite a pleasant drive.

GREAT BRICETT TM0351 **Wattisham Airfield Historical Collection** (off the B1078) Small exhibition related to the adjacent airfield which is now one of the largest helicopter bases in Europe. Disabled access; open pm Sun Apr–Oct; (01449) 728933; free.

GREAT LIVERMERE TL8871 There's a charming shortish walk from the church here, past Ampton Water lake, to Ampton church. A longer path leads through farmland from Livermere to Ixworth.

HADLEIGH TM0242 Old market town with some striking buildings (inc the church, famously painted by Gainsborough); there's a nearby woodland RSPB reserve.

HARTEST TL8352 The village green is attractive; at the end, the Crown is pleasant for lunch. **Giffords Hall** (Shimpling, just SE) 33 acres with vineyard and winery, wild-flower meadows, rare breeds of sheep, pigs and domestic fowl, and a rose garden. It's perhaps best known among gardeners for its sweetpeas, and they have a Rose and Sweetpea Festival the last wknd in Jun. Meals, snacks, shop, disabled access; cl Nov–Easter; (01284) 830464; *£3. They do B & B.

HELMINGHAM HALL GARDENS TM1857 (B1077)

Beautiful gardens pretty much as they were in Tudor times. The grand battlemented house they stand around (not open) is ringed by a moat, over which the drawbridge is still raised each night. Extensive deer park with hundreds of red and fallow deer, as well as Highland cattle and Soay sheep, and magnificent old oak trees. Constable painted several views of the woodlands. Teas, shop (inc Helmingham produce), disabled access; open pm Sun May–early Sept; (01473) 890363; £3.50. The Dobermann at Framsden has good food.

HERRINGFLEET WINDMILL TM4797 Carefully restored, a pretty sight above the river (but rarely open).

HOLTON WINDMILL TM4077 Carefully restored and picturesque (though rarely open for visits).

HORHAM TM2172 The churchyard here has for generations been conserved as natural grassland around its older graves, just scythed for hay in the first week of July; so from spring onwards it's a mass of wild flowers, with plenty of butterflies (and beehives). The Ivy House, in the quiet village of Stradbroke, does good-value lunches.

★ **HORRINGER** TL8261 A serenely attractive village with well spaced, colour-washed buildings. On Suns Mar–Dec you'll usually find various crafts in the Community Centre. **Ickworth** Very untypical stately home, an oval rotunda 30 metres (100ft) high, with 2 curved corridors filled with a fascinating art collection (pictures by Gainsborough among others), and an exceptional array of Georgian silver. The grounds have a deer enclosure, adventure playground and a new family cycle route. Meals, snacks, shop, disabled access (there's a stair-lift); house open 21 Mar–1 Nov, pm daily exc Mon (though open bank hols) and Thurs; garden cl winter wknds; park open all yr; (01284) 735270; £5.20, park and gardens only £2; NT.

IPSWICH TM1644 From the 13th c it flourished as a port sending cloth to the continent; the port is still quite active. Too busy now to consider as a place to stay in, the town has quite a lot to encourage briefer visits (though traffic schemes make getting in and out by car rather slow). Cardinal Wolsey set up a college here, but all that remains is the 16th-c gatehouse in College St. The Ancient House in the Butter Market (now a bookshop) has some 15th-c carvings and exceptionally neat pargeting (decoratively patterned external plasterwork). Dotted about the town are several attractive **medieval churches**, especially the 15th-c St Margaret's (Constable Rd); St Mary at the Elms (Belstead Rd) has the town's oldest cottages behind it. If you're there on a winter's night, 5 medieval churches are nicely floodlit. In the central pedestrian area, the Great White Horse, a former coaching inn, is useful for snacks; the County (opposite County Hall), Old Rep (Tower St) and the Greyhound (Henley Rd) have decent food. **Christchurch Mansion** (Soane St) Perhaps the town's highlight; the original 16th-c house was altered in the following century after a fire, but since then it's escaped any further redevelopment. The rooms are furnished in period style, with a Victorian wing inc servants' quarters, and the Suffolk Artists' Gallery has the best collection of works by Constable and Gainsborough outside London. Shop, disabled access to ground floor only; cl am Sun, Mon (exc most bank hols), 24–26 Dec, 1 Jan, Good Fri; (01473) 253246; free. Another gallery is next door, and the surrounding park has play areas and a bird reserve. **Ipswich Museum** (High St) The natural history section has been painstakingly restored to how it was in its Victorian heyday, and includes the first gorillas brought to Europe in the mid-19th c. Other parts have quite an emphasis on Roman Suffolk. Shop, disabled access to ground floor only; cl Sun, Mon, 24–26 Dec, 1 Jan, Good Fri; (01473) 213761; free. **Tolly Cobbold Brewery** (Cliff Rd) Striking waterside Victorian brewery, with tours. Some particularly interesting old equipment, inc a Victorian steam engine, and tastings in the Brewery Tap (which functions as a separate pub). Shop; tours daily May–Sept at noon, best to check winter times; (01473) 231723;

£3.75 (inc drink). **Peter's Ice Cream Factory** (Grimwade St) A small museum and tours of the factory, and, of course, a café where you can sample the finished product. Tours Mon–Fri, 10am, 12pm, 2pm and 4pm, but best to ring; (01473) 253265; £3.50. **Ipswich Transport Museum** (Lupin Rd) In an old trolley-bus depot, a developing collection of around 100 ancient commercial vehicles built or used here, from fire engines to buses and milk floats. Snacks, shop, disabled access; open Sun and bank hols Easter–Oct, and maybe pm wkdys school hols; (01473) 715666; £2.25.

KEDINGTON CHURCH TL7046 Attractive, with Saxon crucifix.

★ **KERSEY** TM0044 A very pretty one-street village, full of timbering and attractive and colourful plasterwork – though one or two buildings look ready for some attention. It runs from the fine 14th-c church down to a ford with ducks, and up the other side; several craft and antique shops.

KESSINGLAND TM5286 **Suffolk Wildlife Park** (A12) Quite an emphasis on African wildlife at this 100-acre park; some animals are the only examples of their type in the country, inc the wonderfully strange bonteboks (like a cross between a horse and a goat with a bit of cow thrown in). Lots for families in summer, with a bouncy castle beside the play areas, animal demonstrations, birds of prey (usually only Tues and Weds), crazy golf, and games and activities in the summer hols. Feeding times spread through the day (meerkats and otters at 11.30am, lions and cheetahs at 3.15pm, snake-handling at 4pm). The same people run Banham Zoo in Norfolk. Meals, snacks, shop, disabled access; cl 25–26 Dec; (01502) 740291; £5.95. Kessingland's beach is good, though busy in summer, and it's only 3 or 4 miles to Lowestoft.

KNETTISHALL HEATH TL9480 Country park with pleasant strolls – if you're overflowing with energy (and several days' supplies), you may even be tempted northwards on the Peddars Way, waymarked from here all the way to Norfolk's north coast.

LAKENHEATH CHURCH TL7182 Elegant and charming, though now a bit hidden away in the sprawl edging the nearby huge air base.

★ **LAVENHAM** TL9149 One of the finest surviving examples of a small medieval town, this lovely little place has delightfully rickety-looking 14th- and 15th-c timbered buildings wherever you look; many now house teashops, banks or antique shops. **Guildhall** (Market Pl) Picturesque, 16th-c timbered building, at various stages in its career a town hall, prison, workhouse and wool store; its beamed and oak-filled interior has interesting local history displays. Snacks, shop; cl Good Fri, and all Nov–Mar; (01787) 247646; £2.80; NT. **Little Hall** (Market Pl) Delightful 15th-c house, attractively repainted, showcasing the Gayer-Anderson collection of books, pictures and antiques, with a pleasant enclosed garden. Open pm Weds, Thurs, Sat, Sun and bank hols Easter–Oct; (01787) 247179; £1.50. There's a good small commercial art gallery nearby. The old wool hall has been incorporated into the Swan Hotel, itself well worth seeing. Both it (at a price) and the Angel are enjoyable for lunch. The A1141 through Monks Eleigh and then the B1115 through Chelsworth to Hitcham is a pretty drive.

LAXFIELD CHURCH TM2972 Well worth a visit, in tucked-away, quiet surroundings; nearby is a charmingly preserved very old-fashioned pub, and a small museum.

LEISTON TM4462 **Long Shop Museum** (Main St) Big industrial museum in the preserved buildings of Garrett Engineering Co, with steam engines, steam rollers, traction engines, and memorabilia from the nearby World War II air base. Shop, disabled access; cl Nov–Mar; (01728) 832189; £2.50. The Engineers Arms opposite has so much memorabilia it seems almost an extension. The sizeable shopping town has the fragmentary remains of a 14th-c abbey off the B1122, just N.

LETHERINGHAM WATERMILL TM2858 Pretty, and surrounded by nice gardens; maybe open in summer.

★ **LEVINGTON** TM2338 A pleasant spot, with ancient almshouses, a marina below, and the Ship, a good pub (no children) with estuary views.

✝ **LINDSEY** TL9744 **St James's Chapel** Charming, little, thatched, flint and stone chapel, 13th c but inc earlier work too. The White Rose does good food.

LITTLE BLAKENHAM TM1048 **Blakenham Woodland Garden** Woodland garden richly planted with camellias, rhododendrons, magnolias and the like; lovely in May when the bluebells are out. Lots of rare trees and shrubs. Open pm Sun–Fri Mar–Jun; *£1. The Sorrel Horse at Barham has decent food and pleasant walks nearby.

★ ✝ **LONG MELFORD** TL8645 A very nice old place to stroll around: the fine green and exceptionally long main street (Hall St) are lined with buildings from varied eras, many with lovely timbering, and around 20 of them are now antique shops (not cheap, but interesting). The **church** of Holy Trinity is glorious, with ornate carvings and dozens of spectacular windows; especially attractive when floodlit at night. The Bull Hotel, one of the finer old buildings here, does good light lunches, as does the comfortable Black Lion Hotel; the Crown and Hare are also useful for food. *See separate Family Panel on p.591* for **Kentwell Hall**. **Melford Hall** Turreted Tudor house mostly unchanged since the reign of Elizabeth I, when hundreds of servants and courtiers stayed here in 1578; it still has the original panelled banqueting hall. Fine collection of Chinese porcelain; the gardens have a Tudor pavilion. Some disabled access; open pm wknds and bank hols Apr–Oct, plus pm Weds and Thurs May–Sept; (01787) 880286; £4; NT.

✝ **LOWESTOFT** TM5492 Britain's most easterly town and the area's main fishing port, so the harbour always has lots to see. It's developed as a resort thanks to its beaches (South Beach has the best bathing water) and proximity to the Broads. Cobbled streets of old buildings survive in the part known as The Scores, and the early medieval **church** is imposing and attractive. In the High St, the Bayfields Hotel and Volunteer are useful for lunch, as is the seafront Jolly Sailors (Pakefield St). There are regular summer sea **boat trips**, (01502) 523337 for details. The tourist information office on the Esplanade is housed in a rather grand old Pavilion, along with good local history displays and **Discoverig**, a children's play area themed as a North Sea rig; adults free, children £2.20 per hour. **Lydia Eva steam drifter** (Harbour) Last surviving herring drifter, with an exhibition on life aboard. Usually open July–mid-Oct (moored in Great Yarmouth Apr–Jun, when maybe a sidewinder diesel trawler is here instead); free. **Lowestoft Maritime Museum** (Whapload Rd) Housed under the lighthouse; cl Oct–May; 50p. There's a small **Royal Naval Museum** nearby (cl 1–2pm, am Sun, all Sat, mid-Oct–mid-Apr; free). **Pleasurewood Hills Theme Park** (Corton Rd) Lots of rides and family attractions; trains and chairlifts speed up travel round the grounds. Meals, snacks, shop, disabled access; open daily Easter, mid-May–Sept, and wknds Apr–Oct; (01502) 508200; £10.95.

MICKFIELD WATERGARDEN CENTRE TM1461 2 acres of ornamental watergardens and working nursery, with displays of marine and freshwater fish. Wknd teas in summer, garden centre, disabled access; cl 25 Dec; (01449) 711336; free.

✝ **MILDENHALL CHURCH** TL7074 Elegance and style – a beautifully harmonious building.

MONKS ELEIGH TL9747 **Corn Craft** (A1141) Traditional corn dollies and their production (demonstrations by appointment). In Aug and Sept you can walk through the fields and pick the flowers. Snacks, big shop, disabled access; cl 25–26 Dec, 1 Jan; (01449) 740456; free. The Swan Hotel is handy.

✝ ★ **NAYLAND** TL9734 Well rewards a stroll – its fine **church** has an altar painting by Constable; the old White Hart is now a smart pub-restaurant. Constable also painted an altarpiece for nearby Brantham church TM1034.

✝ **NEEDHAM MARKET CHURCH** TM0854 The marvellous

hammerbeam roof has been described as 'a whole church seemingly in the air'.

! NEWMARKET TL6463 The centre of horseracing since James I used to slope off here from 1605, and in the early morning people driving through are quite likely to have to give way to a string of racehorses. The Rutland Arms (across the road from the Jockey Club) and Bedford Lodge Hotel are useful for lunch. **National Horseracing Museum** (High St) The stories and scandals of the sport's development through the centuries, with trophies, videos of classic races, a display on the history of betting, and racing relics from saddles to skeletons. You don't have to be interested in racing to get something out of it. Meals, snacks, shop, disabled access; cl Mon (exc bank hols and July–Aug), and Nov–Feb; (01638) 667333; £3.50. They also organise informative tours of the local breeding and racing scene, with a look at horses at work on the gallops, and visits to a training yard, stud and the handsome Georgian Jockey Club itself; booking essential on (01638) 560622; prices start at £20. **National Stud** (A1304 W) Tours of this Mecca of horse breeding by arrangement (01638) 663464, at 11.15am and 2.30pm wkdys, 11.15am Sat, and 2.30pm Sun, cl Sept–Feb (exc race days); £3.80. The King's Head at Dullingham is a good nearby lunch spot.

ORFORD TM4249 When Henry II commissioned the **castle** here it was right on the shore, but since then the river has silted so much that it's now slightly inland. It has an amazing 18-sided keep rising to 27 metres (90ft), supported by 3 extra towers. Good views from the top (as usual, up a spiral staircase). Shop; cl winter lunchtimes, 24–26 Dec, 1 Jan; (01394) 450472; £2.30. **Dunwich Underwater Exploration Exhibition** (Craft Shop, Front St) The process of coastal erosion well illustrated; cl 25–26 Dec; 50p. The **church** has the ruined chancel arches of a Norman predecessor in the graveyard. There's a long lane down to the shore with its quay and old smugglers' inn, the Jolly Sailor. **Orford Ness** After years of belonging to the Ministry of Defence (who barred access to anyone who wasn't in uniform), this magnificently desolate shingle spit just opposite Orford quay is now owned by the NT and open to the public, though it's more for serious wildlife fans than day-trippers. Ferries leave the quay every 20 mins from 10am till 12.20pm Thurs–Sat Easter–Oct – you can book if you want; (01394) 450057; £5. **Havergate Island** (TM4147) Birdwatchers can arrange whole day trips to this marshy RSPB reserve by writing to the warden, Mr Partridge, at 30 Mundays Lane, Orford, Woodbridge IP12 2LX (with SAE); permits every Thurs and alternate wknds Apr–Aug, then in winter just the 1st Sat of the month; £5 inc boat trip from Orford quay. The road through Iken Heath to Snape is a pleasant drive through quiet pinewoods.

PAKENHAM WINDMILL TL9267 Pretty and carefully restored; open for visits at least summer Suns.

★ **PIN MILL** TM2037 A nice spot much favoured by artists, below the wooded slopes by the River Orwell, with Thames barges on tidal moorings; the Butt & Oyster is attractively placed for a bite to eat.

RIVER BLYTH TM4974 Broad river winding close to the coast nr Southwold, with delightful waterside paths, and marshy and heathy expanses to explore around Walberswick at its mouth (where the waterside scenery has drawn generations of artists).

RIVER DEBEN TM3041 Walks by another river winding along the coast, with bird-haunted sandbanks; best reached from roads off the B1083 S of Shottisham, or the Maybush at Waldringfield.

ROUGHAM GREEN TL9261 **Netherfield Cottage** (Nether St, towards Hessett) Proof that you don't have to have a massive garden to make it very special indeed: hundreds of different herbs, beautifully yet sensibly grouped by how you'd use them, with 2 small knot gardens. Best May–Oct, but a peaceful haven at any time. The cheery owner is happy to chat. Cl Nov–Mar; (01359) 270452; free, guided tours by appointment. The Gardeners Arms over at Tostock is an appropriate place for lunch.

★ ✝ ✿ **SAXMUNDHAM** TM3863
This attractive bypassed village has yet another fine **church**. The Poacher's Pocket, at Carlton just N, has decent food, and nearby Yoxford has a couple of good craft workshops.

SAXTEAD GREEN POST MILL
TM2564 (A1120) Traditional Suffolk windmill dating from 1854, meticulously brought back into perfect working order, but it's a steep climb up the stairs. New audio tour; cl 1–2pm, Sun, and all Nov–Mar; (01728) 685789; £1.75. Attractive surroundings; the Old Mill House over the green has good home-made food.

SHOTLEY GATE TM2434
At the meeting of the Stour and Orwell estuaries, the hub of a rewarding walk with good views across to Harwich and its shipping. Start inland at Shotley and cross the fields either N to the Orwell or S to the Stour, then follow the waterside.

! **SIZEWELL** TM4763
Sizewell Visitor Centre (B1353) Interactive displays and exhibitions on energy and nuclear power, with tours of both the Sizewell A and B power stations (booking essential); cl 25–26 Dec, 1 Jan; (01728) 642139; free. The aptly named Vulcan Arms opposite has good-value food. **Sizewell Beach** Generally virtually deserted out of season, and pleasurable walking ground despite the nuclear power plant in the distance. Agate and other semi-precious stones are common among the pebbles, sometimes even amber after stormy east winds; heathland, an old railway track walk and The Meare (Thorpeness's lake) justify detours inland. **Thorpeness** TM4759 At the S end of Sizewell beach, this curious place was built as a holiday village in a deliberately fanciful olde-worlde style, with quite a few attractive mock-Tudor houses (one even masking a watertower); it has a sizeable artificial but now thoroughly natural-looking picturesque lake, and the **windmill** here was brought over from Aldringham.

★ **SNAPE MALTINGS**
TM3957 The converted 19th-c **maltings** are home of the Aldeburgh Music Festival begun by Benjamin Britten, with other concerts throughout the year. The centre is pleasant to wander around, with unusual shops and galleries, and 1-hour summer **boat trips** down the River Alde. The Plough & Sail just outside is good for lunch; up in the village, the Crown (with a bar re-created in *Peter Grimes*) and Golden Key are both decent places, too.

SOMERLEYTON HALL
TM4997 (B1074) Interesting Jacobean house rebuilt in the Anglo-Italian style in 1840, still very much lived in, with period furnishings and paintings. The lovely gardens have a maze and miniature railway, and live music on bank hol afternoons. Snacks, shop, disabled access; open pm Sun, Thurs and bank hols Easter–Sept, plus Tues and Weds in July and Aug; (01502) 730244; £4.50. The Plough at Blundeston, home of Barkis the carrier in *David Copperfield*, is useful for lunch. N of here, with access from the Hall, is wooded **Fritton Lake**, which attracts numerous wildfowl, particularly in autumn and winter. **Country World** (Church Lane, Fritton) Good for families, with woodland walks, a children's farm, fishing, heavy horse stables, miniature railway, birds of prey (displays at 11.45am and 3.30pm, not Fri), golf, rowing, boat trips and plenty of space for pottering. Snacks, shop, disabled access; cl Oct–Mar; (01493) 488208; £5.

SOUTH ELMHAM TM3385
Medieval St Peter's Hall has in its outhouses the more modern **St Peter's Brewery**, whose excellent bitters, porters and fruit beers are made with water from their own source. Tours take in the whole brewing process, as well as parts of the Hall; a visitor centre is planned for one of the thatched barns. Shop, some disabled access; open Fri–Sun, ring for tour times; (01986) 782322; free entry, *£5 tour.

★ ✝ **SOUTHWOLD** TM5076
Once an important fishing port, now a quite enchanting and civilised little resort with a distinctive lighthouse as its main landmark, an attractive unspoilt green by the sea, and no end of decent

pubs and inns supplied by the local Adnams brewery (their wholesale wine shop has interesting stock). For food, the Crown is outstanding, and though more straightforward the King's Head is good, as is the smart Swan Hotel; the Sole Bay and Lord Nelson have the most atmosphere. The Denes is the best beach. Southwold Jack on the tower of the interesting **church** is worth a look; he's an automaton that rings the bell for services. There are 2 decent museums: the town collections, housed in a 17th-c Dutch gabled cottage on Bartholomew Green (open pm Easter–Sept; free), and a **lifeboat museum** on Gun Hill (open pm daily Jun–Sept; free). Across the golf course or along the breezy sea wall is the harbour, a tidal inlet, with its cheerful mix of beached fishing boats, multitudes of sailing boats, and tall black fishing shacks; the Harbour Inn here is full of character. There's a footbridge over to **Walberswick** – a pleasantly decorous seaside village, popular with artists ever since Wilson Steer's days there in the 1890s. The Bell here is a striking old inn, and the 15th-c church, parts now destroyed and other bits looking shaky, is attractive. (The drive round by car between Southwold and Walberswick is several miles.)

STANTON TL9671
Wyken Hall Gardens Formal herb, knot and woodland gardens, a walled old-fashioned rose garden, copper beech maze, and woodland walk to a 7-acre vineyard. A very nice unspoilt estate, just right for exploring. Meals and snacks in medieval barn, unusual country shop, disabled access; open Thurs, Fri, Sun and bank hols, and some evenings by appointment, cl 25 Dec–5 Feb; (01359) 250240; *£2.50. The Six Bells at Bardwell has good fresh food.

STOKE-BY-NAYLAND TL9836
The lovely 15th-c **church** has a tower familiar from several Constable paintings, and a few handsome Tudor buildings among more ordinary ones; the Angel is excellent for lunch, but get there early.

STONHAM ASPAL
TM1459 Around 30 small businesses based at **Stonham Barns** on the A1120, inc various craft workshops, a bonsai shop, and garden centre. A new **nature centre** has pony rides, pond-dipping, ostriches, lots of goats, rabbits, chickens and guinea pigs; details as British Birds of Prey Centre below. Also here is a **British Birds of Prey and Conservation Centre** which has flying displays Apr–Oct, and every species of British owl; (01449) 711425; cl 25 Dec; £4.50 (inc nature centre).

STOUR ESTUARY WALKS
TM1534 Stutton gives access to a fine stretch of the broad Stour estuary; on its N side, Alton Water is a reservoir recreation area, with a bird reserve. The King's Head (B1080) has good-value food.

STOWMARKET TM0458
Museum of East Anglian Life
(Iliffe Way) Excellent 70-acre open-air museum. Children look at the reconstructed buildings with a genuine sense of astonishment: did people really live like that? Even the room settings from the 1950s seem prehistoric to fresher eyes. The main buildings (which include a watermill, chapel, smithy and wind pump) are quite spread out, so there's a fair bit of walking involved, inc a nice stroll down by the river. There are also a few animals inc Remus the Suffolk punch horse and his friend Blackberry the Shetland pony, and an adventure playground. Often wood-turning or basket-making on Sun. Snacks, shop, disabled access; cl Nov–Mar; (01449) 612229; £3.85. The King's Arms and the Railway at Haughley both have good-value food.

★ **SUDBURY** TL8741
Gainsborough's House
(Gainsborough St) The painter was born here in 1727, and the house has an excellent collection of his work; unexpected finds include his efforts at sculpture. Plenty of period furniture and china too, and contemporary arts and crafts. Shop, disabled access to ground floor only; cl am Sun, all Mon (exc pm bank hols), Christmas wk, Good Fri; (01787) 372958; £2.80. This market town is pleasant, with useful market stalls on Sat; the Waggon & Horses (Acton Sq) has good plain food.

SUTTON HOO TM2849 One of the most famous archaeological sites in the country, where in 1939 the discovery of an Anglo-Saxon ship burial made historians completely reinterpret the Dark Ages. Most of the finds from here are in the British Museum, but you can see the burial mounds, and an exhibition explains the site's importance. At the moment, tours are at 2pm and 3pm wknds and bank hols, Easter–Oct; £2 (arrive in good time, there is a 20-minute walk from the car park to the site). The NT, who took over the site in 1997, have embarked on a £3.6 million Lottery-supported upgrade, which by 2001 should include a new visitor and study centre with a reconstruction of the ship itself. A turn off the B1083 S takes you to the Ramsholt Arms, at Ramsholt, for lunch among waterside pinewoods, with quiet walks along the Deben estuary.

TANGHAM NATURE TRAIL TM3548 A short walk among the plantations off the B1084 towards Woodbridge, specially designed for disabled people; there are also longer walks through the pinewoods here, where red squirrels often show themselves.

THELNETHAM WINDMILL TM0078 Carefully restored and attractive; open for visits at least summer Suns.

† **WENHASTON CHURCH** TM4275 Attractive building, with a 15th-c wall painting (in excellent condition) full of lovely devils; it's a nice peaceful village, too.

WEST STOW COUNTRY PARK TL7971 Attractive, with 125 acres of heath and woodlands bordered by the River Lark. Over 120 different species of bird have been sighted here, and 25 species of animal; the visitor centre often has art exhibitions. The most interesting feature is the reconstructed **Anglo-Saxon Village**, its buildings erected using the same methods and tools as in the 5th c. They plan to open a new visitor centre Easter 1999 to house the original, genuinely Anglo-Saxon finds. Occasional costumed days, and special events such as their Easter Sun market. Snacks, shop; cl 25–26 Dec; (01284) 728718; park free, village £3.20, inc very good Walkman guide. The Red Lion at Icklingham has excellent food.

★ **WESTLETON** TM4369 A pleasant village with an attractive green. The White Horse has good-value food, and just past it **Fisks Clematis Nursery** has many varieties of clematis on show and for sale; cl winter wknds. **Minsmere Reserve** (TM4667) Big RSPB reserve with lots of different species among the heath, woods, marshes and lagoons – good observation hides, and enjoyable walks at any time of year. Meals, snacks, shop, disabled access; cl Tues, and 25–26 Dec; (01728) 648281; £4 for non-RSPB members. The reserve is skirted by public paths, and one hide is free for public use, but you need a permit to enter the rest of the reserve. Approach points are Dunwich and Eastbridge. Outside the reserve, much of the flat formerly heathy land nr the coast is now covered with pine plantations: also pleasant for undisturbed walks, with the chance of seeing red squirrels, and in

Days Out

Stour Valley gems: Clare, Cavendish and Long Melford villages; lunch at the Bull, Long Melford; Gainsborough's House, Sudbury; Stoke-by-Nayland and Nayland churches; Kersey and Lavenham villages.

Sole Bay: Southwold (walk along the shore and river, and across to Walberswick if there's time); lunch at the Crown or King's Head, Southwold; Blythburgh church; the wildlife park at Kessingland.

Anglo-Saxon chronicle: Bury St Edmunds; lunch at the Beehive, Horringer or Red Lion, Icklingham; Ickworth at Horringer, or West Stow Country Park and Anglo-Saxon Village.

summer with that lovely, fresh, foreign, pinewood smell.

WINGFIELD COLLEGE TM2276 Quite a surprise to find a splendid, medieval, timber-framed building behind the Georgian façade. One of its 18th-c owners constructed the Palladian exterior to make his home more fashionable, using false ceilings, floors and windows so skilfully that for 200 years the house's earlier parts were forgotten. Striking Great Hall, and topiary and kitchen gardens. Snacks; open pm wknds and bank hols Easter–Sept; (01379) 384888; £2.80. They also organise Wingfield Arts, a varied programme of events in churches, halls and other everyday buildings all over the region; phone for programme. The De La Pole Arms has good food.

★ **WOODBRIDGE** TM2749 Quietly attractive and rather dignified market town, with many fine buildings and interesting book and antique shops, and a **church** of great style and interest. **Woodbridge Museum** (Market Hill) Looks at the ship burial at nearby Sutton Hoo, as well as the recent Anglo-Saxon finds at Burrow Hill. Cl am Sun, all Mon (exc bank hols), Tues and Weds, and all Nov–Easter; (01394) 380502; 60p (inc free activity sheets for children). **Woodbridge Tide Mill** Restored 18th-c mill on a busy quayside, its wheel usually working when tides allow. Shop, disabled access to ground floor only; open Easter, then daily May–Sept and wknds in Oct; £1. **Buttrums Mill** (Burkitt Rd) 6-storey tower mill, now fully restored, with displays of its history; open pm wknds and bank hols May–Oct; £1. The Wilford Bridge Hotel, at nearby Melton, is a good lunch stop – and well placed for river walks. The Cherry Tree and Seckford Hall Hotel (both off the A12 N) do nice lunches, and in the town the Seckford Arms (Seckford St) is worthwhile. The B1079 and then the B1077 up to Eye is a pleasant drive on an old coach road.

WOOLPIT TL9762 The **church** here has a hammerbeam roof, and a translation of the village tale that in the 1100s 2 slightly strange-looking, green-skinned children were found by a pit that was suddenly blasted in the earth one night; the boy soon died, but the girl lived, and grew up to marry a local lad and have children. She never said more about her origins than that she'd come from a land far far away. More on this at the small but interesting **district museum** (The Institute), which has annually changing local history displays. Shop, disabled access; open pm wknds and bank hols Easter–Sept; donations. The drive to Buxhall is pretty.

WRENTHAM TM4982 **Wrentham Basketware** (London Rd) They make and sell traditional willow baskets and hampers, with up to 320 styles. Cl pm Sun, 25 Dec; (01502) 675628; free.

★ **Other attractive villages,** all with decent pubs, include Bildeston TL9949, Blaxhall TM3657, Blyford TM4277, Boxford TL9640, Chelsworth TL9848, Dalham TL7261, Eastbridge TM4566, Fressingfield TM2677, Haughley TM0262 (its Jacobean manor house in lovely grounds), Hoxne TM1777, Huntingfield TM3374, Ixworth TL9370, Middleton TM4367, Polstead TL9938, Risby TL8066 (with a decent antique centre), and Shimpling Street TL8752.

Where to eat

ALDEBURGH TM4656 **Regatta** *171–173 High St (01728) 452011* Bustling seaside restaurant decorated with pennants and seaside murals, and specialising in fresh local seafood – though they also offer interesting meat dishes and fine puddings; a relaxed atmosphere, friendly service, and a no smoking area; disabled access. **£25**|£5.

BARDWELL TL9473 **Six Bells** *(01359) 250820* Quietly placed, 16th-c pub with heavy beams and timbering, attractive decorations, a snug dining room and a bigger restaurant with conservatory; wide range of interesting food, polite service, real ales, and good wines; seats out in front and on the back lawn; bdrms; cl 25–26 Dec. **£17.50**|£5.

BRAMFIELD TM3973 **Queens Head** *(01986) 784214* Popular pub with a pleasantly relaxed, high-raftered lounge bar, log fire in the impressive fireplace, no smoking side bar, and a family room; wide choice of very good interesting food (super puddings), well kept real ales, decent wines, and maybe home-made elderflower cordial; cl 26 Dec. **£20.50**|£6.95.

BURY ST EDMUNDS TL8564 **Mortimers Seafood Restaurant** *31 Churchgate St (01284) 760623* Airy restaurant with artist Thomas Mortimer's sea pictures on the walls; lots of good fish dishes inc daily specials, and interesting wines from their shop next door; cl am Sat, Sun, 2 wks Aug, 2 wks Christmas, bank hols; disabled access. **£22**|£6.95.

CAVENDISH TL8046 **Bull** *(01787) 280245* Cheerful pub hiding an attractive, 16th-c, beamed interior behind a Victorian frontage, with big standing timbers and fireplaces in the open-plan rooms, and a thriving atmosphere; big range of enjoyable, good food (fresh fish is delivered daily), well kept real ales, and a decent choice of wines by the glass. **£19.50**|£6.

CHILLESFORD TM3852 **Froize** *(01394) 450282* Heavy beams and lots of interesting things to look at in the big, comfortable, open-plan dining bar and no smoking restaurant; very generous helpings of excellent food, an especially wide choice of particularly good fresh fish, super schoolboy puddings, a fine choice of real ales and a decent range of wines by the glass; courteous service and hard-working owners; also, seats in the garden; bdrms; cl Mon (exc bank hols), 3 wks end Feb/beginning Mar; disabled access. **£25.50**|£6.50.

COTTON TM0667 **Trowel & Hammer** *Mill Rd (01449) 781234* Big, friendly, partly thatched and partly tiled white pub; with a sprawling lounge, lots of dark beamery and timber baulks, a big log fire, good and interesting food; a large pretty back garden with swimming pool; cl 25 Dec; no small children in Cotton Club restaurant; disabled access. **£17**|£5.

DUNWICH TM4770 **Flora Tearooms** *(01728) 648433* Extended, former fisherman's hut right on the beach, with great views of the sea and fishing boats; famous for very good fish and chips, but also other snacks, teas and home-made cakes; cl Dec–Feb; disabled access. £4.85.

DUNWICH TM4770 **Ship** *(01728) 648219* Delightful old pub by the sea, with a good bustling atmosphere, and friendly, helpful staff who cope cheerfully with the crowds; wonderfully fresh fish off the boats on the beach, a traditionally furnished bar, conservatory, sunny back terrace, and a well kept garden; the RSPB reserve at Minsmere is close by; bdrms; cl 25 Dec; disabled access. **£16.35**|£5.

ERWARTON TM2134 **Queens Head** *(01473) 787550* Remote and unspoilt little pub with lovely views, a welcoming, unpretentious atmosphere, and a cosy coal fire in the beamed bar; good, well priced bar food inc fresh fish and game in season, a decent-value Sun lunch, well kept real ales, and friendly service; cl 25 Dec; children in restaurant only; disabled access. **£16.50**|£3.75.

FRAMSDEN TM1959 **Dobermann** *(01473) 890461* Charmingly restored thatched pub with a twin-facing fireplace separating the friendly, spotlessly kept bars; good, popular food, and a decent choice of beers and spirits; disabled access; no children. **£19.20**|£7.75.

FRESSINGFIELD TM2677 **Fox & Goose** *(01379) 586247* Early 16th-c timbered inn by the churchyard and duckpond; with a wide choice of upmarket food, and fine wines; new licensees; cl 25–26 Dec. **£30**|£5.50.

HARTEST TL8352 **Crown** *(01284) 830250* Comfortably modernised and brightly lit pink-washed pub by the village green and church (bell-ringing practice pm Thurs), lots of space in the 2 no smoking dining areas and a large conservatory restaurant; reliably good, reasonably priced food inc take-away fish and chips and really good-value Mon, Weds and Fri 2-course lunches, quick and friendly black-tie staff, a chatty local atmosphere, and well kept real ales; also, a big back lawn and side courtyard; disabled access. **£13**|£6.50.

HORRINGER TL8261 **Beehive** *The Street (01284) 735260* Particularly well run and pretty ivy-covered pub with extremely helpful service, a friendly atmosphere, attractively furnished little rambling rooms, and a woodburner; excellent imaginative food with lots of daily specials and a pudding board, well kept real ales and decent wines; disabled access. **£21**|£5.95.

HOXNE TM1877 **Swan** *(01379) 668275* Carefully restored, late 15th-c building with heavy oak floors, fine fireplaces, and lots of atmosphere; good bar food, well kept beer, decent wines, and a tranquil back garden. **£20.50**|£7.

ICKLINGHAM TL7772 **Red Lion** *(01638) 717802* Civilised and rather smart thatched pub with a nice mix of wooden chairs, candlelit tables, fresh flowers, fishing rods and various stuffed animals, an inglenook fireplace and heavy beams; very good food, well kept real ales and country wines; disabled access. **£20**|£4.95.

IPSWICH TM1644 **Mortimers on the Quay** *Wherry Quay (01473) 230225* This is the place to come for really fresh, daily changing fish, simply cooked; a thoughtful French wine list and a relaxed atmosphere; cl am Sat, Sun, 24 Dec–6 Jan. **£20**|£4.35.

IXWORTH TL9370 **Theobalds** *68 High St (01359) 231707* Consistently good and imaginative food (inc a vegetarian choice) in this 17th-c restaurant with log fires, beams and standing timbers in the cosy rooms; very good wine list, and kind service; cl am Sat, pm Sun, Mon, 2 wks Aug; children in evening over 8 only. **£35**|£8.75.

LAVENHAM TL9149 **Great House** *Market Pl (01787) 247431* Restaurant with rooms in an ancient house behind a handsome Georgian façade; bare boards, antiques, open fires (inc an inglenook in the restaurant itself), very good French cooking plus lighter lunches, a super French cheeseboard, and mainly French wines; friendly staff, and an attractive flower-filled courtyard for outside eating; charming beamed bdrms; cl pm Sun, Mon, 3 wks Jan. **£24**|£6.50.

LIDGATE TL7257 **Star** *(01638) 500275* Quaint old place with an interesting small bar, big log fire, handsomely moulded heavy beams, polished oak and pine tables, and a chatty Spanish landlady; big helpings of hugely enjoyable food with Mediterranean hints, good wines and ales, a cosy simple dining room, and tables in front and in the little rustic back garden; cl pm Sun. **£24.50**|£5.50.

LONG MELFORD TL8645 **Chimneys** *Hall St (01787) 379806* Lovely beamed 16th-c building, with very good and carefully prepared, interesting food and a thoughtful wine list; paintings for sale; cl pm Sun; disabled access. **£30**.

NAYLAND TL9734 **White Hart** *(01206) 263382* Smart 15th-c pub/restaurant with an 18th-c coaching frontage, polished tables on wooden floors, comfortable sofa by the log fire, and a glass-floored section over the wine cellar; good, well presented cooking, a wide choice of wines, real ales in straight glasses, and a relaxed atmosphere; popular with businessmen and retired folk; cl 26 Dec, 1 Jan; disabled access. **£21**|£5.10.

NEEDHAM MARKET TM0855 **Bonds** *Bridge St (01449) 720265* Excellent fish and chip shop with an enviable local reputation; can buy fresh fish here too; cl Sun, Mon. £2.25.

ORFORD TM4249 **Butley Orford Oysterage** *(01394) 450277* Simple restaurant with its own oyster beds, fishing boat and smoke house; very popular locally and with yachtsmen for its wonderfully fresh fish, decent wines, and brisk, friendly service; cl 25–26 Dec; disabled access. **£20**|£5.50.

RATTLESDEN TL9758 **Brewers Arms** *(01449) 736377* 16th-c pub with a pleasantly simple beamed lounge and a small lively public bar; very welcoming and friendly service, imaginative food, decent wines, well kept ales, and a magnificent old bread oven in the main eating area; children must be well behaved; disabled access. **£20**|£5.

REDE TL8055 **Plough** *The Green (01284) 789208* Welcoming, partly thatched cottage in a lovely spot, with particularly helpful owners; lots of well presented fresh fish and game in season, imaginative daily specials, a good evening restaurant, decent wine, and a lovely sheltered cottagey garden; disabled access. **£19.95**|£6.95.

SNAPE TM3958 **Crown** *(01728) 688324* Unspoilt smugglers' inn with a relaxed and friendly atmosphere, old brick floors, beams, a big brick inglenook and nice old furnishings; particularly good, interesting and well presented food served by smiling staff, pre- and post-concert suppers, a thoughtful wine list (12 by the glass inc champagne), well kept real ales, and tables in the pretty garden; bdrms; cl 25 Dec, pm 26 Dec; no children; partial disabled access. **£23.95**|£7.50.

SNAPE TM3957 **Plough & Sail** *The Maltings (01728) 688302* Part of the Snape Maltings centre; a relaxed and friendly series of attractively furnished rooms, busy little restaurant, delicious food, well kept real ales and a fine wine list; cl Sun, pm Mon Christmas–Easter; disabled access. **£18.50**|£7.50.

SUDBURY TL8640 **Red Onion Bistro** *57 Ballingdon St (01787) 376777* Bustling, friendly bistro serving good, fairly priced, honest food with dishes from all over the world (usually some French and English choices); helpful service, a select-your-own-wine room, and a sunny garden; cl Sun; disabled access. **£13.25 dinner, £11.50 lunch**|£5.

WINGFIELD TM2276 **De La Pole Arms** *(01379) 384545* Carefully converted village pub with interesting bric-à-brac, comfortable, traditional seats, and a pleasantly civilised feel; enjoyable bar food, well kept ales, and prompt, welcoming service. **£19.75**|£8.50.

Special thanks to C Patton, John Wooll, H M Tobias-Waite, Mrs Woodfield.

We welcome reports from readers

This *Guide* depends on readers' reports. Do help us if you can – in return, we offer a discount on the next edition to people who've helped us with reports for it. Tell us what you think about places already in it, and anything extra you think we should say about them. And send us your ideas for inclusion in the next edition: places to visit, eat at or stay in, attractive drives or walks, maybe even unusual interesting shops you know of. Use the card in the middle, the report forms at the end, or just write – no stamp needed: *The Good Guide to Britain*, FREEPOST TN1569, Wadhurst, E Sussex TN5 7BR.

Suffolk Calendar

Some of these dates were provisional as we went to press. Please check information with the telephone numbers provided.

MARCH

7 **Long Melford** Lambing Days at Kentwell Hall – *till 1 Apr* (01787) 310207
30 **Ipswich** Antiques Fair: about 300 stands at the Showground (01728) 723067

APRIL

2 **Long Melford** Easter Egg Hunt Quiz and Re-creation of Tudor Life at Easter at Kentwell Hall – *till Mon 5* (01787) 310207; **Needham Market** East Anglian Art and Crafts Exhibition and Sale: over 750 paintings – *till Mon 5* (01449) 722202
4 **West Stow** Saxon Living History: demonstrations and costumed Saxons at West Stow Anglo-Saxon Village – *till Mon 5* (01284) 728718
8 **Bury St Edmunds** Beer Festival – *till Sat 10* (01842) 860063
16 **Ipswich** Craft Fair at the Showground – *till Sun 18* (01728) 723067
17 **Clare** Landmark Trust Open Day at Ancient House: not open to the public at any other time of the year (01628) 825925
23 **Ipswich** Garden Show at the Showground – *till Sun 25* (01728) 723067
24 **Otley** Open Weekend at Otley College of Agriculture and Horticulture – *till Sun 25* (01473) 785543

MAY

1 **Long Melford** Tudor May Day Celebrations at Kentwell Hall – *till Mon 3* (01787) 310207
2 **Ipswich–Felixstowe** Historic Vehicle Run from Christchurch Park to Felixstowe Promenade (01473) 715666
3 **Ipswich** Woodbridge Horse Show at the Showground (01728) 723067; **Mendlesham** Street Fair (01449) 766563; **West Stow** Archaeology Day at West Stow Anglo-Saxon Village (01284) 728718
9 **Ingham** South Suffolk Agricultural Show at Ampton Park (01638) 750879
14 **Bury St Edmunds** Festival – *till Sun 30* (01284) 757099
15 **Hadleigh** Agricultural Show (01473) 827920
23 **West Stow** Park Week at West Stow Anglo-Saxon Village: nature trails and costumed craftspeople – *till Mon 31* (01284) 728718
29 **Felixstowe** Drama Festival – *till 5 Jun* (01394) 282126; **Long Melford** Re-creation of Tudor Life at Whitsuntide at Kentwell Hall – *till Mon 31* (01787) 310207; **Mildenhall** RAF Air Fête – *till Mon 31* (01638) 542995
30 **Bury St Edmunds** Flower Market (01284) 757094
31 **Framlingham** Gala (01728) 723857; **Woolpit** Street Fair (01359) 240297

JUNE

2 **Ipswich** Suffolk Show at Suffolk Showground – *till Thurs 3* (01473) 726847
5 **Bury St Edmunds** Carnival (01284) 701216; **Wetherden** Woolpit Steam Rally at Warren Farm (01473) 584349
11 **Ipswich** Fireworks Concert with the Royal Philharmonic at Christchurch Park – *till Sun 13* (01473) 464007; **Snape** Aldeburgh Festival of Music and Arts at the Maltings – *till Sun 27* (01728) 452935

Suffolk Calendar (Cont.)

12 **Long Melford** Country Fair at Melford Hall – *till Sun 13* (01787) 280941
13 **Euston** Country Fair and Old-time Rally at Euston Park and Church Flower Festival (01359) 269265
15 **Ipswich** Antiques Fair: about 300 stands at the Showground (01728) 723067
19 **Ipswich** Maritime Festival – *till Sun 20* (01473) 262052
20 **Bury St Edmunds** Open Gardens (01284) 754993; and Nowton Park Country Fair (01284) 757092; **Long Melford** Re-creation of Tudor Life at Kentwell Hall – *till 11 July* (01787) 310207
26 **Eye** 20 Open Gardens – *till Sun 27* (01379) 870703; **Ipswich** Flower Show at the Showground – *till Sun 27* (01473) 401733
27 **Chelsworth** Open Gardens Day (01449) 740438; **Lowestoft** Classic Vehicle Event (01502) 523004

JULY

9 **Lowestoft** East Point Musical Explosion: rock and folk festival – *till Sat 10* (01502) 523004
10 **Hadleigh** East Anglian Summer Music Festival – *till 1 Aug* (01473) 822596; **Woodbridge** Flower Show – *till Sun 11* (01394) 382180
11 **Nr Halesworth** Country Fair at Heveningham Hall (01986) 798151
16 **Bury St Edmunds** Open-air Concerts at Ickworth House (01625) 575681; **Weeting** Steam Engine Rally at Fengate Farm – *till Sun 18* (01842) 810317
17 **Framlingham** Horse Show at Castle Meadow (01473) 822790; **Lowestoft** Armada Special: family fun day, fireworks (01502) 523004
18 **Stowmarket** Carnival (01449) 676800
21 **Long Melford** Open-air Theatre and Concerts at Kentwell Hall – *till Sun 25* (01787) 310207
24 **Aldeburgh** Suffolk Craft Society Exhibition at Peter Pears Gallery – *till 30 Aug* (01379) 740711
25 **Cowlinge** Open Gardens Day: over 20 gardens (01440) 820204
29 **Lowestoft** Air Show – *till Fri 30* (01502) 523004
30 **Beccles** Regatta Carnival – *till 2 Aug* (01502) 712627

AUGUST

1 **Aldeburgh** Summer Theatre at Jubilee Hall – *till Mon 30* (01728) 454022; **Snape** Proms: folk, jazz, classical, opera and dance at the Maltings – *till Tues 31* (01728) 453543; **West Stow** Anglo-Saxon Festival at West Stow Anglo-Saxon Village: costumed Anglo-Saxons live in the village, with traders, crafts, storytellers and guided tours – *till Mon 30* (01284) 728718
2 **Lowestoft** Carnival Week – *till* carnival on *Sun 8* (01502) 523002
7 **Haverhill** Thurlow Steam Rally and Show – *till Sun 8* (01440) 783457; **Long Melford** Re-creation of Tudor Life at Lammastide at Kentwell Hall – *till Sun 8* (01787) 310207
14 **Ipswich** Carnival (01473) 743861; **Lowestoft** Flower Show – *till Sun 15* (01502) 523004
16 **Aldeburgh** Carnival (01394) 383422
27 **Assington, Boxford** and **Stoke-by-Nayland** Churches take part in the Suffolk Villages Festival – *till Mon 30* (01206) 767895; **Long Melford** Re-creation of Tudor Life in High Summer at Kentwell Hall – *till Mon 30* (01787) 310207

Suffolk Calendar (Cont.)

29 **Eye** Show – *till Mon 30* (01379) 870224; **Walsham le Willows** Gardens Weekend: about 25 gardens – *till Mon 30* (01359) 259450

30 **Oulton Broad** Gala Day (01502) 523004

SEPTEMBER

3 **Ipswich** Garden Show at the Showground – *till Sun 5* (01728) 723067

7 **Ipswich** Antiques Fair: about 300 stands at the Showground (01728) 723067

18 **Nr Blythburgh** Henham Steam Rally – *till Sun 19* (01502) 578523; **Long Melford** Re-creation of Tudor Life at Michaelmas at Kentwell Hall – *till Sun 19* (01787) 310207; **Lowestoft** Horse Trials at Somerleyton Hall – *till Sun 19* (01502) 730224

OCTOBER

1 **Ipswich** Craft Fair at the Showground – *till Sun 3* (01728) 723067

2 **Otley** Open Weekend at Otley College of Agriculture and Horticulture – *till Sun 3* (01473) 785543

Surrey

Enjoyable outings and surprisingly unspoilt scenery, with very good walking.

Surprisingly, Surrey is the most heavily wooded county in England – and includes some lovely villages, especially Shere, Outwood and Chiddingfold. Away from the urban corridors, much of the countryside is beautifully preserved, and quite hilly. The National Trust owns several thousand acres in the finest parts, and walkers have an excellent choice, with relatively free access.

Good family days out here are headed by Chessington World of Adventures and Thorpe Park. Birdworld near Farnham and the zoo at Charlwood are also very enjoyable family days out, the show farms west of Epsom and south of Godstone are very well set up for children, and the rural life centre at Tilford is a family treat.

Adults have some first-rate places to visit – including splendid little-known finds such as the network of tunnels under Reigate castle grounds, the Watts picture gallery at Compton and Hannah Peschar's sculpture garden at Ockley. Better known favourites are the NT properties at East and West Clandon (there's a good-value joint ticket), Denbies vineyard at Dorking, the gardens at Wisley, Brooklands (if you like motor racing), Polesden Lacey near Great Bookham, Claremont garden at Esher, Loseley House near Guildford, Winkworth arboretum at Hascombe and Painshill Park at Cobham. The Derby Day Experience in Epsom delights even people who aren't horseracing enthusiasts.

Where to stay

BAGSHOT SU9062 **Pennyhill Park** *Bagshot GU19 5ET (01276) 471774* **£211.131,** plus special breaks; 105 charming spacious rms. Impressive Victorian country house in 120 acres of well kept gardens and parkland; with friendly and courteous staff, comfortable 2-level lounge with panelling and beams, a little bar, tapestries and fine paintings, and very good, imaginative cooking; outdoor swimming pool, tennis, 9-hole golf course, stabling, game fishing and clay-pigeon shooting – they can arrange riding too; disabled access.

CHERTSEY TQ0466 **Crown** *7 London St, Chertsey KT16 8AP (01932) 564657* **£58w;** 30 comfortable modern rms. Bustling, friendly place with some original features and an open fire in the large bar; conservatory extension, good food, attractive restaurant, and a lovely big garden; disabled access.

CHOBHAM SU9760 **Knap Hill Manor** *Carthouse Lane, Chobham, Woking GU21 4XT (01276) 857962* **£65;** 3 spacious rms with garden views. Really welcoming and relaxing late 18th-c family home with lovely peaceful gardens (tennis and croquet); a big, comfortable sitting room, delicious breakfasts with home-made preserves, and helpful, knowledgeable owners; golf nearby; cl Christmas–Easter; children over 8.

EWHURST TQ0840 **High Edser** *Shere Rd, Ewhurst, Cranleigh GU6 7PQ (01483) 278214* ***£45;** 3 charming rms, shared bthrm. 16th-c timber-framed farmhouse in lovely countryside; with a comfortable residents' lounge, friendly owners, enjoyable food (by arrangement) and an open fire in the dining room; tennis court in the grounds; cl Christmas.

FARNHAM SU8145 **Farnham House** *Alton Rd, Farnham GU10 5ER (01252) 716908* **£74w,** plus special breaks; 25 comfortable rms. Attractive Victorian 'gothick' manor house with oak panelling and open fires in the comfortable public rooms, a split-level restaurant, and tennis court and outdoor heated swimming pool in the 5-acre gardens.

GODSTONE TQ3551 **Godstone** *The Green, Godstone RG9 8DT (01833) 742461* **£55;** 8 rms. Well run, late 16th-c hotel with an open fire in the comfortable residents' lounge, and good, popular food in the attractive, beamed restaurant; summer cream teas, and helpful service from the very welcoming owners.

HASLEMERE SU8931 **Deerfell** *Blackdown Park, Fernden Lane, Haslemere GU27 3LA (01428) 653409* ***£40;** 2 rms with showers. Comfortable, no smoking, stone coach house with wonderful views and good nearby walks; generous meals in the handsome dining room (ordered in advance), an open fire in the sitting room, nice breakfasts, pictures, antiques and old rugs, a sun room, and friendly owners; cl mid-Dec–mid-Jan; children over 6.

HASLEMERE SU9232 **Lythe Hill Hotel** *Petworth Rd, Haslemere GU27 3BQ (01428) 651251* **£137,** plus special breaks; 41 individually styled rms, a few in the original house. Lovely, partly 15th-c building in 20 acres of parkland and bluebell woods (adjoining the NT hillside), with a floodlit tennis court, croquet lawn and jogging track; plush, comfortable and elegant lounges, a relaxed bar, 2 no smoking restaurants (one with French cooking, the other with traditional English), and good, attentive service.

HOLMBURY ST MARY TQ1144 **Bulmer Farm** *Holmbury St Mary, Dorking RH5 6LG (01306) 730210* ***£44;** 8 big comfortable rms, 5 in no smoking barn conversion with own showers. Attractive and welcoming 17th-c farmhouse on a 30-acre beef farm in lovely countryside; with oak beams and an inglenook fireplace in the attractive sitting room, breakfasts with home-made preserves in the neatly kept dining room, and a large garden; self-catering also; children over 12; disabled access.

NUTFIELD TQ2950 **Nutfield Priory** *Nutfield, Redhill RH1 4EL (01737) 822066* **£140,** plus special breaks; 60 rms. Impressive Victorian 'gothick' hotel in 40 acres of parkland; with lovely, elaborate carvings, stained-glass windows, gracious day rooms, a fine panelled library, cloistered restaurant, and even an organ in the galleried grand hall; extensive leisure club with indoor heated swimming pool; disabled access.

We welcome reports from readers

This *Guide* depends on readers' reports. Do help us if you can – in return, we offer a discount on the next edition to people who've helped us with reports for it. Tell us what you think about places already in it, and anything extra you think we should say about them. And send us your ideas for inclusion in the next edition: places to visit, eat at or stay in, attractive drives or walks, maybe even unusual interesting shops you know of. Use the card in the middle, the report forms at the end, or just write – no stamp needed: *The Good Guide to Britain*, FREEPOST TN1569, Wadhurst, E Sussex TN5 7BR.

To see and do

Surrey Family Attraction of the Year

☺ **Chessington World of Adventures** TQ1762 (A243) There's not too much to choose between this and Thorpe Park, but for sheer unadulterated fun Chessington probably has the edge. Outstanding rides are Rameses Revenge, which spins you round 360 degrees at speeds of up to 60mph while plummeting towards a rock-lined pit and water fountains, and the hanging rollercoaster, the Vampire, which flies above rooftops before diving underground. Last year they added a rather jolly and much less intense rollercoaster, the Rattlesnake, loosely themed around a Mexican silver mine. Leaflets and maps explain which age group each attraction is aimed at, with enough to appeal to just about everyone. Younger children enjoy Toytown, the Dragon River log flume, and Professor Burp's Bubbleworks, and a circus show has trapeze artists, clowns and stuntmen. Over on the quieter, greener side of the park is the zoo from which it all developed – perhaps a little lost now among the other attractions, but still popular with children. A monorail gives bird's-eye views of the lions, gorillas and meerkats. The recently opened Creepy Caves show off collections of insects and spiders, and there are sealion and penguin displays at set times throughout the day. It's worth taking advantage of their later opening hours in the summer hols (it's open till 9pm then) as the park isn't so busy later in the day; it can be very busy indeed at weekends. At the end of the season they have entertaining Family Fright Nights, with laser shows and the fun of trying everything out in the dark (best to ring to check dates, and you'll need to get there before 4pm). If you don't like theme parks this probably won't change your mind, but it's all very well organised, with very good facilities. Meals, snacks, shop, some disabled access but best to phone in advance; open late Mar–Oct; (01372) 727227; entry is rather pricey at £19 (£15 children 4–14), but some of their promotional leaflets have coupons that can save up to £20 off the total admission.

★ ✝ **ABINGER COMMON** TQ1245 Charmingly set village, with a pretty church and duckpond surrounded by woodland – popular for walks, with the Abinger Hatch a useful pub.

★ **ALBURY** TQ1547 Attractive village, with glimpses of the Victorian mansion Albury Park – or at least its famous chimneys.

BANSTEAD WOOD TQ2657 Popular strolling-ground, a peaceful escape from suburbia and heavily used trunk roads.

BASINGSTOKE CANAL SU8955 Formerly derelict, this has undergone a tremendous programme of rehabilitation over the last 15 years or so. It does not pass through such fine Surrey scenery as the Wey Navigation, but its towpath has been well restored. **Basingstoke Canal Visitor Centre** (Place Rd, Mytchett) Displays on the canal, and good access to its towpath, with boat trips (wknds, bank hols and daily in school hols, Easter–Nov) and rowing-boat hire. Teas, shop, disabled access; cl Mon (exc bank hols), winter wknds; (01252) 370073; information centre and play areas free; exhibition *£1.50.

★ **BETCHWORTH** TQ2149 Attractive village, with strolls along an annotated trail from a church where *Four Weddings and A Funeral* was filmed, passing a working blacksmith. There's a nice drive via Brockham and Newdigate to Rusper in Sussex.

BOX HILL TQ1751 Surrey's most popular viewpoint, with a summit car park and walks on its steep juniper and boxwood slopes: great views, wild orchids and butterflies in early summer, maybe field mushrooms in early autumn; the King William IV at Mickleham is excellent for lunch.

✝ **CHALDON** TQ3155 Attractive church, particularly worth a visit for its unique wall painting of the Ladder of Salvation.

CHARLWOOD TQ2341 **Gatwick Zoo and Aviaries** (Russ Hill) Hundreds of mammals and birds, many in big naturalistic settings – some of which visitors can walk through, inc the 2 big tropical houses with plants and butterflies from around the world. Meals, snacks, shop, disabled access; cl 25–26 Dec; (01293) 862312; £3.95. The Greyhound in the attractive village has good-value food; the Fox Revived at Norwood Hill is a bigger nearby dining pub.

CHERTSEY TQ0467 Quite a few Georgian buildings in its main streets, the remains of a medieval **abbey**, and pleasant walks by the Thames, for instance from the Boathouse pub (Bridge Rd). **Chertsey Museum** (Windsor St) Late Georgian building, with displays on the abbey, a good costume collection, a new hands-on gallery, and a pleasant little garden; Shop, disabled access to ground floor only; cl am wkdys, all Sun, Mon and bank hols; (01932) 565764; free. **Great Cockrow Railway** (Hardwick Lane, Lyne, slightly NW) Notable miniature steam railway, with a unique signalling system. Snacks, shop; open pm Sun May–Oct; (01932) 565474; £1.50. The Golden Grove on St Ann's Hill, out towards here, is a nice spot for lunch. **Thorpe Park** (A320 N of Chertsey, TQ0368) The area's main draw, a well organised theme park covering 500 acres. Star ride is the bizarrely named X:\No Way Out, a rollercoaster hidden

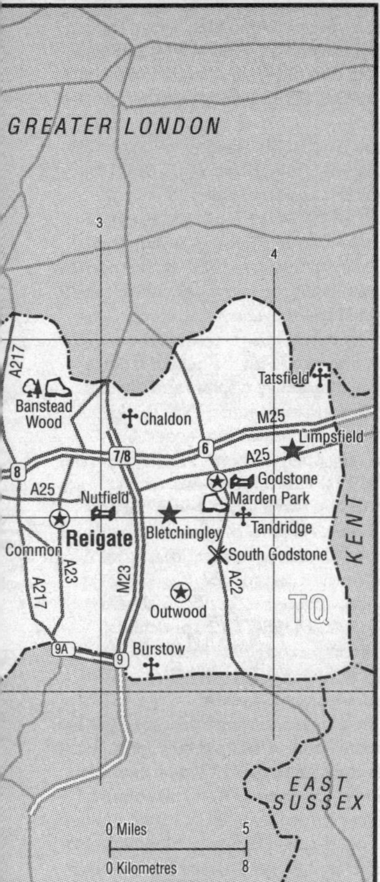

in an enormous pyramid that not only soars up and down in total darkness, but does it all backwards. Tastes have clearly changed since the park opened with its models and rather gentle displays in 1979 (you can still see some of these in Model World, or dotted around the grounds). Other lively features include Thunder River and Calgary Stampede, and there are quite a few water-based rides, inc the highest log flume in the country; you'll need your swimming things if you want to try the latest water slides Wet!Wet!Wet!. Also more sedate play areas, a man-made beach and pools, and a traditional working farm with craft centre, reached by train or waterbus. Staff are friendly, and booking in advance (even a couple of days) can knock quite a bit off the normal price. Meals, snacks, shop, disabled access; cl Nov–mid-Mar; (01932) 562633 or (0990) 880880 for credit card booking; £16.50. Granddad could very happily be dropped off in the nearby Red Lion on Ten Acre Lane.

CHESSINGTON TQ1762 See *separate Family Panel on p.613* for **Chessington World of Adventures**. The Star (A243 towards Leatherhead) is a good place to fortify yourself before or after.

★ † **CHIDDINGFOLD** SU9635 Lovely village in fine surroundings, with one window of its church made up from locally excavated fragments of 13th-c glass made here. The old Crown is a handsome place for lunch or afternoon tea. **Ramster** (A283 S) Splendid Edwardian woodland spring garden. Embroidery exhibition planned for May 1999. Teas (May only), plant sales, disabled access; open mid-Apr–mid-July; (01428) 654167; £2.50.

COBHAM TQ1159 Quite a busy shopping town, with some fine older buildings around the church and in Church St; just SW, Downside Common is a classic cricket green, with cottages scattered around it, and an attractive pub. **Cobham Mill** (Mill Rd) Prettily set working watermill, authentically restored by enthusiastic locals. Open pm 2nd Sun of month Apr–Oct; free. **Cobham Bus Museum** (Redhill Rd, off the A425 W) Private collection of London buses from the 1930s to the present. Open wknds and bank hols; (01932) 868665; free. **Painshill Park** (A425 slightly W) These beautifully restored 18th-c landscape gardens are a continual surprise, with Gothic temples, Chinese bridges, even a Turkish tent and other follies at every turn, and a lake with seemingly endless bays and inlets. Lots of unusual trees and shrubs. Snacks, shop, limited disabled access; usually cl Mon (exc bank hols), and winter Fri; (01932) 868113; £3.50. The Snail brasserie opposite has decent food.

† **COMPTON** SU9547 **Watts Picture Gallery** (Down Lane) Memorial gallery to the Victorian painter and sculptor G F Watts, in his time one of the most celebrated in the

world. Good tearoom (readers report 24 different teas and not a microwave in sight), shop, disabled access; cl all Thurs, am Mon, Tues, Fri and Sun; (01483) 810235; free. Just down the road, the Art Nouveau tomb built by his widow is worth a look, and the village church is attractive.

DEVIL'S PUNCHBOWL SU8936 Spectacular fold of the Downs, with nature trails through mixed woodlands, quiet valleys and sandy heaths with scattered ponds. The area is quite developed but the woods and intricacy of the landscape give it a wholesome rurality, and the footpath network is dense. Gibbet Hill above the A3 gets a view over most of it.

★ ! **DORKING** TQ1649 Pleasant market town with a lot of antique shops, and a local museum (West St, where the 16th-c King's Arms has decent food); the roads S of the A25, W of here, are the county's most rewarding drives, and the steep road up Box Hill N opens a great panorama. **Denbies** (London Rd, Dorking) Britain's biggest vineyard – at 250 acres, bigger than most in France. The tour is unique, with road-train rides round the winery, and a 3-D film where 4 months of vine growth is condensed into 4 minutes, and grapes seem to fly out of the screen. You don't have to be a wine buff to enjoy it. Meals and snacks (in an unusually designed restaurant), big shop, good disabled access; cl am Sun, 25–26 Dec; (01306) 876616; £4.50 (inc tastings). Fine views and walks nearby.

DOWNS LINK PATH TQ0735 Disused railway track through pleasant countryside, increasingly popular for walks and family cycling. The Thurlow Arms, at Baynards Station Yard nr Cox Green, is handy for access.

EAST CLANDON TQ0651 **Hatchlands** Handsome 18th-c brick house with more floors than are visible from the outside, thanks to an ingenious use of false windows. The grand rooms are especially notable for their ceilings and fireplaces, early examples of the work of Robert Adam. A fine collection of keyboard instruments includes a piano once played by Mozart. The garden has a parterre by Gertrude Jekyll. Meals, snacks, shop, disabled access (with notice); open Apr–Oct, house and garden pm Sun, Tues–Thurs and bank hols, plus pm Fri in Aug, park walk daily; (01483) 222482; £4.20, garden and park walk £1.70; NT. A visit here is easily combined with Clandon Park at West Clandon (joint ticket £6). The Queen's Head is useful for lunch.

! **EPSOM** TQ2158 **Derby Day Experience** (Queen's Stand) The Derby (first run in 1780) is still the most prestigious race for 3-year-olds – and a grand social event. At its home racecourse, this re-creates the excitement, with the help of archive film, interactive displays and various relics and mementos. Worth a look even if you're not a racegoer, but usually open only one Sun a month; ring (01372) 726311 for dates; £3.50. **Horton Park Children's Farm** (B280 W) Plenty of animals to feed and cuddle, tractor rides (50p), and an adventure playground. Meals, snacks, shop, disabled access; cl 25–26 Dec; (01372) 743984; £3.30 per child (accompanied adults free).

ESHER TQ1464 **Claremont Landscape Garden** (off the A307) The oldest surviving landscaped garden in the country, laid out by Vanbrugh and Bridgeman before 1720 and extended and naturalised by Kent; 50 colourful acres to lose yourself in. Meals, snacks, shop, disabled access; cl Mon Nov–Mar, 25 Dec, 1 Jan, and maybe some days in July; (01372) 469421; £3; NT. A farm shop has pick-your-own fruit on Winterdown Rd just N.

★ **FARNHAM** SU8346 Handsome town that owed its Georgian heyday to the importance of local corn and hops. Many elegant buildings from this period remain, and there are some even older ones such as the early 17th-c Spinning Wheel. The area around Castle St is especially nice to stroll round. The Spotted Cow (Tilford Rd, Lower Bourne) is popular for lunch. **Farnham Museum** (West St) Excellent local history museum; some William Cobbett memorabilia (his picturesque birthplace in Bridge Sq is now a pub named after him), and a pleasant walled garden. Shop, disabled access; cl Sun and Mon; free. **Farnham**

Castle For 800 years a residence of the Bishops of Winchester. Most of the buildings have been adapted to suit the briefing organisation based here, but the major rooms, inc the Great Hall, can be visited pm Weds; cl Christmas–New Year;(01252) 721194; £1.20. The **castle keep** (administered separately) includes the massive foundations of a Norman tower. Open daily Apr–Sept; (01252) 713393; £2, inc Walkman tour. **Farnham Maltings Gallery** (Bridge Sq) Diverse arts and crafts; cl Sun and bank hols; (01252) 713637; free, although maybe £1 for national exhibitions.

Birdworld (Holt Pound, off the A325, 3m SW – just over the Hants border) A wide variety of birds in 18 acres of garden and parkland – all shapes and sizes from the tiny tanagers to the huge ostrich, with many rare species. Woodland walks and trails. The adjacent **Underwater World** has tropical and other freshwater and marine fish. Meals, snacks, shop, disabled access; cl wkdys Nov and Jan–mid-Feb; (01420) 22838; just Birdworld £5.50, just Underwater World £1.95, both £6.95. The nearby 16th-c Cherry Tree at Rowledge has good food.

FRENSHAM COMMON SU8540 Popular for walks, with heather and woodland around a 13th-c lake made for fish-breeding.

★ **GODALMING** SU9643 Attractive town with quite a few interesting buildings and, because of its narrow streets (part cobbled and pedestrianised), a more old-fashioned feel than most in Surrey. The Inn on the Lake (A3100 S) is good for lunch, and the Star (Church St) has decent snacks. **Godalming Museum** (High St) 15th-c house with local history, and a Gertrude Jekyll-style walled garden; cl Mon, Sun, bank hols; free. The town hall opposite is known affectionately by the locals as the Pepper Pot. **River Wey & Godalming Navigation** This 17th-c canal, passing through some fine scenery, was extended here in 1763. The wharf has some handsome Georgian buildings, and the locks and towpath have been restored for the NT. You can walk all the way to Weybridge, some 20 miles, or hire boats from Farncombe Boat House (01483) 421306. **Busbridge Lakes** (Hambledon Rd, off the B2130) Very pretty spot with 3 lakes in fine parkland – exotic waterfowl, peacocks, ornamental pheasants and many other kinds of bird, as well as follies and grottoes throughout the grounds. Snacks, shop; only open 2–11 Apr, 2–3 and 30–31 May, and 22–30 Aug; (01483) 421955; £3.40.

★ † **GODSTONE** TQ3551 Attractive despite its main roads, spread around a broad green with a duckpond, and a pretty group of houses around the imposing **church**, 14th/15th-c with a Norman tower. The Bell is an enjoyable dining pub. **Godstone Farm** (Tilburstow Hill, S) Friendly 40-acre working farm; children are encouraged to touch the animals (and even climb in with some of them). Very good play areas, snacks, shop, disabled access; cl wkdys (exc school hols) Oct–Mar; (01883) 742546; £3.45 per child (accompanied adults free). **Pilgrim Harps** (Stansted House, Tilburstow Hill Rd) Make and restore harps of all shapes and sizes; appointment preferred, (01342) 893242. The ancient Fox & Hounds out this way has good food (no children inside). **Flower Farm** (Quarry Rd, just off the A22 W of Oxted) Looking up to the Downs, this has organically grown pick-your-own produce and a vineyard. Meals, snacks, shop, disabled access; cl Oct–Apr (exc vineyard open all year); (01883) 744590; free.

GOMSHALL TQ0846 **Gomshall Mill** (A25) Working 2-wheeled watermill dating back to 1086, with riverside gardens, and various craft shops; restaurant (not pm Mon), disabled access; (01483) 202433; free. **Gomshall Gallery** (A25) Contemporary arts and crafts; also a French wine wholesaler, and house plants for sale. Cl Sun and bank hols. The neighbouring Compasses (also with a streamside garden) does good-value lunches, and you can stroll up on wooded Netley Heath.

GREAT BOOKHAM TQ1352 **Polesden Lacey** (S off the A246) Attractive Regency house once at the heart of Edwardian high society, with photographs of notable guests, as well as splendid tapestries, porcelain, old masters and other art. The spacious grounds have a walled rose garden and an open-air theatre. Meals, snacks, shop, disabled access; house open pm Weds–Sun and bank hols Apr–Oct, grounds open all yr; (01372) 458203; £6, grounds only £3; NT. On the other side of the extended commuter village, the attractive Bookham Commons are a mix of thorny scrub (full of birds), small lakes, marshy bits and oakwoods, and nearby **Walton Poor** sell herb, scented and foliage plants Weds–Sun Easter–Oct, and open their pretty garden by appointment (01483) 282273. In Effingham nearby, the Plough and Sir Douglas Haig are reliable food pubs.

GUILDFORD SU9949 The biggest town in the area, and older than you might at first think; what's behind those Georgian frontages is often much older. The sloping High St has attractive parts as well as its briskly modern shops, with interesting buildings inc the **Abbots Hospital** and the **Grammar School** with its notable chained library; Tunsgate Arch is the start for free guided walks – 2.30pm every Sun, Mon and Weds May–Sept (plus 7.30pm Thurs till end Aug). The hill of the ruined 12th-c **castle** has fine views of the town, and a garden in the former castle ditch. Shop; open Easter–Sept; (01483) 444702; 85p keep, grounds free. **Guildhall** (High St) Mainly Tudor, with one of the few existing sets of Elizabethan standard measures. Free guided tours at 2pm and 3pm Tues and Thurs and 3.30pm Weds when you can have tea with the mayor; (01483) 444035; (free but you need a ticket from the Tourist Information Centre for Weds). The cathedral, begun in 1936, is one of only two entirely 20th-c Anglican cathedrals in the country; it's quite austere, but has a cool elegance inside. **Guildford Museum** (Quarry St) Local history, with a display on Lewis Carroll, who died here in 1898 (cl Sun; free). He's buried in the cemetery on the Mount, the continuation of the High St. The handsome **Guildford Boat House** (Millmead) is impressive; you can hire boats here for the Wey Navigation (01483) 504494. Nearby the White House and Jolly Farmer do decent food in a lovely riverside setting. **Loseley House** (off the B3000, 3 miles SW) Most people are familiar with the name from the yoghurts and ice-cream produced here (try the white chocolate and butterscotch versions). The stately Elizabethan country house was built in 1562, and has fine panelling, ceilings, paintings and tapestries. The gardens include a new fountain garden. Trailer rides across the estate on Sats. Meals, snacks, shop, limited disabled access; house and farm open pm Weds–Sat and bank hols May–Aug, gardens open all day (from 11am); (01483) 304440; £4.50 house and gardens, gardens only £2.25, trailer rides £2.75.

! HAMBLEDON SU9639 You can climb inside what's said to be a witch's tree in front of the church here; walk round the tree 3 times and the witch may well appear.

★ HASCOMBE SU9940 A lovely village with an interesting **church**; Dirk Bogarde's old local the White Horse is good for lunch (with a great garden), and the B2130 S and then the Dunsfold–Chiddingfold back road is a pleasant drive. **Winkworth Arboretum** (B2130, just NW) Nearly 100 acres of lovely hillside woodland, with fine views over the North Downs – especially nice in spring, and with flaring autumn colours. Summer snacks and shop, some disabled access; (01483) 208477; £2.70; NT.

HEADLEY HEATH TQ2053 Sandy walks and rides through heather and birchwoods.

HOLMWOOD COMMON TQ1845 Undulating oak and birchwoods, lots of good paths; the Plough at Blackbrook is useful for lunch.

HORSELL COMMON TQ0060 Walks gain a touch of interest from the sandpits which inspired and saw the start of H G Wells's *The War of the Worlds*; the Bleak House at the Anthonys and the Red Lion in Horsell have decent food.

HURT WOOD TQ0943 Large areas of private broadleafed forest around here are open to walkers;

relatively unfrequented and good for spotting birds and wild animals.

HYDON'S BALL SU97453939 Fine viewpoint in unspoilt walking terrain off the road between Loxhill and Hydestile S of Godalming, though rather hard to find (hence our 8-figure map reference).

LEATHERHEAD TQ1656 **Local History Museum** (Church St) In a pretty, 17th-c, timber-framed building, and well worth a visit; open Sat, pm Thurs and am Fri Apr–Christmas; free. The Duke's Head in the pedestrianised High St is pleasant for lunch, and there are riverside walks nearby. **Fire and Iron Gallery** (Oxshott Rd, A244 N) Unusual exhibitions of ornamental metalwork; cl Sun. **Bocketts Farm Park** (A246 S) Working farm in a pretty, historic setting, with traditional and rare breeds, cart rides, pig-racing, falconry and craft demonstrations. Meals, snacks, shop, disabled access; cl 25–26 Dec; (01372) 363764; £3.25.

LEITH HILL TQ1343 Perhaps the best walking in Surrey – which surprises by being England's most wooded county. It has heather, sandy walks, steep pinewoods and tremendous views. An 18th-c tower on top of the hill, the highest point in south-east England, is the best viewpoint of all, with a surprising view of South London – which feels a hundred miles away. It's open, with teas, on pm Weds and Sat, Sun and bank hols, but cl Oct–Mar exc fine wknds – 50p. Attractive Friday Street, with a fine pub and a lake, is one starting-point for switchback routes S through a series of brackeny summits to the tower. Leith Hill can also be approached through attractive farmland from the S, from Ockley or from the Parrot at Forest Green.

LIGHTWATER COUNTRY PARK SU9262 The exemplary visitor centre, with displays on the area's rich natural history (especially the sandy heathlands) recently burned down; they hope to have a new one by May, and there are plenty of nature trails. Snacks, shop, disabled access; park open all year; (01276) 479582; free.

MARDEN PARK TQ3653 Popular strolling-ground, surprisingly peaceful despite nearby suburbia and even the M25.

OCKHAM COMMON TQ0858 **Chatley Heath Semaphore Tower** (via Old Lane, off the A3 to Effingham) Unique tower rather like a lighthouse, the only surviving member of a chain that once sent messages between the Admiralty in London and Portsmouth; excellent views, once up the 88 steps. Round it are 700 acres of heath and woodland, with a nature trail and pleasant walks (inc a 20-minute trek from car park to tower). Shop; open pm wknds and bank hols Apr–Sept, plus Weds in school hols; (01932) 862762; £2. The extraordinary 'gothick' Hautboy (Ockham Lane) has a good brasserie, and Ockham church is attractive.

OCKLEY TQ1439 Some attractive old houses along the Roman road here, with the 15th-c Cricketers Arms doing good-value food; the Scarlett Arms out at Walliswood is a delightful old place. **Hannah Peschar Gallery and Garden** (Black and White Cottage, Standon Lane) Lush garden filled with contemporary sculpture: the watergarden is now more like a tropical rainforest than the cottage garden it started as, and the atmospheric sculptures and ceramics blend perfectly with its unusual design. Some disabled access but no facilities; open Fri, Sat and pm Sun and bank hols May–Oct, other times (exc Mon) by arrangement; (01306) 627269; *£7. There's a good big farm shop with pick-your-own fruit nearby.

★ **OUTWOOD** TQ3245 Spread around an attractive common, with an antique shop, and adjacent NT woodlands ideal for a picnic. The Bell nr the common and the Dog & Duck out towards Coopers Hill are good for lunch. **Outwood Post Mill** Very well preserved, England's oldest working windmill, built in 1665. It's a lovely spot, 120 metres (400ft) up, with ducks, goats and horses all wandering freely around it. In Apr they do bluebell tours in the adjacent woods. Shop, disabled access to ground floor only; open pm Sun and bank hols Easter–Oct; (01342) 843644; £2.

PITCH HILL TQ0842 Largely wooded, but good heathy stretches for walkers, with pleasant views on the relatively open approach from Ewhurst; above the village, the Windmill pub has glorious views from its garden.

RANMORE COMMON TQ1551 Chalk downland with sheep, wild orchids and dense woodlands, within close range of Polesden Lacey. You can walk on the well marked North Downs Way.

REIGATE TQ2548 Below the peaceful castle grounds is a network of old tunnels, notably the intriguingly elaborate **Barons Cave**, an atmospheric passageway with all sorts of myths and stories attached. Usually open at least one Sat a month Apr–Oct for enthusiastic and entertaining tours – ring the Information Office on 01737) 276000 for full details and dates; £1. Among the few surviving original buildings in this mainly modern town are one or two timber-framed houses around the High St. **Reigate Heath** (off the A25 W) The 220-year-old former windmill here was converted into a church in 1882, and still has services at 3pm on the 3rd Sun each month in summer. Disabled access; open all year – if cl, key at the golf clubhouse. There are pleasant walks out here, and the Skimmington Castle is a nice country pub.

RUNNYMEDE TQ0071 A field by a main road; not worth visiting unless you are quite fascinated by Magna Carta, though up the hill beyond the trees, the nearby memorials to John F Kennedy and, with their names, to the aircrew who died during World War II, are dignified and touching.

ST MARTHA'S HILL TQ0348 (E of Guildford) The church on its summit can only be reached on foot, and by starting from attractive Chilworth (where the prettily set pub, the Villagers at Blackheath, has maps for walkers), you can see the long-abandoned gunpowder mills by the Tilling Bourne.

★ **SHEPPERTON** TQ0766 One of the best places to watch the comings and goings on the **River Thames**, with the Wey Navigation joining the river here; the Thames Court Hotel (Shepperton Lock, Ferry Lane), Red Lion (Russell Rd) and Warren Lodge Hotel (Church Sq) all have riverside gardens, and there's a quiet and attractive 18th-c village square.

★ **SHERE** TQ0747 Very picturesque, with 17th-c timber-framed cottages, a grassy-banked stream with ducks and a ford, and lots of interesting corners. In the partly Norman **church**, a quatrefoil blocked hole in the chancel wall marks the spot where a 14th-c anchorite had herself walled in, being fed through another hole outside. The Malt House is a decent local history museum, and the ancient White Horse is a good place for lunch.

STOKE D'ABERNON CHURCH TQ1259 Notable for the earliest surviving memorial brass in Britain, dating from the 13th c; set in the floor of the chancel, it's very well preserved.

★ **THURSLEY COMMON** SU9040 Remote-feeling sandy heathland (easy to lose the way in) with unusual birds and a number of ponds; the best starting-points are attractive Thursley village (with an interesting church, and the handily placed Three Horseshoes), and the Moat car park on the road S of Elstead. The Moat itself is one of the ponds, a habitat for dragonflies, and across the heath is Forked Pond, bright with kingcups. The S part of the heath is a national nature reserve.

TILFORD SU8543 **Rural Life Centre** (Reeds Rd, just W) Carefully displayed private collection of farm implements and machinery, spread over 10 acres of field and woodland, with an arboretum, children's playground, and a miniature railway on Sun. Snacks, shop, disabled access; cl Mon (exc bank hols), Tues, all Oct–Mar; (01252) 795571; *£3. The village has a massive oak tree, thought to be 800 years old; the Barley Mow between the river and the goose-cropped cricket green is a pleasant spot for lunch, and it's not far from here to the remains of Waverley Abbey.

TONGHAM SU8848 **Hogs Back Brewery** (Manor Farm, The Street) Tours of this friendly little brewery, using traditional methods to produce 6 distinctive ales. The shop has over 500 English, Belgian and German beers (as well as their own), also English wines and farm ciders. Tours at 6.30pm Weds, Thurs and Fri, 11am and 2.30pm Sat, 2.30pm Sun, other times by arrangement; shop open daily; (01252) 783000; tour *£5.75 (inc tastings and a commemorative glass). Manor Farm has pick-your-own fruit here Jun–Sept and the **Manor Farm Craft Centre** in adjacent Seale is worth a visit; cl am Sun, and Mon exc bank hols.

★ ⛰ ✝ **WALLISWOOD** TQ1138
Attractive village, with delightful woodland walk from the pub to the 13th-c church.

WEST CLANDON TQ0451
Clandon Park (A247) Grand 18th-c house with unusual collection of porcelain birds, and fine furnishings and paintings; also a regimental museum. Regular concerts in the grand 2-storeyed Marble Hall. The gardens have a Maori house brought over from New Zealand in 1892. Meals, snacks, shop, disabled access to ground floor; open Apr–Oct, house from 11.30am Sun, Tues–Thurs and bank hols, gardens every day; (01483) 222482; £4.20 NT. The smart Onslow Arms is good for lunch, and the 16th-c Bull's Head is popular too.

✝ **WEYBRIDGE** TQ0862
Brooklands Museum (B374)
Exhaustive museum re-creating the racing circuit's 1920s and 30s heyday, with plenty of racing cars, motorbikes and bicycles in the restored clubhouse. Also a restored Wellington bomber and a comprehensive collection of vintage Vickers and Hawker planes. This was the site of the first British Grand Prix, and the first 100mph motor ride. Demonstrations and events most wknds. Snacks, shop, good disabled access; cl Mon (exc bank hols), Good Fri, Christmas wk; (01932) 857381; £6. In the town, the waterside Old Crown (Thames St) does good-value food.

⛰ **WISLEY GARDEN**
TQ0658 (A3) These 300-acre gardens have come a long way since they were set up in 1904 as experimental gardens for the Royal Horticultural Society; lots of unusual plants, shrubs, trees, fruit and vegetables, exemplary glasshouses; also a farm, orchard and woodland. The gardens get very busy (especially at weekends) but are quite big enough to cope. Meals, snacks, shop (lots of hard-to-get gardening/plant books), garden centre (good plants from a wide range of nurseries, but expensive), disabled access; cl Sun (exc to RHS members), 25 Dec; (01483) 224234; £5. The canalside Anchor at Pyrford Lock (turn left down exit road) is well placed for walks along the prettiest section of the **Wey Navigation Canal**, whose towpath gives Surrey's best waterside walks.

★ **Other attractive villages**, all with decent pubs, include Alfold TQ0334, Bletchingley TQ3250 (Norman church), Dunsfold TQ0036 (lovely green and church), Englefield Green SU9970 (handy for Savill Garden in Berks), Holmbury St Mary TQ1144, Hurtwood TQ0845, Leigh TQ2246, Limpsfield TQ4053 (church where Delius is buried), Ripley TQ0556, Shackleford SU9345, Thorpe TQ0268 and Wood Street SU9550.

✝ Beside those mentioned, other **churches** worth a look include Burstow TQ3140, Okewoodhill

Days Out

Surrey's greensand country: Ockley sculpture garden; lunch at the Stephan Langton, Friday Street; walk up to Leith Hill tower; Shere.

Exploring the North Downs: Stroll on Box Hill or Ranmore Common; Denbies vineyard; lunch at the King William IV in Mickleham; Polesden Lacey.

A house and garden theme: Clandon Park, West Clandon; lunch at the Onslow Arms there, or at Michels in Ripley; Wisley Garden.

TQ1337, Tandridge TQ3750, Tatsfield TQ4156 and Wotton TQ1247. You'll usually have to get the key from a local keyholder.

Popular starts or finishes for **walks** include the William IV at Little London TQ0646, the Sportsman at Mogador TQ2452, the Donkey at Charleshill SU8944, the Plough, high on its hill, at Coldharbour TQ1543 and Botley Hill Farmhouse at Warlingham TQ3759 (Limpsfield Rd). Besides places already mentioned for the River Thames, the Swan in Staines TQ0471 (The Hythe) and the Swan, Riverside (both Manor Rd), the Magpie in Sunbury TQ1068 (Thames St), and the Anglers Tavern (off Manor Rd) and the Weir (Sunbury Lane) in Walton-on-Thames TQ1066 all have good views and access to the river. The county council has guided walks all year, exploring historical or, more usually, natural history themes; on a typical Sun there might be 8 or more to choose from. For the current programme ring the Planning Dept, (0181) 541 9463.

! You can book **balloon trips** on (01252) 844222.

Where to eat

BLACKBROOK TQ1846 **Plough** *(01306) 886603* Popular pub with award-winning hanging-baskets and window-boxes; generous helpings of good, imaginative food, very friendly service, marvellous choice of wines by the glass, and well kept real ales; pretty cottagey garden with Swiss play house for children; cl 25–26 Dec, 1 Jan; no children inside; limited disabled access. **£15.95**|£5.25.

CHILWORTH TQ0346 **Villagers** *Blackheath (01483) 893152* Surrounded by quiet woodland and walks, with a pretty terrace and garden, and a path through trees to the cricket green (where Monty addressed thousands of Canadian troops before D-Day – a shame there isn't a commemorative plaque); rambling beamed main bar, small flagstoned room with a big fireplace, good, home-made, often interesting food, well kept real ales, decent house wines, and pleasant young staff; bdrms; disabled access. **£18**|£4.50.

COMPTON SU9547 **Tea Shop** *Down Lane (01483) 811030* Well liked tea shop doing morning coffee, light lunches and afternoon tea; home-made cakes, scones and jams, free-range eggs, a wide range of drinks inc interesting juices, seltzers and fruity mineral waters, lots of Indian, China, herbal and fruit teas, and different coffees; cl 24–31 Dec; partial disabled access. £2.90.

DORKING TQ1649 **Partners & Sons** *2–4 West St (01306) 882826* Heavily beamed 16th-c building with dining rooms on 2 floors; very good, imaginative modern cooking, and a thoughtful wine list; cl Sun, 1st 3 wks Jan; disabled access. **£24.50**.

ELSTEAD SU9043 **Woolpack** *(01252) 703106* Cheerfully old-fashioned pub, bustling and friendly, with huge helpings of good, interesting bar food inc vegetarian choices and lovely home-made puddings; a fair amount of wool trade memorabilia, open fires, well kept real ales, and play area in the garden; cl pm 25 Dec–26 Dec; children in family room or dining room only. **£20**|£4.75.

GOMSHALL TQ0847 **Mulligans** *Station Rd (A25) (01483) 202242* Friendly staff in this attractively decorated and relaxed fish restaurant, with live French café music on Thurs; cl pm 25 Dec, pm 1 Jan; disabled access. **£18**|£7.

HERSHAM TQ1164 **Dining Room** *Village Green (01932) 231686* 5 little rooms with log fires, very good food (half English, half international) inc huge puddings, a relaxed atmosphere, and cheerful, friendly staff; also a shaded terrace garden; cl am Sat, pm Sun, 1 wk at Christmas, bank hols; disabled access by arrangement. **£23**|£6.95.

MICKLEHAM TQ1753 **King William IV** *(01372) 372590* Relaxed and unpretentious pub cut into the hillside; with fine views from the snug front bar, a spacious back bar with log fires and fresh flowers, a wide range of interesting daily specials inc a good vegetarian choice, and well kept ales; lovely terraced garden, and nice nearby walks; no food pm Mon; cl 25 Dec, 31 Dec; children over 12. **£18**|£8.25.

RIPLEY TQ0556 **Michels** *13 High St (01483) 224777* Charming Georgian house, with carefully cooked seasonal food (inc some unusual dishes), a fine range of wines, and good service; cl am Sat, pm Sun, Mon; children over 5. **£23 4-course set dinner**.

SHERE TQ0747 **Kinghams** *Gomshall Lane (01483) 202168* Beamed 17th-c cottage with a relaxed atmosphere; unpretentious surroundings, cheerful service, good sound cooking from a shortish menu inc daily fish dishes and vegetarian choices, and nice puddings; cl pm Sun, Mon, 25–31 Dec; disabled access. **£30**|£8.

SOUTH GODSTONE TQ3549 **Fox & Hounds** *(01342) 893474* Pretty, old-fashioned inn in a pleasant spot; lots of little nooks and crannies, a cosy low-beamed bar with a good mix of seats and woodburner, popular and imaginative food, a restaurant with more elaborate dishes, well kept ales, and an extensive wine list. **£17.75**|£5.75.

TADWORTH TQ2356 **Gemini** *28 Station Approach (01737) 812179* Bustling and popular local restaurant with very good modern cooking using influences from all over the world, super puddings, a mainly French wine list, and courteous service; cl am Sat, pm Sun, Mon, 2 wks Christmas, 2 wks summer; children lunchtime only; disabled access. **£29**|£10.50.

THURSLEY SU9039 **Three Horseshoes** *(01252) 703268* Rather civilised, tile-hung, partly 16th-c pub, with beams and log fires in the dark cosy bar, fine old country furniture, and well kept real ales; good, home-made bar food, a separate back restaurant, and 2 acres of garden; cl pm Sun in winter; children over 5 in lunchtime restaurant only. **£18**|£5.50.

Special thanks to Mrs Rita Cox.

Please let us know what you think of places in the *Guide*. Use the report forms at the back of the book or simply write us a letter.

Surrey Calendar

Some of these dates were provisional as we went to press. Please check information with the telephone numbers provided.

JANUARY

6 **Guildford** Wassailing: Twelfth night pub tour by morris men who perform a mummers' play and drink spiced beer from the wassail bowl (01483) 444751

16 **Wisley** Orchids for All at RHS Gardens – *till Sun 24* (01483) 212387

FEBRUARY

16 **Esher** Antiques Fair at Sandown Park (0171) 249 4050

26 **Guildford** Home Design Exhibition at Loseley Park – *till Sun 28* (01705) 677200

28 **Esher** Road Bike Show at Sandown Park Exhibition Centre – *till 1 Mar* (0117) 907 1000

MARCH

6 **Esher** Toy Fair at Sandown Park (01604) 770025; **Guildford** International Women's Festival – *till Sun 14* (01483) 444333; **Wisley** Garden Crafts at RHS Gardens – *till Sun 14* (01483) 212387; **Woking** Dance Umbrella: international companies and workshops – *till Sun 28* (01483) 726448

7 **Esher** Antiques Fair at Sandown Park (0171) 249 4050

12 **Guildford** International Music Festival – *till Sun 28* (01483) 444333

APRIL

3 **Esher** Craft Fair at Sandown Park – *till Mon 5* (01344) 874787

4 **Woking** Canal Festival at Woking Bridge Barn – *till Mon 5* (01483) 743024

5 **Weybridge** Alternative Power Festival at Brooklands Museum (01932) 857381

20 **Esher** Antiques Fair at Sandown Park (0171) 249 4050

24 **Esher** Gold Cup Racing at Sandown Park (01372) 470047

26 **Guildford** Home Design Exhibition at Loseley Park – *till Weds 28* (01705) 677200

30 **Banstead** Arts Festival – *till 16 May* (01737) 353738

MAY

1 **Guildford** May Day Ceremony: at 5.30am Pilgrim morris men dance to greet the sunrise on St Martha's Hill; later procession carries maypole up the High St to castle green; folk dancing around the pole and elsewhere throughout the day (01483) 444751

8 **Guildford** Motor Show at Loseley Park – *till Sun 9* (01483) 304440

16 **Esher** Spring Plant Fair at Claremont (01372) 467806

20 **Tilford** Bach Festival – *till Sat 22* (01252) 782167

29 **Epsom** Derby Festival in the town and at the Racecourse – *till 6 Jun* (01372) 732341; **Guildford** County Show at Stoke Park (01483) 414651

Surrey Calendar (Cont.)

JUNE

4 **Guildford** Live Crafts at Loseley House and Park Farm – *till Sun 6* (01494) 450405
5 **Epsom** Derby Day at Epsom Racecourse (01372) 470047
12 **Caterham** Carnival (01883) 342008
12 **Abinger** Old Fair: medieval fair with maypole dancing, knights and traditional competitions (01306) 731083; **Great Bookham** Open-air Theatre at Polesden Lacey Open-air Theatre – *till 4 July* (01372) 451596
26 **Guildford** Summer Festival – *till 1 July* (01483) 444333

JULY

2 **East Clandon** Open-air Concerts at Hatchlands – *till Sun 4* (01372) 451596
3 **Redhill** Motor Show at Redhill Memorial Park – *till Sun 4* (01737) 732000
14 **Esher** Fête Champêtre at Claremont: music, dance, storytelling, street theatre, fireworks and themed costume – *till Sat 17* (01372) 451596
19 **Sunbury–Abingdon** Swan Upping on the River Thames: colourful traditional ceremony – *till Fri 23* (01628) 523030
23 **Guildford** Garden Festival at Loseley House and Park – *till Sun 25* (01483) 797332
24 **East Molesey** Metropolitan Police Show and Tournament at Imber Court – *till Sun 25* (0181) 247 5480
25 **Tilford** Rustic Day: traditional crafts and entertainments at Old Kiln Rural Life Centre (01252) 792300
31 **Lingfield** Steam and Country Show – *till 1 Aug* (01293) 771980; **Wisley** Family Fortnight at RHS Gardens – *till 15 Aug* (01483) 212387

AUGUST

6 **Guildford** Folk and Blues Festival – *till Sun 8* (01483) 536270
8 **Guildford** Fireworks Concert at Loseley Park (01625) 575681
14 **Guildford** Classic Car Show and Country Fair at Loseley Park: over 1,000 vintage vehicles, arena events and bands – *till Sun 15* (01372) 842204
24 **Wisley** RHS Flower Show at RHS Gardens – *till Thurs 26* (01483) 224234
29 **Lingfield** Edenbridge and Oxted Agricultural Show at Ardenrun Showground – *till Mon 30* (01737) 645843

SEPTEMBER

24 **Esher** Woodworking Show at Sandown Park – *till Sun 26* (01926) 614101

OCTOBER

10 **Esher** MG Show at Sandown Park (0121) 745 5256
17 **Esher** Triumph Show at Sandown Park (0121) 745 5256
18 **Wisley** Apple Days at RHS Gardens – *till Weds 20* (01483) 212387
23 **Chessington** Fright Nights at Chessington World of Adventures – *till Sun 24* (01372) 729560; **Esher** Craft Fair at Sandown Park – *till Sun 24* (01344) 874787; **Guildford** Book Festival – *till Sun 31* (01483) 444333

Surrey Calendar (Cont.)

30 Chessington Fright Nights at Chessington World of Adventure – *till Sun 31* (01372) 729560

NOVEMBER

12 Guildford Christmas Fair at Loseley Park – *till Sun 14* (01483) 304440
20 Farnham Southern Ceramics Show at the Maltings Gallery – *till Sun 21* (01494) 450504; **Wisley** Christmas at RHS Gardens – *till Sun 28* (01483) 212387
26 Guildford Live Crafts at Loseley House and Park Farm – *till Sun 28* (01483) 304440
28 Esher Mini Show at Sandown Park (0121) 745 5256
30 Esher Antiques Fair at Sandown Park (0171) 249 4050

DECEMBER

16 Epsom Victorian Christmas Evening (01372) 732341

Sussex

A favourite county for many readers – lots to see and do, sunny resorts, attractively varied scenery.

Brighton has elegant Regency architecture, the remarkable Royal Pavilion, good free museums, endless antiques, and also a more raffish and studenty side that gives it a real buzz. While it's a seaside place that refuses to stand still, others here – dignified Eastbourne, sandy Bognor and Worthing – appeal precisely because they have not moved with the times. Rye is an enchanting small town (the new mechanical music museum is fun), and Chichester has plenty to see (Pallant House is outstanding).

Sussex has a lot for children to enjoy. Special favourites include the lively collection of rescued buildings at Singleton, Bodiam Castle, Drusillas zoo near the delightful village of Alfriston, the sheep centre at East Dean, Bentley at Halland, the open-air museum at Amberley, the Bluebell steam line near Sheffield Park, the Foredown Centre near Brighton, and the llama farm at Wych Cross. And even the splendid Roman villas at Bignor and Fishbourne, appealing primarily to adults, are enjoyed by many children.

For many people, it's the county's spectacular gardens which stand out – Leonardslee at Lower Beeding, Wakehurst Place at Ardingly, Nymans at Handcross, Borde Hill near Haywards Heath and Sheffield Park, with many really worthwhile smaller places. Earnley Gardens is rather special for its unusual range of other attractions.

Sussex is also rich in great houses to visit: Uppark at South Harting, Arundel Castle, Goodwood, Parham at Pulborough, and Petworth. Both Arundel and Petworth have a lot to see nearby, and the Goodwood sculpture park is most appealing (but very expensive). Firle has some smaller gems around it.

The Sussex countryside has very varied yet very characteristic scenery: the South Downs with their attractive flint buildings and expansive views, culminating in Beachy Head and its nearby cliffs (good, well organised walks from the visitor centre); the sparsely wooded high sandy heathland of the Ashdown Forest; and the intricate landscapes of the Weald, with its steep slopes and valleys, ancient woods and hedgerows punctuated by great oaks, pretty villages, tile-hung or weatherboarded oast houses and wood and tile Sussex barns with their long 'cats'-slide' roofs. Much of the coast is developed, but the great sea inlet of Chichester Harbour has some very attractive places along its shore.

Where to stay

ALFRISTON TQ5103 **Star** *High St, Alfriston, Polegate BN26 5TA (01323) 870495* **£104,** plus special breaks; 37 rms. Fine hotel with a fascinating, atmospheric front part, built in the 15th c as a guesthouse for pilgrims; lots of medieval carvings, sanctuary post in the bar, decent food and drinks, and excellent service; disabled access.

AMBERLEY TQ0213 **Amberley Castle** *Amberley, Arundel BN18 9ND (01798) 831992* **£170;** 15 very well equipped, charming rms. Magnificent 900-year-old castle with day rooms filled with suits of armour and weapons as well as antiques, roaring fires and panelling; friendly service, imaginative food in the no smoking, 13th-c dining room, and exceptionally pretty gardens; children over 12.

ARLINGTON TQ5507 **Bates Green** *Tye Hill Rd, Arlington, Polegate BN26 6SH (01323) 482039* ***£48;** 3 rms. Originally an 18th-c gamekeeper's cottage, now a no smoking farmhouse on a 130-acre turkey and sheep farm; with beams and log fire in the oak-panelled sitting room, home-made cake and tea on arrival, big breakfasts with home-made preserves, and good Aga-cooked evening meals; sizeable garden (open under the National Garden Scheme), and a fine wood with lovely May bluebells; cl Christmas; no children and no pets.

BATTLE TQ7714 **Little Hemingfold Farmhouse** *Hastings Rd, Battle TN33 0TT (01424) 774338* ***£76,** plus special breaks; 13 rms, most with own bthrm. Partly 17th-c, partly early Victorian farmhouse in 40 acres of woodland, with trout lake, tennis, gardens, and lots of walks (the 2 labradors may come with you); comfortable sitting rooms, open fires, a restful atmosphere and very good food using home-grown produce – either in the style of a dinner party or at your own candlelit table; children can feed farm animals; tennis court; cl 4 Jan–11 Feb; dogs welcome.

BATTLE TQ7217 **Netherfield Place** *Netherfield, Battle TN33 9PP (01424) 774455* **£120;** 14 lovely rms. Handsome Georgian-style hotel in 30 acres of gardens and parkland; with light attractive day rooms, log fire, lovely flowers, a relaxed and friendly atmosphere, and imaginative food using garden's produce; 2 hard tennis courts, croquet and putting green; cl 2 weeks Christmas.

BATTLE TQ7414 **Powder Mills** *Powdermill Lane, Battle TN33 0SP (01424) 775511* **£85,** plus special breaks; 35 rms, some in annexe. Attractive 18th-c, creeper-clad manor house in 150 acres of park and woodland with 4 lakes (trout fishing) and outdoor swimming pool; country-house atmosphere, log fires and antiques in the elegant day rooms, attentive service, and good modern cooking in the Orangery restaurant; children over 10 in evening restaurant; well behaved dogs by prior arrangement; disabled access.

BEPTON SU8618 **Park House** *Bepton, Midhurst GU29 0JB (01730) 812880* ***£130,** plus special breaks; 14 rms. Quietly set country house nr Goodwood and Cowdray Park, with a heated swimming pool, grass tennis courts, croquet and putting; comfortable drawing room, convivial small bar, and good homely cooking in the elegant dining room; disabled access.

BOSHAM SU8005 **Kenwood** *Bosham, Chichester PO18 8PH (01243) 572727* **£50;** 3 large rms. Comfortable and well kept Victorian house, with harbour views, a plushly furnished lounge, pleasant dining room (with useful fridge for your own picnic things), lots of old sporting bats, hockey sticks and tennis rackets, super breakfasts, games room with pool, heated swimming pool, croquet, and free-range poultry; disabled access.

BOSHAM SU8004 **Millstream** *Bosham Lane, Bosham, Chichester PO18 8HL (01243) 573234* ***£112,** plus special breaks; 33 rms. Warm and friendly small hotel in charming waterside village; with an attractive bar and sitting room, open fire and fresh flowers, very good food using fresh local produce, decent wine list, and a streamside garden; disabled access.

BRIGHTON TQ3004 **Dove** *18 Regency Sq, Brighton BN1 2FG (01273) 779222* ***£68,** plus special breaks; 8 rms, 4 with sea view. Lovely, neatly kept, bow-windowed Regency house (being refurbished this year) with warmly welcoming and helpful owners, and very good breakfasts in the light and airy dining room (enjoyable evening meals by prior arrangement); they are kind to families, with toys and babysitting available.

BRIGHTON TQ3004 **Grand** *King's Rd, Brighton BN1 2FW (01273) 321188* **£180,** plus special breaks; 200 handsome rms, many with sea view. Famous Victorian hotel with marble columns and floors and fine moulded plasterwork in the luxurious and elegant day rooms; exemplary service, very good food and fine wines, popular afternoon tea in the sunny conservatory, a bustling nightclub, and health spa with indoor swimming pool.

BRIGHTON TQ3004 **Topps** *17 Regency Sq, Brighton BN1 2FG (01273) 729334* **£84;** 15 lovely comfortable rms, 11 with gas-effect coal fires and many with sea view. Carefully furnished and well kept Regency town house nr seafront; particularly helpful and genuinely friendly owners, really good breakfasts and unpretentious dinners in the attractive basement restaurant, and a library/reception room.

BURWASH TQ6724 **Ashlands Cottage** *Burwash, Etchingham TN19 7HS (01435) 882207* **£36;** 2 rms, shared bthrm. In a lovely spot nr Batemans, this pretty cottage has marvellous views, a homely sitting room, an attractive dining room (no full suppers but pubs nearby), charming owner, and an appealing garden; children over 12.

CHICHESTER SU8604 **Bedford** *Southgate, Chichester PO19 1DP (01243) 785766* **£80,** plus special breaks; 20 attractive rms. Family-run Georgian hotel in the centre, with a friendly atmosphere, and a comfortable, no smoking lounge and restaurant opening on to a quiet terrace.

CHICHESTER SU8604 **Suffolk House** *3 East Row, Chichester PO19 1PD (01243) 778899* ***£88;** 10 rms, some overlooking garden. Friendly Georgian house in the centre, with a homely comfortable lounge, little bar, traditional cooking in the dining room, and a small walled garden; disabled access.

CHIDHAM SU7804 **Old Rectory** *Chidham Lane, Chidham, Chichester PO18 8TA (01243) 572088* **£44;** 4 rms. Handsome country house with an elegant sitting room, friendly owners, good breakfasts (nice pub nearby for evening meals), and croquet and a summer swimming pool in the big garden; may cl Feb.

CLIMPING TQ0000 **Bailiffscourt** *Climping, Littlehampton BN17 5RW (01903) 723511* **£135,** plus special breaks; 32 rms, many with four-poster beds and open log fires in winter, and with super views. Mock 13th-c manor built only 60 years ago but with tremendous character – fine old iron-studded doors, huge fireplaces, heavy beams and so forth – in 22 acres of coastal pastures and walled gardens; elegant furnishings, enjoyable modern English and French food, fine wines, and a relaxed atmosphere; outdoor swimming pool, tennis and croquet.

COOLHAM TQ1023 **Blue Idol Quaker Guesthouse** *Old House Lane, Coolham, Horsham RH13 8QP (01403) 741241* **£43,** plus winter breaks; 4 rms, shared bthrm. Lovely, no smoking, timber-framed house in quiet countryside, with a big garden (dogs welcome), comfortable lounge, enjoyable breakfasts, and helpful, friendly owners; cl Christmas week.

CUCKFIELD TQ3024 **Ockenden Manor** *Ockenden Lane, Cuckfield RH17 5LD (01444) 416111* **£115,** plus special breaks; 22 pretty rms. Dating from 1520, this carefully extended manor house has antiques, fresh flowers and an open fire in the comfortable sitting room, good modern cooking in the fine panelled restaurant, a cosy bar, and lovely views from the neatly kept garden (surrounded by 23 acres of parkland).

EAST GRINSTEAD TQ3634 **Gravetye Manor** *Vowels Lane (off the B2110 SW), East Grinstead RH19 4LJ (01342) 810567* **£240;** 18 lovely rms. Elizabethan manor house in magnificent grounds and gardens – 400 years old last year, and also the 40th year the Herbert family have been at the helm; antiques, fine paintings, and lovely flower arrangements in the spacious panelled public rooms, an excellent restaurant using home-grown produce (inc spring water and free-range eggs) and their own home-smoked fish and meats, an exceptional wine list, exemplary service, and a relaxed, almost old-fashioned atmosphere; children over 7 (but babies welcome).

EAST HOATHLY TQ5116 **Old Whyly** *Halland Rd, East Hoathly, Lewes BN8 6EL (01825) 840216* ***£90;** 3 rms. Handsome and historic 17th-c manor house in a lovely garden with a tennis court and swimming pool and very close to Glyndebourne (hampers can be provided); fine antiques and paintings, and delicious food; plenty of walks; children must be well behaved.

EASTBOURNE TV6097 **Hydro** *Mount Rd, Eastbourne BN20 7HZ (01323) 720643* **£100,** plus special breaks; 85 rms, many with fine sea views. Long-standing hotel with a loyal following, quiet gardens with croquet, putting, heated outdoor pool, and sea views; comfortable, spacious lounges, a tranquil library, courteous, helpful staff, and good reliable food in the elegant restaurant; disabled access.

FAIRLIGHT TQ8611 **Fairlight Cottage** *Fairlight, Hastings TN35 4AG (01424) 812545* ***£40,** plus winter breaks; 3 rms. Comfortable and very friendly house in fine countryside with views over Rye Bay and plenty of rural and clifftop walks; big, comfortable lounge (nice views), good breakfasts in the elegant dining room, and generous, carefully prepared food (by prior arrangement, but not at Christmas); well behaved pets welcome.

FITTLEWORTH TQ0018 **Swan** *Fittleworth, Pulborough RH20 1EN (01798) 865429* **£60;** 10 rms. Attractive 15th-c inn (newly refurbished) with a big inglenook log fire in the comfortable lounge, friendly service, enjoyable food in the beamed restaurant, attractive panelled side room, and a sheltered back lawn; good nearby walks; cl Christmas.

FIVE ASHES TQ5326 **Huggetts Furnace Farm** *Stonehurst Lane, Five Ashes, Mayfield TN20 6LL (01825) 830220* **£55;** 3 rms. Lovely medieval house in quiet countryside, with 120 acres of farmland to walk around, a heated swimming pool, ponds and a river (coarse fishing); beams and inglenooks, a friendly atmosphere, and hearty breakfasts; self-catering cottages; children over 8; cl 24–26 Dec.

FRANT TQ5935 **Old Parsonage** *Church Lane, Frant, Tunbridge Wells, Kent TN3 9DX (01892) 750773* ***£69,** plus special breaks; 3 very pretty rms, 2 with four-posters. Just 2 miles from Tunbridge Wells, this carefully restored, imposing former Georgian rectory has antiques, watercolours and plants in the elegant sitting rooms, a spacious Victorian conservatory, good food in the candlelit dining room, and a balustraded terrace overlooking the quiet 3-acre garden; several nearby walks.

HARTFIELD TQ4737 **Bolebroke Mill** *Perry Hill, Edenbridge Rd, Hartfield TN7 4JP (01892) 770425* **£59;** 5 rms, some in the mill and some in the adjoining Elizabethan miller's barn. A working mill until 1948, this ancient place was mentioned in the Domesday Book, and is surrounded by mill streams and woodland; the internal machinery has been kept intact and steep, narrow stairs lead to bedrooms that were once big corn bins; both this and the barn have their own sitting room, breakfasts are marvellous, light suppers enjoyable, and the owners very friendly; no smoking; cl mid-Dec–end Jan; children over 7.

HELLINGLY TQ5914 **Grove Hill House** *Hellingly BN27 4HG (01435) 812440* ***£42;** 2 spacious, pretty rooms, shared bthrm (one has own lavatory). Lovely, heavily beamed, 17th-c farmhouse in quiet countryside; with charming, friendly owners, a relaxed and restful atmosphere, traditional furnishings inc antiques and family photographs, fresh flowers and an open fire; good hearty breakfasts in the separate dining room, and an attractive, flower-filled garden.

MAYFIELD TQ5826 **Middle House** *Mayfield TN20 6AB (01435) 872146* **£55,** plus special breaks; 8 spacious rms, most with own bthrm. Old-world Elizabethan hotel nr the church; with a lovely panelled restaurant, red leather chesterfields and armchairs by the cosy log fire, chatty locals' bar with a big open fire (maybe spit roasts), and a wide choice of good, interesting bar food; attractive back garden, and pleasant views.

OFFHAM TQ4011 **Ousedale House** *Offham, Lewes BN7 3QF (01273) 478680* **£54,** plus special breaks; 3 pretty rms with shower or bthrm. Victorian country house with good views, and 3½ acres of garden and woodland; friendly owners, a spacious lounge, and traditional cooking using home-grown seasonal produce; no children.

ROGATE SU8022 **Mizzards** *Rogate, Petersfield GU31 5HS (01730) 821656* ***£54;** 3 rms. 16th-c house in quiet country setting, with a comfortable and elegant sitting room, and a vaulted dining room; outside swimming pool, landscaped gardens and lake, and fine farmland views; no evening meals, no smoking; cl Christmas; children over 8.

RUSHLAKE GREEN TQ6218 **Stone House** *Rushlake Green, Heathfield TN21 9QJ (01435) 830553* ***£99.95,** plus winter breaks; 7 rms, some with four-posters. In a thousand acres of pretty countryside (with plenty of walks and country sports) and surrounded by an 18th-c walled garden, this lovely house was built at the end of the 15th c and extended in Georgian times; there are open log fires, antiques and family heirlooms in the drawing room, a quiet library, an antique, full-sized table in the mahogany-panelled billiards room, wonderful food in the panelled dining room, fine breakfasts, and a cosseting atmosphere; cl 24 Dec–1 Jan; children over 9.

RYE TQ9120 **Jeakes House** *Mermaid St, Rye TN31 7ET (01797) 222828* ***£65,** plus special breaks; 12 rms overlooking the rooftops of this medieval town or across the marsh to the sea, 10 with own bthrm. Fine 16th-c building, well run and friendly, with good breakfasts, lots of well worn books, comfortable furnishings, linen and lace, a warm fire, and a lovely peaceful atmosphere.

RYE TQ9220 **Little Orchard House** *West St, Rye TN31 7ES (01797) 223831* ***£64;** 3 rms. Beautifully furnished, fine old house with antiques and personal prints and paintings, Georgian panelling, and a big open fireplace in the study; good generous breakfasts (the friendly owners will make evening reservations at any of the many nearby restaurants), and an unexpectedly wonderful, secluded garden; children over 12.

RYE TQ9220 **Old Vicarage** *66 Church Sq, Rye TN31 7HF (01797) 222119* ***£60,** plus bargain breaks; 5 pretty rms with complimentary newspaper and glass of sherry. Charming, quietly placed, mainly 18th-c house with helpful and friendly owners; comfortable sitting room or small library, a log fire in the elegant dining room, and marvellous breakfasts with free-range eggs, freshly made scones and home-made marmalade; cl Christmas; children over 8.

SHIPLEY TQ1523 **Goffsland Farm** *Shipley, Horsham RH13 7BQ (01403) 730434* ***£38;** 1 family rm. 17th-c Wealden farmhouse on 260-acre family farm, with decent breakfasts and a friendly welcome; good walks.

SLINFOLD TQ1131 **Random Hall** *Stane St, Slinfold, Horsham RH13 7QX (01403) 790558* **£81.50,** plus special breaks; 14 comfortable rms. Restored 16th-c farmhouse with lots of beams, flagstones, copper and brass and a fine inglenook fireplace in the lounge; a friendly, relaxed atmosphere, good breakfasts, and enjoyable modern cooking in the candlelit restaurant (or on the terrace); cl 27 Dec–5 Jan.

STORRINGTON TQ1015 **Little Thakeham** *Merrywood Lane, Storrington, Pulborough RH20 3HE (01903) 744416* **£176.25,** plus special breaks; 9 individually decorated rms with stylish fabrics and early antiques. Splendid combination of a magnificent Lutyens house, delightfully restored Gertrude Jekyll garden, antiques and arts and crafts furniture and objets d'art; log fires, traditional English and French food using local produce, and good French wines; outdoor swimming pool, tennis court, and croquet; cl Christmas/New Year; disabled access.

TILLINGTON SU9622 **Horse Guards** *Tillington, Petworth GU28 9AF (01798) 342332* ***£60;** 3 spacious, clean rms. Neat, friendly and civilised 17th-c pub in a lovely village setting, with a beamed front bar, very good, imaginative food (fresh fish delivered 5 times a week, and excellent puddings), up to a dozen wines by the glass; cl 25 Dec; no children.

UCKFIELD TQ4718 **Horsted Place** *Little Horsted, Uckfield TN22 5TS (01825) 750581* ***£140;** 20 individually decorated, spacious rms. Stately Victorian country house on extensive estate; antiques, flowers and log fires in the luxurious lounges, delicious food and good wine list in the no smoking dining room; croquet, tennis, an indoor heated swimming pool, and reduced green fees at East Sussex National Golf Club; babies or children over 8 in restaurant.

WADHURST TQ6632 **Newbarn** *Wards Lane, Wadhurst TN5 6HP (01892) 782042* **£50;** 3 pretty rms, 2 with own bthrm. Carefully renovated, 18th-c tile-hung farmhouse in marvellous position by Bewl Water (walks, bike hire, boating, etc); very friendly, helpful owners, an inglenook fireplace in the attractive and comfortable sitting room, and good breakfasts with home-made preserves; lakeside gardens; self-catering cottages also; cl Christmas.

WARTLING TQ6509 **Wartling Place** *Wartling, Hailsham BN27 1RY (01323) 832590* **£45;** 3 individually furnished rms. Handsome Georgian house in lovely gardens; with antiques in residents' drawing room, good breakfasts in the elegant dining area (they will arrange a hamper service for picnics), fresh flowers, and helpful owners.

WISBOROUGH GREEN TQ0625 **Old Wharf** *Wharf Farm, Wisborough Green, Billingshurst RH14 0JG (01403) 784096* **£55;** 3 rms with views over farmland and canal. Carefully restored, no smoking, canal warehouse with fine old hoist wheel; comfortable sitting room with a log fire, breakfasts using free-range eggs from the farm, a walled canalside garden, and a friendly atmosphere; cl Christmas/New Year; children over 12; no pets.

To see and do

BRIGHTON TQ3104 Despite its many more modern blocks, huge shopping centre and vast modern sports halls, Brighton still has plenty of glistening white Regency buildings dating from its fashionable days in the 18th c, when the health fad of the time (sea-bathing) sent London's finest scurrying to the coast. Still a thriving resort, its atmosphere gets a real kick from its vigorous young university and from its several language schools for foreign students; there's also a booming gay scene. The most lively part is the Lanes – 17th-c fishermen's cottages squeezed together in narrow twisting byways, now crammed with jewellery and antique shops, restaurants and bars; they're mostly closed to traffic. English's here is entertaining for lunch. The North Laine area is slightly more trendy, with good buskers and cool cafés. Throughout, there's no shortage of simple places to eat, inc the Cricketers (Black Lion St), Greys (Southover St, Kemp Town), Mary Packs Cliftonville (good local fish; Hove Pl), and the lively Font & Firkin (Union St, Lanes). On Sun mornings there's a good **market** by the station approach; you do have to get there well before breakfast for the bargains, as it's become a major source of supply for the countless Brighton antique dealers. Nr here **St Bartholomew's Church** (Anne St) is an odd building, like a huge brick barn. Film buffs will be well satisfied with the Duke of York's cinema at nearby Preston Circus, which shows the kind of movies not always found outside London.

Royal Pavilion Nash's flamboyant Indianesque confection should be top of anyone's itinerary: the most eccentric of all royal palaces, a riot of chinoiserie inside. Queen Victoria was the last monarch to own it, but was hardly its greatest fan; if the town council hadn't bought it from her she might well have demolished it. She would no doubt not have been amused to see her apartments restored to their full overblown glory. The gardens have also been returned to the original Regency plan. The whole building is beautifully floodlit at night. It's less busy after 3pm – and better still out of season, when you may find more going on. Meals, snacks, shop, disabled access to ground floor only; cl 25–26 Dec; (01273) 290900; £4.50. **Museum and Art Gallery** (Church St) The Prince Regent's stables and riding school now house the town's outstanding art nouveau and art deco collection, quite sumptuous in parts, from vases, tapestries and sculpture to shoe heels and Salvador Dali's Mae West lips sofa. Snacks, shop, disabled access to ground floor only; cl am Sun, all day Weds, 24–26 Dec, 1 Jan, Good Fri; (01273) 290900; free.

! Brighton was one of the earliest resorts to have a pier – that rusting original is now being restored; in the meantime the **Palace Pier** is a more than satisfactory replacement, and looks magnificent at night. **Sea Life Centre** (Marine Parade) Lively displays of creatures found off the British coast, with seahorses, touch pools and a new undersea soft play area. Meals, snacks, shop, disabled access; cl 25 Dec; (01273) 604234; £5.25. **Fishing Museum** (King's Rd) The seafront arches across from the Old Ship Hotel used to be occupied by local fishermen, and a couple still are, the rest now given over to little craft shops and artists. One houses a collection of local boats, nets, models and pictures. Disabled access; cl 25–26 Dec, and any day Nov–Apr when the weather is poor; (01273) 723064; free.

Booth Museum of Natural History (Dyke Rd) Superb and well presented collection of animal skeletons (inc some dinosaur bones), as well as the Victorian collection of birds the museum was first built to house. Shop, disabled access; cl am Sun, Thurs; (01273) 292777; free. **Preston Manor** (A23) Entertaining and vivid illustration of life in Edwardian times, with fully furnished period rooms, and pleasant walled gardens. Shop; cl am Sun and Mon, 25–26 Dec, Good Fri; (01273) 292770; £3.

Brighton marina (E of the centre) This modern place is lively in summer, with lots of boutiques, bars, tables out by the water and so forth. Also a large new entertainment centre with 10-pin bowling and American pool. An electric train runs to here along the beach from the pier.

Barlow Collection (Brighton University, Falmer; off the A27 N) Reckoned to be Europe's finest collection of Chinese ceramics. It's usually open 11.30am–2.30pm Tues and Thurs; (01273) 606755; free.

HOVE The quieter half of the resort, just W of Brighton proper. On the way you may be able to visit a **Regency town house** in Brunswick Sq – you'll need to make an appointment on (01273) 206306; or pass **St Andrew's Church** (Waterloo St), designed by Sir Charles Barry – quite dull from the outside, but inside rather elaborate in places. **Hove Museum and Art Gallery** (New Church Rd) This grand Victorian villa houses a fine collection of British painting; cl am Sun, all day Mon, and Christmas wk; (01273) 290200; free.

British Engineerium (Nevill Rd) All sorts of road, locomotive and marine steam engines, as well as tools, models, and a restored Victorian water pumping station. Shop, limited disabled access; cl wk before Christmas, engines in steam 1st Sun in month and bank hols; (01273) 559583; £3.50. A restored windmill on Holmes Ave has local history displays; open pm Sun and bank hols May–Sept; 70p.

! **Foredown Tower Countryside Centre** (Foredown Rd, Portslade) Very well done, with a **camera obscura** (best on bright days) as well as a weather station with satellite images, astronomy displays, and splendid views. They can arrange visits to Portslade Old Manor, a ruined medieval house a short stroll away. Snacks, shop; cl Mon–Weds, 23 Dec–2 Jan; (01273) 292092; £2.

Above Brighton the **South Downs** are open country; arable farming and the presence of pylons rather detract from the pleasure of walking, but the steep northern slopes are still impressive, as at Devil's Dyke TQ2610 (with its tremendous view over Brighton, even more startling at night than by day), Wolstonbury Hill TQ2813 and the Jack and Jill windmills nr Clayton TQ3014.

We welcome reports from readers

This *Guide* depends on readers' reports. Do help us if you can – in return, we offer a discount on the next edition to people who've helped us with reports for it. Tell us what you think about places already in it, and anything extra you think we should say about them. And send us your ideas for inclusion in the next edition: places to visit, eat at or stay in, attractive drives or walks, maybe even unusual interesting shops you know of. Use the card in the middle, the report forms at the end, or just write – no stamp needed: *The Good Guide to Britain*, FREEPOST TN1569, Wadhurst, E Sussex TN5 7BR.

Other things to see and do

Sussex Family Attraction of the Year

SINGLETON SU8713 **Weald and Downland Open-air Museum** (on the A286) Best for families on the activity weekends, when children can try their hand at traditional skills and trades, this is a fascinating collection of over 40 historic buildings rescued from all over the SE, re-erected here to form an authentic-looking village set in 50 acres of attractive countryside. Neatly restored by dedicated volunteers, the buildings include farm and agricultural houses, a Tudor market hall, blacksmith's forge, tollhouse and Victorian schoolroom; some interiors are furnished as they would have been when originally built. A hands-on gallery teaches children ancient building techniques – how to construct a bridge or a house – and, depending on how many volunteers they have around that particular day, there might be demonstrations of candlemaking or spinning. Shire horses and other animals give an authentic feel to the farm (watch out for the cockerel – he can be a bit bossy), and there's a nice spot for picnics by the millpond, where you can feed the ducks. Children get most out of it on the activity weekend in the middle of Aug, or during the Oct half term, when they can have a go at brick-laying or basket-making, and join in traditional games; other events throughout the year include heavy horse and rare breed shows. Undemanding and gently instructive, the museum can engage children's attention for quite a chunk of the day when there's a special event on, but even at other times it's an intriguing place to while away a couple of hours – provided it isn't raining. Dogs are welcome on a lead. You can buy flour from the medieval farmstead's working watermill. Snacks, shop, some disabled access, but the site is rather steep; open daily Mar–Oct, then Nov–Feb just wknds, Weds, and Christmas wk; (01243) 811348; £5.20 (£2.50 children over 5).

★ **ALFRISTON** TQ5102 In a sheltered spot below the Downs, this is one of Britain's most charming villages – at quieter times of year (in high summer the ice-cream eaters, teashops and curio shops somewhat blunt its appeal). Thatched, tiled and timbered houses, and a fine **church** built on a Saxon funeral barrow, by a large green just off the single main street. One of the most engaging buildings is the Star Inn, with its Old Bill, a bright red figurehead lion on one corner taken as a trophy from a 17th-c Dutch ship, and some intricate painted 15th-c carvings among its handsome timbering. The Market Cross, too, is good for lunch. **Clergy House** (The Tye) 14th-c, the first building to be taken over by the NT. Carefully restored, it now gives a faithful impression of medieval life; charming cottage garden. Open daily Apr–Oct (exc Tues and Fri); (01323) 870001; £2.20; NT. **Drusillas Park** (up towards the A27) One of the best organised places for children in Britain, a small zoo keeping only animals that they can provide with everything they'd have in the wild, so no lions, tigers or elephants, but plenty of smaller and arguably more entertaining creatures like meerkats, otters, beavers and parrots, in thoughtfully designed enclosures. You watch the meerkats through a little dome in the floor of their spacious enclosure, and underwater vantage points in Penguin Bay make it look as if the birds are flying above you. The latest arrivals include bats and rats. Excellent play areas (one especially for toddlers), and lots of opportunities for hands-on fun. Nearly half is under cover, and there's also a railway and pottery, with special events like birds of prey or knights, jesters, and jugglers in school hols. Shops and eating areas are just outside in Drusillas Village (along with some delightful gardens); you can visit here free without having to go in the zoo. Good meals and snacks, shops, disabled access; cl 24–26 Dec; (01323) 870234; £6.25. **English Wine Centre** (next to Drusillas) Good cross-section of wines made in this country, as well as regional foods and crafts. Snacks, shop, disabled access; cl 23 Dec–2 Jan; (01323) 870164; free, £4.95 tours and tastings.

★ **AMBERLEY** TQ0212 A delightful thatched village; from the churchyard you can peer into the castle (now a good hotel), and there is public access to the Wild Brooks, a large expanse of watermeadows which form an important habitat for wetland plants and birds; there's also a way up to the Downs here. **Amberley Museum** (by Amberley Stn) A carefully thought out open-air museum covering 36 acres of former chalk quarry and limeworks, with plenty of traditional crafts and re-created workshops. Lots going on, from pottery and cobbling to a working village telephone exchange. Meals, snacks, shop, disabled access; cl Mon and Tues (exc school or bank hols), and Nov–mid-Mar; (01798) 831370; £5.20. Nearby the riverside Bridge Inn at Houghton Bridge is great in summer; the B2139 is a pleasant drive. The unspoilt Black Horse has good food, and there are lovely Downs views from the Sportsman.

ARDINGLY TQ3431 **Wakehurst Place Garden** (B2028) The 'Southern Kew', administered by the Royal Botanic Gardens, with a tremendous variety of interesting trees and shrubs inc many tender rarities. Lakes and watergardens, steep Himalayan glade, woodland walks and fine rhododendron species. Plenty to see all year, and very peaceful. The Millennium seed bank being constructed here will eventually store over 25,000 species from all over the world. Meals, snacks, plant and book sales, disabled access; cl 25 Dec, 1 Jan; (01444) 894066; £4.50 (free to NT members). Wknd guided walks usually start in front of the mansion at 11.30am and 2.30pm (2pm in winter); 0181 332 5585 to check. The Gardeners Arms (children in garden only), Ardingly Inn and Oak all do good lunches. Nearby, **Ardingly Reservoir** offers pleasant strolls by its shores, or you can plan a longer walk around the elevated farmland and woodlands surrounding Wakehurst Place and Balcombe.

★ **ARUNDEL** TQ0107 Dating from pre-Roman days, this is dominated by the magnificent walls and towers of the castle on a mound high over the River Arun. Attractive buildings, inc antique shops and so forth, cluster along the sides of the steep main street climbing from the bridge to the castle. The 19th-c Roman Catholic **cathedral** complements the castle wall, giving rather a French feel to the whole small town. **Arundel Museum** (High St) Local history and heritage; cl am Sun, and all Oct–Mar; *£1. **Arundel Castle** Seat of the Dukes of Norfolk for over 700 years – a magnificent sight, a great spread of well kept towers and battlements soaring above the village and the trees around it. The keep is the oldest part; the rest dates mainly from the 19th c. Excellent art collection, inc portraits by Van Dyck, Reynolds, Lely and Gainsborough, as well as 16th-c furniture, and personal possessions of Mary Queen of Scots. Meals, snacks, shop; cl am, Sat, Good Fri and all Nov–Mar; (01903) 883136; £5.70. The Swan and St Mary's Gate Hotel have decent food. There are public paths along the canalised River Arun and into Arundel Park, with its lakes and woodlands. **Wildfowl and Wetlands Trust** (Mill Rd) 55 acres of well landscaped pens, lakes, and paddocks, home to over 1,000 ducks, geese and swans from all over the world. Hides overlook the various habitats, and there are children's activities in school hols. Meals, snacks, shop, disabled access; cl 25 Dec; (01903) 883355; £4.50. The lane past the Trust ends at a little cluster of houses by an isolated church and former watermill. On the way, the Black Rabbit has a superb location and does food, with summer **boat trips**.

ASHDOWN FOREST TQ4832 A major inland attraction for walkers, part forest, part heathland – sandy tracks, clumps of Scots pines, secretive glades and exhilarating views. Traffic restrictions introduced in 1997 are already making it even more peaceful (the B2026 gives the best views). Don't be put off by the OS map: there are far more walking routes than it suggests (a useful 1:30,000 scale

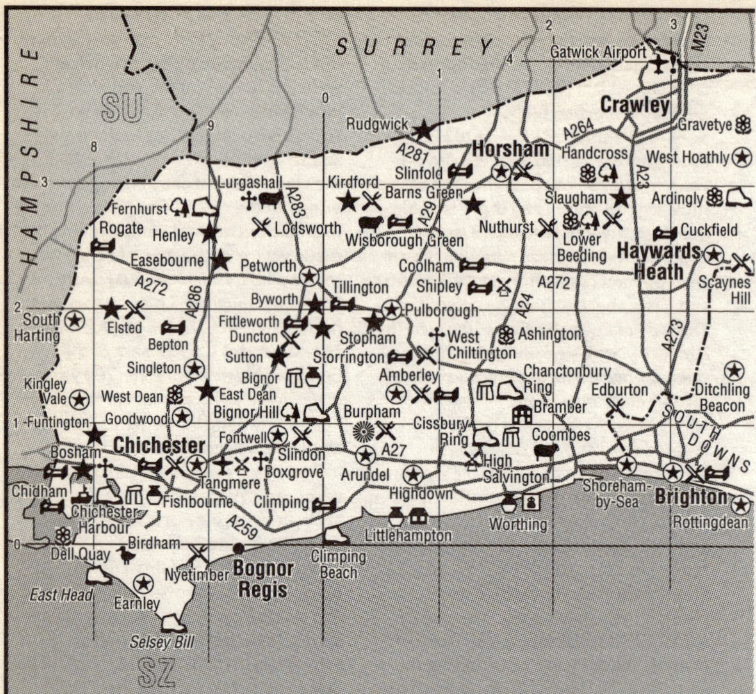

walkers' map issued by the Ashdown Forest Centre shows all the paths and rides and names the car parks – extremely useful, given the Forest's lack of other landmarks). The Forest still looks just like the E H Sheppard drawings for A A Milne's Winnie the Pooh stories, which were set here. Five Hundred Acre Wood is the Hundred Acre Wood of Pooh's world, and with a little searching you can find, SE of Hartfield, the Poohsticks Bridge and, by the B2026, Gills Lap (the 'enchanted place' at the top of the Forest, nr Piglet's house), with its memorial to Milne nr the triangulation point. Handy pubs include the Foresters Arms at Fairwarp, Half Moon at Lye Green and Hatch at Colemans Hatch.

ASHINGTON TQ1317 **Holly Gate Cactus Garden** (Billingshurst Lane) Over 30,000 succulents and cactus plants from both tropical and arid habitats all over the world – a cactus enthusiast's prickly paradise. Plant sales, disabled access; cl 25–26 Dec; (01903) 892930; £1.50. The Franklands Arms at Washington is a useful lunch stop.

BARCOMBE MILLS TQ4316 One of Sussex's secrets, with lazy riverside walks (or boat trips) from the tucked-away Anchor pub.

BARKHAM MANOR VINEYARD TQ4321 (nr Newick) Appealingly set around a striking manor house with B & B; cl Mon exc bank hols; (01825) 724220; £2.50.

BATTLE TQ7515 Takes its name from certainly the most celebrated and perhaps the most disorganised skirmish in English history, thrashed out here in 1066. The main streets (carrying a fair bit of traffic, so not exactly peaceful) have a lot of attractive old buildings, some now antique shops and cafés; beyond them the town extends into spreading new estates. The friendly Olde King's Head has decent food, and the **church** of St Mary has some 13th-c wall paintings. **Battle Abbey** The battlefield itself has a mile-long walk around it with a good audio tour explaining what happened.

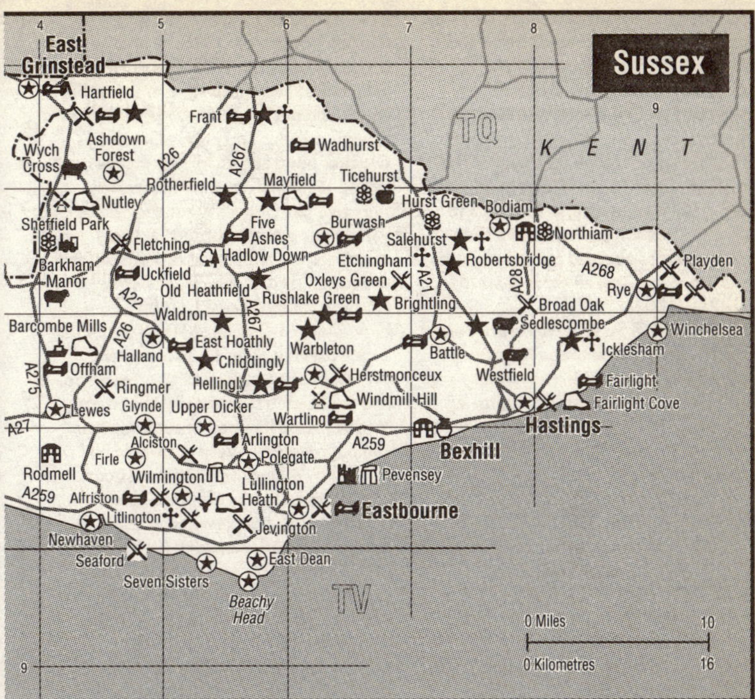

4 years after the bloodshed William built an abbey on the site as penance, the altar reputedly on the very spot where Harold fell. What's left are mostly later remains, inc the monks' dormitory and common room, and the great 14th-c gatehouse which looms over the small market square. Snacks, shop, mostly disabled access; cl 24–26 Dec; (01424) 773792; £4. **Battle Museum** (High St) Good local history inc diorama of the Battle of Hastings and a reproduction of the Bayeux Tapestry (cl am Sun and all Oct–Easter; £1). **Almonry** (High St/Virgins Lane) Ancient building with town model, teas, and a pretty little garden (cl Sun and bank hol Mons, 25–26 Dec; £1). **Buckleys Yesterday's World** (High St) Carefully reconstructed period shops, railway station and the like; lots of hands-on activities, and a nostalgic film show. Snacks, shop; cl 25–26 Dec, 1 Jan; (01424) 775378; £3.95. The B2096 Heathfield road gives views S to Beachy Head from its highest points, nr Netherfield and just before Dallington. Off this road any of the narrow side roads N into the countryside between Burwash and Dallington take you into the most unspoilt part of the steep Wealden woods and pastures.

BEACHY HEAD TV5997 This towering, abruptly cliffy end of the Downs is a landmark for miles around, and the giant of this stretch of cliffy headlands: an unspoilt spot with terrific views, inc the lighthouse dwarfed far below. It's easily reached from Eastbourne. **Beachy Head Countryside Centre** Surprisingly enjoyable hands-on exhibitions, as well as indoor and outdoor play areas, and a full programme of guided walks (best to book for these) around cliffs, beaches and wildflower meadows. Usually open daily Easter–Oct, plus wknds Nov and Dec (may close lunchtime), with walks wknds and school hols – ring for exact dates; (01323) 737273; free, walks £2.

BEXHILL TQ7407 A low-key seaside town with a pebble beach interrupted by cumbersome groins – an unlikely setting for a gem of Bauhaus architecture, the shoreside De La Warr Pavilion designed by Mendelsohn and Chermayeff. The Italian-run café opposite is good value. **Bexhill Museum of Costume and Social History** Set in the delightful grounds of the Old Manor House up towards the tiny 'Old Town', a good look at 18th- to 20th-c fashions, with accessories and other domestic items as well as the clothes. Shop, disabled access; cl Weds (exc Jun–Sept), and all Nov–Easter; (01424) 210045; *£2.

BIGNOR SU9814 **Roman Villa and Museum** One of the largest villas discovered so far, with marvellous mosaics inc the longest in Britain – 25 metres (82ft) long, and still in its original position. Snacks, shop, some disabled access, and largely under cover; cl Mon (exc bank hols and Jun–Sept), and all Nov–Feb; (01798) 869259; £3.25. The White Horse at nearby Sutton has good food (and good-value bedrooms).

BIGNOR HILL SU9813 Here the trees that obscure views for much of the way in this part of the South Downs give way to open ground; Stane St, a Roman road here relegated to a path, arrows off SW through woodland and pasture.

BIRDHAM SU8401 **Sussex Falconry Centre** (Lockacre Aquatic Nursery, Wophams Lane) Originally a breeding and rescue centre, then opened to the public with birds such as falcons, hawks, eagles and owls flown throughout the day. Shop, disabled access; cl Mon (exc bank hols), and Nov–Mar; (01243) 512472; £2.50. This area S of Chichester is flat country, full of nurseries and huge glasshouses; the Lamb towards West Wittering is a popular dining pub.

BODIAM TQ7825 **Bodiam Castle** The perfect picture-book castle, a classic example of 14th-c fortification at its peak, with massive walls rising sheer and virtually complete from the romantic moat, and round drum towers guarding each corner. Built to withstand attack from the French, it was only ever besieged by other Englishmen, and on both occasions was rather weedily handed over without a fight. The interior was destroyed about the time of the Civil War, and wasn't repaired until Lord Curzon bought it in 1916; he left the castle to the NT in 1925. Plenty of space for picnics. They have several enjoyable special events, inc a fun day with donkey rides and Punch and Judy, a Christmas Cracker hunt, and children's story-telling. It's worth reading the leaflet they give you on arriving at the car park – most people fail to spot that the lavatories are at this end rather than at the castle itself. Meals, snacks, shop, limited disabled access; cl Mon Nov–Dec, 24–26 Dec; (01580) 830436; £1 for parking, then £3.30 for castle; NT. Adjacent Knollys is a good teashop, and the Salehurst Halt at Salehurst just W does good lunches. In summer you can put together a very enjoyable full day out by taking the 45-minute boat trip to the castle through peaceful countryside from Newenden (they don't run in bad weather); (01797) 280363 for times; £6.50 return. This can then link with a **steamtrain** on the Kent & East Sussex Railway, from the Tenterden terminus over the Kent border. Up the hill in Ewhurst Green, the White Dog has interesting food, and **Bodiam Bonsai** grow, show and sell these miniature trees.

BOGNOR REGIS SZ9398 An old-fashioned seaside family resort, popular above all for its sandy beaches; the Alex (London Rd) has good-value food.

✝ ★ **BOSHAM** SU8004 The Saxon **church** here figures in the Bayeux Tapestry, and the village is a lovely cluster of old cottages around it, the green, and a broad, almost landlocked, inlet of Chichester harbour, busy with boating in the summer. Don't be tempted to park on the shore – the incoming tide is well known for its trick of lapping around parked cars. Very pleasant to stroll around, with good antique shops and craft galleries, especially on Bosham Lane. The Anchor Bleu, right by the water, is popular for lunch.

✝ **BOXGROVE PRIORY** SU9007 Now the parish church, this 12th-c building is one of the region's most outstanding Early English churches, with a surprising 16th-c painted ceiling, free-standing chantry chapel, and atmospheric monastic ruins outside.

BRAMBER TQ1810 **St Mary's** Striking medieval house, with fine panelling, a pretty garden with topiary, and unusual Elizabethan painted room. Concerts in spring and autumn. Teas, shop; open pm Sun, Thurs and bank hols Easter–Sept; (01903) 816205; *£4. The Bramber Castle has decent food. Adjacent Steyning has some attractive timber-framed and Georgian buildings (and a good Tudor pub, the Chequer).

BURPHAM TQ0309 Great views from this attractive coastal hill village; maybe even bison.

★ **BURWASH** TQ6724 The single main street of this ridge village has many attractively restored tile-hung cottages, inc a good antique centre and teashop, with lime trees along its brick pavement. The graveyard of the Norman-towered church gives fine views over the Dudwell Valley, and the Bell opposite is useful for lunch. Around here the intricate landscapes of the Sussex Weald show steep slopes and valleys, ancient woods and hedgerows punctuated by great oaks, pretty villages, tile-hung or weatherboarded oast houses and wood and tile barns with their long 'cats'-slide' roofs. **Batemans** (signed off the A265) Handsome early 17th-c stonebuilt ironmaster's house, home to Rudyard Kipling 1902–1936. His study is preserved much as it was then, as is the hefty pipework he installed for a pioneer hydro-electric lighting plant. The gardens have a quaint operating watermill, grinding flour every Sat at 2pm. A couple of friendly donkeys are paddocked opposite. New dog crèche, snacks, shop, disabled access to ground floor only; cl Thurs, Fri (exc Good Fri), and Nov–Mar; (01435) 882302; £4.70; NT. Good little-used walks up the wholly unspoilt valley from here, where you can look for Kipling landmarks such as Pook's Hill.

CHANCTONBURY RING TQ1312 One of the great South Downs landmarks, an Iron Age fort, now a prominent hilltop clump of trees, a bracing walk up from Steyning or Washington.

★ † **CHICHESTER** SU8504 Partly pedestrianised and easy to get around, this handsome former Roman city is one of the country's finest examples of Georgian town planning and architecture. The central Nag's Head (St Pancras) is useful for food. **Chichester Cathedral** Mostly Norman, and unusual for rising straight out of the town's streets rather than a secluded close. The spire collapsed in the 1860s (the latest in a long line of structural problems), and was rebuilt, but even now the scaffolding always seems to be up. Highlights include the 14th-c choir stalls, John Piper's Aubusson tapestry, and the window by Chagall. Guided tours (not Sun) at 11am and 2.15pm Easter–Oct. Snacks, shop in the medieval bell tower (23 South St – unusual for being separated from the main building), disabled access; £2 suggested donation. The Bishop's Palace gardens are very pleasant. **St Mary's Hospital** (St Martin's Sq) 13th-c almshouse with some unique misericords in its chapel, and a pretty walled garden; usually open wkdys (exc Weds), but best to check first, (01243) 783377; free. **Guildhall** (Priory Park) Former medieval Grey Friars church, housing the city's archaeological collections; usually open pm Sat Jun–Sept, (01243) 784683 to check; free. The Park Hotel opposite has decent food. **Pallant House** (North Pallant) Interesting Queen Anne town house with Edwardian kitchen and fine furnishings. The gallery has fine Bow porcelain, and an excellent range of 20th-c art – Sutherland, Klee, Leger, Ben Nicholson and the like. Shop; cl am Sun, Mon, bank hols, and 2 wks in Jan; (01243) 774557; £2.80. **Mechanical Music and Doll Collection** (Church Rd, Portfield) A multitude of barrel, fair and Dutch street organs, music boxes and phonographs – all restored and ready to play. Shop, disabled access; open pm exc Sat Easter–Oct, then just pm Sun (not Dec); (01243) 785421; £2. **Pagham Harbour** (off the B2145 S) Peaceful nature reserve, largely silted marshy tidal flats, full of wading birds and wildfowl, especially in spring and autumn; on the way the Blacksmiths Arms at Donnington, packed with bric-à-brac, has a good children's play area. **Centurian Way** Short stretch of disused railway track, now an easy route for cyclists (and walkers) W of Chichester to Mid Lavant.

CHICHESTER HARBOUR SU7702 The most attractive views for walkers are from the shoreside path which skirts the quiet, unspoilt peninsulas of Thorney Island and Chidham. Peter Adams runs **boat trips** around the harbour, full of yachts and dinghies in summer. They leave from Itchenor and are best at high tide; (01243) 786418; £4.50. There's also an hourly passenger ferry between here and the landing at the end of the lane S from Bosham (daily Jun–Aug, wknds only Apr, May and Sept).

CISSBURY RING TQ1308 Huge ramparted Iron Age hill fort, one of the great downland landmarks of the Downs; nr pretty Findon, where the Gun and Village House are both good lunch places.

CLIMPING BEACH TQ0000 This allows an attractive few miles' walk; this bit of coast between Middleton-on-Sea and Littlehampton is the only appreciable undeveloped seaside stretch in W Sussex, apart from Chichester Harbour.

COOMBES TQ1908 **Church Farm** Trailer rides over farmland and through conservation areas – you have to book, but it's great fun, especially in the lambing season. Snacks, shop, disabled access; cl mid-Oct–Feb; (01273) 452028; *£3. They also have a coarse fishing lake.

DELL QUAY SU8303 Attractive waterside hamlet with remains of a Roman quay, harbour views (and fresh fish) from the Crown & Anchor.

Apuldram Roses (Apuldram Lane S) Over 300 kinds of old-fashioned and new roses in harbourside field and gardens made from former orchards. The field is at its best Jun–Sept, after which they have a good end-of-season sale. Snacks, plant sales; cl 24 Dec–7 Jan; (01243) 785769; free.

DITCHLING BEACON TQ3313 Right by the road, with superb views all around, especially out over the villages and towns to the N; a nice walking area of preserved, sheep-cropped, unimproved downland, with chalk hill blue butterflies in summer. The village below is pleasant, with a decent **museum**; the 14th-c Bull has decent food. The B2116 to Offham has good downs views.

! EARNLEY GARDENS SZ8197 (Almodington Lane, Earnley) This 5-acre site is these days quite a busy day out; as well as the long-established 17 themed gardens, exotic birds and free-flying butterflies, they now have a shipwreck display, small animal farm, and a refreshingly informal nostalgia museum, **Rejectamenta**. This takes in thousands of everyday objects from the last hundred years, collected over nearly a quarter of a century by an ex-art student who says she just can't stop. Meals, snacks, shop, disabled access; open mid-Mar to end of Oct; (01243) 512637; £5.50 everything, £3.50 just gardens and butterflies or just nostalgia museum.

EAST DEAN TV5597 **Seven Sisters Sheep Centre** (Gilberts Drive) Very enjoyable family-run downland sheep farm with compact visitor centre, and paved paths between pens of many breeds of sheep. Lambing (mid-Mar–early May), demonstrations of shearing (Jun–mid-July), spinning, milking and cheese-making, and plenty of young animals to cuddle or bottle-feed. The farm shop sells sheep cheeses and yoghurts. Snacks, disabled access; cl am wkdys (exc school hols), all mid-Sept–mid-Mar; (01323) 423302; £3. The village itself is prettily set around a sloping green, with an attractive pub, the Tiger. A lane past the farm continues to the **Birling Gap**, a cleft in the coastal cliffs famous since smuggling days, with a coastguard station and lighthouse (there are plans to move it to save it from coastal erosion); and on to Beachy Head. The Birling Gap Hotel is nicely set just above the shore.

EAST GRINSTEAD TQ3835 **Standen** (off the B2110 W) A fine example of the many talents of the 19th-c Arts and Crafts Movement. Designed by Philip Webb (even down to the unusual light fittings), a friend of William Morris, and little changed since, the interior of the house is decorated with several different William Morris wallpapers, and many of the furnishings are of the period. Snacks, shop, limited disabled access; open pm Weds–Sun mid-Mar–Oct; (01342)

323029; £5, £3 garden only; NT. Nearby **Weir Wood Reservoir** has waterside walks along its N shore, with public paths leading up to Standen. The town itself is really to be avoided, with long weekend traffic queues.

★ ✝ ☗ ⛫ ❃ **EASTBOURNE** TV6198 The Duke of Devonshire still owns much of this civilised and restrained seaside resort; as he prohibits seaside tat the place has a more dignified and solid feel than many of its livelier rivals – fun seekers should head elsewhere, but it's perfect for gentle seafront strolling. The Old Town's **church** is lavish; next to it the Lamb is a nice old pub. **Museum of Shops and Social History** (Cornfield Terr) One of the most comprehensive collections of its type, 20 reconstructed and very well filled shops and rooms, inc an old seafarers' tavern. Shop, disabled access to ground floor only; cl 24–26 Dec; (01323) 737143; £2.50. **Wish Tower** (King Edward's Parade) One of the 103 Martello towers built in case of French invasion; there's a fascinating collection of puppets, some centuries old. Shop; cl Nov–Easter (exc school hols); (01323) 411620; £1.80. **Redoubt Fortress** (Royal Parade) Another splendid tower, housing a more interesting than average military museum. Open-air concerts (usually every Weds and Fri Jun–Aug) always end in a firework display. Snacks, shop; cl early Nov–Easter; (01323) 410300; *£2. **Lifeboat Museum** (Grand Parade) Makes up in enthusiasm what it lacks in size; cl Jan–Easter; free. **Towner Museum** (High St, Old Town) Handsome building, with good temporary exhibitions; cl am, and all day Mon (exc bank hols); charges for some exhibitions.

⛰ **EAST HEAD** SZ7699 A NT-owned promontory on the E entrance of Chichester Harbour, a sandy spit with dunes overlooking the marshes and mudflats.

✝ **ETCHINGHAM CHURCH** TQ7126 Lovely, sturdy and ancient semi-fortified building in honey-coloured stone – quaintly, the station is built to match.

⛰ **FAIRLIGHT COVE** TQ8711 A good destination for walks from Hastings Old Town, by a path climbing on to the sandstone cliffs for a rugged couple of miles. The tumbled appearance of the coast here bears witness to the occasional cliff-falls.

♣ ⛰ **FERNHURST** SU8928 Nicely varied walking country here, often densely wooded, but with some open hillsides such as Woolbeding Common SU8625 and the S tip of Black Down SU9129.

★ ❁ ⛰ ⛫ 🐄 ❀ ✝ **FIRLE** TQ4707 An attractive quiet village, with a good pub, the Ram. **Firle Beacon**, a South Downs landmark, is a lovely walk above the village, with good views. **Firle Place** (off the A27) Beautiful house, essentially Tudor but remodelled in the 18th c, with some treasures of European and English painting, and wonderful furnishings. Meals, snacks, shop, some disabled access; open pm Weds, Thurs and Sun Jun–Sept, as well as Easter, spring and summer bank hols; (01273) 858335; £4. There are longer unguided tours the first Weds in the month, when more rooms are open (and the price is higher). **Middle Farm** (A27 E) Best known for its excellent farm shop, with a huge range of English ciders and perries, farmhouse cheeses, English wines, good sausages, organic meats and other produce. Also children's farmyard, and always lots going on at apple harvest time; cl 25–26 Dec; (01323) 811411; *£1 for farmyard. **Charleston Farmhouse** (A27 Firle–Selmeston) Delightful 17th/18th-c house which was the home of Duncan Grant and Clive and Vanessa Bell; decorated by them, it and its magical garden still evoke the atmosphere of those Bloomsbury days. Teas Sat, shop; open pm Weds–Sun and bank hols Easter–Oct (am too in summer hols), no guided tours Sun and bank hols; (01323) 811265; £5. Longer tours on Fri (when children under 8 aren't admitted). At Alciston, the Rose Cottage has very good home cooking. **Berwick Church** (TQ5205) nr here has 1940s murals by the Bloomsbury Group; the Cricketers Arms is a good lunch place.

⛫ ☗ **FISHBOURNE ROMAN PALACE** SU8304 (Salthill Rd) This magnificent villa with its 100 or so rooms was occupied from the 1st to the 3rd c – Britain's largest known residence of the time. You can see 25 superb mosaic floors (a bigger collection than anywhere else in Europe), and a garden has been laid out according to its 1st-c plan. One theory about the site is that it was a high-class brothel. Snacks, shop, disabled access; cl mid-Dec–mid-Feb; (01243) 785859; £4. The welcoming Bull's Head has a good choice of food.

FONTWELL SU9406
Denmans Garden (off the A27) Colourful series of vistas over 3½ acres, inc exuberantly oriental-feeling areas with a gravel stream, ornamental grasses, bamboos and flowering cherries, as well as a beautiful, richly planted walled garden. Meals, snacks, plant sales, disabled access; cl Nov–Feb; (01243) 542808; £2.80. In the pretty nearby village of **Eartham** there is a small but charming church; the George there is a good place to eat.

★ † **FRANT** TQ5935 Despite the main road, a charming and rather elegant village, with an ancient **church** and handsome green.

† ! **GATWICK AIRPORT** TQ2740
Skyview (South Terminal) Entertaining visitor gallery, with a multi-media show demonstrating a typical airport day, good explanation of cockpit controls, and excellent simulator rides. Splendid runway views. Shop, disabled access; (01293) 502244; £4.50.

GLYNDE PLACE TQ4509
Elizabethan manor house in a beautiful setting, extensively remodelled inside in the 18th c, but outside pretty much unchanged. Portraits and mementos give a good grounding in the family history, while outside are pleasantly wild parklands and lawns. Snacks, shop; open pm Sun and bank hols in May, then pm Weds, Sun and bank hols Jun–Sept; (01273) 858224; £4. There's a neat neo-Palladian **church** nearby, and the Trevor Arms has decent food. The Glyndebourne Festival, with its decidely smart operas and marvellous new auditorium designed by Sir Michael Hopkins, takes place May–Aug.

GOODWOOD HOUSE
SU8808 Unusual-looking house in beautiful downland countryside, especially renowned for its paintings, inc works by Canaletto and Stubbs. There's quite a riding feel – it was acquired by the first Duke of Richmond in 1697 so that he could ride with the local hunt, and the stables added during 18th-c alterations seem grander even than the house. Ring for opening times, (01243) 755040; *£6. The adjacent **racecourse** is the setting for Glorious Goodwood, and as well as around 19 race days a year has monthly antique markets; (01243) 774107 for dates.
Sculpture at Goodwood (Hat Hill Copse, towards East Dean) Excellent changing exhibitions of sculpture in 20 acres of beautiful wooded parkland; it's established an excellent reputation in the few years it's been open, so it's a shame the high admission price limits it to people with more than just a passing interest in the subject. Some disabled access; open Thurs, Fri and Sat Mar–Nov; (01243) 538449; *£10. This is a good area for a country drive; the Anglesey Arms at Halnaker is the best nearby place for a meal.

GRAVETYE TQ3534
Ingwersens (Birch Farm) Very long-established alpine plants specialist nursery; cl 1–1.30pm, wknds Sept–Feb, 2 wks at Christmas; (01342) 810236. Out this way, the White Hart at Selsfield (B2028) and the Crown and cheaper Red Lion at Turners Hill are useful for lunch.

HADLOW DOWN TQ5424
Wilderness Wood (A272) Acres of working woodland, good for learning about forests and their wildlife, or just for a stroll. Several picnic areas and play area, occasional demonstrations of heavy horses and other traditional woodland working methods. Teas, shop (they make chestnut furniture and other goods), some disabled access; (01825) 830509; £1.90. Just along the A272, Buxted has one of the oldest trees in Britain, a yew thought to be 2,479 years old.

HALLAND TQ4815
Bentley Wildfowl and Motor Museum Busy estate centred around Tudor farmhouse converted into Palladian mansion, filled with fine furnishings and paintings, inc 150 watercolours by local artist Philip

Rickman. The motor museum has gleaming veteran, Edwardian and vintage vehicles, while the lakes and ponds that surround it are home to a countless variety of exotic wildfowl. There's also a narrow-gauge railway (summer wknds and bank hols, plus Weds in Aug), so plenty to keep families happy. Meals, snacks, shop, disabled access; open daily mid-Mar–Oct (house cl am), and all exc house also open wknds in Nov, Feb and Mar; (01825) 840573; £4.20, less winter. The Forge is useful for lunch.

HANDCROSS TQ2629 **Nymans** (B2114) Very impressive rare trees, inc magnificent southern beeches and eucryphias, as well as fine camellias, rhododendrons and magnolias, countless other interesting flowering shrubs, a secluded sunken garden, and an extensive, artfully composed wilderness. Meals, snacks, plant sales, shop, disabled access; cl Mon (exc bank hols), Tues, and wkdys Nov–Feb; (01444) 400321; £5; NT. **High Beeches gardens** (B2110) Well worth a look, 20 acres of landscaped woodland, lots of rare plants, watergardens, and wildflower meadows. Plant sales; usually open pm daily exc Weds from Apr–Jun and Sept–Oct, and Mon and Tues July–Aug; (01444) 400589; £3.50. The Chequers at Slaugham is a good nearby dining pub.

★ **HARTFIELD** TQ4735 Pleasant village with some attractive houses. The well stocked shop at Pooh Corner reflects the fact that surrounding Ashdown Forest inspired A A Milne's tales of Winnie the Pooh, and Perryhill Nursery has rare plants.

★ **HASTINGS** TQ8209 The Old Town at the E end is very attractive – 2 medieval churches, a couple of streets with raised pavements, lots of medieval buildings, and relatively unobtrusive more recent infilling. Down below, the fishermen still haul their boats up on to the beach and sell excellent fresh fish by the unusual tall, black, wooden net huts. At each end of the cliffs is an unusual sloping tracked lift down to sea level (70p). The First In Last Out in the Old Town has interesting food and brews its own beer. The rest of the town is a busy shopping town, rather run-down in parts, with 19th-c resort buildings nearer the seafront, seaside hotels and B & Bs, a good prom, and shingle beach. You can fish from the **pier** (30p to walk along it). **Hastings Castle** Bracingly set above crumbling cliffs (and the tracked lift), the evocative Norman ruins are close to the site of William the Conqueror's first English motte and bailey castle. There's a lively audio-visual exhibition on the Battle of Hastings. Shop, some disabled access; (01424) 422964; £2.90. **Fishermen's Museum** (Rock-a-Nore Rd) Interestingly housed in a former fishermen's chapel; cl Good Fri and 25 Dec; free. A few doors along is the **Shipwreck Heritage Centre**; cl Oct–Easter; £2.20. **Sea Life Centre** (Rock-a-Nore Rd) Another in the lively chain, with walk-through underwater tunnel. Snacks, shop, disabled access; usually only cl 25 Dec, but best to check first in winter; (01424) 718776; £4.95. **Hastings Tapestry** This ambitious 73-metre (240-ft) tapestry depicting great events in British history, created by the Royal School of Needlework, can now be seen at the White Rock Theatre; cl Mon and all Mar; *£2. **Smugglers Adventure** (Cobourg Pl) A labyrinth of deep caverns and passages, with models, museum and well done life-size tableaux illustrating life for an 18th-c smuggler. Spooky lighting and sound effects in places. Shop, limited disabled access; cl 25–26 Dec; (01424) 422964; £4.40. **Hastings Museum and Art Gallery** (Johns Pl, Cambridge Rd) A little out of the centre, but worth a look for its American Indian displays; children may prefer the dinosaur gallery. Shop, disabled access; cl 1–2pm Sat, 25 Dec and Good Fri; (01424) 781155; free.

HAYWARDS HEATH TQ3226 **Borde Hill** (Balcombe Rd, N) Lovely 40-acre gardens with woodland walks through rare maples, oaks, conifers and many other fine trees, as well as a lake (you can fish), herbaceous borders and magnificent rhododendrons. There's an adventure playground. Meals, snacks, plant sales (Blooms of Bressingham), disabled access; cl 25 Dec; (01444) 450326; £4.

The White Harte at Cuckfield does good-value lunches.

HERSTMONCEUX TQ6410 (SE of village) Extensive gardens around handsome, 15th-c brickbuilt **castle**, with nature trails, hands-on science centre, and astronomy displays in former buildings of the Greenwich Royal Observatory. You can tour the castle itself by arrangement. Children's play area; snacks, shop, disabled access; cl Nov–Mar; (01323) 834444; £3. **Sussex Trugs** (Hailsham Rd) Thomas Smith demonstrates the local art of trug basket-making; no demonstrations wknds (though shop open Sat); (01323) 832137. The Ash Tree over at Brownbread Street has good old-fashioned home cooking.

HIGH SALVINGTON TQ1206 An 18th-c post mill; open pm 1st and 3rd Sun Apr–Sept, *£1.

HIGHDOWN HILL TQ0903 (A259) Excellent views from this famous garden, which differs from most of the other great Sussex gardens in that it's on very uncompromising chalk – laid out in and around a chalk pit high on the Downs above Angmering; many rarities, inc unusual Chinese plants. Some disabled access; cl wknds Oct–Mar; (01903) 501054; free. Iron Age hill fort nearby, and the Spotted Cow at the foot of the hill does good-value food.

HORSHAM TQ1730 **Museum** Timber-framed Tudor house with well organised local history, and an extraordinary collection of early bicycles. The small but pretty garden has some unusual wild cyclamen. Shop, some disabled access; cl Sun and bank hols; (01403) 254959; free. The town's much developed, but a particularly attractive quiet corner is The Causeway, by the church. The Black Jug (North St) has good food. **Christ's Hospital** (just SW) You may be able to join tours of the refreshingly egalitarian public school, where a remarkable painting by Verrio fills an entire wall of the Dining Hall. Meals, snacks, shop, disabled access; tours from £3.50 – booking essential; (01403) 211293 for dates. S of here, popular bases for local walks include the Bridge at Copsale TQ1725 and Black Horse at Nuthurst TQ1926 (bluebell woods).

HURST GREEN TQ7327 **Merriments** (Hawkhurst Rd) Developing, newish 4-acre demonstration garden with lots of planting ideas, some unusual plants, and a comprehensive nursery inc rare hardy plants. Tearoom, disabled access; garden open Easter–Oct, nursery all year; (01580) 860666; *£2.50.

★ † **ICKLESHAM** TQ8616 Attractive village despite the main road, with a Norman church and country walks.

KINGLEY VALE SU8210 An interesting walk though needing some stamina, whether you approach via the nature trail on the S side or from Stoughton to the N (the Hare & Hounds will fuel you well). This nature reserve is Europe's largest yew forest, a magical place where the trees create eerie pools of darkness on the S slopes of the Downs; above, you can look over Chichester Harbour from a prehistoric burial mound.

LEWES TQ4110 The administrative capital of East Sussex, a pleasantly unrushed country town below the quarried white edge of the South Downs. It has some attractive old buildings, mainly Georgian though with a few older stonebuilt or timber-framed specimens, particularly along its steep main street and in the little narrow alleys and other streets alongside. This is where you'll see Sussex tile-hanging at its best; there's also quite a lot of 'mathematical tiling' – sham bricks over timbered buildings to make them look more progressive. There are several decent antique shops, and an attractive complex of **craft shops** in a former candlemaker's factory in Market Lane; café, cl Sun. The Dorset Arms (Malling St) and more bohemian Snowdrop (South St) are useful for lunch. Local brewers Harveys have a good shop and new pub attached to the brewery on Cliffe High St. **Lewes Castle** Norman, unusual for being built on not one but 2 artificial mounds (Lincoln is the only other such place we know of). The best view of the town is obtained from the roof of the keep, and there's a good archaeological museum. Shop; cl 25–26 Dec; (01273) 486290; £3.40. **Anne of Cleves House** (Southover High St) Henry VIII's fourth wife had this fine 16th-c house as part of her divorce settlement. She probably never came here, but its rooms give a good idea of regional life over the following 2 centuries. Shop; cl am Sun, and all Nov–Feb exc Tues, Thurs and Sat; (01273) 474610; £2.20 (combined ticket with castle £4.50). Guided tours of the ruined Norman **priory** leave here in summer, call (01273) 486290 for details. **Southover Grange** (Southover Rd) Diarist John Evelyn's handsome boyhood home is now the District Registry Office, but you can visit the attractive gardens free. From Bell Lane on the SW edge you can follow the old Juggs Road track, used by the Brighton fishwives, up past Kingston and the downland nature reserve by Newmarket Hill to the outskirts of Brighton itself. There are more public paths than the OS map suggests; from the town centre you can walk up Chapel Hill, through the golf course and on via an unspoilt dry valley to **Mount Caburn**, rather grandiosely named for its size but capped by an Iron Age fort and with views towards the coast; it's also popular with paragliders. A fine 3-mile circuit from Lewes is had by following the Ouse N, then heading under the railway line, through the woods to cross the A275 at Offham, then keeping left to follow a path (not on the OS map) above some spectacularly deep chalk pits; another unmapped path leads along a downland crest past the site of the Battle of Lewes and past the prison to re-enter the town.

LITTLEHAMPTON TQ0202 Little sign here of its age (it was an important port up to the 1500s), but its long sandy beaches make it a popular, simple family resort. **Littlehampton Museum** (Church St) In an early 19th-c manor house; cl Sun and Mon; free. Towards the W, beyond the River Arun, is quite an extensive area of unspoilt dunes between the beach and golf course. The 18th-c Arun View right on the river does decent lunches. **Body Shop factory** (Watersmead, on the A259 N of Littlehampton) You can book to visit – the 90-minute tours are interesting and informative; (01903) 844044. No tours Sun; *£3.95.

† **LITLINGTON** TQ5101 Over the Cuckmere valley from Alfriston, notable for its **church** down a footpath – so small there can scarcely be room in it for a congregation of more than about 15. The Plough & Harrow here is useful.

LOWER BEEDING TQ2225 **Leonardslee Gardens** Enormous Grade I listed garden set in a 240-acre valley with 6 beautiful lakes; marvellous rhododendrons, magnolias, oaks and unusual conifers, delightful rock garden, extensive greenhouse and Japanese garden, bonsai exhibition, and wallaby and deer. The gardens are on the edge of the ancient St Leonards Forest, and there's a summer wildflower walk. Readers get a great deal of pleasure from coming here. Meals, snacks, plant sales, limited disabled access; cl Nov–Mar; (01403) 891212; May £5, other times £4. The Crabtree does excellent food.

LULLINGTON HEATH TQ5401 A rare survival of downland untouched by modern farming practices, and managed as a National Nature Reserve for its chalkland and heathland flora; a good spot for walks, which can be spun out with a diversion to Wilmington for a view of the enigmatic chalk figure, the Long Man of Wilmington.

† **LURGASHALL** SU9327 Attractive small village, with an unusual loggia outside the largely Saxon **church** where parishioners walking in from a distance could eat their sandwiches. The Noah's Ark here is prettily placed for lunch. **Lurgashall Winery** Produces a wide range of traditional country wines, meads and cordials. Tastings, shop, disabled access; cl 25–26 Dec, 1 Jan; (01428) 707292; self-guided tours wknds; £1 per family.

★ **MAYFIELD** TQ5826 One of Sussex's prettiest villages, with interesting shops, and pleasant hilly terrain around it. A reasonable network of paths includes a short waymarked circular walk.

NEWHAVEN TQ4400 **Newhaven Fort** (Fort Rd) Built 120

years ago in case of French attack, this is a big place to explore, with underground installations, period reconstructions and tunnels burrowing into the cliffs, super views from its ramparts, and an assault course for children. Snacks, shop; cl wkdys in Mar, and all Nov–Feb; (01273) 517622; £3.60. You can take the **ferry trip** to Dieppe in France from here. The harbourside Hope has decent food. **Paradise Park and Planet Earth** (Avis Rd) Garden centre with exhibition on the last few million years of evolution, complete with earthquake experience and life-size moving dinosaurs. Also model village with miniaturised Sussex landmarks. Meals, snacks, shops, disabled access, cl 25–26 Dec; (01273) 512123; £3.99.

NORTHIAM TQ8225 **Great Dixter** (off the A28 at the post office) Timbered 15th-c house, carefully restored and added to by Lutyens in the early part of this century. He designed the attractive gardens too; originally arranged as a series of distinct areas, they were later stocked more informally with interesting plants by the gardening writer Christopher Lloyd who lives here. Snacks, plant sales, disabled access; cl am, all day Mon (exc bank hols) and all Nov–Apr; (01797) 252878; £4, £3 gardens only. The Mill (Station Rd) has decent food.

NUTLEY WINDMILL TQ4428 17th-c mill saved by enthusiastic locals before such action became more common; open pm last Sun of month Apr–Sept; free. Nearby **Camp Hill** is one of the best walking areas in the Ashdown Forest.

★ **OLD HEATHFIELD** TQ5920 Charming peaceful hamlet – very different from the sprawly small town of Heathfield nearby which sprang up around the now-defunct railway (the town has a busy Tues morning market, excellent delicatessen specialising in unusual cheeses, and first-class butcher – Pomfrets).

PETWORTH SU9721 The magnificent rooms of splendid **Petworth House** are filled with one of the most impressive art collections in the country, inc Dutch Old Masters and 20 pictures by Turner, a frequent visitor. Other highlights include the 13th-c chapel, grand staircase with frescoes, carved room elegantly decorated by Grinling Gibbons, and contrasting servants' block. You can see extra rooms on Tues and Weds and there may be conservation demonstrations on Mon. Meals, snacks, shop, disabled access; cl am, all day Thurs and Fri, and all Nov–Mar; (01798) 342207; £5; NT. The deer park, with stately trees and prospects still recognisable as those glorified by Turner, is open all year; free. The village has narrow streets of attractive old houses, inc a good few antique shops. The **Doll House Museum** has over 100 dolls' houses, with 2,000 miniature inhabitants; shop, disabled access; open Sun Jan–Oct, plus Thurs–Sat Mar–Oct; (01798) 344044; £3.50. The **Cottage Museum** on the High St has an interesting reconstruction of an estate worker's cottage; cl am, all day Fri and Mon (exc bank hols), £1.50. The Angel Hotel fits in well, and has a good weekend carvery; the Stonemasons has decent food too.

PEVENSEY CASTLE TQ6505 Formidable castle based around huge 4th-c Roman fort, with massive bastions and walls of Roman masonry still up to 9 metres (30ft) high in places. The Norman keep was built for William the Conqueror, and interesting details include fireplaces, dungeons and an oubliette. Shop, some disabled access; cl winter Mon and Tues, 24–26 Dec; (01323) 762604; £2. The Castle Cottage restaurant does decent food, inc light summer lunches in the castle garden.

POLEGATE TQ5602 **Filching Manor Motor Museum** (Jevington Rd, Wannock) Gleamingly restored vintage cars, shown to great effect in the grounds of a striking manor house. Unique panelling in the minstrels' gallery, acres of woodland, and Donald Campbell connections. Snacks, disabled access; open Thurs–Sun plus bank hols Easter–Sept; (01323) 487838; *£3.50. **Cuckoo Trail** Following the route of a former railway Polegate–Heathfield (with plans for extension beyond), good for traffic-free walking or family cycling; the mileposts, sculpted by local artists, each have a cuckoo hidden in their design.

PULBOROUGH TQ0518 The town has some attractive buildings down towards the river; the Waters Edge, with lake views, has a good choice of food. There's an RSPB Reserve nearby. The charmingly placed White Hart at Stopham is another nearby place with good food. **Parham House** Charming Elizabethan house, still a family home, its panelled rooms full of notable portraits, furniture, oriental carpets and rare needlework. The surrounding grounds are really very special – popular with birds, they include a rose garden and a vegetable garden with its produce sold in the shop. Also deer park, and maze designed with children in mind. Lunches in 15th-c kitchen, shop, plant sales; open pm Weds, Thurs, Sun and bank hols Easter–Oct; (01903) 744888; £5, £3 garden only. **Nutbourne Vineyards** (Nutbourne Manor) 18-acre vineyard with tours and tastings, and visitor centre in former windmill; shop; no tours am wkdys and mid-Oct–May; (01798) 815196; free.

RODMELL TQ4206 **Monks House** Just a quiet, lived-in house, in a pleasant village, but a beautifully kept place of pilgrimage for followers of the Bloomsbury Group, as Leonard and Virginia Woolf lived here from 1919 – Leonard until his death in 1969. Open pm Weds and Sat Apr–Oct; (01892) 890651; £2.50; NT. The Juggs at Kingston on the way from Lewes is good for lunch.

ROTTINGDEAN TQ3602 A pretty place, worth a stop. Enthusiastic local volunteers are responsible for preserving both the handsome Georgian grange, now a **museum** (cl am Sun), and the pleasant 2-acre **Kipling Gardens**, well restored Victorian gardens named after the author who lived here for 5 years from 1897. Burne-Jones was a resident for a while too, designing the windows built by William Morris for the Early English **church**.

RYE TQ9321 Enchanting, and still relatively unspoilt despite its many charms. Before the wind and sea currents did their work, the little town was virtually surrounded by sea, and as one of the Cinque Ports played an important part in providing men and ships for coastal defence. It's built on a hill crowned by the partly Norman **St Mary's church** (with a notable churchyard, and very early turret-clock, 2 quarter-jacks by it striking the quarter-hours); up here the largely cobbled streets still follow a 12th/13th-c narrow layout, with most of the houses lining them dating from the 16th c. The town is full of antique shops, book shops and craft shops; Rye Art Gallery (107 High St) is a non-profit trust with several floors selling the best of local art and craft. The views are lovely, and steep Mermaid St in particular is famously photogenic (the Mermaid itself is a handsome old inn). **Rye Heritage Centre** (Strand Quay) A useful introduction, with a sound-and-light show based around an intricate town model. Shop, disabled access; cl 25 Dec; £2. **Lamb House** (West St) Built in 1723 for former mayor James Lamb, and chiefly devoted to mementos of the author Henry James, who lived here from 1898 to 1916; after his death E F Benson, who also became mayor, moved here. Open pm Weds and Sat Apr–Oct; (01892) 890651; £2.50; NT. **Rye Castle Museum** In the striking 13th-c Ypres Tower (as in Wipers), this museum has received a Lottery grant for expansion and hopes to open a second site in East St by Easter 1999; shop, disabled access at East Street; cl winter wkdys; (01797) 226728; £1.50. The Ypres Castle pub just below has good food in a nice setting. **Rye Treasury of Mechanical Music** (Cinque Ports St) An entertaining collection of music boxes, barrel organs and pianolas, and you can hear them all. Shop, disabled access; (01797) 223345; £3. **Rye Harbour**, because of the build-up of shingle along this coast, is now a mile or two from the town, though yachts and fishing boats do still come right up the river to the pretty quay. The Inkerman Arms has good fresh fish (as does the Hope & Anchor up in the town). Tony Easton will take you **sea fishing** for the day; (01797) 252104; from £25. The expanse of shingle stretching around the river mouth is now preserved as a **nature reserve**, with hides to watch the shore birds. **Camber Castle** TQ9218 This massive Tudor fort had the sea lapping up to it when it was built, but is now stranded a mile or so inshore by the encroaching shingle (open wknds July–Sept; £2). Beyond it the Ship on Winchelsea Beach is a welcoming refuge. On the other side of the river **Camber Sands** is a splendid beach, with plenty of room for walking.

★ ✝ **SALEHURST** TQ7424 Attractive tucked-away village with 14th-c church.

★ **SEDLESCOMBE** TQ7719 Attractive village, with an unusual organic vineyard.

SELSEY BILL SZ8592 One of the nicest and cleanest **beaches** along the south coast.

SEVEN SISTERS COUNTRY PARK TV5199 (A259, Exceat) Running down to the sea by the River Cuckmere – protected meadow, saltings, shingle and the flanking chalk headlands; you can hire bikes from the Cuckmere Cycle Co at Granary Barn, (01323) 870310. The chalk cliffs, together with Beachy Head, form the spectacular finale of the South Downs; the South Downs Way long-distance path angles up over them above the flats and past the sea at Cuckmere Haven. For an interesting circular walk you can head inland by Friston Forest, Westdean and East Dean. The roomy Golden Galleon at Exceat does good food.

SHEFFIELD PARK TQ4124 Wonderful 120-acre garden partly landscaped by Capability Brown, since then imaginatively planted with many varieties of tree unknown to him, especially chosen for their autumn colours. Also marvellous rhododendrons, azaleas and water lilies on the lakes. Snacks, shop, disabled access; cl Mon (exc bank hols), Tues mid-Nov–Dec, all late Dec–Feb, and wkdys in Mar; (01825) 790231; £4.20; NT. At nearby attractive Fletching (often Sussex's Best-Kept Village), the Griffin is good for lunch. **Bluebell Line** (Sheffield Park Station, A275) Earliest preserved steam railway in Britain, and one of the best; 9-mile trips through Horsted Keynes to Kingscote (which has period bus connections to main line East Grinstead), with splendid stations decked out with period advertisements and wonderful genuine period carriages. The journey passes woodlands full of bluebells in late spring (usually best in mid-May), hence the name of the line. Part of the station is a museum housing the region's largest railway collection, inc some 30 locomotives. Pullman dining specials, Santa specials, shop, café; trains wknds all year, daily May–Sept and school hols – (01825) 722370 for timetable; £7.40. The Sloop at Scaynes Hill is not far for lunch.

SHIPLEY TQ1422 Smock mill built in 1879, once owned by Hilaire Belloc and now used as the home of BBC's *Jonathan Creek*; open pm 1st and 3rd Sun and bank hol Mon Apr–Oct; £1.50.

✝ ✝ **SHOREHAM-BY-SEA** TQ2106 Though not one of England's more famous ports, this is quite a busy one, with several attractive old buildings around the harbour. Inland, in Old Shoreham, the early Norman **church** is accompanied by some handsome old houses (among them the good 16th-c Red Lion). Just W is striking **Lancing College Chapel**, begun in 1868, with a soaringly handsome nave, and elaborate stained-glass Rose Window. **Marlipins** (High St) Norman building which may once have been a customs house, now a local history museum. Shop; cl 1–2pm, am Sun, Mon, and Oct–Apr; £1.50. **Museum of D-Day Aviation** (Shoreham Airport) Uniforms, engines, artefacts and a replica Spitfire. Meals, snacks, shop, disabled access; cl wkdys in Mar and Nov, all Dec–Easter; (01374) 971971; £3. Housed in England's oldest airport, with an appealing 1930s art deco terminal; tours available (£2), good-value restaurant with uninterrupted views.

SINGLETON SU8713 *See separate Family Panel on p.634* **Weald and Downland Open-air Museum**.

SOUTH HARTING SU7819 A pretty Downland village, with good-value food in the nicely set Ship. **Uppark** (B2146 S of South Harting) Splendid 17th-c house, extensively restored after a disastrous fire in 1989. Incredibly, most of the public treasures were rescued, even the wallpaper, but behind the scenes it's a different story: the family that live here lost almost everything, and one wonders how they feel about the way the Trust has left a few charred floorboards in place – and recycled others into fruit bowls sold in the shop. The grounds, designed by Humphrey Repton, have a woodland walk and fine views towards the Solent. Meals, snacks, shop, disabled access; open pm Sun–Thurs Apr–Oct; (01730) 825857; £5.50; NT. Entrance is by timed ticket, a few of which can be booked in advance – otherwise get there between 11.30am and 1.30pm. The chalk Harting Downs involve no more than a level stroll from the road above the village; the Coach & Horses at nearby Compton is another good base for walks in this area. The roads round here give attractive drives – the B2141 and B2146 S, the Walderton–E Mardon back road between them, and the Downs-foot road E through East Harting, Elsted, Treyford and Cocking.

TANGMERE SU9106 **Military Aviation Museum** (off the A27) Good collection of flying memorabilia based around the former RAF base where H E Bates finished writing *Fair Stood the Wind for France*. Meals, snacks, shop, disabled access; cl Dec–Jan; (01243) 775223; £3. The nearby Bader Arms has more memorabilia; and there's good food at the Anglesey Arms at Halnaker (with the shell of an 18th-c windmill nearby).

TICEHURST TQ7029 **Pashley Manor** (on the B2099) 8 acres of beautifully restored mainly Victorian formal gardens around a handsome house once owned by the Boleyn family. Magnificent old trees, delightfully placed moat and walled garden, views, folly, fine shrubs, roses, herbaceous beds, and clever focal points; very relaxed, charming and peaceful. Tulip festival in May, and a festival of old-fashioned roses in Jun. Snacks, plant sales, limited disabled access; open Tues–Thurs, Sat and bank hols, Apr–Sept; (01580) 200692; £4.50. The village is attractive; up a side road at Three Legged Cross, Maynards has good pick-your-own and the Bull is pleasant for lunch.

UPPER DICKER TQ5509 **Michelham Priory** Charming 16th-c house based around 13th-c Augustinian priory, with 15th-c gatehouse by the moat (which has plenty of waterfowl). Interesting furniture, tapestries and local ironwork, as well as crafts, working watermill, and rope-making museum. Meals, snacks, shop, disabled access to ground floor only; open Weds–Sun and bank hols mid-Mar–Oct, daily in Aug; (01323) 844224; £4. The Plough is useful for lunch.

★ **WARBLETON** TQ6018 Right off the beaten track and as a result very unspoilt – the village has more pre-1750 Sussex barns than anywhere else.

WEST CHILTINGTON CHURCH TQ0918 Beautiful building in lovely downland countryside – this is windmill country, too.

WEST DEAN GARDENS SU8612 Old roses, 100-yard pergola, wild garden, walled kitchen garden and interesting collection of stately mature conifers in park and arboretum; a splendid downland setting, notably peaceful and relaxed. Meals, snacks, shop, some disabled access, plant sales; cl Nov–Feb; (01243) 811303; £3.50. The smart White Horse at Chilgrove or Royal Oak a little N of it would be our choice for lunch.

★ **WEST HOATHLY** TQ3632 Attractive village tucked quietly away from the road, with tremendous views from the lane downhill past the ancient Cat pub. On a clear day you can see the whole sweep of the South Downs between Chanctonbury Ring and the Long Man of Wilmington. **Priest House** Nr the 13th-c church, 15th-c timbered house, now a folk museum with a little cottage garden. Shop; cl am Sun, and Nov–Feb; (01342) 810479; *£2.30. They can arrange guided tours of the village.

WESTFIELD TQ8115 **Carr Taylor Vineyard** One of England's most successful commercial vineyards, producing sparkling wine as well as still; cl 25 Dec–2 Jan, and Suns Jan–Feb; (01424) 752501; trails *£1.50.

WILMINGTON TQ5403 **Long Man of Wilmington** Gigantic chalk-cut figure so far impossible to date – guesses hover anywhere between the early 18th c and the Bronze Age. The

Giant's Rest in the village below has good home cooking.

★ ✝ **WINCHELSEA** TQ9017 Storms and French raids pretty much put paid to this once-flourishing port's importance; today it's a quiet and pleasant little place, dwarfed by the distances between the 3 surviving town gates around it. The **Royal Military Canal** runs from here to Hythe in Kent, a never-used Napoleonic defence that was meant as a sort of glorified coastal moat – now a peaceful spot for coarse fishermen. The New Inn is popular for lunch, and the tranquil **church** of St Thomas is elaborately decorated, with some fine old stained glass and medieval tombs. The Fairlight road has clifftop views.

WINDMILL HILL TQ6412 From here you can follow paths and tracks for an absorbing walk of about 4 miles past Herstmonceux Castle and the former observatory (now the Science Centre). And, yes, there is a windmill.

WISBOROUGH GREEN TQ0526 **Fishers Farm Park** Friendly farm, well equipped for families, with animal show and petting areas, good indoor and outdoor play areas, paddling pool and a go-kart track. Meals, snacks, shop, disabled access; cl 25–26 Dec; (01403) 700063; *£5.75; also holiday cottages and campsite. The Three Crowns, with well priced food, has a more solidly adult appeal.

WORTHING TQ1402 Restrained but rather charming town, with a pleasant seafront; in the same mould as Brighton but altogether quieter and less gaudy. There's an excellent **herb shop** on Field Row, opposite M&S. **Worthing Museum and Art Gallery** (Chapel Rd) Extremely rich archaeological collection, and a sculpture garden. Shop, disabled access; cl Sun, 25–26 Dec, Good Fri; (01903) 239999; free. The formerly separate village of West Tarring has a 250-year-old fig garden by the 14th-c parish hall, a folklore museum in a row of 15th-c cottages, and a welcoming old pub, the Vine.

WYCH CROSS TQ4235 **Ashdown Llama Farm** Unusual working llama farm, with big breeding herds of alpacas; sheep and goats too. Snacks, shop, disabled access (but no facilities); cl Mon (exc bank hols), and all Oct–Mar; (01825) 712040; £2.25. The same people run Barnsgate Manor Vineyard over at Herons Ghyll TQ4828, which has great views from its attractive restaurant.

★ **Other attractive villages**, all with civilised pubs doing decent food, include Barns Green TQ1227, Brightling TQ6921 (the pub is at nearby Oxleys Green), Byworth SU9820, Chiddingly TQ5414, Easebourne SU8922, East Dean SU9013 (not the one mentioned above), Elsted SU8119, Fittleworth TQ0118, Funtington SU7908, Hellingly TQ5812, Henley SU8925, Kirdford TQ0126, Robertsbridge TQ7323, Rotherfield TQ5529, Rudgwick TQ0833, Rushlake Green TQ6218, Slaugham TQ2528, Stopham TQ0218, Sutton SU9715 and Waldron TQ5419 (ancient church).

! British School of Ballooning SU9627 (Ebernoe – just N of Petworth) Organises champagne balloon trips over the Sussex countryside; (01428) 707307; £130.

Days Out

1066 and all that: Bodiam Castle; lunch at Salehurst Halt, Salehurst; Battle Abbey and battlefield – and/or Buckleys Yesterday's World.

Bloomsbury Group mementos: Berwick church paintings; Charleston Farmhouse and Middle Farm, Firle; lunch at the Ram, Firle; Monks House, Rodmell (limited opening); Lewes.

Great gardens and an Arts and Crafts rarity: Leonardslee, Lower Beeding, or Wakehurst Place, Ardingly or Nymans, Handcross; lunch at the Crabtree, Lower Beeding, the Gardeners Arms, Ardingly or the Cat, West Hoathly; Standen, East Grinstead.

Where to eat

ALCISTON TQ5005 **Rose Cottage** *(01323) 870377* In the same family for over 30 years, small, charming wisteria-covered cottage full of harness, traps, ironware and bric-à-brac, as well as Jasper the talking parrot (mornings only); very good promptly served food (especially the simply cooked fresh fish) using organic vegetables and their own eggs, well kept real ales, decent wines, small, no smoking evening restaurant, and seats outside; cl 25–26 Dec; children over 6 in evening. **£20**|£6.50.

ALFRISTON TQ5202 **Moonrakers** *(01323) 870472* Reliably enjoyable evening food (Sun lunch, too) in this cosy little cottage with a log fire, good wine list and friendly staff; cl pm Sun, 2 wks early Jan; children over 8. **£15.95 set 3-course meal.**

AMBERLEY TQ0211 **Bridge** *Houghton Bridge (01798) 831619* Nice old white-painted pub by pretty stretch of the River Arun, relaxed and friendly narrow bar, an attractively furnished 2-roomed dining room leading off, and lots of interesting modern portraits and impressionist-style paintings, generous helpings of good home-made bar food (lots of fresh fish), proper puddings, 4 Sunday roasts, well kept real ales, and friendly, helpful service. **£19.50**|£6.25.

BRIGHTON TQ3104 **Il Teatro** *7 New Rd (01273) 202158* Friendly and enjoyable Italian restaurant next to the Theatre Royal; cl Sun, Mon; reasonable disabled access. **£18**|£5.75.

BRIGHTON TQ3103 **Mock Turtle** *4 Pool Valley (01273) 327380* Delightful, no smoking, traditional English teashop with enjoyable snacks and light lunches (local fish and local sausages), lovely home-made cakes, bread, and so forth, and popular cream teas; cl Sun, Mon, Good Fri, 2 wks spring, a few days over Christmas. **£8**|£4.20.

BRIGHTON TQ3203 **One Paston Place** *1 Paston Pl (01273) 606933* Just off the seafront, enjoyable restaurant with big mural on one wall; very good modern British food inc super fish and game dishes, nice puddings, decent house wines, and a friendly atmosphere; cl Sun, Mon, 1st 2 weeks Jan, 1st 2 wks Aug; children over 5. **£39.**

BRIGHTON TQ3104 **Waikikamookau** *11a Kensington Gardens (01273) 671117* Easygoing and chatty lunchtime restaurant, with interesting contemporary furnishings in the long L-shaped room, particularly good, very cheap vegetarian (and vegan) food, an unusual list of juices, and fresh fruit milk shakes; open all day till 6pm, also Weds–Sat evenings. **£15**|£4.

BRIGHTON TQ3004 **Whytes** *33 Western St (01273) 776618* Popular and attractive cottagey restaurant just off the seafront, with a relaxed, friendly atmosphere; enjoyable food using fresh local produce, and a decent wine list; cl Sun, Mon, end Feb–early Mar. **£25.70.**

BROAD OAK TQ8219 **Rainbow Trout** *Chitcombe Rd (01424) 882436* Pleasant pub with an attractive bustling old bar, and a big restaurant extension; wide range of well cooked food (especially fish) served by friendly waitresses, and well kept real ales; cl 25 Dec, pm 26 Dec; disabled access. **£20**|£4.95.

BURPHAM TQ0308 **George & Dragon** *(01903) 883131* Smartly comfortable dining pub with splendid views down to Arundel Castle and the river; good, promptly served food with unusual specials inc nice vegetarian dishes; elegant restaurant – worth booking; cl pm Sun in winter, 25 Dec. **£17.90**|£6.

CHICHESTER SU8605 **Comme Ça** *67 Broyle Rd (01243) 788724* Busy little restaurant close to the Festival Theatre, with good classic French cooking, popular Sun lunches and children's menu; cl pm Sun, Mon; disabled access. **£28**|£10.25.

CHICHESTER SU8604 **St Martin's Tea Rooms** *3 St Martin's St (01243) 786715* Handsome, brick, Georgian-fronted house with a pretty garden for summer eating, good lunchtime snacks and meals (mainly vegetarian but with some fish dishes) and afternoon teas using organic produce; cl Sun, bank hols; disabled access. £4.20.

DUNCTON SU9517 **Cricketers** *(01798) 342473* Pretty little white house with welcoming staff and jovial landlord; inglenook fireplace, standing timbers and country furniture in the small bar, and a dining room decorated with farm tools; good popular food, well kept real ales, and a charming back garden with proper barbecue; skittle alley; no food pm Sun/Mon; no children. **£19.25**|£7.25.

EASTBOURNE TV6098 **Downland** *37 Lewes Rd (01323) 732689* Pretty, candlelit evening restaurant in a well run small hotel; carefully prepared, innovative food, good vegetables and lovely puddings, a relaxed atmosphere, and friendly service; bdrms; cl 26–30 Dec; children over 10. **£30**.

EDBURTON TQ2211 **Tottington Manor** *(01903) 815757* Cosy country house with particularly good food using fresh seasonal produce in both the bar and restaurant; winter log fire, friendly service and a relaxed atmosphere; bdrms; cl pm Sun, and Christmas–New Year; children over 5. **£28**|£7.

ELSTED SU8320 **Elsted Inn** *(01730) 813662* Victorian roadside pub with a warm and friendly welcome; unpretentious bars with open log fires, lots of original wood, and a candlelit dining room; extremely good, interesting cooking using fresh local ingredients (Weds is theme night), and very well kept real ales; 2 dogs, and a large garden (with dog-free zone); bdrms; disabled access. **£20**|£4.50.

ELSTED SU8119 **Three Horseshoes** *(01730) 825746* Cosy Tudor pub in lovely setting, with fine views of the South Downs from the garden (and good walks); snug rustic rooms with huge log fires, ancient beams and venerable furnishings; very good English country cooking inc lovely puddings, well kept real ales, and decent wines by the glass; cl pm Sun Oct–May; well behaved children welcome. **£23**|£5.50.

FLETCHING TQ4223 **Griffin** *(01825) 722890* Civilised old country inn with blazing log fires in the quaintly panelled rooms, old photographs and hunting prints; very good, innovative food, well kept beers, a decent wine list with lots (inc champagne) by the glass, a relaxed, friendly atmosphere, and a lovely garden; bdrms; cl 25 Dec; disabled access. **£25**|£6.50.

HARTFIELD TQ4735 **Anchor** *Church St (01892) 770424* Relaxed and friendly pub on the edge of Ashdown Forest, with good bar food, quick service, a chatty, heavily beamed bar, dining area, well kept real ales, and popular front verandah; cl 25 pm Dec. **£17.50**|£5.

HASTINGS TQ8209 **Harris** *58 High St (01424) 437221* Relaxed, informal and chatty, reasonably priced, mainly Spanish food (enjoyable tapas), friendly staff in long white aprons, and decent wine; cl Sun (but open all day Sat). **£16.50**|3-course set lunch £6.50.

HASTINGS TQ8009 **Roser's** *64 Eversfield Pl, St Leonards (01424) 712218* Extremely rewarding and generous, imaginative food using top-quality produce inc home-cured, smoked and pickled ingredients in a straightforward-looking little restaurant opposite the pier; fine wines, too; cl am Sat, Sun, Mon, 1st 2 wks Jan, last 2 wks Jun; disabled access. **£21.95 set dinner, £18.95 set lunch**.

HERSTMONCEUX TQ6312 **Sundial** *Gardner St (01323) 832217* Pretty and plush 17th-c cottage, with excellent, carefully cooked food inc lovely vegetables and delicious puddings; a praiseworthy wine list, relaxed atmosphere, formal but warm and friendly service, and a terrace and garden for summer eating; cl pm Sun, Mon, last 2 wks Aug–1st wk Sept; disabled access. **£29**|£10.50.

HORSHAM TQ1730 **Black Jug** *31 North Street (01403) 253526* Most attractively refurbished Edwardian town pub with a relaxed atmosphere, a big airy bar around the central servery, lots of old prints and photographs, and a plant-filled conservatory; very popular, interesting bar food, chilled flavoured vodkas, well kept real ales, decent wines, and small back terrace; no children pm Sat/Sun; cl pm Sun, 26 Dec. **£18.35**|£5.95.

JEVINGTON TQ5601 **Hungry Monk** *The Street (01323) 482178* Long-standing popular candlelit evening restaurant (also Sun lunch) with 3 beamed sitting rooms, bar, a little dining room, and open fires; a friendly, dinner-partyish atmosphere, and good interesting food; cl am Mon–Sat, bank hols, Christmas; children over 5. **£30**.

KIRDFORD TQ0126 **Half Moon** *(01403) 820223* Family-run inn with marvellous fresh fish (the family have had Billingsgate links for 130 years) inc some really unusual ones, well kept real ales, local wine and cider, friendly service, simple neat bars, and a big garden; cl pm 25 Dec; disabled access. **£20**|£4.50.

LITLINGTON TQ5201 **Litlington Tea Gardens** *(01323) 870222* Established 150 years ago, these tearooms still keep their quaint Victorian elegance, with seating on an attractive sheltered lawn under a copper beech or ginko, in renovated beach huts with open fronts, or the tearoom/restaurant; colourful hanging baskets and flowering tubs, and quick, efficient service; morning coffee, light lunches, and cream teas; handy for Alfriston; cl end Oct–end Mar; disabled access. £4.

LODSWORTH SU9321 **Halfway Bridge** *A272 (01798) 861281* Stylish and civilised, warm and friendly family-run pub, with big helpings of delicious and inventive home cooking in the no smoking restaurant or attractively decorated comfortable bar rooms; log fires, well kept real ales, ciders and wines; cl pm Sun in winter; children welcome over 10. **£19**|£8.

LOWER BEEDING TQ2225 **Crabtree** *A281 S (01403) 891257* Very popular dining pub with civilised but simply furnished and cosy beamed bars, and no smoking Jeremy's Restaurant with plenty of character; imaginative, carefully prepared food, good wines, well kept real ales, and prompt, friendly service; pleasant garden; cl Sun, pm bank hols, 25 Dec; disabled access. **£33**|£6.50.

NUTHURST TQ1926 **Black Horse** *(01403) 891272* Warmly welcoming black-beamed pub in lovely walking country; with a log fire in the inglenook fireplace, good, promptly served bar food, very well kept real ales and country wines, friendly service; disabled access. **£19.35**|£6.95.

NYETIMBER SZ8998 **Inglenook** *255 Pagham Rd (01243) 262495* Extended 16th-c hotel with enjoyable food in the attractive, rustic-style restaurant; beamed bars, a comfortable lounge, open fires, real ales, and a garden for light snacks; disabled access. **£23**.

OXLEYS GREEN TQ6921 **Jack Fullers** *(01424) 838212* Cosy and softly lit dining pub, with enjoyable pies and steamed puddings, good side dishes, and some vegetarian choices – all in big helpings; excellent wines (English ones, too), and seats in the pretty flower-filled garden with fine views; cl Mon, Tues; disabled access. **£19.50**|£5.

PLAYDEN TQ9122 **Peace & Plenty** *(01797) 280342* Cottagey dining pub with lots of little pictures, china and lamps and a big inglenook with comfortable armchairs on either side in the cosy bar; 2 intimate dining areas, very well prepared traditional food, well kept ales, and a pretty garden. **£16.90**|£5.95.

RINGMER TQ4313 **Cock** *Uckfield Rd (01273) 812040* Civilised heavily beamed country pub with a log fire in the big inglenook, a fine range of good food, decent wines, 2 lounges (one no smoking), and seats on the terrace and in the attractive fairy-lit garden. **£16**|£6.50.

RYE TQ9220 **Flushing** *4 Market St (01797) 223292* Run by the same family for 38 years, this fine old timber-framed inn serves particularly good local fish and seafood (local meat dishes, too) and holds various gastronomic occasions; note the fine 16th-c wall painting; bdrms; cl pm Mon, Tues, 1st 2wks Jan. **£34**|£10.50.

RYE TQ9220 **Landgate Bistro** *5–6 Landgate (01797) 222829* Simply furnished, beamed bistro (evenings only); good, accomplished cooking, nice puddings, relaxed service, and a carefully chosen little wine list; cl Sun, Mon, Christmas–New Year, 2 wks Jun, 1 wk Oct. **£25**.

RYE TQ9321 **Ypres Castle** *(01797) 223248* Popular, straightforward pub in a fine setting nr 13th-c Ypres Tower, with fairly spartan décor but a particularly warm and friendly atmosphere; enjoyable and interesting food inc fresh local fish and seafood, good fresh vegetables, well kept changing ales, good-value wine with 20 by the glass, and seats on a sizeable lawn with fine views over the River Rother; cl pm 25 Dec. **£18**|£5.50.

SCAYNES HILL TQ3824 **Sloop** *Sloop Lane, Freshfield Lock (01444) 831219* Country pub tucked away in this lovely spot with a sheltered garden and nr Bluebell

Line steam railway; long saloon bar with pine furniture and comfortable old seats, a simple public bar, good bar food (especially the daily specials), well kept real ales, and decent wines; cl 26 Dec; children must be well behaved; partial disabled access. **£20**|£6.95.

SEAFORD TV5199 **Golden Galleon** *Exceat, A259 E (01323) 892247* Big and bustling, popular pub with high, trussed and pitched rafters in the airy bar and dining area, an open fire in a nice little side area, and a conservatory, up to a dozen real ales inc some from their own microbrewery, good food inc lots of Italian dishes (the chatty landlord is from Italy), and good views from tables in the sloping garden; bdrms; cl pm Sun Sept–May. **£15**|£5.

SEAFORD TV4898 **Quincy's** *4 High St (01323) 895490* Enjoyable little cottagey restaurant with homely décor, really friendly service, very good, soundly based, interesting food (fresh fish from Newhaven, and lovely puddings), and a thoughtful wine list; cl pm Sun, Mon, am Tues–Sat, 1st wk Jan. **£29**.

SLINDON COMMON SU9608 **Spur** *London Rd (01243) 814216* Attractive little 17th-c pub with 2 big log fires, a good choice of daily changing food, a sizeable restaurant, well kept ales, friendly dogs, and a pleasant garden; bdrms. **£18**|£7.

STORRINGTON TQ0814 **Old FORGE** *6a Church St (01903) 743402* Good, imaginative food in 500-year-old converted beamed forge; excellent choice of sweet wines to go with the rich puddings and home-made ice-creams; cl am Sat, pm Sun, Mon, am Tues, 2 wks spring, 2 wks autumn; well behaved children welcome; **£28.50**.

Special thanks to Mark Willstatter, Paul Kennedy, Neil Mallon, Mark Holman, Graham James.

We welcome reports from readers

This *Guide* depends on readers' reports. Do help us if you can – in return, we offer a discount on the next edition to people who've helped us with reports for it. Tell us what you think about places already in it, and anything extra you think we should say about them. And send us your ideas for inclusion in the next edition: places to visit, eat at or stay in, attractive drives or walks, maybe even unusual interesting shops you know of. Use the card in the middle, the report forms at the end, or just write – no stamp needed: *The Good Guide to Britain*, FREEPOST TN1569, Wadhurst, E Sussex TN5 7BR.

Sussex Calendar

Some of these dates were provisional as we went to press. Please check information with the telephone numbers provided.

JANUARY

5 **Ardingly** Antiques Fair: up to 4,000 stands at the South of England Showground – *till Weds 6* (01636) 702326

FEBRUARY

2 **Tinsley Green** Marble Championships at the Greyhound (01403) 211661
7 **Chichester** Festival of Music, Dance and Speech – *till 21 Mar* (01243) 785715
15 **Fishbourne** Roman Family Fun Days at Fishbourne Roman Palace – *till Thurs 18* (01243) 785858
19 **Brighton** International Model Festival at Brighton Centre – *till Sun 21* (01273) 202881
23 **Brighton** Sussex Real Ale and Cider Festival at the Town Hall – *till Sun 28* (01903) 692370

MARCH

2 **Ardingly** Antiques Fair – *till Weds 3* (see 5 Jan for details)
21 **Ardingly** Food and Drink Fair at the South of England Showground (01444) 892048; **Brighton** Motorcycle Run, Madeira Drive (01273) 292606

APRIL

3 **Upper Dicker** Medieval Re-enactments and Archery at Michelham Priory – *till Mon 5* (01323) 844224
4 **Eastbourne** Easter at Eastbourne Miniature Steam Railway (01323) 520229; **Herstmonceux** Easter Egg Hunt at the Castle (01323) 834444; **Singleton** Traditional Food Fair at the Weald and Downland Open-air Museum – *till Mon 5* (01243) 811348
6 **Hastings** Old Town Conducted Walks (free) from the top of West Hill Lift – *every Tues, 3pm, till 15 Sept* (01424) 721249
17 **Haywards Heath** Garden Festival at Borde Hill Garden – *till Sun 18* (01444) 450326
24 **Brighton** UK Coach Rally, Madeira Drive – *till Sun 25* (01273) 292606
27 **Ardingly** Antiques Fair – *till Weds 28* (see 5 Jan for details)
30 **Brighton** Horse Driving Trials at Stanmer Park – *till 2 May* (01323) 841641

MAY

1 **Brighton** Festival: over 450 events – *till Sun 23* (01273) 713875; also Festival of Family Fun at Hove Lawns (01273) 292606; **Lower Beeding** Bonsai Weekend at Leonardslee Gardens – *till Mon 3* (01403) 891212
2 **Ardingly** Garden Show at the South of England Showground – *till Mon 3* (01444) 892048; **Bexhill** Festival of Motoring – *till Mon 3* (01424) 730564; **Brighton** Historic Commercial Vehicle Run, Madeira Drive (01273) 292606

Sussex Calendar (Cont.)

3 **Hastings** Jack in the Green Morris Dance Festival: procession, concerts, street entertainment (01424) 712574; **Lewes** Garland Day at the Castle (01273) 486290; **Upper Dicker** May Day Festival at Michelham Priory (01323) 844224

9 **Brighton** MG Regency Run, Madeira Drive (01273) 292606; **Haywards Heath** Children's Animal Fair at Borde Hill Garden (01444) 450326

15 **Brighton** National Museums' Week – *till Sun 23* (01273) 292606; **Singleton** Out of the Wood Show at the Weald and Downland Open-air Museum – *till Sun 16* (01243) 811348

16 **Brighton** Mackerel Fayre at the Fishing Museum (01273) 292606

27 **Firle** Charleston Festival at Charleston Farmhouse – *till Mon 31* (01323) 811626

28 **Brighton** Old Ship Royal Escape Race: yacht race from beach in front of the Old Ship, King's Rd (01273) 329001; **Upper Dicker** Weavers, Potters and Woodturners at Michelham Priory – *till Mon 31* (01323) 844224

29 **Broad Oak** Heathfield Agricultural Show (01825) 713369; **Chichester** Folk Festival – *till Mon 31* (01705) 471929; **Petworth** Craft Fair at Petworth House – *till Mon 31* (01798) 342207

31 **Brighton** Carnival at Hove Park (01273) 292606; **Upper Dicker** Teddy Bears Picnic at Michelham Priory (01323) 844224

JUNE

2 **Arundel** Corpus Christi Carpet of Flowers and Floral Festival at the Cathedral – *till Thurs 3* (01903) 882297

6 **Brighton** Classic Car Show, Madeira Drive (01273) 292606; **Singleton** Heavy Horses at the Weald and Downland Open-air Museum (01243) 811348

9 **Boxgrove** Music at Boxgrove Priory – *till Sat 12* (01243) 536240; **Fishbourne** *Trojan Women* and *Troilus and Cressida* at Fishbourne Roman Palace – *till Sat 12* (01243) 785858

10 **Ardingly** South of England Show – *till Sat 12* (01444) 235475

11 **Battle** Festival – *till Sun 27* (01424) 775275

12 **Eastbourne** International Ladies Tennis Championship – *till Sat 19* (01323) 415442; **Herstmonceux** Open-air Concert at the Castle (01323) 834444; **Pulborough** Parham Park Steam Rally and Country Show – *till Sun 13* (01903) 744888

18 **Goodwood** Festival of Speed at Goodwood House: historic motor sport event – *till Sun 20* (01243) 774107

19 **Crawley** International Festival of Arts – *till 4 July* (01293) 552941; **Haywards Heath** Rose Fair with the National Rose Society at Borde Hill Garden (01444) 450326

25 **Petworth** Open-air Concerts at Petworth House – *till Sun 27* (01798) 342207

26 **Crawley** Folk Festival at the Hawth – *till Sun 27* (01293) 552941; **Lower Beeding** Country Craft Fair at Leonardslee Gardens – *till Sun 27* (01403) 891212

JULY

2 **Chichester** Festival of the Arts – *till Sun 18* (01243) 785718; **Crawley** Fireworks Concert at Tilgate Park – *till Sat 3* (01293) 552941

Sussex Calendar (Cont.)

3 **Ardingly** Smallholders Show at the South of England Showground – *till Sun 4* (01444) 892048; **Crowborough** Sherlock Holmes Festival – *till Mon 5* (01892) 665464; **Haywards Heath** Horse Trials at Borde Hill Garden – *till Sun 4* (01444) 450326

10 **Eastbourne** Carnival (01323) 415442

17 **Eastbourne** Emergency Services Display at Western Lawns – *till Sun 18* (01323) 415442; **Lewes** Open-air Trad Jazz at the Castle (01273) 486290; **Pulborough** Parham House Garden Weekend – *till Sun 18* (01903) 742021

19 **Eastbourne** County Cup Tennis at Devonshire Park – *till Fri 23* (01323) 415442; **Fishbourne** Archaeological Excavations: guided tours and archeologists at Fishbourne Roman Palace – *till 30 Aug* (01243) 785858

20 **Ardingly** Antiques Fair – *till Weds 21* (see 5 Jan for details)

21 **Petworth** Festival – *till Weds 28* (01428) 707658

23 **Worthing** Seafront Fair – *till Sun 25* (01903) 239999

24 **Bodiam** Fireworks Concert at the Castle (01892) 890651; **Brighton** Carnival at Preston Park (01273) 292606; **Ebernoe** Horn Fair (01428) 707587

25 **Singleton** Rare and Traditional Breeds at the Weald and Downland Open-air Museum (01243) 811348

27 **Goodwood** Glorious Goodwood – *till Sat 31* (01243) 755022

31 **Littlehampton** Regatta – *till 1 Aug* (01903) 732063

AUGUST

2 **Eastbourne** Family Festival of Tennis at Devonshire Park – *till Sat 7* (01323) 415442

7 **Burwash** Fireworks Concerts at Batemans – *till Sun 8* (01892) 891001; **Eastbourne** Horse Show at Gildredge Park – *till Sun 8* (01323) 415442; **Hartfield** Summer Flower Show (01342) 822372; **Hastings** Old Town Week: open houses, displays, concerts, street party, carnival – *till Sun 15* (01424) 433142; **Haywards Heath** Fuchsia Society at Borde Hill Garden – *till Sun 8* (01444) 450326; **Worthing** Victorian Seaside Fair – *till Sun 8* (01903) 239999

12 **Upper Dicker** Guild of Sussex Craftsmen in Action at Michelham Priory – *till Sun 15* (01323) 844224

14 **Brasted** The Blues Band at Emmetts Garden (01892) 890651; **Brighton** Brunswick Festival, Brunswick Square (01273) 292606; **Singleton** Children's Activities at the Weald and Downland Open-air Museum – *till Sun 15* (01243) 811348

15 **Bognor Regis** Birdman Competition (01903) 716133

19 **Eastbourne** Airbourne '99 and RAF Show – *till Sun 22* (01323) 410044

20 **Pulborough** Parham House Craft Show – *till Sun 22* (01903) 742021

23 **Eastbourne** South of England Tennis Championship at Devonshire Park – *till Sat 28* (01323) 415442

28 **Hellingly** Festival of Transport at Broad Farm – *till Mon 30* (01323) 484926; **Herstmonceux** Medieval Festival at the Castle – *till Mon 30* (01323) 834444; **Rotherfield** Torchlight Procession (01273) 515451

30 **Worthing** Carnival (01903) 239999

SEPTEMBER

4 **Shoreham** RAFA Air Show – *till Sun 5* (01273) 441545; **Uckfield** Torchlight Procession and Fireworks (01273) 515451

Sussex Calendar (Cont.)

5 **Eastbourne** MG Rally at Western Lawns: over 300 vehicles (01323) 415442; **Upper Dicker** Country Fair at Michelham Priory (01323) 844224

8 **Brighton** Windsurfing World Cup – *till Sun 12* (01273) 292606

11 **Brighton** National Speed Trials, Madeira Drive (01273) 292606; **Crowborough** Torchlight Procession and Fireworks (01273) 515451; **Findon** Sheep Fair at Nepcote Farm (01435) 873999; **Haywards Heath** Autumn Fair at Borde Hill Garden – *till Sun 12* (01444) 450326; **Pulborough** Parham House Country Show – *till Sun 12* (01903) 742021

18 **Fishbourne** Celtic Warriors Re-enactment and Celtic and Roman Crafts at Fishbourne Roman Palace – *till Sun 19* (01243) 785858; **Mayfield** Torchlight Procession and Fireworks (01273) 515451

21 **Ardingly** Antiques Fair – *till Weds 22* (see 5 Jan for details)

25 **Burgess Hill** Torchlight Procession and Fireworks (01273) 515451

OCTOBER

2 **Brighton** Living History Weekend at the Royal Pavilion – *till Sun 3* (01273) 292606; **Hartfield** Autumn Flower Show (01342) 822372

3 **Ardingly** Autumn Show (01444) 892048

9 **Newhaven** Torchlight Procession and Fireworks (01273) 515451

20 **Chichester** Sloe Fair (01243) 775888

23 **Singleton** Autumn Countryside Celebration at the Weald and Downland Open-air Museum – *till Sun 24* (01243) 811348

30 **Littlehampton** Torchlight Procession and Fireworks (01273) 515451

NOVEMBER

2 **Ardingly** Antiques Fair – *till Weds 3* (see 5 Jan for details)

5 **Lewes** Torchlight Procession and Fireworks, best of Britain's bonfire celebrations, town closed to traffic *at 5.30pm*, spectacular celebrations with bands, effigies and burning tar-barrel race (01273) 515451

6 **Brighton and Crawley** London to Brighton Classic Commercial Vehicle Run (01273) 777409

7 **Brighton** RAC Veteran Car Run (01273) 292606

13 **East Hoathly** Torchlight Procession and Fireworks (01273) 515451

18 **Ardingly** Rural Craft Show at the South of England Showground – *till Sun 21* (01444) 892048

DECEMBER

4 **Ardingly** Festive Food and Drink Fair at the South of England Showground – *till Sun 5* (01444) 892048

WARWICKSHIRE (with Birmingham and the West Midlands)

Some great day visits for all ages, and possibilities for an enjoyable short stay.

Birmingham has great scope for day visits, with excellent art collections, lively museums, good botanic gardens, and interesting period houses; many places are free. Coventry also has quite a lot to see on day visits, with its good transport museum trying free admission this year (previously £3.30). The Kingswinford glass museum is an unexpected dazzler, and the Nickelodeon at Ashorne has a fine nostalgic appeal. Striking historic houses include Arbury Hall, Coughton Court, Moseley Old Hall (good guided tours) and Wightwick Manor near Wolverhampton, and the atmospheric ruins of Kenilworth Castle. People get a lot out of the organic gardening centre at Ryton-on-Dunsmore. Stratford is the obvious focus for people on the Shakespeare trail, with plenty to interest them (though prices are high here, and others will find more to enjoy elsewhere); there are further Shakespeare connections in the pretty villages nearby.

This is an excellent area for family outings, topped by Warwick Castle, Cadbury World at Bournville, the sea life centre in Birmingham, and the Black Country living museum in Dudley. Boys (of any age) who like cars will be thrilled by the Heritage Motor Centre at Gaydon. There are a few good farms, and there's always a lot going on at the big crafts village at Hatton.

Warwick has the character and atmosphere to make a short stay enjoyable; its neighbour Leamington Spa still has the gardens, parks and spacious terraces of its heyday as a spa resort. The countryside (which edges into the Cotswolds in the south) is quietly attractive, laced with canals and dotted with charming villages and appealing places to stay.

Where to stay

AVON DASSETT SP4150 **Crandon House** *Avon Dassett, Leamington Spa CV33 0AA (01295) 770652* ***£40,** plus winter breaks; 5 rms. Welcoming farmhouse on small working farm with various livestock, fine views, big garden, comfortable sitting rooms (one with log fire), and fine breakfasts; cl Christmas; children over 10.

BISHOP'S TACHBROOK SP3262 **Mallory Court** *Harbury Lane, Bishop's Tachbrook, Leamington Spa CV33 9QB (01926) 330214* ***£195,** plus special breaks; 18 wonderfully comfortable and luxurious rms. Fine ancient-looking house – actually built around 1910 – with elegant antique and flower-filled day rooms (carefully refurbished this year), attentive staff, excellent food using home-grown produce in panelled restaurant, and 10 acres of lovely gardens with outdoor swimming pool, tennis, squash and croquet; cl 2–9 Jan; children over 9.

BLACKWELL SP2343 **Blackwell Grange** *Blackwell, Shipston on Stour CV36 4PF (01608) 682357* ***£56;** 3 pretty rms. 17th-c Cotswold farmhouse with log fire in comfortable beamed sitting room, large inglenook fireplace in flagstoned dining room, good home cooking using their own free-range eggs (evening meal by arrangement; bring your own wine), pretty garden, and nice country views; cl Jan and Feb; children over 12, but parents with younger children can stay in annexe; good disabled access.

ILMINGTON SP2143 **Howard Arms** *Ilmington, Shipston on Stour CV36 4LT (01608) 682226* **£55;** 2 rms. Neatly kept golden stone 17th/18th-c inn opposite village green with a pleasant, sheltered garden, a beamed and flagstoned bar, open fires, friendly service, very good food, and decent wines.

LEAMINGTON SPA SP2864 **Lansdowne House** *Clarendon St, Leamington Spa CV32 4PF (01926) 450505* **£65.90,** plus special breaks; 14 rms. Enjoyable Regency town house with particularly good service, very attractive public rooms, a tranquil atmosphere, good daily-changing dinners, fine-value wine list, and small prize-winning garden; cl 24–25 Dec; children over 5.

LITTLE COMPTON SP2630 **Red Lion** *Little Compton, Moreton-in-Marsh, Gloucestershire GL56 0RT (01608) 674397* **£38;** 3 rms, shared bthrm. Simple but civilised low-beamed Cotswold stone inn with log fires, a separate dining area, big menu with speciality steaks, extensive wine list, and a large, attractive garden; children over 8.

LOXLEY SP2755 **Loxley Farm** *Loxley, Warwick CV35 9JN (01789) 840265* **£55;** 2 suites in attractive barn conversion. Not far from Stratford, tucked-away, thatched and half-timbered partly 14th-c house with low beams, wonky walls and floors, antiques and dried flowers, an open fire, a helpful and friendly owner, and good Aga-cooked breakfasts; peaceful garden, and fine old village church; cl Christmas/New Year.

SHERBOURNE SP2562 **Old Rectory** *Vicarage Lane, Sherbourne, Warwick CV35 8AB (01926) 624562* ***£58,** plus special breaks; 14 rms, all with antique brass or brass and iron beds, and some in converted stables. Georgian house not far from Warwick, with cosy sitting room, a big log fire, beams, flagstones, and an honesty bar; hearty breakfast and enjoyable evening meals, and pretty walled gardens; no children.

STRATFORD-UPON-AVON SP1954 **Carlton** *22 Evesham Pl, Stratford-upon-Avon CV37 6HT (01789) 293548* **£48;** 6 homely rms, most with own bthrm. Neatly kept and very welcoming no smoking Victorian house, close to theatre and restaurants, with helpful owners, very good breakfasts in airy dining room, and a little garden.

STRATFORD-UPON-AVON SP2054 **Melita** *37 Shipston Rd, Straford-upon-Avon CV37 7LN (01789) 292432* ***£62;** 12 well equipped rms. Friendly family-run Victorian hotel with a pretty, carefully laid-out garden, and a comfortable lounge with an open fire, extensive breakfasts, and some provision for non-smokers; close to town centre and theatre; cl 4 days over Christmas; pets by arrangement; disabled access.

STRATFORD-UPON-AVON SP2055 **Payton** *6 John St, Stratford-upon-Avon CV37 6UB (01789) 266442* **£64;** 5 charming rms. Quietly set no smoking Georgian house, handy for theatre, with caring owners, very good breakfasts in a pretty dining room, and seats in flower-filled courtyard; cl 25–26 Dec.

STRATFORD-UPON-AVON SP2054 **Shakespeare** *Chapel St, Stratford-upon-Avon CV37 6ER (01789) 294771* **£156,** plus wknd breaks; 74 comfortable, well equipped rms. Smart ex-Forte hotel based on handsome lavishly modernised Tudor merchants' houses, with comfortable bar, good food, quick friendly service, tables in back courtyard, and civilised tea or coffee in peaceful chintzy armchairs by blazing log fires; 3 minutes' walk from theatre.

STRATFORD-UPON-AVON SP2056 **Welcombe** *Warwick Rd, Stratford-upon-Avon CV37 0NR (01789) 295252* **£175,** plus special breaks; 68 rms with antiques and luxurious bthrms. Jacobean-style mansion in parkland estate with 18-hole golf course and 2 all-weather floodlit tennis courts, deeply comfortable day rooms inc a fine panelled lounge, open fires and fresh flowers, an elegant restaurant, and good service; disabled access.

SUTTON COLDFIELD SP1394 **New Hall** *Walmley Rd, Sutton Coldfield B76 1QX (0121) 378* 2442 **£136,** plus wknd breaks; 60 lovely rms (the ones in the manor house are the best). England's oldest moated manor house, in 26 beautiful acres, with luxurious day rooms, a graceful panelled restaurant with carefully cooked imaginative food using very fresh (often home-grown) produce, and excellent service; children over 8; disabled access.
WALCOTE SP1258 **Walcote Farm** *Walcote, Alcester B49 6LY (01789) 488264* ***£38;** 2 rms. Attractive 16th-c oak-beamed farmhouse on 75-acre working sheep farm with log fires in inglenook fireplaces, and friendly owners, good breakfasts (several local pubs for evening meals), a pretty garden, and fine surrounding walks; no smoking; cl Christmas/New Year.
WARWICK SP2864 **Forth House** *44 High St, Warwick CV34 4AX (01926) 401512* ***£58;** 2 appealing and spacious suites. Prettily decorated no smoking house with lovely, surprisingly big garden, and good breakfasts (supper trays by prior arrangement); self-catering flat; disabled access.
WILLEY SP4984 **Manor Farm** *Willey, Rugby CV23 0SH (01455) 553143* **£38;** 3 rms, 1 with own bthrm. Tranquil no smoking house with helpful pleasant owner, homely lounge, and good filling breakfasts in relaxed dining room; cl Christmas/New Year; no children.
WILMCOTE SP1658 **Pear Tree Cottage** *7 Church Rd, Wilmcote, Stratford-upon-Avon CV37 9UX (01789) 205889* ***£46;** 7 rms. Charming half-timbered Elizabethan house owned by the same family for 3 generations, with beams, flagstones, country antiques, a cosy atmosphere, good breakfasts, and a sizeable shady garden; self-catering also; cl 24 Dec–1 Jan; children over 3.

To see and do

BIRMINGHAM SP0786 The city has masses of things to see and do. It has a long heritage despite its mainly modern centre, and a rich and varied industrial history taking in everything from guns to chocolate buttons. Reputedly there are more canals here than in Venice, and redevelopment of old canal buildings is bringing a lively new focus to the Gas St/Brindley Pl area. However, the city centre doesn't really have the overall appeal which would encourage long stays; plans to replace the notorious Bull Ring with something more in tune with the city's growing cultural pride seem permanently on hold. So Birmingham's strength is as a place for enjoyable day trips, particularly at weekends – the formidably efficient traffic system which ploughs through its heart makes it easy to penetrate from outside. The city has had a dearth of decent pubs, but now has enough to keep visitors happy, especially around the canal area: Flapper & Firkin (Cambrian Wharf), Tap & Spile (Brindley Wharf), James Brindley (Gas St Basin) and Malt House (Brindley Pl), with the newish Fiddle & Bone (Sheepcote St), owned by 2 members of the City Of Birmingham Symphony Orchestra, the current favourite.

Birmingham Museum & Art Gallery (Chamberlain Sq) Perhaps the best collection of Pre-Raphaelite paintings anywhere, plenty still looking as brilliantly, almost shockingly, fresh and detailed as when they were painted. Other notable paintings too, and lots of coins and archaeology. Meals, snacks, shop, disabled access; cl am Sun, 24–26 Dec, 1 Jan; (0121) 303 2834; free. Local boy Burne-Jones, a leading light in the Pre-Raphaelite movement, was responsible for 4 windows in **St Philip's church** on Colmore Row nearby, since 1905 the city's cathedral.
Ikon Gallery (Oozells Sq, off Brindley Pl) Vibrant modern art newly housed in stunningly converted school building. Meals, snacks, shop, disabled access; cl Mon and bank hols; free.
National Sea Life Centre (Water's Edge, Brindley Pl) The flagship of the excellent Sea Life Centre chain: the hi-tech displays are both fun and instructive, with around 3,000 native British marine and freshwater creatures

shown off in careful re-creations of their habitats, also new themed soft play area and a reconstruction of the *Titanic* wreck. The highlight is a walk-through tube giving the impression of walking along the sea bed, with sharks, rays and other creatures swimming above and around you. Sir Norman Foster designed the building. Meals, snacks, shop, disabled access; cl 25 Dec; (0121) 633 4700; £6.75.

Museum of the Jewellery Quarter (Vyse St) Birmingham is still Britain's biggest producer of gold jewellery, if not as important to the jewellery trade as it used to be. This excellent centre is built around the perfectly preserved workshops of Smith & Pepper Co, still much as they were at the start of the century. There's a good overview of the industry, tours of the factory and demonstrations of jewellery-making techniques. Snacks, shop, disabled access; cl Sun; (0121) 554 3598; *£2. Around 100 jewellery shops nearby, so useful for browsing or repairs. The Rosevilla has decent food.

Soho House (Soho Ave, 2m NW of centre) Elegant former home of Matthew Boulton, who developed the steam engine with James Watt; possibly the first centrally heated house in England since Roman times. Furnished in 18th-c style with Boulton-related displays. Snacks, shop, disabled access; cl am Sun, and all day Mon (exc bank hols); (0121) 554 3598; *£2.

Aston Hall (Aston, 2m NE) Strikingly grand Jacobean mansion with panelled long gallery, balustraded staircase and magnificent plaster friezes and ceilings. Snacks, shop, disabled access to ground floor; cl am, maybe Mon, and all Nov–Mar; (0121) 327 0062; free (and more satisfying than a good many houses you'd have to pay for).

Barber Institute (Birmingham University) Excellent collection of paintings and sculptures, well housed in an attractive gallery – the right size to be enjoyable without being overwhelming. Quite a lot of Impressionist works as well as European masters. Shop, disabled access; cl am Sun, 25–26 Dec, 1 Jan, Good Fri; (0121) 472 0962; free. The university (marked by its huge clock tower) is on the outer fringes of Edgbaston, a couple of miles S of the city centre. This area developed as a smart residential part of town, where industry and commerce gave way to parks and greenery, much of which still remains today.

Birmingham Botanical Gardens (Westbourne Rd, Edgbaston) Outstanding: 15 acres inc a tropical house (with lily pool, bananas and cocoa), palm house, orangery, national bonsai collection and cactus house. The gardens have lots of trees, rhododendrons and azaleas, and bands play on summer Sun and bank hol pms. Meals, snacks, shop, disabled access; cl 25 Dec; (0121) 454 1860; £4, £4.30 summer Suns.

Birmingham Nature Centre (Pershore Rd, Edgbaston) British and European animals in indoor and outdoor enclosures designed to resemble natural habitats. Snacks, shop, disabled access; cl Nov–Mar exc Sun; (0121) 472 7775; *£1.50.

Blakesley Hall (Yardley, 2m E) Timber-framed 16th-c merchant's house, furnished according to an inventory of 1684. Shop, disabled access to ground floor and garden; cl am, and Nov–Mar, and maybe other times in 1999 due to redevelopment, best to check; (0121) 783 2193; free.

Sarehole Mill (Hall Green, 3m SE) Working 18th-c watermill, with several displays explaining the milling process. Tolkien often came here as a child. Shop; cl am, and Nov–Mar; (0121) 777 6612; free. Other local sites that influenced Tolkien are listed on a leaflet available at information centres.

Birmingham Railway Museum (Warwick Rd, Tyseley; on the A41 3m SE) Working railway museum with fully equipped workshop, steam locomotives, and historic carriages and wagons. Trains run along a short track, but rides only in summer, usually 1st Sun of the month. Meals and snacks (wknds only), shop, limited disabled access; cl 25–26 Dec and 1 Jan; (0121) 707 4696; £2.50.

Bournville (on the A441 4m S) A planned village built by the Cadbury family when they moved their factory out of the centre in 1879. Part of the plans for their garden suburb involved re-erecting timber-framed manor houses from elsewhere; 2 survive as the **Selly Manor Museum** (Maple Rd), with herb garden, crafts and various exhibitions. Snacks, shop, disabled access to ground floor only; open Tues–Fri, plus bank hols and maybe some wknds, cl 15 Dec–15 Jan; (0121) 472 0199; *£1.50. **Cadbury World** Attached to the factory, this is hugely enjoyable, with all you could ever want to know about how chocolate is made and marketed. Obviously there's something of a corporate bias (you could be forgiven for thinking nobody else has ever made chocolate apart from the Aztecs and the Cadburys), but the displays and exhibitions have great verve. It's not a factory tour, though you do see demonstrators hand-making and decorating luxury chocolates, and the packaging plant where the more standard bars are wrapped and packed. Children enjoy the alternative view of chocolate-making offered by Mr Cadbury's Parrot at the Fantasy Factory, and Cadabra, a jolly ride through an imaginative chocolate-themed world in a car shaped like a cocoa bean. Older visitors get nostalgic watching TV adverts for Cadbury's products from the last 40 years (some from overseas), and a 1930s-style sweet shop has period wrappers. Elsewhere cars and climbing frames are disguised as Creme Eggs (and a slide as a box of Roses), and there are plenty of samples to satisfy the cravings created by the sumptuous smells. A typical visit lasts about 2½ hours (most under cover), but book in advance – on popular days tickets can be sold out well ahead. Restaurant and picnic areas, good shop (some bargains and unusual varieties), mostly disabled access; open daily Mar–Oct, and usually wknds and at least a couple of other days Nov–Feb; (0121) 451 4180; £6.25.

STRATFORD-UPON-AVON SP2055 Visitors who look at the town just as a town can be disappointed, but if you have any interest in Shakespeare and his plays the whole place comes alive: the interesting buildings seem that bit more interesting, and not so outnumbered by the workaday ones, the overpriced antique shops and the gift shops. The gardens by the River Avon make a memorable setting for the Memorial Theatre. The pub with the most theatrical Shakespeare connections is the Mucky Duck, or more properly White Swan (Southern Way), where RSC actors and actresses drink; the Arden Hotel has the closest bar to the Memorial Theatre, with good snacks. Useful places for lunch include the Brasserie (Henley St), quaint old Garrick (High St), Vintner Wine Bar (Sheep St) and Slug & Lettuce (Guild St/Union St). Tea in the Shakespeare Hotel (Chapel St) is relaxing.

Shakespeare's Birthplace (Henley St) The logical place to start, though despite what they'll tell you, there's no guarantee the playwright really was born here. Even so, there are interesting period features, and good interpretative displays. Shop; cl 23–26 Dec; (01789) 204016; £4.50. If you want to see all the Shakespearian properties it makes sense to buy a joint ticket; this costs £10, for the above and the following 4 houses (all open the same hours). Tickets for just the 3 in-town sites cost £7. A tour bus with commentary links the sites but costs another £8; you'll be better off walking, though may need some form of wheels to get to Mary Arden's house (public transport is rather sporadic).

New Place/Nash's House (Chapel St) Shakespeare died here in 1616; the house was destroyed in the 18th c, but the Elizabethan knot garden remains, and the adjacent house, former home of the writer's granddaughter, has a good collection of furniture and local history; cl 23–26 Dec; (01789) 292325; £3.

Hall's Croft (Old Town) Lovely gabled Tudor home of Dr John Hall, who married Shakespeare's daughter; good displays on the medicine of the time, Elizabethan and Jacobean furniture, and a walled garden. Teas, shop, some disabled access; cl 23–26 Dec; (01789) 292107; £3.

Anne Hathaway's Cottage SP1855 (Shottery, just W) Substantial thatched Tudor farmhouse, the home of Anne Hathaway until her marriage to William Shakespeare. Displays of domestic life at that time, colourful cottage garden. Snacks, shop; cl 23–26 Dec; (01789) 292100; £3.50. There's a craft centre next door, and the Bell is handy for something to eat away from the tourists.

Mary Arden's House SP1658 (Wilmcote, 3m NW) The picturesque home of Shakespeare's mother, with the barns given over to countryside memorabilia. Daily falconry displays, rare breeds. Snacks, shop, some disabled access; cl 23–26 Dec; (01789) 293455; £4. The Swan House, overlooking it in the attractive village, is good for lunch.

† **Holy Trinity church** (Waterside) 15th-c, where Shakespeare was baptised and buried; cl am Sun and for services; *60p to enter the chancel where the grave is. The cosy old Windmill has decent food.

Memorial Theatre (Waterside) Shakespeare's plays are of course still performed here by the Royal Shakespeare Company. You can sometimes book guided tours of the main theatre, and a gallery has temporary exhibitions. Meals, snacks, shop, disabled access; cl am Sun, 24–25 Dec; (01789) 296655; £2 for gallery, tours £4. The RSC productions themselves are performed in repertory, so over a few days you can see several. Advance booking is recommended – (01789) 295623 – though 100 tickets are kept back for each performance and sold on the day from 9.30am; don't leave it much later, as they go pretty fast.

Harvard House (High St) Late 16th-c home of the mother of the man who founded Harvard University – no Shakespeare connection, but a striking example of houses of his day; cl Mon (exc bank hols) and all mid-Oct–Apr; (01789) 204507; free.

! **National Teddy Bear Museum** (Greenhill St) Delightfully displayed, furry friends of all shapes and sizes – mechanical and musical ones, ones that belonged to famous people, and some that are famous themselves. Shop; cl 25–26 Dec; (01789) 293160; *£2.25.

Butterfly Farm & Jungle Safari (Tramway Walk) Stratford's quaintly gabled houses here give way to cascading waterfalls and tropical forests, with up to 1,500 exotic butterflies flying free in a re-created jungle habitat. There's an incredible collection of spiders and insects. Shop, disabled access; cl 25 Dec; (01789) 299288; *£3.25.

☺ **Ragdoll** (Chapel St) They make children's TV programmes like *Teletubbies* and *Tots TV*; the ground floor has a shop, play areas and plenty to amuse small children, who can even talk to their favourite Teletubby on the telephone. Disabled access; cl am Sun, 25–26 Dec, 1 Jan; free.

Shire Horse Centre & Farm Park (Clifford Rd – the B4632 S) Parades and demonstrations of the huge horses, as well as goats, pigs, rare breeds, owl sanctuary, falconry displays and an adventure playground. Readers rate this very highly. Good meals and snacks, shop, disabled access (can be a bit bumpy); cl Thurs and Fri Nov–Feb, and 25 Dec; (01789) 415274; £4.50.

WARWICK SP2864 *See separate Family Panel on p.665* for **Warwick Castle**. The elegant town centre dates largely from Queen Anne's days, though many older buildings survived a major fire in 1694. Some of the oldest structures are to be found around Mill St – very attractive for strolls, with a good few antique shops. The Tilted Wig (Market Pl) and ancient Tudor House (West St, opposite the castle) have good-value food, and the Saxon Mill (Guys Cliffe), a straightforward family dining pub, has charming waterside surroundings.

Mill Garden Delightful plantings in a super setting on the river beside the castle – very nice to stroll through, with plenty of old things to look at along the way. Disabled access; open Easter–mid-Oct; (01926) 492877; £1.

† **St Mary's church** (Old Sq) Splendid medieval church on the town's highest point, with Norman crypt, chapter house and magnificent 15th-c

Beauchamp chapel; in summer the tower is open, for excellent views – small admission charge.

Lord Leycester Hospital (High St) Delightfully wonky half-timbered building built in 1383, still a home of rest for retired servicemen. Fine old guildhall, candlelit chapel, gatehouse and courtyard, and garden with Norman arch and a 2,000-year-old urn from the Nile. Snacks (summer only), shop, disabled access to ground floor only; cl Mon, 25 Dec, Good Fri; (01926) 491422; *£2.75.

St John's House (St John's) 17th-c house with exhibits from the county museum, and several room reconstructions. They plan considerable refurbishment over the next year, so check opening times. Shop, disabled access to ground floor only; cl 12.30–1.30pm, all day Sun (exc pm Apr–Sept) and Mon (exc bank hols) and Christmas week; (01926) 410410; free.

Doll Museum (Castle St) Half-timbered Elizabethan house with comprehensive collection of antique dolls and toys. A fun video shows the exhibits come to life. Shop; cl Nov–Easter exc Sat; (01926) 412500; *£1.

Warwickshire County Museum (Market Pl) In the 17th-c Market Hall, with lots of fossils, and a Sheldon tapestry map of the county. Shop, disabled access to ground floor; cl Sun exc May–Sept, 25–26 Dec; (01926) 410410; free.

Other things to see and do

Warwickshire Family Attraction of the Year

Warwick Castle SP2864 (Castle Hill) Over 800,000 people a year cross the drawbridge of this splendid fortress – one of Britain's most splendid castles. It's a lively place, with several displays showing the influence of the Tussaud's group who own the site, but purists shouldn't be put off by the gloss or waxwork figures; the rooms are excellently preserved, and their fine furnishings and art well worth braving the crowds for. There's a great deal for children to enjoy, especially in summer, when at weekends medieval knights or Tudor mercenaries may engage in jousting or hand-to-hand combat, and most other days (weather permitting) you can join in medieval games or watch traditional craftsmen. The most elaborate display in the castle itself – the Royal Weekend Party – has had a facelift in recent months, and now shows off better than ever the aristocracy at play as the 19th c drew to a close. Another highlight is the medieval experience Kingmaker in the 14th-c vaulted undercroft; sounds, smells and well put together tableaux bring to life the Earl of Warwick's preparations for battle, and you can handle chainmail and weaponry in the armoury, en route to the atmospheric dungeons. You can explore the towers and battlements, and helpful staff are on hand to answer questions (some might be in costume). The marvellous grounds were designed by Capability Brown, and as well as delightful gardens have pleasant strolls along the River Avon; the views from the parklands are stirring stuff. The only thing that might rankle slightly is the price, so try to come when there are extra events and activities, or at least make sure you allow enough time to get value for money. Meals, snacks, shop, disabled access to grounds only; cl 25 Dec; (01926) 406600; £9.95 (£5.95 children). A family ticket (2 adults and 2 children) is £27. All prices are slightly reduced out of high season.

ALCESTER SP0755 **Ragley Hall** (on the A435) Perfectly symmetrical Palladian house in 400 acres of parkland and gardens; excellent baroque plasterwork in Great Hall, fine paintings (inc some modern art), and adventure playground, maze and woodland walks. Good outdoor concerts. Snacks, shop, disabled access; open Thurs–Sun and bank hols, Easter–Sept; (01789) 762090; £5, £4 grounds only. The village is attractive,

STAFFORDSHIRE
SJ
SK
Austrey
M42
M6
10
Wolverhampton
Walsall
Middleton
A5
Sutton Coldfield
A4123
9
Hartshill Hayes
WEST MIDLANDS
Dudley
Kingswinford
8
Castle Bromwich
Arbury
M5
Birmingham
4
M6
Amblecote
Bickenhill
Meriden
Coventry
Hampton in Arden
Berkswell
M42
Barston
Earlswood
M42
3
A452
Stoneleigh
Honiley
Kenilworth
3A
Packwood House
A46
16
Tanworth in Arden
Baddesley Clinton
A445
Stratford-upon-Avon Canal
Lowsonford
Henley-in-Arden
Warwick
WORCESTERSHIRE
SO
M40
Hatton
A4189
Leamington Spa
Wootton Wawen
SP
Sherbourne
Bishop's Tachbrook
Coughton
15
A435
A3400
14
Hampton Lucy
13
Alcester
Aston Cantlow
Charlecote
Ashorne
A46
Walcote
Stratford-upon-Avon
Wilmcote
Lighthorne
Temple Grafton
Exhall
Wellesbourne
Gaydon
Ardens Grafton
R Avon
Welford on Avon
A429
Loxley
Clifford Chambers
A422
Alderminster
Preston on Stour
Windmill Hill
Lower Quinton
Armscote
A422
Blackwell
Middle Tysoe
Ilmington
Honington
Shipston on Stour
Lower Brailes
Sutton-under-Brailes
GLOUCS
A429
Long Compton
0 Miles 5
Great Wolford
0 Kilometres 8
Barton-on-the-Heath
A3400
Little Compton

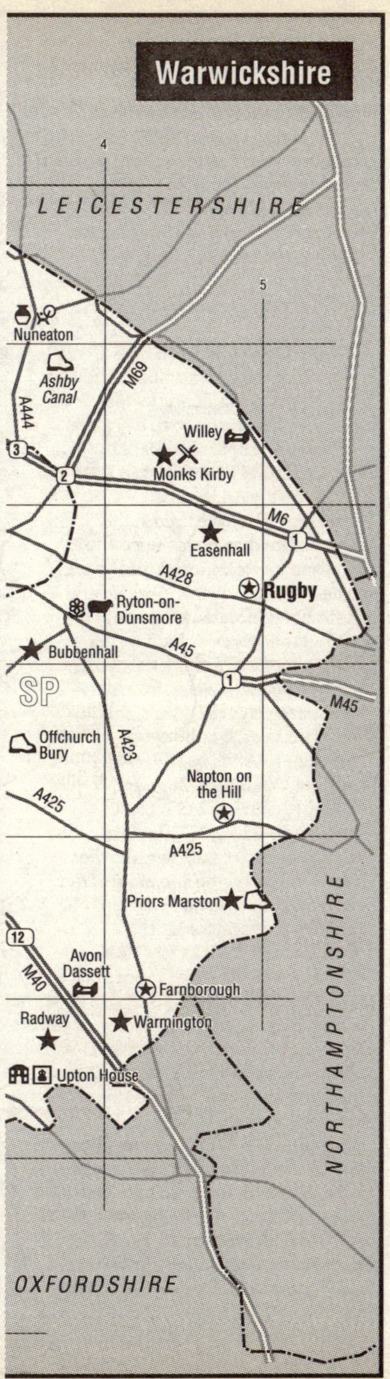

and the Moat House (on the A435 towards Studley) has good food; nearby Arrow village is interesting to stroll around (despite some development), as is the pretty stream that divides the two. Fruit farming around here is rarer than it once was, but you can still find delicious fresh dessert plums in Sept. The county's best drive (partly in Gloucs) circles Alcester, via Walcote, Aston Cantlow, Wilmcote, Temple Grafton, Wixford, Radford, Inkberrow, Holberrow Green, New End and King's Coughton.

AMBLECOTE SO8985 **Royal Doulton** (on the A491) You can tour the factory or visit the factory shop, ¼ mile further N; tours 10am and 11.15am wkdys only (no under-10s), booking recommended; (01384) 552900; free. The Robin Hood here (Collis St) has good-value food.

ARBURY HALL SP3388 (Arbury, off the B4102 just S of Nuneaton) Splendid-looking place, the original Elizabethan house elaborately spruced up in the 19th c as one of the best examples of the Gothic Revival style. The writer George Eliot was born on the estate, and her *Mr Gifgil's Love Story* describes some of the rooms – not unreasonably comparing the dining room to a cathedral. Some work by Wren in the stables (now housing a collection of vintage cycles), and the gardens are a pleasure. Meals, snacks, shop, limited disabled access; open pm Sun and bank hols Easter–Sept; (01203) 382804; £4.50, £2.50 gardens only.

! ARDENS GRAFTON SP1253 **Golden Cross Inn** Unusually decorated with over 250 antique dolls, teddies and toys. Small shop, decent food; cl 3–6pm, all 25–26 Dec.

★ ARMSCOTE SP2444 Picturesque Cotswold stone village.

ASHBY CANAL SP3688 Canal towpaths offer some of Warwickshire's nicest walks, and heading off towards Leics from the Coventry Canal link at Marston Junction on the edge of Bedworth this canal has perhaps the prettiest of them.

! ASHORNE SP3057 **Nickelodeon** (Ashorne Hall, off the B4100) Mechanically played musical instruments inc self-playing harps, drums and violins, and a vintage theatre complete with organ rising from the floor (demonstrated daily at 4.15pm). They show silent comedies and 1950s Pathé newsreels, and have various nostalgic tea concerts and events. There's a miniature railway in the grounds (£1.80 extra). Meals, snacks, shop, disabled access; open pm Sun Mar–Nov, plus Fri and Sat July and Aug, and maybe other days too – worth checking; (01926) 651444; *£6.60. The Cottage has good-value food (maybe cl wkdy lunchtime).

★ **ASTON CANTLOW** SP1461 Charming timbered houses and guildhall, lovely church where Shakespeare's parents married, fine old pub.

★ **AUSTREY** SK2906 Attractive village with black and white timbered houses and cottages, some thatch.

BADDESLEY CLINTON HOUSE SP2072 Romantic 13th-c moated manor house, mostly unchanged since the 17th c. Interesting portraits, priest's holes and garden with chapel and pretty walks. The family history is intriguing. Meals, snacks, shop, some disabled access; open pm Weds–Sun and bank hols Mar–Oct (shop and restaurant open till Christmas); (01564) 783294; £4.80 (timed ticket system), grounds only £2.40; NT. The nearby **church** has a lovely east window, and the canalside Navigation at Lapworth does decent food.

BICKENHILL SP2083 **National Motorcycle Museum** (Coventry Rd) Handy for the NEC, 5 halls displaying over 650 gleamingly restored motorcycles, all British. Incongruously, they also have the biggest theatre organ in Europe. Meals, snacks, shop, disabled access; cl 24–26 Dec; (01675) 443311; £4.50. The White Lion at Hampton in Arden has good-value food.

CASTLE BROMWICH HALL GARDEN SP1489 (Chester Rd) Carefully restored 18th-c formal gardens, with authentic collection of period plants, inc ancient vegetables as well as herbs and shrubs. Snacks, plant sales, disabled access; cl am, all day Fri, and Oct–Easter; (0121) 749 4100; *£2.

CHARLECOTE PARK SP2656 250 acres of parkland, full of deer (Shakespeare is said to have poached some), along with the descendants of reputedly the country's first flock of Jacob sheep. Well furnished Great Hall and Victorian kitchen, and an impressive Tudor gatehouse. Meals, snacks, shop, disabled access; open Fri–Tues Apr–Oct (cl Good Fri); (01789) 470277; £4.80; NT. By the park a charming 19th-c estate village has timbered cottages and a show Victorian church. The Boar's Head in pretty Hampton Lucy does decent food.

★ **CLIFFORD CHAMBERS** SP1952 Pretty black and white timbered houses and cottages, and a Tudor former rectory with some claim to being the true birthplace of Shakespeare.

COUGHTON COURT SP0860 (on the A435) The Throckmortons have lived in this mainly Elizabethan house since 1409; renowned for its imposing gatehouse and beautiful courtyard, it has several priest's holes, notable furniture and porcelain, and an exhibition on the Gunpowder Plot, with a lake, two churches, pleasant walks, formal gardens and play area. Meals, snacks, shop, plant sales, limited disabled access; open wknds mid-Mar–mid-Oct, plus Mon–Weds May–Sept, and Fri July and Aug; (01789) 462435; £5.90, grounds only £3.90; NT. Poppies, at the Court, is a good restaurant, and the Green Dragon on the fine old green at nearby Sambourne and Washford Mill at Studley are good for lunch.

COVENTRY SP3379 Like Birmingham, more a place to dip into than to use as your base for a short holiday. Its most interesting street is Spon St, with one or two ancient buildings that started their lives here and others that have been rescued from elsewhere and rebuilt here (the picturesque Old Windmill does cheap basic lunches). The town's famous Lady Godiva is commemorated best by the Coventry Clock – from which she pops out in the pink every hour. The Royal Court Hotel, Greyhound out at Sutton Stop (Alderman's Green/Hawkesbury) and Prince William Henry and William IV (both Foleshill Rd – authentic Indian) are popular for lunch, and Browns café-bar near the cathedral (Lower Precinct) serves food all day. **Coventry Cathedral** (Priory Row) Bombed in the war, the old cathedral ruins have been carefully preserved, and parts of it such as the 14th-c tower remain intact. These have been joined by the new cathedral designed by Sir Basil Spence. Deliberately different from a conventional church building, it has striking modern art (inc windows by John Piper, tapestry by Graham Sutherland, even holograms); the visitor centre (cl Sun) has more, as well as a full history of its development. Meals, snacks, shop, disabled access; cl 4 days in July and Nov for degree ceremonies; £2 suggested donation, *£1.25 for visitor centre. **Coventry Toy Museum** (Much Park St) Toys from 1740 to 1990, housed in a 14th-c monastery gatehouse. Shop; cl am, and 25 Dec; (01203) 227560; *£1.50. **Herbert Art Gallery & Museum** (Jordan Well) Fine silver and furniture, Chinese art, and a lively interactive history of the city. Meals, snacks, shop, disabled access; cl Christmas; (01203) 832381; free. **Lunt Roman Fort** (Coventry Rd) Fun reconstruction of 1st-c Roman fort, interesting to see such a site in all its glory. Good interpretative displays. Shop, some disabled access; open wknds and bank hols Apr–Oct, plus daily late July–Aug; (01203) 832381; £2.60 (inc audio tour). **Museum of British Road Transport** (St Agnes Lane) Big collection of motor cars (developed in Coventry from the already established sewing machine industry), as well as commercial vehicles and bicycles, and a display of die-cast models. Snacks, shop, disabled access; cl 24–26 Dec; (01203) 832425; free. **St Mary's Guildhall** (Bayley Lane) Very well preserved medieval building, with its minstrels' gallery still, and some Flemish tapestries; usually open Easter–Sept (exc Fri and Sat), provided there aren't any civic functions, but best to check; (01203) 832381. **Midland Air Museum** (Coventry Airport) Civil and military aircraft spanning more than 70 years. Snacks, shop, disabled access; cl 25–26 Dec; (01203) 301033; *£3.25.

DUDLEY SO9591 **Black Country Living Museum** (Tipton Rd, 1m N) Well thought out open-air museum giving a good feel of how things used to be in the Black Country, the heavily industrialised and proudly individual areas in the west part of the Birmingham conurbation. It's an authentically reconstructed turn-of-the-century village, complete with cottages, chapel, chemist, school, baker, pub and old-fashioned fairground, and trips along the canal or even down a mine. All the staff wear period costume, and demonstrations are informative and entertaining. This could easily fill most of a day. Meals, snacks, shop, some disabled access; cl Mon and Tues in Nov–Feb, and 21–25 Dec; (0121) 557 9643; £6.95. The Dudley Canal Trust do **boat trips** along part of a unique network of canal tunnels and limestone mines. Trips Mar–Nov, and some days in Dec – best to ring for times; (01384) 236275; £2.60. **Dudley Zoo** (The Broadway) Based around an impressive **ruined castle**, so the animals enjoy rather special views. Meals, snacks, shop, disabled access; cl 25 Dec; (01384) 215300; £6. **Dudley Museum & Art Gallery** (St James's Rd) Some fine paintings, well displayed geology, and appealing temporary exhibitions. Shop, disabled access but no facilities; cl Sun and bank hol Mon, Christmas and New Year; (01384) 815575; free.

EARLSWOOD SP1074 **Manor Farm craft workshops** (Wood Lane) Furniture restoration, stained glass, print-making, needlework, a new vintage car display, and farm shop with home-made ice-cream. Meals, snacks, shop, disabled access; cl Mon, Christmas wk; (01564) 702729; free. The canalside Bluebell and the Red Lion (past the lakes) are useful dining pubs.

★ **EXHALL** SP1055 Pretty black and white timbering, and some pleasant, gently hilly walks nearby; very quiet.

FARNBOROUGH HALL SP4349 Palladian villa filled with splendid sculptures, paintings and fine rococo plasterwork; the staircase, hall and 2 main rooms are on show. The 18th-c landscaped gardens have a couple of ornamental temples, and views from the terrace walk – less impressive than they were, thanks to the M40. Disabled access to ground floor only; open pm Weds and Sat Apr–Sept, terrace also open pm Thurs and Fri; (01295) 690002; £2.90, £1 terrace walk only; NT. The Butchers Arms has good food.

GAYDON SP3354 **Heritage Motor Centre** (Banbury Rd) Busy centre with the world's biggest collection of historic British cars – 300 in all, starting with an 1895 Wolseley. Also hundreds of drawings, photographs, trophies and models, hi-tech displays and video shows, and a nature reserve. The design of the building is incredible, especially inside. Meals, snacks, shop, disabled access; cl 24–26 Dec; (01926) 641188; £5.50. The Malt Shovel is handy for lunch.

HARTSHILL HAYES SP3194 Country park with mixed woodland, opening out for broad views towards the Peak District. The Coventry Canal below allows more extended rambles.

! HATTON SP2367 **Country World** (Dark Lane) Britain's biggest crafts village, made up of some 3 dozen workshops and still growing; demonstrations most wknds. The 100-acre site also includes a rare breeds farm (with walk-through paddocks), adventure playground and soft play area and antique and plant centres. Meals, snacks, shop, limited disabled access; (01926) 843411; craft village free, farm £3.80. A nature trail leads to the **Stairway to Heaven**, a flight of 21 Grand Union Canal locks over 2 miles. Windmill House Farm nearby has a good farm shop; the Durham Ox at Shrewley is handy for lunch.

★ **HENLEY-IN-ARDEN** SP1565 More small town than village, but a pretty conservation area, with good churches.

★ **HONILEY** SP2472 The village has virtually gone now, and there are only vestiges of the big house, but you can still sense the vanished settlement around the surviving 18th-c church.

★ **HONINGTON** SP2642 Attractive village, its church prettily set on the edge of the lawn of charming late 17th-c Honington Hall (open pm Weds Jun–Aug).

★ † **ILMINGTON** SP2143 Quietly attractive, with peaceful path to partly Norman **church**, lovely inside; pleasant walks on hills above; the Howard Arms is good for lunch.

KENILWORTH CASTLE SP2772 Dramatic castle transformed by John of Gaunt into a spectacular fortress. These are among the finest castle ruins in the country, with a still-impressive keep and several other buildings within the sandstone walls. Also restored Tudor garden, various re-enactments and open-air plays and operas, and children's activities most summer hol wknds. Shop, disabled access (but no facilities); cl 24–26 Dec, 1 Jan; (01926) 852078; £3.10. The town itself has a Norman church and some pleasant strolls, especially around the castle area, where the Clarendon House Hotel has good-value food.

! KINGSWINSFORD SO8888 **Broadfield House Glass Museum** (Barnett Lane) Excellent collection of glass from nearby Stourbridge, displayed to dazzling effect. Clever use of lighting shows off the exhibits quite spectacularly, and even the audio-visual shows create a sense of excitement. One of the area's least expected treasures. Teas, shop; cl Mon (exc bank hols, 24–28 Dec, 1 Jan; (01384) 812745; free. **Crooked House** (off the B4176 E of Himley, SO8991) Extraordinary pub bent by mining subsidence into a 3-dimensional optical illusion that'll have you imagining things roll uphill here, instead of down; perhaps surprisingly, it's a good pub too.

★ **LEAMINGTON SPA** SP2864 Elegant spa resort popularised by the rich who came to take the waters in the 18th and 19th c. Still many fine Regency buildings, though today the town is better seen as a civilised shopping centre, and perhaps as a base for sallies into the surrounding countryside – or into Warwick, across the River Avon. Beautifully laid out **Jephson Gardens** (The Parade) are worth a look, with wild ducks on the lake. The adjoining **Royal Pump Rooms** should reopen in May 1999 after restoration, housing an art gallery, museum and café. The Carpenters Arms (Chandos St) is a decent well restored early Victorian pub.

★ **LONG COMPTON** SP2932 Pleasant Cotswoldy village of thatched stone houses, some antique shops; the Red Lion has good food.

★ ✝ ❁ **LOWER BRAILES** SP3139 Attractive Cotswold-edge village with lovely slender-spired **church**, pretty stone houses, good views.

★ **MERIDEN** SP2482 A cross on the green claims this as England's centre – one stream rising in the village pond ends up in the Severn, the other over in the Humber. The Bull's Head does good-value food.

★ **MIDDLE TYSOE** SP3344 Charming village – with a very traditional cottage bakery.

MIDDLETON SP1797 **Ash End House Farm** (off the A4091) Friendly farm set up specifically for children; animals from shire horses to baby chicks and fluffy ducklings, as well as rare breeds of goats, pigs and sheep. A pony ride is included in the price, and there's plenty under cover for wet days. Snacks, shop, disabled access; cl 25–27 Dec, 1 Jan; (0121) 329 3240; £3.60 children (adults half price). **Middleton Hall** (on the A4091) Varied architecture in the house (being restored), also nature reserve, walled gardens, orchards, woodland, and a good craft centre in the stables. Snacks, shop, some disabled access; house open pm Sun and bank hols Apr–Sept, craft centre open all year exc Mon and Tues; (01827) 283095; £1.50. The Green Man is a decent family dining pub.

★ ❁ **NAPTON ON THE HILL** SP4661 Attractive village on a rounded hill above a curve in the Oxford Canal – perhaps the prettiest canal in this part of the world, with pleasant towpath walks. Great views of 7 counties from the hill. **Church Leyes Farm** Friendly 40-acre family-run organic farm with animals, walks and wild flower conservation headlands by the hedges. Disabled access with prior notice; cl Sat, and Jewish holy days; (01926) 812143; *£1.

NUNEATON SP3691 (Coton Rd) A display on the life of George Eliot can be seen at the **museum**, nicely set in colourful Riversley Park; cl am Sun, all day Mon (exc bank hols), and Christmas; (01203) 350720; free. Good craft centre nearby; the new central Felix Holt pub has decent food all day.

OFFCHURCH BURY SP3565 Attractive riverside parkland, with a pleasant walk winding through from the Stag's Head in Offchurch.

PACKWOOD HOUSE SP1772 (off the A34) Friendly old house starting as a 16th-c farmhouse, carefully restored and not at all commercialised; interesting panelling, furniture and needlework, and yew trees clipped to represent the Sermon on the Mount. Snacks, shop, some disabled access; open pm Weds–Sun and bank hols Apr–Oct; (01564) 782024; £4.20, garden only £2.10; NT. The canalside Navigation at Lapworth has good-value food.

★ **PRIORS MARSTON** SP4857 Attractive old houses around the village green, and unusual blue brick paths; the ancient Holly Bush is a decent pub. There's a walk up Marston Hill behind, and quite a good network of paths around nearby Priors Hardwick taking you down to the Oxford Canal. The old drovers' Welsh Road through here via Southam to Cubbington is a pleasant drive; just before Offchurch it crosses the Fosse Way, a quiet Roman road running dead straight from Brinklow through Stretton-on-Dunsmore and Princethorpe down to Halford.

RUGBY SCHOOL SP5074 Founded in 1567, moving to its current site nearly 200 years later. A **museum** on Little Church St looks at its history and former pupils, such as Rupert Brooke and Lewis Carroll. Shop, disabled access; cl am, all day Sun and Mon, and 2 wks at Christmas; (01788) 574117; £1.50. Guided tours of the school buildings leave here at 2.30pm (not Sun or Mon, 01788 573959), and other times by arrangement; £2, or £3 combined ticket with museum. The game the school invented is commemorated at **Gilberts** nearby, the shop making the standard rugby ball since 1842. You can see them do it, also related displays and collections. Shop, some disabled access; cl Sun and a few days over Christmas; (01788) 542426; free. The Three Horseshoes Hotel (Sheep St) is useful for lunch.

RYTON-ON-DUNSMORE SP3874 **Ryton Gardens** (off the A45, on the Wolston road) Home of the

Henry Doubleday Research Association for organic farming and gardening, so the grounds are landscaped with thousands of organically grown plants and trees; herb garden, rose garden, garden for the blind, and shrub borders among the displays, as well as some free-range farm animals and a new cook's garden where all the plants are edible. Very good meals and snacks in wholefood café, shop, disabled access; cl Christmas wk; (01203) 303517; £2.50 (usually less in winter).

★ **SHIPSTON ON STOUR** SP2540 Small town with quite a busy shopping centre; rewarding to stroll through, with a good church and handsome old stone buildings, antique shops among them.

★ **STONELEIGH** SP3271 Primarily known as the showground for the Royal Show, with an increasing number of permanent displays; the village has an attractive sandstone Norman church, timber-framed houses, and soon to be restored Stoneleigh Abbey.

STRATFORD-UPON-AVON CANAL SP1867 This gives some pleasant towpath walks; the Fleur de Lys at Lowsonford is a good start.

★ **SUTTON-UNDER-BRAILES** SP3037 Attractive stone-built village, with nearby walks in pleasing Cotswold countryside.

TANWORTH IN ARDEN SP1270 **Umberslade Children's Farm** Friendly family-run farm with animals to stroke and feed, and play areas for letting off steam. Also nature trails and walks, and goat-milking area. Snacks, shop, disabled access; cl Nov–mid-Mar and usually some wkdys Oct; (01564) 742251; £2.75.

UPTON HOUSE SP3745 (on the A422 nr Ratley) The exceptional art collection is the main draw, an enormous range of paintings inc works by Bosch, El Greco, Bruegel and Hogarth, all sensibly arranged and displayed. Also Brussels tapestries, Sèvres porcelain, and woodland and terrace walks. The late 17th-c house was remodelled earlier this century. Teas, shop, disabled access; open pm Sat–Weds Apr–Oct (cl Good Fri); (01295) 670266; £5, garden only £2.50; NT. There's a timed ticket system at peak periods. Ratley is a pretty village, with a lovely church and good home cooking in the Rose & Crown; the Castle on Edge Hill is a very interesting place for lunch, with terrific views.

WALSALL SP0199 **Leather Museum** (Wisenmore) Well restored 19th-c leather goods factory with tours of aromatic workshops and leather-making demonstrations (not Sun). Meals, snacks, shop (lots of local leather goods), disabled access; cl am Sun, all day Mon (exc bank hols), 24–26 Dec, 1 Jan, Easter Sun; (01922) 721153; free. The Hammakers Arms (Shaw St/Blue Lane) does good-value food. **Jerome K Jerome Birthplace Museum** (Bradford St) Dedicated to the life and work of the author of *Three Men in a Boat*, with a reconstructed 1850s parlour; cl 12.45–2.15pm, pm Sat, all day Sun and bank hols; free. **Birchills Canal Museum** (Top Lock, Old Birchills) Small museum with a replica boat cabin, and maybe boat trips; cl Mon, pm Tues and Weds, am Thurs–Sun, 25–26 Dec, 1 Jan, Good Fri; (01922) 645778; free.

Days Out

Machine aesthetics: Heritage Motor Centre, Gaydon; lunch at the King's Head, Wellesbourne; watermill there (limited opening); Nickelodeon, Ashorne.

Birmingham at work: Birmingham railway museum; Jewellery Quarter Discovery Centre; lunch at the Rosevilla (Vyse St); Cadbury World.

Black Country heritage: Broadfield House glass museum, Kingswinford; Amblecote for the Royal Doulton factory tour (limited opening); lunch at the Crooked House, Himley; Black Country Museum, Dudley.

WELLESBOURNE SP2854
Wellesbourne Watermill (on the B4086) Historic watermill reopened after heroic works to right 1998 flood damage; still producing flour in secluded rural setting, with striking wooden wheel. Helpful staff, nature trails and traditional crafts. Snacks, shop, some disabled access (but some steep steps); open Thurs–Sun Apr–Sept (daily exc Mon in summer hols), plus pm Sun Oct and Mar; (01789) 470237; £3.
Wartime Museum In the underground HQ of a former RAF base, a collection of aeronautical archaeology and wartime memorabilia, with a restored Vampire. Shop, some disabled access (not underground); open Suns only; *£1.50. The King's Head is a decent pub with tables in the garden facing the church.

WINDMILL HILL SP3343
The walk S from Upper Tysoe over this hill (which does have a windmill) takes you to the church on the edge of Compton Wynyates park, giving views of the attractive Tudor manor – a refreshing bit of brick building, in this Cotswold-edge stone country.

WOLVERHAMPTON
SJ9400 This workaday town has a good **museum** (Lichfield Rd), and Wightwick Manor and Moseley Old Hall on the outskirts are splendid.
Wightwick Manor SO8798 (just off the A454 3m W) Only a century old, but beautifully and unusually designed by followers of William Morris, and a fine testimonial to the enduring qualities of his design principles. Flamboyant tiles, fittings, furnishings and glass, and lots of Pre-Raphaelite art, cannily acquired while it was unfashionable. Also period garden with yew hedges and topiary. Snacks, shop, some disabled access; open pm Thurs, Sat and bank hol wknds, Mar–Dec, garden also open Weds; (01902) 761108; £5.20, garden only £2.40.
Moseley Old Hall SO9304 (Featherstone, off the A460/A449 4m N) Tudor house famed as a hiding place for Charles II after the Battle of Worcester. The façade has altered since, but the furnishings and atmosphere in its panelled rooms don't seem to have changed much, and there's a 17th-c knot garden. Readers particularly enjoy the guided tours. Teas, shop, limited disabled access; open pm Weds, wknds (Apr–May) and bank hols Apr–Oct, plus pm Tues July and Aug and after bank hols, and pm Suns Nov–Christmas; (01902) 782808; £3.60; NT.

★ **Other attractive villages**, almost all with decent pubs, include Barston SP2078, Barton-on-the-Heath SP2532 (no pub), Berkswell SP2479 (pretty Norman church), Bubbenhall SP3672, Easenhall SP4679, Hampton in Arden SP2081, Hampton Lucy SP2557, upmarket Lighthorne SP3355, Lower Quinton SP1847, Monks Kirby SP4683 (huge church), Preston on Stour SP2049, Radway SP3748 (we've had no pub recommendation here yet), Temple Grafton SP1255 (Shakespeare's 'Hungry Grafton'), Warmington SP4147 and Welford on Avon SP1452.

Canals give some of the county's best walking opportunities. Besides places already mentioned, useful canalside pubs include the Anchor at Leek Wootton SP2868, Two Boats at Long Itchington SP4164 (the flight of Stockton Locks just E usually has plenty going on), George & Dragon at the Wharf nr Fenny Compton SP4152 (on the A423 – a popular family pub, with aviaries and so forth) and Dog & Doublet at Bodymoor Heath SP2096 (useful for the Kingsbury Water Park too). There are pleasant walks by the **River Avon** from the Ferry, a good dining pub in Alveston SP2356, and Cottage of Content at Barton SP0950, which has day fishing tickets.

Where to eat

ALDERMINSTER SP2348 **Bell** *(01789) 450414* Very popular and rather civilised dining pub nr Stratford, with excellent imaginative food using fresh local produce (no fried food), several communicating areas with flagstones and wooden floors, fresh flowers, good wines, real ales, obliging service, and no smoking restaurant; cl pms 24 Dec–2 Jan; disabled access. **£22**|£6.50.

BERKSWELL SP2479 **Bear** *(01676) 533202* Handsomely refurbished 16th-c timbered pub with relaxed atmosphere, comfortably snug low-beamed areas, nooks and crannies, beams and panelling, bric-à-brac, well kept ales, decent house wines, and a wide choice of food inc interesting daily specials; seats on back lawn. **£17.35**|£6.25.

GREAT WOLFORD SP2434 **Fox & Hounds** *(01608) 674220* Inviting 16th-c inn with a good mix of locals and visitors in the cosy low-beamed old-fashioned bar; candlelit tables, flagstones and a roaring log fire, really enjoyable imaginative daily specials, over 200 malt whiskies, and a little tap room with several changing real ales. **£20.50**|£7.

LEAMINGTON SPA SP3165 **Phoenix Bar** *Regent Hotel, The Parade (01926) 427231* Extremely popular, elegant and comfortable hotel bar with lovely trompe l'oeil murals, open fire, relaxed atmosphere, very good food and helpful service; also 2 restaurants; disabled access. **£21**|£5.

LOWSONFORD SP1867 **Fleur de Lys** *(01564) 782431* Bustling canalside pub with comfortable civilised atmosphere, smart spreading bar with lots of low black beams, and open fires; good food, well kept real ales, and decent wines by the glass; cl 25 Dec; children in dining room only. **£18**|£7.25.

MONKS KIRBY SP4682 **Bell** *Bells Lane (01788) 832352* Busy pub with warmly chatty Spanish landlord, timbered and flagstoned rambling rooms, cheerful locals, marvellous tapas (Spanish hors d'oeuvres) as well as more usual bar food, a very good wine list, well kept real ales, and quite a few whiskies; cl am Mon, 26 Dec, 1 Jan; disabled access. **£25**|£4.75.

STRATFORD-UPON-AVON SP2054 **Opposition** *13 Sheep St (01789) 269980* Small bustling restaurant with friendly atmosphere, generous helpings of very good interesting food – handy for theatres and open for after-show meals; cl 25–26 Dec. **£20**|£5.95.

STRATFORD-UPON-AVON SP2054 **Russons** *8 Church St (01789) 268822* Cheerful and popular bistro in 17th-c malt house with very good imaginative food (plenty of fresh fish) and good-value simple wine list; pre-theatre meals, too; cl Sun, Mon, 2 wks spring, 2 wks autumn; **£24.50**|£4.95.

STRATFORD-UPON-AVON SP2055 **Slug & Lettuce** *38 Guild St (01789) 299700* Cheerfully friendly and popular, with good food, helpful staff, well kept real ales, decent wine, attractive bar with open fire and newspapers, and pretty back terrace. **£25**|£9.

WOOTTON WAWEN SP1563 **Bull's Head** *(01564) 792511* Charming old black and white timbered building with heavy-beamed bar, low-ceilinged lounge with huge upright timbers, handsome restaurant, generous helpings of good, often unusual food from a sensibly short menu, notably friendly young staff, several wines by the glass, well kept beer; handy for walks by the Stratford Canal; cl 25 Dec; no children. **£20**|£8.

Special thanks to Mrs T Fountain, B M Eldridge, Maureen DuMont, Mark Smith, Philip Turner, Mark Smith, D Haddon, Mrs C Wheeldon, Graham Tayar.

We welcome reports from readers

This *Guide* depends on readers' reports. Do help us if you can – in return, we offer a discount on the next edition to people who've helped us with reports for it. Tell us what you think about places already in it, and anything extra you think we should say about them. And send us your ideas for inclusion in the next edition: places to visit, eat at or stay in, attractive drives or walks, maybe even unusual interesting shops you know of. Use the card in the middle, the report forms at the end, or just write – no stamp needed: *The Good Guide to Britain*, FREEPOST TN1569, Wadhurst, E Sussex TN5 7BR.

Warwickshire Calendar

Some of these dates were provisional as we went to press. Please check information with the telephone numbers provided.

JANUARY

1 **Birmingham** Burne-Jones Exhibition at the Gas Hall – *till Sun 17* (0121) 605 7000
7 **Birmingham** Autosport International at the NEC – *till Sun 10* (0171) 402 2555
10 **Birmingham** Toy & Train Collectors Fair at the NEC (0121) 780 4141
20 **Birmingham** Antiques & Fine Art Fair at the NEC – *till Sun 24* (0121) 780 4141

FEBRUARY

16 **Atherstone** Shrovetide Football: hundreds of locals gather for the game in the Main St (01827) 716410
20 **Birmingham** National Boat, Caravan & Leisure Show at the NEC – *till Sun 28* (01203) 221443

MARCH

6 **Hagley** Food & Country Shopping Fair at Hagley Hall – *till Sun 7* (01509) 217444
11 **Birmingham** Crufts Dog Show at the NEC – *till Sun 14* (0171) 493 7838
17 **Coventry** St Patrick's Day Pageant in the City Centre (01203) 831345

APRIL

5 **Walsall** Easter Fun at the Leather Museum (01922) 653141
17 **Alcester** Gardeners Weekend at Ragley Hall – *till Sun 18* (01625) 573477
24 **Stratford-upon-Avon** Shakespeare Birthday Celebrations: procession and birthday lunch (01789) 204016
30 **Warwick** Classical Music Festival – *till 5 May* (01926) 410747

MAY

1 **Birmingham** National Classic Motor Show at the NEC – *till Sun 2* (0121) 780 4141
2 **Gaydon** Land Rover Day at Heritage Motor Centre (01926) 645042
8 **Solihull** Festival – *till Sat 15* (0121) 704 6961
9 **West Bromwich** Historic Vehicle Parade and Show (0121) 569 3402
10 **Birmingham** World Cup, warm-up game: Warwicks v West Indies at Edgbaston Cricket Ground (0121) 446 4422
11 **Birmingham** World Cup, warm-up game: Warwicks v Zimbabwe at Edgbaston Cricket Ground (0121) 446 4422
13 **Birmingham** National Dog Show at Perry Park, Perry Barr – *till Sun 16* (01536) 791399
16 **Leamington Spa** Dolls Show: houses and miniatures at the Royal Spa Centre (01787) 281855; **Packwood** Plant Fair at Packwood House (01564) 782024

Warwickshire Calendar (cont.)

29 **Birmingham** World Cup: England v India at Edgbaston Cricket Ground (0121) 446 4422

30 **Alcester** Transport Show at Ragley Hall – *till Mon 31* (01789) 762090; **Offchurch** British Falconry, Raptor & Game Fair at Offchurch Bury – *till Mon 31* (01588) 672708

JUNE

4 **Coventry** Godiva Weekend inc live music, street entertainers, stalls at Memorial Park – *till Sun 6* (0500) 777220

5 **Solihull** Carnival (0121) 704 6130; **Walsall** Summer Show inc arena events at Aldridge Airport – *till Sun 6* (01922) 653141

6 **Nuneaton** Transport Spectacular at Arbury Hall (0121) 502 3713

10 **Birmingham** World Cup: super six playoffs at Edgbaston Cricket Ground (0121) 446 4422

12 **Coventry** Hillfields Festival – *till Sun 20* (01203) 831345

16 **Birmingham** BBC *Gardeners' World* at the NEC – *till Sun 20* (0121) 780 4141

17 **Birmingham** World Cup Semi-Final at Edgbaston Cricket Ground (0121) 446 4422

26 **Leamington** Jazz Weekend – *till Sun 27* (01926) 410747; **Warwick** Carnival (01926) 411020

27 **Alcester** Outdoor Concert: Music from the Movies at Ragley Hall (01789) 762090; **Wellesbourne** Raft Race (01789) 841073

30 **Warwick and Leamington** Festival – *till 11 July* (01926) 410747

JULY

2 **Birmingham** International Jazz Festival – *till Sun 11* (0121) 454 7020

3 **Baddesley Clinton** Open Air-opera at Baddesley Clinton House – *till Sun 4* (01564) 783294; **Kenilworth** Carnival (01926) 852595; **Warwick** Fireworks Concert at the Castle – *till Sun 4* (01926) 406600; **Warwick** Street Theatre (01926) 410747

4 **Gaydon** Triumph Day at Heritage Motor Centre (01926) 645042; **Stratford-upon-Avon** Poetry Festival *and every Sun till 22 Aug* (01789) 204016; **Walsall** Classic Car Show at Walsall Arboretum (0121) 502 3713

5 **Kenilworth** The Royal Show at National Agricultural College, Stoneleigh Park – *till Thurs 8* (01203) 696969

10 **Packwood** 1920s Summer Follies: outdoor concert, fireworks, dancing at Packwood House (01564) 782024

11 **Leamington Spa** Street Theatre (01926) 410747

18 **Alcester** Triumph Rally at Ragley Hall (01625) 573477; **Gaydon** Supercar Sunday at Heritage Motor Centre (01926) 645042

19 **Wellesbourne** Warwicks Rural Show at Wellesbourne Watermill (01789) 470237

24 **Coughton** Fireworks Concert at Coughton Court (0500) 661812; **Coventry** Caribbean Festival at Memorial Park (01203) 831345

26 **Stratford-upon-Avon** International Flute Festival – *till 7 Aug* (01789) 269247

Warwickshire Calendar (cont.)

AUGUST

6 **Walsall** Leather Festival at the Leather Museum – *till Sun 8* (01922) 653141
7 **Alcester** Firework & Laser Concert at Ragley Hall (01789) 762090; **Canwell** Show (0121) 323 4057
8 **Gaydon** MG 75th Anniversary at Heritage Motor Centre (01926) 645042
12 **Long Marston** Bulldog Bash: motorcycle rally at Avon Park Raceway – *till Sun 15* (01789) 414119
21 **Alcester** Warwicks & West Midlands Game Fair inc arena events, military bands at Ragley Hall – *till Sun 22* (01588) 672708; **Hatton** Hatton '99 at Hatton Country World – *till Sun 22* (01926) 843411
28 **Kenilworth** Town & Country Festival at National Agricultural College, Stoneleigh Park – *till Mon 30* (01203) 696969

SEPTEMBER

3 **Alcester** Outdoor Concert at Ragley Hall (01789) 762090
11 **Alcester** Garden Fair at Ragley Hall – *till Sun 12* (01789) 762090
12 **Gaydon** Classic Car Show at Heritage Motor Centre (01926) 645042
18 **Walsall** Illuminations at Walsall Arboretum: light and laser show with music, street theatre and live performances – *till 31 Oct* (01922) 653148
19 **Birmingham** International Garden & Leisure Exhibition at the NEC – *till Tues 21* (0121) 780 4141

OCTOBER

3 **Gaydon** Mini 40th Anniversary at Heritage Motor Centre (01926) 645042
10 **Stratford-upon-Avon** Apple Day and Harvest Fair at Mary Arden's House (01789) 204016
15 **Stratford-upon-Avon** English Music Festival – *till Sun 24* (01789) 261561
16 **Warwick** Hog Roast and Mop Fair – *till Sun 17* (01926) 492212
30 **Gaydon** Fireworks Display at Heritage Motor Centre (01926) 645042

NOVEMBER

4 **Birmingham** International Motorcycle Show at the NEC – *till Sun 14* (0121) 780 4141
13 **Birmingham** National Classic Motor Show at the NEC – *till Sun 14* (0121) 780 4141
24 **Birmingham** BBC Good Food, Cooking & Kitchen Show at the NEC – *till Sun 28* (0121) 780 4141

DECEMBER

2 **Warwick** Victorian Evening (01926) 491527
3 **Birmingham** BBC *Clothes Show* Live at the NEC – *till Weds 8* (0121) 780 4141

Wiltshire

Interest for all ages; Salisbury makes a good short break, particularly for older people.

Longleat is a great day out for people of any age. Apart from the enjoyable farms at Cholderton and Teffont Magna, many children enjoy the striking ruins of Old Wardour Castle near Tisbury, and there are particularly good play areas or other children's attractions at several of the places which have a more adult appeal.

Top outings include Stourhead's wonderful grounds, Wilton House and Lacock village and Abbey. Other major draws are Bowood, Lydiard Park (a real bargain), Corsham Court, the intriguing gardens at Tollard Royal and Hazelbury Manor at Box, the waterside ones at Middle Woodford, and the unusual stone-working museum at Great Bedwyn (the extraordinary underground quarry at Corsham has closed to visitors – the price of stone has gone up and they have started quarrying again). Castle Combe is another exceptionally pretty village, and Bradford-on-Avon, Devizes, Marlborough and Malmesbury are attractive small towns with a good deal of character.

The two great prehistoric stone circles, Stonehenge and Avebury, are best appreciated at quiet times of day, out of season (with Stonehenge we'd recommend one of the specially authorised Astral tours). The county has a good many other ancient sites to explore, too.

Salisbury is a splendid small city for a short civilised break, with a lovely cathedral precinct and interesting places to visit tucked quite closely around it.

The most appealing countryside is along the valleys of the southern chalk streams – intimate scenery with stone or flint houses and sparkling rivers now recovering after recent dry summers. The northern part of the county has some quietly attractive drives and walks, especially around Marlborough.

Where to stay

ALDERTON ST8482 **Manor Farm** *Alderton, Chippenham SN14 6NL (01666) 840271* **£56;** 3 rms. Warmly friendly 17th-c house on busy working farm (550 arable acres) with homely lounge and good breakfasts; cl 24–26 Dec; children over 10.

BRADFORD-ON-AVON ST8261 **Bradford Old Windmill** *4 Masons Lane, Bradford-on-Avon BA15 1QN (01225) 866842* ***£75;** 3 rms, one with a giant waterbed, another with a round bed. Interesting and carefully converted windmill with a log fire in the attractive circular lounge (former grain store), lots of books, a friendly atmosphere; good evening meals inc vegetarian dishes from Thailand, Nepal, Mexico and so forth, and fine breakfasts eaten around communal refectory table; pretty cottagey garden; no smoking; cl Jan and Feb; children over 6.

BRADFORD-ON-AVON ST8359 **Widbrook Grange** *Trowbridge Rd, Widbrook, Bradford-on-Avon BA15 1UH (01225) 864750* **£92;** 20 pretty rms, many in carefully converted courtyard cottages. Handsome stone former farmhouse in 11 acres, with comfortable drawing rooms, good food in the elegant dining room, a sunny conservatory, and an indoor swimming pool and exercise machines; disabled access.

BRADFORD-ON-AVON ST8361 **Woolley Grange** *Woolley Green, Bradford-on-Avon BA15 1TX (01225) 864705* **£105,** plus winter breaks; 23 rms, with fruit and home-made biscuits. Civilised Jacobean manor house with relaxed informal atmosphere, lovely flowers, log fires and antiques in comfortable and beautifully decorated day rooms, and a pretty conservatory; delicious food using local (or home-grown) produce, often organic, inc home-baked breads and muffins and home-made jams and marmalades for breakfast; marvellous staff, and very good for children – nursery with full-time nanny, games room, their own sort of food, and outdoor toys; swimming pool, tennis and croquet; limited disabled access.

CALNE ST9871 **Chilvester Hill House** *Chilvester Hill, Calne SN11 0LP (01249) 813981* **£70;** 3 charming spacious rms. Big Victorian house with neat gardens and grounds, particularly helpful friendly owners, comfortable sitting rooms with antiques, good breakfasts and honest no-choice dinners around a large table in the separate dining room (using home-grown produce); plenty of local sights; children over 12 (babies allowed).

CASTLE COMBE ST8477 **Manor House** *Castle Combe, Chippenham SN14 7HR (01249) 782206* **£171,** plus special breaks; 45 lovely rms, some in mews cottage. 26 acres of garden and parkland, inc an Italian garden, around 14th-c manor house with gracious day rooms, panelling, antiques, log fires and fresh flowers; a warm friendly atmosphere, and very good innovative food; 18-hole golf course, croquet, boules, and all-weather tennis court; disabled access.

CHICKSGROVE ST9729 **Compasses** *Lower Chicksgrove, Tisbury, Salisbury SP3 6NB (01722) 714318* **£45;** 2 rms with showers. Lovely thatched house in delightful hamlet with old bottles and jugs hanging from the beams, home-made food, well kept real ales, and peaceful farm courtyard and garden.

COLERNE ST8272 **Lucknam Park** *Colerne, Chippenham SN14 8AZ (01225) 742777* **£197,** plus special breaks; 41 luxurious rms. Noble Georgian house reached by a long beech-lined drive through extensive grounds, with elegant carefully furnished day rooms, a panelled library, lovely flowers, antiques and paintings; excellent food and extremely good service in charming restaurant; leisure spa with indoor swimming pool, gym, beauty salon, hairdresser, snooker and floodlit tennis courts; croquet; equestrian centre; children over 12 in evening restaurant.

CORSHAM ST8770 **Methuen Arms** *High St, Corsham SN13 0HB (01249) 714867* **£60,** plus special breaks; 25 rms. Georgian inn (former nunnery) with mullioned windows and heavy oak beams in 14th-c part, comfortable seats in neatly kept bar, good food and friendly staff; pretty walled garden and fine skittle alley.

CROCKERTON ST8642 **Springfield House** *Crockerton, Warminster BA12 8AU (01985) 213696* ***£52;** 3 rms with garden views. 17th-c house on the edge of Longleat Estate, with tennis in the garden, beams, flowers and open fires, dinner by the inglenook fireplace in candlelit dining room, and lots to do nearby; cl Christmas.

DEVIZES SU0061 **Bear** *Market Pl, Devizes SN10 1HS (01380) 722444* ***£80,** plus special breaks; 24 rms. Very much at the town's heart, this 16th-c inn has an old-fashioned feel, a wide choice of food from snacks to more elaborate meals served in the oak-panelled Lawrence room, 2 more formal restaurants, beams and fresh flowers, and prompt service; cl 25–26 Dec.

DOWNTON SU1821 **Warren** *15 High St, Downton, Salisbury SP5 3PG (01725) 510263* ***£48;** 5 rms with fresh flowers, 2 with own bthrm. Friendly 15th-c house with lots of beams and antique furnishings, a lounge with open fire, and enjoyable breakfasts in lovely oak-panelled room with French windows on to big walled garden; cl 20 Dec–6 Jan; children over 5.

EASTON GREY ST8987 **Whatley Manor** *Easton Grey, Malmesbury SN16 0RB (01666) 822888* **£126,** plus special breaks; 29 rms with antique furniture, 18 in main house, 11 in Court House across courtyard (which are cheaper). Lovely

Cotswold manor house in quiet gardens with riverside paddocks, tennis court, swimming pool, croquet lawn, putting green, billiards, sauna, solarium and Jacuzzi; spacious and rather fine oak-panelled drawing room, pine-panelled lounge, log fires, a relaxed atmosphere, lots of books in the library-bar, and an attractive dining room overlooking garden; partial disabled access.

EBBESBOURNE WAKE ST9924 **Horseshoe** *Ebbesbourne Wake, Salisbury SP5 5JG (01722) 780474* ***£45;** 2 rms. Particularly welcoming pub with beautifully kept little bar, open fire, fresh flowers and interesting bric-à-brac on beams; popular home-made food in the bar or no smoking restaurant, big breakfasts and nice Sunday lunches, well kept real ales; pretty little garden, and pets corner in paddock.

FORD ST8374 **White Hart** *Ford, Chippenham SN14 8RP (01249) 782213* **£75;** 11 rms. Very well run, popular and attractive ivy-covered inn in lovely spot by trout stream, with old-fashioned atmosphere, heavy black beams, big woodburner in ancient fireplace; particularly good imaginative food, well kept real ales, malt whiskies and fine wines, attentive cheerful service, and secluded small swimming pool; disabled access.

GASTARD ST8867 **Boyds Farm** *Gastard, Corsham SN13 9PT (01249) 713146* ***£40,** plus special breaks; 3 rms, 1 with own bthrm. Friendly and handsome 16th-c house on family-run working farm with pedigree Herefords; homely lounge, woodburner, traditional breakfasts; no evening meals (local pubs nearby).

GRITTLETON ST8679 **Church House** *Grittleton, Chippenham SN14 6AP (01249) 782562* ***£56.50,** plus winter breaks; 4 big comfortable rms. Large Georgian rectory on the edge of a lovely village, in 11 acres of gardens and pasture with a heated indoor swimming pool and croquet; a relaxed and friendly house-party atmosphere, open fire, antiques and paintings in the drawing room; very good imaginative food using organic home-grown vegetables and fruit (advance notice required), and breakfasts with their own eggs; children under 1 and over 12.

HEYTESBURY ST9242 **Angel** *High St, Heytesbury BA12 0ED (01985) 840330* ***£49;** 3 comfortable rms. Beautiful little 16th-c coaching inn with armchairs, sofas, and a good fire in cosy homely lounge, a long, beamed bar with woodburner, quite a few prints, good service from friendly staff, well kept real ales, decent wines, and a wide choice of consistently good food in charming back dining room opening on to secluded garden.

HINDON ST9132 **Lamb** *High St, Hindon, Salisbury SP3 6DP (01747) 820573* ***£70,** plus special breaks; 13 rms. Solidly built, welcoming and civilised old inn (once a smugglers' haunt) with log fires in the fine old bar, attractive lounges, imaginative food, friendly helpful service, and no smoking restaurant.

LACOCK ST9168 **At the Sign of the Angel** *Church St, Lacock, Chippenham SN15 2LB (01249) 730230* **£95,** plus special breaks; 10 charming rms. This fine 15th-c house in a lovely NT village is full of character, with heavy oak furniture, beams and big fireplaces, a restful oak-panelled lounge, and good English cooking in 2 candlelit restaurants; cl 1 wk Christmas; disabled access.

MALMESBURY ST9387 **Old Bell** *Abbey Row, Malmesbury SN16 0AG (01666) 822344* **£90,** plus special breaks; 31 rms. With some claim to being one of England's oldest hotels and standing in the shadow of the Norman abbey, this fine wisteria-clad building has traditionally furnished rooms with Edwardian pictures, an early 13th-c hooded stone fireplace, 2 good fires, cheerful helpful service, and attractively old-fashioned garden; very good for families – they have a children's den supervised by nursemaids, baby-sitting/listening service, and thoughtful food.

MILDENHALL SU2168 **Fisherman's House** *Mildenhall, Marlborough SN8 2LZ (01672) 515390* ***£50;** 3 lovely rms, 1 with own bthrm. Extremely pretty house with lawns running down to the River Kennet, fresh flowers and stylish furniture, friendly owners, and good breakfasts in airy conservatory; no children.

NETTLETON ST8377 **Fosse Farmhouse** *Nettleton Shrub, Nettleton, Chippenham SN14 7NJ (01249) 782286* ***£120,** plus special breaks (inc some interesting craft wknds); 6 rms. 18th-c Cotswold stone house extensively restored with decorative French antique furniture and pretty English chintzes; morning coffee, lunch and afternoon cream teas served on the lawns or in the very attractive dining room; antique shop with dried flowers and decorative items in former dairy behind the house.

PURTON SU0987 **Pear Tree** *Church End, Purton, Swindon SN5 9ED (01793) 772100* ***£95;** 18 very comfortable, pretty rms. Impeccably run former vicarage with elegant comfortable day rooms, fresh flowers, fine conservatory restaurant with good modern English cooking using home-grown herbs, and 7½ acres of grounds inc a traditional Victorian garden; cl 26–30 Dec; disabled access.

SALISBURY SU1430 **Farthings** *9 Swaynes Close, Salisbury SP1 3AE (01722) 330749* ***£42;** 4 rms, some with own bthrm. Spotlessly kept no smoking house with friendly owners, good breakfasts, and pretty garden; nr cathedral; no children.

SALISBURY SU1329 **Old Mill** *Town Path, Salisbury SP2 8EU (01722) 322364* ***£75,** plus special breaks; 10 comfortably converted rms. Based on a former mill and warehouse – there's been a mill here since 1135 – with terrace out by mill pool, and meadow walks with classic cathedral views; good honest English cooking in evening restaurant and beamed bar.

SALISBURY SU1429 **Red Lion** *Milford St, Salisbury SP1 2AN (01722) 323334* ***£117.50,** plus special breaks; 54 individually decorated rms. Handsome, family-run 700-year-old hotel with a mix of antique settles, leather chairs and modern banquettes in small 2-roomed panelled bar, spacious old-fashioned lounge with interesting furnishings inc clock with skeleton bellringers, and medieval restaurant; no pets; disabled access.

SALISBURY SU1428 **Rose & Crown** *Harnham Rd, Salisbury SP2 8JQ (01722) 399955* **£149,** plus special breaks; 28 rms in the original building or smart, modern extension. It's almost worth a visit just for the view – well-nigh identical to that in the most famous Constable painting of Salisbury cathedral; elegantly restored inn with friendly beamed and timbered bar, log fire, good bar and restaurant food, and charming Avonside garden; disabled access.

SALISBURY SU1431 **Stratford Lodge** *4 Park Lane, Salisbury SP1 3NP (01722) 325177* **£56,** plus special breaks; 8 rms. Warmly friendly and relaxed Victorian house with antique furnishings, fresh flowers, generous helpings of very good carefully prepared evening food, super breakfasts in conservatory, and quiet garden; cl Christmas; children over 5; limited disabled access.

SUTTON VENY ST9041 **Old House** *Sutton Veny, Warminster BA12 7AQ (01985) 840344* **£68;** 3 rms. Carefully modernised 17th-c thatched house in 4 quiet acres; winter log fires, nice food using home-grown vegetables, and good breakfasts; cl Christmas/New Year; children by arrangement.

TEFFONT EVIAS ST9931 **Howards House** *Teffont Evias, Salisbury SP3 5RJ (01722) 716392* **£115;** 9 rms. Very well run, welcoming and comfortable little hotel in 2 acres of gardens surrounded by quiet countryside; log fire and lots of fresh flowers from the garden in a restful sitting room, delicious food (using their own vegetables and herbs), fine breakfasts, particularly good wines, and extremely good service; cl Christmas.

UPPER MINETY SU0091 **Flisteridge Cottage** *Flisteridge Rd, Upper Minety, Malmesbury SN16 9PS (01666) 860343* ***£42;** 3 rms, 1 with own bthrm. Warmly welcoming and homely cottage with a pretty garden, and a woodburner in the sitting room; good breakfasts with home-made preserves (evening meals by arrangement), and friendly helpful owners; children over 11; well behaved pets by arrangement.

WARMINSTER ST8943 **Bishopstrow House** *Bishopstrow, Warminster BA12 9HH (01985) 212312* **£184,** plus special breaks; 31 sumptuous rms, some with Jacuzzi. Charming ivy-clad Georgian house in 27 acres with heated indoor and outdoor swimming pools, indoor and outdoor tennis courts, fitness centre and beauty treatment rooms, and own fishing on River Wylye; very relaxed friendly atmosphere, log fires, lovely fresh flowers, antiques and fine paintings in the boldly decorated day rooms, and really impressive food.

WARMINSTER ST8744 **Old Bell** *Market Pl, Warminster BA12 9AN (01985) 216611* **£58,** plus special breaks; 20 rms, most with own bthrm. Old-world country-town hotel with traditional bar food, bistro and restaurant, good choice of wines, pretty central courtyard, and friendly service; lots to do nearby.

WEST GRAFTON SU2459 **Rosegarth** *West Grafton, Marlborough SN8 3BY (01672) 810288* ***£40;** 2 rms. Charming 16th-c thatched and half-timbered cottage in 3-acre garden, with comfortable lounge, good breakfasts, and friendly owners; no children.

WINSLEY ST7960 **Burghope Manor** *Winsley, Bradford-on-Avon BA15 2LA (01225) 723557* **£65;** 6 rms. Lovely 13th-c manor house in attractive countryside, with carefully preserved old rooms and interesting fireplace engraved with Elizabethan writing; antiques in the big drawing room, welcoming caring owners, nice breakfasts, and evening meals by arrangement; wknd self-catering in Dower House in grounds; cl Christmas/New Year; children over 10.

WOOTTON BASSETT SU0783 **Marsh Farm Hotel** *Wootton Bassett, Swindon SN4 8ER (01793) 848044* **£70w;** 33 rms. Handsome Victorian farmhouse in landscaped grounds with particularly warm and friendly atmosphere, a comfortable lounge, convivial bar, and enjoyable food in the relaxed restaurant; disabled access.

To see and do

★ **SALISBURY** SU1429 A beautiful and gently relaxed city, with a good many fine old buildings, particularly around the lovely cathedral close. The most extensive in the country, it's always been a distinct area of town, its gates still locked each night. The buildings cover a variety of architectural styles from the 13th c to the present, and while of course its great glory is the elegant cathedral itself, you can't help being struck by how impeccably mown the lawns are. Outside are some interesting antique and other shops, and the broad Market Sq still has a traditional market each Tues and Sat; parking can be tricky then. The Haunch of Venison (Minster St) is a delightful old tavern, while the no smoking New Inn (New St), Red Lion Hotel (Milford St), Kings Arms (St John St) and Avon Brewery (Castle St) are all good for lunch, as is the waterside Old Mill out at West Harnham.

✝ **Salisbury Cathedral** Begun in 1220 and completed in only 38 years – giving a rare uniformity of style. The magnificent spire (added in 1334 along with the tower) is at 123 metres (404ft) the tallest in the country, and many would say the finest in the world; Christopher Wren discovered it was leaning, and managed to put it right. Also notable are the 14th-c clock (the oldest working mechanical clock in the world), and the tomb of the first Earl of Salisbury, who gave the church one of only 4 surviving copies of the Magna Carta; it's still on display (exc in Dec). The cloisters stand out too. Snacks, shop, disabled access; cl during services, and on Good Fri; (01722) 555120; £3 suggested donation. While the west front is being restored, you can don a hard hat and go up in the builder's hoist for a guided tour along the scaffolding, giving a once-in-a-lifetime view of the building's statuary. The knowledgeable guides are full of entertaining local lore. There's a good view of the cathedral from outside the 13th-c **Bishop's Palace**, though the one immortalised by Constable, and still much as then despite road-scheme threats, is from across the meadows by the River Avon over by West Harnham.

Mompesson House (Cathedral Close) Exquisite Queen Anne building, probably the most interesting in the close, with period furnishings, china and paintings, remarkable collection of 18th-c drinking glasses, and interestingly carved oak staircase. Teas, some disabled access; cl am, all day Thurs and Fri, and Nov–Mar; (01722) 335659; £3.40; NT. The NT shop is a couple of minutes' walk away on the High St.

Salisbury & South Wiltshire Museum (65 The Close) Local history and archaeology in lovely building, with excellent Stonehenge gallery, collections of Wedgwood, costume, lace and embroidery, and some beautiful local watercolours by Turner. Meals, snacks, shop, disabled access to ground floor; cl Sun exc pm July and Aug, Christmas; (01722) 332151; £3.

Cathedral Close – other attractions Also worth a look in the close are **St Anne's Gate**, **Malmesbury House** (open bank hols), the regimental museum, and **North Canonry Gardens**, a peaceful place for a stroll nr the river – open certain dates in summer, best to check with the very friendly tourist information centre, (01722) 334956. Nearby, **St Thomas's church** was built for the cathedral workers, so in part is slightly older than the cathedral itself; it's notable for the unusually expansive medieval painting of Doom.

Old Sarum (off the A345 2m N) This substantial and easily defended Iron Age hill fort continued as a town right through the Roman occupation and Dark Ages into Norman times. In the early 13th c there was a general move to the much more fertile site of the present city, and the fort gradually fell into decline, becoming a quarry for the new centre; so there's not much left, but the views are splendid, and the foundations give interesting clues to ancient architecture and styles. Snacks, shop; cl 24–26 Dec, 1 Jan; (01722) 335398; £2.

Other things to see and do

Wiltshire Family Attraction of the Year

! **Longleat** ST8043 (off the A362 4m W of Warminster) Few stately homes can boast as many things for families as this well organised estate, easily a full day's excursion, and great fun for all ages. One of the first lived-in grand houses to open its doors to the public, Longleat has since become firmly geared to visitors, but not so much that the attractive grounds have lost any of their appeal. Children will probably get most excited about the safari park, which as well as the famous lions has rhinos, camels, elephants and a rare white tiger; unusually, you can walk through some parts, the fine beech trees and parkland an appealing backdrop to giraffes, llamas and zebras. The safari park starred in a recent BBC fly-on-the-wall documentary series, *Lion Country*. A bus can take you round if you haven't got your own car (though you'll need to book a place on it fairly quickly), and a boat trip across the lake leads to the Monkey Jungle. Among what seem like hundreds of other attractions are displays of parrots, butterflies, and sea lions, a narrow-gauge railway, collection of doll's houses, and exhibitions based around the worlds of Postman Pat and Doctor Who. Perhaps the most dramatic recent addition is a balloon that gently rises 120 metres (400ft) above the grounds; not in bad weather, and not in the inclusive price given below – it's a very affordable £4.95 extra (£14.95 for a family of 2 adults and 2 children). A splendid big play area is themed around a mock castle, and there's a simulator ride and children's petting zoo. Older visitors may prefer the formal gardens laid out by Capability Brown, and of course the handsome 16th-c house itself, much restored inside, but still with impressively grand formal rooms, and the individual murals of the colourful current Marquis of Bath. He has had several mazes and labyrinths built around the grounds; one is still Britain's longest, another has a slightly saucy shape that can be appreciated only from the Marquis's private roof terrace, and the latest addition is a bewildering knot of mirrors, with animatronic effects adding to the confusion. There's a busy calendar of extra events and activities. Meals, snacks, shop, disabled access; most attractions, inc safari park, are cl Nov–mid-Mar, but the house is open all year (exc 25 Dec); (01985) 844400; you can get individual tickets to each of the attractions (the house on its own is £5, the safari park £5.50, and grounds only £2), but it works out much cheaper to buy the all-in Passport ticket for £12 (£10 for children).

ALTON BARNES SU1061 Here the Kennet & Avon Canal (see below) is close enough to **Pewsey Down nature reserve** for an afternoon's walk to incorporate both features; the spine of the downs here is followed by the Wansdyke, an ancient earthwork which runs across the downs for miles from Morgan's Hill nr Calne nearly as far as the Savernake Forest.

★ ! **ANSTY** ST9526 Pleasant village, notable for England's tallest maypole.

★ **AVEBURY** SU1070 The spectacular **stone circle** shares its setting with the pretty village – where Stones does good vegetarian food, and the Red Lion's position within the circle makes it special too. It's the largest stone circle in Europe, the 200 stones enclosed in a massive earthen rampart nearly a mile in circumference. One of Avebury's main draws has always been the free and open access to the stones, but the number of visitors is beginning to take its toll – it would be a tragedy if this ultimately proved the site's downfall. An interesting **museum** has an important collection of archaeological finds from the area. Shop, disabled access; cl 24–26 Dec, 1 Jan; (01672) 539250; £1.60; NT. **West Kennett Avenue** Leading away from the circle is this imposing 1½-mile avenue of stones – a good stretch has been restored. **West Kennett Long Barrow** (just SE) The prehistoric remains of a 5,000-year-old chambered tomb and barrow, where several dozen people were buried – take a torch if you want to venture in behind the massive entrance stone: the chamber with 2 side chapels runs some 9 metres (30ft) or more into the barrow. The Waggon & Horses at Beckhampton (of *Pickwick Papers* fame) is quite handy. **Windmill Hill** This neolithic enclosure is on a slight rise a mile or so N.

BARBURY CASTLE SU1476 One of Wiltshire's 4,500 recorded ancient sites. Many are scarcely a lump in the ground, but this Iron Age camp at the northernmost point of the Marlborough Downs, splendidly remote and atmospheric, still has formidable ramparts. There is a car park nearby, but you can also walk up to it from Ogbourne St George along Smeathe's Ridge, a preserved stretch of downland (gorse and all). The Castle is on the long-distance Ridgeway Path.

★ † **BISHOPS CANNINGS** SU0364 Attractive village, with an outstanding church.

BOWOOD ST9770 (off the A4 W of Calne) The extensive Capability Brown parkland and colourful pleasure gardens are the glory of Bowood, with their temples, cascades and hermit's cave shielded from the outside world by further miles of partly wooded grounds; in May and Jun a woodland garden is open for rhododendron walks. Much of the main building was demolished in 1955, but there's plenty left, inc the impressive library designed by Robert Adam. Excellent collection of English watercolours, and an outstanding adventure playground. Joseph Priestley discovered oxygen here in 1772. Meals, snacks, shop, garden centre, limited disabled access; cl Nov–Mar; (01249) 812102; £5.20. The Lansdowne Arms nearby at Derry Hill is popular for lunch, and Calne has a **motor museum**.

★ † **BOX** ST8268 An attractive up-and-down village, its interesting parts hidden down the steep valley below the A4, with cottages and houses using the same stone that's been quarried nearby since Roman times. They say that on 9 Apr, Brunel's birthday, the rising sun shines right through the great railway tunnel he quarried through the hill above here (you can see the restored grand entrance from the A4). **Hazelbury Manor** (off the B3109 just E) Richly varied landscaped gardens with a medieval archery alley, stone and yew circles, fountain, waterfall, pond, large rockery, formal areas and laburnum walk, all laid out as a sort of giant maze. Open by appointment, (01225) 812952; £2.80. In Chapel Plaister on the way, look out for the 15th-c **chapel** for Glastonbury pilgrims on the little hilltop green. The Quarryman's Arms tucked away on Box Hill is good for lunch.

★ † **BRADFORD-ON-AVON** ST8260 Attractive hillside town given a distinguished air by the same sort of golden stone as was used in Bath; it's very steep, and has some handsome buildings reflecting its past wealth as a wool town – and quite a few serious antique shops. Near the Norman parish church is a tall narrow late **Saxon church**, unusual for having virtually no later additions. The Bunch of Grapes (on picturesque Silver St) is good for lunch. A medieval **tithe barn** can be seen at nearby Barton Farm down by the river and canal, its massive stone-slab roof supported by an impressive network of great beams and rafters. **Avoncliff** A short walk W along the canal, this quite steep gorge is shared by canal, river and railway, the canal disdainfully stepping over the river by way of an aqueduct. The Cross Guns has remarkable views over it, and is a good place for lunch. **Westwood Manor** (above Avoncliff) Fully furnished 15th-c stone manor house with its original Gothic and Jacobean windows, fine 17th-c plasterwork, and modern topiary garden. Open pm Sun, Tues and Weds Apr–Sept; (01225) 863374; £3.50; NT. The New Inn in Westwood village has decent food, and the **church** has some interesting late medieval stained glass. **Iford Manor** (just past Westwood) Notable for its stylish Edwardian Italianate riverside terraced garden, well liked by readers, with romantic cloisters, colonnade and statues; house not open. Teas wknds and bank hols, May–Aug; open pm Sun and bank hols Apr–Oct, and pm daily (exc Mon and Fri) May–Sept; (01225) 863146; £2.50.

BROKERSWOOD ST8352 **Woodland Heritage Centre & Woodland Park** 80 acres of woodland, with lakes, campsites, conservation displays, summer guided walks, adventure playground, and a little railway. Snacks, shop; park open daily; (01373) 823800; £2.50. The Woolpack at Beckington has good food.

BROMHAM ST9464 **Sandridge Farm** (towards Melksham) They cure bacon and Wiltshire ham using traditional recipes; also summer nature trail through woodland and pig paddocks (wellies recommended). Shop (good bacon and sausages), disabled access; cl Sun; (01380) 850304; free. The Greyhound has good food, especially fish.

★ † **CASTLE COMBE** ST8477 For many the prettiest village in Britain, this has a classic group of stone-tiled Cotswoldy cottages by the turreted **church** at the bottom of a tree-clad hill running down to a trout stream and its ancient stone bridge. Preservation is taken so seriously that you won't even see television aerials on the houses. In past years several villagers have opened their beautifully kept gardens for charity the last wknd of Jun. Best of all during the week out of season; at other times it does get a great many visitors, even though the car park is sited some way up the hill. The Castle Inn (snacks all day, hot meals usual times) is a charming old place. The surrounding country is equally appealing, with attractive paths along deep peaceful valleys.

★ **CASTLE EATON** SU1495 Attractive village, by a quiet stretch of the upper Thames, pleasant for strolling.

CHERHILL DOWN SU0469 Large NT area of ancient downland, with free access for walkers. A range of man-made features of various periods adorn its slopes, inc a figure of a white horse, an Iron Age hill fort (Oldbury Castle), the mid-19th-c Lansdowne Monument, and an assortment of long barrows, tumuli and ancient field systems; the site is rich in chalkland flora such as orchids, and associated butterfly and bird life.

★ **CHICKSGROVE** ST9729 Charming tucked-away hamlet, peaceful walk to Sutton Mandeville church, and back by Nadder Valley.

★ † **CHILMARK** ST9732 Attractive village, with a decent partly 13th-c **church**.

☺ **CHOLDERTON RARE BREEDS FARM** SU2042 (Amesbury Rd, just off the A338) Plenty of friendly animals at this entertaining farm park, especially rabbits: nearly 60 breeds in spacious pens, and younger rabbits for children to stroke. Other animals to pet include pygmy goats and sheep, and you'll probably meet Ebenezer the goat, Hannah the shire horse and Coco the donkey. They have pig racing wknds and school hols (12.30pm and 3.30pm), tractor or

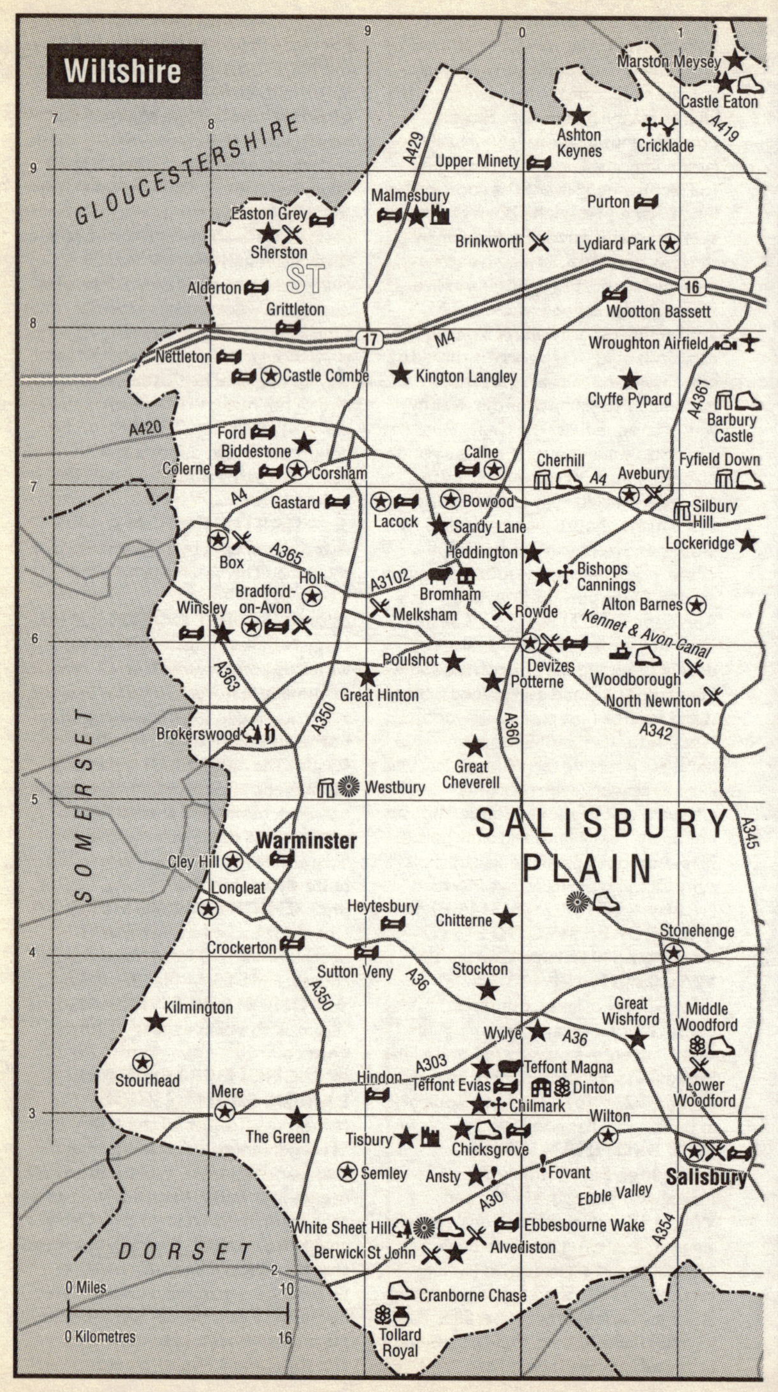

Wiltshire
GLOUCESTERSHIRE
SOMERSET
DORSET
SALISBURY PLAIN
Marston Meysey
Castle Eaton
Ashton Keynes
Cricklade
Upper Minety
Malmesbury
Purton
Brinkworth
Lydiard Park
Easton Grey
Sherston
Alderton
Grittleton
Wootton Bassett
Wroughton Airfield
Nettleton
Castle Combe
Kington Langley
Clyffe Pypard
Barbury Castle
Ford
Biddestone
Colerne
Corsham
Calne
Cherhill
Avebury
Fyfield Down
Gastard
Lacock
Bowood
Sandy Lane
Silbury Hill
Lockeridge
Box
Holt
Heddington
Bishops Cannings
Bromham
Bradford-on-Avon
Winsley
Melksham
Rowde
Alton Barnes
Kennet & Avon Canal
Devizes
Poulshot
Potterne
Woodborough
Great Hinton
North Newnton
Brokerswood
Great Cheverell
Westbury
Warminster
Cley Hill
Longleat
Heytesbury
Chitterne
Stonehenge
Crockerton
Sutton Veny
Stockton
Kilmington
Great Wishford
Middle Woodford
Wylye
Stourhead
Teffont Magna
Hindon
Teffont Evias
Dinton
Lower Woodford
Mere
Chilmark
Wilton
The Green
Tisbury
Chicksgrove
Salisbury
Semley
Ansty
Fovant
Ebble Valley
White Sheet Hill
Ebbesbourne Wake
Berwick St John
Alvediston
Cranborne Chase
Tollard Royal
A429
A419
A4361
A420
A4
A365
A3102
A363
A350
A360
A342
A345
A36
A303
A30
A354
M4
16
17
ST
0 Miles 10
0 Kilometres 16

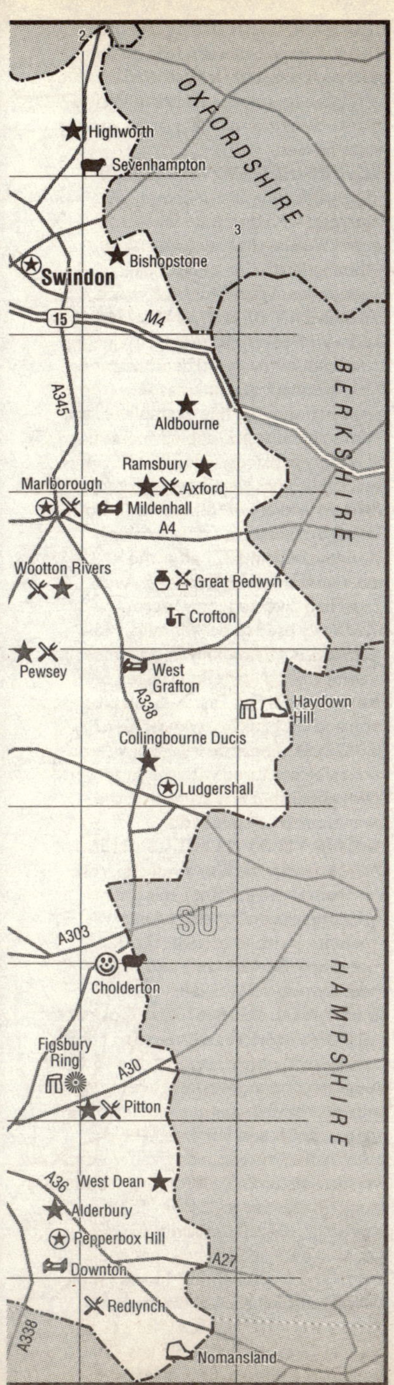

trailer rides, pony rides for children and good adventure playgrounds. The attractive grounds have tranquil carp-filled watergardens, and nature trails through orchards and woodland. Meals and snacks (good cream teas), shop, disabled access; cl Nov–Mar; (01980) 629438; *£3.90. The thatched Crown is useful for lunch.

CLEY HILL ST8344 This steep-sided hill just W of Warminster involves a short, puffy stroll to the Iron Age hill fort at its summit, looking across Longleat Park.

CORSHAM COURT ST8770 Fine house and park begun in 1582, later added to and developed by those busy masters Capability Brown, John Nash, Robert Adam and Humphrey Repton. The paintings are among the best at any stately home, inc works by Caravaggio, Reynolds, Rubens and Van Dyck. In the gardens, the peaceful lake and a Georgian bath-house are patrolled by a number of peacocks – if they haven't decided to wander off into the village. Shop, disabled access; cl am, Mon (exc bank hols), wkdys Nov–Easter and all Dec; (01249) 701610; £4.50. Nearby are some attractive former weavers' cottages; the **church**, on the edge of the park, is largely 12th c, partly Saxon. The town has a surprising number of antique shops, some very fine, and the Methuen Arms is good for lunch.

CRANBORNE CHASE ST9319 Some of Wiltshire's finest walking is to be found here close to the Dorset border, where the county's abundant chalk downland shows at its best. A good example is **Ashcombe Bottom** N of Tollard Royal, a deep remote valley which plunges into the heart of the Chase.

CRICKLADE SU1093 Small town quietly separated from the busy A419, with some attractive buildings and a glorious tower crowning the fine parish **church**. At the end of the High St, just N of the Thames, a path on the left off the slip road heading back towards the A419 leads to a broad **riverside meadow** kept unimproved for decades, and mown only in July after the numerous wild flowers have seeded.

CROFTON BEAM ENGINES SU2662 Still pumping water into the Kennet & Avon Canal, the oldest working beam engines in the world, an 1812 Boulton & Watt, and an 1845 Harveys of Hayle. Snacks, shop; open Easter–Oct, engines usually static, but in steam bank hols and last wknds of Jun and July; (01672) 870300; static £1.50, steam wknds £3.

DEVIZES SU0061 Lots of grand old buildings in this interesting and friendly town, and a good town trail takes most of them in. The 29 locks of the **Kennet & Avon Cànal** coming up Caen Hill from the W form one of the longest flights of locks in the country. The Canal Trust HQ on the Wharf has a museum and information centre; (01380) 729489; £1. **Devizes Museum** (Long St) First-class local history, particularly good on finds from the area's ancient sites (the Bronze Age gallery is especially interesting); art gallery with John Piper window. Shop, some disabled access; cl Sun, bank hols, Christmas; (01380) 727369; *£2 (free on Mons). **Broadleas** (Potterne Rd) Rare plants in secluded dell among rhododendrons and other fine flowering shrubs, unusual trees, spring and autumn colour too. Teas Sun, unusual plant sales; open pm Sun, Weds and Thurs, Apr–Oct; (01380) 722035; *£3. The Bear Hotel, Elm Tree and Castle, all tied to Wadworths the local brewery, are all good for lunch.

DINTON SU0031 **Philipps House & Dinton Park** Fine early 19th-c mansion, until recently HQ of the YWCA, now restored and opened by the National Trust, with interesting Portland stone staircase and underfloor heating system. The surrounding parkland has plenty of scope for a stroll. Some disabled access; house open am Sat and pm Mon Apr–Oct; park open all year; (01985) 843600; house £2, park free.

EBBLE VALLEY SU0024 The valley of the Ebble chalk stream winds prettily through a sleepy string of villages from Odstock SU1526 to Alvediston ST9723 – a delightful drive.

FIGSBURY RING SU1833 Iron Age hill fort with good views over Salisbury.

! **FOVANT** SU0128 **Regimental Badges** Huge chalk carvings on the escarpment (visible from the road), cut by regiments stationed here in World War I – a sight to rival England's various white horses.

FYFIELD DOWN SU1470 Primeval-feeling and unkempt, scattered with outcrops known as sarsen stones, the raw material of Avebury stone circle and of part of Stonehenge; a good spot for walks.

GREAT BEDWYN SU2764 **Bedwyn Stone Museum** Fascinating little open-air museum demonstrating the ancient art of stonemasonry (the nearby church has fine examples of the finished product). Disabled access but a bit bumpy in places; (01672) 870234; free. The Cross Keys has decent food. **Wilton windmill** (off the A338 E of Burbage) Wiltshire's only working windmill, built in 1821 after the construction of the Kennet & Avon Canal had diverted the water previously used to power mills. Now restored, it's beautifully floodlit most evenings. Shop (sells flour milled on site); open pm Sun Easter–Sept, plus Mon and Sat bank hol wknds; (01672) 870427; £1. The little village of Wilton (not to be confused with the larger town nr Salisbury) is attractive; the Swan does enjoyable food.

HAYDOWN HILL SU3156 Reached from the E by a walk up from Vernham Dean in Hants, this has hill fort ramparts bounded by steep gradients on its south side; the 3 counties of Berks, Hants and Wilts meet close by at SU3559.

HOLT ST8661 **The Courts** (on the B3107) Weavers used to come here to settle their disputes; the 15th-c house isn't open, but there are lovely and extensive formal gardens full of yew hedges, pools and borders, with the other half of the grounds given over to wild flowers among interesting trees. Some disabled access; cl am, Sat, and Nov–Mar; (01225) 782340; £3; NT. The Old Bear at Staverton has good food. **Great Chalfield Manor** (N of Holt) Beautiful moated manor house, restored in 1920 and still with its original Great Hall. Open Tues–Thurs Apr–Oct, guided tours only, at

12.15pm, 2.15pm, 3pm, 3.45pm and 4.30pm; (01249) 730141 to book; £3.50; NT. Next door is a small 13th-c **church**.

KENNET & AVON CANAL Recently restored, this runs right across the county, with pleasant boat trips from several places; Devizes SU0061 or Wootton Rivers SU1962 for example, or the notably friendly hire companies at Hilperton ST8559 and Bradford-on-Avon ST8260. In the canal's restoration, a great deal of attention has been paid to the natural environment, so it's attractive for walks alongside; in winter you may even see a kingfisher flashing along it. For a more sedentary view, try the Barge at Seend Cleeve ST9361, Barge at Honeystreet SU1061 or Bridge Inn at Horton SU0563; the Golden Swan at Wilcot SU1461, Crown at Bishops Cannings SU0363 and Hop Pole at Limpley Stoke ST7861 are also useful.

★ ✝ **LACOCK** ST9168 A favourite village of both visitors and film-makers, its grid of quiet and narrow streets a delightful harmony of mellow brickwork, lichened stone and timber-and-plaster. The **church** is 15th-c, and nothing looks more recent than 18th-c. It's remained so remarkably unspoilt because most of its buildings were owned for centuries by the Talbot family, until they left them to the NT in 1944. It gets very busy in summer, but the Trust has preserved it against a surfeit of antique shops (you'll find all you want in the nearby old market town of Melksham). The village does on the other hand have a splendid collection of pubs – the George is the best. **Lacock Abbey** Tranquil spread of mellow stone buildings, around a central timber-gabled courtyard, based on the little-altered 13th-c abbey. Tudor additions include a romantic octagonal tower, and there was a successful 18th-c Gothicisation. Surrounded by quiet meadows and trees, this was the setting for Fox Talbot's experiments which in 1835 led to the creation of the world's first photographic negative – a picture of part of the abbey itself. There's a museum devoted to this in a 16th-c barn at the gates, and the gardens are evidence of Fox Talbot's skills in other fields. Limited disabled access; open daily Apr–Oct (plus grounds only in Mar), abbey cl am and all day Tues; (01249) 730227; £5.50, museum, grounds and cloisters only £3.50; NT. The photography museum may also open some winter wknds. **Lackham Country Attractions** Plenty of family activities, inc farm museum, walled garden and glasshouses, rare breeds farm, pleasant woodland and riverside walks, and a children's playground. The 500-acre estate is the home of the Lackham College of Agriculture, and the old roses are worth catching from May–July. Snacks, shop, plant sales, disabled access; open wknds and bank hols Easter–Oct; (01249) 466800; £3.

☺ **LONGLEAT** ST8043 *See separate Family Panel on p.683* for the estate. The Bath Arms at Horningsham at the south entrance to the park, and the White Hart at Corsley on the north side, are good for lunch. One of England's 3 **Center Parcs** is nearby, a rewarding place to stay with excellent leisure facilities; (0990) 200300.

✝ **LUDGERSHALL** SU2651 The ruins of a royal **castle** and hunting palace, still with some of the original hefty Norman earthworks, as well as the later flint walling; free. The **church** is also Norman. The nearby area is very pretty and unspoilt, with pleasant walks in remote countryside, and the little villages of the Chutes, Tangley and Vernham Dean straddling the Hants border all worth a look (the pubs over that way are worth exploring too).

✝ **LYDIARD PARK** SU1084 (nr M4 junction 16, or the A3102) Painstakingly restored grand Georgian house, with interesting early wallpaper, rare painted glass window, and elegant furnishings much as they would have been when first installed. Extensive lawns, lakes and well wooded parkland, with nature walks and adventure playgrounds. Snacks, shop, disabled access; cl 1–2pm (exc school hols), am Sun, 25–26 Dec, Good Fri; (01793) 770401; car parking £1, house 80p – quite a bargain. The adjacent parish **church** has interesting monuments to the St John family, who lived in the house for 500 years.

★ **MALMESBURY** ST9387 Yet another charming old town, especially around the green facing its serene Norman **abbey**, from the tower of which a medieval monk called Elmer made one of the earliest semi-successful attempts at flight – he covered a couple of hundred yards, but did break both legs when he crash-landed. The picturesque Old Bell is almost as old as the abbey beside it. The B roads radiating from here are all quite pleasant drives.

★ **MARLBOROUGH** SU1868 One of the area's most attractive towns, this has a very pleasing wide High St, scene of the annual autumn Mop Fair (now a funfair) which used to be held in most market towns for the hiring of servants (see *calendar, below*) – there's also a regular market each Weds and Sat. Even the more modern additions don't look obtrusively out of place among the harmonious mix of Georgian and Tudor buildings. The Sun (by St Peter's church where Cardinal Wolsey was inducted as a priest) and Bear are useful for lunch. The Broad Hinton road N gives a good feel of the downs' great open spaces, as does the Manton–Alton Priors road to the SW, passing one of the area's several white horses cut into the chalk, and leading into a pleasant valley drive through Allington and Horton to Devizes. To the E, the quiet road along the Kennet Valley has some attractive views, with good food stops at the Red Lion in Axford and Bell in Ramsbury, and pleasant walks; there are also walks through the surviving miles of **Savernake Forest** woodland.

★ **MERE** ST8132 Attractive village, dominated by its 30-metre (100-ft) church tower, with good views from Castle Hill. **White Sheet Hill** easily reached via a road bridge over the busy A303 (or from Stourton) is lofty chalk downland studded with antiquities inc a Neolithic causewayed camp and Bronze Age barrows. It's a good site for cowslips, orchids and such butterflies as adonis and chalkhill blues.

MIDDLE WOODFORD SU1236 **Heale Gardens** 8 acres of lovely formal gardens beside the Avon chalk stream, with lots of varied plants; the watergarden is especially nice in spring and autumn. Specialist plant sales with many rare types propagated from the main gardens, shop, disabled access; cl Christmas; (01722) 782504; £2.75. The Wheatsheaf in nearby Lower Woodford is popular for lunch, there are lots of walks nearby, and this Salisbury road along the Avon's quieter bank is a pretty drive (as is the continuation N of Amesbury, through Fittleworth and East Chisenbury).

NOMANSLAND SU2517 The Lamb on the edge of the New Forest is a base for pleasant walks in countryside that's unusual for Wiltshire.

PEPPERBOX HILL SU2125 (5m SE of Salisbury) Named after the strangely shaped 17th-c tower on its summit. You can't get into the tower, but the site commands fine views over Salisbury itself, and S as far as Southampton. **Bentley Wood** Beyond East Grimstead N of here, a nature reserve with good walks. The Hook & Glove at Farley has decent food.

SALISBURY PLAIN ST9648 Better for driving over than walking – an almost unbroken expanse of rolling high ground, a mixture of pasture and broad unhedged arable fields intersected by tank-training tracks. The A360 gives a good feel of its emptiness. However, the county council has a leaflet mapping out clearly some 30 miles of way-marked walks around the edges of the army's Imber firing range: generally peaceful countryside with large-scale arable farming, but some wide views and maybe the sight of tank and infantry training.

★ **SANDY LANE** ST9668 Attractive village; the road from here through Bowden Hill is the prettiest approach to Lacock, and the George is good for lunch.

★ † **SEMLEY** ST8926 Another attractive village, with an interesting church, open greens, and hilly walking country around it.

SEVENHAMPTON SU2188 **Roves Farm** The 8-week spring lambing season is the time to come to this friendly sheep farm; trailer rides and shearing in summer. Snacks, shop, disabled access; open Weds–Sun Mar–Sept; (01793) 763939; £3.75. The

Saracen's Head in Highworth has good-value food.

SILBURY HILL SU1068 This towering prehistoric mound, purpose unknown, is the largest man-made mound in Europe – it would have taken a thousand men about 10 years to build. Don't follow the example of the people you'll see clambering all over it – that's how monuments like this are gradually worn away. It's anyway more impressive from down at normal ground level.

STONEHENGE SU1142 (off the A344) One of the most famous prehistoric monuments in the world; everyone knows what it looks like, and how they got the stones here has been pretty much sorted out (the larger ones local, the smaller ones all the way from Wales), but no one's really sure exactly what Stonehenge with its careful astronomical alignments was for. Some experts now reckon it could even have been built by the French. In the interests of conservation, you can't go right up to the stones, but you can get pretty close and the fact that people are kept back means that your photographs won't be cluttered by the crowds. The best views are very early in the morning from the track from Larkhill, on the other side of the A344, or on a cold clear winter evening looking W past the monument towards the sunset; the ancient stones look very impressive silhouetted against the sky. Even in the crowded light of day the place never quite loses its power to inspire awe, although the car park area would definitely benefit from some investment. The busy main roads nearby detract too, but at last it looks as if diversion plans will now go ahead, probably involving a tunnel. Snacks, shop, disabled access; cl 24–26 Dec; (01980) 624715; £3.90 (inc very good Walkman tour); NT. On a handful of dates through the year you can still wander among the stones by joining one of the coach tours of mysterious sites organised by Astral Travels, (01628) 488413; these cost around £60 for a whole day and currently leave only from London, but it's worth it just for the moment when they set you loose in Stonehenge with dowsing rods. Good walks from here around associated ancient monuments (leaflet available in the car park). **Woodhenge** SU1442 The scant traces of another prehistoric monument which consisted of 6 rings of timber posts in a ditch; the positions are now marked by concrete posts, and a cairn marks the central spot where the tomb of a little girl ceremoniously axed to death was found. There's good pick-your-own fruit late Jun–late July at Rolleston Manor Farm on the B3086 NW of Stonehenge.

STOURHEAD ST7835 (Stourton, off the B3092) Marvellous 18th-c gardens, gradually laid out in Italian style by the banker Henry Hoare II following his return from an Italian tour; a beautifully harmonious landscape of temples, lakes, bridges and splendid trees and other plants. Remarkable views into Somerset from Alfred's Tower, the very tall 18th-c folly at the far end, though there are 221 steps (cl Mon and Fri, and winter). The early Georgian Palladian house has some good Chippendale furniture, and the church in the grounds is in a lovely hillside setting. Meals, snacks, shop, disabled access; garden open all year, house pm daily exc Thurs and Fri, Apr–Oct; (01747) 840348; £7.90 for gardens and house, £4.40 for one or the other (less for gardens Nov–Feb) – if you can do only one, make it the gardens; NT. The Red Lion at Kilmington, and Spread Eagle at Stourhead's entrance, are useful for lunch.

SWINDON SU1484 Much older than you might think, this bustling market town and business centre was caught up with a vengeance in the railway age, and in the Railway Village had one of the earliest examples of a planned workers' estate. In the heart of this, the **Great Western Railway Museum** (Faringdon Rd) is excellent, with lots of locomotives and related train memorabilia celebrating this most highly regarded railway. Shop, limited disabled access; cl 1–2pm, am Sun, 24–26 Dec, Good Fri; (01793) 466555; £2.40. Next door, the **Railway Village House & Museum** (34 Faringdon Rd) is a restored foreman's house furnished in typical turn-of-the-century working-class style; it's included in admission to the main museum, or you can just visit here for 85p. Not far from here, the Savoy (Regent St) has affordable food. **Swindon Museum & Art Gallery** (Bath Rd) Includes works by important 20th-c artists such as Moore and Sutherland. Shop, limited disabled access; cl am Sun, bank hols; (01793) 466556; free. **Swindon & Cricklade Railway** (Blunsdon, off the B4553 N of Swindon) One of the only live steam projects in the area, gradually being restored, with occasional trips through the countryside, and a museum. Snacks, shop, disabled access; cl wkdys; (01793) 771615 for train times; £3.

TEFFONT MAGNA ST9832 **Farmer Giles Farmstead** Friendly working dairy farm with 150 cows milked every afternoon; children can feed lambs and other animals, or simply sit and stroke them. Also tractor rides, play areas, old farming equipment, small vineyard. Meals, snacks, shop, disabled access; cl wkdys Nov–Mar; (01722) 716338; *£3.95. The village is very attractive, with charming stone-built cottages and neatly banked stone-walled gardens; the Black Horse has good food.

★ **TISBURY** ST9429 Charming small town, left behind by the main roads so largely unspoilt, with some fine old buildings, riverside church, and just outside to the E an immensely long medieval tithe barn. The lovely old Crown does decent food. **Old Wardour Castle** (a couple of miles S) Remains of a substantial 14th-c lakeside castle. Though badly damaged in the Civil War, its walls still stand to their original 18 metres (60ft), and you can walk almost to the top. It's a lovely peaceful setting, landscaped in the 18th c (and used for Kevin Costner's *Robin Hood* in the 20th). Disabled access to grounds only; cl 1–2pm, winter Mon and Tues, 25–26 Dec, 1 Jan; (01747) 870487; £1.70.

TOLLARD ROYAL ST9517 **Larmer Tree Pleasure Grounds** (off the A354) Attractive Victorian pleasure gardens in the heart of Cranborne Chase. Laid out by General Pitt Rivers, they were the first privately owned gardens open to the public but then closed for almost a century, opening again very recently. Pheasants, peacocks and even macaws wander merrily about, you can play croquet, and the temples and grottoes are an appealing backdrop to the band concerts they have most Suns; also adventure playground and small museum. Teas, disabled access; open Sun–Thurs Easter–Oct; (01725) 516228; £3.

WESTBURY ST8951 To the E you can see the huge Westbury **white horse** cut into the chalk of the downs; late 18th-c, it was an 'improvement' on an altogether older one which may have been Saxon, and which faced in the opposite direction. Above the white horse is an extensive Iron Age hill fort, with good views right down to the Mendips in Somerset.

WHITE SHEET HILL ST9424 The Harepath here is a high track giving sweeping views; you can branch off into a forest plantation. Confusingly, Wiltshire has a second hill with the same name, above Mere.

Days Out

Prehistoric enigmas: Avebury stone circle and stone avenue; Silbury Hill (view from below); West Kennett Long Barrow; lunch at Stones or the Red Lion, Avebury; walk up on to Fyfield Down to see sarsen stones.

Grandeur and charm: Bowood House; drive via Sandy Lane to Lacock; lunch at At the Sign of the Angel there, or in one of the pubs; look round Lacock.

Eye-catchers beneath the downs: A30 SW from Wilton past Regimental Badges nr Fovant; Ansty's maypole; Old Wardour Castle; lunch at the Beckford Arms, Fonthill Gifford, drive through Fonthill park; Wilton House.

WILTON SU0931
Wilton House One of the most satisfying historic houses we know, well organised and friendly, with lots to see. The original house was damaged by a fire in 1647, and superbly redesigned by John Webb and Inigo Jones, the latter responsible for the magnificent double cube room. There's an outstanding art collection inc works by Rubens, Van Dyck and Brueghel, as well as fine furnishings, Tudor kitchen, Victorian laundry, and the Wareham Bears, a collection of 200 dressed teddies. Outside are 21 acres of landscaped parkland, with water and rose gardens, cloister garden, woodland walk, and huge adventure playground. Meals, snacks, shop, disabled access; cl Nov–Easter; (01722) 743115; £6.75. The ornately Italianate 19th-c **church** incorporates all sorts of more ancient treasures, especially its magnificent medieval Continental stained glass and 2,000-year-old marble pillars. Wiltons (Market Pl) is good for lunch, the Pembroke Arms has a good Sun carvery, and the charming Victoria & Albert in nearby Netherhampton is nicely off the tourist track, with a pleasant riverside walk into Salisbury. **Wilton Royal carpet factory** (King St) Surprisingly interesting demonstrations of how they make Wilton weaves and Axminster carpets. Tours 4 times a day between 10.15am and 3.30pm, best to book on (01772) 742733; disabled access; cl 2 wks at Christmas; £4. There's a new **shopping village** next door.

WROUGHTON AIRFIELD SU1379 A branch of London's **Science Museum** houses national collections of aircraft, rockets, hovercraft, and road transport vehicles. Not really aimed at entertaining the general public, it's usually open around 5 times a year, with lively special events or air displays; (01793) 814466 for 1999 dates.

★ **WYLYE** SU0037 Charming village in delightful valley; one lane is called Teapot St.

★ **Other attractive villages**, all with decent pubs, include Aldbourne SU2675, Alderbury SU1827, waterside Ashton Keynes SU0494, Axford SU2370, Berwick St John ST9323 (steep walks nearby), Biddestone ST8773, Bishopstone SU2483, Chitterne ST9843, Collingbourne Ducis SU2453, Clyffe Pypard SU0777, Great Cheverell ST9754, Great Hinton ST9059, Great Wishford SU0735, Heddington ST9966, Highworth SU2092, Kilmington ST7736, Kington Langley ST9277, Lockeridge SU1467 (good walks), Marston Meysey SU1297, Pewsey SU1560, Pitton SU2131 (wood and downland walks), Potterne ST9958, Poulshot ST9559, Ramsbury SU2771, Sherston ST8585, Stockton ST9738, The Green ST8731 (nr East Knoyle), West Dean SU2527, Winsley ST7961 and Wootton Rivers SU1963.

Where to eat

ALVEDISTON ST9723 **Crown** *(01772) 780335* Lovely old thatched inn with 3 charming low-beamed panelled rooms, 2 inglenook fireplaces, lots of bric-à-brac, very good imaginative bar food, well kept ales, and attractive garden; bdrms. **£21.20**|£7.

AVEBURY SU1070 **Stones Restaurant** *(01672) 539514* Excellent vegetarian restaurant in converted farm building opposite the stone circle; local, organic and home-grown produce used in the delicious cooking (lovely cakes and soups), afternoon tea, and friendly service; they sell country wines and organic wines; open all day (not evenings; and during Nov–Mar open only Fri–Sun); cl Jan; disabled access. **£13**|£4.

AXFORD SU2370 **Red Lion** *(01672) 520271* Welcoming brick and flint pub with fine views over valley from sheltered garden or bustling beamed and pine-panelled bar, good popular food in bar and no smoking restaurant (enjoyable daily specials and fresh fish and game), decent wines, and well kept real ales; bdrms and self-catering; cl 25 Dec; disabled access. **£23**|£4.95.

BERWICK ST JOHN ST9422 **Talbot** *(01747) 828222* Well run and friendly village pub with simply furnished heavily beamed bar, huge inglenook fireplace and decent food in bar and restaurant; cl pm Sun; children over 7 in evening. **£20.75**|£6.

BOX ST8369 **Quarryman's Arms** *Box Hill (01225) 743569* Tucked-away unspoilt hillside pub with fine views, 2 small interesting knocked-together rooms with quarrying memorabilia, wide choice of good home-cooked food, well kept real ales, and very friendly staff; bdrms. **£20.50**|£5.50.

BRADFORD-ON-AVON ST8260 **Bridge Tea Rooms** *24a Bridge St (01225) 865537* Old-fashioned no smoking 17th-c tearooms with a large choice of teas, lots of coffees, sandwiches and snacks, lovely home-made cakes and pastries, cream teas; waitresses in mob caps and aprons; cl 25–26 Dec. £4.95.

BRINKWORTH SU0184 **Three Crowns** *The Street (01666) 510366* Friendly atmosphere in villagey pub with imaginative food from a changing menu that covers an entire wall, many wines by the glass, well kept real ales, elegant no smoking conservatory, and garden looking out towards church and rolling country; get there early as they don't take bookings and it is very busy; disabled access. **£25**|£6.

DEVIZES SU0061 **Wiltshire Kitchen** *11 St John's St (01380) 724840* Bustling little no smoking self-service coffee house (open all day) just off the market square, serving breakfast, lunch, and afternoon tea inc good-value OAP 2-course lunches; quite a few coffees, lots of sandwiches, and home-made scones and cakes; evening cellar restaurant, too – cl pm Sun; disabled access. **£20**|£5.

LOWER WOODFORD SU1235 **Wheatsheaf** *(01722) 782203* Friendly pub with indoor goldfish pond (crossed by a miniature footbridge), wide choice of popular food, partly no smoking dining room, well kept real ales, helpful staff, and big walled garden; good disabled access. **£15**|£3.95.

MARLBOROUGH SU1969 **Munchies** *8 The Parade (01672) 512649* Lovely beamed building with marvellous range of really interesting and delicious sandwiches with daily-changing home-made fillings using the freshest ingredients; cl Sun; disabled access. £1.75.

MARLBOROUGH SU1868 **Polly Tearooms** *26–27 High St (01672) 512146* In centre of pretty High St, well known for very good cream teas, with home-made bread, scones, jams and cakes; also light lunches and cooked breakfasts; cl evenings, and 25–26 Dec; disabled access. Teas £4.45.

MELKSHAM ST9164 **Toxique** *187 Woodrow Rd (01225) 702129* Former farmhouse with unusual artwork in colourfully and eccentrically decorated rooms, comfortable armchairs in purple lounge, excellent really adventurous meals, thoughtfully planned and prepared, and a helpfully annotated wine list; good atmosphere, popular themed evenings – and booking essential; cl Mon, Tues, am Weds–Sat, pm Sun; bdrms. **£38**.

NORTH NEWNTON SU1357 **Woodbridge** *on the A345 (01980) 630266* Bustling pub with large garden by the River Avon (boules, play area and space for a few tents/caravans), cheerfully decorated bars, a huge choice of dishes from all over the world inc quite a few Mexican dishes and super puddings, afternoon teas and Sun lunch, real ales, 2 dozen enjoyable wines by the glass, and friendly service from enthusiastic licensees. **£20.20**|£7.95.

PEWSEY SU1660 **London House** *Market Pl (01672) 564775* Elegant, popular restaurant with a relaxed bar, open fire in cosy sitting room, particularly good, interesting, well prepared food, a thoughtful wine list, and professional service; cl Sun, am Mon, 25–29 Dec; children over 7; disabled access. **£35**.

PITTON SU2131 **Silver Plough** *(01722) 712266* Stylish village inn with lots to look at in beamed and comfortable front bar, good bar snacks and more elaborate meals with emphasis on fresh fish and seafood, well kept real ales, country wines, and efficient service; disabled access. **£26**|£5.95.

REDLYNCH SU2120 **Langley Wood** *(01794) 390348* Very good innovative food and decent wines in homely creeper-covered restaurant-with-rooms set in its own grounds; cl Mon, Tues, am Sat, pm Sun; children must behave (small helpings but no special menu); disabled access. **£27.50**|£12.

ROWDE ST9762 **George & Dragon** *(01380) 723053* Interesting old pub with log fire and plenty of dark wood, a simple dining room, exceptional imaginative food (especially Cornish fish and lovely puddings), good-value set lunches, a relaxed atmosphere, friendly efficient service, and well kept real ales; cl Sun, Mon, 25 Dec, 1 Jan. **£19 set lunch**|£5.

SALISBURY SU1429 **New Inn** *(01722) 327679* Very attractive pub, no smoking throughout, with ancient heavy beams, timbered walls, an inglenook fire, panelled dining room, an unpretentious relaxed atmosphere, good range of well presented home-made food with nice daily specials and good hearty puddings, well kept beer, decent wines, friendly helpful licensees and staff, and a pleasant walled garden looking up to the nearby cathedral. **£19.35**|£6.95.

SHERSTON ST8586 **Rattlebone** *Church St (01666) 840871* 16th-c pub with low beams, country furnishings, big dried-flower arrangements, pleasant relaxed atmosphere in several rambling rooms, wide choice of good interesting food, partly no smoking restaurant, decent wines, well kept real ales, lots of malt whiskies, 20 rums, and pretty little garden; cl am 25 Dec; partial disabled access. **£20**|£5.

WOODBOROUGH SU1159 **Seven Stars** *Bottlesford (01672) 851325* Civilised pub in 7 acres of riverside gardens, with attractively moulded panelling in the main bar, a hot coal fire in a range at one end and a big log fire at the other, a pleasant mix of seats and tables, cosy nooks, retired wine bottles on Delft shelves, attractive back dining area, exceptionally good, daily changing Anglo/French cooking (inc marvellous veg), an exemplary wine list with a dozen by the glass, and very friendly owners. **£20**|£6.50.

WOOTTON RIVERS SU1962 **Royal Oak** *(01672) 810322* Prettily thatched 16th-c pub with relaxed atmosphere, L-shaped dining lounge with woodburning stove, comfortably furnished timbered bar, very popular food from a huge menu, well kept beer, decent wines and some interesting whiskies, and friendly service; bdrms with help-yourself breakfasts. **£21**|£7.

Special thanks to Paul Kennedy, Mr and Mrs Lawson, Phyl and Jack Street, M and J Back, B M Eldridge.

We welcome reports from readers

This *Guide* depends on readers' reports. Do help us if you can – in return, we offer a discount on the next edition to people who've helped us with reports for it. Tell us what you think about places already in it, and anything extra you think we should say about them. And send us your ideas for inclusion in the next edition: places to visit, eat at or stay in, attractive drives or walks, maybe even unusual interesting shops you know of. Use the card in the middle, the report forms at the end, or just write – no stamp needed: *The Good Guide to Britain*, FREEPOST TN1569, Wadhurst, E Sussex TN5 7BR.

Wiltshire Calendar

Some of these dates were provisional as we went to press. Please check information with the telephone numbers provided.

APRIL

2 **Devizes** Start of Westminster International Canoe Race (01491) 872042
4 **Wilton** Easter Children's Quiz at Wilton House – *till Mon 5* (01722) 746720
24 **Salisbury** St George's Spring Festival: traditional medieval events and pageantry – *till Sun 25* (01722) 434300
25 **Westbury** Transport Extravaganza at Fitzroy Farm (01373) 827158

MAY

1 **Downton** Cuckoo Fair (01722) 510646
3 **Amesbury** Sarsen Trail Walk and Marathon starting at Avebury *(from 7pm)*, crossing Salisbury Plain (normally closed to the public), ends at Stonehenge (01380) 725670
15 **Marlborough** Savernake Forest Horse Trials – *till Sun 16* (01483) 424637
22 **Salisbury** Festival – *till 5 Jun* (01722) 323888
23 **Rockley** Marlborough Cup (3-mile timber horse race) and Country Fair at Barbury Castle Racecourse (01672) 514428
28 **Chippenham** Folk Festival – *till Mon 31* (01249) 706333
29 **Corsham** Festival: concerts, open gardens – *wknds till 3 July* (01249) 712241

JUNE

4 **Warminster** Horse Trials at Longleat House – *till Sun 6* (01985) 844400
11 **Wilton** Wessex Craft & Flower Show at Wilton House – *till Sun 13* (01722) 743115
19 **Bradford-on-Avon** Peto Garden Centenary Events inc concerts at Iford Manor – *till July* (01225) 866233; **Chippenham** Carnival – *till* procession on *Sat 26* (01249) 706333; **Warminster** Fire Sculpture and Concert at Longleat House (01985) 844400
21 **Stonehenge** Druid Summer Solstice Ceremony *from midnight on Tues 20*, vigil *till dawn* when service celebrates first rays of sun on altar, Presider crowned *at noon* (01458) 850924

JULY

3 **Amesbury** Carnival (01980) 622173; **Heddington** Steam Rally at Home Farm: rural crafts and shire horses – *till Sun 4* (01380) 850885; **Warminster** Proms Concert at Longleat House (01985) 844400; **Wilton** Horse Trials at Wilton House – *till Sun 4* (01722) 743115
10 **Swindon** Old Town Festival – *till Sun 11* (01793) 641033
12 **Marlborough** Festival of Music & Arts inc jazz weekend – *till Sun 25* (01672) 892388
16 **Marlborough** International Jazz Festival – *till Sun 18* (01672) 512656
17 **Wilton** Fireworks Concert at Wilton House (01722) 743115
18 **Teffont Magna** Morris Dancing at the Farmer Giles Farmstead (01722) 716338

Wiltshire Calendar (cont.)

22 **Stourton** Fête Champêtre at Stourhead – *till Sat 24* (01985) 843600; **Trowbridge** West Wilts Show at Civic Hall and Town Park – *till Sat 24* (01225) 770387
23 **Warminster** Balloon Festival and Night Glow at Longleat House – *till Sun 25* (01985) 844400
24 **Salisbury** Country & Garden Show at Hudsons Field – *till Sun 25* (01722) 434238

AUGUST

7 **Wilton** Have a go at Archery at Wilton House – *till Sun 8* (01722) 743115
14 **Warminster** Popular Music Concert at Longleat House (01985) 844400
22 **Teffont Magna** Sheep to Jumper at the Farmer Giles Farmstead (01722) 716338; **Wilton** Teddy Bears' Picnic at Wilton House (01722) 743115
22 **Edington** Music Festival – *till Sun 29* (01373) 827158
30 **Corsley** Show (01373) 832643

SEPTEMBER

5 **Bradford-on-Avon** Wharf Show and Boat Parade (01225) 864378
10 **Warminster** Dog Agility Show at Longleat House – *till Sun 12* (01985) 844400
11 **Teffont Magna** Country Craft Festival at the Farmer Giles Farmstead – *till Sun 12* (01722) 716338; **Westbury** Medieval Fayre (01373) 827158
12 **Marlborough** Carnival inc massed hot air balloons (01672) 515573
18 **Pewsey** Illuminated Carnival Procession (01672) 563378

OCTOBER

1 **Calne** Music & Arts Festival – *till Sun 10* (01249) 815417
9 **Marlborough** Mop Fair: fun fair (01672) 513989 – *also Sat 16*
30 **Warminster** Carnival (01985) 218548

NOVEMBER

6 **Warminster** Craft Fair at Longleat House – *till Sun 7* (01985) 844400

DECEMBER

2 **Salisbury** Christmas Lights Switch On (01722) 434238

Yorkshire

Yorkshire is one of Britain's friendliest areas, very good value for holidays. Many superb new places have opened recently here, and great imagination (and in some cases pots of money) is going into updating existing attractions.

We have divided this vastly rewarding county into the Dales, with which we have included Ripon, the civilised spa town of Harrogate, and their surroundings (virtually all North Yorkshire west of the A19); the Moors and East Yorkshire (North Yorkshire east of the A19 along with the administrative county of East Yorkshire); and the administrative counties of West and South Yorkshire. We start with a section on the city of York – an excellent holiday city.

Each area has a rich variety of interesting places to visit – most of all in West Yorkshire, which has an outstanding range of unusual visitor attractions, especially for families. Many are free. The countryside of the Dales and the Moors is memorable for walkers, and very appealing even to people who never leave their cars. The east coast has plenty to keep children amused.

York

Masses to see and do in delightful, virtually traffic-free surroundings.

York's whole centre, ringed by strollable 13th-c city walls, is virtually traffic-free – the biggest such area in any similarly-sized European city. It has lovely medieval buildings and twisting alleys, tempting shops and lots of lively cafés, pubs and bars. An extraordinary variety of things to interest all ages includes the magnificent Minster (one of Britain's great sights), the outstanding Castle Museum and National Railway Museum, and the Jorvik Centre, Britain's first modern heritage centre and still one of the best. Though it's undeniably a tourist city, with summer queues and crowds at the main attractions, all the other visitors actually seem to add to the atmosphere, rather than detracting from it

The York for Less scheme gets two people discounts on some attractions and restaurants for four days; £3.50, from tourist information centres. Another way to save money – at least in winter – is to come by train; ask for the First Stop York vouchers when you book your ticket, or on arrival at York Station, and you'll usually get half-price entry to most of the city's attractions (and big discounts at some hotels).

York's good racecourse has monthly meetings; the Ebor Festival in August is the biggest event in the northern racing calendar.

You can do the circuit of the 13th-c city walls and their many towers in a couple of hours or so, mostly on top. One of the best stretches, with fine views of the Minster, is between the Monk Bar and Bootham Bar. If you plan on doing the whole circuit it's well worth using one of the Walkman guides rented by the helpful tourist office (Exhibition Sq).

Where to stay

SHIPTON BY BENINGBROUGH SE5458 **Sidings** *Shipton by Beningbrough, York YO6 1BS (01904) 470221* **£97.50,** plus special breaks; 8 rms with showers in 2 converted coaches. A railway enthusiast's paradise, based on restored former railway carriages, with good food served at Pullman-style tables, and a decent wine list; railway viewing platform, models, videos, paintings and artefacts; disabled access.

YORK SE5952 **Arnot House** *17 Grosvenor Terrace, York YO3 7AG (01904) 641966* **£50,** plus winter breaks; 4 rms with brass beds. Friendly, no smoking, Victorian terraced house with lots of original features, antiques and paintings; good breakfasts in the neat dining room (evening meals on request), and a pleasant, relaxed atmosphere; children over 10.

YORK SE5849 **Curzon Lodge** *23 Tadcaster Rd, Dringhouses, York YO2 2QG (01904) 703157* **£65,** plus winter breaks; 10 rms, some in former old coach house and stables. Charming, early 17th-c house in a marvellous spot just S of the city, overlooking Knavesmire racecourse; with an attractive, comfortable drawing room, sunny farmhouse dining room (good breakfasts), and a secluded walled garden; cl Christmas.

YORK SE6050 **Dairy Guesthouse** *3 Scarcroft Rd YO23 1ND (01904) 639367* ***£45;** 5 attractive rms (with thoughtful extras), some with own bthrm. Carefully restored, no smoking, Victorian house with lots of original features and attention to detail; enjoyable breakfasts with vegetarian choices, a warmly hospitable atmosphere, and a flower-filled courtyard; cl mid-Dec–31 Jan.

YORK SE6052 **Dean Court** *Duncombe Pl, York YO1 2EF (01904) 625082* **£115 inc dinner,** plus special breaks; 40 rms. Next to the Minster, this comfortable and neatly kept hotel has fresh flowers and plants in the airy rooms, very helpful, efficient staff, and enjoyable food in the elegant restaurant; good for families, with thoughtful extras; children over 5 in evening restaurant.

YORK SE5952 **Grange** *Clifton, York YO3 6AA (01904) 644744* **£115,** plus special breaks; 30 individually decorated rms with antiques and chintz. Close to the Minster, this Regency townhouse has elegant public rooms, an open fire, newspapers, good breakfasts, excellent restaurant food (there's also a brasserie), and warm, friendly staff; car park; disabled access.

YORK SE6052 **Hazlewood** *24–25 Portland St, Gillygate, York YO3 7EH (01904) 626548* ***£54,** plus winter breaks; 14 recently refurbished rms. Just 4 mins from the Minster, this no smoking, neatly kept Victorian house has quite a few original features; a cosy lounge, an attractive dining room, helpful owners, and a pretty little garden; off-street parking; children over 7.

YORK SE5951 **Holmwood House** *114 Holgate Rd, York YO2 4BB (01904) 626183* **£65,** plus special breaks; 14 pretty rms. Built as 2 19th-c houses, this no smoking hotel is 5 mins from the city walls; with books in the comfortable sitting room, and very good breakfasts; children over 8.

YORK SE5948 **Middlethorpe Hall** *Bishopthorpe Rd, Middlethorpe, York YO23 2GB (01904) 641241* **£161,** plus special breaks; 30 elegant rms, most in the converted stables. Lovely, immaculately restored William III country house just S of the city, with fine gardens and parkland; antiques, paintings and fresh flowers in the comfortable quiet day rooms, and excellent food and service; children over 8.

YORK SE6052 **Palm Court** *17 Huntington Rd, York YO3 7RB (01904) 639387* ***£42;** 8 rms. Quiet and spotlessly kept Victorian house 5 mins from the Minster; with a pleasant sitting room, very good breakfasts, particularly helpful and friendly owners, and evening meals on request; cl Christmas.

YORK SE5951 **4 South Parade** *York YO2 2BA (01904) 628229* **£83,** plus special breaks; 3 lovely rms with Edwardian-style furnishings, original fireplaces and fresh flowers. Beautifully decorated house in a small, elegant, Georgian terrace on a private cobbled street, 15 mins from the Minster and 5 from the station; pretty drawing room, very helpful owners, good breakfasts and candlelit suppers by arrangement in the delightful dining room; no smoking; cl Christmas; no children.

To see and do

York Minster Glorious Gothic architecture, in soft-coloured York stone: Britain's largest medieval building, begun in 1220 and taking a staggering 250 years to build. The richly detailed interior has more medieval glass than any other church in England, housing half of all that's known in the country. Look out for the great east window which shows Genesis and Revelations in 27 panels, the splendid 5 sisters window in the north transept (chapter 6 of Dickens's *Nicholas Nickleby* tells the story), and the beautiful ceilings of the central tower and chapter house. The choir screen has 15 niches with statues of the kings of England from William the Conqueror to Henry VI. There's a display on the church's turbulent history in the Foundations Museum and Treasury. Shop, disabled access; cl am Sun, and occasionally for major services; £1.80 for museum and treasury, also small charges for chapter house and crypt. You can climb the tower for good views of the city (£2). Largely traffic-free, the Close outside is fairly quiet, but not enclosed, and without the tranquil serenity of say Exeter, Salisbury or Winchester. Evening walking tours start from various points around it.

St William's College (College St, opposite the Minster) 15th c, with an exhibition, 3 finely timbered rooms – and a good restaurant. Shop; cl 25–26 Dec, Good Fri, and if they have conferences, so best to phone and check; (01904) 637134; 60p. Another useful nearby food stop is Peels in High Petergate.

Besides the Minster, the city has quite a few other handsome medieval **churches**, though many are no longer used for services. Most were built during the prosperous 15th and 16th centuries, and among the finest are Holy Trinity (Goodramgate, which also contains in Our Lady's Row the city's oldest houses) and St Helen's (St Helen's Sq). All Saints (North St) has fascinating windows showing the world's last 15 days. The spire of 15th-c St Mary's is York's tallest; the church has lively exhibitions on the city's history in the **York Story** (cl 25–26 Dec, 1 Jan; (01904) 628632; £1.90).

Treasurer's House (Chapter House St, next to the Minster) There's been a house here since Roman times – this one dates from the 17th c, and the basement has an exhibition on its history. The timbered hall and period furniture are very fine, and there is a newly restored period kitchen. Good snacks; cl Fri, all Nov–Mar; (01904) 624247; £3.50; NT.

Jorvik Viking Centre (below Coppergate Shopping Centre) Time-cars whisk you through an exact reconstruction of the Viking street, market and quayside that used to stand here, with quite astonishing detail – sounds and smells too; some of the faces were painstakingly reconstructed following actual Viking skulls. At the end are excavated finds from the site. Queues can be horrifically long, but almost everyone finds the wait well worth while (you can book tickets 7 days in advance (01904) 543403). Shop, disabled access; cl 25 Dec; (01904) 653000; £4.99.

ARC (St Saviourgate) Refreshingly accessible archaeology centre; helped by hands-on interactive displays, you can decipher Viking-age writing or learn to make a Roman shoe, with professional archaeologists to give advice. In summer you may be able to watch a dig on Walmgate. Very much on the school-trips circuit, so best out of term-time. It's in a beautifully restored medieval church, with an interesting, old-fashioned garden. Shop, mostly disabled access; cl am Sat, Sun, Good Fri, last 2 wks in Dec; (01904) 654324; £3.60.

Barley Hall (Swinegate) The Archaeological Trust that runs the ARC (and the Jorvik Centre) has almost finished its restoration of this medieval family home. Shop, disabled access to ground floor only; cl Oct–Mar; (01904) 643211; *£3.50. The nearby Punch Bowl has good-value food.

Castle Museum (Tower St) In 18th-c prison buildings on the site of the former castle (part of the outer wall still stands), this is one of Britain's best social history museums, with a huge range of everyday objects from the past 4 centuries shown in convincingly reconstructed real-life settings, from Edwardian streets to prison cells and period living rooms. There's even a watermill, by the river outside. They have one of only 3 Anglo-Saxon helmets in the world, found here in York in the 1980s. Again, best out of term-time. Shop, disabled access ground floor only; cl 25–26 Dec, 1 Jan; (01904) 613161; £4.75.

Clifford's Tower (Tower St) This former castle keep nearby is perhaps York's most interesting building after the Minster. You can walk round the top of the walls, which enclose a garden, and there are good views of the city. It's named for Roger Clifford, who was hanged from the tower in chains. There's an unusual Lowry painting of the tower in the City Art Gallery (*see entry, right*). Shop; cl 24–26 Dec; (01904) 646940; £1.70. The Tudor Masons Arms is a handy stop.

Fairfax House (Castlegate) Magnificently restored mid-8th-c townhouse, probably one of England's finest, its richly decorated rooms fully furnished in period style, with impressive paintings, pottery, clocks and Georgian furniture (much donated by the great-grandson of the confectionery baron Joseph Terry); there's a re-created 18th-c meal. Shop, some disabled access by arrangement (steps at front); cl all Fri (exc Aug and Sept), and Twelfth Night–mid-Feb; (01904) 655543; *£4.

The Shambles Jettied medieval buildings lean towards each other across these alleys, with witty details such as the red printer's devil almost opposite the courtyard entry to the Olde Starre (a touristy pub, but genuinely old, with a view of the Minster from seats in its yard). This area has good bookshops, all sorts of unusual specialist shops, and, especially in Stonegate, nearer the Minster, and in elegant Micklegate, some serious silver and antique shops.

Monk Bar The most striking and best preserved of York's 4 turreted medieval gateways. It now houses the **Richard III Museum**, where displays on the much-maligned monarch (or evil hunchbacked murderer, depending on your point of view) are themed as if he were on trial – put your verdict in the appropriate Guilty or Innocent book on the way out. Shop; cl 25–26 Dec; (01904) 634191; £1.

Micklegate Another of York's medieval gateways, housing social history displays. Cl 25–26 Dec, 1 Jan, mid-Jan–mid-Feb and maybe other times in winter; (01904) 634436; £1.50.

York Brewery (Toft Green) Tours and tastings (not am Sun; £3.50 – inc a pint of their beer). Just along the road from here, the **bar convent** has a museum looking at early Christianity (and decent accommodation).

York City Art Gallery (Exhibition Sq) Well displayed collections running from old masters to the lusciously romantic nudes of William Etty, with some very handsome stoneware pottery. Shop, disabled access; cl am Sun, 25–26 Dec, 1 Jan, Good Fri, maybe other dates for civic events; (01904) 551861; free.

Merchant Adventurers' Hall (Piccadilly) The city's largest timber-framed building – one of the finest in Europe. Built for the powerful Merchant Adventurers' Company in the 1350s and hung with banners of medieval guilds, it has a chapel and undercroft as well as the Great Hall itself. Disabled access; cl Sun Nov–Mar, and Christmas wk; (01904) 654818; *£1.90.

York Guildhall (St Helen's Sq) Exact replica of the original building of 1446, destroyed in a 1940 air raid, using the stone walls of the earlier building as the framework. Disabled access; cl winter wknds (and am Sun in summer), and bank hols; (01904) 613161; free.

Yorkshire Museum (Museum Gardens) A real treasure-trove, crammed with myriad archaeological finds and riches from Roman, Anglo-Saxon, Viking and medieval times, inc the fabulous medieval Middleham Jewel. All set out very sensibly, with the displays effectively put into context. There will be an exhibition on myths and monsters in 1999. Shop, disabled access; cl 25–26 Dec, and am Sun Nov–Mar; (01904) 629745; £3.60, less for York residents.

Outside are 10 acres of botanical gardens by the wall: peaceful and attractive, around a shapely group of ruins inc the Benedictine St Mary's abbey and the Multangular Tower (medieval, on a Roman base), as well as a working observatory.

! **York Dungeon** (Clifford St) Carefully researched exploration of superstition, torture and various forms of death, full of grue and gore. There's an extensive Guy Fawkes Experience and a new exhibition on the Plague. Shop, some disabled access; cl 25 Dec; (01904) 632599; £4.95.

National Railway Museum (not valid for Thomas the Tank Engine events) (Leeman Rd) The great railway age is celebrated here with lots of panache and flair, and the background sounds of steam-era station noises. The centrepiece is the great hall in which 2 sets of tracks and platforms radiate from central turntables, one with a changing display of two dozen great locomotives from the museum's huge collection, the other with all sorts of carriages and waggons, from the humblest and most utilitarian to Queen Victoria's sumptuous royal coach; you can go inside most of them. A mass of material vividly illustrates the history of rail and how it changed the world. Timetabled working demonstrations and rides – one place where the trains are always on time. Meals, snacks, shop, disabled access; cl 24–26 Dec; (01904) 621261; £4.95. The nearby Maltings (Wellington Row) has generous food.

York Model Railway (York Station) Painstakingly re-created miniature town and country landscape, running as many as 20 trains at a time; a second much smaller model shows a typical German town at night. Shop, disabled access; cl 25–26 Dec; (01904) 630169; £2.80.

Murton Park SE6552 (just E) Busy 8-acre park, excellent for children and best known for its **Museum of Farming**, with exhibitions of agricultural equipment, some animals and a Land Army display (museum cl 25 Dec; £2.80). Also here the **Derwent Valley Light Railway** has trips along what was once known as the Blackberry Line, and a reconstructed Dark Age settlement (aimed mostly at children). Meals, snacks, shop, disabled access; open Suns and bank hols Mar–Oct; (01904) 489966; £2.80.

Where to eat

YORK SE6051 **Bettys** *6 St Helen's Sq (01904) 659142* Famous tearooms opened in 1937 with fine teas and coffees (they import their own), good sandwiches, salads and hot specialities, delicious scones, tea breads, and pâtisserie; home-made milk shakes, Alsace wines from family vineyards, and an evening pianist; cl 25–26 Dec. £6.50.

YORK SE6052 **19 Grape Lane** *(01904) 636366* Close to the Minster and under new owners, this neat timbered restaurant serves a good mix of imaginative and traditional dishes (lovely nursery puddings) in a warm and friendly atmosphere; cl pm Sun and Mon. **£25**|£7.50.

YORK SE6050 **Meltons** *7 Scarcroft Rd (01904) 634341* Smart little restaurant with paintings for sale, a cheerful mural and a collection of cookery books; very good, imaginative modern cooking using tip-top ingredients (plenty of vegetarian choice), lovely puddings, fair-value wines, and a relaxed, friendly atmosphere; cl pm Sun, am Mon, 3 wks Christmas–Jan, 1 wk end Aug. **£25.50**|£6.

YORK SE6052 **St William's College Restaurant** *College St (01904) 634830* Lovely 15th-c buildings with an enclosed courtyard for outside summer eating, next to York Minster; enjoyable, varied food, and evening jazz and candlelight; cl Good Fri, 25–26 Dec. **£16.75**|£5.50.

YORK SE6052 **Treasurer's House** *Minster Yard (01904) 624247* Lovely National Trust property, once home to the medieval treasures of York Minster, with a tearoom in the converted cellars; traditional and herbal teas, decent coffee, fruit wines, home-baked cakes and scones, savoury dishes and good puddings, all served by friendly staff; no smoking; cl Fri, cl Nov–Mar. **£19.50**|£4.50.

The Yorkshire Dales, Harrogate and Ripon

Glorious countryside, and really interesting places to visit.

This area is among the finest places in Britain for adults who enjoy at least a bit of fresh air. The Dales' steep stone-walled pastures, majestic moors, wind-carved limestone crags and rushing streams give drivers and particularly walkers a succession of mouth-watering, quickly varying views. Wharfedale (the most visited) and Wensleydale are the most varied, with a string of appealing villages and small towns. Malhamdale, much smaller, has some of Yorkshire's most striking landscape features – a magnet for day visitors. Nidderdale has fewer paths than the other dales, but has the advantage of being rather off the tourist track. Ribblesdale above Settle, and the upper reaches of Swaledale in the north, climb into austere and largely unspoilt scenery with challenging walks.

Skipton Castle and Bolton Abbey are very rewarding indeed, and an enjoyable mix of other places in the Dales includes Jervaulx abbey ruins, the mechanical music museum at Rufforth, Thorpe Perrow garden near Bedale, the cheese creamery in Hawes, lively brewery visits in Masham, the Ingleton show cave, and castle remains at Richmond and Middleham. There are many charming villages; the larger ones and small towns generally have craft shops and the like, and sometimes interesting bookshops. The train trip over the Pennines from Settle to Carlisle is a wonderful ride on a clear day.

Over to the east, Fountains Abbey is a great favourite. Ripley Castle, Newby Hall and Beningborough Hall are also memorable, with grand gardens. The most interesting gardens are those at Harlow Carr just outside Harrogate. The theme park at North Stainley is a fun day out for children.

Harrogate is a civilised, former spa resort with some of Yorkshire's smartest shops – a very comfortable base for touring, in easy reach of both Dales and Moors. Ripon, also strategically placed for touring, is attractive and largely unspoilt, with one of Britain's largest cathedrals; Richmond is appealing, too.

Where to stay

ALDBOROUGH SE4066 **Ship** *Aldborough, Boroughbridge, York YO5 9ER (01423) 322749* **£45;** 5 rms, showers. Friendly and neatly kept 14th-c pub nr an ancient church and Roman town; with a coal fire in the stone inglenook fireplace and old-fashioned seats in the heavily beamed bar, ample food, good breakfasts, well kept real ales, and seats on a spacious lawn.

ARNCLIFFE SD9371 **Falcon** *Arncliffe, Skipton BD23 5QE (01756) 770205* ***£50;** 5 rms, some with own bthrm. Friendly, delightfully basic Georgian inn ideal for walkers; with functional little rooms and a fire, homely front lounge, an airy conservatory, no smoking dining room, and generous, plain lunchtime snacks; no accommodation Nov–Easter; self-catering cottage.

ASKRIGG SD9491 **Kings Arms** *Market Pl, Askrigg, Leyburn DL8 3HQ (01969) 650258* **£79,** plus special breaks; 11 rms. Smart Georgian manor house with a homely, friendly atmosphere in several bars – one used in TV's *All Creatures Great and Small*; attractive furnishings, low beams and oak panelling, open fires, imaginative restaurant dishes, excellent bar food, and very good wines; children over 9 in restaurant.

BAINBRIDGE SD9390 **Rose & Crown** *Bainbridge, Leyburn DL8 3EE (01969) 650225* **£50,** plus special breaks; 12 comfortable rms. 15th-c coaching inn overlooking a lovely green; with antique settles and other old furniture in the beamed and panelled front bar, open log fires, a cosy residents' lounge, big wine list, and home-made, traditional food in both the bar and restaurant; pets welcome by prior arrangement.

BOLTON ABBEY SE0753 **Devonshire Arms** *Bolton Abbey, Skipton BD23 6AJ (01756) 710441* **£155,** plus special breaks; 41 individually furnished rms with thoughtful extras. Close to the priory itself and in lovely countryside, this civilised former coaching inn owned by the Duke of Devonshire has been carefully furnished with fine antiques and paintings from Chatsworth; log fires, impeccable service, beautifully presented, imaginative food in the elegant restaurant, and super breakfasts; health centre; children over 12 in restaurant; disabled access.

BRAFFERTON SE4370 **Brafferton Hall** *Brafferton, York YO6 2NZ (01423) 360352* ***£70;** 4 spacious rms. In a quiet village by the Swale, an 18th-c, no smoking, private house with comfortable lounges, welcoming hosts, enjoyable breakfasts, and good evening meals (if ordered in advance) eaten around a candlelit communal table; disabled access.

BUCKDEN SD9477 **Buck** *Buckden, Skipton BD23 5JA (01756) 760228* ***£72,** plus special breaks; 14 comfortable rms. Busy pub surrounded by moorland views (lots of walkers); with a snug original area and a bustling, extended, open-plan bar, popular food served by smartly uniformed staff in the attractive no smoking dining room, decent wines, and well kept real ales; disabled access.

BURNSALL SE0361 **Red Lion** *Burnsall, Skipton BD23 6BU (01756) 720204* ***£89,** plus special winter breaks; 11 rms. Pretty, 16th-c, family-run ferryman's inn overlooking the river and village green with its tall maypole; an attractively panelled bar with beams and log fires, good food in both the bar and no smoking restaurant, and a decent wine list; also, big gardens and a riverside terrace; 75 yards of private fishing, permits for a further 7 miles; disabled access.

CARPERBY SE0089 **Old Stables** *Carperby, Leyburn DL8 4DA (01969) 663590* ***£45,** plus special breaks; 3 rms, showers. Carefully converted stables in unspoilt moorland country, with warmly welcoming and helpful owners; pleasantly furnished and neatly kept lounge and dining room (glass door to a terrace with fine views), log fire in the inglenook fireplace, and marvellous breakfasts with home-made marmalade; no smoking; cl Dec–Feb (possibly Nov, too); no children or pets.

CHAPEL LE DALE SD7477 **Old Hill** *Chapel le Dale, Carnforth, LA6 3AR (01524) 241256* **£35;** 5 warm, basic but well furnished rms, also 2 bunk rooms with 8 beds in each; shared bthrms. On the Three Peaks walk, this inn is popular with potholers too, and has stripped stone walls, flagstones, old woodwork, a roaring log fire in the cosy back parlour, and popular food inc big breakfasts; live music Fri/Sat nights; camping.

CRAY SD9479 **White Lion** *Cray, Skipton BD23 5JB (01756) 760262* **£50,** plus special breaks; 8 comfortable rms in adjoining barn. Welcoming little pub, spectacularly isolated at 335 metres (1,100ft) up, with super views and lots of nearby walks; traditional feel with flagstones, beams and log fires, good bar food, and decent wines.

DANBY WISKE SE3398 **White Swan** *Danby Wiske, Northallerton DL7 0NQ (01609) 770122* ***£35;** 3 comfortable rms, shared bthrm. Cosy little pub in the middle of nowhere, handy for walkers on the Coast-to-Coast footpath; with very friendly licensees, and a decent choice of good-value food, inc free-range eggs from their chickens.

FEIZOR SD7967 **Scar Close Farm** *Feizor, Austwick, Lancaster LA2 8DF (01729) 823496* ***£45,** plus special breaks; 4 clean, well appointed rms. Friendly converted barn on a working farm, with large guests' lounge, books, magazines and TV, and big breakfasts and homely evening meals – packed lunches, too; lovely, quiet countryside; cl 25–26 Dec; disabled access.

GRASSINGTON SE0064 **Black Horse** *Garrs Lane, Grassington, BD23 5AT (01756) 752770* **£60,** plus special breaks; 15 rms. On the edge of the cobbled square, this is a bustling place with open fires and beams in the comfortable bar, friendly service, and enjoyable food in the attractive little restaurant; sheltered terrace.

HARROGATE SE2955 **Alexa House** *26 Ripon Rd, Harrogate HG1 2JJ (01423) 501988* ***£58,** plus special breaks; 13 rms, some in a former stable block. Attractive Georgian house with friendly staff, a comfortable lounge, good home cooking in the no smoking dining room, and marvellous breakfasts; can use local health club; good disabled access.

HARROGATE SE3055 **Balmoral** *16-18 Franklin Mount, Harrogate HG1 5EJ (01423) 508208* ***£90,** plus special breaks; 20 lovely rms, many with four-posters. In quiet gardens but nr the centre, this popular hotel has a restful drawing room (lots of cat decorations), cosy snug, an interesting Oriental bar, fine food in the elegant restaurant, and helpful, friendly staff; you can use the nearby leisure club; cl Christmas; disabled access.

HARROGATE SE2955 **Old Swan** *Ripon Rd, Harrogate HG1 2SR (01423) 500055* **£90w;** 136 rms. Creeper-covered Victorian hotel, nr the centre, in quiet gardens; with a friendly atmosphere, attractive day rooms, antiques and fresh flowers, good breakfasts in the splendid dining room, and fine modern cooking in the elegant restaurant.

HAWES SD8789 **Cocketts** *Market Pl, Hawes DL8 3RD (01969) 667312* ***£59,** plus special breaks; 8 warm rms. Friendly, hard-working owners make this a most attractive and enjoyable place to stay; a candlelit restaurant, woodburner in the small bar, and a residents' lounge with books; cl Christmas, 2 wks beginning of Feb; children over 10; disabled access.

INGLETON SD6872 **Thorngarth House** *New Rd, Ingleton, Carnforth LA6 3HN (01524) 241295* ***£50,** plus special breaks; 5 comfortable rms. Victorian country house in lovely countryside; with a cosy fire and plenty of books in the sitting room, a small candlelit restaurant with enjoyable, totally home-made food (can take their home-made jam, chutneys, herb oils and vinegars home with you), courteous service, and a tranquil atmosphere; lots to do nearby; cl Nov–Feb; no children.

KILNSEY SD9767 **Tennant Arms** *Kilnsey, Skipton BD23 5PS (01756) 752301* ***£47,** plus special breaks; 10 rms. In a nice spot nr the River Wharfe, this spacious, beamed and flagstoned inn has open fires (one fireplace made from an ornate, carved four-poster), friendly service, good-value food, and views of spectacular overhanging Kilnsey Crag from the restaurant; pets welcome by prior arrangement.

KNARESBOROUGH SE3457 **Dower House** *Bond End, Knaresborough HG5 9AL (01423) 863302* **£81,** plus special breaks; 32 clean, comfortable rms. Creeper-clad, former dower house with attractively furnished public rooms of some character, good food in the Terrace Restaurant, super breakfasts, and helpful service; also, a leisure and health club; disabled access.

LEYBURN SE1190 **Golden Lion** *Market Pl, Leyburn DL8 5AS (01969) 622161* **£60,** plus special breaks; 15 good-value rms. Homely inn with comfortable and quietly friendly, bay-windowed 2-room bar with light squared panelling; good, home-cooked, traditional food in both the bar and evening restaurant, well kept real ales (inc one brewed to their own recipe), and helpful service; self-catering in nearby Hawnby; cl 25–26 Dec; disabled access.

MALHAM SD9062 **Miresfield Farm** *Malham, Skipton BD23 4DA (01729) 830414* ***£46,** plus winter breaks; 14 rms. Spacious old farmhouse, with good, freshly prepared food in the beamed dining room, a pleasant conservatory, 2 lounges, and a lovely garden by the stream and village green; disabled access.

MARKINGTON SE2764 **Hob Green** *Markington, Harrogate HG3 3PJ (01423) 770031* **£90;** 12 well equipped, pretty rms. Lovely gardens and over 800 acres of rolling countryside surround this charming stone hotel; comfortable lounge and garden room, log fires, fresh flowers, a relaxed atmosphere, good food and friendly service.

MASHAM SE2280 **Kings Head** *Market Sq, Masham, Ripon HG4 4EF (01765) 689295* **£71;** 10 rms. Tall and handsome Georgian stone inn on the market square of this attractive small town; with lovely hanging-baskets, 2 opened-up rooms of the neatly kept lounge bar, home-made food from an extensive menu, a separate restaurant, well kept real ales, helpful service, and good breakfasts.

MIDDLEHAM SE1287 **Greystones** *Market Pl, Middleham DL8 4NR (01969) 622016* **£56,** plus special breaks; 4 rms. Friendly, family-run Georgian house with a log fire, books, magazines and TV in the restful lounge, and generous helpings of good, home-made food using home-grown vegetables; also, home-made bread, cakes and sweet and savoury biscuits, and enjoyable breakfasts; cl Dec–Jan exc New Year; children over 5.

MIDDLEHAM SE1287 **Millers House** *Market Pl, Middleham DL8 4NR (01969) 622630* **£76.50,** plus special breaks; 7 pretty rms. Neatly furnished Georgian house with fine views, an open fire in the pleasant lounge, and an attractive restaurant with good, interesting, home-cooked food using vegetables and herbs grown in their garden; lunchtime picnic hampers, and helpful service; cl Jan; children over 10.

NEWTON-LE-WILLOWS SE2189 **The Hall** *Newton-le-Willows, Bedale DL8 1SW (01677) 450210* **£80;** 3 spacious rms. Handsome Georgian house with quiet gardens and acres of paddocks, lots of fine antiques, paintings and wall hangings, a tranquil drawing room with an open fire and French windows into the garden, a cosy snug with another fire, and an honesty bar; good breakfasts in the light breakfast room (home-made fruitcake, tea and coffee always available), enjoyable food in the elegant dining room (by prior arrangement), and a helpful, hospitable owner; no children.

RAMSGILL SE1171 **Yorke Arms** *Ramsgill, Harrogate HG3 5RL (01423) 755243* **£90,** plus special breaks; 14 attractive rms. Enjoyable, small, former shooting lodge with antique furnishings and log fires; particularly good and imaginative cooking in both the brasserie and comfortable dining room, fine wines, courteous service, and lovely surrounding walks; open all day for tea and coffee.

REETH SE0499 **Arkleside** *Village Green, Reeth, Richmond DL11 6SG (01748) 884200* **£62;** 9 pretty rms. Charming small Swaledale hotel with warm, friendly and caring owners; an attractively furnished lounge, airy conservatory bar overlooking the gardens, a relaxing atmosphere, and good Yorkshire cooking in the candlelit restaurant; cl Jan–early Feb; children over 10.

RICHMOND NZ1700 **Millgate House** *Richmond DL10 4JN (01748) 823571* ***£55;** 2 rms overlooking the garden. Georgian townhouse with lots of interesting antiques and lovely plants, a peaceful drawing room, and warm, friendly hosts offering meticulous attention to detail; good breakfasts in the charming dining room which also overlooks the garden; it is this award-winning small garden, with views over the River Swale and the Cleveland hills beyond, that is so special, filled with wonderful roses, ferns, clematis and hostas – they have a booklet listing the plants; children over 10.

RICHMOND NZ1600 **Old Brewery** *29 The Green, Richmond DL10 4RG (01748) 822460* ***£42;** 5 rms. In a pretty corner overlooking the village green and castle ruins is this delightful former inn with Victorian-style renovations and furnishings, a hospitable atmosphere, and a nice garden; dinner by arrangement; cl Dec–Jan; children over 10.

RICHMOND NZ1404 **Whashton Springs Farm** *Whashton Springs, Richmond DL11 7JS (01748) 822884* ***£44;** 8 comfortable rms. Attractive, stone-built Georgian farmhouse on a 600-acre working mixed farm; with a log fire in the comfortable sitting room, good country breakfasts in the attractive dining room (no evening meals), and lovely surrounding countryside; cl Christmas–Jan; children over 5.

RIPLEY SE2860 **Boars Head** *Ripley, Harrogate HG3 1AY (01423) 771888* ***£125,** plus special breaks; 25 charmingly decorated rms. Fine old coaching inn with comfortable sofas in the attractively decorated lounges, a long flagstoned bar, notable wines by the glass, fine food in both the bar and restful dining room, and unobtrusive service; disabled access.

RIPON SE3071 **Ripon Spa** *Park St, Ripon HG4 2BU (01765) 602172* ***£78,** plus special breaks; 40 individually furnished rms, many overlooking the grounds. Neatly kept, friendly and comfortable Edwardian hotel with 7 acres of charming gardens, yet only a short walk from the centre; attractive public rooms, and good food in both the bar and restaurant; disabled access.

SEDBUSK SD8790 **Stone House** *Sedbusk, Hawes DL8 3PT (01969) 667571* ***£70,** plus special breaks; 22 rms, 2 with own conservatories. Small, warm and friendly Edwardian hotel with a country-house feel and appropriate furnishings, in a stunning setting with magnificent views; attractive, oak-panelled drawing room, billiard room, log fires, exemplary service, and good local information available; pleasant, newly extended dining room with excellent wholesome food (special needs catered for) inc super breakfasts, and a reasonable choice of wines; tennis lawn in the grounds, wonderful walks; P G Wodehouse stayed here as a guest of the original owner who employed a butler called Jeeves – it was on him that Wodehouse based his famous character; cl Jan; dogs welcome; good disabled access.

SETTLE SD8162 **Falcon Manor** *Skipton Rd, Settle BD24 9BD (01729) 823814* **£80,** plus special breaks; 19 rms. Quietly set, imposing Victorian hotel in its own grounds, with original features in the spacious public rooms, log fires, fine food and lovely views in the elegant restaurant, and obliging service; a well placed touring base; disabled access.

SHIPTON BY BENINGBROUGH SE5458 **Sidings** *See under York, p. 699.*

SIMONSTONE SD8791 **Simonstone Hall** *Simonstone, Hawes DL8 3LY (01969) 667255* ***£100,** plus special breaks; 18 pretty rms. Carefully restored, warmly welcoming country house in beautiful countryside with fine views; spacious panelled drawing rooms, antiques, paintings and old maps of the area, a convivial bar, and good, carefully cooked food and interesting wines; dogs welcome; disabled access.

STARBOTTON SD9574 **Fox & Hounds** *Starbotton, Skipton BD23 5HY (01756) 760269* **£50;** 2 rms with showers. Prettily placed and rather smart little Upper Wharfedale village inn; warm and welcoming, with flagstones, beams and a big log fire, imaginative food and well kept real ales; cl Jan–mid-Feb.

STUDLEY ROGER SE2970 **Lawrence House** *Studley Roger, Ripon HG4 3AY (01765) 600947* ***£80;** 2 spacious, lovely rms. Attractive Georgian house with 2 acres of garden on the edge of Studley Royal deer park and Fountains Abbey; lovely antiques and fine pictures, log fires, good breakfasts, and delicious evening meals; cl Christmas–New Year; children by arrangement.

THORALBY SE0086 **Scarr House** *Thoralby, Leyburn DL8 3SU (01969) 663654* **£59,** plus special breaks; 3 rms with showers. Relaxed and friendly, no smoking, 18th-c former farmhouse with lovely views; lots of books (no TV), comfortable lounge in a converted hayloft with beams, exposed stonework and an open fire, carefully cooked food (bring your own wine) at candlelit tables, and nice breakfasts; no children.

THORNTON WATLASS SE2385 **Buck** *Thornton Watlass, Ripon HG4 4AH (01677) 422461* **£52,** plus fishing and racing breaks; 7 rms, most with own bthrm. Warm and friendly country pub overlooking the cricket green in a very attractive village; interesting beamed and panelled rooms, open fire, live music weekends in the function room, excellent food inc summer barbecues, and lots of nearby walks (the arboretum is very popular); the inn offers guided walking holidays; cl 25 pm Dec.

WATH IN NIDDERDALE SE1467 **Sportsmans Arms** *Wath in Nidderdale, Harrogate HG3 5PP (01423) 711306* **£60;** 13 rms, most with own bthrm. Friendly, quietly placed 17th-c hotel, refurbished this year, with lovely views; elegant bar, a decent range of wines, excellent food (especially fish) in the no smoking evening restaurant, super lunchtime bar food, and attentive service; particularly good Sun lunch, and lots of fine cheeses; cl 25 Dec.

WEST WITTON SE0688 **Wensleydale Heifer** *West Witton, Leyburn DL8 4LS (01969) 622322* ***£70,** plus special breaks; 15 rms in 2 adjacent old buildings. Friendly, 17th-c stone coaching inn with comfortable furnishings, log fires and oak beams, a cosy bar, and good local game and fresh seafood in the bistro or spacious restaurant; well behaved dogs allowed.

WIGGLESWORTH SD8056 **Plough** *Wigglesworth, Skipton BD23 4RJ (01729) 840243* **£55,** plus special breaks; 12 well equipped rms. Friendly and well run country inn with popular food in the barn/conservatory restaurant and bar; lots of little rooms surrounding the bar area – some smart and plush, others more spartan yet still cosy; friendly service, big breakfasts, packed lunches, and views of the Three Peaks; disabled access.

To see and do

AISKEW SE2787 **Big Sheep and Little Cow Farm** Small-scale dairy farm, with friendly sheep and dexter cows (Britain's smallest), pigs and chicks – the family in charge love talking to visitors. Don't come when it's wet. Snacks, shop selling sheep's milk and home-made sheep's milk ice-cream, some disabled access; cl Sept–Mar; (01677) 422125; *£2.95.

★ ✝ **ALDBOROUGH ROMAN TOWN** SE4066 The northernmost civilian Roman town was on this site, its houses, courts, forum and temple surrounded by a massive 6-metre (20-ft) high wall. All that remain are 2 pavements, the line of the wall and, in the museum, some finds from the site. Shop; open pm Apr–Oct (cl 1–2pm); (01423) 322768; £1.70, free admission to site only in winter. It's a pleasant village with an impressive church (check out the sundial); the Ship opposite is good for lunch.

APEDALE HEAD SE0095 This spectacular viewpoint is reached by a 3-mile plod up tracks NW of Castle Bolton; on fine days it feels like the top of the world, with views over both Wensleydale and Swaledale.

! **ARKENDALE** SE3861 You can book **balloon trips** from the Flight Centre, (01423) 340664 (£125); they also have an authentic Boeing 737 flight-simulator, though you may experience some turbulence paying for the £125 session.

★ **ARNCLIFFE** SD9371 Charming, tucked-away Dales village, well placed for walks. The road up Littondale is pretty, and that to Langcliffe in Ribblesdale runs through dramatic scenery. The Falcon, in the same family for many generations, is an archetypal Dales inn, very simple but warmly welcoming.

★ ✝ **ASKRIGG** SD9491 Delightful collection of elegant stone houses around neat streamside greens, walks to nearby waterfalls, a fine 15th-c church, and good pub, the King's Arms.

★ **AYSGARTH** SE0188 **Waterfalls** The Lower Fall is the most spectacular of this famously romantic series of falls, via a path over the road from the car park. The falls are the National Park's chief visitor honeypot and do get crowded, particularly through Aug (when parking can be a problem). They're better in late spring or early autumn, when there tends to be more water in the river. In severely cold weather they can be stunning, with wonderful ice sculptures building up. There's generally a small charge to see the Upper Fall (it's on private land), but you can see it almost as well without paying, from the bridge on the road. The main car park (around £1 for 3 hours, more at wknds) has a **National Park Centre**, with displays on the Dales, and useful walks, maps, and guides. Café, shop, disabled facilities; cl Mon–Thur Nov–Mar; (01969) 663424; free. You can contrive longer walks along the S bank of the Ure from the delightful village of West Burton. **Yorkshire Carriage Museum** (Yore

Mill) A collection of Victorian coaches and carriages. Meals, snacks; cl Christmas; (01969) 663399; *£2. The George & Dragon is a good place for lunch.

★ **BAINBRIDGE** SD9390 Delightful, its broad sloping green still with the village stocks, and still ringing with the blowing of a buffalo-horn to guide shepherds down through the mists each night at 9pm from the end of Sept till late Feb, as it has done for centuries. **Low Mill** Restored 18th-c **corn mill** with a collection of fully furnished, hand-made dolls' houses, all produced here. Good shop (sells plans to make your own). Open pm Weds July–mid-Sept, maybe bank hols, and by appointment; (01969) 650416; *75p.

BEDALE SE2685 **Thorpe Perrow** (off the B6268 S) Well laid out, 60-acre, landscaped lakeside collection of rare trees and shrubs among some splendid mature specimens that have been growing here for over 400 years. Particularly strong on oaks, ornamental cherries, willows and hazels, and lovely in spring when the bulbs are out. There are plans for a new swamp cypress glade and wild-flower meadows. Snacks, shop, disabled access; (01677) 425323; £3.50. In the town, the convivial Olde Black Swan does good-value lunches.

BENINGBROUGH HALL SE5358 Stately, early 18th-c baroque mansion, with a good collection from the National Portrait Gallery, also a marvellous staircase with balusters carved in imitation of wrought iron, fine carvings, and a big restored Victorian dairy. Regular events for families, and lovely formal gardens. Meals, snacks, shop, disabled access to ground floor only; cl Thurs, Fri (exc July/Aug), and all Nov–Mar; (01904) 470666; £5, garden only £3; NT. The riverside Dawnay Arms at Newton-on-Ouse is handy for lunch.

BISHOPDALE SD9885 One of Wensleydale's tributary dales, broader than the others but still quite dramatic for walkers.

BOLTON ABBEY SE0754 Beautiful spot in lovely, rolling wooded parkland on a knoll above the River Wharfe. Most of the 12th/16th-c priory buildings are in ruins, but the central core of the main church is still used for Sunday services. 19th-c additions such as stained glass (some by Pugin) and murals oddly don't strike a false note. The car park gets rather full in summer. The Devonshire Arms is very fine for lunch. Attractive walks lead off in most directions: the landscape has a lowland beauty, with the abbey, the grassy riverbanks and the oaks of the Strid Wood (nature trail leaflet there). A steep ascent from Howgill SE0659 is rewarded by views from Simon's Seat, perched on the edge of moors.

BRIMHAM ROCKS SE2065 (off the B6265) Spectacular and extraordinarily weathered gritstone pinnacles, tors and boulders facing the winds at a height of 290 metres (950ft), conjuring up people, animal heads and other strange figures, which Victorian tourists found 'grim and hideous' but children now like a lot – Henry Moore said that when he was a boy they strongly influenced his imagination. Information centre, shop and tearoom open wknds and bank hols Easter–Oct, daily Jun–Sept and school hols – weather permitting, the site is open all yr; (01423) 780688; parking £2; NT. The Half Moon on the B6265 is handy for food.

CASTLE BOLTON SE0391 **Bolton Castle** (off the A684) A massive 14th-c structure towering over the tiny village built for it. Considering it was partly dismantled in 1645 and has been empty ever since, it's still in fine shape; great views from the 30-metre (100-ft) towers. Meals, snacks, shop; cl Nov–Feb; (01969) 623981; £3. The King's Arms at Redmire has decent food.

★ **CLAPHAM** SD7469 Attractive village that has turned walking and caving into something of an industry. It has a good **National Park Centre** with an audio-visual show and useful local information; best to check winter opening, usually wknds only; (01524) 251419; parking £1 for 3 hours (more at wknds). The riverside New Inn is useful for lunch (and handy for walkers to stay in). **Ingleborough Cave** One of the most easily visited of

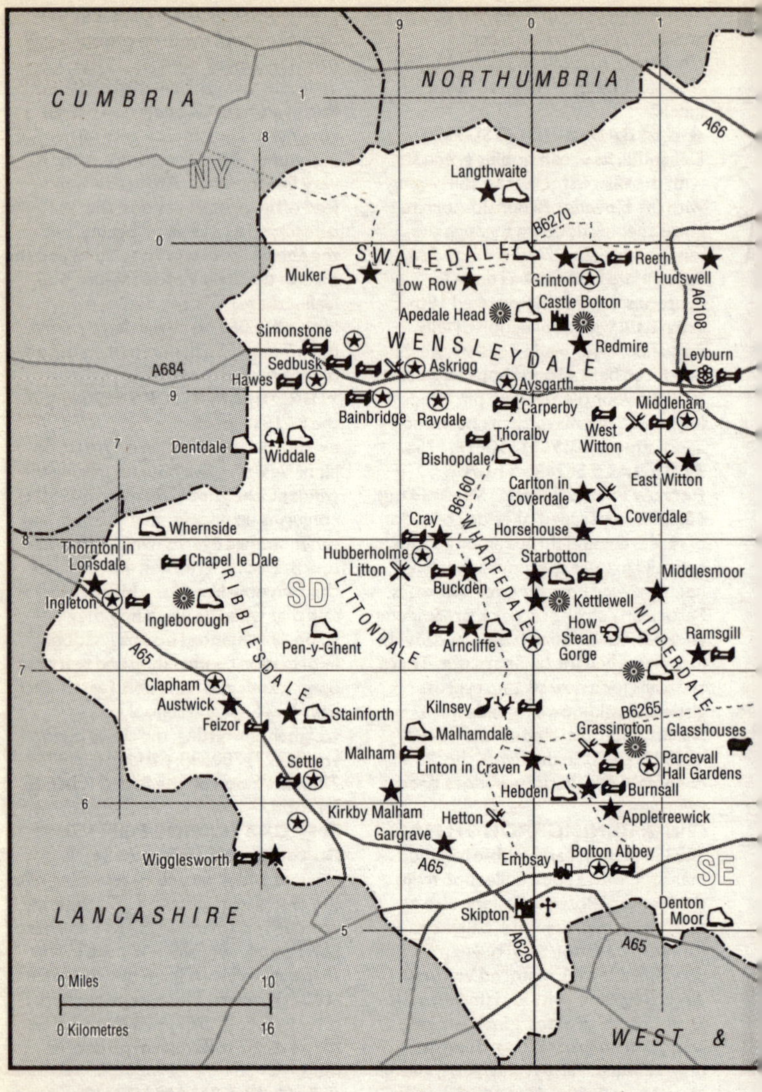

the vast network of caverns plunging into the limestone hills around here; wheelchairs can go all the way through. It's in the grounds of the Ingleborough Hall outdoors centre – formerly the family home of the great plantsman Reginald Farrer, who in his short life introduced and eulogised many notable plants from the Himalayas and China. A nature trail leads past Farrer's woods and a small lake to the cave; unusually, it's a place that looks better in wet weather. Snacks, shop; cl wkdys Nov–Feb; (015242) 51242; *£4.

COVERDALE SE0481
Wensleydale's major side valley is relatively quiet; fairly gentle in its lower reaches, climbing high into a wild and untamed-feeling world of lonely sheep farms.

CRAKEHALL SE2490
Watermill 17th c, on the site of a still earlier one; restored in 1980, it now produces flour again. Even when they're

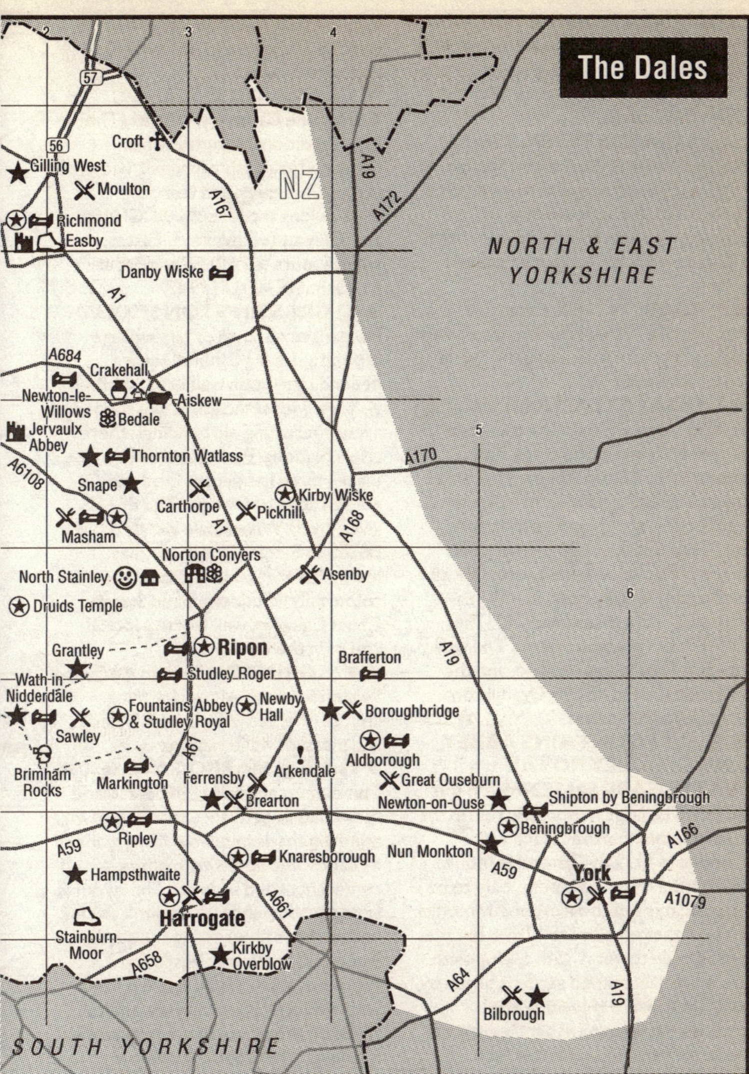

not milling, the wheel should still be turning. Snacks, shop; cl Mon, Fri and Oct–Easter; (01677) 423240; £1. The Bay Horse, in a nice spot on Little Crakehall green, has good-value food.

Museum of Badges and Battledress Not large, but plenty of interest; cl am wknds, Mon (exc bank hols), and Oct–Easter; (01677) 424444; *£1.50.

† **CROFT** NZ2809 Right on the border with County Durham is a pleasant **church**, where Lewis Carroll's father was parson; there's a plaque in memory of the writer, complete with an enamelled White Rabbit, and an unusual family pew reached by a staircase. The key is kept at the hotel across the road. Nice river views.

DENTDALE SD7586 Just on the Cumbrian side of the Yorkshire border, with walks along a lonely green track above the S side of the dale.

DENTON MOOR SE1450 Above the reservoirs S of Blubberhouses, with scope for fairly stretching walks (though nothing to compare with the Dales themselves).

! DRUIDS TEMPLE SE1879 Nr the hamlet of Ilton, a no-through road leads up to woodlands where you can walk to this scaled-down Stonehenge, built by a landowner in the 1820s as work for local unemployed people.

EASBY NZ1800 Extensive remains of a 12th-c Premonstratensian **abbey**, a pretty walk along the Swale from Richmond.

EMBSAY STEAM RAILWAY SE0053 Steamtrips along a track prettily set beneath limestone crags, now extended to Bolton Abbey. There's a ticket office originally from Ilkley, and a collection of old locomotives and carriages. Snacks, shop (remarkable range of books), disabled access (notice preferred); usually open Sun all year, and other days in summer – (01756) 795189 for timetable; £4.50. The well run Elm Tree has good food, and the Wayside Café in nearby Draughton does delicious scones.

FOUNTAINS ABBEY AND STUDLEY ROYAL WATERGARDEN SE2769 (off the B6265) The largest monastic ruin in the country, this romantic place was founded in 1132 by Cistercian monks, in a delightful riverside setting. Said to be haunted by a full choir of ghostly monks, most of the remains are 12th c, but the proud main tower is 15th c. Opposite are lovely landscaped gardens begun by William Aislabie in 1768, with ornamental temples and follies, formal watergardens, lakes aflutter with waterfowl, and 400 acres of deer park. The most beautiful approach is through the extraordinarily ornate Victorian church at the far end (restoration in progress, best to phone for opening), and this 'back-door' entrance is the most tranquil too. A modern visitor centre blends in and doesn't spoil the view. Free guided tours 2.30pm Mar–Oct, plus 11am May–Sept. Meals, snacks, shop, good disabled access; cl Fri Nov–Jan, and 24–25 Dec; (01765) 608888; £4.20, deer park – an excellent strolling ground – free; NT. The very civilised Sawley Arms, in Sawley just W, does good food.

GLASSHOUSES SE1764 **Yorkshire Country Wines** (The Mill) Traditional country wines produced in a 19th-c flax mill, with free tastings, antiques, and tearoom overlooking the River Nidd. Cl Mon and Tues and wkdys Nov–Easter, winery tours (£2.50) Fri and Sat at 11.45am; (01423) 711947.

★ **GRASSINGTON** SE0063 Pleasant small town or large village around a sloping cobbled square, depending a lot on walkers and other visitors, with some attractive shops and a few interesting old buildings; there's also a National Park Centre here. The Black Horse has decent food and comfortable bedrooms. The B6160 gives lovely Wharfedale views, and the B6265 to Pateley Bridge also has memorable views (and passes the colourfully lit, underground Stump Cross Caverns, well worth a look if you're in the vicinity).

★ † **GRINTON** SE0498 Attractive Swaleside village with a charming church (the 'cathedral of the Dales') and pleasant walks nearby.

★ **HARROGATE** SE3054 This elegant and self-confident inland resort has kept its Victorian spa-town atmosphere despite now filling many of its handsome hotels with business conferences and so forth. The layout is very gracious, and you couldn't ask for better shops (interesting antiques and some top-notch specialist shops). Almost every available space is filled with colourful plant displays, as if to shake off the gloom of the dark stone buildings. The first thing a visitor notices is the great swathe of The Stray, open parkland which sweeps right along and through the S side of the centre. What looks like an Italianate mausoleum up here encloses the **Tewit Well**, the original sulphur well discovered in the 16th c and named after the local word for the lapwings which led a local sporting gent to ride into what was then a smelly bog. The elegant buildings of the compact central area run down from here to the pleasantly laid out Valley Gardens, very

Victorian, their curlicued central tea house run by a friendly Italian family. The relaxed tempo of the place, and the clean bracing climate (it's quite high on the moors), have made it a popular retirement area. Besides the places mentioned in the **Where to eat** *section on p.721*, the Drum & Monkey (fish restaurant/wine bar, Montpellier Gardens), Hedleys (wine bar, Montpellier Parade) and the Regency (off East Parade) are all good for lunch or a snack; the café of the Theatre Royal is also pleasant, as is the Lascelles Arms out in Follifoot.

Royal Pump Room Museum (Royal Parade) The central sulphur wells (there are other outlets all over the town) are housed here, cased in glass to contain the reek. You can get a free glass of the water at the original spa counter, now the ticket counter for the museum. The octagonal pump room building has fine 19th-c china and jewellery, as well as bath chairs and other impedimenta of the golden spa days. Shop, disabled access; cl Oct–Mar; (01423) 503340; £1.75. **Mercer Art Gallery** (Swan Rd) Another early spa building, with an excellent collection (cl am Sun, and Mon exc bank hols; free). **Harlow Carr Botanical Gardens** (Crag Lane, on W edge, off the B6162) Ornamental and woodland gardens spread over 68 acres, with streams, pools, rockeries, rhododendrons, spring bulbs and many interesting plants. Also a museum of gardening, model village, scented garden, and a developing rose garden. A place of real peace and fresh moorland air, the finest strolling ground nr Harrogate, and virtually deserted out of season, when the excellent collection of heathers comes into its own. Meals, snacks, plant centre, disabled access; (01423) 565418; £3.50. The adjacent Harrogate Arms is good value.

★ **HAWES** SD8789 Busy in summer with hikers and coach parties, but pretty, and a proper market town, its Tuesday mart alive with sheep in late summer (cattle too, in normal years less overshadowed by BSE). The Crown and White Hart are useful for lunch. **Wensleydale Creamery** (Gayle Lane) This has developed a fascinating visitor centre, with a well set out dairying/cheese museum; you can watch the cheese being made by the traditional method, all by hand. The shop (busy in summer) has samples of their variously flavoured cheeses – our favourite was one with blueberries. Very good café, disabled facilities; cl 25 Dec; (01969) 667644; *£2.50. **Dales Countryside Museum and National Park Centre** (Station Yard) Interesting displays of local crafts and domestic and industrial life, and a new extension with hands-on exhibits, a steam locomotive and displays on transport. Shop, disabled access; cl winter Mon, Tues and Thurs; (01969) 667450; £2. **Outhwaites ropemakers** (A684, Town Foot) They've been making rope for 200 years – see how it's done. Shop (not just great hawsers, useful things too like dog-leads), disabled access; cl wknds (exc summer Sats, Easter and spring bank hol), 10 days at Christmas; (01969) 667487; free. **Hardraw Force** (just N) England's tallest waterfall cascading over a 30-metre (100-ft) lip; it's best after rain (though the paths can be muddy then), and at dry times you may see barely a trickle; small fee at the Green Dragon pub. A longer excursion follows the Pennine Way from Hawes and over the River Ure. The valley above the falls is attractive, and this can be a start for the long day's walk to Great Shunner Fell. The B6255 S to Ribblehead gives fine mountain views, and the Buttertubs Pass northwards through High Shaw over into Swaledale is a spectacular drive (the Buttertubs are deep ferny holes nr the summit where carriers used to cool their butter in hot weather).

HEBDEN LEAD MINES SE0263 There's a rewarding walk from Hebden up Hebden Beck, with its legacy of old lead-mine workings; the route can be extended to take in Grassington and the path along the River Wharfe.

HOW STEAN GORGE SE0874 To the W of Lofthouse, spectacular ravine pocked with potholes and caverns; a footpath snakes between miniature cliffs, with bridges giving views into the gorge; there's also a visitor centre.

★ † ⌂ **HUBBERHOLME** SD9377 Beautifully placed dales hamlet with a good 13th-c **church**, built on an ancient burial site, with a Norman tower, an unusual rood loft and pews by Thompson of Kilburn – with their little carved mouse trademark. The charmingly set George, J B Priestley's favourite pub, has decent food and bedrooms. A walk not to be missed is up to Scar House and along a level turfy terrace, which commands magnificent views down the dale, to Cray (another good inn there). The walk can be expanded to include Buckden – in fact there are fine walks between all the Wharfedale/Littondale places flagged on our map, with enjoyable pub food available in each of them.

⌂ ❋ **INGLEBOROUGH** SD7474 (721 metres; 2,376ft) Best approached along the Reginald Farrer Trail from Clapham, *see entry above*, past Ingleborough Cave (guided visits) and Gaping Gill (a vast pothole); the panorama extends far across Lancashire and into Cumbria.

INGLETON SD7174 **White Scar Cave** (B6255 towards Hawes) The country's biggest show cavern and one of the most spectacular, with underground waterfalls and streams, and an Ice Age cavern. Some amazing sights and atmospheric formations, and stunning stalactites and stalagmites formed over 100,000 years. Wrap up well – the 80-minute guided tour gets chilly. Snacks, shop, disabled access by arrangement; cl 25 Dec (and sometimes after heavy rain); (015242) 41244; £5.95. The Three Horse Shoes and Wheatsheaf are useful pubs, and the B6255/B6479 is a very scenic long way round to Settle. Ingleton Glen is a lovely wooded walk up the River Twiss, over the moor and back down the River Doe, past a series of picturesque waterfalls; not too strenuous, with very varied scenery, it takes 2 or 3 hours – the admission fee is amply justified by the delightful gorge and waterfalls.

JERVAULX ABBEY SE1785 Less imposing than Fountains, Rievaulx and Bolton, but in some ways even more appealing – perhaps because the rough-cropped grass and wild flowers around the shattered walls emphasise the slightly melancholy atmosphere of a place of great worldly wealth and power that's come to nothing. Teas, shop, disabled access; cl am Nov–Dec, and all Jan–Feb; (01677) 460391; £1.50. The Blue Lion at East Witton nearby has superb food.

★ ❋ **KETTLEWELL** SD9672 Attractive and popular with walkers, with 3 decent pubs; exhilarating views from the back roads up into Coverdale, and to Hawes via Hubberholme.

KILNSEY PARK TROUT FARM SD9767 (B6160, Kilnsey) 2 lakes for fly-fishing, plus a fun-fishing area for children, an adventure playground, visitor centre with an aquarium and a sizeable orchid collection, and a good estate shop with fish, oven-ready game and other local produce. You may catch a glimpse of a red squirrel: this is a conservation area for these creatures driven out of much of the country by the grey ones. Good meals and snacks (tasty trout and local cheeses), disabled access; cl 25 Dec; (01756) 752150; £2 for visitor centre, £4.20 for children's fishery (only open wknds and school hols), and proper fishing from £15 per half-day. The Tennant Arms has decent food.

KIRBY WISKE SE3684 **Sion Hill Hall** Splendid mansion, one of the last great country houses to be built before World War I, with period furnishings and masses of antiques, porcelain, paintings and clocks. Also costume and doll collections and a birds of prey centre. Snacks, shop (inc antiques), some disabled access; cl am, all Mon and Tues, and Nov–Mar; (01845) 587206; £4.

★ ! **KNARESBOROUGH** SE3557 The little town itself above the steeply picturesque river gorge, with its spectacular railway viaduct, is pleasant and colourful (especially on Weds market day), with some attractive buildings. The 1720 chemist's shop on the square is said to be the oldest in the country, and still has its original fittings. You can hire **rowing boats** down on the river, and there are pleasant waterside paths and walks: from Abbey Rd for example you should be able to see the intriguing **House in the Rock**, and a 15-minute walk down here brings you to St Robert's Cave, the riverside home of a 12th-c hermit. The Mother Shipton and Yorkshire Lass both have good-value food. **Petrifying well** In the 19th c quite a little tourist industry was concocted for the toffs from Harrogate around the alleged 16th-c prophecies of Mother Shipton. The cave she lived in is pleasantly set in 12 acres of riverside parkland, along with this limestone spring, which quickly coats teddy bears and other unlikely objects in rock so that they can be sold as souvenirs. There are guided tours, and a local history museum, but admission is £4.25 and not everyone comes away feeling it was worth it. Snacks, shop; (01423) 864600; cl 25 Dec. **Knaresborough Castle** All that remains are the 14th-c keep (with a museum and suitably dank dungeon), gatehouse and some of the curtain wall, but it's easy to imagine what an imposing sight it must have made, glowering over the gorge of the River Nidd – a suitable spot for Thomas à Becket's murderers to hide in. Shop; cl Oct–Easter; (01423) 503340; £1.75, also includes entrance to the 14th-c **Old Court**, now a local history museum.

★ ⛰ **LANGTHWAITE** NZ0002 Idyllic Dales hamlet, with good circular walks from the pub – and the Arkengarthdale road up to the remote but very popular Tan Hill Inn is a very fine drive.

★ ❀ **LEYBURN** SE1190 Bustling little agricultural town with a proper country atmosphere and a lively Fri market: the Sandpiper's the nicest pub, and Tennants is Europe's largest auction room for house clearances and antiques. **Constable Burton Hall Gardens** (A684 E, SE1691) A series of fine terraced gardens around a handsome Georgian house (not open); the cyclamen, at the end of the short lime avenue, flower beautifully in early Aug. Some disabled access but no facilities; open 25 Mar–24 Oct; (01677) 450428; £2. Off the A684 W are fine drives: up Coverdale to Kettlewell; up Bishopdale on the B6160 and on down past Cray into Wharfedale; up into the Eden Valley's Cumbrian headwaters on the B6269; and the Carperby–Castle Bolton–Reeth road.

★ **LINTON IN CRAVEN** SD9962 A gem of a Dales village, with lovely stone buildings, set off by lawns running down to a duck-filled stream.

⛰ **MALHAMDALE** SD9062 One of the smaller dales and a magnet for visitors, its upper stretches cut tortuously and deeply out of the limestone by the River Aire and its steep tributaries, leaving spectacular cliffs, extensive bare upland limestone 'pavements', craggy bowls carved out of the overhanging hillsides, and sparkling waterfalls. Malham village has a good National Park Centre, and the Lister Arms is a pleasant refuge. A fine if busy walk leads along the beck to Janet's Foss waterfall, and to the romantic severity of dramatic Gordale Scar, the dale's most memorable natural feature, where a beck makes a spectacular leap from the rocks. The Pennine Way heads N up the side of Malham Cove, a great cliff, then crosses a natural rock pavement and heads over a landscape of limestone scars, disappearing streams and green turf to Malham Tarn, a lovely mountain lake skirted on its E side by a nature trail.

★ ✝ 🏛 ✿ **MASHAM** SE2280 (pronounced Mazzum) Civilised small market town, with an interesting church, and dignified Georgian houses around its broad market square – which comes to life on Weds. The King's Head does good food. **Theakston Brewery Visitor Centre** Next to the brewery, this explains the brewing process behind Theakstons beer, inc their Old Peculier. Shop, disabled access; Open daily Easter–Oct, and wknds and Weds Nov–mid-Dec and Mar–Easter; £2. Enthusiastic tours of the brewery itself (£3), best to book on (01765) 689057; you see more in the mornings; no under-10s. **Black Sheep Brewery** Set up by a breakaway member of the Theakston family a few years back, its beers since proving very popular. The visitor centre has nice food all day, and there are decent children's facilities. Readers enjoy the fun and imaginative tours: best to book, (01765) 689227 – evening tours are best, with more time to enjoy samples at the end; £3.75. **Uredale Glass** (42 Market Pl) Hand-made glassware, with glass-blowing demonstrations (not Sun or Mon); cl Christmas wk; (01765) 689780; free.

★ **MIDDLEHAM** SE1287 Attractive and civilised, basically Georgian, stone-built village, still with the style that came from its days as the country's top racehorse-training centre in the 18th and early 19th centuries. Even now there are times when it seems to have more horses than people: pick up breeding and gallops gossip in the bar of the good Black Swan. **Middleham Castle** This 12th-c structure, for a time home of young King Richard III, dwarfs the village. Only the huge keep and some later buildings remain, but there are marvellous views from the top, and an informative exhibition centre. Snacks, shop, disabled access; cl 1–2pm in winter, winter Mon and Tues, 24–26 Dec; (01969) 623899; £2.20. This is a good area for self-catering accommodation, and fine walking country.

★ **MUKER** SD9197 Attractive Dales hamlet, with a very good woollens shop and well liked tearooms. Between here and Keld, the River Swale enters a deeply cut valley and tumbles over waterfalls, with paths on both sides; or you can take a more upland route over Kisdon above the river.

NEWBY HALL SE3568 (off the B6265 E of Ripon) In beautiful formal gardens covering 25 acres, this late 17th-c mansion, redesigned inside and out by Robert Adam, has an important collection of classical sculpture and Gobelins tapestries, as well as a fine range of Chippendale furniture. In the grounds are a miniature railway, children's adventure garden, paddling pool and a woodland discovery walk. Meals, snacks, shop, some disabled access; house cl am, all Mon (exc bank hols), and Oct–Mar; (01423) 322583; £6, gardens only £4.30. The Ship over in Aldborough is the nearest good place for food.

NIDDERDALE SE1073 This quiet yet beautiful valley has an impressive, solitary grandeur. Just outside the National Park, it and the hills above are less liberally laced with footpaths and open-access moorland than the other dales here, and attract far fewer visitors. There are plenty of relatively unfrequented walks, often on good, paved but untarred tracks. The Nidderdale Way allows a fine, fairly gentle walk of a couple of hours or so, up on to the high pastures (see lambs being born in spring) and moorland at Glasshouses and back, with spectacular views almost all the way. It's well signed; start from Dacre Banks SE1962 and take the lane a couple of hundred yards past the church. The stretch between the attractive small town of Pateley Bridge SE1566 and the hamlet of Lofthouse is dominated by the sheltered 2-mile waters of Gouthwaite Reservoir, serenely set below the hills with some tall trees alongside. From Lofthouse SE1073 a path runs beside the River Nidd, with picturesque tracks among small woods and ruined farmhouses, to Scar House Reservoir, quite exposed at the valley head (there's also a toll road up to it); high, exposed routes line the N side of the dale up here.

☺ **NORTH STAINLEY** SE2876 **Lightwater Valley Theme Park** Family fun from the nostalgic pleasure of a steamtrain to the white-knuckle thrills of one of the world's biggest rollercoasters; another rollercoaster is entirely under ground. Meals, snacks, shop, disabled access; open wknds and school hols (not Christmas) Easter–Oct, and daily Jun–early Sept; (01765) 635321; £11.95. An adjacent factory shopping village is open all year. The Staveley Arms does decent food.

NORTON CONYERS SE3076 (3½ miles N of Ripon) The same family have lived in this late medieval house for 370 years, and the furniture and pictures reflect the fact that it's still very much a family home. Charlotte Brontë used the building as one of her models for Thornfield Hall. Look out for the hoofprint on the stairs. Attractively planted 18th-c walled garden. Shop (with unusual plants and, in season, garden fruits), limited disabled access; open pm bank hol Suns and Mons, then pm Sun 6 Jun–12 Sept, plus pm daily 12–17 July; (01765) 640333; £3. The Freemasons Arms at Nosterfield is useful for lunch.

★ **NUN MONKTON** SE5057 This attractive village is in appearance almost more like France than Yorkshire, with its broad avenue, and the stately meeting of the Rivers Nidd and Ouse.

PARCEVALL HALL GARDENS SE0660 16 acres of woodland gardens charmingly set around an Elizabethan house, on a hillside E of Wharfedale; superb views from the cliff walk. New tea garden, plant sales; cl Nov–Easter exc by appointment; (01756) 720311; £2. The Craven Arms at nearby Appletreewick is good for lunch, with lovely views.

PEN-Y-GHENT SD8473 (694 metres; 2,277ft) Reached from Horton in Ribblesdale; its satisfyingly compact summit is the craggiest feature on the Pennine Way, which nr here passes some potholes inc Hull Pot.

RAYDALE SD9187 The most interesting of Wensleydale's subsidiary valleys for walkers. Its lower neck is quite narrow, but it broadens into a sheltered bowl of valley, with Semer Water, a sizeable glacial lake said to have been conjured up by a wandering beggar to drown a village which had spurned him. It's Yorkshire's third largest natural lake, and has a path along its half-mile-long S side, but for circular routes you have to do some road walking. The walled track (a Roman road) just N has wide-ranging views as it descends to Bainbridge.

★ **REETH** SE0399 Attractive Dales village with a high, wide, sloping green; the King's Arms is a popular dining pub. The village is a centre for rambles ranging from pottering along the meadows by the Swale to hill walks into adjacent Arkengarthdale (where the ascent on to Fremington Edge is memorable). The B6270 through Swaledale is a very scenic drive.

RIBBLESDALE SD7776 Climbing above Settle into severe and grand mountain scenery, the high walking country of Upper Ribblesdale is craggy and remote: a major magnet for walkers on the Three Peaks Walk, 24 miles taking in the summits of Ingleborough, Pen-y-ghent and Whernside. This is a tough undertaking in its entirety, but each of the peaks on its own is a manageable half-day excursion: choose a clear day – not just for the magnificent views but for your own safety. This area is riddled with impressive potholes, some of them gaping chasms of sensational size that can be admired from the surface, as well as the intricate underground passages that make the area so popular with cavers. Up in the loneliest parts, useful refuges are the cheerful cavers' inn, the Old Hill at Chapel le Dale, and the isolated Station Inn at Ribblehead. Below Settle, the valley is less interesting for walkers, and marred by some quarrying.

★ **RICHMOND** NZ1600 A most attractive riverside country town, with steep pretty streets of old stone buildings, and a splendid, broad, sloping market square (still cobbled, and perhaps the biggest in the country; market day is Sat). Scollards Hall, built in 1080, may be the oldest domestic building in Britain. **Richmond Castle** These austere and intricate ruins dominate the town, and overlook the River Swale from a high rocky outcrop. Shop, some disabled access; cl 1–2pm in winter, 24–26 Dec; (01748) 822493; £2.20. **Theatre Royal** (Victoria Rd) The country's oldest working theatre still in its original form, complete with gallery, boxes and pit. Built in 1788, it doesn't look much from the outside but the immaculately restored interior is really special. Shop; guided tours and museum open Easter–Oct; (01748) 823021; *£1.50. **Green Howards Museum** (Market Sq) In a converted 12th-c church, this includes among duller regimental history the blood-stained pistol holsters of the Grand Old Duke of York. Shop, some disabled access; cl wknds in Feb, Sun in Mar and Nov, am Sun Apr–Oct, and all Dec–Jan; (01748) 822133; *£2. The army connection is still strong; nearby Catterick Camp is the biggest in the north. There are attractive riverside walks beneath the castle's towering bulk – E to Easby Abbey, or W through Hudswell Woods, with an extension to Whitcliffe Scar, a cliff above the Swale with an exciting path along its top. The Black Lion in Finkle St is good value.

★ **RIPLEY CASTLE** SE2860 (off the A61) Beautifully picturesque, in the same family for 26 generations. Most of the current building dates from the 16th c, inc the tower with its collection of Royalist armour. For some the main attraction is the splendid gardens, the setting for a national collection of hyacinths and (under glass) fine tropical plants. Also, a birds of prey centre. Meals, snacks, shop, some disabled access; open Tues, Thurs, Sat and Sun Jan–Mar and Nov–Dec, Thurs–Sun Apr–Jun and Sept–Oct, and daily July and Aug; (01423) 770152; *£4, gardens only *£2.50. The attractive village, rebuilt in the 1820s, has a superb delicatessen, and the Boar's Head Hotel is a fine old place for lunch.

★✝ **RIPON** SE3171 On Thurs, colourful stalls fill the attractive and ancient market square (quite a few too on Sat, inc bric-à-brac); it's largely unspoilt, lined with specialist shops and old inns and hotels. At 9pm each night the Wakeman, a red-coated bugler, blows a buffalo horn here, as one has done for centuries. Going from here down one of the town's engagingly narrow old streets, you're rewarded by a magnificent view of the elegant Early English west front of **Ripon Cathedral**. Spectacularly floodlit at night, this is one of the largest half-dozen in the country, with plenty to see inc very fine carving indeed in both stone and wood, and a 7th-c crypt – the oldest surviving part of any British cathedral building (and probably the oldest surviving crypt outside Italy). Shop, disabled access; £2 suggested donation. **Ripon Prison Museum** (St Marygate) Small but interesting – and nicely chilling; cl am (exc July and Aug), and all Nov–Easter; *£1.50. The **Old Workhouse** (Grainger Row) is also worth a look (opening as Prison Museum; £1). The Golden Lion, just off the market square, is useful for a bite to eat.

★ **SETTLE** SD8163 Market day (Tues) around the Shambles is particularly attractive; look out to the right of here for the Folly, an extraordinary 17th-c townhouse. Mary Milnthorpe & Daughter is a good antique jewellery and silver shop, and the Golden Lion has decent food. Just across the Ribble, Giggleswick is a peaceful contrast to the hectic little town. **Settle–Carlisle Railway** A magnificent 70-mile route carved up through Ribblesdale across the wild moors between here and Cumbria, then dropping down through the lovely Eden Valley; (0345) 484950 for times and fares, £13.80 for day return. All year on Sats and some Suns and Weds, there's a programme of walks connecting with the moorland stops; they start quite early (8.45am Sat), with dates and times listed on the timetable. Aside from the setting, it's an ordinary railway line: steamtrains do run most Sats in summer, but only from cities in the south (01543 419472 for routes and times), resulting in the odd situation that you can travel by steam from Norwich or London, but not from the immediate vicinity. The B6479 is not quite comparable to the train, but an enjoyable drive. **Yorkshire Dales Falconry and Conservation Centre** SD7867 (top of Crows Nest, off the A65 N) Well organised, with lots of vultures, eagles, hawks, falcons and owls, and regular flying displays (from noon). Meals, snacks, shop, disabled access; cl 25 Dec, maybe other days too in winter; (01729) 825164; *£4.50.

✝ **SKIPTON** SD9851 On Sat the main street has a colourful market (at least some stalls here most other days too, exc Sun, Tues and Thurs). The 14th-c **church** has a 16th-c rood screen and interesting stained glass. A canal runs through the town, and the Royal Shepherd, in an attractive spot, has good-value, quick food. **Skipton Castle** 12th c, and properly romantic, with sturdy round towers, broad stone steps, and a lovely central flagstoned and cobbled courtyard with a seat around its venerable yew tree. One of the best-preserved medieval castles in Europe; it really is remarkable how much is left, interior and all – very few other castles have kept their roofs and stayed habitable. The original Norman arched gateway still stands. Snacks, shop; cl am Sun, 25 Dec; (01756) 792442; £3.80.

STAINBURN MOOR SE2452 The area E of the Dales really has nothing to compare with the Dales themselves for serious walking, but this moorland W of Harrogate has some possibilities for fairly stretching walks, for instance from the car park by the woods along the side road W from Beckwithshaw.

★ ⛰ **STAINFORTH** SD8167
Attractive village with a gentle Ribblesdale walk from Stainforth Force to Langcliffe.

★ ⛰ **STARBOTTON** SD9574
Delightful, tiny Wharfedale village; a good base for walks, for example along the river to Kettlewell, then back up over the high land; or you can follow less obvious paths W to Arncliffe in Littondale – very similar to Wharfedale itself, though with a flatter damper valley floor.

⛰ **SWALEDALE** SE0098 The northernmost dale, and one of the least visited – giving more chance of getting away from it all even at peak times. Its bold hills, abundant stone barns and extreme tranquillity make it a walkers' favourite. It's grandly austere for the most part, though quite heavily wooded as it drops down towards Richmond. In the steeper parts there are some fine waterfalls. The upper slopes towards the Durham and Cumbrian borders are wild and empty, except for the huge scattered flocks of hardy, clean-limbed, Swaledale sheep with their dark faces, grey muzzles, thick fleeces and curly-horned rams. The meadowland down in the valley and its broad tributary Arkengarthdale is largely unimproved, with slow-growing natural grasses and lots of wild flowers. Many of the area's 1,200 traditional stone hay barns, which are such a distinctive feature here, have been rehabilitated in recent years, with generous National Parks grant aid. Gunnerside SD9598 still has around it many of the 'rushes' where lead-miners dammed streams to form torrents that could break up the lead-bearing rock strata below; this whole area was an important lead centre until Victorian times, and other visible mementos are ruined mill buildings, tunnel entrances and spoil heaps.

★ ⛰ **WATH** SE1467 Attractive Dales hamlet spreading up the valley, with pleasant walks along past the reservoir to Ramsgill – beyond is a splendid moorland drive over to Masham.

⛰ ★ 🏰 **WENSLEYDALE** SD9889
More expansive in character and not quite as dramatic as Swaledale, but richly picturesque; its unspoilt villages and numerous waterfalls make for pleasurable walking. It used to be one of the richest dales, its broad pastures and countless sheep supporting the wealthy abbeys and castles whose ruins now add so much interest to its scenery. Wensleydale sheep are very distinctive, with long, fleecy, dreadlock curls. Upper Wensleydale (around and W of Hawes) is steep and wild; E of here the valley starts broadening out, with richer lower pastures, and more regular farmland below Middleham.

⛰ 🌳 ★ **WHARFEDALE** SD9769
With its tributary valley Littondale and its headwaters up in the steep conifer plantations at the top of Langstrothdale, this is one of England's most popular areas for walkers, and very beautiful indeed in parts. The Dales Way follows the River Wharfe for most of the dale.

Days Out

Southern gateway to the Dales: Embsay steam railway; Skipton Castle; lunch at the Royal Shepherd, Skipton, or at the Angel, Hetton; Grassington; walk through Strid Woods; Bolton Abbey.

Drive through Wensleydale and Swaledale: Hawes; Bainbridge; lunch at the King's Arms, Askrigg, or the George & Dragon at Aysgarth; Aysgarth Falls; Castle Bolton; Reeth, Gunnerside (old lead mines in Gunnerside Gill), Muker (optional walk along the Swale to Keld and return on the Pennine Way); cross Buttertubs Pass to return to Hawes.

Monastic mementos and Georgian follies: Ripon Cathedral; lunch at the Sawley Arms, Sawley; Fountains Abbey and Studley Royal Watergarden.

Upper Wharfedale, above Grassington, has a level floor of sheltered, well drained pastures with the river winding through, a few grey stone barns, and steep sides laced with dry-stone walls, gnarled woodland and occasional austere crags, climbing up to high, fairly level tops some 365 metres (1,200ft) above the valley floor. The smaller villages are delightfully private and unspoilt, their grey or whitewashed stonework blending perfectly with the long scars of the limestone terraces above them. Away from the valley floor, stone-walled grassy tracks are the easiest ways of gaining height. Below Grassington, there's an extremely pretty stretch where the valley winds more sinuously past Burnsall, Appletreewick (good riverside car park – £2) and Bolton Abbey, below hills which though less grand are more varied in shape, with rather sensitively laid out conifer plantations adding a slightly subalpine feel.

WHERNSIDE SD7381 (736 metres; 2,415ft) Sometimes criticised by keen walkers as the boring one of the Three Peaks, this is Yorkshire's highest point, and has an exhilarating ridge section; start from the magnificent Ribblehead Viaduct carrying the Settle–Carlisle railway over the head of the dale (the Station Hotel here is a comfortable halt).

WIDDALE SD8287 Steep-sided and dramatic tributary of Wensleydale, with extensive conifer plantations above.

★ **Other attractive villages** include Appletreewick SE0560, Austwick SD7768, Bilbrough SE5346, Boroughbridge SE3967, Brearton SE3261, Buckden SD9477, Burnsall SE0361, Carlton in Coverdale SE0684, Cray SD9379, East Witton SE1486 (ancient houses, long wide green), Gargrave SD9354 (on the Pennine Way), Gilling West NZ1804, Grantley SE2369, Hampsthwaite SE2659, Horsehouse SE0481, Hudswell NZ1400, Kirkby Malham SD8961, Kirkby Overblow SE3249, Low Row SD9897 (popular with potholers), Middlesmoor SE0874, Newton-on-Ouse SE5160, Ramsgill SE1271, Redmire SE0591, Snape SE2784, Thornton in Lonsdale SD6873 (Conan Doyle was married in the charming church), Thornton Watlass SE2486 and Wigglesworth SD8157.

Where to eat

ASENBY SE3975 **Crab & Lobster** *(01845) 577286* Old, thatched pub/restaurant, relaxed and informal but civilised; interestingly furnished cosy rooms with lots of bric-à-brac, delicious food, and good wines by the glass; bdrms. **£25**|£7.50.

ASKRIGG SD9490 **Rowan Tree** *(01969) 650536* Cosy little candlelit stone barn run by an Irish husband and German wife team; just a few tables so booking advisable, good, imaginative evening meals and a reasonably priced wine list; cl Sun, Mon, and winter Sun–Weds (best to phone for winter opening times); children over 10. **£21 for 5 courses.**

BILBROUGH SE5346 **Three Hares** *(01937) 832128* Smartly refurbished dining pub with a welcoming landlord and staff; traditional bar with lots of polished copper and brass, a no smoking restaurant, very good modern cooking using the freshest local produce, an interesting wine list and well kept real ales; children over 8; cl Mon, 25 Dec, pm 26 Dec, pm 1 Jan; disabled access. **£18.70**|£7.

BOROUGHBRIDGE SE3966 **Black Bull** *St James Sq (01432) 322413* Lovely old inn said to date from the 13th c, with a big stone fireplace in the main bar area (service from an old-fashioned hatch), a cosy traditional snug, and an extended dining room; well presented food – the bread, pasta, sorbets and ice-creams are all home-made – fresh daily fish and lovely puddings, well kept real ales, enjoyable wines with 10 by the glass, afternoon teas (not Sun), friendly and attentive service; also, a plump ginger cat, and classical piped music; bdrms; cl 1 Jan; disabled access. **£20**|£5.

BREARTON SE3260 **Malt Shovel** *(01423) 862929* Unspoilt village pub with hard-working licensees; heavily beamed rooms with open fires and lively hunting prints, very good bar food (super fresh fish and lovely puddings), well kept real ales, and a fine choice of malt whiskies and wines; cl Mon, 1st 2 wks Jan. **£13**|£5.50.

CARLTON SE0684 **Foresters Arms** *(01969) 640272* Friendly, carefully restored inn with log fires, low beams and a nice atmosphere; well kept real ales, a good choice of whiskies, imaginative food in both the bar and restaurant, and friendly, helpful service; good bdrms; no food pm Mon or Sun, 2 wks Jan; children over 12 in restaurant in evening. **£35**|£7.50.

CARTHORPE SE3083 **Fox & Hounds** *(01845) 567433* Pretty little extended village house with an extended bar, 2 log fires and some evocative Victorian photographs of Whitby; attractive, high-raftered, no smoking restaurant with lots of farm and smithy tools, imaginative food (fine daily specials and puddings), decent wines, and helpful service; cl Mon, 1st wk Jan; disabled access. **£15**|£7.95.

EAST WITTON SE1485 **Blue Lion** *(01969) 624273* Stylish and civilised dining pub with a log fire, daily papers, bric-à-brac, and rugs on the flagstones in the distinctive old rooms; exceptionally good and imaginative food, nice breakfasts, decent wines, real ales, and a pretty garden; bdrms; disabled access. **£36**|£7.

FERRENSBY SE3660 **General Tarleton** *Boroughbridge Rd (01423) 340284* Run by the same successful team as the Angel Inn (see *Hetton entry below*), this bustling 18th-c dining pub has 18th-c beams and open fires, a relaxed atmosphere, delicious food inc super puddings, polite service, and plenty of wines by the glass from a good list; cl 25 Dec; disabled access. **£38**|£8.

GRASSINGTON SE0064 **Dales Kitchen** *51 Main St (01756) 753208* Former apothecary's house (no smoking) with lovely cakes, scones and so forth, very good and imaginative light lunches, delicious puddings, and a children's menu; cl Christmas wk; disabled access. **£15**|£4.75.

GREAT OUSEBURN SE4461 **Crown** *(01423) 330430* Cheery and notably friendly village pub (where Ambrose Tiller started his Tiller Girls dancing troupe) and plenty of interest in the welcoming bar; with 2 no smoking, eating areas opening off, serving excellent, well presented food using home-grown herbs and salad, and well kept real ales. **£19.70**|£6.50.

HARROGATE SE3055 **La Bergerie** *11–13 Mount Parade (01423) 500089* Delightful, unassuming, French evening restaurant with freshly prepared and interesting food and very good French staff; cl Sun, 25–26 Dec; disabled access. **£20**.

HARROGATE SE3055 **Bettys** *1 Parliament St (01423) 502746* Famous cake shop run by the same Swiss family that started this small chain in 1919, with special blends of teas and coffees, Alsace wines, wonderful, light, home-cooked meals, and traditional afternoon teas; over 75 different delicious cakes and pastries; they also have 2 tearooms in York, one in Ilkley and one in Northallerton – same details apply to each; cl 25–26 Dec. **£20**|£4.30.

HARROGATE SE2955 **Bistro** *1 Montpellier Mews (01423) 530708* Busy little restaurant in a small mews, with Mediterranean-style décor, good modern cooking using worldwide influences, and mainly French wines; cl Sun, Mon, 1 wk Christmas; disabled access. **£25.95**|£4.50.

HARROGATE SE3055 **Tannin Level** *5 Raglan St (01423) 560595* Very nice basement wine bar with brick walls and country dining chairs; good, often French food, lovely puddings, a fine wine list, and early evening tapas; children allowed but not encouraged; cl Sun. **£22**|£7.50.

HARROGATE SE2954 **William & Victoria** *Cold Bath Rd (01423) 521510* Busy wine bar with an upstairs evening restaurant and hearty helpings of decent country cooking; cl Sun; children over 11. **£17.95**|£5.95.

HETTON SD9658 **Angel** *(01756) 730263* Extremely popular dining pub with old-fashioned, rambling rooms; consistently excellent and imaginative food, very good service from the hard-working, friendly staff, well kept real ales, and over 300 wines; cl 1 wk Jan; disabled access. **£33.75**|£8.50.

LITTON SD9073 **Queens Arms** *(01756) 770208* Welcoming, quietly placed 17th-c inn with popular food; a big collection of cigarette lighters in the main bar, another room with more of a family atmosphere, and 2 coal fires; no food Mon (exc bank hols); pretty bdrms; cl Jan. **£15**|£5.60.

MASHAM SE2280 **Floodlite** 7 *Silver St (01765) 689000* Bustling little candlelit restaurant with lots of bric-à-brac; particularly good, sound cooking using top local ingredients, with an emphasis on fish and game, lovely puddings, and a sizeable, fairly priced wine list; cl Mon, am Tues–Thurs, 2 wks Jan. **£20.57 dinner, £16.75 lunch.**
MIDDLEHAM SE1287 **Waterford House** *Kirkgate (01969) 622090* This most enjoyable restaurant with rooms, close to the market square, is filled with all sorts of antiques, has a friendly atmosphere, a superb wine list (they will offer you a glass from any of their 900 bottles), and delicious food using tip-top produce; bdrms (lovely breakfasts); **£24.50 for 4 courses**|£14.
MOULTON NZ2303 **Black Bull** *(01325) 377289* Decidedly civilised, well run pub with an old-fashioned style and standards of service; memorable bar snacks (excellent smoked salmon), conservatory restaurant or one in the Brighton Belle Pullman dining car, and good wines; cl Sun, 24–26 Dec; children over 7. **£30**|£5.
PICKHILL SE3483 **Nags Head** *(01845) 567391* Deservedly popular old inn with a nice mix of customers, a busy tap room and smarter lounge; a no smoking restaurant with particularly good food inc interesting daily specials and lovely puddings, friendly and efficient staff, a fine wine list and well kept real ales; bdrms; disabled access. **£21**|£4.95.
SAWLEY Sawley Arms *SE2568 (01765) 620642* Rather smart pub with absolutely stunning flowering tubs and baskets, several small rooms with log fires and comfortable furniture, and daily papers; a no smoking restaurant, good, enjoyable bar food (inc interesting soups), and nice house wines; children over 9. **£19.75**|£7.

North York Moors and East Yorkshire

Some classic and unusual places to visit; expansive countryside, interesting coast.

The North York Moors National Park has fewer visitors than the Dales: rich valley pastures, with red-tiled stone farmhouses, twisting rivers, quiet roads, and few villages. The higher moorland is generally very grand and empty, mile after mile of heather scoured by breath-snatching winds, where the few walkers have for company scatterings of hardy sheep and the occasional harsh cry of a grouse. Walkers are helped by the meticulously signed Cleveland Way around the Park's margins.

South of here are the gentle landscapes of the generously wooded Howardian Hills. In the east, the Wolds are quiet agricultural chalk country dissected by dry valleys, with wide views over huge corn fields. The bulk of the off-road walking is found on the well signed 79-mile Wolds Way from Hessle Haven down on the Humber to Filey Brigg on the coast, where it meets the Cleveland Way. Some of the lesser roads are a delight to walk on, with wide verges, good views and virtually no traffic. The B1249 and B1252 out of Driffield and B1253 west of Bridlington give drivers a good sampling (driving throughout this area is a pleasure).

The coast is splendidly cliffy and full of character north of the attractive resort of Scarborough (lots to see and do here), with some delightful little fishing villages. Bridlington is another attractive seaside resort, with a restrained charm and plenty of family amusements. Whitby is a working fishing port of real individuality – an enjoyable place to stay; Hull is a bigger port, but again has a lot to interest visitors.

The ruins of Rievaulx Abbey have a powerful appeal. Unusual experiences include Eden Camp just outside Malton, Beverley's surprisingly enjoyable army transport museum, the Hutton-le-Hole folk museum, the Skinningrove mining museum, and even llama-trekking in Staintondale. Castle Howard is one of England's most magnificent houses, and other great houses include Burton Agnes Hall, Sledmere House and Burton Constable Hall – all in splendid grounds. The Burnby Hall waterlilies are rather special in summer. Children have several good open farms and the Pickering steam railway, as well as the seaside resort amusements.

There are quite a few handsome villages (Coxwold is delightful), and pleasant small towns such as Helmsley and Beverley.

Where to stay

AMPLEFORTH SE5678 **Carr House Farm** *Shallowdale, Ampleforth, York YO6 4ED (01347) 868526* ***£35;** 3 rms. In peaceful undulating farmland and with an acre of garden, this no smoking, 16th-c stone farmhouse has beams and oak panelling, a flagstoned dining room with woodburner in the inglenook, a separate lounge, and good breakfasts using home-made butter and preserves and fresh farm eggs; cl Christmas and New Year; children over 7; no dogs.

BLAKEY RIDGE SE6799 **Lion** *Blakey Ridge, Pickering YO6 6LQ (01751) 417320* **£55,** plus winter breaks; 10 clean rms, most with own bthrm. The 4th highest inn in England, this has spectacular moorland views, characterful rambling bars, blazing fires (a good place to be snowed up in), and generous helpings of decent food served all day; also, good breakfasts, a candlelit restaurant, 8 real ales, and genuinely friendly licensees and staff; fine walking country; disabled access.

CHOP GATE SE5796 **Hillend Farm** *Chop Gate, Bilsdale, Middlesbrough TS9 7JR (01439) 798278* ***£42;** 2 rms. Friendly 17th-c farmhouse with good home cooking, a comfortable lounge and dining room, and fine walks; on the farm is part of one of the last remaining ancient oak forests; cl Nov–Mar.

COXWOLD SE5377 **Fauconberg Arms** *Coxwold, York YO6 4AD (01347) 868214* ***£55;** 4 rms. Civilised old stone inn in a lovely setting; big log fire, some handsome settles and gleaming copper in the 2 cosy and comfortably furnished rooms of the lounge bar, good food in both the restaurant and bar, an extensive wine list, and decent breakfasts.

EGTON BRIDGE NZ8004 **Horse Shoe** *Egton Bridge, Whitby YO21 1XE (01947) 895245* **£45,** plus special breaks; 6 simple rms, most with own bthrm. Beautifully placed inn by the River Esk (stepping stones big enough for children to sit on), lots of friendly wild birds, and a pleasant, sheltered lawn; open fires, attractive and traditionally furnished bars, well cooked food inc excellent breakfasts in the cottagey dining room, and decent wines; no accommodation 25 Dec.

ESCRICK SE6243 **Church Cottage** *Escrick, York YO4 6EX (01904) 728462* **£55;** 8 rms. Family-run guesthouse by the church, in 2 acres of lawn and woodland; with friendly owners, most attractively decorated rooms, and good breakfasts; cl Jan; disabled access.

FLAMBOROUGH TA2270 **Manor House** *Flamborough, Bridlington YO15 1PD (01262) 850943* **£60;** 2 rms, the more expensive room has a 17th-c four-poster. Beautifully restored Georgian house with a log fire and books in the guests' sitting room, lots of antiques (Mrs Berry is an antiques dealer), good breakfasts, and a friendly atmosphere; the old stable block has antiques and intricate, hand-knitted fishermen's sweaters called ganseys for sale; cl Christmas; children over 8.

HAROME SE6481 **Pheasant** *Harome, Helmsley YO6 5JG (01439) 771241* ***£80,** plus special breaks; 12 rms. Family-run hotel with a relaxed, homely lounge and a traditional bar with beams, inglenook fireplace and flagstones; good, very popular food, efficient service, and an indoor heated swimming pool; cl Dec–Feb; children over 10; disabled access.

HARTOFT END SE7592 **Blacksmiths Arms** *Hartoft End, Rosedale Abbey, Pickering YO18 8EN (01751) 417331* ***£70,** plus special breaks; 13 rms. Carefully extended and modernised former farmhouse in lovely surroundings at the foot of Rosedale; with a friendly, traditionally furnished bar, open fires in the cosy and comfortable lounges, and imaginative food in the spacious and attractive restaurant; lovely walks all round.

HAWNBY SE5690 **Laskill Farm** *Easterside, Hawnby, York YO6 5NB (01439) 798268* ***£50;** 4 rms, some in a beamy, converted outside building. Attractive and welcoming, creeper-covered stone house on a big sheep and cattle farm nr Rievaulx Abbey; open fire and books in the comfortable lounge, good food using home-grown produce, and their own natural spring water; self-catering also; cl 25 Dec; partial disabled access.

HELMSLEY SE6183 **Black Swan** *Market Pl, Helmsley YO6 5BJ (01439) 770466* **£120,** plus special breaks; 44 well equipped and comfortable rms. Striking Georgian house and adjoining Tudor rectory with a beamed and panelled hotel bar, attractive carved oak settles and Windsor armchairs, cosy and comfortable lounges with lots of character, and a charming, sheltered garden; disabled access.

HOVINGHAM SE6675 **Worsley Arms** *Hovingham, York YO6 4LA (01653) 628234* ***£80,** plus special breaks; 18 individually decorated bedrooms. Stone-built Georgian inn with comfortable and pretty sitting rooms, fresh flowers and open fires, and very good modern cooking in the elegant restaurant and more informal Cricketers Bistro; also, seats out by the stream; disabled access.

KILBURN SE5179 **Forresters Arms** *Kilburn, York YO6 4AH (01347) 868386* ***£58,** plus special breaks; 10 clean, bright rms. Friendly old coaching inn opposite the pretty village gardens; with sturdy but elegant furnishings made next door at the Thompson furniture workshop, a big log fire, and decent food in both the restaurant and beamed bar; disabled access.

KIRKBYMOORSIDE SE6986 **George & Dragon** *17 Market Pl, Kirkbymoorside, York YO6 6AA (01751) 433334* **£79,** plus special breaks; 19 large luxurious rms in a converted corn mill and former rectory behind. Handsome 17th-c coaching inn, very well run, with excellent food using the best local produce in the elegant restaurant, and a particularly fine choice of wines (the owner used to be a wine merchant) and whiskies; pretty, beamed residents' lounge, warm and friendly staff, log fire in the relaxed, beamed bar, well kept real ales, and peaceful gardens; activity breaks, too.

LASTINGHAM SE7390 **Lastingham Grange** *Lastingham, York YO6 6TH (01751) 417345* **£149,** plus special breaks; 12 rms. Attractive, stone-walled country house in 10 acres of neatly kept gardens and fields – with the moors beyond; relaxed and homely atmosphere in the spacious lounge, an open fire, fine breakfasts and dinners, extremely helpful service, and marvellous nearby walks; cl Dec–Feb.

MIDDLETON SE7887 **Cottage Leas Country Hotel** *Nova Lane, Middleton, Pickering YO18 8PN (01751) 472129* **£74,** plus special breaks; 12 comfortable rms. Delightful 18th-c farmhouse with extensive gardens; comfortable and informal rooms, beamed ceilings, an open log fire in the cosy lounge, and a snug bar; pets by prior arrangement; partial disabled access.

MONK FRYSTON SE5029 **Monk Fryston Hall** *Monk Fryston, Leeds LS25 5DU (01977) 682369* **£98.50,** plus special breaks; 30 comfortable rms. Grand manor house in attractive grounds; with antiques, log fires and fresh flowers in the oak-panelled bar and lounge, friendly staff, and good food in the original manor house dining room; disabled access.

NAFFERTON TA0559 **Wold House** *Nafferton, Driffield YO25 0LD (01377)*

254242 **£55;** 6 rms. Informal and comfortable, early 19th-c country house with panoramic views, friendly service, and traditional English cooking; outdoor pool, putting green, and snooker; cl Christmas.

PICKERING SE7983 **White Swan** *Market Pl, Pickering YO18 7AA (01751) 472288* **£70,** plus special breaks; 12 comfortable rms. Inviting, small and quiet, plush hotel bar, friendly staff and locals, log fires, and antiques in the comfortable, beamed, residents' lounge; good, traditional bar food, attractive restaurant with fine clarets and daily changing food using the best local produce, and breakfasts with home-made marmalade; pets welcome.

ROBIN HOOD'S BAY NZ9504 **Coble** *Covet Hill, Robin Hood's Bay YO22 4SN (01947) 880042* **£38,** plus special breaks; 3 rms, 1 with own shower. 17th-c former coastguard's cottage by the beach, with views over the bay from both the lounge and sun terrace; warm, friendly and caring owners, and huge, first-class breakfasts (8 courses); good nearby walks.

ROBIN HOOD'S BAY NZ9405 **Rounton House** *Mount Pleasant South, Robin Hood's Bay, Whitby YO22 4PD (01947) 880341* **£30;** 3 rms, shared bthrm. Big, friendly, family Victorian house with homely rooms, a relaxed atmosphere, and good breakfasts served at one big table in the dining room; pleasant garden with summerhouse; cl Dec–Jan; well behaved dogs allowed.

ROSEDALE ABBEY SE7296 **Milburn Arms** *Rosedale Abbey, Pickering YO18 8RA (01751) 417312* **£76,** plus special breaks; 11 rms. Friendly 18th-c inn in a village surrounded by fine steep moorland; log fire and books in the comfortable drawing room, traditionally furnished beamed bar, very good English cooking in the attractive restaurant, decent wine list, excellent breakfasts, and helpful staff; cl 18–28 Jan; pets by prior arrangement.

ROSEDALE ABBEY SE7294 **White Horse Farm Hotel** *Rosedale Abbey, Pickering YO18 8SE (01751) 417239* **£75,** plus special breaks; 15 rms. Friendly country hotel, above the village, in 11 acres, with marvellous views; cosy beamed bar with log fire, a comfortable lounge, generously served food, and a decent range of wines and malt whiskies; excellent walks; cl 24–25 Dec; dogs by prior arrangement.

SCARBOROUGH TA0191 **Wrea Head** *Scalby, Scarborough YO13 0PP (01723) 378211* **£115,** plus special breaks; 20 individually decorated rms. Victorian country house in 14 acres of parkland and gardens; with friendly staff, a minstrels' gallery in the oak-panelled hall and lounge, open fires, a bow-windowed library, pretty flowers, and good food in the airy restaurant; disabled access.

WASS SE5579 **Wombwell Arms** *Wass, York YO6 4BE (01347) 868280* **£49,** plus special breaks; 2 individually furnished rms. Attractive, warmly welcoming small inn with a cosy rambling bar, good, imaginative food and decent wines in the comfortable dining rooms (2 are no smoking), and enjoyable breakfasts; cl 2 wks Jan; children over 8.

WHARRAM LE STREET SE8666 **Red House** *Wharram le Street, Malton YO17 9TL (01944) 768455* ***£52,** plus special breaks; 3 rms. Spacious and comfortable, no smoking, country house with friendly owners; log fires in the sitting rooms, good home cooking in the dining room (using home-grown produce where possible), and a lovely garden with tennis court; cl Christmas wk; pets welcome.

WILLERBY TA0230 **Willerby Manor** *Well Lane, Willerby, Hull HU10 6ER (01482) 652616* **£97;** 51 individually decorated rms. Family-owned Victorian house in 3 acres of gardens, with an airy and attractive conservatory dining bar and a more formal restaurant; good food, helpful service, and a health club; cl 25 Dec.

To see and do

❀ ♈ **ACKLAM** NZ4915 **Nature's World** (Ladgate Lane) Thriving environmental demonstration centre, developing all the time, with organic gardens, nature trails, and re-created natural habitats (moorland, wetlands, etc.) under construction. Splendid home-cooked meals and snacks, shop, disabled access; cl 25 Dec; (01642) 594895; £3 (less in winter).

★ ⌂ **BECK HOLE** NZ8202 Charming tucked-away village; Birch Hall here is a unique cross between country tavern and village store. The most rewarding way to get here is walking along the **historic rail trail** on the abandoned line that preceded the current North Yorkshire Moors Railway route, between Grosmont and Goathland.

BEMPTON CLIFFS TA1973 The RSPB **bird reserve** here has England's biggest colony of seabirds – up to a quarter of a million of them nesting in the cliffs. Best views of puffins Jun–July, but plenty of skuas and shearwaters later in summer, with weekend **boat trips** from Flamborough (North Landing) or Bridlington, though what you'll see depends on the weather. Snacks, some disabled access; visitor centre cl all Jan, wknds Dec and Feb; (01262) 851179 – book well ahead for the boats; *£2.50 car parking charge. Local fishermen run early summer weekend boats to the cliffs too.

★ † **BEVERLEY** TA0339 An attractive country town, in a way like a small-scale York, with much the same sort of appeal. It's partly pedestrianised, with many fine Georgian buildings, several antique shops and the like, but unlike York is still a market town rather than a tourist place. Up to 1,000 animals, mainly pigs, are still sold at the Tues and Thurs market, and the racecourse is central to local life. **Beverley Minster** Wonderful 12th–14th-c building, with elegant buttressing and elaborately pinnacled towers. The west front is richly carved yet extraordinarily harmonious. Inside are several delights, inc the intricately carved Percy tomb canopy, the unusual Saxon *fridstol* (one of only two in the country), and the biggest collection of misericords in Britain. Shop, disabled access; guided tours summer only; £1 suggested donation. **St Mary's Church** (Hengate) The town's former wealth can be guessed at from the magnificence of this subsidiary church not far from the Minster; the weather-vane on the south-west turret is said to have been the last design by Pugin, who sketched it on the back of an envelope. Opposite is the White Horse, a quaint, old, gaslit, bare-boarded tavern. The comfortably traditional Beverley Arms and cheap Queen's Head are good for lunch. **Museum of Army Transport** (Flamingate) Huge hangar with all sorts of military vehicles inc planes, tanks and cars, many displayed in realistic settings – down to farm-building camouflage for the Second World War and scratchy sand for the Gulf War. Children can climb into the jeeps and so on. Some vehicles may be demonstrated on summer Suns. Meals, snacks, shop, disabled access; cl 24–26 Dec; (01482) 860445; £4. **Beverley Art Gallery and Museum** (Champney Rd) Includes lots of pieces by Fred Elwell the woodcarver, most famous for his work in the Minster (cl 12.30–1.30pm wknds, all Mon and Tues, 25–26 Dec, 1 Jan; free). The B1248 N has rolling Wolds views. **Beverley Guildhall** (Register Sq) Parts of this mainly Georgian building are open, although changes are afoot and they were unable to give us specific opening times as we went to press; phone (01482) 884471.

★ **BLACKTOFT** SE8424 Attractive Humber-side village; the Hope & Anchor, with tables out by the water, is great for bird watchers, being right by the **RSPB marsh reserve**.

† ! ⌂ **BRIDLINGTON** TA1767 Famous for its bracing image in the heyday of the traditional seaside resort, and the way the country rolls down to the long sands of the shore still gives that feeling. The centre is a quay and small harbour, with the usual summer attractions, but the original core of the town is half a mile in from the sea, with some charming old houses among the more modern ones around the heavily restored **priory church**. A 14th-c gateway gives some idea of how imposing the priory must have been before the Dissolution, and now houses a local history museum (open Tues–Thurs, Jun–mid-Sept; £1.50). **Harbour Museum and Aquarium**

(Harbour Rd) The best place to find out about the town's seafaring heritage; shop, disabled access; cl 25 Dec; (01262) 670148; 40p. **Sewerby Hall** (NE edge) In spacious coastal parkland, with a miniature zoo and aviary (good for children), and a charming garden. The elegant, early 18th-c house has some Amy Johnson memorabilia – the pioneer aviator lived nearby. Snacks, shop, disabled access (but not to the Hall); grounds open daily all year, house open Mar–mid-Jan, though only Sat–Tues out of season; (01262) 673769; £2.80. **Bondville Model Village** (Riviera Drive, Sewerby) Readers enjoy this; disabled access; cl Oct–Apr; (01262) 401736; *£2.50. A walk along the low cliff from here towards Flamborough Head soon brings you to a strip of woodland by a stream; the lane up from here past the car park and along the wood leads to Iron Age earthworks which cut right across the head – making it a pretty impressive defensive position. Broadacres (A165) has reliable family food inc a carvery. The coast to the S is generally much flatter. **Park Rose Pottery** (Carnaby Covert Lane, off the A614 SW) Factory visits and a seconds shop, also 12 acres of strollable parkland with play areas, an owl sanctuary and a new bee exhibition. Meals, snacks, shop, disabled access; cl Christmas wk; (01262) 602823; site entry free, owl sanctuary £1.75, £1.25 per child for play areas. **John Bull's World of Rock** (Carnaby Industrial Estate, off the A614) See how they squeeze the words into the candy, and maybe even personalise your own stick of the seaside favourite. Cl winter wknds, Christmas; (01262) 678525; £1 factory and exhibition.

† **BOLTON PERCY** SE5341 Behind its medieval gatehouse the 15th-c church has a most unusual **churchyard**: over 15 years ago local lecturer Roger Brook set about tackling its profusion of weeds, and since then has transformed it into a splendidly colourful garden, with more than a thousand different types of plant creeping around and over the headstones. Rather like a semi-wild cottage garden, it houses part of the National Collection of dicentra. Open all the time, with regular open days to find out more; (01904) 744213 for dates. The Crown has generous, simple food (not Mon or Tues).

★ **BROMPTON** SE9582 **Wordsworth Gallery** (Gallows Hill) The former home of Mary Hutchinson, who married William Wordsworth at Brompton Church in 1802. The medieval barn has an exhibition on the poet and Samuel Coleridge, as well as an exhibition of paintings and prints. Meals, snacks, shop; cl Mon exc bank hols; (01723) 863298; free. The village is pretty, and the Cayley Arms does good food.

★ † **BUGTHORPE** SE7757 Attractive village, especially in spring, with an interesting **church**.

† **BURTON AGNES HALL** TA1063 Marvellous, richly decorated Elizabethan house, with a fantastically carved Great Hall, 16th-c antiques, and some splendid Impressionist paintings. A fine woodland garden has colourful borders, a pets corner and a topiary walk to an orangery. Meals, snacks, shop, disabled access to ground floor only; cl Nov–Mar; (01262) 490324; £4. Between here and the church is the earlier Norman manor house. Nearby Kilham's attractive **church** has a memorable Norman door; the 18th-c Bell in Driffield is pleasant for lunch.

BURTON CONSTABLE HALL TA1836 (N of Sproatley) The wonderful exterior gives away this delightful house's Elizabethan origins, but the inside was extravagantly remodelled in the 18th c. Around 30 beautifully preserved rooms to see, with a sweeping long gallery and some intriguing collections. Capability Brown landscaped the 200 acres, and there's a riding centre in the stables. Teas, shop, disabled access to ground floor only; cl am, all Fri, and Nov–Easter; (01964) 562400; £4. Camping, caravanning and seasonal fishing. The Cock & Bell down at Preston does good-value lunches.

BYLAND ABBEY SE5478 Jagged ruins of this 12th/13th-c Cistercian abbey. Enough detail survives to show how fine it must have been, inc well preserved floor tiles and carved stone. Good for picnics. Snacks, shop, some

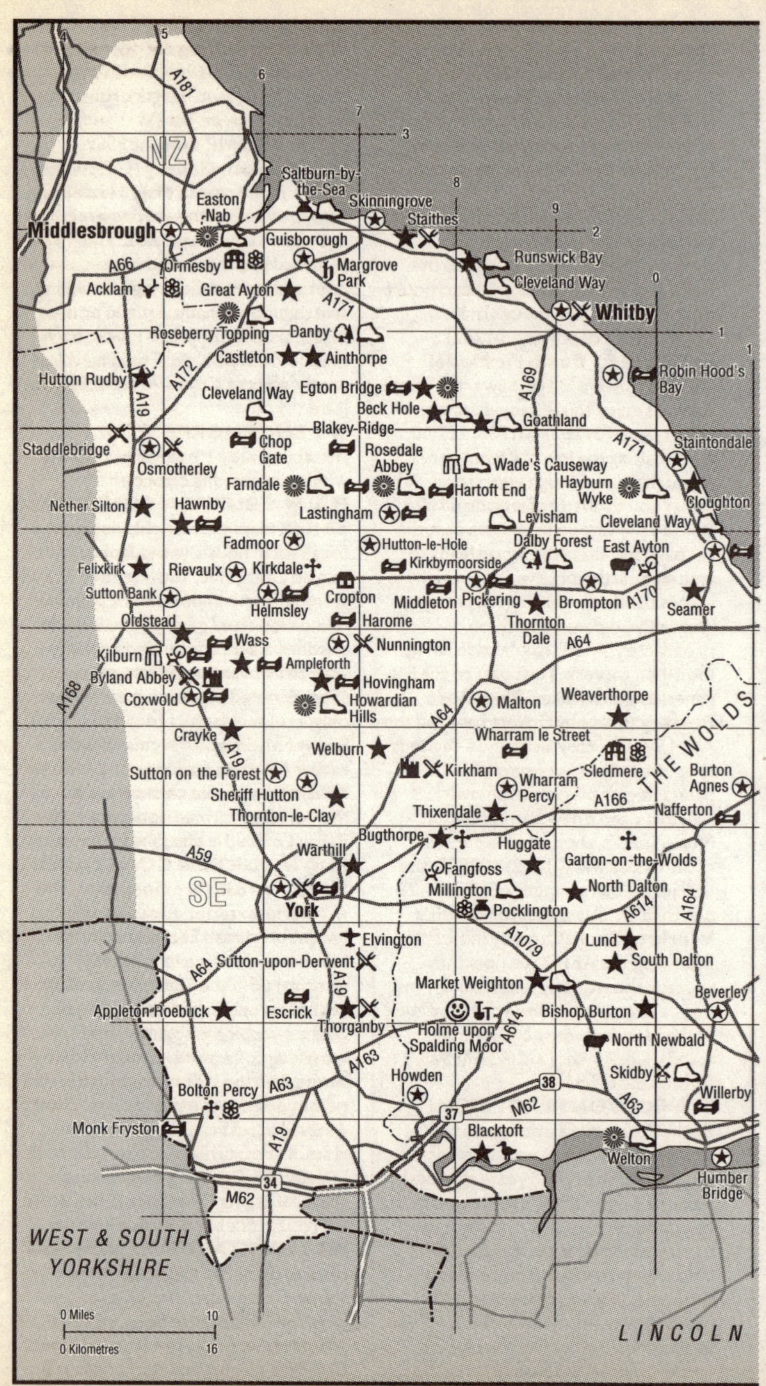
NZ
Saltburn-by-the-Sea
Skinningrove
Staithes
Easton Nab
Middlesbrough
Guisborough
Ormesby
Margrove Park
Runswick Bay
Cleveland Way
Whitby
Acklam
Great Ayton
A171
A66
Roseberry Topping
Danby
Castleton
Ainthorpe
Hutton Rudby
A172
A19
Cleveland Way
Egton Bridge
Beck Hole
Goathland
A169
Robin Hood's Bay
Blakey Ridge
Chop Gate
Rosedale Abbey
Staddlebridge
Osmotherley
Wade's Causeway
A171
Staintondale
Farndale
Hartoft End
Hayburn Wyke
Cloughton
Nether Silton
Hawnby
Lastingham
Levisham
Cleveland Way
Fadmoor
Hutton-le-Hole
Dalby Forest
East Ayton
Felixkirk
Rievaulx
Kirkdale
Kirkbymoorside
Sutton Bank
Helmsley
Cropton
Middleton
Pickering
Brompton
A170
Seamer
Thornton Dale
Oldstead
Harome
Wass
Nunnington
A64
Kilburn
Ampleforth
Byland Abbey
Hovingham
Coxwold
Howardian Hills
Malton
Weaverthorpe
A168
Crayke
A64
Wharram le Street
THE WOLDS
A19
Welburn
Sledmere
Kirkham
Sutton on the Forest
Wharram Percy
Burton Agnes
Sheriff Hutton
A166
Thornton-le-Clay
Thixendale
Nafferton
Bugthorpe
Huggate
Garton-on-the-Wolds
A59
Warthill
Fangfoss
Millington
North Dalton
SE
York
Pocklington
A614
A164
Elvington
A1079
Lund
Sutton-upon-Derwent
South Dalton
A64
A19
Market Weighton
Beverley
Appleton Roebuck
Escrick
Thorganby
Holme upon Spalding Moor
A614
Bishop Burton
North Newbald
A163
Howden
Skidby
Bolton Percy
A63
38
A63
Willerby
Monk Fryston
37
M62
A19
Blacktoft
Welton
Humber Bridge
34
M62
WEST & SOUTH YORKSHIRE
0 Miles 10
0 Kilometres 16
LINCOLN

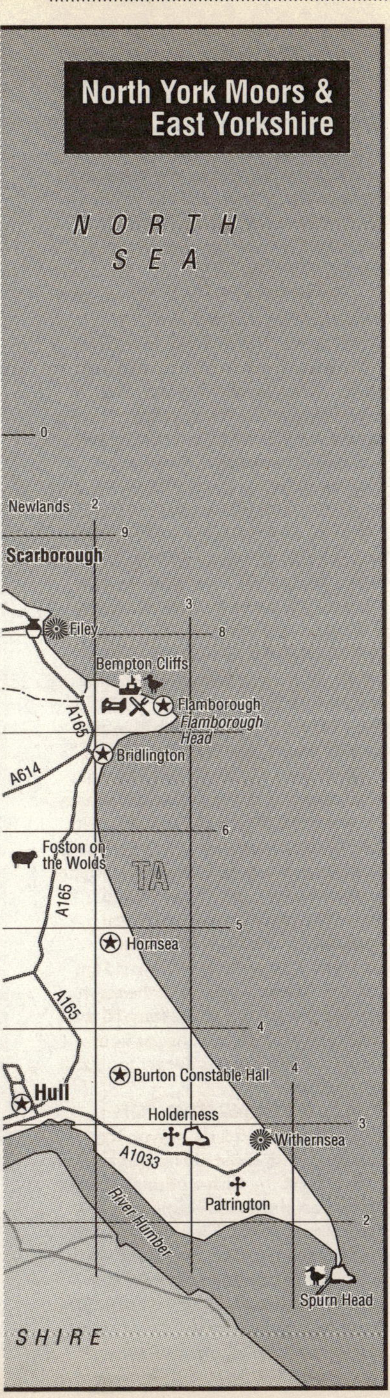

disabled access; cl Nov–Mar; (01347) 868614; £1.50. The nearby Abbey Inn is enjoyable for lunch. The drive past here from Bagby (SE of Thirsk), Kilburn and Coxwold, and on via Wass and Ampleforth to Oswaldkirk is very attractive.

CLEVELAND WAY NZ8215 Along the coast this well marked, long-distance path is consistently interesting – and so much more rewarding than the immediate hinterland that there-and-back walks keeping to the Way itself are more fun than trying to work out circular walks heading inland. A bus service is useful for the section linking Whitby, Robin Hood's Bay and Scarborough. A fine section can be reached off the B1257 N of Chop Gate (where the Buck does good food): the path westwards, on the N slopes of the moors, takes in rocky outcrops.

★ † **COXWOLD** SE5377 Neat and attractive, little stone-built village, very harmonious. Laurence Sterne's quaint **Shandy Hall** has been well restored, the little study much as it must have been when he wrote *Tristram Shandy* here. Outside is a lovely walled garden. Shop with unusual plant sales; open Jun–Sept, house pm Weds and Sun, gardens daily exc Sat; (01347) 868465; £3. Close by is the attractive 15th-c **church** of which Sterne was curate, with the box pews it had in his day. The Fauconberg Arms does good food. **Newburgh Priory** (just S) Charming old house, partly Norman with Tudor and Georgian additions. One of the family married Oliver Cromwell's daughter, who is supposed to have rescued her father's headless corpse and had it reburied here; the room with the tomb is on the tour. Outside, a 40-acre lakeside and riverside garden has a fine collection of dogwoods, splendid formal borders and lots of unusual plants. Snacks; open pm Weds and Sun Apr–Jun and Sun and Mon Aug bank hol wknd; (01347) 868435; £3.50, grounds only £1.50.

CROPTON BREWERY SE7588 The small, family-run brewery has guided tours on the hour 10am–4pm summer (phone for winter times), and samples of their robustly flavoured beers, as well as a children's treasure hunt, and good adjacent pub, the New Inn; disabled access to ground floor; (01751) 417330; £2.50. They sell local walks leaflets.

DALBY FOREST SE8789 The eastern part of the National Park has large forest plantations; this area has colour-coded trails.

DANBY NZ7108 **Moors Centre** (Lodge Lane) Helpful National Park information centre, with exhibitions, guided walks and events, and an adventure playground; terraced riverside and woodland grounds. Meals, snacks, shop, disabled access to ground floor only; cl wkdys Oct–Easter and Christmas; (01287) 660540; free. The area has decent **horse riding** centres, for experts and beginners; the Moors Centre has the full list, and numbers for the area's **cycle hire** firms. The Duke of Wellington has good-value food.

EAST AYTON SE9985 **Honey Farm** (Betton Farm Centre) Exhaustive exhibition on bees and honey-making, with sales of wax and honey-based products. Also animals, craft shops, farm shop and a play area. Meals, snacks, shop, disabled access; (01723) 864001; £2.95. The Londesborough Arms at Seamer has decent food, and the Forge Valley drive to Hackness runs through ancient woodlands.

★ **EGTON BRIDGE** NZ8005 Charming Eskdale village, pleasantly eccentric, twinned with a fictional French one; lovely Esk views, good riverside pub.

✝ **ELVINGTON** SE6748 **Yorkshire Air Museum** Part of a World War II airfield and base preserved as it was then, with fine aircraft, an old control tower and plenty of other memorabilia inc a Halifax Mk III, engines, models and photographs. Meals, snacks, shop, disabled access; open daily in summer, best to check in winter; (01904) 608595; *£4. The St Vincent Arms at Sutton-upon-Derwent is good for lunch.

ESTON NAB NZ5618 Outside the National Park, this gives walkers a massive view over industrial Teesside.

★ ✝ **FADMOOR** SE6789 Attractive village with a good pub, on a charming drive from Kirkbymoorside, on over Rudland Slack and past Cockayne to Helmsley. The graveyard of nearby **Gillamoor church** SE6890 gives a classic view of interlocking moor and valley landscapes.

FANGFOSS SE7653 **Rocking Horse Shop** Splendid collection of antique rocking horses; you can watch replicas being made, and buy either a finished horse or plans for doing it yourself. Open by appointment (not Sun), (01759) 368737.

FARNDALE SE6697 The largest dale in the National Park, with characteristic North York Moors scenery – lush green fields and red-roofed, yellow stone houses beneath the brooding moorland plateau. It's famous for its miles of wild daffodils in Apr, introduced and naturalised here many centuries ago. They're at their best around Low Mill, and any walk to enjoy them gives the chance of coming back down the ancient green lane of Rudland Rigg, for spectacular views. The friendly Feversham Arms at Church Houses, by the daffodil reserve, does good-value food.

★ **FELIXKIRK** SE4684 Attractive village, with a good drive to Kepwith and Nether Silton; nice pub.

FILEY TA1180 Much quieter seaside resort than Scarborough, its neighbour up the coast, with the main road dropping down a steep little valley between the church and the old town (and under a footbridge linking the two) to the beach, where fishermen still haul up their boats. There's a small and attractively homely, summer local **museum** in medieval fishermen's cottages (Queen St; cl 1–2pm and am Sat; £1). The rock reef N of the town beyond the sands is interesting; to the S are holiday camps, and the seafront Coble Landing Bar has decent food and great views.

✝ **FLAMBOROUGH** TA2270 A blowy place, high on the headland, with some old houses at its core around the 15th-c **church**; down below past the holiday camp, the natural rock harbour is well sheltered, with a lifeboat station, and there are fine views of coast and sea from the point of the headland, by the lighthouse. Flamborough Marine sell a local version of guernseys, weatherproof 'ganseys', hand-knitted in the round. The Seabirds is good for lunch, and the B1259 and B1229 are the most interesting coast roads. There is some quite exciting walking, particularly around the N side of Flamborough Head, with the cacophony of thousands of kittiwakes sounding within the inlets; puffins can sometimes be seen on rock ledges. A level mile and a half from the lighthouse along clifftops leads to North Landing (café and car park). A longer walk making the Head the midway point starts from Flamborough village, skirting fields to join the coastal path; to avoid anticlimax, walk the southern cliffs first and keep the real drama for later on. To the N, the path follows the coast closely nearly all the way, and hilly country coming right to the coast makes for interest.

FOSTON ON THE WOLDS TA0855 **Cruckley Farm** Friendly working farm, with lots of animals to fuss over – inc some very strange-looking rare breeds. Daily milking displays (usually around 10.45am). Snacks, shop, disabled access; cl Oct–Apr; (01262) 488337; £2.75. The Trout at Wansford has decent food.

† **GARTON-ON-THE-WOLDS CHURCH** SE9859 12th c, and very High Church inside, with 19th-c mosaics and frescoes.

★ **GOATHLAND** NZ8301 In the heart of the moors, the picturesque setting for TV's *Heartbeat*; filming has been rather intrusive, as have the coachloads of tourists in its wake, but there are interesting walks from here, inc the short one from opposite the church to **Mallyan Spout**, a waterfall which tumbles into a fine, wooded, smooth-rocked gorge. The Mallyan Spout Hotel does popular food.

★ **GUISBOROUGH** NZ6116 **Gisborough Priory** 14th-c ruined church, one huge window rising dramatically from the rest of the more or less foundation-level ruins. The gatehouse is fairly well preserved, and it's an atmospheric spot for a picnic. Shop; cl Mon Oct–Mar, 24 Dec–1 Jan; 80p. The Fox nearby has decent food, and the market town has attractive corners. Out at Newton NZ5713 (A173), the King's Head is a popular dining pub below Roseberry Topping viewpoint.

★ **HAWNBY** SE5489 Attractive village, on the very scenic Rievaulx Abbey–Osmotherley road; good pub.

HAYBURN WYKE TA0096 From the well sited hotel here (good-value Sun carvery), steep Victorian woodland paths wind down to a cliff-sheltered cove; a clifftop path to the S gives fine views.

★ **HELMSLEY** SE6184 Lanes run straight up on to the moors from this attractive small market town (the B1257 is one of the best moorland roads, and the lane at SE6188, a bit more than a mile N of Carlton, gives a classic view of the contrasting moor and valley landscapes). There's a large cobbled square (busy Fri market), and enough antique shops and craft shops to please a visitor without seeming too touristy. A lively and bustling place, with a lot of class. **Helmsley Castle** This 12th-c pile, ruined in 1644, stands within enormous earthworks and dominates the town; good for picnics. Shop; cl 1–2pm, winter Mon and Tues, 24–26 Dec; (01439) 770442; £2.20. **Duncombe Park** Beautifully restored, early 18th-c house, rebuilt after a fire at the turn of this century. The landscaped gardens, with grand terracing, are magnificent, covering around a tenth of the 300 acres of memorable parkland. Meals, snacks, shop, some disabled access; cl winter, best to phone for opening times; (01439) 770213; *£5.75, gardens only £3.50. You can wander through the estate (recently granted nature reserve status) for £2. A rewarding and very varied drive is past Rievaulx Abbey, Old Byland and Cold Kirby to Sutton Bank, left along the A170 then next right turn to Kilburn, Coxwold, Byland Abbey and back via Ampleforth and Oswaldkirk.

† **HOLDERNESS** TA3029 The area between the Wolds, Humber and coast is flat: rich farming country with huge fields and not many buildings, though the fine village churches often with soaring towers or spires reflect the wealth that this fertile land has put into them in the past. The long southern stretch of coast is flat country too, without a great deal of appeal for walkers – except for long, lonely, off-season walks by the edge of the North Sea.

HOLME UPON SPALDING MOOR SE7838 **Major Bridge Park** (Selby Rd) Private collection of working rural equipment, small rare breeds farm and vintage fairground rides (you can go on these), with surrounding nature trails. Snacks, disabled access; open Thurs and Sun May–Sept, daily (exc Sat) in Aug; (01430) 860992; *£1.50. The Red Lion has good food.

HORNSEA TA2145 Sizeable resort with one of the area's most visited attractions, **Hornsea Freeport** (Rolston Rd), a developing leisure centre based around a factory shopping village. Several well known brands and stores (some good bargains), and family features such as butterflies, a model village, a birds of prey centre and an adventure playground. Meals, snacks, shop, disabled access; cl 25–26 Dec; (01964) 534211; site free, £3 for family attractions. Next door is well established, working **Hornsea Pottery**. **Hornsea Museum** (Newbegin) Enthusiastic museum with regular craft demonstrations; cl Nov–Easter; (01964) 533443; *£2. Behind the town, Hornsea Mere, 2 miles long, is the biggest natural lake in this area, with herons and other birds.

★ **HOVINGHAM** SE6675 Attractive village, with a good pub and a pleasant drive S to Sheriff Hutton and Flaxton.

HOWARDIAN HILLS SE6575 A path along the N flank of these gentle generously wooded hills gives intermittent rather patrician views across the plain to the North York Moors.

★ † **HOWDEN** SE7428 Unpretentiously attractive, with cobbled alleys, a fine market hall, majestic **minster** with a tall tower, the ruins of a charming medieval chapter house, and a small marshland country park, down the lane opposite the minster, with ponds and raised walkways. The White Horse is useful for lunch.

★ **HUGGATE** SE8855 Attractive village, with a nice pub and easy walks nearby.

HULL TA1028 Kingston-upon-Hull is the full name of this big port, surprisingly pleasant for visitors now that the former docks have been so well tidied up. The landing stage for the former Humber ferry is now an attractive pedestrian enclave with some solid, well restored Georgian buildings, and pleasing Humber views from the waterfront Minerva (which brews its own beer). Nearby, the original dock has become a yacht marina, with buoyant modern buildings around it. Princes Quay is now a smart shopping centre (with good-value food in the Mission, a converted seamen's mission over in Posterngate). Away from the water, some of the most ancient buildings in the narrow streets of the old town have survived, notably on the High St. One of the most delightful old buildings is the Olde Whyte Harte just off Silver St; it was in its heavily panelled upper room that the town's governor made the fateful decision to lock the town's gate against King Charles in 1642, depriving him of the arsenal that might otherwise have let him win the Civil War. The old town and former docks are separated from each other by good main roads through to the modern container and ferry docks; the traffic just sweeps by, leaving them as self-contained islands – very quiet at weekends.

Hull's enjoyable museums are mostly concentrated in the old town, so it's easy to walk from one to another. **Hull Maritime Museum** (Queen Victoria Sq) This massive yet solidly stylish 3-domed Victorian building has good displays on Hull's maritime history. There's a long-established section on whales and whaling, and the huge skeletons on display were mentioned in *Moby Dick*. Shop, disabled access; cl am Sun; (01482) 613902; £1. **Wilberforce House** (High St) William Wilberforce was born in this 17th-c house, and its Jacobean and Georgian rooms have a interesting exploration of the horrors of the slave trade and the struggle for its abolition; also a notable collection of dolls; cl am Sun, 25 Dec, 1 Jan, Good Fri; (01482) 613921; £1. The Olde Black Boy nearby was the site of slave auctions. **Ferens Art Gallery** (Queen Victoria Sq) Enterprisingly run general collection, with lots of maritime paintings and Dutch old masters; particularly strong on Frank Brangwyn. Snacks, shop, disabled access; cl am Sun, 25 Dec, 1 Jan; (01482) 613902; *£1. **Museum of Transport** (High St) Recently doubled in size, this expanding collection is devoted mainly to local public transport and bicycles, some weird and wonderful, with a few interactive displays inc the new Streetlife exhibition. Snacks, shop, disabled access; cl am Sun, 24–26 Dec; (01482) 613902; £1. **Hull and East Riding Museum** (High St) Fine mosaics and a new medieval section; cl am Sun, 25 Dec, 1 Jan; (01482) 613902; *£1. **Old Grammar School: Hands-on History** (South Church Side) Expanding social history collection; open wknds and school hols (exc am Sun); *£1. **Spurn Lightship** (Princes Dock, Marina) Operating from the 1920s to the 1970s – interesting to go below decks and imagine being confined to this for weeks at a time, not going anywhere, tossed about in storms or blanketed in fog; usually open Apr–Sept, daily exc am Sun, but as we went to press the ship was cl for dry-dock work so best to check; (01482) 613902; *£1. **Maister House** (High St) Only the staircase and entrance hall are open in this mid-18th-c rebuilding (the rest is still used as offices), but the Palladian staircase is splendid, and the doors ornate and finely carved. Cl wknds and bank hols; 80p; NT. **Water Museum** (Springhead Ave) Its main feature is a beam engine that in its day could raise about a million litres of water an hour from the well below. Shop, limited disabled access; open pm Fri–Sun, cl Dec; (01482) 652283; free.

HUMBER BRIDGE TA0224 The world's longest single-span suspension bridge, nearly a mile between the towers, and a very impressive sweep of engineering (there's a footway across as well as the road). At the N end, the **Humber Bridge Country Park** has woodland and clifftop walks, and an old mill. Meals, snacks, shop, good disabled access; (01482) 640852; free.

★ **HUTTON-LE-HOLE** SE7090 Neat and pretty streamside village at the mouth of Farndale; sheep wander the streets – though they won't be alone in the summer months. Its excellent 2-acre **folk museum** is practically a village itself – old buildings from the area re-erected here, inc an Elizabethan manor house, gypsy caravan, and an Edwardian photographic studio; craft demonstrations most Sat–Weds. Shop, disabled access; cl Nov–Mar; (01751) 417367; £3. The Crown is useful for lunch. There's a pleasant walk (an hour or so) over to Lastingham, and the Blakey Ridge road to Castleton is a great drive with classic moorland views.

KILBURN SE5179 This quiet village is home to the Robert Thompson **furniture workshop**, famous for the unobtrusive little mouse carved as a trademark that you'll see all over North Yorks, on church pews and in the better inns and pubs. A visitor centre traces the company history, and you can watch the craftsmen at work. Shop; cl Mon (exc bank hols and Jun–Sept), and Nov–Mar; (01347) 868218; £1.50. They make lovely simple furniture – though not cheap (for a wider choice you might try the Old Mill at nearby Balk, where the craftsmen include an ex-Thompson employee and prices seem lower). The oak they use can be seen all around. Nr the church (with a memorial to Thompson carved by his own craftsmen), the Singing Bird does refreshments, as does the Forresters Arms – full of Thompson work. Above the village, on Roulston Scar, is a **white horse** cut in the turf in 1857 and unique in this part of the country.

† **KIRKDALE CHURCH** SE6686 Saxon, with a unique sundial, and 7th-c Celtic crosses and carved stones.

KIRKHAM PRIORY SE7366 Augustinian priory remains in an attractive quiet spot by the River Derwent; finely sculpted lavatorium, graceful arcaded cloister, and a handsome 13th-c gatehouse with some neatly carved sculptures and shields. Snacks, shop, disabled access; open Easter–Sept; (01653) 618768; £1.50. The Stone Trough overlooking the ruins is good for lunch, and a pleasant path meanders S by a placid stretch of the river, to Howsham Bridge and beyond.

★ † ❋ ⌂ **LASTINGHAM** SE7290 Attractive village, with a former **monastery**, once one of the area's most sacred spots of pilgrimage, with an outstanding 11th-c crypt. The hillside just S gives a classic North Yorks Moors view, and there's a pleasant hour's walk over to Hutton-le-Hole.

⌂ **LEVISHAM** SE8390 A good spot for walkers, with open scenery around it, a track across the blustery moors, and an attractive valley giving separate routes to and from the Hole of Horcum, just below the A169.

MALTON SE7270 **Castle Howard** (off the A64 W of Malton) Quite magnificent 18th-c palace designed by Sir John Vanbrugh, who till then had no architectural experience, but went on to create Blenheim Palace. The striking 90-metre (300-ft) long façade is topped with a marvellous painted and gilded dome, an unforgettable sight beyond the lake as you approach from the N. Splendid apartments, sculpture gallery and long gallery (192ft long to be exact), a glorious chapel with Burne-Jones stained glass, beautiful paintings inc a Holbein portrait of Henry VIII. The impressive grounds are inviting, inc Vanbrugh's domed Temple of the Four Winds, a beautiful rose garden and the family mausoleum designed by Hawksmoor. Also a fantastic collection of period costume, and a good unobtrusive adventure playground. The palace celebrates its tercentenary in 1999 with special displays and events. Meals, snacks, shop, disabled access; cl Nov–mid-Mar; (01653) 648333; £7. A grand public road runs through the grounds, from Slingsby on the B1257; the vast estate is threaded by a few public footpaths which gain glimpses of the great house and the landscaped parts of its grounds. There's decent food at the Bay Horse at Terrington.

Eden Camp (A64/A169 N) Elaborately re-created wartime scenes in a former prisoner-of-war camp, very well done with sounds, smells and even smoke effects. Covers a wide range of World War II experiences, from the rise of the Nazis to the Blitz and Bomber Command ops room. There's a children's commando assault course, but it's perhaps the wartime generation that will get most out of the place. Meals and snacks in NAAFI, shop, disabled access; cl 24 Dec–12 Jan; (01653) 697777; £3.50. **Eden Farm** (Ryton rd, Old Malton) Working farm with animals, trails, a working gin wheel and combine harvester, and daily dog, duck and parrot shows. Snacks, shop, disabled access; cl Sat, and Nov–Mar; (01653) 692093; £2.50.

Malton itself is a comfortable market town with some interesting side streets, in prosperous farming and racehorse-training country. Sat is a busy market day (the lively livestock mart is on Tues and Fri). The Cornucopia (Commercial St, Norton) is a well run dining pub, and the Royal Oak and King's Head do good, generous food. A scenic road towards York is the old coach road parallel to the A64, from Norton to Buttercrambe and Gate Helmsley.

MARGROVE PARK NZ6515 **South Cleveland Heritage Centre** By the moors, with natural history and wildlife exhibitions; can organise walks and nature trails. Meals, snacks, shop, disabled access; cl Fri, Sat and am Sun Apr–Oct, and all Oct–Mar; (01287) 610368; free.

★ ⌂ **MARKET WEIGHTON** SE8741 Neat and pleasant old market town with one or two useful antique shops; the Londesborough Arms has interesting food (and comfortable bedrooms). Here the Wolds Way long-distance path briefly divides in two, allowing walkers a circuit taking in the old railway line, now the Hudson Way, and the villages of Goodmanham and Londesborough, with its fine parkland.

! **MIDDLESBROUGH** NZ4919 Not a particular attraction for visitors, but it does have good places to visit nearby. Its working **Transporter Bridge** (A178) across the Tees is now unique, with the central section serving as a ferry, every 15 mins shuttling cars and pedestrians across the river; cl am Sun, am bank hols, 25–26 Dec, 1 Jan; 80p cars, 30p pedestrians. **Dorman Museum** (Linthorpe Rd) Summer activities for children, as well as interesting changing exhibitions; Shop, disabled access to ground floor; cl am

Sun and all Mon (exc bank hols); (01642) 813781; free. **Captain Cook Birthplace Museum** (Stewart Park, Marton, 3m S) Now open again after a £1.2 million refurbishment, with computers, films and special effects. The sound of creaking ship's timbers accompanies some of the displays, and the impressive grounds have a conservatory with tropical plants, animals and birds. Meals, snacks, shop, disabled access; cl Mon exc bank hols, 25–26 Dec, 1 Jan; (01642) 311211; £2. **Newham Grange Leisure Farm** (Coulby Newham, off the A174 S) Rare breeds and other animals and poultry, an agricultural museum, and a reconstructed vet's surgery and saddler's shop. Snacks, shop, disabled access; cl wkdys Nov–Mar; (01642) 300202; £1.55.

MILLINGTON SE8351 The Wolds Way allows round walks through attractively rolling countryside around here.

NORTH NEWBALD SE9338 **Northern Shire Horse Centre** (Flower Hill Farm) Busy working farm with pedigree shire horse stud. Also farming bygones, decent walks, and plenty of animals inc rare sheep and cattle. Snacks, shop, disabled access; cl Fri, Sat, and Oct–Easter (though you can usually see at least some animals on Suns then); (01430) 827270; *£2.75.

★ † **NUNNINGTON HALL** SE6779 Big 16th/17th-c house nicely set by the River Rye, with fine panelling and a magnificent staircase. A family home for nearly 400 years, with the intriguing Carlisle Collection of miniature rooms, each of them ⅛ th life-size. Snacks, shop, limited disabled access; cl am, all day Mon (exc bank hols) and Tues (exc Jun–Aug), and Nov–Mar; (01439) 748283; £4, garden only £1; NT. In the attractive village, the Royal Oak is good for lunch, and the church has a fine effigy of a knight said to have rid the district of a Loathly Worm.

ORMESBY HALL NZ5317 18th-c elegance with elaborate plasterwork, Victorian laundry and kitchen, a model railway, pleasant gardens and grounds. Snacks, shop, disabled access to ground floor only; cl am, all Mon (exc bank hols), Fri, Sat, and Nov–Mar; (01642) 324188; £3.30, garden and railway only £2; NT.

★ ! **OSMOTHERLEY** SE4597 Perhaps more small town than village, but quietly attractive; the Three Tuns has decent food (and comfortable bedrooms). **Mount Grace Priory** (A19 NW) Carthusian monks took a vow of silence and rarely emerged from their own individual cells; at this ruined 14th-c priory one of these has been fully restored, giving a good illustration of how the monks must have lived. The ruins are better preserved than those of any other Carthusian establishment in England, and in spring an impressive display of daffodils makes it especially attractive. An adjacent 17th-c manor house has an exhibition, and interesting Arts and Crafts connections. Snacks, shop; cl winter Mon and Tues, 24–26 Dec, 1 Jan; (01609) 883494; *£2.70. A lonely stretch of the Cleveland Way long-distance path runs up over the Hambleton Hills from here, with some road access along the way. The **Adventure Centre** just up the road at Ingleby Cross can organise climbing, caving and canoeing; (01609) 882571.

† **PATRINGTON CHURCH** TA3122 Glorious, with lovely carving inside – its graceful spire beckoning you from a long way off.

★ † **PICKERING** SE7984 Another attractive small town, usually very quiet (busier Mon market day), with vividly restored medieval murals in the splendid tall-spired **church**. The White Swan, Black Swan, Bay Horse and Forest & Vale do decent food; the A169 N has sweeping moorland views (up there, the Saltergate Inn is a good stop). **North Yorkshire Moors Railway** 18-mile steamtrain trips through lovely countryside and nostalgically restored stations; the line was originally built by George Stephenson. The Grosmont end has various locomotives and antique carriages, and you can stop off at Goathland. Meals, snacks, shop, disabled access; cl Nov–Mar (exc Nov and Dec wknds); (01751) 472508 for timetable; £8.90 full return journey. **Pickering Castle** Ruins of a 12th-c keep and later curtain walls and towers, with fine views from its imposing castle mound above the town. Snacks, shop, some disabled access; cl winter Mon and Tues; (01751) 474989; £2.20. **Beck Isle Museum** Charmingly set, 17th-c riverside house with a wonderful collection of local bygones and period shops. Shop, limited disabled access; cl Nov–Mar; (01751) 473653; *£2.

POCKLINGTON SE8048 An open-faced market town below the Wolds, with quite a few handsome buildings; the Feathers is popular for lunch (and has decent bedrooms). **Burnby Hall Gardens** (B1247 S) Famous for their waterlilies, with dozens of varieties in 2 lakes; also a splendid rose garden, and an intriguing collection of all sorts of ethnic material and sporting trophies from across the world. Snacks, shop, disabled access; cl Oct–Mar; (01759) 302068; £2.20. From out here, it's not far to the Plough at Allerthorpe (good for lunch). The B1246 Driffield road runs through some quite picturesque hills.

RIEVAULX ABBEY SE5785 Superbly atmospheric ruins of a magnificent and once highly prosperous abbey, among the wooded hills of Rye Dale (the most dramatic views are gained by walking down the dale from the N). The nave, dating from 1135, is one of the earliest built in England. Also among the spectacular 3-tiered remains is a fine 13th-c choir, and a visitor centre has displays on monastic life. The graceful colonnades, arches and lancet windows are especially evocative if you get there early or late on a weekday out of season. Snacks, shop, some disabled access; cl 24–25 Dec; (01439) 798228; £2.90. Besides the many places in Helmsley not far off, the Hare over in Scawton (a pleasant drive) is useful for lunch. **Rievaulx Terrace** This half-mile-long, grass-covered 18th-c terrace overlooks the abbey, with dramatic views. Each end is adorned with a classical temple: a small Tuscan rotunda built to while away the hours in peaceful contemplation, and an elaborate Ionic creation for hunting parties. An ideal picnic spot, with good frescoes and a landscape design exhibition. Snacks, shop, disabled access; cl Nov–Apr; (01439) 798340; £2.80; NT.

★ **ROBIN HOOD'S BAY** NZ9505 Picturesque fishing village, once popular with smugglers and still largely unspoilt (despite the shops and cafés for visitors), its cottages clustered steeply above the rocky shore – a low-tide hunting-ground for fossils, and a surprising expanse of sand exposed beyond the fascinating rock pools. You can walk along a fine section of cliffs to Ravenscar, where a geological trail takes in old alum quarries; an abandoned railway provides an easy walkway back. **Music in Miniature** (Albion Rd church hall) Charming collection of painstakingly created models illustrating English musical history; among the 50 or so doll's house-sized scenes are medieval minstrels, Victorian carol singers, and a 1920s palm court orchestra, all imaginatively put together by one dedicated woman. Shop, disabled access; cl Nov–Easter; (01947) 880512; *£1. The Laurel and Olde Dolphin have enjoyable food. The car park up at the top is quite a climb.

ROSEBERRY TOPPING NZ5712 A memorable viewpoint on the extreme N edge of the moors, reached by a moorland walk from Gribdale Gate car park E of Great Ayton; a popular circuit goes by way of Airy Home Farm, the childhood home of Captain Cook.

ROSEDALE SE7296 With its lush fields and red-roofed, yellow stone houses sheltering warmly below the gaunt moorland, this now seems to typify the quiet pastoral countryside of the area. But until 60 or 70 years ago it was a busy iron-working site: the old railway track that once served the quarries loops around the moor above, and makes an easily followed stroll. The hillside at the top of the dreadfully steep Rosedale Chimney road, heading S over Spaunton Moor, gives motorists too a classic view.

★ **RUNSWICK BAY** NZ8016 Very pretty, harbourless fishing village, pleasant pubs; the Cleveland Way gives good walks to Staithes (or you can begin closer from tiny Port Mulgrave).

SALTBURN-BY-THE-SEA NZ6621 Originally a superior Victorian seaside resort, with traces of those days still in the Italianate valley garden and the water-operated sloping tramway by the pier. **Smugglers Experience** (Whitby Rd) Vivid, interactive exhibition on the town's smuggling heritage, housed in old seaside cottages. Cl Oct–Easter; (01287) 625252; *£1.70. The Ship, a good pub right by the boats pulled up on the beach, is probably the most ancient building. The beach is sheltered by the great headland of Warsett Hill to the S, and a grand section of the Cleveland Way takes walkers over this and beyond.

SCARBOROUGH TA0488 All the usual seaside attractions in a place of some style, its 2 great curves of firm sandy beach separated by the small harbour below a high, narrow headland. Looking down from this, **Scarborough Castle** stands on the site of British and Roman encampments. It was a royal palace of some importance until the reign of James I. Remains include the 13th-c barbican, medieval chapels and house, and the shell of the 12th-c keep; great coastal views from the walls. Shop, disabled access; cl winter Mon and Tues, 24–26 Dec, 1 Jan; (01723) 372451; £1.80. Between castle and cliff are the remains of a 4th-c Roman signal station, one of 5 that warned of approaching raiders. To the S is the older part of the resort, with antique tracked cliff lifts between the promenade and the pleasant upper town, which has a house associated with Richard III (looking a little dilapidated), and a small craft centre in a former 14th-c inn. The station has one of the longest benches in the world; 139 metres (456ft) long, it can seat 228 people. **Rotunda Museum** (Vernon Rd) Georgian local history museum, with a Bronze Age skeleton and displays on the resort's Victorian heyday. Shop; cl Mon, and also cl Weds–Fri Nov–May; (01723) 374839; £1. (£3 joint ticket with Wood End and Art Gallery). **Wood End** (The Crescent) The Sitwells lived here for 60 years from 1870 (Edith was born here); displays of their work and associated memorabilia, also lots of fossils, and a Victorian conservatory with tropical plants – though not the free-flying birds that once mingled with party-goers. Shop; cl Mon, and also cl Tues, Thurs and Fri Nov–May; (01723) 374839; £2. **Scarborough Art Gallery** (The Crescent) Striking Italianate villa with good temporary exhibitions; cl Mon, and also Tues, Weds and Sun Nov–May; (01723) 374839; £2. **Millennium** (harbour) Vivid journey across 1,000 years of the town's history, through Vikings, Normans and the Civil War to the early days of rail and Victorian sea-bathing – very entertainingly done. Shop, limited disabled access; cl 25 Dec; (01723) 501000; *£4.50. **Sea Life Centre** (Scalby Mills) The same lively mixture we've described in several other resorts. Snacks, shop, disabled access; cl 25 Dec; (01723) 376125; £5.50. The handy Old Scalby Mill has decent food all day. The new **Terror Tower** is another wet-day diversion for children, with ghoulish reconstructions of horror film sets and actors adding to the tension. Shop, cl winter wkdys; (01723) 501016; £2.50. Interesting **churches** include medieval St Mary's, where Anne Brontë is buried, and 19th-c St Martin's, with elaborate work by Burne-Jones, William Morris and other Pre-Raphaelites. One entertainingly quaint unique tradition is the summer staging of miniaturised sea battles, with all sorts of special effects among the ducks on the lake of Peasholm Park, in the more seasidey N part of town; 3.30pm Mon and Thurs, May–early Sept. Good views of the bay from the top of Olivers Mount (and harbour views from the Golden Ball on the front).

The **Cleveland Way** S to Filey is an agreeable and well signed few hours' walk, though of less scenic significance than the cliffs further N. Oddly, the Way stops just short of Filey, at the headland of Filey Brigg, although there is nothing to prevent you from walking on into town.

★ **SHERIFF HUTTON** SE6566 Attractive village, with a ruined castle and 12th-c church; good pub.

SKIDBY TA0333 Has a **working windmill** (open wknds and bank hols, plus Wed–Fri in summer hols, mill working Sun only; *£1.50), and gentle country walks nearby; the Half Moon is useful for something to eat.

SKINNINGROVE NZ7119 **Tom Leonard Mining Museum** Good mining museum well demonstrating the reality of work underground. You can see how the stone is drilled, charged with explosives and fired. Snacks, shop; cl am, and all Nov–Mar; (01287) 642877; £2.50. The village is industrial, with a steel-rolling mill – far from picturesque, but it has strong local colour, with its odd shantytown of pigeon-fanciers' sheds spreading over the cliff. Walkers can join the well signed Cleveland Way southwards to ascend monumental Boulby Cliff, the highest point on the E coast, before re-entering the National Park.

SLEDMERE HOUSE SE9365 Grand 18th-c mansion decorated and furnished in period style, with one showpiece room done in Turkish tiling and a library bigger than many public ones; 18th-c walled garden, and an extensive park landscaped by Capability Brown. They usually play their pipe organ pm Weds, Fri and Sun. Cl all Mon (exc bank hols), Sat, and Oct–Easter; (01377) 236637; £4. The Triton is useful for lunch.

SPURN HEAD TA4010 This spit curling like a claw round the mouth of the Humber estuary has a rough track open to cars almost to its end: a bleak place to some but a paradise for birdwatchers, who often wait here in spring and autumn for glimpses of rare migrant species. Thanks to the vagaries of nature the peninsula is gradually becoming an island, so best to check tide times carefully. The estuary itself is usually grey, solemn and grim.

! **STAINTONDALE** SE9998 **Llama-trekking** Bruce Wright organises this, across the moors or along the coast; the llamas hump your bags while you walk beside them. They can do specialist treks with forest rangers or experts on wild flowers or archaeology. All treks include home-made food; (01723) 871234; from £18 for 3 hours. **Shire Horse Farm** Friendly little farm with good demonstrations and talks; as well as horses there are various rabbits, small animals and poultry, nature trails, and bracing clifftop walks along part of the Cleveland Way. Snacks, shop, disabled access; open Sun, Tues, Weds, Fri and bank hols, spring bank hol–Sept; (01723) 870458; £3. The Bryherstones Hotel, off the Cloughton road, has good-value food.

★ **STAITHES** NZ7818 Steep fishing village, unspoilt down by the shore, where little cottages and the storm-battered Cod & Lobster pose fetchingly against the staggering background of a great red sandstone headland, a striking colour picture as the sun comes up.

SUTTON BANK SE5182 This steep escarpment gives an enthralling view, particularly from the very popular section of the Cleveland Way that runs S from the A170, along the level clifftop. Immediately N of the A170, you can combine the path along the top of the slope with a venture down the nature trail into Garbutt Wood, a nature reserve abutting Gormire Lake, the only natural lake in the National Park.

Days Out

Grit and grace: Eden Camp, nr Malton; lunch at the Cornucopia there; Castle Howard.

Seabirds' citadel: Cliff stroll at Flamborough Head; lunch at the Seabirds, Flamborough; boat trip or walk to see Bempton Cliffs.

Backroads of the Wolds: Burnby Hall waterlily gardens; Londesborough, with a stroll into parkland on the Wolds Way; South Dalton and Lund villages; lunch at the Star, North Dalton; Sledmere House (limited opening); Wharram Percy medieval village site.

SUTTON ON THE FOREST SE5864 **Sutton Park** The friendly 1730s manor house itself is now open only Sun and Mon bank hol wknds, but the delightful grounds are open pm daily Easter–Sept, with terraced gardens, a Georgian ice house, lily-pond, and pleasant woodland walks and nature trails. Shop; (01347) 810249; £4, gardens only £2. The village with its broad street is pretty, and the smart Rose & Crown has good food.

★ **THORNTON DALE** SE8383 Despite the main road, one of the most delightful villages in this part of Yorks – with an attractive forest toll road running NW to Langdale End.

WADE'S CAUSEWAY SE8097 Also known as Wheeldale Roman road, this mile-long stretch of broad, paved, Roman road up over the moors is well restored and maintained. It's open to walkers only, and reached easily by the narrow moorland lane S from Egton Bridge (or a longish walk S from Goathland).

WELTON SE9627 Good area for round walks based on the Wolds Way, with fine views over the Humber in places.

WHARRAM PERCY SE8564 The most famous of the medieval abandoned villages of the Wolds, with lots of grassy humps and an evocative ruined church; English Heritage site, free access. From Thixendale (where the Cross Keys has sensibly priced food) a stretch of the Wolds Way gives walkers a view of the village, and takes in a stretch of classic dry valley.

★ ✝ ! **WHITBY** NZ8911 Famous as the port at which Count Dracula came ashore; Bram Stoker got the idea for the book in the fishermen's graveyard of the partly Norman **church**, 199 steps up from the harbour, with lovely woodwork. **Whitby Abbey** Impressive set of 13th-c ruins, newly designated a World Heritage Site, dramatically overlooking the harbour from their windswept clifftop setting. You can see the skeletal remains of the magnificent 3-tiered choir and the north transept, and it's an evocative spot for a picnic (and site of a famous scene in *Dracula*). An earlier building had been the site of the Synod of Whitby, where the dating of Easter was thrashed out in 664. Snacks, shop; cl 25–26 Dec; (01947) 603568; £1.70. Not too far from the abbey on Church Rd is a small but interesting workshop where you can watch jet being crafted into jewellery. Away from the bright waterfront, the town is steep and quite attractive, with picturesque old buildings (now often rather smart shops) and some quaint cobbled alleys at its original core east of the busy harbour, where excellent fresh fish is sold straight from the catch. **Whitby Museum** (Pannett Park) Delightfully old-fashioned and crowded, with the only surviving part of Captain Cook's original journal, Queen Victoria's nightdress, some spectacular fossils and the hand of a murderer used as a candle-holder by superstitious burglars. Shop, some disabled access; cl am Sun, and in winter cl pm Tues and all Mon; (01947) 602908; £1.50. **Captain Cook Memorial Museum** (Grape Lane) In the house where the great explorer lived as an apprentice in the shipping trade from 1746; rooms are furnished in period style with models, letters and drawings from Cook's later voyages. Shop; cl Nov–Easter; (01947) 601900; *£2.60. **Dracula Experience** (Marine Parade) Children probably won't be satisfied until they've visited this vividly spooky re-creation of scenes from the classic tale. Shop; cl winter wkdys; (01947) 601923; £1.95.

Besides excellent fish and chips from the Magpie Café, the Duke of York (Church St, at the foot of the 199 steps) does decent food all day. In the 2 weeks around the summer solstice, the sun both rises and sets above the sea.

WITHERNSEA TA3428 **Lighthouse** Towering above the houses of this little resort, with fantastic views if you climb the 144 steps. Teas, shop, disabled access to ground floor only; open pm wknds and bank hols Mar–Oct, daily mid-Jun–mid-Sept; (01964) 614834; £1.50. The Commercial Hotel has very low-priced food.

★ **Other attractive villages** here, all with decent pubs, include Ainthorpe NZ7008, Ampleforth SE5879 (with its famous school and partly wooded moors), Appleton Roebuck SE5542,

Bishop Burton SE9939, Castleton NZ6908 (high above the Esk Valley), Cloughton Newlands TA0196, Crayke SE5760, Great Ayton NZ5611, Hutton Rudby NZ4706, Lund SE9748, Nether Silton SE4692, North Dalton SE9352, Oldstead SE5380, Rosedale Abbey SE7395, Seamer TA0284, South Dalton SE9645, Thixendale SE8461, Thorganby SE6942, Thornton-le-Clay SE6865, Weaverthorpe SE9771, Welburn SE7268 and Warthill SE6755.

Where to eat

BYLAND ABBEY SE5478 **Abbey** *(01347) 868204* Beautifully placed dining pub opposite the abbey ruins, with an interesting series of rambling old rooms, enjoyable food, decent wines, well kept beers, and a big garden; cl am Mon (exc bank hols), 24–25 Dec; disabled access. **£20**|£6.50.

FLAMBOROUGH TA2270 **Seabirds** *(01262) 850242* Friendly old pub full of shipping memorabilia, with excellent fresh fish and other home-made dishes, lots of wines, and cheerful, hard-working staff; cl pm Mon in winter; partial disabled access. **£15**|£4.

KIRKHAM ABBEY SE7365 **Stone Trough** *(01653) 618713* Quaint, beamed inn with small, cosy and interesting bars, and log fires; good lunchtime bar food, an old-fashioned restaurant with a farmhouse atmosphere, seats outside with valley views; **£18.75**|£7.25.

NUNNINGTON SE6679 **Royal Oak** *(01439) 788271* Attractive little dining pub nr Nunnington Hall; log fires, beams hung with copper jugs, antique keys and earthenware flagons, and carefully chosen furniture; generous helpings of enjoyable, home-made bar food – super daily specials; cl Mon; children over 8. **£19.50**|£8.25.

OSMOTHERLEY SE4597 **Three Tuns** *South End (01609) 883301* Unassuming and popular front bar area, comfortable and stylish back restaurant with an emphasis on fish; good bar food inc interesting daily specials, well kept real ales, and smart, courteous service; tables in the garden with lovely views; bdrms; cl pm Sun. **£15**|£6.50.

STADDLEBRIDGE SE4499 **McCoys** *The Cleveland Tontine (01609) 882671* For over 20 years, 3 brothers have run this rather special brasserie with its bustling, relaxed atmosphere, individual furnishings, very good international modern cooking (super puddings), and a wine list that includes some decent-quality bin ends; bdrms. **£37**|£5.25.

STAITHES NZ7818 **Endeavour** *1 High St (01947) 840825* Popular little quayside restaurant at the bottom of a steep hill; with lovely, fresh local fish dishes (delicious meat and game, and vegetarian dishes, too), super puddings, a good-value wine list, and friendly service; bdrms; cl winter Sun, bank hols, 25–26 Dec, best to check wkdys mid-Jan–mid-Mar; well behaved children only. **£25**|£8.95.

SUTTON-UPON-DERWENT SE7047 **St Vincent Arms** *(01904) 608349* Relaxed atmosphere in the traditional, panelled front parlour with an open fire, high-backed old settles, good, solid, home-cooked food in the spacious dining room, friendly staff, well kept beers and a decent choice of wines; big garden. **£16.70**|£6.50.

THORGANBY SE6941 **Jefferson Arms** *(01904) 448316* Handsome old village inn run by 2 particularly helpful and friendly sisters; with a stylish and relaxed, spacious main bar, delightful beamed lounge with sofas and fresh flowers, a no smoking conservatory festooned with passion flowers and vines, a separate no smoking restaurant, and very good food inc lots of rostis with various toppings; thoughtful wine list and well kept real ales; bdrms. **£17**|£4.90.

WHITBY NZ9011 **Duke of York** *Church St (01947) 600324* Bustling, welcoming pub with a nice outlook over the harbour entrance and western cliff from the comfortable beamed bar (lots of fishing memorabilia); a wide choice of good-value, fresh local fish as well as other things, well kept real ales, fine wines, and quick, pleasant service; bdrms. **£14.70**|£4.95.

WHITBY NZ8911 **Magpie Café** *Pier Rd (01947) 602058* Overlooks the town and river, with lots of wonderfully evocative sepia photographs of old Whitby, and much liked for its delicious, fresh haddock served by cheerful staff; cl Jan, 24–25 Dec. **£15**|£5.

WHITBY NZ8910 **Trenchers** *Newquay Rd (01947) 603212* Neatly kept, big busy diner by the harbour, with delicious fresh fish (and other food), friendly and helpful staff, and a good wine list; cl mid-Nov–mid-Mar; disabled access. **£16.95**|£5.95

West and South Yorkshire

Fascinating places to visit – many of them free, and many specially good for children; lively towns and cities, striking mix of mill towns and moors in the west.

Leeds is lively, individual and interesting, with something for all ages: its Royal Armouries Museum makes an outstanding family day out, Tropical World is very enjoyable (and free), and there's plenty more to fill a short stay.

Sheffield's National Centre for Popular Music and the first phase of the Denaby Main Earth Centre's development (opening in spring) are among the first fruits of really big Lottery money for visitor projects, and it looks as if the many millions spent upgrading Bradford's already excellent film and photography museum will pay off handsomely (both Bradford and Sheffield have other particularly good places to visit). Harewood House is another favourite, with wide appeal.

Other fine places include Brodsworth Hall, the coal mining museum at Middlestown, Bramham Park, Conisbrough Castle, the pioneering industrial village of Saltaire, Nostell Priory, the Bagshaw Museum in Batley, the Colne Valley Museum at Golcar and (out of season) the Brontës' parsonage in Haworth – where the picturesque Keighley & Worth Valley Railway is fun for family outings. Other enjoyable spots for children are the developing Elsecar Heritage Centre, the open farm at Cawthorne, the butterfly house at North Anston, the Eureka! centre in Halifax (an appealing, cleaned-up mill town with lots to see).

Ilkley on the edge of the moors is attractive, and Hebden Bridge is interesting, with good-value, subsidised train links to Bradford and Halifax, also to Saltaire and Huddersfield. The Halifax–Huddersfield journey is through fascinating trouble-up-mill scenery; for a rosier-tinted view, try the new *Last of the Summer Wine* exhibition in Holmfirth.

The west of the area has a real Yorkshire mix of steep stone cottage terraces, remarkable mill buildings and some dramatic moorland coming right up to the towns, with plenty of exhilarating walking.

With the present counties of South and West Yorkshire, we have included the bottom corner of North Yorkshire, below York itself and the A64.

Where to stay

BRADFORD SE1632 **Victoria** *Bridge St, Bradford BD1 1JX (01274) 728706* **£66w,** plus wknd breaks; 60 well equipped rms with CD and video (they have a library). Carefully renovated Victorian station hotel with many original features and lots of stylish character; a bustling bar, popular and informal brasserie serving good modern food, and marvellous breakfasts; disabled access.

FIRBECK SK5688 **Yews Farm** *Firbeck, Worksop S81 8JW (01909) 731458* ***£52;** 2 rms. In an attractive village, this charming, carefully furnished country home dates from the 16th c and has views over woodland and fields; tasty home cooking, and friendly owners; cl Nov–Feb.

GRENOSIDE SK3394 **Whitley Hall** *Elliott Lane, Grenoside, Sheffield S30 3NR (0114) 245 4444* **£70;** 18 rms. 16th-c, creeper-clad hotel in 30 acres; with a relaxed beamed bar, good, popular food in the spacious restaurant, and friendly, helpful service; cl 25–26 Dec.

HALIFAX SE0828 **Holdsworth House** *Holdsworth, Halifax HX2 9TG (01422) 240024* **£114,** plus wknd breaks; 40 pretty, individually decorated rms. Lovely 17th-c house a few miles outside Halifax; with antiques, fresh flowers and open fires in the comfortable lounges, friendly, helpful staff, a very fine oak-panelled dining room with imaginative food and carefully chosen wines, and a garden; dogs by prior arrangement; cl 1st wk Jan; disabled access.

HAWORTH SE0237 **Old White Lion** *Haworth, Keighley BD22 8DU (01535) 642313* **£61,** plus special breaks; 14 rms, many with lovely views. Friendly, warm and comfortable 300-year-old inn with 3 bars, a cosy restaurant with enjoyable food, and an oak-panelled residents' lounge; nr Brontë Museum, parsonage and church, and the Keighley & Worth Valley steam railway.

LEEDS SE3033 **42 The Calls** *42 The Calls, Leeds LS2 7EW (0113) 244 0099* **£98w,** plus special breaks; 41 attractive rms with original features, and lots of extras – CD stereo with disc library, satellite TV, and good views. Stylish modern hotel in a converted riverside grain mill, with genuinely friendly staff, marvellous food in both the restaurant and next-door Brasserie Forty-Four, and fine breakfasts; cl 5 days over Christmas; limited disabled access.

LINTON SE3946 **Wood Hall** *Trip Lane, Linton, Wetherby LS22 4JA (01937) 587271* **£120,** plus special breaks; 43 spacious, well furnished rms. Grand Georgian mansion set in over a hundred acres of parkland overlooking the River Wharfe; comfortable reception rooms, log fire, antiques and fresh flowers, and imaginative cooking in the no smoking restaurant; indoor swimming pool and health centre; disabled access.

OTLEY SE2143 **Chevin Lodge** *Yorkgate, Otley LS21 3NU (01943) 467818* **£97w,** plus special breaks; 50 rms. Built of Finnish logs and with walks through the 50 private acres of birchwood (free mountain bikes too), and good restaurant food; tennis, fishing, and free membership of the nearby leisure club: indoor swimming pool, gym and supervised crèche; disabled access.

ROYDHOUSE SE2112 **Three Acres** *Roydhouse, Shelley, Huddersfield HD8 8LR (01484) 602606* ***£70,** plus special breaks; 20 refurbished, pretty rms. In lovely countryside, this extended 18th-c hotel has a welcoming atmosphere in its traditional bars, good wines and well kept real ales, and excellent food in the 2 restaurants (one with an occasional pianist), using fresh local produce; cl 25 Dec.

SCISSETT SE2408 **Bagden Hall** *Wakefield Rd, Scissett, Huddersfield HD8 9LE (01484) 865330* **£80;** 17 rms. Handsome hotel in 40 acres of parkland, with its own 9-hole par 3 golf course; comfortable, airy public rooms inc a conservatory bar, well prepared French and English food, and quietly efficient service; cl 25 pm Dec; limited disabled access.

SHEFFIELD SK3485 **Charnwood** *10 Sharrow Lane, Sheffield S11 8AA (0114) 258 9411* ***£90,** plus special breaks; 22 comfortable, well equipped rms. Friendly, extended Georgian house with peaceful lounges, a conservatory, and very good food in both the Brasserie and elegant little Henfreys restaurant; cl 24–31 Dec; disabled access.

WENTBRIDGE SE4817 **Wentbridge House** *Old Great North Rd, Wentbridge, Pontefract WF8 3JJ (01977) 620444* ***£85;** 19 rms. Fine hotel dating from 1700 and set in 20 beautiful acres; with attractive public rooms, a relaxed bar, and enjoyable food in the pretty restaurant; cl pm 25 Dec; disabled access.

Please let us know what you think of places in the *Guide*. Use the report form at the back of the book or simply write us a letter.

To see and do

Yorkshire Family Attraction of the Year

! SHEFFIELD SK3281 **National Centre for Popular Music** (Paternoster Row, opposite the station) Better late than never (it was originally meant to be ready in late 1998), this striking £15-million centre had yet to open its doors as we went to press, but so much effort and thought has gone into its development that we'd be very surprised indeed if it wasn't a huge hit when it's finally unveiled in Mar. Distinctively shaped to resemble 4 big drums, its main exhibition areas upstairs use up-to-the-minute techniques to explore the evolution of popular music from classical to hip-hop, with an emphasis on post-1945 sounds. There should be something for everyone, whether you're a Spice Girl or a Rolling Stone, with interactive displays designed to appeal to adults just as much as children. Most fun for younger visitors will be the Making Music section, where you can try your hand at playing instruments, mixing a record, being a DJ, or designing an album cover; one wow is the chessboard-style floor which adds sound effects to your footsteps, and you can press lots of buttons to check out how songs are recorded. In other areas, massive screens show off hi-tech films and videos looking into how music influences our lives and varies across the continents, and a big auditorium has what they promise is the world's first 3-dimensional surround-sound system, to make you feel part of anything from the latest releases to an Amazonian rainforest. Downstairs are temporary exhibition areas (the first focusing on Q magazine), and a café-bar, and they may have bands on special occasions. A couple of hours is likely to be enough to do the place justice, though music buffs may need to be dragged away from a database said to contain details and facts on just about every successful singer and band. Meals, snacks, shop, disabled access; best to ring for exact opening date, then only cl 25 Dec; (0114) 279 8941; *£5.95 (£4 children).

ANSTON BROOK SK5184 Reached on foot from South Anston, this gives walks through a wooded valley that breaks the monotony of the flat farmlands SE of Rotherham. It can be combined with a walk by the derelict Chesterfield Canal.

BATLEY SE2325 **Bagshaw Museum** (Wilton Park) Beautiful Victorian Gothic mansion in a pleasant lakeside park, with one of those excellent miscellaneous collections based on the curio-hunting of an individual enthusiast. Shop, some disabled access; cl am wknds, Good Fri, Christmas; (01924) 472514; free. The Old Hall at Heckmondwike (B6117), once Joseph Priestley's home, is interesting for lunch.

★ † **BRADFIELD** SK2692 Attractive 2-part village, with an interesting church and scenic walks.

† ! **BRADFORD** SE1632 Many buildings survive from what was one of Britain's finest Victorian cities (though horribly knocked about by heavy-handed civic designers in the 1960s and 1970s). These, in a solidly unifying northern stone, are a staggering monument to the days when its wools, woollens and worsteds ruled the world: gigantic and confidently Renaissance-style woollen and velvet mills, the imposing Wool Exchange, the opulent city-centre cliffs of heavily ornate merchants' warehouses in Little Germany behind the mostly 15th-c cathedral, and the florid exuberance of the municipal buildings such as the Gothic city hall, the neo-classical St George's concert hall, even the great Undercliffe cemetery with its sumptuous Victorian memorials (and sweeping Pennine views) – it's been called the most spectacular graveyard in Britain. The city's Asian immigrants have brought a vivid and visible dash of cultural diversity, and there's a feeling of underlying vigour and zest which makes

it exciting to visit. Useful places for a pub lunch include the Fountain (Heaton Rd), the Office (off City St) and Ram's Revenge (Kirkgate), but you might prefer one of the multitude of Indian, Pakistani or Bangladeshi restaurants.

National Museum of Photography, Film and Television (Princes View) Reopening early spring 1999 after a £13-million refurbishment. Previously, it's been one of Britain's best-loved museums – altogether more lively and fun than that word implies, with masses to experience and try your hand at – and from what we hear the changes will make it even more spectacularly enjoyable. Meals, snacks, shop, disabled access; cl Mon (exc bank hols); (01274) 727488; free (charges for the huge IMAX cinema). **Industrial Museum** (Moorside Rd, Eccleshill) Former spinning mill well illustrating the growth of the woollen and worsted textile industry. Horse-drawn trams carry you along a Victorian street complete with workers' cottages and stables with shire horses. Meals, snacks, shop, disabled access; cl am Sun, and all Mon (exc bank hols), 25–26 Dec, Good Fri; (01274) 631756; free. **Colour Museum** (Grattan Rd) Imaginative study of the use and perception of colour, with interactive displays on the effects of light and colour in general, and particularly the story of dyeing and textile printing. Shop, disabled access; cl am (exc Sat), all Mon and Sun; (01274) 725138; £1.50. **Cartwright Hall Art Gallery** (Lister Park) Dramatic, baroque-style building in an attractive floral park, housing the *Brown Boy* by Reynolds and a good representative selection of late 19th- and early 20th-c paintings. Snacks, shop, disabled access; cl am Sun, and all Mon (exc bank hols), 25–28 Dec; (01274) 493313; *free. **Bolling Hall** (off Brompton Ave, S) Classic, mainly 17th-c Yorkshire manor house, now home to the city's collection of local furniture and pictures. Shop; cl Mon (exc bank hols) and Tues; (01274) 723057; *free.

BRAMHAM PARK SE4041 The garden is beautiful, very much in the grand style – Versailles comes to Yorkshire. Long prospects of ornamental lakes, cascades, temples, statuary, grand hedges and stately trees and avenues surround a classical Queen Mary house of great distinction, with lovely period furnishings and paintings. Open pm Sun and Tues–Thurs mid-Jun–mid-Sept, and gardens also open Easter, May and spring bank hol wknds; (01937) 844265; £4, grounds and gardens only £2.50. The Red Lion has decent food.

BRODSWORTH HALL SE5007 Grand house vividly illustrating Victorian life; the family closed off parts as their fortunes waned, inadvertently preserving the contents and décor exactly as they were (right down to the billiard score-book). Richly furnished rooms, lots of marble statues, and a busily cluttered servants' wing. The family commissioned some of the largest and fastest Victorian yachts, and a new exhibition charts the history of these splendid vessels. The marvellous formal gardens and parkland are being restored. Snacks, shop, some disabled access; cl Mon (exc bank hols), and all Nov–Mar; (01302) 722598; £4.50.

CARL WARK SK2581 Hill fort on the edge of the Peak District, set handsomely in a great bowl fringed by gritstone outcrops; a more interesting walk than most in South Yorkshire.

★ **CAWTHORNE** SE2708 **Cannon Hall Open Farm** Unusual animals like wallabies and llamas among the residents at this busy working farm; also baby animals all year, with piglets born every 2 weeks. Good play areas, and mostly concreted so it doesn't get muddy. Meals, snacks, shop, disabled access; cl 25 Dec; (01226) 790427; £2. Cannon Hall itself is now a museum and the grounds an attractive country park. The village is pleasant.

CONISBROUGH CASTLE SK5198 (Castle Hill) Mightily impressive 12th-c castle with a unique 27-metre (90-ft) keep – circular, with 6 buttresses and a curtain wall with solid round towers. An added roof and floors re-create something of the original feel, and there's a good audio-visual show. Summer tours by costumed guides. Snacks, developing craft shop, some disabled access; cl Christmas; (01709) 863329; *£2.80. Scott set much of *Ivanhoe* here, writing it while staying at the Boat at Sprotbrough nearby; then a riverside farm, it's now a popular dining pub.

! ⚓ ❀ ✈ **DENABY MAIN** SK4999 **Earth Centre** A redevelopment of over 400 acres left derelict by the coal industry's decline, this environmental centre was awarded one of the Millennium Commission's biggest grants, and by the time it's finished in 2001 will have cost around £100 million. The first phase is due to open in Apr 1999. The whole place has been designed with sustainability in mind, and the green message will be obvious as soon as you enter the main building under a huge array of solar panels (35 per cent of the centre's energy will come from the sun), but it isn't too preachy: the aim is to promote environmental issues in an enjoyable way, so children's activities in the landscaped gardens will include building dens, grottoes and pond-dipping, as well as trails and play areas. Also woodland walks and displays on water treatment and the possibilities for a greener future. There will be daily processions through the site and entertainments in the 400-seat Earth Arena. Meals, snacks, shop, disabled access; best to phone for opening and admission price details; (01709) 512000.

DONCASTER SE5802 Its race meetings are a draw, and there is some fine architecture, especially around the High St and Market Pl, and a good antiques and junk market on Weds. **Doncaster Museum and Art Gallery** (Chequer Rd) Strong on natural history; shop, good disabled access; cl am Sun; free. **Cusworth Hall** (just W) Excellent museum of South Yorkshire life, in an elegant 18th-c house. Displays on mining, transport, costume and entertainment, and an especially popular gallery of toys and childhood. Snacks, shop, disabled access; cl am Sun; (01302) 782342; free. The Boat at Sprotbrough is a fairly handy waterside dining pub.

ELSECAR HERITAGE SK3899 Developing centre in restored industrial workshops. Lots to see inc a **hands-on science centre**, a **history centre** where you can dress up and star in a Victorian melodrama, a beam engine and **craft workshops**. On summer Suns there's a **steamtrain** to the Hemingfield Basin. Meals, snacks, shop, disabled access; cl 25 Dec–1 Jan; (01226) 740203; £3.25 science centre, £1 history centre, £2.50 train, or £5.25 for all.

✝ ★ **FIRBECK** SK5689 **South Yorkshire Aircraft Museum** (Home Farm) More aviation history, in former RAF officers' mess. Crash relics, 20 aero engines, uniforms, a changing collection of planes and a couple of helicopters. Snacks, shop, disabled access; open wknds and bank hols, or by appointment; (01709) 812168; *£1. In the attractive village, the Black Lion has generous food.

GOLCAR SE0915 **Colne Valley Museum** (Cliff Ash) Enthusiastic museum spread over 3 weavers' cottages, with weaving, spinning and clog-making in gaslit surroundings, and a re-created 1850s living room. Snacks, shop, occasional craft festivals, some disabled access; open pm wknds and bank hols; (01484) 659762; £1. The Scapehouse (High St) has decent food. There's a good year-round walk along the Huddersfield Canal's restored towpath to Marsden in *Last of the Summer Wine* country. The Tunnel End pub there is useful for food, as are the Carriage House and Olive Branch just a little further away.

★ **GOOSE EYE** SE0240 Interesting preserved village; there are good drives around here.

✝ ! ❀ **HALIFAX** SE0925 Another town with an impressive show of former textiles wealth, interesting to drive through on a quiet summer evening or a Sun, and surrounded by a splendid ring of moorland. The centre's been cleaned up and partly pedestrianised, and there are some first-class attractions, with the town now going through something of an artistic renaissance. The medieval **church** has an extremely grand spire and fine carving. Look out for Old Tristram, the life-size painted carving of a beggar which was used to collect alms. The Shears (Paris Gates, Boys Lane), down steep lanes among the mill

NORTH YORKSHIRE
LANCASHIRE
GREATER MANCHESTER
DERBYSHIRE
SD
SK
Askwith
Ilkley
Otley
East Morton
Keighley
Goose Eye
Haworth
Esholt
Saltaire
Stanbury
Leeds
Bradford
Blackshaw Head
Ogden Reservoir
Ogden
Heptonstall
Hebden Bridge
Luddenden
Halifax
Oakwell Hall
Batley
Withens Clough Reservoir
Sowerby
Sowerby Bridge
Norland Moor
Barkisland
Wakefield
Ripponden
Huddersfield
Middlestown
Grange Moor
Golcar
Roydhouse
Honley
Scisset
Meltham
Cawthorne
Holmfirth
Holme
Bradfield
Carl Wark
A65
A660
A650
A658
A6120
A61
A6033
A629
A646
A58
M62
M621
A644
A640
A62
A616
A637
M1
A635
A6024
A628
A57

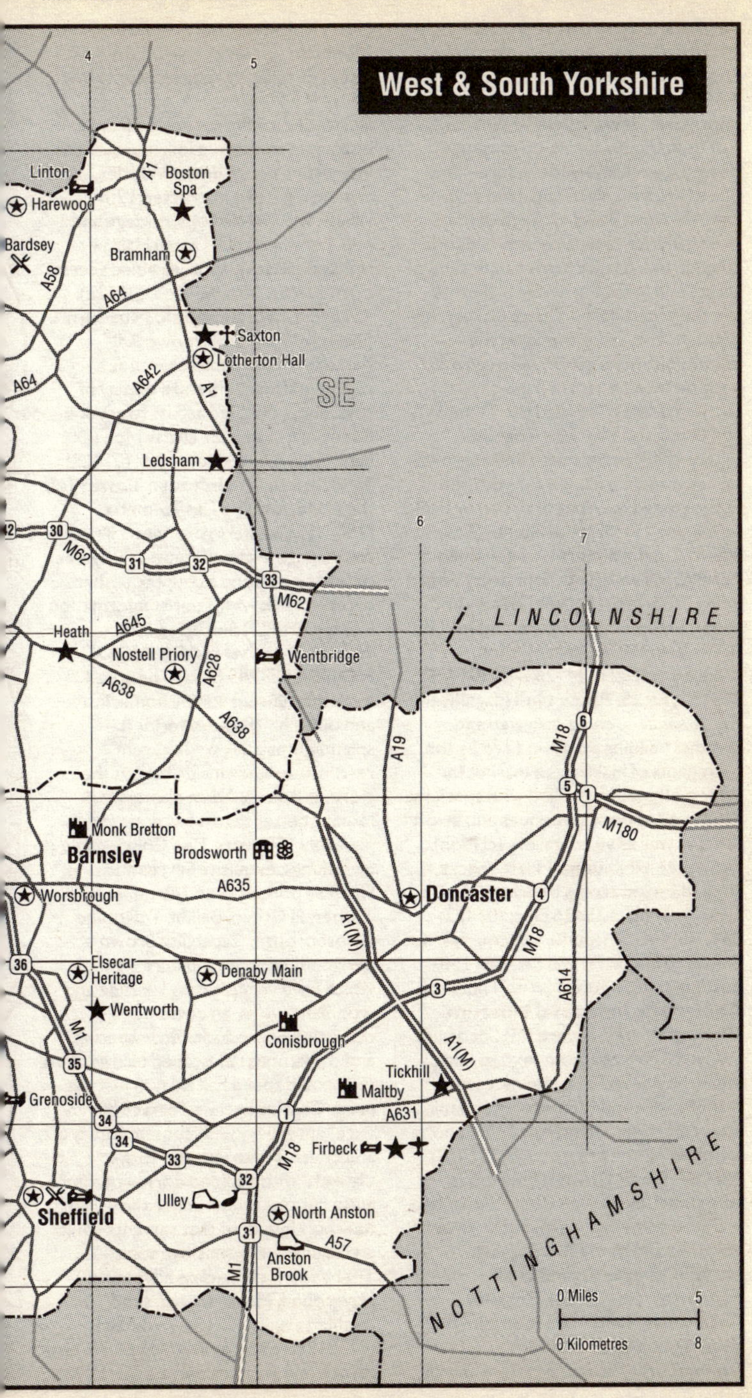
West & South Yorkshire
Linton
Harewood
Boston Spa
Bardsey
Bramham
Saxton
Lotherton Hall
SE
Ledsham
Heath
Nostell Priory
Wentbridge
LINCOLNSHIRE
Monk Bretton
Barnsley
Brodsworth
Worsbrough
Doncaster
Elsecar Heritage
Denaby Main
Wentworth
Conisbrough
Tickhill
Maltby
Grenoside
Firbeck
Ulley
North Anston
Sheffield
Anston Brook
NOTTINGHAMSHIRE
0 Miles 5
0 Kilometres 8

buildings, is a pub that embraces much of Halifax's past and atmosphere; the Sportsman (Lee Lane, Shibden, off the A647) has a good-value carvery and impressive views. **Eureka!** (Discovery Rd) Remarkable hands-on museum designed exclusively for children; few places are as likely to spellbind anyone aged between 3 and 12. Each of the 4 main galleries ostensibly explores one subject, but in fact covers a multitude of topics and ideas. Particular highlights are the broad-based Things Gallery, full of bright colours and images, the communications gallery (you can put your picture on a front page, save a yacht in distress, or read the TV news), and Living and Working Together, where children try their hand at grown-up activities like filling a car with petrol at the garage, working in a shop or bank, or making a meal in the kitchen. Easy to see why in the 6 years it's been open Eureka! has won just about every award going, from Most Parent Friendly and Best Customer Care to several for Loo of the Year. Meals, snacks, shop, disabled access; cl 24–26 Dec; (01426) 983191; £5.25. **Piece Hall** Magnificent, Renaissance-looking, galleried and arcaded building put up in 1775 by the merchants of Halifax as a market for their cloth. Now it's filled with specialist shops selling books, antiques and bric-à-brac, as well as an art gallery (cl Mon) and other exhibitions. Meals, snacks, shop, disabled access by prior arrangement; cl 25–26 Dec; (01422) 368725; free. The Italianate courtyard comes to life on Fri and Sat with 160 bustling stalls; a good few on Thurs too. **Calderdale Industrial Museum** (Central Works, Square Rd) Social and industrial heritage from textiles and steam engines to coal mining, carpet manufacture and cat's-eyes. Reopening after refurbishment in Apr 1999; phone for opening and price details, (01422) 358087. **Dean Clough** Enormous carpet mill, faced with demolition when it closed some years ago, but now well restored and home to a thriving complex of galleries and small businesses; best are the Crossley Gallery and Henry Moore Studio, the latter a good showcase for contemporary sculpture (cl am and all Mon). **Shibden Hall and Folk Museum** (Godley Lane, off the A58, just E) Excellently refurbished, 15th-c house in a 90-acre park, each room illustrating a different period from its history. In the barn, a folk museum has interesting horse-drawn vehicles, while around it is a reconstructed 19th-c village, with workshops, cottage and a pub. For many this is a real Halifax highlight. Snacks, shop, disabled access; cl am Sun, and all Dec–Feb; (01422) 352246; £1.60. **Bankfield Museum** (Ackroyd Park, Boothtown Rd) Textiles and costume, as well as a regimental museum and a display of toys. Shop, disabled access to ground floor only; cl am Sun, all day Mon (exc bank hols), 25–26 Dec, 1 Jan; (01422) 354823; free. **Wainhouse Tower** (off the A646, just W) This 75-metre (250-ft) folly offers good views if you can manage all those steps; usually open only bank hols and a couple of other dates – check with Tourist Information Centre (01422) 368725; £1.20.

HAREWOOD HOUSE SE3245 (A61) The area's most magnificent stately home, inside and out. The 18th-c exterior is splendidly palatial, while recent restoration work inside has left the glorious Robert Adam plasterwork looking better than it has done for probably 150 years. Fine Chippendale furnishings, exquisite Sèvres and Chinese porcelain, and paintings by Turner, El Greco, Bellini, Titian, and Gainsborough. Capability Brown designed the thousand-acre grounds, which have very pleasing lakeside and woodland walks, an outstanding collection of rhododendron species, and the famous landscaped bird gardens (you could spend half a day in just this part). Charles Berry's Terrace has an excellent gallery with contemporary art and crafts. Try to visit the 15th-c **church**, with a splendid array of tombs, and a curious tunnel under the wall of the churchyard, so that servants could arrive unseen by sensitive souls. There's also a first-class adventure playground. Meals, snacks, shop, disabled access; cl Nov–mid-Mar; (0113) 288 6331; everything £6.75, bird garden and grounds only £5.50. TV's

Emmerdale is now filmed on a purpose-built set on the Harewood estate. The Harewood Arms (A61) is a welcoming stop. Just N, Wharfedale Grange have pick-your-own fruit.

HAWORTH SE0237 Plenty of craft shops, antique shops and tea shoppes catering for all the people drawn here by the Brontës (spelt Brunty before father Patrick went posh). A visit out of season catches it at its best, though at any time the steep cobbled main street has quieter, more atmospheric side alleys. Most of the family are buried in the churchyard, except Anne, interred in Scarborough. **Parsonage Museum** Their former home has some 120,000 visitors a year (it was something of a tourist attraction even in Charlotte's days). It is very carefully preserved, with period furnishings, very good changing exhibitions, and displays of the siblings' books, manuscripts and possessions; also the original ink-stained manuscript of *Jane Eyre*, and the sisters' writing table. Shop; cl 11 Jan–5 Feb, 24–27 Dec; (01535) 642323; £3.80. For the most evocative views and atmosphere go up to the moors above town, very grand and not much different from when the Brontës knew them – despite the Japanese footpath signs. The Fleece and Old White Lion are useful for lunch. **Keighley & Worth Valley Railway** Actually begins just N at Keighley (where you can connect with main line trains) but is based here. Run by enthusiastic volunteers, the line was built to serve the valley's mills, and passes through the heart of Brontë country. The Oxenhope terminus has a museum, but the prettiest station is Oakworth (familiar to many from the film *The Railway Children*). Snacks, shop, some disabled access; open wknds all yr, daily Jun–early Sept, and most school hols; (01535) 647777 for timetable; £5.20 return. The A6033 is an interesting drive to Hebden Bridge, and there's a fine old moors road via Stanbury over to the Colne Valley in Lancs.

The Pennine moors around here are a favourite stamping-ground for walkers, with a good walk W through Penistone Hill Country Park SE2403 to the much-visited Brontë Waterfalls SD9935, and on through a remote valley to Withins, the original Wuthering Heights. There are plenty of paths, though finding the way across fields frequently entails searching for unprominent stone stiles over the dry-stone walls.

★ **HEATH** SE3519 Extraordinarily old-fashioned common with gypsy ponies alongside 18th-c mansions (and contrasting views over Wakefield); the gaslit King's Arms here is good.

★ **HEBDEN BRIDGE** SD9927 Engaging small town deep in a valley below the moors, and stepped very steeply up the hillsides, with a lively subculture of art and craft shops. There is a small museum; the Robin Hood (A6033 towards Keighley) has good-value food. At Hebble End are several working craftsmen, with demonstrations of skills inc glass-making, and in summer there are **horse-drawn barge trips** along the canal basin, (01422) 845557. The hold of one barge in the marina has been converted into a **visitor centre** with a traditional boatman's cabin (cl Nov–Easter; free). **Hardcastle Crags** A beauty spot above the wooded river valley, ideal for walks or a picnic. The Nutclough House on the way up also has decent food.

★ **HEPTONSTALL** SD9828 Interesting ancient village, a crippling climb up a fearsomely steep cobbled lane above Hebden Bridge; Sylvia Plath is buried in the churchyard. There's a rewarding scenic path along Heptonstall Crags (the cliffs above the wooded valley of Colden Water). An exhilarating old high road leads out to Widdop and beyond (for fine views and walks), and another runs via Colden and Blackshaw Head.

★ † **HOLMFIRTH** SE1408 Instantly recognisable setting for TV's *Last of the Summer Wine*, with evocative little alleys, several good pubs, and a handsome Georgian **church**. There's an exhibition on the world's longest-running comedy series in **Compo's House** (Huddersfield Rd). Meals, snacks, shop; cl 25 Dec; (01484) 681408; £1.

HUDDERSFIELD SE1416 has a great sense of style in

many of its buildings, especially around the station and central square, and much of the centre is now closed to traffic. **Castle Hill** (Almondbury) 275 metres (900ft) high, giving unrivalled views of the surrounding moors and towards the Pennines and Peak District, best from the top of the 165 steps of the Victoria Tower (open pm May–Sept, plus most bank hols; £1.20). The Castle Hill Inn is another good place to take in the panorama. Also up here is an **art gallery** with a range of 19th-c English paintings (cl Sun, bank hols, Christmas and New Year; (01484) 221964; free. **Tolson Memorial Museum** (Ravensknowle Park) The myths and legends asssociated with Castle Hill are outlined in this former wool baron's mansion, which also has a look at the textile industry, and a collection of horse-drawn vehicles. Shop, disabled access; cl am wknds, Christmas, 1 Jan, Good Fri; (01484) 223830; free. **Transport Museum** (Leeds Rd) One of the better ones we know of; cl 25–26 Dec, 1 Jan; (01484) 559086; £2. The A640 W is a good moorland drive.

★ **ILKLEY** SE1147 Owes its Victorian and Edwardian spaciousness and style to the mid-19th-c and later craze for hydropathic 'cures', which produced quite a rash of luxurious hydros using the town's pure moorland spring water. Their forerunner was the simple little bath-house built a century before around the ice-cold spring up on the moor, just S at **White Wells** – you can still follow the paths the infirm took by donkey. The group of quaintly shaped rocks known as the Cow & Calf up here also makes a pleasant short walk above the town. **Manor House Gallery and Museum** (Castle Yard) One of the few buildings in town to predate the 19th c, an Elizabethan manor house built on the site of a Roman fort, with local history displays. Shop; cl am Sun, all Mon (exc bank hols) and Tues; (01943) 600066; free. The **church** has 3 lovely Saxon crosses, and just beside it are traces of the Roman fort. There are quite a few prehistoric remains around the town, the best known of which is the Bronze Age **Swastika Stone**, a symbol of eternity carved on a flat rock by a moorland path SE of the town, above wooded Heber's Ghyll; the stone is marked on the Ordnance Survey 1:50,000 map, at SE095469. Heber's Ghyll itself is a picturesque ravine with steep Victorian walkways, and the town with its attractive gardens and interesting shops (you can see chocolate being made at Humphreys) makes a nice stop. Useful places for lunch include the Ilkley Moor Vaults (Stockel Rd/Stourton Rd) and Wheatley Arms (Ben Rhydding). Ilkley Moor, S of the town, has potential for satisfying high-level walks (without your hat).

KEIGHLEY SE0542 (pronounced 'Keithly') A busy working town with a pleasant centre. The Grinning Rat nr the 16th-c church is useful for lunch. **Cliffe Castle Museum and Gallery** (Spring Gardens Lane) 19th-c mansion with French furniture from the Victoria & Albert Museum, as well as local ephemera. Though quite nr the centre, it's in a park well above the main road, with an aviary and greenhouses. Shop, disabled access to ground floor only; cl am Sun, all Mon (exc bank hols), 25–26 Dec, Good Fri; (01535) 618238; free. **East Riddlesden Hall** (Bradford Rd, just NE) Interesting, early 17th-c, oak-panelled, stone manor house with attractive plasterwork, period textiles and furniture, and a formal walled garden. There's a medieval monastic fishpond, and a huge medieval tithe barn. Snacks, shop, some disabled access; open pm Sat–Weds Mar–Oct, plus Thurs July and Aug; (01535) 607075; £3.30; NT.

! **LEEDS** SE2934 Now a really rewarding place to visit, with something for all ages: its Royal Armouries Museum makes an outstanding family day out, Tropical World is very enjoyable (and free), and there's plenty more to fill a short stay. A great deal of effort has gone into developing a 24-hour café culture here, and the compact centre, increasingly popular with young people in the evenings (lots of bars and clubs), is ideal for daytime exploring – it's largely free of traffic.

There are lots of splendid covered arcades (Victorian, Edwardian and modern), and all sorts of interesting and engaging Victorian architectural details to spot. Shoppers and theatre-goers are well catered for – the former in the exuberantly Venetian/Oriental glass-roofed **market**, the biggest in Yorks, and the latter by the West Yorkshire Playhouse (a useful meeting-place with fine city views from its good café/bar) and The Grand (home of Opera North). The imposing **town hall** is perhaps the high point of Leeds's essentially Victorian centre; and there are pleasant gardens and open spaces. Whitelocks (Turk's Head Yard, off Briggate) is a marvellous old city tavern, very much a Leeds institution.

The historic Waterfront area has been well developed for visitors in recent years. **Royal Armouries Museum** (Clarence Dock) This stunning £42.5 million complex houses the National Museum of Arms and Armour, previously at the Tower of London. It's almost completely interactive, with hi-tech effects and push-button displays, and plenty of costumed demonstrations showing how weapons were made and used, and affected everyday life; children can try on costumes and helmets, or even test their crossbow aim. Don't miss the breathtaking Hall of Steel, with 3,000 pieces of gleaming arms and armour on the walls. The most spectacular feature is outside: the country's only full-size, authentically re-created tiltyard, with dramatic exhibitions of jousting, fencing and duelling, as well as hunting dogs and birds of prey; phone for dates and times. An inside display area often has martial arts displays, and there are demonstrations of traditional skills in the Craft Court. Meals and snacks, shop, good disabled access; cl winter Mons, 24–25 Dec; (0990) 106666; £7.95 (£4.95 low season). **Tetleys Brewery Wharf** (Waterfront) Small museum, a chance to meet the shire horses and tour the brewery (booking recommended – or at least reserve a place as soon as you arrive; not suitable for under-14s). Indoor and outdoor play areas. Meals, snacks, shop, disabled access to ground floor of museum; cl 24–26 Dec, 1 Jan; (0113) 242 0666; £3.95. Granary Wharf, nr here on Neville St, has interesting shops and weekend events, festivals and entertainment.

Leeds City Art Gallery (The Headrow) Excellent collection of 20th-c British art, as well as English watercolours and a sculpture gallery, inc carefully chosen works by Henry Moore (he had his first exhibition here in 1941). Meals, snacks, shop, limited disabled access; cl am Sun, bank hols; (0113) 247 8248; free. **Henry Moore Institute** (The Headrow) Over a footbridge is this delightful place, with temporary exhibitions of sculpture from Roman times to the present, displayed in quite an unusual building (they don't actually show anything by Henry Moore). Shop, disabled access; (0113) 234 3158; free. Both galleries stay open late on Weds. **Corn Exchange** (Call Lane) This impressive 1860s building is filled with neat little specialist and designer shops, and plenty of places for tea, coffee and so forth, as well as an excellent, fresh, continental bread stall; there's a stamp market here on Sun, and often a small jazz group at teatime. **Leeds City Museum** (Claverley St) Deservedly on the Heritage Secretary's shortlist of excellent museums, of national importance. Cl Sun, Mon and bank hols; (0113) 247 8275; free.

Thackray Medical Museum (Beckett St) Dynamic museum at St James's Hospital, well known from the TV series *Jimmy's*. The emphasis is more on social history than science, but interactive displays show how the body works, and good reconstructions show the progress of medical care in Britain, inc some deliciously gruesome parts on surgery before the development of anaesthetics. Snacks, shop, disabled access; cl Mon (exc bank hols), 25–26 Dec, 1 Jan; (0113) 244 4343; £3.95. **Museum of the History of Education** (Parkinson Ct, Leeds University) Small but interesting, inc text and exercise books going back to the 17th c – it's usually best to book with Dr Foster, (0113) 233 4665 (open pm Mon, Weds, Fri and all Thurs; free). **Armley Mills Museum** (Canal Rd,

Armley) Once the largest woollen mill in the world, now a huge working museum, its floors given over to a massive display of textile machinery. Also a printing gallery, reconstructions of a turn-of-the-century tailor's shop and clothing factory, and demonstrations of static engines, steam locomotives and underground haulage. Snacks, shop, disabled access; cl am Sun, Mon (exc bank hols), 25–26 Dec; (0113) 263 7861; £2.

Middleton Colliery Railway Running from Turnstall Rd to Middleton Park, this is the oldest running railway in the world, and the first to be authorised by Parliament. Later it was the first to succeed with steam locomotives, and in 1960 became the first standard-gauge line run by enthusiasts. With a picnic area, fishing, nature trail and playgrounds as well as the trains, there's plenty for families here. Snacks, shop, disabled access; diesel or steamtrains most wknds Apr–Sept and some other days; (0113) 271 0320 for timetable; *£2. **Thwaite Mills** (Stourton) This water-powered mill was the focus of a tiny island community perched between the River Calder – which drives the mill wheels – and the Aire & Calder Navigation; hourly guided tours. The Georgian mill-owner's house has been restored, with displays on the site's history. Snacks, shop, disabled access; cl am Sun, all Mon (exc bank hols), 25–28 Dec, 1 Jan; (0113) 249 6453; £2.

Roundhay Park (off the A58 N) 700 acres of rolling parkland, well known for concerts and events. On Princes Ave here the **Canal Gardens** are very pleasant and peaceful, with several national flower collections (inc dahlias and violas), lots of roses, and ornamental wildfowl; free. The huge conservatory next door is **Tropical World**, housing the biggest collection of tropical plants outside Kew, along with all sorts of exotic trees, reptiles, fish, birds and butterflies, in careful re-creations of their natural settings. Meals, snacks, shop, disabled access; cl 25 Dec; (0113) 266 1850; *£1. The newly reopened Roundhay dining pub has cheap cheerful food.

Meanwood Valley Urban Farm (Meanwood) Small working farm on regenerated waste land N of the city centre, with rare breeds, an organic garden, and a new environment centre. Meals and snacks (not Mon), shop, good disabled access; (0113) 262 9759; *50p.

Temple Newsam House (5m E, S of the A63) Capability Brown designed the wonderful 1,200 acres of landscaped parkland and gardens in which this house stands, an extraordinary asset for any city. The house itself dates from Tudor and Jacobean times, and has the city's very good collections of decorative and fine art, as well as an exceptional assemblage of Chippendale furniture. Rare breeds in the grounds; picnic areas and a children's play area. Snacks, shop, disabled access to ground floor only; cl am Sun, all Mon, and Jan–Feb; (0113) 264 7321; *£2 (£1 parking).

LOTHERTON HALL SE4436 (B1217 Garforth–Tadcaster road) Edwardian, with displays ranging from Oriental art to British fashion, and paintings, silver and ceramics and some lovely furnishings. There's a bird garden in the restored grounds. Meals, snacks, shop, some disabled access; cl Mon (exc bank hols), am Sun, 1 Jan; (0113) 281 3259; *£2 house, grounds free. The Swan at nearby Aberford is popular for lunch.

★ **LUDDENDEN** SE0426 Interesting village with Brontë connections; the enormous Oats Royd Mill in the valley is a remarkable sight.

MALTBY SK5489 **Roche Abbey** (off the A634 SE) A fine gatehouse to the NW and the still-standing walls of the south and north transepts are all that's left of this 12th-c Cistercian abbey, but they make an impressive sight. Snacks, shop, some disabled access; cl Nov–Mar; (01709) 812739; £1.50.

MIDDLESTOWN SE2416 (Caphouse Colliery, New Rd) Well deserves its many awards for its exploration of life as a coal miner. No simple reconstruction this – they take you 140 metres (450ft) underground, down one of Britain's oldest working mine shafts, where models and machinery show the methods and working conditions of miners from the

1800s to the present. For the faint-hearted (and under-5s), on the surface there are pit ponies, 'paddy train' rides, steam winder, nature trail and an adventure playground. Dress sensibly if you're going underground. Meals, snacks, shop, disabled access and excellent facilities – helpful to arrange it in advance; cl 24–26 Dec, 1 Jan; (01924) 848806; £5.75. The Kaye Arms at Grange Moor is a good smart dining pub.

MONK BRETTON SE3706 The red sandstone remains of an important 12th-c **priory**, with gatehouse, church and other buildings, and some unusually well preserved drains. The ancient Mill of the Black Monks is pleasant at lunchtime (live music for young people most nights).

NORLAND MOOR SE0521 S of Sowerby Bridge, this gives walkers views from the Calderdale Way into adjacent Calderdale, with the Rochdale Canal along its foot.

NORTH ANSTON SK5284 **Tropical Butterfly House** Friendly, with insects, reptiles, snakes, birds of prey and farm animals besides the butterflies; they positively encourage you to touch as well as look. Meals, snacks, shop, disabled access; cl 25–26 Dec; (01909) 569416; £3.50.

NOSTELL PRIORY SE4017 (off the A638) Sumptuous Palladian mansion, with an additional wing built by Adam in 1766, and perhaps the best collection of Chippendale furniture anywhere, all designed for this house. Other highlights include the tapestry room, charming saloon, and a remarkably intricate 18th-c doll's house also said to have been furnished by Chippendale. The most attractive grounds have woodland walks and a lovely rose garden; coarse fishing on the lakes. There's an interesting **medieval church** nr the entrance, and a craft centre in the stables. Snacks, shop, disabled access; open pm wknds and bank hols Apr–Oct, plus pm Mon–Thurs July–early Sept; (01924) 863892; £4 house and grounds, £2.50 grounds only; NT. The Spread Eagle has decent food.

! **OAKWELL HALL** SE2127 (signed off the A651/A652, S of Birkenshaw) Moated Elizabethan manor house, altered in the 17th c, and still furnished to give something of the atmosphere then; look out for the unusual dog gates at the foot of the staircase. Also period formal gardens, extensive country park with an adventure playground, visitor centre and for children the **Discovery Gallery** – a hands-on exploration of the 4 elements. Snacks, shop, limited disabled access; cl am wknds (Discovery Gallery cl every am), Christmas wk; (01924) 326240; £1.20 house, visitor centre and Discovery Gallery free. The Black Bull opposite the ancient Norman church in nearby Birstall, has good-value home cooking.

Red House Museum (Oxford Rd, Gomersal) Vividly re-creates the 1830s in 9 carefully furnished period rooms (they plan to open more). Charlotte Brontë often stayed at the house (which stands out from its stone neighbours for its unusual red brick), and used it as the basis for Briarmains in *Shirley*. The gardens have been restored in 1830s style. Cl am wknds, Christmas wk, Good Fri; (01274) 335100; free.

OGDEN RESERVOIR SE0630 N of Halifax, this is well served with paths for walkers (inc a stretch of Roman road).

★ **OTLEY** SE2045 Archetypal Yorkshire market town with a most attractive atmosphere (helped by its remarkable number of pubs?). The nearby **Chevin** is not a high hill, but gives walkers a grand view of Wharfedale.

★ **RIPPONDEN** SE0318 Rather austerely attractive village, with a medieval pack-horse bridge; the B6113 and B6114 above here are interesting moors roads.

★ **SALTAIRE** SE1337 The pioneering industrial village Titus Salt developed in Shipley in the 1850s. Salt's beautifully thought out, classically designed village was so successful that even now it's a favoured place to live. It's well worth looking around, and you might want to try the antique **cable railway**. There's a splendid flight of locks on the Leeds–Liverpool Canal.

1853 Gallery (Victoria Rd) Taking its

name from the date when the magnificent mill it's housed in was built, probably one of the largest private collections of art in the country, inc around 300 works by David Hockney, with some of his intriguing experiments with photography. Huge bookshop, disabled access; cl 25–26 Dec; (01274) 531163; free. Some good smart shops in the building (inc one selling clothes made in the mill). **Victorian Reed Organ Museum** (Victoria Hall, Victoria Rd) Unique, with some eye-opening exhibits, inc an organ no bigger than a family bible. If you're an organ-player you may get the chance to try some of those on display. Limited disabled access; cl Fri, Sat, 2 wks at Christmas; (01274) 585601; £2.50.

★ ✝ **SAXTON** SE4736 Attractive village with a decent pub; don't miss the magnificent church, with Lord Dacre buried sitting on his war horse – the 1461 Battle of Towton site is just N.

SHEFFIELD SK3281 A vast industrial city, redeveloped extensively in post-war years – you really have to be a local to tap into the increasingly thriving and enjoyable cultural life of the place, but several places are rewarding to visit – though needing a street map and quite a bit of journeying. Best to use the comfortably modern tram to get about; it runs out to the giant indoor shopping mall at Meadowhall. The city's botanic gardens are now being restored, thanks to a hefty lottery grant. *See separate Family Panel on p.743* for **National Centre for Popular Music. Kelham Island Museum** (around Alma St, signed from Sheffield centre) Lively exploration of Sheffield's industrial development, with all sorts of buildings, workshops and machinery collections (inc formidable working engines), and traditional cutlery craftsmen at work. Snacks, shop, disabled access; cl Fri, Sat; (0114) 272 2106; £3. The Fat Cat here has good food. **Sheffield City Museum and Mappin Art** (Weston Park) Firmly traditional, but with some interesting collections, inc fine cutlery and a splendid display of antique Sheffield plate. The excellent gallery has works by Renoir, Cézanne, Turner and even Walt Disney. Meals, snacks, disabled access; cl Mon (exc bank hols), Tues, Christmas; (0114) 276 8588; free. **Graves Gallery** (Surrey St) Well worth a visit, with some fine decorative art; cl Sun and Mon; free. **Ruskin Gallery** (Norfolk St) The collection of Victorian artist and writer John Ruskin, with an adjacent craft gallery; cl Sun and Mon; free. **Bishop's House** (Meersbrook Park, S of the city centre) Striking 15th- and 16th-c yeoman's house, now a good museum of social history. Shop, limited disabled access; cl Mon (exc bank hols), Tues; (0114) 255 7701; £1. **Sheffield Bus Museum** (Tinsley) Diverse collection of buses and even pre-war milk floats, with related memorabilia and a big model railway. Shop, snacks, some disabled access; open pm wknds for restoration work, with open days every couple of months when the displays are more lively; (0114) 255 3010; *£1. **Abbeydale Industrial Hamlet** (Abbeydale Road S) has been closed for redevelopment. It should reopen in Apr 1999; (0114) 2367731 for details; £3.

ULLEY SK4687 Pleasant walks around a reservoir, also good for fishing and watersports; the Royal Oak is in a lovely setting by the church.

✝ **WAKEFIELD** SE3221 A number of handsome buildings, inc its **cathedral**, much restored in Victorian times but with some fine 15th-c masonry and carvings (and a marvellous spire – the tallest in Yorks), its rare 14th-c **bridge chapel** over the River Calder, some Georgian and Regency houses most notably around Wood St and St John's Sq, and its imposing civic buildings. **Wakefield Art Gallery** (Wentworth Terrace) Good collection of 20th-c painting and sculpture, internationally famous for its galleries devoted to local sculptors Barbara Hepworth and Henry Moore. Shop; cl am Sun, all Mon, 25–26 Dec, 1 Jan; (01924) 305796; free. **Wakefield Museum** (Wood St) Unique collection of preserved animals and exotic birds, and an exhibition of 1940s women's costume. Shop; cl for refurbishment for much of 1999; (01924) 305351; free. **Yorkshire Sculpture Park** SE3014 (Bretton Hall College, West Bretton; A637 SE) Carefully and imaginatively displayed series of major contemporary sculpture in fine, 18th-c, landscaped parkland. There are 16 works by Henry Moore in the adjacent country park, often surrounded by grazing sheep. Shop; cl Christmas; (01924) 830579; free (though £1.50 car parking charge).

★ **WENTWORTH** SK3898 Reckoned by some readers to be the prettiest village they've ever seen.

WITHENS CLOUGH RESERVOIR SD9822 S of Hebden Bridge, with a path for walkers – the more energetic can head up to the prominent monument on Stoodley Pike, for the views.

WORSBROUGH SE3503 **Country Park, Farm and Mill Museum** (A61) Hard to believe this peaceful country park was once a busy industrial area; the only sign of those days is the working corn mill, now a museum but still producing stoneground flour. The 200 acres also include nature trails, traditional and rare breeds, and several beehives; lots of events all year, especially on bank hols and summer Suns. Snacks, shop, some disabled access; cl Mon (exc bank hols), Tues, and 19 Dec–2 Jan; (01226) 774527; *50p.

★ **Other attractive or attractively placed villages**, with decent pubs, include Askwith SD1648, Barkisland SE0420, Blackshaw Head SD9527, Boston Spa SE4345, East Morton SE1042, Esholt SE1840, Holme SE1006, Honley SE1312, Ledsham SE4529, Ogden SE 0730, Sowerby SE0423, Sowerby Bridge SE0623, Stanbury SE0037 and Tickhill SK5993 (especially the church and semi-ruined castle).

Other useful pubs in fine positions or with good views include Dick Hudsons on the Otley rd at High Eldwick SE1240 above Bingley, the Castle overlooking the reservoirs nr Bolsterstone SK2796, the Brown Cow by the open-access woods at Ireland Bridge (on the B6429) nearer Bingley, the Strines nr Strines Reservoir above Bradfield SK2692, the Stanhope Arms on Windle Edge Lane nr Winscar Reservoir by Dunford Bridge SE1502, the New Inn at Eccup SE2842, the Cow & Calf up Skew Hill Lane at Grenoside above Sheffield SK3293, the Malt Shovel at Harden SE0838, the Robin Hood at Pecket Well SD9928 outside Hebden Bridge, the Cherry Tree on Bank End Lane at High Hoyland SE2710, the Fleece at Holme SE1006, the Buckstones on the A640 towards Denshaw, high above Huddersfield SE1416, the Blacksmith's Arms on Heaton Moor Rd at Kirkheaton SE1818, the Shepherd's Rest on Mankinholes Rd at Lumbutts SD9523, the Mount Skip nr Midgley SE0027, perched high over Hebden Bridge (on the Calderdale Way footpath), the Hinchcliffe Arms at Cragg Vale, Mytholmroyd SE0126 (the B6188 S is a good moors road), the Hobbit up Hob Lane, Norland SE0723, the Grouse on Harehills Lane, Oldfield, nr Oakworth SE0038, the Causeway Foot on the Keighley rd by Ogden Reservoir SE0631, the Waggon & Horses (on the A6033) and Dog & Gun (off the B6141 towards Denholme), both nr Oxenhope SE0335, the Pineberry on the A644 Keighley rd out of Queensbury SE1030, the Brown Cow

Days Out

Bradford bounce: National Museum of Photography, Film and Television (when it reopens) – or (now free) Bradford's Industrial Museum; stroll through Little Germany, behind the cathedral; lunch at one of the city's Indian restaurants; Saltaire (easiest by train).

Last of the Summer Wine: Holmfirth; lunch at Will's o' Nat's in Meltham; Colne Valley Museum, Golcar; stroll along the Huddersfield Canal towpath.

Leading Leeds: Royal Armouries Museum; lunch at the Brasserie Forty-Four (The Calls); Temple Newsam House.

(on the A672) dramatically overlooking Scammonden Reservoir SE0215, the Clothiers Arms in Station Rd, Stocksmoor, nr Shepley SE1810, the White House (on the B6107) or Rose & Crown up Cop Hill at Slaithwaite SE0813, the Blue Ball nr Soyland SE0120, the Sportsman's Arms at Hawks Stones, Kebcote on Stansfield Moor SD9227, the Ring o' Bells on Hill Top Rd at Thornton SE0933, the Freemason's Arms on Hopton Hall Lane at Upper Hopton SE1918, the Cross Keys overlooking the restored Rochdale Canal at Walsden SD9322, the Delvers on Cold Edge Rd and Withens on Warley Moor Rd at Wainstalls SE0428 and the Pack Horse at Widdop SD9333.

Where to eat

BARDSEY SE3642 **Bingley Arms** *Church St (01937) 572462* Ancient pub decorated in keeping, full of interest and atmosphere, with big fireplace in the spacious lounge (split into intimate areas), a smaller public bar, and an upstairs brasserie; warm and friendly atmosphere, a wide range of fair-value food inc good daily specials, well kept real ales, nice wines, and a charming terrace. **£17.45**|£5.95.

GRANGE MOOR SE2415 **Kaye Arms** *(01924) 848385* Civilised and busy, family-run dining pub with a smart dining lounge; particularly good, imaginative food, exceptional-value house wines from a fine list, decent malt whiskies, and helpful, courteous service; cl Mon, 25–26 Dec; children allowed lunchtime only; disabled access. **£20**|£7.

HALIFAX SE0925 **Design House** *Dean Clough (01422) 383242* Stylish modern restaurant in this thriving, carefully restored carpet mill complex, with enjoyable cooking to match; relaxed and friendly atmosphere, good service, and a thoughtful wine list; cl pm Sun and Mon, 26 Dec, 1 Jan; disabled access. **£17.50**.

HAWORTH SE0237 **Weavers** *15 West Lane (01535) 643822* Charming evening restaurant made up of weavers' cottages, with most enjoyable, hearty (not heavy) food, cheerful service, and lovely puddings; has a good loyal following; bdrms; cl Sun, Mon, 2 wks after Christmas. **£18.25 3-course set meal**.

LEEDS SE3033 **Brasserie Forty-Four** *44 The Calls (0113) 234 3232* Originally a grain mill (below 42 The Calls, *see* **Where to stay** *section on p.742*), this riverside restaurant is simply furnished with modern designs, and serves enjoyable British and Mediterranean food (very good-value early evening set menu); also, a good-value wine list; cl am Sat, Sun, bank hols; partial disabled access. **£29.26**|£5.

LEEDS SE3033 **Leodis** *Victoria Mill, Sovereign St (0113) 242 1010* Stylish modern restaurant on the ground floor of a former Victorian mill, with carefully cooked, popular brasserie food, decent wines, and a bustling buoyant atmosphere; cl Sun, 25–26 Dec; disabled access. **£19.45**|£6.90.

LEEDS SE3033 **Pool Court at 42** *42 The Calls (0113) 244 4242* Cleverly converted quayside grain mill (also incorporating Brasserie Forty-Four and the stylish hotel, 42 The Calls), this is a smart modern restaurant with a calm atmosphere, very accomplished, enjoyable food with French leanings (the set meals are good value), lovely puddings, and an interesting wine list; cl am Sat, Sun, bank hols; disabled access. **£42.50**.

LEEDS SE2736 **Salvos** *115 Otley Rd, Headingley (0113) 275 5017* Welcoming, family-run, Italian restaurant with good modern food (popular and interesting daily specials) and cheerful service; cl Sun, 24–26 Dec; disabled access. **£15**|£5.85.

LEEDS SE2933 **Sous le Nez en Ville** *The Basement, Quebec House, Quebec St (0113) 244 0108* Imaginative and popular food in this fashionable basement restaurant with tiled floors and exposed brick walls; a very good wine list, and efficient service; cl Sun, bank hols. **£14.95 3-course set evening menu**.

MELTHAM SE0912 **Will's o' Nat's** *Blackmoorfoot Rd (01484) 850078* Well run pub, alone in a fine moorland spot; with comfortable seating and lots of interesting old local photographs and drawings in the spacious bar, nice views from the raised, partly no smoking dining extension, a wide choice of popular, good-value food, well kept real ales, and a big collection of malt whiskies; cl pm 25 and 26 Dec, 1 Jan; limited disabled access. **£14**|£4.60.

RIPPONDEN SE0419 **Old Bridge** *(01422) 822595/823722* Well kept, medieval inn by a pretty bridge over the River Ryburn; with interesting rooms, good wines and real ales, and a very popular cold buffet weekday lunchtimes (best to book); charming evening restaurant just over the bridge; no bar food Sat or pm Sun; no children; disabled access. **£16**|£4.75.

SHEFFIELD SK3186 **Smith's of Sheffield** *34 Sandygate Rd (0114) 266 6096* Very popular restaurant, cheerfully decorated in cream and red, with an unusual tented ceiling; a relaxed chatty atmosphere, stylish modern cooking using influences from all over the world, and a good wine list; upstairs is perhaps more serious, with an open-plan kitchen and 6 gourmet courses of the chef's choice; cookery demonstrations, too; cl Sun, Mon. **£29.25**.

Special thanks to Patrick Joseph Hone, Mrs C Mitchell, Mr and Mrs S J Pyke, Margaret and Arthur Dickinson, Duncan Blake, Barbara J Cummins, K V and A A McAnna, E G Parish, A J Clark, Melinda Simmons, L Price, Trevor Knapton, S Clarke, Miss A McDougall, L A McCardie, Mrs Woodfield, Miss N Hurt.

We welcome reports from readers

This *Guide* depends on readers' reports. Do help us if you can – in return, we offer a discount on the next edition to people who've helped us with reports for it. Tell us what you think about places already in it, and anything extra you think we should say about them. And send us your ideas for inclusion in the next edition: places to visit, eat at or stay in, attractive drives or walks, maybe even unusual interesting shops you know of. Use the card in the middle, the report forms at the end, or just write – no stamp needed: *The Good Guide to Britain*, FREEPOST TN1569, Wadhurst, E Sussex TN5 7BR.

Yorkshire Calendar

Some of these dates were provisional as we went to press. Please check information with the telephone numbers provided.

JANUARY

4 **Hubberholme** Land Letting at the George pub, *at 8pm* – ancient auction for church lands grazing (01756) 760223

9 **York** Book Fair at the Barbican Centre (01904) 656688

16 **Goathland** Day of Dance: ancient long sword dance (Norse origin) around the village *from 9am* (01904) 770318

FEBRUARY

13 **Doncaster** Festival of Railway Modelling at the Exhibition Centre – *till Sun 14* (01778) 391109

16 **Scarborough** Shrovetide Skipping Festival *at noon*: ¾ mile of Foreshore Rd closed to traffic till 5pm (01723) 373333

18 **York** Jorvik Viking Festival: warriors' torchlit procession, combat, boat burning and fireworks – *till Sun 21* (01937) 541030

26 **York** Antiques and Collectors' Fair at the Racecourse – *till Sun 28* (01526) 298198

28 **Harrogate** Classic Car Restoration Show at the Great Yorkshire Showground (01484) 660622

MARCH

5 **Bradford** Film Festival – *till Sun 21* (01274) 394540

6 **Whitby** Eskdale Festival of the Arts: competitive event – *till Sat 13* (01947) 601249

7 **Harrogate** National Classic Bike Show at the Great Yorkshire Showground (01484) 660622

15 **Elsecar** National Week of Science and Technology at Elsecar Heritage – *till Sun 21* (01226) 740203

22 **Hull** International Festival – *till 5 Apr* (01482) 615624

27 **Nunnington** John Ives Exhibition at Nunnington Hall –*till 28 Apr* (01439) 748283

APRIL

1 **Doncaster** Easter Egg Rolling at Cusworth Hall Museum of South Yorkshire Life (01302) 782342

2 **Harrogate** International Youth Music Festival – *till Fri 9* (01306) 744360; **Hebden Bridge** Pace Egg Plays: old custom (01422) 843831; **Keighley** Children's Events – *till Sun 4* at East Riddlesden Hall (01535) 607075

3 **Hull** Easter Street Organ Festival in the city centre (01482) 615625; **York** Model Railway Show: almost 40 layouts – *till Tues 6* (01653) 694319

4 **Carlton** Selby Game Fair at Carlton Towers – *till Mon 5* (01757) 618333

5 **Elsecar** Easter Country Fayre at Elsecar Heritage: animals, brass and folk bands (01226) 740203; **Ossett** World Coal-carrying Championship (01924) 218990

16 **Harrogate** National Model Engineering and Modelling Exhibition at the Showground – *till Sun 18* (01751) 473780

Yorkshire Calendar (cont.)

17 **Great Ouseburn** Festival of Springtime: open gardens and flower festival – *till Sun 18* (01423) 330833

21 **Beningbrough** Members Day at Beningbrough Hall: conducted tours behind the scenes for NT members only (01904) 470002

22 **Harrogate** Spring Flower Show – *till Sun 25* (01423) 536880

23 **Whitby** Gothic Weekend – *till Sun 25* (0115) 949 7659

24 **Marsden** Cuckoo Day at Marsden Mechanics Hall, and village procession, with maypole and morris dancing (01484) 847071

25 **Horton in Ribblesdale** Three Peaks Race (01423) 712000

30 **Bridlington** Arts Festival inc street entertainment, ballet and concerts – *till 9 May* (01262) 671400; **Cleethorpes** Beer Festival at the Winter Gardens – *till 3 May* (01472) 692925

MAY

2 **Elsecar** Classic Car Show at Heritage Centre – *till Mon 3* (01226) 740203; **Gawthorpe** Maypole Procession (01924) 305000; **Halifax** Farming Fun at Snibden Hall (01422) 352246; **Hovingham** Rare Plant Sale at Hovingham Hall (01904) 608332

8 **Bishop Burton** Gardens Open Day at Bishop Burton College (01964) 553000; **Sheffield** Chamber Music Festival – *till Sat 22* (0114) 221 2182; **Sowerby Bridge** Waterways and Town Festival – *till Sun 9* (01422) 831627

9 **Headingley** World Cup Cricket Warm-up, Yorkshire v India (0113) 278 7394; **Settle** Sheep Show inc sheepdog trials and craft workshops (01729) 822989

12 **Headingley** World Cup Cricket Warm-up, Yorkshire v Scotland (0113) 278 7394; **Whitby** Planting of the Penny Hedge (corruption of penance hedge): a tradition since 1159 (01947) 602674

15 **Haworth** 40s Weekend: music and military vehicles – *till Sun 16* (01535) 644407

16 **Beningbrough** Plant Fair at Beningbrough Hall (01904) 470666; **Keighley** Plant Fair at East Riddlesden Hall (01535) 607075; **Mytholmroyd** World Dock Pudding Championships (01422) 883023; **Nunnington** Plant Fair at Nunnington Hall (01439) 748283

22 **Otley** Show (01943) 462541; **York** Busking Festival (01904) 551677

23 **Headingley** World Cup Cricket: Australia v Pakistan (0113) 278 7394

27 **Beverley and East Riding** Early Music Festival – *till Mon 31* (01904) 645738; **Keld** Tan Hill Show at Tan Hill Inn (01833) 628246

28 **Elsecar** Enid Blyton Fun Weekend at Elsecar Heritage – *till Mon 31* (01226) 740203; **Scarborough** Fair, and International Morris and Folk Festival – *till 6 Jun* (01723) 379220; **Swaledale, Wensleydale and Arkengarthdale** Festival: classical music, folk and jazz – *till 13 Jun* (01969) 622217

29 **Harewood** Spring Festival: fashion, fine art and crafts sale at Harewood House – *till Mon 31* (01273) 833884; **Sewerby** Horse Pageant: shire horses, carriage events, horse show with 190 classes at Sewerby Hall and Gardens – *till Mon 31* (01262) 851052

30 **Leeds** Steam Spectacular at Temple Newsam – *till Mon 31* (01751) 473780; **York** Motor and Leisure Show at York Racecourse – *till Mon 31* (01904) 48888

Yorkshire Calendar (cont.)

JUNE

2 **Heptonstall** Pennine Spring Music Festival – *till Sat 5* (01799) 530643
4 **Robin Hood's Bay** Folk Festival – *till Sun 6* (01947) 602674
5 **Hull** Lord Mayor's Parade and Gala (01482) 615625
6 **Cawthorne** Children's Events at Cannon Hall (01226) 790270; **Headingley** World Cup Cricket: super six (0113) 278 7394
10 **Bramham** International Horse Trials and Country Fair at Bramham Park – *till Sun 13* (01937) 844265
11 **Helmsley** Antiques Fair at Duncombe Park – *till Sun 13* (01423) 522122
12 **Halifax** Procession (01422) 368725; **Hebden Bridge** Arts Festival – *till 11 July* (01422) 842684; **Knaresborough** Bed Race (01423) 866886; **Whitby** Festival – *till Sun 20* (01947) 602674; **York** Outdoor Chess Festival – *till Sun 13* (01904) 554433
13 **Headingley** World Cup Cricket: super six (0113) 278 7394
18 **Grassington** Festival: classical, jazz and comedy – *till 3 July* (01756) 752774; **Horton in Ribblesdale** Terrier and Stick Show (01729) 860289
19 **Leeds** Lord Mayor's Parade (0113) 245 1101; **Nunnington** Outdoor Concert at Nunnington Hall (01439) 748283; **Wetherby** Agricultural Show (01937) 833299; **York** Cycling Rally inc vintage displays, sales, and arena events – *till Sun 20* (01483) 417217
20 **Bishop Burton** Town and Country Day at Bishop Burton College (01964) 553000; **Elsecar** Classic Motorbike and Car Rally at Elsecar Heritage (01226) 350239; **Great Ouseburn** Twelve Open Gardens (01423) 330394; **Mirfield** Vintage Vehicle Display (01924) 490833; **Walkington** Hay Ride to Bishop Burton (01482) 868955
24 **Fountains Abbey** Open-air Shakespeare at Fountains Abbey – *till Sat 26* (01765) 608888
25 **Bradford** Festival: street theatre, music, dance and Asian Mela – *till 18 July* (01274) 309199
26 **Filey** Edwardian Festival – *till 4 July* (01723) 516142; **Keighley** Outdoor Concert at East Riddlesden Hall (01535) 607075; **Nidderdale** Festival – *till 2 July* (01423) 711532; **South Otterington** North Yorkshire County Agricultural Show at Otterington Hall (01609) 773429
27 **Halifax** People's Park Festival: multicultural event (01422) 347392

JULY

1 **Malton** Agricultural Show at Scampston Park (01653) 693382; **Whitby** Angling Festival – *till Sat 10* (01287) 660118
2 **Cleckheaton** Folk Festival – *till Sun 4* (01924) 404346; **York** Early Music Festival – *till Sun 11* (01904) 645738
3 **Helmsley** Steam Fair at Duncombe Park – *till Sun 4* (01439) 770213; **Northallerton** Historic and Classic Car Rally (01642) 722791; **York** Street Art Festival – *till Sun 4* (01904) 554433
4 **Alne** Vintage Vehicle and Machinery Event (01429) 268760; **Halifax** Irish Festival at Piece Hall (01422) 358087; **Holmfirth** Art Week at the Civic Hall: approx 1,800 amateur and professional exhibits – *till Sat 10* (01484) 683211; **Oxenhope** Straw Races: teams in fancy dress race between 5 pubs carrying a bale of straw (01535) 644298
9 **Fountains Abbey** Music by Moonlight at Fountains Abbey – *till Sat 10* (01765) 608888

Yorkshire Calendar (cont.)

13 Harrogate Great Yorkshire Show at the Yorkshire Showground – *till Thurs 15* (01423) 541000
16 Hornsea Carnival inc classic cars, bands and arena events – *till Sun 18* (01964) 536404
18 Bramhope Arthington Show (0113) 275 9335; **Middlesbrough** Family Asian Arts Day in Albert Park (01642) 263839
19 Hull International Festival – *till 1 Aug* (01482) 615624
22 Harrogate International Festival – *till 7 Aug* (01423) 562303
23 Fountains Abbey Open-air Opera at Fountains Abbey – *till Sat 24* (01765) 608888
24 Elsecar Garden Weekend at Elsecar Heritage – *till Sun 25* (01226) 740203; **Middlesbrough** Eisteddfod Parade and events at the Town Hall – *till Thurs 29* (01642) 263839
25 Flask Sports, Gymkhana and Working Hunter Show (01947) 880441; **Fountains Abbey** Music Day at Fountains Abbey (01765) 608888
27 Rye Dale Show (01653) 697820
28 Whitby Sneaton and Hawsker Agricultural Show at Russel Hall Farm (01947) 602674
30 Pickering Traction Engine Rally – *till 1 Aug* (01751) 473780
31 Leeds Rhythms of the City: largest street theatre festival in the North – *till 29 Aug* (0113) 213 7800

AUGUST

1 Halifax Yorkshire Day at Piece Hall (01422) 358087; **Keighley** Children's Theatre – *till Weds 4* at East Riddlesden Hall (01535) 607075
3 Egton Bridge Old Gooseberry Show at St Heddas School: since 1800, tastings *from 5pm*, music (01947) 810009; **Halifax** Shakespeare Festival – *till Tues 10* at Piece Hall (01422) 358087; **Littlebeck** Garden Fête and Rose Queen Ceremony (01947) 810759
4 Hull Jazz Festival – *till Sun 8* (01482) 615624
6 Middlesbrough Stockton International Riverside Festival – *till Sat 7* (01642) 263839; **Saltburn-by-the-Sea** International Folk, Music, Dance and Song Festival – *till Sun 8* (01947) 840928
7 Elsecar Model Engineering Gala at Elsecar Heritage – *till 8 Sept* (01226) 740203; **Fountains Abbey** Watergarden Revels at Fountains Abbey (01765) 608888
11 Keighley Storytelling in the Garden at East Riddlesden Hall (01535) 607075
13 Castle Bolton Son et Lumière: re-enactment of the history of the castle from the 14th c to the 17th c, inc siege and fireworks at Bolton Castle (01969) 623981
14 Whitby Regatta and Carnival – *till Mon 16* (01947) 602674
15 Halifax South Asian Festival at Piece Hall (01422) 358087; **Ripley** Classic Car and Motorcycle Rally inc arena display and stands (01484) 660622
17 York Races: Ebor Festival at the Racecourse – *till Thurs 19* (01904) 620911
21 West Witton Burning of the Bartle: effigy of legendary outlaw, and fun day – *till Sun 22* (01969) 622034; **Whitby** Folk Week – *till Fri 27* (01947) 820408
25 Egton Show (01947) 895281
28 Elvington Air Spectacular at the Airbase – *till Mon 30* (01904) 554455; **Leyburn** Wensleydale Agricultural Show (01969) 640261

Yorkshire Calendar (cont.)

29 **Halifax** Live Crafts Weekend at Piece Hall – *till Mon 30* (01422) 358087
30 **Burniston** Horticultural and Agricultural Show (01723) 870049; **Epworth** Show (01427) 872571

SEPTEMBER

2 **Hull** International Sea Shanty Festival: music and classic boat regatta – *till Sun 5* (01482) 615624
4 **Elsecar** Classic Car Show at Elsecar Heritage – *till Sun 5* (01226) 740203; **Keighley** and District Agricultural Show (01535) 643206; **Sowerby Bridge** Rushbearing Festival – *till Sun 5* (01422) 831896
11 **Castleton and Danby** Agricultural Show (01287) 660409; **Whitby** Heritage Week – *till Sun 19* (01947) 602674
12 **Hardraw Scar** Brass Band Competition at the Green Dragon Inn (01430) 423451
17 **Harrogate** Autumn Flower Show – *till Sun 19* (01423) 561049; **York** National Book Fair at the Barbican Centre – *till Sat 18* (01904) 656688
18 **York** Festival of Food and Drink – *till Sun 26* (01904) 653655
25 **Keighley** Civil War Living History at East Riddlesden Hall – *till Sun 26* (01535) 607075

OCTOBER

8 **Hull** Fair: huge funfair – *till Sat 16* (01482) 615624
16 **Wetherby** Festival: amateur and professional drama, opera and art exhibitions – *till Sun 31* (01937) 583221
20 **Rievaulx** Apple Week at Rievaulx Terrace – *till Sun 24* (01439) 798340
29 **Whitby** Gothic Weekend – *till Sun 31* (0115) 949 7659

NOVEMBER

5 **Helmsley** Country Fair at Duncombe Park – *till Sun 7* (01923) 788517
10 **Hull** Literature Festival – *till Sun 21* (01482) 615624
17 **Huddersfield** Contemporary Music Festival – *till Sun 28* (01484) 425082
25 **York** St Nicholas Fair: crafts, choirs – *till Sun 28* (01904) 632257

DECEMBER

3 **Fountains Abbey** Christmas Concerts at Fountains Abbey – *also on Sat 4, Fri 10 and Sat 11* (01765) 608888; **Holme upon Spalding Moor** Christmas Market and Craft Fair (01430) 860201
11 **Elsecar** Christmas Fair at Elsecar Heritage (01226) 740203; **Keighley** Christmas Fair at East Riddlesden Hall – *till Sun 12* (01535) 607075
24 **Dewsbury** Old Custom: tolling the Devil's knell (01484) 223200

London

More visitors than ever – and more to see and do, with the approaching Millennium prompting all sorts of developments.

One of the great things about London is that almost everything worth visiting or looking at is concentrated in the relatively small centre, and it seems likely that in the next year or two more of the central tourist places such as Trafalgar Square will be closed to most traffic.

With London prices so high, it's important to note that some of the most outstanding places to visit are free: the National Gallery, National Portrait Gallery and Wallace Collection (West End), the Tate Gallery (Westminster), Leighton House (Kensington), the Geffrye Museum, Museum of Childhood and Guildhall (City), the British Museum (despite pressure on it to introduce charges), the British Library and the extraordinary Sir John Soane's Museum (Bloomsbury), Kenwood (Hampstead) and the Horniman Museum (Forest Hill). The big three South Kensington museums are now free again – if you go after 4.30pm – as is the Imperial War Museum (south of the river). And several places have free entertainment – most notably, Covent Garden, the Barbican Centre and the South Bank.

Among places that do charge admission, you get a real feeling of value for money from the new London Balloon (the world's largest tethered balloon – south of the river), the Museum of the Moving Image (MOMI), the Museum of London (City; its admission ticket is valid for 3 months), Britain at War, and the Imperial War Museum (south of the river; the War Museum's free after 4.30pm), and the toy and model museum at Lancaster Gate (West End). The remarkable London Aquarium (south of the River) is a great family outing, and the House of Detention (City) is a really good new look at the grimmer side of London's past. The Rugby Experience out at Twickenham is immensely popular with people hooked by the game.

There are plenty of ways to save money on attractions: one of the best is the London White Card, which covers entry to 15 of the top museums (including the Science Museum, MOMI, and the V&A) for £16, provided you can squeeze them all into 3 days. The London for Less scheme gives discounts on some attractions (including the high-priced Madame Tussaud's), restaurants, theatres and hotels: quite a bargain, it covers 4 people for 8 days for £12.95, and is on sale at the tourist information centre at Victoria and at bookshops such as Dillons and WH Smith. A one-day Travelcard is an excellent investment for visitors; you can even buy them in advance from newsagents. It's valid on buses, tube and rail trains, for as many journeys as you want to make during the day (not the morning rush hour). For only slightly more, you can get a Travelcard for the whole weekend, or a book of 10 individual tickets. If you're coming up to London by train, you can add a one-day Travelcard to the rail fare at a big discount. Tickets on some rail routes allow discounts at a few London attractions.

London's Tube, the underground railway, is the most straightforward way of getting around, and easy for even first-time visitors. Around rush hour and late at night, though, the underground becomes rather unpleasant, with infrequent trains and overcrowded carriages. Buses have the advantage of letting you sight-see as you go (there are also several hop-on hop-off tour buses, day or night, with commentaries). Pocket tube and London Transport bus route maps are free from ticket offices. In the text, we have grouped most things to see and do under the heading of the most convenient tube station, using the ⊖ symbol – or the ⇌ symbol if it's surface rail instead.

If you're going to be wandering around, you should have an A–Z street guide; even people who've lived here for years carry one almost wherever they go.

Central London is fun to explore on foot, though the traffic and stop-start rhythm can be wearying. There is no end of potential walks concentrating on particular interests – architecture, history, Royalty or whatever. One of the best overviews of the capital is had by walking along the south bank of the Thames from Lambeth Bridge to Tower Bridge, giving mostly traffic-free panoramic views of the West End, St Paul's Cathedral, the City, the Tower of London and, finally, the Docklands. Quite a number of people lead guided walks. We have found Original London Walks, (0171) 624 3978, consistently good over the last few years, with a choice of 9 or 10 walks a day. Walks last about 2 hours, usually starting from a tube station; you don't need to book, and the cost is around £4.50.

A point to note is that food in London pubs (as opposed to the better ones elsewhere) tends to be very ordinary indeed; few, apart from those we mention, are worth considering for a decent bite to eat.

All the places to stay that we include are within reasonably easy reach of the centre, and many of them are actually part of it.

Where to stay

22 JERMYN STREET *22 Jermyn St SW1Y 6HL (0171) 734 2353* **£233.83;** 5 rms and 13 suites – spacious with deeply comfortable seats and sofas, flowers, plants, and antiques. Stylish little hotel owned by the same family for over 80 years and much loved by customers; no public rooms, wonderful 24-hour service, helpful notes and suggestions from the friendly owners, in-room light meals, and a warm welcome for children; disabled access.

BASIL STREET HOTEL *8 Basil St SW3 1AH (0171) 581 3311* **£206,** plus special breaks; 93 pretty, decent-sized rms, most with own bthrm. Handy for Harrods and Hyde Park, this very civilised, privately owned Edwardian hotel has a relaxed atmosphere, antiques, fine carpets and paintings in the public rooms, a panelled restaurant with reliably good food, cellar wine bar, afternoon teas in the lounge, and ladies' club (named after a parrot who had to go when his language became inappropriate); helpful, courteous service – many of the staff have been here for years, the manager for over 40; children free in parents' rm.

CAPITAL *22–24 Basil St SW3 1AT (0171) 589 5171* **£287.98;** 48 luxury rms with lovely fabrics, fine paintings, marble bthrms, and complimentary extras. Exclusive little hotel nr Harrods, with a warm welcome and log fire in the reception, an intimate panelled bar with good nibbles, and a small lounge; exemplary service, and exceptional, French-inspired food in the chandelier-lit restaurant; disabled access.

CHESTERFIELD *35 Charles St W1X 8LX (0171) 491 2622* **£223.25;** 110 well equipped, pretty rms. Charming hotel with particularly courteous, helpful staff; afternoon tea in the panelled library, a relaxed club-style bar with resident pianist, and fine food in the attractive restaurant or light and airy Terrace Room; disabled access.

CLARIDGES *Brook St W1A 2JQ (0171) 629 8860* ***£295 inc champagne and chocolates,** plus luxury breaks; 197 excellent rms. Grand hotel long used by Royalty and heads of state; with liveried footmen, lift attendants and valets, elegant and comfortable day rooms, and a civilised colonnaded foyer where the Hungarian Quartet plays; lovely formal restaurant with mirrored mural and terrace, more intimate, smaller restaurant called the Causerie, and dinner-dance Fri–Sat evenings; free golf at Wentworth (and tennis at the Vanderbilt Racquet Club); disabled access.

CLAVERLEY *13–14 Beaufort Gdns SW3 1PS (0171) 589 8541* **£120,** plus special breaks; 30 individually and recently decorated rms, most with own bthrm. Friendly, privately owned Edwardian house with a comfortable lounge, panelled reading room, and good breakfasts in the cheerful dining room.

CONNAUGHT *Carlos Pl W1Y 6AL (0171) 499 7070;* 90 lovely, individually decorated rms inc 24 suites. A very special place with fine old-fashioned dignified values – there's no brochure, no price list; elegant, restful day rooms filled with lovely flowers and antiques, fine panelling, exemplary service, and outstanding food in the 2 formal restaurants; disabled access.

CONRAD *Chelsea Harbour SW10 0XG (0171) 823 3000* **£206.38;** 160 suites with a light and spacious living-room area (many have sofa-beds so 2 small children could stay with parents at no extra cost). American-owned, Europe's first purpose-built luxury 'suite hotel' is tucked away in the quiet modern enclave of the Chelsea Harbour development and overlooks its small marina; good food in the Brasserie (marina views) or the Long Gallery, friendly service, evening pianist, and a health club; disabled access.

COVENT GARDEN HOTEL *10 Monmouth St WC2H 9HB (0171) 806 1000* **£247.65;** 50 big, individual bdrms with smart bthrms. Stylish luxury hotel nr theatres; wrought-iron staircase from the foyer to the panelled upstairs drawing room and library filled with richly coloured, interesting furniture; small ground-floor brasserie.

DURRANTS *George St W1H 6BJ (0171) 935 8131* **£136.50;** 92 well equipped rms, with own bthrms; the quietest are at the back. Managed by the same family for over 70 years, this surprisingly quiet central hotel, set behind a delightful Georgian façade, has fine paintings and antiques, a clubby bar, and relaxing lounges; cosy panelled restaurant with essentially English cooking, and helpful, pleasant staff; disabled access.

FIELDING *4 Broad Court WC2B 5QZ (0171) 836 8305* **£96;** 24 rms, with showers. Carefully renovated and well run, small 18th-c hotel opposite the Royal Opera House site and charmingly lit at night by the preserved 19th-c gas lamps; with a residents' bar (watched over by Smokey the African grey parrot), and good breakfasts; cl 1 wk over Christmas; children over 12.

GORING *15 Beeston Pl, Grosvenor Gdns SW1W 0JW (0171) 396 9000* **£247.38,** plus special breaks; 75 individually decorated rms, some with balconies overlooking a pretty garden. Built in 1910 by the grandfather of the present Mr Goring, this family-run, impeccably kept and very English hotel has a particularly welcoming atmosphere (many staff have been there for years); very good, enjoyable cooking in the elegant restaurant, a super wine list, comfortable lounge for afternoon tea, airy cocktail bar, and staunchly loyal customers; disabled access.

HALKIN *5 Halkin St SW1X 7DJ (0171) 333 1000* **£327.62,** plus special breaks; 41 stylish, well equipped rms, with wonderful marble bthrms. Despite its Georgian exterior, the décor and furnishings here are ultra-modern but enjoyable; there's a particularly good Milanese restaurant overlooking the garden, fine breakfasts, and really charming staff; much liked by the business community, too – lots of facilities for them; disabled access.

HAZLITTS *6 Frith St W1V 5TZ (0171) 434 1771* **£208.50;** 23 rms with 18th- or 19th-c beds and free-standing Victorian baths with early brass shower-mixer units. Behind a typically Soho façade of listed early Georgian houses, this is a well kept and comfortably laid-out little hotel, which could scarcely be handier for the West End; good continental breakfasts served in your bedroom, snacks in the sitting room, lots of restaurants all around; kind, helpful service; cl 25–26 Dec; disabled access.

KNIGHTSBRIDGE GREEN *159 Knightsbridge SW1X 7PD (0171) 584 6274* **£154,** plus special breaks; 27 rms, most suites with sitting room. Friendly, family-owned hotel, carefully refurbished and neatly kept; with very good in-room breakfasts (no restaurant), bar service, free coffee and tea in the lounge, and helpful, efficient staff; cl 24–26 Dec.

L'HOTEL *28 Basil St SW3 1AS (0171) 589 6286* ***£164.50;** 12 well equipped rms. Small, family-owned, French-style city hotel, nr Harrods and above the neatly kept, well run Metro wine bar where English and continental breakfasts are served, as well as good, modern French café food; friendly staff; disabled access.

LEONARD *15 Seymour St W1H 5AA (0171) 935 2010* **£243.50;** 31 rms – mainly luxury suites – with fine paintings, antiques, lovely fabrics, fresh flowers, videos, satellite TV, and hi-fi system. Smart 18th-c town house, with marvellous staff, light modern meals all day in the café bar, and a compact exercise room.

LE MERIDIEN PICCADILLY *21 Piccadilly W1V 0BH (0171) 734 8000* **£199w,** plus special breaks; 266 comfortable, well equipped rms. The very best in modern French hotel-keeping; attractive and quiet public rooms with professional and friendly service, popular afternoon tea, fine restaurant food, and free membership of the good health club downstairs; one child under 12 free in parents' room; disabled access.

RUBENS *39–41 Buckingham Palace Rd SW1W 0PS (0171) 834 6600* **£135.12,** plus special breaks; 175 well equipped rms. Opposite Buckingham Palace and nr Victoria Stn, this attractive hotel has comfortable day rooms inc an airy lounge with views of the Royal Mews, and a restful library; open fire in the bar, and an attractive, split-level restaurant with good food.

ST GEORGE'S *Langham Pl W1N 8QS (0171) 580 0111* **£232,** plus special breaks; 86 light rms with marvellous views over London. Popular modern hotel, a stone's throw from Oxford Circus; with afternoon tea in the bar and lounge, a fine rooftop restaurant and dinner-dance every Fri and Sat.

STAKIS ST ERMIN'S *2 Caxton St SW1H 0QW (0171) 222 7888* **£158;** 290 rms. Opulent Edwardian hotel with fine staircase, ornate plasterwork, antiques and elegant furniture in the luxurious day rooms; fine food in 2 restaurants, and helpful staff.

SWISS HOUSE *171 Old Brompton Rd SW5 0AN (0171) 373 2769* ***£87;** 16 rms. Festooned with ivy and flower-boxes, this is a warmly friendly and good-value, family-run hotel, relaxed and tidy inside, with very good buffet continental breakfasts – English breakfasts available, too.

TOPHAMS BELGRAVIA *28 Ebury St SW1W 0LU (0171) 730 8147* **£130;** 40 cosy rms, most with own bthrm. Small, charmingly old-fashioned hotel made up of several town houses, with a friendly country-house atmosphere; downstairs bar, attractive lounges, good food in the elegant restaurant, and decent wines; cl Christmas.

WILBRAHAM *Wilbraham Pl, Sloane St SW1 9AE (0171) 730 8296* **£112;** 45 simply furnished rms. Privately owned, nicely old-fashioned and friendly hotel with pretty public rooms, and good breakfasts and decent food in the bar-cum-buttery.

WINDERMERE *142–144 Warwick Way SW1 4JE (0171) 834 5163* **£85;** 23 pleasant modern rms, 19 with own bthrm. Small private hotel with a cosy lounge; decent breakfasts and evening meals in the attractive, no smoking dining room, and a friendly and informal atmosphere.

The West End

World-famous for its shopping and window-shopping, from the daunting bustle of Oxford St, through the bookshops around Charing Cross Rd, the specialist food and cookery shops of Soho, and the elegant stores of Regent St and Piccadilly, to the ultra-smart clothes shops of South Molton St and Bond St. There are great opportunities for window-shopping in the auction houses and fine art galleries. The West End is synonymous with theatre; it's worth knowing that on Leicester Square a half-price ticket booth sells off surplus tickets for that day's performances: open around 12–2 pm for matinee tickets, then from about 2.30pm for evenings – there's usually a queue so it's worth getting there earlier. Highlights here include the National Gallery and Trafalgar Square, Piccadilly with the Royal Academy, and Covent Garden. The BBC Experience up by Oxford Circus is great for anyone interested in what goes into TV or radio, not just what comes out, and the toy and model museum out at Lancaster Gate is well worth tracking down. Chinatown is a vivid enclave, and Neal St is a focus for vegetarian restaurants and rather alternative shops.

To see and do

London Family Attraction of the Year

! London Transport Museum (The Piazza, Covent Garden) On the site of the former flower market, this has greatly increased its appeal to families in recent years. The new 'Kids Zones' – 15 interactive stations aimed at 5 to 12 year olds – proved very popular with our party. You can race a tram and a bus, delve into feely boxes, design your own bus and see why a steamtrain doesn't suit the Underground. You're given a card at the entrance to punch or stamp at each station. There's also a 'Fun Bus' for the under-5s with a soft play area and lots of levers to pull, bells to ring, buttons to push, wheels to spin and lights to switch on and off. The main exhibition is quite traditional, but they don't mind if you climb aboard some of the buses, trams and tube trains. On our visit, younger children got a real buzz from sitting in the driving seat of a London bus, while the older ones liked the challenge of driving a computerised Tube train (the knack is to close the doors just as you see people trying to get on). The interactive touch screens throughout are much more enticing for children than traditional information boards, although they did work a bit slowly for the most impatient members of our party. Costumed actors tell nostalgic transport tales, and there might be story telling, face painting or craft workshops in school holidays. Snacks, interesting shop, disabled access; cl 24–26 Dec; (0171) 836 8557; £4.95 (£2.95 children aged 5–15). A family ticket for 2 adults and 2 children costs £12.85 and an all-year family pass is £19.95.

⊖ CHARING CROSS The tube station here extends under **Trafalgar Square**, which many think of as the heart of central London: distances to and from central London used to be measured from the Cross on the Strand. There are elaborate plans to pedestrianise at least part of it so as to make it even more accessible to visitors. Named for the great naval victory of 1805, it was designed by Nash and completed in 1841; the fountains were added a century later. The centrepiece, **Nelson's Column**, stretches up 56 metres (185ft), its base guarded by 4 huge identical lions. Look out for the gifted roller-skaters who perform in the evenings around the base – and, of course, for the innumerable pigeons; Nelson has a special coating to protect him from their droppings.

National Gallery This magnificent building, right on the square, houses the national collection of Western European painting, with around 2,000 pictures dating from the 13th c to the end of the 19th. You'll enjoy it most if you're firm and restrict yourself to just a few of the galleries, rather than trying to see everything. It's hard to pick out highlights (the whole collection is worth studying), but don't miss the Sainsbury Wing, which gives perfect lighting and viewing conditions for its treasure-trove of early Renaissance works. The gallery gets very busy, especially on a Sat, or at any time around the Impressionist works. The hi-tech audio tour, with a CD rather than a cassette (so you can skip to whichever bit you want), is well worth the cost, with a commentary on every single picture in the main gallery. Meals, snacks, shop, disabled access; cl am Sun, 24–26 Dec, 1 Jan, Good Fri; (0171) 747 2885; free, charges for some exhibitions.

National Portrait Gallery (St Martin's Pl, just round the corner) Grandly illustrates British history, with paintings of kings, queens and other notable characters arranged in chronological order from the top floor (medieval) to the present. Recent extensions have greatly broadened the gallery's appeal (creating space for some delightfully varied temporary exhibitions), and there are more on the way. Snacks, shop (where computer technology now lets them print you a poster of any painting in the gallery), disabled access; cl am Sun, 24–26 Dec, 1 Jan, Good Fri, May Day bank hol; (0171) 306 0055; free, charge for some special exhibitions (their photography ones are excellent).

Theatres abound around here, with a group based around the S end of the Charing Cross Rd, and another up along the Strand. Marked out by the globe on top of the building, the Coliseum (St Martin's Lane) is the home of the English National Opera, though they plan to move elsewhere early next century; in the meantime, you can usually get decently priced seats on the day, from 10am. (London's more famous Covent Garden Opera House is closed all year for restoration – financial as much as architectural – and extension.) Almost next door to the Coliseum, the Chandos is a good pub with food all day (upstairs is best), down past the Post Office the underground Tappit Hen is an atmospheric wine bar, and there's no end of smart little coffee shops and cafés near by – Gabys (30 Charing Cross Rd) does perfect hot salt-beef sandwiches.

† **St Martin-in-the-Fields** This elegant church has frequent lunchtime and evening concerts; (0171) 930 0089 for programme. Unmistakable for its blue clock-dial – the only clock in this part of London that seems always to keep the right time – the church has a busy, but very well liked coffee bar in its crypt, with frequent art exhibitions; also brass-rubbing centre, shop (inc all the Academy of St Martin-in-the-Fields CDs) and afternoon craft market, useful for bargains. Every night the church is used as a shelter for the homeless, but even so, as you make your way home from the theatre, you're likely to see plenty of bodies huddled in shop doorways in these streets – a sadly common sight all over London, but especially obvious around here.

COVENT GARDEN *See separate Family Panel on p.767* for the **London Transport Museum**. Partly pedestrianised, the former vegetable, fruit and flower market with its elegant buildings is now made over to smart café-bars, boutiques and stalls, such as those in the covered piazza, selling good but expensive handmade clothes and craft items. There's a bustling cosmopolitan atmosphere and good street entertainers. The Jubilee Market specialises in different wares on different days. The many bars and restaurants are always lively at night, but not cheap. A delight of this area is its range of unusual or specialist **shops**. In nearby streets, Knutz (Russell St) has everything for the practical joker, and Penhaligons (Wellington St) sell lovely old-fashioned toiletries. On the other side of the market, N of the tube station, interesting and unusual shops are set in a labyrinthine network of attractively rejuvenated alleys and streets; you will get lost, but wandering around is great fun, and they all lead back to roughly the same area. Neal St is rewarding for its small craft and specialist shops, and Neal's Yard is full of healthy living – delightful in summer with its fresh paint and tubs of flowers. Floral St has elegant and expensive clothes and shoe shops (plus the Tintin shop – paradise for the Tintin fan). The Africa Centre on King St may have exhibitions of African art and culture. No shortage of places to eat around here, but useful pubs for lunch or refreshment include the Marquess of Anglesey on Bow Street, with a good-value upstairs restaurant, and the Lamb & Flag on Rose St, an attractive 300-year-old pub with decent snacks, its back room still much as Dickens described it.

! Cabaret Mechanical Theatre Tucked away in the heart of the former market buildings, an appealing collection of unique hand-made working automata, operated by the touch of a button or by inserting a coin. Great fun – though several exhibits are quite bizarre, notably the incredible *Last Judgement* by Paul Spooner. Shop, some disabled access; cl 25–26 Dec; (0171) 379 7961; *£1.95.

Theatre Museum (Tavistock St) Exhaustive look at events and personalities on the stage over the last few hundred years. Posters, puppets and props are among the permanent collection, which although astonishingly comprehensive is arranged a little confusingly; it's easy to find yourself going round backwards. The very good temporary displays leave the deepest impression: they sometimes have free stage make-up demonstrations. Shop, disabled access; cl Mon, 25–26 Dec; (0171) 836 7891; £3.50.

Theatre Royal (Drury Lane) The oldest working theatre in the world, first opened in 1663 (Nell Gwynn was one of its earliest performers), but rebuilt several times over the next few centuries. Tours show backstage features inc the intriguing hydraulic lift beneath the stage, still in use. Meals, snacks, shop, disabled access; 4 tours a day (exc on Weds and Sat when only 2 because of matinée), 10.30am, 1pm (12.30pm Weds and Sat), 2.30pm and 5.30pm, (12noon, 2pm and 3.30pm Sun); (0171) 494 5091; £4.

† **! St Paul's Church** (Covent Garden) The actors' church, full of interesting memorials to performers. Pepys watched the first-ever Punch and Judy show here in 1662. Outside its back gate, facing the covered market, the theatrical tradition continues, with jugglers, clowns, mountebanks and unusual musicians performing on the cobbles.

⊖ **LEICESTER SQUARE** All central London's attractions are within easy walking distance of here, with several of the more interesting theatres little more than 5 minutes' stroll. The tube station's various exits are a favourite with Londoners stuck for a place to meet; hordes mill around, anxiously looking for the friends they finally discover they've been standing next to for half an hour. Around the bustling edges of the pedestrian square, attractively cleaned up in recent years, are several huge cinemas, pricy but with excellent sound; you can see films more cheaply at the Prince Charles in Leicester Pl, leading off the square (where Notre Dame de France has an impressive Jean Cocteau mural). The well run Moon Under Water is much more reasonably priced than most pubs around here. Leicester Sq is also very handy for Soho, described below under Tottenham Court Rd.

Bookshops are the Charing Cross Rd trademark, specialist and general, new and secondhand. Foyles is the biggest, but trying to find what you want is time-consuming; Waterstones is very friendly and relaxed, with informed staff. The side alleys between here and St Martin's Lane have good secondhand bookshops, several with specialisations such as crime, the occult, antique children's books, or the theatre;

Cecil Court is perhaps the best. 2 distinctively designed pubs round here are the good-value Moon Under Water opposite Blackwells on the Charing Cross Rd, and the Salisbury on St Martin's Lane, a splendid Victorian pub, all velvet and cut glass. Not far away on Long Acre is Stanfords, the best map and guidebook shop in Britain, with helpful, knowledgeable staff, and books and maps covering all corners of the globe.

Chinatown, marked out by its dramatic ornamental gate, has developed its own character, inviting despite the locals' cool indifference to outsiders; the supermarkets and shops along pedestrianised Gerrard St and in neighbouring streets are fascinating, with their weird and wonderful vegetables, strange squidgy things in little cellophane packets, and odd-smelling dried meats and fish. Plenty of authentic Chinese restaurants, as well as less convincingly adapted telephone boxes.

⊖ PICCADILLY CIRCUS Another lively hub of London life, with famous streets radiating off, each quite different in character; handsome Piccadilly roughly to the W, the theatres of bustling Shaftesbury Avenue to the E, with smarter ones on Haymarket to the S, Regent St coolly curving N towards Oxford Circus – and, of course, the famous statue of Eros, where all the foreign students sit to be photographed.

Shopping is the main thing around here. On opposite sides of the traffic islands in Piccadilly Circus are Tower Records, 3 floors of pop, classical and jazz (open till midnight), and Lillywhites, the long-established sports clothes and equipment store. On Piccadilly, friendly Hatchards is a nicely old-fashioned bookshop where the staff can still sometimes turn vague requests into actual books. Almost next door, Fortnum's (Fortnum & Mason) has superior if expensive clothes, as well as the foods for which they're world-famous. Nearby, the Burlington Arcade is an elegant Regency covered arcade of expensive but good shops (excellent cashmere and knife/scissors shops, for instance), with a delightful set of rules, still enforced, that stop people whistling, singing or running in its confines. The Ritz is gorgeously flamboyant inside: well worth the high price of having a frogged and liveried waiter bring you a cup of tea or a perfectly mixed whisky sour. Simpson's, with several floors of good classic British clothes, for men and women, is sadly set to be closed by its Japanese owners very early in 1999. Behind Piccadilly's S side is Jermyn St, where among other splendid but top-of-the-range shops you can buy fine cheeses at Paxton & Whitfield, briar pipes at Astleys, hand-made shoes at Tricker's, hand-made shirts from Turnbull & Asser, flat hats at Bates, and old-fashioned toiletries at Floris. The Red Lion in Duke of York St, just off here, is a little gem of a pub, with decent snacks (but very busy on wkdy lunchtimes). A landmark on Haymarket is one of the 2 branches of Burberrys the mac-makers (the other's in Regent St).

Royal Academy of Arts (Burlington House, Piccadilly) Splendid building with excellent changing exhibitions for most of the year, then from 13 Jun–22 Aug its famous (often notorious) Summer Exhibition of works by living artists great and small (see calendar at the end of this chapter for other exhibitions). Meals, snacks, shop, disabled access; cl 25 Dec, Good Fri; (0171) 439 7438; admission charge varies – usually between £5 and £8.

☺ **Segaworld** (Trocadero, Piccadilly Circus) Mammoth attraction as the central redevelopment of the vast preserved Trocadero building. When it first opened a couple of years ago it had a splendid cover-all entrance charge, but now you have to pay for each ride individually, so it's more like a glorified amusement arcade. The best ride, Aqua Planet, has remarkable 3-D graphics, there's a 7-storey high IMAX cinema, and you can take part in your own winter olympics in the only virtual reality bobsleigh outside Japan.

! Rock Circus (London Pavilion, Piccadilly Circus) Exuberant romp through the history of rock and roll with ingenious headset sound accompaniment; more fun than its stablemate Madame Tussaud's, but still alarmingly high-priced considering its comparative brevity. Wax figures from Elvis to Bono, some interesting archive film, and a finale with moving animatronic models. Snacks, shop; cl 25 Dec – it's open most nights till 9 or even 10 pm; (0171) 734 7203; £7.95.

⊖ **TOTTENHAM COURT RD** is handy for **Soho** and its often heady mix of the tawdry and the fashionable, its coffee bars and cafés swarming with colourful young people in the evenings. Many of Soho's Georgian terraces are rather run-down, with peepshows and naughty video shops stuffed into basements and ground floors. But there are parts that have had much of their original quiet charm restored, like Soho Sq and Meard St, and it's still good for restaurants, and for shops connected with food or cooking. Old Compton St, central London's gayest st, has a good few interesting shops – Italian delicatessens (I Camisa is the best, with fabulous salamis), the Algerian Coffee Store, which also sells lots of fruit teas, and 2 cheap but good wines and spirits shops. Milroys in Greek St has a wonderful collection of hundreds of different malt whiskies. Berwick St has a daily fruit and vegetable market – the lower half is more expensive but has better produce; at Simply Sausages down here you can watch them making some of their 43 different varieties of sausage, inc vegetarian and seafood ones. The little Dog & Duck in Frith St and Coach & Horses in Poland St (the *Private Eye* pub) are 2 of the nicest Soho locals; in Romilly St another Coach & Horses is also on the well known Soho characters circuit, and Kettners, now part of the Pizza Express chain, is a very entertaining old building. The area as a whole forms a sort of square, with the tube stations at Leicester Sq, Piccadilly Circus, Tottenham Court Rd and even Oxford Circus all just as handy.

⊖ **OXFORD CIRCUS** The heart of the city's busiest shopping areas, busy and noisy Oxford St to the left and right, and altogether nicer Regent St to the S. **Oxford St** doesn't have much character, but has broad pavements and good stores such as Selfridges, John Lewis (the self-service restaurant is good for lunch), Marks & Spencer (2 major outlets), the 2 giant music shops HMV and Virgin Megastore, and the usual high street chains. South Molton St and St Christopher's Pl on either side of Oxford St are full of designer clothes shops and smart cafés; St Christopher's Pl also has quite an interesting antiques market. **Regent St** is one of the grandest streets in the whole area, with a splendid curve as it reaches Piccadilly Circus. A harmonious street of considerable character, with the fine shops definitely enhancing its appeal, even if all you want to do is browse. Liberty's is a splendid art nouveau timbered building, full of gorgeous soft furnishings and clothes, oriental and leather goods, jewellery and a good gift department. Other high points include Mappin & Webb for fine china, glass, and jewellery; Hamleys, a marvellous toy shop (not cheap, though); Aquascutum, great for expensive English classic clothes; Garrard's the Royal jewellers; and Waterford/Wedgwood, for lovely china and glass in quite a wide range of prices. The Old Coffee House in Beak St, around the corner from here, and the Red Lion in Kingly St, are useful for lunch. Carnaby St, tucked away behind, has some rather florid men's shops and good street-fashion houses, but is mainly full of small boutiques with trendy accessories, leather goods and tacky souvenirs; not really worth seeking out.

! BBC Experience (Portland Pl) Below the imposing yet rather bullying bulk of Broadcasting House, this excellent visitor centre celebrates the work and programmes of the BBC over the last 75 years, with a mixture of multi-media exhibitions and hands-on displays. You can try your hand at directing *Eastenders*, or presenting the TV weather or sport, while the radio sections offer an interactive *Desert Island Discs*, and the chance to make a 3-minute play. Plenty for families, but also a great deal to please nostalgic-minded adults, and you'll come out with a much better idea of how programmes are put together. Snacks, big shop, disabled access; (0870) 603 0304; £5.75.

⊖ **BOND ST** W of Regent St and N of Piccadilly (where Green Park tube station is just as handy for it), **Mayfair** is mostly a quietly discreet area of elegant town houses, smart, well established hotels, and richly unobtrusive offices. Despite their famous names, Berkeley Sq and Grosvenor Sq don't have any special appeal for visitors – though you might want to stroll down Brook St to see the neighbouring blue plaques commemorating Handel and Jimi Hendrix living there (part of Handel House may become a museum). Bond St, with its continuation New Bond St, is the focus for **shopping**, though unless you want to spend a great deal of money on top-notch designer clothes and shoes, jewellery or oriental rugs this is likely to be confined to the window. Plenty of art and antique galleries, and a good indoor antique market (124 New Bond St). Asprey's is a remarkable place, famous for its opulent luxury goods and glittering with an awesome tonnage of gems and precious metals. Sotheby's auction rooms are fascinating to wander around. Other small and prestigious art galleries are dotted throughout Mayfair, particularly in nearby Dover St and Cork St; Grays antique market, off 58 Davies St, has hundreds of indoor stalls. South Audley St has Hobbs of Mayfair, a delicious smart delicatessen, and Goode's, a magnificent glass and china shop. Higgins in Duke St is the Queen's coffee-man. The best Mayfair pub is the Red Lion in Waverton St.

Wallace Collection (Hertford House, Manchester Sq – across Oxford St) Excellent art collection beautifully displayed in an elegant 18th-c house. It's visually very seductive, with probably the best collection of 18th-c French paintings in the world, inc luscious offerings from Watteau, Boucher and Fragonard. Also great Canalettos, fine works by Rembrandt, Rubens and Van Dyck, works by British painters, furniture (mostly 18th-c French), a notable assemblage of Sèvres porcelain, and an amazing array of arms and armour, both oriental and European. It's rarely busy, and in places feels more like an historic home than a museum. Shop, disabled access with prior warning; cl am Sun, 24–26 Dec, Good Fri, 1 Jan, May Day bank hol; (0171) 935 0687; free. The Devonshire Arms (Duke St) is a handy lunch stop.

! **⊖ MARBLE ARCH** Striking in itself, originally a grand entrance for Buckingham Palace, it was moved here decades ago, and is gleaming after its recent restoration. Over the road **Speakers Corner**, on the edge of Hyde Park, is where every Sun morning you can still hear impassioned diatribes on all sorts of causes. Traditional debating methods have practically disappeared, and disputes between rival fundamentalist groups have been known to become extremely heated, with the result that extra police armed with hidden cameras now patrol this famous bastion of free speech. Also on Sun it has probably the longest free open-air art exhibition in the world, with the work of 300 artists and craftsmen laid out along the park railings on Bayswater Rd; the Swan opposite gives a pleasant break. The tube station – with so many exits it's a real initiative test finding your way out – is also handy for Oxford St.

Hyde Park Riding Stables (Bathurst Mews) They can organise horse-riding in the park; (0171) 262 3791; £25 an hour (not Mon).

⊖ LANCASTER GATE London Toy and Model Museum (Craven Hill) Particularly fine collection of toys, dolls, models and trains spread over 20 themed galleries, from Roman dolls to the latest from Japan. Much appeals to adults more than children, but they've put a lot of effort into making it fun for younger visitors – some interactive displays, for instance, and a steamtrain and a carousel in the walled garden. Many exhibits are working; hang around a bit if they're not moving when you first go past. A collection of working Victorian slot-machines downstairs is one of the most popular features, and there's an amazing miniature town. Good activities and events in school hols. Snacks, shop; cl 25–26 Dec; (0171) 402 5222; £5.50 (for sale as we went to press, so best to check).

Westminster

This centre of Court and Government is a pleasant area to walk around, much of it with only light traffic, and with few shops to add extra people to the wide pavements. The Abbey's admission charge has brought back some space and tranquillity to its chapels and cloisters. London's other great centrepiece, Buckingham Palace, is just the other side of St James's Park – a fine walk between the two. The Tate Gallery, Westminster Cathedral and the RHS flower shows are also highlights here.

To see and do

ST JAMES'S PARK

Buckingham Palace A marvellous position, surrounded by Royal Parks and looking commandingly along the stately Mall towards Admiralty Arch. At the grand front palace gates the guards still keep their unflinchingly solemn positions: you can watch the **Changing of the Guard** each day Apr–Aug (every other day in winter) at 11.30am; the ceremony may be late or even cancelled in exceptionally wet weather.

Buckingham Palace tour Now firmly established as one of London's most visited attractions, usually drawing around 400,000 visitors in the 8 weeks it's open. The main appeal is that this is where the Queen actually lives – her official London residence, and where she meets other Heads of State; the Royal Standard flies above it when she's home. But beyond that, while perhaps not the most satisfying of the Royal Palaces, it does pile a magnificent series of opulent sights into your walk through the state rooms. Highlights include the beautiful Picture Gallery, 46-metres (150-ft) long and filled with paintings from the Royal collection, the spectacular Grand Staircase, and the throne room with its predominant impression of gold, red and splendour. Tours are unguided, and there aren't many clues to help you, so it's definitely worth buying the guide book. Theoretically, you see everything at your own pace, but in practice you're likely to be carried along in the stream of other people, without much chance to linger. Tickets are sold from a little booth opposite the palace by the entrance to Green Park, though you can book in advance on (0171) 839 1377 – ask for the Visitor Office. Busy shop, disabled access (with notice); open Aug–Sept; £9.50.

Queen's Gallery (Buckingham Palace Rd) The former Palace chapel, now showing further magnificent paintings from the Royal collection. Shop; cl between exhibitions; £4.

Royal Mews (Buckingham Palace Rd) Contains the State Coaches, private driving carriages and even sleighs of the Royal Family, as well as the immaculately turned out Windsor greys and Cleveland bay carriage horses. The longest painting in the Royal collection is here too, a 36-metre (120-ft) canvas of William IV's Coronation procession. Shop, disabled access; open pm Tues–Thurs all year, all day Mon–Thurs Aug–Oct; (0171) 839 1377; £4 (a joint ticket with the Gallery is £6.50).

St James's Park This is the best approach to the Palace (you can get there more quickly, though less attractively, from Victoria). The oldest of London's Royal Parks, it was drained and converted into a deer park for Henry VIII, redesigned in the style of Versailles by order of Charles II (who often went for walks through it), and then re-created by Nash for George IV – this is the park which we see today, its relaxing lakeside environment particularly enjoyed by lunch-breaking office workers (and by hundreds of more or less exotic waterfowl), and with a brass band in summer. It's beautifully floodlit at night, and on Sun traffic is barred from its roads. **The Mall** Running along the park, this ⅔ mile-long ceremonial route was laid out from 1660 for Charles II, with the Palace at one end and the magnificent Admiralty Arch at the other. In between, as well as various grand buildings and government departments, there are a couple of good contemporary art galleries, with various changing exhibitions at the **Mall Galleries** ((0171) 930 6844 for exhibition information; *£2), and a wonderfully informal little restaurant and bar at the **ICA**, which, with exhibitions and cinemas too, is an excellent place to spend an afternoon – and possibly the evening as well (cl am; (0171) 930 0493; £1.50 day membership).

⊖ GREEN PARK The park itself is the smallest of the parks in Central London. It's not a formal garden but, watered by the underground Tyburn stream, stays genuinely green even in hot summers when London's other grassy spaces are dry and dusty. It's a short stroll to **Shepherd Market**, a colourful place where Mayfair lets its hair down, no longer a market but busy with cafés, good wine bars and pubs (the Bunch of Grapes and King's Arms), and little lanes to wander down.

Spencer House (St James's Pl) Overlooking Green Park, this gleaming, gilt-filled town house was built for the first Lord Spencer in the mid-18th c. Its sumptuous rooms, restored to their full glory, were among the first neo-classical interiors in Europe. Disabled access; open for guided tours every Sun (exc Jan and Aug), best to book on (0171) 499 8620; *£6.

St James's Palace Though comparatively domestic-looking, this is exceptionally harmonious and carries a real feel of old London. It's not open to the public (its apartments are used by members of the Royal Family and their officials), but does provide another good spot for the **Changing of the Guard**, with guardsmen leaving here at 11.15am to go to the Palace, and coming back at around 12.10pm.

Clubland The area around St James's St and Pall Mall seems to have more gentlemen's clubs than anything else, along with the interesting and upmarket **shops** that their members might use: hand-made shoes at Lobb's, hats at Lock's, wonderful antiques and antiquities at Spink's, fishing equipment at Hardy's, and fine wines at Berry's, or Berry Bros & Rudd to give it its full name. This last is the only shop in London still to look both inside and out just as it did in the early 19th c (they've only just taken down the full-screen shutters), and they are very helpful even if you want just one humble bottle. Farlow's on Pall Mall have everything you might need for that expedition up the Limpopo or into the Gobi Desert. Christie's auction galleries are on King St (the friendly Red Lion off here in Crown Passage is useful for a snack), and there are some other top-of-the-market antique and book shops nearby, especially up Duke St.

† ⊖ WESTMINSTER

Westminster Abbey One of the most impressive pieces of architecture to survive from the Middle Ages: Edward the Confessor transformed it into the crowning place of English kings, and his body now lies in the great shrine of the present building, erected in the 13th c on the site of his original. Recent restoration work has left the exterior looking almost as good as new (in fact, some bits *are* new), and a quite different colour from the one visitors had become used to, with monthly hawk patrols now deterring pigeon nesting. Pretty much every king and queen up to George II is buried here; Henry VII's chapel is particularly impressive, and there are splendid tombs erected by James I for his mother Mary, Queen of Scots, and his predecessor Elizabeth I, under whose orders Mary had been executed. Perhaps it's in revenge for this that Elizabeth was lumped in with her sister Mary I, with whom she never got on. The loosely named Poets Corner takes in a wide range of cultural figures. There's a brass-rubbing centre and a small medieval garden in the charming, tranquil cloisters. Snacks, shop, disabled access (but not to Henry VII chapel); Royal chapels cl Sun, and between 2.45pm and 3.45pm Sat; £5. The **museum** in the Norman undercroft has effigies of many ancestors of the Royal Family made from their death masks, and often wearing their own clothes; £2.50 (which also includes entry to the Chapter House and Pyx Chamber); £7 inc audio tour and entry to all areas of the Abbey.

✝ **St Margaret's Church** (Parliament Sq) The official church of the House of Commons, worth a look particularly for its exceptional 16th-c Dutch stained glass; Sir Walter Raleigh is buried here.

Houses of Parliament Across the road from St Margaret's church, these buildings are now, of course, the main seat of British government, but until Henry VIII moved to Whitehall Palace in 1529, the site was the main residence of the monarch – when they answer the phone today they still call it the Palace of Westminster. The present 19th-c building was designed by Charles Barry, though the Gothic detail which has given so much life to what would otherwise be rather a tiresomely deadpan, classical façade is by Pugin. One end of the extraordinary 286-metre (940-ft) structure finishes in a lofty Victorian tower (which flies the Union Jack when Parliament is in session), and the other in the clock tower which contains **Big Ben**, the 3½-ton bell whose sonorous hourly rings are one of the best known sounds in the world. Inside, over 2 miles of passages link the central hall and two chambers – the Houses of Lords and Commons to the N and S of the building respectively. The Commons sits from 2.30 pm Mon–Thurs, and from 9.30am on Fri; to gain entrance to the Strangers' Galleries, you'll need to queue by St Stephen's Gate (on the left for the Commons, right for the Lords) – or arrange it first with your MP. A letter from your MP can also give access to what's called the Line of Route, going through both Houses and the Members' Lobby and Divisions Lobby, to Westminster Hall, from 1224 to 1882 the chief law court of the country. It witnessed such trials as those of Sir Thomas More and Charles I, and organising admission is worth the trouble even just to admire the magnificent hammerbeam roof, the earliest surviving example of its kind. The Westminster Arms in Storeys Gate across the square is a good pub, and you're likely to see politicians in the imposing Albert on Victoria St.

Jewel Tower (Parliament Sq) Across the road from the statue of Oliver Cromwell (whose attitude towards Parliament when he was Lord Protector was not unlike that of Charles I – they were more trouble than they were worth), this 14th-c building has an exhibition on Parliament's history. It was originally a huge treasure chest for Edward III; cl 24–26 Dec, 1 Jan; (0171) 222 2219; £1.50.

Cabinet War Rooms (King Charles St, just off Whitehall) An intriguing series of 21 rooms built to provide Sir Winston Churchill, the War Cabinet and his Chiefs of Staff with a safe place to run the 1939–45 war effort. The Cabinet Room, Map Room and Prime Minister's Room were preserved intact from the end of the war, and the other rooms have been authentically restored since. Quite basic, they're very evocative, with sound effects adding to the atmosphere. Shop, disabled access; cl 24–26 Dec; (0171) 930 6961; £4.60.

Cenotaph (Whitehall) Designed by Lutyens, a sombre reminder of this century's two world wars, standing indomitably in the centre of the road. An original wooden structure had been intended as a temporary symbol, but public opinion demanding something permanent brought the present stone monument.

Downing St Famous as the residence of the Prime Minister at No 10 and the Chancellor of the Exchequer at No 11. You can't get past the gates, but you can at least have a passing look at its surprisingly modest buildings.

Banqueting House (Whitehall) The only surviving part of the Palace of Whitehall (which used to sprawl all the way between Parliament Sq and Trafalgar Sq), designed by Inigo Jones and built in 1619; it was a Royal residence until late that century. Charles I was executed here, and it was also the site of his son's restoration. The severely classical hall is pretty much all there is to see, but an entertaining Walkman tour and good audio-visual exhibition keep up your interest for quite some time. The highlight is the wonderful ceiling painted by Rubens, commissioned by Charles I to glorify the Stuart monarchy. Mirrored tables let you study the detail without straining your neck; don't lean on these though – they're on wheels and liable to speed off like errant supermarket-trolleys. Snacks, shop; cl Sun, 24–26 Dec, 1 Jan, Good Fri, bank hols, and for some government functions; (0171) 839 7569; £3.25. The partly 13th-c Silver Cross is an interesting old pub, and the huge and very ornate Lord Moon of the Mall is another good refuge.

Mounting the Guard (Whitehall) A survival of the kind of Royal pageantry this area was once full of can be seen in this daily ceremony at Horse Guards Parade, 11am Mon–Sat and 10am Sun.

✝ ❁ ⊖ **VICTORIA Westminster Cathedral** (just off Victoria St) Built in 1903, the red-brick Roman Catholic building is an astonishing structure, very un-English, with handsome mosaics and marble work in its richly ornamental interior. At night its black ceiling seems almost to disappear in the darkness. Its Byzantine splendour is a welcome relief from the glassy governmental cliffs of Victoria St. It offers great views over Central London from its tall tower (lift; cl Mon–Weds in winter; £2).

❀ **Royal Horticultural Society** (Vincent Sq) Regular flower shows, filled with beautifully arranged displays by specialist nurserymen; (0171) 828 1744 for information.

⊖ **PIMLICO Tate Gallery** (Millbank) Designed in classical style to house the collection of Sir Henry Tate, the sugar refiner, and now containing the national collection of British art. It covers all important British artists for the past 450 years, with a large number of works by Turner and Constable, and plenty of contemporary sculpture. A hi-tech audio guide looks rather like a mobile phone, and at the push of a button murmurs comments on what you're looking at. Meals, snacks, shop, disabled access; cl 24–26 Dec; (0171) 887 8000; free (exc for special exhibitions). Though the Tate Gallery restaurant is particularly good, you might find the Morpeth Arms nearby useful, with its views of the glossy MI6 ziggurat across the river.

Knightsbridge, Chelsea and Kensington

The 3 great South Kensington museums between them have something for everyone: the visually spectacular collections of the V&A, or Victoria & Albert (fingers crossed that the batty proposal to change its name is quietly dropped); and the lively Natural History and Science Museums, both favourites for children. After 4.30pm they are free. The revamped Commonwealth Experience has plenty for younger children. There's grandeur in Kensington Palace, the less visited but free Leighton House, and, across Hyde Park, the excellent Apsley House. The Albert Memorial is once again a sight really worth seeing. Harrods seems irresistible to most visitors, though shopping in the Portobello Rd can be more fun. The Roof Gardens on High St Kensington are a surprise. Down towards the Thames, the Chelsea Physic Garden and the nearby free National Army Museum are both rather special. A placid grid of clean-cut, subdued Georgian terraced houses contrasts with the ostentatious bustle of the King's Rd in the S and the hubbub of the Portobello Rd market in the N.

To see and do

HIGH ST KENSINGTON
This is a good area for shopping, especially if you consider yourself young and fashionable. An unusual haven from the crowds is the **Roof Gardens** above BHS on the High St; these extraordinary gardens are usually open every day, but are often closed for private functions, so check first on (0171) 937 7994; free. Kensington Church St has some interesting antique shops. Decent food pubs include the Ladbroke Arms (Ladbroke Rd), Windsor Castle (Campden Hill Rd; excellent courtyard garden) and the Churchill Arms (Kensington Church St).

Kensington Palace (Kensington Gardens) Once-humble town house remodelled by Sir Christopher Wren and then enlarged by William Kent, the birthplace of Queen Victoria, and principal private Royal residence until the death of George II. Diana Princess of Wales lived here until her death (people still leave flowers at the gates), and it's still the home of Princess Margaret and Prince and Princess Michael of Kent. Some of the rooms are quite magnificent, with elaborate furnishings and décor, while others are interesting for their comparatively restrained understatement; a couple of the older ones could even be described as downright poky. Make sure you look up at the ceilings: some are exquisitely painted, inc an effective trompe-l'oeil dome (a couple of patterns transfer very nicely to stationery in the gift shop). Also pictures and furniture from the Royal collection, and a court dress collection. Snacks, shop, disabled access to ground floor only; cl all Apr and winter Mon and Tues; (0171) 937 9561; £7.50 – quite a steep increase since last year.

Kensington Gardens
Surrounding the Palace, and well worth a wander. There are controversial plans to turn a large part into a garden memorial to Diana, but for now it's a place where local Londoners come to enjoy themselves. There's a toy boats' lake, playground, a fetching statue of Peter Pan, and a tree trunk carved with all sorts of little painted animals. On a sunny day you could be forgiven for thinking you'd stumbled on a beach club, as the grass is covered with prone bodies soaking up the radiation.

Serpentine Gallery (Kensington Gardens) Reopened after extensive renovation in 1998. Often has some of London's most interesting exhibitions, concentrating on younger, contemporary artists (and on our most recent visit showed the big boost to park users' art appreciation given by a rainstorm); (0171) 823 9727 for what's on; free.

Albert Memorial (S side of Kensington Gardens) Now open to view again after 8 years of painstaking English Heritage restoration (under the tallest, free-standing scaffolding in Europe), marvellously grand yet intricate Victoriana, especially the mosaics, and the golden statue of Prince Albert (had been black since World War I – when the gold was stripped off to prevent moonlight glinting on it as a night-time landmark for Germans).

Commonwealth Experience (Kensington High St) The Commonwealth Institute continues to shake off its dated image. A helicopter simulator ride was the first stage, and in Jan 1999 it will reopen with the second stage of its relaunch, incorporating an interactive approach to the displays on each of the Commonwealth countries; (0171) 603 4535 for opening details.

Holland Park One of London's lesser-known open spaces, a wooded park with peacocks, a summer open-air theatre and an airy restaurant.

Leighton House (12 Holland Park Rd) This splendid 19th-c house is a uniquely opulent monument to High Victorian art, its lavish décor and collections assembled by the first owner, Lord Leighton, former President of the Royal Academy. The centrepiece Arab Hall has a fountain and an almost dazzling assemblage of Islamic tiles, and there's a fine collection of paintings by Millais, Burne-Jones, and Leighton himself; cl Sun and bank hols; (0171) 602 3316; free.

Linley Sambourne House (18 Stafford Terrace) The 19th-c home of the celebrated *Punch* cartoonist, unchanged since – a fascinating example of a Victorian town house, with a fine collection of his work. Shop; open Weds and pm Sun, Mar–Oct; (0171) 937 0663; £3.

SOUTH KENSINGTON Natural History Museum (Cromwell Rd) This elaborate Romanesque building covers 4 acres, with a huge range of informative and entertaining displays and activities. It's been very successfully jazzed up in recent years; museum purists may feel some of the grandeur of the place has been lost, but families will find plenty to keep them busy for a good chunk of the day. It's long been a place where people have come to see the dinosaurs, but while that used to mean fossils and skeletons, it now involves a hi-tech exhibition that even has robotic versions of the monsters. The revamped Earth Galleries are a current highlight – an escalator whisks you up towards a revolving metal globe, and there's an earthquake simulator. Meals, snacks, shops, disabled access; cl 23–26 Dec; (0171) 938 9123; £6 (free after 4.30pm wkdys, 5pm wknds).

Science Museum (Exhibition Rd) No problems getting children interested in this amazing place: over 600 working exhibits whizz you through all aspects of science and industry, with the highlight perhaps the very successful Launch Pad, a hi-tech interactive gallery where you can have great fun carrying out your own experiments. Exhibits elsewhere range from Stephenson's Rocket to the Apollo 10 space capsule, with lively displays on food, flight and pharmaceuticals. Various temporary exhibitions, and special events like their all-night camp-ins – which enthrall children. Meals, snacks, shop, disabled access; cl 24–26 Dec; (0171) 938 8080; £6.50 (free after 4.30pm wkdys and 5pm wknds).

Victoria & Albert Museum (Cromwell Rd) Britain's national museum of art and design, one of the finest in the world; it was founded in 1851 by Prince Albert, and houses all manner of decorative arts, from all ages and countries. The galleries run to over 7 miles, inc a spectacular glass gallery (with touch-screen computer displays), a dazzling silver gallery, and the world's greatest collection of Constables. They have ambitious plans for extensions and improvements, and a new photographic gallery opened last year. Meals and snacks (inc a good Sunday brunch with jazz), shop, disabled access; cl am Mon, 24–26 Dec; (0171) 938 8500; £5 though free after 4.30pm, and any time for the unwaged.

† **Brompton Oratory** Roman Catholic, and heavily magnificent – sombre despite the pallor of its marble.

† **Holy Trinity Brompton** London's most fashionable and perhaps most lively church, currently spearheading a popular if controversial evangelical movement. Its gardens lead you into a very peaceful corner of residential London, with a decent pub in Ennismore Mews (the Ennismore Arms, which does Sun lunches).

Royal Albert Hall (Kensington Gore) The home of the summer Promenade Concerts and many other concerts throughout the year; completed in 1871, this huge oval arena was built in honour of Prince Albert. Below its massive metal and glass dome a terracotta frieze shows the progress of Man in the arts and sciences throughout the ages. Before modern technology (in the form of giant suspended mushrooms) got to grips with its acoustics, the hall used to be famous for its echo – it was said that this was the only hall where you could hear the works of modern composers twice.

KNIGHTSBRIDGE Harrods A wonderful place to browse, it has most things anyone could want – there's even a personal shopper available to help you choose. But it's the food halls that even top restaurateurs envy; they're divided into fruit and vegetables, an interesting delicatessen, grocery, meat, poultry, fish (the display of fresh fish at the end of the room is legendary), bread and cakes, flowers, and wines – and the downstairs pantry is not as expensive as you might think. The Scotch House, almost opposite, is not cheap but does have lovely cashmeres, fine woollens, kilts and so forth.

Sloane St Headed by Harvey Nichols, a long-standing fashion store now split into numerous famous-brand boutiques; its 5th-floor food store is superb, alongside a very good bar/restaurant. The street stretching down from here has had something of a renaissance recently, with international designers jostling to open very expensive new stores. In the handsome terraces E of here can be found the charming Grenadier (Wilton Row; no food in the bar, but a snug little restaurant) and the surprisingly countryish Nag's Head (Kinnerton St).

HYDE PARK CORNER

The 340 acres of **Hyde Park** used to be a Royal hunting park, and in 1851 it was the site of the Great Exhibition. Now very much a city central park, complete with cycle lanes, roller-bladers, summer sunbathing and a boating lake: you can hire boats (around £6 an hour), or swim in parts. At the Park's bottom corner there is a relentless torrent of traffic around Hyde Park Corner; the subway can bring you up nr the glittering neo-baroque gates erected in honour of the Queen Mother.

Apsley House (Hyde Park Corner) The Duke of Wellington's elegant former home, designed by Robert Adam. It soon became known as Number One London, as it was the first house beyond a toll gate at the top of Knightsbridge. The magnificent building has been painstakingly restored; everything gleams and looks as good as new, and works by Correggio, Rubens and Velasquez, amassed by Wellington as the spoils of war, are back as he had them (not always to their best advantage). Sumptuous furnishings, décor and sculpture – inc a statue of Napoleon by Canova that has him looking quite different from the usual image. Shop; cl Mon (exc bank hols), 1 Jan, Good Fri, May Day bank hol, 24–26 Dec; (0171) 499 5676; £4.50.

SLOANE SQUARE The heart of Chelsea, with Peter Jones, the mecca of the Sloanes, on the square itself (a sister department store of John Lewis, it's good value). Just around the corner, the Antelope in Eaton Terrace is a useful lunch stop. The bottom end of Sloane St has 2 interesting though expensive shops: Partridges, a fancy food shop, and the General Trading Company, with a fine collection of oddities, besides stylish kitchenware, soft furnishings, antiques, glass and so forth.

King's Rd Not what it used to be in the '60s and '70s, but you can still find some really individual clothes and shoe shops, and good antique markets. On your way along, refresh yourself at Henry J Beans (197 King's Rd; an American-style bar with good quick snacks), La Bersagliera (a pleasantly clattery, matriarchal pizza house just past Beaufort St) or the Sporting Page (Camera Pl/Limerston St). S from here, it's quite a short-cut through to the Thames.

Carlyle's House (Cheyne Row) The home of the writer from 1834 till his death, with lots of letters and personal possessions, and an early piano played by Chopin. There's a charming little Victorian walled garden. Open Weds–Sun and bank hols Apr–Oct; (0171) 352 7087; £3.20; NT. The nearby King's Head & Eight Bells, across a green and a busy road from the Thames, is almost villagey; at the far end of the green, Old Church St past the elegant Chelsea Old Church takes you quickly to a good food pub, the Front Page.

Royal Hospital (Royal Hospital Rd) Christopher Wren's most glorious secular building, which still houses some 400 Chelsea Pensioners; cl 12–2pm, am Sun (though you can go to the full dress service in chapel at 11am on Sun); free. The spacious and calm adjacent riverside Ranelagh Gardens are the site of the Chelsea Flower Show.

National Army Museum (Royal Hospital Rd) Surprisingly little visited but well and honestly presented – the history of the men of the British, Indian and Colonial armies from 1485, told with photographs, models, uniforms, prints and other mementos, and portraits by Gainsborough and Reynolds. Also the collections of the former Museum of the Women's Royal Army Corps. Snacks, shop, disabled access; cl 24–26 Dec, 1 Jan, Good Fri, May Day bank hol; (0171) 730 0717; free.

Chelsea Physic Garden (Royal Hospital Rd) If you're tired of the braying crowds of Chelsea, take refuge here. A real haven of peace, it was started in 1673 to study the plants used in medicine by the Society of Apothecaries. It's still used for botanical and medicinal research (there's a unique garden of medicinal plants), but is also full of lovely and unusual plants which thrive here in Thames-side London's warm microclimate. Snacks, shop, disabled access; open pm Weds and Sun Apr–Oct; (0171) 352 5646; £3.50.

Pimlico Rd An interesting collection of antique and other small shops (and Peter's Restaurant, a very good-value, all-day, Italian-run café which has been a taxi-drivers' haunt for about 30 years). The Orange Brewery here is a pub brewing its own beers, with decent food. Keep on along to Ebury Bridge for a classic photographic view of partly dismantled Battersea Power Station, beyond a sinuous network of railway lines.

FULHAM BROADWAY The best tube station for the clutch of good value **antique shops** towards the bottom end of the Fulham Rd. You can quickly cut through to the interesting series of more specialised antique shops on the New King's Rd, some of which yield unexpected treasures: lovely old clocks, imposing model ships, garden furniture, and ornaments going back to the 16th c. 2 shops specialise expensively but magnificently in mirrors, and there's also Christopher Wray's enormous lighting shop, which largely fuelled the vogue in Tiffany-style lamps and has almost any sort of lamp fitting you could possibly want. The tube station is also handy for the unfrequented, rather melancholy tranquillity of the somewhat overgrown **Brompton Cemetery**. The countrified Fox & Pheasant in Billing St is a pleasant break.

Chelsea Harbour (Lots Rd) This modern development includes a striking modern covered mall (mainly luxurious, top-of-the-range, international soft furnishings specialists), with popular Deals Restaurant, the stylish Canteen, the smart but relaxed Matt's café, and an adjacent marina. Children like the glass-sided lifts which swoop up into the big dome, and on pm Suns they often have jazz by the marina.

NOTTING HILL GATE Damien Hirst's restaurant Pharmacy (150 Notting Hill Gate) caused a shiver – and a prosecution for calling itself a pharmacy – when it opened here last year, with the waiters dressed in surgical garb, and surroundings of swabs and operating instruments. Nearby **Portobello Rd** is famous for its market – fruit and vegetables during the week, antiques on Sat from 6am; with well over a thousand dealers, you can still pick up a bargain. The quality and prices are higher at the Notting Hill end; it's more bric-à-brac as you get towards Ladbroke Grove.

The City and East End

The Tower of London is a favourite for children, and other highlights here include St Paul's, the Museum of London, Geffrye Museum and Museum of Childhood, and the highly individualistic 18 Folgate Street. The recently opened Lothbury Gallery has a good art collection, the Tower Bridge Experience is something that bit different, and the House of Detention has loads of atmosphere.

The City's most typical financial buildings are mainly Victorian and Edwardian, and its landmark churches are mostly elegant classical designs, but the ground-plan follows the narrow twisting streets and alleys of medieval times – though because of the Great Fire of 1666 only a handful of buildings are medieval or Tudor (it was rebuilding after the Great Fire that gave the City its host of glorious churches). Around St Paul's and the Tower, the layout is more open – and far less affected by the City's human tides: most of the rest of the area is packed with worried financial workers during weekdays, then when they leave goes into a catatonic trance in the evening and at weekends. For every person who actually lives in the City, another 60 or 70 flood in each day to work there, then flood out again at night.

Originally, particular streets came to be associated with particular crafts and trades, and this is reflected in street names throughout the City – Carter Lane, Hosier Lane, Cloth Fair, Ropemaker St, Milk St, Silk St, Coopers Lane and so forth. The great Livery Companies representing the various trades have effectively run local government in the City for 800 years or more, and it's only now that the franchise is to be widened to allow more modern financial institutions a share in local government here. Many guilds have only a tenuous connection with the original crafts involved in their trades. But in Billingsgate Market, still controlled by the ancient Fishmongers Company, you can still see the fish trade being carried on in much the same way as ever (West India Dock Rd, early morning Tues–Sat). Though the halls of the City Livery Companies may have been rebuilt since they were first established in the Middle Ages, they still house some remarkable treasures. Some are open to visit by prior arrangement: book well ahead, through the City of London Information Centre, St Paul's Churchyard, EC4; (0171) 332 1456.

The liveliest glimpse of East End life nowadays is to be had on Sunday mornings in Brick Lane market.

To see and do

TOWER HILL Tower of London (Tower Hill) Picturesque classic castle, the most notable building to survive the Great Fire of London. A lot of fun to look at even superficially, it dates back to the late 11th c, though the site had been used as a defensive position by the Romans much earlier. Almost every period of English history has witnessed gruesome goings-on here, with not even the highest or mightiest safe from imprisonment or even execution: Walter Raleigh, Lady Jane Grey and 2 of Henry VIII's wives spent their last days in the Tower. The mass of things to see includes enough armour and medieval weaponry to glut the most bloodthirsty small boy's appetite, the Crown Jewels, the Beefeaters and the ravens. You can walk along the elevated battlements. The Jewel House shows off the Crown Jewels to dazzling effect; on the busiest days those tempted to linger are gently drawn along by moving floorways. Two towers that were part of Edward I's medieval palace are furnished in period style, and peopled with appropriately costumed, helpful guides; one room in this part has been left untouched to show what a difficult job the restoration was. A reorganisation of the oldest part, the White Tower, has revealed that the inside of the fortress when built was much less imposing than was suggested by the formidable exterior – they were clearly just trying to intimidate the locals. You need a fair bit of time to see everything properly. Shop, some disabled access; cl 24–26 Dec, 1 Jan; (0171) 709 0765; *£9.50.

Tower Bridge Experience Inside the landmark bridge, with wonderful views from its glass-covered walkways, 43 metres (142ft) above the Thames;

animatronic characters and hi-tech displays present the view at various other dates in the bridge's history, with lively multi-media shows designed to leave you feeling proud to be British. The bridge is unusual not just for its design, but because it's still fully operational, raising the roadway from each side drawbridge-style to let ships pass; you can see some of the Victorian machinery that does the work. Snacks, shop, disabled access; cl 24–26 Dec, 1 Jan, 27 Jan; (0171) 403 3761; £5.95.

† ❋ ⊖ **ST PAUL'S St Paul's Cathedral** Despite the attempts of brasher, taller modern buildings to take over, this masterpiece still asserts itself proudly as the area's real landmark, its unmistakable shape repeatedly looming out above the crowded streets. Its huge dome is a pleasing shape after the stolid self-satisfaction of the Victorian and Edwardian masonry which dominates this area. Originally, the cathedral was Gothic in style, with a towering 150-metre (500-ft) spire. It fell into disrepair and Wren was assigned to work on its renovation. He didn't relish the job, and no doubt was delighted when the Great Fire of London swept the old church away, letting him build something entirely new. His mainly classical design is unlike any other cathedral in Britain, and took just 35 years to build. The setting for various state occasions, it's full of interesting monuments – the one to John Donne was the only complete figure to be salvaged from the Great Fire. Look out for the wonderful exterior carving – some by Grinling Gibbons, who also did the choir stalls. Other highlights include the dizzying Whispering Gallery, the panoramic views from the top (quite a walk), and the crypt, full of tombs and memorials to notable figures from British history. Snacks, shop, disabled access; virtually cl Sun; (0171) 236 4128; £4 (£3.50 more to climb the dome). The City Pipe by the tube station is an enjoyable weekday wine bar.

Guildhall (off Gresham St) 15th c, where the Court of Common Council, over which the Lord Mayor presides, administers the City of London. The Lord Mayor's Banquet is held in the Great Hall, hung with the banners and shields of the City's 90-odd livery companies. Underneath is the largest 15th-c crypt in the City, and there's also a clock museum, and library with an unrivalled collection of City-related manuscripts and books. Disabled access; cl Sun Oct–Apr, and for civic occasions; guided tours, must book, (0171) 606 3030 ext 1460; free.

† **St Anne and St Agnes Church** (Gresham St) Particularly worth knowing for the Bach cantatas that may grace its Lutheran Sun services; (0171) 606 4986 for programme.

† **St Mary le Bow Church** (Cheapside) With the famous Bow Bells, and also Thurs lunchtime early-music concerts; (0171) 248 5139.

❋ ⊖ **MONUMENT** The **Monument** itself (Monument St) is a fluted Doric column designed by Wren and Hooke at an exact height of 62 metres (202ft) to mark the spot where the Great Fire of London began – in Pudding Lane 202ft from its base. The views of the city from the top are tremendous, though there are 311 steps up (coming down, your feet seem to want to rush you down into that swirling spiral). The viewpoint was designed as a cage to prevent people jumping off. Cl some bank hols, and occasional other dates; (0171) 626 2717; £1.50.

⊖ **BANK** Some of the City's finest buildings are around here, though with most you'll have to content yourself with looking at just the outside. Besides the Bank of England itself, handsome or interesting buildings include the neo-classical Custom House on Lower Thames St, Lloyds of London on Lime St, and the Renaissance-style Royal Exchange on Cornhill. If you apply in writing in advance, you should be able to see inside the **Mansion House** (Bank), the Lord Mayor's official residence, with its suite of sumptuous 18th-c rooms inc the fabulous Egyptian Hall.

Bank of England (Bartholomew Lane) This neo-classical fortress does still contain oodles of gold – though you can't see it, let alone get your hands on it. There's a small but interesting **museum**, which even shows how computerised currency speculators work. Disabled access; cl wknds and bank hols; (0171) 601 5545; free.

Lothbury Gallery (Lothbury) The NatWest Bank's excellent collection of

17th- to 20th-c paintings. See it while you can – shareholders after bigger dividends have now started getting other institutions to cash in their art; open wkdys; (0171) 726 1642; free.

Leadenhall Market (Whittington Ave, off Gracechurch St) Victorian iron and glass covered market, vibrant with Cockney humour yet quite smart, and filled with seafood, game, vegetables and fruit; cl afternoonish, and wknds. The Lamb's top-floor dining bar gives good views of the market activity.

BARBICAN Could be called the North Bank's answer to the South Bank Centre, and on an aesthetic par. This complex includes theatres, exhibition halls, galleries, and what some would say is the city's most comfortable cinema. There's often free entertainment in the foyers.

Museum of London (London Wall) No other city museum in the world is quite as comprehensive as this; anyone with just a passing interest in history will find it compelling. London's development is told through chronological reconstructions and period clothes, music and various remains, from a medieval hen's egg to an early (and quite different) tube map – ever heard of the station called Post Office? The 18th-, 19th- and 20th-c sections have almost too much to take in. Under a 7-year redevelopment programme, excellent new galleries cover Roman London (the building adjoins a stretch of original Roman wall) and 'London Bodies', based on research on 672 bodies from a 14th-c Black Death cemetery nr the Tower. Meals, snacks, shop, disabled access; cl am Sun, all day Mon (exc bank hols), 24–26 Dec; (0171) 600 0807; £5 – ticket valid for 3 months, and it's certainly a place to come back to.

LIVERPOOL ST In the mainline station, Hamilton Hall is an extraordinarily grand ex-ballroom pub.

! 18 Folgate St Guided tours of a quite remarkable house – be warned, this is no ordinary guided tour. It doesn't do the place justice to say that it's been furnished and decorated in period style – to all intents and purposes you really are back in the 18th c, with candles and firelight flickering away, food and drink laid out on the table, even urine in the chamber-pots. Dennis Severs the owner, who lives here, spends hours getting everything ready, and goes to extreme lengths to immerse people in the experience – it's not unusual to be locked in a cold dark cellar, and he's been known to throw people out if he doesn't like them. Open 2–5pm the first Sun of each month; (0171) 247 4013; £7. Elaborate candlelit tours the first Mon evening of the month (no children), £10.

OLD ST Geffrye Museum (Kingsland Rd) One of London's most friendly and interesting museums, yet least known; 18th-c almshouses converted to show the changing style of the English domestic interior – a sort of historical *Through the Keyhole*. Displays go from lovely 17th-c oak panelling and furniture through elegant Georgian reconstructions and Victorian parlours to art deco fashions, though not all is as it seems – out of sight inside the shell of a vintage radio, for example, there's actually a distinctly modern CD player. Notable herb garden, and an excellent programme of exhibitions, special events, talks and activities. Well worth tracking down. New galleries showing 20th-c interiors should be open by the time this book reaches the shops. Snacks, shop, disabled access; cl am Sun, all day Mon (exc pm bank hols), 24–26 Dec, 1 Jan, Good Fri; (0171) 739 9893; free.

† Wesley's House (49 City Rd) The father of Methodism had his house and chapel built here in 1778, and they're still much as they were then, with plenty of his possessions. You can see his tomb in the chapel, and the crypt has a museum on the history of Methodism. Shop, disabled access – limited in house, but good in museum; cl bank hols, Thurs lunchtime and limited opening Sun (when services); (0171) 253 2262; £4.

FARRINGDON Museum of the Order of St John (St John's Lane) In a 16th-c gatehouse and 12th-c crypt, silver, paintings and furniture belonging to the medieval Order, and displays relating to its more modern offshoot, the St John's Ambulance Brigade. Shop, some disabled access; cl Sun, Christmas, Easter, bank hol wknds;

(0171) 253 6644; free, £3.50 guided tours of the gatehouse and priory church on Tues, Fri and Sat at 11am and 2.30pm. The Eagle in Farringdon Rd/Bakers Row has outstanding food.

House of Detention (Clerkenwell Close) Well put together displays on crime and punishment in a former prison's underground cells. Atmospheric without the sensationalised gore of other similar attractions; cl 25 Dec; (0171) 253 9494; *£5.

† **St Bartholomew the Great Church** (west Smithfield) Partly Norman, with a 13th-c gateway into the market precincts, lunchtime recitals and choral evenings; (0171) 606 5171 for details.

! **ALDGATE EAST** Once the terror-stricken haunt of Jack the Ripper, Whitechapel around here is still one of London's poorest areas. **Brick Lane market** London's biggest and most atmospheric street market, a riot of colour, smells and sound, with very entertaining market patter. There are plenty of bargains for early risers (and things to avoid – we've even seen someone specialising in secondhand felt-tip pens). The community is largely Asian, so much of the food and other wares are quite exotic; Sun 5am–2pm. Nearby **Columbia St market** is devoted to garden and house plants; bargains as it closes around 1pm on Sun.

BETHNAL GREEN Museum of Childhood (Cambridge Heath Rd) This very special little museum houses the V&A's collection of toys, dolls, dolls' houses, games, puppets and children's costumes. Excellent programme of events, theatre shows, and children's activities (most Sats and several school hols) – most completely free. Snacks, shop, disabled access with prior notice; cl am Sun, all day Fri, 24–26 Dec, 1 Jan, May Day bank hol; (0181) 980 2415; free.

! **DOCKLANDS** Once the heartland of Britain's trade-based Empire, these 8½ square miles over the last decade became the largest redevelopment site in Europe, the old warehouses imaginatively converted into smart apartments and office blocks. 244-metre (800-ft) Canary Wharf is an all-too-obvious landmark – mostly offices, with ground-level shops. Many of the buildings around it were designed to give a taste of the 21st c. While they're undoubtedly striking, there's sometimes a soullessness about the place that's positively eerie; on a wknd or holiday Docklands seems even more deserted than the rest of the City. Most parts are reached and seen best by the **Docklands Light Railway**; the best bit is between West India Quay and Island Gardens, where you can get off and walk through the foot tunnel under the Thames to Greenwich (see *Further Afield* section below). The earliest docks to be redeveloped are the most visitor-friendly: St Katharine's Dock (Tower Hill tube station is quite handy), which has a lively marina, a quite cheerful pastiche of a Victorian pub, and lots going on, and Tobacco Dock, with an American-style factory shopping centre. Further E down river is the gigantic closeable **Thames Flood Barrier**, built to protect the city from freak tides; a Visitor Centre is on Unity Way, Woolwich SE18; cl 24–26 Dec; (0181) 854 1373; £3.40. Boats down here from Westminster Pier now stop at Canary Wharf too; (0171) 930 3373, £6.70 return).

Bloomsbury, Holborn and Regent's Park

The British Museum is almost synonymous with Bloomsbury. With Holborn, this civilised and genteel if slightly faded area of Georgian squares, gardens and courts between the City and Westminster is academic and legal London. The Sir John Soane's Museum here is one of London's little-known treasures, not to be missed, and the new British Library is at last open. Right down on the southern fringes of the area, Somerset House is becoming a handsome centre for major art collections.

To the west, Bloomsbury merges into a more genteel area, over towards Marylebone (inc Madame Tussaud's), with smart Regent's Park (and the Zoo) on its northern border; away from the shopping streets of Marylebone High St and Baker St this is largely residential, and the capital of private medicine and dentistry.

Bloomsbury does have a large number of hotels, especially for the more budget-conscious visitor, though many are on the tawdry side. Ones which can be recommended include the Academy (17 Gower St WC1E 6HG (0171) 631 4115), the Morgan (24 Bloomsbury St WC1B 3QJ (0171) 636 3735) – both handy for the British Museum – and the George (60 Cartwright Gdns WC1H 9EL (0171) 387 6789).

To see and do

RUSSELL SQUARE British Museum (Great Russell St) Monumental 19th-c building housing spectacular collections of priceless man-made objects from all over the world, some over 3,000 years old. The range is staggering, in which just a few highlights are the Elgin Marbles, the log-book of Nelson's *Victory*, the wonderful and intriguing Egyptian galleries, the comprehensive galleries of Greek vases, the oriental antiquities, and the Amaravati sculpture. Now that the books have gone to the new British Library, there's room to show the fascinating collections of non-Western art and culture that were farmed out to the temporary Museum of Mankind. Don't try to take it in all at once – decide what interests you most and stick to that, or your head will start reeling before you've got even a tenth of the way through. Ambitious redevelopment is planned over the next few years: work has started on the transformation of the museum's currently hidden centre courtyard into a covered public square. Try to arrive early as it can get very busy. Meals, snacks, shop, disabled access; cl am Sun, 24–26 Dec, 1 Jan, May Day bank hol, 2 Apr; (0171) 636 1555; free exc for special exhibitions. Just up Gower St, Dillons is a first-class serious bookshop, and in Museum St the Museum Tavern does decent food all day.

Dickens' House (48 Doughty St) Dickens lived here during his 20s, when he wrote the *Pickwick Papers*, *Oliver Twist* and *Nicholas Nickleby*. The drawing room has been reconstructed as it was then, and there are original manuscripts and first editions, pictures and personal possessions. His wife's sister died here in 1837, an event which the writer later used as the model for the death of Little Nell in *The Old Curiosity Shop*. Shop; cl Sun and some public hols; (0171) 405 2127; £3.50.

GOODGE ST Pollock's Toy Museum (1 Scala St) Housed in a rather charming setting, a wide range of playthings from all over the world and from all periods, almost as if lots of enthusiastic children had just left them scattered through these little rooms. Mechanical and optical toys, teddy bears, furniture, board games and model theatres, and a proper toy shop downstairs. Disabled access to ground floor only; cl Sun and bank hols; (0171) 636 3452; £2.50.

HOLBORN This is legal London, and you'll usually find a good number of lawyers in the splendid Cittie of York (22 High Holborn), an enormous and very atmospheric basement pub with little private booths down one side. Other fine pubs in this area are the opulent Victorian gin palace, the Princess Louise (208 High Holborn), and the classic Lamb in Lamb's Conduit St. Dom Vitos Sandwich Bar on Kingsway has superb sandwiches. **Lincoln's Inn Fields** A perfect example of the area's tranquil architecture – a large open space with trees and lawns surrounded by handsome houses, also tennis courts and summer band concerts; it's a pleasant place to spend a summer afternoon. Nearby, the Gothic **Royal Courts of Justice** are impressive, and you can also stroll through the gardens of **Gray's Inn**, said to have been laid out by Francis Bacon around 1600.

Sir John Soane's Museum (13 Lincoln's Inn Fields) One of London's hidden highlights, built by the architect for his splendid collection of pictures, books and antiquities. It's most eccentric, full of architectural tricks and mirrors, which form a complex natural-lighting system for the antiquities covering most of the walls. There's a lovely picture by Turner and an Egyptian sarcophagus, but the highlight is Hogarth's acid series on *The Rake's Progress* and *The Election*. When you've seen them the guide swings open the hinged 'walls' and further treasures emerge, inc choice Piranesi drawings and a scale model of the Bank of England. The house is built around a central courtyard monument to his dog ('Alas, poor Fanny!'); you ring the bell to get in, and sign a visitors' book. The guides are very friendly and helpful, and the guidebook is well worthwhile. Shop; cl Sun, Mon and Christmas, open 1st Tues evening of every month; (0171) 405 0175; free (donations welcome). The breakfast room of Soane's first house, no 12 next door, can also be visited.

TEMPLE Courtauld Institute Galleries (Somerset House, Strand) Outstanding collection of Impressionist and Post-Impressionist paintings inc works by Monet, Renoir, Degas and Cezanne, also Michelangelo, Rubens, Goya and other masters. Snacks, shop, disabled access; cl am Sun; (0171) 873 2526; £4.

Gilbert Collection (Somerset House) Spectacular collection of over 800 pieces of silver made for the rich and famous over the past 500 years, from cups, bowls and soup tureens to a massive wine cistern weighing nearly 36kg and even a pair of silver chamber pots. After a nationwide tour it should be housed here by late 1999; phone for details, (01787) 282288. Other parts of Somerset House are set be opened up to visitors over the next few years.

TEMPLE Of all the Inns of Court, this is perhaps the most impressive, and boasts many famous literary figures among its former members. Most of the buildings date from after the reign of Elizabeth I or the Great Fire, but the name points to an older history: the land was owned by the Knights Templar from about 1160. **Middle Temple Hall** is a fine example of Tudor architecture, with a double hammerbeam roof and beautiful stained glass. There is a table made from timber from Sir Francis Drake's ship the *Golden Hind* – he was a member of the Middle Temple – while a single oak tree from Windsor Forest supplied the wood for the 9-metre (29-ft) long High Table. Open 10-am–noon Mon–Fri exc bank hols, during Aug, and over some vacations – best to check first, (0171) 427 4800; free. The Inner Temple has an unusual round church.

Dr Johnson's House (17 Gough Sq) A perfect example of early 18th-c architecture, just as Dr Johnson himself was a perfect example of 18th-c barbed, slightly flawed gentility. Between 1749 and 1759 he wrote his great *English Dictionary* here, and a first edition of this is on display, along with various memorabilia from his learned life. Shop; cl Sun and bank hols; (0171) 353 3745; £3. The passages and walkways around here are a good reminder of how London's streets used to be laid out; the 17th-c Olde Cheshire Cheese nearby is a splendid old tavern.

St Bride's Church (Fleet St) A Wren masterpiece, its splendid steeple the influence for today's traditional 3-tiered wedding cake; good Sun choir and frequent short lunchtime recitals; (0171) 353 1301 for programme. There's an interesting **museum** in the partly Roman crypt (cl bank hols; free). Caxton set up his first printing press alongside, and ever since St Bride's has been the parish church for anyone involved in the press. This was useful in the days when adjoining Fleet St was the hub of newspaperland; today it's really just a passage between the law courts and the City – but look out for relics of the newspaper kingdoms such as the black-glass former Daily Express Building. The opulent Old Bank of England is now a magnificent pub.

BAKER ST Madame Tussaud's (Marylebone Rd) Almost half of overseas visitors place this famous waxworks museum at the top of their list of things to do in London, which explains why the queues can be so long and slow-moving (and perhaps why German TV presenters and Japanese sumo wrestlers now crop up among more familiar simulacrums). Some of the models are uncannily realistic, others rather less so; several members of the Royal Family spring to mind. They've successfully reworked the famous Chamber of Horrors (it no longer has that rather unpleasant emphasis on real-life crime), and the Spirit of London finale is entertaining – you sit in a black cab and are whisked through a cheery interpretation of the city's history. This part is excellently put together, and in places rather witty, but is over a little quickly – like the waxworks as a whole. As you can be in and out of the museum in little over an hour, you're paying more per minute here than practically anywhere else in Britain. Meals, snacks, shop, disabled access; cl 25 Dec; (0171) 935 6861; £9.25.

London Planetarium (Marylebone Rd, next door to Madame Tussaud's) A satisfying place, showing off one of the most advanced star projectors in the world. Surround-sound gives its enjoyable presentations an added sense of realism. Make sure you get to each show on time – stragglers barely have a moment to find a seat before the lights are dimmed. Plenty of interactive displays – you can see how much you'd weigh on another planet. Meals, snacks, shop, disabled access; cl 25 Dec; £6.35 (less in winter); joint ticket with Madame Tussaud's available. Opposite, the café of St Marylebone Church has good-value, simple vegetarian meals.

Sherlock Holmes Museum (221b Baker St) To many people the world over, Baker St calls to mind only one thing – Conan Doyle's great detective. This famous address has various Holmes paraphernalia, and something of the atmosphere of the books re-created – though 'The Case of Why They Charge So Much To See It' might have baffled even brother Mycroft. Shop; cl 25 Dec; (0171) 935 8866; *£5.

KING'S CROSS British Library (Euston Rd) This vast new library has good exhibition space for its national treasures such as the Lindisfarne Gospels and Magna Carta, and will change its displays frequently, as well as mounting special exhibitions; the entrance courtyard has a gigantic bronze of a crouching Sir Isaac Newton, by Paolozzi after William Blake, and impressive entrance gates. Open daily; (0171) 412 7111; free. The Euston Flyer opposite, open all day, has decent food.

REGENT'S PARK (Great Portland St tube station is also handy) Covering over 400 acres, this is the culmination of a glorious swathe of Regency terraces designed by John Nash, which can be seen almost all around it; the buildings of Park Crescent are among the finest. The park was originally intended to be the setting of a palace for the Prince Regent, after whom it was named: now it contains an open-air theatre where Shakespeare and other plays are performed in the summer, the lovely Queen Mary's Rose Garden, the spectacular Avenue Garden (now restored to its 1864 glory), a boating lake, bandstand concerts on summer Suns, and plenty of paths to stroll along.

London Zoo (Camden Town tube station is even closer) In the N corner of the Park, they opened the listed Mappin Terraces as a sort of animal playground shared by deer, peacocks, monkeys and bears in 1997. Other areas show that the last few years haven't been the zoo's easiest, and despite the presence of lions, elephants and rhinos it's with the smaller creatures that the zoo currently excels: there's a fascinating insect house, and other highlights are the irresistible children's zoo, where you can get right up to the animals (and maybe help feed the pigs at lunchtime), the biggest reptile house of any British zoo, and the spellbinding Moonlight World, where day and night are reversed so that you can watch nocturnal creatures such as vampire bats. The 1930s architecture of the penguin pool remains quite something. Meals, snacks, shop, disabled access; cl 25 Dec; (0171) 722 3333; £8.50.

Primrose Hill Once part of the same hunting park as Regent's Park, now a popular strolling ground for this sober residential area. The modest rounded summit gives eye-opening views of the city.

Regent's Canal This offers an excellent walk from Little Venice to Camden Lock, passing by Regent's Park and Primrose Hill; boat cruises also operate along here – one-way tickets available. The London Waterbus Company – one of several companies who now run along the stretch of Regent's Canal between Little Venice and Camden Lock – make a stop for passengers who want to get off at the zoo; (0171) 482 2550 for timetable.

South of the River

South of the river has some very strong draws for visitors: the London Aquarium, Museum of the Moving Image (MOMI), Imperial War Museum and Britain at War – these last two are by no means just for warmongering types. Children particularly like MOMI, and the expensive London Dungeon. Though small, the Old Operating Theatre is eye-opening, and the Design Museum is interesting. The buildings of the South Bank arts centre have been largely humanised inside (though not out), with pleasant bars and so forth, and usually something going on in their foyers – inc free entertainment. The magnificent reconstruction of Shakespeare's Globe Theatre has performances through the summer, and other new projects are livening up other parts of the South Bank. A stroll along its walkways gives marvellous views across the river – the best views of the Houses of Parliament are from the quiet riverside walk between Westminster Bridge and the ancient palace of the Archbishop of Canterbury by Lambeth Bridge.

To see and do

WESTMINSTER London Aquarium (County Hall – a pleasant walk across Westminster Bridge) This £25 million show is one of Europe's biggest collections of underwater life, housed in around 2 million litres of water. If you come at a sensible time there isn't much congestion around the main Atlantic and Pacific tanks, spectacular in their sheer size, giving great views of the sharks, stingrays and conger eels swimming round Easter-Island-style giant heads (and occasional divers – often more entertaining than the fish). The rest of the displays – arranged in different areas representing rivers, coral reefs and rain forests – are a more conventional size, so you may have to wait a couple of minutes to get right up to them. Some areas make good use of sound and light effects, and of course the fish and sea life are quite spectacular, with breath-taking colours and patterns; some species haven't been seen in Britain before. Well sized touch-tanks let you stroke a ray or gingerly handle a crab, and the Ford Ka aquarium is a novel diversion. To avoid queues at weekends and school holidays, try to come early or late (they're open till 7.30pm in summer). Meals, snacks, big shop, disabled access; cl 25 Dec; (0171) 967 8000; £7. Great views of the Houses of Parliament and river from outside.

County Hall Besides the Aquarium, this grandiose home of the former Greater London Council also has simulator rides, video games and ten-pin bowling, a couple of new hotels and a McDonalds. This is also where the huge Ferris wheel to mark the

Millenium will be – a 'working sculpture' rather than a fairground attraction.

WATERLOO Quite a few recent projects have brightened up the South Bank: relaxed **Gabriel's Wharf** (Upper Ground) has cheery designer and craft workshops, along with cafés, events, and Fri craft market, and the **Oxo Tower Wharf** offers great views over the City from the top of the lavishly restored art deco tower with its landmark logo. Though the South Bank and its attractions are well signed from Waterloo, if you have time to spare the walk is more pleasant over Blackfriars Bridge, or from Westminster. Nr the Old Vic, just S of Waterloo, La Barca (Lower Marsh St) is an enjoyably theatrical Italian restaurant, and Livebait (The Cut) is renowned for its fish. The café of the Young Vic (The Cut) does very good-value light lunches, but you'll feel centuries old if you're out of your 20s.

South Bank Centre These theatres, cinemas and galleries contain all sorts of cultural treasures – they fairly boast that it's the biggest arts complex in the world. Externally, it's not appealing. Exciting plans to float a spectacular 'crystal wave' over the complex to bring some charm and warmth to the uninviting space around these rather dismal blocks of stained concrete have been delayed, if not scuppered by the recent diversion of Lottery money into non-arts projects. In the meantime occasional open-air festivals, with stalls of books, clothes and jewellery going down to the river, are a well meaning substitute and can be pleasant on a sunny day. Inside there are frequent free performances and interesting small exhibitions in the foyers of the various halls. The National Theatre, as well as the excellent productions in its 3 different-sized auditoria, has interesting artistic exhibitions, guided tours behind the scenes, and good places to eat – often accompanied by live music in the foyer of the Olivier Theatre; (0171) 452 3400 to book a tour (£4; they don't do them on Sun). The National Film Theatre has good themed screenings and events, as well as a new riverside café. The Hayward Gallery specialises in world-class art exhibitions. The Royal Festival Hall has a full programme of music and dance; its People's Palace is a good modern restaurant and bar. It's a short walk from here to the London Aquarium (a rather longer one to the Imperial War Museum).

! Museum of the Moving Image (South Bank Centre) MOMI, as it's usually called, provides a romp through cinematic history which everyone really enjoys. Lively displays trace moving pictures from magic lanterns to today's hi-tech special effects, taking in clips from favourite films, TV shows and cartoons along the way. You can learn how to operate a television studio, read the news or fly like Superman, and older visitors find the montage of old Pathé newsreels particularly nostalgic. The costumed actors work really hard with their performances, and there are temporary themed exhibitions. One of London's best attractions, and a visit can easily last several hours. Meals, snacks, shop, disabled access – contact reception when you get there; cl 24–26 Dec; (0171) 401 2636; £6.25.

LONDON BRIDGE

Bankside is very much on the up, with quite a bit of redevelopment going on in the old buildings, and plenty more to come (the Tate are to open a £106 million modern art gallery in the old Bankside power station). Riverside promenades offer good Thames and City views – Wren is said to have watched the building of St Paul's from here, and Pepys certainly did watch London burning down in the Great Fire, from nr the interesting old Anchor tavern. One of the best cross-river views of St Paul's is from the modern Founders Arms pub. For centuries this was London's entertainment centre, full of theatres, bars and licensed brothels. Clink St has the medieval remains of the Bishop of Winchester's palace, once said to be the biggest building in Europe but now reduced to a single wall and atmospheric rose window. A full-size replica of Francis Drake's *Golden Hind* is moored nearby; cl 25 Dec; (0171) 403 0123; *£2.30.

! Globe Theatre The most famous of Southwark's 1600s theatres,

Shakespeare's Globe, has been reconstructed on its original site, where it was open from 1599 to 1642 (when the Puritans shut it down). The late Sam Wanamaker's ambitious project was derided when first mooted, but the theatre has now enjoyed 2 very successful seasons. It couldn't be more different from the West End: shaped like an O, the 3-tiered open-topped theatre is 30 metres (100ft) in diameter, seating audiences of 1,500 with a further 500 promenaders. Shakespeare's works are performed almost the way they were in the early 1600s – no spotlights, canned music or elaborate sets, lots of audience/actor interaction. Anyone who tells you the seats are uncomfortable has rather missed the point (and you can hire cushions). There are entertaining tours during the day, and there's an exhibition on the Globes old and new – a good substitute if you can't make a performance. Shop, disabled access; museum cl 24–25 Dec; (0171) 902 1500; tours £5. The 17th-c galleried George in Borough High St, back past London Bridge station, gives another idea of how the area's buildings used to look back then; NT.

† **Southwark Cathedral** Off the busy main road and quite a contast to the buildings cluttered all around it, well worth a passing look, with parts over 600 years older than the present late 19th-c nave; interesting memorials to William Shakespeare (whose brother is buried here) and John Harvard, the founder of the American university. They generally have free music Mon lunchtime, and sometimes Tues too.

♁ **Old Operating Theatre** (St Thomas St) The church of St Thomas has a unique reconstructed operating theatre in its roof, and a developing museum looking at the history of surgery and herbal medicine. *The Madness of King George* was filmed here. Shop, cl some Mons, 24 Dec–5 Jan; £2.90.

♁ ! **London Dungeon** (Tooley St) A sensationalised look at London's seamy underside, so better for unsqueamish children, with witchcraft, torture, black magic and death in ghoulishly life-like waxwork scenes. The Jack the Ripper Experience has a computer-controlled fireball blasting towards visitors as its climax, and there's an entertaining water ride, Judgement Day. The whole place is very atmospheric and well laid out, though families may find the scariest thing about it is the rather high price. Snacks, shop, disabled access; cl 25 Dec; (0171) 403 0606; *£8.95.

♁ ħ **Britain at War** ⊞ (Tooley St) A splendidly put together re-creation of Blitz-hit London, from reconstructed streets and air-raid shelters to a BBC radio station and GI club. The special effects are suitably dramatic, with lots of smoke, smells and noise. Also authentic period newsreels and front pages, a fully stocked shop and bombed-out pub, and lots of fascinating little details. Shop, disabled access; cl 24–26 Dec; (0171) 403 3171; £5.95.

Hays Galleria (off Tooley St) An old dock attractively converted into a shopping arcade, with several places to eat inc a good river-view pub, and a fascinating, whimsical pirate-ship working sculpture by David Kemp.

☸ **HMS *Belfast*** (E side of Southwark Bridge) Docked permanently in the Pool of London, this is the largest preserved Royal Navy cruiser. Its 7 decks are now a floating naval museum, with sound and light displays and various exhibitions. Anyone with even a passing interest in naval life and history should get a lot out of this, and there's plenty to see, from the ship's gun decks to its dental surgery. Meals, snacks, shop, limited disabled access; cl 24–26 Dec; (0171) 407 6434; *£4.70.

♁ **Design Museum** (Butlers Wharf) Intriguing museum showing how design is used in the mass production of everyday objects, from cars and furniture to graphics and ceramics. An exhibition looking at the early Modern Movement in Britain runs from 19 Jan–18 July. Meals, snacks, interesting if pricey shop, disabled access; cl 25–26 Dec; (0171) 403 6933; £5.25.

♁ **Bramah Tea and Coffee Museum** (Maguire St, Butlers Wharf) Almost scholarly but surprisingly interesting, meticulously charting the history of these two favourite commodities, with around 1,000 teapots, and lots of ceramics, silver and prints. Teas (good stuff – they're not fans of the tea bag), snacks, shop, disabled access; cl 25–26 Dec; (0171) 378 0222; £4. Nearby the Anchor Tap (just off Shad Thames) is a handy refreshment stop.

LAMBETH NORTH Imperial War Museum (Lambeth Rd) This top-notch museum uses very up-to-date presentation techniques to give a vibrant and sometimes even nerve-racking exploration of aspects of all wars involving Britain and the Commonwealth since 1914. The Blitz Experience vividly re-creates London's darkest days, and a Trench Experience gives World War I the same treatment. Small boys of all ages love it, though the tone isn't all gung-ho: the interesting archive recordings of people's experiences of war can leave a deep impression, as do some of the harrowing paintings by official war artists. Meals, snacks, shop, disabled access; cl 24–26 Dec; (0171) 416 5000; £4, free after 4.30pm. It's housed in the former lunatic asylum known as Bedlam, the name a corruption of Bethlehem: the site was originally a hostel set up in the 13th c by the bishop of that town. There's a clutch of useful tapas bars and the like up past here, around the junction of Kennington Rd and Kennington Lane, and on Waterloo Rd the Fire Station does good food.

† **Lambeth Palace** (S end of Lambeth Bridge) The official residence of the Archbishop of Canterbury, with a charming late 15th-c red-brick exterior; though there are twice-weekly tours of the partly early medieval interior, they're fully booked for the whole of this year – and well into next. The adjacent **Church of St Mary** has the tombs of several archbishops, and Captain Bligh of the *Bounty* is buried here too. Just by the south gateway is a little **Museum of Garden History** founded in memory of John Tradescant, Charles I's gardener (also buried in the church), with a small area planted with plants grown in his time. Snacks, shop, some disabled access; cl Sat, and early Dec–early Mar; (0171) 401 8865; free.

Florence Nightingale Museum (St Thomas's Hospital, Lambeth Palace Rd) On the site of the first School of Nursing, a re-created Crimean War hospital ward, and various artefacts and possessions of the Lady with the Lamp. 1999 is the museum's 10th anniversary, with special events all year. Shop, disabled access; cl Mon (exc bank hols), Good Fri, Easter Sun, 24–25 Dec, 31 Dec–1 Jan; (0171) 620 0374; £3.50.

! ELEPHANT & CASTLE Bermondsey market (Bermondsey St/Long Lane) Get up very early on Fri for the bargains: when the antique-dealers start arriving around 5am, other dealers literally pounce on the choice items while they're being set out, and by 8am or 9am things are more ordinary. It's probably the biggest primary source of antiques and bric-à-brac in London, and can be the most exciting. Take a torch in winter.

! VAUXHALL London Balloon (Spring Gardens) Soar 150 metres (500ft) above London in 'Big Bob', the world's largest tethered balloon. Surprisingly affordable, and giving a truly unique view of the capital. Snacks, shop, disabled access; cl Nov–Mar and in bad weather; (0171) 587 1111; £12.

Further Afield

We include here only those places which, despite being away from the centre, appeal so much at least to some people that, for them, even a short stay in London would be incomplete without them. The most generally appealing are Greenwich and Kew, and elsewhere the lively RAF Museum in Colindale is excellent, Kenwood is a Hampstead highlight, the unusual Horniman Museum makes Forest Hill well worth a family expedition, and the Saatchi Gallery in St John's Wood is right on the cutting edge of young British art.

Other parts of London do have many treasures tucked away, and though we don't list them they are well worth Londoners themselves tracking down: prime among them are the Whitechapel Gallery in Whitechapel High St, E of the City, and, out in west London, Osterley Park, Sion House, Chiswick Mall (18th-c Thames-side village), Chiswick Park (the first true example of English naturalistic landscaping, with Chiswick House, an early 18th-c partying pavilion), and perhaps Hogarth's House.

To see and do

CAMDEN TOWN A bohemian's idyll, with a very wide variety of unusual shops from radical bookshops to fashion workshops, from comic shops to one of London's best brassware and ironmongery shops. Lots of restaurants and cafés too, and good delis serving the area's Italian and Greek communities; try the Parkway Deli for Italian, and Chris Milia (Pratt St) for Greek. The area's biggest draw is its weekend series of lively **markets**, particularly the interesting craft, hand-made fashion and other stalls around the attractively converted former warehouses of Camden Lock. There's also a covered market on Camden High St, the Inverness St market for fruit and vegetables, and the Stables, where the best food stalls are to be found. Go and browse, but be warned that you may never again see such huge crowds – the markets here draw 200,000 people every weekend. The Princess of Wales up towards Primrose Hill (Chalcot Rd/Regent's Pk Rd) does good bistro food.

Jewish Museum (129 Albert St) Excellent look at Jewish life, history and religion, with a particularly fine collection of ceremonial art, portraits and antiques, and various audio-visual displays. Shop, disabled access; cl Fri, Sat, all bank and Jewish hols; (0171) 388 4525; £3. Another branch on East End Rd, Finchley, (0181) 349 1143, traces the history of Jewish immigration and has a moving exhibition on the Holocaust.

GREENWICH The sort of place you can come back to time and time again; some of our contributors rate Greenwich more highly than anywhere else in the country. Once a favoured residence of the Royal Family, Greenwich has a long and illustrious maritime heritage, still reflected in the museums, boats and grand old ships you can visit. A weekend market has some excellent antiques, junk and secondhand books, also arts and crafts. College Approach has a good weekend covered craft market. You should be able to get boat trips from the Pier up to Westminster (around £5). The Cutty Sark pub (Lassell St) is an attractive old place for lunch; other reliable Thames-view pubs here are the Trafalgar (Park Row) and Yacht (Crane St). The almost constantly controversial Millennium Exhibition, with its centrepiece riverside Dome, is to be staged here, the projected cost climbing towards an uncomfortably millenary £1,000 million. Three of the best attractions, the Queen's House, National Maritime Museum and Royal Observatory, can be visited on a joint ticket for a bargain £5. You'll still pay this even if you can visit only one of them, but you don't have to do them all on the same day.

Royal Naval College With the Queen's House as its focal point, this glorious group of buildings was designed initially by Webb in the late 17th c, then augmented in succession by Wren, Vanbrugh, Hawksmoor and Ripley. It's a magnificently preserved part of old London. Visitors can see an interesting chapel and a notable painted hall; the Navy are leaving in Dec 1998, so phone to check the details under the new administration; (0181) 858 2154. The view from across the river (there's a pedestrian tunnel under the Thames here) looks like an 18th-c print come to life.

Queen's House (Romney Rd) On the site of the original magnificent Royal palace; all that's left of that is the vaulted crypt beneath what's now called Queen Anne's Block. The new building was designed in the early 17th c by Inigo Jones for Anne of Denmark, and finished for the wife of Charles I, Queen Henrietta Maria. The first Palladian-style villa in the country, it's been grandly refurbished to show how it was when first built. Sumptuous silks and furnishings, as well as a collection of Dutch seascapes; good Walkman commentary. Shop, limited disabled access; cl 24–26 Dec; (0181) 858 4422; £5 joint ticket.

National Maritime Museum (Romney Rd) Good fun, telling the story of Britain and the sea, with plenty of boats, details of past Royal fleets and vessels, great masterpieces of naval battles and an impressive exhibition on Nelson. Parts will be closed for restoration in 1999; details as Queen's House.

Greenwich Park Wonderful views from this carefully landscaped park, sloping down towards the river; a great place for a picnic. A herd of deer graze in a smallish area of woodland and wild flowers known as the Wilderness, and there's the largest children's playground in any Royal Park (as well as the preserved trunk of a tree in which the young Elizabeth I is said to have played).

Old Royal Observatory (Greenwich Park) The original home of Greenwich Mean Time – standing as it does on zero meridian longitude. The brass line marking the meridian is still there set in the ground: standing over it with one foot in the western hemisphere and one in the east is almost irresistible. As you do so you can check your watch against the big clock counting down the days left to the Millennium. The Wren-built observatory was founded by Charles II in 1675, and now houses a comprehensive collection of historic instruments for time-keeping, navigation and astronomy. Good views from the top. The Time Ball is rather confusing – it can go down and up so fast that you barely notice it. Meals, snacks, shop; details as Queen's House.

Cutty Sark Moored not far from Greenwich Pier, this 1896 clipper was the fastest of her time – she once sailed 363 nautical miles in a single day. On board, you can watch a video telling her story, and there's an impressive collection of ships' figureheads. Shop; cl am Sun, 24–26 Dec; (0181) 858 3445; £3.50.

Fan Museum (12 Crooms Hill) Unique collection of around 3,000 fans and related items from all over the world. They even do fan-making classes. Shop, disabled access (with notice); cl am Sun, and all day Mon; (0181) 858 7879; *£3.50.

Ranger's House (Chesterfield Walk, Blackheath) Lovely stately home with fine furnishings, portraits and a collection of musical instruments. In the 19th c it was the official residence of the Greenwich Park ranger – and Blackheath opposite is a civilised place, good for a pleasant stroll. Cl winter Mon and Tues, 24–26 Dec; (0181) 853 0035; £2.50.

HAMPSTEAD Prides itself on its villagey atmosphere, and off the main streets its maze of twisting lanes is very picturesque and seductively charming. It's home to artistes of all kinds, and well heeled bohemians in general; in some streets a commemorative blue plaque on the front of the house is almost compulsory. Particularly attractive parts include early Georgian Church Row, and Squires Mount (where the Regency-looking house at the end on the left, in fact built in the 1950s, belonged to Richard Burton and Elizabeth Taylor). The gaslit Holly Bush, prettily tucked away up Holly Mount, is a good pub, as is the Flask in Flask Walk (a long-standing favourite of local actors).

Sigmund Freud's House (20 Maresfield Gardens) Extraordinary collection of antiques from various ancient cultures, as well as Freud's library, papers and indeed his desk and couch. Shop, some disabled access; open pm Weds–Sun; (0171) 435 2002; *£3. The monumental seated statue of Freud by Oscar Nemon can now be seen outside the Tavistock Clinic on nearby Belsize Lane.

Fenton House (Windmill Hill) Fine William and Mary merchant's mansion, set in a walled garden, with Oriental, English and European china and an exceptional collection of early keyboard instruments. Their period-music concerts on some summer Weds evenings are well worth catching. Open pm Weds–Sun Apr–Oct, plus pm wknds in Mar; (0171) 435 3471; £4; NT.

2 Willow Rd The first Modern Movement house acquired by the National Trust. Designed and built by the architect Erno Goldfinger, with a good range of work by artists and intellectuals who lived around Hampstead in the 1930s – as well as the only working TV on show in any NT property. Guided tours from noon Thurs–Sat Apr–Oct; (0171) 435 6166; £4; NT.

Hampstead Heath North London's best open space, with woody glades and hollows, lakes, hilly prospects, and some wonderful views of the city skyline – Parliament Hill has a direction-finder pointing out various landmarks. On one edge the ancient Spaniard's Inn, still as popular as when Dickens made it famous in the *Pickwick Papers*, faces an 18th-c toll booth, notorious for the way its road-narrowing blocks the traffic here.

Kenwood (Hampstead Lane) Achieved its present splendid proportions in the 18th c at the hands of Robert Adam. The house contains a fine collection of paintings, inc old masters and 18th- and 19th-c portraits by Reynolds and Gainsborough, and efforts are being made to reacquire its original contents. The grounds are lovely, and in summer there are concerts out here, idyllic when it's fine, with the music drifting across the lake with its Japanese bridge, and sometimes a fireworks finale (virtually impossible to park anywhere near – a free shuttle bus runs from East Finchley tube from 5pm then). Meals, snacks, shop, disabled access; cl 24–25 Dec; (0181) 348 1286; free.

HAMPTON COURT An amazing place, just as a Royal palace should be. Begun by Cardinal Wolsey in the early 16th c, the house's splendour soon so pricked Henry VIII's jealousy that Wolsey felt compelled to present it to his king in an attempt to appease him. Successive monarchs have left their architectural marks: the hammerbeamed hall and kitchens were Henry's addition, the Fountain Court was designed by Wren for William and Mary, and much comes from the work of the Victorians (the chimneys mostly date from then). The rooms have managed to keep their distinctive styles, from the starkly imposing Tudor kitchens (themselves taking up 50 rooms) to the elaborate grandeur of the Georgian chambers. The King's Staircase is wonderfully over the top, and the Picture Gallery has the finest Renaissance works from the Royal collection, inc Bruegel the Elder's fascinating *Massacre of the Innocents*. Look out too for the carvings by Grinling Gibbons and the cartoons by Mantegna in the Lower Orangery. There are several audio guides you can pick up and listen to as you go along, with no extra charge. Tudor Christmas activities 27 Dec–3 Jan. Meals, snacks, shops, disabled access; cl 24–26 Dec; (0181) 781 9500; £9.25.

Hampton Court Gardens Worth a visit in their own right, especially since the restoration of William III's Privy Garden, damaged in the Palace's 1986 fire – the last time these gardens looked as they do now was in 1702. The elaborately landscaped grounds also include the famous maze, and the annual flower show here is one of the world's biggest. Open as for the Palace; gardens only £2.10. The King's Arms, next to the Lion Gate, is useful for something to eat.

River Thames There are pleasant Thames-side walks around Hampton Court, and summer cruise boats from here back down to Westminster, (0171) 930 4721; around £8.

Bushy Park Another Royal Park, formerly reserved for hunting. Wren laid out its famous double chestnut avenue, which runs from Teddington Gate to the great house.

HIGHGATE An easy walk across the Heath from Hampstead, this dates largely from the Victorian period and still keeps a villagey atmosphere, centred as it is around the High St. The village is dominated by Highgate School (which Betjeman attended and where

T S Eliot taught). There are lots of pubs in this area, and some smart little cafés. The Grove, a row of very elegant Victorian houses, is home to such diverse musicians as Yehudi Menuhin and Sting.

! Highgate Cemetery (Swains Lane) The most impressive of a series of landscaped and formal cemeteries started in the early decades of Victoria's reign on the outskirts of the city, very well restored over the last 20 years, and still in use. You'll find it hard to miss the tomb of Karl Marx – a monstrous head, frequently daubed with paint and slogans. It's more difficult to search out the graves of Christina Rossetti and George Eliot in the wonderfully atmospheric tangle of trees, shrubs and crumbling, ivy-covered monuments. The east cemetery is open all year (exc 25–26 Dec), the west by guided tour only (not wkdys Dec–Feb), (0181) 340 1834 for times; east cemetery £1, west cemetery £3.

KEW Kew Gardens Started in 1759 by George III's mother as 9 acres landscaped by Capability Brown. By 1904, they had grown to cover 300 acres, with the foundations of the present wonderful collection firmly laid. The glasshouses include the magnificent modern Princess of Wales range and the remarkable restored Victorian Palm House, as well as an Evolution House displaying plants from up to 400 million years ago. The gardens nr the entrance are largely formally arranged, and drift into attractively landscaped woodland, glades and tree collections further out. The museum has now reopened after extensive renovation, but the modest 17th-c Dutch-style Kew Palace is closed till 2000. There's also a gallery, and on some summer evenings jazz concerts with fireworks. A wonderful place you can come back to time and time again – always discovering something new. Meals, snacks, shop, disabled access; cl 25 Dec, 1 Jan; (0181) 332 5622; £5. The Flower & Firkin next to Kew main line and tube stations does decent simple food. In summer you can come to Kew by cruise boat from Westminster – see the numbers we give for Hampton Court and Richmond.

Queen Charlotte's Cottage (Kew Gardens) This rusticated summerhouse was built for the Royal Family in the 18th c, its interior designed to look like a tent; it's usually open wknds and bank hols Apr–Sept; free with admission to the gardens.

Kew Bridge Steam Museum (Green Dragon Lane) Over the bridge from the gardens, by Kew Bridge mainline station, this splendid old pumping station houses 5 Cornish beam engines – one of which you can walk through while it's working. Also a miniature railway, and a surprisingly interesting exhibition on the development of London's water supply: there are peepholes into the sewers. Wknd snacks, shop, some disabled access; cl Christmas, Good Fri; (0181) 568 4757; £3.80 wknds (when engines in steam), £2.80 wkdys.

Musical Museum (368 Brentford High St, just W of the Bridge) Worth a look if you have the time, with a fascinating collection of continuously playing automatic musical instruments. Shop, disabled access; open pm wknds Apr–Oct, plus pm Weds July and Aug; (0181) 560 8108; £3.20.

Towpath walks by the Thames between here and Putney have train stations at either end; you have to cross the river a few times, and can take in Chiswick Mall, Chiswick Park (a necessary diversion from the river at a point where there is no towpath on the N bank), and Strand on the Green, as well as Kew Gardens. The towpath can also be combined with a walk in Richmond Park and to Ham House.

RICHMOND Agreeable if much extended Thames village, with lots of fine 18th-c houses especially around the Green and up Richmond Hill. There are quite a few good dining pubs, inc the riverside White Cross, and the White Swan (Old Palace Lane), Orange Tree (Kew Rd) and Rose of York (Petersham Rd). The river here is really attractive for strolls, and there are summer cruise boats from here back down to Westminster, stopping at Kew and Putney (more fine riverside walks) on the way; (0171) 930 2062.

Richmond Park The most country-like of all London's parks, with great rolling spaces and wildlife (inc herds of deer), model boats on Adam's Pond, and fishing in the 18-acre Pen Ponds. There's a good formal garden at Pembroke Lodge, and the Isabella Plantation's rhododendrons and azaleas are a must-see in season.

Ham House (Petersham) A pleasant 2-mile walk W along the river from Richmond to this outstanding Stuart mansion, recently wonderfully restored. A new ghost guide takes you on a tour of haunted rooms (Mon 3pm). Meals, snacks, shop, disabled access; open pm Sat–Weds Apr–Oct; (0181) 940 1950; £5, £1.50 garden only; NT. If you happen to be in Twickenham you can get a ferry across.

More Specialised Expeditions

CAMDEN PASSAGE (⊖ Angel) This and the surrounding streets have a great collection of **antique shops**, well worth the expedition if that interests you. The nearby Island Queen (Noel Rd) does good food in its bar and upstairs restaurant.

CHISLEHURST CAVES (off Caveside Close nr the Bickley Arms, B264; ⇌ Chislehurst) Atmospheric 45-minute lamplit tours of labyrinthine tunnels and passageways carved out of the rock over 8,000 years. They've been used by flint-knappers, druids, and as an air-raid shelter during the war. Longer, more adventurous tours on Suns and bank hols at 2.30pm. Snacks (wknds and school hols), shop; cl Mon and Tues (exc school hols); (0181) 467 3264; *£3 (£5 longer tour).

★ **DULWICH** (⇌ West Dulwich) The village still is villagey, with imposing 18th-c houses, a duckpond, good pub, the Crown & Greyhound, and an almost rural feel (there's even a toll road). There are good walks, in Dulwich Park (best in rhododendron time), and through Dulwich Wood to adjacent Sydenham Hill Wood – the largest fragment of ancient woodland in inner London, and a most surprising place (just big enough to lose your way in), with woodpeckers among the oaks and hornbeams. The best of the wood is a nature reserve jealously guarded against developers by the London Wildlife Trust; a trail starts from the Crescent Wood Rd entrance on the Sydenham side. The excellent Dulwich Picture Gallery is closed till 2000.

ESTORICK COLLECTION OF MODERN ITALIAN ART (Northampton Lodge, 39A Canonbury Sq; ⊖ Highbury & Islington) This outstanding collection of modern Italian art opened early last year. Fine futurist works by artists inc Balla and Boccioni, as well as later figurative works by Modigliani and Sironi. Meals, snacks, shop, disabled access; cl Mon, Tues and am Sun; (0171) 704 9522; £2.50.

HORNIMAN MUSEUM (London Rd; ⇌ Forest Hill) Art nouveau building with eclectic, mainly ethnographic collections inc a fine group of mummies, religious artefacts, and exotic folk art; also a remarkable musical instrument collection (interactive computers let you hear some of the extraordinary instruments), lots of stuffed animals, very well laid out aquarium/ecosystem; children love it, despite the old-fashioned feel (£10 million of Lottery money awarded in 1998 will bring more space and even better displays). Friendly small farm animals in the gardens outside. Snacks, shop, some disabled access; cl am Sun, 25–26 Dec; free wknd talks/concerts; (0181) 699 1872; free.

LORD'S CRICKET GROUND (St John's Wood Rd; ⊖ St John's Wood) Tours of the famous club and grounds, and the excellent MCC Museum, with an exhaustive collection of cricket memorabilia, inc the Ashes urn and 18th-c paintings of the game. As this is a private club, visits are by appointment only, (0171) 432 1033 (usually at 12 and 2pm), though you can also see the museum if you're watching a cricket match during the season. Shop, disabled access by prior arrangement; £5.80 (£2 for museum on match days). Down in Aberdeen Pl, Crockers is a remarkably opulent Victorian pub with decent food.

✝ **RAF MUSEUM** (Grahame Park Way; ⊖ Colindale) The story of flight from early times, with 80 full-size aeroplanes, dramatic simulators, films and hands-on exhibits (you can have a go at the controls of a modern jet trainer), lively Battle of Britain Experience, and an interesting examination of the impact of flight on history and politics. Excellent for enthusiasts and flying-minded children (with a new interactive Fun 'n' Flight gallery), and warmly recommended by several of our contributors. Meals, snacks, shop, disabled access; cl 24–26 Dec, 1 Jan; (0181) 205 9191; £6.50.

SAATCHI GALLERY (Boundary Rd; ⊖ St John's Wood) Challenging modern art inc works by Marcus Harvey, Richard Wilson and a shark in formaldehyde by Damien Hirst. Shop; cl am, Mon–Weds, and all August; £4.

! TWICKENHAM EXPERIENCE (Rugby Rd; ⇌ Twickenham) Combines tours of the 75,000-seat home of Rugby Union with an excellent museum of related memorabilia under the East Stand; interactive displays and period reconstructions illustrate the game's history, and there's plenty of classic match footage. Snacks, shop, disabled access; cl Mon (exc bank hols), am Sun, 24–26 Dec, Good Fri and 2 days before and after match days; 4 tours a day (only 2 on Sun), best to book on (0181) 892 2000; £4, £2.50 for either the museum or tour only.

! WEMBLEY STADIUM (Empire Way; ⊖ Wembley Central) Tours of the most famous football stadium in the land, going from the dressing-rooms through the players' tunnel and onto the pitch itself, with an audio-visual show and displays of trophies and related memorabilia. You can receive the Cup or sit in the Royal Box. Snacks, shop, some disabled access (with notice); cl 25–26 Dec, during occasional special events and permanently from June 1999 – they are demolishing the stadium to make way for the new national stadium; (0181) 902 8833; £7.45.

WILLIAM, MORRIS GALLERY (Lloyd Park, Forest Rd; ⊖ Walthamstow Central) William Morris lived here 1846–1858, and the house has an excellent collection of his work: fabrics, furnishings and wallpaper, much of it still fashionable today. Pre-Raphaelite works upstairs include pictures by Burne-Jones and Rossetti. The attractive grounds are ideal for picnics. Shop, disabled access to ground floor only with prior notice – though this is where the main exhibition is; cl 1–2 pm, all day Mon, and Sun (exc first Sun in month); (0181) 527 3782; free.

WIMBLEDON LAWN TENNIS MUSEUM (Church Rd; ⊖ Southfields) The only museum of its type, with trophies, pictures and other tennis memorabilia tracing the development of the game through this century. Also highlights of past Wimbledon Championships, an interesting display on the changes in tennis fashions, and of course the famous Centre Court outside. Snacks, shop, disabled access; cl am Sun, all day Mon, and every day during the Championship fortnight (unless you've gone to watch the tennis); (0181) 946 6131; *£3. If you're in London during the Wimbledon fortnight it's always worth popping along to the club in the early evening around 5.30 or 6pm – lots of people leave then and their seats are resold cheaply. Wimbledon Common, with its ponds and striking **windmill** on Windmill Rd (open pm wknds and bank hols Easter–Oct; *£1), is one of the best strolling grounds among south London's numerous commons and parks. There's an attractive old core around it.

South London walks The SE fringes of London give way to surprisingly rural North Downs countryside, still within the London borough of Bromley, around Knockholt, High Elms and Downe; paths are plentiful and well maintained. Only the view over S London from behind Knockholt church shows how close you are to the capital.

Where to eat

ALASTAIR LITTLE *49 Frith St W1 (0171) 734 5183* Uncluttered, almost starkly furnished restaurant with very good, simple modern food from a sensibly short menu – plenty of strong flavours – enjoyable puddings, and an interesting small wine list; cl am Sat, Sun, bank hols. **£39 dinner, £31 lunch**|£7.

APPRENTICE *Butlers Wharf Chef School, Cardamon Building, 31 Shad Thames SE1 (0171) 234 0254* The school is a charitable organisation for hopeful chefs and front-of-house personnel; long, simple restaurant and good-value modern meals in an enjoyable atmosphere; weekend courses; cl Sat, Sun, Christmas, bank hols; disabled access. **£22.50**|£9.50 for 2 courses.

BANK *1 Kingsway WC2 (0171) 379 9797* Very modern restaurant with décor to match (the slanted glass decorations hanging from the ceiling are quite a sight), an open kitchen, and interesting food from a very varied menu (as well as lunch and dinner, they also serve breakfasts, from 7am, pre-theatre meals, and weekend brunches that includes a children's menu); cl bank hols; disabled access. **£29.50**|£9.50.

BIBENDUM *81 Fulham Rd SW3 (0171) 581 5817* Magnificent art deco Michelin building housing a light and spacious restaurant; with exceptionally good, French-style cooking (more elaborate in the evening), a marvellous wine list, and courteous, well trained staff; the unpretentious downstairs oyster bar is a fine place for a lighter (and cheaper) meal; cl 25–26 Dec; disabled access. **£45**.

BISHOPS FINGER *9–10 West Smithfield EC1 (0171) 248 2341* Swish little bar-cum-restaurant with fresh flowers on elegant tables that are set on polished bare boards, and comfortably cushioned chairs under a wall lined with prints; distinctive food from an open kitchen, well kept real ales, a wide choice of wines, and friendly service; upstairs evening restaurant. **£18.35**|£6.95.

BLOOMS *130 Golders Green Rd NW11 (0181) 455 3033* Strictly kosher Jewish restaurant with enjoyable food – most fun on Sun lunchtime when it's packed with Jewish families; cl Fri evening, am Sat, and Jewish hols (they are open bank hols); disabled access. **£20**|£5.

BLUEBIRD *350 King's Rd SW3 (0171) 559 1000* The Bluebird Garage, built in 1923, has been converted to house the King's Rd Gastrodrome with a foodmarket offering all sorts of delicious specialist products (inc ready-made dishes), flower market, wine merchant, kitchenware shop, and private dining club, plus the huge, airy 1st-floor restaurant with its kite-like artwork hanging from the ceiling, and dark green limestone floor; stainless-steel bar at one end with a shellfish bar the other, open-plan kitchen with a big woodburning oven, and good modern British cooking served by friendly staff; pre-theatre meals and weekend brunches; cl 25 Dec; disabled access. **£26.50**|£12.75.

BLUE ELEPHANT *4–6 Fulham Broadway SW6 (0171) 385 6595* Luxurious Thai food among waterfalls and exotic jungle greenery, with produce flown in weekly from Thailand; the set meals are better value; cl am Sat, 24–26 Dec; disabled access. **£38**|£12.

BOMBAY BRASSERIE *Courtfield Close, Courtfield Rd SW7 (0171) 370 4040* Grand colonial-style furnishings in big restaurant and conservatory; very good Indian food using recipes from all over India (lots of vegetarian dishes), and courteous, helpful staff; cheaper at lunchtime when there's a buffet; cl 25–26 Dec; children over 10; disabled access. **£31**|£15.95 buffet lunch.

CAFÉ FISH *36–40 Rupert St W1 (0171) 287 8989* This bustling, well run fish restaurant has become so popular that they have moved to bigger premises, and now have a brasserie with light meals and an upstairs restaurant; super fresh fish, fine French cheeses, and a fair wine list. **£28.90**.

CAFÉ IN THE CRYPT *St Martin-in-the-Fields, Trafalgar Sq WC2 (0171) 930 0089* Popular place under the lovely arches of the church, with a relaxed atmosphere, good, freshly prepared daily changing food; shop, free lunchtime concerts, candlelit evening concerts, brass-rubbing; cl 25 Dec, am Good Fri. **£13.75**|£5.50.

CAFÉ DU JARDIN *28 Wellington St WC2 (0171) 836 8769* Well liked by theatre-goers and Covent Garden shoppers, this busy brasserie serves very good modern European food inc plenty of really fresh fish and nice puddings; a decent choice of wines and efficient service; disabled access. **£35**.

CANTEEN *Chelsea Harbour SW10 (0171) 351 7330* Some tables overlook the marina in this smart modern restaurant, with its excellent European food inc delicious puddings, and good service; cl am Sat, pm Sun; disabled access. **£33**|£15.50 2-course lunch.

CHAPEL *48 Chapel St NW1 (0171) 402 9220* Attractively refurbished pub with a civilised but relaxed feel, and a light and spacious main room dominated by the open kitchen; very good modern cooking, prompt, efficient service, smart but simple furnishings, real ales, and a good range of interesting wines and teas. **£23**|£8.

CHEZ NICO AT NINETY PARK LANE *90 Park Lane W1 (0171) 409 1290* Comfortable, elegant restaurant run by Nico Ladenis, one of the country's best-known chefs, serving impeccable food (the set lunch is marvellous value) and fine wines (at a price); cl am Sat, Sun, 23 Dec–2 Jan, Easter and bank hols; children over 6; disabled access. **£65 dinner not inc wine, lunch £34 for 3 courses**.

CHUTNEY MARY *535 King's Rd SW10 (0171) 351 3113* Very good, interesting Anglo-Indian food served in light conservatory and 2 dining rooms, plus a verandah bar, a good choice of drinks, and knowledgeable staff; buffet only Sun, cl pm 25 Dec, 26 Dec; some disabled access. **£32**|£12.50 2-course lunch.

CITY RHODES *1 New St Sq EC4 (0171) 583 1313* Airy and light restaurant serving good modern and inventive British food cooked by the well known TV chef; enjoyable puddings, helpful, efficient service, and an interesting if pricey wine list; cl Christmas, New Year, bank hols; disabled access. **£45**|£18.

COAST *26b Albemarle St W1 (0171) 495 5999* Light, airy and rather smart restaurant with a huge window overlooking the street, and stylish, simple furnishings; very friendly service, delicious modern cooking, and a good wine list; may cl 1 wk Christmas; free Sun brunch for accompanying children. **£37**.

CORK & BOTTLE *44–46 Cranbourn St WC2 (0171) 734 7807* Basement wine bar we've liked for over 25 years, nr West End theatres – good food inc interesting salads, cold buffet and unusual hot dishes, excellent wines, and cheerful service; cl 25–26 Dec, 1 Jan. **£18**|£6.95.

DEALS *Chelsea Harbour SW10 (0171) 795 1001* Bustling café-restaurant with good food ranging from hamburgers to sizzle platters, generous glasses of decent house wine, good cocktails and very friendly service; best at lunchtime when it's less frenetic; good for children on Sun lunchtime (must book); cl 25–26 Dec, 1 Jan; disabled access; other branches. **£25**|£8.

EAGLE *159 Farringdon Rd EC1 (0171) 837 1353* Particularly good Mediterranean-style food in this popular, stylish pub where the open kitchen forms part of the bar; well kept real ales, lots of wine by the glass, properly made cocktails, a lively and chatty atmosphere (lots of young media folk), and simple furnishings; cl pm Sun, bank hols, Easter, 1½ wks Christmas. **£26**|£7.50.

EBURY WINE BAR *139 Ebury St SW1 (0171) 730 8206* Said to be London's first wine bar (established in 1959) with a loyal following, an excellent list of wines by the glass, and very good modern cooking; they have another bar restaurant called Carriages opposite the Royal Mews in Buckingham Palace Rd; cl 3 days at Christmas. **£30**|£6.50.

FIRE STATION *150 Waterloo Rd SE1 (0171) 401 3267* Remarkable conversion of a former fire station; with 2 chatty front rooms, plenty of wooden pews, chairs and long tables, some brightly red-painted doors, modern art on the walls, newspapers to read, very good, imaginative food, a decent choice of wines, and well kept real ales. **£21.25**|£5.25.

FOOD FOR THOUGHT *31 Neal St WC2 (0171) 836 9072* Long-established and consistently good, unlicensed vegetarian restaurant with take-away service upstairs and communal eating at long tables downstairs – you can also eat at tables outside; no corkage; cl pm Sun, Christmas/New Year, and Easter Sun. **£8.50**|£3.80.

FOOTSTOOL *St John's Smith Sq SW1 (0171) 222 2779* Partly no smoking restaurant in the church crypt below the concert hall, with plants, pictures and stripped brick, and good food from a monthly-changing menu; lighter lunchtime buffet; cl am Sat–Sun; disabled access. **£20.50**|£5.95.

FORTNUM & MASON *181 Piccadilly W1 (0171) 734 8040* Famous store with elegant 4th-floor St James's Restaurant (must book), Fountain Restaurant (ground floor), Patio Restaurant and newly opened salmon and champagne bar (on the mezzanine) offering good breakfasts, morning coffee, lunches, fine afternoon tea and pre-theatre meals; cl Sun, bank hols, 25–26 Dec and Easter; disabled access. **£26**|£7.20

LE GAVROCHE *43 Upper Brook St W1 (0171) 408 0881* This put London on the eating map when it was opened by the Roux brothers 30 years ago; drinks and delicious canapés are served in the cosy lounge, and the quietly decorated, club-like restaurant with its pictures and table flowers is in the basement; cooking is exemplary classic French with modern touches (lovely puddings and perfect cheeses, too), service from the French staff is attentive and professional, and the wine list is classy but expensive (some wines reach four figures); the set lunch is incredible value; cl Sat, Sun, 23 Dec, 2 Jan. **£100 dinner, £40 lunch**.

GAY HUSSAR *2 Greek St W1 (0171) 437 0973* Very long-standing and happily unchanging Hungarian restaurant with bags of atmosphere (downstairs has the most), good, generous and authentic food, friendly service; cl Sun, bank hols. **£23 3-course lunch**.

HANOVER SQUARE WINE BAR *25 Hanover Sq (0171) 408 0935* Under the same enthusiastic ownership as the popular long-standing Cork & Bottle in Leicester Sq, this bustling wine bar offers a constantly changing cold buffet plus daily hot dishes and charcoal grills, and a particularly good and interesting wine list; cl Sun, bank hols. **£25**|£6.95.

KALAMARES MICRO *66 Inverness Mews W2 (0171) 727 5082* (Not to be confused with its larger sister restaurant at No 76). Tiny, close-packed, authentically Greek restaurant with very good cheap food and friendly service; unlicensed, take your own wine; cl Sun, am, and bank hols; **£18**|£6.50.

MON PLAISIR *21 Monmouth St WC2 (0171) 836 7243* Bustling French bistro with super atmosphere, good-value, well prepared food, decent wines, and friendly staff; cl am Sat, all day Sun, bank hols, Christmas, New Year and Easter; disabled access. **£30**|£13.95 popular 3-course pre-theatre meal.

MORO *34–36 Exmouth Market EC1 (0171) 833 8336* Simply decorated restaurant with smart bentwood chairs on bare boards, cream and green walls, a side bar with high stools, and an open-plan kitchen; thriving atmosphere, interesting modern Spanish cooking with influences from North Africa and the Middle East, nice tapas, a short, thoughtful wine list, and informal but punctilious service; cl wknds, Christmas, Easter; disabled access. **£30**|£11.50.

L'ODEON *65 Regent St W1 (0171) 287 1400* Long restaurant reached by a rather fine staircase, with 9 big semi-circular windows overlooking Piccadilly Circus, and lots of tables and banquettes; a bustling atmosphere, classic French provincial cooking with modern additions, good puddings, a light menu in the bar, afternoon tea, and a well chosen wine list; pre-theatre meals; cl bank hols; disabled access. **£35**|£10.

ODETTES *130 Regent's Park Rd NW1 (0171) 586 5486* Smart front dining room with lots of gilded mirrors, airy back conservatory, and slightly cheaper downstairs wine bar offering good modern English and more unusual dishes; friendly service, and a thoughtful wine list; cl am Sat, pm Sun, 1 wk Christmas; limited disabled access. **£33**|£10 3-course set menu.

OXO TOWER *Barge House St SE1 (0171) 803 3888* Briskly modern brasserie and restaurant on the 8th floor of this South Bank redevelopment; light and airy, with a busy open kitchen, lots of functional tables and chairs, and promptly served, modern English food; what stands out, of course, is the panoramic view over the Thames and City – best in summer from tables on the outside terrace; restaurant cl am Sat. **£60 dinner, £32.75 set lunch in restaurant; £40 dinner, £25 lunch in brasserie**.

POONS *27 Lisle St WC2 (0171) 437 4549* Atmospheric unlicensed and unmodernised Chinese restaurant with extremely good-value tasty barbecued and wind-dried food; cl Good Fri, 24–26 Dec. **£15**|£5.50. Other branches (more modern and expensive) at 4 Leicester St WC2 (0171) 437 1528, 50 Woburn Place, Russell Square WC1 (0171) 580 1188, and 2 Minster Court, Mincing Lane EC3 (0171) 626 0126.

QUAGLINOS *16 Bury St SW1 (0171) 930 6767* Fashionable restaurant with a big stone staircase to the antipasti bar overlooking the huge dining room with its flamboyantly painted pillars, fine flowers, highly modern attractive furnishings, and buoyant, buzzing atmosphere; lovely fresh fish and other modern cooking, good wine list, and efficient service; cl pm 24–25 Dec, am 26 and 31 Dec, am 1 Jan; no children in bar in evening; disabled access. **£30**|£13.

RAINFOREST CAFE *20 Shaftesbury Ave W1 (0171) 434 3111* Exciting big restaurant on 3 floors with amazing special effects such as mist, wildlife noises, thunder and lightning storms, waterfalls, live tropical parrots and aquariums, animatronic trumpeting elephants, gorillas, fluttering butterflies, life-size splashing crocodile and so forth, and 'jungle-esque'-type food (burgers, pizzas, pasta, sandwiches, salad, and appetizers); cl Christmas. **£18**|£6.95.

REBATO'S *169 South Lambeth Rd SW8 (0171) 735 6388* Busy and attractive high-ceilinged bar with friendly barman and waiters, a good choice of tapas (plenty of fresh fish), and lots of Spanish wines; also Spanish restaurant; cl am Sat, Sun, Christmas. **£20.20**|£4.

RSJ *13a Coin St SE1 (0171) 928 4554* Handy for the South Bank, this relaxed and friendly restaurant serves fine modern British and Mediterranean cooking and exceptional Loire wines in simple surroundings; cl am Sat, Sun. **£23 3-course set lunch**.

RULES *35 Maiden Lane WC2 (0171) 836 5314* One of London's oldest restaurants, smart and very British, with good English food inc fine seasonal game and oysters; interesting history; cl 4 days over Christmas. **£35**|£13.95.

SIMPSONS IN THE STRAND *100 Strand WC2 (0171) 836 9112* Marvellously old-fashioned, with traditional English cooking inc nursery puddings, and roasts carved as you want them at your table on silver-domed trolleys; all very decorous – the surroundings and atmosphere are more memorable than the food; cl 25–26 Dec, 1 Jan; disabled access. **£42**|£13 for 2 courses.

SOTHEBY'S CAFE *34 New Bond St W1 (0171) 293 5077* Very small but very classy café with simple, high-class food inc lovely puddings and good cheeses, a carefully chosen little wine list, and courteous staff; cl Sat, last 2 wks Aug, 24 Dec–2 Jan. **£24**|£10.

STEPHEN BULL *12 Upper St Martin's Lane WC2 (0171) 379 7811* Useful for pre-theatre meals, this simply decorated restaurant serves enjoyable and innovative European food inc good puddings, and reasonably priced wines; service is efficient and friendly, and there are branches in Blandford St W1 and 71 St John St EC1; cl am Sat, Sun, 1 wk Christmas, bank hols; partial disabled access. **£35**.

TANTE CLAIRE *Wilton Pl, SW1 (0171) 823 2003* As we went to press, this fine restaurant was moving into a wing of the Berkeley Hotel. Exceptional and beautifully presented French cooking – more relaxed at lunchtime when the set menu is very good value; courteous service, and some good-value French country wines; jacket and tie required; best to phone for opening times. **£80 dinner, £28 set lunch**.

TAPPIT HEN *5 William IV St WC2 (0171) 836 9839* Cosy and atmospheric little wine bar, very old-fashioned feeling, with good snacks and good-value wines – more for lunchtimes (when the smoked salmon sandwiches are lovely), though you can book for upstairs in the evening; cl Sat, Sun. **£16**|£6.50.

TURNERS *87–89 Walton St SW3 (0171) 584 6711* Most enjoyable, elegantly furnished restaurant run by the warm and friendly TV cook Brian Turner; with extremely good food based on sound, classic French techniques, lovely puddings, very good service, and a mainly French wine list; very good-value fixed price meals;

cl am Sat, Christmas, bank hols; no children in evening; disabled access. **£36 dinner, £22 lunch**|£12.50 2 courses.

WAGAMAMA *4 Streatham St WC1 (0171) 580 9365* You will have to queue to get into this trendy, simply furnished Japanese basement restaurant with its long tables and benches for communal eating; very friendly, cheerful service, noisy and informal atmosphere, good healthy food – raw salads, ramens (huge bowls of noodles with meat, vegetables and Japanese additions), rice dishes, sake, grape and plum wines, beer, and free green tea; exceptionally good value; cl 25–26 Dec; another branch at 101a Wigmore St. £5.50.

ZAFFERANO *15 Lowndes St SW1 (0171) 235 5800* Wonderful Italian food served in 2 simply furnished little rooms; marvellous fresh pasta, good chargrilled dishes (super fish), lovely puddings, lots of Italian wines, and considerate service; cl Sun, Easter, Aug; disabled access. **£32.75**|£16.50 2 courses.

Special thanks to Paul Kennedy, Annabella Martin, Sheila Keene, Bob and Maggie Atherton.

We welcome reports from readers

This *Guide* depends on readers' reports. Do help us if you can – in return, we offer a discount on the next edition to people who've helped us with reports for it. Tell us what you think about places already in it, and anything extra you think we should say about them. And send us your ideas for inclusion in the next edition: places to visit, eat at or stay in, attractive drives or walks, maybe even unusual interesting shops you know of. Use the card in the middle, the report forms at the end, or just write – no stamp needed: *The Good Guide to Britain*, FREEPOST TN1569, Wadhurst, E Sussex TN5 7BR.

London Calendar

Some of these dates were provisional as we went to press. Please check information with the telephone numbers provided.

JANUARY

1 **Westminster Bridge to Berkeley Square** London Parade *from 12am*: Lord Mayor, marching bands from over 40 countries, vintage cars (0181) 566 8586
8 **Earls Court** International Boat Show – *till Sun 17* (01784) 473377
9 **London** International Mime Festival – *till Sun 24* (0171) 637 5661
14 **Kensington Town Hall** West London Antiques and Fine Art Fair: 60 stands – *till Sun 17* (01444) 482514
15 **Olympia** Adventure, Travel and Sports Show – *till Sun 17* (01795) 844400
19 **Westminster** Botanical Painting Show at RHS Halls – *till Weds 20* (0171) 821 3351
20 **Business Design Centre, N1** Art '99: new young designers – *till Sun 24* (0171) 359 3535
23 **Piccadilly** Monet in the 20th c at the Royal Academy of Arts – *till 18 Apr* (0171) 439 7438
27 **Alexandra Palace** Road Racing and Superbike Show – *till Sun 31* (01440) 707055; **Park Lane** Drawings and Watercolours at the Dorchester Hotel – *till Sun 31* (0171) 411 3166
31 **St James's Palace to Banqueting House** Charles I Commemoration Ceremony: procession of members of the society of King Charles and Royal Stuart Society in 17th-c costume (0171) 730 3450

FEBRUARY

7 **Wembley Conference Centre** Masters Snooker Tournament – *till Sun 14* (0171) 243 7102
16 **Westminster** Botanical Painting Show at RHS Halls – *till Wed 17* (0171) 821 3351
18 **Royal College of Art** Art on Paper Fair – *till Sun 21* (0181) 742 1611
20 **Twickenham** Five Nations: England v Scotland Rugby International (0181) 892 2000
21 **Royal National Hotel** WC1 Napoleonic Fair (0181) 458 6314; **Soho** Chinese New Year Celebrations: Lion Dances (0171) 734 5161
23 **Olympia** Fine Art and Antiques Fair – *till Sun 28* (0171) 370 3188

MARCH

6 **Alexandra Palace** Sailboat and Surf Show – *till Sun 7* (01703) 627425; **Twickenham** Five Nations: Ireland v England Rugby International (0181) 892 2000
12 **Chelsea Old Town Hall** Antiques Fair – *till Sun 21* (01444) 482514
17 **Olympia** BBC Good Food Show – *till Sun 21* (0181) 948 1666
18 **Earls Court** Ideal Home Exhibition – *till 11 Apr* (0181) 515 2079
19 **Westminster** London Orchid Show at RHS Halls – *till Sun 21* (0171) 821 3351
20 **Alexandra Palace** London Classic Motor Show – *till Tues 23* (01296) 631181; **Twickenham** Five Nations: England v France Rugby International (0181) 892 2000

London Calendar (cont.)

23 London Handel Festival – *till 26 Apr* (0181) 563 0618
24 Business Design Centre, N1 Country Living Spring Fair: talks, walks, cookery, gardening – *till Sun 28* (0171) 490 1005
25 Chelsea Old Town Hall 20th-c Show: design and furniture – *till Sun 28* (01444) 482514
27 Battersea Contemporary Art Fair at Battersea Arts Centre – *till Sun 28* (0171) 228 0741; **Mortlake to Putney** Head of the River Race on the Thames (01932) 220 401
28 London International Book Fair – *till Tues 30* (0171) 371 3333

APRIL

3 Alexandra Palace Fine Art and Crafts Show – *till Mon 5* (01273) 833884; **Putney to Mortlake** Oxford v Cambridge Boat Race (0171) 379 3234
5 Battersea Park Harness Horse Parade: extensive display of horse-drawn vehicles (01733) 234451
9 Business Design Centre, N1 Health Show – *till Sun 11* (01923) 840044
11 Twickenham Five Nations: Wales v England Rugby International (0181) 892 2000
15 Piccadilly Kandinsky Exhibition at the Royal Academy of Arts – *till 27 Jun* (0171) 439 7438
18 Greenwich to the Mall London Marathon (0171) 620 4117
22 Chelsea Old Town Hall Art Fair: works from 47 galleries – *till Sun 25* (01444) 482514

MAY

1 Wembley Rugby League Challenge Cup Final (0113) 2329111
8 Richmond Green May Fair (0181) 948 4464
14 Lord's Cricket Ground World Cup Cricket: England v Sri Lanka (0870) 6061999
15 Dulwich Festival – *till Sat 22* (0181) 299 1011; **Kensington Town Hall** London Dollshouse Festival – *till Sun 16* (0171) 932 2041; **Twickenham** Rugby Football Union Cup Final (0181) 892 2000
19 Tower of London Anne Boleyn's Memorial (0171) 709 0765
22 Covent Garden Festival – *till 5 Jun* (0171) 379 8070; **Wembley** FA Challenge Cup Final (0171) 402 7151; **Westminster** Mind-Body-Spirit Festival at RHS Halls – *till Mon 31* (0171) 938 3788
25 Chelsea Royal Hospital Flower Show – *till Fri 28*, members only *Tues 25 and Weds 26* (0171) 649 1885
29 Horse Guards Parade First Rehearsal: Trooping the Colour (0171) 414 2357

JUNE

Westminster Festival of Baroque Music at St John's, Smith Square – *throughout Jun* (0171) 228 6388
2 Horse Guards Parade Beating Retreat: Massed Guards of the Household Division – *till Thurs 3* (0171) 414 2271
3 Olympia Fine Art and Antiques Fair – *till Sun 13* (0171) 370 8188
5 Colindale Emergency Services Weekend at RAF Museum – *till Sun 6* (0181) 205 2266; **Horse Guards Parade** Second Rehearsal: Trooping the Colour (0171) 414 2357

London Calendar (cont.)

6 **South Bank** Coin Street Festival: free events and music at Gabriel's Wharf, Bernie Spain Gardens and Oxo Tower Wharf – *till 5 Sept* (0171) 401 2255; **Syon Park and Crystal Palace Park** London to Brighton Classic Car Run (01296) 631181
7 **West Kensington** Tennis Championships at Queen's Club – *till Sun 13* (0181) 876 0044
9 **Grosvenor House Hotel** Art and Antiques Fair – *till Tues 15* (0171) 499 6363; **Lord's Cricket Ground** World Cup Cricket: super six play-offs (0870) 6061999; **Spitalfields** Festival – *till Weds 30* (0171) 377 0287
10 **Hampton Court Palace** Music Festival – *till Sat 19* (0181) 233 5800
11 **Park Lane Hotel** International Ceramics Fair and Seminar – *till Mon 14* (0171) 734 5491
12 **Horse Guards Parade** Queen's Birthday Parade: Trooping the Colour (tickets in advance only from The Brigade Major, Household Division, HQ London District, Horse Guards, Whitehall, London, SW1A 2AX) (0171) 414 2357; **Islington** International Festival – *till Tues 29* (0171) 354 2535
13 **Piccadilly** Royal Academy Summer Exhibition: large open contemporary art exhibition – *till 22 Aug* (0171) 439 7438
14 **London** International Festival of Theatre – *till 4 July* (0171) 247 4667
20 **Lord's Cricket Ground** World Cup Cricket Final (0870) 6061999
21 **Wimbledon** Lawn Tennis Championships – *till 4 July* (0181) 946 2244
22 **City of London** Festival – *till 15 July* (0171) 377 0540
24 **Olympia** House and Garden Fair (0171) 453 5340
26 **Middlesex Showground** Middlesex Show – *till Sun 27* (01895) 252131
30 **Earls Court** *Tomorrow's World* Live Event – *till 4 July* (0171) 402 2555

JULY

1 **Hampton Court Palace** Flower Show inc British Rose Festival – *till Sun 11*, members only *Tues 6 and Weds 7* (0171) 834 4333; **Hays Galleria** Summer Festival of Music: jazz every Tues evening, classical every Thurs evening – *till 31 Aug* (0171) 940 7700
9 **Greenwich and Docklands** Festival – *till Sun 18* (0181) 305 1818
16 **Royal Albert Hall** Henry Wood Promenade Concerts – *till 11 Sept* (0171) 765 4296
20 **Earls Court** Royal Tournament – *till 1 Aug* (0171) 370 8206

AUGUST

3 **Olympia** CAMRA Great British Beer Festival – *till Sat 7* (01727) 867201
29 **Notting Hill** Carnival: largest carnival in Europe – *till Mon 30* (0181) 964 0544

SEPTEMBER

2 **Alexandra Palace** Mind-Body-Spirit Festival – *till Sun 5* (0171) 938 3788
3 **Hays Galleria** Oyster and Seafood Fair – *till Sun 5* (0171) 940 7700
4 **Beside the River Thames** Thames Festival: between Westminster Bridge and Southwark Cathedral, and Putney Bridge and Hampton Court – *till Sun 19* (0171) 928 0960; also Great River Race: Chinese dragon boats and lots more between Richmond and Greenwich (0181) 398 9057
7 **City** Flower Show at the Guildhall – *till Weds 8* (0181) 472 3584
14 **Westminster** Great Autumn Show at RHS Halls – *till Weds 15* (0171) 821 3351

London Calendar (cont.)

16 **Chelsea Old Town Hall** Antiques Fair: 40 stands – *till Sun 26* (01444) 482514; **Piccadilly** Van Dyck Exhibition at the Royal Academy of Arts – *till 16 Dec* (0171) 439 7438

18 **London** Open House Weekend: free access to many sites of cultural and natural interest, some not always open to the public – *till Sun 19* (0191) 341 1371

22 **Royal College of Art** Twentieth Century British Art Fair – *till Sun 26* (0181) 742 1611

23 **Soho** Jazz Festival – *till 3 Oct* (0171) 437 6437

25 **Piccadilly** Sir John Soane Exhibition at the Royal Academy of Arts – *till 12 Dec* (0171) 439 7438

29 **Wembley** Horse of the Year Show – *till 3 Oct* (0181) 900 9282

OCTOBER

London Dance Umbrella – *from mid-Oct till mid-Nov* (0181) 741 4040

3 **Trafalgar Square** Pearly Kings' and Queens' Service at St Martin-in-the-Fields: since the 19th c, best occasion to see Kings and Queens in traditional button-covered costumes (0171) 930 0089

7 **City Road** Antiques Fair at Armoury House – *till Sun 10* (01444) 482514

8 **Olympia** Festival of Fine Wine and Food – *till Mon 11* (0171) 453 5340

14 **City Road** Art Fair: mainly 20th-c works at Armoury House – *till Sun 17* (01444) 482514

23 **Earls Court** London Motor Show – *till 1 Nov* (0171) 370 8213

24 **Trafalgar Square** Trafalgar Day Parade: naval parade in memory of the Battle of Trafalgar (0171) 928 8978

28 **Kensington Town Hall** Fine Art and Antiques Fair: 80 stands – *till Sun 31* (01444) 482514

29 **Kensington** International Exhibition of Early Music at the Royal College of Music – *till Sun 31* (01274) 393753; **Olympia** Ski and Snowboard Show – *till 7 Nov* (0181) 515 2000

NOVEMBER

2 **Westminster** Botanical Painting Show at RHS Halls – *till Weds 3* (0171) 821 3351

7 **Hyde Park** London to Brighton Veteran Car Run (01753) 681736

11 **Kensington Town Hall** National Honey Show – *till Sat 13* (01303) 254579; **Westminster** Mind-Body-Spirit Festival at RHS Halls – *till Sun 14* (0171) 938 3788

13 **City** Lord Mayor's Show: from Guildhall to the Royal Courts of Justice (0171) 606 3030

14 **Whitehall** Remembrance Day Service and Parade at the Cenotaph (0171) 414 2357

DECEMBER

2 **Trafalgar Square** Christmas Tree and Carol Singing – *till 6 Jan* (0171) 211 6393

3 **Alexandra Palace** Christmas Craft Fair – *till Sun 5* (01273) 833884

14 **Westminster** Christmas Show at RHS Halls – *till Weds 15* (0171) 821 3351

London Calendar (cont.)

16 **Olympia** International Showjumping Championships – *till Mon 20* (0171) 370 8206

31 **Battersea Park** Firework Display; **Greenwich** Multimedia Sound and Light Show at the Dome; **St Paul's Cathedral** Watchnight Service; **Trafalgar Square** New Year's Eve Celebrations: all (0171) 932 2041

We welcome reports from readers

This *Guide* depends on readers' reports. Do help us if you can – in return, we offer a discount on the next edition to people who've helped us with reports for it. Tell us what you think about places already in it, and anything extra you think we should say about them. And send us your ideas for inclusion in the next edition: places to visit, eat at or stay in, attractive drives or walks, maybe even unusual interesting shops you know of. Use the card in the middle, the report forms at the end, or just write – no stamp needed: *The Good Guide to Britain*, FREEPOST TN1569, Wadhurst, E Sussex TN5 7BR.

Scotland

With quite a few new places opening, Scotland is gearing itself up for the Millennium; a major project is the Millennium Link, reopening canals between Edinburgh and Glasgow, which are to be linked at Falkirk by a giant wheel that will lift boats some 25 metres (80ft).

South Scotland is the major destination for first-time visitors. It includes many of the most enjoyable places to visit, as well as Edinburgh (a great city for a short break) and Glasgow (lots to see here, too). It also has charming and very peaceful countryside towards the Borders and the south-west corner. A three-hour drive will get anyone living north of Manchester or York well into South Scotland. Beyond that, you really need a longer stay to make the driving worth while. Rail and air, of course, bring Scotland much closer. The fastest trains do the London–Edinburgh run in around four hours.

East Scotland also has a mass of interesting places to visit, with a marvellous variety of scenery from Highland grandeur to placid lochs and rich valleys, from intimate fishing villages and sandy beaches to rugged cliffs. The fastest roads run up this side.

West Scotland has a glorious and intricate series of mountain and coastal landscapes, with magnificent gardens, at their best in May and June. There are interesting family outings, though not nearly so many as in the south and east. We've defined this area as north of the Clyde and south of the Great Glen, with Loch Lomond marking its eastern edge.

North Scotland, everything north of the Great Glen, has fewer places to visit (and fewer visitors – but as one reader told us, once you've been once you may be hooked for ever); there is magnificent scenery on the west coast and on Skye, a quieter sandy east coast, and some wild and desolate places in the north.

For non-mountaineers the Highlands (included in our East, West and North areas) can be tantalising but problematic: compared to the uplands of England and Wales there are few obvious walking routes (OS maps show hardly any), and the scale of the scenery is often so vast that you need to walk for hours before the views change. The high peaks are mostly for the dedicated (and fit) enthusiast. There is an informal tradition of allowing general access to the mountains, but there are few rights of way, and areas are often closed for at least part of the grouse-shooting season (12 Aug–10 Dec), particularly its first few weeks, or the deer-stalking season (1 July–20 Oct for stags, 21 Oct–15 Feb for hinds). We note in the text many of the best spots for walking – but even if you never leave your car, you can still see some breathtaking scenery.

Outside Edinburgh, Glasgow and areas within easy reach of them, many places close for the winter, and others change to shorter winter opening hours in September, rather than October (the usual month for a change in England). For the scenery, the best time to visit is May and June, when the days are very long, the weather is generally at least as fine as in high summer, the roads are not yet clogged by summer crowds, and (as the **Calendar** shows) there's lots going on.

The Scottish Tourist Board is working hard to attract autumn visitors, and does a card that will save money then on flights, trains, accommodation and attractions, as well as getting two-for-one entry to the properties of the National Trust for Scotland and Historic Scotland.

This second organisation looks after most of the castles and abbeys we list. A good-value Explorer ticket admits you free to all their properties, for £12.50 (one week) or £17 (two weeks); from tourist information centres, or in advance (0131) 668 8800. Some local tourist boards sell passes covering a round at that area's finest golf courses – such as the Freedom of the Fairways passport available in the Borders.

Direct flights connect London and some regional airports with Edinburgh, Glasgow, Inverness and Aberdeen, with some local connections from there.

South Scotland

Outstanding sightseeing, with Edinburgh excellent for short city breaks; the extreme south is very quiet and relaxing.

Edinburgh is a city of great visual appeal, with lots of interesting places within a pleasant walk of each other; the Festival is in August (when to go if that appeals, a time to avoid otherwise). New things to visit here include the spectacular new Dynamic Earth Centre, and the Royal Yacht *Britannia*. There are some great things to visit in Glasgow, too – almost all free.

This part of Scotland has an abundance of ancient and evocative castles, romantic ruined abbeys, and some glorious gardens and grand houses such as Culzean Castle, Traquair, Manderston at Duns and Mount Stuart on Bute. There are plenty of enjoyable family outings, most notably at New Lanark and in Dalkeith and Largs; Edinburgh Zoo is a great favourite.

The Borders countryside, grand without being austere, has plentiful solitary hill-walking. The Southern Upland Way (which covers 212 miles coast-to-coast from Portpatrick to Cockburnspath) is a good basis for day walks, though the distances involved often make it hard to find focal points for rambles. The gentler south-west corner is one of Britain's friendliest areas, with relatively few tourists.

Where to stay

AUCHENCAIRN NX8249 **Balcary Bay** *Auchencairn, Castle Douglas, Kirkcudbrightshire DG7 1QZ (01556) 640217* **£98,** plus special breaks; 17 rms with fine views. Once a smugglers' haunt, this charming and much-liked hotel has wonderful views over the bay, neat grounds running down to the water, comfortable public rooms (one with log fire), a relaxed friendly atmosphere, good enjoyable food inc super breakfasts, and lots of walks; cl mid-Nov–Feb.

BEATTOCK NT0603 **Auchen Castle** *Auchen, Beattock, Moffat, Dumfriesshire DG10 9SH (01683) 300407* **£95,** plus special breaks; 26 pleasantly decorated rms, some in lodge. Smart but friendly country-house hotel in lovely quiet spot with a trout loch and spectacular hill views; good food, and peaceful comfortable bar; disabled access.

BONNYRIGG NT3263 **Dalhousie Castle** *Bonnyrigg, Midlothian EH19 3JB (01875) 820153* ***£135,** plus special breaks; 28 rms, some of great character. Turreted red sandstone castle with some fine historic features such as the dungeon restaurant and oak-panelled library bar; children under 12 free if in parents' room and meals half-price; cl 2 wks Jan; disabled access by arrangement.

CANONBIE NY3976 **Riverside** *Canonbie, DG14 0UX (01387) 371512/371295* **£78;** 7 chintzy rms, 2 in cottage. Civilised little inn with friendly owners, comfortable communicating bar rooms, open fire, attractive furnishings, good imaginative food with home-made breads and preserves and using top-quality produce, a fine wine list, and marvellous breakfasts; cl 2 wks Feb; children over 8.

CLARENCEFIELD NY0768 **Comlongon Castle** *Clarencefield, Dumfries DG1 4NA (01387) 870283* **£90;** 12 rms. 15th-c castle keep with 18th-c mansion house adjoining – suits of armour and a huge fireplace in oak-panelled great hall, good food in Jacobean dining room, and a relaxing drawing room; dungeons, lofty battlements, archers' quarters and haunted long gallery – candlelit tour before dinner if you like; disabled access.

EDINBURGH NT2573 **Balmoral** *Princes St, Edinburgh EH2 2EQ (0131) 556 2414* **£150,** plus special breaks; 184 luxurious rms. Splendid Victorian hotel with wonderfully opulent entrance hall, elegant day rooms, lovely flowers, particularly friendly helpful staff, and very good food in several restaurants; excellent leisure facilities; good disabled access.

EDINBURGH NT2374 **Channings** *South Learmonth Gardens, Edinburgh EH4 1EZ (0131) 312 3232* ***£155,** plus special breaks; 48 pretty rms. Privately owned hotel carefully converted from 5 Edwardian townhouses, with a cosy atmosphere, lots of original features, antiques and open fires in the peaceful lounges, good food in downstairs brasserie, and friendly service; cl 24–28 Dec.

EDINBURGH NT2574 **Drummond House** *17 Drummond Pl, Edinburgh EH3 6PL (0131) 557 9189* ***£100;** 4 charming rms. Georgian townhouse in handsome square with antiques and fine rugs in elegant rooms, a warmly welcoming atmosphere, and good Scottish breakfasts; cl Christmas; no children.

EDINBURGH NT2572 **Elmview** *15 Glengyle Terrace, Edinburgh EH3 9LN (0131) 228 1973* ***£85;** 3 large rms. Quietly placed in fine Victorian terrace overlooking a park 15 minutes' walk from the castle and centre; elegantly furnished, good breakfast and welcome; no children.

EDINBURGH NT2674 **Greenside** *9 Royal Terrace, Edinburgh EH7 5AB (0131) 557 0022* ***£65;** 15 individually decorated rms. Family-run hotel in Georgian terrace with friendly atmosphere, big lounge, hearty breakfasts, and quiet terraced garden.

EDINBURGH NT2574 **Howard** *34 Great King St, Edinburgh EH3 6QH (0131) 315 2220* ***£198,** plus special breaks; 15 luxurious rms. Fine civilised 18th-c hotel with comfortable, elegant public rooms, courteous efficient service and good food; cl 24–28 Dec.

EDINBURGH NT2776 **Malmaison** *1 Tower Pl, Edinburgh EH6 7DB (0131) 555 6868* **£116;** 60 stylish rms with CD players and satellite TV. Converted baronial-style seamen's mission in the fashionable docks area of Leith with very good food in the downstairs French brasserie, a cheerful café/bar, gym, and friendly service; free parking; pets by arrangement; disabled access.

EDINBURGH NT2574 **Sibbet House** *26 Northumberland St, Edinburgh EH3 6LS (0131) 556 1078* **£100;** 5 good rms. Lovely little Georgian house with warmly friendly owners, comfortable public rooms filled with antiques, delicious breakfasts, and suppers on request; self-catering flats also; partial disabled access.

ETTRICK VALLEY NT3017 **Tushielaw** *Ettrick Valley, Selkirk TD7 5HT (01750) 62205* ***£42,** plus special breaks; 3 small but well furnished rms. Friendly little inn in lovely spot on Ettrick Water, with good imaginative restaurant food, intimate bar, fine views, own loch, and shooting and fishing (as well as birdwatching and walking); cl Mon–Weds from Nov–Mar.

GATEHOUSE OF FLEET NX5954 **Cally Palace** *Gatehouse of Fleet, Castle Douglas, Kirkcudbrightshire DG7 2DL (01557) 814341* **£84,** plus special breaks; 56 rms. 18th-c country mansion with marble fireplaces and ornate ceilings in the public rooms, a relaxed cocktail bar, enjoyable food in elegant dining room (smart dress required), evening pianist and Sat dinner dance, helpful friendly staff, 18-hole golf course, croquet and tennis, indoor leisure complex with heated swimming pool, private fishing/boating loch; cl Jan, and wkdys in Feb; disabled access.

GIFFORD NT5367 **Tweeddale Arms** *Gifford, Haddington, East Lothian EH41 4QU (01620) 810240* ***£65,** plus special breaks; 16 rms. Civilised old inn in quiet village with comfortable sofas and chairs in tranquil lounge, gracious dining room, wide choice of good daily-changing food, and charming service; disabled access.

GLASGOW NS5965 **Babbity Bowster** *16–18 Blackfriars St, Glasgow G1 1PE (0141) 552 5055* **£65;** 7 clean simple rms, showers. Warmly welcoming, rather continental place with decent breakfasts (served till late), attractively decorated airy bar, and a cheery first-floor restaurant which hosts a gallery as well as a programme of musical and theatrical events; cl 25 Dec–1 Jan.

GLASGOW NS5865 **Malmaison** *278 West George St, Glasgow G2 4LL (0141) 221 6400* ***£116;** 70 smart rms. Stylishly converted Nonconformist church with striking central wrought-iron staircase, friendly young staff, enjoyable food in the basement brasserie, café/bar with all-day snacks, gym, and a relaxed no-frills atmosphere; disabled access.

GLASGOW NS5567 **One Devonshire Gardens** *Glasgow G12 0UX (0141) 339 2001* **£165;** 27 huge, opulent rms. Elegant cosseting hotel a little way out from the centre, with luxurious Victorian furnishings, fresh flowers, exemplary staff, and fine modern cooking in the stylish restaurant; disabled access.

GULLANE NT4983 **Greywalls** *Duncar Rd, Gullane, East Lothian EH31 2EG (01620) 842144* **£190;** 23 individually decorated rms. Overlooking Muirfield golf course, this beautiful family-run Lutyens house has antiques, open fires and flowers in its comfortable lounges and panelled library, very good food and fine wines in the restaurant, impeccable service, and lovely garden; cl Nov–Mar; disabled access.

INNERLEITHEN NT3336 **Traquair Arms** *Innerleithen, Peeblesshire EH44 6PD (01896) 830229* **£70,** plus special breaks; 7 comfortable rms. Very friendly inn with interesting choice of good food in attractive dining room, cosy lounge bar, friendly service, the superb local Traquair ale on handpump, and nice breakfasts; cl 25–26 Dec, 1–2 Jan.

LOCKERBIE NY1283 **Dryfesdale Hotel** *Lockerbie, Dumfriesshire DG11 2SF (01576) 202427* **£84,** plus wknd breaks; 15 rms, 6 on ground floor. Relaxed and comfortable former manse in 5 acres, open fire in homely lounge, good food in pleasant restaurant, and lovely surrounding countryside; good disabled access.

MAYBOLE NS3103 **Ladyburn** *Kilkerran, Maybole, Ayrshire KA19 7SG (01655) 740585* **£145,** plus special breaks; 6 rms. Quietly set family home in lovely wooded countryside with antiques, books and open fires in comfortable day rooms, and friendly staff; shooting and fishing can be arranged; self-catering flat also; cl 2 wks Nov, 4 wks Jan–Mar; no children.

MELROSE NT5433 **Burts Hotel** *Melrose, Roxburghshire TD6 9PN (01896) 822285* **£82,** plus special breaks; 20 rms. Welcoming 18th-c inn in delightfully quiet village, close to abbey ruins; coal fire in bustling bar, residents' lounge, consistently popular imaginative food, exceptional breakfasts, and a decent wine list; cl for accommodation 24–26 Dec.

MELROSE NT5434 **Dunfermline House** *Buccleuch St, Melrose, Roxburghshire TD6 9LB (01896) 822148* ***£48;** 5 rms. Neatly kept Victorian terraced house nr abbey ruins, with good breakfasts and friendly owners.

MINNIGAFF NX4165 **Creebridge House** *Minnigaff, Newton Stewart, Wigtownshire DG8 6NP (01671) 402121* ***£95,** plus special breaks; 20 rms.

Attractive country-house hotel in 3 acres of gardens with relaxed friendly atmosphere, open fire in comfortable drawing room, cheerful bar, and big choice of delicious food inc fine local fish and seafood; disabled access.

NENTHORN NT6938 **Whitehill Farm** *Nenthorn, Kelso, Roxburghshire TD5 7RZ (01573) 470203* ***£46;** 4 rms, 3 with shared bthrm. Comfortable farmhouse on mixed farm with fine views, big garden, log fire in sitting room, and good home cooking; cl Christmas/New Year.

PEEBLES NT2344 **Cringletie House** *Cringletie, Peebles EH45 8PL (01721) 730233* **£120,** plus special breaks; 13 pretty rms. Surrounded by 28 acres of garden and woodland and with fine views, this turreted baronial mansion, run by the same couple for over 20 years, is very welcoming and quiet, with delicious food using home-grown vegetables, extensive Scottish breakfasts, and excellent service.

PORTPATRICK NW9954 **Crown** *Portpatrick, Stranraer, Wigtownshire DG9 8SX (01776) 810261* **£72;** 12 attractive rms. Atmospheric harbourside inn with rambling and interestingly furnished old-fashioned bar, airy art deco dining room, good food with an emphasis on local seafood, excellent breakfasts, and carefully chosen wines.

PORTPATRICK NX0252 **Knockinaam Lodge** *Portpatrick, Stranraer, Wigtownshire DG9 9AD (01776) 810471* **£180 incl dinner,** plus special breaks; 10 individual rms. Lovely very neatly kept little hotel with comfortable pretty rooms, open fires, wonderful food, and friendly caring service; the surroundings are dramatic, with lots of fine cliff walks; children over 12 in evening restaurant (high tea at 6pm); disabled access to restaurant only.

QUOTHQUAN NT0040 **Shieldhill** *Quothquan, Biggar, Lanarkshire ML12 6NA (01899) 220035* **£114,** plus special breaks; 16 pretty rms. Partly 13th-c hotel in fine setting, with comfortable oak-panelled lounge, open fires, library, particularly good food in no smoking restaurant, and warm friendly service.

SWINTON NT8347 **Wheatsheaf** *Swinton, Duns, Berwickshire TD11 3JJ (01890) 860257* ***£75,** plus special breaks; 6 rms, most with own shower. Warmly friendly inn with exceptionally good food, a pleasantly decorated and relaxed main lounge plus small pubby area, separate locals' bar, and no smoking front conservatory; garden play area for children; cl 25 Dec, 1 Jan.

TURNBERRY NS2005 **Turnberry** *Turnberry, Ayrshire KA26 9LT (01655) 331000* **£250,** plus special breaks; 132 stylish and comfortable rms. Grand Edwardian country house in spectacular 360-acre coastal setting with 2 championship golf courses that are ranked among the best in the world. Elegant reception rooms, quite a choice of places to eat inc very good restaurant using tip-top local produce – and plenty of sporting activities: 12-hole pitch and putt (plus the 2 18-hole golf courses), indoor swimming pool, health spa, gym, sauna, solarium, squash, and tennis courts; disabled access.

UPHALL NT0571 **Houstoun House** *Uphall, Broxburn, West Lothian EH52 6JS (01506) 853831* ***£130,** plus wknd breaks; 72 comfortable rms, 26 in new extension. 17th-c house divided into 3 distinct buildings: fine food in 3 wood-panelled dining rooms, vaulted bars (one with a fire that burns nearly all year), quiet lounge, lovely grounds, and leisure complex with swimming pool, sauna, gym, tennis courts and bistro; disabled access.

We welcome reports from readers

This *Guide* depends on readers' reports. Do help us if you can – in return, we offer a discount on the next edition to people who've helped us with reports for it. Tell us what you think about places already in it, and anything extra you think we should say about them. And send us your ideas for inclusion in the next edition: places to visit, eat at or stay in, attractive drives or walks, maybe even unusual interesting shops you know of. Use the card in the middle, the report forms at the end, or just write – no stamp needed: *The Good Guide to Britain*, FREEPOST TN1569, Wadhurst, E Sussex TN5 7BR.

To see and do

EDINBURGH NT2573 Edinburgh is one of Britain's most rewarding cities for visitors, whether it's your first visit or you've been dozens of times before. And this year there are some exciting new places to visit: the Dynamic Earth Centre, and the Royal Yacht *Britannia* now moored at Leith (see below). The city is dominated by the ancient silhouettes of Edinburgh Castle on its castle cliff and of the long erratic line of tall, narrow Old Town buildings beside it. Up here narrow streets and alleys with steep steps between them and courtyard closes leading off have a real flavour of the distant past, with a good many interesting ancient buildings (and a lot of the city's antiquarian bookshops and other interesting specialist shops). When the authorities decided to redevelop the city in the 18th c, they did it not by knocking down the medieval buildings, but instead by creating an entirely new part of the city, working from scratch. The resulting New Town is a masterpiece of spacious Georgian town planning, stretching out handsomely below the steep crag of Castle Rock and its medieval skyline. There's a hop-on hop-off tour bus, and the ticket gives discounts to some of the places to visit. Evening walking tours are often led by students. The regular bus services have good-value daily and weekly passes, and it is worth getting used to the public transport: the city council has come up with a radical road-pricing scheme to ease congestion and cut pollution, which they hope will be running by 2000. The Edinburgh for Less scheme (£2.50 from information centres) gives discounts at some restaurants and attractions inc the castle for up to 4 days. Edinburgh does put on its best clothes and best events for its August Festival; it's easier to see, and truer to itself, at other times of year. If you do visit the Festival, make sure you've got accommodation sorted out well in advance. Edinburgh's pubs and bars are a special delight, chatty places often of great character. Among the best for atmosphere are the Bow Bar (Victoria St), Bannerman's (Cowgate), Bennet's (Leven St), Guildford Arms (West Register St), Cumberland (Cumberland St), Athletic Arms (Angle Park Terrace/Kilmarnock Rd), Kays (Jamaica St W) and Jolly Judge (James Court, off Lawnmarket); for food too, the Abbotsford, Kenilworth and Milnes (all Rose St), Starbank (Laverockbank Rd), Golf Tavern (Wright's Houses), Braidwoods (West Port) and Ship on the Shore (The Shore, Leith). The corner lobby bar of the Balmoral Hotel is a relaxing spot at the hub of the town. For a fuller meal, the city has a remarkable number of good-value bistro-style restaurants (as well as the places we mention in the **Where to eat** section, below). There are lots of good shops dotted around town, especially on or near **Princes St** – its tall, mainly Georgian buildings lining just the one side, giving an expansive view across the sunken gardens to the castle. Parallel is **George St**, with some superior shops and the new Dome complex (a handsome place for refreshment), while Rose St, an alley between the two, has plenty of pubs and cafés. More bars around the **Grassmarket** and **Lawnmarket**, a lively area of the Old Town; Victoria St here has interesting shops, notably that of Ian Mellis, who specialises in Scottish, Irish and English farm cheeses. Valvona & Crolla on Elm Row is a dazzling delicatessen.

Edinburgh Castle A place of great magnetism; it's been a fortress since at least the 7th c, and excavations show there's been a settlement here for 4,000 years. The oldest building today is the beautiful St Margaret's Chapel, thought to have been built in the 12th c and little changed since. Other highlights include the apartments of Mary, Queen of Scots, Mons Meg (the 15th-c Belgian cannon with which James II cowed the Black Douglases), the Scottish Crown Jewels (centuries older than the English ones), and for romantics the Stone of Destiny or Scottish coronation stone, now returned by England which had seized it 700 years ago. Glorious views from the battlements, over the Firth of Forth to Fife beyond. You can wander around on your own, but the official guides are a great bonus – they leave from the drawbridge, several times a day. Meals, snacks, shop, disabled access; cl 25–26

South Scotland
WEST SCOTLAND
EAST
Dumbarton
Bearsden
Greenock Cut
Langbank
Glasgow
Coatbridge
Bathgate
Linlithgow
BUTE
Largs
Paisley
Uddingston
Lochwinnoch
NS
Blantyre
Larkhall
Lanark
Quothquan
Irvine
Kilmarnock
New Lanark
Symington
ARRAN
Sorn
FIRTH OF CLYDE
Alloway
Wanlockhead
Culzean Castle
Maybole
Turnberry
Old Dailly
NX
Thornhill
Ellisland Farm
Dumfries
RHINNS OF KELLS
Minnigaff
New Abbey
Kirkcowan
Creetown
Castle Douglas
Kirkbean
Stranraer
Glenluce
Gatehouse of Fleet
Kippford
Kirkcudbright
Portpatrick
RHINNS OF GALLOWAY
Cardoness Castle
GALLOWAY FOREST PARK
Auchencairn
Rockcliffe
Port Logan
Dundrennan
Whithorn
SOLWAY
Mull of Galloway

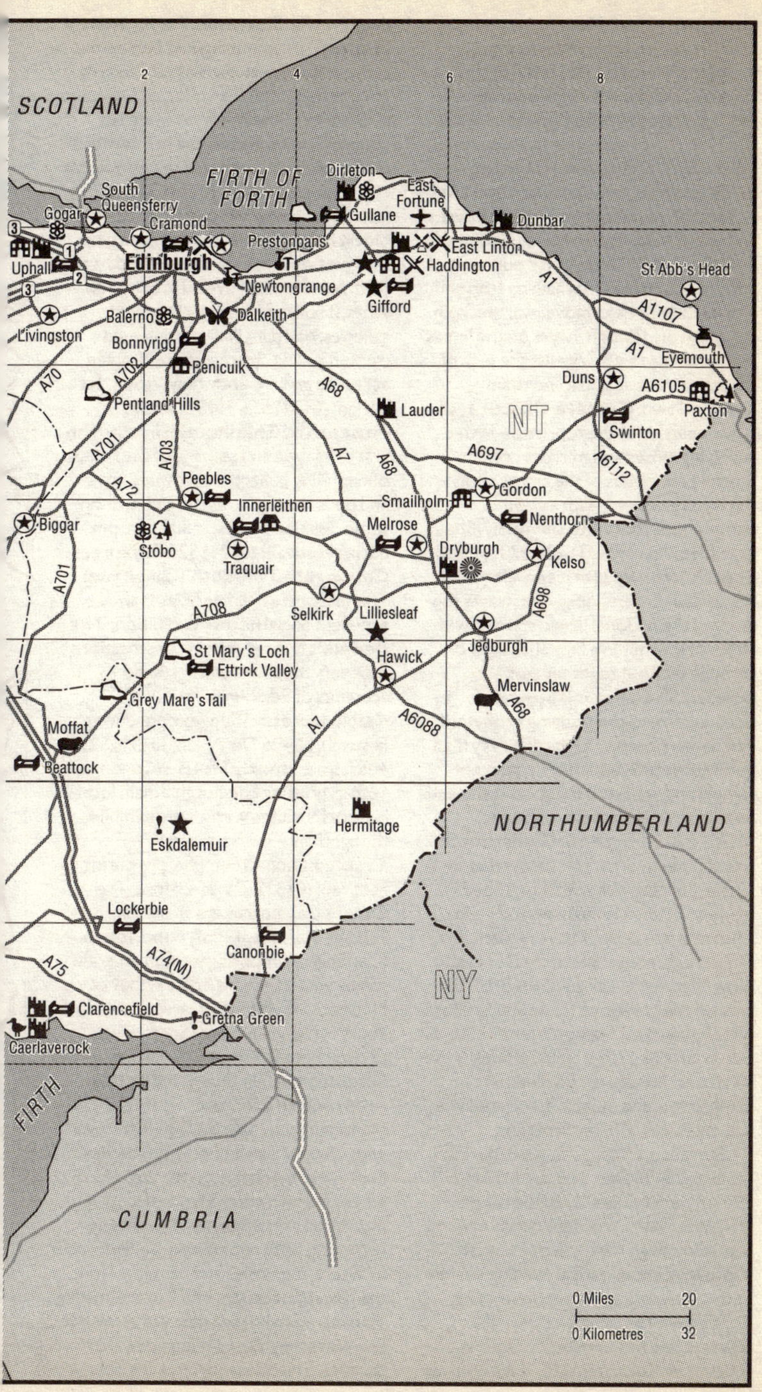
SCOTLAND
FIRTH OF FORTH
Dirleton
East Fortune
South Queensferry
Gogar
Cramond
Gullane
Dunbar
Prestonpans
East Linton
Edinburgh
Uphall
Haddington
Newtongrange
Gifford
St Abb's Head
Balerno
Dalkeith
Livingston
Bonnyrigg
Penicuik
Eyemouth
Duns
A6105
Paxton
Pentland Hills
Lauder
NT
Swinton
A697
Peebles
Smailholm
Gordon
Innerleithen
Nenthorn
Biggar
Melrose
Stobo
Dryburgh
Kelso
Traquair
Selkirk
Lilliesleaf
A708
Jedburgh
St Mary's Loch
Ettrick Valley
Hawick
Mervinslaw
Grey Mare's Tail
Moffat
Beattock
NORTHUMBERLAND
Hermitage
Eskdalemuir
Lockerbie
Canonbie
A74(M)
A75
NY
Clarencefield
Gretna Green
Caerlaverock
FIRTH
CUMBRIA
0 Miles 20
0 Kilometres 32

Dec; (0131) 225 9846; £6 (inc audio tour). If you're around at lunchtime, look (and listen) for the firing of the One o'Clock Gun from the parapet.

Royal Mile Between Castle and Holyrood Palace (for most people Edinburgh's 2 must-sees) is this largely medieval street, around which you'll find all sorts of interesting or historic houses and features, and quaint lanes leading off in all directions. Usefully, it's punctuated with cafés and bars in which to stop and work out your next move, starting with the old-world Ensign Ewart on the left as you leave the castle. We list the pick of the attractions as you'll find them heading down. **Camera Obscura** (Castlehill) Up at the top, these 19th-c revolving lenses and mirrors create unique panoramas of the city as soon as the lights go down, with a good commentary; best on a sunny day. Shop; cl 25 Dec, 1 Jan; (0131) 226 3709; £3.85. **Scotch Whisky Heritage Centre** (Castlehill) Entertainingly illustrates the story of the national drink, starting with a shortish journey in a barrel-shaped car through well put together sets and tableaux. The full tour is a useful introduction to the distilling process; if you haven't been to a real distillery it's a good substitute, and there's a decent sample and well stocked shop at the end. Snacks, disabled access; cl 25 Dec; (0131) 220 0441; £4.95. **Gladstone's Land** (Lawnmarket) 6-storeyed early 17th-c building, still with its arcaded front, and refurnished in period style. The walls and ceilings have remarkable tempera paintings. Shop; cl am Sun, and Nov–Mar; (0131) 226 5856; £3; NTS. **Lady Stair's House** (Lady Stair's Close, off Lawnmarket) Named after its 18th-c occupant, this 17th-c building houses the **Writers' Museum**, a collection of manuscripts and objects associated with Robert Burns, Walter Scott and R L Stevenson. Shop; cl Sun exc during Festival, 25–26 Dec, 1–3 Jan; (0131) 529 4901; free. **St Giles' Cathedral** (High St) The Royal Mile widens briefly around Scotland's High Kirk, the city's most impressive ecclesiastical building, mainly 15th-c, but dating from around 1120. Topped with an ornate crown-like tower, it has monuments to famous Scots from Knox (minister here until his death) to R L Stevenson. **Parliament House** (Parliament Sq) Just behind the cathedral, this was the seat of Scottish government until the Union of 1707, and now houses Scotland's supreme law courts. Don't miss the fine hammerbeam roof in the Hall. Limited disabled access; cl 1–2pm and wknds; (0131) 225 2595; free. **John Knox House** (High St) The oldest house on the Royal Mile, where the great reformer is supposed to have died. Now looking every bit of its 500 years, it still has its original timber galleries, oak panelling and splendid painted ceiling. Snacks, shop, disabled access to ground floor only; cl Sun, 1st wk Jan; (0131) 556 9579; £1.95. **Museum of Childhood** (High St) The first of its type and still one of the best, an outstanding collection of games, toys and dolls from all over the globe. Shop, some disabled access; cl Sun (exc pm during Festival); (0131) 529 4142; free. **Canongate Tolbooth** (Canongate) This elaborate building houses an excellent social history exhibition, **The People's Story**, with reconstructions built very much around firsthand accounts of Edinburgh life. Shop, disabled access; cl Sun (exc pm during Festival), 25–26 Dec, 1 Jan; (0131) 529 4057; free. **Huntly House** (Canongate) 16th-c, housing Edinburgh's main local history museum, with all the exhibits thoughtfully – even artistically – arranged. Shop; cl Sun (exc pm during Festival); (0131) 529 4143; free. The Canons Gait nearby is a smart bar.

Palace of Holyroodhouse (Canongate) Imposing yet human-scale palace with its origins in the Abbey of Holyrood, founded by David I. Later the court of Mary, Queen of Scots, it was used by Bonnie Prince Charlie during his occupation of Edinburgh, and is still a royal residence for part of the year. The oldest surviving part is James IV's tower, with Queen Mary's rooms on the second floor, where a plaque on the floor marks where her secretary Rizzio was murdered in front of her. The throne room and state rooms have period furniture, tapestries and paintings from the Royal Collection. Much more inviting than many English palaces, and in the last few years they've really improved visitor facilities. The palace gardens are open

Apr–Oct. Shop, limited disabled access by prior arrangement; cl Good Fri, 25–26 Dec, and occasional other dates (if the Queen is in residence, for example) – check first on (0131) 556 1096; £5.30.

! **Our Dynamic Earth Centre** In a spectacular new building opposite Holyrood and the site for the new Scottish Parliament building, this stunning exhibition uses state-of-the-art technology to provide a lively exploration of the earth. You can see a volcano erupt, experience an earthquake, watch animals swinging through the trees in a rainforest, take a helicopter ride over the glacial valleys of Norway and touch and feel ice sculptures. Set to open Easter 1999, it looks certain to be a major addition to the city's attractions. Meals, snacks, shop, disabled access; opens Easter 1999, then cl winter Mon and Tues, 25–26 Dec; (0131) 550 7800; £5.50.

Royal Museum of Scotland (Chambers St) A tremendous variety of collections, covering virtually anything you might care to poke around in. Children enjoy its intricate working models of early engines, but it has something for everyone – in a gloriously light and spacious Victorian building. Meals, snacks, shop, disabled access; cl am Sun, 25 Dec; (0131) 225 7534; £3.

National Gallery of Scotland (The Mound) Fine neo-classical building with particularly good examples of most European schools and periods. Plenty of Scottish paintings too, with many great works by Ramsay, Raeburn, Wilkie and McTaggart. Some art critics objected to changes in the look of the gallery under its current director, but few would dispute that it's undoubtedly still one of Britain's best. Look out for the rather incongruous portrait of one of the donors' dogs – it has to be hung here as a condition of the donation of other pictures. Shop, disabled access; cl am Sun, 25–26 Dec; (0131) 624 6200; free (exc major exhibitions).

Royal Scottish Academy (The Mound) Founded in 1826, in a second neo-classical temple next door, with good changing exhibitions. Shop, disabled access; cl am Sun, and between exhibitions; (0131) 225 6671 for what's on; £2 for annual exhibition Apr–July. On either side, like a broad moat for the castle (this was a loch before the New Town was built), are well tended gardens.

Scottish National Portrait Gallery (Queen St) The history of Scotland through a huge collection of portraits in a variety of media. Meals, snacks, shop, disabled access; cl am Sun, 25–26 Dec; (0131) 624 6200; free. The new **Museum of Scotland** opens soon in the same building, with a fine collection of antiquities.

Georgian House (Charlotte Sq) Archetypal period house, part of Robert Adam's magnificent terrace along the north side. The rooms and servants' quarters have been refurbished in the style of 1800. Shop, disabled access to ground floor only; cl am Sun, and Nov–Mar; (0131) 225 2160; £4.20; NTS. Close by, nr Queen St, beyond a further strip of gardens, is another Georgian area with some interesting shops. Hoggs in the alley behind stately Great King St has a wide choice of malt whiskies at low prices.

! **Edinburgh Dungeon** (Shandwick Pl) All too realistic scenes recalling the darker moments in Scottish history, from the body-snatching of Burke and Hare to witches burned at the stake on Castle Hill. As we went to press they were closed after a fire but hoped to be fully operational by the time this book reaches the shops. Shop; cl 24–26 Dec, 1–2 Jan; (0131) 225 1331; £4.

World of Communications (Cambridge St) Lively and interactive new look at telecommunications; open Tues–Sat and pm summer Sun; free.

Scott Memorial (Princes St) After the castle, probably Edinburgh's most memorable building: remarkably ornate, with its handsome if mucky exterior. The historic crypt of St John's episcopal church on Princes St has interesting vegetarian and vegan food.

! **Calton Hill** Dominating the east end of Princes St, with magnificent views over the city. An unusual sight up here is a romantic Doric colonnade, intended to be a full replica of the Parthenon (until the money ran out). The **Nelson Monument** up here gives the best views of Edinburgh – if you can face the 31-metre (102-ft) climb to the top. Every day at 1pm (exc Sun) the time ball drops as the gun at the castle goes off. Shop; cl am Mon; £1.50. **Edinburgh Experience** in a nearby observatory has a 20-minute 3D history of the city (they provide special glasses); cl Nov–Mar; (0131) 556 4365; £2.

Scottish National Gallery of Modern Art (Belford Rd) Breathtaking collection inc outstanding range of Surrealist works, and great works by Picasso, Barbara Hepworth and Lichtenstein. Meals, snacks, shop, disabled access; cl am Sun, 25–26 Dec, 1 Jan; (0131) 624 6200; free (maybe charges for temporary exhibitions).

Royal Botanic Garden (Inverleith Row, N of centre) Founded as a physic garden in 1670 at Holyrood and then transplanted here in the early 19th c. Covering 72 acres, it has various splendid themed areas, with a woodland garden, peat garden, arboretum and the Glasshouse Experience, inc palm houses, fern house and aquatic house. They keep the most comprehensive rhododendron collection in Britain, and grow many other rare Asiatic plants to perfection – particularly primulas and lilies and their more awkward relatives. Guided tours leave from inside the West Gate at 11am and 2pm Apr–Sept. Meals, snacks, shop, disabled access; cl 25 Dec, 1 Jan; (0131) 552 7171; free (tours £2).

! **Royal Observatory Visitor Centre** (Blackford Hill) Good range of often lively astronomy displays, inc videos, computer games, and the biggest telescope in Scotland. In winter some telescopes are open till 9pm. Shop, limited disabled access; cl am Sun, 24 Dec–2 Jan; (0131) 668 8405; *£3. Blackford Hill is virtually a mountain within the city, giving walkers glorious views down over the capital, and even as far as the Braid Hills.

! **Edinburgh Zoo** (Corstorphine Rd, the A8 W) Best known for its Penguin Parade each day at 2pm (Apr–Oct), but plenty of other rare and odd-looking animals around the attractive grounds. Children enjoy the yew-hedge maze loosely themed around Darwin's theory of evolution, with several fountains along the way that periodically shoot out jets of water (summer only). Extra events and activities in summer hols. Meals, snacks, shops (special penguin and polar bear shops in summer), disabled access (though a little hilly); open every day (inc 25 Dec); (0131) 334 9171; £6.50.

Royal Yacht *Britannia* (Ocean Drive, Leith Docks) The chance to explore 5 decks of the ship in which the Queen and Prince Philip have cruised the world, and an onshore visitor centre with displays about the yacht and its regal past. Snacks, shop, disabled access; cl 25 Dec; (0131) 555 8800; £6.50.

Water of Leith W of the centre and well worth exploring, often very picturesque and ravine-like. By its banks is the quaint little Dean Village, surprisingly close to the heart of the city, yet unaffected by all the New Town building above it. There's a fine series of Georgian crescents around Moray Pl. The river eventually winds down to Leith itself (a once prosperous and separate dockland area now swallowed up by the city, its waterfront reviving again with trendy bars). The Scottish Malt Whisky Society (Giles St), dedicated to cask strength top-quality malt whiskies, has a downstairs bar/restaurant.

Clan Tartan Centre (Leith Mills, Bangor Rd) Displays of various clans and their costume, computers that allow you to trace your own Scottish heritage, and a factory shop with good-value Pringle knitwear and tweeds. Meals, snacks, shop, disabled access; cl 25 Dec; (0131) 553 5161; free.

Arthur's Seat Out beyond Holyrood in Holyrood Park is this saddleback mountain, a great volcanic mass giving a wonderful panorama over the city, and a pleasant place for wandering, with a hill fort on top and the largely unspoilt Duddingston village below it (the Sheep Heid is a good pub).

GLASGOW NS5865 There's a real zing and vitality about this proud city, which is making great strides in its efforts to shake off its rather rough image. It's the UK City of Architecture and Design 1999 and in the centre smart shops and galleries seem to be springing up all the time. Besides the excellent art galleries and interesting museums, which the local director of museums has fought hard to keep free, it houses the Royal Scottish Orchestra (with a fine-sounding concert hall), the Scottish Opera and the Scottish Ballet. Though there are many places to see and visit, a snag for visitors is that they are scattered around this sprawling city: the Burrell Collection, the most interesting place of all, is out in the suburbs. It's worth investing in a Day Tripper ticket, which allows virtually unlimited bus and train travel not just in the city but as far out as Ayr and Lanark. Besides the restaurants and bars mentioned in the **Where to eat** section, below, Glasgow is full of places to eat out in, formal and informal; interesting and undaunting pubs and bars include the Auctioneers (St Vincent Pl), Blackfriars (Bell St), Bon Accord (North St), Brewery Tap (Sauchiehall St) and Cask & Still (Hope St).

Merchant City The area around George Sq and Buchanan St was built on a grid plan in the 19th c, and visually has something in common with New York City – Americans are said to feel at home here. With its proud Victorian buildings cleaned back to their warm sandstone, this smart shopping quarter is the city's most comfortable area to stroll around. The City Chambers (George Sq) is a spectacular monument to 1880s civic pride, marble everywhere; free tours. The Counting House is a splendid new pub in an opulent converted bank nearby. There are café/bars and bistros off Princes Sq, and antique stalls in Victorian Village (West Regent St). On the south-east edge of this area, between Gallowgate and London Rd past the Tolbooth, the **Barras** (barrows) is an entertaining weekend flea-market. With around 800 stalls it's one of the biggest covered markets in the world, great for bargains or just passing time; try the plump fresh clappie doos (mussels). **Gallery of Modern Art** (Queen St) Glasgow's latest big gallery, concentrating on art by living British artists – not just Scottish. Lively café/bar (open some evenings too), shop, good disabled access; cl 25–26 Dec, 1–2 Jan (0141) 229 1996; free. **Tenement House** (145 Buccleuch St) is a one-floor late 19th-c flat giving a vivid impression of life for many Glaswegians at the turn of the century. The same woman lived here from 1911 to 1965 and in that time scarcely changed a thing; its time-capsule quality was preserved by a subsequent owner, and then the flat, still with its original furnishings and fittings, was left to the National Trust for Scotland. Open pm Mar–Oct; (0141) 333 0183; £3; NTS.

Cathedral area Just NE of the centre, this is Glasgow's oldest area, though not the most interesting. The **cathedral** is 12th c, dedicated to St Mungo, the founder of the city. It's very well preserved, though most fittings date from the 19th c; best parts are the crypt, a gracefully vaulted affair built in the mid-13th c, and the Blackadder aisle. The spectacular Necropolis graveyard is closed for restoration, but there's a fine overview from the cathedral. **St Mungo Museum of Religious Life & Art** (Cathedral Precinct) Unique collection of art from all the world's major religions – and some rather obscure ones too. Everything from an Egyptian mummy mask to Dali's *Christ of St John of the Cross*, and in the grounds Britain's only permanent Zen garden. Meals, snacks, shop, disabled access; cl Tues until May 1999, 25–26 Dec, 1–2 Jan; (0141) 553 2557; free. **Provan's Lordship** (Castle St) Glasgow's oldest house, used by the Prebend of Provan – a canon of the cathedral. Dating from 1471, it's been carefully restored and furnished according to several period styles. Shop, disabled access to ground floor only; cl Tues until May 1999, 25–26 Dec, 1–2 Jan; (0141) 552 8819; free.

People's Palace (Glasgow Green) Very enjoyable and recently refurbished social history museum looking at Glaswegians over the centuries, in a park just SE of the centre; it was temporarily closed as we went to press but should be open again by the time this book reaches the shops; cl am Sun; (0141) 5540 223; free. The museum's café is in the adjacent **Winter Gardens**, a massive conservatory with huge tropical plants.

Glasgow's museum quarter NW of the centre, the West End, Kelvingrove and the university quarter have some elegant streets, the main concentration of museums, and the botanic gardens. **Hunterian Museum** (Hillhead St) Scotland's oldest museum, housing the university collections of ethnographic, palaeontological and anthropological material, along with lots of archaeology, and a coin display. Shop; cl Sun and public hols; (0141) 330 4221; free. The exhibitions were founded by Dr William Hunter, the 18th-c physician. **Hunterian Art Gallery** (Hillhead St) Dr Hunter also bequeathed the core of fine paintings which form the basis of this beautifully hung collection. A grand range of works by Whistler, interesting and well chosen contemporary British art and sculpture, and an amazing re-creation of the home of Charles Rennie Mackintosh (cl 12.30–1.30pm), the designer/architect whose exuberant yet very disciplined and clean-lined art nouveau buildings stand out among the more traditional solidity of much of Glasgow. Shop, disabled access with prior notice; cl Sun, public hols; (0141) 330 5431; free. **Glasgow Art Gallery & Museum** (Kelvingrove Park) Huge Victorian building with remarkably rich collection of paintings, especially strong in works by the French Impressionists, Post-Impressionists, and Scottish artists from the 17th c. Also sculpture, silver, porcelain, armour, ethnography and natural history. Meals, snacks, shop, disabled access; cl 25–26 Dec, 1–2 Jan; (0141) 287 2699; free. **Glasgow Museum of Transport** (Kelvin Hall) Comprehensive collection of vehicles, from trams to ships, very well displayed; the walk-through car showroom is arranged as if some were for sale, with original prices displayed on the windscreens. Meals, snacks, shop, disabled access; cl Tues until May 1999, 25 Dec, 1 Jan; (0141) 287 2720; free. **University of Glasgow Visitor Centre** (University Ave) Interactive displays on the history and life of the university (founded in 1451), with tours around some of its grander features, such as the Lion & Unicorn Staircase, Bute and Randolph Halls and Memorial Chapel. Snacks, shop, disabled access; cl Sun Oct–Apr, 25–26 Dec, 1–2 Jan; (0141) 330 5511; visitor centre free, tours (11am and 2pm Weds, Fri and Sat May–Sept; Oct–Apr just 2pm Weds) £1.50. You can stay in some of the university buildings during vacations. **Glasgow Botanic Gardens** (730 Great Western Rd) Sloping gently down to the River Kibble, famous for their fantastic glasshouses, particularly the ½-acre Kibble Palace, with its soaring tree ferns interspersed with Victorian sculpture. Disabled access; main glasshouse cl am wknds; (0141) 334 2422; free. Sauchiehall St, one link between the museum/university and the centre, is an ordinary shopping street, but well worth the walk for the ground-breaking designer and architect Charles Rennie Mackintosh's most famous building, the **Glasgow School of Art** (Renfrew St, just off; the tours are highly recommended, (0141) 332 9797), and the decoratively mirrored **Willow Tea Room** (open till 5pm), furnished to his designs, too. As well as other places we mention with Mackintosh connections, you can buy works after him at the Glasgow Style Gallery on Great Western Rd. **McLellan Galleries** (Sauchiehall St) Spacious and well lit, these have good changing art exhibitions; shop, disabled access; cl between shows; (0141) 331 1854; charge varies according to exhibitions.

Scotland Street School Museum (S of centre) Designed by Mackintosh, this spectacular building originally had a capacity of 1,250 pupils in 21 classrooms. It now houses a lively education museum, with reconstructed classrooms. You can be measured in the medical room and even peek into the headmaster's office. Snacks, shop; cl am Sun, 25–26 Dec, 1–2 Jan; (0141) 429 1202; free.

Burrell Collection (Pollok Country Park, south-west Glasgow) A couple of miles out in the suburbs, but not to be missed – and rarely gets too crowded. Splendidly and imaginatively housed in a modern building created to show its different parts to perfection, the huge collection – far too much to see at one go – includes Egyptian alabaster,

Chinese jade, oriental rugs, remarkable tapestries, medieval metalwork and stained glass, even medieval doorways and windows set into the walls, as well as paintings by Degas, Manet and Rembrandt among others. Good meals and snacks, shop, disabled access; cl Tues until May 1999, 25–26 Dec, 1–2 Jan; (0141) 649 7151; free, though you may have to pay for parking. **Pollok House** (Pollok Country Park) Treasures here include silver, ceramics and porcelain, but it's the paintings that stand out, with a collection of Spanish masters such as Goya and El Greco cannily acquired in the days when they were greatly undervalued. Snacks, shop; cl 25–26 Dec, 1–2 Jan; (0141) 616 6410; £3.20 Apr–Oct, other times free; NTS. The park itself is one of the best of the several parks and gardens you'll find around Glasgow, with waterside and woodland trails, guided Sun afternoon walks, rose garden, shire horses, and a herd of Highland cattle.

Provan Hall (Auchinlea Park; on the B806 E) Mansion house virtually unchanged since the 16th c, in a pleasant park with various formal and informal gardens inc a herb garden. Disabled access; cl wknds and public hols; (0141) 771 4399; free; NTS.

Bellahouston Park NS5463 (SW) The Empire Exhibition of 1938 was held on these 171 acres, which now have a walled garden, sunken garden and sweeping lawns. An additional attraction is the Charles Rennie Mackintosh-designed **House for an Art Lover** built here to his 1901 plans. There's an exhibition on Mackintosh and contemporary art exhibitions. Meals, snacks, shop, disabled access; (0141) 353 4449; £3.50.

Rouken Glen Park NS5458 (Thornliebank, SW) A place of tranquil beauty, with a walled garden, gorgeous lawns, and woodland walks to a waterfall at the head of the glen.

Victoria Park NS5467 (Victoria Park Drive N, NW) Tree-lined park where the fossil remains in the Fossil Grove, some of them 230 million years old, were discovered by workmen digging a path in the late 19th c.

Linn Park NS5859 (Cathcart/Castlemilk, S) Lots to do – riverside walks, nature trails, children's zoo, golf course, and collections of British ponies and Highland cattle, as well as a ruined 14th-c castle, and an adventure playground for the disabled (prior arrangement preferred). Visitor centre open pm wknds only; (0141) 637 1147; free.

Greenbank Garden NS5656 (Flenders Rd, Clarkston; off the A726 S) Aims to encourage and help owners of small gardens, so has lots of different shrubs and flowers to spark ideas. Also garden and greenhouse designed to meet the needs of disabled gardeners, with advice on specially designed tools. Summer teas, shop, disabled access; cl 25–26 Dec, 1 Jan; (0141) 639 3281; £3; NTS.

Mugdock Country Park NS5577 (NW outskirts) Good strolling ground, with two castle ruins, a view over Glasgow, and an attractive loch. The West Highland Way long-distance path starts here nr Milngavie, giving level walks. The determined can press on along glen routes right up to Fort William – the scenery getting better all the way.

Clyde walks NS5069 A walkway tracks along the Clyde now that its waterfront has been cleaned up. The veteran pleasure steamer *Waverley* makes some runs from here Jun–Aug – (0141) 221 8152 for times. Some Clydeside pubs well outside Glasgow with decent food and good sea views include the Cardwell at Cardwell Bay in Gourock and the Spinnaker there, and the Lookout down in Troon Marina.

Other things to see and do

ALLOWAY NS3318 A key stop on the Burns Trail: the poet was born here in 1759. The associated local sites are grouped together under the name **Burns National Heritage Park** and the introductory visitor centre at Murdochs Lane has been brightly revamped. Rechristened the **Tam o' Shanter Experience**, its main feature is a multi-media show bringing Burns's famous poem vividly to life. Up the road you can explore the tiny rooms of the poet's birthplace, thatched **Burns Cottage**, and there's an adjacent museum of his life, with a good collection of manuscripts and letters. In the other direction, S of the centre, the **Burns Monument** was built in 1823 to a fine design by Thomas Hamilton Jr, and is adorned with characters from Burns's poems sculpted by James Thorn. Snacks, shop, disabled access; cl 25–26 Dec, 1 Jan; (01292) 443700; £4.25 for all 3 sites, £2.50 for the monument plus either of the other 2.

ARRAN NS0037 This island is just under an hour by ferry from Ardrossan (2 ferries a day in winter, more in season; a popular public-transport day trip from Glasgow), with summer ferries from Claonaig on Kintyre too; (01475) 650100 for ferry enquiries. It has a marvellous variety of scenery from subtropical gardens to mountain deer forest – and highly regarded (and beautifully set) golf courses. Brodick the main settlement has several places to hire bikes. **Brodick Castle** Fine old castle, in lovely surroundings between the sea, hills and majestic mountain of Goatfell. Partly 13th c, and extended in 1652 and 1844, it's very fierce-looking from the outside, but comfortably grand inside – even a little homely in places. There are almost a hundred antlered heads on the walls of the main staircase. It's surrounded by magnificent formal gardens, with the highlight the woodland garden started in 1923 by the Duchess of Montrose, inc many lovely rare and tender rhododendrons. Meals, snacks, shop, disabled access; castle cl Nov–Mar, garden and country park open all year; (01770) 302202; £4.80, garden and country park only £2.40; NTS. **Arran Heritage Museum** This 18th-c croft farm has well presented local history. Meals, snacks, shop, disabled access; cl Nov–Mar; (01770) 302636; £2. The Kingsley on Brodick esplanade has decent home cooking, and the Ormidale Hotel has good-value food. On the opposite side of the island nr Machrie are several intriguing Bronze Age stone circles. Arran has a good circular walk up and down Goatfell, prominent for miles around, and you can follow the shore right around the northern tip, the Cock of Arran. Up near here the waterside Catacol Hotel has decent food. There's a good walk on the west coast, from Blackwaterfoot to the King's Cave, which supposedly sheltered Robert the Bruce.

★ **AUCHENCAIRN** NX7951 Attractive village, with a lane down to sandy Balcary Bay, where **Balcary Point** NX8149 on the west side makes for a good peaceful walk.

BALERNO NT1666 **Malleny House Garden** (off the A70) Charming gardens that are home to a national collection of 19th-c shrub roses (best in late Jun), as well as 4 clipped old yew trees – the survivors of a dozen planted in 1603. Limited disabled access; open all year; (0131) 449 2283; £1; NTS. The handsome Johnsburn House Hotel does good lunches.

BATHGATE NS9970 **Cairnpapple Hill** (just E of Torpichen, off the B792) One of the most important prehistoric sites in Britain, a stone circle and series of successive burial cairns that seems to have been used for around 3,000 years from Neolithic times to the first century BC, and especially during the second millennium BC. Extraordinary views from this raw and atmospheric hilltop site, known locally as 'windy ways'.

BEARSDEN NS5472 **Roman Bath House** (Roman Rd) Probably the best surviving visible Roman building in Scotland, built in the 2nd c for the garrison at Bearsden Fort, part of the Antonine Wall defences; free. The appropriately named Fifty-Five BC (Drymen Rd) has decent food, as does the Beefeater (Station Rd).

! **BIGGAR** NT0437 Several good museums here: with admission to one you get a 20% discount to all the others. **Gladstone Court Museum** (North Back Rd) Houses an entire reconstructed village street (cl am Sun, and all mid-Oct–mid-May; £1.80). **Greenhills Covenanters House** (North Back Rd) 17th-c farmhouse originally at Wiston but moved piece by piece and reassembled here, with rare breeds of sheep and poultry (cl am, and all mid-Oct–mid-May; £1). **Moat Park Heritage Centre** Good local history collections, and the centrepiece of the town's several worthwhile museums (cl am Sun, and all mid-Oct–Easter; £2.40). **Gasworks** (Gasworks Rd) This striking old building is now a museum on the coal-gas industry (open pm Jun–Sept; £1). **Biggar Puppet Theatre** (just off the A702) Very jolly; when they're not doing shows they sometimes do backstage tours. Teas, shop, disabled access (tel first – they have to remove some seats in the theatre); cl 25 Dec, 1 Jan, and maybe winter Suns; (01899) 220631 for programme and booking; shows £4.40.

BLANTYRE NS6958 **David Livingstone Centre** (Station Rd, off the A724) The birthplace of the famous explorer, with a museum on his life and work. An African pavilion looks at the continent today, with contemporary crafts, and there's an adventure playground in the landscaped grounds. Meals, snacks, shop, some disabled access; cl am Sun, and limited opening Nov–Mar – best to check first then; (01698) 823140; £2.95. The Cricklewood at Bothwell (on the B7071) is a good dining pub.

BUTE NS0864 This popular Glasgow holiday island is a ½-hour ferry trip from Wemyss Bay/Skelmorlie; a mix of fresh air and ebullient summer entertainments. In Rothesay the island's main town the seafront Black Bull has good food. There's lovely open country in the N, and its southern tip is rewarding too, with the **Monastery of St Blane**, a ruined Norman chapel in a delightful spot, a short way uphill from the road – just sheep and the occasional walker. **Mount Stuart House & Gardens** (off the A844, just E of Upper Scoulag) In this bracingly bleak landscape, the spectacular Victorian 'gothick' mansion is quite a shock; the elaborate rooms are splendidly over the top too. The 300 acres of landscaped grounds and woodland include several pretty gardens, as well as a pinetum of mature conifers and a nicely isolated stretch of sandy beach, reached via a lime tree avenue. Meals, snacks, shop, disabled access; cl Tues, Thurs, and Oct–Apr; (01700) 503877; £6, garden only £3.50. Scotrail do a special ticket (£15) inc entrance and train, ferry and bus travel from Glasgow. Rothesay has a 13th-c **castle** (cl am Sun, and in winter pm Thurs and all day Fri; £1.80), and a decent **museum** on Stuart St (cl Sun exc summer pms, and Mon Oct–Mar; £1.20). The gents' at the harbour, built in 1899, has ornate wall tiles and fine ceramic mosaic floors. There are grand sea views from the Kames Inn, which has food all day.

CAERLAVEROCK CASTLE NY0265 13th-c, protected not just by its moat but by the wild swampy marshes around it, it has an unusual triangular inner courtyard, and elaborate projecting tops for dropping missiles on assailants. Snacks, shop, some disabled access; cl 12.30–1.30pm Nov–Mar, 25–26 Dec, 1–2 Jan; (01387) 770244; £2.30. **Wildfowl & Wetlands Trust** The salt marshes are a reserve with outstanding hide facilities and observation towers. Countless wildfowl flock here, especially barnacle geese; between Oct and Apr there are generally around 13,000 of them, very dramatic when they're all in flight. Snacks, shop, some disabled access; cl 25 Dec; (01387) 770200; £3.25 – discounts if you turn up by bike, foot or public transport. The Nith at Glencaple has good-value food.

CARDONESS CASTLE NX5955 (on the A75) Well preserved 15th-c 4-storey tower house, overlooking the Water of Fleet; interesting fireplaces. Shop; cl winter wkdys; (01557) 814427; £1.80. A mile NE, Gatehouse of Fleet has places to eat.

CASTLE DOUGLAS NX7560 **Threave Garden** (1m W off the A75) The National Trust for Scotland's horticulture school, with plenty to see all year in its walled garden and glasshouses; in spring, don't miss the massed display of over 200 varieties of daffodil. Meals, snacks, shop, some disabled access; visitor centre cl Nov–Mar; (01556) 502575; £4; NTS. The Royal Hotel has good-value food. **Threave Castle** (off the minor road from Bridge of Dee–Townhead) The

Black Douglas, Archibald the Grim, built this in the 14th c; 4 storeys high, it stands on an islet in the River Dee and you have to get a ferry across (ring the bell and the custodian will come to get you). Shop; cl Oct–Mar; (0831) 168512; £1.80, inc ferry.

CLARENCEFIELD NY0669 **Comlongon Castle** (on the B725) 15th-c, unusually well preserved and recently carefully renovated, with interesting original features inc dungeons, kitchen, great hall and even privies; cl pm; (01387) 870283; £2.

COATBRIDGE NS7265 **Summerlee Heritage Trust** (West Canal St) Ambitious centre looking at the local iron, steel and engineering industries. Lots going on, spread over 25 acres of a former iron works; the din from the working machines creates a real feeling of authenticity. Meals, snacks, shop, limited disabled access; cl 25–26 Dec, 1–2 Jan; (01236) 431261; free (tram 60p). **Time Capsule** (Buchanan St) Fun – swimming pools and leisure centre with a loose historic theme: water chutes whizz you through the origins of man, and a woolly mammoth holds court in the centre of the ice rink; (01236) 449572.

★ **CRAMOND** NT1877 Charming preserved former fishing village, the once-humble cottages now snapped up by Edinburgh's professionals. **Lauriston Castle** Interesting, with mostly Edwardian décor and antiques; cl Fri, and wkdys Nov–Mar; (0131) 336 2060; £4. There's a pleasant walk from the Cramond Brig Hotel NT1775 (on the A90) along the wooded River Almond valley to Cramond; cross the Almond by ferry, then go along the shore past Dalmeny House, and finish below the Forth Bridge at South Queensferry. There are frequent buses back to the start, and to Edinburgh.

CREETOWN NX4759 **Gem Rock Museum** (Chain Rd) Enormous private collection of gemstones and minerals, some displayed in an atmospheric crystal cave. Also an unusual fossilised dinosaur egg. Snacks, shop, disabled access; cl wkdys Dec–Feb; (01671) 820357; £2.75.

CULZEAN CASTLE NS2310 (pronounced 'Cullane') A day here is one of the most popular outings in the region. The 18th-c mansion is one of great presence and brilliance, and the 563 acres of grounds are among the finest in Britain, lushly planted and richly ornamental, with woods, lake, an abundance of paths, bracing clifftop and shoreline walks, and an 18th-c walled garden. The house was splendidly refashioned by Robert Adam, and has been well restored to show off his work to full effect. Meals, snacks, shop, disabled access; house open Easter–Oct, park all year; (01655) 760274; £6.50 park and castle, £3.50 park only; NTS. You can stay in rather smart self-contained apartments on the top floor.

DALKEITH NT3167 **Edinburgh Butterfly & Insect World** (Dobbies Nursery, off the A720 at the Gilmerton junction) Gloriously coloured exotic butterflies, as well as scorpions and tarantulas, bee garden, and rainforest frogs. Handling sessions mean you can get even closer to some of the animals. Meals, snacks, shop, disabled access; cl 25–26 Dec, 1–2 Jan; (0131) 663 4932; £3.75. The Sun (Lothianbridge – on the A7 S) has good-value food.

DIRLETON CASTLE NT5184 (on the A198) Grandly rebuilt after a siege in 1298, only to be destroyed again in 1650. It has a charming garden planted in the 16th c, with ancient yews and hedges around a bowling green; cl am Sun, 25–26 Dec, 1–2 Jan; (01620) 850330; £2.30. The Castle Hotel and Open Arms in this pleasant golfing village are both good for lunch.

DRYBURGH ABBEY NT5932 Remarkably complete ruins of one of David I's monasteries, in a lovely setting among old cedars by the River Tweed – its graceful cloisters are very peaceful. Walter Scott is buried here (and on the B6356 N **Scott's View** is idyllic). Shop, some disabled access; cl am Sun, 25–26 Dec, 1–2 Jan; (01835) 822381; £2.30. The Buccleuch Arms at St Boswells is a civilised place for something to eat.

DUMBARTON CASTLE NS4074 (on the A82) Perched on a rock 73 metres (240ft) above the River Clyde, with dramatic views of the surrounding countryside. Most of what can be seen dates from the 18th and 19th c, though there are some earlier remains. Snacks, shop; open daily in summer, cl winter am Sun, pm Thurs and all day Fri, 25–26 Dec, 1–2 Jan; (01389) 732167; *£1.80. The Ettrick in the picturesque Clydeside village of Old Kilpatrick has good-value food.

DUMFRIES NX9775
Another place with close Burns connections (you can get a ticket covering all the related attractions). **Robert Burns Centre** (Mill Rd) Exhibition and audio-visual display, as well as an interesting scale model of the town at the time he wrote. Snacks, shop, disabled access; cl 1–2pm in winter, am Sun (all day in winter), and winter Mons; (01387) 264808; £1.20 for audio-visual exhibition. **Burns House** (Burns St) Where he lived for the 3 years before his death, with original letters and manuscripts, and the chair in which he wrote his last poems and songs. Shop; cl am Sun (all day in winter), winter lunchtimes and winter Mons; (01387) 255297; free. The **Globe Tavern** (off the High St) has 2 rooms still very much as they were when this was his regular haunt (Anna Park, a barmaid here, bore his child). **Burns Mausoleum** (St Michael's churchyard) Neatly rounding off the tale is this tomb of Robert Burns, his on-and-off wife Jean Armour, and their 5 sons; you can usually make an appointment to visit at the Burns House. **Dumfries Museum** (Church St) In the tower of an 18th-c windmill, this has a **camera obscura** and local history. Shop; cl am Sun (all day in winter), winter lunchtimes and winter Mons; camera obscura cl Oct–Mar; (01387) 253374; museum free, camera obscura £1.20.

DUNBAR NT6779 Pretty harbour, picturesquely jagged fragments of the medieval castle in the John Muir Country Park, and pleasant walks nearby, along the cliffs and by the marshy inlets of Belhaven Bay; the Eagle is good value. Quite a few decent clean beaches near here, notably Belhaven, nearby Whitesands Bay, and the one at Thorntonloch a few miles down the coast.

DUNDRENNAN ABBEY
NX7547 (on the A711) Ruined Cistercian abbey famous as the place Mary, Queen of Scots is thought to have spent her last night in Scotland; cl am Sun, winter wkdys; (01557) 500262; £1.50.

DUNS NT8155
Manderston (2m E, off the A6105) Splendidly lavish house built for the plutocrat racecourse owner Sir James Miller; he told the architect to spare no expense, so ended up with the world's only silver staircase. Other gloriously extravagant parts are the painted ceilings, and a ballroom decorated in Miller's racing colours. Also fine formal gardens, and an unusual biscuit-tin museum. Teas, shop, limited disabled access; open pm Thurs and Sun mid-May–Sept; (01361) 883450; £5, £2.50 grounds only. The Wheatsheaf at Swinton isn't far, for a very good meal. **Crumstane Farm Park** just across the road is a cheerful place well liked by children; cl Tues and all Oct–Easter; (01361) 883268; *£2. Off the A6112 is **Edin's Hall Broch**, one of very few such Iron Age strongholds in the Lowlands.

EAST FORTUNE NT5578
Museum of Flight (East Fortune Airfield, on the B1347) Good range of aircraft, with 35 aeroplanes from a Spitfire to a Vulcan bomber, and displays on famous flyers and air traffic control. Snacks, shop, disabled access; cl wknds Nov–Mar; (01620) 880308; £3.

EAST LINTON NT5875 **Hailes Castle** (on a minor rd SW) Another brief stopping point for Mary, Queen of Scots, now in ruins, but lovely in spring, with wild flowers along the stream; free. **Preston Mill** (on the B1407) One of the oldest working water-driven oatmeal mills surviving in Scotland. It's a pretty spot with geese and ducks, and an old dovecot nearby. Snacks, shop, limited disabled access; cl 1–2pm, am Sun, wkdys in Oct, and all Nov–Apr; (01620) 860426; £2; NTS. The Drovers Inn has good food.

ELLISLAND FARM
NX9283 (off the A76) Robert Burns lived here from 1788 to 1791, trying unsuccessfully to introduce new farming methods. There are displays of material associated with the poet (who

wrote *Tam o' Shanter* and *Auld Lang Syne* while living here), and cattle and sheep wander around much as they must have done then. Lovely riverside walk. Shop, some disabled access; cl am Sun, and in winter all day Sun and Mon; (01387) 740426; *£1.50.

★ ! **ESKDALEMUIR** NY2597 Beautifully set mountain village, famous for its cruel winter weather; it also has an unexpected Tibetan Buddhist temple and monastery.

EYEMOUTH NT9464 Understated family holiday seaside town around busy but pretty fishing harbour, with a decent beach, and a good local history **museum** with a magnificent tapestry commemorating the great east coast fishing disaster of 1881 when 189 fishermen were lost at sea (cl am Sun and pm too in Oct, all Nov–Easter; £1.75). The Ship overlooking the harbour has reasonable food.

FIRTH OF FORTH NT4682 Excellent shoreside walks along the sands from Aberlady to North Berwick, with stop-off possibilities at Dirleton and Gullane; a good bus service connects the shoreside villages between North Berwick and Edinburgh, though the hinterland is dull.

GALLOWAY FOREST PARK NX3672 Attractive and easily accessible, taking in around 100 lochs, 300 miles of river, great views, and thousands of hectares of forest, mountain and moorland. Many of the trees are fairly recent replantings, the original woodland having from the 15th c onwards fallen victim to the demand for timber. Many of the lochs are ringed by waymarked walks and trails, and there are plenty of scenic drives and cycle routes. Visitor centres (open Apr–Sept) at Kirroughtree, Glen Trool (Merrick NX4285, the highest point in south-west Scotland, is a worthwhile but long and strenuous walk up from here) and Clatteringshaws all have exhibitions and information to help you make the most of the forests, inc details of where you can camp or fish, and the best places to spot wildlife. Stones mark 14th-c battles between Scotland and England, and the 1680s Killing Time, when Scottish covenanters were hunted down and killed in the government's attempts to impose bishops on the Scottish church. There are particularly attractive trails around **Loch Trool** NX4180, and a memorial stone here commemorates a 1307 battle between Robert the Bruce and the armies of Edward I. The Wood of Cree NX3771 is one of the best surviving stretches of ancient forest, with an **RSPB reserve** among its trees and marshes.

GLENLUCE ABBEY NX1858 Ruined Cistercian abbey founded in the late 12th c, in beautiful surroundings. Limited disabled access; cl am Sun, and usually wkdys Oct–Mar; (01581) 300541; £1.50.

GOGAR NT1770 **Suntrap Garden & Advice Centre** (off the A8 nr Edinburgh Airport) Splendidly informative as well as sumptuous to look at, with several different gardens (Italian, Japanese, rock, peat, herbaceous and woodland), and free advice and tips. Plant sales (wkdys only); cl wknds Oct–Mar; (0131) 339 7283; *£1; NTS. The Bridge at Ratho is a good canalside family dining pub.

GORDON NT6439 **Mellerstain House** (just W, off the A6089) William and Robert Adam both worked on this striking Georgian house, which has impressive plasterwork and furnishings, and paintings by Van Dyck and Gainsborough. Every house in Scotland seems to have something that belonged to Bonnie Prince Charlie – this one has his bagpipes. Very pleasant terraced gardens and parkland, with fine views towards the distant hills. Meals, snacks, shop; cl am, all day Sat, and Oct–Apr; (01573) 410225; *£4.50. The Gordon Arms has decent food.

GREENOCK CUT NS2472 Part of an elaborate abandoned water scheme for Greenock below, this allows a level walk meandering around a hillside terrace giving views into the Highlands.

! **GRETNA GREEN** NY3167 Though a surprising number of people still come to be wed in this little village, it's more tourists than runaway couples now that flock to the Old Blacksmith's Shop. More people come here than to just about any other Scottish attraction outside Edinburgh, despite the fact that there's really very little to see. An exhibition centre looks at the village's marriage story; cl 25 Dec, 1 Jan; (01461) 338224; £1.50.

GREY MARE'S TAIL NT1814 Spectacular **waterfalls**, a pretty walk from the A708 car park NE of Moffat, up a narrow glen. You can continue beyond them along Tail Burn to Loch Skeen.

★ **HADDINGTON** NT5173 A pretty market town; the comfortable George and Maitlandfield House hotels, and the aptly named Waterside Inn, all have above-average food. **Lennoxlove** (on the B6369, 1 m S) The Duchess of Lennox (La Belle Stuart) gave this old house its unusual name in memory of her dead husband. Among reminders of other members of her family are the casket and death mask of Mary, Queen of Scots. In the grounds the Cadzow herd of white park cattle are said to be descended from the sacrificial cattle of the Druids. Meals, snacks; open pm Wed, Sat and Sun Easter–Oct; (01620) 823720; £3.50.

HAWICK NT5014 **Drumlanrig's Tower** (Towerknowe) Fearsome-looking 16th-c tower with state-of-the-art displays of Borders history, some quite gripping. Shop, disabled access; cl Nov–Mar; (01450) 377615; £2. **Hawick Museum** (Wilton Lodge Park) Made considerably more appealing by its setting, a park with riverside walks and gardens; cl 12.30–1.30pm, am Sat and all day Sun; (01450) 373457; £1.25.

HERMITAGE CASTLE NY4995 Almost perfect from the outside, the well restored but very forbidding remains of a 14th-c Borders stronghold reeking of dire deeds. Shop; cl am Sun, and all Nov–Mar; (01387) 376222; £1.50.

INNERLEITHEN NT3336 **Robert Smail's Printing Works** (High St) Fully restored Victorian printer's shop, with water-powered press; you can try your hand at metal typesetting and hand-print your own bookmark. Shop, limited disabled access; cl 1–2pm, am Sun, and all Oct–Apr (exc Oct wknds); (01896) 830206; £2.40; NTS. The Traquair Arms is the place to eat.

IRVINE NS3238 **Glasgow Vennel Art Gallery & Burns Heckling Shop** Art gallery and museum, and behind, a reconstruction of the Heckling Shop where, as a young man, an unwilling Burns tried to learn the filthy trade of flax dressing. Happily for him, during a New Year's Eve party his aunt knocked over a candle and burnt the building to ashes. Disabled access; cl 1–2pm, all day Sun, Mon (exc Jun–Sept), Weds; (01294) 275059; free. **Scottish Maritime Museum** (Gottries Rd) Down by the harbour, very much a working museum, with lots of restoration work on the good range of historic vessels. Snacks, shop, some disabled access (not to boats); cl Nov–Mar; (01294) 278283; £2. The nearby Keys has decent food (all day wknds).

JEDBURGH NT6521 **Jedburgh Abbey** The most complete of the ruined 12th-c Borders monasteries founded by David I, and an impressive sight, despite its town setting. Imposing 26-metre (86-ft) tower, splendid west door, and audio-visual show in visitor centre. Snacks, shops, disabled access; cl am Sun, 25–26 Dec, 1–2 Jan; (01835) 863925; £2.80. **Mary Queen of Scots House** (Queen St) Charming 16th-c fortified dwelling where Mary had to prolong her 1566 stay because of a near-mortal fever (she was later to say she wished she'd died here). There's a good interpretation of her life. Shop; cl Dec–mid-Mar; (01835) 863331; £2. **Castle Jail** (Castlegate) Now a local history museum (cl am Sun, and all Nov–mid-Mar; *£1.25). The Pheasant has good food (and makes a point of having good-value pheasant in season). Just off the A68 S of town are the ruins of **Ferniehurst Castle**.

★ **KELSO** NT7233 The town is attractive to wander round, and its Sept ram sales are altogether more fun than you could imagine. The Cobbles (Beaumont St) and Queen's Head (Bridge St) both have good food. **Kelso Abbey** The greatest and wealthiest of the 4 famous Borders abbeys, though today not much of the building remains.

Floors Castle (1 m NW) Magnificent building designed by William Adam in 1721, much embellished in the next century, and Scotland's biggest inhabited house, with a window for each day of the year. Splendid collection of tapestries and French furniture, and wonderful walled garden (best July–Sept). Good home-made meals and snacks, shop, disabled access; cl Nov–Apr; (01573) 223333; £4.50.

KILMARNOCK NS4339 **Dean Castle** (off Glasgow Rd) Very well restored family home, with a wonderful collection of medieval arms and armour, musical instruments, tapestries, and a display of Burns's manuscripts. It's surrounded by 200 acres of woodland, with nature trails, deer park, riding and other activities. Snacks, shop; cl am, and wkdys Oct–Mar; (01563) 522702; £2.50. The 18th-c Wheatsheaf in the pretty village of Symington on the other side of town has good original food.

★ **KIPPFORD** NX8355 Charming yachting place, usually plenty to watch in summer.

KIRKBEAN NX9857 **Arbigland Gardens** (off the A710) Extensive woodland, formal and water gardens based around a lovely sandy bay. The US Admiral John Paul Jones worked here as a boy (his father was the gardener), and his birthplace nearby has been turned into a little museum. Snacks, shop, some disabled access; cl am, all day Mon exc bank hols, and all Oct–Apr; (01387) 880283; *£2. The Steamboat at Carsethorne has good home cooking and sea views.

LANGBANK NS3673 **Finlaystone** (on the A8, 1m W) Some say the garden here is the finest in Scotland – formal and walled, with woodland walks and adventure playgrounds. They have recently renovated some of the greenhouses, making them more accessible to the disabled. The house has connections with Robert Burns and John Knox (unlikely partners), as well as displays of dolls, Victorian flower books and Celtic art. Snacks (summer only), shop, disabled access; gardens open all year, house pm Sun Apr–Aug; (01475) 540505; £2.50, house £1.20 extra. The modern Langbank Lodge nearby has sensibly priced food (inc afternoon tea and scones) and incredible Clyde views.

☺ **LARGS** NS2059 The pick of the traditional Clydeside resorts, with boats across the narrow strip of water to the island of Great Cumbrae. The pleasure steamer *Waverley* (see Glasgow entry, above) calls here in summer, and Nardinis (Esplanade) is a vintage tearoom – or rather tea palace, with acres of immaculate tables and smartly aproned motherly waitresses. **Vikingar!** (Barrfields Centre, Greenock Rd) Lively look at the Vikings in Scotland, from their arrival to their defeat at the Battle of Largs. Very much an 'experience', with lots of interactive displays, and a multi-media show as the centrepiece. There's an adjacent swimming pool. Meals, snacks, shop, disabled access; cl 25–26 Dec, 1–2 Jan; (01475) 689777; £3.50.

LAUDER NT5347 **Thirlestane Castle** (off the A697) Charming old castle with recently restored assemblage of pictures, interesting collection of old toys (some which children can touch), and outstanding plasterwork in the 17th-c state rooms. The bedchamber was opened for the first time in 1998. Snacks, shop; open pm Easter wk, then pm Weds, Thurs, Sun and Mon May–Sept, and pm daily (exc Sat) July and Aug; (01578) 722430; £4, grounds only £1.50. The Eagle and Lauderdale Hotel are useful for lunch.

LINLITHGOW PALACE NT0077 The birthplace of Mary, Queen of Scots, a magnificently sombre lochside ruin. You can still see the chapel, great hall and a quadrangle with fountain. Shop, limited disabled access; (01506) 842896; £2.30. In the town a pleasant old tavern, the Four Marys, is named for her maids-in-waiting Mary Livingstone, Mary Fleming, Mary Beaton and Mary Seton, with relevant memorabilia. **House of the Binns** (3m E, off the A904) The home of the Dalyell family since the 17th c, with some splendid plaster ceilings and a varied collection of furniture and porcelain. Limited disabled access; cl am, all day Fri, and Oct–Apr; (01506) 834255; £3.70; NTS.

LIVINGSTON NT0366 **Almond Valley Heritage Centre** (off the A705) Friendly 16-acre museum, with lots to see inc working farm, watermill, and underground shale mine. Also trailer rides (summer wknds and summer hols), adventure playground, and demonstrations of milking and other seasonal activities. Meals, snacks, shop, disabled access; cl 25–26 Dec, 1–2 Jan; (01506) 414957; £2.20.

LOCHWINNOCH NATURE CENTRE NS3558 (Largs Rd) RSPB bird reserve with fine views, good woodland and marsh nature trails, and several observation hides – one specially for disabled visitors. Wknd snacks (wkdys too July and Aug), shop, disabled access; cl Christmas and New Year; (01505) 842663; *£2. The Mossend is a useful dining pub.

MELROSE NT5434 The ruins of the **abbey** are among the finest in Britain – best in moonlight, as Scott says (though he admitted he never saw them thus himself). Look out for the wonderful stonework on the 14th-c nave (and the pig playing the bagpipes). Archaeological investigations now leave little doubt that this was the burial place of Robert the Bruce's heart. Shop; limited disabled access; cl am Sun, 25–26 Dec, 1–2 Jan; (01896) 822562; £2.80. The new **Harmony Garden** opposite has lovely views of the abbey and the Eildon Hills; cl am Sun, and all Oct–Mar; (01721) 722502; £1; NTS. **Priorwood Garden** (Abbey St) Specialises in flowers suitable for drying, with a herb garden and display orchard illustrating apples through the ages. Shop, disabled access; cl am Sun, and 24 Dec–Easter; (01896) 822493; £1; NTS. **Teddy Melrose** (they will admit 2 children free with each voucher; must be accompanied by 2 paying adults) (The Wynd) Unusually comprehensive and informative teddy bear museum, with resident bear-maker. Snacks (inc award-winning coffee), shop, disabled access; cl 1–2pm, all day Thurs and all Oct–May; (01896) 823854; *£1.50 Besides the Burts Hotel, the Kings Arms is useful for lunch. **Abbotsford House** (on the B6360, 3m W) Set grandly on the River Tweed, this was Walter Scott's home until his death in 1832. You can still see his mammoth 9,000-volume library, and several of the historical oddities he liked to collect, like Rob Roy's sporran. Snacks, shop, disabled access; cl am Sun (Mar–May and Oct), plus all Nov–mid-Mar; (01896) 752043; £3.50. **Eildon Hills** Above the town, these are splendidly compact, giving a very pleasing ridge walk along the top.

MERVINSLAW NT6713 **Jedforest Deer & Farm Park** (on the A68) Working hill farm with deer as well as other animals inc hawks and several rare breeds. Good for children, and peaceful walks and trails nearby. Snacks, shop, some disabled access; cl mid-Oct–Apr; (01835) 840364; £3.

MOFFAT NT0804 Tweedhope Sheepdog Centre (Hamerlands Farm, Selkirk Rd) Friendly place with demonstrations of working sheepdogs (11am and 3pm), and an exhibition. Shop, some disabled access; open wkdys Apr–Oct (wknds by appointment); (01683) 221471; *£2.50. The small town nearby still has some of the poise of its former days as a spa; the Black Bull, Star (Britain's narrowest hotel) and Moffat House Hotel all do decent food.

MULL OF GALLOWAY NX1530 Beautifully unspoilt, Scotland's south-west toe; good coastal walking.

NEW ABBEY NX9666 **Sweetheart Abbey** (on the A710) One of the most romantic ruins in the area, with a lofty arched nave open to the sky, and a touching story attached. Shop; cl am Sun, winter pm Thurs and all day Fri; (01387) 850397; £1.20. Abbey Cottage Tea Rooms here make a pleasant stop. **Shambellie House of Costume** (on the A710) Much extended in recent years, often dazzling displays of costume, thoughtfully arranged in appropriately furnished rooms. Shop; cl Nov–Mar; (01387) 850375; £2.50. The pretty village also has a restored 18th-c **corn mill**; cl winter am Sun, pm Thurs and all day Fri; (01387) 850260; £2.30. The summit of the **Criffel** just SW gives walkers an astonishing view of the English Lake District over the Solway Firth.

NEW LANARK NS8842 (off the A73) Founded in 1785 and now the subject of a major conservation programme, this is Scotland's best example of an industrial village, with plenty to keep families amused for a good chunk of the day. Many of the old millworkers' buildings have been interestingly converted to modern accommodation, so it's very much a living village rather than a museum. The village can be busy at wknds; try and visit during the week if you can. In Lanark itself the Crown (Hope St) has a decent restaurant. **New Lanark Visitor Centre** (off the A73) Award-winning dark ride looking at life here in the 1820s (lots of special effects), as well as various other displays and working machinery. Included in the visitor centre ticket are a nature reserve, craft workshops, and period shop and house; a little extra gets you a classic car collection, and Scotland's biggest model railway. Snacks, shop, disabled access; cl 25 Dec, 1–2 Jan; (01555) 661345; £3.75. **Falls of Clyde** The countryside around here is spectacular, with a short walk snaking around river cliffs through a verdant gorge to these falls that used to power the mill; a visitor centre here has lots of information on badgers (open pm wknds Nov–Easter, then daily till Oct; cl all Jan). The falls are dramatic when the hydro-electric station upriver opens the sluices.

NEWTONGRANGE NT3363 **Scottish Mining Museum** (Lady Victoria Colliery, on the A7) Vivid re-creation of mining days, both at the well restored pithead and back home, even in the tearooms. Home-baked snacks, shop, limited disabled access; cl Nov–Mar; (0131) 663 7519; *£3.

OLD DAILLY NS2401 **Bargany Gardens** Fine ornamental trees, woodland walks winding through springtime glades of snowdrops, bluebells and daffodils, and a lily pond enveloped by azaleas and rhododendrons. Disabled access; cl Nov–Mar; (01465) 871249; donations.

! PAISLEY NS4863 **Museum & Art Gallery** (High St) Paisley is not just a place but a pattern, so as well as a very wide range of 19th-c art, the appealing museum has a marvellous collection of antique and more modern Paisley shawls, along with the looms on which they were made. Shop, some disabled access; cl am Sun and all day Mon (exc bank hols); (0141) 889 3151; free. The Anchor (Glasgow Rd) does decent lunches. **Coats Observatory** (High St) Displays on astronomy, meteorology and space flight. Shop; cl am Mon, Tues, and Thurs (open till 7.45pm these days), and all day Sun and bank hols; (0141) 889 2013; free.

PAXTON HOUSE NT9352 (on the B6461) Built in 1758 by the lovestruck Patrick Billie, who hoped to marry a daughter of Frederick the Great; the marriage never took place, but the result was a splendid neo-Palladian mansion, designed and later embellished by the Adam family, and furnished by the Chippendales. Also woodland and riverside walks, huge herd of Highland cattle, and adventure playground designed by the Territorial Army. Meals, snacks, shop, disabled access; cl Nov–Mar, plus house cl am; (01289) 386291; £4, £2 gardens only.

★ **PEEBLES** NT2540 Attractive if sedate Borders town, with quite a lot for visitors; the old-fashioned Tontine Hotel has reliable food. **Neidpath Castle** (off the A72 just W) Spectacularly set, converted from the original 14th-c tower in the late 16th and early 17th c. There's a rock-hewn well, small museum (children like the mummified rat), period kitchen, and a pit prison – not much chance of escape, as some of the walls are 3½ metres (11ft) thick. Super views from the parapets. The castle was used for the filming of the recent film version of *King Lear* with Brian Blessed. Shop, limited disabled access; cl am Sun, and all Oct–Easter; (01721) 720333; *£2.50. **Kailzie** (on the B7062, 2m SE) Extensive grounds with lovely old trees flanked by azaleas and rhododendrons, formal rose garden, walled garden, and small art gallery. Meals, snacks, shop, disabled access; restaurant and gallery cl Nov–Easter; (01721) 720007; *£2.50 (less in winter).

PENICUIK NT2360 **Edinburgh Crystal Visitor Centre** (Eastfield) Demonstrations of glass-blowing, cutting and engraving, with an exhibition on the crystal's history. Meals, snacks, shop, disabled access; tours Mon–Fri all year and wknds Apr–Sept (last wknd tour 2.30pm, wkdys 3.30pm), cl 25–26 Dec, 1–2 Jan; (01968) 675128; £2. They run a free minibus service from Waverley Bridge in Edinburgh (on the hour, Apr–Sept only). The Horseshoe out on the Peebles road is a civilised dining pub.

PENTLAND HILLS NT1558 Within easy reach of Edinburgh, genuine uplands with some good high-level walks and attractive reservoirs.

PORT LOGAN NX0942 **Logan Botanic Garden** (off the B7065) A specialist garden of the Royal Botanic Garden of Edinburgh, containing a wide range of plants from the warm temperate regions of the southern hemisphere. Snacks, shop, plant sales, disabled access; cl Nov–Feb; (01776) 860231; £2. The village itself has a natural sea pool where fat fish will eat from your fingers; the Inn does good food.

★ **PORTPATRICK** NW9954 Attractive harbour town, usually with something going on down by the water.

PRESTONPANS NT3874 **Industrial Heritage Museum** (on the B1348 Prestongrange Rd) Based around the oldest documented coal-mining site in Britain. Reconstructed coalface and colliery workshop, as well as displays on other local industries, from brick and pipe making to brewing and weaving. Lots going on, especially at wknds. Snacks, shop, disabled access; cl late Oct–Mar; (0131) 653 2904; free.

RHINNS OF GALLOWAY NX0650 This hammerhead of land in the extreme W of the area is largely empty even in high summer, a very peaceful place, with cliffs (especially on the southern point), rocks and small coves.

RHINNS OF KELLS NX7274 This ridge has energetic hill walking from Forrest Lodge NW of New Galloway.

★ **ROCKCLIFFE** NX8453 Attractive yachting village, with a good peaceful walk to Castle Hill Point headland, and beyond by vast stretches of tidal sands.

★ **ST ABBS** NT9167 A steep and pretty little seaside village on the east coast, with a sandy beach and old fishing harbour, little used now. **St Abb's Head** The best of the east-coast scenery for walkers; walk from Eyemouth or St Abbs, with a good path along the cliffs – noisily crowded with breeding seabirds in late spring, and there's a **lighthouse**.

ST MARY'S LOCH NT2320 A pretty spot for walks, tracked by the Southern Upland Way along its east shore; the Tibbie Shiels Inn is a handy stop.

SELKIRK NT4628 A decorous town, good for bargain-hunting for the tweeds, woollens and cashmeres which are woven and knitted here; the Queen's Head has freshly cooked food. There's an exhibition on Walter Scott in the former courtroom where, as sheriff, he dispensed justice (cl am Sun and all Nov–Mar, *£1); not that gripping, but easily combined with Abbotsford nr Melrose. **Selkirk Glass** (off the A7 just N) Demonstrations of paperweight-making; snacks, factory shop; cl am Sun, no glass-making wknds; (01750) 20954; free. **Bowhill House** (off the A708, 3m W) Outstanding collection of paintings, inc works by Canaletto, Van Dyck, Gainsborough and Claude, as well as impressive furnishings and porcelain, and memorabilia relating to Scott and Queen Victoria. Also restored Victorian kitchen, adventure playground, very active little theatre, and surrounding country park. Snacks, shop, disabled access; grounds open pm May–Aug (exc Fri), house pm in July only; (01750) 22204; £4 house, £1 park.

SMAILHOLM NT6334 **Border Tower House** (just S, signed off the B6404 NE of St Boswells) Classic 15th-c Borders tower house, very well preserved – all 17 metres (57ft) of it. Display based on Walter Scott's book *Minstrels of the Borders*, and an exhibition of dolls. Shop; cl Oct–Mar; (01573) 460365; £1.80.

SOUTH QUEENSFERRY NT1378 Notable for its views of the 2 great Forth bridges on either side, with piers to potter on; the Hawes Inn, famous from *Kidnapped*, is still going strong. **Hopetoun House**

(off the B904, 2m W) This huge place is probably Scotland's best example of the work of William and Robert Adam. The magnificent reception rooms have a wonderful art collection with works by Canaletto and Gainsborough, while the superb grounds include a deer park and a flock of rare sheep. You can play croquet on the lawn, or climb to the rooftop for wonderful views. Meals, snacks, shop, some disabled access; cl Oct–Easter; (0131) 331 2451; £4.70, £2.50 grounds only. **Dalmeny House** (on the B924, 3m E) Despite its Tudor Gothic appearance, this splendidly placed house dates only from the 19th c – there's a superb hammerbeamed roof, as well as fine furnishings, porcelain and portraits. Good walks in the grounds and on the shore. Snacks, disabled access; open Mon, Tues and pm Sun, July–Aug; (0131) 331 1888; *£3.80. **Inchcolm Abbey** Out in the Forth (a lovely ½-hour seal-spotting ferry trip from Aberdour), this Augustinian abbey founded by Alexander I is better preserved than any other in Scotland, with a fine 13th-c octagonal chapter house and a wall painting from the same period. Ferries usually 11am, 1pm and 3pm, summer only, but best to check on (0131) 331 4857; £7.50 inc ferry.

STOBO NT1534 **Dawyck Botanic Garden** (on the B712) Another specialist garden of the Royal Botanic Garden, particularly noted for its arboretum rich in mature conifers (inc a larch believed to have been planted in 1725), with notable Asiatic silver firs and many rarities. Snacks, shop, limited disabled access; cl Nov–Feb; (01721) 760254; £3.

STRANRAER NX0760 **Castle Kennedy Gardens** (on the A75, 4m E) Prettily set between 2 lochs (with lots of good walks around), these gardens were first laid out in the early 18th c, then after years of neglect were restored and developed in the 19th. They're particularly admired for their walled garden and flowering shrubs. Snacks, shop, limited disabled access; cl Oct–Mar; (01776) 702024; £2.

THORNHILL NX8599 **Drumlanrig Castle** (off the A76) Spectacular and rather unusual pink sandstone castle built in the late 17th c, with a glory of fine panelling and furnishings (mainly Louis XIV), and splendid paintings by Leonardo, Holbein, Rembrandt and Murillo; you can see what's said to be Bonnie Prince Charlie's campaign kettle. Also craft workshops, adventure playground, peacocks wandering over the lawn, birds of prey, and extensive woodland walks. You can hire bikes. Snacks, shop, disabled access; cl Oct–Apr; (01848) 330248; £6.

TRAQUAIR HOUSE NT3336 (on the B709) One of the longest-inhabited and most romantic houses in Britain; no less than 27 English and Scottish kings have stayed here. The Bear Gates have stayed shut since

Days Out

Edinburgh's Old Town: From Edinburgh Castle, walk down the Royal Mile past the Camera Obscura and Gladstone's Land; walk along Victoria St, Grassmarket and Candlemaker Row; snack at Bannerman's Bar (Cowgate); Royal Museum of Scotland; rejoin the Royal Mile, and continue past John Knox's House and Canongate Tolbooth to Holyrood Palace; Our Dynamic Earth Centre; Arthur's Seat.

Some of Glasgow's contrasts: Burrell Collection, and Pollok House; snack at the Willow Tea Room (Sauchiehall St); Tenement House; City Chambers, perhaps the Gallery of Modern Art; if you have time, the People's Palace, then walk along the Clyde Walkway.

Kidnapped country: Hopetoun House, South Queensferry; lunch at the Hawes Inn there, and look at the Forth bridges; boat to Inchcolm Abbey.

1745 when Bonnie Prince Charlie passed through them for the last time – they won't open again unless the Stuarts regain their place on the throne. An 18th-c brewery still produces tasty beers; you can try them between 3 and 4pm on Fri Jun–Sept. Traquair is particularly popular with our contributors, and with a maze, art gallery, and antique and craft shops (best on Weds and Thurs) as well as the house and gardens, there's plenty to see. Meals, snacks, shop, some disabled access; cl am (exc Jun–Aug), and all Oct–mid-Apr (exc pm Fri-Sun in Oct); (01896) 830323; £4.50, grounds only £1.75. The Traquair Arms is good.

UDDINGSTON NS6862 **Glasgow Zoo** (Calderpark) Growing open-plan zoo, specialising in cats and reptiles (snake-handling every day), with other rare mammals and birds, children's farm, orienteering course, and wknd car boot sales. Falconry and parrot flying displays in winter; Snacks, shop, disabled access; cl 25 Dec; (0141) 771 1185; £4.50 (less in winter). **Bothwell Castle** Picturesquely set by the river: now ruined, but once the finest stone castle in Britain; in winter cl pm Thurs and all day Fri; £1.80.

WANLOCKHEAD NS8713 **Museum of Lead Mining** (on the B797) Guided tours of an 18th-c lead mine, heritage trail and miners' cottages furnished in the styles of 1740 and 1890. You can have a go at panning for gold. Meals, snacks, shop, limited disabled access; cl Nov–Mar; (01659) 74387; £3.50. This remote village is Scotland's highest.

★ **WHITHORN** NX4440 Scotland's first-recorded Christian settlement was established here by St Ninian 1,500 years ago. There have been several churches on the site since, the last of the line the ruined 13th-c priory you can see today. Archaeologists have been hard at work here for some time, and you can generally watch the dig's progress during the summer. An excellent visitor centre and museum have plenty of the finds, with some fine Celtic crosses. Shop, disabled access; museum and visitor centre cl Oct–Easter (though you may still be able to wander round the priory ruins then); (01988) 500508; £2.70. **Isle of Whithorn** NX4736 Picturesque mainland harbour with **boat trips** and lots of yachtsmen: the Steam Packet has good local fish.

★ **Other attractive villages** with decent pubs include Gifford NT5368, Kirkcowan NX3260, Kirkcudbright NX6851 (particularly enjoyable), Larkhall NS7651, Lilliesleaf NT5325, Sorn NS5526 and Symington NS3831. Pubs with a decent bite to eat and particularly well placed for walkers, drivers or just strollers in these parts include the Murray Arms, Masons Arms and Angel at Gatehouse of Fleet NX5956, Golf Hotel and Old Clubhouse at Gullane NT4882, Breadalbane Hotel at Kildonan NS0231, Swan at Kingholm Quay NX9773, Border at Kirk Yetholm NT8328, Gordon Arms at Mountbenger NT3125 and Buccleuch Arms at St Boswells NT5931.

Where to eat

BEARSDEN NS5472 **Fifty-Five BC** *128 Drymen Rd (0141) 942 7272* Friendly little place with reliably good, honest cooking, and pleasant staff; cl 1st Jan; disabled access. **£25**|£5.

EAST LINTON NT5977 **Drovers** *5 Bridge St (01620) 860298* Comfortable 18th-c inn with atmospheric and pubby main bar, prints and pictures for sale, cosy armchairs, a basket of logs by the woodburner, hops around the bar, very good interesting food (more elaborate in the evening), a good range of real ales, and partly no smoking upstairs restaurant; cl 25 Dec, 1 Jan. **£20.20**|£7.

EDINBURGH NT2473 **Atrium** *10 Cambridge St (0131) 228 8882* Next to Usher Hall and Traverse Theatre, unusually modern restaurant with wire sculptures, railway sleepers, dim lighting from glass torches, cheerful friendly staff, interesting wine list, and very good imaginative modern Scottish food – lunchtime snack menu, too; cl Sun, 10 days Christmas; disabled access. **£30**|£6.50.

EDINBURGH NT2672 **Kalpna** *2–3 St Patrick Sq (0131) 667 9890* Extremely good Indian restaurant with carefully cooked very fresh Gujerati vegetarian food (super lunchtime buffets) and efficient service; cl Sun and Christmas/New Year; disabled access. **£14.50**|£4.50.

EDINBURGH NT2776 **Ship on the Shore** *26 The Shore, Leith (0131) 555 0409* Lovely old pub with charming ship model for its hotel sign, a bar with old painted company signs, ship's lanterns and nautical equipment, popular food (especially the bargain 3-course lunches), plenty of fish and well liked Sunday breakfasts; children over 8. **3-course lunch £11**.

EDINBURGH NT2676 **Vintners Rooms** *The Vaults, 87 Giles St, Leith (0131) 554 6767* Bustling restaurant – former fine old saleroom, above ancient wine vaults – with most enjoyable French provincial cooking plus more modern dishes, super puddings, and a good wine list; you can also choose to eat in the more informal bar; cl Sun, 2 wks from Christmas; partial disabled access. **£35**|2-course lunch £11.

GLASGOW NS5667 **Di Maggios** *61 Ruthven Lane (0141) 334 8560* A Glasgow institution with good Italian and other food, and a cheerful atmosphere; cl Christmas–1 Jan; disabled access. **£16**|£5.50.

GLASGOW NS5965 **Rogano** *11 Exchange Pl (0141) 248 4055* Long-standing restaurant in splendid 1930s ocean liner style with quite an emphasis on fish – vegetarian and meaty dishes, too; Café Rogano (downstairs) is open all day for lighter meals. **£36 in restaurant, £22 in café**|£6.95.

GLASGOW NS5667 **Ubiquitous Chip** *12 Ashton Lane, Byres Rd (0141) 334 5007* Friendly and informal restaurant (no chips, hence the name) in Victorian coach house with interesting modern Scottish cooking, outstanding wines, and no smoking areas; disabled access; cl 25 Dec, 31 Dec, 1 Jan. **£28.60 lunch, £36.60 dinner**|£4.95. Upstairs is similar but less expensive.

GLASGOW NS5865 **Willow Tea Room** *217 Sauchiehall St (0141) 332 0521* Beautifully restored from the 1903 art deco original with careful reproductions of the stylish furniture, this tearoom (and the newly opened downstairs Gallery) has pastries and cakes, good sandwiches, toasties, filled croissants and bagels, and salads; herbal, fruit and loose teas, quite a choice of coffees, and milk shakes; cl 25 Dec, 1–2 Jan. £4.

GLASGOW NS5865 **Yes** *22 West Nile St (0141) 221 8044* Stylish bustling restaurant with a relaxed, if fashionable, feel, and very good modern cooking taking ideas from all over the world using first-class local produce; courteous service, and a short well chosen wine list; cl Sun, all public hols. **£31.50**|£18 2 courses.

HADDINGTON NT5173 **Waterside** *(01620) 825674* In a really lovely spot on a sunny day with a fine view across the water, this long 2-storey white house has 2 plush rooms, a woodburner, a more formal stripped-stone conservatory, very good bistro-style food, real ales, and a good range of wines. **£19.65**|£6.95.

LANARK NS8843 **La Vigna** *40 Wellgate (01555) 664320* Imaginative Italian menu with good basics, more imaginative dishes and lots of fresh fish; cl am Sun; disabled access. **£25.50**|£8.25.

LINLITHGOW NT0378 **Champany** *(01506) 834532* Wonderful Aberdeen Angus beef as well as lovely fresh fish (they also have their own smoke-house), home-made ice-creams, and good wines; cheaper bistro-style meals in their Chop & Ale House next door; children over 8 in restaurant; disabled access. **£30**|£14.50.

East Scotland

Plenty to see and do, with great variety of picturesque scenery.

The best scenery here is in the north: both Highland, and the valleys – the well known Spey, Dee and Don, and lesser-known places such as the Angus glens of Glen Clova, Glen Esk and Glen Isla. Further south, the Trossachs are a sort of Highlands in miniature, with lovely if small-scale landscapes of loch, river, forest, moor and mountain, but not the grandeur of the true Highlands. The coast is attractive, with appealing fishing villages in Fife, and a little-known but charming stretch from Nairn to Aberdeen, with good sands, quaint little coves and awesome cliffy crags such as Slains Castle and the nearby Bullers of Buchan.

The Blair Drummond safari park and Kincraig wildlife park are both excellent family outings, and other good varied family attractions include the deep-sea centre at North Queensferry, a very enjoyable new look at the past at Oyne, Landmark Park at Carrbridge, the lively science and technology centre in Aberdeen, the unique collection of great land birds and other creatures at Collessie, and (for some children at least) the Fraserburgh lighthouse museum. The new exploration of the jute industry in Dundee is surprisingly interesting; both this town and Aberdeen have lots to see, and the area has plenty of other rewarding days out, from a splendid range of historic smaller towns and villages to glorious castles, palaces and great houses.

The relatively few roads through the best parts do tend to make them feel crowded in high summer; to get a feeling of peace, June (when it's still light as midnight approaches) is much better.

Where to stay

ABERDEEN NJ9305 **Ferryhill House** *169 Bon Accord St, Aberdeen AB11 6UA (01224) 590867* **£75;** 9 rms. Well run small hotel with comfortable and spacious communicating bar areas, well over 100 malt whiskies, real ales, friendly staff, a wide choice of food in bar and restaurant and lots of tables on neat, well sheltered lawns.

ABERFELDY NN8249 **Farleyer House** *Aberfeldy, Perthshire PH15 2JE (01887) 820332* ***£150,** plus winter breaks; 19 pretty rms. Charming country house with fine Tay Valley views, log fires, antiques and flowers in library and drawing room, excellent food in airy and elegant restaurant and Scottish bistro; use of nearby leisure club; disabled access.

ALLOA NS8794 **Gean House** *Gean Park, Tullibody Rd, Alloa, Clackmannanshire FK10 2HS (01259) 219275* **£140,** plus special breaks; 7 luxury rms. Carefully restored mansion house in mature parkland with views of the Ochil Hills; elegant drawing room with inglenook fireplace, minstrels' gallery and marvellous windows, cosy library, and very good food in no smoking walnut-panelled dining room overlooking the rose garden.

ARDEONAIG NN6635 **Ardeonaig** *Ardeonaig, Killin, Perthshire FK21 8SU (01567) 820400* ***£87;** 14 rms. Extended 17th-c farmhouse on south shore of Loch Tay with log fire in snug and lounge, library with fine views, and good food using plenty of fish and game; salmon fishing rights on the loch – as well as fishing for trout and char – a drying and rod room, and boats and outboards; shooting and stalking can be arranged, lots of surrounding walks, and pony trekking; cl Nov–Mar.

AUCHTERARDER NN9211 **Gleneagles** *Auchterarder, Perthshire PH3 1NF (01764) 662231* **£260,** plus special breaks; 229 individually decorated rms. Grand hotel in lovely surroundings with attractive gardens and outstanding leisure facilities: golf courses (inc a championship one designed by Jack Nicklaus), shooting, riding, fishing, health spa, tennis, squash, bowling green, croquet and even falconry; comfortable, elegant high-ceilinged day rooms, a fine bar, exceptional service, pianists, good food using local produce (much is home-grown) in 4 restaurants; disabled access.

AVIEMORE NH8810 **Lynwilg House** *Lynwilg, Aviemore, Inverness-shire PH22 1PZ (01479) 811685* **£60;** 4 rms, 3 with own shower. Attractive quietly set 1930s-style house in 4 acres of landscaped gardens with open fire in spacious lounge, lovely breakfasts with their own free range eggs and home-baked bread, super dinners using home-grown produce, and charming friendly owners; plenty to do nearby; cl beginning Nov–28 Dec.

BALLATER NO3696 **Auld Kirk** *Braemar Rd, Ballater, Aberdeenshire AB35 5RQ (01339) 755762* ***£52,** plus winter breaks; 6 attractive rms. 19th-c church converted to a hotel in 1990, still with bell tower (the bell is in the main entrance), stained glass and exposed rafters; lacy dining room has original pillared pine ceiling, homely décor in public rooms with lots of knick-knacks, home cooking; cl 25 Dec–1 Jan.

BALLATER NO3696 **Balgonie Country House** *Braemar Pl, Ballater, Aberdeenshire AB35 5NQ (01339) 755482* ***£105,** plus special breaks. 9 pretty rms. Quietly set and spotless Edwardian house with fine views from 4 acres of mature gardens, particularly helpful friendly owners, fresh flowers, games and books in lounges, and most enjoyable food using the best local produce in charming dining room; cl Jan–mid-Feb; dogs by arrangement (away from public rooms).

BALQUHIDDER NN4318 **Monachyle Mhor** *Balquhidder, Lochearnhead, Perthshire FK19 8PQ (01877) 384622* ***£65;** 10 rms with fine views overlooking Voil and Doine lochs. Remote 18th-c farmhouse/hotel several miles W of Balquhidder on 2,000-acre estate with prettily furnished rooms and good food using own game and herbs; private fishing and stalking for guests; no children.

BLAIRGOWRIE NO1345 **Kinloch House** *Blairgowrie, Perthshire PH10 6SG (01250) 884237* ***£195 full board,** plus special breaks; 21 individually decorated rms. Creeper-covered 19th-c country house in 25 acres of parkland with Highland cattle and fine views; relaxed lounges, comfortable bar, pretty conservatory with lots of plants, and fine choice of carefully prepared food in an elegant dining room; popular sportsmen's room with own entrance, drying facilities, gun cupboard, freezer, game larder and so forth; cl 20–30 Dec; no children under 7 in dining room; disabled access.

BRIDGE OF CALLY NO1451 **Bridge of Cally** *Bridge of Cally, Blairgowrie, Perthshire PH10 7JJ (01250) 886231* **£55,** plus winter breaks; 9 rms. In an acre of grounds along the River Ardle, this former drovers' inn is a friendly family-run place with good-value home-made food using seasonal game in restaurant and comfortable bar; cl 25–26 Dec; pets welcome.

BRIDGE OF MARNOCH NJ5950 **Old Manse of Marnoch** *Bridge of Marnoch, Huntly, Aberdeenshire AB54 7RS (01466) 780873* ***£94,** plus special breaks; 9 light, well equipped rms, some in new wing. Neat Georgian country house in 3 acres of gardens on the River Deveron, with antiques in comfortable sitting room, a friendly and informal atmosphere, imaginative 4-course set dinner in elegant dining room, carefully chosen wine list, and superb breakfasts; liked by fishing people; cl 2 wks Nov; children over 12.

CALLANDER NN6208 **Poppies** *Leny Rd, Callander, Perthshire FK17 8AL (01877) 330329* ***£44,** plus special breaks; 8 rms. Small private hotel with excellent food in popular and attractive candlelit dining room, convivial bar with RAF theme, comfortable lounge, helpful friendly owners, and seats in the garden; cl Oct–end Mar; disabled access.

CALLANDER NN6208 **Roman Camp** *Main St, Callander, Perthshire FK17 8BG (01877) 330003* **£110,** plus special breaks; 14 individually decorated pretty rms with garden views. Extended over the years since it was built as a hunting lodge in 1625, this pink-painted turreted house has warm open fires and lovely fresh flowers, an elegant drawing room, tranquil library, very good food in candlelit dining room, and 20 acres of grounds; disabled access.

CRIANLARICH NN3726 **Allt-Chaorain Country House** *Crianlarich, Perthshire FK20 8RU (01838) 300283* ***£70,** plus special breaks; 7 rms. Comfortable small hotel with homely atmosphere, log fire in lounge, honesty bar, sunroom with marvellous views, and good home-cooked food in panelled dining room; lots of fishing, golf and walks nearby; cl 1 Nov–1 May; children over 7; disabled access.

DALCROSS NH7451 **Easter Dalziel Farm** *Dalcross, Inverness IV1 2JL (01667) 462213* ***£38,** plus special breaks; 3 rms with shared bthrm. Early Victorian farmhouse on 210 acres of family-run mixed farm (beef cattle and grain) with friendly helpful owners, log fire in lounge, good Scottish breakfasts in big dining room and – when farm commitments allow – evening meal using own beef, lamb and vegetables; holiday cottages, too; cl Christmas/New Year.

DUNBLANE NN7806 **Cromlix House** *Kinbuck, Dunblane, Perthshire FK15 9JT (01786) 822125* **£185,** plus special breaks; 14 rms inc 8 spacious suites. Walking, loch and river fishing or shooting on 3,000 acres around this rather gracious country house; relaxing day rooms with fine antiques and family portaits, an informal atmosphere, very good food using estate game and local meats and fish in 2 dining rooms, and courteous service; cl 2 Jan–1 Feb.

DUNKELD NN9849 **Kinnaird House** *Kinnaird Estate, Dunkeld, Perthshire PH8 0LB (01796) 482440* ***£235,** plus special breaks; 9 spacious, individually decorated rms. 18th-c country-house hotel on 9,000-acre estate with very restful civilised atmosphere in deeply comfortable antiques-filled rooms, lovely flowers, family mementos and pictures, log fires, good creative food in no smoking dining room with early 19th-c hand-painted frescos, and a fine wine list; excellent fishing on River Tay and 3 hill lochs, and shooting; cl Mon–Weds during Jan and Feb; children over 12.

EAST HAUGH NN9656 **East Haugh House** *East Haugh, Pitlochry, Perthshire PH16 5JS (01796) 473121* ***£58,** plus special breaks; 12 rms, 4 in converted bothy. Turreted stone house with lots of character, delightful conservatory bar, house-party atmosphere, helpful cheerful owners, and very good popular food inc local seafood and game in season; excellent shooting, stalking and salmon and trout fishing on surrounding local estates.

ELGIN NJ2163 **Mansion House** *The Haugh, Elgin, Moray IV30 1AW (01343) 548811* **£120,** plus special breaks; 22 rms. Relaxed and friendly Scottish baronial mansion with prettily furnished public rooms, fresh flowers, lovely food inc fine breakfasts, and good wine list; country club facilities; disabled access.

FINTRY NS6287 **Culcreuch Castle** *Fintry, Glasgow G63 0LW (01360) 860228* **£108,** plus special breaks; 10 individually decorated rms with lovely views. Scotland's oldest inhabited castle, nearly 700 years old, in beautiful 1,600-acre parkland and surrounding hills and moors, with log fires and antiques in the public rooms, good freshly prepared food in candlelit panelled dining room, and a friendly relaxed atmosphere; 8 modern Scandinavian holiday lodges, too.

GLENDEVON NN9904 **Tormaukin** *Glendevon, Dollar, Clackmannanshire FK14 7JY (01259) 781252* **£75,** plus special breaks; 10 rms, some in converted stable block. Comfortable neatly kept inn in good walking country, with loch and river fishing, lots of golf courses within reach, beamed dining room and softly lit bar, very good food (soup and coffee all day), and fine breakfasts; cl 2 wks early Jan; disabled access.

GLENROTHES NO2803 **Balbirnie House** *Balbirnie Park, Markinch, Glenrothes, Fife KY7 6NE (01592) 610066* **£170,** plus special breaks; 30 rms. Fine Georgian country house in 400-acre park landscaped in Capability Brown style, with fresh flowers, open fires and antiques in gracious public rooms, extremely good inventive food, and a big wine list; disabled access.

GRANTOWN-ON-SPEY NJ0227 **Culdearn House** *Woodlands Terrace, Grantown-on-Spey, Moray PH26 3JU (01479) 872106* ***£126 full board,** plus special breaks; 9 rms. Victorian granite stone house with homely décor and local watercolours, a friendly chatty atmosphere, and enjoyable Scottish food; packed lunches on request; cl 1 Nov–28 Feb; children over 10; disabled access.

INVERNESS NH6245 **Bunchrew House** *Bunchrew, Inverness IV3 6TA (01463) 234917* ***£110,** plus special breaks; 11 individually decorated rms. Warmly friendly 17th-c mansion W of town by Beauly Firth with fine views and landscaped gardens, log fire in the elegant panelled drawing room, and traditional cooking using local produce and local game and venison.

KINCLAVEN BY STANLEY NO1336 **Ballathie House** *Kinclaven by Stanley, Perth PH1 4QN (01250) 883268* **£150;** 38 pretty rms, some luxurious. On a vast estate with fine salmon fishing on the River Tay (special facilities for fishermen) and plenty of sporting opportunities, this turreted mansion has a comfortable and relaxed drawing room, separate lounge and bar, good enjoyable modern Scottish cooking, and tennis, croquet, and putting; disabled access.

KINGUSSIE NH7200 **Hermitage** *Spey St, Kingussie, Inverness-shire PH21 1HN (01540) 662137* **£40;** 5 rms. Welcoming house in large garden with fine Cairngorm views, log fires in comfortable lounge, enjoyable home-made set dinners, and hearty Scottish breakfasts; fishing, golf, walking, climbing and birdwatching close by; disabled access.

KINNESSWOOD NO1702 **Lomond Country Inn** *Main St, Kinnesswood, Kinross KY13 7HN (01592) 840253* ***£62;** 12 comfortable rms, 8 in an extension. Attractive little inn in the centre of the village with views across Loch Leven (nice sunsets), open fires, an informal bustling bar, well kept real ales, and good reasonably priced bar and restaurant food using local produce; disabled access.

KIRKTON OF GLENISLA NO2160 **Glenisla** *Kirkton of Glenisla, Blairgowrie, Perthshire PH11 8PH (01575) 582223* **£99 inc dinner,** plus special breaks; 6 rms. Attractively placed peaceful 17th-c coaching inn, prettily restored with natural unpainted wood throughout, happily unmatched furniture, bar with open fire and 2 real ales, good food, very attentive owners and a cheerful warm atmosphere; nice garden; cl 20–27 Dec; dogs welcome.

MONYMUSK NJ6815 **Grant Arms** *Monymusk, Inverurie, Aberdeenshire AB51 7HJ (01467) 651226* **£65;** 17 rms, some with own bthrm. Smart old inn with dark-panelled lounge bar divided in two by a log fire in the stub wall, simpler public bar, and exclusive right to 15 miles of good trout and salmon fishing on the River Don; ghillie available; disabled access.

NAIRN NH8756 **Clifton House** *Viewfield St, Nairn IV12 4HW (01667) 453119* ***£100,** plus special breaks; 12 individually decorated comfortable rms. Lovely, civilised, flower-filled old family hotel (the present owner has lived in this elegant Victorian house all his life and has been running it as a hotel since 1952), individually furnished with antiques, paintings and sculptures; extremely good food using local eggs, fish, meat and game, fine breakfasts with home-made jams, bread, and oatcakes, and an exceptional wine list; during the winter they stage some 20 concerts, plays and recitals; cl Christmas/New Year; pets welcome.

PEAT INN NO4509 **Peat Inn** *Peat Inn, Cupar, Fife KY15 5LH (01334) 840206* ***£140,** plus special breaks; 8 luxurious rms. Famous restaurant with rooms: beams and white plaster walls, log fires and comfortable sofas, friendly service, fine interesting food using the best local produce inc plenty of game and seafood, and an excellent wine list; cl Sun, Mon; disabled access.

PITLOCHRY NN9162 **Killiecrankie** *Pitlochry, Perthshire PH16 5LG (01796) 473220* **£100 inc dinner,** plus special breaks; 10 spotless rms. Comfortable country hotel in spacious grounds with putting course and croquet lawn, splendid mountain views, mahogany-panelled bar with stuffed animals and fine wildlife paintings, spacious sitting room with books and games, a relaxed atmosphere, very friendly owners, and excellent well presented food in elegant restaurant; cl Jan and Feb.

ROTHES NJ2650 **Rothes Glen** *Rothes, Elgin, Moray NV38 7AH (01340) 831254* **£110;** 16 individually decorated, spacious rms. Fine baronial mansion in 10 acres with fishing, croquet and putting, lots of original features in the tranquil public rooms, good modern Scottish cooking using local game and fish in attractive no smoking dining room, a fine wine list, and helpful friendly staff; children over 7.

SCONE NO1526 **Murrayshall House** *Scone, Perth PH2 7PH (01738) 551171* ***£120,** plus special breaks; 28 rms, plus lodge which sleeps 6. Handsome mansion in 300 acres of parkland, very popular with golfers (it has its own course); comfortable elegant public rooms, warm friendly staff, a relaxed atmosphere, imaginative food, good wines; dogs welcome; disabled access.

SPEAN BRIDGE NN2591 **Letterfinlay Lodge** *Spean Bridge, Inverness-shire PH34 4DZ (01397) 712622* **£76,** plus special breaks; 12 rms, most with own bthrm. Secluded and genteel family-run country house with picture window in extensive modern bar overlooking loch; elegantly panelled small cocktail bar, good popular food, friendly attentive service; grounds run down through rhododendrons to the jetty and Loch Lochy; fishing can be arranged; cl Nov–Mar.

SPITTAL OF GLENSHEE NO0971 **Dalmunzie House** *Spittal of Glenshee, Blairgowrie, Perthshire PH10 7QG (01250) 885224* **£94;** 18 rms, 16 with own bthrm. Old-fashioned former Victorian shooting lodge, off the A93, peacefully set in huge estate among spectacular mountains, plenty of walks within it, and own golf course; it has made a gentle transition to a hotel, keeping a family-run atmosphere, and serves good local food; cl end Nov–28 Dec; disabled access.

WHITEBRIDGE NH4413 **Knockie Lodge** *Whitebridge, Inverness IV1 2UP (01456) 486276* **£100,** plus special breaks; 10 rms. In a wonderful setting by Loch Knockie above Loch Ness, this Georgian hunting lodge has plenty of outside pursuits, a warmly friendly and relaxed house-party atmosphere, lovely flower arrangements, log and peat fires, antiques, and comfortable day rooms; delicious evening meals, and super breakfasts; billiards; cl Nov–Apr; children over 10; dogs by prior arrangement.

To see and do

Scotland Family Attraction of the Year

Blair Drummond Safari & Leisure Park NS7498 (on the A84) Odd as it sounds, there's enough going on at this enjoyable and well organised place to keep even those who don't like animals busy for quite some time. Plenty of other activities are included in the price, from gentle rides for younger children to the exhilarating Flying Fox slide over the lake. You can explore part of the water in pedal-boats, there's a good-sized astroglide, and they'll provide charcoal and equipment for barbecues in the attractive grounds (you just need to bring the food – and utensils if you're not inspired to copy the wildlife). As for the animals, the drive-through safari takes in elephants, rhinos, giraffes and other wild and exotic creatures, there's timed lion and penguin feeding, sea lion shows 4 times a day, and a pets farm where children can meet donkeys, piglets, wallabies and other creatures face to face. Boat trips circle Chimpanzee Island leaving the monkeys to enjoy their natural habitat undisturbed. A few children's activities, such as face-painting and dodgems, are extra. The play areas are good, with toddlers' corners as well as an adventure playground. Plenty of space for picnics, with some areas under cover (inc the sea lion shows if it's raining). If you haven't got a car a bus can take you round the safari part, and there are kennels to leave dogs in nr the entrance. Meals, snacks, shop, disabled access; cl Oct–mid-Mar; (01786) 841456; £8 (£4 children 3–14) – not bad value if you bring a barbie and make a half-day of it.

★ ! **ABERDEEN** NJ9305 Scotland's third-largest city, with a large and interesting harbour, well worth pottering around (especially its early morning Fishmarket). The granite centre has wide, orderly streets not unlike Edinburgh's New Town in places, and parks. Leafy Seaton Park is famous for its 14th-c Brig (or bridge) o' Balgownie. The Ferryhill House Hotel (Bon Accord St), Royal Hotel (Bath St) and Athol (King's Gate, W of centre) are useful for lunch, and the Prince of Wales (St Nicholas Lane) is the best proper pub in this part of Scotland. **Satrosphere** (Justice Mill Lane) Lively hands-on science and technology centre – everything is there to be touched, and they have lots of changing displays and exhibitions. Great fun. Snacks, shop, disabled access; cl Tues (exc school hols) and am Sun; (01224) 213232; £3.90. **Aberdeen Maritime Museum** (Provost Ross's House, Shiprow) In the town's third-oldest building (very striking), with very good displays on the city's nautical heritage. Meals, snacks, shop, disabled access; cl 25–26 Dec, 1–3 Jan; (01224) 337700; £3.50. **Provost Skene's House** (Guestrow) Named after its most famous resident, a stately well restored 16th-c house with refurbished period rooms, and remarkable painted ceilings.

Meals, snacks; cl Sun, 25–26 Dec, 1–2 Jan; (01224) 641086; £2.50. **Tolbooth** (Castle St) Good civic history collection in 17th-c building (cl 12–2pm, am Sun and Wed, all day Tues, and all Oct–May; free). **Aberdeen Art Gallery** (Schoolhill) First-class collection of Scottish and English painting since the 16th c, especially strong on contemporary works (cl am Sun, 25–26 Dec, 1–2 Jan; free). **Marischal College** (Broad St) The later Protestant rival to King's (see below), though the two were joined to form Aberdeen University in the last century. A splendid neo-Gothic structure, it has a decent **museum**; cl Sat, am Sun, (01224) 274301; free. **Aberdeen Old Town** N of the centre, really too far to walk, this part above the River Don seems quite separate. It has some charming old streets to explore, and attractive buildings; its pedestrianised villagey High St is dominated by the university, especially the very Oxbridge-like **King's College** (High St), founded in 1495. The chapel is one of the most complete examples of a medieval collegiate church in Britain. A visitor centre outlines the history. Meals, snacks (in barrel-vaulted former library), shop, disabled access; cl 2 wks at Christmas; (01224) 273702; free. **St Machar's Cathedral** An austere mainly 15th-c church notable for its painted wooden heraldic ceiling. It's the only granite cathedral in the world. **Cruickshank Botanic Garden** (St Machar Drive) 11 acres first planted in the 19th c, and divided into various smaller gardens – rock, water, rose and herbaceous – as well as trees and shrubs and a small terrace garden; cl winter wknds; (01224) 272704; free.

★ **ABERFELDY** NN8549 This quiet and pleasant small Highland shopping town has a fine 18th-c stone bridge designed by William Adam. There's a well restored **watermill** on Mill St (still mills oatmeal; all parts open to visit), and just S of town the delightful verdant 1½-mile walk along to the oak-lined Den and Falls of Moness inspired Burns's song *The Birks of Aberfeldy*. Weem, for a good lunch at the Ailean Chraggan, is close by.

ABERFOYLE NN5200 Lots of woollen shops, and in the heart of Queen Elizabeth Forest Park, so lovely scenery around; you can hire bikes. **Scottish Wool Centre** The story of Scottish wool from sheep to shop, entertainingly told by a live sheep show in the amphitheatre (11am, 12, 2pm, 3pm). They have demonstrations of spinning and weaving. Meals, snacks, good shop, disabled access; cl 25 Dec, 1 Jan; (01877) 382850; £2.50.

ALFORD NJ5815 **Grampian Transport Museum** (on the A944) Big collection of vintage vehicles, from horse-drawn sledges and carriages to motorcycles, cars and steamers; always plenty going on. Snacks, shop, disabled access; cl Nov–Mar; (01975) 562292; £3. Next door the **Alford Valley Railway** is a narrow-gauge passenger railway with trips in 2 one-mile sections, and a good static display at the station. Shop, disabled access; trains in steam wknds Apr–Oct and pm daily Jun–Aug; (01975) 562326; £1.50. There's a dry ski slope on Greystone Rd, and the Forbes Arms at Bridge of Alford has decent home cooking.

★ **ANSTRUTHER** NO5603 Pretty East Neuk fishing village; from May–Sept (weather permitting) you can get boat trips out to the nature reserve of the **Isle of May** (home to countless puffins and seals in summer). **Scottish Fisheries Museum** Nicely evocative, in a little cobbled courtyard by the harbour; cl am winter Sun; £3.50.

ARBROATH ABBEY NO6441 Substantial remains of 12th-c abbey, connected with Thomas à Becket and Robert the Bruce. Shop, disabled access to ground floor only; cl 25–26 Dec, 1–2 Jan; (01241) 878756; £1.80.

AVIEMORE NH8912 Uncompromisingly modern ski-resort village. There are plenty of places to get something to eat in this sizeable tourist development (the Olde Bridge is our current recommendation); it's a useful springboard for the Cairngorms, with the ski-lift from Glen More giving walkers an easy way up to the summits. **Strathspey Steam Railway** 5 miles of great scenery between here and Boat of Garten. Snacks, shop, limited disabled access; usually open daily Jun–Sept, plus other dates and wknds – best to ring for timetable; (01479) 810725; £5.

BALMEDIE COUNTRY PARK
NJ9820 Along a constantly shifting stretch of coast, this is splendidly bleak-feeling despite the closeness of Aberdeen. Visitor centre cl winter wknds. The beaches are clean and safe.

BALMORAL CASTLE
NO2693 (off the A93) The royal family's Highland residence. Prince Albert bought the property 4 years after he and Queen Victoria had first rented it in 1848, and had a new castle built here by 1855. You can't go inside, but can explore the wonderful gardens and woodlands, and there are various exhibitions in the ballroom. Also pony trekking and pony cart rides. Snacks, shop, disabled access; open daily 12 Apr–31 July (exc Sun Apr and May); (013397) 42334; *£4.

BEN LAWERS NN6341
This towering bulk, well over 1,200 metres (nearly 4,000ft), dominates Loch Tay, and is an interesting spot, with alpine wild flowers not found elsewhere in Britain and a quite different feel from other Highland mountains; a steep road leads up the side.

BEN VENUE NN4706 Allows some good mountain walks comparable in difficulty to some of the fells of the English Lake District.

BEN VORLICH NN6218 This too gives good mountain walks, on a par with Lakeland fell walking.

BENNACHIE NJ6623 On the eastern edge of the Grampians nr Inverurie, this is not that high but gives walkers tremendous views over lowland Grampian; the gently rolling moorland top has several colour-coded Forestry Commission trails (the lower slopes are forested).

BLAIR ATHOLL
NN8665 **Blair Castle** (off the A9) Nestling among forests and heather-clad hills, this is Scotland's most visited privately owned house, dating back to the 13th c, though largely renovated in the 18th. You can see 32 of the rooms, and they recently opened an 18th-c walled garden. A new display charts the history of the Atholl Highlanders – the Duke of Atholl's unique private army that turns out here for its annual parade in May. A piper outside every day in summer adds to the atmosphere. Meals, snacks, shop, disabled access to ground floor only; cl Nov–Mar; (01796) 481207; £5.50, plus grounds charge of £2 per car. Friendly little **folk museum** beside the turn-in for the White Horse; cl am May–mid-Oct (exc wkdys July–Sept) and all mid-Oct–Apr; *£2. Readers enjoy visiting the nearby **House of Bruar** (Glen Atholl, on the A9), a country shopping complex with fine specialist foods and clothing.

BLAIR DRUMMOND NS7498
See separate Family Panel on p.839 for **Safari & Leisure Park**.

BO'NESS NS9880
Kinneil Estate Includes the interesting if not extensive remains of a Roman fortlet, as well as a few later ruins and remains. The converted stables of adjacent Kinneil House have a museum on the site's history, with lots of local pottery. You can still see the workshop where James Watt developed the steam engine, and there are pleasant woodland walks. Shop, disabled access; cl am and all day Sun; (01506) 778530; free. **Bo'ness & Kinneil Railway** Re-creation of the days of steam complete with relocated railway buildings and Scotland's largest collection of locomotives and rolling stock. The 7-mile round trip takes passengers to the woodlands of the Avon Gorge at Birkhill, where there are tours of an old clay mine. Snacks, shop, disabled access to railway only; trains usually run wknds Apr–mid-Oct, and daily (exc Mon) July and Aug, though you can see the locomotives all year; (01506) 822298; £7.30 mine and railway, £3.90 train only.

BRAEMAR NO1491 One of the best-known Highland villages, with a good **Heritage Centre** (Mar Rd) showing useful films on the area's history and scenery (inc an interesting look at the building of Balmoral Castle), and on Braemar's famous Highland Gathering. Shops, disabled access; (01339) 741944. **Braemar Castle** (on the A93 NE) Highly unusual and charming exterior. Shop; cl Fri, and all Nov–Easter; (01339) 741219; £2.50. The Fife Arms (very much on the coach routes) is good for lunch. A steep path

East Scotland
Moray Firth
NORTH SCOTLAND
LOCH NESS
NH
NN
NS
WEST SCOTLAND
Inverness
Nairn
Fort George
Dalcross
Culloden
Cawdor
Clava Cairns
Brodie Castle
Forres
Elgin
Rothes
Craigellachie
Cardhu
Glenfarclas
Glenlivet
Tomatin
Grantown-on-Spey
Dulnain Bridge
Carrbridge
Glenmore
Aviemore
Loch an Eilein
Whitebridge
Kincraig
Kingussie
Balmoral
Braemar
Dalwhinnie
Glen Roy
Spean Bridge
Loch Ericht
Spittal of Glenshee
Killiecrankie
Blair Atholl
Kirkton of Glenisla
Pitlochry
Loch Rannoch
East Haugh
Bridge of Cally
Weem
Aberfeldy
Blairgowrie
Ben Lawers
Kenmore
Dunkeld
Loch Tay
Kinclaven by Stanley
Ardeonaig
Scone
Deil's Cauldron
Kinnoull Hill
Loch Earn
Perth
St Fillans
Crianlarich
Balquhidder
Crieff
L Voil
Ben Vorlich
THE TROSSACHS
Muthill
Auchterarder
Collessie
Kilmahog
Lomond Hills
Loch Katrine
Callander
Ochil Hills
Ben Venue
Dunblane
Kinross
Glendevon
Aberfoyle
Doune
Kinnesswood
Port of Menteith
Alloa
Blair Drummond
Castle Campbell
Stirling
Culross
Dunfermline
Fintry
Glencoyne
North Queensferry
Falkirk
Bo'ness
A96
A9
A939
A93
A82
A85
M90
8
0
6
4
2

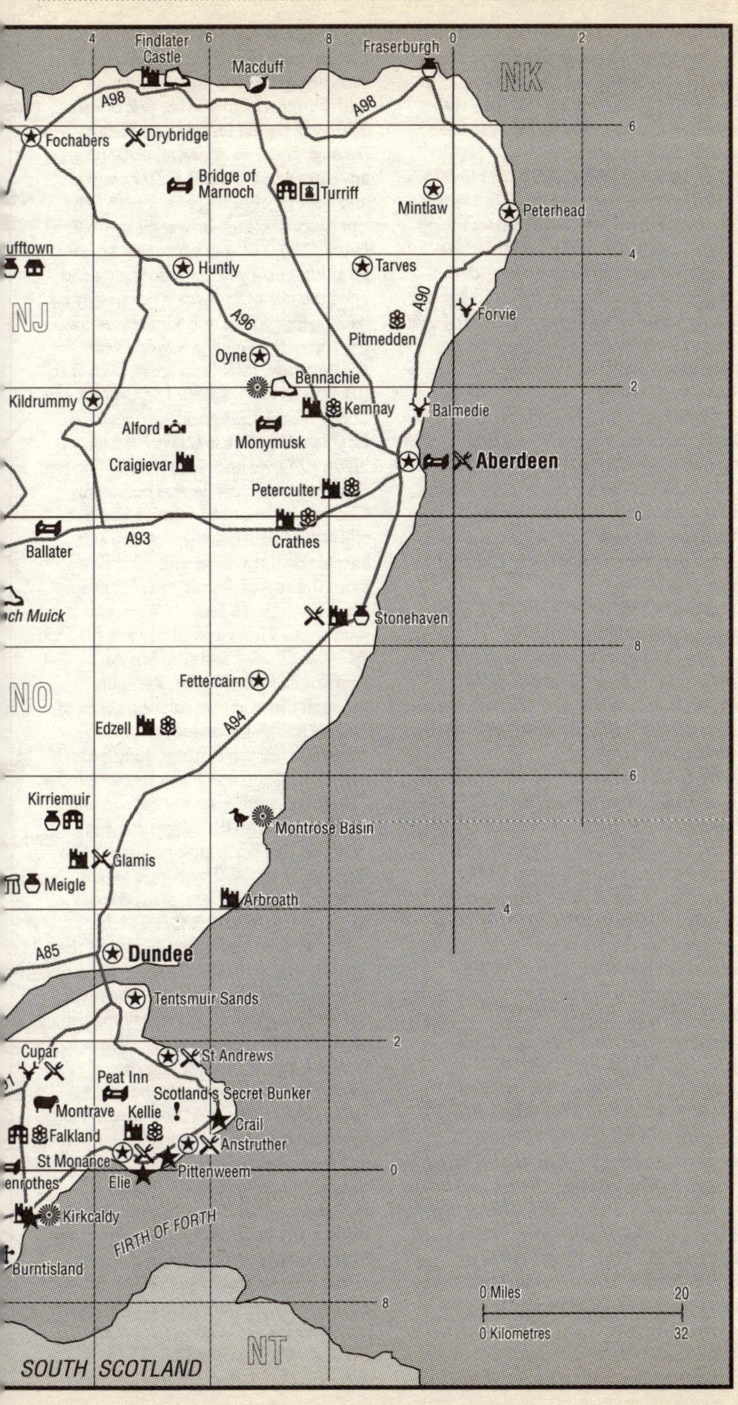

Findlater Castle
Macduff
Fraserburgh
NK
A98
A98
Fochabers
Drybridge
Bridge of Marnoch
Turriff
Mintlaw
Peterhead
ufftown
Huntly
Tarves
NJ
A96
A90
Forvie
Pitmedden
Oyne
Bennachie
Kildrummy
Kemnay
Balmedie
Alford
Monymusk
Craigievar
Aberdeen
Peterculter
A93
Crathes
Ballater
ch Muick
Stonehaven
Fettercairn
NO
Edzell
A94
Kirriemuir
Montrose Basin
Glamis
Meigle
Arbroath
A85
Dundee
Tentsmuir Sands
Cupar
St Andrews
Peat Inn
Scotland's Secret Bunker
Montrave
Kellie
Crail
Falkland
Anstruther
St Monance
enrothes
Elie
Pittenweem
Kirkcaldy
FIRTH OF FORTH
Burntisland
0 Miles
20
0 Kilometres
32
NT
SOUTH SCOTLAND

up Morrone takes the most determined walkers along a route used for a race in the Gathering. The **Linn of Dee** NO0689 gives long gentler glen walks into the Cairngorms along Glen Dee and the Lairig Ghru.

BRODIE CASTLE NH9757 (off the A96) Handsome gabled castle with extensive art collection featuring 17th-c paintings of the Dutch school, English watercolours and French Impressionists. Before the NTS took it over in 1980 it had been the seat of the same family since 1160. Outside are woodland walks and wildlife observation hides, and beautiful daffodils in spring. Snacks, shop, disabled access; cl am Sun, wkdys in Oct and all Nov–Mar; (01309) 641371; £4.20; NTS. Their occasional evenings of traditional Scottish music are enjoyed by readers. The nearest really good place for a meal is the Clifton Hotel in Nairn.

† **BURNTISLAND** NT2385 Once famous for shipbuilding (and shipbreaking), now a popular little resort, with an unusual octagonal **church** where the decision was made to produce the Authorised Version of the Bible in 1601.

CALLANDER NN6207 Quite a busy tourist town, popular in Victorian times thanks to the works of Walter Scott, and later this century for its appearances in the original *Dr Finlay's Casebook*. **Rob Roy & Trossachs Visitor Centre** (Ancaster Sq) The story of Scotland's most whitewashed rascal (or brave supporter of the downtrodden, depending on your point of view), well told with hi-tech displays. Also information on the beautiful surrounding countryside. Shop, disabled access; cl wkdys Jan–Feb; (01877) 330342; £2.50. **Kilmahog Woollen Mill** (just N) Restored watermill with 250-year-old working wheel, selling tweeds, tartans and other woollen gifts; also maybe whisky tasting. Meals, snacks, shop, some disabled access; cl 25 Dec, 1 Jan; (01877) 330268; free. There is usually a piper outside and Highland dancing some days in summer. The Lade Inn out here and the Byre at Brig o' Turk out in the Trossachs are both good food places.

CARRBRIDGE NH9022 **Landmark Highland Heritage & Adventure Park** Good family day out, with films on Highland life (inc one in 3D), well signed forest trails (one through the tree-tops), an elaborate adventure playground, water coaster, and Forestry Heritage Park with fully operational steam-powered sawmill (Apr–Oct). You can sometimes have a go at log-cutting or bark-stripping and Fred the giant Clydesdale horse may be hauling logs to the mill. Great views from the top of the viewing tower. Meals, snacks, shop, disabled access; cl 25 Dec; (01479) 841614; £6.20. The Dalrachney Lodge Hotel does good lunches.

CASTLE CAMPBELL NS9699 Once known as Castle Gloom, this late 15th-c castle was burned by Cromwell's troops in the 1650s, but still has its courtyard, great hall and barrel roof, as well as splendid views from the tower. Meals, snacks, shop; cl am Sun, 25–26 Dec, 1–2 Jan, and in winter pm Thurs and all day Fri; (01259) 742408; £2.30. **Dollar Glen** An amazing short track takes you up through these spectacular 60 acres of Arthur Rackham-esque woodland – catwalks, rock overhangs, jungle-thick vegetation, and a swirling stream below. Take care, some paths are steep and narrow, and can be dangerous after rain. But this is a gripping approach to Castle Campbell. The King's Seat in Dollar has good home-made food.

CAWDOR CASTLE NH8449 (on the B9090) Home of the Thanes of Cawdor since the 14th c, this splendid old house is one of the most entertaining as well as interesting places to visit in the whole area. Look out for the tree inside a tower and the freshwater well inside the house, as well as the more usual fine tapestries, furnishings and paintings (inc Dali's odd interpretation of the Macbeth tale). The busy grounds have several pretty gardens, craft and wool shops, nature trails, and a little pitch-and-putt course. Meals, snacks, shop, disabled access; cl mid-Oct–Apr; (01667) 404615; £5.20, grounds only £2.80. The nearby Cawdor Tavern is good for lunch.

CLAVA CAIRNS NH7544 A group of circular burial cairns from around 1600 BC surrounded by 3 concentric rings of great stones, on the banks of the River Nairn.

COLLESSIE NO2712 **Ostrich Kingdom** (on the B937) Unique collection of ostriches, emus and rheas – they have birds of all ages (inc maybe newly hatched ones in the incubator house), as well as videos, play area, and animals like lambs, pigs, and wallabies. Meals, snacks, shop, good disabled access; (01337) 831830; £3.

CRAIGELLACHIE NJ2944 **Speyside Cooperage Centre** (Dufftown Rd) Working cooperage and visitor centre, with a viewing area to watch the craftsmen. A reconstructed Victorian cooperage has life-size models speaking in the local dialect, and various improvements this year include an enlarged tasting area. Shop (wide range of wood goods), disabled access to exhibition only; cl Sun, winter Sats, 2 wks Christmas; (01340) 871108; £2.25. The little Fiddichside Inn (Keith Rd) is a charmingly old-fashioned fishing pub.

CRAIGIEVAR CASTLE NJ5609 (on the A980) Perhaps the most fairytale-romantic of the area's castles, this picturesque early 17th-c multiple tower dotted with erratically shaped windows soars to a mushrooming of corbels, turrets and crow-stepped gables. Inside, a warren of narrow staircases climbs through a rich series of ornately beamed and plastered rooms. The NTS are worried that too many people come here, so try to avoid busy times – it's not a place to absorb coach parties comfortably. Castle cl am May–Sept, and all Oct–Apr, grounds open all year; (013398) 83635; £5.80, grounds only £1; NTS.

★ **CRAIL** NO6107 One of the prettiest of the East Neuk fishing villages – the East Neuk being the local name for the east part of the Fife coast.

CRATHES CASTLE NO7596 (on the A93) Beautiful 16th-c tower house with wonderful interiors – especially its ceiling paintings, filled with wise old sayings in a mixture of Scots and English. Best of all are the surrounding gardens, inc a 4-acre walled garden with a remarkable series of carefully toned colour borders. Meals, snacks, shop, some disabled access; cl Nov–Mar; (01330) 844525; £4.80, garden only £4; NTS.

CRIEFF NN8621 A pleasant airy town, perched on the edge of the Highlands. A modern visitor centre (on the A85) has a pottery, plant centre and demonstrations of paperweight making, and there's a Stuart Crystal factory shop on Muthill Rd. **Glenturret Distillery** (off the A85 NW) Scotland's oldest distillery, dating from 1775 and using the pure water of the Turret Burn. There's a statue of the distillery cat Towser, who died in 1987 but still holds the record as world mousing champion – challengers have 28,899 to beat. Good meals and snacks, shop, some disabled access; cl am Sun, all wknds Jan, 25–26 Dec, 1–2 Jan; (01764) 656565; £3.50. The Knock of Crieff, a wooded hill just above, gives walkers a good viewpoint.

CULLODEN NH7445 (on the B9006) The bleak site of the gruesome massacre in which the 25-year-old Duke of Cumberland destroyed the Highland army of Bonnie Prince Charlie. On the moor a cairn marks this last bloody battle fought on mainland Britain. You can see the Graves of the Clans and the Wells of the Dead, as well as the Old Leanach Cottage around which the battle was fought, now refurbished in period style. Meals, snacks, shop, disabled access; visitor centre cl Jan; (01463) 790607; £3; NTS. The Coach House (Stoneyfield, on the A96) does food.

★ **CULROSS** NS9885 (off the A985) Fascinating small town on the Forth, virtually unchanged since the 16th/17th c. Until the 1930s this was because no one could afford any improvements, and since then its red pantiled-roofed houses have been carefully restored and preserved by the National Trust for Scotland (they are still lived in). **Culross Palace** The laird's house was the first building the Trust purchased here. It's fully furnished in 17th-c style, and they're creating a period garden. Guides are good at pointing out those small but fascinating details that make the difference between just another building and a real experience. Snacks, shop; cl wkdys in Oct, and all Nov–Mar;

(01383) 880359; £4.20; NTS. The price includes admission to the Trust's 2 other main properties here, the **Town House** (a good visitor centre), and the **Study**, with a Norwegian painted ceiling in the drawing room. There are the remains of a 13th-c abbey.

CUPAR NO3313 **Scottish Deer Centre** (Bow of Fife, on the A91 just W) You can stroke the deer and feed the young fawns at this friendly place, and there are also nature and heritage trails, aerial walkways and observation platforms, and an adventure playground. There's an adjacent holiday shopping courtyard. Snacks, shop, disabled access; cl 25 Dec, 1 Jan; (01337) 810391; *£2.95.

DEIL'S CAULDRON NN7624 Beauty spot reached by a signed circular walk through Glen Lednock from Comrie (where the Earthquake House records tremors).

DOUNE CASTLE NN6901 (on the A84) A 14th-c stronghold with 2 fine restored towers on the River Teith. Strong associations with Bonnie Prince Charlie and Walter Scott, and the Knights of Ni – the castle was used in *Monty Python and the Holy Grail*. It's the 25th anniversary of the making of the film in 1999, with celebrations likely here. Shop; in winter cl pm Thurs and all day Fri; (01786) 841742; £2.30. The village's bridge is said to have been built out of spite by James IV's tailor when the ferryman refused him passage.

DUFFTOWN NJ3240 **Glenfiddich Distillery** (on the A491, slightly N) The only Highland distillery where you can follow the entire whisky production process from barley to bottle; most other distilleries bottle elsewhere. Tastings, shop, disabled access; cl winter wknds, Christmas; (01340) 820373; free. Dufftown has a useful museum.

DULNAIN BRIDGE NH9823 **Speyside Heather** (Skye of Curr, off the A95) Over 300 different types of heather growing in ornamental landscaped garden, along with exhibition on its various uses, and shop with wide range of heather-based goods. Home-made meals and snacks, garden centre, disabled access; cl Jan (exc by appointment); (01479) 851359; 75p exhibition.

DUNBLANE NN7801 A small town of ancient origin, its name now tragically familiar all over the world. Plenty of old buildings in its narrow streets, especially around the close of its elegant 13th-c **cathedral**. This incorporates a much older tower, and has a beautiful oval window that you can see only from outside. There's a **museum** nearby (cl 12.30–2pm, all day Sun, some Sats, and Oct–May; free) and the Stirling Arms has good food.

DUNDEE NO3929 Beneath the straightforward modern wrappings of this bustling city, you can uncover signs of its distinguished heritage in a number of museums. **Discovery Point** (Docks) Excellent lively visitor centre with hi-tech displays on the Royal Research Ship *Discovery*, moored here, which was the first British purpose-built research vessel, commissioned for Scott's ill-fated expedition to the Antarctic; displays too on him and others who used the ship. Snacks, shop, disabled access; cl 25 Dec, 1–2 Jan; (01382) 201245; £4.50. You can get a joint ticket with **Verdant Works** (West Hendersons Wynd) a lively look at the jute industry, once an important part of the local economy. Snacks, shop, disabled access; cl 25 Dec, 1–2 Jan; (01382) 225282; £4.50. **Frigate *Unicorn*** (Victoria Dock) This 1824 vessel is the oldest British-built warship afloat, now with a new audio-visual presentation and a museum of naval life in her days in commission. Snacks, shop, limited disabled access; cl wknds Nov–Mar; (01382) 200900; *£3. **McManus Galleries** (Albert Sq) Important works by 19th-c Scottish and English artists, and a splendid hall with vaulted ceiling and stained glass; cl Sun, 25–26 Dec, 1–2 Jan; (01382) 434000; free. **Mills Observatory** (Balgay Park) Exhibits on space research and astronomy, as well as a small planetarium (by prior arrangement only), and splendid 10-inch refracting telescope. Shop; best to ring for opening times, which vary depending on when the sun sets – in autumn and winter for example they're open 4–10pm (not wknds or Mon); (01382) 435846; free. **Camperdown**

Country Park (off the A90) 400 acres of fine parkland with golf course, nature trails, woodland footpaths, and wildlife centre with indigenous animals from wolves to wildcats. Also adventure play area themed around the defeat of the Dutch at the 1797 Battle of Camperdown. Snacks, shop, disabled access; (01382) 432689; free, £1.65 wildlife centre. **Broughty Castle Museum** (Broughty Ferry, off the A930 4m E) 15th-c seaside castle rebuilt in the 19th c to defend the estuary, now a maritime museum. Plenty of harpoons and whaling exhibits – whaling used to be one of Dundee's major industries. Shop; cl 1–2pm, all day Sun (exc pm summer) and Fri, 25–26 Dec, 1–2 Jan; (01382) 436916; free. The Fisherman's Tavern and Ship (fantastic view upstairs) are good. The Number 10 (South Tay St), Royal Oak (Brook St), Mercantile (Commercial St) and Number 1 (Constitution Rd) all do good-value food.

DUNFERMLINE NT0987
Quite a prosperous light-industry town with a distinguished distant past – it was once Scotland's capital. **Dunfermline Abbey** The remains of a Benedictine abbey and later church buildings are pleasantly set in quiet precincts away from the busy centre. The foundations of the original 11th-c church underlie the more elaborate Norman nave, and the grave of King Robert the Bruce is marked by a modern brass in the choir stalls. The Palace is the birthplace of Charles I. Shop, mostly disabled access; cl am Sun, plus in winter pm Thurs and all day Fri; (01383) 739026; £1.80. **St Margaret of Scotland** A major figure in Dunfermline's history; her shrine is outside the abbey nr the East Gate. There's an exhibition on her life in **Abbot House** on Maygate (cl 25 Dec, 1 Jan; (01383) 733266; £3), and the cave she used to pray in is 84 steps below the Glen Bridge car park (cl Oct–Easter; free). **Dunfermline Museum** (Viewfield Terrace), Looks at the local manufacture of damask linen (cl 12.30–1pm and wknds; free). **Pittencrieff House Museum** (Pittencrieff Park) Fine 17th-c mansion in lovely rugged glen, with costume displays (free). **Andrew Carnegie Museum** (Moodie St) Focuses on the man who from humble origins in this house made a fortune in Pittsburgh steel, then gave away over $350 million – all the while claiming he didn't believe in charity (cl am Sun, am daily in winter; *£1.50). Handloom weaving demonstrations the first Fri of each month, May–Oct.

DUNKELD NO0242
Charming small town by the River Tay; the Atholl Arms is a useful stop. The **cathedral** has the tomb of the notorious Wolf of Badenoch, Alexander Stewart (the illegitimate son of English king Richard II). There are pretty preserved cottages (NTS), and riverside forest walks through NTS land around the waterfalls nr the **Hermitage**, an 18th-c folly, and so-called Ossian's Cave; there may be bat tours and other ranger-led walks in summer. Nearby **Birnam** is a pleasant tiny town, a 15-minute walk from Dunkeld on the opposite bank of the River Tay. A small garden next to the Birnam Institute re-creates the house of Mrs Tiggywinkle and Peter Rabbit's burrow (cl am Sun and all Sept–May; free); Beatrix Potter spent holidays here. Birnam Wood (of *Macbeth* fame) has a venerable oak, and there's plenty of stirring walking country around. Walkers can also ascend Birnam Hill.

EDZELL CASTLE NO5969
(on the B966) Some unique features at this pretty old place – the walled garden planted here in 1604, and the charming series of heraldic and mythical sculptures that decorate the walls around it; these alternate with recesses for flowers and nests for birds. They claim to have captured on camera the castle's rather active ghost. Shop, disabled access; in winter cl pm Thurs and all day Fri; (01356) 648631; £2.30. The Ramsay Arms in Fettercairn has decent food, and just N there's a lovely drive up Glen Esk, passing a wayside folk museum.

★ **ELGIN** NJ2263
Shopping town of some poise, with some handsome ancient buildings and handy for the coast; Thunderton House has decent food. **Elgin Cathedral** Founded in 1224, and known as the Lantern of the North and the Glory of

the Kingdom because of its extraordinary beauty and fine-traceried windows. There's still quite a lot to see of the ruins: the 15th-c nave has some ancient Celtic cross slabs with Pictish symbols, and you can go inside the spires. Snacks, shop, some disabled access; in winter cl pm Thurs and all day Fri; (01343) 547171; £1.80. **Elgin museum** (High St) World-famous fossil collection (cl am Sun, and all Nov–Mar; £1.50). **Elgin Motor Museum** (Bridge St) Decent little place, in a converted mill (cl Oct–Mar; £2.50). **Spynie Palace** (on the A941, 2m N) Former residence of the Bishops of Moray, the biggest tower house in Scotland, with good views over Spynie Loch. Shop, disabled access; cl winter wkdys; (01343) 546358; £1.80. **Pluscarden Abbey** NJ1457 (nr Barnhill, 5m SW) Fascinating; built in the 13th c, it gradually fell to ruin, but was rebuilt this century by monks from Prinknash Abbey in Gloucs – they now sing recently rediscovered chant which may well have been sung by St Columba himself; (01343) 890257; free.

★ **ELIE** NT4999 Attractive fishing village set around a broad bay – the beach is notably clean and safe (and has a good pub, the Ship, virtually on it).

FALKIRK NS8979 **Callender Park** (on the A803 just E) This huge park, with woodland walks and lots of summer activities, includes **Callender House**, a striking old house used briefly as an HQ by Oliver Cromwell. Remodelled in the last century to look like a French chateau, it's now a museum, with costumed guides interpreting its history. Part of the Antonine Wall, the Roman Empire's farthest frontier, runs through the grounds. Meals, snacks, shop, disabled access; house cl winter Suns; (01324) 503770; house *£2.50, park free. **Rough Castle** NS8479 (6m W) One of the best preserved sections of the Antonine Wall; not too much is left of the Roman fort that once stood here, but you can see the ramparts and ditches; free.

FALKLAND PALACE NO2507 Lovely Renaissance palace of the Stuart kings and queens, set below the Lomond Hills on the main street. Not all is as old as it looks, but it doesn't really matter – accurate restoration work has created a comfortably cosy and genuinely lived-in feel. Pleasant gardens and grounds, with the 1539 tennis courts said to be the oldest in Britain. Shop; cl am Sun, and all Nov–Mar; (01337) 857397; £4.80, garden only £2.40; NTS. Parts of the village are delightful and were Scotland's first conservation area – the Hunters Lodge has decent food.

FETTERCAIRN NO6475 **Fasque** (just N) Prime Minister William Ewart Gladstone lived here 1830–1851, and it still belongs to the Gladstones. The main rooms look as if they've scarcely been changed (let alone modernised) since he moved to Wales, and it's quite cluttered with homely odds and ends. In summer 1997 a parcel of shooting targets turned up behind a chair posted from London in the 1920s and covered with 'Urgent' stickers – but not yet even opened. There's a touching gallery of servants' portraits and lots of Gladstone memorabilia. Shop, disabled access; cl Oct–Apr; (01561) 340569; £3.50. **Fettercairn Distillery** (Distillery Rd) One of Scotland's oldest licensed distilleries, with tours, tastings, and good audio-visual show. Shop, disabled access to visitor centre only; cl Sun, and Oct–Apr; (01561) 340205; free. In Fettercairn itself the square has a magnificent archway erected to commemorate a visit by Queen Victoria, and the Ramsay Arms has decent food. The drive along the twisting and climbing B974 Fettercairn–Banchory is good, with spectacular views from **Cairn o' Mount** at the top – and when the water's high enough salmon jumping nr the Dee bridge as you enter Banchory.

FINDLATER CASTLE NJ5467 This windswept cliff-edge ruin makes a good destination for a walk; walkers can enjoy other stretches of this coast around Banff, with the bus service along the main road a useful method of return. The Cullen Bay Hotel has good-value food.

FOCHABERS NJ3458 The small town has a very good **folk museum** on the High St (cl 1–2pm, free), and the Gordon Arms is a reliable food stop. **Baxters Visitor Centre** (on the A96 just W) Explores how the grocery shop set up by George and Margaret Baxter grew into a company whose food is now sold all over the world. Tours (not wknds), landcaped gardens and woodland walk. Meals, snacks, good shops, some disabled access; cl 25–26 Dec, 1–2 Jan; (01343) 820393; free.

FORRES NJ0559 **Sueno's Stone** (E end of town) Mysterious 9th- or 10th-c stone that may have been erected to commemorate a forgotten battle. It's 6 metres (20ft) high, carved with a cross on one side and groups of warriors on the other. **Falconer Museum** (Tolbooth St) Good fossil collection; cl Sun all year and Sat Oct–Apr; free. In summer you can usually climb the **Nelson Tower** in Grant Park for good views of the Moray Firth; free. **Dallas Dhu** (2m S) Perfectly preserved Victorian distillery, which you can wander around on your own. Animatronic models explain what's happening. Shop (nearly 200 different types of whisky), disabled access; in winter cl pm Thurs and all day Fri; (01309) 676548; £2.30.

FORT GEORGE NH7656 One of the finest examples of an 18th-c artillery building, one of 3 fortresses built after 1745, when the Hanoverians were taking no risks in keeping this area firmly under their thumb. Very big, with quite a bit to see. Snacks, shop, disabled access; cl Christmas and New Year; (01667) 462777; £3. Just off from the fort in the Moray Firth you may be lucky enough to see one of the very few inshore schools of dolphins around the British coast.

FORVIE NATURE RESERVE NK0029 The fifth-largest sand dune system in Britain – and the one least disturbed by people, so lots of wildlife. You have to stick to the footpaths so as not to disturb the birds and other wildlife. Disabled access; visitor centre cl winter wknds; (01358) 751330; free.

FRASERBURGH NJ9967 **Scottish National Lighthouse Museum** (Quarry Rd) Based around a lighthouse working up to 1991; guided tours take you to the top and demonstrate how everything works. Snacks, shop, limited disabled access; cl 25–26 Dec, 1–2 Jan; (01346) 511022; £2.75.

GLAMIS CASTLE NO3847 (on the A94) The family home of the Earls of Strathmore, and the childhood home of the Queen Mother; a splendid creation, utterly suitable as the setting for Shakespeare's murder of Duncan in *Macbeth*. Notable features include the chapel with its painted panels and ceiling, and of course there are those stories about what's locked away in one of the towers. Meals, snacks, shop, limited disabled access; cl Nov–Mar; (01307) 840393; £5.20. The Strathmore Arms is good for lunch.

GLEN ROY NN3088 The glen and its curious Parallel Roads (not actually roads but the tubmarks of a former glacier) can be seen from an easily walked track along its bottom, a spectacular 4-mile route from Brae Roy Lodge (return the same way).

GLENMORE NH9809 **Cairngorm Reindeer Centre** (on the A951) Mingle with free-ranging reindeer in their natural surroundings, a pretty stretch of the Cairngorms; you can feed and stroke them too. Guided walks leave the visitor centre every day at 11am, weather permitting (maybe 2.30pm too in summer). Shop, disabled access to visitor centre only (though usually reindeer down here too); cl 25 Dec, 1 Jan; (01479) 861228; £4.

HUNTLY NJ5240 The original medieval **castle** here was destroyed and rebuilt several times, once by Mary, Queen of Scots. Reconstructed for the last time in 1602, the ruins are worth a look for their ornate heraldic decorations. Shop; in winter cl pm Thurs and all day Fri; (01466) 793191; £2.30. In the square is a little local history **museum**, and a ski centre can teach you how to cross-country ski through the local forest. **North East Falconry Centre** NJ4544 (Cairnie, off the A96 N) 4 flying displays a day in a richly meadowed glade, as well as a herd of red deer. Snacks, shop, disabled access; cl Nov–Feb; (01466) 760328; *£3.75.

INVERNESS NH6645 The biggest town up here, and the main

shopping town for the whole of the N of Scotland (Melvens is a good book shop). It has an attractive riverside setting and is a handy centre without being at all touristy. Nicky Tams (Ness Bank Rd) has decent food, and the Blackfriars (Academy St) is good for local colour. **Castle Stuart** NH7449 Looking over the Moray Firth a few miles E, this was built for the Earl of Moray in 1621 when his family, the Stuarts, ruled Great Britain; it was soon abandoned for nigh on 3 centuries, but has been restored to reflect its days of glory. So much celebration of Bonnie Prince Charlie is quite poignant just 3 miles from the scene of his final downfall. You can stay here by appointment. Shop; best to check opening times; (01463) 790745; £4. A good way of seeing the Highland scenery is the cross-Highland **railway** to Kyle of Lochalsh, in 2½ hours – the last minutes of which are much the best.

KELLIE CASTLE NO5205 (on the B9171) Fine example of 16th- and 17th-c domestic architecture, though parts date from the 14th c, with good collections of plasterwork, panelling and furniture. Also 4 acres of gardens inc a Victorian walled garden. Snacks, shop; cl am, wkdys in Oct, and all Nov–Apr (exc Easter), grounds open all year; (01333) 720271; £3.70, garden only £1; NTS.

KEMNAY NJ7212 **Castle Fraser** (off the A944) Once one of the grandest castles of Mar, the z-shaped building incorporates the remains of an earlier one, and there are excellent formal gardens. Snacks, shop; cl wkdys in Oct, and all Nov–Apr (exc Easter), grounds open all year; (01330) 833463; £4.20, £2 grounds only; NTS.

★ **KENMORE** NN7544 Attractive estate village; the good village inn has a poem in Burns's own handwriting on the wall of the lounge bar. **Scottish Crannog Centre** Interesting new reconstruction of a prehistoric loch dwelling. Snacks, shop, disabled access; cl Nov–Mar; (01887) 830583; £2.80.

KILDRUMMY CASTLE NJ4516 Now in ruins, though still with its original 13th-c round towers, hall and chapel, as well as some later remains; cl am Sun, plus pm Thurs and all day Fri when quiet, and all Oct–Mar; (01975) 571331; £1.80. **Kildrummy Gardens** (on the A97) Very beautiful indeed and of some botanical interest. There's an alpine garden in an old quarry, a watergarden, walks in the woods and a video showing the changes through the seasons. Shop, disabled access; cl Nov–Mar; (01975) 571203; £2. The ruins provide a spectacular backdrop.

KILLIECRANKIE NN9162 Queen Victoria was just one of the people to have found this romantic spot beguiling, but it wasn't always so serene. In 1689 it was the site of a fierce battle when the Highlanders routed the troops of William IV, and a **visitor centre** tells the tale. Snacks, shop, disabled access; cl Nov–Mar; (01796) 473233; £1; NTS. The Killiecrankie Hotel, with good food, is an attractive place.

KINCRAIG NH8305 **Highland Wildlife Park** (on the B9152) Owned by the same charity as Edinburgh Zoo, this 260-acre wildlife park somehow manages to seem a bit wilder than most animal attractions; perhaps it's because they specialise in species once native to the area, so you really get a feeling that the animals could have wandered out of the surroundings woods and mountains. You drive safari-style around enclosures of reindeer, bears, wildcats and enormous bison. The most exciting feature at the moment is the wolf territory, where a walkway takes you to a safe vantage point right in the heart of the enclosure. Plenty of rare breeds, inc the wild Przewalksi's horses, one of the world's rarest mammals, and you may see red squirrels feeding in the forest; daily talks and wknd face painting. Snacks and shop in visitor centre (cl winter), disabled access; cl Nov–Mar in bad weather; (01540) 651270; £6.

KINGUSSIE NH7500 **Highland Folk Museum** (Duke St) The first folk museum in Britain, originally opened on Iona in the 1930s. Still a good range of exhibits, inc craft demonstrations and a reconstructed Isle of Lewis Black House. Shop, disabled access; cl am Sun, wknds Sept–Oct and all Nov–Mar; (01540) 661307; £3 (inc admission to the folk park below). **Highland Folk Park**

(on the A86 E, nr Newtonmore) Demonstrates the life and work of crofters at the turn of the century; you may be able to help with some of the farming activities. Also a museum of Highland sport, which explains why so many of the area's golfers are left-handed. Usually open wkdys May–Aug; (01540) 673551; £3 (inc admission to the folk museum above). The Royal is useful for lunch.

KINNOULL HILL NO1423 Just outside Perth, this offers walkers forest tracks and paths, and two folly 'castles' above the River Tay.

KINROSS NO1301 **Lochleven Castle** Reached by ferry from Kinross jetty, the islet fortress where Mary, Queen of Scots was imprisoned for a while; she was rowed to freedom by a page boy, but only after she had been persuaded to abdicate in favour of her infant son. Shop; limited disabled access; cl Oct–Mar; (0131) 668 8800; £2.80 (inc ferry). **Loch Leven** itself is serene rather than dramatic: in the winter the evening flights and sounds of the thousands of ducks and geese here are very moving. An **RSPB reserve** at the south end of the lake has good facilities for watching the birds; cl Christmas and New Year; (01577) 862355; £2. **Kinross House Gardens** Rather fine and formal, with yew trees, roses and herbaceous borders. Disabled access; cl Oct–Apr; (01577) 863467; £2. The Muirs has good-value food, as does the Lomond Hotel at Kinnesswood with its quiet views over Loch Leven.

KIRKCALDY NT3093 This busy resort and shopping town is not too interesting to visitors, but has some charming old wynds and houses in the eastern suburb of Dysart, which has its own picturesque little harbour. Between here and the main town is 15th-c **Ravenscraig Castle**, perhaps most notable for its symmetrical shape. Great views over the Firth of Forth. Snacks, limited disabled access; free.

KIRRIEMUIR NO3854 **Barrie's Birthplace** (Brechin Rd) The birthplace of the writer of *Peter Pan* in 1860: the upper floors are furnished in the style of the period, and next door are displays relating to his work, both literary and theatrical. Teas, shop, disabled access; open Easter, daily May–Sept (exc am Sun), wknds in Oct; (01575) 572646; £2; NTS.

LOCH AN EILEIN NH8907 A draw for walkers, nestling beneath the Cairngorms on the Aviemore side; a forest track encircles this delightful little loch, with its castle romantically placed on an isle – great echoes here.

LOCH EARN NN5924 With a trunk road alongside, so not one of Scotland's quieter lochs – and is largely given over to water-skiing and that sort of thing. Lochearnhead offers a round walk along a nature trail into Glen Ogle and back via the trackbed of an abandoned railway.

LOCH ERICHT NN6284 Very peaceful but does involve foot-slogging to make the most of it. The road from Dalwhinnie on the A9 at the north end runs along the foot of a steep forested slope; the south end of the loch has more varied scenery, but no road once you reach the end of the little road off the B846 at Bridge of Ericht.

LOCH KATRINE NN4009 A lovely stretch of water that inspired Scott's *Lady of the Lake*, and has a Victorian steamer in summer. The main approach to the east end through the Trossachs does bring a fair bit of summer traffic, but the central part of the loch is served by just a narrow back road, so is fairly peaceful even then.

LOCH MUICK NO2984 Nestling below the summit of Lochnagar, this has paths around its shores, with a car park at the end of the Glen Muick road from Ballater.

LOCH RANNOCH NN6257 Among the quieter and more beautiful lochs, wooded for much of its length. There are peaceful walks from the back road along the southern shore.

LOCH TAY NN7745 Remarkably long, with the view seeming to change moment by moment as the clouds flit across the sky. It has a quiet road along its southern side. There are easy walks at the east end of the loch, along the River Tay, or into the adjacent forest to a viewpoint over the loch.

LOCH VOIL NN5220 Served by just a narrow back road, so fairly peaceful even in summer; it's famous for having Rob Roy's grave at Balquhidder. It's worth keeping on the road beyond the far end of the loch; there's some striking scenery around the picnic site at its end.

LOMOND HILLS NO2206 A level walk from the car park by the road above Falkland gives some pleasant rambles – not to be confused with Loch Lomond, this upland gives views over most of south-east Scotland.

MACDUFF NJ7064 The **Marine Aquarium** (High Shore) here has a unique design with a huge central tank containing more than 400,000 litres and open to the sky. The emphasis is on fish native to the Moray Firth and there are touch pools and an audio-visual presentation. Snacks, shop, disabled access; (01261) 833369; £2.75.

MEIGLE NO2844 **Museum** Outstanding collection of Celtic Christian **sculptured stones**, all found in or around the churchyard. Shop, disabled access; cl 12.30–1.30pm, and all Nov–Mar; (01828) 640612; £1.50.

MINTLAW NJ9847 **Aden Country Park** More than 200 acres of lovely woodland and farmland, criss-crossed with nature trails and with plenty of wildlife. The **Aberdeenshire Farming Museum** here illustrates 2 centuries of farming history, with seasonal open-air demonstrations and tours. Meals, snacks, shop, disabled access; park open all year, museum cl Oct–Apr; (01771) 622906; free.

MONTRAVE NO3806 **Praytis Farm Park** (on the A916) An indoor putting green and crazy golf in addition to the usual farm animals and walks; also deer park, play areas, and big farm shop with venison and smoked salmon. Home-made meals and snacks, some disabled access; cl Jan and Feb; (01333) 350209; £4.

MONTROSE BASIN NO6856 This enclosed estuary is a rich feeding ground for thousands of native and migrant birds, inc oystercatchers, curlews and eider ducks. There's a good **wildlife centre** (on the A934) with great views, interactive displays and high-powered telescopes. Snacks, shop, disabled access; cl 25–26 Dec, 1 Jan; (01674) 676336; *£2.50.

MUTHILL NN8616 **Drummond Castle Gardens** (on the A822) Majestic formal gardens originally laid out in 1630 by the 2nd Earl of Perth. Lovely views from the upper terrace, splendid early Victorian parterre, and centrepiece sundial designed and built by the master mason of King Charles I; cl am Jun–Oct, and all Nov–May; (01764) 681257; *£3.

★ **NAIRN** NH8856 A quiet, relaxed and rather discreet old-fashioned resort, with good clean sheltered beaches.

NORTH QUEENSFERRY NT1380 **Deep-Sea World** One of the most elaborate aquariums we know; moving walkways take you through an incredible transparent viewing tunnel as long as a football pitch, surrounded by a million gallons of water and sharks and exotic fish from all around the world. You can go round as often as you like. Meals, snacks, shop, disabled access; cl 25 Dec; (01383) 411411; £6.15. The Ferrybridge Hotel has good-value food.

OCHIL HILLS NS9099 A range of green mountains which rise without preamble from the lowland plain – a striking textbook example of the Highland Fault. A path from Tillicoultry up Mill Glen takes you to Ben Cleuch, the highest point of the range.

OYNE NJ6725 **Archaeolink** This lively new centre is a fun exploration of the past. A remarkable turf-roofed building houses an audio-visual presentation, there's an exhibition on myths and legends and you can try out ancient crafts such as weaving, grinding and arrow-making. Outside are the remains of an Iron Age hill fort, a reconstructed Iron Age farm, a new Roman marching camp and a sandpit play area, where younger members of the family can dig for the past. Meals, snacks, shop, disabled access; (01464) 851500; £3.90.

PERTH NO1223 Spaciously laid out along the broad River Tay, with an excellent specialist rhododendron nursery at Glendoick Gardens (on the A85). There are a couple of decent museums and galleries, and the Greyfriars and Timothy's are popular for lunch. **Branklyn Garden** (116

Dundee Rd) Only about 2 acres but seems much bigger, thanks to a remarkable planting of interesting rhododendrons, small trees, Asiatic primulas, meconopsis, lilies and the like. Shop, disabled access; cl Nov–Feb; (01738) 625535; £2.50; NTS. **Caithness Glass** (Inveralmond Industrial Estate, northern edge) Displays of paperweight-making, with audio-visual theatre, collectors' museum and factory shop. Meals, snacks, disabled access; cl am Sun Nov–Mar, 25–26 Dec, 1–2 Jan, no glass-making wknds (exc July and Aug); (01738) 637373; free. **Huntingtower Castle** (just W) The main thing to see is its interesting painted ceiling; in winter cl pm Thurs and all day Fri; £1.80.

PETERCULTER NJ7900 **Drum Castle** (off the A93) Still looks out over what's left of the medieval forest granted the family by Robert the Bruce. Mainly a much-altered Jacobean mansion, the house is based around a 13th-c keep, one of the 3 oldest tower houses in Scotland. There's a historic rose garden in the grounds. Snacks, shop, limited disabled access; cl am, wkdys in Oct, and all Nov–Easter; (01330) 811454; £4; NTS. The Lairhillock Inn at Netherley a few miles S is good for lunch.

PETERHEAD NK1246 One of Europe's busiest fishing ports, with a bustling market and smartened up marina. There's a good local history **museum** on St Peter St (cl pm Wed, Sun and bank hols; free) and a new **heritage centre** (South Rd) with interactive displays on the fishing industry (cl am Sun and winter wkdys; £2.50). The ancient **Ugie Fish House** sells a good range of salmon and trout, caught from the adjacent river in season (cl pm Sat, all day Sun; (01779) 476209).

PITLOCHRY NN9458 An inland resort town for a good long time, beautifully set in fine countryside; a happy sort of place, with a comfortable feel. There's lovely woodland on the banks of man-made Loch Faskally, with walks and nature trails. The hydro-electric power station has a **visitor centre** (cl Nov–Mar; £1.80) where you may be able to see salmon leaping up the fish ladder. The Moulin Inn (which brews its own beer) and the Westlands have decent food. **Edradour** (on the A924 E) Scotland's smallest distillery, founded in 1825 and virtually unchanged since Victorian times. Guided tours, tastings, shop, some disabled access; cl am Sun, and all Nov–Mar (exc shop); (01796) 472095; free.

PITMEDDEN GARDEN NJ8828 (on the A920) Originally planted in the 17th c and pretty much unchanged since, with sundials, fountains and pavilions among the elaborate formal gardens. Meals, snacks, shop, limited disabled access; cl Oct–Apr; (01651) 842352; £3.70; NTS. The Redgarth Hotel over at Oldmeldrum has decent food (and good bedrooms).

★ **PITTENWEEM** NO5402 Attractive East Neuk fishing village, with some pretty crow-gabled houses (the gables in steps which seagulls rather than crows sit on here).

PORT OF MENTEITH NN5700 **Inchmahome Priory** Famous as the refuge of the infant Mary, Queen of Scots in 1543, this Augustinian priory was founded in 1238 on an island in the middle of the lake, and in spring and summer you can get a boat across. Robert the Bruce prayed here before the Battle of Bannockburn. Snacks, shop; cl Oct–Mar; (01877) 385294; £2.80 inc ferry.

ROTHES NJ2749 **Glen Grant Distillery** Founded in 1840 by the brothers Grant, whose malt whisky was one of the first to be bottled and sold as a single malt. Guided tours, tastings, shop, some disabled access; cl am Sun, and all Nov–mid-Mar; (01542) 783318; £2.50.

ST ANDREWS NO5116 This civilised university town doubles as rather a dignified seaside resort, with clean safe beaches. It's outstanding for golfers, though to play on the hallowed greens of the Old Course, you'll need to ring the St Andrews Links Trust on (01334) 466666 before 2pm the day before you want to go, and you'll be entered into a daily ballot; after that you'll have to tee up £70. **St Andrews Castle** 13th-c, the scene of Bishop Beaton's murder during a wave of anti-Catholic feeling in 1546. It was largely demolished in the 17th c, but some substantial ruins remain. Shop, disabled access; cl am Sun, 25–26 Dec, 1–2 Jan; (01334) 477196; £2.30. **St Andrews Cathedral** Impressive twin-towered Norman remains; in its time this was the largest cathedral in Scotland, but angry locals sacked it in the 16th c. Shop, disabled access; cl 25–26 Dec, 1–2 Jan; (01334) 472563; £1.80. You can get a joint ticket with the castle. Beside it the very tall and narrow Romanesque **St Rules Tower** is part of the older church the cathedral was built to replace (perhaps pre-Conquest), and if you can face over 150 steps gives wonderful views from the top. There are a few interesting **museums** on the city's history, some quite lively, and a number of fine buildings belonging to Scotland's oldest university – especially St Leonard's and St Mary's colleges. South St is worth strolling along: attractive riggs or small courts and alleys off, the ancient West Port gateway at the end, and **Holy Trinity Church** where John Knox preached his first sermon in 1547. **British Golf Museum** (Bruce Embankment) Fascinates anyone keen on the game, with interactive and audio-visual displays going right through its 500-year history. Assorted memorabilia include lots of glamorous golfing gear, and the technology is some of the most up-to-date you'll find in any museum. Shop, disabled access; cl Tues and Weds mid-Oct–Easter, and all mid-Dec–1 Jan; (01334) 478880; £3.75. **Sea Life Centre** (The Scores) 3 resident seals, and lots of other examples of British native marine life, well displayed in realistic re-creations of the sea bed. Meals, snacks, shop, limited disabled access; phone for winter opening; (01334) 474786; £4.35. **St Andrews Botanic Garden** (just off Canongate) Around 18 pleasantly landscaped acres, with a good range of trees and shrubs, and several glasshouses. Disabled access; (01334) 477178; £1.50. You can arrange fishing trips with Mr Thomas on (01334) 870957; rod and tackle provided. The Vine Leaf, Ma Bells (pleasant seafront views outside), St Andrews Wine Bar and (1 m S) the Grange are all good eating places.

SCONE PALACE NO1126 (off the A93) Pronounced 'Scoon', the seat of government in Scotland from Pictish times, though the current building is largely 16th-c behind an 18th-c castellated façade. It was the site of the Stone of Destiny – the famous coronation stone – until it was seized by the English in 1296 (it's at last returned to Scotland, though to Edinburgh Castle). Good displays of porcelain, furniture, clocks and needlework, and pleasant grounds. Meals, snacks, shop, some disabled access; cl mid-Oct–Good Fri; (01738) 552300; £5.40.

★ ✝ **ST MONANCE** NO5201 One of the most attractive East Neuk fishing villages, with an unusual fishermen's church and a restored 18th-c windmill (the Cabin has good seafood and sea views).

! SCOTLAND'S SECRET BUNKER NO5608 (on the B940 4m W of Crail) Beneath an innocuous-looking farmhouse is a network of underground rooms and corridors from where the government would have run the country in a nuclear attack (cl Oct–Easter; £5.95).

✝ **STIRLING** NS7994 Strategically placed on the Firth of Forth, this is a very unstuffy place, with the university students putting quite a bit of buzz into the atmosphere. **Stirling Castle** Provides magnificent views from its lofty hilltop site. It became very popular with the royal family in the 15th and 16th c, and most of the buildings date from that period. The finest features are the Chapel Royal built by James VI (and I of England), and the Renaissance palace built by James V. Snacks, shop; cl 25–26 Dec, 1–2 Jan; (01786) 450000; £4.50. There's a good visitor centre in a restored building next door. Whistlebinkies (St Mary's Wynd), formerly part of the ancient castle stables, has decent food. Dropping down the steep hill on which the castle stands is an attractive and interesting network of old streets, with a lot of character in their old-to-ancient buildings; **Argyll Lodgings** is an interesting ruined Renaissance-style mansion, and the **Church of Holy Rood** was where

Mary, Queen of Scots and James VI were crowned as babies. **Smith Art Gallery** (Dumbarton Rd) Good changing exhibitions; cl am Sun, all day Mon; (01786) 471917; free. **Wallace Monument** (top of Abbey Craig, just NE) Perhaps Stirling's most satisfying attraction, a huge 67-metre (220-ft) Victorian tower with dramatic views from the top of its 246 spiralling steps. Each floor has lively audio-visual displays, one looking at Sir William Wallace, another examining other Scottish heroes. There is a statue of Wallace as portrayed by Mel Gibson in *Braveheart* in the new car park. Snacks, shop; cl Christmas and New Year; (01786) 472140; £3. **Bannockburn Heritage Centre** (on the A872 S) Plenty of information on Robert the Bruce's finest hour, inc an audio-visual show on the battle itself. Shop, disabled access; cl Jan and Feb; (01786) 472140; £2.40.

STONEHAVEN NO8785 An old fishing town, with its more seasidey but discreet Victorian streets in the upper part; the harbourside Marine has good, reasonably priced food. There's a good local history museum in the old **Tolbooth** on the quay; cl 12–2pm, am Weds and Sun, all day Tues, and all Oct–May; (01779) 477778; free. **Dunnottar Castle** (just S) On a precipitous sea-girt crag stands this bleak and battered but still extensive and well preserved 14th-c ruin, used for the filming of Mel Gibson's *Hamlet*. It sheltered the Scottish Crown Jewels during the Civil War, but has seen much darker episodes in its time. Shop; cl winter wknds, 25–26 Dec, 1 Jan; (01569) 762173; £3.

TARVES NJ8634 **Haddo House** (off the B999) Wonderfully grand yet still very much a family home; designed by William Adam, and refurbished in the 1880s in the Adam Revival style. The chapel has stained glass by Burne-Jones. Its choral society is renowned, holding concerts and operas in the adjacent hall; (01651) 851770 for what's on. Meals, snacks, shop, disabled access; house open Easter, then pm May-Sept and wknds in Oct, gardens open all year; (01651) 851440; £4.20; NTS. Surrounding the house is a 150-acre country park, with wildlife exhibition and guided walks, and a shop selling produce from the estate, and local salmon, venison, whisky and crafts. There's an interesting medieval tomb in Tarves churchyard. **Tolquhon Castle** (off the B999 S) Impressive remains of a 15th-c castle (cl winter wkdys, £1.50). Nearby, the decidely unstuffy **Tolquhon Gallery** has contemporary Scottish art and crafts (cl am Sun, all day Thurs, and wkdys Jan and Feb; free).

TENTSMUIR SANDS NO5024 5 miles of shore walking from Kinshaldy car park on the Fife coast; you may see common and grey seals on the sandbanks, and there are good clean beaches – shorter routes back through the forest.

THE TROSSACHS NN5007 The Highlands in microcosm, famously popular for their dense conifer forests, steep glens and beautifully framed lochs. Perhaps surprisingly, not brilliant for low-level walks unless you like forests; the route on to **Callander Crags** from Callander is one of the best.

Days Out

Villages of the East Neuk: St Andrews; Crail; lunch at the Cellar, Anstruther; Pittenweem; Kellie Castle, or Scotland's Secret Bunker.

Cairngorm encounter: Strathspey Steam Railway, Aviemore; lunch at the Olde Bridge there; Highland Wildlife Park, Kincraig, or chairlift up to Cairngorm summit and/or walk round Loch an Eilein.

Castles of Royal Deeside: Braemar Castle; lunch at the Fife Arms, Braemar; drive past Balmoral, then up Glen Muick for a walk round Loch Muick; Crathes Castle or Craigievar Castle.

TURRIFF NJ7639 **Fyvie Castle** (off the A947) Each of the 5 towers of this magnificent palace was built in a different century by the family that lived here throughout; the oldest parts date back to the 13th c, and the whole building is one of the most fantastic examples of Scottish baronial architecture. Collections of armour and tapestry, and paintings by Romney and Gainsborough. Snacks, shop, limited disabled access; cl am (exc July and Aug), wkdys in Oct, and all Nov–Easter; (01651) 891266; £4.20; NTS. The Towie Tavern does good food.

Working malt whisky distilleries open for tours and tastings include **Cardhu** NJ1943 (on the B9102 nr Knockando), cl wknds exc July–Sept; £2; **Dalwhinnie** NN6384 Scotland's highest, cl wknds; **Glencoyne** NS5086 (on the A81 nr Killearn); **Glenfarclas** NJ2138 (Marypark), cl wknds exc Jun–Sept; £2.50; **Glenlivet** NJ1928 (Ballindalloch) the first Highland distillery to be licensed, (01542) 783220 for opening times; £2.50; and **Tomatin** NH7929, cl wknds exc summer Sats.

Worthwhile inns in good spots for walkers, drivers or just strollers (besides those we've mentioned as places to eat at or stay in) include the lochside Achray at St Fillans NN6924, seaview Creel at Catterline NO8778, Loch Ericht Hotel at Dalwhinnie NN6384, Dores Hotel at Dores by Loch Ness NH5930, Clachan overlooking pretty Drymen's green square NS4788, Anchor at Dunipace NS8083, Old Smiddy at Errol NO2523, Hungry Monk at Gartocharn NS4286, Clova Hotel in Glen Clova NO3373, Old Mill at Killearn NS5285, Cross Keys at Kippen NS6594 (pretty village), Trossachs Hotel nr Loch Achray NN5106, Corriegour Lodge nr Altrua on Loch Lochy NN2390, Loch Tummel Hotel above Loch Tummel NN8460, Meikleour Inn at Meikleour NO1539 (handy for the 30-metre (100-ft) high beech hedge planted in 1746), Pennan Inn in the pretty seaside *Local Hero* village of Pennan NJ8465, Potarch Hotel at Potarch NO6097, Sheriffmuir Inn on wild Sheriff Muir NN8202 and Tomdoun Hotel at Tomdoun NH1501.

Where to eat

Many places in the **Where to stay** section, above, also have very good food.

ABERDEEN NJ9305 **Q Brasserie** *9 Alford Pl (01224) 595001* On the second floor of a former religious training college, this bustling place has bold modern paintings, simple contemporary furniture on bare boards, a bar in what was the altar, innovative brasserie-style cooking, super puddings, and a decent little wine list; cl am Sat, Sun. **£30**|£6.

ABERFOYLE NN5300 **Braeval** *on the A821 S (01877) 382711* TV chef Nick Nairn's small country restaurant in a converted mill with stone walls and flagstones, fresh flowers and a woodburner, serving particularly good imaginative modern cooking from a daily-changing set menu, fine French cheeses, good-value wine list, and helpful friendly staff; cl pm Sun, Mon, Tues, 1 wk Feb/June/Oct; children over 10; disabled access. **£31.50 4-course dinner**.

ANSTRUTHER NO5603 **Cellar** *24 East Green (01333) 310378* Off a little courtyard nr the harbour, with beams, stone walls, and peat fires – and wonderful fresh fish, good wines; cl Sun, am Mon, Tues, 25 Dec, 1 Jan. **£35**|£8.50.

BLAIRGOWRIE NO1845 **Cargill's** *Lower Mill St (01250) 876735* Busy bistro, part of a complex that includes a crafts gallery and coffee shop, antiques warehouse and upholstery business; good varied food inc nice puddings, and several teas and coffees; bright, helpful staff; cl Mon; disabled access. **£22**.

CUPAR NO3714 **Ostlers Close** *25 Bonnygate (01334) 655574* Cosy, unpretentious, much liked restaurant with lovely food using the best local fresh produce, game and fish, and home-grown herbs; a reasonably priced wine list, and friendly owners; cl Sun, Mon, 2 wks June; children welcome lunchtime but must be over 6 in evening. **£33 dinner, £23 lunch**|£9.50.

DRYBRIDGE NJ4362 **Old Monastery** *(01542) 832660* Lovely views from former monastery – as well as very good fish, game and Aberdeen Angus beef, reasonably priced wines and friendly service, cl Sun, Mon, 2 wks Nov, 3 wks Jan; children over 8. **£27**|£4.50.
GLAMIS NO3846 **Strathmore Arms** *(01307) 840248* Picturesque unspoilt village with simply decorated old inn, well presented delicious food inc wonderful puddings, roaring log fire in lounge, and good caring service; disabled access. **£20**|£7.50.
KILMAHOG NN6008 **Lade Inn** *(01877) 330152* Well run place in lovely wooded surroundings with beamed and partly panelled main bar, Highland prints, no smoking room opening on to terrace and attractive garden, a wide choice of interesting bar food, decent wine list and real ales. **£18.40**|£6.40.
KINGUSSIE NH7500 **The Cross** *(01540) 661166* No smoking friendly tweed mill beside a stream offering fine Scottish cooking based on the best local produce, an excellent wine list (popular wine wknds), and super breakfasts; bdrms; cl pm Tues, 1–26 Dec, 10 Jan–25 Feb; children over 12; disabled access. **£35 for 5 courses.**
PERTH NO1223 **Let's Eat** *77 Kinnoull St (01738) 643377* Very popular restaurant in what was the Theatre Royal with a relaxed friendly atmosphere, enjoyable modern cooking inc proper old-fashioned puddings, and a short selective wine list; cl Sun, Mon, 2 wks Jan, 2 wks July; disabled access. **£27**|£6.50.
ST ANDREWS NO5016 **Vine Leaf** *131 South St (01334) 477497* Warm welcome in attractively laid-out dining room overlooking walled herb garden, very good food, unobtrusive service and decent wines; evenings only; cl Sun, Mon and Jan; disabled access. **£25**.
ST FILLANS NN6924 **Four Seasons** *(01764) 685333* Long white family-run hotel with wonderful Loch Earn views, generous helpings of very good Scottish food inc super fish and game dishes; lunchtime snacks, too; you can eat in Tarken Bar, on terrace or in smarter restaurant; comfortable bdrms and chalets; cl Dec–Mar; partial disabled access. **£23**|£6.50.
ST MONANCE SO5201 **Cabin** *West End (01333) 730327* Immaculate, snug and cosy inside, with seafaring models and mementos on illuminated shelves, plenty of well polished light wood panelling, plainer locals' bar, very good modern cooking inc excellent seafood in no smoking back restaurant, and good enjoyable bar food; cl Mon, 3 wks Jan. **£25**|£2-course lunch £11.95.
STONEHAVEN NO8595 **Lairhillock** *Netherley, 6m N (01569) 730001* Relaxed and friendly extended 18th-c country pub with a wide choice of good, popular and imaginative food, well kept real ales, lots of malt whiskies and wines, nice views from the cheerfully atmospheric beamed bar, central fire in spacious lounge, and airy conservatory; cl 25–26 Dec, 1–2 Jan; disabled access. **£33.95**|£4.65.
WEEM NN8449 **Ailean Chraggan** *(01887) 820346* Small friendly inn with lovely views, very good food inc plenty of fresh fish and enjoyable puddings – you can eat in bar or restaurant – and a very good wine list; comfortable bdrms; cl 25–26 Dec, 1–2 Jan. **£17**|£3.75.

West Scotland

Mainland Scotland's finest scenery, especially on the coast.

Roads winding slowly along the intricate coast make driving here a succession of glorious sea-and-mountain views. Inland too has its delights: Loch Lomond, with the Trossachs nearby in East Scotland, is to become Scotland's first National Park, early in the new millennium. Places to visit are mostly low-key, suiting the relaxed pace of life here – the great gardens are the high point for most people, and are at their peak in May and June. That's a glorious time to visit this part, with very long days and lots of wild flowers. In high summer the traffic on the twisting roads in the most scenic parts can make driving painfully slow, and the midges become a menace. In autumn the Highland heather's still gorgeous and the weather can be very kind, but the days are shortening dramatically. In winter most hotels here do remain open, and the coast stays very mild, but the days are too short to make much of – and most of the attractions close; a time to do some brisk walking, then cosset yourself indoors in one of the many comfortable places to stay, looking forward to an evening meal with some of the area's magnificent seafood.

Oban is quite lively, Inveraray is interesting, and Dunoon has all you'd expect of a long-standing summer resort; all three have things to keep children entertained, as does Glencoe.

Where to stay

ARDUAINE NM7910 **Loch Melfort** *Arduaine, Oban, Argyll PA34 4XG (01852) 200233* **£105,** plus special breaks; 27 rms, gorgeous sea views. Comfortable hotel popular in summer with passing yachtsmen (hotel's own moorings), nautical charts and marine glasses in airy modern bar, own lobster pots and nets so emphasis on seafood; pleasant foreshore walks, outstanding springtime woodland gardens; cl mid-Jan–mid-Feb; disabled access.

BALLACHULISH NN0459 **Ballachulish House** *Ballachulish, Argyll PA39 4JX (01855) 811266* **£40;** 8 rms with views. Remote 18th-c house with a friendly atmosphere, spacious antique-furnished elegant rooms, log fires, honesty bar, hearty helpings of good food using local fish and beef, and billiard room; cl Oct–Mar; children over 8.

CRINAN NR7894 **Crinan Hotel** *Crinan, Lochgilphead, Argyll PA31 8SR (01546) 830261* **£210 inc dinner,** plus special breaks; 22 rms. Rather smart hotel by start of canal to Lochgilphead, marvellous views from stylish formal top-floor restaurant, nautical decorations in lounge bar, lots of local fish and large wine list; disabled access.

DERVAIG NM4449 **Druimard Country House** *Dervaig, Tobermory, Island of Mull PA75 6QW (01688) 400345* **£115 full board,** plus special breaks; 6 rms. Peaceful Victorian country house with wonderful views across the glen and River Bellart, friendly helpful owners, a comfortable lounge and conservatory with lots of pictures, books and magazines, good breakfasts, and excellent food using the best local produce; the Mull Little Theatre is in the grounds; cl Nov–Mar; dogs welcome.

ELLANBEICH NM7417 **Inshaig Park** *Ellanbeich, Easdale, Oban, Argyll PA34 4RF (01852) 300256* **£62;** 6 rms. Solid family-run stone building on Seil island (bridge to mainland), a hotel since Victorian times, with stunning sea views, good food inc fresh local seafood, friendly bar, and warm welcome.

ERISKA NM9042 **Isle of Eriska Hotel** *Ledaig, Eriska, Oban, Argyll PA37 1SD (01631) 720371* **£195,** plus winter breaks; 17 rms. In a wonderful position on small island linked by bridge to mainland, impressive baronial hotel with very relaxed country-house atmosphere, log fires and pretty drawing room, excellent really enjoyable food, exemplary service, and comprehensive wine list; leisure complex with indoor swimming pool, sauna, gym and so forth, lovely surrounding walks, and 9-hole golf course, windsurfing or waterskiing, clay pigeon shooting, pony-trekking, and golf – and plenty of wildlife inc tame badgers who come nightly to the library door for their bread and milk; cl Jan; children over 5 in evening restaurant (high tea provided) and pool; disabled access.

FORT WILLIAM NN0973 **Grange** *Grange Rd, Fort William, Inverness-shire PH33 6JF (01397) 705516* ***£72;** 4 rms. Charming Victorian house in quiet landscaped gardens with log fire in comfortable lounge, fine breakfasts in dining room overlooking Loch Linnhe, and helpful hard-working owners; cl Nov–Easter; children over 12.

GIGHA ISLAND NR6448 **Isle of Gigha Hotel** *Gigha Island, Argyll PA41 7AA (01583) 505254* **£84,** plus special breaks; 13 rms, most with own bthrm. Attractive traditional family-run small hotel with lots of charm, bustling bar (popular with yachtsmen and locals), neatly kept and comfortable residents' lounge, and local seafood in restaurant; cottages also; cl end Nov–Feb.

KILBERRY NR7164 **Kilberry Inn** *Kilberry, Tarbert, Argyll PA29 6YD (01880) 770223* ***£67;** 3 ground-floor, no smoking rms. Homely and warmly welcoming inn on west coast of Knapdale with fine sea views, old-fashioned character, entertaining owner, and outstanding country cooking – everything home-made, from soups and breads to chutney and marmalade; cl mid-Oct–Easter; well behaved children over 8.

KILCHRENAN NN0421 **Taychreggan** *Kilchrenan, Taynuilt, Argyll PA35 1HQ (01866) 833211* **£104,** plus special breaks; 19 rms. Civilised and extensively refurbished hotel with fine garden running down to Loch Awe, comfortable airy bar with stuffed birds and fish, attractively served lunchtime bar food, polite efficient staff, good freshly prepared food in no smoking dining room, careful wine list, dozens of malt whiskies, and pretty inner courtyard; no children.

KILFINAN NR9279 **Kilfinan Hotel** *Kilfinan, Tighnabruaich, Argyll PA21 2EP (01700) 821201* **£82,** plus special breaks; 11 rms. Friendly former coaching inn, popular locally, in fine scenery with sporting activities such as shooting, fishing and stalking; very good restaurant food, decent bar food, and log fires; cl Feb; children over 12.

KILNINVER NM8724 **Knipoch** *Kilninver, Oban, Argyll PA34 4QT (01852) 316251* **£154;** 16 rms. Elegant and very well kept Georgian hotel in lovely countryside overlooking Loch Feochan; fine family portraits, log fires, fresh flowers and polished furniture in comfortable lounges and bars, carefully chosen wines and malt whiskies, and marvellous food inc their own smoked salmon; cl 2 Dec–1 Mar.

OBAN NM8529 **Dungallan House Hotel** *Gallanach Rd, Oban, Argyll PA34 4PD (01631) 563799* ***£80,** plus special breaks; 13 rms, most with own bthrm. Victorian house in neat grounds with fine views over the bay to Mull and Lismore; marvellous food in elegant no smoking dining room, relaxed lounge bar and reading room, warm coal fires, and helpful friendly owners and staff; cl Nov and Feb; limited disabled access.

ONICH NN0461 **Allt-Nan-Ros** *Onich, Fort William, Inverness-shire PH33 6RY (01855) 821210* **£105,** plus special breaks; 20 rms. Victorian shooting lodge with fine Scottish food, a friendly atmosphere, bright airy rooms, and magnificent views across Loch Linnhe and the gardens; cl mid-Nov–28 Dec.

PENNYGHAEL NM5226 **Pennyghael** *Pennyghael, Island of Mull, Argyll PA70 6HB (01681) 704288* **£98.90 inc dinner;** 6 rms. Beautifully placed converted byre by Loch Scridain with comfortable little lounge, generous breakfasts, lovely (if limited in choice) evening food using local fish and venison, and really friendly owners and staff; cl end Oct–1 May.

PORT APPIN NM9045 **Airds Hotel** *Port Appin, Appin, Argyll PA38 4DF (01631) 730236* **£236 inc dinner,** plus winter breaks; 12 lovely rms, plus 4 cheaper rooms in Linnhe House 60 yards away. Instantly relaxing 18th-c inn with lovely views of Loch Linnhe and the island of Lismore, blissfully comfortable day rooms, professional courteous staff, and charming owners; the food is exceptional (as is the wine list) and there are lots of surrounding walks, with more on Lismore (small boat every 2 hours); cl 10–31 Jan; dogs by arrangement.

STRACHUR NN0802 **Creggans** *Strachur, Cairndow, Argyll PA27 8BX (01369) 860279* ***£95;** 19 rms. Smart inn in extensive grounds overlooking sea loch and hills (deer-stalking, fishing and pony-trekking arranged), with attractive lounge, conservatory and cocktail bar, lively locals' bar, particularly fine cooking and

carefully chosen wines, coffee bar, and gift shop.
TARBERT NR8768 **Columba** *East Pier Rd, Tarbert, Argyll PA29 6UF (01880) 820808* **£65.90,** plus special breaks; 10 rms. In a peaceful position on Loch Fyne with views of the surrounding hills, this family-run hotel has log fires in the friendly bar and lounge, an informal and relaxed atmosphere, enjoyable food using fresh local produce, and quite a few malt whiskies; cl 24–26 Dec.
TARBERT NR8671 **Stonefield Castle** *Tarbert, Argyll PA29 6YJ (01880) 820836* **£130 inc dinner,** plus special breaks; 33 rms. With wonderful views and surrounding wooded grounds, this Scottish baronial mansion has comfortable public rooms and decent restaurant food; snooker room, sauna and solarium; heated swimming pool open in summer only; disabled access.

To see and do

ALTNAFEADH NN1557 Good start for walks from the top of Glencoe. The West Highland Way takes a zigzag route N up the Devil's Staircase and through the mountains to Kinlochleven; another hill walk from Altnafeadh heads E up Beinn a' Chrulaiste, one of Glencoe's more manageable peaks.
ARDUAINE NM7910 (on the A816) The seaside **gardens** here, a very sheltered spot with lovely views of the islets and islands, are almost subtropical, with many rarities beside the rhododendrons, camellias and magnolias which flourish so in this part of the world. Open all year; (01852) 200366; £2.40; NTS. The comfortable Loch Melfort Hotel, with great sea views, does good bar lunches.
AUCHINDRAIN TOWNSHIP OPEN-AIR MUSEUM NN0102 (on the A83) The only communal tenancy township to have remained on its ancient site much in its original form. All the buildings have been excellently restored and simply furnished in period style, so you get a real feeling of stepping back into the past. Snacks, shop; cl Oct–Mar; (01499) 500235; *£3.
BARCALDINE NM9240 **Sea Life Centre** (on the A828) Lively underwater centre (part of a chain with several in England and one in St Andrews), with hi-tech face-to-fish-face displays of native marine life inc jelly fish, and playful seal puppies. Also nature trails and woodland adventure playground. Meals, snacks, shop, limited disabled access; phone for winter opening; (01631) 720386; £5.50. The Lochnell Arms and Falls of Lora down at Connel are reliable lunch stops.
BEN LOMOND NN3602 The southernmost Munro (see next entry), with a good ascent for walkers from Rowardennan on the east side of Loch Lomond.
BEN NEVIS NN1671 Though Britain's highest mountain, this is one of the more easily managed summits, with a long safe path up: expect crowds in season. Munro-baggers say it's far from being the best viewpoint mountain; a 'Munro' is any 3,000ft peak (914 metres), named for Sir Hugh Munro, who first tabulated them (in 1997 climbers relaxing after a lifetime of gaining them all were shocked by publication of a new list adding several more).
BENMORE NS1391 **Younger Botanic Garden** (on the A815) An outstation of the Royal Botanic Garden in Edinburgh, with attractive woodland and glorious rhododendrons. Some enormously tall and magnificent conifers here, and a good many rarities. Nice views too. Meals, snacks, shop, disabled access; cl Nov–mid-Mar; (01369) 706261; £2.
CAIRNDOW NN1710 **Ardkinglas Woodland Garden** (off the A83) On a hillside overlooking Loch Fyne, the pinetum here includes the tallest tree in Britain, a grand fir well over 61 metres (200ft) and still shooting upwards. Also rhododendrons, azaleas and other exotic plants, and daffodils in spring. Disabled access; open all year; £2. The same people run the **Tree Shop** (about 2m N at the top of the loch), which specialises in specimen trees, indigenous Highland trees, and shrubs.

Also lots of well crafted woodware (inc some lovely toys and puzzles); cl Jan; (01499) 600263. Next door the Loch Fyne Oyster Bar is renowned for its fresh shellfish, which you can eat in the restaurant or buy in the shop; the Cairndow Hotel with a waterside garden is also good.

CALEDONIAN CANAL NN1177 From Corpach there are straightforward towpath walks NE, up a flight of locks known as Neptune's Staircase, with mountain backdrops. There's good access to the locks from the Moorings Hotel (good-value basement wine bar) at Banavie.

★ **COLINTRAIVE** NS0374 This attractive village spreads along the shore of the sea loch, with lovely views (for example from the well run Colintraive Hotel) across the narrow Kyles of Bute. There's a short ferry crossing to Rhubodach on Bute.

CONIC HILL NS4292 Less than half Ben Lomond's height and more accessible, a straightforward but rewarding climb from Balmaha at Loch Lomond's south-east corner.

CORPACH NN0976 **Treasures of the Earth** (Mallaig Rd) Award-winning collection of gemstones, crystals and minerals, imaginatively displayed in carefully lit rock cavities. Shop, disabled access; cl 25–26 Dec, 3–31 Jan; (01397) 772283; £3.

CRINAN CANAL NR7894 Cut through the top of the Kintyre peninsula at the end of the 18th c, to save coastal sailors many miles of dangerous waters; the end at Crinan is attractive, usually with one or two yachts or even a rare fishing boat waiting to enter the first lock, and the Crinan Hotel is a comfortable lunch stop. The canal towpath allows gentle strolls.

DUNOON NS1878 Brought in easy reach of Glasgow by frequent ferries from Gourock, this late Victorian resort has pleasant views from its fine long promenade; very busy in Aug.

FORT WILLIAM NN1174 A largely Victorian town that manages to combine its role as a regional centre with its other life as a holiday base, particularly for solid Ben Nevis which rises above it, and for the Caledonian Canal which leads on up into the Great Glen and across eventually to the North Sea. **West Highland Museum** (Cameron Sq) Recently refurbished, especially good on Jacobite relics: a secret portrait of Prince Charlie requires a curved mirror to decode it. Shop, disabled access; cl Sun (exc July and Aug), (01397) 702169; £2. The Alexandra and Nevis Bank hotels are useful for food, as is the upstairs part of the Grog & Girvel pub; the Nevisport is the place for walking and climbing chat. In summer you can take steamtrain journeys on the **West Highland Line** from here – it goes right up into the Highlands and the views are quite superb. **Inverlochy Castle** (north-east edge) Partly 13th-c ruins (usually under scaffolding), site of the 1645 battle between Montrose and the Campbells; free.

GIGHA NR6551 3 miles offshore, linked by frequent ferries from Tayinloan on the A83 down the west coast of Kintyre, the island is a perfect place for really getting away from it all. Apart from the small hotel, there are rooms at the post office and other places, and you can hire bicycles to explore it properly. Try to see the strange old stones, some of which are supposed to have mysterious powers; (01583) 505254 for ferry times. **Achamore Gardens** Created by Sir James Horlick, who bought the island in 1944; a garden of woodlands filled with rhododendrons and azaleas, many plants brought from his home in Berkshire in laundry baskets. Lots of subtropical plants – the climate and soil are perfect for them. Snacks, shop, limited disabled access; open all year; *£2.

GLEN ETIVE NN1651 Reached from Glencoe by a squelchy walk along glens (or a long track from the A82 E of Glencoe), with close-ups of mighty peaks for reward.

GLEN NEVIS NN1468 (nr Fort William) Probably the best-known Highland valley, with splendid gorge scenery for an easy long mile's walk to Steall Falls. The Pap of Glencoe and the succession of peaks in the largely unwooded Mamore Forest (access

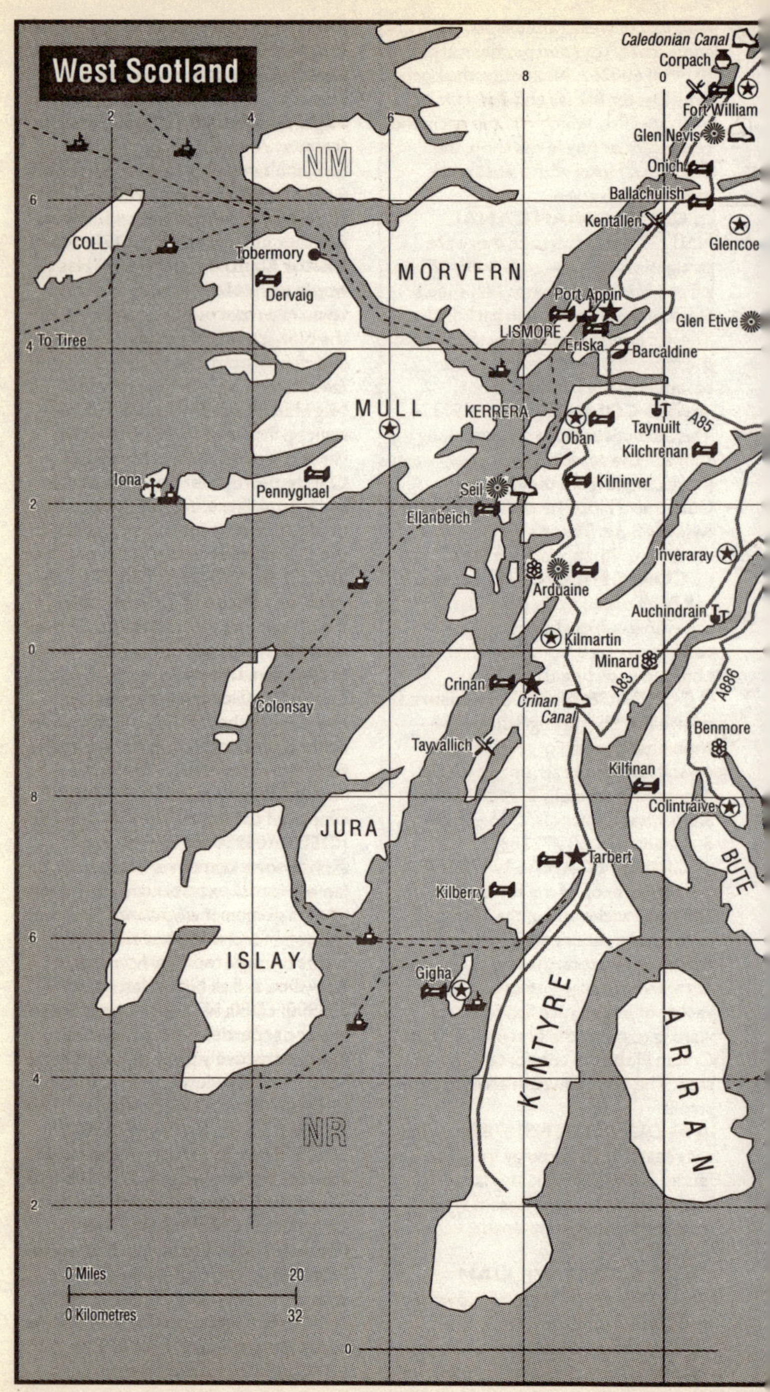
West Scotland
NM
NR
COLL
To Tiree
Tobermory
Dervaig
MORVERN
MULL
Iona
Pennyghael
KERRERA
LISMORE
Caledonian Canal
Corpach
Fort William
Glen Nevis
Onich
Ballachulish
Kentallen
Glencoe
Port Appin
Glen Etive
Eriska
Barcaldine
Oban
Taynuilt
A85
Kilchrenan
Kilninver
Seil
Ellanbeich
Inveraray
Arduaine
Auchindrain
Kilmartin
Minard
A83
A886
Crinan
Crinan Canal
Colonsay
Tayvallich
Benmore
Kilfinan
Colintraive
JURA
BUTE
Tarbert
Kilberry
ISLAY
Gigha
KINTYRE
ARRAN
0 Miles 20
0 Kilometres 32

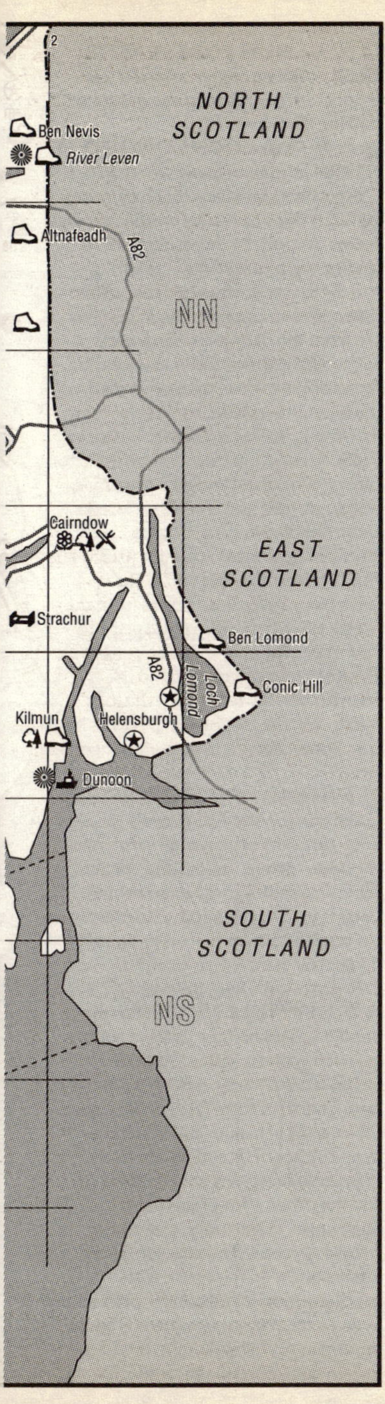

from the glen) are interesting viewpoint summits; they don't need rock-climbing expertise, just fitness and plenty of time.

! **GLENCOE** NN1557 The scenery around here is some of Scotland's most beautiful and wild. It's understandably popular with walkers and climbers, who share it with deer, wildcats and golden eagles. **Glencoe Visitor Centre** (on the A82) Has the whole story of the massacre of 1692, when billeted troops tried to murder all their MacDonald hosts, as well as useful local information (and fishing permits). Snacks, shop, disabled access; cl Nov–Mar; (01855) 811307; 50p, free parking all day; NTS. **Highland Mysteryworld** (Glencoe village) Children enjoy the spooky local myths and legends here. There may also be outdoor theatre here. Meals, snacks, shop, disabled access; cl Nov–mid-Mar; (01855) 811660; £4.95. The Clachaig and King's House do food. A forest walk runs from the hospital by Glencoe village past a lochan (small loch) above Loch Leven. **Lost Valley** (NN1455) This secret Glencoe pasture-ground was used by the MacDonalds for stolen cattle in times of clan warfare; a good walk involves an ascent from the Meeting of the Three Waters NN1756.

HELENSBURGH NS2983 **Hill House** (Upper Colquhoun St) In an area short of many great houses, this is a wonderful example of the work of Charles Rennie Mackintosh; there's an exhibition on his life, and the gardens are being restored. Snacks, shop; cl am Apr–Oct, and all Nov–Mar; (01436) 673900; £5.80; NTS – it's one of their busier properties. The dignified resort town, attractively placed on the Clyde, has some good views from its broad streets.

★ † **INVERARAY** NN0908 Beautifully placed and rather self-consciously elegant, this was built as an estate village in the 18th c, and is now a magnet for visitors. **All Saints Church** The bell tower has the world's second-heaviest ring of 10 bells, installed in 1931. Even if there's no one ringing them you should be able to hear a recording; cl 1–2pm, and all Oct–Apr; (01499) 302259; £2 for tower, exhibition free. **Inveraray Castle** Built in 1743, and still the home of the Duke and Duchess of Argyll, it has particularly impressive state rooms, and a striking hall. Snacks, shop, disabled access to ground floor only; cl 1–2pm (exc July and Aug), am Sun, all day Fri (exc July and Aug), and mid-Oct–Mar; (01499) 302203; £4.50. **Inveraray Jail** (Church Sq) Excellent prison museum, with costumed guides really bringing the place to life. You can watch a trial, try your hand at hard labour, and even experience being locked up in one of the sparse little cells. By 1999 there should also be some animated surprises. Shop; cl 25 Dec, 1 Jan; (01499) 302381; £4.40. Nearby woodland trails include a view over Loch Fyne from Dunchuach Tower. The Loch Fyne Hotel is pleasant for lunch, with stunning views; the George is popular too. **Argyll Wildlife Park** (Dalchenna; on the A83 SW) A collection of local or once-local animals, from wild boars to wildcats – with some eminently tame wild creatures wandering around. Snacks, shop, disabled access; cl Dec–Mar; (01499) 302264; £3.75.

IONA NM2824 (off Mull) Lovely island, filled with a sense of spirituality as well as its tangible remains of ancient shrines; Scotland's first kings were buried here (as is former Labour leader John Smith).

KILMARTIN NR7487 The **church** here is plain and Victorian, but has a stunning 10th-c cross; the graveyard has interesting carved medieval tombstones. The archeology of the local area is explained at **Kilmartin House** (open daily; *£3.90), and a short walk away tracks link the well signed North, Mid and South Cairns (impressive prehistoric burial mounds – you can climb into the North one via trapdoor and ladder, to see cup-and-ring carvings), and the Templewood stone circles. The simple Kilmartin Hotel is useful for lunch. **Dunadd** (3m S) This prehistoric hill fort was one of the ancient capitals of Dalriada from which the Celtic kingdom of Scotland was formed. Look out for the carvings nearby of a boar and a footprint, which probably mark the spot where early kings were invested with royal power.

KILMUN FOREST NS1781 Good walks among rare conifers, an arboretum of great beauty, and some striking gum-trees.

LOCH LOMOND NS3884 In spite of being so close to Glasgow and on every coach company's hit list, it does have a serene beauty that seems unspoilt by the visitors. Wee birdies sing and wild flowers spring – and the water is often calm enough to reflect the mountains. The best views are from the narrower north end. Surprisingly, there aren't many paths: the shoreline track, partly metalled, on the quieter east side, comes closest to the water. **Balloch Castle Country Park** A useful introduction, with visitor centre, woodland and meadow trails, walled garden, and fine views. Snacks, shop, disabled access; cl some lunchtimes, all late Oct–Apr; (01389) 758216; free. Cruises round the lake leave from Balloch, as well as from the pretty village of Luss, a good place to hire a boat for pottering about (there's a visitor centre here too, and the Inverbeg Inn is useful). Past the loch's north end, the Inverarnan Drovers Inn is an entertaining and very idiosyncratic stop.

MINARD NR9799 **Crarae Gardens** (on the A83) Lovely gardens noted for rare ornamental shrubs and rhododendrons, azaleas and conifers, set in a beautiful gorge overlooking Loch Fyne. Snacks, shop, and interesting plant sales (all summer only), limited disabled access; visitor centre cl Oct–Easter; (01546) 886614; *£2.50.

MULL NM5055 For most people this island takes a bit of getting to, but if you are within reach its unspoilt coasts are certainly a dramatic lure. There's a good ferry service from Oban and Lochaline (and in summer from Kilchoan). A couple of castellated mansions, one going back to the 13th c and the other 19th-c, and a small museum in Tobermory, give some rainy-day scope. The interior is less interesting than the coast, with brackeny moors and conifer plantations over much of it, though there is some mountainous hill walking in the S (as usual, not many defined paths). On the west coast at Fionnphort is a new **visitor centre** dedicated to St Columba, and you can get boats to Iona. At nearby Bunessan children can cuddle some very fluffy bunnies at the **Isle of Mull Angora Rabbit Farm**; cl Sat and all Nov–Mar; £2. The Keel Row at Fionnphort has decent food, overlooking Iona.

★ **OBAN** NM8530 This bustling coastal town is a busy ferry port and popular with holidaymakers, with a good cheerful atmosphere; the Oban Inn is fun, and the Lorne has decent food inc fresh local fish. Besides the main ferries, there are boats to Lismore and (just a hop really) Kerrera, for shoreside walks with the odd ruined fort. **Dunstaffnage Castle** (off the A485, 4m N) Beautifully set, this was once the prison of Flora MacDonald. It's now in ruins, but you can still see its gatehouse, round towers and massively thick walls. Shop, disabled access to visitor centre only; cl Thurs and Fri; (01631) 562465; £1.80. **Oban Rare Breeds Farm** (on the A816 Oban–Kilmore) A collection of very visitor-friendly animals. Teas, shop, some disabled access; cl Nov–Easter; (01631) 770608; £4. A little way S at Cologin, the countrified Barn is useful for lunch, and often has evening folk music.

★ **PORT APPIN** NM9045 An attractive little settlement, very peaceful, where you can pick wild blueberries by the roadside, catch a boat across to Lismore, or just sit by the water keeping your eyes open for the seals that are so common around here. This is *Kidnapped* country, with the scene of the Appin Murder not far off, and a monument marking where James of the Glens was wrongly hanged at Ballachulish to the N (the Ballachulish Hotel has decent food and wide views).

RIVER LEVEN NN1861 The glen gives a fine walk through semi-wooded terrain, from Kinlochleven to the dam of the gigantic Blackwater Reservoir – with an awesomely bleak view ahead of empty hills.

SEIL NM7819 This little island is linked to the mainland by a short bridge that people call the Bridge over the Atlantic. The Tigh an Truish inn by the bridge is a pleasant stop, and there's an attractive walk over to the anchorage on the far side which looks out to Jura.

★ **TARBERT** NR6182 Quite picturesque small harbourside town; the West Loch Hotel (on the A83 W) does good local seafood.

TAYNUILT NN0031 **Bonawe Iron Furnace** (off the A85) The most complete remaining charcoal-fired ironworks in Britain, worked until 1876. Iron produced here was used for cannonballs for Nelson's ships. Shop; cl Oct–Mar; (01866) 822432; £2.30. The Polfearn Hotel on the lochside does good food.

Inns with decent food, in good places for drivers, walkers or strollers, include the Ardentinny Hotel by Loch Long at Ardentinny NS1887, Galley of Lorne at Ardfern NM8004, Village Inn at Arrochar NN2904, Kilchrenan Inn at Kilchrenan by Loch Awe NN0222, Portsonachan Hotel on the opposite side of that loch NN1227, Whistlefield Hotel by Loch Eck NS1493, Loch Gair Hotel on Loch Gair NR9190 and Oystercatcher at Otter Ferry NR9384.

Days Out

On the shores of Loch Fyne: Inveraray Jail and village; lunch at the Loch Fyne Hotel there; Inveraray Castle, or walk up to Dunchuach Tower; Auchindrain Township, or Crarae Gardens.

Island walkabout: Dunstaffnage Castle; lunch at the Oban Inn, Oban (North Pier); boat to Kerrera, or visit Oban Rare Breeds Farm.

The grandeur of the glens: Stroll in Glen Nevis, or along the Caledonian Canal at Neptune's Staircase; Glencoe Visitor Centre; lunch at the Clachaig there; drive on the A82 through Glencoe to Rannoch Moor, with a walk up to the Lost Valley or up the Devil's Staircase.

Where to eat

Many places in the **Where to stay** section, above, also have very good food.

CAIRNDOW NN1710 **Loch Fyne Oyster Bar** *Clachan Farm (01499) 600264* Relaxed restaurant in converted farm buildings by Loch Fyne, serving good seafood and smoked fish (they have their own smokehouse); reasonably priced wine list and a warm welcome; cl 25–26 Dec, 1 Jan; disabled access. **£20**|£6.

FORT WILLIAM NN1074 **Alexandra** *The Parade (01397) 702241* Popular hotel in town square with meals and snacks in the Great Food Stop (open all day) and evening restaurant; disabled access. **£18 in restaurant**|£5.

KENTALLEN NM9957 **Ardsheal House** *(01631) 740227* Particularly good food in attractive conservatory dining room of fine hotel in 900 acres; very comfortable rooms, antiques, and relaxed atmosphere; lovely bdrms; cl Christmas. **£33 4-course dinner**.

KENTALLEN NN0057 **Holly Tree** *(01631) 740292* Super food in carefully converted railway station; cosy public rooms, lovely shoreside setting; best to book in winter; bdrms; cl Dec–Feb; disabled access. **£28.50**|£6.

TAYVALLICH NR7487 **Tayvallich Inn** *(01546) 870282* Simply refurbished pub overlooking yacht anchorage with quite superb local seafood (other decent dishes too), dining conservatory (no smoking), and friendly service; cl Mon during Nov–Mar; limited disabled access. **£22.50**|£5.

North Scotland

Sensational scenery in the west and on Skye, solitude in the north, good golf and empty beaches on the east coast.

There are a few interesting places to visit scattered through the area, but its main draw is unquestionably the scenery – and the feeling of getting away from it all. The west coast has glorious vistas of sea, mountains and islands. Long empty sandy beaches (and good golf courses) make the east coast suit a quiet summer holiday. The north coast is relatively wild and empty: addictive to some people, harsh and inhospitable to others. Skye is idyllic in good weather.

The area is usually at its best between late May and early July, while the days are very long and before the midges have really got into their stride.

Where to stay

ACHILTIBUIE NC0208 **Summer Isles** *Achiltibuie, Ullapool, Ross-shire IV26 2YG (01854) 622282* ***£110;** 13 comfortable rms. Beautifully placed above the sea towards the end of a very long and lonely road, a warm, friendly and well furnished hotel with delicious set menus using fresh ingredients (in which it's largely self-sufficient), a choice of superb puddings and an excellent array of uncommon cheeses; pretty watercolours and flowers; cl mid-Oct–Easter; children over 6.

APPLECROSS NG7144 **Applecross** *Applecross, Strathcarron, Ross-shire IV54 8LR (01520) 744262* ***£50;** 5 rms with breathtaking sea views over Sound of Raasay, shared bthrms. Gloriously placed informal inn with tables out by shore, simple comfortable and friendly bar, log or peat fire in lounge, lively landlord, small restaurant with excellent fresh fish and seafood; cl Christmas and New Year; no children.

ARDVASAR NG6303 **Ardvasar** *Ardvasar, Island of Skye IV45 8RS (01471) 844223* **£70,** plus special breaks; 9 rms. Comfortably modernised 18th-c inn with spectacular views and friendly new owners – all the staff have stayed on; nice residents' lounge and cocktail bar, popular locals' bar, open fire, enjoyable food inc local fish and shellfish, and very good breakfasts; may cl Nov–Feb.

ARISAIG NM6984 **Arisaig House** *Beasdale, Arisaig, Inverness-shire PH39 4NR (01687) 450622* **£150,** plus special breaks; 14 most attractive rms with wonderful views, and 2 suites. Beautifully furnished extremely comfortable hotel in attractive wooded and terraced grounds nr the shore; elegant drawing room, cosy morning room, lovely flowers, and very good imaginative food using fresh local produce; billiards room, croquet; cl Nov–Apr; children over 10.

CROMARTY NH7867 **Royal** *Marine Terrace, Cromarty, Ross-shire IV11 8YN (01381) 600217* ***£55,** plus special breaks; 10 rms. Traditional waterfront hotel with friendly owners and staff, attractive lounges, bars and sun lounge, and Scottish dishes in dining room; gets very busy in summer.

DRUMNADROCHIT NH5029 **Benleva** *Drumnadrochit, Inverness IV3 6UH (01456) 450288* ***£60;** 8 rms. Run by particularly helpful and friendly owners, this small family-run hotel is in a fine spot nr Loch Ness with plenty of outside pursuits (the owners will help organise fishing trips); comfortable residents' lounge with open fire, well stocked bar, and homely dining room with a good choice of tasty food using local meat and fish; pets welcome.

DRUMNADROCHIT NH5129 **Borlum Farmhouse** *Drumnadrochit, Inverness IV3 6XN (01456) 450358* **£58;** 6 rms, 2 with own bthrm. Traditional stone farmhouse with marvellous views over Loch Ness, warm comfortably furnished sitting room with log fire, summer conservatory sitting room, friendly atmosphere, and good Scottish breakfasts; BHS-approved riding centre, and you can help with animals on the farm; good provision for families; self-catering and caravan/camping also.

DRUMNADROCHIT NH4731 **Polmaily House** *Drumnadrochit, Inverness IV3 6XT (01456) 450343* **£110,** plus special breaks; 14 light, pretty rms. Very relaxing and homely hotel in 18 acres, with comfortable drawing room and library, open fires, and excellent food in the no smoking restaurant (wonderful packed lunches too); a happy place for families with well equipped indoor play area with lots of supervised activities, baby sitting and listening, hundreds of children's videos, plenty of ponies and pets, swimming pool, tennis, croquet, fishing, and boating; disabled access.

GARVE NH3969 **Inchbae Lodge** *Inchbae, Garve, Ross-shire IV23 2PH (01997) 455269* ***£66,** plus special breaks; 12 rms, 6 in chalet. Former hunting lodge – under new owners – in lovely Highland setting with comfortable homely lounges, winter log fires, small bar (liked by locals), and good fixed-price evening meals using fresh local produce; lots of wildlife, marvellous walks; cl Christmas; pets by prior arrangement; disabled access.

GLENELG NG8119 **Glenelg** *Glenelg, Kyle, Ross-shire IV40 8JR (01599) 522273* **£128 inc dinner,** plus special breaks; 6 individually decorated and comfortable rms, all with fine views. Overlooking Skye across its own beach, this carefully refurbished homely hotel has a relaxed bar, comfortable sofas and blazing fires, friendly staff and locals, good food using local venison, local hill-bred lamb and lots of wonderfully fresh fish and seafood, and quite a few whiskies; the drive to the inn involves spectacular views from the steep road; cl Nov–end Feb; disabled access.

HARLOSH NG2841 **Harlosh House** *Harlosh, Dunvegan, Island of Skye IV55 8ZG (01470) 521367* **£160 inc dinner;** 6 rms, 5 with own bthrm, and most with lovely views. One of the oldest buildings on north-west Skye, this 18th-c house is on a small peninsula jutting into Loch Bracadale; lochside gardens and lots of wildlife, wonderfully quiet homely lounge, home-made breads, imaginative cooking using fresh local produce in evening restaurant, and fine breakfasts; cl late Oct–Easter.

ISLE ORNSAY NG7015 **Kinloch Lodge** *Island Ornsay, Island of Skye IV43 8QY (01471) 833214* ***£116,** plus special breaks; 10 rms. Surrounded by rugged mountain scenery at the head of Loch Na Dal, this charming little white stone hotel has a relaxed atmosphere in its comfortable and attractive drawing rooms, antiques, portraits, flowers, log fires, and good imaginative food; cookery demonstrations; cl 23 Dec-22 Jan.

ISLE ORNSAY NG6912 **Tigh Osda Eilean Iarmain** *Isle Ornsay, Island of Skye IV43 8QR (01471) 833332* ***£100,** plus winter breaks; 12 individual rms (best in main hotel), all with fine views. Sparkling white hotel with Gaelic-speaking staff and locals, big cheerfully busy bar, pretty dining room with lovely sea views, and very good food.

LYBSTER ND2436 **Portland Arms** *Lybster, Caithness KW3 6BS (01593) 721208* **£68;** 24 comfortable rms. Staunch old granite hotel with really friendly staff, attractive dining room, generous helpings of good fresh food and fine breakfasts, small cosy panelled lounge bar, and informal locals' bar; shooting/fishing can be arranged; disabled access.

MELVICH NC8864 **Melvich Hotel** *Melvich, Thurso, Caithness KW14 7YJ (01641) 531206* **£60,** plus special breaks; 14 rms with showers (4 bthrms in addition). Small traditional hotel in lovely spot with homely furniture and peat fires in the civilised lounge, cosy bar, very relaxing atmosphere, friendly owners and staff, good food (especially local seafood and wild salmon), and fine views over Melvich Bay.

PLOCKTON NG8033 **Plockton** *41 Harbour St, Plockton, Ross-shire IV52 8TN (01599) 544274* ***£60,** plus special breaks; 8 rms (more planned in next-door cottage). Small notably friendly hotel in a row of elegant houses by a shore lined with palm trees and flowering shrubs, looking over the sheltered anchorage to rugged mountains, with comfortably furnished lively lounge bar, separate public bar, enjoyable food in little no smoking restaurant, good breakfasts, a good choice of whiskies, and attentive owners; good disabled access.

PORTREE NG4843 **Craiglockhart** *Beaumont Crescent, Portree, Island of Skye IV51 9DF (01478) 612233* ***£44;** 9 rms, 3 with own bthrm. Small family-run guesthouse overlooking harbour with fine views through picture windows in lounge and dining room and good breakfasts.

PORTREE NG4843 **Rosedale** *Beaumont Crescent, Portree, Island of Skye IV51 9DF (01478) 613131* **£80,** plus special breaks; 23 rms, many with harbour views. Built from 3 fishermen's cottages with lots of passages and stairs, this waterfront hotel has 2 traditional lounges, small first-floor restaurant with freshly cooked popular food, lots of whiskies in the cocktail bar, helpful staff, harbourside garden and marvellous views; cl mid-Oct–May.

RAASAY NG5641 (off Skye) **Isle of Raasay** *Raasay, Kyle of Lochalsh, Ross-shire IV40 8PB (01478) 660222* ***£50,** plus special breaks; 12 rms, plus 6 beds in bunkhouse. Family-run Victorian hotel with marvellous views over the Sound of Raasay to Skye, popular with walkers and birdwatchers; home-made food with an emphasis on fresh fish; no petrol on the island; disabled access.

SCARISTA NG0192 **Scarista House** *Scarista, Harris, Western Isles HS3 3HX (01859) 550238* **£110;** 5 rms, some in annexe. Marvellously wild countryside and empty beaches surround this isolated small hotel with its homely rooms, warm friendly atmosphere, plenty of books and records (no radio, TV or newspapers), and good food in candlelit dining room using home-grown veg and herbs, hand-made cheeses, their own eggs, home-made bread, cakes, biscuits, yoghurt and marmalade, and lots of fish and shellfish; excellent for wildlife, walks and fishing; cl Oct–Apr; dogs allowed.

SCOURIE NC1641 **Eddrachilles** *Badcall Bay, Scourie, Lairg, Sutherland IV27 4TH (01971) 502080* ***£79,** plus special breaks; 11 comfortable rms. Well run hotel in its own 320 acres overlooking Badcall Bay, with wonderful island views; popular with nature-lovers – bird sanctuary nearby, seals, fishing and walking; cl Nov–end Feb; children over 3.

SHIEL BRIDGE NG9319 **Kintail Lodge** *Shiel Bridge, Kyle of Lochalsh, Ross-shire IV40 8HL (01599) 511275* ***£74,** plus special breaks; 12 good-value big rms, most with own bthrm. Pleasantly informal and fairly simple former shooting lodge on

Loch Duich, with magnificent views, 4 acres of walled gardens, residents' lounge bar and comfortable sitting room, good well prepared food inc wild salmon, and fine collection of malt whiskies.

SHIELDAIG NG8153 **Tigh an Eilean** *Shieldaig, Strathcarron, Ross-shire IV54 8XN (01520) 755251* **£100;** 11 rms. Attractive hotel in outstanding position with lovely view of pine-covered island and sea, within easy reach of NTS Torridon Estate and Beinn Eighe nature reserve; pretty, comfortable residents' lounge with well stocked honesty bar, modern dining room with delicious food, warmly friendly owner; private fishing and sea fishing arranged; cl end Oct–Apr.

SKEABOST NG4148 **Skeabost House** *Skeabost, Portree, Island of Skye IV51 9NP (01470) 532202* **£88,** plus special breaks; 26 rms, 5 in annexe in Garden House. Smart, friendly little hotel with lawn running down to Loch Snizort (good salmon fishing), spacious no smoking lounge (marvellous buffet table), Victorian-style dining conservatory, lovely afternoon tea, log fires, high-ceilinged bar off stately hall, and billiards room; bog-and-water garden, 9-hole golf course; cl Nov–Mar.

STRONTIAN NM8161 **Kilcamb Lodge Hotel** *Strontian, Acharacle, Argyll PH36 4HY (01967) 402257* **£140 inc dinner,** plus special breaks; 11 rms. Warmly friendly little hotel in 30 acres by Loch Sunart, with log fires in 2 lounges, carefully cooked food using fresh local ingredients, fine choice of malt whiskies in small bar, and a relaxed atmosphere; cl Dec–end Feb, open New Year; children over 8 in dining room.

TARBERT NB1301 **Leachin House** *Tarbert, Harris, Western Isles HS3 3AH (01859) 502157* ***£80,** plus special breaks; 2 comfortable rms. Meaning 'house among the rocks', this neat and peaceful Victorian stone house on the loch shores (wonderful sunsets) is a haven for nature lovers and walkers – guided trips to look for seals, otters and eagles, fishing, and fine wild flowers in spring and early summer; friendly helpful owners, interesting nautical memorabilia, open fire in the drawing room, and particularly good food using delicious local seafood and lamb, served around a communal table in dining room with original 19th-c hand-painted French wallpaper; cl 18 Dec–18 Jan; children over 10.

TORRIDON NG8854 **Loch Torridon** *Torridon, Ashnasheen, Ross-shire IV22 2EY (01445) 791242* **£110,** plus special breaks; 21 comfortable rms. Built in 1887 as a shooting lodge in 58 acres at the foot of Ben Damph by Upper Loch Torridon, this turreted stone house has unusual ornate ceilings and panelling, log fires and innovative cooking; children over 12 in dining room; disabled access.

ULLAPOOL NH1192 **Altnaharrie** *Ullapool, Ross-shire IV26 2SS (01854) 633230* ***£330 inc dinner;** 8 rms. Across Loch Broom and reached by a 10-minute boat journey, this carefully restored house was originally built for drovers: 2 lounges with lots of books, an open fire, a mix of Scandinavian and English furnishings, marvellously quiet relaxing atmosphere, room service (they think tea-making facilities in rooms are a sign of neglect), perhaps the best food in Scotland – 5 set courses with much of the food home-grown or caught locally – and very good wine list; no smoking; cl Nov–Easter; children over 8.

ULLAPOOL NH1293 **Ceilidh Place** *Ullapool, Ross-shire IV26 2TY (01854) 612103* ***£110,** plus special breaks; 13 rms, most with own bthrm, plus 10 in annexe across the road. White-painted hotel in quiet side street with attractive conservatory dining room, stylish café/bar with attractive modern prints and plants, good food, decent wines and cognacs, and a relaxed friendly atmosphere.

To see and do

ACHILTIBUIE NC0208
Hydroponicum Bizarre indoor garden of the future – without any soil. Fascinating guided tours show how plants such as figs, lemons and bananas grow quite happily using the nutrients from the soil, but not the soil itself. Good home-made meals and snacks, shop; hourly tours Easter–Sept; (01854) 622202; *£4.

AUCKENGILL ND3664
Northlands Viking Centre (Old

School) Interesting displays on how the Norsemen came from Scandinavia to Shetland, Orkney and Caithness, with a Viking longship and other relics. Shop, disabled access; cl early Sept–May; (01955) 607771; £1.40.

BALMACARA NG8028 (on the A67) Huge crofting estate surrounding the Kyle of Lochalsh, with challenging walks through breathtaking scenery; you can still see traditional crofting at Drumbuie and Duirnish. The landscape is interspersed with lochs and impressive landmarks like the Five Sisters of Kintail (a fine target for hardened walkers) and Beinn Fhada. **Lochalsh House** (on the A87, 3m E of Kyle of Lochalsh) Wonderful woodland gardens, with peaceful walks, collections of rhododendrons, hydrangeas, fuchsias and other plants, and views towards Skye. Open all year; (01599) 566325; *£2; NTS. Nearby **Plockton** NG8083 is an idyllic waterside village, with palm trees along the village street; the TV series *Hamish Macbeth* was filmed here. The Plockton Hotel has good generous food.

BALNAKIEL NC3967 The most north-westerly part of mainland Britain, a wild and remote spot with spectacular scenery, and a little **craft village** (some bits cl Sun, and limited opening in winter; (01971) 511277; free).

BEINN EIGHE NG9963 One of the easier mountain ascents, with a well marked mountain trail making a circular route above Loch Maree.

BETTYHILL NC7062 **Strathnaver Museum** A good informative memorial to the notorious Clearances of the Highlands (cl 1–2pm and all day Sun, best to phone for winter opening; (01641) 521418; £1.50), with a finely carved 9th-c Celtic stone in the churchyard outside. The Bettyhill Hotel does decent food. Just S is a wonderful **nature reserve**, and the beach nearby is attractive.

CAPE WRATH NC2674 This stormy tip of coast is guarded by a lonely lighthouse. In summer you can make an adventurous expedition here from Durness nr the beautiful sea loch of Eriboll, by boat across the Kyle of Durness and then along a very long rough track to the lighthouse itself. Durness also has atmospheric boat tours of the **Smoo Cave** and its underground waterfall; cl Nov–May; (01971) 511259; £2.50.

CROMARTY NH7867 **Dolphin Ecosse** (Bank House) **Boat trips** out to see the local bottlenose dolphins: they can't guarantee sightings, but 9 out of 10 of their trips do come across dolphins, and they point out various seabirds and local landmarks along the way. Very friendly and informal, and rated very highly by readers. Whale-watching trips too in Aug and Sept – best to book on (01381) 600323; *£15. Cromarty itself is a delightfully sleepy place with lots of unspoilt buildings in its well restored core and a surprisingly good little **museum**. The friendly Royal Hotel has good-value food and lovely views.

DORNIE NG8826 **Eilean Donan Castle** (off the A87) Connected to the mainland by a causeway, and unforgettably beautiful. First built in 1220, destroyed in 1719, and then restored at the beginning of this century, it's perfectly positioned at the meeting point of Lochs Long, Duich and Alsh. New visitor centre with teas and shop; cl Nov–Mar; (01599) 555202; £3.50.

! DRUMNADROCHIT NH5330 The best place to begin exploring Loch Ness. You can generally take **boat trips**, some equipped with sonar for monster-spotting. **Official Loch Ness Monster Exhibition** (Drumnadrochit Hotel) Walk-through multi-media experience tracing the legend from its beginnings in Highland folklore to the scientific investigations of recent years. There's a kilt-maker on site. Meals, snacks, shop, disabled access; cl 25–26 Dec, 1 Jan; (01456) 450218; £4.50. **Urquhart Castle** (just SE) 14th-c remains, once the biggest castle in Scotland. A piper plays here every day Jun–Sept. Snacks, shop; cl 25–26 Dec, 1–2 Jan; (01456) 450551; £3.50.

DUNCANSBY HEAD ND4073 A grand spot on a fine day, with an absorbing cliff walk S for a good view of the spectacular Stacks of Duncansby, 60-metre (200-ft) offshore rock pinnacles.

DUNNET HEAD ND2074 Mainland Britain's furthest point N, with views to Orkney. A lovely spot on a clear early summer's day, with spring flowers in the close turf, and puffins pottering around – wild and unforgiving when the weather changes.

ELPHIN NC2110 **Highland & Rare Breeds Farm** (on the A835) Traditional Scottish farm animals close up, on a family-worked croft in attractive setting. They sell fleeces and hand-spun wool. Snacks, shop, some disabled access; cl Oct–mid-May; (01854) 666204; £3.25.

FALLS OF GLOMACH NH0125 Tremendous waterfall in a wilderness setting, a fine destination for walkers on Kintail.

FALLS OF MEASACH NH1978 With a mighty drop of 60 metres (200ft), these are the highlight of the mile-long, sheer-sided Corrieshalloch Gorge, owned by the NTS and equipped with a viewing platform.

FALLS OF SHIN NH5799 (on the B864 S of Lairg) There's a good chance of seeing **salmon leaping** here in Jun or early July, especially if there's been a dry spell followed by rain so that the river is in spate.

GAIRLOCH NG8076 The enthusiastically run **Gairloch Heritage Centre** is perhaps the best of the several heritage museums in the Highlands. Meals, snacks, shop, disabled access; cl Sun, and all Oct–Mar exc by arrangement; (01445) 712287; £2.50. The Old Inn here is a useful stop, and Gairloch is a useful base for hikers.

GLEN AFFRIC NH2124 One of the most majestic inland glens, with a walking route along its floor.

GLENFINNAN NM9080 **Jacobite Monument** (on the A830) Built in 1815 to commemorate the Highlanders who fought and died for Bonnie Prince Charlie, in a commanding position at the head of Loch Shiel. A visitor centre has exhibitions on the prince. Good snacks, shop, limited disabled access; visitor centre cl Oct–Easter and some lunchtimes; (01397) 722250; £1.50; NTS.

GOLSPIE NC8500 **Dunrobin Castle** (on the A9) Splendid castle – a gleaming turreted structure with views out to sea and gardens modelled on those at Versailles. The family home of the Earls and Dukes of Sutherland for longer than anyone can remember – it was named after Earl Robin, responsible for the 13th-c square keep. Drastically renovated in the 19th c, it has fine collections of furnishings and art, inc several Canalettos, and a unique collection of Pictish stones. Snacks, shop; cl am Sun, and mid-Oct–Mar, gardens open all year; (01408) 633177; *£6.

HELMSDALE ND0315 **Timespan Visitor Centre** (Dunrobin St) Recently extended centre with reconstructions of scenes in Highland history (with sound effects), art exhibitions and interesting herb garden. Teas, shop, disabled access; cl am Sun, and mid Oct-Easter; (01431) 821327; £2.75.

JOHN O' GROATS ND3773 Gets its share of visitors under the mistaken impression that it's the most northerly point on mainland Britain. Increasingly developed for tourists, though much less than Land's End in Cornwall, and still a pleasant spot. The hotel on the harbour looking across to the Orkneys has decent food.

KINLOCHBERVIE NC2156 A friendly village with decent beaches, mountains and scenery around; it's most lively around 6pm on Mon–Thurs (2pm Fri), when the fishing boats return to the pier and auction their catch. There may be boat trips round the harbour.

KIRKHILL NH5543 **Moniack Castle** (on the A862) Former fortress of the Lovat chiefs, now producing traditional country wines – also meat and game preserves, and an interesting apricot, almond and banana jam. There are tastings and tours. Snacks, shop; cl Sun, 25 Dec; (01463) 831283; £2.

KNOYDART NG8100 A real west-coast Highland wilderness, glorious roadless country that's irresistible to hardened walkers – given good weather, full equipment and strong legs.

LOCH NESS NH5224 A place of great beauty, a striking 24-mile loch with the largest volume of fresh water of any lake in the British Isles; up to 215

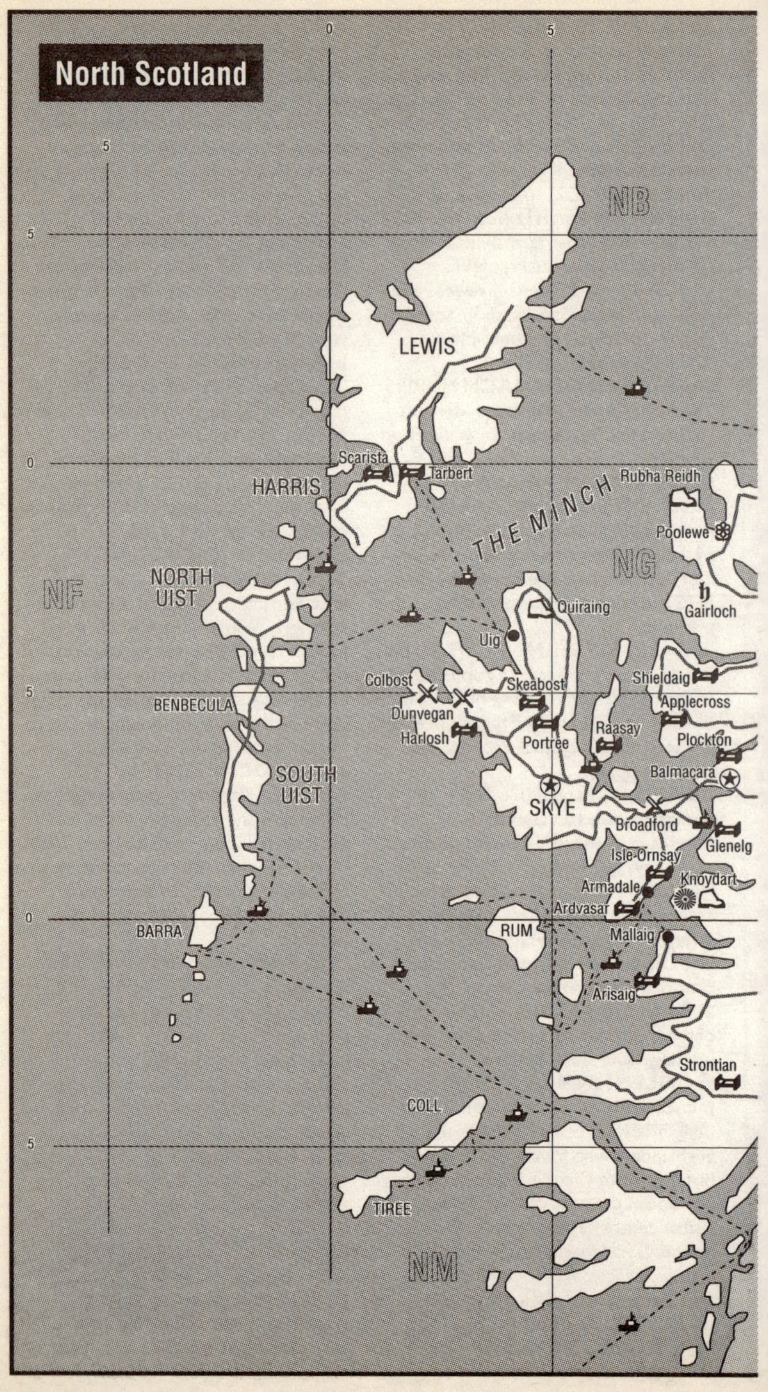
North Scotland
0
5
5
5
0
5
0
5
NB
NG
NF
NM
LEWIS
HARRIS
Scarista
Tarbert
Rubha Reidh
THE MINCH
Poolewe
NORTH UIST
Quiraing
Gairloch
Uig
Colbost
Skeabost
Shieldaig
BENBECULA
Dunvegan
Applecross
Harlosh
Raasay
Portree
Plockton
SOUTH UIST
Balmacara
SKYE
Broadford
Glenelg
Isle Ornsay
Armadale
Knoydart
Ardvasar
BARRA
RUM
Mallaig
Arisaig
Strontian
COLL
TIREE

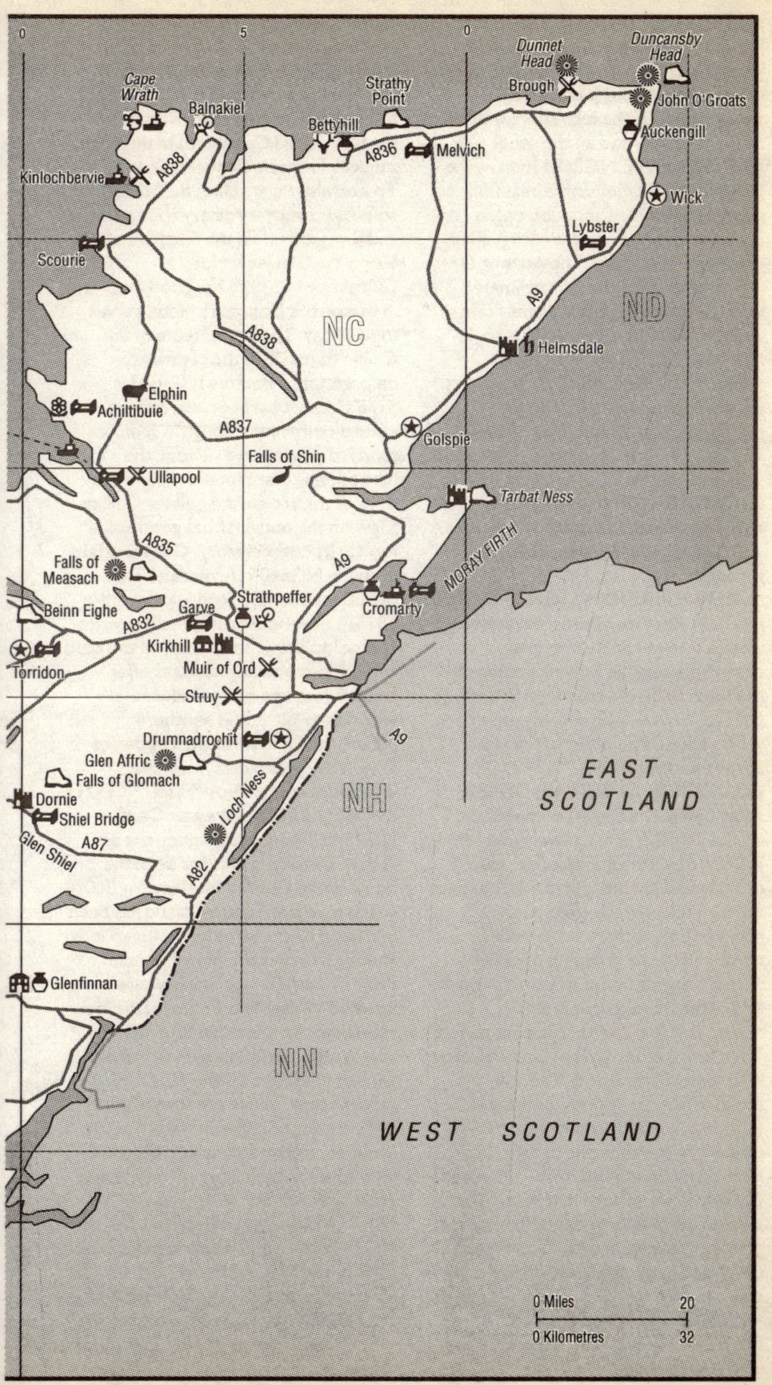

Cape Wrath
Balnakiel
Kinlochbervie
A838
Scourie
Strathy Point
Bettyhill
A836
Melvich
Dunnet Head
Brough
Duncansby Head
John O'Groats
Auckengill
Wick
Lybster
A9
ND
NC
A838
Helmsdale
Elphin
Achiltibuie
A837
Golspie
Falls of Shin
Ullapool
Tarbat Ness
A835
Falls of Measach
A9
MORAY FIRTH
Strathpeffer
Cromarty
Beinn Eighe
Garve
A832
Kirkhill
Torridon
Muir of Ord
Struy
A9
Drumnadrochit
Glen Affric
Falls of Glomach
Dornie
Shiel Bridge
Loch Ness
NH
EAST SCOTLAND
Glen Shiel
A87
A82
Glenfinnan
NN
WEST SCOTLAND
0 Miles 20
0 Kilometres 32

metres (700ft) deep in places, so it's not hard to see why stories spring up of what is hidden in its waters. The calmest drive along it is the B862, though it leaves the loch shore more than the trunk road on the other side.

POOLEWE NG8681 **Inverewe** (on the A832) Unmissable beautiful gardens full of rare and subtropical plants, with a magnificent background of mountain scenery. The Atlantic Drift is responsible for the microclimate which lets these unusual plants flourish even though this is further N than Moscow. Guided walks wkdys at 1.30pm, Apr–Sept. Meals, snacks, shop, disabled access; visitor centre and restaurant cl Nov–mid-Mar; (01445) 781200; £4.80; NTS. Choppys has good well priced food.

QUIRAING NG4569 (north-east Skye) A fascinating tumbled rock mass, with a surprisingly manageable path through it.

RUBHA REIDH LIGHTHOUSE NG7391 Remote outpost several miles along a track N of Melvaig; they organise enjoyable walking holidays in the splendidly wild countryside around; B & B or hostel-style rooms – don't worry about the colour of the water, it's just peaty; (01445) 771263.

SKYE NG4829 After Lewis, the biggest of the islands off the Scottish coast, now linked to the mainland by a bridge: islanders who'd campaigned for the bridge didn't expect the high tolls (which were later reduced), and others were initially unnerved by the prospect of easier access bringing floods of visitors and the end of the island's unique air of romance – so far neither has happened. The closing of the Kyle of Lochalsh ferry is lamented (though you can still emulate Bonnie Prince Charlie and Flora MacDonald on one from Mallaig, or the tiny summer one to Kylerhea from past Glenelg NG8119 – where the Glenelg Inn is an excellent stop). The coasts have plenty of opportunities for gentle pottering, and for finding quiet coves and bays, especially on the west coast, where for instance Tarskavaig NG5810, or the good Stein Inn NG2556 in the N, are lovely spots to watch the sun go down. There may be summer boat trips to the lonely and dramatic inlet of Loch Coruisk from Elgol NG5114. One of the island's lovely shoreside walks runs from Elgol to Loch na Creitheach at the heart of the formidable Cuillin mountain range, a mecca for rock-climbers. The Trotternish Peninsula in the NE has some quite extraordinary rock scenery and formations like the Old Man of Storr; the Glenview Hotel at Culnaknock up here has good food, and in season the Flodigarry Hotel serves food all day. The jagged teeth of the Cuillin to the SE of the centre are unforgettable. Portree NG4843 is Skye's busiest harbour, attractive and quite picturesque, though in summer it tends to swarm with visitors; the harbourside Pier Hotel is right in the thick of the action, the quieter Cuillins View on the outskirts has good-value food in its conservatory. **Clan Donald Centre** NG6404 (Armadale) The castle was built for Lord Macdonald in 1815; it now houses an excellent visitor centre looking at the history of the clan, and the surrounding 40 acres offer beautiful walks among gardens and woodlands. Sleat, this southern peninsula, is known as the Garden of Skye. Very good restaurant, shop, disabled access; cl Nov–Easter; (01471) 844305; £3.50. **Dunvegan Castle** NG2449 Dramatically set on the sea loch of Dunvegan, this has been the home of the Chief of Macleod for 800 years; no other Scottish castle has been inhabited by the same family for so long. Among its relics is a lock of Bonnie Prince Charlie's hair. Staying here inspired Walter Scott's *Lord of the Isles*. Meals, snacks, shops, limited disabled access; open daily but best to check in winter; (01470) 521206; £5, £3.50 gardens only. There are several good self-catering cottages in the attractive grounds, and **boat trips** go from the jetty to a nearby colony of brown and great grey Atlantic seals (Easter–Oct; £8). The **Museum of Island Life** NG2547 (Kilmuir) is also worth a look (cl Sun, and all Nov–Easter; £2). Besides places mentioned in the **Where to stay** and **Where to eat** sections, the Misty Isle at Dunvegan, Sligachan Inn at the junction of the A850 and A863 in the middle of the island, Struan Grill at Struan and waterside Old Inn at Carbost (handy for the Talisker distillery, which can be visited) all do decent food. Raasay NG5537 is a very peaceful island off Skye, an ideal place for gentle pottering without lots of competition from other visitors – and for some quite stiff hill walks if that's what you prefer.

STRATHPEFFER NH4858 Originally a fashionable 19th-c spa resort, this has quite a different feel from the rest of the area, with its rather continental appearance of dignified hotels and villas stepped up among its wooded slopes; some call it the Harrogate of the North. **Highland Museum of Childhood** In the restored Victorian railway station, with several craft workshops in summer. Snacks, shop; disabled access; cl am Sun, and all Nov–Feb (exc by appointment); (01997) 421031; *£1.50.

STRATHY POINT NC8269 (W of Thurso) With a lighthouse at the end of a narrow peninsula, a pleasant stroll along the little road from its car park.

TARBAT NESS NH9487 Jutting from the S side of Dornoch Firth, this is rather isolated, but worth the journey for the walk around the peninsula, from Portmahomack, past the lighthouse, and then along the south coast past a ruined castle to reach Rockfield.

TORRIDON COUNTRYSIDE CENTRE NG9055 (junction of the A896 and the Diabaig road) Gateway to a huge area of nature reserve in stunning mountain scenery – some say the best in Scotland. It has displays on the scenery and wildlife, as well as a deer park and deer museum. Visitor centre cl am Sun, and all Oct–Apr; (01445) 791221; £1.50; NTS. Nearby at the Mains there are herds of red deer. Torridon is wonderful for challenging walks, and there are a few outstanding easier ones, based, for example on Loch Torridon's shores. The Kinlochewe Hotel (on the A896 E) has decent food; to reach anywhere N of here by car from the S, incidentally, it's much quicker to go by Inverness than to make your way all the way up the west coast.

ULLAPOOL NH1294 A good centre, with quite a busy harbour, a lot going on for a small place – and good eating (besides the places we've picked out in the **Where to stay** and **Where to eat** sections, the fish and chip restaurant is very good, with surprisingly presentable white wines, and the Ferry Boat is useful). You can get a ferry out to the Summer Isles.

WICK ND3650 The history of the town is well presented in the **Wick Heritage Centre**, in 8 buildings by the harbour; cl Sun, and all Oct–May; (01955) 605393; *£2. **Caithness Glass Factory** (Wick Airport industrial estate) has glass-making demonstrations (not wknds), and factory seconds. Meals, snacks, shop, disabled access; cl Sun Jan–Easter; (01955) 602286; free. **Castle of Old Wick** (just S) Ruined 4-storey square tower, probably dating from the 12th c.

Days Out

Highland drama: Beinn Eighe nature reserve/mountain trail; lunch at the Kinlochewe Hotel near Torridon; the Countryside Centre there; drive to Applecross.

Sea lochs of the far north-west: Ullapool; lunch at the Morefield Motel there; drive on the A835 SE to the Falls of Measach; take the A832 to Inverewe garden, Poolewe; Gairloch Heritage Museum.

Skye's changing moods: Portree; drive round Trotternish peninsula, past the Old Man of Storr and the Quiraing; lunch at Skeabost House, Skeabost; Dunvegan Castle, Armadale; boat trip to spot seals, or the Museum of Island Life (cl Sun).

Inns doing a decent bite to eat are very much at a premium in this part of the world, and a welcome sight indeed after miles of empty road. Besides those listed elsewhere, ones we can recommend for their positions include the Aultbea Inn at Aultbea NG8689, Aultguish Hotel NH3570 on the A835 nr Loch Glascarnoch, Badachro Inn at Badachro NG7773, Northern Sands at Dunnet ND2170, Lock at Fort Augustus NH3709, Cluanie by the loch (walks and maybe eagles) in Glen Shiel NH0711, Garvault Inn extraordinarily isolated on the B871 N of Kinbrace NC8732, Kylesku Hotel at Kylesku NC2234 (the boatman here has taken readers for fascinating 4-hour boat tours), Lewiston Arms at Lewiston NH5029, Loch Carron Hotel on Loch Carron NG9039, Glenuig Hotel at Lochailort NM7682, Inver Lodge Hotel overlooking Lochinver harbour NC0923, Scrabster Inn at Scrabster ND0970, Ben View at Strontian NM8161, Loch Maree Hotel at Talladale NG8970 and Ben Loyal Hotel at Tongue NC5957. Almost all have bedrooms.

Where to eat

BROADFORD NG6323 **Fig Tree** *Island of Skye (01471) 822616* Enjoyable home-made food inc fresh fish and vegetarian choices in friendly little place; cl Sun, and end Nov–1 Mar; disabled access. **£17**|£3.50.

BROUGH ND2273 **Dunnet Head Tearoom/Restaurant** *(01847) 851774* Small traditional unpretentious cottage with good reasonably priced food and snacks served by warmly friendly owners – fair choice of vegetarian dishes, fresh salmon, local seafood, and local beef; take your own wine; bdrms; open 3–8pm (last orders then), tearoom cl Oct–Easter; children must be well behaved. **£12**|£4.

COLBOST NG2050 **Three Chimneys** *Island of Skye (01470) 511258* No smoking crofter's cottage nr sea with cosy feel in 2 stone-walled rooms, open fires, friendly owners, thoughtful wine list, and most enjoyable food with a strong emphasis on fish (though plenty of game and vegetarian choices, too); morning coffee and afternoon teas; bdrms planned; cl Nov–Mar; children over 10 in evening restaurant (any age at lunchtime). **£30**|£5.75.

DUNVEGAN NG2449 **Macleod's Table** *Dunvegan Castle, Island of Skye (01470) 521310* Decorated with pine throughout, popular family restaurant with very reasonably priced generous morning coffee, snacks and full meals, and afternoon teas; friendly helpful staff; loch cruises, sea colony, castle gardens and craft shops; cl 31 Oct–mid-Mar; disabled access. **£17**|£5.

KINLOCHBERVIE NC2455 **Old School House** *Inshegra (01971) 521383* Very good food in old school building with school-related items like photographs, maps, notebooks on tables; home-grown vegetables, local fish and venison, enjoyable puddings, and very good service; bdrms in newish building; disabled access; cl 25–26 Dec, 1 Jan. **£16**|£3.50.

MUIR OF ORD NH5251 **Dower House** *(01463) 870090* Very good modern cooking in attractive hotel restaurant, fine wines, and friendly service; lovely gardens; bdrms; children over 5 in restaurant. **£35**|£3.50.

STRUY NH3939 **Struy Inn** *(01463) 761219* Clean, pleasant and friendly small restaurant with very good fairly priced food, and good range of malt whiskies; in winter cl Mon and Tues; disabled access. **£19.75**|£4.

ULLAPOOL NH1294 **Morefield Motel** *(01854) 612161* Large helpings of exceptionally fresh enterprisingly cooked fish and seafood (owners are ex-fishermen and divers), Aberdeen Angus steaks and roast beef, and vegetarian dishes in smart restaurant of basic hotel, also bar food; restaurant cl 25–26 Dec, 1 Jan; disabled access. **£20**|£5.

Special thanks to David Lintonbor, G and J Dundas, Mrs M Burgess, Graham McIntosh, Mrs A Storm, John Brooks, Mr and Mrs K McAnna, Mr and Mrs B Cutt, Gerald Slocock.

Scotland Calendar

Some of these dates were provisional as we went to press. Please check information with the telephone numbers provided.

Highland Games take place all over Scotland and include ancient traditional sports: putting the stone, throwing the hammer and tossing the caber, as well as athletics, Highland dancing, piping and carnival entertainments.

Glasgow UK City of Architecture & Design: festivals, exhibitions, displays and open buildings *throughout the year* (0141) 287 7346 for brochure

JANUARY

1 **Edinburgh** Ruskin Exhibition at the Scottish National Portrait Gallery – *till 7 Mar* (0131) 624 6200; also Turner Watercolours at the National Gallery of Scotland – *till Sun 31* (0131) 624 6200; **Kirkwall** Boys' and Men's Ba' Games: 200-year-old mass football game with tussles lasting up to 6 hours (01856) 872961; **Stonehaven** Fireball Festival: old tradition of swinging fireballs (01569) 762635

2 **Edinburgh** Handel's *Messiah* at the Festival Theatre (0131) 529 6000; **Glasgow** New Year Concert at the Royal Concert Hall (0141) 287 5511

11 **Burghead** Burning of the Clavie: old Scottish New Year, burning tar barrel procession (01343) 835773

14 **Glasgow** Celtic Festival – *till Sun 31* (0141) 332 6633

15 **Scalloway** Fire Festival: torch procession and burning galley (01595) 880345

22 **Aviemore** Sled Dog Racing in Glenmore Forest – *till Tues 26* (01604) 686281

25 Robert Burns Day: commemoration of Scotland's national poet around the country; **Greenock** Inverclyde & Renfrew Musical Festival – *till 6 Feb* (01475) 727139

26 **Lerwick** Up-Helly-Aa: traditional Viking Fire Festival – *till Weds 27* (01595) 693434

27 **Aberdeen** Exhibition: etchings by Simon Fraser exploring Celtic legends at the Aberdeen Art Gallery – *till 27 Mar* (01224) 646333

FEBRUARY

3 **Glasgow** Outdoor Leisure Exhibition – *till Sun 7* (0141) 248 3000

6 **Edinburgh** Rugby International: Scotland v Wales (0131) 346 5000

19 **Glasgow** Frank Lloyd Wright Exhibition at the Art Gallery & Museum – *till 11 Apr* (0141) 287 1999

22 **Inverness** Music Festival – *till Sat 27* (01463) 233902

23 **Inverurie** Royal Northern Highland Aberdeen Spring Show at Thainstowe Agricultural Centre (01224) 790613

27 **Aviemore** Try A Snow-Sport – *till Sun 28* (01479) 861261

MARCH

1 **Glenshee** Snow Fun Week – *till Mon 8* (01575) 582213

12 **Milnathort** Folk Festival – *till Sun 14* (01577) 864164

Scotland Calendar (cont.)

19 **Aviemore** Cairngorm Snow Festival – *till Sun 21* (01479) 861261; **Edinburgh** Rugby International: Scotland v Ireland (0131) 346 5000
24 **Glasgow** Interior Design Show – *till 28 Apr* (0141) 287 3000
26 **Gatehouse of Fleet** Festival of Music, Arts & Crafts – *till Sun 28* (01557) 814030

APRIL

1 **Edinburgh** Folk Festival – *till Sun 4* (0131) 554 3092
3 **Edinburgh** Science Festival – *till Sun 18* (0131) 220 3977; **Elgin** Great North of Scotland Model Railway Show – *till Sun 4* (01343) 549341
4 **Edinburgh** Easter Treasure Trail at the Zoo – *till Mon 5* (0131) 334 9171
9 **Auchterarder** Gleneagles Spring Festival of Show-Jumping – *till Sun 11* (01764) 665307; **Edinburgh** International Youth Rugby Final at Murrayfield (0141) 644 5463
10 **Scotland** PGA National Golf Week: free lessons (0131) 663 8038
16 **Ayr** Scottish Grand National – *till Sat 17* (01292) 264179; **Speyside** Scotch Whisky Festival – *till Mon 19* (01309) 690073
17 **Brodie Castle** Double Daffodil Show at the Castle – *till Sun 18* (01309) 641371; **Culloden** Annual Service of Commemoration of the battle of 1746 (01463) 790607; **Oban** Fiddlers Rally (01631) 710488
26 **Glasgow** Big Big Country: music festival – *till 5 June* (0141) 553 1055
29 **Island of Bute** Jazz Festival – *till 3 May* (01700) 502151; **Orkney** Country & Irish Music Festival – *till 2 May* (01856) 761204
30 **Oban** Highlands & Islands Music & Dance Festival – *till 2 May* (01631) 710201; **Perth** Food Festival – *till 9 May* (01738) 638353

MAY

1 **Melrose** International Sevens Rugby Tournament (01890) 822993
8 **Dumfries** Book Fair (01556) 670395; **Kintyre** Landmark Trust Open Day at Saddell Castle and Tangy Mill: properties not usually open to the public (01628) 825925
9 **Gourock** Highland Games (01475) 714850
20 **Perth** Festival of the Arts – *till Sun 30* (01738) 475295
21 **Highlands & Islands** Festival – *till 5 June* (01463) 719000; **Islay** Festival – *till Sat 29* (01496) 302418; **Strichen** Buchan Heritage Festival – *till Sun 23* (01224) 288813
22 **Loch Fyne** Seafood Fair – *till Sun 23* (01786) 445222; **Thornhill** Country Fair at Drumlanrig Castle – *till Sun 23* (01350) 723226
24 **Edinburgh** Cricket World Cup: Scotland v Bangladesh (0171) 432 1200; **Island of Skye** Story-Telling Festival – *till Sat 29* (01470) 511340
27 **Loch Fyne** Scottish Series National Yacht Race – *till 1 Jun* (0141) 221 2774; **Orkney** Traditional Folk Festival – *till Sun 30* (01856) 872856
28 **Dumfries & Galloway** Arts Festival – *till 6 Jun* (01387) 260447; **Inverness** Highland Food Festival – *till 5 Jun* (01463) 724262
29 **Bathgate** and West Lothian Highland Games (01506) 654507; **Blackford** Highland Games (01764) 682314; **Blair Atholl** Atholl Highlanders Parade at Blair Castle (01796) 481207; **Loch Fyne** Seafood Fair – *till Sun 30* (01499) 600217; **St Andrews** Country Fair at Craigtoun Park – *till Sun 30* (01334) 412200
30 **Blair Atholl** Highland Gathering at Target Park (01796) 481355
31 **Edinburgh** Cricket World Cup: Scotland v New Zealand (0171) 432 1200

Scotland Calendar (cont.)

JUNE

4 **Motherwell** National Gardening Show at Strathclyde Country Park – *till Sun 6* (01698) 252565

5 **Lockerbie** Gala and Riding of the Marches (01576) 202674; **Strathmiglo** Highland Games (01337) 860467

6 **Turriff** Pipe Band Contest (01224) 288813

7 **Island of Arran** Folk Festival – *till Sun 13* (01770) 302623

10 **Dumfries** RSAC Scottish Rally: motorsport event – *till Sat 12* (0141) 204 4999; **Lanark** Lanimer Day: street tableaux, beating retreat, checking of old burgh boundaries (01555) 661661

11 **Keith** Traditional Music & Song Festival – *till Sun 13* (01542) 810222

12 **Dumfries** Festival Week – *till re-enactment of the granting of the Royal Charter in 1186 and crowning of the Queen of the South on Sat 19* (01387) 254805; **Glasgow** West End Festival inc Midsummer Carnival Parade – *till Sun 27* (0141) 341 0844; **Stirling** Show (01786) 445222; **Strathpeffer Spa** Victorian Gala (01997) 421214

14 **Paisley** Festival – *till 3 July* (0141) 889 3151

17 **Burgie** International Horse Trials – *till Sun 20* (01343) 850281

18 **Killin** Traditional Music Festival – *till Sun 20* (01567) 820224; **Orkney** St Magnus Festival – *till Weds 23* (01856) 872669

19 **Aberdeen** Highland Games in Hazelhead Park (01224) 522190; **Helensburgh** Faslane Fair: helicopters, ships, dancing (01436) 674321; **Oldmeldrum** Sports and Highland Games (01224) 288813; **Stonehaven** Vintage Vehicle Rally – *till Sun 20* (01224) 288813

24 **Dunkeld & Birnam** Arts Festival – *till Sun 27* (01350) 727688; **Edinburgh** Royal Highland Show at Ingliston Showground – *till Sun 27* (0131) 333 2444

25 **Dingwall** Highland Traditional Music Festival – *till Sun 27* (01349) 830388

27 **Beauly** Highland Games (01463) 782239

30 **Glasgow** International Jazz Festival – *till 4 July* (0141) 552 3552

JULY

3 **Annan** Riding of the Marches (01461) 202708; **Doune** and Dunblane Agricultural Show (01786) 202708; **Forres** Highland Games (01309) 673289; **Paisley** Sma' Shot Day: celebration of Paisley's weaving heritage (0141) 889 3151; **Perth** Scottish Game Conservancy Fair at Scone Palace – *till Sun 4* (01620) 850577; **Portsoy** Scottish Traditional Boat Festival: racing, music, drama – *till Sun 4* (01261) 843598

7 **Luss** Loch Lomond World Invitational Golf Championship – *till Sat 10* (0990) 661661

9 **Thornhill** Horse Driving Trials at Drumlanrig Castle – *till Sun 11* (01848) 200441

10 **Alva** Highland Games (01786) 813523; **Dingwall** Highland Gathering (01349) 862024; **Glamis** Transport Rally at Glamis Castle – *till Sun 11* (01307) 462496

11 **Stirling** Highland Games (01259) 761735

12 **Skye & Lochalsh** Festival – *till Fri 23* (01471) 844207

14 **Stornoway** Hebridean Celtic Music Festival at Lews Castle – *till Sat 17* (01851) 701828

Scotland Calendar (cont.)

15 **Armadale** Hebridean Music, Theatre and World Music – *till Sat 24* (01471) 844207; **Carnoustie** Open Golf Championship – *till Sun 18* (01334) 472112

16 **Stonehaven** Folk Festival – *till Sun 18* (01569) 765063

17 **Elgin** Highland Games (01343) 541856; **Lochcarron** Highland Games (01520) 722554; **Tomintoul** Highland Games (01807) 580407

18 **Stonehaven** Highland Games (01569) 768358

24 **Glamis** Grand Scottish Prom at Glamis Castle (01307) 840393; **Inverness** Highland Games (01463) 724262; **Largs** International Celtic Watersports Festival – *till Sat 31* (01475) 689899; **Lochearnhead** Highland Gathering (01567) 830229

25 **Alford** Cavalcade: arena events, over 200 exhibits at Grampian Transport Museum (019755) 62292; **Castle Douglas** Civil Week – *till 1 Aug* inc parade *on Sat 31* (01556) 502839

26 **Gatehouse of Fleet** Gala – *till 2 Aug* (01557) 874765; **Inverness** Tattoo – *till Sat 31* (01463) 234511

28 **Stranraer** Show (01776) 870207

30 **Edinburgh** International Jazz & Blues Festival – *till 8 Aug* (0131) 225 2202; **Greenock** Cutty Sark Tall Ships Race: over 100 tall ships – *till 2 Aug* (01475) 551256; **Langholm** Common Riding: ceremonial procession, Highland dancing, sports (01387) 380428

31 **Callander** World Highland Games – *till 1 Aug* (01877) 330919; **Dufftown** Highland Games (01340) 820487; **Inverness-shire** World Orienteering Championships and Highland Championships – *till 8 Aug* (01463) 714712; **Palnackie** World Flounder Trampling Championships at Glen Sand: winner tramps the heaviest flounder (01556) 600234

AUGUST

1 **Maybole** Classic Vehicle Show at Culzean Castle (01655) 760269; **Patron Village** Scottish Alternative Games (01557) 814030

2 **Auchterarder** WPGA Golf Tournament at Gleneagles – *till Sun 8* (01764) 662231; **Turriff** Agricultural Show – *till Tues 3* (01224) 288813

4 **Aberdeen** International Youth Festival – *till Sat 14* (0181) 946 2995; **Island of Skye** Highland Games (01478) 612608

5 **Speyside** Speyfest: pan-Celtic festival of traditional music and song – *till Sun 8* (01343) 820951

6 **Edinburgh** Military Tattoo at Edinburgh Castle: massed piped bands, display teams, dancers – *till Sat 28* (0131) 225 1188; **St Andrews** Lammas Fair – *till Tues 10* (01334) 412200

7 **Aberlour** Highland Games (01340) 871325; **Aboyne** Highland Games (013398) 87132

8 **Edinburgh** Festival Fringe – *till Mon 30* (0131) 226 5257

9 **Lerwick** Cutty Sark Tall Ships Race: over 100 tall ships – *till Thurs 12* (01595) 694335

12 **Ballater** Highland Games at Monaltrie Park (013397) 55377

13 **Sanquhar** Riding of the Marches – *till Sat 21* (01659) 58287

14 **Arbroath** Seafest – *till Sun 15* (01674) 664000; **Aviemore** Highlands & Islands Beer Festival – *till Weds 18* (01479) 812060; **Edinburgh** Book Festival – *till Mon 30* (0131) 228 5444; **Glasgow** World Pipe Band Championships (0141) 221 5414

15 **Edinburgh** International Film Festival – *till Sun 29* (0131) 228 4051; **Edinburgh** International Festival – *till 4 Sept* (0131) 473 2001

19 **Annan** National Sheepdog Trials – *till Sat 21* (01234) 352672

Scotland Calendar (cont.)

20 Glenisla Highland Gathering (01575) 582349; **Lauder** Scottish Championship Horse Trials at Thirlestane Castle – *till Sun 22* (01896) 860242

21 Brodie Castle Family Fun Day at the Castle (01309) 641371; **Edinburgh** Langholm & Eskerdale Festival of Music & the Arts – *till Sun 29* (013873) 80914; **Kirkmichael** Strathardle Highland Gathering (01250) 881337

22 Crieff Highland Games (01764) 652578

25 Oban Argyllshire Gathering and Highland Games – *till Thurs 26* (01546) 602615

27 Dunoon Cowal Highland Gathering: world's largest Highland games – *till Sat 28* (01369) 703206; **Kirkcudbright** Arts Festival – *till 11 Sept* (01557) 332301

28 Aviemore Scottish Balloon & Harley Davidson Festival – *till Sun 29* (01479) 861261; **Lonach** Highland Gathering and Games (01224) 288813; **Peebles** Arts Festival – *till 12 Sept* (01721) 720371; **Strathdon** Lonach Highland Gathering and Games (019756) 51302

SEPTEMBER

3 Dundee Flower Show: over 500 exhibits at Camperdown Country Park – *till Sun 5* (01382) 433815

4 Blairgowrie Braemar Night: fireworks, live bands (01250) 872960; **Braemar** Royal Highland Gathering (01339) 755377; **Loch Lomond** Scottish Pipe Band Championships at Balloch Castle Country Park (01389) 737269

5 Blairgowrie Highland Games (01828) 627253; **Dumfries & Galloway** Doors Open Day: free access to many sites of cultural and natural interest, some not always open to the public such as Buittle Tower (jousting and re-enactments); complete list from (01387) 247543

10 Aberdeen Festival of Science & Family Activities – *till Sun 19* (01224) 273161; **Dalnaglar** British Horse Trials Association at Dalnaglar Castle (01250) 872960; **Hawick** Borders Festival of Jazz & Blues – *till Sun 12* (01750) 377278

11 Leuchars RAF Battle of Britain Airshow: over 100 aircraft (01334) 839000; **Nairn** International Amateur Golf Tournament at Nairn Golf Club – *till Sun 12* (01667) 453208

17 Creetown Country Music Festival – *till Sun 19* (01671) 820251

18 Carrbridge World Porridge Championships (01479) 841240; **Glenrothes** Fife Garden Festival at Rothes Halls – *till Sun 19* (01592) 412341

23 Oban Seafood Festival – *till Weds 29* (01631) 563122

OCTOBER

8 Lochaber Royal National Mod: Highland gaelic meeting for music and poetry – *till Fri 15* (01463) 231226; **Mull** Rally: top UK rally crews – *till Mon 11* (01688) 302133

15 Aberdeen Alternative Festival – *till Sun 24* (01224) 635822

20 Glasgow Big Big World: music festival – *till Sat 30* (0141) 204 4400

21 Alloa Real Ale Festival – *till Fri 22* (01259) 452486

Scotland Calendar (cont.)

NOVEMBER

5 Inverness Fireworks at Bught Park (01463) 724224
6 Island of Skye Fireworks: pipe band, torchlit procession at Dunvegan Castle (01470) 521206
24 St Andrews Festivities Week celebrating St Andrew's Day – *till Tues 30* (01334) 477872

DECEMBER

24 Aviemore Torchlight Procession (01479) 810624
25 Kirkwall Boys' and Men's Ba' Games (*see 1 Jan for details*)
27 Aviemore Mid-Winter Festival – *till 1 Jan* (01479) 810188; **Edinburgh** 7 Day Millennium: 7 days of family events – *till 3 Jan* (0131) 473 3898
29 Edinburgh Hogmanay – *till 1 Jan* (0131) 473 3800
31 Biggar Ne'erday Bonfire: Druid ceremony, torchlight procession, pipe band (01899) 220661; **Comrie** Flambeaux Procession: traditional Pagan event (01764) 652578; **Dumfries** Millennium Ball at Easterbrook Hall (01387) 770531; **Inverness** Hogmanay and Winter Festival – *till 1 Jan* (01997) 421160; **Stonehaven** Fireball Festival: old tradition of swinging fireballs (01569) 762635

We welcome reports from readers

This *Guide* depends on readers' reports. Do help us if you can – in return, we offer a discount on the next edition to people who've helped us with reports for it. Tell us what you think about places already in it, and anything extra you think we should say about them. And send us your ideas for inclusion in the next edition: places to visit, eat at or stay in, attractive drives or walks, maybe even unusual interesting shops you know of. Use the card in the middle, the report forms at the end, or just write – no stamp needed: *The Good Guide to Britain*, FREEPOST TN1569, Wadhurst, E Sussex TN5 7BR.

WALES

Tourist Board advertising in 1998 showing Wales's empty beaches and lonely mountains infuriated some Welsh holiday firms – they thought the emptiness would suggest that no-one wanted to go. But the beauty of Wales for visitors is that it does indeed have this glorious unspoilt scenery – alongside plenty of enjoyable and interesting places to visit. This combination is particularly powerful in North Wales (which gets the lion's share of summer visitors). West Wales has the most attractive coastline, with lovely walks along it – even in bad weather when upland areas are more or less a write-off, the coast preserves a gloomy magnificence. Mid Wales has fewer tourist attractions: its strength is the grand scenery, which includes the Brecon Beacons National Park, the empty and lonely Cambrian Mountains (wonderful high-level drives here), and the 'Welsh lake district' of the Elan Valley reservoirs. The chief appeal of South Wales is its good choice of interesting days out, but here too there is fine scenery – especially parts of the Gower Peninsula, and the gorge of the lower Wye Valley, graced by Tintern Abbey.

Wales is famous for its medieval castles and spectacular private railways. All sorts of other enjoyable outings run from dramatic show caves to grand houses and gardens, from animal parks to Celtic myth-making, from engrossing see-how-we-lived-and-worked centres to lively alternatives for the future.

We have mentioned a handful of the Roman and prehistoric sites in which the area abounds. You can get more information from CADW (Welsh Historic Monuments Commission), (01222) 500200, which is also responsible for the care of the great majority of the historic castles and other monuments here: if you plan to visit many of their sites, an Explorer Pass (about £15 for a week, less for 3 days) from tourist information centres or CADW direct is good value as it admits to all.

You can cut down on transport costs with a 7-day Freedom of Wales Rover train pass (around £59), covering train trips round all of Wales and out to Chester.

North Wales

Great landscapes, with lots to do and see.

North Wales has a splendid range of places to stay in, many in superb countryside. There are good long beaches, attractive traditional family resorts, and also plenty of places where you can get away from the crowds even at the height of summer – particularly on the shores of the very Welsh Lleyn Peninsula. The landscape varies richly, from majestic mountain expanses to the intricate and rather intimate landscapes of Clwyd, the luscious Vale of Conwy and the peace of Anglesey – twice the size of the Isle of Wight with just half the population. Dramatic Snowdonia gives plenty of fine walking, both gentle and taxing – somewhere to justify a walking holiday. The much less visited Berwyn Hills further inland also give memorable scenic drives.

A wide choice of places to visit and things to do includes tremendous castles, and lots of picturesque railway lines – the one up Snowdon is stunning. While some Welsh mining museums have closed this year, the slate mining museum above Llanberis has been a major beneficiary of lottery cash. Among great houses, Erddig is particularly enjoyed by readers, Bodelwyddan Castle makes for a very good family visit, and Plas Mawr in Conwy is remarkable. Bodnant Garden is glorious, and there are many other enjoyable family days out.

Where to stay

ABERSOCH SH3225 **Porth Tocyn** *Bwlch Tocyn, Abersoch, Pwllheli, Gwynedd LL53 7BU (01758) 713303* **£83,** plus special breaks; 17 attractive rms, some with sea views. On a headland overlooking Cardigan Bay, this is a lovely place to stay – with a refreshingly sensible and helpful approach to families (though not solely a family hotel); very friendly, hard-working owners and staff, several cosy interconnecting sitting rooms with antiques and fresh flowers, most enjoyable traditional cooking in the restaurant (lots of options such as light lunches, high teas for children as they must be over 7 for dinner in the restaurant, and imaginative Sun lunches), and a happy atmosphere; lots of space in the pretty garden, heated swimming pool in summer, hard tennis court; cl mid-Nov–wk before Easter; disabled access.

BEAUMARIS SH6076 **Olde Bulls Head** *Castle St, Beaumaris, Anglesey, Gwynedd LL58 8AP (01248) 810329* ***£81,** plus special breaks; 15 rms with antiques and brass bedsteads. Partly 15th-c pub nr the castle; with snug alcoves, low beams and an open fire in the quaint rambling bar, interesting decorations, popular bar food, very good restaurant food (especially fish), fine wines, and cheery service; the entrance to the pretty courtyard is through the biggest single-hinged door in Britain; cl 25–26 Dec, 1 Jan; children over 7 in restaurant in evening.

BEDDGELERT SH5948 **Sygun Fawr Country House** *Beddgelert, Caernarfon, Gwynedd LL55 4NE (01766) 890258* ***£57,** plus special breaks; 10 rms. Marvellous views of the Gwynant Valley and the Snowdon range from this secluded 17th-c hotel, and lots of surrounding walks; comfortable sitting room, well-stocked bar, and home cooking in the candlelit, traditionally furnished dining room; sauna.

BETWS-Y-COED SH7955 **Ty Gwyn** *Betws-y-coed, Gwynedd LL24 0SG (01690) 710383* ***£56,** plus special breaks; 12 lovely rms, most with own bthrm. Welcoming 17th-c coaching inn with interesting old prints, furniture and bric-à-brac (owners own the antique shop next door), good food and friendly service; pleasant setting overlooking the river and a very handy base for the area; children free if sharing parents' rm; cl Mon–Weds in Jan; disabled access.

BLAENAU FFESTINIOG SH7045 **Queens** *1 High St, Blaenau Ffestiniog, Gwynedd LL41 3ES (01766) 830055* **£50,** plus special breaks; 12 individually decorated rms. By the famous narrow-gauge railway and surrounded by Snowdonia National Park, a most attractively refurbished Victorian hotel, with real ales in the convivial lounge bar, good all-day food in the bistro (converts to a more formal evening restaurant with imaginative dishes), and swift, friendly service; lots to do nearby; cl 25 Dec.

BRYNSIENCYN SH4868 **Plas Trefarthen** *Brynsiencyn, Llanfairpwllgwyngyll, Isle of Anglesey, Gwynedd LL61 6SJ (01248) 430379* **£44;** 9 rms, 7 with own bthrm. Happy and comfortable family house with panoramic views of Caernarfon Castle and Snowdonia; full-size snooker table, table tennis, and home-cooked food using produce grown on the farm; Mrs Roberts is a well known soprano soloist for Welsh choirs; self-catering also; cl Christmas.

CAERNARFON SH5163 **Seiont Manor** *Llanrug, Caernarfon, Gwynedd LL55 2AQ (01286) 673366* **£130,** plus special breaks; 28 luxurious rms. Fine hotel built from the original farmstead of a Georgian manor house, in 150 acres of mature parkland; open fires and comfortable sofas in the lounge, restful atmosphere in the library and drawing room, imaginative food in the restaurant's 4 interconnecting areas; leisure suite with swimming pool, gym, sauna and solarium.

CAPEL COCH SH4581 **Tre-Ysgawen Hall** *Capel Coch, Llangefni, Isle of Anglesey, Gwynedd LL77 7UR (01248) 750750* **£120,** plus special breaks; 19 lavish rms. Handsome Victorian stone mansion with landscaped gardens; plushly comfortable bar, carefully decorated lounge, friendly staff and fine food in the conservatory-style restaurant; clay-pigeon shooting; cl 24–25 Dec; disabled access.

CAPEL GARMON SH8156 **Tan-y-Foel Country House** *Capel Garmon, Betws-y-coed, Gwynedd LL26 0RE (01690) 710507* **£120,** plus special breaks; 7 recently upgraded rms. Charming, partly 16th-c, no smoking manor house N of the village, with mature gardens and marvellous surrounding countryside; 2 spacious lounges, one with winter log fire, warm, friendly and relaxing atmosphere, very good food using the freshest produce inc local lamb and home-made bread, and an interesting wine list; cl Christmas, limited opening Jan; children over 7; no pets.

CAPEL GARMON SH8155 **White Horse** *Capel Garmon, Llanrwst, Gwynedd LL26 0RW (01690) 710271* ***£56,** plus special breaks; 6 simple rms (those in the newish part are quietest). Comfortable, homely, low-beamed inn with a friendly atmosphere, winter log fires, very good home-made food in both the bar and little no smoking restaurant (some traditional Welsh meals), and marvellous breakfasts; magnificent views, delightful surrounding countryside; children over 12.

CONWY SH7877 **Castle** *High St, Conwy, Gwynedd LL32 8DB (01492) 592324* ***£90,** plus special breaks; 29 rms. In the heart of the historic town, this early 16th-c inn has fine original oil paintings in the public rooms, good food in the pretty restaurant, and a proper pubby bar (popular with locals); friendly, helpful staff, decent breakfasts, and car parking.

GELLILYDAN SH6939 **Tyddyn Du Farm** *Gellilydan, Ffestiniog, Gwynedd LL41 4RB (01766) 590281* ***£38;** 5 rms with views of hills and mountains, most with own bthrms, 2 in private cottage suites. 400-year-old farmhouse on a working farm in the heart of Snowdonia; beams and exposed stonework, big inglenook fireplaces in the residents' lounge, and wholesome home-made food using their own free-range eggs; you can help with the lambs, goats, ducks, sheep and pony; fine walks, inc a short one to their own Roman site; cl 25 Dec; partial disabled access.

HANMER SJ4639 **Buck Farm** *Hanmer, Whitchurch, Clwyd SY14 7LX (01948) 830339* ***£36,** plus special breaks; 2 rms, shared bthrms. 16th-c half-timbered farmhouse in rolling dairy country; with a well stocked library, very good and imaginative food using only fresh produce (often organic), nice breakfasts with home-made muesli, and a pretty little garden; lots to do in the area; no smoking.

LLANABER SH5919 **Llwyndu Farmhouse** *Llanaber, Barmouth, Gwynedd LL42 1RR (01341) 280144* ***£58,** plus special breaks; 7 charming rms, some in a nicely converted 18th-c barn. Most attractive 16th-c farmhouse set just above Cardigan Bay; with a warm welcome, big inglenook fireplaces, oak beams, little mullioned windows, relaxing lounge, enjoyable breakfasts, and good, imaginative food in the candlelit dining room.

LLANARMON DC SJ1532 **West Arms** *Llanarmon DC, Llangollen, Clwyd LL20 7LD (01691) 600665* ***£70,** plus special breaks; 12 rms. Charming and civilised old place with heavy beams and timbers, log fires in inglenook fireplaces, a lounge bar interestingly furnished with antique settles, sofas in the old-fashioned entrance hall, and a comfortable locals' bar; good food and a friendly, quiet atmosphere; the lawn runs down to the River Ceiriog (fishing for residents); disabled access.

LLANDRILLO SJ0337 **Tyddyn Llan** *Llandrillo, Corwen, Clwyd LL21 0ST (01490) 440264* **£98,** plus special breaks; 10 pretty rms. Restful Georgian house with fresh flowers and antiques in the elegantly furnished and comfortable public rooms; charming staff and very good, inventive food (using their own herbs); 3 acres of lovely gardens, fishing on 4 miles of the River Dee (ghillies available) and fine forest walks (guides available) – they can arrange riding and shooting too; dogs by prior arrangement.

LLANDUDNO SH7979 **Bodysgallen Hall** *Pentywyn Rd, Llandudno, Gwynedd LL30 1RS (01492) 584466* **£168,** plus special breaks; 35 deeply comfortable rms, 19 in hotel, the rest in cottages in the grounds. Fine 17th-c house in its own parkland, with mullioned windows, oak panelling, a lovely entrance hall and first-floor drawing room, open fires, and very good, imaginative food in the no smoking dining room; an 18th-c walled rose garden and knot garden; tennis, croquet, swimming pool, sauna, gym and beauty salon; children over 8; dogs allowed in cottage suites; disabled access.

LLANDYRNOG SJ1264 **Berllan Bach** *Llandyrnog, Denbigh, Clwyd LL16 4LR (01824) 790732* **£45,** plus special breaks; 3 rms with French windows on to individual patios. Carefully converted cottage and barns at the foot of hills in the Vale of Clwyd; with a woodburner in the comfortable sitting room and good food in the dining conservatory; marvellous nearby walks, well behaved dogs welcome.

LLANERCHYMEDD SH4284 **Llwydiarth Fawr Farm** *Llanerchymedd, Isle of Anglesey, Gwynedd LL71 8DF (01248) 470321* ***£50,** plus special breaks; 3 rms in main house, 2 cottage suites in grounds. Handsome Georgian farmhouse on an 850-acre cattle and sheep farm; with a particularly warm, homely atmosphere and welcome, comfortable lounge with antiques, log fire, books and lovely views, and very good home-made food using farm and other fresh local produce; terrace, lake for private fishing, nature walks, birdwatching; no smoking; cl Christmas; partial disabled access.

LLANFAIR DC SJ1355 **Eyarth Station** *Llanfair DC, Ruthin, Clwyd LL15 2EE (01824) 703643* ***£44,** plus special breaks; 6 pretty rms. Carefully converted old railway station with quiet gardens and wonderful views; a friendly and relaxed atmosphere, log fire in the airy and comfortable beamed lounge, good breakfasts and enjoyable suppers in the dining room (more lovely views); sun terrace and heated swimming pool, and lots of nearby walks; dogs by prior arrangement; disabled access.

LLANFIHANGEL-YNG-NGWYNFA SJ0815 **Cyfie Farm** *Llanfihangel, Llanfyllin, Powys SY22 5JE (01691) 648451* **£46;** 4 rms inc 3 suites with lovely views. Carefully restored, 17th-c Welsh stone longhouse on 178 acres of cattle and sheep farm (guests welcome to take an interest in the lambs, shearing and hay-gathering); timbered and beamed rooms with fine family furniture, log fire in the residents' lounge, hearty farmhouse cooking in the attractive dining conservatory, and a relaxed, friendly atmosphere; cl Jan–Feb.

LLANGOLLEN SJ2044 **Abbey Grange** *Llantisilio, Llangollen, Clwyd LL20 8DD (01978) 860753* **£46;** 8 comfortable rms. Cosily converted, former quarrymaster's house in a beautiful spot, with superb views, nr Valle Crucis abbey; decent food, good wine list and efficient, courteous service.

LLANGOLLEN SJ2541 **Bryn Howel** *Llangollen, Clwyd LL20 7UW (01978) 860331* **£102.80,** plus special breaks; 36 rms. Extended Victorian mansion in the lovely Vale of Llangollen; with comfortable lounges, a panelled bar, small cocktail bar, open fires, and good food using home-grown herbs and fresh local produce in the restaurant; neat grounds, sauna and solarium, and private salmon and trout fishing on the River Dee; disabled access.

LLANNEFYDD SH9870 **Hawk & Buckle** *Llaneffyd, Denbigh, Clwyd LL16 5ED (01745) 540249* ***£55;** 10 modern rms, lovely views. Pleasant 17th-c stone inn, 215 metres (700ft) up in the hills, with remarkable vistas; decent choice of food using fresh local produce, neatly kept, beamed and knocked-through lounge bar; a good base for exploring the area – by horse, car or on foot; cl 25 Dec; children over 8.

LLANSANFFRAID GLAN CONWY SH8075 **Old Rectory** *Llanrwst Rd, Glan Conwy, Colwyn Bay, Clwyd LL28 5LF (01492) 580611* **£139,** plus special breaks; 6 deeply comfortable rms. Georgian house in pleasant gardens, with fine views over Conwy estuary, Conwy Castle and Snowdonia; delightful public rooms with flowers, antiques and family photos, and after introductions over cocktails you can enjoy the delicious food and marvellous wines; good Welsh breakfasts, and warm, friendly staff; cl 20 Dec–1 Feb; children under 9 months or over 5; small, well behaved dogs and smokers are both welcome in the coach house only.

LLANWDDYN SJ0219 **Lake Vyrnwy** *Llanwddyn, Oswestry, Powys SY10 0LY (01691) 870692* **£115;** 35 rms, the ones overlooking the lake are the nicest – and quietest. Large, impressive, Tudor-style mansion overlooking the lake from the hillside, in 24,000 acres of forestry, with lots of sporting activities (especially fishing); log fires and sporting prints in the comfortable and elegant public rooms, a relaxed atmosphere, clubby bar, and good food using home-made preserves, chutneys, mustards and vinegars and home-grown produce from their own kitchen garden; nice teas, too.

MAENTWROG SH6640 **Grapes** *Maentwrog, Blaenau Ffestiniog, Gwynedd LL41 4HN (01766) 590208* ***£50;** 8 rms. Bustling, cheery and family-run, 17th-c pub with interesting lamps, guns and blowlamps, lots of varnished pine and stripped stone walls in the relaxed and friendly bars; enjoyable food in both the bar and new restaurant, refurbished verandah with café-bar, big breakfasts, and good views from the terrace and garden; can arrange mountain bike weekends.

NANT GWYNANT SH6655 **Pen-y-Gwryd** (junction of the A498/A4086) *Nant Gwynant, Llanberis, Caernarfon, Gwynedd LL55 4NT (01286) 870211* **£52;** 16 comfortably basic rms, some with own bthrm (one with an unusual Edwardian bath). Wonderfully cheery climbers' inn in a magnificent setting below the mountains; with a rugged, slate-floored bar that doubles as a mountain rescue post; lots of climbing mementos and equipment, a charming, panelled sitting room, good lunches ordered through a hatch, hearty communal evening meals in the no smoking restaurant, and sherry from their own solera; sauna in the trees, table tennis; book well ahead; cl Nov–Dec, wkdys Jan–Feb; disabled access.

PENMAENPOOL SH6818 **George III** *Penmaenpool, Dolgellau, Gwynedd LL40 1YD (01341) 422525* **£94,** plus special breaks; 11 low-beamed rms, some in an award-winning, converted railway station. Cosy 17th-c inn on the Mawddach estuary; with good lunchtime food, an imaginative evening restaurant, snug lounge with log fire, a beamed and partly panelled bar (real ales), and fine nearby walks; free salmon and trout fishing permits for residents; disabled access.

PORTMEIRION SH5937 **Portmeirion Hotel** *Penrhyndeudraeth, Porthmadog, Gwynedd LL48 6ET (01766) 770228* **£139** in hotel (14 rms), **£119** in village (17 rms), plus special breaks. On the edge of an estuary and surrounded by beaches and woods (and traffic-free), this is a remarkable place; the hotel down by the water is quite luxurious – elegant rooms with marble, gilt and rich colourful fabrics; while behind and in the steeply landscaped grounds above it is a well dispersed, very colourful Italianate village, luscious to look at, inc all sorts of characterful cottage bedrooms tucked into the hillside; very romantic when the day visitors have left; lots to do; cl 10–23 Jan; disabled access.

SARON SH4557 **Pengwern** *Saron, Caernarfon, Gwynedd LL54 5UH (01286) 831500* ***£40,** plus special breaks; 3 rms. In 130 acres running down to Foryd Bay, this spacious, no smoking farmhouse has marvellous views of Snowdonia; delicious food using home-produced beef and lamb in the attractive dining room; cl Dec–Jan.

TALSARNAU SH6135 **Maes-y-Neuadd** *Talsarnau, Gwynedd LL47 6YA (01766) 780200* **£173 inc 5-course dinner,** plus special breaks; 16 luxurious rms. Looking out across Snowdonia, this attractive, extended 14th-c mansion is set in 8 acres of landscaped hillside; flowers, plants, antiques and open fires, a peaceful atmosphere, very good food (herbs and vegetables from their own garden), friendly dogs and cats, and charming staff; children over 7 in evening restaurant; disabled access.

TAL-Y-BONT SH7669 **Lodge** *Tal-y-Bont, Conwy, Gwynedd LL32 8YX (01492) 660766* **£60,** plus special breaks; 10 rms. Friendly little modern hotel in over 3 acres on the edge of Snowdonia; with an open fire, books and magazines in the comfortable lounge, generous helpings of popular food using lots of home-grown produce in the no smoking restaurant, and good service; lots of walks; well behaved pets welcome; good disabled access.

TREMEIRCHION SJ0771 **Bach-y-Graig** *Tremeirchion, St Asaph, Clwyd LL17 0UH (01745) 730627* ***£40;** 3 rms, 2 with brass beds. Wales's first brick-built house with a date-stone of 1567, in a 200-acre dairy farm at the foot of the Clwydian Hills; inglenook fireplace in the big lounge, home cooking using home-produced beef and lamb and their own free-range eggs, and a warm welcome; you can join in farm activities or walk their woodland trail; cl Christmas–New Year.

TUDWEILIOG SH2336 **Lion** *Tudweiliog, Pwllheli, Gwynedd LL53 8ND (01758) 770244* **£38;** 4 basic rms. Extended, 300-year-old village pub, with good-value, home-made food in the comfortable bar and dining rooms; a welcome for families, play area, and lovely views; 10 minutes' walk to the beach.

To see and do

ABERFFRAW SH3270 **Barclodiad y Gawres** Some 5,000 years old, this 6-metre (20-ft) underground passage tomb at the top of the cliff is notable for the patterns carved by the entrance and in the side chambers, shown up by a good torch; it's sealed, but you can ask for a key at the Wayside Café in Llanfaelog, about a mile away. Hard to believe now, but Aberffraw was once the Welsh capital. There are some lovely unspoilt coves and beaches nearby; the beach up the road at Rhosneigr is particularly good (and clean).

BANGOR SH5872 Quiet university town with a pedestrianised High St, a recently restored pier, and a yacht harbour that adds a lively touch in summer. The Nelson nr the harbour has decent food, as do the Antelope and Union. **Bangor Cathedral** Founded 70 years before the one at Canterbury; the present building is restored 13th/15th-c, and has an interesting 16th-c carving of Christ bound and seated on a rock, as well as some fine Victorian stained glass. The Bible Garden has only plants mentioned in the Scriptures. Opposite is a little museum of Welsh rural life (cl Mon and Sun; free). **Penrhyn Castle** (1m E) Splendid 19th-c, neo-Norman fantasy built by a slate magnate: the interior is in suitably grand style, with remarkable often bizarre panelling, decoration and furnishings. The cathedral-like Great Hall is heated by the Roman method of hot air under the floor, and one of the beds weighs over a ton – carved from slate. An unexpectedly rich collection of paintings includes works by Rembrandt and Canaletto. In the stableyard is a museum of early locomotives, and there's a walled garden and adventure playground. Meals, snacks, shop, disabled access; cl am (exc July and Aug), all Tues, and Nov–Mar; (01248) 353084; £4.80, garden only £3; NT.

★ **BEAUMARIS** SH6076 The most attractive town on Anglesey, with a good deal of character, several old buildings, and a busy waterfront. The 15th-c **church** of St Mary and St Nicholas – easy to spot by its robust square tower – houses the stone coffin of Joan, daughter of King John and wife of the Welsh leader Llewelyn the Great. The Olde Bull's Head and Sailor's Return are reliable for lunch. **Beaumaris Castle** One of the most impressive and complete of those built by Edward I, despite the struggle over it with Owain Glyndwr in the early 1400s, and the later plundering of its lead, timber and stone. Beautifully symmetrical, it took from 1295 to 1312 to build (though the money ran out before it could be finished). Shop, good disabled access; cl 24–26 Dec, 1 Jan; (01248) 810361; £2.20. **Beaumaris Courthouse** Unique Victorian survival: you can stand in the dock and imagine you're just about to be sentenced. Open Easter–Sept, exc when court in session; (01248) 811691; £1.50. **Beaumaris Gaol** Paints a vivid picture of the harshness of the 19th-c prison system, especially in the dank poky cells. Shop, limited disabled access; open as courthouse, or by appointment, (01248) 810921; £2.75, joint with courthouse £3.25. **Marine World** (Seafront) The sea life of the Menai Strait; cl 25 Dec; (01248) 810072; £2.25.

★ **BEDDGELERT** SH5948 A quiet village which dreamed up the myth that it was the resting place of Llewelyn's faithful mastiff over a hundred years ago and has been living off it ever since. The Prince Llewelyn does good-value food, and there's fine Snowdonia walking around the Aberglaslyn Pass (A498 S). **Sygun Copper Mine** (A498 NE) Interesting tours through often spectacular underground mine workings, with magnificent stalactites and stalagmites and traces of gold and silver in the copper ore veins. There's a wonderful view of the mountains when you come up at the end. Snacks, shop, some disabled access; best to check winter opening; (01766) 510101; *£4.75.

BETWS-Y-COED SH7956 19th-c inland resort village in a beautiful wooded gorge at the head of the Vale of Conwy, on the road to Bangor (and thence Ireland) as well as to Snowdon. Surrounded by picturesque woodland walks, the village has over a century of catering to visitors behind it. One of the best strolls is along the old riverside railway track by the Afon Llugwy W: the raging Swallow Falls and Fairy Glen just W of the village are 2 of the area's finest beauty spots. Several interesting bridges nearby, as well as the bizarre Ugly House, which looks like a series of boulders thrown haphazardly together. The Royal Oak Hotel (open all day – afternoon teas, too), Glan Aber Hotel and Ty Gwyn have worthwhile food. **Conwy Valley Railway Museum** (Old Goods Yard) Good look at the narrow- and standard-gauge railways of North Wales, with railway stock and other memorabilia, model railway layouts, a steam-hauled model railway in the 4-acre grounds, and a 15in-gauge tramway to the woods. Meals, snacks, shop, disabled access; cl wkdys Nov–Feb; (01690) 710568; *£1.

BLAENAU FFESTINIOG SH6946 This straggle of village is dwarfed by the vast spoil slopes from the slate mines all around it – once the slate capital of Wales, now with the passing of the industry like a living museum. **Llechwedd Slate Caverns** (A470) Very busy and popular, with exciting underground train journeys through the caverns; one of the 2 routes re-creates the world of the Victorian miner, while the other (along Britain's steepest railway) ends with a walk through 10 atmospheric chambers, each with its own sound and light show. Plenty on the surface too, inc a railway museum, slate mill and a complete Victorian village. Meals, snacks, shop, disabled access with prior warning; cl 25–26 Dec, 1 Jan; (01766) 830306; single tour £6.50, both £9.95, surface attractions free. **Pumped Storage Power Station** (Tanygrisiau, off the A496 S) Guided tours of the first hydro-electric pumped storage scheme in the country, with dramatic views towards the peaks of Snowdonia. Meals, snacks, shop; cl Sat (exc mid-July–Aug), and all Nov–Easter; (01766) 830310; *£2.75. From the information centre there's an attractive (if slightly hairy) drive into the mountains to Stwlan Dam, which also gives super views. The Grapes at Maentwrog is fairly handy for lunch.

† **BODELWYDDAN CASTLE** SH9974 (off the A55) The walled gardens surrounding this showy white limestone castle include a glorious mix of woodland walks, flowering plants, aviary and water features. The house (older than its 19th-c exterior suggests) has been very well restored as a Victorian mansion, with furniture from the Victoria & Albert Museum, and photographs and portraits from the National Portrait Gallery. Plenty for children, inc a woodland adventure playground, and entertaining exhibitions of puzzles, games and optical illusions. Snacks, shop, disabled access; cl Fri (exc July and Aug), and Mon too Nov–Mar; (01745) 584060; £4.30, grounds only £1. In the village itself, the 19th-c **Marble Church** built entirely of locally quarried stone is an unusual and quite splendid sight. The Kinmel Arms at St George has good, interesting food.

BODNANT GARDEN SH7972 (off the A470 at Tal-y-Cafn) Started in 1875 but improved in 1900 (and indeed ever since, in the hands of the green-fingered family which has owned them), these gardens are among Britain's greatest. Part of the 80-acre grounds have a beautiful woodland garden in a sheltered valley, notable for its rhododendrons and azaleas, while below the house are 5 terraces in the Italian style, with a canal pool, reconstructed pin mill and an open-air stage on the lowest. Many fine rare plants inc unusual trees and shrubs. Meals, snacks, shop, disabled access (but it is steep in places); cl Nov–mid-Mar; (01492) 650460; £4.60; NT. The Tal-y-Cafn Inn is useful for lunch, and the Olde Bull, in a delightful setting on the hillside opposite at Llanbedr-y-Cennin, does good, imaginative food; the Holland Arms at Trofarth is also useful.

BODORGAN SH4272 **Henblas Park** Good range of family activities, from sheep-shearing, falconry and farm animals, through magic shows and juggling workshops, to tractor rides and a Neolithic burial chamber. Meals, snacks, shop, disabled access (but no facilities); open Easter hols, May bank hol wknd, and Sun–Fri late May–Sept; (01407) 840440; *£3.75.

BRYNSIENCYN SH4765 **Anglesey Sea Zoo** (A4080 just S) Excellent collection of local marine life, in tanks giving as unrestricted and natural an environment as possible. Also a walk-through shipwreck, touch pools, adventure playground, and home-made fudge and ice-cream. Meals and snacks (their oysters are guaranteed to contain a pearl), shop, disabled access; cl 18–26 Dec, 1 wk in Jan; (01248) 430411; £4.95. **Foel Farm Park** Friendly working farm with daily sheep-milking, tractor rides, and more home-made ice-cream. Snacks, shop, disabled access; cl Nov–Mar; (01248) 430646; £3.85. The Mermaid at Foel Ferry is quite useful for lunch. At Gwydryn Hir Farm, you can pick your own fruit and veg in view of Snowdonia; open Jun–Oct; (01248) 430344. A couple of miles NW of Brynsiencyn, by the back road towards Llangaffo, is what looks like a Stone Age hut, but is actually a burial chamber from which the covering earth has been eroded over the millennia.

CAERNARFON SH4763 Surviving lengths of its 13th-c town walls still crowd in its quaintly narrow streets (quaint, that is, unless you're trying to drive through). The town harbour is busy with yachts in summer, and you can explore a restored **steam-powered dredger** moored here. The Black Boy and Palace Vaults do decent food. **Caernarfon Castle** The largest of Edward I's Welsh castles, built after the defeat of Llewelyn the Last, and still quite spectacular. Finished in 1328, it's unusual both for its octagonal towers and for the bands of colour decorating the walls. Edward's son was born here and presented to the people, setting the precedent for future Princes of Wales. A big lottery grant is funding major redevelopment of the Royal Welch Fusiliers exhibit in the Queen's Tower and Chamberlain Tower. Shop, some disabled access; cl 24–26 Dec, 1 Jan; (01286) 677617; £4. In the square outside, around the statue of former PM David Lloyd George, there's a busy Sat market. **Segontium** (A4085) Roman fort dating from AD78. Excavations have exposed the remains of various rebuildings during its 3 centuries of importance, and a museum shows some of the finds. There's a tradition that Constantine the Great was born here (and the walls of the nearby castle used to be thought to be modelled partly on the walls of Constantinople). Shop, some disabled access; cl am Sun, 24–26 Dec, 1 Jan; (01286) 675625; *£1.25. **Air World** (Caernarfon Airport, off the A499 nr Llandwrog, SH4358) They encourage you to climb aboard some of the helicopters and aeroplanes here; also a great many model aeroplanes, and pleasure flights. Meals, snacks, shop, disabled access; cl Nov–Feb (exc by appointment); (01286) 830800; £4.

★ **CAPEL CURIG** SH7258 This attractive village is a useful for base for enjoyable Snowdonia rambles around the pleasantly landscaped reservoirs to the north.

CASTELL DINAS BRAN SJ2243 The place for walkers to head for from Llangollen. This hill fort commands views over the vale and is close to the Panorama Walk (actually a surfaced minor road); walks can be linked to the canal towpath below.

CHIRK SJ2938 The quiet little town, important as a staging-post on the former road to Ireland, has something of a bypassed-by-time feel now; the Hand and (on the B5070 S) the Bridge are quite useful for lunch. **Chirk Castle** (just W) One of the lucky few of Edward I's castles to survive as an occupied home rather than fall to ruin. The exterior is still much as it was when built 700 years ago, with its high walls and drum towers, though there have been lots of alterations inside: most of the medieval-looking decorations were by Pugin in the 19th c, the elegant stone staircase dates from the 18th c, and the Long Gallery is 17th-c. The wrought-iron entrance gates are particularly fine, and the formal gardens are magnificent. Meals, snacks, shop, some disabled access; cl am, all Mon (exc bank hols) and Tues, and Nov–Mar; (01691) 777701; £4.60; NT. It's right by a well preserved stretch of the earthworks of Offa's Dyke.

COED Y BRENIN SH7226 The name means King's Forest, and it was so called to commemorate the Silver Jubilee of King George V. Some beautifully varied sights and landscapes, as well as wildlife observation hides, and over 50 miles of walks. The **Forest Park and Visitor Centre** (Maesgwn) is an excellent introduction. Snacks, shop, disabled access; cl wkdys Nov–Easter; (01341) 440666; free, £1 parking. You can hire bikes here.

COLWYN BAY SH8480 Though this busy summer seaside resort has all that's wanted for a family beach holiday, it's rather eclipsed by Llandudno just along the coast. The quieter end at Rhos-on-Sea has a **puppet theatre**; mainly open just school hols; (01492) 548166 for programme. The Rhos Fynach opposite the small harbour at this end, once Captain Morgan's home, does decent food. **Welsh Mountain Zoo** (Flagstaff Gardens, Old Highway, SH8378) Lots of exotic animals in natural-looking habitats, but what really distinguishes this 37-acre zoo from any other is the quite magnificent view over the bay. Also, a penguin parade and falconry displays. Meals, snacks, shop, mostly disabled access; cl 25 Dec; (01492) 532938; *£5.95. In summer, a free minibus service usually runs here from the town station. The Mountain View at Mochdre has good-value food.

★ **CONWY** SH7877 Cheerful old town dominated by its **castle**, one of the best-known in Wales, and one of the most important examples of military architecture in the whole of Europe. Built for Edward I in 1283–9, it's very well preserved, still looking exactly as a medieval fortress should – despite the ravages of the Civil War and beyond. There's an exhibition on Edward and the other castles he built, as well as a scale model of the castle and the town in the early 14th c. The top of the turrets offer fine panoramic views; the most dramatic views of the castle itself are from the other side of the estuary. Shop; cl 24–26 Dec, 1 Jan; (01492) 592358; £3.50. The castle was a key part of the town's elaborate defensive system – 21 (originally 22) towers linked by walls some 9 metres (30ft) high, still the most complete town wall in Wales, with craggy old town gates. You can walk along some parts, looking down over the narrow little streets that still follow their medieval layout. **Aberconwy House** (Castle St) The only house in the town which survives from the 14th c, once the home of a prosperous merchant. Rooms are furnished in period style and there's an interesting audio-visual show. Shop; cl Tues, and Nov–Mar; (01492) 592246; £2; NT. **Plas Mawr** (High St) Elaborate Tudor mansion reopened after a lengthy restoration, its splendid plasterwork, flagstone floors and huge fireplaces all now looking as good as when they were new. Shop; cl Mon (exc bank hols) and all Nov–Apr; (01222) 500200; £4. **Smallest House** Nicely placed on the quayside is Britain's smallest house, barely 2 metres (6ft) wide and its front wall only 3 metres (10ft) high. Squeezed into the 2 rooms (one up, one down) are all the comforts of home, or at least most – there's no lavatory. Shop, limited disabled access; cl Nov–Mar, Good Fri; (01492) 593484; 50p. There's also a little **aquarium** by the quay, and you can usually go on summer **boat trips**. **Teapot World** (Castle St)

Splendidly silly collection of unusually shaped teapots from the last 300 years – everything from wigwams to cauliflowers. Shop; cl Nov–Easter; (01492) 593429; *£1.50. The Castle Hotel is a civilised place for lunch. The suspension bridge over the river built by Telford in 1826 has been restored by the National Trust, who have also opened up its **toll house**, the rooms furnished as they would have been in the last century; cl Tues (exc July and Aug) and all Nov–Mar; (01492) 573282; £1. The other, tubular bridge was built by Stephenson in 1848. **Butterfly Jungle** (Bodlondeb Park) By the river, with butterflies and exotic plants and birds in a re-created jungle

environment. Shop, disabled acess; cl Nov–Mar; (01492) 593149; £3.

Conwy Mountain Just W of the town, pleasant walking; not a real mountain but with views of Anglesey worthy of mountain status.

† **CORWEN** SJ0744 **Rhug Chapel** (1m N) 17th c, not inspiring from the outside, but inside is a riot of colour, almost every available piece of woodwork covered with cheery patterns and paintwork. Cl 2–3pm (when the custodian opens nearby Llangar Church, *see below*), all Sun and Mon (exc bank hol wknds), and Oct–Mar; (01490) 412025; £2.

Llangar Church (B4401 S) Built in the 13th c, with remarkable paintings of the

7 deadly sins; it's usually visited only at 2pm, from Rhug Chapel (and covered by the same ticket). The Crown in Corwen has good-value food. **Derwen Church** SJ0750 (off the A494 a few miles N) Interesting medieval building with an elaborately carved rood screen and loft, some old wall paintings, and an excellent Celtic cross in the churchyard.

CRICCIETH SH4937 Restrained resort with a good sheltered, sandy beach. The Prince of Wales is a reliable food pub. **Criccieth Castle** 13th-c remains on a rocky, mounded peninsula above the little town, giving superb views over Tremadog Bay. Parts of the inner walls are well preserved, and there's an impressive gatehouse. A cartoon video looks at Gerald of Wales and other Welsh princes. Shop, disabled access; cl Nov–Mar; (01766) 522227; *£2.20.

† **DENBIGH CASTLE** SJ0566 Largely ruined, but the 13th-c gatehouse is still impressive, with its trio of towers and a superb archway; the figure on the summit is thought to represent Edward I. Among other remains are what's left of an ambitious church built by the Earl of Leicester, favourite of Elizabeth I. Shop, limited disabled access; cl 24–26 Dec; £1.70 (free in winter). A museum on the High St has interesting finds from nearby Bronze Age sites, and the riverside Brookhouse Mill is popular for lunch, as is the Lion out at Gwytherin (B5384 W).

DINAS MAWDDWY SH8513 **Meirion Mill** Nestling among riverside woods below the mountains on the S fringes of Snowdonia is this charmingly set working woollen mill, in the grounds of the old Mawddwy railway station. Meals, snacks, shop (lots of locally made goods), disabled access; cl Jan–Feb; (01650) 531311; free. Nearby is a picturesque pack-horse bridge, and the waterside Dolbrodmaeth has decent food.

† **DOLWYDDELAN CASTLE** SH7352 Picturesquely set on a lightly wooded crag, these old ruins were reputedly the birthplace of Llewelyn the Great. You can still see a restored keep from around 1200 and a 13th-c curtain wall. Cl 24–26 Dec, 1 Jan; (01690) 750366; £1.70. The village church is attractive.

FLINT CASTLE SJ2473 Another fine 13th-c castle, the first built by Edward I to subdue the natives. Parts of the walls and corner towers survive, but the most impressive bit is the great tower or donjon, which is separated by the moat. Overlooking the River Dee, it has a role in Shakespeare's *Richard II*. Cl 24–26 Dec, 1 Jan; free. The Britannia in nearby Halkyn is good for lunch, with nice Dee estuary views from its conservatory.

† **GRESFORD** SJ3454 The **church** has some wonderful medieval stained glass, and its bells are often described as one of the Seven Wonders of Wales. A yew tree outside is reputed to be 1,400 years old. The Pant-yr-Ochain has decent food.

HARLECH CASTLE SH5831 Splendid-looking structure built in 1283–90 by Edward I, its rugged glory the massive twin-towered gatehouse. It was starved into capitulation by Owain Glyndwr in 1404, and later dogged defence inspired the song *Men of Harlech*. Before the sea retreated there was a sheer drop to the water on one side, but it now stands above dunes, with wonderful battlement views of Snowdonia. Shop; cl 24–26 Dec, 1 Jan; (01766) 780552; £3. The village around it has all that the crowds of summer visitors to the castle and the good beach could want. The riverside Victoria at Llanbedr does worthwhile food.

HOLYHEAD SH2482 Long-established fishing town on little Holy Island, now an unassuming resort with some burial chambers and ancient sites not far away. The Victorian breakwater protecting the harbour is Britain's longest. Across the old Four Mile Bridge at Valley, the Bull has good-value food.

HOLYHEAD MOUNTAIN SH2183 A dramatic hill giving good walks at the western tip of Holy Island, with an Iron Age fort and Roman watchtower site.

! **HOLYWELL** SJ1876 **St Winefride's Well** Source of the holy spring that turned the spot into a centre of pilgrimage – it's supposed to have healing powers. There are pleasant walks from here through the valley to the coast. **Greenfield Valley Heritage Park** SJ1977 (A548) Farm museum, and an increasing number of buildings rescued from their original sites and rebuilt here, inc a 17th-c cottage, Victorian farmhouse, and a school, all furnished in period style. Also the remains of a Cistercian abbey and a good few relics of the Industrial Revolution. Snacks, shop, disabled access; cl Nov–Mar; (01352) 714172; £1.80.

LAKE VYRNWY SJ0119 This massive century-old reservoir supplies Liverpool with 57 million gallons of water a day. It's an attractive spot to wander, with a visitor centre, waymarked trails, cycle hire, bird hides and a new sculpture trail. When the water is low you can see the remains of the original village of Llanwddyn, drowned long ago; (01691) 870245; free.

LAVAN SANDS SH6473 (nr Aber) Much of the North Wales coast is built on or ribboned by roads, but this is a notable exception: walks by a vast stretch of tidal sands, with flocks of wading birds.

LLANAELHAEARN SH3744 **Tre'r Ceiri Hill Fort** Off the B4417, just up the hill, a signed path leads to this evocative place, occupied from the Bronze Age through to the Dark Ages; a massive stone wall, lots of hut foundations, and fine views. At Morfa Nefyn nearby, the Bryncynan and (overlooking a lovely sandy bay) the Cliff Hotel do decent lunches.

LLANALLGO SH4986 **Din Llugwy Ancient Village** The remains of a 4th-c village: a pentagonal stone wall surrounds 2 circular and 7 rectangular buildings; free. The Parciau Arms at Marianglas is the best place for a meal.

LLANBEDR SH5826 **Maes Artro** (A496) Imaginatively converted wartime RAF camp, with an original air-raid shelter complete with light and sound effects, a 'Village of Yesteryear', log fort playground, marine aquarium, and nature trails through the woodland. Meals, snacks, shop, disabled access; cl Sept–Easter; (01341) 23467; £3. The Victoria in the village is useful for a family lunch. **Shell Island** A causeway leads over the sands to this near-island, appropriately named – after winter storms and high tides it's excellent for beach-combing; there are also wild birds and flowers, and you can fish here. Snacks, shop; (01341) 241453; £4 a car.

LLANBERIS SH5760 Plenty of B & Bs, small hotels, shops and cafés for the summer visitors here for Snowdon, and quite a few craft shops dotted along the High St. **Snowdon Mountain Railway** (A4086) The best ascent of Snowdon: Britain's only public rack-and-pinion railway, operated by vintage Swiss steam and modern diesel locomotives. It follows the route of an old pony track, and on a good day takes passengers up over 915 metres (3,000ft) right to the summit – where, in clear weather, glorious, breathtaking views might include the Isle of Man and the Wicklow Mountains in Ireland. It's without a doubt one of the most spectacular train journeys in the country. Trains leave when there are more than a couple of dozen people on board – so if there aren't many people about you may have to wait for it to start, and if there are you may have to queue (there is a sort of booking service). It can be chilly, so wrap up well. Meals, snacks, shop, disabled access (with notice); open mid-Mar–Oct, though always best to ring first – of the 241 operational days in 1996, it was only possible to reach the summit on 138; (01286) 870223; £14.80 return. Just N of town is a modern working **pottery**; cl 2 wks at Christmas; (01286) 872529; free. Pen-y-Gwryd Hotel (Nant Gwynant, A4086/A498 SE) is a good spot for Snowdon walks; also for lunch. **Lake Railway** (Padarn Country Park, off the A4086) 4-mile trips along the shore of Llyn Padarn, using steam locos dating from 1889 to 1948. Ideal for those who want the steamtrain experience but don't want to spend too long getting it. Snacks, shop, disabled access; cl Nov–Easter; (01286) 870549 for timetable; £4.10. The station is set in a super lakeside park with walks through ancient woodland. **Welsh Slate Museum** (Padarn Country Park, off the A4086) Once one of the biggest quarries in the country, stepped steeply into the mountain. Lottery funding means that there will be considerable improvements over the next year, inc a period refurbishment of the Chief Engineer's House, the restoration of a slate-carrying incline and a new hands-on play and discovery area for children. The quarry workshop has been preserved largely in its original state, with working craftsmen and machinery. Its waterwheel is one of the largest in the world. Snacks, shop, disabled access; cl wknds Oct–Easter; (01286) 870630; £3.50. **Electric Mountain** Various changing exhibitions, then a coach whisks you off for a tour of the spectacular Dinorwic hydro-electric power station (one of Europe's biggest), deep in the mountain. Best to book, (01286) 870636. Snacks, shop, disabled access (with notice); cl Mon–Weds in Jan and Feb, and 2 weeks at Christmas; £5. **Dolbadarn Castle** (A4086, at the foot of Llanberis Pass) Built in the early 13th c by Llewelyn the Great – it has a fine round keep; free.

LLANDANIEL FAB SH5069 **Bryn Celli Ddu** Restored Neolithic passage burial chamber built over a previous stone circle, at the end of a long tunnel, with a carved stone over a burial pit; locked, but key at the nearby farmhouse; free. Take a torch.

★ ☺ ♪ ❋ ✝ ⌂ !

LLANDUDNO SH7882 The area's main holiday town, and though it does have a long, well sheltered curve of good pebbly beach, a promenade and a range of resort entertainments, it doesn't feel at all brash. There are charming little shops and boutiques, a well restored pier (where you can fish), and cable-cars as well as the famously steep quaint tramway up the massive Great Ormes headland which protects the main beach – there's a quieter but more exposed beach on the far side. You can walk all the way up, too; a café en route has views to justify stopping. At the top there's a 12th-c church, a visitor centre with local geology exhibits, and more good walking. **Great Orme Mines** 4,000-year-old copper mine nr the summit of Great Ormes, the biggest such site so far discovered. It's also the only prehistoric mine open to the public, with displays of finds, and guided underground walks through the cavernous workings themselves. Teas, shop; cl Nov–Jan; (01492) 870447; *£4.20. On the way down, a dry ski slope also has a toboggan run. **Rabbit Hole** (Trinity Sq) Jolly exhibition devoted to Alice in Wonderland, with life-size animated tableaux; the real Alice holidayed in Llandudno as a child. Shop, disabled access; cl winter Suns; (01492) 860082; £2.95. The Queen's Head at Glanwydden, off the Colwyn Bay road, does very good food. **Conwy Valley Railway** Main line from Llandudno to Blaenau Ffestiniog, through magnificent scenery, with several useful stops en route.

⌂ **LLANDDWYN ISLAND** SH3863 Really a peninsula, making a satisfying walk from Newborough Warren over the lovely beach.

❋

LLANFAIRPWLLGWYNGYLL SH5372 The record books and tongue-twisting schoolchildren add another 39 letters (gocherychwyrndrobwllllantysili ogogogoch) to this village's name, but locals cut it even shorter, to Llanfair PG, or Llanfairpwll. Excellent views of Snowdonia and the Menai Strait from the top of the Marquess of Anglesey's Column, built in 1816 to commemorate the military achievements of Wellington's second-in-command at the Battle of Waterloo. The nearby village of Penmynydd was the ancient home of the Tudor family. The Liverpool Arms at Menai Bridge is the nearest good place for lunch. **Plas Newydd** (A4080, 2 miles S) Fine mountain views from the creeper-covered former home of the Marquess of Anglesey, an elegant 18th-c mansion best known for its mural by Rex Whistler. Other works by the painter as well, along with a collection of relics from Waterloo, and a nice spring garden with rhododendrons (Apr–Jun only). Meals, snacks, shop, disabled access; cl am, Fri and Sat, all Nov–Mar; (01248) 714795; £4.20; NT.

LLANGEFNI SH4576 Right in the centre of Anglesey, and its 'capital', with a big open-air market every Thurs. **Oriel Ynys Mon** (Rhosmeirch, B5111 N) Excellent gallery with imaginative changing displays on Anglesey's history, and a collection of wildlife paintings by C F Tunnicliffe. You can spend a surprising amount of time here. Snacks, shop, disabled access; cl Mon (exc bank hols), Christmas wk; (01248) 724444; *£2.

! **LLANGOLLEN** SJ2142 Not special in itself despite a number of solid and gracious Georgian and Victorian villas; what makes it attractive is its charming valley setting above the River Dee. It has discreet hotels that cater for the generally older people to whom the area most appeals – though it comes vividly alive during the *eisteddfod*. The Abbey Grange, Royal and Wild Pheasant hotels do decent lunches. **Pontcysyllte aqueduct** (off the A5/A539 E of Llangollen) Very spectacular to cross – by boat or on foot; the Sun Trevor at Trevor Uchaf above here has good food and spectacular views. **Valle Crucis Abbey** (A542 2m N) Substantial remains of the early 13th-c abbey church, and some beautifully carved grave slabs. Shop, limited disabled access; cl Oct–Apr; (01978) 860326; £1.70. The ruins stand at the bottom of the Horseshoe Pass, a nerve-rackingly steep but extremely scenic mountain drive; the Britannia Inn just above the abbey has exceptional views. **Plas Newydd** Lady Eleanor Butler and Sarah Ponsonby, the 'Ladies of Llangollen', lived here 1780–1831. The beautiful half-timbered house has stained glass, leather wall coverings and domestic paraphernalia of the period. Pleasant gardens. Shop; cl Oct–Mar; (01978) 861314; *£2. **Llangollen Railway** (Abbey Rd) Now running 8 miles, this used to be part of the Great Western Railway; steam and diesel trains go from the pleasantly preserved station to the village of Glyndyfrdwy up the Dee (the Bedwyn Arms, in a lovely setting above the river, does food). Meals, snacks, shop, special coach for the disabled (you have to book); (01978) 860951 for timetable; £7 full return fare, less for shorter trips. From Llangollen Wharf there are **horse-drawn boat trips** along the Vale of Llangollen; Apr–Oct; (01978) 860702; £3. The Sarah Ponsonby close by has decent food. **Motor Museum and Canal Exhibition** Classic cars and motorcycles and an exhibition on the canal network. Snacks, shop, disabled access; cl Mon and all Nov–Feb; (01978) 860324; £2. **Lower Dee Exhibitions Centre** New centre housing a large display of model railways and a collection of memorabilia from the *Dr Who* series, inc many of the monsters bent on exterminating him. You can also visit a toy factory here. Meals, snacks, shop; (01978) 860584; toy factory £1, model railways £3.50, Dr Who £4.75, all 3 £7.95.

! LLANGYBI SH4241 **St Cybi's Well** Known to the Welsh as Fynnon Gybi, this has been reckoned to have healing properties for over a thousand years. Look out for the corbelled beehive vaulting inside the roofless stone structure, which is ancient Irish in style.

★ † LLANRWST SH7961 Pretty little town with an old stone bridge over the Conwy river, said to be the work of Inigo Jones. **Gwydir Chapel**, added by the influential Wynn family to the parish church in the 17th c, has a stone coffin reputedly that of Llewelyn the Great, as well as a magnificent rood screen from the ruins of Maenan Abbey. The Wynns also built the nearby **Gwydir Uchaf Chapel**, with intriguing ceiling paintings.

LLANUWCHLLYN SH8829 **Bala Lake Railway** Some of the carriages on trains using this delightful 4½-mile route are open to the elements, which seems to make the views of the lake and mountains more vivid. The locomotives were once used to haul slate in the local quarries. Snacks, shop, disabled access (but no facilities); cl most Mons and Fris Apr–Jun and Sept, and all Oct–Easter; (01678) 540666 for timetable; £6. The Eryrod, with panoramic views, has good-value food; and you can walk along the shores of the Lake itself.

LLANYSTUMDWY SH4738 **Lloyd George Memorial**

Museum (A497) Audio-visual displays and memorabilia relating to Lloyd George, whose family moved here from Manchester when he was a boy. They lived in nearby Highgate Cottage, which has been restored to how it was then, and has a neat Victorian garden. Shop, disabled access; cl wknds (exc in summer), and all Nov–Mar (exc by appointment); (01766) 522071; £2.50. The old-fashioned bar opposite is good value. It's a short stroll from here to the site where he's buried. **Rabbit Farm** (just off the A497) Children enjoy this: around 700 rabbits, with other animals and pony rides. Open May–Sept; (01766) 523136; *£3.

LLEYN PENINSULA Very unspoilt, this peninsula has some good coastal walks around its tip, starting W from Aberdaron SH1726, with fine windswept views from Mynydd Mawr (bird reserve nearby), and E of here is the spectacular bay of Hell's Mouth SH2626; the beaches along here have clean bathing water. For a stiffer walk, try Yr Eifl SH3644 (the Rivals), a 563-metre (1,849-ft) mountain nr the coast.

LLYN IDWAL SH6460 This superbly sited Snowdonia lake beneath Glyder Fach gives pleasant walks along a signed nature trail.

MENAI BRIDGE SH5571 The village takes its name from Thomas Telford's magnificent iron suspension bridge linking Anglesey to the mainland, the first such bridge in the world. The waterside Liverpool Arms has good-value, fresh food. **Butterfly Palace** (A5025) Exotic butterflies from all over, as well as a bird house, insectarium, reptile house, and adventure playground. Meals, snacks, shop, disabled access; cl Jan and Feb; (01248) 712474; £3.75.

MOEL FAMMAU SJ1662 The highest point of the Clwydian Range, a bulging massif with clearly marked paths; walk up from the car park on the minor road E of Llanbedr DC through colour-coded forest trails or over open land, for views of much of Snowdonia, the edge of the Peak District and the Wirral.

MOLD SJ2364 A very good theatre, and a richly decorated parish **church** built to commemorate the victory of Henry Tudor at Bosworth Field in 1485. The Druid Arms, in a lovely setting at Llanferres, out on the Ruthin road has decent food.

PENMACHNO SH8052 **Penmachno Woollen Mill** Timeless watermill powered by the River Machno, with local weavers explaining and demonstrating the history and craft of the cottage weaving industry. The setting is lovely. Snacks, good shop; cl 25 Dec and maybe winter Sun and Mon; (01690) 710545; free. **Ty'n y Coed** Reached by a pleasant walk along the river from the mill's car park, a fully furnished 19th-c farmhouse, good for showing the traditional way of life in this area. Open pm Thurs, Fri and Sun Apr–Oct; (01690) 760229; £2; NT. **Ty Mawr** (Wybrnant, forest road NW) Picturesque, lonely thick-walled, medieval cottage, birthplace of Bishop William Morgan who first translated the Bible into Welsh (*see St Asaph entry on p.900*). Shop; open pm Thurs–Sun Apr–Oct (cl Sat in Oct); (01690) 760213; £2; NT.

PENMAENPOOL SH6717 Its small waterside nature reserve has a useful nature information centre pointing out promising places throughout this whole area, a good region for walks. One is the walk along the old railway track beside the Mawddach estuary to Fairbourne, giving magnificent views. The George III is a pleasant place for lunch. **Pony-trekking centre** (A493, about a mile SW) Will take beginners out on ponies for an hour over scenic routes; (01341) 422377; from £9. You can stay at the farm too.

PLAS YN RHIW SH2328 Charming if unassuming little manor house, worth a visit for the gardens and woodland, inc a waterfall, spring snowdrop wood and subtropical specimens. Shop, very limited disabled access; cl am, Tues and Weds Apr–mid-May, and all Oct–Mar; (01758) 780219; £3.20; NT. The setting is lovely, overlooking one of the area's wildest coasts. The beautifully placed Sun over at Llanengan does decent food.

PORTHMADOG SH5638 Quite a busy shopping town of low slate-roofed houses, with a spacious harbour and a long causeway road (5p toll) across the estuary. The Ship has decent food, and nearby Black Rock Golden Sands is one of the area's finest beaches. **Ffestiniog Railway** (Harbour Stn) The famous narrow-gauge railway opened in 1836 to carry slate from Blaenau Ffestiniog to Porthmadog by gravity. Closed in 1946, it reopened in 1955 and has gradually been extended to climb the 13¼ miles to Blaenau Ffestiniog; further extensions are planned. Stop off at stations along the way for good walks and views. The railway links with the main line Cambrian Coast Line, hugging the coast from Pwllheli to Machynlleth, with many stops along the way. Meals, snacks, shop, some disabled access; limited winter service, best to phone; (01766) 512340; full return fare £12.80. The adjacent **museum** tells the story of the railway, with exhibits inc a 4-wheeled hearse converted from an old quarryman's coach, and one of the original steam locos from 1863; cl Jan and Feb; donations. **Welsh Highland Railway** (opposite Porthmadog main line station) Overshadowed by its more famous neighbour in size but certainly not in spirit, this enthusiastically restored line runs trains daily in the summer hols and most Suns Apr–Oct; (01766) 513402 for timetable; £2. **Porthmadog Pottery** (Snowdon St) Demonstrations, and the chance to make a pot yourself, as well as try out other crafts, and a mural illustrating the town's history. Snacks, shop, very good disabled access; cl most wknds, best to check winter opening; (01766) 512137; free, though may be charges for some activities.

★ ! **PORTMEIRION** SH5837 On the steep wooded shores of an inlet from Tremadog Bay, this fairy-tale holiday village, designed by Welsh architect Sir Clough Williams-Ellis, is set in 175 acres of lush coastal cliff and woodland gardens. Quite charming, it's an Italianate folly – pastel-washed cottages interlaced with grottoes and cobbled squares, a bell tower, castle and lighthouse, and long picturesque flights of steps zigzagging down to the water, which at low tide dries to miles of sand. Enveloping the village are the 60 acres of Gwyllt gardens, with fine displays of rhododendrons, azaleas, hydrangeas and subtropical flora; good wild woodlands, too. You have to pay a toll to enter the village, but once in can see the house where Noel Coward wrote *Blithe Spirit* and the locations for the cult TV series *The Prisoner*; children can play in the playground, on a make-believe schooner apparently moored by the hotel, or, tide permitting, on the beach. A lovely relaxing place, quite unlike anywhere else. Meals, snacks, shops (one specialising in Portmeirion pottery), some disabled access; (01766) 770000; £4, less Nov–Mar. No dogs – though there's a touching dog cemetery in the woods nearby. **Plas Brondanw** (Llanfrothen, A4085 N of Penrhyndeudraeth) The ancestral home of Sir Clough Williams-Ellis, and you can visit the architectural garden he designed there – great views; (01766) 771136; £1.50.

PRECIPICE WALK SH7321 Signposted N of Dolgellau, this is an attractive Snowdonia walk.

PRESTATYN SJ0683 Bustling seaside resort standing at one end of the 168-mile route of Offa's Dyke, marked by a stone pillar above the main beach.

† **RHUDDLAN CASTLE** SJ0278 Fine old castle, adapted by Edward I from an earlier Norman structure, to guard what was once a busy port (now a sleepy little town). Overlooking the river, it's a pretty spot. Cl Oct–Apr; (01745) 590777; £1.70. **Bodrhyddan Hall** (A5151 towards Dyserth) Lovely doll's-house front, and some wonderfully elaborate fireplaces in the drawing room. Also a formal French garden and an interesting well-house built by Inigo Jones. Teas, shop, disabled access to ground floor only; open pm Tues and Thurs Jun–Sept; (01745) 590414; £3. **Dyserth Church** Partly 13th c, with a Jesse window; not far from a plunging 18-metre (60-ft) **waterfall**.

RHYL SJ0081 Rather brash seaside resort; if you're passing with children, the Knights Cavern, a lively interpretation of Welsh history, should amuse them. **Sea Life Centre** (East Parade) One of the very good centres that we've described in several English resorts, with a dramatic Shark Encounter as well as the usual walk-through underwater tunnel. Meals, snacks, shop, disabled access; cl 25 Dec; (01745) 344660; £4.50.

ST ASAPH CATHEDRAL SJ0374 To match its tiny little city, this is the smallest in Britain, founded in 537. A column in the grounds commemorates its most famous cleric Bishop Morgan (*see Penmachno entry on p.898*) and his work translating the Bible into Welsh. A little museum has finds from the site, open by appointment; shop, disabled access; (01745) 583429; free. The Farmer's Arms (The Waen) does proper food.

SNOWDON SH6455 This whole area has plenty of fine walking, both gentle and taxing, to fill a walking holiday. Snowdonia's main mountain group soars dramatically, many of its peaks having easily identifiable shapes (when you can see them through the mist). Snowdon itself is the highest mountain in England or Wales. The summit has the highest postbox in Britain, and a café that Prince Charles dubbed 'the highest slum in Wales'; certainly one of the less succesful works of Portmeirion architect Sir Clough Williams-Ellis, it's likely to be replaced in the next few years. The National Trust, with massive help from the actor Sir Anthony Hopkins, is currently buying much of the surrounding land. A number of walks up range from the easy path alongside the mountain railway from Llanberis to the enthralling Horseshoe Route, which makes its way along knife-edge ridges; the Pyg Track and Watkin Path are among the favourites. For a taste of the mountain without actually going up it, follow the start of the Miners Track (from the Pen-y-pass car park on the A4086), which really is a track as far as Glaslyn, the last of 4 lakes passed. Sherpa Buses run a good service up the mountain (you can get them from several of the North Wales resorts).

SOUTH STACK SH2182 The spectacular cliffs nr the lighthouse are full of seabird breeding colonies, and there's a 780-acre **RSPB reserve**, where you may be able to see guillemots, razorbills and puffins (especially around May, Jun and July). Lots of colourful wild flowers too, and maybe the odd seal. The visitor centre has closed-circuit TV of nesting birds; guided walks leave here at 2pm Tues and Sat May–Aug. Visitor centre cl Oct–Easter; (01407) 764973; free. Nearby is a large group of the foundations of **hut circles**, probably around 2,000 years old, still with some visible traces of stone sleeping slabs. The RSPB have now opened a second seabird centre at the South Stack lighthouse; cl Oct–Easter; (01248) 724444; £2.

TAN-Y-BWLCH SH6945 **Plas Tan-y-Bwlch** (off the A487) The grounds of the Snowdonia National Park's study centre have rewarding strolls through extensive woodland; in places the paths cross the Ffestiniog Railway (and you can buy tickets for it here). Woods open all year, gardens summer only; (01766) 590324; donations.

TREFRIW WOOLLEN MILL SH7863 (B5106) The same family

Days Out

Medieval town planning and seaside Victoriana: Conwy; lunch at the Castle Hotel there, or the Queen's Head, Llandudno Junction; tram up Great Ormes Head from Llandudno, or visit Bodnant Garden.

Around the Welsh Everest: Caernarfon Castle; lunch at Y Bistro, Llanberis; Snowdon Mountain Railway, Welsh Slate Museum or the Electric Mountain there.

Italianate fantasy and slate city: Portmeirion; lunch there, or at the Ship, Porthmadog; Llechwedd Slate Caverns at Blaenau Ffestiniog.

have run this woollen mill for 135 years; 2 hydro-electric turbines are driven by the fast-flowing Afon Crafnant, and there's a weaver's garden (best Jun–Sept). Weaving demonstrations in the turbine house wkdys all year (even Nov–Easter when the mill itself is closed), plus wknds in summer. Maybe spinning demonstrations too in summer, so worth checking first to see exactly what's going on. Snacks, shop (selling tapestries and tweeds made here), disabled access; cl Sun (exc bank hols and late May–Sept); (01492) 640462; free. Trefriw used to be a spa, and you can still see the **wells** on the N outskirts of the village (the water is said to treat rheumatism, indigestion, and homesickness). The village also has a 14th-c church; the Prince's Arms has decent food.

WREXHAM SJ3350 Mostly an industrial town, but its 15th-c **church** is worth a look, with its magnificent steeple. **Erddig** (well signed S) Superb late 17th-c house, especially interesting for the way you can explore the life of those 'upstairs' and 'downstairs' equally as thoroughly; the gallery of servants' portraits is especially touching. Enlarged and improved in the early 18th c, the house is filled with splendid original furnishings, inc a magnificent state bed in Chinese silk. Restored outbuildings include a laundry, bakehouse, estate smithy and sawmill, and the surrounding parkland is very pleasant to stroll through. It's one of the most attractive places to visit in Wales. Meals, snacks, shop, some disabled access; open pm Sat–Weds Easter–Sept; (01978) 313333; £5.60, garden and below-stairs tour only £3.60; NT. The Red Lion in Marchwiel has decent food. **Farm World** (adjacent to Erddig) Well liked by readers, a 300-acre working dairy farm with all the necessary ingredients. Cl Nov–Feb; (01978) 840697; *£3.95. **Bersham Industrial Heritage Centre** (B5099/B5098 W) Well re-created 18th-c ironworks, with a good overview of other local industries, and demonstrations of various traditional skills. Snacks, shop, limited disabled access; ironworks cl all Oct–Easter and wkdys in Apr; (01978) 261529; heritage centre free, ironworks £1.

! Y FELINHELI SH5367 **Greenwood Centre** (off the B4366 NE of Caernarfon) An unexpected delight, a lively look at trees and wood from trunks and rainforests to Ethiopian wooden pillows. You can handle most of the exhibits, and there's 17 acres of woodland to explore. Mostly indoors so ideal for rainy days, but worth popping into at any time. Teas, shop, disabled access; open daily in summer, best to ring for winter opening; (01248) 671493; £3.95. The Vaynol Arms at Pentir has good food.

★ **Attractive villages** in the area, all with decent pubs and in general tending to appeal for their surroundings more than for the beauty of their buildings, include Betws-yn-Rhos SH9174, Cilcain SJ1865, Erbistock SJ3542, Halkyn SJ2172, Hanmer SJ4639, Llanarmon DC SJ1633, Llanarmon-yn-Ial SJ1956, Llanasa SJ1082, Llandwrog SH4456, Llanelidan SJ1150, Llangedwyn SJ1924 in the Tanat Valley, Llanrhaeadr-ym-Mochnant SJ1226 (where *An Englishman Who Went Up A Hill* was filmed), Llansannan SH9466, Pontblyddyn SJ2761, Porth Dinllaen SH2741 (an idyllic seaside spot, but you have to walk to it) and St George SH9576.

Other pubs and inns in attractive areas or with notable views include the Porth Tocyn Hotel above the sea at Abersoch SH3225 (excellent clean beach for families here), Castell Cidwm at Betws Garmon SH5458, Sportsman's Arms up on the A543 S of Bylchau SH9863, White Horse and Bryn Tyrch at Capel Garmon SH8255, the Grouse at Carrog SJ1144, T'yn y Groes at Ganllwyd SH7224, Eagle & Child in the hilltop village of Gwaenysgor SJ0881, the Druid at Llanferres SJ1961 (doing well under new management), Cross Foxes on the Dee at Overton Bridge SJ3643, the Ship by acres of sand on the shore of Red Wharf Bay SH5281, Cwellyn Arms at Rhyd-ddu SH5753 (big playground), White Eagle on Holy Island at Rhoscolyn SH2676 and Caerffynon Hall at Talsarnau SH6236.

Where to eat

BALA SH9236 **Neuadd-y-Cyfnod** (Old School Restaurant) *High St (01678) 521269* Relaxed and informal restaurant in an attractive old building (it can trace its history back to 1600); with huge helpings of good-value food (morning coffee, lunch, tea and dinner), pleasant service, and nice furnishings; Welsh lamb a speciality; disabled access; cl beginning Nov–beginning Apr. **£15**|£4.50.

BEAUMARIS SH6076 **Sailors Return** *Church St (01248) 811314* Bright and cheerful, more or less open-plan, with a collection of car-shaped teapots, naval memorabilia, maps and old prints; comfortable furnishings in rich colours, a good mix of customers, well kept real ales, and enjoyable food inc daily specials. **£18.15**|£5.95.

BODFARI SJ0970 **Dinorben Arms** *(01745) 710309* Carefully extended building with warmly welcoming beamed rooms, and 3 open fires; a huge collection of whiskies, well kept real ales and plenty of good wines, popular lunchtime smorgasbord, Fri/Sat carvery, and a help-yourself farmhouse buffet Weds/Thurs; disabled access. **£14**|£4.45.

GRESFORD SJ3352 **Pant-yr-Ochain** *Chester Rd (01978) 853525* Attractively and interestingly decorated spacious pub with country furnishings, open fires, a big dining area set out as a library, and a no smoking room; consistently good, interesting food, a decent range of wines, well kept real ales, polite and efficient service, and a civilised atmosphere. **£22.45**|£5.25.

LLANBERIS SH5760 **Y Bistro** *43–35 High St (01286) 871278* Friendly, no smoking restaurant with good local produce used in the Welsh and English cooking – fine fish and enjoyable puddings; cl Sun, Mon in winter. **£29**.

LLANDUDNO JUNCTION SH8180 **Queens Head** *Glanwydden (01492) 546570* Busy but comfortable dining pub with a spacious and comfortable modern lounge bar; carefully prepared and imaginative food using lots of fine seafood, delicious puddings, real ales, and decent wines; cl 25 Dec; children over 8. **£21**|£5.95.

LLANGEDWYN SJ1924 **Green** *(01691) 828234* Very well run, ancient place in a lovely spot in the Tanat Valley; with lots of nooks, alcoves and crannies, a blazing log fire, a nice mix of furnishings, and a pleasant, upstairs, no smoking restaurant; impressive range of tasty bar food, half-a-dozen real ales, and a good choice of malt whiskies and wines; attractive garden over the road, with picnic sets by the river, and fishing permits. **£16.95**|£4.90.

LLANRWST SH7961 **Ty-Hwnt-i'r-Bont** *(01492) 640138* Charming little 500-year-old cottage by a bridge, run by the Holt family for 26 years; with nice old country furniture under the beams and joists, interesting knick-knacks, light lunches, home-made cakes, shortbread and scones for enjoyable afternoon teas, and quite a choice of teas, coffees and milk shakes; home-made mustards to take away; also, old books and bric-à-brac upstairs; cl Mon (exc bank hols), cl 1st Sun in Nov–Tues before Easter; partial disabled access.£4.50.

PWLLHELI SH3535 **Plas BODEGROES** off the A497 *(01758) 612363* Lovely Georgian manor house in tree-filled grounds; with comfortably restful rooms, good food using superb fresh local produce (especially fish) and a very fine wine list; bdrms; cl Mon, Dec–Feb. **£40 for 5 courses**.

RED WHARF BAY SH5281 **Ship** *(01248) 852568* Solidly built old pub looking over miles of cockle-sands; with enterprising bar food, big old-fashioned bars, coal fires, friendly, cheerful service, a no smoking dining room and cellar room, well kept real ales, quite a few whiskies, and plenty of seats outside; disabled access. **£18.90**|£5.25.

TY'N-Y-GROES SH7772 **Groes** *(01492) 650545* Particularly well run family pub with wonderful views from the airy, no smoking conservatory, rambling, low-beamed and thick-walled rooms with a welcoming atmosphere and interesting old furnishings, winter log fires; a fine range of good traditional country cooking, well kept real ales, and efficient, friendly service; bdrms; children over 10 in restaurant; disabled access. **£25**|£6.

West Wales

Lovely unspoilt coast, great for a quiet holiday.

This part of Wales has lots of castles, a fair spread of other places to visit, and quite a lot to keep children amused – the leisure park near Narberth is particularly good, though the area has virtually no bright-lights attractions. Tenby, showing its medieval origins still, is an enjoyably civilised small resort. St David's Cathedral is a real surprise in such rural surroundings, and there are a good few things to look at nearby.

The coast is relatively gentle in the south, with level cliffs, sinuous estuaries and some lovely sandy beaches. In the west and north, it's much more rugged, with seals and dolphins. The Pembrokeshire Coast Path snaking round the intricate seaboard makes for notable walks. Outstanding stretches are between St David's and Strumble Head near Fishguard – largely unspoilt, full of rocky coves and exhilarating cliff walks; around St Brides Bay – low cliffs flanking surfing beaches; by the attractive fishing villages of Solva and Little Haven; and in the wild places around Marloes.

The best of the inland scenery is around Brechfa and Abergorlech, with steep forests and plunging ravines, and other good spots include the blustery Prescelly Hills and the secluded and intimate Gwaun Valley; but other parts of Wales are better for scenic drives.

Where to stay

BROAD HAVEN SM8616 **Druidstone** *Broad Haven, Haverfordwest, Dyfed SA62 3NE (01437) 781221* **£70** plus special breaks; 9 rms, some with sea views, shared bthrms. Alone on the coast above an effectively private beach, with exhilarating cliff walks, this roomy and very informal, friendly hotel, with something of a folk-club and Outward Bound feel at times, is extremely winning and relaxing if you take to its unique combination of good, wholesome and often memorably inventive food, slightly fend-for-yourself approach amid elderly furniture, and glorious seaside surroundings; self-catering cottages, 2 with wheelchair access. Unusual sporting activities inc sand-yachting; cl Mon–Weds mid-Nov–mid-Dec (fully open from then on), and then Mon–Weds beginning Jan–mid-Feb; disabled access (see above).

CAREW SN0403 **Old Stable Cottage** *Carew, Tenby, Dyfed SA70 8SL (01646) 651889* **£48;** 3 rms. Originally a stable and carthouse for the castle, this attractive place has an inglenook fireplace with original bread oven, a games room, and a conservatory overlooking the garden; good, Aga-cooked food; may cl Dec–Feb (best to phone); children over 3.

CRUGYBAR SN6437 **Glanrannell Park** *Crugybar, Llanwrda, Dyfed SA19 8SA (01558) 685230* ***£76**, plus special breaks; 8 rms. Surrounded by lawns and overlooking a small private lake in 23 acres of parkland, this peaceful hotel has 2 comfortable lounges and a small library, a well stocked bar, good food using fresh local produce where possible, and friendly, helpful staff; excellent area for walks and especially birdwatching, also lots of wildlife, pony-trekking, and fishing nearby; cl Nov–Mar.

FISHGUARD SM9736 **Gilfach Goch Farm** *Fishguard, Dyfed SA65 9SR (01348) 873871* ***£52,** plus special breaks; 6 rms. Traditional, carefully modernised, 18th-c

Welsh stone farmhouse on a 10-acre smallholding with sheep, donkeys, a Vietnamese pot-bellied pig, dogs, cats and fowl; lovely views and nr Pembrokeshire Coast Path; log fires, a homely lounge, good country cooking using many home-produced ingredients, and a safe garden for children; no smoking; self-catering also; cl end Oct–beginning Apr; disabled access.

FISHGUARD SM9537 **Manor House** *Fishguard, Dyfed SA65 9HG (01348) 873260* ***£54,** plus special breaks; 6 comfortable rms, most with sea views. Georgian house with fine views of the harbour from the sheltered garden; well planned basement restaurant with a good choice of home-made food using fresh local produce; cl Christmas.

GLYNARTHEN SN3049 **Penbontbren Farm** *Glynarthen, Llandysul, Dyfed SA44 6PE (01239) 810248* **£74;** 10 rms in converted stone outbuildings. Run by a friendly Welsh-speaking family, this Victorian farmhouse is in lovely countryside with nature trails, horse riding, a little farm museum, and nearby beaches; period pine furnishings in the bar, lounge and well liked restaurant, good hearty dinners inc some regional dishes, bar lunches, and decent breakfasts; cl 25 Dec; disabled access.

LLANDELOY SM8527 **Lochmeyler Farm** *Llandeloy, Haverfordwest, Dyfed SA62 6LL (01348) 837724* **£60,** plus special breaks; 16 rms. Attractive 16th-c farmhouse on a 220-acre working dairy farm; 2 lounges (one no smoking), log fires, traditional farmhouse cooking in the pleasant dining room, a mature garden, and Welsh cakes on arrival; you can walk round the farm trails; disabled access.

NEVERN SN0840 **Trewern Arms** *Nevern, Newport, Dyfed SA42 0NB (01239) 820395* **£45;** 10 rms. Creeper-clad old inn in a pleasant riverside hamlet; interestingly decorated, slate-floored bar, a comfortable lounge bar, decent food, well kept real ales, and a quiet garden.

PENALLY SS1199 **Penally Abbey** *Penally, Tenby, Dyfed SA70 7PY (01834) 843033* **£100;** 12 pretty rms, many with four-posters, and 4 in coach house. 'Gothick'-style country-house hotel in 5 acres of gardens and woodland, with fine views across the golf course and Carmarthen Bay; open fire in the comfortable lounge, a tiny bar, conservatory, very good food in the elegant, candlelit restaurant, and delicious breakfasts; small indoor swimming pool, snooker and croquet; children over 7 in restaurant; disabled access.

PONTFAEN SN0533 **Tregynon Country Farmhouse** *Pontfaen, Fishguard, Dyfed SA65 9TU (01239) 820531* **£64,** plus special breaks; 6 rms. Peacefully set, 16th-c farmhouse on the edge of the Gwaun Valley, in lovely unspoilt countryside with lots of wildlife and walks; big inglenook fireplace in the beamed lounge, a friendly welcome, and very good, imaginative, additive-free food using produce from their own own and neighbouring farms; home-smoked meats and home-made preserves; cl 2 wks winter – best to phone; children over 8.

RHYDLEWIS SN3447 **Broniwan** *Rhydlewis, Llandysul, Dyfed SA44 5PF (01239) 851261* **£40;** 3 pretty rms, 2 with own bthrm. Grey stone house with pine-panelled windows, on a small farm surrounded by beech and pine trees, with fine views of the Prescelly Hills in the distance; lots of wildlife, and you can help with the calves, hens and cows; stone barn with games, table tennis and books, a woodburner in the comfortable sitting room, a separate dining room, and good, naturally produced food from both the garden and farm; no smoking; children over 7.

ST DAVID'S SM7524 **Warpool Court** *St David's, Haverfordwest, Dyfed SA62 6BN (01437) 720300* ***£110,** plus special breaks; 25 rms. Originally built as St David's cathedral school in the 1860s and bordering NT land, this popular hotel has lovely views over St Brides Bay; Ada Williams's collection of lovely hand-painted tiles can be seen in the public rooms, food in the spacious, elegant restaurant is imaginative (good for vegetarians too), and staff are helpful and friendly; quiet gardens, heated summer swimming pool, tennis, exercise room, table tennis, pool, croquet, and free golf at St David's golf club; cl Jan.

SPITTAL SM9822 **Lower Haythog** *Spittal, Haverfordwest, Dyfed SA62 5QL (01437) 731279* **£50;** 6 rms. Centuries-old farmhouse on a working dairy farm in 250 acres of unspoilt countryside; with a comfortable lounge, log fire, books and games, traditional breakfasts, good cooking in the dining room, and friendly owners; swing and slide in the garden, trout ponds in the woods.

To see and do

★ **ABERAERON** SN4562 The line of colour-washed houses facing the harbour is very pretty; there's a good craft centre, and the Harbourmaster and Hive on the quay are good for food.

AMROTH SN1607 The beach here is lovely, and the New Inn facing it has good home cooking inc local seafood. **Colby Woodland Garden** (off the A477 nr Amroth) Beautiful woodland gardens in a sheltered valley with a pretty cascading stream – very pleasant and colourful, especially in autumn. A walled garden has a 'gothick' gazebo and colourful herbaceous plants. Snacks, shop; cl Nov–Mar; (01834) 811885; £2.80; NT.

★ **BEGELLY** SN1109 **Folly Farm** (A478) Busy working dairy farm, with the chance to milk a cow – or watch the more modern methods in the milking parlour. Everyone gets a chance to bottle-feed some of the friendly animals. Also an indoor traditional fairground, good play areas and go-carts. Meals, snacks, shop, disabled access; cl Nov–Feb; (01834) 812731; £3.75. A working **pottery** is nearby, (01834) 811204. Nearby **Saundersfoot** is a relaxed, extended, seaside village, with a lighthouse on the spit sheltering the harbour and sandy beach; nice fresh fish at the Royal Oak (which has heaters for its outside tables).

BURRY PORT SN4100 **Pembrey Country Park** Good for families to unwind, with 100 acres of woodland, summer falconry and orienteering, an adventure playground, visitor centre, dry ski slope, toboggan run, a minature railway and 8 miles of clean sandy beach (no dogs in summer). Meals, snacks, shop, disabled access; park open all yr, though most attractions cl winter; (01554) 833913; parking £4, considerably less in winter; charges for some attractions.

CAREW CASTLE AND TIDAL MILL SN0403 Magnificent Norman castle (the setting for the Great Tournament of 1507), with an especially handsome, ivy-clad, south-east tower. The mill is one of just 3 restored tidal mills in Britain, with records dating back to 1558. Shop; cl Nov–Easter; (01646) 651782; £2.50 both, £1.70 each. By the good Carew Inn nearby is the Carew Cross, an impressive 4-metre (13-ft) Celtic cross dating from the 11th c.

CARMARTHEN SN4120 Busy regional market town, according to legend the birthplace of Merlin, with the remains of a 13th-c castle, and on Priory St an unusual 2nd-c Roman amphitheatre. **Carmarthen Museum** (Abergwili, just E) Good museum in a former palace of the Bishop of St David's, in 7 attractive acres. Snacks, shop, disabled access to ground floor only; cl Sun, 25–26 Dec, 1 Jan; (01267) 231691; free. **Gwili Railway** (Bronwydd, A484 N) Short steamtrain trips along a scenic standard-gauge branch line of the old Great Western Railway. Snacks, shop, disabled access; trains daily in Aug, and most Suns and some Weds May–Sept; (01267) 230666 for timetable; £3.50. The Cresselly Arms, along the A40 E in the pretty village of Pont ar Gothi (pleasant riverside walks), is reliable for lunch.

CARNINGLI COMMON SN0637 (Mynydd Carningli, S of Newport) Pleasant walks with some interesting views, on largely unspoilt moorland capped by ancient cairns and other antiquities.

CASTELL HENLLYS SN1138 (signed off the A487 E of Newport – where the Llwyngwair Arms surprises with its authentic Indian food) Iron Age hill fort in beautiful countryside overlooking the River Gwaun, with interesting reconstructions of 3 big conical roundhouses. Also a forge, smithy, primitive looms and a herb garden. Snacks, shop, some disabled access; cl Nov–Mar; (01239) 891319; £2.50.

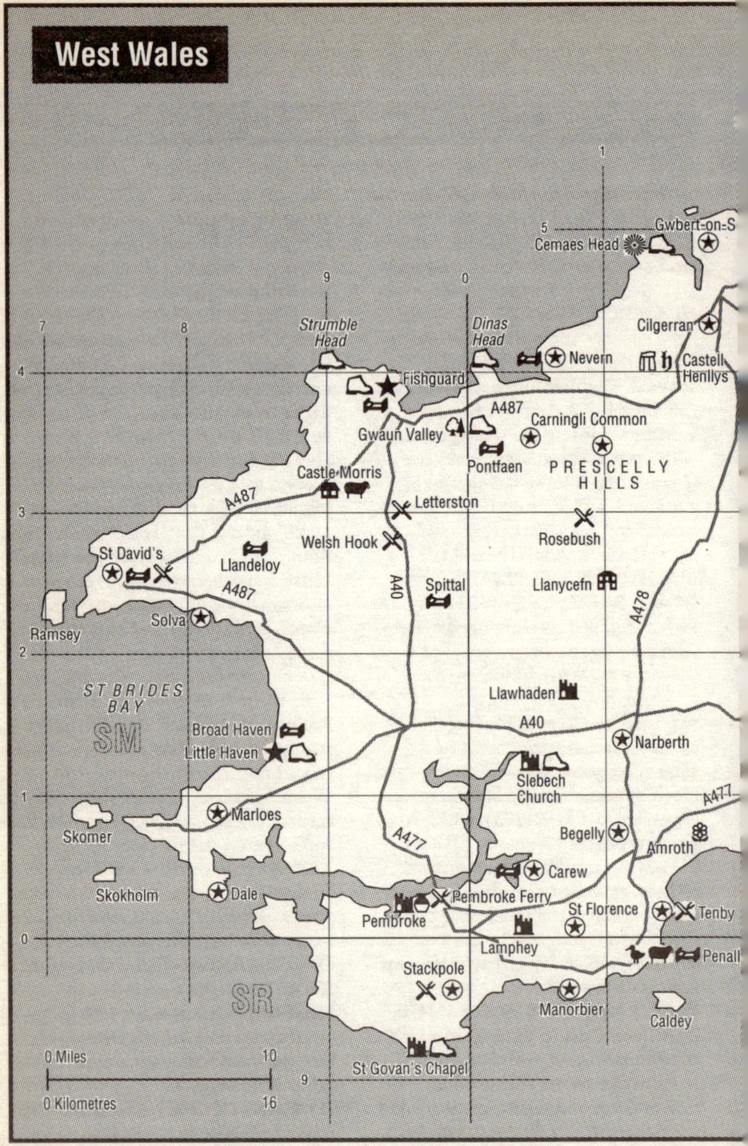

CASTLE MORRIS SM9032 **Llangloffan Farmhouse Cheese** (just N) Delicious, traditional farmhouse hard cheeses are hand-made here, and you can watch the whole process (which stage depends on the time of day you visit) and even meet the cows. Before Mr Downey set up the farm (run entirely on organic principles) he was a viola player in the Hallé Orchestra; his award-winning cheeses now go all over the world. Snacks, shop, disabled access; cheese-making am only, phone to check times, farm shop open daily exc Sun; (01348) 891241; *£1.75. The excellent-value fish restaurant at Letterston is handy.

CEMAES HEAD SN1249 Gives walkers good views over the

mouth of the Teifi estuary and out over the Irish Sea.

CENARTH SN2641 **National Coracle Centre** Unique collection of small hand-made boats from all over the world; they may have demonstrations of how they're made, and there are also various tools used for poaching. A medieval bridge and a pretty waterfall provide the backdrop. Snacks, shop, disabled access; cl Sat, and all Nov–Mar; (01239) 710980; *£2. Nearby **Newcastle Emlyn** has an attractive main st leading down to an ancient bridge; the Bunch of Grapes and Pelican do decent food.

CILGERRAN CASTLE SN1943 (off the A484) On a

picturesque crag above the River Teifi, this twin-towered Plantagenet fortress has fine views from its towers and high walls, though, as usual, you have to go up a spiral staircase. Shop (not Sat), disabled access; (01239) 615007; £1.70. The ancient Pendre is good for lunch. **Welsh Wildlife Centre** (signed off the A478 and A487) Covering 350 acres, one of the richest areas of wetland in the district; the reed bed is the second biggest in Wales. You'll probably see more towards dusk, but even then some bashful creatures might not emerge; a video shows the species you may have missed. Meals, snacks, shop, disabled access; open Easter–Oct half-term; (01239) 621600; £2.50.

DALE SM8104 Normal base for the National Park boats to the 3 islands named below; sailing times (usually Apr-Oct only) from Dale Sailing Co, (01646) 601636. The Griffin overlooking the anchorage is useful for lunch. This peninsula at the entrance to the huge natural harbour of Milford Haven has gentle, level-topped terrain giving walkers a bird's-eye view of the shipping activities, reducing the giant oil tankers to a pleasantly toy-like scale. **Skomer** SM7209 720 acres of spectacular wild scenery with countless birds (inc breeding pairs of short-eared owls) and flowers, as well as seals playing on the shore – maybe common seals briefly in Jun or July, more likely grey seals and their pups in Sept and Oct; it's also remarkable for the easily traced remains of the Iron Age settlement here – there's a well laid out trail. **Grassholme** SM5909 Notable for its 30,000 pairs of gannets: on a clear sunny morning even from the coast you can see it's white with them. **Skokholm** SM7304 Home of Britain's first bird observatory.

DINAS HEAD SN0039 The circuit of this nice miniature headland gives about an hour's walk.

DRE-FACH FELINDRE SN3539 **Museum of the Welsh Woollen Industry** (off the A484) Working museum with textile machinery and tools dating back to the 18th c. Also factory trails, and demonstrations of fabric-making – you may be able to try your hand at spinning. Snacks, shop, disabled access to ground floor; cl Sun, and Sat Nov–Mar; (01559) 370929; *£2.60. There are decent places to eat in Newcastle Emlyn.

★ **FISHGUARD** SM9537 The old fishing harbour is surrounded by appropriately small streets of terraced cottages (the Ship here has lots of atmosphere); there's an entirely separate big commercial harbour used by the Irish ferries. In between, the upper town has some attractive old buildings and is pleasant to saunter through. The Royal Oak has decent food. You can drive or walk up on to the high headland which protects the harbour; its cliffs are quite grand, particularly where the seas boil through the narrow neck cutting off the rock on which Strumble Head lighthouse stands. Down on the rocks there you quite often see seals even in the spring, though they're more common in late summer.

GWAUN VALLEY SN0034 Pretty walks along the lushly wooded river either upstream or downstream of Pontfaen.

GWBERT-ON-SEA SN1648 **Cardigan Island Coastal Farm Park** Most notable for its fine clifftop setting overlooking Cardigan Island; there are quite a few friendly animals for children, as well as plenty of wild flowers, and a coastal walk to caves where seals breed (best Mar–Nov). You may even see dolphins leaping out of the sea. Open all yr; (01239) 612196; £1.50.

KIDWELLY CASTLE SN4007 When this was built in the 12th c, the sea used to wash against the steep slope below. 4 massive towers, the tremendous gatehouse and much of the impressive outer walls still remain, with steps up to the battlements and turrets. From the walls, the narrow medieval street layout of Kidwelly itself is very obvious. Shop, some disabled access; cl 24–26 Dec, 1 Jan; (01554) 890104; £2.20 (inc audio tour). **Kidwelly Industrial Museum** (Mynyddygarreg, NE) Looks at 2 great Welsh industries: coal and tin-mining. The original tinplate-working buildings are still here, and there's an exhibition of coal-mining with pithead gear and a winding engine. Snacks, shop, disabled access; open Easter, then wkdys and pm wknds May–Aug; (01554) 891078; free. The riverside Gwenllian Court Hotel out this way has decent food.

LAMPHEY PALACE SN0101 (A4139) Ruined 13th-c palace once belonging to the Bishops of St David's. Some disabled access; cl 25 Dec; (01222) 500200; £1.70.

LAUGHARNE SN3011 **Dylan Thomas's Boat House** (Dylan's Walk) Wales's best known recent poet lived here while he was writing *Under Milk Wood*, and there are still some of his family photographs and furniture. The writing shed he used for so many poems is nearby. Snacks, shop; cl 25 Dec; (01994) 427420; *£2.50. **Laugharne Castle** The ruin Dylan Thomas described as 'brown as owls' is a massive battlemented compilation of styles from the 12th to the 16th c; it has Victorian and Georgian gardens and good views over the estuary. Cl Oct–Apr; (01994) 427906; £2. The setting on the Taf estuary makes this a rewarding spot for wandering – past Laugharne Castle and Boat House and along the cliff walk (known as Dylan's Walk); in the other direction there's a pleasant walk via Roche Castle. Thomas and his wife are buried in the village churchyard, their grave marked by a simple white cross.

★ **LITTLE HAVEN** SM8512 An attractive village, with boats pulled up on to the sand, and a good base for seaside walks on the Pembrokeshire Coast Path. There are some pleasing sandy-floored rock coves to explore at low tide around here and around the Druidstone Hotel to the N, with a good cliff walk northwards from there to the long sweep of sand and surf at Newgale Sands (food all day from the Duke of Edinburgh).

★ **LLANDEILO** SN6222 An attractive sloping town; the Plough at Rhosmaen just N is a favourite local dining pub. **Dinefwr Park** (20 minutes' walk from the riverside lodge on the S edge of town; follow Dyfed Wildlife Trust path) Pleasant walks through wooded Capability Brown parkland around an isolated, largely 13th-c castle. Plenty of deer, but no trace of the medieval town which is known to have stood outside the walls. Meals, snacks, disabled access; cl Tues, Weds, and Nov–Mar; (01558) 823902; £2.80. **Gelli Aur Country Park** (3m W, off the B4300) Very relaxing: 60 acres of wooded parkland around a splendid mansion, with an arboretum, nature trails, and specimen trees and shrubs. Meals, snacks, shop, disabled access; cl 25–26 Dec; (01558) 668885; parking charge £1.20.

LLANELLI SN5001 **Parc Howard Art Gallery and Museum** In pleasant parkland, the largest collection of the distinctive local pottery, as well as local history, and pictures by local artist J Dickson Innes. Snacks; cl 1–2pm, and 25–26 Dec; (01554) 772029; free. The Stepney (Park St) is handy for lunch. **Wildfowl and Wetlands Trust** (3 m E) By Wales's main estuary for wildfowl and waders, with plenty of observation hides and special walkways. Many of the birds will feed from your hand, and at their summer Duckery you can hear ducklings cheeping inside their eggs. Meals, snacks, shop, disabled access; cl 24–25 Dec; (01554) 741087; *£4.

★ **LLANGRANOG** SN3154 Attractive fishing village with a nice family beach backed by cliffs; there's a pleasant stroll to a headland to the N (otherwise, Cardiganshire lacks a coast path for much of the way). Further N, Cwmtydu cove is pretty – spectacular at sunset.

LLANSTEPHAN CASTLE SN3410 Sprawling 11th/13th-c ruin, majestically overlooking the Tywi estuary and Carmarthen Bay from an isolated ridge high over the water. Impressive gatehouse with a fine vaulted ceiling – and slots for drenching intruders with boiling fat or lead; free.

LLANYCEFN SN1024 **Penrhos Cottage** (off the B4313) There can't have been many housing problems around here if local tradition is to be believed; anyone who built a house overnight on common land was entitled to claim it, and this old cottage was such a one, frantically constructed by friends and family. Small shop, disabled access; open by appointment only, (01437) 731328; donations.

LLAWHADEN CASTLE SN0617 12th-c ruins ringed by a deep moat, with remains of the 13th/14th-c bishop's hall, kitchen and bakehouse; free. The Post Office nearby sells guides and cards.

★ **MANORBIER CASTLE** SS0697 Still in the hands of the family who have owned it for over 300 years, this impressive, partly 12th-c fortress looking down to the beach has massive medieval outer walls and an early round tower, with a 13th-c chapel and other buildings, and more modern constructions within the walls. Snacks, shop; cl Oct–Easter; (01834) 871394; *£2. The quiet village is attractive, with a particularly good clean beach, and there's a striking view of the castle from the church. The Castle Inn (open all day in summer) is useful for lunch. Springfields Farm (off the A4139) has pick-your-own strawberries and a decent farm shop; (01834) 871746.

MARLOES DEER PARK SM7508 Not actually a deer park, but a cliffy headland a couple of miles W of Marloes, joined to the mainland by quite a narrow isthmus showing steep Iron Age defences; a place to watch birds (choughs breed here) and maybe seals on the offshore rocks. The Lobster Pot in Marloes is a useful, informal, family pub, and the beaches are safe for bathing as well as gloriously remote. The gentle terrain above the cliffs, giving views of Skomer Island, has memorable walkers' routes that need only minimal inland walking to complete the circuit.

★ **NARBERTH** SN1014 Pleasant little town on the imaginary Landsker line separating the 'Little England' of South Pembrokeshire from the more properly Welsh areas to the N. The Angel and Coach & Horses are useful for lunch. **Landsker Visitor Centre** (High St) Enjoyable look at local facts and fancies (one of its local yarns involves a man who tried to hang a pregnant mouse), but as we went to press its future was uncertain; best to check on (01834) 860061. **Blackpool Mill** (Canaston Bridge, 3m W) Striking 3-storeyed former corn mill with working machinery, and pleasant walks along the fish-filled river that powers it. As we went to press the adjacent caverns were cl for refurbishment, but may reopen during 1999. Snacks, shop; cl Nov–Mar; (01437) 541233; £1. **Oakwood** (A4075 W) The only real theme park in Wales, and a good one too, especially in the summer holidays when they stay open till 10pm, rounding off every night with a firework display. There's a real mix of things to do, from Europe's biggest wooden rollercoaster to live Wild West saloon shows. Younger children have their own little rollercoaster (there's another medium-sized one aimed at families), as well as a small farm area, and carousels and the like. The real talking point is the sky-coaster, Vertigo, the Ride We Most Want Not To Go On: you're strapped in a harness and winched to a height of up to 40 metres or more (140ft), then freefall at 60mph towards the ground – just before which you'll start swinging like a frantic pendulum. This nightmare cross between bungee-jumping and a parachute drop obviously wouldn't suit everyone, so rather than bump up the entry price, there's an extra charge (£30 for up to 3 people, the maximum number that can go on it at once). This has proved enormously popular, so if you want to try it in peak periods you'll need to get there fairly early to book in. Meals, snacks, shop, disabled access; cl Oct–Easter (exc around Christmas, when special events); (01834) 891373; £9.95. **CC2000** (next door) 10-pin bowling, amusements and a reconstruction of TV's *Crystal Maze*; cl 25–26 Dec; (01834) 891622; separate charges for individual attractions. **Cwm Deri Vineyard** SN0310 (Martletwy, off the A4075 SW) Self-guided walks, rare breeds, a small collection of teddy bears hidden in a shed, and tastings. Maybe cl winter wkdys, and all Jan and Feb (though worth giving them a ring if you're passing); (01834) 891274; free.

† ! **NEVERN** SN0839 Interesting old riverside village with a medieval bridge over the Nyfer. The **church** has a tall, 10th-c carved Celtic cross and other carved stones, some with Viking patterns, in the graveyard, where the massive yew trees are reputed to weep tears of blood if the priest is not Welsh-speaking. The

Trewern Arms is handy for lunch. The nearby Garden of Eden is a 'liberated' nudist club centred around a big subtropical glasshouse. **Pentre Ifan Burial Chamber** (SE, towards Brynberian) One of the most impressive ancient monuments in Wales: a striking, former long barrow, with the enormous capstone still held up by 3 of the 4 surviving great upright megaliths. Super valley views.

PEMBROKE SM9801 The birthplace of Henry VII and thus the Tudor dynasty, the impressive 13th-c **castle** is largely intact, and its endless passages, tunnels and stairways are great fun to explore. The 23-metre (75-ft) tower is one of the finest in Britain. Summer snacks, shop, disabled access; cl 25–26 Dec, 1 Jan; (01646) 684585; *£3 (guided tours by arrangement, Jun–Aug exc Sat, 50p extra). **Museum of the Home** (Westgate Hill) Intriguing private collection of all sorts of everyday objects from the past 300 years, in a pleasant domestic setting. No under-5s; open Mon–Thurs May–Sept; (01646) 681200; *£1.20. The Pembroke Ferry pub, by the water at the foot of the bridge over the estuary, does good fresh fish.

PENALLY SS1199 **Stepaside Bird and Animal Park** (A477) A friendly place with exotic birds, snakes, reptiles and meercats. Lots going on through the day inc crocodile-taming demonstrations and spider and snake handling. Snacks, shop, disabled access; cl Nov–Mar; (01834) 811710; *£3.50.

PENDINE SN2307 **Museum of Speed** The hard flat sand on the beaches here made it a favourite spot for attempting new speed records (and even 1998 saw a determined assault on the electric car world record here). In 1926 J G Parry Thomas and his 27-litre car *Babs* set a short-lived land-speed record of 168mph, but the careers of both ended the following year in a grisly accident. The car spent the next 40 years buried in the sand but has now been restored, and in July and Aug (maybe longer) forms the centrepiece of this small museum overlooking the beach. Also local and natural history; (01994) 453488; free.

PRESCELLY HILLS SN0529 (*Mynydd Preseli*) Pleasant walks with interesting views, on largely unspoilt moorland capped by ancient cairns and other antiquities – for example, the intriguing Carn Arthur and a hill fort, both reached from the back road along the E side.

! PUMSAINT SN6639 **Dolaucothi Gold Mines** (off the A482) 2,000 years of gold-mining are the focus of this unusual mine, in use since Roman times; tours of both the Roman adits and the deeper 1930s workings, complete with miners' lamps and helmets. Good visitor centre, woodland walks, and the chance to have a go at panning for gold. Stout footwear recommended. Meals, snacks, shop, disabled access; site open Apr–Sept (cl Thurs and Fri exc July and Aug), underground tours (no under-5s) mid-May–late Sept; (01558) 650359; £3, tours £3.50 (£2 NT members); NT. Get there early for the underground tours, especially in summer hols. The nearby Brunant Arms in fine scenery at Caio has decent food.

★ ! **ST DAVID'S** SM7525 The cathedral here has had a community in residence around it for longer than any other in Britain, but thanks to the relative isolation of the place it's stayed undeveloped, so that St David's today is little more than a village – with lots of colourful flowers in spring. **St David's Cathedral** The Norman church had largely collapsed by the 15th c and elaborate repairs had to be made; the resulting roof is an impressive lace-like oak affair, and oak features in most of the rest of the church too. There's a fine collection of Celtic sculptured crosses. Shop, disabled access; donations. **Bishop's Palace** Now a series of impressive ruins, this was clearly once very grand: plenty of quadrangles, stairways and splendid arcaded walls, with all sorts of intricate and often entertaining details (like the carvings below the arcaded parapets). Very atmospheric and tranquil, particularly out of season when you may have it largely to yourself. Shop, limited disabled access; cl am winter Suns, 24–26 Dec, 1 Jan; (01437) 720517; £1.70. **Oceanarium** (New St) Excellent insight into sea and shore life;

highlights include the shark tank and rock pool. Talks and demonstrations for children during school hols. Snacks, shop, limited disabled access; cl 25–26 Dec; (01437) 720453; *£3. **St David's Farm Park** (NE edge, off the A487) Big collection of rare breeds, as well as rides on either a tractor or one of their shire horses. Highly praised by readers. Meals, snacks, shop (with their own wool, and spinning demonstrations), disabled access; cl Sept–Easter; (01437) 721601; £3.50. **Adventure Days** can organise well supervised abseiling, canoeing, rock-climbing and other activities – ideal for offloading active children for the day (no under-8s); (01437) 721611. The Old Cross Hotel nr the cathedral is a civilised place for lunch, and the Farmer's Arms is cheap and cheerful. The beach at Whitesands Bay is good. In summer there are **boat trips** from the lifeboat station to rocky Ramsey Island, where seabirds nest in great numbers. **St Non's Chapel** (about ½ mile N) Reputed birthplace of St Non, St David's mother; lovely sea views from the very scant ruins of the simple coastal chapel, signed down a track from the useful St Non's Hotel, with a holy well nearby. The walk from St David's is pleasant. **St David's Head** Good walking in rugged coastal scenery, spectacular in autumn with both heather and gorse out. There are Neolithic burial chambers, ramparts of prehistoric hill forts right on the point, overlooking Caerfai Bay, and from the top of Carn Ledi, the moorland hill close by the coast path, you can often see Ireland. Another nice coastal walk is W to St Justinian (another chapel here, looking over Ramsey Island).

ST FLORENCE SN0802 **Manor House Wildlife and Leisure Park** (B4318) Around 35 acres of wooded grounds and gardens with exotic birds, reptiles and fish, a pets corner, playground, model railway and falconry displays (2pm); also a new natural history museum. Meals, snacks, shop, disabled access; cl Oct–Easter; (01646) 651201; £4. The Old Parsonage Farm does quick family food.

ST GOVAN'S CHAPEL SR9692 (past Bosherston, towards St Govan's Head) A simple reroofed 14th-c ruin, dramatically set halfway down the sea cliffs, and reached via rough rock steps; the former holy well just below has now dried up.

SLEBECH CHURCH SN0215 (off the A40, 5 miles E of Haverfordwest) Gloriously isolated, ruined 12th-c church, formerly a temple of the Knights Hospitaller, by the tidal waters of the East Cleddau. Though there is a track from the main road, it's more enjoyable to turn down the A4075, take the next right turn and park by the mill, walk over the bridge and down the track through the woods above the river. In Haverfordwest, George's (Market St) does good food.

★ **SOLVA** SM8024 One of the prettiest coastal villages, with a great deal of character. From the harbour a good, interesting, shortish path runs E to Dinas Fawr, the opposite headland. This high crag (enclosed by the ramparts of an Iron Age fort) gives pretty views of the fishing village and coast. The

Days Out

Cathedral village: Solva; lunch at the Cambrian Arms there, or the Old Cross Hotel or the Farmer's Arms in St David's; St David's Cathedral and Bishop's Palace; boat trip to Ramsey Island, or walk from Whitesand Bay to St David's Head.

Lily-ponds behind the beach: Pembroke Castle; lunch at the Armstrong Arms, Stackpole, or the Ferry at Pembroke Ferry; Bosherston lily-ponds, St Govan's Chapel.

Harnessing the tide: Tenby; lunch at the Carew Inn, Carew; Carew Castle and Tidal Mill.

Cambrian Arms does decent food.

STACKPOLE SR9896 (off the B4319) This spectacular 2,000-acre estate is a delight to wander through, with lakes, woodlands, cliffs, dunes and beaches offering a range of landscapes to suit every taste and mood. Barafundle Bay is a lovely relatively undiscovered beach. Footpaths lead past a quarry and assorted wildlife over the lake to Bosherston lily-ponds SR9694 – ancient elongated ponds, a fine sight when in bloom in summer, and well worth a walk; (there are several car parks). Snacks (at Stackpole Quay); (01646) 661359; free, NT. The Armstrong Arms does good food, and the St Govan's pub is useful too.

STRUMBLE HEAD SM8941 Typifies the rocky, big-dipper coastline of North Pembrokeshire; walkers can use the car park nr the lighthouse.

TALLEY ABBEY SN6332 (off the B4302) Ruins of a once-magnificent 12th-c abbey, still very fine, especially the 2 pointed archways; (01558) 685444; free.

★ ! **TENBY** SN1300 Pleasantly restrained family resort, with sheltered beaches and rock coves. It's a walled town, the splendidly preserved 13th-c wall still with many of its towers surviving, as well as a magnificent 14th-c arched barbican gateway; a moat used to run the whole length of what is now a tree-lined street. The medieval Plantagenet House, and Coach & Horses and Lamb are all pleasant lunch places. There are some remains of the 13th-c **castle** on the headland above the yachting harbour. Within the castle site is a local history and geology **museum**, with prehistoric finds and an art gallery with a collection of Augustus and Gwen John. Shop; cl winter wknds and Christmas wk; (01834) 842809; £1.70. **Tudor Merchant's House** (Quay Hill) Fine example of gabled 15th-c architecture, with a good Flemish chimney and the remains of frescos on 3 walls; also a small herb garden. Shop; cl Weds, and all Nov–Mar; (01834) 842279; £1.80; NT. **St Mary's Church** Interesting 13th-c building with a huge steeple, and a plaque commemorating a local invention that many of us use every day – the equals sign. **Caldey Island** Reached by summer boat trips from Tenby harbour (May–Sept wkdys, weather permitting, £6), still a monastic island, where the Cistercian monks have good cream and honey for sale, as well as more durable crafts and old-fashioned perfume. Besides the modern abbey, there's a 13th-c church with a simple cobbled floor, still in use, on one side of the small cloister of the original priory; these ancient priory buildings (which you can see from outside but not enter) give a better sense of the past than almost anywhere else in West Wales. Sailing times from the tourist information centre, (01834) 842404. **Hoyles Mouth Cave** (off the A4139 just SW; Trefloyne Lane towards St Florence – short path through wood on left after 500 yds) Running more than 30 metres (100ft) back into the hillside, this spooky place has yielded Ice Age mammoth bones, as well as human tools dating back over 10,000 years. Take a torch, but don't go in winter – you'd disturb the hibernating bats. **Dino's Den** (Great Wedlock Farm, Gumfreston – B4318 W) Fun for families, and an unusual example of farm diversification. The woods are filled with very well constructed, life-size dinosaurs, some of which roar or spit. A visitor centre is designed to look like fossilised dinosaur ribs. Meals, snacks, shop, disabled access; open daily Easter–Sept, and wkdys in Oct; (01834) 845272; £3.50.

★ **TRESAITH** SN2751 Attractive coastal village down steep roads, with a decent pub (and a waterfall to its beach).

Pubs and inns doing food that are noteworthy for their fine positions include the Black Lion at Abergorlech SN5833 (lots of good walks nearby), Forest Arms at Brechfa SN5230, Cresselly Arms by the water at Cresswell Quay SN0406, Denant Mill at Dreenhill SM9214 (includes a Goan restaurant), Stanley Arms on the Cleddau estuary opposite Picton Castle at Landshipping SN0111, the Sloop in the pretty seaside village of Porthgain SM8132 and Cennen Arms at Trapp SN6518. The Teifi Netpool at St Dogmaels SN1645 is handy for a walk along to Poppitt Sands.

Where to eat

ABERAERON SN4562 **Hive on the Quay** *Cadwgan Pl (01545) 570445* Cheerful harbourside place on the wharf, based around a family honey business (their home-made honey ice-cream is delicious); with a lunchtime buffet, popular café, and good, unfussy evening meals relying heavily on organic produce – quite an emphasis on fish from their own boat; also a bee exhibition and shop; cl mid-Sept–spring bank hol. **£18.50**|£6.50.

LETTERSTON SM9429 **Something Cooking** A40, 5m S of Fishguard *(01348) 840621* Enthusiastically run and very friendly fish restaurant with truly outstanding fresh fish, served by neat, uniformed waitresses – very reasonable prices too; cl pm Sun, 2 wks Christmas; disabled access. **£13.75**|£4.25.

PEMBROKE FERRY SM9704 **Ferry** *(01646) 682947* Former sailors' haunt by the water below Cleddau Bridge (not by the new ferry), with an extensive range of very fresh fish dishes – non-fishy things too; nautical décor, good views, a relaxed pubby atmosphere, well kept real ales, decent malt whiskies, and efficient service; restaurant cl Sun, pm Mon; children allowed in restaurant only. **£17.80**|£5.25.

ROSEBUSH SN0630 **New Inn** NW of village *(01437) 532542* Very attractively restored, 17th-c drovers' inn with 3 cosy rooms; simple antique oak country furniture on handsome slate flagstones, a relaxed atmosphere, good wide-ranging bar food using carefully chosen local ingredients, half-a-dozen real ales, well selected wines, and friendly staff; cl 2nd wk Jan. **£26**|£7.

ROSEBUSH SN0729 **Old Post Office** *(01437) 532205* Quaint bistro with lots of local photos, farming tools and teapots on the ceiling; good-value lunches, well prepared, traditional cooking in the candlelit dining room, and coffee and afternoon tea; bdrms; some disabled access. **£18**|£5.25.

ST DAVID'S SM7525 **Morgan's Brasserie** *20 Nun St (01437) 720508* Smart little brasserie specialising in good fresh fish, from a shortish menu supplemented by daily specials and using fresh local produce; friendly service, and good-value wines; cl Jan; partial disabled access. **£25**.

STACKPOLE SR9896 **Armstrong Arms** *Jasons Corner (01646) 672324* Charming, rather Swiss-looking dining pub, run by a mother and daughter team, with neat oak furnishings and glossy beams in 4 rambling areas; particularly good, interesting food (more elaborate in the evening), well kept real ales, cheerful, uniformed waitresses, and seats in the flower-filled garden; must book pm Sat, am Sun; cl winter Sun pm. **£19.20**|£4.95.

TENBY SN1300 **Celtic Fare Tearooms** *Vernon House, St Julian St (01834) 845258* Cosy tearoom with jugs and teapots hanging from the beams, an open fire and gas lamps, quite a few teas, and really good home-made cakes, scones and pastries; disabled access. **£16.65**|£4.25.

WELSH HOOK SM9327 **Stone Hall** *(01348) 840212* 14th-c house with imaginative French food and fine wines in a beamed restaurant (evenings only), a characterful bar, and lovely grounds; bdrms; disabled access for meals only (not accommodation). **£24**.

Mid Wales

Splendid unspoilt scenery – the undiscovered heart of Wales.

This is one of Britain's best areas for really getting away from it all. It's the scenery which counts for most. The countryside is spectacular. Though it doesn't quite match the very best of Snowdonia or the West Wales coast, you're not sharing it with as many other visitors. It has very good walking, and little-used former drovers' roads give glorious scenic drives, threading through the huge tracts of forest and moorland around the Llyn Briane reservoir, the Cambrian Mountains and the reservoirs above the Elan Valley. Other kinder ranges of hills tempt out more people, most notably the western Black Mountain, the Brecon Beacons and the eastern Black Mountains. The area's river valleys are among the finest in Wales: the friendly Usk, the rather more imposing Upper Wye, and above Aberystwyth, the beautiful Vale of Rheidol.

Sparsely populated, with far more sheep than people, Mid Wales doesn't have that many places to visit, but those we include do suit its distinctive character. Celtica in Machynlleth and the nearby Centre for Alternative Techology are both particularly worth going to, families find King Arthur's Labyrinth at Corris fun, and the new Judge's Lodgings in the attractive town of Presteigne is interesting. The towns are friendly and untouristy, and include a string of dignified, slightly old-fashioned, inland spa towns.

There are some very comfortable places to stay in, with glorious countryside more or less on their doorsteps.

Where to stay

ABERDOVEY SN6195 **Bodfor** *Bodfor Terrace, Aberdovey, Gwynedd LL35 0EA (01654) 767475* **£58.76,** plus special breaks; 16 rms with showers, most with sea views. Small, family-run, seafront hotel with a bar, comfortable lounge, good restaurant food, and helpful service; dogs welcome; cl 20 Dec–2 Jan.

ABERDOVEY SN6195 **Penhelig Arms** *Terrace Rd, Aberdovey, Gwynedd LL35 0LT (01654) 767215* ***£70,** plus special breaks; 10 comfortable rms. Carefully refurbished building in a fine spot overlooking the sea; with a cosy bar, newly decorated dining room, open fires, very good food with an emphasis on daily delivered, fresh local fish, extensive wine list with 14 by the glass (champagne, too), splendid breakfasts, and friendly service; lovely views of the Dyfy estuary.

ABERHAFESP SO0595 **Dyffryn** *Aberhafesp, Newtown, Powys SY16 3JD (01686) 688817* ***£46;** 3 rms. Carefully restored, half-timbered barn on a 100-acre sheep and beef cattle farm; with a residents' lounge overlooking the stream, traditional cooking in the dining room, and friendly owners; no smoking; babysitting by arrangement, children's play area and a nature trail.

CARNO SN9697 **Aleppo Merchant** *Carno, Caersws, Powys SY17 5LL (01686) 420210* ***£45;** 6 rms, most with shower. Warm and friendly 17th-c inn in a rural setting; with a comfortably modernised, beamed lounge bar, an open fire in the small adjoining lounge, a fair choice of well liked food, helpful service, and well kept real ales; children over 12.

CHURCH STOKE SO2689 **Drewin Farm** *Church Stoke, Montgomery, Powys SY15 6TW (01588) 620325* ***£40;** 2 rms. Attractive 17th-c farmhouse with lovely views; a warm welcome, comfortable lounge, dining room and games room with snooker table in the converted granary; Offa's Dyke footpath runs through the mixed farm of sheep, cattle and crops; cl Nov–Feb.

CRICKHOWELL SO2118 **Bear** *Crickhowell, Powys NP8 1BW (01873) 810408* **£56;** 35 rms, the back ones are the best, and some have Jacuzzis. Particularly friendly coaching inn with a civilised atmosphere, excellent food using local produce and home-grown herbs (some Welsh specialities), fine wines and ports, well kept real ales, and prompt, attentive service; lots of antiques, deeply comfortable seats, and a roaring log fire in the heavily beamed lounge; children over 5 in restaurant; dogs welcome; disabled access.

CRICKHOWELL SO1719 **Gliffaes Country House** *Crickhowell, Powys NP8 1RH (01874) 730371* **£81,** plus special breaks; 22 rms. Run by the same family since

1948, an imposing house in 33 acres of wonderfully peaceful grounds with fine rare trees; an enjoyably informal and relaxed atmosphere, a comfortable big sitting room, elegant drawing room, pleasant conservatory, and glorious Usk Valley views from the terrace; good cooking and cheerful staff; fishing, hard tennis court, golf practice net, and a putting and croquet lawn.

EGLWYSFACH SN6796 **Ynyshir Hall** *Eglwysfach, Machynlleth, Powys SY20 8TA (01654) 781209* ***£150,** plus special breaks; 8 individually decorated rms. Carefully run Georgian manor house in 14 acres of landscaped gardens adjoining the Ynyshir coastal bird reserve; with particularly good service, antiques, log fires and paintings in the light and airy public rooms, extremely nice food using home-grown vegetables, and delicious breakfasts; lots to do nearby; cl 5–20 Jan; children over 9.

GLADESTRY SO2355 **Royal Oak** *Gladestry, Kington, Herefordshire HR5 3NR (01544) 370669* ***£40,** plus special breaks; 5 well equipped rms, some with own bthrm. Unpretentious and welcoming inn on Offa's Dyke; with beams and flagstones, a quiet relaxing atmosphere, good, home-cooked bar food (inc nice breakfasts), a comfortable lounge, separate bar, and picnic sets in the lovely secluded garden behind.

GUILSFIELD SJ2110 **Lower Trelydan** *Guilsfield, Welshpool, Powys SY21 9PH (01938) 553105* ***£46;** 3 rms. Charming black and white farmhouse on a beef-cattle and sheep farm; with lovely, heavily beamed ceilings, fine antiques and comfortable seating, a cosy licensed bar, a warm and friendly atmosphere, and delicious farmhouse cooking; pretty garden; self-catering also in barn conversion; cl Christmas; disabled access.

HAY-ON-WYE SO2342 **Old Black Lion** *26 Lion St, Hay-on-Wye, Herefordshire HR3 5AD (01497) 820841* **£55,** plus special breaks; 10 rms, some in modern annexe. Smartly civilised old hotel with low beams and black panelling, and a convivial bar; wide choice of carefully prepared food in both the bar and candlelit, no smoking, cottagey restaurant, and an extensive wine list; close to fishing (private salmon and trout fishing) and riding; children over 5; disabled access.

KNIGHTON SO3172 **Milebrook House** *Stanage, Milebrook, Knighton, Powys LD7 1LT (01547) 528632* ***£73,** plus special breaks; 10 spacious rms, 4 in a newer smart wing. Charming 18th-c house in 3 acres, surrounded by really unspoilt countryside and with River Teme trout fishing; log fires, a residents' sitting room, bar (where light lunches are served), and good sound cooking using home-grown vegetables; children over 8.

LLANDEFALLE SO1034 **Trehenry Farm** *Llandefalle, Brecon, Powys LD3 0UN (01874) 754312* ***£40;** 4 rms. 18th-c farmhouse on a 200-acre farm with lovely views of the Black Mountains and Brecon Beacons; inglenook fireplaces, beams, TV lounge, good food, and a large garden; self-catering also; cl Christmas.

LLANDEGLEY SO1263 **Ffaldau Country House** *Llandegley, Llandrindod Wells, Powys LD1 5UD (01597) 851421* ***£44;** 4 rms. Carefully restored, heavily beamed, 16th-c country house with flower-filled, landscaped gardens; log fire in the comfortable lounge, a residents' bar, upstairs sitting room with games and books, enjoyable dinners in the charming dining room, and fine breakfasts; dogs by prior arrangement; children over 10.

LLANGAMMARCH WELLS SN9447 **Lake** *Llangammarch Wells, Powys LD4 4BS (01591) 620202* **£140;** 19 charming, pretty rms with fruit and a decanter of sherry. Particularly well run, turn-of-the-century, half-timbered hotel in 50 acres, with plenty of wildlife, a well stocked trout lake, clay-pigeon shoots, and tennis; deeply comfortable, tranquil drawing room with antiques, paintings and a log fire, wonderful afternoon teas (in summer under the chestnut tree overlooking the river), courteous, discreet service, fine wines and very good modern British cooking in the elegant, candlelit dining room, and liberal breakfasts; children over 7 in evening dining room; disabled access.

LLANWRTYD WELLS SN8746 **Carlton House** *Dolycoed Rd, Llanwrtyd Wells, Powys LD5 4RA (01591) 610248* ***£60,** plus special breaks; 7 well equipped rms. Warm, friendly owners run this comfortable, Edwardian restaurant with rooms;

there's a relaxing sitting room with original panelling, log fire, plants and antiques, and an attractive little dining room serving exceptionally good, modern British cooking using top quality local produce (delicious puddings, home-made canapés and petit fours) and a thoughtful wine list; nice breakfasts with home-made bread and marmalade; cl Christmas.

LLYSWEN SO1337 **Griffin** *Llyswen, Brecon, Powys LD3 0UR (01874) 754241* **£70,** plus special breaks; 7 rms. Old-fashioned and warmly welcoming, family-run sporting inn; imaginative fresh food in the no smoking restaurant (brook trout and salmon caught by the family, local game in season), good breakfasts, an interesting, comfortable bar with a huge inglenook, and helpful service; fishing and shooting courses.

LLYSWEN SO1239 **Llangoed Hall** *Llyswen, Brecon, Powys LD3 0YP (01874) 754525* **£185,** plus special breaks; 23 very pretty rms with luxurious touches. Fine, largely Jacobean mansion, beautifully converted into a first-class hotel with a lovely house-party atmosphere; handsome hall, elegant and spacious public rooms with antiques, wonderful pictures, fresh flowers and views over the grounds, imaginative modern cooking in the charming restaurant, and very good Welsh breakfasts; marvellous surrounding countryside; children over 8.

MONTGOMERY SO2296 **Dragon** *Market Sq, Montgomery, Powys SY15 6PA (01686) 668359* **£72,** plus special breaks; 20 rms. Attractive, black and white timbered small hotel with a pleasant, grey-stone tiled hall; comfortable residents' lounge, a beamed bar, and restaurant using local produce; indoor swimming pool, live jazz pm Weds.

NEWTOWN SO1292 **Lower Gwestydd** *Aberbechan, Newtown, Powys SY16 3AY (01686) 626718* ***£40;** 3 rms. Traditional, 17th-c, black and white half-timbered house on 200 acres of mainly sheep and arable farmland, in lovely countryside; comfortable lounge and dining room, and good food with their own fruit and vegetables, chicken and lamb; you can wander around the farm; cl Christmas.

PENNAL SH6799 **Gogarth Hall Farm** *Pennal, Machynlleth, Powys SY20 9LB (01654) 791235* **£38;** 2 rms. 17th-c house on a working farm of suckler cows and sheep, with marvellous views of the Dovey estuary – guests are welcome to walk around the farm; dining room and lounge, enjoyable breakfasts and evening meals, and a utility room for children to use in wet weather; babysitting available; dogs by arrangement; self-catering also.

PRESTEIGNE SO3164 **Radnorshire Arms** *Presteigne, Powys LD8 2BE (01544) 267406* **£79;** 16 rms. Rambling, handsomely timbered, 17th-c hotel with old-fashioned charm and an unchanging atmosphere; elegantly moulded beams and fine dark panelling in the lounge bar, latticed windows, enjoyable food (inc morning coffee and afternoon tea), a separate no smoking restaurant, well kept real ales, and politely attentive service.

RHANDIRMWYN SN7843 **Royal Oak** *Rhandirmwyn, Llandovery, Dyfed SA20 0NY (01550) 760201* **£56;** 5 rms, most with own bthrm. Homely, friendly, family-run pub in the foothills of the Cambrian Mountains, with fine views, superb walking and the RSPB Dinas Bird Reserve nearby; simple furnishings, a log fire, well kept real ale, decent food, and a warm welcome; dogs by prior arrangement.

RHAYADER SN9969 **Beili Neuadd** *Rhayader, Powys LD6 5NS (01597) 810211* **£40,** plus special activity breaks; 3 rms. Charming, partly 16th-c, stone-built farmhouse in quiet countryside (they have their own trout pools and woodland); with beams, polished oak floorboards and log fires in the renovated rooms, and evening meals by arrangement; golf, pony-trekking and guided walks nearby; cl Christmas; children over 8.

TAL-Y-LLYN SH7109 **Minffordd Hotel** *Tal-y-llyn, Tywyn, Gwynedd LL36 9AJ (01654) 761665* ***£73,** plus special breaks; 6 rms. 17th-c drovers' inn in a lovely valley at the foot of Cadair Idris, surrounded by sheep pastures; warmly welcoming and relaxed, open fires in the cosy little rooms, good, Aga-cooked food in the beamed dining room, and super breakfasts; lots of outdoor pursuits; cl Dec–end Feb; children over 3.

TAL-Y-LLYN SH7109 **Tynycornel** *Tal-y-llyn, Tywyn, Gwynedd LL36 9AJ (01654) 782282* **£94;** 17 rms. Low white hotel, peacefully set overlooking a charming lake and surrounded by mountains – lots of nearby walks; civilised and friendly atmosphere, deep armchairs and sofas around a central log fire, big picture windows looking out to the water, big bird prints and local watercolours on the walls, enjoyable food, afternoon tea, a no smoking restaurant, conservatory, and helpful staff; sauna, outdoor swimming pool, boats and fishing.

To see and do

Wales Family Attraction of the Year

! ⛹ **Centre for Alternative Technology** (A487 3m N of Machynlleth) SH7504 A revelation for anyone who thinks recycling newspapers is enough to save the world, this remarkable 7-acre site is at once fascinating, surprisingly good fun, and worryingly thought-provoking. They've been thinking up and showing off all sorts of solutions to environmental problems for over 20 years now, with constantly updated demonstrations of wind power, wave power, solar energy, and a lot more besides. Everything has some sort of green bent, and we really do mean *everything* – even the phone box is wind-powered, and sensitive souls might not want to know what happens if you visit their quaint little lavatories (they're happy to show anyone who does). The fun cliff railway (one of Britain's steepest; Easter–Oct only) works by 'water-balancing', a seemingly innocuous maze explores burning issues such as whether diesel is less polluting than petrol, and the wood in the adventure playground all comes from trees grown on-site. They look after children particularly well, and there's plenty to maintain their interest, notably the Mole Hole, where you can feel what it's like to live underground, squeeze through tiny gaps as though you're an animal, and even pop your head out of the ground like a mole. The energy-saving house is best in winter when you can feel how snugly effective the super-insulating system is, and though they don't have animals or the cliff railway at that time of year there's still enough going on to make an out-of-season visit worthwhile. The centre is on the site of an old slate quarry, with fine views over neighbouring Snowdonia National Park. A short introductory video gives the overall flavour of the place. There may be extra activities in the summer holidays. As they should, they take it all very seriously, but the non-stop environmentally sound message is never overbearing or preachy, and most visitors leave with plenty to mull over on their way home. Wholesome vegetarian restaurant, good bookshop, disabled access; cl 24–26 Dec, 1 Jan, and 3 wks mid-Jan; (01654) 702400; £5.70 inc cliff railway, £4.95 without. They do good-value family tickets, and you can save 10 per cent off the entry cost if you arrive by bus, or 50 per cent if you come by bike; you can also halve the cost of hiring a bike from Greenstiles in Machynlleth, (01654) 703543.

★ **ABERDOVEY** SN6196 Attractive, restrained resort with pleasant sheltered beaches but none of the crowds or tat they usually bring. Legend has it there's a lost city beneath the sea, inundated by the crashing waves in a great storm 1,500 years ago. Sometimes at night imaginative people can hear the mournful tolling of its bells. Besides the Penhelig Arms Hotel, the Britannia does good food and has great views.

ABERYSTWYTH SN5981 Low-key resort, scarcely changed in 20 years, with long shingle beaches and a sedate cliff railway to a large camera obscura high above (all that remains of extensive Victorian pleasure gardens). Quite a scholarly university town, too, with a good **museum**, and one of the very few of Edward I's castles in this part of Wales. The university has a large agricultural college attached and as well as the usual sheep you may see llamas in some of the surrounding fields. **National Library of Wales** Imposing neo-classical building overlooking the town, with exhibitions of fine early Welsh and Celtic manuscripts and more modern art. Cl Sun, bank hols and first full wk in Oct; (01970) 632800; free. **Vale of Rheidol Railway** (next to Aberystwyth station, Alexander Rd) The town's main attraction for families, with steamtrains for several miles along the picturesque twists of the Rheidol Valley to the dramatic beauty-spot gorge of Devil's Bridge. You can use the railway for attractive round-trip walks. Snacks, shop, limited disabled access; trains run most days Easter–Oct, (01970) 625819 for timetable; £10.50 full return fare. There's a pleasant walk along the straight coast to Borth; you can use the train for the other half of a round trip.

BLACK MOUNTAIN SN8123 The westernmost range in the Brecon Beacons National Park – not to be confused with the Black Mountains to the E. Much of the high terrain is a long way from the road, so this part suits the committed long-distance walker. The craggy ridge known as Carmarthen Fan protrudes dramatically above the moors and provides the high point of a long but rewarding walk from the N.

BLACK MOUNTAINS SO2632 Making up the E part of the Brecon Beacons National Park, these are finger-shaped ridges with steep-sided valleys in between. Most of the best views are from the Offa's Dyke Path along the eastern flanks: the land eastwards slopes abruptly down to low-lying agricultural Herefordshire, and views far into England give you a feeling of true border country. Circular walks here tend to be long and hefty, often with 2 major ascents to get you up on to the different ridges, but the scenic Gospel Pass road from Hay-on-Wye lets you drive to within reasonable striking distance of Hay Bluff (670 metres, 2,200ft). Twmpa (690 metres; 2,263ft) is better known by its intriguing English name of Lord Hereford's Knob; though it's not itself on the Offa's Dyke Path, it is nearby, and you can combine it with Hay Bluff in a longer walk. Llanthony Abbey, with a pub, makes a beautiful objective in the valley below, where diligent map-reading is needed for a cross-fields route from Cwmyoy, with extensions on to the Offa's Dyke Path on the ridge to complete a satisfying circuit.

BRECON SO0428 Enjoyable and interesting small town, despite too much traffic, with some fine old buildings around its main square and narrow streets, and a bustling livestock market on Tues and Fri. The striking Norman priory was grandly restored in the 19th c and became a cathedral in 1923. Also the rather sad remnants of a castle, and a couple of decent little museums, the best of which is **Brecknock Museum** (Captain's Walk) with the town's excellently preserved assize court, a new interpretative exhibition, lots of love spoons and some interesting Celtic crosses. Cl 1–2pm Sat, am Sun (all Sun in winter), Good Fri, 25–26 Dec, 1 Jan; (01874) 624121; £1. The George (George St) has good-value food. Some of the highest peaks in the area are a short drive away. The Brecon Beacons Mountain Centre (just S) is a useful National Parks Visitor Centre (cl 25 Dec; free); they can advise on local walks, inc how to get to the spectacular waterfalls nr Glyn Neath. From the centre there's free access to the surrounding area known as Illtud Common, with fine views of the Beacons and an Iron Age hill fort to make for; this can also be used as a starting-point for walking up to Craig Cerrig-gleisiad a Fan Frynach National Nature Reserve SN9522, home to Arctic/alpine flora and some 80 bird species. **Cantref Riding Centre** (Upper Cantref, just S) can organise pony-trekking through this attractive landscape (£13 for half a day), and does B & B too; ring Mrs Evans on (01874) 665223.

BRECON BEACONS NATIONAL PARK SO0517 The southern parts of the Park, within easy reach of South Wales, have gentle forest walks in large conifer plantations, where waterfalls and a series of attractive reservoirs are the main features. The abrupt transition from the industrial valleys into this empty wildness is startling. The Beacons themselves are a pair of graceful pointed summits connected by a short ridge that seems to be visible from most of South Wales, and that gives a magnificent high-level walk along the crest, with massive drops on the northern side. Pen-y-Fan (886 metres, 2,906ft) is the highest Welsh summit outside Snowdonia, and the main E–W upland spine effectively stretches about 5 miles. The most popular walk up from Pont ar Daf SN9819, from the A470 to the W, is straightforward enough although there has been some serious footpath erosion, but the N approaches are more exciting and surprisingly little walked.

★ △ **BUILTH WELLS** SO0451 Pleasant small spa town, with good walks in attractive scenery.

△ **CADAIR IDRIS** SH7112 This great peak in the S of Snowdonia offers walkers various ways up its friendly slopes. Good spots are the Arthog waterfalls and nearby lakes on the lower slopes.

♜ **CARREG CENNEN CASTLE** SN6619 (nr Trapp, SE of Llandeilo) Few castles can boast as excellent a setting as these old ruins, dramatically dominating their limestone crag high above the river, and overlooking the unspoilt countryside towards the Black Mountains. Rebuilt in the 13th c (and again in the 19th – you can easily distinguish the new stonework), the castle has a mysterious passage in the side of the cliff. Readers enjoy coming here and the staff are very friendly. Meals, snacks, shop; cl 25 Dec; (01558) 822291; *£2.50. The Cennen Arms nearby has good, simple food.

△ ⛫ ✝ ❁ **CEFNLLYS CASTLE** SO0861 A good walk from Llandrindod Wells to this impressively sited hill fort with a lonely church below, nr Shaky Bridge (no longer shaky); a nature trail here takes you along the banks of the River Ithon.

★ ✿ ⛴ ☺ ! **CORRIS** SH7408 Attractive and nicely set beneath the towering crags of Cadair Idris, with lakes and pine forests in the surrounding valley. The whole village seems to be made of slate. **Corris Craft Centre** (off the A487 towards Corris Uchaf) Craft workshops inc a potter, toy-maker, goldsmith and candle-maker, with a restaurant, picnic area and play area; best to check winter opening; (01654) 761249; free. **King Arthur's Labyrinth** (next to the craft centre) Fun for families; a boat trip takes you to the heart of the underground tunnels and caverns, then it's a half-mile walk through passageways punctuated with scenes from the local version of the Arthurian legends. Wrap up well: it can get cold down here. Shop; cl Nov–Mar; (01654) 761584; £4.10.

☺ ! 🐄 ❁ ✿ △ **CRAIG Y NOS** SN8415 **Dan yr Ogof Showcaves** (A4067 just N) Fascinating series of caves, well lit to emphasise the extraordinary rock formations. The Cathedral Cave is the largest single chamber open to the public in any British showcave, while 3,000 years ago Bone Cave was lived in by humans. There's also a dinosaur park, an Iron Age farm, shire horse centre and an artificial ski-slope, so lots to see. Meals, snacks, shops; cl Nov–Mar (though maybe open Christmas and Feb half-term, phone to check); (01639) 730284; £6.50. The Tafarn y Garreg just N does decent food. **Craig y Nos Country Park** Ideal for a picnic or a stroll: 40 acres of woodland, lake and meadow, landscaped and developed last century by the opera singer Adelina Patti. Interactive displays in the visitor centre, and a wild flower maze. Shop, limited disabled access; cl 25 Dec; (01639) 730395; park free, though £1 parking. The riverside Gwyn Arms has a good range of food.

✿ **DEVIL'S BRIDGE** SN7477 Pretty bridges and a dramatic waterfall, tucked away in an atmospheric wooded gorge. The oldest bridge gave this beauty spot its name, when it was built by the Devil to trap an old woman into giving him her soul; she outwitted him. Wordsworth was inspired to write a sonnet after a visit here. The entertaining Halfway Inn at Pisgah on the A4120 to Aberystwyth is good for lunch.

❁ 🐦 △ **ELAN VALLEY** SN9365 These 4 lakes W of Rhayader are the best and most famous of the many man-made reservoirs in Wales. Built at the turn of the last century, they have weathered in well now – even the dams look good, and there are splendid valley and Cambrian Mountain views, especially from the high-level trackways. It's a good spot for birdwatching, particularly in summer, and among the many species you may see red kites. **Elan Valley Visitor Centre** (Elan village) Informative opening to this attractive area, with an audio-visual show and displays. Cl Nov–mid-Mar; (01597) 810880; free. Outside is a statue of Shelley, who lived in a house now lost beneath the water. Low-level walks from here include forest walks and strolls along the old railway track by the water's edge – very attractive. The Elan Valley Hotel (B4518) has decent food.

FAIRBOURNE SH6112 **Fairbourne & Barmouth Steam Railway** (Beach Rd) Running the spectacular 2½ miles to the end of the peninsula and the Barmouth ferry, this started life in 1890 as a horse-drawn railway bringing building materials for the seaside resort. Meals, snacks, shop, good disabled access; cl Nov–Easter, (01341) 250362 for timetable; £3.80. The Fairbourne Hotel is quite useful for lunch, as is the 15th-c Last Inn on Barmouth harbour. The attractively set George III along the estuary at Penmaenpool is quite handy too. Fairbourne and Barmouth both have good clean beaches.

GILFACH NATURE RESERVE SN9671 (just N of Rhayader) Includes farmland virtually unchanged in 200 years amid fine craggy mountain backdrops; several paths have been freshly signposted and some new ones opened, inc the Monks' Trod and the nature trail from Gilfach Farm – leading across a defunct railway and close to the otter-populated River Marteg, eventually emerging on the A470 by Pont Marteg, a delightful shady place with a footbridge over the River Wye.

★ **HAY-ON-WYE** SO2342 This pleasant small town has become a world centre for secondhand and antiquarian books. There's a growing number of junk and antique shops too, as well as a rather jolly puzzle and teddy bear shop on Broad St. Hay Bluff nearby has lovely walks, and it's within easy reach of the Black Mountains, the Golden Valley over the English border, and the attractive, unspoilt countryside just over the Gwent border that we mention in the South Wales section. Besides the fine Old Black Lion, the Kilvert Court, tel (01497) 821042, can be recommended both for food and as a place to stay. Black Mountain Activities just up the road (technically in Herefordshire) can arrange all sorts of exertions; (01497) 847897.

† **LLANBISTER** SO1073 The **church** here is interesting, with a chimney instead of the usual tower, and presumably a warmer congregation. Nearby **Llananno Church** is also remarkable, with an astonishingly elaborate rood screen that wouldn't be out of place in a cathedral.

★ **LLANDRINDOD WELLS** SO0661 Civilised inland resort below the hills, a largely intact gem of the railway age, with imposing buildings on broad avenues and terraces, wrought-iron frills everywhere, elegant flower displays and Victorian parks, antique shop-fronts and little canopies along the shopping streets. It was clearly a resort for temperance – though there are places to drink, they're tucked discreetly away. The former spa pump room has been reopened, and there are sedate walks around a very old-fashioned boating lake. **Radnorshire Museum** (Temple St) Charming district museum, well worth a look; cl 12.30pm–2pm, all Weds, and winter wknds exc am Sat; *£1. **National Cycle Exhibition** (Automobile Palace) New, with over 120 cycles and reconstructions of Victorian and Edwardian cycle shops. Meals, snacks, shop, disabled access; (01597) 825531; £2.50. The atmospheric old Llanerch has good home cooking, and the Metropole Hotel generally does some food all day.

LLANFAIR CAEREINION SJ1006 **Welshpool & Llanfair Light Railway** (A458) Colonial and Austrian steam locomotives are among the wide variety that run along this pretty 8-mile line, and the Welshpool

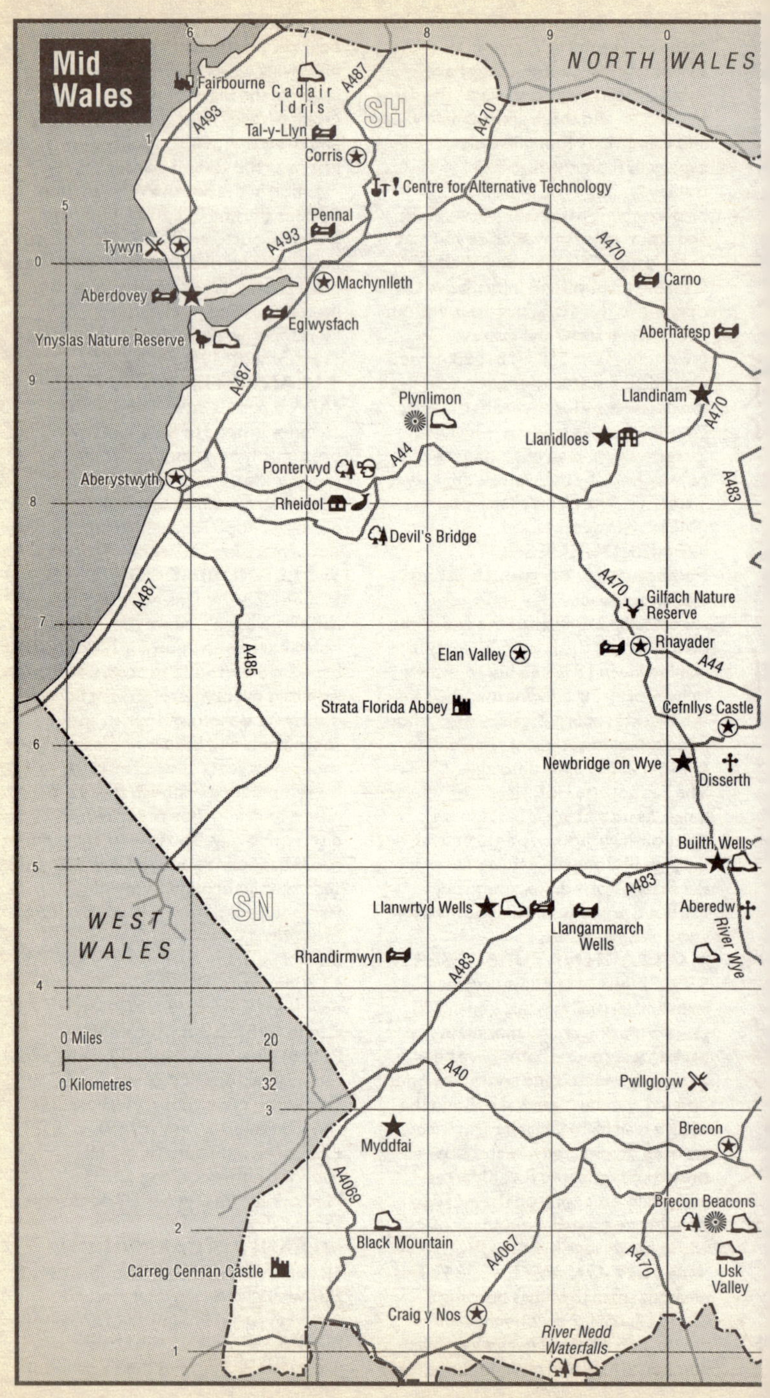
Mid Wales
NORTH WALES
WEST WALES
SH
SN
Fairbourne
Cadair Idris
Tal-y-Llyn
Corris
Centre for Alternative Technology
Pennal
Tywyn
Aberdovey
Machynlleth
Eglwysfach
Ynyslas Nature Reserve
Carno
Aberhafesp
Llandinam
Plynlimon
Llanidloes
Aberystwyth
Ponterwyd
Rheidol
Devil's Bridge
Gilfach Nature Reserve
Rhayader
Elan Valley
Strata Florida Abbey
Cefnllys Castle
Newbridge on Wye
Disserth
Builth Wells
Llanwrtyd Wells
Llangammarch Wells
Aberedw
River Wye
Rhandirmwyn
Pwllgloyw
Myddfai
Brecon
Brecon Beacons
Black Mountain
Usk Valley
Carreg Cennan Castle
Craig y Nos
River Nedd Waterfalls
0 Miles
20
0 Kilometres
32
A493
A487
A470
A44
A483
A485
A40
A4069
A4067

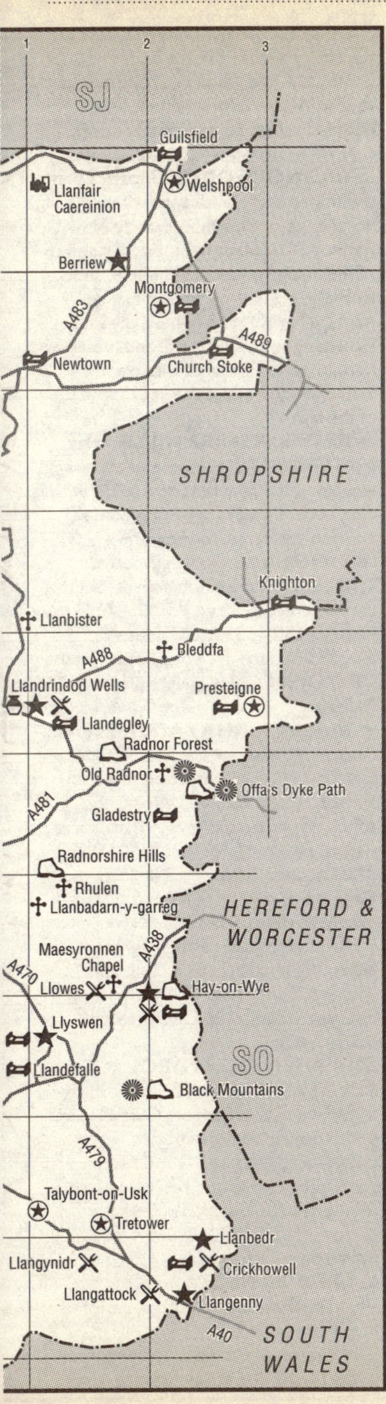

end has an award-winning station reconstruction. Snacks, shop, disabled access (with prior notice); cl Oct–Mar exc December Santa Specials; (01938) 810441 for timetable; £7.50. The Goat is useful for lunch.

★ **LLANIDLOES** SN9584 Attractive small town, with a unique, Elizabethan timbered market hall.

★ **LLANWRTYD WELLS** SN8746 Pleasant spa town, said to be Britain's smallest town, with good walks in attractive scenery; the Stonecrodt has wholesome food.

! ★ **MACHYNLLETH** SH7400 *See separate Family Panel on p.918* for nearby **Centre for Alternative Technology**. Wide main street with a handsome, 24-metre (78-ft), 19th-c clock tower (you can hire bikes from the nearby shop), and a very relaxed feel. The White Lion does decent lunches, inc vegetarian. **Celtica** Very enjoyable look at the history and legends of the Celts, in an 18th-c mansion. There's a traditionalish museum upstairs, but more fun is the lively walk-through exhibition on the ground floor, special effects bringing ancient villages and druids' prophecies vividly to life; also a good themed indoor play area for the under-8s. It's popular with school trips the last couple of weeks of term. Meals, snacks, good shop, disabled access; cl Christmas; (01654) 702702; *£4.70. **Parliament House** Local history museum in a 16th-c building, with the emphasis on the rebellion of Owain Glyndwr (it's on the spot where he held parliament). Brass rubbing centre, shop, disabled access; cl 1–1.30pm, Sun, and all Oct–Easter; (01654) 702827; free.

★ **MONTGOMERY** SO2793 Tiny town, rewarding for a short exploration on foot, with great views from its castle perched above. Montgomeryshire consists of the quintessential sheep-grazed lands of rural Wales – generally not prime walking country, lacking major objectives for walkers, with few major peaks and fair distances between villages.

OFFA'S DYKE PATH SO2455 The major walkers' attraction in this part of Wales; on its coast-to-coast route over the Welsh Marches it takes in some very attractive hill-farm country between Hay-on-Wye and Knighton SO2872, inc Hergest Ridge (in Herefordshire, but easily reached from the Welsh side) and some well preserved stretches of Offa's 9th-c boundary marker between Knighton and Kington. The George & Dragon in Knighton is worth knowing.

† ❋ **OLD RADNOR CHURCH** SO2559 Handsome screen and roof, Britain's oldest organ-case and font; delightful surroundings, with hilltop views.

❋ **PLYNLIMON** SN7687 These windswept often boggy uplands and the surrounding Cambrian Mountains, though not endowed with the friendliest of climates, can be magnificently exhilarating for hardy walkers.

PONTERWYD SN7380 **Llywernog Silver-Lead Mine** (on the A434 just W) Busy and lively, against a beautiful sweeping mountainside backdrop. Regular displays of silver panning, sound and light tableaux in the caves and tunnels along the expanded underground tour, and working waterwheels; you can try panning for Fool's Gold or dowsing for mineral veins. Wear sensible shoes in wet weather. Snacks, shop, some disabled access; open mid-Mar–Oct; (01970) 890620; £4.50. **Bwlch Nant-Yr-Arian Forest Visitor Centre** (A44 just W) Good starting point for exploring the forest, with walks and a few activities for children. You may see otters in the adjacent lake. Snacks, shop, disabled access; cl Nov–Feb; (01974) 261404; free (parking £1). The Dyffryn Castell in the spectacular valley to the E is handy for lunch. There's an eye-opening mountain drive N past the partly wooded Nant-y-moch reservoir below the slopes of Plynlimon, and on to Tal-y-bont.

★ † **PRESTEIGNE** SO3164 Attractive small town with some fine black and white timbering and a handsome **church**; the Radnorshire Arms is good value. **Judge's Lodgings** Good restoration of the judge's living quarters in what used to be the county town of Radnorshire. Unlike in most historic reconstructions you can sit on the chairs and try out the beds for comfort. A lively audio tour leads you to trial in the Victorian court. Shop, disabled access to ground floor only; cl Nov–Feb; (01544) 260650; £3.50.

RADNOR FOREST Mostly open walking country, with conifers on the northern slopes. Walks include New Radnor SO2160 to the modest summit of the quaintly named Whimble, and from the A44 between Llanfihangel-nant-Melan SO1858 (where the Red Lion has good-value food) and New Radnor to Water-break-its-neck waterfall (don't miss the path at the top of the fall).

RADNORSHIRE HILLS Away from Offa's Dyke, Radnorshire is less well known than it deserves to be, with old drovers' tracks providing some enjoyable escapist walking, and a reasonable network of field paths. There are few major objectives, but the part between Aberedw SO0847, Glascwm SO1553 and Gladestry SO2355 (where the Royal Oak is on the Offa's Dyke Path) is all very pleasant walking.

★ ❋ **RHAYADER** SN9768 Pleasant little town; the Bear, Castle and Cornhill are useful food stops. **Welsh Royal Crystal** Workshop tours; no glass-making wknds, or some wkdys, best to check first on (01597) 811005, shop cl 25 Dec, 1 Jan; £2. **Gigrin Farm** (just S) Farm trail with excellent views; from mid-Oct–mid-Apr also has a red kite centre with hides (the birds are fed daily at 2pm). Also B & B and camping. Snacks, shop, disabled access; cl 25 Dec; (01597) 810243; £2.50.

RHEIDOL HYDRO-ELECTRIC SCHEME SN7079 (off the A44 at Capel Bangor) Guided tours of this power station with an unexpected fish farm. Good nature trails, scenic lakes and reservoirs, trout fishing. Snacks, disabled access; cl Nov–Mar; (01970) 880667; free, fishing permits from £6.

RIVER NEDD WATERFALLS SN9007 A series of mighty waterfalls with few rivals in Britain grace the deep wooded gorges of the Nedd, Hepste and Mellte, just inside the southern Brecon Beacons park boundary (within easy reach of South Wales, too). An easy path from Pontneddfechan SN9007 nr Glyn Neath leads along the River Nedd, and Porth yr Ogof car park SN9212 nr Ystradfellte is convenient for the Mellte. Dire warning notices ward you off getting too close to the edge (it is certainly hazardously slippery), but you can accompany the river most of the way to its junction with the Hepste. Here, a path actually crosses the river by going behind the curtain of Sgwd yr Eira waterfall – a rock ledge holds you in safely, but it's an excitingly damp experience. The Old White Horse in Pontneddfechan does generous food.

RIVER WYE SO0847 Pleasant escapist walks around Aberedw and Boughrood, with a reasonable network of field paths.

STRATA FLORIDA ABBEY SN7465 Little is left of this once-important centre of learning, except the ruined church and cloister, but the surroundings are lovely. 14th-c poet Dafyd ap Gwilym is thought to be buried here. Teas, shop, disabled access; cl Oct–Mar; (01974) 831261; £1.70. From Tregaron down the B4343 a steep road climbs through the pine forests into the mountains, eventually reaching the Llyn Brianne reservoir.

★ **TALYBONT-ON-USK** SO1122 An attractive village, with friendly boat hire on the Monmouthshire & Brecon Canal, opposite the Travellers Rest (generous food). It's on the Taff Trail waymarked path.

★ **TRETOWER COURT AND CASTLE** SO1821 (off the A40) The medieval manor house dates from the 14th c, though it has been developed over the centuries; beside it is the substantial ruin of an 11th-c motte and bailey, with massively thick walls and a 3-storey tower. Shop, limited disabled access; cl Nov–Feb; (01222) 500200; £2.20. The Nantyffin Cider Mill is a nice, handy place for lunch. Nearby Crickhowell is a pleasant, village-sized 'town', with an excellent inn in the Bear, and a fine ancient bridge over the Usk (which the good Bridge End Inn overlooks).

TYWYN SH5800 **Tal-y-Llyn Railway** This railway journey affords glorious views, climbing from the little seaside resort up the steep sides of the Fathew Valley and stopping for passengers to admire Dolgoch Falls and visit the Nant Gwernol Forest (there's a waterfall 2 minutes away from the platform at this end). The 27in-gauge railway, the oldest of this gauge in the world, was built in 1865 to serve the slate mine at Abergynolwyn (where the Railway Inn does decent food in a lovely setting). Snacks, shop, disabled access with prior notice; cl Nov–mid-Feb (exc December Santa specials); (01654) 710472 for timetable; full return £8. A museum at the Tywyn Station shows locomotives, wagons and signalling equipment whenever the railway is running.

Days Out

The railway that served the mines: Aberystwyth; snack at the Mill (Mill St) there; Devil's Bridge by the Vale of Rheidol Railway; or by car, then drive via the Llywernog silver mine, Ponterwyd, and on past Nant-y-Moch reservoir to Talybont – if time, stroll on the nearby Ynyslas seaside nature reserve.

Ascent from bookshop town: Hay-on-Wye; drive up the Gospel Pass; lunch at the Abbey Hotel, Llanthony; walk there (leaflets in car park); Cwmyoy and Partrishow churches.

Brecon Beacons waterfall country: Brecon; take the A470 past the slopes of Pen-y-fan; walk from Brecon Beacons Mountain Centre on to Mynydd Illtud common, or in the Mellte/Hepste gorges; either picnic en route, or lunch at the Gwyn Arms, Craig y Nos; Dan yr Ogof caves at Craig y Nos.

⛰ **USK VALLEY** SO1519 Walkers can enjoy the lusher swathes, along the towpath of the 33-mile Monmouthshire & Brecon canal.

WELSHPOOL SJ2106 **Powis Castle** (A483, 1m S) In magnificent gardens with splendid 18th-c terraces, this dramatic-looking castle was built in the 13th c, but far from falling into decay like so many others, has developed into a grand house over the years. It's been constantly occupied since its construction, once by the son of Clive of India – there are displays about his father's life. Snacks, shop; cl Mon (exc bank hols), Tues (exc July and Aug), and Nov–Mar (castle and museum cl am); (01938) 554336; £7.50, gardens only £5; NT. The King's Head at Guilsfield does good home cooking. **Powysland Museum** (Canal Wharf) Respectable local history museum, with canal material too; cl 1–2pm, Weds; *£1. The Raven and Royal Oak both have decent food.

YNYSLAS NATURE RESERVE SN6094 (just N of Borth) A major scenic highlight of the coast, with watery views across the vast sands of the Dovey estuary, lots of birds, and an important dune system, habitat for orchids. You can walk round the tip of land jutting into the mouth of the Dovey and then along the shore.

★ **Attractive villages and small towns** in the area, all with decent pubs, include Berriew SJ1801, Llanbedr SO2420, Llandinam SO0388, Llangenny SO2417, Llyswen SO1337, Myddfai SN7730 and Newbridge on Wye SO0158.

Other pubs doing food that are particularly worth noting for their positions include the Admiral Rodney at Criggion SJ2915, Farmers Arms at Cwmdu SO1823, Dolfor Inn at Dolfor SO1187, White Swan at Llanfrynach SO0725, Coach & Horses above the canal at Llangynidr SO1519 (lovely walks), Stables Hotel at Neuadd Fawr SO2322 (good hill walking) and the canalside Royal Oak at Pencelli SO0925.

✝ Some unspoilt and humble rustic **churches** in beautiful settings include Aberedw SO0847, Bleddfa SO2168 (the Hundred House is a good base for walkers), Disserth SO0358, Llanbadarn-y-garreg SO1148, Maesyronnen Chapel SO1740 NW of Hay, and Rhulen SO1349.

Where to eat

Many of the places listed in the **Where to Stay** section *on p.915* serve very good food too.

CRICKHOWELL SO1920 **Nantyffin Cider Mill** (A40 NW) *(01873) 801775* Handsome pink-washed dining pub with a striking, raftered restaurant, a smart, relaxed atmosphere, fresh and dried flowers, a woodburner, comfortable tables and chairs; beautifully presented, imaginative food (much organic produce), well kept real ales, good wines, and charming views; cl Mon; disabled access. **£21**|£5.95.

HAY-ON-WYE SO2342 **Kilverts** *Bullring (01497) 821042* Friendly town pub with an informal and relaxed atmosphere in the airy, high-beamed bar, candles on the tables, some stripped stone walls and standing timbers; good, interesting food (especially the daily specials), well kept real ales, local Welsh wines, and efficient, easy-going service; bdrms. **£22**|£7.95.

LLANDRINDOD WELLS SO0561 **Llanerch** *Waterloo Rd (01597) 822086* Cheerful, 16th-c town local with old-fashioned settles in the beamed main bar, communicating lounges (one no smoking), good-value and popular, straightforward bar food, well kept real ales, and prompt service; peaceful mountain views from the back terrace, and boules and an orchard in the garden; disabled access. **£17.50**|£3.50.

LLANGATTOCK SO2117 **Vine Tree** *(01873) 810514* Friendly, well run dining pub with a comfortable bar, carefully prepared and often imaginative food, well kept real ales, and seats outside. **£21.65**|£5.45.

LLANGYNIDR SO1519 **Coach & Horses** *(01874) 730245* Friendly, well run and bustling pub, with tables on the small lawn running down to a lock on the narrow Monmouth & Brecon Canal (moorings); spacious lounge with a big winter fire, no smoking area in the restaurant, enjoyable food inc lots of fresh fish, and well kept real ales; bdrms; disabled access. **£15**|£5.95.

LLOWES SO1941 **Radnor Arms** *(01497) 847460* Small, modest and very old place with a log fire in the bar, neat little cottagey dining room, enjoyable food (nice puddings), friendly staff, and tables in the imaginatively planted garden; cl pm Sun, Mon (exc bank hols); partial disabled access. **£21**|£6.75.

PWLLGLOYW SO0333 **Seland Newydd** *Gerhonddu (01874) 690282* Popular with a good mix of people, this former pub has a comfortable lounge, a huge fireplace in the bar, and an attractive dining room with most enjoyable, flavoursome food; a thoughtful little wine list; cl am Tues and Weds in winter; disabled access. **£27**|£6.50.

TYWYN SH5800 **Proper Gander** *High St (01654) 711270* Popular little pink tea shop on 2 floors, with morning coffee, lunches and good aftenoon teas; a more elaborate evening restaurant, and a worthwhile Sun lunch; disabled access. **£25 dinner, £15 lunch**|£5.20.

South Wales

The most interesting outings in Wales.

South Wales has plenty of interesting and enjoyable places to visit, for all age groups and tastes. We'd particularly pick out the excellent Techniquest in Cardiff, the Welsh Folk Museum just outside, the very entertaining Llancaiach Fawr at Nelson, and the Rhondda Heritage Park at Porth (perhaps the best of all the mining places for family visits; the Big Pit at Blaenavon is also a very good 'tourist mine'). There are spectacular castles. Children like the friendly animal centres at Penally, Cilfrew and Cwmbran, and Monmouth and Chepstow are small towns of great character.

This area includes the most built-up and industrialised parts of Wales, but there are attractive and unspoilt parts too, for example around the further edges of the Gower Peninsula (almost like a mini-Pembrokeshire), the cliffs at Nash Point near St Donats, the hills on the edge of the Brecon Beacons above the former mining valleys, and the fine gorge of the lower Wye Valley (magnificent in autumn). The Black Mountains on the edge of this area are discribed in the **Mid Wales** section.

Where to stay

GILWERN SO2413 **Wenallt Farm** *Twyn-Wenallt, Gilwern, Abergavenny, Gwent NP7 0HP (01873) 830694* **£44;** 10 rms. Friendly and relaxing 16th-c Welsh longhouse on 50 acres of farmland; with oak beams and an inglenook fireplace in the big drawing room, a TV room, good food in the dining room, and lots to do nearby; dogs welcome; disabled access.

GOVILON SO2513 **Llanwenarth House** *Govilon, Abergavenny, Gwent NP7 9SF (01873) 830289* ***£78,** plus special breaks; 4 spacious, comfortable rms. Fine, family-run, 16th-c manor house in quiet grounds; with a gracious sitting room, log fires, antiques and fresh flowers, fine food using local game and fish and home-produced meat, poultry and garden vegetables in the elegant, candlelit dining room, and friendly, helpful staff; lots to do nearby; croquet; cl mid-Jan–beginning Mar; children over 10; disabled access.

LLANFIHANGEL CRUCORNEY SO3120 **Penyclawdd Court** *Llanfihangel Crucorney, Abergavenny, Gwent NP7 7LB (01873) 890719* ***£74,** plus special breaks; 3 rms with mountain views. Interesting Tudor manor house below Bryn Arw mountain in the Brecon Beacons, with an Elizabethan knot garden, herb garden, Norman motte and bailey, and a developing yew hedge maze; careful renovation, underfloor heating (to avoid unsightly radiators) and no electricity in dining room (breakfast and dinner by candlelight), as well as flagstones, beams and sloping floors; decent breakfasts, good evening meals (and Tudor feasts), and a friendly, relaxed atmosphere; children over 12.

MONMOUTH SO5012 **Riverside** *Cinderhill St, Monmouth, Gwent NP5 3EY (01600) 715577* **£68,** plus special breaks; 17 rms. Comfortably refurbished and warmly welcoming, bustling hotel overlooking the River Monnow and the 13th-c fortified gatehouse; with good-value bar meals, an extensive restaurant menu, and a conservatory; disabled access.

MUMBLES SS6087 **Hillcrest House** *Higher Lane, Mumbles, Swansea SA3 4NS (01792) 363700* ***£65,** plus special breaks; 7 individually decorated rms, each themed to represent a different country. Friendly white house with a stone terrace, 2 minutes from the beach yet handy for Swansea; informal and welcoming atmosphere, thoughtful and individual service, a comfortable lounge, imaginative seasonal dishes, and a new bar-cum-restaurant with an African gamehide theme; cl some dates Jan/Feb.

OXWICH SS5086 **Oxwich Bay** *Oxwich, Swansea, West Glamorgan SA3 1LS (01792) 390329* ***£60,** plus special breaks; 13 rms. Comfortable hotel on the edge of the beach in a lovely area; with dedicated and friendly staff, food served all day, a restaurant/lounge bar with panoramic views, a summer outdoor dining area with weekend barbecues, and a welcome for families; cl 24–25 Dec.

REYNOLDSTON SS4691 **Fairyhill** *Reynoldston, Swansea, West Glamorgan SA3 1BS (01792) 390139* **£110,** plus special breaks; 8 rms. 18th-c hotel in 24 wooded acres with croquet, trout stream and wild duck on the lake; log fire in the comfortable drawing room, a cosy bar, lovely food in the attractive dining room, hearty breakfasts, afternoon tea on a leafy terrace, and personal, friendly service; children over 8; cl 3 days at Christmas.

ST BRIDES WENTLOOG ST2982 **West Usk Lighthouse** *St Brides Wentloog, Newport, Gwent NP1 9SF (01633) 810126* ***£70;** 4 rms. Unusual former lighthouse – squat rather than tall – that was on an island in the Bristol Channel (the land has since been reclaimed); modern stylish furnishings, lots of framed record sleeves (Mr Sheahan used to work for a record company), an informal atmosphere, good big breakfasts, and a small, dinner-partyish, vegan restaurant; flotation tank, aromatherapy and psychotherapy sessions available; lots of nearby walks.

TINTERN PARVA SO5301 **Parva Farmhouse** *Tintern Parva, Chepstow, Gwent NP6 6SQ (01291) 689411* ***£68,** plus special breaks; 9 comfortable rms. Friendly stone farmhouse rebuilt in the mid-17th c; with leather chesterfields, woodburner and honesty bar in the large beamed lounge, books (no TV downstairs), and very good food and wine (inc wine using home-grown grapes) in the cosy restaurant; 50 yards from the River Wye and lovely surrounding countryside; free accommodation for children in parents' rm.

WHITEBROOK SO5306 **Crown at Whitebrook** *Whitebrook, Monmouth, Gwent NP5 4TX (01600) 860254* **£80,** plus special breaks; 10 neat rms. Small modernised hotel with a 17th-c core, in the beautiful Wye Valley; friendly, caring service, a relaxed atmosphere, and comfortable lounge and bar; small cosy restaurant with fine wines and excellent food combining Welsh ingredients and French style, very good breakfasts; cl 2 wks Jan and 2 wks Aug.

To see and do

ABERDULAIS FALLS SS7799 (A465) Since the 16th c this splendid waterfall has been used to power a range of industries from copper smelting to tinplate. A magnificent waterwheel now generates electricity. Wknd snacks, shop, disabled access (right to the top of the falls thanks to a lift powered by the electricity generated on site); open Apr–Oct, and wknds in Mar; (01639) 636674; £2.80; NT.

ABERGAVENNY SO2914 There are some attractive ancient buildings in Nevill St and particularly Market St, with its busy Tues and Fri market. The **church** has a remarkable collection of memorials.

Abergavenny Castle 12th/14th-c remains inc the walls, towers and rebuilt gatehouse; the early 19th-c keep and an adjoining house now contain a local history museum. Shop; cl 1–2pm, all Sun (exc pm in summer); (01873) 854282; *£1. The Greyhound is a good dining pub, while outside, the Lamb & Flag (B4598 SE) and Llanwenarth Arms (Brecon road) are also popular.

AFON LWYD VALLEY SO2703 Interesting example of post-mining land reclamation between Cwmbran New Town and Blaenavon, with plantings designed for the re-establishment of nature.

BARRY ST1166 Lively seaside resort which, along with its jutting-out peninsula Barry Island, grew as a centre for the coal industry. Remains of a 13th-c castle, and the usual fairground attractions for children. Nearby, the Star in Dinas Powis is good for lunch.

Welsh Hawking Centre (Weycock Rd) Cheery centre with over 200 birds of prey. Regular flying demonstrations (12pm, 2.30pm, 4pm), baby birds (May–July), an adventure playground, and animals for children to fuss. Snacks, shop, some disabled access; cl 25 Dec; (01446) 734687; *£3.

BETTWS NEWYDD CHURCH SO3605 Largely unaltered from the 15th c, with a choir gallery and fine screen.

BLAENAVON SO2308 **Big Pit Mining Museum** (B4248) Sample the life of a miner by donning a safety helmet and descending 90 metres (300ft) in the cage into the Big Pit, which closed as a working coal mine in 1980. Also a reconstructed miner's cottage, and an exhibition in the old pithead baths. Good fun – the guides are former miners so they have plenty of anecdotes; you'll need sensible shoes and warm clothing. Children must be over 1 metre tall to go underground. Meals, snacks, shop, disabled access with prior warning; usually cl Dec–Feb – but worth checking; (01495) 790311; £5.50. The Goose & Cuckoo over the hill at Rhyd-y-Meirch, just off the A4042, does good home cooking.

BRIDGEND SS9079 **Newcastle** Ruined 12th-c castle with surviving rectangular tower, a richly carved Norman gateway and massive curtain walls; collect key from the nearby corner shop. The prosperous industrial town below isn't much of a place for visitors, but nearby Merthyr Mawr, with its interesting warren of high sandhills, is attractive, as are Southerndown and Ogmore. **Ewenny Priory** SS9177 This riverside ruin is one of the finest fortified religious buildings in Britain. **Bryngarw Country Park** (just N) Unexpectedly tranquil refuge from the M4, with woodland walks, formal gardens, ornamental lakes and a Japanese garden. Playground, snacks, shop, disabled access; cl 25–26 Dec; (01656) 725155; free (£1.50 parking school hols and wknds).

CAERLEON ST3490 **Roman Fortress, Baths, Ampitheatre and Barracks** One of the best examples of an amphitheatre in the country, alongside a similarly well preserved bath-house, now under cover. Also the foundations of barrack lines and parts of the ramparts, and the remains of the cookhouse and latrines. Shop, disabled access; cl 24–26 Dec, 1 Jan; (01554) 890104; £2. **Roman Legionary Museum** (High St) Gives some idea of the daily life of the garrison; quite a few hands-on activities at weekends. Shop, disabled access; (01633) 423134; £3.30. You can get a

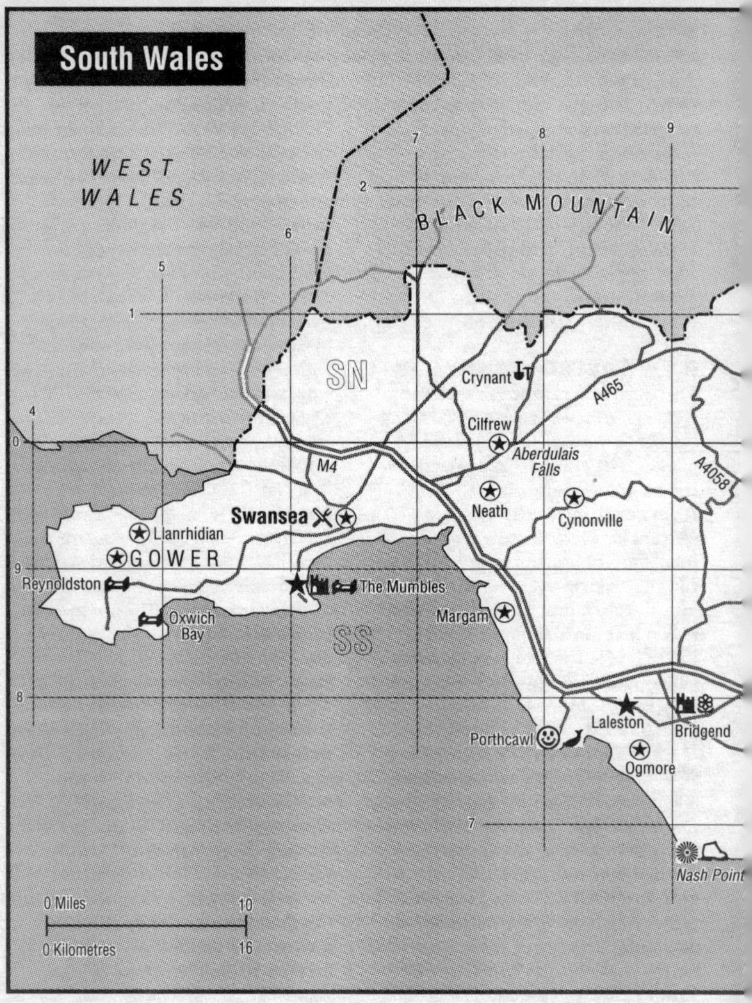

joint ticket for the museum and the baths. Caerleon is reckoned in these parts to have been the site of the court of King Arthur. The Tourist Information Centre on the High St has a little art gallery and various craft workshops; the Hanbury Arms has generous food.

CAERPHILLY CASTLE ST1587 The largest in Wales, with extensive land and water defences. Rising sheer from its broad outer moat, it's a proper picture-book castle, pleasing for this reason to the most casual visitor. It also enthrals serious students of castle architecture with its remarkably complex design of concentric defences. Look out for the incredible leaning tower, which appears ready to topple any second. Shop, disabled access to ground floor; cl 24–26 Dec, 1 Jan; (01222) 883143; £2.40. In the oddly strung-out small town, the ancient Courthouse overlooking the castle has a useful quick carvery.

CAERWENT ROMAN WALLS ST4790 These massive walls, still some 4½ metres (15ft) high in places, enclosed the large site of Venta Silurum – over 40 acres, enough for a sizeable

town, though none of that's left now; free. The Carpenters Arms up in the attractive village of Shirenewton does good-value food.

CALDICOT CASTLE
ST4888 (off the B4245) Well preserved 12th/14th-c castle restored as a family home in the 1880s, and lived in until 20 years ago – since when it's been a local museum, surrounded by a country park. Snacks, shop, limited disabled access; cl am Sun, lunchtimes Oct and Mar, and all Nov–Feb; (01291) 424447; £1.50.

! CARDIFF
ST1876 The civic centre has a range of grand, 20th-c, white stone civic, governmental or museum buildings around formal Cathays Park. The old city centre is closer to Cardiff Castle, which has Capability Brown's 18th-c landscaped park between it and the river. In the centre, parts are pedestrianised (for example around the fine church of St John the Baptist), and there are many covered shopping arcades, Victorian and modern; multi-ride bus tickets are good value for getting around. A new national stadium will host the 1999 Rugby World Cup. The Cottage and Philharmonic (both St

Mary's St) and Golden Cross (Custom House St) are quite useful for lunch. **Cardiff Castle** (Castle St) Despite their fairy-tale medieval appearance, the main buildings are largely 19th c, when the Marquess of Bute employed William Burges to rebuild and restore the place, adding richly romantic wall paintings, tapestries and carvings. Some parts are much older, and in the grounds there's even a piece of a 3-metre (10-ft) thick Roman wall. The Norman keep survives, and there's a 13th-c tower – these 2 look like proper castle architecture, perched on a little mound. Also 2 military museums. Snacks, shop; cl 25–26 Dec, 1 Jan; (01222) 878100; £4.80 for full guided tour, grounds only £2.40. **National Museum of Wales** (Cathays Park) Considerably enlivened in recent years, with interactive displays and exhibitions on subjects as diverse as ceramics, coins and prehistoric sea monsters. The east wing has an impressive collection of paintings, with notable French Impressionists, and there's an excellent section on the evolution of the Welsh landscape. Meals, snacks, shop, disabled access; cl Mon exc bank hols; (01222) 397951; £4.25. **Techniquest** (Stuart St) Fun as well as interest at this high-tech science centre, with around 160 hands-on exhibits and activities, a planetarium, and even a realistic dragon conjured up by laser. All exceptionally well done, it's an excellent family excursion. Meals, snacks, shop, very good disabled access; cl 24–26 Dec; (01222) 475475; £4.75. **Cardiff Bay Development Area** Ambitious rejuvenation of the Inner Harbour and Docklands, explained in a space-age-looking **visitor centre** (cl 25–26 Dec; 01222 463833; free); the area includes Techniquest, and also a slightly incongruous Norwegian timbered church. **Craft in the Bay** (Bute St) has demonstrations by potters, jewellers and glass-workers as well as a large gallery and shop; free. The docklands New Sea Lock (Harrowby St) may be Cardiff's most unspoilt pub, the smarter Wharf (Atlantic Wharf) is right on the water's edge. **Llandaff Cathedral** (W of city centre) Rebuilt several times; it includes some delightful medieval masonry, Pre-Raphaelite works, a marvellous modern timber roof, and a central concrete arch that you may think a mistake. The nearby green has an attractive collection of buildings around it. **Welsh Folk Museum** (St Fagans, 4m W on the A4232) Excellent 100-acre open-air museum, with a variety of reconstructed buildings from castles to cottages illustrating styles and living conditions down the ages. Buildings have come from all over Wales, with some remarkable exhibits inc a homely gas-lit Edwardian farmhouse and an entire Celtic village. You can buy things from a period grocery store. Also crafts and lots of seasonal events – there's plenty to fascinate here. Meals and snacks (in a 1920s tearoom), shop, disabled access; cl 25–26 Dec, 1 Jan; (01222) 573500; £5.25.

CHEPSTOW ST5294
A steep but civilised small town, still with its battlemented 13th-c town gate. **Chepstow Castle** The first recorded Norman stone castle, proudly standing on an easily defended spot above the Wye, overlooking the harbour. Splendid gatehouse with portcullis grooves and ancient gates, and exhibitions on siege warfare and the English Civil War. Shop, limited disabled access; cl 24–26 Dec, 1 Jan; £3. Stuart Crystal have a museum and workshop opposite the castle, and there's a working pottery on Lower Church St (cl 1–2pm). **Chepstow Museum** (Bridge St) Good local history; cl 1–2pm, am Sun; £1. The civilised Bridge and Castle View hotels are both good for lunch.

! CILFREW SS7699
Penscynor Wildlife Park (off the A465) Lots of animals in a charming setting, inc meerkats, parrots, tropical birds and 25 species of monkey. Also a farmyard and a playground. You can feed rainbow trout or take a ride in the chairlift to the clifftop – coming down again on an exciting bobsleigh ride. Meals, snacks, shop, disabled access; cl Oct–Feb; (01639) 642189; £5; bobsleigh £1.

CRYNANT SN7904 **Cefn Coed Colliery Museum** (Blaenant Colliery, A4109) On the site of a former colliery, the story of mining in the Dulais Valley. It still has a steam winding-engine, though the winding gear is now run by electricity. Also a simulated underground mining gallery, boiler house and compressor house. Shop, mostly disabled access; cl Nov–Mar; (01639) 750556; *£3.

CWM DARRAN SO1203 (Rhymney Valley, nr Bargoed) Interesting example of post-mining land reclamation, which now provides a wide variety of natural habitats for wildlife and plants, with scenery ranging from the valley floor through forest areas to upland moors giving walkers superb views of the Brecon Beacons.

CWMBRAN ST2795 **Greenmeadow Community Farm** (1m W) Founded to protect one of the encroaching new town's last green areas, this friendly farm has a wide range of animals – traditional, rare and cuddly – as well as a deer enclosure, bluebell wood, and craft workshops. Meals, snacks, shop, disabled access; cl 25–26 Dec; (01633) 862202; *£3.25. Up towards Pontypool the canalside Open Hearth (Griffithstown) has good food.

CYNONVILLE SS8194 **Afan Forest Park** (A4107) 9,000 tranquil acres of forest, with trails for walking or cycling (you can hire mountain bikes in summer), and a visitor centre; free, though £1.15 parking charge. The **Welsh Miners' Museum** here illustrates life as a miner with coal faces, pit gear and mining equipment among the displays. Meals, snacks, shop, disabled access; cl 25–26 Dec; (01639) 850564; *60p.

EBBW VALE SO1508 **Victoria Park** (Victoria, 2m S on the A4046) The site of the 1992 Garden Festival, still full of the lakes, gardens, wetlands and woodland from then. Much of the site is being developed as an ambitious garden village, and it's fascinating watching the project's progress. Pleasant walks and trails, interesting exhibitions, and some quite extraordinary sculptures, one made from 30,000 individually modelled clay bricks. Also a large factory shopping centre. Snacks, shop, disabled access; centre cl 25 Dec; (01495) 350010; free (charge for land train).

GOVILON SO2414 A walk along the **Monmouthshire & Brecon Canal** to Llanfoist SO2813 can tie in with a return along the track of the former Abergavenny–Merthyr Tydfil railway line, making a level 4 miles in all.

THE GOWER SS4990 This peninsula stretching W of Swansea has quite a bit of off-putting ribbon development along the roads entering it, but it's well worth persevering. Once beyond the creeping urbanisation W of Swansea, it encapsulates on a small scale many different types of Welsh landscape, with lots of walking opportunities, and parts of the coast are lovely (but the N coast is attractive only at its western end). Busy in summer (quite a young feel in parts), even the main places tend to be virtually empty out of season. The King Arthur at Reynoldston, Joiners Arms at Bishopston and the Greyhound at Oldwalls are well placed for food. **Rhossili Down** SS4288 This rounded, windswept, rough-cropped moorland seems a million miles from Swansea (yet as the crow flies is only about 10 from the outskirts); it offers walkers breathtaking coast views. From here walks can also take in the long surfers' sands of the bay. There's an informative NT visitor centre at Rhossili; cl Mon–Tues Nov–Dec, wkdys Feb–Mar, all Jan. **Whiteford Burrows** SS4495 An extensive nature reserve, with sand dunes, marshy slacks and pine trees – worthwhile walks. **Burry Holms** SS4092 Islet with a ruined chapel and an Iron Age fort; you can walk out across the sands at low tide. **Worms Head** SS4087 Nature reserve where you may see seals on the tidal rocks in late summer; walks here can also take in Mewslade Bay, where the south-facing sands are enclosed by limestone cliffs. **Port Eynon Point** SS4684 Interesting, with a huge medieval rock-dove dovecot in the cliff (birds still use it), and cliff walks on either side; wind-surfing below. **Oxwich Bay** SS5086 Dunes and broad sands, presided over by Oxwich Point on its W side; good walking. It's also suitable for windsurfing – you can hire wet suits from a wind-surfing school at Oxwich Bay – though the water will never be more than what might euphemistically be called invigorating. **Threecliff Bay** SS5388

From the NT car park nr Penmaen church, a good walk follows the lane down to this bay, then heads W along the coast as far as Nicholaston Farm to end with the mild ascent of Cefn Bryn, a rounded moorland hill giving breathtaking views of both – or all 3 – Gower coasts. **Brandy Cove** SS5887 This tiny cove makes an attractive destination for a walk down the wooded Bishopston Valley.

LLANRHIDIAN SS4792 **Weobley Castle** 12th/14th-c fortified manor house with an exhibition on the area's history, and superb views. Cl 24–26 Dec, 1 Jan; (01792) 390012; £1.70. The Welcome to Town is in a lovely spot above the estuary, and the long glistening cockle sands – full of interest for walkers.

LLANTHONY PRIORY SO2827 Graceful ruins of a 12th-c priory, the money for its construction put up by Hugh de Lacey when he decided he'd had enough of being a bold bad baron and was thinking of retiring into these lonely hills. It's very romantic, with nothing much but the noise of the sheep to disturb the peace. The remains cover a variety of architectural styles; free. The very ancient crypt bar below the Abbey Hotel, right among the priory buildings, is useful for a snack lunch – a most unusual place. This is a good start or objective for Black Mountains walks. **Cwmyoy Church** SO2923 (Llanthony Valley road) Repeated landslips have left the medieval church twisted, and its tower leans at an angle that makes the Tower of Pisa look positively sober. **Partrishow Church** SO2722 Remarkable building, with a musicians' gallery and a mural of a figure of Death wielding a shovel.

★ † **LLANTILIO CROSSENY** SO3914 Attractive village with a lovely view of the 13th-c church from the former moat of Hen Cwrt nearby; the Halfway House and Hostry are good for lunch. **White Castle** (NW) The remains of the most substantial of the trio of moated castles Hubert de Burgh built to defend the Welsh Marches; £1.70. The others stand at Skenfrith SO4621 (the Bell has good-value food) and Grosmont SO4024, an attractive hillside village with another 13th-c church (the Angel here is also worthwhile).

★ † **LLANVAPLEY** SO3614 Interesting village, with a **church** dating from 860.

MARGAM PARK SS8086 (A48) Pretty country park based around a splendid 'gothick' mansion, its 850 acres full of natural and historic features and various themed areas, inc a scaled-down nursery-rhyme village for young children. Also a ruined abbey and Iron Age hill fort, marked walks among the parkland and forests, giant maze, deer and cattle, and an adventure playground. Meals, snacks, shop, disabled access; cl winter Mon and Tues; (01639) 871131; £3.50, less in winter, when none of the attractions is open (though they have various special events).

MERTHYR TYDFIL SO0511 **Brecon Mountain Railway** (off the A465) The route of this narrow-gauge railway starts at Pant Station, 3m N, where there's a display of various engines inc vintage locomotives and others from around the world. The journey takes you into the beautiful Brecon Beacons as far as the Taf Fechan reservoir. Snacks, shop, disabled access; cl Nov–Easter exc over Christmas; (01685) 722988 for timetable; £5.90. On a disused railway line, the Dowlais Viaduct is a striking sight, well worth a detour. **Cyfarthfa Castle** (Cyfarthfa Park) Impressive, early 19th-c, castellated 'gothick' mansion, set in beautiful gardens. Recently restored to their full Regency glory, the state rooms contain a museum with displays on Egyptology and archaeology. Meals, snacks, shop, disabled access; cl am winter wknds, 24 Dec–2 Jan; (01685) 723112; £1.50. **Joseph Parry's Cottage** (Chapel Row, Georgetown) The composer of Myfanwy was born here, and the ground floor has been restored and decorated in the style of the 1840s. Shop, limited disabled access; open pm Thurs–Sun Easter–Sept; (01685) 723112; 60p. The Butchers Arms up at Pontsticill has good home cooking. **Garwnant Forest Centre** SO0111 (5m NW, off the A470) Looking out over the Llwyn-On reservoir on the southern edge of the Brecon Beacons, carefully restored old farm buildings with displays on forestry, wildlife and conservation, and information on nature trails and cycle routes (you can hire bikes). Also a discovery centre for children. Meals, snacks, shop, disabled access; (01685) 384060; £1 car parking charge.

★ **MONMOUTH** SO5113 Attractive market town of considerable character; below the remains of the 12th-c castle where Henry V was born, and the 17th-c Great Castle House (built with enormous blocks of masonry in its precincts), the main Agincourt Sq is surrounded by handsome buildings, inc the imposing central Shire Hall with its arcaded market floor. **Nelson Museum** (Priory St) Tremendous collection relating to Nelson, inc letters, medals and best of all his fighting sword. Nelson has nothing to do with Monmouth, but the collection was originally put together by Lady Llangattock who lived nearby. Shop, some disabled access; cl 1–2pm, am Sun, 24–26 Dec, 1 Jan; (01600) 713519; £1. The town nestles in the crook formed by the River Wye and the River Monnow, with a splendid 13th-c gatehouse bridge over the Monnow. The Punch House is the most enjoyable place here for lunch, and the Gockett (B4293 towards Trelleck) is also worthwhile. **Fairview Rock** SO55514 This lofty crag nr the Biblins suspension bridge makes a good riverside walk from Monmouth, with a level track giving an easy route along the picturesque Lower Wye gorge.

★ **MUMBLES** SS6287 Pleasantly unspoilt resort with a collection of traditional Welsh love spoons – (01792) 360132; cl Sun – and a surprisingly active night-life; 14 pubs line the stretch of Mumbles Rd nr Mumbles Head, and students like to 'go mumbling' between them. The White Rose does good value food. **Oystermouth Castle** Very complete ruins of the de Breose family castle, in a small park overlooking the bay. The gatehouse, chapel and Great Hall date from the 13th–14th c. Cl Oct–Mar; *£1.

NANTGARW CHINA WORKS ST1285 (Treforest Industrial estate, off the A470) For a brief period early in the 19th c, Nantgarw porcelain was among the finest in the world. They still make pots and clay pipes, and you can watch the craftsmen. Snacks, shop; cl Mon, plus winter Tues and Weds; (01443) 841703; *£1.

NASH POINT SS9168 The curious striped cliffs of the Glamorgan coast look over the Bristol Channel to Exmoor. It is worth getting down to shore level to see the cliffs in their full glory.

NEATH ABBEY SS7397 Remains of a Cistercian abbey founded in 1130 by Richard de Grainville. Disabled access; cl am Sun, 25–26 Dec; free. **Neath Borough Museum** (Gwyn Hall, Orchard St) Includes finds from a nearby Roman fort. Shop, disabled access; cl Sun, Mon (exc bank hols); (01639) 645741; free. **Gnoll Estate** (B4434 NE) Landscaped grounds beautifully restored by the borough council. The visitor centre will have you believe they're the finest in Europe, and though this is something of an exaggeration, with some of the features it's not too wide of the mark. Snacks, shop, disabled access; cl 24 Dec–2 Jan; (01639) 635808; free.

! **NELSON** ST1196 **Llancaiach Fawr** (B4254) Splendidly entertaining and carefully organised living history museum, the Elizabethan manor's Civil War days brought vividly to life by costumed guides who rarely step out of character – they even speak in 17th-c style. Children don't mind visiting a stately home when it's like this – not only are there no ropes or barriers (it's all firmly hands-on), but they can try on historic clothes, handle armour, or even languish in the stocks for a while. Extra activities summer wknds. Meals, snacks, shop, some disabled access (not to upper floors of house); cl am Sun in winter, and Christmas wk; (01443) 412248; £4.10.

NEWPORT ST3187 **Museum and Art Gallery** (John Frost Sq) Worthwhile collections – inc a mass of teapots (cl Sun and bank hols; free). **Tredegar House** (Coedkernew; off the A48, SW edge)

Magnificent 17th-c house and gardens set in 90-acre landscaped park on the edge of this industrial town. The Morgans, later Lords Tredegar, lived here for 5 centuries, and the household's above and below stairs activities are well illustrated in the 30 or so rooms on show. In the grounds are carriage rides, self-guided trails, craft workshops, an Edwardian sunken garden, boating and an adventure playfarm. Meals, snacks, shop, disabled access; cl Mon and Tues (exc Aug), Oct wkdys, and all Nov–Easter; (01633) 815880; £3.95. Past here on the B4239, the Lighthouse Inn at St Brides Wentloog has good food upstairs, and great Severn views.

OGMORE CASTLE SS8876 3-storeyed 12th-c keep with a preserved hooded fireplace, a dry moat surrounding the inner ward and a surviving 12-metre (40-ft) west wall. The setting of this ruin is attractive: odd to think that what this impressive fortress was built to defend was the row of stepping stones which still cross the river; free. The Pelican is good for lunch, and the cheery Three Golden Cups, along the road at Southerndown, gives sea views to Devon on a clear day. Just past it, there's a car park by the interestingly preserved remains of the seaside gardens of entirely demolished Dunraven Castle, with walks by the cliffs over the sands and rock pools, and around to the fragmentary remains of an Iron Age promontory hill fort above the sea.

★ **PENARTH** ST1971 An unspoilt seaside resort of some charm, with the usual attractions. **Turner House** (Plymouth Rd) Changing exhibits from the National Museum of Wales; disabled access to ground floor; cl am Sun, all Mon (exc bank hols), and between exhibitions; (01222) 708870; £1.25 (free pms Sun). **Cosmeston medieval village** (Lavernock Rd, S towards Sully) Living museum of medieval life, reconstructed on the site of an actual village deserted during the 14th c. Hens and sheep wander between the cottages. Meals, snacks, shop, disabled access; cl 25 Dec; (01222) 708686; £3. It's in the Cosmeston Lakes country park, with lakes, woodland and wildlife.

PENHOW CASTLE ST4290 (A48) The oldest lived-in castle in Wales, with tours of the restored rooms taking you from the 12th-c ramparts and Norman bedchamber through the 15th-c Great Hall with its minstrels' gallery to the Victorian housekeeper's room. There's a choice of several good Walkman tours, one for children, and others concentrating on a particular topic, such as the musical or domestic history of the building. You can stay here. Snacks; cl Mon (exc bank hols), Tues, and all Oct–Mar exc Weds and pm occasional Suns; (01633) 400800; £3.35.

PONTYPOOL SO2801 **Torfaen Museum** (Park Rd) Pretty much perfectly preserved 18th-c ironworks; cl am Sun and all Oct–Apr; (01495) 752036; £1.20. **Valley Inheritance** (Pontypool Park, off the A4042) The story of a typical South Wales valley, well shown in the Georgian stable block of Pontypool Park House. Snacks, shop, disabled access; cl am Sun, all Jan; (01495) 752036; £1.20. The surrounding country park is a microcosm of the Welsh valleys scenery: patches of conifer plantation and rather scrappy moorland rising high above the industrial valleys – not exactly pretty, but its gruff sense of place appeals to some. The Open Hearth just below the canal at Griffithstown is good for lunch.

PORTH ST0290 **Rhondda Heritage Park** (off the A470) Based in the last colliery buildings in the area, a very good developing centre with lively multi-media exhibitions re-creating the days when coal was king. Sights, sounds and smells from the life and work of the miners, and an excellent underground tour showing what it was like to work a shift; the noise and heat are uncannily realistic. It ends with an exciting dark ride back to the surface. Unusual features include the gallery with art by locals, a section on the role of women, and an authentic valley chapel. With a good themed play area for children, this is a fulfilling family day out. Meals, snacks, shop, disabled access; cl winter Mons, and 25–26 Dec; (01443) 682036; £5.25. The Bunch of Grapes in

Pontypridd (Ynysangharad road) is useful for food.

PORTHCAWL SS8176 Still developing summer resort, with broad sandy beaches, a well placed golf club, fairground, fishing from the pier, and what's said to be the largest caravan park in Wales (some say Europe); it's quieter on the W side of the harbour.

RAGLAN CASTLE SO4108 Quite magnificent ruins of a 15th-c castle, particularly notable for its Yellow Tower of Gwent. Its intricate history is displayed in the closet tower and 2 rooms of the gatehouse. Shop, some disabled access; cl 24–26 Dec, 1 Jan; (01291) 690228; £2.40. The Clytha Arms (Abergavenny road) has good food.

★ **ST HILARY** ST0171 **Beaupre Castle** Well preserved, ruined Elizabethan courtyard mansion with an extraordinarily elaborate 3-storey Italianate porch; free. The Bush is handy for lunch, and the village with its thatched houses is pretty.

ST NICHOLAS ST0971 **Dyffryn Gardens** (off the A48) Small themed gardens and seasonal bedding displays help break up the 50 acres of rare plants and shrubs which make up these lovely gardens. Also extensive plant houses, inc a large temperate house and a succulent house, and an arboretum. Summer snacks (open-air theatre then too), shop, disabled access; open daily in summer, best to check in winter; (01222) 593328; £3.

SWANSEA SS6593 Largely post-industrial and commercial, so there are few buildings of any age or great appeal to visitors, but there's a good fresh-food covered market with cockles and laverbread, and long sandy beaches have made it something of a family summer resort. Among some high spots is the 1934 **guildhall**, containing the Brangwyn Hall with its 16 huge British Empire murals painted by Sir Frank Brangwyn for the House of Lords – Wales's gain, as they were judged too controversial. There are some castle ruins (you can't go inside, but can see them from outside), inc a striking 14th-c first-floor arcade. The Dylan Thomas Centre (Somerset Pl, Marina) is devoted to Welsh literature, with exhibitions, restaurant, and a good bookshop/café (you can peruse the books over your coffee). The Hanbury in Kingsway is popular for lunch. **Swansea Museum** (Victoria Rd, Maritime Quarter) The oldest in Wales, with local history exhibits and replicas of the oldest human bones found in Wales (cl Mon exc bank hols; free). **Maritime and Industrial Museum** (Museum Sq, Maritime Quarter) In the heart of the revitalised docks, with its summer collection of historic ships the biggest and most varied assemblage of floating maritime exhibits in Wales. Also a complete working woollen mill. Lots of thought is put into the displays. Summer snacks, shop, disabled access; cl Mon (exc bank hols), 25–26 Dec, 1 Jan; (01792) 650351; free. **Glynn Vivian Art Gallery and Museum** (Alexandra Rd) Displays of porcelain from Swansea's all-too-brief but brilliant period of production between 1814 and 1824, and paintings, drawings and sculptures by British, French and,

Days Out

Lower Wye tour: Chepstow Castle; lunch at the Castle View Hotel or the Bridge Hotel there; view from Wynd Cliff; Tintern Abbey; Monmouth.

The great buildings collection: Castell Coch, Tongwynlais; Llandaff Cathedral; lunch at the Maltsters Arms there; Welsh Folk Museum at St Fagans (like Llandaff, described under Cardiff).

An industrious past: Stroll along the Monmouthshire & Brecon Canal between Gilwern and Govilon, back along the old railway track; lunch at the Drum & Monkey, Clydach; Big Pit Mining Museum at Blaenavon.

above all, Welsh artists – especially the locally born Ceri Richards. Good changing exhibitions. Shop, some disabled access; cl Mon (exc bank hols), 25–26 Dec, 1 Jan; (01792) 655006; free. The new **Egypt Centre** (University Campus, off Oystermouth Rd) is also well worth a look, with an important collection of Egyptian artifacts. Shop, disabled access; cl Sun and Mon; (01792) 295960; free. **Plantasia** (Parc Tawe) Tropical and desert plants in a big, futuristic, landscaped glasshouse, also an aviary, reptiles and various creepy-crawlies. Snacks, shop, disabled access; cl Mon, 25–26 Dec; (01792) 474555; £1.95.

TINTERN ABBEY SO5300 (off the A466) Remarkably well preserved, these 14th-ruins were considered an essential visit for 18th-c artists and poets, lying as they do in a lovely part of the steeply wooded Wye Valley. Wordsworth was just one of many to find inspiration here. Shop, disabled access; cl 24–26 Dec, 1 Jan; (01291) 689251; £2.20. The **Abbey Mill** nearby has been converted into a little craft centre, with demonstrations and a decent coffee shop; cl 25–26 Dec; free. A **visitor centre** at Tintern Old Station can help you make the most of the surrounding hills and woodland.

TONGWYNLAIS ST1382 **Castell Coch** (off the A470) This spectacular triangular hillside landmark, designed in 1875 by William Burges for the Marquis of Bute, is actually based on a 13th-c castle in spite of its improbable appearance, something by Disney out of Wagner – red sandstone, conical towers, drawbridge and portcullis. Though never finished, it's a very successful pastiche, and inside is just as impressive: an astonishingly elaborate mock-medieval idyll of gilt, gorgeous colours, statues, murals and carvings. Lady Bute's bedroom is decorated on the theme of Sleeping Beauty. Shop, disabled access to ground floor only; cl 24–26 Dec, 1 Jan; (01222) 810101; £2.50.

★ **USK** SO3700 **Gwent Rural Life Museum** (New Market St) Interesting collection, housed in an old barn; cl am wknds and all Nov–Mar; £1.50. The little town is attractive.

WYND CLIFF ST5297 This Wye Valley viewpoint gives walkers an extensive panorama, a short detour up steps. Elsewhere, the Wye Valley Walk between Chepstow and Tintern gives only occasional views down to the river, which in the picturesque Lower Wye gorge makes the boundary with England.

★ **Other attractive villages or small towns**, all with decent pubs, include Bedwellty SO1600, Cowbridge SS9974 and Laleston SS8879. The church and churchyard of Llancarfan ST0570 are worth a look.

Pubs or inns elsewhere which are particularly useful for their attractive surroundings or views include the Lamb & Flag out on the Brecon road from Abergavenny SO2515, Bridgend by the canal at Gilwern SO2414, Old Glais at Glais SN7000, Prince of Wales nr the sand dune nature reserve at Kenfig SS8383, Old House at Llangynwyd SS8588, the Greyhound at Llantrisant ST3997, Brynfynnon at Llanwonno ST0295, Plough & Harrow at Monknash SS9270, Rowan Tree at Nelson ST1195, Halfway House at Tal-y-coed SO4115, the Trekkers at The Narth SO5206 and the Fountain at Trelleck Grange SO4902.

Where to eat

CARDIFF ST1876 **Le Monde** *60 St Mary St (01222) 387376* Bustling open-plan restaurant with a big choice of delicious fish and shellfish, decent wines, and friendly, efficient service; cl Sun, 25–26 Dec. **£20.25**|£5 2-course lunch.

LLANDEWI SKIRRID SO3416 **Walnut Tree** *(01873) 852797* Comfortable, stylish dining pub run by the same licensees for over 27 years; marvellously relaxed atmosphere (you can pop in for just a drink or a one-course meal), outstanding, imaginative and carefully prepared food using tip-top quality produce (wonderful puddings and fine cheeses), an attractive choice of wines (particularly strong on Italian ones), and efficient, friendly service; cl Sun, Mon, 1 wk Christmas, 2 wks Feb; disabled access. **£35**|£15.

RAGLAN SO3608 **Clytha Arms** *Clytha*, (3m W) *(01873) 840206* Fine old country inn with a tasteful and solidly comfortable bar, and cheerful, helpful staff; carefully prepared food inc delicious puddings and a good-value Sun lunch in the no smoking restaurant, log fires, well kept real ales, and a neat garden; bdrms. **£18.30**|£4.25.

SWANSEA SS6592 **Number One Restaurant** *1 Wind St (01792) 456996* Small, bistro-style restaurant with a relaxed and friendly atmosphere, helpful staff, and really good food using local produce – lots of fish and game and lovely puddings; cl Sun, Mon, 24 Dec–1 Jan. **£25.75 dinner, £14.75 lunch**|£7.

TAL-Y-COED SO4115 **Halfway House** *(01600) 780269* Pretty, neat and clean 17th-c cottage with a huge wisteria; cosy little no smoking dining room, a snug main bar, lots of Wills cigarette cards, well kept real ales, carefully presented bar food, welcoming service, and a tidy garden; children must be well behaved; disabled access. **£18.50**|£6.20.

Special thanks to Mrs H Woodfield, M and J Back, David I Roberts, E G Parish, Jackie Orme, D and N Toulson, E G Parish, Anita Wagner, Amanda Smith, Melanie Thompson, D A Willis.

We welcome reports from readers

This *Guide* depends on readers' reports. Do help us if you can – in return, we offer a discount on the next edition to people who've helped us with reports for it. Tell us what you think about places already in it, and anything extra you think we should say about them. And send us your ideas for inclusion in the next edition: places to visit, eat at or stay in, attractive drives or walks, maybe even unusual interesting shops you know of. Use the card in the middle, the report forms at the end, or just write – no stamp needed: *The Good Guide to Britain*, FREEPOST TN1569, Wadhurst, E Sussex TN5 7BR.

Wales Calendar

Some of these dates were provisional as we went to press. Please check information with the telephone numbers provided.

JANUARY

1 **Cardiff** New Year's Day Concert at St David's Hall (01222) 878500; **Saundersfoot** New Year's Day Swim from the beach (01834) 812448
9 **Llanwrtyd Wells** Roman Festival inc a chariot race – *till Mon 11* (01591) 610236

FEBRUARY

27 **Trehafod** Celtic Festival at the Rhondda Heritage Park – *till Sun 28* (01443) 682036

MARCH

5 **Llanwrtyd Wells** Folk Weekend – *till Sun 7* (01591) 610327
12 **Llandudno** North Wales Country Music Festival – *till Sun 14* (01492) 879771
26 **Conwy** Seed Fair (01492) 650851

APRIL

4 **Newport** Costumed Events at Tredegar House – *till Mon 5* (01633) 815880
10 **Swansea** Model Boat Festival at the Maritime and Industrial Museum – *till Sun 11* (01792) 650351

MAY

1 **Swansea** Clyne in Bloom inc bands, walks and talks, every Sun – *till Sun 30* (01792) 636424; **Wrexham** Arts Festival – *till Sat 15* (01978) 297442
3 **Bodedern** and District Festival inc wakes, a stagecoach, moral play and concerts – *till Mon 10* (01407) 740858
8 **Cardiff** Cricket World Cup, warm-up: Glamorgan v Australia (01222) 343478
11 **Cardiff** Cricket World Cup, warm-up: Glamorgan v Kenya (01222) 343478
14 **Llangollen** International Jazz Festival – *till Sun 16* (0151) 339 3367; **Newport** Folk Festival at Tredegar House – *till Sun 16* (01633) 815880
15 **Llanelwedd** Smallholder Weekend at the Royal Welsh Showground – *till Sun 16* (01454) 299187
20 **Cardiff** Cricket World Cup: Australia v New Zealand (01222) 343478; **Llantilio Crossenny** Festival of Music and Drama – *till Sun 23* (01873) 856928
22 **Chepstow** Horse Trials – *till Sun 23* (01291) 622260
28 **Hay-on-Wye** Literature Festival – *till 6 Jun* (01497) 820144
29 **St David's** St David's Cathedral Music Festival – *till 6 Jun* (01437) 720271
30 **St Donats Castle** Crafts in Action at St Donats Arts Centre – *till Mon 31* (01446) 794848; **Swansea** City and County of Swansea Show – *till Mon 31* (01792) 635428
31 **Lampeter** National Eisteddfod – *till 5 Jun* (01269) 845705

Wales Calendar (cont.)

JUNE

6 **Cardiff** Singer of the World – *till Sat 12* (01222) 878444
12 **Llanwrtyd Wells** 20th Man v Horse Race (01591) 610666
17 **Gregynog** Festival – *till Sun 20* (01686) 650224
19 **Barmouth** Yacht Race to Fort William – *till Fri 25* (01341) 280298; **Llantwit Major** Victorian Fair Day (01446) 794217; **Llanwrtyd Wells** Drovers' Challenge Walk (01591) 610666; **Newport** Motor Show at Tredegar House – *till Sun 20* (01633) 815880
20 **Swansea** Festival of Transport (01792) 635427
22 **Criccieth** Festival – *till Sun 27* (01766) 522680
25 **Cardiff** Folk Dance Festival – *till Sun 27* (01222) 653989; **Carmarthen** Festival – *till 5 July* (01267) 238148

JULY

1 **Newport** Tour of the Garden and Park with the curator and warden *every Thurs in July* at Tredegar House – *till Thurs 29* (01633) 815880
2 **Conwy** North Wales Bluegrass Music Festival – *till Sun 4* (01492) 580454; **Llanwrtyd Wells** Morris in the Forest Festival –*till Sun 4* (01591) 610666
3 **Ely** Festival – *till Sun 11* (01222) 578368; **St Donats Castle** Welsh International Festival of Storytelling at St Donats Arts Centre – *till Sun 4* (01446) 794848
6 **Llangollen** International Musical Eisteddfod: cosmopolitan gathering at the Royal International Pavilion – *till Sun 11* (01978) 860236
10 **Welshpool** Mid Wales Festival of Transport at Powis Castle – *till Sun 11* (01938) 553680
13 **Saundersfoot** in Bloom Flower Festival – *till Sat 17* (01834) 812880
15 **Cardiff** Welsh Proms at St David's Hall – *till Sat 24* (01222) 878500
17 **Llanwrtyd Wells** Annual Mountain Bike Bog Snorkelling World Championships (01591) 610666; **Newport** Last Night of the Proms at Tredegar House (01633) 815880
19 **Caernarfon** Festival – *till Sat 24* (01286) 677227; **Gower** Festival – *till Sat 31* (01792) 419449; **Llanelwedd** Royal Welsh Show at the Showground – *till Thurs 22* (01982) 553683
23 **Swansea** Dylan Thomas Festival at the Dylan Thomas Centre – *till 15 Aug* (01792) 463980
24 **Fishguard** Music Festival – *till Sat 31* (01348) 873612
29 **Abergele** National Sheepdog Trials – *till Sat 31* (01234) 352672
30 **Llanwrtyd Wells** Festival Weekend – *till 1 Aug* (01591) 610666
31 **Caernarfon** North Wales Agricultural Show at Wern Ddu Fields (01286) 881632; **Llanbedrgoch** Royal National Eisteddfod of Wales – *till 1 Aug* (01222) 763777

AUGUST

1 **Gower** Agricultural Show (01792) 884967; **Swansea** Botanics in Bloom inc entertainments every Sun at the Botanical Gardens, Singleton Park – *till Tues 31* (01792) 636424
6 **Knighton** Teme Valley Vintage Club Annual Rally at Llanshay Farm (01568) 708446; **Llanwrtyd Wells** Mountain Bike Festival – *till Mon 9* (01591) 610666

Wales Calendar (cont.)

7 **Brecon** County Show (01568) 708760; **Wrexham** Fireworks Concert and Open-air Opera at Erddig Hall – *till Sun 8* (01978) 355314
8 **Hay-on-Wye** Vintage Steam Rally at Boatside Farm (01874) 711110
10 **Gwalchmai** Anglesey Show at the Showground – *till Weds 11* (01407) 720072
12 **Carmarthen** United Counties Agricultural Show – *till Fri 13* (01267) 232141
13 **Brecon** Jazz Festival: over 80 international performers – *till Sun 15* (01874) 625557
14 **Chepstow** Agricultural Show (01291) 627655; **Eglwysbach** Show (01492) 650739; **Llangurig** Llangurig and District Show (01686) 413214
17 **Haverfordwest** Pembrokeshire County Show at the County Showground – *till Thurs 19* (01437) 764331
19 **Denbigh** Agricultural Show (01352) 712131
20 **Pontardawe** Festival: 5 stages, torchlight procession – *till Sun 22* (01792) 830791
21 **Llandrindod Wells** Victorian Festival – *till Sun 29* (01597) 823441; **Llanfairpwll** Open-air Jazz at Plas Newydd (01248) 714795
22 **Machynlleth** Festival – *till Sun 29* (01654) 703355
26 **Ruthin** Festival – *till Sat 28* (01824) 703832
26 **Monmouth** Monmouthshire Show at Vauxhall Fields (01291) 691160; **Presteigne** Festival of Music and the Arts – *till Tues 31* (01544) 267800
28 **Pren-gwyn** Sheepdog Trials and Show (01559) 362850
30 **Llanwrtyd Wells** World Bog Snorkelling and Mountain Bike Leaping Championships (01591) 610666

SEPTEMBER

4 **Llandysul** Agricultural Show (01559) 362850; **Llangollen** Hot-air Balloon Festival at the Royal International Pavilion – *till Sun 5* (01492) 531731
5 **Barmouth** Arts Festival – *till Sat 11* (01341) 280392
9 **Trawsgoed** International Sheepdog Trials – *till Sat 11* (01234) 352672
11 **Gwernesney** Usk Show (01291) 672379; **Wales** European Heritage Open Days: free access to up to 90 properties, some not usually open to the public, such as Dyffryn Gardens in **Barry**, Cwmgwili House in **Carmarthen**, **Cardiff** Crown Court and Mansion House, **Denby** Town Walls, St David's College in **Lampeter**, Round House Tower in **Nantyglo** and Tredegar House in **Newport** – *till Sun 12* (01222) 484606; **Newport** Jazz in the Park at Tredegar House (01633) 815880
13 **Conwy** Honey Fair (01492) 650851
19 **St Asaph** North Wales Music Festival in the Cathedral – *till Sat 25* (01745) 584508

OCTOBER

1 **Cardiff** Rugby World Cup Festival – *till 6 Nov* (01222) 781999
2 **Swansea** Festival – *till Weds 20* (01792) 205318
8 **Llandudno** October Festival – *till Sun 17* (01492) 872000; **Porthcawl** South Wales Miners' Eisteddfod – *till Sat 9* (01656) 642684
13 **Swansea** Rambert Dance Company at the Grand Theatre – *till Sat 16* (01792) 475715
23 **Cardiff** Rugby World Cup Quarter-finals (01222) 781999
29 **Newport** Halloween at Tredegar House – *till Sat 30* (01633) 815880

Wales Calendar (cont.)

NOVEMBER

4 **Cardiff** Rugby World Cup Play-off (01222) 781999
5 **Swansea** Fireworks at St Helen's Rugby Ground (01792) 635427
6 **Cardiff** Rugby World Cup Final (01222) 514732
12 **Cardiff** Welsh International Film Festival – *till Sun 21* (01970) 617995

DECEMBER

7 **Llanelwedd** Royal Welsh Agricultural Winter Fair at the Royal Welsh Showground (01982) 553683
31 **Cardiff** Fireworks and Party at Cardiff Bay (01222) 667773; **Llanwrtyd Wells** New Year Walk-in, *at 11pm* in the square: torchlight walk with a horse's skull (Welsh tradition) (01591) 610236

This index includes the main places in the **To see and Do** sections. Numbers in *italic* refer to entries included in suggestions for **Days Out**.

London Index

Report Forms

Please report to us: you can use the tear-out card in the middle of the book, the forms on the following pages, or just plain paper – whichever's easiest for you. We need to know what you think of the places mentioned in this edition – especially, whether you think we should add to or change our descriptions of them. We need to know about other places worthy of inclusion. We need to know about ones that should not be included. We try to answer all letters, and readers who send us reports will be offered a discount on the price of the next edition that benefits from their help.

If you are recommending a new entry, the more detail you can put into your description, the better. This will help not just us but also your fellow-readers gauge its appeal. A description of its character and even furnishings is a tremendous boon. Imagine you're writing about it for the *Guide* itself, and put in the sorts of things you'd want to know yourself before deciding whether to choose it.

The atmosphere and character of a holiday hotel or simpler place to stay, or of a restaurant, are very important to us – why it would, or would not, appeal to people who don't know it. But, of course, the quality and type of its food matter a lot, too, so please tell us about that as well. A full address and telephone number is an enormous help.

We'd also very much like you to let us know of places you've enjoyed visiting – anything from a little village to a stately home, from a shop selling unusual things to a factory visit, from an outstanding plant nursery to a hot-air balloon festival, from a hidden-away country church to a cathedral, from a peaceful wood or a nature reserve or a stretch of unspoilt coastal cliff to a theme park or a zoo or a pleasure beach. We're also particularly interested in enjoyable walks and drives. Whatever it is, if you've enjoyed it, please tell us about it.

The card in the middle of the book is a general purpose one for any recommendation. There are also different forms on the following pages: one for endorsement of existing entries; and three forms for more detailed descriptions of places to visit, hotels or restaurants.

When you go to a hotel, restaurant, or anywhere else, don't tell them you're a reporter for *The Good Guide to Britain*; we do make clear that all inspections are anonymous, and if you declare yourself as a reporter you risk getting special treatment – for better or for worse! When you write to *The Good Guide to Britain*, FREEPOST TN1569, WADHURST, E. Sussex TN5 7BR, you don't need a stamp in the UK. We'll gladly send you more forms (free) if you wish. The information you send us will be stored in our computer files.

Though we try to answer letters, we do have other work to do, besides producing this *Guide*. So please understand if there's a delay. And from June well into autumn, when we are fully extended getting the next edition to the printers, we put all letters and reports aside, not answering them until the rush is over (and after our post-press-day autumn holiday). The end of May is pretty much the cut-off date for reasoned consideration of reports for the next edition – and the earlier the better, if they're suggestions of new entries.

We'll assume we can print your name or initials as a recommender unless you tell us otherwise.

The Good Guide to Britain: Endorsement Form

I have been to the following hotels/restaurants/attractions/places in *The Good Guide to Britain 1999* in the last few months, found them as described, and confirm that they deserve continued inclusion:

PLEASE GIVE YOUR NAME AND ADDRESS ON THE BACK OF THIS FORM

Your own name and address (*block capitals please*)

Please return to:

The Good Guide to Britain
FREEPOST TN1569
WADHURST
E. Sussex
TN5 7BR

The Good Guide to Britain: Report Form

Please use this form to tell us about anything which *you* think should or should not be included in the next edition of *The Good Guide to Britain*. Just fill it in and sent it to us – no stamp needed.

ALISDAIR AIRD

☐ *Please tick this box if you would like extra report forms.*

Report on (*its name*)

Its address:

Postcode: Telephone:

What is this? (e.g. *hotel, restaurant, garden, village, drive, walk)*

Description/why it appeals

PLEASE GIVE YOUR NAME AND ADDRESS ON THE BACK OF THIS FORM

Your own name and address (*block capitals please*)

Please return to:

The Good Guide to Britain
FREEPOST TN1569
WADHURST
E. Sussex
TN5 7BR

The Good Guide to Britain: Report Form

Please use this form to tell us about anything which *you* think should or should not be included in the next edition of *The Good Guide to Britain*. Just fill it in and sent it to us – no stamp needed.

ALISDAIR AIRD

☐ *Please tick this box if you would like extra report forms.*

Report on (*its name*)

Its address:

Postcode: Telephone:

What is this? (e.g. *hotel, restaurant, garden, village, drive, walk)*

Description/why it appeals

PLEASE GIVE YOUR NAME AND ADDRESS ON THE BACK OF THIS FORM

Your own name and address (*block capitals please*)

Please return to:

The Good Guide to Britain
FREEPOST TN1569
WADHURST
E. Sussex
TN5 7BR

The Good Guide to Britain: Report Form

Please use this form to tell us about anything which *you* think should or should not be included in the next edition of *The Good Guide to Britain*. Just fill it in and sent it to us – no stamp needed.

ALISDAIR AIRD

☐ *Please tick this box if you would like extra report forms.*

Report on (*its name*)

Its address:

Postcode: Telephone:

What is this? (e.g. *hotel, restaurant, garden, village, drive, walk)*

Description/why it appeals

PLEASE GIVE YOUR NAME AND ADDRESS ON THE BACK OF THIS FORM

Your own name and address (*block capitals please*)

Please return to:

The Good Guide to Britain
FREEPOST TN1569
WADHURST
E. Sussex
TN5 7BR

If you would like to order a copy of
The Good Pub Guide 1999 (£14.99),
edited by Alisdair Aird;
The Good Hotel Guide 1999 Great Britain & Ireland (£13.99),
edited by Caroline Raphael & Hilary Rubinstein; or
The Good Hotel Guide 1999 Continental Europe (£14.99),
edited by Caroline Raphael & Hilary Rubinstein,
direct from Ebury Press (postage & packing free),
please call our credit-card hotline 8.30am–5.30pm,
Mon–Fri on **01206 255800**

Alternatively send a cheque/postal order made payable to
Ebury Press, plus your name, address and order, to
**TBS Direct, Frating Distribution Centre, Colchester Road,
Frating Green, Essex CO7 7DW**

We welcome reports from readers

This *Guide* depends on readers' reports. Do help us if you can – in return, we offer a discount on the next edition to people who've helped us with reports for it. Tell us what you think about places already in it, and anything extra you think we should say about them. And send us your ideas for inclusion in the next edition: places to visit, eat at or stay in, attractive drives or walks, maybe even unusual interesting shops you know of. Use the card in the middle, the report forms, or just write – no stamp needed: *The Good Guide to Britain*, FREEPOST TN1569, Wadhurst, E Sussex TN5 7BR.

Symbols Guide

We repeat here the symbols we have used in the **To see and do** sections and on the maps in this book, so that you can refer to them quickly. You will find a more detailed explanation of the symbols in the Introduction on p. xvi.

- ★ Attractive village or town
- Interesting house – anything from an intimate cottage to the stateliest of stately homes
- Castle, ruined abbey or other romantic ruin
- More or less archaeological site such as Roman remains, Neolithic stone circles, early medieval maze, Iron Age hill fort
- † Church, cathedral, minster, inhabited abbey
- Watermill, windmill or other type of mill
- Nature conservation, including wildlife reserves
- Bird reserve, bird centre (including falconry)
- Zoo, safari park, anywhere keeping exotic animals
- Farm animals, farm park, country centre, farm museum; also a vineyard
- Anything to do with fish, including both fishing and aquariums
- Butterfly park
- Garden, plant centre, arboretum, landscaped park
- Walk
- Wood, forest
- Viewpoint
- Orchard, fruit farm, pick-your-own
- Cave, cavern
- Museum
- Art gallery, sculpture park, notable painting collections
- Boat museum
- Air museum
- Motor museum
- Open-air museum (including industrial museums)
- Heritage centre such as Jorvik Centre in York
- Steam locomotives, railway
- Boat trip
- ☺ Amusement park, theme park, leisure park, permanent funfair
- Craft centre or craft workshop: potters, glass-blowers, weavers, etc
- Factory visit (including power station visits and breweries)
- ! Anything odd, unusual or decidedly different
- London Underground
- Surface rail – former British Rail
- Our special offer discount (see details on p. xiii and on the tear-out card in the middle of the book)

On the maps:

- Recommended place to stay
- ✕ Recommended place to eat
- Used when there are three or more different attractions in a locality